Congress and the Nation

Congress and the Nation

VOLUME XII • 2005–2008

POLITICS AND POLICY IN THE 109TH AND 110TH CONGRESSES

A Division of SAGE
Washington, D.C.

CQ Press
2300 N Street, NW, Suite 800
Washington, DC 20037

Phone: 202-729-1900; toll-free, 1-866-4CQ-PRESS
(1-866-427-7737)

Web: www.cqpress.com

Cover design: Jeff Miles Hall, ION Graphic Design Works
Cover photo: Interior of the Rotunda of the U.S. Capitol with statue of George Washington. *Andrew Prokos*
Composition: C&M Digitals (P) Ltd.

♾ The paper used in this publication exceeds the requirements of the American National Standard for Information Sciences—Permanence of Paper for Printed Library Materials, ANSI Z39.48-1992.

Printed and bound in the United States of America

14 13 12 11 10 1 2 3 4 5

ISBN: 978-0-87289-485-3
ISSN: 1047-1324

Summary Table of Contents

Contents

CHAPTER 5 Defense Policy

CHAPTER 6 Transportation, Commerce, and Communications

CHAPTER 7 Energy and Environment

CHAPTER 8 Agriculture

CHAPTER 9 Health and Human Services

CHAPTER 10 Education

Tables, Figures, and Boxes

Introduction

The eight years between 2001 and 2009, most of the first decade of a new century, were remarkable for the Republican Party's extended period of control of the federal government. Except for two years, 1952 and 1953, when Dwight D. Eisenhower was in the White House, the GOP had not controlled all the levers of legislative and executive power in Washington since the 1920s. Republicans aggressively seized this opportunity to implement an agenda that had in many respects eluded previous GOP administrations.

Even with this long-sought advantage, Republicans—under the leadership of President George W. Bush—rode a political roller coaster from triumph and success to, in the presidency's latter days, defeat and unpopularity. During this ride, Republicans put into effect—through legislation and executive actions—an array of programs and undertakings, many reflecting historical GOP priorities and philosophy but others breaking with traditional party thinking. In all, the Republican years from 2001 to 2009, when the Democrats regained congressional majorities, were as significant and controversial as any since the mid-1960s under President Lyndon B. Johnson. Supported by commanding Democratic majorities in Congress, Johnson had pushed through far-reaching domestic programs while foundering in a misbegotten war, much as history may judge Bush's years.

Congress and the Nation Vol. XII, like its predecessor volumes, is framed by a presidential term but its content is informed deeply by the entire events of Bush's eight years in office. Most of the content of this volume is devoted to presidential and congressional actions in the four legislative years from 2005 to 2009, the 109th and 110th Congresses. But three overarching events from the eight years Bush occupied the White House dominate the story. The first two came in Bush's first term: the terrorist attacks on September 11, 2001, which destroyed the World Trade Center in New York City and severely damaged the Pentagon outside Washington, D.C. The second came in 2003 when Bush authorized the invasion of Iraq to topple the regime of Saddam Hussein that was believed to be harboring, or developing, weapons of mass destruction. Both events set into motion continuing controversies still very much alive as Bush left office, including balancing national security and civil liberties, the appropriate role of the United States in world affairs, the rule of law in treating individuals who came into U.S. custody as part of the Iraq and related conflicts, the appropriate manner of paying the costs of waging war, and many more.

The third central event came in the last years of Bush's tenure when the United States, and nearly the entire world, were plunged into a deep recession that was the most serious economic contraction since the Great Depression of the 1930s and that threatened to become another true worldwide depression. The economic crisis had its roots in a vast housing bubble in which home prices always seemed to go higher, until they no longer did, and in exotic financial activities created in Wall Street investment houses, major banks, and in what essentially was a shadow banking system of hedge funds and other financial structures, many overseas and outside the reach of usual U.S. regulation. When the economic downturn came, starting with declining housing prices in 2007, it resulted by 2008 in the near collapse of huge investment houses, insurance companies, and regular banks—and the actual collapse of a few key ones and many smaller institutions. While a wholesale disaster was prevented only by vast bailouts from the federal government costing billions of dollars, the subsequent economic recession was accompanied by unemployment rising above 10 percent by 2009.

In an irony that was missed by none, it fell to a Republican administration, with impeccable free-market credentials and deeply held antiregulation philosophy, to lead the federal government's initial efforts to prevent a vast economic meltdown. It required the Bush administration—albeit with help from the Democratic-controlled Congress—to pour billions into financial institutions and even American auto manufacturers, essentially taking public ownership of some of the nation's largest firms. The administration's willingness to do this was illustrated in financial aid to banks and investment houses, in return for equity rights that portended government control; in the seizure of some institutions, including the nation's two largest underwriters of the mortgage market; and, in late 2008, during Bush's final weeks in office, in extending loans of up to $9.4 billion to General Motors and $4 billion to Chrysler, with the possibility of additional amounts in 2009. All of the money, which came from a $700 billion program approved by Congress, was intended to rescue the sprawling auto companies from almost certain bankruptcy within weeks. Bankruptcy eventually came to both automakers but in a carefully choreographed manner under the federal government's oversight that brought both companies back to life, free of many crushing debts and with an opportunity to regain their former role in American manufacturing.

The accounts of that two-year period that began to emerge after Bush left office, including some by participants, portrayed an administration acting against its basic economic principles because the alternative of not acting was almost certainly going to end in an economic catastrophe.

The economic crisis may remain, for historians, the premier example of the triumph of political practicality over political philosophy in a fundamentally conservative administration. But there were other examples of Republicans deviating from traditional beliefs when their agenda required it. One example came early in Bush's first term when GOP majorities in Congress pushed through deep tax reductions but without corresponding cuts in spending, resulting in yet more deficits and federal borrowing—traditionally anathema to Republicans. A second example occurred in 2003 when the Republican Congress enacted a significant expansion of Medicare, the health care program for seniors, by creating a prescription drug plan. This action substantially broadened one of the nation's largest and most expensive entitlement programs, which—even without the drug plan—faced long-term financial shortages that were predicted to drive it into bankruptcy eventually unless major changes were undertaken. The irony was not lost here, either: Republicans historically had been vocal critics of entitlement programs.

BUSH II: FROM HEIGHTS TO DEPTHS

The settled themes of Bush's first term continued into, and defined, his second: two wars, primarily in Iraq but also in Afghanistan; an assertive and muscular foreign policy, which began to soften toward the end of his term; the policy aftermath to the 2001 attacks in what Bush described as a war on terror; and continued Republican efforts to reverse or significantly modify long-standing programs—largely delivered through government—that had become in the previous half century deeply woven into the nation's social and economic fabric. In addition, the administration continued to advance a theory of government known as the unitary presidency or unitary executive, which assumed extraordinary powers vested in the president by the Constitution to control the entire executive branch that, in the process, subordinated the role of Congress. This was often stated through signing statements by the president at the time legislation was signed into law in which the president asserted he would enforce the law's provision in the context of his understanding of the president's constitutional role, often as commander in chief—thus in effect saying he had the authority to ignore congressional language in a bill that he did not agree with under the cover of his presumed constitutional powers.

All of these themes continued to build controversy around the Bush administration, but none more than the continuing, and increasingly violent, war in Iraq. Nevertheless, Bush won reelection in 2004 by a margin that left little doubt—unlike 2000—that his victory was convincing and legitimate. Republicans also strengthened their hold on Congress. With this renewed political strength Bush put forward an expansive vision of the appropriate role of government that differed starkly from the central pillars of Democratic theory. In this Republican vision, individuals would have more freedom to make decisions on their own—on housing, education, health care, business opportunities—with less intrusive government intervention and with lower taxes. Bush gave this view of the future a special name: an ownership society.

Although Bush's ownership society touched on an array of activities, none drew more attention than his desire to change the nation's biggest entitlement program—Social Security—by permitting younger workers to use some of their pay to fund private savings accounts, which the president argued would strengthen the program's long-term solvency and help future generations as baby boomers went into retirement and started to draw benefits.

Social Security, however, epitomized a fundamental divergence between the political philosophies of the two parties, with Democrats anchored in the belief that government was the proper vehicle to assure Americans a secure future and Republicans equally certain that citizens would be better off making their decisions free of government involvement on such matters as retirement, health care, and education. Bush's Social Security changes went nowhere, caught up in fierce opposition not only to the

HOW TO USE THIS BOOK

Readers can access information from several avenues. The sixteen chapters are listed in the Summary Table of Contents *(p. v)*. An outline of each chapter, including boxes, tables, graphs, and other related material, is provided in the detailed Table of Contents *(p. vii)*.

For specific topics turn to the two indexes at the end of the volume. The full Index *(p. 1205)* provides the most comprehensive roadmap while Supplementary Indexes *(p. 1197)* provide a quick guide to legislation. Throughout the book page references to related subjects in other chapters are provided. These page "flags" are designed to speed research across an array of subjects.

The Introduction provides an overview of political and legislative activity and an expanded description of each chapter's content.

substance of the proposal but, as important, in the growing disillusionment of voters with his administration over the seemingly endless Iraq commitment, an inept federal response to 2005's devastating Hurricane Katrina, and a cascade of scandals in Congress—both personal and financial—that mostly involved Republicans.

Nevertheless, Bush could look with satisfaction on many accomplishments. Perhaps most long lasting was the opportunity to solidify conservative control of the Supreme Court. When Chief Justice William Rehnquist died of cancer in September 2005, Bush replaced him with a much younger but equally conservative jurist, John G. Roberts Jr. (who had initially been nominated to replace Sandra Day O'Connor after she announced her intention to retire at the end of the 2004–2005 term of the Court). The major change, however, came with the nomination of a replacement for O'Connor, who had been a key swing vote on the Court, often voting with Court liberals on contentious social issues. Bush replaced her with a justice, Samuel A. Alito Jr., who in his early years proved by his votes to be a staunch member of the Court's conservative wing. He too was young, thus increasing the likelihood that the conservative tilt of the Court would continue for years, possibly decades.

Bush also won legislative approval of long-sought GOP goals, including bankruptcy law reform, that critics said tilted heavily toward financial institutions at the expense of consumers; a limitation on class-action lawsuits; an energy bill that critics said was based mainly on new resource extraction rather than conservation; and steadfast—and largely successful—opposition to domestic program proposals of Democrats. In one notable instance, however, Bush emerged from his consistent conservative vision to aggressively urge a far-reaching immigration reform bill, joining with many Democrats in the effort and alienating many in his party who opposed any legislation that would offer a path to citizenship and who preferred instead to focus on removing illegal immigrants from the nation's borders. Bush lost this battle as his usual allies split between business groups, which needed the relatively inexpensive labor provided by immigrants, and socially conservative groups—a vital part of the GOP base—that saw illegal immigrants as flaunting U.S. laws, taking away needed jobs, contributing to a raft of social ills, and even changing the basic ethnic structure of the population.

Although Bush could point to a legislative record in his first six years that was, in many respects, impressive, voter discontent grew after the GOP's 2004 electoral success and led, in fall 2006, to Democrats recapturing control of both houses of Congress, essentially ending hope of any further major legislative victories. Much of that discontent grew from the Iraq War but it also was fed, initially, by a stumbling federal response to the damage from Hurricane Katrina that devastated states on the Gulf Coast, as well as controversies over alleged torture of enemy combatants captured in Iraq and elsewhere, and wiretapping American phone lines without a court's authorizing warrant. The financial crisis that engulfed Bush's last two years in office merely added to his—and the GOP's—unpopularity leading up to the 2008 national elections. In the voting that fall, Democrats built on their 2006 success, and the plummeting popularity of Bush and fellow Republicans, to expand their majorities in Congress and to win control of the White House.

CONTROL OF CONGRESS

Republicans controlled the House during all of Bush's first six years in office and the Senate for more than four of those years. Although they lost the 2000 elections, Democrats improbably took control of the Senate in June 2001 when a disgruntled GOP senator became an independent and caucused with the Democrats, giving them a razor-thin majority of one vote.

For most of this period, Congress was a loyal follower of the White House, reflecting the GOP's ascendancy to power and the opportunity to enact its agenda. Even Democratic control of the Senate in the 109th Congress was limited by the party's slim majority and by the inclination of both parties to unite behind the president in the wake of the September 2001 terrorist attacks. The House was under a disciplined leadership that produced the votes for Republican legislation when needed or kept bills off the floor when agreement in their caucus was lacking. The Senate's Republican leaders were less effective—no surprise in a chamber that favors individuality and deliberation over unity and efficiency—but they still managed to find the votes to pass important bills favored by the White House.

Missing during the first six years of the Bush administration was Congress exercising its watchdog role of oversight of the executive branch. Republicans were little interested in probing the actions of their president, much less in pushing back against administration initiatives they favored. This was reflected in the fact that Bush did not veto a single bill until 2006 and only one in that year.

The administration's unitary presidency theory also affected the balance of power between the White House and Congress during this period. Many viewed Congress, even under Republican control, as a less than equal branch of the federal government.

This compliant time for Congress ended when Democrats took charge in 2007 after the 2006 midterm elections. Congressional committees then aggressively began to conduct oversight investigations, causing significant troubles for the administration involving both programs and administration officials, one of whom—Attorney General Alberto Gonzales—was in effect forced to resign. Moreover, Congress no longer went along quietly with the administration's legislative preferences, instead putting the Democratic majority's stamp on bills. This, too, was reflected in Bush's veto record. In his last two years in office, he vetoed eleven bills; four of the vetoes were overridden. Still, Democrats often were limited by the lack of the supermajority needed in the Senate to block filibusters.

LEGISLATION AND POLITICS: 2005–2009

This book continues a series begun in 1965 with the publication of *Congress and the Nation* Vol. I, which covered national government and politics from 1945 to 1964. Subsequent volumes, published every four years, covered the same subjects over the two Congresses of each succeeding administration. As with the preceding volumes, this edition is divided into a series of chapters focusing on such substantive subjects as commerce, law and justice, and health and welfare. This volume, as with recent ones, contains sixteen chapters, an extensive appendix, and a comprehensive index. Following are brief summaries of the chapters and the highlights of events described in them.

Chapter 1 Politics and National Issues

This chapter is an overview of the four-year period 2005 to 2008. The major legislative and political events noted here are covered in more detail in subsequent chapters.

Chapter 2 Economic Policy

This chapter, in four parts, begins with an overview of economic events followed by descriptions of congressional action on budgeting and taxation, financial regulation, and trade issues.

In a continuation of a pattern developing for a number of years, budgetary gridlock characterized congressional sessions from 2005 through 2008 as legislators' constitutional control of spending and taxing authority nearly collapsed. Congress completed action on regular appropriations bills only once, in 2005. In spite of admonitions from President Bush, Congress refused to grapple with looming financial crises in Medicare and Social Security. The economic crises that engulfed the nation in 2007 and 2008 forced emergency spending of billions of dollars that sent the federal deficit spiraling.

The development and consequences of that financial crisis are described in substantial detail in the subchapter on economic policy and regulation. The crisis is described in a separate essay discussing the origins of the housing bubble, old and new systemic problems, and the economic fallout when the bubble imploded and financial institutions worldwide face collapsed. The report provides a chronology of governmental actions over the two-year period, 2007 and 2008, and into 2009.

In its most important action, Congress, in late 2008—with the financial system teetering on collapse—passed a $700 billion bill known as the Troubled Asset Relief Program (TARP). The vast sum of money was intended primarily to stabilize the financial sector of the economy, although it came to be used for many other purposes. The effort was roundly criticized by some, who saw it as a bailout for Wall Street while average Americans on Main Street suffered. Voter rage was so great that the House at first rejected the TARP bill, which in turn sent the stock market into its steepest dive ever recorded, nearly 800 points on the Dow-Jones average. Congress, thoroughly spooked by the reaction of the financial markets, quickly reconsidered and passed the bill, which had been sweetened by the addition of a number of unrelated provisions advocated by different interest groups.

The TARP money then became the primary vehicle for rescuing not only failing banks but also, in one of Bush's last major actions, the automakers General Motors and Chrysler, which were about to collapse in the face of disastrously declining auto sales as the recession worsened.

Trade, seldom a popular subject in Congress, was caught up in the deteriorating domestic employment picture as unemployment rose from the recession. Many people, especially trade unions, also believed that globalization was shipping U.S. jobs overseas. As a result Bush was denied much of his second-term trade agenda.

Chapter 3 Homeland Security

The legislative branch became more skeptical of the executive branch's national security prerogatives, and members of Congress pushed back against White House claims of executive privilege, which the executive branch used to cloak details of national security efforts.

Bush in 2005 had to negotiate with renegade Senate Republicans over renewal of his signature anti-terrorism law, the USA PATRIOT Act, and was challenged over allowing American telecommunication companies to eavesdrop on American citizens without first obtaining a court order. Inept handling of the disaster that unfolded in New Orleans in 2005 after Hurricane Katrina made lawmakers wonder if the administration had become too focused on emphasizing international threats while ignoring serious problems at home.

Congress did eventually approve a broad range of national security measures, however, including bills to protect U.S. ports, distribute first responder grants, secure the nation's southwest border, prevent bioterrorism attacks, and safeguard chemical plants.

Chapter 4 Foreign Policy

The Iraq War dominated foreign policy debate in Bush's second term, as the conflict approached its sixth anniversary when the 110th Congress adjourned in 2008. Legislators and the president dealt with many significant issues—including North Korea, Iran, Cuba, Sudan, China, the Middle East, foreign aid, HIV/AIDS, nuclear power—but none dominated as did Iraq. Through it all President Bush urged Americans to "stay the course" in Iraq. Democratic efforts to wind down the war came to naught, even as public sentiment went from support to skepticism to outright opposition. Voter discontent was a key factor in returning control of Congress to the Democrats in 2006 and expanding that majority and electing a Democrat to the White House in 2008. Bush himself late in his term agreed to a timetable to end most U.S. involvement.

Congress nevertheless did act on many foreign policy issues. Both parties united to insist on more congressional involvement in a nuclear power agreement with India, which became one of Bush's most important foreign policy accomplishments. Over White House protests, legislators made deep cuts in Bush's signature foreign aid program, the Millennium Challenge Account, but approved billions more than requested for a popular global HIV/AIDS program.

Chaper 5 Defense Policy

The conduct and end-point of the U.S. war in Iraq overshadowed all other defense issues during Bush's second term. Democrats, with a few notable exceptions, tried unsuccessfully to assert congressional influence on the conflict, but Bush won all the important battles. By the end of his term, antiwar congressional Democrats and their limited number of GOP allies had become a chastened lot, unable to force the president's hand on the war.

Bush and Congress did reach an agreement to revamp rules and standards for trials and treatment of accused terrorists. The compromise action was forced by a 2005 Supreme Court decision in, *Hamdan v. Rumsfeld,* which found that military tribunals at Guantánamo Bay, Cuba, violated U.S. and international law.

Chapter 6 Transportation, Commerce, and Communications

Congress produced a substantial amount of legislation on transportation and communication issues during Bush's second term, compared to meager enactments in his first. Legislators approved a variety of major legislative bills on transportation, television, consumer product safety, Internet use and availability, and money to keep highway construction from running out of funds. The White House, after frequently grumbling about the costs of some bills, often changed its tune to accept the work of the legislators—sometimes grudgingly and sometimes with praise. One of Congress's first and most noteworthy actions was passage of a $286.5 billion, six-year surface transportation bill that legislators had been wrestling with since the basic transportation authorization, dating from 1998, expired in 2003.

Chapter 7 Energy and Environment

Congress approved a major energy bill in 2005 reflecting long-standing Republican preferences for business-oriented efforts to spur domestic production of energy from both renewable and traditional sources. Critics said the law largely subsidized traditional producers of oil and natural gas and would do little to curb Americans' appetite for fuel. Just two years later, in the 110th Congress, newly empowered Democrats cleared a more targeted bill aimed at reducing energy use, which included a long-sought increase in vehicle fuel efficiency standards.

Lawmakers also turned to other legislative vehicles to pass energy priorities. The 2008 farm bill contained popular tax breaks for ethanol and other biofuels. A major tax bill in 2008 contained a number of incentives for renewable energy conservation that were offset with revenue increases on the oil and gas industry.

During Bush's second term, however, Republicans failed to win approval for drilling in Alaska's Arctic National Wildlife Refuge. Environmental issues settled into something of a stalemate, as neither Republicans, who wanted to relax federal regulations, nor Democrats, who wanted to respond to the threat of climate change, could win passage of significant legislation.

Chapter 8 Agriculture

Congress passed, over a presidential veto, a major agricultural bill extending and revising basic farm laws. Bush, critical of farm spending, sought reductions in crop subsidies, but ran headlong into the blunt political fact that agricultural spending remained vital to many members of Congress. The final bill boosted spending on nutrition programs, preserved the existing approach to crop subsidies, and expanded conservation programs. The legislation also set up a permanent disaster fund to quickly help farmers hit by floods and droughts.

Chapter 9 Health and Human Services

No major medical initiatives were enacted during Bush's second term, but Congress approved important bills reforming the Food and Drug Administration, reducing medical errors, extending mental health insurance coverage, preventing employers and insurers from discriminating on the basis of genetic information about workers and patients, and funding preparations for a possible flu pandemic. Congress also gave a temporary extension, to 2009, to the popular program of federal health insurance for low-income children (CHIP) and reauthorized for the first time in nearly a decade the Head Start early childhood development program.

Chapter 10 Education

Education legislation played a smaller role in Bush's second term. Congress passed nothing comparable to the No Child Left Behind Act of his first term, but legislators extended and expanded higher education and vocational education aid programs. In 2006 Congress reauthorized the popular vocational education program for high school students, which Bush tried unsuccessfully to kill to get funds for No Child Left Behind. In 2007 legislators approved sweeping changes to federal student aid and loan programs despite veto threats from the president. In 2008 Congress reauthorized the Higher Education Act for the first time in a decade and included many new requirements intended to keep down the cost of college education while increasing federal financial aid to students.

Chapter 11 Housing and Urban Aid

Congress responded to the bursting of the housing bubble with legislative packages designed to help homeowners facing foreclosure, strengthen federal oversight powers, and protect overall market stability. These included:

- Providing a backstop for the Federal National Mortgage Association (Fannie Mae) and the Federal Home Loan Mortgage Corporation (Freddie Mac) and establishing a new regulator for the two mortgage finance giants. Legislation also help borrowers who could not afford their mortgage payments to stay in their homes.
- Allowing the Treasury Department to buy assets from Fannie Mae and Freddie Mac, essentially expanding their existing line of credit with the government, or to buy stock in the companies to keep them capitalized and boost the confidence of their private investors. The Treasury later put both companies into conservatorships and began funneling billions of dollars into them to keep them functioning.
- Providing federal grants to states to help low-income people pay their heating and cooling bills and weatherize their homes.

Chapter 12 Labor and Pensions

Several important labor and pension bills were enacted in Bush's second term: the national minimum wage was increased for the first time in nearly ten years; pension security laws were reformed to protect workers' retirement money; significant changes were made in mine safety rules after a series of fatal accidents in early 2006; and unemployment compensation benefits for workers who had exhausted their normal payments were extended twice.

Chapter 13 Law and Justice

President Bush solidified conservative control of the Supreme Court by appointing a new chief justice, John G. Roberts Jr., and an associate justice, Samuel A. Alito Jr. Alito replaced retiring Court member Sandra Day O'Connor, who often was the swing vote between the liberal and conservative blocs.

Congressional Democrats, once back in power in 2007, stepped up oversight of the executive branch, uncovering scandals and forcing the resignation of controversial attorney general Alberto R. Gonzales.

In one of its most important actions, Congress in 2006 extended expiring provisions of the 1965 Voting Rights Act. Congress also cleared bills to limit class-action lawsuits and the legal liability of firearms makers and dealers, and legislators extended and expanded the landmark Americans with Disabilities Act. Congress, however, could not agree on President Bush's top-priority plan to revise immigration laws, despite considerable support from Democrats as well as Republicans.

Republicans took a public relations hit when in 2005 they passed legislation to help parents keep alive their brain-damaged daughter, Terri Schiavo, prompting a national debate about end-of-life medical care. Opinion polls showed strong public disapproval of congressional intervention in this private family case. Courts eventually decided the issue by allowing her husband to have her feeding tube removed.

Chapter 14 General Government

Devastating hurricanes Katrina and Rita hit the coasts of Louisiana, Mississippi, and Alabama in August 2005, flooding New Orleans and resulting in vast swaths of disaster throughout these states. The destruction, and the federal government's inept response, prompted congressional investigations and quick approval of more than $62 billion for recovery and rebuilding in the Gulf Coast region.

Chapter 15 Inside Congress

The Republican Party was raked with scandals and criminal prosecutions in the 109th Congress, tarnishing the GOP's claim to continuing control of the institution and helping Democrats win back the majority in the 110th. Ethics inquiries continued throughout the four-year period in both chambers.

Congress approved a plan to ensure that the legislative branch would continue even if many of its members were killed or incapacitated, a pressing concern since the September 11, 2001, attacks. The legislation pertained only to the House, the chamber in which replacing members with new elections is a more cumbersome process as compared to the Senate, where most governors can quickly make appointments.

Chapter 16 The Bush Presidency

President Bush, in his second term, imploded in a way rarely seen in American history. The same man who once scored a 90 percent approval rating in the Gallup opinion polls a few weeks after the September 11, 2001, attacks—the highest rating in the history of the Gallup poll, which started when Franklin D. Roosevelt was president—had plummeted to a 25 percent approval rating by October 2008. Only two other presidents, Harry S. Truman and Richard Nixon, had received lower Gallup scores at the depth of their unpopularity.

It was a stunning turn of events rooted in the continuing war in Iraq, a decision made in his first term. Bush's presidency continued to unravel in a series of disasters and misjudgments, including a slow and ineffective response to Hurricane Katrina. Various scandals, from the outing of an undercover CIA agent to the firing of several U.S. attorneys, depicted a level of political vindictiveness within the administration that seemed unusual even by Washington standards. The financial meltdown that started in his final years seemed to be just another catastrophe that happened on his watch, although the president—often against his own political philosophy—helped summon the resources of the federal government to prevent an economic depression.

Appendix

The Appendix contains a variety of supplementary material, including key Senate and House votes (highlighted in boldface in the legislative chapters) during the four-year period, with charts showing how each member voted; a glossary of congressional terms; an explanation of how a bill becomes law; lists of committee and subcommittee chairs; biographical data on members of Congress between 2005 and 2009; presidential vetoes; and major presidential speeches and messages to Congress as well as other important documents. In addition, the Appendix includes extensive political charts, including presidential, House, Senate, and gubernatorial election returns for the period. Other tables record members who died or switched parties and special elections that were held. Finally, the Appendix includes a complete list of public laws enacted during the four years.

This volume has been prepared under the direction of editors at CQ Press, a division of SAGE. The chapters and the appendix were prepared and edited by a group of veteran reporters, many of whom covered Congress for Congressional Quarterly Inc. and other Washington, D.C., news organizations. The principal contributors were John Felton, Martha Gottron, David Hosansky, Ken Jost, Kerry Kern, Chris Lawrence, Colleen McGuiness, David Nather, Ann O'Connor, Julie Rovner, and David Tarr, who also served as volume editor for this edition. Judy Schneider at the Congressional Research Service in the Library of Congress reviewed, corrected, and expanded the glossary of legislative terms that appears in the Appendix.

At CQ Press Andrea Cunningham ably shepherded the manuscript through review and compilation to the editing and production team. Bringing the material together to make an actual book was efficiently directed by Belinda Josey. The index to the volume was prepared by Indexing Partners LLC. Doug Goldenberg-Hart at CQ Press was the sponsoring editor.

CQ Press editors also wish to express their thanks to those dedicated reporters and editors on the *CQ Weekly* magazine and the *CQ Almanac* for their assistance in preparation of this edition.

Congress and the Nation

CHAPTER 1

Politics and National Issues

Politics and National Issues

After the 2004 elections Republicans were riding high. President George W. Bush had won a second term, and the GOP had added significant numbers to their majorities in both the House and the Senate. Bush proclaimed that he had accumulated much political capital that he planned to spend advancing his goal of an "ownership society," and Republican leaders in Congress were confident that they could deliver. House Majority Leader Tom DeLay, R-Texas, declared that the foundations had been laid for a "permanent" Republican majority in Congress.

Two years later the Republicans lost that congressional majority. Voters in 2006 gave Democrats control of both chambers of Congress for the first time since 1995. In 2008 voters completed the transition with the election of the country's first African American president, Democrat Barack Obama. Democrats also added to their numbers in both chambers of Congress. As president, Obama inherited two major issues that contributed heavily to voter rejection of the Republican Party: the worst economic recession in decades (and on some measures the worst since the Great Depression of the 1930s), and continuing U.S. military conflicts in Iraq and Afghanistan. Even before Obama was inaugurated on Jan. 20, 2009, it seemed likely that history's judgment of his presidency would be deeply informed by how well he managed the fallout from both continuing crises.

To succeed in righting the economy, successfully ending the two wars, and advancing his agenda that included reform of the nation's health care system, Obama had to overcome a polarization that characterized much congressional action. Each party was more unified in opposition to the other party than any time in recent decades. Moreover, both parties were often divided internally, making it difficult for the party leadership to move forward on some legislation. Even in the few instances where the president and Republican and Democratic leaders worked together, factions in one or the other party, sometimes both, were strong enough to delay or kill the legislation. Sometimes differences between the two chambers proved to be the stumbling block. Little solid evidence from the 2008 election results or the first months of the Obama administration suggested that the divisiveness had eased.

Newly elected House Speaker Nancy Pelosi smiles as President Bush delivers his annual State of the Union address to a joint session of Congress on Capitol Hill in Washington on January 23, 2007.
Source: AP Photo/Larry Downing

THE GOP'S UNRAVELING

With their strengthened numbers, congressional Republicans in 2005 quickly passed several major pieces of legislation that had been blocked in previous years, including new limits on class-action lawsuits and a rewrite of the nation's bankruptcy law that made it more difficult for bankrupt individuals to walk away from their debts. Bush also won approval of energy policy legislation that he had been seeking since 2001, and Congress reauthorized a massive highway and mass transit program. For the first time since 2001, Congress passed all its regular appropriations bills without resorting to an omnibus spending measure, and for the first time since 1997 it passed legislation making cuts in mandatory entitlement spending.

But Bush's vision of an ownership society faded within months of his second inauguration. His plan to partially privatize Social Security for younger workers was quietly shelved after much of the public, Democrats, and even many Republicans voiced opposition to the proposal. A report by a special panel Bush commissioned to make recommendations on simplifying the tax code was also put aside shortly after it was completed, and his proposals to give people more control over their health care plans never gained traction in Congress.

Then, on Aug. 29, 2005, Hurricane Katrina struck Alabama, Louisiana, and Mississippi, killing about 2,000 people and causing an estimated $80 billion in property damage. Most of the deaths and much of the damage occurred in New Orleans, which was 80 percent flooded. Americans watched seemingly endless television coverage showing thousands of stranded people waiting for help that did not come for days. Although state and local governments were equally unprepared to handle such a massive emergency, the federal government's slow and mismanaged response to the storm drew especially heavy criticism as it became clear that four years after the terrorist attacks of Sept. 11, 2001, the government was still not prepared to react quickly or effectively to a major disaster.

Public shock over the government's incompetent handling of the hurricane fed into growing voter dismay over the continuing war in Iraq. Bush had launched the war in 2003 to rid the country of the weapons of mass destruction that its leader Saddam Hussein was thought to have stockpiled. The military action quickly toppled Hussein's regime, but by the time the administration acknowledged that there were no weapons of mass destruction, Iraq was caught up in bloody sectarian violence fueled by a growing number of terrorists drawn to the unstable nation. With Iraqi civilian and U.S. military casualties rising, public support for the war was rapidly eroding and Bush's conduct of the conflict came under serious question. Revelations that the administration, in its efforts to detect and deter terrorist attacks aimed at the United States, had secretly eavesdropped on the conversations of thousands of Americans further damaged support for the president. So too did news that the administration had secretly detained and perhaps tortured suspected terrorists in violation of international conventions.

At the same time that these external events were chilling Republicans' standing with the public, the party was plagued by a series of ethical issues that the Democrats were later to portray to voters as a "culture of corruption." The most damaging to the GOP was an indictment in September 2005 in Texas of House Majority Leader Tom DeLay, for alleged violations of campaign finance laws. DeLay stepped aside temporarily, pledging to return to power after clearing his name. However, he was closely tied to lobbyist Jack Abramoff, who in January 2006 agreed to cooperate with prosecutors looking into favors he traded for help from members of Congress. Just days before Abramoff's plea bargain was announced, DeLay said he would not try to regain his leadership position, and in June he resigned from the House. His departure meant that the House GOP lost its most effective leader in decades. Known as the "Hammer," DeLay was famous for lining up and delivering the votes his party needed to enact much of Bush's agenda after 2001. His successors simply lacked the capacity to replicate DeLay's leadership.

DeLay's downfall was not the only Republican scandal. Rep. Bob Ney of Ohio, who had earlier been tied into the Abramoff investigation, gave up his committee chair in January 2006 while maintaining his innocence against accusations of influence peddling. Some months later, Ney pleaded guilty to two federal counts of conspiracy and false statements and gave up his House seat just weeks before the 2006 midterm election. Rep. Randy "Duke" Cunningham, a California Republican, resigned his seat in December 2005 after pleading guilty to bribery and tax evasion. Cunningham admitted accepting at least $2.4 million in bribes to use his position on the House Appropriations Committee to steer funds to defense contractors. He was later sentenced to eight years and four months in prison. *(Congressional ethics, pp. 838, 882)*

Then, little more than a month before the 2006 elections, Rep. Mark Foley, R-Fla., resigned following revelations of inappropriate e-mails and instant messages sent over several years to current and former teenage male pages. The episode was particularly difficult for the party not only because of the homosexual implications but because it left the impression that the Republican leadership, from the Speaker on down, had known of Foley's conduct for some time and had done nothing to stop it.

All of these events—the president's unpopularity, dissatisfaction with the conduct of the war in Iraq, dismay over the inept response to Hurricane Katrina, the congressional ethics scandals, and a shortage of legislative accomplishments—combined with a growing sense that middle America was not fully participating in the economic recovery that followed a mild recession in late 2000 and early 2001. Although the aggregate figures showed relatively strong growth and productivity and low inflation, job growth lagged, and the soaring price of gasoline and heating fuel and rising costs of health care were taking their toll on many Americans' pocketbooks.

Democrats realized they had their best chance in years to knock the Republicans out of power and they seized it, fielding strong, well-funded candidates who promised to end the Iraq War, rid the Capitol of the "culture of corruption" they said the GOP had created, and generally keep the Bush administration in check by providing the aggressive oversight they argued the Republicans had never delivered. On Election Day 2006, voters responded by giving the Democrats control of both chambers of Congress.

In the House, the Democrats successfully retained every seat they defended—a feat neither party had accomplished in nearly seventy years—and gained thirty seats from the

GOP. The Democrats would take control of the House for the first time in twelve years, under the leadership of Rep. Nancy Pelosi of California, the first woman in history to become Speaker of the House.

The Democratic margin of control in the Senate was much more precarious. Although Democrats gained six seats in the Senate, they were tied forty-nine seats to forty-nine-seats with the Republicans and won control only because two independents, Bernard Sanders of Vermont and Joseph I. Lieberman, a former Democrat and vice-presidential candidate in 2000, agreed to caucus with the party. That fifty-one vote majority was far from the sixty votes needed to cut off filibusters in the Senate, a fact that Democrats would be reminded of repeatedly during the next two years.

JUDICIAL TRANSITION

One transition in the 109th Congress worked in favor of Republicans. That was the nomination and confirmation of two youthful and conservative Supreme Court justices. In what could prove to be the most important legacy of President Bush and his GOP allies in the 109th Congress, these new justices held out renewed hope to conservatives that their long-sought goal of moving the Court further to the political right was now within their grasp. *(New justices, p. 728)*

The first change was the confirmation of John G. Roberts Jr. as chief justice. That chair had been held since 1986 by William H. Rehnquist, who died Sept. 3, 2005. Roberts, who had spent just two years on the U.S. Circuit Court of Appeals for the District of Columbia, was well-respected among both Democrats and Republicans and won confirmation Sept. 29, 2005, on a **key vote of 78–22 (R 55–0; D 22–22; I 1–0)**. Because both Rehnquist and Roberts were conservatives, however, the change did not immediately affect the Court's alignment. *(2005 key votes, p. 915)*

The next appointment did. On July 1, 2005, Sandra Day O'Connor, the first woman on the Court, announced her retirement. O'Connor had become the key swing vote on the Court, siding with the four liberal justices on some cases and with the four conservatives on others—much to the frustration of conservatives nationwide. (Originally, Roberts was nominated to replace her; when Rehnquist died, Bush changed Roberts's nomination to chief justice.) Once Roberts was confirmed, Bush named his White House counsel Harriet Miers to O'Connor's seat, then withdrew the nomination in the face of loud opposition from conservatives who said too little was known about Miers's views on specific issues to ensure that she would be a reliable conservative justice.

Bush then turned to Samuel A. Alito Jr., a judge on the Court of Appeals for the Third Circuit, who, like Roberts, had impeccable conservative credentials. Because Alito was thought likely to provide a crucial fifth conservative vote on the Court, his nomination was opposed by liberals and Democrats, who said Alito was hostile to abortion rights, civil rights, and workers' rights and would favor big business and government over individual rights. Although opponents attempted a filibuster, it was easily put down in January 2006 by a 72–25 vote, and Alito was confirmed Jan. 31 by a **key vote of 58–42 (R 54–1; D 4–40; I 0–1)**. *(2006 key votes, p. 937)*

One reason the filibuster against Alito's confirmation was so weak may have been an unusual collaboration between seven Republican and seven Democratic senators who had allied to stop the filibusters that had prevented confirmation of dozens of judicial nominations both in Bush's first term and in his predecessor Bill Clinton's presidency. Matters reached a breaking point at the beginning of the 109th Congress when the president renominated seven controversial candidates that Democrats had successfully filibustered in the previous Congress. At the same time, Senate Majority Leader Bill Frist, R-Tenn., threatened to resort to the "nuclear option"—a parliamentary maneuver that would effectively eliminate the filibuster as a tool for thwarting judicial nominees—if Democrats persisted in their opposition. On the evening before the Senate was scheduled to vote on the nuclear option, the so-called Gang of Fourteen announced an agreement that averted the crisis. *(Filibusters and Gang of Fourteen, p. 820)*

In essence the seven Democrats agreed that judicial nominations should be filibustered only under "extraordinary circumstances," a term that was left undefined, while the seven Republicans agreed to oppose any change in the rules that would eliminate the judicial filibuster unless Democrats mounted a filibuster in what Republicans considered less than extraordinary circumstances. The agreement, one of the few bipartisan accords reached during the 109th Congress, somewhat eased a source of high tension between the two parties.

DEMOCRATS' LIMITED CONTROL

Although Democratic congressional leaders faced different problems in the 110th Congress than GOP leaders did in the 109th, Democrats found, as the Republicans had before them, that there were definite limits to their exercise of power. For one thing, the one-vote margin in the Senate meant that Republicans could fairly easily block any legislative action they did not like. More important, Bush was still the president, and though his popularity was greatly reduced even among members of his party, he still was capable of wielding significant power by threatening use of his presidential veto pen.

Overriding those factors, however, was the 2008 presidential election. For the first time since 1928, neither a sitting president nor a sitting vice president was running for the nation's highest office. The race to succeed Bush started earlier than ever, with most major presidential contenders from both sides of the aisle announcing their candidacies in late 2006 or early 2007. The stakes in the 2008 congressional races were also high, with Republicans intent on regaining control of the Senate and at least paring back the

Democratic majority in the House, and the Democrats eager to bolster their numbers in both chambers. As a result, electoral politics tinged, and in many cases drove, much of the legislative action in Congress.

As the Republicans had in 2005, Democrats acted quickly to enact some of their long-sought legislation, such as the first increase in the minimum wage in ten years. In other major action during the 110th Congress, they increased fuel economy standards for new cars for the first time in thirty-two years, reauthorized farm support programs over two vetoes, approved a measure requiring insurers to offer mental health benefits equal to traditional medical benefits, and passed the biggest expansion of veterans' education benefits in twenty-five years, among other achievements. Democrats also began the oversight investigations they had promised during the 2006 campaign. One of those, involving allegations that the several U.S. attorneys had been fired for political reasons led to the resignation of Attorney General Alberto R. Gonzales in September 2007.

But Democrats were unable to push through some of their top priorities in the face of determined GOP opposition. Perhaps their most frustrating loss was their inability to fulfill their campaign promise to end U.S. military involvement in Iraq. Immediately after the 2006 election, President Bush said that he had "heard" the voters and he fired his defense secretary, Donald H. Rumsfeld, who had become the main target of public criticism of the mismanaged war. Barely two months later, in January 2007, Bush announced that he was sending thousands of additional U.S. troops to Iraq in a "surge" intended to quell the insurgency there. The controversial decision drew outraged protests from Democrats, who cleared a spending measure for the war in April that would have required the president to begin withdrawing U.S. troops from Iraq in about six months.

Bush vetoed that bill, and House Democrats were unable to override it. Democratic leaders then had to decide whether to send the president the same bill, risking not only another veto that they would be unable to overcome but also charges that they were delaying needed military supplies for the troops. Party leaders decided to back down, but the pattern was set. Later attempts during the year to force a troop withdrawal also failed, and by 2008 Democrats, hopeful that one of their own would soon occupy the White House, had all but abandoned the effort.

Democrats also engaged the Republican president in a year-long battle over spending priorities, which ended shortly before Christmas 2007, with Democrats giving in to the president's spending limit. They were able to steer some funding toward their domestic priorities, but with Republicans backing the president's veto threats, the new majority had to choose between paring back the amount of spending it had hoped to spread to a broad range of domestic programs or leaving for the year without completing work on the spending bills, something they had railed against the Republicans for doing in 2006. In 2008 Democratic leaders opted not to reengage in what they knew would be a losing battle and instead packaged that year's appropriations bills into a continuing resolution that temporarily froze most funding for domestic programs at the previous year's levels.

The controversy that most came to symbolize the Democrats' inability to have their way, however, was the drawn-out and rancorous debate over the State Children's Health Insurance Program. Democrats, with the support of some powerful Republican allies, started out the year hoping to expand the popular program to ensure that it covered economically stressed middle-class families. Bush, who opposed a broad expansion of government health care, fought Congress all the way, twice vetoing versions of the measure that the Democrats were unable to override. In the end, Congress simply extended the existing program through March 2009, when a new president would be in the White House.

ECONOMIC CRISIS

Given the high-stakes presidential election campaign under way, neither party in Congress had much interest in doing anything in 2008 that the other party could turn against them on the campaign trail. However, beginning in the middle of the year, the nation was confronted with a financial and economic crisis that threatened to be the worst since the Great Depression of the 1930s. To prevent a full-scale collapse of the economy, Congress and Bush were forced to take a series of actions that were likely to reverberate economically and politically for years to come.

The crisis had its origins in the housing boom that ran from 2002 until early 2006, when real estate prices began to decline across the country, throwing construction workers out of their jobs and leaving many homeowners owing more on their mortgages than their homes were worth. Most affected was the subprime mortgage market, where often unscrupulous lenders had given mortgages to people with inadequate assets and income to be homeowners. In late 2006, these borrowers began to default on their mortgages. Eventually the cascade of foreclosures spread to many better-qualified homeowners who also found themselves overextended as housing prices fell, the stock market plummeted, and their personal financial worth shrank.

The housing crisis, bad enough on its own, turned into a broader crisis when the value of billions of dollars in mortgage-based securities came under question. Wall Street banks and other financial firms had created and sold the securities based on a complicated and opaque intermingling of mortgages, including subprime mortgages. When the housing market was booming, investors large and small snapped up the securities, apparently on the assumption that home prices would continue to rise, returning a handsome profit. When the housing market collapsed, the mortgage-based securities also lost value, but because of the way they were packaged it was nearly impossible to distinguish between those securities that might still hold some value and those that were "toxic" and essentially worthless. That uncertainty led to a lack of confidence in which banks around the world were unwilling to lend even to other banks for fear that the loans were at risk. That in turn precipitated a worldwide credit crunch, where even borrowers with good credit ratings were unable to secure loans at reasonable prices, bringing a worldwide contraction in economic growth.

An officially declared recession began in late 2007, but even before then many Americans were feeling the economic pinch of rising food and fuel prices and slow job growth. The "Big Three" American automakers—General Motors (GM), Ford, and Chrysler—once the symbol of American manufacturing might, now became the symbol of economic distress as they laid off thousands of workers and renegotiated union contracts that allowed them to pay some new employees half of starting wages in the past. As economic conditions deteriorated, Congress and the president negotiated a $151.7 billion economic stimulus bill that was signed into law in February 2008. It focused on tax rebates for families and individuals.

Meanwhile, the Federal Reserve, often in concert with the central banks of other countries, was pumping billions of dollars into the financial system to prevent its total collapse. Although slow to grasp the seriousness of the crisis, both Congress and the Bush administration took some small steps in 2007 to ease the housing crisis. But in July 2008 Treasury Secretary Henry M. Paulson Jr. appealed to Congress to give him open-ended authority to shore up the government-backed mortgage giants Freddie Mae and Fannie Mac, which held or guaranteed about $5 trillion in mortgages, many of them subprime. At the time Congress acted, Paulson said he did not think he would have to use the authority. But on Sept. 7, 2008, with both mortgage lenders on the brink of failure, the federal government seized control of the two agencies and said it would funnel as much as $200 billion to them to keep them solvent.

A week later the emergency worsened when the Lehman Brothers, one of the most aggressive packagers of mortgage-backed securities, filed for bankruptcy after the government declined to bail out the venerable Wall Street investment bank. With other banks near collapse and credit markets frozen around the world, the Bush administration determined it had no choice but to take bold action. On Sept. 18, Paulson and Federal Reserve Chairman Ben S. Bernanke appealed to Congress for authority to spend up to $700 billion to acquire presumably worthless mortgage-based assets from financial companies and buy stock in those companies to prevent total collapse. Congress approved the measure, called the Troubled Asset Relief Program (TARP), but only after the House at first rejected it amid widespread constituent anger over bailing out huge financial firms believed to be the cause of the problems. Together the bailouts of Wall Street and the two mortgage agencies represented the largest intervention of the federal government into private business in the nation's history.

Later in the year Republicans in the Senate balked at approving a multibillion assistance package to keep afloat the three American auto companies. Although Ford was in a little better financial shape than GM or Chrysler, all three companies encountered plummeting car sales as the recession deepened and credit dried up. To prevent the loss of tens of thousands of jobs throughout the auto industry, President Bush pledged $17.4 billion to the carmakers from the TARP program. Bush said at the time that under ordinary circumstances, he would have preferred that the companies proceed through an orderly bankruptcy process, but "these aren't normal circumstances.... That's the problem."

PRESIDENTIAL TRANSITION

If inheriting the worst financial crisis in decades can be considered a good thing, one beneficiary of the economic crisis may have been Democratic presidential nominee Sen. Barack Obama of Illinois. At the height of the bailout debate in Washington, the Republican nominee, Sen. John McCain of Arizona, told campaign audiences that the fundamentals of the economy were sound, only to suspend his campaign a few days later to rush to Washington to try to broker a deal on the bailout. When a White House summit that McCain had requested broke up in partisan rancor, and after his fellow Republicans voted against the bailout package in the House, McCain looked ineffective to many voters. Obama, who had remained calm and deliberate throughout the bailout debate, took a lead in the polls in late September that carried him through to victory on Election Day.

Obama's election to the White House was remarkable on many fronts. He was virtually unknown to most voters before he delivered what was widely regarded as a riveting speech at the 2004 Democratic National Convention and winning election later in the year to the U.S. Senate. Three years later he threw his hat in the ring against several more experienced Democratic politicians, including front-runner Sen. Hillary Rodham Clinton of New York, the former first lady and the first woman in either party to mount a viable campaign for the presidential nomination. In a well-organized and well-funded campaign that took full advantage of Internet social networking communications, Obama steadily whittled away at Clinton's lead, winning several primaries, losing others by relatively close margins, but winning most of the Democratic caucuses. Obama appealed to a wide variety of voters, white and black, with his message of "hope" and call for "change" in such areas as health care, climate change, and education. As the long primary campaign continued, more and more Democratic officials endorsed Obama, and Clinton finally conceded the nomination early in June.

By that time, it was clear the GOP nominee would be John McCain, the Republican maverick who had lost a run for the nomination to George Bush in 2000. A generation older than Obama, McCain was widely respected as a former prisoner of war who had been tortured at the hands of his Vietnamese captors and as a senator who worked "across the aisle" with Democrats on several important issues. But McCain's campaign, highly disorganized at the beginning, never caught fire with the voters. His selection of Sarah Palin, governor of Alaska, as his running mate enhanced his support among conservatives but did not draw independent voters or women as he had hoped. On Nov. 7, Obama won 53 percent of the popular vote and 365 electoral votes to McCain's 173. Obama's coattails also helped Democrats bolster their margins in both the House and Senate. When all the votes were finally counted, the party held 257 House seats and 59 Senate seats.

PARTISAN POLITICS

Whether those majorities would be enough for the Democrats to overcome the bitter polarization that had taken hold in Washington remained to be seen. The relative comity that had prevailed in Washington since the end of World War II began to fade in the 1980s and by the 1990s had disappeared almost completely. In 2001, when George W. Bush arrived in Washington to begin his first term as president, he promised to work with both parties to achieve common goals. "I'm a uniter, not a divider," he famously claimed. By the end of his second term in January 2009, he had presided over the most polarized period in the Capitol since Congressional Quarterly began quantifying partisanship in the House and Senate in 1953. In that period, Democrats in the House were never more unified than they were during the four years of Bush's second term. Democrats in the Senate and Republicans in both chambers did not set unity records, but they came close all four years.

Particularly in the Senate, where neither party had the sixty votes required to cut off debate, the minority party was able to block many initiatives promoted by the majority or to force changes that made the legislation more to its liking. In one notable case, Democrats in the Senate voted against a hike in the minimum wage that they supported in order to deny Republicans a reduction in the estate tax, which was packaged in the same bill. In many cases, opposition by the minority party kept the majority party from even trying to bring a piece of legislation to the Senate floor.

Internal divisions in both parties, and divisions between the House and Senate exacerbated the partisan differences, sometimes thwarting bipartisan efforts. A majority of House Republicans voted against their president to kill the initial financial bailout bill weeks before the 2008 elections. In 2006 GOP conservatives in the House killed an immigration reform bill Bush supported when they refused to go to conference with the Senate. Internal party divisions were also a major factor preventing either party from completing action on its most basic job—deciding how to spend taxpayer dollars. Only in 2005 was Congress able to complete action of the annual congressional budget resolution and all regular spending bills before the end of the calendar year. In the other three years, government agencies were funded either through continuing resolutions that generally kept spending at the previous year's level or by a mammoth omnibus spending resolution that allowed little adequate oversight of funding decisions.

Partisanship in Congress, 2005–2008

This table shows the percentage of times that the majority of one party voted against the majority of the other. House Democrats voted together 92 percent of the time in both 2007 and 2008 against a majority of House Republicans. These percentages were the highest party unity scores recorded in the House since Congressional Quarterly began keeping track of party unity in 1953. The House Republican high was 91 percent, recorded in 2003. The high for Senate Democrats was 89 percent, set in 1999 and 2001; while the record high for Senate Republicans was 94 percent, set in 2003.

Party unity	*2005*	*2006*	*2007*	*2008*
House Democrats	88	86	92	92
House Republicans	90	88	85	87
Senate Democrats	88	86	87	87
Senate Republicans	88	86	81	83
Partisan votes (% of total)				
House	49	55	62	53
Senate	63	57	60	52

Legislating is always about compromise. But the compromises that leaders of both parties made in Bush's second term often resulted in unwieldy legislation covering disparate subjects carefully crafted to produce the necessary votes for passage. The inevitable outcome of the push and pull of the election calendar and special interests, these balancing acts nonetheless raised questions about the ability of Congress to legislate meaningful responses to several longer-term threats to the nation's well-being. Chief among these challenges were helping to stimulate the economy and managing the budget deficit that had nearly tripled in the face of the federal response to the recession, coordinating with the rest of the world on ways to slow harmful climate change, and ensuring the financial stability of the Social Security and Medicare systems. Political scientists cautioned, however, that the period of relative comity that Congress and the nation enjoyed in the mid-1900s might have been the exception to the rule and that the partisanship of the early 2000s could well be a return to traditional American party politics.

2005

The Legislative Year

Republicans opened the 109th Congress brimming with confidence from their 2004 election victories, which gave President George W. Bush a second term and expanded the party's majorities in both chambers. "We begin the new Congress with a sense of purpose and optimism. It's been a long time since Republicans have had this much power in Washington," Rep. David Dreier, R-Calif., chairman of the House Rules Committee told his colleagues Jan. 4, 2005, the first day of the session.

But the new majorities were not enough to ensure the sweeping changes GOP leaders had hoped would occur. Democrats reacted by becoming more unified than ever, and the Republican leadership often found itself navigating between conservatives and the party's small moderate wing.

Nor were the Republican majorities enough to offset the sagging popularity of President Bush. After his reelection Bush said he had a "lot of political capital" and pledged to use it to advance several domestic programs, including partially privatizing Social Security. But whatever political capital he might have had was blown away in the winds of Hurricane Katrina. The administration's inept response to the emergency created by the storm that devastated much of the Gulf Coast, including the city of New Orleans, could not have come at a worse time for the president. Bush was already facing dwindling support from a public concerned about mounting American casualties in the war in Iraq and mounting gasoline prices and other economic woes at home.

At the same time troubles of another kind were brewing for the Republicans, as ethics problems surrounded a number of House Republicans, notably Majority Leader Tom DeLay of Texas. By the end of the session the Republican caucus seemed to be unraveling, and Democrats were growing more confident that they would win the House in the 2006 midterm elections and perhaps even gain control of the Senate.

A HOPEFUL BEGINNING

The Republicans began the 109th Congress with 232 House seats and 55 Senate seats, enough, the leadership hoped, to allow the party to overcome the nearly united Democrats who had blocked several top Republican priorities in the previous Congress. *(Congress and the Nation Vol. XI, pp. 18–19, 21)*

The GOP had some early success. A business-backed bill that limited plaintiffs' ability to pursue class action lawsuits in sympathetic state courts had been a centerpiece of the GOP "tort reform" agenda for years. Senate Majority Leader Bill Frist, R-Tenn., had pulled the measure off the floor in 2004 when he was unable to get the sixty votes needed to stop a Democratic filibuster. In 2005 the fifty-five vote GOP majority in the Senate enabled him to fend off Democratic amendments and send a clean bill to the House. *(Class action lawsuits, p. 695)*

The enlarged Senate majority also enabled Frist to defeat an amendment that had prevented enactment of a bankruptcy overhaul prized by the credit card and financial services industry. Supporters had been trying to clear the legislation for eight years. The Senate had also been the graveyard for another top Republican priority: an energy policy overhaul that Bush had been seeking since 2001. The Senate easily cleared the energy bill in late July, after the House dropped the provision that had been the deal breaker in the Senate in 2004. At White House insistence, DeLay backed off a demand that the bill protect manufacturers of the gasoline additive methyl tertiary butyl ether (MTBE) from liability suits over water contamination. *(Bankruptcy, p. 142; Energy, p. 447)*

In a major victory for Bush's free-trade policy, legislation to implement a trade agreement with five Central American countries and the Dominican Republic cleared in late July. But the largely unified Democratic opposition forced Republican leaders and the White House to make deals to win solid backing from their own party, and it was the last significant free-trade agreement approved in Bush's second term, as skepticism mounted about the benefits of liberalized trade. *(Trade pacts, p. 197)*

CONGRESS IN 2005

The first session of the 109th Congress convened at noon on Jan. 3, 2005, as required by the Twelfth Amendment and federal law, and ended at 8:04 p.m. on Dec. 22, when the Senate adjourned *sine die*. The House had adjourned *sine die* at 4:36 p.m. the same day. The session stretched over 354 days. The Senate met on 159 days, for a total of 1,222 hours; the House met on 140 days, for a total of 1,067 hours.

A total of 8,319 bills and resolutions were introduced during the 2005 session, compared with 3,656 in 2004 and 7,014 in 2003. Congress cleared 169 bills in 2005 that were signed into public law. For the fifth year in a row, President George W. Bush did not issue any vetoes. *(Public laws table, p. 16; Presidential vetoes, p. 1039)*

During 2005, the House took 669 recorded votes (not including two quorum calls). That was 126 more recorded votes than it took in 2004. The Senate took 366 recorded votes in 2005, 150 more than in 2004. *(Recorded votes table, p. 21)*

Perhaps the biggest breakthrough, however, came on Bush's nominees for federal court appointments. In the 108th Congress Democrats had successfully filibustered ten federal appeals court nominees that they considered too conservative or otherwise unqualified for the federal bench. As the 109th Congress opened Frist appeared ready to follow through on his threat to employ an arcane parliamentary maneuver, dubbed the "nuclear option," to deny Democrats the ability to continue filibustering Bush's court picks, The crisis was averted at the last moment when a group of seven senators from each party, who became known as the Gang of Fourteen, struck a deal to let all but a few of the Bush nominees Democrats found most objectionable win confirmation. *(Judicial filibusters, p. 820)*

There were a few bumps in the road as well. The Senate began the year by confirming all but one of Bush's nominees for high-level jobs in his second term. The exception was John R. Bolton, whose nomination as ambassador to the United Nations was blocked by Senate Democrats. Bush subsequently sent Bolton to the United Nations as a recess appointment. The newly confirmed cabinet members included Alberto R. Gonzales, the first Hispanic to serve as attorney general; Condoleezza Rice, the national security adviser in Bush's first term who became secretary of state; and Michael Chertoff, who became the second head of the Department of Homeland Security.

Despite a full-bore effort Bush failed to persuade the public, most Democrats, and many Republican legislators to support his proposal to overhaul Social Security by creating personal investment accounts for younger workers. The matter was put on a back burner early in the session, where it was left for the remainder of Bush's term. *(Social Security, p. 662)*

In addition, polls showed that Congress's decision early in the year to intervene in the case of a brain-damaged woman named Terry Schiavo, contrary to public sentiment, had left many voters feeling that the government was out of touch with their interests.

Still, Republicans left Washington for the August recess in 2005 with an ample list of bragging rights—and a full agenda for the fall. Items on that agenda included a package of mandatory spending cuts, renewal of the 2001 antiterrorism law known as the Patriot Act, and confirmation of a new Supreme Court justice, as well as completion of the annual appropriations bills and the defense authorization bill. *(USA Patriot Act, p. 222, Supreme Court justice, p. 728)*

KATRINA: THE START OF A PERFECT STORM

Before lawmakers could return to Washington, however, Hurricane Katrina ripped through coastal areas of Louisiana, Mississippi, and Alabama on Aug. 29, leaving staggering problems in its wake. The levees that protected New Orleans were breached, and the rising water flooded 80 percent of the city. More than 1,300 people were killed, and tens of thousands of people who had not fled the city sought temporary shelter in the Superdome sports stadium and the city's convention center, where food, water, and sanitation were soon in short supply. The federal government was caught unprepared, and Americans watched round-the-clock coverage as people sought help that did not come. The public seemed to know more about the deteriorating conditions than did the federal government. Disillusionment and anger grew over the slow response by governments at all levels.

Lawmakers cut short their vacations and returned to Washington. Within ten days of the disaster, two supplemental spending bills totaling $62.3 billion were enacted (PL 109-61; PL 109-62). In addition lawmakers enacted many bills—either individually or as parts of other measures that became law—aimed at cutting red tape and addressing myriad problems facing hurricane victims, from housing evacuees, to education for relocated students, to health care for poor people who no longer had addresses, to the need to relocate federal courts and provide temporary identification for those whose possessions were lost in the disaster. Republican leaders in both the House and Senate announced hearings or investigations to look into government actions before and after Katrina. Democrats boycotted the panels, arguing that an outside, impartial commission should be created. "The Republican Congress will not investigate this Republican administration," House Minority Leader Nancy Pelosi, D-Calif., predicted. *(Katrina, pp. 79, 80, 787, 789)*

In many ways Katrina blew in a perfect storm for Republican legislators. Almost everything that lawmakers would do for the rest of the year would be colored in some way by Katrina and by Hurricane Rita, which hit the Texas and Louisiana Gulf Coast a month later on Sept. 24, doing major damage to the nation's oil and gas infrastructure. Republicans faced the added danger that public dismay over the Bush administration's response to the calamity would converge with the growing disillusionment over war in Iraq and anger at the climbing cost of gasoline. For nearly two years public opinion polls had shown growing dissatisfaction with the war and with the direction the country was headed. Bush's approval rating fell from just above 50 percent in January 2005 to the low 40s in September.

It did not help that DeLay had to step aside as majority leader Sept. 28, following his indictment by a Texas grand jury in a campaign fund-raising scandal. DeLay vowed to return to power after he cleared his name of what he said were baseless charges. Along with several other Republicans and some Democrats, DeLay was also being questioned in the media about his connections to Washington lobbyist Jack Abramoff who was already under investigation by the Justice Department. By the end of the year DeLay's political future seemed to be in serious doubt.

In the wake of Katrina and mindful of midterm elections coming in 2006, Republican lawmakers, whether moderate or conservative, began looking to their political futures, and fissures in the party came into the open.

CONGRESSIONAL LEADERSHIP, 2005–2009

109th Congress

Senate

President Pro Tempore: Ted Stevens, R-Alaska
Majority Leader: Bill Frist, R-Tenn.
Majority Whip: Mitch McConnell, R-Ky.
Republican Conference Chair: Rick Santorum, R-Pa.
Republican Conference Secretary: Kay Bailey Hutchison, R-Texas

Minority Leader: Harry Reid, D-Nev.
Minority Whip: Richard J. Durbin, D-Ill.
Democratic Conference Secretary: Debbie Stabenow, D-Mich.

House

Speaker of the House: J. Dennis Hastert, R-Ill.
Majority Leader: Tom DeLay, R-Texas/John A. Boehner, R-Ohio[1]
Majority Whip: Roy Blunt, R-Mo.
Chair of the Republican Conference: Deborah Pryce, R-Ohio

Minority Leader: Nancy Pelosi, D-Calif.
Minority Whip: Steny H. Hoyer, D-Md.
Democratic Caucus Chairman: Robert Menendez, D-N.J./James E. Clyburn, D-S.C.[2]

110th Congress

Senate

President Pro Tempore: Robert C. Byrd, D-W.Va.
Majority Leader: Harry Reid, D-Nev.
Majority Whip: Richard J. Durbin, D-Ill.
Democratic Caucus Vice Chairman: Charles E. Schumer, D-N.Y.
Democratic Policy Committee Chairman: Byron L. Dorgan, D-N.D.

Minority Leader: Mitch McConnell, R-Ky.
Minority Whip: Trent Lott, R-Miss./John Kyl, R-Ariz.[3]
Republican Conference Chairman: John Kyl, R-Ariz./Lamar Alexander, R-Tenn.[3]

House

Speaker of the House: Nancy Pelosi, D-Calif.
Majority Leader: Steny H. Hoyer, D-Md.
Majority Whip: James E. Clyburn, D-S.C.
Democratic Caucus Chairman: Rahm Emanuel III, D-Ill.

Minority Leader: John A. Boehner, R-Ohio
Minority Whip: Roy Blunt, R-Mo.
Republican Conference Chairman: Adam H. Putnam, R-Fla.

NOTES: [1] DeLay announced on Jan. 7, 2006, that he was permanently stepping down from his position as majority leader (he had temporarily stepped aside in September 2005 after being indicted by a Texas grand jury on conspiracy charges associated with campaign financing). DeLay was succeeded by Boehner who was elected majority leader by the Republican caucus on Feb. 2, 2006.

[2] After winning election as New Jersey governor in November 2005, former senator Jon R. Corzine appointed Menendez to the Senate seat that Corzine had left vacant. Menendez took his seat on Jan. 18, 2006, and was elected to a full six-year term in November 2006. He was succeeded as House Democratic Caucus chairman by Clyburn.

[3] Lott, who had been minority whip in 2007, resigned his Senate seat officially on Dec. 18, 2007, to avoid new lobbying rules for former members of Congress that went into effect January 2008. The Senate Republican caucus Dec. 6, 2007, elected Kyl to replace Lott as minority whip and elected Alexander to succeed Kyl as conference chairman.

With Democrats demanding, and for the most part getting, strict adherence to party discipline, GOP leaders had to keep their caucus in tight lockstep—a feat they could not always accomplish, especially in the Senate. Toward the end of the year the Republican caucus was badly fragmented and scrambling for direction and a unified message.

Democrats meanwhile sought to take political advantage of the Republicans' problems, particularly the growing dissatisfaction with the administration's conduct of the Iraq War, and to call attention to the "culture of corruption" they said the GOP had spawned in the nation's capital.

RESHAPING THE SUPREME COURT

Nevertheless, Republicans were able to win some significant victories in the last half of the year, notably confirmation of two new justices to the Supreme Court. *(Court nominations, p. 728)*

After Sandra Day O'Connor, the first woman on the Court, announced her retirement on July 1, the president chose John G. Roberts Jr., a federal appeals court judge, to replace her. Hearings on his confirmation were scheduled for Sept. 6, but on Sept. 3 ailing chief justice William H. Rehnquist died. Bush quickly nominated Roberts to serve as the seventeenth chief justice, and the Senate easily confirmed Roberts on Sept. 29.

Roberts's smooth confirmation was a much-needed victory for Bush, but within days the president undercut himself by announcing his selection of White House counsel Harriet Miers to take O'Connor's seat on the Court. Miers, a Texas lawyer before she followed Bush to the White House in 2001, had little in her background to indicate where she stood on most issues. Democrats criticized the choice, pointing out that Miers lacked any background in constitutional law. Those on the political right, who had been counting on Bush to pick a proven conservative with a clear record on issues such as abortion, were outraged. Bush was ultimately forced to withdraw the nomination. It was the most emphatic rejection yet from a Republican-run Congress that had mostly deferred to Bush and his agenda throughout his presidency. The implosion of Miers's nomination also revealed disarray and divisions within the broader GOP coalition, with Bush looking more and more like a lame duck president just months after his reelection.

Bush moved quickly to assuage his allies on the right by tapping conservative federal appellate judge Samuel A. Alito Jr. to replace O'Connor. Although liberals were not happy with the appointment, Alito had a sound legal record, and he was confirmed in January 2006.

WAR WEARINESS

In no area was the growing disconnect between Bush and congressional Republicans more evident than on the conduct of the war in Iraq and the administration's secrecy about the war on terrorism. On Nov. 15, 2005, the Senate voted overwhelmingly to adopt a Republican leadership amendment to the defense authorization bill requiring the president to send Congress quarterly unclassified reports on the course of the war and on progress toward withdrawing U.S. forces there. The amendment also stated that 2006 should be a turning point in the war. The Republican amendment was offered as an alternative to a Democratic proposal that was nearly identical except for an additional provision requiring the Pentagon to set a schedule for a phased withdrawal from Iraq. That amendment was rejected 58–40. The Republican version passed on a **key vote of 79–19 (R 41–13; D 37–6; I 1–0)** Passage of the Republican amendment was widely seen as a signal that senators in both parties, a majority of whom had authorized the intervention, were beginning to have concerns about the course of the war. *(2005 key votes, p. 915)*

Tension over the war ratcheted up two days later, when Rep. John P. Murtha of Pennsylvania, the ranking Democrat on the House Defense Appropriations Subcommittee and a decorated former marine who had voted for the war, called for a withdrawal of troops over the next six months. "The military has done everything that has been asked of them. The U.S. cannot accomplish anything further in Iraq militarily," Murtha said. "It is time to bring them home." Murtha's comments were widely seen as putting new political pressure on the administration to start bringing at least some troops home before the November 2006 midterm elections.

Meanwhile, reports of abuse at military detention centers had prompted the Senate in early October to add language to the fiscal 2006 defense appropriations bill calling for a ban on "cruel, inhuman, or degrading" treatment of detainees. Sen. John McCain, R-Ariz., the author of the amendment and a former prisoner of war who had been tortured by the North Vietnamese, also succeeded in attaching the language to the defense authorization bill. Despite intense White House pressure, including a visit by Vice President Dick Cheney, McCain refused to back down.

With House leaders opposed to the amendment and the White House threatening to veto any legislation that contained it, Senate leaders held back the two defense bills. Then, on Dec. 14, the House on a **key vote of 308–122 (R 107–121; D 200–1; I 1–0)** instructed its conferees to accept the McCain amendment. The next day Bush reversed course and accepted the language in an Oval Office meeting with McCain, who agreed to add protections for U.S. interrogators who were performing "officially authorized" actions. *(2005 key votes, p. 915)*

Administration secrecy about its actions in its "global war on terror" also sparked controversy. In early November the Senate voted to demand a classified report on U.S.-run secret detention facilities overseas. The move came in response to a *Washington Post* report about a secret Central Intelligence Agency (CIA) system of overseas prisons for terrorists. The House voted to add the provision to the defense authorization bill, but it was dropped in conference.

In mid-December the *New York Times* ran a story revealing that the president in 2002 had authorized the National Security Agency to monitor, without court permission, overseas telephone calls by U.S. citizens. Angry reaction spilled into Senate debate on a bill to reauthorize the provisions of the Patriot Act that focused on enhanced surveillance powers. Four Republicans joined nearly all Democrats to reject cloture, blocking a vote on the conference report on the reauthorizing legislation in that chamber. With the Patriot Act provisions set to expire at the end of the year, Bush and Frist reversed an earlier refusal to consider a short-term bill and settled for a five-week extension. The conference report was passed early in 2006 after the White House agreed to three relatively minor changes.

APPROPRIATIONS, SPENDING CUTS

For the only time in Bush's second term, Congress managed to approve a budget and pass all the regular appropriations bills before adjourning for the year. Tight limits on discretionary spending made it particularly difficult to muster support for the labor, health, and human services, and education spending bill (PL 109-149). House leaders suffered an embarrassing defeat shortly before Thanksgiving, when twenty-two Republicans joined Democrats in rejecting the conference report on the bill. Members were angry over the elimination of their individual earmarks and reduced spending for health care and education. Congress eventually passed a slightly modified version of the measure. The defense spending bill also did not pass until the last minute. Still, when all the spending bills were finished, Congress had made the first reduction in nondefense discretionary spending since the administration of Ronald Reagan.

Congressional Republicans also pushed through the first cuts in entitlement spending since 1997. The biggest savings came from changes to federal student loan programs, Medicare, and Medicaid. With Democrats almost uniformly opposed to the cuts, GOP leaders had to walk a fine line between their conservatives who wanted even deeper cuts and moderate Republicans who opposed reduction in Medicaid and other aid for the poor. The final bill (PL 109-171), which was not cleared until early 2006, cut mandatory spending by about $39 billion over five years, far less than conservatives wanted and the White House had requested.

CHAOTIC END TO THE SESSION

The session became increasingly chaotic as it dragged into December. House Democrats remained united on vote after vote, leaving the interim Republican leadership to assemble separate majorities for each roll call, trading provisions in one bill for votes on another. One casualty was the long-stymied GOP goal of opening portions of Alaska's Arctic National Wildlife Refuge (ANWR) to oil and gas drilling. The budget resolution passed early in the year had included language to prevent a Senate filibuster of the ANWR provisions, and the Senate version of the mandatory spending cut bill contained the provisions. But House leaders concluded they could not get enough voters from moderate Republicans to get the conference report on entitlement cuts through their chamber as long as the provisions remained. An attempt to move the ANWR provisions to the defense spending bill also failed, killing the issue for yet another year. *(ANWR, p. 474)*

An unexpected addition to the year-end mix was an immigration bill, introduced in the House on Dec. 6, marked up by the House Judiciary committee on Dec. 8, and passed on the House floor on Dec. 16. The bill, which focused on border security and criminal penalties for illegal immigrants, highlighted deep divisions between legislators, both Republicans and Democrats, on the question of immigration and presaged a bitter debate that would take place in 2006.

The Political Year

Three special elections were held to fill House vacancies in 2005, but there were no partisan turnovers. The Republicans held two of the seats, the Democrats one. One Senate vacancy, created when Democrat Jon Corzine was elected governor of New Jersey, was filled in early 2006 by a Democrat. In the only other gubernatorial race in 2005, Democrats held on to the governorship of Virginia. One vacancy in the House remained to be filled at the end of the year; it was created when Rep. Randy "Duke" Cunningham, R-Calif., resigned, effective Dec. 1, after pleading guilty to bribery and tax evasion. Cunningham was subsequently sentenced to more than eight years in prison. *(Membership changes table, p. 993)*

House Special Elections

In Ohio's 2nd District Republican Jean Schmidt, president of Right to Life of Greater Cincinnati, won an Aug. 2 special election with 52 percent of the vote against Democratic attorney Paul Hackett, a marine veteran of the Iraq War who had sharply criticized Bush's handling of that conflict. Because the district had been reliably Republican, Democrats viewed Schmidt's narrow victory as an indicator of weakening support for the president and his policies. Schmidt, whose election brought the number of women in the House to a record sixty-seven, replaced Rob Portman, who had resigned on April 29 upon his confirmation as the U.S. trade representative.

Two special elections were held in California in 2005. Democrat Doris Matsui won a special election on March 8 with 69 percent of the vote against eleven opponents in the 5th District. Her husband, Robert Matsui, had represented the district until his death on Jan. 1, 2005. Matsui became the forty-fourth widow—thirty-six in the House and eight in the Senate—to directly succeed a husband in Congress. Born in a World War II internment camp for Japanese Americans, she also brought the number of Asian Americans in the 109th Congress to six, a record.

In California's 48th District Republican John Campbell won a Dec. 6 special election to replace Christopher Cox, who had held the seat since 1989 but resigned on Aug. 2 after winning Senate confirmation to serve as the chairman of the Securities and Exchange Commission. Campbell won only 45 percent of the vote in the three-way race. Jim Gilchrist, a co-founder of the Minuteman Project that solicited volunteers to conduct surveillance along the Mexican border, won 25 percent running under the banner of the American Independent Party. Democrat Steve Young, an attorney, won 28 percent of the vote.

Gubernatorial Elections

Democrat Tim Kaine won the Virginia governor's seat with 52 percent of the vote against Republican Jerry Kilgore, a former state attorney general. Kaine succeeded Mark Warner, also a Democrat, who was ineligible to run for another term.

In New Jersey, Sen. Jon Corzine won election as governor with 53 percent of the vote, nine percentage points ahead of his opponent, Republican businessman Doug

Forrester. Corzine was only the sixth person since 1913, when the direct election of senators began, to leave the Senate in the middle of his term to take up a governorship. The two most recent members of the group were Frank H. Murkowski of Alaska in 2002 and Pete Wilson of California in 1990. As a member of that tiny club, Corzine also had the extraordinary power to pick his senatorial successor.

On Dec. 9, 2005 Corzine announced that he had chosen Rep. Robert Menendez, a fellow liberal who had been chairman of the House Democratic Caucus since 2003, to fill the final year of the Senate term. When Menendez took office on Jan. 18, 2006, he became only the sixth Hispanic senator in U.S. history, and the third in the 109th Congress. Republican Mel Martinez of Florida and Democrat Ken Salazar of Colorado joined the Senate in 2005.

2006

The Legislative Year

With the midterm election and control of the next Congress on lawmakers' minds, the second session of the 109th Congress was a time of partisan posturing and limited accomplishments. Indeed, several measures that had been stalled before the election recess were cleared in the final days of the lame duck session, after the election, which turned control of both chambers over to the Democrats. Some of the more significant pieces of legislation cleared during the regular session were holdovers from 2005 that had been all but completed before the clock ran out that year.

Republican leaders were dealt a tough hand, starting with the unpopularity of their standard bearer, President George W. Bush, and the deepening public dismay over the war. The year also opened with an unpleasant reminder of the ethics problems that had dogged them in 2005: Tom DeLay of Texas announced that he would not try to reclaim his job as House majority leader, a post he had surrendered in September 2005 after being indicted in Texas for alleged political fund-raising violations. DeLay had used his leadership position to keep his troops in line and to drive much of the Republican agenda. His replacement, John A. Boehner of Ohio, an architect of the original Republican revolution in 1993, had to hit the ground running, and the new House leadership never gained the kind of control DeLay had exerted over the sometimes fractious GOP rank and file.

Democrats, on the other hand, were united. That was particularly noticeable in the House, where the rules for debate favor the majority. Minority Leader Nancy Pelosi, D-Calif., held her rank and file together and was able to force Republicans to come up with a majority for legislation within their fractured caucus. Although Republicans still prevailed most of the time in party unity votes—those in which a majority of one party voted against a majority of the other—Democrats in both chambers voted as a unanimous bloc more often than did Republicans. It was the first time that had happened in the House since 1986.

The GOP leadership's job became more difficult as the year went on, sometimes because of its own missteps. Republican lawmakers became increasingly independent and divided as they looked to their political needs in advance of the election. Republicans backed off on issues they had said were top priorities, starting with an overhaul of their lobbying and ethics rules, and they all but ignored some issues that their constituents made clear they considered vital, such as the continuing increase in health care costs. House and Senate leaders sometimes seemed not to coordinate or to recognize what was politically necessary or legislatively possible in the other chamber. Decisions about issues to focus on and how to use floor time came back to haunt them. "They spent so much time on issues like gay marriage that they knew weren't going to pass," said James A. Thurber, director of the Center for Congressional and Presidential Studies at American University. "Boy, wouldn't they like to have that week back?"

Their sparse record damaged Republicans' hopes in the fall election. Voters in November closed the books, for the immediate future, on an era of GOP control of the Capitol—one that had lasted a dozen years, except for eighteen months in 2001 and 2002 when the Democrats held a slight edge in the Senate. It also ended the Speakership of J. Dennis Hastert of Illinois, who held the job longer than any House Republican in history.

BUDGET BREAKDOWN, APPROPRIATIONS COLLAPSE

The widening rift between Republican conservatives and moderates that would limit their options, especially on fiscal issues, for the entire year became apparent in February, as the House tried to clear a $38.8 billion five-year package of cuts to entitlement programs (PL 109-171) that had been all but finished at the end of the first session in 2005. Nearly every Democrat and some Republican moderates opposed the bill because it cut programs for the poor, and Senate Democrats had used a procedural ploy to force it back to the House for one last vote. With no Democratic support, the leadership was barely able to corral enough Republicans to win a 216–214 victory.

CONGRESS IN 2006

The second session of the 109th Congress began at noon on Jan. 3, 2006, and ended when the Senate adjourned *sine die* at 4:39 a.m. on Dec. 9. The House had adjourned *sine die* at 3:17 a.m. earlier the same day. The session lasted 341 days. The Senate met on 138 days, for a total of 1,028 hours. The House met on 101 days, for a total of 850 hours.

There were 4,753 bills and resolutions introduced during the 2006 session, compared with 8,319 in 2005 and 3,656 in 2004. Congress cleared 248 bills in 2006 that were signed into public law. President George W. Bush vetoed one bill, the first of his presidency. *(Public laws table, p. 16; Presidential vetoes, p. 1039)*

During 2006, the House took 540 votes (not counting quorum calls), 129 fewer than in 2005. The Senate took 279 recorded votes, 87 fewer than in 2005. *(Recorded votes table, p. 21)*

The fiscal 2007 budget resolution ran into the same political crosswinds. The House version (H Con Res 376) barely survived a floor vote in May. To get it through, House leaders had to promise additional funding for labor, health, and education programs demanded by moderates. Fiscal conservatives insisted on tighter budget rules, including limits on supplemental spending (which did not count against spending targets), as their price for support. Republican appropriators, however, fiercely resisted any restrictions on their discretion over supplemental appropriations.

The Senate adopted its budget resolution (S Con Res 83) in March, after stretching the discretionary spending limit by $9 billion and allowing another $7 billion in advance appropriations that did not count against the cap. The Senate version also counted on $3 billion in revenue from opening the Arctic National Wildlife Refuge to oil drilling, a proposal that was anathema to enough GOP moderates that it could not have survived in the House.

Recognizing the deep party splits, Republican leaders did not even try to hold a conference. Instead, each chamber separately adopted an $872.8 billion limit for fiscal 2007 discretionary spending, which allowed them to proceed with the appropriations process.

But on its most basic task—allocating the taxpayers' money through the regular appropriations bills—Congress came close to a meltdown. GOP leaders managed to clear just two of eleven bills, those for the Defense Department (PL 109-289) and the Homeland Security Department (PL 109-295). They left the other nine—for domestic programs, foreign operations, and military construction—for the Democrats to handle in the 110th Congress. A short-term bill (PL 109-383) kept the affected departments and agencies operating through Feb. 17, 2007.

The House passed all but one of its spending bills by the end of June. The last one—for the Departments of Labor, Health and Human Services (HHS) and Education—had multiple problems, the biggest of which was a minimum wage increase, attached by the Appropriations Committee, that guaranteed opposition from Republican conservatives. House leaders might have been able to pass it with a combination of Democratic and moderate Republican votes, but they were not willing to do that.

Senate appropriators could not fit their bills under the $872.8 billion spending cap and still hope to pass them. The Appropriations Committee approved all eleven of its bills by cutting about $9 billion from defense to fill out the domestic spending measures.

Although the Senate bills were ready in July, Majority Leader Bill Frist, R-Tenn., did not schedule much floor time for them; the Homeland Security bill was the only one to pass before the August recess. September was devoted to national security legislation in both chambers, which brought final action on the homeland security and defense spending bills.

Number of Public Laws Enacted, 1975–2008

Year	*Public Laws*	*Year*	*Public Laws*
1975	205	1992	347
1976	383	1993	210
1977	223	1994	255
1978	410	1995	88
1979	187	1996	245
1980	426	1997	153
1981	145	1998	241
1982	328	1999	170
1983	215	2000	410
1984	408	2001	136
1985	240	2002	241
1986	424	2003	198
1987	242	2004	300
1988	471	2005	169
1989	240	2006	248
1990	410	2007	175
1991	243	2008	285

But to avoid a threatened veto of the defense bill, Senate appropriators had to agree to restore $5 billion of the $9 billion they had borrowed for domestic programs. That left them with the task of shaving $5 billion from domestic bills such as labor-HHS-education, which would have significantly undercut support for them. Frist opted to hold off. In the end, the Senate passed only one more fiscal 2007 bill—for military construction and veterans affairs.

After the election, the appropriators planned to resume work, assembling at least some of the bills into an omnibus package. But conservative Senate Republicans blocked the military construction-Veterans Affairs (VA) appropriations bill to keep it from turning into an omnibus stuffed with earmarks. The result was the decision to put much of the budget on autopilot and hand the problem to the next Congress.

A FEW SUCCESSES

Bush and the Republicans had one early victory on Jan. 31, when the Senate confirmed Samuel A. Alito Jr. to replace retiring justice Sandra Day O'Connor on the Supreme Court. Liberals were unhappy with Alito's conservative record as a federal appeals court judge, but his proven competence on the bench gave them little traction, and he was confirmed 58–42.

Congress also cleared a $70 billion, five-year tax cut package in May (PL 109-222), after months of negotiations aimed at accommodating the priorities of the conservative and moderate wings of the GOP. The bill mainly extended tax benefits enacted in the 2001 and 2003 laws. It also included an extension of lower tax rates on capital gains and dividends, which was the House Republicans' top priority, and a "patch" to prevent millions of middle-class taxpayers from falling under the alternative minimum tax

(AMT), which was intended to target the wealthy. The AMT proposal was critical to Senate Democrats and GOP moderates.

The only other tax bill that cleared was a set of extensions for popular tax credits, deductions, and other benefits for businesses and individuals. Several attempts to send Bush a permanent reduction in the estate tax were unsuccessful.

In July Bush signed a twenty-five year reauthorization of the landmark Voting Rights Act of 1965 in a ceremony on the South Lawn of the White House. The act was not due to expire until August 2007, but Republican leaders wanted to renew it before the 2006 midterm election. *(Voting rights passage, p. 696)*

The reauthorization began as a bipartisan effort, but it nearly foundered in the House, where it was delayed for several months by southern Republicans and opponents of bilingual voter assistance. The bill came to the floor only after leaders decided to allow opponents to offer four amendments, any one of which, if adopted, might have killed the bill. All the amendments were voted down, although some fell only because Democrats voted with the Republican leadership. A majority of Republicans voted for three of the amendments against the wishes of their leaders, reflecting the relative weakness of the GOP leadership after the departure of DeLay, whose iron grip on the Republican caucus had usually crushed such internal discord.

Also before the August recess, lawmakers overcame months of painful conference negotiations to clear a measure requiring that companies fully fund their pension plans and pay higher premiums to the Pension Benefit Guaranty Corporation (PBGC), the government agency that insured private pensions and that was facing record deficits.

IMMIGRATION DIVIDE

Few, if any, issues divided Republicans in the 109th Congress more than immigration. Despite GOP control of both chambers, the intraparty split doomed an immigration overhaul that was a White House priority. The issue pitted probusiness Republicans, who said the nation's economy depended on immigrant labor, against cultural and social conservatives, who said illegal immigrants stole American jobs, threatened security, and eroded the nation's predominant culture.

The House had passed a bill (HR 4437) in December 2005 that focused exclusively on border security and criminal penalties for illegal immigrants and those who aided them. Bush, however, made it clear he wanted Congress to send him a broader bill.

In January a coalition of business, labor, religious, and health care organizations led by the lobbying group, the U.S. Chamber of Commerce, called on the Senate to reject the House plan and pass a comprehensive measure that included a temporary guest-worker program and offered some means for the estimated 12 million illegal immigrants in the United States to earn permanent legal status. In major cities around the country, tens of thousands of Hispanics and others marched to protest the House proposals.

After six markups and two weeks of floor debate, the Senate passed a bipartisan bill (S 2611) in May that combined border security and workplace enforcement with a guest-worker program and a path to citizenship for most of the illegal immigrants in the country. John McCain, R-Ariz., and Edward M. Kennedy, D-Mass., joined forces to shepherd the bill through the Senate, where it won the support of twenty-three Republicans and all but four Democrats.

House Republicans quickly labeled the bill "amnesty" for illegal immigrants and called it the work of Democrats. They refused to convene a conference to negotiate a final bill and instead held two-dozen field hearings around the country during the August recess. When they returned to Washington, they declared that they would not accept the Senate bill. With broad legislation off the table, House GOP leaders instead pressed for a bill to build a physical and electronic fence along large stretches of the U.S.-Mexican border. The measure cleared just before lawmakers left Washington to campaign (PL 109-367).

REPUBLICAN OVERREACHING

House Republicans sacrificed, or came close to sacrificing, several goals because they were unwilling to settle for what they could get from the Senate.

A case in point was legislation to limit teenage abortions. The Senate passed a bill (S 403) in July to make it a federal crime to take a minor across state lines for an abortion in violation of her home state's parental consent laws. It was a breakthrough for abortion-rights opponents: the Senate had declined to take up similar, House-passed bills in previous Congresses. Moreover, the Senate passed the bill with sixty-five votes, more than enough to end a filibuster.

However, in what turned out to be a tactical mistake, House leaders chose not to clear the Senate bill. Instead, the House sent it back with a new section requiring that doctors give parents twenty-four hours' notice before performing an abortion. The additional language lost the support of centrist Senate Democrats, who said it would not give enough protection to girls who were victims of incest or parental abuse, and the measure died when the Senate was unable to choke off a filibuster. Republicans had to leave for the campaign trail without the abortion bill, which was a priority for social conservatives.

A bill to open sections of the Gulf of Mexico to oil drilling nearly met a similar fate. The House passed an ambitious measure (HR 4761) in June that would have opened most of the nation's coastline to drilling. Just before the August recess, the Senate passed a narrower bill that would

REPUBLICAN "AMERICAN VALUES" AGENDA

With the 2006 midterm election in mind, Republican leaders held votes on a trio of measures that were dear to the party's socially conservative base but had no prospects of making it through the Congress. Two were proposed constitutional amendments: to ban flag burning and prohibit same-sex marriages. The third was a bill to bar most federal courts from hearing challenges to the Pledge of Allegiance. *(Details, pp. 707, 708, 709)*

To become part of the Constitution, an amendment first must pass by a two-thirds majority in both chambers. Then three-quarters of the states, or thirty-eight, must ratify it within seven years.

Flag Desecration

A proposed constitutional amendment to give Congress the power to prohibit desecration of the U.S. flag (S J Res 12) died at the end of the session, after the Senate fell one vote shy of the required two-thirds majority. The House had passed a virtually identical resolution in 2005 (H J Res 10).

Conservatives had been pushing for such an amendment since 1990, when the Supreme Court, in *United States v. Eichman,* struck down a federal law (PL 101-131) that banned flag desecration. The 1990 law had been enacted after the high court ruled in 1989, in *Texas v. Johnson,* that the conviction under a Texas state law for desecration of a flag by a protester at the 1984 Republican National Convention in Dallas violated the First Amendment.

Supporters argued that an amendment was necessary to wrest control of the Constitution from unelected judges. Opponents, mainly Democrats, decried the debate as politically motivated. Although the president has no formal role in the constitutional amendment process, the White House issued a supportive statement calling the flag "a cherished symbol of national unity."

The House had passed similar resolutions six times since 1995; the lowest level of support for the amendment came in 2005, when the measure passed, 286–130. The Senate had not voted on a flag-burning amendment since 2000, when the measure fell four votes short of the two-thirds margin required. Though the 2006 resolution attracted the largest number of "yeas" yet in the Senate, the 66–34 vote on June 27 was not enough.

Gay Marriage

Supporters of a constitutional amendment aimed at banning gay marriage fell eleven votes short of the number needed to overcome a procedural hurdle in the Senate in June 2006. The House rejected a companion measure in July. The proposed constitutional amendment would have defined marriage as "the union of a man and a woman."

Senate proponents could not muster the three-fifths majority required to limit debate on a motion to take up the resolution (S J Res 1). The vote on June 7 was 49–48. Seven Republicans voted against invoking cloture, or limiting debate; two Democrats voted in favor of doing so. Proponents made a net pickup of one vote from the last time the chamber had held a procedural vote on the issue, in 2004.

Despite the defeat of the measure in the Senate, House Republican leaders put their chamber's resolution—(H J Res 88), sponsored by Marilyn Musgrave, R-Colo.—to a vote in July as part of the GOP's American "values" agenda. The measure was brought up under an expedited procedure that allowed no amendments but required a two-thirds vote. It was rejected 236–187 on July 18, falling forty-six votes short of the threshold for passage.

Pledge of Allegiance

The House passed a bill (HR 2389) to bar most federal courts, including the Supreme Court, from hearing constitutional challenges to the Pledge of Allegiance. The legislation was aimed at preventing federal judges from ruling that the phrase "under God" in the pledge was unconstitutional. The bill, however, went no further and died at the end of the session.

In 2002 the U.S. Court of Appeals for the Ninth Circuit ruled that the phrase "under God," which Congress inserted in the pledge in 1954 (PL 83-396), amounted to an unconstitutional establishment of religion. The Supreme Court reversed the Ninth Circuit in June 2004 on technical, not constitutional, grounds.

The House passed the bill 260–167 on July 19, 2006, after the Judiciary Committee deadlocked 15–15 over sending the measure to the floor.

The Senate, which was reluctant to consider legislation to strip federal courts of jurisdiction over other hot-button issues, did not consider the bill.

open 8.3 million acres in the eastern Gulf of Mexico, ban exploration until at least 2022 within 125 miles of the Florida panhandle, and direct a portion of the revenue from new leases to coastal states and a federal conservation fund. Protection of the Florida coast was particularly important because the state had blocked past efforts to expand drilling in the Gulf out of concern for its beaches and tourist industry.

Senate negotiators said the bill represented a delicate balance between competing interests that would collapse if the House tried to amend it. Trade groups representing the agriculture, petrochemical, and utilities industries joined oil and gas interests in pressuring House leaders to accept the Senate bill, arguing that it was the best deal they could get. Gulf Coast lawmakers and organizations also pushed for the Senate bill because of the promised revenue for their states.

But House negotiators held out, saying the Senate version would accomplish little more than what the Bush administration had already proposed doing administratively. Finally, with the session coming to a close, they agreed to attach a version of the Senate bill to the tax and trade package that cleared Dec. 9 (PL 109-432). It was the only significant energy legislation enacted during the year.

Frist and Hastert both took out time for other legislation that they knew would never clear but that was important to the party's conservative base. Frist set aside time on the floor in June to allow conservatives to go on record favoring constitutional amendments to ban flag desecration and to prohibit same-sex marriages. The Senate rejected both measures. In July, Hastert held a vote on a companion gay marriage proposal, which was defeated, and passed a bill to bar most federal courts from hearing constitutional challenges to the Pledge of Allegiance, which was not considered in the Senate. *(Social legislation box, p. 18)*

Bush's First Veto

In mid-July, the Senate cleared a bill (HR 810) to lift restrictions on federal funding for embryonic stem cell research, which the House had passed in 2005. Bush had left no doubt that he would veto the legislation, which was anathema to social conservatives who equated the destruction of embryos with abortion. It was also clear that neither chamber had the votes to override him.

In a carefully planned series of events, the Senate passed a second bill that made it illegal to perform research on embryos that were created for that purpose on "fetal farms," although the sponsors acknowledged that such farms did not exist. The House cleared the fetal farms bill the same day. Bush vetoed the bill and signed the fetal farms measure on July 19. The same day, the House fell fifty-one votes short of the two-thirds needed to override the president, and the embryonic stem cell bill died. The veto was the first in Bush's presidency; he issued only twelve in his eight years in office. *(Veto list, p. 1039)*

NATIONAL SECURITY MONTH

With national security issues on voters' minds, and polls showing Democrats within striking distance of taking over the House, Frist and Hastert pushed national security to the top of their agenda when Congress returned after Labor Day. The GOP focus coincided with the fifth anniversary of the Sept. 11, 2001, attacks, and Bush made a series of speeches recalling that day and underscoring Republicans' national security credentials.

The leadership succeeded in clearing the defense and homeland security spending bills, along with a $532.8 billion authorization bill for Pentagon programs and Energy Department nuclear weapons activities (PL 109-364).

But the centerpiece of the month's activities in Congress turned out to be a high-profile battle among Republicans over rules for trying terrorist suspects. Although it ended in success for the White House, the battle raised questions about the conduct of the war in Iraq and highlighted differences within the GOP. Democrats were content to sit back and watch.

The issue landed in Congress's lap after the Supreme Court ruled in June that the military tribunal system Bush had created to try terrorist suspects held at Guantánamo Bay, Cuba, violated both U.S. and international law. Bush, who previously had claimed that as president he had the authority to set up the tribunals, turned to Congress and outlined his proposal in a speech Sept. 6. *(Details, pp. 336, 364, 400, 730)*

The plan won immediate endorsement from GOP leaders in both chambers, who made enactment before the election a top priority. But a trio of influential Republicans on the Senate Armed Services Committee—McCain, John W. Warner of Virginia, and Lindsey Graham of South Carolina—were not ready to sign on. They objected to a plan to reinterpret U.S. obligations under the Geneva Convention. Also at issue were provisions that would allow prosecutors to use classified evidence that the accused could not see, permit trials in which the defendant was not present, and allow the use of evidence obtained through coercion unless a judge said it was unreliable.

Unable to find common ground with the White House, the three marked up their own bill in the Armed Services Committee. The White House launched an intensive lobbying campaign on behalf of its approach, with top officials visiting Capitol Hill and phoning lawmakers. It made for a dramatic standoff: three staunch Republicans with impeccable national security credentials—a Vietnam POW, a former Navy secretary who fought in World War II and Korea, and a former Air Force Reserve military judge—versus the president of the United States.

Finally, with less than ten days before lawmakers were set to leave to campaign, the White House and the three senators reached a deal. The final bill (PL 109-366) dropped Bush's proposals to reinterpret the Geneva Convention and allow defendants to be tried and convicted on the basis of classified evidence they could not see. Bush, however, got much of what he wanted, above all protection for CIA agents who interrogated top terrorist suspects in clandestine overseas facilities. Among provisions that Democrats condemned were the denial of *habeas corpus* rights to detainees and permission to use coerced confessions so long as the treatment occurred before Dec. 30, 2005, and the judge determined that the statements were reliable.

Lawmakers made less progress on another priority: legislation to establish ground rules for a National Security Agency warrantless electronic surveillance program that began in 2002 but only became public in late 2005. The

House passed a bill in September that gave Republicans something to use in the campaign to highlight differences with Democrats. A companion measure approved by the Senate Judiciary Committee never came to the floor.

MORE SCANDAL FOR REPUBLICANS

Although DeLay's departure from Congress early in the year removed a prominent symbol of the Republicans' ethics problems from the public eye, two later incidents kept Republican scandals alive just as legislators were heading out to campaign in what had become a nose-to-nose race for control of the next Congress.

The first involved Rep. Bob Ney, R-Ohio, who had already been implicated in the investigation into the influence-peddling activities of lobbyist Jack Abramoff. Ney had stepped down as chairman of the House Administration Committee in January 2006 under pressure from Hastert. After maintaining his innocence for months, Ney subsequently did an abrupt turnaround in September and pleaded guilty to two federal counts of conspiracy and false statements in the Abramoff investigation.

The more damaging blow for the GOP, however, came from an unexpected direction. On Sept. 29, Rep. Mark Foley, a six-term Republican legislator from Florida, announced his resignation from the House after news organizations disclosed sexually explicit e-mail messages that he had sent to teenage boys who had served as House pages. The scandal quickly moved beyond Foley to envelop the GOP leadership, raising questions about whether the response to earlier evidence of Foley's inappropriate behavior had been timely or assertive, and casting doubts on the ability of Hastert and others to manage the party.

After a year of scandals, the Foley affair seemed to be the last straw, especially for social conservatives who were the GOP's base of support. In a *Time* magazine poll released Oct. 5, 64 percent of respondents said they thought Congress tried to cover up the situation and 25 percent said it would make them "less likely" to vote Republican in the midterm congressional election. In December, after Democrats claimed control of both the House and Senate for the first time since 1994, the House Committee on Standards of Official Conduct concluded its investigation of the Foley incident, finding that Hastert and others had broken no laws or House rules.

ORGANIZING THE 110TH CONGRESS

A week after the 2006 election, legislators returned to Washington to organize for the next Congress. For the most part, the caucus votes suggested that rank-and-file lawmakers in both chambers wanted proven leadership teams made up of veteran members.

House Democrats unanimously elected Nancy Pelosi, a nine-term California representative and minority leader since 2002 to become the first woman Speaker of the House. The caucus then defied Pelosi by voting 149–86 to make their whip, Steny H. Hoyer of Maryland, the new majority leader. Pelosi had endorsed and lobbied vigorously for John Murtha of Pennsylvania because, she said, she thought it would help end the war in Iraq. Murtha's reputation soared in 2005 after he called for a speedy withdrawal of U.S. troops from Iraq. But his long tenure in the House had included a stint as an unindicted co-conspirator in the 1980s Abscam scandal, and he was also a leading procurer of earmarks for his district, a controversial practice in which members wrote funding into spending bills for specific projects. After lambasting Republicans about corruption throughout the campaign, Democrats did not want to start out with even a hint of an ethics problem. *(Abscam scandal, Congress and the Nation Vol. V, p. 931; Congress and the Nation Vol. VI, p. 804; Congress and the Nation Vol. VII, p. 879; Earmarks box, p. 74)*

House Republicans voted to make Boehner the minority leader and Ray Blunt of Missouri the minority whip. Blunt had served as interim majority leader when DeLay first stepped down from that position and lost the election to make the appointment permanent to Boehner earlier in the year. In electing Boehner and Blunt, the Republican caucus rejected leaders of the party's conservative wing by wide margins.

In the Senate, both Harry Reid, D-Nev., and Mitch McConnell, R-Ky., were unopposed in their races to serve as the majority and minority leader, respectively. Democrat Richard J. Durbin of Illinois became the majority whip. Trent Lott, R-Miss., won the job of minority whip, prevailing over Lamar Alexander, R-Tenn., 25–24. Lott's victory was sweet redemption for a man whose long public career had been derailed four years earlier. Just weeks after Republicans voted to return him to the post of majority leader after the 2002 election, he was pressured out of the job after making an off-the-cuff suggestion that the country would have been better off had former senator Strom Thurmond, R-S.C. (1954–2003), won the presidency in 1948 running on his segregationist Dixiecrat platform. Lott contemplated retiring at the time but decided that he could still help funnel much-needed federal largesse to Mississippi, one of the nation's poorest states. Lott eventually resigned from Congress in December 2007.

FINAL FLURRY

A flurry of activity at the end of the 109th Congress, while Republicans were still in control, led to final passage of eight measures on the last day of the session, nearly all of which had been stalled before the election.

In addition to the offshore drilling legislation and the tax break extensions, Congress cleared overhauls of the U.S. Postal Service and the fisheries law, a reauthorization of a law to cope with a bioterrorist attack, renewal of the nation's safety net program for low-income HIV and AIDS patients, a restructuring of the National Institutes of Health, and a measure allowing the administration to go forward with final negotiations on a nuclear cooperation treaty with India.

Recorded Vote Totals

Following are the recorded vote totals between 1953 and 2008. The figures do not include quorum calls. Congress in 2007 set a new record for the highest number of recorded votes ever taken in a single year: 1,619. The year was also the high mark for the House, which took 1,177 recorded votes. The high mark for the Senate was 688 recorded votes in 1976. The 95th Congress (1977–1979) held the record for the most votes taken in a two-year Congress: 2,691.

Year	*House*	*Senate*	*Total*
1953	71	89	160
1954	76	171	247
1955	76	87	163
1956	73	130	203
1957	100	107	207
1958	93	200	293
1959	87	215	302
1960	93	207	300
1961	116	204	320
1962	124	224	348
1963	119	229	348
1964	113	305	418
1965	201	258	459
1966	193	235	428
1967	245	315	560
1968	233	281	514
1969	177	245	422
1970	266	422	688
1971	320	423	743
1972	329	532	861
1973	541	594	1,135
1974	537	544	1,081
1975	612	602	1,214
1976	661	688	1,349
1977	706	635	1,341
1978	834	516	1,350
1979	672	497	1,169
1980	604	531	1,135
1981	353	483	836
1982	459	465	924
1983	498	371	869
1984	408	275	683
1985	439	381	820
1986	451	354	805
1987	488	420	908
1988	451	379	830
1989	368	312	680
1990	510	326	836
1991	428	280	708
1992	473	270	743
1993	597	395	992
1994	497	329	826
1995	867	613	1,480
1996	454	306	760
1997	633	298	931
1998	533	314	847
1999	609	374	983
2000	600	298	898
2001	507	380	887
2002	483	253	736
2003	675	459	1,134
2004	543	216	759
2005	669	366	1,035
2006	540	279	819
2007	1,177	442	1,619
2008	688	215	903

The Political Year

Anger over the war in Iraq, President George W. Bush's unpopularity, several ethics scandals in the Republican-led Congress, and the shortage of congressional accomplishments led voters on Nov. 7, 2006, to turn over control of both chambers of Congress to the Democrats. In a stunning victory, House Democrats won a thirty-seat edge over Republicans, who had controlled that chamber since the party's "conservative revolution" brought the GOP to power in the 1994 elections. In the Senate, Democrats barely eked out a majority, which included two senators who ran and won as independents.

Midterm elections were usually about local politics. Turnover was typically low, and most incumbents seeking reelection, especially in the House, could count on winning. But the war in Iraq and a series of corruption scandals involving Republican legislators allowed Democrats to "nationalize" the 2006 elections to an unusual degree. At a news conference on Nov. 8, President George W. Bush said he was "disappointed" with the results and admitted that he shared "a large part of the responsibility" for his party's losses. Bush also announced that Secretary of Defense Donald H. Rumsfeld was resigning. Rumsfeld's tenure had grown increasingly controversial as the secretary refused to acknowledge publicly that the war in Iraq was not going well.

Meanwhile, the Republicans' ethics scandals had allowed Democrats to brand the GOP as the party of corruption. Democrats, political pundits, and many voters also said the Republican Party had lost its direction in its effort to maintain itself in power. Republicans who had once championed smaller government, these critics said, had enacted a prescription drug entitlement for seniors—the largest expansion of Medicare since it was established in the 1960s—and they had abandoned fiscal responsibility to spend billions on pork barrel projects. Many public opinion polls showed that a majority of the respondents thought the Democrats would do a better job than the Republicans in dealing with the war, immigration, and high gasoline prices, among other issues.

Senate Elections

Going into the 2006 campaign season, Democrats seeking to retake control of the Senate were looking at a seemingly impossible task. They had to win six of the eight at-risk Republican seats, hold on to three seats that Democrats were vacating, and successfully defend fifteen of their incumbents, including four who appeared highly vulnerable. Campaigning largely on dissatisfaction with the president and the Republican-led Congress, Democrats managed to win a one-seat margin. That included forty-nine Democrats, and two men who had run as independents: Vermont's Bernard Sanders, who had always caucused with the Democrats during eight terms in the House and was expected to continue to do so in the Senate;

nnecticut's Joseph I. Lieberman, who lost the cratic primary but won the general election on his independent ballot line and said he would remain a oyal Democrat and should be counted in their ranks.

The election represented the first time since 1994 that Democrats won control of the Senate through the ballot box. Their short-lived majority for part of 2001 and all of 2002 came from the postelection defection of Vermont Republican James M. Jeffords.

The Senate races were so close in Montana and Virginia that the outcome hung in the balance for two days before the Republican incumbents conceded on Nov. 9, erasing the specter of recounts that could have left the two contests in limbo for weeks if not months. All six of the Democratic victories came out of a strategy by Charles E. Schumer, N.Y., chairman of the Democratic Senatorial Campaign Committee, to nationalize the issues and ask voters: Do you want more of the same? "The message of this election came down to one word: change," Schumer said a day after the election. Two years later, that same message would carry a Democrat, Barack Obama, into the Oval Office at the White House.

Montana's Republican senator, Conrad Burns, was the senator most endangered by his ties to convicted lobbyist Jack Abramoff, the central figure in a sweeping influence-peddling scandal that had helped end the congressional career of Tom DeLay, the former powerful House majority leader. Burns's own proclivity for colorful statements did not help his case, and he narrowly lost his reelection bid to organic farmer and state senator Jon Tester. Colorful comments also were a major factor in Republican George Allen's defeat in Virginia. Allen had been a popular one-term governor before his election to the Senate in 2000 and was touted by some as a presidential contender for 2008. Initially, Allen was expected to cruise through a reelection race against his upstart opponent, former Navy secretary Jim Webb. But Allen came under fire for comments deemed racially insensitive by some, and those remarks combined with general disapproval of Congress to give Webb a narrow margin of victory.

Public disapproval of the Republican-led Congress appeared to be the primary factor in the other four Democratic takeovers: Claire McCaskill's defeat of Sen. Jim Talent in Missouri; Rep. Sherrod Brown's victory over Sen. Mike DeWine in Ohio; Bob Casey's ouster of Sen. Rick Santorum in Pennsylvania; and Sheldon Whitehouse's defeat of Sen. Lincoln Chafee in Rhode Island.

Republicans also managed to hold on to their one open seat. Republican Bob Corker, the former mayor of Chattanooga, defeated Democratic representative Harold E. Ford Jr. in a highly competitive race to succeed Bill Frist, the GOP majority leader who said when he won his seat in 1994 that he would stay only two terms. Ford was hoping to become the first African American from the South to win a Senate seat. (A black senator from the South was appointed during Reconstruction.)

The four Democratic seats thought to be vulnerable were in New Jersey, Maryland, Nebraska, and Washington. In New Jersey, Sen. Robert Menendez won a full-term in the Senate against a vigorous challenge by Thomas H. Kean Jr., son of a popular two-term governor. Menendez had been appointed to the Senate seat in January by Democrat Jon Corzine, the previous occupant, who resigned to take over the governor's mansion. In the contest for the open Senate seat in Maryland, where Democrat Paul S. Sarbanes was retiring, ten-term Democratic representative Benjamin L. Cardin defeated Republican lieutenant governor Michael Steele. The first African American elected to statewide office in Maryland, Steele had won the support of several top black Democratic officials who crossed party lines publicly to back him, but their support was not enough to give the Republican the edge in the strongly Democratic state.

Nebraska Democrat Ben Nelson handily defeated Pete Ricketts, a former Ameritrade chief executive officer, to win a second term. In Washington State, Maria Cantwell, who won her 2000 race with just 49 percent of the vote, held on to her seat by defeating Republican businessman Mike McGavick.

Buoyed by their victories in 2006, Democrats were hopeful of strengthening their majority in the 2008 elections when they had to defend just twelve seats against the Republicans' twenty-one.

House Elections

Although the party lineup in the House—233 Democrats to 202 Republicans—was not final until mid-December, it was clear on election night that Democrats had wrested control of the House from the Republicans for the first time since 1994. In doing so, the Democrats successfully retained every seat they defended—a feat neither party had accomplished in nearly seventy years.

Illustrating the depth of voter frustration with the Bush administration and scandal-tainted congressional Republicans, the Democrats registered seat gains across the nation. The Democratic upswing even spread to reliably Republican-leaning states such as Kansas, where Rep. Jim Ryun lost his reelection bid two days after President Bush campaigned for him in Topeka. "From sea to shining sea, the American people voted for change," a jubilant Nancy Pelosi said.

The Democratic gains were particularly notable in the Northeast. In New Hampshire both Republican incumbents were swept out of office, giving the state's two House seats to Democrats for the first time since 1912. In New York Democrats defeated two Republican incumbents, nearly defeated three others, and won the seat of a retiring GOP moderate. Only six Republicans remained in the twenty-nine member New York House delegation after the election. The Democrats also unseated four GOP House members from Pennsylvania.

Republican moderates bore a disproportionate brunt of the party's losses. Rep. Jim Leach, a thirty-year House veteran and one of the party's most prominent and widely respected moderates was defeated by Democratic college professor David Loebsack in a Democrat-leaning district in Iowa that had nonetheless reelected Leach by handsome margins in most of his previous fifteen elections. Other GOP moderates who lost reelection included Nancy L. Johnson and Rob Simmons of Connecticut and Michael G. Fitzpatrick of Pennsylvania. Fitzpatrick was defeated by lawyer Patrick Murphy, one of a handful of Iraq War veterans who were victorious on Election Day.

Several seats held by Republicans caught up in corruption scandals were also turned over to the Democrats. The top prize might have been the suburban Houston seat once held by former House majority Leader DeLay. The seat was won by former Democratic representative Nick Lampson, who had been a casualty of a DeLay-engineered redistricting map in 2004. Democrat Zack Spence, an elected municipal attorney, won the seat in Ohio that had been held by Republican Bob Ney. The Republican pleaded guilty in August to federal corruption charges that stemmed from an investigation of his ties to the Abramoff scandal, but Ney did not resign his seat until just weeks before the election.

In Pennsylvania Democrats picked up the seat held by Republican Don Sherwood, whose reputation had been marred by an extramarital affair. Sherwood had admitted to the affair but denied the woman's allegations of physical abuse. In Florida Democrat Tim Mahoney won the seat that Republican Mark Foley resigned in September after disclosures that he sent inappropriate messages to teenage boys who had served as House pages. Mahoney would lose the seat just two years later after being caught in his own sex scandal. One Democrat caught up in a federal corruption probe held onto his seat. William J. Jefferson won a ninth term in his New Orleans district despite being forced to give up his seat on the powerful House Ways and Means Committee in the wake of bribery allegations. Jefferson would eventually lose his seat in the 2008 Democratic primary elections.

Statehouse Elections

Democrats also ran well in gubernatorial races, picking up six seats formerly held by Republicans. When all the ballots were counted, Democrats held the governorships in twenty-eight states—their first gubernatorial majority since 1994. The elections broadened the Democratic base and, potentially, the party's regional influence.

Only one incumbent was defeated: Maryland Republican governor Robert L. Ehrlich Jr. lost to Baltimore mayor Martin O'Malley. Among the newly elected governors were Democrat Patrick Duval of Massachusetts, who became the second African American ever elected governor (the first was L. Douglas Wilder of Virginia in 1989), and Democrat Eliot Spitzer of New York, the former state attorney general who was active in suing polluters and moving against abuses in Wall Street brokerage houses and insurance companies. (Spitzer resigned in March 2008 after he was caught up in a prostitution scandal; he was succeeded by Lt. Gov. David Paterson, an African American Democrat.)

Democrats also increased their representation in state legislatures, particularly in the Midwest. After the 2004 elections, the two parties essentially split the control of state legislatures. In 2007 Democrats would have a majority of both houses in twenty-two states, compared with the Republicans' fifteen. Control in twelve states was split between the two parties. One state, Nebraska, had a nonpartisan, unicameral legislature.

Special House Elections

Two special House elections were also held on Nov. 7. In Texas, Republican Shelley Sekula Gibbs won a special election to fill out the remaining two months of DeLay's term even as she lost the general election to Lampson. In New Jersey, Democrat Albio Sires won a special election and the general election to replace Democrat Robert Menendez, who earlier had been appointed to the Senate seat vacated by Democrat Jon Corzine, who became governor.

In the only other special election in 2006, Brian P. Bilbray, a former House Republican, defeated Democrat Francine Busby by four percentage points to win the San Diego seat left vacant by Randy "Duke" Cunningham, who resigned after his conviction on bribery and tax evasion charges. Bilbray, who was first elected to Congress in 1994 but lost his seat in 2000, defeated Busby a second time in 2006, when he won the general election in November to serve a full term.

2007

The Legislative Year

The 110th Congress opened with Democrats in control of both chambers for the first time in twelve years. Energized by their victories in the 2006 midterm elections, party leaders laid out an ambitious agenda that included setting a timetable for ending the U.S. war in Iraq, pumping up spending on domestic programs such as education and health care, and cleaning up what they had characterized during the election campaign as a "culture of corruption" on Capitol Hill under the Republicans.

Democrats came away with victories on a number of signature issues. They also made history with the first roll call vote of the year when they installed Democrat Nancy Pelosi of California as the first woman to serve as Speaker of the House.

But the party's slim majority and the refusal of President George W. Bush and congressional Republicans to yield ground enabled the minority to defeat many Democratic measures or extract significant concessions on matters that were important to the GOP electoral base. Bush, who had vetoed only one bill in his first six years in office, rejected seven in 2007.

The partisan jockeying in the narrowly divided Congress was intensified by the 2008 presidential campaign, which was already underway when Congress convened in January. Both parties forced votes they knew they could not win for the purpose of making life uncomfortable for the opposition and shaping issues for the 2008 election.

The biggest frustration for the Democrats was their inability to set a timetable for withdrawing troops from Iraq. The leadership considered the 2006 election results a mandate to end the war, but they never found a way to satisfy the party's antiwar caucus and still win the support of enough moderates in both parties to override a promised presidential veto or in some cases even get the measure through the Senate. Democrats also could not overcome the combined resistance of the White House, the GOP minority, and many of their own fiscal conservatives to major funding increases for several domestic programs. *(Iraq war, pp. 270, 303)*

There were other disappointments as well. Twice Democrats failed to override Bush's veto of a measure to expand the State Children's Health Insurance Program (SCHIP), which provided medical coverage to poor children. Despite support from Republicans, Democrats for the second year in a row were unable to muster the two-thirds majority necessary to override the president's veto of a bill expanding federal funding for stem cell research. Finally, despite the president's support, Democrats for the second year in a row were unable to overcome resistance from Republican legislators to enact an overhaul of U.S. immigration policy. *(CHIP, p. 558; Stem cell, pp. 542, 573; Immigration, pp. 686, 711)*

Both Congress and the president were slow to recognize the potential severity of the approaching economic crisis, triggered in 2006 when the air began to go out of the once-booming housing bubble. By mid-2007 millions of mortgages were in foreclosure. Many of them were so-called subprime mortgages for borrowers, often with spotty credit histories, who were unable to make the monthly payments required after low introductory rates on adjustable-rate mortgages reset at higher levels. In November the House passed a major mortgage regulation measure to overhaul such tactics, and one was under consideration in the Senate, but neither measure offered much immediate help to struggling homeowners. Meanwhile, the stability of the financial system was coming under threat as the value of securitized mortgages plummeted. These were individual mortgages that were bundled together in packages that then were sold in pieces to investors, thus clouding the true ownership of the mortgage debt and raising questions about the value of securities. *(Economic crisis, pp. 51, 136, 151, 163; Housing, pp. 149, 153, 625, 630, 639, 640, 641, 642)*

CONGRESS IN 2007

The first session of the 110th Congress began at noon on Jan. 4, 2007, and ended at 10 a.m. on Dec. 31, when the Senate adjourned *sine die*. The House had adjourned *sine die* at 7:36 p.m. on Dec. 19. The session lasted 362 days. The Senate met on 189 days, for a total of 1,376 hours. The House met on 164 days, for a total of 1,478 hours.

A total of 9,227 bills and resolutions were introduced during the 2007 session, compared with 4,753 in 2006 and 8,319 in 2005. Congress cleared 175 bills in 2007 that were signed into public law during the session. President George W. Bush vetoed seven bills, including one he called a pocket veto. Congress overrode one of the vetoes. *(Public laws table, p. 16; Presidential vetoes, p. 1039)*

During 2007, the House took 1,177 recorded votes (not counting quorum calls), 637 more than in 2006 and 310 more than the 867 votes taken in 1995, the previous high mark for recorded votes in the House. The Senate took 442 recorded votes, 163 more than in 2006. The total of 1,619 was the most recorded votes ever taken by Congress in a single year.

DEMOCRATIC UNITY, GOP RESISTANCE

The year was one of the most partisan in Congress in at least half a century. Congressional Quarterly's annual study of party unity votes—those on which a majority of one party opposed a majority of the other—found that 62 percent of House votes fell into that category, the highest percentage since the record-setting year in 1995. Party voting was almost as frequent in the Senate in 2007, with the parties split on 60 percent of the votes.

When Democrats scored victories, it was a consequence of Pelosi and Senate Majority Leader Harry Reid of Nevada working to hold their ranks together. Pelosi maintained unprecedented unity in her caucus; House Democrats on average voted with the party on 92 percent of the party unity votes. She also used the majority's ability to control the rules for floor debate to block GOP initiatives and save party members from casting politically difficult votes. In the more independent-minded Senate, Reid held his caucus together on 87 percent of the party votes, about the average for the previous ten years.

Republicans stuck together less often on party unity votes, but they often rallied when it counted. House Republicans were able to obstruct, and occasionally halt, Democratic legislation, succeeding twenty-one times in ordering bills returned to committee for changes more to their liking—an extremely rare event. During their previous twelve years in the minority, House Democrats moved 276 times to recommit bills and prevailed only four times.

But it was in the Senate that Republicans had the most significant influence. Mitch McConnell of Kentucky, serving in his first year as Republican Senate minority leader, became adept at using that chamber's procedures to kill or force major revisions to Democratic bills. The key to his success was savvy use of amendments and prolonged debate to force Reid to hold cloture votes, a method of limiting debate that required sixty votes to succeed. Holding just fifty-one seats, counting two independents whose support they secured most, but not all, of the time, Democrats won just half the sixty-two cloture votes held during the year.

Reid had his own reasons for holding so many votes on limiting debate: success not only prevented time-consuming filibusters but also gave him a chance to avoid amendments on which his caucus might fracture. Similar to time-consuming votes on chamber rules in the House, cloture votes in the Senate were generally seen as loyalty votes on which party members fell in behind their leaders.

The overall result was a record number of roll call votes and a remarkably small number of substantive legislation enacted into law. The House took a record 1,177 roll call votes in 2007 and the Senate took 442, for the most roll calls ever taken in a single session of Congress. Just 75 public laws were enacted; of those, fifty-four—39 percent—renamed post offices.

Age Structure of Congress, 1949–2009

Following are the average age of members at the beginning of each Congress.

Year	*House*	*Senate*	*Congress*
1949	51.0	58.5	53.8
1951	52.0	56.6	53.0
1953	52.0	56.6	53.0
1955	51.4	57.2	52.2
1957	52.9	57.9	53.8
1959	51.7	57.1	52.7
1961	52.2	57.0	53.2
1963	51.7	56.8	52.7
1965	50.5	57.7	51.9
1967	50.8	57.7	52.1
1969	52.2	56.6	53.0
1971	51.9	56.4	52.7
1973	51.1	55.3	52.0
1975	49.8	55.5	50.9
1977	49.3	54.7	50.3
1979	48.8	52.7	49.5
1981	48.4	52.5	49.2
1983	45.5	53.4	47.0
1985	49.7	54.2	50.5
1987	50.7	54.4	52.5
1989	52.1	55.6	52.8
1991	52.8	57.2	53.6
1993	51.7	58.0	52.9
1995	50.9	58.4	52.2
1997	51.6	57.5	52.7
1999	52.6	58.3	53.7
2001	55.4	59.8	54.4
2003	54.0	59.7	55.5
2005	55.0	60.4	56.0
2007	56.0	61.2	57.1
2009	57.0	63.1	58.2

FIRST 100 HOURS

The year started well enough for House Democrats, who pushed to passage—with a significant number of GOP votes—Speaker Pelosi's "Six for '06" platform well within the self-imposed deadline of the first one hundred legislative hours of the year. Three of the agenda items eventually became law: the first increase in the federal minimum wage in a decade; enactment of most of the recommendations for improving homeland security made in 2004 by the independent Sept. 11 commission; and lower interest rates on student loans. *(Minimum wage, pp. 661, 686; Homeland security recommendations, p. 245; Student loans, pp. 607, 612, 615)*

The House also imposed new ethics rules as the session began; although not strictly part of the Six for '06 program, the ethics rules symbolized the Democrats promise to clean up after the Republicans. The Senate ethics rules were altered under a law enacted later in the year. The rules provided greater transparency on earmarks inserted in funding measures, required more disclosure of members' contacts with lobbyists, severely restricted members' travel that could be paid for by outsiders, and lengthened the time period before former members or some staff members could take jobs lobbying their former colleagues. *(Ethics rules, p. 829)*

But the other three elements of the House package ran into obstacles. The House quickly passed a bill redirecting billions of dollars from the oil and gas industry to alternative energy sources. It was eventually jettisoned to win Senate passage and avert a veto of the first increase in car and truck fuel efficiency standards in thirty-two years. For the second time in two years, President Bush vetoed a measure that would have allowed federal funding of research on stem cells discarded by fertility clinics; with no prospect of securing the two-thirds vote needed, no override was attempted. Senate Democrats were unable to muster the sixty votes needed to end debate on a measure allowing the government to bargain with pharmaceutical companies to lower the prices of Medicare prescription drugs. The Senate action killed the measure for the remainder of the 100th Congress. *(Energy, fuel standards, pp. 484; Stem cells, pp. 542, 573; Drug prices, pp. 556, 578)*

IRAQ WITHDRAWAL TIMETABLE

By the November congressional elections, an increasing number of Americans were becoming disillusioned with the U.S. war plan for Iraq as widening sectarian violence and growing casualties among U.S. troops and Iraqi civilians seemed poised to plunge the nation into a civil war. Voters sent Democrats to a majority in both chambers of the 110th Congress in important part on the strength of their promise to end U.S. military involvement in Iraq. As the new Congress convened, there was some hope that the administration would adopt the proposals of a bipartisan Iraq Study Group, which recommended beginning a U.S. troop withdrawal and stepped-up diplomatic efforts in the region.

Instead President Bush greeted the new Congress with a nationally televised address announcing that he was ordering a "surge" of U.S. forces in Iraq to secure neighborhoods in Baghdad and other cities and give local authorities "breathing room" to promote political reconciliation among the country's warring sects.

Pelosi, Reid, and other Democrats reacted angrily, saying Bush had not listened to the voters. With strict discipline from the leadership, House Democrats passed at least seven bills with some form of antiwar language and prevailed on a dozen or more antiwar votes. But Republicans blocked the legislation in the Senate, mostly through filibusters that Democrats lacked the votes to overcome.

The longest fight came in the first half of the year, when Democrats tried to tie emergency supplemental spending for the war to a timetable for winding down the U.S. presence in Iraq. Although the original House language was stronger, Congress managed to send Bush a bill that would have required the Pentagon to begin redeploying troops by Oct. 1.

As promised, Bush on May 1 vetoed the bill; House leaders fell sixty-two votes short of the two-thirds needed to override him. With the Memorial Day recess approaching and Bush escalating the rhetoric about troops needing supplies, Democratic leaders backed down, sending Bush a new version of the supplemental bills without a withdrawal timetable. He signed it the next day (PL 110-28). *(Details, p. 383)*

By then the pattern had been set. Democrats continued trying to force votes on the war, but their slim Senate majority doomed any measure with teeth. Although Democratic leaders vowed there would be no more money without strings for the war, they conceded again in December, providing $70 billion more in funding as part of the price for winning enactment of the fiscal 2008 omnibus spending bill.

DOMESTIC SPENDING SHOWDOWN

The other price Democrats paid for passage of the omnibus spending bill (PL 110-161) was acceptance of the president's overall cap on discretionary appropriations for domestic programs. Democrats had made it clear early in the year that they planned to confront Bush on domestic spending, approving a budget resolution that was $21.3 billion more than the president requested. When Bush threatened vetoes for most of the bills, Democrats tried to bundle higher spending for the Labor, Health and Human Services (HHS), and Education departments with outlays for military construction and veterans, hoping the president could not afford politically to veto funding for veterans. Senate Republicans blocked that maneuver, however, and the Democrats passed a stand-alone spending bill for the Labor-HHS-Education departments, which Bush promptly vetoed. An attempt to override the veto failed. *(Details, pp. 111, 112; Veto message, p. 1065)*

That was the turning point, demonstrating clearly that Democrats lacked the votes to win a face-off with Bush over domestic spending. Despite having to live within Bush's spending caps, the Democrats found ways to increase funding for some of their top priorities, including increased funding for veterans' programs and relief for victims of Katrina and other 2005 hurricanes and for coping with wildfires in the western states.

RESTORING OVERSIGHT

Gaining the majority in Congress gave Democrats the opportunity to probe executive branch activities that had been subject to almost no congressional oversight while Republicans were in control. Democrats undertook the job enthusiastically, often to little immediate avail.

The most dramatic outcome of the committee investigations was the resignation of Attorney General Alberto R. Gonzales in September. Gonzales had lost credibility with lawmakers of both parties following embarrassing revelations about his involvement in the administration's firing of nine U.S. attorneys and a probe of the National Security Agency's warrantless wiretapping program. *(Gonzales's resignation, p. 680; Attorney firings, p. 721)*

The Democrats were frustrated, however, in their efforts to compel testimony from other high-ranking administration officials. Nor could Democrats persuade the administration to hand over secret memos on techniques used in interrogating Iraqi and other detainees. Michael B. Mukasey, who replaced Gonzales as attorney general, refused to answer a series of questions from the Senate Judiciary Committee about the CIA's destruction of videotapes showing the interrogation of detainees, and the Justice Department advised the CIA not to cooperate with a similar probe by the House Select Intelligence Committee.

Numerous committees held hearings on the Iraq War and the impact of the troop surge. Other investigations looked into corruption by the Iraqi government, waste and fraud in the reconstruction of Iraq, and the readiness of military forces trained by continuing deployments in Iraq.

The session ended as it had begun, with partisanship in full swing.

The Political Year

Ten seats in Congress became vacant in 2007, eight in the House and two in the Senate. It was the largest midterm turnover in a single year since 1974. Three of the seats remained vacant at the end of the year; the other seven had all been filled by members of the same political party as the preceding occupant.

GOP Leadership Resignations

Two veterans of the GOP leadership quit before their terms were complete. J. Dennis Hastert, the Speaker of the House from 1999 until his party lost its majority in the 2006 midterm election, resigned in November 2007 and said he was retiring from public life. In his farewell speech, Hastert expressed concern about the "breakdown of civility" in the political process and told members they could not find solutions in a "pool of bitterness."

Hastert, who was the longest-serving Republican Speaker in U.S. history, was elected to an eleventh term from his Illinois district in 2006 even as Democrats were wresting control of the House from the GOP. In 2007 he became the first ex-Speaker to serve in the House in four decades. The last was fellow Republican Joseph W. Martin Jr. of Massachusetts, who served as minority leader from 1939 until 1958, except when the GOP controlled the House in 1947–1949 and 1953–1955, when he served as Speaker. Martin was ousted as minority leader after the Republicans' devastating election losses in 1958, though he remained in Congress until 1968. A special election to fill Hastert's seat did not take place until March 2008.

The second GOP leader to resign was Sen. Trent Lott of Mississippi. Lott had served as his party's floor leader from 1996 through 2002, when he was forced to step down after he made an off-the-cuff remark suggesting support for segregation. He was the first Senate floor leader forced from his post since the leadership jobs took their current form in the early twentieth century.

Lott had planned to retire from the Senate in 2006, but when Hurricane Katrina laid waste to the Gulf Coast in 2005, including destroying his waterfront Pascagoula home, he decided to stay to help secure as much federal money as possible to rebuild the state. When Majority Leader Bill Frist of Tennessee retired in 2006 and Kentucky's Mitch McConnell moved up from whip to the top spot, Lott launched a comeback bid, defeating Lamar Alexander of Tennessee for the whip post by a single vote.

Less than a year later, he announced his retirement on Nov. 26, 2007, insisting he did not have a new career planned. But in January 2008 he announced the formation of a lobbying partnership with former senator John B. Breaux, D-La. (1987–2005), and their sons. That decision made Lott the first member of Congress to resign midterm to become a lobbyist. Lott's timing was also critical to his new career choice. Under an ethics and lobbying law enacted in September 2007, Lott, as a former senator, would have been subjected to a two-year cooling-off period before he could lobby his former colleagues. As long as he resigned before Jan. 1, 2008, however, he was subject to only a one-year break.

On Dec. 31, Republican Mississippi governor Haley Barbour appointed Republican representative Roger Wicker to fill the Senate seat until a special election in November 2008. A special election to fill the House vacancy caused by Wicker's move to the Senate was set for April 2008.

Other Special House Elections

Five special elections were held to fill vacant House seats in 2007.

- In Georgia's 10th District, Republican physician Paul Broun bested former state senator Jim Whitehead, a fellow Republican who had the backing of the GOP establishment, to take the seat left open on Feb. 13 with the death of Republican Charlie Norwood. A dentist, Norwood had become an influential GOP congressional voice on health care policy.
- Democratic state representative Laura Richardson took 67 percent of the vote in California's 37th District, to win the Aug. 21 special election to replace fellow Democrat Juanita Millender-McDonald, who died of cancer on April 22. Millender-McDonald, chairman of the House Administration Committee, was one of two African American women to head House committees in the 110th Congress. The other

was Stephanie Tubbs Jones, D-Ohio, who chaired the Committee on Standards of Official Conduct and who died of an aneurysm in 2008.

- Democrat Niki Tsongas, a community college dean, took 51 percent of the vote to win an Oct. 16 special election in the Massachusetts 5th District. Tsongas, the widow of Paul E. Tsongas, a Democrat who served in both the House and Senate, replaced Democrat Martin T. Meehan, who resigned his House seat to become chancellor of the University of Massachusetts at Lowell.
- The vacancy in Ohio's 5th District, caused by the death of Republican Paul E. Gillmor after a fall in his home, was filled in a Dec. 11 special election by GOP state representative Bob Latta, who won 57 percent of the vote. Latta was the son of Delbert L. Latta, who held the seat from 1959 until his retirement in 1988.
- Republican state representative Rob Wittman took 61 percent of the vote to win a Dec. 11 special election for Virginia's 1st District. Wittman took the seat previously held by Jo Ann Davis, the first Republican woman to represent Virginia in Congress. Davis died Oct. 6 of breast cancer.

Another House vacancy was created on Dec. 15 when Democrat Julia Carson, who represented Indiana's 7th District, died of lung cancer; two weeks earlier she had announced that her illness was terminal and she would not seek another term. A special election was scheduled for March 2008. Carson was only the second black woman to represent her state in Congress.

Senate Appointment

Republican senator Craig Thomas of Wyoming died June 4 of leukemia. Thomas had just been elected to a third term in November 2006 and was diagnosed with the disease a short time later. On June 22, state senator and orthopedic surgeon John A. Barrasso, a Republican, was appointed to fill Thomas's seat for the rest of the 110th Congress. In November 2008, Barrasso won election to the remaining four years of Thomas's term with 73 percent of the vote.

2008

The Legislative Year

Elections and the economy dominated lawmakers' attention in 2008. With a presidential election in November, a quiet year was expected on Capitol Hill. Democrats did not want to risk their new majority in Congress by doing anything dramatic. Republicans did not want to give the Democrats any large victories upon which to campaign. Moreover, even if President George W. Bush had wanted to boost his legacy by pushing Congress on some major issue, he lacked the political capital to do so. Democrats even decided to postpone action on domestic spending until 2009 rather than risk a political showdown with the president like the one they had in 2007.

"Everybody was trying not to make a mistake that would affect the election," said former representative Charles W. Stenholm, D-Texas, who served twenty-six years in the House before being defeated in 2004.

However, a series of economic crises intervened, leading to some of the most dramatic legislative moments in recent memory and forcing lawmakers to take actions that many feared would come back to haunt them on Election Day. Republicans who usually favored keeping the government out of private business consented to a federal takeover of the giant mortgage lenders Fannie Mae and Freddie Mac and to a multibillion-dollar bailout of the financial industry. In the face of rapidly rising oil and gasoline prices, Democrats reversed a long-held stance and agreed to end a ban on drilling for oil and gas off the intercontinental shelf.

ECONOMIC STIMULUS

Efforts to stimulate the flagging economy began in January, when House leaders and the White House agreed on legislation to jump-start the economy. Just two weeks were required for legislators to clear a $151.7 billion bill (PL 110-185) that provided tax rebate checks to individuals and families and investment incentives to businesses. *(Rebates, p. 151; Financial crisis background, p. 163)*

Work also continued on mortgage relief legislation. The House had passed a bill in 2007, and the Senate took up the legislation in spring 2008. The central element of the bill was a $300 billion trust fund for the Federal Housing Administration to help borrowers refinance loans they could no longer afford. During the next few months, senators worked to alleviate concerns about the legislation voiced by members and President Bush. The bill took on unexpected urgency in July when Treasury Secretary Henry M. Paulson Jr. announced that the government needed immediate authority to protect Fannie Mae and Freddie Mac from collapsing. Paulson wanted Congress to allow the Treasury to buy assets from the companies, including their mortgage holdings and shares of their stock, and extend new credit to them. *(Housing, pp. 153, 630)*

Lawmakers agreed and passed the bill (PL 110-289) in late July. Conservatives complained about the bill's cost and the government's new authority to bail out the enterprises, which owned or guaranteed about half of all U.S. mortgages. About six weeks later, in early September, the government used its new authority to take over the two agencies, injecting new capital into each and guaranteeing their debt in return for controlling ownership of the two agencies.

That takeover came amid mounting fears of a widespread credit crunch and bank collapses. Just a week later on Sept. 15, Lehman Brothers, one of Wall Street's largest investment banks, filed for bankruptcy, sending panic through global financial systems. Warning that the economic downturn could become the worst since the Great Depression, Paulson and the administration pleaded with congressional leaders to allow a government bailout of the financial services industry.

The plan would give the Treasury secretary the authority to use as much as $700 billion to buy up troubled mortgage-related securities in an attempt to reopen frozen credit markets and improve the balance sheets of banks and other financial institutions on the edge of collapse. Coming little

CONGRESS IN 2008

The second session of the 110th Congress began at noon on Jan. 4, 2008. The House adjourned *sine die* at noon on Jan. 3, 2009. The Senate adjourned *sine die* at 10 a.m. on Jan. 2, 2009. Although the session lasted 366 days (2008 was a leap year), both chambers met for many fewer days and hours than they had in 2007. In 2008 the Senate met on 184 days, for a total of 988 hours, whereas the House met on 119 days, for a total of 891 hours.

A total of 4,815 bills and resolutions were introduced during the 2008 session, compared with 9,227 in 2007 and 4,753 in 2006. Congress cleared 285 bills in 2008 that were signed into public law during the session. President George W. Bush vetoed four bills, three of which Congress overrode. *(Public laws table, p. 16; Presidential votes, p. 1039)*

During 2008, the House took 688 recorded votes (not counting quorum calls), 489 fewer than in 2007 but 148 more than in 2006. The Senate took 215 recorded votes, 227 fewer than in 2007 and 64 fewer than in 2006.

more than a month before the elections, the proposal set off an intense political struggle on Capitol Hill.

The debate also created political dilemmas for the Democratic and Republican presidential candidates, both of whom, as members of the Senate, would have to vote on the final product. Democrat Barack Obama staked out a cautious approach, supporting the idea of a bank rescue but calling for restrictions on pay of bank executives. Republican John McCain took a big gamble on Sept. 24, announcing that he would suspend his campaign so he could help congressional negotiators reach a deal. McCain's gamble backfired, however, after he came to a White House negotiating session but played no significant role.

Shaken by Paulson's dire description of the state of the economy, congressional leaders in both parties went along with the Troubled Asset Relief Program (TARP). Congress and the Bush administration, however, underestimated the extent of constituent anger over what was widely viewed as a bailout of wealthy financial giants. A bipartisan coalition in the House defeated the plan on the floor in a vote that stunned stock markets globally. On Sept. 29, the day of the vote, the Dow Jones Industrial Average declined 777 points, the biggest point loss in a single day in its 112-year history.

The Senate then took over and combined a slightly sweetened bailout package with a multipurpose measure to renew a variety of expiring tax breaks, add a one-year fix for the alternative minimum tax, and require insurance companies to offer benefits for treating mental illness and addictions on par with those provided for other health issues. The Senate easily passed the legislation, and the House followed suit, albeit with continued grumbling from many members. *(TARP passage, p. 154)*

Even with the TARP in place, banks continued to report enormous losses for the rest of the year. Job losses quickly mounted as companies of all sizes contracted or went out of business. On Dec. 1 the National Bureau of Economic Research, a nonprofit think tank, confirmed what everyone already knew: the economy was in a recession. Most economists were surprised, however, by the bureau's finding that the recession had begun a year earlier, in December 2007.

After the elections, Democrats talked about another stimulus bill focused on spending for job-creating projects such as infrastructure improvements. But because Republican lawmakers and President Bush showed little interest in the idea, Democrats decided to wait until January, when they would have control of the White House and larger majorities in both chambers.

Congressional Republicans also blocked emergency funding for the American auto industry. Late in 2008, the heads of the auto companies (Chrysler, Ford, and General Motors) went to Washington twice—first by corporate jet and then, after being criticized for traveling in luxury to ask for taxpayer money, driving their own products—to plead for additional federal assistance to help them avoid bankruptcy. In September Congress had agreed to a $25 billion loan program to help the companies. But by December, with polls showing Americans reluctant to support another bailout of the private sector, many legislators were reluctant to approve more federal funds to help the beleaguered automakers.

Congressional Democrats and the Bush White House put together a $15 billion rescue proposal for the auto industry, announced on Dec. 8. That proposal quickly fell apart in the Senate where Republicans demanded deeper wage cuts by unionized auto workers as the price for injecting tax dollars into the companies. Many of the Republicans represented southern states where foreign auto companies had built large, nonunionized plants. Stymied by resistance from his party, Bush on Dec. 19 did what he previously had said he would not do: divert money from the bank bailout program to the auto industry. The president announced he had approved $17.4 billion in direct loans for General Motors and Chrysler. Corporate chiefs at Ford insisted that company could survive without government aid.

BUSH VICTORIES

The degree of compromise between Bush and congressional Democrats on the economic rescue legislation was remarkable, given the president's general disinclination to bargain with Congress. The administration cut a deal with House leaders from both parties on the economic stimulus bill that passed in January, and again in September in drafting the TARP bill.

Entering his final year in office with some of the lowest job approval ratings ever recorded and with little ability to press his legislative agenda, Bush was forced to abandon his domestic policy goals. He made no progress in making his earlier tax cuts permanent or in overhauling the tax code. Nor was he able to reform the nation's immigration laws or limit punitive damages in medical malpractice lawsuits. Moreover, the president was embarrassed when the first bailout bill collapsed in the House because he could not persuade enough Republicans to vote for it and again at the end of the year when he was unable to persuade Republicans to sign on to the auto bailout bill he had worked out with the Democrats.

Despite his political weakness, Bush succeeded on some of the biggest issues of the year. The administration secured more money to fight AIDS globally and completed a controversial nuclear-cooperation agreement with India. Bush was successful most often using threatened vetoes and the Senate filibuster to avoid significant changes to his Iraq policies, major restrictions on intelligence-gathering tactics, and removal of tax breaks for oil and gas companies. Unable to force the president's hand on the Iraq War in 2007 after they took control of Congress, Democrats in 2008 backed away from any serious efforts to force a deadline for withdrawing most combat troops from that nation. Instead, antiwar Democrats settled for a few provisions placing restrictions on U.S. funding of reconstruction programs for Iraq.

DEMOCRATIC ACCOMPLISHMENTS

Democrats did complete several reauthorization measures, some of which Republicans had not passed for several years. Among them were bills reauthorizing Amtrak for the first time since 1997 and reauthorizing the Higher Education Act for the first time in a decade.

Congress also overrode three Bush vetoes. The first two were on a $289 billion, five-year farm bill; the third was on legislation that blocked a scheduled cut in pay rates for physicians who participate in the Medicare Health care program for the elderly and disabled. The Democrats also laid the foundation for future legislation, initiating debates on climate change, workplace discrimination, and tobacco regulation that they hoped to pass in the 111th Congress.

The Political Year

On Nov. 4, 2008, Barack Obama became the first African American president in the nation's 220-year history. In an election campaign that was more civil and positive in tone than some in the recent past, Obama, a Democratic senator from Illinois, won a decisive victory over John McCain, a Republican senator from Arizona. Obama's victory returned the White House to the Democratic Party after the tumultuous and ultimately unpopular eight-year presidency of Republican George W. Bush.

Bush's unpopularity, Obama's convincing margin, recruitment of strong candidates, and abundant campaign finances all combined to help congressional Democrats strengthen the majorities they had won in the House and Senate in 2006. In the House Democrats netted twenty-one seats; the party lineup after the election was 257 Democrats to 178 Republicans. In the Senate Democrats gained a net of seven seats; counting two independents who caucused with the Democrats, the party effectively had fifty-eight seats, with one race still undecided at the time but which later went to a Democrat. (In April 2009 a Republican—Pennsylvania's Arlen Specter—switched to the Democrats, giving that party sixty votes including the two independents.)

The Democrats also gained a governorship in the Nov. 4 election and made gains in state legislatures.

The Presidential Election

Barack Obama's election as the forty-fourth president of the United States capped an amazingly rapid political rise. He was a state legislator, little known outside his constituency on Chicago's South Side, just four years earlier when he burst onto the national stage with a stirring keynote address at the 2004 Democratic National Convention and then three months later won a landslide victory to take a U.S. Senate seat left open by the retirement of a Republican incumbent.

Obama's ranking among the nation's chief executives, and his prospects for winning a second term in 2012, were expected to depend heavily on his handling of the enormous challenges that awaited him following his inauguration Jan. 20, 2009. These included a deep recession, rapidly rising unemployment, and rising federal budget deficits, long-standing problems in national priorities such as health care and education, and the U.S. military engagements in long-running wars in Iraq and Afghanistan. But no delay was needed to acknowledge the historic breakthrough Obama achieved the moment he declared victory at a massive outdoor election night rally in Chicago's Grant Park: the first black elected to hold the nation's highest office. *(2008: A Year of Firsts, p. 32)*

The son of a black father from Kenya and a white mother from Kansas, Obama had already made history on Aug. 27, 2008, by formally winning the Democratic nomination at the party's national convention in Denver. No nonwhite candidate had ever come close to winning the nomination of one of the two major parties. In winning that nomination, Obama defeated the first woman to have run a competitive campaign for the presidential nomination, Hillary Rodham Clinton, a senator from New York and the former first lady. Clinton had been the Democratic front-runner as the campaign season began.

Elected at age forty-seven, Obama was born in Hawaii on Aug. 4, 1961, just two years before the March on Washington, when the Rev. Martin Luther King Jr. delivered his "I Have a Dream" speech; three years before the enactment of the 1964 Civil Rights Act; and four years before passage of the Voting Rights Act. In contrast to many black politicians, who were veterans of that civil rights movement and who received most of their support from blacks, Obama personified a younger generation of black politicians who practiced what many analysts described as "postracial" politics. From the beginning of the campaign Obama's themes of "change" and "hope" attracted support from millions of white Americans, with special appeal to younger voters.

Obama's emergence came at a time when a huge majority of respondents told pollsters they believed the country was on the wrong track. Instead of following the example of every presidential candidate since Ronald Reagan and declaring government to be the problem, Obama pledged to use the agencies of the federal government to help turn around the sputtering economy, address issues raised by climate change, and overcome what he described as chronic shortcomings in the nation's health care, education, and infrastructure systems.

The message gained cogency in the final weeks of the general election campaign, when the financial sector, undermined by badly flawed mortgage lending practices that had fueled a mid-decade economic boom, unraveled and pushed the economy into a recession that Obama and many in both parties characterized as the worst economic

2008: A YEAR OF FIRSTS

Democratic presidential candidate Sen. Barack Obama, D-Ill., and Republican presidential candidate Sen. John McCain, R-Ariz., talk during the presidential debate Wednesday, October 15, 2008, at Hofstra University in Hempstead, N.Y.
Source: AP Photo/Gary Hershorn, Pool

When the 2008 votes were tallied, the people of the United States had elected Democrat Barack Obama, an Illinois senator, as the first African American president, an outcome that most observers thought inconceivable a quarter century earlier. But even before the votes for president were counted in November 2008, that year's election already had become renowned.

Although Obama's election made 2008 "one for the books," in the words of many political commentators, by the time the primaries and caucuses ended and candidates were anointed at the conventions, the "firsts" of the 2008 presidential election cycle had become an impressive list.

- Most remarkable of all firsts was Obama's capturing the nomination of a major political party.
- The 2008 race was the first since 1928 that no incumbent president or vice president sought the nomination, and was the first since 1952 that neither the incumbent president nor vice president was running on the final ticket.
- The presidential race started earlier than any other in history, when Democrat Tom Vilsack, who was stepping down as Iowa's governor after two terms, became the first candidate of either party to formally announce that he was seeking the presidential nomination. Vilsack's announcement came on November 2006—two full years before the election. Vilsack remained in the race for fewer than four months, withdrawing in February 2007 for lack of funding.
- The initial front-runner in the Democratic contest was Sen. Hillary Rodham Clinton, the first woman in U.S. history to run a competitive race for the nomination. That Democrats were choosing between a woman and an African American male was a matchup that virtually no one could have imagined in previous national elections.
- For the first time ever, both major party candidates had been born outside the continental United States, Obama in Hawaii on Aug. 4, 1961, to a white woman from Kansas and a black man from Kenya; and his opponent, Sen. John McCain, an Arizona Republican, at a U.S. naval base in the Panama Canal Zone on Aug. 29, 1936.
- Two sitting members of the U.S. Senate were the major party candidates, the first time this had ever occurred. It also was the first time since 1960 that a sitting senator was elected. That year Sen. John F. Kennedy, D-Mass., defeated outgoing vice president Richard Nixon.
- For only the second time in U.S. history a woman was selected to run on a major party ticket as the vice-presidential candidate. McCain selected Gov. Sarah Palin of Alaska. In 1984 Geraldine A. Ferraro was the Democratic vice-presidential candidate, but she was on the losing ticket headed by former senator and vice president Walter Mondale.

crisis since the Great Depression. Almost from the moment of his election, the president-elect and his aides were working to develop policy responses to the crisis that would see the federal government become more intertwined with private enterprise than at any time since the depression of the 1930s. *(Financial crisis, pp. 51, 163, 192)*

THE RACE FACTOR

While most of Obama's detractors refrained from direct reference to race, there was a concerted effort to portray him as exotic or radical. Much was made of the fact that his African father was born a Muslim, and some Republicans relished enunciating the candidate's full name, Barack Hussein Obama, leaving unsaid the implied reference to Saddam Hussein, the Iraqi dictator overthrown by President Bush's invasion of that country in 2003. Conservatives also made much of a comment in February by Michelle Obama, the candidate's wife, that "for the first time in my adult life I am really proud of my country, because it feels like hope is finally making a comeback."

The effort to caricature the Obamas was captured by a cover drawing for the *New Yorker* magazine. It portrayed Michelle Obama—a conservatively coiffed, Princeton-educated lawyer—bearing an AK-47 rifle, sporting an outsize Afro, and fist-bumping her turban-topped husband in the Oval Office beneath a portrait of the al Qaeda leader

Osama bin Laden. The magazine's editors said its intent was to ridicule the descriptions of the Obamas as radicals being spread through the right-wing rumor mill. Democrats decried the cartoon as promulgating the very negative issue the magazine was trying to mock.

During the primary campaign, Obama made a major address on race relations to deflect a controversy that arose over his former pastor, the Rev. Jeremiah Wright, who had made a series of inflammatory comments about race. In his speech, which was widely praised, Obama distanced himself from Wright's comments, but he also sought to explain the anger that many blacks felt at continuing racial disparities in American society and called on Americans of all races and religions to work together to end those inequalities. In the fall Republicans tried to get political mileage out of Obama's past work on education panels in Chicago with William Ayers, a 1960s leftist radical turned college professor. Obama said he and Ayers were not personally close. However, the Republican vice-presidential nominee, Gov. Sarah Palin of Alaska, took to describing Obama as "palling around with terrorists."

There was some irony, then, in another frequent criticism of Obama: that he had a cerebral and overall cautious approach to addressing complex policy questions. While the soaring rhetoric he employed in his speeches inspired his supporters, his answers to questions in debates and television interviews at times appeared hesitant and less than heartfelt.

REPUBLICAN VULNERABILITY

The Democrats had an advantage going into the election. For the first time since 1928, neither a sitting president nor vice president was running for the presidency, and President George W. Bush and Vice President Dick Cheney were leaving office with some of the lowest public opinion rankings ever recorded.

As recently as 2004, the Republican Party appeared to be on the ascent, with Bush winning reelection while the GOP maintained control of the House and expanded its Senate majority by four, for a total of fifty-five seats. But the party's standing was already beginning to unravel by the time Bush was sworn in for his second term.

Both of the principal rationales that Bush, Cheney, and other administration officials had used to justify the 2003 invasion of Iraq—stockpiled weapons of mass destruction and close ties between Iraqi dictator Saddam Hussein and the al Qaeda terrorist network that perpetrated the attacks of Sept, 11, 2001—had been proved wrong. Poor planning for postvictory pacification resulted in a conflict that was growing longer, bloodier, and much more expensive than Bush and fellow Republicans had predicted.

Bush's popularity already was shrinking when a slow and widely criticized federal response to Hurricane Katrina's devastation in New Orleans in August 2005 sent his job approval rating into a rapid decline from which it never recovered. These setbacks, along with early signs that the economy was slowing and a spate of corruption scandals involving Republican legislators, cost the GOP thirty House seats, six Senate seats, and control of both chambers in the 2006 midterm elections. Analysts immediately predicted, accurately, substantial additional congressional losses for the GOP in the 2008 contests.

By the onset of the presidential campaign, Bush's approval ratings were below 30 percent, and opinion polls showed the Democrats favored by significant margins on nearly all issues. Even the Republicans' traditional advantages on national and homeland security issues were reduced. To overcome these handicaps, the GOP needed an exceptionally strong nominee running a nearly flawless presidential campaign. McCain, despite his significant political strengths, came up short of that threshold on Election Day.

DEMOCRATIC PRIMARY CAMPAIGN

With no incumbent seeking reelection, the presidential election began earlier than ever—nearly two years before the election—and with a crowded field of candidates in both parties. The Republicans settled on their standard bearer relatively quickly once the formal primary season began, but the Democratic nominee was not finally determined until nearly all the primaries and caucuses had been held.

Obama announced that he was running for president Feb. 10, 2007, in Springfield, Ill. The event, held at the Old State House where Abraham Lincoln famously declared before the Civil War, "A House divided against itself cannot stand," drew the large crowds and media presence that would come to characterize his public appearances across the country. But on that frigid morning there was little to suggest that Obama was anything more than an ambitious and fast-rising star in American politics. Clinton was widely regarded as a nearly prohibitive favorite to win the Democratic nomination.

Clinton's low-key announcement, three weeks earlier, exuded the confidence of a front-runner: she posted a video on her Web site that had been made while she sat on a couch in her home off Washington's Embassy Row. That confidence appeared well-placed. Though controversy and even an impeachment had tarnished Bill Clinton's tenure in the White House and had fueled intense partisan divisions within the country, most Democrats remained fond of the forty-second president and appeared open to a sort of dynastic restoration through the nomination of his wife, the only first lady to have won elective federal office.

A USA Today–Gallup poll taken Feb. 9–11, 2007, a period that included Obama's announcement, showed Clinton leading Obama 40 percent to 21 percent. Third, with 14 percent, was Al Gore, Bill Clinton's vice president and the party's unsuccessful nominee in 2000, who ultimately decided not to run in 2008. John Edwards, the 2004 vice-presidential nominee and a former North Carolina senator, had 13 percent.

Stuck in single digits, and bound for early elimination from the nominating contest a year later, were Gov. Bill

Richardson of New Mexico, who sought to become the first Hispanic president; Senate Foreign Relations Committee Chairman Joseph R. Biden Jr. of Delaware, who ran briefly for the 1988 nomination and was ultimately chosen by Obama as his running mate; Sen. Christopher J. Dodd of Connecticut, chairman of the Senate Banking, Housing, and Urban Affairs Committee and a former national party chairman; Rep. Dennis J. Kucinich of Ohio, who was running as an antiwar candidate as he had in 2004; and former senator Mike Gravel of Alaska, who cast himself as an iconoclastic outsider.

Clinton sought to create the impression that her nomination was inevitable, suggesting in an initial series of Democratic debates that the other candidates were focusing their criticism on her because she was so clearly in the lead. Yet weaknesses emerged that would prevent Clinton from clearing the field and eventually would knock her off her front-runner's perch. Although she was a strong critic of Bush's handling of the Iraq War, she angered party liberals by refusing to renounce her Senate vote in 2002 to authorize the initial invasion of the country. In contrast, Obama, who was a state senator at the time, had spoken out against going to war.

Clinton also fell short of gaining the support of the party establishment, which at the outset appeared to be hers for the asking. Party rules gave hundreds of seats at the August 2008 convention in Denver to party operatives and elected officials. Clinton had counted on these superdelegates rallying to her early in the primary season. Instead, most deferred their endorsements until after the caucuses and primaries began.

Obama's surge into contention was helped by several factors. From the start, he exhibited the rhetorical talents that first brought him to national attention, displaying a sense of stagecraft and an ability to draw big audiences. Perhaps even more important were Obama's prodigious fund-raising skills and instincts for grassroots political organizing.

Once a community organizer who counseled laid-off steel workers in Chicago, Obama applied those organizing principles to his campaign. He teamed with chief advisers David Axelrod and David Plouffe, both veterans of Chicago politics, to build a vast network of campaign offices across the nation—including some in conservative-leaning states in the South, Midwest, and Mountain West where Democrats had not vigorously competed in presidential elections for many years. The campaign also broke new ground in using high-tech tools, both at its national headquarters in Chicago and at the local level, for identifying and contacting potential Obama voters, "mining" data such as e-mail addresses and cell phone numbers to promote frequent communications, generate campaign support, and ultimately increase voter turnout.

The Obama fund-raising operation, a significant share of it Internet-based, ultimately shattered previous records by raising about $750 million overall. To the consternation of some, he became the first candidate to opt out of the public financing system for presidential general elections (which included spending limits) since it took effect with the 1976 election.

EARLY SETBACK FOR CLINTON

Clinton's image of inevitability was shattered when the first votes of the nomination season were cast. Obama won 38 percent of the precinct delegates in the Jan. 3 Iowa caucuses; Clinton came in third, with 29 percent to Edwards's 30 percent.

Suddenly the commentary turned from how quickly Clinton would clinch the nomination to whether her campaign could survive the New Hampshire primary just five days later. Clinton fought back with renewed emphasis on her experience in national affairs, which she asserted made her ready "from day one" to fulfill the duties of the presidency. She also challenged Obama's claim to be the true agent of change, saying that he was a relative newcomer and outsider, while she had spent more than three decades working to better the lives of Americans. Clinton was victorious in New Hampshire, winning 39 percent to Obama's 36 percent, with Edwards finishing a distant third, with 17 percent, a showing that pushed him to the brink of elimination.

Clinton scored only two more victories in January, however, and both wins—in Michigan and Florida—were tainted by a dispute between the state parties and the Democratic National Committee (DNC) over the timing of their primaries, and the DNC had threatened to deny both states their delegates to the national convention.

Meanwhile, Obama fought Clinton to a virtual draw in the Jan. 19 caucuses in Nevada, a harbinger of his subsequent successes in organizing at the grassroots in the states that held caucuses instead of primaries. His twenty-eight-point margin of victory in the Jan. 26 South Carolina primary showed that Obama could both generate enormous support among black voters and cut into Clinton's support among whites. Obama prevailed despite an aggressive and at times combative involvement in that primary by Bill Clinton, starting a long-running debate within the Clinton camp about the strategically appropriate campaign role for the former president.

The next milestone came Feb. 5, "Super Tuesday," designed by the party to be the climax of a front-loaded primary and caucus schedule that would surely yield a prohibitive front-runner for the nomination. It did not work that way in 2008. Clinton, whose campaign was built on an expectation that she would dominate most of the day's contests, won ten, including primaries in California and New York, the day's biggest delegate prizes. But Obama won thirteen states, including a primary landslide in his home state of Illinois. Beyond that, he exposed one of Clinton's crucial miscalculations—making little effort to organize in caucus states, under the presumption that her front-runner status would be sufficient to push her to the nomination. Obama capitalized on that decision by winning six of the day's seven caucuses by lopsided margins.

A LONG HOME STRETCH

It quickly became apparent that Clinton's team lacked a plan for waging a competitive campaign after Super Tuesday. Obama won the next ten primaries and caucuses, spurring a wave of superdelegate endorsements and putting pressure on Clinton to concede so that Obama could start focusing on a general election contest against McCain, who had clinched his party's nomination in early March. But while Obama was ahead of Clinton in the delegate count, he remained well short of the necessary majority.

Clinton won the next two big primaries, on March 4. Support among working-class white voters propelled her to an eight-point margin of victory in Ohio, and strong support from Hispanics helped her claim a four-point win in Texas. Her pivotal levels of support from these two demographic groups, both vitally important in the general election, gave Clinton an opening to argue that she would have a better shot in November than would Obama.

The six weeks leading up to the April 22 Pennsylvania primary—the longest lull in the primary campaign—were the most difficult for Obama. Allegations of media favoritism toward Obama allowed Clinton's supporters to decry what they viewed as sexism in the media coverage. The Clinton campaign also began to run its most effective television ad of the campaign. Hoping to underscore her view of her superior experience, it showed children sleeping when the White House phone rings, signaling a crisis. "It's 3 a.m., and your children are safe and asleep. Who do you want to answer the phone?"

Even more damaging to Obama were the videos that gained wide circulation in mid-March showing Rev. Wright, Obama's former pastor, engaging in inflammatory rhetoric about race relations. Obama's speech on race, delivered in Philadelphia, quelled much of the furor, although some detractors continued throughout the campaign to try to link Obama to Wright's views.

Obama committed his biggest campaign gaffe just before the contest in Pennsylvania, home to a large population of white, blue-collar voters. In remarks made at a private event in San Francisco but leaked to a political Web site, Obama said many working-class people who experience economic distress "get bitter" and "cling to guns or religion or antipathy to people who aren't like them." Clinton's campaign sought to capitalize on the comment, portraying Obama as an elitist. This issue, too, would get a second airing in the general election campaign.

Clinton won the Pennsylvania primary, 55 percent to 45 percent, but because Democrats divide their delegates proportionally among primary candidates, her delegate gain was small. She was set further back on May 6 when Obama easily won in North Carolina and held Clinton to a one-point victory in Indiana, another state with a large working-class population.

MINNESOTA STANDOFF

The 2008 election year ended without an official winner in the Minnesota Senate contest between incumbent Republican Norm Coleman, who was seeking a second term, and Democrat Al Franken, a liberal talk-radio host and satirical author who initially gained fame as an actor and writer with NBC's *Saturday Night Live*.

The race appeared to be a toss-up throughout the fall. Coleman's campaign was hampered by questions about his ethics and complicated by the strong support in the state for Democratic presidential candidate Barack Obama (who carried the state by 10 percentage points in November). But no one was expecting the race to be as close as it was or to drag on as long as it did.

On Nov. 18, two weeks after Election Day, a statewide canvassing report had Coleman ahead by 215 votes, out of 2.4 million cast. Because the margin separating Coleman and Franken was less than half a percentage point, a state law required a hand recount, which began Nov. 19. Both candidates gained votes in the recount, but Franken's gains were sufficient to overcome Coleman's lead, and the Democrat pulled ahead by 225 votes.

The recount was certified Jan. 5, 2009, and Franken declared victory. Coleman, however, contested the outcome in state court, alleging inconsistencies in the vote count. A court-ordered examination of rejected absentee ballots put Franken ahead by 312 votes, and the state trial court ruled in April that Franken was the winner. Coleman appealed the decision to the state supreme court, which upheld the state trial court decision on June 30. Coleman conceded the race hours later. Saying that "further litigation" would damage the "unity of the state," Coleman added that he joined "all Minnesotans in congratulating out newest senator, Al Franken." Franken was sworn in on July 7, 2009, eight months after the election. The Senate seat had been vacant since the 111th Congress was convened on Jan. 3.

For the next several weeks, the candidates traded wins. Clinton sustained a final blow, however, when the DNC and the state Democratic parties in Florida and Michigan resolved their conflict over the disputed January primaries in a manner that diminished the importance of her victories in the two states.

Obama declared victory the night of June 3, after the final primaries that produced a win for him in Montana and a win for Clinton in South Dakota. Clinton did not leave questions lingering about whether she would support

Obama. In a June 7 speech in Washington, she conceded the nomination and urged her supporters to back Obama.

REPUBLICAN PRIMARY CAMPAIGN

Like Clinton, John McCain came into the primary season ahead of the pack. He had been the consensus front-runner in mainstream political circles since President Bush won a second term in 2004. But McCain had to cross several hurdles before he could claim the Republican nomination in 2008, which he won in part because he was able to revive many of the political assets he had brought to his first bid for the White House, which he lost to Bush in the 2000 primaries.

McCain's greatest asset was a personal story that spoke of strength and character: a Navy aviator, shot down over North Vietnam and seriously injured, who survived more than five hellish years in prison camps. That background also provided McCain with an image of expertise on defense and foreign policy issues—the central focus of his political career—that he conveyed during the 2008 campaign. McCain was a strong supporter of Bush's decision to go to war in Iraq and an early advocate of the "surge" of additional U.S. troops that Bush instituted in 2007. McCain described Obama, who opposed the Iraq War, as naive and unprepared to serve as commander in chief.

The other credential that McCain made a central element of his campaign was his reputation for defying party orthodoxy. His campaign lionized him as the "Original Maverick." The reputation was well earned. While his overall record was conservative, McCain had broken with most Republicans on several important issues. Perhaps the most significant were his alliance with Sen. Edward M. Kennedy, D-Mass., in proposing immigration reform legislation that included a program to assimilate many of the nation's millions of undocumented workers; his crusade for enactment in 2002 of a law tightening federal campaign finance, which many conservatives view as an infringement on their freedom of speech; and his conclusion, early among Republicans, that global climate change was a major environmental problem that should be met with assertive federal intervention.

In a society that seemed fixated on youth, McCain's one big disadvantage was his age—he was seventy-two in August 2008 and would have been the oldest president at the time of his inauguration. But he sought to allay concerns by campaigning with vigor, often aboard a bus he dubbed the "Straight Talk Express," as he had during his unsuccessful bid in 2000.

McCain's wide recognition among voters and his populist image convinced many in the party that he could reach beyond the GOP base to win over independents and some Democrats. But McCain had alienated many conservative activists when he waged a serious challenge to Bush for the 2000 nomination. During that contest, he described Pat Robertson and Jerry Falwell, longtime leaders of the Christian conservative movement and crucial supporters of Bush, as "agents of intolerance." Although McCain heartily endorsed Bush for reelection in 2004 and reached out to the Christian right, the senator was still regarded with a great deal of suspicion by many on the Republican right.

McCain's campaign got off to a rocky start after his official entry into the race in April 2007 when he enlisted so many enthusiastic consultants that his campaign grew top-heavy and quickly burned through millions of dollars. By July the organization was nearly broke, and McCain was compelled to make some serious changes, which appeared to stabilize the operation.

But the senator had slipped badly in the polls. A CBS News survey from Aug. 8–12, 2007, showed former New York City mayor Rudolph Giuliani with the support of 38 percent of GOP respondents, followed in second place, with 18 percent, by former senator Fred Thompson of Tennessee, whose other career as an actor led some Republicans to hope that, like Reagan, he could become a rallying figure for conservatives. Third, with 13 percent, was Mitt Romney, the former governor of Massachusetts, who once was seen as a center-right Republican but who was campaigning for president on a strongly conservative platform. McCain was fourth with 12 percent. Later in the year, this top tier of candidates was joined by Mike Huckabee, a former governor of Arkansas who rose quickly in the polls because his role as a Southern Baptist minister appealed to many conservatives.

Joining these five in the race for the GOP nomination was Rep. Ron Paul of Texas, a libertarian Republican who was alone in the GOP field in opposing the war in Iraq. Paul developed a fervent though relatively small following and remained in the race through the end of the primary schedule in early June 2008. Five others joined the race but quickly dropped out. They were former governors Tommy G. Thompson of Wisconsin and James S. Gilmore III of Virginia; Sen. Sam Brownback of Kansas, and Reps. Duncan Hunter of California and Tom Tancredo of Colorado.

AN EARLY WINNOWING

McCain skipped the Jan. 3, 2008, kickoff event in Iowa, which he had no chance of winning. The gamble paid off. Romney invested heavily in Iowa but finished second, with 27 percent to 30 percent for Huckabee. Thompson took 12 percent, the same share McCain won without campaigning.

Romney faced a must-win situation five days later in New Hampshire, which neighbors his home state. But his emphasis on Iowa had provided an important opportunity to McCain, who had focused on New Hampshire, an open-primary state (allowing voters registered in one party to vote in another party's contest). McCain in New Hampshire had scored a stunning upset of Bush in 2000. In 2008 McCain won the primary again with 37 percent to 32 percent for Romney. Huckabee slipped to 12 percent.

The next big contest was the Jan. 15 primary in Michigan, the state where Romney was born and where his father had been an auto company chief executive and governor in the 1960s. Although McCain had won the state in 2000, he was given little likelihood to do so again in 2008, especially after he angered many voters there with his "straight talk" assessment that "there are some jobs that aren't coming back to Michigan." Romney won, 39 percent to McCain's 30 percent.

But the race permanently turned in McCain's favor four days later with his victory in the South Carolina primary. Eight years earlier McCain had suffered a defeat by Bush in the state that all but ended his hopes. This time he won with a modest plurality of 33 percent, which topped Huckabee's 30 percent, ending the Arkansan's hopes of establishing himself as the candidate of the South. Thompson made a last-stand bid for a foothold on that same turf, but he finished with 16 percent and quit the race. Romney scored only 15 percent in the state.

It was during this period that McCain stirred some controversy by declaring that he would not vote again for the immigration bill he had written with Kennedy but instead work for border security—a position held by many conservatives eager to crack down on illegal immigration. McCain also pushed hard to exploit his principal rival's biggest weakness: the opinion of many conservatives that Romney was not altogether trustworthy and was a campaign-season convert to positions important to the party's right-wing. McCain's advertisements raised questions about Romney's fealty to tax cuts and the Iraq War, prompting Romney to protest that McCain had unfairly distorted his record. Romney's Mormon religion also may have hindered him from building support among mainstream Christian Republicans.

The Jan. 29 Florida primary further slowed Romney, who lost to McCain, 36 percent to 31 percent. That primary also eliminated Giuliani from the race. The former mayor of New York had remained first in the polls through most of 2007, but his backings dropped as voters grew weary of continual reference to his widely praised role as mayor following 2001 terrorist attacks and as social conservatives learned more about his three marriages and his more liberal position on social issues. With dwindling support, Giuliani had decided to wager his entire campaign on winning Florida, a state with a sizable population of transplanted New Yorkers. Instead he finished third with 15 percent.

MCCAIN MOMENTUM

McCain's momentum gave him a significant advantage going into Super Tuesday on Feb. 5. He won nine of the day's twenty-one contests, including the big delegate prizes of California, New York, Illinois, New Jersey, and Missouri. Romney won seven, but most were in smaller states with fewer delegates. Four days later, Romney ended his campaign in a speech at the annual Conservative Political Action Conference in Washington.

Although he had a dominant lead, McCain had not yet secured a majority of convention delegates. Huckabee, who had won five Super Tuesday contests, kept his campaign going in hopes that conservatives who were not thrilled with McCain might rally around him. He received some encouragement by winning Feb. 9 contests in Kansas and Louisiana, but those were his final victories. McCain's wins in four states on March 4 put him over the top and prompted Huckabee to concede.

The strong finish that enabled McCain to wrap up the nomination early overshadowed an imbalance in voter turnout that worried GOP strategists. The Democratic nominating contest between Obama and Clinton was drawing many more voters than the Republic side, producing discussion that the Republicans were suffering from an "enthusiasm gap."

McCain's hopes for victory in November appeared heavily dependent on the winner of the Democratic contest being irreparably damaged by the prolonged battle to win the nomination. Instead, Clinton endorsed the victorious Obama, and they achieved a reconciliation much quicker than had seemed plausible during their long and often acrimonious contest. Meanwhile, from early March to early June, McCain, with his primary campaign funds mostly spent, sat on the sidelines, his visibility reduced for three months as the voters and the media focused on the race between the two Democrats.

CHOOSING RUNNING MATES

Shortly after Obama locked up the nomination, his campaign unveiled a strategy for the general election campaign focused on "spreading the playing field" by competing not only for the electoral votes of traditional battleground states—among them Ohio, Pennsylvania, Florida, Iowa, and New Mexico—but in long-standing Republican presidential strongholds such as Virginia, North Carolina, and Colorado.

Republicans scoffed that the Obama campaign was blowing smoke in an effort to bait McCain and his party into unnecessarily spending time and money defending states that should be securely in their column. But the Republicans underestimated Obama's determination to follow through on his plan, the ability of his well-endowed campaign to do so, and the underlying weakness of the GOP's case for retaining the White House in the political atmosphere of 2008.

McCain campaigned on standard Republican arguments that he would be a better steward of voters' tax dollars and a stronger defender of national security. But his efforts to slow Obama's momentum involved a series of shifting and at times contradictory tactical moves, which contrasted, mostly unfavorably, with the Democrat's steady and unflappable demeanor—a calmness that earned him the nickname "No Drama Obama."

Obama, after absorbing a steady barrage of criticism from McCain about his lack of experience in foreign relations, embarked on a heavily publicized foreign tour in July that took him to the war zones of Afghanistan and

Iraq and to several European capitals where Bush's foreign policies were highly unpopular. The highlight was an outdoor speech before a huge and enraptured throng in the German capital of Berlin.

Although Obama received mainly positive coverage from the U.S. press, the McCain campaign launched an ad at the end of July that derided Obama as "the world's biggest celebrity" and juxtaposed a photograph of him with images of socialite Paris Hilton and pop star Britney Spears. It turned out to be the most successful ploy of McCain's campaign, raising questions about Obama's depth. The Republicans returned to the theme after Obama accepted the Democratic nomination on Aug. 28 before a crowd of 84,000 that filled Denver's pro football stadium.

Yet the very next day, after hammering Obama for months as inexperienced and the political equivalent of a superficial rock star, McCain announced that he had chosen Gov. Sarah Palin of Alaska as his running mate. Palin, who at forty-four was younger than Obama, had been governor for less than two years. Her political experience before that consisted of two years on a state regulatory board and six years as the mayor of an Anchorage suburb of fewer than 10,000 people. Introduced to most Americans for the first time at the Republican Convention in St. Paul the first week of September, the charismatic and staunchly conservative Palin quickly proved a magnet for huge crowds of Republican loyalists. Seeing her effect in animating McCain's campaign events, the campaign began to tout her as an even bigger celebrity than Obama.

Palin was only the second woman—and the first Republican woman—on a national, major-party ticket. (The other was Rep. Geraldine Ferraro of New York, the 1984 Democratic vice-presidential nominee.)

Despite Palin's splashy start, her choice turned out to be, at best, a wash for McCain. While her popularity among conservatives addressed one of his biggest chronic weaknesses, she did not appeal to a crucial bloc of moderate Republican and independent voters. She also was unable to appeal to more liberal women who had supported Hillary Clinton and were disappointed that she had not won the Democratic nomination. Moreover, Palin's stumbling performances in interviews and her Obama-bashing partisanship became fodder for comedians, most notably Tina Fey of NBC's *Saturday Night Live*, whose dead-on impersonation of Palin was matched by her uncanny physical resemblance.

Obama had moved from the outset toward a much more conventional choice for vice president. In the end, the finalists were Biden, Sen. Evan Bayh of Indiana, and Gov. Tim Kaine of Virginia. Of the three, Biden had far and away the most foreign policy experience and was chosen in part to counteract voters' concerns about Obama's relative lack of experience in this area. Biden's modest upbringing in the Pennsylvania city of Scranton and his long rapport with white working-class voters were also expected to help seal off another of Obama's political weaknesses.

POLITICS AND THE ECONOMIC CRISIS

The near collapse of the financial sector in September boosted Obama into a lead in the polls that he would maintain to election day. While McCain was hobbled by the fact that the economic tailspin occurred on the watch of a Republican president, his own actions underscored the downside of his improvisational approach to politics.

After first drawing heat by telling a campaign audience that "the fundamentals of the economy are sound," McCain described the situation as a crisis. On Sept. 24, two days before his first scheduled debate with Obama, McCain said he would suspend his campaign to return to Washington to help broker a deal on a rescue bill for the financial industry. He then prevailed upon Bush to convene a summit at the White House that included both presidential candidates and congressional leaders of both parties. Obama, saying that voters expected a potential president to be able to handle more than one responsibility at a time, rejected the idea of suspending his campaign. McCain's strategy backfired when the summit dissolved into partisan rancor. House Republicans, whom McCain had tried to persuade to vote for the legislation, instead sent it to an embarrassing defeat. A revised version was enacted a few days later.

The traditional presidential debates—three between Obama and McCain on Sept. 26 at the University of Mississippi in Oxford, Oct. 7 at Belmont University in Nashville, and Oct. 15 at Hofstra University in Hempstead, N.Y.; and one between Biden and Palin on Oct. 2 at Washington University in St. Louis—did little to change the dynamic of the race. By the middle of October, Obama was maintaining a steady lead in national polls of mid- to high-single digits. More ominously for McCain, Obama moved into big leads in several states that had been expected to produce competitive races.

THE PRESIDENTIAL VOTE

When all the votes were counted, Obama captured nearly 53 percent of the popular vote and 365 electoral votes to 173 for McCain. But neither candidate waited for the count to be completed to acknowledge the victor. Late in the evening of Nov. 4, Election Day, when it was clear that Obama had won a majority of the electoral college votes, McCain conceded and Obama appeared with his family before a joyous crowd in Chicago's Grant Park. It was clear that the president-elect was already thinking about the challenges he and the country would face starting the next day. "The road ahead will be long. Our climb will be steep. We may not get there in one year or even in one term," he said to a worldwide audience riveted by his achievement. "But, America, I have never been more hopeful than I am tonight that we will get there. I promise you, we as a people will get there."

Although Obama's election was not a landslide of the sort enjoyed by Franklin Delano Roosevelt in 1936 or

Lyndon B. Johnson in 1964, it was widely considered a substantial majority that Obama could legitimately consider a mandate for a different approach to national and international issues than had prevailed under his predecessor. Obama would take office in January with 257 Democrats in the House and at least fifty-six in the Senate. With the votes of two independents who caucused with the Democrats, the conversion of veteran Pennsylvania senator Arlen Specter from Republican to Democrat in April 2009, and the declaration in July 2009 that Democrat Al Franken had won the closely contested Minnesota Senate race, Obama had, at least on paper, the sixty votes needed to cut off filibusters in the Senate. Whether he could muster that number on the numerous controversial issues likely to come before the Senate was a different question, however.

About 131.3 million Americans cast a vote for a presidential candidate on Nov. 4, the most in history. Thanks in part to the Democrats' registration and voter turnout drives, Obama received 69.5 million votes, or 52.9 percent of all votes cast, to McCain's 59.9 million votes (45.7 percent). Other candidates, including perennial third-party candidate Ralph Nader, received 1.8 million votes (1.4 percent).

According to a report from the Census Bureau released in July 2009, 63.6 percent of the nation's eligible voters went to the polls in 2008, down a fraction from the 63.8 percent that voted in 2004. The biggest drop in turnout came among white voters; 66 percent voted in 2008 compared with 67 percent in 2004. Sixty-five percent of eligible black voters cast ballots in 2008, a five-percentage point increase over 2004. Hispanics and Asians also increased their turnout, each reaching a turnout of almost 50 percent. Almost one of every four ballots was cast by a minority, making the 2008 electorate the most diverse in the nation's history.

Obama received more votes than any presidential candidate in history, easily topping the 62 million votes that Bush won in his 2004 reelection campaign. Obama's share of the popular vote was also the largest for a presidential candidate since 1988, when Republican George H.W. Bush took 53.4 percent of the vote to win his first and only term. It was the highest for a Democratic candidate since 1964, when Johnson won with 61.1 percent of the vote. Obama's margin of victory of 7.2 percentage points was the largest for a nonincumbent Democratic presidential candidate since 1932, when Roosevelt unseated President Herbert Hoover by nearly 18 points.

Obama swept the nineteen states that Democrat John Kerry won in 2004 as well as nine states that Bush had carried—three in the South (Florida, North Carolina, and Virginia), three in the Midwest (Indiana, Iowa, and Ohio), and three in the West (Colorado, Nevada, and New Mexico). Indiana and Virginia had last voted Democratic for president in 1964.

The twenty-eight states that Obama won had a cumulative 364 electoral votes, but the electoral college tally was 365–174 because Obama won one of five electoral votes in Nebraska; McCain outpolled Obama statewide, but Obama won more votes in the congressional district that included Omaha. Nebraska was one of two states—the other was Maine—that did not use a winner-take-all system of awarding electoral votes but rather a district-based system that awarded two electoral votes to the statewide winner and one electoral vote for each congressional district a candidate carried. Among the fifty states, Obama took his largest vote share in his birth state of Hawaii (71.8 percent); McCain's best-performing state was Oklahoma (65.5 percent).

Presidential Vote by Region

Democrat Barack Obama received more votes in 2008 than any other presidential candidate in history, winning 69.5 million votes to Republican John McCain's 59.9 million. Obama's margin of victory was nearly 9.5 million votes, or 7.2 percentage points. Obama improved the Democrats' share of the presidential vote in all four regions of the country, including the South, where he won three states (Florida, North Carolina, and Virginia) that Democrat John Kerry lost in 2004. Obama also won three states in the Midwest (Indiana, Iowa, and Ohio), and three in the West (Colorado, Nevada, and New Mexico) that Kerry lost, as well as the nineteen states that Kerry claimed.

	2004			
	Popular vote		*Electoral vote*	
Region	*Kerry*	*Bush*	*Kerry*	*Bush*
East	56%	43%	117	5
Midwest	48	51	58	66
South	42	57	0	168
West	50	49	77	47
National	48	51	252	286
	2008			
	Popular vote		*Electoral vote*	
Region	*Obama*	*McCain*	*Obama*	*McCain*
East	59%	37%	117	5
Midwest	54	45	97	27
South	46	53	55	113
West	55	42	96	28
National	53	46	365	173

THE TRANSITION

Obama's victory celebration was short. The very next day the president-elect and his transition team began work by appointing key White House staff and cabinet members and beginning to devise policy proposals. Among his first appointments: John D. Podesta, chief of staff in the Clinton White House, as head of his transition team, and Illinois representative Rahm Emanuel as his chief of staff.

Obama also made the appointment of his economic team a top priority. In a Nov. 24 news conference in Chicago, where he spent most of his time before his inauguration, Obama named Timothy F. Geithner his choice to succeed Henry M. Paulson Jr. as Treasury secretary.

Geithner, the president of the New York Federal Reserve Bank, had worked closely with Paulson and Federal Reserve Chairman Ben S. Bernanke on the bailout of the financial system, and Geithner's nomination had been widely expected. Other key members of the Obama's economic team included Lawrence Summers, Clinton's Treasury secretary and the former president of Harvard University, named as chairman of the White House National Economic Council; Peter R. Orszag, director of the Congressional Budget Office, named director of the White House Office of Management and Budget; and Christina D. Romer, an economics professor at the University of California at Berkeley, named chairman of the Council of Economic Advisers. On Nov. 26, Obama announced the creation of an Economic Recovery Advisory Board, to be chaired by former Federal Reserve chairman Paul A. Volcker.

Obama also said he expected to have the broad outlines of a stimulus package ready for Congress to consider when it convened on Jan. 3, 2009. Typically, when a president takes office, Congress convenes on or shortly after Jan. 3 and then leaves town until Inauguration Day. In 2009, however, Democratic leaders of both houses kept their chambers in session and working for much of the period. Less than a month after taking office, Obama signed a $780 billion stimulus package into law (PL 111-5).

Other key appointments included Hillary Clinton as secretary of state and Gov. Janet Napolitano of Arizona as secretary of homeland security. Robert Gates, who succeeded Rumsfeld as secretary of defense in 2007, agreed to remain in that position in the Obama administration. Other members of the Obama national security team included James L. Jones, a retired four-star marine general, as national security adviser, and former representative Leon Panetta of California as director of the CIA.

Although the Obama transition team had promised to do a careful vetting of all potential nominees, several of Obama's key appointments were forced to withdraw their nominations in the face of ethics questions. Perhaps the most disappointing for Obama was the withdrawal of Tom Daschle as secretary of health and human services. Daschle, a well-respected former Senate majority leader, was expected to head Obama's drive to secure health care reform legislation but withdrew his resignation after it was revealed that he had failed to pay some back taxes. Kansas governor Kathleen Sebelius was later given the job. Tax issues also dogged Geithner's nomination, but he was ultimately confirmed on a 60–34 vote.

New Mexico governor Bill Richardson withdrew his nomination for commerce secretary amid a federal "pay for play" probe involving a campaign donor; Richardson was later cleared of any involvement in the matter. Obama then named Judd Gregg, a moderate Republican senator from New Hampshire to the post, but after saying he would take the position, Gregg changed his mind, citing "irreconcilable differences" with Obama on economic stimulus and the conduct of the 2010 Census, which is a responsibility of the Commerce Department. Obama then named former governor Garry Locke of Washington to the post; Locke was easily confirmed.

Obama's cabinet was the most diverse in presidential history. It included five women—Clinton, Sebelius, Napolitano, Labor Secretary Hilda Solis, and EPA administrator Lisa Jackson—and two Republicans, Gates and Transportation Secretary Ray LaHood, a former U.S. representative from Illinois. Two Hispanics—Solis and Interior Secretary Ken Salazar, a senator from Colorado—joined three Asian Americans—Locke; Eric K. Shinseki, former Army chief of staff, named secretary of veterans affairs; and Steven Chu, a Nobel Prize winner and the director of the Lawrence Berkeley National Laboratory, named energy secretary—and three African Americans—Jackson; Eric Holder, deputy attorney general in the Clinton administration, named attorney general; and Ron Kirk, the former mayor of Dallas, named U.S. trade representative.

Obama was helped in the transition by the unusual cooperation offered by President Bush and top members of his staff. Bush set up a formal transition council to help transfer power, and his staff helped expedite security checks for Obama's appointees. While President Bush took some policy actions that Obama was thought likely to try to overturn, the outgoing president also made a few unpopular decisions before he left office, relieving Obama of the need to deal with them in his first days in office. These included agreeing to use bailout funds for loans to General Motors and Chrysler to help the automakers stave off bankruptcy and asking Congress to release the second half of the $700 billion financial bailout.

Senate Elections

Democrats dominated the Senate balloting for the second election in a row, gaining a total of eight seats in the 2008 election (although the outcome of the Minnesota race was not determined until July 2009). Counting the two independents who had caucused with the Democrats, the new majority stood at fifty-nine seats. The new Democratic majority was the largest for either party since 1994, just before Republicans gained eight seats and control of the Senate.

But the final lineup was not clear for several months. The results of several Senate contests were not finalized until days or even weeks after the election. In Minnesota, nearly eight months elapsed before the victor was declared. Al Franken, the humorist and radio talk show host, ultimately defeated one-term Republican Norm Coleman by 312 votes but was not sworn in until July 7, 2009, after Coleman's legal challenge failed and he conceded the election. Meanwhile, Republican senator Arlen Specter of Pennsylvania switched parties in April 2009, fearing that he would lose the 2010 Republican primary to a more conservative GOP opponent. Specter's defection to the

Democrats gave the party its potential sixtieth vote, necessary to cut off filibusters. *(Minnesota race, p. 35)*

In addition to Coleman, four Republican incumbents were turned out. In New Hampshire, John E. Sununu, who was finishing his first term, lost to former governor Jeanne Shaheen, who had lost to Sununu in 2002 by four percentage points. Shaheen, a moderate on fiscal and social issues, had wide support from the state and national parties and led Sununu in the polls throughout most of the year, despite Sununu's attempts to distance himself from President Bush and the national Republican Party.

In North Carolina, Kay Hagen, a moderate state senator, shocked Republicans by trouncing Elizabeth Dole, who had held cabinet posts in two Republican administrations before succeeding conservative icon Jesse Helms in the Senate in 2002. In Oregon, Gordon Smith, seeking a third term, emphasized his generally moderate and independent voting record, including his support for environmentalist causes and gay rights. That was not enough to overcome an increasingly strong Democratic trend in the state, which was backing Jeff Merkley, speaker of the state house. Smith did not concede the race until Nov. 6, two days after the election; Merkley won with 49 percent of the vote to Smith's 46 percent.

The fourth turnover came in Alaska, when Ted Stevens, the longest-serving Republican senator in history, conceded that he had lost his campaign for a seventh full term on Nov. 18. Unofficial Election Day returns put Stevens slightly ahead of Democrat Mark Begich, the mayor of Anchorage—a surprising result, given that Stevens had been politically wounded by his conviction in federal court a week earlier on seven felony counts of failing to report

Incumbents Reelected, Defeated, or Retired, 1946–2008

Year	Retired[1]	Total seeking reelection	Defeated in primaries	Defeated in general election	Total reelected	Percentage of those seeking reelection
House						
1946	32	398	18	52	328	82.4%
1948	29	400	15	68	317	79.3
1950	29	400	6	32	362	90.5
1952	42	389	9	26	354	91.0
1954	24	407	6	22	379	93.1
1956	21	411	6	16	389	94.6
1958	33	396	3	37	356	89.9
1960	27	405	5	25	375	92.6
1962	24	402	12	22	368	91.5
1964	33	397	8	45	344	86.6
1966	23	411	8	41	362	88.1
1968	24	408	4	9	395	96.8
1970	30	401	10	12	379	94.5
1972	40	392	14	13	366	93.4
1974	43	391	8	40	343	87.7
1976	47	384	3	13	368	95.8
1978	49	382	5	19	358	93.7
1980	34	398	6	31	361	90.7
1982	31	387	4	29	354	91.5
1984	22	409	3	16	390	95.4
1986	38	393	2	6	385	98.0
1988	23	408	1	6	401	98.3
1990	27	407	1	15	391	96.1
1992	65	368	19	24	325	88.3
1994	48	387	4	34	349	90.2
1996	49	384	2	21	361	94.0
1998	33	402	1	6	395	98.3
2000	32	405	3	6	396	97.8
2002	35	398	8	8	382	96.0
2004	29	404	2	7	395	97.8
2006	27	404	2	22	380	94.1
2008	32	403	4	19	380	94.3

Year	Retired[1]	Total seeking reelection	Defeated in primaries	Defeated in general election	Total reelected	Percentage of those seeking reelection
Senate						
1946	9	30	6	7	17	56.7%
1948	8	25	2	8	15	60.0
1950	4	32	5	5	22	68.8
1952	4	31	2	9	20	64.5
1954	6	32	2	6	24	75.0
1956	6	29	0	4	25	86.2
1958	6	28	0	10	18	64.3
1960	4	29	0	1	28	96.6
1962	4	35	1	5	29	82.9
1964	2	33	1	4	28	84.8
1966	3	32	3	1	28	87.5
1968	6	28	4	4	20	71.4
1970	4	31	1	6	24	77.4
1972	6	27	2	5	20	74.1
1974	7	27	2	2	23	85.2
1976	8	25	0	9	16	64.0
1978	10	25	3	7	15	60.0
1980	5	29	4	9	16	55.2
1982	3	30	0	2	28	93.3
1984	4	29	0	3	26	89.7
1986	6	28	0	7	21	75.0
1988	6	27	0	4	23	85.2
1990	3	32	0	1	31	96.9
1992	7	28	1	4	23	82.1
1994	9	26	0	2	24	92.3
1996	13	21	1	1	19	90.5
1998	4	30	0	3	27	90.0
2000	5	29	0	6	23	79.3
2002	5	28	1	3	24	85.7
2004	8	26	0	1	25	96.2
2006	4	29	1	6	23	79.3
2008	5	30	0	5	25	83.3

SOURCES: Norman J. Ornstein, Thomas E. Mann, and Michael J. Malbin, *Vital Statistics on Congress, 2001–2002* (Washington, D.C.: American Enterprise Institute, 2002); *CQ Weekly*, selected issues; Richard Scammon, Alice McGillivray, and Rhodes Cook, *America Votes* (Washington, D.C.: CQ Press, 2001) various editions; Harold W. Stanley and Richard G. Niemi, *Vital Statistics on American Politics, 2009–2010* (Washington, D.C., CQ Press, 2009).

NOTE:[1] Does not include persons who died or resigned before the election except, in the case of deaths, for candidates whose name remained on the ballot.

LENGTHY SENATE ABSENCES

Often in presidential election cycles, Senate leaders must cope with extended absences of members who are seeking the presidency. That was the case in 2007 and 2008 when four Democrats—Barack Obama, Ill., Hillary Rodham Clinton, N.Y., Joseph R. Biden Jr., Del., and Christopher Dodd, Conn.—and two Republicans—John McCain, Ariz., and Sam Brownback, Kan.—were campaigning for the White House. House absences occur but less often. In 2008 Democrat Dennis Kucinich of Ohio and Republicans Duncan Hunter of California, Tom Tancredo of California, and Ron Paul of Texas were absent for periods to seek their parties' presidential nominations.

Typically, campaigners return if their vote might affect an outcome. Because the Senate is smaller, the absence of a single member is more likely to make a difference. That was the case, for example, when both Obama and McCain left their campaigns in September 2008 to vote on financial bailout legislation in the midst of a severe economic crisis.

Serious illness or incapacitation can present similar challenges to Senate leaders. In July 2008 while fighting a brain tumor, Edward M. Kennedy, D-Mass., returned to help end a Republican filibuster on a Medicare bill; he returned again in February 2009 to help end a GOP filibuster of economic stimulus legislation. Kennedy made only a few other visits to the Capitol after his illness was announced May 20, 2008, most notably for the inauguration of President Obama on Jan. 20, 2009. Kennedy had a long reputation as a legislative dealmaker and tactician. Although he was involved from his home in helping to write the landmark 2009 health care reform legislation, colleagues and others said it was not the same as if Kennedy had been on the scene personally to make the deals necessary to forge a measure with broad appeal to both Democrats and Republicans. Five months after his last Senate vote, Kennedy died on Aug. 29, 2009.

In some cases, illness or incapacity has threatened the Senate's party balance. In December 2006 Democrat Tim Johnson, South Dakota's senior senator, underwent emergency surgery to stanch bleeding on the brain from a condition known as arteriovenous malformation. He then underwent months of rehabilitation and did not return to the Senate until Sept. 5, 2007. Had Johnson died or resigned, the state's Republican governor was expected to name a Republican to take his place, leaving the Senate in a 50–50 tie, with Republican vice president Dick Cheney in a position to break any tie votes.

Nothing in the Constitution or Senate rules requires a senator to resign in the event of a debilitating illness, and long-term absences have not been unusual. South Dakota's Karl E. Mundt, for example, was away for more than three years after a stroke. Nor have lengthy absences affected the electoral status of a sitting senator. Johnson, for example, was elected to a third Senate term in 2008 with more than 62 percent of the vote.

Illness sometimes produced dramatic moments in Senate history. One came on two 1964 votes a week apart by Clair Engle, D-Calif., to end a Republican filibuster of the 1964 Civil Rights Act and then for passage of the legislation. Engle, suffering the final stages of a brain tumor, was wheeled on to the Senate floor. Unable to speak, he pointed to his eye, and the clerk duly recorded his vote as an "aye."

Ironically the civil rights debate figured in another extended absence from the Senate. After making his first major Senate speech, in support of the civil rights legislation, Kennedy was almost killed when the private plane in which he was returning to Massachusetts crashed. Kennedy sustained back injuries that left him bedridden for several months.

Following are notable extended Senate absences dating to 1942, according to Senate historian Richard A. Baker:

- Styles Bridges, R-N.H.: January 1942 to June 1942. Bridges fractured a hip in a fall on Dec. 31, 1941.
- Carter Glass, D-Va.: June 1942 until his death at the age of eighty-eight on May 28, 1946. Glass was absent because of the infirmities of old age, despite holding the posts of president pro tempore (1941–1945) and chairman of the Appropriations Committee. He was reelected in November 1942.
- Robert F. Wagner, D-N.Y.: January 1947 until his resignation June 28, 1949. Wagner had a heart ailment that prevented him from attending any sessions in the 80th or 81st Congresses.
- Arthur H. Vandenberg, R-Mich.: October 1949 until his death April 18, 1951. After major surgery to remove a tumor on his lung in October 1949, Vandenberg returned to the Senate briefly in January and February 1950, then was absent for most of 1950, with a second surgery in April and another brief return to the Senate in May of that year.
- Joseph R. Biden Jr., D-Del.: Feb. 12, 1988 until Sept. 7, 1988. Biden had surgery for a brain aneurysm.
- Al Gore, D-Tenn.: On the opening day of the baseball season, April 3, 1989, Gore and his four-year-old son, Albert Gore III, were leaving the baseball stadium in Baltimore when the younger Gore was struck by an automobile and seriously injured. The senator and his wife alternately remained at Johns Hopkins Hospital with their son until his release. Gore returned to the Senate on May 1, 1989.
- David Pryor, D-Ark.: April 15, 1991, until Sept. 10, 1991. Pryor suffered a heart attack in Washington, D.C.

expensive gifts from home-state business interests. But a count of thousands of absentee ballots put Begich on top by about 4,000 votes. Stevens's conviction was set aside in April 2009 after the Justice Department asked for a dismissal, citing prosecutorial misconduct and said the department was mounting an investigation. *(Stevens's trial, p. 838)*

Democrats also won three open seats that had been held by Republicans: Colorado, New Mexico, and Virginia. The seats in Colorado and New Mexico were taken by two first cousins, who were moving up from the House. Rep. Mark Udall benefited from a nearly decade-long Democratic surge in Colorado to take the seat formerly held by Wayne Allard, while Rep. Tom Udall won handily to take the seat in New Mexico relinquished by Pete Domenici after thirty-six years in office.

In Virginia, Mark Warner, a popular centrist governor from 2002 through 2005 who entered the Senate race after considering a run for the Democratic presidential nomination, won by thirty-one points over another former governor, James S. Gilmore III, who was a distinct underdog throughout the race. Warner's election coincided with Obama's victory in the state, the first by any Democratic presidential nominee since 1964.

Democrats almost turned out another Republican senator, Saxby Chambliss of Georgia, who did not receive the 50 percent required in the state to claim outright victory over Democratic opponent Jim Martin on election night. In a runoff election on Dec. 2, Chambliss decisively outpolled Martin, who found it difficult to replicate turnout, especially among African Americans, without Obama on the ballot. Democrats had been determined to defeat Chambliss ever since his winning 2002 campaign, when his ads impugned the patriotism of the Democratic incumbent and Vietnam War veteran Max Cleland.

Republicans put together a strong challenge against only one incumbent Democrat, Mary L. Landrieu of Louisiana, and it failed. She won a third term by six percentage points. Of the eleven other Democratic senators on 2008 ballots, only New Jersey's Frank R. Lautenberg was reelected with less than 60 percent of the vote. Democrats had also targeted three Republican incumbents—Mitch McConnell of Kentucky, Susan Collins of Maine, and Roger Wicker in Mississippi—all of whom won reelection.

THE DEMOCRATIC ADVANTAGE

Democrats had many of the same advantages in the Senate campaigns as Obama did in his presidential campaign: money, public disillusionment with Republicans, and carefully calibrated candidates. The international financial crisis that emerged late in the campaign solidified Democratic chances.

The Democratic Senatorial Campaign Committee had almost twice as much in campaign contributions as the National Republican Senatorial Committee, raising $163 million in the two-year election cycle, compared with $94 million for the Republicans. That imbalance allowed the Democrats to spend heavily in states where Republican candidates otherwise would have had a substantial money edge over their opponents.

Republicans, meanwhile, not only suffered from President Bush's low approval ratings and the accumulated mistakes of his administration, but they also were forced to defend more territory—twenty-three of the thirty-five Senate seats up for election. Moreover, five Republican senators did not seek reelection in 2008, while Democrats did not have a single retirement in their ranks.

In addition to the advantages of money and number of incumbents at stake, experts said the Democrats were able to recruit stronger candidates. The seven Democratic senators first elected in 2008 were a politically experienced bunch: two former governors, two U.S. House members, a state House Speaker, a state senator, and a mayor of his state's biggest city.

APPOINTED DEMOCRATS

In addition to those elected in November, four more Democrats were headed to the Senate as freshmen in 2009, starting with the appointed successors to the newly elected president and vice president. Barack Obama's Illinois Senate seat was taken by Roland W. Burris, a former state attorney general and state treasurer. In a highly controversial appointment, Burris was tapped for the seat on Dec. 29, 2008, by Illinois governor Rod R. Blagojevich, who had been arrested in early December on federal corruption charges that included an allegation that he tried to trade the Senate seat for money. Democratic Senate leaders initially resisted seating Burris but ultimately relented. Burris replaced Obama as the Senate's only African American. The Illinois Legislature in January 2009 removed Blagojevich from office. In July 2009 Burris announced that he would not seek election to a full Senate term in 2010.

Joseph R. Biden Jr. of Delaware, the vice president–elect, was succeeded by Ted Kaufman, his former Senate chief of staff. Kaufman's appointment was announced Nov. 24 by outgoing Delaware governor Ruth Ann Minner. Kaufman said that he would not run in the 2010 special election to fill the remaining four years of the six-year term Biden won with 65 percent of the vote on the same day he was elected vice president. Biden was sworn in for his seventh term in January 2009 and resigned from the Senate five days before his inauguration as vice president. Kaufman was sworn in on Jan. 16.

After Clinton said Dec. 1 that she had accepted Obama's offer to become secretary of state, it took New York governor David A. Paterson nearly eight weeks to decide on a successor. He settled Jan. 23, 2009, on Rep. Kirsten E. Gillibrand, a Democrat who in November 2008 won a second term to an upstate New York district surrounding Albany. Paterson considered appointing Caroline Kennedy, the daughter of President John F. Kennedy, but she took herself

Women in Congress, 1947–2009

Congress	*Senate*	*House*
80th (1947–1949)	1	7
81st (1949–1951)	1	9
82nd (1951–1953)	1	10
83rd (1953–1955)	1	12
84th (1955–1957)	1	17
85th (1957–1959)	1	15
86th (1959–1961)	1	17
87th (1961–1963)	2	18
88th (1963–1965)	2	12
89th (1965–1967)	2	11
90th (1967–1969)	1	10
91st (1969–1971)	1	10
92nd (1971–1973)	1	13
93rd (1973–1975)	1	16
94th (1975–1977)	0	17
95th (1977–1979)	2	18
96th (1979–1981)	1	16
97th (1981–1983)	2	19
98th (1983–1985)	2	22
99th (1985–1987)	2	22
100th (1987–1989)	2	23
101st (1989–1991)	2	28
102nd (1991–1993)	3	29
103rd (1993–1995)	7	48
104th (1995–1997)	8	48
105th (1997–1999)	9	51
106th (1999–2001)	9	56
107th (2001–2003)	13	59
108th (2003–2005)	14	59
109th (2005–2007)	14	64
110th (2007–2009)	16	71
111th (2009–2011)	17	74

NOTE: House totals reflect the number of members at the start of each Congress and exclude nonvoting delegates.

out of the running after initially pursuing the appointment. Gillibrand planned to run in a 2010 special election to serve the final two years of Clinton's term. Gillibrand's House seat was narrowly won in March 2009 by Democrat Scott Murphy.

Michael Bennet, the superintendent of the Denver public school system, was appointed on Jan. 3, 2009, by Colorado governor Bill Ritter Jr. to take the seat vacated when Ken Salazar resigned to head the Interior Department. Bennet took office on Jan. 22 after Salazar's nomination was confirmed by the Senate.

House Elections

Democrats solidified control of the House on Nov. 4, the second consecutive election in which the party gained a significant number of House seats. Democrats had a net gain of twenty-one seats to augment the thirty-seat gain in the 2006 midterm elections, when Democrats ended a dozen years of GOP control in the House.

Democrats unseated fourteen Republican incumbents and captured twelve open districts that had been held by Republicans. The Republicans won just five Democratic seats, defeating incumbents in each. That, however, was a significantly better performance than two years earlier, when the GOP did not take a single seat away from the Democrats.

Democrats entered Election Day with effective control of 236 districts, counting a vacant, heavily Democratic district in Ohio that the party easily retained, compared with 199 seats for the GOP. The 2008 results gave Democrats 257 seats, their largest caucus since early 1994, when they effectively controlled 259 seats.

House Democratic offices described the election as an unmitigated success, pointing to the rarity of the same party making substantial gains in the House in consecutive election years. The Republicans lost House seats in 1996, two years after their watershed election, and the Democrats also sustained losses in 1984, two years after they made big gains midway through President Reagan's first term. Not since 1952 had a party gained at least twenty House seats in an election after winning at least as many in the previous election.

Democrats ran in a political environment that was at least as favorable to their party as in 2006, when voters were angry about Bush's Iraq War policy and about corruption scandals involving House Republicans. Those issues were less of a factor in the 2008 campaign. But they were replaced by the deteriorating economy, an issue that also weighed heavily against the party holding the White House. Throughout the election cycle, voters gave the Bush administration poor marks on handling economic policy, and the GOP bore the lion's share of the blame from voters for the turmoil in the financial markets.

The public unhappiness with the Republicans allowed Democrats to thrive in candidate recruitment and expand the number of competitive districts. Democrats mounted especially vigorous challenges in many generally Republican-leaning districts that had voted decisively for Bush in 2004. Of the twenty-six Democratic candidates who prevailed in GOP-held seats, twelve were from districts that voted for Republican John McCain for president, and all but three were from districts that went for President Bush in 2004.

The Democratic campaign efforts also were aided by a lopsided partisan disparity in the districts where incumbents were not seeking reelection, either because they were retiring or seeking other offices or because they were defeated in primary elections. Of those thirty-five seats, Republicans were defending twenty-nine and the Democrats just six.

Democrats made gains in virtually every region of the nation. In Connecticut, Chris Shays, a moderate Republican, lost his bid for reelection to a Democratic investment banker, leaving Republicans without a single House seat in

New England for the first time in the party's history. A Democratic gain of three seats in New York put the party in control of twenty-six of the state's twenty-nine congressional districts, including all thirteen that included parts of New York City.

Democrats also registered major gains in the Mountain West, a fast-growing, generally politically independent region. They came out of the election with control of all three House seats in New Mexico, five of Colorado's seven seats, and five of eight seats in Arizona. A high turnout from strongly Democratic African American voters, energized by Obama's presence at the top of the ticket, helped Democratic challengers displace Republicans in one district in North Carolina, one in Ohio, and two in Virginia; all four districts were more than one-fifth black.

Republicans held down their net loss by unseating five Democratic incumbents, four of them freshmen from districts that normally voted Republican, one of whom, Tim Mahoney of Florida, was caught up in a sex scandal that came to light in the waning weeks of the campaign. The fifth Democrat unseated was William J. Jefferson of Louisiana, who had been indicted in 2007 on federal corruption charges and who lost in his party's primary. (Jefferson was convicted on several of those charges in August 2009 but said he would appeal.)

It was clear well ahead of the November balloting that Democrats were headed for gains in the House. Throughout the campaign, public opinion surveys showed that voters preferred a Democratic-run Congress. Bush's poor approval rating was a major hindrance to House Republican campaign efforts and motivated Democrats to air commercials linking GOP candidates to the unpopular president and his policies. There were also warning signs in the spring, when the Democrats won three special elections in GOP-leaning districts that Republicans vacated.

Special House Elections, 2008

Eight special elections for House seats foreshadowed the rough time Republicans would face in November 2008. Democrats picked up three seats from the Republicans, the first time in thirty years that one political party took that many seats away from the opposing party during a single Congress. Democrats also maintained control of four seats, in California, Indiana, Maryland, and Ohio, while Republicans held on to one, in Louisiana.

The first turnover came in the Illinois district that had been represented since 1986 by J. Dennis Hastert, who served as the Republican Speaker of the House from 1999 through 2006 and who resigned in November 2007. Democrat Bill Foster, a scientist and first-time candidate, won with 53 percent of the vote in the district that President Bush had won in 2004 with 55 percent of the vote.

The other two Democratic pickups came in Louisiana, where state representative Don Cazayoux won a seat that had been held for twenty-one years by the same Republican (Cazayoux lost the seat in the November election), and Mississippi, where Travis W. Childers upset the Republican to replace Rep. Roger Wicker, who had been appointed to the Senate in December 2007 to succeed fellow Republican Trent Lott, who had resigned. Bush had won 66 percent in the district in 2004, and the GOP spent more than $1 million trying to hold onto the seat.

Obama Appointments

In addition to the special election in New York to fill the seat left vacant when Kirsten E. Gillibrand was appointed to succeed Hillary Rodham Clinton in the Senate, three Democratic House vacancies were created when members resigned to take positions in the Obama administration.

Rep. Rahm Emanuel of Illinois resigned his House seat on Jan. 2, 2009, to become White House chief of staff. Democrat Mike Quigley handily won a special election in March to replace Emanuel.

Blacks in Congress, 1947–2009

Congress	*Senate*	*House*
80th (1947–1949)	0	2
81st (1949–1951)	0	2
82nd (1951–1953)	0	2
83rd (1953–1955)	0	2
84th (1955–1957)	0	3
85th (1957–1959)	0	4
86th (1959–1961)	0	4
87th (1961–1963)	0	4
88th (1963–1965)	0	5
89th (1965–1967)	0	6
90th (1967–1969)	1	5
91st (1969–1971)	1	9
92nd (1971–1973)	1	12
93rd (1973–1975)	1	15
94th (1975–1977)	1	16
95th (1977–1979)	1	16
96th (1979–1981)	0	16
97th (1981–1983)	0	17
98th (1983–1985)	0	20
99th (1985–1987)	0	20
100th (1987–1989)	0	22
101st (1989–1991)	0	24
102nd (1991–1993)	0	26
103rd (1993–1995)	1	39
104th (1995–1997)	1	38
105th (1997–1999)	1	37
106th (1999–2001)	0	37
107th (2001–2003)	0	36
108th (2003–2005)	0	39
109th (2005–2007)	1	40
110th (2007–2009)	1	41
111th (2009–2011)	1	41

NOTE: House totals reflect the number of members at the start of each Congress and exclude nonvoting delegates. Senate figure for 111th Congress is as of Jan. 15, 2009.

Hilda Solis of California resigned her House seat after being confirmed as secretary of labor in February 2009. Democrat Judy Chu won the seat in a July 14, 2009, special election.

Ellen O. Tauscher resigned her California seat in June to become undersecretary of state for arms control and international security. A Democrat, John Garamendi, California's lieutenant governor, won the seat in a Nov. 3, 2009, election.

Statehouse Elections

In addition to winning the White House and expanding their majorities in the U.S. House and Senate, Democrats continued their slow march to dominance of state-level politics, adding to their majorities among governorships and legislatures. Democrats carried seven of eleven governorships in play in 2008, for a net gain of one. The state that changed political hands was Missouri, where the Democratic attorney general, Jay Nixon, was elected to succeed Republican Matt Blunt, who decided not to see a second term. As a result of that turnover, Democrats controlled twenty-nine governorships, the most since 1994.

In other notable elections, Washington's incumbent Democratic governor Christine Gregoire prevailed by eight percentage points against Dino Rossi, a former state senator. In 2004 Gregoire had defeated Rossi by just 133 votes after several controversial recounts. In North Carolina, Democratic lieutenant governor Beverly Perdue won a narrow victory over Pat McCrory, the mayor of Charlotte. Perdue was clearly aided by the Obama campaign's organizational efforts in the state. Two Republican governors, Mitch Daniels of Indiana and Jim Douglas of Vermont, both easily won contests that at one time looked like they might be competitive.

The Democratic Party also made gains in state legislatures, particularly in the Northeast, where they won the New York senate and the Delaware house. Those wins gave the Democrats control of every legislative chamber east of Ohio and north of Virginia except for the Pennsylvania senate. Republican victories came primarily in the South. Republicans won the Tennessee house for the first time since 1970 to hold both chambers simultaneously for the first time since Reconstruction. The GOP also carried the Oklahoma senate for the first time ever.

After a long period of divided control, legislatures were becoming increasingly one-sided affairs, with Democrats controlling twenty-seven chambers outright, for a gain of four. Republicans held fourteen legislatures, while just eight states were divided between the two parties: Alaska, Indiana, Kentucky, Michigan, Montana (where the GOP controlled the state senate but the state house was evenly divided between the two parties), Ohio, Pennsylvania, and Virginia.

Hispanics in Congress, 1947–2009

Congress	*Senate*	*House*
80th (1947–1949)	1	1
81st (1949–1951)	1	1
82nd (1951–1953)	1	1
83rd (1953–1955)	1	1
84th (1955–1957)	1	1
85th (1957–1959)	2	0
86th (1959–1961)	2	0
87th (1961–1963)	2	1
88th (1963–1965)	1	3
89th (1965–1967)	1	4
90th (1967–1969)	1	4
91st (1969–1971)	1	5
92nd (1971–1973)	1	6
93rd (1973–1975)	1	6
94th (1975–1977)	1	6
95th (1977–1979)	0	5
96th (1979–1981)	0	6
97th (1981–1983)	0	7
98th (1983–1985)	0	10
99th (1985–1987)	0	11
100th (1987–1989)	0	11
101st (1989–1991)	0	11
102nd (1991–1993)	0	11
103rd (1993–1995)	0	17
104th (1995–1997)	0	17
105th (1997–1999)	0	18
106th (1999–2001)	0	18
107th (2001–2003)	0	19
108th (1993–2005)	0	24
109th (2005–2007)	2	23
110th (2007–2009)	3	23
111th (2009–2011)[1]	3	23

NOTE: Totals reflect the number of members at the start of each Congress and exclude nonvoting delegates.

[1] Hispanic Ken Salazar (D-Colo.), who was a member of the Senate when the 111th Congress convened, resigned on Jan. 21, 2009, to become secretary of the interior in the cabinet of President Barack Obama. Salazar's replacement, appointed by the Colorado governor, was not Hispanic.

(In the New York senate, Democrats held a two-seat margin until June 8, 2009, when Republicans, in the minority for the first time in four decades, persuaded two Democrats to switch parties, putting the GOP in control—until one of the defectors returned to the Democratic side of the aisle, leaving each party with thirty-one seats and senate business virtually in a deadlock.)

There was no discernible trend on state ballot measures, except perhaps that voters were slightly more inclined than usual to vote them down. Bans on same-sex marriage passed in all three states where they were on the ballot: Arizona, California, and Florida. The California ban was particularly hard fought, and its passage sparked angry demonstrations from gay rights activists. Gays had been allowed to marry in the state since May when the state supreme court struck down a constitutional amendment, enacted in 2000, banning such marriages. Altogether, supporters and opponents of same-sex marriages spent

$74 million on the ballot initiative, at least double the combined amount spent in more than a score of the states where gay measures had been at issue. Most other social-issue measures failed, however, including a strict ban on abortion in South Dakota, a near-replay of a 2006 fight meant to create a test case to challenge *Roe v. Wade,* the landmark Supreme Court that upheld a woman's right to an abortion.

Voters also said no to taxes—both increases and cuts. Massachusetts voters rejected a measure that would have repealed the state income tax, Colorado voters turned down a proposal to end a tax rebate program, and North Dakota voters stopped a measure to cut corporate and personal income taxes. Voters in four states, however, approved proposals to create or expand state gambling operations.

CHAPTER 2

Economic Policy

Economic Policy

President George W. Bush left office on Jan. 20, 2009, in the midst of a financial crisis many experts predicted was likely to be the deepest economic crisis the United States had experienced since the Great Depression of the 1930s. Although indications of a slowdown had been apparent for some time, the seemingly imminent near-collapse of the U.S. financial system in late 2008 precipitated a worldwide financial crisis that abruptly slowed economic activity around the world. In the United States, millions lost their jobs, millions were facing foreclosure on their homes, and millions more saw their nominal net worth plunge as both housing prices and the stock markets fell to their lowest levels in years.

The crisis thrust the U.S. government into the unaccustomed—and for many politicians, highly uncomfortable—role of bailing out the nation's financial institutions, acquiring ownership stakes in several of the country's largest banks, two mortgage finance giants known as Fannie Mae and Freddie Mac, and the global insurance company American International Group. In early 2009 the government also acquired ownership shares in General Motors and Chrysler in an effort to prevent the two American carmakers from going out of business. Together the bailouts represented the largest direct federal intervention in the nation's market in history. In addition, the Federal Reserve pumped some $1 trillion directly and indirectly into the economy to shore up the financial system and keep credit flowing, and Congress passed two economic stimulus bills: a modest one in 2008, and a much larger one in early 2009, costing nearly $1 trillion.

By late 2009 it was still too soon to determine the effects of these and other extraordinary actions taken by the federal government to keep the economy running. There were signs that segments of the economy had begun to grow again, albeit slowly, but other indicators, most dramatically the jobless rate, suggested that the situation was still fragile. Many economists warned that the country might be in for more hard economic times before the economy truly stabilized. Economists and politicians sharply disagreed with each other and among themselves on whether more stimulus was needed, on how to disengage the government from the marketplace without causing more disruption, and on whether and how the financial industry should be regulated to prevent similar disasters in the future. Barack Obama, the Democratic president who succeeded Bush in the middle of the crisis, and the Democratic-led Congress were also confronted with the largest federal budget deficit since 1945. Failure to reduce the deficit significantly and in a timely fashion was likely to slow, perhaps even jeopardize, economic recovery.

BEFORE THE STORM

When Bush took office in 2001, the longest peacetime expansion in the nation's history was drawing to a close. Democrat Bill Clinton was president during most of that expansion. During his eight years in the White House, economic growth averaged 4 percent a year; more than 22.5 million jobs were created, mostly in the private sector; unemployment and poverty fell to their lowest levels in thirty years; inflation averaged 2.5 percent; and the federal budget deficit, which had reached $290 billion the year before Clinton took office, turned into a large surplus by 1998.

But by Inauguration Day on Jan. 20, 2001, the high-tech bubble that had fueled much of the growth in the 1990s had burst and the economy slowed, growing at a

REFERENCES

Discussion of economic policy for the years 1945–1964 may be found in *Congress and the Nation Vol. I*, pp. 337–458; for the years 1965–1968, *Congress and the Nation Vol. II*, pp. 119–182, 253–305; for the years 1969–1972, *Congress and the Nation Vol. III*, pp. 53–145; for the years 1973–1976, *Congress and the Nation Vol. IV*, pp. 49–149; for the years 1977–1980, *Congress and the Nation Vol. V*, pp. 205–287; for the years 1981–1984, *Congress and the Nation Vol. VI*, pp. 27–120; for the years 1985–1988, *Congress and the Nation Vol. VII*, pp. 27–136; for the years 1989–1992, *Congress and the Nation Vol. VIII*, pp. 31–161; for the years 1993–1996, *Congress and the Nation Vol. IX*, pp. 31–148; for the years 1997–2001, *Congress and the Nation Vol. X*, pp. 33–170; for the years 2001–2004, *Congress and the Nation Vol. XI*, pp. 35–167.

pace of only 0.3 percent in the first quarter of 2001. Then the al Qaeda terrorist attacks of Sept. 11, 2001, brought much of the economy to a standstill. Although many aspects of the economy returned to near normal within a week or two, a loss of investor confidence led to the worst week on Wall Street since the Great Depression. Between the opening bell on Sept. 17, 2001, and the closing bell on Sept. 21, stocks lost about $1.4 trillion in value. Uncertainty about the direction of the economy continued in October as the United States invaded Afghanistan in an effort to wipe out the leaders of the al Qaeda terrorist organization thought to be hiding there. By late November the administration acknowledged that as a result of the economic slowdown and the invasion of Afghanistan, the federal government was likely to run a budget deficit for at least the next three years.

One of Bush's first acts as president was to push through Congress a massive tax cut he said would stimulate the economy by encouraging investment and spending. Less than six months after taking office, Bush signed a $1.4 trillion, ten-year tax cut into law. The Federal Reserve also moved to stimulate the economy, initiating a series of cuts in the federal funds interest rate (the rate financial institutions charged each other on overnight loans) that reduced the rate from 6.5 percent at the end of 2000 to 1.75 percent at the end of 2001. In retrospect both of these actions may have served to spur the economy in the short term, but they may also have contributed to continual budget deficits and to the housing boom that eventually proved unsustainable.

The Business Cycle Dating Committee of the National Bureau of Economic Research, which dated the beginning and end of recessions, later said the nation had experienced a mild recession that lasted from March through November 2001. Had it not been for 9/11, the committee said, the decline in the economy might not have qualified as a recession. In any event, from the end of 2001 until near the end of 2007 the economy grew, if somewhat fitfully and modestly. The annual increase in the nation's gross domestic product (GDP), the value of all goods and services produced in the United States, rose from 1.8 percent in 2002 to 3.6 percent in 2004 before slowly declining to a rate of 2.1 percent in 2007. Overall, annual economic growth in the first seven years of Bush's presidency averaged 2.4 percent.

Even as economic growth began to recover in late 2001, job growth lagged far behind, and analysts began to talk of a "jobless recovery." From its low point in the Bush administration of 4.2 percent in February 2001, the unemployment rate reached 5 percent in September 2001 and remained at or above 5 percent until December 2005, when it gradually began to decline again, reaching as low as 4.4 percent in March 2007. Many factors contributed to the economy's failure to create jobs, including the loss of thousands of manufacturing and service jobs to overseas labor markets, heightened labor productivity at home made possible by technological advances that enabled more efficient ways to build and store inventory, and consumer spending on imported goods that had once been made domestically.

Chairman of the Federal Reserve Ben S. Bernanke, right, delivers his opening remarks on the ongoing mortgage foreclosure problems before the House Financial Services Committee hearing with Housing and Urban Development Secretary Alphonso Jackson, center, and Treasury Secretary Henry M. Paulson Jr., left, on September 20, 2007.
Source: AP Photo/Susan Walsh

The economy was also buffeted by a series of events, including Hurricanes Katrina and Rita that in 2005 devastated much of the Gulf Coast from Alabama to Texas at great loss of life and property. The storms also affected offshore oil production in the gulf that contributed to the spike in oil and gasoline prices. The Bush administration's decision to invade Iraq in March 2003, to rid that country of the weapons of mass destruction it turned out not to have, developed into a bloody and costly military operation that further destabilized the Middle East, pushed oil prices up, and added to the federal budget deficit. Booming economies in China, Brazil, and many eastern European countries that were once part of the former Soviet Union also pushed up the prices of commodities such as oil and steel and diverted some investment away from the United States.

HOUSING BOOM AND BUST

In the United States, consumers continued to drive economic growth, thanks in large part to a boom in the housing market that began in 2002. Fueled by historically low interest rates, government policies encouraging home ownership, and aggressive lending practices, nominal housing prices rose 51 percent from 2000 through 2005. In the hottest markets, such as California, south Florida, Nevada, and Arizona, housing prices doubled over the five-year period. Lulled by low interest rates and the belief that home values would continue to rise indefinitely, many renters became homeowners for the first time, while people who already owned homes tapped into their home equity to buy a more expensive house or to pay for other things, such as college educations, new cars, and other consumer goods.

The relatively easy money also increased economic incentives for lenders to make, and borrowers to take, risky, unconventional mortgages. Many of these mortgages were made in the "subprime" market, meaning that borrowers lacked the income to qualify for conventional loans. Many loans required no down payment, others offered adjustable-rate mortgages with low "teaser" interest rates that ballooned in the second or third year. In some cases borrowers were not required to document their ability to repay the loan. By 2005 the Government Accountability Office estimated that these unconventional loans accounted for three of every ten mortgages.

Another factor that contributed to the housing boom was the increased "securitization" of home mortgages—the bundling of mortgages, including subprime mortgages, into securities that were then sold to investors. By 2006 two-thirds of all new mortgages, worth a total of $2 trillion, were put into securities. That freed up more money for lenders to issue new mortgages, but it also spread the risk if the mortgages underlying the securities went bad.

And that is what happened, starting in 2006, when the air began going out of the housing bubble, and home prices began to level off. By mid-2007 the housing market was in decline across much of the country; in some places prices dropped so much that homeowners were "underwater," meaning they owed more on their mortgages than their houses were worth. At the same time millions of homeowners with adjustable rate mortgages suddenly faced monthly payments that had risen by 10 to 40 percent. The portion of homeowners that fell behind on their mortgages began to increase significantly in 2006. By mid-2009, according to the Center for Responsible Lending, lenders had foreclosed on 1.5 million homeowners and another 2 million holders of subprime loans were delinquent and in danger of losing their homes. One projection estimated that between the end of 2008 and 2014, 13 million mortgages of all types would be in default.

FINANCIAL CRISIS

On its own the collapse of the housing market would have been bad enough, but in this case, it also precipitated the near-collapse of the financial system. Wall Street had packaged many of the mortgage-based securities in such a way that their worth could not easily be evaluated. As long as real estate prices were rising, however, investors seemed willing to overlook the risk inherent in securities based on mortgages, including subprime mortgages. Demand for these securities was high; many investors borrowed heavily to buy the securities in the belief that the returns they earned would allow them to pay off their loans and still realize a handsome profit. When the housing bubble burst and the foreclosures began to mount, the risks inherent in these mortgage-backed securities began to appear.

The seriousness of the situation began to come clear in April 2007, when a major subprime lender in California was suspended because of losses in defaulted mortgages and subsequently filed for bankruptcy. That summer, two hedge funds created by the Wall Street investment firm Bear Sterns went broke, after losing $20 billion in value because of heavily leveraged investments in failed securities based on subprime mortgages. The failures badly shook the financial world, which began to question the value of similar securities in other portfolios. By the end of 2007, according to one report, twenty large international banks had written down or posted losses totaling $93 billion in mortgage-backed assets, many banks had stopped making and securitizing subprime loans, and U.S. banks had laid off 10,000 employees.

Like the financial markets, both the White House and Congress were slow to realize the magnitude of the pending crisis. President Bush announced a program to help homeowners refinance their mortgages rather than default, and congressional committees also worked on mortgage relief legislation but with little apparent sense of urgency. By the end of the year, as worries mounted that the financial situation might propel the economy into recession (and as the 2008 presidential election drew closer), both political parties began to discuss passage of economic stimulus legislation. In a bipartisan effort rare during Bush's presidency, the administration and leaders of the two parties in both chambers of Congress reached agreement on a stimulus bill. The $151.7 billion measure that cleared on Feb. 7, 2008, was aimed at individual tax rebates, which began reaching taxpayers that spring; the stimulus was later judged to have given a small but temporary boost to the economy.

But the stimulus did little to stem the rising tide of losses in the financial markets both at home and abroad. By mid-2008 investments once thought safe had become "toxic assets" jeopardizing the balance sheets of banks, pension funds, college endowments, state and local governments, and other investors. Also vulnerable were the two huge housing agencies—Freddie Mae and Fannie Mac—that owned or guaranteed about $5 trillion worth of the $12 trillion in mortgages issued on U.S. houses.

In mid-2007 the share price for both companies had been above $60, but by mid–July 2008 it had dropped to $10 as frightened investors withdrew their money. That prompted Treasury Secretary Henry M. Paulson Jr. to ask Congress for immediate authority to protect the two mortgage giants from potential collapse. The House and Senate

ECONOMIC LEADERSHIP

Little did President George W. Bush realize when he named a new Treasury secretary and a new chairman of the Federal Reserve Board in early 2006 that his legacy as president might well be shaped by how successful these two appointees were in steering the country through its worst economic crisis in recent decades. Treasury Secretary Henry M. Paulson Jr. and Federal Reserve Chairman Ben S. Bernanke, along with Timothy F. Geithner, the president of the Federal Reserve Bank of New York (and later Treasury secretary under President Barack Obama), led the day-to-day response to the crisis that saw the near-collapse of the world financial system and the largest federal intervention in the private markets in U.S. history. While generally credited with staving off an even worse financial and economic crisis, the three men nonetheless were likely to face continuing scrutiny of their decisions for years to come.

Treasury Secretary

Paulson, the chairman and chief executive officer of the investment bank Goldman Sachs, a leading Wall Street firm, was nominated to the Treasury post May 30, 2006, and confirmed by voice vote June 28. He replaced John W. Snow, a former executive with CSX, who had little experience with Wall Street and little power within the White House. Paulson reportedly refused the Treasury job at first but changed his mind after heavy lobbying from White House chief of staff Joshua B. Bolten, a former Goldman Sachs executive, and after Bush promised Paulson that he would be allowed to run the Treasury Department without interference from White House economic policy advisers. Paulson later told the *Washington Post* that during the financial crisis the president had assured him of White House backing for whatever steps he felt it necessary to take.

At the time neither Bush nor Paulson knew that within months, Paulson would be pushing the limits of his authority and taking unprecedented steps to prevent a financial crisis from growing deeper. These actions ranged from prodding independent regulatory agencies to change some regulations, including imposing a temporary ban on the practice of "short selling" stocks; to insisting that Bank of America take over the ailing investment firm Merrill Lynch; to winning authority from Congress to nationalize all or parts of mortgage giants Fannie Mae and Freddie Mac and several of the nation's biggest banks at a cost of hundreds of billions of dollars.

Several of Paulson's actions were sharply criticized, including his role in the Bank of America–Merrill Lynch merger. Other criticisms involved the ad hoc nature of the government's bank rescue plans as well as their terms, which some said were too generous. In an interview with the *Post* in November 2008, Paulson said his biggest regret was not understanding the severity of the financial crisis sooner. "But," he added, "even if we had been more clairvoyant, we wouldn't have been able to do much differently than what we have done."

Federal Reserve

Bernanke succeeded the legendary Alan Greenspan, who was first appointed Fed chairman in 1987 and who was required by law to leave the Fed in January 2006.

Greenspan, a Republican who favored small government and light regulation, had extraordinary economic and political influence in Washington. He was widely respected for manipulating interest rates to keep inflation and unemployment low, especially after the recessions of 1990–1991 and 2001. But with the collapse of the housing market, which began shortly after he left the Fed, Greenspan was blamed in some quarters for fueling the housing bubble by keeping interest rates too low for too long.

By coincidence, Bernanke was uniquely qualified to head the Fed as it dealt with the financial crisis. As an economics professor at Princeton, Bernanke had specialized in the Great Depression and the conditions that caused it. Like others, Bernanke could be faulted for reacting slowly to the housing crisis but not for failing to take bold action once the credit crunch precipitated by the housing collapse began to emerge. Under his direction, the Fed lent hundreds of billions of dollars to banks and businesses, supported the federal takeover of Fannie Mae and Freddie Mac, and backed the federal bailout known as the Troubled Asset Relief Program.

had been wrangling over legislation to provide a new regulator for the beleaguered agencies and to provide new relief for stressed homeowners, but those differences were quickly negotiated in the face of the new emergency. The legislation was quickly passed, complete with the requested authority. In a pattern that would be repeated subsequently, a majority of Republicans in the House opposed the bailout and voted against the wishes of their president, citing fears that the government might be saddled with the two companies' debt.

Although Paulson had told Congress that he hoped to avoid using Treasury's new authority, on Sept. 7 the

Although Bernanke said in August 2009 that the economy might be coming out of recession, the Fed still had before it the difficult task of unwinding its emergency actions in a way that neither slowed recovery nor set off inflation. But his handling of the emergency was sufficient for President Barack Obama to nominate him for a second term as Fed chairman. In his Aug. 25, 2009, announcement, Obama praised Bernanke for his "out-of-the-box thinking" that helped prevent a second Great Depression. He was confirmed by the Senate on Jan. 28, 2010, by a vote of 70–30.

Office of Management and Budget

Bush had three directors of the Office of Management and Budget in his second term. The first was Joshua B. Bolten, who had run OMB since 2003. Bolten mastered the art of diplomacy in dealing with Budget and Appropriations Committee members, thereby winning the respect of most lawmakers even if they disagreed with his policy positions. Perhaps the Bush administration's largest budget victory came under Bolten's watch, when Congress in 2006 cleared legislation making the first cuts in entitlement programs since 1997.

In a major shake-up of the White House staff, Bolten left OMB in April 2006 to become Bush's chief of staff. To replace him, Bush named Rob Portman, a former six-term U.S. representative from Ohio who had been serving as Bush's chief trade official since May 2005. Portman's accessibility, his eager pursuit of bipartisanship, and his command of complex policy details had won him trust in both Republican and Democratic circles on Capitol Hill, and he was easily confirmed by voice vote on May 26, 2006. He resigned just a year later, six months after Democrats took control of Congress and in the midst of major gridlock between the two parties over the fiscal 2007 appropriations bills. Portman said he wanted to spend more time with his family; he was considered a strong contender in 2010 for either the Ohio governorship or the Senate seat held by retiring Republican George V. Voinovich.

To succeed Portman, Bush chose former U.S. representative Jim Nussle, R-Iowa, (1991–2007) who until January 2007 had served as chairman of the House Budget Committee. Nussle was confirmed on Sept. 4, 2007, by a vote of 69–24 and remained in the post until the end of Bush's term.

A fiscal conservative, Nussle was not afraid to aggressively take on Democrats during his years in Congress, excoriating them for not holding down federal spending. As OMB director, he stood by the president, vigorously lobbying his former colleagues to support the $700 billion financial bailout bill and other measures aimed at preventing the financial system from collapsing

National Economic Council

The National Economic Council was established by President Bill Clinton to coordinate the administration's economic policies. In Bush's second term, the office was headed by Allen B. Hubbard, a classmate of the president at Harvard Business School, an Indiana businessman, a deputy chief of staff to Vice President Dan Quayle in the 1990s, and a major financial contributor to the Bush presidential campaigns. Hubbard was the president's point man on the failed proposal to partially privatize Social Security. Hubbard, who in 2005 replaced Stephen Friedman, a former chairman of Goldman Sachs, resigned in 2007 and was replaced by his deputy Keith Hennessey, formerly a top budget aide to then Senate Majority Leader Trent Lott. Hennessey served from November 2007 until the end of Bush's term.

Council of Economic Advisers

The Council of Economic Advisers was created in 1946 to advise the president on national economic policy; it is the body responsible for the president's annual economic report. Bush had three council chairmen during his second term. Harvey S. Rosen, a Princeton professor specializing in public finance, held the post for the first part of 2005. It was taken in June 2005 by Ben Bernanke, who resigned in January 2006 when he was appointed Fed chairman. Bernanke was succeeded by Edward Lazear, a professor at Stanford Graduate School of Business and a senior fellow at the Hoover Institute, who remained at the council through the end of Bush's presidency.

government took control of Fannie Mae and Freddie Mac, pledging to provide the two mortgage agencies with new capital as needed and to guarantee the companies' $5 trillion in debt. In return the government became the controlling owner of the two companies, and many Republicans felt their fears had been justified.

A week later, two of the largest Wall Street investment firms, Merrill Lynch and Lehman Brothers, were on the verge of collapse. Treasury and Federal Reserve officials worked frantically to find buyers for the two companies, which had invested heavily in now unmarketable securities related to subprime mortgages. After an intense weekend

A Look at the Economy, 1988–2008

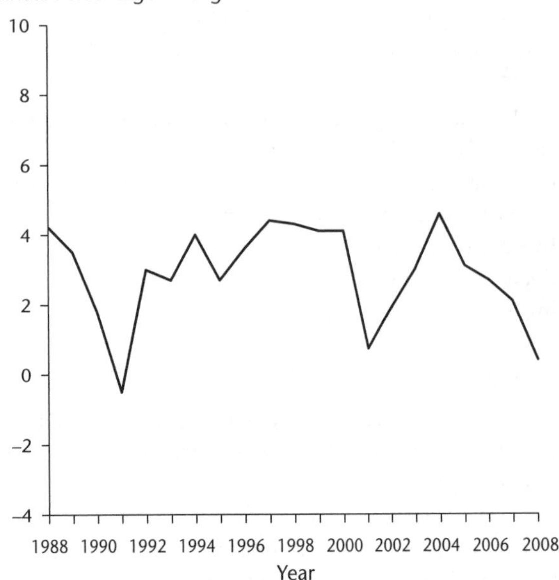

. . . declined during the 1990–1991 recession but a prolonged recovery followed that lasted nine years, from 1992 to 2000. President George W. Bush's first term was marked by a mild recession, followed by a mild recovery. In his second term, economic growth slowed gradually until December 2007, when the country entered the deepest recession since at least World War II. In the first quarter of 2009 the economy contracted 6.4 percent.

Growth: Annual changes in the gross domestic product (GDP).

SOURCE: Commerce Department, Bureau of Economic Analysis.

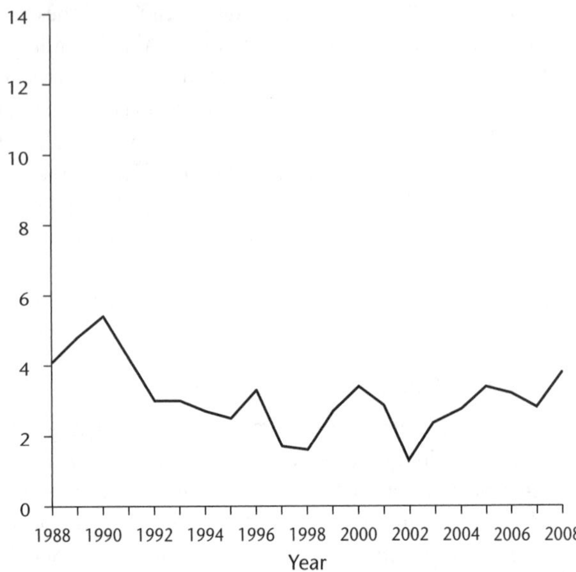

. . . before the 1990–1991 recession did not reach the historically high levels it did leading up to the recession of the early 1980s. For the rest of the 1990s and the first years of the 2000s, inflation has stayed relatively consistent and tame, despite hikes in oil and gasoline prices in the mid-2000s.

Inflation: Annual change in the consumer price index for all urban consumers, expressed as an annual average rate.

SOURCE: Labor Department, Bureau of Labor Statistics.

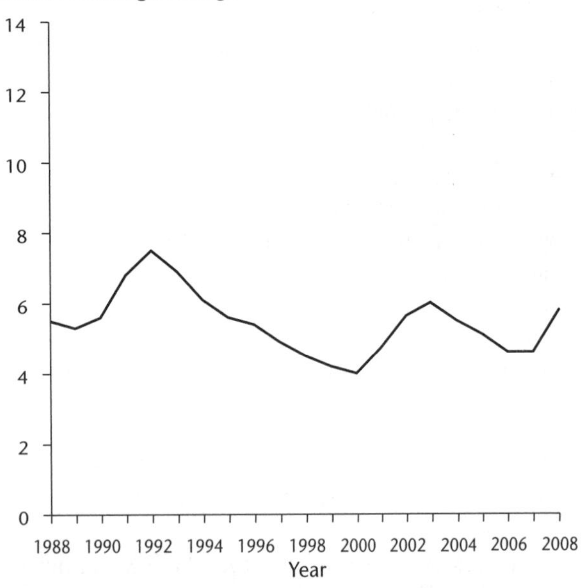

. . . surged after the 1990–1991 recession but then steadily declined until the early 2000s, when it experienced a slight uptick before settling in at about 5 percent. As recession took hold in 2008, unemployment began to rise, reaching 9.8 percent in September 2009, and went over 10 percent by the end of that year.

Unemployment: Annual rate of unemployment for all civilian workers (does not include the military).

SOURCE: Labor Department, Bureau of Labor Statistics

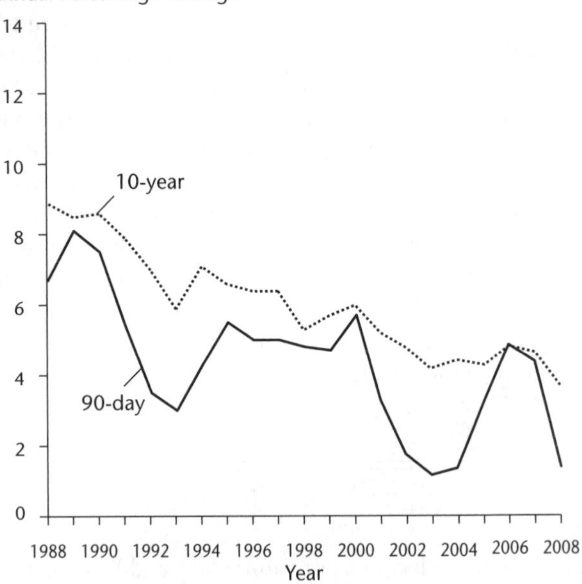

. . . on short-and long-term Treasury securities fell in 2003 to their lowest levels in almost thirty years, then rose slightly as the Federal Reserve tried to engineer a "soft landing" for the booming housing market. When the housing market collapsed, precipitating a global credit crisis in late 2008, interest rates fell again.

Interest rates: Annual average for new issues or 90-day Treasury bills and 10-year Treasury notes, adjusted for constant maturities.

SOURCE: Treasury Department.

of discussions, Bank of America agreed to purchase Merrill Lynch, but no buyer was found for Lehman Brothers, which declared bankruptcy on Sept. 15.

The Lehman Brothers collapse provoked panic in financial markets around the world. It was later seen as the crucial turning point in the financial crisis that was to envelope the world. Investors worldwide immediately withdrew billions of dollars from money market funds, the stock markets, and from any other investment perceived to carry even the slightest degree of risk. Among other things the panic caused a credit crisis throughout the world, with banks all but refusing to lend new money to anyone, and slowing economic activity throughout the world.

On Thursday, Sept. 18, Paulson, Federal Reserve Chairman Ben S. Bernanke, and other senior officials met with congressional leaders to urge them to give Treasury the authority to spend up to $700 billion on a program that would help banks clean up their balance sheets and begin lending again. By most accounts, the warnings about the imminent collapse of the economy were the strongest veteran legislators had ever heard. At one point, Bernanke was quoted as saying that if the government failed to shore up the troubled banks, "we may not have an economy on Monday."

Coming just six weeks before the presidential election, the unprecedented bank rescue proposal, known as the Troubled Asset Relief Program (TARP), touched off an intense political battle. Many legislators worried that taxpayers could end up being saddled with billions in debt if banks were unable to repay the loans. Republicans and some Democrats were philosophically opposed to such a massive government intervention into private markets. Angry voters asked why middle America was being asked to bail out wealthy Wall Street firms; in response Democrats sought to cap pay for top bank officials.

The two presidential candidates, both U.S. senators, also got caught up in the frenzy. Democrat Barack Obama tried, with a fair amount of success, to stay above the fray. He supported the bailout but also called for pay caps for bank officials. Republican John McCain, on the other hand, announced he was suspending his campaign to return to Washington to help congressional negotiators reach a deal on the rescue package. The effort fell apart after Republican legislators backed away from an agreement in principle and negotiators had to go back to the drawing board, leaving McCain looking ineffectual.

President Bush and his economic team set aside their own ideological preferences and lobbied strenuously for the rescue package, warning repeatedly of the dire economic consequences Americans could face if the bailout failed to pass. Their arguments failed to convince House Republicans. On Sept. 29, with nearly two-thirds of GOP legislators opposed, the House rejected the bailout legislation by a vote of 205 to 228. Reaction to the House vote was swift—the Dow Jones Industrial Average fell 777 points, the largest single-day point drop in its history.

Congressional negotiators went back to work and produced a new bill that answered some of the criticisms raised on the first bill and added several unrelated provisions to win over reluctant legislators. The Senate passed that version Oct. 1 74–25 and the House followed Oct. 3, clearing it by a vote of 263–171, with most of the no votes cast by Republicans. The measure gave the Treasury secretary wide latitude to spend the bailout funds however he saw fit, so long as the goal was restoring fiscal stability. Paulson initially said the funds would be used to buy troubled assets. In mid-October, however, Paulson announced the department was investing a portion of the TARP money directly into several major banks, acquiring partial ownership in the banks—a controversial step that was still being debated well into 2009.

RECESSION ON MAIN STREET

The remainder of Bush's term was marked by a steady rain of economic bad news. Banks continued to report enormous losses; Citigroup, for example, had posted losses of $65 billion by November and received a second infusion of taxpayer aid under the TARP program. The insurance giant American International Group, or AIG, was a particular target of taxpayer ire. Faced with having to pay out on billions of dollars of insurance it had written on the debts of banks and other troubled companies, AIG itself was on the verge of collapse and threatening to drag many other companies down with it. A day after allowing Lehman Brothers to file for bankruptcy, the Federal Reserve extended the company a line of credit to keep it afloat, again in return for an ownership stake in the company. Three more times over the next five months, the government was required to extend financial help to AIG to keep the company from going under. When it was later revealed that the company planned to pay its executives $165 million in bonuses, public outrage threatened to undercut support for the government's broader efforts to shore up the financial system.

In addition, the downturn in the housing, construction, and financial industries was spreading through the rest of the economy, resulting in company closures and job losses in virtually every segment of the economy. By the end of December the jobless rate stood at 7.2 percent. The Labor Department reported that 3.6 million jobs had been lost since the recession began in December 2007, 1.9 million of them just in the last four months of 2008.

One particularly hard-hit industry that sought help from Congress to no avail in 2008 was the auto industry, or more precisely the Big Three domestic automakers: General Motors, Ford, and Chrysler. The entire auto industry had been hurt by high gasoline prices, but the effects were greatest for the domestic carmakers that were more reliant on sales of fuel-extravagant light trucks and sports utility vehicles and that were also burdened by union wages and pension costs that put them at a disadvantage against more nimble foreign makers, such as Toyota and Honda. The top executives of the Big Three came to Washington shortly after the November elections to request federal aid but were instead scolded for flying from Detroit in their luxurious corporate jets and for failing to bring detailed business plans to make the companies viable. The executives returned, by car, in December with the requested plans, and the Bush administration and congressional Democrats quickly worked out a $15 billion rescue proposal. But Senate Republicans objected and the plan died. Days later, with both General Motors and Chrysler on the verge of declaring bankruptcy, Bush did what he had once said he would not do and approved $17.4 billion in direct loans from the TARP funds for the two companies. Bush said allowing the companies to collapse in the midst of a financial crisis and a recession was "not a responsible course of action."

Throughout the crisis, Bush relied heavily on Paulson, a former chief executive of the giant New York investment bank of Goldman Sachs, to guide the administration's response to the crisis. Fed Bernanke, a recognized academic expert on the Great Depression, also played a significant role, coordinating closely with Paulson and working with central banks in other countries to stabilize the financial markets. During the four months between the presidential election and Obama's inauguration, the Bush administration also worked closely with Obama's team to ensure as smooth a transition during the crisis as possible. Obama's first order of business upon taking office in January 2009 was to win congressional approval of an ambitious, economic stimulus package aimed at creating or saving 3.5 million jobs and increasing spending through individual and business tax cuts. Barely a month later, on Feb. 17, he signed the $787 billion measure into law, but in a move that signaled the determination to oppose the new president, Republicans voted no. Not a single Republican in the House and only three in the Senate supported the bill.

A LOST DECADE

At the end of October 2009, the Department of Commerce reported that the economy had grown at an estimated annual rate of 3.5 percent in the third quarter of the year, a number many analysts took to mean that the recession had probably ended sometime in the summer. (The number was later revised down to 2.2 percent. But even that was significantly better than earlier quarters.) *(Details, p. 185)*

Home prices had also been rising for several months, an indication that the housing bust might have reached bottom and begun turning around. But few people were uncorking the champagne yet. Although consumer spending accounted for about two-thirds of the growth in the third quarter, much of that was attributable to the "Cash for Clunkers" federal program that paid consumers for turning in their older, gas-guzzling cars for more-fuel-efficient vehicles. Car sales soared in July and August 2009 but sagged again in September when the program ended. Home sales were also up, but most analysts attributed the increase to a federal program that gave first-time homebuyers a tax credit of up to $8,000. That program was scheduled to expire in November 2009, although Congress extended it into 2010. Without the federal incentives, it was still unclear how much the economy was growing. It seemed all but certain that months and probably years would pass before the economy would grow enough to bring the jobless rate down to more normal levels. The Department of Labor in late 2009 announced that unemployment reached 10.2 percent in October and 10 percent in November.

Whatever the economic future held, it was already clear that the financial and economic crises had erased most of the economic gains the country had made during Bush's two terms as president. Some of the greatest losses in dollar terms were in the stock market and in household net worth, a measure of a household's assets minus its liabilities. For most people, their major assets were their pension and retirement savings and the equity in their homes—and the value of both plunged in the recession. The last low for the stock market had been in the aftermath of the Sept. 11 attacks, when the Dow Jones Industrial Average lost 14.3 percent of its value in just a week. From that low period, the Dow climbed fitfully for several years; in early 2006 it broke through the 11,000 barrier for the first time since January 2001. Over the next eighteen months, the Dow soared, closing above 14,000 for the first time in its history in October 2007 and making even middle-class Americans whose pensions or retirement accounts were invested on Wall Street feel well off.

By the end of 2008, those feelings of well-being had dissipated. Overall, U.S stockholders lost $7 trillion during 2008, wiping out all the gains that had been made since the 2001 recession. The losses were especially hard for many retired Americans who suddenly found their incomes reduced, while many other Americans nearing retirement began recalculating whether they could afford to retire or would have to keep working for a few more years. (The Dow reached a low of 6,547 on March 9, 2009, before beginning to climb again slowly, reaching 10,000 by October before falling back into the 9,000-point range. It resumed its climb in 2009, ending the year at 10,428.)

Housing prices also declined sharply. According to the National Association of Realtors, the median price for an existing single-family home in a metropolitan area fell from $221,900 in 2006 to $196,600 in 2008. On a monthly comparison, the median price in January 2009 was $170,300, down nearly 15 percent from January 2008. Although housing sales had begun to improve during the year, median prices had not shown much improvement as of September 2009.

As a result of the losses in the stock market and housing prices, American households lost $11 trillion, or 18 percent, in 2008, erasing four years of gains. According to the Federal Reserve, it was the largest loss since the Fed began tracking household net wealth after World War II. Thanks largely to gains on Wall Street, household net wealth rose $2 trillion in the second quarter of 2009, its first increase in two years, according to the Federal Reserve.

Other aggregate measures of well-being were also bleak. The poverty rate as calculated by the Census Bureau reached 13.2 percent in 2008, up from 12.5 percent in 2007 and the highest level since 1997. According to the bureau's annual report, 39.8 million Americans lived below the poverty line in 2008, which was defined as an income of $22,025 for a family of four. Median family incomes in 2008 fell to $50,303, down from $52,163 in 2007. The decline wiped out the gains of the previous three years, and when adjusted for inflation the median family income in 2008 was lower than it had been in 1998. Given the spike in unemployment since the data for the 2008 report were collected, many analysts expected the 2009 report to show even more people in poverty.

The share of Americans who said they did not have health insurance remained the same in 2008 as in 2007, at 15.4 percent, or 46.3 million people. But the number of people who relied on government health insurance programs, such as Medicare, Medicaid, children's health insurance program, and military insurance, increased, while the number of people with private or employer-sponsored insurance declined. This shift continued an eight-year trend. In addition the share of children with health insurance dropped by 1.1 percent, to 9.9 percent, apparently the result of government's efforts to reach low-income children, while the share of adults aged eighteen to sixty-four without insurance rose to 20.3 percent in 2008, from 19.6 percent in 2007. Although many Americans, especially younger ones, chose not to buy insurance, many others did not buy it because they said they could not afford it.

UNCERTAIN FUTURE

How quickly the economy would recover and begin to recoup these losses was a subject of considerable debate as 2009 drew to a close. Many analysts predicted that recovery would be slow, in large part because consumers, at least for the time being, seemed more focused on paying down their debts and building up their savings than on resuming the spending that drove nearly 70 percent of the economy during the Bush presidency. But unless and until something filled the gap, a lingering drop in consumption could limit economic growth as well as job growth in the immediate future.

State and local governments, most of which could not under their constitutions cushion bad years with deficit spending, were also likely to face continuing hard times. Some of Obama's stimulus package went to these governments, but few were able to avoid cutbacks that weakened services for the most vulnerable citizens and that threw thousands of government employees out of work. Many states were predicting that even more drastic spending cuts would be required in 2010.

In Washington, the president and Congress faced the immediate challenge of nurturing the recovery while at the same time withdrawing the extraordinary supports it had given to the private sector. Over the long haul, the greater challenge was likely to be reducing the federal budget deficit. Already at a record dollar amount of $455 billion in fiscal 2008, the deficit tripled in fiscal 2009 to $1.4 trillion—equal to 9.9 percent of the nation's economic activity, the highest percentage recorded since 1945. Although the deficit was expected to decline in the short term as recovery took hold, revenues increased, and government stimulus actions wound down, it was projected to start growing again in the medium-term as an aging population made increasing demands on Social Security and Medicare. The actions that Congress and the president took over the remainder of Obama's term—not only on the recovery but a host of other issues such as the wars in Afghanistan and Iraq, health care reform, and Bush's tax cuts, many of which were set to expire in 2010—would help determine just how difficult grappling with the long-term deficits would be.

Chronology of Action on Budget and Tax Policy

Introduction

The Constitution gives Congress authority to appropriate federal monies and direct how they should be spent. But in the partisan atmosphere that characterized the 109th and 110th Congresses from 2005 through 2008, the exercise of that authority nearly collapsed. In only one of the four years, 2005, did Congress complete action on the regular annual appropriations bills. In 2008 Democratic leaders did not even try to pass individual bills, instead packaging the appropriations for the year into one omnibus measure that left annual spending for most domestic programs uncertain until early 2009.

The gridlock over spending decisions reflected ideological differences not only between the Democrats and Republicans but within each political party and between the Senate and House as well. In many cases, ideological principles gave way to maneuvering for political gain, with both parties seeking to deny the other anything it could claim as a victory. Disarray in 2006 over appropriations among Republicans, particularly in the Senate, contributed to the public's sense that the GOP had lost its way on fiscal discipline and helped thrust the Democrats into power in both chambers in that year's midterm elections.

Democratic leaders, however, fared little better in the 110th Congress against a Republican president determined to hold the line on discretionary spending and congressional Republicans unwilling to take any action that could be seen as benefiting Democrats in a presidential election year. In 2007 all eleven of the nondefense bills were put together in one package and signed into law the day after Christmas, and in 2008 the Democrats gave up trying to enact individual spending bills and instead relied on stopgap funding measures to keep most of the government running until after the newly elected president, Democrat Barack Obama, took office in 2009.

The same gridlock also affected tax policy. President George W. Bush repeatedly called on Congress to make permanent the massive tax cuts enacted during his first term—a request that was a nonstarter in a Congress closely divided between the parties, particularly in the Senate, where neither the Republicans in the 109th nor the Democrats in the 110th had enough votes on their own to stop filibusters. Indeed, it was all that leaders in either Congress could do to assuage competing interests long enough to

REFERENCES

Discussion of tax policy for the years 1945–1964 may be found in *Congress and the Nation Vol. I*, pp. 397–442; for the years 1965–1968, *Congress and the Nation Vol. II*, pp. 141–182; for the years 1969–1972, *Congress and the Nation Vol. III*, pp. 77–96; for the years 1973–1976, *Congress and the Nation Vol. IV*, pp. 83–106; for the years 1977–1980, *Congress and the Nation Vol. V*, pp. 231–251; for the years 1981–1984, *Congress and the Nation Vol. VI*, pp. 63–82; for the years 1985–1988, *Congress and the Nation Vol. VII*, pp. 75–107; for the years 1989–1992, *Congress and the Nation Vol. VIII*, pp. 87–112; for the years 1993–1996, *Congress and the Nation Vol. IX*, pp. 83–107; for the years 1997–2000, *Congress and the Nation Vol. X*, pp. 87–119; for the years 2001–2008, *Congress and the Nation Vol. XI*, pp. 86–122.

Discussion of federal budget policy for the years 1945–1964 may be found in *Congress and the Nation Vol. I*, pp. 387–395; for the years 1965–1968, *Congress and the Nation Vol. II*, pp. 127–140; for the years 1969–1972, *Congress and the Nation Vol. III*, pp. 63–75; for the years 1973–1976, *Congress and the Nation Vol. IV*, pp. 57–81; for the years 1977–1980, *Congress and the Nation Vol. V*, pp. 211–230; for the years 1981–1984, *Congress and the Nation Vol. VI*, pp. 33–61; for the years 1985–1988 *Congress and the Nation Vol. VII*, pp. 33–74; for the years 1989–1992, *Congress and the Nation Vol. VIII*, pp. 37–86; for the years 1993–1996, *Congress and the Nation Vol. IX*, pp. 37–82; for the years 1997–2000, *Congress and the Nation Vol. X*, pp. 40–86; for the years 2001–2004, *Congress and the Nation Vol. XI*, pp. 44–85.

The Federal Budget, Fiscal 1993–Fiscal 2008
(billions of dollars)

Year	Revenues	Outlays	On-budget	Social Security	Total Surplus (Deficit)[1]	Public Debt
1993	$1,154.5	$1,409.5	$–300.4	$46.8	$–255.1	$3,248.4
1994	1,258.7	1,461.9	–258.8	56.8	–203.2	3,433.1
1995	1,351.9	1,515.8	–226.4	60.4	–164.0	3,604.4
1996	1,453.2	1,560.6	–174.0	66.4	–107.4	3,734.1
1997	1,579.4	1,601.3	–103.2	81.3	– 21.9	3,772.3
1998	1,722.0	1,652.7	–29.9	99.4	69.3	3,721.1
1999	1,827.6	1,702.0	1.9	124.7	125.6	3,632.4
2000	2,025.5	1,789.2	86.4	151.8	236.2	3,409.8
2001	1,991.4	1,863.2	–32.4	163.0	128.2	3,319.6
2002	1,853.4	2,011.2	–317.4	159.0	–157.8	3,540.4
2003	1,782.5	2,160.1	–538.4	155.6	–377.6	3,913.4
2004	1,880.3	2,293.0	–568.0	151.1	–412.7	4,295.5
2005	2,153.9	2,472.2	–493.6	173.5	–318.3	4,592.2
2006	2,407.3	2,655.4	–434.5	185.2	–248.2	4,829.0
2007	2,568.2	2,728.9	–342.2	186.5	–160.7	5,035.1
2008	2,523.6	2,978.5	–638.1	180.2	–454.8	5,802.9

[1]Includes surplus (deficit) for the Postal Service.

SOURCE: Congressional Budget Office, *The Budget and Economic Outlook: Fiscal Years 2009–2019,* January 2009.

enact annual legislation that prevented tax increases for a large group of middle-class taxpayers—even though both parties would have suffered politically if the increases had not been prevented.

The upshot was a further hardening of each side's position, making it increasingly difficult for legislators either to bridge ideological differences or resolve serious budgetary issues facing the country in the coming years. The most immediate of these was the soaring budget deficit that resulted from the multi–billion-dollar spending Congress authorized in late 2008 to prevent the collapse of the financial system and ease the hardships caused by economic recession.

But the 111th Congress that began in 2009 was also facing a decision about whether to extend some, none, or all of the Bush tax cuts, which were to expire at the end of 2010. Also in the near future, the country would face significantly larger deficits as benefits paid out of the Medicare and Social Security programs began to outpace the taxes paid into them. How Congress and the president dealt with these problems—or failed to deal with them—was likely to have major consequences for the economic growth and well-being of Americans for decades to come.

THE FEDERAL BUDGET DEFICIT

When President Bush first entered the White House in 2001, he inherited a budget surplus from his predecessor, President Bill Clinton (1993–2001) that the Congressional Budget Office (CBO) projected would average $800 billion a year by fiscal 2009, assuming policy and the economic situation remained the same. The surplus disappeared almost immediately, however, eroded by a mild recession that Bush also inherited and made worse by the economic downturn that followed terrorist attacks on Sept. 11, 2001. Policy decisions during Bush's first year, including large tax cuts enacted in 2001 and the decision to use military force against al Qaeda and the Taliban in Afghanistan, added to a steadily growing federal budget deficit. In one year the federal budget plunged from a $128 billion surplus in fiscal 2001 to a $158 billion deficit in fiscal 2002.

Over the next three years, a start-and-stop economic recovery continued to dampen federal revenues, while the Republican-led Congress enacted two more sizable tax cuts, drew up a new entitlement program giving seniors a prescription drug benefit at a projected ten-year cost of $400 billion, and voted to go to war in Iraq. By the end of fiscal 2004 the deficit had climbed to almost $413 billion.

In his second term, Bush held the line on domestic spending, effectively using his veto authority to prevent passage of appropriations bills containing spending he deemed too high. Continuing demands from the Iraq and Afghanistan wars, the federal recovery and relief efforts following Hurricane Katrina and several other damaging storms in 2005, as well as flooding in the Midwest and wildfires along the West Coast added to the deficit. By the end of Bush's presidency, an estimated $854 billion had been approved for the wars in Iraq and Afghanistan, according to figures compiled by the Congressional Research Service. The CRS numbers included costs connected with the wars—such as veterans health care, embassy costs, and reconstruction—as well as outlays for actual military activity.

For the first three years of the second term, however, the country was enjoying strong economic growth, and federal revenues began to climb again. (The Bush administration claimed that was a result of the stimulus provided by the tax cuts in the first term; detractors noted that revenues would be higher still had the tax cuts not been enacted.) Even though the annual federal budget deficit was high in dollar terms, it was steadily declining, from $318 billion in fiscal 2005 to $161 billion in 2007. As a percentage of the gross domestic product (GDP), the total of all goods and services produced in the economy, the deficit was at some of its lowest levels in four decades (not counting the years around the surplus in the late 1990s). *(Federal budget table, this page; Deficit history table, p. 62)*

That was before the housing bubble burst. When this event took hold it precipitated a crisis in the financial sector that came to a head in September 2008 and a recession that most experts said was the worst downturn since the Great Depression of the 1930s. By September 2009 there were signs that the economy was beginning to turn around. But in the interim the federal budget deficit exploded to $455 billion in fiscal 2008 and to an estimated $1.6 trillion in fiscal 2009. With business profits falling and the jobless rate rising to its highest level in

Deficit History, 1929–2008

(Fiscal years in billions of dollars)

Fiscal Year	*Receipts*	*Outlays*	*Surplus or Deficit(–)*	*Surplus/ deficit as % of GDP*
1929	$3.9	$3.1	$0.7	—
1933	2.0	4.6	–2.6	–4.5%
1939	6.3	9.1	–2.8	–3.2
1940	6.5	9.5	–2.9	–3.0
1945	45.2	92.7	–47.6	–21.5
1950	39.4	42.6	–3.1	–1.1
1955	65.5	68.4	–3.0	–0.8
1960	92.5	92.2	0.3	–0.1
1965	116.8	118.2	–1.4	–0.2
1969	186.9	183.6	3.2	–0.3
1970	192.8	195.6	–2.8	–0.3
1975	279.1	332.3	–53.2	–3.4
1980	517.1	590.9	–73.8	–2.7
1981	599.3	678.2	–79.0	–2.6
1982	617.8	745.7	–128.0	–4.0
1983	600.6	808.4	–207.8	–6.0
1984	666.5	851.9	–185.4	–4.8
1985	734.1	946.4	–212.3	–5.1
1986	769.2	990.4	–221.2	–5.0
1987	854.4	1,004.1	–149.7	–3.2
1988	909.3	1,064.5	–155.2	–3.1
1989	991.2	1,143.8	–152.6	–2.8
1990	1,032.1	1,253.1	–221.2	–3.9
1991	1,055.1	1,324.3	–269.2	–4.5
1992	1,091.3	1,381.6	–290.3	–4.7
1993	1,154.5	1,409.5	–255.1	–3.9
1994	1,258.7	1,461.9	–203.2	–2.9
1995	1,351.9	1,515.8	–164.0	–2.2
1996	1,453.2	1,560.6	–107.4	–1.4
1997	1,579.4	1,601.3	–21.9	–0.3
1998	1,722.0	1,652.7	69.3	0.8
1999	1,827.6	1,702.0	125.6	1.4
2000	2,025.5	1,789.2	236.2	2.4
2001	1,991.4	1,863.2	128.2	1.3
2002	1,853.4	2,011.2	–157.8	–1.5
2003	1,782.5	2,160.1	–377.6	–3.5
2004	1,880.3	2,293.0	–412.7	–3.6
2005	2,153.9	2,472.2	–318.3	–2.6
2006	2,407.3	2,655.4	–248.2	–1.9
2007	2,568.2	2,728.9	–160.7	–1.2
2008	2,523.6	2,978.5	–454.8	–3.2

SOURCE: Executive Office of the President, Office of Management and Budget, *Budget of the United States Government, Fiscal Year 2010, Historical Tables* (Washington, D.C.: Government Printing Office, 2009), Table 1.1.

GDP: Gross domestic product.

nearly thirty years, reaching over 10 percent in late 2009, federal tax receipts fell while spending on federal safety net programs, such as unemployment compensation, increased. Congress in 2008 sought to ease some of the pain of economic recession by giving $600 tax rebates to individual taxpayers, at an estimated cost of $168 billion. That number paled in comparison to the $700 billion bank bailout package a reluctant Congress approved in September 2008 and a $787 billion economic stimulus package that the Democrats passed in February 2009 with almost no Republican support. The federal takeover of the government-sponsored mortgage giants Fannie Mae (formally, the Federal National Mortgage Association) and Freddie Mac (the Federal Home Loan Mortgage Corp.) in September 2008 was estimated to cost another $291 billion.

In May 2009 the new administration of Democrat Barack Obama estimated that the fiscal 2009 deficit would exceed $1.8 trillion. Five months later, both the Obama administration and CBO were projecting that the fiscal 2009 budget deficit would be slightly lower, at $1.6 trillion—largely because some of the banks had already returned the bailout money they had received. Still, a $1.6 trillion deficit would equal 11.2 percent of GDP, the highest level since World War II. Obama's first full budget, released in January 2010, forecast a deficit of $1.6 trillion for fiscal year 2010, 10.6 percent of GDP.

LONGER-TERM PROBLEMS

Both the White House and CBO expected the deficit to decline as the economic emergency eased. But years of continuing budget deficits were increasing the public debt—the amount the federal government owed to its bondholders—at a quickening pace. From 33 percent of GDP in fiscal 2001, it had reached 40.8 percent in fiscal 2008; the CBO in August 2009 projected the public debt would reach 53.8 percent of GDP in fiscal 2009 and to climb to 68 percent by the end of fiscal 2019.

Although those medium-term projections were subject to significant change depending on policy changes and economic conditions, those would be the highest levels since the years following World War II.

Economists and some politicians continued to caution that pressures from rising public debt, combined with mounting claims from an aging population for Social Security, Medicare, and Medicaid benefits, could stifle economic growth. Because the federal government was required to borrow more and more to meet these obligations, interest rates would likely rise, diverting the amount of capital available for investment and eventually lowering wages and living standards. Most mainstream economists argued that without significant changes, federal budget policy was on an unsustainable path.

Although critics in and out of Congress complained about the size of the budget deficit for much of Bush's second term, lowering the deficit never took on the urgency that the issue did in the late 1990s when President Clinton and Congress took steps that helped turn a perennial deficit into a surplus, albeit a short-lived one. In part that was because until fiscal 2009, the red ink was always well within the historical tolerances as a share of the total economy. In addition, interest rates for much of the period were at historically low levels, as was inflation, easing any

Federal Budget Receipts

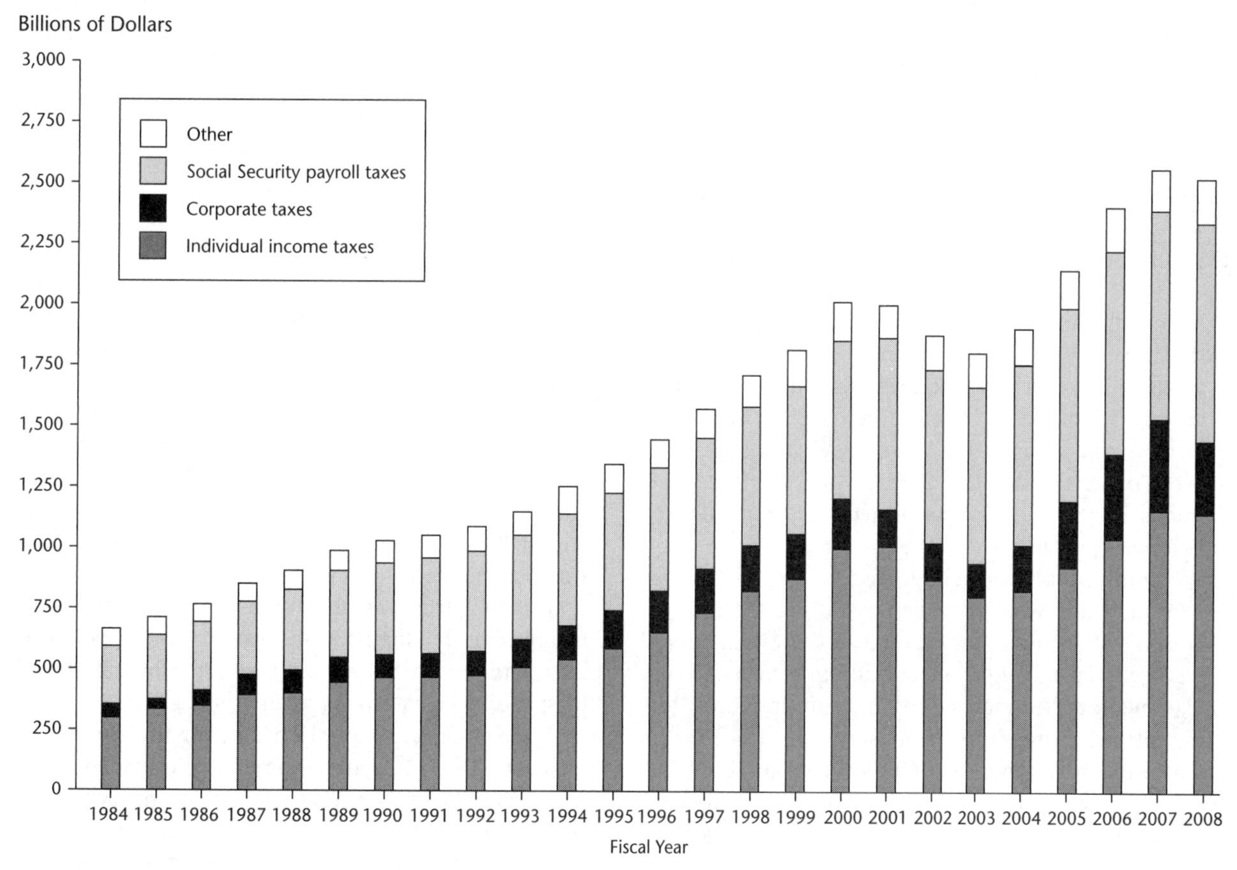

SOURCE: Office of Management and Budget, *Historical Tables, Budget of the United States Government: Fiscal Year 2010* (Washington, D.C: U. S. Government Printing Office, 2009), Table 2.1.

significant pressures that might have come from the business community to lower the deficit.

Moreover Congress, like Wall Street, had a short time horizon; most legislators were unwilling to take votes on issues that could hurt them in the next election to deal with a problem that might not fully develop until they were out of office. In Bush's second term, it was those short-term political instincts that ultimately came to the fore.

PARTISAN GRIDLOCK

Concerned that rising deficits on their watch could hurt them at the polls in 2004, Republicans pulled together that year to keep nondefense spending to an increase of just 1 percent above the previous year's level. In 2005 Republican congressional leaders held their caucus together again, passing a budget resolution (with no Democratic support) and enacting all the regular spending bills by the end of the year. (Deficit hawks noted, however, that Congress appropriated more than $200 billion in emergency supplementals, which did not count against the spending limits. Much of it was for the wars in Iraq and Afghanistan and hurricane relief and recovery.) The Republican leadership also managed to enact the first cuts in mandatory spending since 1997, with no help from the Democrats, as well as to make another $70 billion in tax cuts over five years.

But the discipline of 2004 and 2005 evaporated in 2006. The House and Senate passed budget resolutions that were so different the two chambers did not even try to reconcile them. With no agreement on spending priorities, the appropriations process fell into chaos. Conservative Republicans wanted to cut spending to hold down the budget deficit, whereas GOP moderates wanted more money for health, education, and labor programs. Time was lost during the first part of the year as Congress finished up the mandatory spending and tax cut bills from 2005 and enacted emergency supplemental funding for the two wars. Republican Majority Leader Bill Frist of Tennessee was blamed by members of his own party for not making time to bring the appropriations bills to the Senate floor. By the end of 2006, following Democratic election victories that returned the party to control of both houses of Congress, legislators had passed only two of the regular spending bills and packaged the rest into a stopgap spending resolution, effectively leaving it to the new Democratic leadership to finish the job in 2007.

The Democrats, however, had perhaps an even more difficult time managing the budget process in the 110th Congress than the Republicans did in the 109th. Not only did they face a Republican president determined to hold the line on spending, and who used his veto and the threat of veto to great effect. In the House the Democratic leadership also had to deal with dissension from fiscally conservative Blue Dog Democrats who made up one-fifth of the party's House members after the 2006 elections and who fought to hold down spending. The Blue Dogs scored a major victory in 2007 by persuading the House to accept pay-as-you-go budget rules requiring that any discretionary tax cuts or spending increases be offset by spending decreases or revenue increases. Those rules may have held down the deficit a fraction but they also contributed to the general air of rancor that permeated congressional proceedings in Bush's last term.

So too did Republican use of procedural moves to tie up the floor and otherwise get their way on the specifics of legislation. In the House, for example, one GOP member, Arizona's Jeff Flake, in 2007 offered fifty-one amendments to strike members' earmarks—specific appropriations for specific entities or programs—from spending bills.

As a result the budget resolutions passed in 2007 and 2008 were largely pro forma. In both years Democrats packaged most or all of the regular spending bills into omnibus packages that did relatively little to reorient spending toward their own domestic priorities.

The real boost to the budget deficit in fiscal 2008 and 2009 came from the steps Congress took to deal with the financial and economic emergencies, and these votes too were highly partisan. The mortgage relief and bank bailout measures pushed by the Republican administration would not have passed had it not been for substantial Democratic support; a majority of Republicans in the House voted against both bills. The initial economic stimulus package in 2008 carried with strong bipartisan support, but the much larger stimulus package pushed by President Obama in 2009 passed with no Republican support in the House and only three Republican votes in the Senate.

TAX POLICY

Partisan politics also affected tax policy during Bush's second term. Having succeeded in his first term in making substantial cuts in both individual and corporate taxes, Bush offered few new tax initiatives in his second term. In what became an annual mantra, the president regularly asked Congress to make the tax cuts permanent and Congress just as regularly failed to oblige. As he began his second term, Bush pledged to overhaul and simplify the tax code, but then did not follow through on the recommendations of his own presidential tax force.

Instead the president and Republicans in Congress repeatedly locked horns with Democrats over annual legislation seeking to extend popular corporate tax breaks and to exempt most middle–class taxpayers from having to pay the alternative minimum tax, a tax designed in 1969 to ensure that the rich paid at least some taxes. Toward the end of Bush's second terms, each of the annual measures was held hostage to a variety of competing interests in both parties, from members who wanted to give tax breaks to promote development and use of alternative forms of energy to those who insisted that any tax breaks be offset by spending cuts or increases in other taxes.

Meanwhile, the expiration date for most of the Bush tax cuts—Dec. 31, 2010—loomed ever closer and became a central issue in the presidential campaign, with Obama promising to extend individual tax cuts for all but the most wealthy and Republican candidate Sen. John McCain arguing that the current tax rates should be left alone.

By the end of 2008 it seemed likely that the need to curb the soaring budget deficit could have a profound effect on American tax policy and politics, requiring the president and Congress alike not only to raise taxes but to consider alternatives to the traditional income tax system. "The gap between federal spending and federal revenues going forward is really a serious problem that is going to have to be dealt with once the economy gets back on a firm footing," said Michael J. Graetz, a professor at Yale Law School who favored shifting from an income tax to a consumption tax.

2005–2006

For the only time in the four-year period, Congress in 2005 adopted a budget resolution and approved the eleven regular appropriations bills and several supplementals, including war funding. The Republican-controlled legislature also completed all but final passage on a bill making the first cuts in mandatory spending programs since 1997 and on a $70 billion tax-cut package that extended relief to middle-income taxpayers from the alternative minimum tax for another year. Both bills were cleared and signed into law early in 2006.

But if 2005 demonstrated what could be done when Republicans worked together, 2006 showed what could happen when party leaders were unable to overcome intraparty feuds. For the fourth time since the Budget Act of 1974 created the modern congressional budgeting process, the House and Senate were unable to agree on a common approach, although each chamber passed its own version. Congress passed only two of the regular eleven appropriations bills and funded the rest of the government through continuing resolutions, the final one of which was enacted in 2007, after the Democrats reclaimed the majority after the 2006 elections, and reflected Democratic spending priorities such as increases for education and veterans' health care.

Because there was no common budget resolution in 2006, there were no reconciliation bills dealing with taxes or mandatory spending cuts. Talk about overhauling the budget process to instill more fiscal discipline was supported but with little action. Although the federal budget deficit was declining, Congress still had to raise the debt ceiling in March 2006, the fourth increase of George W. Bush's presidency. *(Debt ceiling, box, p. 68)*

Fiscal 2006 Budget Resolution

Congressional Republicans produced a budget resolution in 2005 that was adopted by slim margins in both chambers, without a single Democratic vote. The measure set a cap of $843 billion on discretionary spending in fiscal 2006. It also called for $34.7 billion in cuts from entitlement programs over five years, which was the first significant attempt to slow the growth in mandatory spending programs since a bipartisan budget-balancing deal was reached in 1997. *(Glossary of budget terms, p. 66)*

Adoption of the budget resolution (H Con Res 95) was a high priority for GOP leaders, who had been unable to complete a budget in 2004. Although they controlled both chambers, they could not resolve an intraparty dispute over whether to reinstate so-called pay-as-you-go rules requiring that tax cuts or new entitlement spending be offset with other revenue or spending cuts. It was only the third time in thirty years that Congress had not completed a budget resolution. *(Congress and the Nation Vol. XI, p. 77)*

The budget was a congressional document that did not go to the president for his signature, but it was important to the leadership because of the limit it set on discretionary spending and the special protection it could provide for subsequent bills that sought to alter taxes and entitlement programs.

The limit on discretionary spending in the fiscal 2006 budget resolution mirrored President George W. Bush's budget request, as calculated by the Congressional Budget Office (CBO). Any fiscal 2006 appropriations bill that exceeded the allocation in the budget resolution would be subject to a point of order on the floor. In addition, the budget assumed that at least $50 billion in fiscal 2006 emergency funds would be appropriated for the wars in Iraq and Afghanistan; spending designated as an emergency was not subject to the spending cap.

The resolution instructed House and Senate authorizing committees to find specific savings in mandatory programs, which would be bundled together into a spending-cut reconciliation bill. It also called for two other reconciliation bills: one to reduce taxes by $70 billion and the other to increase the ceiling on federal borrowing. Reconciliation bills, which can only arise as a result of a budget resolution, are subject to special Senate rules that prohibit filibusters and bar amendments unrelated to the budget. The no-filibuster rule means that a reconciliation bill can be passed by a simple majority in the Senate, rather than requiring the sixty votes needed to halt a filibuster. *(Mandatory spending bill, p. 81; Tax cuts, p. 105, Debt limit, p. 68)*

The central issue in House-Senate negotiations on a final budget resolution was how much to cut mandatory spending, especially for Medicaid, the health care program for the poor. To get a conference report on the budget through the Senate, House GOP leaders had to accept much less than the $69 billion in entitlement cuts that the House had initially passed. The final resolution also included a Senate provision intended to pave the way for oil and gas drilling in portions of Alaska's Arctic National Wildlife Refuge (ANWR)—a GOP priority because it would allow authorization for such energy exploration to be part of a filibuster-proof reconciliation bill. *(ANWR debate, p. 474)*

HIGHLIGHTS

Following are the main features of the fiscal 2006 budget resolution, H Con Res 95:

Discretionary spending. Set a cap of $843 billion on discretionary spending, the one-third of the budget distributed annually through the appropriations bills. The budget recommended $438.9 billion for national defense and $29.1 billion for homeland security, a 4 percent increase over fiscal 2005 for each department. Appropriations outside of defense and homeland security would

A BUDGET GLOSSARY

Appropriations. A bill that gives legal authority to spend or obligate money from the U.S. Treasury. The Constitution prohibits money to be drawn from the Treasury "but in Consequence of Appropriations made by Law."

By congressional custom, an appropriations bill originates in the House. It is not supposed to be considered by the full House or Senate until a related measure authorizing the funding is enacted. An appropriations bill grants the actual budget authority approved by the authorization bill, though not necessarily the full amount permissible under the authorization.

Budget authority. The authority for federal agencies to spend or otherwise obligate money, accomplished through the enactment of appropriations bills.

Budget outlays. Money that is actually spent in a given fiscal year, as opposed to money that is appropriated for that year. One year's budget authority can result in outlays over several years, and the outlays in any given year result from a mix of budget authority from that and other years.

Budget resolution. A concurrent resolution that is adopted by both chambers of Congress but does not require the president's signature. The measure sets a strict ceiling on discretionary budget authority, along with nonbinding recommendations about how the spending should be allocated. The budget resolution may also contain "reconciliation instructions" requiring authorizing and tax-writing committees to propose changes in existing law to meet deficit-reduction goals.

Continuing resolution. A joint resolution, cleared by Congress and signed by the president, to provide new budget authority for federal agencies and programs whose regular appropriations bills have not been enacted. These resolutions, also known as CRs or continuing appropriations, are used to keep agencies operating when, as often happens, Congress does not complete action on the regular appropriations process by the beginning of the fiscal year; if uncovered by either a regular appropriation or a CR, a federal agency must shut down.

Discretionary spending. Programs that Congress can finance as it chooses through appropriations (usually within the parameters set by authorization bills). About a third of the federal budget is financed by discretionary funding (the rest is financed by mandatory spending). Examples of discretionary spending include all federal agencies, Congress, the White House, the federal courts, the military, and activities from space exploration to child nutrition.

Emergency spending. Spending that the president and Congress have designated as an emergency requirement. Emergency spending is not subject to limits on discretionary spending set in the annual budget resolutions or to pay-as-you-go rules. The designation is intended for unanticipated spending, such as funding needed to respond to disasters. However, most of the appropriations for the Iraq war were designated as emergency spending, and Congress from time to time will designate spending as "emergency" to escape the discretionary spending limits.

Fiscal year. The budget year, which runs from October 1 of one calendar year through September 30 of the next.

Mandatory spending. Spending on programs, made up mostly of entitlements, whose eligibility requirements are written into law. Anyone who meets those requirements is entitled to the money until Congress changes the law. Examples include Social Security, Medicare, Medicaid, unemployment benefits, food stamps, and federal pensions.

Another major category of mandatory spending is the interest paid to holders of federal government bonds. Social Security and interest payments are permanently appropriated. Although budget authority for some entitlements is provided through the appropriations process, appropriators have little or no control over the money. Mandatory spending accounts for about two-thirds of federal spending.

Reconciliation. The process by which tax laws and spending programs are changed, or reconciled, to reach outlay and revenue targets set in the congressional budget resolution. Special rules in the Senate limit debate on reconciliation bills and prohibit extraneous or nongermane amendments. Established by the 1974 Congressional Budget Act, reconciliation was first used in 1980.

Revenues. Taxes, customs duties, some user fees, and most other receipts paid to the federal government. Some receipts and user fees show up as "negative outlays," however, and do not count as revenue.

---

have to be cut by 1 percent for fiscal 2006 and would essentially be frozen through fiscal 2010.

Supplemental war spending. Assumed that an additional $50 billion in fiscal 2006 discretionary funds would be needed for the wars in Iraq and Afghanistan, pending a larger supplemental spending request from the White House.

Mandatory spending cuts. Set a net reduction of $34.7 billion over five years in the anticipated cost of entitlement programs, to be achieved through a reconciliation bill. Entitlement spending accounted for about 54 percent of the federal budget.

Tax cuts. Set a total of $70 billion over five years in tax reductions, also to be achieved through a reconciliation bill. The budget resolution authorized an additional $36 billion in tax cuts but did not protect them from a Senate filibuster.

Deficit. Assumed an anticipated fiscal 2006 deficit of $382.7 billion, with declining deficits over the succeeding four years, reaching $254.4 billion in fiscal 2008 and $210.9 billion in fiscal 2010. That would beat by one year Bush's often-stated goal of cutting the deficit in half by 2009, using as a baseline the administration's initial fiscal 2004 deficit projection of $521 billion. If, however, Social Security surpluses were not counted to offset deficits in the rest of the budget, the fiscal 2010 deficit was projected to reach $470.8 billion.

Debt limit increase. Increased the debt limit. Under House rules, upon adoption of the budget by both chambers, the House was automatically considered to have passed a joint resolution increasing the statutory limit on the public debt, in this case from $8.2 trillion to $9.0 trillion, an exact increase of $781 million.

PRESIDENT'S BUDGET REQUEST

President Bush sent lawmakers the most austere fiscal blueprint of his presidency to date on Feb. 7, 2005. The $2.6 trillion budget for fiscal 2006 called for the first nominal cut in domestic spending since fiscal 1996, when a confrontation between President Bill Clinton (1993–2001) and the GOP majority in Congress led to two government shutdowns. Bush also proposed the first reductions in politically sacrosanct entitlement programs such as Medicaid and crop subsidies since 1997. *(Shutdowns, Congress and the Nation Vol. IX, pp. 37–40, 929; Entitlement cuts, Congress and the Nation Vol. X, pp. 3, 40, 43–45)*

The White House Office of Management and Budget (OMB) said the budget would produce a $390 billion deficit in fiscal 2006 and keep Bush on track to cut the annual deficit in half by 2009. However, Bush's budget did not include future costs of military activity in Iraq and Afghanistan beyond Sept. 30, 2006, the end of the fiscal year. The proposed budget also left out the cost of widely expected legislation to modify the alternative minimum tax, as well as his proposal to overhaul Social Security—neither of which was enacted in 2005. *(AMT, p. 91; Social Security, pp. 131, 662)*

The budget relied almost entirely on domestic spending restraint to achieve the deficit reduction. Bush requested increases for defense and homeland security and proposed $1.4 trillion in new tax cuts over ten years.

Republican budget writers on Capitol Hill embraced Bush's call for domestic spending cuts, though they acknowledged the plan would be tough to implement. "Obviously, this is a budget which is going to cause some significant angst amongst my colleagues, to be kind," said Judd Gregg, R-N.H., chairman of the Senate Budget Committee. "But the fact that everyone's probably going to be upset by it, because everyone's ox gets gored, including defense, by the way . . . probably means they've done a good job."

Democrats generally blasted Bush for continuing to run up huge deficits through tax cuts while trying to slash domestic spending. Rep. John M. Spratt Jr. of South Carolina, ranking Democrat on the House Budget Committee, said domestic discretionary accounts represented less than 20 percent of the overall budget. "No one can argue that these programs are the source of the deficit, because they've barely increased over the last several years," Spratt said. "Cuts like this hurt, but in the end they barely make a dent in the deficit."

The CBO published its annual recalculation of the president's budget in March. Congress traditionally used CBO's revised numbers in preparing its own budget resolution, although lawmakers said they were not required to do so. Bush called for capping discretionary spending at $804 billion in fiscal 2006, a 2.1 percent increase over the previous fiscal year not counting supplementary appropriations. Of that, he said, $419 billion would go to defense, $32 billion to homeland security, and $389 billion to nondefense, non–homeland-security programs. CBO said Bush's proposals would cap discretionary spending at $843 billion, a 1.7 percent increase. Either way, the growth in discretionary accounts would be well below the projected 2.5 percent rate of inflation.

According to CBO, Bush's discretionary proposals included $439 billion for defense, a 4.4 percent increase over fiscal 2005 spending but less than the 6.8 percent boost the Pentagon got the previous year. The extra funding was primarily for personnel and maintenance accounts, while the Pentagon's procurement budget would be frozen at existing levels. The budget request also included a net total for homeland security of $29 billion, plus an additional $3 billion to $4 billion to be covered by offsetting user fees. The president asked for $375 billion for nondefense, non–homeland-security programs, a 0.7 percent cut from fiscal 2005 levels. Several accounts within this category were slated for increases, further reducing the funds that would be available for the remaining domestic programs. For example, Bush proposed what CBO said was an increase of $3.8 billion, or 12.8 percent, for international affairs, about $1.5 billion of which was for his Millennium Challenge Corporation. Medicare was expected to need a discretionary increase of $1.1 billion, or 26.5 percent, for the extra costs of administering the new prescription drug program, which was set to begin in 2006.

Many of Bush's proposed cuts to discretionary programs—such as trimming Army Corps of Engineers water projects and eliminating $1.5 billion in anticrime grants to state and local governments—had been tried before and ignored by a Republican Congress. The administration proposed eliminating ninety-nine discretionary programs for a savings of $8.8 billion. Congress had rejected more than half those terminations before.

The president's budget also proposed net savings of $61.6 billion over five years and $137 billion over ten years from entitlement programs. Later in the year, the White

DEBT CEILING RAISED SEVEN TIMES UNDER BUSH

During President George W. Bush's second four-year term in the White House, Congress four times raised the legal limit on the federal debt, once in 2006, once in 2007, and twice in 2008. Over his eight years in office the limit had been raised a total of seven times, to $11.3 trillion when he left the White House. At the time of the first increase, in 2002, the ceiling was just over $5.9 trillion. *Congress and the Nation Vol. XI, pp. 63, 76, 84*)

The increases reflected both conscious decisions by the administration and Congress to cut taxes and to increase expenditures, particularly on wars in Iraq and Afghanistan, and unanticipated events, including a financial crisis that began in 2007 and hurricane relief efforts dating from 2005.

Background

Periodically, government borrowing came close to exceeding the debt ceiling. Because a default was unthinkable, Congress had no choice but to increase the limit. But lawmakers often took the opportunity to try to score political points about deficit spending or to use must-pass debt limit bills to advance other legislation. The need to lead the drive to approve an increase in the debt limit was particularly awkward for Bush and congressional Republicans, who regularly castigated Democrats as big spenders.

To take some of the political sting out of the process, the House in 1979 adopted a special procedure stipulating that the House was automatically deemed to have passed a debt limit increase when both chambers adopted the annual budget resolution. The procedure was known as the Gephardt rule after its author Richard A. Gephardt, D-Mo., and it was frequently derided by Republicans as a ruse to avoid direct responsibility for the nation's debt. Although the rule remained in place in the GOP-controlled 104th, 105th, and 106th Congresses, it was not used when the limits were raised in 1996 and 1997.

The House GOP leadership repealed the provision in the 107th Congress but revived it at the start of the 108th after nearly failing to pass the 2002 debt limit bill. The House cleared that measure (PL 107-199) by a one-vote margin as the Treasury was approaching unprecedented default on U.S. obligations.

Congress was required to raise the debt ceiling again in 2003 and in 2004. The timing of the 2004 request proved awkward. The administration in August said it expected to run out of money in mid-November and asked Congress to act before recessing in October, just weeks before election day. When it became apparent that a lame-duck session would be necessary, GOP congressional leaders postponed the vote until after the election, in which Democratic contender Sen. John Kerry of Massachusetts had tried to make the record budget deficits under Bush a major campaign issue. Even then it was close call, with the Senate approving the increase 52–44 and the House approving it 208–204 on the day that Treasury had set as the deadline for congressional action.

2006 Action

The Senate narrowly cleared a $781 billion increase in the federal debt limit on March 16, 2006, averting a government default and allowing House Republicans to escape a politically unpopular vote in an election year. The Senate vote was 52–48. All forty-four Democrats, Independent James M. Jeffords of Vermont, and three conservative Republicans opposed the measure. The House had passed the measure in 2005. President Bush signed the increase March 20 (H J Res 47—PL 109-182).

The legislation brought the statutory ceiling on the cumulative federal debt to just under $9 trillion. It was the fourth such increase since Bush took office; together, they raised the debt ceiling by a total of $3 trillion. The federal debt includes bonds held by the public (the public debt) and money owed to government trust funds such as Social Security.

Congress had no choice but to act. Treasury Secretary John W. Snow had warned the week of March 13 that he had already taken "all prudent and legal actions" to stay under the cap. To avoid a default, Snow had temporarily tapped civil service retirement and disability funds, among other actions. Without an increase, the Treasury would have been unable to pay interest on existing notes and bonds, redeem maturing securities, or borrow additional funds.

The House had passed the debt limit measure in 2005, after the Treasury Department alerted Congress that it

House said the budget would result in "gross" savings—not counting proposed increases in some mandatory programs—of $83.9 billion over five years and $187 billion over ten years. CBO said Bush's policy proposals would produce net savings of about $51 billion over five years and $140 billion over ten years, if some refundable credits were not counted.

A major piece of the savings cited by the White House came from $60 billion in cuts from projected spending over ten years for Medicaid, the joint federal-state health insurance program for the poor, which had been immune to budget cuts since 1997. The budget also proposed putting about $15 billion back into Medicaid and children's health programs, reducing the net savings to about $45 billion.

thought it would need more borrowing authority before the end of the year. House passage occurred automatically under the Gephardt rule, when both the House and Senate adopted the conference report on the fiscal 2006 budget resolution (H Con Res 95) on April 28. The resulting legislation (H J Res 47) proposed to increase the $8.2 trillion federal debt limit by $781 billion to nearly $9 trillion. *(Budget resolution, p. 65)*

Congress put off further action after the Treasury Department wrote lawmakers in August 2005 to say that a smaller-than-expected deficit attributed to a surge in federal tax revenue meant the debt ceiling would not have to be raised until sometime in the first quarter of 2006. The federal government ended fiscal 2005 with a deficit of $318.3 billion, about $100 billion less than projected at the start of the year.

Once Snow informed them the government was on the verge of default, Senate GOP leaders still delayed the unpopular vote until the day before the scheduled March 2006 recess, in an effort to minimize chances that amendments would be adopted. Any amendment would have sent the measure back to the House, forcing representatives to cast a roll-call vote, which Republicans hoped to avoid.

2007 Action

A year and a half later, President Bush signed legislation (H J Res 43—PL 110-91) on Sept. 29, 2007, increasing the statutory limit on the nation's cumulative debt by $850 billion to $9.8 trillion. It was the fifth increase since 2002, totaling more than $3 trillion.

Treasury Secretary Henry M. Paulson Jr. informed Congress in July 2007 of the need to raise the debt limit sometime in October. He followed in September with a letter asking for action by Oct. 1.

The Senate cleared the debt limit increase (H J Res 43—S Rept 110-184) by a vote of 53–42 on Sept. 27. Democrats used the latest increase to criticize what they said were the risky fiscal policies of the White House and the Republicans who controlled Congress in the first six years of Bush's presidency. Democrats particularly blamed Bush's 2001 and 2003 tax cuts, which were not offset by spending cuts or tax increases elsewhere in the budget. *(Bush tax cuts, Congress and the Nation Vol. XI, pp. 89, 105)*

Republicans argued that those tax cuts helped the economy gain strength after a short recession earlier in the decade. They blamed most of the deficit growth on the end of the 1990s' economic surge; on increased national security spending after the Sept. 11, 2001, terrorist attacks; and on the cost of the war in Iraq. Democrats had hammered Republicans on war spending as part of their broader opposition to Bush's Iraq policy.

The House did not take a separate vote. Under the Gephardt rule, the House was considered to have passed legislation boosting the debt limit when Congress adopted its annual budget resolution (S Con Res 21), which specified the size of the increase. *(Budget resolution, p. 108)*

2008 Action

Congress raised the limit twice in 2008, to $10.6 trillion at the end of July and to $11.3 trillion at the beginning of October. Both times the increase was enacted as part of legislation aimed at shoring up major financial institutions to keep the economy from slipping into deep recession, even though that occurred in any event by 2009.

In contrast to past years, when the two parties used the need to raise the debt limit to attack each other's fiscal policies, there was little debate in 2008, as Congress engaged in the larger debate over the government's unprecedented and costly efforts to help the struggling financial industry and unfreeze credit markets. *(Financial crisis, pp. 51, 163)*

Congress first raised the debt ceiling in July, by $800 billion to $10.6 trillion, as part of a law (PL 110-289) that gave the government the authority to take over mortgage giants Fannie Mae and Freddie Mac. The debt ceiling probably would have had to be raised regardless, but the expectation that the Treasury would use the authority provided in the law to shore up the two companies necessitated an increase in the amount of federal debt the government could carry. *(Fannie Mae, Freddie Mac assistance, p. 625)*

In October, Congress cleared a bill (PL 110-343) authorizing the Treasury Department to spend $700 billion as part of an effort to unfreeze credit markets and keep the financial sector from collapsing. The expectation that the Treasury would use this money required increasing the statutory ceiling by $700 billion to $11.3 trillion. *(Financial industry assistance, p. 154)*

Bush called for a net total of $1.5 trillion in tax cuts in fiscal 2005 through 2014, according to the Joint Committee on Taxation, whose calculations were used by Congress and by the CBO. Most of the estimated revenue loss was from Bush's proposal to make his earlier tax cuts permanent (most were scheduled to expire in 2010). These included reduced tax rates for dividends and capital gains, reduced income tax brackets, and repeal of the estate tax, among other things.

The president also proposed new lifetime savings accounts that would allow tax-free earnings and withdrawals, five new tax breaks for health care costs, including a refundable credit of up to $3,000 for health insurance premiums for taxpayers who were not covered through their employers, and a $500-per-employee small business credit for employer contributions to new Health Savings Accounts; and a permanent extension of a 20 percent tax credit for company research and development costs above a specified level.

HOUSE ACTION

Reflecting the influence of fiscal conservatives, the House Budget Committee approved a fiscal 2006 budget resolution (H Con Res 95—H Rept 109-17) that called for $68.6 billion in cuts to mandatory programs over five years—about $18 billion more than Bush had requested in his budget. The resolution, drafted by Chairman Jim Nussle, R-Iowa, was approved 22–15 on March 9.

The House adopted the budget resolution March 17 by a narrow vote of 218–214, but only after GOP leaders had quelled a revolt by conservative members of the Republican Study Committee (RSC), who insisted on a new mechanism to stop spending bills that exceeded budget limits.

The conservatives, led by RSC Chairman Mike Pence of Indiana, threatened to withhold their votes on the budget resolution unless they were satisfied. In the end, they settled for a promise from GOP leaders to amend House rules to create a new, though mostly redundant, point of order. It would apply when the House stripped fees or rescissions from a bill during floor debate, causing the remaining appropriation to exceed the discretionary allocation for the bill.

Some GOP authorizers expressed concern over the mandatory spending cuts that their committees were expected to deliver. Education and the Workforce Chairman John A. Boehner, R-Ohio, for example, acknowledged he would have difficulty producing the $21.4 billion in savings called for in the resolution. He was supposed to achieve a significant part of that through increases in premiums paid by companies to the financially troubled Pension Benefit Guaranty Corporation (PBGC).

The Blue Dog Coalition, which usually offered a budget substitute, did not do so this time. But three Democratic substitutes were rejected. One, by David R. Obey of Wisconsin, the ranking member on the Appropriations Committee, would have increased the fiscal 2006 discretionary spending cap by $15.8 billion to allow extra funding for a variety of programs, including education, veterans, and health care. The proposal was rejected 180–242. A second, offered by Spratt, would have eliminated all mandatory spending cuts and increased taxes by $159 billion over five years, promising a balanced budget by 2012. It was rejected 165–264. Illustrating divisions among Democrats, thirty-six members of the caucus voted against their leadership's alternative.

The third substitute, offered by the Congressional Black Caucus, was rejected 134–292. The amendment would have increased fiscal 2006 discretionary spending by $36.3 billion, focused mainly on education, job training, homeland security, and veterans' programs while rescinding tax cuts for wealthy individuals.

SENATE ACTION

Across Capitol Hill, the Senate Budget Committee approved its version of the budget (S Con Res 18) by a vote of 12–10 on March 10, the day after the House committee acted. Unlike his House counterpart, Gregg, the newly installed Senate Budget chairman, had to work overtime to negotiate a plan that could appeal to moderate Republicans and win acceptance from GOP authorizers without completely alienating the fiscal conservatives. Powerful Republicans, such as Saxby Chambliss, R-Ga., who ran the Agriculture Committee, and Michael B. Enzi, R-Wyo., chairman of the Health, Education, Labor, and Pensions panel, used their leverage to limit the demands upon them to produce savings.

The committee-approved resolution included an $843.4 billion discretionary spending limit, $400 million higher than the House recommended. But the major difference from the Senate was in mandatory spending cuts. The Senate committee proposed cutting a total of $32 billion from entitlement programs over five years, significantly below the $51 billion sought by Bush and less than half the $68.6 billion proposed by the House. Gregg scaled back Bush's proposals to curb farm subsidies and raise PBGC premiums, but he stood firm on Medicaid, saying it was crucial for Congress to demonstrate a willingness to at least begin addressing the spiraling growth of entitlement programs. The resolution instructed the Finance Committee to find $15 billion in savings over five years, with the assumption that $14 billion of that would come from Medicaid.

The resolution also instructed the Finance Committee to report a bill by Sept. 7 that would cut taxes by $70.2 billion over five years. Gregg said that tax-writers would be able to extend several tax cuts that were enacted in 2003 (PL 108-27) but slated to expire before 2010, including those on stock dividends, capital gains, small-business expensing, tuition costs, and state and local sales taxes. To offset some of the cost of the tax cuts, the resolution assumed as part of its reconciliation instructions that the government would receive $2.4 billion in leasing revenues from drilling in ANWR.

The Senate approved its budget resolution 51–49 March 17, just hours after the House had acted. Before final passage, however, moderate Republicans teamed up with Democrats to shrink the mandatory spending cuts to $17 billion from the $32 billion approved by the committee—mainly by eliminating $14 billion in Medicaid reductions proposed by Bush.

During a marathon session that featured voice or roll call votes on fifty-nine amendments, the Senate adopted 52–48 an amendment by Gordon H. Smith, R-Ore., to strip the reconciliation instructions to the Finance Committee. Instead, the amendment called for a presidentially appointed commission to study ways to overhaul Medicaid. The vote, which had the support of seven Republicans and all Senate Democrats, stung Gregg, who had made Medicaid cuts the centerpiece of his budget. A furious lobbying effort by Majority Leader Bill Frist, R-Tenn., and administration officials failed to sway key moderates such as Susan Collins, R-Maine, who ended up as the decisive vote.

"What we have said with this vote is that Congress is unwilling to curb spending in any of the areas where explosive growth is occurring," Gregg said. "We are effectively kicking the can down the road for maybe another decade, because I predict if we don't get these savings done this year, it will be a long time before we have another real opportunity."

The Medicaid vote took some of the shine off two significant GOP wins by Gregg and Frist on the divisive issues of pay-as-you-go rules and drilling in ANWR. The amendment to eliminate the ANWR provision, offered by Maria Cantwell, D-Wash., was rejected 49–51. The vote was a reversal for drilling opponents, who had won a 52–48 vote to strike a similar provision in 2003.

The Senate also rejected on a 50–50 tie an attempt by Russ D. Feingold, D-Wis., to add pay-as-you-go budget language requiring that any tax cut or new entitlement spending proposal be fully offset or face a sixty-vote point of order in the Senate. Feingold had succeeded 51–48 on a similar amendment in 2004. Republicans Lincoln Chafee of Rhode Island, Olympia J. Snowe of Maine, and George V. Voinovich of Ohio supported the amendment and subsequently voted against the budget.

FINAL ACTION

The House adopted the conference report on the budget resolution (H Rept 109-62) by a vote of 214–211 on April 28; the Senate adopted the report 52–47 later that day.

The final budget closely resembled the version Gregg had put before his committee. The $34.7 billion in savings from mandatory programs over five years was only slightly larger than the $32 billion in the Senate committee bill but about half the $69 billion in the House version. The House agreed to take the Senate's proposal for a five-year, $70 billion tax cut reconciliation bill. Panels were told to report both the tax and spending cut bills in September.

An overriding desire to finish the budget resolution prompted House Republican leaders to make concessions to the small but well-positioned band of Senate GOP moderates who took a stand against future cuts in programs aimed at the poor or unemployed.

During several weeks of talks with the White House and Senate GOP leaders, Sen. Gordon Smith agreed to accept $10 billion in Medicaid cuts if a presidential study commission was created to recommend ways to wring savings from the program without hurting beneficiaries. But he balked when he discovered that budget negotiators also expected the Finance Committee to propose an additional $6 billion in cuts coming from other programs such as Supplemental Security Income, which provides cash grants to the poorest of the poor.

In the end, Nussle and GOP leaders agreed to drop the extra $6 billion. They said taking the first step to cut mandatory spending was more important than standing firm on the higher figure. "The [budget] still maintains its basic integrity, which is the need to move forward to try to address major entitlements in the out years," Gregg said.

Senate GOP moderates were not the only ones to play a strong hand in limiting the entitlement cuts. Chambliss made it plain he would not accept significantly more than the $2.8 billion in cuts to farm subsidies and food stamp programs included in the Senate budget. Conferees settled on $3 billion. The House called for $9 billion. Meanwhile, business groups lobbied hard to fend off an increase in PBGC premiums. Although the House proposed to raise $18 billion through such an increase, the final budget called for $6.6 billion in additional PBGC receipts.

The final budget instructed the House Resources and Senate Energy and Natural Resources committees to find $2.4 billion over five years for deficit reduction, with the assumption that the funding would come from leasing drilling rights in ANWR.

Despite the political pain encountered in even talking about entitlement cuts, the reductions assumed in the budget resolution amounted to just 0.4 percent of the $9.1 trillion total spending for such programs expected in fiscal 2006 through 2010.

POSTSCRIPT

In the fall, Republican Speaker J. Dennis Hastert of Illinois called on the House to revise the budget resolution to require deeper cuts in mandatory spending and across-the-board reductions in discretionary programs. Hastert was reflecting a determined push by fiscal conservatives to offset a portion of the mounting relief and reconstruction costs following hurricanes Katrina and Rita in the Gulf Coast.

But Hastert and acting majority leader Roy Blunt, R-Mo., abandoned the idea after running into resistance from Republican moderates. The Senate leadership refused to consider such a change in their chamber, arguing that it was unnecessary and would take too much time. House leaders instead persuaded their authorizing committees to approve additional savings as part of a spending-cut reconciliation bill without relying on a new budget resolution.

Fiscal 2006 Regular Appropriations

For only the third time in a decade Republican leaders succeeded in clearing all of the regular fiscal 2006 appropriations bills by the end of 2005 without resorting to an omnibus spending package. Previously Congress had

GROWING PUBLIC DEBT

The public debt is the amount owed to the public, American or foreign, through individual or institutional purchase of government securities such as bonds. The remainder of the federal debt is the amount the government has borrowed from government trust funds such as Social Security. The latter is an intragovernmental transaction but is still an obligation that must be paid someday and carries interest the same as debt owed to the general public.

(In millions of dollars)

Fiscal Year	Total Public Debt	As a of GDP%	Fiscal Year	Total Public Debt	As a % of GDP
1990	$ 2,411.6	42.0%	2000	$3,409.8	35.1%
1991	2,689.0	45.3	2001	3,319.6	33.0
1992	2,999.7	48.1	2002	3,540.4	34.1
1993	3,248.4	49.4	2003	3,913.4	36.2
1994	3,433.1	49.3	2004	4,295.5	37.3
1995	3,604.4	49.2	2005	4,592.2	37.5
1996	3,734.1	48.5	2006	4,829.0	37.1
1997	3,772.3	46.1	2007	5,035.1	36.9
1998	3,721.1	43.1	2008	5,802.7	40.8
1999	3,632.4	39.8	2009*	8,531.4	59.9

* Estimated
GDP: Gross domestic product

SOURCE: Executive Office of the President, Office of Management and Budget, *Budget of the United States Government, Fiscal Year 2010, Historical Tables* (Washington, D.C.: Government Printing Office, 2009), Table 7.1.

managed to do so only in 1997 and 2001. In addition, the bills stayed within the $843 billion limit on discretionary spending set by President George W. Bush and ratified by Congress in its fiscal 2006 budget resolution. The chairmen of the Appropriations committees gave their subcommittees a little breathing space under the discretionary caps by cutting some money from the amounts Bush wanted for defense and using it for domestic programs. *(Budget resolution, p. 65)*

In other action, however, Congress cleared more than $200 billion in emergency supplemental spending during the year—much of it for fiscal 2005. Under the budget rules, none of that counted against the spending caps. In addition to funding the Iraq and Afghanistan wars through supplemental appropriations rather than the regular defense bill, Congress also provided emergency funding during 2005 for veterans' health care, preparations for a potential flu pandemic, and relief and recovery efforts following hurricanes Katrina and Rita.

Reorganization in the House and Senate pared the number of regular spending bills from thirteen to eleven. One consequence was that in several cases, companion House and Senate bills covered slightly different accounts, a problem that was sorted out only when the bills reached conference.

All but two of the bills were ready for Bush by Thanksgiving. The last two did not clear until Dec. 21. House members were so dissatisfied with the spending limits in the labor, health and human services, and education bill—particularly the elimination of earmarked projects for their districts—that they shocked the leadership by rejecting the first conference report in mid-November.

The must-pass defense spending bill was also held up. The main obstacle was a dispute over language by Sen. John McCain, R-Ariz., to bar "cruel, inhuman, or degrading" treatment of military detainees. From September on, the White House threatened to veto the bill if the provision remained. The administration did not give in until Dec. 15, a day after the House strongly supported the language. The defense bill then became the vehicle for several emergency supplementals including funding for the Gulf Coast relief and veterans' health care as well as a 1 percent across-the-board cut in discretionary spending in all the regular fiscal 2006 spending bills except veterans' programs and emergency war funding.

Because only two of the appropriations bills had cleared when fiscal 2006 began Oct. 1, Congress also had to clear a series of three short-term continuing resolutions to tide the government over while lawmakers finished the rest of the bills. None of the three—PL 109-77, signed Sept. 30; PL 109-105, signed Nov. 19; and PL 109-128, signed Dec. 18—was controversial.

Following are highlights of the eleven regular appropriations bills and three supplementals enacted in 2005.

LABOR, HHS, EDUCATION

The Senate cleared the largest of the fiscal 2006 spending bills—for the Departments of Labor, Health and Human Services, and Education—on Dec. 21 as one of its last acts before adjournment. President Bush signed the bill (HR 3010—Pl 109-149) into law on Dec. 30.

The bill's difficult path through Congress resulted largely from tight spending limits that left many lawmakers dissatisfied.

The $609.1 billion was $105.1 billion over the fiscal 2005 version, but the difference was attributable entirely to growth in mandatory spending. Funding to pay for the new Medicare prescription drug benefit, scheduled to begin on Jan. 1, 2006, was responsible for about half the mandatory spending increase. Funding for discretionary programs, those over which appropriators have control, shrank by about $200 million from fiscal 2005, to $142.5 billion. *(Medicare prescription drugs, Congress and the Nation Vol. XI, p. 496)*

The House passed its version of HR 3010 on June 24 by a 250–151 vote. In the Senate, Arlen Specter, R-Pa., chairman of the Labor-HHS-Education Appropriations Subcommittee, used several bookkeeping maneuvers to create more room for discretionary funding including an additional $1.1 billion for the National Institutes of Health (NIH), one of Specter's longtime priorities. During floor debate, senators also added nearly $8 billion in emergency funding for development and production of a vaccine to combat avian flu. An outbreak of a new strain of the virus in several Asian countries had sparked fears of a pandemic. The Senate then passed HR 3010 on Oct. 27 with only three dissenting votes.

In conference, House appropriators rejected most of the Senate's efforts to expand spending under the bill, including Specter's funding shift and the funds to combat avian flu. Congress eventually included $3.8 billion for flu protection in the defense appropriations bill (HR 2863—PL 109-148). Conferees said, among other things, that the tight spending caps forced them to scrap $1 billion worth of earmarks for members.

Elimination of the earmarks was a sticking point for many in the House, which caught the GOP leadership off guard on Nov. 17 when it rejected the conference report on the bill (H Rept 109-300) on a vote of 209–224. Legislators also complained about cuts in rural health care programs and the level of spending for education. *(Earmarks box, p. 74)*

The House narrowly adopted a revised conference report (H Rept 109-337) on the bill Dec. 14 on a vote of 215–213. The second conference report contained only a few adjustments, including an increase in funding for rural health care. Although the changes were enough to win House adoption, several senators, including Specter, said they would vote against the conference report because it shortchanged NIH and other programs. Specter ultimately agreed to support the bill, noting that the programs would get even less money if Congress kept them operating through a long-term continuing resolution, and the Senate cleared the bill by voice vote as part of an effort to complete its work and adjourn for the year.

DEFENSE DEPARTMENT

Often one of the first spending bills to be enacted, the defense appropriations bill was the last of the regular fiscal 2006 funding measures approved, and arguably the most contentious. The measure, which appropriated $453.5 billion in defense spending, was held up initially over language banning abuse of detainees in U.S. custody. That dispute was not resolved until late in the year, when the bill (HR 2863) then became a magnet for a host of unrelated legislation including an across-the-board cut in discretionary spending of 1 percent and a provision, added in conference, to allow oil and gas drilling in Alaska's Arctic National Wildlife refuge (ANWR). That provision was ultimately removed from the bill, which did not clear until Dec. 21. President Bush signed it into law (PL 109-148) on Dec. 30.

The House easily approved HR 2863 (H Rept 109-119) on June 20 but the measure stalled in the Senate. Typically legislators complete action on the annual defense authorization bill before taking up the defense spending bill, but a series of disputes delayed action on the authorization bill. One of the disputes involved McCain's amendment to ban the use of torture on enemy combatants held in U.S. custody. The amendment also required military interrogators to use the Army field manual, which outlined specific interrogation techniques that complied with the Geneva Conventions on treatment of war prisoners.

President Bush, who argued that the Geneva standards applied to state-sponsored, uniformed soldiers but not to terrorists, threatened to veto the bill. The White House repeatedly told lawmakers they must not pass any legislation that would tied the president's hands in the war on terror.

Despite the veto threat and frequent phone calls and personal visits to legislators by Vice President Dick Cheney, the Senate adopted McCain's amendment Oct. 5 on a **key vote of 90–9 (R 46–9; D 43–0; I 1-0).** The Senate then passed its version of HR 2863 (S Rept 109-141) on Oct. 7 with no dissenting votes. (A month later, the Senate added the McCain amendment to the defense authorization bill by voice vote.) *(2005 key votes, p. 915)*

With such strong bipartisan support, the vote on the McCain amendment was the most direct slap to the administration on the moral conduct of the war on terror since it began after the Sept. 11 attacks in 2001. Nonetheless, the White House continued to oppose the language until Dec. 14, when an overwhelming majority of the House

EARMARKS: A CONTINUING CONTROVERSY

The controversy over the practice of earmarking—appropriations or tax breaks inserted into legislation by individual legislators for the benefit of specific organizations, businesses, or projects in their home districts or states—steadily ratcheted up during the 109th and 110th Congress. Although both the House and Senate adopted a series of new rules to govern earmarks, legislators opposed to the practice insisted the rules were not strong enough and vowed to push for stronger controls if not outright elimination.

Earmarks were a relatively new phenomenon in Washington. Just a few decades earlier, "pork barrel politics" played out informally, and in only a few of the Capitol's backrooms, where a handful of committee chairmen had the power to secure votes for their bills by adding on hometown projects for wavering members.

Starting in the late 1970s and early 1980s, however, as power in Congress grew more diffuse and procedures more democratic, rank-and-file members began to expect the same amenities that the power players received. Over time, party leaders, who wanted to maintain broad constituencies as a means of holding power, capitalized on those longings by turning an informal system into an institutionalized earmark industry, in which members make formal requests or follow the bureaucratic procedures set out by the Appropriations Committees. By the 109th Congress, the promise of earmarks—and the threat of withholding them—had become one of the most powerful tools party leaders used to build legislative coalitions and enforce party discipline.

Several watchdog groups and some legislators in both parties had long complained that earmarks were spinning out of control, distorting spending decisions and possibly leading to excesses. Two events in 2005 that seemed to confirm those criticisms helped fasten public attention on the practice. One was the plea bargain by Rep. Randy "Duke" Cunningham, R-Calif., in which he admitted receiving bribes in exchange for earmarks and federal contracts for four co-conspirators. Allegations that other legislators had accepted bribes or campaign contributions in return for earmarks were rife, as were allegations that some lawmakers steered earmarks to relatives and friends and used earmarks to increase the value of their real estate holdings. *(Cunningham ethics scandal, p. 823)*

The Bridges to Nowhere

The second evolved out of passage of legislation reauthorizing the nation's surface transportation programs (PL 109-59). Among other things, the measure authorized $223 million for construction of a bridge connecting Ketchikan, Alaska, to the tiny population on Gravina Island. A second bridge, running from Anchorage to lightly populated Knik, was also authorized. The two bridges, quickly dubbed the "bridges to nowhere," came to symbolize fiscal irresponsibility on Capitol Hill later in 2005 after Sen. Tom Coburn, R-Okla, tried unsuccessfully to strip funding for them from the fiscal 2006 transportation appropriations bill and use the funding instead to repair the Interstate 10 bridge in New Orleans that had been torn apart in August 2005 by Hurricane Katrina. *(2005 Surface Transportation reauthorization, p. 407)*

"What I am here to tell you," Coburn said during debate on his amendment, "is that the rumble against spending is getting louder. People are fed up. All across the country, Americans are rising up against government overspending."

Coburn's move touched off a vehement defense of the bridges, and of earmarks in general, by senators who had made a career out of returning money to their constituents. In a tirade on the Senate floor, Alaska's senior senator, Republican Ted Stevens, a former chairman of the Appropriations Committee, threatened to resign from the Senate if funds for the two bridges were cut. "This amendment is an offense to me" Stevens shouted. "If one senator can decide he will take all the money from one state to solve a problem of another, that is not a union. That is not equality."

A majority of the Senate agreed with Stevens, rejecting Coburn's amendment on a **key vote of 15–82 (R 11–43; D 4–38; I 0–1).** *(2005 key votes, p. 915)*

During the House-Senate conference on the spending bill, however, negotiators quietly included language "unearmarking" the money for the bridges but allowing the Alaska Legislature to retain the money to spend as it chose. (The issue of who stopped funding for the bridge would come up again in the 2008 presidential campaign, when Alaska's governor, Sarah Palin, the Republican vice presidential nominee, famously claimed credit for stopping the bridge, saying she told the federal government "thanks but no thanks" for the funding. However, she had championed the building of the bridge during her 2006 gubernatorial campaign and opposed it only after it became a national scandal.)

Fearing voter backlash from a series of corruption scandals involving lobbying, both the House and Senate debated legislation in 2006 to tighten ethics and lobbying rules, but were unable to reconcile their differences. The House did change its rules in September to require members to identify earmarks they inserted into appropriations bills in committee or in conference; undisclosed earmarks would be subject to a point of order. The rule, passed by a vote of 245–171 over the objections of Republican appropriators, did not have much effect because the House had already passed all but one of the fiscal 2007 spending bills.

After losing control of both chambers of Congress in 2006, GOP fiscal conservatives later said a leading cause was the party's failure to do anything meaningful about earmarks during their twelve-year tenure.

New Democratic Rules

When they came to power in 2007, Democrats in the House, who had campaigned against what they called the GOP "culture of corruption," moved quickly to adopt a package of rules changes (H Res 6) that included a requirement that earmarks be specified and their sponsors be named. The earmark provision was tied to a pay-as-you-go-provision, requiring revenue-raising offsets to any new entitlement spending or tax cuts. Together the two provisions represented the new Democratic majority's intent to distinguish itself from its Republican predecessors by promoting fiscal responsibility and discipline. The rule was adopted Jan. 5, 2007, on a **key vote of 280–152 (R 48–152; D 232–0).** *(Pay-as-you-go rules, p. 118; 2007 key votes, p. 955)*

The Senate included two earmark rules changes in its version of a lobbying and ethics bills (S 1—PL 110-81). One mirrored the House rule requiring disclosure of earmarks and their sponsors, and the other created a point of order against "airdropped" earmarks—set-asides added in conference without being included in either chamber's version of the legislation being negotiated. The goal of the rule was to make it easier to remove earmarks inserted in conference because they could not stand on their own. But the language of the rule quickly proved to be problematic as senators used it or threatened to use it to break apart conference agreements that bundled whole bills together into a single package. For example, to avoid the rule late in 2007, an omnibus spending measure (HR 2764) that incorporated eleven unfinished bills was created by sending amended versions back and forth between the chambers rather than creating a conference committee where the merger of several bills could be subject to a point of order.

The new rules on earmark disclosure added an unprecedented level of transparency to the appropriations process—and to the workloads of appropriators and their staffs. For example, a study of the fiscal 2008 House-passed spending bills conducted by Congressional Quarterly based on data compiled by Taxpayers for Common Sense found that almost one-third of the $4.2 billion credited to individual lawmakers were sponsored by just twenty members, many of whom were on the House Appropriations Committee. Leading the list, with sixty-nine earmarks worth nearly $180 million, was John P. Murtha of Pennsylvania, who held the top Democratic slot on the Defense Appropriations Subcommittee. Second was Murtha's Republican counterpart, C. W. Young of Florida, who also had sixty-nine earmarks worth $128.5 million.

In the final analysis, however, the rule had little effect on the amount of money specified for special projects. According to the Office of Management and Budget, the tally for the fiscal 2008 appropriations measures was 11,737 earmarks costing about $17 billion (including earmarks jointly credited to several lawmakers and to President George W. Bush). That compared to 13,492 earmarks costing nearly $19 billion in the fiscal 2005 spending measures.

An Unresolved Issue

Earmarks became a campaign issue not only because of controversy about Palin's claims about the bridge to nowhere but because GOP presidential nominee, Sen. John McCain of Arizona, was one of the few members of Congress who refused to request earmarks and supported a moratorium on the practice—a position that so far neither chamber or party was willing to endorse.

During the campaign his rival Sen. Barack Obama of Illinois said he would overhaul the practice. Once in office, however, Obama signed into law an omnibus spending bill for fiscal 2009, left over from 2008, that included, by one count, more than 8,500 earmarks at a cost of $7.7 billion. Republicans had urged Obama to veto the omnibus, but instead after signing the omnibus bill (HR 1105) on March 11, he offered a package of earmark reforms. It included requiring members to post their earmark requests on their Web sites; holding public hearings on earmark requests, "where members will have to justify their expense to the taxpayer"; and competitively bidding any earmark for a for-profit company.

The House and Senate appropriations panels had already announced at the start of 2009 that members would have to post requests on their Web sites. They also announced a plan to limit the growth of earmarks by keeping the amount of funding devoted to the projects to less than 1 percent of overall discretionary spending—still a significant amount in a budget where discretionary spending totaled some $1 trillion.

On March 11 House Democratic leaders announced further changes to the earmarking process. They said that executive agencies would be given twenty days to review an earmark request after it is made "to ensure that the earmark is eligible to receive funds and meets goals established in law." They also echoed Obama's call to require competitive bidding on earmarks targeted to for-profit companies.

voted to instruct House conferees to retain the McCain amendment in negotiations with the Senate. The **key vote was 308–122 (R 107–121; D 200–1; I 1–0).** *(2005 key votes, p. 915; McCain amendment details, pp. 364, 365)*

Although the House vote resolved the dispute over the McCain amendment, the bill had become a vehicle for several unrelated provisions, including $29 billion for aid to victims of Hurricane Katrina, $3.8 billion to protect against a potential flu pandemic, and a spending cut of 1 percent in most of the government's discretionary spending. The most controversial provision was the amendment added in conference by Ted Stevens, R-Alaska, chairman of the Senate Defense Appropriations Subcommittee, to open ANWR to oil and gas exploration, which Stevens pursued for years.

The House adopted the conference report on HR 2863 (H Rept. 109-359), including the ANWR language, on Dec. 19. When the conference report came to the Senate floor on Dec. 21, however, Democrats successfully blocked a cloture vote to limit debate on the bill on a **key vote of 56–44 (R 52–3; D 4–40; I 0–1).** *(2005 key votes, p. 915)*

Through a series of negotiated procedural steps, the Senate voted to instruct congressional clerks to strip the ANWR provision from the cleared spending bill and then voted to clear the bill. The following day, the House agreed by voice vote to strip the ANWR provision from the cleared bill. *(ANWR details, p. 474)*

Overall the defense spending bill provided $123.6 billion for operations and maintenance, $76.5 billion for procurement, $97 billion for military personnel, including a $3.1 billion military pay raise, and $72.1 billion for research, development, testing and evaluation of new weapons systems. Spending in the bill was $4.4 billion less than President Bush had requested

The bill also appropriated $50 billion in emergency supplemental funding for the wars in Iraq and Afghanistan, bringing the amount Congress had voted to spend for military operations and related activities in the two countries since 2003 to approximately $362 billion. Of the $50 billion total, $8 billion was earmarked to replace equipment lost in combat; $1.4 billion was designated for testing and fielding new equipment to thwart roadside bombs.

HR 2863 provided funding for 10,000 more personnel for the active-duty Army, for a new total, of 512,400, and funding to increase Marine Corps personnel by 1,000, to 179,000.

AGRICULTURE

Congress Nov. 3 cleared a bill (HR 2744—PL 109-97) appropriating $101 billion in fiscal 2006 for the Department of Agriculture, the Food and Drug Administration, and rural development programs. President Bush signed it Nov. 10.

Although funding in the bill exceeded fiscal 2005 spending by $11.5 billion, or 13 percent, virtually all of the increase was attributable to the growth of mandatory programs such as food stamps and crop subsidies. The $17 billion in the bill for discretionary programs represented an increase of about 1 percent over fiscal 2005, less than the rate of inflation. The legislation delayed until 2008 an Agriculture Department rule that required country-of-origin labeling of meat, produce, and peanuts, a victory for meatpackers and retailers who complained that the labels would cost too much money with little benefit for consumers. For the third straight year, House and Senate conferees bowed to a veto threat and dropped a House provision that would have allowed individuals and wholesalers to import prescription drugs from Canada and other countries. *(Food labeling, pp. 514, 517, 526 and Congress and the Nation Vol. XI, p. 467; Prescription drug imports, pp. 556, 578 and Congress and the Nation Vol. XI, p. 508)*

COMMERCE, JUSTICE, SCIENCE, STATE

Congress Nov. 16 provided a total of $61.8 billion in fiscal 2006 for the Departments of Commerce, Justice, and State, their related agencies, and science programs, including NASA and the National Science Foundation (HR 2862—PL 109-108). President Bush signed it Nov. 22.

Of the total, $57.9 billion was discretionary funding, a 3 percent increase over fiscal 2005 and 4 percent less than President Bush requested. In negotiating the final bill, conferees stripped out several controversial provisions, including a House amendment that would have limited the FBI's ability to access library and bookstore records under the 2001 antiterrorism law known as the Patriot Act (PL 107-56). The amendment, which the House adopted in June by a 238–187 vote, had drawn a veto threat. Conferees also removed a proposal to give the Drug Enforcement Administration the power to control the entry of new prescription painkillers into the market. *(USA Patriot Act, Congress and the Nation Vol. XI, p. 187; USA Patriot Act extended, p. 222)*

DISTRICT OF COLUMBIA

The District of Columbia government received $603 million for fiscal 2006 as part of the regular transportation-Treasury-housing appropriations bill (HR 3058—PL 109-115). The bill cleared Nov. 21 and was signed by the president Nov. 30.

The total was a $47.5 million increase over the previous year and nearly $30 million more than the president requested. The funding is mainly a payment in lieu of taxes, which the federal government does not pay. A controversial amendment to prevent enforcement of the city's gun control law, considered by many to be the most restrictive in the nation, was dropped from the final bill. Two other initiatives pushed by conservative Republicans were included. One established a $3 million pilot program aimed at reducing the number of children raised out of wedlock, while the other included $14 million for vouchers that could be used to send children to private schools.

ENERGY, WATER

Congress cleared a $30.5 billion fiscal 2006 spending bill (HR 2419—PL 109-103) for the Department of Energy, the Army Corps of Engineers, and related water programs on Nov. 14. President Bush signed the legislation Nov. 19.

Appropriators allowed just $450 million for the planned nuclear waste dump at Yucca Mountain in Nevada, 21 percent less than fiscal 2005 spending and about 31 percent less than the president requested. Even supporters of the controversial program accepted the cut with little resistance, saying that the project did not need as much money as agency officials originally anticipated because the administration was still dealing with legal and administrative delays. The bill also included $50 million in new funding for the Energy Department to plan a facility to recycle nuclear waste.

The bill provided $5.4 billion for the engineer corps, about $57 million less than the agency got in fiscal 2005, but the 2005 total included $400 million in emergency supplemental funding approved after Hurricane Katrina struck in August. The corps played a leading role in repairing levees damaged from the storm. *(Hurricane supplemental, p. 79)*

FOREIGN OPERATIONS

Congress provided $21 billion for foreign aid programs in fiscal 2006, an increase of $2.4 billion over fiscal 2005 but $1.9 billion less than requested. The legislation (HR 3057—PL 109-102) cleared Nov. 10 and was signed by the president Nov. 14.

The measure provided $1.8 billion for the Millennium Challenge Corporation, the president's signature foreign aid initiative. The president had requested $3 billion for the program that channeled aid to developing countries that established policies to promote investment, combat corruption, protect human rights, and ensure free elections. Congress increased Bush's request for funding for programs to prevent, treat, and control global HIV/AIDS, malaria, and tuberculosis by $268 million for a total of $2.8 billion.

Bush got only $61 million of the $459 million he sought for programs to help the Iraqi government deliver basic services, improve security, and develop a free market economic system. The conference report (H Rept 109-265) said that $3.5 billion remaining from the original $18.4 billion Iraq reconstruction package enacted in 2003 could be used for that purpose.

HOMELAND SECURITY

Congress Oct. 7 cleared a bill (HR 2360—PL 109-90) appropriating $31.9 billion for homeland security activities in fiscal 2006. President Bush signed the legislation Oct.18.

Republicans said they wrote a "threat-based bill" focused on the top priorities: border security and protecting the country against the dangers of weapons of mass destruction. Two agencies, Customs and Border Protection and Immigration and Customs Enforcement, received funding boosts of 10 percent and 35 percent, respectively, over fiscal 2005 and soaked up nearly one-third of the discretionary funding in the bill. The bill also provided $1.5 billion, a 35 percent increase, for the Homeland Security Department's research and development arm, which conducted most of the government's work on defenses against chemical, biological, and nuclear weapons.

The increases for border security came at the expense of grants to police, firefighters, and other first responders. State and local aid, including first-responder grants, was cut by 16 percent, to $3.3 billion. In what was hailed as a major breakthrough, the bill also allowed the department to distribute some of the first responder grants based on risk of a terror attack rather than on population.

The bill also provided $7.8 billion for the Coast Guard, $3.9 billion for the Transportation Security Administration, and $2.6 billion for the Federal Emergency Management Agency (FEMA). Although the bill represented a 4 percent increase over the budget request, Democrats said the bill still underfunded key priorities, including first responders and rail security.

The measure largely accommodated a reorganization plan for the department, announced in July. It included splitting off FEMA's preparedness functions into a new division and making FEMA a stand-alone agency within the department that will focus on recovery and response. The reorganization was a direct response to FEMA's inept handling of the government's response to Hurricane Katrina. *(FEMA reorganization, p. 236)*

INTERIOR, ENVIRONMENT

The $26.2 billion spending bill for the Interior Department, the Environmental Protection Agency (EPA), and other agencies, cleared July 29, was the first of the regular fiscal 2006 appropriations bills to become law (HR 2361—PL 109-54). The president signed it Aug. 2.

Its early enactment reflected a lack of controversy on substantive issues. It also made an attractive vehicle for $1.5 billion in supplemental fiscal 2005 funds to cover a shortfall in veterans' health care funding. *(Details, p. 78)*

Not counting veterans' health care, spending in the bill was 3 percent under fiscal 2005 spending but 2 percent higher than requested. Agencies sustaining the largest cuts were the EPA, which received $7.7 billion, a 4 percent cut from fiscal 2005, and the Agriculture Department's Forest Service, which received $4.3 percent, an 11 percent cut from fiscal 2005 when emergency firefighting funds for 2005 are counted. The EPA's Clean Water State Revolving Fund, which provided loans for state and local water and sewage treatment projects, was cut by more than 17 percent to $900 million.

LEGISLATIVE BRANCH

Congress July 29 cleared appropriations of $3.8 billion for fiscal 2006 (HR 2985—PL 109-55) to pay for its own operations, as well as for affiliated agencies such as the

Library of Congress, the Government Accountability Office, and the Government Printing Office. The president signed the bill Aug. 2.

The final version continued the so-called continuity of Congress provisions, enabling states to fill House vacancies in the event of a catastrophe. It also provided $44 million for construction of the Capitol Visitor Center if the project was completed by the target date of September 2006. Many members had expressed frustration with the over-budget and past-due project. The cost of the project had nearly doubled, from an original estimate of $265 million to at least $522 million. *(Continuity of Congress, p. 819; Capitol Visitor Center, pp. 821, 837)*

MILITARY CONSTRUCTION, VETERANS AFFAIRS

The Senate Nov.18 cleared an $82.6 billion fiscal 2006 spending bill (HR 2528—PL 109-114) for military construction and the Department of Veterans Affairs (VA) and the president signed it Nov. 30. The action came after lawmakers agreed to add $1.2 billion in emergency funding to help cover a shortfall in the VA's health care budget. That funding was added after the disclosure in June and July of budget shortfalls for VA health care that totaled nearly $3 billion. VA officials blamed the shortfall on outdated forecasts that underestimated the rising cost of long-term health care, as well as on a rapid increase in the number of patients seeking treatment, including many veterans of the Iraq and Afghanistan wars. HR 2528 appropriated $22.5 billion for medical services, including $1.2 billion in emergency funds that could be spent only if the president declared an emergency. In separate action Congress attached $1.5 billion in emergency supplemental funds to the fiscal 2006 interior-environment bill (PL 109-54) to cover the portion of the shortfall in VA health care funding that fell in fiscal 2005. *(Veterans supplemental, p. 79)*

TRANSPORTATION, TREASURY

After taking steps to eliminate or modify provisions President Bush had threatened to veto, Congress Nov. 21 cleared a $137.6 billion fiscal 2006 spending bill for the Departments of Transportation, Treasury, and Housing and Urban Development (HR 3058—PL 109-115). The president signed it Nov. 30. The legislation also contained funding for the District of Columbia. The final bill included $65.9 billion in discretionary appropriations, 4 percent more than in fiscal 2005 and almost 9 percent more than the administration had requested. *(District of Columbia spending, p. 76)*

Funding for Amtrak was controversial, as it had been for several years. President Bush requested no money for the passenger rail system and threatened to veto the bill if it contained funding for Amtrak without language overhauling the way Amtrak conducted business. Congress appropriated $1.3 billion for Amtrak along with several conditions on its business operations. Another high-profile controversy involved a provision adopted by both chambers that would have made it easier to sell agricultural products to Cuba. The provision was dropped from the final bill in the face of a veto threat. *(Amtrak details, p. 431; Cuba embargo, pp. 294, 324)*

Conferees also dropped two House provisions that had drawn veto threats: one that would have prevented most government agencies from contracting out federal jobs, and another that would have prevented the Federal Aviation Agency from implementing an existing contract for flight-service stations. The bill renewed existing language that banned the use of funds to pay for abortions through federal employee health plans, except in the case of rape, incest, or danger to the life of the woman. Conferees removed a Senate provision that would have blocked an automatic cost-of-living increase in congressional salaries. *(Congressional pay, p. 849)*

FISCAL 2005 WAR SUPPLEMENTAL

Congress cleared a fiscal 2005 emergency supplemental on May 10, 2005, that appropriated $82 billion, nearly all of it to pay for operations in Iraq and Afghanistan. The president signed it May 11. The bill (HR 1268—PL 109-13) also included $907 million for victims of the December 2004 tsunami in South Asia and contained several broad changes in immigration law. The funding was in addition to $25 billion that Congress had already provided as "bridge funding" in the fiscal 2005 defense appropriations bill (PL 108-287), pending the president's fuller request. *(Fiscal 2005 defense spending bill, Congress and the Nation Vol. XI, p. 354; War spending, table, p. 387)*

The final bill provided about $900 million more than Bush had requested for military operations in Iraq and Afghanistan through the end of fiscal 2005. It also provided about $635 million more than requested for border security and other homeland security needs, including funds to pay for an additional 500 border patrol agents. Bush had not requested the immigration policies either, but they were a high priority for House Republicans and were retained in conference. The provisions imposed tougher requirements on foreigners seeking asylum in the United States and created national standards for state driver's licenses. *(Immigration changes, pp. 686, 711)*

House fiscal conservatives initially succeeded in blocking funds for a new U.S. embassy in Iraq. But conferees agreed with the Senate and included $459 million of the $658 million that Bush requested for the purpose.

Fiscal 2005 Veterans Supplemental

Congress appropriated $1.5 billion in supplemental spending to make up an unexpected shortfall in fiscal 2005 funding for veterans' health care programs. The emergency money was attached to the fiscal 2006 interior-environment spending bill, which President bush signed into law on Aug. 2 (HR 2361—PL 109-54). In late June officials from the Department of Veterans Affairs told stunned lawmakers about the shortfall, saying the fiscal 2005 budget had been based on forecasts that predated the Iraq War and did not account for the spiraling costs of long-term care or the higher-than-expected number of returning veterans seeking care. In addition to the emergency fiscal 2005 funding, Congress also appropriated $1.2 billion in emergency fiscal 2006 veterans' health care funding that would be used only if the president declared an emergency.*)*

Hurricane Supplementals and Related Aid

Hurricane Katrina, which wreaked havoc on New Orleans and the Gulf Coast in August 2005, was the costliest natural disaster the federal government had ever faced. Congress quickly cleared a pair of emergency supplemental appropriations bills totaling $62.3 billion to begin paying for relief and cleanup. At the end of December—after an intense lobbying by the Mississippi delegation—lawmakers came up with a $29 billion package to help the hurricane-ravaged states with urgent infrastructure needs. About $23.4 billion of that was money reallocated from the earlier emergency measures. *(Katrina, pp. 781, 787, 788, 790)*

$10.5 BILLION "DOWN PAYMENT"

After the hurricane struck Aug. 29, congressional leaders cut short their summer recess and returned to Washington to clear a $10.5 billion emergency supplemental to meet immediate needs. The measure gave $10 billion to the Federal Emergency Management Agency (FEMA) and $500 million to the Defense Department. The House passed the bill and the Senate cleared it, both on voice votes, on Sept. 2. President Bush, who had requested the funds, signed the bill into law a few hours later (HR 3645—PL 109-61). During a tour of the region that day, he called it "a small down payment on the cost of this effort." Although accurate loss projections were impossible to make in the immediate aftermath of the storm, congressional leaders predicted that costs to the government would reach $150 billion to $200 billion.

SECOND SUPPLEMENTAL

Less than a week later, the administration sent Congress a second supplemental request, this one for $51.8 billion. The House passed and the Senate cleared HR 3673 on Sept. 8, and the president signed it the same day (PL 109-62). The second supplemental provided $50 billion for FEMA, $1.4 billion for the Defense Department and $400 million for the Army Corps of Engineers. Although Congress included $15 million for an audit of the spending by the inspector general, the supplemental essentially was a government piggy bank with few restrictions.

FEMA spending slowed dramatically in the weeks that followed, however. Even Hurricane Rita, which hit southeastern Texas and southwestern Louisiana on Sept. 24, did not put a large dent in FEMA's disaster relief funds. On Oct. 7 Congress reallocated $750 million in previously appropriated FEMA funds to a community disaster loan program that provided loans to local governments for maintaining government services such as police and fire (PL 109-88). Louisiana's two senators said their state needed the money before Congress started the weeklong Columbus Day recess to prevent more layoffs of government employees. At that time, more than $42 billion of the $62.3 billion Congress had appropriated had yet to be spent or allocated to hurricane relief efforts.

BILLION END-OF-YEAR PACKAGE

In October, the administration sent Congress a $17.1 billion reallocation request to redirect FEMA money to a variety of agencies, largely for repairing and replacing critical infrastructure such as highways, levees, and military facilities. But Senate Appropriations Chairman Thad Cochran, R-Miss., said it would not be enough. Along with Mississippi's influential Republican governor Haley Barbour, Cochran pressed for $35 billion and eventually persuaded House GOP leaders to agree in late Dec. to a $29 billion package. The spending, which was enacted as part of the conference report on the fiscal 2006 defense appropriations bill (PL 109-148), reallocated $23.4 billion in funds originally granted to FEMA. The additional funds were financed in part by an across-the-board spending cut in almost all fiscal 2006 discretionary programs except those for veterans and emergency war funding. The cut was also enacted as part of the defense bill. *(Defense appropriations, pp. 73, 102, 116, 400)*

The huge cost of the relief and reconstruction efforts had led fiscal conservatives—the 100-plus member Republican Study Committee in the House and a smaller band of senators—to call for funding offsets elsewhere in the federal budget. Republican leaders and the administration rejected many of the suggestions, such as delaying the Medicare prescription drug benefit. But the fiscal conservatives pushed GOP leaders to call for deeper-than-planned cuts in mandatory spending programs in the year-end budget-reconciliation bill. That bill totaled $38.8 billion in savings over five years (PL 109-171). *(Budget reconciliation, p. 81)*

Hurricane Tax Relief Bills Enacted

Congress in 2005 cleared two bills to provide tax relief to the victims of Hurricane Katrina, which devastated the Louisiana, Mississippi, and Alabama coasts the week of Aug. 29, and subsequent hurricanes Rita and Wilma that also hit the region.

The first, a $6.1 billion collection of provisions mainly to aid individuals and businesses hurt by Katrina, was enacted in September with little difficulty. The second, a $7.8 billion package of incentives for investment in the hurricane disaster zones, was signed in December but only after the two chambers reached an uneasy compromise on a controversial provision that would have barred gambling casinos and some other businesses from receiving the tax breaks.

IMMEDIATE KATRINA RELIEF

Congress Sept. 21 cleared a $6.1 billion package of tax breaks aimed at individuals and corporations in the hurricane-ravaged Gulf Coast region. President George W. Bush signed the measure into law Sept. 23 (HR 3768—PL 109-73).

The House and Senate passed slightly differing versions of the legislation by voice vote Sept. 15. After a brief tussle over the scope of tax breaks aimed at encouraging corporations to retain and hire victims of Katrina and at spurring more charitable contributions, House and Senate tax writers resolved their differences Sept. 20, avoiding a drawn-out formal conference on the legislation.

The House adopted a special rule (H Res 454) by a vote of 422–0 on Sept. 21 that had the effect of amending and passing the bill, sending it back to the Senate. The Senate cleared the bill by voice vote that evening.

Major provisions

The bill included provisions to:

- Allow individuals to withdraw up to $100,000 from their individual retirement accounts without paying the 10 percent federal penalty, provided they restored the funds to the account within three years.
- Allow Katrina victims to use their 2004 income in claiming the earned income tax credit or child tax credit on their 2005 tax returns. This was to ensure that those displaced by the hurricane did not lose benefits because of a change in their living situation.
- Allow firms with fewer than 200 employees to claim a 40 percent tax credit for up to $6,000 in wages paid to a worker between Aug. 28 and Dec. 31. This was a scaled-back version of a Senate provision aimed at encouraging businesses in the disaster area that could not operate to continue paying their workers.
- Make the "work opportunity" tax credit—used by employers of workers who received welfare benefits or food stamps—available for two years to those in disaster zones who hired people displaced by Katrina, and through the end of 2005 for employers outside the disaster area.
- Allow individuals in disaster zones to gain access to mortgage revenue bonds typically issued by state and local governments to help first-time homebuyers finance homes. Up to $150,000 of the proceeds from mortgage revenue bonds could be used to repair homes damaged by Hurricane Katrina.
- Allow S-corporations, partnerships, and sole proprietorships to claim a deduction on charitable contributions of food inventory through the end of the year. It also allowed corporations to claim a deduction through the end of 2005 for donations of educational books to public schools.
- Temporarily increase deduction limits for cash donations made by individuals and corporations. The increased deduction for individuals applied to all charitable contributions, not just those related to Hurricane Katrina.

STIMULATING INVESTMENT

Congress cleared a $7.8 billion package of tax incentives Dec. 16, 2005, that was intended to spur investment in the Gulf Coast region. President George W. Bush signed the measure into law Dec. 22 (HR 4440—PL 109-135).

Final House and Senate passage marked a delayed victory for Louisiana and Mississippi lawmakers, who had worked for months to secure a second round of tax breaks to help rebuild their states. The bill was the product of a week of informal House-Senate negotiations that allowed tax writers to avoid a formal conference and expedite action as lawmakers prepared to leave for the holidays.

Major Provisions

The centerpiece of the bill was the creation of "Gulf Opportunity Zones" to spur business investment in devastated areas of Alabama, Louisiana, and Mississippi, with tax breaks and bond provisions that totaled $6.2 billion over five years. They included:

- A "bonus depreciation" deduction for businesses equal to 50 percent of the cost of new property investments made in the disaster zone. The cost to the Treasury would be $2 billion over five years.
- An additional tax-exempt bond authority for Louisiana, Mississippi, and Alabama at a cost of $478 million over five years.
- A change in federal law to allow one additional "advance refunding" of debt for each state at a cost of $493 million over five years. Advance refunding allowed municipalities to issue new bonds to pay off outstanding bonds. Existing law allowed only one advance refunding of tax-exempt bonds.
- A 50 percent deduction for the costs of site cleanup and demolition from Aug. 27, 2005, through Dec. 31, 2007, at a cost of $121 million over five years.
- A 50 percent federal guarantee for up to $3 billion in bonds to aid local governments in Alabama, Louisiana, and Mississippi that had lost revenue or lacked access to capital to help fund infrastructure projects or operating expenses.

The bill also expanded tax breaks enacted in the earlier hurricane tax relief law to apply to individuals and businesses affected by hurricanes Rita and Wilma, as well as Katrina.

Legislative Action

The Senate included a $7.1 billion package of Gulf Coast tax relief in its tax reconciliation bill (S 2020) passed Nov. 18, but House-Senate negotiations on that legislation were put off until 2006. *(Tax reconciliation, p. 89)*

The House on Dec. 7 then passed 415–4 a $7.1 billion version of HR 4440. After a week of House-Senate negotiations aimed at avoiding a formal conference, the Senate took up HR 4440 on Dec. 16, amended it with a compromise $7.8 billion tax cut package and passed it by voice vote. The House cleared the bill by voice vote later the same day.

The key sticking point in the negotiations was a House-passed provision to prohibit public and private golf courses, country clubs, massage parlors, hot tub facilities, tanning salons, liquor stores, horse and dog racetracks, and gambling facilities from taking advantage of any of the new tax benefits. The language was added at the insistence of a group of more than thirty social conservatives.

The provision drew a sharp rebuke from Mississippi Republican Trent Lott, a member of the Senate Finance Committee whose state's economy relied on casino revenue. Lott said he would not agree to a bill that did not benefit the gambling industry. The White House agreed, saying tax benefits should be available to all industries.

In the end, Senate tax writers engineered a complicated compromise that slightly watered down the House language. The final bill was written so that only the portion of gambling and racetrack facilities directly related to gambling room equipment and construction would be denied tax breaks. The hotel and restaurant portions of casinos, for example, could still receive the benefit of the "bonus depreciation" deduction. Gambling facilities smaller than 100 square feet also would be afforded tax benefits—a provision that would ensure that stores with video gambling machines would not be denied the tax breaks.

Mandatory Entitlement Spending Cuts

Congress completed work in February 2006 on a budget reconciliation bill that promised to reduce spending on entitlement programs by $38.8 billion over five years—the first reduction in mandatory spending since 1997. The bill was a top priority for the Republican leadership and President George W. Bush, but it faced near-unanimous opposition from congressional Democrats. Although Democrats could not stop the bill, they raised a procedural hurdle at the last moment that forced final action on the measure from 2005 into 2006. The bill cleared Feb. 1, 2006, and Bush signed it into law Feb. 8 (S 1932—PL 109-171).

The biggest savings came from changes to federal student loan programs, Medicare, and Medicaid. The bill also required higher premiums for the federal pension guarantee agency and counted on additional funds from auctioning portions of the electromagnetic spectrum. Those funds were used to offset some mandatory spending and to help pay for new expenditures that were included in the bill.

Republicans paved the way for the spending-cut package early in the year, when they adopted a fiscal 2006 budget resolution (H Con Res 95) that included instructions for a reconciliation bill that would reduce mandatory spending by $34.7 billion over five years. Reconciliation legislation has special protections in the Senate, where it is not subject to a filibuster. That meant that GOP leaders could count on passing the spending cuts with a simple majority, rather than the sixty votes that would be needed to cut off a filibuster. *(Budget resolution, p. 65)*

The leadership left the difficult work of actually putting such a bill together for the crowded end of the session in 2005. By that point Hurricane Katrina had altered the dynamic. The devastating storm generated new concern about the poor, whose suffering in New Orleans captured the nation's attention, but it also led fiscal conservatives to demand even deeper spending cuts to offset some of the tens of billions of dollars needed to cope with the Gulf Coast calamity. Within two weeks of the Aug. 29 storm, Congress had cleared $62.3 billion in emergency relief, and more was expected. *(Hurricane supplementals, p. 79)*

The Senate passed its reconciliation bill on Nov. 3, proposing to cut entitlement spending by a net $35 billion over five years. Fiscal conservatives wanted deeper cuts, but influential Senate GOP moderates, including Gordon H. Smith of Oregon, refused to support more than $10 billion in cuts to Medicaid and held fast against other cuts to programs for the poor. The Senate bill also included provisions to open a portion of Alaska's Arctic National Wildlife Refuge (ANWR) to oil and gas drilling.

Two weeks later, after repeated starts and stops, the House passed a bill that included $50 billion in net cuts to mandatory programs. When they returned from the Thanksgiving break, House and Senate negotiators managed to settle on a $38.8 billion five-year package. The ANWR language was removed, however, after House GOP leaders concluded its removal was the only way they could get the conference report through their chamber. The ANWR provisions were attached to the fiscal 2006 defense appropriations bill (PL 109-148) instead but were eventually dropped. *(ANWR, p. 474)*

Democrats generally denounced the final bill, saying it would bring pain to the poor to help finance Republican tax cuts for the wealthy. No Democrat voted for the conference report in either chamber.

Republicans said they were doing the hard work to overhaul mandatory spending programs such as Medicare, Medicaid, and student loans that accounted for 55 percent of the budget and were growing automatically. They said their efforts were targeted at making the programs more efficient, with a minimal effect on beneficiaries.

However, Republicans included billions in new spending in the package in an effort to sway enough centrist votes to enact it. That reduced the net savings and drew the ire of GOP conservatives, who argued for omitting new spending provisions and concentrating on deficit reduction.

The final bill cut $5 billion more than required in the budget resolution and was expected to reduce federal spending by less than 0.3 percent over five years.

The package promised net savings of $4.7 billion over five years from projected spending on Medicaid, $6.4 billion from Medicare, $11.9 billion from mandatory student loan subsidies, $2.7 billion from farm programs, and $1.5 billion from child support enforcement. New receipts included $3.6 billion from increased pension premiums and about $10 billion from auctioning off broadcast spectrum remaining from the transition to digital television.

Sweeteners added to gain votes included $7.3 billion to avert a scheduled 4.4 percent cut in doctors' Medicare reimbursements, about $1 billion to extend expired milk subsidies, $1 billion in budget authority for heating subsidies for the poor, $1 billion in budget authority for child care subsidies and $3.7 billion for new math, science and engineering scholarships. Last-minute deals to secure votes included removing any cuts to sugar subsidies and nixing a $1.9 billion cut to Medicare reimbursements for durable medical equipment.

The new law also reauthorized the 1996 welfare overhaul bill through fiscal 2010 at the existing level of $16.5 billion a year for basic block grants. *(Welfare, p. 579)*

HIGHLIGHTS

Following are major elements of the reconciliation law, PL 109-171. Savings are in outlays over a five-year period (fiscal 2006 through 2010) as estimated by the Congressional Budget Office (CBO). The basis for comparison is a baseline projection issued by CBO in March that showed what existing programs would cost, adjusted for inflation.

Agriculture. Net savings of $2.7 billion from reducing advances on direct subsidy payments to farmers and from reducing funding for mandatory conservation, research, and rural development programs. The total included a two-year extension of the expired milk subsidy program, at a cost of $998 million.

Student loans. Savings of more than $20 billion, combined with about $9.3 billion in new spending, resulting in net savings of $11.9 billion over five years. The biggest savings came from provisions that reduced yields for lenders, increased interest rates for parents' loans, and eliminated mandatory funding for the administrative costs of student loan programs.

Medicaid. A net reduction of $4.7 billion over five years from the projected growth in spending for Medicaid, the federal-state health care program for the poor. CBO said the final bill included a net of $6.9 billion in Medicaid savings, but of that total, $2.1 billion was reallocated to help with Medicaid costs in states most affected by Katrina. The bill reduced the price Medicaid paid for prescription drugs, increased cost sharing for Medicaid beneficiaries, and allowed states to reduce benefits. It also tightened asset transfer rules to make it more difficult for people to qualify for long-term care coverage, for a savings of $2.4 billion. The law included about $3.6 billion in new Medicaid spending.

Medicare. A net $6.4 billion reduction over five years in the growth of spending on Medicare, the federal health care program for the elderly and disabled. The biggest savings came from reducing Medicare payments for some imaging services, accelerating plans to charge premiums for some beneficiaries, reducing payments to home health care providers, and reducing payments to "disproportionate share" hospitals, which have a large number of low-income patients.

The net savings came after the measure eliminated a scheduled 4.4 percent reduction in Medicare payments to physicians in 2006, instead freezing funding for one year at the 2005 level. Had Congress gone ahead with the reduction, it would have saved another $7.3 billion.

Child support. $1.5 billion in savings over five years through changes to the child support enforcement program, mainly by eliminating federal matching funds to states in 2008 for the funds they use as incentive payments on child support enforcement.

Supplemental Security Income. $712 million in savings over five years from two changes in the Supplemental Security Income (SSI) program, which provides payments to poor, elderly, and disabled individuals.

Spectrum auction. A net $7.4 billion in new revenue from auctioning off analog frequencies vacated by television broadcasters as they switch to all-digital transmissions. That money was counted as an offset to entitlement spending. The law set Feb. 17, 2009, as the deadline for television stations to complete their transition from analog to digital transmission. The auction was expected to generate about $10 billion, but $2.6 billion was to be spent on other programs, including up to $1.4 billion in outlays to help consumers pay for equipment to keep their analog sets working after the digital transition and $1 billion to help first-responders acquire interoperable communications systems.

Pension insurance. $3.6 billion in savings over five years as a result of increased premiums paid by employers to the Pension Benefit Guaranty Corporation (PBGC), the federal agency that insures private pension plans. The annual flat-rate premiums paid by companies with pension plans increased to $30 from $19 per plan participant for single-employer plans and to $8 from $2.60 per worker for multi-employer plans. The law also established a new premium to be paid by companies that terminated their pension plans while in bankruptcy. Once a company emerged from bankruptcy, it was required to pay the PBGC $3,750 over three years for each plan participant. *(Details, p. 654, 656, 658)*

Deposit insurance. A net $250 million in savings over five years from increasing the total premiums paid by banks and savings associations to the Federal Deposit

Insurance Corporation (FDIC). The law merged the FDIC's Bank Insurance Fund and the Savings Association Insurance Fund, into a single fund, the Deposit Insurance Fund. It allowed risk-based premiums for insured institutions and increased the amount covered in certain types of individual retirement accounts and 401(k)s to $250,000 from $100,000. The FDIC could increase the $100,000 deposit insurance available on most bank accounts to compensate for inflation starting in 2010. *(Details, p. 148)*

LIHEAP. An additional $250 million in spending in fiscal 2007 for the Low-Income Home Energy Assistance Program (LIHEAP), plus an extra $750 million for assistance to offset higher-than-anticipated energy costs caused by hurricanes Katrina and Rita. None of the money could be spent after the end of fiscal 2007. *(LIHEAP, p. 628)*

TANF. Reauthorization through fiscal 2010 of the welfare program known as Temporary Assistance for Needy Families (TANF) at the existing level of $16.6 billion a year for basic block grants. Supplemental grants were reauthorized for three years at the existing level of $319 million a year. The law also made some cuts, including eliminating bonuses that had been given to states for actions such as moving TANF recipients into jobs, saving $755 million over five years. A new grant program to promote healthy marriage was estimated to cost $604 million over five years. The net effect of all TANF provisions was a $374 million spending increase over five years.

Antidumping rule. $300 million in savings over five years from phasing out a trade law (PL 106-387) known as the Byrd amendment, under which antidumping and countervailing duties collected by the government were distributed to the domestic companies that were hurt by the imports. Instead, the funds were to be kept in the Treasury Department. The World Trade Organization had ruled that the Byrd amendment violated international trade laws.

BACKGROUND

Under the fiscal 2006 budget resolution, House and Senate authorizing committees were instructed to submit mandatory savings provisions to their respective budget committees by Sept. 16. These two panels were responsible for assembling the proposals and taking the resulting bill to the floor. In reality, the Senate bill was not introduced until Oct. 27. House Budget Chairman Jim Nussle, R-Iowa, did not introduce his version until Nov. 7.

The House leadership had an especially difficult time. In an effort to quell a revolt by GOP conservatives over the mounting costs of hurricane recovery, Speaker J. Dennis Hastert, R-Ill., in early October called for the first midsession amendment to a budget resolution since 1977. He said the leadership wanted to increase the requirement for mandatory savings to $50 billion and require across-the-board cuts in discretionary spending. But Hastert and Roy Blunt, R-Mo., (who had recently replaced Tom DeLay, R-Texas, as majority leader) ran into resistance from Republican moderates and ultimately abandoned the idea.

In the Senate, Budget Chairman Judd Gregg, R-N.H., and Majority Leader Bill Frist, R-Tenn., pressed ahead with plans to find hurricane offsets without trying to change the budget resolution. Frist called on the authorizers to make voluntary cuts beyond the required $34.7 billion, though most committees did not.

SENATE ACTION

The Senate Budget Committee voted 12–10 along party lines Oct. 26 to approve a bill (S 1932) that promised $39.1 billion in net savings over five years. The package included $71 billion in gross savings and $32 billion in new spending. The bulk of the proposed savings were from Medicare, Medicaid, and student loan programs, combined with new receipts from auctioning off analog spectrum and leasing drilling rights in parts of ANWR. The biggest controversies were over how much to allocate reductions between Medicare and Medicaid, and whether to include the ANWR provisions.

The Senate passed the bill 52–47 on Nov. 3 after defeating an attempt to strip out the ANWR provisions on a vote of 48–51. Before passage, the Senate adopted a series of amendments that added billions in new spending, reducing the net savings to $35 billion from the $39.1 billion proposed by the authorizing committees. The Senate rejected a proposal by Kent Conrad of North Dakota, ranking Democrat on the Budget panel, to restore pay-as-you-go rules that would prevent passage of tax cuts or new mandatory spending without offsets. Supporters failed 50–49 to waive a point of order, which required sixty votes for passage.

On passage, the leadership lost five moderate Republicans—Olympia J. Snowe and Susan Collins of Maine, Mike DeWine of Ohio, Norm Coleman of Minnesota, and Lincoln Chafee of Rhode Island. Two moderate Democrats, Ben Nelson of Nebraska and Mary L. Landrieu of Louisiana, voted for the bill. Landrieu voted "yes" after billions of dollars in hurricane relief funds were added on the Senate floor.

President Bush praised passage of the bill, although two days earlier the White House had issued a veto threat over the proposed elimination of the stabilization fund for the Medicare prescription drug program. Frist called the vote "a victory that we're going to relish here for a while."

Democratic leaders said the bill's savings would not even pay for a planned $70 billion tax cut package—the other half of Republicans' budget reconciliation strategy—let alone make a dent in the budget deficit, which CBO estimated at $1.6 trillion over five years.

HOUSE ACTION

Even as Senate leaders cheered their hard-fought victory, House GOP leaders were scrambling to salvage their bolder budget-cutting plan in the face of a backlash by moderates.

The House Budget Committee approved a $53.9 billion net savings package (HR 4241—H Rept 109-276) Nov. 3

on a near party-line vote of 21–17. Nussle rejected Democrats' assertions that the cuts would cause significant pain, noting the savings would equal less than one-half of 1 percent of total mandatory spending over five years.

But before they could take the bill to the floor, Blunt and Hastert still had to negotiate changes to appease a group of moderates upset over oil drilling provisions as well as the cuts to Medicaid, food stamps, child-support enforcement, and farm aid. Multiple closed-door meetings with rank-and-file members failed to yield the 218 votes needed for passage. "I fully expect we'll have 100 percent of Democrats voting against the reconciliation bill," said House Minority Leader Nancy Pelosi, D-Calif. "We'll make this budget very hot for the Republicans to handle."

The House bill differed from the Senate version in a number of major ways. Because House GOP conservatives refused to touch Medicare, their bill got all of its health care savings from Medicaid ($9.5 billion). In the Senate, where GOP moderates insisted on avoiding changes that would affect Medicaid recipients, the bill split the savings between Medicaid ($4.3 billion) and Medicare ($5.7 billion).

As part of the Medicaid cuts, the House committee proposed giving states greater flexibility to impose cost sharing on Medicaid beneficiaries and to limit benefit packages. The Senate bill included no changes to Medicaid cost sharing. Nor did it include Senate provisions eliminating the stabilization fund created under the Medicare law and allowing an increase in the payment rate for Medicare doctors in 2006.

House GOP leaders eked out a narrow 217–215 victory shortly before 2 a.m. Nov. 18 for a somewhat smaller version of the bill totaling $49.9 billion in savings. Passage was in doubt until the final moments. Republican leaders managed to corral just enough moderates with tweaks to the package and persuaded conservatives to vote for it despite the removal of the ANWR provision. No amendments were allowed.

Republican leaders agreed to a number of demands late Nov. 17 to win over the votes of leading GOP moderates such as Sherwood Boehlert of New York, who had derided the package as a recipe for the party to lose its majority in the House, and Delaware's Michael N. Castle. "Moderates feel we have been heard, we have been listened to," Boehlert said.

In addition to eliminating the ANWR provisions, the changes allowed people with incomes up to 150 percent of the poverty level who were receiving noncash aid under TANF to remain eligible for food stamps, and allowed children receiving such services to remain eligible for school lunch programs. Seniors were allowed to retain up to $750,000 in home equity, up from $500,000 in the committee version, and still be entitled to Medicaid coverage for nursing home care, and an attempt to increase to $5 from $3 the cap on Medicaid copayments for individuals with incomes below the poverty line was scuttled.

An appeal to party loyalty also rounded up Republican votes. Steven C. LaTourette, R-Ohio, switched from "nay" to "yea." "As lousy as I thought this bill was, I am in the majority, and it's my responsibility to help the majority govern," LaTourette said. He said he was offered nothing in exchange for his support.

Jeff Flake of Arizona, a member of the conservative Republican Study Committee, said his group accepted the bill even though the cuts were slightly less than they asked for and expressed hope that other parts of Hastert's plan for offsetting hurricane costs would be passed as well. "Our expectations are lowered these days," Flake said. "It was important to make this small step."

FINAL ACTION

Only with great difficulty did House and Senate negotiators manage in nearly three weeks of negotiations to bridge their differences over spending and ANWR and file a conference report (H Rept 109-362) in the early morning hours of Dec. 19. The way was cleared in the House when Sen. Ted Stevens, R-Alaska, agreed to remove the Senate-passed ANWR provisions. House leaders had said GOP moderates would reject the conference report if it included ANWR. Instead, the language was included in the fiscal 2006 defense appropriations bill (HR 2863), although it ultimately was dropped from that bill as well.

Conferees also made several changes to satisfy Senate supporters, including removing cuts to sugar subsidies, which secured Coleman's vote, and reducing cuts to Medicare equipment supplies, which appeased Ohio Republican George V. Voinovich by protecting an Ohio manufacturer of oxygen tanks for the elderly.

House leaders moved quickly once the conference report was filed, securing a vote in favor of the agreement just after 6 a.m. on Dec. 19. The agreement was approved on a **key vote of 212–206 (R 212–9; D 0–196; I 0-1).** *(2005 key votes, p. 915)*

But expectations of quick Senate action were dashed when Democrats in that chamber succeeded in stripping several provisions on procedural grounds. The Senate leadership managed to salvage the rest of the conference agreement, but only with the tie-breaking vote of Vice President Dick Cheney. That sent the measure back to the House for final approval in 2006.

Although the reconciliation bill was considered under special rules that protected it from a filibuster, Senate Democrats managed to use another rule to halt action. On Dec. 21, Conrad raised objections that three provisions of the conference agreement violated the Byrd rule, which dated from 1985 and prohibited the inclusion in a reconciliation bill of provisions having only an incidental effect on the budget. One of the provisions would have made hospitals immune from malpractice liability if they refused to treat poor Medicaid recipients who could not afford a copayment. The two others were technical in nature.

Gregg's attempt to waive Conrad's objections failed on a 52–48 vote, well shy of the sixty votes needed. By upholding Conrad's objections, the Senate effectively nullified the conference report and gave opponents of the savings package yet another chance to modify or kill it.

Approval of the conference agreement, minus the three stricken provisions, came Dec. 21 on a **key vote of 50–50 (R 50–5; D 0-44; I 0-1)** when Vice President Cheney cast a "yea" vote to break the tie. Cheney had returned from a trip to Pakistan to cast his seventh tie-breaking vote since the start of the Bush presidency in 2001. *(2005 key votes, p. 915)*

The Senate action had the effect of returning the measure to the House for a final vote. House GOP leaders wanted to accomplish that without bringing all members—most of whom had already left for the holidays—back to the floor. But Pelosi demanded a roll call vote "in the light of day"—a reference to the predawn House vote on the conference report—that was not possible before the end of the year.

Bush congratulated both chambers on voting for the legislation in a Dec. 21 statement that did not mention that Congress failed to clear the measure before adjourning. "The Senate vote to reduce entitlement spending is a victory for taxpayers, fiscal restraint and responsible budgeting—and it will help keep us on track to cut the deficit in half by 2009," Bush said.

Although the measure was expected to clear when Congress reconvened in 2006, GOP leaders still had to work to round up the last few votes. The House narrowly cleared the bill 216–214 on Feb. 1, 2006. President Bush signed it on Feb. 8.

MAJOR PROVISIONS

Following are the main provisions of the Deficit Reduction Omnibus Reconciliation Act of 2005; PL 109-171.

Agriculture programs

Changes to agriculture and rural development programs were expected to yield net savings of $2.7 billion over five years.

Crop payments. Advances to eligible farmers on their annual direct payments for certain crops were reduced to 40 percent in the 2006 crop year, down from 50 percent under prior law. The advance could be no more than 22 percent for 2007. The law affected only the timing of the direct payment, not the amount. (Savings: $1.5 billion in 2007.)

Cotton subsidy. The upland cotton Step-2 subsidy, which was successfully challenged by Brazil in the World Trade Organization, was eliminated. (Savings: $282 million over five years.)

Milk income loss contract. The popular milk subsidy program, which primarily aided small- and medium-size dairy farms, was extended through Sept. 30, 2007. (Cost: $998 million over five years.)

Conservation programs. The law limited funding for the Watershed Rehabilitation program, which provided aid to communities to rehabilitate aging local dams; the Natural Resources Conservation Service, which assisted projects to upgrade or remove dams; the Conservation Security Program, which provided financial and technical assistance to promote conservation on land used for agriculture production; and the Environmental Qualities Incentive Program, which provided financial and technical assistance to promote conservation on land used for agriculture production. (Savings: $934 million over five years.)

Rural Development, Energy, and Research. The law canceled, eliminated, or limited funding for rural development programs, unused funds for rural development programs (including rural broadband grants, value-added agricultural product development grants, rural business grants, rural firefighter grants, and rural community grants). Funds were also canceled for a competitive research grant program for agriculture and for a program that made loans and grants to farmers to purchase renewable energy systems or make energy efficient improvements. (Savings: $1.0 billion over five years.)

Deposit insurance

Changes to the deposit insurance system that increased coverage for depositors and allowed the Federal Deposit Insurance Corporation (FDIC) to alter the premiums it charged banks and savings and loan associations were expected to produce a net savings of $250 million over the next five years. Most of the changes would have negligible effect until after 2010. *(Details, p. 148)*

Digital TV

Provisions allowing the Federal Communications Commission (FCC) to auction analog spectrum vacated by television broadcasters were projected to bring in about $10 billion. The law directed $2.6 billion of the proceeds to other uses, leaving $7.4 billion over five years to be used for deficit reduction. *(Details, p. 419)*

Reclaiming spectrum. The law set a deadline of Feb. 17, 2009, for full-power television stations to return the frequencies used for analog broadcasts to the FCC. The stations had other spectrum for broadcasting digital signals.

Spectrum auctions. The FCC was required to begin the process of auctioning off the reclaimed spectrum to wireless carriers and others by Jan. 28, 2008.

Converter box subsidies. Up to $1.5 billion in spectrum proceeds would be set aside to subsidize digital-to-analog converter boxes for the roughly 21 million Americans who still relied on over-the-air television broadcasts and would otherwise see their television screens go dark after the transition. The Commerce Department was authorized to distribute up to two $40 coupons per household to help cover the cost of converter boxes.

Other uses of proceeds. The law also allocated up to $156 million to build a unified national emergency alert and tsunami warning system, $44 million to upgrade 911 emergency phone systems, $65 million to help eligible low-power television stations purchase equipment to upgrade from analog to digital operations, and $10 million to help eligible low-power television stations purchase digital-to-analog conversion devices that would allow them to convert incoming digital signals to analog format.

Medicare

Changes to Medicare, the federal health care program for the elderly and disabled, were projected to achieve $6.4 billion in net savings over five years.

Hospital quality improvement. Hospitals that did not submit required quality data would get a lower increase in payments beginning in fiscal 2007. Their increase would drop by 2 percent, rather than 0.4 percent under previous law. (Savings: $300 million over five years)

Disproportionate share hospitals. Inpatient hospital stays for patients who were covered by Medicaid for other services, but not for hospital inpatient services, would not count as Medicaid days for the purposes of calculating the additional payments Medicare made to hospitals that served a large number of low-income patients. (Savings: $1.2 billion over five years.)

Skilled nursing facilities. Medicare was to reduce the percentage of its payments to skilled nursing facilities for uncollected debts from 100 percent to 70 percent. Unpaid debts incurred by beneficiaries eligible for both Medicare and Medicaid would be paid at 100 percent.

Durable medical equipment. Beneficiaries would be required to assume ownership of rental durable medical goods (excluding oxygen equipment) after thirteen months of rental. For oxygen equipment, ownership would be required after thirty-six months. Medicaid could pay for service and maintenance if it was determined necessary. (Savings: $700 million over five years)

Imaging services. The law reduced the reimbursement rate for imaging services by $2.8 billion over four years. Reimbursement rates for imaging services conducted in a physician's office could not be greater than the rate paid to hospitals for the same service. (Savings: $2.8 billion over five years)

Ambulatory surgical centers. The law reduced Medicare payments to ambulatory care surgical centers to the rate Medicare paid to hospitals, if the hospital payment rates were lower. (Savings: $300 million over five years)

Physician payments. The law froze Medicare payments to physicians for 2006 at the 2005 level. Under prior law, the payments would have fallen by 4.4 percent as of January 2006. (Cost: $7.3 billion over five years)

Means testing in Part B premiums. The law accelerated the phase-in of a scheduled increase in Medicare Part B premiums for beneficiaries with incomes above certain levels. The phase-in was to begin in 2007 and be completed by 2009, instead of 2011. (Savings: $1.6 billion over five years)

Home health payments. The law eliminated a scheduled 2.8 percent increase in home health care payments for 2006, although it provided for a one-year, 5 percent additional payment to rural home health providers in 2006. Starting in 2007, home health care providers would have their payments reduced by 2 percentage points if they did not report required health care quality data to the Department of Health and Human Services (HHS).

Risk adjustment. Starting in 2007, payments to Medicare Advantage plans would be altered to take into account the health status of the beneficiaries served in each plan, paying higher amounts for care of sicker patients. (Savings: $6.5 billion over five years)

Medicaid

Changes to Medicaid, the federal-state health program for the poor, were expected to reduce mandatory spending by a net $6.9 billion over five years, while paying for $3.6 billion in new spending.

Asset transfers. The law was projected to save $2.4 billion over five years by increasing the penalties on people who transferred their house or other assets for less than fair market value to qualify for nursing home care.

Five-year look-back. States would look back five years, rather than three, when determining whether a senior applying for Medicaid-funded nursing home care had transferred assets below fair value to qualify for Medicaid. Beneficiaries who made improper transfers would be penalized with a period of ineligibility for certain long-term care services. Individuals could apply for a waiver of the penalty because of undue hardship.

Home equity limits. The law excluded individuals with more than $500,000 in home equity from eligibility for nursing home or other long-term care coverage paid for by Medicaid. States could raise the limit to $750,000. Starting in 2011 the amount would increase each year based on the consumer price index.

Prescription drugs. Changes to payments for prescription drugs—mainly reducing Medicaid reimbursements to pharmacies—were expected to reduce spending by $3.9 billion over five years.

Fraud, waste, and abuse. Provisions to reduce fraud, waste and abuse were expected to save $822 million over five years; $528 million of that was to be spent on education and other steps to improve the integrity of the program. Among other steps, the law required states to do more to find a party responsible for paying outstanding claims instead of relying on Medicaid as the payer of last resort. The law also stipulated that the government would not reimburse states for a beneficiary who had not given a state proof of U.S. citizenship. Immigrants who were eligible for benefits were exempt from this provision.

Cost sharing and benefit reductions. Allowing states to set higher premiums and cost-sharing payments and to offer limited benefits for some in Medicaid was projected to reduce outlays by $3.2 billion over five years.

Premiums and cost sharing. The law permitted states to charge premiums and require cost sharing by beneficiaries at or above the poverty level, with some restrictions. Under prior law, premiums and enrollment fees were generally prohibited and nominal cost sharing was limited to $3.

Under the new law, beneficiaries with incomes between 100 percent and 150 percent of the federal poverty line could not be charged a premium. Cost sharing could not exceed 10 percent of the cost of the service for families with incomes between 100 percent and 150 percent of the poverty level, and 20 percent for families with incomes above 150 percent. Total payments for the year could not exceed 5 percent of the family income. Certain groups could not be subject to cost sharing for some services, such as pregnancy-related care and preventive care for children under age eighteen.

Enforcement. States could allow providers to refuse to offer service or dispense a drug if cost-sharing payments were not made at the time of service. If a beneficiary failed to pay premiums for sixty days, a state could terminate coverage.

Prescription drugs. States were allowed to waive or lower copayments for "preferred drugs" and could not require cost sharing from beneficiaries who otherwise were exempt from cost sharing. For drugs not designated as preferred drugs on a state's formulary, a state could set higher cost sharing and co-payments and could impose cost sharing on any beneficiary, even those who were otherwise exempt from cost sharing in the program. For beneficiaries with family incomes below 150 percent of poverty, cost sharing could not exceed a set nominal amount. For beneficiaries with family incomes above 150 percent of poverty, cost sharing could not exceed 20 percent of the cost of the drug.

Indexing. The nominal rate for cost sharing, previously $3, would be indexed to the medical cost component of the consumer price index.

Emergency room. States were allowed to increase cost sharing for certain beneficiaries who used the emergency room for nonurgent care. The law provided $50 million in mandatory funds for payments over four years to states to make nonemergency health services available and accessible.

Alternative benefit packages. The law allowed states to replace the traditional Medicaid benefits package with a reduced-benefit, or "benchmark" plan, for certain populations. The plans had to provide basic services, such as physician and hospital coverage, and be actuarially equivalent to one of the following benchmarks: standard Blue Cross/Blue Shield Plan offered in the Federal Employees Health Benefit Plan, health coverage offered to state employees, coverage offered by the largest commercial health maintenance organization in the state, or a different coverage plan approved by the HHS. States could not require certain beneficiaries to participate in the benchmark plans, including seniors who were poor enough to qualify for Medicaid and who qualified for Medicare because they were over sixty-five. Other exempted groups included pregnant women who had to be covered by state Medicaid programs, patients in Medicaid-funded hospice facilities or receiving long-term care, some children in foster care and blind or otherwise disabled individuals.

State financing. Changes to the rules for state financing of Medicaid programs, which affected the amount of federal grants, were estimated to save $1.2 billion over five years. The major change required states that levied taxes on Medicaid managed care organizations, and used the proceeds to help pay the state's share of Medicaid spending, to apply the tax to all managed care organizations, not just those that served Medicaid recipients. Generally, the organizations that paid the taxes got the money back in the form of increased Medicaid payments. But the increased payments also generated increased federal matching funds, and the states often kept the difference.

Spending increases. The law included a number of provisions that were projected to increase spending under Medicaid by a combined total of $3.6 billion over five years.

Medicaid buy-in. Children with disabilities whose families earned more than the cut-off for Supplemental Social Security Income, but less than 300 percent of the poverty level, would be eligible for Medicaid benefits beginning in 2008. States choosing to offer these benefits were allowed to charge a premium and parents would be required to enroll in any available employer-sponsored coverage for themselves while the child was on Medicaid. (Cost: $1.4 billion over five years.)

Home and community-based care. Up to ten states could participate in a five-year demonstration project to provide home and community-based services to children who would be hospitalized otherwise. (Cost: $766 million over five years.)

Health information centers. The law increased funding for health information centers that assisted families of children with special needs by a total of $22 million over five years.

"Money follows the person" demonstration. The law authorized a demonstration project under which the federal government would pay a higher share of costs than under existing law for the first twelve months of long-term care services provided in the home or community for a person who was formerly in a nursing home. (Cost: $340 million over five years.)

Health Opportunity Accounts. Up to ten states were allowed to participate in a demonstration program to set up health opportunity accounts that could be used by Medicaid beneficiaries who volunteered for the program to pay for medical treatment. Once a deductible was reached, beneficiaries would be covered under the state Medicaid program. States could not set a deductible that was higher than 110 percent of the state contribution to the account. States could contribute up to $2,500 for each adult and $1,000 for each child into a family's account. The programs had to disclose the cost of the care and encourage prevention and discourage overuse of health services. If beneficiaries became ineligible for Medicaid, they could keep the accounts for future health care costs. States could also choose to allow the beneficiaries to use the accounts to pay for job training.

Medicaid transformation grants. The HHS secretary could provide extra funding to state Medicaid programs that adopted innovative methods for reducing medical errors; improving collection of payments and reducing fraud, waste, and abuse; increasing the use of generic drugs; implementing a medication risk management program for beneficiaries who use a number of prescription drugs; and increasing the use of university-based hospitals and clinics by the uninsured.

Katrina Relief

The law appropriated $2.1 billion to be used by the HHS secretary to help with health care costs for residents of states evacuated because of Hurricane Katrina.

Welfare

The law reauthorized the 1996 Temporary Assistance for Needy Families (TANF) law (PL 104-193) at a projected cost of $374 million over five years. Viewed over a ten-year period, however, the changes were projected to save $344 million. The main TANF block grant to states was reauthorized through fiscal 2010 at the existing level of $16.5 billion per year. Supplemental grants were reauthorized through fiscal 2008 at $319 million per year. The law retained a thirty-hour-per-week work requirement for individuals, but it altered what was known as the caseload reduction credit so that states would have to ensure that at least 50 percent of their welfare recipients were engaged in work.

The law extended grants to states to provide child care subsidies to low-income families through 2010 and increased funding by a total of $1 billion over five years, for total funding of $2.9 billion per year. It also authorized grants of $150 million per year to states through fiscal 2010 for activities to promote "healthy marriage" and "responsible fatherhood."

Child support

Changes to child support enforcement were expected to save a net $1.5 billion over five years. Beginning in 2008 the law barred states from using federal incentive payments to receive matching child support enforcement funds. States were still required to spend the incentive awards on child support services, but they could not also count the money as a match for additional federal funds. (Savings: a net $1.6 billion over five years.) The law also provided incentives to encourage states to give TANF families more of the child support payments collected on their behalf.

Child Welfare

Changes to child welfare programs were projected to save a net $320 million over five years. However, the law increased spending on two programs—funding for family courts and a program intended to keep troubled families together, or if that was impossible to promote adoption of abused and neglected children.

Supplemental Security Income

Disability reviews. The Social Security Administration was directed to review at least 20 percent of disability claims approved by state-level Disability Determination Service offices in fiscal 2006, rising to 40 percent in fiscal 2007 and 50 percent in fiscal 2008. (Savings: $287 million.)

Retroactive benefits. The threshold for paying retroactive benefits owed to the disabled because of delays in approval was lowered. Any lump sum greater than three times the maximum monthly benefit would be subject to payments in installments, except under certain conditions, such as terminal illness. (Savings: $425 million.)

Higher Education

Changes to federal student loan programs were expected to save a net $11.9 billion over five years, mainly by reducing the amounts received by lenders and increasing some borrower costs.

Student loan reauthorization. The law reauthorized the government's two college loan programs through 2012. The Federal Family Education Loan program provided government guarantees for loans made by private lenders. The William D. Ford Direct Loan Program provided government loans to students and their families. So-called consolidation loans that enabled students to lock in prior year interest rates and combine multiple loans into a single payment were reauthorized through 2012.

Parent loan rate increase. The fixed interest rate charged for guaranteed loans made to parents was changed to 8.5 percent starting in July 2006, rather than at 7.9 percent as under prior law.

"Excess interest." Lenders earning more than the fair market return on student loans were required to rebate the "excess interest" paid by students and parents to the federal government. Prior law allowed the lender to receive the higher of the market rate or the amount paid by the borrower. (Combined savings under this and the parent loan rate provision: $14.3 billion over five years.)

9.5 percent loans. The law eliminated a provision of prior law that allowed lenders making loans backed by certain tax-exempt bonds to receive up to a 9.5 percent return from the government. An exception allowed nonprofit lenders with less than $100 million in outstanding 9.5 percent loans to make new loans under the system for five years. (Savings: $1.8 billion over five years.)

Administrative costs. The law eliminated mandatory funding for the costs of administering student loan programs beginning in fiscal 2007. After that, administrative costs would have to be paid through discretionary appropriations. (Savings: $2.2 billion over five years.)

Guaranty agency fees. Loan guaranty agencies were required to pay the government a 1 percent default insurance premium on guaranteed loans, which they could charge to student and parent borrowers. Previously, guaranty agencies had the option of charging such a fee, but they often waived it. (Savings: $1.5 billion over five years)

Federal lender insurance. The law reduced the portion of a defaulted loan for which the lender was reimbursed to 97 percent from 98 percent for most lenders, and to 99 percent from 100 percent for "exceptional" lenders. (Savings: $505 million over five years.)

Schools as lenders. Colleges were prohibited from lending to undergraduates or to people who were not their students and were limited to the loans they could make to their graduate students. Schools had to award contracts for financing, servicing, or administering their loans on a competitive basis. Schools were required to offer lower interest rates or lower origination fees, or both, than either private lenders or the government can. The permissible default rate for a lending school was reduced to 10 percent from 15 percent. Annual audits had to be submitted to the government. Schools were required to use proceeds from interest paid by borrowers, subsidies from the government or sales of loans to increase need-based student grants. They were forbidden to use those proceeds to supplant federal grant money.

Increased loan limits. The maximum amount of subsidized loans was increased to $3,500 from $2,625 for first-year students, and to $4,500 from $3,500 for second-year students, beginning in fiscal 2007. The limit for each year of graduate school was increased to $12,000 from $10,000. (Cost: $1.5 billion over five years.)

Origination fees. The 3 percent origination fee for Stafford loans would be phased out by 2010 for guaranteed loans and reduced to 1 percent by 2010 for direct loans. (Cost: $4 billion over five years.)

New grant programs. The law created two new mandatory grant programs for college students who were eligible for Pell grants. The first was available to first- and second-year college students who had completed a "rigorous" high school education. The second program aided third- and fourth-year students who were pursuing degrees in the physical, life, or computer sciences; math, technology, or engineering; or one of several foreign languages considered critical for national security. The grants were $750 for a first-year student, $1,300 for a second-year student and $4,000 for third- and fourth-year students. The law appropriated $790 million in fiscal 2006 for the grants, rising to $1 billion in fiscal 2010. (Cost: $3.7 billion over five years.)

Teacher loan forgiveness. The law reauthorized an existing provision that allowed the government to forgive up to $5,000 in loans to highly qualified teachers of math, science, or special education. Private school teachers who were exempt from state certification requirements could benefit from the provision in some cases.

Pension Plan Insurance

An increase in the premiums that companies paid to the Pension Benefit Guaranty Corporation, the federal agency that insured worker retirement plans, was expected to bring in a total of $3.6 billion over five years.

Single-employer plans. Payments to the PBGC by individual corporations that offered their workers defined benefit pension plans, which pay retirees a set amount, usually based on years of service and earnings, were $30 per employee starting in 2006, an increase from $19. Future premium levels would be indexed to account for increases in average wages. (Receipts: $2.3 billion over five years.)

Multiemployer plans. Premiums paid to cover pension plans that applied to multiple employers were $8 per year for each participant, up from $2.60, beginning in 2006. After 2006 the premium would be increased to account for gains in average wages. (Receipts: $300 million over five years.)

Termination premium. Companies that attempted to terminate their pension plans while in bankruptcy between the end of 2005 and the start of 2011 would have to pay a special annual premium of $1,250 per participant for three years after the termination of the plan. The special premium also applied to cases in which the PBGC moved to terminate a plan. If a company was assessed the premium while in bankruptcy, it would not have to make the payment until after it exited from bankruptcy protection. The provision did not apply to companies that started bankruptcy proceedings prior to Oct. 18, 2005. (Receipts: $1 billion over five years.)

Other Provisions

CHIP. The law provided an additional $283 million in funds under the State Children's Health Insurance Program for states that faced funding shortfalls in 2006. No additional states were allowed to use CHIP funds to cover adults without children.

LIHEAP. The law added $1 billion in fiscal 2007 to the Low Income Home Energy Assistance Program. Of that amount, $750 million was reserved for emergency needs. A law (PL 109-204) advancing that funding to fiscal 2007 was enacted in March 2006. *(LIHEAP, p. 628)*

Antidumping duties. The law phased out a 2000 statute that directed antidumping and countervailing duties, which were assessed as a trade penalty, to be distributed to the domestic companies that were hurt by the unfair trade. Starting in fiscal 2008, the revenue would stay in the Treasury instead. (Savings: $300 million over five years.)

Fiscal 2006 Tax Reconciliation Bill

After months of negotiations that stretched over two congressional sessions, Republican leaders handed President George W. Bush a victory in May 2006, when legislators cleared a $70 billion, five-year tax cut package. The bill mainly extended tax breaks that were enacted in Bush's

2001 and 2003 tax laws. Bush signed the measure into law May 17 (HR 4297—PL 109-222).

The tax package was one of two reconciliation bills called for in the fiscal 2006 budget resolution (H Con Res 95). The other bill, which cut a net $38.8 billion from mandatory spending programs over five years, was signed Feb. 8 (PL 109-171). *(Budget reconciliation, p. 81)*

The $70 billion five-year cost of the tax cuts was the maximum amount permitted for a tax reconciliation bill in the budget resolution. Two items accounted for nearly three-fourths of the total: a two-year extension of lower tax rates on capital gains and dividends, and a one-year extension of provisions that prevented the alternative minimum tax (AMT)—intended to target the wealthy—from reaching millions more middle-class taxpayers.

The two chambers passed significantly different versions of the bill in late 2005, highlighting divisions over tax policy within the GOP.

The Senate passed a $57.8 billion, five-year bill Nov. 18 that was built around the broadly popular AMT "patch." At the insistence of GOP moderates, it did not include an extension of the capital gains and dividend rates, which mainly benefited upper-income taxpayers and were not scheduled to expire until the end of 2008. Part of the overall cost was offset by provisions estimated to bring $18.8 billion into the Treasury over five years.

The House passed a narrower tax bill Dec. 8 that focused primarily on extending the capital gains and dividends rates. Those provisions were too costly to allow room in the bill for the AMT exemption, which the House passed separately (HR 4096). The House tax reconciliation bill had no revenue raisers.

Both the House and Senate bills also proposed extending a list of popular temporary tax breaks, such as the research and development credit; a deduction for small businesses of up to $100,000 in the first year for capital investment; a deduction for state and local sales taxes in lieu of state income taxes; a deduction for college expenses; a full deduction of certain nonrefundable tax credits under the AMT; and welfare-to-work and work opportunity credits.

In the end, these tax break extensions were removed from the bill to make room for both the ATM patch and the capital gains reductions. The House subsequently passed the tax break extensions as part of an estate tax–minimum wage measure (HR 5970), but that bill was pulled from the Senate calendar Aug. 3 after an attempt to bring it up was blocked. The tax extensions were then passed in a stand-alone bill cleared on the final day of the 2006 session. *(Estate tax, p. 96; Tax break extensions, p. 105)*

The Senate bill, but not the House version, also carried a $7 billion package of tax incentives for Gulf Coast states hit by hurricanes Katrina and Rita in 2005. The House passed a separate bill giving $7.1 billion worth of tax breaks for Gulf Coast rebuilding (HR 4440). That bill was cleared and became law in December 2005 (PL 109-135). *(Hurricane relief tax incentives, p. 80)*

Republican leaders originally had planned to clear the tax reconciliation bill in 2005, but they decided to push it into 2006 rather than try to reach a compromise in the midst of delicate negotiations over the mandatory spending cut bill and other end-of-session legislation. When Congress reconvened in 2006, the Senate quickly passed a revised version of its bill that increased the net total for the tax cuts to $70 billion and opened the way for a conference with the House.

The chief quandary for House and Senate negotiators was finding a way to include both chambers' priorities and still stay within the cost limit set in the budget resolution. To make the numbers work, they included revenue raisers and agreed to move some of the other popular tax cut extensions to a separate bill.

The two largest revenue-raising provisions had not been in either bill: a 3 percent withholding tax that federal, state, and local governments were supposed to subtract from certain payment for services and property, and the elimination in 2010 of existing income limits on converting traditional individual retirement accounts (IRAs) to Roth IRAs—a change that critics said might bring in money in the short run but would have a huge cost over time.

Enactment of HR 4297 marked the third time under the Bush administration that Congress used budget reconciliation rules to move a package of tax cuts. The process made passage easier because reconciliation bills could not be filibustered in the Senate, allowing supporters to prevail with a simple majority rather than the sixty votes needed to limit debate. The earlier tax reconciliation bills were the $1.3 trillion tax cut package enacted in 2001 (PL 107-16) and a $330 billion measure (PL 108-27) enacted in 2003. *(Congress and the Nation Vol. XI, pp. 89, 105)*

The Joint Committee on Taxation (JCT) estimated that the bill would reduce revenue by a total of $73.1 billion over the five years from fiscal 2006 through 2010, and by $90.9 billion over the ten-year period through fiscal 2015. To keep within the $70 billion cap in the budget resolution, the measure contained provisions expected to raise $3.1 billion over five years and $21.8 billion over ten years.

HIGHLIGHTS

The following are major provisions of the new tax law:

Tax Cuts

Capital gains and dividends. A two-year extension, through 2010, of the maximum 15 percent tax rate on capital gains and dividends. The provisions, enacted in 2003, had been scheduled to expire in 2008. Without an extension, the top tax rate on capital gains—profits from the sale of assets such as stocks or property—would have returned to 20 percent. Dividends—corporate profits distributed to shareholders—would have been taxed at the same rate as the taxpayer's regular income. (Estimated cost: $20.6 billion over five years, $50.7 billion over ten years.)

AMT "patch." A one-year extension, through 2006, of a provision that increased the amount individual taxpayers could subtract from their taxable income before determining whether they owed additional taxes under the AMT. The AMT was intended to prevent high-income individuals from using deductions and other benefits to avoid paying income tax, but it was not adjusted for inflation. The exemption was increased to $42,500 for individuals and to $62,550 for couples filing joint returns. (Estimated cost: $31 billion over five and ten years.)

The bill also extended for one year a provision that allowed taxpayers to claim certain nonrefundable tax credits—such as the dependent care credit, the credit for the elderly and disabled, and the credit for energy-efficient residential property—to the full extent of their regular tax and AMT liability. (Estimated cost: $2.8 billion over five and ten years.)

Increased expensing for small businesses. A two-year extension, through 2009, of an expiring tax cut that allowed small businesses to deduct up to $100,000 in depreciable assets in a single year. (Estimated cost: $7.3 billion over five years, negligible over ten years.)

Taxes on foreign subsidiaries. A two-year extension, through 2008, of an expiring provision that allowed U.S. banking and insurance firms to delay paying taxes on overseas profits. (Estimated cost: $4.8 billion over five and ten years.)

Corporate estimated taxes. A shift in several due dates for corporate estimated tax payments. Although the provision did not increase total tax payments, it concentrated an extra $11.4 billion in payments in fiscal 2012, helping to offset an anticipated bulge in the cost of the capital gains and dividend breaks in that year. (Estimated cost: $5.6 billion over five years, revenue-neutral over ten years.)

Revenue Raisers

Withholding tax on government payments. A requirement that, beginning in 2011, federal, state, and local governments withhold for tax purposes 3 percent from payments made for property or services. The provision did not apply to needs-based government assistance. (Estimated revenue: $7 billion over ten years.)

Roth IRA conversions. The elimination, beginning in 2010, of the existing income limits for taxpayers who wanted to convert traditional IRAs to Roth IRAs. Traditional IRAs typically allow some tax-free contributions, but the individual has to pay taxes on the money when it is withdrawn. The change was expected to generate revenue as individuals withdrew money from their traditional IRAs to put it into Roth IRAs. But federal revenue was expected to fall, potentially by a much larger amount, in years beyond the ten-year window when the same taxpayers took tax-free withdrawals from their Roth IRAs. (Estimated revenue: $447 million over five years, $6.4 billion over ten years.)

Other revenue raisers. The bill also required taxpayers to submit partial payments when they presented compromise offers for repaying back taxes; the provision was expected to raise $2 billion over ten years. The bill expected to raise $2.1 billion over ten years by changing the rules for taxing the unearned income of minors to generally cover children younger than eighteen. It also changed the rules for excluding income earned abroad to raise $2.1 billion over ten years, and it repealed provisions that allowed certain companies to keep export subsidies after the repeal of the extraterritorial income (ETI) exclusion, raising $502 million over ten years. Also, it required certain large oil companies to write off geological and geophysical costs over five years instead of the two-year period enacted in the 2005 energy policy overhaul (PL 109-58), a move that was expected to raise $189 million over ten years.

BACKGROUND

Middle-class relief from the reach of the alternative minimum tax and a reduction in tax rates on capital gains and dividends were the two major subjects discussed in the tax cut legislation.

The AMT was created in 1969 to ensure that high-income individuals and corporations could not use deductions, credits, and other provisions to avoid paying at least some taxes. Taxpayers whose liability was greater under the AMT than under the regular tax system had to give up certain credits and deductions and so ended up paying higher taxes. To protect middle-income taxpayers from having to pay the alternative tax, the tax code exempted a certain amount of income from the AMT. But because the levels were not adjusted for inflation, more people were pushed into the AMT each year. According to the Joint Committee on Taxation, while fewer than 1 percent of taxpayers were subjected to the tax before 2000, projections showed it could affect 29 million people, 20 percent of all taxpayers, by 2010.

To protect more taxpayers from the AMT, Congress provided short-term increases to the exemption levels. Completely eliminating the AMT was considered too expensive. The Joint Tax Committee estimated it would cost nearly $611 billion over ten years.

The 2001 tax law raised the exemption to $35,750 for single taxpayers (from $33,750) and $49,000 for joint filers (from $45,000); the provision expired at the end of 2003. The 2003 tax law extended the exemption for two years and increased it to $40,250 for individuals and $58,000 for married couples. A 2004 tax law (PL 108-311) extended those levels for an additional year, through 2005. *(PL 108-311, Congress and the Nation Vol. XI, p. 112)*

If the exemption levels were not extended, they would return to pre-2001 levels in 2006. According to the Joint Tax Committee, 19 million taxpayers, including a larger number of middle-income taxpayers, would be subject to the alternative tax. An estimated 3.6 million taxpayers were liable for the tax in 2005.

The 2003 tax law reduced tax rates on capital gains and dividends. It capped the rates for individuals at 15 percent. The rate for taxpayers in the two lowest brackets—the 10 percent and 15 percent brackets—was 5 percent through 2007, dropping to zero in 2008.

The provisions were due to expire after 2008. At that point, the maximum rate for capital gains would return to the pre-2003 level of 20 percent (10 percent for the lower brackets). Dividends would be taxed at the same rate as ordinary income.

SENATE ACTION IN 2005

The Senate Finance Committee approved a $59.6 billion tax cut package by a vote of 14–6 on Nov. 15, but only after conservatives agreed to drop a proposed extension of the capital gains and dividends tax breaks. Democrats were expected to oppose any measure that would have extended the reductions; when Sen. Olympia J. Snowe, R-Maine, the moderate swing vote on the closely divided committee, indicated that she too would oppose the extension, committee conservatives grudgingly agreed to remove the provisions. But several said they would seek to restore the extension during the House-Senate conference.

Majority Leader Bill Frist, R-Tenn., also pledged that he would not bring a conference report back to the Senate without the capital gains and dividends language. "I will insist that negotiators include an extension of the capital gains and dividend tax relief," he said.

The Senate passed the bill 64–33 on Nov. 18. GOP leaders again insisted they would restore the extension of the capital gains and dividend rates when they negotiated a conference agreement with House Republicans.

As passed, the bill provided about $76.5 billion in tax breaks over five years and included $18.8 billion in revenue-raising offsets for a net cost of $57.8 billion. Included in the tax breaks were $7 billion in tax incentives designed to spur economic activity on the hurricane-damaged Gulf Coast. Although the budget resolution allowed a $70 billion tax cut bill to move on the Senate floor under special reconciliation rules, it specified that a $35 billion package of mandatory spending cuts had to be cleared first. Until that happened, the Senate tax bill could not exceed a net cost of $60 billion. (The spending cut bill did not clear until 2006.)

Senate GOP leaders beat back almost two dozen amendments, most offered by Democrats. The floor debate also served as a forum for members of both parties to score political points at the expense of oil and gas companies, which were reaping huge profits amid high oil prices. Among the rejected amendments was one, offered by Byron L. Dorgan, D-N.D., to impose a 50 percent excise tax on oil company profits when crude oil prices exceeded $40 per barrel, unless the company invested the profits in new production. The proceeds would be used for consumer rebates. The proposal drew fierce opposition from oil-state senators, who called it a disincentive to domestic oil production.

HOUSE ACTION IN 2005

The House Ways and Means Committee voted 24–15 on Nov. 15 to approve a $56.1 billion tax bill (HR 4297—H Rept 109-304) that included no revenue offsets. But having just barely won a close floor victory on the mandatory spending cut bill, House GOP leaders postponed a floor vote on the tax cuts until lawmakers returned from the Thanksgiving recess the week of Dec. 5.

Unlike the Senate measure, the House bill included a two-year extension of the capital gains and dividends tax breaks, which cheered securities industry lobbyists and conservatives. It did not include the AMT extension.

The House passed the bill on Dec. 8 234–197 after passing two separate measures on Dec. 7 to extend the AMT and provide tax relief for Gulf Coast rebuilding.

During the floor debate on the tax cut measure, the House rejected 192–239 a Democratic substitute to eliminate the capital gains and dividends extensions, as well as extensions of tax cuts that were not due to expire in 2005. It also rejected 193–235 a motion to send the bill back to the committee with instructions to strike the capital gains and dividend tax breaks and add a new section to provide AMT relief.

LEGISLATIVE ACTION IN 2006

Eager to get the tax bill to conference, GOP leaders brought a revised version to the Senate floor Feb. 1, the second day of the 2006 session. After two days of debate, the Senate on Feb. 2 passed HR 4297, as amended to reflect the new Senate bill, by a vote of 66–31, opening the door to formal conference negotiations with the House. Republicans wanted to reach a final deal on the bill before Congress adopted a new fiscal 2007 budget resolution. Once that occurred, the reconciliation protections afforded the tax bill in the fiscal 2006 resolution would end. *(Budget resolution, p. 97)*

As passed by the Senate, HR 4297 was similar to the version the Senate passed in 2005, but it included about $18.4 billion in additional tax cut extensions and totaled a net $69.4 billion over five years, compared with $57.8 billion in the 2005 bill. Under Senate budget rules, the tax cuts in that bill could not exceed $60 billion because the entitlement savings bill had not been enacted. When the mandatory spending bill cleared Feb. 1, the Senate was able to provide $10 billion more in net tax cuts. In addition, the $7 billion worth of Hurricane Katrina–related tax incentives in the original Senate bill had been enacted in separate legislation (PL 109-135) at the end of 2005.

Senate Finance Chairman Charles E. Grassley, R-Iowa, and the panel's ranking Democrat, Max Baucus of Montana, agreed to use the additional room in the bill to extend a number of the popular tax breaks for two years instead of one, as called for in the 2005 version.

The largest revenue-raiser in the bill was an oft-proposed provision that would clarify the judicial doctrine of economic substance, requiring that business activities be performed for a profitable purpose and not simply to lower taxes. The bill also included a one-year prohibition on the use by the nation's five largest oil companies of an accounting method known as "last in, first out" (LIFO), which allowed companies to show less income by calculating sales profits based on the cost of the newest portion of their inventories. The Senate bill called for the five oil companies to calculate profits based on the cost of their oldest oil.

It took negotiators more than two months to reach a final agreement on the bill. The House adopted the conference report (H Rept 109-455) May 10, 2006, on a largely party-line **key vote of 244–185 (R 229–2; D 15–182; I 0–1).** The Senate cleared the bill the following day on a **key vote of 54–44 (R 51–3; D 3–40; I 0–1).** The vote illustrated the significance of treating the measure as a reconciliation bill in the Senate; supporters did not appear to have the sixty votes that would have been needed to cut off debate on a regular bill. *(2006 key votes, p. 937)*

Despite intense White House pressure for a deal, Grassley and his House counterpart, Ways and Means Chairman Bill Thomas, R-Calif., had bickered for weeks over the content of the final bill. The chief issue was how to handle the AMT and capital gains provisions. The GOP leadership in both chambers wanted to include the capital gains and dividend extension, although it was expected to lose votes for the conference report in the Senate. House negotiators proposed putting the AMT provision into a separate bill, but Grassley said he could not round up fifty-one votes in the Senate for a bill with the investment tax breaks unless it also carried the AMT provision.

A bill with both an AMT patch and capital gains breaks required offsetting revenue raisers under a Senate rule. Thomas was philosophically opposed to many of the offsets in the Senate bill, which he saw as tax increases. Most were dropped, including the proposals to clarify economic substance rules and to bar big oil companies from using LIFO accounting rules. He was more receptive to a new proposal: the elimination of income limits on converting to a Roth IRA.

As part of the talks, conferees agreed to move provisions that would extend less-controversial tax benefits, such as the research credit and educational deductions, into a separate bill, leaving room for both the AMT and capital gains provisions. Negotiations dragged on for several days after the reconciliation bill was complete, while Grassley and Thomas tried unsuccessfully to finish the second bill.

In the end, Grassley signed the conference report, saying he was confident they would get a deal on the separate tax breaks extension bill. For several months, Grassley sought to attach the provisions to pension overhaul legislation; he said Thomas and GOP leaders had assured him that they would be included. Although that plan also failed, the so-called extenders finally cleared on the last day of the 2006 session (PL 109-432). *(Pension overhaul, pp. 654, 658; Tax extenders, p. 105)*

MAJOR PROVISIONS

Tax Extensions and Reductions

The law extended a number of existing tax provisions and made other changes that were estimated to reduce revenue collections by $73 billion over five years (fiscal 2006 through 2010), and $90.9 billion over ten years, through fiscal 2015.

Capital gains and dividends. The law extended the maximum 15 percent rate on capital gains and dividends for two years, through 2010. It also extended for two years a zero percent rate that was set to come into effect in 2008 for those taxpayers whose total income put them in the two lowest tax brackets: 10 percent and 15 percent. The 15 percent rate on capital gains and dividends, enacted in the 2003 tax act, had been scheduled to expire after 2008. (Estimated cost: $20.6 billion over five years; $50.8 billion over ten years.)

Without the extension, the top rate on dividends would have reverted to the 20 percent maximum under previous law (10 percent for those in the lower income tax brackets). Dividends would have been taxed at higher rates as if they were ordinary income.

Alternative minimum tax exemption. The law increased the amount of income exempt from the AMT in 2006 to $42,500 for individuals and to $62,550 for couples filing joint returns. Taxpayers could subtract that amount from their taxable income before calculating whether they owed additional tax under the alternative system. The AMT is intended to prevent high-income individuals from using deductions, credits, and other benefits to avoid paying any income tax. (Estimated cost: $31 billion over both five and ten years.)

Use of credits under the AMT. The law also extended through 2006 a list of nonrefundable credits that taxpayers could use to reduce their tax liability under the AMT. (Estimated cost: $2.8 billion over five and ten years.)

Small-business expensing. The law extended for two years, through 2009, provisions that allowed small-business owners to deduct up to $100,000 in the first year for purchases of depreciable assets. The deduction was phased out for businesses with total investments over $400,000 and eliminated if investments exceeded $500,000. (Estimated cost: $7.3 billion over five years; $271 million over ten years.)

Without the extension, the limit on first-year expensing would have reverted to $25,000 and the deduction would have begun phasing out when total purchases exceeded $200,000.

Controlled foreign corporations. The law extended for two years, through 2008, a provision that exempted income from banking and insurance activities from a requirement that income earned by foreign subsidiaries of U.S. companies be subject to tax immediately, even if it had not been repatriated to the United States. (Estimated cost: $4.8 billion over five and ten years.)

U.S. law exempted "active" source income from the immediate taxation rule that applied to most ordinary business activity, but investment earnings and the like were typically considered "passive" income. The new exemption granted banking and insurance income essentially the same benefit granted to manufacturing income, which meant profits were subject to tax only when they were returned to the United States.

The law also provided a three-year exception for dividends, interest, rents, and royalties transferred between related foreign subsidiaries to ensure that those payments were exempt from immediate taxation through 2008. (Estimated cost: $746 million over five and ten years.)

Corporate estimated tax payments. Companies with assets of at least $1 billion were required to make certain quarterly estimated tax payments early in 2006, 2012, and 2013, then reduce their following payment by the extra amount paid. In 2006 affected companies were required to pay 105 percent of the amount due in July, August, or September, then reduce the next quarterly payment accordingly. In 2012 the companies had to pay 106.25 percent of the amount due in July, August, or September; in 2013 they had to pay 100.75 percent. (Revenue-neutral over five and ten years.)

In addition, the law allowed corporations to postpone 20.5 percent of estimated payments due on Sept. 15, 2010, until Oct. 1, 2010, and postpone 27.5 percent of estimated payments due on Sept. 15, 2011, until Oct. 1, 2011. (Estimated cost: $5.6 billion over five years; revenue-neutral over ten years.)

Environmental settlement funds. Environmental cleanup settlement funds were to be treated as government-owned and thus not liable for taxation if certain standards were met. Previously, income earned by such funds was taxable to the company that contributed the money. The provision applied to accounts or funds established through 2010. (Estimated cost: $44 million over five years; $116 million over 10 years.)

Expenditure limits for certain small-issue bonds. The law accelerated to Dec. 31, 2006, an existing provision that increased the capital expenditure limit to $20 million for certain tax-exempt small-issue bonds. It applied to bonds issued by state and local governments to finance private business manufacturing facilities or land and acquisition for farmers. Previous law limited the maximum capital expenditures in a municipality or county funded by the bonds to $10 million, but it allowed $10 million in expenditures to be disregarded, thus increasing the total available amount to $20 million, for bonds issued after Dec. 31, 2009. (Estimated cost: $44 million over five years; $136 million over ten years.)

Tonnage tax. More U.S.-flagged vessels engaged in foreign trade could choose to participate in an alternative tax regime known as the "tonnage tax," which based tax owed on the tonnage of the fleet instead of on income. The law lowered the threshold for participating in the tax regime from 10,000 deadweight tons under the 2004 corporate tax law (PL 108-357) to 6,000 deadweight tons in taxable years 2006 through 2010. (Estimated cost: $17 million over five years; $20 million over ten years)

Revenue-Raising Provisions

The law included provisions estimated to raise a net $3.1 billion in the five-year period from fiscal 2006 through 2010, and $21.8 billion through 2015. This was necessary to keep the net cost of the legislation from exceeding $70 billion over five years, as required in the reconciliation instructions and to prevent the provisions from increasing the deficit in years beyond the five-year budget resolution, which was a requirement in the Senate.

Tax withholding on government payments. Federal, state, and local governments were required to withhold 3 percent for tax purposes from payments made for property or services after Dec. 31, 2010. The provision included payments by government voucher or certificate. Political subdivisions of a state, such as a city or county, were exempt if they spent less than $100 million a year on property or services.

A number of payments were excluded from the withholding requirement, including government assistance based on need or income testing, wages or other payments already subject to withholding requirements, payments of interest, payments to tax-exempt entities or foreign governments, and payments made under a classified or confidential contract. (Estimated revenue: zero over five years; $7 billion over ten years, almost all of it in 2011.)

Roth IRA conversion. The law removed income limits, beginning in 2010, for taxpayers who wanted to convert a traditional individual retirement account to a Roth IRA. The law also eliminated a provision that prevented married taxpayers from converting their traditional IRAs to Roth IRAs. Taxes owed on conversions made in 2010 could be paid in equal installments in 2011 and 2012, if the taxpayer chose to do so. (Estimated revenue: $6.4 billion over ten years, with significantly decreased revenue in later years.)

With a traditional IRA, qualified taxpayers could make pretax contributions, but they owed taxes on the money when they withdrew it. Money contributed to a Roth IRA was subject to tax, but no taxes were owed on either the contributions or earnings when money was withdrawn from the account. Single filers with adjusted gross incomes of less than $95,000 and joint filers with incomes of less than $150,000 could make full contributions to a Roth IRA. Single filers with incomes up to $105,000 and joint filers with incomes up to $160,000 could make partial contributions.

Previously, taxpayers could convert a traditional IRA to a Roth IRA only if they had an income of $100,000 or less. Married taxpayers filing separate returns were not eligible.

Children's unearned income. Beginning in 2006, the law increased the age of minors whose unearned income was subject to taxation at their parents' tax rate. If a child had unearned income, such as interest and dividends, above a specific amount ($1,700 in 2006) and was required to file a tax return, the portion of the child's income that exceeded the specified amount was taxed at the same rate as the parent's, assuming that parent's rate was higher than the child's. Previously, this rule applied to children younger than fourteen; the law increased the age to eighteen. It exempted minors who were married and filed a joint return, and it created exceptions for income from certain disability trusts, treating such money as earned income. (Estimated revenue: $776 million over five years; $2.1 billion over ten years.)

Offers in compromise. The law required taxpayers who were proposing to settle an outstanding tax bill at less than the total amount to submit a partial payment while the IRS considered their proposal. Any offer that did not meet these guidelines was to be returned as unprocessable. The law also required the IRS to make a decision on the offer within two years; if it did not, the offer was deemed accepted. (Estimated revenue: $715 million over five years; $2 billion over ten years.)

Repeal of export subsidy provisions. Two provisions that were remnants of broad U.S. export subsidies ruled illegal by the World Trade Organization (WTO) were repealed.

The first was enacted in 2000 (PL 106-519), when Congress repealed the foreign sales corporation (FSC) law. The FSC law, which allowed U.S. companies to avoid paying taxes on income from certain foreign operations, was ruled a prohibited subsidy by the WTO. However, Congress kept the tax break in place for transactions that involved a "binding contract" in effect on Sept. 30, 2000. *(Congress and the Nation Vol. X, p. 118)*

The successor to the FSC—known as the extraterritorial income (ETI) exclusion—also was ruled a prohibited subsidy by the WTO and triggered international sanctions by the European Union. In 2004 Congress agreed to phase out the ETI over a two-year period as part of the corporate tax law. But it kept the ETI exclusion for transactions that involved a binding contract in effect on Sept. 17, 2003, including contracts held by Boeing Inc. In early 2006 the WTO appellate body ruled that both the grandfather clauses and the two-year phase-out rules for the ETI were illegal subsidies. Although the new law eliminated the grandfather clauses, it did not affect the two-year phase-out. (Estimated revenue: $467 million over five years; $502 million over ten years.) *(Congress and the Nation Vol. XI, p. 115)*

Amortization of oil exploration costs. The law stretched from two years to five years the period over which large integrated oil companies could amortize, or write off, the cost of geological and geophysical expenditures related to oil and gas exploration in the United States. The provision applied to companies with production in excess of 500,000 barrels per day, gross receipts that exceeded $1 billion for the taxable year ending during 2005, and at least a 15 percent ownership interest in a crude-oil refiner. The provision applied to amounts paid or incurred after enactment. The two-year amortization period was enacted as part of the 2005 energy policy overhaul (PL 109-58). (Estimated revenue: $160 million over five years; $189 million over 10 years.) *(2005 energy policy, p. 447)*

U.S. citizens living abroad. The law changed the way that foreign earned income and housing costs for U.S. citizens living and working abroad were treated for tax purposes. Because U.S. citizens who earned income abroad were also subject to taxation by the foreign country, federal law generally allowed the foreign government to have the primary right to tax the citizen. The tax code allowed citizens or residents who lived abroad to exclude from their U.S. taxable income certain foreign earned income or housing costs.

The new law provided for inflationary adjustments beginning in 2006, rather than 2008 as under prior law, in the maximum amount of foreign income that a taxpayer could exclude from his or her U.S. taxable income. It also changed the way taxpayers calculated how much of the housing costs paid by a foreign employer they could deduct. Finally, it included a so-called stacking rule, under which the excluded income had to be taken into consideration when determining the tax rate for the income not excluded from taxation. (Estimated combined revenue: $903 million over five years; $2.1 billion over ten years)

Tax-exempt entities. The law established penalties for tax-exempt entities that became involved in a prohibited tax-shelter transaction. Tax-exempt organizations that were a party to a tax-shelter transaction had to adhere to certain disclosure requirements and were subject to higher penalties if they did not do so. (Estimated revenue: $123 million over five years; $428 million over ten fiscal years.)

Earnings-stripping rules. The law codified regulations drafted by the Treasury Department to clarify existing law, which limited the ability of companies to use so-called earnings-stripping transactions to reduce their tax liability. In such transactions, corporations typically transferred large portions of their earnings to tax-exempt persons or entities, such as foreign subsidiaries. The law limited how much interest could be deducted based on debt-equity ratios and net interest expenses. (Estimated revenue: $106 million over five years; $284 million over ten years.)

The Treasury regulations affected corporations that directly or indirectly owned a stake in a partnership and counted the company's share of the interest earned or paid by the partnership, as well as its share of the partnership's liabilities, as belonging to the company itself when applying the earnings-stripping rules.

Section 199 wage limits. The law changed the manner in which wages were calculated for the purposes of a provision in the 2004 corporate tax law. That provision allowed companies to deduct from their tax liability a portion of their "qualified production activities income," which reflected the gross receipts from production activities minus the costs of goods sold and other expenses and losses. The provision gradually increased the percentage of activities that could be claimed, but the deduction was limited to 50 percent of the wages paid during a calendar year by the company.

The new law allowed companies to include only wages that could be applied to the domestic production gross receipts. It also repealed a special rule for pass-through entities. (Estimated revenue: $43 million over five years; $181 million over ten years.)

Distributions by controlled corporations. The law prevented certain "spin-offs," or controlled corporations, from being considered tax-free if the controlled corporation or the corporation that controlled the spin-off was considered a "disqualified investment corporation" because its investment assets constituted more than 75 percent of its assets in the first year after enactment, or two-thirds of its total assets thereafter. (Estimated revenue: $46 million over five years; $116 million over ten years.)

Pooled financing bonds. The law set new conditions for pooled financing bonds to qualify for tax-exempt status. Pooled financing bonds are issued by state and local governments to help finance activities or projects of two or more third parties, which are known as "conduit borrowers." The law required the issuer to obtain written commitments from the ultimate borrowers to cover 30 percent of the proceeds of the bonds before the bonds were issued. There was an exception for bonds issued by states or their subdivisions for local governments and state entities that provided financing for water infrastructure projects through the State Revolving Fund Program, sponsored by the Environmental Protection Agency.

The law also required that at least 30 percent of the net proceeds from the bonds be used to make loans within one year of issuance. It required issuers to use proceeds from bonds that had not been lent to a third party within a specified period to redeem outstanding bonds. Finally, it eliminated a provision in previous law that allowed pooled financing bonds to be disregarded when determining whether the issuer was exempt from a requirement that it send certain rebates to the federal government. (Estimated revenue: $172 million over five years; $417 million over ten years.)

Reporting interest on tax-exempt bonds. The measure subjected interest paid on tax-exempt bonds after Dec. 31, 2005, to the same reporting requirements as interest paid on taxable obligations. (Estimated revenue: $9 million over five years; $24 million over ten years.)

Estate Taxes

Republicans were optimistic that their four-seat gain in the Senate in the 2004 elections would finally enable them to do away with the estate tax or at least permanently reduce it. The House passed one bill in 2005 and two in 2006 to get rid of the tax, but in all three cases, the Senate GOP leadership was unable to overcome procedural hurdles, and the measures died.

Labeled the "death tax" by its opponents, the estate tax was a perennial target of GOP tax cutters and their allies in the business community. The 2001 tax law (PL 107-16) set in motion a gradual phase-out of the tax, culminating in a full repeal in 2010. But because of budget constraints, the repeal was good for only one year, and the estate tax was set to revert to the 2001 level in 2011. At that point, unless the repeal was extended or made permanent, estates faced a 55 percent tax when the owners died and the estates were passed on to heirs. The first $675,000 in assets, scheduled to increase to $1 million in 2006 were exempt from the tax. *(Congress and the Nation Vol. XI, pp. 89, 98)*

Opponents of repeal, including most congressional Democrats, argued that making the repeal permanent would be an expensive giveaway to the wealthy and would greatly increase the federal deficit. "Permanent repeal of the estate tax would benefit only a few very large estates," said the liberal-leaning Center on Budget and Policy Priorities, "but would cost more than $1 trillion over the first ten years in which its cost would be fully felt, 2012–2021." The Urban Institute-Brookings Institution Tax Policy Center estimated that the estate tax would affect only about 7,000 estates worth more than $3.5 million each by 2009.

The House had voted in 2002 and 2003 to extend the one-year repeal indefinitely, but each time the effort died in the Senate. GOP leaders said the "sunset" clause in the 2001 law was wreaking havoc with the ability of small-business owners to plan for the future. *(Congress and the Nation Vol. XI, pp. 103, 112)*

2005 ACTION

On April 13, 2005, the House once again passed a bill to delete the sunset date, making the one-year repeal permanent. The bill (HR 8) passed 272–162, with forty-two Democrats joining almost all Republicans present in supporting the repeal. The full repeal would cost $290 billion in its first ten years, according to the Joint Committee on Taxation.

In the Senate, Majority Leader Bill Frist, R-Tenn., was under pressure from conservatives to hold a vote on the issue before senators left for the August recess. But Frist faced a crowded agenda, plus resistance from the Senate's top GOP tax writer, Charles E. Grassley of Iowa. Grassley, chairman of the Finance Committee, said a rushed vote could doom compromise talks that were going on between the lead Senate supporter of a repeal, Republican Jon Kyl of Arizona, and Max Baucus of Montana, the top Democrat on the Finance Committee. Kyl and Baucus both supported lowering the estate tax rate and increasing the exemption—the level below which estates are not taxed. But Democrats remained skittish about the cost, and the business community was divided on what might constitute an acceptable compromise.

On July 29 Frist filed a motion for cloture to limit debate on the House-passed estate tax repeal. The Senate was expected to vote on the motion shortly after returning from its August recess. But the September cloture vote was never held. Before members returned from the recess, Hurricane Katrina devastated the Gulf Coast and totally remade the congressional agenda. With hurricane victims suffering in Louisiana, Mississippi, and Alabama, Senate GOP leaders canceled the estate tax vote. Meanwhile, Republican moderates were increasingly concerned about voting for more tax cuts at a time when Congress was considering cuts to mandatory programs and worrying about the enormous costs of the hurricane relief effort. The estate tax vanished from the congressional agenda for 2005. *(Hurricane Katrina, pp. 787, 788)*

2006 ACTION

It was not until June 8, 2006, that Frist decided to try again to cut off debate on the House-passed measure, but that effort fell three votes short of the sixty needed to invoke cloture. The tally on this **key vote was 57–41 (R 53–2; D 4–38; I 0-1)**. After the loss, Frist conceded that he did not have the votes for full repeal and asked House Speaker J. Dennis Hastert, R-Ill., to send him a compromise bill. *(2006 key votes, p. 937)*

Two weeks later, the House passed a new bill (HR 5638) that proposed an indefinite estate tax reduction, rather than a repeal. Despite a brief revolt by House conservatives, the bill passed by a vote of 269–156 on June 22. No amendments were allowed.

The bill, which was similar to the bipartisan proposal discussed in the Senate, would exclude the first $5 million of an individual's assets ($10 million for couples) from taxation, starting in 2010. Additional assets up to $25 million would be taxed at the capital gains rate, and those above $25 million would be taxed at double that rate. The existing capital gains tax rate was 15 percent, but it was set to expire after 2010. If Congress did not extend it, assets between $5 million and $25 million would be taxed at 20 percent; assets above $25 million would be taxed at 40 percent.

House conservatives warned they would not accept Senate changes. "This is not a first offer," Thomas said during the floor debate. "It is the only offer." Rep. Mike Pence, R-Ind., a leader of House conservatives, added: "Don't come back with anything else. These are the parameters." The White House said the bill would provide "significant relief" but added that a full repeal would still be needed.

Frist pledged to bring the bill to the Senate floor before the July Fourth recess, but he was stymied by the combined opposition of Democrats who opposed any big reduction in the estate tax and conservative Republicans who wanted nothing less than total repeal. On June 27, Frist announced that he was postponing action.

With the month-long Aug. recess days away, House leaders hastily assembled a bill (HR 5970), the so-called trifecta, that combined an estate tax reduction with a popular set of tax cut extensions, which were a high priority for the business community, and the first minimum wage increase since 1997. The combination was just enough to win the support of thirty-four Democrats and all but twenty-one Republicans. The House passed the bill 230–180 on July 29 and then left town.

The main aim of the exercise seemed to be nailing down a few last-minute accomplishments so Republicans would not go into the August recess empty-handed, as well as mending some growing rifts within the GOP. Conservatives, for example, wanted to show that they were continuing to push on the estate tax. A growing faction of GOP moderates in close races was demanding a vote on a minimum wage increase, worried that otherwise they would be pilloried in Democratic attack ads. Rank-and-file conservatives demanded that the leadership balance any wage increase with measures they thought would cushion the blow to businesses.

Under the estate tax provisions, the first $3.8 million in an individual's estate would be excluded from the tax in 2010, rising annually until the exclusion reached $5 million in 2015. After that, the level would be adjusted annually for inflation. For married couples, any unused exemption would carry over to the surviving spouse.

As in the earlier House-passed bill, additional assets up to $25 million would be taxed at the capital gains rate, and assets above $25 million would be taxed at double that rate.

The gamble of tying the estate tax cut prized by Republicans to the minimum wage increase, a Democratic priority, did not help in the Senate. On Aug. 3, the Senate rejected a motion to limit debate on the three-part bill by a vote of 56–42. Frist voted "no" as a procedural move to allow him to ask for another vote when the Senate returned in the fall, although he never did.

Cloture was opposed by most Democrats and two Republicans. Majority Whip Mitch McConnell, R-Ky., called the Democratic opposition a "block and blame" strategy. "I think this is an excuse to make this a 'do-nothing' Congress," charged Sen. Kay Bailey Hutchison, R- Texas. Democrats insisted it was Frist who miscalculated and said they would press him in September to reconsider bringing up the minimum wage increase and tax cut extensions separately.

The tax cut extensions were enacted in December, but the minimum wage proposal died at the end of the Congress. *(Tax extenders, p.105; Minimum wage, p. 664)*

Fiscal 2007 Budget Resolution

The House and Senate adopted significantly different budget resolutions for fiscal 2007 but made no effort to reconcile the two Republican-written measures. Instead, each chamber separately set a limit of $872.8 billion on fiscal 2007 discretionary spending, which allowed them to proceed with the appropriations process.

BUDGET PROCESS OVERHAUL PROPOSALS

There was much talk in Congress in 2006 about ways to improve fiscal discipline and reduce the size of the federal budget deficit, with few results. The only law enacted was a measure to set up a federal database to track spending. Lawmakers considered proposals such as expedited line-item recession authority for the president and "sunset" commissions to eliminate wasteful and duplicative federal programs, but none of them were enacted into law.

Spending Database

Web surfers would be able to track billions in government contracts and grants under legislation cleared by the House on Sept. 13, 2006. The bill (S 2590—PL 109-282) required the Office of Management and Budget to create a database of federal contracts and grants allowing users to type in key words that would bring up exactly how much money any particular recipient had received. Approximately 30,000 entities each year received federal grants worth more than $25,000, and that information would appear in the database. All contracts worth more than $25,000 also would be entered into the database.

Republican leaders held up the bill as an example of their zeal to make the workings of government more open to outsiders. House Majority Leader John A. Boehner, R-Ohio, said enactment of the bill demonstrated a commitment "to bring more accountability and transparency and help fundamentally change the way Congress spends taxpayer dollars."

Introduced in the Senate by Republican Tom Coburn of Oklahoma and Democrat Barack Obama of Illinois, the bill won easy approval from the Homeland Security and Government Operations Committee in late July. It came to the Senate floor in September, however, only after liberal and conservative bloggers exposed anonymous "holds" on the legislation placed by two senior appropriators, Republican Ted Stevens of Alaska and Democrat Robert C. Byrd of West Virginia. Once the holds were dropped, the Senate passed S 2590 by voice vote on Sept. 7.

In June the House had passed a narrower version of the measure (HR 5060) by voice vote that would have required creation of a federal database that would focus only on grants, not contracts. Watchdog groups had criticized the narrow focus of that bill.

Line-Item Rescissions

The House June 22 passed 244–172 a modified version of the expedited line-item rescission authority (HR 4890—H Rept 109-505, Part 1) that President George W. Bush requested in his January State of the Union address. Unlike the line-item veto struck down by the Supreme Court in 1998 (PL 104-130), the House bill would not have allowed the president to cancel spending items unilaterally. Instead, Congress would have to pass a new law incorporating the president's proposed cuts, which would be considered under expedited procedures that allowed no amendments or filibusters.

An effort to bring up line-item rescission authority fell short in the Senate, where it was opposed by key Republicans on the Appropriations Committee as well as most Senate Democrats. Supporters said the line-item rescission was an important check against wasteful spending, particularly earmarks, but opponents said it would tilt the balance of power on spending decisions too far toward the executive branch.

Sunset Commissions

The House Government Reform Committee approved two sunset commission bills (HR 3282, HR 5766), but vehement opposition from Democrats and moderate Republicans prevented any further action. HR 3282 would have eliminated federal departments and agencies unless Congress acted affirmatively at least once every twelve years to reauthorize them. HR 5766 would have authorized bipartisan commissions to study the efficiency of federal programs and agencies and determine whether they should be reorganized, consolidated, expanded, transferred, or abolished. Congress would have had to act on the recommendations under expedited procedures.

Differences among Republicans over fiscal policy nearly prevented House leaders from getting a budget resolution to the floor at all. Any attempt to agree on a conference report would likely have deepened the painful intraparty rifts, which pitted moderates against fiscal conservatives, and appropriators against those seeking new budget controls.

The annual budget resolution, required under the 1974 Budget Act, was an internal document meant to give Congress a framework for the year's actions on taxes and spending. In 2006 there were not sufficient incentives for GOP leaders to try to force a deal. It was the fourth time since 1974 that Congress did not reach a bicameral agreement on the budget.

One of the main objectives of a budget resolution is to set a binding limit on discretionary spending for the year. Spending that exceeds the cap is subject to a point of order on the floor. In addition, without a new discretionary spending limit the Senate would have been required to operate under the previous year's budget resolution, which had a tighter cap than either chamber wanted. Both the House and Senate got around the problem by including language in other legislation "deeming" a fiscal 2007 discretionary cap of $872.8 billion to be in place as if the two chambers had agreed on a final budget resolution.

The lack of any major new tax bills or mandatory spending cuts on the GOP leaders' agenda reduced the pressure for a deal. Getting such measures through the Senate usually required protection that only a budget resolution can offer. With the blessings of the budget resolution, tax provisions and changes in entitlement spending can be incorporated into a reconciliation bill, which is not subject to a filibuster and can pass by a simple majority instead of the sixty votes needed to limit debate in the Senate. Republicans had used the reconciliation process to enact more than $2 trillion in tax cuts since George W. Bush took office in 2001. But the appetite for more tax cuts had diminished as Republicans focused on the deficit and the need to find ways to cut spending.

HIGHLIGHTS

Following are the major features of the House- and Senate-adopted budget resolutions:

Discretionary limit. The House approved a cap of $872.8 billion on nonemergency spending, equivalent to the limit proposed in President Bush's budget as scored by the Congressional Budget Office (CBO). The Senate stretched the limit, increasing the cap by $9 billion and allowing another $7 billion in advance appropriations that did not count against the cap.

Entitlement savings. The House resolution included instructions for a $6.8 billion package of entitlement savings in a reconciliation bill, protected from filibusters in the Senate. The savings were not to come from Medicare, Medicaid, or student loans.

ANWR. The only reconciliation instructions in the Senate resolution were for a stand-alone bill to open portions of Alaska's Arctic National Wildlife Refuge (ANWR) to oil and gas drilling, generating an estimated $3 billion in revenue. The House did not include the ANWR provisions, which were anathema to two dozen House Republicans—more than enough to sink a budget that contained it.

Budget rules. Under the House resolution, the Budget Committee or its chairman would have had to approve any nondefense emergency spending beyond a limit of $6.5 billion. The measure also called for the deficit to be calculated on an accrual basis as well as a cash basis. The budget deficit appeared much larger using accrual accounting because mounting future obligations to pay Social Security and other benefits were included.

The Senate resolution would have triggered pay-as-you-go rules for mandatory spending, but not tax cuts, once 45 percent or more of the Medicare program became subsidized by general revenue, a situation that was viewed as possible within the next five years. It also provided for a Senate budget point of order against emergency spending that exceeded $90 billion. Fiscal conservatives argued that emergency spending was a backdoor way to evade spending limits because it did not count against the discretionary cap.

PRESIDENT'S BUDGET REQUEST

President Bush Feb. 6, 2006, released a $2.8 trillion fiscal 2007 budget that called for significant increases in defense and homeland security spending, coupled with reductions for most domestic programs. Bush again proposed to make permanent a number of tax cuts enacted earlier in his administration that were set to expire by the end of 2010.

For the second straight year, Bush sought an absolute cut in discretionary spending outside of defense and homeland security. He also called on Congress to pass new legislation to reduce the growth of entitlement spending, particularly in the Medicare program. The cuts would have been in addition to a $38.8 billion package of reductions in mandatory spending over five years that he signed into law Feb. 8 (PL 109-171). *(Budget reconciliation, p. 79)*

The budget request called for an $877.7 billion cap on discretionary spending and an increase of $43 billion in fees over five years, including many increases that Congress had rejected previously. The White House said Bush's budget would produce a $354 billion deficit in fiscal 2007.

As scored by CBO, the budget proposed an $872.8 billion cap on discretionary spending, the money that appropriators could allocate as they chose. That was a 3.6 percent increase over fiscal 2006, excluding supplemental appropriations for Iraq and Afghanistan. Bush's proposals to boost spending for defense and homeland security meant cuts in most domestic programs. The discretionary total included $460 billion for defense, an increase of 6.4 percent over fiscal 2006 appropriations, excluding supplemental spending. The request also included $50 billion for operations in Iraq and Afghanistan, a fraction of what the war was expected to cost in fiscal 2007. The administration continued funding the war primarily through supplemental appropriations bills that did not count against discretionary spending caps.

The request also included $29 billion for homeland security, a 6.6 percent increase, not counting supplemental spending, and $383 billion in discretionary funding for all other domestic programs, virtually the same as fiscal 2006 spending.

Major increases proposed for some programs left others with big cuts. For example, Bush requested $35.2 billion for international affairs, a 12 percent increase. The extra funds were mainly for his Millennium Challenge Corporation, an aid program for countries that agreed to promote economic growth, democracy, and human rights, and for Bush's global HIV/AIDS Initiative. Funding for veterans' benefits and services would increase by nearly 9 percent to $2.9 billion. But support for education and training would fall by 11 percent to $11.7 billion. For natural resources and the environment, Bush requested $28.2 billion, nearly 7 percent below the amount appropriated for fiscal 2006.

Bush proposed a net reduction of $57 billion in the growth of entitlement programs over five years, including $32 billion in cuts to Medicare payments to hospitals, nursing homes, and other institutional health care providers. Bush defended the proposed Medicare savings, saying they would limit growth in the program to 7.7 percent a year, down from 8.1 percent. "That's not a cut. It's slowing down the rate of growth," he said.

Among the proposals certain to be controversial in Congress were a $16.7 billion increase in pension insurance premiums paid by corporations, $5 billion carved from agricultural subsidies, and smaller cuts in food stamps and federal employee health benefits. The plan also assumed $4 billion in revenue from opening up Alaska's Arctic National Wildlife Refuge to oil exploration.

CBO estimated that Bush's budget would result in a fiscal 2007 deficit of $335 billion, or 2.4 percent of the gross domestic product (GDP). However, CBO noted that the budget included only $50 billion for the wars in Iraq and Afghanistan and said that if the pace of operations remained the same as in the previous year, the fiscal 2007 deficit would be closer to $355 billion, or 2.6 percent of GDP. It said Bush's proposals for supplemental spending would bring the fiscal 2006 deficit to $371 billion, 2.8 percent of GDP.

Bush reiterated his call for Congress to provide new budget controls, particularly a line-item veto that would give the president the authority to strike individual items from spending bills, and statutory limits on discretionary spending enforced by across-the-board cuts. Congress had enacted a line-item veto in 1996 (PL 104-130), but it was declared unconstitutional by the Supreme Court two years later. The White House said it had developed legislation that would pass muster with the courts without requiring a constitutional amendment. *(Congress and the Nation Vol. IX, pp. 76–80; Vol. X, pp. 64–65)*

SENATE COMMITTEE ACTION

The Senate Budget Committee started first, approving its budget resolution (S Con Res 83) on an 11–10 party-line vote March 9. The committee approved an $872.5 billion discretionary limit, in line with Bush's budget, but chairman Judd Gregg, R-N.H., disappointed fiscal conservatives by abandoning plans to seek another package of savings from entitlement programs such as Medicare and Medicaid. Gregg cited election-year resistance within the GOP ranks. "We didn't have the votes on the floor," he said. Only a month earlier, in February 2006, Congress had cleared a 2005 budget reconciliation bill that cut $38.8 billion from mandatory spending over five years (PL 109-171). *(2005 budget reconciliation, p. 79)*

The only reconciliation instructions called for a bill to allow drilling in portions of ANWR, bringing in an estimated $3 billion in leasing revenue. In 2005 the Senate's budget reconciliation bill included the leasing, but GOP leaders dropped it in conference to get the final package (PL 109-171) through the House. Although no reconciliation protection was provided, the resolution assumed that expiring provisions of Bush's 2001 and 2003 tax cuts (PL 107-16; PL 108-27) would be extended at a cost of $227 billion over five years.

The budget resolution allowed for $90 billion in fiscal 2007 emergency spending, including $50 billion for the war in Iraq and Afghanistan; $2.3 billion for pandemic flu preparation; and $2 billion for border security. The total was $37.7 billion more than Bush assumed in his budget.

During the markup, the committee rejected 10–11 a proposal by ranking committee Democrat Kent Conrad of North Dakota to require that new mandatory spending and tax cut proposals be offset. Such pay-as-you-go budget rules had been enacted in 1990 and existed in various forms until they lapsed in 2002 after four years of budget surpluses, allowing tax cuts and the new Medicare prescription drug benefit (PL 108-173) to be enacted without offsetting budget cuts or revenue increases. Conrad said the requirement should be restored to ensure fiscal discipline. *(Medicare prescription drugs, Congress and the Nation Vol. XI, p. 496)*

SENATE FLOOR ACTION

Ignoring Bush's call for belt-tightening, Senate Republicans added $17 billion to the budget resolution before adopting it 51–49 on March 16. Vice President Dick Cheney was on hand in case of a tie, but his vote was not needed. As adopted, the measure raised the discretionary spending cap for fiscal 2007 to about $882 billion and added an additional $7 billion in advance spending.

Senate leaders made multiple deals to win enough votes without dropping the highly contested ANWR drilling language. Among other things, Senate leaders agreed to use some of the ANWR lease revenue for Gulf Coast hurricane relief, to allow Medicare to negotiate drug prices, and to add billions of dollars for low-income energy subsidies, and health and education programs. Attempts to restrain spending or cut the growth in entitlement programs were turned down, as was an attempt to restore the pay-as you-go budget rules, which was defeated on a 50–50 vote.

HOUSE COMMITTEE ACTION

The House Budget Committee approved its own budget resolution (H Con Res 376—H Rept 109-402) on a party-line 22–17 vote March 29. The panel endorsed Bush's discretionary cap of $872.8 billion. But in a nod to GOP election-year jitters, chairman Jim Nussle, R-Iowa, proposed only a modest $6.8 billion in savings from mandatory accounts over five years, sparing politically sensitive programs such as Medicaid and Medicare. Bush had asked for $65 billion in entitlement cuts, with more than half coming from Medicare.

The House allowed for an additional $50 billion in emergency spending for the wars in Iraq and Afghanistan, and an additional $4.3 billion to cover emergencies other than wars. Nussle included a change in House rules that would make nondefense supplemental spending beyond $4.3 billion subject to approval by the Budget Committee or its chairman. Additional war funding could be appropriated without such approval. Appropriators balked at the idea of having to seek such permission, but conservatives insisted on an upper limit to curb the explosive growth of supplemental spending, which they maintained had created a parallel appropriations process that bypassed the limits in the budget resolution.

HOUSE FLOOR ACTION

After months of false starts and GOP infighting, House Republican leaders managed to win adoption of the budget resolution (H Con Res 376—H Rept 109-402) on a 218–210 vote just after 1 a.m. on May 18. To reach that point, leaders promised to find an additional $3.1 billion for labor, health, and education programs sought by Republican moderates.

Party moderates who were holding out for additional funds for health and education programs eventually agreed to support the budget plan, after winning language stating that the president's request for the labor, health and human services, and education bill needed to be increased by at least $7.2 billion. The amendment specified that $1 billion should come from unobligated funds for reconstruction in Iraq, with the rest offset by unidentified cuts elsewhere in the budget. The moderates said they had received assurances that the money would not come from programs such as Medicare, Medicaid, or other programs for the needy.

To appease members of the Appropriations Committee who were furious about the Budget Committee's cap on supplemental spending, GOP leaders ultimately agreed to increase from $4.3 billion to $6.5 billion the amount of nondefense supplemental spending that could be appropriated without approval from the Budget Committee or its chairman. Appropriators still opposed the limit.

Passage of the resolution was a victory for Majority Leader John A. Boehner, R-Ohio, who had struggled for weeks to bring the budget resolution to a vote in the face of intraparty feuds. The deal cleared the way for the House to move forward on the annual appropriations bills. "It's almost impossible for us to do an appropriations process without a budget," Boehner said. Adoption of the budget resolution also spared the party leadership from being the first to fail to get a budget through the House since the enactment of modern budget rules in 1974.

FINAL ACTION

After the House vote, House and Senate leaders talked bravely of reaching a conference agreement on the budget, but most lawmakers thought the two chambers were too far apart to reach a compromise.

Shortly after approving the budget resolution, the House voted to deem the $872.8 billion cap in its version of the budget to be in effect in the absence of a final budget resolution. The language was part of the rule (H Res 818) for consideration of the fiscal 2007 Interior-Environment appropriations bill (HR 5386). That allowed the House to avoid a messy backup scenario that would have involved trying to deem separate spending caps to be in effect for each of the fiscal 2007 bills.

The Senate had a more difficult problem. In the absence of a conference report on the fiscal 2007 budget resolution, Senate appropriators were required to operate under the fiscal 2006 budget resolution (H Con Res 95), which set an $866 billion discretionary spending cap for fiscal 2007, $7 billion below the House level and $23 billion below the level adopted by the Senate. The cap would apply to the final bill of the year, expected to be the labor, health and human services, and education bill, creating a huge end-of-session mess.

To avoid that situation, Senate appropriators managed to attach an $872.8 billion fiscal 2007 cap to the conference report on a fiscal 2006 supplemental spending bill for Iraq, enacted June 15 (PL 109-234). *(Details, p. 105)*

Fiscal 2007 Appropriations

Shortage of time and intraparty divisions among Republicans led to an impasse over fiscal 2007 appropriations that Republican leaders were unable to surmount. Congress passed just two of the eleven regular appropriations bills—for the defense and homeland security departments—before the end of the year and cleared a $94.5 billion supplemental spending bill, mainly for the wars in Iraq and Afghanistan. They left the rest, including all the domestic spending bills, for the 110th Congress beginning in 2007.

Democrats, who were to take control of both chambers in 2007 as a result of the 2006 midterm elections, said they would clear a year-long continuing resolution for all nine bills. To keep programs and agencies operating in the meantime, Congress passed a series of three continuing resolutions. The third funded the programs through Feb. 15, 2007, at the lower of the House-passed, Senate-passed, or fiscal 2006 level.

The session was one of the shortest in recent history, and the Senate often voted only three days a week. In addition, the administration's use of supplemental appropriations to fund the wars took up considerable time from February to June. "When you have to do these supplementals, they drain an enormous amount of staff energy and member time away from the regular process," said James W. Dyer, a former GOP staff director of the House Appropriations Committee. Also, Senate leaders used the crucial months of July and September for other legislation.

But more time would not have resolved the growing rift between GOP conservatives, who were angry over high deficits and demanded spending cuts, and moderates, who insisted on protecting social programs. Their disagreements had scuttled any hopes of completing a fiscal 2007 budget resolution. Instead, each chamber separately set a discretionary spending limit of $872.8 billion, not counting emergency funds, which allowed them to proceed with the spending bills.

Fitting the funds for domestic programs under that cap, however, proved impossible. For example, moderate Republicans demanded an extra $7 billion for social programs only to trigger a veto threat from President George W. Bush when the appropriators tried to meet the demand by taking money out of the defense bill.

The House managed to pass all but the toughest measure—labor, health and human services, and education bill—by the end of June. The Appropriations Committee had approved a spending bill that not only was $4.1 billion more than Bush requested but also included a minimum wage increase promoted by the Democrats. GOP moderates in tight election races refused to accept the bill without the minimum wage, but many conservatives said they would not vote for the legislation if the provision remained. To win passage, GOP leaders would have had to ignore their conservatives and rely on Democratic and moderate Republican votes, something they were not prepared to do.

In the Senate, no spending bills were ready for the floor when the supplemental was finished in mid-June. To make up for lost time, the appropriators got six appropriations bills ready for floor debate by July 1, and all of them were ready three weeks later.

But Majority Leader Bill Frist, R-Tenn., allowed little floor time for floor action on the bills in the crucial month of July, passing only the homeland security measure. After the August recess, with pre-election polls looking increasingly ominous for Republicans, Frist and his House counterparts decided to devote much of September—a month typically filled with action on appropriations bills—to national security, an issue that had played well for them at the polls in the past. The defense and homeland security bills cleared before the election, but that was all.

Typically, appropriators assembled unfinished appropriations bills into an omnibus package at the end of a session. No longer limited by rules that govern regular appropriations bills, the package often absorbed members' pet projects and other last-minute legislation. But when Congress returned in November, a defiant band of conservative GOP senators stepped in to shut down the appropriations process. They blocked the appointment of conferees on the military construction-veterans affairs bill, warning that if it went to conference, it would become the vehicle for a bloated omnibus spending package.

Bowing to the conservatives, Frist told Minority Leader Harry Reid, D-Nev., on Nov. 20 that Republicans planned to pass a continuing resolution that would put the rest of the government's funding on autopilot and defer final decisions until the next Congress. Conservatives were pleased at being able to avoid last-minute earmarks. Democrats denounced the move as an abdication of responsibility.

Following are brief descriptions of the fiscal 2007 spending bills.

DEFENSE

In one of its final acts before recessing for the November elections, Congress cleared legislation (HR 5631—PL 109-289) appropriating $447.6 billion in fiscal 2007 spending for the Defense Department, one of only two regular appropriations bills lawmakers managed to clear in 2006.

The defense bill included $70 billion in emergency supplemental spending, nearly all of it for the wars in Iraq and Afghanistan. That brought the total for emergency spending for military and related operations in the two countries to $140.4 billion for fiscal 2007 and to about $500 billion since Sept, 11, 2001, according to the Congressional Research Service. The other $70 billion for fiscal 2007 was contained in an emergency war supplemental that Congress passed in June. *(War supplemental, p. 105)*

Not counting the emergency funds, HR 5631 appropriated a total of $377.6 billion for the Defense Department, all but $256 million of it discretionary spending under the annual control of Congress. That was an increase of nearly $19.2 billion, or 5 percent, over fiscal 2006 funding.

The House bill, passed in June, was $4.1 billion, or 1 percent, less than requested, a reduction that drew a rebuke from the White House. The Senate version, passed in early September, was $5 billion less than the House version. Threatened with a veto, Senate conferees agreed to accept the smaller House cut. The House adopted the conference report (H Rept 109-676) 394–22 on Sept. 26. The Senate cleared the bill Sept. 29, 100–0, and the president signed it into law later in the day. *(PL 109-289 details, p. 358)*

The final bill included $119.8 billion for operations and maintenance, $86.4 billion for military personnel; $80.9 billion for weapons procurement, and $75.7 billion for research and development. Congress made a number of changes to Bush's requests for specific weapons systems, including appropriating $2.7 billion for the Air Force to buy twenty F-22A Raptor warplanes in fiscal 2007, almost double the request, plus $687 million in advance funds for twenty more in fiscal 2008. Congress also insisted on providing more than the president sought for the Army National Guard.

Congress prohibited the use of any of the money in the bill to establish permanent U.S. bases in Iraq; a similar provision had been dropped from the final version of the supplemental war spending bill passed in June.

HOMELAND SECURITY

The only other regular fiscal 2007 appropriations bill Congress cleared during the year appropriated $34.8 billion for the Department of Homeland Security. The measure (HR 5441—PL 109-295) included $1.8 billion in emergency funds and $1.1 billion in mandatory appropriations for Coast Guard retiree pay. The total was more than either chamber initially approved and was about 10 percent more than Congress appropriated for the department in fiscal 2006. The total was also about 8 percent more than the president had requested, in part because Congress rejected a White House proposal for a fee increase that would have offset about $1.2 billion in spending.

Of the emergency funding, $1.2 billion was designated for construction of a "fence" along the Mexican-U.S. border that combined physical infrastructure such as vehicle barriers with sensor technology. Congress had approved construction of the fence after failing to reach agreement on an overhaul of U.S. immigration policy. Despite the emergency funding for the border fence, completion of the bill was delayed by a House GOP effort to incorporate several additional House-passed border security measures. The only one of those provisions included in the final bill established criminal penalties for tunneling under the border. *(Immigration policy, pp. 686, 711; Border security, p. 679)*

A dispute over the future of the Federal Emergency Management Administration (FEMA) was resolved, at least temporarily, when Congress agreed to keep the agency within the Homeland Security Department but to give it more autonomy. FEMA was widely criticized in 2005 for being unprepared to deal with Hurricane Katrina. *(FEMA overhaul, p. 236)*

Another policy provision included in the conference report allowed individuals to import small amounts of approved prescription drugs for personal use. The House inserted into its agriculture spending bill (HR 5384) a broader measure that would allow drug wholesalers to import cheaper pharmaceuticals from abroad, but the Senate never acted on that bill. The White House steadfastly threatened to veto any measure opening the U.S. prescription drug market to foreign imports. *(Drug imports, pp. 556, 578)*

The House passed HR 5441 (H Rept 109-476) on June 6 and the Senate passed its version (S Rept 109-273) on July 13. The House adopted the conference report (H Rept 109-699) on Sept. 29, and the Senate cleared it later that day. President Bush signed the bill on Oct. 4.

OTHER REGULAR APPROPRIATIONS BILLS

None of the other nine regular appropriations bills cleared during the session. Funding for the programs funded by the nine regular spending bills was extended through a series of stopgap funding bills. *(Continuing appropriations resolution, pp. 105, 107)*

Following are highlights of the nine bills that did not pass.

Agriculture

The House passed a $93.6 billion appropriations bill (HR 5384—H Rept 109-463) on May 23. The House-passed bill proposed $18.5 billion for discretionary programs, slightly more than the Senate committee version. The bills contained several controversial provisions likely to make a conference difficult. For example, the House would have allowed drug wholesalers to import cheaper pharmaceuticals from abroad, an initiative the White House strongly opposed. Another controversial provision involved peanuts. A provision in the Senate bill would have paid peanut farmers to store their crops for another year, probably ensuring the survival of the peanut subsidy when Congress took up a rewrite of the 2002 farm bill, expected in 2007. A similar provision, however, was removed from the House bill on a point of order.

Commerce, Justice, Science, State

In June, the House passed a fiscal 2007 spending bill (HR 5672 (H Rept 109-520) totaling $62.6 billion for the Departments of Commerce, Justice, and State and for science programs. The Senate Appropriations Committee version, approved in July, appropriated $54.7 billion, but its version did not include funding for the State Department, which the Senate covered in a separate bill. Among the biggest differences between the two versions was an extra $1 billion in emergency spending in the Senate to reimburse NASA for costs incurred as a result of Hurricane Katrina and the 2003 destruction of the space shuttle *Columbia.*

During floor debate, the House rejected several contentious provisions, including one to raise the federal minimum wage. The House voted to bar funding to enforce a law requiring that all handguns be sold with trigger locks. The requirement had been added to a bill (S 397—PL 109-92) passed in 2005 that limited the legal liability of firearms makers and dealers. *(Minimum wage, pp. 661, 664; Handgun liability, p. 699)*

Energy, Water

The House passed a $30.5 billion energy and water spending bill (HR 5427—H Rept 109-474) for fiscal 2007 in May; the Senate Appropriations Committee approved an amended version (S Rept 109-272) in June that totaled $31.2 billion. The major difference was over how to dispose of spent fuel rods that were piling up at commercial nuclear reactors around the country. The federal government was charged by law to take charge of the nuclear waste and secure it in a permanent repository. At issue was a White House proposal intended to reduce the volume of waste by reprocessing spent fuel for reuse in a new generation of nuclear reactors. Fearing that the new technology was too risky, the House voted to cut the proposed budget for the program from the $250 million requested to $120 million but to fully fund the $545 million request for the planned permanent repository at Yucca Mountain in Nevada. The Senate committee took nearly the opposite approach, cutting the Yucca Mountain request by $50 million while fully funding the reprocessing program. *(Nuclear waste, p. 476)*

Foreign Operations

The House passed a $21.3 billion foreign operations bill (HR 5522—H Rept 109-4886) on June 9. The Senate Appropriations Committee followed broadly in the House's footsteps, approving a $31.5 billion version that included $49.7 billion for the State Department, which the House covered in a separate bill. Both versions were significantly less than the $23.2 billion the president had requested. Both bills would have fully financed several significant requests, including funding for international HIV/AIDS relief and for aid to Israel and Egypt. Both bills also proposed sizable cuts to Bush's signature foreign aid program, the Millennium Challenge Account, which offered aid to countries that followed free-market principles. Earlier concerns about management of the program declined during the year, but with a tight cap on overall discretionary spending, resistance to providing the full request remained.

Interior, Environment

The House in May passed a $25.9 billion fiscal 2007 spending bill (HR 5386—H Rept 108-465) for the Interior Department, the Environmental Protection Agency (EPA), and related agencies. The Senate committee version (S Rept 109-275), approved in June, was slightly higher, at $26.1 billion. Legislators in both chambers said the measure was woefully short of funding for longstanding programs, such as loans to state and local governments to upgrade aging sewer systems, as well as for new initiatives, including some authorized by the 2005 Energy Policy Act (PL 109-58). *(2005 energy measure, p. 447)*

Both versions of HR 5386 carried language aimed at forcing oil companies to pay royalties to the federal government for certain offshore leases negotiated in the late 1990s. The leases, signed when crude oil prices were depressed, waived royalty payments and did not require that they be reinstated when oil prices rose. The House version also carried several controversial provisions, including language to bar logging in Alaska's Tongass National Forest and to prevent the EPA from relaxing some reporting requirements for companies that used toxic substances.

Labor, Health and Human Services, Education

Neither chamber approved the fiscal 2007 spending bill for the Departments of Labor, Health and Human Services, and Education, although both appropriations committees approved differing versions of the bill. The House committee bill (HR 5647—H Rept 109-515) approved $605 billion, including $141.9 billion in discretionary funds; the Senate committee approved $605.5 billion in a separate bill (S 3708—S Rept 109-287), including nearly $1 billion more in discretionary funds than the House version.

The main delay came in the House on an amendment narrowly added in committee that to increase the federal minimum wage by $2.10 over two years, to $7.25 an hour. Although the amendment was pushed by Democrats, many moderate Republicans facing tough reelection fights said they would vote against the bill if it did not contain the wage increase. Many conservatives, already unhappy with the cost of the bill, said they would not support the bill if the minimum wage increase remained in it. *(Minimum wage, pp. 661, 664)*

Legislative Branch

The House passed a $3 billion fiscal 2007 appropriations bill (HR 5221—H Rept 109-485) in June, and the Senate Appropriations Committee approved a $4 billion version later in the month. By tradition the House version of the spending bill does not contain funding for Senate operations; of the $1 billion the Senate committee added, $841 billion was for the chamber's operations. Action on the measure was held up not because of disagreements over funding or policy but because of members' reluctance to be seen as funding their own branch before the rest of government.

Military Construction, Veterans Affairs

Both chambers voted to significantly increase funding for the Department of Veterans Affairs (VA) and military construction in fiscal 2007, but fears that the measure would become an end-of-the-year vehicle for other spending bills blocked final action.

The House passed HR 5385 (H Rept 109-464, Part 2) on May 19, appropriating $136.1 billion. The Senate version (S Rept 109-286), passed on Nov. 14 during the lame-duck session, was lower, at $94.3 billion, but did not contain three major programs included in the House bill because of jurisdictional differences between the two Appropriations committees. Both bills included $77.9 billion for the VA. The differences between the two versions were not large, making it the one spending measure sure to be enacted before Congress adjourned. But a defiant band of conservative Republican senators placed a hold on the appointment of conferees, eliminating the possibility that the conference report would become the basis for an omnibus spending bill and pushing the appropriations process into 2007. *(Continuing resolutions, p. 107)*

Transportation, Treasury, Housing

The House passed a $139.2 billion spending bill for the Treasury, Transportation, and Housing and Urban Development departments (HR 5576—H Rept 109-495) in June. The Senate Appropriations Committee approved a $141.2 billion version (S Rept 109-281) in July. For jurisdictional reasons the House version, but not the Senate version, contained funding for the District of Columbia; Senate appropriators separately approved $597 million for the District, which was essentially a payment to the city in lieu of taxes. As usual, the measure provided a forum for disputes over several controversial issues. Disagreements arose in 2006 over funding for Amtrak, foreign ownership of U.S.

airlines, agricultural trade with Cuba, and the merits of individual earmarks. Transportation advocates also complained that the delay in enacting the spending bill was stalling work on needed infrastructure repairs and improvements. *(Earmarks, box, p. 74)*

CONTINUING RESOLUTIONS

One of the last actions lawmakers took before adjourning the 109th Congress was to clear the third fiscal 2007 continuing resolution since the Oct. 1 start of the new fiscal year. The measure (H J Res 102—PL 109-383) provided funding through Feb. 15, 2007, for all federal programs covered by the nine unfinished appropriations bills. Funding for departments and programs covered in the unfinished bills was provided at the lowest of the House-passed, Senate-passed, or fiscal 2006 level.

Congress had completed action on only two of the regular fiscal 2007 spending bills, for the Departments of Defense (PL 109-289) and Homeland Security (PL 109-295 before recessing at the end of September to campaign for the midterm elections, where Democrats took control of both chambers from the Republicans. The Senate returned after the election to pass the military construction and veterans' affairs bill (HR 5385), but a group of fiscal conservatives blocked the appointment of Senate conferees, saying they feared the bill could become a legislative vehicle for a bloated omnibus spending bill.

Democrats accused the Republicans of abdicating responsibility by refusing to finish the spending process on their watch. But the fiscal conservatives maintained that a continuing resolution was preferable to an earmark-filled omnibus funding package and blamed Appropriations Committee members for their insistence on retaining member projects in the spending bills. *(Earmarks, box, p. 74)*

On Dec. 11, the incoming Democratic chairmen of the Appropriations committees announced plans to pass a year-long fiscal 2007 continuing resolution for the nine remaining bills, with "limited adjustments" and without earmarks. *(Details, p. 107)*

The House passed H J Res 102 on Dec. 8, 370–20; the Senate passed it later in the day by voice vote; and President Bush signed it into law on Dec. 9. Earlier Congress had cleared two other stopgap spending measures. The first provided funding from the start of the fiscal year until after the election, through Nov. 17, and was tacked onto the defense spending bill, which cleared on Sept. 29. The second funded programs through Dec. 8 (PL 109-369).

Fiscal 2006 War and Disaster Supplemental

Congress in June cleared a $94.5 billion emergency supplemental appropriations bill for fiscal 2006 (HR 4939—PL 109-234), providing money for the wars in Iraq and Afghanistan, hurricane recovery, and pandemic flu preparation. To reach the final version, conferees had to make large cuts in the Senate-passed bill, which totaled $108.9 billion and included significantly more funding for hurricane aid and largely unrelated items. President George W. Bush helped keep the total down, vowing repeatedly to veto the bill if it exceeded $94.5 billion.

Most of the money—$70.4 billion—was for ongoing military operations in Iraq and Afghanistan and related State Department and foreign aid activities. That brought to more than $400 billion the amount of supplemental funds appropriated to cover war-related expenses since Sept. 11, 2001. None of these supplemental funds, all designated as emergency funding, counted against Congress's discretionary spending limits.

Despite the desire of the Appropriations Committee chairmen to clear the bill before the Memorial Day recess, and the Pentagon's insistence that the funding was urgently needed, Congress did not complete action until mid-June. Among the final sticking points were funding levels for agriculture relief, fisheries, the Federal Emergency Management Agency disaster-relief fund, the distribution of homeland security money, and the fate of assorted earmarks. The final version eliminated or substantially pared back funding for these items.

The bill also served as a vehicle for a "deeming resolution" that set a fiscal 2007 discretionary spending limit of $873 billion in the Senate, a move necessitated after the Senate was unable to complete action on its budget resolution. The House passed HR 4939 (H Rept 109-388) on March 16; the Senate approved its version (S Rept 109-230) on May 4. The House adopted the conference report (H Rept 109–494) on June 13, the Senate cleared it on June 15, and the president signed it later that day. *(Budget resolution, pp. 97, 101)*

Tax Breaks Extended

Shortly before adjourning Dec. 9, 2006, the Senate cleared a package of popular tax break extensions, including the research and development credit and the deduction for college tuition. The bill also provided a last-minute ride for several unrelated provisions on trade, oil drilling, and Medicare payments to doctors. President George W. Bush signed the package into law Dec. 20 (HR 6111—PL 109-432).

Congress regularly extended the credits and deductions in the package, but never for very long because the cost would have invited greater scrutiny. Also, the so-called extenders had broad support and were useful as engines for getting other, more controversial legislation through Congress.

The 2006 bill extended about two dozen expiring and expired tax breaks for companies and individuals at an estimated cost of $35.9 billion over ten years, according to the Joint Committee on Taxation.

The most expensive provision was a two-year extension of the research and development credit, estimated to cost

$16.5 billion over ten years. The credit had lapsed at the end of 2005, and businesses with large research components, such as technology companies, had lobbied for retroactive renewal. The bill extended the credit in its existing form through 2006, then expanded and simplified it in 2007, allowing a company to base the credit on an average of its research expenses over the previous three years. Half of those expenses would be eligible for the 12 percent credit.

As cleared, the bill also included permanent normalization of trade relations with Vietnam, trade benefits for Haiti and other countries, and language to allow offshore drilling in 8.3 million acres in the Gulf of Mexico. It also blocked a 5 percent cut in Medicare physicians' payments that was scheduled to take effect in 2007, paid for largely by reducing the Medicare stabilization fund. *(Trade, p. 197; oil drilling, p. 471; Physician payments, pp. 553, 571)*

Other provisions included a package of tax benefits related to energy production, provisions to broaden tax benefits for health savings accounts in an effort to expand their use, and expansion of the abandoned coal mine reclamation program at an estimated ten-year cost of $3.9 billion. *(Health savings accounts, p. 554)*

Attempts to enact the tax extenders began early in the year. Many of the provisions were included in a tax reconciliation bill the Senate passed in February. When conferees put together the final $70 billion tax reconciliation measure (PL 109-222), they agreed that the tax extenders made the package too expensive and decided to put them in a separate bill. Senate Finance Chairman Charles E. Grassley, R-Iowa, a chief proponent of the tax extensions, agreed to drop them from the reconciliation bill after he got a commitment from House Ways and Means Chairman Bill Thomas, R-Calif., that they would be attached to other legislation, probably a pension overhaul. *(Pension overhaul, pp. 654, 658)*

But bickering over the tax provisions slowed conference negotiations on the pension bill (PL 109-280), and in late July GOP leaders decided to put the provisions into a new three-part bill (HR 5970) that also included an indefinite reduction in the estate tax and an increase in the federal minimum wage. They hoped the tax breaks for business would make the minimum wage more palatable to conservative Republicans.

The House passed that bill July 29, but Senate supporters could not collect the sixty votes needed to break a Democratic filibuster. *(Estate tax, p. 96, Minimum wage, pp. 661, 664)*

As Congress scrambled to adjourn in December, Grassley and Thomas struck a deal designed to move the tax extenders along with the other sidetracked bills that wound up in the package. The House passed HR 6111 by a vote of 367–45 on Dec. 8. In its last roll call vote of the 109th Congress, the Senate cleared the bill 79–9 on Dec. 9.

(Technically, the votes were a bit more complicated: The House vote was on a motion to concur in a Senate amendment with a House amendment; the House amendment was the text of the bill. Trade provisions were attached to the bill in a separate vote, and the Senate then concurred in all of the House changes.)

HIGHLIGHTS

Following are the main tax provisions, with estimated costs over ten years.

R&D credit. A two-year extension, through fiscal 2007, of a credit that allowed businesses to deduct a percentage of research and development expenses. (Cost: $16.5 billion.)

State sales tax deduction. A two-year extension, through fiscal 2007, of an opportunity for those who itemized their deductions to deduct amounts paid for state and local sales taxes in place of state income taxes. The provision was beneficial to taxpayers in states with no income tax. (Cost: $5.5 billion.)

College tuition deduction. A two-year extension, through fiscal 2007, of a deduction of up to $4,000 a year for higher education expenses, regardless of whether the taxpayer itemized. (Cost: $3.3 billion.)

Leasehold improvements. A two-year extension, through fiscal 2007, of a provision allowing a depreciation period of fifteen years, instead of thirty-nine years, for improvements to leased nonresidential property and restaurants. (Cost: $5.2 billion.)

Welfare-to-work and work opportunity tax credits. A two-year extension, through fiscal 2007, of credits for employers who hired individuals on long-term assistance, high-risk youths, and other hard-to-place employees. In the second year, the programs were to be combined. (Cost: $1 billion.)

Energy taxes. Extension of a list of energy credits and deductions. The most expensive was a credit for electricity produced from renewable sources that was estimated to cost $2.9 billion over ten years. (Total cost: $3.4 billion.)

Health savings accounts. An expansion of health savings accounts, including a repeal of the annual limit on tax-deductible contributions. (Cost: $1 billion.)

2007–2008

Democrats in control of the 110th Congress had little more success in setting and passing their budget priorities than they did when they were the minority party in the 109th Congress. Eager to show their fiscal responsibility and contrast themselves with Republicans, who had been unable to pass budget resolutions in three of the past five years, Democrats in May 2007 passed a $3.0 trillion budget resolution for fiscal 2008 that contained $21.3 billion more in discretionary funding for domestic programs than President George w. Bush had requested.

But after a yearlong showdown in which the president repeatedly made good on his veto threats, the Democrats ultimately backed down, agreeing to Bush's spending limits and, at the GOP's insistence, adding additional funding for a war they opposed. Congress passed only one regular appropriations bill in 2007—for the Defense Department. Funding for the remaining federal departments and programs was bundled into an omnibus package that cleared Congress just before the session ended in late December.

With elections looming—and the possibility of a Democrat in the White House in 2009—Democrats decided early in 2008 that they would not get caught in the same spending showdown. Congress adopted the fiscal 2008 budget resolution in a process that did little more than highlight the differences between the two parties on tax and spending issues. Democrats also dispensed with most of the regular fiscal 2009 appropriations bills, passing only a single annual spending bill in the House and none in the Senate. Instead appropriators packaged fiscal 2009 spending for three security-related bills—defense, homeland security, and military construction and veterans' affairs—in a single measure, together with stopgap funding for the rest of the federal government that ran through March 6, 2009, about six weeks after the new president would take office.

Election campaigning also effectively prevented the Democrats from seriously challenging funding for the war in Iraq, which many Democrats opposed. The 110th Congress passed three emergency supplemental appropriations providing funding for the wars in Iraq and Afghanistan among other things.

By the end of Bush's presidency, an estimated $854 billion had been approved for the wars in Iraq and Afghanistan, according to figures compiled by the Congressional Research Service. *(War costs, box, p. 387)*

Democrats exacted a price for their acquiescence, winning, in 2007, the first increase in the federal minimum wage in nearly ten years and, in 2008, the first major overhaul of the GI education benefits bill in twenty-five years.

Republican opposition to the Democrats' pay-as-you-go rule, which required revenue-raising offsets to tax cuts or increases in entitlement, killed a measure to extend some popular tax breaks in 2007 and forced the Democrats to abandon the rule in order to enact a law providing millions of middle-class taxpayers temporary relief from the alternative minimum tax. In 2008 the dispute over the pay-as-you-go rule repeated itself until the Senate attached the tax break and AMT relief legislation to the $700 billion bank rescue package, forcing the House to accept a version that had far fewer offsets in it than House Democrats wanted.

Taxes and Other Revenues as Percentage of Gross Domestic Product, 1935–2008

Fiscal Year	*Individual Income*	*Corporate Income*	*Social Insurance*	*Excise*	*Other*	*Total*
1935	0.8	0.8	—	2.1	1.6	5.2
1940	0.9	1.2	1.8	2.0	0.7	6.8
1945	8.3	7.2	1.6	2.8	0.5	20.4
1950	5.8	3.8	1.6	2.8	0.5	14.4
1955	7.3	4.5	2.0	2.3	0.5	16.6
1960	7.9	4.2	2.8	2.3	0.8	17.9
1965	7.1	3.7	3.2	2.1	0.8	17.0
1970	8.9	3.2	4.4	1.6	0.9	19.0
1975	7.8	2.6	5.4	1.1	1.0	17.9
1980	9.0	2.4	5.8	0.9	1.0	19.0
1985	8.1	1.5	6.4	0.9	0.9	17.7
1986	7.9	1.4	6.4	0.7	0.9	17.4
1987	8.4	1.8	6.5	0.7	0.9	18.4
1988	8.0	1.9	6.7	0.7	0.9	18.2
1989	8.3	1.9	6.7	0.6	0.9	18.4
1990	8.1	1.6	6.6	0.6	1.0	18.0
1991	7.9	1.7	6.7	0.7	0.9	17.8
1992	7.6	1.6	6.6	0.7	0.9	17.5
1993	7.8	1.8	6.5	0.7	0.8	17.6
1994	7.8	2.0	6.6	0.8	0.8	18.1
1995	8.1	2.1	6.6	0.8	0.9	18.5
1996	8.5	2.2	6.6	0.7	0.8	18.9
1997	9.0	2.2	6.6	0.7	0.8	19.3
1998	9.6	2.2	6.6	0.7	0.9	20.0
1999	9.6	2.0	6.7	0.8	0.9	20.0
2000	10.3	2.1	6.7	0.7	0.9	20.9
2001	9.9	1.5	6.9	0.7	0.9	19.8
2002	8.3	1.4	6.7	0.6	0.8	17.8
2003	7.3	1.2	6.6	0.6	0.7	16.4
2004	7.0	1.6	6.3	0.6	0.7	16.3
2005	7.6	2.3	6.5	0.6	0.7	17.6
2006	8.0	2.7	6.4	0.6	0.8	18.5
2007	8.5	2.7	6.4	0.5	0.7	18.8
2008	8.1	2.1	6.3	0.5	0.8	17.7

NOTE: The Social Insurance category includes Social Security, Medicare, railroad and other retirement programs, and unemployment insurance. The Other category principally includes estate and gift taxes and customs duties.

SOURCE: Office of Management and Budget, *Historical Tables, Budget of the United States Government: Fiscal Year 2010* (Washington, D.C.: U.S. Government Printing Office, 2009). Table 2.3

Fiscal 2007 Continuing Resolution

Before appropriators could start work on the spending bills for fiscal 2008, they had to clear out the unfinished fiscal 2007 bills left over from the previous Congress. Thirteen

Cabinet departments and numerous agencies were operating under a stopgap spending bill that would expire Feb. 15, 2007. With one day remaining, the new Democratic-controlled Congress cleared a year-long continuing resolution that wrapped together the nine unfinished spending bills. President George W. Bush signed the measure into law Feb. 15 (H J Res 20—PL 110-5).

The bill was a compromise worked out by Rep. David R. Obey, D-Wis., and Sen. Robert C. Byrd, D-W.Va., the chairmen of the House and Senate Appropriations committees, respectively. The two had announced in December 2006 that they would package the spending in a single long-term continuing resolution, rather than considering the bills separately, in order to save time and move on to the fiscal 2008 appropriations cycle.

A series of three continuing resolutions had kept the government operating since the start of fiscal 2007, with funding provided at the lowest of the House-passed, Senate-passed, or fiscal 2006 spending level. The third was enacted shortly before the 109th Congress adjourned, after Republican leaders decided to let the new Democratic majority take charge of dealing with the unfinished bills when they came to power in January. *(Details, p. 105)*

The full-year measure provided a total of $463.5 billion in discretionary funds. The Congressional Budget Office said that together with the two bills that had cleared the previous year for the Departments of Defense (PL 109-289) and Homeland Security (PL 109-295), the measure brought total discretionary spending for fiscal 2007 to $872.8 billion. That was the cap that Bush and Congress had agreed to in 2006.

Byrd and Obey set aside the unfinished fiscal 2007 bills. Instead, the continuing resolution kept most programs going at fiscal 2006 levels, but with numerous additions for Democratic priorities such as veterans' health care and education. Most programs also got additional funds to cover the cost of pay increases and to maintain staffing levels. The chairmen said they had explicitly eliminated any new earmarks. The resolution also cut more than sixty programs below fiscal 2006 levels and rescinded some unobligated balances to free up roughly $10 billion that Democrats distributed elsewhere in the bill. The measure blocked a scheduled congressional pay raise from taking effect.

Republicans sharply criticized the additional Democratic spending. They also chafed under a Democratic-controlled process that did not allow amendments.

"You forfeited any right to squawk about how we cleaned up your mess," Obey retorted.

The White House praised the package for keeping fiscal 2007 discretionary spending within the spending ceiling and for avoiding new earmarks. But the White House statement of administration policy criticized the structure of the measure and the "formulaic approach" used by Democratic appropriators.

LEGISLATIVE HISTORY

The bill went directly to the House floor, where it passed by a vote of 286–140 on Jan. 31, 2007. House Republicans complained because Democrats used a rule for floor debate that barred amendments. The characterization of the measure as earmark-free also rankled some Republicans. House Minority Leader John A. Boehner of Ohio said Democrats had included "hundreds of millions of dollars' worth of funding for earmarked pork projects." Although Obey and Byrd did not include new earmarks, the measure did not wipe out funding for projects approved in previous spending bills.

To register their dissatisfaction, Republicans forced a number of procedural votes that delayed but did not prevent final passage. In the end, fifty-seven Republicans supported passage, recognizing that a "no" vote could put them in the politically awkward position of having to explain why they voted to shut down the government.

The Senate cleared the bill by a vote of 81–15 on Feb. 14. A day earlier, a motion to invoke cloture and limit the debate was adopted 71–26. Majority Leader Harry Reid, D-Nev., then used a parliamentary maneuver known as "filling the amendment tree" to block other amendments, citing the need to enact the bill before the short-term continuing resolution expired.

Fiscal 2008 Budget Resolution

Congressional Democrats adopted a fiscal 2008 budget resolution in May 2007 that set up a showdown with the White House over domestic spending, especially for social programs such as education and health care, while also creating barriers to extending President George W. Bush's signature tax cuts.

The budget (S Con Res 21), the first written by Democrats since fiscal 1995, totaled $3.0 trillion in fiscal 2008. It allowed Congress to appropriate $21.3 billion more in discretionary spending than President Bush wanted, all of it for domestic programs. It assumed that Congress would provide the full amount that Bush requested for defense, including extra funds for the wars in Iraq and Afghanistan.

House Budget Chairman John M. Spratt Jr., D-S.C., and Senate Budget Chairman Kent Conrad, D-N.D., put the fiscal 2008 deal together. The main differences between the House and Senate versions concerned how much to increase domestic spending above Bush's budget, whether to allow tax cuts without requiring offsets and whether to call for a reconciliation bill. As had become the pattern in recent years, it garnered virtually no support from the minority party.

Democrats hailed the agreement for allowing higher spending for certain domestic priorities while projecting a $41 billion surplus in 2012, and characterized it as a crucial corrective to years of Republican stewardship. The budget "addresses our nation's critical needs on national security, education, health care, the environment, and many other areas, while also making a 180-degree turn away from the most reckless fiscal policies in the history of our nation," said House Majority Leader Steny H. Hoyer, D-Md.

Republicans condemned the spending increases, failure to address growing entitlements, and what they said would be "massive tax hikes," noting that a surplus would occur only because most of Bush's 2001 and 2003 tax cuts (PL 107-16, PL 108-27) would be allowed to expire as scheduled in 2010. The tax cuts could be extended only if they were offset with other revenue. Sen. Judd Gregg of New Hampshire, ranking Republican on the Senate Budget Committee, chided both chambers for endorsing what he called "the largest tax increase in U.S. history, billions in new spending, and no attempt to address the long-term fiscal crisis posed by entitlement programs."

Even before Democrats produced the final version, Rob Portman, director of the Office of Management and Budget, said he would recommend a veto for any spending bills that exceeded the president's request. Democrats shrugged off the White House's veto threat and Republican criticism of the budget plan, arguing that administration policies had led to the huge deficit. "They have about zero credibility when it comes to fiscal responsibility," Conrad said.

MAJOR PROVISIONS

Following are the highlights of the fiscal 2008 budget resolution.

Discretionary cap. The measure set a $954.1 billion discretionary spending limit—$21.3 billion, or 2 percent, above Bush's request as calculated by the Congressional Budget Office (CBO). It recommended that $503.8 billion of the total be used for defense, equal to the president's request, although the specific allocations in the budget resolution were only advisory. In addition, it allowed for $2 billion in advance appropriations.

Emergency war spending. The budget resolution also allowed Congress to appropriate $145.2 billion in emergency funds for the wars in Iraq and Afghanistan in fiscal 2008 and $50 billion in fiscal 2009. That would have brought the overall total for discretionary fiscal 2008 spending to $1.1 trillion, but the emergency spending did not count against the discretionary cap.

Mandatory spending. In addition to reflecting automatic annual increases to keep mandatory programs such as Medicare and crop subsidies running, the budget resolution included "reserve funds" to accommodate possible legislation to expand some entitlement programs—including $20 billion for a new farm bill and $50 billion for the expansion of the State Children's Health Insurance Program (CHIP) through 2012. Such legislation, however, had to be offset by cuts in other mandatory spending or by revenue increases. *(Farm bill, p. 514; CHIP expansion, p. 558)*

Reconciliation. One committee in each chamber—House Education and Labor and Senate Health, Education, Labor and Pensions—was instructed to report legislation by Sept. 10 that would save $750 million over six years by cutting projected mandatory funding, presumably from student loan programs. The resulting reconciliation bill would benefit from special rules in the Senate that barred filibusters, allowing supporters to prevail with fifty votes instead of the sixty that would otherwise be needed to limit debate. *(Student loan programs, p. 612)*

Taxes. The resolution assumed that $179.8 billion in middle-class tax cuts—such as the child tax credit, the 10 percent income tax bracket, and equalized treatment for married couples—would be extended without offsets. It allowed for a one-year revision of the alternative minimum tax (AMT) to limit its reach into the middle class; the cost, however, had to be fully offset. If left unchanged, the AMT, which was meant to prevent the wealthy from escaping taxes, was expected to hit an estimated 23 million more taxpayers when they filed their 2007 taxes. The budget also assumed the extension of the college tuition deduction, with the costs offset. Other Bush tax cuts, such as those for dividends and capital gains, could be extended after 2010 only if matched by comparable revenue increases or program spending cuts. *(AMT extension, pp. 118, 131)*

Budget enforcement. The resolution reinstated pay-as-you-go rules in the Senate: All tax cuts and mandatory spending increases had to be offset by tax increases or entitlement cuts; sixty votes were required to waive the rule. The requirements were comparable to ones the House had adopted in its rules package at the beginning of the session. The resolution also created a separate "trigger" mechanism to block tax cuts in the House if the surplus projected for fiscal 2012 did not materialize. *(Pay-as-you-go rules, p. 118)*

Debt limit. By adopting the conference agreement on the budget, the House triggered what was known as the Gephardt Rule, which deemed the House to have passed a bill (H J Res 43) raising the statutory ceiling on the federal debt by $850 billion to $9.8 trillion. The Senate cleared the bill in September (PL 110-91). *(Debt limit, p. 68)*

PRESIDENT BUSH'S REQUEST

President Bush sent Congress a $2.9 trillion fiscal 2008 budget request Feb. 5 that offered few concessions to the new Democratic majority. Bush proposed to squeeze domestic programs, long favored by Democrats, by holding domestic discretionary spending essentially flat, and he called for deeper cuts in the growth of Medicare and Medicaid than he had sought when Republicans controlled Congress. As in the past, he proposed devoting spending increases to defense and homeland security. He proposed an 11 percent increase in regular defense spending, plus $236 billion in emergency funds for the rest of fiscal 2007 and 2008 to continue the wars in Iraq and Afghanistan.

He also reiterated his call for a permanent extension of tax cuts enacted in 2001 and 2003, a goal that had eluded Republicans when they were in the majority in Congress. CBO released its annual calculation of the president's budget in March; its estimates were subsequently used by Bush and Congress in their budget negotiations. They are used in this account as well.

While the White House's Office of Management and Budget (OMB) said Bush's budget plan would eliminate the deficit by 2012 and yield a small surplus, CBO concluded that there would still be a small deficit.

Bush included a number of initiatives in the budget that GOP-led Congresses had rejected, such as allowing oil drilling in the Arctic National Wildlife Refuge and imposing new or increased fees for veterans' health care.

Democratic leaders sharply criticized the proposed cuts in domestic programs. They said Bush's plan relied on overly optimistic revenue projections and faulty assumptions, such as not accounting for the long-term costs of modifying the alternative minimum tax and assuming that spending on the wars in Iraq and Afghanistan would stop by the end of fiscal 2009. "We're concerned that you have overstated revenues and understated the costs, particularly war costs," House Budget Chairman John Spratt told Portman, the OMB director, at a hearing Feb. 6, 2007.

Bush called for a $932.8 billion cap on fiscal 2008 discretionary spending, an increase of $51 billion, or 6 percent, over fiscal 2007 funding, not including emergency funds for the wars in Iraq and Afghanistan. Almost all of the proposed increase was for security spending, including defense, homeland security, and international relations. The request included $504 billion for the regular defense budget, an 11 percent increase over fiscal 2007; $32 billion for homeland security, a 3 percent increase; and $397 billion for nondefense, non-homeland-security programs, slightly less than fiscal 2007 funding. The total included increases of $3.8 billion, or 11.5 percent, for international affairs, and $3.1 billion, or 8.5 percent, for veterans' programs. Some other programs were slated for significant cuts. Funding for education, training, employment, and social services, for example, would be cut by $3.8 billion, about 5 percent below fiscal 2007 levels.

In addition, the president requested emergency funding for operations in Iraq and Afghanistan—$94 billion in fiscal 2007 and $142 billion in fiscal 2008. Congress had been demanding that Bush include requests for the war in the regular budget. The administration made it clear, however, that this was only part of the money that would be needed in fiscal 2008.

Bush made his most ambitious attempt yet to slow the growth of entitlement programs, with Medicare and Medicaid the principal targets. He called for cutting Medicare by $58 billion over five years and by $232 billion over ten years, with proposed cuts in payments to hospitals and other providers generating most of the savings. The budget also proposed higher premiums for wealthier beneficiaries.

Bush called for a net reduction of $535.9 billion in tax revenue over five years and $1.8 trillion over ten years, according to Congress' Joint Committee on Taxation. The proposals included an indefinite extension of the 2001 and 2003 tax cuts and a one-year extension of the exemption for the AMT.

The economic assumptions underlying Bush's budget were roughly in line with congressional and private forecasts, although they assumed faster economic expansion and slightly higher inflation than did other estimates, particularly for 2007. Economists said the administration's expectations stemmed in part from stronger-than-anticipated economic data released in the weeks before the budget came out. They also noted, as did some Democratic lawmakers, that the rosier assumptions allowed the White House to be more optimistic about bringing in revenue and reducing the deficit. Questions about the economic assumptions were muted, however, a departure from previous years when critics suggested that the Bush administration was intentionally low-balling its forecast so it could take credit later when the economy beat expectations.

SENATE ACTION

The Senate Budget Committee approved its fiscal 2008 budget resolution (S Con Res 21) on a 12–11 party-line vote March 15 after rejecting a string of Republican amendments. The proposal, drafted by Conrad, set discretionary spending for fiscal 2008 at $948.8 billion, $16 billion more than Bush had requested. The measure also allowed for various deficit-neutral changes, including increases in mandatory spending of up to $50 billion for CHIP and $15 billion for agriculture programs. Gregg blasted the $50 billion as a backdoor effort to nationalize health insurance. Democrats countered that it was a disgrace that millions of American children lacked health insurance.

Republicans argued for concrete steps to cut the growth of entitlement spending. Conrad said he supported the concept of slowing entitlement growth but maintained that it should be done as part of a separate, bipartisan effort rather than in a budget resolution that was not likely to have much Republican support. "I don't think either party can do this on its own," Conrad said.

The committee also agreed to a two-year revision of the AMT, with the costs offset. It also reinstated Senate pay-as-you-go rules through 2017, with new sixty-vote points of order against a number of possible legislative actions: reconciliation bills that would increase the deficit or reduce the surplus; all emergency designations; legislation that would increase deficits before the Social Security Trust Fund had been actuarially sound for seventy-five years; legislation that would increase deficits by $5 billion in any decade between 2018 and 2057; and any income tax increase.

The committee defeated a series of Republican amendments to reduce the discretionary total, shave entitlement spending, or prevent tax increases, virtually all of them on 11–12 party-line votes.

The Senate adopted the budget resolution 52–47 on March 23, 2007. A single Democratic amendment, adopted 97–1, allowed Congress to use about $180 billion between fiscal 2010 and 2012 to extend certain tax provisions, including small-business and estate tax provisions and the elimination of the so-called marriage penalty, and to devote $15 billion to the proposed $50 billion expansion of CHIP.

Finance Chairman Max Baucus, D-Mont., wrote the amendment in consultation with Democratic leaders and with Conrad's backing. The intent was to unify the caucus so that a series of Republican amendments aimed at using the surplus to extend all of the 2001 and 2003 tax cuts would fail. The amendment added to the projected deficits for fiscal 2010 and 2011 and absorbed all but about $700 million of the projected 2012 surplus. Although the amendment did not require offsets, any legislation to enact the new spending and tax cut extensions without offsets would have bumped up against pay-as-you-go rules in the resolution, which required sixty votes to waive.

Democrats turned back several Republican amendments that would have assumed extensions of all of Bush's tax cuts, including reduced rates on capital gains and dividends, which Republicans contended had led to years of economic growth. Conrad maintained that wholesale extensions of Bush's tax cuts would "blow a hole in the budget" and drive it back into deficit.

HOUSE ACTION

The House Budget Committee approved its version of the budget (H Con Res 99—H Rept 110-69) by a vote of 22–17 on March 22, 2007, a week after the Senate committee acted.

The committee capped discretionary spending at $954.8 billion, $22.1 billion more than the president had requested and $6 billion more than the Senate version. The budget recommended major spending increases for veterans' benefits, education, environmental initiatives, health care, and homeland security. It included provisions for additional mandatory spending similar to those in the Senate measure, and it agreed to a one-year patch for the AMT, with the revenue loss having to be offset. Unlike the Senate version, the measure contained instructions for a reconciliation bill, requiring the Education and Labor Committee to report a bill by Sept. 10 that would achieve $75 million in savings over six years.

The House adopted the budget March 29 on a narrow 216–210 vote after turning back alternatives by Republicans, liberal Democrats, and the Congressional Black Caucus. A dozen Democrats—almost all of them conservative Blue Dogs—voted no on passage; most of them waited to cast their votes until the roll call was almost complete and adoption was ensured. No Republicans supported the measure.

FINAL ACTION

On May 16, 2007, House and Senate conferees announced they had resolved all their differences. The following day, the House adopted the conference report (H Rept 110-153) by a **key vote of 214–209 (R 0–196; D 214–13).** The Senate followed less than a half-hour later, adopting the report 52–40. *(2007 key votes p. 955)*

No House Republican voted for the budget; thirteen Democrats voted against it. Several moderate Democrats, including Gene Taylor of Mississippi and Brad Ellsworth of Indiana, cast their "no" votes with just moments left in the roll call. Taylor, who had voted for the original House version of the budget, was the only lawmaker to switch sides on the conference report.

In the Senate, Maine senators Olympia J. Snowe and Susan Collins were the only Republicans to vote with the chamber's Democrats and two independents in favor of the resolution.

The $954.1 billion limit on discretionary spending agreed to in conference was $1.7 billion less than the House sought but $5.3 billion more than the Senate proposed. Like the Senate version, the conference report also included $145.2 billion in emergency fiscal 2008 war spending.

One of the main issues resolved in conference concerned the Senate's plan to allow a six-year, $179.8 billion extension of middle-class tax cuts without offsets. The proposal made Spratt and House Democratic fiscal conservatives uncomfortable because it violated the spirit of the House pay-as-you-go rule and would use a surplus that had not been realized. But Senate support for the amendment had been nearly unanimous, and Baucus said that if it were dropped it might be tough to win Senate adoption for the final resolution.

To get around the problem, Spratt agreed to allow the tax cuts but with a "trigger" that made any legislation containing such cuts subject to a point of order in the House unless it included language making them contingent on the Office of Management and Budget certifying, shortly before they were to go into effect, that their cost would not exceed $179.8 billion through fiscal 2012 or eat up more than 80 percent of any surplus then projected for 2012. The dispute was largely one of principle. The House Ways and Means and Senate Finance committees had no plans to advance such legislation in 2007 because the provisions were not scheduled to expire until after 2010.

Fiscal 2008 Spending Bills

In their first year back in control of Congress, Democrats' quest to appropriate billions more in funding for a variety of domestic programs ran up against a Republican president willing to use the full powers of his office to hold the line on spending. In the end, the president won, but the end came only with the last vote of the 2007 session, when Congress cleared an eleven-bill omnibus spending package (PL 110-161) that accepted President George W. Bush's overall cap on discretionary appropriations. Congressional Democrats who wanted to bring the war in Iraq to a close also were unsuccessful in blocking inclusion of emergency spending for military operations in Iraq and Afghanistan. The omnibus contained one of two fiscal 2008 emergency war supplementals passed during the year.

The 2008 budget resolution, passed in May with no Republican support in the House and only two Republican votes in the Senate, limited appropriators to $854.1 billion in discretionary budget authority for all twelve annual spending bills—$21.3 billion more than the president wanted. (A reorganization of the Appropriations Committees after the Democrats came to power resulted in increasing the number of regular annual spending bills from eleven to twelve; the new bill covered financial services.)

The appropriators used the extra budget authority for domestic programs, allocating about $10 billion to the bill for the Departments of Labor, Health and Human Services (HHS), and Education. Programs scheduled for major increases included the National Institutes of Health (NIH), heating assistance for low-income households, Pell grants, and programs to improve the quality of teachers.

The planned spending levels drew veto threats for all the nondefense bills except for military construction and veterans' affairs (VA) and the legislative branch. Bush said any excess in the former would have to be offset by cuts in the others.

The House proceeded anyway, passing the twelve fiscal 2008 bills before the August recess. The Senate passed one before the recess, three more in September, and another three in October. By November, Democrats were scrambling to find some way to get past Bush's veto threats. Their main ploy was to combine the conference reports on the bills for labor, health and human services, education, military construction, and the VA bills, hoping Bush could not afford to veto veterans' funding. When the Senate rejected that maneuver, Democrats cleared a stand-alone labor, health and human services and education bill (HR 3043), which Bush promptly vetoed. An attempt in the House to override the veto failed.

That was a turning point, demonstrating clearly that Democrats lacked the votes to win a face-off with Bush over domestic spending. In December they agreed to wrap all but the defense bill, which had been enacted separately (PL 110-116), into an omnibus package.

Congress also passed a series of short-term resolutions that kept the government operating while Congress continued to work on the spending bills. The first, H J Res 52—PL 110-92, was cleared Sept. 27, 2007. The second was attached to the defense spending bill (HR 3222—PL 110-116), which cleared Nov. 8. The third, H J Res 69—PL 110-137, cleared Dec. 13.

Fiscal 2008 Omnibus Appropriations

The showdown between President George W. Bush and the Democratic-controlled Congress over fiscal 2008 spending ended shortly before Christmas 2007, when Congress combined eleven unfinished spending bills into an omnibus measure containing $555 billion in regular and emergency discretionary funding. HR 2764 (PL 110-161) cleared on Dec. 19, the last day of the session. In the end, Democrats chose to accept Bush's spending limit for domestic programs rather than leave for the year without completing work on the appropriations bill. President Bush signed HR 2764 on Dec. 26.

In total, the omnibus package provided $473.5 billion for eleven regular spending bills; $11.2 billion in emergency funding for such things as veterans' programs, border security, and drought relief; and $70 billion in emergency funding for military operations in Iraq and Afghanistan. The defense bill (PL 110-116), signed into law Nov. 13, provided $459.3 billion in discretionary spending for defense programs. Another war supplemental had cleared in May. *(Details, p. 116)*

Democrats began the year planning to add funds for domestic programs they argued had withered during the first six years of the Bush administration, when the GOP-dominated Congress directed most funding boosts to defense and homeland security programs. Bush, however, threatened to veto appropriations bills if they exceeded his bottom-line total of $933 billion in discretionary spending for all twelve regular appropriations bills, including defense. The Democrats' original budget plan called for $23 billion more than that, and they worked all year to build support for their spending bills. In late fall, as the White House stood firm, the Democrats began considering legislative moves they hoped could prompt Bush to sign legislation with funding boosts for at least some of their top priorities, including education and health programs.

That strategy failed, however, in November, when Democrats tried to combine the spending bill for the Departments of Labor, Health and Human Services (HHS), and Education with the spending bill for military construction and veterans' affairs. The Democrats hoped that public support for veterans and health care would make it politically difficult for Bush to veto the labor, health and human services, and education bill, which was $10 billion over the president's budget. Senate Republicans objected to combining the two measures, and a stand-alone labor, health and human services, and education bill was sent to the president, who promptly vetoed it. The House failed to override the veto, and the Democrats decided to back down. Although they stayed within the president's spending caps, they were able to steer some funding to their chief priorities by paring money from other programs, by putting some spending in emergency measures that did not count against the spending caps, and by using tactics to redirect funding to favored programs.

The omnibus also represented a last, unsuccessful attempt in 2007 by congressional Democrats to force the president to bring an end to the war in Iraq. Repeated efforts during the year to put constraints on the president's conduct of the war had failed. A White House request that Congress add $70 billion in emergency funding for the wars in Afghanistan and Iraq to the omnibus gave Democratic leaders one more chance to show their opposition to the war. The drama began in the House, which passed HR 2764 on Dec. 17 by adopting an amendment adding ten other regular spending bills to the State-foreign operations appropriations measure and adopting another amendment, 206–201, that would add $31 billion for the war in Afghanistan and bar any use of that money for the war in Iraq.

In the Senate, however, all but one Republican and almost half of the Democrats who voted refused to go along with the House and instead on Dec.18 by a **key vote of 70–25 (R 48–1; D 21–23; I 1–1)** substituted a $70 billion unrestricted appropriation for use in both Iraq and Afghanistan. *(2007 key votes, p. 955)*

The Senate action put House Democrats in the untenable position of insisting on their approach—and risking that there would be no full-year appropriations for most federal activities and limiting their ability to influence at least some spending priorities for nondefense programs—or allowing the Senate, House Republicans, and the president to prevail. Consequently, in the final roll call of the year, the House cleared the omnibus spending bill as amended by the Senate, with almost all Republicans and a third of the Democrats voting "yes." The Dec. 19 **key vote was 272–142 (R 194–1; D 78–141).** *(2007 key votes, p. 955)*

MAJOR PROVISIONS

Following are highlights from the eleven regular appropriations bills for fiscal 2008 that were folded into an omnibus package at the end of the session.

Agriculture

Overall, the agriculture section of the omnibus spending bill appropriated $91 billion for the Agriculture Department and the Food and Drug Administration, $10.1 billion below the fiscal 2007 level but $1.2 billion over the president's request. The appropriators included $18.1 billion in discretionary spending, mainly for nutrition, food safety, and conservation programs, plus an additional $1 billion in emergency spending for child nutrition programs and for farmers who lost crops to floods. The other 80 percent of the bill was for mandatory accounts, such as farm subsidies and nutrition programs.

Lawmakers dropped from the final bill two provisions that would almost certainly have drawn a veto. One, contained in the House-passed bill (HR 3161—H Rept 110-258), would have allowed individuals, pharmacies, and wholesalers to import prescription drugs from Canada and other countries. The other, added to the Senate committee bill (S 1859—S Rept 110-134), would have allowed travel to Cuba for agricultural purposes. *(Drug imports, pp. 556, 578; Travel to Cuba, pp. 294, 324)*

Commerce-Justice-Science

The commerce-justice-science portion of the omnibus provided $53.7 billion for fiscal 2008, which exceeded the fiscal 2007 appropriation by 2 percent and Bush's request by almost as much. The bill included $51.8 billion in discretionary spending, and $286 million in emergency funds for border and cybersecurity. It did not include $1 billion in emergency spending for NASA to make up for shortfalls caused by the explosion of the space shuttle *Columbia* in 2003. The final version also omitted Senate language that would have barred the Equal Employment Opportunity Commission from taking legal action against organizations with an English-only work rule. Members of the Congressional Hispanic Caucus objected to the provision, as well as to language also dropped from the omnibus that would have extended an exemption from the national cap in H-2B visas for returning seasonal workers. Members of the caucus said they preferred to deal with the issue as part of a broader bill overhauling immigration policy (that bill died in June 2007). *(Immigration legislation, pp. 686, 711)*

Both the House and Senate passed versions of the commerce-justice-science spending measure (HR 3093—H Rept 110-240; S 1745—S Rept 110-124), but the dispute over the immigration-related provisions prevented further action on the measure, and it was ultimately folded into the omnibus.

Energy-Water

The energy-water portion of the omnibus appropriated $31.5 billion for the Energy Department, the Army Corps of Engineers, and other agencies. That was $579 million more than Bush requested, but about $600 million less than the House had approved in July (HR 2641—H Rept 110-185, Parts 1 and 2). The Senate Appropriations Committee approved a $32.8 billion version (S 1751—S Rept 110-127) in June, but the full Senate never acted.

Major differences between the two chambers and between Congress and the president came over nuclear energy and weapons programs. The omnibus provided $179 million for the Global Nuclear Energy Partnership, a White House initiative for expanding nuclear energy internationally and securing the world's nuclear fuel supply. The amount was less than half the $405 million Bush had requested. The final version also gave Bush less than he requested for the Energy Department's nuclear weapons program and for basic research into technologies for recycling nuclear waste into fuel for a new generation of reactors.

Financial Services

The financial services section of the omnibus provided $20.6 billion in discretionary spending, $1.1 billion less than Bush had requested. Counting mandatory spending, much of it for federal employee retirement plans, the total came to $43.3 billion. Several controversial riders in the House-passed bill (HR 2829—H Rept 110-207) were also dropped from the omnibus, including one that would have blocked the Treasury Department from enforcing a rule, adopted in 2005, that limited agricultural sales to Cuba. The omnibus retained a policy change that allowed the District of Columbia to use city dollars to fund a needle-exchange program to combat the spread of HIV. About one in twenty D. C. residents was HIV-positive.

The Senate Appropriation Committee approved its version of the bill (S Rept 110-129), but the full Senate never acted. The bill was a result of a restructuring of the Appropriations committees at the beginning of the 110th Congress; it included funding for the Treasury Department, the federal judiciary, the White House executive offices, various other federal agencies, and the District of Columbia.

Homeland Security

Both chambers passed homeland security spending bills before the August recess, but further action stalled in the face of White House warnings that Bush would veto them because of their spending levels. The spending totals in the House- and Senate-passed bills (HR 2638—H Rept 110-181; S 1644—S Rept 110-84) were about the same, except that the Senate bill also contained emergency spending of $3 billion for border security that did not count against the spending limits. The final version incorporated into the omnibus cut the discretionary total for homeland security to $35.1 billion, just $606 million more than Bush had requested, but it kept $2.7 billion in emergency funds for border security. Combined with mandatory spending, that brought the grand total to $38.7 billion.

The omnibus contained several policy riders, including a provision delaying a requirement that U.S. citizens carry passports for land and sea travel to Canada, Mexico, the Caribbean, and Bermuda. Another provision required the Homeland Security Department to regulate the production, sale, and purchase of ammonium nitrate, a common component of fertilizer that could be used to make explosives, including the bomb that killed 168 people in Oklahoma City in 1995. The omnibus also allowed states to impose tougher security regulations on chemical plants than those enforced by the federal government, a provision opposed by the White House. *(Passports, p. 225; Ammonium nitrate, p. 259; Chemical plant regulations, p. 260)*

Interior-Environment

The omnibus contained $26.9 billion in fiscal 2008 spending for the Interior Department, the Environmental Protection Agency, the U.S. Forest Service, and various other agencies. That was about $1.2 billion more than Bush had requested, but less than the $27.6 billion the House has passed (HR 2643—H Rept 110-187) and the $27.2 billion approved by the Senate Appropriations Committee (S 1696—S Rept 110-91).

On policy issues, the omnibus omitted language from the House bill that would have forced oil and natural gas companies to renegotiate leases for which they were granted royalty relief in the 1990s. The intent was to restore revenue to taxpayers now that fuel prices were much higher, but the White House strongly opposed the provision. Appropriators also dropped a provision from the House-passed bill that would have provided $50 million for a new commission on climate-change mitigation and adaptation. The omnibus retained House language expressing the sense of Congress in support of mandatory limits on greenhouse gas emissions.

Labor-HHS-Education

The Democratic challenge to Bush's spending limits came to a climax over the fiscal 2008 spending bill (HR 3043—H Rept 231; S 1710—S Rept 110-424) for the Departments of Labor, Health and Human Services, and Education in November, but Bush vetoed it because it exceeded his discretionary spending request by nearly $10 billion. The bill, which is often considered a legislative hassle no matter which party controls Congress, glided to passage in 2007 with bipartisan support, in part because the Democratic authors of the bill took steps to defuse several potential GOP objections before they could arise. One of the more important of these was a provision removed from the original Senate committee version that would have expanded federal funding for embryonic stem cell research; Bush had threatened to veto any measure that carried such a provision. *(Stem cell research, pp. 542, 573)*

Still the final version was $9.8 billion over Bush's request, and he vetoed it as promised. The House Nov.15, 2007, rejected the motion to override the veto on a **key vote of 277–141 (R 51–141; D 226–0).** Although the tally fell just two votes short of the two-thirds majority needed for an override, the vote made clear that the Democrats could not win their battle with Bush on raising the overall amount of discretionary spending for the year. *(2007 key votes, p. 955)*

A slimmed-down version included in the omnibus still contained more money than Bush wanted and favored Democratic priorities. The version of the bill that became law appropriated $600.1 billion, including $144.8 billion in regular discretionary funds—$3.9 billion more than Bush had requested but only $320 million more than fiscal 2007 spending. Democrats rejected cuts proposed by Bush to several programs, including special education grants, the National Institutes of Health, teacher quality programs, and Pell college tuition grants.

Legislative Branch

Lawmakers included $4 billion for legislative branch operations in the omnibus fiscal 2008 spending measure. The House passed its version of the measure (HR 2771—H Rept 110-198) in June, but the full Senate never acted on the Senate committee version (S 1686—S Rept 110-89). The omnibus version included $3.9 million to fund elements of a "Greening of the Capitol" initiative pushed by House Speaker Nancy Pelosi, D-Calif., aimed at reducing the Capitol's complex carbon footprint. The legislation also created an inspector general to oversee the Office of the Architect of the Capitol, which was managing the construction of the beleaguered Capitol Visitor Center, a cavernous underground addition that was plagued by delays and cost overruns. *(Capitol Visitor Center, pp. 821, 837)*

Military Construction–Veterans Affairs

The military construction and VA fiscal 2008 spending bill (HR 2642—H Rept 110-186; S 1645—S Rept 110-85) was incorporated into the omnibus after Democrats tried unsuccessfully to join the stand-alone bill with the labor, health and human services, and education appropriations bill in hopes of making it difficult for Bush to veto the latter bill, which contained nearly $10 billion more than he had requested. The House adopted the combined conference report (H Rept 110-424), but the Senate objected and stripped out the military construction and VA portion. The stand-alone labor, health and human services, and education bill was then cleared and sent to the president, who vetoed it. Trimmed-down versions of both measures were then rolled into the omnibus.

The omnibus provided $108.4 billion for military construction and veterans' affairs, including $3.9 billion in emergency funding for the VA that Bush could spend if he chose. Democrats had pushed all year to boost funding for the VA, but the White House said the president would not accept the additional funding unless Congress offset it with cuts in discretionary spending elsewhere in the budget. Democrats made the funding "contingency emergency" spending, which did not count against the discretionary caps and would be spent only if Bush requested it. He did so on Jan. 18, 2008. Counting the emergency funding, the Veterans' Health Administration received $37.2 billion in fiscal 2008 funding, $2.6 billion more than the president's request. Most of the additional funding was for VA health care accounts, including medical and prosthetic research, medical services for injured and ill veterans, and construction of new medical facilities. The bill offset some of those increases by cutting back on the military construction portion of the bill, notably by taking money out of the Base Realignment and Closure account.

In addition to the VA funding in the omnibus bill, Congress included $3.6 billion for veterans' health programs in the year-long continuing resolution (PL 110-5), which took the place of nine unfinished fiscal 2007 appropriations bills. The VA also received $1.8 billion as part of the Iraq War supplemental (PL 110-28) enacted in May 2007. *(Continuing resolution, p. 107; War supplemental, p. 117)*

State and Foreign Operations

The final version of the fiscal 2008 State-foreign operations bill, which served as the vehicle for the omnibus, totaled $35.3 billion, 3 percent more than either chamber recommended and about 1 percent more than Bush proposed. Appropriators were able to do that by designating $2.4 billion of the total as emergency spending not subject to the caps on discretionary spending. That trimmed discretionary spending to $32.8 billion, 4 percent less than in either chamber's bill and 6 percent less than the president's request. Democrats cut the president's request for his signature foreign aid program, the Millennium Challenge Corporation in half, from $3 billion to $1.5 billion. The program used the funds to reward developing counties that adopted democratic and open-market institutions.

To avert a veto, appropriators dropped language to loosen the so-called Mexico City restrictions, which barred federal money to groups that provide or promote abortion. The final bill also barred contracts with the Iraqi government to establish permanent U.S. military bases in Iraq, and it prohibited the use of money in the bill to "support or justify the use of torture, cruel or inhumane treatment by any official or contract employee of the United States government." *(Mexico City policy, pp. 284, 287, 314; Iraq war policy, pp. 270, 303; Debate on torture, pp. 364, 399, 724)*

The House passed HR 2764 (H Rept 110-197) in June, and the Senate passed an amended version (S Rept 110-128) in September. The texts of the other ten regular spending bills were then added, and the omnibus measure was eventually cleared for the president on Dec. 19.

Transportation-HUD

The final version of the fiscal 2008 spending bill for the Departments of Transportation and Housing and Urban Development, included in the omnibus bill, totaled $103.6 billion, including $48.9 billion in discretionary funding—about $2 billion less than conferees had agreed to in November but $2.2 billion over fiscal 2007 spending. Much of the increase was for the highway program. The omnibus also provided $1 billion for bridge repair and inspections and $195 million in emergency funding to help fix the I-35 bridge in Minnesota that collapsed in August 2007. Funding for the controversial Amtrak passenger rail system remained at fiscal 2007 funding levels, as did funding for HOPE VI, the public housing replacement program, which Bush wanted to eliminate. The bill also contained language preventing the administration from proceeding with a controversial program allowing up to 100 Mexican trucking companies to operate vehicles more than twenty-five miles inside the U.S. border.

The House passed its original version of the bill (HR 3074—H Rept 110-238) in July, and the Senate acted on its version (S 1789—S Rept110-131) in September. The House adopted the conference report on HR 3074 (H Rept 110-446) in November, but the final measure was not cleared until after it was made part of the omnibus.

Fiscal 2008 Defense Appropriations

The $460.3 billion fiscal 2008 defense appropriations bill (HR 3222—PL 110-116) was the only annual spending measure enacted separately rather than as part of the omnibus package. Not counting emergency fiscal 2008 funds, discretionary funding in the bill totaled $459.3 billion, which was about 1 percent less than President George W. Bush had requested but about 9 percent more than comparable fiscal 2007 spending.

The bill contained $11.6 billion in emergency funding for mine-resistant vehicles to protect troops in Iraq from improvised explosive devices. Democratic leaders did not include $196.4 billion in emergency fiscal 2008 funds that Bush requested for operations in Iraq and Afghanistan, preferring to consider them separately. Whether to include supplemental funding for the war in Iraq was hotly debated within the Democratic leadership. Most Democrats were reluctant to approve additional money for the war unless it was accompanied by major changes in policy, including firm withdrawal dates. As a result, the conferees decided to postpone consideration of the Iraq funding, easing passage of the basic defense spending bill. *(War supplementals, this page)*

HR 3222 also carried the second continuing appropriations resolution (CR) for fiscal 2008 enacted since Oct. 1, 2007, the start of the fiscal year. Attached to the conference report, the CR funded the government through Dec. 14, 2008. It included a provision to allow the Pentagon to spend prorated portions of a $70 billion bridge fund for Iraq operations that had been included in the fiscal 2007 defense spending bill (PL 109-289). It also included emergency appropriations of $3 billion to assist housing for victims of hurricanes Katrina and Rita, $2.9 billion for the Federal Emergency Management Agency, and $500 million for wildfire suppression.

Congress rearranged some of Bush's spending priorities. The bill provided more than requested for combat equipment depleted in Iraq, for operational training, for National Guard and reserve battle gear, and for more support services for military families. To offset those increases, the measure provided 11 percent less than requested for the Army's next generation of combat vehicles and weapons and 4 percent less for missile defense.

For the basic defense budget, not counting emergency funding, the bill provided $140.1 billion for operations and maintenance, $105.3 billion for personnel; $98.2 billion for weapons procurement, $77.3 billion for research and development, and $23.5 billion for the Defense Health Program.

AIRLINES WIN HELP WITH PENSION PAYMENTS

The fiscal 2007 emergency spending supplemental for costs related to the conflicts in Iraq and Afghanistan (HR 2206—PL 110-28) included several technical changes to the 2006 pension overhaul (PL 109-280), the most significant of which was requested by American and Continental airlines. The changes gave the air carriers seventeen years to fund their pension plans instead of ten and allowed them to use a different interest-rate calculation that allowed them to add less money to their plans than previously required. *(2005 pension overhaul, pp. 654, 658)*

The changes put the two airlines on the same footing as Delta and Northwest airlines, both of which had filed for bankruptcy protection. Lawmakers from Texas, home to American and Continental, backed the provision.

Once leaders postponed debate on Iraq war funding, action on the defense spending measure went relatively smoothly. The House passed its version of HR 3222 (H Rept 110-279) 395–13 on Aug. 5. The Senate passed an amended version (S Rept 110-155) by voice vote on Oct. 3, 2007.

With little difference in funding levels in the two versions, negotiations on the final version were not difficult. In addition, conferees effectively shifted billions from the base defense bill to a future supplemental bill to help meet overall spending limits. Conferees reached agreement on a bill Nov. 6. The House adopted the conference report (H Rept 110-434) by a vote of 400–15, and the Senate cleared the bill by voice vote later that day. President Bush signed it into law on Nov. 13.

War Supplementals

Despite the protests of many Democrats, Congress in 2007 cleared two emergency appropriations bills for the wars in Iraq and Afghanistan. The first, a $120 billion fiscal 2007 supplemental, was enacted in May after the House failed to override Bush's veto of a supplemental that contained deadlines for withdrawing troops from Iraq. The second, which provided a $70 billion "bridge" fund, cleared on the last day of the session as part of an eleven-bill omnibus appropriations package for fiscal 2008 (PL 110-161). According to the Congressional Research Service, the two supplementals brought the total cost of the two conflicts and related antiterrorism operations since Sept. 11, 2001, to $700 billion. *(Omnibus spending bill, p. 112)*

The first supplemental also carried several unrelated provisions, including a long-sought Democratic priority to raise the federal minimum wage to $7.25 an hour, from $5.15 an hour, over two years, and a $4.84 billion package of business tax cuts that were fully offset. *(Minimum wage, p. 664, Tax cuts, p. 120)*

Democrats became the majority party in both chambers of the 110th Congress in part on the strength of their campaign pledge to end U.S. military involvement in Iraq. But the party did not have the sixty votes in the Senate necessary for cutting off filibusters, and most Republicans either supported the war or were reluctant to buck President George W. Bush on the issue. As a result, Democratic efforts to constrain the war effort were largely unsuccessful in 2007.

FIRST WAR SUPPLEMENTAL

The main battle came on Bush's request for $103.1 billion in fiscal 2007 emergency supplemental funding. Of that, $91.6 billion was for the wars in Iraq and Afghanistan, $8 billion was for related homeland security activities, and $3.4 billion was for rebuilding efforts in Gulf Coast areas ravaged by Hurricane Katrina and other storms in 2005. Moving quickly, a divided Congress cleared a supplemental measure (HR 1591) on April 26 that provided about $20 billion more than requested, including $95.5 billion for the two military operations, $16.9 billion for hurricane relief, and additional funding for a variety of unrequested items such as disaster aid for farmers and money for children's health insurance and wildfire control.

In addition, the bill would have required the Pentagon to begin redeploying U.S. troops from Iraq by Oct. 1—earlier if the president did not certify that Iraq was making progress in meeting a series of benchmarks such as quelling sectarian violence, sharing oil revenue, and holding local elections. The goal was to complete the redeployment within 180 days, with U.S. forces continuing in only limited roles.

Bush had made it clear from the outset that he would not accept a bill that contained deadlines for withdrawing troops from Iraq, and he vetoed HR 1591 on May 1, within hours of receiving it, citing the withdrawal language, limits on remaining troops, and what he called "billions of dollars of non-emergency spending."

After falling sixty-two votes short of the two-thirds majority required to override the veto, House Democratic leaders quickly introduced and passed a new bill (HR 2206) that would have appropriated the war funds requested by the president but fenced off more than half the money until July. Release of those funds would have been contingent on Bush certifying that the Iraqi government had met certain benchmarks, followed by a vote of approval in both chambers.

Not eager to provoke a second veto, the Senate stripped the House-passed measure of all its provisions, substituted language expressing support for U.S. troops, and sent it back to the House as a placeholder for further negotiations. Under pressure to send the president a funding bill by Memorial Day, House leaders gave up trying to tie the funding to developments in Iraq. Instead, the House substituted a two-part compromise version of the bill that set no deadlines. The Senate cleared the amended bill and sent it to the president, who signed it into law (PL 110-28) on May 25. *(Iraq war debate, pp. 270, 303)*

MAJOR FUNDING PROVISIONS

Major funding components of HR 2206—PL 110-28 follow. *(Minimum wage provisions, p. 664; Tax provisions, p. 120; Airline help, box, p. 116)*

Iraq. Required the president to report to Congress by July 15 and Sept. 15, 2007, on the Iraqi government's progress in meeting a series of eighteen "benchmarks" and goals, based on objectives that Bush outlined Jan. 10 in a speech announcing a "surge" in U.S. forces in Iraq. The president was allowed, but not required, to withhold U.S. reconstruction aid if the objectives were not met.

The benchmarks included adoption of a broadly accepted hydrocarbon law that equitably shared oil revenue among all Iraqis; passage of legislation necessary to conduct provincial and local elections, a revision of Iraqi laws governing the de-Bathification process, and allocation and initial expenditure, on any equitable basis, of $10 billion in Iraqi revenues for reconstruction projects, including delivery of essential services.

Defense. Appropriated $94.7 billion for Pentagon activities in support of military operations, mainly in Iraq but also in Afghanistan. The total was $3.2 billion, or 3 percent, more than Bush requested.

Base closings. Appropriated $3.1 billion in unrequested funds for the 2005 round of base realignment and closure.

Veterans. Appropriated $41.8 billion in unrequested funds for the Department of Veterans Affairs, including $1.3 billion for veterans' health care.

State Department and foreign aid. Appropriated $5.7 billion, including about $1.6 billion ($500 million less than requested) for economic reconstruction and State Department operations and other programs in Iraq, and $910 million ($189 million more than requested) for humanitarian, reconstruction, embassy operations, and related assistance for Afghanistan. The overall total was about equal to Bush's request.

Homeland Security. Appropriated $1.1 billion in unrequested funds for antiterrorism expenses of the Homeland Security Department, including $395 million for the Transportation Security Administration.

Gulf Coast recovery. Appropriated $6.3 billion for continued assistance to areas affected by the 2005 hurricanes; that was $2.9 billion, or about 85 percent, more than requested. The total included $4.4 billion for the Federal Emergency Management Agency; Bush had requested $3.4 billion. It also included $1.4 billion in unrequested funds for the Army Corps of Engineers for work on levees and other projects.

Agriculture disaster assistance. Appropriated $3 billion in unrequested funds for crop and livestock disaster assistance.

Other domestic programs. Other unrequested funds in the bill included:

- $650 million to eliminate the fiscal 2007 shortfall in funding for the State Children's Health Insurance Program, the federal health insurance program for children in low-income families not eligible for Medicaid. Fourteen states needed additional funding to be able to continue their program at existing levels. Of the total, $250 million was offset, bringing the net funding to $400 million.
- $465 million for wildfire suppression.
- $425 million for the Secure Rural Schools program, a revenue-sharing program that distributed 25 percent of Forest Service receipts to the states, mainly for community schools and roads.

Pay-as-You-Go Rules

After promising fiscal responsibility during the 2006 midterm election campaign, Democrats moved quickly in 2007 to establish "pay-as-you-go" budget rules, requiring that new mandatory spending or tax cuts—beyond the base budget—be offset by spending cuts or tax increases. The goal was to prevent Congress from increasing the size of the budget deficit, and the rules served their purpose for much of the year. But faced with a tight deadline and the need for an expensive bill to prevent the alternative minimum tax (AMT) from reaching further into the middle class for the 2007 tax year, the majority relented, clearing a bill that cut taxes without revenue-raising offsets.

The House adopted the pay-as-you-go restriction as part of its rules package (H Res 6) in January on a **key vote of 280–152 (R 48–152; D 32–0).** The Senate acted in May, when the rules change was made as part of the fiscal 2008 budget resolution (S Con Res 21). Both rules required Congress to offset the costs of newly implemented priorities over two time periods: the next six years and the next eleven years. Both chambers also adopted new rules to limit the use of earmarks that targeted specific appropriations to specific recipients. *(2007 key votes, p. 955; House rules, p. 828; Earmarks box, p. 74)*

Throughout the year, the rules sparked frequent and difficult searches for offsets on issues as disparate as the farm bill (HR 2419), energy legislation (HR 6, HR 3221), changes to the Freedom of Information Act (HR 1309), reauthorization of terrorism insurance (HR 2761, S 2285), and the temporary fix for the AMT (HR 3996). Democrats maneuvered carefully to avoid breaking the rules, and they survived most of the year without formally abandoning the concept. But that ended in December, when the Senate ignored the rule in order to pass the AMT bill. House members initially balked, but eventually accepted the bill and sent it to the president. *(AMT action, p. 131)*

Republicans argued that pay-as-you-go rules create an artificial straitjacket, pointing in particular to the scheduled expiration in 2010 of the 2001 and 2003 tax cuts (PL 107-16, PL 108-27). Because the budget baseline was based on current law, it assumed that the tax cuts would disappear or be fully offset if extended; either option severely constrained discretionary spending under the pay-as-you-go rules.

The GOP also charged that Congress was in many instances following the letter but not the spirit of what is also known as PAYGO. For instance, Democrats found farm bill offsets by shifting the dates when certain payments would be made, a change that did not save money in the long run. Budget watchdogs lauded Democrats for reinstating the rule but also echoed GOP complaints about the use of accounting maneuvers to technically comply with the law.

Democrats responded that the GOP had essentially abandoned the rule when the party backed President George W. Bush's tax cuts in 2001 and the Medicare prescription drug benefit (PL 108-173); those measures each cost hundreds of billions of dollars and had no offsets. The new majority also argued that Republicans had no right to complain after adding $3 trillion to the national debt during Bush's presidency. *(Debt limit, p. 68)*

Short-Term AMT "Patch"

After a year of discussing more far-reaching proposals, lawmakers cleared a simple one-year "patch" to the alternative minimum tax (AMT) on the final day of the session. President George W. Bush signed the bill (HR 3996—PL 110-166) on Dec. 26, 2007.

The legislation was needed to prevent an additional 23 million taxpayers from paying the alternate tax, which was originally designed to make sure the wealthy could not use legal deductions and credits to avoid all income taxes.

The final bill marked a serious setback for Democrats, who had to abandon their pay-as-you-go budget rules for the first time all year to pass it. Senate Republicans and Bush pledged to block any AMT patch that included revenue-raising offsets.

Republican opposition also doomed a Democratic attempt to cancel tax breaks for oil and gas companies to help pay for a package of tax incentives to promote alternatives to fossil fuels. Democrats in the Senate were unable to muster enough votes to cut off debate on the proposal and were finally forced to abandon the effort. Congress subsequently passed an energy overhaul bill (HR 6—PL 110-140) that raised fuel-economy standards for cars and trucks for the first time in three decades and mandated the use of at least 36 billion gallons of biofuels annually by 2022. *(Energy bill, p. 484)*

BACKGROUND ON AMT

The AMT was first enacted in 1969 (PL 91-172) after reports that 155 wealthy people paid no income taxes. The AMT was designed to prevent such tax avoidance. As subsequently amended, it required taxpayers with relatively large incomes and a number of credits and deductions to recalculate their taxes without many of those tax benefits. The law set a specific amount that would be exempt in calculating the alternative tax. If the taxpayer owed more under the AMT than under the regular tax, then that person was required to pay the higher amount.

The reach of the AMT was growing so rapidly that the 27 million people who would be subject to the tax in 2007 was six times the number of people who paid it in 2006. The expansion was occurring both because the exemptions used to determine who had to pay the tax were not indexed for inflation and because Bush's earlier tax cuts (PL 107-16, PL 108-27) provided larger credits and lower tax rates, reducing the amount many people owed under regular rates and pushing more of them into the AMT.

Congress routinely passed bills that increased the exemption, but they were temporary. Repealing the law was estimated to cost $872.3 billion over eleven years. The previous one-year law expired at the end of 2006 (PL 109-222). Under existing law, the exemptions for 2007 tax returns were $33,750 for individuals and $45,000 for married couples. *(2006 extension, p. 91)*

The bill passed in 2007 increased the AMT exemption for the 2007 tax year to $44,350 for individuals and $66,250 for married couples. It also continued rules that allowed taxpayers to offset their liability under the AMT using nonrefundable personal tax credits. The Joint Committee on Taxation said the cost would be $50.6 billion, all of it falling in 2008.

HOUSE ACTION

Early in the year, House Democrats, led by Ways and Means Committee Chairman Charles B. Rangel, D-N.Y., talked about a far-reaching, long-term overhaul of the AMT that would prevent the need for future patches. Rangel introduced his huge tax code overhaul (HR 3970) in late October. Estimated to cost $1.3 trillion over ten years, it included a repeal of the AMT; expanded benefits for middle-income taxpayers such as a higher standard deduction and an enhanced child credit; higher income taxes for the wealthy; a corporate tax rate cut; and an array of tax-raising provisions to make the entire package revenue-neutral.

It was clear by then, however, that Congress would have to pass another short-term bill to protect taxpayers in 2007, so Rangel also produced a one-year AMT patch, combined with extensions of a number of expiring tax provisions and enough revenue raisers to cover the full cost, an approach consistent with the pay-as-you-go rules that Democrats had reinstated at the start of the 110th Congress. Those rules required any tax cuts or mandatory spending increases to be offset by tax increases or spending cuts.

The House Ways and Means Committee approved the short-term bill (HR 3996—H Rept 110-431) on Nov. 1. The House passed the bill Nov. 9 by a vote of 216–193, without the support of any Republicans.

Democrats presented the bill as an example of fiscal responsibility, saying the government should not cut revenue without making up the difference. Republicans argued the AMT was never intended to reach middle-class taxpayers and that fixing a mistake in the tax code was not the same thing as a tax cut requiring offsets. They also argued that the tax increase could stifle business innovation and investment.

SENATE ACTION

In a significant concession to the Republican minority, Senate Democrats agreed in December to a "clean" AMT extension that dropped the offsetting tax increases and extensions of popular tax breaks. The Senate passed the amended House bill 88–5 on Dec. 6.

Senate Democratic leaders abandoned the pay-as-you-go principles they had followed all year only after it became clear that Republicans would block any AMT bill with revenue increases. Hours before passing the stripped-down measure, the Senate rejected an attempt by Majority Leader Harry Reid, D-Nev., to bring up the original House-passed version. The 46–48 vote against cloture was led by Republicans.

"What we want everyone to know is that we've tried every alternative possible to do this," said Reid, who strongly opposed dropping the offsets. "We've tried to have it paid for, which I support. We've tried it partially paid for, which I support."

SECOND HOUSE BILL

Despite the Senate action, House leaders remained determined to follow the pay-as-you-go rules. On Dec. 12 the House passed a new, slimmed-down bill (HR 4351) that dropped a number of provisions but included $55.7 billion in revenue-raising offsets to pay for curbing the reach of the AMT in 2007. The bill, introduced by Rangel, passed by a vote of 226–193, again with no Republicans voting in favor.

Senate Minority Leader Mitch McConnell, R-Ky., issued a statement saying the House vote was a "partisan dead end." The White House issued a fresh veto threat the same day, arguing that the House's "stubbornness" in insisting on the offsets had created administrative challenges for the IRS "and all but assured a late filing season and delays for tens of billions of dollars in refund checks."

FINAL ACTION

Pressured by House Democratic leaders to make one more attempt at passing a fully offset AMT fix, Reid brought the new House bill to the Senate floor. Again,

Republicans successfully resisted the attempt. On Dec. 18, the Senate voted on whether to attach the House provisions to the fiscal 2008 omnibus appropriations package (HR 2764). The amendment, which by Senate agreement required sixty votes, failed, 48–46. This time, Republicans Olympia J. Snowe of Maine and George V. Voinovich of Ohio voted with the Democrats.

The Senate's inability to pass the House-passed bill left House Democratic leaders with a choice between enacting AMT relief or sticking with the pay-as-you-go rules that Democrats had championed all session. The trade-off was particularly acute for members representing suburban, predominantly Democratic districts in the Northeast and California that were home to many of the taxpayers who would be affected if the exemption was not expanded.

In the end, the chamber chose to limit the AMT bill. On the last day of the session, the leadership brought the Senate's stripped-down version of the bill to the floor under suspension of the rules, which allowed no amendments but required a two-thirds majority for passage.

The bill passed on a **key vote of 352–64 (R 195–0; D 57–64)** on Dec. 19. House Speaker Nancy Pelosi, D-Calif.; Majority Leader Steny H. Hoyer, D-Md.; and the entire House Democratic leadership team voted against it, along with many conservative Democrats and some liberals. The coalition of fiscally conservative Blue Dog Democrats protested vociferously, calling the final bill irresponsible because it would increase the deficit. But most members found the prospect of allowing the AMT to increase the taxes of millions of their constituents too unappealing. *(2007 key votes, p. 955)*

Small Business Tax Breaks

Congress in 2007 enacted a package of tax breaks for small businesses in one of the most convoluted legislative dances of the year. The tax breaks totaled $7.1 billion over six years and $4.8 billion if the period was extended to eleven years. As required by House rules adopted at the start of the 110th Congress, the costs were completely offset.

The tax package was signed into law as part of the fiscal 2007 supplemental appropriation funding military operations in Iraq and Afghanistan (HR 2206—PL 110-28), which President George W. Bush signed into law on May 25. PL 110-28 also raised the federal minimum wage for the first time in nearly ten years. *(Supplemental, p. 117; Iraq debate, pp. 270, 303; Minimum wage, pp. 661, 664)*

Democrats had pledged in the 2006 midterm election that one of the first orders of business if they took control would be an increase in the minimum wage. The House got off to a quick start, passing a stand-alone minimum wage bill (HR 2) as the second item on the Democrats' "first 100 hours" agenda. In the Senate, however, where Democrats held a bare majority and needed GOP votes to pass legislation, leaders paired the minimum wage increase with an $8.3 billion package of tax breaks to benefit small businesses. The Senate passed the amended bill Feb. 1. Hoping to avoid tough battles on the revenue offsets that would be required, the House Ways and Means Committee responded with a smaller, $1.3 billion tax package (HR 976), which the House passed Feb. 16.

With the two chambers far apart on the tax proposals. The House tried an alternative route, inserting minimum wage and tax cut provisions into its version of the fiscal 2007 supplemental spending bills for the wars in Iraq and Afghanistan. From that point on, the fate of both the tax package and the minimum wage increase was caught up in the fight between Democrats and the White House over setting a timetable to pull U.S. troops out of Iraq.

Bush vetoed the first supplemental (HR 1591) over the war provisions and nondefense spending. Democrats subsequently pulled back from their war demands, and Bush signed a second supplemental bill (HR 2206) that carried the minimum wage and tax proposals to enactment.

SMALL BUSINESS TAX PROVISIONS

Following are the main tax-related provisions of HR 2206 (the Joint Committee on Taxation estimated the cost of the provision based on a six-year period (fiscal 2007 through 2012) and an eleven-year period (fiscal 2007 through 2017).

Work opportunity tax credit. Extended, through Aug. 11, 2011, the credit for businesses that hired certain low-income workers, including food-stamp recipients, those on welfare, and some high-risk youth. The bill also expanded eligibility criteria to include veterans disabled after Sept. 1, 2001, and some other groups. Businesses could qualify for the credit for employees hired between Jan. 1, 2008, and Aug. 31, 2011. (Cost: $2.2 billion over six years; $2.6 billion over eleven years.)

Small-business expensing. Extended for one year, through 2010, provisions that allowed small business owners to deduct an extra amount in the first year for purchases of deductible assets. The bill also increased the maximum deduction to $125,000 from the existing, inflation-adjusted deduction of $112,000. The deduction was phased out for businesses that purchased more than $500,000 of such assets over the year, allowing a greater number of businesses to qualify. The previous level was $450,000. Both the expensing limit and the phase-out threshold were indexed for inflation. (Cost: $3.5 billion over six years; $68 million over eleven years.)

Tip credit. Permitted businesses to use the old $5.15 minimum wage as the basis for calculating their "tip credit"—a credit for Social Security taxes that they paid on tips that brought an employee's wage above minimum wage. Without the provision, the minimum wage increase would have significantly reduced the credit available to restaurant owners and others. (Cost: $185 million over six years; $457 million over eleven years.)

Use of credits under the AMT. Allowed taxpayers—individuals as well as businesses—to claim the work opportunity tax credit and the tip credit against their liability under the alternative minimum tax (AMT). The provision applied to all taxable years beginning after Dec. 31, 2006. (Cost: $581 million over six years; $617 million over eleven years.)

S-corporations. Changed certain rules regarding S-corporations, which "pass through" much of their income and losses to their shareholders, who include the income and losses on their individual tax returns. (Cost: $366 million over six years; $892 million over eleven years.)

Hurricane-related tax breaks. Extended low-income housing credits, special small business expensing rules, and other tax relief for areas affected by the 2005 hurricanes along the Gulf Coast, including Katrina, Rita, and Wilma. (Cost: $246 million over six years; $239 million over eleven years.)

Corporate estimated tax payments. Shifted quarterly estimated tax payments to require companies with more than $1 billion in assets to increase their payments due for the fourth quarter of fiscal 2012 by 8 percent and to reduce their payments due for the first quarter of fiscal 2013 by the same amount. The result was to shift $5 billion in revenue from fiscal 2013 to fiscal 2012, thus offsetting the cost of the revenue-losing provisions in the fiscal 2007–2012 period. (Revenue: $5 billion over six years; revenue neutral over eleven years.)

IRA notification deadline. Extended the IRS deadline for notifying taxpayers who owed unpaid taxes to thirty-six months from the due date of a tax return. The previous deadline was eighteen months. If the deadline was not met, the IRS had to suspend any interest or penalty on the unpaid taxes until twenty-one days after a notice had been sent to the taxpayer. The thirty-six month extension allowed the IRS to collect more interest and penalties. (Revenue: $1.2 billion over six years; $2.4 billion over eleven years.)

"Kiddie tax." Increased the age of minors whose unearned income was subject to their parents' tax rate. If a child had unearned income, such as interest or dividends) above a specified amount ($1,700 in 2007) and was required to file a tax return, then the portion that exceeded the specified amount was taxed at the same rate as the parents', assuming that the parents' rate was higher than their child's. Previously the rule applied to children under age eighteen. The bill raised it to nineteen and expanded the rule to cover children under twenty-four who were full-time students and provided less than half of their support with earned income. The rule did not apply to minors who were married and filed joint returns. (Revenue: $608 million over six years; $1.4 billion over eleven years.)

Fiscal 2009 Budget Resolution

House and Senate Democrats agreed in May 2008 to a $3 trillion fiscal 2009 budget resolution (S Con Res 70), allowing appropriators to begin a largely symbolic effort to assemble the annual spending bills.

The resolution, written by the Democratic majority and adopted with virtually no Republican support, set a $1 trillion limit on fiscal 2009 discretionary spending—$20.1 billion more than President George W. Bush requested. Democrats wanted all of the increase to go to domestic programs.

A similar decision in 2007 resulted in a showdown with Bush and congressional Republicans over appropriations that the president ultimately won. In 2008, however, Democratic leaders responded to warnings that Bush would veto the bills by indicating they would hold them until after the presidential election in November, which they hoped would put a Democrat in the White House. "The president really had us over a barrel last year on the appropriations bills," Senate Majority Leader Harry Reid, D-Nev., said early in the 2008 budget season. "But he doesn't" this year, Reid continued, because a Democrat "will be the president in less than a year." He indicated that Congress could pass a short-term continuing resolution to keep the government running until Inauguration Day. *(Fiscal 2009 appropriations bills, p. 124)*

Although the annual budget did not require the president's signature or become law, it established guidelines for congressional spending and tax decisions.

HIGHLIGHTS

Following are highlights of the conference report (H Rept 110-659) on the fiscal 2009 budget resolution as adopted by both chambers.

Discretionary appropriations. The $1 trillion cap on discretionary appropriations set the amount of money appropriators could divide among the twelve regular fiscal 2009 appropriations bills for allocation to specific programs and functions. It was about $20.1 billion more than Bush had requested.

The resolution also allowed $28.9 billion in advance fiscal 2010 appropriations, $3.5 billion more than Bush sought, plus nearly $1 billion for "program integrity" initiatives to counter fraud and tighten spending. Counting those funds, the resolution allowed $24.5 billion more than Bush sought for discretionary budget authority.

Of the total, the resolution agreed with Bush's request for $537.7 billion in nonemergency defense spending, a category that included nuclear weapons activities at the Energy Department.

Deficit. The budget resolution included a deficit number of $340.4 billion in fiscal 2009, decreasing to $209.8 billion in 2010 and $73 billion in 2011 before being replaced by a $21.9 billion surplus in 2012. According to the Congressional Budget Office, Bush's budget would have resulted in a $342.3 billion fiscal 2009 deficit turning into a balanced budget in fiscal 2012. The subsequent financial and economic crises made these projections meaningless. The federal deficit for fiscal 2008 reached a record high of $458 billion, and in August 2009 the White House and Congressional Budget Office projected that the deficit for fiscal

2009, ending on Sept, 30, 2009, would be $1.6 trillion—largely a result of several emergency measures that were enacted to deal with the economic situation. In October, the government reported that the actual deficit for fiscal 2009 was slightly lower: $1.4 trillion.

Taxes. The revenue levels in the budget resolution were based on the assumption that most of the 2001 and 2003 tax cuts would expire, as scheduled, in 2010. If they were extended beyond that date, it assumed that the costs would be fully offset through tax increases or spending cuts. CBO estimated that allowing the tax cuts to expire would increase revenue by $683 billion over five years.

The resolution assumed that Congress would pass a one-year bill to limit the expansion of the alternative minimum tax, which otherwise would reach a growing number of middle-class taxpayers; it also assumed the resulting revenue loss would be offset.

Mandatory spending. The final resolution assumed $1.945 trillion in outlays for mandatory programs in fiscal 2009, which anticipated the effects from passage of the 2008 farm bill (PL 110-246). It ignored cuts proposed by Bush in the Medicaid program, assumed that funding for Medicare would follow the CBO baseline, and rejected Bush's proposed private accounts for Social Security. It also did not include House provisions that would have required authorizing committees to find savings in mandatory programs that could be packaged into a reconciliation bill.

Budget enforcement. The resolution assumed that spending and tax bills would be subject to House and Senate pay-as-you-go budget rules, which required that any legislation reducing federal revenue or increasing mandatory spending be offset by reductions in other mandatory spending or increased federal revenue. If pay-as-you-go rules were waived, it was assumed that the resulting deficit would instead be offset through efforts to improve tax collections and end abusive tax shelters.

Debt limit. The resolution set the stage for raising the statutory debt limit by $800 billion, to $10.615 trillion by the end of the year. When the financial crisis hit in September, Congress was forced to raise the debt limit by an additional $700 billion. *(Debt limit, p. 68)*

PRESIDENT'S BUDGET REQUEST

President Bush sent his last full budget to Capitol Hill on Feb. 4, 2008, requesting $3.1 trillion for the federal government in fiscal 2009. The event elicited familiar protests from Democrats who had scoffed at Bush's budget recommendations for seven years but were unable to change the broad outlines beyond minor tinkering at the edges.

Bush once again proposed that domestic discretionary spending be frozen at nearly existing levels while seeking significant increases for defense, homeland security, and foreign assistance. He called for some reductions in the expected costs of Medicare, Medicaid, and other entitlement programs. He also recommended that his signature tax cuts—the centerpiece of his economic agenda in his first term—be made permanent before they expired in 2010.

Bush again proposed cuts in a number of programs popular with Democrats, such as transportation and sewage treatment projects and local law enforcement grants. Overall, he proposed eliminating or reducing spending on 151 programs for a savings of $18.2 billion in fiscal 2009, but Congress had rejected many of these same proposals in the past.

Bush also requested some increases in domestic spending for administration priorities, such as renewal of the 2002 education law known as the No Child Left Behind Act, for which he requested $14.3 billion, a 3 percent increase, for Title I programs that funded most of the initiative's efforts.

Democrats criticized the budget for omitting several major items that affected the federal budget deficit. For example, the administration assumed a one-year provision to restrict the reach of the alternative minimum tax (AMT) in 2008. But it did not assume further limits on the tax in later years (thereby increasing potential revenue), an unrealistic assumption because it meant Congress would have deliberately allowed the AMT to affect millions of additional middle-class taxpayers. *(AMT patch, pp. 91, 131)*

Also, the administration included $70 billion for war operations in Iraq and Afghanistan for fiscal 2009 and nothing for later years. Moreover, the $70 billion was likely to be a placeholder for the real costs. In fiscal 2008 Bush had requested a total of $196.4 billion for the two wars.

Highlights of Bush's Budget

Although the White House Office of Management and Budget wrote the president's budget, Congress traditionally used the numbers that the Congressional Budget Office (CBO) provided in its analysis of the president's budget; those are the numbers used in the following description.

Discretionary spending. Bush called for a $991.6 billion cap on discretionary spending. The total, which did not include emergency war funding or disaster aid, was $37 billion, or 3.8 percent, more than fiscal 2008 spending. The request included $537.8 billion for defense (not counting emergency war money), a 7.2 percent increase over fiscal 2008; $37 billion for homeland security, a 7.8 percent increase; and $453.9 billion for domestic programs (excluding emergency funds), a $13 billion, or 3 percent, increase. A few programs were singled out for big increases, leaving deep cuts in many domestic accounts. For example, Bush proposed a 16 percent increase for international affairs and 14 percent more for veterans' programs but a 6.5 percent cut for natural resources.

War funds. The budget called for $70 billion in fiscal 2009 as partial funding for operations in Iraq and Afghanistan and related activities.

Mandatory spending. CBO said Bush's proposed changes in entitlement programs would reduce net mandatory spending by $11 billion in fiscal 2009 and $143 billion over ten years (fiscal 2009 through fiscal 2018), compared with the costs projected for existing programs. The biggest reduction—$481 billion over ten years—was from proposed changes to Medicare, including rate reductions for many of the services covered by hospital insurance (Part A) and supplementary medical insurance (Part B) programs and from premium increases to higher-income beneficiaries for Part B services and the prescription drug benefit (Part D).

At the same time, the budget included increases in mandatory outlays for other programs, such as a $126 billion increase for the refundable portions of the earned income and child tax credits going to people who made too little money to owe taxes.

Tax cuts. Bush's proposed tax cuts, which would cost $94 billion in fiscal 2009 and a net $2.1 trillion over ten years, included making permanent many of the individual tax cuts that were scheduled to expire Dec. 31, 2010. These included reduced individual tax rates, elimination of the so-called marriage penalty, a 15 percent rate on dividends and capital gains, repeal of the estate tax, and a child credit of $1,000. Congress took no action on these proposals in 2008.

He also asked for a one-year extension through 2008 of provisions that exempted millions of middle-income taxpayers from the AMT, a system intended to ensure that the wealthy did not escape paying their taxes, as well as for a permanent, modified 20 percent tax credit for business costs for research and development above a certain level. Congress approved the AMT extension for 2008 and extended the research and development tax credit through 2009 but did not make it permanent. *(AMT, tax extenders, p. 131)*

Economic Outlook

An indicator of the government's failure to anticipate the severity of the economic downturn was the relatively optimistic economic outlooks forecast by OMB, CBO, and the private Blue Chip Consensus. The White House projected 2.7 percent growth in GDP in fiscal 2008, compared with CBO's January prediction of 1.7 percent. The Blue Chip Consensus, an average of about fifty top private economists, forecast economic growth of 2.2 percent. In actuality, economic growth increased just 0.4 percent for the year, according to revised figures published by the Bureau of Economic Statistics in July 2009.

HOUSE ACTION

The House Budget Committee approved its version of the resolution (H Con Res 312—H Report 110-543) March 6 on a party-line vote of 22–16. The committee set a cap of $1.014 trillion on fiscal 2009 discretionary spending, $22.4 billion more than the president requested, plus $27.6 billion in advance appropriations, $2.2 billion more than Bush proposed.

Revenue levels were based on the assumption that any changes to the AMT would be fully offset. The resolution also instructed the Ways and Means Committee to report a reconciliation bill allowing a one-year adjustment in the AMT, offset by revenue increases through 2013. The conservative Blue Dog wing of the Democratic Caucus pushed hard to ensure that offsets for the AMT patch could move through the reconciliation process to protect it from a filibuster in the Senate. They had been frustrated in 2007 at their inability to offset the cost of a similar bill despite the pay-as-you-go rules that Democrats had instituted as evidence they would govern in a fiscally responsible manner.

The full House adopted the resolution 212–207 on March 13, after rejecting substitutes offered by Republicans, the Congressional Black Caucus, and the Congressional Progressive Caucus. No Republicans voted for the measure. The House subsequently agreed to adopt S Con Res 70 after substituting its own text, a step needed in order to go to conference with the Senate.

SENATE ACTION

The Senate Budget Committee approved its version of the budget (S Con Res 70—S Print 110-39) by a vote of 12–10 on March 6, the same day the House panel acted. The vote came at the end of a two-day markup. The chief differences concerned the total for discretionary spending and whether to require offsets for a one-year AMT fix. The committee agreed to a discretionary spending cap that was $5.5 billion lower than the amount the House committee approved. The Senate resolution allowed a one-year AMT patch without requiring offsets. It also provided for a $35 billion economic stimulus package, leaving the door open for possible housing relief, unemployment insurance benefits, infrastructure projects, and expansion of the food stamp program. Congress had already cleared a $151.7 billion fiscal 2008 stimulus bill earlier in the year. *(Stimulus bill, p. 151)*

The Senate adopted the resolution 51–44 early March 14 after voting on dozens of amendments in a marathon fifteen-hour session. All 100 senators were on hand for a lengthy string of roll call votes, including Senate Appropriations Chairman Robert C. Byrd, D-W. Va., who was released from the hospital the night of March 12 in time to attend the session.

In a high-profile debate, senators rejected a one-year moratorium on individual members' spending projects, or earmarks, although many members had previously pledged to cut the number of earmarks in annual appropriations bills. The amendment, by Jim DeMint, R-S.C., was defeated on a procedural vote, 29–71. *(Earmarks box, p. 74)*

FINAL ACTION

Agreement on a conference report was held up over an argument about offsets for the AMT patch. Senate Budget Committee Chairman Kent Conrad, D-S.D., said he did not have the votes for any budget that contained reconciliation instructions because of opposition from Maine Republicans Olympia J. Snowe and Susan Collins, whose support was necessary for the Democrats to be able to cut off a filibuster.

The breakthrough came in late April 2008, when Conrad and House Budget Chairman John M. Spratt Jr., D-S.C., reached a deal with the Blue Dogs that revenue levels in the final budget plan would reflect an assumption that an AMT bill will be offset, but that will not be put into reconciliation instructions. Under the deal, a Senate provision making room for a non-offset $35 billion stimulus package was dropped from the final resolution, and a new Senate point of order was created that could be raised against bills that are not offset and cost more than $10 billion. (In the end, the Blue Dogs lost their battle for a second year in a row, when legislation containing the AMT patch without offsets was attached to the $700 billion financial services bailout bill in October.) *(AMT legislation, pp. 118, 131)*

The Senate adopted the conference report (H Rept 110-659) on S Con Res 70 by a vote of 48–45 on June 4. Snowe and Collins were the only two Republicans to support the measure. The House followed suit the next day, adopting the report 214–210, again with no Republican support.

Fiscal 2009 Continuing Resolution

Congress in 2008 dispensed with most of the fiscal 2009 appropriations bills by punting them into 2009. Just before the start of the fiscal year on Oct. 1, 2008, appropriators packaged three security-related bills—defense, homeland security, and military construction–veterans' affairs—together with stopgap funding through March 6, 2009, for the rest of the federal government. Funding for the unfinished bills was largely frozen at fiscal 2008 levels, although a few programs, such as Pell education grants and home energy assistance, were singled out for increases. (In March 2009 Congress enacted an omnibus spending bill, PL 111-8, to provide funding for the remainder of the fiscal year for State Department and domestic programs funded under the continuing resolution.) *(2009 action, box, p. 124)*

The continuing resolution, signed into law Sept. 30 (PL 110-329), also provided $22.9 billion in emergency funds for disaster assistance to states that had suffered hurricane damage, flooding, and other natural disasters, and $7.5 billion to fund a $25 billion loan program for automakers. *(Auto loans, p. 159)*

Democrats served notice early in the year that they did not intend to repeat the appropriations showdown of 2007,

FISCAL 2009 OMNIBUS BILL

Congress closed out work on appropriations for fiscal 2009 more than five months after the fiscal year began when the Senate cleared an omnibus bill (HR 1105) on March 10, 2009, that covered spending for a multitude of domestic and State Department programs not addressed in legislation enacted in 2008. President Barack Obama signed the legislation into law (PL 111-8) on March 11.

The measure provided for a total of $1.05 trillion, of which $410 billion was in discretionary funding. It contained the nine spending bills that were never enacted in the 110th Congress. The Senate cleared the bill by voice vote after first agreeing 62–35 to a cloture motion that ended debate on the bill. The vote came almost two weeks after the House passed the bill and a day before a stopgap spending measure (PL 111-6) keeping the government in operation expired.

The earmarks in the bill—more than 8,500 totaling $7.7 billion, according to Taxpayers for Common Sense—had become an embarrassment for Obama, who said during the campaign that he wanted to overhaul the earmark process, which had come under fire in recent years because of its perceived excesses and related criminal convictions of lawmakers and aides. *(Earmark box, p. 74)*

The White House tried to distance itself from the omnibus bill, arguing that it was last year's business. "I am signing an imperfect omnibus bill because it is necessary for the ongoing functions of government," Obama said. "But I also view this as a departure point for more far-reaching change." Republicans had urged Obama to veto the omnibus, but the president defended most of the spending in the measure and added, "I also find it ironic that some of those who railed the loudest against this bill because of earmarks actually inserted earmarks of their own—and will tout them in their own states and districts."

The omnibus provided about $31 billion, or 8 percent, more than the total discretionary funding in the fiscal 2008 versions of the nine bills in the package. The spending figure was $19 billion more than President George W. Bush requested.

It also made several changes in policy that no doubt would have sparked a veto fight with Bush, such as relaxing some travel and trade restrictions with Cuba and ending a school voucher program for the District of Columbia unless it was reauthorized by Congress and the District government.

in which President George W. Bush made good on his threat to veto spending bills that exceeded his budget request. "I'm not about to waste the time of this committee or of this Congress ... with a needless eight-month squabble over numbers if the president simply intends to stick by his original budget, not changing a dollar," House Appropriations Committee chairman David R. Obey, D-Wis., told his panel in February.

Nonetheless, appropriators in the House continued to work on their spending bills until June 26, when Republicans on the Appropriations Committee disrupted a planned markup of a bill to fund the labor, health and human services, and education spending bill in an attempt to force a vote on offshore oil drilling. The move was part of a campaign by Republicans to put Democrats on the spot over GOP proposals to increase domestic drilling at a time when gas prices were rising and voters were increasingly receptive to producing more oil at home.

Obey abruptly adjourned the session and refused to have additional full committee markups. "It's stunts like this that make people hate Washington," he said, adding, "I'll see them in September on a CR," a reference to the continuing resolution. In a victory for Republicans and the White House, however, Democrats were ultimately forced to allow new oil and gas drilling off the East and West coasts. A moratorium prohibiting such drilling had been extended every year since it was first enacted in 1982 in the interior-environment appropriations bill but was allowed to expire on Oct. 1. The continuing resolution also allowed the expiration of a ban on drilling in the Rocky Mountain West for oil shale.

When it stopped working, the House committee had approved five of the twelve regular fiscal 2009 spending bills, and the full House had approved one, for military construction and the Veterans Affairs Department. The Senate panel approved nine spending bills, but none of them was taken up on the Senate floor.

To bypass some procedural obstacles, Democrats ended up using the fiscal 2008 homeland security bill (HR 2638), which had never been cleared for President Bush's signature, as the vehicle for the continuing resolution and the trio of security bills. The House 370–58 approved the stopgap spending package as an amendment to HR 2683 on Sept. 24. The Senate cleared the bill 78–12 on Sept. 27 and the president signed the measure into law on Sept. 30, one day before the start of fiscal 2009.

Following are summaries of the main decisions House and Senate appropriators made in each of the twelve regular appropriations bills before they were enacted as PL 110-329.

AGRICULTURE

This measure provided spending for the Department of Agriculture, the Food and Drug Administration (FDA), the Commodity Futures Trading Commission, and other agencies. The House Appropriations Agriculture Subcommittee and the Senate Appropriations Committee had both approved versions (House draft; S 3289—S Rept 11-426) of the legislation that included about $2.5 billion more in discretionary funding than in fiscal 2008, but no further action was taken.

Most accounts received the same amount under the stopgap law as they did in fiscal 2008, although several significant programs were singled out for extra funding.

The continuing resolution authorized the FDA to spend an additional $150 million in fiscal 2009 funds that were appropriated under the war supplemental (PL 110-252) enacted in June. Support for the increase was widespread in the aftermath of a nationwide salmonella scare and deaths tied to contaminated doses of the blood-thinning drug heparin made in China.

The Women, Infants and Children (WIC) nutrition program got a $1.1 billion increase above the fiscal 2008 level, bringing the total for WIC to $6.7 billion. The program supplements the diets of low-income pregnant and postpartum women and their children. Meanwhile, the Commodity Supplemental Food Program, a nutrition program for low-income seniors that the president proposed to eliminate received $163 million.

The continuing resolution also provided $403 million in emergency funds for disaster recovery, mainly for conservation programs.

COMMERCE-JUSTICE-SCIENCE

The fiscal 2009 commerce-justice-science spending bill (House draft; S 3182—S Rept. 110-397) did not advance beyond the committee level in either chamber. Both committees would have increased spending for the Commerce and Justice departments, NASA, and several agencies by at least 10 percent over fiscal 2008 funding. The Justice Department would have been the biggest beneficiary of the additional funding. Both committees also rejected attempts by the Bush administration to rescue or eliminate several popular law enforcement grant programs.

Legislators agreed to an increase in the continuing resolution for the Census Bureau, which was funded at an annual level of $2.9 billion, about $1.7 billion above fiscal 2008 spending, to help it prepare for the 2010 census.

DEFENSE

The fiscal 2009 defense appropriations bill was approved by House and Senate subcommittees but went no further. Instead, a compromise version was bundled—along with the fiscal 2009 homeland security and military construction–veterans affairs bills—in a short-term continuing resolution (PL 110-329) that kept the rest of the government operating through March 6, 2009.

The defense portion of the package largely followed the president's request, although discretionary funding was pegged at $487.7 billion, $4 billion less than the president requested but 6 percent above the fiscal 2008 level, not counting emergency spending. The bill met the president's request for most weapons programs, including $2.9 billion for the Air Force to buy twenty F-22 Raptor fighters, and $14.1 billion for shipbuilding, spread out over eight ships rather than the nine the administration sought. Almost no war policy language was included, although the bill called for a report on options for closing the detention center at Guantánamo Bay, Cuba, and it continued a ban on torture. *(Fiscal 2009 defense appropriations, p. 116)*

The bill increased soldiers' pay raises for fiscal 2009 from the requested 3.4 percent to 3.9 percent and added $1.2 billion to offset administration attempts to increase soldiers' fees to use the military's Tricare health care system. Congress provided $1 billion more than requested for defense health care, bringing the total to $25.8 billion.

Many lawmakers complained that the expedited and secretive nature of the process used to produce the legislation compromised oversight and accountability and limited the transparency of the approximately $5 billion worth of earmarks in the bill.

ENERGY-WATER

The House and Senate Appropriations committees approved versions of the energy-water spending bill (House draft, S 3258) in June and July, but the legislation went no further. Instead, funding for the Department of Energy, the Army Corps of Engineers, and the Interior Department's Bureau of Reclamation was extended at fiscal 2008 levels through March 6, 2009, under the continuing resolution. One exception was the Energy Department's weatherization program to help low-income families reduce energy costs. Congress added $250 million to the $200 million program, one that Bush had proposed to eliminate.

Both committees called for $33.3 billion in discretionary spending for programs under the bill. That was $2.4 billion, or nearly 8 percent, more than provided under the fiscal 2008 law, and $2.1 billion more than Bush had requested. The panels proposed similar amounts for most programs.

The major difference between the two chambers, as in past years, was over funding of nuclear weapons programs at the national laboratories. House appropriators wanted to cut the account by about $600 million from fiscal 2008 levels, while Senate appropriators wanted to maintain funding.

FINANCIAL SERVICES

The House and Senate Appropriations committees each approved a version of the fiscal 2009 financial services spending bill (House draft; S 3260—S Rept 110-417), but neither measure went any further and spending for programs covered by the annual bill were extended through March 6, 2009, at fiscal 2008 levels under the stopgap funding resolution. The financial services bill covered a diverse array of federal agencies, including the Treasury Department, the federal judiciary, the White House, and the District of Columbia. The House version approved spending of $44.3 billion; the Senate committee, $44.8 billion. About half of the spending was mandatory funding, much of it for federal retiree pension programs.

Both versions contained controversial provisions to expand travel to Cuba, including allowing family members of Cubans to travel to the communist-controlled country once a year, instead of every three years as under existing law. Both bills also prohibited the IRS from using funds in the bill for a program that allowed private debt collectors to pursue some unpaid taxes. The two sets of provisions had been left out of the fiscal 2008 spending bill in the face of White House opposition. *(Cuba travel, pp. 294, 324)*

Both bills called for a 3.9 percent cost-of-living increase for federal civilian employees, a boost over Bush's 2.9 percent increase. They also would have continued a policy set in the fiscal 2008 law of allowing the District of Columbia to use its own local funds on a needle-exchange program for drug users. Bush opposed the program. *(Needle exchange, p. 804)*

The House bill barred spending to implement a Federal Communications Commission ruling allowing one company to own both a newspaper and a television or radio station in the same market.

HOMELAND SECURITY

The homeland security spending bill was one of only three regular appropriations bills to receive full funding for fiscal 2009. It together with the spending measures for the Defense Department and for military construction and the Veterans Affairs Department were enacted as part of the continuing resolution (HR 2638—PL 110-329) that funded other government programs only through March 6, 2009.

The measure appropriated $41.2 billion for the Department of Homeland Security in fiscal 2009, $2.4 billion more than the president requested. The department was also gaining access to $2.2 billion for the Bioshield program, which had been appropriated in fiscal 2004 (PL 108-90) on the condition that it not be released until fiscal 2009. Project Bioshield was an initiative enacted in 2004 to develop and stockpile vaccines and medications to combat a terrorist attack. Trouble with that initiative led Congress to establish, in 2006, a Biomedical Advanced Research and Development Authority to coordinate research and production of vaccines for potential plagues and bioweapons. *(Congress and the Nation Vol. XI, p. 213; 2006 law, p. 226)*

Most of the additional money in the final bill was used to increase funding for state and local grants that helped governments prepare for and respond to terrorist attacks. That brought the total for the grants to $4.2 billion, about double Bush's request. Bush and many Republicans argued that the states already had received billions of dollars in homeland security funding and a slowdown in spending was warranted. Democrats said the funding was needed because states and cities were the front-line defense against terrorists.

The bill also provided $745 million for border fencing and related technology projects, as well as $404 million for shipping container security. Funding for an additional 4,361 border-protection personnel and 1,400 additional beds for illegal alien detention facilities was also included. Most divisions in the department received more funding than Bush requested.

The bill provided about 4 percent more than requested for Customs and Border Protection, 5 percent more for Immigration and Customs Enforcement, 3 percent more for the Coast Guard, and 7 percent more for the Transportation Security Administration. However, Congress also provided less than Bush sought for some programs, such as the US-VISIT, which screened foreigners entering and exiting the United States, and the Domestic Nuclear Detection Office.

The House and Senate Appropriations committees both approved versions of the bill in June (HR 6947—H Rept 110-862; S 3181—S Rept 110-396) but neither measure reached the floor, and a negotiated version was included in the continuing resolution.

INTERIOR-ENVIRONMENT

A fiscal 2009 bill to fund the Interior Department, Environmental Protection Agency, U.S. Forest Service, Smithsonian, and other cultural institutions won subcommittee approval in the House, but no further action was taken and funding for programs covered by the bill was extended at fiscal 2008 levels through March 6, 2009.

The fiscal 2009 draft approved by the House Appropriations Subcommittee on Interior, Environment and Related Agencies would have provided $27.9 billion in discretionary funding. That was $1.3 billion, or 5 percent, more than appropriated in fiscal 2008. Bush had asked for a 3 percent cut from the previous year.

The draft included a controversial provision that would have forced oil and natural gas companies to renegotiate offshore-drilling leases for which they were granted royalty relief in 1998 and 1999, costing taxpayers billions. Lawmakers had repeatedly tried to add this language to the spending bill in recent years.

The bill never made it to the full House Appropriations Committee. Chairman David R. Obey, D-Wis., halted the committee's markups after Republicans tried to amend a pending appropriations bill with the text of the interior spending bill, which would have opened a path for them to offer an amendment to expand domestic energy production, including oil and gas drilling off the Pacific and Atlantic coasts. Republicans accused Democrats of delaying the markup out of fear hat the amendment would pass—a likely outcome given voters' worries about high gas prices.

In the end, larger disputes between Democrats and the White House over funding levels for all domestic programs led Democratic leaders to put off finishing the bills until a new administration took office. The price for clearing the continuing resolution to keep funds flowing to government programs through March 6, 2009, was the lifting of the ban on offshore drilling. *(Drilling moratorium, pp. 471, 497)*

LABOR-HHS-EDUCATION

House and Senate appropriators began work in June on the fiscal 2009 spending bill for the Departments of Labor, Health and Human Services (HHS), and Education, but the measures never made it to the floor in either chamber. Instead, spending for most programs was frozen at fiscal 2008 levels through March 6, 2009, under the continuing resolution.

The labor-health and human services-education bill was at the center of the breakdown in the fiscal 2009 appropriations process that grew out of conflicts between Democrats and Republicans over lifting a moratorium on offshore oil and gas drilling and between Democrats and President Bush over domestic funding. House Democratic leaders pulled the plug on further action on fiscal 2009 appropriations measure in late June in an effort to block Republicans from offering an amendment to lift the moratorium. Democrats were ultimately forced to give in to Republicans as the price for enacting the continuing resolution. Democrats were also unwilling in an election year to engage in a veto battle with Bush over funding.

The House Labor-HHS-Education Appropriations Subcommittee approved a $626.5 billion draft of the measure that included $153.1 billion in discretionary spending, $7.8 billion more than Bush requested and about $8 billion above the fiscal 2008 law. The cost alone set the measure up for an almost-certain veto. Increases included $1.2 billion for the National Institutes of Health (NIH) and $3.1 billion above the fiscal 2008 level for Pell grants to low-income college students.

The Senate Appropriations Committee approved a similar bill (S 3230—S Rept. 110-410) with approximately the same bottom line. Senate Democrats further antagonized the administration by including a provision that would have negated a controversial administrative directive, sent to state health directors in August 2007, establishing new requirements for receiving federal funding for their children's health insurance programs. Many states saw the new mandates as onerous and lobbied Congress to step in. *(Children's health insurance, p. 558)*

The short-term funding provided in the continuing resolution froze most accounts through early March 2009, but some programs did receive increases, including Pell education grants, which went up by $2.5 billion, and the Low Income Home Energy Assistance Program, which assisted the poor with home energy bills, which also went up by $2.5 billion. A Senate provision to add $1 billion to that program was dropped from the fiscal 2008–2009 war supplemental bill (PL 110-252). There was no increase for the NIH. *(Home energy aid, p. 628)*

LEGISLATIVE BRANCH

Neither the House nor the Senate Appropriations Committee marked up a fiscal 2009 version of the annual legislative branch spending measure. Like most of the rest of the government, the House, the Senate, and other legislative branch agencies were operated at fiscal 2008 levels under the continuing resolution. The fiscal 2008 spending level was $3.9 billion; House and Senate legislative branch appropriators had informally agreed on roughly $4.4 billion for fiscal 2009.

MILITARY CONSTRUCTION–VETERANS

Providing care for the nation's veterans in wartime was a top priority for Congress, which made the pending bill for military construction and the Department of Veterans Affairs (VA) one of only three full-year fiscal 2009 spending bill completed before the end of the year. The measure was enacted as part of a continuing resolution that kept most other government agencies operating through March 6, 2009.

The spending bill provided $119.6 billion, including $72.9 billion in discretionary appropriations. The other $46.7 billion was mandatory spending, mainly for veterans' pensions and other benefits. The discretionary total was about $3.5 billion, or 5 percent more than President Bush requested, and $4.2 billion, or 6 percent, above fiscal 2008 funding, counting emergency funds.

Most of the discretionary funding above the president's request was directed to the VA, which was slated to receive $47.6 billion, a $2.8 billion increase. Counting mandatory spending, VA spending for fiscal 2009 totaled $494.4 billion. Veterans' health programs were the chief beneficiary, receiving nearly $41 billion, an increase of $1.8 billion over the president's request. Congress included $510 million for trauma and other research aimed at improving the quality of life for injured an aging veterans. The Veterans Health Administration estimated that it would treat more than 5.8 million patients in 2009, including at least 333,275 veterans of the Iraq and Afghanistan conflicts.

The bill provided $25 billion for military construction projects, about $650 million, or 3 percent, above Bush's request.

The military construction-VA bill was the only regular fiscal 2009 appropriations to come to the floor in either chamber. The House passed HR 6599 (H Rept 110-775) on Aug. 1. The Senate Appropriations Committee approved its version (S 3301—S Rept 110-428) in July, but no further action was taken. Instead, a negotiated version of the bill was adopted as an amendment to the continuing resolution.

STATE-FOREIGN OPERATIONS

Before work stopped on individual fiscal 2009 appropriation bills, the Senate Appropriations Committee and the House Appropriations State-Foreign Operations Subcommittee approved versions of the spending measure for the State Department of U.S. foreign aid (S 3288—S Rept 110-425; House draft). Funding for operations covered under the bill was extended through March 6, 2009, by the continuing resolution. Although spending under the stopgap measure was frozen at fiscal 2008 levels, Congress in June had included $8.8 billion in supplemental spending for foreign assistance in fiscals 2008 and 2009. *(Details, p. 407)*

Both the House and Senate fiscal 2009 spending bills would have provided a 12 percent increase in spending over fiscal 2008 but 4 percent less than President Bush requested. The funding levels reflected Democrats' impatience with Bush's signature foreign aid program, the Millennium Challenge Corporation, a bilateral aid program aimed at fostering democracy and free-market economies. Bush had requested $2.2 billion, the Senate version called for just $254 million, while the House version kept funding at the fiscal 2008 level of $1.5 billion. Critics said the program had been too slow to spend money and was sitting on hefty reserves.

Both bills also would have provided more funding for, and loosened restrictions on, international family planning programs. The Senate version, but not the House draft, would have overturned the so-called Mexico City policy, which barred funding for groups that performed or promoted abortions overseas. Bush had threatened to veto past spending bills that tried to overturn the policy. The Senate and House bills would also have provided $5.1 billion and $5.5 billion, respectively, for global AIDS activities. Congress would have to boost those numbers significantly to keep up with funding levels committed in the five-year, $48 billion global AIDS reauthorization law enacted in July (PL 110-293). *(Details, pp. 284, 287, 314)*

TRANSPORTATION-HUD

Like spending for most other domestic programs, fiscal 2009 funding for the Departments of Transportation and Housing and Urban Development (HUD) was included in the stopgap continuing resolution, enacted on Sept. 30.

Before work stopped on the regular spending bills, the Senate Appropriations Committee approved a bill (S 3261—S Rept 110-418) in July that would have appropriated $109.4 billion for the two departments. The measure included $53.3 billion in discretionary funds, $4.5 billion, or 9 percent, more than provided in fiscal 2008 and $2.7 billion, or 5 percent, more than President Bush requested. The House Transportation-HUD Appropriations Subcommittee approved a $108.7 billion draft bill in June that advanced no further.

Most of the mandatory funding in the bill came from trust funds, primarily the highway trust fund, which was fed by fuel excise taxes, notably a tax of 18.4 cents on a gallon of gasoline. The trust funds were then distributed to the states to be used for maintaining highways and bridges. Funding levels for those programs were guaranteed in the 2005 surface transportation law (PL 109-59). *(Details, p. 407)*

However, gasoline tax revenues were not expected to keep pace with inflation or growing transportation demands, and a shortfall of $3.7 billion was anticipated in fiscal 2009. The Bush administration wanted to borrow $3.2 billion from a small trust fund account for mass transit, but transportation advocates dismissed that approach as "robbing Peter to pay Paul." Instead the continuing resolution provided $850 million in emergency spending for the Federal Highway Administration to help repair roads and bridges damaged by disasters. Congress subsequently cleared a separate bill (PL 110-318) that transferred $8 billion from the general fund to the highway account. *(Details, p. 439)*

Much of the debate during the Senate markup involved an embattled transportation pilot program that allowed some Mexico truck companies to send vehicles more than twenty-five miles across the U.S. border. The committee approved an amendment to prohibit the department from using any money in the bill to carry out the program, which critics said would cost Americans jobs and allow Mexican trucks to skirt U.S. safety laws. The fiscal 2008 spending bill had blocked the administration from proceeding with the program during that year, but the Transportation Department had been accused of ignoring the prohibition. (*Congress and the Nation Vol. XI, p. 371*)

Fiscal 2008 War Funding Supplemental

Congress in June 2008 cleared a $186.5 billion supplemental spending bill, primarily for U.S. operations in Iraq and Afghanistan. The war funding measure also served as a vehicle for Congress to add supplemental funding for several other nondefense purposes. President George W. Bush, who prevailed in a battle over the contents of the bill, signed HR 2642 into law on June 30, 2008 (PL 110-252).

Final action on the fiscal 2008–2009 measure was hastened, in part, by warnings from the Defense Department that it would run out of funds for war operations and personnel in early July. *(Details, p. 387)*

The bill provided $161.8 billion for Pentagon operations in Iraq and Afghanistan, including $65.9 billion in "bridge" funds for the first few months of fiscal 2009. Another $24.7 billion went to domestic programs, foreign aid, military construction, and disaster relief. The spending was treated as emergency funding and did not count against congressional limits on discretionary appropriations.

Democrats also attached unrelated legislation to expand education assistance for veterans, extend federal unemployment benefits by thirteen weeks, and postpone seven proposed Medicaid regulations for a year. The cost of those provisions was accounted for separately.

Bush's request for emergency funds totaled about $183.9 billion. It included $166.1 billion for the war operations and $5.8 billion for levee reconstruction in Louisiana.

The measure was divided into three separate pieces that were treated as amendments to an unneeded fiscal 2008 appropriations bill (HR 2642). Two of the amendments dealt with the war funding and policy in Iraq; the third centered on the domestic and other programs. The tactic was designed to allow antiwar Democrats to vote against the war funding while supporting the domestic funding.

The amendments went back and forth between the chambers until a bipartisan group of House leaders reached an agreement with the White House shortly before the Memorial Day break. The House deal met the president's demands, giving him the war funding he requested without the House's proposed restrictions on troop deployments in Iraq and without a number of domestic spending items approved by the Senate.

HIGHLIGHTS

Following are the main components of the supplemental.

War funding. $161.8 billion to cover costs related to operations in Iraq and Afghanistan—$95.9 billion for the remainder of fiscal 2008 and $65.9 billion for the first part of fiscal 2009.

Iraq policy provisions. A requirement that reconstruction aid from the U.S. Agency for International Development be matched dollar for dollar by the Iraqi government. The bill also prohibited the use of funds to establish permanent U.S. bases in Iraq, and it prohibited the use of funds for a U.S.-Iraq agreement that subjected U.S. forces to the jurisdiction of the Iraqi courts. *(Iraq war, policy disputes, pp. 270, 303)*

Disaster aid. $5.8 billion to strengthen New Orleans levees and $2.7 billion for relief from floods and tornadoes in the Midwest. *(Hurricane damage, p. 787)*

Military construction. $4.6 billion, $1.6 billion more than requested, for military construction, including base-closing costs. *(Military construction, p. 389)*

Other domestic programs. $1 billion in unrequested funds for the Food and Drug Administration, the Federal Bureau of Prisons, census cost overruns, and other programs.

Global food aid. $1.2 billion over two years for international food aid through the PL 480 program, about $500 million more than requested.

Bilateral aid. $8.8 billion over two years for refugee assistance in Iraq and elsewhere, drug enforcement aid in Central America and Mexico, embassy security, and international economic support. The total was $165 million more than requested.

Veterans education benefits. Expanded education benefits for service members who had served on active duty since Sept. 11, 2001. It was the largest expansion of the GI Bill program since World War II. The cost was put at $796 million for fiscal 2008 and 2009. *(Veterans, p. 593)*

Unemployment benefits. Up to thirteen additional weeks of federal employment benefits for workers who had exhausted their existing compensation. The extension was estimated to cost a total of $12.6 billion in fiscal 2008 and 2009. *(Extension, p. 667)*

Medicaid. A moratorium on seven Medicaid regulations issued by the Bush administration that were aimed at narrowing certain services, limiting others eligible for federal reimbursement, and ending some accounting maneuvers used by the states.

HOUSE FLOOR ACTION

To expedite action, House leaders brought the measure directly to the floor, bypassing the committee stage. The division of the measure into three separate amendments was designed to allow Democrats to oppose the war while supporting other spending, but the complex strategy also gave Republicans an opportunity to foil the Democratic leadership.

Instead of voting "yes" on the war funding, as the Democrats had expected, many Republicans voted "present," forcing Democrats to rely on their own majority to adopt the amendment. But with many Democrats opposed to further war funding, the amendment failed 141–149 with 132 Republicans voting "present." As a result, the legislation went to the Senate without the core funding provisions.

The second amendment, on Iraq war policy, was adopted 227–196, with almost all Democrats supporting it and almost all Republicans opposed. Among other things the amendment would have required the president to begin withdrawing combat troops from Iraq within thirty days of enactment, required that troops sent to Iraq be "fully mission capable," prohibit troops from being deployed longer than Pentagon guidelines recommended, and prohibited the establishment of permanent U.S. bases in Iraq. It also required that U.S. reconstruction costs be matched by the Iraq government and that Iraq partially reimburse the United States for the cost of fuel used by U.S. forces.

The amendment also called for ratification by the Senate of any agreement with the Iraqi government that committed U.S. forces. This provision was directed at a status-of-forces agreement that the Bush administration was negotiating with Iraq to provide a legal basis for continued presence of U.S. forces there after the U.S. Security Council mandate expired on Dec. 31, 2008.

Finally, the amendment prohibited interrogation techniques not authorized by the relevant Army field manual and required that the International Red Cross be given access to military detainees.

The third amendment was adopted 256–166, with almost all Democrats and thirty-two Republicans supporting it. This amendment contained the expanded veterans' education benefits, together with a 0.47 surtax on modified adjusted gross income above $500,000 ($1 million for joint filers) to offset the cost. The surtax was crucial for House "Blue Dogs," forty-nine fiscally conservative Democrats, who had delayed action on the bill and threatened to defect if it included new veterans' benefits without paying for them. The amendment also contained the jobless benefit extension, military construction spending, and disaster relief.

SENATE COMMITTEE ACTION

As the House was voting on its amendments May 15, the Senate Appropriations Committee was marking up a version of the bill that added billions for domestic programs. Democratic leaders had tried to avoid a Senate markup, but Appropriations Committee chairman Robert C. Byrd, D-W. Va., insisted on putting his panel's stamp on the bill.

Unlike the House, the Senate appropriators did not attempt to stay within Bush's aggregate request totals of $183.9 billion. Although Byrd asked for restraint in the markup, the committee adopted more than 220 provisions that added both policy language and at least another $1.1 billion to the bill's cost.

The amendment funding domestic and other programs included, among other things, the expansion of veterans' education benefits; a delay in implementing the seven Medicaid regulations; even more expanded jobless benefits; and disaster relief, along with $1 billion for the Low Income Home Energy Assistance program, $1.3 billion for global food aid, and $1.2 billion for science programs at NASA, the National Science Foundation, the National Institutes of Health, and the Energy Department; funding for state and local law enforcement assistance grants; and a set of immigration provisions making adjustments in visas for agricultural and other seasonal workers.

The war funding amendment proposed $168.9 billion for operations in Iraq and Afghanistan, while the Iraq war policy amendment included a requirement that units deployed for combat be fully mission-capable; a time limit on combat deployments; a prohibition on permanent bases in Iraq; a statement that the U.S. mission in Iraq should shift to counterterrorism, training and supporting Iraqi forces, and force protection by June 2009; and a requirement that Iraq provide partial reimbursement for fuel used by U.S. troops.

SENATE FLOOR ACTION

On May 22 the Senate passed a revised version of the bill that was assembled on the floor and that left out some of the committee's most controversial provisions. The convoluted process was orchestrated by Democratic leaders in what they said was an effort to reach across the aisle and get enough votes to send the measure back to the House. The Senate never took an actual vote on passage. Rather it agreed to the House amendments, with further amendments.

In a surprise move, Democrats raised a point of order against their own committee's amendment on domestic programs, effectively killing it. Senators then agreed 75–22 to a scaled-back amendment written by the leadership that dropped much of the committee-approved authorizing language, such as the long list of immigration provisions and the funding for science programs.

The leadership combined the committee's war funding and Iraq policy prescriptions into a single amendment, which the Senate rejected 34–63. Having demonstrated that the policy restrictions could not survive a filibuster in the Senate, the leadership then put forward a war-funding-only amendment that called for $164.5 billion for the two wars. The amendment had virtually no restrictions on how the funds were spent, calling instead for a number of reports to Congress. It was adopted 70–26.

COMPROMISE, FINAL ACTION

After weeks of negotiations, and with the Pentagon running short of money, House Democrats struck a deal the week of June 16 with the White House and the chamber's GOP leadership. The bill included the president's entire request for war funding, without any of the House's proposed restrictions on the deployment of U.S. troops in Iraq. Senate leaders were not involved in the negotiations, and most of the Senate's domestic spending add-ons were dropped.

The House agreed to the compromise June 19 in the form of two amendments. It voted 268–155 to adopt the war spending amendment, which provided $165.4 billion, as the Senate had proposed. The second amendment, adopted 416–12, provided $24.7 billion for a range of domestic, foreign aid, and military construction accounts. It reduced the war funding total by $3.6 billion, bringing the total into line with the president's request. The amendment also included unemployment provisions that were less generous than either the original House or Senate versions, and it approved the expansion of the GI Bill education benefits but not the surtax to pay for them.

Blue Dog Democrats were not happy with that decision, nor with a decision to allow veterans to transfer the education benefit to family members, which was likely to add $10 billion to its costs. But most of them chose to express their opposition by voting against the rule (H Res 1284) governing floor debate and not against the supplemental itself.

The Senate did not need to vote on the first amendment because it was identical to the one senators had adopted May 22. The chamber adopted the second amendment 92–7 on June 26, clearing the bill for the president.

AMT and Tax "Extenders"

After nearly two years of skirmishing over revenue-raising offsets, Congress cleared a $107 billion tax package that extended popular tax breaks, created new incentives for the production and use of alternative energy, and approved another one-year fix for the alternative minimum tax (AMT). The tax package was enacted only after it was attached to a $700 billion financial services rescue bill. President George W. Bush signed the measure into law Oct. 3, 2008 (HR 1424—PL 110-343).

Lawmakers from both parties agreed on many of the tax breaks, but they had been locked in a fight over whether to pair them with revenue raisers to offset the cost. House Democrats instituted a pay-as-you-go rule at the beginning of the 110th Congress that required offsets for any new tax cuts or entitlement spending, and they insisted that any tax package comply.

Republicans rejected the idea, arguing that the extension of existing tax provisions was not the same as enactment of new tax cuts and did not need to be offset. Republicans were outvoted in the House, but the Democrats' narrow majority in the Senate and the need for sixty votes to prevent a filibuster enabled Senate Republicans to make their position stick. In 2007 the GOP position prevailed over Democrats, who ultimately abandoned their efforts to offset the costs of extending the AMT as well as a package of tax incentives for alternative types of energy. *(2007 AMT, p. 113; Energy tax provisions, pp. 493, 494)*

But the debate was renewed early in 2008, when the House passed a tax bill to encourage investment in alternative energy that was fully offset by repealing some tax breaks for fossil fuel companies. The fight, which eventually encompassed another extension of the AMT "patch," devolved into a procedural stalemate: House Majority Leader Steny H. Hoyer, D-Md., refused to consider any tax bill that did not comply with the pay-as-you-go rule, while Senate Republicans forced repeated cloture votes to stop House-passed tax bills from reaching the Senate floor. The battle ended only when the Senate added its provisions to the must-pass financial services rescue bill, forcing House Democrats to accept far fewer offsets than they wanted. The final bill provided about $149.2 billion in tax breaks, offset by $42.2 billion, which brought the total of $107 billion.

Three main categories of tax benefits were central to the debate and the final legislation:

"Extenders." Debate over so-called tax extenders was a leftover from 2007, when Congress adjourned without renewing popular tax breaks such as the research and development tax credit and the optional deduction for state sales taxes beyond their Dec. 31, 2007, expiration date. Some provisions affected businesses and others benefited individuals. They routinely expired after one or two years, and Congress almost always extended them—retroactively if the expiration date had already passed. The final version of the 2008 tax package did just that, at a total cost of $48.4 billion.

The extensions were partially offset by a single provision that was expected to bring in an estimated $25.2 billion by curtailing the ability of senior executives such as hedge fund managers to avoid taxes on large amounts of money by receiving it as deferred compensation in offshore tax havens.

Energy incentives. Another set of tax breaks was aimed at encouraging the production and use of alternative energy sources. Some were extensions of expiring benefits, such as a tax credit for producing electricity from wind and solar power and a tax benefit for purchasing energy-efficient appliances. Other proposals were new, such as assistance for state energy conservation projects and a tax credit for plug-in hybrid cars. The total cost of $16.9 billion was fully offset with a variety of revenue raisers, many of which targeted the oil and gas industry.

AMT. Limiting the reach of the AMT had become a perennial issue for Congress in recent years. The alternative tax was created to prevent the rich from paying minimal or no taxes, but because the alternative tax calculations had not been adjusted for inflation, the AMT covered an increasing number of middle-class taxpayers each year. In

2008 the tax was expected to reach an additional 22 million couples or individuals. As a result, lawmakers felt compelled to provide an annual "patch" that raised the exemption for the tax, thus allowing most taxpayers to avoid falling under the AMT. *(AMT background, p. 119)*

The final version provided a one-year AMT patch for the 2008 tax year at an estimated cost of $64.1 billion from the loss of anticipated tax revenue. As in 2007 none of the costs were offset.

LEGISLATIVE ACTION

Several different pieces of legislation containing various combinations of tax extensions, tax breaks, and offsetting revenue raisers bounced back and forth between the House and Senate during the year before the final package was assembled.

House Energy Taxes

The House started the ball rolling early, when it passed a bill (HR 5351) on Feb. 27 that was designed to encourage investment in renewable-energy technologies. The bill proposed $17.6 billion in tax breaks, fully offset by changes in tax breaks targeted at oil and gas companies. The vote was 236–182, with all but seventeen Republicans voting "nay."

For the Democrats the timing of a measure to spur alternative energy was ideal. Oil futures topped $102 a barrel for the first time on the day the bill passed, before closing at $99.64 on the New York Mercantile Exchange. The average price of a gallon of regular gasoline was $3.13, with experts predicting it could rise to $4 by spring. But the administration threatened to veto the bill, calling it a "targeted tax increase" that was unfair to the oil and gas industry, and the Senate did not take up the measure.

Senate Energy Taxes

Democrats on the Senate Finance Committee had tried in January to include an energy tax package in an economic stimulus bill (HR 110-185), but under pressure from Republicans and the White House, they removed it from the final version of that legislation. *(Economic stimulus, p. 151)*

In April, however, the Senate agreed to attach an $8.3 billion package of energy tax breaks to a high-profile bill (HR 3221) aimed at relieving the mortgage crisis. Unwilling to budge from its pledge to offset any new taxes, House Democrats stripped out the energy provisions before passing an amended version of the mortgage relief bill and sending it back to the Senate. *(Mortgage relief, p. 630)*

House Energy Taxes, Tax Extenders

Two weeks later, the House combined energy tax breaks and the extension of other expired or expiring tax breaks into a $54.1 billion (HR 6049—H Rept 110-658) that was fully offset. The measure passed 263–160 on May 21. Thirty-five Republicans supported the bill, but in the Senate Republicans declared it "dead on arrival."

House Republicans tried to force changes in the bill, moving to recommit it with instructions to add an AMT patch, lengthen the extension of several tax breaks, and strip out the offsets. The motion failed 201–220. Republican Jim McCrery of Louisiana said the offsets "would lead to a huge tax increase over the next ten years." The White House also opposed the bill, issuing a veto threat.

House AMT Bill

The partisan wrangling over offsets continued in June, when the House passed a one-year AMT patch (HR 6275—H Rept 110-728) that was fully offset. The bill passed by a vote of 233–189 on June 25, with ten Republicans joining virtually all Democrats to vote for it.

Most Republicans, however, said the offsets would raise taxes and hurt the struggling economy. Before passage, the House rejected 199–222 a GOP motion to recommit the bill with a requirement that the offsets be dropped. The White House also issued a veto threat on this bill, citing its tax increases.

Senate Energy, Extenders, AMT Bill

After a summer of failed cloture votes on proceeding to the House tax-extenders bill (HR 6049), the Senate voted overwhelmingly Sept. 23 in favor of a bipartisan tax package that combined the tax break extensions with energy incentives and AMT relief and was partially offset. The Senate substituted its compromise package for the text of the House bill, which it then passed 93–2.

The bill, which contained many of the same provisions included in the other bills, was broken into two parts. The first was a fully offset set of energy tax incentives. The second part combined a partially offset extenders section, which pushed expiration dates to the end of 2009, and a one-year AMT patch and disaster relief that had no offsets. The bill also included a variety of provisions designed to please particular lawmakers, including mental health parity legislation; the extension of a rural county payments program; and tax breaks for oil-shale refining, Alaska fisherman, and farming equipment. *(Mental health parity, p. 569)*

"I would hope when this matter goes to the House of Representatives, that they take [account]. . . of how difficult it has been for us to get this passed," Majority Leader Harry Reid, D-Nev., said. "I say to my friends on the other side of the Capitol, don't send us back something else. We can't get it passed."

House Four-Bill Response

Rejecting the pleas, House Democrats quickly pulled the Senate compromise apart and sent a four-bill barrage back to the Senate.

On Sept. 23 the House passed a mental health parity bill (HR 6983) by a vote of 376–47. On Sept. 24 the House passed an AMT patch (HR 7005) with no offsets by a vote of 393–30. The House then passed 419–4 a set of tax breaks (HR 7006) for individuals and businesses hit by natural disasters, mainly from storms and flooding in the Midwest. It too had no offsets. Both bills were considered under suspension of the rules, which meant Democrats did not have to formally waive the House's pay-as-you-go rule.

On Sept. 26 the House passed the most expensive of the bills (HR 7060), a $60.3 billion measure that combined about $14.3 billion in incentives for renewable energy with the extension of numerous expired or expiring tax breaks, at a cost of $42.1 billion, and some miscellaneous tax provisions, at a cost of $3.9 billion. The vote was 257–166. The tax breaks and benefits were fully offset by a series of revenue-raising proposals, which prompted another veto threat from the White House.

Final Bill

On Sept, 29, as the House prepared to leave for the election campaign, the House majority leader reiterated that he would not consider the Senate-passed bill. But just hours later, the House inadvertently handed the Senate an opportunity to emerge victorious from the two-year tax policy fight. In a vote that stunned financial markets, the House rejected a $700 billion rescue package (HR 3997) that the administration said was critical to addressing the nation's financial crisis. The bailout bill was rejected on a **key vote of 205–228 (R 65–133; D 140–95).** That moved action to the Senate, where Democratic leaders added the Senate's energy tax, tax extension, and AMT provisions to a revised bailout bill (HR 1424) as sweeteners intended to make the bailout more palatable to House opponents. *(HR 3997 rejection, p. 154)*

The Senate passed the bill Oct. 1 by a **key vote of 74–25 (R 34–15; D 39–9; I 1–1)** giving the House a take-it-or-leave-it choice. House Democrats reluctantly accepted the Senate's version as the price for completing the bailout bill, and the House cleared the measure Oct. 3 on a **key vote of 263–171 (R 91–108; D 172–63).** *(2008 key votes, p. 972)*

Fiscal conservatives were not the only ones in the House frustrated by being forced to vote on the Senate's tax package. Liberal Democrats were disgruntled, particularly over the Senate's tax provisions, which contained more incentives for coal than they wanted and provided a new break for oil-shale refining. Those provisions had been absent from House versions of the energy-tax legislation.

The House also lost on the disaster-relief provisions. The House version would have provided a consistent set of tax breaks for disaster victims from 2008 through 2011, regardless of where they lived. The Senate bill created a national disaster program, but only for 2008 and 2009. The Senate bill also gave Midwest flood victims a more generous collection of tax assistance, modeled on the legislation (PL 109-73) enacted shortly after Hurricane Katrina in 2005. Residents of the hurricane-battered Gulf Coast also got additional tax breaks beyond the national program.

Perhaps most important for House members, who carefully guarded their tax-writing prerogative, was the fact that the Senate strategy succeeded. "I hope that this Senate gamble is not accepted as some new constitutional attitude by their leadership," Ways and Means Chairman Charles B. Rangel, D-N.Y., said in a statement. "We have a process in the House. . . . Apparently, in the Senate, they just decide what can get sixty votes and insist the House follow suit."

TAX PROVISIONS

Following are the major tax provisions attached to the financial services rescue bill enacted Oct. 3, 2008 (HR 1424—PL 110-343). Cost and revenue estimates are for ten years (fiscal 2009 through fiscal 2018) as calculated by the Joint Committee on Taxation.

Alternative Minimum Tax

One-year AMT patch. Provided a temporary increase in the amount of income that was exempt when individuals calculated whether they had to pay the alternative minimum tax (AMT) rates, rather than regular rates. The exemption was increased from $33,750 in 2007 to $46,200 in 2008 for unmarried individuals and from $45,000 to $69,950 for married couples filing jointly. (Cost: $61.8 billion in 2008.)

Incentive stock options. Provided a $2.3 billion provision to help taxpayers affected by a quirk in the AMT in which many taxpayers paid taxes on paper gains from exercising incentive stock options, even if they received little cash. A 2006 law (PL 109-432) allowed those taxpayers to reclaim the extra taxes paid over five future years when they did not make enough to pay the AMT. The new law allowed that process over two years and waived penalties and interest associated with this scenario.

Energy Tax Incentives

Production tax credit. Extended the main tax incentive for generating electricity from wind and refined coal for one year, applying to projects placed in service by Dec. 31, 2009. Allowed other energy sources, including geothermal power, hydropower, and trash combustion, a two-year extension, through the end of 2010. Made energy generated from tides and waves eligible for the tax credit.

Solar energy. Extended a 30 percent investment tax credit for solar energy and certain fuel cells for eight years, applying to projects placed in service through 2016. Removed a $2,000 cap on a similar credit for residential scale solar projects and allowed residential wind turbines (capped at $4,000) and geothermal pumps (capped at $2,000) to become eligible for the tax credit.

Coal production. Provided $1.5 billion in tax credits for projects that produced electricity from coal and met targets for sequestering the resulting carbon dioxide. Required advanced coal electricity projects, to qualify for the credit, to sequester 65 percent of their carbon, and coal gasification projects to sequester 75 percent. Created a tax crediting for capturing carbon dioxide—$10 per ton if it was injected into wells to recover oil and $20 per ton if it was permanently stored. Provided producers of coal used to make coke for steel production a new tax credit of $2 per barrel-of-oil equivalent.

Fuels. Extended a $1-per-gallon credit for production of biodiesel through 2009. Extended through 2010 a 30 percent tax credit for fueling station pumps that dispense natural gas or ethanol and expanded the credit to cover electric-recharging stations. Allowed certain investments in many cellulosic biofuels, not just ethanol, to qualify for a 50 percent write-off.

Bond authority. Allocated $800 million in Clean Renewable Energy Bonds, to provide tax-advantaged financing for facilities owned by electric cooperatives, public power companies, and state and local governments that produced electricity from renewable sources. Created a category of tax-advantaged bonds, setting aside $800 million for state and local governments to use for projects designed to reduce greenhouse gas emissions. Both types of bonds provided investors with tax credits.

Refineries. Extended for two years, through 2013, a 2005 provision that allowed refinery owners to deduct half the cost of capital improvements that increased refinery capacity or that allowed certain nonconventional fuels to be processed, and added oil shale and tar sands to the fuels eligible for the refining credit.

Energy efficiency. Provided a series of provisions to encourage energy efficiency and conservation, including extensions of a tax credit for energy-efficient improvements to existing homes through 2009, a similar initiative for commercial buildings through 2014, a program for energy-efficient appliances through 2010, and one for energy-efficient new homes through 2009.

Smart meters. Allowed electric meters that provided more detailed information about consumption to be depreciated on a ten-year schedule, instead of a twenty-year schedule, giving an incentive to utility companies that wanted to deploy the new meters.

Recycling. Permitted companies that bought equipment for collecting and processing certain recyclable materials an accelerated depreciation, allowing them to recover their costs more quickly.

Plug-in vehicles. Included a new tax credit for plug-in vehicles that typically ranged from $2,500 to $7,500. The credit would be reduced after the 250,000th such vehicle was produced.

Offsets for Energy Tax Benefits

Oil and gas offsets. Most of the cost of the energy tax breaks was offset by revenue increases targeting the oil and gas industry. A manufacturing deduction scheduled to jump from 6 percent of profits to 9 percent in 2010 was frozen at 6 percent for income from oil and gas activities, raising an estimated $4.9 billion. The oil spill liability tax was increased from five cents a barrel to eight cents through 2016, and then up to nine cents in 2017, raising $1.7 billion. The law also altered the treatment of oil companies' foreign income in a way that would force higher taxes on income earned from transporting and refining oil, generating another $2.2 billion.

Securities basis reporting. Required securities brokers, starting with certain stocks purchased in 2011, to report their customers' basis, or cost of purchasing the stocks, to the IRS. (Revenue impact: expected to raise $.7 billion over ten years by preventing investors from overstating their cost basis and thus underestimating their profit subject to capital gains taxes.

Other offsets. Extended through 2018 a coal excise tax of $1.10 a ton from underground mines and fifty-five cents a ton from surface mines, raising $1.3 billion to replenish the Black Lung Disability Trust Fund. Extended a 0.2 percent surtax under the Federal Unemployment Tax Act for one year, bringing in $1.5 billion.

Business Extensions

Research and development. Extended the research and development tax credit through 2009 and modified the credit, increasing the credit percentage under an alternative structure from 12 percent to 14 percent in 2009 and repealing a different alternative structure. (Cost: $19.1 billion.)

Restaurant and retail depreciation. Extended accelerated depreciation for certain leased retail and restaurant space through 2009 and provided a fifteen-year depreciation schedule (instead of thirty-nine years for most real estate) for retail owners and new restaurants starting in 2009. (Cost: $8.7 billion.)

Active-finance exception. Allowed financial services companies that operated overseas and manufacturers with overseas financing arms to continue to treat their income as active in 2009, allowing them to defer taxes on that income. (Cost: $4 billion.)

Straight extensions. Included extensions through 2009 of dozens of provisions that benefited a variety of targeted groups, including companies that cleaned up contaminated "brownfields," owners of motor sports tracks, homebuyers in the District of Columbia, and short-line railroads.

Individual Tax-Break Extensions

Sales tax deduction. Allowed taxpayers to deduct sales taxes, according either to a formula or to actual receipts, for two additional years (2008 and 2009) as an alternative to deducting state and local income taxes, benefitting states with no income taxes. (Cost: $43.3 billion.)

Tuition. Extended through 2009 a deduction of up to $4,000 for tuition and related expenses. (Cost: $5.3 billion.)

Teachers. Extended through 2009 a $250 deduction for teachers who spent their own money to purchase classroom equipment. It and the tuition deduction were subtracted before calculating gross adjusted income. (Cost: $410 million.)

IRAs. Allowed people over age 70 1/2 to continue to make up to $100,000 in tax-free charitable contributions from their individual retirement accounts in 2009. (Cost: $795 million.)

Property taxes. Extended through 2009 an earlier 2008 law (PL 110-289) providing an additional homeowner deduction for taxpayers who did not itemize property taxes of up to $500 ($1,000 for married couples). (Cost: $1.5 billion.)

Deferred-compensation offset. To partially pay for the extensions, required people with certain offshore deferred-compensation arrangements to count that compensation as income at the time the money was set aside for them, rather than waiting until they took the money out. The arrangements, often used by hedge fund managers, were set up in countries with little or no taxation. (Revenue increase: $25.2 billion.)

Disaster-Related Provisions

National program. Created a standardized national program of disaster tax assistance to take effect automatically whenever the president declared a natural disaster, applicable to disasters in 2008 and 2009. Previously, Congress was required to pass an emergency bill to provide the tax relief. Allowed victims more flexibility to deduct casualty losses and write off demolition costs.

Midwest flood response. Allowed victims of floods in ten Midwestern states a separate set of tax breaks modeled after the government's response to Hurricane Katrina (PL 109-73), included more flexible use of money in retirement accounts, additional low-income housing tax credits, extra tax-advantaged bonds for reconstruction efforts, benefits for businesses that paid employees while they were closed, and looser rules for charitable contributions.

Gulf Coast. Targeted provisions for victims of Hurricane Ike along the Gulf Coast, including low-income housing tax credits and more tax-exempt bonds for reconstruction.

Other Provisions

Child tax credit. Temporarily expanded the refundable child tax credit to low-income families even if they owed no income taxes.

County payments. Reauthorized and funded a program of payments to rural counties with significant amounts of federal land. The payments, designed to replace a portion of federal timber revenues and help counties shift to new funding sources, was sought by lawmakers from Western states. The law allocated $3.3 billion to extend the program through 2011.

Film and TV production. Extended for one year an existing $15 million deduction for domestic film and television production—$20 million if production occurred in economically distressed areas, and expanded the deduction to apply to bigger-budget productions and broadened the criteria for companies that could receive tax breaks for domestic investment.

Farm equipment. Allowed certain farming equipment purchased in 2009 to be depreciated over five years instead of seven.

Wooden arrows. Exempted certain wooden arrows used by children for target practice from an excise tax on arrows.

***Exxon Valdez* assistance.** Allowed commercial fishermen and others receiving money from legal action related to the 1989 oil spill to average their income over three years, reducing their tax burden, and to contribute up to $100,000 to a retirement account.

Chronology of Action on Economic and Regulatory Policy

Introduction

Until very late in the presidency of George W. Bush, the term "financial regulation" was not fashionable on Capitol Hill. Members of Congress in both parties for many years had been receptive to the arguments of bankers and others in the financial services industry that government regulation tended to have more negative than positive results and should be applied lightly except, possibly, under extreme circumstances. Indeed, one of the few significant pieces of financial services regulation legislation enacted by Congress in either the 109th or 110th Congresses was intended specifically to reduce regulatory burdens on a wide range of banks, credit unions, and savings and loans.

Extreme circumstances arrived in 2007 and 2008, when a bubble in the housing market burst and led to a near-collapse of the credit markets and, ultimately, the worst worldwide recession since World War II. The most expert government officials, including the Treasury secretary and the Federal Reserve chairman, feared at one point that the entire economy was only, literally, hours away from collapse.

These broad economic events exposed numerous shortcomings in government regulations of the financial services industry at nearly all levels. Even so, Washington policymakers were so focused on pulling the economy out of the ditch—during an election year, no less—that serious action to revamp the regulatory failings would have to wait until future years. *(Economic collapse details, p. 163)*

The 109th Congress passed important legislation affecting the financial services industry, notably a major revision of bankruptcy laws and an updating of the Federal Deposit Insurance Corporation. The most important action during the 110th Congress did not occur until after the financial crisis was well under way, and that legislation was crisis-driven and carried few long-term remedies. One major piece, the Housing and Economic Recovery Act of 2008 (HR 3221—PL 110-289), essentially set the stage for the government to bail out and take over the two mortgage giants, Fannie Mae and Freddie Mac. These companies, known as "government-sponsored entities" because of their origins, had gotten into deep trouble by buying too many of the risky mortgage-backed securities that were at the heart of the financial crisis.

An even more important, indeed historic, piece of legislation emerged from Congress right in the midst of the worst weeks of the financial crisis—and just weeks before the 2008 elections. This was a $700 billion measure (HR 1424—PL 110-343) to rescue the banks that had created the financial meltdown with excessively risky lending practices.

REFERENCES

Discussion of financial regulation activity for the years 1945–1964 may be found in *Congress and the Nation Vol. I,* pp. 337–386; for the years 1965–1968, *Congress and the Nation Vol. II,* pp. 253–279; for the years 1969–1972, *Congress and the Nation Vol. III,* pp. 135–145; for the years 1973–1976, *Congress and the Nation Vol. IV,* pp. 107–117; for the years 1977–1980, *Congress and the Nation Vol. V,* pp. 253–265; for the years 1981–1984, *Congress and the Nation Vol. VI,* pp. 83–93; for the years 1985–1988 *Congress and the Nation Vol. VII,* pp. 109–136; for the years 1989–1992, *Congress and the Nation Vol. VIII,* pp. 113–161; for the years 1993–1996, *Congress and the Nation Vol. IX,* pp. 109–148; for the year 1997–2000, *Congress and the Nation Vol. X,* pp. 120–144; for the years 2001–2004, *Congress and the Nation Vol. XI,* pp. 123–144.

Although the Bush administration requested the bill and insisted it was essential to avoid a deep economic crisis, possibly even a new depression, Democrats carried most of the political burden of getting it through Congress. This was particularly true in the House, which at first rejected the measure because of near-solid Republican opposition. Congress cleared the bill on October 3, 2008, after the administration made just enough changes to win over wavering House members in both parties. In political terms if nothing else, passage of one of the most expensive measures in the nation's history—rescuing the very private companies that were largely responsible for the country's economic troubles—was a remarkable achievement. Nevertheless, the action went down poorly with a wide swath of Americans, many of whom even a year later remained deeply angry with what they saw as bailing out irresponsible bankers.

Within weeks after Congress acted, Treasury Secretary Henry M. Paulson Jr. radically altered how the $700 billion would be used. Paulson had sold the bill to Congress as a way of rescuing the financial system by buying questionable securities (popularly known as "toxic assets") from the banks, thus cleaning up their balance sheets and putting them on the road to financial health. Instead, Paulson said on Nov. 12 he would invest the $700 billion directly in troubled banks, a step he said would be a quicker and surer way of making sure the banks would survive and begin lending again. In essence, the financial crisis had resulted in the deepest government intervention in the banking system since the Great Depression—and reversed, at least temporarily, a decades-long consensus in Washington that the financial sector was most efficient and successful when the government largely kept its hands off. (Just how protean the $700 billion program would be became even more obvious toward the end of 2009 when the new administration of President Barack Obama was mulling using some of the funds that had not been spent for activities to lower the unemployment rate, which by then had reached 10 percent, and threatened the future employment of many members of Congress—mainly Democrats.)

REGULATORY ISSUES

By the time the financial crisis got into full swing in late 2008, there was broad agreement in Washington, and even on Wall Street, that the government's regulation (at all levels) of banks and other financial institutions had been inadequate both to catch systemic market failures and to prevent those failures from causing severe damage to the broader economy. Numerous high government officials acknowledged that their faith in the self-correcting nature of private marketplaces had been misplaced. Most notable among these mea culpas was a statement by former Federal Reserve Board chairman Alan Greenspan before the House Oversight Committee on October 23, 2008. Greenspan, who had been one of the nation's most prominent advocates of allowing wide leeway to the markets, said the failure of banks to act in ways that protected their own interests had deeply surprised him. He said that "those of us who have looked to the self-interest of lending institutions to protect shareholder's equity (myself especially) are in a state of shocked disbelief."

Representatives of the banking industry—including those who had long sought to ward off regulations—also acknowledged that government regulation had been inadequate to prevent systemic problems within their industry. Testifying to the Senate Banking, Housing, and Urban Affairs Committee on March 3, 2009, Steve Bartlett, the president and chief executive officer of the Financial Services Roundtable (a major industry lobbying group), said one root cause of the financial crisis was "a clear breakdown in policies, practices, and processes at many, but not all, financial services firms. Poor loan underwriting standards and credit practices, excessive leverage, misaligned incentives, less than robust risk management and corporate governance are now well known and fully documented."

In hindsight, many experts across the ideological spectrum cited two overall problems with the government's complex system of regulating financial institutions as having contributed to the financial crisis. One was the complexity of the regulatory regime itself. Responsibility for overseeing various institutions was fragmented among numerous regulatory agencies at the federal and state levels—essentially meaning that no one had a broad enough overview to catch serious risks to the entire financial system. A second, and related problem, was the inability of government regulators to keep pace with rapid changes in the financial industry. By the middle 2000s the government lacked the manpower and technical expertise to monitor mammoth financial institutions that operated worldwide and the arcane financial instruments (some of bewildering complexity) that those institutions had developed to spread risks and increase profits.

REGULATORY FRAGMENTATION

As of 2008, according to the General Accountability Office, the United States had some 16,000 depository institutions subject to five federal regulatory bodies. Among those banks were some 5,200 state-chartered banks that faced scrutiny both at the state level and by the Federal Deposit Insurance Corporation. Financial institutions (such as investment banks and brokerages) that did not accept deposits from individual customers were subject to regulations by some of the same agencies or by different agencies. Complicating things even further, some financial institutions were regulated by several different agencies, each of which looked at one or possibly two lines of the company's business but had no responsibility for evaluating the company as a whole. This latter situation developed largely as a result of the 1999 Gramm-Leach-Bliley Act (PL 101-102), which repealed Depression-era regulations that had prohibited banks from engaging both in commercial business (such as accepting deposits and making loans) and investment business (such as buying and selling securities). *(Congress and the Nation Vol. X, pp. 122, 130)*

Many other businesses that provided financial services—in some cases services virtually identical to some of those provided by traditional banks—were not regulated at all, or at most were regulated by state authorities. These businesses included mortgage brokers, payday lenders, and automobile finance agencies. The only federal agency with any oversight for these companies was the Federal Trade Commission, and it was limited to enforcing consumer protection laws, which had little teeth in terms of financial services. In addition, hedge funds (which became major financial players only since the 1990s) faced virtually no regulation and simply were urged (not even required) to register with the Securities and Exchange Commission.

The result of more than 150 years of federal policy and legislation was a confusing patchwork of regulation that was fully understood only by some bankers and regulators and by a handful of academic experts on the subject. Most members of the public tended to believe that, with the enactment of Depression-era reforms, banks generally were safe places to put money and reliable sources of loans. Periodic crises, such as a partial collapse of the savings and loan industry in the 1980s and the failure of a major hedge fund (Long Term Capital Management) in 1998 temporarily shook investor and public confidence in the system. Confidence, indeed overconfidence, quickly returned during eras of prosperity, one of which was the housing boom of the early 2000s.

FAILURE TO KEEP UP WITH THE MARKET

A second overall problem with financial services regulations—one that did not become blindingly obvious until the collapse of the housing bubble—was that government regulations and regulators failed to keep pace with rapid changes in the marketplace. One trend involved the many mergers of banks into giant financial institutions that operated not just across state lines but worldwide; keeping track of such businesses was difficult enough for the companies themselves, and was all but impossible for regulators charged with enforcing just U.S. law. In addition, no single regulatory body was charged with monitoring the financial system as a whole to determine where broad risks might be and what could be done to minimize those risks.

A related trend was the development since the late 1980s of extremely complex financial instruments, including derivatives such as "collateralized debt obligations" and "credit default swaps." Financial service companies paid enormous salaries to specialized experts who developed these securities, which became popular because they were supposed to spread risk while generating steady profits.

Regulatory bodies, which often struggled with budget shortfalls and could not compete with the highly paid expertise of the private sector, were in a weak position to evaluate the safety of these complex securities on behalf of the broader public. That task was left to the private credit rating agencies, which proved not up to the task either. In a March 2007 report, for example, the Government Accountability Office noted that the Office of Thrift Supervision had only one insurance expert to help it monitor the insurance giant American International Group (AIG), some of whose operations came under that agency's supervision because of a regulatory quirk.

Moreover, public officials at very high levels often insisted there was little or no need for government intrusion into the marketing of complex securities. A notable struggle over the matter, at the end of President Bill Clinton's second term (1997–2001) resulted in legislation in 2000 barring the Commodities Futures Trading Commission from regulating the very type of derivatives that were at the heart of the financial crisis eight years later. A similar example was a 2004 decision by the Securities and Exchange Commission to exempt the brokerage business of large investment banks from requirements to hold large reserves of capital to cushion against possible investment losses. This decision, in effect, made the banks responsible for voluntarily monitoring the riskiness of their own investments. Four years later, after enormous losses put nearly all major investment banks under intense financial pressure and one of the largest (Lehman Brothers) collapsed, the SEC revoked its rule. Chairman Christopher Cox, who had advocated a regulatory "light touch" by his agency, acknowledged: "The last six months have made it abundantly clear that voluntary regulation does not work."

OTHER REGULATORY FAILURES

Academic experts, industry analysts, politicians, and others cited numerous other problems with the nation's regulations—but there was little consensus about the extent and damage caused by each of these problems. Many consumer protection advocates, for example, insisted the federal government did have regulatory powers that could have reduced the impact of the financial crisis but had chosen not to use those powers. A prime example was the sweeping authority Congress gave the Federal Reserve Board in 1994 (under the Home Ownership and Equity Protection Act, PL 103-325), to protect a wide range of mortgage borrowers, including the so-called "subprime" borrowers whose loans caused much of the difficulty in the financial crisis. These borrowers were people without adequate income or assets to borrow as much as bankers were allowing in order to purchase homes. However, the Fed declined to use that authority (and Congressional Republicans blocked legislation to force the Fed to use it) until late in 2007, when the crisis was well under way.

Critics also said state and federal regulators, including the Federal Trade Commission, failed to enforce consumer protection laws that might have prevented unscrupulous lenders from pushing unwary borrowers into taking out loans they could not afford. Independent mortgage brokers, who wrote the majority of subprime mortgages that ultimately failed, faced no federal regulation and only spotty regulation at the state level—but state and federal regulators could have used consumer protection laws to prevent the worst abuses by these brokers, according to some experts.

Some bankers complained that politicians also shared in the blame because they were so interested in promoting "home ownership" as a societal virtue that they put pressure on banks to make loans to unworthy borrowers. According to this line of reasoning, political pressure to make it easier for low-income borrowers to get into their own homes led to a cascading series of developments: lenders made loans they probably should not have, Fannie Mae and Freddie Mac were under pressure to buy questionable loans on the secondary market, and the entire housing market floated on expectations that prices would continue to rise because the economy was booming and a larger share of the population was able to become homeowners rather than renters.

BAILING OUT FANNIE AND FREDDIE

The one major regulatory step Congress took in response to the financial crisis came in July 2008, when it enacted the Housing and Economic Recovery Act (HR 3221—PL 110-289). The chief aim of this bill was to shore up Fannie Mae and Freddie Mac, which were in danger of collapse because of over-exposure to the risky loans at the heart of the financial crisis. The legislation also created a new office, the Federal Housing Finance Agency (FHFA), to oversee Fannie and Freddie and the Federal Home Loan Banks.

Two months after this legislation was enacted, the Bush administration used the new powers to place Fannie and Freddie in conservatorship, under the control of the new Federal Housing Finance Agency. As of late 2009, the government had used authorities from PL 110-289 to invest $110.6 billion directly into Fannie and Freddie to keep them—and thus the housing market—limping along on life support. Many experts said the two agencies would need billions of dollars in additional help at least through 2010 and probably for years to come.

"NONTRADITIONAL" LOANS

For observers outside the professional housing and finance communities, one of the most surprising aspects of the financial crisis was the extent to which it was caused by excessively risky lending to subprime borrowers: people whose incomes and assets raised serious questions about their ability to repay their loans. The riskiness of subprime lending was no secret among those doing it, however, nor apparently was it unknown to state and federal regulators, some of whom warned about potentially negative consequences. Even so, government agencies did little until late in the housing bubble to control the growth and riskiness of subprime lending.

The government's only concerted action came on Sept. 29, 2006, when the five major federal regulators issued a document called "Guidance on Nontraditional Mortgage Product Risks." The regulators were the Federal Reserve Board, the Comptroller of the Currency, the Federal Deposit Insurance Corporation, the Office of Thrift Supervision, and the National Credit Union Administration.

The agencies had first suggested guidelines in December 2005, provoking an outcry from the banking industry, which said federal intervention would stifle innovation and make it difficult for people to buy their homes. In response to such complaints, the agencies narrowed the scope of the guidelines, making them apply only to loans that allowed borrowers to defer repayment of principal or interest rather than to the broader category of "subprime" loans to risky borrowers. Moreover, because the guidance was nonbinding, banks were free to ignore it.

PAULSON REGULATORY PROPOSAL

On March 31, 2008, as the credit crisis was deepening but had not yet reached its full depth, Treasury Secretary Paulson launched what many observers believed was a preemptive effort to steer the inevitable debate about fixing regulations of the financial services industry. If it also was intended to ensure that Congress would not rush through new regulations in the midst of the crisis, it was successful in that regard, since Congress essentially punted major regulatory issues into 2009 or even beyond.

Paulson called his plan a "Blueprint for Regulatory Reform," and it fit the description, including both detailed proposals and broader concepts. Paulson acknowledged that the government's regulations had not kept pace with changes in the financial services industry, but he also insisted the regulatory structure was not to blame for the financial crisis.

At the core of Paulson's blueprint was a realignment of the federal government's five financial regulators into just three, which he described as "a regulator focused on market stability across the entire financial sector, a regulator focused on safety and soundness of those institutions supported by a federal guarantee, and a regulator focused on protecting consumers and investors." Paulson suggested that the Federal Reserve Board was the natural fit for the first role; an agency similar to (but not necessarily the same as) the Office of the Comptroller of the Currency should take on the role of supervising the safety and soundness of most financial institutions; and a combination of the Securities and Exchange Commission and the Commodities Futures Trading Commission should protect consumers and investors.

Paulson had a mixed message on the complex question of how to regulate the various entities that "originated" (or wrote) mortgages. Many of these entities, particularly independent mortgage brokers, were free of federal rules and faced little or no supervision by states, which technically had authority over them. Paulson recommended keeping the states in charge of mortgage practices, but he also called for a Mortgage Origination Commission, led by a presidential appointee, which would set minimum standards and licensing requirements for those who wrote mortgages. To put some pressure on the states to tighten their standards, Paulson also proposed that the commission should "evaluate, rate, and report on each state's adequacy for licensing and regulation of participants in the mortgage origination process." Investors could use this information to help them evaluate the soundness of mortgages written within each state.

Paulson acknowledged that his proposal would generate controversy and would take time for Congress to consider. He might have been disappointed on the first count; after an initial flurry of criticism from nearly all quarters, Paulson's blueprint quickly receded into the background as the financial crisis escalated and took priority. Congress did not begin work on any serious regulatory reform until well into 2009; even then, it was unclear when, or if, the lessons learned from the financial crisis would be translated into real changes in the government's laws and rules.

MADOFF SCANDAL

Early in December 2008, just as it seemed that the news from Wall Street and the financial industry could not get any worse, word came of a major new financial scandal, one that equaled or even exceeded the impact of giant corporate scandals of the early part of the decade. On Dec. 11 government agents in New York arrested hedge fund manager Bernard L. Madoff on charges of running a giant Ponzi scheme that had defrauded investors of billions of dollars. Initial estimates of Madoff's fraud ranged around $50 billion, but later estimates in 2009 put total losses of investors at nearly $65 billion. Madoff had given his investors detailed reports about investments supposedly made on their behalf; in truth, nearly all these investments were shams.

Madoff on March 12, 2009, pleaded guilty to criminal charges of defrauding his investors by using the proceeds from new investors to pay previous ones—the classic device in a Ponzi scheme. However, he refused to cooperate with investigators by providing details or naming co-conspirators. A federal judge on June 29, 2009, sentenced Madoff to 150 years in prison, the maximum penalty allowed. He began serving his term in July.

Hundreds of individual investors and several dozen charitable foundations lost enormous sums in the collapse of Madoff's firm; several of the charities were forced to close their doors. U.S. officials began an extensive effort to collect as much money as possible from Madoff's personal and business assets to compensate investors, but this work was expected to take several years and result in only modest compensation for the vast majority of victims.

The Madoff scandal caused widespread upheaval, starting on Wall Street but spreading globally, for several reasons. First, of course, was the enormity of the crime. One man, allegedly with help from only a handful of aides, managed to steal a sum of money that rivaled the annual budgets of several states or the gross domestic products of several small countries. Another reason was that Madoff was well-known and highly respected on Wall Street, in part because he was a former chairman of the NASDAQ exchange. Madoff also had built his reputation through a mystique that he accepted only a small number of clients, many of whom turned out to be well-heeled members of the Jewish communities in the New York area and Florida. The scandal also came at an exceptionally sensitive time, with the nation still reeling from the financial crisis.

This scandal exposed yet another flaw in federal regulations. The Securities and Exchange Commission, which had authority over Madoff's line of investments, had received several tips about potential fraud but had conducted investigations that failed to dig beneath the surface. The SEC and other agencies finally acted only after Madoff's two sons effectively turned him in by reporting his own admission to them that his business was fraudulent.

In a Dec. 16, 2008, statement, SEC Chairman Cox acknowledged that the agency had received numerous complaints about Madoff since 1999, none of which went beyond the staff level. "I am gravely concerned by the apparent multiple failures over at least a decade to thoroughly investigate these allegations or at any point to seek formal authority to pursue them," Cox said. "Moreover, a consequence of the failure to seek a formal order of investigation from the Commission is that subpoena power was not used to obtain information, but rather the staff relied upon information voluntarily produced by Mr. Madoff and his firm."

A lengthy investigation by the SEC's inspector general concluded in September 2009 that "the SEC received more than ample information in the form of detailed and substantive complaints over the years to warrant a thorough and comprehensive examination and/or investigation of Bernard Madoff and BMIS [his company] for operating a Ponzi scheme, and that despite three examinations and two investigations being conducted, a thorough and competent investigation or examination was never performed."

Mary L. Schapiro, who took over from Cox in 2009, launched numerous reforms of SEC procedures in an attempt to prevent a recurrence of the agency's failure to catch Madoff's wrongdoing. Among other things, Schapiro reorganized the Enforcement Division (which had conducted the inadequate investigations of Madoff) and created new procedures to handle tips, such as repeated tips by one investor that proved to be remarkably accurate about the extent of Madoff's fraud but had been dismissed by the SEC staff.

2005–2006

Buoyed by their 2004 election victories, congressional Republicans in early 2005 quickly passed an overhaul of the nation's bankruptcy law that they had been trying to enact since 1997. The rewrite, which was supported by banks and credit card companies, was written to force more individuals to repay their debts over several years rather than wipe the debts off the books altogether. In previous years, the bill had been killed in the Senate by an amendment aimed at preventing abortion clinic protestors from avoiding court fines or fees by declaring bankruptcy. A combination of more Republicans in the Senate and a handful of Democratic defectors defeated the amendment in 2005, and the measure then easily passed both chambers.

Another long-sought goal, this one a reform of the Federal Deposit Insurance Corporation (FDIC), came to fruition in the 109th Congress as part of a much larger effort to cut mandatory spending. But legislators who had been pushing for several years to tighten regulation of the mortgage giants Fannie Mae and Freddie Mac came up empty-handed once again, stalled by partisan tensions in the Senate.

Bankruptcy Reform

An eight-year drive to rewrite bankruptcy law ended April 20, 2005, when President George W. Bush signed a far-reaching bankruptcy overhaul bill into law (S 256—PL 109-8). Enactment was a victory for the credit card and financial services industries, which had been pushing the legislation since 1997.

The centerpiece of the new law was the establishment of a means test aimed at forcing more consumers to file under Chapter 13 of the bankruptcy code, rather than Chapter 7. Under Chapter 7, individuals could have much of their debt discharged, or erased, whereas Chapter 13, in contrast, required debtors to enter into a court-ordered plan to repay their debts over several years.

The new law also bolstered the legal rights of creditors, required potential bankruptcy filers to receive credit counseling, and increased the fees and paperwork requirements related to filing for bankruptcy.

Supporters argued the changes would help stem the rise in personal bankruptcy filings and prevent abuse of the system by wealthy filers who could repay their debts but used the bankruptcy system, in the words of critics, as a financial planning tool. Opponents said the measure was a windfall for the credit card industry and faulted the bill for not addressing corporate bankruptcy in the wake of accounting scandals at Enron Corp. and WorldCom Inc. They also criticized the bill for putting the burden of proof on those attempting to file under Chapter 7 to show they were not abusing the law. They said the provisions would force filers to pay additional lawyers' fees and complete paperwork tied to the means test, potentially worsening their financial woes. *(Accounting scandals, Congress and the Nation Vol. XI, p. 124)*

The legislation was first introduced in 1997. Supporters tried to win enactment through four Congresses, but each time the bill was derailed. The primary stumbling block was an amendment by Senate Democrat Charles E. Schumer of New York intended to prevent violent protesters from escaping court-ordered judgments or fines by filing for bankruptcy protection.

Because it was originally aimed at antiabortion protesters, the amendment was anathema to conservative Republicans, and it doomed the legislation in both the 107th and 108th Congresses. Supporters of the bill were able to overcome the Schumer amendment in 2005 because of the increased Republican majority in the Senate following the 2004 elections and the defection of a small group of Senate Democrats that waylaid efforts by opponents to filibuster. Once the Senate passed the bill, House GOP leaders steered the same measure through their chamber without amendment, avoiding the need for a House-Senate conference, and another round of votes on the legislation.

HIGHLIGHTS OF BANKRUPTCY REVISION

Means test. Established a means test to determine how a debtor would be treated in bankruptcy proceedings. The means test was created to determine whether an individual was eligible to file for protection under Chapter 7 or had to file under Chapter 13. Filers generally were not eligible for Chapter 7 if they earned more than their state's median income and if their income, after deducting allowable expenses, was sufficient to repay up to $6,000 over a five-year period. In general, anyone whose income exceeded this threshold was considered to be abusing the law, and it was up to the individual to show that his or her finances had not crossed the threshold. Under previous law, debtors could use Chapter 7 even if they could repay their debts.

Homestead exemption. Limited the home equity a debtor could protect during bankruptcy proceedings to $125,000 for a home purchased within forty months of the bankruptcy filing.

Nondischargeable debts. Made certain debts nondischargeable, meaning they could not be erased. These included alimony and child support, certain money owed for luxury goods, qualified student loans, fines or penalties under federal election laws, and any debt incurred while paying a debt that was nondischargeable: for example, a credit card charge that was used to pay state or local taxes.

Repeat filers. Generally made it more difficult for individuals to file repeated bankruptcy claims.

NEW FEDERAL RESERVE CHIEF CONFIRMED

Ben S. Bernanke took over as chairman of the Federal Reserve Board of Governors on Feb. 1, 2006, ushering in a new era at the agency responsible for the nation's monetary policy. Bernanke replaced Alan Greenspan, who stepped down Jan. 31 at the end of his fifth term. Greenspan was first appointed as Fed chairman by President Ronald Reagan in 1987.

The Senate confirmed Bernanke's nomination by voice vote Jan. 31.

President George W. Bush had announced the nomination Oct. 24, 2005, tapping Bernanke for a fourteen-year seat on the central bank's Board of Governors and a four-year, renewable term as chairman. Bernanke said his first priority would be "to maintain continuity with the policies and policy strategies established during the Greenspan years." Groups such as the Mortgage Bankers Association, the American Insurance Association, the National Association of Manufacturers, and the Bond Market Association endorsed the nomination.

Bernanke was educated at Harvard University and the Massachusetts Institute of Technology. He taught at Princeton University from 1985 to 2002 and served as a member of the Fed's Board of Governors from 2002 to 2005. He had become head of the Council of Economic Advisers in June 2005. During his academic career, Bernanke thought and wrote extensively about the Great Depression, scholarship that would prove central to his actions as he helped guide the country through the financial crisis and subsequent economic recession that struck at the end of Bush's second term.

The Senate Banking Committee approved the nomination by voice vote Nov. 16, 2005, a day after a hearing at which Bernanke faced little opposition. Banking Chairman Richard C. Shelby, R-Ala., and panel member Christopher J. Dodd, D-Conn., each called the nomination "superb." In response to Democratic concerns that he not carry water for the White House, Bernanke promised to be "strictly independent of all political influences."

During the floor debate, other senators generally praised Greenspan and his successor. Bernanke is "erudite; he is smart," said Charles E. Schumer, D-N.Y., who also said Bernanke was "not an ideologue." Tim Johnson, D-S.D., who like Schumer sat on the Banking Committee, said in a statement, "Bernanke's credentials, both academic and professional, are exemplary."

Bernanke in 2009 was nominated for a second four-year term by President Barack Obama, but this time the confirmation approval was anything but smooth. Bernanke became the focus, along with a few other high-level Obama financial officials, of congressional and public anger over the financial crisis and the by-then soaring unemployment rate. Critics in Congress on both the left and right political spectrum said Bernanke contributed materially to the crisis by not using Fed powers earlier to prevent the risky financial activity that led, eventually, to the crisis. Nevertheless, Obama stood by the nomination and the Senate confirmed Bernanke Jan. 28, 2010, by a 70–30 vote. The margin, although substantial, was the closest ever for a Fed chairman: fourteen votes worse than the previous closest approval for the position.

Consumer education. Included a number of provisions aimed at increasing a debtor's knowledge about bankruptcy and money management including requiring consumers to get credit counseling before filing for bankruptcy and allowing their debts to be canceled only if they took a course to learn to better manage their finances.

Consumer protection. Required credit card companies to include a number of new sections in billing statements such as an example of the time it would take to repay the balance at a specified interest rate, warnings that paying only the minimum payment would increase the minimum amount of interest that had to be paid, and a toll-free number for consumers to get information on how long it would take to repay a credit card balance if only the minimum was paid.

Business provisions. Required small-business debtors—those with less than $2 million in debts—to file a reorganization plan within 180 days of filing for bankruptcy and to file periodic financial reports after that. Created a new chapter of the bankruptcy code to address transnational bankruptcy cases.

BACKGROUND

The campaign to rewrite the bankruptcy code began in the late 1990s in response to a significant increase in consumer bankruptcy filings, which peaked at nearly 1.4 million in 1998. This increase prompted a coalition of credit card companies, banks, and retailers to argue that the code needed tightening to prevent rampant abuse by borrowers who could afford to repay some of their debts but instead took advantage of permissive bankruptcy rules. Consumer advocates, on the other hand, blamed much of the rise in bankruptcies on aggressive marketing by credit card companies and opposed what they said were attempts to help the banks at the expense of low-wage workers.

Consumer filings dropped in 1999 and 2000 and then began to pick up again, reaching nearly 1.7 million in 2003.

Experts said the increase stemmed from a combination of an economy that was just pulling out of a recession and a market blitz by bankruptcy lawyers who warned debtors to file for protection before the law was changed.

Bankruptcy overhaul legislation had come close to enactment three times before. In 1998, 2000, and 2002, the House and Senate completed negotiations on conference reports. The first one died in the Senate where Democrats were angry over the watering down of consumer protections. The second one was pocket-vetoed by President Bill Clinton (1993–2001), who cited deletion of an earlier version of the provision aimed at antiabortion protestors. He also said the homestead exemption in that bill was too lenient.

In 2004 protests by a group of House Republicans opposed to abortion forced GOP leaders to abandon their plans to bring the conference report to the House floor before the August recess. The leadership tried again late in the year, but the opponents managed to defeat the rule for debate on the measure. The House then removed the antiabortion protest provision and passed the conference report. The bill died in the Senate after Democrats made clear they would not support the measure without the abortion provision.

A similar scenario played out in the 108th Congress. The House handily passed the legislation early in 2003, but action stalled in the Senate where Republican leaders worried that the Schumer antiabortion protest language could be adopted in the closely divided chamber. *(Congress and the Nation Vol. X, pp. 16, 142; Vol. IX, pp. 129, 141)*

SENATE ACTION

The Senate Judiciary Committee approved S 256 by a vote of 12–5 on Feb. 17, 2005. The bill largely mirrored the legislation that had died in the previous Congress. Democrats held many of their most contentious amendments for the floor, in part out of respect for the wishes of Chairman Arlen Specter, R-Pa., who had announced the previous day that he had an advanced form of Hodgkin's disease. But they offered enough amendments, virtually all of which were rejected, to presage the nearly two weeks of sometimes vitriolic debate that occurred on the Senate floor, before the Senate passed the bill 74–25 on March 10.

With House leaders signaling that any amendments would jeopardize the measure's chances in their chamber, GOP leaders held their caucus together to defeat dozens of Democratic amendments aimed at exempting certain groups from the means test and placing new restrictions on the credit card industry. Only one exemption from the means test prevailed: disabled veterans whose debts occurred primarily while they were on active duty or performing homeland defense duties passed 99–0. The Senate also agreed to an amendment allowing bankruptcy courts to consider a call to active duty as a "special circumstance" when deciding whether a person who did not meet the means test could still file under Chapter 7.

Republicans and some Democrats held firm against other proposed exemptions, rejecting amendments that would have exempted debtors whose financial troubles resulted from medical expenses; those who went into debt paying medical costs for a family member or took a lower-paying job to have time to care for a family member; and victims of identity theft.

The Senate also rejected Democratic attempts to limit the interest that companies could charge on extended credit, require credit card companies to increase disclosure to consumers, and discourage predatory lending. Democrats were also defeated in their efforts to create special homestead exemptions for the elderly, those with high medical expenses, and eligible members of the military.

The long-awaited vote on the Schumer amendment came March 8. As in 2002, the amendment was broadened to bar all violent protesters, not just those protesting abortion, from escaping court-ordered fines or judgments by filing for bankruptcy protection. In an impassioned floor speech, Schumer said the Senate should not "protect those who use violence" and warned his colleagues that a vote against his amendment was a vote "against the rule of law."

Senate Republicans attacked the amendment on two fronts. They said it was unnecessary and, more immediately, that it would once again prevent Congress from overhauling federal bankruptcy law. Sen. Jeff Sessions, R-Ala., characterized the Schumer amendment as the "most perfect example of a "poison pill" he had ever seen. Sen. Orrin G. Hatch, R-Utah, argued that bankruptcy courts had made clear they would not allow debtors to escape fines and judgments for willful, violent actions.

Those arguments helped the Republicans defeat the amendment on a **key vote of 46–53 (R 4–51; D 41–2; I 1–0)**. The main factor in the defeat of the Schumer amendment was the unified Republican strength on the vote. *(2005 key votes, p. 915)*

With that hard-won victory in hand, Republicans easily prevailed on a cloture motion later the same day. With the support of fourteen Democrats, the Senate voted 69–31 to limit debate and block any effort to filibuster, clearing the way for passage.

HOUSE ACTION

House Judiciary Committee chairman F. James Sensenbrenner Jr., R-Wis., urged the panel to "vigorously oppose" all amendments to avoid the need for a conference. Committee Republicans followed his wishes, approving the Senate-passed bill without change March 16 by a mostly party-line vote of 22–13.

The House passed the bill 302–126 after about two hours of debate April 14, clearing it for the president, who signed it into law on April 20. Many Democrats were outspoken in their opposition to the bill and to the strategy GOP leaders used in pushing it through. The leadership-controlled Rules

Committee had approved a closed rule for floor debate that barred any amendments.

MAJOR PROVISIONS

As enacted, PL 109-8 overhauled the federal bankruptcy law, generally making it more difficult for individuals who could afford to pay at least some of their debts from filing a successful claim for bankruptcy. The measure also codified some consumer protections and creditor rights, added provisions to curb abuse of personal bankruptcy laws, and reformed business bankruptcy law.

Individual Bankruptcy

Means test and definition of "abuse." Barred individuals from eligibility for Chapter 7 relief if their "current monthly income" was at or above the median income in their state and, when multiplied by sixty, was equal to or greater than 25 percent of their nonpriority unsecured claims or $6,000. Secured claims were those involving collateral, such as a house. Priority claims were paid before other unsecured debts. If the individual exceeded this threshold, there was a "presumption of abuse," which would result in the case being dismissed or converted to Chapter 13. Under previous law, there was a presumption in favor of granting relief under Chapter 7.

Definition of "current monthly income." Defined current monthly income as the debtor's average monthly income from all sources in the six months preceding a bankruptcy filing, including both taxable and nontaxable income, including any amount paid on a regular basis by outside sources for the household expenses of a debtor or the debtor's dependents. Excluded from the calculation were Social Security benefits and payments to victims of war crimes, crimes against humanity, or international or domestic terrorism.

Allowable monthly expenses. Allowed a person filing for bankruptcy, in calculating current monthly income, to first deduct a number of expenses, including applicable monthly expenses as defined by the Internal Revenue Service. Eligible expenses included food and clothing; "reasonably necessary" expenses to protect the debtor and his family from certain types of violence; and some expenditures for health insurance, disability insurance, and health savings accounts. Bankruptcy filers in a Chapter 13 case were also allowed to deduct the administrative expenses stemming from the administration of a court-ordered repayment plan.

Filers could also deduct "reasonable and necessary" expenses for the care or support of any elderly, chronically ill, or disabled household members, as well as up to $1,500 per dependent child for public or private elementary or secondary school education. The school expenses could be deducted only if they were documented and the debtor could show why they were necessary and were not already accounted for by the IRS standards.

Secured debts. Allowed filers to deduct payments on secured debts from their current monthly income figure. For Chapter 13 filings, the debtor could deduct any additional payments necessary to maintain possession of a house, vehicle, or other property needed to support themselves or their dependents if it is collateral for secured debts.

Exceptions. Allowed filers that exceeded the income threshold to still use Chapter 7 under special circumstances such as a serious medical condition or a call to active duty in the armed forces, but only if those circumstances justified additional expenses or reductions in monthly income. To be eligible, a filer had to provide the bankruptcy court with a detailed explanation of the special circumstances and testify under oath as to the accuracy of the claims.

Creditor rights. Allowed for the first time "parties of interest," such as creditors, to seek to have a Chapter 7 bankruptcy filing dismissed or converted to Chapter 13. Under existing law, only the bankruptcy courts or a U.S. trustee could seek to have a case dismissed and then only if the court found that the Chapter 7 filing was a "substantial abuse" of the bankruptcy system. Under the new law, the standard was reduced to "abuse."

Safe harbor provisions. Stipulated that if a debtor's current monthly income is less than the state median, only a judge, federal trustee, or bankruptcy administrator—not a creditor—could seek to dismiss a Chapter 7 filing for abuse. No motion for dismissal based on a debtor's ability to pay could be filed by any party if the debtor's income was below the state median income threshold. Disabled veterans whose bankruptcy occurred primarily during a time when they were on active duty or performing a homeland defense activity are exempted from the means test.

Bad-faith provision. Required the court in cases where a filer did not meet the means-test threshold, to consider whether the Chapter 7 filing was made in bad faith or the debtor's overall financial situation suggested some sort of abuse.

Attorney sanctions. Made a debtor's attorney liable for civil penalties and administrative costs if a bankruptcy filing is found to be false or abusive. The attorney could be required to reimburse a bankruptcy trustee for trial costs if the bankruptcy court or a creditor made such a request and the request was granted. Additionally, creditors or the court could make a motion to assess civil penalties against an attorney representing a bankruptcy filer.

Creditor sanctions. Allowed the court to award the debtor reasonable costs, including applicable attorney fees, if a creditor filed a motion claiming abuse by the debtor and the motion was not granted. In such situations, the court could determine whether the party of interest, typically a creditor, or the lawyer that actually filed the motion, did so to coerce the debtor into waiving his or her rights or entering into a repayment plan.

Nonqualification. Required the clerk of the bankruptcy court, in cases where a debtor did not qualify for Chapter 7 based on the means test, to notify all of the debtor's creditors within ten days after the beginning of the case that the "presumption of abuse" applied. Such notice would give creditors the opportunity to file a motion to dismiss the bankruptcy filing or push the debtor into a Chapter 13 repayment plan.

Chapter 13 disposable income. Allowed the court in a Chapter 13 case, under certain circumstances, to force a debtor to pay all his "disposable income" to unsecured creditors. Disposable income was calculated by taking into account all of the debtor's income and deducting all expenses for the support of the debtor and his dependents, child support payments, charitable contributions that do not exceed 15 percent of annual gross income, and payments to operate a business. Debtors could deduct the cost of health insurance for themselves and their dependents if they documented the cost and the court determined the cost was reasonable.

Mandatory credit counseling. Required a debtor, to be eligible for relief, to have had to have received credit counseling during the six months before filing for bankruptcy. The counseling had to be provided by an approved nonprofit agency and had to include either an individual or group briefing on opportunities for available credit counseling and assistance in performing a budget analysis. The briefing, which could occur over the telephone or Internet, was not required if the bankruptcy trustees determined that adequate credit counseling was not available in the district where the debtor lived.

Financial management instruction. Allowed a bankruptcy court to discharge remaining debts under Chapter 7 only if the debtor completed a financial management training course.

Consumer Protections

Creditor's refusal to negotiate. Allowed a bankruptcy court to reduce an unsecured consumer claim by up to 20 percent if the debtor could show the creditor refused to negotiate a reasonable alternative repayment plan that was approved by an approved credit counseling agency on the debtor's behalf.

Mandatory disclosure for reaffirmation agreements. Required certain disclosures and explanations for any reaffirmation agreement that a debtor signed with a creditor. A reaffirmation agreement is an agreement for the repayment of a particular debt that would otherwise be discharged during the bankruptcy proceedings. Typically, the debts a debtor agrees to repay in such an agreement are secured by collateral that could be repossessed or foreclosed on in the absence of an agreement. The reaffirmation agreement had to include a statement of the total amount of debt the debtor agreed to pay, the annual percentage rate for the agreement, any lien on goods or property under the agreement, and a long statement clarifying the possible repercussions to the debtor of signing a reaffirmation agreement. The debtor's attorney was required to certify that the debtor voluntarily agreed to the agreement and that it would not impose an undue hardship.

Enforcement. Required the attorney general to appoint a U.S. attorney for each judicial district and an FBI agent for each field office to oversee the enforcement of laws pertaining to abusive reaffirmation agreements and "materially fraudulent" statements made in bankruptcy filings. Required bankruptcy courts to develop a procedure for referring bankruptcy cases to the U.S. attorney in cases where a fraudulent filing was made.

Child support payments. Stipulated that a debtor had to pay all legally settled support payments before a court could approve a debt repayment plan, and made child support obligations nondischargeable. The section was intended to make child support payments a priority claim during bankruptcy proceedings.

Discharge of qualified educational loans. Allowed for the discharge of debts for certain types of qualified educational loans if repayment would impose an undue hardship on the debtor or dependents.

Bankruptcy filing preparers. Created a number of new rules for bankruptcy petition preparers who were not attorneys, including a requirement that they notify debtors they cannot practice law or give legal advice. The section was intended to protect consumers from unscrupulous bankruptcy filing services.

Protection of retirement savings. Allowed an individual debtor to exempt from bankruptcy proceeding certain types of tax-exempt retirement funds that had not already been offered as collateral for the extension of credit. Placed a $1 million cap on the exemption, with periodic adjustments for inflation. Made debt owed to a pension, profit-sharing, stock bonus, or other retirement plan nondischargeable in the bankruptcy proceedings.

Protection of education savings. Amended existing law to protect educational individual retirement accounts in bankruptcy proceedings but specified that the debtor's child, stepchild, grandchild, or step-grandchild had to be the beneficiary of the account, and the funds were protected only if they were placed in the account more than a year before the bankruptcy filing. Specified that funds deposited between 720 days and 365 days before the filing were only protected up to $5,000.

Restrictions on debt relief agencies. Included a number of provisions aimed at controlling the behavior of debt relief agencies, organizations that provided bankruptcy assistance for a fee. Prohibited these firms from encouraging an "assisted person" to make false or misleading statements in a bankruptcy filing and from encouraging debtors to take on additional debt while filing for bankruptcy relief or to pay the agency fees for preparing a bankruptcy case.

Discouraging Bankruptcy Abuse

Filing abuse. Included provisions to discourage abuse of the bankruptcy system, including penalties for debtors who filed more than one case within a year or who filed a claim in a deliberate effort to defraud creditors.

Homestead exemption. Included limitations on the ability of debtors to use state homestead exemption laws to shield their assets. Required a debtor to be a resident of a state for at least two years before being eligible to claim that state's homestead exemption, making it more difficult to benefit from the laws in those states that have unlimited homestead exemptions. Capped the amount of home equity that could be protected in a bankruptcy proceeding at $125,000 if the home was bought within forty months of filing but allowed the limit to be waived if it involved the primary residence of a family farmer.

Luxury goods. Required a debtor to pay any amount over $500 owed to a single creditor for luxury goods purchased within ninety days of a bankruptcy filing; the previous limit was $1,075 for goods bought within sixty days of the filing. Required the debtor to repay all cash advances that totaled $750 or more and were made within seventy days; the previous limit was $1,075. The provision was intended to make it more difficult to escape paying for luxury goods bought on credit.

Frequency of bankruptcy relief. Increased the limit on a filer entering Chapter 7 a second time to eight years of the original discharge from the existing six years. Denied a Chapter 13 discharge to any debtor who received a discharge under Chapter 7, 11, or 12 within the preceding four years, or under Chapter 13 within the previous two years.

Filing fees. Increased fees to file for Chapter 7 relief to $200 from $155 for an individual case. Reduced the fee for filing a Chapter 13 case to $150 from $155. Increased the Chapter 11 fee to $1,000 from $800. The budget reconciliation bill signed into law in February 2006 (PL 109-171) raised the fee to $245 for Chapter 7 filings and to $235 for Chapter 13. *(Reconciliation, p. 79)*

Business Bankruptcy

Business bankruptcies were governed by Chapter 11 of the Bankruptcy Code, which allowed businesses to reorganize themselves, giving them an opportunity to restructure debt and escape from some leases and contracts. A business was usually allowed to continue operating while it was in Chapter 11 under the supervision of the bankruptcy court. Family farmers were covered under Chapter 12. The measure made several technical changes, including:

Securities regulations. Specified that the automatic stay, in the case of a business filing for bankruptcy, did not prevent a self-regulatory securities organization or securities exchange from taking enforcement actions against a debtor or from delisting the debtor's securities.

Reorganization time limit. Limited the time period available for a debtor to file a Chapter 11 reorganization plan to eighteen months or less after an order for relief in the case, and required debtors to obtain acceptance of the plan from creditors within twenty months after the order for relief.

Small-business debtors. Defined in most situations a small-business debtor as a business with less than $2 million in secured and unsecured debt when it filed for bankruptcy protection. Urged the adoption of standardized disclosure statements and reorganization plans for small-business debtors, as well as for uniform national reporting requirements aimed at providing sufficient information without excessive costs to the business. Required small-business debtors to file a reorganization plan within 180 days after filing for bankruptcy and to file additional financial reports periodically at the direction of the court.

Permanent Chapter 12 protection. Made permanent Chapter 12 of the bankruptcy code, created in 1986 to provide bankruptcy relief for family farmers that had a regular income. Chapter 12 required farmers to reorganize their debts pursuant to a repayment plan but was generally thought to be less complex and expensive than other sections of the bankruptcy code.

Definition of a family farmer. Broadened the definition of a family farmer for bankruptcy purposes to allow an eligible farmer to have up to $3.2 million in debt, at least 50 percent of it from farming, and allowed the limit to be adjusted periodically for inflation. To qualify for Chapter 12 protection under existing law a farmer could have no more than $1.5 million in debt, 80 percent of which had to come from farming. Allowed farmers to have received 50 percent of their income from farming in one of the three years prior to filing rather in one year before filing under existing law.

Family fishermen. Extended Chapter 12 bankruptcy relief to include "family fishermen" with regular income. Defined a family fisherman as any individual involved in a commercial fishing operation that had debt up to $1.5 million, at least 80 percent of which stemmed from the fishing operation, and specified that at least 50 percent of the individual's income had to come from fishing in the year prior to filing for bankruptcy.

Consumer credit studies. Directed the Federal Reserve to study whether credit card companies indiscriminately offered credit without making any effort to ensure that the consumers would be able to repay their debt. Allowed the Fed to write regulations requiring additional disclosures to consumers, and directed it to take steps to ensure that credit industry practices were responsible and helpful in preventing consumer debt and insolvency.

Directed the Fed to study and report to Congress on the type of information credit card companies provided to consumers, and on existing consumer protections from identity theft and other unauthorized uses of credit cards. Required the Fed to report to Congress on the effect of credit card offers to dependent college students on the number of federal bankruptcy cases.

New consumer disclosures. Included various provisions to ensure that consumers were better informed about open-ended credit plans, such as those offered by most credit card firms. Required billing statements for such plans had to include an example of the time it would take to pay the balance at a specified interest rate; a toll-free number consumers could call to receive an estimate of the time it would take to pay the balance if only the minimum was paid, and warnings that paying only the minimum amount on a balance would increase the minimum amount of interest that had to be paid.

Required additional disclosures regarding introductory interest rates on credit cards, Internet-based credit card offers, and late payment deadlines and penalties. Barred creditors from terminating an open-end account before its expiration date solely because a consumer paid off the balance consistently.

Effective date. Made the bankruptcy law changes effective 180 days after the date of enactment, which was April 20.

Deposit Insurance

Legislation to overhaul the Federal Deposit Insurance Corporation (FDIC) was incorporated into the fiscal 2006 budget reconciliation that President George W. Bush signed into law Feb. 8, 2006 (S 1932—PL 109-171). The reforms gradually increased coverage for depositors, merged the separate funds that protected bank and savings and loan depositors, and allowed the FDIC to alter the premiums it charged those financial institutions. The changes were expected to produce a net savings of $250 million over the following five years. Most of the changes were expected to have little effect until after 2010. *(Reconciliation, p. 79)*

Passage concluded a multiyear effort to reform the agency that insured individual bank deposits against bank failure. A string of bank failures and a steady erosion of deposit insurance reserves in the early 2000s prompted efforts in both chambers of Congress to increase insurance coverage for depositors The House passed legislation in both the 107th and 108th Congresses to increase deposit insurance coverage to $130,000, from $100,000, but the Senate did not act. Senate Banking Committee chairman Sen. Richard C. Shelby, R-Ala., opposed the increase, saying the change could put taxpayers at risk if there was a crisis in the banking industry, and refused to consider the legislation.

In 2005 the House passed the legislation again, approving a bill (HR 1185) on May 4, with only ten dissenting votes. The Senate Banking Committee did not act until late in the year, when it was faced with the need to make cuts in mandatory spending. On Oct. 18 it approved a measure (S 1562), which maintained the $100,000 limit on coverage but adjusted that level for inflation every five years starting in 2010, and sent the bill to the Senate Budget Committee to be merged into the Senate's reconciliation measure.

The House Financial Services Oct. 27 voted to send legislation to the House Budget Committee that was identical to the FDIC reform measure the House had passed in May. During negotiations on the final FDIC language, Shelby agreed to support other aspects of the bill, and House negotiators agreed to Shelby's approach of indexing the insurance ceiling for inflation.

The FDIC and the federal deposit insurance system were established in 1934 to stabilize the nation's banking system in the wake of a nationwide run on banks and thrifts. Under the system, the federal government guaranteed the funds of bank depositors in the event of a bank failure. Initially the FDIC insured deposits up to $2,500. Congress periodically increased the limit. The last increase before 2006 was in 1980, when the $40,000 limit was raised to $100,000 per account (PL 96-221). *(Congress and the Nation Vol. V, p. 261)*

MAJOR PROVISIONS

Merging BIF and SAIF. Required the FDIC to merge the separate funds that protected bank and savings and loan depositors no later than the start of the calendar quarter ninety days after enactment, which occurred Feb. 8, 2006. Transferred the assets and liabilities of the Bank Insurance Fund and the Savings Association Insurance Fund to a new Deposit Insurance to cover all insured banks and thrifts.

Increased deposit insurance amounts. Required the FDIC together with the National Credit Union Administration (which insured credit union depositors), beginning in April 2010 and every five years after, to determine whether an increase in deposit insurance levels to cover inflation was warranted. Directed the agencies to consider the financial health of the Deposit Insurance Fund, economic conditions, and whether an increase would cause the amount of insurance fund reserves to fall below 1.15 percent of estimated insured deposits. Specified that if an increase was deemed warranted, it would be calculated by the change in the personal consumption expenditures price index published by the Commerce Department, but limited the increase to increments of $10,000 and applied them to all covered accounts. Made any increase effective Jan. 1 of the following year, unless Congress acted by July 1 to block it.

IRA deposit insurance. Increased deposit insurance coverage for individual retirement account holdings to $250,000 from $100,000, and permitted inflationary increases after 2010 for these accounts.

Deposit insurance premiums. Permitted the FDIC to adjust collections of insurance premiums to keep the value of the Deposit Insurance Fund between 1.15 percent and 1.5 percent of estimated insured deposits (compared with the previous requirement of a flat 1.25 percent ratio). Required the FDIC, in setting the insurance fund's ratio of assets to deposits, to consider the potential for losses based on historical patterns and estimates for the future and on general economic conditions. Authorized the FDIC, in setting premium assessments for banks and thrifts, including assessments based on the riskiness of specific institutions, to consider the effect of assessment levels on the earnings and capital of insured institutions and any other factor deemed appropriate. Allowed the FDIC to grant a one-time credit to banks and thrifts that paid assessments before 1997, which could be used to cover future assessments.

Mortgage Regulation

Efforts to tighten the regulation of mortgage finance giants Fannie Mae and Freddie Mac were unsuccessful for the third straight year in 2005, derailed by partisan disagreements over proposals to restrict the firms' investment portfolios and to set up an affordable housing fund.

The House passed a version of the overhaul legislation (HR 1461—H Rept 109-171) on Oct. 26, 2005. A Senate committee approved a companion bill (S 190) in July, but that measure never reached the floor, and both bills died at the end of the 109th Congress in 2006. *(Details, pp. 625, 641)*

Lawmakers in both chambers began pushing for stronger oversight of Fannie Mae and Freddie Mac as multibillion-dollar accounting scandals came to light, leading to the ouster of a number of executives. As recently as December 2004, Fannie Mae chairman Franklin D. Raines was removed, and the firm's chief financial officer, J. Timothy Howard, resigned after the Securities and Exchange Commission forced the company to restate its earnings by as much as $9 billion. *(Background, Congress and the Nation Vol. XI, p. 143)*

But aggressive lobbying by the two firms and the inability of lawmakers and the Bush administration to agree on a new regulatory framework stymied the congressional efforts.

Both the House and Senate bills called for a new regulator for the two government-sponsored enterprises and the twelve Federal Home Loan Banks. Lawmakers agreed that the new regulator would be independent of existing agencies, would exist outside the appropriations process, and would have broader authority to oversee the firms than the existing regulator, the Office of Federal Housing Enterprise Oversight. The chambers differed, however, on how to regulate the firms' trillion-dollar investment portfolios and whether to require them to set aside a percentage of their profits to create an affordable housing fund.

The inclusion of affordable housing fund language in the House bill allowed supporters to win easy bipartisan approval in the Financial Services Committee in May. But objections from the conservative Republican Study Committee delayed floor action and led sponsors to add language that would strictly limit the groups that would be eligible for grants from the fund.

The Senate Banking, Housing, and Urban Affairs Committee approved its version of the bill in late July, but the bill advanced no further. The Senate measure, championed by Banking Chairman Richard C. Shelby, R-Ala., included portfolio restrictions but not the affordable housing fund. Democrats were opposed to the portfolio restrictions and also disappointed that the legislation did not include the affordable housing provisions.

During the lame duck session after the November 2006 election in which the Democrats won control of both chambers, top GOP and Democratic lawmakers on the House Financial Services Committee, aided by the Treasury Department, pushed a last-minute compromise that would not set portfolio limits but instead allow a new regulator to draft rules governing the investment portfolios based on safety and soundness concerns. No formal action was taken, but Rep. Barney Frank, D-Mass., who was in line to chair the Financial Services Committee, as well as other members, said they were hopeful that they had laid the groundwork for a compromise on the issue in the 110th Congress.

Credit Rating Agencies Regulation

Congress enacted legislation in 2006 that supporters insisted would increase competition among, and investor confidence in, the national credit agencies that rated corporate and municipal bonds. The legislation was, in part, a response to corporate accounting scandals of previous years, notably those involving the energy giant Enron and the telecommunications company WorldCom, which went bankrupt despite having earned top-flight "investment grade" ratings from the credit agencies. Those scandals, and similar ones involving major companies early in the twenty-first century, brought substantial criticism of the credit rating industry, which was dominated by Standard & Poor's and Moody's Investors Service. *(Congress and the Nation Vol. XI, p. 124)*

Congressional action on the credit rating agencies controversy began in the House, where the Financial Services Committee on July 7, 2006, reported HR 2990 (H Rept. 109-546). The bill established rules under which the Securities and Exchange Commission (SEC) would give official recognition to the credit agencies, also called Nationally Recognized Statistical Rating Organizations (NRSROs). The full House passed the bill on July 12 by a 255–166 vote, with the opposition coming from Democrats who argued that it would make it too easy for rating agencies to gain SEC recognition, and thus reduce the reliability and value of those agencies.

The Senate Banking, Housing and Urban Affairs Committee on Sept. 6 approved a companion bill (S 3850) giving the SEC several oversight powers that had not been included in the House bill. Among these were requirements for additional public disclosures by the credit agencies and power for the SEC to reject applicants that did not have adequate resources.

The full Senate adopted S 3850 by voice vote on Sept. 22. The additional oversight powers included in the Senate version helped clear the way for action in the House, which passed the Senate bill on Sept. 27 under suspension of the rules, thus clearing it for President George W. Bush, who signed it into law (PL 109-291) on Sept. 29.

PROVISIONS

The central provisions of the new law established requirements for a credit rating agency to meet when it applied to the SEC for recognition as a Nationally Recognized Statistical Rating Organization. Among these requirements were providing information about the twenty largest securities the agency had rated and at least ten institutional investors who had used the agency's ratings services in the previous three years. The law gave the SEC the ability to reject applicants that lacked "adequate material and financial resources" to produce ratings with integrity. However, the SEC was barred from regulating the methodologies or substance of ratings issued by the agencies.

The SEC adopted rules implementing the new law on June 18, 2007. Despite the new rules, the credit agencies came under new, and even more intense, criticism during the financial crisis of 2008 when it became clear that they had given investment grade ratings to numerous financial instruments without adequately evaluating the soundness of those securities. *(Financial crisis, p. 163)*

Financial Services Regulatory Relief

Various elements of the financial services industry—national and community banks, savings and loans, and federally charted credit unions—won promises of significant relief in 2006 from what they regarded as obsolete or excessively intrusive federal regulations.

With broad bipartisan support in both chambers, Congress approved the Financial Services Regulatory Relief Act of 2006, which reduced or repealed numerous regulations that financial services lobbyists said imposed onerous and unnecessary burdens on their industry. Just two years later, however, the financial crisis forced Congress and the executive branch to examine whether regulations for at least some sectors of the financial services industry had been too weak or vague rather than too strong, as the industry and its many political supporters had long insisted.

Congressional committees had begun work in 2004 on the regulatory changes sought by the industry, but the Senate did not act on a proposal passed by the House. Prospects for the legislation appeared to brighten in December 2005 when the House Financial Services Committee approved (H Rept 109-356, Part I) a sweeping measure (HR 3505) clearing away dozens of regulatory requirements for nearly all segments of the industry. The House Judiciary Committee gave its approval on Feb. 16, 2006 (H Rept 109-356, Part II), and the full House approved the bill on March 8 by a vote of 415–2.

In the meantime, the Senate Banking, Housing and Urban Affairs Committee completed its work on a narrower measure, S 2856, which left in place many of the regulations that would have been dropped under the House bill. The committee approved that bill on May 18 (S Rept 109-256), and the full Senate gave its approval on a voice vote on May 25.

House-Senate negotiators worked out a compromise version of the Senate bill in late September. The House adopted the compromise by a 417–0 vote on Sep. 27, and the Senate gave its approval by voice vote on Sept. 30. President George W. Bush signed the measure into law (PL 109-351) on Oct. 13.

Despite the numerous provisions meeting the requests of the banking industry, lobbyists said the bill did not go far enough in reducing regulations. The bill "is just the beginning of what needs to be done," Floyd Stoner, a lobbyist for the American Bankers Association, said in a statement.

MAJOR PROVISIONS

- Gave the Federal Reserve increased latitude to reduce the amount of capital many banks would need to keep in reserve to hedge against investment losses. Authorized the Fed to reduce or even eliminate the reserve requirement to zero percent in come cases, as opposed to the previous reserve minimums ranging from 3 percent to 14 percent. Authorized the Fed to pay interest to banks on funds they held at the Fed. Made both provisions effective on Oct. 1, 2011.
- Directed the Securities and Exchange Commission and the Federal Reserve to adopt the new banker-broker rules jointly, in consultation with other banking regulators. The provision sought to resolve a longstanding dispute over SEC rules on when banks must register as security brokers that arose after Congress in 1999 passed the Gramm-Leach-Bliley Act (PL 106-102) allowing banks to emerge as so-called "full service" financial services. The SEC had proposed rules that some banks had insisted were unduly burdensome.
- Increased the number of small banks eligible to be examined by federal regulators every eighteen months, as opposed to annually.
- Allowed Federal credit unions to provide services such as check-cashing and money orders to any person eligible for membership, regardless of whether that person was a member of the credit union.
- Repealed or modified several regulations governing national banks, thus giving banks greater organizational flexibility but not changing their basic legal structure. One such change repealed a statutory formula for when national banks could declare dividends and instead allowed bank directors to use their own judgment in declaring dividends.

2007–2008

Both Congress and the White House were slow to respond to the growing housing crisis that led to the country's worst financial crisis since the Great Depression and propelled the economy into recession. Although legislation was being considered in both chambers in 2007 to provide some mortgage relief to homeowners threatened with foreclosure, the talks seemed to have little urgency behind them. Toward the end of the year, as it became clear that the crisis on Wall Street was beginning to have an impact on Main Street, lawmakers started to think about an economic stimulus package, but little action occurred. In 2008, however, Congress and the administration could delay no longer and both moved actively to help forestall economic catastrophe.

Prompted by a decline in consumer spending in December 2007 and the first monthly job loss in more than four years, Democratic and Republican leaders in the House reached a deal with the White House early in 2008 to send rebate checks to taxpayers in an effort to stimulate the economy. The package, which was expected to add $276 billion to the budget deficit, was cleared for the president's signature on Feb. 8, less than three weeks after it was introduced.

Congress again acted quickly in July 2008 when Treasury Secretary Henry M. Paulson Jr. asked Congress for the authority to protect mortgage giants Fannie Mae and Freddie Mac from imminent collapse, including authority to take them over if necessary. Congress had been debating legislation to tighten regulation of the two troubled companies for several years but had not been able to overcome differences between the two chambers and the two parties. In the wake of Paulson's announcement, however, and a reluctant agreement by the administration to acquiesce on mortgage relief provisions, Congress cleared legislation granting Treasury the bailout authority. Paulson had said he did not think the government would have to take over the two companies, but on Sept. 7, it did just that and announced that it would spend up to $200 billion to keep the companies solvent. *(Financial crisis of 2007–2008, p. 163)*

Then, on Sept. 15, 2008, Lehman Brothers, one of the country's largest investment banks, went into bankruptcy, sparking a worldwide panic in the financial markets. To calm those markets and unfreeze credit, which had become unavailable at almost any cost, Paulson and Federal Reserve Chairman Ben S. Bernanke implored Congress to take the unprecedented step of granting the Treasury Department authority to spend as much as $700 billion to bail out troubled financial institutions.

The Troubled Asset Relief Program (TARP) was not universally applauded. Many Republicans opposed the idea of such vast federal intervention in private markets, while many Democrats said the big financial institutions did not deserve a bailout. The House initially rejected it, which sent stock markets plunging as investors panicked. With the prospect of a global financial collapse becoming more likely as the clock ticked, ideological and political preferences faded for the moment: the bailout was approved and signed into law on Oct. 3, just fifteen days after Paulson and Bernanke made their first request to congressional leaders on Sept. 18.

Congress took up one final bailout request in 2008, this one to aid the three struggling domestic automakers, two of which, General Motors and Chrysler, were on the verge of bankruptcy. After an intense lobbying campaign, Congress in September agreed to appropriate funds for a $25 billion loan program for carmakers that had been enacted in 2007 but not funded.

But when the executives came back to Congress after the elections in November asking for an additional $25 billion, they discovered they had worn out their welcome. Many lawmakers balked at giving yet more money to an industry that they said was in trouble largely because of poor business decisions. After Congress refused to act, the White House stepped in, announcing short-term loans from TARP funds to GM and Chrysler to help with restructuring their businesses. The decision about a more comprehensive program to aid the automakers was left to the incoming administration of President-elect Barack Obama.

Economic Stimulus Package

Congressional leaders of both parties claimed victory in February 2008 for their roles in quickly clearing a short-term stimulus package designed to put money in Americans' pockets and boost the sagging economy. President George W. Bush signed the bill into law Feb. 13 (HR 5140—PL 110-185). The stimulus package was expected to increase the federal budget deficit by $151.7 billion in fiscal 2008 and a total of $124.5 billion in fiscal 2009 through 2018.

The package was the result of a deal negotiated by House Speaker Nancy Pelosi, D-Calif., House Minority Leader John A. Boehner, R-Ohio, and Treasury Secretary Henry M. Paulson Jr. The central element of the bill called for the Treasury to send checks of up to $600 for individuals and $1,200 for couples who paid income taxes in 2007 or 2008. The tax credits were refundable, which meant that people whose incomes were so low that they paid little or no taxes would also receive the payments.

The bill also provided write-off incentives to encourage businesses to invest in new equipment. In addition, it increased the size of mortgages that Fannie Mae and Freddie Mac could purchase and that the Federal Housing Administration (FHA) could insure to assist some families in refinancing their mortgages and to help stabilize the housing market, which was collapsing as a result of the subprime mortgage crisis. That crisis arose from several years of aggressive mortgage lending by financial companies to prospective home buyers who had neither adequate incomes nor financial strength to meet normal lending standards. Thousands of these homes went into foreclosure within two years. *(Additional details, p. 163)*

The bipartisan agreement between House leaders and the White House, announced Jan. 24, was a notable exception to the partisan dueling that dominated Congress in the presidential election year. The compromise was driven not only by the housing market crisis but also by slowing economic growth and rising unemployment, which were stoking fears of economic recession. In January the nation lost jobs for the first time in more than four years, and consumer spending, the main engine driving economic growth, slowed sharply in December, according to government reports. Leaders of both parties said that taxpayers and markets around the world were waiting for the U.S. government to take action.

"We know throughout the households of America that many people are living paycheck to paycheck, and they need this economy to turn around," Pelosi said. "Now we see across the world that the state of the economy [in the United States] is having an impact [abroad] as well, so the urgency we feel at home is now even more urgent as we see the impact of our markets on others."

MAJOR PROVISIONS

Following are the major provisions of the stimulus law, with cost estimates from the Congressional Budget Office and the Joint Committee on Taxation.

Individual refunds. Provided payments to individuals totaling $15.7 billion in fiscal 2008 and $9.8 billion in fiscal 2009, allocated as follows:

- Checks of up to $600 for individuals ($1,200 for couples filing jointly) who paid income taxes on wages and investment income in 2007 or 2008. Eligibility for the rebate began phasing out for individuals with more than $75,000 in gross income ($150,000 for couples).
- Checks of $300 for individuals ($600 for couples) who earned at least $3,000 in qualifying income in 2007 and filed a return but had no tax liability. Qualifying income included wages, Social Security benefits, and payments to disabled veterans or their survivors.
- An additional $300 for each dependent child under age seventeen for workers receiving either of the two types of credit.
- A requirement that taxpayers include a valid Social Security number on their tax returns to prevent illegal immigrants from receiving checks.

Business tax deductions. Provided businesses with tax benefits that were expected to cost $44.8 billion in fiscal 2008, declining to $7.5 billion by 2018. The benefits included:

- A bonus depreciation that allowed companies to deduct an additional 50 percent from their taxable income in fiscal 2008 for the cost of items that would be subject to depreciation over twenty years or less. The equipment had to be purchased and put into service in 2008. The remaining value of the investment would be depreciated over the life of the item.
- An increase to $250,000 from $128,000 in the amount small businesses could "expense," or deduct in full in fiscal 2008 for new property, mainly equipment. The amount was gradually reduced after a company's total investments for the year reached $800,000; previously the phase-out began at $410,000.

Mortgage relief. Provided two changes in federal mortgage law that had no net cost and that provided for:

- An increase in the size of individual mortgage loans that Fannie Mae and Freddie Mac could purchase to 125 percent of the median home price in the local market or $729,750, whichever was less. The previous limit was $417,000. The increase applied to loans originated between July 1, 2007, and Dec. 31, 2008.
- An increase in the limit on the Federal Housing Administration mortgage loans to 125 percent of the median home price in the local market or $729,750, whichever was less. The previous loan limit was $362,000. The FHA could increase the limit by $100,000 if it was warranted by market conditions. The provision applied to loans approved before Dec. 31, 2008.

LEGISLATIVE ACTION

Pelosi and Boehner brought the negotiated bill directly to the House floor, bypassing the committee process, and called on their members to line up behind the package. The House passed the bill Jan. 29 by a lopsided 385–35 vote, one day after Bush urged support for the bipartisan agreement in his State of the Union address.

Despite intense pressure to clear the House bill, senators—particularly Democrats—insisted that the Senate have its say on the package. On Jan. 30 the Senate Finance Committee produced a broader bill with expanded rebates, more options on tax breaks for businesses, energy tax breaks, and an expansion of unemployment benefits.

After more than a week of partisan jousting, however, Senate Democrats gave up their efforts to pass a broader bill, settling instead for a few changes to the House's measure. The turning point came on Feb. 6 when Democrats fell one vote short of the sixty needed to invoke cloture, thereby limiting debate, on the Finance Committee's version.

After the cloture motion failed, Majority Leader Harry Reid, D-Nev., and Minority Leader Mitch McConnell,

R-Ky., reached a deal that preserved some provisions sought by the Finance Committee, including expanding eligibility for the rebates to include low-income senior citizens, disabled veterans, and survivors of veterans. Among the provisions left out of the bill were the temporary extension of unemployment benefits and an extension of renewable energy credits. Unemployment benefits were subsequently extended twice, once in June and again in November. *(Details, p. 667)*

The Senate adopted the agreed amendment 91–6 on Feb. 7, and then passed the revised House bill on a **key vote of 81–16 (R 33–16; D 46–0; I 2–0).** The House cleared the measure later the same day on a **key vote of 380–34 (R165–28; D 215–6).** *(2008 key votes, p. 972)*

Mortgage Relief, Financial Reform

Five months after Congress passed an economic stimulus measure giving rebates to American taxpayers, it cleared a foreclosure relief bill that provided a multimillion-dollar lifeline for troubled mortgage finance giants Fannie Mae and Freddie Mac.

An essentially open-ended grant of authority to the Treasury Department to shore up Fannie and Freddie was added to a mortgage relief bill—which already contained a new regulatory regime for the two companies—after government officials warned that they could fail amid the housing slump and tightened credit markets. President George W. Bush signed the measure into law July 30 (HR 3221—PL 110-289).

Fannie Mae and Freddie Mac were government-sponsored enterprises that played a critical role in creating a secondary housing market. They purchased mortgages from banks, which gave the banks the money to make new loans at lower rates than might otherwise be available. Fannie and Freddie bundled the mortgages into packages that became the basis for mortgage-backed securities. Over time they had become involved in more complicated transactions that critics said put the two operations at higher risk than necessary. The management of the two companies also raised problems: accounting scandals in 2003 and 2004 had forced out the top executives in both companies.

Lawmakers had tried repeatedly for several years to impose new rules on Fannie and Freddie but failed in the face of disagreements over the shape of the regulation and the companies' powerful lobbying ability. In May 2007 the House once again passed a measure to establish a strong new federal regulator (HR 1427—H Rept 110-142). The Senate did not act on the bill, in part because in the fall of 2007 lawmakers' priority shifted to stabilizing the collapsing housing market by getting credit flowing to homeowners and providing some relief for homeowners facing foreclosure.

In the fall of 2007, both chambers passed bills (HR 1852, S 2338) aimed at expanding the ability of the Federal Housing Administration (FHA) to guarantee mortgage loans. The House also passed a broad overhaul of the nation's mortgage laws (HR 3915) that included a nationwide licensing registry for mortgage brokers, minimum standards for home loans, and a requirement that firms that packaged, or securitized, the loans for sale on the secondary market share in the liability.

In February 2008 the two chambers began writing increasingly broad legislation to ease the mortgage crisis. After nearly three months of maneuvering and negotiations, the Senate voted in April to pass a mortgage relief bill (HR 3221) that was devoted mainly to overhauling FHA lending practices and providing tax benefits to businesses hurt by the mortgage crisis. The bill dropped proposed language to allow bankruptcy judges to modify subprime mortgages, including reducing the outstanding principal.

The House passed a much broader version of HR 3221 in May that included a new strong independent regulator for Fannie Mae and Freddie Mac, an affordable housing fund, an expanded FHA program to help borrowers threatened with foreclosure on their primary residence refinance to new mortgages, and a set of provisions designed to relieve the tax burden on new and struggling homeowners.

The Senate took up HR 3221, as amended by the House, in mid-June and replaced most of the text with a compromise substitute that provided a new regulator for Fannie Mae and Freddie Mac and the FHA and an affordable housing fund similar to that in the House version but rejected the House tax relief provisions for new homeowners.

Significant differences remained in the two versions of HR 3221. But on a Sunday afternoon in mid-July 2008, House and Senate wrangling over those differences—and vigorous opposition from the White House to elements of the measure—was swept away when Treasury Secretary Henry M. Paulson Jr. announced that the government needed immediate authority to protect the two mortgage giants from potential collapse. Fannie and Freddie owned or guaranteed about $5 trillion of the $12 trillion in mortgages issued in the United States. The price per share for both companies, which had exceeded $60 in mid-2007, had dropped to $20 in mid-June as frightened investors withdrew their money. The price stood at $10 when Paulson made his announcement, cutting the market capitalization for the two companies in half in a month and raising concerns about bankruptcy.

Paulson lobbied hard for the bailout authority, which gave the Treasury authority to buy assets from the companies, including their mortgage holdings and shares of their stock, and to extend new credit to them. Lawmakers agreed with Treasury to impose no new dollar limit on the lending to Fannie or Freddie or on purchases of their stock. But costs associated with the bailout were limited by the overall ceiling on government borrowing, which the bill raised by $800 billion to $10.6 trillion. *(Debt ceiling details, p. 68)*

As part of the bargain to add the bailout of Fannie and Freddie to the mortgage relief legislation, the White House dropped its objections to the broader measure. Some conservative Republicans worried that the government could end up being exposed to the two companies' huge liabilities, but their objections were not strong enough to derail the aid. The House passed the bailout authority July 23 on a **key vote of 272–152 (R 45–149; D 227–3).** The Senate cleared the measure on July 26 on a **key vote of 72–13 (R 27–13; D 43–0; I 2–0).** The bill became law on July 30, less than three weeks after Paulson's surprise announcement. *(Background of mortgage crisis, p. 163; Details of the legislation, p. 630; 2008 key votes, p. 972)*

Paulson said at the time that he did not think it would be necessary for the government to actually give the companies money. The Congressional Budget Office also said there was a strong likelihood that the money would not have to be used, and it estimated the likely cost to taxpayers at $25 billion. The mortgage market continued to deteriorate, however, and enactment of the bailout did little to reassure investors, especially those that had loaned more than $1.5 trillion to Fannie and Freddie. Barely five weeks after enactment, on Sept. 7, the Treasury announced it had put both Fannie and Freddie into conservatorships and said it would funnel as much as $200 billion into the companies to keep them functioning.

A new HOPE for Homeowners program, created under the bill to help borrowers avoid foreclosure by refinancing mortgages at lower rates, turned out to be too complicated and never got off the ground. As of Feb. 3, 2009, only 451 people had applied for relief under the program.

Financial Sector Aid: TARP

In an extraordinary response to events that were threatening to become the worst financial and economic crisis since the Great Depression of the 1930s, Congress granted the Treasury Department authority to spend as much as $700 billion to stabilize a battered financial sector crippled by losses on housing-related assets. President George W. Bush signed the unprecedented legislation into law Oct. 3, 2008 (HR 1424—PL 110-343).

As originally conceived, the program would have purchased seemingly worthless mortgage-based assets from financial companies. But Treasury officials soon abandoned that plan in favor of buying stock in troubled financial institutions.

The plan drew strong opposition from both sides of the aisle, not to mention the public. The House at first rejected it outright. But Congress sent Bush a finished bill just fifteen days after receiving the request from Treasury Secretary Henry M. Paulson Jr., whose warnings of a global financial collapse left lawmakers stunned.

The legislation was the third broad effort by Congress in 2008 to address the worsening economy; it followed a tax-driven stimulus bill and a measure to stem rising home foreclosures. This third effort grew out of a late-night meeting with congressional leaders on Sept. 18, led by Paulson and Federal Reserve Chairman Ben S. Bernanke, who pleaded for new emergency powers to respond to the deepening crisis. *(Stimulus, p. 151; Mortgage finance overhaul, pp. 153, 630)*

During the two weeks preceding the request, the Treasury had taken control of mortgage giants Fannie Mae and Freddie Mac. The fourth-largest investment bank, Lehman Brothers Holdings, Inc., had been allowed to go bankrupt. The Fed and Treasury had bailed out the country's largest insurance company, American International Group, Inc. And global financial conditions had deteriorated further, threatening banks, pension funds, and individual investors. *(Details of the financial crisis, p. 163)*

Many credit markets were frozen, largely because lenders held hundreds of billions of dollars in mortgage-related securities whose value had fallen sharply in the wake of rising number of foreclosures and because the number of subprime home loans that were in danger of default remained large. As a result, banks tightened their lending standards, refusing to do business even with one another. Paulson and Bernanke warned that the resulting evaporation of credit would cripple the entire economy.

PAULSON'S PLAN

On the evening of Thursday, Sept. 18, 2008, Paulson and Bernanke held a closed-door Capitol Hill meeting with congressional leaders, in which they outlined the depth of the economic problems. They asked for approval of a comprehensive, if not clearly defined, plan to allow the government to purchase the bulk of the essentially worthless assets of damaged banks and investment firms. "The ultimate taxpayer protection will be the stability this troubled asset relief program provides to our financial system, even as it will involve a significant investment of taxpayer dollars," Paulson, a former chairman of the investment bank Goldman Sachs, said at a news conference the following morning.

Two days after the meeting, a three-page proposal from Paulson was circulated on the Hill. Paulson wanted a free hand to purchase $700 billion worth of so-called toxic assets from financial institutions, though the plan included provisions that would allow the Treasury to buy almost any financial instrument with the bailout money.

Treasury hoped to buy the assets through a reverse auction process, allowing market participants to set the price the government would pay for the troubled assets. After buying the assets, Treasury would hold them until the market stabilized, when it would then sell the assets and recover at least some of the taxpayers' dollars.

Lawmakers balked at Paulson's opening bid, saying it would give the Treasury secretary nearly unfettered authority to spend huge sums of taxpayer money as he saw fit. Complaints ranged from the lack of details in the proposal to the need to protect taxpayers to the absence of oversight.

Many Republicans objected strongly to giving the government such a major role in the private sector.

However, given the urgency of the situation, bipartisan leaders from the House and Senate sat down with Treasury officials and others to put together a deal. The plan that came out of the talks called for the creation of the Troubled Asset Relief Program (TARP). Treasury would receive an initial $250 billion for the program and an additional $100 billion following a certification from the president that the money was needed. A further $350 billion would be available if the president requested it and Congress agreed, using an expedited process.

The delicate compromise essentially left intact the broad asset-buying powers Paulson sought for the Treasury, while providing some assurances to nervous lawmakers that taxpayer investments would be paid back. Safeguards included an oversight panel and authority for the Treasury to take equity positions in companies receiving assistance. The negotiated agreement also included some restrictions on executive pay for companies that received money from the bailout fund.

TENSE NEGOTIATIONS

The intense and speedy deal-making that led to the compromise proposal was by all accounts torturous. "We've had a lot of pleasant words, and some that haven't always been pleasant," Senate Majority Leader Harry Reid, D-Nev., said after the agreement was reached Sept. 28.

Selling the proposal to skeptical lawmakers was difficult from the outset. The administration spent the week of Sept. 21 trying to persuade legislators to support the TARP, sending Vice President Dick Cheney and White House Chief of Staff Joshua B. Bolten to the Capitol to cajole balky Republicans. Paulson and Bernanke implored lawmakers to give them the go-ahead, both in testimony on Sept. 22–23 and in private meetings with legislators on both sides of the Hill.

Senate Banking chairman Christopher J. Dodd, D-Conn., sharply criticized the Treasury proposal, calling Paulson's initial three-page draft "stunning and unprecedented in its scope and lack of detail." The proposal, Dodd said, "would do nothing to help even a single family save a home, at least not up front.... And it would allow [Paulson] to act with utter and absolute impunity—without review."

Most Senate Republicans expressed cautious support for the bailout package, but Richard C. Shelby of Alabama, the ranking Republican on the Banking Committee, made it clear that he was not persuaded, adding that Congress needed more time to develop a proper plan.

President Bush went on national television Sept. 24 to build support for the proposal. "I know that an economic rescue package will present a tough vote for many members of Congress," he said in his first prime time broadcast speech in more than a year. But, he added, "the government's top economic experts warn that, without immediate action by Congress, America could slip into a financial panic, and a distressing scenario would unfold."

"More banks could fail, including some in your community," the president continued. "The stock market would drop even more, which would reduce the value of your retirement account. The value of your home could plummet. Foreclosures would rise dramatically. And if you own a business or a farm, you would find it harder and more expensive to get credit. More businesses would close their doors, and millions of Americans could lose their jobs."

The urgency of action on the financial crisis was underscored by news of the largest bank failure in U.S. history. The Federal Deposit Insurance Corporation on Sept. 25 seized Washington Mutual Inc. and sold its bank assets to JP Morgan Chase & Co. for $1.9 billion. Mortgage-related losses at the Seattle-based thrift, the nation's largest savings and loan, had led to near panic, with the thrift experiencing withdrawals of $16.7 billion since Sept. 16.

Still, congressional opposition to the bailout grew throughout the week, particularly among conservative Republicans who objected to the wholesale government intervention in the workings of the financial sector. Rank-and-file lawmakers from both parties were caught between the potential for a financial meltdown and the anger of constituents who viewed the administration plan as a veritable lifeboat for risk-happy Wall Street executives and speculators.

In a surprise move, the Republican presidential nominee, Sen. John McCain, suddenly announced that he was suspending his campaign and returning to the Senate to help manage the deal. He challenged his opponent, Democrat Sen. Barack Obama, to do the same. Obama reluctantly returned to Washington after Bush invited both candidates to join with congressional leaders in a White House meeting on Thursday afternoon, Sept. 25.

The White House gathering was designed to smooth the way for a bipartisan deal based on the administration's core plan of buying mortgage-backed securities and other risky assets from financial institutions. Hours earlier, the chief congressional negotiators from both parties announced they had reached an agreement in principle.

But House Republicans caught the negotiators off guard at the White House meeting by calling instead for the government to offer insurance to holders of risky mortgage-backed securities, with the holders financing the plan through premium payments. Within hours, Paulson returned to the Hill, and negotiators began working to get the talks back on track.

Throughout the negotiations that followed, the underlying concept for the TARP never changed. But reaction on the Hill and in home districts grew so negative that negotiators gathered late Saturday, Sept. 27, to make sure the bill they would bring to the House and Senate floors appealed to a bipartisan majority of lawmakers. The congressional side of the negotiating table included a bipartisan, bicameral representation of leadership: Reid; House Speaker Nancy

Pelosi, D-Calif.; Rep. Barney Frank, D-Mass., chairman of the House Financial Services Committee; and Sen. Judd Gregg, R-N.H., the ranking Republican on the Senate Budget Committee.

Shortly after midnight on Sunday, Sept. 28, the negotiators triumphantly announced that they had reached an accord. Leaders on both sides of the aisle expressed confidence that they had the votes, and House leaders scheduled a vote for the next day. The Senate was expected to clear the measure on Wednesday, after a one-day break for the Jewish holiday of Rosh Hashanah, after which lawmakers would go home to campaign for the Nov. 4 elections.

HOUSE REJECTS BILL; STOCK MARKET TANKS

The hopefulness expressed by leaders hours earlier evaporated Monday, Sept. 29, when the $700 billion bailout (HR 3997) was defeated in the House. Resounding opposition from conservative Republicans, who said the intervention violated free market principles, and liberal Democrats, who argued that Wall Street executives did not deserve a bailout, scuttled the rescue package, on a **key vote of 205–228 (R 65–133; D 140–95).** Traders on the floor of the New York Stock Exchange watched in disbelief, first as the House rejected the plan and then as the Dow Jones Industrial Average fell 777 points, the largest point decline in a single day in its 112-year history. *(2008 key votes, p. 972)*

Refusing to ask their members to shoulder the burden of passing the bill by themselves, Democratic leaders had demanded support from a majority of the GOP members, pressuring House Minority Leader John A. Boehner of Ohio to produce the necessary votes. The lobbying to win GOP votes for the plan came from all sides. McCain called fifty to sixty House Republicans. The U.S. Chamber of Commerce, a lobbying voice often heeded by the GOP, warned that the vote would be on its annual scorecard. President Bush worked the phones, and his budget director, Jim Nussle, a former House Republican, kept up the push during the vote from the back of the House chamber.

But lawmakers were also listening to the voters, and nothing in the deal assuaged concerns that the plan was anything more than a taxpayer bailout of Wall Street. The blizzard of negative telephone calls and e-mail messages from angry constituents continued to bombard legislators in both parties right up to the vote. Democratic leaders kept the roll call open for about thirty minutes, fifteen minutes longer than normal, trying to change the outcome, but in the end, two-thirds of House Republicans voted against the plan, while three-fifths of the Democrats voted for it.

A breakdown of the House vote showed a broad and varied opposition to the legislation. Most members of the conservative Republican Study Group voted against HR 3997 and against their Republican president. Members of specific Democratic groups—the fiscally conservative "Blue Dogs," the Hispanic and black caucuses, the Progressives, and New Democrats—split their votes almost evenly. Most members who were in highly competitive reelection races—nineteen Republicans and seventeen Democrats—voted against the bill. Members of the leadership in both parties held together and voted for the measure.

SENATE TAKES THE REINS

Sobered by the Wall Street losses in response to the House vote, Senate leaders quickly stepped in to try to salvage the bailout. "We're going to stay here until we get this done," Gregg said.

Bipartisan Senate negotiations produced a package that preserved the core of Paulson's plan but added several items to attract additional House votes: a mental health parity plan; a package of energy tax breaks and extensions of popular but expiring tax benefits; and an increase in the limit on federal insurance for bank deposits, to $250,000 for each bank account, up from $100,000. The tax and mental health provisions had been stalled. *(Mental health parity, p. 569; Tax extensions, p. 131)*

Few senators were enthusiastic about the bailout, but most saw no alternative. To underline the gravity of the moment, Reid asked that all members remain seated and cast their votes from their desks, a formality used on the most momentous of occasions. On Oct. 1, the Senate agreed, on a **key vote of 74–25 (R 34–15; D 39–9; I –1),** to insert the package into the mental health parity bill (HR 1424). The Senate then passed the bill by the same tally. Presidential candidates Obama and McCain returned to Washington for the votes; the absent senator was Edward M. Kennedy, D-Mass, who was recovering from treatment for a brain tumor. *(2008 Key votes, p. 972)*

HOUSE CLEARS THE BILL

With some trepidation about the outcome of a vote, but with evidence mounting that the economy was in recession, the House took up HR 1424 on Oct. 3, and cleared it on a **key vote of 263–171 (R 91–108; D 172–63).** Thirty-three Democrats and twenty-five Republicans who had voted against the original bill switched their vote to yea on the revised version. *(2008 key votes, p. 972)*

Several of the vote switches cited the new elements in the Senate package and fresh signs that the Main Street economy was under stress. Although many members said they continued to receive a high volume of negative calls from voters, the stock market's plunge after the first vote appeared to rattle constituents worried about the effect the crisis was having on their retirement savings, particularly stock-based mutual funds and 401(k) plans. Business lobbyists also mobilized, warning that they were facing increasing difficulty in obtaining credit to finance their day-to-day operations.

"I think the biggest reason for the change here," said Frank, "is the damages that started coming in ... the reality of the economic damage." Still most of those in both parties who voted against the original bill were not swayed to switch by either the new version or the economic news.

SHIFT IN BAILOUT PURPOSE

Less than two weeks after the bill was signed, the rescue program began to evolve. Originally described as a plan to buy up troubled assets, the TARP was used mostly to inject capital directly into banks by purchasing stock. That policy, first announced Oct. 14, made the government a stockholder in troubled banks, rather than relieving the banks of toxic mortgage-backed securities.

Paulson explained the shift Nov. 12, saying that by the time the bill was enacted on Oct. 3, market conditions had "worsened considerably," making it clear that Treasury had to act quickly. "Purchasing troubled assets—our initial focus—would take time to implement and would not be sufficient given the severity of the problem," he said. The most timely approach, he said, was "to strengthen bank balance sheets quickly through direct purchases of equity in banks." Treasury used the first $250 billion of the TARP funds to buy shares in the largest U.S. banks and in several smaller ones. Left for the next administration to deal with in 2009 and later were the estimated $2 trillion of toxic mortgage-backed assets still on the balance sheets of dozens of banks.

MAJOR PROVISIONS

Following are the major provisions of the financial services rescue bill enacted Oct. 3, 2008 (HR 1424—PL 110-3430). The legislation also included a package of tax provisions and a mental health parity bill, which are covered separately in this volume. *(Taxes, p. 131; Mental health parity, p. 569)*

Troubled Asset Relief Program

Program created. Authorized the Treasury Department to establish a program, called the Troubled Asset Relief Program (TARP), to purchase troubled assets from financial institutions on terms and conditions determined by the secretary under the legislation.

Authorization. Authorized purchase up to $700 billion in troubled assets. Made $250 billion available for immediate release upon enactment and another $100 billion available if the president certified the need for it to Congress. Allowed Congress the option, if the president requested the final $350 billion, of passing a joint resolution, to be considered on an expedited basis, disapproving the release of funds. Specified the $350 billion would be released fifteen days after the president's request if no disapproval resolution was enacted.

Eligible assets. Authorized the Treasury to buy residential and commercial mortgages and any mortgage-backed securities, obligations, or other instruments that were originated before March 14, 2008. Authorized the Treasury to buy "any other financial instrument" if deemed necessary to "promote financial market stability," after consulting with the Federal Reserve Board and notifying Congress.

Eligible institutions. Specified that a financial institution, to be eligible to sell assets to the government, had to have significant operations in the United States and could not be owned by a foreign government.

Purchase price. Barred the Treasury from buying assets from an institution for more than that institution originally paid for them.

Consultation. Required the Treasury to consult with the Fed, the Federal Deposit Insurance Corporation (FDIC), the Comptroller of the Currency, the Office of Thrift Supervision, and the Housing and Urban Development Department (HUD) in exercising its new authorities.

Sunset. Terminated Treasury's authority to buy assets Dec. 31, 2009. Allowed the Treasury secretary to extend the buying authority for up to two years after enactment after reporting to Congress on reasons the extension was necessary to assist American families and stabilize financial markets and on how much the extension was expected to cost taxpayers.

Management and sale of assets. Authorized the Treasury to manage troubled assets purchased under the program, including selling the assets or repackaging them for sale to private investors at any time and price and under any conditions the Treasury secretary determined. Required proceeds be used to reduce the federal debt. Specified these provisions were not subject to the expiration requirement.

Recouping losses. Required the Office of Management and Budget, in consultation with the Congressional Budget Office, five years after enactment to submit a report to Congress on the net amount in the TARP. Required the president, if there was a shortfall, to submit legislation to Congress to recoup the loss from the financial services industry.

Insurance of troubled assets. Required the Treasury Department, after setting up the TARP, to establish the Troubled Assets Insurance Financing Fund to guarantee the assets originated or issued before March 14, 2008, including mortgage-backed securities. Directed the Treasury to develop guarantees for troubled assets still held by financial institutions. Allowed financial institutions to request that the Treasury guarantee the timely payment of the principal and interest on such assets in amounts not to exceed 100 percent of the payments.

Insurance premiums. Authorized the Treasury Department to collect premiums from the financial institutions participating in the insurance program to cover anticipated claims, based on an analysis of the risk involved.

Warrants. Required the Treasury to take warrants in a company that sold its assets into the program, allowing the government to take a nonvoting equity stake in the company and providing Treasury with a share of any profits if the company made money after the government bought the troubled assets.

Executive compensation. Required any financial institution that sold troubled assets directly to the program to abide by limits on executive compensation. Specified that the limits, set by the Treasury, were to include a ban on "golden parachutes," such as severance pay, bonuses, stock options, or any combination of those. Specified that the limits would also include a requirement that a participating firm pay back bonuses that turn out to be based on incorrect earnings statements—known as a claw-back provision—and a ban on compensation incentives for executives who took excessive risks.

Prohibited an institution that sold more than $300 million in assets to the Treasury through an auction from signing any new employment contracts for a senior executive officer that provided a golden parachute in the event of an involuntary termination, bankruptcy filings, insolvency, or receivership.

Tax penalties. Made an institution that sold more than $300 million in assets to the Treasury subject to additional taxes, including a 20 percent excise tax on golden-parachute payments triggered by events other than retirement. Prohibited those institutions from deducting more than $500,000 in compensation per executive from the company's taxable income.

Oversight

Oversight board. Established a board, the Financial Stability Oversight Board, to review Treasury activities. Authorized the board to make recommendations and to appoint a credit review committee to evaluate how the Treasury exercises its authority to buy troubled assets. Specified the following would be board members: the chairman of the Federal Reserve, the Treasury secretary, the director of the Federal Home Finance Agency, the chairman of the Securities and Exchange Commission (SEC), and the secretary of housing and urban development.

Reports to Congress. Required the Treasury to report to Congress sixty days before it began exercising its new authority to buy financial instruments and every thirty days thereafter. Required the reports to include an overview of actions taken by the department, the actual obligation and expenditure of the funds provided for administrative expenses, and a detailed financial statement. Required the Treasury, after it bought $50 billion worth of troubled assets, to provide another report describing all of the transactions made during the reporting period, how prices were set for the transactions, and a justification for the purchase price. Required the Treasury to review the state of the financial markets and the regulatory system and report to Congress on its findings.

GAO oversight. Charged the Government Accountability Office (GAO) with conducting ongoing oversight of the activities and performance of the program and to report to Congress every sixty days, and to determine the extent to which financial institutions' leveraging, or borrowing, and sudden deleveraging were factors behind the existing financial crisis.

Inspector general. Established a special inspector general for the program who would be nominated by the president and confirmed by the Senate. Provided $50 million to conduct, supervise, and coordinate audits and investigations. Required the inspector to submit a quarterly report to Congress summarizing the programs' activities.

Congressional oversight. Established a five-member Congressional Oversight Panel to review the state of the financial markets and the regulatory system. Required the panel to submit a special report on regulatory reform before Jan. 20, 2009, that analyzed the state of the regulatory system and its effectiveness at overseeing the financial system and protecting consumers. Required the report to include recommendations for improvement and existing gaps in consumer protections. Specified that four appointments would be made by the House Speaker, the House minority leader, and the Senate majority and minority leaders, with the fifth member appointed by the Speaker and Senate majority leader after consultation with the two minority leaders.

Deposit Insurance Increase. Increased, through Dec. 31, 2009, the limit on FDIC and National Credit Union Administration deposit insurance to $250,000 for each account, from $100,000. The limit had not been increased since 1980. *(Earlier FDIC reforms, p. 148)*

Foreclosure mitigation. Required the Treasury Department to implement a plan to mitigate foreclosures and to encourage lenders to modify loans or mortgages that supported mortgage-backed securities acquired under the program. Authorized the Treasury to use loan guarantees and credit enhancement to avoid foreclosure. Directed the department to coordinate with other federal agencies that held troubled assets in order to identify opportunities to modify loans.

Homeowner assistance. Required certain other federal agencies that held mortgages, mortgage-backed securities, and other assets secured by residential real estate to carry out plans to maximize assistance for homeowners. Directed the agencies to encourage servicers of the underlying mortgages to take advantage of the HOPE for Homeowners Program and other available programs to minimize foreclosures. Applied the provision to the FDIC, the Federal Housing Finance Agency, and the Federal Reserve Board.

Taxes, Other Provisions

Community Banks. Allowed community banks to deduct losses from investments purchased before April 1, 2008, in mortgage finance giants Fannie Mae and Freddie Mac, which were taken over by the Treasury in September. The Joint Committee on Taxation (JCT) estimated that the provision would reduce federal revenue by more than $3 billion through fiscal 2018.

Forgiven mortgage debt. Included a three-year extension of a provision that allowed taxpayers who had their mortgage loans reduced to avoid paying taxes on up to $2 million of the forgiven debt. The exclusion, enacted in 2007 (PL 110-142), originally applied to mortgage debts discharged through the end of 2009. The Taxation Committee estimated the cost to the Treasury at more than $362 million through fiscal 2018. *(2007 legislation, p. 639)*

Mark-to-market accounting. Restated the Securities and Exchange Commission's authority to suspend the application of mark-to-market accounting rules if it determined that doing so would serve the public interest and protect investors. Required the SEC, in consultation with the Fed and Treasury, to conduct a study on mark-to-market standards, including the effects on balance sheets and the impact on the quality of financial information, and report to Congress within ninety days of enactment. Mark-to-market rules required companies to calculate the value of their holdings using the current market price, not the price they paid to acquire them.

Debt limit increase. Increased the statutory limit on the public debt to $11.3 trillion from the previous limit of $10.6 trillion. The $700 billion increase was needed to accommodate the potential cost of the new bailout program.

Auto Industry Assistance

Struggling domestic automakers persuaded Congress in late 2008 to finance a $25 billion loan program as part of the fiscal 2009 stopgap spending bill enacted on Sept. 30 (HR 238—PL 110-329). But legislators rebuffed the companies when they returned after the November elections seeking an immediate bailout aimed at staving off potential bankruptcies.

Given the precarious state of the American auto industry and projections of large-scale layoffs, President George W. Bush reluctantly intervened in December to provide $17.5 billion in immediate short-term loans, leaving difficult decisions about the industry's future to his successor, President-elect Barack Obama.

BACKGROUND

Many of the problems facing U.S. car manufacturers, all headquartered in Michigan, had been in the making for decades. Critics had long complained that the American companies were hurting themselves by focusing too much on vehicles that were highly profitable at the expense of developing cars that would compete well with the foreign-based sedans and small cars that many buyers were increasingly turning to in making purchase decisions.

During the oil crisis of the 1970s and the economic slowdown that followed, American buyers started buying the more fuel-efficient, reliable Japanese cars that were just beginning to be imported into the United States. The Big Three—General Motors Corp. (GM), Ford Motor Co., and Chrysler—found themselves in financial trouble as they scrambled to deal with new fuel economy, clean air, and safety regulations while also retooling their factories to follow the "lean production" patterns of their foreign rivals.

With the general pickup in the economy in the mid-1990s, domestic automakers increasingly left the markets for small and luxury cars to their foreign competitors and concentrated on building and selling popular and highly profitable pickup trucks and sports utility vehicles, which were in considerable demand from car buyers at the time. The companies all offered sedans and smaller vehicles but with some exceptions few were considered fully competitive in quality, features, design, and other standards with foreign vehicles—many from Japan but also luxury cars from Germany. This left the American firms heavily dependent on the large trucks and sports utility vehicles that at the time buyers were purchasing.

When increases in world oil prices in the early and mid-2000s pushed the price of gasoline above $2 a gallon and then over $3 and $4 a gallon—and in some places upwards of $5 a gallon, the U.S. car manufacturers had few smaller, fuel-efficient cars to offer buyers, and purchasers began to rethink their love affairs with trucks and SUVs that typically got under 15 miles per gallon.

Another problem for the American automakers was their wage and benefit structure. Union wages at the domestic car companies' factories were roughly twice as high as those at nonunion factories, mainly in the South, run by foreign makers. Unions, defending the contracts negotiated over the years, argued that actual wages of current workers were negligibly higher than nonunionized plants of foreign car companies.

But the cost of the companies' generous pension and health benefit plans, often negotiated with unions in lieu of wage increases, had mounted as their large workforce aged and retired; these costs weighed heavily on the financial structure of the American firms. By the mid-2000s, the three companies had run up huge "legacy" costs, which they said added about $1,800 to the price of every new car. Much of this obligation was unfunded, leading to a lowering of their credit ratings, which in turn made it more expensive for them to borrow money to invest in plants and new development.

Starting in 2005, each of the Big Three announced restructuring plans that entailed laying off tens of thousands of workers and closing dozens of plants in the United States and Canada. The companies also won concessions from their unions on retiree health care, and they offered buyouts that led to early retirement for thousands of workers. In 2007 the companies negotiated a new four-year contract with the United Auto Workers (UAW) that allowed the automakers to shed many of their legacy costs over time and to lower wages for new workers.

$25 BILLION LOAN

Congress in 2007 passed legislation (HR 6—PL 110-140) raising the fuel-efficiency standards for cars and trucks and authorizing loans to the automakers to help them retool to produce more fuel-efficient vehicles and meet the new federal mileage standards. The loans were unfunded then, but by 2008 the companies' long-standing problems were compounded by the deepening U.S. recession and the reduced availability of credit. *(Energy overhaul, p. 484)*

In August the car companies began talking with key Democrats and members of the Michigan delegation about funding the loans. In September the companies' three top executives—G. Richard Wagoner Jr., chairman and CEO of GM; Robert Nardelli, chairman and CEO of Chrysler LLC; and Alan Mulally, president and CEO of Ford, came to Capitol Hill urging lawmakers to act by the end of the month.

The lobbying blitz came just as lawmakers were trying to absorb the impact of unprecedented government intervention in the financial markets that included takeovers of the mortgage giants Fannie Mae and Freddie Mac and the country's largest insurance company, American International Group Inc., and a campaign by the Bush administration for Congress to approve a $700 billion rescue package for the financial services industry.

The automakers and their allies took pains to separate themselves from these bailouts, stressing that they were asking for a loan that would be repaid. Democratic leaders supported them, arguing that the loans were necessary to save jobs. "This is very, very important to an important industry in our country, said House Speaker Nancy Pelosi, D-Calif. "It's about jobs, jobs, jobs." Not all legislators were so enthusiastic. Sen. Judd Gregg of New Hampshire, the top Republican on the Senate Budget Committee, opposed funding the loans but noted they were likely to be approved. "Politics wins over policy every time in a presidential [election] year," he said.

House Democratic leaders included the $25 billion loan in the fiscal 2009 continuing resolution, which was brought directly to the House floor without committee action. The House easily passed it by a vote of 370–58 on Sept. 24. The Senate cleared the measure 78–12 on Sept. 27. *(Continuing resolution, p. 124)*

MORE AID SOUGHT

With the jobless rate reaching 6.6 percent in October and the auto industry in increasingly dire straits, Democratic leaders put aid to carmakers at the top of their agenda for the lame-duck session following the November elections, which began Nov. 17. Help for the Big Three was one of the first things President-elect Barack Obama called for after his victory, which was aided by Michigan's seventeen electoral college votes; the state also added Democrats to the House majority.

The plan was to tap into the $700 billion financial industry bailout enacted in October (PL 110-343) to give Detroit a quick infusion of money. Although Congress had activated the $25 billion direct-loan program at the end of September, the money was not expected to reach the companies for some time because it was tied to specific plans for retooling factories and could not be used for other purposes.

Questions remained, however, about whether the federal government should intervene to save the automakers. Critics on both the right and left pointed out that the companies had been troubled for decades and said they had done too little to control costs and produce products that satisfied consumer demand. The Bush administration and congressional Republicans were united in opposing the use of the Troubled Assets Relief Program (TARP) to assist the companies. The White House said Congress should instead relax the restrictions on the $25 billion Energy Department loan.

There was precedent for the bailout. In late 1979 Congress approved $1.5 billion in federal loan guarantees to Chrysler to help the ailing company stave off bankruptcy. In return Chrysler officials agreed to several conditions, including winning wage concessions from its unions; obtaining new credit from banks, dealers, and suppliers; and selling some of the company's assets or other equity. The bailout was a major controversy, raising questions about the federal government's role in propping up private enterprises. But most lawmakers reluctantly agreed to the plan, convinced that the federal government had no choice but to try to save what was at the time the country's tenth-largest corporation. The government was fully repaid its loans by 1983. *(Congress and the Nation Vol. V, p. 280)*

NOVEMBER HEARINGS

In hearings held by the House and Senate banking committee Nov. 18–19, the auto company executives said vehicle sales were plunging to levels not seen since World War II and that the companies were burning through cash reserves at a rate that would leave them bankrupt within months. They were armed with projections that, given the industry's symbiotic relationship with parts suppliers, dealers, and associated businesses, a collapse of the Big Three could result in the loss of almost three million jobs and $150 billion in personal income in 2009 alone.

But the executives did little to show that they had credible plans for restructuring their companies into viable businesses or that government aid would be anything more than a short-term fix. In a public relations blunder that seemed to underscore their lack of awareness of the mood in Congress and the country, they arrived in Washington in separate corporate luxury jets. A typical response came from Republican Patrick T. McHenry of North Carolina. "I'm not an opponent of private flights by any means,"

McHenry said, "but the fact that you flew in on your own private jet at tens of thousands of dollars of cost just for you to make your way to Washington is a bit arrogant before you ask the taxpayers for money."

As the lame-duck session came to an end on Nov. 20, Pelosi, Senate Democratic leader Harry Reid of Nevada, and other key Democrats said they would give each of the three car companies until Dec. 2 to submit a proposal showing a path to viability that would protect taxpayers and autoworkers. If they did, committees in both chambers would hold hearings, with floor action possible the week of Dec. 8.

DECEMBER HEARINGS

The three CEOs returned to Washington—in hybrid cars—for a second round of hearings Dec. 4–5. This time they came with individual restructuring plans that focused on cost cutting and on developing new, more fuel-efficient product lines. The UAW also announced concessions on a health-care trust fund and on payments to laid-off workers.

GM requested a total of $18 billion in loans and credit but said it needed an immediate $4 billion loan to stay solvent through March. Chrysler said it needed $7 billion by the end of the year to avoid bankruptcy. Although Ford requested $9 billion in long-term loans, it said it might not need to use them.

The executives, joined by UAW president Ron Gettelfinger, implored the lawmakers not to consider bankruptcy as an option, arguing that the public would not buy vehicles from a company going through bankruptcy. "Time is of the essence," Gettelfinger said. "I believe we could lose General Motors by the end of this month.

As the hearings went into a second day, the Labor Department announced that the economy had lost 533,000 jobs in November, the steepest decline in thirty-four years. The unemployment rate rose to 6.7 percent, up from 6.6 percent in October, the highest level since 1993.

LEGISLATION SHELVED

House and Senate leaders called members back into session the week of Dec. 8 to consider legislation granting assistance to the domestic automakers. On Dec. 10, the House voted to make a $14 billion short-term bridge loan available. The bill (HR 7321) passed on a **key vote of 237–170 (R 32–150; D 205–20).** Most of the Republicans who supported the measure came from states heavily dependent on manufacturing, many in the Midwest region known as the Rust Belt, likely to be significantly affected if the domestic automakers were to go bankrupt. *(2008 key votes, p. 972)*

The measure was the result of intense negotiations between Democratic leaders and the White House, spurred by the enormity of the November job losses. With the administration adamant in its refusal to use any of the TARP funds for the automakers, Democrats relented on redirecting the $25 billion loan.

Under HR 7321, the president was directed to choose one or more administrators from the executive branch who would be authorized to disburse the bridge loans to the three auto companies. The administrators would bring together the companies, unions, creditors, and other stakeholders to negotiate long-term restructuring plans, which the companies would have to submit by March 31, 2009. If the administrators had not approved a company's plan by the deadline, the company's loans would be recalled immediately.

But Senate Republicans, especially those from states that were home to foreign-owned auto plants, were staunchly opposed to the bill, and White House attempts to sway them fell flat. When it was clear the House bill would not pass, senators spent a day in tense bargaining sessions trying to agree on an alternative proposed by Republican Bob Corker of Tennessee, which was home to both union and nonunion auto plants. When those talks deadlocked, Reid decided to bring the effort to a close. "We are not going to get to the finish line," he said on the Senate floor. "That is just the way it is. There is too much difference between the two sides."

On Dec. 11, the Senate rejected, on a **key vote of 52–35 (R 10–31; D 40–4; I 2–0),** a motion to invoke cloture on proceeding to a House tax bill (HR 2005) that was to serve as a shell for the Senate's auto bailout language. The vote was eight shy of the sixty votes needed to prevail. Immediately after the roll call, Reid said the Senate would adjourn until January. "I dread looking at Wall Street tomorrow," Reid said, "It's not going to be a pleasant sight." *(2008 key votes, p. 972)*

THE PRESIDENT STEPS IN

Before the markets opened the next day, however, the White House announced that it was considering stepping in to prevent a collapse of the automakers.

Seven days later, on Dec. 19, Bush announced that the administration would immediately make available $13.4 billion in low-interest, short-term loans to GM and Chrysler in return for concessions and restructuring. Among other things, he said, that meant "putting their retirement plans on a sensible footing" and "persuading bondholders to convert their debt into capital."

In an about-face, Bush said the funds would come from the TARP money, adding that the administration was acting only because Congress had failed to do so. The White House said an additional $4 billion would become available in February if Congress gave Treasury access to the second $350 million tranche of the TARP funding.

Of the initial $13.4 billion, Treasury officials said, $9 billion would go to GM and $4 billion to Chrysler. The second round of $4 billion would all go to GM. The plan paralleled much of the House-passed bill, giving the companies until March 31, 2009, to put restructuring plans in place or pay back the loans immediately. Under the plan, the government would take warrants in the participating companies, and the companies would have to accept restrictions on their executive compensation and issue no dividends for the life of the loans.

Obama quickly supported the administration, saying its "actions are a necessary step to help avoid a collapse in our auto industry that would have devastating consequences for our economy and our workers." The day before Bush made his announcement, the president said at a Washington think tank forum that he wanted to avoid leaving Obama with a major catastrophe that would further rattle financial markets. "I'm worried about a disorderly bankruptcy and what it would do to the psychology of the markets," Bush said. In response to a question, Bush said that under normal circumstances, he thought a court-supervised Chapter 11 bankruptcy reorganization was "the best way to sort through credit and debt and restructuring.... These aren't normal circumstances. That's the problem."

Economic Crisis Hits United States: 2007–2009

A credit crunch that surfaced in August 2007—but that had been in the making for several years—gradually became more serious and led to the worst economic downturn globally since the Great Depression of the 1930s. By the time President George W. Bush left office in January 2009, the United States had been in a recession for more than a year, many other major economies also were in recession or headed toward it, and most economists were predicting that a full recovery from the global economic downturn would be slow in coming.

The immediate cause of the economic crisis was the collapse of a bubble in the housing market, starting in the United States. Fueled by speculation and historically low interest rates, the housing market had boomed from 2002 through early 2006, in many locations recording annual sales price increases of 20 percent or more. All such bubbles burst eventually, and this one did so starting in mid-2006, when housing prices began to level off in the United States. The housing market declined in much of the country by mid-2007, a trend that accelerated, and spread globally, throughout 2008 and continued into 2009.

This decline, the first widespread downturn in housing prices since the Great Depression, was extraordinarily damaging because much of the financial system had become dependent on rising real estate prices. In particular, Wall Street banks had made enormous profits by creating securities based on mortgages, including so-called "subprime" mortgages taken out by borrowers who did not qualify for conventional lending. The banks sold billions of dollars worth of these mortgage-backed securities but also kept many of them on their own books.

When housing prices fell, many borrowers were in trouble because their mortgages now exceeded the value of their homes, a condition known as being underwater. By the end of 2008 an estimated one-sixth of all borrowers in the United States faced this predicament. In addition many homeowners were unable to meet their monthly payments when they lost their jobs or when interest rates increased significantly after the expiration of short-term "teaser" loans. The impact on individuals, and society as a whole, was worsened by the failure of most Americans to save for such a rainy day. Indeed, the U.S. personal savings rate, which had been declining for a decade, had dipped into negative territory in 2005—meaning that the average American family was spending more than its annual income.

Banks foreclosed on millions of borrowers, flooding the market with houses and depressing prices even further. This collapse of the U.S. housing market reverberated into financial markets globally because of the impact on mortgage-backed securities that banks and investment firms had packaged and sold to investors worldwide. Few investors had bothered to investigate, or even fully understand, the inherent risks in these complex securities, relying instead on overly optimistic assessments from credit rating agencies and assuming that the mortgages would be paid and the housing market would keep rising.

The sudden tide of foreclosures exposed the latent risks and made clear that many of these mortgage-backed securities were now worth a fraction of their face value. By late 2008, securities that investors once had snapped up were becoming known instead as "toxic assets"—nearly worthless junk that posed dangers to the balance sheets of all investors, including the banks that had created the assets and often held onto them.

One after another, major financial institutions fell into deep trouble. The pivotal moment came in mid-September 2008 when the federal government allowed the collapse of Lehman Brothers, a venerable Wall Street investment firm that had been one of the most aggressive packagers of now-toxic mortgage-backed securities. The failure of Lehman Brothers, coinciding with the near-collapse of even-bigger Merrill Lynch, froze the global credit system, which had already become sluggish. With businesses and individuals suddenly unable to borrow money, it became clear that a half-decade of mild economic expansion had come to a crashing end.

The economic consequences were severe. By early 2009 most economists were saying the recession was the worst the United States had faced since the Great Depression, although that appeared to be an exaggeration. For example, the unemployment rate as of April 2009 had reached 8.9 percent, about one-third of the peak of the Depression and below the rate of over 10 percent at the height of a downturn in 1982–1983, the most recent deep recession. However, by the end of 2009 the unemployment rate had topped 10 percent.

But a broader view revealed the substance behind the economists' anxieties. Just about every economic measure in the United States turned downward starting in the second half of 2007. One of the most startling was the Federal Reserve Board's calculation of the net worth of households and nonprofit organizations (in other words, the excess of total assets to total liabilities). This measurement had reached a record $64.4 trillion in mid-2007 but slid downward at an accelerating rate. By the end of 2008, American households and nonprofits had lost $12.9 trillion in net assets in just eighteen months—a 20 percent decline. Much of this was the result of losses in the stock markets, which dropped in value by more than 30 percent during the final months of 2008.

On an even broader scale, the latest recession stretched around the world, momentarily cooling even the rapidly growing economies of China and India. The freezing of the international financial system threatened to delay or weaken a recovery because it hampered the ability of businesses and individuals to access credit.

Indeed, many observers said the financial crisis was the first major test of globalization: the decades-long process by which the world's economies had become increasingly interdependent through trade in goods and financial services. "There is a strong case to be made that that the current crisis is in the strictest sense a crisis of globalization, fostered and transmitted by the rapid and deep integration of very different economies," the *Financial Times* reported in March 2009. "Fast-growing developing countries with undeveloped financial systems were exporting savings to the developed world for packaging and re-export to them in the form of financial products." All this was based on the assumption that financial centers in New York, London, and elsewhere "could create the financial products efficiently and without blowing up. They could not."

Governments in the United States and Europe led the response to the crisis with such steps as bailing out troubled financial institutions and lowering interest rates. Governments elsewhere followed, notably in China, where leaders feared social unrest if the world's hottest economy cooled too much, too fast.

In the United States, the Bush administration and Congress, along with the Federal Reserve Bank, implemented extraordinary measures as part of an increasingly frantic effort to counteract the immediate consequences of the financial crisis. These steps included repeated rescues of major banks from failure, unprecedented injections of billions of dollars into the financial system, and adoption by Congress in October 2008 of a $700 billion banking bailout. *(Legislative action, p. 154)*

The new president, Barack Obama, who took office in January 2009, convinced Congress to approve a $787 billion "stimulus" program injecting money directly into the economy, mostly in the form of subsidies for government programs, but also in billions of dollars worth of tax cuts. Obama's administration also took its own steps to bolster the financial system.

The net impact of these actions was unclear well into 2009, but senior officials insisted that a generalized collapse of the financial sector had been averted. It was clear, however, that the global economy remained in deep distress and much of the burden of attempting to right the sinking U.S. economy, and thus the global economy, would fall to Obama.

The Housing Bubble

Historically low interest rates; government policies encouraging home ownership; aggressive lending practices, particularly by lightly regulated financial institutions; and a widespread attitude that housing prices were destined to rise forever were among the primary factors that led to the rapid expansion of housing markets in the United States and in many other countries from 2000 through 2005. This in turn lulled nearly everyone from homebuyers to those who traded and evaluated securities based on the housing market into believing that their investments were inherently safe. A sudden cooling of the housing market beginning in 2006 proved the assumption false and had ripple effects that eventually led to the sharp downturn of the global economy.

The statistics documenting the housing boom at the beginning of the new millennium were simply astonishing. Nationwide, housing prices rose at least 63 percent between January 2000 and July 2006 (according to one measure by the Federal Housing Finance Agency) and 106 percent (according to Standard and Poor's Case-Schiller index of sales in twenty major metropolitan areas).

The national figures disguised an even more robust boom in the hottest markets, including California (with an average 111 percent increase over five years), south Florida (112 percent), Nevada (105 percent) and Arizona (97 percent). Put in dollar terms, such increases meant that a California house that in 2000 sold for $200,000 might have sold for more than $400,000 just five years later.

The boom in housing prices was fueled by several factors, starting with infusions of hundreds of billions of dollars into the U.S. economy from China and other developing countries, which were attracted by the strong dollar. The cash enabled the Federal Reserve to keep interest rates at exceptionally low levels. Low rates, in turn, made it much cheaper for people to borrow, not just to buy homes but to tap the equity in their homes for more transient purposes such as buying cars or taking vacations. The ability to borrow at low rates also reduced the incentive for individuals and families to save for a rainy day.

The era of relatively easy money also increased economic incentives for lenders to make, and borrowers to take, risky loans. Investors and financial institutions were eager to find returns that would be more profitable than conventional mortgages. Wall Street banks found one route to greater short-term profits by packaging many kinds of mortgages, including risky ones, into securities that could be marketed as solid investments seemingly guaranteed to deliver high rates of return.

Fundamentally, during this period many people saw real estate, and the financing of it, as safe and easy ways to make money. With house prices on the rise, many families felt pressure to get into homes sooner rather than later, and the financial industry was eager to help them get there.

SUBPRIME AND ALTERNATIVE MORTGAGES

Lenders offered a variety of financing options that were intended to encourage new buyers into the housing market. Among these options were interest-only loans (on which buyers paid interest but no principal for the first several years); loans with exceptionally low "teaser" rates that ballooned much higher in subsequent years; and no-down payment loans that allowed buyers to avoid this often-costly upfront expense, or even to borrow the down payment amounts.

Many of these mortgages were taken out by people in what bankers called the "subprime" market, meaning that the borrowers lacked the income to qualify for conventional "prime" mortgages. Subprime borrowers were assumed to be more likely than borrowers with stronger financial qualifications to fall behind on their payments or even default altogether. In the past, most banks had avoided the subprime market, generally by charging extra-high rates for such loans. But with the Bush administration promoting what it called an "ownership society," of which home ownership was a key element, pressure mounted to get a wide range of buyers into their own homes. Between the early 1990s and 2007, the overall rate of homeownership in the United States rose from 64 percent of households to 68 percent, translating into millions of families who shifted from renting to owning.

Even while this push toward home ownership was under way, the boom in housing prices meant that owning a home became more difficult for working-class families, whose real, after-inflation, incomes stagnated or rose only marginally over the same period. The standard 20 percent down payment on a $200,000 house in the year 2000 would have been $40,000, a substantial amount for all but the wealthiest families. By 2005, making a 20 percent down payment on the same house, now priced at $400,000, would have required $80,000. Mortgage lenders thus argued that giving buyers more options, such as reducing or even eliminating down payment requirements, was essential to getting average families into homes.

In the definitive book on the subject, *Subprime Mortgages: America' Latest Boom and Bust*, completed early in 2007 before the worst of the financial crisis hit, former Federal Reserve Board member Edward M. Gramlich noted that subprime lending in the United States rose from $35 billion in 1994 (representing 5 percent of that year's total mortgage lending) to $625 billion in 2005 (representing 20 percent of the total).

Gramlich said the boom in subprime lending was "good news" in the sense that it helped millions of people get into homes they could not otherwise have afforded. But in a warning that later seemed prescient, he said the bad news was that some of the new homeowners were "stretched thin, vulnerable to the least shock, saving very little, with high levels of consumer debt, at the mercy of predatory lenders, being forced to sell their houses early, and often ending up in foreclosure."

A central element in the boom in subprime lending was the increasing use of unconventional mortgages, often described as "alternative" lending. Among these were "no documentation" loans given to borrowers who claimed, but were not required to prove, incomes that met or exceeded the minimum standards. Over time, as some of these borrowers fell behind on their payments and went into default, these type of mortgages acquired a new name: "liars' loans." By 2005, the Government Accountability Office (GAO) estimated that all forms of unconventional lending (including both subprime and alternative loans) constituted about 30 percent of the total U.S. mortgage market.

Some lenders actually preferred subprime mortgages over prime mortgages because they earned higher upfront commissions and fees on them. Independent mortgage brokers often steered buyers into subprime loans even though they might have qualified for prime loans. One way of doing this was by urging borrowers to take out no-documentation loans (for which they paid higher rates) even after the borrowers had presented income documentation.

Millions of low-income borrowers were especially attracted by low, short-term "teaser" rates, often with no down payments required. In many cases, numerous studies have shown, buyers were misled by unscrupulous mortgage brokers into believing they could afford houses that, under standard practices, would have been beyond their means. Among the mortgages that proved especially problematic for low-income borrowers were those known as 2/28 and 3/27 loans. In the first type, the interest rate remained at a low level for two years then could rise (but never decline) for each of the subsequent twenty-eight years; in the second type, the rate was low for three years then rose during the next twenty-seven years.

When the introductory rates expired and higher rates kicked in (in some cases resulting in 30 to 40 percent increases in monthly payments), many borrowers could no longer afford their mortgages, and banks foreclosed. The result was a tragedy for the families involved because they lost their homes. For those mortgages brokers interested only in profits, however, each foreclosure represented yet another opportunity to make money by collecting fees from subsequent sales.

The Center for Responsible Lending, a nonprofit group that advocated on behalf of low-income borrowers, said in 2008 that "independent brokers played a particularly destructive role in the subprime market" because they had incentives to steer borrowers into riskier, more expensive loans. In a speech delivered in September 2007, just before he died from cancer, former Federal Reserve official Gramlich asked this question: "Why are the most risky loan products sold to the least sophisticated borrowers? The question answers itself—the least sophisticated borrowers are probably duped into taking these products." Other critics of the banking industry noted that subprime borrowers often were given incomplete and misleading information about their loans; some lenders even refused to provide any of the important details about loans until borrowers had paid nonrefundable deposits.

In response to such criticism, representatives of the banking industry acknowledged that many, but not all, banks failed to adhere to appropriate lending standards and took excessive risks. They also insisted that abusive lending was practiced only by independent, unregulated brokers.

U.S. GOVERNMENT BAILOUT AND STIMULUS SPENDING

Depending on who did the counting, and when, and what was included, various agencies of the federal government spent or promised to spend between $4 trillion and nearly $13 trillion on investments, loans, guarantees, tax breaks, and government programs between late 2007 and early 2009 to shore up the financial system and stimulate the U.S. economy. Not all of the government programs involved actual spending of tax dollars; in fact, most of the money was created by the Federal Reserve Board or was committed by the Fed and other agencies in the form of guarantees that might never be called into action.

In nominal dollar terms, these efforts represented the largest U.S. government economic support effort in history. As a percentage of the overall economy, they constituted the largest programs since the Great Depression in the 1930s and World War II during the 1940s.

Following is a list of the major programs created by Congress, the Treasury Department, the Federal Reserve, and other government agencies from December 2007 through May 2009:

2008 Stimulus Bill (PL 110-185)

Congress on Feb. 7, 2008, cleared for the president a bill (HR 5140) that provided tax rebates of up to $600 for individuals and $1,200 for married couples, as a stimulus to the economy. Other measures in the bill included tax breaks for businesses to buy equipment and increases in the amount of mortgages purchased by housing agencies Fannie Mae and Freddie Mac and purchased by the Federal Housing Administration.

The Congressional Budget Office estimated that the bill would cost $151.7 billion in fiscal 2008, $16.3 billion in fiscal 2009, and a net of $133.9 billion over six years. *(Stimulus passage, p. 151)*

Troubled Asset Relief Program, TARP (PL 110-343)

Congress on Oct. 3, 2008, cleared for the president a massive bill (HR 1424) appropriating up to $700 billion for the Treasury Department to purchase so-called "toxic assets," or any other assets, from financial institutions.

As of April 30, 2009, $645 billion had been committed to banks, other financial institutions, and the auto industry, and to support other government programs to bolster the financial industry. The government expected that much, but not all, of this money eventually would be returned to the taxpayers through repayments by the banks, dividend payments, and other proceeds.

Major allocations of TARP funding as of April 2009 included: $168 billion for the Capital Purchase Program (CPP) to buy shares in banks other than Bank of America and Citigroup; $70 billion for American International Group (AIG); $55 billion for the Term Asset-Backed Securities Loan Facility (TALF), to purchase securities backed by consumer and small business loans; $52.5 billion for Bank of America; $50 billion for Citigroup; $50 billion under the Public-Private Investment Fund (PPIF) to purchase toxic assets; $50 billion for the Homeowner Affordability and Stability Plan; $29.9 billion in loans to Chrysler, General Motors, and GMAC; and $15 billion for the Unlocking Credit for Small Business program. *(TARP passage, p. 154)*

Federal Reserve Programs

As of April 1, 2009, the Federal Reserve Board had increased its own balance sheet by approximately $1.5 trillion to enable it to make various forms of credit to banks and other financial institutions under several new programs developed to counter the financial crisis. None of these programs directly affected the government's budget because the Fed was able to create money as necessary. Most of the profits (if any) from the Fed's loans would be sent to the Treasury.

Following is a list of the Fed's major programs and their costs:

- **Term Auction Facility.** Created by the Fed on Dec. 12, 2007, to allow banks to bid for short-term secured loans (up to twenty-eight days). The amount of outstanding loans on any given day ranged from $100 billion to $450 billion, as of April 2009.
- **Term Securities Lending Facility.** Created by the Fed on March 11, 2008, to allow so-called "primary dealers" (large Wall Street financial firms) to borrow a total of $200 billion for short-term loans (up to twenty-eight days) secured by various assets, such as mortgage-backed securities or Treasury bills.
- **Primary Dealer Credit Facility.** Created by the Fed on March 16, 2008, to allow primary dealers to borrow from the Federal Reserve, but on an overnight basis. Daily borrowing under this program ran as high as $50 billion, and as low as zero.
- **Asset-Backed Commercial Paper Money Market Liquidity Facility.** Created by the Federal Reserve on Sept. 19, 2008, to loan money to banks to purchase short-term debt (called commercial paper) issued by large companies. This program was superseded on Oct. 7, 2008, by the Commercial Paper Funding Facility, which had broader leeway to make loans for the purchase of commercial paper; this facility loaned as much as $300 billion in 2008.

- **Term Asset-Backed Securities Loan Facility (TALF).** Created by the Federal Reserve on Nov. 25, 2008, to loan loans money to U.S. companies to buy securities backed by assets such as auto loans, student loans, credit card debt, and small business loans. The Fed set a $200 billion limit on these loans. The TALF began operation on March 1, 2009.
- **Money Market Investor Funding Facility.** Created by the Federal Reserve on Oct. 21, 2008, to loan up to $540 billion to encourage money market funds to purchase commercial paper.
- **Fannie Mae and Freddie Mac.** The Federal Reserve said on Nov. 25, 2008, that it would purchase up to $100 billion in bonds issued by each of these government-sponsored enterprises, and up to $500 billion worth of mortgage-backed securities guaranteed by these companies and Ginnie Mae, a similar company. The Fed in March 2009 increased to $200 billion each the amount of bonds it would purchase from Fannie and Freddie, and up to $1.3 trillion the amount of mortgage-backed securities backed by Fannie, Freddie, and Ginnie.
- **Bear Stearns purchase.** In a deal announced on March 16, 2008, and completed on June 26, the Federal Reserve provided $28.8 billion in a ten-year loan to a limited liability corporation, called Maiden Lane, that it had created to enable JP Morgan Chase to buy the assets of failed investment bank Bear Stearns for $29.9 billion (JP Morgan put up the remaining $1.2 billion).
- **AIG loans.** In four separate announcements between September 2008 and March 2009, the Federal Reserve participated in the government's bailout of American International Group (AIG), the giant insurance company. The net effect of these transactions, as of mid-April 2009, was to provide AIG $86.7 billion in loans from the Fed (in addition to $70 billion in Treasury Department investments under the TARP program); AIG used most of the money to pay claims against it by other companies.
- **Citigroup guarantees.** In the first step of a broader, multi-step process of rescuing Citigroup, the government announced on Nov. 23, 2008, that it would guarantee a pool of up to $306 billion in the bank's assets, such as mortgages and consumer and corporate loans. The total was reduced to $301 billion when an agreement was finalized on Jan. 16, 2009. The deal was complex. Citigroup would incur the first $29 billion in losses, the TARP program would incur the next $5 billion, the FDIC would incur the next $10 billion, and the Fed would incur the remainder (approximately $257 billion) in the form of a loan to Citigroup. In return, the government received preferred and common stock in Citigroup valued at $9.7 billion as of Jan. 16, 2009. In addition to this guarantee, the government purchased $50 billion in Citigroup stock through the TARP program (see above).
- **Bank of America guarantees.** On the same day (Jan. 16, 2009) as its latest bailout of Citigroup was completed, the government announced a broad bailout of Bank of America, which had run into trouble after purchasing the investment bank Merrill Lynch. Under this deal, the government guaranteed a $118 billion pool of Bank of America assets, including mortgage-backed securities. The bank itself would incur the first $10 billion of losses and the next $10.8 billion of any subsequent losses; the Treasury Department and the FDIC would split the next $10 billion in losses; and the Federal Reserve would incur any of the remaining $87.2 billion in losses. As payment, Bank of America gave the government $4 billion in preferred stock and warrants for the purchase of $2.4 billion worth of common stock.

Federal Deposit Insurance Corporation

As of March 31, 2009, the FDIC had guaranteed $336.3 billion in debt held by banks and other financial institutions, under its Temporary Liquidity Guarantee Program (TLGP). The FDIC also guaranteed deposits in member banks up to $250,000 for each account, an increase over the previous $100,000 deposit guarantee (the guarantee was scheduled to revert to $100,000 at the end of 2009). *(FDIC passage, p. 148)*

2009 Stimulus Bill (PL 111-5)

Congress on Feb. 13, 2009, cleared for the president the largest-ever program intended to stimulate the economy through government spending and tax cuts. The bill's total of $787 billion included roughly $463 billion for spending programs and $326 billion for tax individual and business tax cuts.

SOURCES: *Assessing Treasury's Strategy: Six Months of TARP,* Congressional Oversight Panel, April 7, 2009. http://cop.senate.gov/reports/library/report-040709-cop.cfm

Financial Turmoil: Federal Reserve Policy Responses, Congressional Research Service, April 9, 2009.

The Budget and Economic Outlook: Fiscal Years 2008 – 2018, Congressional Budget Office, January 2009. http://www.cbo.gov/ftpdocs/89xx/doc8917/01-23-2008_BudgetOutlook.pdf

"Eye on the Bailout," ProPublica.org http://bailout.propublica.org/

Also central to the boosting of subprime lending were Fannie Mae (Federal National Mortgage Association) and Freddie Mac (Federal Home Loan Mortgage Corporation), two firms established by the federal government (and later converted into private companies) with missions of making housing more affordable for Americans. Neither company made loans directly to home buyers, but both were in the business of buying mortgages from lenders and, for a fee, guaranteeing them.

Under pressure from the mortgage industry, members of Congress, and the Bush administration, both companies stepped up their purchases of subprime loans at the height of the housing boom in 2005. By September 2008 it was clear that both Fannie and Freddie were in deep financial trouble because so many of the mortgages they owned had gone bad. The government took control once again, pumping up to $100 billion into each of them to prevent even more damage to the financial system.

BUNDLING MORTGAGES

The risks posed by subprime mortgages were serious enough by themselves, but the risks were magnified exponentially when those mortgages reached the financial markets. In the past, many banks viewed the mortgages they wrote as long-term investments. In recent decades, however, an increasing number of banks sold their mortgages on the financial markets, often to the government-sponsored enterprises Fannie Mae and Freddie Mac but also to private investors and even other banks.

Wall Street firms began bundling mortgages into securities during the 1970s, for the most part using only prime mortgages because they were seen as safe. Searching for higher profits and new markets, however, Wall Street firms in the 1980s began including subprime mortgages in bundles of mortgage-backed securities, called "collateralized mortgage obligations." Each of these securities was divided into parts called tranches, which investors could buy according to their appetites for risk. Tranches composed of prime mortgages were less risky, and also less profitable, than those composed of subprime mortgages.

In 1997, according to the Congressional Research Service, just under one-half of all mortgages were placed into securities; these "securitized" mortgages totaled $423 billion. By 2006, two-thirds of all mortgages, with a total value of $2 trillion, were put into securities. Fannie Mae and Freddie Mac played a significant role in this trend, particularly during the height of the housing boom when they bought several hundred billion dollars worth of securities based on subprime mortgages. Fannie's CEO at the time, Daniel Mudd, told congressional panels late in 2008 that he had agreed to these riskier investments under competitive pressure from the larger financial industry which, he said, was threatening to make the company "irrelevant" if it stayed out of that market.

The increased securitization of mortgages boosted the overall amount of money available for homebuyers because banks no longer tied up their money with mortgages held on their books; instead, they used the revenue from the sale of old mortgages to make new ones. The downside was that the pain was spread when mortgages went bad: Banks, pension funds, college endowments, state and local governments, and even entire countries suddenly lost money on investments they had believed to be safe. It was only after the credit crisis took hold that many investors realized they had not scrutinized these securities carefully enough to assess all the potential risks.

Systemic Problems: Old and New

A number of other factors worked together to ensure that this financial crisis, and the resulting economic downturn, would be more severe than previous ones since the 1930s. Sudden losses on subprime mortgages, by themselves, might not have caused the financial system to freeze up. But coupled with the role these mortgages played within an increasingly complex and opaque financial system, the impact of losses was magnified because investors and institutions quickly realized they did not know the true risks they had assumed. In the ensuing panic, individual and institutional investors dumped all kinds of investments and fled to the relative safety of Treasury bills. The result was the collapse or near-collapse of once-mighty companies and the rapid plunge of economies worldwide.

The damage was so widespread because banks and other financial institutions, which provided the lending that was necessary for all economic activity, were among the chief culprits in the subprime mortgage boom and also among the chief victims of its collapse. By late 2008, the total debt held by the financial sector in the United States represented 117 percent of the country's gross domestic product (GDP), according to *Financial Times* economics columnist Martin Wolf. This suggested that the failure of even a small portion of the banking sector would have serious consequences for the economy. Indeed, it had become clear that a large portion of the banking sector was in deep trouble.

Of all the root causes of the 2007–2008 financial crisis and resulting global recession, perhaps the simplest and most obvious was that people in all walks of life sought to cash in on the latest boom—in this case, a boom in housing. Homeowners began to view their homes as major financial investments, not just as places to live. Bankers sought to capitalize on demand for financing as the perceived value of houses skyrocketed. And investors across the globe saw financial instruments associated with housing as a sure route to higher returns than were available in other types of investments.

The drive for higher returns was particularly strong because major central banks had kept interest rates exceptionally low in the wake of the economic downturns following the collapse of the high-technology bubble in 1999–2000 and then the Sept. 11, 2001, terrorist attacks against the United States. To lure those investors, hedge funds and even banks began using ever-riskier forms of financial instruments, including those based on the housing market.

"Investors said, 'I don't want to be in equities [stocks] anymore and I'm not getting any return in my bond positions,'" William T. Winters, co–chief executive of JP Morgan's investment bank, told the *New York Times* in November 2008. "Two things happened. They took more and more leverage, and they reached for riskier asset classes. Give me yield, give me leverage, give me return."

UNDERESTIMATION OF RISK

The investors to whom Winters referred reached increasingly for complex financial instruments that went by various names, among them collateralized mortgage obligations and collateralized debt obligations. Basically, these were giant securities—some valued at billions of dollars—that bundled together various assets, such as mortgages, and that were bought and sold like any other commodity.

One big advantage of these securities was that they transferred risks from one institution to another. When a bank sold a pool of mortgages to investors, for example, the investors took on whatever risks were inherent in those mortgages. The disadvantage was that these large combinations of assets made it more difficult for investors to determine where the ultimate risk actually lay. Over time it became clear that few investors, even including supposedly sophisticated money managers, truly understood these products and instead took it on faith that risk levels were low or that risks would be assumed by someone else. Governments, which were supposed to oversee the financial system to ensure that problems did not get out of hand and endanger the entire economy, appeared to share the view that any risks could be managed. Credit rating agencies, which were paid to evaluate risk, also failed in their jobs.

Summarizing this phenomenon, the *Financial Times* reported on August 3, 2008: "Policymakers thought that because the pain of any potential credit defaults was spread among millions of investors, rather than concentrated in particular banks, it would be much easier for the system to absorb shocks than in the past." Some central bankers had doubts about this and argued that "risk dispersion might not always be benign. However, such warnings were largely kept out of public view, partly because the U.S. Federal Reserve was convinced that financial innovation had changed the system in a fundamentally beneficial way."

The Institute of International Finance described this same trend in a July 2008 report setting out "best practices" for banks, which made up the institute's membership. The "buoyant environment" of the housing boom, the report said, "in some cases adversely affected senior management's ability to attend fully to recommendations by the risk management departments and encouraged some banks to operate with a false sense of confidence regarding their ability to curtail any excessive risk encountered before it was too late."

In other words, investors across the board appeared to lose their fear of risk. They demonstrated this not only by buying subprime mortgages but even by declining to demand higher rates of interest for risky investments. During the middle part of the decade, the interest rate spread between junk bonds (risky corporate debt) and presumably safe U.S. Treasury securities was very low by historical standards.

The first significant indication that many investors had underestimated risk came in June 2007 when Bear Stearns, a large Wall Street investment firm, said two of its hedge funds, which had invested heavily in mortgage-backed securities, were in trouble. The company said the securities had lost 28 percent of their value overall since the beginning of the year. Although the amount of money involved was relatively small (only about $600 million), the news caused investors to question whether they understood the risks inherent in similar mortgage-backed securities. The announcement also raised doubts about the stability of other hedge funds, which also had highly leveraged investments in these types of securities. Over the next year, it became increasingly clear that risks, which had been ignored or underplayed, had in fact existed all along.

LEVERAGE AND SHORT-TERM BORROWING

Another significant aspect of the financial crisis, according to nearly all independent assessments, was an excessive reliance on leverage to acquire assets. Basically, financial institutions, notably the large investment banks on Wall Street and in other financial capitals, borrowed too much of the money they used to acquire assets, such as mortgage-backed securities. On average, investment banks had leveraged their investments by a 25 to 1 ratio at the time the financial crisis hit; that meant they had built their investment portfolios by putting down only 4 percent of the purchase price with the remainder from borrowed money. This was more than twice the leverage of the large commercial banks, which faced greater government regulation of their investments.

This extensive use of leverage made it possible for the investment banks to expand their holdings—and thus potential profits—but it also had enormous consequences during an economic downturn. By putting down an average of only 4 percent of the value of its investments, a bank stood to lose all of those investments, and thus its capital base, if the market values declined by just 5 percent. When markets, particularly the market for mortgage-backed securities, fell much more dramatically between 2007 and 2008, Bear Stearns, Lehman Brothers, and other investment banks suddenly found that their portfolios were worth less money than the money they had borrowed to build them.

The risks inherent in leverage were compounded by an over-reliance on short-term borrowing to make investments. In good times, the banks easily could borrow new funds, on a daily basis if needed, to pay off previous loans they had used to build their portfolios. However, when the financial crisis began to take hold in late 2007 and the value of investments came into question, banks with highly leveraged investments were forced to pay higher and higher interest rates on these short-term loans. Ultimately, even some large and respected institutions could not borrow at all on the private markets and had to turn to the government for help or face insolvency when that help was not forthcoming.

COMPLEX FINANCIAL INSTRUMENTS

At the core of the financial crisis was a relatively new model of handling securities called "originate-and-distribute." In its simplest terms, this model meant that one institution would develop (or "originate") assets, such as mortgages, and then distribute a portion of both the income and the risks of those assets among investors in the form of securities. This was a dramatic shift from the long-established previous model under which banks made loans, usually to customers they knew, and tended to keep them on their own books (a process known as "originate-and-hold").

One form of the securities based on the originate-and-distribute philosophy was given the unwieldy title of "collateralized debt obligations" or CDOs. A typical CDO might include thousands of assets, for example, mortgages. Some mortgages might be prime (and thus relatively low-risk) and others might be subprime (and thus relatively high-risk). An investment bank would assemble these mortgages and other assets into a CDO, then divide the CDO into groups, called tranches, based on the presumed profitability and risk of those assets. Credit rating agencies were supposed to evaluate the inherent risk of each tranche of each CDO, and investors would buy a tranche or an entire CDO based on that rating. An investor who wanted higher returns and was willing to accept higher risks might be attracted to a tranche heavily laden with subprime mortgages; a more risk-adverse investor might settle for the lower returns promised by a tranche composed mainly of prime mortgages.

CDOs were part of a broader form of investment called "derivatives" because their inherent value derived from underlying assets, which the investor never actually owned. A simple form of derivative was the typical household insurance policy; it had a value that could be traded based on the value of the premiums and the risk that the house might burn down. During the closing decades of the twentieth century Wall Street firms developed increasingly complex types of derivatives. Financial institutions that created these derivatives appeared to be the big winners because they charged hefty fees at each step of the process in assembling and selling the new financial products, even as they spread the risks of these products to those who bought them.

One flaw in the theory of risk-dispersion, however, was that many banks held on to the CDOs they had created. They did this in some cases by leaving the CDOs on their books, and in other cases by transferring them to off-the-books entities known as "structured investment vehicles." In either case, a bank would get profits generated by the mortgages and other assets within each CDO. By retaining rather than spreading the inherent risk, however, a bank stood to lose when subprime mortgages went into default.

Despite their wide acceptance, derivatives remained controversial because they were complex and few investors took the time to understand what they were buying. The most famous, and most prescient, criticism of derivatives came in 2003 from billionaire investor Warren Buffett. In his annual letter to investors in his company, Berkshire-Hathaway, Buffett summarized numerous problems with derivatives in this widely quoted sentence: "In my view, derivatives are financial weapons of mass destruction, carrying dangers that, while now latent, are potentially lethal." Despite this warning, Buffett's own company continued trading in derivatives, as Buffett ruefully acknowledged in his March 2009 letter to investors reporting record losses by the company.

Buffett's warning also had little impact on other investors. In 2005, according to the *New York Times*, firms issued \$178 billion in mortgage and other asset-backed CDOs, compared with just \$4 billion worth of CDOs based on safer, high-grade corporate bonds (which had lower returns). In 2006, issuance of mortgage and asset-backed CDOs totaled \$316 billion, versus \$40 billion backed by corporate bonds.

CREDIT DEFAULT SWAPS

Before the latter months of 2008, it was unlikely that many people outside of financial circles had ever heard of credit default swaps. The near-collapse of insurance giant American International Group (AIG) in September 2008 quickly elevated public awareness of, if not regard for, this type of complicated financial instrument that had played a central role in the events leading to the credit crisis.

A credit default swap essentially was an insurance policy intended to spread the risk that a business could default on its credit obligations. For example, if Company A sold a bond to (in essence, took out a loan from) Company B, then Company B could buy a credit default swap from Company C to protect itself from the possibility that Company A would default on its obligations. Company B would pay a fee to Company C for its services, one of which was to use its own good credit rating to elevate the status of the underlying bond. Even if Company A was not seen as a particularly good risk by the credit rating agencies, financial markets assumed that the insurance provided by Company C would reduce the risk to Company B.

Based in New York but with operations around the world, AIG was by far the biggest Company C in the credit default swap business. A major reason was AIG's long success as a business; AIG not only was the biggest insurance company in the world, it was one of the few companies of any type with a rock-solid AAA rating from the big credit rating agencies. In effect, when a Company B bought a credit default swap from AIG, it was also borrowing AIG's AAA rating as a guarantee against a default by Company A.

At its peak, according to *New York Times* business columnist Joe Nocera, AIG wrote credit default contracts with a total value of $450 billion; it was guaranteeing the credit of other companies for up to that amount. Even though it was the biggest single player in the credit default business, AIG by no means was alone. According to the Bank for International Settlements, the total value globally of credit default swaps (a figure known as the "notional value") was $57.9 trillion as of December 2007. No one expected all of those swaps to go bad at once, so the estimated "market value" of them was only about $2 trillion; this was the amount that AIG and other insurance companies could be expected to pay in the case of defaults.

Credit default swaps played a significant role in the subprime mortgage market because banks and other institutions used them as insurance when they bought and sold mortgage-backed securities. When banks did this, they assumed they were simply spreading the risk should some of the underlying mortgages go into default. Virtually no one anticipated what eventually happened: that a large number of subprime mortgages would go into default, thus setting off the cascading series of events that would affect not only the banks but also the companies, such as AIG, that had issued the credit default swaps.

One key element of the credit default business that contributed to the financial crisis was that insurance companies, such as AIG, were not required to set aside capital reserves to cover potential losses as they would have if the credit default swaps were traditional insurance policies. The reason was that credit default swaps were not closely regulated by the government.

As a result, when subprime mortgages went into default, and securities containing those mortgages went bad, AIG and other companies that had issued the credit default swaps guaranteeing those securities found themselves without the reserves to make good on their guarantees. By September 2008, credit rating agencies had downgraded AIG's once-sterling rating; this forced the company to set aside billions of dollars in collateral for the default swaps it had guaranteed, and it caused panic among the dozens of companies that had done business with AIG because of its strong credit rating. For the second quarter of 2008, AIG posted losses of $25 billion on its credit default swap business.

When Lehman Brothers, one of AIG's trading partners, collapsed in September 2008, AIG suddenly seemed to be in danger of failing itself, thus threatening to take down untold numbers of its clients. The Federal Reserve stepped in on Sept. 16, lending AIG $85 billion in exchange for warrants for nearly 80 percent of the company's stock. It was to be the first of four rescues of AIG, totaling up to $180 billion in taxpayer funds, over the next five months.

Although enormous in scale, these bailouts attracted little public controversy until March 2009, when Andrew Cuomo, the New York state attorney general, revealed that AIG intended to pay $165 million in bonuses to executives of the subsidiary responsible for the credit default swaps (the total bonus figure later was reported to be $218 million). The scale of the bonuses (seventy-three of which were more than $1 million each), paid out by a company that was kept in business only by virtue of taxpayer-funded bailouts, ignited a populist firestorm that temporarily threatened to undercut public support for the government's broader efforts to shore up the financial system. The House of Representatives responded on March 19 by passing legislation (HR 1586) imposing a 90 percent tax on the bonus income of highly paid employees of any firm receiving U.S. government bailouts of at least $5 billion. The tax proposal died in the Senate, and the furor gradually died down, in part because some AIG employees, including most of those who had received the highest pay, gave back their bonuses.

CREDIT RATING AGENCIES

One reason investors across the board underestimated the risks in complex securities was that they relied on advice from the major credit rating agencies, whose job was to evaluate the chances that a financial investment, or an entire company, could go bad. The three major U.S.-based credit rating agencies—Moody's, Standard & Poor's, and Fitch—had strong reputations for integrity and financial savvy. It turned out, however, that the agencies' reputations were stronger than their performance.

The credit rating agencies received fees to rate securities based on information provided by the firms issuing the securities. That information, in turn, was based on models for determining risk, models that turned out to be inaccurate, particularly when markets began to fall. Moreover, the rating agencies appeared to have little understanding of how instruments such as credit default swaps would respond under crisis conditions.

Over the course of 2007 and 2008, the agencies were forced to downgrade their ratings of hundreds of securities. The reason was simple: many of these securities were based on subprime mortgages that once seemed safe because housing prices were rising, but were now endangered because of the collapse of the housing bubble. One example, cited in a Dec. 7, 2008, report by the *New York Times* was a $165 million pool of mortgages contained in a broader security issued two years earlier by Goldman Sachs. Moody's and Standard & Poor's gave this mortgage pool their highest AAA ratings. In August 2007, Moody's downgraded this mortgage pool to its lowest investment-grade level (Baa), then four months later gave it a "junk" rating.

Officials at the rating agencies defended their actions, saying no one could have foreseen the combination of developments that led to the financial crunch starting in 2007. Critics, however, said the agencies, which once had been independent monitors paid by investors, sought to maximize their own profits by changing their business model to earn the bulk of their fees from the companies whose securities they evaluated. Thomas J. McGuire, a former director of corporate development at Moody's, told the *New York Times* that his old firm, which once had been a "good watchdog," by the 1990s had been "muzzled and gelded. It was told to turn into a lapdog."

The Role of Regulation

Private credit rating agencies were not the only institutions that failed to alert investors and the general public to the gathering dangers posed by giant financial instruments based on subprime mortgages. Government agencies, which many people thought were keeping a close watch on the financial industry, also were caught napping or, in some cases, simply did not have the authority to supervise key segments of the industry.

Once the financial crisis accelerated, experts inside and outside government identified two central problems with the nation's regulatory structure. First, about one-half of all subprime mortgages were originated by independent mortgage brokers who were largely free of regulation at the state and national levels. Some of these brokers used deceptive practices to persuade gullible buyers to take out mortgages they could not afford over the long-term. Although some of these practices were illegal, the brokers did not have to answer to any regulators, and so they were able to pocket profits from writing mortgages they knew, or should have known, could go bad.

Second, much of the business of packaging and selling financial products, formerly dominated by closely regulated banks, had been taken over by investment banks and other institutions (often called "nonbanks") that faced lighter regulation. As a result, the overall financial system had become more opaque, not just to the general public but even to knowledgeable investors.

Federal Reserve Board Chairman Ben S. Bernanke put it this way in a March 10, 2009, address to the Council on Foreign Relations: ". . . I do think that this crisis has revealed some rather shocking gaps in our regulatory oversight. I mean, who was overseeing the subprime lenders, for example? Who was overseeing AIG? There simply wasn't enough adequate oversight in those cases." The Federal Reserve, which Bernanke had headed since February 2006, had responsibility for regulating major banks, but no single agency looked at the entire picture of the financial industry.

Bernanke's predecessor, Alan Greenspan, frequently insisted he and other regulators could not have prevented the housing bubble or the resulting financial crisis. However, he did acknowledge a flaw in his own fundamental belief in the self-correcting tendencies of private markets. Testifying to the House Oversight Committee on Oct. 23, 2008, Greenspan said the failure of banks to act in ways that protected their own interests had come as a surprise to him. He said that "those of us who have looked to the self-interest of lending institutions to protect shareholder's equity (myself especially) are in a state of shocked disbelief." Asked by committee chairman Henry Waxman, D-Calif., if his free-market ideological inclinations had prevented him from understanding this failure, he said it had. "That's precisely the reason I was shocked, because I had been going for forty years or more with very considerable evidence that it [his view of how the world worked] was working exceptionally well."

The Bush administration on March 31, 2008, released detailed proposals for new regulations to close some of the gaps that had become obvious since the onset of the financial crisis. Election-year concerns meant that these proposals received minimal consideration on Capitol Hill, however, and the administration made little effort to push for their enactment. The incoming Obama administration said it would seek a comprehensive regulatory reform, but only after the immediate crisis had passed. A central question was whether to give one regulatory agency broad authority over the financial industry, and, if so, which agency that should be. Some experts and members of Congress said the obvious answers were: yes, one agency should be able to oversee the bulk of the industry, and the Federal Reserve Board was the obvious choice. Others agreed on the need for at least some consolidation of regulatory power but suggested the Fed already had too much on its hands. By the end of 2009, the House had passed a wide-ranging revamp of financial services regulation, but similar legislation had yet to move out of committee in the Senate.

DEREGULATION AND NONREGULATION

Ever since Margaret Thatcher rose to power as British prime minister in 1979 and Ronald Reagan was elected U.S. president the following year, government regulation of business had become unfashionable in many world capitals. Business leaders and politicians across much of the ideological spectrum decried what they called the stranglehold of government red tape and argued that free markets offered the only true path to economic growth.

The rise of this ideology had many consequences, one of the most important of which was a broad consensus that financial institutions should have wide latitude to develop innovative products to meet the needs of the increasingly complex global economic system. Among the resulting products were the mortgage-backed securities and credit default swaps that ultimately played such a major role in the financial crisis and faced only limited scrutiny by government regulators.

During much of the previous decade, the financial services industry had devoted a considerable political effort to reducing regulations already on the books and heading off new ones. One notable success came in the 1999 repeal of the Depression-era Glass-Steagall act, which had limited the kinds of businesses in which banks could engage. Repeal of the law meant that even regulated banks could use a holding company structure to own securities and insurance businesses. Banks also could hold risky positions in "special purpose entities"—investment vehicles that might, or might not, be reflected directly on banks' balance sheets but ultimately affected the bottom line.

One of the most significant results was the creation of Citigroup, a mammoth company combining the former Citibank with Travelers Insurance Company in 1998 into a firm that then-chairman Sanford Weill liked to describe as "one stop shopping" for financial services. The new freedom made Citicorp and other banks potentially more profitable in flush times but exposed them to a greater range of risks when the economy turned sour. This definitely was the case with Citigroup, which survived 2008 only with the help of large-scale government bailouts and guarantees.

In addition to enabling banks to enter new lines of business, the government, starting in the 1990s, allowed banks to cut their capital reserves—their holdings against possible losses—even though most banks were entering into increasingly risky ventures. "People really believed that the world was different," said Larry Fink, head of the private investment firm BlackRock. "There was this huge trust in the intellectual capital of Wall Street—and that appeared to be supported by the fact that banks were making so much money."

Several press reports late in 2008 recalled a brief bureaucratic battle during the administration of President Bill Clinton (1993–2001) over the regulation of derivatives, such as the CDOs that included mortgage-backed securities. Starting in 1997, the Commodity Futures Trading Commission, under its chairman Brooksley E. Born, pushed to begin regulating derivatives. That effort was headed off by a high-powered trio of then-Fed chairman Greenspan, Treasury Secretary Robert E. Rubin, and Securities and Exchange Commission (SEC) chairman Arthur Levitt. At their request, Congress in 2000 stripped Born's agency of any regulatory authority over derivatives.

Thereafter, the subject of derivatives was rarely mentioned in governmental policymaking circles. Even so, some experts maintained that derivatives had become so important that the world's financial system was beholden to them; this warning proved prophetic when banks and other institutions faced huge losses on derivatives gone sour.

REGULATING MORTGAGES

Yet another aspect of the regulatory picture involved the mortgage industry, only part of which was subject to serious government oversight. About one-half of subprime mortgages were originated by independent mortgage companies that were subject to minimal federal regulation and patchwork state regulation; another 30 percent were originated by subsidiaries of banks and thrifts that faced lesser regulation than the parent institutions.

Mortgage brokers—intermediaries between borrowers and lenders—were subject to virtually no regulation. Subprime expert Edward M. Gramlich, a former member of the Federal Reserve Board, called the environment in which these brokers operated the "Wild West." These brokers, he said in a September 2007 speech, acted "without any skin in the game—they would just place a mortgage, collect their fee, and move on."

Congress in 1994 gave the Federal Reserve broad powers to step up consumer protections in mortgages written by all types of mortgage lenders, not just commercial banks; it did this in the Home Ownership and Equity Protection Act (PL 103-325). *(Congress and the Nation Vol. IX, p. 116)*

That law enabled the Fed to prevent a range of unfair or deceptive lending practices and even to require the revision of loans that abused borrowers. According to numerous subsequent reports, however, Fed Chairman Greenspan refused to make use of this power, arguing that increased regulations of the banking industry were unnecessary because the financial markets were self-correcting. Subsequent attempts in Congress to require the Federal Reserve to make use of its new powers were stymied by the House Republican leadership at the time. Nearly thirty states imposed stronger regulations to ban predatory lending, but these rules did not apply to federally chartered financial institutions.

Other federal bank regulators—notably the Comptroller of the Currency, which regulated national banks, and the Office of Thrift Supervision, which oversaw savings and loans—also failed to impose or force regulations that might have limited the boom in risky loans. In addition, federal agencies used their authority to preempt state laws barring predatory lending by federally chartered financial institutions, thus leading to demands by state-chartered institutions that they should also be freed of regulations.

Describing the lack of comprehensive regulations, University of Connecticut professor Patricia A. McCoy told the Senate Banking, Housing, and Urban Affairs Committee in March 2009: "The result was a system in which lenders could shop for the loosest laws and enforcement. This shopping process, in turn, put pressure on regulators at all levels—state and local—to lower their standards or relax enforcement. What ensued was a regulatory race to the bottom."

As the subprime crisis was unfolding, the Federal Reserve in December 2007 proposed new rules making use of the powers it had spurned since 1994. For subprime loans, the Fed rules barred lenders from making loans without determining the borrower's ability to repay or determining the borrower's income and assets, and barred prepayment penalties for most adjustable rate mortgages (many borrowers had lost their homes because they could not afford the prepayment penalties that kicked in if they tried to renegotiate a loan after their mortgage payments rose). After the required period of public comment, the Federal Reserve adopted those rules on July 14, 2008, effective on Oct. 1, 2008.

REGULATING INVESTMENT BANKS

The consequences of the collapse of Lehman Brothers in September 2008 brought to public attention, as no incident had previously, the vital role in the economy of Wall Street's investment banks and the relatively lax regulation of those banks by the federal government. These banks had led the trend toward bundling subprime mortgages and other questionable assets into giant pools of securities that were given investment-grade ratings and then sold to investors.

Lehman Brothers was one of the five major investment banks that had dominated Wall Street since periods of consolidation in the industry over the previous three decades. The others were Goldman Sachs, Morgan Stanley, Merrill Lynch, and Bear Stearns. At the end of 2008, none of these firms still existed as traditional investment banks. Bear Stearns had been taken over by JP Morgan Chase; Lehman Brothers had filed for bankruptcy and its profitable assets were taken over by Barclays Bank in Britain; Merrill Lynch was taken over by Bank of America; and Goldman Sachs and Morgan Stanley had transformed themselves into commercial banks that took consumer deposits, and thus fell under tighter federal regulations.

Under the government's division-of-regulatory-labor, investment banks were regulated by the Securities and Exchange Commission because their primary role was to buy and sell securities. Following the failures of Bear Stearns and Lehman Brothers, newspaper investigations appeared to demonstrate that one major decision by the SEC allowed the banks to take the excessive risks that led to their demise.

The decision was made on April 28, 2004, when the SEC agreed to a request by the investment banks that their brokerage units (the heart of their business) be exempted from requirements to hold large reserves of capital to cushion against possible investment losses. With no dissent and virtually no public debate, the commission unanimously exempted the banks from the reserve requirements, known as the "net capital rule," and thus freed up billions of dollars for the banks to make risky investments. Under the commission's ruling, the banks were responsible for monitoring the riskiness of their investments, and the SEC was given new powers to review the banks' claims.

In subsequent years, the investment banks used their new freedom to load up on credit default swaps, mortgage-backed securities, and other risky investments without the inconvenience of having to set aside reserves to cover potential losses. The SEC—according to investigations by the *New York Times*, the *Wall Street Journal*, and other newspapers—never stepped in to prevent the banks from getting themselves into trouble. The SEC's inspector general, H. David Kotz, came to a similar conclusion. In a Sept. 25, 2008, report, Kotz said SEC officials had known that Bear Stearns was taking excessive risks with some of its investments but had done nothing about it.

The SEC rescinded its 2004 rules the day after receiving Kotz's report. In a statement accompanying the commission's action, Chairman Christopher Cox said: "The last six months have made it abundantly clear that voluntary regulation does not work."

The Bubble Collapses

For a few years in the first decade of the twenty-first century, millions of people came to believe that housing prices were always going to rise, or at the very least had reached some kind of a permanent plateau. This was true not just for ordinary citizens who saw their homes as their principal investments but even for many experts—bankers, economists, real estate industry officials, and Wall Street investors—who should have known better. History suggested an endless rise in home values was impossible and that, sooner or later, the bubble was going to burst. A handful of experts began warning in 2005–2006 that the boom would not last, but their warnings were largely discounted, certainly by the financial markets.

The warnings proved correct in 2006 when home prices began falling in parts of the country. During 2007, according to the National Association of Realtors, sale prices of existing homes fell slightly in all regions except for the Northeast (where they kept rising). By 2008, however, sale prices had fallen in every region, by a 21 percent decline in western states (notably the high-boom areas in California, Arizona, and Nevada). Nationally, sale prices eventually declined by about 11 percent between 2006 and 2008, the real estate association said.

Falling prices meant that many homeowners found themselves owing more in mortgages than their houses were now worth, a status that bankers described as being "underwater." The Center for Responsible Lending estimated that one in six homeowners were in this predicament; among those who bought their homes during the 2000s, the ratio was about one in three.

The problems faced by homeowners in this situation often were compounded by increased monthly mortgage costs once their original two- or three-year adjustable rate mortgages reset to higher rates. Millions of homeowners suddenly faced mortgage payments that had risen by 10 percent to 40 percent even as the values of their homes had declined by similar rates. In such situations, many homeowners fell behind on their monthly payments; once that happened, their financial situations often deteriorated rapidly until the lender foreclosed on the mortgage.

The portion of subprime borrowers who were seriously delinquent (more than 90 days past due) on their variable rate loans began to rise sharply from just under 10 per cent in late 2005 to nearly 30 percent in 2008. During the first half of 2007, banks began the foreclosure process on some 650,000 homes, according to the Mortgage Bankers Association; one year later, that number had nearly doubled to 1.2 million homes.

The foreclosure rate was still high in the early months of 2009. According to RealtyTrac Inc., a private research firm, lenders filed a record of 803,489 foreclosure notices in the first three months of 2009. Among states, California and Florida were the hardest hit, particularly the urban areas in those states; among the twenty-five cities with the highest rates of foreclosure, thirteen were in California and eight were in Florida. Las Vegas topped the urban list, with 4.5 percent of households having been in some state of foreclosure as of mid-April 2009, RealtyTrac said.

Overall, the Center for Responsible Lending estimated in January 2009 that about 8.1 million homeowners would lose their homes due to foreclosure over a four-year period, with the heaviest losses occurring from late 2008 through 2009. The center said these foreclosures would undermine the values of another 40.6 million neighboring homes at a cost of $352 billion. In some cities, particularly in the former boom areas of California, Arizona, and Florida, entire neighborhoods were devastated by foreclosures.

Behind these numbers were hundreds of thousands of tragic stories of families who lost their homes. Some of these foreclosures resulted from irresponsible decisions borrowers had made willingly, but many others were the result of buyers being duped by predatory lenders into taking mortgages they could not afford once the teaser rates expired. Other homeowners quickly fell into financial distress once they lost their jobs after the recession began in late 2007.

MOUNTING LOSSES, FAILING BANKS

After subprime mortgages began defaulting at exceptionally high rates, some leaders in the financial industry acknowledged that they faced problems but insisted the housing and mortgage markets remained strong. "The housing boom lasted so long that consumers, rating agencies and investors all got too aggressive" in taking on too much risk, Michael Perry, the CEO of IndyMac Bancorp, a large California lender, told Bloomberg news service in July 2007. "So at the end of the cycle we all did some stupid things, but once you pay for the cost of those stupid things there's still a fundamentally sound business left." One year later, IndyMac failed and was taken over by the FDIC; it was the second largest bank failure to that point in U.S. history.

For the American public, one of the first signs that the bursting of the housing bubble—and the resulting surge of defaults in subprime mortgages—would have broad ramifications came in mid-March 2007. That was when trading in shares of New Century Financial, a major subprime lender in California, was suspended because of losses in defaulted mortgages. Three weeks later the bank filed for bankruptcy and announced it was under investigation for financial irregularities.

In stages over the next three months, investors learned that two hedge funds created by the Wall Street investment firm Bear Stearns had gone bust, having lost nearly $20 billion in value because of heavily leveraged investments in failed securities based on subprime mortgages. By themselves, the Bear Stearns funds were relatively small, but the admission by one of Wall Street's largest firms that its bets on mortgage-backed securities had gone bad shook the financial world. If the Bear Stearns securities, which had been given investment-grade ratings by the major ratings agencies, were proving to be risky, similar securities held by other funds might be risky as well. In July 2007, one of the rating agencies, Standard & Poor's, cut its ratings for about $6.4 billion in bonds backed by subprime mortgages.

With losses mounting at several large institutions in the United States and Britain, Federal Reserve Chairman Bernanke issued his first public warning. He told congressional committees in July 2007 that losses in the subprime market could be "fairly significant" and reach $50 billion to $100 billion. Subsequent events proved that estimate to be wildly optimistic. Bernanke's comments, coupled with a forecast that the economy was slowing, helped stop what had been a steady rise in the stock markets; July 2007 had seen the high water mark on Wall Street, where the Dow Jones Industrial Average topped 14,000 for the first time.

The moment at which the global ramifications of losses in U.S. subprime mortgages became clear was on August 9, 2007, when the large French investment bank BNP Paribas froze investments in three of its hedge funds with a combined value of $2.2 billion. The bank said the funds were at the point of failure because of a "complete evaporation of liquidity in certain segments of the U.S. securitization market." This was a reference to subprime mortgage-backed securities, which the bank's funds had bought because they were given top credit ratings despite the inherent risks. The BBC's business editor, Robert Peston, said the collapse of the BNP Paribas funds suggested that "investors have bought the financial equivalent of poisoned mutton dressed as prime lamb."

The bank's warning led to a sudden freezing of short-term credit markets worldwide because of heightened concerns that many other funds weighted with mortgage-backed securities could also be in trouble. Seeking to contain the damage, the European Central Bank pumped $131 billion into the markets by lending to banks that could not access funds through traditional overnight borrowing. Other central banks (including the Federal Reserve) also acted to

TROUBLED FINANCIAL INSTITUTIONS

More than sixty banks and other financial institutions in the United States shut their doors or were forced into the arms of competitors between September 2007 and early 2009, nearly all of them as a direct result of the subprime mortgage meltdown. Most of the failed institutions were small, community-based banks, particularly in states (such as California and Nevada) where the housing boom had been most intense. More than a dozen large institutions, some with international reach, also were affected.

Here is a partial list of the major institutions involved in the credit crisis:

New Century Financial New Century was a large California lender that had written $76 billion in subprime mortgages. It filed for Chapter 11 bankruptcy in April 2007 after revealing that it was under a federal investigation for insider trading and "accounting errors." The company continued operating under supervision of a bankruptcy court.

Countrywide Financial Countrywide was a major national mortgage lender that had written $97 billion in subprime mortgages. When it ran into serious financial trouble in mid-2007 because of losses it was taken over by Bank of America in July 2008 for $2.8 billion.

Bear Stearns Bear Stearns, the world's fifth largest investment bank, began posting losses on mortgage-backed securities held by two of its hedge funds in the summer of 2007. The bank was taken over by JP Morgan Chase in March 2008 at a deep discount in a deal made possible by nearly $30 billion in lending by the Federal Reserve.

IndyMac IndyMac, a large California bank, was taken over by FDIC in July 2008, making it the second-largest bank failure to that point in U.S. history. The government continued running the bank as IndyMac Federal Bank until March 19, 2009, when the sale of the bank, for $16 billion, was completed to OneWest Bank, a newly formed federal savings bank organized by a consortium of private investors under the name of IMB HoldCo LLC.

Fannie Mae and Freddie Mac These two government-chartered but privately owned companies bought mortgages from direct lenders, thereby allowing lenders to make new mortgages. They were taken into conservatorship by the government in September 2008. The Treasury pledged to inject up to $100 billion into each company, then later said the total could reach $200 billion for each company. As of May 2009, Fannie Mae had received $34.2 billion and Freddie Mac $44.6 billion.

Lehman Brothers This firm, one of the most venerable on Wall Street, had underwritten $106.4 billion in mortgage-backed securities in 2005–2006. It posted a loss of $3.9 billion for the second quarter of 2008. The government on Sept. 15, 2008, allowed the investment bank to declare bankruptcy, after failing to find a buyer. Parts of the company were later acquired by Barclays Bank in London.

Merrill Lynch CEO Stanley O'Neal resigned in October 2007 after the company revealed its exposure to $7.9 billion in bad debt. The company agreed to be taken over by Bank of America in September 2008 for $50 billion; the merger was completed in December.

American International Group (AIG) AIG was the world's largest insurance company at the time it faced collapse in September 2008 after losing at least $20 billion on credit default swaps (similar to insurance) it had written guaranteeing transactions by other companies. The government announced a $85 billion rescue package on Sep. 16, 2008, in exchange for a controlling interest in the company. As of May 2009 the government's total bailout of the company had reached $180 billion.

Wachovia Wachovia was a North Carolina-based bank that had written $17 billion in subprime mortgages. The government initially arranged a purchase by Citigroup, but Wells Fargo Bank stepped in with a higher offer and bought the company without government aid.

Washington Mutual Commonly known as WaMu, the Seattle-based bank was closed down by regulators and sold to JP Morgan Chase for $1.9 billion in September 2008. It was the largest U.S. bank failure to that point.

Citigroup One of the world's largest banks, Citigroup revealed its first subprime losses (nearly $9 billion) in October 2007, but within six months the losses had reached $40 billion. The government invested $45 billion in Citigroup in October and November 2008 and also guaranteed the bulk of $301 billion in mortgage-backed assets held by the bank.

SOURCES: FDIC, Federal Reserve, Treasury Department, Center for Public Integrity, ProPublica.

restore liquidity and, in the Fed's case, to lower interest rates. In an August 17, 2007, statement, the Federal Reserve's Open Market Committee for the first time expressed serious worries about the fallout from failing subprime mortgages. "Financial market conditions have deteriorated, and tighter credit conditions and increased uncertainty have the potential to restrain economic growth going forward," the committee said.

August 2007 also saw a series of financial institutions announce that they were getting out of the businesses of making subprime mortgages and bundling them into securities. Goldman Sachs, Capital One, Lehman Brothers, and

Lehman Brothers Holdings Inc. Chief Executive Richard S. Fuld Jr., testifies before the House Oversight and Government Reform Committee on Capitol Hill on October 6, 2008, on the collapse of Lehman Brothers.
Source: AP Photo/Susan Walsh

Wachovia were among the major banks halting new business in the subprime sector or acknowledging losses from investments in mortgage-backed securities.

President Bush on Aug. 31, 2007, announced a series of measures, including tax changes, intended to help homeowners refinance their loans rather than go into default. "Recent disturbances in the subprime mortgage industry are modest, modest in relation to the size of our economy," he said. "But if your family's one of those having trouble making the monthly payments, this problem doesn't seem modest at all."

Another shock came early in September 2007 when a major British mortgage lender, Northern Rock, failed because its source of funds, the money markets, was drying up. The bad news escalated in the United States with the release in October of reports for the third quarter of 2007. The biggest, most negative revelation came from the huge investment bank Merrill Lynch, which said it was writing down $8.4 billion worth of investments because of losses in mortgage-backed securities. Merrill's board ousted CEO Stanley O'Neal but gave him a departing gift of $161 million, on top of $70 million in compensation he had been paid during his four years at the helm. Less than a week after O'Neal was shown the door, Citigroup's board forced out its chairman, Charles O. Prince III, because the company's losses had ballooned to more than $8 billion.

Other major banks reporting large losses on subprime mortgages during late 2007 included Bank of America, Credit Suisse, HSBC (a large British bank), Morgan Stanley, Wachovia, and Washington Mutual. By the end of 2007, twenty large international banks had written down or posted losses totaling $97 billion worth of mortgage-backed assets, according to Bloomberg news. Some analysts were suggesting prospective losses could range as high as $400 billion. In one of many attempts to stanch damage to their balance sheets, U.S. banks laid off more than 10,000 employees during the year; this was just a hint of the bigger layoffs to come.

CASCADING PROBLEMS IN 2008

If anyone seriously hoped that 2008 would bring a turnaround, such hopes were shattered quickly in January as banks all over the world reported continuing, and in many cases increasing, losses from subprime mortgages during the fourth quarter of 2007. By late January banks had reported losses of more than $130 billion. The biggest single jolt came from Citigroup, which said it was writing down $18.1 billion in subprime mortgage losses; this was more than double the $8 billion estimate that had led to the ouster of Prince as chief executive just two months earlier.

In anticipation of the U.S. general elections later in the year, the Bush administration announced plans for a $145 billion "stimulus" plan that included tax rebates for individuals and investment tax credits for businesses. Rather than optimism, that plan stimulated even more pessimism in the financial markets, which tumbled sharply on Jan. 21, 2008. One day later, the Federal Reserve slashed interest rates by 0.75 percent, the central bank's biggest single cut since August 1982. Saying that financial markets "remain under considerable stress," the Fed cut rates by another one-half percent just one week later.

By late January some experts, including the International Monetary Fund, were estimating that total subprime losses eventually would approach or exceed $1 trillion. The bearish economist Nouriel Roubani, of New York University, offered an even grimmer estimate of $2 trillion. Roubani had acquired a reputation as Dr. Doom, and his pessimistic forecasts had been widely dismissed. By early 2008, however, Roubani's brand of pessimism had proven generally accurate and was becoming more widely accepted than in the past. On Feb. 10, finance ministers of the Group of Seven industrialized nations acknowledged that losses resulting from collapse of the U.S. housing market could reach $400 billion.

Congress cleared the economic stimulus bill (PL 110-185) on Feb. 7; it was the result of remarkably friendly bipartisan negotiations among the administration and leaders of the two parties in both chambers. Pegged at a cost of $151.7 billion in fiscal year 2008, the bulk of the bill was aimed at individual tax rebates, which began reaching taxpayers during the spring. Most economists later said the bill provided a small, temporary boost to the economy during the second quarter of the year. *(Details, p. 151)*

The government's first major rescue of a failing financial institution came in March 2008, when the Federal Reserve worked with JP Morgan Chase to salvage what remained of Bear Stearns. The Wall Street investment firm had been one of the most aggressive speculators in subprime mortgages; officials worried that its sudden collapse would dump billions of dollars of questionable securities on the market.

The Fed on March 14, 2008, agreed to loan Bear Stearns $13 billion, with the money channeled through JP Morgan because Bear Stearns was not a member of the Fed system. When that move failed to stem market demands on Bear Stearns, the Fed worked out a deal under which JP Morgan bought Bear Stearns for $2 a share (the price later was raised to $10), a fraction of the company's claimed book value of $80 a share. The Fed made this deal possible by agreeing to purchase assets that Bear Stearns had valued at $30 billion but that JP Morgan did not want to take onto its own balance sheet.

More than any other action to that point, the failure of Bear Stearns appeared to signify just how serious the financial crisis had become. A $2 bill taped to the front door of the company's office building in New York illustrated graphically that mighty Wall Street banks were suffering the consequences of bad decision making.

For a while, it appeared that the Fed's intervention to prevent the total collapse of Bear Stearns was having the desired effect of calming the financial system and the equity markets. Even so, banks in the United States and Europe continued to report losses in the subprime market; those losses topped $320 billion by early May and jumped to $500 billion by late August, according to the Bloomberg financial service.

The next major financial institution to collapse was IndyMac, a California bank that had bet heavily on subprime mortgages. The FDIC took control of the bank on July 11, 2008, and in January 2009 announced plans to sell it as a thrift holding company. Also in July, Bank of America took over Countrywide Financial, a large mortgage lender, which had been in serious trouble since 2007 because of its large portfolio of troubled subprime mortgages.

ADDRESSING FORECLOSURES

With the economic crisis taking place in an election year, members of Congress felt under pressure to do something that appeared to address the collapse of the housing industry. This perceived need for action was shared by members of both parties, one of the rare examples of bipartisan agreement in a Congress noted for partisan gridlock on matters large and small. There was less agreement, however, on exactly what Congress should do, and so it was not until late July that Congress gave final approval to a heavily revised version of a bill (HR 3221) that had been debated for months.

As cleared by Congress on July 26, and signed into law (PL 110-289) by Bush four days later, the bill included numerous provisions intended to stanch the flood of foreclosures. *(Details, p. 153)*

The centerpiece was a program, known as HOPE for Homeowners, that allowed the Federal Housing Administration (FHA) to insure up to $300 billion in mortgages voluntarily refinanced by banks and distressed homeowners; under this provision, banks were encouraged to write down the balance of existing loans so borrowers could avoid foreclosure by refinancing with loans through the FHA. The bill also increased loan limits for mortgages originated by FHA or purchased by Fannie Mae and Freddie Mac; and created a new regulatory body (the Federal Housing Finance Agency) to supervise Fannie Mae and Freddie Mac. Other provisions of the bill ultimately made it possible for the government in September to take over Fannie and Freddie.

At the time of its passage, members of Congress and the Bush administration estimated that the HOPE for Homeowners provisions would help about 400,000 homeowners refinance their loans and avoid foreclosure. Banks were reluctant to use the voluntary refinance provisions, however, even after the administration reduced some requirements that bankers had opposed. By early 2009 only a handful of mortgages had been refinanced under the law.

COLLAPSE OF LEHMAN BROTHERS

Then came September 2008, when the broad contours of the financial problems became frighteningly obvious. The first major development came on Sept. 7, when the government took control of the mortgage giants Fannie Mae and Freddie Mac. The government did this through the new regulator for the two so-called government-sponsored enterprises, the Federal Housing Finance Agency, which placed them in conservatorship. The government pledged to provide the two agencies with new capital as needed and to guarantee about $5 trillion worth of debt. In return, the government received warrants equal to 79.9 percent of the stock in each company, making the government the controlling owner.

Fannie and Freddie had been started by the government in the mid-twentieth century to promote home buying but were later spun off as private entities, chartered by the government. Their basic role was to buy mortgages from commercial banks, which could use the proceeds to make more loans; neither Fannie nor Freddie made mortgage loans directly, however. By early September, both companies had lost much of their capital value in the marketplace and their balance sheets were deteriorating rapidly because of questions about the worth of the mortgages and mortgage-related securities they held. The Federal Housing Finance Agency said it intervened because the companies "cannot continue to operate safely and soundly and fulfill their critical public mission, without significant action" to shore up their finances.

Just one week after its rescue of Fannie Mae and Freddie Mac, the government made what turned out to be one of its most fateful decisions in the entire history of the financial crisis. Over the weekend of Sept. 14–15 it became clear that two of the largest Wall Street investment firms were on the verge of collapse: Lehman Brothers and Merrill Lynch. The balance sheets of both firms were heavily laden with unmarketable securities related to subprime mortgages.

Treasury and Federal Reserve officials found a buyer for Merrill Lynch in Bank of America. That bank was itself the creation of several previous mergers and was widely assumed, at the time, to be relatively solid.

Despite a frantic weekend of searching, the government could not find a willing buyer for Lehman Brothers, which had been one of Wall Street's most aggressive marketers of, and investors in, securities based on subprime mortgages. At one point on Sept. 13 it appeared that the British giant, Barclays Bank, might be willing to step in as Lehman Brothers savior, but authorities in London were unwilling to waive regulations that stood in the way of a rapid takeover. Without a buyer, the U.S. government lacked the legal authorization to take over Lehman Brothers and rescue it directly, according to subsequent statements by Treasury Secretary Henry M. Paulson Jr. and Federal Reserve Chairman Bernanke. Lehman Brothers promptly declared bankruptcy, on Sept. 15. Barclays Bank later took over the company's marketable assets, at bargain-basement prices.

It did not take long for the full ramifications of the Lehman Brothers collapse to become clear. Investors worldwide immediately withdrew billions of dollars from money market funds and the stock markets—from any place, in fact, where they perceived even the slightest degree of risk. Much of this money was dumped into U.S. Treasury bills, where the interest fell close to zero percent.

The effect on money market funds was particularly dramatic and affected nearly everyone with any kind of savings, not just Wall Street financiers. The nation's oldest money market fund, the Reserve Fund, suffered such rapid losses because of Lehman Brothers' collapse that it could no longer guarantee that a $1 investment was still worth $1—a process known as "breaking the buck." This frightened investors even more, posing such a threat to the entire financial system that the government quickly stepped in to guarantee money market investments.

In retrospect, nearly every expert said the collapse of Lehman Brothers marked the key turning point in the financial crisis: the moment at which nervousness and uncertainty suddenly swelled into outright panic, not just in the United States but worldwide. If an institution as large and well-connected as Lehman Brothers could fail—and, just as important, be allowed to fail—what about other financial institutions, both big and small?

Overnight, the risks that investors and financial institutions had ignored or played down took on a new urgency. "After the failure of Lehman Brothers . . . institutional investors have said they would prefer to stay home," Bill Gross, the head of the giant bond fund manager Pimco, said. "Instead of risking their money [it] goes into that figurative mattress."

One of the companies that fell the hardest during this rush away from risk was the insurance giant, American International Group. With the near-collapse of Fannie Mae and Freddie Mac, and the actual collapse of Lehman Brothers, AIG suddenly faced enormous losses on billions of dollars in credit default swaps it had written. The failure of AIG would have reverberated across the financial system—perhaps even more than had the bankruptcy of Lehman Brothers—because the debts of many other companies were tied to the insurance AIG had provided. Even companies that had kept current on their debt payments would face higher interest expenses, possibly leading to default, if AIG could no longer provide the insurance that underwrote their debt.

To prevent the collapse of yet another giant firm, the Federal Reserve announced on Sept. 16 that it was providing a $85 billion line of credit to AIG. In exchange for its loan, the government received warrants enabling it to take an ownership stake of 79.9 percent in AIG, representing a controlling share. As AIG's finances continued to spiral downward in subsequent months, the government took three more actions to shore up AIG through early March 2009. Each step got the government deeper into the hole as AIG's treasurer, to a total tune of $180 billion.

BAILING OUT THE BANKS

On Thursday, Sept. 18, four days after Lehman Brothers filed for bankruptcy and the same fate threatened AIG, Treasury Secretary Paulson, Federal Reserve Chairman Bernanke, and other senior officials went to Capitol Hill to meet with key congressional leaders. Participants later described the dramatic evening session as a wake-up call during which Bernanke offered a frightening description of what could happen to the financial system, and thus to the economy, if the government failed to shore up troubled banks. "If we don't do this," the *New York Times* later quoted Bernanke as saying, "we may not have an economy on Monday." Several veteran legislators said they had never before heard such dire warnings from the nation's top economic officials.

In separate news conferences the next morning, Sept. 19, Bush and Paulson offered the broad outlines of a plan under which the government would spend up to $700 billion on a program that would allow the banks to clean up their balance sheets and give them the confidence to begin lending again. Under this program, Paulson said, the government would buy "illiquid assets that are weighing down our financial institutions and threatening our economy." Such a step, he added, represented "decisive action to fundamentally and comprehensively address the root cause of our financial system's stresses."

The government took other steps on the same day to shore up confidence in the financial system. In addition to the Treasury Department's action to guarantee investments in money market funds, the Securities and Exchange Commission temporarily banned so-called short-selling (betting that stock prices would fall) in the shares of some 800 financial firms, and the government said Fannie Mae and Freddie Mac would increase their purchases of mortgage-backed securities.

The Treasury Department released a draft of the administration's proposal for the $700 billion bank rescue plan—formally known as the Troubled Asset Relief Program (or TARP) on Sept. 20. It showed that Paulson wanted almost total discretion to spend the money as he saw fit. That proposal angered many on Capitol Hill, notably Democrats who demanded that any step to rescue the banks also include provisions capping the pay of senior bank executives and providing some kind of aid to struggling homeowners.

Testifying before the Senate Banking Committee on Sept. 23, Paulson rejected suggestions by some Democrats that the government should take partial ownership stakes in major banks rather than try to buy the so-called "toxic assets" from them. Putting capital in banks is "what you do when you have failure," he said, adding that the administration's plan was "about success."

The administration's unprecedented bank rescue plan set off an intense political struggle on Capitol Hill. The struggle produced odd alliances, with most Democrats generally supporting the plan of the Republican administration (with conditions, notably pay caps for top bank officials) while most Republicans opposed it.

Coming just a little over one month before the elections, the debate also created political dilemmas for the Democratic and Republican presidential candidates, both of whom were members of the Senate and therefore would be called on to vote on the final product. Democrat Barack Obama took a cautious approach, supporting the idea of a bank rescue but calling for restrictions on pay of bank executives. Republican John McCain took a big gamble on Sept. 24, announcing that he would suspend his campaign so he could help congressional negotiators reach a deal; McCain also said he wanted to postpone the first of three televised debates with Obama, scheduled for Sept. 26. McCain's gamble backfired, however, when Obama said the financial crisis made having the debate more important than ever and after McCain showed up at a White House negotiating session but played no significant role. The presidential debate went ahead as scheduled, with Obama appearing more sure-footed than his opponent.

Even as Congress and the presidential candidates were debating their next steps, the red ink continued to flow in the financial markets. The government on Sept. 25 seized Seattle-based Washington Mutual, which became the largest bank ever to fail in U.S. history, and sold it to JP Morgan Chase for $1.9 billion. Four days later, the Federal Deposit Insurance Corporation (FDIC) acted to help Citigroup acquire, for $2.2 billion, the Charlotte-based Wachovia, another large bank that had lost billions in the subprime market. This deal was superseded just a few days later when Wells Fargo bid $15 billion for Wachovia.

The first congressional vote on the bailout plan (HR 3997) took place on Sept. 29 and proved disastrous for the administration. With Republicans nearly united in opposition, the House rejected the proposal crafted by the bipartisan leadership, 228–205. Stock markets plunged on the news even though, on the same day, the Federal Reserve and other central banks injected $330 billion into the global financial system.

Congressional negotiators went back to work and produced a new version of the bailout legislation that answered some of the criticisms that had been offered by members of both parties. The revision also included numerous provisions intended to win over reluctant legislators, notably several tax breaks for businesses and individuals. The Senate approved the revised version (HR 1424) on Oct. 1 by a 74–25 vote, and the House followed on Oct. 3 by an unexpectedly wide margin of 263–171. Bush signed the bill into law (PL 110-343) the same day. *(Details, p. 154)*

The bailout bill established the TARP program with a pool of up to $700 billion. Congress divided the money into two tranches: $350 billion was available immediately to the administration, with the second $350 billion available after the president requested it and Congress had a chance to block its release. The administration could use the money to purchase a wide range of assets from financial institutions, including mortgages and mortgage-related assets, or any other asset the purchase of which would help restore financial stability. Other provisions gave the Treasury secretary broad authority to spend the money, so long as the goal was restoring financial stability. The bill also imposed limits on the pay of top officials of banks receiving taxpayer funds.

Any hope that the extraordinarily rapid, if politically contentious, congressional action would calm the financial markets was quickly dashed. The following week proved to be one of the worst ever for financial markets around the world. In the midst of that market turmoil, British prime minister Gordon Brown announced a major injection of government funds into his country's banks, a move that set the stage for similar actions by other countries.

At regularly scheduled meetings in Washington over the weekend of Oct. 10–12, finance ministers and central bank leaders agreed that no more major banks could be allowed to collapse and that governments should act to rescue their own banking systems. European leaders, meeting in Paris, agreed on a $2.5 trillion rescue plan for their banks. Bush administration officials said Washington, too, would seek to bolster the financial system by investing directly in U.S. banks—the very step Paulson had rejected as a "failure" just three weeks earlier.

THE GOVERNMENT BUYS INTO BANKS

On Oct. 13, Paulson met at the Treasury Department with the leaders of the country's largest banks and, in effect, forced them to accept government investments totaling $125 billion from TARP funds. The banks, and the initial amount of taxpayer funds invested in them, were: Citigroup, $25 billion; Bank of America (including Merrill-Lynch, which it was acquiring), $25 billion; JP Morgan Chase, $25 billion; Wells Fargo, $25 billion; Goldman Sachs, $10 billion; Morgan Stanley, $10 billion; Bank of New York, $3 billion; and State Street Bank, $2 billion. News of the investments sent the stock markets soaring; the Dow-Jones Industrial Average, which had been plunging for weeks, shot up by 11 percent, the largest single-day gain since the 1930s.

Paulson formally announced the investments the following day, saying they were part of a Capital Purchase Program, which would use a total of $250 billion of the total TARP money. That total included the $125 billion in the eight big banks, plus $125 billion to be invested later in smaller banks.

"Government owning a stake in any private U.S. company is objectionable to most Americans, me included," Paulson said. "Yet the alternative of leaving businesses and consumers without access to financing is totally unacceptable." Paulson specifically linked the investments to expanded lending by the banks, saying: "At a time when events naturally make even the most daring investors risk averse, the needs of our economy require that our financial institutions not take this new capital to hoard it, but to deploy it." The goal, he added, was "to see a wide array of healthy institutions sell preferred shares to Treasury and raise additional private capital so that they can make more loans to businesses and consumers across the nation."

In return for the taxpayer money, the banks were required to give the government preferred shares (the equivalent of loans) paying 5 percent annual dividends and to accept limits on compensation for their top executives, plus a ban on so-called "golden parachutes" for executives who were forced out for failed performance.

Over the next month, the government held open the possibility that it might use at least some of the TARP money for the original purpose of buying troubled assets. That stance changed on Nov. 12 when Paulson said he had concluded the remaining TARP funds would be better used to continue recapitalizing banks and supporting markets that bought up consumer credit. Pumping money directly into banks was a "more powerful" way to bolster the financial system than buying the toxic assets, he said. Asked why he had abandoned a program that he and other officials just weeks earlier had described to Congress as vital, Paulson said: "I will never apologize for changing an approach or strategy when the facts change," he said. The facts that had changed, he noted, were the economic forecasts, all aspects of which had continued to deteriorate since Congress enacted the TARP legislation.

BAD NEWS, AND MORE BAD NEWS

The final four months of the Bush administration—the interregnum between the elections and the inauguration of Obama as the new president—saw an endless succession of bad economic and financial news. The gloom was offset only by hope that Obama's administration would find more creative and more effective ways of dealing with the economic crisis than Bush's team had developed so far.

On the financial front, banks continued to report enormous losses. By November, Citigroup had posted losses of $65 billion, about one-half from mortgage-backed securities that had gone bad and the rest in write-downs of assets and other charges. The losses at Citigroup were so severe that the government on Nov. 24 announced a second infusion of taxpayer aid to the bank (in addition to the $25 billion TARP investment just five weeks earlier): a $20 billion investment and federal guarantees of the bulk of $306 billion in troubled investments (later recalculated at $301 billion). Merrill-Lynch, which was in the process of being acquired by Bank of America, dumped tens of billions of dollars in toxic securities, in some cases for less than one-third of their face value. For the first nine months of 2008, the company lost nearly $15 billion on its collateralized debt obligations.

From the perspective of the general public, the gloom coming from Wall Street was overshadowed by a succession of announcements of job cuts by companies both large and small. On Nov. 10, for example, the shipping carrier DHL announced it was cutting 9,500 jobs in the United States, the majority of them at its hub in the small town of Wilmington, Ohio. The electronics retailer Circuit City announced on the same day that it was filing for Chapter 11 bankruptcy. Dismal earnings reports over the next few weeks from Sun Microsystems, Target, Starbucks, and dozens of other companies demonstrated that the economic stress was both broad and deep. The Labor Department reported early in December that employers had cut 533,000 jobs in November—the single worst month in thirty-four years (this number was later revised to 597,000).

A broad context for the grim economic numbers emerged on Dec. 1, when the National Bureau of Economic

Research, a nonprofit think tank, said it had concluded that the United States had been in a recession since December 2007. Nearly all economists had said the nation would enter a recession at some point, but until this announcement few had suggested that a recession already had been under way for so long. The stock markets, which had climbed in previous days on the expectation of a major government stimulus package, suddenly plunged again but then see-sawed up and down for the rest of the year.

DETROIT ASKS FOR HELP

For a brief period between late November and mid-December, the focus of attention shifted from the bad news on Wall Street to the even worse news in Detroit. With sales of nearly all types of vehicles in free-fall, the top executives of the Big Three domestic automakers—Chrysler, Ford, and General Motors—appeared on Capitol Hill on Nov. 19 to request federal aid for the industry. Specifically, the executives asked for immediate access to $25 billion that Congress had appropriated earlier for development of fuel-efficient vehicles.

This appeal turned into a public relations disaster for the industry, however. Lawmakers hammered the executives for flying from Detroit to Washington in luxurious corporate jets and then failing to offer specific plans for how they would use taxpayer money to restore their companies to health. House Speaker Nancy Pelosi, D-Calif., and Senate Majority Leader Harry Reid, D-Nev., said the next day that Congress would consider direct aid to the auto industry only after the companies presented detailed business plans. "It's all about accountability and viability," Pelosi said at a news conference. "Until we can see a plan where the auto industry is held accountable and a plan for viability for how they go into the future—until we see the plan, until they show us the plan, we cannot show them the money."

Auto executives returned to Capitol Hill on Dec. 4—this time in automobiles, not private jets—with plans that were more detailed than before and that included wage and other concessions from the United Auto Workers union. Based on the new plans, congressional Democrats and the Bush White House put together a $15 billion rescue proposal for the auto industry, announced on Dec. 8. That proposal quickly fell apart in the Senate, where Republicans demanded deeper wage cuts by unionized auto workers as the price for injecting tax dollars into the companies. Many of the Republicans represented southern states where foreign auto companies had built large, nonunionized plants.

Stymied by resistance from his own party, Bush on Dec. 19 did what he previously had said he would not do: divert money from the bank bailout program to the auto industry. The president said he had approved $13.4 billion in direct loans, including $9.4 billion for General Motors and $4 billion for Chrysler. Bush said another $4 billion could be provided to one or both companies the following February. If the companies had not become "financially viable" by March 31, 2009, a White House statement said, the money would have to be returned to the Treasury. Officials at Ford insisted that company could survive without government aid.

Bush said his preference, in "ordinary" times, would have been to allow market forces to work their will with the car companies. But current times were not ordinary, he said, so "in the midst of a financial crisis and a recession, allowing the U.S. auto industry to collapse is not a responsible course of action."

STOCK MARKETS TUMBLE

Stock markets in the United States and overseas reacted warily to the grim news from the banking and housing sectors during 2007 and the first two-thirds of 2008. Sharp declines one day often were followed by similar rises the following day as investors tried to fathom the impact of economic and financial developments that generally, but not always, were negative.

The collapse of Lehman Brothers in mid-September 2008, the near-collapse of AIG, and the host of other troubles in the financial sector heightened the volatility in the stock markets. At year's end the *New York Times* quoted Howard Silverblatt, an index analyst at Standard and Poor's, as noting that the S&P index of 500 stocks had moved up or down by more than 5 percent on eighteen days during the last four months of the year; there had been only seventeen such days in the previous fifty-three years, Silverblatt said.

By Dec. 31, the Dow-Jones Industrial Average (a composite of the stocks of thirty so-called "blue chip" companies) was down 34 percent, and the broader S&P 500 index was down 38 percent. The NASDAQ composite index, heavily laden with the stock of high-tech firms, fell 41 percent, the worst year since that exchange was formed in 1971. A different measure put the results in an even worse light: during 2008 U.S. investors lost $6.9 trillion in the value of their stock holdings, an amount equal to all of their gains in the six years since the previous recession, which resulted in part from the collapse of a bubble in the high-technology industry.

Millions of Americans whose retirement plans were invested heavily in stocks saw the results of the year's calamity in quarterly reports from their investment firms—assuming they were willing to look at the reports. The gallows humor joke was that a 401(k) retirement account (named after the section of the tax code dealing with such accounts) had become a 201(k) account.

The 2008 results on international markets, for the most part, were even worse than in the United States: stocks were down by 41 percent in Brazil, by 42 percent in Japan, and by 40 percent in Germany, for example. Globally, stock markets were down by an average of 48 percent.

Markets in the United States and most other countries continued to tumble early in 2009, appearing to reach a bottom in the first week of March before starting a slow climb that lasted, with occasional setbacks, through the rest of 2009. Investors and economists debated whether the upswing represented a new bull market or merely a temporary bear market rally, preceding yet another swing downward.

Yet another blow to the economy came on Dec. 11 when government agents in New York arrested hedge fund manager Bernard L. Madoff on charges of running a giant Ponzi scheme that had defrauded investors of an estimated $50 billion. Some reports put the losses as high as $65 billion. Madoff on March 12, 2009, pleaded guilty to criminal charges of defrauding his investors by using the proceeds from new investors to pay previous ones—the classic structure of a Ponzi scheme, which was named for Charles Ponzi who by 1920 had defrauded thousands of small investors. However, Madoff refused to cooperate with investigators by providing details or naming co-conspirators. Hundreds of individual investors and several dozen charitable foundations lost enormous sums in the collapse of Madoff's firm. (In June 2009 Madoff, 71, was sentenced to a total of 150 years in prison on several criminal charges, including securities fraud, money laundering, and perjury. He began serving the term on July 14.)

OBAMA'S ECONOMIC STIMULUS PLAN

Obama had suggested during the election campaign that he would offer a program to "jump start" the economy through a large-scale infusion of tax dollars, but he was careful not to offer specifics. The first concrete evidence of the thinking of the new team came on Nov. 23, 2008, when news organizations reported that Obama's aides and key Democrats in Congress were discussing a plan for $700 billion in spending to boost the economy over the next two years.

In the weeks following the elections, Obama at first expressed hope that the newly expanded Democratic majority in Congress (which would take office two weeks before his inauguration) would pass an economic stimulus bill that he could sign on, or shortly after, inauguration day. It quickly became clear that Congress could not move that quickly, however, and Obama's aides shifted to a goal of having the legislation ready within a few weeks of inauguration.

Obama did achieve a legislative victory of sorts during the transition period when President Bush (at Obama's request) asked Congress to release the second $350 billion in funding under the TARP bill. The key action on this request took place on Jan. 15, 2009, when the Senate, by a vote of 42–52, defeated a motion to deny the funds; this freed up the funds because, under the TARP legislation, action by both chambers of Congress was necessary to block use of the money.

The Senate's approval came despite growing unease in Congress about the Bush administration's use of the TARP money. Reports by two bodies charged with monitoring the TARP program—an independent inspector general within the Treasury Department and a special Congressional Oversight Panel—suggested that Paulson's Treasury Department had attached very few strings when handing out billions of dollars to dozens of banks. Many of the recipient banks refused to disclose publicly how they were using the money. The few bank officials who did speak for the record said they had no plans or obligations to step up lending as a consequence of the injection of taxpayer funds, despite Paulson's statements that stimulating such lending was a main goal of the investments.

Obama's first order of business, upon taking office on Jan. 20, 2009, was to get Congress to adopt his ambitious economic "stimulus" plan, which he said would pump billions of taxpayer dollars into the economy to help replace lagging private investments. Rather than submitting his own detailed proposal for such a plan, Obama offered general guidelines to both houses of Congress, which then developed their own specific bills. The process began in the House, where Appropriations Committee Chairman David Obey, D-Wis., wrote a massive spending bill, totaling $819 billion, that relied heavily on grants to states and municipalities and included tax cuts for about 90 percent of individual taxpayers, a central promise of Obama's presidential campaign. Obey's bill also kept two other promises by Obama: it was "transparent" in that key details were posted on the Internet before the House voted on it, and it contained no specific "earmarks," or pet projects sponsored by individual members.

The House adopted Obey's bill (HR 1) on Jan. 28 by a vote of 244–188, without a single Republican voting in favor. Republicans decried the measure as bloated with government programs that would crowd private borrowing from the economy, inflate the federal deficit, and do little to create jobs. The administration had marginally more success in getting bipartisan support in the Senate, where, on Feb. 10 three moderate Republicans joined in supporting an even bigger bill totaling $838 billion. One major change was the addition of a so-called "patch" for the alternative minimum tax, which originally was intended to capture taxes from high earners but in recent years had threatened to boost taxes even for middle-income individuals. The patch eliminated the tax's potential impact on the middle class, but at an estimated cost of $70 billion.

The three moderate Republicans—Susan Collins and Olympia Snowe of Maine and Arlen Specter of Pennsylvania—proved to be the key figures in congressional action on the bill because Democrats needed their votes to overcome a threatened Republican filibuster. They joined top Democratic leaders in negotiating a final bill and insisted on cutting the overall total, but otherwise pushed for the main provisions of the Senate version rather than the original House measure.

Both chambers adopted a somewhat stripped-down (at $787 billion) final version of the bill. The House acted on Feb. 13 and the Senate cleared the bill early in the morning of Feb. 14. Again, not a single Republican in the House voted for the bill, while Collins, Snowe, and Specter were the only Republicans supporting it in the Senate. Obama traveled to Denver to sign the bill into law (PL 111-5) on Feb. 17. It represented a major accomplishment for the new president, fulfilling some of his top campaign promises in less than one month after he took office.

The bill Obama signed consisted of two major portions: $463 billion in spending for transportation and other infrastructure projects, education aid to states and localities, improved energy efficiency, health care, and housing; and $326 billion for individual and business tax cuts. Democrats and administration officials insisted the bill would save or create about 3.5 million jobs, which had been one of Obama's key promises. An analysis by the Congressional Budget Office suggested this result might be possible by late 2010. One unusual component of the bill was a series of requirements for transparency: agencies were required to post details on the Internet showing how they used the money, and a high-level board, chaired by Vice President Joseph R. Biden, had authority to oversee the stimulus program and issue reports on waste and abuse.

DEALING WITH BANKS AND FORECLOSURES

Obama's economic stimulus plan was a first step to deal with the consequences of the nation's economic plight. The early months of the new president's tenure also saw a series of proposals to address the underlying causes of the recession, including lingering problems at the largest banks and the continuing tide of foreclosures against homeowners unable to meet their mortgage payments. The administration put off until later in the year the equally vexing question of how to revise government regulations of the financial industry to prevent a recurrence of the credit crisis.

One of the first issues on the administration's plate involved the estimated $2 trillion of toxic mortgage-backed assets still on the balance sheets of dozens of banks. These were the same assets that the Bush administration originally had planned to buy with the TARP funds approved by Congress in October 2008 but were left untouched when Paulson decided instead to invest taxpayer money in banks.

Obama's Treasury secretary, Timothy Geithner, unveiled an approach, which he called a financial stability plan, on Feb. 10, 2009. The multistep plan, he said, "will help restart the flow of credit, clean up and strengthen our banks, and provide critical aid for homeowners and for small businesses." Geithner acknowledged that the public had lost much of its confidence in the government's handling of the financial crisis, notably because billions of dollars in TARP funds had gone to "the same institutions that help caused the crisis, with limited transparency and oversight" and because some banks had "continued to award rich compensation packages and lavish perks to their senior executives."

Geithner's plan consisted of several elements, starting with financial examinations (known as "stress tests") of the largest financial institutions, defined as those with assets of more than $100 billion. The purpose of these tests, to be conducted by federal regulators, was to determine which banks needed additional capital in the event the overall economy continued to deteriorate. A second program was a public-private investment fund, in which the government would put up an unspecified amount of money, to be leveraged with funds from private investors, with the goal of buying $500 billion to $1 trillion worth of the toxic assets that remained on the balance sheets of banks. A third program, called the consumer and business lending initiative, promised to use $100 billion in government funds to stimulate up to $1 trillion in new bank loans for consumers and small businesses. Geithner also promised increased "transparency" in future uses of money under the TARP program, and he announced a $50 billion program to help middle-class homeowners faced with foreclosures on their mortgages.

Although Geithner's plan contained several important proposals, the financial markets reacted negatively because it lacked key details and fell short of the dramatic reworking of the nation's financial system that Obama had appeared to promise during a White House news conference just the day before. In previous weeks, economists had debated a range of possible actions for the government to take, including creating a "bad bank" that would buy all the toxic assets from banks and the even more extreme step of forcing the weakest banks into bankruptcy. Geithner's middle-of-the-road plan thus satisfied few of those who had advocated some other action. Stock markets in the United States and other countries fell sharply, and many commentators suddenly began questioning whether Geithner (who had been head of the New York Federal Reserve Bank during the Bush years) was up to the monumental job Obama had given him.

Six weeks later, on March 23, Geithner returned with a more fleshed-out plan for the public-private investment fund that came closer to meeting the expectations of financial markets and other experts. This revised plan dealt in more detail with procedures the government would use to work with private investors to purchase what Geithner called "legacy assets"—a euphemism for unmarketable securities based on subprime mortgages. Under the plan, the government would use $75 billion to $100 billion from remaining TARP funds, along with private investments, to buy at least $500 billion worth of the toxic securities still held by banks, and possibly as much as $1 trillion. The investors would manage the assets for sale at a time of their choosing.

This plan won much broader praise than had Geithner's earlier version, and stock markets in the United States and globally continued an upward swing that had begun two weeks earlier. Even so, some critics noted that private investors could reap one-half of any profits from the sale of the toxic assets, while the taxpayers would be liable for nearly all of any potential losses. Others suggested Geithner's plan was still inadequate to meet the challenge of undercapitalized banks.

The Obama administration took its first crack at another key element of the financial crisis—the foreclosure threat faced by millions of homeowners—with a broad-scale program announced by the president on Feb. 18. Speaking in Mesa, Arizona, Obama said the government would commit up to $275 billion to help as many as 9 million homeowners refinance their mortgages or take other steps to avoid foreclosure. Of this amount, $75 billion would be in direct spending and the remainder financial guarantees for Fannie Mae and Freddie Mac. "This plan will not save every home, but it will give millions of families resigned to financial ruin a chance to rebuild," Obama said.

Unlike Geithner's original banking plan announced just eight days earlier, this mortgage-rescue plan was more comprehensive than most experts had expected, and so it drew wide praise, including even from some Republicans who had been skeptical of Obama's other economic policies. Nevertheless, no one saw the plan as a cure-all for the still-ailing housing and mortgage industries, in part because of limitations that Obama himself acknowledged were necessary to keep costs down. For example, the plan would not help homeowners who had kept current on their mortgage payments but still owed more money than their homes currently were worth. Nor would it help homeowners whose mortgage balances exceeded the current value of their homes by more than 5 percent—a problem faced by the majority of homeowners in financial trouble, according to some experts.

In the early months of the Obama presidency Congress also approved two pieces of legislation designed to directly help homeowners, one to assist persons facing foreclosure and the other to strengthen protections against mortgage fraud. Both were signed by Obama in May 2009.

The first, approved overwhelmingly in both chambers, sought to ease application and eligibility requirements for a foreclosure prevention program. The bill also raised the federal deposit insurance coverage by the Federal Deposit Insurance Corp. and the National Credit Union Administration. The limit on coverage for each account with one of these agencies had been raised to $250,000 the previous fall, from $100,000, but the increase was scheduled to expire at the end of 2009. The bill extended the period to the end of 2013.

The second bill extended federal fraud law to apply to mortgage lenders not directly regulated or insured by the federal government as well as to cover the money paid out in the financial assistance programs approved earlier, including TARP and the economic stimulus package passed earlier in 2009.

Economic Consequences

If the U.S. housing market had cooled, beginning in mid-2006, but the financial system had remained relatively intact, the economic consequences might have been modest and of short duration. However, the combination of the collapse of the housing bubble and the implosion of the system that financed the bubble meant that the U.S. economy would contract sharply, and along with it much of the rest of the world economy. The consequences were still being felt in mid-2009, when some forecasts suggested the situation would stabilize by year's end, with minimal growth possible in 2010.

By some individual measures (such as unemployment in the United States, which reached 9.8 percent in September 2009 and exceeded 10 percent by the end of the year), the recession of 2007–2009 was severe but not of historic proportions. The cumulative impact of the downturn on all aspects of the economy, however, led most observers to conclude that the recession was the worst on a global scale in many decades.

In a report issued on March 9, 2009, the World Bank forecast that the global economy would shrink in 2009 for the first time since World War II. The report also said the recession would hit developing countries even harder than the industrialized world, noting that 94 out of 116 developing countries already had experienced economic downturns.

THE RECESSION

The United States had experienced ten recessions of varying magnitude and duration since World War II, but none of them had the sweeping consequences of the downturn that began in late 2007.

According to the Commerce Department's Bureau of Economic Analysis, the U.S. gross domestic product (GDP) contracted in the fourth quarter of 2007, grew slightly in the first half of 2008, then shrank dramatically in the last quarter of 2008 through the first quarter of 2009. Noting several indicators suggesting that growth was returning, the Fed's Bernanke said on Sept. 15 that the recession "is very likely over at this point." Even so, he added, "it is still going to feel like a very weak economy for some time as many people still find their job security and their employment status is not what they wish it was."

The seasonally-adjusted, annualized figures for "real" (after inflation) GDP growth released by the bureau on Dec. 22, 2009, were:

Fourth Quarter 2007: -0.2 percent
First Quarter 2008: +0.7 percent
Second Quarter 2008: +1.5 percent
Third Quarter 2008: -2.7 percent
Fourth Quarter 2008: -5.4 percent
Full year 2008: +0.4 percent
First quarter 2009: -6.4 percent
Second quarter 2009: -0.7 percent
Third quarter 2009: +2.2 percent

The results for late 2007 through early 2009 met the technical definition of a recession, as established by the National Bureau of Economic Research (NBER): ". . .[A] recession is a significant decline in economic activity spread across the economy, lasting more than a few months, normally visible in real GDP, real income, employment, industrial production, and wholesale-retail sales." That private agency determined that the United States had gone into recession in December 2007; under its definition, the country remained in the economic dumps through the early months of 2009. (By fall 2009 many economists believed the recession had technically ended, although when that actually occurred would not be known for some time when the NBER had sufficient evidence to declare it over. However, economists and others said that the recovery, whenever it actually began, was expected to be exceptionally slow and unemployment would remain high for well into 2010 and possibly longer.)

At least three aspects of this recession demonstrated its historic nature: as of April 2009, it had lasted seventeen months, making it the longest since World War II (the previous post-war record-holders, the recessions in 1973–1975 and 1981–1982, had each lasted sixteen months); the fourth-quarter 2008 contraction was the worst for any quarter since 1982 and was the third-worst quarter since a recession of 1957–1958; and this was the first time since the 1957–1958 recession that the U.S. economy had contracted by more than 4 percent in two consecutive quarters.

"This recession is broader, deeper and more complicated than virtually anything we have ever seen," Wachovia Corp. economist Mark Vitner told the Associated Press in early March 2009. "The whole evolution of the credit markets resulted in all sorts of complex financial instruments that are difficult to unwind. It's like trying to unscramble scrambled eggs. It just can't be done that easily. I don't know if it can be done at all."

Just two months later in May 2009, many economists were expressing modest optimism that the worst of the recession had passed and the economy might stabilize by year's end and even begin to grow again in 2010. The evidence supporting such optimism was fragile, indeed. Although the unemployment rate rose in April 2009, the rate of job losses in the United States appeared to be slowing. Home sales were starting to pick up, and consumer confidence was on the rise for the first time in more than a year. Moreover, the Obama administration's stress tests of the nineteen largest banks, which found ten of the banks needing new injections of capital, produced better results than many experts had predicted. "The winds are still howling, but I think we can see the sunlight on the distant horizon," Mark Zandi, chief economist at Moody's Economy .com told the Associated Press on May 8. "Clearly, the job losses are moderating."

EMPLOYMENT

For most people, the true measure of a recession was not a decline in Gross Domestic Product or some other macroeconomic metric but the level of unemployment. Job losses began hitting the United States in late 2007 and continued unabated through the first half of 2009. The damage was particularly intense because, in terms of employment, Americans had never fully recovered from the previous recession of 2001. Employment rose by 8 million jobs between 2002 and 2007, according to the Labor Department, but the low point in unemployment during that growth period (4.4 percent in October 2006 and again in March 2007) was still higher than the previous low of 2.8 percent in April 2000.

The U.S. economy began shedding jobs in January 2008 but the unemployment rate did not begin its steady climb until that May, when it jumped 0.5 percent in that month to 5.5 percent. The unemployment suddenly leapt up to 6.6 percent in October 2008 after credit markets froze in the wake of the collapse of Lehman Brothers. Each subsequent month saw dramatic rises in unemployment as the economy shed jobs at alarming speed. The unemployment rate reached 7.2 percent in December 2008, and then in 2009 went to 7.6 percent in January, topped 8 percent in February, and hit 8.9 percent in April before reaching 10.2 percent in October and 10 percent in November.

Overall, the economy lost nearly 7.8 million jobs between December 2007 and November 2009. Most of the job loss came in the six months between November 2008 and April 2009. In its report for November 2009, the Bureau of Labor Statistics said nearly 15.4 million Americans were out of work. Although some measures of economic activity did suggest the economy began to improve late in 2009, nearly all economists warned that job losses would continue for a period, as had happened in most previous recessions, and were proven correct as job loss figures came out.

These unemployment figures from the Labor Department told only part of the story. When two other categories were counted—"discouraged workers" who had given up looking for jobs, and part-time employees who wanted to work full-time—the total rate soared to 15.8 percent by April 2009 and to 17 percent in the fall months. In other words, about one in six adult Americans either was unemployed or could not find enough work. The unemployment figures also were much worse than the national average for some groups, notably blacks, Hispanics, and persons with fewer years of formal education; unemployment rates for such groups were nearly twice the overall average.

Over the long term, many experts said, the shedding of jobs in key parts of the economy was likely to be a permanent fact of life. Financial services, manufacturing, and retail were the three sectors hardest hit by the recession, and none of them were likely to recover fully anytime soon, if ever. "These jobs aren't coming back," John E. Silvia, chief economist at Wachovia Corp., told the *New York Times* in March 2009, after the government reported that 651,000 jobs had been cut in February. "A lot of production either isn't going to happen at all, or it's going to happen somewhere other than the United States. There are going to be fewer stores, fewer factories, fewer financial service operations. Firms are making strategic decisions that they don't want to be in their businesses."

The rapid shrinking of the American auto industry was the most visible of these strategic decisions. For 2009, analysts were expecting that Americans would buy about 9 million cars—just over one-half of the high-water mark of 17 million in 2007. General Motors and Chrysler in 2008 and early 2009 closed factories and shed tens of thousands of jobs, even as they appealed for federal funding to avert bankruptcy. Despite these efforts, Chrysler was pushed into bankruptcy on April 30, 2009, with its ultimate fate dependent on an alliance with the Italian automaker, Fiat. The Obama administration in March 2009 also forced out General Motors chief G. Rick Wagoner Jr. as the price for continued federal aid to that company. Then, like Chrysler, GM too was forced to go through a swift bankruptcy.

Thousands of other firms, both big and small, were deciding to cut their losses when doing so was still possible. Some large retail companies went into bankruptcy and liquidation, including Circuit City, Linens 'n Things, Sharper Image, and Mervyns. Other firms drastically scaled back their overall operations or dumped entire parts of their businesses. Retailers laid off more than 500,000 workers in the twelve months ending in February 2009.

Along with manufacturing and retail, financial services was the sector of the economy most damaged by the recession—and the most likely to have trouble recovering. The collapse of Bear Stearns, Lehman Brothers, Washington Mutual, and more than one dozen smaller firms in 2008 and early 2009 sliced tens of thousands of jobs, particularly in and near New York City.

The newspaper industry was another significant casualty of the downturn. Even some of the nation's largest and most respected newspapers, including the *New York Times*, the *Washington Post*, the *Los Angeles Times*, and the *Chicago Tribune*, were forced to trim staffs and reduce news coverage, and in the case of the Tribune company, which owned both the Chicago and Los Angeles papers, to go into bankruptcy. Several urban newspapers closed altogether, or switched to Internet-only versions, or even cut back their print versions to a few days a week. Newspapers were hit by two simultaneous trends: they lost advertisers to the recession, and they lost readers (and thus more advertisers) to the Internet, which offered readers quick and free access to news.

MARKET LOSSES

Since the 1980s, millions of Americans who had never set foot on Wall Street had become investors in the stock markets through their pension funds or personal retirement accounts (many of them invested in mutual funds). By 2006, with the stock markets at historic highs and housing prices at their peak, many middle-class Americans suddenly felt wealthy; investments in their tax-sheltered 401k retirement plans and the perceived equity in their homes seemed to be on an endless upward track, offering the prospect of a rosy future.

Reality began to set in by late 2007, when it became clear that housing prices could, in fact, decline. With housing prices dropping by 20 percent or more in some areas, many homeowners realized their homes were no longer the golden investments they had imagined; indeed, the millions of homeowners who fell behind on their mortgages and faced foreclosures had lost money in the housing market.

The reality grew even grimmer in late 2008 when the stock markets plunged in the wake of the collapse of Lehman Brothers. All U.S. stock indices fell by more than 30 percent in the last four months of the year. Overall, U.S. stockholders lost $7 trillion during 2008, wiping out all the gains that had been made since the previous recession of 2001.

The markets continued to tumble until the middle of March 2009, when they were down from their peak by about 40 percent. The markets had recouped some of those losses as 2009 progressed, but only the most optimistic of market bulls were expecting that average investors would be certain to regain and hold on to their former portfolio worth anytime soon.

INFLATION AND DEFLATION

Inflation, which cursed the U.S. economy and much of the rest of the world throughout the 1970s, had been tamed by the deep recession of 1981–1982 that resulted in part from the deliberate imposition of high interest rates by the Federal Reserve. During the next two decades, inflation always was considered a threat, but the Fed's monetary policy helped keep it in check. Energy and food prices did fluctuate wildly during 2007–2008, creating public perceptions of raging inflation even though the "core" inflation (which discounted such fluctuations) rose only gradually and remained low by recent historical standards. The broadest measure of inflation, the GDP Price Index, went from 2.2 percent in 2000 to a high of 3.3 percent in 2005, then retreated to 2.2 percent in 2008.

As the most recent recession became worse in late 2008, many economists suddenly began worrying not about inflation but its opposite: deflation, or a decline in wages and prices as the economy contracted. Japan had suffered a serious bout of deflation during its "lost decade" of economic malaise in the 1990s (a downturn that also had resulted from the collapse of a real estate bubble), and that experience offered a sobering reminder for the rest of the world about the dangers of economic stagnation.

The worries about deflation seemed to abate in the early months of 2009, however, as economists saw modest signs of a possible economic recovery later in the year. During its March meeting, the Federal Reserve's Open Market Committee (which set interest rates), agreed that inflation was "likely to remain subdued" in the near-term and might even "persist below desirable levels." Even so, the minutes of the committee's meeting made no mention of a concern about deflation. The Fed continued to keep interest rates low all through 2009, suggesting that it had no immediate concerns about inflation. At year's end, however, most observers were expecting the Fed to begin a gradual process of interest rate hikes by the middle of 2010 as a hedge against inflation as the economy began to grow.

IMPACT ON STATE AND LOCAL GOVERNMENTS

State and local governments were hit by the recession just as much, and in some cases even more severely, than was the private sector. Declining economic activity led directly to declining tax revenues; unlike the federal government, states and localities could not print money or, in most cases under their constitutions, run budget deficits.

As of April 2009, the National Conference of State Legislatures said that forty-two of the fifty states were facing budget shortfalls in the current fiscal year and the same number (though, in some cases different states) were expected to face shortages in fiscal 2010. In most of the states, the fiscal 2009 shortages were expected to represent less than 10 percent of each state's general fund, but in six states the shortages were estimated to be as high as 15 percent. The outlook for fiscal 2010 was much gloomier, with twenty-one states expected to have shortfalls of greater than 10 percent, and most of them falling short by more than 15 percent.

The highest profile state budget crisis was in California, the largest state, which had faced chronic financial problems over the past decade. Governor Arnold Schwarzenegger and the legislature battled for weeks in early 2009 over how to close an estimated $42 billion budget gap. A hard-fought deal, signed into law on Feb. 20, included budget cuts and an increase in the state sales tax but also presumed a big boost from the federal economic stimulus plan.

Nearly every other state, along with cities and towns across the country, also was cutting spending (while avoiding tax increases for the most part) to keep budgets balanced. These cuts contributed to increased unemployment, which, according to some economists, slowed the prospects for economic growth necessary for the governments to get back on track for the long term.

FEDERAL BUDGET DEFICITS

Over the long term, many experts said, one of the most potentially damaging consequences of the recession was the enormous rise in the federal budget deficit. The government had run deficits during most of the Bush administration, after a brief period of surplus in the final years of President Clinton's second term. The cumulative effect of the government's numerous programs to spur the economy—notably the $700 billion TARP program, Obama's $787 billion stimulus plan, and a $3.6 trillion budget Obama requested for fiscal year 2010—was to boost the deficit to record levels, in dollar terms if not in relation to the overall size of the U.S. economy.

The administration on May 11, 2009, estimated that the deficit would top $1.8 trillion for fiscal 2009, then fall to about $1.3 trillion the next year and diminish progressively over the next five years before rising again in fiscal 2016. In relation to the overall economy, these projected deficits would be high but nowhere near record levels. The projected fiscal 2009 deficit, for example, represented 12.9 percent of the gross domestic product, and the 2010 deficit would comprise 8.5 percent of the total economy. (The actual deficit for fiscal 2009, reported in the fall, turned out to be $1.4 trillion. Although slightly under earlier predictions it still was vastly higher than the $455 billion deficit for fiscal 2008. The projection for 2010, released in January that year, was $1.6 trillion.)

Critics of the Obama administration, particularly Republicans in Congress, denounced the projected deficits as fiscally irresponsible and damaging to the prospects for long-term economic recovery. Democrats said the Republicans were conveniently forgetting that two of their own presidents, Ronald Reagan and George W. Bush, had presided over the fastest increases in the deficit in modern times.

INTERNATIONAL IMPACT

The financial crisis originated in the United States and led to a deep recession there, but the impact was greater in many other countries, including developing countries with fragile economies and even some developed countries that were especially reliant on international finance. The Bush and Obama administrations both attempted to lead and coordinate global responses to the downturn overseas, with limited success.

Some economists had warned, as early as 2006, that the global economy could suffer if, or more likely when, the extraordinary boom in the U.S. housing market came to an end. The reason was simple: global financial markets had become so interconnected that even a hiccup in the world's largest economy was felt almost immediately across the world. Subprime mortgages written in Arizona or California were bundled into securities not only by Wall Street banks but by financial institutions in London, Frankfurt, Zurich, and other financial capitals. The investors who bought these securities included individuals, banks, pension funds, mutual funds, government agencies, and other entities internationally as well as in the United States.

Despite the obvious implications for a potential collapse of the U.S. housing market, the concerns of a handful of economists were not widely understood—even by experts and top international officials—until it was too late. In his Jan. 16, 2007, report to his board of directors, Rodrigo de Rato, the outgoing managing director of the International Monetary Fund, boasted of a "benign global economic environment."

The environment turned decidedly less benign just seven months later, on Aug. 9, 2007, when several major European banks reported severe losses by their hedge funds that had invested heavily in securities based on U.S. mortgages. This set off a cascade of problems at banks, notably in Europe but also in other regions, that mirrored the onset of the financial crisis in the United States.

Several countries were candidates for the dubious distinction of being hardest hit, but one of the strongest claims could be put forth by Iceland. In an attempt to diversify its maritime-based economy, this small island country in the North Atlantic had deregulated its banks, which invested heavily in mortgage-backed securities from Britain, the United States, and other countries. Iceland's three largest banks essentially collapsed in early October 2008 and were taken over by the government, which negotiated a $2.1 billion long-term rescue loan from the International Monetary Fund. By early 2009, according to the *Economist* magazine, half of Iceland's businesses were technically insolvent and the country's economy was projected to shrink by 10 percent in 2009. Angry voters in April punished the conservative party that had implemented the free-market policies allowing the banks to become so heavily dependent on global finance.

Among the other countries hardest hit by the recession were Ireland (where the economy had boomed during the 1990s) and several counties that had been part of the Soviet bloc during the cold war, including Estonia, Hungary, Latvia, Lithuania, and Ukraine. Japan, which had never fully recovered from its decade-long economic malaise during the 1990s, also went into a deep recession.

The global downturn hit even some of the countries whose economies had been expanding rapidly in recent years, notably China, the world's emerging economic superpower. Driven largely by exports to the United States, Japan, and other countries that had shed much of their manufacturing industries, China's economy had been surging at an average annual pace of about 10 percent since the late 1980s. By May 2009, most forecasts suggested China's economy would grow "only" about 6.5 percent during the year. This was still an incredibly fast pace by world standards but well below what China needed to achieve to keep pace with population growth and pull hundreds of millions of its citizens out of poverty.

The first attempt at a concerted international effort to deal with the financial crisis came on Nov. 15, 2008, right after the U.S. elections, when President Bush hosted leaders from the so-called Group of 20 (G-20) countries—those with the world's largest economies. In the past, such a meeting might have been restricted to the Group of Seven leading industrialized countries (the United States, Canada, Japan, and leading European nations). This meeting was expanded to a much broader group in recognition of the growing importance of Brazil, China, India, Russia and other countries whose economies often were described as "emerging." The leaders issued a communiqué that had few concrete proposals, aside from a pledge to meet again the following April. The communiqué was long on rhetoric about confronting the global crisis and reforming the financial system, including the IMF and World Bank.

The G-20 leaders held their follow-up meeting in London on April 2, 2009. The advance publicity suggested a likely conflict between the new Obama administration (which wanted European countries to develop economic stimulus programs similar to the one Congress had just approved), and European leaders who were divided about the wisdom of stimulus programs but did agree generally on the need to step up government regulation of their financial markets. Once again, the leaders issued a bold statement about confronting the economic downturn with a "concerted fiscal expansion," but they offered few details for how this might be done. The leaders did promise to triple the IMF's resources, from $250 billion to $750 billion, so that agency could better respond to the needs of troubled developing countries. It was unclear when, if ever, this pledge would be carried out. Even so, most observers attributed significance to the fact that world leaders were endorsing a major role for the IMF, which just a few years earlier had been widely written off as an agency whose function as rescuer-of-last-resort supposedly had been outdated by the globalized economy.

One of the IMF's undisputed functions remained the issuing of economic forecasts, which had become increasingly gloomy since Rato's sunny observations at the beginning of 2007. The IMF in late April 2009 said most industrialized countries would remain in recession through the first half of the year and possibly well into the second half. The agency also said the United States and major European nations would continue running large budget deficits into the foreseeable future as governments tried to boost their economies and provide unemployment benefits and other social services to their citizens. In October, the IMF said the global economy "appears to be expanding again," driven by resumed growth in China and other Asian countries. However, the IMF projected global economic growth to be only about 3 percent in 2010 (well below pre-recession levels) because of continuing concern about prospects in the United States and other industrialized countries.

Reviews of the Government's Actions

By any historical standards, the U.S. federal government took extraordinary actions in 2008 and early 2009 to contain the damage caused by the credit crunch and resulting recession. The Bush administration and the Federal Reserve acted with particular vigor following the collapse of Lehman Brothers in mid-September 2008, and the new Obama administration in 2009 managed to speed up the pace of activity. Indeed, federal agencies rolled out so many programs that only experts and a handful of dedicated journalists were able to keep track of them all.

The Bush administration's $700 billion Troubled Assets Relief Program (TARP) became widely known because congressional approval of it had been fraught with partisan controversy just weeks before the 2008 elections. President Obama's economic stimulus plan also earned wide attention because of its eye-catching price tag of $787 billion and its potential impact. Both of these programs became increasingly unpopular during 2009, for different but related reasons. Many in the public came to view the TARP measure as an unjustified bailout of the banks that had caused the financial crisis; this view gained strength when several of the bailed out firms announced plans for significant bonuses for their top executives. Obama's stimulus bill came in for criticism because it was seen as slow-acting (much of the money was not to be spent until 2010) and because Congress had larded it with provisions that benefited special interests or that had no apparent connection to reviving the economy.

Other programs—such as the FDIC's Temporary Liquidity Guarantee Program, and Federal Reserve programs known as the Money Market Investor Funding Facility, the Asset-Backed Commercial Paper Money Market Mutual Fund Liquidity Facility (AMLF), the Term Securities Lending Facility (TSLF), and the Term Asset-Backed Securities Loan Facility (TALF)—also committed the government to spend or guarantee hundreds of billions of dollars but were virtually unknown among the general public. The basic goal of all these new programs was to keep the banking system intact, in some cases by investing directly in banks and other financial institutions and in other cases by guaranteeing various forms of private debt.

In addition to establishing new programs, federal agencies used existing authorities to intervene directly in the economy. Examples included the Federal Reserve's repeated lowering of interest rates (to stimulate borrowing) and frequent injections of billions of dollars directly into the financial markets, often in conjunction with other central banks.

The government also imposed or altered some regulations in hopes of fixing some of the problems that had led to the financial crisis. The Securities and Exchange Commission was particularly active in this belated closing of the barn door. Days after the collapse of Lehman Brothers, the SEC temporarily barred so-called "short-selling" of stocks in financial firms (in essence, betting that stock prices would fall) and reversed its 2004 rule that had allowed the brokerage units of Wall Street investment banks to escape requirements to hold large reserves of capital to cushion against possible investment losses. Further regulatory changes were likely in later years.

The net impact of all this motion was not entirely clear even by late 2009, and some experts said it might be years before a serious analysis could show exactly how the government's actions had affected the course of the recession. It was not too early, however, for the participants themselves, and their critics, to draw their own conclusions.

Federal Reserve Chairman Bernanke, one of the most visible and active government officials during both the Bush and Obama administrations, made only limited claims. An expert on past economic downturns, notably the Great Depression, Bernanke said the government had no alternative to acting aggressively; standing by would have allowed the situation to deteriorate much faster and more severely, he said. Testifying to congressional committees in February 2009, Bernanke argued that "measures taken by the Federal Reserve, other U.S. government entities, and foreign governments since September have helped to restore a degree of stability to some financial markets." As examples of stability, he cited the reduction of short-term interest rates, an improved climate for borrowing by corporations, and a stabilization of money market funds.

In the final months of 2008 one of the biggest controversies about the government's role involved something the Bush administration did not do: rescue Lehman Brothers, one of Wall Street's largest and most interconnected investment banks. The government allowed numerous commercial banks to fail (or be bought by other banks) without broad consequences, but the collapse of Lehman Brothers on Sept. 15 was widely seen as the pivotal moment when the worldwide financial system seized up.

Some critics said the government should have done something, almost anything, to keep Lehman Brothers afloat—just as it had already done with Fannie Mae and Freddie Mac and would do with the insurance giant AIG and other banks such as Citigroup. Letting Lehman Brothers fail "was a colossal error, and many people said so at the time," former Fed vice chairman Alan S. Blinder, a professor of economics and public affairs at Princeton University, wrote in the Jan. 25, 2009, *New York Times.*

In response, Bernanke and Treasury Secretary Paulson insisted they could not have saved Lehman Brothers because the government did not have the power, at the time, to buy the company's assets prior to its collapse, and no other buyers were willing to step in. This explanation failed to satisfy some of the critics, who noted that the Federal Reserve acted to prop up a subsidiary of Lehman Brothers on the same day the government allowed the larger company to fail.

Two other aspects of the federal government's response to the financial crisis generated broad controversy and were likely to be studied for decades to come. The first was the Bush administration's entire handling of the $700 billion TARP program, and the second was the new Obama administration's approach to major banks that remained in trouble even after the injection of TARP funds.

Congress in October 2008 gave Treasury Secretary Paulson broad discretion to use the TARP money, and his handling of that authority generated widespread criticism. Critics across the ideological spectrum faulted Paulson for selling Congress on one version of TARP (buying troubled assets from the banks, at a discount, to improve their financial positions and thus encourage them to start lending again), then switching almost immediately to the different approach of investing federal money directly into the banks. Some members of Congress complained that they had been subjected to a "bait and switch" by the Treasury secretary. Some economists worried that the administration was neglecting the very problem—the supposedly toxic assets on the banks' balance sheets—that remained most urgent.

Paulson responded to such criticisms by saying he had acted to deal with the situations as he found them. When he proposed the TARP program, he said, removing the toxic assets from bank balance sheets seemed the most urgent matter. Weeks later, however, it became clearer that some banks urgently needed to improve their capital positions, and injecting taxpayer money directly into them was the necessary solution.

"Seven hundred billion [dollars] wouldn't go far enough in my judgment," Paulson told National Public Radio on Nov. 13. "So you get much more leverage by putting capital into the banks. What we were looking to do was to stabilize the system and encourage banks to lend more. And the quickest and most powerful way to do that was with capital."

Paulson's Treasury Department also faced widespread criticism for the way it handed out billions of TARP dollars to the banks. The government, according to these criticisms, failed to get assurances that the banks would start lending again and allowed the banks to keep their use of the taxpayer money secret. Among those offering this criticism were the Government Accountability Office (GAO), which said in several reports it could get neither the government nor the banks to reveal how the cash infusions had been spent, and a special Congressional Oversight Panel, which had been created by the TARP legislation. The latter body also raised related questions about Treasury's use of the TARP money to buy capital shares in the banks. In a Feb. 6, 2009, report, the panel said a study it commissioned suggested that the government had paid "substantially more for the assets it purchased under the TARP than their then-current market value."

The Obama administration, early in 2009, faced criticism from both ends of the ideological spectrum. With their near-unanimous opposition to Obama's $787 billion economic stimulus plan, Republicans on Capitol Hill clearly decided that their political interests lay in handing responsibility for the economy over to the new president. Voting against the stimulus legislation gave Republicans the freedom to criticize Obama for his reliance on big-government programs and offered them the opportunity to say "I told you so" if the economy still languished at the time of the 2010 mid-term elections.

Obama, and particularly Treasury Secretary Geithner, also faced broad criticism from the left. Some liberal Democrats in Congress and influential liberal economists argued that too much of the $787 billion stimulus bill was composed of tax breaks that were included in a generally unsuccessful attempt to lure Republican votes but would do little to boost the economy. In particular, critics worried that $70 billion of the bill was devoted to a popular revision of the Alternative Minimum Tax, to reduce its impact on middle-class taxpayers. This provision was guaranteed to pass in separate legislation, the critics said, so including it in the stimulus bill soaked up $70 billion that could have gone to direct investments in the economy.

Other critics, notably Princeton University economist Paul Krugman (also a columnist for the *New York Times* and the 2008 recipient of the Nobel prize in economics), objected to what they considered the administration's unnecessarily soft treatment of troubled banks. Krugman and others argued early in 2009 that the government should simply nationalize several of the most troubled banks, such as Citigroup, and hold onto their assets for resale when the economy improved.

The administration rejected such an approach as premature and counterproductive, arguing that investing in the banks to bolster their financial positions was a better strategy. The release on May 7, 2009, of the results of the government's so-called "stress tests" of the nineteen largest U.S. banks was widely seen as validating the administration's approach, at least for the moment. Geithner said the tests showed that nine banks were strong enough to survive an even deeper recession, while ten banks needed $75 billion in extra capital—a large amount, to be sure, but much smaller than many bankers and economists had been expecting.

"With the clarity that today's announcement will bring, we hope banks are going to get back to the business of banking," Geithner said. The fate of the U.S. economy, and of much of the rest of the world's economy, rested in large part on whether Geithner's hope would turn into reality.

Chronology of Federal Responses to the Financial Crisis

The federal government took an extraordinary range of actions to deal with the credit crunch, which became evident in August 2007, and the resulting recession. Following is a chorological list of some of the major steps taken by Congress and executive branch agencies from late 2006 through early 2009.

2006

Oct. 4 Federal regulators, known collectively as the Federal Financial Institutions Examination Council, issue guidance on alternative mortgages. The guidance requires banks to tighten their underwriting standards and give more complete disclosure to borrowers, in plain language, of the costs they would pay. The guidance applies to regulated banks but not to nonbank lenders in the subprime sector (for example, independent mortgage brokers). However, the guidance specifically rejects the so-called "doctrine of suitability," which would have required lenders to determine that a mortgage is suitable to the borrower's financial circumstances and goals.

2007

Aug. 9 Responding to a sudden fall in international financial markets, the Federal Reserve joins the European Central Bank and the central banks of Australia, Canada, and Japan in injecting money into the credit markets; this is the first such coordinated action since the immediate aftermath of the Sept. 11, 2001, terrorist attacks against the United States.

Aug. 17 The Federal Reserve cuts the discount rate (paid by banks to borrow directly from the Fed) from 6.25 to 5.75 percent; move is another attempt to calm financial markets.

Sept. 18 The Federal Reserve cuts federal funds target rate by one-half percent to 4.75 percent; this was the first of ten rate cuts that resulted in an effective rate of zero percent by mid-December 2008.

Oct. 15–17 Government backs a plan by a consortium of U.S. banks (Bank of America, Citigroup and JP Morgan Chase) for a $100 billion "superfund" to buy and unwind structured investment vehicles.

Nov. 15 The House passes the Mortgage Reform and Anti-Predatory Lending Act of 2007 (HR 3915), tightening regulations over mortgage lending. The bill is referred to Senate Banking Committee, where it dies. *(Details, p. 640)*

Dec. 6 President George W. Bush signs the Mortgage Forgiveness Debt Relief Act of 2007 (PL 110-142), which freezes interest rates on the mortgages of a limited number of mortgage debtors. *(Details, p. 639)*

Dec. 12 The Federal Reserve creates the Term Auction Facility, a new window for lending to banks, many of which had been reluctant to borrow from the Fed's discount window because doing so was seen as a sign of weakness. Similar actions are taken by the central banks of Canada, the European Union, Switzerland, and the United Kingdom.

2008

Jan. 21 The Federal Reserve cuts federal funds target rate by 0.75 percent, the biggest single reduction in twenty-five years.

Feb. 13 Bush signs into law a $168 billion (over fiscal years 2008–2009) "economic stimulus" bill (PL 110-185), featuring tax rebate checks of $600 for individuals or $1,200 for families. *(Details, p. 151)*

March 7 The Federal Reserve injects $100 billion into currency markets to maintain liquidity and keep the federal funds rate near its target.

March 11 The Federal Reserve creates the Term Securities Lending Facility, with a pool of $200 billion for security swaps of up to twenty-eight days with the large Wall Street investment banks known as primary dealers. This is a significant step, aimed at rescuing the troubled firm Bear Stearns, because primary dealers were not regulated by the Fed and previously were not able to borrow directly from it.

March 14 With Bear Stearns facing intense liquidity pressure, the New York Federal Reserve Bank grants a twenty-eight-day emergency loan (via its discount window) of $13 billion to Bear Stearns through JP Morgan Chase.

March 16 The government arranges for JP Morgan Chase to buy Bear Stearns for $2 a share; the Federal Reserve makes the deal possible by lending $28.8 billion to a limited liability corporation created to purchase $29.9 billion in mortgage-backed securities from Bear Stearns (thus taking them off the bank's books). The LLC will repay the Fed using assets generated by its sale of these assets. JP Morgan Chase later agrees to increase its purchase price to $10 a share. JP Morgan Chase also repays the $13 billion loan made by the Fed two days earlier.

The Fed also creates the Primary Dealer Credit Facility, to make overnight loans at the discount rate to primary dealers; this is a departure from its previous practice of lending only to commercial banks. The Fed also cuts the discount rate by 25 basis points to 3.25 percent.

March 31 Treasury Secretary Henry M. Paulson Jr. proposes a broad overall of the government's system of financial regulations, including giving new powers to the Federal Reserve and possibly merging the Securities and Exchange Commission (SEC) and the Commodity Futures Trading Commission. Congress does not act on his proposals.

May 2 The Federal Reserve increases, from $50 billion to $75 billion, the amount of its lending to banks under its Term Auction Facility and allows Wall Street investment banks to put up riskier collateral under its new lending program for such banks. In addition, the Fed boosts the value of its currency swap arrangements with the European Central Bank and the Swiss National Bank.

June 30 Bush signs into law a military construction bill (PL 110-252) containing $110 million for supplemental unemployment compensation under an Emergency Unemployment Compensation program that provides up to twenty additional weeks of coverage to certain workers who had exhausted their rights to regular unemployment benefits. This is extended again in November. *(Details, pp. 387, 667)*

July 11 FDIC takes control of IndyMac, a major commercial bank in Pasadena, California, after it fails, the second-largest bank failure in U.S. history to that point.

July 14 The Federal Reserve adopts rules (which had been announced in December 2007 and would become effective on Oct. 1) barring several of the abusive lending practices that had led to the escalation in subprime mortgages that borrowers could not afford. Applying both to banks and nonbanks (such as mortgage brokers), the rules placed restrictions on the use of prepayment penalties for mortgages with introductory periods and required disclosures for mortgages with adjustable rates.

July 30 Bush signs the Housing and Economic Recovery Act of 2008 (PL 110-289), which, among other things, contained a voluntary plan to allow banks to write down balances on existing mortgages to allow borrowers to refinance under FHA to avoid foreclosure. The law also created a new regulatory body (the Federal Housing Finance Agency) for the Federal National Mortgage Association (Fannie Mae), the Federal Home Loan Mortgage Corporation (Freddie Mac), and the Federal Home Loan Banks, and gave Treasury some of the authorities it later used in its bailouts of Fannie, Freddie, and American International Group (AIG), as well as its use of the Troubled Assets Relief Program. *(Details, pp. 153, 630)*

Sept. 7 The new Federal Housing Finance Agency, created by legislation signed July 30, places Fannie Mae and Freddie Mac under conservatorship, effectively seizing control of them. The Treasury agrees to inject up to $100 billion in each company through stock purchases. The Treasury also agrees to make open-market purchases of up to $5 billion in mortgage-backed securities issued by both companies.

Sept. 14–15 The government allows Lehman Brothers to fail; it files for bankruptcy. The government also arranges for the sale of Merrill Lynch to Bank of America for $50 billion.

Sept. 16 The Federal Reserve lends AIG $85 billion in exchange for 79.9 percent of its stock. This comes one day after Standard and Poor's cuts AIG's credit rating because of its mounting losses in credit default swaps.

Sept. 17 SEC adopts rules prohibiting "naked short-selling" (betting against a stock without owing even an option to buy it).

Sept. 18 Federal Reserve joins other central banks (in Canada, Europe, and Japan) in injecting up to $180 billion into markets.

Treasury Secretary Paulson, Federal Reserve Chairman Ben S. Bernanke, and other top officials meet with congressional leaders to warn them about the seriousness of the financial crisis.

Sept. 19 Bush and Paulson announce plan to use $700 billion in taxpayer funds to buy troubled assets from financial firms; few details are offered.

The SEC temporarily bans all short-selling in stocks of about 800 financial firms. The SEC also expands an investigation into credit default swaps.

The Treasury says Fannie and Freddie will increase their purchases of mortgage-backed securities.

The Federal Reserve announces creation of the Asset-Backed Commercial Paper Money Market Mutual Fund Liquidity Facility (AMLF), to make nonrecourse loans to banks to purchase asset-backed commercial paper.

The Treasury announces plan to protect investments in money market funds. In effect, the plan guarantees investments held as of Sept. 19 in all funds that apply for the guarantee. This is the first time the government has guaranteed money market holdings and is a direct response to the failure four days earlier of Reserve Primary Fund (the country's oldest money market fund) to maintain the $1 per share face value of its holdings, a failure directly tied to the collapse of Lehman Brothers.

Sept. 21 The Federal Reserve allows Goldman Sachs and Morgan Stanley to convert themselves into bank holding companies (under Fed regulation, with access to the Fed's discount loan window), thus ending their status as investment banks and bringing them under tighter regulations.

Sept. 22 The SEC adds 100 financial companies to the list of those protected temporarily from short-selling of their stock.

The Treasury revises its promise to back investments in money market funds; says it will only protect existing investments (to prevent a rush of transfers from bank accounts).

Sept. 23 Bernanke, Paulson, and other officials open testimony to Congress on behalf of the bailout legislation.

The FBI opens inquiry into whether fraud was involved in recent collapses of financial institutions.

Sept. 25 Negotiations at the White House fail to produce bipartisan agreement on a bailout bill; House Republicans balk.

Federal regulators seize control of Washington Mutual; it's the largest bank failure in U.S. history. The government immediately sells most of the bank's assets to JP Morgan Chase for $1.9 billion.

Sept. 26 The House passes the Job Creation and Unemployment Relief Act of 2008 (HR 7110), which would have provided $61 billion for a variety of programs, including highway construction, mass transit, state Medicaid programs and food stamps, as well as another extension of federal unemployment insurance. Senate Republicans block action on a companion measure (S 3604) on the same day.

Sept. 26 The SEC ends its Consolidated Supervised Entity program, which since 2004 had allowed Wall Street investment banks to minimize their capital reserves against losses.

Sept. 29 The House narrowly rejects the $700 billion bailout bill.

The FDIC brokers a deal for Citicorp to take over the troubled Wachovia bank; Wells Fargo later steps in with a higher offer and takes over the bank without government aid.

The Federal Reserve and other central banks inject $330 billion into world financial markets in response to new bank troubles in Europe.

The SEC and Justice Department launch investigations into accounting procedures, disclosure, and governance matters at Fannie and Freddie since January 2007.

Sept. 30 The SEC and the Financial Accounting Standards Board "clarify" stringent "mark to market" accounting standards, in effect allowing banks to inflate the value of some assets on their banks.

The FDIC asks Congress for a temporary increase, to $250,000 from $100,000, in the limit on guarantees for bank deposits; Congress approves this as part of the Emergency Economic Stabilization Act.

Oct. 1 After the bailout bill is revised, the Senate approves it by a wide margin.

Oct. 2 The Justice Department says it will seek criminal charges against individual brokers and corporate officers, rather than entire companies, in its investigations.

Oct. 3 The House approves, and Bush immediately signs into law (PL 110-343), the Emergency Economic Stabilization Act, authorizing the $700 billion Troubled Assets Relief Program (TARP), along with dozens of other provisions. The law also authorizes the government to provide guarantees for troubled assets in return for premiums paid by the companies involved, and authorizes the government to take equity stakes in companies participating in the asset purchase program. *(Details, p. 154)*

Oct. 6 The Federal Reserve funnels an additional $900 billion into the banking system.

Oct. 7 The Federal Reserve says it will buy short-term debt of banks and corporations; it will create a new entity, the Commercial Paper Funding Facility, a special purpose vehicle (SPV) that would borrow from the Fed to purchase all types of three-month, highly rated U.S. commercial paper, secured and unsecured, from issuers.

Oct. 8 The Federal Reserve loans AIG an additional $37.8 billion (guaranteed by investment-grade securities held by its insurance subsidiaries), bringing total aid to the company so far to $122.7 billion. In addition, AIG says it has been approved to borrow up to $20.9 billion from the Fed's new Commercial Paper Facility.

The Federal Reserve and five other major central banks around the world (including the European Central Bank and the Bank of England) announce emergency interest rate cuts of one-half percent, a coordinated step Bernanke later said was "unprecedented." The U.S. cut is from 2 percent to 1.5 percent.

Oct. 10 Paulson and other Group of Seven finance ministers issue a coordinated plan to rescue the finance industry, generally endorsing a British proposal for governments to take large stakes in banks.

Oct. 13 Following the worst week on global stock markets in recent decades, Paulson meets with heads of the nation's largest banks and tells them to accept U.S. direct investments totaling $125 billion.

The Fed says it will make dollars available to support moves by European governments to invest in their banks.

Oct. 14 Paulson announces the investments in the large banks as part of what he calls a Capital Purchase Program, under which the Treasury would use $125 billion in TARP funds to purchase preferred stocks of banks rather than mortgage-backed assets. Treasury says it planned to use another $125 billion for investments in smaller banks.

FDIC announces the Temporary Liquidity Guarantee Program, which would guarantee new unsecured debt issued by financial institutions and provide full deposit insurance, through 2009, of non–interest bearing deposit accounts (such as business payroll accounts), regardless of amount. The latter step is intended primarily to help smaller banks, which had been losing these accounts to larger banks.

Oct. 21 The Federal Reserve says it will make up to $540 billion available to buy assets from money market funds to protect them against cash shortages; it creates the Money Market Investor Funding Facility.

Oct. 24 The Treasury says it is working on broadening the $700 billion bailout to include insurance companies.

Oct. 27 The Federal Reserve begins buying short-term commercial debt; General Electric is among the companies benefiting.

Oct. 29 The Federal Reserve cuts the federal funds target rate to 1 percent, a one-half percent reduction.

The Treasury and FDIC say they are developing a plan to guarantee up to 3 million mortgages.

The Federal Reserve says it will, for the first time, lend money to central banks in Brazil, Mexico, Singapore, and South Korea.

Nov. 10 The Federal Reserve and Treasury announce a second "restructuring" of the aid program for AIG; the changes increase the government's total aid to the company to $150 billion by reducing the Fed's loan from $85 billion to $60 billion, over five years (previous limit had been two years) and at a lower interest rate than previously announced; $40 billion in share purchases through TARP; $52.5 billion in Fed asset purchases through two limited liability corporations; and the previously announced $20.9 billion in potential loans from the Fed's new commercial paper facility.

Nov. 11 Government and mortgage industry announce plan to simplify the process of modifying hundreds of thousands of mortgages owed by borrowers facing hardships.

Nov. 12 Paulson announces an about-face on use of the TARP money; says none of it will be used to buy toxic securities as was originally planned, but instead will be used solely to support banks and commercial lenders. Purchasing the toxic assets, Paulson said, was "not the most effective way to use TARP funds."

The Federal Reserve, Treasury, and FDIC issue a statement calling on banks "to fulfill their fundamental role in the economy as intermediaries of credit to businesses, consumers, and other creditworthy borrowers" and "to work with existing borrowers to avoid preventable foreclosures."

Nov. 14 Treasury announces a second round of cash injections into banks totaling $33.6 billion for twenty-one banks.

Nov. 19 Senate Republicans block move by Democrats to call up legislation extending unemployment benefits and providing $25 billion, from the TARP fund, in aid to automakers.

Nov. 20 Congressional leaders say heads of the Big Three auto companies failed to make the case for a $25 billion bailout; demanded a "plan" before the money can be approved. House Speaker Nancy Pelosi, D-Calif., and Senate Majority Leader Harry Reid, D-Nev., outline conditions in a letter sent to the automakers the next day.

Nov. 21 FDIC seizes control of three banks, including a large California thrift, the Downey Savings & Loan.

Nov. 21 Bush signs into law the Unemployment Compensation Extension Act Of 2008 (PL 110-449), increasing and extending unemployment benefits. *(Details, p. 668)*

The Treasury says it will be the buyer of last resort for the Reserve U.S. Government Fund, a private money market fund that had been hit by waves of customer withdrawals.

Nov. 23 Following a sharp drop in Citigroup's stock value, the Treasury, the Federal Reserve, and FDIC announce plan to support Citigroup; it includes a $20 billion direct investment (in addition to $25 billion earlier under TARP) and federal guarantees for $249.3 billion of the bank's $306 billion in problem securities backed by residential and commercial mortgage "and their associated hedges" (a revised calculation reduced this figure to $301 billion on Jan. 16, 2009). The deal includes limits on dividends and executive compensation, plus Citigroup will pay the government a fee in the form of preferred stock.

Nov. 24 Treasury extends its guarantee of deposits in money market funds through April 30, 2009; this is the guarantee announced on Sept. 19.

Nov. 25 The Federal Reserve and Treasury announce that they are committing up to $800 billion to support lending to consumers and businesses, and to lower interest rates. Of the total, $600 billion is to support mortgage-backed securities held by Freddie Mac, Fannie Mae, and Ginnie Mae (thus for the first time making the Fed an indirect lender to homebuyers). The Fed creates the Term Asset-Backed Securities Loan Facility (TALF), initially with up to $200 billion to purchase AAA-rated asset-backed securities (assets including student loans, auto loans, credit card loans, and SBA-backed loans). Of the TALF funding, $20 billion is to come from the TARP program. These actions led to an immediate reduction in mortgage interest rates, which generally fell below 6 percent (for thirty-year fixed mortgages). The Fed later expanded the TALF to a total of $1 trillion and began lending from it in March 2009.

Dec. 16 The Federal Reserve drops its targeted funds rate from 1 percent to a range of between zero and 0.25 percent, effectively putting it at zero because that had become the rate in recent sales. The Fed also says it will use "all available tools to promote the resumption of sustainable growth and to preserve price stability." This includes increasing planned purchases of securities issued by Fannie Mae and Freddie Mac. Fed also said it was considering purchasing longer-term Treasury securities.

Dec. 19 Following failure by Congress to act, Bush announces short-term loans to GM and Chrysler using TARP funds: up to $9.4 billion in a secured loan to GM and up to $4 billion in a secured loan to Chrysler, through March 2009. Bush held out the possibility of another $4 billion to be determined by the Obama administration. The money comes from the TARP program and is conditioned on restructuring by the companies. In addition, the government provides $6 billion to GM's former finance unit, GMAC (a $5 billion investment and $1 billion loan through GM). The auto companies are required to give the government a detailed plan, by March 31, 2009, for returning to profitability.

2009

Jan. 15 Senate refuses to block release of the second half ($350 billion) of the TARP funds, thus making it available for spending by the incoming Obama administration.

Jan. 16 Federal agencies announce a bailout of Bank of America similar to an earlier one for Citigroup. It includes an additional $20 billion investment using TARP funds and federal guarantees of $118 billion in troubled assets, most of them assumed by the bank when it bought Merrill Lynch.

Feb. 10 Treasury Secretary Timothy Geithner announces broad outlines of a sweeping plan to support the banking industry, using up to $2 trillion in funds from the government and the private sector. Geithner's plan lacks the details Wall Street had been expecting, prompting a sharp fall in the stock markets.

Feb. 17 President Obama signs into law (PL 111-5) an economic "stimulus" bill totaling $787 billion, including $464 billion in spending on infrastructure and other projects and $326 billion worth of tax breaks for individuals and businesses.

Feb. 18 Obama announces the Homeowner Affordability and Stability Plan, which he says will help up to 9 million homeowners refinance their mortgages so they can stay in the homes and avoid foreclosure. The plan is launched on March 4.

Geithner announces that the Treasury will provide up to $200 billion each to Fannie Mae and Freddie Mac to insure that the companies stay in business. This represents a commitment, not an actual infusion of cash.

Feb. 27 The government says it will convert its preferred shares in Citigroup into common stock, raising the government's ownership stake to 36 percent. This is the third rescue of the giant bank since the previous October.

March 2 The Federal Reserve and Treasury announce a third revision of the AIG bailout, this time providing up to $30 billion more for a total commitment of $180 billion.

March 3 The Federal Reserve and Treasury formally launch the Term Asset-Backed Securities Loan Facility (TALF), which had been created in November 2008 to revive consumer credit markets, with a potential impact of up to $1 trillion.

March 18 The Federal Reserve announces that it might purchase an additional $750 billion in mortgage-backed securities from Fannie, Freddie, and Ginnie Mae, in addition to $500 billion already purchased.

March 23 Geithner announces details of the government's new plan to rescue banks, using a public-private partnership to purchase toxic assets from banks. Wall Street reacts favorably, consolidating a rally already under way.

March 30 Obama lays out conditions for further government aid to General Motors and Chrysler.

April 30 The Treasury says the government will loan up to $6 billion to a new alliance of Chrysler and the Italian automaker Fiat; Chrysler enters bankruptcy because a minority of bondholders reject terms of a debt-for-equity deal.

May 7 The Treasury and The Federal Reserve release results of so-called "stress tests" of nineteen major banks. Nine banks are found to have adequate capital to meet potentially worse economic conditions, but the government tells ten other banks to secure a total of $75 billion in additional capital by November; the biggest shortage is at Bank of America, which needs $34 billion. Several of the banks immediately begin raising the capital.

June 1 General Motors enters bankruptcy; the company emerges from bankruptcy on July 5 as a slimmed-down, government-owned entity known as the "New GM."

SOURCES: Federal Reserve Board; Treasury Department; White House; news reports.

Chronology of Action on Trade Policy

Introduction

Growing skepticism about the economic benefits of globalization combined with a steadily worsening domestic jobs picture and a highly partisan Congress to deny President George W. Bush much of his second-term trade policy agenda. Congress endorsed only one major trade agreement that the Bush administration had negotiated. That agreement was with five Central American countries and the Dominican Republic. Congress also voted to normalize trade relations with Vietnam and approved bilateral trade accords with a handful of other countries, including Bahrain, Oman, and Peru.

Left on the table at the end of Bush's presidency in 2009 was a pending agreement with South Korea, a significant U.S. trading partner, as well as agreements with Colombia and Panama that were much smaller in scope. The Democratic-led 110th Congress also declined to extend the president's "fast-track," or trade promotion, authority, a procedure under which Congress could approve or reject a trade pact but not amend it. Both U.S. and foreign trade representatives considered fast-track authority critical in ensuring that carefully negotiated agreements could not be undone by a congressional majority unhappy with specific parts of the pact. *(Congress and the Nation Vol. XI, p. 150)*

Multilateral negotiations on an agreement aimed at leveling the trading field between developed and developing countries in agriculture, services, intellectual property, and other trade matters did not fare much better. The Doha Development Round talks under the auspices of the World Trade Organization hit repeated stumbling blocks during the period, and as Bush left office, their ultimate success remained in doubt. The talks were named after the location of the initial meeting in Doha, Qatar, in 2001.

SHIFTING GLOBAL LANDSCAPE

Trade talks at both the domestic and multilateral level during Bush's presidency were set against a shifting perception of the benefits of globalization as well as changes in the relationships between developed and developing countries, particularly those such as Brazil, China, and India that were emerging as economic powers in their own right. Initially, globalization—the expansion of trade and investment among countries that began in the late twentieth century with the collapse of communism and the widespread adoption of free market principles—was touted for its benefits. Especially in the industrialized world, companies had more markets in which to sell their goods, consumers had more choices than ever before, and buyers enjoyed lower prices from increased competition.

In the developing world, too, expanded trade and investment spurred economic growth and development. Driven by exports to the United States, Japan, and elsewhere, China became the world's fastest-growing economy, with a vast demand for raw materials and finished goods produced in other regions of the world. India and other countries became bustling hubs for "back office" service operations for companies in countries halfway around the world. The spread of technology and new shipping techniques that allowed corporations and investors to move money, goods, and services around the world efficiently and seamlessly seemed poised to bring significant and lasting economic benefits to even the poorest countries.

Yet globalization was faulted for failing to spread its benefits evenly, for creating losers as well as winners.

REFERENCES

Discussion of trade action for the years 1945–1964 may be found in *Congress and the Nation Vol. I,* pp. 172–207; for the years 1965–1968, *Congress and the Nation Vol. II,* pp. 49–116; for the years 1969–1972, *Congress and the Nation Vol. III,* pp. 119–134; for the years 1973–1976, *Congress and the Nation Vol. IV,* pp. 125–137, for the years 1977–1980, *Congress and the Nation, Vol. V,* pp. 267–276; for the years 1981–1984; *Congress and the Nation Vol. VI,* pp. 95–112; for the years 1985–1988, *Congress and the Nation Vol. VII,* pp. 139–166; for the years 1989–1992, *Congress and the Nation Vol. VIII,* pp. 165–200; for the years 1993–1996, *Congress and the Nation Vol. IX,* pp. 151–184; for the years 1997–2000, *Congress and the Nation Vol. X,* pp. 147–170; for the years 2001–2004; *Congress and the Nation Vol. XI,* pp. 145–167.

Trade Balance

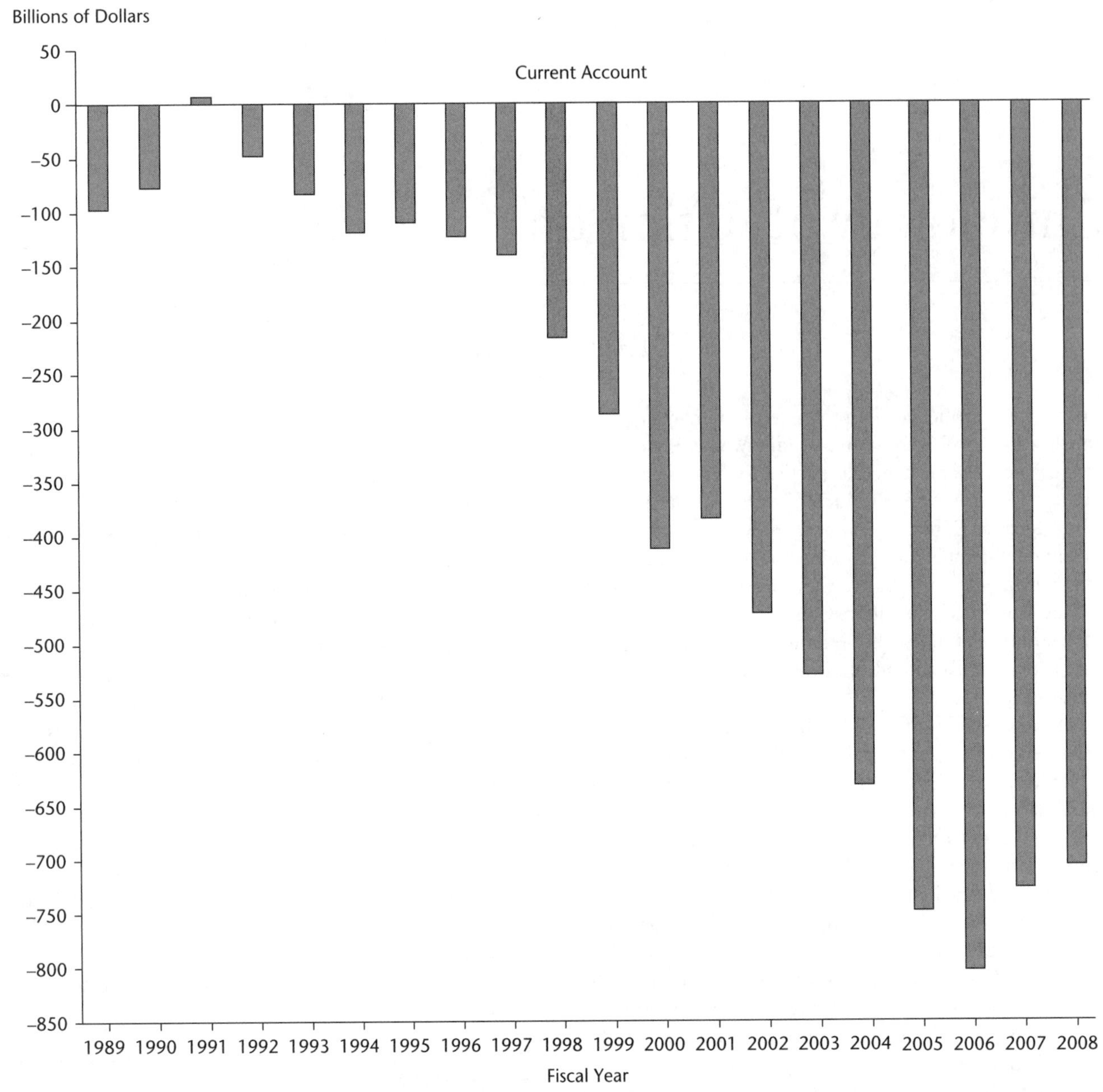

SOURCE: Bureau of Economic Analysis, Department of Commerce, "U.S. International Transactions."

NOTE: The current account balance includes the balances on trade in goods and services, income, and net unilateral transfers such as private remittances. The trade balances are by far the largest component of the current account balances.

Workers in the United States and other developed countries complained that good-paying manufacturing and service jobs were being lost to developing countries where pay and labor standards were lower. Weaker environmental standards in developing countries resulted in greater air and water pollution and the loss of irreplaceable natural resources. Multinational corporations were blamed for exploiting human and natural resources for profit. Developing countries complained that tariffs and nontariff barriers in the developing world hurt their ability to compete in the global marketplace. Developed countries made similar accusations about developing countries.

As the world became more integrated and developed, the vulnerability of many nations to problems in a few countries or even a single country grew. That became starkly clear in 2008 when the collapse of the housing market in the United States led to a credit crisis in the world financial system that dried up trade and investment and slowed economic growth throughout the world. Reforming the operations of the financial sector to prevent such global meltdowns in the future required unprecedented cooperation from the world's leading economies. This fact was recognized in September 2009 when the Group of Eight leaders of the industrialized world formally turned

U.S. TRADE REPRESENTATIVES

President George W. Bush named two U.S. trade representatives during this second term. In March 2005, after Robert B. Zoellick left the post to become deputy secretary of state under Condoleezza Rice, Bush picked Rob Portman, a Republican U.S. representative from Ohio as his trade czar. The Senate confirmed Portman by voice vote on April 29, after Sen. Birch Bayh, D-Ind., dropped a hold he had placed on the nomination designed to showcase the frustration of several Democratic and Republican senators with what they saw as foot dragging by the Bush administration in confronting China on its trade practices.

Portman's long-standing and close ties to the president, his position as a member of the House GOP leadership, and his reputation as an effective mediator and deal maker helped him maneuver the Central American Free Trade Agreement (CAFTA) through a skeptical Congress in 2005. Portman also forged important ties with world trade leaders around the world. But he remained in the job for less than a year. On April 18, 2006, Bush announced that he was making Portman director of the White House Office of Management and Budget. At the same time, he nominated Portman's deputy trade representative, Susan C. Schwab, to replace him.

Schwab began her career as a USTR agricultural trade negotiator, and served as an aide to Sen. John C. Danforth, R-Mo., (1976–1995) and in several government, private, and academic positions before rejoining the trade office as its deputy in November 2005. The Senate confirmed her to the top job by voice vote on June 8, 2006, after Sen. Charles E. Schumer dropped a hold he had placed on her nomination because he feared she would not be aggressive enough in curbing what he said were China's unfair trade practices.

During her tenure positions hardened on both domestic and world trade policies. Multilateral talks in the Doha Development Round, intended to open world markets to developing countries, stalled repeatedly. The Bush administration won congressional approval of a bilateral trade pact with Peru after reaching an agreement with congressional Democrats on labor and environmental standards to be included in all trade pacts. But the House leadership subsequently blocked consideration of a controversial trade agreement with Colombia, which also left pending agreements with Panama and South Korea in limbo. Fast-track authority for trade pacts was also allowed to lapse.

Schwab resigned her post at the end of Bush's term. President Barack Obama's nomination to replace her was Ron Kirk, the former mayor of Dallas, who promised to review the three pending trade pacts. "We're not going to do deals just for the sake of doing so," he said at his March 9 confirmation hearing. Kirk was confirmed March 18, 2009, on a 95–2 vote.

over stewardship for coordinating policy on economic policy to the Group of Twenty, which also included leaders from the major developing countries. Solutions to global problems such as climate change were also likely to be successful only if they drew the cooperation of developing as well as developed countries. That kind of global cooperation would require a realignment of the power structure among countries that had prevailed for decades.

Perhaps nowhere was the political difficulty of making that adjustment more apparent than in the Doha multilateral talks, where developing countries were demanding a voice at the table. Led by India and Brazil, among others, delegates from developing countries refused to compromise on their own agricultural tariffs and other trade barriers until the United States and the European Union agreed to significant changes in their domestic agricultural subsidies that made it difficult for farmers in poor countries to compete against U.S. and European producers. The stand-off on this and related trade issues had repeatedly moved the Doha talks to the edge of collapse, most recently in July 2008. Low-level formal talks were renewed in September 2009 in hopes that newly appointed trade delegates in key countries might help move the talks forward.

BUSH TRADE POLICY

With multilateral trade issues tied up in the on-again, off-again Doha talks since they began in November 2001, the Bush administration turned to bilateral trade agreements both as a way of broadening U.S. trade and as a means of achieving its political goals in various regions of the world. While Bush was able to forge agreements with several individual countries, his hopes for building regional trading partners fell short.

For example, after the al Qaeda attacks of Sept. 11, 2001, the Bush administration sought to use bilateral trade with Middle Eastern countries as a weapon in the war on terror. Agreements with Jordan, approved by Congress in 2001; Morocco (2004), Bahrain (2005), and Oman (2006), while of negligible economic value to U.S. commercial interests, were seen as ways to improve economic ties with Muslim countries, cement political connections, and push for democratic reforms. The strategy was not always successful, however. The administration stopped free-trade talks with Egypt in early 2006 after President Hosni Mubarak suspended municipal elections. *(Congress and the Nation Vol. XI, pp. 150–163)*

Trade negotiations were a success story of sorts in Latin America. Bush had to put aside his goal of a hemisphere-wide Free Trade Area of the Americas, which was stymied by many of the same North-South disagreements that stalled the Doha talks. But the administration forged ahead with bilateral talks to counter the rising influence of Venezuelan president Hugo Chavez and other leftist leaders in this increasingly left-leaning region. The United

States signed individual agreements with Chile, Peru, Colombia, and Panama. Talks with Ecuador were stopped in May 2006 after that country terminated its contract with Occidental Petroleum Corp., and were not resumed.

Although Congress approved the agreements with Chile (in 2003), five Central American Countries and the Dominican Republic (in 2005), and Peru (in 2007), the House in 2008 delayed indefinitely any action on the Colombia agreement, leaving both it and the Panama agreement in limbo. Democrats objected to the Colombia agreement because they said the Colombian government had not done enough to reduce violence targeted at labor union leaders in the country.

The House action also left in limbo an exceptionally controversial agreement the Bush administration had negotiated with South Korea, the United States' seventh largest trading partner. Although many U.S. companies supported the accord, two of the three American automakers, Chrysler and Ford, opposed it, saying it did not ensure that South Korea would remove the nontariff barriers, such as tax and regulatory rules, that discouraged Koreans from buying American-made cars. (General Motors bought South Korea's Daewoo in 2002 and remained neutral in the debate.)

The administration had hoped the agreement with South Korea would increase the U.S. trade presence in Asia as a counter to China's growing influence in the region. In addition, countries throughout Asia were increasingly trading with one another under scores of regional and bilateral agreements to which the United States was not party—a situation that was costing American companies market share and economic influence throughout one of the fastest growing regions in the world.

SHIFTING POLITICAL DYNAMICS

The Bush administration's struggle to win congressional approval for even modest bilateral trade agreements reflected a shift in the dynamics of the trade debate in Washington. Trade agreements were often controversial in Congress and with the public, especially organized labor concerned about the implications for American workers, and specific businesses or industries concerned about whether their new trading partners might gain a competitive edge. But in the first years of globalization, the potential for economic gain seemed to outweigh more traditional concerns, and politicians looked to trade agreements to further that potential.

In 1992 Bush's father, President George H. W. Bush, negotiated a trade agreement with Canada and Mexico, the United States' two largest trading partners, that eliminated most trade barriers between the three countries. The following year President Bill Clinton used much of his influence as a new president to get the North American Free Trade Agreement through Congress, publicly denouncing the anti-NAFTA tactics of his labor union allies. After months of pleading, pushing, and bargaining, significant numbers of Democrats joined a majority of Republicans in both chambers to approve the agreement. *(NAFTA passage, Congress and the Nation Vol. IX, p. 155)*

Passage of NAFTA was hailed as a political landmark, placing the United States on the leading edge of the new global economy. Pointing to the prosperity of the 1990s, free-traders, including many Democrats, cited the treaty as a key factor in the country's enhanced standing in the global marketplace.

However, the treaty also sparked a sizable backlash, not only from traditional nationalists but also among a newly energized anti-trade coalition on the Democratic Party's left wing that complained that the agreement was costing American industrial workers their jobs and at the same time failing to improve pay and working conditions for cheaper foreign labor. Although many industrial job losses actually were the result of a large technological shift to a more productive and service-oriented economy, complaints about free trade and globalization grew louder throughout the 1990s and 2000s as more and more American companies moved their manufacturing and services operations overseas and bought raw materials and intermediate goods from foreign suppliers.

In 1997 Democrats showed their displeasure with NAFTA by denying Clinton renewal of the fast-track authority he had used to negotiate the treaty and get it through Congress without change. Despite a strong lobbying effort by the White House, Clinton failed to win enough support from his own party in the House to merit a floor vote. Fast-track negotiating authority lapsed until 2002, when President Bush managed to get the authority renewed over Democratic objections after promising expanded assistance for dislocated workers. *(Congress and the Nation Vol. XI, p. 150)*

Democrats increasingly opposed the bilateral trade agreements the Bush administration negotiated, arguing that the agreements were modeled on basic NAFTA provisions that were in need of change. The administration not only was not doing enough to help displaced American workers, they claimed, but the trade agreements were also failing to protect foreign workers from low pay and bad working conditions. Some Democrats also argued that trade agreements should include environmental protections for water, air, and natural resources. Nor, they said, was the administration enforcing those trade conditions that were set out in the treaties. These objections, combined with objections about specific provisions of the treaties from other quarters, made votes on approving trade pacts increasingly precarious. The Central American Free Trade Agreement (CAFTA), for example, passed by narrow margins in the House.

By 2007, when the Democrats took control of both the House and Senate, Democrats were divided over pending trade agreements. The leadership in both chambers sought to establish a feasible framework for approving already negotiated deals. But a cohort of populist Democrats, many of them freshmen elected in part because of their trade stance, called for stricter labor standards and more aggressive enforcement of trade agreements. Thirty-nine of the forty-two freshman Democrats signed a letter addressed to Ways and Means Committee chairman Charles B. Rangel, D-N.Y., stating their intention "to take a vocal stand against the administration's misguided trade agenda and offer our voters real, meaningful alternatives to the job-killing agreements, such as CAFTA, that the majority of our opponents supported."

Democratic leaders thought the split might have been smoothed over in May 2007, when they reached an agreement with the White House to amend pending trade deals to require the United States and its trading partners to meet international labor standards that prohibited forced and child labor, guaranteed workers' rights to organize and bargain collectively, and barred employment discrimination.

Not long after that agreement was completed, however, the Democrats saw the populist anti-trade flank of their caucus help rally a majority of House Democrats to vote against a pending trade accord with Peru. Although that deal eventually passed the House and cleared the Senate in December 2007, it was clear that the other three pending agreements, particularly those with Colombia and South Korea, were facing an uphill battle.

Congressional Democrats, including the leadership, opposed the Colombia agreement, arguing that it should not go forward until the Colombian government had shown a serious intention to restrain violent attacks on union leaders. Despite warnings that there were not enough votes to approve the implementing legislation without making some changes in it, Bush followed through on a threat to force the issue, sending the pact to Congress for approval in April 2008. Because the treaty had been negotiated under fast-track authority, Bush's action meant that Congress had ninety days to vote the treaty up or down. However, the House Democratic leadership introduced a resolution to change House rules and suspend fast-track procedures for the pact; the change passed (with most Democrats voting for it and most Republicans voting against), effectively delaying action on the treaty indefinitely.

That vote put the remaining pending treaties in limbo for the rest of the year. It also meant there was no chance that Congress would renew the president's fast-track authority, which had expired as of July 1, 2007. Although the Bush administration formally requested that Congress renew the authority, the president made no serious effort to persuade Congress to act on it.

Democrats were also stymied in their efforts to expand trade adjustment assistance, which provided benefits and retraining for manufacturing workers who had lost their jobs or had their pay cut because of increased imports or because production was shifted overseas. Facing strong opposition from Republicans and a veto threat from the president, Democrats were forced to settle for a simple extension of the legislation, and vowed to try again in the 111th Congress, when a Democrat would be in the White House and the Democratic majority in Congress would be swelled by several new members whose anti-trade campaigns helped them win election.

CHINA, TRADE DEFICITS, AND RECESSION

Many legislators, Democrat and Republican, were agreed on one trade issue: China's alleged unfair trade practices. China, the second largest source of American imports and the third largest destination for American exports, was the United States' second largest trading partner, behind Canada and ahead of Mexico. But the benefits of the relationship—huge job growth and wealth creation for Chinese companies and cheap goods—were overshadowed by the huge imbalance between the countries. In 2008 the United States imported $268 million more in goods from China than it had exported there, accounting for about one-third of the total U.S. merchandise trade deficit.

Lawmakers on Capitol Hill, especially those from states that accounted for large volumes of manufacturing exports, had long complained that China artificially suppressed the value of its currency to help its own exporters. As a result, U.S.-made goods were less competitive on price. After prodding by the Bush administration and others, the Chinese in July 2005 began to allow its currency to appreciate slowly. It had gained about 21 percent against the dollar, when the rise stopped in mid-2008 as the economic slowdown began to be felt. U.S manufacturers and the unions that represented their workers said that a much bigger appreciation was still needed.

Trade tensions between the two countries also flared over the safety of some Chinese imports, including high-profile cases of contaminated pet food, toothpaste, and seafood that were imported into the United States. American companies also continued to complain of unfair trade practices in various sectors; one notable dispute involved what Americans said was the Chinese government's refusal to protect intellectual property against commercial piracy. The Bush administration filed a complaint with the World Trade Organization in 2007, which sided with the United States in an August 2009 ruling.

Despite these and other trade disputes, the United States and China had grown increasingly dependent on each other in just a few years. China looked to the United States as a market for the exports that helped keep its economy growing and a source of U.S. dollars, while the United States depended on China to continue to finance America's national debt; as of early 2009 China held about $768 billion in U.S. Treasury securities—more than any other country.

Overall U.S. trade deficits reached a high point in 2006, when the country imported $701.4 billion more in goods and services than it exported. The trade deficit fell to $695.9 billion in 2008, as economic recession markedly slowed consumer spending in the United States. Imports and exports both continued to decline in the first months of 2009, before beginning to rise again mid-year. Analysts saw this turnaround as another indication that the worst of the recession may have passed. But there were also signs that the recession may have strengthened protectionist sentiments, both in the United States and elsewhere. Turned into policies or more trade disputes, such sentiments could hamper the pace of recovery.

2005–2006

President George W. Bush succeeded in winning the approval of the 109th Congress for four trade pacts that his administration had negotiated, but in three cases it was an uphill battle. An accord with Bahrain passed with little fanfare. But on the other three accords—with five Central American countries and the Dominican Republic, with Vietnam, and with Oman—concern that American workers were losing jobs to workers in countries with lax labor and environmental standards combined with partisan politics to make passage difficult. With Democrats set to take control of both chambers in 2007, the prospects for further action on Bush's trade agenda looked bleak.

In July 2005 the administration won approval of the controversial Central American agreement by just two votes in the House and only after offering several sweeteners to persuade reluctant legislators to support the measure. Democrats almost uniformly opposed the agreement, citing concerns that American workers were losing jobs to countries that had lax labor and environmental standards, while some Republicans were concerned about the agreement's effect on the American sugar and textile industries.

The House initially voted down the Vietnam pact under suspension of the rules, which require a two-thirds majority to pass. This time GOP conservatives questioned Vietnam's human rights record while Democrats again expressed concern about labor standards. The loss was an embarrassment to the president, coming in November 2005 just before he left for an economic summit in Hanoi. Both chambers subsequently approved the agreement after it was added to a popular package of tax breaks. The Oman agreement ran into similar headwinds, with members of both parties citing national security concerns along with concerns about labor standards.

Central American Free Trade Accord

Partisan loyalty and one-on-one negotiations enabled the White House and Republican leaders in Congress to win just enough votes to put the long-stalled Central America Free Trade Agreement (CAFTA) into law. Congress cleared a bill implementing the pact July 28, 2005, and President George W. Bush signed the measure into law Aug. 2 (HR 3283—PL 109-53).

Although enactment was a major victory for the president's free trade policy, the bitter battle and narrow House and Senate tallies underscored growing skepticism about the benefits of free trade. Especially in the House, where the pact was approved by just two votes, the vote was also seen as a test both of the president's power and GOP party loyalty amid growing congressional partisanship.

The agreement involved Costa Rica, El Salvador, Guatemala, Honduras, and Nicaragua, and a linked accord with the Dominican Republic. It was completed in 2004, but opposition from U.S. labor groups and the sugar industry made passage a difficult challenge for the administration.

The pact eliminated most tariffs and some other barriers to cross-border economic activity. It phased out over ten years customs duties on originating goods between participating countries, while eliminating nearly all textile and clothing duties. It also eliminated export subsidies for agricultural goods traded among CAFTA nations. It specifically regulated the import of sugar into the United States, maintained the U.S. duty on sugar imports that exceeded a certain quota, and allowed the United States to provide compensation to a participating nation in place of sugar imports.

The benefits to the United States were expected to be more political than economic. The six Central American and Caribbean economies together generated a little more than $200 billion a year, about the same as the economy of Missouri. Proponents mainly argued that CAFTA would have a positive effect on national security, immigration, and regional stability. The Office of the U.S. Trade Representative (USTR) also said that more than 80 percent of the imports from Central America and the Dominican Republic already entered the United States duty-free, so the agreement "levels the playing field for Americans."

Congress considered the bill to implement CAFTA under special fast-track procedures enacted in the 2002 Trade Promotion Authority Act (PL 107-210). Once the White House submitted the bill, lawmakers had ninety legislative days to consider it—forty-five days for House committees, fifteen days for House floor action, and fifteen days each for Senate committee and floor votes. Congress could only accept or reject the bill; it could not amend it. The expedited process was intended to assure U.S. trade partners that lawmakers would not alter a trade agreement once it had been signed. In return, the administration was required to consult with Congress and keep the appropriate committees informed as it negotiated the pact and wrote the bill. *(PL 107-210, Congress and the Nation, Vol. XI, p. 150)*

Supporters and foes of the administration's trade policy offered competing views of what the outcome meant for future trade pacts. "The House rejected isolationism," John Engler, president of the National Association of Manufacturers and a former Republican governor of Michigan, said in a statement. "It affirmed that America's economic future lies with open markets and a level playing field for international trade." Opponents of administration policy portrayed the closeness of the vote and the degree to which the White House and GOP leaders had to scramble as evidence of a growing bipartisan bloc that was opposed to free trade for its own sake.

TRADE WITH CHINA

Before casting their votes on the highly politicized Central American Free Trade Agreement (CAFTA), House lawmakers first got caught up in a partisan struggle over an issue on which there is generally broad bipartisan agreement: the desire to address alleged unfair trade practices by China.

Republican leaders brought to the House floor a bill (HR 3283) that would more aggressively monitor and seek changes in China's currency policy, enhance the U.S. government's ability to impose duties on highly subsidized Chinese goods, and provide federal agencies with more resources to enforce trade rules.

Sponsored by Rep. Phil English, R-Pa., the China measure had the support of Rep. Bill Thomas, R-Calif., chairman of the House Ways and Means Committee, which has jurisdiction over trade issues. Both parties viewed action on the China bill as an attempt by GOP leaders to secure votes needed for passage of the CAFTA implementing bill (HR 3045). English later estimated that as many as ten lawmakers had joined him in supporting CAFTA because of the China bill.

The House passed the China bill July 27 by a vote of 255–168, before the final debate on CAFTA began later that day. It was the second time the China measure had been brought to the floor in two days. On July 26, it failed on a 240–186 vote, short of the two-thirds majority needed for passage under suspension of the rules. A majority of Democrats voted against the measure both times. Democrats protested that the bill was inadequate to address concerns that members of both parties had about China's trade practices, and they said it was being given inadequate attention.

The Senate took no further action on the House bill. Nor did either chamber act on several alternative pieces of legislation introduced in the 109th and 110th Congress aimed at forcing China to change its trade and currency valuation policies.

HIGHLIGHTS

The target date for implementation of the trade agreement was Jan. 1, 2006. Following are highlights of the pact provisions to which the six nations agreed:

Manufactured goods. Eliminated tariffs immediately on about 80 percent of U.S.-made consumer and industrial goods and phased out the remaining tariffs over ten years. Phased out auto and auto parts tariffs over five years.

Farm products. Eliminated tariffs immediately on about 50 percent of U.S. farm goods going to the six countries—particularly high-quality beef, soybeans, cotton, and wheat. Exempted agricultural products designated as sensitive—such as corn, milk, potatoes, and onions—from tariff reduction, or specified that such tariffs would be phased out over lengthy periods up to twenty years.

Textiles. Allowed textiles and apparel made in participating countries with U.S.-produced yarn and fabric to be shipped tariff-free to the United States, retroactive to Jan. 1, 2004. (The region already was the second-largest consumer of U.S. yarn and fabric. Some Central American goods made with Canadian or Mexican yarn and fabric also would enter the United States tariff-free.)

Sugar. Increased quotas for U.S. sugar imports for CAFTA countries only, thereby permitting increased imports from the region equal to about 1.2 percent of existing U.S. production in the first year, rising to about 1.7 percent in fifteen years.

Services. Removed or reduced countries' trade barriers in the six CAFTA nations in the fields of telecommunications, computers, package delivery, tourism, transportation, construction and engineering, financial services and insurance, and entertainment.

Intellectual property. Increased patent, copyright, and trademark protections for software, music, videos, written works, and other intellectual property in the Central American countries and the Dominican Republic.

Government procurement. Required the six CAFTA countries to enact anticorruption measures for government contracting and permit U.S. companies to bid to provide a range of goods and services to those governments.

Worker rights. Required the countries to enforce their existing laws guaranteeing worker rights, but specified that trade sanctions could not be used to require compliance. (The agreement did not require the countries to enact laws meeting International Labor Organization standards.)

Environment. Agreed that participants would enforce existing environmental protection laws, but did not require changes and did not have a mechanism to require compliance.

LEGISLATIVE ACTION

The fate of the Central American Free Trade Agreement was uncertain from the start. The Bush administration secured the agreement in 2004 only after several fits and starts, but nearly a year lapsed before Congress took up the issue. Among the biggest issues were bipartisan worries among sugar-state lawmakers that their states would suffer from CAFTA's sugar provisions, concern from Democrats that CAFTA would not fully safeguard Central American workers' rights, and fears that CAFTA could cost U.S. jobs.

In June 2005 the congressional committees with jurisdiction over trade—House Ways and Means and Senate Finance—approved draft versions of a measure to implement the pact after holding informal mock markups of a draft administration bill, which allowed members to recommend technical changes or signal concerns to the administration before it formally submitted the bill. The

White House, however, was not bound to follow the recommendations when writing the final implementing bill.

The sessions highlighted issues that would dominate the CAFTA debate and made clear that the White House still had work to do, especially with regard to sugar.

Even on the morning of the Finance mock markup June 14, the White House was unsure there were enough votes to approve a draft without significant amendments that might have called for renegotiation of sections of the agreement. "My expectations were not high, and they were exceeded today," U.S. Trade Representative Rob Portman said after the panel's vote.

That narrow victory became possible only when Republican Sen. Craig Thomas of Wyoming, concerned about CAFTA's effect on his state's sugar beet growers, gave his tentative support. Thomas acted only after the administration agreed to continue talks with reluctant sugar-state lawmakers. He said he still might oppose the final measure if talks involving lawmakers, industry officials, and the White House yielded no agreement to strengthen the long-term global position of domestic sugar producers.

In both markups, Democrats voiced concerns that CAFTA would not fully safeguard Central American workers' rights. But Republicans insisted that CAFTA provided better worker protections than previous trade agreements and ruled out renegotiating sections of the pact. The administration had laid out steps to reinforce U.S. commitments to monitor labor practices and provide resources to CAFTA countries to enforce labor laws. Still, votes in both committees reflected Democrats' skepticism.

The Finance Committee rejected on a 10–10 tie vote an amendment by Democratic Sen. John Kerry of Massachusetts to allow the United States to impose sanctions if CAFTA countries failed to enforce labor laws. During their mock markup June 15, House Ways and Means members turned back a similar proposal offered by the panel's ranking Democrat, Charles B. Rangel of New York, on a 17–24 party-line vote.

The effect of the agreement on U.S. workers also entered the debate. Finance members adopted by voice vote a proposal by Sen. Ron Wyden, D-Ore., to expand trade adjustment assistance to include service-sector workers. The program, which aids workers who lose jobs because of expanding trade, was currently aimed primarily at manufacturing workers. In the House Bill Thomas, R-Calif., Ways and Means Committee chairman, would go no further than inserting language calling for a study of the idea. *(Trade adjustment assistance, p. 213)*

SENATE ACTION

The Bush administration sent implementing legislation June 23 to Congress, making no substantial changes from the drafts approved in nonbinding committee sessions the week of June 13.

Supporters decided to seek a vote first in the Senate, where its prospects were considered somewhat better than in the House. The first task facing the administration was to secure a majority in the Senate Finance Committee, where several of the panel's typically pro-trade members were still concerned about the effects the agreement would have as a result of increased sugar imports.

To address those concerns, U.S. Trade Representative Rob Portman and Agriculture Secretary Mike Johanns pledged to use provisions allowed under commodity trading rules to keep sugar imports permitted under CAFTA and other trade deals out of U.S. markets for the remaining two years of the current farm bill (PL 107-171). They also agreed to study the feasibility of government initiatives to spur production of ethanol made from sugar.

To address labor concerns, the White House pledged a multiyear commitment to strengthen enforcement and monitoring of labor and environmental standards in Central America and to aid farmers there. Portman said the White House would seek $40 million a year from fiscal 2006 through fiscal 2009 to aid CAFTA countries in monitoring and enforcing labor and environmental protections.

The Senate on June 30, 2005, approved the agreement on a **key vote of 54–45 (R 43–12; D 10–33; I 1–0).** *(2005 key votes, p. 915)*

HOUSE AND FINAL ACTION

A larger hurdle came in the House, where passage of the identical measure (HR 3045—H Rept 109-182) was in doubt until the final seconds of the vote. The House passed the bill early July 28 on a **key vote of 217–215 (R 202–27; D 15–187).** *(2005 key votes, p. 915)*

The roll call was held open for an hour and stretched after midnight as jockeying for votes continued. House GOP leaders had to cut numerous deals to win passage.

Opposition was especially strong in textile- and sugar-producing states, and not all Republicans from those districts were satisfied with administration pledges to contain CAFTA's potential effect on U.S. jobs. Phil English, R-Pa., pressed for floor action on a bill (HR 3283) aimed at China's alleged unfair trade practices. English said as many as ten Republican lawmakers agreed to vote for CAFTA after the House passed the China bill July 27. *(China bill, box, p. 203)*

Bush made a rare appearance on Capitol Hill the morning of the House debate to rally rank-and-file Republicans. He challenged them to put aside parochial concerns in some cases and to seize what he argued was a unique opportunity to advance the cause of democracy in the hemisphere. Bush was joined at the rally by Vice President Dick Cheney, National Security Adviser Stephen J. Hadley, and Portman. By the end of the day, Agriculture Secretary Johanns and Commerce Secretary Carlos Gutierrez had also met with small groups of lawmakers off the floor as the debate unfolded.

GOP leaders still did not have the votes in hand when the electronic tally boards lit up in the House chamber shortly after 11 p.m. on July 27 for a scheduled fifteen-minute vote. A half-hour later, the count was frozen at 214–211 in favor of the bill. Over the next half-hour, Portman said later, Republicans had to sort out "who gets to vote no," while still securing a victory for the party and the president.

Many undecided members finally gave in to the arguments made by GOP leaders and administration officials about CAFTA's potential effect on their districts.

For example, Robin Hayes, R-N.C., issued a statement after the vote saying he had decided that administration pledges to address concerns of textile makers were adequate. Earlier in the week, Portman promised to go back into the accord and amend three textile provisions to better ensure that U.S.-made fabric, not fabric from China, would be used in duty-free apparel assembled in Central America.

Only fifteen Democrats voted for the pact, a sharp contrast to the 102 Democrats who had answered President Bill Clinton's call to vote for the North American Free Trade Agreement with Mexico and Canada more than a decade earlier. Democrats' opposition was based in part on their concerns about what they regarded as a lost opportunity to improve on the NAFTA model, which many Democrats believed had fallen short of promised outcomes. But Republicans claimed that those "no" votes were simply a partisan effort to weaken President Bush.

Final action on the measure came later in the day July 28, when the Senate cleared the House-passed bill by a vote of 55–45 and sent it to the president.

Bahrain Trade Pact

Little of the acrimony that attended the CAFTA debate spilled over into consideration of a free trade agreement with Bahrain that Congress approved later in 2005 (HR 4340—PL 109-169). Supporters hoped the pact would help improve economic and political relations in the Middle East. Located just east of Saudi Arabia in the Persian Gulf, Bahrain was not a large U.S. trading partner, but the White House said the trade agreement would help it achieve a longer-term goal of establishing a Middle East Free Trade Area.

Trade between the two countries totaled about $782 million in 2005, with Bahrain exporting aluminum, chemicals, textiles, and fertilizer to the United States. In return the small nation bought U.S. machinery, aircraft, and medical equipment.

The trade agreement was considered under fast-track procedures (PL 107-210) that required an up-or-down vote on the implementing legislation with no amendments allowed. The House acted first, voting in favor of the measure 327–95 on Dec. 7. Some House members who voted against the agreement raised concerns about Bahrain's commitment to improving its labor protections. Democrats on the Ways and Means Committee initially withheld their support for the measure during the committee's consideration of a preliminary draft of implementing legislation but relented after receiving more specific assurance that Bahrain would follow through with its commitments to workers' rights. Still, some Democrats remained unsatisfied, saying the labor protections should have been spelled out in the agreement itself. "I support trade, but it has to be fair before it can be free," said Pete Stark, D-Calif., during floor debate.

The Senate cleared the agreement by voice vote on Dec. 13. President George W. Bush signed the agreement into law on Jan. 11, 2006.

WTO Membership

The House on June 9, 2005, overwhelmingly rejected a proposal for the United States to pull out of the World Trade Organization (WTO) after a debate that highlighted bipartisan concern about the direction of U.S. trade policy. The WTO was the international body set up by member countries in 1995 to provide a framework for negotiating and supervising multilateral trade treaties as well as a dispute resolution process for settling trade disputes. The 86–338 vote to defeat the resolution (H J Res 27) preempted the need for a Senate vote and meant the United States would remain in the WTO.

Though the outcome of the vote was never in doubt, lawmakers used the opportunity to criticize the U.S. approach on trade. Bernard Sanders, I-Vt., who with Ron Paul, R-Texas, sponsored the resolution, declared in floor remarks that "our trade policies have failed the American worker." Congress should "take a tough look" at U.S. policy, Sanders said, because "the middle class in the United States of America is collapsing. Poverty is increasing. Our trade deficit is soaring." While many colleagues said they shared his concern about jobs, unfair trade practices, outsourcing and competition with China, they argued that leaving the WTO was not a solution.

The debate on U.S. membership in the organization was clearly a warm-up for more immediate trade decisions, such as an upcoming vote on the Central American Free Trade Agreement (CAFTA) and a linked pact with the Dominican Republic. That agreement won narrow approval from Congress in July. *(CAFTA, p. 202)*

The George W. Bush administration said the WTO vote boded well for passage of CAFTA. But opponents of U.S. trade policy viewed the debate and vote on WTO membership as a sign that lawmakers were more uneasy than ever about trade, which could make passage of CAFTA difficult. In 2000, the House voted 56–363 to reject a resolution to pull out of the WTO. The addition of thirty votes in 2005 in favor of withdrawal was a signal of growing discontent with the WTO and the effects of U.S. trade policy.

Under the law that helped establish the WTO (PL 103-465), Congress could take up a resolution to end U.S. membership in the body every five years.

Oman Free Trade Agreement

Legislation to implement a free-trade pact with the tiny Persian Gulf state of Oman cleared in July 2006. The accord was another step in a White House effort, announced in May 2003, to create a Middle East Free Trade Area by 2013. President George W. Bush signed the bill into law Sept. 26 (HR 5684—PL 109-283). Congress in late 2005 had cleared a similar trade pact with Bahrain, which Bush signed in January 2006 (PL 109-169). A bill to implement a free-trade agreement with Morocco was enacted in 2004 (PL 108-286). *(Bahrain pact, p. 205; Morocco agreement, Congress and the Nation, Vol. XI, p. 166)*

However, the resistance that the Oman pact encountered at every step in Congress seemed to presage trouble for other trade agreements that the Bush administration negotiated and for the renewal of fast-track trade authority, which was set to expire in 2007. That authority allowed the president to negotiate trade deals that Congress had to accept or reject without amendment.

Negotiations on the U.S.-Oman free-trade agreement began in November 2004 and were concluded one year later. The agreement was signed Jan. 19, 2006. Trade between the United States and Oman, a nation of 3 million located at the tip of the Arabian Peninsula near the strategically important Straits of Hormuz, totaled a relatively modest $1.1 billion in 2005. Oman had significant oil resources and exported metals and textiles.

The trade agreement provided for the immediate elimination of customs duties on all U.S. consumer and industrial goods and 87 percent of U.S. agricultural products entering Oman. It also provided safeguards for the textile and apparel industry if, as a result of the duty-free treatment, the volume of an Omani product being imported into the United States became so large as to injure or threaten the domestic industry.

LEGISLATIVE ACTION

Legislative action in both chambers began with "mock markups," an element of the fast-track procedure that allowed the committees to weigh in on the administration's draft of the bill before it was formally submitted. The committee recommendations were nonbinding, but they gave the administration an opportunity to assess support for, or opposition to, various provisions before sending the final legislation to the Hill. Once the White House formally submitted the bill, lawmakers had ninety legislative days to either accept or reject the amendment.

The House Ways and Means Committee approved the draft implementation bill May 10, 2006, by a party-line vote of 23–11 after Democrats raised concerns about Oman's labor standards. The Senate Finance Committee endorsed the administration's draft 9–0 on May 18 after adopting an amendment by Kent Conrad, D-N.D., to prohibit products manufactured by companies that engaged in human trafficking or indentured labor from receiving free-trade protections. A U.S. trade representative at the markup said Oman's labor laws already prohibited forced labor, but Conrad said the laws were "not being appropriately enforced."

Bush formally submitted his legislation to Congress on June 26. The Ways and Means Committee approved the implementing bill (HR 5684—H Rept 109-574) by a party-line vote of 23–15 on June 29. The Senate Finance Committee approved an identical bill (S 3569—S Rept 109-364) by a 10–3 vote June 28 but only after an angry debate over the administration's decision not to include Conrad's committee-approved language on forced labor. Max Baucus of Montana, the committee's ranking Democrat, said the administration "has disrespected the process here." Baucus warned that ignoring the committee's unanimous request was "another nail driven into the coffin" of fast-track negotiating authority, which was scheduled to expire in July 2007.

The Senate passed S 3569 60–34 on June 29. Democrats again attacked the agreement for failing to incorporate international labor standards, chastised the administration for ignoring Conrad's amendment in the informal markup, and warned that, as a result, Bush might have trouble securing renewal of fast-track trade negotiating authority in 2007.

The House narrowly endorsed its bill July 20 in a vote that signaled trouble ahead for the administration's trade agenda. For a time, it looked as though the bill would be defeated, but Republican leaders held the vote open while they rounded up enough holdouts to secure passage on a 221–205 tally. Twenty-eight Republicans opposed the measure. Critics from both parties cited concerns about national security, Oman's labor standards, and enforcement of existing trade agreements.

Some Democrats expressed concern that the pact could lead to the takeover of U.S. ports by foreign government-owned companies, such as DP World, the Dubai-based company that was at the center of a ports controversy earlier in 2006. But the U.S. Trade Representative's office rejected that argument, stating that the Oman agreement "provides no new 'right' to supply port-related services." Supporters said the trade pact would not alter the existing process for reviewing sensitive foreign acquisitions. *(Ports controversy, p. 243)*

Because trade bills must originate in the House, the Senate still had to clear the House-passed version (HR 5684). The Senate did so Sept. 19, on a vote of 62–32. Democrats used the second round of debate to renew their criticism of the administration's trade agenda just weeks before the midterm election. Supporters again praised the pact as a means of advancing U.S. political goals in the Middle East and noted Oman's role as an ally in the war against terror.

Vietnam Trade Relations

Over the objections of conservative Republicans, Congress cleared legislation in 2006 sought by President George W. Bush to normalize trade relations with Vietnam. To get the measure to the president's desk, GOP leaders attached it to an end-of-session bill that renewed a series of popular expiring tax breaks. Bush signed the package into law Dec. 20 (HR 6111—PL 109-432).

The bill allowed the president to extend low tariffs to products from Vietnam without requiring an annual waiver of cold war–era restrictions against trading with communist countries. Bush declared the new trade status in effect for Vietnam on Dec. 29, 2006.

The measure also included an extension of the Generalized System of Preferences, a trade program that allowed duty-free entry into the United States for products from more than 100 developing countries as a means of promoting economic growth, as well as of trade provisions for Haiti and four nations of the Andes.

Bush wanted the bill enacted before he made a Nov. 17–20 trip to Vietnam to attend the Asia-Pacific Economic Cooperation Summit. But GOP conservatives and lawmakers from textile states were able to scuttle the initial effort in the House, and Bush went to Hanoi empty-handed.

The White House continued to push for the legislation, however, and in the final days of the session, Republican leaders succeeded in clearing it as part of the larger package of tax and trade provisions.

The bill lifted restrictions imposed by a section of the 1974 Trade Act (PL 93-618) known as the Jackson-Vanik amendment, which at one time restricted trade with virtually all communist countries. Since 1998 the United States had maintained trade relations with Vietnam through annual waivers of Jackson-Vanik. Under the bill, conditional trade ties with Vietnam were no longer necessary. *(Jackson-Vanik amendment, Congress and the Nation Vol. IV, p. 131)*

Vietnam was the fastest-growing market for U.S. exports in Asia. Exports to Hanoi had increased by over 150 percent since 2001. In 2005 alone, they grew by 24 percent to $1.2 billion. The United States and Vietnam had agreed in May to a bilateral trade agreement that promised lower trade barriers for a range of U.S. industrial and agricultural goods and services. The Bush administration was eager to take advantage of those trade benefits, but that required permanent normal trade relations.

The U.S.-Vietnam trade agreement also helped clear the way for Vietnam's entry into the World Trade Organization (WTO). Hanoi was formally invited to join the world body on Nov. 7, 2006, which meant it would be extending mutual low tariffs to all WTO countries. If the United States had not been able to take advantage of the trade benefits, U.S. companies would have had difficulty maintaining their share of the Vietnamese market.

The legislation also was important to the administration at a time when it was trying to forge bilateral free-trade deals with other Asian nations, including Malaysia and South Korea, and counter China's growing trade presence in the region.

PROVISIONS

Following are the major provisions in HR 6111 related to trade.

Trade with Vietnam. Normalized trade relations with Vietnam by stating that the Jackson-Vanik amendment prohibiting trade with communist countries no longer applied to Vietnam.

Trade with Haiti. Granted the Caribbean nation of Haiti duty-free access to the U.S. market for its apparel exports even if it used fabric from third world countries and China.

GSP extension. Extended for two years the Generalized System of Preferences, which was set to expire Dec. 31, 2006. The GSP provided duty-free treatment to imports from more than 100 developing countries. The language allowed the president to make exceptions for "supercompetitive" products that amount to annual imports of greater than $180 billion.

Andean trade. Extended duty-free access to the U.S. market for six months for four Andean countries: Peru, Bolivia, Ecuador, and Colombia. Allowed benefits to be renewed for another six months if the United States and the Andean nations completed the legislative process to implement free-trade pacts.

Sub-Saharan Africa access. Allowed sub-Saharan African countries to continue duty-free access through 2012 to the U.S. market for textiles that include third-country fabrics.

Miscellaneous trade provisions. Suspended or reduced tariffs on imports of more than 500 products that generally were otherwise not available in the United States. These provisions originally had been part of a miscellaneous trade bill that was typically passed every year.

LEGISLATIVE HISTORY

The Senate Finance Committee approved a bill (S 3495—S Rept 109-321) on July 31 stating that Jackson-Vanik no longer applied to Vietnam. The vote was 18–0, and the bill was expected to move through both chambers before Bush's trip in November. When House Ways and Means Chairman Bill Thomas, R-Calif., tried to whisk the measure through the House in November, however, the plan backfired, dealing an embarrassing setback to Bush as he was heading to Hanoi.

Lawmakers were just returning Nov. 13 from the midterm election when Thomas brought the bill up under suspension of the rules, an expedited procedure that requires a two-thirds majority for passage and is reserved for bills that have little or no opposition.

In this case, however, GOP conservatives voiced concerns about Vietnam's human rights record and its communist government. Democrats questioned the potential effect on U.S. jobs, as well as the way the Republicans had rushed the vote. Lawmakers from textile-producing states complained about the possible effects of increased Vietnamese imports. The upshot was a 228–161 vote that was thirty-two votes short of the 260 votes needed to pass under suspension of the rules. Ninety-four Democrats and sixty-six Republicans voted against the bill; forty-three House members did not vote.

Clearly caught by surprise, House leaders discussed getting the Rules Committee to provide a rule for floor debate, which would have allowed the measure to pass with a simple majority. But faced with strong opposition even within their own ranks, they pulled the bill Nov. 14 and announced it would not be considered until December.

When lawmakers returned for a week in December to wind up the 109th Congress, GOP leaders orchestrated a complicated set of maneuvers that resulted in enactment of the Vietnam trade legislation along with a broad package of tax, trade, and other last-minute provisions.

Thomas put the Vietnam language into a trade bill (HR 6406) that also included a two-year extension of the Generalized System of Preferences, which was due to expire Dec. 31, and trade provisions for Haiti and the Andean countries. The House passed the measure 212–84 on Dec. 8. To help the trade bill clear the Senate, where several members were unhappy about the potential effect on textiles, House leaders had it automatically attached to the must-pass tax legislation (HR 6111) under the rule that governed the floor debate. The Senate took up the combined package and cleared it 79–9 in its last roll call vote before adjourning Dec. 9. *(Tax extensions, p. 131)*

2007–2008

The Democratic-led 110th Congress faced off with President George W. Bush over trade policy, giving him very little of what he wanted. Democrats had long been frustrated with Bush's trade policy, claiming the administration did not do enough to protect American workers from trade-related job losses or to ensure that U.S. trading partners abided by international labor and environmental standards. The administration had run into significant problems in the 109th Congress rounding up Republican votes for trade pacts that narrowly passed. By 2007, with the president's popularity sagging, legislators preparing for the 2008 elections, and jobs and the economy a potent political issue, the administration all but conceded the field.

Although the president formally requested renewal of fast-track, or trade promotion, authority, which expired as of July 1, 2007, the administration did not make a concerted push to get it passed. The authority required Congress to either approve or disapprove trade agreements without amending them. Without it, neither U.S. nor foreign trade negotiators could be sure that any agreements they reached would be left unchanged by Congress. That was a significant stumbling block in the multilateral Doha Development Round talks that were grappling with extremely difficult issues surrounding American and European agricultural subsidies. Little progress was made in those talks during 2007 and 2008.

A breakthrough of sorts came in 2007 when the Bush administration and Democratic leaders agreed on a package of labor and environmental protections to be added to pending and future agreements. That helped win approval of a long-stalled trade agreement with Peru at the end of 2007. But the president suffered a major loss in early 2008 when he sent a free-trade agreement to Congress for approval over Democratic objections that it did not have enough votes to pass. Rather than take an up-or-down vote, the House voted to put off action on the trade pact indefinitely, effectively leaving it and two others, one with Panama and a highly controversial one with South Korea, in limbo for the rest of the year. With the election of Democrat Barack Obama to the presidency, it seemed likely that at least parts of the three pending agreements would have to be renegotiated before coming to Congress for approval.

Fast-Track Authority

The president's fast-track negotiating authority for trade pacts expired on June 30, 2007, without Congress or the White House making a serious bid to renew it. Called trade promotion authority by the Bush administration, fast-track authority allowed Congress to approve or disapprove, but not amend, trade agreements negotiated by the administration. With fast-track authority in place, both domestic and foreign trade negotiators could be relatively certain that Congress would not try to amend a trade agreement after it had been signed, forcing new rounds of negotiations. In recent years, Congress had approved only one trade pact, with Jordan in 2001, that was not protected by fast-track authority.

When the authority expired in 2007, trade advocates warned that its absence would hinder negotiation of new trade deals and allow other countries to gain competitive advantages for their businesses. Those on the other side charged that trade agreements negotiated under the fast-track rules had harmed, rather than helped, many U.S. workers and businesses. Fast-track opponents contended that rebuilding political support for trade required a variety of policy changes, including the operation of the fast track system.

Democrats, who gained control of Congress at the beginning of 2007, had long sought changes in the Bush administration approach to trade and had shown little interest in a quick renewal of the authority (PL 107-210). The Bush administration, which had urged Congress to extend the authority in 2005, two years before the expiration but when Republicans were in control, did not push hard for action once the Democrats took over.

Some trade experts thought a more timely renewal was a possibility after congressional leaders and the administration announced a deal on trade policy May 10. In the agreement, the administration made concessions to Democrats to include labor and environmental standards in trade deals, most immediately with pending pacts with Peru and Panama. *(Labor, environmental standards, box, p. 212)*

Trade backers said the administration made the concessions with an eye to extending fast track. But in the 2006 midterm election, criticism of Bush trade policies worked well for Democrats in many congressional districts, helping them win control of Congress, and the party had little interest in removing what could be an important political tool as they entered the 2008 presidential election period.

Peru Free-Trade Agreement

Long-stalled legislation to implement a free-trade agreement with Peru became law in late 2007 after the George W. Bush administration revised sections on labor and environmental protections as part of a deal to gain Democratic support. President Bush signed the measure into law Dec. 14, 2007 (HR 3688—PL 110-138).

However, fewer than half of House Democrats voted for the bill, reflecting continued party concerns about such trade pacts. The lack of Democratic support boded ill for Bush's chances of winning congressional approval of other pending trade agreements. Also, despite provisions added to protect labor, the pact received little support from U.S. unions, which argued that workers' rights in Peru would still be limited.

The trade pact reduced most tariffs and duties affecting trade between the United States and the South American country, reduced barriers to services trade, and increased protections for intellectual property. Most of the provisions related to U.S. exports to Peru because Peru already received duty-free treatment on 98 percent of its exports to the United States under the Andean Trade Preference Act and other agreements. The pact was expected to increase U.S. exports, including beef, cotton, wheat, and soybeans, by $1 billion annually. *(Andean pact, p. 213)*

The Bush administration originally signed the pact with Peru in April 2006, but the president's trade agenda stalled when the Democrats took over Congress in 2007. That changed in May, after Democrats and the White House agreed to add stronger protections for labor and the environment to the text of pending and future trade agreements. Supporters called it the model for a new era of trade deals. *(Labor, environment protections, box, p. 212)*

On June 25, 2007, the United States and Peru agreed on legally binding amendments to the pact that reflected the bipartisan agreement. Two days later, Peru's Congress endorsed the revisions. In its report on the bill, the Ways and Means Committee called the resulting pact "the strongest free trade agreement ever to be considered by the committee with regard to basic internationally recognized labor standards and basic protections for the environment."

Despite the changes, a significant segment of Democrats, including a number of freshmen, still opposed the pact. Nevertheless, the implementation bill moved through Congress with relative ease.

The agreement was considered under "fast-track" rules, an expedited procedure developed to assure U.S. trading partners that Congress would not change any agreement they had reached with U.S. trade negotiators. Under the procedure, lawmakers could suggest changes to a trade bill before it was introduced. Once it was introduced, however, Congress had ninety days to consider it and had to vote it up or down, without amendments. The 2002 law expired June 30, 2007, but it still applied to agreements reached before that date. The administration had also signed trade agreements with Colombia, Panama, and South Korea before its fast-track authority expired.

MAJOR PROVISIONS

The trade agreement, as revised in June:

Industrial and consumer goods. Granted duty-free access for 80 percent of U.S. industrial and consumer exports to Peru. Duties on an additional 7 percent would be phased out within five years, with the remainder eliminated within ten years.

Agriculture. Granted immediate duty-free access for two-thirds of U.S. agricultural exports to Peru, with the remaining tariffs phased out within seventeen years. Items receiving immediate duty-free treatment included beef, cotton, wheat, soybeans, key fruits and vegetables, and many processed food products.

Textiles and apparel. Granted immediate duty-free and quota-free access for all textile and apparel products if all processing from the yarn stage to the final product took place in the United States, Peru, or both. Gave duty-free status to handmade, hand-loomed, or traditional folklore goods. Included special safeguard relief procedures for textile and apparel imports that unduly affected domestic industries.

Services. Provided market access for most service sectors including e-commerce, audiovisual, express delivery, telecommunications, computer and related services, distribution, and trucking, and for services incidental to construction, architecture, and engineering.

Financial services. Provided greater protection for U.S. financial services firms. Gave banks, insurance, and securities companies the right to establish subsidiaries and joint ventures in Peru with strong regulatory transparency. Allowed U.S.-based firms to offer cross-border services to Peruvians in such areas as insurance, data processing, and financial advisory services.

Telecommunications. Gave access to and use of public telecommunications networks and services to all firms, thereby preventing local firms from having preferential or first right of access to telecom networks in either country.

Intellectual property. Improved standards for protection and enforcement of intellectual property rights consistent with U.S. and international standards. Included flexibility aimed at enabling Peru to develop and provide access to general medicines.

Investment protections. Provided a secure, predictable legal framework for U.S. investors operating in Peru covering all forms of investment, including enterprises, debt, concessions and similar contracts, and intellectual property.

Labor. Established enforceable obligation by both countries to enact and enforce internationally recognized labor standards as defined by the International Labor Organization, including freedom of association, recognition of the right to collective bargaining, elimination of all forms of forced or compulsory labor, effective abolition of child labor, and elimination of discrimination in employment and occupation.

Environment. Required both countries to effectively enforce domestic environmental laws and to fulfill obligations under seven multilateral environmental agreements, and included specific steps to maintain biodiversity and forests.

LEGISLATIVE HISTORY

Once the Democrats and the White House reached agreement on labor standards and the Peruvian government agreed to new language in the trade pact, congressional approval came relatively swiftly and easily. Following fast-track procedure for trade agreements, the committees with jurisdiction over trade, House Ways and Means and Senate Finance, began by holding informal sessions in late September to consider a draft of the bill provided by the administration. The "mock," or advisory, markups allowed the committees to propose changes to the implementing legislation before it was formally submitted and the fast-track clock started. Although individual members of both parties registered displeasure with the agreement, both committees easily approved the agreement as modified to reflect the agreement Democrats had made with the White House on labor and environmental standards.

The administration then formally submitted the legislation implementing the trade agreement, on Sept. 27, and both committees again handily approved identical versions of the measure. The Senate Finance Committee approved its bill (S 2113—S Rept 110-249) by voice vote Oct. 4. The House Ways and Means Committee approved its bill (HR 3688—H Rept 110-421) by a vote of 39–0 on Oct. 31.

The House passed the implementing bill on Nov. 8, on a **key vote of 285–132 (R 176–16; D 109–116).** The vote was seen as evidence that the bipartisan agreement on labor and environmental standards was widely acceptable, at least in this one case. Some critics said the lack of Democratic support suggested that the other pending free-trade pacts Bush negotiated would not be able to win congressional approval. *(2007 key votes, p. 955)*

On Dec. 4, the Senate cleared the bill 77–18, with twenty-nine Democrats supporting it and sixteen opposed.

U.S.-Colombia Trade Pact

In a significant loss for the White House, the House in April 2008 delayed indefinitely any congressional action on a free-trade agreement with Colombia, leaving that and other international trade deals negotiated by trade officials in President George W. Bush's administration stalled in Congress for the remainder of the year.

The U.S. Colombia Free Trade Agreement promised to eliminate tariffs on more than 80 percent of U.S. industrial and consumer goods bound for Colombia. Colombia, Bolivia, Ecuador, and Peru already received duty-free treatment on many of their U.S.-bound exports because of recently renewed trade preferences for the Andean nations (PL 110-191). Although the trade pact would benefit American businesses seeking to export to Colombia, it faced strong opposition from Democrats and labor groups, who said the Colombian government had not done enough to reduce violence against union members in the country. Colombia, along with GOP supporters of the pact, said Bogotá had met every objection that opponents raised.

Two other trade pacts, one with Panama and one with South Korea, remained in limbo after the White House said it would not send any more trade agreements to Capitol Hill until Congress dealt with the Colombia pact. The Panama agreement was seen as relatively noncontroversial. But the U.S.-Korea pact faced criticisms from lawmakers of both parties who represented manufacturing states, who argued that the agreement still left the South Korean market closed to many U.S. imports. The American carmakers, Chrysler and Ford, were particularly opposed to the agreement (General Motors, which owned the Korean carmaker Daewoo, remained neutral in the debate.)

Early in 2009 the new Obama administration said it would seek "new benchmarks" before supporting passage of the Colombia trade agreement. Although the administration did not specify what those benchmarks might be, one was thought to be a sharp reduction in the murders of labor leaders in the country. Ron Kirk, Obama's nominee as U.S. trade representative, said in March that the South Korea pact was "simply unfair" and that the administration was "prepared to step away from" it unless it was reworked.

LEGISLATIVE ACTION

The trade agreement was negotiated under fast-track procedures, which required Congress to cast an up-or-down vote on the pact without amendment. The agreements had been negotiated in 2006; in 2007 Congress let the authority for the president to use fast-track procedures expire. Although the fast-track procedure was controversial, it had been used repeatedly over the years for trade agreements both large and small, and Congress had never before rejected a trade pact under the procedure. But House leaders considered the opposition to the pact to be sufficiently large that they did not want to take a chance that the agreement would be rejected outright. Such a rejection was likely to be interpreted around the world as a signal that the United States was backing away from general support for opening trade between countries. *(Fast-track authority, p. 209)*

House Speaker Nancy Pelosi, D-Calif., asked President Bush to withhold sending Congress legislation implementing the agreement until changes could be made in the pact that would satisfy its opponents. Bush, however, sent the implementing legislation to Capitol Hill on April 8, which started the clock ticking under the fast-track authority, which required Congress to affirm or reject a trade deal within ninety days of receiving the implementing legislation.

Under fast-track authority, however, the procedures and timetable were rules of the House and Senate that could be changed by either chamber, and Pelosi immediately introduced a resolution to change House rules and suspend fast-track procedures for the Colombia trade pact. The resolution was adopted April 10, 2008, on a near–party-line **key vote of 224–195 (R 6–185; D 218–10).** Most of the Democrats voting against the resolution were members of the conservative Blue Dog Coalition. Six Southern Republicans voted with the majority for the resolution. *(2008 key votes, p. 972).*

LABOR STANDARDS AGREEMENT

Congressional Democrats and the White House reached an agreement on labor standards in May 2007 that ended, at least temporarily, a stalemate over trade. The agreement, announced on May 10 after months of negotiations, required that enforceable, internationally recognized labor and environmental standards be added to pending trade pacts before Congress voted on them. The requirements also need ratification in a legally binding way by the other parties to the trade accords.

Democrats had long sought to ensure that trade pacts include enforceable labor and environmental standards. Critics argued that any trade agreement that required countries to adopt, maintain, and enforce core labor and environmental standards would apply to the United States as well and could be used to challenge existing U.S. labor and environmental law.

With their victories in the 2006 midterm election, the Democrats were able to implement the standards goal. Once they were in control of both chambers of Congress, the George W. Bush administration needed support from Democratic leaders to advance pending trade bills. In addition, some thirty newly elected Democrats won their races in part by challenging free-trade orthodoxy. The Democratic dominance, including the freshmen, meant there was little chance of winning approval of free-trade agreements that did not include the standards.

Flanked by Treasury Secretary Henry M. Paulson Jr., U.S. Trade Representative Susan C. Schwab, and top lawmakers, House Speaker Nancy Pelosi, D-Calif., said the agreement "takes us to a place where we can have a bipartisan consensus on trade but only with the recognition of the importance and centrality of labor . . . and environmental principles." The White House praised the agreement, saying it provided "a clear path for advancing our proposed free-trade agreements with Peru, Colombia, Panama, and South Korea."

The agreement required both parties to a trade agreement to "adopt, maintain, and enforce in their laws and practice" the five labor standards set out in the 1998 International Labor Organization declaration, which the United States had signed. The agreement referred to principles that prohibit all forms of forced and child labor, guarantee workers' rights to organize unions and bargain collectively, and bar employment discrimination.

Under the agreement with the White House, trade pacts also would include enforceable environmental standards and call back intellectual property protections for pharmaceutical companies as they pertained to generic medicines. Democrats said that provision was intended to give the poor in developing countries access to life-saving medicines.

The only trade agreement to clear before the end of 2008 was a pact with Peru (HR 3688—PL 110-138), which was revised to contain the standards as agreed. The pending agreement with Panama was considered noncontroversial but was never taken up in either chamber. *(Peru agreement, p. 209)*

The other two agreements were controversial, however. Allegations of human rights abuses in Colombia, including the murder of union leaders, concerned many Democrats in Congress; President-elect Barack Obama had also expressed concerns about it. The House blocked action on the agreement in April 2008. President Bush pressed Democratic lawmakers to approve the deal during the lame-duck session after the November 2008 elections, but that session was cut short and the agreement was never taken up. The pact with South Korea faced stiff opposition from U.S. automakers, who contended that nontariff barriers effectively kept the Korean markets closed to imports of U.S. cars. With American car manufacturers struggling for survival, there seemed little likelihood that agreement would be approved without modification.

Democrats said the vote would not necessarily kill the trade deal. But they were frustrated that Bush sent the pact to Congress in the midst of the heated election campaign and without securing support from their party leadership. Trade legislation was politically sensitive, especially in the House, and Pelosi said that "if brought to the floor immediately, it would lose."

Democratic leaders also viewed the Colombia trade pact as leverage to force Bush to compromise with them on trade adjustment assistance and other measures designed to help laid-off workers and struggling homeowners in a slumping economy. "I said we'll take back the leverage to ourselves," Pelosi told reporters after the vote. "All the leverage was with the White House. Now we can talk."

During floor debate, Republicans decried the Speaker's unprecedented procedural move, saying it would weaken a strong U.S. ally in the region and empower neighboring Venezuelan president Hugo Chavez and his anti-American policies. Most House Democrats opposed the trade agreement, however, saying the Colombian government had not taken sufficient steps to reduce violence against union members. Republicans countered that Colombia had worked hard to crack down on right-wing paramilitary groups blamed for much of the violence. *(Andean trade pact, p. 213)*

The House action was decisive, because legislation involving revenue—including trade agreements—must originate in that chamber. Despite a push from the administration in the lame-duck session after the election, House leaders declined for the rest of the year to say when they might restore the fast-track process or bring up the Colombia trade pact for consideration.

Trade Adjustment Assistance

Democrats in both the House and the Senate had hoped to revise and expand the Trade Adjustment Assistance (TAA) program during the 110th Congress, but were blocked by Republicans. Instead Congress enacted two simple extensions of the program that provided retraining and wage and health insurance subsidies to workers who lost their jobs as a result of boosted imports or production shifts by foreign competitors.

The House in October 2007 by a vote of 264–157 passed a bill (HR 3920) to reauthorize the program through fiscal 2012. The bill also expanded the program's benefits to service workers, and increased a health care tax credit to pay for 85 percent of premiums, up from the existing 65 percent. But the White House threatened to veto the measure, saying an expansion of the program would send costs skyrocketing and open the door to covering many more laid-off workers.

With the Trade Adjustment Assistance act set to expire at the end of 2007, the House then passed a bill (HR 4341) authorizing a short-term extension of the assistance through March 2008. When Republicans blocked that bill in the Senate over an unrelated matter, Congress in December 2007 included an extension of the TAA program in the fiscal 2008 omnibus appropriations bill (PL 110-161).

In the Senate, Finance Committee chairman Max Baucus, D-Mont., introduced a bill (S 1848) similar to the one passed in the House. Senate Democrats sought to use the Colombia trade agreement as leverage to force a White House compromise on displaced worker aid and other measures designed to help laid-off workers and struggling homeowners in a slumping economy. But the efforts were stymied by Republicans, who demanded that a vote on the Colombia deal take place first. Instead, the House passed and the Senate cleared an extension of the TAA program as part of the continuing funding resolution (PL 110-329) that kept government agencies operating through March 6, 2009. *(Continuing resolution, p. 124)*

Andean Trade Pact

Congress in 2008 cleared two extensions of the Andean trade pact, which provided duty-free treatment for most goods from Bolivia, Colombia, Ecuador, and Peru. The second extension also extended the Generalized System of Preferences (GSP), a trade program that allowed duty-free entry into the United States for products from more than 100 developing countries as a means of promoting economic growth.

The Senate cleared the first extension, through 2008, of the Andean trade pact, by voice vote Feb. 28, 2008. The House had passed the bill a day earlier, also by voice vote. President George W. Bush signed the measure into law on Feb. 29 (HR 5264—PL 110-19), the day the trade preferences for the four South American countries would have expired if the extension had not been enacted. The bill was expected to reduce revenues from customs duties by an estimated $82 million in fiscal 2008 and $37 million in fiscal 2009, according to the Congressional Budget Office.

Congress cleared the second extension of the Andean pact and the GSP extension in October 2008. Sen. Charles E. Grassley, R-Iowa, had held up the bill for several months out of dissatisfaction with antidrug efforts in Bolivia and Ecuador. He eventually agreed to a compromise that renewed trade benefits for the countries for six months with an additional six-month extension if they cooperated with antidrug efforts. The Senate added the language to the bill (HR 7222) and passed the bill by voice vote on Oct. 2. The House cleared the bill by voice vote on Oct. 3, and President Bush signed it into law (PL 100-436) Oct. 16. On Nov. 28 the president suspended Bolivia's benefits under the Andean trade pact because of its lack of cooperation in antidrug efforts.

Myanmar Sanctions

Congress in July 2008 cleared a resolution (H J Res 93—PL 110-287) extending trade sanctions against Myanmar's military junta for one year.

The House on July 23, 2008, passed the resolution by voice vote. The Senate followed suit by voice vote the next day. The Senate Finance Committee had approved a companion measure (S J Res 41) by voice vote on July 23.

The resolution renewed the sanctions first put into place in 2003 (PL 108-61) and extended every year since then. The sanctions barred all U.S. imports from Myanmar, formerly known as Burma, until its regime improves its record on human rights, moves toward a democratic government, and complies with antidrug treaties.

During a brief House debate, supporters noted the government's use of lethal force against demonstrators in September and its efforts to block international relief efforts after Cyclone Nargis left nearly 150,000 killed or missing earlier in 2008.

The Senate on July 22 also cleared a bill (HR 3890—PL 110-286) by voice vote to bar imports of gems originating in Myanmar. Ninety percent of the world's rubies and fine-quality jade come from Myanmar, though only 3 percent of rubies entering the United States are claimed to originate there.

Despite the import restrictions imposed in 2003, gems from Myanmar continued to arrive in the United States via a third country, where they were cut and exported. The legislation was meant to stop that practice. The measure also made regime leaders and their family members ineligible for U.S. visas.

CHAPTER 3

Homeland Security

Homeland Security

After the terrorist attacks of Sept. 11, 2001, Congress and President George W. Bush had worked closely to shore up the nation's defenses and strengthen the hand of domestic law enforcement agencies. During the course of Bush's second presidential term from 2005 to 2009, however, the legislative branch became more skeptical of the executive branch's national security prerogatives. Bush found members of Congress pushing back against the White House's claim of executive privilege, which the administration used to cloak details of its national security efforts.

Bush in 2005 found he had to negotiate with a renegade band of Senate Republicans over the renewal of provisions in his signature antiterrorism law, the USA PATRIOT Act. He was also challenged when it came to light that his administration was using U.S. telecommunication companies to eavesdrop on American citizens without first obtaining a court order. Moreover, his administration's inept handling of the disaster that unfolded in New Orleans in 2005 after Hurricane Katrina made many lawmakers wonder if the administration was too focused on emphasizing international threats while ignoring serious problems here at home. *(Katrina details, pp. 791, 797)*

The broad range of measures that were needed to keep the nation secure also gained congressional attention. The legislators passed measures designed to protect U.S. ports, distribute first-responder grants, secure the nation's southwestern border, prevent bioterrorism attacks, and safeguard chemical plants. In addition some members of Congress feared that the Department of Homeland Security, created after the 2001 terrorist attacks to focus on homeland protection, was too large and unwieldy to provide the necessary leadership needed to keep the nation safe. Bush also ran into difficulty in the second half of his second term when the Democrats regained control of both the House and Senate. The new congressional leaders were less willing to go along with Bush's vision of actions and legislation needed for the nation's security.

RETHINKING THE USA PATRIOT ACT

One of the first measures to be enacted after the Sept. 11 attacks was the USA Patriot Act, which expanded the federal government's ability to investigate, prosecute, and punish terrorism. Five years after its passage, lawmakers began to question the reach of the law.

The Patriot Act included many provisions long sought by law enforcement agencies, including creation of "one-stop shopping" for court orders, which would allow a single judge to issue a search warrant or approve surveillance that would be valid across the country. The law also made it easier for investigators to track Internet communications.

When sixteen provisions of the law were set to expire in 2006, Bush made the law's reauthorization a cornerstone of his second term. The administration and its Republican allies wanted to make all sections of the law permanent and give law enforcement agencies additional legal tools. But these proponents of the reauthorization came up against a bipartisan coalition of senators who wanted more protections for civil liberties and time limits on some of the more contentious provisions in the sweeping law.

House and Senate conferees reached agreement in December 2005 on a bill to reauthorize the sixteen provisions of the 2001 law, but a steady drumbeat of dissenters, led by civil liberties groups, almost scuttled the reauthorization measure's chances in the Senate. Republican dissenters, led by Sen. John E. Sununu of New Hampshire, retooled the measure with the White House and the renewal was eventually cleared with additional protections against records seizures by the Federal Bureau of Investigation (FBI).

GOVERNMENT MONITORING

There also was growing congressional disillusionment over the Bush administration's expanded use of executive power to monitor overseas telephone calls by U.S. citizens that the White House said could be terrorist activity. The *New York Times* reported in December 2005 that Bush had secretly authorized domestic surveillance of U.S. citizens

REFERENCES

Discussion of homeland security policy for the years 2001–2004 may be found in *Congress and the Nation Vol. XI*, pp. 175–225.

President George W. Bush, right, shakes hands with Attorney General Alberto Gonzales after promoting the USA PATRIOT Act at the Ohio State Highway Patrol Academy in Columbus, Ohio, on June 9, 2005.
Source: AP Photo/Charles Dharapak

without first obtaining federal court approval. As a result of the article, members of both parties introduced bills to establish oversight of the National Security Agency (NSA) program, which reportedly monitored overseas telephone calls and e-mails of U.S. citizens.

But it was not until July 2008 that a measure cleared Congress overhauling the 1978 Foreign Intelligence Surveillance Act (FISA), which required the government to get approval from a special court outside of criminal statutes before beginning electronic surveillance within the United States. Bush had argued that his constitutional status as commander in chief enabled him to bypass federal laws on domestic surveillance as part of his war on terrorism.

While Democrats agreed that FISA needed to be overhauled, they generally wanted more restrictions to protect the civil liberties of U.S. citizens. However, Democratic leaders were not able to resolve differences between the two chambers over the exact role of the FISA court. Bush also wanted the legislation to give immunity to the telecommunications firms that had assisted in the warrantless wiretapping program.

Some Democrats opposed giving companies such as AT&T immunity for their work with the NSA, expressing concern about the legal precedent and the effect such immunity might have on potential court scrutiny of the program. The Bush administration threatened to veto any bill that did not include such immunity, saying that leaving it out could discourage private-sector cooperation with future spying programs.

The legislation eventually revamped FISA to establish new rules for the use of electronic surveillance to collect foreign intelligence, including monitoring communications involving parties on U.S. soil. The bill did not explicitly grant retroactive legal immunity to the telecommunications companies, but it came close enough to satisfy the White House by creating conditions for the courts to dismiss lawsuits against the companies.

DEPARTMENT OF HOMELAND SECURITY

By the start of Bush's second term, the Department of Homeland Security had been in operation for three years. Created after the Sept. 11, 2001, terrorist attacks, the new federal agency had received mixed reviews for its effort to graft twenty-two separate agencies and more than 170,000 employees into a single umbrella organization tasked with keeping U.S. citizens safe against all enemies, foreign and domestic.

The agency was seen as particularly ineffective after Hurricane Katrina extensively damaged New Orleans in August 2005. The lack of a coordinated response on the Gulf coast in the aftermath of the storm prompted Republicans and Democrats alike to call for a new level of accountability for dealing with domestic disasters. A number of lawmakers were ready to return the Federal Emergency Management Agency (FEMA), a cornerstone of the new department, to status as an independent agency to prevent such large-scale management mistakes again. Congress did take a careful look at FEMA but ended up leaving it in the Department of Homeland Security, while making it more independent.

Aside from FEMA's travails, the Homeland Security Department generally had an exceptionally friendly relationship with the Republicans who controlled the department's oversight committees for its first four years. But when the Democrats gained control of Congress in 2007, they were not as patient with the department as their GOP

HOMELAND SECURITY LEADERSHIP

At the start of George W. Bush's second term, a new secretary of the Department of Homeland Security (DHS) took over as head of the huge agency. Federal Appeals Court judge Michael Chertoff was confirmed by the Senate on Feb. 15, 2005, by a unanimous vote of 98–0. Former Pennsylvania governor Tom Ridge, the first DHS secretary, had stepped down in late 2004. Chertoff had previously served in the Bush administration as assistant attorney general in the Department of Justice's criminal division from 2001 to 2003.

Bush's surprise selection of Chertoff reflected a desire to have a DHS secretary who brought a hard-nosed, prosecutorial edge to the job. Sen. Charles E. Schumer, D-N.Y., said Chertoff was ideally suited for the job "given his law enforcement background and understanding of New York's and America's neglected homeland security needs." The state's other senator, Hillary Rodham Clinton, was more neutral, mainly because Chertoff served as Republican counsel for the Senate Whitewater Committee during the presidential administration of her husband, Bill Clinton. That investigation became part of a larger examination of Clinton's conduct in office by the Republican-led Congress that resulted in the president's impeachment and eventual acquittal. *(Clinton impeachment, Congress and the Nation Vol. X, pp. 797, 813)*

Chertoff, a rabbi's son and former clerk to Supreme Court justice William O. Brennan, had already been confirmed three times by the Senate: in 1990 to be assistant U.S. attorney for New Jersey; in 2001 to run the Justice Department's Criminal Division; and in 2004 to be a judge on the U.S. Court of Appeals for the Third Circuit in Philadelphia.

Generally lost in the debate over Chertoff's administrative qualifications—except by liberal critics—were his aggressive tactics in pursuit of potential al Qaeda "sleeper agents" after the Sept. 11, 2001, terrorist attacks. Chertoff devised the "material witness" legal strategy for the indefinite, anonymous detention of more than 1,100 individuals suspected of having terrorist links "until we find out what's going on." None of them were convicted of terrorism by the time of his DHS nomination.

Together with Alberto R. Gonzales, who was then White House legal adviser and later attorney general, Chertoff helped devise the legal defense of torture that surfaced in the wake of the Abu Ghraib prison scandal. All this drew the wrath of liberals, such as Rep. Jerrold Nadler, D-N.Y., who called Chertoff's record on civil liberties "abominable," and a "black mark" on the United States. Others glimpsed something in Chertoff that they said made him the right choice to run the troubled DHS. For example, Chertoff had pushed the White House to strip the department of its authority to conduct terror finance investigations, ceding the job to the Justice Department. *(Abu Ghraib, torture controversy, pp. 369, 399)*

Two other key players in the debates over homeland security during 2005–2008 were former New Jersey governor Thomas H. Kean and former Democratic representative Lee H. Hamilton of Indiana. The two men were chair and co-chair, respectively, of the bipartisan National Commission on Terrorist Attacks Upon the United States, or the Sept. 11 Commission. Established by Congress in 2002, the commission was charged to examine and report on the facts and causes relating to the 2001 terrorist attacks and make recommendations for improving the nation's preparedness and response capabilities. The commission's final report, released in July 2004, concluded that the U.S. government had been unprepared for the attacks and that the intelligence community had not been properly organized to identify the plotters.

Kean had served two terms as governor of New Jersey from 1982 to 1990, winning his second term by the largest margin in state history. Afterward Kean was president of Drew University for fifteen years until his retirement in spring 2005. Hamilton served as chairman of the House Committee on Foreign Affairs and of the Permanent Select Committee on Intelligence, during his thirty-four years in the House (1965–1999). After leaving Congress, he was the director of the Center on Congress at Indiana University, a nonpartisan educational institution seeking to improve the public's understanding of Congress and encourage civic engagement. Hamilton also served as president and director of the Woodrow Wilson International Center for Scholars in Washington, D.C.

counterparts had been. Democrats raised concerns over the many crucial vacancies in top Homeland Security management positions and port security measures that continued to miss congressional deadlines.

PORT SECURITY

Congress tackled the issue of enhanced port security before recessing for the 2006 midterm elections. The bill was spurred by security concerns raised in February when DP World, a company based in Dubai (one of seven emirates composing the United Arab Emirates), acquired operational control of six U.S. port terminals through a deal it made with a British firm. The Bush administration had approved the deal. Under congressional pressure, the company ultimately decided to sell its interest in the ports.

The measure codified a number of programs at the Homeland Security Department aimed at securing U.S. ports and the estimated 11 million containers that enter them each year. Only 5 percent of the containers arriving at U.S. seaports were examined in 2005, causing some members of Congress to call for inspections of all U.S.-bound containers. The measure required the twenty-two largest U.S. ports to scan all incoming containers for radiological weapons by the end of 2007. The conference report also served as a last-minute vehicle for provisions aimed at reducing Internet gambling. *(Internet gambling, p. 422)*

9/11 COMMISSION RECOMMENDATIONS

After Democrats regained the majority in Congress in 2007, one of their first priorities was to enact some of the remaining recommendations from the bipartisan National Commission on Terrorist Attacks Upon the United States, or 9/11 commission. Congress had established the 9/11 commission in 2002 to study the events surrounding the 2001 terrorist attacks. Many of the recommendations had already been enacted as part of the 2004 law that reorganized the intelligence community.

Among its myriad provisions, the bill required that federal first-responder grants be distributed largely on the basis of risk, greatly expanded the scrutiny of cargo for nuclear devices and other dangerous contraband, and created a new grant program to improve the interoperability of emergency communications.

Some of the provisions were watered down to avoid a presidential veto, however. For example, the White House had threatened to veto the Senate bill over a provision to give airport screeners collective bargaining rights, so Democrats agreed to drop the provision from the final bill. The measure also left undone one of the 9/11 commission's principal recommendations: strengthening congressional oversight of homeland security and intelligence.

BIOTERRORISM AND CHEMICAL PLANTS

Lawmakers also cleared legislation in 2006 reauthorizing a post-Sept. 11 law intended to prepare the nation for an attack by bioterrorists. The bill included provisions to establish a Biomedical Advanced Research and Development Authority to coordinate research and production of vaccines for potential plagues and bioweapons. The new biomedical authority would coordinate all federal efforts to research and produce vaccines and cures for potential plagues and weapons and was also authorized to award grants and contracts for the work.

Lawmakers also became concerned about security at the nation's chemical plants, and the issue was ultimately addressed in the fiscal 2008 Homeland Security appropriations bill. The chemical plant provision allowed states to impose tougher security regulations on chemical plants than those enforced by the federal government. The White House had opposed the provision, saying it would harm the Homeland Security Department's ability to set and enforce a single national security standard for chemical plants.

Chronology of Action on Homeland Security

2005–2006

Lawmakers during the 109th Congress, 2005–2006, began to pay more attention to the question of whether the emphasis on national security by the administration of George W. Bush was curtailing U.S. civil liberties. This concern was made clear when certain provisions of the 2001 antiterrorism law known as the USA PATRIOT Act expired in 2005. The administration and its Republican allies wanted to make all sections of the law permanent and give law enforcement additional legal tools. But proponents of reauthorizing the Patriot Act came up against a bipartisan coalition of senators who wanted more protections for civil liberties and time limits on some of the more contentious provisions in the sweeping antiterrorism law. Congress eventually cleared a renewal of the act but not before four GOP holdouts won White House agreement to three additional changes on records seizures by the Federal Bureau of Investigations (FBI) that they believed violated Americans' civil liberties. There was also growing congressional disillusionment over the Bush administration's expanded use of executive power to monitor overseas telephone calls by U.S. citizens to track what the White House said could be terrorist activity.

Homeland security took on a more domestic focus in the fall of 2005 as Hurricanes Katrina and Rita roared through the coastal areas of Louisiana, Mississippi, and Alabama. During Katrina, the levees that protected New Orleans were breached and water flooded 80 percent of the city. Americans watched dramatic television news coverage of the city being swept away as residents remained stranded on their roofs or were forced to hunker down in the city's Superdome. The federal government appeared clueless and inept. Lawmakers returned hurriedly to Washington that fall and much of what they did through the rest of the year, and into 2006, was suddenly driven by the lack of federal response to the hurricanes.

The American public began to question how the federal government would deal with domestic natural disasters instead of just guarding against ones from overseas. The fact that the federal agency charged with responding to domestic emergencies, the Federal Emergency Management Agency (FEMA), appeared as confused as the rest of the government as the disaster was unfolding in New Orleans led Congress to reorganize the agency in 2006. The central issue was whether to remove the once-independent agency from the Homeland Security Department, which had absorbed it in March 2003. Many lawmakers complained that FEMA was buried under layers of a departmental bureaucracy that focused on terrorism and was not as nimble as it needed to be when responding to domestic disasters. Those who supported keeping FEMA in the department countered that removing the agency would create new, duplicative layers of bureaucracy. Ultimately, lawmakers decided to keep FEMA within Homeland Security, but to give it independent, autonomous status, similar to the Coast Guard.

Lawmakers also were uneasy about the level of administration secrecy on the war on terrorism. When the *New York Times* reported in December 2005 that President Bush had secretly authorized domestic surveillance of U.S. citizens without first obtaining court approval, members of both parties introduced bills to establish better oversight of the National Security Agency (NSA) program. The NSA had reportedly monitored overseas telephone calls and e-mails of U.S. citizens in an effort to obtain terrorist communications.

The White House maintained that Bush had the authority to order the eavesdropping under the 2001 law that authorized the use of force in response to the Sept. 11 terrorist attacks. But critics said the domestic surveillance program was illegal because it did not comply with the Foreign Intelligence Surveillance Act (FISA), a 1978 law that required the government to get approval from a special court before beginning electronic surveillance within the United States outside of criminal statutes. But congressional efforts to establish new rules to govern the NSA program were unsuccessful by the end of the 109th Congress.

On the last day of September 2006, Congress cleared a bill authorizing more than $2 billion over five years for U.S. port and container security programs. The port security bill codified a number of programs at the Homeland

Security Department aimed at securing the nation's 361 ports and the estimated 11 million cargo containers that enter them each year. The conference agreement also extended an existing ban on interstate gambling to include Internet communications. *(Gambling provisions, p. 422)*

Concern over port security had escalated in February 2006 with news that the Bush administration had approved a transaction giving operational control of six key U.S. ports to DP World, a Dubai-owned company. Members of Congress, prodded by constituent complaints about the deal and concerns about the antiterrorism record of the United Arab Emirates (which was composed of seven emirates including Dubai), pressed to reverse the deal. The company quickly volunteered to sell off its U.S. port assets, but with the vulnerability of ports in question both chambers pushed legislation shoring up port defenses against attacks.

Congress also cleared legislation in 2006 authorizing the construction of 700 miles of fencing along the southwestern border with Mexico, as well as a "virtual fence" of cameras, sensors, unmanned aerial vehicles, and other surveillance technology along the entire U.S.-Mexico border. After nine months of intense disagreement over proposals to overhaul federal immigration policy, Republican leaders decided in advance of the November elections to focus on a relatively narrow bill to build a border fence and leave the rest of the debate for the 110th Congress. *(Border fence, immigration, pp. 686, 694, 711)*

USA PATRIOT Act

Congress struggled for over a year on whether to extend the 2001 antiterrorism law known as the USA PATRIOT Act when sixteen of its key provisions were set to expire on Dec. 31, 2005. After much debate and many revisions, the issue was finally resolved on March 2, 2006, when the Senate voted overwhelmingly to clear a reauthorization bill. President George W. Bush, who had made renewing the law a priority, signed the measure at a White House ceremony on March 9 (HR 3199—PL 109-177).

BACKGROUND

The 2001 antiterrorism law (PL 107-56) was enacted less than two months after the Sept. 11 attacks. It gave the federal government expanded powers under the Foreign Intelligence Surveillance Act (PL 95-511), known as FISA, to conduct searches and seizures and carry out electronic surveillance of people with suspected links to terrorism. To address concerns about civil liberties and citizens' rights to privacy, Congress had included the Dec. 31, 2005, expiration date for sixteen of the provisions, meaning that Congress would need to revisit them after four years. The Bush administration had opposed the "sunsets" but accepted them as the price of getting the legislation through Congress *(2001 antiterrorism law, Congress and the Nation Vol. XI, p. 187; FISA, Congress and the Nation Vol. V, p. 720; 110th Congress action on FISA, pp. 249, 251)*

(The antiterrorism law's name was commonly written as the "Patriot Act" but more formally it was the USA PATRIOT Act, which was an acronym that stood for its official name: Uniting and Strengthening America by Providing Appropriate Tools Required to Intercept and Obstruct Terrorism Act.)

The administration and its Republican allies wanted to make all sections of the law permanent and give law enforcement additional legal tools. But they came up against a bipartisan coalition of senators who wanted more protections for civil liberties and time limits on some of the more contentious provisions in the sweeping law. Republican senators Larry E. Craig of Idaho, Lisa Murkowski of Alaska, and John E. Sununu of New Hampshire repeatedly joined Democratic senators Richard J. Durbin of Illinois, Russ Feingold of Wisconsin, and Ken Salazar of Colorado to seek more limits on the powers conferred in the law.

The group succeeded in brokering a compromise bill sponsored by Senate Judiciary Chairman Arlen Specter, R-Pa., which easily passed that chamber in July. The bill proposed four-year sunsets for two of the most controversial expiring provisions—giving the FBI power to seek "roving wiretaps" and get access to a wide array of business records—and further restrictions on the FBI's threshold for acquiring records and search warrants. The bill also included a four-year extension of a provision in the 2004 intelligence overhaul law (PL 108-458) that allowed law enforcement to seek warrants against "lone wolf" terrorists who were not connected to a foreign power. *(2004 intelligence law, Congress and the Nation Vol. XI, p. 263)*

The White House's antiterrorism policies fared better in the House, which passed a bill supported by Judiciary Chairman F. James Sensenbrenner Jr., R-Wis., that included ten-year reauthorizations for the two most controversial provisions and no sunset on the lone wolf provision.

The provision in the Patriot Act that drew the most scrutiny was a section that allowed federal agents to get court orders for access to "any tangible thing"—mainly business records—related to an authorized terrorism investigation. The language amended FISA, which was originally aimed at giving the government tools to combat foreign spying.

The provision drew fire from an unusual alliance of liberals and some conservatives who feared that it could be used to gain access to a seemingly unlimited range of private records, including library and bookstore records. Librarians across the country vociferously opposed the language, saying it could be used for broad requests for their patron records. FBI Director Robert S. Mueller III assured lawmakers in April that the FBI had not used the provision to obtain library records because libraries had been voluntarily cooperating with requests for information.

HOUSE COMMITTEE ACTION

The House Judiciary Committee amended and approved Sensenbrenner's bill (HR 3199—H Rept 109-174, Part 1) on a 23–14 party-line vote July 13. As amended, the bill proposed to make fourteen of the sixteen provisions permanent and extend the roving wiretap and business records provisions for ten years, through 2015.

Sensenbrenner's bill originally would have made all sixteen provisions permanent, but he agreed to support an amendment by Dan Lungren, R-Calif., to set the two expiration dates. "I support, reluctantly, the longer sunset provision," Sensenbrenner said. The amendment was adopted 26–2. Democratic attempts to terminate the provisions sooner—in 2009 or 2011—were rejected.

The committee rejected nearly all of the more than forty amendments offered by Democrats, many of them aimed at further restricting or demanding more information from law enforcement officers conducting surveillance, requesting records, or entering homes without notifying the target of the investigation. A proposal by New York Democrat Jerrold Nadler to add sunsets to the other fourteen expiring provisions failed 12–21. "The one thing sunsetting says is we should not get too comfortable with expanded police powers," Nadler said.

Democrats were not alone in their concerns. Republicans offered and won several new limitations. The committee agreed to proposals to allow recipients of requests for information under the business records provision to consult with a lawyer and challenge the request in court; to require investigators to notify a judge every time they planned to tap a new communications device within ten days of a new wiretap being approved; to require the attorney general to submit a report to Congress showing all cases in which communications service providers handed over records, such as e-mail; to require the Justice Department to review the detention of material witnesses held without charges; and to make it a federal crime to survey, photograph, videotape, diagram, or otherwise collect information with intent to plan or assist a terrorist attack against mass transit.

The Select Intelligence Committee also amended and approved Sensenbrenner's bill July 13 (H Rept 109-174, Part 2) on a voice vote, with one change: The committee added a sunset date of 2010 on the lone wolf provision.

HOUSE FLOOR ACTION

The House passed the bill July 21 by a vote of 257–171. Democrats tried to limit the expiration dates on all sixteen provisions to just four years, but a motion to recommit the bill with instructions to do so was narrowly defeated 209–218. Nine Republicans voted in favor of the motion. "Emergency powers should not become the standard once the threat is gone," said Dana Rohrabacher, R-Calif. "Let's stand up to the principles our Founding Fathers talked about: limiting government."

Sensenbrenner said he found no record of abuse of the law and therefore saw no need to put expiration dates on all sixteen provisions. The White House issued a statement supporting the House bill but also expressed disappointment with the decision to include the expiration dates on the two provisions, calling the sunsets "unnecessary and detrimental."

SENATE COMMITTEE ACTION

The Senate Judiciary Committee voted 18–0 on July 21 to approve a compromise bill (S 1389) to make the same fourteen sections permanent, but set four-year expiration dates on the roving wiretap and record search provisions. The committee also included a four-year sunset for the lone wolf provision, which had been permanently reauthorized under the House bill.

The unanimous vote in the notoriously fractious committee signaled that the bill would go to the Senate floor with a built-in bipartisan unity that would be hard to break. The Senate panel had prepared dozens of amendments, and Senator Specter and aides worked through the night before the markup to fashion a compromise the committee could accept. Specter hailed the eleventh-hour deal as "a very, very significant accomplishment."

The measure contained many of the same provisions that were added to the House bill, but it sometimes went further to curb government powers. For instance, it required the FBI director or deputy director to sign off on any attempt to obtain medical or gun sales records, as well as records from libraries or booksellers. It proposed a higher threshold for business records searches, requiring authorities to demonstrate reasonable grounds, in a statement of fact, showing that the information sought was relevant to the activities of a foreign power, or that it pertained to an individual in contact with or known to a suspected agent of a foreign power.

Senators from both parties said they would keep pushing for more restrictions on law enforcement's powers. "There is still a lot of uneasiness about this legislation in middle America, and I think we need to pay attention to that," said Republican Tom Coburn of Oklahoma. Coburn favored making the entire antiterrorism law, not just the sixteen expiring provisions, temporary.

SENATE FLOOR ACTION

In striking contrast to the House, the Senate passed HR 3199 on July 29 without debate or roll call votes. Senators passed the bill by voice vote after substituting the text of the Judiciary Committee measure. Senators who had indicated they would offer amendments on the floor acquiesced in the unanimous consent necessary to consider the bill on short notice and pass it by voice vote.

"The alacrity of the bill's passage is a testament to the significant work that preceded its introduction and the intense efforts of many in the days that followed," Specter said. "The bill has been refined and improved to address the concerns of those on both sides of the political aisle."

CONFERENCE ACTION

When the House-Senate conference on the bill began in the fall of 2005, Sensenbrenner pressed Senate Republicans to accept a deal favored by the Justice Department that would have extended the two provisions for seven years.

Specter tentatively agreed despite some concerns, and the bill seemed headed for completion in late November. A bipartisan group of six senators, however, threatened to block action unless several changes were made to increase civil liberties protection.

After that, the White House became more involved, and Vice President Dick Cheney entered the negotiations in early December. Within hours of Cheney joining the talks, Sensenbrenner agreed to the Senate's demand for four-year expirations on the roving wiretap and business records provisions, and the conference report was filed.

House and Senate conferees completed work on the bill Dec. 9. While the House adopted the conference report (H Rept 109-333) 251–174 on Dec. 14, the Senate was not ready to go along. The six senators who wanted more civil liberties protections—Republicans Craig, Sununu, and Murkowski, and Democrats Feingold, Salazar, and Durbin—led a filibuster that prevented the Senate from clearing the bill. Despite five days of intense pressure from Senate Republican leaders and the White House, Craig, Murkowski, and Sununu, along with Republican Chuck Hagel of Nebraska, refused to help the leadership invoke cloture and bring the conference report to a vote.

An attempt by Senate Majority Leader Bill Frist, R-Tenn., to secure the sixty votes needed to limit debate failed on Dec. 16, 2005, on a **key vote of 52–47 (R 50–5; D 2–41; I 0–1)**. Four Republicans joined forty-one Democrats and Vermont Independent James M. Jeffords in voting against cloture on the conference report. Frist changed his vote to "no" at the end to preserve his right to offer a motion to reconsider at a later date. *(2005 key votes, p. 915)*

SHORT-TERM EXTENSION

Frist then insisted that he and Bush would rather let the 2001 antiterrorism law expire Dec. 31 than give in to demands for a short-term extension to break the bipartisan filibuster. But with the deadline looming and sentiment growing within the GOP caucus to protect the sixteen provisions, Frist on Dec. 21 waved a white flag and supported a six-month extension bill (S 2167), which passed by voice vote.

Sensenbrenner objected to an extension for that long, and with the agreement of the House leadership, he amended the bill to shorten the extension to five weeks. The House then passed the bill by voice vote Dec. 22. With few good options left, the Senate cleared the revised short-term bill (S 2167—PL 109-160) a few hours later. John W. Warner, R-Va., was the only senator in the chamber to conduct what was the final legislative act of the session.

2006 COMPROMISE

Despite repeated warnings from the chief negotiators that the conference on the reauthorization bill was over, the four Republicans and their Democratic allies continued to seek revisions when they returned to Washington, D.C., in January 2006. This group mainly targeted the provisions concerning national security letters, the seizure of business records, and delayed-notification search warrants. While they negotiated with White House staff, the Senate on Feb. 2 voted 95–1 to clear a second short-term reauthorization to March 10 (HR 4659—PL 109-170).

Senator Sununu met with White House and Justice Department officials and in February won support for three changes to the provisions dealing with records seizures. On Feb. 9, the renegade Republicans announced they had reached a deal that satisfied enough of their concerns. They were joined at a news conference by Minority Whip Durbin, who said he supported the deal. Minority Leader Harry Reid, D-Nev., issued a statement calling it a "step in the right direction." Dianne Feinstein, D-Calif.—also a member of the Judiciary Committee—said the deal was "a substantial improvement" over the conference report.

Sununu then introduced a new bill (S 2271) that changed the records seizures language in the broader bill. The new provisions included:

- **Gag orders.** Allowed recipients of an FBI order to produce "tangible" items, such as business records, to challenge the secrecy of the order in court. The 2001 antiterrorism law broadened the use of such orders in terrorism cases and barred the recipients from disclosing to anyone that they had received such an order. In reauthorizing the provision, Congress allowed the recipient to consult an attorney and challenge the order in court but still barred disclosure to anyone else. Under Sununu's revision, the recipients could challenge the gag order in a FISA court. However, recipients had to wait for one year, and the gag order would stand if the attorney general, deputy attorney general, an assistant attorney general, or FBI director certified that disclosure might endanger national security—unless a judge found that the certification was made in bad faith.
- **Naming attorney.** Eliminated a requirement that recipients of a FISA order or a national security letter—which could be used to seize records without court approval—disclose the name of any attorney they consulted. However, they were required to report the names of anyone other than an attorney to whom they had disclosed information about the existence of the letter or order.
- **Library records.** Specified that libraries that operated in traditional roles, including allowing patrons access to the Internet, were not subject to national security letters unless they were acting as providers of Internet services.

One of the main revisions that critics wanted but were unable to get was language that would have required the FBI to tie FISA orders and national security letters directly to a terrorist suspect or a case of espionage. The conference report required a "statement of facts" showing "reasonable grounds to believe" that the records or other items sought were relevant to an authorized investigation to protect against international terrorism or espionage. Sununu said the White House and Justice Department thought the terrorist-connection language was too narrow a standard. "I think it's an area where there is an agreement to disagree," he said.

FINAL ACTION

The Senate passed Sununu's bill 95–4 on March 1, which only included the changes sought by the senators. Once that was resolved, clearing the broader measure was all but guaranteed. Senators voted 84–15 to invoke cloture, ending the filibuster that had commenced eleven weeks earlier. The following day, March 2, the Senate cleared the conference report (H Rept 109-333) by **a key vote of 89–10 (R 55–0; D 34–9; I 0–1).** *(2006 key votes, p. 937)*

Not all of the critics were satisfied. Sen. Russ Feingold, D-Wis., the only senator to vote against the original law in 2001, called the changes a "fig leaf" that did little to alter the legislation. "I'm mystified why everybody can say this is OK when we did not get any real changes," Feingold said.

The House cleared Sununu's bill 280–138 on March 7 under suspension of the rules, a process that bars amendments, limits debate, and requires a two-thirds majority for passage—in this case, 279 votes. Sununu visited the House floor during the vote to lobby members. His primary audience was House Democrats, many of whom dismissed the changes as trivial and expressed frustration at being barred from amending the legislation.

But the opposition could not overcome the support of the Republican majority, led by Sensenbrenner. By supporting the bill, Sensenbrenner honored the deal Sununu sealed Feb. 9 that ended a filibuster of the broader conference report on the legislation.

A week later, Bush signed the two measures together: the reauthorization (HR 3199—PL 109-177) and Sununu's bill (S 2271—PL 109-178).

MAJOR PROVISIONS

As signed into law March 9, 2006, HR 3199 (PL 109-177) included the following major provisions:

Temporary Extensions

Extended for four years, through 2009, the remaining two provisions—dealing with roving wiretaps and acquiring records—that were set to expire at the end of 2005:

- **Roving wiretaps.** Section 206, which authorized roving wiretaps on terrorism suspects, or orders that do not specify a single telephone or residence to be put under surveillance, but rather allowed taps on multiple phones and computers if a suspect changes communications methods or locations.
- **Acquiring records.** Section 215, which allowed federal law enforcement to seek a court order for "any tangible thing," such as business, bookstore, and library records that law enforcement officials deemed related to a terrorism investigation. The original conference report would have put a gag order on people who received requests for information under this provision, only allowing them to consult with a lawyer in order to challenge the request in court.

Under compromise language negotiated with the White House, the law allowed recipients to challenge such gag orders in court after one year. The gag order would stand if the attorney general, deputy attorney general, an assistant attorney general, or director of the FBI certified that disclosure may endanger national security unless a judge finds that the certification was made in bad faith.

In two final changes to the measure made in a compromise struck with the White House, the reauthorization removed a requirement that recipients of national security letters, which do not require court approval, disclose the name of attorneys they consult or intend to consult. It also clarified language in the 2001 law to ensure libraries that operate in traditional roles and not as Internet service providers are not subject to national security letters.

Permanent Extensions

The law permanently extended fourteen provisions of the antiterrorism act that were set to expire at the end of 2005, including the following:

- **Wiretaps.** Section 201, which allowed law enforcement authorities to use wiretaps and other surveillance measures to investigate suspected acts of terrorism.
- **Computers.** Section 202, which added computer fraud felonies to the list of violations that justify a federal wiretap.
- **Information sharing.** Sections 203 (b) and 203 (d), which allowed law enforcement and intelligence officers to share information in matters of national security.
- **Pen registers and trap devices.** Section 204, which clarified that the law governing the installation and use of pen registers and trap devices will not interfere with certain foreign intelligence activities that fall outside of electronic surveillance.
- **Extended wiretaps and warrants.** Section 207, which extended the duration of wiretaps and search warrants from 90 days to 120 days, with renewals extended for a maximum of one year. Orders and extensions required permission of a federal judge.

- **Voice mail seizure.** Section 209, which permitted stored voice mail to be obtained by a search warrant rather than a wiretap order, making the procedure for obtaining voice mail messages consistent with the procedure for obtaining answering machine messages.
- **Disclosure of customer records.** Section 212, which allowed electronic communications services providers to disclose either customer records or the content of customers' communications to a government entity in emergency situations involving immediate danger or death or serious physical injury.
- **Electronic surveillance.** Section 214, which made it easier under FISA to issue pen-register and trap-and-trace orders, which can be used to track telephone calls and Internet communications.
- **Computer hacking.** Section 217, which allowed victims of computer hacking to obtain law enforcement assistance in intercepting the electronic communications of a computer trespasser that have been transmitted to, from, or through a protected computer under limited circumstances.
- **FISA warrants.** Section 218, which lowered the threshold for law enforcement officers seeking search warrants under FISA. Before the law was enacted, agents could request a warrant only for the purpose of investigating foreign intelligence activity.
- **Warrants for electronic evidence.** Section 220, which allowed federal judges with jurisdiction over a particular investigation to issue search warrants for electronic evidence stored anywhere in the country.
- **Recompense.** Section 223, which allowed individuals to sue the federal government for money damages if a federal official discloses sensitive information without authorization.
- **Disclosure.** Section 225, which immunized from civil liability individuals who disclose information to the government in compliance with a FISA order.

Additional Antiterrorism Provisions

The law also provided several additional antiterrorism provisions, including:

- **Lone wolf terrorists.** Extended, until 2009, a provision in the 2004 intelligence overhaul law that allowed law enforcement to seek warrants from the Foreign Intelligence Surveillance Court against lone wolf terrorists not connected to a foreign power.
- **Duration of surveillance of foreign agents.** Extended the maximum duration of court-ordered electronic surveillance or physical searches targeted against agents of foreign powers to 120 days. The provision also extended the duration of surveillance that captures outgoing and incoming telephone numbers to one year in cases where such monitoring is likely to yield foreign intelligence information.
- **Delayed notices of search warrant.** Permitted the delay, for thirty days, of notifying an individual of a "sneak and peek" search resulting in the seizure of any property or material that constituted evidence of a criminal offense. It allowed that delay to be extended by up to ninety days if determined necessary by a judge.
- **Port security.** Set new criminal penalties for crimes relating to smuggling goods through ports, unauthorized entrance to ports, tampering with the Coast Guard's navigational devices, and theft or destruction of ships or seaport facilities.
- **Money laundering.** Increased criminal penalties for financing terrorist activities, and added certain illegal money-transferring businesses to the list of terrorism-related offenses that could be considered money laundering.

Bioterrorism Law

Congress in 2006 cleared a measure to renew a bioterrorism law enacted after the Sept. 11, 2001, terrorist attacks, which was due to expire that fall. President George W. Bush signed the bioterrorism bill into law Dec. 19 (S 3678—PL 109-417).

The 2002 Public Health Service Act (PL 107-188) had authorized the creation of a national stockpile of vaccines and medical devices for use in a catastrophe and established a position to coordinate the government's response to a public health emergency. *(Congress and the Nation Vol. XI, p. 206)*

In addition to renewing the 2002 law, the 2006 legislation created a new agency within the Department of Health and Human Services (HHS) to coordinate the research and production of vaccines for potential pandemics and biological weapons. The agency was called the Biomedical Advanced Research and Development Authority.

BACKGROUND

Intending to help Americans better prepare for a public health crisis or pandemic flu, North Carolina Republican senator Richard M. Burr introduced S 3678 in July 2006. Burr was chairman of the Senate Health, Education, Labor and Pensions (HELP) Subcommittee on Bioterrorism and Public Health Preparedness.

Burr also was reacting to the government's chaotic response to Hurricane Katrina in the fall of 2005, which had devastated New Orleans. The measure put HHS in charge of the medical response to a disaster by clarifying the lines of authority in an emergency. The HELP Committee approved the bill (S 3678) in July, but efforts to bring it to the floor were stalled by partisan maneuvering related to the midterm elections that fall.

Burr's subcommittee found that since 2002, several studies revealed how the public health law could be improved. Data from the Department of Homeland Security revealed that 68 percent of the states were not completely confident their health disaster plans would adequately manage a catastrophe, according to the report filed on the bill. Likewise, a 2005 RAND study concluded that local public health agencies were still unprepared to respond to a crisis quickly.

Congress had tried in 2004 to create a single federal entity to be responsible for coordinating all federal efforts to research and produce vaccines and cures for potential plagues and weapons through a law known as Project Bioshield (PL 108-276). The law authorized $5.6 billion over ten years to stockpile vaccines and other countermeasures against the most severe biological threats. But the pharmaceutical industry had proved reluctant to invest in drugs that might never be needed. Critics argued that the government was slow to establish priorities for responding to bioterrorism threats and to identify which products it wanted to buy. *(Congress and the Nation Vol. XI, p. 213)*

SENATE COMMITTEE ACTION

The HELP Committee easily approved Burr's bill by voice vote July 19, 2006. The measure, which Burr drafted with Edward M. Kennedy, D-Mass., proposed to reauthorize the 2002 law for five years, through 2011. While committee Democrats generally supported the measure, some believed it did not go far enough. Connecticut Democrat Christopher J. Dodd said he was disappointed that the committee did not include provisions addressing liability protections for vaccine manufacturers and compensation for people harmed by vaccines. Sen. Patty Murray, D-Wash., likewise backed the bill but said she had hoped the measure would also ensure that states could use funds to enter into agreements with Canada during public health emergencies.

In its report on the bill (S Rept 109-319), the committee cited the "uncoordinated and inadequate" local, state, and federal responses to Hurricane Katrina. It said one conclusion of the White House report on the lessons learned from that experience was that emergency medical responses "should be managed and overseen by HHS, which has the greatest health experience and expertise."

HOUSE ACTION

The Energy and Commerce Committee gave voice vote approval on Sept. 20 to a bipartisan bill (HR 5533—H Rept 109-686) aimed at solving some of the problems that were seen as limiting the effectiveness of Project Bioshield. Mike D. Rogers, R-Ala., the bill's sponsor, said he hoped it would entice companies to invest in biodefense. As with S 3678, the bill designated the HHS secretary as the lead federal official in charge of emergency public health and medical response, and transferred the National Disaster Medical System from the Department of Homeland Security to HHS. Energy and Commerce Committee members said that in light of what many termed the botched federal government response to Hurricane Katrina, the system would be most effective under a different department.

The House passed HR 5533 by voice vote with little debate on Sept. 26.

SENATE, FINAL ACTION

On Dec. 5, the Senate passed Burr's bill by voice vote after agreeing to an amendment by Burr to add the House provisions. Kennedy summed up the purpose of the legislation, saying it would "increase our medical surge capacity, strengthen our public health infrastructure and clarify the responsibilities of federal officials." No one spoke against the measure.

But the bill still faced one more hurdle. House Energy and Commerce Chairman Joe L. Barton, R-Texas, persuaded GOP leaders to hold off floor action and used the bill as leverage to get the Senate to clear separate legislation (HR 6164) he had written to restructure the National Institutes of Health (NIH). Barton also held up a bill to reauthorize the federal assistance program for low-income people with AIDS (HR 6143). After reaching an agreement Dec. 8, the Senate passed the NIH legislation Dec. 9, and the House cleared the bioterrorism bill, along with the two other measures, shortly before adjourning the same day. *(AIDS bill, p. 312; NIH, p. 545)*

MAJOR PROVISIONS

As signed into law Dec. 19, 2006, S 3678 (PL 109-417):

- Designated the HHS secretary as the lead federal official in charge of emergency public health and medical response, building on existing law.
- Transferred the National Disaster Medical System from the Department of Homeland Security to HHS.
- Renamed the assistant secretary of Health and Human Services for public health emergency preparedness as the assistant secretary for preparedness and response. (Among many responsibilities, that person oversaw the advanced development and procurement of countermeasures and managed the Strategic National Stockpile.
- Required the HHS secretary, beginning in 2009, to prepare and implement a national preparedness and response strategy to deal with major public health crises, followed by revised assessments every four years.
- Reauthorized $1 billion each year in federal grants to states for public health and medical preparedness. Required states and hospitals that receive federal resources and cooperative grants to meet minimum standards and to conduct regular exercises.
- Required the HHS secretary to establish a near real-time nationwide public health awareness network to better detect outbreaks and inform the public. Called on the HHS secretary to collaborate with state and local officials to create a voluntary electronic tracking network to monitor influenza vaccines that are available for distribution.
- Created the Biomedical Advanced Research and Development Authority within HHS to handle the development of drugs and vaccines in response to natural outbreaks and bioterrorism.

Coast Guard Authorizations

After failing to finish a bill in 2005, Congress finally cleared fiscal 2006 Coast Guard reauthorization legislation in June 2006, but a measure authorizing funds for fiscal 2007 remained stalled at the end of the 109th Congress. President George W. Bush signed the fiscal 2006 measure (HR 889—PL 109-241) on July 11.

BACKGROUND

The Coast Guard's role and its finances had received increased attention from Congress since the Sept. 11, 2001, terrorist attacks. Lawmakers were concerned that the maritime agency's transfer to the Homeland Security Department decreased its focus on security missions other than that for the homeland. A Government Accountability Office (GAO) report released in February 2003 said several of those missions, such as law enforcement, remained well below pre-Sept. 11, 2001, levels.

The two chambers disagreed over the level of funding for the Coast Guard. The House fiscal 2006 bill was a one-year, $8.7 billion authorization, while the Senate passed a two-year authorization of $8.2 billion in fiscal 2006 and $8.9 billion in fiscal 2007.

Beyond the money, the two chambers also differed over the Coast Guard's Deepwater modernization program, its long-term plan to update its fleet of cutters, aircraft, communication systems, and other equipment, and whether foreign crews should be allowed to work on some U.S.-flagged vessels.

On the crew issue, Don Young, R-Alaska, chairman of the House Transportation and Infrastructure Committee, championed a provision in the House bill to allow cruise and freighter operators to hire foreign workers for certain support positions such as wait staff, entertainment, and maintenance. Unions that represented sailors and marine engineers argued that the provision would weaken national security because it would water down citizenship requirements for the crew. Proponents argued that it would simply codify existing practices. The Senate bill did not contain the worker provision.

The 2006 bill, which ultimately authorized $8.7 billion for the Coast Guard in fiscal 2006, was enacted almost three-quarters of the way through the fiscal year, after both chambers agreed to alter language that would have blocked a wind-generating facility off the Massachusetts coast. Proposed by Young, the aim of the language was to block Cape Wind Associates from erecting 130 giant windmills off the coast of Massachusetts.

The project was opposed by state officials led by Sen. Edward M. Kennedy, D-Mass., whose Cape Cod home was just miles from the proposed windmill project, and by the state's governor, Republican Mitt Romney. The original language gave a veto over the project to the governor. Before being sent to the president, the bill was altered to give the final decision to the commandant of the Coast Guard, a change to which Kennedy and Young as well others opposed to the windmill project agreed.

HOUSE COMMITTEE ACTION

The House Transportation and Infrastructure Committee approved a one-year reauthorization bill by voice vote May 18, 2005 (HR 889—H Rept 109-204, Part 1) that recommended $8.7 billion for the Coast Guard in fiscal 2006.

The committee approved a substitute amendment by Frank A. LoBiondo, R-N.J., the chairman of the panel's Coast Guard and Maritime Transportation Subcommittee, that increased the authorized funding level for the Deepwater program to $1.6 billion. The increase was intended to address concerns about a Coast Guard plan to stretch out the program from its twenty-year schedule to as much as twenty-five years. Lawmakers said the longer timetable could result in construction of fewer vessels. The committee's total for Deepwater included $1.3 billion to acquire and build new vessels and aircraft and $284 million to maintain existing ones.

To help the Coast Guard maintain maritime security, the bill proposed redefining U.S. "navigable waters" to include territorial waters as far as twelve nautical miles offshore and allowing the Coast Guard to provide technical assistance to foreign maritime authorities.

HOUSE FLOOR ACTION

The House easily passed the bill 415–0 on Sept. 15, 2005, after agreeing by voice vote to authorize an extra $60 million to reimburse the Coast Guard for the cost of saving and rescuing about 33,500 people stranded by Hurricane Katrina, which had devastated New Orleans and the Gulf Coast on Aug. 29.

The bill also extended temporarily existing mariners' licenses and vessel certificates, many of which had been left in the Coast Guard's New Orleans office. Coast Guard personnel affected by the hurricane also would be deemed eligible for property losses under the bill.

During floor debate, the House adopted by voice vote Young's amendment to allow foreign workers to work in support jobs on U.S. cruise ships and freighters. The House also adopted by voice vote an amendment by Vito J. Fossella, R-N.Y., to require ferries that carried more than 399 passengers to be equipped with a "black box" recording device similar to those on commercial airliners. The provision was in response to the 2003 crash of a Staten Island ferry in which eleven passengers died and seventy more were injured.

SENATE COMMITTEE ACTION

The Senate Commerce, Science, and Transportation Committee gave voice vote approval June 23, 2005, to a two-year bill (S 1280—S Rept 109-114) to authorize $8.2 billion in fiscal 2006 and $8.9 billion in fiscal 2007.

The committee rejected the Coast Guard's plan to stretch out the timetable for replacing aging ships and aircraft under its Deepwater program. "The Coast Guard's revised plan is falling far short of the mark," said Olympia J. Snowe, R-Maine. "We are putting our men and women in harm's way." Snowe said previous studies, including the Coast Guard's data, "do not buttress" the revised Deepwater plan.

The bill directed the Coast Guard to write a new plan that accelerated the completion date to between ten and fifteen years and to meet a number of new reporting requirements. The authorization included $1.1 billion in fiscal 2006 and $1.2 billion in fiscal 2007 for the program.

The committee proposed stiffer civil penalties for violating maritime laws and enhanced tools for the Coast Guard to enforce those laws. As recommended by the U.S. Commission on Ocean Policy, it directed the Coast Guard to develop a process for determining when damaged vessels could seek refuge in the United States. The bill also instructed the Coast Guard to take steps to improve the detection and interdiction of foreign vessels that violated fishing regulations.

SENATE FLOOR ACTION

Senators called up HR 889 on Oct. 27, 2005, then struck its language and inserted the text of the companion bill S 1280. The Senate then passed the bill by voice vote.

The Senate's version authorized $1.1 billion in fiscal 2006 and $1.2 billion in fiscal 2007 for Deepwater. It also required the Coast Guard to complete the program in ten to fifteen years. Senators also adopted an amendment addressing the aftermath of hurricanes Katrina and Rita. The amendment extended annual leave for Coast Guard participants in the disaster relief effort. It also authorized the Coast Guard authority to extend temporarily the expiration date of merchant marine licenses and vessel inspection certifications if documents were lost or damaged during the hurricanes.

CONFERENCE, FINAL ACTION

Although both the Senate and House promptly appointed conferees, no agreement between the two chambers was reached until April 2006. Conference negotiations were delayed by the amendment dealing with the Massachusetts "wind farm." Young's amendment, which gave the governor of Massachusetts veto authority on the windmill project, made it into the conference report but was later changed when both chambers adopted a joint resolution, after the conference report was approved, that gave the final decision to the Coast Guard commandant rather than the Massachusetts governor.

Young said the wind farm could create a navigational hazard in Nantucket Sound. Other critics argued that the windmills would blight the scenery and deter tourism, costing the region jobs. Environmentalists were split: some said the blades could kill migrating seabirds, while others supported the project, saying it would generate enough clean energy to power 75 percent of Cape Cod, Nantucket, and Martha's Vineyard.

On the Deepwater program, conferees adopted the House figure of $1.6 billion for fiscal 2006. However, fiscal 2006 funds had already been appropriated, and Deepwater received only $933 million. While they did not include the time line directive in the Senate version, conferees said the $1.6 billion authorization level would have been enough to accelerate the program's completion. *(Fiscal 2006 Homeland Security appropriations, p. 77)*

The conference report on the bill also included the contentious provision to permit cruise and freighter operators to hire foreign support and maintenance workers for up to sixty days annually. Young had inserted the measure into the House bill. Meanwhile, the conferees omitted provisions to address "critical port security shortfalls" that Snowe sought to add after the recent flap over foreign control of U.S. port facilities. *(Port security, p. 237)*

Conferees also included a provision in the House bill to raise the oil spill liability limits in the Oil Pollution Act of 1990. The cap on what owners or operators of vessels must pay in the case of accidents was supposed to be adjusted to reflect changes in inflation every three years. Nonetheless, the cap had never been updated.

The conference report (H Rept. 109-413) was agreed to in the House by a vote of 413–0 under suspension of the rules on June 27, 2006. The Senate adopted the conference report the next day.

FISCAL YEAR 2007 APPROPRIATIONS

On the same day that the Senate cleared the fiscal 2006 Coast Guard authorization—June 28, 2006—the House Transportation and Infrastructure Committee approved legislation (HR 5681) by voice vote authorizing $9 billion for the Coast Guard in fiscal 2007.

The panel gave the bill the green light after adopting two amendments by voice vote. One, by subcommittee chairman LoBiondo, accelerated the Deepwater program by ordering completion of the program in fifteen years. The amendment increased Deepwater's funding to about $1.7 billion, from $1.1 billion in the original bill.

LoBiondo incorporated into his amendment changes to the legislation sought by his colleagues on both sides of the aisle, including a provision that would make the Coast Guard the primary federal entity responsible for providing maritime security for nuclear facilities located on navigable waters.

Sue W. Kelly, R-N.Y., who represented an area of the Hudson Valley just north of New York City that included the Indian Point nuclear power facility, sought the provision. Kelly said efforts to protect nuclear facilities from terrorist attacks were inadequate.

The underlying legislation made permanent a 500-person increase in the number of authorized Coast Guard officers, to 6,700. The agency was granted a temporary increase after the Sept. 11, 2001, terrorist attacks.

HOUSE ACTION

The House passed the fiscal 2007 bill (HR 5681—H Rept 109-614), by voice vote Sept. 28, 2006. It authorized $9 billion for the Coast Guard and directed the service to complete the Deepwater program in fifteen years, rather than twenty-five. It included provisions to increase the Coast Guard's responsibility to help safeguard nuclear power facilities, in part by allowing the service to provide enhanced security at nuclear plants near navigable waters. Coast Guard officers could be assigned as liaisons to the Nuclear Regulatory Commission (NRC).

Other provisions sought to make permanent a temporary increase in Coast Guard commissioned officers to 6,700 from 6,200, and to allow service members to carry firearms, make arrests without warrants and, in some cases, seize property. The Senate did not consider the measure in 2006.

The day after the House passed the Coast Guard measure, Congress cleared the fiscal 2007 Homeland Security spending legislation (HR 5441) that provided fewer funds for the Coast Guard than HR 5681 authorized. The fiscal 2007 spending bill (PL 109-295), which became law on Oct. 4, 2006, provided $8.4 billion for the Coast Guard, with $1.4 billion of that allocated to fund the Deepwater program. *(Fiscal 2007 Homeland Security spending bill, p. 102)*

Homeland Security Department

A measure to reauthorize the Department of Homeland Security was approved by the full House in 2005 and by the House Homeland Security Committee in 2006, but the Senate did not act on either bill. The measures were largely symbolic as funding for the national security agency was received through its annual appropriations measure. *(Homeland Security appropriations, pp. 77, 102, 114, 126)*

The House on May 18, 2005, passed the first-ever reauthorization bill (HR 1817) for the Department of Homeland Security, but the committee responsible for the legislation in the Senate pushed consideration to 2006 because it was preoccupied with an investigation into the government's response to Hurricane Katrina.

BACKGROUND

The force behind House passage of the fiscal 2006 reauthorization bill was Christopher Cox, R-Calif., who chaired the House Homeland Security Committee until Aug. 2, when he resigned his seat to become chairman of the Securities and Exchange Commission (SEC). Cox argued that by producing annual bills similar to those that authorize the Department of Defense, Congress would affirm the status of the three-year-old Homeland Security Department as an important part of the federal government's national security apparatus.

In the Senate, Maine Republican Susan Collins, who chaired the Homeland Security and Governmental Affairs Committee, started out with the intention of waiting until 2006 to mark up an authorization bill to give her panel time to study the issues. Then in July, Homeland Security Secretary Michael Chertoff announced plans for restructuring the department. Collins said she was inclined to move the timetable up a year to address elements of Chertoff's plan that needed congressional approval and to incorporate her proposals on the structure and policies of the department. But Collins's plans were interrupted following Hurricane Katrina when Majority Leader Bill Frist, R-Tenn., tasked her committee to lead the Senate inquiry into the government response to the hurricane.

Meanwhile, House and Senate negotiators reached agreement on the fiscal 2006 Homeland Security appropriations bill (PL 109-90), which accommodated nearly all of Chertoff's restructuring proposals. These included the creation of a centralized intelligence office and a new consolidated preparedness division that would allow the Federal Emergency Management Agency (FEMA) to focus strictly on recovery and response to disasters. *(FEMA, p. 236)*

HOUSE COMMITTEE ACTION

In a testament to the tangle of overlapping responsibilities in Congress for authorizing and overseeing homeland security programs, the reauthorization bill had to make its way through three House committees before going to the floor. Five other panels could have weighed in, but agreed not to do so.

In the Homeland Security Committee, Cox won approval for his $34.2 billion authorization measure on April 27, 2005 (HR 1817—H Rept 109-71, Part 1). The committee acted by voice vote.

The bill called for the hiring of 2,000 Border Patrol agents and included provisions to refine the department's much-maligned color-coded terror alert system, instructing the department to provide more-specific directions for responding to increases in the warning level. It also prescribed remedies to boost its frequently struggling intelligence wing. The authorization was in line with President George W. Bush's budget request for the department.

The Homeland Security Department had the fifth-highest discretionary budget in the federal government, and Cox said it should be authorized annually. But Cox also had another goal: sealing the legitimacy of the committee itself. The House rules package that made his committee permanent in January included language to allow chairmen of at least ten other committees to claim jurisdiction over legislation that would affect various agencies and policies of the department.

To circumvent potential conflicts with other committees, Cox fended off most major amendments to the bill during the markup. Democrats initially sought an additional $7 billion, as well as language on port security, aviation security, and other topics not covered by the legislation. In the end, Cox won their support.

The House Energy and Commerce Committee approved the bill by voice vote May 11, 2005 (H Rept 109-71, Part 2), after rewriting significant portions of a cybersecurity provision.

The panel agreed by voice vote to an amendment to strip some of the new powers the Homeland Security Committee wanted to confer on the department's top cybersecurity official. Chairman Joe L. Barton, R-Texas, said he also wrote language to ensure that nothing in the bill would intrude on the powers of other agencies that protected computer networks.

The bill created an assistant secretary for cybersecurity to oversee a National Cybersecurity Office and the National Communications System. Barton's amendment left in place the assistant secretary position but eliminated the National Cybersecurity Office and deleted any new cybersecurity initiatives.

The House Judiciary Committee approved the bill by voice vote May 12 (H Rept 109-71, Part 3), after adopting an amendment to clarify the definition of "terrorism prevention" to mean border and infrastructure security, information dissemination, and first-responder preparedness.

HOUSE FLOOR ACTION

The House passed the bill by a vote of 424–4 on May 18, 2005.

Democrats, led by the ranking member on the Homeland Security Committee, Bennie Thompson of Mississippi, fought unsuccessfully to expand the scope of the measure with proposals that would have added $6.9 billion to the authorization and covered a broader sweep of homeland security. Their substitute amendment was rejected, 196–230.

The House Rules Committee barred more than sixty amendments from coming to the floor, provoking complaints from lawmakers on both sides of the aisle who intended to offer changes. The House still considered two dozen amendments and adopted more than half of them, including a proposal by Cox and House Judiciary Chairman F. James Sensenbrenner Jr., R-Wis., adopted by voice vote, to authorize $40 million to help state and local officials enforce federal immigration laws.

HOMELAND SECURITY REAUTHORIZATION

In a largely symbolic gesture, the House Homeland Security Committee in 2006 approved a $34.7 fiscal 2007 authorization bill for the Department of Homeland Security (HR 5814—H Rept 109-713, Part 1) on July 19. The vote was 30–1.

Rep. Peter King, R-N.Y., who took over as chairman of the committee after Cox left, did not have the bill on his agenda at the start of 2006, arguing that the panel should concentrate on legislation, such as port security, that had a realistic chance of being enacted. *(Port security, p. 237)*

King's Senate counterpart, Republican Susan Collins of Maine, also had other priorities: leading the Senate inquiry on the handling of Hurricane Katrina and preparing legislation to overhaul FEMA. Her committee did not consider an authorization bill. *(FEMA, p. 236; Hurricane Katrina, pp. 791, 797)*

But the Democrats on King's panel complained publicly about the chairman's decision, arguing that an authorization bill was vital to establishing the jurisdiction of the committee, which was formed as a select committee in 2002 and did not gain status as a standing committee of the House until 2005. Shortly thereafter, the panel's subcommittees began approving an array of mini-authorization measures, which were combined into the department-wide bill the committee approved in July.

The measure would have revised the formula for distributing state and local grants, basing them more on risk. It would have authorized most aspects of a departmental reorganization that Homeland Security Secretary Chertoff had carried out in 2005 and would have abolished the Management Directorate, allowing the chief operating officers to report directly to the secretary. The bill also included an amendment to require annual reports to Congress on a controversial database of high-risk infrastructure sites maintained by the department.

"Being a new committee, it's more of an obligation," King said of the measure. However, the committee's approval came after the House had passed the fiscal 2007 appropriations bill for the Homeland Security Department, giving it little chance of influencing the funding levels.

Domestic Warrantless Surveillance

The *New York Times* in December 2005 reported that President George W. Bush had secretly authorized domestic surveillance of U.S. citizens without first obtaining court approval. As a result of the article, members of both parties introduced bills to establish oversight of the National Security Agency (NSA) program, which reportedly monitored overseas telephone calls and e-mails of U.S. citizens in an effort to obtain terrorist communications.

But congressional efforts to establish new rules to govern the NSA program were unsuccessful. The House passed a bill in September 2006 to provide a legal basis for the warrantless surveillance. The Senate Judiciary Committee approved several proposals, none of which reached the floor, and the legislation died at the end of the 109th Congress.

BACKGROUND

The White House maintained that President Bush had the authority to order the eavesdropping under the 2001 law (PL 107-40) that authorized the use of force in response to the Sept. 11 terrorist attacks. Bush also claimed that his constitutional status as commander in chief enabled him to bypass federal laws on domestic surveillance as part of his war against terrorism.

Critics, however, said that the domestic surveillance program was illegal because it did not comply with the Foreign Intelligence Surveillance Act (FISA, PL 95-511), a 1978 law that required the government to get approval from a special FISA court before beginning electronic surveillance within the United States outside of criminal statutes. The law stated that the FISA procedure was the "exclusive means" to govern such surveillance. At the time, the Senate Judiciary Committee said the provisions were necessary to "curb the practice by which the executive branch may conduct warrantless electronic surveillance on its own unilateral determination that national security justifies it." *(FISA, Congress and the Nation Vol. V, p. 720; 110th Congress action on FISA, pp. 249, 251)*

The Bush administration had briefed congressional leaders and top members of the Intelligence committees on the NSA program but balked at widening that circle. Eventually, on the eve of a Senate Intelligence confirmation hearing for Gen. Michael V. Hayden to head the Central Intelligence Agency (CIA), the administration agreed to brief all members of the two committees.

The most prominent legislative effort came from Senate Judiciary Chairman Arlen Specter, R-Pa., who had not been briefed on the details of the NSA program. Specter held a series of high-profile hearings on the issue before introducing legislation (S 2453) in March that became the main Senate legislative vehicle.

Specter negotiated critical changes to his bill with the Bush White House before winning approval from the Judiciary Committee in September. The Senate panel also approved two competing bills, but none of the three measures reached the floor. Intelligence chairman Pat Roberts, R-Kan., indicated that his panel would weigh in, but the committee never marked up legislation.

The House got a later start but made more progress on its legislation, sponsored by Heather A. Wilson, R-N.M. The House bill (HR 5825) sought to give the president greater flexibility to authorize warrantless surveillance in times of war or attack but also required that more members of Congress be privy to more information about warrantless spying conducted in the United States. The Judiciary and Intelligence committees approved separate versions of the bill in September, and the House passed a compromise version later that month, but the bill went no further.

In January 2007 Attorney General Alberto R. Gonzales notified top members of the Senate Judiciary Committee that the FISA court had issued orders Jan. 10 authorizing the surveillance. As a result, he said, President Bush would not reauthorize the warrantless NSA program. The Justice Department declined to describe the specifics of the FISA court orders, such as whether they were narrowly tailored or gave the government broad surveillance authority, but said the FISA court had issued more than one order.

By involving the special court, Bush appeared to bow to the program's congressional critics. But the move also helped the White House undercut congressional oversight of the program and possibly judicial review by regular federal courts.

SENATE COMMITTEE ACTION

After numerous delays, the Senate Judiciary Committee approved Specter's bill (S 2453) 10–8 on Sept. 13, 2006. Specter, whose overarching goal was to engineer judicial review of the NSA surveillance program, had spent months negotiating changes to pick up support from other Republicans on the committee, including conservatives who did not want to restrict Bush.

As introduced, the bill required the attorney general to get approval for the surveillance program from the FISA court. The court could authorize surveillance for up to forty-five days and renew the order for another forty-five days after a fresh request.

At a June 8 committee meeting, Specter won voice vote approval for a substitute that included several significant changes bolstering the president's claim of broad executive authority to conduct the activity. Specter said he was conceding temporarily to other panel Republicans, particularly Jon Kyl of Arizona, to move his bill out of the committee, but he added that he would seek changes on the Senate floor.

Specter's substitute dropped the requirement that the administration get approval from the FISA court. It provided that if the attorney general did not seek approval for the surveillance, federal judges would have to direct legal challenges to the program to the FISA court if there was a "at least a substantial question" that the challenging party had come under surveillance. The substitute also provided significant changes to the 1978 law, including deleting the language that established the law as the exclusive means to govern such surveillance outside criminal statutes.

Specter delayed further committee action while negotiating with the White House. On Aug. 3, the Judiciary Committee by voice vote approved a substitute incorporating terms of a deal Specter had reached with Bush. Although not required under the substitute, Specter said Bush pledged to submit the NSA program to the FISA court if Congress did not make any further changes to the bill that the president disliked.

Committee Democrats used a variety of delaying tactics to slow further committee consideration of the bill. They said Specter had agreed to legislative language that would help Bush win in court by putting a congressional imprimatur on his argument that his constitutional status as commander in chief gave him the authority to conduct warrantless surveillance. In addition to deleting the exclusive-means language from the statute, Specter's substitute explicitly bowed to "the constitutional authority of the president" to conduct such surveillance. Russ Feingold, D-Wis., described Specter's bill as "a dramatic expansion of presidential power."

The committee also approved two other bills:

- **S 2455.** A bill by Mike DeWine, R-Ohio, to subject the NSA program to more congressional oversight and give the administration the option of seeking approval from the secret court for surveillance of particular targets. The committee approved it 10–8 along party lines.
- **S 3001.** An alternative bill by Specter and Dianne Feinstein, D-Calif., to streamline FISA procedures and reiterate that FISA and criminal statutes were the exclusive means for conducting electronic surveillance on American citizens in the United States. The vote was 10–8.

Senate Minority Whip Richard J. Durbin of Illinois indicated that Democrats would try to assemble a majority of votes for Feinstein's proposal. Specter, who predicted he had the votes in the Senate to pass his own bill, said he might seek to incorporate some of the Specter-Feinstein provisions.

Majority Leader Bill Frist, R-Tenn., introduced a revised version of Specter's main approach, both as a stand-alone bill (S 3931) and combined with legislation authorizing military tribunals for terrorism suspects (S 3929). The Senate eventually acted on a stand-alone military tribunals bill (S 3930) but never took up Specter's bill. *(Military detainees, p. 399)*

HOUSE COMMITTEE ACTION

The House Intelligence Committee approved its version of the bill (HR 5825—H Rept 109-680, Part 1) by voice vote Sept. 20, 2006, after voting 9–8 to adopt a substitute by Wilson. Her original legislation, which remained largely intact in the Intelligence panel, proposed to extend the number of days the administration could conduct emergency surveillance without a warrant from three to five, when an application had to be submitted for approval to the FISA court. The bill also gave the executive branch longer periods of time for warrantless surveillance in the event of a terrorist attack.

Wilson's substitute amendment, drafted with committee chairman Peter Hoekstra, R-Mich., added provisions to authorize expanded warrantless surveillance for fixed, renewable periods before an "imminent attack," as the administration wanted, as well as after an attack. Wilson said she left the term loosely defined to give the administration discretion to conduct surveillance on terrorist plots that would cause "serious injury" or "substantial economic damage."

The bill required the president to notify the congressional Intelligence committees and the FISA court. The chairmen of the House and Senate Intelligence panels were allowed to share the substance of the administration's reports on electronic surveillance with all members of the committees.

Committee Democrats charged that Republicans did the White House's bidding by expanding presidential power and that the bill "allows for broad eavesdropping on Americans in violation of the Fourth Amendment." After a testy debate, the House Judiciary Committee approved an amended version of the bill (HR 5825—H Rept 109-680, Part 2) by a vote of 20–16 on Sept. 20.

Before approving the bill, the committee adopted several GOP amendments including:

- A proposal by Chairman F. James Sensenbrenner Jr., R-Wis., that deleted two sections of the bill concerning surveillance authority after the country was attacked. Sensenbrenner said that "the mission of the government is to prevent another attack" rather than simply reacting after an attack had occurred. It was adopted by voice vote.
- A twenty-five-page amendment by Dan Lungren, R-Calif., that narrowed many of the bill's provisions. Lungren said that although the original measure went "in the right direction overall," it "probably went too far." After the markup, Lungren said that his amendment, adopted 17–2, incorporated several changes sought by the administration. Democrats objected that they had not seen Lungren's lengthy proposal before he offered it. "This sounds like a 'trust me' amendment," said John Conyers Jr., D-Mich.
- An amendment by Chris Cannon, R-Utah, to bar courts from imposing any penalties "relating to any alleged intelligence program involving electronic surveillance" if the attorney general or a designee certified that the program was intended to prevent a terrorist attack. Democrats said Cannon's amendment, adopted 22–16, would allow the attorney general to grant immunity for illegal activity.
- An amendment by Jeff Flake, R-Ariz., adopted by voice vote, to insert a congressional finding that the Constitution gives Congress "clear authority to regulate the president's inherent power to gather foreign intelligence." But an attempt by Flake and Adam B. Schiff, D-Calif., to streamline the FISA application process and underscore that FISA was the exclusive means for conducting foreign intelligence surveillance on U.S. soil was rejected on an 18–20 vote.

HOUSE FLOOR ACTION

The House passed a measure based on an agreement by the two committees that largely tracked the version reported by the Intelligence panel. The House approved the bill Sept. 28 on a **key vote of 232–191 (R 214–13; D 18–177; I 0–1).** *(2006 key votes, p. 937)*

Under the bill, the president could authorize warrantless electronic surveillance for up to ninety days in the case of an armed attack against the United States, a terrorist attack against the country or an imminent threat that was likely to cause death or widespread harm. The administration would have to notify the House and Senate Intelligence committees and the FISA court of such surveillance.

The amount of time that the government could conduct emergency warrantless surveillance before seeking FISA court approval was extended to seven days. A warrant to conduct electronic surveillance on a specific suspect within the United States remained effective if the suspect left the country and then returned. The chairmen and ranking members of the Intelligence committees could share the contents of the administration's reports with all members of the committees on a bipartisan basis.

Democrats argued that the bill yielded too much discretion to the executive branch and threatened constitutional rights. "It is a White House dream," said Anna G. Eshoo, D-Calif. "It is a blank check for the president."

The House rejected, 202–221, a motion by Flake, Schiff, Jane Harman, D-Calif., and Bob Inglis, R-S.C., to recommit the bill and substitute language reiterating that the existing FISA law was the exclusive means to govern the surveillance. The motion authorized additional resources and procedural changes in an attempt to speed processing of FISA warrant applications. After some ambivalence, the White House announced its support for the bill just hours before the House passed it.

Driver License Restrictions

House Republicans in February 2005 won quick enactment of legislation to crack down on illegal immigrants and tighten U.S. border security. Although the House initially passed the provisions as a separate bill, most of them became law as part of an $82 billion supplemental spending bill for operations in Iraq and Afghanistan. President George W. Bush signed that bill May 11 (HR 1268—PL 109-13). *(HR 1268 details, pp. 78, 348)*

As passed by the House, the original bill (HR 418) made it harder for illegal immigrants to seek asylum or get driver's licenses and removed some obstacles to the construction of physical barriers along portions of the U.S.-Mexico border. The driving force behind the legislation was House Judiciary Committee Chairman F. James Sensenbrenner Jr., R-Wis., who said his intent was to "prevent another 9/11-type terrorist attack by disrupting terrorist travel." *(2006 border fence legislation, p. 694)*

Most of the provisions had been included in the 2004 intelligence overhaul bill (PL 108-458), but House Republican leaders agreed to drop them as the price of getting the measure through the Senate. To placate an infuriated Sensenbrenner, GOP leaders promised that the provisions would be included in the first must-move piece of legislation in 2005. *(2004 Intelligence overhaul, Congress and the Nation Vol. XI, p. 263)*

Senate Majority Leader Bill Frist of Tennessee had tried to keep the immigration language out of the supplemental in his chamber for fear it would cause major delays. But House leaders were insistent, and the Senate ended up adding its proposal to allow more temporary seasonal workers into the country. Most of Sensenbrenner's language survived in the war supplemental, though conferees tweaked some of the provisions to make them more acceptable in the Senate. The Senate amendment also was included.

HOUSE FLOOR ACTION

In one of its first major legislative actions of the year, the House passed Sensenbrenner's bill (HR 418), which he called the Real ID Act, by a vote of 261–161 on Feb. 10, 2005. The White House issued a statement the day before the vote saying it "strongly" supported the Sensenbrenner asylum bill. President Bush was promoting a policy that stressed border security and a guest-worker visa program that would allow immigrants to fill low-skill jobs. His support for the asylum bill was seen as part of his effort to woo reluctant Republicans who opposed any initiatives they saw as giving "amnesty" to lawbreakers.

The National Conference of State Legislatures opposed the driver's license provisions, saying they would be costly and burdensome for states to implement. But many lawmakers, particularly those from states that would not see dramatic changes under the legislation, said the language made sense. Ten states did not require people to show they had a lawful presence in the United States before issuing them driver's licenses. An eleventh state, Tennessee, issued separate driver's licenses and certificates for those who could prove legal residency and for those who could not.

A month after the House passed Sensenbrenner's bill, GOP leaders added the immigration provisions to the supplemental (HR 1268) as part of the rule for floor debate (H Res 151). The rule was adopted by voice vote. The House passed the supplemental, 388–43 on March 16.

Despite Frist's statements that he preferred to handle the crackdown on illegal immigrants in a separate bill, House Republicans said they were confident that the provisions would eventually be included in the supplemental sent to the president.

SENATE FLOOR ACTION

Senate appropriators pointedly excluded immigration provisions from their version of the supplemental (HR 1268—S Rept 109-52), but senators immediately began offering amendments once the bill reached the floor. The debate sidetracked action on the spending bill for nearly a week, but in the end the only major amendment adopted was a proposal to allow more seasonal workers into the country.

The amendment, by Barbara A. Mikulski, D-Md., exempted seasonal workers who had worked in the United States in previous years from a cap on the number of so-called H-2B visas issued nationwide. Amendment backers said the cap of 66,000 had been reached early in the fiscal year, leaving an insufficient workforce for the summer tourism and seafood harvesting seasons. Hotels, restaurants, and the crab and lobster industries were particularly dependent on temporary immigrants. The amendment was adopted 94–6. The Senate passed the supplemental spending bill 99–0 on April 21.

CONFERENCE, FINAL ACTION

House and Senate conferees began meeting on the supplemental in late April under intense pressure from the Pentagon, which said troops in Iraq would run out of money after the first week of May. They reached agreement on a conference report May 3. The House adopted the report (H Rept 109-72) 368–58 on May 5, after rejecting a motion by David R. Obey of Wisconsin, the ranking Democrat on the Appropriations Committee, to return it to the conference committee with instructions to adopt the higher Senate funding level for immigration and customs enforcement. Obey's motion was rejected 201–225. The Senate cleared the measure 100–0 on May 10.

The conference agreement on the supplemental spending bill kept the House immigration provisions largely intact. Sensenbrenner credited the White House with ensuring that the language was included in the final bill. Senate conferees won a few concessions that softened some House language, but sponsors and opponents agreed they made changes only at the margins. "Democrats were shut out of all negotiations in conference, and none of our concerns were addressed," said John Conyers Jr. of Michigan, the ranking Democrat on House Judiciary.

MAJOR PROVISIONS

As signed into law May 11, 2005, HR 1268 (PL 109-13) included the following major provisions:

- **Federal use.** Prohibited driver's licenses that did not meet the requirements set out in the law from being used by federal agencies for any official purpose, beginning three years after enactment. Required state-issued driver's licenses or identification cards that did not satisfy the requirements to indicate on the face of the card that it was not acceptable for federal identification or other purposes. Required such licenses to use a unique design or color to indicate that they were not acceptable for federal purposes. (Other than the three-year deadline the law did not set a time for states to comply with the new requirements.)
- **License physical features.** Required licenses to include the driver's full legal name, date of birth, gender, driver's license or identification card number, digital photo, address of principal residence, and signature. Required the licenses to have "physical security features" designed to prevent anyone from changing or duplicating them, and to use a common machine-readable technology.
- **Issuance requirements.** Required an applicant for a license to present, and states to verify, the authenticity of a photo identity document, documentation showing the applicant's date of birth, proof of a Social Security number, and documentation showing the applicant's name and address of principal residence. Required applicants to provide valid documentary evidence that they were lawfully in the United States as citizens; were immigrants lawfully admitted for permanent or temporary residency; were recipients of or applicants for conditional permanent status, asylum, or refugee status; or that they had a valid unexpired nonimmigrant visa.
- Permitted applicants who had a pending asylum application or pending approval for temporary protected status, had approved deferred action status, or had a pending application for adjustment of status to permanent residency to be issued a temporary driver's license or temporary identification card.
- Allowed temporary licenses and identification cards to remain valid only during the time the applicant was authorized to stay in the United States, or for one year in instances in which the period was indefinite. Permitted their renewal only if the applicant's stay was extended by the Department of Homeland Security. Specified that licenses that were not temporary could not be valid for more than eight years.
- **Document verification.** Required states, before issuing a license or identification card, to verify the validity and completeness of all documents with the agencies that issued them. Prohibited states from accepting any foreign documents other than official passports. Required states, by Sept. 11, 2005, to agree to routinely use an automated system, the Systematic Alien Verification for Entitlements, maintained by the Department of Homeland Security, to verify the legal presence of persons other than U.S. citizens. Required applicants' Social Security numbers to be confirmed with the Social Security Administration.
- **Record maintenance and access.** Required states to retain digital copies of documents presented by applicants and take digital pictures of them, and to retain the digital copies for ten years, or paper copies for seven years. Required states to provide other states with electronic access to their motor vehicle database that contained all the data printed on the driver's licenses or identification cards as well as the license holders' histories of violations and suspensions.
- **Counterfeits.** Made it a crime to traffic in either false or actual authentication features used in false documents. Provided that information about persons convicted of using false driver's licenses at airports would be included in aviation security screening databases.
- **Funding.** Authorized the Homeland Security secretary to make grants to help states conform to the new driver's license standards. Authorized "such sums as may be necessary" but did not specify a dollar amount.

Library and Bookstore Records

The House, but not the Senate, in 2005 sought to limit the FBI's ability to access library and bookstore records under the 2001 antiterrorism law known as the USA PATRIOT Act (PL 107-56). The provision was added to a $61.8 billion fiscal 2006 spending bill for the Departments of Commerce, Justice, and State (HR 2862) in November 2005. The Senate did not include the provision and conferees removed it from the final version. President George W. Bush signed HR 2862 on Nov. 22 (PL 109-108). *(2001 USA PATRIOT Act, Congress and the Nation Vol. XI, p. 187; HR 2862 details, p. 76; USA PATRIOT Act reauthorization, p. 222)*

The House language was added by Independent Bernard Sanders of Vermont and barred the use of funds in the bill to search library circulation records, library patron lists, book sales records, or book customer lists under the Foreign Intelligence Surveillance Act (FISA, PL 95-511). The power to conduct such searches was originally granted under the Patriot Act. *(FISA, Congress and the Nation Vol. V, p. 720)*

Sanders's amendment was adopted June 15, 2005, by a **key vote of 238–187 (R 38–186; D 199–1; I 1–0).** *(2005 key votes, p. 915)*

Thirty-eight Republicans supported Sanders despite a White House warning that Bush would likely veto the bill if it contained the restriction. Adoption of the amendment was seen as a sign of bipartisan unease about portions of the sweeping antiterrorism law. The White House had urged Congress to swiftly renew and make permanent the powers provided in the antiterrorism law. Howard Coble, R-N.C., and other critics of Sanders's amendment said investigators need all tools to combat terrorism and noted the authority granted has never been directed at either booksellers or libraries.

But the provision became a magnet for criticism across the political spectrum as an example of excessive power granted by the antiterrorism law. "A number of conservatives voted conservatively today and 'conservative' means limited government," said Sanders, who pumped his arm in the air to Democratic applause as he left the chamber.

But when the Commerce, Justice, State appropriations bill was considered in conference in early November, the committee stripped Sanders's language from the bill. The House adopted the conference report (H Rept 109-272) by a vote of 397–19 on Nov. 9. The Senate cleared the bill 94–5 on Nov. 16.

FEMA Overhaul

The future of the Federal Emergency Management Agency (FEMA) was the subject of extensive debate during the 109th Congress after the agency's widely criticized response to Hurricane Katrina in the fall of 2005. The central issue was whether to remove the once-independent agency from the Homeland Security Department, which had absorbed it in March 2003. *(Homeland Security Department, Congress and the Nation Vol. IX, p. 176)*

Congress eventually cleared legislation to retool the nation's troubled disaster-response agency while leaving it in the Department of Homeland Security. The overhaul of FEMA was enacted as part of the fiscal 2007 Homeland Security appropriations bill (HR 5441), which President George W. Bush signed into law Oct. 4, 2006 (PL 109-295). *(HR 5441 appropriations, p. 102)*

After the devastation of New Orleans by Hurricane Katrina and the lack of a coordinated federal response to the events, many lawmakers complained that FEMA was buried under layers of departmental bureaucracy that focused on terrorism and was not nimble enough in responding to natural disasters. Those who supported keeping FEMA within Homeland Security countered that removing the agency would further disrupt it and create new, duplicative layers of bureaucracy.

SENATE FLOOR ACTION

FEMA's status was debated in both the House and Senate in 2006. Sen. Trent Lott, R-Miss., who lost a home to Katrina, was one of the most vocal advocates in the Senate for returning FEMA to an independent status. In late June, however, Maine Republican Susan Collins, who chaired the Senate Homeland Security and Governmental Affairs Committee, convinced Lott otherwise. Drawing on the recommendations of a report on the hurricane issued by her panel in May, Collins and Lott introduced a bill (S 3595) to give FEMA more autonomy but keep it within the Homeland Security Department. The revamped agency would have independent, autonomous status within Homeland Security, similar to the Coast Guard. The primary recommendation of Collins's committee staff, which for seven months studied the response to Katrina, was the creation of a new agency that combined national preparedness and response. The committee report said the agency should be housed within the Homeland Security Department but be able to report directly to the president during a crisis.

With limited time to get legislation through the Senate in an election year, Collins attached an amendment to the Senate's version of the Homeland Security appropriations bill that incorporated many of the changes proposed in her separate bill. It was adopted July 11 on a **key vote of 87–11 (R 51–2; D 36–8; I 0–1).** The House version of the bill did not contain a similar provision. *(2006 key votes, p. 937)*

The amendment gave FEMA more autonomy and its director more power to advise the president on disasters. Proponents compared the director's enhanced position to that of the chairman of the Joint Chiefs of Staff, who advises the president on defense issues.

Under the legislation, the FEMA administrator was required to have five years of executive experience and an emergency management background, a provision aimed at avoiding the appointment of another FEMA administrator such as Michael D. Brown, who was head of the agency during Katrina. Brown had strong political credentials but lacked the emergency management experience to deal with the devastation of the hurricane. Bush took exception to that provision, contending in an October signing statement that he did not have to obey the requirement in appointing an administrator.

HOUSE ACTION

The House Homeland Security Committee approved a bill (HR 5351—H Rept 109-712, Part 1) 28–0 on May 17 that proposed to keep FEMA in the Homeland Security Department but restore its preparedness role and have it report directly to the president during a crisis. Committee members said taking the agency out of the department would not solve the problems seen during Katrina but would create a new level of bureaucracy that could cause redundancy and confusion during disasters.

The House Transportation and Infrastructure Committee approved a competing bill (HR 5316) offered by its chairman, Don Young, R-Alaska, to separate FEMA from the department and make it a cabinet-level agency with responsibilities for preparedness and response. The bill also called for establishing a National Emergency Preparedness System and returning disaster preparedness and response functions to FEMA.

The committee approved the measure by voice vote May 17 (H Rept 109-519, Part 1), after adopting a manager's amendment to ensure that FEMA response teams worked with state and local officials during a crisis and to make it easier for people who spoke limited English to receive disaster information.

Rep. Bill Shuster, R-Pa., one of the sponsors, said he would be willing to work with other committees to incorporate solutions to strengthen FEMA, but he said anything short of removing the agency from the department would be "just treating the symptoms of FEMA's disease" and would be a deal-breaker. "It needs to be an agency that's sitting at the right hand of the president during an emergency," he said.

The Government Reform Committee approved Young's bill by voice vote May 18 (H Rept 109-519, Part 2). Members said it was a mistake to lump FEMA in with the Department of Homeland Security to begin with, pointing to FEMA's historic performance during natural disasters as evidence that it functioned better on its own.

The House had approved the fiscal 2007 Homeland Security measure (HR 5441—H Rept 109-476) on June 6. The House spending bill did not have FEMA provisions. None of the individual measures considered by the three House committees was considered by the full House.

FINAL ACTION

The House and Senate appropriations conference did not begin until September, but negotiations in August had produced an agreement in principle between Young and House Homeland Security Chairman Peter T. King, R-N.Y., to keep a more autonomous FEMA within the Homeland Security Department. Details were worked out in mid-September. The appropriations bill also provided $2.5 billion for FEMA preparedness and response activities in fiscal 2007.

The Senate amendment was largely included in the conference report on the spending bill. The House adopted the conference report (H Rept 109-699) 412–6 on Sept. 29, and the Senate cleared the bill by voice vote the same day.

MAJOR PROVISIONS

As signed into law Oct. 4, 2006, HR 5441 (PL 109-295):

- Reconstituted FEMA to incorporate most of the Preparedness Directorate, as well as all of its previous offices, and gave the agency responsibility to "prepare for, protect against, respond to, recover from, and mitigate against" risks of both natural disasters and terrorist acts.
- Gave FEMA the status of a distinct agency within the department and prohibited the secretary from transferring responsibilities, capabilities, or major funding to another part of the department.
- Authorized a system of ten regional FEMA offices that, among other responsibilities, would oversee multiagency strike teams drawn from federal, state, and local government and the private sector and be ready to respond quickly in a disaster.
- Made the FEMA administrator the principal adviser to the president, the Homeland Security Council, and the Homeland Security secretary for all matters relating to emergency management. Specified that the administrator was to report directly to the secretary, could be given cabinet status in an emergency, and could provide emergency management recommendations directly to Congress.
- Required the administrator to create a Surge Capacity Force that could rapidly provide search and rescue capabilities, food, water, medicine, housing, medical care, evacuation capacity, staffing, "and other resources necessary to save lives and protect property during a catastrophic incident."
- Authorized 10 percent funding increases for the agency in fiscal 2008 through 2010.

U.S. Ports Security

On the last day of September 2006, Congress cleared a bill authorizing more than $2 billion over five years for U.S. port and container security programs. The conference report also served as a last-minute vehicle for provisions to reduce Internet gambling. President George W. Bush signed the measure Oct. 13 (HR 4954—PL 109-347).

The port security bill codified a number of programs at the Homeland Security Department aimed at securing the nation's 361 ports and the estimated 11 million cargo containers that enter them each year. It required the twenty-two largest U.S. ports to scan all incoming containers for radiation by the end of 2007, established protocols to resume trade in the event of a catastrophic incident, and offered new benefits for trusted shippers.

The conference agreement extended an existing ban on interstate gambling to include Internet communications, and prohibited banks, credit card companies, and other financial institutions from processing transactions related to illegal Internet gambling. *(Internet gambling, p. 422)*

BACKGROUND

Concern over port security escalated in February 2006 with news that the Bush administration had approved a transaction giving operational control of six key U.S. ports to DP World, a Dubai-owned company. Members of Congress, prodded by constituent complaints about the deal and concerns about the antiterrorism record of the United Arab Emirates (which was composed of seven emirates including Dubai), pressed to reverse the deal. The company quickly volunteered to sell off its U.S. port assets, but with the vulnerability of ports in question both chambers pushed legislation shoring up port defenses against terrorist attacks. *(Foreign investment, pp. 243, 257)*

The House passed legislation in May to authorize $5.5 billion over six years and focused almost exclusively on port security. The Senate Homeland Security Committee, chaired by Sen. Susan Collins, R-Maine, approved a port security bill in May, but became embroiled in a jurisdictional fight with the Commerce, Science, and Transportation Committee, headed by Sen. Ted Stevens, R-Alaska.

Stevens's committee had approved a broader transportation security bill (S 1052) in 2005 that included provisions on port security. It authorized random inspections of cargo entering the United States, promoted new technologies and technical standards for inspections, and authorized $729 million over three years for port security. Stevens claimed jurisdiction, and Senate Majority Leader Bill Frist, R-Tenn., indicated that the two panels would have to resolve their dispute before he would bring legislation to the floor. In addition, the Finance Committee asserted its jurisdiction over customs and trade. *(2005 transportation bill, p. 407)*

The three committees did that and sent a compromise bill to the floor in September. Before passing the bill, the Senate expanded its scope by adding more than $4.5 billion for rail and mass transit security programs. The Senate bill also proposed an extension of customs fees to help pay for some of the programs.

In advance of the November 2006 election, Democrats used the bill to highlight what they said were shortcomings in the Bush administration's homeland security planning. They made inspection of 100 percent of cargo containers bound for the United States a central proposal of their election year security agenda and criticized the existing rate of U.S. inspections, about 5 percent, as dangerously low. The Democrats' complaints promoted considerable debate but they were unable to get the provision included in the bill.

Eager to finish the bill before leaving to campaign, House and Senate GOP conferees agreed to drop the rail and mass transit security funding and the customs fee extensions, returning the bill to its original focus of port security. In the meantime, the Homeland Security appropriations bill, enacted Oct. 4 (PL 109-295), provided $4.3 billion for port, container, and cargo security in fiscal 2007. *(Homeland Security appropriations, p. 102)*

HOUSE ACTION

The House Homeland Security Economic Security, Infrastructure Protection, and Cybersecurity Subcommittee approved a port security measure March 30. The six-year measure (HR 4954) proposed to authorize $801 million annually in fiscal 2007 through 2012. The bill required the Department of Homeland Security to develop a timeline for installing radiation-screening equipment at all U.S. ports, hire a director of cargo security policy, and establish procedures for restoring port traffic in the event of a disaster. It also codified several existing programs.

Before approving the bill, the subcommittee agreed to add $20 million in fiscal 2007 to speed implementation of a process to issue transportation security cards to port workers with access to secure areas. In the interim, the Department of Homeland Security would be required to check port workers against terrorism watch lists.

During the markup, Republicans voted down a proposal by Rep. Edward J. Markey, D-Mass., to require 100 percent inspection of cargo containers entering the United States from a foreign port.

The full Homeland Security Committee approved the port security bill (H Rept 109-447, Part 1) 29–0 on April 26, after Republicans fended off another Democratic bid to require 100 percent inspection of cargo containers arriving from foreign ports. The total authorization in the bill for port security programs jumped to $5.5 billion over six years, including $400 million annually for risk-based grant programs. A $1.9 billion authorization for the Coast Guard was also added.

The bill required the evaluation of next-generation cargo scanning technology to determine the feasibility of deploying it at foreign ports, but it did not require that all cargo bound for the United States be scanned and sealed. It required the department to deploy nuclear and radiological detection systems at twenty-two U.S. seaports by Sept. 30, 2007, set deadlines for developing regulations for a transportation security card for port employees, and codified and authorized $196 million annually for the Container Security Initiative program.

The committee rejected 16–18 Markey's amendment to again set deadlines for 100 percent scanning of incoming cargo containers for radiation and density. Committee members instead adopted 33–0 an alternative proposal by Rep. Ginny Brown-Waite, R-Fla., to require the Homeland Security secretary to evaluate next-generation cargo scanning technology to determine the feasibility of deploying it at foreign ports.

The House passed the bill 421–2 on May 4. During the floor debate, the House rejected 202–222 a motion by Jerrold Nadler, D-N.Y., to send the bill back to the committee with instructions to add language setting a timetable for achieving 100 percent inspection of cargo containers arriving from foreign ports.

SENATE COMMITTEE ACTION

The Senate Homeland Security and Governmental Affairs Committee voted 14–2 on May 2 to approve a $5 billion, six-year authorization of port and cargo security programs. The bill (S 2459) was sponsored by the panel's chair, Susan Collins, R-Maine, and cosponsored by Sen. Patty Murray, D-Wash.

The bill authorized $835 million per year for port security in fiscal 2007 through 2012; gave statutory authorization to the Customs-Trade Partnership Against Terrorism, a voluntary program that rewarded trusted shippers with benefits such as reduced inspections and priority processing; formally authorized the Container Security Initiative; and established protocols for resuming trade after a catastrophic incident. It also required a pilot project to test "100 percent scanning" systems at three foreign ports to screen all cargo bound for the United States.

SENATE FLOOR ACTION

The Senate substituted its legislation for the House's (HR 4954) and passed the legislation 98–0 on Sept. 14, after adding more than $4.5 billion in rail and mass transit programs, which were later dropped in conference.

The Senate Sept. 13 approved 95–3 an amendment to mandate screening of high-risk cargo containers. The amendment required all cargo containers arriving at a U.S. port to be screened to identify high-risk containers, and that 100 percent of those identified as high-risk must be scanned before leaving the port facility.

CONFERENCE, FINAL ACTION

Republican negotiators, pushing to clear the legislation before recessing for the midterm elections, agreed on a $2 billion measure that focused almost exclusively on port security. The House adopted the conference report (H Rept 109-711) by a vote of 409–2 in the early morning hours of Sept. 30, and the Senate cleared it by voice vote immediately afterward.

The main question that stymied the conference was whether to include the $4.5 billion for rail, mass transit, hazardous materials, and pipeline security. House conferees refused to accept the $4.5 billion for rail and other transportation security, and the provisions were dropped.

The conference report included several provisions sought by senators, including a requirement that Homeland Security draft a security plan for small and rural airports that received federal subsidies for commercial airline service. The conference report also directed the Transportation Department to begin instituting a program that required anyone applying for a commercial driver's license to provide proof of citizenship or legal residency, information that previously was required only of truckers who applied for a commercial hazardous materials certification. It also directed the department to crack down on fraudulent commercial drivers and allow roadside inspections of commercial driver's licenses.

MAJOR PROVISIONS

As signed into law Oct. 13, 2006, HR 4954 (PL 109-347) included the following major provisions:

Port Security

Authorized $400 million annually from fiscal 2007 through 2011 for a dedicated grant program to assist ports on the basis of risk and need.

Required the Homeland Security Department to:

- Establish protocols for resuming port operations after a transportation security incident that suspended trade operations.
- Verify the effectiveness of each port's security plans at least twice a year, including at least one unannounced inspection, and assess antiterrorism measures at foreign ports every three years.
- Establish a network of Interagency Operational Centers at appropriate seaports and authorize $60 million annually from fiscal 2007 through 2012 for their operations.
- Create a program to help train port security officers, law enforcement, and the private sector to prepare for and respond to port security incidents.
- Finalize regulations by Jan. 1, 2007, for biometric transportation security cards for eligible port workers, merchant mariners, and truck drivers. Directed the department to establish a risk-based priority list of U.S. ports and to ensure that workers at the ten ports at highest risk received the cards by July 1, 2007. Required workers at the next forty ports on the list to receive cards by Jan. 1, 2008, and all other ports by Jan. 1, 2009.

Cargo Security

Gave statutory authority to the Container Security for forty-four foreign ports and required host nations to share shipping data before a vessel reached U.S. shores.)

Other Provisions

Required the Homeland Security Department to:

- Create an Office of Cargo Security Policy to coordinate cargo policies and consult with other agencies in developing standards and regulations.

- Ensure 100 percent screening of cargo containers originating outside the United States to identify high-risk containers, and ensure that 100 percent of those containers were scanned or inspected for radiation before leaving the seaport facility.
- Conduct a pilot project at three overseas ports similar to the Integrated Container Inspection System in Hong Kong, which used radiation scanners and gamma-ray detectors to screen every cargo container that entered two of the port's terminals.
- Ensure that by Sept. 30, 2007, all containers arriving through the twenty-two busiest U.S. seaports from outside the United States were scanned for radiation, and develop plans to expand the system to all U.S. ports. Directed the department to implement plans for random physical inspections of shipping containers.

Trusted shippers. Authorized the Customs-Trade Partnership Against Terrorism (C-TPAT), a voluntary program that rewarded trusted shippers with benefits such as reduced inspections and priority processing. Provided a new "tier three" of additional preferences to shippers that exceeded the voluntary standards in order to free up more resources to focus on higher-risk and unknown shippers.

Funding. Authorized $213 million over three years for the program.

Terrorism Insurance

The House cleared a two-year extension of a federal terrorism insurance program after more than a year of intense lobbying by business groups. President George W. Bush signed the measure into law (S 467—PL 109-144) Dec. 22, 2005, nine days before the original program's Dec. 31 expiration date.

The 2002 Terrorism Risk Insurance Act (PL 107-297), or TRIA, created a three-year program to help stabilize the commercial property and casualty insurance markets following the Sept. 11, 2001, terrorist attacks. The program, which expired on Dec. 31, 2005, was meant to encourage insurers to provide affordable coverage for terrorism while giving the industry time to develop a market-based system for absorbing the risks. TRIA guaranteed that the federal government would cover much of the terrorism-related losses once they exceeded a specific trigger level. Total federal responsibility was capped at $100 billion per year. *(TRIA, Congress and the Nation Vol. XI, p. 203)*

The Sept. 11 attacks had resulted in an estimated $40 billion in insured claims. The commercial property and casualty insurers reacted by lobbying for federal assistance, saying they would be unable to continue to insure against terrorism in the absence of a federal backstop. The insurance lobbyists started the push for a TRIA extension in 2004, but Senate Banking Chairman Richard C. Shelby, R-Ala., resisted pressure to act until a Treasury Department study of the program was released in June 2005.

The Treasury report found that TRIA had ensured the availability of affordable terrorism insurance, but it also said the program was inhibiting development of private alternatives. Treasury Secretary John W. Snow said the program should not be extended unless it was significantly scaled back.

SENATE ACTION

Sen. Christopher J. Dodd, D-Conn., introduced S 467 on Feb. 18 as a straightforward two-year extension of the program. When the Banking Committee considered the bill, Shelby said the bill did not mesh with the Republican ideal of limited government, and he would not support a simple extension. During the committee markup, Shelby offered a substitute to make private insurers shoulder more of the terrorism risk insurance. The committee approved the bill by voice vote on Nov. 16. The White House released a statement on Nov. 17 praising the Senate measure, saying the legislation "sends the proper signal to the marketplace that the Terrorism Risk Insurance Program was envisioned to be temporary."

The Senate passed the measure by voice vote on Nov. 18.

HOUSE ACTION

The House Financial Services Committee approved a TRIA extension (HR 4314—H Rept 109-327) by a vote of 64–3, also on Nov. 16. The House bill required insurers to take on a greater share of the financial risk, and it also expanded the program to new areas of insurance.

The House proposal, drafted by Financial Services Chairman Michael G. Oxley, R-Ohio, added group life insurance coverage and expanded coverage to include attacks perpetrated by domestic terrorists. It also required companies to offer coverage for nuclear, biological, chemical, and radioactive attacks. In its Nov. 17 statement on the measure, the White House said it would "strongly oppose" any efforts to add lines of coverage, such as life insurance, or further expand the program.

The House passed S 467 by a 371–49 vote on Dec. 7, after substituting the text of HR 4314. In addition to the coverage for group life insurance, the House bill also established a public-private commission to develop long-term solutions for dealing with terrorism risk and created deductibles for different categories of insurance.

FINAL ACTION

At Shelby's insistence, the Senate did not appoint conferees, putting pressure on the House to accept the Senate version. In informal negotiations, Shelby and Oxley agreed to an amended bill that closely tracked the Senate approach.

Rep. Barney Frank of Massachusetts, the ranking Democrat on the House Financial Services Committee, criticized the Senate's unwillingness to hold a formal conference. "They have forced us to deal with it in a constricted and inappropriate way," Frank said on the House floor.

The final negotiations hinged on how much insurance companies would be required to repay the federal government for financial assistance through the program. Under the agreement, the amount insurers would have to repay in 2006 increased to $25 billion from $17.5 billion in the original Senate bill. That figure would increase to $27.5 billion in 2007. The House bill would have required 100 percent repayment of federal assistance, but it was likely it would take companies years to repay the government.

The final measure also increased the amount of risk taken on by insurers, raising the level of industry-wide losses that would trigger the assistance to $50 million in 2006 and $100 million in 2007. Under the original law, the trigger was $5 million. The Bush administration had sought to raise the trigger to $500 million.

Left out of the final version was the House provision creating a public-private commission to seek private-market solutions for insuring against terrorism risk. The House provisions expanding the program by adding group life insurance as well as attacks perpetrated by domestic terrorists were also dropped.

Oxley said the amended bill excluded "any real reform." He added, "In this shortsighted legislation, we have missed a golden opportunity to frame the TRIA program more effectively and to move to a more market-based solution."

The Senate passed the amended version of S 467 on Dec. 16, and the House cleared the amended legislation the next day.

MAJOR PROVISIONS

As signed into law Dec. 22, 2005, S 467 (PL 109-144):

- Required insurance companies to shoulder a larger share of the cost of insuring against terror attacks by increasing the trigger level, or the cost of an attack at which the federal government would potentially provide aid, from $5 million in insured losses to $50 million in 2006 and $100 million in 2007.
- Maintained the $100 billion cap on the federal government and insurers' annual liability.
- Limited the number of insurance lines covered by the program, excluding commercial automobile insurance, burglary and theft insurance, surety insurance, professional liability insurance, and farm owners multiple peril insurance, which were covered under previous TRIA law.
- Increased the deductibles for insurers before the federal share contributes from 15 percent of prior year premiums to 17.5 percent in 2006 and 20 percent in 2007.
- Required insurers, once the deductible was reached, to pay 10 percent of the costs in 2006, the same level previously required, and 15 percent in 2007.
- Maintained the federal share of the compensation for insured losses at 90 percent in 2006 but reduced the government's share to 85 percent for 2007.
- Required recoupment of at least a portion of the federal compensation through policyholder premium surcharges in the event that the federal government provided compensation for insured losses for an act of terrorism under the program.
- Codified a federal regulation that required insurers to seek Treasury's advance approval of certain settlements involving insured losses.
- Required the president's Working Group on Financial Markets to conduct a report by Sept. 30, 2006, on the long-term availability and affordability of terrorism risk insurance, including group life coverage and coverage for chemical, nuclear, biological, and radiological events.

Chinese Purchase of Unocal

Lawmakers were stunned in June 2005 when the China National Offshore Oil Corp. (CNOOC), a company that was majority-owned by the Chinese government, outbid the U.S. oil giant Chevron Corp. by $2 billion to take over California-based Unocal Corp. Unocal owned significant oil and natural gas properties around Asia. CNOOC officials said they were making a "friendly" bid to buy Unocal for $18.5 billion in cash, much of it provided by the Chinese government.

The proposed sale raised immediate concerns on Capitol Hill, and the House voted twice the week after the announcement to show its displeasure with the deal. Shortly after the House action, and in the face of rising opposition, CNOOC withdrew its bid, and Chevron made the acquisition.

BACKGROUND

The Unocal purchase sparked an outcry in Congress, based on oil's status as a strategic resource and the Chinese government's 70 percent stake in CNOOC. No proposed business transaction in recent memory had drawn such a swift and unambiguous response from lawmakers.

Foreign investments in the United States were reviewed by the Committee on Foreign Investment in the United States (CFIUS). This somewhat secretive interagency body was charged with reviewing investments in U.S. companies by foreigners and recommending that such transactions be stopped or redesigned if they might compromise national security. *(CFIUS background box, p. 242)*

Its mission was to steer clear of political anxieties in examining acquisitions, and to navigate the twin imperatives of national security and open commerce. Since 1988, CFIUS had evaluated more than 1,500 acquisitions that might harm U.S. defense production capability, result in the spread of sensitive technology, or compromise the strategic advantage of the United States in aerospace and other fields. Because the group had to avoid blurring defense readiness with protecting U.S. industries from

CFIUS: MANDATE AND HISTORY

The Committee on Foreign Investment in the United States (CFIUS) is responsible for reviewing the acquisition of U.S. assets by foreign-owned, and particularly foreign-government-owned, enterprises to ensure that national security is not compromised.

What Is CFIUS?

President Gerald R. Ford established CFIUS by executive order in 1975. It was created as an interagency body, led by the Treasury Department, to review foreign-owned acquisitions in the United States. The 1988 trade law PL 100-418)) contained the so-called Exon-Florio provision that gave the president authority to suspend or block a merger or acquisition if "there is credible evidence that the foreign entity exercising control might take action that threatens national security" and if no other law would protect national security. Deliberations were to be confidential to protect proprietary information. Notice of a proposed acquisition begins a thirty-day agency review, which could trigger a formal forty-five-day investigation and report to the president if a threat to national security were found. The fiscal 1993 defense authorization bill (PL 102-484)) expanded the law to require a formal investigation and presidential determination in cases where a foreign government controls the acquirer and the acquisition could affect national security.

Who runs CFIUS?

The Treasury Department was designated the lead agency in the twelve-member group that included the president's national security adviser; the director of the National Economic Council; the U.S. trade representative; and representatives of the Departments of State, Commerce, Defense, Justice, and Homeland Security; and officials of the Office of Management and Budget, the Council of Economic Advisers, and the Office of Science and Technology Policy.

Past Activity

Between 1988 and 2005, CFIUS evaluated more than 1,500 proposed acquisitions, and on some occasions companies agreed to alter deals to satisfy concerns. In 2005 CFIUS cleared the sale of IBM's personal computer unit to the Chinese Lenovo Group, after the parties agreed to create procedures to protect potentially sensitive information held by IBM. Of the acquisitions reviewed, twenty-five triggered formal investigations. Of those, thirteen proposed acquisitions were withdrawn and twelve reached the president's desk. In only one case, in 1990, President George H. W. Bush ordered a company owned by the Chinese Aerospace Industry Ministry to divest an interest in MAMCO Inc., a Seattle-based manufacturer of aircraft components that could have either commercial or military use.

competition, CFIUS resolved some cases with agreements from companies to alter deals; it recommended that just one be undone.

With global trade on the rise, President Gerald R. Ford established CFIUS by executive order in 1975 to monitor, review, and coordinate U.S. policy on foreign investment. Its size was expanded to include the secretary of the Treasury, who is chairman, and officials from a dozen agencies, including the Departments of Defense, Commerce, Justice and Homeland Security, and the U.S. trade representative.

Japan's rise as an economic power in the 1980s increased anxiety about U.S. technological competitiveness, and a rewrite of trade law in 1988 ultimately gave CFIUS added authority to recommend that the president block or restructure foreign acquisitions of U.S. companies by executive order if they might undermine national security.

Under the law, companies contemplating an acquisition involving a foreign entity may notify CFIUS voluntarily, and CNOOC said July 1 that it had filed notice of its intention to buy Unocal. However, the interagency group may review any deal that comes to its attention.

HOUSE ACTION

House lawmakers on June 30 voted 333–92 to add a provision to the Transportation-Treasury-Housing appropriations bill (HR 3058) to prohibit the Treasury Department from using any funds to favorably recommend the sale of Unocal Corp. to CNOOC. The amendment was aimed at blocking regulatory approval of the merger. *(HR 3058, p. 78)*

That same night, the House voted 398–15 in favor of a resolution (H Res 344) stating that if the proposed takeover went through, U.S. national security could be impaired. The nonbinding resolution called on President George W. Bush to order a review of the proposed sale.

The House votes were intended to pressure CFIUS to block the purchase. In late June, more than forty House members had sent a letter to Treasury Secretary John W. Snow, urging him to block the sale if it would hurt U.S. industry or threaten national security.

The Chinese oil company sent a letter to Congress urging lawmakers not to block its "friendly and open offer," and then the Chinese foreign minister issued a stronger statement July 4 that told lawmakers to "stop interfering." But the anger in Congress proved to be too much, and the Chinese company withdrew its bid in July, paving the way for the purchase by Chevron.

Foreign Investment: U.S. Ports

When news began to filter out in late January 2006 of a deal to give a Dubai government-owned company (Dubai was one of the seven emirates making up the United Arab Emirates) operational control over six major U.S. ports, the House and Senate each passed bills to overhaul the process for reviewing foreign investment in the United States. But lawmakers were split over the proper balance between protecting security interests and maintaining an open climate for foreign investment, and the legislation died at the end of the 109th Congress. *(110th Congress action, p. 257)*

The bills were inspired by news that became public in February that Dubai's DP World was acquiring a British company that had long operated U.S. port facilities. Lawmakers were outraged to learn that the deal had been approved by the Committee on Foreign Investment in the United States (CFIUS), an interagency panel whose job was to review and potentially block foreign acquisitions that could compromise national security. Top administration officials and members of Congress were not aware of the CFIUS review until after the purchase had been approved.

Under pressure from Congress, the company pulled out of the deal on March 9, 2006, but concerns with the regulation of foreign investments persisted. Lawmakers insisted that they should have been informed during the approval process, not afterward. They also complained that the administration of George W. Bush had failed to follow a 1992 law (PL 102-484) that required a full investigation of any acquisition involving a foreign government-owned company. CFIUS did not take that step in the DP World case.

In late July, both the House and Senate passed bills to give a statutory basis to CFIUS. This interagency committee was established in 1975 by executive order. Both bills codified a process to subject sensitive acquisitions to a preliminary thirty-day review by CFIUS, which was to be followed by a full-scale forty-five-day investigation in cases where a potential security threat was identified. Where a clear threat was found, the president could bar the transaction or even require the undoing of an acquisition completed without U.S. government knowledge.

BACKGROUND

The operations of CFIUS had always been relatively obscure to members of Congress. A wave of concern over the increase in foreign takeovers in the United States led in 1988 to approval of authority allowing the president to block foreign acquisitions that threatened U.S. national security, known as the Exon-Florio provision after its principal congressional sponsors. President Ronald Reagan gave CFIUS the job of reviewing foreign investments, investigating those that might affect U.S. interests and recommending appropriate action. Reagan's executive order gave the committee thirty days for a review and forty-five days for an investigation. *(1988 law, PL 100-418, Congress and the Nation Vol. VII, p. 148)*

CFIUS was further strengthened in 1992 under a provision known as the Byrd amendment (PL 102-484) requiring a full investigation of any transactions that involved a foreign government and that could affect U.S. national security. It was this mandate that lawmakers said CFIUS ignored in the Dubai case. *(1990 law, Congress and the Nation Vol. VIII, p. 177)*

In July 2006, both chambers passed competing proposals to overhaul CFIUS. The Senate measure (S 3549) stiffened CFIUS reviews and gave Congress a larger role in approving transactions. Richard C. Shelby, R-Ala., chairman of the Banking, Housing and Urban Affairs Committee—and a longtime critic of CFIUS—was the bill's sponsor.

The less restrictive House bill was written largely by the Financial Services Committee, whose chairman, Michael G. Oxley, R-Ohio, was a vigorous supporter of foreign investment and one of the few prominent lawmakers to defend the Dubai deal.

SENATE COMMITTEE ACTION

After the news broke of the possible ownership of the U.S. ports by DP World, Shelby quickly drafted a bill aimed at tightening CFIUS reviews. Shelby had held hearings on CFIUS in late 2005 and ordered a Government Accountability Office (GAO) report on the agency, which found numerous problems.

The Banking Committee approved Shelby's bill (S 3549—S Rept 109-264) by a vote of 20–0 on March 30. The committee changed two provisions in the draft to make it more palatable to businesses and other committee members. The panel sought to balance national security interests with business interests, which had resisted the legislation because, they argued, it would prolong the process for businesses trying to acquire U.S. assets.

The Senate bill approved by the committee mandated a formal forty-five-day national security investigation of all transactions that affected critical infrastructure and carried potential national security concerns. The legislation also mandated the forty-five-day investigation on all cases involving a foreign government. The bill required that relevant congressional panels and leaders be notified of the reviews.

The Senate bill also required CFIUS to notify Congress of all acquisitions submitted to it for review and allowed lawmakers broad access to transaction-related documents that are generally considered proprietary. The House bill, however, required notice to Congress only at the conclusion of a forty-five-day national security investigation.

The Senate measure also allowed any CFIUS member to extend the initial thirty-day review to sixty days; the House version did not provide for extensions. The forty-five-day period for a national security investigation would have been doubled only if two-thirds of the members of CFIUS voted to do so.

SENATE FLOOR ACTION

The Senate passed its bill by voice vote with almost no debate July 26. Sen. John McCain, R-Ariz., criticized the requirement that CFIUS report to Congress on every transaction it reviewed, saying it would open the process to inappropriate political influence. He also objected to a requirement that an investigation be opened if there was "any possible impairment to national security," which he said was too broad. McCain said Shelby had assured him that he would work to resolve those concerns in conference.

HOUSE COMMITTEE ACTION

The House Financial Services Committee approved its bill (HR 5337—H Rept 109-523, Part 1) by a vote of 64–0 on June 14, after adopting by voice vote a substitute amendment by Deborah Pryce, R-Ohio, that added reporting requirements and altered the role of the national intelligence director in the review process.

The House Energy and Commerce Committee then gave voice-vote approval July 12 to an amended version of the bill (H Rept 109-523, Part 2) that aimed to increase the panel's jurisdiction over the review process. The changes were backed by Chairman Joe L. Barton, R-Texas, and the panel's ranking Democrat, John D. Dingell of Michigan.

The changes designated the commerce secretary, not the Treasury secretary, as the CFIUS chairman, added the energy secretary as a member, and eliminated the vice president. It also specified that CFIUS reports to Congress would go to the Energy and Commerce Committee, among others.

Several business groups, including the U.S. Chamber of Commerce, Business Roundtable, Financial Services Forum, and Organization for International Investment, sent a letter to panel members July 12 opposing the provision to make the commerce secretary chairman. "Doing so would serve no policy benefit and would send a confusing message as to U.S. investment policy," they wrote.

HOUSE FLOOR ACTION

The House passed HR 5337 by a vote of 424–0 on July 26, just hours after the Senate acted. HR 5337 was essentially a revised version of the legislation passed by the House Financial Services Committee. House leadership inserted a few changes into the bill before the measure went to the floor.

The Treasury secretary remained as chairman of CFIUS under the revised bill, but the commerce secretary was elevated to the role of vice chairman, a position to be shared with the secretary of homeland security. The energy secretary was added to CFIUS, and the bill specified that Energy and Commerce be among the committees that would receive reports. Also, the thirty-day review period would end with a roll call vote, and a single member of CFIUS could send the transaction to a forty-five day review. The House bill also did not require that Congress receive notification of all transactions that CFIUS considers, only those with national security implications.

"We must protect our national security, but national security includes economic security," Oxley said on the floor. "Our friends in the other body should understand that no bill would be a preferable alternative to a bad bill, and we in the House will not sacrifice American prosperity and job growth when there is no real improvement to American security."

GOP leaders in both chambers were unable to clear a final version before the November midterm elections. When Congress returned, there was little interest on the part of the White House or lawmakers in reconciling and completing the legislation.

Meanwhile, the Treasury Department, which chaired CFIUS, made some changes aimed at addressing lawmakers' concerns. These included improving congressional notification, giving the director of national intelligence a more formal role, and creating an in-house manager for the CFIUS process.

2007–2008

The November 2006 midterm election turned out to be far better for the Democrats than they had dared to hope. Democrats claimed total control of Congress for the first time since 1994, although the margin in the Senate was very narrow.

One of the first acts of the new Democratic majority in the 110th Congress (2007–2008) was to clear a measure to enact recommendations from a bipartisan commission on homeland security that was formed after the Sept. 11, 2001, terrorist attacks. Many of the recommendations had already been enacted as part of the 2004 law that reorganized the intelligence community, but Democrats promised during the 2006 election campaign that they would finish the job. The final bill did not implement all of the remaining recommendations and some of the provisions were watered down to avoid a veto. For example, the White House had threatened to veto the Senate bill over a provision that would have given airport security screeners collective bargaining rights. Democrats agreed to drop the provision in exchange for President George W. Bush's approval.

Congress also easily cleared bipartisan legislation to overhaul the process for reviewing foreign investments that might affect U.S. national security. The 2007 enactment of the measure marked a quiet legislative finale to the issue of the foreign company DP World, which had hoped to acquire operational control of six U.S. port terminals through a deal with a British firm. Both chambers wanted to overhaul the Committee on Foreign Investment in the United States (CFIUS), a secretive multiagency panel charged with reviewing the national security risks posed by proposed foreign acquisitions, but House and Senate negotiators could not agree in 2006 on how to protect national security while still maintaining an open environment for foreign investment. In 2007 the two chambers worked more closely, producing similar bills from the outset. Both chambers' bills established CFIUS in statute for the first time, and required a full-blown national security investigation of foreign bids by state-owned companies.

During the 110th Congress, lawmakers also returned to the issue of domestic surveillance. In 2008 Congress cleared a White House–backed bill overhauling the 1978 Foreign Intelligence Surveillance Act (FISA) after Democrats failed to block key administration goals for electronic surveillance laws. The legislation gave Bush the two things he wanted most: enhanced executive branch spying authority and dismissal of lawsuits against telephone companies that had assisted in a warrantless wiretapping program conducted under presidential authority by the National Security Agency. While Democrats agreed with the Bush administration on the need to overhaul FISA, Democratic congressional leaders generally wanted more restrictions to protect Americans' civil liberties.

Congress also agreed in 2007 to a seven-year extension of a federal terrorism insurance program created to help stabilize the commercial real estate market in the wake of Sept. 11, 2001, terrorist attacks. The Terrorism Risk Insurance Act (TRIA) was enacted in 2002 at a time when the property and casualty insurance industry was thrown into disarray by the heavy losses suffered in 2001. Without continued terrorism insurance coverage, mortgages for big projects would have been far too costly.

Sept. 11 Commission Recommendations

Legislation to enact recommendations from a bipartisan commission on homeland security was cleared by Congress on July 27, 2007. President George W. Bush signed the bill (HR 1—PL 110-53) into law Aug. 3. The bill's designation as HR 1 reflected the high priority Democrats gave to the legislation.

Among its myriad provisions, the bill required that federal first-responder grants be distributed largely on the basis of risk, greatly expanded the scrutiny of cargo for nuclear devices and other dangerous contraband, and created a new grant program to improve the interoperability of emergency communications.

The legislation was a response to the recommendations of the bipartisan Sept. 11 commission, which Congress established in 2002 to study the events surrounding the 2001 terrorist attacks in New York City and outside Washington, D.C. Many of the recommendations had already been enacted as part of the 2004 law that reorganized the intelligence community. Democrats promised during the November 2006 midterm election campaign that they would finish the job. *(Intelligence reorganization, Congress and the Nation Vol. XI, p. 263)*

The final bill did not implement all of the remaining recommendations—especially proposals to strengthen congressional oversight of homeland security and intelligence—and some of the provisions were watered down to avoid a veto. For example, the White House had threatened to veto the Senate bill over a provision that would have given airport screeners collective bargaining rights. Democrats agreed to drop the provision in exchange for Bush's approval. But the measure still won praise from the leaders of the commission.

BACKGROUND

The ten-member bipartisan National Commission on Terrorist Attacks Upon the United States, better known as the Sept. 11 or 9/11 commission, was created under the fiscal 2003 intelligence authorization law (PL 107-306), signed in November 2002. The commission's purpose was to examine and report on the facts and causes relating to the 2001 terrorist attacks and make recommendations for improving the nation's preparedness and response capabilities. *(Congress and the Nation Vol. XI, p. 243)*

The 9/11 commission's final report, released in July 2004, concluded that the U.S. government had been unprepared for the attacks and that the intelligence community was not properly organized to identify the plotters. Its recommendations included an overhaul of the intelligence community and congressional oversight of homeland security and intelligence, additional tools for first-responders and emergency personnel, and enhanced diplomatic efforts to combat terrorism. *(Congress and the Nation Vol. XI, p. 275)*

After the report was released, the Republican-led Congress in 2004 cleared the most extensive overhaul of the U.S. intelligence community since World War II (PL 108-458). As the 9/11 commission recommended, the law created a new director of national intelligence to oversee intelligence agencies, authorized additional U.S. Border Patrol agents, created uniform security-clearance procedures, and included provisions related to transportation security and efforts to combat money laundering and terrorist financing. *(Congress and the Nation Vol. XI, p. 263)*

The 2004 law, however, did not include all of the commission's recommendations. For example, it did not fully enact a recommendation that the director of national intelligence be given wide-ranging authority over all intelligence agency budgets and personnel, leaving most Defense Department intelligence programs—accounting for approximately 80 percent of all intelligence spending—under the control of the Pentagon. The law did not declassify the total amount of money spent each year for the intelligence community. It also did not include language to change the distribution of grants for first-responders.

In 2005 the 9/11 Public Discourse Project, a successor organization to the 9/11 commission, released a "report card" on the government's success in enacting the commission's recommendations. It gave several low or failing grades, including an "F" for airline passenger prescreening, a "D" for checked-baggage and cargo screening, a "D" for international collaboration on borders and document security, a "D" on efforts to prevent terrorists from acquiring weapons of mass destruction, and an "F" for failing to declassify the top-line number for the intelligence budget. The project also gave the government an "F" for failing to provide homeland security grant funds on the basis of risk, but it said that enactment of pending legislation would result in an "A."

HOUSE FLOOR ACTION

The House passed HR 1 299–128 on Jan. 9 as its first legislative act of the 110th Congress. It was the part of the new Democratic leadership's top priorities to be completed in the House's first 100 hours of legislative business. Under rules set up the first week of January under an organizing resolution (H Res 6), no amendments were offered to the bill. *(House rules package, p. 812)*

The bill included stiff cargo inspection requirements that drew opposition from shipping and retail industry officials who said they would impose new costs on shippers and manufacturers. The bill required within three years, at larger ports, that all maritime cargo bound for the United States be scanned for radiation and density before being placed on a ship in a foreign port. A five-year deadline was set for smaller ports. Both could be extended a year if the necessary technology was unavailable.

The bill also required that within three years of enactment 100 percent of the cargo carried on passenger planes be screened, phased in over three years. The White House said the screening proposals were "neither executable nor feasible" but did not promise a veto. The administration, however, threatened to veto the bill over another provision granting Transportation Security Administration (TSA) screeners collective-bargaining rights on par with other federal workers.

The House bill proposed reducing the minimum amount guaranteed to each state to 0.25 percent of overall funding for state homeland security grants, law enforcement terrorism-prevention grants, and urban area security grants. Also, border states would receive a guarantee of 0.45 percent of overall funding, a provision not retained in the final bill.

A principal criticism of the bill was the absence of specific funding for all but one of its initiatives.

SENATE COMMITTEE ACTION

The Senate Homeland Security and Governmental Affairs Committee approved a companion bill (S 4) by voice vote Feb. 15. The core of the bill was a substitute amendment by Chairman Joseph I. Lieberman, I-Conn., adopted by a vote of 16–0.

The committee proposed to authorize $1.3 billion per year in fiscal 2008 through 2010 for risk-based grants to high-risk urban areas. An additional $913 million per year would go to state homeland security grants, and the state guarantee would be reduced to 0.45 percent from 0.75 percent, leaving more money to be distributed according to risk. Another $913 million would go to states in emergency management performance grants for all types of hazards, including natural disasters; each state would receive at least 0.75 percent of that total, with the remainder distributed on the basis of population.

The bill authorized $3.3 billion over five years for a new grant program administered by the Federal Emergency Management Agency (FEMA) to improve operability and interoperability at local, regional, state, and federal levels. Each state would get a minimum of 0.75 percent of the total funds.

Unlike the House version, the bill included a provision requiring the president and Congress to reveal the total amount appropriated for the intelligence community each year. During the markup, the committee also added language similar to that in the House bill to extend collective-bargaining rights and whistleblower protections to TSA screeners. The amendment, sponsored by Lieberman, was adopted 9–0 with the committee's Republicans opposing it.

SENATE FLOOR ACTION

After more than two weeks of debate, the Senate passed its bill by a vote of 60–38 on March 13, ignoring a White House threat to veto the measure because of the TSA collective-bargaining language.

Before passage, the Senate agreed by voice vote to a substitute amendment by Majority Leader Harry Reid, D-Nev., that authorized more than $4 billion for rail and mass transit security, in addition to the $12.8 billion in the underlying bill. The substitute incorporated several bills that the Science and Transportation Committee had approved by voice vote Feb. 13. These bills were:

- A rail security bill (S 184—S Rept 110-29) that authorized $1.1 billion in fiscal 2008 through 2011 to safeguard people and cargo on rail, bus, and other means of surface transportation. The bill also authorized systemwide security upgrades on the Amtrak train system as well as specific funding for Amtrak's Northeast corridor and freight railroads.
- A bill (S 509—S Rept 110-31) that required the TSA to develop within three years of enactment a system for screening all cargo on passenger aircraft and proposed removing the existing hiring cap of 45,000 for TSA screeners.
- An emergency communications bill (S 385—S Rept 110-30) that contained new eligibility guidelines for a $1 billion communications grant program administered jointly by the Commerce and Homeland Security departments. The program was to be funded by proceeds from the federal government's auction of the analog radio spectrum.

Floor debate on the bill was complicated by an impasse over amendments that would be allowed. The deadlock was broken March 9 when the Senate rejected an attempt to limit debate on a multipart amendment by John Cornyn, R-Texas, aimed at terrorists in the United States. It contained provisions to make it a crime to recruit terrorists, to allow the deportation of suspected terrorists whose visas had been revoked and to toughen penalties for those who tortured U.S. soldiers or their families. The Senate then agreed 69–26 to limit debate on Reid's substitute.

One of the biggest battles was over the provisions to give airport screeners collective-bargaining rights. The turning point came March 6 when the Senate voted 51–46 to table, or kill, an amendment by Jim DeMint, R-S.C., to strip the language from the bill.

Democrats said the issue was one of equity because the screeners should have the same rights and whistleblower protections as other Homeland Security employees, including Border Patrol and immigration officers. Bush and Senate Republicans countered that permitting screeners to have collective-bargaining rights would make labor unions a party to fundamental national security decisions, potentially making it more difficult for the department to respond in emergencies.

TSA screeners had been pushing for collective-bargaining rights since 2001, when the president signed an aviation security law (PL 107-71) that gave the agency flexibility to set the terms and conditions of the screeners' employment. *(Congress and the Nation Vol. XI, p. 198)*

HOUSE ACTION, BUS AND RAIL SECURITY BILL

Ten days after the Senate acted, the House passed a separate bill (HR 1401—H Rept 110-65) authorizing more than $6.1 billion over four years for surface transportation security, including $2.5 billion for rail, $3.4 billion for urban mass transit, and $87 million for buses. The aim was to establish a House position on those issues before conference negotiations on the 9/11 commission bill. The House passed the bill 299–124 on March 27, after adding compromise language by Thompson and James L. Oberstar, D-Minn., chairman of the Transportation and Infrastructure Committee.

Both House committees had written their own versions of rail-security legislation, and disagreement over whether Homeland Security or the Transportation Department should distribute mass transit security funds had stalled the bill for weeks.

The compromise amendment, which was adopted by a vote of 222–197, gave the Transportation Department the power to administer transit security grants, though the grants still would be technically housed in the Homeland Security Department, which would conduct vulnerability assessments and make funding recommendations. Both departments would monitor and audit the programs.

The amendment also included language designed to strengthen whistleblower protections, drawing a White House veto threat. The administration said the provision would erode the government's ability to protect sensitive information. The expanded protections, modeled after whistleblower provisions included in a bill (HR 985) the House had passed March 14, specifically barred retribution—including revocation of security clearances—against whistleblowers and those who assisted them.

CONFERENCE, FINAL ACTION

After months of delay over the TSA collective-bargaining language, the House and Senate appointed conferees in mid-July, and the negotiators completed a deal on the legislation July 25. Most Republican conferees signed the conference report (H Rept 110-259) after winning adoption of a provision that gave liability protection to individuals who reported suspicious activity to authorities, which had been added to HR 1401 in the House.

The Senate adopted the conference report 85–8 on July 26. The House cleared the bill 371–40 the following day.

The following are some of the main agreements on the legislation:

- **Collective bargaining.** Senate Republicans refused to allow the appointment of conferees as long as the TSA collective-bargaining language remained in the bill. The GOP lifted their objections the week of July 9, after Democrats promised to drop the provisions. Minority Leader Mitch McConnell, R-Ky., who had repeatedly spoken against the collective-bargaining provisions, declared victory.
- **Cargo screening.** Conferees accepted the more aggressive House requirement that all U.S.-bound maritime cargo containers be scanned. But instead of requiring compliance within three years for major ports and five years for the rest, they agreed to a proposal by Thompson to set a deadline of July 1, 2012, for all ports and allowed the Homeland Security secretary to extend the deadline indefinitely by two-year increments if certain conditions were not met. Republicans, including Collins, fiercely opposed the language.

The conferees extended the House deadline for 100 percent of cargo carried on passenger planes to be screened, to August 2010. The deadline had been September 2009. The final bill defined screening as "a physical examination or nonintrusive methods of assessing whether cargo poses a threat to transportation security."

- **Intelligence budget.** Conferees struck a deal that required the government to disclose the totals for fiscal 2007 and 2008 but allowed the president to waive the disclosure requirement starting in fiscal 2009 if he explained to Congress why revealing the spending would jeopardize national security. Lieberman said the compromise responded to the administration's concern that a significant increase in expenditures would indicate to the nation's enemies that "we're doing something surprisingly different."
- **Liability shield.** The liability protection for "good faith" informants of terrorist activity on transportation systems was added in conference. It had not been in either chamber's version of the bill, although it was part of the House-passed rail and mass transit security bill (HR 1401). It was a response to an incident at the Minneapolis airport in 2006, in which six Muslim men were forced to leave an airplane because passengers complained of suspicious behavior. The men filed a lawsuit against those who complained and US Airways. Representative King, R-N.Y., was among those who pushed hardest for the provision. "In a post-9/11 world, vigilance is essential to security," King said in a statement praising the final language on civil immunity. "I'm proud to announce that common sense has prevailed and heroic Americans who report suspicious activity will be protected from frivolous lawsuits."

The provision applied to actions that posed a threat to a passenger transportation system, passenger safety, or passenger security, or that involved an act of terrorism. The suspicious activity had to be directed against a passenger transportation system.

MAJOR PROVISIONS

The principal provisions of HR 1 (PL 110-53), signed into law Aug. 3, 2007, included the following major provisions:

Grant distribution. Changed the distribution of the main homeland security grant programs, reducing the minimum amounts guaranteed for each state to 0.35 percent from 0.75 percent and requiring that the rest of the money be distributed primarily on the basis of risk. (The change benefited major metropolitan areas such as New York and Washington, D.C.)

Intelligence budget. Required the government to disclose the total amount appropriated each year for intelligence programs, but allowed the president to postpone or block the requirement for national security reasons beginning in fiscal 2009.

Cargo screening. Required all U.S.-bound seaborne cargo containers loaded in foreign ports to be scanned by July 2012, but allowed the deadline to be extended in two-year increments if the Homeland Security Department reported to Congress that adequate technology was not available.

Aviation security. Required that, within three years of enactment, all air cargo placed on passenger aircraft be screened. Authorized additional funding for aviation security needs, including $250 million annually for airport checkpoint screening, $450 million annually for baggage screening, and $50 million annually for four years for aviation security research.

Surface transportation. Authorized $4 billion over four years for rail, mass transit, and bus security grant programs under the Homeland Security Department. Required the development of risk assessments and security plans, set training requirements for workers, and extended whistleblower protections to transit employees.

Emergency communications. Established a grant program under the Homeland Security Department to improve the interoperability of state and local emergency communications and authorized $1.6 billion for it over five years.

Civil liberties. Made the Privacy and Civil Liberties Oversight Board, created under the 2004 intelligence overhaul law, an independent agency in the executive branch rather than a unit in the executive office of the president as it had been.

Liability shield. Provided immunity from civil lawsuits in federal, state, and local courts for individuals who in good faith reported suspicious activities relating to passenger safety, and provided officials who responded to their warning similar immunity.

Visa waivers. Expanded the visa-waiver program, under which nationals of certain allied countries could enter the country for short periods without visas.

Nonproliferation. Repealed limits on the aid that could be given to former Soviet states for nuclear nonproliferation and antiterrorism activities.

Electronic Surveillance: FISA Reforms 2007

Under pressure from the White House and congressional Republicans, Democrats agreed before the August 2007 recess to a six-month law that loosened rules for electronic surveillance by the government (S 1927—PL 110-55). Democratic leaders expected a new bill after the recess to scale back the temporary law. The House passed a bill in November, but the Senate put off action until 2008. *(2008 activity, p. 251)*

A congressional debate over electronic surveillance had simmered on Capitol Hill since December 2005, when the *New York Times* revealed that President George W. Bush had ordered the National Security Agency (NSA) to eavesdrop on Americans without court orders as a counterterrorism tactic.

BACKGROUND

On Jan. 17, 2007, Attorney General Alberto R. Gonzales told lawmakers that henceforth any electronic surveillance would be conducted subject to the approval of the secret court created under the 1978 Foreign Intelligence Surveillance Act (FISA) (PL 95-511). *(FISA, Congress and the Nation Vol. V, p. 720)*

FOREIGN INTELLIGENCE SURVEILLANCE BACKGROUND

The original Foreign Intelligence Surveillance Act (FISA) became law in 1978 in response to public outcry over the extensive use of wiretapping by the administration of President Richard Nixon (1969–1974), as well as revelations by what became known as the Church Committee—a select congressional committee charged with investigating forty years of covert activities—that every administration since Franklin D. Roosevelt's (1933–1945) had authorized the use of warrantless electronic surveillance. *(FISA, Congress and the Nation Vol. V, p. 720)*

The law (PL 95-511) required the government to obtain a warrant from a special FISA court before it could conduct foreign surveillance in which one of the parties was a U.S. citizen. The FISA court did not have jurisdiction over intelligence operations that took place completely outside the United States. Cases that came before the court were sealed and generally were not revealed even when subsequent court cases were based on evidence obtained through the warrants.

The president could authorize electronic surveillance to collect foreign intelligence without first getting court approval for up to three days in an emergency and fifteen days after a declaration of war by Congress. The government also could conduct warrantless surveillance for up to a year if the activity involved communications only among foreigners and if communications of U.S. citizens or residents were unlikely to be collected.

In December 2005 the *New York Times* revealed that the National Security Agency (NSA) had been secretly monitoring international telephone calls and e-mails of U.S. residents without warrants. The secret program, authorized by President George W. Bush in the year following the Sept. 11, 2001, terrorist attacks, monitored thousands of U.S. citizens, permanent residents, tourists, and foreigners in the country to track possible links to terrorist groups, including al Qaeda. In January 2007, after Democrats took control of both chambers of Congress, the Bush administration announced that the NSA surveillance program had been submitted to the FISA court for approval and that the court had granted several orders. Subsequent reports indicated some effort by the court to limit surveillance of foreign communications that were routed through the United States.

On May 1, 2007, National Intelligence Director Michael McConnell called on Congress to update FISA to reflect the widespread advances in communications technology by making the law "technologically neutral." He told the Senate Select Intelligence Committee that the law should be changed to allow warrantless surveillance of foreign terrorism suspects without regard to whether they were communicating with people in the United States—essentially, one of the activities that the administration had conducted through the NSA program. On July 28, 2007, Bush called on Congress to send him a bill that would authorize U.S. intelligence agencies to cope with "sophisticated terrorists" who used disposable cell phones, the Internet, and other technologies that were not available when FISA was written. On Aug. 4, 2007, Congress cleared a Republican-written bill that gave the government significant latitude under FISA, but the law lasted temporarily for six months.

In March the Senate Select Intelligence Committee told the administration it would assess whether legislation was still needed. The administration submitted a legislative proposal in April and began lobbying urgently for a new law in late July. A few days before the House and Senate were to begin the August recess, President Bush, Gonzales, and Director of National Intelligence Michael McConnell suddenly ramped up their demand for an expansion of the executive branch's authority to eavesdrop without a warrant on foreign targets, whether or not the target was communicating with someone in the United States. They said the change was necessary to prevent a possibly imminent terrorist attack from occurring.

The White House said a secret FISA court ruling had dangerously impaired the government's ability to conduct counterterrorism-related electronic surveillance. In arguing for the bill, House Minority Leader John A. Boehner, R-Ohio, revealed that the ruling had limited the government's ability to spy without warrants on foreign-to-foreign communications that passed through the United States.

Democrats argued that the FISA law had been updated many times since it was enacted and that any further changes should ensure a court check on the government's surveillance of U.S. citizens. House and Senate Democrats put together legislation to allow warrantless surveillance of foreign-to-foreign communications and, in some circumstances, of communications between U.S. citizens and targets overseas. But Democrats could not get the legislation through either the House or Senate.

Under intense White House pressure, Democratic leaders agreed to a six-month law written by the administration. This bill allowed the administration to immediately begin conducting warrantless surveillance of foreign targets, whether or not the target was communicating with someone in the United States. The bill required the attorney general, in consultation with the director of national intelligence (DNI), to write procedures for collecting the information. Those procedures would later be subject to FISA court approval.

After House passage of the temporary bill, Speaker Nancy Pelosi, D-Calif., directed the chairmen of the Intelligence and Judiciary committees to send the House a bill after the recess that would scale back the temporary law. Senate Majority Leader Harry Reid, D-Nev., followed suit. Bush, meanwhile, called for a comprehensive overhaul of the FISA law, including language that would make the existing provisions permanent and protect telecommunications companies against lawsuits for their alleged past role in the NSA's warrantless surveillance program.

SIX-MONTH BILL

Democrats spent days trying to negotiate changes to the plan being advanced by the White House, but in the end they were able to secure only the promise that it would be kept short-term, with an expiration date six months from enactment. The bill (S 1927) did not include retroactive immunity provisions.

Democratic leaders reluctantly accepted the administration bill after their efforts to pass legislation more to their liking failed. House Democrats brought their own bill (HR 3356) to the floor Aug. 3 under expedited procedures that required a two-thirds majority. The 218–207 tally fell sixty-six votes short of the number needed.

The Senate passed the White House bill (S 1927) by a **key vote of 60–28 (R 43–0; D 16–27; I 1–1),** also on Aug. 3, once Republicans agreed to the six-month expiration date. The Senate then rejected a version of the Democrats' bill (S 2011) by a vote of 43–45. *(2007 key votes, p. 955)*

The House cleared the administration bill Aug. 4 on a **key vote of 227–183 (R 186–2; D 41–181).** Bush signed the bill into law Aug. 5.

HOUSE COMMITTEE ACTION

The House Select Intelligence and Judiciary committees worked together after the August recess to produce their legislation (HR 3773) designed to scale back the executive branch's spying authority.

The Judiciary Committee approved the bill (H Rept 110-373, Part 1), introduced by Chairman John Conyers Jr., D-Mich., by a vote of 20–14 on Oct. 10. Conyers argued that it provided the tools to both "go after terrorists and protect vital rights of Americans." Republicans said it gave too many rights to terrorists and would harm national security.

The bill contained provisions to clarify that government officials would not have to seek court orders to spy on foreign-to-foreign communications. It permitted the DNI and the attorney general to apply to the FISA court for surveillance of targets or groups of foreign targets reasonably believed to be located outside the United States when the surveillance could involve individuals in the United States. The DNI and attorney general would have to certify that the targets were not reasonably believed to be "United States persons" and that a significant purpose of the surveillance was to obtain foreign intelligence information.

The application also would have to describe the so-called minimization procedures the government would use to lessen the aggregation and retention of sensitive information about U.S. citizens. The procedures would have to bar the dissemination of nonpublic information gleaned from Americans that was not necessary to foreign intelligence gathering or law enforcement. The order would be for one year and could be extended for an additional year.

The measure also allowed the DNI and attorney general to conduct electronic surveillance for up to seven days before submitting an application to the FISA court. They could conduct warrantless surveillance for up to forty-five days in an "emergency situation" if certain criteria were met.

The bill did not include retroactive liability protection for telecommunications firms that allegedly participated in the NSA program.

The Select Intelligence Committee approved an amended version of the bill (H Rept 110-373, Part 2), 12–7, also on Oct. 10. Both votes were along party lines. Democrats won adoption of several amendments requiring more court and congressional oversight. The committee adopted 12–7 an en bloc amendment by Rush D. Holt, D-N.J., to reaffirm that FISA was the only basis for conducting domestic surveillance; to require the administration to "fully inform" Congress on any surveillance programs put into place since the Sept. 11, 2001, attacks; to increase the number of FISA court judges and personnel handling FISA warrants; and to require that the FISA court examine and approve how guidelines were applied for surveillance targeting. Holt had been at the forefront of a revolt against the Conyers legislation by Democrats who were focused on strongly protecting civil liberties.

HOUSE FLOOR ACTION

The House took up a merger of the two bill versions (HR 3773). Floor action began Oct. 17 and was slated to finish after a brief recess. Democratic leaders, however, abruptly pulled the measure in the face of a threatened GOP procedural move that would have effectively killed the bill. Republicans planned to offer a motion to recommit the bill to committee for an amendment to ensure that the measure would not prevent any form of surveillance of Osama bin Laden, al Qaeda, or any other designated terrorist organization.

Typically, motions to recommit legislation, if adopted, result in an immediate floor amendment. But the instructions in this motion were to report back "promptly" rather than "forthwith." That important procedural distinction would have removed the bill from the floor, requiring its return to committee for formal action. Voting against the motion would have opened members to charges that they were weak on terrorism.

Majority Leader Steny H. Hoyer, D-Md., said the leadership would bring the surveillance bill back to the floor quickly and disputed reports that it was pulled because Democrats lacked the votes to pass it. But the legislation did not return to the House floor until November. When it did, Republicans tried to send it back to the Intelligence and Judiciary committees with instructions to clarify that it would not confer rights on state sponsors of terrorism or their agents. Democrats had added language to the bill clarifying that illegal immigrants would not be ensured rights under the bill in an attempt to head off similar GOP motions to recommit. The House rejected the motion 194–222 and then passed HR 3773 by a vote of 227–189 on Nov. 15, despite a White House veto threat. All but five Republicans voted against the measure.

SENATE COMMITTEE ACTION

Two Senate committees marked up versions of a companion bill.

The Senate Select Intelligence Committee voted 13–2 on Oct. 18 to approve a surveillance bill (S 2248—S Rept 110-209) that included retroactive legal immunity. The bill, written by Chairman John D. Rockefeller IV, D-W.Va., and Vice Chairman Christopher S. Bond, R-Mo., permitted warrantless surveillance targeting foreigners overseas regardless of whether they were communicating with someone in the United States. But it gave the secret FISA court the power to approve several aspects of warrantless surveillance of targets reasonably believed to be outside the United States. The bill provided that the legislation would expire Dec. 31, 2013.

Before approving the bill, the Intelligence Committee adopted 8–7 an amendment by Russ Feingold, D-Wis., and Ron Wyden, D-Ore., calling for more oversight by the Justice Department inspector general, along with semiannual reports to Congress. The committee also adopted 9–6 an amendment by Wyden, Feingold, and Sheldon Whitehouse, D-R.I., to require FISA court approval for surveillance of a U.S. citizen who was overseas.

On Nov. 15, the Senate Judiciary Committee voted 10–9 to approve a substitute amendment, offered by Chairman Patrick J. Leahy, D-Vt., to S 2248 that dropped the retroactive immunity. While the spying provisions were similar to Rockefeller's approach, the Judiciary panel sought to place more restrictions on the executive branch. The Judiciary measure would sunset the bill on Dec. 31, 2011.

SENATE FLOOR ACTION

Brokering a compromise between Rockefeller and Leahy proved impossible for Reid. As part of his effort, Reid introduced two bills on Dec. 10 (S 2440, S 2441) that mixed the Rockefeller and Leahy approaches. In the end, Reid tried to bring Rockefeller's bill to the floor in the final week of the session, with the Judiciary amendment as the pending business.

On Dec. 17, 2007, the Senate voted 76–10 to invoke cloture on the motion to proceed to Rockefeller's bill. But opponents, particularly critics of retroactive immunity, refused to waive the required thirty hours of postcloture debate. Reid pulled the legislation from consideration when opponents showed they would use Senate procedures to delay action.

FISA Reforms 2008: Electronic Surveillance

Congress in 2008 cleared a White House–backed bill overhauling the 1978 Foreign Intelligence Surveillance Act (FISA), after Democrats failed to block key administration goals for electronic surveillance laws. President George W. Bush signed the bill into law (HR 6304—PL 110-261) July 10.

The legislation gave Bush the two things he wanted most: enhanced executive branch spying authority and

DOMESTIC SURVEILLANCE TIMELINE

The debate over how to regulate domestic surveillance focused on two distinct questions: How much spying power should the president have? And should telecommunications companies have legal immunity for their alleged participation in the administration's warrantless wiretapping program?

- **Fall 2001.** After the attacks of Sept. 11, 2001, the National Security Agency (NSA) started a surveillance program that did not seek warrants under the Foreign Intelligence Surveillance Act (FISA). The surveillance involved international calls where one party was in the United States. The *New York Times* reported the program's existence in 2005, prompting an outcry about invasion of privacy and lawsuits against telecommunications carriers. Republicans, who were in control of Congress, however, moved no legislation.
- **Winter 2007.** When Democrats regained control of Congress, the administration said it put its program under the supervision of the secret FISA court. The court then issued a secret order, according to officials, limiting the government's ability to spy without a warrant on calls between foreigners that were routed through U.S. telecommunications hardware, creating a backlog of new warrant applications.
- **Spring 2007.** After the backlog was disclosed, many congressional Republicans pressed Democrats to move a bill that would effectively authorize the warrantless wiretapping program. Democrats wanted to address only the "foreign to foreign" issue.
- **Summer 2007.** To hasten a bargain, the administration set aside its desire to immunize telecommunications companies from past lawsuits and pushed hard for the broad authorization, warning that terrorist plots might otherwise go undetected. Facing a split among Democrats and pressure to start their August recess on time, lawmakers acquiesced and cleared a bill allowing warrantless wiretapping for six months (PL 110-55).
- **Fall 2007.** After several liberal groups attacked the Democratic majority, party leaders vowed to improve on the six-month law. The administration requested that the spying powers be made permanent and renewed its demands for retroactive immunity for the telecommunications companies.
- **November 2007.** The House passed a bill (HR 3773) that omitted the immunity language. Democratic leaders had to make adjustments to win over liberal members, who pushed for individualized warrants but settled for a bill that would ultimately allow "basket" warrants for conducting surveillance of large numbers of targets at once that might be communicating with people in the United States. The Senate did not take up the bill.
- **Summer 2008.** Congress cleared legislation overhauling the 1978 Foreign Intelligence Surveillance Act. The bill allowed enhanced executive branch spying authority and dismissal of lawsuits against telephone companies that had assisted in the warrantless wiretapping program. President George W. Bush signed the bill into law (HR 6304—PL 110-261) July 10.

dismissal of lawsuits against telephone companies that had assisted in a warrantless wiretapping program conducted under presidential authority by the National Security Agency (NSA).

The legislation revamped FISA to establish new rules for the use of electronic surveillance to collect foreign intelligence, including monitoring communications involving parties on U.S. soil. FISA was scheduled to expire Dec. 31, 2012. The bill did not explicitly grant retroactive legal immunity to the telecommunications companies, but it came close enough to satisfy the White House by creating conditions for the courts to dismiss the lawsuits. Dozens of lawsuits had been brought against the telecommunications firms over their participation in the program.

While Democrats agreed with the Bush administration on the need to overhaul FISA, they generally wanted more restrictions to protect Americans' civil liberties. However, they were not able to resolve differences between the two chambers over the exact role of the FISA court and whether to grant retroactive immunity. Some Democrats opposed giving companies such as AT&T immunity for their work with the NSA, expressing concern about the legal precedent and the effect such immunity might have on potential court scrutiny of the program. The administration threatened to veto any bill that did not include such immunity, saying that leaving it out could discourage private-sector cooperation with future spying programs.

BACKGROUND

When the Senate cleared the bill on July 9, it ended a congressional standoff that had begun in December 2005 when the *New York Times* revealed that Bush had secretly ordered surveillance that could involve U.S. citizens without first obtaining approval from the FISA court.

Critics said the domestic surveillance program was illegal because it did not comply with FISA (PL 95-511), which required the government to get approval from a special FISA court before beginning electronic surveillance outside of criminal statutes within the United States. The law stated that the FISA procedure was the "exclusive means" to govern such surveillance. *(FISA, Congress and the Nation Vol. V, p. 720)*

The White House maintained that President Bush had the authority to order the eavesdropping under a 2001 law (PL 107-40) that authorized the use of force in response to the Sept. 11, 2001, terrorist attacks. Bush also claimed that his constitutional status as commander in chief enabled him to bypass federal laws on domestic surveillance as part of his war against terrorism. Bush had made a FISA rewrite a legislative priority for his administration. Unable to agree on a long-term overhaul, Democrats consented in August 2007 to a six-month law (PL110-55) that effectively authorized the program as Bush sought. *(2007 action, p. 249)*

The House passed a more lasting FISA bill (HR 3773) in November 2007, but the Senate still had not completed its own version by February 2008 when the temporary law was set to expire. The House bill specified that no warrant would be required for electronic surveillance of communication between parties that were not known to be "United States persons" and were reasonably believed to be located outside the country—"without respect to whether the communication passed through the United States or the surveillance device was located within the United States." Except in emergencies, the FISA court would have to approve the procedures being used before the surveillance could begin.

Warrants would still be required for electronic surveillance of foreign targets who were communicating with someone in the United States, although intelligence agencies could get "blanket" warrants covering entire groups of people. The bill did not include retroactive immunity for the telecommunications providers.

Democrats indicated they needed more time to finish a long-term bill, and President Bush reluctantly agreed to a fifteen-day extension (HR 5104—PL 110-182). The Senate then passed its version of a FISA overhaul.

The chief differences between the House and Senate versions of the bill concerned retroactive immunity for the telecommunications companies, and rules for authorizing electronic surveillance. The Senate bill included retroactive immunity provisions; the House version did not. The Senate measure allowed warrantless surveillance of foreign targets even if they were communicating with someone in the United States. The House version would have required the administration to apply to the FISA court for an order permitting spying on a large number of foreign targets that might be communicating with people in the United States.

With those differences to resolve, Democrats argued for another extension, against Bush's wishes. But every House Republican combined with a number of Democrats—some who opposed any extension, and some who sided with Bush—to reject the extension (HR 5349). The temporary law expired, and Republicans initially refused to negotiate with Democrats on a compromise, insisting that the Senate bill, favored by Bush, was the only acceptable legislation.

SENATE FLOOR ACTION

The Senate passed Feb. 12 a comprehensive FISA overhaul (S 2248) 68–29 after rejecting a series of amendments that would have turned the White House against the measure. The most significant amendments eliminated the retroactive immunity provisions. Nineteen Democrats and one independent joined forty-eight Republicans in support of the bill; no GOP senators voted against it. After passage, the Senate inserted the text into the bill (HR 3773) the House had passed the previous November.

Floor debate stretched over three weeks. Majority Leader Harry Reid, D-Nev., started with legislation favored by Republicans and the White House that was drafted by the Intelligence Committee. It included retroactive immunity and warrantless surveillance of foreign targets regardless of whether they were communicating with someone in the United States. If the FISA court later found that statutory procedural requirements were not being met, the court could order the government to correct the problems within thirty days or stop the surveillance. The bill would expire on Dec. 31, 2013.

The Senate tabled, or killed, an amendment to substitute a Judiciary Committee version, which omitted the retroactive-immunity provisions and imposed more limits on executive branch spying, including oversight authority by the FISA court. The White House warned that such an amendment could result in a veto of the bill. The vote was 60–36.

The debate then stalled in a partisan feud over floor procedures as Democrats sought ways to remove the immunity language. An effort to invoke cloture failed, largely on a party-line vote of 48–45, twelve short of the sixty needed.

In floor action in February, the Senate rejected a number of Democratic amendments, including one by Christopher J. Dodd, D-Conn., to strike the immunity provision from the bill. It was rejected 31–67. Finally, on Feb. 12, the Senate voted 69–29 to limit further debate on the bill, clearing the way for passage.

HOUSE FLOOR ACTION

House Democratic leaders reworked their bill from November 2007, and on March 14 the chamber adopted it 213–197. A mix of twelve liberal and conservative Democrats joined every Republican in voting against the bill, which still defied the president in the way it dealt with the telecommunications companies that had cooperated in the administration's eavesdropping operations. As with the November version, the bill would have expired Dec. 31, 2009.

Republicans did everything they could to force the House to accept the Senate bill, even walking out of the chamber as a group at one point. Bush castigated Democrats and said he would delay the start of a planned trip to Africa over the weekend if it would help quickly clear long-term legislation.

The rule for floor action allowed no amendments. Debate on the bill broke along party lines, with Democrats arguing that it would grant the intelligence community all the authority it needed to spy on foreign terrorist suspects while protecting Americans' civil liberties. Republicans assailed the bill for too many restrictions on surveillance and for the absence of immunity provisions.

The day before the vote on passage, the House held its first secret session in twenty-five years, at the request of the Republicans who said they wanted to discuss classified material that would help lawmakers understand the need to clear the Senate-passed legislation. Democrats derided the secret session; Republicans defended it and blamed Democrats for not getting more out of the meeting. But members of both parties said it was unlikely to change the outcome of the vote on the bill.

FINAL ACTION

Three months after the House vote, Congress cleared a new FISA overhaul bill (HR 6304) that was based on a bipartisan agreement announced June 19 and backed by the White House.

House Majority Leader Steny H. Hoyer, D-Md., said pressure from conservative House Democrats to adopt the Senate bill had forced Democratic leaders into a reluctant compromise. Hoyer and Blunt from the House struck the deal with Rockefeller and Christopher S. Bond, R-Mo., from the Senate. Supporters said the measure was an improvement over the Senate-passed bill, which would have required less court and congressional oversight.

Bush and congressional Republicans praised the legislation. "It will help our intelligence professionals learn our enemies' plans for new attacks," Bush said. "It ensures that those companies whose assistance is necessary to protect the country will themselves be protected from liability for past or future cooperation with the government."

But the final bill proved a bitter pill for many Democrats. House members who voted against it said the expansion of executive branch surveillance powers would gut Fourth Amendment protections against unreasonable search and seizure. "This bill scares me to death," said Barbara Lee, D-Calif. "It's not a happy occasion, but it's the work we have to do," said Speaker Nancy Pelosi, D-Calif. She said the debate on the legislation was "valuable for making the bill better, if not good enough, but certainly preferable to the alternative we have."

The House passed the bill (HR 6304) June 20 on a **key vote of 293–129 (R 188–1; D 105–128).** *(2008 key votes, p. 972)*

On July 9, twenty-one Senate Democrats joined all Republicans to clear the measure 69–28. Before clearing the bill, the Senate voted down a trio of amendments. Dodd and Russ Feingold, D-Wis., had managed to delay the final vote until after the Fourth of July recess, giving opponents one last chance to derail the legislation.

But an overwhelming vote of 80–15 on June 25 to limit debate on a motion to proceed to the legislation made it all but certain that they would not succeed. All three of the Democrats' amendments were aimed at modifying or eliminating the retroactive immunity. They were:

- A proposal by Feingold and Dodd to strip out the immunity provisions rejected on July 9 on a **key vote of 32–66 (R 0–48; D 31–17; I 1–1).** *(2008 key votes, p. 972*
- An amendment by Arlen Specter, R-Pa, defeated 37–61, to deny retroactive immunity to a telecommunications company that aided in government surveillance activities if the court found that the intelligence activities violated the Constitution.
- An amendment by Jeff Bingaman, D-N.M., defeated 42–56 to stay pending lawsuits against the phone companies until ninety days after Congress received an inspectors general report, required by the bill, on the warrantless surveillance program.

The White House opposed all three amendments, insisting any provision that jeopardized or delayed retroactive legal immunity threatened future private-sector cooperation with spying programs. Rockefeller said the bill would prevent a repeat of Bush's warrantless surveillance program by strengthening court review and congressional oversight. Senate Judiciary Chairman Patrick J. Leahy, D-Vt., disagreed. "This bill would dismiss ongoing cases against the telecommunications carriers that participated in that program without allowing a judicial review of the legality of the program," he said.

Concessions to Democrats in the final bill included:

- The requirement for prior court review of electronic surveillance procedures and provisions to limit the information that could be retained and disseminated on U.S. citizens.
- A stronger statement that FISA and the bill were the only means by which the executive branch could conduct surveillance related to foreign intelligence and that the act could be modified only by a new statute directly addressing the executive branch's foreign intelligence surveillance authority.
- The requirement that inspectors general report to Congress within a year on the president's warrantless surveillance program.

MAJOR PROVISIONS

As signed into law July 10, 2008, HR 6304 (PL 110-261) included the following major provisions:

Warrantless surveillance. Allowed the attorney general and director of national intelligence (DNI) to jointly authorize up to one year of surveillance of parties that they reasonably believed were not Americans and were located outside the country. Specified that no FISA warrant was required, even if the communications were routed through the United States.

FISA review. Required the attorney general and DNI, before such surveillance could begin, to secure approval from the FISA court of the procedures to be used, but not of the targets. Allowed the surveillance to start prior to the FISA court review if the need was deemed urgent. Gave the court thirty days to determine whether the procedures met statutory guidelines on providing reasonable assurance that the target was outside the United States, preventing the targeting of communication with anyone known to be in the United States, and minimizing possible disclosure of any information acquired about an American. Required the agencies to comply with the procedures if the court withheld approval or terminate the surveillance.

Domestic surveillance. Required FISA court warrants for surveillance that targeted anyone located in the United States, as required by previous law. Required a FISA warrant for surveillance of Americans located outside the country.

Lawsuit waivers. Required federal and state courts to dismiss existing lawsuits against companies that assisted the Bush administration's warrantless surveillance program if there was "substantial evidence" the companies had received written assurances that the program was legal and authorized by the president.

Surveillance rationale. Included language stating that FISA, as modified by the new law, was "the exclusive means by which electronic surveillance and the interception of domestic wire, oral, or electronic communications may be conducted." Specified that any variations or modifications could be made only through a new statute directly addressing FISA.

Program reviews. Required the inspectors general for the Justice Department, DNI, NSA, and Defense Department to review the president's warrantless surveillance program and report within a year. Required the administration to file periodic reports to Congress on the execution of the new law, disclosures of FISA court orders, and other information.

Passport Requirements

During consideration of the fiscal 2008 Homeland Security appropriations measure (HR 2764—PL 110-161), lawmakers addressed the thorny issue of whether passports should be required when traveling to neighboring nations. Congress in the bill cleared in late 2007 decided, in a policy rider on the spending bill, to delay a requirement that U.S. citizens carry a passport for land and sea travel to Canada, Mexico, the Caribbean, and Bermuda. The Homeland Security and State departments were told to postpone the program until three months after they met a series of certification requirements or until June 1, 2009, whichever was later.

The administration of President George W. Bush had opposed the provision, saying it would inhibit the work of Customs and Border Protection. The fiscal 2007 Homeland Security appropriations law (PL 109-295) had allowed but did not require the departments to delay the passport requirement for up to fifteen months. *(Fiscal 2007 Homeland Security spending bill, p. 102)*

BACKGROUND

Congress rewrote the rules for documentation and travel within North America at the end of 2004. One major provision took effect Jan. 20, 2007, when airlines began requiring passports or other proof of citizenship from all passengers on flights linking the United States to Canada, Mexico, and the Caribbean. Canada was upset over the next phase, which extended the national identification requirements to all land travelers at the start of 2008.

Before this new requirement, Americans who crossed the U.S.-Canadian or U.S.-Mexican borders in either direction needed to show a driver's license and birth certificate, but Congress accepted the Bush administration argument that those were inadequate documents to guard against terrorism because a driver's license does not prove citizenship and birth certificates are not secure documents.

The Government Accountability Office (GAO) had cautioned in 2006 that requiring passports would pose "broad and extensive challenges" for implementation. Sen. Patrick J. Leahy, D-Vt., got a provision added to the Homeland Security Department's fiscal 2007 spending bill providing the department with an eighteen-month extension, to June 2009.

Canadian business interests along with many American businesses near the Canadian border opposed the passport requirement arguing that it would stifle tourism and trade, potentially costing billions for businesses in both countries.

LEGISLATIVE ACTION

The Senate Appropriations Committee June 14 approved by voice vote a package of amendments by Leahy to the Homeland Security spending bill that included a delay in the passport requirement for U.S. citizens traveling by sea and land to and from Canada, Mexico, the Caribbean, and Bermuda. The measure barred the Homeland Security and State departments from beginning the passport program until three months after the departments had met a series of certification requirements or by June 1, 2009, whichever was later.

Leahy cited recent troubles with passport processing, which previously caused the Homeland Security Department to delay the implementation of a similar requirement for air travel, which finally took effect in January. "The administration is walking blithely toward a cliff with this program, and they're threatening to take millions of Americans with them," Leahy said.

The House passed the $37.4 billion Homeland Security spending bill 268–150 on June 15, 2007, with significant GOP support. Before passage, Democrats agreed to add money for border fencing and to delay the controversial new passport requirements for U.S. citizens traveling in the Western Hemisphere.

The language targeting the passport requirements was adopted 379–45 in an amendment by Steven C. LaTourette, R-Ohio. The amendment barred the department from spending money to implement the new passport rules for Western Hemisphere travel before June 2009. Congress already had extended the deadline from September 2007 to Jan. 1, 2008, for those who could show that they had applied for a passport but had not yet received one because of delays in processing.

The Homeland Security Department subsequently issued rules phasing in the new passport requirements for land and sea travel, with full implementation due by June 1, 2009.

Terrorism Insurance

Congress agreed in 2007 to a seven-year extension of a federal terrorism insurance program created to help stabilize the commercial real estate market in the wake of the Sept. 11, 2001, attacks. President George W. Bush signed the measure into law Dec. 26, 2007 (HR 2761—PL 110-160).

BACKGROUND

The Terrorism Risk Insurance Act (TRIA) was enacted in 2002 at a time when the property and casualty insurance industry was thrown into disarray by the heavy losses suffered in the 2001 terrorist attacks. Lobbyists for the industry said insurers would pay claims from the attacks but that they could not continue to offer terrorism insurance unless the federal government stepped in to share the risk. The reinsurance industry, which had played that role in the past, said it could no longer do so because it had no way to estimate the likelihood or costs of such attacks.

Without terrorism insurance coverage, mortgages for big projects would have been too costly. Mortgage lenders would have had to factor in the risk that the building could be destroyed and the borrower could be left with no money to pay the mortgage or rebuild.

The 2002 program required insurance firms that sold commercial property and casualty insurance to offer clients insurance coverage for damages caused by foreign terrorist attacks. The government was responsible for paying 90 percent of the claims arising from a terrorist attack once insurers' aggregate losses exceeded a certain threshold, beginning at $5 million and rising annually after that. The government's responsibility was capped at $100 billion per year.

TRIA was initially seen as a temporary backstop to give the industry time to create a market-based system to absorb the risks. The original law (PL 107-297) was good through the end of 2005. Insurers and the real estate industry won a two-year extension through Dec. 31, 2007 (PL 109-144), which also raised the threshold to $50 million in 2006 and $100 million in 2007. *(TRIA, Congress and the Nation Vol. XI, p. 203)*

With that law due to expire at the end of 2007, the insurers and realtors lobbied for a long-term extension, arguing that private companies could not shoulder risks from both domestic and foreign terrorism. The idea of a long-term extension had considerable Democratic support, particularly in the House. But many Republicans opposed it, arguing that market forces should be left to determine the solutions for insuring against risks of terrorist attacks.

HOUSE ACTION

The House Financial Services Committee approved a long-term extension and expansion of the terrorism insurance program by a vote of 49–20 on Aug. 1, 2007. The bill (HR 2761—H Rept 110-318), sponsored by committee chairman Barney Frank, D-Mass., included provisions to extend TRIA for fifteen years, through Dec. 31, 2022, and added group life insurance to the lines of coverage included under the program. Frank's bill also required insurers to make coverage available to property and casualty and group life insurance policyholders for losses resulting from domestic, as well as foreign, terrorism. The measure also lowered the threshold for federal intervention to $50 million.

Conservative Republicans opposed the bill, saying it would expose taxpayers to potentially huge costs and prevent the development of private-market solutions. Democrats and some Republicans countered that the issue was one of national security, which required a shared burden among all taxpayers, not just those in high-risk areas.

The White House had warned two days earlier that Bush's advisers would recommend a veto. The statement said TRIA "should be phased out in favor of a private market for terrorism insurance" and that the administration strongly opposed expanding the government's role. Despite the veto threat, the House easily passed the fifteen-year extension by a vote of 312–110 on Sept. 19. Eighty-eight Republicans joined most Democrats in supporting the measure.

Before the vote, House leaders wrote a last-minute change to require that a future Congress expressly approve, under expedited procedures, any spending for the program after an attack. The legislation would bypass committee action and would not be limited by budget rules.

The change was necessary to comply with pay-as-you-go budget rules that Democrats had put in place at the start of the Congress. Under the rules, any new mandatory spending or tax cuts had to be fully offset. In a report released

Sept. 6, the Congressional Budget Office (CBO) had said the fifteen-year extension of the program would increase the budget deficit by $3.5 billion over the next five years and $8.4 billion over the next decade.

The leadership's solution drew fire from insurers, who complained that they needed a guaranteed federal backstop.

SENATE ACTION

The Senate Banking, Housing and Urban Affairs Committee approved a narrower, seven-year reauthorization bill (S 2285—S Rept 110-215) by a vote of 20–1 on Oct. 17. The measure kept the existing $100 million trigger for coverage and did not propose expanding the kinds of risks that would be covered.

"Nearly all of the experts say that the insurance industry alone cannot insure against" terrorist attacks, Senate Banking Chairman Christopher J. Dodd, D-Conn., said. Dodd, whose state was home to significant insurance interests, made it clear that he favored making the TRIA program permanent. That was not an option for him, however, given the strong opposition of Senate Republicans, particularly that of ranking Republican Richard C. Shelby of Alabama.

Shelby agreed to the Senate version, despite longstanding objections to the program, but his office said he did not support the House language. Treasury Secretary Henry M. Paulson Jr. said on the day of the markup that the Bush administration would not oppose the Senate version of the bill.

The Senate passed HR 2761 by voice vote Nov. 16, after inserting the text of its own version. To solve pay-as-you-go issues that had stalled floor action, negotiators worked out a plan to accelerate annual payments by the insurance industry. The payments, already required by law, were to reimburse the government for coverage, up to a certain level.

HOUSE ACTION

With the two chambers at an impasse, Frank won passage of a modified bill (HR 4299) that accepted the seven-year extension but retained other provisions to expand the program. But Shelby rejected the revised measure, and the White House threatened to veto both House bills.

Facing the Dec. 31 expiration of the program, Frank ultimately accepted the narrower Senate bill. Still, the insurance industry, along with several lawmakers, said Frank's aggressive push for a broad bill helped make the case for a lengthy extension and pushed Shelby to accept a longer reauthorization than he originally wanted.

Expressing frustration at what he called the Senate's "take it or leave it" approach, Frank shepherded a modified version of his bill through the House in the hope of prodding senators to negotiate. The House passed the new measure (HR 4299) by a vote of 303–116 on Dec. 12.

Frank made several concessions to the Senate, accepting an extension of seven years rather than fifteen and dropping efforts to significantly expand the program's scope. But the bill still proposed to add group life insurance coverage to the program, lower the trigger for federal intervention from $100 million to $50 million, and reduce deductibles in areas already hit by a terrorist attack, a provision supported by many New York Democrats.

After the vote, Frank said it was "not likely" the Senate would take up the new bill, but he said, "They're going to get a lot of heat." Shelby refused to bend; the White House renewed its veto threat.

With the session drawing to a close and the previous law about to expire, the House yielded to the Senate, clearing the narrower Senate-passed bill (HR 2761) by a vote of 360–53 on Dec. 18, 2007.

Foreign Investment

Early in the 110th Congress, Congress easily cleared bipartisan legislation to overhaul the process for reviewing foreign investments that might affect U.S. national security. President George W. Bush signed the bill into law July 26, 2007 (HR 556—PL 110-49).

The signing of the measure marked a quiet legislative finale to an issue that had roiled Washington in 2006, after DP World—a company based in Dubai (one of seven emirates composing the United Arab Emirates—won approval from the Bush administration to acquire operational control of six U.S. port terminals through a deal with a British firm. The arrangement had been approved by the Committee on Foreign Investment in the United States (CFIUS), a secretive multiagency panel charged with reviewing the national security risks posed by proposed foreign acquisitions. *(CFIUS background box, p. 242)*

BACKGROUND

CFIUS was created by executive order in 1975, and its powers were expanded in 1988. Congress had expressed concerns about oversight in the past, but it was only after the administration approved the Dubai ports deal that the calls for an overhaul led to attempts at legislative action.

The news that a foreign government would own six U.S. ports caught lawmakers unaware and the subsequent congressional outcry put an end to the deal. Even though DP World pulled out of the investment on March 9, 2006, concerns with the regulation of foreign investments persisted. Lawmakers insisted that they should have been informed during the approval process, not afterward. They also complained that the Bush administration had failed to follow a 1992 law (PL 102-484) that requires a full investigation of any acquisition involving a foreign government-owned company. CFIUS did not take that step in the DP World case. *(1992 law, Congress and the Nation Vol. VIII, p. 395)*

Both chambers passed bills in 2006 to overhaul CFIUS, but House and Senate negotiators could not agree on how to protect national security while still maintaining an open environment for foreign investment. Business groups said elements of the Senate bill, such as a requirement that CFIUS notify Congress of every acquisition submitted to it for review, could chill foreign investment. The legislation died at the end of the 109th Congress. *(2006 CFIUS legislation, p. 243)*

In 2007 the two chambers worked more closely, producing similar bills from the outset. Massachusetts Democrat Barney Frank, chairman of the House Financial Services Committee, got off to an early start, winning House passage in February of a bill very similar to the one the chamber had passed in 2006. Christopher J. Dodd, D-Conn., chairman of the Senate Banking, Housing and Urban Affairs Committee, and the panel's ranking Republican, Richard C. Shelby of Alabama, took the House-passed bill as a starting point and made modest changes, which the House accepted and cleared in July.

Both versions proposed establishing CFIUS in statute for the first time, requiring a full-blown national security investigation of foreign bids by state-owned companies and formalizing the role of the national intelligence director in such reviews. The Senate-passed bill, however, included narrower congressional reporting mandates and focused more on threats to critical infrastructure. The business community generally supported the legislation, saying it would provide needed certainty in the review process.

HOUSE COMMITTEE ACTION

The House Financial Services Committee approved its bill (HR 556—H Rept 110-24, Part 1), based on the previous year's measure, by voice vote Feb. 13. The bill was sponsored by Carolyn B. Maloney, D-N.Y.

Before approving the bill, the committee adopted 40–29 an amendment by Tom Price, R-Ga., that was opposed by the Bush administration and a majority of Democrats. It added language requiring presidential approval for any transaction involving a foreign government or national from a country designated as a state sponsor of terrorism. The State Department listed five countries—Cuba, Iran, North Korea, Sudan, and Syria—in that category. Under existing law, the president made the final decision only when CFIUS agencies could not reach consensus after a second-stage investigation or the panel recommended blocking a deal.

To enhance congressional oversight of the secretive review process, the bill proposed establishing the panel in statute and requiring CFIUS to report to Congress within five days of final action in a case. It also proposed formalizing the role of the national intelligence director in the review process and elevating the Homeland Security secretary to vice chairman of the panel, a new position, along with the Commerce secretary. The Treasury secretary would lead the committee.

The bill required a second-stage, forty-five day investigation if the proposed acquisition threatened to impair national security and if efforts to modify the deal to remove the threat had been unsuccessful. A full investigation also was required if the deal involved a foreign government. That step could be waived if the heads of Treasury, Homeland Security, and Commerce certified that the case presented no security risks and would require no mitigation agreements, contingencies that CFIUS sometimes required before approving a deal. CFIUS had approved the DP World deal without launching a second-stage investigation.

HOUSE FLOOR ACTION

The House passed the bill 423–0 on Feb. 28, 2007. During floor consideration, Frank said the goal was to prevent the DP World debacle "from leading to bad public policy that would extend to restricting and discouraging foreign direct investment in general." Spencer Bachus of Alabama, the ranking Republican on the Financial Services panel, agreed, saying the bill "modernizes the way CFIUS does business" without pushing the United States toward protectionism.

The House adopted several amendments by voice vote, including a manager's amendment with changes sought by Duncan Hunter of California, the ranking Republican on Armed Services. In one of the new provisions, CFIUS would be required to develop ways to monitor companies' compliance with risk-mitigation agreements and to report annually to Congress on those methods.

The White House endorsed the bill in a statement of administration policy but expressed concerns about procedural requirements, such as roll call votes, "ill-suited" for a body that could "deter the full and open interagency discussion that is required."

SENATE COMMITTEE ACTION

The Senate Banking, Housing and Urban Affairs Committee approved its version of the bill (S 1610—S Rept 110-80) by voice vote May 16, 2007. Compared with the House version, the bill generally focused more power in the Treasury secretary and loosened the congressional reporting requirements. "With this new law, a Dubai Ports World would not be able to happen," said Charles E. Schumer, D-N.Y., who was among those who caused DP World's deal to unravel.

Among the modifications to the House bill, the Senate measure added a requirement for a forty-five-day investigation if the deal would result in foreign control of any critical infrastructure.

The Senate measure also made the Homeland Security secretary the only vice chairman, a position that would have been shared with the Commerce secretary under the House bill. It also allowed CFIUS to decide against a full investigation of a transaction involving a foreign government based on certification from the Treasury secretary and the lead agency—omitting the Homeland and Commerce secretaries. The Senate bill also dropped the House amendment requiring that the president approve any transactions that involved countries on the watch list.

FINAL ACTION

The Senate passed the legislation (HR 556) by voice vote June 29 after substituting the text of its own version, with some technical changes. The House accepted the Senate changes, clearing the bill by a vote of 370–45 on July 11.

Dodd emphasized the new role of the intelligence director in the review process and the bill's clarification "that the president has the ultimate authority to suspend or prohibit a covered transaction if there is credible evidence that U.S. national security is at risk."

Shelby called the Senate version "a reasonable compromise that achieves the primary objective of safeguarding our nation's security without unnecessarily restricting the flow of direct foreign investment that is critical to the U.S. economy."

MAJOR PROVISIONS

As signed into law July 26, 2007, HR 556 (PL 110-49) included the following major provisions:

CFIUS statutory authorization. Established CFIUS, which had been created by executive order in 1975, in statute. Specified that the Treasury secretary would chair the committee and that the Homeland Security secretary would be the vice chairman. Specified that other members would be the secretaries of Labor, Commerce, Defense, Energy, and State; the attorney general; the director of national intelligence; and the heads of any other agency the president chose to add.

Authorization. Authorized $10 million per year in fiscal 2008 through 2011 for the Treasury Department to pay for CFIUS operations.

Reviews. Required CFIUS to conduct a review to determine the national security implications of any transaction that might result in foreign control of a company engaged in interstate commerce and to conduct the review in no more than thirty days.

Investigations. Required CFIUS to carry out a full forty-five-day investigation if the review found that the transaction threatened to impair national security and the threat was not mitigated during the review; if the transaction involved a company owned by a foreign government; or if it involved critical infrastructure and national security concerns that had not been resolved during the review.

Congressional oversight. Required CFIUS and the lead agency on any transaction to notify Congress upon completing a review and to submit a certified written report on the results of any full-blown investigation "as soon as is practicable" after it was completed. Specified that the notices and reports were to be sent to the Senate majority and minority leaders, the House Speaker and minority leader, and the chairmen and ranking members of the Senate Banking and House Financial Services committees. Also specified the report would go to the senators and representative from the state and district where the business was headquartered if the transaction involved critical infrastructure.

Required CFIUS to submit an annual report to the chairmen and ranking members of the committees of jurisdiction in Congress on all the transactions reviewed and investigated during the previous twelve months. Allowed a member of Congress to request and receive a classified briefing after final action on any transaction.

Presidential action. Authorized the president to suspend or prohibit any transaction that threatened to impair national security. Required the president to announce whether or not he decided to take such action within fifteen days after an investigation was completed.

National security agreements. Allowed CFIUS to enter into agreements with the parties to a transaction to mitigate any threats to national security. Required CFIUS to name an appropriate lead federal agency to monitor the compliance with any agreement, negotiate any changes in an agreement, and report back to CFIUS on compliance and any modifications.

Intelligence analysis. Required the director of national intelligence to provide an analysis to CFIUS of the security implications of any transaction under review.

Ammonium Nitrate Controls

Congress in 2007 approved new regulations to control ammonium nitrate, a highly explosive chemical commonly found in agriculture fertilizers. The chemical was used in the 1995 Oklahoma City federal building bombing.

The measure required the registration of anyone who owned or purchased ammonium nitrate. The Homeland Security secretary could issue fines of up to $50,000 if someone sold the chemical without registering with the department. The bill also required buyers of the chemical compound to undergo a terrorist watch-list check, which had to be done within seventy-two hours.

The legislation was introduced in the House by Homeland Security Committee Chairman Bennie Thompson, D-Miss., (HR 1680) in March 2007. The House approved the bill in October 2007 but the provisions eventually ended up being folded into that year's Homeland Security appropriations bill (HR 2764). *(Homeland Security appropriations bill, pp. 112, 114)*

In fall 2007 the Homeland Security appropriations bill, like ten other fiscal 2008 appropriations measures, became ensnared in the Democrats' battle with the White House over nondefense spending. In the end, Democratic appropriators trimmed the spending bill and folded it into a year-end omnibus package. President George W. Bush signed the omnibus into law Dec. 26 (HR 2764—PL 110-161)

BACKGROUND

Bills to regulate ammonium nitrate had been introduced since the 108th Congress, yet only a bill by former representative Curt Weldon, R-Pa., introduced in the 109th Congress, showed potential for passage. The House Homeland

Security Committee reported the measure favorably in June 2006, but the bill did not receive floor consideration.

Ammonium nitrate, or its chemical formula, NH_4NO_3, is commonly used in high-nitrogen fertilizers, favored by farmers because they are fast acting and inexpensive. Besides its widespread agricultural use, ammonium nitrate is also an ingredient in other household items, including instant cold packs.

The chemical compound has highly explosive qualities when mixed with a hydrocarbon, such as diesel fuel or kerosene. Terrorist groups have used the volatile mixture in improvised explosive devices. On April 19, 1995, Timothy McVeigh and Terry Nichols used 108 fifty-five-pound bags of ammonium nitrate fertilizer and three fifty-five-gallon drums of diesel oil to bomb the Alfred P. Murrah Federal Building in Oklahoma City, killing 168 people. In a June 2006 sting operation, the Royal Canadian Mounted Police arrested members of a suspected terrorist cell after they ordered 6,600 pounds of ammonium nitrate as part of an alleged plot to blow up Canadian national monuments.

HOUSE ACTION

The Homeland Security Committee's Emerging Threats, Cybersecurity, and Science and Technology Subcommittee approved HR 1680 by voice vote on March 29, 2007. Thompson said the purpose of the bill was "to keep [the] valuable fertilizer available to farmers across the country, and at the same time take the necessary measures to help provide additional security for ammonium nitrate fertilizer and not unduly burden agricultural professionals or farmers who use this fertilizer for legitimate use."

The House Homeland Security Committee approved the bill by voice vote April 26. The committee amended the bill to include a provision sought by Dan Lungren, R-Calif., making buyers of the chemical compound subject to the terrorist watch-list check. When Lungren first proposed the amendment during an April 17 markup, Democrats argued that the amendment could place a burden on owners of small farms that use the fertilizer.

The committee then approved a compromise version of Lungren's amendment. The new language, which followed conditions set forth in an April 20 American Farm Bureau letter, required that the Homeland Security Department issue or deny registration numbers within seventy-two hours of receiving an application. The compromise also required the department to resolve appeals on watch-list matches within seventy-two hours.

The legislation also required ammonium nitrate facility owners to maintain a record of all sales transactions for two years after the sales. The measure did not preempt state ammonium nitrate laws unless they were not as strong as the federal law. The bill required the Department of Homeland Security to designate the concentration of ammonium nitrate in compounds, such as fertilizer, that should be subject to regulation.

Thompson backed the revised Lungren amendment. The only Democrat to continue objecting to the terror watch list requirement was Sheila Jackson-Lee, D-Texas, who advocated further study of the system. She said its "faults may overcome its good intentions."

The House passed the bill by voice vote under suspension of the rules Oct. 23, 2007. Jackson-Lee even delivered a House speech in support of the bill. The following day HR 1680 was referred to the Senate Homeland Security and Governmental Affairs Committee. Instead of marking up the bill, however, the language was included in the Homeland Security spending bill, which ended up being folded into the end-of-the-year fiscal 2008 omnibus appropriations bill.

Chemical Plant Regulation

Congress in 2007 gave the Department of Homeland Security permanent regulatory power over the chemical industry and established an Office of Chemical Facility Security in the department in an effort to better guard against terrorist threats. The legislation started as a bill (HR 5577) approved in March by the House Homeland Security Committee, but the legislation was never voted on by the full House. The issue of chemical plant security was ultimately addressed in the fiscal 2008 Homeland Security appropriations bill, which was rolled into an omnibus spending package signed by President George W. Bush on Dec. 26, 2007 (HR 2764—PL 110-161).

The chemical plant provision in the omnibus bill allowed states to impose tougher security regulations on chemical plants than those enforced by the federal government. The White House opposed the provision, saying it would harm the Homeland Security Department's ability to set and enforce a single national security standard for chemical plants. *(Fiscal 2008 Homeland Security spending bill, pp. 112, 114)*

BACKGROUND

Congress began to focus attention on chemical plants as potential terrorist targets because of the Sept. 11, 2001, terrorist attacks. A study (leaked to the *Washington Post*) that was conducted one month after the Sept. 11 attacks by the Army surgeon general found that up to 2.4 million people could be killed or wounded by a terrorist attack on a single chemical plant. The FBI's National Infrastructure Protection Center warned Feb. 12, 2003, "al Qaeda operatives also may attempt to launch conventional attacks against the U.S. nuclear/chemical-industrial infrastructure to cause contamination, disruption, and terror."

The Environmental Protection Agency (EPA) identified about 120 chemical facilities in 2001 where an accident or attack could threaten more than a million people. Proponents of increased regulation cautioned against lethal possibilities of chemical plants that lack strict regulations.

Chemical plant security regulations were also attached to the fiscal 2007 Homeland Security spending legislation (PL 109–295), but unlike HR 5577, the spending bill contained no language allowing the federal government to preempt state and local laws governing chemical plants. The provisions in the fiscal 2007 appropriations measure authorized the Homeland Security Department to issue regulations for high-risk chemical plants and to shut down plants for noncompliance. The new regulations were to expire after three years. A group of thirty-four senators, led by George V. Voinovich, R-Ohio, unsuccessfully sought to limit the regulations to the "highest risk" facilities and allow them to continue indefinitely. *(Fiscal 2007 Homeland Security spending bill, p. 102)*

HOUSE ACTION

The House Homeland Security Committee on March 6 approved HR 5577 15–7 to give the Homeland Security Department permanent regulatory power over the chemical industry. The department already exercised that power through the Chemical Facility Anti-Terrorism Standards established in the fiscal 2007 Homeland Security appropriations bill but the authority was set to expire in October 2009. No companion legislation was introduced in the Senate.

During the committee markup, members from both parties negotiated an agreement on a controversial plan to require high-risk chemical plants to compare their employees' names against criminal records, the terrorist watch list, and immigration databases. Ed Perlmutter, D-Colo., proposed the amendment after working with Republicans to add new language to ensure that employees would have access to a redress process and guarantee they would not be fired for false-positive background checks. Ginny Brown-Waite, R-Fla., had proposed the background checks at a subcommittee markup, saying it was the one way to ensure that chemical plants remain safe.

CHAPTER 4

Foreign Policy

Foreign Policy

The Iraq War was approaching its second anniversary when the 109th Congress convened and closing in on its sixth anniversary when the 110th Congress adjourned. In the intervening years lawmakers had dealt with a variety of significant foreign policy issues: North Korea, Iran, Cuba, Sudan, China, the Middle East, foreign aid, HIV/AIDS, and nuclear power. But none dominated as did Iraq.

Many people had expected the war to be over by then. Instead, it slogged on and the situation on the ground for a time worsened dramatically. Sectarian violence spiraled upward and Iraq appeared to be moving—careening—toward civil war. Casualties in dead and wounded mounted. Confidence in the war began to erode, and American public opinion went from support to skepticism to outright opposition. Surveys began to show that a majority of Americans thought the war had been a mistake and troops should be brought home.

Voters took those opinions into the voting booths and in the middle of President George W. Bush's second term transferred control of Congress from the Republicans to the Democrats. Two years later they did the same with the White House.

Through it all President Bush urged Americans to "stay the course" in Iraq. That is basically what the nation did, as antiwar members of Congress found themselves unable to change that course, no matter which party was in control of the legislative branch. The reasons for that ranged from practical to political to constitutional to strategic. They did not have the votes. Republicans did not want to cross their party's president. It is difficult to challenge a commander in chief during wartime. Bush's decision to increase the number of troops in Iraq started to pay off. So, ultimately, it was Bush who, along with the Iraqi leadership, set a timetable for withdrawing the United States from Iraq.

But Congress's scorecard during the second Bush administration was far from blank when it came to foreign policy.

Both parties, for example, joined forces to insist on greater congressional involvement in a nuclear power agreement being drafted with India. The White House would have preferred to see Congress on the sidelines, but lawmakers insisted on a more active role.

Over protests from the White House, members made deep cuts in President Bush's signature foreign aid program, the Millennium Challenge Account. On the other hand, they approved many billions more than requested for a popular global HIV/AIDS program, and the White House went along.

Lawmakers also approved measures strengthening sanctions on trouble spots around the world.

A NATION AT WARS

In the wake of the Sept. 11, 2001, terrorist attacks in which nearly 3,000 people perished, the United States had gone to war on three fronts: a retaliatory war against Afghanistan, a preemptive war against Iraq, and an open-ended war against terrorism on U.S. soil and abroad.

Approval of the use of force against those responsible for the Sept. 11 attacks and those who had harbored them had come easily as Congress gave its overwhelming support. Within weeks the United States went to war against Afghanistan, closing terrorist training camps and banishing the Taliban leadership for having given safe haven to the presumed mastermind of the Sept. 11 plot, Osama bin

REFERENCES

Discussion of foreign policy for the years 1945–1964 may be found in *Congress and the Nation Vol. I,* pp. 91–232; for the years 1965–1968, *Congress and the Nation Vol. II,* pp. 49–116; for the years 1969–1972, *Congress and the Nation Vol. III,* pp. 853–948; for the years 1973–1976, *Congress and the Nation Vol. IV,* pp. 847–912; for the years 1977–1980, *Congress and the Nation Vol. V,* pp. 31–95; for the years 1981–1984, *Congress and the Nation Vol. VI,* pp. 123–197; for the years 1985–1988, *Congress and the Nation Vol. VII,* pp. 169–251; for the years 1989–1992, *Congress and the Nation Vol. VIII,* pp. 203–297; for the years 1993–1996, *Congress and the Nation Vol. IX,* pp. 187–250; for the years 1997–2000, *Congress and the Nation Vol. X,* pp. 173–231; for the years 2001–2004, *(Congress and the Nation Vol. XI,* pp. 229–300.

Outlays for International Affairs

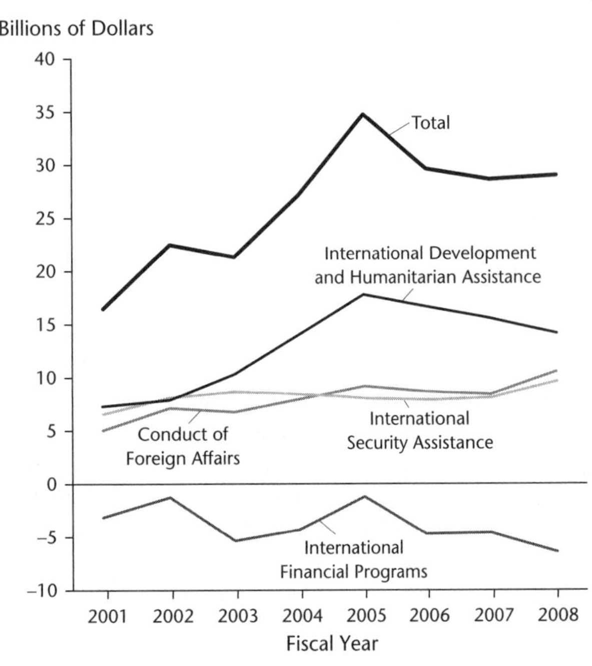

SOURCE: Office of Management and Budget, *Historical Tables, Budget of the United States Government: Fiscal Year 2010* (Washington, D.C.: U. S. Government Printing Office, 2009), Table 3.2.

NOTE: Total line includes some expenditures not shown separately.

Laden, and his al Qaeda terrorist network. The United States stayed on in Afghanistan, but the Iraq War soon became its focus. As a result, some observers claimed Afghanistan had become the forgotten war—forgotten, that is, until the resurgence of the Taliban late in the decade. Regional and military experts said the U.S.-led war effort in Afghanistan was woefully underfunded and undermanned after the president turned his attention to war in Iraq.

Members of Congress had more difficulty authorizing military action against Iraq. But with the White House raising the specter of Iraqi leader Saddam Hussein in possession of weapons of mass destruction, bipartisan majorities eventually gave the president the authority he needed to wage a preemptive war to disarm Saddam.

Bush's third war—the more amorphous war on terrorism—in time set off passionate debates over national security and civil liberties. Battles were fought over everything from abusive interrogations of detainees in U.S. custody to the legal status of enemy combatants to whether the National Security Agency could conduct within the United States warrantless electronic surveillance of the overseas communications of American citizens.

THE IRAQ WAR

Fears and misgivings about the war in Iraq had only deepened when no weapons of mass destruction were found. The Bush administration insisted that the war was still justified because of Saddam's oppression of his people and his presumed support of terrorism.

The latter point seemed to be a self-fulfilling prophecy. Soon al Qaeda terrorists and other Islamic militants flocked to Iraq to fight alongside the Sunnis, the faction thrown out of power with Saddam. Bush recast Iraq as the "central front" in the war on terror and the place to showcase his policy of democratizing the Middle East.

But critics of the war became more vocal, partisan differences more pronounced, while the defeat of terrorism and the flowering of democracy seemed increasingly remote.

Public support of the war quickly eroded. A Gallup poll several days after the war began in March 2003 showed 75 percent of those surveyed supported the decision to send troops to Iraq. That was the highest approval rating of the war seen in the ongoing Gallup polling during the Bush presidency. Several polls taken just months later in the summer of 2004 showed for the first time that a majority of those polled thought the war was a mistake. The polls fluctuated for a while, but after 2005 they did not show a majority in favor of the war for the duration of Bush's term.

Those polls reflected the grim news coming out of Iraq. At the top of that list were the tallies of war casualties.

By the beginning of 2005, 1,332 Americans had died in the Iraq War—1,032 had been killed in action or died of their wounds. Another 10,421 had been wounded in action. By the end of 2008, the death toll had reached 4,212, of which 3,394 had been killed in action or died of their wounds. The number of wounded in action had reached 30,940. Those were just the U.S. numbers. Countless more died or were maimed in the war-ravaged country.

"Grave and Deteriorating" Situation

The invasion of Iraq in 2003 had gone swiftly and smoothly. Baghdad was taken and Saddam fled into hiding. But as the occupation of Iraq stretched on, U.S. and coalition troops from other nations found themselves increasingly vulnerable. Soldiers patrolling city streets and crowded neighborhoods were targeted by insurgent snipers and suicide bombers. When they drove in the cities and countryside, their thin-skinned military vehicles were blasted by crude roadside bombs.

As criticism of the war mounted, the White House focused on its strategy of "Iraqification," or making Iraqi troops the dominant security force in their country. "As the Iraqis stand up, we will stand down," Bush told soldiers at Fort Bragg, N.C., in June 2005. In November of that year in a speech at the U.S. Naval Academy, the president said: "We will never back down. We will never give in. And we will never accept anything less than complete victory."

But the situation in Iraq continued to deteriorate, overshadowing political achievements in that country, including the holding of elections and formation of a new Iraqi government. The insurgency against U.S. occupation forces

Senate Majority Leader Harry Reid, center, urges President Bush to sign the war funding bill just passed by Congress on Capitol Hill in Washington on April 26, 2007.
Source: AP Photo/Dennis Cook

grew stronger and more lethal. Adding to the turmoil was sectarian violence between the Shiite and Sunni factions that seemed to be exploding across Iraq, raising fears that the country was teetering on the brink of a civil war.

Even Republicans, perhaps with an eye on the November 2006 congressional elections, began to push the White House to spell out its plan for transferring responsibilities to the Iraqi military and withdrawing U.S. forces.

Dissatisfaction with Bush's handling of the war was seen as the key factor in the Democratic victory in those 2006 midterm elections. Democrats easily won a majority of House seats in the next Congress, ending twelve years of Republican control, and won enough Senate seats to take control of that chamber as well.

As Washington debated strategy in Iraq and potential exit strategies, much hope was placed on a high-level Iraq Study Group that had been established at the urging of both Democratic and Republican members of Congress. In its report in December 2006 the group found the situation in Iraq "grave and deteriorating" and confirmed what everyone knew already: there were no magic formulas or easy answers. The bipartisan panel recommended new regional diplomatic initiatives—that would include Iran and Syria—to end the conflict. It also called for U.S. forces to assume a supporting role aimed at getting the Iraqi army to take prime responsibility for combat operations and, as they proceeded, to start moving U.S. troops out of Iraq.

The White House was guarded in its reaction to the report, but on Jan. 10, 2007, the president gave his response. Just days after the Democratically-controlled 110th Congress had convened, Bush in an address to the nation called the continuing violence "unacceptable" and said that it was "clear that we need to change our strategy in Iraq." To that end, he said he was sending additional troops to Iraq to rid Baghdad of terrorists and insurgents, to train Iraqi security forces, and to bolster U.S. forces in the mostly Sunni Anbar province, a stronghold of al Qaeda.

Bush called it a "surge." Critics called it escalation.

The new Democratic leaders looked as if they had been blindsided. House Speaker Nancy Pelosi of California and Majority Leader Harry Reid of Nevada complained about not having any input in the president's planning. Pelosi characterized a meeting at the White House the afternoon of Bush's speech as "notification, not consultation."

It was no surprise that the White House had not consulted the Democratic leaders.

Congressional Action

Opponents of the war—mostly Democrats—had been trying for some time to change the direction of U.S. policy in Iraq but there were a number of factors working against them.

For starters, Democrats often had trouble agreeing among themselves on a course of action. Views ranged across the spectrum from those who wanted to start a phased withdrawal within a few months to those who opposed any kind of specific timetable for rotating troops out of Iraq. Republican leaders tried their best to exploit and spotlight the divisions within the Democratic Party.

Also, the Democrats did not hold a majority in either chamber of the 109th Congress. Even after they took control in the 110th Congress, they did not have the votes to pass controversial antiwar proposals. Senate Democrats held control of their chamber in the 110th Congress by a margin that was too slim to overcome a GOP filibuster. Moreover, they usually could not count on enough, if any, stray Republican votes to help them reach the sixty votes needed to open debate or in some cases, depending on the agreement governing debate, even to adopt an amendment. It was far easier to pass measures on the House side, thanks to its procedures and bigger majority. But still the votes were not necessarily there to override a presidential veto—a move that required a two-thirds majority.

Ultimately, when it comes to foreign policy and military strategy, the commander in chief holds most of the cards. Congress has tools at its disposal—the most potent being its ability to cut off funding for the war—but few on Capitol Hill advocated such a drastic move. It was doubtful that such a move would have succeeded, but even proposing to do it would have left advocates open to charges of undermining military commanders, of not protecting American troops, of—as the Republicans liked to put it—"cutting and running." Those were not charges members wanted to have leveled at them, particularly in election years.

Iraq Proposals

All attempts to legislate a withdrawal from Iraq or require even estimated dates for a pull-out were doomed to fail. Such proposals died a number of different deaths—they were defeated outright, were blocked by a Senate filibuster, fell victim to a presidential veto, lost out to a Republican alternative acceptable to the White House, or split the Democrats too much to survive.

Democrats and some Republicans attempted to challenge the president's decision to send more troops to Iraq. After forty-five hours of debate, the House passed a resolution voicing its opposition, but a bipartisan Senate measure that said much the same thing was blocked by a filibuster.

With withdrawal proposals stymied, Democrats put their hopes in proposals that would have required a set amount of time in between a service member's deployments in Iraq. Some saw the proposals as an end-run around the troop-withdrawal issue. While the language would not have mandated troop shifts, most thought it would have resulted in a drawdown in forces because, with the mandatory time at home, there would not have been enough troops to maintain set levels of deployment. But after U.S. generals argued that the requirement would tie the military's hands in Iraq and Afghanistan, it lost key GOP support and was blocked by a filibuster.

Democrats and Republicans did find some areas of agreement. One was in the setting of benchmarks for the Iraqi government. In 2007 Congress cleared and the president signed a bill that included eighteen legislative, security, and economic benchmarks and required the president to report to Congress on Iraq's progress toward meeting them. Later that year Bush submitted two reports with mixed findings. Congress also asked the Government Accountability Office, a support agency within the legislative branch, to report as well. The GAO was harsher in its assessments.

Signs of Progress

By the fall of 2007 there were nascent signs of progress in Iraq. The top military and civilian leaders in Iraq, Army Gen. David H. Petraeus and Ambassador Ryan C. Crocker, reported significant if fragile military results from the surge and the president announced that U.S. troop levels would return to pre-surge levels by the next summer. This was not nearly enough for congressional Democrats—and some Republicans—but that was as far as the administration would go at that time.

But the level of violence continued to decline and economic activity began to return in Iraq, so much so that by the summer of 2008 Bush, who had battled every Democratic attempt to set a timetable for withdrawal, accepted in principle an Iraqi proposal that most combat forces would be pulled out of cities and villages by the summer of 2009 and out of the country by the end of 2011. That agreement on U.S. withdrawal was formalized in a Security Agreement signed by the U.S. ambassador and the Iraqi foreign minister in November 2008, several weeks after the American electorate had chosen war opponent Barack Obama as their next president. Bush signed the agreement again in December during a visit to Baghdad.

The president considered the Security Agreement to be an executive agreement that did not have to be submitted to Congress for approval. Democrats objected—to no avail.

U.S.-INDIA NUCLEAR AGREEMENT

Congress had better luck making its influence felt when the administration negotiated a nuclear cooperation agreement with India.

The White House viewed the agreement as the means of forging an important partnership with a country that was both the world's largest democracy and a key counterweight to China. It was seen as a way of bringing the South Asian nuclear power into the global nonproliferation framework and providing it with energy security.

However, to proceed with the pact the president needed legislation that would waive provisions of the 1954 Atomic Energy Act (PL 83-703) in order to permit exports of nuclear materials, equipment, and technology. Along with the waivers, the White House proposal would have allowed the agreement to take effect after ninety days unless both chambers of Congress opposed it.

But lawmakers wanted a more significant role—and they got it. The waiver bill they passed required that Bush submit the agreement to Congress for an up-or-down vote before it could take effect. It also required the administration to report to Congress on the final negotiations and on India's nuclear programs. A number of members wanted to make sure that India's close ties with Iran did not lead India to assist Iran's nuclear program.

Passage of the bill in 2006 was a major foreign policy victory for the White House. It was for the 109th Congress, too.

The 110th Congress approved the final agreement, but again with provisions for greater safeguards and congressional oversight.

FOREIGN ASSISTANCE

In the wake of the Sept. 11 attacks, foreign assistance programs—a favorite punching bag for many on Capitol Hill—enjoyed something of a renaissance after it came to be seen as an important tool in the war on terrorism.

To this end, Bush made the Millennium Challenge Account his signature foreign aid program. Its goal was to target assistance to poor countries that were committed to democracy, human rights, and open-market economies. Congress approved billions of dollars, but the program was slow getting off the ground. Lawmakers pointed to the program's mounting reserves to justify the deep cuts they made in the administration's requests.

Members did the opposite when it came to Bush's global HIV/AIDS program. He asked for $30 billion and they gave him $48 billion. Lawmakers wanted to do more than just reauthorize the existing program. They wanted to shift it from its original "emergency" purpose toward a long-term, sustainable plan that would expand its focus to include food aid, health care worker recruitment, and special outreach to women and girls. Bush went along, signing it into law in 2008. It was a rare display of bipartisanship in the overheated election year.

SANCTIONS

Congress kept up the pressure on the government of Sudan to put an end to the violence in the Darfur region of that country. Hundreds of thousands of people had been killed and several million more had been displaced in fighting that many were calling "genocide." The 109th Congress cleared legislation imposing sanctions on Sudanese officials and others considered responsible for the genocide. The next Congress intensified the pressure with a bill authorizing state and local government to divest themselves of assets in companies doing business with several sectors of the Sudanese economy, including its oil industry.

Congress strengthened existing sanctions against Iran to punish that country for pursuing a nuclear weapons program. Members primarily had Iran in their sights when they stiffened penalties on companies doing business with countries deemed a threat to U.S. national security, although they pointed to Sudan, Cuba, and North Korea as targets as well.

The Iran Nonproliferation Act was extended to cover Syria, too. The sanctions were aimed at preventing Syria from exporting or importing technology to develop weapons of mass destruction.

Reflecting the ups-and-downs in the United States' relationship with North Korea, the 109th Congress expanded the Iran and Syria Nonproliferation Act to include North Korea, thereby imposing sanctions on entities transferring to or from North Korea the technology for weapons of mass destruction and missile programs. Then in the next Congress lawmakers approved a Bush request for legislation waiving certain sanctions to allow the United States to assist North Korea in dismantling a nuclear reactor.

But there would be no lifting of sanctions against Cuba while Bush was in office. A number of attempts were made but none advanced to become law, illustrating once again that the U.S. relationship with Communist leader Fidel Castro's Cuba remained one of the most sensitive issues in U.S. politics. It would take a new occupant of the White House—Obama—for changes to be made.

LOSS OF CLOUT

The Senate Foreign Relations Committee and the House Foreign Affairs Committee continued to cede power to the Appropriations committees. The House passed a foreign relations authorization bill in 2005, but the Senate bill stalled after becoming a magnet for amendments dealing with everything from abortion to trade with Cuba. Congress had not cleared a stand-alone State Department authorization bill since 2002 or a separate foreign aid authorization since 1985. Because of that, the foreign policy committees had lost a key tool for affecting policy. Their loss was the Appropriations panels' gain, as authorizations were folded into funding bills.

The House and Senate Intelligence committees began to feel the foreign policy committees' pain when for four fiscal years in a row no intelligence authorization bill was enacted. Reasons varied, but the result was the same: the Intelligence panels lost their voice in setting policies and funding levels for the intelligence community, while the Appropriations committees picked up the slack.

Chronology of Action on Foreign Policy

2005–2006

The Iraq War was the major foreign policy issue facing the 109th Congress. Death tolls were mounting, the situation on the ground seemed to be deteriorating almost daily, and polls showed public opinion turning increasingly against the war. The George W. Bush administration called on the country to "stay the course" to fight terrorists and secure a democratic future for the Iraqi people—and not "cut and run," in terms often used by Republicans. The GOP majority in Congress, looking increasingly vulnerable as the midterm elections approached, began to press the White House for its withdrawal strategy. Democrats on Capitol Hill pushed for a change in policy but could not agree on what that should be: some wanted a firm withdrawal timetable while others wanted something more flexible. Everyone was hoping the Iraq Study Group, a bipartisan panel set up by Congress, would come up with answers. But the panel's report in December 2006 only confirmed the obvious: there were no easy answers. A weary electorate, however, wanted change and voted to turn over control of the next Congress to the Democrats in hopes of getting it.

Lawmakers did manage to flex their muscles on another significant foreign policy proposal: a civilian nuclear cooperation agreement with India. To proceed with the agreement President Bush needed Congress to allow him to waive provisions of an existing atomic energy statute. The White House had hoped Congress would give him that authority and then basically move to the sidelines. Congress, however, insisted on an up-or-down vote on the final agreement and required a series of reports. Of particular interest to some members was India's role in stopping Iran from getting nuclear weapons.

Democratic opposition twice doomed Senate approval of John R. Bolton to be the U.S. representative to the United Nations. Bolton, however, did serve in the position for sixteen months, under a recess appointment.

President Bush had mixed results on his foreign assistance priorities. Funding for his signature foreign aid program, the Millennium Challenge Account, was cut dramatically. On the other hand, Congress increased aid for another priority, HIV/AIDS programs.

Attempts to pass a foreign affairs authorization bill went the way of most attempts in recent years: nowhere. This left the foreign policy committees of Congress once again without a valuable tool to affect programs and policies. The Intelligence committees suffered a similar loss of influence when the 109th Congress failed to clear any intelligence authorization bills.

Congress strengthened sanctions on Sudan and Iran, and expanded the Iran sanctions statute to cover North Korea and Syria. But an attempt to impose sanctions on military sales to China failed. Provisions to loosen sanctions on Cuba failed as well.

Lawmakers responded to the political upheaval in the Middle East with policy resolutions and restrictions on aid to the Palestinian Authority.

Iraq War Policy

Debate over President George W. Bush's Iraq War policies intensified during the 109th Congress, as violence in that country escalated and war casualties mounted. With American public opinion turning increasingly against the war, Congress grappled with how to respond.

Republicans, for the most part, stayed united behind the president, but some, especially in the Senate, did begin to push for the White House to spell out its plan for transferring responsibilities to the Iraqi military and drawing down U.S. forces. Democrats demanded a plan as well but were divided over the question of whether to set a specific timetable for withdrawal from Iraq. In the end, no major policy initiatives emerged from the partisan clashes that ensued.

With their competing proposals meeting expert and military skepticism, both Republicans and Democrats were hopeful that the bipartisan Iraq Study Group might have answers when it issued its report in December 2006. The panel, however, came up with no magic formula for the situation in Iraq. Their report painted a grim picture of the deteriorating situation in Iraq and the limited options available. They called for greater diplomatic efforts to stabilize Iraq and the region—including working with Iran and Syria—and for the United States to adjust its role to encourage the Iraqis to take control of their destiny, so U.S. troops could be withdrawn responsibly. *(Iraq Study Group, p. 274)*

The clearest response to Iraq came from the American people. In the November 2006 midterm elections, with the war as the dominant issue, voters chose to end Republican control on Capitol Hill and install Democratic majorities in both chambers in the next Congress.

BACKGROUND

In October 2002, Congress cleared a resolution (PL 107-243) authorizing President Bush to use U.S. forces "as he determines to be necessary and appropriate in order to (1) defend the national security of the United States against the continuing threat posed by Iraq; and (2) enforce all relevant United Nations Security Council resolutions regarding Iraq." The House had passed the measure by a vote of 296–133, and the Senate had cleared it by a 77–23 margin. *(2002 resolution, Congress and the Nation Vol. XI, p. 238)*

Five months later, on March 19, 2003, Bush launched a war to eliminate what he said were Iraqi president Saddam Hussein's weapons of mass destruction. No such weapons were ever found. After that, however, followers of al Qaeda—the terrorist network responsible for the Sept. 11, 2001, attacks on the United States—and other Islamic militants flowed into Iraq to fight alongside the Sunnis, the group thrown out of power when the United States ousted Saddam. This prompted Bush to recast Iraq as the "central front" in the war on terror and the most important laboratory for his policy of democratizing the Middle East.

But growing sectarian violence in Iraq put those plans to establish a full-blown democracy on hold. After U.S. forces had toppled Saddam's regime, sectarian loyalties sharpened among Iraq's Sunnis, Shiites, and Kurds, the country's three major religious and ethnic groups. Despite elections and the formation of a new Iraqi government, those allegiances remained strong among the Kurds, who wanted autonomy and maintained their own militia, and among Sunnis, who made up most of the insurgents. Increasing communal violence between Sunnis and Shiites—including wholesale massacres of men by one religious group or the other—outpaced the political milestones that the Iraqis achieved and strained the country to the breaking point. Middle East experts and lawmakers began to warn that the sectarian violence could simply push Iraq into a civil war—the worst of all possibilities for Bush.

Between the administration's vision of a stable, fully democratic Iraq and the nightmare scenario of civil war, some observers said that the administration still had an opportunity to salvage the situation by speeding up the training of Iraqi troops and giving the country's new leaders breathing room to peacefully resolve their sectarian differences. But building an Iraqi force capable of taking over the fight and policing a nation of 26 million people proved more difficult than expected, given the ferocity of insurgents and the deep ethnic divisions.

In a major speech Nov. 30, 2005, President Bush tried to reassure a skeptical nation that the war in Iraq was on track and appealed for patience. He acknowledged the mission in Iraq had encountered "setbacks," but he insisted that troops had to remain until military commanders said conditions had improved. "We will never back down. We will never give in. And we will never accept anything less than complete victory," he said. To achieve such a victory, Bush released a plan calling for helping Iraqis build and train their security forces, rebuild their economy, and achieve a functioning democratic government. While several Republicans hailed Bush's remarks as a display of leadership, lawmakers from both sides of the aisle said the administration had to do more to inform the public of progress in Iraq and set clearer benchmarks showing success.

Republicans were buoyed in mid-2006 with the formation of a permanent Iraqi government and the elimination of terrorist leader Abu Musab Al Zarqawi. The new government was hailed with optimistic pronouncements of how the country's security would improve in line with political events. Bush's announcement June 8 that U.S. military forces a day earlier had killed Zarqawi, the brutal leader of al Qaeda in Iraq responsible for the deaths of scores of U.S. soldiers and thousands of Iraqis—led to broad praise in Congress for the U.S. military and strong Republican affirmations of Bush's stay-the-course policy in Iraq. The news provided GOP leaders with what they saw as a fresh opportunity to portray themselves as the true stewards of the nation's security and Democrats as the weak-kneed liberals who could not wait to "cut and run" from Iraq.

But the sectarian violence continued and just a few months later, in August, Senate Armed Services Committee Chair John W. Warner, R-Va., said Congress might need to pass a new resolution to authorize the continued use of U.S. military force in Iraq if a civil war broke out between the Shiites and Sunnis. The grim specter of Iraq falling apart had been raised by top U.S. military commanders in testimony before Warner's committee.

In an Aug. 31, 2006, speech, Bush called the Iraq War the "ideological struggle of the twenty-first century" and said it would be "absolutely disastrous" if the United States pulled out before Iraq could defend itself. In an Aug. 29 speech, Defense Secretary Donald H. Rumsfeld enraged Democrats when he suggested that critics of the administration's Iraq policies were similar to those who appeased Adolf Hitler before World War II.

FOREIGN POLICY LEADERSHIP

Secretary of State

Condoleezza Rice was confirmed to succeed Colin L. Powell as secretary of state by a vote of 85–13 on Jan. 25, 2005. Rice had been George W. Bush's closest foreign policy adviser since his first presidential campaign and had served as the White House national security adviser during Bush's first term. Previously, she had been provost of Stanford University and a professor of political science.

During her two days of confirmation hearings, Rice outlined a new path for U.S. global policy, making a passionate pitch for diplomacy, multilateral alliances, and nation building. This represented a departure from Bush's first-term focus on the need to act unilaterally at times, with or without the approval of other nations. While Rice insisted on looking forward during her testimony before the panel, committee Democrats wanted to reexamine the administration's Iraq policy, given that Rice had been one of the architects of that war. Democrats dominated the hearings, trying to dissect many of the nominee's past statements about the justification of going to war in Iraq. In the most heated exchange, Barbara Boxer, D-Calif., accused Rice of shifting the reasons for going to war and Rice tersely asked the senator to refrain from impugning her integrity. But Rice held her ground and avoided specifics on Iraq as well as other foreign policy issues. The Senate Foreign Relations Committee approved Rice's nomination by a vote of 16–2 on Jan. 19.

Some Democrats, acknowledging that Rice's qualifications were never in question, sought instead to turn the floor debate on the nomination into a referendum on the Iraq war, but at the end of the nine-hour debate, they had mustered just thirteen votes against Rice—twelve Democrats and one independent. Still, the 85–13 tally represented the most votes cast against a secretary of state nominee since Henry Clay was confirmed 27–14 in 1825.

Intelligence Community

Legislation signed into law in December 2004 (PL 108-458) had mandated the most comprehensive overhaul of the intelligence community since the end of World War II. The position of director of central intelligence—and, as such, the head of the Central Intelligence Agency (CIA)—was abolished and in its place the law created two new positions: a cabinet-level position of director of national intelligence (DNI) to serve as head of the U.S. intelligence community and a separate position of director of the CIA. *(Intelligence system overhaul, Congress and the Nation Vol. XI, p. 263)*

Director of National Intelligence

President Bush nominated John D. Negroponte to be the first DNI. Negroponte, a career diplomat, had been Bush's first ambassador to the United Nations from 2001 until 2004 and then had served as U.S. ambassador to Iraq for fourteen months. Bush also nominated Air Force Lt. Gen. Michael V. Hayden, the director of the National Security Agency (NSA) since 1999, to be Negroponte's top deputy. Both Republicans and Democrats praised the nominations, saying Negroponte would use his considerable diplomatic skills to bring credibility to the new intelligence job, while Hayden would provide the technical know-how gained from running one of the nation's largest and most secretive intelligence agencies. *(Negroponte U.N. appointment, Congress and the Nation Vol. XI, p. 235)*

Negroponte's confirmation was never in doubt, but the nominee still faced tough questioning from the Senate Select Intelligence Committee at his confirmation hearing on April 12, 2005. The nominee was pressed by the Democrats about allegations that he was indifferent to human rights abuses in Honduras in the early 1980s when he was ambassador there. He was also challenged by senators of both parties about what he would do to improve the performance of the fifteen U.S. spy organizations. The panel approved Negroponte's nomination 14–1 on April 14, along with Hayden's nomination to be his deputy, which was approved unanimously. The full Senate gave Negroponte an overwhelming vote of confidence when it confirmed him by a 98–2 vote on April 21. The Senate also confirmed Hayden by voice vote. The two were sworn in later that day

After his reelection in November 2004, President Bush had claimed the confidence of the American people in his Iraq War policy. But in November 2006 the voters had another chance to deliver their verdict on the war and on Bush's accountability and the result this time was seen as a strong vote of no confidence. Democrats easily swept to victory in the House and won an uphill battle to gain control of the Senate.

A November 2006 nationwide survey by the Pew Research Center for the People & the Press found that 64 percent of those polled thought the situation in Iraq was not going well and 51 percent thought the war was the wrong decision. On the question of whether U.S. troops should be withdrawn, 46 percent thought the troops should be kept in Iraq and 48 percent thought they should be brought home.

In the wake of the election, Rumsfeld, who had come to symbolize the botched planning for the war, was on his way out. His abrupt dismissal the day after the election was widely seen as a preemptive move to take some of the bite out of the new majority's oversight efforts on Iraq in the next Congress.

in the Oval Office and the Office of the DNI began operations the next morning.

Negroponte served as DNI until Feb. 13, 2007, when he became deputy secretary of state and Michael McConnell replaced him. McConnell had retired from the Navy as a vice admiral in 1996, after four years as director of NSA. During the Persian Gulf War he had been the top intelligence officer to the Joint Chiefs of Staff chair, Army Gen. Colin L. Powell. McConnell was returning to government after a decade as a senior executive at the consulting firm Booz Allen Hamilton. The Senate Select Intelligence Committee approved McConnell's nomination unanimously on Feb. 6 and the full Senate confirmed him the next day by voice vote.

CIA Director

Porter J. Goss, in his job as the director of central intelligence, had headed up the CIA from September 2004 until April 21, 2005, when the restructuring of the intelligence community went into effect. Under the new organizational scheme, Goss was the director of the CIA and, as such, had a subordinate role to the new DNI who took over the CIA director's old job of giving the president daily intelligence briefings. Goss continued in that position until May 26, 2006. *(Goss 2004 confirmation, Congress and the Nation Vol. XI, p. 234)*

Michael Hayden left his job as deputy DNI to replace Goss as CIA director. As a chief architect and defender of the Bush administration's controversial domestic surveillance program, Hayden was the perfect target for angry and frustrated senators, who turned his public confirmation hearing before the Senate Intelligence panel on May 18 into a forum for a broad debate over civil liberties, warrantless eavesdropping, and national security in wartime. But Hayden held his own in defending the surveillance program, which was initiated while he headed NSA, as essential in the war on terrorism. He said he had been told by administration attorneys that the program was legal. Despite sometimes terse exchanges, the Intelligence Committee voted 12–3 on May 23 to approve the nomination. The full Senate confirmed Hayden on May 26 by a vote of 78–15.

U.N. Representative

In January 2005 John C. Danforth, a former GOP senator from Missouri, cited personal reasons for resigning as U.S. representative to the United Nations after serving only seven months in the job. *(Danforth U.N. appointment, Congress and the Nation Vol. XI, p. 235)*

John R. Bolton, the under secretary of state for arms control and international security, was nominated in March to succeed Danforth. But Democrats claimed Bolton's combative, preemptory style was a poor match for a sensitive diplomatic post and worked to block the nomination. After senators twice in 2005 voted against invoking cloture to limit debate on Bolton's nomination, the president used his constitutional recess appointment powers to install Bolton at the United Nations during the Senate's August recess. Bolton's interim appointment was good until the end of the 109th Congress in January 2007. Bush resubmitted the Bolton nomination, but the Senate in 2006 again rebuffed the president's attempt to win Bolton's confirmation. After the Democrats won the 2006 midterm election, Bush resubmitted the nomination but Bolton resigned in December. *(Bolton nomination, p. 280)*

By contrast, the Senate in 2007 easily confirmed Bush's next choice for the U.N. job. Zalmay Khalilzad, who had been serving most recently as the U.S. ambassador in Iraq, had a smooth confirmation hearing in the Senate Foreign Relations Committee on March 15, won that panel's endorsement on March 28, and was confirmed by a voice vote of the full Senate on March 29. Lawmakers thought Khalilzad's service as the U.S. ambassador in Baghdad since 2005 and in Afghanistan from 2003 to 2005 made him well-suited for the U.N. post, given that the after-effects of the U.S. invasions of those two countries were among the top issues the United Nations faced. Khalilzad was originally from Afghanistan before immigrating to the United States.

By the end of 2006, nearly 3,000 Americans had died in Iraq and more than 22,750 had been wounded. The cost of military operations in Iraq totaled about $288 billion by the end of fiscal 2006, according to Congressional Research Service estimates. *(Iraq war casualties, p. 306; war costs, p. 387)*

2005 LEGISLATIVE ACTION

Under pressure from their constituents and with an eye on the 2006 elections, some members began to express more of their frustrations with the ongoing war in Iraq.

Defense Authorization Bill

Lawmakers used the annual defense authorization bill (HR 1815—PL 109-163) as the main vehicle for their efforts to reassert their role in overseeing the Iraq War.

The House on May 25, 2005, rejected 128–300, a Lynn Woolsey, D-Calif., amendment to HR 1815 to express the sense of Congress that the president should develop a plan for withdrawing U.S. military forces from Iraq and submit it to the appropriate congressional committees.

IRAQ STUDY GROUP REPORT

The bipartisan Iraq Study Group, created at the request of Congress in early 2006, issued a widely anticipated report Dec. 9, 2006, that set out in stark terms the conditions confronting the United States in Iraq and the relatively limited options for U.S. policy.

The 142-page report described the situation in Iraq as "grave and deteriorating" and warned that "no one can guarantee that any course of action ... at this point will stop sectarian warfare, growing violence, or a slide toward chaos." But it also acknowledged an enormous U.S. stake in finding a successful outcome.

The study group offered two main recommendations that it said were equally important. The first was to undertake immediate diplomatic initiatives, including talking to Syria and Iran, to help resolve the violence that had overtaken Iraq. The second was "a change in the primary mission of U.S. forces in Iraq that will enable the United States to begin to move its combat forces out of Iraq responsibly."

The panel's seventy-nine recommendations were nonbinding, and White House officials signaled they would review the findings along with other studies by the National Security Council and the Joint Chiefs of Staff. President George W. Bush was noncommittal after receiving the report, saying, "We will take every proposal seriously and we will act in a timely fashion."

Reaction to the report was more positive on Capitol Hill, where many Republicans and Democrats seized on recommendations they believed validated previously held positions, and expressed hope that the report would provide a path to ending the conflict. Republicans, in particular, were pleased that the recommendations did not include establishing a firm timetable for a withdrawal but rather set a goal of withdrawing U.S. combat troops by early 2008.

The document, titled "The Iraq Study Group Report: The Way Forward--A New Approach," was prepared by a ten-member panel co-chaired by James A. Baker III, who served as secretary of state under President George H.W. Bush, and former Democratic representative Lee H. Hamilton of Indiana (1965–1999). Besides Baker and Hamilton, the members of the bipartisan group included Lawrence S. Eagleburger, who also served as secretary of state under the first President Bush; Vernon E. Jordan, who was an adviser to President Bill Clinton; Edwin Meese III, who was President Ronald Reagan's attorney general; former Supreme Court justice Sandra Day O'Connor; former representative Leon Panetta, D-Calif. (1977–1993), who was Clinton's White House chief of staff; Clinton secretary of defense William Perry; former senator Charles S. Robb, D-Va. (1989–2001), and former senator Alan Simpson, R-Wyo. (1979–1997).

Baker and Hamilton announced the formation of the study group at a Capitol Hill meeting March 15 attended by members of both parties. The initiative came from a bipartisan group in Congress, led by Rep. Frank R. Wolf, R-Va., who called for "fresh eyes" to assess the situation in Iraq. Congress appropriated $1 million for the group through the fiscal 2006 supplemental spending law (HR 4939—PL 109-234).

The following are highlights from the Iraq Study Group report:

But the story was quite different when the Senate took up its version of the fiscal 2006 defense authorization (S 1042). The Senate, in fact, used the bill to make the most powerful statement of congressional oversight on Iraq policy since the 2003 invasion. By a **key vote of 79–19 (R 41–13; D 37–6; I 1–0)** on Nov. 15, 2005, senators approved a proposal, offered by Armed Services Committee Chair Warner and Majority Leader Bill Frist, R-Tenn., to add language requiring the president to send Congress quarterly unclassified reports on the course of the war that would spell out for the first time how conditions in Iraq were linked to goals for withdrawing U.S. troops. *(2005 key votes, p. 915)*

The reports were to include details on the number of Iraqi battalions that would have to be able to fight independently before U.S. troops could withdraw. They were also to include a schedule for meeting the various conditions set out in the provision and the reasons for any subsequent changes to that schedule. The proposal included nonbinding "sense of the Senate" language declaring 2006 as the year that Iraqis should take the lead in their security. It called on the administration to tell Iraqis to make the compromises necessary for political progress and to explain the president's "strategy for successful completion of the mission in Iraq" to Congress and the American people.

The Warner-Frist amendment was offered as an alternative to a Democratic proposal that was nearly identical except for language requiring the Pentagon to set "a campaign plan with estimated dates for the phased redeployment of United States Armed Forces from Iraq as each condition is met...." Republicans accused Democrats of advocating a "cut-and-run" strategy and said the "estimated dates" section—which the GOP called a "timetable"—would tip

- **Situation in Iraq.** "Violence is increasing in scope and lethality. It is fed by a Sunni Arab insurgency, Shiite militias and death squads, al Qaeda, and widespread criminality. Sectarian conflict is the principal challenge to stability." The report said the democratically elected government in Iraq was "not adequately advancing national reconciliation, providing basic security, or delivering essential services. Pessimism is pervasive."
- **Potential consequences.** "If the situation continues to deteriorate, the consequences could be severe. A slide toward chaos could trigger the collapse of Iraq's government and a humanitarian catastrophe. Neighboring countries could intervene. Sunni-Shia clashes could spread. Al Qaeda could win a propaganda victory and expand its base of operations. The global standing of the United States could be diminished."
- **Diplomacy.** "The United States should immediately launch a new diplomatic offensive to build an international consensus for stability in Iraq and the region. This diplomatic effort should include every country that has an interest in avoiding a chaotic Iraq, including all of Iraq's neighbors. Iraq's neighbors and key states in and outside the region should form a support group to reinforce security and national reconciliation within Iraq, neither of which Iraq can achieve on its own."
- **U.S. military mission.** "The primary mission of U.S. forces in Iraq should evolve to one of supporting the Iraqi army, which would take over primary responsibility for combat operations. By the first quarter of 2008, subject to unexpected developments in the security situation on the ground, all combat brigades not necessary for force protection could be out of Iraq.

  "At that time, U.S. combat forces in Iraq could be deployed only in units embedded with Iraqi forces, in rapid-reaction and special operations teams, and in training, equipping, advising, force protection, and search and rescue. Intelligence and support efforts would continue. A vital mission of those rapid-reaction and special operations forces would be to undertake strikes against al Qaeda in Iraq."
- **Iraqi milestones.** "It is clear that the Iraqi government will need assistance from the United States for some time to come, especially in carrying out security responsibilities. Yet the United States must make it clear to the Iraqi government that the United States could carry out its plans, including planned redeployments, even if the Iraqi government did not implement [its] planned changes.

  "The United States must not make an open-ended commitment to keep large numbers of American troops deployed in Iraq....

  "The United States should work closely with Iraq's leaders to support the achievement of specific objectives—or milestones—on national reconciliation, security, and governance. Miracles cannot be expected, but the people of Iraq have the right to expect action and progress.

  "The Iraqi government needs to show its own citizens—and the citizens of the United States and other countries—that it deserves continued support."

off the Iraqi insurgents as to how long they would have to hold out. The Senate rejected the Democratic amendment, offered by Carl Levin, D-Mich., by a vote of 40–58.

Republicans insisted that the Warner-Frist amendment was not a change in policy but rather a continuation of oversight the Senate had been conducting for years. Bush joined in, saying he welcomed the vote. But most saw its approval as a major change. Until then, the Senate, like the House, had given the president almost everything he asked for in the war effort.

House-Senate conferees on the bill retained most of the Warner-Frist amendment in the final version (H Rept 109-360). However, where the Senate required a "schedule" for achieving the conditions necessary for a U.S. withdrawal, conferees substituted the vaguer word "plan." *(2006 defense authorization, p. 336)*

Murtha Calls for Withdrawal

On Nov. 17, 2005—two days after the Senate approved the Warner-Frist amendment—Rep. John P. Murtha of Pennsylvania, the ranking Democrat on the House Defense Appropriations Subcommittee and a decorated ex-Marine who had voted for the Iraq War, called for a withdrawal of troops from that country over the next six months. Until then, Murtha had never wavered in his support for the war effort; his only concern had been for the troops that he felt were not getting the armor and supplies they needed. Now, he said, he was convinced their mere presence in Iraq was making things worse by inviting insurgent attacks.

Although no one would have mistaken Murtha for a liberal, Republicans tried to paint him as one, anyway. House Speaker J. Dennis Hastert, R-Ill., said he was "saddened" that Murtha and other Democrats "want us to wave the white flag of surrender to the terrorists of the world." White House press secretary Scott McClellan compared Murtha with liberal filmmaker Michael Moore.

House Republicans tried to embarrass Murtha by putting a resolution based on his proposal on the House floor for a vote Nov. 18. But it turned out the GOP resolution (H Res 571) was not actually what he had proposed. Murtha had called for redeploying U.S. troops "at the earliest practicable date," but H Res 571 would have ended the deployment "immediately." That made it easy for Democrats to vote against the resolution, too, and it was rejected 3–403.

Other Legislation

Conferees on the fiscal 2005 war supplemental bill (HR 1268—PL 109-13), which was enacted in May 2005, called on the Bush administration to provide Congress with "a more comprehensive set of performance indicators and measures of stability and security in Iraq than is currently available." The conference report directed the secretary of defense to provide a report to Congress that identified "security, economic, and Iraqi security force performance standards and goals, accompanied by a notional timetable for achieving these goals." The report also was to include—in a classified annex, if necessary—an assessment of U.S. military requirements, including planned force rotations, through the end of 2006. *(2005 war supplemental, p. 348)*

During House International Relations Committee action on a foreign relations authorization bill (HR 2601), the panel adopted an amendment asking Bush to provide a plan for the establishment of a stable Iraqi government that would permit a U.S. drawdown there. The Democratic amendment was backed by thirteen Republicans, including the committee chair, Henry J. Hyde, R-Ill. On the floor, the House adopted a nonbinding amendment 291–137 on July 20, stating that it was U.S. policy not to withdraw prematurely from Iraq, but to do so only when it was clear that U.S. national security and foreign policy goals relating to a free and stable Iraq had been or were about to be achieved. Sponsor Ileana Ros-Lehtinen, R-Fla., warned that setting a date for withdrawal would "embolden" terrorists. House Democrats called the amendment "unnecessary and inflammatory" but failed in their bid to have it withdrawn and reintroduced as a stand-alone resolution. The House also rejected 203–227 a Democratic attempt to recommit the bill to committee to add language asking the president for his benchmarks for a successful strategy in Iraq and stating that it was U.S. policy to, among other things, bring stability to Iraq so that the responsibility for Iraq's security could be transferred to the Iraqi people as soon as possible. *(Foreign relations authorization, p. 287)*

A bipartisan group of six House members introduced a resolution (H J Res 55) in June 2005 that stated it to be U.S. policy that a plan for withdrawal of U.S. forces be announced by the end of 2005 and that troops begin coming home by October 2006, one month before the midterm election. The resolution required the president to implement the policy by taking certain steps to prepare Iraq for the transfer of responsibilities. But the resolution never got out of committee. A discharge petition attracted 124 signatures of the 218 signatures required for further action.

2006 LEGISLATIVE ACTION

In June 2006 Congress held its first major debates on the Iraq War since the 2003 invasion. Ultimately, however, the debates in both chambers were fiercely partisan with little genuine deliberation over the war and the policies that guided it. Democrats, deeply divided over whether troops should be withdrawn, focused on the mistakes they saw, ranging from the faulty intelligence on Saddam Hussein's alleged weapons of mass destruction to the insufficient number of troops sent to occupy Iraq. Despite the public's growing disillusionment with the president's stay-the-course Iraq policy, Republicans fell in line with Bush and focused on the progress they saw in the elimination of Zarqawi and the formation of a permanent Iraqi government.

House Resolution

Lawmakers in the House held more than twelve hours of debate on a Republican resolution (H Res 861) that pledged support for winning the "war on terror," rejecting any "arbitrary dates" for the withdrawal of U.S. forces from Iraq, and finishing the U.S. mission there.

House Speaker Hastert opened the debate on June 15, 2006, with an appeal for national steadfastness in the face of a war in which the U.S. death toll reached 2,500 on that same day. Many Republicans equated the fighting in Iraq with the broader war on terror, warning that a withdrawal of U.S. forces from Iraq—as many antiwar Democrats had demanded—would result in more Sept. 11-style terror attacks inside the United States. Republicans also returned to a political theme that helped them in the 2002 and 2004 elections: the accusation that Democrats did not have the toughness required to be trusted with the nation's security.

Many Democrats protested when the House Rules Committee, which was controlled by GOP leaders, refused to allow any amendments to the resolution. They said the resolution was a "trap" that falsely conjoined the fight against terrorism with the fight in Iraq and accused Republicans of avoiding a real debate on the war. Responding to the Republicans' call for continued resolve in Iraq, Rep. Murtha said, "That's rhetoric. Rhetoric doesn't solve the problem....We need a plan. It's not enough to say 'stay the course.'"

On June 16, after several more hours of debate, the House passed H Res 861 by a **key vote of 256–153 (R 214–3; D 42–149; I 0–1).** *(2006 key votes, p. 937)*

The forty-two Democrats who voted for the resolution underscored the divisions in the party. Some wanted to avoid being portrayed during the 2006 election campaign as weak on terrorism. House Minority Leader Nancy Pelosi,

D-Calif., had not told the Democrats in her caucus how to vote.

Senate Amendments

In the Senate, the debate over Iraq erupted during consideration of the fiscal 2007 defense authorization bill (S 2766). Republicans rallied around Bush's policy to stay the course in Iraq, defeating several Democratic amendments aimed at reducing U.S. troop strength.

The debate highlighted one of the major fault lines within the Democratic Party over Iraq. While most Senate Democrats believed that setting a date for beginning a pullback from Iraq would goad the Iraqis into making political compromises and improving their security forces, they differed on setting a date for completing that withdrawal, with many believing the date should be determined by events in Iraq, not in Washington. This moderate approach also reflected political concern among Democrats that Republicans would be able to accuse them of "cutting and running" if Democrats pushed legislation requiring a firm date for pulling out of Iraq. *(2007 defense authorization, p. 354)*

The Senate on June 15 agreed 93–6 to table (kill) an amendment that would have required a withdrawal of U.S. forces from Iraq by Dec. 31, 2006. Democratic leaders had persuaded John Kerry, D-Mass., not to offer such an amendment out of concern that it would highlight disagreements within the party. Prominent Senate Democrats such as Minority Leader Harry Reid of Nevada, Hillary Rodham Clinton of New York, and Levin did not support a deadline for a U.S. troop withdrawal. But Majority Whip Mitch McConnell, R-Ky., seeing a chance to embarrass Democrats and expose their divisions, scratched out Kerry's name on the amendment and offered it as his own on the floor. Unhappy with the maneuver, Reid offered the motion to table.

On June 22 the Senate defeated 13–86 a revised proposal by Kerry and Russ Feingold, D-Wis., to require the withdrawal of most U.S. forces from Iraq by July 2007 with the exception of those needed to train Iraqi troops, protect Americans, and target terrorists. The proposal was still too precipitous for many Democrats, and after hours of debate thirty-one Democrats joined all fifty-five Republicans in voting no.

Next the Senate defeated by a **key vote of 39–60 (R 1–54; D 37–6; I 1–0)** a far milder proposal by Levin and Jack Reed, D-R.I., that contained nonbinding language stating the president should begin the phased withdrawal of U.S. troops from Iraq in 2006 and send Congress a plan by the end of the year with estimated dates for the continued phased redeployment of U.S. forces from Iraq, "with the understanding that unexpected contingencies may arise." *(2006 key votes, p. 937)*

When the Senate took up the fiscal 2007 defense appropriations bill (HR 5631—PL 109-289) in September, the administration's conduct of the Iraq War triggered another combative debate. Democrats attempted to attach nonbinding sense-of-the-Senate language calling for a "change of course in Iraq," including the replacement of Defense Secretary Rumsfeld. After more than four hours of debate, Republicans were able to block a vote by raising a point of order that the proposal was not germane to the bill. They generally offered tepid support for Rumsfeld, however, focusing instead on the need to win the war in Iraq and warning against any withdrawals. *(2007 defense appropriations, p. 358)*

U.S.-India Nuclear Agreement

Congress in 2006 approved legislation (HR 5682—PL 109-401) giving the president authority to complete a civilian nuclear cooperation agreement with India. It marked a major foreign policy victory for the White House. However, Congress insisted on being far more involved in the process than the administration had wanted, and retained the right to approve or disapprove a final agreement.

The legislation allowed the president to waive parts of the 1954 Atomic Energy Act (PL 83-703) to permit exports of nuclear materials, equipment, and technology to India. In return, India promised to open its civilian nuclear sites to inspection by the International Atomic Energy Agency (IAEA) for the first time and to continue negotiations with the United States on a fissile material cutoff treaty, among other requirements.

President George W. Bush and Prime Minister Manmohan Singh announced the agreement on civilian nuclear cooperation March 2, 2006, during a visit by Bush to New Delhi. The administration maintained that bringing India into the global nonproliferation framework and providing the South Asian giant with energy security were payoffs that far outweighed any risk that India might regress to the days of its first nuclear explosion in 1974 or subsequent nuclear tests.

To finalize a nuclear cooperation pact with India, however, the president needed legislation that exempted the deal from some restrictions on nuclear exports under the Atomic Energy Act. Because India had never signed the Nuclear Non-Proliferation Treaty, it was officially treated as a non–nuclear-weapons state and fell under various requirements of the act. Bush could have asked for annual waivers from Congress, but that would have conflicted with his aim of building a global partnership with India.

The initial White House proposal would have allowed an agreement with India to take effect after ninety days unless both chambers of Congress opposed it. But Henry J. Hyde, R-Ill., and Richard J. Lugar, R-Ind.—chairs, respectively, of the House International Relations and Senate Foreign Relations committees—insisted that Congress have a significant role.

As a result, both the House and Senate bills required passage of a joint resolution of approval before a final U.S.-India nuclear agreement could take effect. They also specified that the deal was off if India exploded a new nuclear weapon or broke other commitments to promote nonproliferation. They also added a variety of reporting requirements to keep Congress informed of the final negotiations and of India's nuclear programs.

Even with the enactment of the legislation, the United States and India still had a number of steps left before they would have a full-fledged agreement. They had to negotiate a final pact, which in turn had to be approved by the IAEA and by the forty-five-nation Nuclear Suppliers Group, an international body overseeing trade in nuclear reactors and fuel. Finally, it would have to be approved by Congress.

That approval came in the next Congress, with the enactment in October 2008 of legislation (HR 7081—PL 110-369) signing off—albeit, with additional safeguards and continued oversight requirements—on the final agreement reached with India. *(U.S.-India nuclear agreement, p. 311)*

BACKGROUND

U.S. nuclear relations with India went back to the mid-1950s, when Washington actively promoted nuclear energy cooperation by helping India to build nuclear power reactors and allowing Indian scientists to study at U.S. nuclear laboratories. Although India participated in negotiations of the 1968 Nuclear Non-Proliferation Treaty, it refused to sign the pact on grounds that it discriminated against the nuclear have-nots. Under the treaty, only the United States, Russia, China, France, and Britain could possess nuclear weapons. Most other countries, except for Pakistan, India, and Israel, signed the agreement, promising not to develop nuclear weapons in return for getting civilian nuclear technology. *(1968 treaty ratification, Congress and the Nation Vol. III, p. 201)*

India tested its first nuclear device in 1974, using plutonium extracted from spent fuel imported for use in its energy sector. Pakistan, India's neighbor and bitter rival, followed soon after with its own nuclear weapons program. The developments contributed to enactment in 1978 of the Nuclear Non-Proliferation Act (PL 95-242). The act amended the 1954 Atomic Energy Act (PL 83-703) to strengthen the requirements for U.S. nuclear exports to non–nuclear-weapons states. Among other restrictions, it prohibited nuclear exports to any country that did not have full IAEA safeguards on all its nuclear facilities or that detonated a nuclear explosive device or engaged in activities related to acquiring or manufacturing nuclear weapons. In addition, the United States created the international Nuclear Suppliers Group in 1975 to implement nuclear export controls worldwide. *(1978 legislation, Congress and the Nation Vol. V, p. 147)*

The controls limited the export of low enriched uranium fuel for India's reactors. After 1980, all nuclear exports from the United States were cut off under the terms of the Nuclear Non-Proliferation Act. In 1998, India conducted a series of underground nuclear tests, followed within two weeks by Pakistan's first nuclear explosion. The Clinton administration punished both countries with economic sanctions. With some lawmakers arguing that the sanctions hurt American farmers and businesses and did little to deter nuclear proliferation, Congress in 1999 gave the president authority to waive those sanctions (PL 106-79). *(India, Pakistan sanctions, Congress and the Nation Vol. X, p. 223)*

U.S. relations with India gradually had warmed in the aftermath of the cold war, due in part to growing economic ties as well as to India's role as a strategic counterweight to China. After the Sept. 11, 2001, terrorist attacks on the United States, Washington perceived India as a natural ally in the global war on terrorism. Bush lifted sanctions against both India and Pakistan in 2001 as he prepared to invade Afghanistan.

A joint U.S.-India statement on July 18, 2005, outlined plans for a new global partnership that would include civil nuclear cooperation. To that end, India agreed to separate its fourteen civilian nuclear sites from its eight military sites and to sign a protocol with the IAEA opening the civilian sites to inspection. India also agreed to continue a moratorium on nuclear weapons testing, not to transfer nuclear technology to third parties, and to work with the United States toward the conclusion of a treaty to stop the production of fissile material for nuclear arms purposes. During Bush's March 2006 trip to India, the two leaders announced they had reached agreement on the nuclear cooperation deal.

HOUSE ACTION

The House passed HR 5682 on July 26, 2006, by a **key vote of 359–68 (R 219–9; D 140–58; I 0–1).** The House International Relations Committee had reported the bill (H Rept 109-590) on July 21. *(2006 key votes, p. 937)*

To underline the fact that Congress intended to remain involved in the process, Hyde had brought a newly drafted measure to the committee markup in place of the original administration proposal. Unlike the administration plan, the bill required a joint resolution of approval by both chambers for a nuclear cooperation agreement with India to enter into force. The bill also set certain preconditions that India would have to meet and required the White House to consult with Congress.

Committee approval came after a lengthy and sometimes heated debate. While most committee members enthusiastically supported the measure, several were vehemently opposed. The panel rejected a string of amendments aimed at adding restrictions to nuclear cooperation, including several efforts by Howard L. Berman, D-Calif., to demand that India halt its production of fissile material for nuclear weapons before the United States entered any agreement.

Berman continued his battle when the bill reached the floor—again without success. The full House rejected

184–241 his amendment to restrict exports of uranium and other types of nuclear reactor fuel to India until the president determined that India had halted the production of fissile material for use in nuclear weapons. The House also rejected 155–268 a Brad Sherman, D-Calif., amendment to require that before any nuclear cooperation with India proceeded, and every year thereafter, the president certify that India had not increased the level of domestic uranium it sent through its weapons program.

The House rejected 192–235 a motion by Edward J. Markey, D-Mass., to send the bill back to committee to add language making the waiver of the Atomic Energy Act conditional on the president determining that India was fully and actively supporting U.S. efforts to prevent Iran from acquiring weapons of mass destruction.

An administration statement issued ahead of the vote had warned that an amendment on Iran would disrupt the whole deal and noted that India had twice voted to report Iran to the U.N. Security Council for noncompliance with IAEA safeguards. The statement also voiced opposition to requiring a fissile material cap, saying India would not agree to such a requirement unless Pakistan and China did so as well. The White House said it already was involved in discussions with India on a multilateral fissile material cutoff treaty and was "pressing for substantial progress in that context."

SENATE ACTION

The Senate, by a vote of 85–12 on Nov. 16, passed HR 5682, after inserting the text of its companion bill (S 3709). The Senate Foreign Relations Committee had reported S 3709 (S Rept 109-288) on July 20.

The Senate version was similar to the House bill. But, at the request of the administration, a new section had been added to implement an agreement with the IAEA—called the Additional Protocol—to give international inspectors enhanced authority to inspect U.S. nuclear sites. U.S. implementation of the protocol was seen as a reciprocal step for India's submission to inspections and an encouragement to other nations to follow suit.

Most Foreign Relations members wholeheartedly supported the bill, but several voiced concern about the spread of nuclear weapons and material, and voted against reporting the bill.

Passage by the full Senate was delayed for months by differences over how many Democratic amendments to allow as well as a scarcity of floor time and competing priorities in advance of the November elections.

Lugar urged his colleagues not to adopt any of a batch of floor amendments that could have killed the agreement as far as India was concerned. Lugar and Joseph R. Biden Jr. of Delaware, the ranking Democrat on Foreign Relations, did accept an amendment by Tom Harkin, D-Iowa, to make the president's waiver authority contingent on a determination that India was "fully and actively participating" in U.S. and international efforts to halt Iran's nuclear program. The Senate adopted the amendment by voice vote.

In other action, the Senate:

- Rejected 26–73 a Jeff Bingaman, D-N.M., amendment to block nuclear exports to India unless the president determined that specific steps had been taken toward a fissile material cutoff treaty and that India had halted production of fissile material for nuclear weapons.
- Rejected 27–71 a Byron L. Dorgan, D-N.D., amendment stating, among other things, that it is U.S. policy to support a U.N. Security Council resolution requiring India to adhere to all nonproliferation, arms control, and disarmament agreements.
- Rejected 27–71 a John Ensign, R-Nev., amendment to impose tighter restrictions on IAEA inspections in the United States.
- Rejected 25–71 a Russell D. Feingold, D-Wis., amendment to require, as a precondition, that the pact not assist India to manufacture or acquire nuclear weapons or other nuclear explosive devices.
- Rejected 38–59 a Barbara Boxer, D-Calif., amendment to require, as a precondition, that India suspend military cooperation with Iran until Iran ceased support for international terrorism.

CONFERENCE, FINAL ACTION

The House adopted the conference report (H Rept 109-721) by a vote of 330–59 on Dec. 8. The Senate cleared the bill by voice vote early the next day.

When appointing conferees Dec. 5, the House had agreed by voice vote to instruct its negotiators to keep Senator Harkin's amendment regarding India's cooperation on Iran. The administration, however, strongly opposed the restriction and urged that it be dropped. Secretary of State Condoleezza Rice sent a letter to Congress saying that making such a requirement a prerequisite could prompt India to seek to renegotiate agreements on other issues such as opening its civilian nuclear sites to international inspection.

Conferees agreed not to make cooperation on Iran a precondition. Instead, they required the president to include as part of his annual report to Congress an assessment of whether India was fully and actively participating in international efforts on Iran.

MAJOR PROVISIONS

As signed into law Dec. 18, HR 5682:

Presidential Waivers

Permitted the president to exempt a U.S.-India nuclear agreement from several restrictions in the Atomic Energy Act, including requirements that a country have all its nuclear facilities under IAEA safeguards and that it not test a nuclear weapon. The testing requirement was waived for India's actions prior to July 18, 2005.

Preconditions

Provided that the waivers were conditional on the president reporting to Congress that he had made the following determinations:

- India had provided the United States and the IAEA with a credible plan to separate its civilian and military nuclear facilities, materials, and programs.
- India and the IAEA had concluded all legal steps needed prior to signing an agreement that would require India to place all its civilian nuclear facilities under permanent IAEA safeguards.
- India and the IAEA were making substantial progress toward concluding an Additional Protocol giving inspectors expanded access to India's civilian nuclear program. At that time, 112 countries had signed Additional Protocols.
- India was working actively with the United States for the early conclusion of a multilateral fissile material cutoff treaty.
- India was supporting U.S. and international efforts to prevent the spread of enrichment and reprocessing technology.
- India was taking the necessary steps to secure nuclear and other sensitive materials and technology, including the enactment and enforcement of comprehensive export control legislation.
- The Nuclear Suppliers Group had agreed to allow India to be supplied with nuclear items covered by the group's guidelines.

Congressional Approval

Required a joint resolution of approval by Congress for a nuclear cooperation agreement with India to enter into force, and provided expedited procedures for considering such legislation.

Termination

Stated that the nuclear agreement would be terminated automatically if India were to test a nuclear device.

The bill did not affect provisions of the Atomic Energy Act that required termination of a treaty if India should interfere with or violate the IAEA safeguards, violate the cooperation agreement with the United States, or engage in an unauthorized transfer of nuclear material or technology. Conferees noted in their report that they rejected a White House proposal to waive those provisions.

Reports to Congress

Required a series of presidential reports related to nuclear cooperation with India, including:

- A detailed explanation of the determinations made by the president as a condition of waiving the Atomic Energy Act, including a description of what India had done to aid U.S. and international efforts to prevent Iran from acquiring weapons of mass destruction.
- Information to keep Congress "fully and currently informed" of the facts and implications of any significant nuclear activities in India.
- A wide-ranging implementation and compliance report, due within 180 days of the agreement entering into force and annually after that. Among the topics to be covered: any additional nuclear facilities that India had put under IAEA safeguards, any significant nuclear commerce between India and other nations, an assessment of India's role in stopping Iran from getting weapons of mass destruction, and an assessment of whether the agreement was assisting India's nuclear weapons program in any way.

Additional Protocol

Implemented an Additional Protocol between the United States and the IAEA that would give international inspectors carefully regulated access to U.S. nuclear sites. The Senate had approved the ratification of the protocol (Treaty Doc 107-7) on March 31, 2004, but U.S. laws had to be modified before it could take effect.

Bolton Nomination

The nomination of John R. Bolton to be the U.S. representative to the United Nations was blocked in the Senate in 2005 and again in 2006. Although never confirmed by the Senate, Bolton did serve in the position for sixteen months after President George W. Bush sidestepped Congress and gave him a recess appointment.

Bush on March 17, 2005, had nominated Bolton to replace John C. Danforth, a former GOP senator from Missouri who had resigned for personal reasons in January 2005 after serving only seven months at the United Nations. Bolton was under secretary of state for arms control and international security at the time.

Democrats immediately denounced the nomination, portraying Bolton as an outspoken critic of multilateral organizations who was too abrasive to make a good diplomat. Secretary of State Condoleezza Rice countered that Bolton was the sort of "tough-minded diplomat" who was ideally suited to fight for the Bush administration's proposals for changes at the U.N., which included measures to change the U.N. Human Rights Commission, create a stronger internal investigative division to combat corruption, and create a mechanism for reviewing and eliminating obsolete mandates.

Personality became the main issue during Bolton's confirmation hearings before the Senate Foreign Relations

Committee in April 2005, when some of Bolton's former government colleagues charged that he was abusive and tried to bully subordinates into altering intelligence to justify his ideological preconceptions. The investigation into Bolton's career and management style involved interviews with twenty-nine witnesses, 830 pages of documents and memos, and seven hours of questioning of the nominee, who also answered 100 written questions for the committee.

On May 12, the committee voted 10–8 to send the nomination to the full Senate "without recommendation," only the third time in twenty-two years that the panel had forwarded a nominee without an endorsement. The neutral vote was the best GOP leaders could hope for after one Republican, George V. Voinovich of Ohio, signaled he was ready to side with the Democrats who wanted a negative recommendation. Voinovich delivered a scathing fifteen-minute rebuke of Bolton in which he labeled him "the poster child of what somebody in the diplomatic corps should not be."

On May 26, Republican leaders tried to win a cloture motion and shut off debate on the nomination but lost on a **key vote of 56–42 (R 53–1; D 3–40; I 0–1),** four votes short of the sixty votes required to invoke cloture. *(2005 key votes, p. 915)*

Democrats denied they had filibustered the nomination, saying they wanted more information from the White House about how Bolton handled intelligence on Syria and top-secret National Security Agency (NSA) documents while he was the State Department's senior arms control official. Bolton's Senate GOP supporters said the request was a tactic to divert attention from the minority party's efforts to scuttle the nomination. After some balky negotiations, the administration refused to turn over the information, and on June 20 the Republicans failed a second time to win cloture, 54–38.

Those cloture votes amounted to the most direct rejection of a cabinet-level nominee since 1989, when the Senate voted against confirming former Texas Republican senator John Tower as President George H. W. Bush's defense secretary. *(Tower nomination, Congress and the Nation Vol. VIII, p. 339)*

On Aug. 1, 2005, the first weekday after Congress began its summer break, Bush gave Bolton a recess appointment, a maneuver that allowed the president to bypass the Senate when it did not act on a nominee while in session. Under the terms of a recess appointment, Bolton's appointment would expire in January 2007 at the end of the 109th Congress, unless he was renominated for a full term and confirmed by the Senate.

President Bush renominated Bolton in September 2005. The Foreign Relations Committee took up the nomination again in July 2006. Bolton's prospects for confirmation seemed to have improved when Voinovich—a pivotal committee opponent in 2005—said he had changed his mind about Bolton's qualifications for the job after watching him at the United Nations over the course of a year. But Democrats continued to oppose the nomination and found ways to derail it, especially with their renewed demands for NSA transcripts, which they said would shed light on alleged attempts by Bolton to intimidate his political opponents at the State Department. With several Republicans undecided about whether to support Bolton, Foreign Relations Chair Richard G. Lugar, R-Ind., on Sept. 7 put off a vote and the nomination never made it out of committee.

The White House stood by Bolton as its nominee even after the November midterm election gave Democrats control in the 110th Congress. Bush resubmitted the nomination on Nov. 9, 2006, but Bolton was convinced that he would not win Senate confirmation in the new Congress and announced his resignation on Dec. 4.

2005 Supplemental Appropriations

Congress in 2005 cleared a fiscal 2005 emergency supplemental appropriations bill (HR 1268—PL 109-13) that primarily funded the wars in Iraq and Afghanistan but also provided some money for other programs, including international assistance. *(2005 war supplemental, p. 348)*

The $5.1 billion appropriated in HR 1268 for foreign affairs activities was $464 million less than President George W. Bush had requested. A $1 billion rescission of previously appropriated but unused aid to Turkey brought the net total to $4.1 billion. The final bill included money for, among other things, reconstruction in Afghanistan, international peacekeeping in the Darfur region of Sudan, and a new U.S. Embassy compound in Baghdad.

In addition to the foreign affairs money, the bill also provided nearly $1 billion in aid to the victims of the December 2004 tsunami that struck twelve countries in the Indian Ocean. More than 275,000 were thought to have died in the five most affected countries—India, Indonesia, the Maldives, Sri Lanka, and Thailand—according to U.N. and International Red Cross agencies. Beyond the loss of life, the economic and social impact was massive as coastal areas were destroyed and millions of people lost their homes and livelihoods.

LEGISLATIVE ACTION

The House passed HR 1268 (H Rept 109-16) on March 16, 2005, by a vote of 388–43. The $81.4 billion version included a net total of $3.3 billion for foreign affairs activities. Another $992 million in nonemergency funds was offset by the unused aid to Turkey. The funds for Turkey, provided under a fiscal 2003 war supplemental (PL 108-11), had not been obligated because the Turkish parliament had never ratified an agreement not to deploy forces to the Kurdish region of northern Iraq.

Despite objections voiced during markup, the House Appropriations Committee had approved $592 million of

$658 million requested for a new U.S. Embassy in Baghdad. Critics questioned the need to fund the embassy in the supplemental rather than through the regular State Department appropriations bill, but Republicans said money to begin construction of a highly secure compound was needed immediately. When the bill reached the floor, however, a majority from both parties voted 258–170 to adopt an amendment by Fred Upton, R-Mich., to bar use of funds in the bill for embassy construction. The vote was part of a concerted effort by budget hawks to curb what they said was reckless spending in light of a growing budget deficit.

In other floor action, the House adopted by voice vote an amendment by Jesse L. Jackson, D-Ill., to add $100 million for disaster relief and refugee assistance for Sudan and other African countries.

On April 21, the Senate passed HR 1268 (S Rept 109-52) by a vote of 99–0. The Senate's $81.2 billion version included $5.1 billion for foreign affairs activities. The unused Turkey aid reduced the net total to $4.1 billion.

The Senate bill included $592 million for construction of a U.S. Embassy in Iraq. A floor amendment offered by Tom Coburn, R-Okla., to reduce the embassy funding to $106 million was tabled (killed) by a vote of 54–45.

The Senate agreed by voice vote to a Jon Corzine, D-N.J., amendment to dedicate $90.5 million in funding for international peacekeeping specifically to help stop genocide in Sudan and to provide food aid for the Darfur region. In other action, the Senate adopted by voice vote an amendment by Herb Kohl, D-Wis., to increase food aid to $470 million.

House-Senate conferees were under intense pressure from the Pentagon to move quickly on the war supplemental. The House adopted the conference report (H Rept 109-72) by a vote of 368–58 on May 5. The Senate cleared the bill 100–0 on May 10.

MAJOR PROVISIONS

As signed into law May 11, HR 1268 included $5.1 billion for international activities. The rescission of $1 billion in unused aid to Turkey brought net funding for international activities to $4.1 billion, all of it emergency appropriations.

In addition to that money, HR 1268 also provided $907 million in aid to victims of the Dec. 26, 2004, tsunami in South Asia.

Specific appropriations included:

- $680 million for assessed contributions for international peacekeeping programs in the Darfur region of the Sudan, as well as in Cote D'Ivoire, Haiti, and Burundi.
- $240 million for other countries' efforts in support of the U.S. war on terrorism. Conferees eliminated funding for a similar but separate account called "Global War on Terror Partners Fund."
- $592 million for a new U.S. Embassy compound in Baghdad.
- $200 million for economic development in the West Bank and Gaza Strip. The conference report allocated the funds to specific programs, including $50 million dedicated to Israeli border control to ease the flow of goods and people between the two sides. The funding was subject to an existing prohibition of providing funds directly to the Palestinian Authority (PL 108-447), although that law allowed the president to waive the restriction if it was in the national security interest of the United States.
- $1.1 billion in economic assistance for Afghanistan.
- $400 million for humanitarian assistance in Africa, including about $238 million for Darfur.

2006 Aid Appropriations

Congress in 2005 cleared legislation (HR 3057—PL 109-102) appropriating $21 billion for foreign aid and related programs in fiscal 2006.

The bill's total appropriation represented an increase of about $2.4 billion over the previous year's regular appropriations, excluding supplemental spending for the wars in Iraq and Afghanistan. But it was still about $1.9 billion less than President George W. Bush had requested. Congress cut back on the administration's request for the Millennium Challenge Account (MCA), the president's signature foreign aid initiative for the world's poorest countries, and it provided more than Bush sought for programs to combat HIV/AIDS, tuberculosis, and malaria.

Congress also provided only a fraction of the money requested for reconstruction in Iraq. Lawmakers said the request could be covered by previously appropriated money.

Under the threat of a veto, House-Senate conferees resolved a perennial dispute over restrictions on funding for international family planning programs by dropping a Senate provision that would have lifted the restrictions.

The foreign operations bill funded most U.S. foreign assistance—including bilateral economic aid provided by the U.S. Agency for International Development (USAID), military aid, contributions to multilateral aid institutions, and export assistance.

HOUSE ACTION

The House passed a $20.3 billion version of HR 3057 by a vote of 393–32 on June 28, 2005. The House Appropriations Committee had reported the bill (H Rept 109-152) on June 24.

The House bill was about 11 percent less than Bush had requested. Foreign Operations Subcommittee Chair Jim Kolbe, R-Ariz., said that he had been constrained by the $20.3 billion discretionary spending cap the full committee had placed on the bill.

Kolbe's panel made its most controversial cut in the president's request for MCA, which Kolbe said was the White House's highest priority in the bill. The bill provided $1.75 billion instead of the requested $3 billion. *(MCA background, Congress and the Nation Vol. XI, p. 289)*

The panel also rejected a request for $459 million for Iraq reconstruction because, Kolbe explained, ongoing reconstruction needs could be met from the approximately $3.5 billion remaining from the original $18.4 billion Iraq reconstruction package (PL 108-106) enacted in 2003. *(Congress and the Nation Vol. XI, p. 291)*

Also left out of the bill was the $108 million requested for the Global Environmental Facility (GEF), an independent organization that provided aid for environmental programs in developing countries. Kolbe said the group had not established a "performance-based" system for giving out money.

The House bill included $2.7 billion for HIV/AIDS spending, $131 million more than requested.

The president's requests for $2.5 billion for Israel and $1.8 billion for Egypt were included in the bill, despite the concerns of some Democratic appropriators that Egypt had not embraced democracy and modernization. The committee did earmark $50 million of the economic aid to Egypt for democracy and human rights and $50 million for education programs. Appropriators also agreed to a $150 million request for economic assistance for the West Bank and Gaza but, reflecting their concerns about corruption, they mandated that the money had to flow through USAID, with no funds going directly to the Palestinian Authority.

During the floor debate, the House adopted 313–114 an amendment to effectively prohibit the Export-Import Bank from loaning $5 billion to help the British-owned nuclear division of the Westinghouse Co. provide nuclear power technology to help China build four nuclear plants. The amendment was offered jointly by Bernard Sanders, I-Vt., one of the most liberal members of the House, and conservative Republican Dana Rohrabacher of California.

An amendment by Anthony Weiner, D-N.Y., to prohibit any financial aid for Saudi Arabia was adopted 293–132. The vote was symbolic because the bill had included only $25,000 for Saudi Arabia. An amendment by Nathan Deal, R-Ga., to bar use of the bill's funds to aid any country that had an extradition treaty with the United States but refused to extradite certain accused criminals was approved 294–132. Deal said his amendment was aimed at Mexico.

The House rejected 87–326 a Joe Pitts, R-Pa., amendment to shift $750 million from military aid to Egypt to USAID child survival and health accounts. Also rejected 189–234 was a Jim McGovern, D-Mass., amendment to cut $100 million from Andean Counterdrug Initiative funding.

SENATE ACTION

The Senate passed its $31.8 billion version of HR 3057 on July 20 by a vote of 98–1. The Senate Appropriations Committee had reported the bill (S Rept 109-96) on June 30.

The much larger Senate version not only included more for foreign aid than the House bill—$22.1 billion as compared to the House bill's $20.3 billion—but it also contained $9.7 billion for the State Department and related agencies, which the House covered in a separate spending bill.

The Senate bill included $1.8 billion for the MCA, slightly more than in the House bill but still $1.2 billion below Bush's request. The bill, however, did include—unlike the House bill—the administration's requests for Iraq reconstruction and the GEF. The Senate bill also called for $2.9 billion to fight HIV/AIDS, malaria and tuberculosis, more than both the House and the president had proposed.

Two days before Senate passage, the White House issued a statement calling on Congress to increase the MCA funding, saying it was "a critical part of the president's foreign assistance program."

That White House statement also warned that the president would veto any bill that contained language lifting abortion-related restrictions on family planning aid. The Senate bill sought to overturn the so-called Mexico City policy embraced by the Bush administration, which prohibited U.S. funding for any organization that provided or actively promoted abortion as a method of family planning, even if it did so with its own money. The bill also would have weakened the Kemp-Kasten amendment, a provision of law that extended the prohibition to any organization that "participates in the management" of a program of coercive or forced sterilization. These provisions had typically resulted in the withholding of money appropriated for the U.N. Population Fund (UNFPA). On Sept. 17, 2005, the State Department announced that it was withholding the $34 million provided as part of the fiscal 2005 appropriations bill (PL 108-447). *(Background, Congress and the Nation Vol. XI, p. 247, p. 294)*

Despite the veto threat, the provisions to end the restrictions remained in the Senate-passed version. During floor action, the Senate adopted by voice vote a Patrick J. Leahy, D-Vt., amendment to specify that U.S. family planning aid for the UNFPA be limited to six specific uses. The bill already required that the organization keep the money in a separate account and spend none of it for abortions or programs in China. Like the House bill, the measure included $35 million for the UNFPA.

In other floor action, the Senate adopted 86–12 a Saxby Chambliss, R-Ga., amendment to withhold funding from any country that refused to extradite criminal suspects facing capital charges in the United States. The amendment was aimed at certain Latin American countries, including Nicaragua, Mexico, and Costa Rica, that refused to extradite a suspect to the United States if the suspect might face the death penalty or even life in prison.

The Senate adopted by voice vote an amendment by Sam Brownback, R-Kan., to specify that $50 million of economic aid to Egypt be devoted to education. The bill already set aside $35 million for promoting democracy.

Unlike the House, the Senate rejected 37–62 an attempt by Tom Coburn, R-Okla., and Barbara Boxer, D-Calif., to block an Export-Import Bank loan to help build nuclear power plants in China.

CONFERENCE, FINAL ACTION

The House adopted the conference report on HR 3057 (H Rept 109-265) by a vote of 358–39 on Nov. 4. The Senate cleared the bill on Nov. 10 by a vote of 91–0.

Conferees agreed to drop the Senate bill's funding for the State Department and to follow instead the outlines of the House bill. Fiscal 2006 State Department funding was included in the Commerce-Justice-Science appropriations bill (HR 2862—PL 109-108). The difference in handling the State Department had been the result of separate reorganizations in the House and Senate Appropriations committees early in 2005.

Conferees settled on a $21 billion bill, after resolving the two chambers' differences over funding for the MCA, HIV/AIDS programs, and reconstruction in Iraq, among other things.

Senate provisions that would have ended the Mexico City policy and modified the Kemp-Kasten amendment were dropped, as was the Senate amendment outlining acceptable uses for the UNFPA money.

Conferees also dropped a House provision that sought to block the Export-Import Bank from loaning money for nuclear power plants in China.

Conferees added waivers to provisions on aid to Saudi Arabia and extradition that were adopted during House and Senate floor action.

MAJOR PROVISIONS

As signed into law on Nov. 14, HR 3057 appropriated $21.0 billion for foreign aid and related programs in fiscal 2006. The total included $1.3 billion for the World Bank and other international institutions, $14.6 billion for bilateral economic assistance, and $4.8 billion for military assistance.

The appropriations totals did not reflect a 1 percent across-the-board cut in most discretionary appropriations enacted as part of the fiscal 2006 defense spending bill (HR 2863—PL 109-148). HR 3057 contained $20.94 billion in discretionary spending.

Millennium Challenge Account

Provided $1.77 billion.

HIV/AIDS Assistance

Provided $2.8 billion to fight HIV/AIDS, malaria, and tuberculosis. The total included about $2 billion for President Bush's State Department-run Global HIV/AIDS Initiative, of which $200 million was to go to the Geneva-based Global Fund to Fight AIDS, Tuberculosis, and Malaria. Another $250 million through USAID brought the total for the international organization to $450 million.

Middle East

Provided $2.5 billion for Israel, including $240 million in economic assistance.

Provided $1.8 billion for Egypt, including $495 million in economic aid. The bill earmarked $50 million of Egypt's economic aid for education and $50 million to promote democracy.

Provided $150 million for the West Bank and Gaza, but only for USAID projects, not direct assistance to the Palestinian Authority. No funds could go to the Palestinian Authority unless the president certified that it was in the national security interests of the United States.

Afghanistan, Pakistan, Iraq

Provided $931 million for Afghanistan, including $430 million for economic assistance. The bill stipulated, however, that no more than $225 million of the economic funds was to be made available until the secretary of state certified that Afghan officials were cooperating with programs to eradicate opium-poppy cultivation and interdicting narcotics trafficking. The president could waive the certification requirement if it was deemed to be in the interests of national security. The bill also provided $235 million in counternarcotics funding.

Provided $638 million for Pakistan, including $300 million for economic assistance, $300 million for military aid, and $38 million for counternarcotics funding.

Provided $61 million for reconstruction programs in Iraq.

Global Environmental Facility

Provided $80 million.

Family Planning

Provided $432 million for bilateral family planning programs. The bill allocated $34 million for the United Nations Population Fund (UNFPA). Family planning aid was subject to the abortion-related restrictions contained in the Mexico City policy and the Kemp-Kasten amendment.

Andean Counterdrug Initiative

Provided $734.5 million.

2006 SUPPLEMENTAL

A supplemental appropriations bill (HR 4939—PL 109-234) enacted into law in June 2006 provided almost another $4 billion for State Department operations and international assistance in fiscal 2006.

The bulk of the money in the $94.5 billion bill—$65.8 billion—was for military operations in Iraq and Afghanistan. HR 4939 also included funding for hurricane relief, flu preparedness, border protection, and agriculture disaster assistance. *(2006 war supplemental, p. 350)*

The international operations portion of the bill provided:

- $3 billion for Iraq, about $210 million less than requested. The total included $1.1 billion for the U.S. Embassy, as requested; and $1.6 billion for "stabilization assistance," about $20 million less than requested. The total was within $50 million of both the House and Senate versions.
- $96.5 million for aid to Afghanistan, $6 million less than requested, according to the Congressional Research Service.
- $66 million for pro-democracy forces in Iran, about $9 million less than requested.
- $618 million for humanitarian aid and peacekeeping operations in Darfur and southern Sudan, an increase of $104 million over the request. The House proposed $618 million, the Senate $624 million.
- $126 million, as requested, to pay for earthquake relief to Pakistan.
- $64 million for Liberia, an increase of $50 million over the request, as recommended by both chambers.

Reflecting members' concern over the victory of Hamas—branded by the United States as a terrorist group—in the January 2006 Palestinian parliamentary elections, the bill also tightened restrictions on aid to the Palestinian Authority. *(Details, Middle East policy, p. 297)*

The House passed its $91.9 billion version of HR 4939 by a vote of 348–71 on March 16, 2006. The House Appropriations Committee had reported the bill (H Rept 109-388) on March 13.

The Senate passed a $108.9 billion version by a vote of 77–21 on May 4. The Senate Appropriations Committee had reported the bill (S Rept 109-230) on April 5.

The House adopted the conference report (H Rept 109-494) by a vote of 351–67 on June 13. The Senate cleared the bill 98–1 on June 15 and President Bush signed it into law that same day.

2007 Aid Appropriations

The fiscal 2007 foreign operations appropriations bill was one of nine spending measures left unfinished at the end of the 109th Congress. The House passed an aid appropriations bill (HR 5522) in 2006, but that measure never made it to the floor in the Senate. Three short-term continuing resolutions kept aid programs—along with programs in the other eight unfinished funding bills—operating through early 2007. As the third stop-gap spending bill was about to expire, Congress cleared another resolution (H J Res 20—PL 110-5) that continued funding until the end of fiscal 2007.

President George W. Bush had requested $23.7 billion for foreign operations, an increase of $3 billion over fiscal 2006 spending, not counting supplemental appropriations. He focused his request for additional funds on a few specific programs—mainly the Millennium Challenge Account (MCA), the Global HIV/AIDS Initiative, and reconstruction in Iraq. The MCA was Bush's signature foreign aid program, created to reward developing countries that embraced market-based economic growth, democracy, and human rights. The HIV/AIDS Initiative was a bilateral program targeting fifteen countries with the most severe HIV/AIDS problems.

Lawmakers in both chambers made it clear that they planned to give the president significantly less than he requested. Although they acknowledged that foreign aid could pay dividends in both humanitarian terms and for the U.S. economy and security, they said that the billions of dollars going to the wars in Iraq and Afghanistan, combined with electoral pressure to meet homefront needs, made it difficult to provide as much for foreign programs as Bush wanted.

In June 2006 the House passed its version of HR 5522, appropriating $21.3 billion for foreign operations. Later that month the Senate Appropriations Committee followed broadly in the House's footsteps, approving $21.8 billion for foreign aid. The Senate committee's version also included $9.7 billion for the State Department, which the House covered in a separate bill.

Both bills would have fully funded several of the president's most significant requests, including HIV/AIDS relief and aid to Israel and Egypt, although Egypt came under fire in both chambers for its human rights record. And both bills proposed hefty cuts in the MCA. Earlier concerns about management of the MCA fell away during the year, but with a tight cap on overall spending, resistance to approving the full request remained.

H J Res 20, the year-long continuing resolution that was ultimately enacted, kept most programs funded at the fiscal 2006 levels, although there were some additions. A major increase came in funding for HIV/AIDS programs. *(2006 aid appropriations, p. 282)*

HOUSE ACTION

The House passed HR 5522 by a vote of 373–34 on June 9, 2006. The House Appropriations Committee had reported the bill (H Rept 109-486) on June 5.

The bill's $21.3 billion total reflected spending allocations determined by Appropriations Committee leaders, who decided to provide $2.4 billion, or 10 percent, less than requested for foreign aid, and use the money for domestic programs instead.

Under the bill, funding for the MCA would have been reduced to $2 billion, one-third less than requested.

Cuts were also made in aid to Iraq, Afghanistan, and Pakistan. A portion of the aid for Afghanistan was to be withheld pending certification that Kabul was providing sufficient help for U.S. antidrug efforts. In its report, the Appropriations Committee expressed concern over human rights, especially women's rights, and democratic governance in Pakistan.

The bill included the president's request for $3.4 billion to fight HIV/AIDS, although it increased the allocation of money for the Global Fund to Fight AIDS, Tuberculosis, and Malaria, an international organization, while reducing the amount going to the State Department's separate Global HIV/AIDS Initiative.

Aid to Egypt provoked controversy during both committee and floor action. David R. Obey of Wisconsin, the Appropriations Committee's ranking Democrat, tried to convince the panel to withhold $200 million of the military aid to Egypt until Congress passed a bill to release it. He said Egypt's backsliding on democracy and human rights should not be rewarded by unquestioning congressional support. But opponents of Obey's amendment argued that the aid helped to anchor the Israel-Egypt peace treaty, a central pillar of U.S.-Middle East policy since it was signed in 1979. They said the military aid in particular was critical to cementing Egypt's contributions to U.S. military operations in the region, such as allowing U.S. combat aircraft to traverse Egypt's skies and U.S. warships to pass through the Suez Canal. Secretary of State Condoleezza Rice also voiced her opposition. The amendment was rejected, although the panel did agree to rescind $200 million in previously appropriated but unspent aid to Egypt until the country met certain benchmarks for financial reform. Obey attributed the defeat of his proposal more to lawmakers' parochial interests than other strategic concerns, given the big weapons contracts that U.S. defense contractors received from the Egyptian government.

Obey's luck did not improve when the bill reached the floor. The House rejected 198–225 his attempt to cut $100 million in economic aid for Egypt and use the funds to fight AIDS globally and to assist the Darfur region of Sudan. The amendment—by Obey, House International Relations Committee Chair Henry J. Hyde, R-Ill., and Tom Lantos of California, the ranking Democrat on the International Relations panel—was supported by a majority of Democrats and opposed by most Republicans.

During floor consideration, the House rejected two amendments offered by Jim McGovern, D-Mass. A proposal that would have shifted $30 million from the Andean Counterdrug Initiative, a program aimed at combating the drug trade in Colombia, to refugee assistance programs was rejected 174–229. His second amendment, rejected 188–218, would have prohibited spending for the Western Hemisphere Institute for Security Cooperation at Fort Benning, Ga., previously known as the School of the Americas.

The House did adopt 312–97 an Anthony Weiner, D-N.Y., amendment to bar use of any funds in the bill to provide aid to Saudi Arabia.

SENATE ACTION

The Senate Appropriations Committee reported its $31.5 billion version of HR 5522 (S Rept 109-277) on July 10. The bill provided $21.8 billion for foreign aid and $9.7 billion for the State Department and related agencies.

The Senate version would have cut the request for MCA to $1.9 billion.

The bill included the requests for aid to Afghanistan and Pakistan but reduced the aid requested for Iraq, although not as much as the House had.

The Senate committee approved the president's overall $3.4 billion request for HIV/AIDS programs but agreed to provide more to the international Global Fund than requested or in the House version.

Like the House bill, the Senate version included the requests for Israel and Egypt but rescinded $300 million in unused economic aid to Egypt.

The Senate bill proposed to consolidate all health-related programs into one account, called the Child Survival and Health Programs Fund, and consolidate all democracy programs into a single Democracy Fund. The idea behind the consolidation was to keep better track of how those programs were administered.

CONTINUING RESOLUTIONS

The Senate bill never reached the floor. With the November 2006 elections approaching, members focused their attention on domestic issues and felt little pressure to wrap up the foreign aid bill in the regular session. When lawmakers returned in November, Republican leaders quickly decided to leave the foreign operations funding bill and the eight other unfinished appropriations bills to the Democrats, whose electoral victories guaranteed them control in the next Congress. Members kept the aid programs operating through Feb. 15, 2007, at the lower of the House-passed or fiscal 2006 levels under a short-term continuing resolution signed into law Dec. 9, 2006 (H J Res 102—PL 109-383).

Democratic leaders—eager to save time and move on to the fiscal 2008 appropriations cycle—decided to pull together the nine unfinished spending bills from fiscal 2007 into a resolution that would continue funding until the end of fiscal 2007. Congress cleared the year-long continuing resolution on Feb. 14, 2007, and President Bush signed it into law the following day (H J Res 20—PL 110-5).

Under H J Res 20, most programs were to be continued at the fiscal 2006 appropriations levels, with additions to cover pay increases and to maintain staffing levels. Other increases reflected Democratic priorities. The resolution, for example, boosted funding for bilateral and multilateral HIV/AIDS programs by nearly $1.3 billion. *(2006 aid appropriations, p. 282)*

MAJOR PROVISIONS

Under the series of continuing resolutions, fiscal 2007 appropriations for the State Department and foreign operations ultimately totaled $37.13 billion, including $31.28 billion in discretionary spending. The overall total included $10.9 billion for State Department operations, $19.6 billion for bilateral economic assistance, $5.4 billion for foreign military aid, and $1.3 billion for international financial institutions.

Major provisions of H J Res 20:

Millennium Challenge Account

Provided $1.75 billion.

HIV/AIDS Assistance

Provided $3.2 billion for the State Department's Global HIV/AIDS Initiative and $712 million for the Child Survival and Health Programs Fund of the U.S. Agency for International Development. From these funds, $625 million was for the U.S. contribution to the Global Fund to Fight HIV/AIDS, Tuberculosis, and Malaria. (The Health and Human Services section of the continuing resolution contained additional funds: $494 million, of which $99 million was for the Global Fund.)

Middle East

Provided $2.34 billion in military aid and $120 million in economic assistance for Israel.

Provided $1.3 billion in military aid and $455 million in economic assistance for Egypt.

Andean Counterdrug Initiative

Provided $721.5 million.

2007 SUPPLEMENTAL

Congress cleared a fiscal 2007 supplemental appropriations bill (HR 2206—PL 110-28) in May 2007. The bill was primarily aimed at funding military operations in Iraq and Afghanistan, although it did include some money for other programs. Among those appropriations was $5.7 billion for the State Department and foreign aid, about what Bush had requested. *(2007 war supplemental, pp. 117, 383, 664)*

That total included about $1.6 billion ($500 million less than requested) for economic reconstruction and State Department operations and other programs in Iraq. It also included $910 million ($189 million more than requested) for humanitarian, reconstruction, embassy operations, and related assistance for Afghanistan.

Foreign Relations Authorization

The House passed a foreign relations authorization bill in 2005, but the Senate's version stalled on the floor and there was no further action on the legislation in the 109th Congress.

The two bills were very different. The House-passed bill (HR 2601) authorized $20.8 billion for State Department operations and some foreign aid programs over two years. The Senate bill (S 600) proposed $34 billion over two years for the State Department and for U.S. foreign aid programs, including many that were not in the House version. Both bills reauthorized a variety of State Department and foreign aid programs, including the Peace Corps and the Millennium Challenge Account, President George W. Bush's signature effort to promote development and democracy in poor countries.

But each chamber added special provisions and restrictions reflecting the priorities of individual members. The House bill contained a number of provisions that the White House opposed, and the Senate bill became a magnet for amendments dealing with everything from abortion to trade with Cuba.

Such controversy was nothing new. Congress had last cleared a stand-alone State Department authorization bill (PL 107-228) in 2002, but that was the only time it had done so since 1994. The last time it passed a separate foreign aid authorization bill was 1985. Because foreign affairs legislation was so unpopular and controversial, Congress usually opted to waive the requirement that funds be authorized before appropriated and instead continued funding various programs through appropriations bills. As a result, over the years the foreign policy committees in Congress had ceded much of their clout to the appropriators. *(Previous action, Congress and the Nation Vol. XI, p. 294)*

SENATE ACTION

The Senate Foreign Relations Committee reported S 600 (S Rept 109-35) on March 10, 2005. The panel had approved the bill on a bipartisan 18–0 vote, but only after Republicans narrowly defeated a Democratic effort to reduce the $3 billion in the bill for the Millennium Challenge Account (MCA) in favor of shoring up more traditional aid programs.

When the bill reached the floor in early April, Foreign Relations Committee Chair Richard G. Lugar, R-Ind., found his hopes of putting an imprint on a range of foreign policy issues frustrated once again. The bill was met with a deluge of amendments and was pulled after two days of debate when Lugar was unable to reach an agreement to limit debate or amendments.

One amendment adopted before the bill was pulled called for repealing the so-called Mexico City policy, which barred U.S. aid to international family planning organizations that performed abortions or provided consultations for abortion, even if they used their own funds. President Ronald Reagan first enunciated the policy at a conference in Mexico City in 1984. The Bush White House threatened to veto any legislation that lifted the ban. The amendment, sponsored by Barbara Boxer, D-Calif., had been adopted by a 52–46 vote on April 5. *(Background, Congress and the Nation Vol. XI, p. 247)*

The Senate also adopted by voice vote a Lugar amendment to delete a provision that would have made permanent a 27.1 percent cap on U.S. contributions for United Nations peacekeeping. The Senate rejected 40–57 an attempt by Joseph R. Biden Jr., D-Del., to maintain the cap for calendar years 2005 through 2007. The administration favored a two-year extension.

In other action, the Senate voted 65–35 to table (kill) an amendment by Byron L. Dorgan, D-N.D., to reduce funding for international broadcasting operations and prohibit the use of funds for television broadcasts to Cuba.

Amendments still pending when the bill was pulled from the floor included proposals to impose tariffs on Chinese imports if China did not revalue its currency, to reverse a Treasury Department ruling requiring advance payment for agricultural shipments to Cuba, and to lift cold war-trade restrictions on the Ukraine. An attempt to table the Chinese tariffs amendment had been rejected 33–67.

HOUSE ACTION

The House passed HR 2601 on July 20, 2005, by a vote of 351–78. The House International Relations Committee had reported the bill (H Rept 109-168) on July 13, after approving it earlier by a 44–0 vote.

A White House statement issued the day of the House floor vote criticized various provisions, saying they would undermine the administration's foreign policy. One proposal would have scaled back military aid to Egypt in favor of economic and education assistance. An attempt to strike that provision from the bill was rejected during committee consideration. The administration also objected to a provision in both the House and Senate bills that in effect recognized Jerusalem as Israel's permanent capital—an issue the White House said should be settled by Israel and the Palestinians.

During the floor debate, the House adopted 226–195 an amendment offered by International Relations Committee Chair Henry J. Hyde, R-Ill., to withhold up to half of U.S. dues to the United Nations until the secretary of state certified that the organization had made certain changes in its operations. The House had passed similar provisions in a separate bill (HR 2745) in June. *(United Nations dues, p. 302)*

The House also accepted by voice vote a Hyde amendment to mandate sanctions against companies or countries in the arms business with China. The amendment was a toned-down version of a bill (HR 3100) that had been rejected the previous week, when it was considered under suspension of the rules and failed to win the required two-thirds majority vote. *(Military sales to China, p. 296)*

Debate on HR 2601 often strayed from State Department operations to the war in Iraq and the treatment of detained terror suspects. Language asking Bush to provide a plan for establishing a stable Iraqi government that would permit a U.S. drawdown there had been added to the bill in committee with bipartisan support, but only after the provision was modified so as not to indicate whether such a plan had or had not been submitted already. On the floor, the House adopted 291–137 a nonbinding amendment by Ileana Ros-Lehtinen, R-Fla., that opposed any "premature withdrawal" of U.S. troops from Iraq, and it rejected 203–227 a Democratic attempt to recommit the bill to committee to add language asking the president for his benchmarks for a successful Iraq strategy and calling for, among other things, a policy to provide adequate equipment for U.S. troops. The House also adopted 304–124 a nonbinding amendment by Dana Rohrabacher, R-Calif., stating that the detention and interrogation of alleged terrorists at Guantánamo Bay, Cuba, was essential to winning the war against terrorism. *(Iraq war policy, pp. 270, 303)*

Pre–Iraq War Intelligence

The Senate Select Committee on Intelligence in 2006 released the first two reports in its "Phase II" inquiry into the intelligence available to the Bush administration and how it was used in the run-up to the Iraq War.

The committee concluded in one report that the intelligence community—albeit with some exceptions—had erred in assessing Saddam Hussein's weapons of mass destruction capabilities. The inquiry also found that the Iraqi leader had been suspicious of the al Qaeda terrorist network and had refused to assist or deal with it.

The second report stated that the Iraqi National Congress, an exile group led by Ahmed Chalabi and funded with U.S. contributions, fed false information to intelligence analysts, who used the information to produce erroneous assessments.

Although the vote on Sept. 7, 2006, to make the reports public was unanimous, their release triggered a new round of preelection partisan fighting.

"Administration officials cherry-picked, exaggerated, or ignored intelligence to justify the decision they had already made to go to war with Iraq," said Democrat John D. Rockefeller IV of West Virginia, the committee's vice chair.

But the panel's Republican chair saw things differently. "The reports are little more than a vehicle to advance election year political charges," said Pat Roberts of Kansas, who had led the committee's multiphased investigation. He acknowledged that some of the intelligence was flawed but disputed some of the Democrats' claims.

Their comments reflected the partisan tension that had surrounded the probe since the Senate panel began its review in June 2003.

BACKGROUND

The Senate Intelligence Committee's initial inquiry had culminated in the July 2004 release of Congress's first detailed report on the faulty intelligence on Iraq's alleged weapons of mass destruction (WMD). It primarily criticized the CIA for its failings. *(Details, Congress and the Nation Vol. XI, p. 282)*

Republicans preferred that the inquiry stop there, insisting that the panel should examine only the quality of the intelligence and not its use. But Democrats were equally insistent that the committee examine whether the Bush administration exaggerated and manipulated the intelligence to makes its case for war. Ultimately, Roberts and Rockefeller struck a deal for a second phase of the probe that would examine the administration's use of the intelligence and would also probe two Pentagon offices that had provided intelligence on possible ties between Iraq and al Qaeda.

But Democratic leaders became impatient as the probe continued through 2005. To call attention to what Rockefeller described as "only token work, at best, ... on phase II since it was authorized," Minority Leader Harry Reid, D-Nev., on Nov. 1, 2005, resorted to a rarely used parliamentary tactic to force the Senate into a private session. It was the first secret session since the 1999 impeachment proceedings against President Bill Clinton.

The lights went down, Capitol Police cleared the galleries, and then apparently not too much happened on the Senate floor for more than two hours, while outside in the hallway senators took turns going before the television cameras to decry the Democrats' bad manners or the Republicans' bad politics. Pushed by the unusual but easy maneuver—it took only one senator to move for a private session and another to second the motion—Republicans and Democrats agreed to appoint three senators each to evaluate progress made on the intelligence investigation and report on their findings in two weeks.

The inquiry continued and in early August 2006 the Intelligence Committee approved the first two reports. But it still had to work out with the Bush administration what would be made public. After the declassification issues were resolved, the committee on Sept. 7 voted unanimously to release the reports, which it did the next day.

Senate Democrats took to the floor to accuse the administration of deliberately misusing intelligence that boosted the case for war even though analysts had discredited the information. Republicans chastised Democrats for trying to score political points and played down the reports as old news.

Three additional reports were to be released as part of the Phase II inquiry. *(Pre–Iraq War intelligence, 110th Congress, p. 318)*

SADDAM HUSSEIN REGIME

The Intelligence Committee's report that compared postwar findings about Iraq's alleged WMD capabilities and ties to al Qaeda with prewar intelligence assessments (S Rept 109-331) was approved by a 14–1 committee vote on Aug. 3, 2006. The report included one section with the additional views of three Republicans and another section with additional and minority views of four Republicans.

The committee reported that postwar findings had not supported the 2002 National Intelligence Estimate (NIE) judgments that Iraq was reconstituting its nuclear weapons program, had acquired aluminum tubes for that purpose, and was trying to procure uranium from Africa; or that it had biological weapons and mobile facilities to produce them, and was developing an unmanned aerial vehicle that was probably intended to deliver them; or that it had chemical weapons. The report noted entities within the intelligence community that had dissented from some of the NIE assessments.

On the issue of whether Iraq had ties to al Qaeda, the committee reported that postwar findings had indicated that Saddam Hussein was distrustful of al Qaeda and had viewed Islamic extremists as a threat to his regime. He had refused all requests from al Qaeda for material or operational support. The report said that postwar information supported prewar assessments by the intelligence community that there was no credible information that Iraq was involved in the Sept. 11, 2001, terrorist attacks on the United States.

IRAQI NATIONAL CONGRESS

The report on the intelligence community's use of information supplied by Chalabi's Iraqi National Congress (S Rept 109-330) was approved by an 11–4 vote on Aug. 2, 2006. Various Republican senators added three sections of additional views and two of minority views, while all seven Democrats signed an additional views section.

The CIA had begun working with Chalabi, an Iraqi Shiite who had been in exile since 1956, in the early 1990s as part of an effort to encourage and influence factions interested in removing Saddam Hussein from power. Iraqi opposition leaders created the Iraqi National Congress in 1992 and Chalabi became its head.

The Intelligence Committee's examination of the group's role in providing prewar intelligence ended in heated controversy. The final report concluded, among other things, that false information from sources affiliated with the Iraqi National Congress had been used to support key intelligence community assessments on Iraq and was widely distributed in intelligence products prior to the Iraq War. The group was also said to have attempted to influence U.S. policy on Iraq by providing, through defectors, false information aimed at convincing the United States that Iraq possessed WMDs and had links to terrorists.

These, however, were not the conclusions that had been reached by the committee's staff. At a closed meeting Aug. 2, the panel's Democrats had won adoption of an entirely new set of conclusions for the report. The amendment, offered by Rockefeller, was adopted by a vote of 9–6. Two Republicans joined all seven Democrats in approving the change. Committee members were divided—bitterly—on the question of whether the Iraqi National Congress information supported enough key judgments to suggest that it significantly influenced the case for war.

Chair Roberts hotly denounced the move, arguing that Democrats blithely overturned the judgment of "committee analysts"—aides deemed officially nonpartisan—that Chalabi's organization was not a decisive force in hyping the WMD threat. "Very simply, the conclusions are misleading and are not supported by the facts," he said. "I am disappointed that some of my colleagues have twisted the facts to reach conclusions that support other agendas."

But Rockefeller countered that the staff analysts were anything but impartial. They were essentially appointees of the majority—just as, Rockefeller conceded, the staff members that drafted the conclusions ultimately adopted were employed by the minority.

The two moderate Republicans who voted for the Democrats' amendment—Olympia J. Snowe of Maine and Chuck Hagel of Nebraska—said they had followed their own best, and disinterested, judgment. "After reviewing thousands of pages of evidence, I voted for the conclusions that most closely reflect the facts in the report," Snowe said.

Even though he disowned the Democratic-drafted conclusions, Roberts said he voted to release the report because the findings of fact were valuable to the public.

2006 Intelligence Authorization

Congress in 2005 failed to clear a fiscal 2006 intelligence authorization bill because of disputes over the Bush administration's handling of intelligence and its treatment of foreign detainees. The House passed its bill (HR 2475) in June, but the Senate's version (S 1803) never reached the floor after an unidentified Republican member used senatorial prerogative to put a hold on the measure.

The largely secret annual bill set funding levels for intelligence programs and policy prescriptions for covert action, spy satellites, and other intelligence activities. Failure to pass the authorization bill, however, did not interfere with U.S. intelligence activities because the authorization ultimately was included in defense appropriations legislation instead.

Although total spending for the nation's intelligence agencies was classified, it was believed to be more than $40 billion for fiscal 2006. Despite objections from the White House, both the House and Senate bills had proposed scaling back some expensive spy satellite and airborne surveillance programs while expanding and upgrading human intelligence gathering, according to congressional aides. In its influential report released in 2004, the commission created to investigate the Sept. 11, 2001, terrorist attacks on the United States had criticized U.S. intelligence agencies for having inadequate numbers of intelligence analysts and collectors with the right skills to penetrate Islamic terrorist cells. *(Independent Sept. 11 commission, Congress and the Nation Vol. XI, p. 275)*

HOUSE ACTION

The House passed HR 2475 on June 21, 2005, by a vote of 409–16. The House Select Committee on Intelligence reported the bill (H Rept 109-101) on June 2.

The main controversy in the House committee markup had been over a GOP-backed provision to limit the authority of the new director of national intelligence (DNI), a position created by a 2004 overhaul of the intelligence community (PL 108-458). *(Intelligence system overhaul, Congress and the Nation Vol. XI, p. 263)*

Under the committee bill, the DNI was required to notify Congress and receive a response before transferring personnel to any of the new intelligence centers authorized under the 2004 overhaul. The provision had the backing of the Pentagon, which had been suspicious of the DNI's power over military intelligence agencies from the outset. Critics of the provision argued that it would undermine the DNI's authority. A Democratic attempt to kill the provision fell on a party-line vote in committee.

But the controversial DNI provision was removed from the bill when it reached the House floor. The rule (H Res 331) governing floor action on the bill automatically struck the provision. Although he had supported the language in committee, Intelligence Committee Chair Peter Hoekstra, R-Mich., said it had become too much of a distraction and should be removed. House Armed Services Committee Chair Duncan Hunter, R-Calif., objected and temporarily blocked the bill. Hunter relented after John D. Negroponte, the DNI, promised to consult on major personnel transfers.

The rule also removed, at Hunter's behest, a provision that would have given the DNI the power to coordinate all overseas intelligence, including military intelligence operations. Hunter had fought against creating a DNI in the first place, and he opposed giving the position any power over military intelligence.

According to the committee report, HR 2475 also ordered the DNI to give Congress a complete inventory of highly secretive "special access programs" operating at U.S. intelligence agencies. These highly compartmentalized programs existed outside normal intelligence channels and few officials had access to the information. The Bush administration opposed the creation of such an inventory.

SENATE ACTION

The Senate version of the intelligence authorization was marked up by two committees. The Senate Select Committee on Intelligence reported S 1803 (S Rept 109-142) on Sept. 29 and the Senate Armed Services Committee reported it (S Rept 109-173) on Oct. 27.

The Intelligence panel's version would have expanded the authority of the DNI, giving him access to all information gathered by intelligence operatives throughout the federal government. The Armed Services Committee amended the measure to preserve the independence of

A PRIMER ON THE U.S. INTELLIGENCE COMMUNITY

Director of National Intelligence

Serves as the head of the intelligence community and is the principal adviser to the president, National Security Council, and Homeland Security Council for intelligence matters related to national security. Oversees the National Intelligence Program and coordinates intelligence matters related to the Defense Department with the under secretary of defense for intelligence.

Civilian Organizations

Central Intelligence Agency

Collects, analyzes, and disseminates foreign intelligence to assist government policymakers in making decisions related to national security. (The CIA is the only intelligence agency not within a Cabinet department.)

Justice Department

Federal Bureau of Investigation—An intelligence and law enforcement agency responsible for counterterrorism. Focuses on terrorist organizations, foreign intelligence services, weapons of mass destruction proliferators, and criminal enterprises.

Drug Enforcement Administration—Has an intelligence program that collects, analyzes, and shares drug-related information acquired during its drug enforcement duties.

State Department

Bureau of Intelligence and Research—Analyzes global developments and contributes to the National Intelligence Estimates and other products. Serves as the focal point within the State Department for all policy issues and activities involving the intelligence community.

Energy Department

Office of Intelligence and Counterintelligence—Assesses worldwide nuclear terrorism threats, nuclear proliferation, and foreign technology threats.

Homeland Security

Office of Intelligence and Analysis—Focuses on threats related to border security, weapons of mass destruction and health, critical infrastructure, extremists within the United States, and travelers entering the country.

Coast Guard Intelligence—Focuses on maritime security, including protecting ports, along with its other missions of search and rescue, maritime safety, counternarcotics, and alien migration interdiction.

Treasury Department

Office of Intelligence and Analysis—Responsible for tracking finances of people and organizations considered a national security threat. Also collects information that may affect U.S. fiscal and monetary policies.

Defense Department Organizations

- **Military service intelligence**—The Army, Navy, Air Force, and Marine Corps have their own intelligence organizations which focus on concerns related to their specific missions.
- **National Security Agency**—Cryptologic organization responsible for protecting the government's information systems and producing foreign signals intelligence information.
- **Defense Intelligence Agency**—Collects and analyzes foreign military intelligence, providing assessments of foreign military intentions and capabilities to U.S. military commanders and civilian policymakers.
- **National Reconnaissance Office**—Designs, builds, and operates the nation's signals and imagery reconnaissance satellites.
- **National Geospatial-Intelligence Agency**—Serves as the military's mapping agency, using information from satellites and other intelligence sources for navigation, national security, U.S. military operations, and humanitarian efforts.

Defense Department operatives responsible for gathering the tactical intelligence used by troops in the field. The committee also specified that the DNI would not be allowed to bypass the armed forces' chain of command by seeking direct access to intelligence used to support military operations.

An unidentified Republican put a hold on the bill, preventing it from coming up for debate on the floor in mid-December. Democrats said the senator wanted to block consideration of three amendments. One amendment required the Bush administration to provide Congress with the president's daily intelligence briefings for the period preceding the 2003 invasion of Iraq. Another amendment called on the administration to submit periodic reports to the Intelligence committees on the health and status of suspected terrorists held by the CIA in any "clandestine prison or detention facility operated by the United States government." The *Washington Post* reported on Nov. 2, 2005, that the CIA maintained a covert prison system abroad to hold terrorism suspects. A third amendment required a detailed classified report to Congress on such facilities.

The Bush administration said that it considered the daily intelligence briefings privileged information and probably would veto any effort by Congress to secure access to them. Administration officials did not comment on secret CIA prisons abroad, the existence of which they had not confirmed.

2007 Intelligence Authorization

Congress in 2006 failed to clear a fiscal 2007 intelligence authorization bill. The House passed a measure (HR 5020), but the Senate never brought its bill (S 3237) to the floor because of Republican opposition to several war-related amendments that Democrats planned to offer. An attempt in 2007 to bring another fiscal 2007 intelligence authorization bill (S 372) to a vote on the Senate floor failed as well.

This marked the second consecutive fiscal year Congress had not cleared legislation to reauthorize the nation's intelligence programs, after having cleared one every year since 1978.

Both chambers' bills set policies and funding levels for the Office of the Director of National Intelligence (DNI) and the federal intelligence agencies, including the CIA, the Defense Intelligence Agency, the FBI, and the National Security Agency (NSA), as well as foreign intelligence activities of the State Department, Homeland Security Department, and other agencies. As in previous years, the details were mostly classified, including the amount of the intelligence budget, which was reported to total approximately $44 billion. An overall total close to that figure was in fact confirmed by the DNI the following year. *(Intelligence budget totals, box p. 322)*

One of the main effects of skipping an authorization bill for two straight years was to further reduce the Intelligence panels' influence. Without it, the committees had no say in providing the intelligence community with strategic and financial guidance, and funding decisions fell mainly to defense appropriators. *(2006 intelligence authorization, p. 290)*

HOUSE ACTION

The House passed HR 5020 on April 26, 2006, by a vote of 327–96. The House Select Committee on Intelligence reported the bill (H Rept 109-411) April 6.

One of the declassified provisions of the bill was aimed at limiting the growth of the office of the DNI, created under the 2004 intelligence overhaul law (PL 108-458) to coordinate intelligence activities government-wide. Committee chair Peter Hoekstra, R-Mich., and ranking Democrat Jane Harman of California stressed their concern that the office would become too bureaucratic and impede rather than facilitate collaboration. Though Harman did not mention DNI John D. Negroponte by name, she made clear that she thought he was not yet exerting sufficient control over the intelligence agencies. *(Intelligence system overhaul, Congress and the Nation Vol. XI, p. 263)*

A key issue during both committee and floor consideration was the *New York Times'* disclosure in December 2005 that President George W. Bush had ordered a secret NSA program to conduct warrantless wiretaps of Americans in an effort to gain information about terrorism. The Intelligence Committee was particularly concerned about government leaks that led to that story. HR 5020 required the DNI to study the possibility of revoking the pension of anyone who leaked information.

Some committee Democrats argued that the bill should address the NSA program itself. But a Democratic attempt to withhold 20 percent of the NSA's funding until the Bush administration informed Congress about the cost of the top-secret eavesdropping activities was defeated on a 9–10 vote of the committee. Democrats hoped to continue the battle when the bill reached the floor, but the Rules Committee refused to allow consideration of an amendment seeking greater oversight of the NSA program. The House rejected 195–230 a motion by Adam B. Schiff, D-Calif., to send the bill back to committee with instructions to add language stating that the NSA program had to be approved by a special court set up under the Foreign Intelligence Surveillance Act (PL 95-511) or receive explicit authorization from Congress.

SENATE ACTION

The Senate Select Committee on Intelligence reported S 3237 (S Rept 109-259) on May 25 and the Senate Armed Services Committee reported it (S Rept 109-265) on June 21.

Intelligence Committee Democrats, joined by two Republicans, succeeded in attaching to the bill amendments that would have required public disclosure of the total amount of the nation's intelligence budget and more inclusive briefings of lawmakers by the administration. Also approved was an amendment requiring reports from the administration on secret CIA prisons and its compliance with provisions of the 2006 defense authorization law that governed treatment of detainees (HR 1815—PL 109-163). Another amendment would have increased penalties for disclosing the identities of covert intelligence agents. Special Counsel Patrick J. Fitzgerald was conducting a criminal probe into who disclosed the identity of CIA agent Valerie Plame, wife of former U.S. ambassador Joseph C. Wilson IV. *(2006 defense authorization, p. 290)*

But the bill went no further. Senate Majority Leader Bill Frist, R-Tenn., decided not to bring the bill to the floor in order to avoid giving Democrats a platform to debate the Iraq War, in advance of the midterm election. As in 2005, Senate Democrats were prepared to offer amendments to require Bush to give Congress closely held information about the conduct of the war and about the handling of detainees.

The top Democrat and Republican on the Senate Intelligence Committee—Chair John D. Rockefeller IV, D-W.Va., and Vice Chair Christopher S. Bond, R-Mo.—moved early in the next Congress to revive the fiscal 2007 authorization. Their panel reported S 372 (S Rept 110-2) on Jan. 24, 2007. The Armed Services Committee reported it (S Rept 110-5) on Feb. 8.

S 372 was nearly identical to the previous year's bill, S 3237, and its fate was much the same as well. The White House issued a statement in which it objected to the bill on twenty different grounds, including the requirement that the total amount of the intelligence budget be made public. *(Intelligence budget totals, box p. 322)*

Hopes for quick action were stymied in March when a senator put a hold on the bill. S 372 finally came to the floor in April, but Senate Republicans succeeded in blocking Democratic attempts to end debate on the bill. Senators voted 41–40 for a cloture motion on April 16 and 50–45 for a cloture motion the next day—well short of the sixty votes needed.

There was no further action, as the Intelligence committees turned their attention to writing a fiscal 2008 bill.

Sudan Sanctions

Congress in 2006 cleared legislation (HR 3127—PL 109-344) to impose sanctions on Sudanese officials and others considered responsible for war crimes and acts of genocide in the Darfur region of Sudan. Violence in that region had left perhaps as many as 400,000 dead and had driven some two million people from their homes since 2003.

Previous U.S. sanctions had focused on the government of Sudan, but the new legislation was aimed at individuals. It directed the president to freeze the assets of and deny visas for individuals thought to be involved in the Darfur atrocities, along with any family members and associates they had transferred assets to after mid-2002. The president could waive the restrictions if he notified the appropriate committees of Congress that it was in the national interests of the United States.

HR 3127 also expressed the sense of Congress that the president should immediately impose the same sanctions on Arab militia commanders who impeded the peace process or committed atrocities.

The bill authorized additional assistance to the African Union Mission in Sudan (AMIS), which had about 7,000 peacekeeping troops in Darfur, and it urged the president to work with NATO allies to provide the peacekeepers with logistical support, transport, and training. President George W. Bush already had called for doubling the number of international peacekeepers in Darfur while increasing NATO involvement in the region.

HR 3127 also encouraged the president to block Sudanese cargo ships and oil tankers from entering U.S. ports in a move to deny the government of Sudan access to oil revenues until it honored its peace commitments. The bill allowed some exceptions, such as shipments necessary to carry out elements of a peace agreement.

The bill continued existing sanctions against the government of Sudan.

BACKGROUND

Darfur, a drought-stricken region of western Sudan, erupted into violence in February 2003. Ironically, the catalyst was the start of U.S.-brokered peace negotiations to end a two-decade civil war between Sudan's Muslim leaders and the largely Christian or animist south, which had taken as many as two million lives. Fearful of being left out of power and resource-sharing arrangements, Darfur's rebels launched their own war, killing government soldiers, taking hostages, and looting munitions warehouses.

By the end of 2003, the Sudanese government had unleashed a full-scale counteroffensive. Government soldiers formed an alliance with nomadic Arab Muslim herders who had long competed for resources with Darfur's African Muslim farmers. Mounted on camel and horseback, and sometimes backed by government aircraft, Arab militias, known as Janjaweed, slaughtered African men, raped women, and burned villages. Until early 2004, the Sudanese government blocked most international aid to the region, as tens of thousands died and hundreds of thousands fled.

Officials in Khartoum began allowing humanitarian agencies to help the thousands gathered in makeshift camps, under an agreement signed in April 2004 that also authorized the African Union troops to monitor a truce.

But the killing continued. In July 2004, the U.N. Security Council passed the first of several resolutions against Sudan. The resolutions called on Sudan to disarm the militias, barred arms sales to Darfur, imposed a travel ban on officials accused of atrocities, and provided for the referral of human rights cases to the International Criminal Court in the Hague.

Congress passed twin resolutions in July 2004 declaring that genocide was occurring in Darfur. In September of that year, Secretary of State Colin L. Powell became the highest administration official to use the term, telling the Senate Foreign Relations Committee: "Genocide has occurred and may still be occurring in Darfur." Congress also stepped up humanitarian assistance to the region. *(Sudan relief assistance, Congress and the Nation Vol. XI, p. 298)*

When Powell testified, the death toll stood at about 50,000. By early 2006, estimates of those killed ranged from 300,000 to 400,000. Millions more had been displaced and were living in camps where they survived on donated food and were protected by ill-equipped peacekeepers.

LEGISLATIVE ACTION

HR 3127 was reported first by the House International Relations Committee on March 14, 2006 (H Rept 109-392, Part 1) and then by the Judiciary Committee on March 29 (Part 2). The full House passed it on April 5 by a 416–3 vote.

The Senate passed an amended version of HR 3127 by voice vote Sept. 21, after dropping a controversial House provision to allow states to prohibit the investment of state funds, including state pension funds, in Sudan. The provision had raised questions about whether it interfered with the president's authority to conduct foreign policy and whether federal sanction laws on Sudan preempted states from acting in this area, according to Sen. Richard G. Lugar, R-Ind., chair of the Senate Foreign Relations Committee.

The House cleared the compromise bill on Sept. 25 by voice vote and President Bush signed it into law Oct. 13.

Cuba Sanctions

Proposals to ease restrictions on U.S. relations with Cuba surfaced during debates on several bills in the 109th Congress, but none of the proposed amendments was enacted into law. Their failure indicated that the question of how the United States should deal with Communist leader Fidel Castro's Cuba remained one of the most sensitive issues in U.S. politics—an issue that pitted Democrats and moderate Republicans, especially those from farm and ranching states, against the anti-Castro Cuban-American community and their supporters in Congress and the Bush administration.

Although there had been some easing of the decades-long trade embargo against Cuba during the Clinton administration, President George W. Bush had vowed to veto any bill that would weaken it further. He backed up that threat by tightening rules governing both travel to the island and the limited U.S. exports that were allowed.

Of particular interest in the 109th Congress was a 2005 Treasury Department ruling that required advance payment for agricultural shipments to Cuba.

BACKGROUND

U.S. efforts to topple the Castro regime—ranging from the unilateral embargo the United States had imposed on Cuba in 1962 through steps taken in the 1990s to tighten the embargo—failed to achieve their goal. Even with the fall of communism in the Soviet Union and Eastern Europe and Cuba's subsequent loss of crucial financial support from that region, Castro remained in power.

Critics denounced U.S. policy toward Cuba as ineffective and called for a more open approach. President Bill Clinton in 1999 took several small steps to increase contacts. Congress in 2000 ended sanctions on food and medicine (PL 106-387) over the bitter opposition of conservative Republicans and Cuban-American legislators. The trade-off for members' support of the amendment easing the sanctions was the inclusion of language barring public or private U.S. financing of Cuban agricultural purchases and writing into law restrictions on travel to Cuba that previously had been implemented by executive order. *(PL 106-387, Congress and the Nation Vol. X, p. 224)*

Efforts in the 107th and 108th Congresses to further loosen restrictions on trade with and travel to Cuba proved unsuccessful. *(Details, Congress and the Nation Vol. XI, p. 260, p. 299)*

Opponents of any easing up on Cuba found a fierce supporter in President Bush. After taking office, Bush strengthened restrictions on travel to Cuba. He eliminated a loophole in the law that technically prohibited U.S. citizens from spending money in Cuba but did not bar traveling to the island itself. That put an end to trips financed by Cubans.

On Feb. 22, 2005, the Treasury Department's Office of Foreign Assets Control, in interpreting rules governing the limited exports to Cuba that were allowed, determined that U.S. exporters had to receive payment in advance of shipment of goods to Cuba. It had become common practice for goods to leave a U.S. port before cash payment was in hand. Critics of the Treasury Department action maintained that such a strict interpretation would hurt U.S farmers and ranchers but not Castro's regime. Since the 2001 law began permitting the limited sales, U.S. agricultural sales to Cuba had grown from roughly $7 million to more than $400 million by 2004.

TRANSPORTATION-TREASURY-HOUSING

Issues surrounding trade with and travel to Cuba were a perennial source of conflict during consideration of the annual Transportation-Treasury-Housing appropriations bill because it funded the Treasury Department office that investigated and punished violations of sanctions against Cuba.

During consideration of the fiscal 2006 funding bill (HR 3058—PL 109-115), lawmakers bowed to a White House veto threat by rejecting several Cuba-related amendments. During House action on June 30, 2005, the House defeated 208–211 a Jim Davis, D-Fla., amendment to repeal a 2004 Treasury Department regulation curtailing the number of visits Americans could pay to immediate family in Cuba. The regulation allowed such visits only once every three years for two weeks. Previously, Americans could visit Cuban relatives, including aunts, uncles, and cousins, once a year without a time limit. In other action, the House rejected a Barbara Lee, D-Calif., amendment to nullify a 2004 regulation that curtailed educational travel to Cuba by a 187–233 vote and a Charles B. Rangel, D-N.Y., amendment to end the economic embargo on Cuba by a vote of 169–250. Another Cuba-related amendment was ruled out of order. On the Senate side, Byron L. Dorgan, D-N.D., withdrew an amendment to lift the prohibition on travel to Cuba after John Ensign, R-Nev., offered a second-degree amendment that would have toughened abortion laws.

However, the underlying bills passed by both chambers contained language aimed at blocking enforcement of the February 2005 Treasury rule requiring advanced payment before agricultural goods could be shipped to Cuba. But just like the other amendments, that language had drawn a veto warning and it was dropped in conference. Supporters of the language were not happy. "The administration is simply flat, dead wrong on that one," said Christopher S. Bond, R-Mo., chair of the Senate Transportation-Housing-Education Appropriations Subcommittee. "The Treasury has imposed an impossible restriction on sales to Cuba."

Efforts to block the ruling on advanced payment resumed during consideration of the fiscal 2007 Treasury appropriations bill. The House adopted by voice vote a Jerry Moran, R-Kan., amendment barring enforcement of the ruling. "Unilateral sanctions by the United States are only harmful to our own agriculture sector, to our own farmers, at a time in which drought affects much of the country," Moran argued. But Ileana Ros-Lehtinen, R-Fla., responded: "These requirements were put in place to protect American producers, to protect American taxpayers, so that they will in fact get paid by the Cuban regime." The Senate Appropriations Committee approved a similar amendment offered by Byron L. Dorgan, D-N.D. But neither provision went further because the fiscal 2007 Transportation-Treasury-Housing bill (HR 5576) was one of nine spending bills left to be completed by the next Congress.

COMMERCE-JUSTICE-STATE

During floor action on the fiscal 2006 Commerce-Justice-State appropriations bill (HR 2862—PL 109-108), the House on June 15, 2005, rejected 210–216, an attempt by Jeff Flake, R-Ariz., to relax the trade embargo against Cuba to allow the shipment of gift parcels. Opponents said the goods would wind up in the hands of the Castro regime and the White House had warned that such a provision might trigger a veto.

INTERIOR-ENVIRONMENT

During floor action on the fiscal 2006 Interior-Environment appropriations bill (HR 2361—PL 109-54), the Senate on June 29, 2005, rejected, on a procedural vote, an attempt by Dorgan to offer an amendment that would have allowed travel to Cuba to visit immediate family members for funerals and other humanitarian purposes. The vote was 60–35; Dorgan needed a two-thirds majority (sixty-four in this case) to suspend the rule against legislating on an appropriations bill. Subsequently, a point of order was made and the amendment fell.

FOREIGN RELATIONS AUTHORIZATION

During floor action on the State Department and foreign aid authorization bill (S 600), the Senate on April 6, 2005, agreed 65–35 to table (kill) a Dorgan amendment prohibiting the use of funds for television broadcasts to Cuba. Dorgan argued that they were a waste of money because Cuba routinely jammed the broadcasts—known as TV Marti. TV Marti began its broadcasts in 1990.

Another Cuba-related amendment was pending when the bill was pulled from the floor. This one, proposed by Montana Democrat Max Baucus, would have reversed the Treasury ruling on advanced payment and also would have allowed direct payments between Cuban financial institutions and U.S. banks. Such direct transactions were prohibited under existing law, so Cuban payments to U.S. farmers were routed through third-party banks in other countries, often delaying payment. *(Foreign relations authorization, p. 287)*

AGRICULTURE

The Agriculture spending bill was one of the nine fiscal 2007 appropriations measures left unfinished when the 109th Congress adjourned. Both the House and Senate versions of the legislation (HR 5384) contained several provisions that would have led to disputes and made a conference difficult. Among them was a Senate amendment, offered by Dorgan during committee action, that would have allowed travel to Cuba for the purposes of selling agricultural products or medicine.

North Korea Policy

North Korea's nuclear ambitions prompted several actions by Congress in 2006, a year that saw that country test-fire long-range missiles and conduct its first nuclear weapons test.

The fiscal 2007 defense authorization bill (HR 5122—PL 109-364) included a provision requiring the administration to appoint a new coordinator for North Korea policy and to report to Congress on North Korea's nuclear and missile capabilities. But President George W. Bush found language in the provision intrusive on his foreign policy prerogatives and when he signed the defense bill he indicated he would treat it as optional.

Congress also cleared a bill (S 3728—PL 109-353) imposing sanctions on entities transferring to or from North Korea the technology for weapons of mass destruction and missile programs.

BACKGROUND

Cycles of agreements and aggressiveness had made the North Korean government one of the most difficult on Earth to deal with. President Bill Clinton nearly went to war with the country in 1994 after he learned that the North Koreans were preparing to reprocess nuclear reactor fuel rods into bomb-grade plutonium, expel international inspectors, and withdraw from the Nuclear Non-Proliferation Treaty. But Clinton averted a war by negotiating with the North Koreans a formal accord called the Agreed Framework, under which North Korea agreed to freeze its nuclear program in return for two light-water reactors for electricity and a large supply of fuel oil. The United States, Japan, and South Korea set up the Korean Peninsula Energy Development Organization (KEDO) to implement the agreement. Other countries later joined KEDO. *(North Korea nuclear capacity, Congress and the Nation Vol. IX, p. 221)*

But North Korea's relations with the outside world remained troubled. Particularly worrisome was North

Korea's development and export of ballistic missile technology. Negotiations failed to rein in North Korea's missile program, as was illustrated in 1998 when the regime fired a multi-stage rocket into the Pacific, thus demonstrating that it could strike Japan.

President Bush was never shy about showing his distaste for North Korean leader Kim Jong Il. He once told a reporter he "loathed" the dictator, whom he compared to Adolf Hitler. In his January 2002 State of the Union message he labeled North Korea a member of an "axis of evil" (along with Iraq and Iran) for "arming with missiles and weapons of mass destruction, while starving its citizens."

In October 2002 the Bush administration asserted that North Korea had admitted to a U.S. envoy that it had a secret nuclear weapons program, although North Korea subsequently denied it. The following month the United States, Japan, and South Korea—KEDO's executive board—halted oil shipments promised under the 1994 agreement. In response, North Korea extracted nuclear fuel rods and began reprocessing them into weapons-grade plutonium. The regime expelled international inspectors and announced its withdrawal from the Nuclear Non-Proliferation Treaty.

In April 2003 North Korea upped the ante, telling the United States in talks in Beijing that it had nuclear weapons. The Bush administration decided to pursue a diplomatic solution through six-party talks, which included the United States, North Korea, and North Korea's immediate neighbors—China, Russia, Japan, and South Korea. Those talks began in August 2003 but stalled in November 2005 after Washington imposed sanctions on North Korea's offshore bank accounts, claiming they were being used to spread counterfeit U.S. currency. Negotiations remained stalled for months.

The KEDO executive board decided at the end of May 2006 to terminate the already-suspended project to build the light-water reactors in North Korea.

On July 4 and 5, 2006, in what many observers saw as a sign of continuing defiance, the North Koreans tested seven ballistic missiles, including a long-range Taepodong-2 that failed. Then on Oct. 9 North Korea conducted its underground nuclear weapons test. The United States condemned the test and won approval of U.N. Security Council Resolution 1718, which imposed sanctions.

But the Bush administration also continued to pursue negotiations. The six-party negotiations resumed in December.

POLICY COORDINATOR

During floor action on its fiscal 2007 defense authorization bill, the Senate on June 22, 2006, adopted by voice vote an amendment offered by Minority Leader Harry Reid, D-Nev., requiring the president to appoint a new coordinator for North Korea policy and to report regularly to Congress. In a press release the next day Democrats accused the White House of allowing North Korea "to grow ever more dangerous" in the four years since it was branded as part of the axis of evil. They said the Senate's action was a vote of "no confidence" in the Bush administration's policy and hailed passage of their provision to fix the "failing" policy.

House conferees agreed to the provision with a clarifying amendment. The final version required the appointment within sixty days of a senior coordinator for North Korea policy, who was to conduct a comprehensive policy review and report back to the president and Congress within ninety days. Other duties of the coordinator were to consult with foreign governments, including the parties to the six-party talks, and provide policy direction for negotiations with North Korea on nuclear weapons, ballistic missiles, and other security matters. The president also was required to provide semiannual reports to Congress on North Korea's nuclear and missile programs.

When he signed HR 5122 into law on Oct. 17, 2006, President Bush added a number of conditions on how he would execute some of the bill's provisions. Regarding the North Korea provision, he took note of language requiring the executive branch to consult with foreign governments and to take certain steps in formulating and carrying out U.S. foreign policy and said the White House would construe the provision "in a manner consistent with the President's constitutional authorities to conduct the Nation's foreign affairs and to supervise the unitary executive branch." *(2007 defense authorization, p. 354)*

SANCTIONS LEGISLATION

In the wake of North Korea's tests of medium- and long-range missiles, the Senate on July 25, 2006, passed by voice vote S 3728, a bipartisan bill to extend the provisions of the Iran and Syria Nonproliferation Act (S 1713—PL 109-112) to North Korea. The House cleared the bill by voice vote Sept. 30 and the president signed it into law Oct. 13.

As enacted, S 3728:

- Authorized the president to apply sanctions to persons and entities, including foreign governments, that transferred weapons of mass destruction and missile technology to or from North Korea.
- Renamed the law the Iran, North Korea, and Syria Nonproliferation Act. *(Syria sanctions, p. 301)*
- Urged all governments to comply promptly with U.N. Security Council Resolution 1695, adopted on July 15, 2006, requiring all member states to prevent both the transfer of missiles or missile-related materials or technology to or from North Korea and the transfer of financial resources related to such activities.

Military Sales to China

The House in 2005 rejected legislation (HR 3100) aimed at monitoring and sanctioning European governments or companies that sold military hardware or technology to China. The bill's defeat came after an intense barrage of last-minute lobbying by defense firms and other business groups that feared U.S. companies might be harmed by the measure.

Sponsors had hoped HR 3100 would discourage the European Union (EU) from lifting a sixteen-year-old ban on weapons sales to China. Both the United States and European nations had imposed an embargo on military trade with China in June 1989, following China's bloody crackdown on pro-democracy demonstrators in Beijing's Tiananmen Square. By 2005, however, Europeans were arguing that lifting the embargo would engage Beijing and make China more flexible in its international dealings. EU officials also said that such a move would not dramatically affect China's arms purchases because the embargo was toothless to begin with.

The Bush administration strongly opposed ending the ban, and a bipartisan group of supporters in Congress seemed to agree. HR 3100 would have required annual reports on European companies making arms-related sales to China and on European countries that condoned such sales. Companies that violated the embargo would have been subjected to sanctions, including revocation of export licenses, although the president could have waived those sanctions.

House leaders expected action on HR 3100 to be routine. After all, the House on Feb. 2, 2005, adopted 411–3 a resolution (H Res 57) urging the European Union to maintain the arms embargo. On May 25 the House passed a defense authorization bill (HR 1815) that included a provision that would have forced western arms suppliers to choose between doing business with China or with the United States. On June 30, just two weeks before HR 3100 came to the floor, the House voted overwhelmingly to express its opposition to allowing a government-controlled Chinese energy company to buy U.S. oil company Unocal. *(2006 defense authorization, p. 336; Unocal controversy, p. 241)*

HR 3100 had evoked little debate in the House International Relations Committee, which reported it (H Rept 109-165) on July 12. It was brought to the floor two days later under suspension of the rules, a procedure reserved for noncontroversial legislation that requires a two-thirds vote for passage.

What happened next, however, was far from routine or noncontroversial. The bill's sponsors watched their legislation killed in a frenetic vote-switching episode in which Republican and Democratic opponents went member-to-member trying to turn votes. At the end of the twenty-three-minute roll call—which was supposed to last only five minutes—the bill had been killed by a **key vote of 215–203 (R 118–106; D 96–97; I 1–0)** on July 14. This was far short of the two-thirds vote—in this case, 279 votes—needed for passage. *(2005 key votes, p. 915)*

House leaders had underestimated the intensity of the opposition from the defense industry and their supporters in Congress who feared that the bill could unintentionally punish defense contractors who might be part of the supply chain for European companies that sold aircraft and other hardware to China.

Less than a week later the House attached a toned-down version of HR 3100 to a foreign relations and State Department authorization bill (HR 2601). This amended version still would monitor European governments or companies that sold military hardware or technology to China, but it would punish U.S. companies only if they had known their products would ultimately be used for military purposes. HR 2601 passed the House but died in the Senate. *(Foreign relations authorization, p. 287)*

The related provision in the defense authorization bill was dropped during conference action.

Middle East Policy

The 109th Congress demonstrated its strong support for Israel in the wake of significant political and military developments in the Middle East.

The 2006 Palestinian parliamentary election victory of Hamas—branded by the United States and others as a terrorist group—triggered a series of reactions on Capitol Hill. Through policy resolutions, appropriations provisions, and legislative restrictions, Congress made clear its opposition to aiding Hamas, unless, among other things, it recognized Israel's right to exist.

Congress also voiced support for Israel in its war with Hezbollah in southern Lebanon later in 2006.

BACKGROUND

Early 2006 was a time of major upheaval on the political landscape of the Middle East.

On Jan. 4, 2006, Israeli Prime Minister Ariel Sharon was incapacitated by a massive stroke. As one of President George W. Bush's most influential tutors, Sharon had convinced Bush that the threat Israel faced was the same violent brand of Islamic extremism that Bush had targeted in his global war against terrorism. In recognition of their common cause, Bush pursued the most pro-Israel policies of any U.S. president.

For years Sharon had supported Jewish settlements in the West Bank and Gaza Strip, in what he thought was a drive to bolster the nation's security. But with prodding from Ehud Olmert—his finance minister and the designated acting prime minister—Sharon decided that if Israel retained control over the territories, the Palestinians there eventually would outnumber Israelis, threatening both the Jewish and democratic nature of Israel. Sharon also believed that the weak Palestinian leadership could not deliver on a negotiated peace. So he embarked on a third way: withdrawing Israeli troops and settlers unilaterally from the territories and drawing new lines that would favor Israel's security. Most important, he persuaded Bush to go along with his plan, while voicing support for the Middle East "Road Map." The Road Map was a plan put forward by representatives of the United States, United Nations, European Union (EU), and Russia—a group collectively known as the Middle East Quartet—that called for a negotiated settlement and a two-state solution to the Israeli-Palestinian conflict.

The uncertainty after Sharon's stroke threatened to light a fuse in the increasingly lawless West Bank and Gaza Strip, where the moderate and secular Palestinian president Mahmoud Abbas had proved incapable of imposing order. Among those rising to challenge Abbas's leadership was Hamas (an Arabic acronym for "Islamic Resistance Movement"), an extremist group that had called for Israel's destruction and replacement by an Islamic state in all of Palestine. Capitalizing on the corruption and inefficiency of Abbas's Fatah movement, Hamas won a majority of the seats in parliamentary elections on Jan. 25, 2006.

Hamas's stunning victory presented the United States and the West with a major dilemma. The group had claimed credit for numerous suicide bombings inside Israel and had refused to abide by previous agreements between Israel and the Palestinian Authority that included mutual recognition and commitment to a two-state solution. The United States and the EU had branded Hamas a terrorist organization.

But at the time of their election victory, Hamas had been upholding its end of a truce with Israel, refraining from further attacks. It had run on a platform that did not promise more violence but focused instead on eliminating the corruption within the Fatah-led government and rebuilding the Palestinian Authority's economic and social institutions. As far as Israel and the West were concerned, Hamas said it would operate on the basis of reciprocity: any softening of its positions would depend on what the other side was offering.

A statement on Jan. 30 by the Middle East Quartet congratulated the Palestinians on their "free, fair, and secure" electoral process. It went on to state their view that all members of a future Palestinian Government must be committed to the three principles of "nonviolence, recognition of Israel, and acceptance of previous agreements and obligations, including the Road Map."

Many experts, including some Israelis, said it was worth engaging the new Hamas government in an effort to moderate its views. But the Bush administration opted for a policy of isolating Hamas and demanded that the Quartet's three principles be met before Hamas could be considered a partner in the peace process. Hamas indicated that it was willing to negotiate such demands, but with the United States offering nothing in return—such as more pressure on Israel to halt illegal settlement activity—the group turned down Bush's take-it-or-leave-it offer.

On April 7, Secretary of State Condoleezza Rice announced that the United States was suspending its $411 million in aid to the Palestinian Authority. Three days later, the EU followed suit, suspending its $600 million in assistance. Together the $1 billion made up the authority's annual budget. Rice said the administration would provide $245 million in humanitarian aid, to be distributed through the United Nations and nongovernmental groups.

RESTRICTIONS ON AID

In the wake of the Hamas election, the Senate and House adopted a resolution (S Con Res 79) expressing the sense of Congress that no U.S. aid should be provided to the Palestinian Authority if the party that held a majority of its parliamentary seats called for the destruction of Israel. The Senate adopted the resolution by voice vote Feb. 1, 2006, and the House approved it 418–1 on Feb. 15.

Lawmakers backed up their views with tighter restrictions on U.S. assistance. In the regular fiscal 2006 foreign operations appropriations bill (HR 3057—PL 109-102), which was enacted in November 2005, Congress had provided $150 million for aid to the West Bank and Gaza but had barred direct assistance to the Palestinian Authority unless the president found the aid to be in the national security interests of the United States.

Members attached further restrictions on aid as part of a fiscal 2006 supplemental appropriations bill (HR 4939—PL109-234) enacted in June 2006. The supplemental made aid contingent on a determination by the secretary of state that the Palestinian Authority had met the Quartet's three principles of renouncing violence, recognizing Israel, and accepting previous agreements. The bill would have allowed some assistance to the office of the president of the Palestinian Authority as long as it was not controlled by Hamas, and if it was determined to be in the national security interest of the United States and Congress was consulted fifteen days prior to the exercising of the waiver authority. The bill also required the secretary of state to consult with Congress before obligating any Economic Support Fund aid for the West Bank and Gaza. In signing HR 4939, Bush took issue with the prior consultation requirements and said he would construe them as requiring only notification. *(2006 aid appropriations, p. 282)*

In December 2006 Congress cleared another measure (S 2370—PL 109-446) with similar restrictions on U.S. aid to the Palestinians. It was also aimed at promoting Palestinian democracy. As in the 2006 supplemental appropriations bill, S 2370 barred aid to the Hamas-controlled Palestinian government unless it accepted the Quartet's three principles. It exempted humanitarian aid and democratization funds for the Palestinian people and certain aid to the non-Hamas president of the Palestinian Authority. The bill's restrictions could be waived if it was determined to be in the United States' national security interest and if the proposed recipient was not a member of or controlled by Hamas. The bill provided $20 million for a fund promoting Palestinian democracy and Israeli-Palestinian peace.

S 2370 also included restrictions on the issuing of visas to representatives of the Hamas-controlled government, as well as on their travel or establishment of offices in the United States. It prohibited State Department funds from being used to negotiate with Hamas or other terrorist organizations unless the three principles were met and the group dismantled its terrorist infrastructure.

The House had passed a more stringent version (HR 4681—H Rept 109-462, Parts I and II) by a vote of 361–37 on May 23. The Senate passed S 2370 by voice vote June 23. The House agreed to the Senate bill, clearing it by voice vote Dec. 7. The president signed S 2370 on Dec. 21, despite finding a number of the provisions intrusive on his executive prerogatives. In his signing statement, Bush indicated that he would construe them as advisory or in a manner consistent with his foreign policy powers.

ISRAELI-HEZBOLLAH CONFLICT

In mid-2006 the White House and Congress lined up squarely with Israel in its month-long military campaign against Hezbollah, the radical Shiite Muslim militia based in Lebanon.

Dismissing the diplomacy that previous administrations used to tamp down repeated flare-ups along the Israel-Lebanon border, Bush opted to give Olmert, who had succeeded Sharon as prime minister, the green light to crush Hezbollah. In the process he abandoned any pretense of even-handedness in the Arab-Israeli conflict, essentially turning the conflict in Lebanon into a proxy confrontation between Israel and the United States, on one side, and Hezbollah's patrons, Syria and Iran, on the other.

Both the Senate and House approved resolutions condemning Hamas and Hezbollah attacks against Israel and expressing support for Israel's right to defend itself. The Senate adopted S Res 534 by voice vote July 18, 2006, and the House adopted H Res 921 by a vote of 410–8 on July 20.

But when a UN-brokered ceasefire went into effect after thirty-four days of warfare, Israel appeared to be in a weakened position, having been unable to eliminate the threat that Hezbollah posed to Israel's northern border.

Iran Sanctions

Congress in 2006 cleared legislation (HR 6198—PL 109-293) to strengthen existing sanctions against Iran as a way of punishing that country for pursuing a nuclear weapons program. The bill was also aimed at promoting democracy in Iran.

The original sanctions law, passed in 1996, also had applied to Libya. But HR 6198 eliminated those sanctions from the law because Libya had renounced terrorism and weapons of mass destruction. The United States resumed full diplomatic relations with Libya in May 2006 and in June rescinded Libya's designation as a state sponsor of terrorism.

Lawmakers also approved several policy statements on Iran and attached Iran-related provisions to other pieces of legislation in the 109th Congress.

BACKGROUND

Prior to passage of the 1996 Iran-Libya sanctions law (PL 104-172), the United States already had in place strict unilateral sanctions barring all U.S. companies from trading with those two countries. The United States saw both as rogue regimes that posed a threat to U.S. interests—Iran because of its efforts to develop nuclear and other weapons of mass destruction and Libya because of its support for terrorist attacks against U.S. citizens.

But U.S. efforts to isolate Iran and Libya were undercut as other industrialized nations continued to trade with them. When Iran decided in the mid-1990s to open its petroleum and gas markets to foreign investment, Congress moved to put teeth into the U.S.-orchestrated embargo and penalize foreign firms that assisted the oil industries in both Iran and Libya.

PL 104-172 required the president to impose at least two out of a list of six possible sanctions on foreign firms that invested more than $20 million a year in Iran's energy sector or $40 million a year in Libya's. Sanctioned firms could be denied access to Export-Import Bank credits, U.S. military exports, U.S. bank loans, or U.S. government contracts. The president could waive the sanctions if he determined that doing so was in the national interest. *(PL 104-172, Congress and the Nation Vol. IX, p. 239)*

Congress in 2001 approved a five-year extension of the sanctions law (PL 107-24). The new law lowered the threshold for investment in Libya to $20 million. It also closed a loophole that had allowed companies with oil contracts in Libya or Iran before the 1996 law had gone into effect to amend those contracts without being subject to sanctions. *(PL 107-24, Congress and the Nation Vol. XI, p. 254)*

Britain, France, and Germany—acting on behalf of the European Union—launched a diplomatic push in 2003 to persuade Iran to abandon its nuclear programs. In October 2003, Iran promised that it would halt enriching uranium. Less than a year later international inspectors determined that Tehran had broken that pledge. Under a second agreement with the European Union in November 2004, Tehran again promised to halt its uranium enrichment while insisting on maintaining its nuclear energy programs, which it said were strictly for peaceful purposes.

With no final pledge by Iran to abandon its nuclear programs altogether, the agreement failed to allay international suspicions, particularly those of the United States and Israel. European diplomats and analysts said President George W. Bush's refusal to take part in talks with Iran undermined negotiations and reduced their chances for success. For example, they said, the Europeans wanted to promise Iran access to some less sensitive nuclear energy technologies, such as light-water reactors, or pledge foreign investments in its oil and gas industry in exchange for abandoning its nuclear programs. But any European firms that provided such assistance risked violating the Iran sanctions law. Though the law had never been enforced, it was said to have had a chilling effect on the negotiations.

The Europeans' concerns were well founded. A State Department official said Iran "would have to clean up its act on support for terrorism and nuclear ambitions before we would consider a deal that gave them more economic resources to spread bloodshed and mayhem." The Bush administration said its arm's-length approach to the negotiations provided the Europeans with the threat they needed to persuade Iran to abandon its nuclear research.

The 2005 election of hardliner Mahmoud Ahmadinejad as Iran's president further inflamed the situation. After he took office in August 2005, Iran's nuclear program accelerated as Iran began a program of uranium "conversion," which is the step before enrichment. Ahmadinejad gave the program a menacing cast in October of that year when he called for Israel to be "wiped off the map."

Iran's resumption of uranium enrichment activities in January 2006 prompted the International Atomic Energy Agency to report Iran to the United Nations Security Council. When subsequent negotiations failed to lead to a pledge from Iran to halt uranium enrichment, the U.N. Security Council on Dec. 23, 2006, adopted Resolution 1737 prohibiting the sale or transfer of equipment, goods, and technology that could contribute to Iran's "enrichment-related, reprocessing or heavy water-related activities, or to the development of nuclear weapon delivery systems." It also required member states to freeze the assets of certain entities and persons said to be involved in those programs.

SANCTIONS BILL

The House on April 26, 2006, approved by a vote of 397–21 a bill (HR 282) to stiffen sanctions on foreign companies that invested in Iran's petroleum industry. The House International Relations Committee had reported HR 282 on April 25 (H Rept 109-417).

In its report on HR 282, the House panel had some strong words for the White House. The committee stated its belief that existing laws and prior executive actions had proven inadequate in ending Iran's efforts to produce weapons of mass destruction or its threats to American national interests. The committee went on to say it was "deeply dismayed that the current Administration, like the prior Administration, has not acted to sanction a single enterprise for investing in Iran, but has delayed its decisions on 'alleged' investments well past the point of failing the 'laugh test.'"

But the White House found HR 282 too restrictive. A State Department official said that the Bush administration opposed the bill because it could hinder U.S. efforts to build international support for joint action against Iran. As work continued on a revised bill, Congress on July 31 cleared a short-term extension of the existing sanctions law that kept it in force until Sept. 29, 2006 (HR 5877—PL 109-267).

The House approved a modified sanctions bill (HR 6198) by voice vote on Sept. 28 and the Senate approved it by voice vote Sept. 30. President Bush signed it into law later that day.

Major provisions of HR 6198:

- Codified existing U.S. sanctions against Iran that had been imposed by executive order.
- Authorized the president to waive sanctions under the 1996 Iran and Libya Sanctions Act for up to six months, if the president certified to the appropriate congressional committees that the waiver was "vital to the national security interests." This raised the threshold for waivers from the level of "important to the national interest" in the original law. A waiver could be renewed for subsequent periods of not more than six months each.
- Required the president to impose sanctions on anyone found to have helped Iran acquire or develop chemical, biological, or nuclear weapons or related technologies, or destabilizing numbers and types of advanced conventional weapons.
- Added the requirement that Iran must be determined to pose no significant threat to United States national security, interests, or allies before sanctions could be terminated.
- Dropped references to Libya and renamed the law the Iran Sanctions Act of 1996. The law was extended until Dec. 31, 2011.
- Authorized assistance to individuals and entities working to promote democracy for Iran, and set eligibility conditions for such assistance.
- Stated the sense of Congress that the United States should not enter into a nuclear cooperation agreement with any country that was assisting the nuclear program of Iran or was transferring advanced conventional weapons or missiles to Iran unless the president determined that the country had suspended such assistance or that Iran had halted its enrichment activities.
- Included a provision aimed at preventing money laundering by those involved in the proliferation of weapons of mass destruction or missiles.

OTHER LEGISLATION

Both the Senate and House adopted resolutions strongly condemning anti-Israel sentiments expressed by Ahmadinejad on Oct. 26, 2005. In addition to saying that Israel should be "wiped off the map," the Iranian president described Israel as "a disgraceful blot [on] the face of the Islamic world" and declared that anyone who recognized Israel "will burn in the fire of the Islamic nation's fury." The Senate adopted S Res 292 by voice vote Oct. 27 and the House adopted H Res 523 by a vote of 383–0 on Oct. 28.

In the wake of Iran's resumption of enrichment activities in January 2006, both chambers approved resolutions condemning Iran's move and calling on the U.N. Security Council to take action. The Senate approved S Con Res 78 by voice vote on Jan. 27 and the House approved H Con Res 341 by a vote of 404–4 on Feb. 16.

Iran's nuclear ambitions surfaced during consideration in 2006 of a nuclear cooperation agreement between the United States and India. The White House strongly opposed congressional attempts to require the president to determine that India was cooperating with efforts to halt Iran's nuclear program as a precondition. The administration insisted that India was cooperating and that the amendment would disrupt the deal. It was dropped from the final bill. *(U.S.-India nuclear agreement, pp. 277, 311)*

Congress in 2005 had to amend another sanctions law (PL 106-178) in order to pay Russia for ferrying U.S. astronauts to and from the International Space Station. That law, enacted in 2000, had prohibited NASA from paying Russia for shuttling U.S. astronauts unless the White House certified that Moscow was cooperating in preventing Iran from acquiring weapons of mass destruction and the missile systems to deliver such weapons.

Because President Bush had not made that certification, an exemption to the law was needed for the United States to avoid losing its access to the space station. Under international agreements, a spacecraft had to remain docked at the space station to provide astronauts with a means of escape in the event of an emergency. Russia had been keeping one of its spacecraft docked at the space station, but after spring 2006 Russia would no longer have to provide emergency transportation for U.S. astronauts. That would mean that the U.S. space shuttle would have to be docked there whenever U.S. astronauts were at the space station in case of an emergency evacuation. Moreover, with the United States scheduled to retire its space shuttle in 2010 and not expected to have a replacement ready until at least 2012, the United States would need Russia to provide transportation to and from the space station during the interim period. NASA and the White House were anxious for lawmakers to approve an exemption that would allow the United States to pay Russia for its services. Congress approved an exemption until 2012 in a bill that also expanded the reach of PL 106-178 to include dealings with Syria (S 1713—PL 109-112). *(Syria sanctions, this page; PL 106-178, Congress and the Nation Vol. X, p. 221)*

Syria Sanctions

Congress in 2005 approved sanctions aimed at preventing Syria from exporting or importing technology to develop weapons of mass destruction (S 1713—PL 109-112). The provision amended a 2000 statute (PL 106-178) that had applied similar sanctions to those assisting Iran's nuclear ambitions, most especially Russia.

The Syria-related language had not been in the original version of S 1713. As passed by the Senate, the bill had simply amended PL 106-178—the Iran Nonproliferation Act—in order to allow the United States to pay Russia to shuttle American astronauts to and from the International Space Station. *(Iran sanctions, pp. 299, 326; Russia sanctions, Congress and the Nation Vol. X, p. 221)*

But, spurred by the assassination of Lebanon's ex-prime minister Rafik Hariri, whose death was tied to Syrian and Lebanese officials, the House added the Syria sanctions to the underlying bill. The Senate agreed to the change.

The provisions of the Iran and Syria Nonproliferation Act were extended to North Korea in 2006. *(North Korea policy, p. 295)*

BACKGROUND

After a bomb killed Hariri in Beirut in Feb. 14, 2005, the Bush administration was relentless in its pressure on Syria to end its twenty-nine-year-long military presence in Lebanon. The assassination of Hariri, an outspoken critic of the Syrian occupation who had resigned as prime minister in October 2004, not only raised suspicions of a Damascus-ordered hit to silence him but also provided President George W. Bush with a recognizable event to point to in his campaign to spread democracy in the Middle East. Together with France, the administration constantly called attention to a 2004 U.N. Security Council resolution that had called for the withdrawal of all foreign forces from Lebanon.

That pressure, coupled with demonstrations in Beirut against the Syrian presence, forced President Bashar al-Assad to withdraw his troops from Lebanon in April 2005. In May of that year, Lebanon held its first parliamentary elections since 1976 in which Syrian troops were not overseeing the vote.

Bush also pressured Assad to halt the flow of Islamic insurgents from Syria into Iraq, but the infiltration continued. Despite calls on Assad to liberalize his country both politically and economically, Syria remained an authoritarian state with a creaking centralized economy.

Lawmakers and others called for a tougher policy toward Syria, but the administration, still struggling with the consequences of regime change in Iraq, adhered to existing policy—strong public demands on Assad's regime and economic sanctions enacted in 2003. That law (PL 108-175) had required the president to impose at least two sanctions on Syria unless the president waived them in the interest of national security. The sanctions included a ban on U.S. exports to Syria, with the exception of food and medicine, and on U.S. investment in Syria. *(Syria sanctions, Congress and the Nation Vol. XI, p. 295)*

Hariri's assassination and an October 2005 United Nations report pointing to Lebanese and Syrian involvement in his death provided the impetus to strengthen sanctions against Syria.

LEGISLATIVE ACTION, PROVISIONS

The Senate on Sept. 21, 2005, passed by voice vote S 1713 to allow payments to Russia for travel to and from the International Space Station. The House added Syria sanctions to the bill and passed it by voice vote on Oct. 26. The Senate agreed to the House amendment and cleared S 1713 by voice vote on Nov. 8. The president signed the bill into law on Nov. 22.

The sanctions-related provisions:

- Extended the provisions of the Iran Nonproliferation Act of 2000 to cover Syria as well as Iran and renamed the law the Iran and Syria Nonproliferation Act.
- Applied the law's provisions to transfers of weapons technology both *to* and *from* Iran and Syria. (The original law applied only to transfers *to* Iran.)
- Broadened the definition of people and entities that could be sanctioned to include foreign governments.

CONGRESSIONAL VISITS

In December 2006 a bipartisan commission, known as the Iraq Study Group, issued sweeping recommendations for resolving the war in Iraq. Among the group's proposals was a call for new diplomatic initiatives, including working with Iran and Syria. *(Iraq Study Group, box p. 274)*

In the wake of that report, several senators, ignoring criticism from the White House, made diplomatic visits to Syria. When Sen. Bill Nelson, D-Fl., met with Syrian president Assad in Damascus a week after the study group's report was issued, White House press secretary Tony Snow called the visit "inappropriate" and a "PR victory" for the Syrians. Snow's reaction failed to deter three other senators—Christopher Dodd, D-Conn., John Kerry, D-Mass., and Arlen Specter, R-Pa.—from meeting with Assad over the next few weeks.

A visit to Syria by House Speaker Nancy Pelosi, D-Calif., in April 2007 triggered even higher-level criticism, with both President Bush and Vice President Dick Cheney weighing in on the trip.

United Nations Dues

The House in 2005 passed a bill (HR 2745) mandating that hundreds of millions of dollars in U.S. dues to the United Nations be withheld unless the international organization made sweeping changes in how it conducted business. There was no further action on the legislation in the 109th Congress.

The bill came amid continued investigations into allegations that contractors received kickbacks as part of the U.N. Oil-for-Food program that had permitted an embargoed Iraq to sell oil in exchange for food and medical supplies. HR 2745 would have withheld up to 50 percent of U.S. dues unless the secretary of state certified that the United Nations had made specific changes in its finances, ethics systems, peacekeeping missions, and investigative functions. It also would have directed the United States to vote against peacekeeping missions if a series of changes were not made.

The measure was somewhat of a swan song for International Relations chair Henry J. Hyde, R-Ill., who planned to retire at the end of the 109th Congress and wanted his legacy to include a tough legislative revamp of how the United States dealt with the United Nations, an organization he had frequently criticized.

Hyde's committee reported the bill (H Rept 109-120) on June 10, 2005, and the full House passed it June 17 by a vote of 221–184. A substitute amendment offered by Tom Lantos, D-Calif., which would have given the secretary of state the authority to withhold dues instead of mandating such action, was rejected 190–216.

The bill drew a sharp rebuke from the White House, which in a rare public disagreement with a Republican committee chair, issued a statement saying the measure would "distract from and undermine our efforts" to get the United Nations to overhaul itself. After the Sept. 11, 2001, terrorist attacks on the United States, the Bush administration had worked hard to repair U.S. relations with the United Nations and complete the repayment of dues the United States owed the international organization in order to win diplomatic support for the war on terrorism. *(U.N. debt repayment, Congress and the Nation Vol. XI, p. 253)*

On July 19, 2005, the House voted 226–195 to add an amended version of Hyde's proposal to the fiscal 2006–2007 foreign relations authorization bill (HR 2601). *(Foreign relations authorization, p. 287)*

2007–2008

Against a backdrop of mounting violence and casualties in Iraq, American voters had turned out the Republican majority and put the Democrats in charge of the 110th Congress. Hopes were high that a change in leadership would translate into a change in U.S. policy. There was, indeed, a change in policy, but it was not what war opponents had in mind. Just days into the new Congress President George W. Bush announced his decision to send additional troops to Iraq. This left Democrats not only trying to legislate a withdrawal from Iraq but also contending with the more immediate goal of blocking the so-called troop surge. But without the sixty votes in the Senate needed to shut down filibusters, that was beyond the new leadership's reach. The 110th Congress did, however, agree on a list of benchmarks to measure the Iraqi government's progress and more reporting requirements.

Congress gave President Bush an important foreign policy victory when it approved the civilian nuclear cooperation agreement between the United States and India. Still, lawmakers did attach a few strings, requiring specific safeguards and ongoing congressional oversight.

Another of the president's foreign policy priorities—a five-year extension of the president's global HIV/AIDS program—was approved as well. But Congress put its own stamp on the program when it authorized $18 billion more than had been requested. In return for inclusion of the higher amount, Democrats agreed to drop language that conservatives saw as an opening to funding abortions overseas.

The abortion issue played a significant role during foreign aid debates in the 110th Congress, as it had so many times in the past. In the end nothing changed and the so-called Mexico City policy barring aid to family planning groups that provided or promoted abortion, even if it used its own money, remained intact during the Bush administration. The policy, however, was repealed in the early days of Barack Obama's presidency in 2009.

Congress made deep cuts in Bush's signature foreign aid program—the Millennium Challenge Account—over the objections of the White House and the agency in charge of the program. Lawmakers pointed to the program's large unspent reserves in defense of the reduced funding.

As in the previous Congress, no intelligence authorization measure was enacted in either session of the 110th Congress. One bill fell to a presidential veto over, among other things, Congress's attempt to rein in the intelligence community's methods of interrogating detainees in Bush's war on terror. A bill for the next fiscal year never made it to the Senate floor. The Senate Intelligence Committee wrapped up its probe of pre–Iraq War intelligence, albeit amid the partisan charges and countercharges that had surrounded much of its inquiry.

Congress dealt with a variety of sanctions issues. Members stepped up pressure on Sudan to end the conflict in Darfur by approving a measure that allowed state and local governments to divest themselves of assets in companies doing business in several sectors of the Sudanese economy, including the oil sector. Congress targeted Iran, along with such states as Sudan, Cuba, and North Korea, with legislation to stiffen penalties on companies doing business with countries deemed a threat to U.S. national security. But members did agree to the administration's request for authority to waive certain sanctions on North Korea to facilitate the dismantling of a nuclear reactor and disposal of radioactive material.

President Bush's veto threats blocked attempts in the 110th Congress to weaken restrictions on trade with and travel to Cuba. But an omnibus appropriations bill—put off until 2009 when there would be a new president in the White House—did make several key changes in Cuba policy.

An administration plan to sell advanced weapons to Saudi Arabia alarmed pro-Israel members. Their attempt to block the sale failed, but Congress did increase aid to Israel and required the administration to assess the effect of proposed arms sales on Israel.

Iraq War Policy

Despite repeated attempts by Democrats on Capitol Hill, the 110th Congress did not set troop withdrawal timetables or impose any other conditions on President George W. Bush's prosecution of the Iraq War.

Voters gave Democrats majorities in both chambers of the 110th Congress in large part on the strength of candidates' pledge to end U.S. military involvement in Iraq. However, the Democrats did not win sixty seats in the Senate and therefore lacked the minimum number of votes needed for overcoming filibusters. With Republicans for the most part reluctant to oppose the White House on the war, they could not count on GOP support to reach the requisite number of votes.

As a result, Bush not only prevailed on his war policy but also proceeded in 2007 to send additional troops to Iraq to quell the mounting violence. The announcement of the so-called troop surge came just days after the 110th Congress convened.

Democratic hopes of stopping the surge went nowhere, as did other legislative efforts to influence Iraq policy. Congress did succeed, however, in requiring reports on Iraq's success in meeting a series of benchmarks.

In the end, it would be President Bush, in conjunction with the Iraqi government, who would set a timetable for U.S. withdrawal in 2011.

WHITE HOUSE, GAO REPORT ON IRAQ'S PROGRESS ON BENCHMARKS

The fiscal 2007 supplemental appropriations law (HR 2206—PL 110-28) required President George W. Bush to report to Congress his administration's assessment of the Iraqi government's progress toward meeting eighteen legislative, security, and economic benchmarks listed in the law. The benchmarks reflected commitments made by the Iraqi government. The first report was due by July 15, 2007, and a second report by Sept. 15, 2007. The law also required the U.S. Government Accountability Office (GAO), a congressional support agency, to report its assessment by Sept. 1, 2007. GAO noted in its report that the State and Defense Departments disagreed with some of its assessments.

Following are the benchmarks with the White House and GAO assessments:

1. Forming a Constitutional Review Committee and then completing the constitutional review.

July 12, 2007 White House report:	Satisfactory
Sept. 14, 2007 White House report:	Satisfactory
Sept. 4, 2007 GAO report:	Not met

2. Enacting and implementing legislation on de-Baathification.

July 12, 2007 White House report:	Unsatisfactory
Sept. 14, 2007 White House report:	Satisfactory
Sept. 4, 2007 GAO report:	Not met

3. Enacting and implementing legislation to ensure the equitable distribution of hydrocarbon resources of the people of Iraq without regard to the sect or ethnicity of recipients, and enacting and implementing legislation to ensure that the energy resources of Iraq benefit Sunni Arabs, Shia Arabs, Kurds, and other Iraqi citizens in an equitable manner.

July 12, 2007 White House report:	Unsatisfactory
Sept. 14, 2007 White House report:	Unsatisfactory
Sept. 4, 2007 GAO report:	Not met

4. Enacting and implementing legislation on procedures to form semi-autonomous regions.

July 12, 2007 White House report:	Satisfactory
Sept. 14, 2007 White House report:	Satisfactory
Sept. 4, 2007 GAO report:	Partially met

5. Enacting and implementing legislation establishing (a) an Independent High Electoral Commission; (b) provincial elections law; (c) provincial council authorities; (d) a date for provincial elections.

July 12, 2007 White House report:	Satisfactory on (a); Unsatisfactory on rest
Sept. 14, 2007 White House report:	Satisfactory on (a) and (c)
Sept. 4, 2007 GAO report:	(a) Met; rest Not met

6. Enacting and implementing legislation addressing amnesty.

July 12, 2007 White House report:	No rating
Sept. 14, 2007 White House report:	No rating
Sept. 4, 2007 GAO report:	Not met

7. Enacting and implementing legislation establishing a strong militia disarmament program to ensure that such security forces are accountable only to the central government and loyal to the Constitution of Iraq.

July 12, 2007 White House report:	No rating
Sept. 14, 2007 White House report:	No rating
Sept. 4, 2007 GAO report:	Not met

8. Establishing supporting political, media, economic, and services committees in support of the Baghdad Security Plan [the U.S. "surge" in troops].

July 12, 2007 White House report:	Satisfactory
Sept. 14, 2007 White House report:	Satisfactory
Sept. 4, 2007 GAO report:	Met

9. Providing three trained and ready Iraqi brigades to support Baghdad operations.

July 12, 2007 White House report:	Satisfactory
Sept. 14, 2007 White House report:	Satisfactory
Sept. 4, 2007 GAO report:	Partially met

10. Providing Iraqi commanders with all authorities to execute this plan and to make tactical and operational decisions, in consultation with U.S. commanders, without political intervention, to include the authority to pursue all extremists, including Sunni insurgents and Shiite militias.

July 12, 2007 White House report:	Unsatisfactory
Sept. 14, 2007 White House report:	Satisfactory on pursuit of extremists; Unsatisfactory on political interference
Sept. 4, 2007 GAO report:	Not met

11. Ensuring that the Iraqi Security Forces are providing even-handed enforcement of the law.

July 12, 2007 White House report:	Unsatisfactory
Sept. 14, 2007 White House report:	Satisfactory on military; Unsatisfactory on police
Sept. 4, 2007 GAO report:	Not met

12. Ensuring that, according to President Bush, Prime Minister Nouri al-Maliki said "the Baghdad Security Plan will not provide a safe haven for any outlaws, regardless of [their] sectarian or political affiliation."

July 12, 2007 White House report:	Satisfactory
Sept. 14, 2007 White House report:	Satisfactory
Sept. 4, 2007 GAO report:	Partially met

13. (a) Reducing the level of sectarian violence in Iraq and (b) eliminating militia control of local security.

July 12, 2007 White House report:	Satisfactory on (a); Unsatisfactory on (b)
Sept. 14, 2007 White House report:	Same as in July
Sept. 4, 2007 GAO report:	Not met

14. Establishing all of the planned joint security stations in neighborhoods across Baghdad.

July 12, 2007 White House report:	Satisfactory
Sept. 14, 2007 White House report:	Satisfactory
Sept. 4, 2007 GAO report:	Met

15. Increasing the number of Iraqi Security Forces units capable of operating independently.

July 12, 2007 White House report:	Unsatisfactory
Sept. 14, 2007 White House report:	Unsatisfactory
Sept. 4, 2007 GAO report:	Not met

16. Ensuring that the rights of minority political parties in the Iraqi legislature are protected.

July 12, 2007 White House report:	Satisfactory
Sept. 14, 2007 White House report:	Satisfactory
Sept. 4, 2007 GAO report:	Met

17. Allocating and spending $10 billion in Iraqi revenues for reconstruction projects, including delivery of essential services, on an equitable basis.

July 12, 2007 White House report:	Satisfactory
Sept. 14, 2007 White House report:	Satisfactory
Sept. 4, 2007 GAO report:	Partially met

18. Ensuring that Iraq's political authorities are not undermining or making false accusations against members of the Iraqi Security Forces.

July 12, 2007 White House report:	Unsatisfactory
Sept. 14, 2007 White House report:	Unsatisfactory
Sept. 4, 2007 GAO report:	Not met

SOURCES: Text of PL 110-28; Kenneth Katzman, *Iraq: Politics, Elections, and Benchmarks*, Congressional Research Service, June 2, 2009; *Securing, Stabilizing, and Rebuilding Iraq: Iraqi Government Has Not Met Most Legislative, Security, and Economic Benchmarks*, U.S. Government Accountability Office, Sept. 4, 2007.

U.S. WAR CASUALTIES, 2001–2008

War in Iraq

Year	Deaths Total	Killed in Action/ Died of Wounds	Accidents/ Other Deaths	Wounded in Action
2003	486	319	167	2,416
2004	846	713	133	8,005
2005	844	673	171	5,944
2006	820	704	116	6,411
2007	903	764	139	6,112
2008	313	221	92	2,052
Total	4,212	3,394	818	30,940

War in Afghanistan and War on Terrorism*

Year	Total Deaths	Killed in Action/Died of Wounds	Accidents/ Other Deaths	Wounded in Action
2001	11	3	8	33
2002	49	18	31	74
2003	45	17	28	99
2004	52	25	27	214
2005	98	66	32	268
2006	98	65	33	401
2007	117	83	34	752
2008	155	132	23	790
Total	625	409	216	2,631

*Figures are for "Operation Enduring Freedom" and as such include not only casualties in the War in Afghanistan but also War on Terrorism casualties in the Philippines, Southwest Asia, and other locations. Most, however, occurred in and around Afghanistan, including casualties in Pakistan and Uzbekistan.

SOURCE: Department of Defense, Defense Manpower Data Center, August 2009.

BACKGROUND

In a prime-time address on Jan. 10, 2007, President Bush told the American people that "it is clear that we need to change our strategy in Iraq" and that the continuing violence was "unacceptable." Bush announced a new strategy over the next twelve to eighteen months that included more U.S. troops in some areas, more reconstruction aid, a set of requirements for Iraq's government to meet, and a greater regional approach.

Specifically, he said he was sending another 21,500 combat troops. Of that number, 17,500 troops were to work alongside Iraqi forces to rid Baghdad neighborhoods of insurgents and terrorists and to train Iraqi security forces to continue such protection after U.S. troops left. Another 4,000 Marines were being sent to bolster U.S. forces in Anbar province, a mostly Sunni region, to work with Iraqi and tribal forces to fight al Qaeda terrorists who had made the province a stronghold. Support troops and military police would bring the overall total of additional forces being sent to 28,500.

Democrats considered the plan an escalation of the war. To House Speaker Nancy Pelosi, D-Calif., and Senate Majority Leader Harry Reid, D-Nev., it was as if the president had not been listening to the voters who put Democrats in power and to the bipartisan Iraq Study Group, which had called for the beginning of a withdrawal of U.S. troops and stepped-up diplomatic efforts in the region. *(Iraq Study Group Report, p. 274)*

But Democratic challenges to the surge policy were unsuccessful and the expanded deployment went forward.

In time the administration's hand was strengthened by events on the ground in Iraq. Status reports by the commander of coalition forces in Iraq, Gen. David H. Petraeus, and the U.S. ambassador to Iraq, Ryan Crocker, outlining the progress that was being made helped to hold GOP support and thwart antiwar legislation. By 2008 the levels of violence had dropped significantly and economic activity began to return to the country's war-ravaged cities and towns.

The relative stability in Iraq was the result of several factors. Sunni gunmen, once the backbone of the anti-American insurgency, had grown tired of the religious fanaticism and wanton brutality of their al Qaeda allies and had turned against them, joining forces with U.S. troops instead. Another factor was the ceasefire that had been declared by the powerful Shiite cleric Moqtada al Sadr. Also, the additional U.S. troops had employed a new counterinsurgency strategy that stressed the protection of local populations and they were equipped with high-tech tools that enabled them to more accurately identify and track insurgents. *(Background, 109th Congress, p. 271)*

Perhaps the clearest sign of progress was a decision by Bush, who had always opposed timetables for withdrawal, to accept in principle in the summer of 2008 an Iraqi proposal that most U.S. combat forces should be sent home by the end of 2011.

The Dec. 31, 2011, date for withdrawal was formally agreed to as part of a Security Agreement between the United States and Iraq. An interim deadline of June 30, 2009, for the withdrawal of U.S. combat forces from major populated areas in Iraq was also set. Ambassador Crocker and Iraqi foreign minister Hoshyar Zebari signed the Security Agreement and a Strategic Framework Agreement on Nov. 17, 2008. President Bush and Iraqi prime minister Nuri al-Maliki signed the agreements again on Dec. 14, during a Bush trip to Baghdad.

Congressional Democrats demanded the right to ratify the Security Agreement as a treaty, but Bush considered it to be an executive agreement and did not submit it to the Senate for approval.

2007 LEGISLATIVE ACTION

Congressional committees largely left out the issue of the Iraq War when they wrote the fiscal 2008 defense authorization and appropriations bills. Instead, lawmakers considered the issue in floor amendments to those measures, in supplemental spending legislation, and in standalone bills.

House Democrats, with a bigger majority and procedures that gave them an easier path to victory, passed several troop withdrawal bills. Similar efforts in the Senate generally fell short because of Democrats' inability to curtail GOP filibusters.

Policy Resolutions

Three senior senators took the first major step toward challenging the president's surge strategy, introducing a nonbinding resolution (S Con Res 2) stating that Bush's decision to send more troops was contrary to the U.S. "national interest." They were Foreign Relations Committee Chair Joseph R. Biden Jr., D-Del., Armed Services Committee Chair Carl Levin, D-Mich., and Chuck Hagel, R-Neb., a member of the Foreign Relations Committee. Biden's panel reported S Con Res 2 by a largely party-line vote on Jan. 24, 2007.

John W. Warner, R-Va.—former Senate Armed Services Committee chair and a highly respected voice on defense matters in Congress—introduced a rival resolution (S Con Res 4) stating that lawmakers "disagree" with the president's strategy. Three Republicans joined six Democrats in cosponsoring Warner's resolution. But many conservative Republicans said they would reject any resolution that criticized Bush's Iraq strategy, even Warner's milder proposal.

Next Warner and Levin agreed on a compromise resolution (S Con Res 7) that altered Warner's original language to strengthen the Senate's opposition to the troop surge, opposed cutting funding for troops in the field, encouraged the administration to establish benchmarks for the Iraqi government, and advocated a clear line of command between Iraqi and U.S. military forces. The new resolution won the support of the sponsors of S Con Res 2.

But the Democratic leadership's decision to put S Con Res 7 in bill form (S 470) threatened to derail the compromise. The leaders said it was a procedural step that would allow the proposal to move more quickly through the Senate and that the measure would be turned back into a nonbinding resolution as soon as it was passed. But Republicans saw it as an attempt to prevent amendments to the measure. A motion to invoke cloture on S 470 was rejected 49–47 on Feb. 5, far short of the sixty votes needed to adopt the resolution and begin debate on S 470. Only two Republicans supported the motion; Warner was not one of them.

With the Senate seemingly deadlocked, the House proceeded with its resolution. On Feb. 16, the House agreed 246–182 to adopt H Con Res 63. Unlike S 470, which listed twenty-two findings and twelve "sense of Congress" points, the House resolution made two statements: one supporting the troops and one disagreeing with the president's plan to increase U.S. forces in Iraq. The vote capped forty-five hours of debate in which more than 390 members spoke on both sides of the question. In the end, seventeen Republicans joined almost all of the chamber's Democrats in approving H Con Res 63. The measure was sponsored by Armed Services Committee Chair Ike Skelton, D-Mo., and Foreign Affairs Committee Chair Tom Lantos, D-Calif., as well as Republican Walter B. Jones of North Carolina. No floor amendments were allowed.

Attention reverted to the Senate, where a rare Saturday vote had been scheduled on a new measure (S 574) that was virtually identical to the House-passed resolution except that it also would have required additional reports from the president. A motion to invoke cloture was rejected 56–34 on Feb. 17.

After more than a month of negotiations, the Senate on March 15 voted on three Iraq War resolutions. Senate leaders had agreed that all three resolutions would require sixty votes to pass, although in the end that threshold was not crucial to any of the votes. By 48–50, senators voted down a binding resolution (S J Res 9), sponsored by Majority Leader Reid, to scale back the Iraq mission within 120 days of its enactment. It also set a goal—but not a requirement—that combat troops be pulled out by March 31, 2008.

The Senate then voted overwhelmingly for two nonbinding resolutions (S Res 107 and S Con Res 20) that essentially said the Senate supported U.S. troops.

Supplemental Appropriations

Democrats set out early in 2007 to link emergency money for the Iraq War to time limits on the deployment of U.S. troops. The time limits, in turn, were linked to the Iraqi government's progress in meeting certain military and political benchmarks such as quelling sectarian violence, disarming militias, sharing oil revenue, allocating reconstruction money, and scheduling local elections. The issues of troop readiness and lengths between deployments also were part of the debate.

The House voted 218–212 on March 23 in favor of a fiscal 2007 supplemental spending bill (HR 1591) with language requiring that most troops leave Iraq either by December 2007 if the president did not certify that Iraq was making substantial progress on all benchmarks or by August 2008 if he did make the certifications. The House bill also included troop readiness requirements and a number of policy prohibitions, including on the establishment of permanent U.S. military bases and on U.S. control over any oil resource in Iraq. *(2007 supplemental appropriations, p. 383)*

The Senate compromised on a more modest version of the bill to set as a goal—but not require—the withdrawal of most troops by the end of March 2008, the date recommended in 2006 by the Iraq Study Group. An amendment by Thad Cochran, R-Miss., to remove the war language from the bill lost by a vote of 48–50. The Senate passed the bill 51–47 on March 29. The Senate bill also called for a diplomatic strategy that included working with Iraq's neighbors.

Recognizing that the tougher bill could not make it through the Senate, House Democrats reluctantly agreed to a conference report with language similar to the Senate's goal-setting provisions. The compromise stated that if the president could not certify to Congress by July 1 that the Iraqi government was making progress in meeting the benchmarks, a phased redeployment was to begin immediately, with a goal of completing it by year's end. If the Iraqis were making progress, U.S. withdrawal would begin on Oct. 1, with a goal of completing it by the end of March 2008. Half the funds for reconstruction would be withheld until the president certified to Congress that Iraq had actually met specified benchmarks. The conference bill also included House-authored requirements for troop readiness and time between deployments. The House adopted the report by a **key vote of 218–208 (R 2–195; D 216–13)** on April 25. The Senate cleared the bill 51–46 on April 26. *(2007 key votes, p. 955)*

House Appropriations Committee Chair David R. Obey, D-Wis., said the bill was intended to send a message to political leaders in Iraq that the U.S. presence there would not be permanent. In the end, he said, it would be necessary for the president and Congress to find "a mutually agreed way of extricating ourselves from what has most assuredly become an Iraqi civil war." Many Republicans, however, said that setting a timetable for withdrawal was tantamount to surrender, and also argued that terrorism had to be confronted in Iraq.

Bush vetoed the bill May 1, saying the bill infringed on his powers as president and would restrict commanders in the field with its micromanagement, and that the "mandated withdrawal in this bill could embolden our enemies—and confirm their belief that America will not stand behind its commitments." The next day the House rejected an attempt to override him by a vote of 222–203, far short of the required two-thirds majority.

The Democratic leadership had to decide whether to send Bush a second bill with similar language, risking another veto they could not reverse, or give him a bill he would sign. The House tried passing a bill that had no timetable but would have withheld 55 percent of the funds until Bush sent Congress a report on the Iraqi government's progress in meeting benchmarks; then Congress would have had to vote on releasing the money. The House passed the bill (HR 2206) 221–205 on May 10. Earlier that day the House had defeated 171–255 a bill (HR 2237) that called for troop withdrawals, with limited exceptions, to start within ninety days of enactment and be completed 180 days after that. Defeat of HR 2237 was anticipated, but the total in favor of that bill exceeded supporters' expectations.

With the Memorial Day recess approaching and Bush escalating the rhetoric about troops in need, Democratic leaders ultimately backed down. On May 24, the House adopted an amendment to HR 2206 that included eighteen benchmarks for the Iraqi government and required the president to report on progress toward meeting them; the vote was 280–142. The Senate cleared the bill 80–14 the same day, and Bush signed it May 25 (PL 110-28). *(Benchmarks, box p. 304)*

House Democrats tried again in November, passing a fiscal 2008 emergency-spending bill (HR 4156) to provide $50 billion in "bridge" funding to carry the Pentagon into 2008. The measure, which passed 218–203 on Nov. 14, required withdrawals to begin within thirty days, with a goal of withdrawing most troops by Dec. 15, 2008. Like most of the other withdrawal plans, it stipulated that the Pentagon could leave troops in Iraq to conduct counterterrorism efforts, to protect U.S. personnel, and to train Iraqi security forces. *(2008 supplemental appropriations, p. 386)*

The Pentagon was barred from sending into battle troops who were not fully trained and equipped. All U.S. personnel, including those from the CIA, were required to follow strict rules against torture techniques specified in a recently updated Army Field Manual. *(Detainees, pp. 364, 399)*

But the measure died in the Senate on Nov. 16, when a motion to invoke cloture on proceeding to the bill failed 53–45, seven votes short. A cloture motion to proceed to consideration of a GOP alternative (S 2340) was also rejected, 45–53.

Bush demanded that Congress act on his request for emergency war funds before the end of the session, and he threatened to veto a year-end omnibus spending package unless Democrats relented.

On Dec. 17, the House voted 206–201 to add $31 billion to the fiscal 2008 omnibus appropriations bill (HR 2764) but specified that it was for military operations in Afghanistan and could not be used in Iraq.

The Senate on Dec. 18 agreed by a **key vote of 70–25 (R 48–1; D 21–23; I 1–1)** to a reworked provision that replaced the Afghanistan-only funding with $70 billion that the Pentagon could spend in both Iraq and Afghanistan. Two last-gasp attempts in the Senate to add language calling for a phase-down of the war failed. A Russ Feingold, D-Wis., amendment to require a phased deployment from Iraq within ninety days and to bar the use of funds for most deployments after nine months was rejected 24–71. A Levin amendment to express the sense of Congress that the U.S. armed forces in Iraq should transition to a more limited role by the end of 2008 was rejected 50–45. The Senate had agreed to require sixty votes for both amendments.

The Senate voted 76–17 to send the amended bill back to the House, and the House cleared it by a **key vote of 272–142 (R 194–1; D 78–141)** on Dec. 19. *(2007 key votes, p. 955)*

Defense Authorization

In one of the hardest-fought war votes of the year, the Senate on July 18 rejected 52–47 a motion to invoke cloture on what was seen as the centerpiece of the Democrats' strategy to force Bush to change course on Iraq—an amendment to the defense authorization bill (HR 1585) offered by Levin and Jack Reed, D-R.I., to require redeployment to begin within 120 days and most units to be withdrawn by April 30, 2008. *(2008 defense authorization, p. 373)*

The vote on the Levin-Reed amendment followed an all-night session arranged by Majority Leader Reid that coincided with an antiwar rally outside the Capitol. To prepare for the highly publicized overnighter, leaders had a dozen cots set up and provided pizza and toothbrushes for their colleagues. Senators traded half-hour speeches all night repeating their talking points. Amendment supporters said the war had dragged on long enough. But despite their growing qualms about the war, Republicans for the most part heeded Bush's appeal to wait until September, when General Petraeus and Ambassador Crocker were slated to give a progress report.

Before the cloture vote on Levin-Reed, action in the Senate included:

- Rejecting 56–41 a motion to invoke cloture on an amendment by Jim Webb, D-Va., to set minimum intervals between deployments of U.S. troops. Specifically, it required that active-duty forces be given at least as much time at home as they had in Iraq or Afghanistan before being sent back to war and that National Guard and reservists be given three years at home between deployments. The vote was four short of the sixty votes needed. The language did mandate troop shifts, but by all accounts it would have resulted in a drawdown in forces. The White House had threatened to veto the bill if it included the Webb amendment or any other language dictating missions for U.S. forces in Iraq.
- Rejecting 52–45 a Hagel amendment to limit the length of deployments in Iraq. The president could waive the provision in times of national emergency. Again, sixty votes were needed.
- Rejecting 41–55 a Lindsey Graham, R-S.C., amendment to express the sense of Congress on specified goals for leave time between deployments.
- Adopting 94–3 a John Cornyn, R-Texas, amendment expressing the sense of the Senate that it should commit itself to a strategy that "will not leave a failed state in Iraq."

Petraeus and Crocker gave their much-awaited testimony before four House and Senate committees Sept. 10 and Sept. 11. They reported that the surge of U.S. forces in Iraq had produced significant if fragile military results. Petraeus recommended the withdrawal of those additional forces and a return to the pre-surge level of around 130,000 troops by July 2008. He said force reductions would continue but that he could not discuss specifics until mid-March 2008. Over an unspecified period of time, the U.S. mission was to evolve from leading security, to working with Iraqi forces on such operations, to eventually just an observation role.

In a national address Sept. 13, Bush endorsed Petraeus's recommendations. Democrats generally criticized the plan, saying it did not include a sufficient change in mission.

The Senate's Iraq debate resumed a few days later, when the defense authorization bill was brought back to the floor. Democrats thought their best chance seemed to lie in another vote on Webb's proposal to set requirements on the length of time between deployments. They were hopeful that this time they were within striking distance of the sixty votes the Senate had agreed would be needed to approve the amendment. But Webb was unable to improve on the fifty-six votes he had won on the July motion to invoke cloture on his proposal, and his amendment was rejected by a **key vote of 56–44 (R 6–43; D 49–0; I 1–1)** on Sept. 19. The pivotal moment had come when Warner publicly opposed the amendment after hearing from U.S. generals who argued it would tie the military's hands in Iraq and Afghanistan. *(2007 key votes, p. 955)*

Among other Iraq-related votes on HR 1585, the Senate:

- Rejected 47–47 (sixty votes required), a Levin-Reed amendment requiring withdrawal of an unspecified number of troops from Iraq to begin ninety days after enactment, with most troops to be withdrawn within nine months.
- Rejected 55–45 (sixty votes required), a John McCain, R-Ariz., amendment expressing the sense of Congress that the Pentagon should establish the Webb guidelines as policy "as soon as practicable" and "consistent with wartime requirements."
- Rejected 28–70 a Feingold amendment to require that most troops be withdrawn by June 30, 2008, and that funding be cut off for most operations after that date. (The amendment was also rejected when Feingold attempted to attach it to the fiscal 2008 defense appropriations bill—HR 3222—on Oct. 3. The vote that time was 28–68.)
- Adopted 75–23 a Biden amendment expressing the sense of Congress that the United States should call for Iraq to be divided into Shiite, Kurdish, and Sunni federal regions and that the regions should share oil revenues.

The version of HR 1585 that emerged from conference contained no troop withdrawal requirements or limitations on U.S. policy in Iraq. Yet, Bush unexpectedly vetoed the bill anyway, after the Iraqi government objected to language that would have allowed individuals to sue nations designated as sponsors of terrorism. Iraq faced claims from several American victims of the Saddam Hussein regime, and the White House said the provisions would allow plaintiffs to freeze Iraqi assets during litigation, resulting in harm to the Iraqi government's reconstruction and stabilization efforts. Congress in January 2008 cleared a bill (HR 4986—PL 110-181) nearly identical to HR 1585, except for language effectively exempting the Iraqi government from litigation stemming from Saddam's regime.

Other Iraq Votes

Other efforts in 2007 to alter the conduct of the war met a similar fate: House Democrats could pass a variety of measures, but the Democrats' slim Senate majority doomed any plans with teeth.

Senator Warner proposed tying economic aid to the Iraqi government's progress in meeting benchmarks, although the president could waive the requirement if he submitted written justification to Congress. Warner had offered the amendment to an unrelated water resources bill (HR 1495), but an attempt to limit debate failed 52–44 on May 16. An attempt to limit debate on a Feingold amendment to the same bill that would have required a withdrawal of most U.S. troops from Iraq by March 31, 2008, also failed that day, 29–67.

The House on July 12 passed a bill (HR 2956), sponsored by Armed Services Chair Skelton, that would have required the defense secretary to begin redeploying U.S. troops and contractors out of Iraq within 120 days of enactment and pull most troops out by April 1, 2008. Skelton's bill, which passed 223–201, went no further.

The House weighed in on the troop-relief issue, when it passed a bill (HR 3159) similar to Webb's amendment, mandating minimum rest periods at home for U.S. military units between deployments to Iraq. HR 3159 was reported by the House Armed Services Committee (H Rept 110-282) on July 31 and passed by the full House 229–194 on Aug. 2, but there was no further action.

The House on Oct. 2 passed a bill (HR 3087—H Rept 110-283) to require regular reports on "the status of planning for the redeployment of the armed forces from Iraq." As the vote, 377–46, indicated, the legislation was a rarity in the 110th Congress: a war question on which most members of both parties could agree. There was no Senate action.

2008 LEGISLATIVE ACTION

Bruised from the battles of 2007, Democrats began the session knowing they should not try to repeat that year's strategy. Some resisted the retreat, if only for a while. Senate Majority Leader Reid looked in February 2008 as if he would press for a vote on a Feingold bill (S 2633) that called for a withdrawal within four months. But Reid soon yanked the bill from the floor, and it never resurfaced.

Pulling back from legislative action on the war soon became the norm. The proposal by Senate Democrats Levin and Reed to set a withdrawal timeline that had been a fixture of the 2007 debate did not come up for a vote in 2008. Levin, the Armed Services chair, kept the withdrawal language out of the defense authorization bill (S 3001) that emerged from his committee, and the provision never came up as a floor amendment to the bill. Likewise, in the House, Armed Services Committee Chair Skelton kept withdrawal language out of the House version (HR 5658) both in committee and on the floor.

In both chambers, the fiscal 2009 defense appropriations bill—legislation ultimately attached to a continuing resolution (HR 2638—PL 110-329)—was devoid of Iraq withdrawal provisions.

The frustration of many Democrats over their inability to make significant changes in the war policy itself was reinforced by President Bush's April 10 decision to order an indefinite suspension of U.S. troop withdrawals from Iraq after July. That would leave about 140,000 troops there, 10,000 more than before the surge. The president's decision had been foreshadowed on April 8 and 9 when General Petraeus and Ambassador Crocker testified before the Armed Services and Foreign Affairs committees in the House and Senate.

Supplemental Appropriations

The closest that war critics came in 2008 to legislating troop withdrawal deadlines was during consideration of the fiscal 2008–2009 supplemental war spending bill (HR 2642—PL 110-252) that was enacted in June. Even then, the vote was not close. *(2008–2009 supplemental appropriations, p. 387)*

On May 15, the House approved by a **key vote of 227–196 (R 8–183; D 219–13)** a war policy amendment that would have:

- Required that combat troop withdrawals begin within thirty days of enactment, with a goal of having most troops out by Dec. 31, 2009.
- Required that troops sent to Iraq met the Pentagon definition of "fully mission capable," prohibited troops from being deployed longer than Pentagon guidelines recommended, and required the Pentagon to abide by its policies on home time between deployments.
- Required that any U.S.-Iraq security pact governing the presence of U.S. troops in Iraq after 2008 be ratified by the Senate and specifically authorized in law. The Bush administration was trying to negotiate a status-of-forces agreement with Iraq to provide a legal basis for the continued presence and operation of U.S. armed forces in that country once the existing U.N. Security Council mandate expired on Dec. 31, 2008.
- Required the Iraqi government to match U.S. reconstruction aid dollar for dollar and partially reimburse the United States for the cost of fuel used by U.S. troops.

- Prohibited the establishment of permanent U.S. bases in Iraq.
- Prohibited interrogation techniques not authorized by the relevant Army Field Manual, and required that the International Red Cross be given access to military detainees. *(Military detainees, pp. 364, 399; 2008 key votes, p. 972)*

But the Senate did not even take up the House's set of war policy riders. Instead, the Senate first voted down 34–63 an amendment that combined war funding and the Senate Appropriations Committee's milder Iraq policy prescriptions. The Senate amendment would have:

- Expressed the nonbinding "sense of Congress" that troop withdrawals should be completed, with certain exceptions, by June 2009.
- Required that units deployed for combat be fully mission-capable and would have set a time limit on combat deployments
- Prohibited permanent U.S. bases in Iraq.
- Required that Iraq provide partial reimbursement for fuel used by U.S. troops.

After the Senate rejected the war policy amendment, Reid put forward a war-funding amendment with virtually no restrictions on war funds, calling instead for a number of reports to Congress. It was adopted 70–26.

The final bill had no policy restrictions on how the war funding could be spent—a key concession to the White House. The bill included a requirement that State Department and U.S. Agency for International Development reconstruction aid be matched dollar for dollar by the Iraqi government and a prohibition on the use of military construction funds to establish permanent bases in Iraq. Most of the proposed restrictions on a status-of-forces agreement were also dropped, although the bill prohibited the use of funds for a U.S.-Iraq agreement that subjected U.S. forces to the jurisdiction of the Iraqi courts.

Defense Authorization

The only other Iraq-related language of any significance enacted in 2008 was found in the fiscal 2009 defense authorization law (S 300—PL 110-417). But nothing in it would have ended U.S. military involvement in Iraq any sooner than the Bush administration had planned. *(2009 defense authorization, p. 390)*

The defense policy law banned Defense Department funding of Iraqi infrastructure projects, with certain exceptions. It required the U.S. government to begin negotiating a cost-sharing agreement for U.S.-Iraq military operations. It also required Washington to act to ensure that Baghdad paid for its own security costs.

Heeding a presidential veto threat, members writing the final bill backed away from a House-passed requirement that a U.S.-Iraq security pact come to Congress for approval either as a treaty or a bill enacted into law. Instead, they mandated a report on the subject. But House and Senate managers of the bill said that it was already "well-established" that such an agreement would have to be approved by Congress. The original House provision, an amendment offered by Barbara Lee, D-Calif., to the House defense bill (HR 5658), had been approved by a vote of 234–183 on May 22.

Lawmakers kept other provisions opposed by the administration, as well as language aimed at continuing congressional oversight of the wars. Those included the ban, similar to a Senate proposal, on funding infrastructure projects and the requirement that steps be taken toward cost sharing with the Iraqis.

The final bill also contained a ban on using funds authorized by the bill to establish permanent military bases in Iraq or control over Iraqi oil facilities. Both the Senate and House bills had had versions of that ban.

U.S.-India Nuclear Agreement

Congress in 2008 approved a civilian nuclear cooperation agreement between the United States and India. Enactment of the legislation (HR 7081—PL 110-369) cleared the way for the two countries to put the pact into force and provided President George W. Bush with a foreign policy victory as his term was drawing to a close.

The agreement allowed nuclear trade between the two countries. India agreed to a number of preconditions required by international regulators and U.S. law to engage in such trade. Among the most important was an agreement to separate its military and civilian nuclear facilities and to place the civilian, but not military, program under international oversight. The deal was a significant step forward for India after having been gradually excluded from the global nuclear industry since its first nuclear test in 1974.

Congressional supporters, including leaders of both parties, said the U.S.-India deal would open opportunities for U.S. businesses that would otherwise go to other nations and would cement ties with a nation that was both the world's largest democracy and a key counterweight in the region to China. Critics warned that the deal could give rogue nations a rationale for developing their own nuclear programs and that India could use the imported nuclear fuel to feed its civilian energy program while diverting its own nuclear fuel to weapons production. A number of lawmakers also expressed concern that India's close ties to Iran might lead New Delhi to assist the Iranian nuclear program.

In the end, most members of Congress supported the agreement as part of a strategic global partnership with India, but they also insisted on including in HR 7081 specific safeguards and ongoing congressional oversight, particularly on any subsequent agreement with India on reprocessing nuclear fuel.

President Bush had been able to proceed with negotiations after Congress in 2006 approved legislation (HR 5682—PL

109-401) allowing him to exempt India from certain restrictions on nuclear exports under the 1954 Atomic Energy Act (PL 83-703). Lawmakers, however, had insisted on being much more involved in the process than the White House had wanted, including requiring the administration to win congressional approval of the final agreement before it could go into effect. *(109th Congress action, p. 277)*

LEGISLATIVE ACTION

The House passed HR 7081 on Sept. 27, 2008, by a vote of 298–117 under suspension of the rules, a procedure that barred amendments and required a two-thirds majority.

Howard L. Berman, D-Calif., chair of the House Foreign Affairs Committee, had voiced concern that India might assist Iran with its nuclear program. He considered combining the India legislation with provisions to strengthen sanctions against Iran, but he dropped the idea after receiving assurances from Secretary of State Condoleezza Rice that she would seek a global ban on transferring enrichment and reprocessing technology to countries that did not already have it.

The Senate passed HR 7081 by a **key vote of 86-13 (R 49–0; D 36–12; I 1–1)** on Oct. 1. The Senate Foreign Relations Committee had reported an identical bill (S 3548—no written report) on Sept. 23. *(2008 key votes, p. 972)*

During Senate floor debate, senators rejected by voice vote an amendment by Byron L. Dorgan, D-N.D., and Jeff Bingaman, D-N.M., to require a cutoff of nuclear supplies to India if that country conducted another nuclear test. Richard G. Lugar of Indiana, the ranking Republican on the Foreign Relations Committee, echoed the State Department view when he said that existing law already offered the same protections.

MAJOR PROVISIONS

As signed into law on Oct. 8, HR 7081:

Approval

Gave Congress's approval to the United States-India Agreement for Cooperation on Peaceful Uses of Nuclear Energy.

Additional Safeguards

Before the Nuclear Regulatory Commission could issue licenses for the sale of nuclear-related goods and services to India, required the president to certify to Congress that:

- India had provided the International Atomic Energy Agency (IAEA) with a credible plan to separate civilian and military nuclear facilities, materials, and programs and had filed a declaration regarding its civilian facilities with the agency.
- The required agreement between India and the IAEA on the inspection of India's nuclear facilities, which was reached Aug. 14, 2008, had entered into force.

Reprocessing

Gave Congress the explicit right to review and disapprove of any subsequent agreement to permit India to extract plutonium and uranium from spent reactor fuel that originated in the United States. Congress would have thirty days within which to adopt a joint resolution of disapproval. Also, the president was required to inform the appropriate congressional committees "at the earliest possible time" after any request by the Indian government to negotiate reprocessing arrangements.

Under the U.S.-India accord, before India could reprocess nuclear material, it had to set up a new reprocessing facility for civilian nuclear material, and it had to reach an agreement with Washington on the procedures to be used at the new facility.

Future Agreements

Specified that Congress could reject a presidential decision to resume nuclear trade with any country that had detonated a nuclear explosive device by adopting a joint resolution of disapproval within sixty days of the decision.

HIV/AIDS Assistance

Congress in 2008 cleared a five-year, $48 billion reauthorization and expansion of President George W. Bush's global HIV/AIDS program (HR 5501—PL 110-293). The bill also authorized another $2 billion for programs to assist American Indians.

The program, first enacted in 2003 (PL 108-25), had provided treatment to 1.4 million people, supported care for 6.6 million, and earned bipartisan praise as a foreign policy success. The original law had authorized $15 billion for the first five years. As of Sept. 30, 2007, Congress had appropriated about $19 billion. *(PL 108-25, Congress and the Nation Vol. XI, p. 296)*

President Bush had proposed a $30 billion reauthorization. But a bipartisan compromise among Democrats, Republicans, and the White House allowed all sides to sign on and take credit for the much larger final bill. In exchange for the higher funding level, Democrats dropped language to tie family planning groups more closely to HIV/AIDS services, which conservatives said would open a back door to funding abortion overseas.

In addition to the funding boost, the bill was designed to shift the program from its original "emergency" purpose toward a long-term, sustainable plan, which included expanding the program's focus to include food aid, health care worker recruitment, and special outreach to women and girls.

The new law bore the names of two deceased chairs of the House Foreign Affairs Committee who had been instrumental in formulating the legislation: Tom Lantos, D-Calif. (1981-2008), who had drafted the reauthorization bill, and Henry J. Hyde, R-Ill. (1975-2007), who had guided the 2003 law to enactment.

HOUSE ACTION

The House passed HR 5501 by a vote of 308–116 on April 2, 2008. The House Foreign Affairs Committee first reported the bill (H Rept 110-546, Part I) on March 10 and then, because of a technical error, reported it again the next day (Part II).

The administration supported the House measure, although the committee proposed to authorize $50 billion over five years, $20 billion more than Bush sought. Democrats, implementing groups, and even some Republicans said Bush's request would sustain existing efforts but would not expand the program.

The bill reflected the bipartisan compromise reached by the Foreign Affairs Committee. Without it, the panel would have faced a battle between Democrats pushing to get rid of requirements for abstinence-only education and restrictions on family planning groups and Republicans who said such changes would funnel money to abortion providers overseas. House Republicans and the White House had balked at an earlier Democratic draft that would have made sweeping changes to social-policy provisions in existing law.

No significant changes were made on the floor, and a GOP motion to recommit the bill to lower its cost to the requested $30 billion failed 175–248.

SENATE ACTION

The Senate passed a revised version of HR 5501 by a vote of 80–16 on July 16. The Senate Foreign Relations Committee had reported its version (S 2731—S Rept 110-325) on April 15.

The Senate committee bill was similar to the House-passed version, authorizing $50 billion over five years. Lawmakers had hoped to get the bill to the president by the July 7 start of the Group of Eight summit in Japan so that he could use it to get commitments from other countries. But several months of behind-the-scenes wrangling, three days of debate, and consideration of ten amendments deprived Bush of the chance to use the bill as a talking point at the G8 meeting.

Sen. Tom Coburn, R-Okla., had held up the bill since the committee markup in March, demanding that more than half the program's bilateral aid go toward AIDS treatment and care. Committee leaders in July unveiled a compromise that included Coburn's language.

In the only sizable change made on the floor, senators adopted by voice vote an amendment that trimmed the original $50 billion authorization to $48 billion and directed the other $2 billion to programs for American Indians. The Senate rejected 31–64 an attempt by Jim DeMint, R-S.C., to cut the bill's total authorization to $35 billion.

The Senate adopted amendments by voice vote aimed at increasing oversight of the Global Fund and encouraging cost-sharing and transition strategies as part of agreements with recipient countries. Several GOP amendments were rejected on roll-call votes.

FINAL ACTION

The House cleared the Senate-passed bill July 24 by a **key vote of 303–115 (R 75–114; D 228–1)** and the president signed it into law on July 30. *(2008 key votes, p. 972)*

MAJOR PROVISIONS

As enacted HR 5501 contained the following major provisions.

Authorizations

Provided $48 billion for global HIV/AIDS programs for fiscal 2009 through 2013, including:

- $5 billion for malaria programs.
- $4 billion for tuberculosis programs.
- Up to $2 billion in fiscal 2009 for the Geneva-based Global Fund to Fight AIDS, Tuberculosis, and Malaria and unspecified sums in fiscal 2010 through 2013. The measure continued a provision in existing law that limited the U.S. contribution to 33 percent of the total amount contributed to the fund from all other sources.

Provided $2 billion for health care, clean water, and law enforcement programs for American Indians.

Abstinence Education

Repealed a law that required that one-third of prevention money be spent on abstinence education. Instead, the bill required a report to Congress if abstinence and fidelity programs fell below half of U.S. funds spent on prevention in a given country.

Prostitution

Preserved an existing requirement that, to be eligible for aid, organizations have an explicit policy opposing prostitution.

Aid Distribution

Required that more than half the program's bilateral aid go toward AIDS treatment and care; 10 percent had to go to orphans and vulnerable children.

Targeted Results

Set goals of preventing 12 million new HIV infections worldwide and supporting treatment for 12 million individuals infected with HIV/AIDS. The number was to increase with spending and the decline of drug costs. The bill also set a target of reaching 80 percent of pregnant women for prevention of mother-to-child transmission of HIV in countries with U.S. programs.

Nutrition and Staff

Linked AIDS prevention and treatment programs to nutrition programs and included a goal of recruiting 140,000 new health care workers.

Ban on HIV-Positive Visitors

Repealed language in a 1987 law (PL 100-71) that made HIV infection grounds for barring prospective immigrants, foreign students, refugees, and tourists from entry into the United States.

Faith-Based Organizations

Strengthened the "conscience clause," a provision of law that allowed faith-based organizations to opt out of endorsing or using any prevention or treatment method to which they had a religious or moral objection. The bill stated that faith-based groups would not be required to integrate with or refer people to other programs to which the organizations objected, and it barred government discrimination against faith groups based on their refusal to refer people to organizations to which they objected. The conscience clause was also extended to programs that cared for those affected by AIDS.

2008 Aid Appropriations

Congress in 2007 cleared legislation (HR 2764—PL 110-161) appropriating $35.3 billion for the State Department and foreign aid programs in fiscal 2008. The bill served as the vehicle for an omnibus package that included ten other unfinished spending bills as well.

The funding in the State-foreign operations section of the bill amounted to 3 percent more than in either chamber's original bill and about $240 million more than President George W. Bush had requested. It was also a 5 percent increase over fiscal 2007 spending. Appropriators were able to increase funds while still fitting the bill within Bush's discretionary spending limit by designating $2.4 billion of the money as emergency funding, which was not subject to discretionary caps.

Although the original House and Senate bills had proposed less than requested—both called for $34.4 billion, with $34.2 billion in discretionary budget authority—the White House had issued a strong veto threat, saying the president would reject them because they would relax federal restrictions on abortion. Both bills would have allowed the government to supply contraceptives, but not money, to family planning groups whether or not the groups supported abortion. Under the so-called Mexico City policy, first announced by President Ronald Reagan at a population conference in Mexico City in 1984, the U.S. Agency for International Development (USAID) was barred from providing aid to international family planning groups that provided or promoted abortion, even if it used its own money. President Bill Clinton rescinded the Mexico City policy, but Bush reinstated it shortly after taking office and repeatedly warned that he would veto any effort to alter it. The Senate bill would have repealed the policy altogether. The issue dominated the debates in both chambers, but in the end it was dropped from the final bill.

The combined State-foreign operations bill was the result of a realignment of the House and Senate Appropriations subcommittees at the start of the 110th Congress. In the previous Congress, the State Department was in a different appropriations bill.

HOUSE ACTION

The House passed HR 2764 by a vote of 241–178 on June 22, 2007. The House Appropriations Committee reported the bill (H Rept 110-197) on June 18.

The Appropriations Committee approved the president's requests for military assistance to Israel and Egypt but proposed withholding $200 million from Egypt until the State Department certified that the country was improving its justice system and reducing the smuggling of weapons from Egypt to Gaza. The bill provided $1.8 billion for the Millennium Challenge Corporation—$1.2 billion less than requested. It contained $5.1 billion for global HIV/AIDS programs, including the $4.2 billion Bush sought for his bilateral initiative. Appropriators pointed to funds in other bills to explain why HR 2764 contained none of the $400 million Bush had requested for Iraq.

State-Foreign Operations Subcommittee Chair Nita M. Lowey, D-N.Y., defended the bill's controversial contraceptive aid, arguing that the provision would not affect the Mexico City policy ban on other assistance and that providing contraceptives would reduce abortions by reducing unwanted pregnancies. But the provision produced heated debate when the bill reached the House floor.

The House adopted 223–201 an amendment by Lowey to clarify that the provision would not change the ban on federal funds to groups that supported abortion. Lowey said the provision would not remove the basic Mexico City policy but would only create an exception to allow the United States to provide contraceptives for family planning groups to distribute in developing countries.

Abortion opponents said the provision could open the door for U.S. funding of overseas abortions. But the House rejected by a **key vote of 205–218 (R 180–12; D 25–206)** an amendment offered by Christopher H. Smith, R-N.J., and Bart Stupak, D-Mich., to strike the contraceptive exception from the bill, restoring the original Mexico City policy. *(2007 key votes, p. 955)*

The House rejected 200–226 an amendment by Joe Pitts, R-Pa., to continue a requirement through fiscal 2008 that one-third of HIV/AIDS prevention funding be used to promote abstinence and fidelity. Some public health officials criticized the policy, saying it tied the hands of aid organizations. The bill allowed Bush to continue existing spending on abstinence programs but did not require it.

In other action, the House adopted 355–69 an amendment by Christopher Shays, R-Conn., to provide $1 million to reestablish the Iraq Study Group so it could review its findings and offer any revisions based on the current situation. Members rejected 205–219 a Frank R. Wolf, R-Va., to add $158 million for a variety of programs in Iraq. *(Iraq Study Group, p. 274)*

An amendment by Lincoln Diaz-Balart, R-Fla., to increase democracy programs for Cuba from $9 million to the requested $45.7 million was adopted 254–170.

The House rejected 74–343 a Charles Boustany Jr., R-La., amendment to strike the bill's restrictions on $200 million in military aid to Egypt.

Members adopted 390–30 a Mike Pence, R-Ind., amendment to prohibit the disbursement of $63.5 million in the bill for the Palestinian Authority unless the U.S. government certified that the authority met oversight requirements in distributing the aid. Lawmakers voiced concern about the State Department's move to lift an embargo on aid to the Palestinian Authority after President Mahmoud Abbas sacked the Hamas-led government and formed an emergency cabinet.

SENATE ACTION

The Senate passed an amended version of HR 2764 by a vote of 81–12 on Sept. 6. The Senate Appropriations Committee reported the bill (S Rept 110-128) on July 10.

The committee made even deeper cuts in the funding for the Millennium Challenge Corporation, recommending $1.2 billion. State Department-Foreign Operations Subcommittee Chair Patrick J. Leahy, D-Vt., said the program would be able to meet its commitments with previous funding that remained unspent. But the corporation released a statement saying the reduction would jeopardize funding for new agreements with developing countries.

Like the House, the Senate committee bill included $5.1 billion for global HIV/AIDS programs. The bill contained the requested amounts for military aid to Israel and Egypt. It included no economic aid for Iraq but allowed the administration to draw Iraq funding from a pool of economic aid not specified for any particular country.

The full Senate decided to go beyond the bill's contraceptive aid provision and voted 53–41 to adopt a Barbara Boxer, D-Calif., amendment repealing the Mexico City policy. Senators then rejected 40–54 a Sam Brownback, R-Kan., amendment to drop the contraceptive aid exception and insert the full Mexico City policy restrictions into the bill. The Senate did adopt 48–45 another Brownback amendment restoring language dropped from the bill that prohibited money to organizations that supported coerced abortion or forced sterilization. The longtime policy, known as Kemp-Kasten (PL 99-88), was aimed in part at denying money to the U.N. Population Fund because of its aid to China. *(Background, Congress and the Nation Vol. XI, p. 247, p. 294)*

In other action, the Senate adopted by voice vote a Mel Martinez, R-Fla., amendment to boost money for the promotion of democracy in Cuba from $15 million to $45.7 million. Senators approved 92–1 a Tom Coburn, R-Okla., proposal to bar funding for the U.S. contribution to the United Nations unless copies of all grants, contracts, and other financial and procurement-related information were posted on a publicly available website. Multilateral institutions such as the U.N. and the World Bank came in for heavy criticism for corruption and lack of transparency.

FINAL ACTION

The House passed HR 2764, amended with the text of the omnibus appropriations package, by a vote of 253–154 on Dec. 17. In a second vote that day the House voted 206–201 to add $31 billion for operations in Afghanistan and bar the funds from being used for operations in Iraq.

On Dec. 18 the Senate voted 70–25 to replace the $31 billion with $70 billion that could be used in both Afghanistan and Iraq. After rejecting an amendment related to the alternative minimum income tax, the Senate approved the bill 76–17.

The House cleared the bill the next day by a vote of 272–142.

MAJOR PROVISIONS

As signed into law on Dec. 26, 2007, HR 2764 appropriated $35.3 billion for the State Department, U.S. Agency for International Development (USAID), global health, and foreign military and economic aid. Within that total was $2.4 billion in emergency funding.

The total included $11.5 billion for State Department operations, $17.6 billion for bilateral economic assistance, $4.9 billion for foreign military aid, and $1.3 billion for international financial institutions.

Millennium Challenge Account

Provided $1.5 billion.

HIV/AIDS Assistance

Provided $5.1 billion for global programs to fight HIV/AIDS. Of that total, $4.7 billion was for President Bush's State Department-run Global HIV/AIDS Initiative, including $550 million that was designated as a contribution to the Geneva-based Global Fund to Fight AIDS, Tuberculosis, and Malaria. The other $350 million was for USAID's international AIDS programs.

In addition, the Labor-Health and Human Services-Education section of the omnibus bill provided $300 million for the multilateral Global Fund. Bush had requested these funds but had not sought funding for the Geneva organization in the foreign operations appropriation.

Middle East

Provided $2.4 billion in military assistance to Israel.

Provided $1.3 billion in military assistance and $415 million in economic assistance to Egypt. The bill withheld $100 million of the aid until Egypt took certain steps, including implementing judicial reforms and changes in police training to curb abuses. The restriction could be waived if it was determined to be in the national security interest of the United States. (Although it involved only a small amount of money, the restriction proved to be a major irritant in U.S. relations with Egypt and the Bush administration subsequently waived it.)

Provided about $218 million for assistance in the West Bank and Gaza but made the use of any of the aid for the Palestinian Authority contingent on requirements about the use, fiscal management, and auditing of the funds.

Afghanistan, Iraq

Provided about $1.1 billion in economic and military aid to Afghanistan but specified that no more than $300 million of the economic aid could be disbursed until the State Department certified that the Afghan government was cooperating in efforts to eradicate the poppies that were a major world source of heroin.

Provided none of the $400 million in economic aid requested for Iraq but allowed the administration to dip into the Economic Support Fund account for specified uses in Iraq. The bill allocated $3 billion for the Economic Support Fund, which provided economic aid to strategic allies.

Family Planning

Specified that no money could be used on any program that coerced women into having abortions or used involuntary sterilization as a form of family planning.

Allocated $40 million for the United Nations Population Fund (UNFPA). The funds were not to be made available unless UNFPA kept the money in a separate account and did not fund abortions. None of the money was to be used by UNFPA for a country program in the People's Republic of China.

Darfur

Provided about $1 billion in Darfur-related aid, including $550 million to support the U.N. peacekeeping mission in that region of Sudan.

Andean Counterdrug Initiative

Provided $327.5 million.

2008–2009 SUPPLEMENTAL

Congress in June 2008 cleared a fiscal 2008–2009 supplemental appropriations bill (HR 2642—PL 110-252) that included an additional $10.1 billion for foreign assistance.

The $186.5 billion measure was primarily a war supplemental, providing $161.8 billion for U.S. operations in Iraq and Afghanistan. But it did include another $24.7 billion for foreign aid as well as domestic programs, military construction, and disaster assistance. *(2008–2009 war supplemental, p. 387)*

The foreign aid portion of HR 2642 provided $1.2 billion over two years for global food aid through the PL 480 program—$850 million for fiscal 2008 and $395 million for fiscal 2009. It amounted to about $500 million more than requested.

The bill also appropriated $8.8 billion over two years for bilateral aid, including refugee assistance in Iraq and elsewhere, drug enforcement in Central American and Mexico, embassy security, and international economic support. Of that total about $5.2 billion was slated for fiscal 2008 and $3.7 billion for fiscal 2009. It was about $165 million more than requested.

To move the bill along, House leaders skipped committee consideration and attached the supplemental funding to an unneeded fiscal 2008 appropriations bill. The bill's war funding and domestic spending were divided, so members could vote for them separately. After weeks of back and forth between the two chambers over the two parts of the bill, agreement was finally reached and HR 2642 cleared June 26. President Bush signed it into law June 30.

2009 Aid Appropriations

A fiscal 2009 State Department-Foreign Operations appropriations bill never got beyond the committee stage in either chamber in 2008. An omnibus fiscal 2009 spending package (HR 1105—PL 111-8) was finally enacted in March 2009, providing $36.8 billion for the State Department, the U.S. Agency for International Development (USAID), and foreign military and economic aid.

Democrats had decided early in 2008 that they preferred to wait until a new president took office in January 2009 rather than engage in another round of veto fights with President George W. Bush. As a result, work on most of the appropriations bills ground to a halt mid-year.

Just before the end of the fiscal year, the 110th Congress approved a catch-all fiscal 2009 spending measure (HR 2638—PL 110-329) that provided continued funding—generally at fiscal 2008 levels—through March 6, 2009, for programs covered by nine regular appropriations bills, including the foreign operations measure.

Some additional fiscal 2009 foreign assistance funding was included in a supplemental appropriations bill (HR 2642—PL 110-252) enacted in June 2008 and another one (HR 2346—PL 111-32) enacted in June 2009.

2008 COMMITTEE BILLS

The House State-Foreign Operations Subcommittee approved a draft fiscal 2009 spending bill on July 16, 2008. The full Senate Appropriations Committee reported its bill (S 3288—S Rept 110-425) on July 18. There was no further action on either bill.

Both versions would have appropriated $36.8 billion, of which all but about $150 million was discretionary spending. The total was about 4 percent more than the $35.3 billion appropriated in fiscal 2008 (HR 2764—PL 110-161) and 4 percent below Bush's request of $38.4 billion. *(2008 aid appropriations, p. 314)*

Reflecting Democrats' impatience with Bush's signature foreign aid program, the Millennium Challenge Account (MCA), both bills included significantly less than the $2.2 billion that Bush had requested. The House subcommittee bill contained $1.5 billion for MCA—$700 million less than requested—and the Senate bill had only $254 million. Critics said the bilateral aid program, which was aimed at fostering democracy and free-market economies, had been too slow to spend money and was sitting on hefty reserves. *(Background, Congress and the Nation Vol. XI, box p. 289)*

Meanwhile, conservatives in both chambers raised concerns over proposed increases for the United Nations Population Fund, known as the UNFPA, which they said helped fund abortions in countries including China. They also objected to legislative language that would have relaxed some of the restrictions on the funding. Both bills would have left in place a long-standing law known as Kemp-Kasten (PL 99-88) that allowed the administration to bar money from going to organizations that supported coerced abortion or forced sterilization. But the measures would have made exceptions for certain UNFPA activities, such as supplying emergency obstetric care, preventing unintended pregnancy, and opposing genital mutilation. Since 2002, the Bush administration had withheld $235 million from the UNFPA based on the Kemp-Kasten restriction. The Senate bill would have gone further by overturning the so-called Mexico City policy, which prohibited funding for groups that performed or promoted abortion overseas. *(Background, Congress and the Nation Vol. XI, box p. 247)*

CONTINUING, SUPPLEMENTAL FUNDING

HR 2638, the continuing resolution signed into law Sept. 30, 2008, essentially froze funding at fiscal 2008 levels.

However, HR 2642, the supplemental spending bill that had been signed into law June 30, had an extra $10.1 billion for foreign assistance for fiscal 2008 and 2009. The fiscal 2009 portion included $3.7 billion for bilateral aid and $395 million for global food aid through the PL 480 program.

The bill provided $170 million in fiscal 2009 military financing for Israel, keeping the United States on track to meet a ten-year, $30 billion security agreement with Israel signed in August 2007. The $170 million made up the difference between $2.38 billion provided in the continuing resolution and the $2.55 billion that the pact called for in fiscal 2009.

Also included in HR 2642 was $465 million for a three-year, $1.4 billion counternarcotics program with Mexico, Central America, the Dominican Republic, and Haiti. The program—known as the Merida Initiative—was the result of a 2007 meeting between President Bush and Mexican president Felipe Calderon in the Mexican city of Merida. The two leaders had initialed an agreement pledging U.S. assistance to the Mexican government in its fight against the drug cartels, most of which were getting their weapons from U.S. arms dealers. HR 2642 allocated $400 million for Mexico and dropped some restrictions that Mexican officials viewed as an infringement on their sovereignty. The measure, however, withheld some money contingent on a report to Congress on human-rights issues in Mexico and the other participating countries.

The supplemental also allowed the president to waive the 1994 Glenn amendment (PL 103-236) to the Arms Export Control Act, thereby allowing the use of U.S. equipment and funding in dismantling North Korea's nuclear reactor at Yongbyon and disposing of its radioactive material.

2009 ACTION

The House passed the fiscal 2009 omnibus bill (HR 1105) by a vote of 245–178 on Feb. 25, 2009. The Senate cleared it by voice vote on March 10 and President Barack Obama signed it into law the next day.

The bill provided $36.8 billion for the State Department and foreign operations, of which all but $157 million was discretionary spending.

The Millennium Challenge Account saw the most significant cuts among State Department and international affairs programs. Its budget was slashed more than 40 percent from $1.5 billion in fiscal 2008 to $875 million in fiscal 2009. President Bush had requested $2.2 billion for fiscal 2009. Congress maintained that the program had enough money to implement its current agreements. The Millennium Challenge Corporation had spent roughly 5 percent of the $7.5 billion appropriated since fiscal 2004, but insisted that it had to have money in the bank to guarantee long-term commitments to anxious foreign governments.

The foreign operations section of the bill appropriated $5.5 billion for international AIDS prevention and treatment programs. Legislation (HR 5501—PL 110-293) enacted in 2008 had reauthorized and expanded President Bush's global AIDS program. *(HIV/AIDS assistance, p. 312)*

The measure was silent on the Mexico City restrictions on international family-planning funding that were lifted by Obama on Jan. 23, 2009. The president also said at that time that he looked forward to restoring funding for UNFPA. HR 1105 included $30 million for the organization.

Major provisions of HR 1105:

Millennium Challenge Account

Provided $875 million.

HIV/AIDS Assistance

Provided about $5.5 billion for programs to fight AIDS and other diseases overseas, including a $600 million contribution to the Global Fund to Fight AIDS, Tuberculosis, and Malaria.

In addition, the Labor-Health and Human Services-Education section of the bill provided $300 million for the multilateral Global Fund.

Middle East

Provided $2.4 billion in military assistance to Israel.

Provided $1.3 billion in military assistance and $200 million in economic aid to Egypt. Unlike the previous year, no restrictions were placed on any of the aid.

Provided $75 million in economic support assistance for Palestinians in the West Bank and Gaza but prohibited the funds from being used to support Hamas.

Afghanistan, Iraq

Provided $1 billion for assistance to Afghanistan, including $100 million for programs for women and girls. The measure withheld a portion of the $732 million in economic support funds until the secretary of state certified that the national and local governments were fully cooperating with U.S.-funded narcotics eradication and interdiction efforts.

Barred economic assistance to Iraq except for removal and disposal of land mines and other weapons, and required that Iraq match U.S. contributions.

Family Planning

Provided $30 million for the United Nations Population Fund.

Darfur

Provided $762 million for assistance to Sudan, including $414 million for U.N. peacekeeping operations in and around Darfur.

Counterdrug Initiatives

Provided $405 million for the Merida Initiative for counternarcotic and law enforcement programs in Mexico, Central America, the Dominican Republic, and Haiti.

Provided $315 million for the Andean Counterdrug Initiative in Colombia, Peru, Bolivia, and other Andean nations.

2009 SUPPLEMENTAL

Congress on June 18, 2009, cleared a fiscal 2009 war spending supplemental (HR 2346—PL 111-32) that appropriated $105.9 billion. President Obama signed it into law on June 24.

While the bulk of the money in HR 2346 was for military operations in Iraq and Afghanistan, it did include $10.4 billion for international affairs. But even some of that money was war-related. HR 2346 provided economic and stabilization assistance in areas affected by the wars, including $1.4 billion for Afghanistan, $2.4 billion for Pakistan, and $958 million for Iraq.

The bill included additional economic aid and/or security assistance for countries in the Middle East, including $660 million for the West Bank and Gaza, $300 million for Jordan, $310 million for Egypt, $555 million for Israel, and $69 million for Lebanon.

Also in the bill was another $100 million for the Global Fund to Fight AIDS, Tuberculosis, and Malaria in order to address a shortfall in funding for grants to several key countries, including Haiti, the Democratic Republic of the Congo, and Afghanistan.

The bill also included $5 billion that Obama had requested to leverage $108 billion in additional lending by the International Monetary Fund to countries struggling with the worldwide economic downturn.

Pre–Iraq War Intelligence

During the 110th Congress the Senate Select Committee on Intelligence brought to an end its five-year investigation into pre–Iraq War intelligence. The panel released the final three reports in its "Phase II" inquiry—one in 2007 and two in 2008.

The first of these, released in May 2007, examined the intelligence community's prewar estimates of what Iraq would be like after the conflict.

The other two, released in June 2008, dealt with the most controversial of the topics examined. One report delved into whether the public statements on Iraq by U.S. government officials were substantiated by the intelligence available at the time. The other report looked at intelligence-gathering activities of the Office of the Under Secretary of Defense for Policy.

The first phase of the panel's investigation had culminated in a 2004 report that primarily criticized the CIA for its failings. Partisan fighting slowed the second phase and the first two of its five reports were not released until September 2006. *(Details and background, p. 288)*

2007 REPORT

The Intelligence Committee released its report on prewar intelligence assessments of postwar Iraq (S Rept 110-76) on May 25, 2007. Two Republicans—Chuck Hagel of Nebraska and Olympia J. Snowe of Maine—had joined all of the committee's eight Democrats in approving the report by a 10–5 vote on May 8. Partisan differences on the panel were also reflected in the report's two Democratic "additional views" sections and three Republican "minority views" sections.

Among other assertions, the report concluded that intelligence officials anticipated that:

- Iraq lacked the "social underpinnings" to support democracy, and a lengthy American occupation would fuel the politicization of the Islamic religion,

increase funding for terrorist groups, and lead to factional strife;
- al Qaeda would use the war as an excuse to launch terror attacks against U.S. forces in Iraq and reestablish itself in Afghanistan while the United States was preoccupied with the new conflict;
- Elements of the Iranian government would exploit the war to enhance Iran's regional standing, and toppling Saddam Hussein would not persuade other countries to abandon their weapons of mass destruction (WMD) programs;
- There would be a "fine line" between eliminating rogue elements within Hussein's security forces and preserving the strength of those forces;
- A Baghdad-centered military operation could displace almost a million people and create nearly 1.5 million refugees.

The report listed high-ranking officials, including those in the White House, who received the intelligence products.

"Sadly, the administration's refusal to heed these dire warnings, and worse, to plan for them, has led to tragic consequences for which our nation is paying a terrible price," said Chair John D. Rockefeller IV, D-W.Va

Vice Chair Christopher S. Bond, R-Mo., said that Democrats had presented a distorted picture of what was given to policymakers by focusing on aspects that "seem to be important now." He faulted the committee for refusing to add a conclusion that said the intelligence community had not highlighted an insurgency as a potential postwar challenge. He also objected to including the names of officials who had received the intelligence, saying it was a break from established tradition.

2008 REPORTS

The Intelligence Committee released the final two reports on June 5, 2008. They had been approved by a 10–5 vote, with Hagel and Snowe again siding with the Democratic majority.

Prewar Statements

The first report (S Rept 110-345) examined how the statements of government officials matched up with the intelligence available on Iraq. The report included five "additional views" sections—three from Democrats and two from Republicans—and three "minority views" sections from Republicans.

Conclusions about prewar statements by various members of the Bush administration included the following:

- Statements by President George W. Bush, Vice President Dick Cheney, and other officials regarding a possible Iraqi nuclear weapons program were generally substantiated by available intelligence estimates but did not convey the substantial disagreements that existed in the intelligence community.
- Statements on Iraq's possession of biological and chemical weapons were substantiated. But Bush and Cheney statements prior to the October 2002 National Intelligence Estimate regarding Iraq's chemical weapons production capability and activities did not reflect uncertainties within the intelligence community as to whether such production was ongoing.
- Statements by Bush, Cheney, and others regarding Iraq's possession of WMDs were generally substantiated, although statements prior to late 2002 about ongoing production did not reflect some of the uncertainty in the intelligence community.
- Secretary of Defense Donald H. Rumsfeld's statement that the Iraqi government had underground WMD facilities that were not vulnerable to conventional airstrikes was not substantiated by available intelligence.
- Statements and implications by Bush and Secretary of State Colin L. Powell suggesting that Iraq and the al Qaeda terrorist network had a partnership, or that Iraq had provided al Qaeda with weapons training, were not substantiated.
- Statements by Bush and Cheney indicating that Hussein was prepared to give WMDs to terrorist groups for attacks against the United States were contradicted by available intelligence.
- Statements by Bush and Cheney regarding the postwar political, security, and economic situation in Iraq did not reflect the concerns and uncertainties expressed in the intelligence products.

At the time of the report's release, Rockefeller said, "In making the case for war, the administration repeatedly presented intelligence as fact when in reality it was unsubstantiated, contradicted, or even nonexistent. As a result, the American people were led to believe that the threat from Iraq was much greater than actually existed."

But the Republican vice chair accused committee Democrats of playing election-year politics and complained that Republicans had been cut out of the writing of the final report. Bond said: "It is ironic that the Democrats would knowingly distort and misrepresent the committee's findings and the intelligence in an effort to prove that the administration distorted and mischaracterized the intelligence." He also emphasized that Senate Democrats had seen the same intelligence as the administration and had characterized Iraq as a dangerous threat to the United States.

Defense Policy Office

The final report (S Rept 110-346) was entitled: "Intelligence Activities Relating to Iraq Conducted by the Policy Counterterrorism Evaluation Group and the Office of Special Plans within the Office of the Under Secretary of Defense for Policy." Four Republicans joined in writing a "minority views" section.

The committee examined secret meetings in Rome in 2001 and Paris in 2003 between Pentagon officials and Iranian informants. The meetings were facilitated in part by Michael Ledeen and included Iranian exile Manucher Ghorbanifer, two figures from the Iran-contra affair of the mid-1980s. The report faulted Defense Department officials for keeping the meetings secret and not sharing "potentially useful and actionable intelligence information." *(Iran-contra affair, Congress and the Nation Vol. VII, p. 253)*

The committee recommended that the director of national intelligence (DNI) determine whether there was a need to clarify the requirements for Defense Department policy officials to coordinate their activities with the intelligence community. It also recommended that the DNI have a report prepared on policies and procedures for contacts between foreign agents or entities and U.S. government employees.

A committee press release stated: "The report found that the clandestine meetings between Pentagon officials and Iranians in Rome and Paris were inappropriate and mishandled from beginning to end.... The involvement of Manucher Ghobanifer [sic] and Michael Ledeen in the meetings was inappropriate. Potentially important information collected during the meetings was withheld from intelligence agencies by Pentagon officials."

Dissenting Republicans argued that this probe was unrelated to Iraq and had violated the original agreement about what the committee would examine. They also noted in their minority views: "The majority report shows that there was nothing unlawful about DoD's [Department of Defense's], or any other entity's, role in or conduct during the Rome meetings.... Ironically, after all the allegations of unlawful activities, rather than state this prominently as one of the eight main conclusions, this most significant finding is buried in a summary paragraph."

2008 Intelligence Authorization

Congress in early 2008 finally cleared a fiscal 2008 intelligence authorization bill (HR 2082), but the bill died when lawmakers were unable to override President George W. Bush's veto. The administration's main objection was to a provision in HR 2082 requiring the intelligence community—including the CIA—to abide by specific limits on the methods used in interrogating detainees.

This was the third consecutive fiscal year for which an intelligence authorization bill had not been enacted. After

CONGRESSIONAL OVERSIGHT OF INTELLIGENCE

The House in 2007 adopted a rules change that established a new intelligence oversight panel within the House Appropriations Committee. The resolution (H Res 35) was adopted 239–188 on Jan. 9, 2007.

The action was taken in response to recommendations made in 2004 by the National Commission on Terrorist Attacks Upon the United States. The 9/11 commission, as it was better known, had branded congressional oversight of intelligence and counterterrorism as "dysfunctional" and had called for Congress to improve its oversight by either creating a joint House-Senate committee on intelligence or empowering the Intelligence committees with both authorizing and appropriating powers. *(Congress and the Nation Vol. XI, intelligence system overhaul, p. 263, and congressional oversight of intelligence, p. 274)*

But the recommendations hit a wall of resistance on Capitol Hill. Although Congress approved broad changes in the executive branch's intelligence apparatus, it was reluctant to tackle existing committee jurisdictions and set off turf battles among powerful committee chairs. As a result, none of the major structural changes recommended by the 9/11 commission was made.

Both chambers did establish oversight subcommittees within their Intelligence committees.

The Senate in 2004 adopted a resolution (S Res 445) that, in part, called for the creation of an intelligence subcommittee within the Appropriations Committee, but none was established. In 2007 the Senate included in legislation implementing some of the 9/11 commission's recommendations (HR1—PL 110-53) a "sense of the Senate" provision suggesting that its Intelligence Committee recommend changes to the structure of intelligence oversight. Fourteen of the fifteen members of the Intelligence panel on March 6, 2008, sent a letter to Senate leaders recommending that either they give the Intelligence Committee appropriations powers or create a new appropriations subcommittee on intelligence. Leaders of the Appropriations Committee rejected both suggestions. *(HR 1, p. 245)*

On the House side, the appropriations subcommittee created under H Res 35 was given no actual appropriations power. Instead, the subcommittee—composed of both appropriators and Intelligence Committee members—was to review budget requests for intelligence activities, make recommendations to the relevant appropriations subcommittees, and prepare an annual report with observations and recommendations for the Defense Appropriations subcommittee to use in preparing the classified annex to the defense appropriations bill.

passing a bill every year since 1978, members found the legislation increasingly stymied by battles related to the Iraq War and intelligence tactics in the post-Sept. 11 world. No intelligence authorization bill had been enacted in the 109th Congress, and that fate continued in the 110th Congress as well. *(2006 intelligence authorization, p. 290; 2007 intelligence authorization, p. 292; 2009 intelligence authorization, p. 322)*

HR 2082 would have authorized funding and prescribed policies for the sixteen national intelligence agencies and the Office of the Director of National Intelligence (DNI). The agencies included the CIA, the Defense Intelligence Agency, the FBI, the National Security Agency (NSA), and the National Reconnaissance Office (NRO), as well as the foreign intelligence activities of the Departments of State and Homeland Security. Although funding levels were classified, the budget for the intelligence community was estimated to be in the $44 billion- to $45 billion-range.

The failure of an intelligence authorization bill was a lost opportunity for the Intelligence committees to influence and shape the intelligence community. Funding, however, was continued in defense appropriations bills.

HOUSE ACTION

The House passed HR 2082 by a vote of 225–197 on May 11, 2007. The House Permanent Select Committee on Intelligence had reported the bill (H Rept 110-131) on May 7.

The decision to incorporate portions of the president's fiscal 2008 supplemental intelligence request in the regular fiscal 2008 authorization helped make what Intelligence Committee Chair Silvestre Reyes, D-Texas, said was the largest intelligence authorization bill ever written by the panel. Reyes said the bill would "streamline acquisition" and eliminate "wasteful spending." HR 2082 required reports or audits on Iran's and North Korea's nuclear programs, the use of intelligence contractors, the CIA's covert activities, and the national security threat posed by climate change.

Committee Republicans tried, but failed, to strip out the global warming estimate requirement and to deauthorize $40 million for the National Drug Intelligence Center, a facility located in the district of John P. Murtha, D-Pa., a member of the Intelligence panel and the chair of the Defense Appropriations Subcommittee. In recent budget proposals, Bush had tried to end funding for the facility.

During floor action, the House adopted 245–178 an amendment offered by Adam B. Schiff, D-Calif., and Jeff Flake, R-Ariz., stating that domestic electronic surveillance to collect foreign intelligence could only be conducted under the purview of the Foreign Intelligence Surveillance Act (FISA). The vote was a setback for the Bush administration, which was trying to persuade Congress to expand surveillance authority beyond the existing law. *(Electronic surveillance, pp. 249, 251)*

The House also adopted 297–122 a Mike Rogers, R-Mich., and Alcee L. Hastings, D-Fla., amendment to cap the number of employees at the DNI at existing levels. Some lawmakers argued that the growth of personnel within the DNI was creating a cumbersome layer of bureaucracy.

SENATE ACTION

The Senate passed HR 2082 by voice vote Oct. 3, after incorporating its version of the bill (S 1538). The Select Committee on Intelligence had reported S 1538 (S 1538—S Rept 110-75) on May 31 and the Armed Services Committee had reported it June 26 (S Rept 110-92).

Leaders of the Intelligence panel said the measure included several provisions to scrutinize or modify how the intelligence community spent its money. They said it also contained provisions opposed by the Bush administration, including a proposal to declassify the total of the intelligence budget and another to require additional reporting to Congress on intelligence activities. Another provision required the CIA to release a declassified summary of a report by its inspector general on the Sept. 11, 2001, terrorist attacks.

The Senate bill also included provisions to grant the DNI new personnel authorities and require an overhaul of the intelligence community's strategy for acquiring satellite and aerial photography, known as imagery intelligence. It also established an annual reporting system on major acquisitions and the use of contractors, and instituted several steps to nudge the intelligence community toward producing financial statements that could be audited.

During floor action on S 1538, the Senate removed or weakened several provisions opposed by Republicans, including a requirement that the president hand over Iraq-related intelligence briefing documents dating to the period before the war began and a requirement that the administration provide summaries of all intelligence activities to every member of the Intelligence panels. Also omitted was a requirement that the administration hand over any legal documents from the previous five years pertaining to NSA's warrantless surveillance program. Instead, the bill required only that some congressional committees be notified of FISA orders within forty-five days.

The Senate agreed to the changes by unanimous consent.

CONFERENCE ACTION

Setting up a showdown with the White House, negotiators from the two chambers approved a conference report (H Rept 110-478) that included new language to bar all U.S. intelligence agencies, including the CIA, from using harsh interrogation tactics. Under the provision, all spy agencies—not just those at the Defense Department—would have been required to comply with the rules for interrogation set forth in the Army Field Manual on Human Intelligence Collector Operations. Sen. Dianne Feinstein, D-Calif., said the amendment would ban eight specific techniques, including "waterboarding," or simulated drowning. *(Interrogation of detainees, pp. 364, 399)*

Republicans protested the late addition of the provision and warned of a veto. A Dec. 2 White House policy statement said the provision would "prevent the United States from conducting lawful interrogations of senior al Qaeda terrorists to obtain intelligence needed to protect Americans from attack."

A summary of the conference agreement indicated the bill fully funded or provided increased funding for human spying, counterterrorism operations, counterproliferation, analysis, language skills, research and development, and aging spy agency infrastructure. It also created an annual reporting system to guard against cost overruns and required extensive reports to Congress on the use of contractors.

The conference bill also created an inspector general for the entire intelligence community and required Senate confirmation for the directors of NSA and NRO. The Justice Department was required to provide to Congress the legal justifications for the administration's detention and interrogation policies.

The House approved the conference report on Dec. 13 by a vote of 222–199, a margin well short of the two-thirds majority required to override a veto.

On the Senate side, Lindsey Graham, R-S.C.—reportedly among others—put a hold on the conference report, pushing final action off until the next session of Congress. The Senate adopted the conference report by a vote of 51–45 on Feb. 13, 2008, clearing it for the White House.

VETO, OVERRIDE ATTEMPT

President Bush vetoed the bill on March 8. In his veto message, Bush insisted that it was "vitally important" for the CIA to maintain a separate and classified interrogation program. He said that the attorney general had determined that the CIA methodology was "lawful under existing domestic and international law." *(Veto message, p. 1071)*

Bush cited other provisions as well, including the requirement that the directors of the NSA and NRO be subject to Senate confirmation, in explaining his veto.

The House on March 11 rejected an attempt to override the veto by a vote of 225–188, well short of the two-thirds majority—276 in this case—that was needed.

INTELLIGENCE BUDGET TOTALS MADE PUBLIC

Congress in 2007 approved legislation (H—PL 110-53) requiring the government to disclose the total amount appropriated for the National Intelligence Program (NIP) in fiscal years 2007 and 2008. The requirement could be waived or postponed in subsequent years if the president informed the House and Senate Intelligence committees that the disclosure would damage national security and stated the reasons for that finding.

In complying with the new law, the Director of National Intelligence (DNI) in an Oct. 30, 2007, press release reported that the aggregate amount appropriated to the NIP for fiscal 2007 was $43.5 billion. According to an Oct. 28, 2008, press release, the aggregate total for fiscal 2008 was $47.5 billion. Additional money was spent on the Military Intelligence Program (MIP) under the Defense Department, but HR 1 did not require that figure to be made public.

HR 1 implemented some of the recommendations of the National Commission on Terrorist Attacks Upon the United States or, as it was better known, the 9/11 commission. The commission in 2004 had called for making public the total amount spent on intelligence while keeping specific programs secret. As part of a 2004 overhaul of the intelligence system (PL 108-458), the Senate had approved that disclosure, but House Republicans and the White House opposed the move and the provision had been removed during conference committee action. *(HR 1, p. 245—Homeland Security chapter; Independent 9/11 commission, Congress and the Nation Vol. XI, p. 275; Intelligence system overhaul, Congress and the Nation Vol. XI, p. 263)*

2009 Intelligence Authorization

Congress in 2008 failed to clear a fiscal 2009 intelligence authorization bill. This was the fourth fiscal year in a row in which legislation authorizing funding and prescribing policies for the sixteen national intelligence agencies and the Office of the Director of National Intelligence (DNI) was not enacted.

The House passed a bill (HR 5959) in 2008, but a Senate version (S 2996) never got beyond committee approval. S 2996 included the same controversial provision on the interrogation of detainees that had triggered a presidential veto of a fiscal 2008 authorization bill (HR 2082) and the Senate leadership was unwilling to put it on the abbreviated pre-election schedule in the fall. The White House had threatened to veto both the House and Senate bills. *(2008 intelligence authorization, p. 320)*

Funding was continued under defense appropriations bills, but the failure to enact an annual authorization bill deprived the Intelligence committees of a key mechanism for ensuring their oversight of the intelligence community.

SENATE ACTION

The Senate Select Committee on Intelligence reported S 2996 (S Rept 110-333) on May 8, 2008.

The panel courted another presidential veto when it renewed its efforts to rein in administration interrogation practices. By a 9–6 vote, the panel added a provision prohibiting the intelligence agencies from using any interrogation techniques not authorized in the United States Army Field Manual on Human Intelligence Collector Operations. The manual specifically prohibited harsh interrogation methods, such as simulated drowning, known as waterboarding. *(Interrogation of detainees, pp. 364, 399)*

The panel also adopted amendments to bar the CIA from using contractors for interrogations and to require the intelligence community to disclose detainees' identities to the International Committee of the Red Cross and give that agency access to the detainees.

In addition, the bill proposed creating posts for an inspector general and chief financial officer for the intelligence community, requiring Senate confirmation of several top intelligence officials, and requiring annual reports for major acquisition programs.

S 2996 went no further. Democratic leaders never set aside floor time for the legislation. Passing the bill would have been difficult, given GOP opposition, and would have meant a prolonged floor battle in a year shortened by the elections.

HOUSE ACTION

The House passed HR 5959 by voice vote July 16. The House Permanent Select Committee on Intelligence had reported the bill (H Rept 110-665) on May 21 and filed a supplemental report (Part II) on July 10.

Unlike the Senate committee, House committee members rejected an attempt to add language requiring all federal agencies, including the CIA, to comply with the Army Field Manual. An aide said Silvestre Reyes, D-Texas, the committee chair, preferred to send President George W. Bush a bill he would sign. But the panel did agree to an amendment to block CIA contractors from interrogating detainees.

Lawmakers adopted several other amendments when the bill reached the floor. Among them was a Peter Hoekstra, R-Mich., proposal, adopted 249–180, that effectively barred federal agencies from prohibiting or discouraging the use of certain terms, including "Islamic terrorists." Hoekstra saw the agencies' action as political correctness, while opponents of his amendment stressed the need to not inflame public opinion among moderate Muslims.

On a vote of 200–225, Democrats turned aside a Hoekstra motion to recommit the bill to add language requiring a study of the national security implications of high gasoline prices. Democrats said they supported the idea but thought sending the bill back to committee would essentially kill it.

Even without the Army manual provision, the White House objected to HR 5959, targeting various accountability and reporting provisions that it said represented overzealous congressional interference in the workings of the intelligence community. In a statement, the administration criticized the provision that would have barred the CIA from using contractors to conduct interrogations, even though the DNI could have waived the provision. Also cited, among others, were provisions to require additional information from the White House and to create a statutory inspector general for the intelligence community.

Sudan Sanctions

Congress in 2007 cleared legislation (S 2271—PL 110-174) authorizing state and local governments to divest themselves of assets in companies doing business with several sectors in Sudan. The goal of the measure was to intensify pressure on Sudan to end the conflict in the Darfur region of that country.

Since 2003, Arab militias acting on behalf of the Sudanese government had attacked, raped, and killed Darfuri civilians with impunity to put down local rebellions over discrimination against non-Arab farmers. According to the Congressional Research Service, estimates in 2007 indicated as many as 450,000 people had been killed, 2 million displaced, and more than 234,000 forced into neighboring Chad.

Congress had branded the conflict as genocide and had imposed sanctions aimed at punishing the Sudanese government. Lawmakers went further in 2006 when they approved sanctions (HR 3127—PL 109-344) aimed at punishing Sudanese officials and other individuals considered responsible for the ongoing violence. *(Background, Sudan sanctions, p. 293)*

OTHER LEGISLATION

The 110th Congress kept up the pressure on Sudan.

Among the resolutions adopted to condemn the conflict were two that called on China to use its influence and economic leverage to stop the violence. The House passed H Res 422 by a 410–0 vote on June 5, 2007. The Senate passed S Res 203 by voice vote July 30. China was one of Sudan's biggest trade partners and a major importer of Sudanese oil. While China had taken some steps to help quell the killings, appointing a Darfur envoy and committing a small team of army engineers to the peacekeeping force, it had used its U.N. Security Council seat to resist more robust action against Khartoum

Congress also included in foreign aid appropriations bills many millions of dollars for African Union peacekeepers and for aid and reconstruction in Darfur and southern Sudan. *(2008 aid appropriations, p. 314; 2009 aid appropriations, p. 316)*

Although Iran got most of the attention, Sudan was also one of the targets of a bill (S 1612—PL 110-96) enacted in 2007 to increase fines on companies doing business with countries seen as a threat to U.S. national security. *(Iran sanctions, p. 299)*

DIVESTITURE LEGISLATION

Both chambers moved on divestiture legislation in 2007.

The House went first, approving HR 180 by a vote of 418–1 on July 31, but there was no further action on that bill.

The Senate Banking, Housing, and Urban Affairs Committee reported S 2271 (S Rept 110-213) on Oct. 31 and the full Senate passed an amended version on Dec. 12. The House cleared the Senate bill by a vote of 411–0 on Dec. 18.

The legislation, S 2271, included these major provisions:

- Authorized state and local governments to divest assets in companies doing business in four sectors of the Sudanese economy: power production, mineral extraction, oil, and military equipment production. The U.S. Department of Justice was to be notified of such decisions.
- Allowed private asset fund managers to divest as well, so long as they fulfilled their fiduciary responsibilities and abided by laws and regulations.
- Required federal contractors to certify that they were not conducting business in the sectors of Sudan's economy cited in the bill. The president could waive this requirement if it was in the national interest.
- Required the secretaries of state and Treasury to submit to the appropriate congressional committees a report on the effectiveness of U.S. sanctions imposed on Sudan.

When President George W. Bush signed S 2271 into law on Dec. 31, he issued a statement declaring his view that he could ignore its provisions in the name of other U.S. foreign policy interests. Specifically, he said while he shared Congress's deep concern over the continued violence in Darfur, the bill risked "being interpreted as insulating from Federal oversight State and local divestment actions that could interfere with implementation of national foreign policy."

Rep. Michael E. Capuano, a Massachusetts Democrat who chaired the congressional caucus on Sudan, called Bush's signing statement "ridiculous" and said it undermined the administration's own case that the killings amounted to genocide.

Cuba Sanctions

Attempts to weaken restrictions on trade with and travel to Cuba were thwarted throughout the 110th Congress. As in previous Congresses, veto threats from President George W. Bush and the fierce opposition of Cuban American and conservative lawmakers meant such proposals never emerged from conference, if they even got that far.

But the Democratic leadership's decision to halt action in mid-2008 on nine of the fiscal 2009 appropriations bills until there was a new president increased the odds for those advocating changes to Bush-era restrictions. The Financial Services appropriations section of the fiscal 2009 omnibus spending bill (HR 1105—PL 111-8) enacted in March 2009 called for new regulations governing travel to Cuba to sell agricultural and medical goods. It also barred funding to enforce regulations that had placed restrictions on payments for such goods and on family visits to relatives in Cuba. *(Background, Cuba sanctions, p. 294)*

FINANCIAL SERVICES

In 2007, provisions to loosen Cuba trade and travel restrictions were dropped from the final version of the fiscal 2008 financial services appropriations bill (HR 2764—PL 110-61).

During consideration of its financial services funding bill (HR 2829—H Rept 110-207), the House on June 28, 2007, adopted by voice vote an amendment to block enforcement of a controversial 2005 rule that required Cuba to pay for U.S. goods before a ship left port rather than, as the previous rule had allowed, before the goods were handed over. The amendment's sponsor, Jerry Moran, R-Kan., said the issue was important for farm groups and questioned the wisdom of restricting trade with Cuba when the United States had normal trade relations with countries such as China.

The Senate Appropriations Committee included even broader language in the version of HR 2829 (S Rept 110-129) it reported on July 13. The Senate provisions not only restricted enforcement of the rule but also made it easier to travel to Cuba to sell agricultural and medical goods. Under existing law, such travel had to be authorized on a case-by-case basis by a specific license. A provision of the Senate bill allowed such travel to be authorized by general license.

In a June 26, 2007, statement, the White House had put Congress on notice that President Bush would veto the bill if it included language that loosened sanctions on Cuba. "Lifting the sanctions now, or limiting our ability to enforce them, would provide assistance to a repressive regime at the expense of the Cuban people," it said. The provisions were stripped out of the bill before it was folded into an omnibus spending package.

But the battle resumed in 2008 when Congress took up the fiscal 2009 financial services appropriations bill. The House Appropriations Committee approved a draft bill on June 25, 2008, and finally reported it (HR 7323—H Rept 110-920) Dec. 10. The bill included provisions loosening restrictions on family visits to relatives in Cuba and reversing the 2005 rule on when Cuba had to pay for agricultural imports. The Senate Appropriations Committee reported a bill (S 3260—S Rept 110-417) July 14 with similar provisions, as well as one authorizing travel for the sale of agricultural and medical goods. There was no further action on either bill after the Democratic leadership's decision to postpone final action on the appropriations bills.

Action resumed in 2009. The financial services section of the omnibus spending package (HR 1105—PL 111-8) signed into law by President Barack Obama on March 11, 2009, included three changes in U.S. policy toward Cuba. Those provisions:

- Directed the secretary of the Treasury to issue regulations allowing, by general license, travel to Cuba to market and sell agricultural and medical goods.
- Prohibited funding to enforce 2004 regulations that had restricted travel to visit relatives in Cuba. The modification allowed relatives to visit family members once a year, instead of once every three years, and expanded the definition of "close relative."
- Prohibited funding to enforce the 2005 regulation requiring all agricultural goods sold to Cuba to be paid for before they were shipped from the United States.

AGRICULTURE BILLS

During consideration of a farm bill reauthorization (HR 2419—PL 110-234), the House on July 27, 2007, rejected 182–245 an amendment by Charles B. Rangel, D-N.Y., that would have made it easier for Cuba to buy crops by allowing U.S. exporters to accept payment after crops were shipped, allowing U.S. banks to accept payments directly from Cuban banks, and permitting visas for Cuban nationals coming to the United States to conduct activities related to agricultural purchases. Ileana Ros-Lehtinen, R-Fla., a leader of the anti-Fidel Castro bloc in Congress who represented many Cuban-Americans in Miami, called the proposal an effort to "support state-sponsored terrorism."

The Senate Appropriations Committee in 2007 approved a bipartisan amendment to a fiscal 2008 Agriculture appropriations bill (S 1859—S Rept 110-134) that would have authorized general licenses for travel to Cuba for the marketing and sale of agricultural and medical goods. A similar amendment had been included in Senate Agriculture appropriations bills for fiscal years 2004, 2005, 2006, and 2007, but the provisions had triggered veto threats and had never made it into law. The Senate's fiscal 2008 provision suffered the same fate.

The Senate Appropriations Committee included the provision in its fiscal 2009 Agriculture funding bill (S 3289—S Rept 110-426) as well, but this time its fortunes changed. It was one of the three Cuba-related provisions included in the Financial Services section of HR 1105, the fiscal 2009 omnibus spending bill enacted in 2009.

SANCTIONS BILL

Although most of the attention was on Iran, Cuba was one of the targets of legislation (S 1612—PL 110-96) enacted in 2007 to stiffen penalties on companies doing business with countries deemed a threat to U.S. national security. *(Iran sanctions, pp. 299, 326)*

North Korea Policy

Congress included in a war supplemental appropriations bill (HR 2642—PL 110-252) enacted in 2008 a provision allowing the president to waive certain sanctions against North Korea. The waiver would allow the United States to assist North Korea in dismantling a nuclear reactor.

Lawmakers also cleared in 2008 a bill (HR 5834—PL 110-346) to extend refugee and human rights programs in North Korea.

SANCTIONS WAIVER

A 1994 amendment (PL 103-236) to the Arms Export Control Act (PL 90-629) prohibited many U.S. dealings

RETHINKING NORTH KOREA

How the United States removed a spoke from the "Axis of Evil":

January 2002 In his State of the Union address, President George W. Bush grouped North Korea, Iran, and Iraq as an "axis of evil" that must not obtain weapons of mass destruction.

October 2002 North Korea admitted to a secret weapons program in violation of a 1994 agreement with the United States, Japan, and South Korea. Washington halted shipments of heavy oil to Pyongyang.

January 2003 North Korea withdrew from the Nuclear Nonproliferation Treaty, saying that it only intended to use nuclear technology for "peaceful purposes"; a few months later, it relaunched its nuclear enrichment program.

August 2003 The first of several six-party talks aimed at eliminating North Korea's nuclear program was held in Beijing, but round one failed to deliver a compromise.

February 2005 North Korea announced it had nuclear weapons and refused further disarmament negotiations. That September, it agreed to give up its weapons but then demanded the United States provide it with a nuclear reactor for civilian use.

October 2006 Pyongyang staged a successful nuclear test. In February 2007, it agreed to begin nuclear disarmament in exchange for fuel. The deal was finalized the following October.

October 2008 The State Department formally removed North Korea from its "state sponsors of terrorism" list, four months after Bush announced he would do so.

with state sponsors of terrorism that illegally developed nuclear arms. The provision was known as the Glenn Amendment for its sponsor, Sen. John Glenn, D-Ohio (1974–1999).

The Bush administration requested a waiver of the amendment as applied to North Korea, arguing that the restrictions hampered its efforts to dismantle the North Korean nuclear reactor at Yongbyon and dispose of its radioactive material. Administration officials and their allies on Capitol Hill said waiving the restrictions would allow the Energy Department to move ahead with purchasing and delivering the necessary equipment, and paying the salaries of North Koreans, to dismantle the reactor without benefiting the regime. Because of North Korea's October 2006 nuclear test, only a small State Department fund could be used at that time for these activities, and supporters of the waiver said it was insufficient. *(Background, North Korea policy, p. 295)*

The House on May 15, 2008, approved by voice vote a bill (HR 5916) giving President George W. Bush the waiver authority he sought. The House Foreign Affairs Committee had reported the bill (H Rept 110-626) May 12. The Senate, however, did not act on the bill.

Congress ultimately included the waiver authority in HR 2642, the fiscal 2008–2009 war supplemental that was signed into law on June 30, 2008.

REFUGEE PROGRAMS

Congress passed HR 5834 to reauthorize through fiscal 2012 several human rights and democracy programs in North Korea that were set to expire Sept. 30, 2008. The measure authorized $2 million each year for those programs. *(North Korea aid, Congress and the Nation Vol. XI, p. 300)*

The legislation also reauthorized humanitarian assistance to North Korean refugees at $20 million annually over the same period. It required reports listing State Department efforts to process North Koreans seeking asylum in the United States. Critics said the efforts had been inadequate. According to the bill's sponsor, Ileana Ros-Lehtinen, R-Fla., of 150,000 refugees the United States had settled since 2004, the United States had admitted fewer than fifty North Koreans.

The House passed HR 5834 (H Rept 110-628) by voice vote on May 15, 2008. The Senate passed an amended version by voice vote Sept. 22. The House accepted the Senate changes, clearing the bill by voice vote the next day. The bill was signed into law Oct. 7.

Iran Sanctions

Congress in 2007 cleared legislation (S 1612—PL 110-96) to stiffen penalties on companies doing business with countries deemed a threat to U.S. national security. S 1612 was aimed, in part, at punishing Iran for its nuclear program and its sponsorship of groups on the U.S. list of terrorist organizations. The measure's targets also included such states as Sudan, Cuba, and North Korea.

By making the penalty commensurate with the scope of a crime, S 1612 was meant to increase pressure on firms that viewed the relatively small fines in existing law as part of the cost of doing business. It increased the maximum penalty for civil violations from $50,000 to $250,000 or twice the amount of the transaction, whichever was greater. Criminal penalties were increased from $250,000 and ten years in jail to $1 million and up to twenty years' imprisonment.

BACKGROUND

The new law was an update of the 1977 International Emergency Economic Powers Act (PL 95-223), which authorized the president to impose economic sanctions against countries or groups that posed an "unusual and extraordinary threat." The president could regulate and prohibit foreign exchange transactions, bank payments, or credit transfers, and the importing or exporting of currency or securities.

The Treasury Department said that most companies met their sanctions obligations, steering clear of countries and groups designated as threats to the United States. If they did not comply, the Office of Foreign Assets was responsible for enforcing the sanctions.

Prior to the enactment of PL 110-96, a single illegal transaction had brought a fine of $50,000, regardless of the size of the transaction. The civil penalties had been increased to that $50,000 level under the 2006 reauthorization of the Patriot Act (HR 3199—PL 109-177). *(USA Patriot Act reauthorization, p. 222)*

LEGISLATIVE ACTION

The Senate passed S 1612 on June 26, 2007. The Senate Banking, Housing, and Urban Affairs Committee had reported the bill (S Rept 110-82) on June 13. The House Foreign Affairs Committee approved the bill Sept. 26 and the full House passed it by voice vote on Oct. 2. S 1612 was signed into law on Oct. 16.

The House had passed a tougher sanctions bill (HR 1400) by a vote of 397–16 on Sept. 25, but the Senate did not take up that measure. HR 1400, which was reported by the House Foreign Affairs Committee on Aug. 2 (H Rept 110-294, Part I), was aimed directly at Iran, and floor action on HR 1400 had been hastily scheduled to coincide with a visit to the United States by Iranian president Mahmoud Ahmadinejad. The bill eliminated the president's ability to waive sanctions enacted in 2006 (HR 6198—PL 109-293) and expanded the list of industries that could have been penalized. It would have banned all imports from Iran and expanded curbs on exports to that country.

HR 1400 also called on the president to declare Iran's Revolutionary Guard a terrorist group and authorized him to block the assets of any company that supported it. On Sept. 26—a day after the House passed HR 1400—the Senate adopted by a vote of 76–22 a nonbinding amendment, offered by Republican Jon Kyl of Arizona and Independent Joseph I. Lieberman of Connecticut, to the fiscal 2008 defense authorization bill that, among other things, urged the president to designate the Revolutionary Guard as a terrorist organization. The language was included in a nonbinding sense-of-Congress provision in the final version of the defense bill (HR 4986—PL 110-181).

Middle East Arms Sales

The George W. Bush administration's decision in 2007 to sell sophisticated weapons to Saudi Arabia alarmed many pro-Israel members of Congress. More than one hundred House members signed a resolution (H J Res 76) disapproving the sale, but there was no further action on the measure.

Congress did clear a bill (HR 7177—PL 110-429) authorizing increased aid to Israel and requiring the president to assess the effect of proposed arms sales on Israel.

The Saudi sale was part of a ten-year plan to sell reportedly up to $20 billion worth of weapons to Saudi Arabia and other Persian Gulf states, and to provide military assistance totaling $30 billion to Israel and $13 billion to Egypt. The State Department said the agreements were meant to send a strong signal of support for the security concerns of U.S. partners in the region. The threat posed by Iran was said to be one of the factors in the decision.

But pro-Israel and antiwar members of Congress argued that the weapons would reward Saudi Arabia, which they portrayed as a two-faced sponsor of global terrorism and violence in Iraq, and would do little to pacify threats like Iran. They vowed to use congressional power to stop the deal, but their chances of success were weakened by the fact that Israel chose not to oppose the deal.

Under the Arms Export Control Act of 1976 (PL 94-329), Congress could block major arms sales if both chambers passed a resolution of disapproval within thirty days of being notified of an impending sale. The measure would then require the president's signature, effectively meaning that Congress would need two-thirds of both the House and Senate to override a likely presidential veto.

Congress was formally notified on Jan. 14, 2008, of the first installment of the sale: an estimated $123 million in Joint Direct Attack Munitions, which enabled satellites to guide bombs precisely to targets. H J Res 76 was introduced the next day. The House Foreign Affairs Committee did not take action on the measure.

But Congress could still pass legislation affecting the sale up to the time the arms were delivered. Both the Senate and House later attempted to link the Saudi arms sales to its oil production. Resolutions introduced in both chambers (S J Res 32 and H J Res 87) in May 2008 would have prohibited the issuance of a letter of offer for various arms sales to the Saudis unless within thirty days of enactment they increased their oil production by one million barrels per day and maintained that level for ninety days. There was no further action on either resolution.

HR 7177 was passed by voice votes of the House on Sept. 27, 2008, and the Senate on Oct. 1, and was signed into law on Oct. 15. The bill, among other things, required the president to carry out ongoing assessments of the extent to which Israel possessed a qualitative military edge over military threats to it. The assessments were to be used in considering proposed arms sales to countries in the Middle East. HR 7177 also amended the Arms Export Control Act to require certification that a proposed arms sale would not adversely affect Israel's qualitative military edge.

The bill authorized an additional $150 million in aid to Israel to allow the United States and Israel to stay on track to meet the ten-year, $30 billion security agreement signed in August 2007. HR 7177 also stipulated that Israel could use $670.7 million in fiscal 2009 assistance to procure advanced weapons systems.

CHAPTER 5

Defense Policy

Defense Policy

War in Afghanistan. War in Iraq. War on terrorism. War—in all its forms—dominated the defense agenda during the two Congresses of President George W. Bush's second term. U.S. forces were in their fourth year of fighting wars when Bush was inaugurated for a second time, in their eighth year when he left.

The Iraq War was, of course, the focal point. With insurgents becoming increasingly violent, Iraq seemed at times to be teetering on the brink of civil war. As U.S. troops engaged the insurgents, war casualties spiraled up and public support for the conflict steadily declined. War opponents on Capitol Hill tried repeatedly to change administration policy and start bringing U.S. troops home. But with Republicans remaining loyal to the president's policy and Democrats divided, the president was able to pursue his war strategy pretty much as he wanted. In the end it would be Bush who would set the timing for the withdrawal of U.S. forces, not Congress.

Lawmakers, however, did exert influence on other war-related issues. Although unable to bring the troops home sooner, members worked together to try to make them safer. Billions of dollars were allocated for equipment and vehicles that would protect them from roadside bombs, the enemy's weapon of choice. Billions more were appropriated to make sure they had proper care when they sustained the devastating injuries so typical of the Iraq conflict.

The war's toll on the overall combat readiness of the armed forces was a major concern of Congress. Democratic attempts to make deployments contingent on troop readiness failed, but, as it became increasingly obvious that the war had worn out vast quantities of vehicles and equipment, members did make their repair and replacement a high priority.

By the end of the Bush administration, Congress had provided $854 billion for military operations in Iraq and Afghanistan. *(War costs, box, p. 387)*

Despite all the war costs, Congress still found plenty of money left to allocate for the military's next-generation programs for aircraft, ships, vehicles, and the like. Members impacted these programs with their funding increases or cuts, and occasional defiance of Pentagon plans to shut down a program.

Lawmakers challenged the administration policy on the treatment of enemy detainees—and won. When the Senate and House presented a united front on banning cruel and inhuman treatment of prisoners, the White House backed down and signed the ban into law. A majority of Congress did side with the president on what legal rights should be given to the detainees, after the Supreme Court threw out Bush's initial plan for trying them.

Democrats who wanted a change of direction in Iraq called for Secretary of Defense Donald H. Rumsfeld to step down, but it would take an angry electorate in the 2006 elections to bring that about. The day after the American people voted to return control to the Democrats in the 110th Congress, his departure was announced.

CHANGING NATURE OF WAR

The commander of U.S. forces in Iraq, Gen. David H. Petraeus, at an April 2007 news conference described the Iraq conflict as "the most complex and challenging I have ever seen."

It certainly was not what the Bush administration had anticipated. When Rumsfeld became defense secretary at the start of the Bush presidency, he had set out to transform

REFERENCES

Discussion of defense policy for the years 1945–1964 may be found in *Congress and the Nation Vol. I,* pp. 237–334; for the years 1965–1968, *Congress and the Nation Vol. II,* pp. 827–890; for the years 1969–1972, *Congress and the Nation Vol. III,* pp. 191–252; for the years 1973–1976, *Congress and the Nation Vol. IV,* pp. 153–197; for the years 1977–1980, *Congress and the Nation Vol. V,* pp. 125–176; for the years 1981–1984, *Congress and the Nation Vol. VI,* pp. 201–257; for the years 1985–1988, *Congress and the Nation Vol. VII,* pp. 273–340; for the years 1989–1992, *Congress and the Nation Vol. VIII,* pp. 335–412; for the years 1993–1996, *Congress and the Nation Vol. IX,* pp. 253–323; for the years 1997–2000, *Congress and the Nation Vol. X,* pp. 235–311; for the years 2001–2004, *Congress and the Nation Vol. XI,* pp. 303–366.

Outlays for National Defense

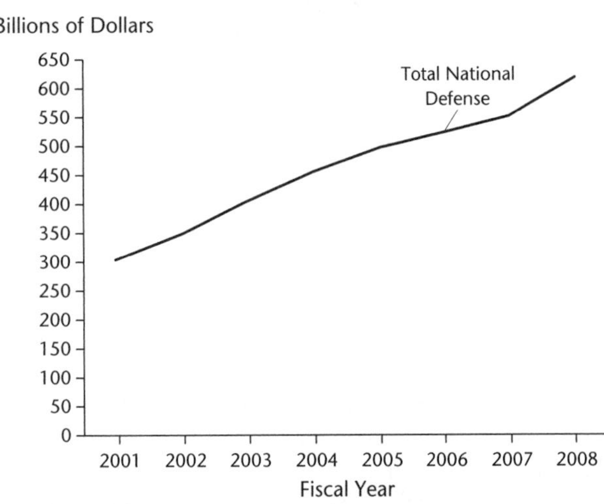

SOURCE: Office of Management and Budget, *Historical Tables, Budget of the United States Government: Fiscal Year 2010* (Washington, D.C.: U. S. Government Printing Office, 2009), Table 3.2.

NOTE: Most of the expenditures, approximately 95 percent, were for military activities of the Department of Defense. Atomic energy defense activities accounted for most of the remainder.

the ponderous U.S. Army of the cold war into a highly-mobile, high-technology ground force that could dominate any battlefield. The quick toppling of Iraqi leader Saddam Hussein and capture of Baghdad went according to plan—but what came after did not.

What had not been foreseen was a guerrilla war in the ancient streets of Baghdad. The asymmetric strategy used by insurgents allowed a relatively weak force to tie down a stronger one by exploiting its vulnerabilities rather than meeting it head-on in conventional combat. The insurgents blew up cars near checkpoints and crowds. They hid snipers in Baghdad's alleys. They detonated powerful improvised explosive devices (IEDs), or roadside bombs, which ripped through the lightweight vehicles in which troops were traveling.

U.S. troops also found themselves involved in stability operations, otherwise known as nation building. This was a major reversal not only for the military but also for the Bush administration and other Republicans who for years had reviled the idea that U.S. soldiers should do anything but fight wars. Nonetheless, it became a core part of the military's mission. In Iraq, service members found themselves doing jobs they were ill-prepared for: negotiating with local leaders, managing municipal governments, fixing sewers, defusing mobs, keeping the electricity on, and having to understand tribal and religious quarrels.

U.S. military leaders came to recognize in the Iraq experience that the nature of warfare itself was changing from conventional conflicts between nations to "small wars"—counterinsurgency, counterterrorism, religious and ethnic strife.

STAYING THE COURSE

It was a painful lesson to learn.

After the United States toppled Saddam in early 2003, the divisions among the country's three major ethnic and religious groups—the Shiites, Sunnis, and Kurds—became more pronounced. The minority Sunnis—the ruling party that had been ousted along with Saddam—took the fight to the streets. Members of al Qaeda—the terrorist network responsible for the Sept. 11, 2001, terrorist attacks on the United States—and other Islamic militants joined them. Sectarian violence between the Sunnis and Shiites escalated. It was soon a full-blown insurgency bordering on what many feared would become a civil war.

U.S. casualties escalated as well, as troops tried to quell the violence. President Bush urged the nation to "stay the course" in Iraq. GOP lawmakers exhorted war opponents not to "cut and run." But the news from Iraq made it difficult for the American people to stay loyal to the cause. Public opinion polls showed dramatic drops in support for the war. The depth of their opposition was shown in the 2006 midterm elections when they voted to return control of both houses of Congress to the Democrats for the first time since 1994.

Democratic proposals calling for a plan for withdrawal from Iraq went nowhere in the 109th Congress. Besides being the minority party, Democrats could not agree among themselves whether it was a good idea to set a firm deadline for withdrawal or not.

Their fortunes did not change in the next Congress, although they were now in control of both chambers. Just days after the 110th Congress convened, President Bush announced that he was sending additional troops to Iraq. Democrats found themselves powerless to stop what became known as "the surge" or, indeed, to alter the administration's strategy. After their proposals to set any kind of timetable for withdrawal failed, Democrats tried other tacks. One proposal would have barred the deployment of any troops who were not fully trained and equipped. Another would have required minimum intervals between deployments of U.S. troops. But Republicans saw such proposals as end-run attempts to limit deployments and managed to block them as well.

The situation on the ground gradually began to improve. Things were so much better by the summer of 2008 that the Bush administration was willing to accept in principle an Iraqi proposal for the withdrawal of U.S. combat troops by the end of 2011. President Bush signed the agreement in Baghdad in December 2008.

SUPPORTING THE TROOPS

The well-being of the men and women serving in Iraq and Afghanistan was one war-related issue that could bring members of both parties together. As the insurgency in Iraq took hold, U.S. casualties rose dramatically. By the end of 2004, 1,032 Americans had been killed in action and 10,421 had been wounded. By the end of 2008, 3,394 had

U.S. Joint Chiefs chairman Gen. Richard Myers, right, accompanied by Defense Secretary Donald H. Rumsfeld, center, and Gen. John Abizaid, commander of the U.S. Central Command, speak with reporters on Capitol Hill on May 18, 2005, after a closed-door meeting with members of Congress to discuss the situation in Iraq.
Source: AP Photo/Lauren Victoris Burke

been killed in combat and 30,940 had been wounded. More than half of U.S. casualties in Iraq were attributed to roadside bombs, and Congress pushed hard to do something about that.

Stories in the early years of the Iraq War of soldiers hammering scavenged steel plates to their thin-skinned vehicles—called "hillbilly armor"—outraged members and the American public alike. Congress added more than $1 billion to one war supplemental for additional equipment, with much of the increase targeted for force protection measures such as truck and body armor, "up-armored" Humvees, night-vision goggles, and electronic jammers to block detonation of remote-controlled roadside bombs. In another supplemental Congress provided almost nine times the amount requested to upgrade Abrams tanks and Bradley fighting vehicles—both first used in the 1980s but now proving helpful in Iraq's urban warfare—and doubled what was requested for upgraded Humvees. Congress added to another war measure upwards of $1 billion more than requested for new Mine Resistant Ambush Protected vehicles.

Members also wanted to make sure that the troops and their families had adequate pay and benefits. The 109th Congress approved the president's requests for military pay raises each year, but the next Congress added half a percentage point to the proposed pay hike in both years. Lawmakers authorized death payment increases, life insurance coverage, and higher hardship duty pay. They protected military personnel from high-interest loans. Against the wishes of the White House, they expanded government-subsidized access to Tricare, the military health care system, to cover almost all reservists. Members repeatedly blocked Bush's proposed increases in enrollment fees, deductibles, and pharmacy copayments for Tricare participants.

Congress made health care for wounded service members returning from Iraq and Afghanistan a top priority after a shocking February 2007 *Washington Post* article highlighted problems of neglect at Walter Reed, the Army's premier medical facility in Washington, D.C. The newspaper revealed that soldiers were receiving substandard care, recovering patients were being put up in deteriorating housing, and service members were having months-long waits for care. Problems throughout the military health-care system and in the Department of Veterans Affairs (VA) medical system subsequently came to light as well. The VA was faulted especially for providing inadequate screenings and care for patients with head wounds, which had become a signature injury in the Iraq and Afghanistan wars.

The stories sparked a public outcry and led to the resignations of Walter Reed's commanding general, the Army's chief medical officer, and the secretary of the Army. Some Democratic lawmakers said the problems at Walter Reed were another example of the administration's lack of prewar planning.

A very angry Congress enacted what was known as the Wounded Warrior Act. The measure called for helping patients and their families navigate the military's medical bureaucracy—a typically daunting experience—by establishing a single point of contact for them. The law required the Pentagon and the VA to work together to develop a comprehensive policy on patient care, management, and transition from the Defense Department's medical system to the VA's. This was to include setting up an interoperable electronic health records system. Semiannual inspections of housing facilities for recovering service members were mandated. The new law also called for a comprehensive policy to address the kinds of injuries increasingly seen in patients, including traumatic brain injury, post-traumatic stress disorder, other mental health conditions, and military eye injuries. It required the creation of centers to focus on the prevention, diagnosis, treatment, and rehabilitation of those conditions.

EQUIPPING THE MILITARY

The erosion of U.S. military preparedness was a major concern on Capitol Hill.

After years of war in Afghanistan and Iraq, many experts worried that the United States would have difficulty responding quickly and effectively to the next crisis abroad or at home.

Army generals indicated in 2006 that two-thirds of their forty-two active brigades were unready to perform their missions because of personnel and equipment shortages. They also said that about 85 percent of the Army's twenty-eight reserve units were unready as well. A report on the issue in September 2006 by Democrats on the House Appropriations Committee said the biggest cause of readiness problems was a shortage of tanks, armored personnel carriers, and trucks, many of which had been worn down, destroyed, or left behind in Iraq. Such equipment shortages were said to have affected training as well.

Critics noted that the declining readiness ratings did not mean that the United States might lose a war—military units preparing to deploy would be outfitted with gear and staffed with enough people to perform their missions. But such quick, last-minute preparations would take time and money.

Lawmakers allocated billions of dollars for "reset" costs to repair, refurbish, or replace equipment damaged or destroyed in the fighting. In a fiscal 2007 funding bill, they appropriated nearly $23 billion for Army and Marine reset costs after the services made urgent requests to Congress for more money to recover from equipment losses. Conferees on the bill noted that the funds had not been formally requested and urged the Defense Department to include reset needs in its future budget requests.

Despite such rising war-related costs, the Pentagon's budgets for research, development, and procurement were not neglected. Lawmakers generously funded the military's next-generation programs.

The costs of those programs were steadily rising. In 2001, the Pentagon made a list of its eighty-five top weapons and estimated that it would cost $790 billion to buy all of them over the expected life that their procurement contracts would run. Some had been in production for years; others were only just being ordered. In 2005, when the Pentagon drew up a comparable list, it found that the eventual total cost had nearly doubled, to $1.5 trillion.

Among the big-ticket items in the pipeline was the F-35 Joint Strike Fighter, which was being built for the Air Force, Navy, and Marine Corps, as well as international customers. Estimated at as much as $300 billion, the program was said to be the costliest in Pentagon history. Adding to the bottom line was Congress's insistence that a second, alternative engine be developed, despite objections from the White House. Members argued that the competition and redundancy would prove cost-effective in the long run and pointed to studies that showed similar second-engine programs for the F-15 and F-16 warplanes had improved performance and production costs for those fighters, which had been Air Force workhorses since the 1970s. The debate was no small matter, for both fiscal policy and military readiness. A modern jet warplane was essentially a collection of weaponry, wings, and a cockpit strapped to an engine. If the engine did not function properly, there would be no warplane to fly.

Cost estimates for another major program—the Army's Future Combat Systems—ran as high as $200 billion. The program called for reorganizing the Army into smaller units that would be equipped with a whole family of ultramodern vehicles, aircraft, robots, weapons, radios, and computers, which were being designed and purchased as one big project. The program had become so costly and complicated that even some of its supporters began questioning its viability.

There were several reasons for the significant jump in weapons costs. In general, the new weapons were more complicated than their predecessors and were designed to meet higher goals. More of them had to work together in communications networks and tactical frameworks. At one time, for example, a tank was just a tank. But a modern tank might be part of a larger weapons system that included other vehicles, support equipment, and data networks. Making those complex systems work under battlefield conditions increased development time and costs.

Another factor driving up the price tag was the Defense Department's effort to reduce the number of people required to operate its ships, tanks, and planes. Developing automated systems to replace people was costly. Also adding to the bottom line were programs that were pushed into development before their basic technologies were ready to be incorporated. Problems could be encountered and the required resources could be understated.

But tightening the reins on defense spending was not easy. Members regularly resisted Pentagon efforts to cut weapons systems, at least in part out of parochial interest and political imperative. Defense contractors deliberately spread the work on major weapons systems across several states and districts, knowing that lawmakers could be counted on to block the termination of programs that would cost their constituents jobs.

The C-17 transport plane provided a good example. The Pentagon in 2006 requested what supposedly were the last C-17 planes it would need and asked Congress for funds to shut down the C-17 production line. But members insisted that the Air Force needed a larger strategic airlift force and instead continued to allocate money to purchase more planes. To critics, the C-17 earmarks symbolized the directed spending that was consuming an ever-larger share of the annual defense budget as lawmakers looked out for home-state industries and jobs.

The C-17s were built by some 700 contractors in forty-two states, chiefly in California, Missouri, Georgia, and Arizona.

Parochial interests, however, were not always enough to save a program. The Future Combat Systems program was said to have 479 contractors in 195 congressional districts and thirty-six states. Nonetheless, members started to raise concerns over the program's escalating costs, slipping deadlines, and heavy investment in technologies before they were sufficiently proven. The program would in fact be restructured by the next administration.

TREATMENT OF DETAINEES

Debate over how the United States treated its enemy detainees continued to roil Washington. Detainee abuse scandals at Guantánamo Bay, Cuba, and Abu Ghraib prison outside of Baghdad had shocked the American people, embarrassed the military, and damaged U.S. prestige abroad. The secretary of defense had been directed to develop a new policy on the humane treatment of detainees, but the issue was far from resolved.

The Bush administration remained adamant that the Geneva Convention, the international treaty governing the treatment of prisoners of war, did not apply to those now being detained—nonuniformed foreign fighters who committed acts of terrorism. The president threatened to veto any legislation that attempted to say otherwise.

Increasing numbers on Capitol Hill disagreed. Leading the way on the issue was Sen. John McCain, R-Ariz., who had been held and tortured by the North Vietnamese for five-and-a-half years during the Vietnam War. McCain and his key Senate supporters argued that it was important to hold the high moral ground and that if the United States did attempt to redefine the Geneva Convention, such a move could give other countries an excuse to mistreat U.S. troops who might be taken prisoner in future wars.

President Bush backed away from his veto threat when the House sided with the Senate on banning "cruel, inhuman or degrading treatment" of detainees in U.S. custody. The language enacted also required Defense Department interrogators to follow standards set in an Army field manual that complied with the Geneva Convention.

A majority in Congress did give the president the authority he asked for to use military tribunals to try unlawful enemy combatants and to deny detainees the right to bring *habeas corpus* petitions in federal court to challenge the legality of their detention. The Supreme Court subsequently declared the denial of *habeas corpus* to be unconstitutional, as it had in previous cases.

NEW LEADERSHIP

Presiding over the wars and the expanding defense budgets in President Bush's second term were two very different Pentagon chiefs—first, Rumsfeld and then, Robert M. Gates.

As a holdover from Bush's first term, Rumsfeld would become the second longest serving member of Bush's Cabinet, surpassed only by Bush's secretary of labor Elaine Chao. After the Sept. 11 attacks, Rumsfeld was held in high esteem. The alarms that he and other so-called neoconservatives had been sounding for years about the gravity of the terrorist threat had been proven correct, and Americans saw in him a decisive, smart leader.

In those early years, his popularity soared. The nation tuned in to his almost daily Pentagon news briefings to watch him toss back reporters' questions with wit and bravado. But his standing with the American people would parallel the troubled war in Iraq—as it became deeply unpopular, so did he.

He had an especially rancorous relationship with Democrats on Capitol Hill. His popularity was not improved any by an August 2006 speech in which he compared critics of the war effort to those who sought to appease Adolf Hitler before the outbreak of World War II. Democrats were infuriated. Several weeks later top House Democratic appropriators introduced a sharply worded resolution calling for Rumsfeld's immediate resignation for the "good of the country." On the Senate side, Democrats attempted to attach to a defense funding bill language calling for a "change of course" in Iraq, including Rumsfeld's replacement. A vote on the resolution was blocked by a point of order, but not until the Senate had spent more than four hours arguing over the administration's conduct of the Iraq War and Rumsfeld's job performance.

The American people would deliver the final verdict. When the voters in the 2006 midterm elections turned over control of the next Congress to the Democrats, opposition to the war in Iraq was widely believed to have been the key factor. As the most public face on the war—besides, of course, President Bush and Vice President Richard Cheney—Rumsfeld had to go. The day after the election President Bush announced Rumsfeld's decision to resign.

It was obviously not a spur-of-the moment decision, since the president announced at the same time his nomination of Gates to succeed Rumsfeld. Gates, a former director of the CIA, had none of Rumsfeld's divisiveness. At his Senate confirmation hearing, members were appreciative of his openness and willingness to consider positions at odds with ones long espoused by the Bush administration. Carl Levin, D-Mich., the incoming chair of the Senate Armed Services Committee, described Gates's testimony as "a welcome breath of honest and candid realism about the situation in Iraq that's been missing, I'm afraid, up to now, from the administration."

During the remaining two years of the Bush administration, Gates earned a reputation as a practical executive with a steady hand on the helm. The decision of President-elect Barack Obama to ask Gates to stay on at the Pentagon was testimony to the secretary's sharp skills and winning political ways.

Chronology of Action on Defense Policy

2005–2006

The war in Iraq was the overriding issue in defense debates in the 109th Congress. As the insurgency escalated and the support of the American people declined, members of Congress grappled with what they should—or could—do about the war.

Democratic lawmakers were clear about one thing—they did not want to stay the course in Iraq as the White House and Republican members of Congress urged. But all of their attempts to change that course by legislating a withdrawal timetable were rejected. Members of both parties did find common ground in what was regarded as the most powerful statement of congressional oversight since the war began in 2003. A provision in the 2006 defense authorization bill included a list of military, political, and economic benchmarks for the Iraqi government and a requirement that President George W. Bush report to Congress on Iraq's progress in meeting them. It also declared the sense of Congress that 2006 would be a "period of significant transition" when Iraqi forces should take the lead on their security.

The 109th Congress made another powerful statement when it took on the issue of how the United States should treat the prisoners it captured in Iraq, in Afghanistan, and in the broader war on terror. The Bush White House insisted that the detainees were "unlawful enemy combatants" who were not entitled to protections under the Geneva Convention. But the Senate defied the president's veto threats and went along with Republican senator John McCain of Arizona—a prisoner of war himself during the Vietnam War—in writing legislation that banned "cruel, inhuman or degrading treatment" of enemy detainees in U.S. custody. When the House sided with the Senate, President Bush gave in and agreed to the language.

Congress also included in the bill limited legal rights for detainees but, despite Supreme Court rulings to the contrary, denied them the right to petition in federal court for *habeas corpus*—that is, to challenge the legality of their detention. And the following year, in response to another Supreme Court decision, Congress approved legislation authorizing military tribunals to try detainees being held at Guantánamo Bay, Cuba. The Court had ruled that an earlier process the Bush administration had set up violated domestic and international law, hence the need for new legislation.

The well-being of U.S. troops was a top priority for members of Congress. Lawmakers increased funding for equipment to protect soldiers from the roadside bomb blasts that were killing and maiming so many of them. They approved pay raises, increased benefits, and recruitment bonuses, and gave reservists some access to the military's health-care system.

Billions of dollars were allocated to the task of repairing, upgrading, or replacing equipment damaged or destroyed in the wars in Iraq and Afghanistan. But Congress still found plenty of money to fund the next-generation programs of the armed forces, although it did shift some funds from futuristic programs to more immediate needs.

The 109th Congress went through another round of military base realignments and closings. The 2005 process called for twenty-two closures (one later was given a reprieve) and thirty-three major realignments. The changes were estimated to save more than $35 billion over twenty years, but that did not make it any less painful for those members whose home districts and states were affected.

Fiscal 2006 Defense Authorization

Congress in 2005 cleared a $491.5 billion fiscal 2006 defense authorization bill (HR 1815—PL 109-163). That total included $441.5 billion for Pentagon programs and for nuclear weapons programs under the Energy Department—about $290 million less than President George W. Bush had requested. In addition, the bill authorized $50 billion in emergency funds for military operations in Iraq and Afghanistan as a "bridge" until the president sent Congress another supplemental request for the wars in early 2006.

Final action on the bill came after more than six months of often rancorous debate in both chambers. As late as mid-December 2005, the White House still was threatening to veto the measure because of a provision that prohibited "cruel, inhuman or degrading treatment" of enemy detainees in U.S. custody. Under the provision, military interrogators would be required to follow standards set in an Army field manual that complied with the Geneva Convention. The administration argued that it would tie the president's hands in the war on terror. But in the end Bush relented on the language—which had been pushed steadfastly by Sen. John McCain, R-Ariz., a prisoner of war for five years during the Vietnam War—and the bill was wrapped up quickly.

In addition to the detainee abuse provision, the bill barred detainees held at the U.S. military prison at Guantánamo Bay, Cuba, from suing for *habeas corpus*, though they gained a limited right to appeal their detention.

Lawmakers also used the annual authorization bill to assert Congress's role in overseeing the war in Iraq. HR 1815 required the president to submit quarterly reports on progress in the Iraq war and on economic, political, and military benchmarks leading to a U.S. troops drawdown. The measure called for 2006 to be a "significant period of transition" in which Iraqi forces would take over security responsibility from U.S. troops. Senate passage of the Iraq amendment had been seen as a milestone in the political debate over Iraq, a subtle but clear statement that Congress would not sit by silently as the public turned against the war.

HR 1815 took care of the troops fighting in Iraq and elsewhere. It increased their pay for the seventh year in a row, by a requested 3.1 percent, and added other special payments and recruitment bonuses. It also gave reservists some access to the military's Tricare health care system.

The recruiting inducements were considered vital to meeting the goals established in the new law for the number of people in uniform. The Army was allowed, but not required, to add another 10,000 active-duty personnel and the Marine Corps could increase by 1,000.

While Congress authorized most of what Bush wanted for weapons, it made efforts to control costs and included provisions to rein in spending and check reported mismanagement in the Pentagon. The prices of several new ships—the DD(X) destroyer, the Virginia-class submarine, and the Littoral Combat Ship—were capped. The Army was required to justify more fully to Congress its plans for the Future Combat Systems program, the Army's next generation of combat vehicles and weapons systems, before it could spend all the money appropriated for the program. The Pentagon was required to provide a comprehensive report on its plans to revamp its financial management systems before it could conduct any more financial audits.

Congress gave the president what he requested for ballistic-missile defense programs.

HOUSE COMMITTEE ACTION

The House Armed Services Committee reported HR 1815 (H Rept 109-89) on May 20, 2005.

The committee agreed to give the Pentagon much of what it wanted in the way of spending. The bill authorized a total of $490.6 billion—$441.6 billion in regular defense spending and another $49.1 billion in emergency supplemental spending for the wars in Iraq and Afghanistan.

But the bill also set guidelines on how the money should be used. Republicans included language in the committee report aimed at improving oversight of the military's accounting for big-ticket items. Beginning in fiscal 2006, the Pentagon would be required to evaluate and monitor changes to its initial cost estimates for major defense acquisition programs, and to provide Congress and the defense secretary with alternatives if a program exceeded its original baseline cost by 15 percent or more. The committee said programs were allowed to get too far along before problems were acknowledged. "This committee strongly believes that Congress should be given alternatives to the traditional approach of either funding or terminating a program with significant costs overruns," the panel added.

The committee bill cut the president's $3.4 billion request for the Future Combat Systems program by $499 million. But it included Bush's requests for $3.7 billion for procurement of the F-22A Raptor, the Air Force's controversial fighter intended to replace the F-15, and $4.9 billion for development of the Joint Strike Fighter, a next-generation multi-role fighter aircraft for all services based on a common airframe.

The bill added $2.1 billion to Bush's $8.7 billion for shipbuilding and increased the number of ships to be purchased from the four requested to seven. The committee also called for a major restructuring of the Navy's shipbuilding program. The committee proposed a $1.7 billion per ship limit on future procurement costs for the DD(X) destroyer, a move that would have effectively killed the program, given that the Navy expected to spend nearly twice that amount on the first ship. It zeroed out the money requested for advance procurement and cut funding for continued research and development. The committee said the cost of the ships had escalated to the point that it would be difficult, if not impossible, to fund construction of the existing ship design in quantities needed to meet force requirements. It recommended that the Navy establish a program that would result in an affordable next-generation destroyer with capabilities equal to or greater than the existing *Arleigh Burke*-class guided missile destroyer. The bill also required the Navy to maintain no fewer than eleven aircraft carriers.

Bush had requested $4 million for an Energy Department study of the Robust Nuclear Earth Penetrator, also known as the bunker buster, but the House bill gave the research money to the Pentagon instead. The committee said the study of the weapon, which was designed to burrow deep in the ground to strike hidden targets, would evaluate both conventional and nuclear penetrator options. Although the administration insisted it only wanted research funds, Democrats had expressed fears that the

DEFENSE LEADERSHIP

Secretary of Defense

Donald H. Rumsfeld

As President George W. Bush made plans for his second-term Cabinet, some called for him to replace Donald H. Rumsfeld as secretary of defense. But Rumsfeld continued to have Bush's support and confidence, and was asked to stay on. *(First term nomination, Congress and the Nation Vol. XI, box p. 313)*

Much would change in the next two years. Rumsfeld was a primary architect of the Iraq War, and as U.S. casualties in Iraq mounted and more people questioned U.S. military strategy, Rumsfeld became a lightning rod for criticism of the conflict.

That he was unpopular among Democrats was no surprise. Democratic lawmakers called for a change of course in Iraq, including a new secretary of defense. Rumsfeld did not improve his popularity among Democrats on Capitol Hill when in an August 2006 speech he compared critics of the war effort to those who sought to appease Adolf Hitler before the outbreak of World War II.

But it was not just the Democrats who were criticizing Rumsfeld. Earlier in 2006 at least half a dozen war generals under Bush had called for Rumsfeld to step down, citing incompetence and a stubborn unwillingness to heed the military's advice. They had retired by the time they began to publicly criticize their one-time boss.

Even in his own party, there were signs of waning support. Although the embattled secretary managed to escape a "no confidence" vote during a combative Senate debate in September 2006, Republicans seemed to offer only tepid support for him, focusing instead on the need to win the war in Iraq.

Rumsfeld was a quick casualty of the Democratic wins in the November 2006 congressional elections, which most attributed to antiwar sentiment. The day after the election Bush accepted Rumsfeld's resignation. Rumsfeld, one of the longest serving members of Bush's Cabinet, agreed to stay on until his successor was in place.

Robert M. Gates

At the same time he announced that Rumsfeld was stepping down, President Bush named Robert M. Gates as his choice to head the Defense Department.

At the time of his nomination, Gates was president of Texas A&M University and also a member of the Iraq Study Group, an independent bipartisan panel Congress created to offer new ideas on Iraq. *(Iraq Study Group, box p. 274)*

Gates had served as CIA director from 1991–1993 for Bush's father, President George H. W. Bush, and had worked at the CIA for twenty-five years before that. His first nomination to serve as director of the CIA, in 1987, had been derailed because of outrage in Congress over the Iran-contra scandal, which had tainted Gates. The scandal was a complicated one involving secret U.S. arms sales to Iran and the diversion of some of the profits to U.S.-backed "contra" rebels in Nicaragua. Investigators strongly believed Gates had been "less than candid" about his level of involvement, and the controversy over his role caused Gates to ask that the nomination be withdrawn. He stayed on as deputy director of the CIA, and by the time he was next nominated to head the agency, in 1991, the Iran-contra scandal was not as much of an issue. *(Congress and the Nation Vol. VII, p. 253, p. 1050)*

---

program could trigger a new nuclear arms race or lower the threshold for use of a nuclear weapon.

The panel made cuts in two space programs, providing $436 million instead of the $836 million sought for the Transformational Satellite Communications System (TSAT) and $100 million instead of $226 million for the Space Radar program. Air Force officials had presented both programs as essential to future war fighting, but the committee expressed concerns that the programs were in danger of falling behind schedule and promising more than they could offer.

The bill authorized an increase of 10,000 Army and 1,000 Marine active-duty personnel in fiscal 2006 to support the missions in Iraq and Afghanistan. It also included a 3.1 percent pay increase and a permanent increase from $12,420 to $100,000 in the death gratuity paid to families of service members killed in the line of duty. Over the objections of Personnel Subcommittee Chair John M. McHugh, R-N.Y., the nearly evenly divided full committee adopted a Gene Taylor, D-Miss., amendment to authorize $180 million for one year to extend the military's Tricare health care coverage to reservists who were not deployed. Under existing law, reservists had access to Tricare only when they were called to active duty. McHugh said that "we simply can't afford it" because of its estimated price tag of $3.8 billion over five years.

The committee stirred up another controversy when it adopted a McHugh amendment to put into law an eleven-year-old Pentagon policy restricting women from serving in direct ground combat or in units that had to accompany others into battle. McHugh's subcommittee had approved more restrictive language barring women from joining specific combat-support units in the Army. Duncan Hunter, R-Calif., chair of the full Armed Services Committee,

During his tenure at the CIA, some critics accused him of being loyal to administration policy to a fault. But during the Dec. 5, 2006, hearing on his nomination to be secretary of defense, Gates stressed that he would be an independent voice and quickly demonstrated the point by telling senators that the United States was not winning the war in Iraq even if U.S. troops were winning the battles they fought. He also questioned several of the Bush administration's critical decisions during the conflict and said he was open to all options for a change in strategy.

Although he opposed setting a timetable for withdrawing U.S. troops, he indicated at his hearing that a Democratic proposal to begin withdrawal in the coming months would be considered. Gates said that he wanted to talk to the military commanders before making decisions on Iraq strategy, but he made it clear he was committed to changing the course somehow, saying that was why the president had nominated him.

Following the day-long hearing, the Armed Services Committee approved the nomination 24–0. The full Senate voted to confirm Gates by a 95–2 vote on Dec. 6 and he was sworn in as secretary of defense on Dec. 18.

On Dec. 1, 2008, Democratic President-elect Barack Obama announced that Gates would continue as defense secretary in his administration.

Joint Chiefs Chairman

Gen. Peter Pace

Marine Corps Gen. Peter Pace was nominated to succeed Air Force Gen. Richard B. Myers as chairman of the Joint Chiefs of Staff, the most senior job in the armed services and the military adviser to the president. Pace was confirmed by voice vote of the Senate on July 15, 2005, and was sworn in on Sept. 30, the day of Myers's retirement. He was the first Marine to hold the post.

Pace had been serving as vice chairman of the Joint Chiefs of Staff under Myers since Oct. 1, 2001. He previously had been chief of the U.S. Southern Command, which had responsibility for Latin America. He had fought in Vietnam and Somalia.

Pace was not renominated to a second two-year term in 2007. As vice chairman and then chairman of the Joint Chiefs since just weeks after the Sept. 11, 2001, terrorist attacks, Pace had become closely identified with the wars in Iraq and Afghanistan and with the policies of former defense secretary Rumsfeld. Gates, Rumsfeld's successor, asked the president to replace Pace rather than risk a contentious and possibly unsuccessful Senate confirmation battle over a second term for Pace. Gates said that he had talked with both GOP and Democratic lawmakers before making his decision.

Adm. Michael G. Mullen

President Bush nominated Adm. Michael G. Mullen to succeed Pace. Mullen was confirmed by voice vote of the Senate on Aug. 3, 2007, and was sworn in on Oct. 1.

At the time of his nomination, Mullen was serving as the chief of naval operations and, as such, was one of the Joint Chiefs. During his career, Mullen had commanded three ships, an aircraft carrier battle group, and the U.S. Second Fleet. He had also served as commander of the NATO Joint Force Command Naples and of all U.S. naval forces in Europe, and as vice chief of naval operations.

---

backed the tougher language, but House Democrats and Army officials strongly opposed it. Democrats opposed even McHugh's watered-down proposal, which they said could result in unnecessary restrictions at a time when recruiting and retention in the military were suffering.

Attempts by Jeb Bradley, R-N.H., to halt or delay the 2005 Base Realignment and Closure (BRAC) round were rejected. *(Military base closings, p. 369)*

HOUSE FLOOR ACTION

The House passed HR 1815 by a vote of 390–39 on May 25.

During floor debate, the House adopted 428–1 a manager's amendment from Hunter that sidestepped the controversial provision added in committee on the role of women in combat. The substitute language called on the Pentagon to review the matter and give Congress at least sixty legislative days' advance notice if it planned to open or close any jobs to women.

The full House also dealt with the Tricare issue. Although the Armed Services Committee had approved Taylor's amendment to extend Tricare coverage to all reservists, Hunter subsequently removed it from the bill on the grounds that its cost would push the bill over its allocation for mandatory spending. The Congressional Budget Office (CBO) estimated the provision would cost the Pentagon $4.6 billion through 2010, assuming that many federal employees who were also reservists would abandon their health care plans and flock to Tricare because of its lower premiums. Taylor insisted that he could change his amendment to bar federal employees from signing up for Tricare, but with stiff opposition from Hunter, Taylor's motion to return the bill to committee to have his amendment restored was rejected 211–218.

SECRET CIA PRISONS OVERSEAS

In late 2005 the *Washington Post* revealed that the CIA was detaining suspected terrorists in secret prisons overseas. It would be nearly a year before President George W. Bush confirmed their existence.

The news story triggered strong reactions on Capitol Hill. Angry Republican leaders called for an investigation to find those responsible for leaking the information to the press. Many members wanted more information from the administration on the CIA program and attempted to use the fiscal 2006 defense authorization bill (HR 1815—PL 109-163) to press their demands.

The Nov. 2, 2005, article said that for nearly four years the CIA had been operating a covert prison system with sites at various times in eight countries—Thailand, Afghanistan, and several democracies in Eastern Europe—as well as a small center at the U.S. military's Guantánamo Bay prison in Cuba. According to the article, the CIA had used the secret facilities—known as "black sites"—to hide and interrogate some of its most important prisoners linked to al Qaeda, the terrorist network responsible for the Sept. 11, 2001, attacks on the United States. The story said the prisons had been built with appropriated funds, but that no members of Congress had been briefed on the program other than the chairs and top-ranking minority members of the House and Senate Intelligence committees.

Dana Priest, the *Post* reporter who wrote the article, attributed her information to unnamed "U.S. and foreign officials familiar with the arrangement," to "current and former intelligence officials and diplomats from three continents," and to "several former and current intelligence officials and other U.S. government officials." She said she was not revealing the location of the sites in Eastern Europe "at the request of senior U.S. officials." (Priest would win a Pulitzer Prize in 2006 for her reporting for this article and others on the government's counterterrorism campaign.)

Senate Majority Leader Bill Frist, R-Tenn., and House Speaker J. Dennis Hastert, R-Ill., called for an investigation by the House and Senate Intelligence committees of the leak, which they characterized as a "dangerous trend." In their letter to the Intelligence panels, the GOP leaders wrote: "The unauthorized release of classified information is serious and threatens our nation's security."

Democratic leaders were skeptical of the value of such an investigation. The Republican leaders' request had come after a drumbeat of Democratic criticism of the Bush administration for the disclosure of the identity of a CIA operative—Valerie Plame—and of congressional committees for their refusal to investigate that incident. Democrats had been doing all they could to draw attention to the Oct. 28 indictment of I. Lewis "Scooter" Libby, Vice President Dick Cheney's former chief of staff, on charges of obstruction of justice, perjury, and making false statements regarding the leak of Plame's connection with the CIA. *(Plame case, p. 855)*

House Minority Leader Nancy Pelosi, D-Calif., said any investigation of the information in the *Post* story should be broad in scope and include "the possible manipulation of prewar intelligence on Iraq, and the disclosure for political purposes of classified information involving the identity of the CIA officer."

However, after it was reported that the CIA had referred the matter to the Justice Department, the bipartisan leadership of the Senate Intelligence panel indicated that they would not attempt to compete with a Justice Department probe of the leak.

In the meantime, a number of members wanted more information on the CIA prisons. During action on its fiscal 2006 authorization, the Senate voted 82–9 on Nov. 10 to approve a John Kerry, D-Mass., amendment that required the director of national intelligence (DNI) to provide a classified report on the prisons to the House and Senate Intelligence committees within sixty days of the bill's enactment. On Dec. 16 the House adopted 228–187 a nonbinding motion to instruct the defense authorization conferees to accept the Senate-passed provision.

But one day after the overwhelming House vote, conferees finished work on a final version of HR 1815 that did not include the CIA reporting provision. Rep. Duncan Hunter, R-Calif., chair of the House Armed Services Committee, confirmed that the provision had been stripped from the bill, saying, "That's a classified portion that is within the jurisdiction of the Intelligence Committee."

The Intelligence committees did take up the issue of classified leaks during consideration of their respective fiscal 2007 intelligence authorization bills. Several provisions aimed at punishing those who leaked classified material were added to the legislation. Sentiments on the issue had been further inflamed in December 2005 when the *New York Times* reported that the administration had ordered a secret program to conduct warrantless wiretaps of Americans to gain information about terrorism. The Senate version of the intelligence authorization (S 3237) also would have required the DNI to report to the Intelligence committees on the clandestine prison program, but the bill never reached the floor, and no intelligence authorization was enacted in 2006. *(2007 intelligence authorization, p. 292; warrantless surveillance, p. 252)*

President Bush acknowledged the existence of the CIA prison program on Sept. 6, 2006, and said that the fourteen men being held in those prisons at that time—including Khalid Sheikh Mohammed, thought to be the key architect of the Sept. 11 attacks—were being transferred to the military's detention facility at Guantánamo Bay. Although their transfer meant there was no one left in the CIA-run prisons, Bush retained the option of using the program in the future.

Lawmakers adopted by voice vote a proposal by Donald Manzullo, R-Ill., to prohibit the secretary of defense from waiving a so-called Buy American provision requiring that at least 50 percent of the cost of a military purchase consist of U.S.-built components.

The House rejected 128–300 an amendment by Lynn Woolsey, D-Calif., to express the sense of Congress that the president should develop a plan for withdrawing U.S. military forces from Iraq.

Members also rejected a Bradley amendment to postpone the 2005 BRAC round by a vote of 112–316 and a Susan A. Davis, D-Calif., amendment to allow military personnel and their dependents overseas to use their own funds to obtain abortion services in overseas military hospitals by a vote of 194–233.

SENATE COMMITTEE ACTION

The Senate Armed Services Committee reported its version of the fiscal 2006 defense authorization bill (S 1042—S Rept 109-69) on May 17. The Senate bill authorized $491.6 billion—$441.6 billion in regular defense spending and $50 billion in emergency supplemental war funds.

Unlike the House version, S 1042 included Bush's $3.4 billion request for the Future Combat Systems. It gave the president the requested amounts for the F-22A Raptor and Joint Strike Fighter programs as well, as the House bill had.

The panel approved $9.1 billion for Navy shipbuilding, not as much as in the House version but still $355 million above Bush's request. This area was a priority for Chair John W. Warner, R-Va., a former Navy secretary whose state had one of the country's largest shipbuilding facilities. Warner's committee did not propose a major restructuring of shipbuilding programs as the House bill did nor did it cut funds for the DD(X) destroyer program as the House had. On the contrary, it increased funds and required that the Navy maintain two shipyards to build the destroyers. The Navy had wanted to hold a winner-take-all competition pitting General Dynamics' Bath Iron Works in Maine against Northrop Grumman Ship Systems' Ingalls Operations in Pascagoula, Miss. The Navy said it could save as much as $3 billion, but lawmakers from shipbuilding states banded together to prevent what they said could result in the closing of one of the shipyards.

S 1042 also directed the Navy to retain twelve aircraft carriers until 180 days after completion of the Quadrennial Defense Review in early 2006 and to take steps to extend the life of the carrier USS *John F. Kennedy*, which the Navy had planned to mothball.

The Senate panel approved Bush's $4 million request for the Energy Department to continue studying the nuclear bunker buster.

The committee cut funding for space programs but not as deeply as the House bill had. It authorized $636 million for the Transformational Satellite and $151 million for the Space Radar programs.

S 1042 authorized an increase of 20,000 in Army troop levels but made no mention of an increase in Marines. The bill approved the same increases in pay and death gratuity payments that were in HR 1815.

SENATE FLOOR ACTION

The Senate passed S 1042 by a vote of 98–0 on Nov. 15 and then inserted the text into HR 1815 and passed that bill by voice vote.

Before passing the bill, the Senate adopted a series of amendments aimed at forcefully asserting Congress's role in overseeing the war in Iraq and the treatment of enemy detainees in U.S.-run prisons.

S 1042 had first come to the Senate floor in late July. But the number of amendments—and the volatility of several—led Majority Leader Bill Frist, R-Tenn., to put it on the back burner until an agreement could be reached on a limited number of relevant amendments. An attempt to invoke cloture to limit debate failed 50–48 on July 26, well short of the sixty votes needed.

By the time the Senate returned to the bill in early November, the public mood on the Iraq war had changed markedly. Domestic polls showed that nearly two-thirds of Americans disapproved of Bush's handling of the war, while international polls showed that reports of torture in U.S.-run prisons abroad had hurt the nation's standing in the world.

In what was viewed as the most powerful statement of congressional oversight on the Iraq war since it began in 2003, the Senate adopted a Warner-Frist amendment that required quarterly unclassified reports from the president on the course of the war and on progress toward drawing down U.S. forces. Senators and aides said this would force the administration for the first time to spell out how conditions in Iraq were linked to goals for withdrawing U.S. troops. The fact that the reports would be unclassified was expected to give the public more of a window onto the debate. The amendment also included nonbinding "sense of the Senate" language that declared 2006 as the year in which the Iraqis should take the lead in their security. The Senate adopted the amendment by a **key vote of 79–19 (R 41–13; D 37–6; I 1–0)**, after rejecting 40–58 a Democratic alternative that would have gone further by requiring the Pentagon to set a schedule for a phased withdrawal from Iraq. *(Details, Iraq war policy, pp. 270, 303; 2005 key votes, p. 915)*

McCain won voice vote approval on Nov. 4 of his detainee abuse amendment. His plan to add the language to the authorization bill despite a veto threat from the White House had been one of the reasons Frist had pulled the legislation in July. With S 1042 stalled, the Senate had agreed to attach the amendment to the defense appropriations bill (HR 2863—PL 109-148). The Senate also adopted 84–14 a Lindsey Graham, R-S.C., amendment to S 1042 on the legal rights of detainees. *(Detainee policies, p. 399)*

In another sign the war was changing the political climate on Capitol Hill, the Senate adopted 82–9 an amendment by John Kerry, D-Mass., to require the director of national intelligence (DNI) to provide the congressional intelligence committees with "a full accounting" of U.S.-run secret detention facilities. The secretary of defense also would be required to report on what he knew about the facilities. The amendment was in response to a *Washington Post* report about a secret overseas system of CIA prisons for suspected terrorists. *(Secret CIA overseas prisons, box p. 340)*

The Senate approved several amendments to improve benefits for military personnel. Members adopted by voice vote an amendment offered by Graham and Hillary Rodham Clinton, D-N.Y., to extend Tricare health care coverage to all reservists. Graham estimated the cost of their proposal to be $3.8 billion over five years—less than past proposals—because it would have limited access to those on standby for deployment and would have charged covered reservists a significant premium.

The Senate also adopted by voice vote an amendment by Evan Bayh, D-Ind., and Richard J. Durbin, D-Ill., to make up income lost by reservists who experienced frequent or extended mobilizations. Their proposal aimed at eliminating what they called "the patriot penalty" on reservists who had been called up to active duty for more than six months and had suffered a cut in pay of at least $50 per month. The amendment set a ceiling of $60 million on obligations under the provision in fiscal 2006, with no such payment to a reservist to exceed $3,000 per month.

The Senate rejected 47–51 an amendment by Frank R. Lautenberg, D-N.J., to close a legal loophole that allowed foreign subsidiaries of U.S. companies to do business with countries such as Iran and Syria that were subject to U.S. sanctions. The Senate instead adopted 98–0 a less restrictive amendment by Susan Collins, R-Maine, to strengthen existing laws, including increasing fines and granting subpoena authority to investigate cases of U.S. companies engaging in business in sanctioned states.

A Byron L. Dorgan, D-N.D., proposal to establish a special Senate committee to investigate the handling of contracts in Afghanistan and Iraq was rejected 44–53.

CONFERENCE ACTION

The House adopted the conference report on HR 1815 (H Rept 109-360) on Dec. 19 by a vote of 374–41. The Senate agreed to it by voice vote on Dec. 21, clearing the bill for the president.

The bill had been declared all-but-dead at several points. By far the longest delay resulted from negotiations among McCain, the White House, and House Armed Services Chair Hunter over the detainee abuse provision. For months, President Bush and Hunter had flatly rejected the language. The turning point came Dec. 14 when the House endorsed the proposal with an overwhelming vote of 308–122 on a motion to instruct House conferees to include the language in the final bill. The following day Bush reversed course and accepted the language in an Oval Office meeting with McCain and Warner. McCain agreed to add some protections for U.S. interrogators. The same language was included in the defense appropriations bill.

Conferees retained most of the Senate amendment limiting detainee legal rights. The conference version added a requirement for reporting on procedures used to determine the status of detainees held by the U.S. military in Afghanistan and Iraq.

Conferees dropped the Senate's requirement that the administration report to Congress on secret CIA prisons overseas, despite a House vote of 228–187 on Dec. 16 to adopt a nonbinding motion instructing House conferees to keep the amendment.

Conferees retained most of the Warner-Frist amendment requiring quarterly reports from the president on progress in Iraq. However, where the Senate required a "schedule" for achieving the conditions necessary for a U.S. drawdown, conferees substituted the vaguer word "plan."

The House provision requiring an analysis of alternatives for any major weapons system that exceeded the original cost by 15 percent was modified to require a less formal analysis of such programs that exceeded the baseline by 50 percent.

Conferees authorized $8.9 billion for shipbuilding, $177 million more than Bush requested but considerably less than the House wanted. And they rejected the House attempt to restructure the Navy shipbuilding program. They followed the Senate's lead in increasing funding for the DD(X) next-generation destroyers and dropped the House plan to authorize funds for two additional *Arleigh Burke*-class destroyers. The final bill retained the Senate ban on choosing a single shipyard to build the new destroyers.

Conferees dropped the House plan to cut $499 million from the request for the Army's Future Combat Systems and restructure the program, and instead authorized $3.4 billion, $50 million less than requested.

Conferees went along with the lower House-approved authorizations for the Transformational Satellite Communications System and Space Radar program.

Conferees included the 3.1 percent pay raise in the final bill, plus a variety of increased benefits, including modified versions of provisions to expand Tricare health insurance coverage and to provide payments to reservists who lost income when they were deployed.

Conferees dropped House provisions that would have denied the defense secretary waiver authority on Buy American requirements and would have prohibited purchases from foreign companies that were government subsidized or that sold restricted items to China.

The final bill authorized funding for a study by the Pentagon of a bunker buster weapon but not the $4 million requested for an Energy Department study of the Robust Nuclear Earth Penetrator. On Oct. 25, the chair of the Senate Energy and Natural Resources Committee, Sen. Pete V. Domenici, R-N.M., released a statement saying the administration wanted to focus on studying non-nuclear weapons for destroying deeply buried targets. At the Energy Department's request, conferees dropped the $4 million from the fiscal 2006 energy and water appropriations bill (HR 2419—PL 109-103).

MAJOR PROVISIONS

As signed into law on Jan. 6, 2006, HR 1815 authorized $491.5 billion for defense spending in fiscal 2006. Of that, $441.5 billion was authorized for the Pentagon and nuclear weapons programs under the Energy Department, and the remaining $50 billion was an emergency funding authorization for military operations in Iraq and Afghanistan.

Iraq, Afghanistan Wars

Authorized $50 billion in emergency funding as a "bridge fund" for the wars in Iraq and Afghanistan.

Required the president to submit quarterly reports on progress in the Iraq war and on military, political, and economic benchmarks that would lead to a U.S. troop drawdown. The reports were to include the president's "plan" for meeting certain conditions related to training Iraqi forces and police to take the lead in maintaining law and order and fighting the insurgency. The reports were to be unclassified "to the maximum extent practicable," with a classified annex if necessary.

Stated the "sense of Congress" that "calendar year 2006 should be a period of significant transition to full Iraqi sovereignty," with Iraqi forces taking the lead on security, thereby creating conditions for a phased redeployment of U.S. forces from Iraq.

Detainee Abuse

Prohibited "cruel, inhuman or degrading treatment" of detainees in U.S. custody, regardless of where they were held. Military interrogators were required to follow standards set in the Army field manual that complied with the Geneva Conventions.

Provided certain protections for U.S. interrogators who might be prosecuted for actions that were "officially authorized and determined to be lawful at the time that they were conducted." Government personnel could use the fact they believed the acts were lawful as a defense, and the government could provide them with counsel.

Required the Pentagon to ensure that all U.S.-trained Iraqi military personnel received training on internationally guaranteed human rights.

Detainee Legal Rights

Required a report to Congress on the procedures used by military tribunals or review boards in determining the status of detainees held at Guantánamo Bay. The report was also to cover procedures used to determine the status of detainees held by the U.S. military in Afghanistan and Iraq.

Barred detainees from filing *habeas corpus* suits contesting their treatment or detention, while giving them limited ability to appeal their detentions and certain sentences handed down by the tribunals.

Required that the civilian official overseeing the tribunals had to be confirmed by the Senate.

Required a tribunal to assess "to the extent practicable" whether statements were obtained under coercion, though using such evidence was not ruled out.

Military Personnel

Authorized $108.9 billion.

Authorized an additional 10,000 personnel for the active-duty Army in fiscal 2006, for a new total of 512,400, and an additional 1,000 personnel for the Marine Corps, for a total of 179,000.

Authorized an average 3.1 percent pay increase.

Increased the re-enlistment bonus for active-duty members to $90,000, from $60,000, and increased the enlistment bonus for new recruits to $40,000, from $20,000. It established a pilot program to grant $1,000 bonuses to service members who encouraged new recruits to enlist. The maximum enlistment age for active duty was increased to forty-two, from thirty-five.

Authorized a permanent increase in the death gratuity to $100,000 from $12,420, retroactive to Oct. 7, 2001; $150,000 in life insurance coverage for personnel serving in Iraq and Afghanistan; and up to $750 per month in hardship duty pay, up from $300.

Authorized access to the military's Tricare health insurance for all reservists who committed to continued service. It also authorized Tricare access for nondeployed reservists who were unemployed or ineligible for employer-provided health insurance.

Extended authority for several special payments and bonuses for reserve personnel through Dec. 31, 2006.

Authorized payments of up to $3,000 per month to make up the income lost by reservists who were involuntarily mobilized and served for eighteen continuous months or a similar extended period.

Operations and Maintenance

Authorized $125.7 billion.

Facilities

Authorized $12.2 billion for military construction and family housing.

Missile Defense

Authorized the requested $7.8 billion for ballistic-missile defense programs.

Ground Forces

Authorized $3.4 billion for the Army's Future Combat Systems. The Army was required to justify more fully to

Congress its plans for the system before it could spend all the money appropriated for the program.

Aviation Forces

Authorized $3.7 billion to procure twenty-four F-22A Raptors.

Authorized $4.9 billion for development of the Joint Strike Fighter.

Authorized $2.8 billion to procure thirty-eight Navy F/A-18E/F Super Hornet fighter jets.

Naval Forces

Authorized $1.1 billion for research and development on the DD(X) destroyer and $766 million for advance procurement of two of the destroyers. The bill set a limit of $2.3 billion per DD(X) and banned selecting a single shipyard to build the destroyer.

Authorized $764.5 million to procure two T-AKE dry cargo ships.

Authorized $50 million for the LHA(R) amphibious assault ship.

Required the Pentagon to maintain twelve aircraft carriers, rather than eleven as the Navy had wanted, and authorized $288 million to extend the life of the USS *John F. Kennedy*.

Nuclear Weapons

Authorized $16.4 billion for Energy Department defense-related activities. The bill did not include the $4 million requested for an Energy Department study of the Robust Nuclear Earth Penetrator but did authorize a related study by the Defense Department.

Space Programs

Authorized $436 million for the Transformational Satellite Communications System and $100 million for the Space Radar program.

Fiscal 2006 Defense Appropriations

Congress in 2005 cleared a fiscal 2006 Defense Department appropriations bill (HR 2863—PL 109-148) providing for $403.5 billion in regular defense spending. In addition, the measure included $50 billion in emergency supplemental funds for the wars in Iraq and Afghanistan, money that was intended to tide over the Pentagon until President George W. Bush submitted a new war supplemental request in early 2006.

The bill included provisions reallocating money for hurricane relief and appropriating emergency funding for a potential flu pandemic. It also mandated a 1 percent across-the-board cut in all fiscal 2006 discretionary spending except for veterans and emergency war funding.

HR 2863's total for defense—excluding the supplemental war funding—was $4.4 billion below President Bush's request and was expected to squeeze the military's modernization and procurement accounts during wartime, making the Pentagon even more reliant on supplemental spending than in the past. And the 1 percent cut shaved about another $4 billion from regular defense programs, bringing the overall total appropriation—excluding the supplemental funds—down to $399.4 billion.

Congress agreed to the administration's request for the Navy's next-generation DD(X) destroyer but trimmed funds for other modernization programs, including the Army's Future Combat Systems, the Transformational Satellite Communications System, and the Joint Strike Fighter, a next-generation multi-role fighter aircraft for all services based on a common airframe.

The defense appropriations bill was usually one of the first spending bills to clear Congress. But the fiscal 2006 measure became one of the last—and arguably the most contentious—regular appropriations bill enacted. Action on HR 2863 slowed in the Senate because lawmakers wanted to wait until the chamber finished its stalled defense authorization bill (HR 1815—PL 109-163). Among the problems holding up the authorization was White House opposition to a pending amendment by John McCain, R-Ariz., to ban abusive treatment of terror suspects in U.S. custody. However, with the Pentagon repeatedly warning that it would soon run out of money, the Senate proceeded to pass HR 2863, after agreeing overwhelmingly to attach McCain's amendment. After the House signaled its broad support for the McCain proposal, Bush dropped his opposition and the provision was enacted in both defense bills. *(2006 defense authorization, p. 336; Detainee policies, p. 399)*

McCain's amendment was not the only last-minute obstacle HR 2863 faced. As pressure mounted to finish the bill, especially the $50 billion for troops in Iraq and Afghanistan, the measure turned into a magnet for other legislation. The hurricane relief and pandemic funding provisions were added, as well as the across-the-board spending cut. Then the GOP leadership attached provisions to open Alaska's Arctic National Wildlife Refuge (ANWR) to oil and gas drilling. Senate Democrats balked, refusing to clear the bill until the ANWR provisions had been removed. Congress finished the bill four days before Christmas.

In addition to the money in HR 2863, Congress appropriated nearly $12.2 billion (before the across-the-board cut) to the Defense Department for military construction, family housing, and the Base Realignment and Closure (BRAC) process in the fiscal 2006 military construction-Veterans Affairs funding bill (HR 2528—PL 109-114). Another $16.4 billion (before the across-the-board cut) in the Energy-Water appropriations bill (HR 2419—PL109-103) was slated for defense activities associated with maintaining U.S. nuclear weapons and reducing the threat from weapons of mass destruction. *(2006 military construction, p. 352)*

HOUSE ACTION

The House passed HR 2863 by a vote of 398–19 on June 20, 2005. The House Appropriations Committee had reported the bill (H Rept 109-119) on June 10.

The House version appropriated $404.9 billion in regular defense spending and $45.3 billion in emergency funds for operations in Iraq and Afghanistan. Because of a committee reorganization earlier in 2005, the bill no longer covered several accounts, including the Defense Health Program, which had been moved to the military construction and Veterans Affairs bill.

The House bill generally met or exceeded the administration's request for major weapons, with the exception of the new DD(X) destroyer. Citing cost increases and technical problems with the program, the Appropriations Committee approved $757 million to continue development of the DD(X) as compared with the $1.1 billion requested. The committee also deleted $716 million that Bush requested for advance procurement and rescinded $304 million in fiscal 2005 advance procurement funding. The recommended funding levels were consistent with HR 1815, the House defense authorization bill. The panel also included $1.4 billion in unrequested funds to procure one DDG-51 *Arleigh Burke*-class guided-missile destroyer, bringing the total provided for the ship in the bill to $1.6 billion. The DDG ships were supposed to be replaced by the DD(X), but the committee said the new DDG would be needed because of delays in developing the DD(X).

The House bill included White House requests for $3.7 billion to procure twenty-four F-22A Raptor fighter jets and $4.9 billion for research and development on the Joint Strike Fighter. House appropriators provided $321 million for four Marine Corps KC-130J tanker/transport planes instead of the $1.1 billion requested for twelve of the aircraft. But they did include $744 million for the Air Force to purchase nine C-130J transport planes that were not in Bush's budget. The Pentagon had said it wanted to cancel the C-130J program after fiscal 2006—a decision ultimately reversed under congressional pressure.

House appropriators provided $3 billion for research and development of the Future Combat Systems program, a $449 million cut from the president's request. The committee said the reduction was due to development and contract delays, and instructed the Army to report by Dec. 1, 2005, with a detailed list and description of the systems included for each stage of development.

HR 2863 provided $7.6 billion for missile defense programs, $144 million less than Bush wanted.

During markup, the Appropriations panel adopted by voice vote an amendment by full committee ranking member David R. Obey, D-Wis., to condemn "coercive and abusive religious proselytizing" at the Air Force Academy in Colorado and require the Air Force to submit a plan to address the reported problem. Accounts of proselytizing by Evangelical Christians at the academy were the subject of an Air Force investigation. But the amendment sparked protracted debate when the bill reached the floor. Ultimately, the full House agreed by voice vote to an amendment by Duncan Hunter, R-Calif., chair of the House Armed Services Committee, to substitute language requiring the Air Force secretary to develop a plan "to maintain a positive climate of religious freedom and tolerance" at the academy. The House rejected 198–210 an attempt by Obey to restore language similar to his committee amendment.

The House adopted by voice vote an Edward J. Markey, D-Mass., amendment stating that none of the funds in the bill could be used to break laws or rules implementing the United Nations Convention Against Torture. The bill already contained language expressing Congress's reaffirmation that the torture of prisoners of war and detainees was illegal and did not reflect the policies of the U.S. government or the values of the people of the United States.

Minority Leader Nancy Pelosi, D-Calif., tried to add language to require the president to outline criteria for withdrawing U.S. troops from Iraq, but her amendment was ruled out of order on the grounds that it was an attempt to legislate on an appropriations bill. *(Iraq war policy, pp. 270, 303)*

SENATE ACTION

The Senate passed its version of HR 2863 on Oct. 7 by a vote of 97–0. The Senate Appropriations Committee had reported the bill on Sept. 28 and filed its report (S Rept 109-141) the next day.

The Senate bill provided $400.95 billion for the regular Pentagon budget. That was $7 billion below the president's request and as a result triggered a White House veto threat. Appropriators had shifted most of the $7 billion to domestic spending bills. The legislation appropriated another $51.3 billion in emergency funds for the wars in Iraq and Afghanistan.

The Senate was far more generous toward the DD(X) destroyer program than the House had been. The Senate version provided the requested $1.1 billion for research and development, $371 million more than in the House bill. The House bill had no DD(X) advance procurement funds, while the Senate version provided $766 million, $50 million more than requested. The Senate bill allocated $30 million for the DDG-51, compared with the $1.6 billion in the House bill.

The Senate approved $3.7 billion for procurement of twenty-four F-22A Raptors, as the House had, and $4.6 billion for research and development of the Joint Strike Fighter, $276 million less than the House. Senate appropriators also included $516 million for seven Air Force C-130Js and $447 million for six Marine Corps KC-130Js, a different mix than in the House bill.

Other allocations included $3.3 billion for the Future Combat Systems, $298 million more than in the House bill, and $7.8 billion for missile defense, $207 million above the House figure. Both chambers' bills allowed for a 3.1 percent military pay raise.

When the bill reached the Senate floor, members quickly added by voice vote another $5.2 billion in emergency supplemental funding—$3.9 billion to prepare for a potential flu outbreak and $1.3 billion for new National Guard equipment.

Senators on Oct. 5 overwhelmingly approved McCain's amendment requiring that combat detainees be treated in accord with the Geneva Convention. The White House had threatened to veto any bill that included McCain's language, saying it would restrict the president's authority to protect the public against terrorism. But the Senate was not deterred, approving the amendment by a **key vote of 90–9 (R 46–9; D 43–0; I 1–0)**. The Senate reaffirmed its support for the amendment Nov. 4, when it added it to the defense authorization bill as well. *(Detainee policies, p. 399; 2005 key votes, p. 915)*

An attempt by John W. Warner, R-Va., chair of the Armed Services Committee, to attach the stalled authorization bill to HR 2863, along with two "manager's packages" containing a total of nearly 100 provisions, was rebuffed. After a heated debate that crossed party lines and pitted appropriators against authorizers, the Senate voted 49–50 to reject Warner's claim that the amendment was germane to the bill.

In other action, the Senate adopted by voice vote an amendment by Richard J. Durbin, R-Ill., to make up the difference in salaries of federal employees who were members of the National Guard or reserves and were called to serve in combat. Durbin had attached a similar provision to the fiscal 2005 Iraq supplemental (HR 1268—PL 109-13) but it was dropped in conference. This Durbin amendment would be dropped as well.

Senators also approved by voice vote a Mark Dayton, D-Minn., amendment to appropriate an additional $100 million for family assistance programs and National Guard counterdrug activities.

Among amendments defeated during the floor debate was a Tom Coburn, R-Okla., proposal to block funding for a Defense Department Web-based travel system. Coburn said the program was not worth the high price tag because the military would not own the software, but Warner and Carl Levin, D-Mich., successfully argued that it would ultimately save resources. Coburn's amendment was tabled (killed) 65–32.

The Senate struck down 48–51 a Debbie Stabenow, D-Mich., amendment to establish a formula to allow funding for veterans' health care programs to keep pace with inflation and population growth.

CONFERENCE ACTION

The House agreed to the conference report (H Rept 109-359) on Dec. 19 by a 308-106 vote. The Senate approved it Dec. 21 by a 93–0 vote, clearing the bill for the president.

Senate approval had come after a bitter dispute that forced GOP leaders to drop the controversial section added in conference that would have opened a part of ANWR to drilling. The Senate had already approved the provisions as part of its budget reconciliation bill (S 1932—PL 109-171), but House Republican leaders said they could not get that measure through their chamber with the ANWR language. So Ted Stevens, R-Alaska, chair of the Defense Appropriations Subcommittee, added it to the defense conference report instead, successfully bypassing opposition from House GOP moderates. Stevens argued that ANWR was related to national security because drilling would reduce reliance on foreign oil, and, in a bid to sweeten the deal, he earmarked part of the future profits from ANWR drilling for additional hurricane recovery on the Gulf Coast and for border security. But opponents would have none of that, insisting that including the ANWR language violated Senate rules because it was not germane to the bill and the provisions had not been part of either the House- or Senate-passed versions.

On Dec. 21, senators rejected by a **key vote of 56–44 (R 52–3; D 4–40; I 0–1)** a motion to limit debate on the conference report as long as it included the ANWR language. Sixty votes were needed to approve cloture. Because most House members already had departed for the holidays, Senate GOP leaders agreed to use an enrolling resolution (S Con Res 74) to get rid of the ANWR package. The Senate on Dec. 21 first adopted the resolution 48–45 and then cleared HR 2863. The House adopted the enrolling resolution by voice vote the following day.

Before the eleventh-hour fight over ANWR, completion of the conference report had been stalled by disagreements over the McCain detainee abuse amendment and over plans by House GOP leaders to attach across-the-board cuts in discretionary spending. Leaders from both chambers also negotiated behind closed doors over adding aid for hurricane victims as well as funds to prepare for a possible flu pandemic at a time of growing concern about avian flu.

McCain's amendment presented a particularly thorny problem. Since September, the White House had threatened to veto any bill that included it. But on Dec. 14, the House by a **key vote of 308–122 (R 107–121; D 200–1; I 1–0)** adopted a motion offered by John P. Murtha, D-Pa., to instruct House conferees to include the McCain amendment in the conference report. Although it was nonbinding, the vote sent a powerful signal to the White House that both chambers wanted a clear codification of the ban on detainee abuse. Faced with such opposition, as well as growing unease among U.S. allies overseas, Bush backed down Dec. 15 and accepted virtually all of McCain's language, clearing the way for its inclusion in both the defense appropriations and authorization bills. The compromise added provisions to protect U.S. interrogators. The conference agreement also included an amendment prohibiting detainees held at Guantánamo Bay, Cuba, from suing for *habeas corpus*, though they gained a limited right to appeal their detention.

Conferees agreed to appropriate $403.5 billion for regular Pentagon spending—an amount that was closer to the House bill's total than to the Senate's.

Conferees followed the Senate's lead in giving the president what he requested for the DD(X). Since the final version included the full amount for the DD(X), conferees dropped the House-added funding for a DDG-51 destroyer.

Like both chambers, conferees agreed to the Air Force's request for the F-22A Raptor aircraft, the most expensive jet fighter ever built up to that time. But they cut $232 million from the Joint Strike Fighter request.

Conferees cut $240 million from the Army's request for the Future Combat Systems program. They funded most of the administration's request for major space programs, although they did cut $400 million from the $836 million requested for the Transformational Satellite Communications System, saying the Pentagon had not acknowledged the risks associated with the program.

The final bill did not include $4.5 million originally requested to research the feasibility of modifying a nuclear weapon to tunnel into the earth and destroy reinforced underground command posts and weapons arsenals. However, conferees provided $4 million for the Air Force to work on a non-nuclear version of the so-called bunker buster, and $7 million for the Navy to study using submarine-launched intermediate range ballistic missiles to penetrate such targets.

Republican appropriators agreed to include $3.8 billion for use in preparing for a flu pandemic. Senate Majority Leader Bill Frist, R-Tenn., added a last-minute provision in conference that granted liability protection to vaccine manufacturers, a move that infuriated House Democrats.

MAJOR PROVISIONS

As signed into law Dec. 30, HR 2863 appropriated $403.5 billion for regular fiscal 2006 military spending. Because the bill also mandated a 1 percent across-the-board cut in fiscal discretionary spending—except for veterans' and emergency war funding—that total was reduced to $399.4 billion.

In addition, HR 2863 appropriated $50 billion in emergency supplemental funds for the wars in Iraq and Afghanistan.

The bill also reallocated $29 billion in emergency funds for hurricane relief for Gulf Coast areas hit by hurricanes Katrina and Rita, including $5.8 billion for the Pentagon, and appropriated $3.8 billion in emergency funding for preparations for a potential flu pandemic. The estimated savings of $8.5 billion from the 1 percent across-the-board cut were used to offset part of the hurricane relief and flu preparation activities.

War Supplemental

Included in the $50 billion emergency supplemental for the wars in Iraq and Afghanistan was $8 billion earmarked to buy equipment lost in combat, including Humvees, trucks, radios, electronic jammers, Tomahawk cruise missiles, and ammunition. The package also included $1.4 billion for testing and fielding new equipment to thwart roadside bombs, and $1 billion in emergency funding for Army Air National Guard and Army Reserve equipment.

Combat Detainees

Prohibited "cruel, inhuman or degrading treatment" of detainees in U.S. custody and required military interrogators to follow standards set in an Army field manual that complied with the Geneva Convention. The bill included provisions to protect U.S. interrogators in lawsuits based on activities that were officially authorized and deemed lawful at the time they were conducted, and to allow the government to pay attorney fees in such a suit.

Prohibited detainees held at Guantánamo Bay, Cuba, from suing for *habeas corpus*, though they were given a limited right to appeal their detention.

Military Personnel

Appropriated $97 billion for military personnel.

Included an average 3.1 percent military pay raise.

Allowed for 10,000 more personnel for the active-duty Army, for a new total of 512,400, and for 1,000 more in the Marine Corps, for a new total of 179,000.

Operations and Maintenance

Appropriated $123.6 billion.

Missile Defense

Appropriated $7.8 billion for ballistic missile defense programs, including funds for the initial deployment of a national missile defense system based in Alaska and California.

Ground Forces

Appropriated $3.2 billion for the Future Combat Systems, the Army's next generation of combat vehicles and weapons systems that were part of a plan to transform the Army into a lighter, more mobile force.

Appropriated $881 million to procure 240 Stryker armored vehicles.

Aviation Forces

Appropriated $3.7 billion to procure twenty-four F-22A Raptor jet fighters.

Appropriated $4.7 billion for research and development of the next-generation multi-role Joint Strike Fighter for use by the Air Force, Navy, and Marine Corps.

Naval Forces

Appropriated $1.1 billion for development and $716 million for procurement of the Navy's next-generation surface combat ship, the DD(X) destroyer.

Appropriated $2.4 billion for procurement of a *Virginia*-class attack submarine.

Appropriated $477 million to procure three LCS Littoral Combat Ships—two ships and $440 million more than requested.

Air and Sea Transport

Appropriated $690 million for eight Air Force C-130Js and $384 million for five KC-130Js for the Marines in fiscal 2006, and a total of $138 million in advance procurement funding for those same quantities for fiscal 2007.

Appropriated $380 million for one T-AKE dry cargo ship.

Space Programs

Appropriated $437 million for the Transformational Satellite Communications System and $100 million for the Space Radar.

Fiscal 2005 Supplemental War Appropriations

Congress in 2005 appropriated an additional $75.9 billion in emergency supplemental funding for the wars in Iraq and Afghanistan. The money was part of an $82 billion fiscal 2005 supplemental appropriations bill (HR 1268—PL 109-13).

Congress had already provided $25 billion in supplemental fiscal 2005 funds as part of the fiscal 2005 defense appropriations bill (PL 108-287) that cleared in 2004. *(2005 defense appropriations, Congress and the Nation Vol. XI, p. 354)*

The Army was the big winner in HR 1268, understandably so since it had the greatest need for additional funding. To tide the Army over until the bill could be signed into law, the Pentagon had shifted $1.1 billion of existing funds into Army coffers, saying the funding was "critically needed" to prevent exhausting operations and maintenance accounts. HR 1268 gave the Army $17 billion for general operations and maintenance, $459 million for aircraft, $310 million for missiles, and $2.6 billion for weapons and tracked combat vehicles.

President George W. Bush had requested $82 billion in supplemental funding for fiscal 2005, including $75 billion for the Defense Department, $5.6 billion for foreign affairs activities, $418 million for homeland security efforts, and $950 million for victims of the tsunami that had caused widespread destruction in South Asia in December 2004.

While Congress was willing to meet the overall request total, both chambers sought to change the way it would be allocated. The final bill allocated about $900 million more that Bush requested for military operations in Iraq and Afghanistan. It also provided about $766 million more than he sought for border security and homeland security needs. Lawmakers made up the difference mainly by shaving about $500 million from the proposed funding for foreign policy activities and paying for another $1 billion by rescinding previously appropriated spending. The final bill also provided $907 million in tsunami relief. *(For details, see 2005 supplemental appropriations, foreign policy chapter, p. 265; Border security, p. 679)*

HR 1268 also included a package of immigration-related provisions that had been a priority for House Republicans. The provisions tightened requirements for foreigners seeking asylum in the United States and established national standards for state driver's licenses. *(Immigration provisions, pp. 679, 684, 686, 711)*

HOUSE ACTION

The House passed HR 1268 on March 16, 2005, by a vote of 388–43. The House Appropriations Committee had reported the bill (H Rept 109-16) on March 11.

The House-passed bill appropriated a total of $81.4 billion in fiscal 2005 emergency supplemental funding. That total included $76.8 billion for the Pentagon—$1.9 billion more than requested. The bill recommended $18.2 billion—$2.1 billion more than Bush sought—for procurement, primarily for equipment to safeguard Army troops in Iraq. The bill also included provisions on military death benefits. Nonmilitary appropriations in the bill included money for foreign affairs programs, homeland security, and tsunami relief.

During floor action on war-related amendments, the House adopted by voice vote an amendment by James P. Moran, D-Va., urging the Pentagon to tell Congress its criteria for success in Iraq. The House rejected 191–236 an amendment by John F. Tierney, D-Mass., and Jim Leach, R-Iowa, to create a special committee to investigate the use of taxpayers' money in Iraq and Afghanistan reconstruction. Amendment supporters questioned how the Defense Department had spent funds it had already gotten, and noted that the Pentagon had failed to submit at least two reports on war costs required under previous laws.

The House voted on nonmilitary amendments as well, including one that added the set of immigration-related provisions.

SENATE ACTION

The Senate passed HR 1268 by a vote of 99–0 on April 21. The Senate Appropriations Committee had reported the bill (S Rept 109-52) on April 6.

The Senate-passed bill appropriated $81.2 billion in fiscal 2005 emergency supplemental funding. Of that total, $74.8 billion was for the Pentagon—$2 billion less than in the House version. Senate appropriators focused on priorities similar to the House's—such as replacing battle-damaged equipment and force-protection items—but with less cash. For instance, senators included less than half the money the House did to pay for the devices intended to thwart roadside bombs. Like the House bill, the Senate measure included provisions on military death benefits. The Senate bill also included money for foreign assistance, homeland security, and tsunami relief.

Senate appropriators used the bill as an opportunity to redirect Pentagon policy by prohibiting the use of funds to enforce a strategy of using only one shipyard to build the Navy's next-generation destroyer, the DD(X). Lawmakers with naval facilities in their home states wanted the Navy to divide work on the destroyer between Bath Iron Works in Maine and Northrop Grumman Ship Systems in Mississippi. Thad Cochran, a Republican from Mississippi, chaired the Senate Appropriations Committee.

During floor action on war-related proposals, the Senate adopted 61–39 an Evan Bayh, D-Ind., amendment to add $213 million for heavily armored Humvees. An amendment offered by Larry E. Craig, R-Idaho, to provide seriously injured troops with additional coverage under the military's life insurance plan was adopted by voice vote. The Senate also adopted 61–31 a Robert C. Byrd, D-W.Va., amendment expressing the sense of the Senate that future funding requests for operations in Afghanistan and Iraq should be included in the president's regular annual budget, and that the president should submit an amended fiscal 2006 budget detailing war costs.

On other defense issues, the Senate adopted 58–38 a John W. Warner, R-Va., amendment to require the Navy to maintain twelve aircraft carriers until certain conditions were met. Warner, chair of the Armed Services Committee and a former Navy secretary with shipbuilding facilities in his home state, successfully argued that the Navy's plans to retire an aircraft carrier would limit the Pentagon's reach in the Pacific Ocean at a time when China was building up its military. The Senate also adopted by voice vote a Saxby Chambliss, R-Ga., amendment to prohibit the Pentagon from using money in the bill to terminate the C-130J Hercules transport plane, which was made by Lockheed Martin Corp. in the senator's home state.

Several votes were taken on military benefits issues. Two attempts by Patty Murray, D-Wash., to offer amendments cosponsored by more than a dozen other Democrats to add $2 billion to the bill to pay for veterans' health care were rejected by 46–54 votes. The Senate did adopt by voice vote a John Kerry, D-Mass., amendment to lengthen the time family members could remain in military housing after a service member died and to expand the "death gratuity" benefit to cover any service member killed while on active duty, not just those killed inside combat zones. Ted Stevens, R-Alaska, chair of the Senate Defense Appropriations Subcommittee, tried to table (kill) Kerry's proposal on the grounds that it would cost too much, but his motion was rejected 25–75.

The Senate also adopted by voice vote a Richard J. Durbin, D-Ill., amendment to make up the difference in salaries of federal employees who were members of the National Guard or reserves and were called to serve in combat. Durbin estimated that reservists lost an average of $368 per month when serving on active duty. Stevens's attempt to table the proposal was rejected 39–61.

The Senate, like the House, dealt with other nondefense issues as well during floor action. Indeed, Senate action on HR 1268 was sidetracked for nearly a week by a debate on immigration.

CONFERENCE ACTION

House and Senate conferees began meeting in late April under intense pressure from the Pentagon, which said troops in Iraq would run out of money after the first week of May. The conference committee reached an agreement on May 3.

The House adopted the conference report (H Rept 109-72) on May 5 by a vote of 368–58. The Senate agreed to it 100–0 on May 10, clearing the bill for the president.

Conferees provided $900 million more than President Bush had requested to equip Army troops in Iraq and Afghanistan—roughly splitting the $2 billion difference between the initial House and Senate figures. Lawmakers on both sides of the aisle lobbied to include extra dollars for equipment that would protect soldiers, including $60 million for electronic jammers to thwart roadside bombs and $308 million for heavily armored Humvees. John P. Murtha of Pennsylvania, ranking Democrat on the House Defense Appropriations Subcommittee, and other lawmakers said that although the bill did not cover all of the Army's shortages, it went a long way toward correcting serious problems.

Conferees included Bush's requests for funds for Iraqi and Afghan security forces but did not fully accept Bush's request to shift control over the funds from the State Department to the Pentagon. Both departments were given specific responsibilities. Conferees kept the Senate provisions calling for war costs to be included in the president's regular budget and prohibiting the Navy from retiring an aircraft carrier, terminating the C-130J cargo plane, or selecting a single naval yard to build the DD(X) destroyer.

Conferees agreed to expand military benefits but dropped the Senate provision that would have made up the difference between military and civilian pay of federal employees called to active duty as reservists.

Conferees settled on $5.1 billion for international activities—$43 million more than the Senate recommended and $866 million more than in the House bill—and $1.2 billion for homeland security—slightly less than the Senate wanted but more than three times what the House proposed. House provisions on immigration were kept largely intact.

MAJOR PROVISIONS

As signed into law on May 11, HR 1268 appropriated $82 billion in fiscal 2005 emergency supplemental funding. The measure:

Defense Spending

Appropriated $75.9 billion for the Pentagon, virtually all of it for the wars in Iraq and Afghanistan, including:

- $37.1 billion for military operations in Iraq and Afghanistan. Included in the total was $5.7 billion to train and equip security forces in Iraq and $1.3 billion for security forces in Afghanistan. The bill divided control over the security funds: the State Department was required to sign off on such expenditures and the Pentagon had to notify congressional committees five days in advance of the spending and provide them with quarterly reports.

- $17.4 billion to replace equipment and munitions expended during the war in Iraq and other antiterrorist operations. That was $1.2 billion more than requested and much of the increase was for Army and Marine Corps force-protection measures, including additional trucks, truck and body armor, night-vision goggles, and electronic roadside-bomb jammers. The total included $611 million for add-on vehicle armor kits and $150 million for up-armored Army Humvees, both of which were needed to provide additional protection from antitank and antipersonnel mines.
- $17.4 billion for military personnel.
- $1.1 billion for military construction, mainly for facilities in Iraq, Afghanistan, and nations providing support for U.S. operations.

Military Benefits

Increased the amount of life insurance a service member could purchase from $250,000 to $400,000, and increased death benefits to a service member's survivors from $12,240 to $100,000.

Included a new insurance rider for traumatic injury protection of up to $100,000.

Provided a one-year extension of the basic housing allowance for dependents of those who died in Iraq and Afghanistan.

Other Provisions

Appropriated $5.1 billion for international activities. *(Details, 2005 supplemental appropriations, p. 348)*

Appropriated $1.2 billion for homeland security. Appropriated $907 million to aid victims of the December 2004 tsunami in South Asia.

Included immigration-related provisions that set tighter restrictions for state driver's licenses and for asylum, and waived state environmental laws to allow completion of a fourteen-mile U.S.-Mexico border fence near San Diego. *(Details, Immigration restrictions, pp. 234, 679)*

Fiscal 2006 Supplemental War Appropriations

Congress in 2006 appropriated an additional $65.8 billion in emergency supplemental funding for ongoing military operations in Iraq and Afghanistan. The money was part of a $94.5 billion fiscal 2006 supplemental appropriations bill (HR 4939—PL 109-234).

Congress had already appropriated $50 billion in emergency war spending for fiscal 2006 as part of the annual defense appropriations bill (HR 2863—PL 109-148). The new infusion of money was for the remainder of the fiscal year. *(2006 defense appropriations, p. 344)*

HR 4939 continued the policy of the George W. Bush administration of paying for the wars in Iraq and Afghanistan outside the regular Defense Department budget. By designating the money as emergency spending, it did not count against Congress's discretionary spending limits.

The $65.8 billion was within $100 million of Bush's request, but Congress made numerous changes in the allocation of the funds. In one of the biggest changes, the bill provided $4.9 billion for the Iraqi and Afghan security forces, $1 billion less than Bush had requested. Congress provided almost nine times the amount requested to upgrade Abrams tanks and Bradley fighting vehicles, and double what was requested for upgraded Humvees.

In addition to the $65.8 billion for war operations, HR 4939 appropriated $235 million for military construction, mostly in Iraq and Afghanistan. The bill also provided funding for international operations, including $3 billion for U.S. embassy operations and reconstruction and other aid in Iraq.

Also in the bill was funding for agriculture disaster assistance, flu pandemic preparations, hurricane relief, and border security.

HOUSE ACTION

The House passed HR 4939 on March 16, 2006, by a vote of 348–71. The House Appropriations Committee had reported the bill (H Rept 109-388) on March 13.

The House-passed bill appropriated a total of $91.9 billion in fiscal 2006 supplemental funding, including $67.6 billion for military operations in Iraq and Afghanistan.

The total for the wars was close to what the administration had originally requested—$67.9 billion. Later, however, after House passage, Bush would reduce his request to $65.9 billion to make room for a $1.9 billion request for border security.

But House appropriators proposed to allocate the money differently. In a move criticized by Defense Secretary Donald H. Rumsfeld, the House Appropriations Committee cut $1 billion from Bush's $5.9 billion request for Iraqi and Afghan security forces. The panel noted that money previously provided for Iraqi forces had not been spent as quickly as expected and was still available.

Appropriators, on the other hand, included over $1 billion in unrequested funds to upgrade or replace Abrams tanks, Bradley fighting vehicles, and armored Humvees. They boosted procurement accounts for the military services by hundreds of millions of dollars, offset by numerous cuts to Bush's proposals. The committee also proposed keeping open the production lines for the C-17 transport plane.

When the bill reached the floor, the Republican leadership managed to beat back dozens of amendments, including those from fiscal conservatives who wanted to offset the spending. While the vote for final passage was overwhelming, it still showed increasing uneasiness about the administration's heavy reliance on supplemental spending for the wars in Iraq and Afghanistan. Of the seventy-one "no" votes, nineteen came from Republicans, including a small group of fiscal conservatives. The previous year, only three Republicans had joined forty others in voting against the fiscal 2005 war supplemental (HR 1268—PL 109-13). *(2005 war supplemental, p. 348)*

During floor action on war-related matters, the House adopted by voice vote a Barbara Lee, D-Calif., amendment to prohibit the use of funds in the bill to enter into a basing rights agreement with Iraq that would lead to a permanent U.S. presence in the country. An attempt by John Salazar, D-Colo., a member of the Veterans' Affairs Committee, to add $630 million for veterans' medical services and general expenses for the Department of Veterans Affairs was ruled out of order as legislating on an appropriations bill. Salazar and other Democrats argued that health care for veterans was a legitimate cost of the war.

SENATE ACTION

The Senate passed an amended version of HR 4939 by a vote of 77–21 on May 4. The Senate Appropriations Committee had reported the bill (S Rept 109-230) on April 5.

The Senate version appropriated a total of $108.9 billion in emergency supplemental funding for fiscal 2006—$17 billion more than the House had approved and $16.7 billion more than Bush had requested. The Senate Appropriations Committee had approved a $106.5 billion version and—over the protests of the White House, Republican leaders in the House, and GOP conservatives in the Senate—another $2.4 billion was added on the floor. The combination of "must-pass" war funding and the fact that it was an election year made the bill a magnet for add-ons.

The Senate-passed version included $65.7 billion for the Iraq and Afghanistan wars. The Senate Appropriations Committee had recommended $67.6 billion, the same as in the House bill, although Senate panel chair, Thad Cochran, R-Miss., had found offsets that made room for additional money for tanks, heavily armored Humvees, and military personnel. During floor action, the total for the wars was reduced to $65.7 billion, after the Senate adopted 59–39 an amendment offered by Budget Committee Chair Judd Gregg, R-N.H., to add $1.9 billion for border security and offset it by cutting the bill's Defense Department spending. An attempt by Minority Leader Harry Reid, D-Nev., to provide the extra money without the offset was rejected 44–54. President Bush subsequently submitted a formal request to the House for the $1.9 billion for border security.

CONFERENCE ACTION

The House adopted the conference report (H Rept 109-494) on June 13 by a vote of 351–67. The Senate cleared the bill on June 15 by a vote of 98–1.

The wide disparity between the House and Senate bills had made negotiations difficult, but the Pentagon kept up the pressure, warning that it was having to reprogram other appropriations to cover war costs. House negotiators insisted that the final bill not exceed the president's request, and they were backed by Bush, who stated publicly that he would veto the measure if it provided more than $94.5 billion—his initial request plus $2.3 billion for pandemic flu preparations.

After weeks of talks, House and Senate conferees managed to bridge their $17 billion gap and settle on the final $94.5 billion bill. The deepest cuts came in Senate-approved hurricane relief and agriculture assistance provisions, and not in the sections appropriating supplemental funds for military operations in Iraq and Afghanistan and for foreign assistance.

The final bill appropriated $65.8 billion for the wars. That total included $37.9 for operations and maintenance, $935 million more than in the House bill but $1.3 billion less than recommended by the Senate. It also included $15 billion for procurement, $2.8 billion less than in the House bill and $548 million less than in the Senate version. Within the procurement total was $1.3 billion, as requested, for up-armored Humvees that provided additional protection to soldiers from antitank and antipersonnel mines. But conferees devoted two-thirds of the money to new vehicles, although the Pentagon would have put a larger portion into retrofitted vehicles that lawmakers believed provided less protection. Conferees included $400 million in unrequested funds for Abrams tanks, as well as funds to keep the production lines open for the C-17 transport plane.

FINAL PROVISIONS

As signed into law on June 15, HR 4939 appropriated $94.5 billion in fiscal 2006 emergency supplemental spending. The measure:

Defense Spending

Appropriated $65.8 billion for military operations in Iraq and Afghanistan, including:

- $37.9 billion for operations and maintenance. This category included $4.9 billion for Iraqi and Afghan security forces—$3 billion for Iraq and $1.9 billion for Afghanistan. It also provided $2 billion for the Joint Improvised Explosive Device (IED) Defeat Fund.
- $15 billion for procurement. Funds were provided to continue production of the C-17 transport plane.
- $10.3 billion for pay and allowances for active-duty soldiers and members of the National Guard and reserve.
- $1.2 billion for the Defense Health Program to provide health care for activated reservists and their families, and to contract for civilian medical staff to fill in for deployed active-duty medical staff at military treatment facilities.

Gave the Pentagon authority to transfer $2 billion among accounts in the supplemental.

Appropriated in a separate section of the bill $235 million for military construction for the global war on terrorism. Most of the money was for projects in Iraq and Afghanistan.

Other Provisions

Appropriated nearly $4 billion for international operations. Included in that total was $3 billion for U.S. Embassy operations and reconstruction and other aid in Iraq. *(Details, 2006 aid appropriations, p. 282)*

Appropriated $19.3 billion for hurricane recovery in the Gulf Coast region. *(Details, hurricane aid, p. 79)*

Appropriated $2.3 billion to prepare for the possibility of an avian flu pandemic. The fiscal 2006 defense appropriations bill (HR 2863—PL 109-148) had already provided $3.8 billion for flu readiness. *(Flu preparations, p. 556)*

Appropriated $1.9 billion for homeland security and border protection. *(Border protection, p. 679)*

Appropriated $500 million to aid farmers whose livelihood was hurt by hurricanes in the Gulf Coast region in 2005.

Included statutory language setting a cap of $872.8 billion for fiscal 2007 discretionary spending in the Senate, equal to the House limit. *(Budget resolution, p. 97)*

Fiscal 2006 Military Construction Appropriations

Congress in 2005 appropriated $12.2 billion for military construction in fiscal 2006—$866 million more than the previous year. The money was part of an $82.6 billion fiscal 2006 spending bill that also funded Department of Veterans Affairs (VA) programs (HR 2528—PL 109-114).

The military construction portion of the bill included $6.2 billion for military construction, $4 billion for construction and maintenance of family housing, and $1.8 billion for Base Realignment and Closure (BRAC) accounts.

About 85 percent of the bill—$70.2 billion—was for the VA. That included $29.1 billion for the Veterans Health Administration and $37.4 billion for the Veterans Benefits Administration. The bill designated $1.2 billion of the funding as emergency spending for veterans' health care in order to keep the bill below the cap on discretionary spending. Earlier in the year Congress had appropriated $1.5 billion in fiscal 2005 supplemental spending for veterans' healthcare programs as part of the fiscal 2006 Interior-environment spending bill (HR 2361—PL 109-54).

The structure of HR 2528—combining military construction and VA funding—was something new, the result of a reorganization earlier in the year by the House and Senate Appropriations committees. The initial House-passed bill included other defense accounts such as the $20 billion Defense Health Program and the Pentagon's housing allowance for military personnel. The Senate approved funding for those programs as part of its defense appropriations bill. House and Senate negotiators ultimately agreed to alternate each year between the House and Senate structures for the bill.

The totals for military construction did not reflect the 1 percent across-the-board cut in most discretionary programs—except those for veterans and emergency war costs—that would be enacted a month later in the fiscal 2006 defense appropriations bill (HR 2863—PL 109-148).

LEGISLATIVE ACTION

The House passed HR 2528 by a vote of 425–1 on May 26, 2005. The House Appropriations Committee had reported the bill (H Rept 109-95) on May 23.

The House-passed bill would have appropriated $121.8 billion in all. Of that total, $12.3 billion was for military construction, including $5.8 billion for military construction, $4.2 billion for family housing, and $1.9 billion for BRAC.

During floor action, the House narrowly defeated, 213–214, a Charlie Melancon, D-La., amendment to add $53 million for veterans' programs, while cutting $169 million from the 2005 BRAC account. Members also rejected 171–254 an amendment by Earl Blumenauer, D-Ore., to add $351 million to complete all environmental remediation at bases closed during the 1988 BRAC round, offset by an equal cut to the 2005 BRAC account.

The Senate passed an $83 billion version of HR 2528 by a vote of 98–0 on Sept. 22. The Senate Appropriations Committee had reported the bill (S Rept 109-105) on July 21.

The Senate version appropriated $12.1 billion for military construction, including $5.9 billion for construction, $4.1 billion for family housing, and $1.9 billion for BRAC. In its report, the Senate Appropriations Committee reiterated Congress's concern that the Pentagon integrate its decisions about base closings, the planned redeployment of overseas troops to home bases, and the need for housing facilities and base infrastructure to support the returning troops.

CONFERENCE ACTION

On Nov. 18 the House agreed to the conference report (H Rept 109-305) by a vote of 427–0 and the Senate cleared the bill by voice vote.

Once the House agreed to put funding for such accounts as the Defense Health Program and the basic housing allowance in the separate Defense Department appropriations bills, the House and Senate versions of HR 2528 were not that different. The House measure totaled $80.5 billion and the Senate bill $81 billion, plus $2 billion in emergency funds to help cover a shortfall in the veterans' health care budget. Conferees settled on the $82.6 billion total, including $1.2 billion in emergency funding.

Conferees had to settle differing funding levels for more than 100 military construction projects—many of them requested by lawmakers rather than the administration. A dispute over a $45 million family housing project at the Spangdahlem Air Base in Germany delayed final passage of the bill. House appropriators eventually won the funding for what they said was a needed upgrade to dangerously dilapidated housing, but only in return for a Senate-required report on the cost-effectiveness of the project.

In other action, conferees agreed to let the Navy keep $300 million from land sales to pay for environmental cleanup at closed bases, rather than putting the funds in a general Pentagon account. They required the Defense Department to notify Congress of military exercises that involved more than $100,000 in construction costs. Conferees also rescinded $29 million in previously appropriated funds for improvements to an air base in Uzbekistan. The Uzbek government had asked U.S. forces to leave after the administration criticized the Uzbeks over human rights abuses.

The final bill prohibited the construction of new bases in the United States without a specific appropriation and barred the construction of new overseas bases without the prior notification of Congress. It barred the use of funds in the bill for military construction, land acquisition, or family housing projects at a military installation approved for closure in 2005. The Pentagon also was barred from transferring funds appropriated for such projects or land acquisitions to another account, or to use such funds for another purpose without congressional approval.

MAJOR PROVISIONS

As signed into law on Nov. 30, 2005, HR 2528:

Military Construction

Appropriated $6.2 billion—$867 million more than requested—for military construction. The total included $5.1 billion for active-duty forces and $1.1 billion for the National Guard and reserve forces.

Family Housing

Appropriated $4 billion—$223 million less than requested—for the construction and maintenance of family housing.

Base Closing

Appropriated $1.8 billion—$499 million less than requested—for BRAC accounts. The total included $1.5 billion for the 2005 round and $255 million for environmental cleanup remaining from the 1990 round. *(Military base closings, p. 369)*

IRAQ RECONSTRUCTION OVERSIGHT

The 109th Congress had a mixed response in 2006 when it pondered the future of the office overseeing billions of dollars in contracts for rebuilding Iraq. Members first agreed to terminate the office in 2007 but later decided on an extension of perhaps another year beyond that date.

A provision of the fiscal 2007 defense authorization law (HR 5122—PL 109-364) had set Oct. 1, 2007, as the expiration date for the Iraq inspector general's term. The office's mandate was then to be transferred to investigators at the State and Defense departments, as well as to the inspector general at the U.S. Agency for International Development.

But some contended that a 2007 date was premature. According to the Senate Homeland Security and Governmental Affairs Committee, the office—occupied by Stuart W. Bowen Jr. since 2004—was overseeing $32 billion in Iraq reconstruction contracts and was providing a $25 benefit for every dollar spent on oversight. After his nomination to be defense secretary, Robert M. Gates said he supported continuing the inspector general's term, and the Iraq Study Group's report recommended that "the authority of the Special Inspector General for Iraq Reconstruction should be renewed for the duration of assistance programs in Iraq." *(Iraq Study Group, box p. 274)*

Sen. Susan Collins, R-Maine, introduced legislation (S 4046) to cancel the October 2007 expiration date and extend the inspector general's term until ten months after 80 percent of Iraq reconstruction funding had been spent. That threshold was expected to be reached in late 2008.

By a voice vote on Nov. 14, 2006, the Senate agreed to amend Collins's proposal to the fiscal 2007 military construction-Veterans Affairs (VA) appropriations bill (HR 5385). To ensure passage in one form or another, the Senate Homeland Security panel moved forward with the stand-alone bill as well, reporting S 4046 on Nov. 16 (no written report). When the military construction-VA spending bill stalled, the Senate on Dec. 6 passed S 4046 by voice vote. The House passed the measure by voice vote on Dec. 8 and the president signed it into law on Dec. 20 (PL 109-440). *(2007 military construction, p. 363)*

The following year the fiscal 2008 defense authorization bill (HR 4986—PL 110-181) provided that the office of inspector general should terminate after there was less than $250 million remaining to be spent on reconstruction.

Fiscal 2007 Defense Authorization

Congress in 2006 cleared a $532.8 billion fiscal 2007 defense authorization bill (HR 5122—PL 109-364). That total included $462.8 billion for Pentagon programs as well as for Energy Department nuclear weapons programs—about $500 million less than President George W. Bush had requested. In addition, the bill authorized $70 billion in emergency funds for military operations in Iraq and Afghanistan—$20 billion more than requested—as a "bridge" fund for the first six months of fiscal 2007.

While endorsing much of what the White House had requested, Republicans who controlled the House and Senate Armed Services committees openly challenged the administration on several high-profile issues related to military personnel, the conduct of the war in Iraq, and plans for purchasing weapons.

HR 5122 made substantial increases in the administration's request for overall troop levels and, despite White House objections, provided more health care benefits. The bill also included, as requested, a 2.2 percent average pay increase for military personnel.

Members made a point of targeting funds for new armor to protect the troops and their vehicles, especially from roadside bomb blasts. The extra $20 billion in supplemental funding for the wars in Iraq and Afghanistan had been added to allow enough money to refurbish, upgrade, or replace military equipment worn down in battle, a problem that had undermined the readiness of many Army, Marine, and National Guard units. "The theme of the bill this year was troop protection," said Duncan Hunter, R-Calif., chair of the House Armed Services Committee.

HR 5122 authorized less than President Bush wanted for some of the more futuristic weapons programs, such as the Army's Future Combat Systems and the F-35 Joint Strike Fighter, and authorized unrequested funding for new ships, submarines, and warplanes.

The bill included the president's request for missile defense.

This was the fifth year in a row that the defense authorization measure was completed after the defense appropriations bill (HR 5631—PL 109-289). Unlike the preceding few years, however, agreement on the conference report had been held up largely by nondefense issues, such as how chaplains should pray and how U.S. courtrooms should be secured. Once those disputes were overcome, the bill cleared easily. *(2007 defense appropriations, p. 358)*

HOUSE COMMITTEE ACTION

The House Armed Services Committee reported HR 5122 (H Rept 109-452) on May 5, 2006.

The committee bill authorized a total of $512.9 billion, including the requested $50 billion in emergency funding for war operations. In drafting the measure, the Republicans who controlled the panel's six subcommittees showed streaks of independence uncharacteristic during the Bush administration, calling for more military personnel and different priorities in some weapons procurement. "We cannot short-change the current force for a promised future capability," said Curt Weldon of Pennsylvania, the second-ranking Republican on the panel.

For military personnel, the committee approved a 2.7 percent increase in basic pay, a half-percent more than Bush sought, at an additional cost of $300 million. The panel blocked a Pentagon plan to raise annual enrollment fees, deductibles, and drug copayments for military retirees under the age of sixty-five who participated in the military's Tricare health care network. Lobbying groups representing millions of active and retired military personnel had been working to sink the administration's proposals. The bill also extended discounted Tricare benefits to almost all reservists.

The committee bill increased active-duty end-strength beyond Bush's request by 30,000 for the Army, 5,000 for the Marines, and 17,100 for the National Guard.

The panel approved $4.4 billion for research and development on the F-35 Joint Strike Fighter—$408 million more than requested in order to continue development of a second engine from a competing contractor, which the committee said could bring down costs. It also agreed to $1 billion for advance procurement, $236 million less than requested, saying it wanted to slow production of the aircraft, which was intended for use by the Air Force, Navy, and Marine Corps, as well as eight allied nations. The General Accounting Office had described the Pentagon's approach as one that "invests heavily in production before testing has demonstrated an acceptable level of performance of the aircraft" and testified that the "program expects to begin low-rate initial procurement in 2007 with less than 1 percent of the flight test program completed." The Armed Services Committee expressed concern that "concurrent development and production of the F-35 is likely to result in further cost increases and schedule delays."

The bill included $3.6 billion for the F-22 Raptor, the Air Force's next-generation premier fighter, including $2.9 billion—$1.4 billion more than requested—to fully fund the purchase of twenty aircraft in fiscal 2007. The committee approved the Air Force's multiyear strategy to procure three lots of planes, each consisting of twenty aircraft, between fiscal years 2008 and 2010. However, it rejected the Air Force's plan to provide incremental funding over three years for each of the lots, saying it presented "an unacceptable budget risk." With rare exceptions, Congress authorized planes on an annual basis, not over several years.

The panel provided $3.2 billion to procure fifteen C-17 cargo planes—$300 million and three planes more than requested. The bill effectively halted Pentagon plans to shut down production of the C-17, thanks to the efforts of the "C-17 caucus," a group of committee members who represented districts where the planes and their engines were manufactured or where the planes were based. The bill also blocked plans to retire U-2 spy planes and some B-52 bombers.

For shipbuilding, the committee approved $2.9 billion to procure a *Virginia*-class attack submarine, including $400 million in unrequested advance procurement funds for a second sub to be purchased in fiscal 2009. The panel called for the Pentagon to maintain an attack submarine fleet of forty-eight vessels, which would force the Navy to step up its purchases of the subs. Members also approved $2.6 billion to fund a single next-generation DD(X) destroyer, rather than splitting the funds between two of the destroyers as the Navy wanted. The committee said it did not believe the DD(X) was affordable, and it authorized $200 million in unrequested funds to modernize the older *Arleigh Burke*-class destroyers.

The bill authorized $3.4 billion—$326 less than requested—for the Future Combat Systems, the Army's program to build a new generation of ultramodern vehicles, aircraft, robots, weapons, and computers. Citing escalating costs, technical uncertainties, and slipping deadlines, the committee included language requiring the Defense Acquisition Board to make a "go/no go" decision on the program no later than Sept. 30, 2008.

The committee bill authorized $9.1 billion for missile defense, down from the president's $9.3 billion request.

The bill also included various "Buy American" provisions pushed by Hunter. The Senate had routinely blocked the House committee chair's efforts in this area, arguing that they would drive up costs and were not feasible in an age of global commerce.

HOUSE FLOOR ACTION

The House passed HR 5122 by a vote of 396–31 on May 11.

On the day of the vote the White House issued a statement opposing many of the House Armed Services Committee's proposals, including increased military pay and benefits and the alterations to Bush's plans for purchasing future weapons and equipment. The statement also warned that Bush advisers would recommend a veto if the Buy American provisions were in the final bill.

Lawmakers were not intimidated. They said it was their right and duty to take care of men and women in uniform. As Ike Skelton, D-Mo., put it: "We are not a rubber stamp." And Hunter defended the Buy American provisions, saying that if the United States was going to supply weapons to defend the free world, it was "only equitable" that U.S. workers would make those weapons.

During the floor debate, the House accepted by voice vote a Gene Taylor, D-Miss., amendment to require that by the end of fiscal 2007 all wheeled military vehicles outside of compounds in Iraq and Afghanistan carry improvised explosive device (IED) jammers. Members also adopted an Adam B. Schiff, D-Calif., amendment requiring regular reports to Congress on roadside bomb threats and on the Pentagon's progress in developing systems to defeat them.

In other action, the House adopted 252–171 a Virgil H. Goode Jr., R-Va., proposal to authorize the assignment of troops to assist in U.S. border security under certain circumstances such as a threat to national security. The House rejected 191–237 a proposal by California Democrats Loretta Sanchez, Susan A. Davis, and Jane Harman to allow overseas military hospitals to provide privately funded abortions for women who were in the service or were military dependents.

SENATE COMMITTEE ACTION

The Senate Armed Services Committee reported its fiscal 2007 defense authorization bill (S 2766—S Rept 109-254) on May 9. Its version authorized $517.7 billion, including $50 billion in emergency war funds.

The committee challenged the president on a number of fronts, but it also deviated significantly from the House panel in some areas. For example, the Senate bill did not include the House's Buy American provisions, its larger-than-requested pay raise for military personnel, or its proposal to extend discounted health care benefits to nearly all reservists. On the other hand, Senate authorizers went much further than the House in challenging the F-35 program.

In other military personnel matters, the Senate panel did agree with the House end-strength troop levels and with its decision to reject the administration proposal to increase Tricare deductibles and enrollment fees for certain military retirees.

The Senate bill authorized virtually the same amount as in the House bill for development of the F-35, but it proposed delaying production of the first five aircraft for one year, providing only $60 million of the $1.3 billion requested for advance procurement. The panel criticized the overlap of testing and production, saying it had been risky in other cases such as the F-22A Raptor, which had experienced major cost overruns and delivery delays. The bill authorized $3.6 billion for the F-22A program, including $2.9 billion to fully fund the purchase of twenty planes in fiscal 2007. Like the House, the panel prohibited incremental funding, but unlike the House, it also rejected a multiyear procurement contract. John McCain, R-Ariz., and Armed Services Chair John W. Warner, R-Va., said the Air Force had not yet demonstrated that such a deal would result in major savings.

The panel rejected retirement of any B-52 bombers until the committee received a report on the bomber fleet.

Like the House, Senate authorizers chose to keep the C-17 production lines going, authorizing $2.9 billion to buy fourteen C-17 transport planes, two more than requested.

The panel authorized the requested $2.5 billion to procure a *Virginia*-class attack submarine, but unlike the House, it did not add funds for advance procurement of a second sub. It also disagreed with the House on funding for the DD(X) destroyer. The bill included the $2.6 billion for partial construction of two DD(X) destroyers to be built at separate shipyards, as had been requested by the Navy but rejected by the House. Senate authorizers also added $1.6 billion in unrequested funds to procure one LPD-17 amphibious ship that was not authorized under the House bill. The bill repealed a requirement that twelve aircraft carriers had to be maintained. The Navy strongly favored eleven aircraft carriers.

In other action, the committee reduced the authorization for the Future Combat Systems by $254 million, still less than the House bill had.

The Senate bill provided the requested amount for missile defense.

SENATE FLOOR ACTION

The Senate passed S 2766 by a vote of 96–0 on June 22 and then by voice vote inserted the text into HR 5122 in preparation for a conference with the House. The total authorization in the Senate version amounted to $519.4 billion.

Passage had come after two weeks of debate—much of it focused on issues related to the war in Iraq.

The Senate agreed 98–0 to require that the president request funding for the war as part of the annual budget rather than as supplemental spending, beginning with fiscal 2008. The amendment, which was offered by McCain, had a bipartisan list of sponsors that included Warner; Ted Stevens, R-Alaska, chair of the Senate Defense Appropriations Subcommittee; and Minority Leader Harry Reid, D-Nev. McCain and his allies noted that the emergency appropriations being used to finance the war were not subject to Congress's spending caps and did not have to be offset by spending cuts elsewhere. McCain said lawmakers were acting as if it were free money when it was not. Amendment sponsors also said that the must-pass emergency spending bills attracted billions of dollars in earmarks, and that the documents the administration provided to justify supplemental spending were scant compared to those submitted for regular budget requests. The House bill had no similar language.

Republicans rallied around Bush's policy to stay the course in Iraq, defeating several Democratic amendments aimed at reducing U.S. troop strength. An amendment that would have required U.S. withdrawal from Iraq by the end of 2006 was tabled (killed) by a 93–6 vote. A proposal to require withdrawal of most U.S. forces from Iraq by July 2007 was rejected 13–86. A milder proposal that contained nonbinding language stating that the president should begin a phased withdrawal from Iraq in 2006 and send Congress his plan with estimated dates for the continued phased withdrawal was defeated by a **key vote of 39–60 (R 1–54; D 37–6; I 1–0)**. *(Details, Iraq war policy, pp. 270, 303; 2006 key votes, p. 937)*

In other war-related action, the Senate agreed by voice vote to a Joseph R. Biden Jr., D-Del., proposal to prohibit the use of funds authorized in the bill to establish permanent military bases in Iraq or to control the country's oil resources. Senators rejected 44–52 a Byron L. Dorgan, D-N.D., amendment to set up a special committee to investigate contracting improprieties in Iraq and Afghanistan.

The Senate set up a point of controversy with the House and the Pentagon when it gave voice vote approval to an amendment by Christopher S. Bond, R-Mo., and Patrick J. Leahy, D-Vt., to make the head of the National Guard a four-star general instead of a three-star lieutenant general. The two sponsors wanted to make the National Guard chief a member of the Joint Chiefs of Staff as well, but they dropped that element to increase support for their amendment.

In separate action, the Senate agreed by voice vote to a proposal by John Ensign, R-Nev., to authorize temporary use of the National Guard to assist in border security along the U.S. southern border.

Senators adopted 70–28 a Saxby Chambliss, R-Ga., amendment to authorize a multiyear commitment to purchase sixty F-22As and their engines over the next three years, as the Air Force wanted, on the grounds that it would save taxpayers money.

The Senate agreed by voice vote to a Frank R. Lautenberg, D-N.J., amendment to block an administration proposal to increase the price of drugs purchased in retail pharmacies by Tricare participants.

A Reid amendment that required the president to appoint a coordinator for policy on North Korea and that set reporting requirements was adopted by voice vote.

CONFERENCE ACTION

The House agreed to the conference report on HR 5122 (H Rept 109-702) by a vote of 398–23 on Sept. 29. The Senate concurred by voice vote the next day, clearing the measure for the president.

For a time it seemed as if HR 5122 would join the long list of legislation that was being postponed until Congress reconvened in a lame-duck session after the November midterm elections. But Warner, in particular, wanted final action before lawmakers departed Sept. 30 for the campaign trail. The conference had been held up, in part, by a House provision that would have allowed chaplains to use sectarian language in delivering prayers at official functions. The provision was a reaction to the issuing of military guidelines that allowed only nonsectarian prayer at military functions. When it became clear the dispute could not be resolved in the short time that was left, conferees agreed to drop the provision but include language in the report requiring the Army and Navy to withdraw the recent guidelines.

With the conferees primed for final action on the bill, House Speaker J. Dennis Hastert, R-Ill., raised a new obstacle: He insisted that provisions aimed at keeping courtrooms secure and combating gang violence by illegal immigrants be added to the conference report. The House had already passed stand-alone measures containing Hastert's provisions (HR 6094, HR 1751). Warner warned of a bipartisan revolt in the Senate if immigration and courthouse security provisions were attached to the defense bill, and in the end Hastert backed off all his demands.

On the substance of the bill, conferees agreed to authorize $20 billion more than either chamber had approved for emergency war funding. The additional money allowed Congress to provide $23.7 billion in "reset" money to repair, upgrade, or replace equipment in order to bring units back to full combat readiness. Although Congress had not received a formal request for the reset funding, senior military officials had made their needs clear to the Armed Services committees.

In resolving differences between the two bills on aircraft, conferees agreed with the House in authorizing multiyear procurement of the F-22A fighter and in allowing initial production of the F-35 in fiscal 2007. They also authorized the procurement of more C-17 cargo planes than either chamber had approved.

On shipbuilding authorizations, the conference committee agreed with the Senate in allowing the Navy to use the funding for two ships rather than for a single destroyer as the House had wanted. Conferees also went along with the Senate's decision to reduce the minimum number of aircraft carriers to eleven. They agreed with the House in authorizing money for advance procurement of a second *Virginia*-class sub and they dropped money added by the Senate to procure a LPD-17 amphibious ship a year early.

The final bill, like the Senate measure, included the full amount requested for missile defense.

Conferees dropped the Senate proposal to make the head of the National Guard a four-star general, which the Pentagon had opposed. Instead, they directed the Commission on the National Guard and Reserves, a congressionally mandated panel, to assess this and other proposals.

In the area of pay and benefits, conferees rejected the House proposal to increase military pay by 2.7 percent instead of the requested 2.2 percent but they adopted the House provision extending discounted health care benefits to most non–active-duty reservists.

The final bill included the Senate proposals to require war-funding requests to be part of the regular annual budget and to require the appointment of a senior envoy to coordinate U.S. policy on North Korea.

MAJOR PROVISIONS

As signed into law on Oct. 17, 2006, HR 5122 authorized $532.8 billion for defense spending in fiscal 2007. Of that, $462.8 billion was for Pentagon spending and Energy Department nuclear weapons programs, and the remaining $70 billion was authorized as emergency funding for the wars in Iraq and Afghanistan.

Iraq, Afghanistan Wars

Authorized $70 billion in emergency war funds for the first six months of 2007. An extra $20 billion had been added to the $50 billion request so that $23.7 billion could be used for reset costs—$17.1 billion for the Army and $6.6 billion for the Marine Corps. Some $2.9 billion of the Army reset money was meant for the Army Guard and Reserve.

Specified that $36.6 billion of the emergency funding be used for operations and maintenance, $8.1 billion for personnel costs, $16.6 billion for additional procurement, $869 million for health care, and $2.5 billion for classified activities. Within those totals, $1.4 billion was for additional regular and "up-armored" Humvees (Humvees reinforced with steel plating and ballistic-resistant glass) for the Army; $1.4 billion for Bradley armored vehicles; $520 million for armored Humvees for the Marines; and $80 million for Predator drones. Also included was $1 billion for personnel protective gear such as body armor; $2.1 billion to counter improvised explosive devices (IEDs); and $1.4 billion for Afghanistan security forces and $1.7 billion for Iraq security forces. The Pentagon was allowed to transfer $2.5 billion to accounts other than those specified in the bill.

Required the defense secretary to ensure that by the end of fiscal 2007 all U.S. military wheeled vehicles used in Iraq and Afghanistan outside secure military operating bases be protected by IED jammers.

Prohibited money authorized by the bill from being used to establish permanent military installations in Iraq.

Required the president to request funds for ongoing military operations in Iraq and Afghanistan as part of the regular annual budget, and to provide an estimate of all the funds that would be needed during the fiscal year.

Military Personnel

Authorized $110.1 billion.

Authorized 512,400 active-duty Army personnel (30,000 above the president's military end-strength request); 175,000 Marine Corps personnel (5,000 more than requested); and 350,000 Army National Guard personnel (17,100 more than requested).

Authorized a 2.2 percent average pay increase.

Extended discounted benefits under the military Tricare health network to almost all non–active-duty reservists, with a requirement that they pay 28 percent of the premium. (Health care benefits were not extended to reservists who were eligible for health insurance as government employees.)

Prohibited increases in Tricare premiums, deductibles, copayments, or other charges from April 1, 2006, through Sept. 30, 2007.

Protected military personnel from high-interest loans, capping annual interest rates at 36 percent.

Operations and Maintenance

Authorized $129 billion.

Facilities

Authorized $13.3 billion for construction at military bases and $4.1 billion for military family housing.

Missile Defense

Authorized $9.3 billion for ballistic-missile defense programs.

Ground Forces

Authorized $3.5 billion for development of the Army's Future Combat Systems program. The bill required a detailed Pentagon assessment of whether the program to build a new generation of ultramodern vehicles, aircraft, robots, weapons, and computers should be continued or terminated.

Aviation Forces

Authorized $2.9 billion to procure twenty F-22A Raptor warplanes. The bill authorized multiyear procurement but included conditions that the Air Force had to meet first.

Authorized $4.4 billion for development of the F-35 Joint Strike Fighter and $998 million for procurement. It required an independent cost analysis that included a one-time firm-fixed-price contract, to be submitted to the Armed Services committees by March 15, 2007.

Authorized retirement of up to eighteen B-52-H bombers but required a minimum of forty-four combat-ready B-52s and barred the Air Force from retiring additional aircraft until a long-range replacement with equivalent capabilities was ready.

Barred retirement of the U-2 spy plane in fiscal 2007.

Naval Forces

Authorized $2.6 billion to allow the Navy to start building two DDG-1000 *Zumwalt*-class guided missile destroyers. [The DDG-1000 was previously known as the DD(X) until its name was changed in April 2006.]

Authorized $2.9 billion for a *Virginia*-class submarine, including $400 million for advance procurement of a second ship.

Authorized $794 million to begin advance procurement of key components for the Navy's next generation aircraft carrier, the CVN-21.

Reduced from twelve to eleven the minimum number of aircraft carriers required, and set conditions on retiring the aircraft carrier USS *John F. Kennedy*.

Air Transport

Authorized a total of $4.6 billion for procurement of twenty-two C-17 cargo planes—$2.5 billion in regular funding had been authorized for twelve of the planes and another $2.1 billion in emergency war funding was added in conference to authorize ten more C-17s.

Required the Pentagon to maintain a minimum strategic airlift force of 299 aircraft beginning in fiscal 2009.

Nuclear Weapons

Authorized $15.8 billion for Energy Department defense-related activities.

Space Programs

Authorized $867 million for development of the Transformational Communications Satellite System and $266 million for development of the Space Radar program.

Other Provisions

Required the president to appoint a senior envoy to coordinate U.S. policy on North Korea. The president also was required to submit semiannual reports to Congress on the nuclear and missile programs of North Korea.

Required that Congress receive a comprehensive National Intelligence Estimate on Iran.

BUSH'S SIGNING STATEMENT

In signing the bill into law, President Bush said he would consider several of the provisions "optional" if he concluded that they would "impinge on the president's right to carry out other responsibilities." He specifically said he would regard the requirement to appoint a coordinator for North Korea policy as optional. He said he would regard conditions placed on retiring the aircraft carrier USS *John F. Kennedy* as "advisory." He also cited a number of requirements that reports and information be supplied to Congress, saying that he would "construe such provisions in a manner consistent with the president's constitutional authority to withhold information the disclosure of which could impair foreign relations, the national security, the deliberative processes of the executive, or the performance of the executive's constitutional duties."

Fiscal 2007 Defense Appropriations

Congress in 2006 cleared a fiscal 2007 Defense Department appropriations bill (HR 5631—PL 109-289) that included $377.6 billion in regular defense spending and $70 billion in emergency supplemental funding for the wars in Iraq and Afghanistan.

The total for basic defense funding in the final bill was $4 billion less than President George W. Bush had requested. Although the White House earlier had raised the possibility of a veto when the House passed its version with $4 billion in cuts and the Senate approved a bill that cut $9 billion, the bill was signed into law.

But while cutting the regular budget, lawmakers approved a substantial increase in the bill's emergency spending. The House had gone along with the president's request for $50 billion, but the Senate approved $66 billion and House-Senate conferees took it up to $70 billion.

At issue during work on the bill was how much money would count against the overall cap on discretionary spending that both chambers had adopted for fiscal 2007. By increasing the amount counted as emergency spending, appropriators were trying to leave more room under the cap for domestic programs and thereby ward off some of the administration's proposed cuts in those programs.

This was the third year in a row that Congress had included emergency supplemental war funds in the annual defense bill. Concerned that the Pentagon might run short before the beginning of the new fiscal year, members again turned to the must-pass defense bill to provide bridge funding. HR 5631 was one of only two appropriations bills (the Department of Homeland Security bill was the other) to clear by the Oct. 1 start to fiscal 2007. It also served as the vehicle for a continuing resolution that provided interim funding for departments covered by the nine other fiscal 2007 bills that were not enacted on time.

Members made a number of changes to Bush's requests for specific weapons systems. For example, HR 5631 almost doubled the request for procurement of Air Force F-22A Raptor warplanes but slashed procurement funding for the Joint Strike Fighter in order to slow that program to allow for further testing. Appropriators rejected the Air Force's plans to shut down the C-17 transport plane production line and provided money for additional aircraft.

The final bill prohibited the use of any of the money to establish permanent U.S. bases in Iraq. A similar provision had been dropped from a fiscal 2006 war supplemental (HR 4939—PL 109-234) several months earlier. *(2006 war supplemental, p. 350)*

HR 5631 put the brakes on a Pentagon proposal to convert existing nuclear missiles into conventional ones out of concern that they could trigger false alarms of a nuclear attack.

HOUSE ACTION

The House passed HR 5631 on June 20, 2006, by a vote of 407–19. The House Appropriations Committee had reported the bill (H Rept 109-504) on June 16.

The House version appropriated $377.5 billion in regular defense spending—$4 billion less than requested—and $50 billion in supplemental funding as requested for the wars in Iraq and Afghanistan. Appropriators made many of the cuts in the regular funding by paying for programs with the supplemental money. The administration issued a statement on the day of the House floor vote, objecting strongly to the reduction in funds and to the shift of about $2 billion in basic Pentagon funding to the emergency funding section of the bill. A veto threat was issued.

In a rebuff to President Bush, House appropriators substantially increased funds for the National Guard, subtracted hundreds of millions of dollars from the request for costly new weapons, and added funds for some programs that were not administration priorities. They also rejected the administration's request to provide partial funding for the purchase of two big weapons systems—the DD(X) destroyer and the F-22A fighter program. "The use of incremental funding," the House Appropriations Committee said in its report on the bill, "mortgages the future of the procurement budget of the Defense Department in a manner that is not acceptable to the committee."

Basic funding for the Pentagon closely followed the House-passed defense authorization bill (HR 5122), reflecting a long-standing relationship between defense authorizers and appropriators that was not seen in many other subject areas. An exception, however, could be seen on the issue of military pay. HR 5631 included the requested 2.2 percent increase in military pay and not the 2.7 percent pay raise called for in the House authorization bill.

The appropriations bill included $3.4 billion for development of the Army's Future Combat System, $326 million less than requested.

The House version appropriated $926 million to begin procurement of the F-35 Joint Strike Fighter, a cut of $334 million that eliminated funding for one of the first five Lockheed Martin aircraft Bush had requested and for parts of eight aircraft that would be completed in subsequent years. The bill provided $4.2 billion for research and development, including an extra $200 million not in Bush's budget for continued development of a backup engine from an alternative source. Citing cost and redundancy, the Pentagon had sought to eliminate the second engine, but lawmakers and allied nations planning to buy the fighter plane protested the move.

The bill provided $3.6 billion, $1.4 billion more than requested, to fully fund the purchase of twenty F-22A Raptor warplanes.

Appropriators rejected the Pentagon's plan to shut down production of Boeing's southern California C-17 cargo plane at the end of fiscal 2007, eliminating $390 million requested for that purpose. Instead, they allocated $2.5 billion to purchase twelve C-17s, plus $798 million in emergency funds to replace three war-damaged C-17s.

The bill included $2.6 billion to fully fund the purchase of one Navy DD(X) destroyer instead of splitting the money to provide partial funding for two destroyers as Bush had wanted.

The bill provided $9 million for missile defense, $355 million less than requested.

House appropriators added $500 million in unrequested funds for National Guard and Reserve equipment. They also added $251 million in emergency funds to the $4.7 billion in the bill to bring the Army National Guard to an end-strength total of 350,000, as authorized. Bush had requested funding for 333,000, reflecting an Army proposal to maintain twenty-eight National Guard combat brigades, down from a previously planned thirty-four units. Lawmakers said that was not enough to enable the National Guard to serve both its international and home-state roles.

Floor action on HR 5631 included a lengthy, passionate debate on the program of warrantless surveillance that was being carried out by the National Security Agency (NSA). By a largely party-line vote of 207–219 the House rejected an amendment by Adam B. Schiff, D-Calif., to bar funding for such surveillance except as specified under the Foreign Intelligence Surveillance Act or other criminal wiretapping statutes. The secret NSA program had been revealed by the *New York Times* in December 2005. *(Warrantless surveillance, pp. 231, 249, 251)*

An attempt by Steve King, R-Iowa, to strike from the bill a John P. Murtha, D-Pa., committee amendment barring the use of funds in the bill to establish permanent military bases in Iraq was rejected 50–376. There had been no opposition to Murtha's amendment during committee consideration because, according to Defense Subcommittee Chair C.W. Bill Young, R-Fla., "we have no intention of establishing permanent bases."

The House adopted by voice vote a Kay Granger, R-Texas, amendment to drop a provision barring the sale of F-22A Raptors to foreign governments. Also adopted by voice vote was an amendment by Edward J. Markey, D-Mass., to bar use of funds in the bill in violation of the U.N. Convention Against Torture.

The House rejected eight amendments by Jeff Flake, R-Ariz., aimed at removing members' pet projects from the bill.

SENATE ACTION

The Senate passed an amended version of HR 5631 by a vote of 98–0 on Sept. 7. The Senate Appropriations Committee had reported the bill (S Rept 109-292) on July 25.

The Senate-passed bill appropriated $414.8 billion in regular defense spending and another $66.2 billion in emergency supplemental funding for the wars in Iraq and Afghanistan. (The total for the bill was not directly comparable to that of the House-passed version. Because of jurisdictional differences between the House and Senate Defense Appropriations subcommittees, the Senate bill included several additional accounts, the largest of which was the $21.4 billion Defense Health Program. House appropriators put those items in the military construction-VA appropriations bill.)

The bill included $3.5 billion for the Army's Future Combat Systems—$254 million below the request but $87 million above the House bill. The Senate Appropriations Committee had expressed concern about the program's long-term affordability.

Senators included $4.3 billion for research and development of the F-35 Joint Strike Fighter, including $340 million to develop a backup engine. But—with the Appropriations Committee warning against "buying before flying" and calling for more testing—there was no F-35 procurement money in the bill.

Like the House, Senate appropriators rejected the Air Force's plan to spread the cost of purchasing twenty F-22A Raptor warplanes over several years. The bill included $3.5 billion—$1.4 billion more than requested—to fully fund the purchase.

Again like their House counterparts, Senate appropriators rejected Pentagon plans to shut down the C-17 production line. The bill included $2.6 billion for twelve of the cargo planes, slightly more than in the House bill, plus $640 million in emergency funds to purchase and modify additional planes.

The bill included the requested $2.6 billion for partial funding of two DD(X) destroyers, rather than requiring that it be spent to fully fund one ship as the House version had.

The bill included the administration's requests for $9.3 billion for missile defense and a 2.2 percent increase in military pay.

The Senate Appropriations Committee added $340 million in unrequested money for Guard and Reserve equipment. The committee bill also included $214 million as part of the emergency war appropriations to enable the Army National Guard to brings its end-strength up to 350,000 soldiers.

When the bill reached the floor, the Senate approved a series of amendments that added $16.2 billion in emergency spending to the $50 billion in supplemental funding already in the bill.

The largest component of that additional supplemental funding was $13.1 billion for the repair and replacement of equipment worn out in Iraq and Afghanistan. That total included $7.8 billion for the Army—in addition to $2.5 billion in the underlying bill—and $5.3 billion for the Marine Corps. The money was proposed in an amendment offered by Defense Appropriations Subcommittee Chair Ted Stevens, R-Alaska, and adopted by voice vote. Because military officials had issued a series of warnings of a shortfall in funds for those items and wanted $17 billion to cover it, the Senate subsequently agreed 97–0 to a Christopher Dodd, D-Conn., amendment that allowed the Pentagon to shift $6.7 billion, if needed, to make up the difference. The Senate also agreed by voice vote to a bipartisan proposal by Christopher S. Bond, R-Mo., and Patrick J. Leahy, D-Vt., to devote $2.4 billion of the total to the Army National Guard and Reserve for the repair and replacement of their war-torn equipment.

The additional supplemental money also included $1.8 billion to build 370 miles of triple-layer fencing and 500 miles of vehicle barriers along the U.S.-Mexico border. The amendment by Jeff Sessions, R-Ala., was adopted 94–3. The Senate had authorized the fencing and barriers as part of its immigration overhaul bill (S 2611).

The extra $16.2 billion emergency money also included $200 million to create a new intelligence unit to hunt down al Qaeda terrorist leader Osama bin Laden, $700 million to fight opium production in Afghanistan, and $275 million to fight wildfires in the West. These additions were made in separate amendments.

During a combative debate over the Iraq War, Republicans managed to block a Democratic nonbinding sense-of-the-Senate provision calling for a "change of course in Iraq." But the Senate did approve several other Iraq-related amendments. With sectarian violence on the rise in Iraq, the Senate agreed by voice vote to an Edward M. Kennedy,

D-Mass., amendment requiring the administration to produce within ninety days of the bill's enactment a new National Intelligence Estimate (NIE) on conditions in Iraq. A proposal by Barbara Boxer, D-Calif., to prohibit any agreement with the Iraqi government that would allow U.S. troops serving in Iraq to be tried under that nation's criminal justice system was adopted 97–0. The Senate also approved by voice vote a Joseph R. Biden Jr., D-Del., amendment to prohibit the use of funds in the bill to establish U.S. military installations in Iraq or exercise U.S. control over Iraqi oil resources. *(Iraq War policy, pp. 270, 303)*

In action on other amendments, the Senate adopted 96–1 a Tom Coburn, R-Okla., amendment requiring the Defense Department to publicly report the costs and recipients of any items put into the bill by individual members of Congress. Most earmarks typically came from the appropriators.

The Senate rejected 31–67 an attempt by Jeff Sessions, R-Ala., to dedicate $77 million in Navy research and development funds to demonstrate the feasibility of modifying Trident missiles to carry conventional warheads. Military leaders said the program would be a way to make use of cold war weapons and provide quick-strike capabilities around the world, and Bush had requested $127 million for that purpose. But the Appropriations Committee left the money out of the bill, saying that basic issues about the use of the weapons had to be addressed first.

CONFERENCE ACTION

The House approved the conference report (H Rept 109-676) on Sept. 26 by a vote of 394–22. The Senate agreed to it Sept. 29 by a vote of 100–0, clearing the bill for the president.

Faced with a White House veto threat, appropriators agreed to restore about $5 billion of the $9 billion in discretionary funding that the Senate had cut from Bush's request. They also added to the emergency section of the bill, bringing total emergency spending to $70 billion.

That $70 billion included $22.9 billion for Army and Marine "reset" costs—money to repair and replace equipment damaged or lost in the fighting in Iraq and Afghanistan. Conferees noted that they were providing the funds without a formal request from the administration and urged the Pentagon "to include funding in future budget requests to address reset requirements and ensure that readiness goals are achieved."

The final bill barred the use of funds to establish permanent military bases in Iraq, as both chambers' bills had. It also included the Senate provision barring any U.S. troops from being tried under the Iraqi criminal justice system and the House provision barring the use of funds in violation of the U.N. Convention Against Torture.

Conferees went along with both chambers' bills in fully funding the purchase of twenty F-22A Raptor planes. They rejected the Senate plan to block procurement of the Joint Strike Fighter for a year, but they agreed to provide only about 55 percent of the funding requested in order to allow the program to proceed "but at a more modest rate." The bill also included unrequested funds for the continued development of a second, competing engine for the Joint Strike Fighter and called for an independent cost analysis of the alternative engine program. As recommended by both chambers, conferees rejected the Air Force's proposal to shut down the C-17 transport plane production line after fiscal 2007.

The conference committee agreed with the Senate to provide the requested partial funding for two DDG-1000 destroyers—the new name for the DD(X)—rather than supplying full funding for a single ship, as the House had wanted. Conferees stressed in their report that this was a one-time exception to the policy of full funding.

Conferees included money to fight wildfires in the West, although less than in the Senate bill. They dropped the Senate bill's extra money to capture Osama bin Laden. They provided $100 million of the $700 million proposed by the Senate for counternarcotics efforts in Afghanistan; basic Defense Department funding also included $978 million for drug interdiction activities. Money for border fencing was provided in the Homeland Security spending bill (HR 5441—PL 109-295).

The conference committee rejected the administration's request for funding to demonstrate the feasibility of using existing Trident II missiles for conventional strikes, saying "fundamental issues about the requirement for and use of this weapon must be addressed prior to determining the efficacy of this program." Instead, conferees provided $5 million for the National Academy of Sciences to study alternative global strike options and $20 million for the Navy to examine which Trident technologies could be used for those alternatives.

The Senate bill's requirement for a new NIE on Iraq was dropped from the bill. However, conferees noted that a new estimate was being drafted and urged that it follow the outlines of the Senate amendment, which included topics such as whether a stable and effective unity government was being created in Iraq, the prospects for controlling severe sectarian violence that could lead to civil war, and whether Iraq was succeeding in creating effective security forces.

The conference bill included $290 million in unrequested nonemergency funds for Army National Guard and Reserve equipment. It also added $296 million in unrequested emergency money, more than in either chamber's bill, to increase the end-strength of the Army National Guard to 350,000—17,000 more than requested. Conferees explained that their review of a Pentagon proposal to reduce the number of Army National Guard combat brigades to twenty-eight had indicated that the National Guard would have difficulty meeting its obligations at home and abroad.

MAJOR PROVISIONS

As signed into law on Sept. 29, HR 5631 appropriated $377.6 billion for regular fiscal 2007 military spending.

In addition, the bill included $70 billion in emergency supplemental money that was almost entirely for the wars in Iraq and Afghanistan.

The bill also included $200 million to fight wildfires in the West. The money was to be split between the Interior Department's Bureau of Land Management and the U.S. Forest Service.

War Supplemental

Included in the $70 billion emergency supplemental was:

- $44.3 billion for operation and maintenance accounts, including $1.9 billion to test and field new jammers to counter improvised explosive devices (IEDs), and $3.2 billion to train and equip Iraqi and Afghan security forces.
- $19.8 billion for various procurement accounts to replace equipment lost in the fighting, including $1.6 billion for additional up-armored Humvees, $214 million for fragmentation and gunner protection kits, $1.3 billion for Abrams tanks, and $1.4 billion for Bradley Fighting Vehicles. The total also included $2.1 billion for ten C-17 transport planes.
- $5.4 billion for military personnel.

Allowed up to $500 million in supplemental money to be used for the Commanders' Emergency Response Program, which provided funds for use by commanders in Iraq and Afghanistan for small humanitarian and reconstruction projects.

Specified that $2.9 billion of the Army's funds be set aside for the Army National Guard and Reserve.

Included $296 million to bring Army National Guard troop levels to 350,000.

Allowed the Pentagon to shift up to $3 billion among accounts through regular reprogramming procedures.

War-Related Provisions

Barred use of funds in the bill to establish permanent military bases in Iraq or to exercise control over that country's oil reserves.

Barred any agreement with the Iraqi government that would have allowed U.S. troops serving in Iraq to be tried under that nation's criminal justice system.

Barred use of the bill's funds in violation of the U.N. Convention Against Torture and Other Cruel, Inhuman or Degrading Treatment or Punishment.

Military Personnel

Appropriated $86.4 billion.

Included a 2.2 percent average pay raise.

Operations and Maintenance

Appropriated $119.8 billion.

Missile Defense

Appropriated $9.4 billion.

Ground Forces

Appropriated $3.4 billion for the Army's Future Combat Systems, a collection of manned and unmanned ground and aerial systems.

Appropriated $799 million for Stryker armored vehicle procurement.

Aviation Forces

Appropriated $3.4 billion for Air Force F-22A Raptor warplanes, including $2.7 billion to buy twenty of the aircraft in fiscal 2007 and $687 million in advance funds for twenty more in fiscal 2008. The bill continued a prohibition on overseas sales of the fighter, which was intended to replace the F-15 and designed to have both air-to-air and air-to-ground fighter capabilities.

Appropriated $4.3 billion for development of the F-35 Joint Strike Fighter, including $340 million to continue the development of a second, alternative engine. The bill directed the Defense Department to sponsor an independent cost analysis of the alternative engine program and report the findings to Congress by March 15, 2007. The bill also provided $699 million for procurement.

Appropriated $2.6 billion for the Navy and Marine Corps to purchase thirty-four of the most advanced F/A-18 Super Hornet fighter aircraft.

Naval Forces

Appropriated $2.6 billion for partial payment for two DDG-1000 destroyers, which was formerly known as the DD(X).

Appropriated $2.5 billion for one *Virginia*-class submarine.

Appropriated $521 million for two Littoral Combat Ships (LCS).

Appropriated $792 million to begin advance procurement of key components for a next-generation aircraft carrier, the CVN-21, which was not to be ready until 2014.

Air and Sea Transport

Appropriated a total of $4.4 billion to purchase twenty-two Boeing-built C-17 transport planes. Regular defense funding included $2.3 billion for twelve aircraft. The emergency supplemental portion of the bill had $2.1 billion to buy ten more. Conferees barred reprogramming that emergency money for purposes other than C-17 production without the approval of Congress and directed the Pentagon to continue funding C-17 production in the fiscal 2008 budget.

Appropriated $455 million for one Navy T-AKE cargo ship.

Space Programs

Appropriated $737 million for the Transformational Satellite Communications System and $186 million for the Space Radar.

Fiscal 2007 Military Construction

No regular fiscal 2007 military construction-Veterans Affairs appropriation bill cleared Congress in 2006, although both the House and Senate passed versions of a spending bill (HR 5385). Accounts in the bill were funded instead through a series of continuing resolutions that extended through the end of fiscal 2007. Additional money was included in a fiscal 2007 supplemental appropriations bill (HR 2206—PL 110-28).

Ultimately, $97.6 billion was appropriated in fiscal 2007 for accounts usually funded by the bill—$17.9 billion for Defense Department military construction costs and $79.6 billion for the Veterans Affairs (VA) Department health and benefits programs.

The defense portion included $7.7 billion for military construction, $4 billion for family housing, and $5.9 billion for Base Realignment and Closure (BRAC).

LEGISLATIVE ACTION

The House passed HR 5385 by a 395–0 vote on May 19, 2006. The House Appropriations Committee had reported the bill (H Rept 109-464, Part I) on May 15 and a supplemental report was filed the next day (Part II).

The House-passed bill would have appropriated a total of $136.1 billion. During floor action, fiscal conservatives won a fight to strip $507 million in emergency funds for some twenty military construction projects that appropriators had included in the bill. Jeb Hensarling, R-Texas, lodged successful budget points of order against the funding. He and his allies said the emergency designation for the money was a budget gimmick used by appropriators to dodge the House-passed budget resolution (H Con Res 376), which they said reflected fiscal responsibility. Republican leaders could have protected the emergency spending in the Rules Committee by barring points of order against it, but they did not. Angry supporters of the rejected projects vowed to restore the funding, which they said was vital during wartime.

The Senate passed a $94.3 billion version of HR 5385 by voice vote on Nov. 14. The Senate Appropriations Committee had reported the bill (S Rept 109-286) on July 20.

During floor action, the Senate approved by voice vote a Susan Collins, R-Maine, amendment to extend the term of the inspector general responsible for overseeing how Iraq reconstruction money was being spent. Under the fiscal 2007 defense authorization bill (HR 5122—PL 109-364), the official's term was set to expire Oct. 1, 2007. The term extension ultimately was enacted in a stand-alone bill (S 4046—PL 109-440). *(Iraq reconstruction oversight, box p. 353)*

The Senate bill was much smaller than the House version mainly because of differences in jurisdiction between the House and Senate Appropriations subcommittees responsible for the bills. Unlike the Senate version, the House measure also included the Defense Health Program for active-duty personnel, basic housing allowances, and environmental restoration funding. In 2005 appropriators had agreed to alternate each year between the House and Senate structures for the bill. They had followed the Senate formula that year.

The main differences between the House- and Senate-passed bills were in the area of military base construction and BRAC costs. The differences, however, were not large and, even though the Senate had not passed the bill until the week before Thanksgiving, HR 5385 seemed sure to clear before the 109th Congress adjourned.

But a defiant band of conservative GOP senators placed a hold on the appointment of Senate conferees, effectively bringing work on this and all the other remaining appropriations bills to a halt. The fiscal conservatives—led by Jim DeMint of South Carolina, Jeff Sessions of Alabama, and Tom Coburn of Oklahoma—feared the bill could become a vehicle for an earmark-laden omnibus spending package.

In a last-minute attempt to save the bill, Kay Bailey Hutchison, R-Texas, chair of the Military Construction-VA Appropriations Subcommittee, threatened to add the text of HR 5385 to the next continuing funding resolution. That led to talks with GOP leaders and the conservatives, who agreed on Dec. 6 to go to conference and allow enactment of a stand-alone bill. But with Congress aiming to adjourn Dec. 8, House appropriators said it was too late.

On Dec. 9, 2006, Congress cleared another stopgap spending law (H J Res 102—PL 109-383)—the third thus far—to continue funding for programs covered by nine unfinished fiscal 2007 appropriations bills, including the military construction-VA measure. And early in the next year Congress cleared a continuing resolution (H J Res 20) covering the nine bills through the end of the fiscal year.

MAJOR PROVISIONS

Military construction accounts in fiscal 2007 were funded through continuing resolutions and a supplemental appropriations measure rather than a regular appropriations bill. A series of four continuing resolutions—three stopgap measures approved in 2006 and a year-long resolution (H J Res 20—PL 110-5) signed into law Feb. 15, 2007—and a fiscal 2007 emergency supplemental appropriations bill (HR 2206—PL 110-28) signed into law May 25, 2007:

Military Construction

Appropriated $7.7 billion for military construction, including $1.7 billion in emergency supplemental funding. That total provided $6.8 billion for active-duty forces and $851 million for National Guard and reserve forces. President George W. Bush initially had requested $6.4 billion for military construction and later asked for another $1.7 billion in supplemental spending.

Family Housing

Appropriated $4 billion for construction and maintenance of family housing. Bush had requested $4.1 billion.

Base Closing

Appropriated $5.9 billion for Base Realignment and Closure (BRAC), including $3.1 billion in emergency supplemental funding. Bush had requested $5.8 billion. *(Military base closing, p. 369)*

Detainee Policies

How the United States should treat terror suspects in its custody and how—or whether—they should be brought to trial were dominant questions in debates on defense legislation during the 109th Congress.

In a move to answer those questions, Congress approved the 2005 Detainee Treatment Act requiring adherence to certain standards of interrogation and treatment of prisoners, as part of the fiscal 2006 defense authorization and appropriations acts (HR 1815—PL 109-163 and HR 2863—PL 109-148).

And the following year lawmakers approved the Military Commissions Act (S 3930—PL 109-366) authorizing a new legal framework for trying terror suspects after the Supreme Court ruled that the military commissions set up by President George W. Bush for that purpose violated U.S. and international law.

BACKGROUND

The legal status and treatment of suspected terrorists had been hotly debated since November 2001, when President Bush authorized their detention and trial by military tribunals.

The administration decided that since terrorist organizations, such as al Qaeda—the terrorist network responsible for the Sept. 11, 2001, attacks on the United States—were not states, and since Afghanistan at the time of the 2001 U.S. invasion was a "failed state," those detained were "unlawful enemy combatants" not protected by the Geneva Convention for the treatment of prisoners of war, though they should be treated humanely. Moreover, since almost all of the detainees were captured and held outside the United States, the administration also argued that they were not entitled to protest their detention in U.S. federal courts. *(Background on wars in Afghanistan and Iraq, Congress and the Nation Vol. XI, pp. 234–241)*

The Geneva Convention was a package of four treaties signed in 1949 to govern the treatment of wartime captives. Common Article 3 of the Geneva Convention—so called because it was common to all four treaties—forbade torture as well as "humiliating and degrading treatment" and required that sentences come from "a regularly constituted court affording all the judicial guarantees which are recognized as indispensable by civilized peoples."

Nothing would focus the attention of Congress, the American people, and the world on the treatment of detainees more than the April 2004 publication of photos of the abuse of Iraqi prisoners in U.S. custody in the Abu Ghraib prison near Baghdad. The shocking pictures of prisoners stripped naked, covered with hoods, threatened by dogs, sexually abused, provoked outrage and disgust and triggered investigations. *(Wartime prisoner abuse, Congress and the Nation Vol. XI, p. 359)*

The fiscal 2005 defense authorization law (PL 108-375) set minimum criteria for a new policy to be drafted by the defense secretary to ensure humane treatment of detainees. It also required the secretary to certify the proper training of those who handled or interrogated detainees, including training on the Geneva Convention.

Despite repeated assurances from Bush and his administration, the images from Abu Ghraib would not fade away. The White House was embarrassed further when it was revealed that the CIA had clandestine prisons abroad where it detained and interrogated prisoners. *(Secret CIA prisons overseas, box p. 340)*

The legal rights of detainees continued to be debated as well. In a series of rulings in 2004, the U.S. Supreme Court upheld the right of detainees to appeal their detentions through *habeas corpus* petitions, which are used to challenge the legality of a person's confinement. *(Supreme Court decisions: prisoners of war, Congress and the Nation XI, pp. 664–665)*

2005 DETAINEE LEGISLATION

In 2005 Congress gave a broader response to the previous year's revelations of the brutal treatment of detainees. After months of battling the White House, agreement was reached to include the Detainee Treatment Act in both HR 1815 and HR 2863—the defense authorization and spending bills for fiscal 2006.

The act banned "cruel, inhuman or degrading treatment" of detainees in U.S. custody, and required that Defense Department interrogators rely on standards set in an Army field manual that complied with the Geneva Convention. The prime mover behind the legislation was Sen. John McCain, R-Ariz., a Navy pilot who was captured and tortured by the North Vietnamese for five-and-a-half years during the Vietnam War.

Threatening to veto any bill containing McCain's amendment on detainee treatment, Bush continued to argue for distinguishing between prisoners captured as uniformed military personnel fighting on behalf of a nation and detainees held as unlawful enemy combatants. The administration said the latter category applied to nonuniformed foreign fighters who committed acts of terrorism—and that the Geneva Convention did not apply to them. McCain said he did not oppose Bush's attempts to distinguish between regular soldiers and enemy combatants and to treat them differently, but he insisted that Congress should spell out the rules for the treatment of all detainees.

Ultimately the House sided with the Senate in supporting the McCain amendment, and the White House backed down.

Legislative Action

McCain had planned to offer his amendment when the Senate's version of the defense authorization bill (S 1042) first came to the floor in late July 2005. However, Senate Majority Leader Bill Frist, R-Tenn., pulled the bill off the floor until agreement could be reached on several amendments, including McCain's. In a statement of policy issued July 21, the administration threatened to veto the bill if it included the detainee amendment, saying it would restrict the president's ability to conduct the war on terror. Vice President Dick Cheney tried without success to persuade McCain to make an exemption for U.S. intelligence personnel.

With the authorization bill stalled, McCain turned to HR 2863, the defense appropriations bill. On Oct. 5 the Senate adopted his amendment to the spending bill by a **key vote of 90–9 (R 46–9; D 43–0; I 1–0)**. *(2005 key votes, p. 915)*

The authorization bill returned to the Senate floor in early November. The Senate on Nov. 4 adopted the McCain amendment again, this time by voice vote. In other action on the bill, the Senate on Nov. 8 rejected 43–55 a proposal by Carl Levin, D-Mich., to create an independent commission to investigate the treatment of detainees in the period since the Sept. 11, 2001, terrorist attacks. On Nov. 15 the Senate adopted 84–14 an amendment offered by Lindsey Graham, R-S.C., along with Levin and Jon Kyl, R-Ariz., that restricted access to the U.S. courts by detainees held at Guantánamo Bay by barring the courts from hearing *habeas corpus* claims. The courts had received more than 160 *habeas corpus* petitions contesting more than 300 detentions since the Supreme Court ruled in a 2004 case, *Rasul v. Bush,* that U.S courts had jurisdiction to hear challenges on behalf of foreigners held at the Guantánamo detention center.

Bush, along with House Armed Services Chair Duncan Hunter, R-Calif., continued to flatly reject the language of the McCain amendment. But the breakthrough for McCain and his allies came on Dec. 14, when the House, by a **key vote of 308–122 (R 107–121; D 200–1; I 1–0),** instructed its conferees on the appropriations bill to include the McCain amendment in the conference bill. After that overwhelming show of support, Bush backed down and accepted the language during an Oval Office meeting the next day with McCain and John W. Warner, R-Va., the chair of the Senate Armed Services Committee. McCain did agree to add provisions to protect U.S. interrogators who might be prosecuted for actions that had been officially authorized and were considered lawful at the time they were conducted.

Nearly identical versions of McCain's amendment were included in the final authorization and spending bills. *(2006 defense authorization, p. 336; 2006 defense appropriations, p. 344)*

Major Provisions

As signed into law on Dec. 30, 2005, as part of HR 2863, and again on Jan. 6, 2006, as part of HR 1815:

Cruel Treatment Ban. Prohibited "cruel, inhuman or degrading treatment or punishment" of an individual in the custody or under the physical control of the U.S. government, regardless of nationality or physical location.

Army Field Manual. Prohibited any person in the custody or under the effective control of the Defense Department or who was being detained in a Defense Department facility from being subjected to any treatment or technique of interrogation not authorized by and listed in the Army Field Manual of Intelligence Interrogation.

Protections for Interrogators. Provided protection in any civil action or criminal prosecution for U.S. military or U.S. government personnel engaged in interrogations that were officially authorized and determined to be lawful at the time they were conducted. Government officials could use their belief that the actions were lawful as a defense, and the government could provide them with counsel.

Training for Iraqi Forces. Required the secretary of defense to ensure that any U.S. training of Iraqi Security Forces included instruction on the humane treatment of detainees, including protections afforded under the Geneva Convention and the Convention Against Torture.

Status of Detainees. Required the secretary of defense to submit to the appropriate congressional committees a report setting forth the procedures used by military tribunals or administrative review boards for determining the status of detainees held at Guantánamo Bay and to provide an annual review to determine the need to continue to hold a detainee. The report was also to cover the procedures used to determine the status of detainees held by the Defense Department in Afghanistan and Iraq.

Civilian Overseer. Required that the person overseeing the decisions of tribunals or review boards be a civilian officer of the Defense Department who was appointed by the president and confirmed by the Senate.

Statements Obtained Through Coercion. Required tribunals or boards to assess "to the extent practicable" whether a statement from a detainee was obtained as a result of coercion and what was the probative value, if any, of the statement.

Legal Appeals, Reviews. Barred courts, justices, and judges from hearing or considering *habeas corpus* applications by detainees at Guantánamo or any other action against the United States relating to any aspect of their detention. However, the legislation did give the United States Court of Appeals for the District of Columbia Circuit exclusive jurisdiction to review a tribunal's decision that an alien has been properly detained at Guantánamo as an enemy combatant. Those sentenced by a tribunal to death or more than ten years in prison would have their sentences automatically reviewed by the appellate court.

2006 TRIBUNALS LEGISLATION

Congress in 2006 cleared legislation (S 3930—PL 109-366) setting new rules for trying accused terrorists held at the Guantánamo detention facility. The legislation was a direct response to the Supreme Court's June 29, 2006, ruling that the tribunals Bush had established by military order in November 2001 were illegal and violated international law.

The Court's decision in *Hamdan v. Rumsfeld* was a major setback for Bush. The president had resisted congressional involvement in setting up the tribunal system, saying that he already had the authority to act both in his constitutional role as commander in chief and under the congressional resolution (PL 107-40) that authorized the use of force after the Sept. 11 attacks. But the Supreme Court ruling made it clear that the tribunals had to be authorized by Congress. *(Hamdan v. Rumsfeld, pp. 730, 764)*

The Court also ruled that the tribunals violated international law because they did not comply with Common Article 3 of the Geneva Convention. In particular, the Court pointed to the fact that defendants were not guaranteed the right to attend the proceedings or to see all of the evidence against them, and that the prosecution could introduce hearsay evidence, unsworn testimony, and evidence obtained through coercion.

Also rejected was the Bush administration's argument that the Supreme Court lacked jurisdiction because the 2005 Detainee Treatment Act had barred courts from hearing *habeas corpus* challenges by Guantánamo detainees. The Court said that provision did not apply because the *Hamdan* case was pending before the detainee act became law—a decision that could be extended to the hundreds of other detainees who had filed such challenges before the law's enactment.

The ruling left the Bush administration with the choice of operating the tribunals under existing military court-martial rules or getting congressional authorization. In either case, the tribunals would have to meet the standards of Article 3.

Bush turned to Congress. Speaking on Sept. 6 to a White House audience that included relatives of victims of the Sept. 11 terrorist attacks, the president asked Congress to send him legislation authorizing the military commissions. He said that fourteen top terror suspects detained by the CIA—including Khalid Sheikh Mohammed, believed to be the al Qaeda mastermind of the Sept. 11 attacks—had been transferred to Guantánamo Bay, where they would be tried "as soon as Congress acts to authorize the military commissions I have proposed."

Bush's proposal won quick endorsement from Republican leaders in both chambers, and enactment became a top GOP priority in advance of the November midterm election, which was expected to turn largely on national security concerns. Senate Majority Leader Frist filed a bill reflecting the president's plan and the House Armed Services Committee approved a similar measure (HR 6054) the following week.

But a trio of influential Republicans on the Senate Armed Services Committee—Warner, McCain, and Graham—took exception to several provisions in Bush's proposal. They singled out in particular a proposal to reinterpret U.S. obligations under the Geneva Convention, which they said could invite other countries to do the same in ways that could put U.S. military and intelligence personnel captured in future wars in greater danger.

Also at issue were proposals by Bush to allow the use of classified evidence that the accused could not see; to allow a trial without the defendant present, if that was judged necessary to protect national security; and to allow the use of evidence obtained through coercion unless the judge found it to be "unreliable or lacking in probative value." The senators generally preferred to follow procedures used for U.S. courts-martial, making exception where necessary, rather than creating a separate system as Bush proposed.

Unable to reach a compromise with the White House, the three senators won the Armed Services Committee's approval of their bill (S 3901). The Bush administration launched an intensive lobbying campaign for its approach, but it was facing staunch Republicans with impeccable national security credentials and media savvy—Warner, a former Navy secretary who fought in World War II and Korea; McCain, a former POW; and Graham, a former Air Force Reserve military judge.

Finally, a deal was reached. Bush's main concessions were to drop his insistence on reinterpreting the Geneva Convention and on allowing defendants to be tried and convicted on the basis of classified evidence they would never see. The White House reportedly was satisfied that a list of war crimes that would be considered "grave breaches" of Common Article 3 was sufficient. Plus, the new bill (S 3930) gave the president much of what he wanted—above all, protection for CIA agents who interrogated top terrorist suspects in clandestine overseas facilities.

The compromise retained provisions that most Democrats and a few Republicans found objectionable, such as the elimination of *habeas corpus* rights for detainees and the inclusion of language allowing a judge to permit the use of coerced confessions as long as the treatment occurred before Dec. 30, 2005 (when the 2005 Detainee Treatment Act was signed into law as part of HR 2863), and the judge determined that the statements were reliable. After winning control of both chambers of Congress in the November elections, Democrats predicted that they would revisit the legislation in the next Congress, perhaps at the direction of the courts.

Indeed, the Supreme Court in 2008 ruled that denying military detainees held at Guantánamo the right to file a *habeas corpus* petition in federal court was unconstitutional. *(Details, p. 730)*

Legislative Action

After Bush asked Congress for the tribunal authorization, the House Armed Services Committee rallied behind the president and reported a bill (HR 6054—H Rept 109-664, Part I) on Sept. 15. The measure authorized the president to create military commissions to try "alien unlawful enemy combatants," created a Court of Military Commission Review to automatically review any case that resulted in a guilty verdict, and allowed for appeals to the U.S. Court of Appeals for the District of Columbia Circuit and ultimately the Supreme Court.

Controversial elements of HR 6054 included allowing a military judge to exclude a detainee from portions of the trial and prevent the person from seeing classified evidence in order to protect national security (defense counsel could be present but could not reveal the evidence to the accused, who would see only a redacted transcript and, if possible, a summary); allowing hearsay and testimony obtained through coercion unless it was ruled unreliable or lacking in probative value; providing that compliance with the Detainee Treatment Act fully satisfied U.S. obligations under Common Article 3; barring courts from hearing *habeas corpus* petitions of detainees; and amending the War Crimes Act to enumerate nine actions that would be punishable as violations of Article 3.

A closely divided House Judiciary Committee reported the bill (H Rept 109-664, Part II) Sept. 25. In its report, the panel lambasted the Supreme Court for taking the *Hamdan* case in the first place, saying it had no authority to hear the case after enactment of the Detainee Treatment Act. It added that HR 6054 had been drafted carefully "so that the court can fully understand that it applies to both pending and later-filed cases."

The Senate Armed Services committee reported S 3901—the Warner-McCain-Graham bill—on Sept. 14 (no written report). One more Republican and all the Democrats on the committee joined in supporting the bill. The sponsors' decision to go forward did not sit well with the White House or the Senate GOP leaders. National Intelligence Director John D. Negroponte called reporters to say that the proposal would "not allow for the CIA high-value terrorist detention program...to go forward." In a rare visit to the House, Bush and Cheney spoke with Republicans for forty-five minutes behind closed doors. And GOP leaders allowed an anonymous senator to block the Senate committee's markup meeting by invoking an obscure Senate rule. The block was eventually lifted and the markup continued.

For the three Senate sponsors, the most important difference between their bill and what Bush had proposed and the House had approved was the fact that they did not seek to define or limit compliance with the Geneva Convention. In addition to barring the use of evidence obtained through torture, the Senate bill banned statements obtained through cruel, inhuman or degrading treatment as outlawed by the Detainee Treatment Act. It allowed statements obtained through coercion if the judge found that they were reliable and of probative value, and that the interests of justice were best served by allowing the evidence. Hearsay evidence could be used under certain circumstances. The accused could be removed from the courtroom only to ensure someone's physical safety or to prevent the defendant from disrupting the proceedings. In listing the violations of Common Article 3 that would be punishable as war crimes, the Senate bill gave a somewhat broader definition of cruel treatment than in the House bill. S 3901 also would not have created a new review court. Under the bill, the denial of access to U.S. courts for *habeas corpus* or other claims would have applied to alien enemy combatants who were detained outside the country.

With the midterm election fast approaching and the Warner-McCain-Graham proposal gaining ground, the White House began trading new compromise proposals with the three senators. Meanwhile, the public impasse was creating an embarrassing distraction for Republicans, who wanted to highlight their national security credentials heading into the November election.

According to Senate aides, the chief sticking point was the White House's insistence on a provision stating that compliance with the Detainee Treatment Act "shall fully satisfy U.S. obligations with respect to the standards for detention and treatment" under the Geneva Convention. Warner, McCain, and Graham said the 2005 law was never intended to define—or limit—U.S. compliance with the Geneva Convention.

In the compromise that was finally reached on Sept. 21, Bush backed away from his insistence on reinterpreting the Geneva Convention and on allowing trials and convictions on the basis of classified evidence the defendants were not allowed to see. A late change to the bill broadened the definition of "unlawful enemy combatants" to cover not only those who engaged in hostilities against the United States and its allies but also those who "purposely and materially" aided and supported them.

The Senate passed the compromise—introduced as a new bill (S 3930)—by **a key vote of 65–34 (R 53–1; D 12–32; I 0–1)** on Sept. 28. *(2006 key votes, p. 937)*.

Bush made another rare visit to Capitol Hill that day to urge Senate Republicans to push the bill over the finish line. During two days of debate, the Senate:

- Rejected 48–51 an amendment by Arlen Specter, R-Pa., chair of the Judiciary Committee, to strike the *habeas corpus* language. Specter won the backing of all but one Democrat as well as that of three other Republicans, but most Republicans agreed with the Bush administration that the United States had no obligation to give such rights to terror suspects.
- Rejected 43–54 an attempt by Levin to scrap the compromise in favor of the bill that the Armed Services Committee had approved.

- Rejected 46–53 an amendment by John D. Rockefeller IV of West Virginia, ranking Democrat on the Select Intelligence Committee, to require the CIA to report quarterly to Congress on its detention and interrogation program.
- Rejected 47–52 a proposal by Robert C. Byrd, D-W.Va., to sunset the bill after 2011.
- Rejected 46–53 an attempt by Edward M. Kennedy, D-Mass., to specify types of interrogation tactics barred under the bill.

While the Senate was debating its bill, the House passed an identical bill (HR 6166) by a vote of 253–168 on Sept. 27. Before passage, the House rejected 195–228 a motion by Ike Skelton, D-Mo., ranking Democrat on the House Armed Services Committee, to send the bill back to committee with instructions to add language establishing a process for expedited judicial review of any challenge to the law and sunsetting it after three years. Two days later, on Sept. 29, the House cleared S 3930 by a vote of 250–170. Both times the bill was considered under a closed rule that prohibited amendments.

Major Provisions

As signed into law on Oct. 17, 2006, S 3930, the Military Commissions Act:

Military Tribunals. Authorized the president to establish military commissions to try "alien unlawful enemy combatants engaged in hostilities against the United States," and laid out their rules, composition, and powers. The commissions were authorized to impose penalties, including death or life in prison, on those found guilty. The law defined an "unlawful enemy combatant" as "a person who has engaged in hostilities or who has purposefully and materially supported hostilities against the United States or its co-belligerents" in the war on terrorism. The law stated that the commissions complied with the requirements of Common Article 3 for "judicial guarantees which are recognized as indispensable by civilized peoples."

Habeas Corpus. Specified that no U.S. court had jurisdiction to consider a *habeas corpus* petition of an alien in U.S. custody who was found to be an unlawful enemy combatant or who was awaiting such determination. There was no time limit on making a determination. The provision was retroactive to Sept. 11, 2001. (A *habeas corpus* petition, if granted, required that the prisoner be brought to the court so the court could determine whether the individual had been imprisoned legally or should be released.)

Rights of the Accused. Provided that the accused had the right to be informed of the charges, to be presumed innocent until determined guilty, to refuse to self-incriminate or testify, to present evidence, and to cross-examine witnesses.

Presence of the Accused. Required that proceedings be conducted in the presence of the accused detainee, with the exception of times when the commission was voting, deliberating, or performing certain other procedural functions. A defendant also could be removed if the person's behavior disrupted the proceedings or threatened anyone's safety.

Classified Evidence. Directed the military judge to protect classified evidence if disclosure would be detrimental to national security, and to protect sources and methods. But the law did not authorize the use of classified evidence that was not disclosed to the defendant. In place of such evidence, the judge was directed "to the extent practicable" to allow summaries, redacted copies, or statements of relevant facts that the classified information would tend to prove. The trial counsel was obligated to provide the accused with any evidence that tended to prove his innocence.

Evidence Obtained Through Torture, Coercion. Provided that statements obtained by torture were not admissible, but evidence obtained through "coercion" could be used if the military judge found that the "totality of the circumstances" made it reliable and of probative value. For evidence obtained after Dec. 30, 2005, the date the Detainee Treatment Act was signed into law, the judge also would have to find that the methods used did not amount to cruel, inhuman, or degrading treatment barred by the act.

Appeals. Directed the secretary of defense to establish a Court of Military Commission Review. A detainee convicted by a military commission could appeal the decision to the review court and then to the U.S. Court of Appeals for the District of Columbia Circuit and the Supreme Court.

War Crimes Act. Limited the offenses punishable as war crimes under U.S. statutes. Previously, the 1996 War Crimes Act (PL 104-192) defined as a war crime any conduct "which constitutes a violation of Common Article 3." The Military Commissions Act narrowed that to conduct "which constitutes a grave breach of Common Article 3," defined as one of nine specific acts. These were: torture, cruel or inhuman treatment, performing biological experiments, murder, mutilation or maiming, intentionally causing serious bodily injury, rape, sexual assault or abuse, and taking hostages. The offenses did not include "humiliating and degrading treatment" as referred to in Article 3.

Geneva Convention. Specified that the Geneva Convention could not be used as a "source of rights" in any U.S. court. (The law did not contain language originally sought by the administration stating that adherence to the Detainee Treatment Act satisfied U.S. obligations under Common Article 3 of the Geneva Convention.)

Counsel for U.S. Personnel. Amended the Detainee Treatment Act to provide, rather than simply allow, government counsel for U.S. interrogators who were prosecuted for authorized actions and extended coverage of this provision to include actions taken from Sept. 11, 2001, through Dec. 30, 2005.

Military Base Closings

Congress in 2005 allowed a new round of military base closings and realignments to go forward. A House resolution (H J Res 65) to block the proposals failed, and no resolution of disapproval was filed in the Senate.

The purpose of the process was to close or consolidate unneeded or redundant facilities. A total of 182 closures or realignments were approved in 2005, including twenty-two major closures and thirty-three major realignments. (Subsequently one base slated for closure was given a new mission and allowed to stay open.) The specially appointed commission that made the closure and realignment recommendations estimated the total savings that would result over the next twenty years at $35.6 billion. *(Major closures, realignments box, p. 370)*

The Defense Department estimated that about 18,000 civilian jobs would be lost. The biggest loser was Virginia, with a projected loss of about 10,840 jobs. The biggest winner was neighboring Maryland, which stood to gain about 7,770 jobs.

The 2005 round was the fifth to take place, following earlier rounds in 1988, 1991, 1993, and 1995. The first four rounds closed ninety-seven major facilities and had net estimated savings (total savings minus costs) of about $29 billion through fiscal 2003, according to a May 2005 Government Accountability Office report. *(1995 round, Congress and the Nation Vol. IX, p. 319)*

BACKGROUND

Decisions to close or realign military bases were nearly always highly controversial because of their economic impact on the communities in which they were located. Members of Congress representing those communities adamantly opposed the closings. Many were also suspicious that the White House used political criteria in making base closing decisions.

To insulate the decision making from congressional pressures to keep bases open, a special process was first enacted in 1988 (PL 100-526). A similar process to cover the next three rounds was enacted in 1990 (PL 101-510). President George W. Bush called for another round in 2003, but, because of congressional opposition, it was put off until 2005. The new round was authorized in 2001 in the annual defense authorization bill (PL 107-107). (*Congress and the Nation Vol. VII, p. 335; Vol. VIII, p. 353; Vol. XI, p. 315)*

Under the procedures mandated by the legislation, the president was to appoint and the Senate confirm a Base Realignment and Closure (BRAC) Commission comprised of a chair and eight members. The Pentagon was to submit a list of recommended closures and consolidations to the commission, which would then evaluate the proposals.

In making its recommendations, the commission was to weigh certain factors, with the military value of a proposal to be given priority consideration. The criteria the 2005 commission used were:

- Current and future mission capabilities and the impact on operational readiness.
- Availability and condition of land, facilities, and airspace at both existing and potential receiving locations.
- Ability to accommodate contingency, mobilization, surge, and future total force requirements at both the existing and potential receiving locations to support operations and training.
- Cost of operations and manpower implications.
- Extent and timing of potential costs and savings.
- Economic impact on existing communities in the vicinity of military installations.
- Ability of the infrastructure of both the existing and potential receiving communities to support forces, missions, and personnel.
- Environmental impact.

After completing its deliberations, the commission was to submit a final list to the president. The president would have fifteen days to review the report and approve the list in its entirety and send it to Congress or reject it. If rejected, the commission could amend it and resubmit the report to the president. If he approved the list and sent it to Congress, it automatically would become law unless Congress cleared a joint resolution blocking it. Congress would have forty-five legislative days to clear a resolution, and it would require the president's signature to go into force.

Once approved the Defense Department was required to start closures within two years and complete them within six years.

COMMISSION APPOINTMENTS

On March 4, 2005, President Bush nominated Anthony J. Principi, his former secretary of Veterans Affairs (2001–2005), to be a member of the BRAC Commission and said that he would designate him chair once he was confirmed. The president submitted the other BRAC nominations—a mix of former members of the House, retired military, and former executive branch officials—to the Senate on March 15. The two former representatives were James H. Bilbray, D-Nev. (1987–1995), and James V. Hansen, R-Utah (1981–2003).

The Senate Armed Services Committee agreed by voice vote March 17 to send Principi's nomination to the floor but put off action on the other nominees until after Congress's spring recess. The nominations, however, went no further in the Senate, after Sen. Trent Lott, R-Miss., a strong opponent of BRAC, announced his intent to block them for as long as possible. Lott, whose state had several potential candidates for closure, had been the principal sponsor in 2004 of an amendment that would have limited the 2005 round to U.S. bases overseas and permitted no domestic closures before 2007. Lott's proposal had been defeated 47–49 during consideration of the fiscal 2005

MAJOR CLOSURES, REALIGNMENTS UNDER 2005 BRAC PROCESS

The 2005 Base Realignment and Closure (BRAC) recommendations that went into effect on Nov. 9, 2005, called for a total of 182 closures or realignments. Twenty-two major military installations were to be closed. (The number was subsequently reduced to twenty-one.) There were also thirty-three major realignments. These are listed below by military service. At the end of the list are major closure and realignment proposals that were rejected by the BRAC Commission.

Major Closures

Army (12)

Riverbank Army Ammunition Plant, CA

- Fort Gillem, GA
- Fort McPherson, GA
- Newport Chemical Depot, IN
- Kansas Army Ammunition Plant, KS
- Selfridge Army Activity, MI
- Mississippi Army Ammunition Plant, MS
- Fort Monmouth, NJ
- Umatilla Chemical Depot, OR
- Lone Star Army Ammunition Plant, TX
- Deseret Chemical Depot, UT
- Fort Monroe, VA

Navy (5)

- Naval Air Station, Atlanta, GA
- Naval Station Pascagoula, MS
- Naval Air Station Willow Grove, PA
- Naval Station Ingleside, TX
- Naval Air Station Brunswick, ME

Air Force (5)

- Kulis Air Guard Station, AK
- Onizuka Air Force Station, CA
- Brooks City Base, TX
- General Mitchell Air Reserve Station, WI
- Cannon Air Force Base, NM*

Major Realignments

Army (6)

- Walter Reed National Military Medical Center (at Bethesda), DC
- Rock Island Arsenal, IL
- Fort Knox, KY
- Army Reserve Personnel Center, St. Louis, MO
- Fort Eustis, VA
- Red River Army Depot, TX

Navy (13)

- Naval Base Ventura City, CA
- Naval Base Coronado, CA
- Naval Medical Center San Diego, CA
- Naval District Washington, DC
- Naval Air Station Pensacola, FL
- Naval Station Great Lakes, IL
- Naval Support Activity Crane, IN
- Naval Air Station Corpus Christi, TX
- Naval Medical Center Portsmouth, VA
- Naval Air Station Oceana, VA
- Naval Support Activity, New Orleans, LA
- Naval Weapons Station Seal Beach Concord Detachment, CA

Air Force (12)

- Eielson Air Force Base, AK
- Elmendorf Air Force Base, AK
- Mountain Home Air Force Base, ID
- Pope Air Force Base, NC
- Grand Forks Air Force Base, ND
- Lackland Air Force Base, TX
- Sheppard Air Force Base. TX
- McChord Air Force Base, WA
- Otis Air National Guard Base, MA
- W.K. Kellogg Airport Guard Station, MI
- Niagara Falls International Airport Air Guard Station, NY
- Pittsburgh International Airport Air Reserve Station, PA

Defense Agencies/Multiple Services (2)

- National Capital Region leased locations, DC
- Defense Finance and Accounting Service Arlington, VA

Proposed Closures Rejected by the Commission

- Hawthorne Army Depot, NV
- Naval Support Activity, Corona, CA
- Submarine Base New London, CT
- Naval Shipyard Portsmouth, ME
- Ellsworth AFB, SD

Proposed Realignments Rejected by the Commission

- Naval Air Station Brunswick, ME**
- Maxwell Air Force Base, AL
- Portland International Airport Air Guard Station, OR
- Defense Finance and Accounting Service Cleveland, OH

*Closure recommendation was to go into effect if the secretary of the Air Force had not designated a new mission for the installation by Dec. 31, 2009. The base stayed open after the Air Force announced on June 20, 2006, that a new special operations mission would be established at the base effective Oct. 1, 2007.

**Commission recommended closure instead.

SOURCE: *2005 Defense Base Realignment and Closure Commission Report.*

defense authorization bill (PL 108-375). *(2004 Senate key votes, Congress and the Nation Vol. XI, p. 856)*

Bush took advantage of the congressional recess to thwart Lott's effort. On April 1 the White House announced that all nine nominees to the commission had been given recess appointments. This meant that they could serve without Senate confirmation until the end of the Senate's next session in 2006. Senate Armed Services Committee Chair John W. Warner, R-Va., praised the president for his action.

BRAC PROCESS, LEGISLATIVE ACTION

The Pentagon announced its recommendations and sent them to the commission on May 13. After nearly four months of investigative hearings, base visits, regional hearings, community meetings, and deliberations, the BRAC Commission sent its report to President Bush on Sept. 8. A week later—on Sept. 15—Bush approved the recommendations and sent them to Congress.

The House on Oct. 27 voted 85–324 to reject H J Res 65 which would have blocked the proposed base closures and realignments. The resolution, offered by Ray LaHood, R-Ill., had been adversely reported by the House Armed Services Committee (H Rept 109-243) on Sept. 29. There was no action in the Senate.

Earlier during consideration of the fiscal 2006 defense authorization bill (HR 1815—PL 109-163), the House had defeated a proposal to postpone the 2005 BRAC recommendations until, among other things, overseas bases had been restructured and a substantial number of troops had returned from Iraq. That amendment, offered by Jeb Bradley, R-N.H., was rejected on May 25 by a vote of 112–316. The White House had warned that such an amendment would cause Defense Secretary Donald H. Rumsfeld and other senior advisers to recommend that Bush veto the defense bill. Two Bradley amendments to halt the BRAC process had been rejected during committee consideration as well.

Defense Reviews

Defense Secretary Donald H. Rumsfeld released his congressionally-mandated Quadrennial Defense Review in early 2006—in the fifth year of what he described as "a long war" against a global network of violent terrorists.

The previous defense review had been released just weeks after the Sept. 11, 2001, terrorist attacks—before the United States had gone to war in Afghanistan and Iraq. In the intervening years, Rumsfeld said the Pentagon had been at work making U.S. forces "more agile and more expeditionary." He said that the military had moved away from "a static defense in obsolete cold war garrisons" and placed emphasis instead on the ability to move troops quickly to trouble spots around the world. The secretary also noted technological advances, "including dramatic improvements in information management and precision weaponry." *(2001 review, Congress and the Nation Vol. XI, p. 334)*

The fiscal 1997 defense authorization act (PL 104-201) had required the defense secretary to report every four years on the results of a comprehensive examination of the national defense strategy, force structure, force modernization plans, infrastructure, budget plan, and other elements of the defense program and policies. The 2006 report was officially sent to Congress on Feb. 6, 2006, the same day the administration sent its proposed fiscal 2007 budget to Capital Hill.

Anticipating that the United States would be fighting Islamic extremism around the world for many years, the Pentagon's review called for a 25 percent increase in the number of Special Forces—to 60,000—over the next five years, as well as new weapons systems for these troops, such as unmanned aerial drones to collect intelligence and Navy vessels that could track terrorists and insurgents in coastal areas.

HOUSE COMMITTEE REPORT

But Pentagon officials stopped short of seeking broad increases in military force structure or equipment. That was not what House Armed Services Committee Chair Duncan Hunter, R-Calif., had wanted to hear. Rather, he had hoped the review would call for a larger force and the addition of billions in weapons spending.

Duncan's committee had begun its own defense review in September 2005, hoping it would be a counterweight to the Pentagon's review. It was meant to be a bipartisan effort and it was for much of the time, but in the end Democrats backed away from the final report, which recommended a massive military expansion that could have cost trillions of dollars.

The GOP report said that the U.S. armed forces did not have enough troops or equipment to both meet current missions and confront emerging threats. Specifically, it called for increasing the number of Army brigade combat teams, Marine Corps infantry battalions, Navy carrier battle groups, and Air Force expeditionary wings. The report said the expanded force would require heavy investments in new equipment, including additional aircraft carriers, submarines, fighter aircraft, and tanks and other armored vehicles. The report warned against retiring existing weapons too soon. It also called for overhauling the acquisition process and backed a robust national missile defense system.

Democrats on the committee declined to endorse the final report and were caught off-guard when Hunter released it on Nov. 30, 2006. A Democratic committee spokesperson said lawmakers from both parties had worked on the report in "good faith," but Democrats disagreed with the final report's calls for a large military buildup.

Hunter said in a memorandum sent to all committee members along with the report that he was publishing it because of the "significant investment" of time and energy put into producing it. A committee aide conceded that funding all the recommendations would cost trillions of dollars and said that the report was meant to serve less as a budget blueprint and more as a measuring stick for determining what could be done to reduce threats to the United States.

NEW REQUIREMENTS

Lawmakers in 2006 included in the fiscal 2007 defense authorization (HR 5122—PL 109-364) several provisions pertaining to the Quadrennial Defense Review (QDR). One required, among other things, that the report's analysis and recommendations not be "constrained" to comply with the president's budget. It also required that a panel be appointed to conduct an independent assessment of the QDR and report its findings to the appropriate congressional committees. Another provision mandated quarterly reports from the secretary of defense on the implementation of his 2006 recommendations.

2007–2008

Defense bills continued to be battlegrounds over Iraq policy. Democrats opened the 110th Congress with high hopes for change. Voter anger over the war was considered the main reason they were now in control of Congress for the first time since 1994.

The change that came, however, was not at all what they had expected. Just days into the new Congress, President George W. Bush announced a "surge" in U.S. forces in Iraq with the mission of quelling the escalating violence and training Iraqi security forces. Democrats were stunned, but found they could not stop it. The same would be true of their other attempts to influence Iraq policy. Congress did write into law a series of benchmarks to measure the progress of the Iraqi government. But an earlier attempt to link that progress to the question of how long U.S. troops would stay brought a presidential veto. Ultimately, the only timetable the president was willing to accept was one proposed by the Iraqis in the summer of 2008, when Bush agreed in principle that most American troops would be out of Iraq by 2011.

So Congress again focused on war-related issues that it could affect. The well-being of service members was at the top of their list. Lawmakers shifted billions of dollars to purchase vehicles that would protect troops from improvised explosive devices, the enemy's weapon of choice. Congress also worked hard to make sure that those who came home from the war with devastating physical and mental injuries would receive the proper treatment.

Nothing would enrage members more than a 2007 *Washington Post* article revealing that injured soldiers at Walter Reed, the Army's premier medical facility, were receiving substandard treatment and living in shabby housing while they recovered. Subsequent articles would reveal that this was not an isolated problem in the military's medical system and that the medical system of the Veterans Affairs (VA) Department had problems as well. The Wounded Warrior Act was Congress's response. The new law instituted a system of electronic health records so that patients' cases could be better managed and better coordinated between the Pentagon and the VA. Another provision created a single contact point to help service members and their families navigate the medical system instead of being overwhelmed by it. The law also required a comprehensive policy to deal with the kinds of injuries sustained in Iraq, such as traumatic brain injury and post-traumatic stress disorder.

Congress also gave service members higher pay raises than the president had requested, and it routinely dismissed his request to raise fees for participants in the military health care system.

Wide concern that the war in Iraq had taken a toll on the military's combat readiness prompted lawmakers to rearrange some of the administration's priorities and provide more money for combat equipment depleted in Iraq. Members were also generous in providing funding for the needs of the National Guard and reserves.

Cuts were made in missile defense and futuristic programs to offset some of these increases. But Congress still found plenty of money for next-generation aircraft, ships, and weapons systems in the pipeline.

It also found money for some programs the White House wanted to end. The C-17 transport plane was a good example. The Air Force wanted to shut down the C-17 production line, but Congress continued to appropriate funding for additional aircraft.

Fiscal 2008 Defense Authorization

Congress in early 2008 cleared a $696.4 billion fiscal 2008 defense authorization bill (HR 4986—PL 110-181). That total included $507 billion for Pentagon accounts and Energy Department nuclear weapons programs, as well as $189.4 billion in emergency supplemental spending for the wars in Iraq and Afghanistan. President George W. Bush amended his request several times, ultimately requesting $694.8 billion for national defense, including $189.3 billion in supplemental funding for the wars.

HR 4986 was the largest defense authorization bill since World War II in real dollar terms, and the first since the Sept. 11, 2001, terrorist attacks to authorize emergency funding for an entire fiscal year of operations in Iraq and Afghanistan.

President Bush had unexpectedly vetoed the first version of the bill (HR 1585), which cleared in December 2007, because of a single provision opposed by the Iraqi government. Congress sent him a revised bill in January 2008 that allowed him to waive application of the provision to Iraq. *(Bush vetoes, p. 1039)*

That final hurdle was but one of several the bill faced during its prolonged consideration. Although Congress regarded the authorization as must-pass legislation, especially in wartime, the fiscal 2008 bill became caught up in acrimonious debates over the war in Iraq and how far Congress should go in trying to direct its conduct. The result was a drawn-out process that began with the first markups and lasted until the end. Even after conferees reached agreement on the defense portions of the bill, a final bill did not emerge until Senate Democrats reluctantly dropped their insistence on an unrelated provision to extend protection against hate crimes.

The companion defense appropriations bill (HR 3222—PL 110-116) had been enacted in November 2007, but the authorization bill had to be signed into law before such items as a 3.5 percent pay raise for U.S. troops along with major improvements in their medical care and other benefits could take effect. The pay raise was higher than Bush

WOUNDED WARRIOR ACT

Congress included in the fiscal 2008 defense authorization bill (HR 4986—PL 110-181) a series of provisions aimed at improving conditions for service members wounded in Iraq and Afghanistan after they returned home to military health care facilities. Changes ranged from instituting electronic health records to focusing on the kinds of injuries being sustained in the wars to creating a single point of contact for patients and their families.

The push for the overhaul—known as the Wounded Warrior Act—was triggered initially by a February 2007 *Washington Post* article suggesting that injured soldiers at the Army's premier medical facility were receiving substandard care. The *Post* reported that buildings housing injured soldiers at the Walter Reed Army Medical Center in Washington, DC, had physically deteriorated and that many soldiers faced months-long delays in receiving care. More news stories followed, and revelations of poor patient care throughout the military's health care system, including problems experienced in navigating the military's medical bureaucracy, subsequently came to light.

More than 25,000 service members had been wounded in Iraq and Afghanistan at that time, according to the Pentagon. The news reports on the poor quality of care they were receiving back home set off a public outcry and bipartisan outrage on Capitol Hill. During highly charged hearings in the wake of the media reports, lawmakers criticized long delays experienced in outpatient treatment, a lack of caseworkers and patient advocates, and the failure of officers who were made aware of problems at Walter Reed to fix them.

By mid-March 2007 the revelations had led to the resignations of Walter Reed's commanding general, the Army's chief medical officer, and the secretary of the Army.

The Department of Veterans Affairs (VA) came under fire as well, particularly for providing inadequate screenings and care for head wounds, which had become the signature injury in the Iraq and Afghanistan wars.

Legislative Action

The House gave Congress's initial response to the controversy with the passage of HR 1538 by a vote of 426–0 on March 28, 2007. The House Armed Services Committee had reported the bill (H Rept 110-68) on March 23.

HR 1538 added caseworkers and counselors to the military's medical system and required the Pentagon and VA to better coordinate the transfer of service members between the two bureaucracies, at a cost of at least $300 million over the next five years, according to the Congressional Budget Office (CBO). The CBO warned, however, that the cost could total "billions of dollars" if, instead of improving their existing computer systems, the Pentagon and VA decided to build a new common computer system for their medical files in order to comply with a provision requiring interoperability between the two departments.

Democrats had blamed the Bush administration for problems at Walter Reed and elsewhere in the military's health system and some said it was another example of the lack of prewar planning. But the White House said President George W. Bush generally supported the House bill, although he considered it premature. The president on

had wanted, and members rejected the higher fees proposed by the administration for participants in the military's health care network.

Both chambers agreed to shift money on the margins from future weapons technology, such as proposed missile defense sites in Eastern Europe, to battlefield needs. The measure paid special attention to equipment used to protect U.S. forces from roadside bombs in Iraq and Afghanistan. Congress shifted billions of dollars to purchase more Mine Resistant Ambush Protected (MRAP) vehicles, which the House Armed Services Committee said could reduce the casualties in vehicles from improvised explosive devices (IEDs) by as much as 80 percent. The Army chief of staff indicated that purchasing MRAP vehicles was a top priority.

The bill also made a number of changes to the way the Pentagon oversaw its contractors, bought weapons and services, and took care of wounded personnel. Many of the provisions were spurred by scandals arising from the war in Iraq.

HOUSE COMMITTEE ACTION

The House Armed Services Committee reported its defense authorization bill (HR 1585—H Rept 110-146, Part I) on May 11, 2007. A supplemental report was filed on May 14 (Part II).

The bill authorized $648.6 billion—$503.8 billion for regular defense and nuclear weapons programs and $141.8 billion in emergency war funds. The measure called for billions more than requested for equipment such as new armored vehicles, as well as a considerable supply of aircraft and ships to fuel job growth back home. It also endorsed a 3.5 percent pay raise instead of the 3 percent hike the administration sought and extended from fiscal 2009 through fiscal 2012 a law requiring military basic pay levels to exceed the civilian norm by at least half a

March 6 had appointed his own commission to study problems in the military's medical system and wanted Congress to wait until after the commission's report, due by the end of July, before passing legislation. Former senator Bob Dole, R-Kan. (House, 1961–1969; Senate, 1969–1996), and Donna Shalala, secretary of health and human services in the Clinton administration, had been chosen to lead the nine-member panel. (In its July report the commission called for, among other things, restructuring disability and compensation systems, improving care for those with post-traumatic stress disorder and traumatic brain injury, strengthening support for families, and creating a fully interoperable information system.)

On June 18 the Senate Armed Services Committee unanimously reported its bill (S 1606—no written report) to address inadequacies in the care of wounded service members and veterans. The full Senate passed an amended version of HR 1538 by voice vote on July 25.

A compromise version of the two bills was folded into the fiscal 2008 defense authorization bill. Conferees acknowledged that there was additional work to be done and vowed to "work to achieve the vision of our Nation's founders—to manifest not only appreciation and gratitude toward those who have borne the battle, but also to provide the highest quality care to U.S. service members and their families."

Major Provisions

As signed into the law on Jan. 28, 2008, the Wounded Warrior Act title of HR 4986:

- Created the Wounded Warrior Resource Center to serve as a single point of contact for service members, their families, and primary caregivers to help them get needed care and to navigate the military's health-care bureaucracy.
- Required semiannual inspections of housing facilities for recovering service members.
- Required the Defense and the Veterans Affairs (VA) departments to jointly develop a comprehensive policy on the care and management of members of the armed forces, including the creation of fully interoperable electronic health records.
- Mandated the establishment of new Defense Department standards for processing medical evaluations and for training and qualifying staff to perform the evaluations. This included assigning independent medical advisers to assist recovering service members and families.
- Mandated the establishment of new department standards for processing disability evaluations in order to reduce discrepancies between the Defense Department assessments and those conducted by the VA and to ensure consistent decisions among the military departments.
- Required a comprehensive policy to address traumatic brain injury, post-traumatic stress disorder, other mental health conditions, and military eye injuries, as well as the creation of centers of excellence focused on those conditions.

percentage point. The House panel rejected Bush's request to increase annual enrollment fees, deductibles, and drug copayments for military retirees in the Tricare health network.

To help pay for those initiatives, the new Democratic majority, in control of the bill for the first time in a dozen years, proposed to scale back some of the administration requests.

The panel, for example, approved $2.7 billion—about $870 million less than requested—for research and development of the Future Combat Systems (FCS), the Army's top modernization program. The program was aimed at fielding a set of vehicles, aircraft, weapons, radios, and computers by 2015 at a total price that could surpass $200 billion. It had drawn criticism for investing too heavily in technologies before they were sufficiently proven. The full committee's report on the bill said that the situation had changed dramatically since the weapons system was first conceived in 1999, and that given the Army's many competing demands, "the committee does not believe that the FCS program is on a sustainable or realistic path." The panel urged pursuing elements of the program that would "get useful equipment into the hands of soldiers on a realistic timeline," while delaying features that would not be ready for years or were redundant given existing Army capabilities.

Cuts also came in the authorization for missile defense. The panel approved $8.1 billion for the Missile Defense Agency, a $764 million reduction from Bush's budget. Authorization levels for building missile defense locations in Poland and the Czech Republic were substantially reduced, amid criticism from NATO allies that they had not been sufficiently consulted about the move. The committee agreed to allow the administration to move forward with the sites once agreements were reached with the host countries and NATO was further engaged.

HR 1585 included $74 million, $45 million less than requested, for the Reliable Replacement Warhead, a new nuclear warhead for long-range missiles.

The House committee agreed to the administration's requests to authorize $2.7 billion for procurement of the F-35 Joint Strike Fighter and $3.5 billion for research and development on the aircraft, but with $480 million of the research money dedicated to the development of a second engine from a competing contractor. The administration wanted to save money by developing only one engine, but lawmakers argued that competition would result in a better engine. The F-35 was intended for use by the Air Force, Navy, and Marine Corps, and several allied nations.

The bill authorized the requested $4.3 billion for the F-22 Raptor, the next-generation Air Force fighter, including $3.6 billion to purchase twenty aircraft and $744 million for research and development. Members brushed off the Air Force's request for funds to help pay for shutting down the C-17 production line and instead authorized $2.4 billion in unrequested funds to purchase ten of the long-range cargo planes. The panel also expressed strong opposition to Air Force plans to reduce the B-52 fleet and included money to modernize and upgrade seventy-six B-52s—twenty more than requested.

The House committee bill added $1.5 billion to Bush's shipbuilding requests. The bill authorized $3.1 billion for the *Virginia*-class submarine, $588 million more than requested, with the extra funds dedicated to advance procurement of items with long lead times. It also authorized $912 million to procure two T-AKE cargo ships, twice what Bush requested. The bill included the request for $3 billion for procurement of two next-generation DDG-1000 destroyers (previously known as the DD(X) destroyer) started in fiscal 2007. The panel approved $711 million to procure two Littoral Combat Ships, down from the $911 million requested to buy three ships.

The House committee bill restored collective-bargaining and appeal rights of Pentagon civilian employees covered by the new National Security Personnel System, while preserving the department's ability to implement a pay-for-performance system.

The bill also included a "Buy American" provision that barred the Pentagon from buying from foreign companies that received government subsidies—a provision that some observers saw as a way to protect Boeing from EADS North America, the U.S. holding company of European Aeronautic Defense and Space, which was competing to build refueling aircraft for the Air Force. *(Aerial refueling tankers, box p. 392)*

HOUSE FLOOR ACTION

The House passed HR 1585 by a vote of 397–27 on May 17.

Passage came after heated debates on such topics as military modernization, nuclear posture, and health care, training, and pay for troops then in the fifth year of the Iraq War. The White House warned of a veto over the bill's proposed bargaining rights and appeals process for civilian Pentagon workers and its Buy American provision, as well as provisions on the detention of enemy combatants that the administration saw as micromanaging.

During the floor debate, the House adopted on a largely party-line vote of 220–208 a James P. Moran, D-Va., amendment to require the Pentagon for the first time to report on its plan to try, transfer, or continue to detain each prisoner at Guantánamo Bay, Cuba. The amendment also directed the Defense Department to explain what it planned to do with eighty-two prisoners who were scheduled for release. But the House rejected 199–229 a Rush D. Holt, D-N.J., amendment to require videotaping of prisoner interrogations.

The House rejected two amendments aimed at barring military action in Iran. An amendment offered by Robert E. Andrews, D-N.J., that would have prohibited the use of funds authorized by the bill to plan contingency operations in that country was rejected 202–216. A Peter A. DeFazio, D-Ore., amendment to require Bush to get specific authorization to attack Iran, unless that country attacked the United States first, was rejected 136–288.

In other action, the House rejected 199–226 a Trent Franks, R-Ariz., proposal to restore funds the House Armed Services Committee had cut from missile defense.

The House agreed 394–30 to a procedural move by Duncan Hunter, R-Calif., the ranking Republican on House Armed Services, to recommit the bill to the committee with instructions to add language expanding a ballistic missile defense system with Israel. It proposed authorizing $205 million for the system and directing the Pentagon to decide where the offsets would come from.

SENATE COMMITTEE ACTION

The Senate Armed Services Committee reported its version of the bill (S 1547—S Rept 110-77) on June 5. The Senate Select Committee on Intelligence reported the bill (S Rept 110-125) on June 29.

The bill authorized a total of $648.3 billion, which included $129.8 billion for the wars in Iraq and Afghanistan after the committee shifted some war costs to the regular defense budget.

The Senate panel approved the same amount as the House had for procurement of the F-35 Joint Strike Fighter but added $440 million more for research and development, while agreeing with the designation of $480 million for a second engine. The committee also went along with the House committee on the authorization for the F-22 Raptor and on directing the Air Force to keep at least seventy-six B-52s in its fleet, but it did not agree on authorizing funds to keep the C-17 production line, despite pressure to do so from some senators.

S 1547 authorized about $980 million more for the Future Combat Systems than the House bill had. The

House decision to cut more than 25 percent from Bush's request had led to a fierce lobbying campaign by the Army and Boeing, the program's main contractor. Reflecting the differences between the committees, the Senate report called the program "the centerpiece of Army transformation and modernization."

The Senate bill authorized $2.6 billion less than the House for shipbuilding. S 1547 authorized the same amount as HR 1585 for two DDG-1000 destroyers and just $118 million less for a *Virginia*-class attack submarine. The Senate panel approved $480 million toward procurement of two Littoral Combat Ships, $230 million less than the House recommended, and $456 million for one T-AKE cargo ship, half what the House proposed.

S 1547 called for $10.1 billion for missile defense, including $8.5 billion for the Missile Defense Agency.

The Senate panel went along with the House on military benefits and pay as well as labor relations guarantees for Pentagon civilian employees. But in contrast to the House panel, the Senate committee sought to repeal an existing "Buy American" requirement that the Pentagon report to Congress on the "essential items" it procured and identify where they came from.

S 1547 called for a process for reviewing the status of military detainees at Guantánamo Bay that would require legal representation for detainees and prohibit the use of statements obtained through cruel and inhuman treatment. The House bill did not include the provision.

The bill also called for more regulation of contractors performing private security functions in combat areas. In its report, the Armed Services Committee noted that there had been reported incidents of contractor employees exchanging or threatening to exchange fire with U.S. forces. It further stated: "Moreover, misconduct by even a few armed contractor employees may reflect badly on the United States and could undermine the chances of success for military missions."

SENATE FLOOR ACTION

The Senate passed HR 1585 by a vote of 92–3 on Oct. 1, after nineteen days of debate punctuated by mostly unsuccessful Democratic attempts to set a timeline for withdrawing U.S. forces from Iraq.

HR 1585 ran aground in the Senate in July after a contentious debate over the Iraq War. Unable to get the sixty votes needed to limit the debate, Majority Leader Harry Reid, D-Nev., pulled the bill from the floor. Some senators worried aloud that the Senate might never pass it.

Debate on the bill, however, resumed in mid-September. After returning from the August recess, Democrats had been hopeful that weariness with the war would finally enable them to win enough Republican support to add some policy restrictions to HR 1585. But a report of limited progress by the U.S. commander in Iraq, Army Gen. David H. Petraeus, and comments by President Bush indicating some troops could be home by July 2008 put some wind back in GOP sails. After a test vote on a war amendment failed, Reid agreed to move forward on the authorization bill, winning a cloture vote 89–6 that made further Iraq amendments nongermane. *(Details, Iraq War policy, pp. 270, 303)*

In action on other amendments, the Senate considered several dealing with Iran. The Senate adopted 90–5 a Jeff Sessions, R-Ala., amendment to make it official U.S. policy to develop and deploy a defense against the ballistic missile threat from Iran as soon as technologically possible and in conjunction with U.S. allies and other nations. The Senate also adopted 76–22 a Jon Kyl, R-Ariz., amendment expressing the sense of the Senate that the United States should prevent Iran from expanding its influence among Shiite militants in Iraq. The Kyl amendment was debated while Iranian President Mahmoud Ahmadinejad was in New York to attend the U.N. General Assembly session in September.

The Senate voted 60–39 to invoke cloture on an amendment by Edward M. Kennedy, D-Mass., to expand hate crimes law to cover crimes based on the victim's gender, sexual orientation, or disability. The amendment was subsequently adopted by voice vote. The Senate also adopted 96–3 a proposal by Orrin G. Hatch, R-Utah, to require the comptroller general to collect data on the prevalence of hate crimes and authorize the attorney general to provide assistance and make grants to state and local governments to aid in the prosecution of hate crimes.

In other action, the Senate adopted 51–44 a Kennedy amendment on private contracting of federal work. The amendment, which was similar to a House provision, required that any outside contract save the government at least $10 million or 10 percent of the personnel costs, and specified that contractors could not lower their bids by reducing health and retirement benefits. The Office of Management and Budget could not require the Pentagon to bid out specific jobs, and federal workers would have the right, as contractors did, to appeal outsourcing decisions to the Government Accountability Office (GAO).

An amendment by Jack Reed, D-R.I., to authorize the expenditure of about $1.2 billion for the procurement of parts for a new attack submarine made partly by workers in his home state was adopted by voice vote. Also approved by voice vote was an amendment offered by Jim Webb, D-Va., and Claire McCaskill, D-Mo., calling for a commission to study and investigate contracting in the Iraq and Afghanistan war zones and issue a series of reports recommending changes in the oversight process.

CONFERENCE, FINAL ACTION

The House agreed to the conference report on HR 1585 (H Rept 110-477) by a vote of 370–49 on Dec. 12. The Senate cleared the bill Dec. 14 by a vote of 90–3.

The agreement of Senate Democrats to drop the Senate's hate crimes amendment had allowed the bill to go forward.

The House prevailed on the issue of whether to authorize additional C-10 cargo planes. Although the Senate had not wanted to buy any new planes, the emergency war section of the conference bill authorized funds to buy eight of the ten planes proposed by the House. Conferees split the difference on the research and development authorization for the Joint Strike Fighter.

The Senate largely prevailed on the Future Combat Systems, getting most of what it wanted for development.

The bill also largely followed the Senate version of shipbuilding authorizations. The biggest difference had been over the LPD-17 amphibious ship, which ended up with $1.4 billion, close to what the Senate recommended but about $1.7 billion less than the House had sought. The final bill authorized funds for one Littoral Combat Ship (LCS), less than either chamber proposed. The LCS program had been beset by cost overruns and delays.

The final bill authorized funds for a new nuclear warhead but barred use of the funds for anything beyond the design phase. It also established a congressionally appointed bipartisan commission to examine U.S. nuclear policy.

Lawmakers reduced funds for more technologically advanced defense against prospective long-range missile threats while adding funds for defenses against short-range and medium-range missiles that already were being deployed and could strike U.S. forces overseas. The conference report expressed support for an effective defense against Iranian missile threats and cooperation with Israel on missile defense. A Senate provision limiting ground-based missile interceptors in Alaska was dropped.

Conferees dropped the House "Buy American" provision.

The House provision requiring a report on plans for dealing with detainees at Guantánamo was included in the bill, but conferees dropped the Senate provision requiring legal representation for detainees and prohibiting the use of statements obtained through cruel and inhuman treatment.

Similar to the House bill, the measure required the GAO to report on contracts in Iraq and Afghanistan The final bill also included the Senate provision setting up a special commission to probe contracting there.

Conferees included Senate provisions on the regulation of private security guards in combat zones. The provisions came in the wake of reports that Blackwater Worldwide and other firms had been charged with crimes, including manslaughter, in Iraq. "We are going to give the commanders in the field control over the contractors and try to get the Blackwaters under control," said Carl Levin, D-Mich., chair of the Senate Armed Services Committee.

The conference report also included both bills' requirement that any outside contract save the government at least $10 million or 10 percent of the personnel costs. Lawmakers said the bill would prevent contractors from scrimping on health care and retirement costs to keep their bids low.

VETO, NEW BILL

President Bush surprised everyone by vetoing HR 1585 on Dec. 28. The Iraqi government had objected to provisions that gave individuals enhanced rights to sue nations designated by the State Department as sponsors of terrorism. Iraq faced claims by several of Saddam Hussein's victims, including former prisoners of war from the 1990–1991 Gulf War. U.S. officials feared that Iraqi assets in U.S. capital markets, totaling some $25 billion, could be frozen during litigation if HR 1585 became law. The Bush administration said a potential freeze of those assets would harm Iraq's reconstruction and stabilization efforts. *(Veto message, p. 1066)*

When Congress returned in January 2008, members moved quickly to clear a revised fiscal 2008 defense authorization (HR 4986—PL 110-181) that contained language effectively exempting the Iraqi government from litigation stemming from the regime of Saddam Hussein.

The House passed the revised bill 369–46 on Jan. 16, 2008, and the Senate cleared it 91–3 on Jan. 22.

MAJOR PROVISIONS

As signed into law on Jan. 28, 2008, HR 4986 authorized $696.4 billion for Defense Department programs and Energy Department nuclear weapons programs in fiscal 2008. That total included an authorization of $189.4 billion in emergency funding for the wars in Iraq and Afghanistan.

Iraq, Afghanistan Wars

Included in the $189.4 billion in fiscal 2008 emergency spending were authorizations of:

- $1 billion for a Strategic Readiness Fund that could be used for critical equipment shortages.
- $17.6 billion for the purchase of Mine Resistant Ambush Protected (MRAP) vehicles, which were troop transports with V-shaped hulls, raised chassis, and various other features designed to resist attacks with improvised explosive devices (IEDs). (Congress had added $4.6 billion to the president's request, $4.1 billion of which had been shifted from what were considered to be lower-priority items.)
- $18.4 billion for the Army and $8.6 billion for the Marines to meet "reset" costs to repair, refurbish, or replace equipment damaged or destroyed by the wars in Iraq and Afghanistan.
- $4.8 billion for the Joint IED Defeat Organization.
- $1.2 billion for personal body armor for U.S. troops.
- $3.3 billion for up-armored High Mobility Multipurpose Wheeled Vehicles (Humvees).
- $1.5 billion for vehicle add-on armor to protect against IEDs.
- $1.1 billion for the Defense Health Program.

Required the defense secretary to set regulations for the selection, training, and conduct of private security personnel in combat zones, not including intelligence personnel.

Established an eight-member Commission on Wartime Contracting to review federal contracts for reconstruction, logistical support, and security functions in Iraq and Afghanistan, and assess the extent of any waste or fraud under the contracts. The commission was to report its findings and make recommendations for improvements.

Required an annual Government Accountability Office (GAO) report to Congress on contracts in Iraq and Afghanistan.

Detainee Policies

Required the defense secretary to report to the congressional defense committees on plans for dealing with each of the detainees being held at Guantánamo Bay.

Military Personnel

Authorized $119.7 billion.

Authorized a 3.5 percent military pay raise.

Authorized an increase of 13,000 Army troops for a total of 525,400, and an increase of 9,000 for the Marines for a total of 189,000.

Authorized $23.1 billion for the Defense Health Program.

Included in a separate "Wounded Warrior" section of the bill a number of overhauls aimed at improving conditions for personnel wounded in battle after they returned home to military health care facilities. *(Wounded Warrior provisions, box p. 374)*

National Guard

Authorized nearly $6.7 billion for National Guard and reserve equipment, $980 million more than requested.

Elevated the general who headed the National Guard to four-star rank but did not make him a member of the Joint Chiefs of Staff.

Created a bipartisan Council of Governors to advise the president on how best to use the National Guard for civil support missions.

Operations and Maintenance

Authorized $142.8 billion.

Facilities

Authorized $10.3 billion for military construction and $2.9 billion for family housing.

Authorized $8.3 billion for Base Realignment and Closure (BRAC). *(Military base closings, p. 369)*

Missile Defense

Authorized $9.7 billion for ballistic-missile defense programs. That total included $8.3 billion for the Missile Defense Agency.

Restricted expenditures from the $225 million authorized to develop a missile-defense site in Eastern Europe until the governments of Poland and the Czech Republic gave final approval.

Stated that it was U.S. policy to develop, test, and deploy an effective defense against Iranian ballistic-missile threats and to encourage NATO to accelerate its missile defense efforts.

Expressed the sense of Congress that the United States should have an active program of ballistic missile defense cooperation with Israel.

Ground Forces

Authorized $3.6 billion for development of the Future Combat Systems, the Army's top modernization program.

Aviation Forces

Authorized $3.6 billion for procurement of twenty F-22 Raptor warplanes, the next-generation Air Force fighter, and about $400 million for development costs.

Authorized $3.7 billion for research and development on the F-35 Joint Strike Fighter. Of that, $480 million was set aside to continue development of a second engine from a competing contractor.

Directed the Air Force to maintain a fleet of no fewer than seventy-six B-52 bombers.

Naval Forces

Authorized $3.1 billion for procurement of a *Virginia*-class submarine, with $588 million of that dedicated to advance procurement of items with long lead times.

Authorized $3 billion for procurement of two of the next-generation DDG-1000 *Zumwalt*-class guided missile destroyers. (The DDG-1000 was known as the DD(X) until its name was changed in April 2006.)

Authorized $340 million for one Littoral Combat Ship.

Prohibited the Defense Department from using any fiscal 2008 funds to deploy a conventional explosive warhead for the Trident submarine. Instead, the bill authorized $100 million to develop a Prompt Global Strike capability that would be distinct from the Trident to avoid the risk that others nations would mistake a launch for a nuclear strike.

AIR AND SEA TRANSPORT

Authorized $2.2 billion in emergency funding for the purchase of eight C-17 cargo planes.

Authorized $756.1 million for the T-AKE cargo ship program—$456.1 to procure one ship and the rest for advance procurement of long-lead items for three ships.

Nuclear Weapons

Authorized $17.1 billion for Energy Department defense-related activities.

Barred use of the $66 million authorized for the Reliable Replacement Warhead—a new nuclear warhead for long-range missiles—for anything beyond the design phase.

Established a congressionally appointed bipartisan commission to examine U.S. nuclear policy and strategic posture as a "prerequisite to any major decisions on the size and composition of the nuclear weapons stockpile."

Other Provisions

Required that any outside contract save the government at least $10 million or 10 percent of the personnel costs. The law specified that contractors could not lower their bids by reducing health and retirement benefits.

Restored collective-bargaining and appeal rights for civilian employees under the Pentagon's new National Security Personnel System, which had not included such rights.

BUSH'S SIGNING STATEMENT

When he signed HR 4986 into law, President Bush said that he reserved the right to disregard several provisions of the bill that he saw as impinging on his powers as chief executive and commander in chief. One of those was the provision setting up a special commission to probe contracting fraud in Iraq and Afghanistan. Bush also objected to a provision barring funds for permanent bases in Iraq—something administration officials had said was not their goal—or for any action that exercised U.S. control over Iraq's oil resources. Also cited were sections that expanded protections for whistleblowers who worked for government contractors and that required U.S. intelligence agencies to promptly respond to congressional requests for documents.

Fiscal 2008 Defense Appropriations

Congress in 2007 cleared a fiscal 2008 Defense Department appropriations bill (HR 3222—PL 110-116) that included $459.6 billion in regular defense spending and $11.6 billion in emergency supplemental funding for mine-resistant vehicles to protect troops in Iraq.

The total for basic defense funding in the final bill was $3.5 billion less than President George W. Bush had requested. The president had also requested $189.3 billion in emergency fiscal 2008 funds for the wars in Iraq and Afghanistan, but Democratic leaders decided not to include the supplemental war funds in HR 3222, preferring to consider them in a separate measure. *(2008 war supplemental, p. 386)*

Although the bill's total was only 1 percent below the president's budget—not counting the war funding request—HR 3222 rearranged some of the administration's spending priorities. It provided more than requested for combat equipment depleted in Iraq, more for operational training, more for National Guard and reserve battle gear, and more support services for military families. To offset those increases, the measure provided 11 percent less than requested for the Army's next generation of combat vehicles and 4 percent less for missile defense.

HR 3222 included sufficient funds for an average 3.5 percent pay increase for military personnel in fiscal 2008, half a percentage point more than the president's 3 percent request. It also continued a prohibition on raising the costs for most participants in Tricare, the military's health care system, as the administration had proposed to do.

The defense spending bill was used as a vehicle for a continuing resolution to fund the government through Dec. 14, while lawmakers continued to work on appropriations bills in other areas. As it turned out, the defense bill was the only separate fiscal 2008 appropriations bill enacted. The eleven other funding bills were folded into a year-end omnibus appropriations package (HR 2764—PL 110-161). *(Continuing resolution, pp. 111, 314)*

HOUSE ACTION

The House passed HR 3222 by a vote of 395–13 on Aug. 5, 2007. The House Appropriations Committee had reported the bill (H Rept 110-279) on July 30.

The House bill appropriated $459.6 billion in regular defense spending—almost exactly the amount in the final bill. But like the companion House authorization bill (HR 1585), the measure proposed to shift money from futuristic weapons systems and failing technology programs to health care for the military, pay raises, base infrastructure, and needed near-term equipment. *(2008 defense authorization, p. 373)*

The House version appropriated $3.1 billion for research and development of the Army's top modernization program, the Future Combat Systems—about $470 less than the $3.6 billion Bush requested but still a reprieve from the deeper reduction called for in the House authorization bill. On the other hand, HR 3222 appropriated $1.9 billion to procure Stryker armored vehicles—about $875 million more than requested. The Appropriations Committee specified that $1.1 billion was unrequested money for an eighth Stryker brigade, saying in its report that "the greatest increase in overall Army readiness can be gained by adding a Stryker brigade to the Army force structure."

The House bill included the $2.7 billion request toward procurement of twelve F-35 Joint Strike Fighters, as well $4.2 billion for ongoing F-35 research and development, about $690 million more than requested. That total included an extra $480 million not in Bush's budget for continued development of a backup engine from an alternative source, something the Pentagon opposed. The bill included the requested amount—$3.6 billion—for procurement of twenty F-22A Raptor warplanes—the Air Force's next-generation premier fighter intended to replace the F-15—but cut the amount for development nearly in half, recommending $380 million instead of the $744 million requested.

The bill included $3.1 billion for the *Virginia*-class submarine—$1.8 billion as requested for procurement, and $1.3 billion, a $588 million increase, for advance procurement of items that had long lead times, with a goal of enabling the Navy to procure two subs per year by 2012.

The bill also provided $1.9 billion, or $1.4 billion more than requested, to procure four T-AKE cargo ships, three more than Bush sought. House appropriators said they were favoring ships "with proven design and construction processes."

The House bill provided $8.5 billion for the Missile Defense Agency, a $298 million cut from Bush's request, including a $139 million reduction from the $310 million requested for missile defense sites in Europe. The proposed sites had strained relations with Russia, which feared that they could be used for offensive purposes, as well as the host nations and NATO, which felt they had not been sufficiently consulted. House appropriators said it was "premature to provide full funding for the European component, given the uncertainty surrounding the program."

The bill added an unrequested $925 million for National Guard and reserve equipment.

For the Defense Health Program, the bill included $23 billion, an increase of $416 million over Bush's request. House appropriators rejected the administration's renewed proposal to boost fees and premiums by $1.9 billion for military personnel under the Tricare health care system.

The bill continued existing prohibitions against the use of torture and establishment of permanent U.S. bases in Iraq.

During floor debate, the House adopted by voice vote a Darrell Issa, R-Calif., amendment to reverse a congressional decision to make public the aggregate budget total for all U.S. intelligence agencies. The provision had been included in legislation (HR 1—PL 110-53) implementing some of the recommendations of the commission that investigated the Sept. 11, 2001, terrorist attacks. The vote on the Issa amendment came the day after HR 1 was signed into law. *(Intelligence budget totals, box p. 322)*

The House also adopted by voice vote an amendment by Jay Inslee, D-Wash., to prohibit the use of funds for the embattled National Security Personnel System, which was aimed at moving the Pentagon's civilian workforce toward performance-based pay and away from the old general schedule system. The new system had faced numerous court challenges from workers' groups contending that it robbed employees of collective-bargaining rights. Those rights were subsequently restored with the enactment of the fiscal 2008 defense authorization bill (HR 4986—PL 110-181).

SENATE ACTION

The Senate passed HR 3222 by voice vote Oct. 3. The Senate Appropriations Committee had reported an amended version of the bill (S Rept 110-155) on Sept. 14.

The Senate-passed bill appropriated $460.4 billion in regular defense spending. The bill also included another $3 billion in emergency funding for border security that had been added during the floor debate.

In an effort to smooth the way to passage, Defense Appropriations Subcommittee Chair Daniel K. Inouye, D-Hawaii, had successfully fended off attempts by fellow Democrats to include Iraq policy and funding amendments. The White House had threatened to veto a bill that restricted the president's war policies.

Like the House version, the Senate bill shifted money from weapons programs to health care, pay raises, and equipment for troops. But it did not include the House provision on the National Security Personnel System. The White House and Pentagon had issued another preemptive veto threat not to include that language even before the Appropriations Committee had acted on the bill.

Unlike the House bill, the Senate version included the requested amounts for the Future Combat System and Stryker vehicles. The Senate did not call for another Stryker brigade.

Senate appropriators agreed to the administration's F-35 Joint Strike Fighter procurement request but increased the research money from the requested $3.5 billion to $3.7 billion, including an extra $480 million for development of a second engine. They approved the requested amount for procurement of F-22A Raptor warplanes but reduced development money to $611 million, $132 less than requested.

The Senate bill provided $3 billion for the *Virginia*-class submarine, only $118 million less than in the House version. But Senate appropriators did not go along with the House plan to add $1.4 billion for three additional T-AKE cargo ships and instead provided $456 million for one. Citing "significant cost growth and schedule slip," Senate appropriators provided no fiscal 2008 procurement funds for the Littoral Combat Ship (LCS) and rescinded $300,000 in fiscal 2007 funding. The bill did include $75 million for advance LCS procurement and $300 million for development, an $83 million increase.

The Senate went along with the House in providing $8.5 billion for the Missile Defense Agency.

Senate appropriators also agreed with the House on a 3.5 percent military pay raise and on rejecting administration plans to increase military healthcare fees. The Senate bill provided $23.5 billion for the Defense Health Program—$949 million more than requested and $533 million more than the House proposed.

The Senate bill included $1 billion in unrequested funds for National Guard and reserve equipment, $75 million more than in the House bill.

The extra $3 billion in emergency border security funds was added by a vote of 95–1 during floor debate. Amendment sponsor Lindsey Graham, R-S.C., had said that he would attach his proposal to every possible vehicle in order to give it the greatest chance of being enacted. *(Border security, p. 679)*

The Senate also agreed by voice vote to a Jeff Sessions, R-Ala., amendment to add $794 million to continue the presence of 6,000 National Guard troops on the border with Mexico through the end of fiscal 2008.

By a vote of 53–41 senators agreed to table (kill) a Barbara Boxer, D-Calif., amendment that would have kept certain convicted felons from enlisting in the armed forces.

CONFERENCE ACTION

The House adopted the conference report on HR 3222 (H Rept 110-434) by a vote of 400–15 on Nov. 8. The Senate cleared the bill by voice vote later that same day.

Negotiations on the substance of the final bill were relatively noncontentious. Funding levels for most programs did not differ greatly in the House and Senate version. In addition, conferees effectively shifted billions from the base defense bill to a future supplemental bill to help meet overall spending limits.

But the question of whether to include supplemental funding for the wars in Iraq and Afghanistan was hotly debated. Democrats were reluctant to approve additional money unless it was accompanied by major changes in policy, including concrete withdrawal dates. They preferred to deal with war funding later as a separate bill. Republicans, however, wanted to include in HR 3222 bridge funds to pay for the wars into the next year. Ted Stevens of Alaska, the ranking Republican on the Senate Defense Appropriations Subcommittee, angrily threatened to invoke a new Senate rule that would have allowed the chamber to remove the continuing resolution that conferees had attached to the bill to provide continued funding of the government until mid-December. When the Democratic leadership threatened to withhold a vote on Michael B. Mukasey's nomination to head the Justice Department unless Republicans cooperated on the defense bill, Stevens relented and the bill moved forward.

House-Senate conferees split the difference on funding the Future Combat System and provided less than either chamber had recommended for Stryker vehicles. Conferees required a report from the Army on whether an additional Stryker brigade—as recommended by the House—was needed.

The conference bill provided funding to buy one T-AKE cargo ship and advance components for three more. In settling on funding to procure one Littoral Combat Ship and not the three requested, conferees said they were "extremely concerned" with the state of the program, calling it "a classic example of the way things could go wrong when construction was started prior to the design being complete."

The conference bill included $8.6 billion for the Missile Defense Agency, about $120 million more than either chamber recommended. But conferees cut $85 million from the $310 million request for missile defense activities in Europe. The cut was to prevent construction from beginning on a missile site in Poland, pending firm agreement from the host nation.

In other action, conferees roughly split the difference between the two chambers when they provided $980 million in unrequested funds for National Guard and reserve equipment. They also included $247 million, about a third of the amounted added by the Senate, for National Guard personnel on the U.S.-Mexican border.

Conferees went along with the Senate in providing $15 million of the $30 million requested for the Reliable Replacement Warhead—the House had provided nothing.

Conferees included in the final bill House provisions that continued existing prohibitions against the use of torture and the establishment of permanent bases in Iraq.

MAJOR PROVISIONS

As signed into law Nov. 13, HR 3222 appropriated $459.6 billion in regular defense spending for fiscal 2008. That total included $10.9 billion for future military retiree health benefits provided under a permanent appropriation.

The bill included another $11.6 billion in emergency money for mine-resistant vehicles to be used in the war in Iraq.

Continuing Resolution

HR 3222 also contained a continuing resolution (CR) to fund the government through Dec. 14, 2007. The CR included a provision allowing the Pentagon to spend prorated portions of a $70 billion bridge fund for Iraq operations that was included in the fiscal 2007 defense appropriations law (HR 5631—PL 109-289). The CR in HR 3222 was the second since the Oct. 1 start of the new fiscal year; the first CR (H J Res 52—PL 110-92) had appropriated $5.2 billion for mine-resistant vehicles in fiscal 2008. *(2007 war supplemental, p. 383; 2008 war supplemental, p. 386)*

Military Personnel

Appropriated $105.3 billion.

Allowed for a 3.5 percent military pay raise.

Appropriated $23.5 billion for the Defense Health Program and prohibited raising the costs for most participants in Tricare, the military's health care system.

Operations and Maintenance

Appropriated $140.1 billion.

Missile Defense

Appropriated $8.6 billion for the Missile Defense Agency

Ground Forces

Appropriated $3.4 billion for development of the Future Combat Systems, the Army's program to build a new generation of ultramodern vehicles, aircraft, robots, weapons, and computers.

Appropriated $925 million for Stryker armored vehicle procurement. The Army was required to deliver a report by March 2008 on the need for an additional Stryker brigade in the context of overall Army needs.

Aviation Forces

Appropriated $3.9 billion for development of the F-35 Joint Strike Fighter. That total included $480 million to develop a second engine from a competing contractor. The bill also provided $2.7 billion for production costs.

Appropriated $3.6 billion to procure twenty F-22A Raptor warplanes and $611 million for continued development.

Naval Forces

Appropriated $2.9 billion for the Navy to start building two DDG-1000 destroyers, formerly known as the DD(X).

Appropriated $3.1 billion for a *Virginia*-class submarine, including $588 million in advance procurement funding.

Appropriated $339 million for procurement of one Littoral Combat Ship (LCS) and $340 million for LCS research and development.

Appropriated $2.8 billion for advance procurement of the CVN-21, the Navy's next-generation aircraft carrier.

Air and Sea Transport

Appropriated $442 million for procurement of the Air Force's C-17 transport plane and $182 million for research and development.

Appropriated $756 million for procurement of one T-AKE cargo ship and advance procurement of long-lead time material and advance construction on three additional ships.

Nuclear Warhead

Appropriated $15 million for development of the Reliable Replacement Warhead, a new nuclear warhead.

Fiscal 2007 Supplemental War Appropriations, Minimum Wage

Congress in 2007 approved $94.7 billion in fiscal 2007 supplemental funding for the wars in Iraq and Afghanistan. The war money was part of a $120 billion fiscal 2007 supplemental (HR 2206—PL 110-28) that also included funding for such things as hurricane recovery and agriculture disaster assistance and was the legislative vehicle for a hike in the minimum wage. *(Minimum wage, pp. 661, 664)*

The war funding was in addition to $70 billion in emergency war funding that had been included in the regular fiscal 2007 defense appropriations bill (HR 5631—PL 109-289) in 2006. *(2007 defense appropriations, p. 358)*

Enactment of HR 2206 came after bruising battles over U.S. policy in Iraq. President George W. Bush had made it clear from the outset that he would not accept a bill that contained deadlines for withdrawing troops from Iraq, and most Republican lawmakers staunchly supported him. Most Democrats, on the other hand, favored setting some kind of deadlines for withdrawal, although Democratic leaders continually had to fight defections from liberals, some of whom opposed appropriating any more money for the war, and from conservative Democrats who opposed hard and fast deadlines.

The Democrats' first try (HR 1591), which would have set deadlines for withdrawal from Iraq starting in 2007, fell to a presidential veto within hours of arriving at the White House. In the end, Democrats backed off from their demands for setting deadlines and Congress cleared a revised bill—HR 2206—that required the president to report on Iraq's progress in meeting a series of benchmarks but did not impose consequences if the Iraqi government failed to meet the objectives. *(Iraq's progress on benchmarks, box p. 304)*

LEGISLATIVE ACTION: ROUND I

House Action

The House passed HR 1591 by a vote of 218–212 on March 23, 2007. The House Appropriations Committee had reported the bill (H Rept 110-60) on March 20.

The House bill appropriated $124.3 billion in supplemental funds, including $95.5 billion for the wars in Iraq and Afghanistan, and required the removal of most U.S. combat troops from Iraq by August 2008.

Specifically, HR 1591 required the president to report to Congress by July 1 and Oct. 1, 2007, on the Iraqi government's progress in meeting certain benchmarks, such as quelling sectarian violence, sharing oil revenue, allocating reconstruction money, and scheduling local elections. If the president did not certify by July 1 that Iraq was making substantial progress on all benchmarks, U.S. forces would have to begin an immediate redeployment to be completed no later than the end of December 2007. If the president could not certify by Oct. 1 that the Iraqi government was meeting certain additional benchmarks, U.S. forces were to begin an immediate redeployment to be completed by the end of March 2008, the date recommended in 2006 by the Iraq Study Group. In addition, the bill held back 50 percent of various reconstruction funds for Iraq until the Oct. 1 certification was made. *(Iraq Study Group, box p. 274)*

Under the bill, if the president reported progress on all benchmarks, the Pentagon would be given until March 1, 2008, to begin redeployment and the end of August 2008 to complete it. The bill allowed some U.S. troops involved in training, protection, and counterterrorism operations to remain in Iraq. The bill had no provision to cut off funding if the requirements were not met.

The House bill also barred deployment of any unit of the armed forces to Iraq unless the Pentagon certified in writing to the Appropriations and Armed Services committees that it was fully mission capable. The president could waive the requirement after reporting to Congress on his need for a unit that was not fully ready. John P. Murtha, D-Pa., chair of the House Defense Appropriations Subcommittee, had added the readiness requirements to the bill.

An attempt to strike the withdrawal provisions from HR 1591 failed during committee consideration. In addition—much to the frustration of Republicans—when the bill reached the floor, it was considered under a closed rule, which meant no amendments were allowed.

The White House had issued a statement March 19 warning the president would veto the measure because of the Iraq provisions and the "excessive and extraneous non-emergency spending." The bill's total was $21.3 billion more than Bush had requested, with almost all of the additional funds directed to nondefense activities.

Senate Action

The Senate passed an amended version of HR 1591 by a vote of 51–47 on March 29, after four days of debate. The Senate Appropriations Committee had reported its own bill (S 965—S Rept 110-37) on March 22.

The Senate-passed bill appropriated $122.8 billion, including $93.5 billion for the wars. The bill included a requirement that U.S. troops begin withdrawing from Iraq within four months of enactment, and it set a goal—but not a requirement—of completing the withdrawal of most troops by March 2008. It required regular reports from the president on the progress of redeployment. It did not include the House bill's troop readiness requirements.

During floor action, an amendment offered by Thad Cochran of Mississippi, the ranking Republican on the Appropriations Committee, to remove the troop withdrawal language lost by a vote of 48–50. In another war-related vote, the Senate adopted 98–0 a Joseph R. Biden Jr., D-Del., amendment to add $1.5 billion to procure 2,500 additional military vehicles with extra protection from mines and improvised explosive devices (IEDs). Senators approved by voice vote an amendment by John W. Warner R-Va., to require an independent study of the readiness of the Iraqi security forces, at a cost of $750,000.

The Senate also adopted amendments dealing with the minimum wage, timber revenue, and the salaries of federal judges.

Conference, Final Action

The House adopted the conference report on HR 1591 (H Rept 110-107) by a **key vote of 218–208 (R 2–195; D 216–13)** on April 25. The Senate cleared the bill 51–46 the next day. *(2007 key votes, p. 955)*

Spending in the bill totaled $124.2 billion, $21.2 billion more than Bush requested. The spending levels generally were closer to those of the House-passed bill.

But conferees hewed closely to the Senate's approach of setting goals for withdrawal from Iraq, rather than adopting the firm deadlines in the House bill. They agreed to tie U.S. military deployments in Iraq to the Baghdad government's record on a series of benchmarks. If the president could not certify to Congress by July 1 that the Iraqi government was making progress in meeting the benchmarks, a phased redeployment would begin immediately, with a goal of completing it by year's end. If the president determined that the Iraqis were making progress, withdrawal would begin three months later, on Oct. 1, with a goal of completing it by the end of March 2008. Half the funds for reconstruction would be withheld until the president certified to Congress that Iraq had actually met specified benchmarks.

The commander of U.S. forces in Iraq, Army Gen. David H. Petraeus, had urged lawmakers during closed-door sessions April 25 to allow the administration strategy more time to work. The following day, before the Senate cleared the bill, he told reporters at an hour-long Pentagon news conference that the Iraq conflict was "the most complex and challenging I have ever seen." Petraeus predicted a long and difficult struggle ahead in Iraq. "We are just getting started with the new effort," he said. "This effort may get harder before it gets easier." He also said that the Iraqi government's lack of political unity could make it difficult to achieve its political, economic, and security benchmarks.

The conference bill included the House readiness provision that required troops to receive full training and proper equipment before they could be deployed to Iraq. The bill required at least one year between deployments for Army, Army Reserve, and National Guard troops and 210 days for Marine and Marine reserves. The president could waive the requirements on a unit-by-unit basis.

Funding was also included for hurricane recovery, disaster aid for farmers, children's health insurance, and fighting wildfires.

Veto, Override Attempt

President Bush vetoed HR 1591 on May 1. It was only the second veto of his presidency. *(Veto message, p. 1063)*

In his veto message, Bush objected to the bill's "arbitrary date for beginning the withdrawal of American troops without regard to conditions on the ground" and said it would "micromanage the commanders in the field in restricting their ability to direct the fight in Iraq." He also found unacceptable the "billions of dollars of spending and other provisions completely unrelated to the war."

The following day the House Democratic leadership attempted to override the veto but failed on a 222–203 vote. A two-thirds majority, 284 votes in this case, was required for the override. With the failed attempt in the House, there was no point to a Senate vote.

LEGISLATIVE ACTION: ROUND II

House Action

On May 10, House Democratic leaders tried again, splitting the vetoed bill into a pair of emergency supplemental measures. The first (HR 2206)—which included the funding for the Pentagon, hurricane recovery, and the bulk of other items in HR 1591's conference report—passed 221–205. The disaster aid for farmers and the firefighting money, which opponents had derided as pork, were put in a second bill (HR 2207), which passed by a much wider margin of 302–120. Under the rule governing the debate, HR 2207 was immediately folded into HR 2206.

Unlike the vetoed bill, HR 2206 did not set a timetable for troop withdrawal. Instead, $42.8 billion—enough to support military operations in Iraq for two or three months—was to be immediately available to the Pentagon. The remaining $52.8 billion, or 55 percent, would be withheld until the president reported to Congress on the Iraqi government's progress toward meeting specific benchmarks and goals.

Like the vetoed bill, the measure also barred the United States from establishing permanent military bases in Iraq and included Murtha's troop readiness provisions, along with a sense of Congress that as each battalion of Iraqi security forces became ready for combat, a U.S. unit of comparable size should be withdrawn.

Senate Action

Senate leaders were lukewarm to the House's defiant approach and were less willing to ensure another White House veto. With senators proposing a variety of approaches, the Senate on May 17 inserted placeholder language into HR 2206 and passed it by voice vote to allow a formal conference with the House to begin.

The Senate-passed bill appropriated no money. Instead, it incorporated a resolution (S Res 107) that the Senate had adopted 96–2, on March 15, expressing the sense of the chamber that Congress should not undermine the safety of the armed forces.

To appease Democrats who wanted some antiwar language in the supplemental, Senate leaders arranged a series of votes on Iraq-related amendments to a water resources bill (HR 1495). All of the votes, which were on cloture motions and needed sixty votes to succeed, were defeated. *(Iraq war policy, pp. 270, 303)*

Final Action

Meanwhile, lawmakers and the White House struggled to find common ground. Top Republican and Democrats met with White House officials May 18 but made no discernible progress.

Faced with unrelenting Republican resistance, Democratic leaders finally settled on a $120 billion spending measure that set eighteen benchmarks for the Iraqi government and required the president to report on progress toward meeting them. It did not set a withdrawal timetable, standards for troop readiness, or binding consequences for failing to meet the benchmarks.

House leaders divided the provisions into two separate amendments that were adopted May 24. The first, providing $22.2 billion in mostly unrequested domestic and security-related spending, was adopted 348–73. The second, providing $97.8 billion primarily for war operations and including the benchmark language, was adopted 280–142. Scores of Democrats voted "no" on the second amendment because there was no withdrawal timetable.

The Senate cleared the bill by a vote of 80–14 later that day.

The final bill appropriated $4.2 billion less than in the version Bush vetoed. Negotiators made small cuts to several programs, including agriculture disaster relief and wildfire suppression. They eliminated money for the Low Income Energy Assistance Program and pandemic flu preparations. Some domestic items remained untouched, such as funding for a secure schools program and children's health insurance.

The bill dropped language that would have barred federal preemption of state and local laws on chemical plant security.

MAJOR PROVISIONS

As signed into law by President Bush on May 25, HR 2206 appropriated $120 billion in emergency supplemental funding for fiscal 2007.

Defense Spending

Appropriated $94.7 billion—$3.2 billion more than requested—for Pentagon activities in support of military operations mainly in Iraq but also in Afghanistan, including:

- $50 billion—about $104 million less than requested—for operations and maintenance. Included in that total were $5.9 billion for Afghan security personnel and the new Afghan army, and $3.8 billion to train and equip Iraqi security forces.
- $25.6 billion—$776 million more than requested—for new weapons procurement. That included nearly $1 billion for various Abrams tank upgrades, $636 million for upgraded Bradley fighting vehicles, and $2.1 billion for new trucks. The measure appropriated $3 billion for a new Mine Resistant Ambush vehicle and $2.4 billion to develop and procure countermeasures to the roadside bombs and mines that accounted for more than half of U.S. casualties in Iraq.
- $13.5 billion—$1.4 billion more than requested—for military personnel.
- $3 billion—$1.9 billion more than requested—for the Defense Health Program. The total included $410 million to ensure that service members did not have to pay extra out-of-pocket copayments for private sector care, and $900 million for research and treatment of post-traumatic stress disorder and traumatic brain injury.

Appropriated $3.1 billion in unrequested funds for the 2005 round of Base Realignment and Closure (BRAC).

Iraq Benchmarks

Required the president to report to Congress by July 15 and Sept. 15, 2007, on the Iraqi government's progress in meeting eighteen benchmarks and goals, based on objectives that Bush listed in his Jan. 10, 2007, speech announcing a "surge" in U.S. forces in Iraq. The president was allowed, but not required, to withhold U.S. reconstruction aid if the objectives were not met. *(Benchmarks, box p. 304)*

Other Provisions

Appropriated $1.8 billion in unrequested funds for the Department of Veterans Affairs, including $1.3 billion for veterans' health care.

Appropriated $5.7 billion for the State Department and foreign aid. *(2007 aid appropriations, p. 285)*

Appropriated $1.1 billion in unrequested funds for antiterrorism expenses of the Homeland Security Department.

Appropriated $6.3 billion, about $2.9 billion more than requested, for continued Gulf Coast recovery from the 2005 hurricanes.

Appropriated $3 billion in unrequested funds for agriculture disaster assistance.

Appropriated $650 million in unrequested funding to eliminate a fiscal 2007 shortfall in funding for the State Children's Health Insurance Program (CHIP).

Appropriated $465 million in unrequested funding for wildfire suppression.

Appropriated $425 million in unrequested funding for the Secure Rural Schools program.

Increased the minimum wage to $7.25 an hour from $5.15 over two years and contained a $4.84 billion package of business tax cuts that were fully offset.

Made several technical changes to the 2005 pension overhaul (HR 4—PL 109-280). The most significant of these were requested by American and Continental airlines. The changes, which put the two airlines on the same footing as Delta and Northwest airlines, gave them seventeen years to fund their pension plans instead of ten, and allowed them to use a different interest-rate calculation that required them to add less money to their plans than previously required. *(Pension overhaul, pp. 654, 658)*

Fiscal 2008 Supplemental War Appropriations

Congress in 2007 appropriated $70 billion in fiscal 2008 emergency supplemental funding for the wars in Iraq and Afghanistan as part of an omnibus appropriations bill (HR 2764—PL 110-161). President George W. Bush had threatened to veto the funding package, which included eleven unfinished fiscal 2008 spending bills, if the war funds were left out.

Many Democrats, particularly in the House, had vowed to provide no further money for the Iraq War without setting conditions aimed at forcing a pullout of combat troops. In an attempt to do just that, the House first passed a stand-alone funding bill (HR 4156) that would have required a shift in Iraq War policy. But the measure died in the Senate when the Democratic leadership in that chamber failed to muster enough votes to cut off debate. Senate Republicans made the war funding—unencumbered by policy directives—the price for their cooperation in clearing the omnibus bill.

The $70 billion in HR 2764 was less than half what the White House had requested for the wars. Another $95.9 billion for the remainder of fiscal 2008 would be included in a fiscal 2008–2009 supplemental appropriations bill (HR 2642—PL 110-252) enacted in June 2008. *(2008–2009 war supplemental, p. 387)*

Additional fiscal 2008 supplemental appropriations for war-related costs had been included in two earlier measures. A continuing funding resolution (H J Res 52—PL 110-92) enacted in September 2007 provided $5.2 billion in emergency funding for Mine Resistant Ambush Protected (MRAP) vehicles to protect troops in Iraq. The regular fiscal 2008 defense appropriations bill (HR 3222—PL 110-116) enacted in November 2007 included another $11.6 billion in emergency funding for the MRAP vehicles.

LEGISLATIVE ACTION

President Bush had requested a total of $189.3 billion in fiscal 2008 emergency war funding.

The House passed its emergency supplemental bill, HR 4156, by a vote of 218–203 on Nov. 14. The measure would have provided $50 billion in "bridge" funds to tide the military over until a larger infusion of funds was enacted in 2008. It would have required U.S. troop withdrawal from Iraq to begin within thirty days of enactment, with a goal of pulling most troops out by Dec. 15, 2008. A limited troop presence would have been allowed after that for such purposes as the protection of U.S. diplomatic facilities and citizens, training of Iraqi forces, and counterterrorism operations.

HR 4156 also contained a troop readiness requirement that would have barred use of funds in the bill for the deployment of a unit unless the president certified to the appropriate congressional committees that it was "fully mission capable." The provision could be waived if the president certified that it was for reasons of national security.

On the Senate side, Republicans introduced their own bill (S 2340) to appropriate $70 billion in emergency funds for the Pentagon, with no strings attached. Senate Democratic leaders agreed to hold cloture votes to determine whether there were sixty votes to limit debate on proceeding to either HR 4156 or S 2340. As expected, supporters of both measures failed to reach the sixty-vote threshold in back-to-back votes on Nov. 16. The motion to proceed to consider S 2340 was rejected 45–53. Then Democrats fell seven votes short, when the Senate rejected 53–45 a motion to proceed to consider the House bill.

The administration warned that inaction would bring dire consequences. Defense Secretary Robert M. Gates said that without bridge funding, he would have to start planning by mid-December for domestic base closures and layoffs.

With the date for adjournment looming, Democrats returned to the war funding issue in December knowing they would have to give in. The House went first, agreeing to add $31 billion to the omnibus bill but the money would be for military operations in Afghanistan only. To allow antiwar Democrats a chance to vote against the war funding, House leaders put it in a separate amendment, which was adopted 206–201, on Dec. 17.

After several last-ditch attempts to add policy amendments failed, the Senate by a **key vote of 70–25 (R 48–1; D 21–23; I 1–1)** replaced the House provision with one that appropriated $70 billion in unrestricted money for military activities in both Iraq and Afghanistan. *(2007 key votes, p. 955; Iraq war policy, p. 303)*

On Dec. 18 the Senate voted 76–17 to approve the amended bill. The House went along, clearing the bill the next day by a **key vote of 272–142 (R 194–1; D 78–141)**.

MAJOR PROVISIONS

As signed into law on Dec. 26, 2007, HR 2764 appropriated $70 billion in emergency supplemental funding for the wars in Iraq and Afghanistan in fiscal 2008. That total included:

- $1.1 billion for military personnel.
- $61.1 billion for operations and maintenance, including $1.4 billion for the Afghan security forces, $1.5 billion for Iraq security forces, and $4.3 billion for the Joint Improvised Explosive Device Defeat Fund.
- $6.1 billion for procurement, including $1.4 billion for Army procurement of weapons and tracked combat vehicles such as the Abrams tank and the Bradley fighting vehicle.
- $576 million for the Defense Health Program.

The bill also required the defense secretary to report to Congress within sixty days after the bill's enactment and then every ninety days through the end of the fiscal year on Iraq's progress on a comprehensive set of measurements of military and political stability.

Provisions in the State Department and foreign operations portion of the omnibus bill barred the use of funds for a permanent basing rights agreement with Iraq or in support of the use of torture, cruel, or inhumane treatment by any U.S. official or contract employee.

MILITARY COSTS: AFGHANISTAN, IRAQ, ENHANCED SECURITY

The following chart shows Congressional Research Service (CRS) estimates of how much Congress appropriated for military operations in Afghanistan and Iraq, by fiscal year, as well as for military costs related to homeland security such as for enhanced security at defense installations, combat air patrols, and reconstruction of the Pentagon after the Sept. 11, 2001, terrorist attacks. It includes regular and supplemental appropriations measures enacted from fiscal 2001 through fiscal 2009. (The latter includes a fiscal 2009 supplemental enacted in 2009 that is not covered in this *Congress and the Nation* volume.) CRS based its calculations on public laws, congressional reports, and Defense Department data.

Fiscal Year	Afghanistan	Iraq	Enhanced Security, Other Expenses
	(in billions of dollars of budget authority)		
FY2001–2002	$ 20.0	—	$ 13.0
FY2003	$ 14.0	$ 50.0	$ 8.0
FY2004	$ 12.4	$ 56.4	$ 3.7
FY2005	$ 17.2	$ 83.4	$ 2.1
FY2006	$ 17.9	$ 98.1	$ 0 .8
FY2007	$ 37.1	$126.8	$ 0.5
FY2008	$ 40.6	$138.3	$ 0.1
FY2009	$ 51.1	$ 90.6	$ 0.2
TOTAL	$210.2	$643.6	$ 28.5

SOURCE: Chart adapted from Table 3, pp. 13–14, in "The Cost of Operations in Iraq, Afghanistan, and Other Global War on Terror Operations Since 9/11," by Amy Belasco (Congressional Research Service Report for Congress, RL33110, Sept. 28, 2009).

Numbers may not add due to rounding.

Fiscal 2008–2009 Supplemental War Appropriations

Congress in 2008 appropriated an additional $161.8 billion for military operations in Iraq and Afghanistan as part of a $186.5 billion fiscal 2008–2009 supplemental spending bill (HR 2642—PL 110-252).

War funding in HR 2642 included $95.9 billion in supplemental money for the remainder of fiscal 2008 and $65.9 billion in supplemental "bridge" funds for the first few months of fiscal 2009. Final action on the measure was hastened, in part, by warnings from the Defense Department that it would run out of funds for operations and personnel in early July 2008. The measure was signed into law on June 30.

The bill also appropriated supplemental money for foreign aid, military construction, and domestic programs, including disaster assistance. Unrelated legislation expanding veterans' education benefits, extending unemployment benefits, and placing a moratorium on certain Medicaid regulations were included as well, although the costs of those provisions was accounted for separately and not included in the bill.

President George W. Bush had requested emergency funds totaling about $183.9 billion, including $166.1 billion for the Pentagon. Because the money appropriated by HR 2642 was treated as emergency funding, it did not count against congressional limits on discretionary appropriations.

The process by which Congress considered HR 2642 was complicated and convoluted, and ended up requiring weeks of negotiations before final agreement was reached.

HOUSE ACTION

To expedite action, House leaders brought the supplemental measure directly to the floor, bypassing the committee stage and using an unneeded fiscal 2008 appropriations bill (HR 2642) as a vehicle. In a process that would be repeated several times, the leadership divided the provisions into separate amendments, a tactic that allowed antiwar Democrats to vote against the war funds while supporting the extended unemployment benefits, extra spending for domestic programs, and other provisions.

Democratic leaders assumed that many House Republicans would oppose the non–war-funding amendment but would provide enough votes to pass the war funds. Republicans were not always willing to oblige.

War Funding

The first amendment would have provided $162.5 billion for Pentagon operations in Iraq and Afghanistan—$96.6 billion for fiscal 2008 and $65.9 billion for fiscal 2009.

Much to the Democrats' surprise, the amendment went down to defeat on a 141–149 vote when 132 Republicans voted "present." The GOP strategy had been devised by Mike Pence of Indiana and members of the conservative Republican Study Committee (RSC). It was purely symbolic—the Senate was expected to restore the funding—but the RSC wanted to demonstrate just how dependent Democrats were on GOP votes to keep money for the troops flowing. House Republican leaders apparently had been apprehensive, but they acquiesced.

Appropriations Committee Chair David R. Obey, D-Wis., maintained that the Democrats had won because most of them opposed further funding of the war anyway.

Iraq Policy

The second amendment focused on war policy. It included provisions on troop withdrawal, troop readiness and length of deployment, a status-of-forces agreement with Iraq, cost-sharing with Iraq, permanent bases in Iraq, and interrogation techniques. *(Details, Iraq war policy, pp. 270, 303)*

The amendment was adopted by a **key vote of 227–196 (R 8–183; D 219–13)**. *(2008 key votes, p. 972)*

Domestic, International Programs

The third amendment, adopted 256–166, dealt with both domestic and international programs. It expanded veterans' education benefits—and proposed a surtax on higher incomes to pay for them. It extended unemployment benefits and put a moratorium on seven Medicaid regulations. It appropriated money for New Orleans levees, international aid, and military construction.

SENATE ACTION

The Senate responded to the House action with its own set of amendments.

Senate leaders had hoped to avoid committee markup of the bill, as the House had, but West Virginia Democrat Robert C. Byrd, chair of the Appropriations Committee, insisted on putting his panel's stamp on the bill. That was exactly what the committee did, as members approved numerous policy provisions and spending items.

Some of the committee's most controversial provisions were dropped when HR 2642 reached the Senate floor. A revised bill was assembled on the floor through a convoluted process that Democratic leaders said was an effort to reach across the aisle and get enough votes to send the measure back to the House. The Senate never took an actual vote on passage. Rather, it agreed to the House amendments—with further amendments.

War Funding, Iraq Policy

The Senate Appropriations Committee had proposed an amendment that would have appropriated $168.9 billion for the wars in Iraq and Afghanistan. A separate amendment set forth policy prescriptions dealing with troop readiness, length of deployments, permanent bases in Iraq, changing the U.S. mission in Iraq, and reimbursement by Iraq for some fuel costs. *(Details, Iraq war policy, pp. 270, 303)*

The Senate leadership combined the committee's war-funding and Iraq policy provisions into a single amendment, which the Senate rejected 34–63. Having demonstrated that the war restrictions could not pass in the Senate, Majority Leader Harry Reid, D-Nev., then proposed a war-funding-only amendment that called for $165.4 billion in supplemental funds—$95.5 billion in fiscal 2008 and $65.9 billion in fiscal 2009. With the policy prescriptions replaced by report requirements, the amendment passed easily 70–26 on May 22.

Domestic, International Programs

The Senate Appropriations Committee approved an expansive version of the third House amendment that included elements of the House proposal along with funding for low-income home energy assistance, science programs, law enforcement agencies, the Federal Highway Administration's emergency relief program, tracking unregistered sex offenders, and fighting drug crimes. It also had a lengthy section of immigration provisions.

But, in a surprise move during floor debate, Democrats raised a point of order against their own committee's amendment, effectively killing it. Senators then agreed 75–22 to a scaled-back amendment written by the leadership that dropped much of the committee-approved authorizing language, such as the long list of immigration provisions, as well as $1.2 billion that had been added for science programs.

The leadership version retained, among other things, the House provisions on veterans' education benefits, unemployment benefits, and delaying the Medicaid regulations. The amendment also included money for hurricane recovery, energy assistance, and international aid. But, in a major difference, it dropped the proposed surtax.

COMPROMISE, FINAL ACTION

After weeks of negotiations, and with the Pentagon running short of money, House Democrats struck a deal with the White House and the chamber's Republican leadership.

The bill included the president's entire request for war funding, without any policy restrictions on how the money could be spent—a key concession to the White House. Senate leaders were not involved with the negotiations, and most of the Senate's domestic spending add-ons were dropped.

The House agreed to the compromise June 19 in the form of two amendments. It voted 268–155 to adopt the war spending amendment, which provided $165.4 billion, as the Senate had proposed. The second amendment, adopted 416–12, provided $24.7 billion for a range of domestic, foreign aid, and military construction accounts. It included the unemployment benefits, Medicaid, and veterans' education provisions. It also reduced the war funding total by $3.6 billion.

The Senate did not need to vote on the first amendment because it was identical to the one it had adopted May 22. The chamber adopted the second amendment 92–6 on June 26, clearing the bill for the president.

MAJOR PROVISIONS

As signed into law on June 30, HR 2642 appropriated $186.5 billion in fiscal 2008–2009 emergency supplemental spending. That total included $161.8 billion for the wars in Iraq and Afghanistan and $24.7 billion for military construction, international aid, and domestic programs.

Defense Spending

Appropriated $161.8 billion for Pentagon operations in Iraq and Afghanistan—$95.9 billion for the remainder of fiscal 2008 and $65.9 billion for the first part of fiscal 2009.

Appropriated $4.6 billion for military construction, including $1.3 billion to support the 2005 round of base realignment and closure (BRAC) and about $980 million for military hospitals. *(Military base closings, p. 369)*

Iraq Policy Provisions

Required Iraq reconstruction aid from the U.S. Agency for International Development be matched dollar for dollar by the Iraqi government.

Prohibited the use of funds to establish permanent bases in Iraq.

International Aid

Appropriated $10.1 billion for international food aid and bilateral assistance. *(Details, 2008 aid appropriations, p. 314)*

Domestic Provisions

Appropriated $5.8 billion to strengthen New Orleans levees and $2.7 billion for relief from floods and tornadoes in the Midwest.

Appropriated $1 billion for the Food and Drug Administration, the Federal Bureau of Prisons, census cost overruns, and other programs.

Expanded education benefits for veterans. *(Details, p. 667)*

Extended unemployment benefits up to thirteen weeks. *(Details, p. 667)*

Placed a moratorium on seven Medicaid regulations.

Fiscal 2008 Military Construction Appropriations

Congress in 2007 appropriated $20.6 billion for Defense Department military construction and related accounts in fiscal 2008. The money was included in the $108.4 billion military construction-Veterans Affairs (VA) section of a year-end omnibus spending package (HR 2764—PL 110-161).

The defense money included $9.9 billion for military construction, $2.9 billion for family housing,; and $7.5 billion for Base Realignment and Closure (BRAC) costs. The total for BRAC was significantly less than what Congress had approved in an earlier conference bill that died in the Senate.

Congress approved an additional $4.6 billion for military construction accounts in fiscal 2008 as part of a war supplemental spending bill (HR 2642—PL 110-252) that cleared in June 2008.

LEGISLATIVE ACTION

The House passed a $109.2 billion military construction-VA bill (HR 2642) by a vote of 409–2 on June 15, 2007. The House Appropriations Committee had reported it (H Rept 110-186) on June 11. The bill included $21.4 billion for military construction accounts—about $207 million more than requested.

The Senate passed a $109.3 billion version of HR 2642 by a 92–1 vote on Sept. 6. The Senate Appropriations Committee had reported its bill (S 1645—S Rept 110-85) on

June 18. The Senate bill largely mirrored the House bill, although it provided slightly more—$21.6 billion—for military construction.

House and Senate negotiators agreed on a version that would have provided $109.2 billion, including $21.5 billion for the Defense Department accounts. But rather than filing a separate conference report on the bill, Democratic appropriators agreed Nov. 1 to attach their compromise to a conference report on an appropriations bill for the Labor, Health and Human Services (HHS), and Education departments (HR 3043—H Rept 110-424). Their hope was that the veterans' funding would make it harder for Bush to carry out his threat to veto domestic spending bills if they were not cut enough to offset a $3.7 billion increase in veterans' funding. The labor-HHS-education bill was $9.8 billion more than requested.

The House adopted the combined conference bill 269–142 on Nov. 6. But when it reached the Senate the next day, Republicans raised a point of order and Democrats were unable to gain the sixty votes necessary to waive it. The vote was 47–46. The Senate then passed an amended version of the labor-HHS-education bill, after dropping the military construction-VA provisions.

With Veterans' Day approaching, the administration stepped up its pressure on Democrats to clear a stand-alone military construction-VA bill. But Democrats were still unwilling to do that because it would leave the other spending bills exposed to Bush's veto threat. Democrats also said the VA had enough money in the short run.

The military construction-VA bill was ultimately folded into HR 2764, the omnibus spending package. In trimming the bill as part of an effort to stay within Bush's discretionary limit for the omnibus bill, appropriators cut from administration priorities, such as the BRAC account, while providing as much or more than they had in the original conference agreement for veterans' health programs by using emergency appropriations. The final bill's funding for military construction was close to what the earlier conference agreement had provided and the funding for family housing was exactly the same, but the BRAC funding was $805 million less.

MAJOR PROVISIONS

As signed into law Dec. 26, the military construction-Veterans Affairs section of HR 2764 appropriated $87.6 billion for the VA and $20.6 billion for the Defense Department in fiscal 2008. The VA money included $3.7 billion in "contingent emergency" funding that could be spent only if the president sent Congress a separate request to release the extra money. Bush did so on Jan. 17, 2008.

The Defense Department provisions:

Military Construction

Appropriated $9.9 billion for construction on military bases, $376 million more than requested.

Family Housing

Appropriated $2.9 billion for the construction and maintenance of military family housing, $65 million less than requested.

Base Closing

Appropriated $7.5 billion for previous rounds of Base Realignment and Closure (BRAC), $863 million less than requested.

2008 SUPPLEMENTAL

Congress appropriated another $4.6 billion for military construction in a fiscal 2008–2009 war supplemental appropriations bill (HR 2642—PL 110-252). The extra funding included $1.3 billion for the 2005 round of BRAC and about $980 million for military hospitals. *(Military base closings, p. 369)*

HR 2642 was the original fiscal 2008 military construction-VA appropriations bill and, because it was no longer needed, it was used as the vehicle for the war supplemental.

Fiscal 2009 Defense Authorization

Congress in 2008 cleared a $611.1 billion fiscal 2009 defense authorization bill (S 3001—PL 110-417). That total included $542.5 billion for Pentagon accounts and Energy Department nuclear weapons programs, as well as $68.6 billion in emergency supplemental spending for the wars in Iraq and Afghanistan.

President George W. Bush had requested $612.5 billion for national defense, $70 billion of which was for war-related activities. Virtually all of the $1.4 billion difference between his request and the final bill was the result of the smaller amount provided for operations in Iraq and Afghanistan. No major conditions were placed on the war funding, which was intended to last through June or July of 2009.

S 3001 did not eliminate any major weapons programs, but it did authorize less than requested for missile defense and other futuristic programs, such as the Army's Future Combat Systems, which had become so complex and expensive that even some supporters questioned its viability. The measure also shifted funds to replace equipment depleted by the war in Iraq, including new combat vehicles and new battle gear for the Army National Guard and reserves. Increases also went to military pay raises and shipbuilding.

In addition, in what had become an annual ritual, Congress rejected Bush's proposal to pay for part of the cost of military health care services through a $1.2 billion increase in fees, premiums, and drug copayments charged to participants in Tricare, the military's health care network for active duty service members, National Guard and reserve members, retirees, and their dependents.

The final bill diluted most provisions that had drawn veto threats, such as proposals to sharply limit the use of contractors in Iraq and to require congressional approval of any agreement on the continued presence of U.S. forces in that country. Other provisions that the White House opposed but did not threaten to veto remained, including language barring the Defense Department from using funds for most infrastructure projects in Iraq.

Although legislation (HR 2638—PL 110-329) providing fiscal 2009 defense appropriations had already been enacted a few weeks early, passage of the authorization bill was essential in order for a 3.9 percent pay raise—half a percentage point more than the president had proposed—and new troop levels to go into effect. *(2009 defense appropriations, p. 396)*

HOUSE COMMITTEE ACTION

The House Armed Services Committee reported its version of the bill (HR 5658—PL 110-652, Part I) on May 16, 2008, and filed a supplemental report (Part II) on May 20.

The bill authorized $612.5 billion—$542.5 billion for the base budget and $70 billion in war funding. Included in the $70 billion was an unrequested $3.9 billion to buy fifteen C-17 cargo planes.

The committee proposed shifting billions of dollars requested for futuristic weapons systems to more immediate battlefield priorities and the pay and health care needs of military families.

The panel also allowed room for billions of dollars in earmarks for ship and aircraft programs that would create jobs in members' districts. The bill also included a provision stating that the measure was exempt from President Bush's January 2008 executive order directing federal agencies to disregard earmarks unless they were specified in the enacted text of a bill.

HR 5658 authorized $3.4 billion, $200 million less than requested to continue development and procurement of the Army's Future Combat Systems. But the Armed Services Committee said in its report that the concerns it had expressed the previous year had "only grown more acute," citing schedule delays, the escalating cost, and the competing need for funds for other Army programs. *(2008 defense authorization, p. 373)*

The committee made some significant changes in the president's shipbuilding requests. Instead of approving the requested $2.6 billion to buy the next DDG-1000 destroyer, the panel agreed to authorize only $400 million to be used either for procurement of long-lead materials for the next DDG-1000 or to restart procurement of two DDG-51-class destroyers. Instead of approving about $100 million to shut down the production line for the LPD-17 amphibious ship as the administration had requested, committee members authorized $1.8 billion to buy another one. The panel approved $4.1 billion for construction and long-lead components for the next ships in the *Virginia* class of submarines, after adding to the president's request $722 million for advance procurement to move up the construction of a second sub to fiscal 2010. Also in the bill was an authorization of $840 million for Littoral Combat Ship procurement, $80 million less than requested.

Aircraft authorizations included $3.1 billion for twenty F-22 Raptor fighters, equal to the request, plus an unrequested $523 million to procure parts for twenty more planes, pending a decision by the next president. The bill authorized the requested $832 million to begin systems design and demonstration of the aerial refueling tanker but included none of the $62 million requested for advance procurement because Air Force officials said they did not need the money in fiscal 2009.

The bill authorized $24.7 billion for the Defense Health Program, with none of the $1.2 billion in increased fees that Bush had proposed.

HR 5658 included $582 million, $372 million less than requested, for missile defense weapons and facilities in Poland and the Czech Republic. Money authorized by HR 5658 and by subsequent authorizations could not be spent to deploy or operate these missiles until the two European governments had ratified agreements for the deployment and until the Pentagon had certified that the interceptor missiles had a high probability of success.

HOUSE FLOOR ACTION

The House passed HR 5658 by a vote of 384–23 on May 22.

The White House issued a statement of administration policy on the day of the House vote that included a long list of provisions and potential amendments that would result in a veto of the bill. The House adopted some of the amendments anyway.

Two of those amendments were aimed at setting ground rules for a status-of-forces agreement being negotiated with Iraq to replace the U.N. mandate, which was due to expire at the end of 2008. One, offered by Democrats John Yarmuth of Kentucky and Ron Klein of Florida and adopted by voice vote as part of a package of amendments, required that a U.S.-Iraq agreement specify that Iraq would have to pay for certain costs of the U.S. military presence there. The other amendment, offered by Barbara Lee, D-Calif., and adopted by a 234–183 vote, required congressional authorization for any agreement obligating the U.S. military to defend Iraq. Lee said the Iraqi parliament was expected to ratify the agreement, and that it was only right that U.S. legislators do the same.

The administration also objected to an amendment by Rush D. Holt, D-N.J., and Ellen O. Tauscher, D-Calif., to require that interrogations of detainees be videotaped. It was adopted 218–192. Also on the veto-triggering list was a David E. Price, D-N.C., amendment, adopted 240–168, to bar the use of contractors as interrogators.

AIR FORCE TANKER CONTRACT

The saga of attempts to award a $35 billion contract for a new aerial refueling tanker lived on in the 110th Congress, and after. After years of twists and turns, the Air Force thought it had reached the end of the tortuous road in 2008 when it selected a contractor to build the tanker, only to have the decision reversed a few months later by the Government Accountability Office (GAO). Then, in early 2010, one of the prime bidders for the plane dropped out of competition entirely.

The Air Force had selected a consortium made up of Northrop Grumman Corp. and the North American division of the European Aeronautic Defence and Space Co. (EADS). But the chief competitor, Boeing Co., filed a protest with GAO, which ultimately recommended that the competition be done over.

The stakes were high and Congress was deeply involved in the process through it all. Authorization to build the tankers was written into law and funds were appropriated. Lawmakers took sides, aligning themselves with the competitor that could bring business—and jobs—to their home districts or states. That one of the competitors was a foreign company also introduced into the mix the highly-charged issue of U.S. jobs going overseas.

Background

The aerial refueling contract had been mired in controversy from the beginning. In the wake of the Sept. 11, 2001, terrorist attacks, the commercial aviation industry was in dire straits. To assist the industry, several key senators turned to an earlier proposal put forward by Boeing Co. to have the Air Force replace its aging fleet of KC-135 refueling tankers with leased aircraft. The idea caught on and a provision of the fiscal 2002 defense appropriations bill (PL 107-117) allowed the Air Force to lease 100 Boeing 767 passenger jets that had been modified to become KC-767 tankers. The Air Force had not requested the new planes but, given that many of its tankers were built in the 1950s Eisenhower era, it quickly became an advocate for the plan. *(Background, Congress and the Nation Vol. XI, box p. 348)*

Critics decried the plan as a sweetheart deal for Boeing. Sen. John McCain, R-Ariz., called it "corporate welfare" and "war profiteering" and argued that the Air Force document establishing the need for the tankers had been written to suit the Boeing KC-767 tanker. He said the planes were not needed and that leasing them was the costliest way to obtain them anyway. At that time the estimated cost was $20 billion over ten years. McCain's criticism started to gain traction.

Supporters, however, argued that it was a fair deal that would help an important member of the aviation industry at a difficult time. The next Congress approved legislation (PL 108-136) that allowed the Air Force to lease no more than twenty aircraft and buy no more than eighty.

But soon the heated debate was overtaken by a full-scale scandal. On the same day PL 108-136 was signed into law—Nov. 24, 2003—Boeing revealed that it had fired two of its top executives: chief financial officer Mike Sears and missile-defense executive Darleen Druyun. A week later Boeing's chief executive, Phil Condit, stepped down. Druyun, a former top Air Force procurement official who had gone to work for Boeing, admitted to favoring the company for several contracts while she was with the government in return for Boeing hiring her and some of her relatives. Druyun and Sears, with whom she had colluded, ultimately were sentenced to jail terms.

The criminal investigation opened Boeing to more scrutiny, resulting in more delays in the program. The next year the congressional defense committees attempted to get the project back on track but with different ground rules. A new law (PL 108-375) allowed the Air Force to purchase, not lease, tankers, but stipulated that the Air Force could not acquire them under the terms of PL 107-117, the statute that had allowed negotiations with Boeing alone.

Members of Congress continued to argue over whether that meant a new contract with competitive bids or just a new contract with Boeing. In the end, the contract was opened up to competitive bids.

A New Contract

EADS leaped in, hoping to end Boeing's near monopoly in the tanker market. But EADS knew that it would be unprecedented for so large a Pentagon contract to go to a foreign company unless it had a U.S. company as its partner. Los Angeles-based Northrop Grumman Corp. teamed up with EADS to compete against Boeing for the new contract. In its September 2005 announcement of the joint effort, EADS described itself as a teammate and principal subcontractor on the Northrop Grumman KC-30 advanced tanker project.

The Air Force announced Feb. 29, 2008, that it had accepted the consortium's bid to develop and build up to 179 tankers. EADS planned to assemble the aircraft, which was to be based on the Airbus A330 passenger jet, at a new facility in Mobile, Ala. EADS, which owned Airbus, said at least 58 percent of the aircraft would come from U.S. parts and labor.

A bipartisan group of senators and House members reacted angrily to the announcement. They were upset that Boeing had been passed over and that some work that might have been done in the United States would now be sent overseas. At a sometimes emotional hearing on March 5, members of the House Defense Appropriations Subcommittee expressed worries that the decision would imperil U.S. jobs, defense industrial capability, and even sensitive technology. "It's outsourcing our national security," said Republican Todd Tiahrt of Kansas, one of the states where the Boeing tanker would have been built.

GAO Review

Boeing Co. filed a protest with the GAO on March 11, citing "irregularities" in the competition.

The GAO, known as the auditing arm of Congress, had been adjudicating disputes between government contractors for many decades. For most of the twentieth century, this was an informal process done at the request of agencies. But since 1985, the GAO had had a specific role under the Competition in Contracting Act (PL 98-369). The law was enacted in 1984 in the wake of embarrassing publicity over some government purchases—including exorbitantly expensive Pentagon parts such as toilet seats and coffeepots. The high costs were at least partly due to a lack of competition in military procurement. The law established competition as the rule in government contracting and permitted sole-source deals as a rare exception. It set up processes intended to make the competitions full and open.

The GAO was authorized to review protests of the ground rules used in bid solicitations and award decisions. The review process was considered beneficial not only because it could be expedited, but also because it was conducted outside the courts, where procedural delays might arise, and outside Congress, where political considerations might carry the day. At that time the agency was issuing about 300 decisions a year.

Under the review process, a losing bidder had to file a protest within ten days of being briefed by the government on the grounds for its decision. The GAO had to make a decision within 100 days of the filing, although it could use a sixty-five-day express option if it saw fit. Under most circumstances, the contract was frozen until the review was completed.

GAO Decision

On June 18, the GAO ruled in Boeing's favor. The agency found that the Air Force had "made a number of significant errors" in soliciting and weighing the tanker bids. Those mistakes were big enough to have affected the competition's outcome in a way that was not fair to Boeing, the GAO said. The Air Force, it determined, did not assess the competing proposals in accordance with criteria set forth in the contract solicitation, misled Boeing about whether its proposal had met a key performance objective, and improperly assessed Boeing's costs.

"We recommend that the Air Force reopen discussions with the offerors, obtain revised proposals, reevaluate the revised proposals, and make a new source selection decision, consistent with our decision," the GAO said.

The Air Force had sixty days to respond to the decision. In July Defense Secretary Robert M. Gates said the competition would be restarted, but that the under secretary for acquisition would oversee the competition instead of the Air Force. The Defense Department was expected to award the new contract by the end of 2008.

But on Sept. 10, 2008, Gates announced that the Pentagon would leave it to the next administration to resolve. He said there was not enough time left in the administration of President George W. Bush to effectively conduct the competition.

In the meantime, Congress continued to approve funding for the tanker program. *(2009 defense authorization, p. 390; 2009 defense appropriations, p. 396)*

Northrop Grumman Withdraws

The contracting process resumed after Barack Obama took office as president in 2009. The Pentagon released its draft request for proposals in September 2009 and its final request for proposals the following February. Less than two weeks later, on March 8, 2010, Northrop Grumman Corp. announced that it was withdrawing from the competition after concluding that the government had written its solicitation in a way that favored Boeing's smaller refueling tanker. Although Northrop Grumman thought it had grounds to protest the bidding process, it said it would not do so because "America's service men and women have been forced to wait too long for new tankers" and to delay the process further would "not be acting responsibly." This left the Pentagon and Congress with the decision of whether to allow the huge Air Force tanker contract to go to a sole bidder.

While objecting to it, the White House did not include in its veto threat a John M. Spratt Jr., D-S.C., amendment, adopted by voice vote, to require the director of national intelligence to send Congress an annual update of intelligence findings on Iran's nuclear weapons program.

Other items cited in the veto warning included provisions that placed a moratorium on public-private competition for Defense Department jobs, restricted the Pentagon's ability to procure goods and services from foreign sources, rejected Bush's executive order on earmarks, and made substantial cuts in the administration's request for missile defense programs, including the system in Poland and the Czech Republic.

Democrats turned back a number of Republican amendments. Among them was a proposal by Trent Franks, R-Ariz., rejected 186–229, to restore the $719 million cut from the missile defense request and direct the funds toward medium-range antimissile systems, rather than the European system or programs aimed at intercepting intercontinental missiles. Also rejected 145–271 was a Steve Pearce, R-N.M., amendment that would have restored a $10 million request for the Reliable Replacement Warhead, a next-generation nuclear weapon.

SENATE COMMITTEE ACTION

The Senate Armed Services Committee reported its bill (S 3001—S Rept 110-335) on May 12.

The bill authorized the same amount as HR 5658—$542.5 billion for the regular defense budget and $70 billion for war costs.

The Senate measure divided the $70 billion into separate accounts, with $49.6 billion authorized for Iraq, $19.9 billion for Afghanistan, and $500 million for war-related military construction. The total also included $2.1 billion to buy six C-17s. The committee wrote language in the bill to bar Pentagon spending on major reconstruction work in Iraq and to lay the groundwork for Baghdad to start paying its own military bills, as well as some of Washington's expenses.

The bill included the requested amount for the Future Combat Systems.

The committee allowed $3.5 billion for construction and long-lead components for the next *Virginia*-class sub, plus $79 million to prepare for two subs per year; $2.6 billion, as requested, to buy one DDG-1000 destroyer; and $273 million for partial procurement of a LDP-17 amphibious ship and none of the funds Bush requested to close down the ship's production line.

S 3001 authorized $3.5 billion for the F-22, including $497 million that could be used either for parts for new F-22s or to begin closing down the production line. It also included $893 million to begin development of the new aerial tanker.

S 3001 authorized $24.8 billion for the Defense Health Program and made up for the $1.2 billion in extra fees, premiums, and drug copayments assumed by Bush but not included in the bill.

Like the House committee, the panel rejected Bush's executive order regarding earmarks. S 3001 included a provision stating that members' projects listed in the committee report were to be considered as authorized by the bill and were "binding on agency heads."

The Senate bill also included the provision prohibiting the Defense Department from conducting a public-private competition before expanding the civilian workforce to address gaps in the number and skills of the workforce.

SENATE FLOOR ACTION

The Senate passed S 3001 by a vote of 88–8 on Sept. 17.

Carl Levin, D-Mich., chair of the Senate Armed Services Committee, had attempted to bring the bill to the floor in late July, but wrangling over Republicans' insistence on offering domestic oil drilling amendments prevented the leadership from getting enough votes to proceed before the August recess. On Sept. 8—their first day back—senators agreed 83–0 to invoke cloture and take up the bill.

The next day the White House issued a veto warning. Among the items cited were provisions to restrict the use of contractors as security guards in combat zones, bar the use of contractors to interrogate detainees, require changes in the structure of military intelligence operations, and limit public-private competition for Pentagon jobs.

As lawmakers began to dispense with amendments, a dispute over the bill's earmark language surfaced as the main obstacle to passage. Jim DeMint, R-S.C., attempted to delete the provision specifying that earmarks listed in the report were part of the bill. DeMint—backed by the Senate's top Republican, Mitch McConnell of Kentucky, and Tom Coburn, R-Okla., a leading anti-earmark crusader—promised to hold up work on the bill until he got a vote on his amendment. Levin said he would be willing to print the earmarks in the bill itself but that it would take at least four days to accomplish, putting the chances of finishing before Congress adjourned in jeopardy.

The bill's fate was not clear until Sept. 16, when Majority Leader Harry Reid, D-Nev., mustered just enough votes to invoke cloture, thereby limiting the remaining debate to thirty hours. The vote was 61–32, one more than the sixty needed. With the time about to run out, senators skipped hundreds of amendments that had been filed and passed the bill the next day.

In earlier action, the Senate had adopted 94–2 an amendment by Bill Nelson, D-Fla., to repeal a requirement in existing law that the survivors of military personnel killed in action had to offset the amount of benefits they received from the Defense Department by the amount they got from the Department of Veterans Affairs. The Senate had passed the provision repeatedly but it had been deleted in conference because of its cost: $6.9 billion over a decade in mandatory spending. The provision would suffer the same fate this time, too, and would not be in the final bill.

The Senate adopted by voice vote an amendment by Patrick J. Leahy, D-Vt., to extend from three years to five years the statute of limitations on contractor fraud in theaters of war, including the conflicts in Iraq and Afghanistan.

The Senate rejected 39–57 an amendment by David Vitter, R-La., to authorize an additional $271 million for testing and procuring parts for antimissile systems.

FINAL ACTION

The House agreed to an amended version of S 3001 by a vote of 392–39 on Sept. 24. The Senate cleared the bill by voice vote on Sept. 27.

Because Senate Republicans had objected to holding a formal conference, senior members of the House and Senate Armed Services committees negotiated the final version of the bill in informal sessions. The compromise they reached took the form of a House amendment to S 3001. House Democratic leaders took the unusual step of bringing the measure to the floor on Sept. 24 under suspension of the rules, which barred amendments and required a two-thirds vote for passage.

The negotiators eliminated or rewrote a number of provisions cited in the White House veto threats.

The language in both bills to ban the use of private contractors to interrogate detainees held in U.S. military facilities was replaced with a nonbinding sense-of-Congress provision. A House requirement that all intelligence interrogations of detainees be videotaped was also replaced with a sense-of-Congress provision, as was a provision in both bills prohibiting private security contractors from performing "inherently governmental functions" in combat zones.

The president was required to report to Congress on any status-of-forces requirement with Iraq. The House provision requiring congressional approval of such an agreement was dropped, although the managers' statement on the bill said that it was already "well-established" that such an agreement had to be approved by Congress.

The committee leaders also dropped both bills' prohibitions on public-private competition for Pentagon jobs.

The lawmakers, however, included other provisions opposed by the administration, as well as language aimed at continuing congressional oversight of the wars. These included provisions on paying for Iraq infrastructure projects, detention operations, permanent military bases in Iraq, control over Iraqi oil facilities, Iran's nuclear weapons program, and members' earmarks.

The final bill contained $410 million less than requested for various missile defense programs. No funds were provided for a proposed Space Test Bed to develop and test space-based interceptors.

Lawmakers shifted the $10 million requested for the Reliable Replacement Warhead, a next-generation nuclear weapon, to other programs.

MAJOR PROVISIONS

As signed into law Oct. 14, S 3001 authorized $611.1 billion for Pentagon programs and Energy Department nuclear weapons activities in fiscal 2009. The total included an authorization of $68.6 billion in emergency funding for the wars in Iraq and Afghanistan.

Iraq, Afghanistan Wars

Included in the $68.6 billion emergency funding for the wars were:

- $10.4 billion to repair and rebuild Army and Marine Corps equipment worn down by fighting in Iraq and Afghanistan.
- $1.7 billion for Mine Resistant Ambush Protected vehicles.
- $2.2 billion for continued research to combat roadside bombs.
- $2.1 billion for six C-17 cargo aircraft.

Required the president to send Congress a report on any pact with Iraq on the future of U.S. forces in that country.

Required the U.S. government to begin negotiating a cost-sharing agreement for U.S.-Iraqi combined operations and to act to ensure that Iraq paid for the costs of its security forces. The provision also banned the use of Pentagon funds for most Iraq infrastructure projects.

Required the Pentagon to submit a detailed report to the Armed Services committees on detention operations at international facilities and reintegration centers in Iraq.

Banned the use of funds authorized by the bill to established permanent military bases in Iraq or control over Iraqi oil facilities.

Expressed the sense of Congress that certain functions should not be carried out by private security contractors in an area of combat operations.

Detainee Policies

Expressed the sense of Congress that one year after enactment the Pentagon should have developed the resources needed to ensure that all interrogations of detainees held in U.S. military facilities could be conducted by government personnel rather than contract employees.

Expressed the sense of Congress that all strategic intelligence interrogations of detainees who were in the custody or under the effective control of the military or in a Defense Department facility should be videotaped.

Military Personnel

Authorized $128.7 billion.

Authorized a 3.9 percent military pay raise.

Authorized, as requested, an increase of 7,000 Army troops for a total of 532,400, and an increase of 5,000 for the Marines for a total of 194,000. The bill also increased the full-time manning level for the Army National Guard to 32,060 and the Air National Guard to 14,360.

Authorized $25 billion for the Defense Health Program. The bill barred for a year any increases in fees, premiums, and drug copayments for participants in the military's Tricare health care system.

Operations and Maintenance

Authorized $154.3 billion.

Facilities

Authorized $15.4 billion for military construction and family housing.

Authorized $9.5 billion for Base Realignment and Closure (BRAC), mainly for ongoing costs of the 2005 round. *(Military base closings, p. 369)*

Missile Defense

Authorized $10.5 billion for missile defense programs, including $8.8 billion for the Missile Defense Agency. The total included funding for deployment of a long-range missile defense system based in Alaska and California.

Included in the total was $708 million to build a third interceptor site in Eastern Europe. Construction could begin only after it was approved by the host nations—Poland and the Czech Republic—and deployment could not occur until the defense secretary certified that the interceptors worked.

Ground Forces

Authorized $3.6 billion for continued development of the Army's Future Combat Systems, planned as an integrated set of vehicles, aircraft, radios, and computers. The bill continued a requirement that the Government Accountability Office (GAO) and other independent consultants review the program. It set numerous other requirements as well.

Aviation Forces

Authorized $3.4 billion for twenty F-22 Raptors, the Air Force's next-generation fighter with both air-to-air and air-to-ground fighter capabilities. The bill dedicated about $525 million of the total to be used either for advance procurement of twenty more aircraft in fiscal 2010 or to shut down the production line, depending on what the next president wanted to do.

Authorized $3.4 billion to procure fourteen F-35 Joint Strike Fighter aircraft, a next-generation, multirole fighter based on a common airframe and components for use by the Air Force, Navy, and Marine Corps. The bill also authorized $3.6 billion for development, $495 million of which was to be used to continue development of a second, competitive engine.

Authorized $832 million to be placed in a tanker replacement fund for development of a new Air Force aerial refueling tanker. The bill included no money for advance procurement in fiscal 2009. *(Aerial refueling tanker, box p. 392)*

Naval Forces

Authorized $3.7 billion for the next ship in the *Virginia* class of attack submarines, which were replacing retiring *Los Angeles*-class submarines and were expected to constitute the bulk of the attack submarine force in the future. The bill also authorized $300 million to purchase components in preparation for building two subs per year.

Authorized $2.6 billion for a third DDG-1000, which at one time had been considered to be the Navy's next-generation battleship. But the bill also included $349 million for spares or advance procurement of the older DDG-51 destroyer. The Navy told Congress in July 2008 that it wanted to halt the DDG-1000 program after the completion of two prototype vessels and restart the DDG-51 program, but it subsequently indicated its support of completing the third DDG-1000.

Authorized $920 million for two Littoral Combat Ships, which were small, specialized ships tailored for fighting close to shore.

Authorized $600 million for advance procurement for two LPD-17 *San Antonio*-class amphibious ships.

Nuclear Weapons

Authorized $16.3 billion for national security programs carried out by the Energy Department.

Other Provisions

Prohibited public-private competition for Pentagon jobs.

Stated that members' projects listed in the statement of managers on the bill were "authorized by law to be carried out to the same extent as if included in the text of the act, subject to the availability of appropriations." The Government Printing Office had indicated that it would not be able to incorporate the tables into the bill in time for Congress to finish the measure before adjournment.

Required an annual report to Congress on Iran's nuclear weapons capabilities. The president also was required to notify Congress if Iran resumed its nuclear weapons program.

BUSH´S SIGNING STATEMENT

In signing the bill, President Bush issued a "signing statement" indicating that he reserved what he described as the executive branch's right to disregard certain provisions. These included the ban on the use of funds authorized in the measure "to exercise control of the oil resources of Iraq" and a requirement that the U.S. government initiate negotiations with Baghdad on sharing costs of combined military operations.

Fiscal 2009 Defense Appropriations

Congress in 2008 approved $488 billion in fiscal 2009 defense appropriations as part of a year-end continuing resolution (HR 2638—PL 110-329). The bill funded the regular Pentagon budget and did not include emergency funding for operations in Iraq and Afghanistan.

HR 2638 provided $4 billion less than President George W. Bush had requested and generally followed the fiscal 2009 defense authorization bill (S 3001—PL 110-417). It provided generously for weapons programs, soldiers' pay and benefits, and readiness and equipment needs, while leaving major program decisions to the next administration. It provided more than was requested for equipment depleted by the war in Iraq, including new combat vehicles and new battle gear for the Army National Guard and reserve, while appropriating less than Bush sought for missile defense and futuristic programs. *(2009 defense authorization, p. 390)*

The clock had run out for attempts to pass a regular stand-alone defense bill. Appropriations subcommittees in both chambers approved versions of the bill, but the measures went no further. Democratic leaders had put off action on the defense bill and ended up not having the time to finish it before the new fiscal year began Oct. 1. Instead, they attached full-year fiscal 2009 funding for the Pentagon, as well as for the departments of Homeland Security and Veterans Affairs, to a continuing resolution that froze most funding for the rest of the government through March 6, 2009.

Republicans decried their exclusion from the process of drafting the final package, but they said the defense portion was written in a bipartisan manner and did not change much from what the defense appropriations subcommittees had decided. Most of the substantive work on appropriations bills is typically done at the subcommittee level anyway.

HOUSE SUBCOMMITTEE ACTION

The House Defense Appropriations Subcommittee approved a $487.7 billion draft bill in a closed-door session July 30, 2008.

The bill fully funded the president's $6.7 billion request for the Joint Strike Fighter program but shifted $785 million away from production, with $430 million devoted to the continued development of a second engine—which the administration opposed—and $320 million used to allow additional testing. The bill provided funds to procure twenty F-22 fighters and an extra $523 million to buy long-lead items for twenty additional aircraft. Without that money, the F-22A production line was due to close after 2009.

The subcommittee bill also allocated $893 million for the Air Force's troubled aerial refueling tanker program and directed the Pentagon to consider "industrial base concerns" in their evaluation of competitors to build the tanker, a nod to Boeing Co., which argued that its selection would bolster national security by keeping more jobs and production from going overseas. *(Aerial refueling tanker, box p. 392)*

President Bush's $3.6 billion request for the Army's Future Combat Systems was fully funded.

The subcommittee made some significant changes in the administration's shipbuilding budget. The bill included $1.6 billion in unrequested funds for an LPD-17 amphibious transport ship and $398 million in unrequested funds for advance procurement of an additional *Virginia*-class submarine. It provided none of the $2.5 billion requested for a third DDG-1000 destroyer, after the Navy said it wanted to halt production following the completion of two prototype vessels, but it did include $450 million in advance procurement funds. It also included the requested $920 million for the Navy's Littoral Combat Ship program, which had faced overruns and delays.

For military personnel, the subcommittee bill funded a 3.9 percent pay raise—0.5 percent more than requested—and added $600 million for a new initiative that would give a salary bonus to all personnel who had been held involuntarily past the end of their enlistments through the Pentagon's stop-loss program. Each soldier affected since October 2001 would receive an extra $500 per month. The bill also added $1.2 billion to make up for jettisoning the administration's plan to increase fees and copayments for the Tricare health care system.

On the policy side, the bill called for a report from the defense secretary on his plans to close the detention facility at Guantánamo Bay, Cuba, and move those prisoners to U.S. facilities. It also required that war costs be included in the regular fiscal 2010 budget request, a requirement that had become law in the fiscal 2007 defense authorization bill (HR 5122—PL 109-364) but had been met only partially by the Bush administration. *(2007 defense authorization, p. 354)*

Other war policy amendments were expected to be added during full Appropriations Committee consideration but the bill went no further. John P. Murtha, D-Pa., chair of the House Defense Appropriations Subcommittee, said he had been promised a full committee markup and floor time for his bill in early September. But by then it was clear that there would not be enough time to pass the bill in both chambers and reconcile the differences before the month was over.

SENATE SUBCOMMITTEE ACTION

The Senate Defense Appropriations Subcommittee approved its unnumbered $487.7 billion draft bill on Sept. 10.

The bill fully funded the Future Combat Systems and added $750 million to the request for intelligence, surveillance, and reconnaissance capabilities. It funded fourteen of the sixteen F-35 fighters that Bush had requested and added $495 million for a second engine. It provided unrequested funds for advance procurement to keep open productions lines for the F-22A fighter and the DDG-51 destroyer. But, unlike the House appropriators, the Senate panel included full funding for a third DDG-1000 destroyer.

Overall, the bill was said to largely mirror the president's request and the bulk of the debate at the subcommittee markup was over two amendments. Pete V. Domenici, R.N.M., successfully added language to limit the amount of enriched uranium that Russia could export commercially to the United States. Domenici stressed the importance of the United States developing its own uranium resources and not be so dependent on Russia.

An amendment by Byron L. Dorgan, D-N.D., to rescind some funds previously appropriated for Iraqi reconstruction in light of Iraqi oil surpluses lost by one vote.

Senate Majority Leader Harry Reid, D-Nev., said he was looking for ways to get the bill done in September, but he never scheduled floor time.

FINAL ACTION

With the end of the fiscal year approaching, Democratic leaders attached a compromise version of the bill, worked out by House and Senate appropriators, to the continuing resolution.

The House voted 370–58 on Sept. 24 to adopt the entire continuing resolution as an amendment to HR 2638, the Homeland Security funding bill. The Senate cleared the bill 78–12 on Sept. 27.

MAJOR PROVISIONS

As signed into law on Sept. 30, the defense section of HR 2638 appropriated $488 billion for fiscal 2009 defense spending. That total included $487.7 billion in discretionary funds—counting nearly $10.4 billion in permanently appropriated funds for retiree health benefits—and $279 million in mandatory spending for CIA retirement and disability benefits.

HR 2638 also included funding for the Homeland Security and Veterans Affairs departments, military construction, and emergency supplemental disaster assistance, as well as continuing appropriations for the rest of the government through March 6, 2009.

Military Personnel

Appropriated $114.4 billion.

Allowed for a 3.9 percent military pay raise.

Provided $72 million for an initiative to pay $500 for every month service members had their term of service involuntarily extended in 2009.

Appropriated $25.8 billion for the Defense Health Program. The bill allocated $300 million for traumatic brain injury and mental health programs.

Operations and Maintenance

Appropriated $152.9 billion.

Missile Defense

Appropriated $10.6 billion, including $8.9 billion for the Missile Defense Agency. The total included funding for the deployment of a national missile defense system in Alaska and California and a third interceptor site in Eastern Europe.

Ground Forces

Appropriated $3.6 billion for the Future Combat Systems, the Army's next generation of combat vehicles and weapons systems.

Aviation Forces

Appropriated $2.9 billion for twenty F-22A Raptors, the Air Force's next-generation, premier fighter, intended to replace the F-15 and designed to have both air-to-air and air-to-ground fighter capabilities. The bill also provided $523 million for advance components for an additional lot of twenty aircraft in fiscal 2010.

Appropriated $6.7 billion for development and procurement of the F-35 Joint Strike Fighter, which was planned as an affordable, next-generation, multirole fighter based on a common airframe and components to be used by the Air Force, Navy, and Marine Corps. Congress allocated funds to buy fourteen planes and set aside $430 million for a program to develop a second, competing engine for the plane. The program had experienced huge cost overruns.

Appropriated $894 million for a new Air Force refueling tanker to replace the KC-135. Of that total, $23 billion was for development and the rest was put into a tanker replacement fund that could be used once a new manufacturer was chosen.

Naval Forces

Appropriated $3.5 billion for procurement of a *Virginia*-class submarine, which was slated to replace retiring *Los Angeles*-class subs and constitute the bulk of the future attack-submarine force.

Appropriated $1.5 billion of the $2.5 billion requested for fiscal 2009 procurement of a third DDG-1000 destroyer. Congress directed that the other $1 billion be requested in the fiscal 2010 budget. The DDG-1000 had been planned as the Navy's next-generation destroyer, but the Navy indicated in 2008 its preference for resuming the older DDG-51 destroyer program instead. The final bill included $200 million for advance procurement for the DDG-51 program.

Appropriated $3.9 billion for long-lead procurement of the CVN-21, the Navy's next-generation nuclear aircraft carrier that was scheduled to be delivered to the fleet in 2014.

Appropriated $933 million for a tenth LPD-17 *San Antonio*-class amphibious ship.

Appropriated $1 billion for two Littoral Combat Ships, which were small, coastal-combat ships.

National Guard

Appropriated $750 million in unrequested funds for National Guard and reserve equipment.

Other Provisions

Required the defense secretary to report to Congress within 180 days of enactment on plans for a potential closure of the detention facility at Guantánamo Bay, Cuba.

Provided $750 million in unrequested funds for urgent intelligence, surveillance, and reconnaissance needs identified by the defense secretary's intelligence task force.

Appropriated $266 million for a headquarters for a new U.S. Africa Command. A location had not been found at that time.

Renewed provisions in the fiscal 2008 defense appropriations law (HR 3222—PL 110-116) prohibiting torture.

Barred the use of the bill's funds to establish permanent bases in Iraq.

Included provisions limiting the importation of enriched uranium from Russia.

Fiscal 2009 Military Construction Appropriations

Congress in 2008 appropriated $119.6 billion for veterans' programs and military construction accounts as part of a continuing resolution (HR 2638—PL 110-329) that was signed into law just in time for the start of fiscal 2009. The total included $25 billion for the Defense Department accounts.

The military construction-Veterans Affairs (VA) appropriations bill was one of only three fiscal 2009 measures completed before Congress adjourned. The other two—for the departments of Defense and Homeland Security—were enacted in the continuing resolution as well. HR 2638 continued funding for the nine other appropriations bills at fiscal 2008 levels.

The money for veterans—$94.4 billion—was the driving force behind the military construction-VA bill, making it the only fiscal 2009 spending measure passed as a separate bill by either chamber. An increase in the number of veterans wounded in Iraq and Afghanistan continued to put financial strain on veterans' health programs. In addition, medical improvements and innovations enabled seriously wounded veterans to survive in greater numbers than before, further raising the costs of the health care system. *(Veterans' health care, p. 590)*

Members also stressed the importance of the military construction portion of the bill in providing better housing and modern facilities for the troops and their families. The final bill provided $12.1 billion for military construction, $3.2 billion for family housing, and $9.2 billion for ongoing costs of the military Base Realignment and Closure (BRAC) process. *(Military base closings, p. 369)*

President George W. Bush had requested a total of $115.3 billion, including $90.8 billion for veterans' programs and $24.4 billion for the Defense Department accounts.

LEGISLATIVE ACTION

The Senate Appropriations Committee reported its bill (S 3301—S Rept 110-428) on July 22, 2008. S 3301 appropriated a total of $119.7 billion, including $94.8 billion for the VA and $24.7 billion for the Defense Department.

The House Appropriations Committee reported its version (HR 6599—H Rept 110-775) on July 24 and the full House passed it 409–4 on Aug. 1. HR 6599 called for spending totaling $118.7 billion—$93.7 billion for the VA and $24.8 billion for the Defense Department.

The White House had issued a statement July 30 that fell just short of threatening a veto. As it had the previous year, the Office of Management and Budget (OMB) warned that if Congress increased funding in the bill above the president's request, it had to reduce spending on other appropriations bills.

"This bill is laden with costly earmarks and contains overall excessive spending, as well as other objectionable provisions," a statement from OMB said. But an attempt by Jeff Flake, R-Ariz., to delete 103 military construction earmarks totaling $621.8 million was rejected by the House 63–350.

Also rejected during the House floor debate were most Republican attempts to attach oil and gas drilling amendments to the bill.

With the end of the fiscal year approaching, Democratic leaders attached a $119.6 billion version of the military construction-VA measure, along with the Defense and Homeland Security bills, to the continuing resolution. The leaders had assumed all along that final action on domestic spending would be put off until the following year to avoid Bush's promised veto. But they put the security bills on a separate track to avoid election-year charges that they were ignoring national security needs.

The House voted 370–58 on Sept. 24 to adopt the entire continuing resolution as an amendment to HR 2638. The Senate cleared the bill 78–12 on Sept. 27.

MAJOR PROVISIONS

As signed into law on Sept. 30, the military construction-VA section of HR 2638 appropriated $94.4 billion for the VA and $25 billion for the Defense Department.

The main Defense Department accounts in the bill:

Military Construction

Appropriated $12.1 billion for construction and maintenance of military facilities on bases—$755 million more than requested.

Family Housing

Appropriated $3.2 billion for construction and maintenance of military family housing—$46 million less than requested.

Base Closing

Appropriated $9.2 billion for the ongoing costs of Base Realignment and Closure (BRAC), particularly for the 2005 round—$235 million less than requested.

Detainee Policies

Members of the 110th Congress continued to grapple with questions surrounding the detention of suspected terrorists. Even after approving major legislation in the previous Congress on the interrogation and legal rights of detainees, there were still unresolved issues.

A key issue was whether detainees held at Guantánamo Bay, Cuba, had the right to bring *habeas corpus* petitions in federal court to challenge the legality of their imprisonment. Many congressional Democrats argued that they did have the right, while President George W. Bush and most Republicans on Capitol Hill insisted they did not.

The Republican-led Congress thought it had put the issue to rest in 2006 with the passage of the Military Commissions Act (S 3930—PL 109-366), which included a provision denying detainees the right of *habeas corpus*. But, in a major setback for the administration and its congressional allies, the Supreme Court in 2008 ruled the provision unconstitutional, as it had in earlier cases. *(Detainee policies, 109th Congress, pp. 364, 399)*

Other issues surfaced in defense policy debates. Such questions as to whether interrogations should be videotaped, whether contract employees should conduct interrogations, and whether CIA interrogation techniques should be restricted were among them.

Whether the Guantánamo detention center should be closed was another significant question being debated. Guantánamo had become a symbol of the larger issues of rules for interrogation, detention, and trial of suspected terrorists. Both 2008 presidential candidates—Democratic senator Barack Obama of Illinois and Republican senator John McCain of Arizona—had vowed to shutter the controversial facility.

Most detainee policy provisions, however, never made it as far as enactment, and, if they did, it was usually in a watered-down version that would avoid a presidential veto.

A final word from the 110th Congress on the topic of detainees came as lawmakers were wrapping up their work for the year. The Senate Armed Services released a report in December 2008 that blamed President Bush and former defense secretary Donald H. Rumsfeld for the abusive treatment of detainees.

HABEAS CORPUS PETITIONS

The Supreme Court ruled in 2004 that detainees held at Guantánamo Bay had the statutory right to bring *habeas corpus* petitions. When a petition was granted, the detainee had to be brought into federal court to determine whether the individual had been imprisoned legally or should be released. *(Terrorism cases, box, p. 730)*

Congress responded in 2005 with legislation (HR 2863—PL 109-148 and HR 1815—PL 109-163) that eliminated statutory *habeas* jurisdiction for the courts.

The Court ruled in 2006 that it nevertheless had jurisdiction to hear pending *habeas* challenges. In September of that year, Congress cleared the military commissions legislation that included new provisions stripping the courts' right to hear *habeas corpus* petitions.

Champions of *habeas corpus* rights did not give up, despite staunch GOP opposition to their efforts. On June 26, 2007, the Senate Judiciary Committee reported a bill (S 185—S Rept 110-90), sponsored by Arlen Specter, R-Pa., to repeal the relevant *habeas corpus* language in all three laws. Specter then turned his measure into an amendment to the fiscal 2008 defense authorization bill (HR 1585). But an attempt to limit debate on the Specter amendment failed by a **key vote of 56–43 (R 6–42; D 49–0; I 1–1)** on Sept. 19. Sixty votes were required to invoke cloture. Legislation was introduced in the House as well, but none of the bills advanced beyond the subcommittee stage. *(2007 key votes, p. 955)*

The issue returned to the Supreme Court in the case of *Boumediene v. Bush.* Oral arguments were heard in December 2007 and the Court issued its decision the following June. The Court ruled 5–4 on June 12, 2008, that limits posed by Congress in 2005 and 2006 on the ability of detainees held as enemy combatants at Guantánamo to challenge their detentions in federal court were unconstitutional. The majority held that provisions of the 2005 laws providing status review for detainees were "not an adequate and effective substitute for *habeas corpus*" and that the 2006 law "operates as an unconstitutional suspension of the writ."

Senate Judiciary Chair Patrick J. Leahy, D-Vt., called the decision "a stinging rebuke of the Bush administration's flawed detention policies." He said: "Congress made a grave error when, for the first time in its history, it voted to strip *habeas corpus* rights, instead leaving in place hopelessly flawed procedures to determine whether detainees can be held indefinitely with no meaningful court review merely by the executive's decree."

But Sen. Lindsey Graham, R-S.C., a former military prosecutor and judge advocate, called the decision "a tremendously dangerous and irresponsible ruling." Graham had been a key sponsor of the statutory language denying *habeas corpus* rights to detainees.

In writing for the majority, Justice Anthony M. Kennedy seemed to leave the door open a crack to possible legislative changes that might pass constitutional muster. He carefully avoided giving a "comprehensive summary" of what would constitute an adequate substitute for *habeas* proceedings, but he said any process should include the assistance of counsel and that an appellate court should be able to consider new exculpatory evidence, correct any errors in the initial review process, and order the release of a detainee.

In July Attorney General Michael B. Mukasey called on the 110th Congress to pass new legislation to codify the ground rules for *habeas corpus* challenges by detainees. But with only about six weeks left before members would head home to campaign for the November 2008 elections, Democratic leaders dismissed the suggestion. "The Congress must not rush to pass yet another piece of ill-conceived legislation," Leahy said.

OTHER ISSUES

Although Congress had passed legislation in 2005 setting standards for interrogating and treating prisoners, some issues had still not been put to rest.

During consideration of the fiscal 2008 defense authorization (HR 4986—PL 110-181), an amendment to require the videotaping of prisoner interrogations was offered, but the House rejected it 199–229. The Senate-passed version would have required legal representation for detainees and prohibited the use of statements obtained through cruel and inhuman treatment, but the provisions were dropped in conference. The final bill included a House provision that required the defense secretary to report on plans for dealing with each of the detainees being held at Guantánamo. *(2008 defense authorization, p. 373)*

By the time the fiscal 2009 defense authorization (S 3001—PL 110-417) was under consideration, a majority in the House was willing to support an amendment requiring that all intelligence interrogations be videotaped, voting 218–192 to adopt it. The House also agreed 240–168 to bar the use of contractors as interrogators. The private contractor language was in the Senate bill as well. But with the White House threatening a veto because of these provisions and others, the two requirements were replaced with nonbinding sense-of-Congress language. The final bill did require the Pentagon to report to the Armed Services committees on detention operations at international facilities and reintegration centers in Iraq. *(2009 defense authorization, p. 390)*

The fiscal 2009 appropriations bill (HR 2638—PL 110-329) required the defense secretary to report to Congress within 180 days of enactment on plans for a potential closure of the detention facility at Guantánamo Bay. *(2009 defense appropriations, p. 396)*

President Bush vetoed the fiscal 2008 intelligence authorization bill (HR 2082) mainly because of a provision that would have limited all intelligence agencies, including the CIA, to the interrogation techniques allowed by the Army Field Manual on interrogations. The manual prohibited eight harsh methods, such as the simulated drowning technique known as waterboarding. The president said that it was "vitally important" for the CIA to be allowed to have a separate, classified interrogation program and that the attorney general had determined that the CIA program was "lawful under existing domestic and international laws, including Common Article 3 of the Geneva Conventions." He also noted in his March 8, 2008, veto message that his disagreement with the provision was not over any particular technique, such as waterboarding. He went on to say that waterboarding was "not part of the current CIA program." *(2008 intelligence authorization, p. 320; Veto message, p. 1071)*

Interrogation methods had been front-page news, when the *New York Times* on Oct. 4, 2007, reported the existence of a secret 2005 Justice Department memo, later acknowledged by the administration, that provided the legal rationale for the use of various techniques on detainees. The memo reportedly authorized the combined use of harsh interrogation tactics such as waterboarding, head slapping, and frigid temperatures, despite a public statement by the Justice Department in 2004 that torture was "abhorrent." Leaders of the House and Senate Judiciary, Intelligence, and Armed Services committees pressed the Bush administration for the document but were unsuccessful.

SENATE REPORT

The Senate Armed Services Committee on Dec. 11, 2008, released portions of a still-classified report on the use of abusive interrogation techniques. The report, the result of more than eighteen months of investigation, concluded that President Bush's determination that the Geneva Convention did not apply to the detainees and Defense Secretary Rumsfeld's approval of aggressive interrogation techniques for detainees at Guantánamo had led to abuses of detainees not only in Guantánamo but also in Iraq and Afghanistan.

A press release from Armed Services Committee Chair Carl Levin, D-Mich., said the panel had "concluded that the authorization of aggressive interrogation techniques by senior officials was both a direct cause of detainee abuse and conveyed the message that it was okay to mistreat and degrade detainees in U.S. custody."

The report said that the Defense Department had based its interrogation methods on a training program designed to prepare U.S. service members to endure torture. The program, Survival Evasion Resistance and Escape, had grown out of the U.S. military's attempt to understand the techniques used by Chinese interrogators on U.S. prisoners during the Korean War.

The methods at issue—including waterboarding, forced nudity, stress positions, extreme temperatures, sleep deprivation, and the use of dogs—had migrated from Guantánamo Bay to U.S.-run prisons in Afghanistan and Iraq, according to the report.

Ranking committee Republican McCain, who had been imprisoned and tortured by the North Vietnamese during the Vietnam War, said that the report "details the inexcusable link between abusive interrogation techniques used by our enemies who ignored the Geneva Conventions and interrogation policy for detainees in U.S. custody. These policies are wrong and must never be repeated."

CHAPTER 6

Transportation, Commerce, and Communications

Transportation, Commerce, and Communications

Compared to President George W. Bush's first four years in office, Congress produced a substantial amount of legislation on transportation and communication issues during his second term from 2005 to 2009. His first term produced a limited record of action in these areas, partly because of administration focus on other issues—particularly the 2001 terrorist attacks and the war in Iraq launched in 2003—but also because these policy areas presented complicated and contentious issues that directly affected a wide swath of businesses and nearly all American consumers.

The two congresses of Bush's second term, the 109th and 110th, enacted a variety of major legislative bills that dealt with transportation, television, consumer product safety, Internet use and availability, and money to replenish highway building funds. The administration, after frequently complaining about the cost of parts of some bills, often changed tune to accept the work of the legislators—sometimes grudgingly and sometimes with praise.

Transportation issues were an important part of the legislative mix during the period. Highways, which received the lion's share of transportation funding, were a rapidly expanding concern—crises in the opinion of many state and local officials—as existing roads and bridges deteriorated, traffic congestion worsened, and the financing system in effect since the mid-1950s was tottering. Revenue for the Highway Trust Fund, financed in large part by gasoline taxes, was declining as vehicles became more efficient and auto owners drove less as gas prices soared. By the latter years of Bush's presidency the nation was spending about $90 billion annually on transportation, but an extensive study commissioned by Congress said the need was for about $225 billion annually for half a century to create a modern highway and transit system.

Finding that kind of money was a daunting task that Congress was not ready to address by 2009. The basic revenue source was an 18.4 cents per gallon gasoline tax, which had not been increased in fifteen years. The congressional study recommended an increase to 40 cents. Other new ideas were beginning to emerge, including greater use of toll roads, various arrangements between public and private entities to provide new and refurbished roads, and so-called congestion pricing where drivers would pay more during high use times. Another idea that was being debated was charging drivers for the distances they drive, made theoretically possible by advances in global positions systems technology.

One of Congress's first and most noteworthy actions was passage of a $286.5 billion, six-year surface transportation bill that legislators had been wrestling with since the basic transportation authorization, dating from 1998, expired in 2003.

The bill—with the unwieldy name of the Safe, Accountable, Flexible and Efficient Transportation Equity Act: A Legacy for Users, or SAFETEA-LU—was of vital interest to members of Congress who counted on highway and other transportation projects to impress their constituents who, members hoped, would remember them at the next election. To this end, the bill contained more than 5,000 earmarks, designations for spending on specific projects in a state or congressional district.

Transportation also was at the forefront when Congress, for the first time in more than a decade, reauthorized Amtrak, the national rail passenger line, and provided billions in dollars to help it become a vital mode of transit. This action went against the administration's grain. Bush repeatedly proposed that Amtrak receive little funding and

REFERENCES

Discussion of transportation, commerce, and communications policy for the years 1945–1964 may be found in *Congress and the Nation Vol. I,* pp. 517–562, 1159–1185; for the years 1965–1968, *Congress and the Nation Vol. II,* pp. 227–251, 281–305, 779–823; for the years 1969–1972, *Congress and the Nation Vol. III,* pp. 147–187, 659–700; for the years 1973–1976, *Congress and the Nation Vol. IV,* pp. 146–147, 433–451, 505–555; for the years 1977–1980, *Congress and the Nation Vol. V,* pp. 291–362; for the years 1981–1984, *Congress and the Nation Vol. VI,* pp. 261–286, 289–329; for the years 1985–1988, *Congress and the Nation Vol. VII,* pp. 357–413; for the years 1989–1992, *Congress and the Nation Vol. VIII,* pp. 415–464; for the years 1993–1996, *Congress and the Nation Vol. IX,* pp. 327–398; for the years 1997–2000, *Congress and the Nation Vol. X,* pp. 318–338; for the years 2001–2004, *Congress and the Nation Vol. XI,* pp. 371–405.

Outlays for Transportation

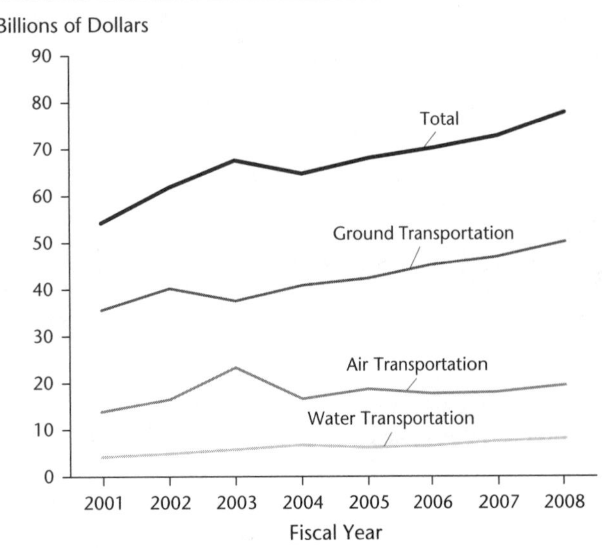

SOURCE: Office of Management and Budget, *Historical Tables, Budget of the United States Government: Fiscal Year 2010* (Washington, D.C: U. S. Government Printing Office, 2009), Table 3.2.

NOTE: Total line includes some expenditures not shown separately.

be sold to private interests. But, like highway spending, members of Congress had always turned a deaf ear to privatization because none wanted to lose a rail line running through their district. The legislation that reauthorized Amtrak also contained provisions intended to improve rail safety, including $1.6 billion in new funding for programs requiring improved train controls systems, limiting rail workers on-duty time, and improving rail grade crossings.

During Bush's second term Congress also passed important telecommunications bills, although a much touted rewrite of the basic law from the 1990s did not pass because of the complicated crosscurrents in the technology business and the vocal complaints of consumer groups.

Congress did finally end analog broadcasting of televisions signals, which had been used since TV first started, and replaced it with digital signals. The end for analog would come during the 111th Congress in June 2009 after repeated delays in the switch to digital. The change was made to free up spectrum that could be sold by the government to raise revenue and to take advantage eventually of the much higher quality pictures from digital broadcasting. However, the switch meant that many viewers who owned older televisions sets would get no signal unless they purchased a converter box that turned digital signals back to analog. This required a mammoth education task and eventually substantial government subsidies to persons who bought the boxes. Even then, many viewers did not take action until their sets went black in 2009.

Congress also significantly expanded penalties on broadcasting of programming considered indecent under federal rules, a goal long pushed by critics of sexual and violent content on television. However the penalties did not extend to broadcasting over cable or from satellites, considered by critics to be prime sources of indecent programs.

In what promised to be one of the more important actions in this area, Congress cleared legislation requiring the federal government to vastly increase information about broadband usage in the nation, and to compare the information with similar data from other nations. A number of studies showed the United States falling significantly behind other nations, particularly in Asia and Scandinavia, in usage and cost of broadband services. Advocates of the legislation said this boded very ill for American competitiveness as use of the Internet continued to expand.

Chronology of Action on Transportation, Commerce, and Communications

2005–2006

The 109th Congress, 2005–2006, the last Congress fully under Republican control, was noteworthy primarily for enacting a huge spending bill on surface transportation that had eluded legislators during President George W. Bush's first term. Even though federal transportation funding is one of the most popular legislative activity for members who want a steady flow of spending into their states and districts. The bill, $286.5 billion for six years, included more than 5,000 earmarks by individual legislators that directed spending on specific projects. The authorization was particularly important because the basic transportation authorization expired in 2003 and was kept alive only by temporary extensions.

Although dwarfed by the transportation bill, other bills cleared Congress during the two years. These included:

- A final deadline to end analog television in order to convert broadcasting to digital format, which occurred in June 2009;
- A substantial increase in fines for broadcasting content on over-the-air television that was deemed indecent under Federal Communication Commission (FCC) standards, although the penalties were not extended to cable and satellite as many advocates urged;
- A ban on Internet gambling.

The most significant issue not resolved was an overhaul of the nation's telecommunications law, which dated from 1996. Both chambers began the Congress with firm commitments to rewrite that and related outdated laws to encourage the expansion of high-speed fiber-optic networks that could deliver voice, video, and broadband Internet services. These efforts, however, ran aground in disputes between the various technology companies, communications businesses, and active consumer groups. Yet the 110th Congress passed an important bill to gather a vast array of data about broadband use in the United States to create a baseline of information to guide future action on telecommunications.

Surface Transportation Authorization

Congress in 2005 passed a $286.5 billion, six-year surface transportation bill that legislators had been trying to get into law since the basic transportation authorization, dating from 1998, had expired in 2003. An array of controversies, many anchored in disputes between states seeking more money from the Highway Trust Fund, had prevented Congress from finishing a bill in the 108th Congress, in 2004. *(Congress and the Nation Vol. XI, p. 387; 1988 law, Congress and the Nation Vol. X, p. 318)*

In 2005 Congress had to pass six stopgap extensions of the 1998 law, on top of the six passed in 2004, to keep programs operating while a conference committee struggled to work out a compromise. That agreement was reached in late July when the bill (HR 3) was cleared for President George W. Bush's approval. He signed it into law (PL 109-59) Aug. 10 in a ceremony held in the district of House Speaker J. Dennis Hastert, R-Ill. "Our economy depends on us having the most efficient, reliable transportation system in the world," Bush said at the signing ceremony. "If we want people working in America, we've got to make sure our highways and roads are modern. We've got to bring up this transportation system into the 21st century." *(Bill highlights, p. 411; Major provisions, p. 413)*

The bill—the Safe, Accountable, Flexible and Efficient Transportation Equity Act: A Legacy for Users, or SAFE-TEA-LU—authorized $244 billion for surface transportation programs in fiscal 2005 through 2009. Funding previously appropriated for fiscal 2004 brought the six-year total to $286.5 billion. The last authorization bill for highway, public transportation, and traffic safety programs—the 1998 Transportation Equity Act for the 21st Century, or TEA-21 (PL 105-178)—expired Sept. 30, 2003.

COMMERCE, TRANSPORTATION, COMMUNICATIONS LEADERSHIP

Norman Y. Mineta, the only Democrat in the first cabinet of President George W. Bush, continued his role for an additional eighteen months of the president's second term. He served from Jan. 25, 2001, until July 7, 2006, the longest term of any secretary in the Transportation Department's history. He earlier served six months as President Bill Clinton's outgoing secretary of commerce. With that service, Mineta held a cabinet position for nearly six continuous years. He joined a public relations firm in Washington, D.C., after leaving government.

Mineta, who had been confirmed by a 100–0 Senate vote in 2001, was a widely respected former House member from 1975 to 1995 where he gained extensive experience with transportation issues. Mineta issued the order to ground all airplanes in U.S. airspace in the immediate aftermath of the terrorist attack on Sept. 11, 2001, in which hijacked airliners were flown into the twin towers of the World Trade Center in New York City, the Pentagon outside Washington, D.C., and an empty field in southwestern Pennsylvania.

Mineta was succeeded by Mary Peters, who served as transportation secretary from Oct. 17, 2006, until the end of Bush's term on Jan. 20, 2008. She had been confirmed by the Senate Sept. 29, 2006, by voice vote. Peters had been director of the Arizona transportation department before serving in the Federal Highway Administration from 2001 to 2005. As secretary, she supported the Bush administration's preference for encouraging selling or leasing roads to private concerns, using tolls to pay for highways, and opposing increases in gasoline taxes. She also backed the administration's opposition to an effort in 2008 in the Democratic-controlled Congress to shore up the Highway Trust Fund, which was running out of money, by transferring about $8 billion to the fund. But in September of that year, she said the fund would be broke in October if action was not taken immediately, and she indicated the administration would accept the transfer, which Congress quickly approved.

Bush also named a new secretary of commerce in his second term. The original secretary, Donald Evans, resigned in late 2004 as part of an overall remaking of the cabinet. In his place Bush named Carlos Gutierrez, who left his position as head of the Kellogg cereal company. Gutierrez was confirmed by a Senate voice vote on Jan. 24, 2005. He remained as secretary through all of Bush's second four years. His appointment was something of a surprise because he had no prior experience in public office. Democrats used his confirmation hearings to criticize Bush administration trade policies, which organized labor in particularly said sent American jobs overseas. The commerce secretary's usual role is to promote U.S. business interests in trade.

Bush's choice to head the Federal Communications Commission (FCC) was Kevin J. Martin. Bush named him as a commissioner in 2001 and promoted him to chairman on March 16, 2005, on the resignation of his predecessor, Michael K. Powell, who was Bush's first FCC chairman. Bush named Martin to a new five-year term on May 25, 2006; Martin was confirmed by the Senate on Nov. 17, 2006. He resigned from the commission on Jan. 20, 2009, as Bush's presidency ended.

Martin came to office and the chairmanship with a public reputation of favoring much stronger controls over programming that critics said carried substantial sexual and violent content. Martin at one point supported tougher penalties and extension of fines to cable and satellite broadcasting as well as traditional television.

Martin's tenure, however, played out in a broader way than many critics expected. Even Larry Cohen, president of the Communications Workers of America, said Martin had been surprisingly open to labor's ideas. The decade in which Martin served saw a growing battle in telecommunications policy that pitted consumer groups, Internet companies, telephone companies, entertainment businesses, and others against one another on some occasions and working together on others.

Near the end of his tenure, Martin pointed to a variety of positions he took on the commission that did not support initial critics of Bush's choice as largely a supporter of business interests. Martin supported, unsuccessfully, consumer complaints against cable companies' pricing structure, arguing that viewers should be able to buy only the channels they wanted to watch. He generally supported efforts to keep Internet pipelines free of control by companies that controlled them and open new radio-wave spectrum to any wireless company whether or not a specific company owned that spectrum. He vocally supported network neutrality when two major carriers, Verizon and Comcast, were caught trying to control the speed and content of some material over their networks.

Martin, however, also developed an unfavorable image as being overly concerned about controlling access to information, both to members of Congress and with other commissioners. His nearly decade on the FCC, however, came during a period in which broadband usage in the United States—as measured by the number of people subscribing to high-speed service—fell dramatically compared to other nations, particularly in Asia and Scandinavia. In 2001, the United States ranked fourth out of thirty leading nations in broadband usage, but the nation had fallen to fifteenth place by 2006. That led Congress in 2008 to require an extensive new examination of broadband use in the United States and other advanced nations.

President Bush and Speaker of the House of Representatives Dennis Hastert, R-Ill., hold the transportation bill Bush signed at the Caterpiller factory in Aurora, Ill., on August 10, 2005. Rep. Jim Oberstar applauds at left with Sen. Barack Obama at right. *Source: AP Photo/J. Scott Applewhite*

The effort to write a new six-year highway bill was caught from the outset between record demands on the nation's transportation grid and White House insistence that the final bill not rely on a tax increase or spending beyond amounts in the Highway Trust Fund, financed mainly through an excise tax on gasoline. In early 2003, Bush set a bottom line of $247 billion over six years; he increased it to $256 billion the following year.

Disagreements over total spending left several influential Republicans in the unaccustomed position of leading the opposition to the administration's position. Republican Don Young of Alaska, chairman of the House Transportation and Infrastructure Committee, introduced an initial proposal in the fall of 2003 that called for $375 billion in transportation spending over six years, funded in part by an increase in the gasoline tax. That plan never saw serious consideration, but the House and Senate passed bills in 2004 that drew veto threats because they still called for significantly more spending than Bush requested. The House bill totaled $283.2 billion; the Senate version reached $318.9 billion.

An even more challenging conflict pitted "donor" states—those that contributed significantly more in excise taxes to the Highway Trust Fund than they got back in highway aid—against "donee" or recipient states, which received more than they collected. House and Senate conferees worked for months in 2004 but could not come up with a plan that could satisfy the donor states—mainly fast-growing states in the South and Southwest—and still win even grudging acceptance from the other states and the White House. Donee states did not oppose a higher guarantee for donors as long as it did not reduce their own highway funds. Under the 1998 law, all states were guaranteed a 90.5 percent rate of return. Donor states aimed to increase that to 95 percent. The final agreement guaranteed that by fiscal 2008 every state would get back at least 92 cents in federal highway funds for each dollar it paid into the Highway Trust Fund, and included members' projects as part of the calculation.

In addition to the rate of return, donor states such as Arizona, California, Florida, North Carolina, and Texas wanted to increase the scope of the guarantee—the range of programs to be included when calculating each state's share. The billions of dollars in projects requested by individual members were part of the calculation under the 1998 law, but the bill passed by the House in 2004 did not include them in the pot of money to be distributed by the formula. They were included, however, in 2005. More than 5,000 of these so-called earmarks for highway and transit projects found their way into the final bill, a far higher number than in previous highway bills. These earmarks accounted for about 8 percent of all funding.

A change in the tax treatment of ethanol fuels enacted in 2004 (PL 108-357) that was estimated to bring $18.9 billion into the Highway Trust Fund paved the way for the Bush administration to increase its bottom line for the bill in early 2005 to $283.9 billion over six years. The House passed a revised surface transportation bill in March that reflected the White House limit, but the Senate bill, passed in May, exceeded it by $11.1 billion. *(PL 108-357, Congress and the Nation XI, p. 432)*

The final bill authorized $2.5 billion more than the administration had said was acceptable, but much less than lawmakers, particularly in the Senate, wanted. In other provisions legislators agreed on changes in environmental reviews and planning procedures that proponents said would lead to faster, and sometimes less costly, completion of highway projects. Environmentalists were angered by these changes, fearing they would push transportation projects rapidly at the expense of environmental concerns.

The final legislation allowed more private-sector involvement in financing, building, and operating portions of the transportation grid, a key administration objective. Many transportation experts said the 2005 law could be the last of its kind. The law contained a mechanism through which Congress would get expert advice on the next authorization effort, which was expected to include recommendations on new ways to fund transportation projects and perhaps a new role for the federal government.

HOUSE COMMITTEE ACTION

The House Transportation and Infrastructure Committee gave voice vote approval March 2, 2005, to a $283.9 billion surface transportation bill (HR 3—H Rept 109-12, Parts 1, 2). With the benefit of nearly a year's worth of negotiations on many of the provisions in 2004, the markup proceeded quickly with only a few amendments offered. Because the committee and the White House had come to terms on the total in advance, the previous year's air of confrontation with the administration was no longer present.

However, Young was still not ready to put forward a formula for distributing highway money among the states. The committee bill retained the 90.5 percent rate of return, but it included a "re-opener" clause from the 2004 House bill that would force Congress to increase the rate in the next few years. The provision proposed to freeze highway funds at fiscal 2005 levels until Aug. 1, 2006, unless a new law was enacted that guaranteed a 92 percent return in fiscal 2006 rising to 95 percent in 2009.

The bill included a consolidated planning process for highways and public transportation projects for metropolitan areas and states, and a new process for environmental impact reviews on proposed transportation projects. The bill also called for making the Transportation Department the lead agency in the review process, with tighter deadlines for public and agency comments, the resolution of disputes among agencies and judicial review.

Young won voice vote approval for a largely technical manager's amendment reflecting bipartisan consultations that added several new programs and inserted more than 3,315 highway and transit projects requested by members.

HOUSE FLOOR ACTION

The House passed the bill by a vote of 417–9 on March 10, 2005. The nine "no" votes were almost all from Republican fiscal conservatives.

Even as the debate began, Young was still trying to find enough support for an agreement to increase the minimum guarantee for each state. The resulting deal, which was added to the bill by voice vote as part of a manager's amendment, increased the amount of highway money to be distributed to states by formula to include about $11 billion in High Priority Projects earmarked by individual lawmakers.

Young left the actual rate of return to the House-Senate conference. Young's amendment also added tax and Highway Trust Fund provisions that the Ways and Means Committee had approved as a separate bill (HR 996—H Rept 109-13) on March 3. The language extended the excise taxes that fed the trust fund through fiscal 2011.

Although the bill's bottom line was the same as the president's request, the White House issued a statement of administration policy March 8 warning that the re-opener clause would trigger a veto.

SENATE COMMITTEE ACTION

The Senate version of the bill was written by four committees in early March, with the Environment and Public Works Committee, chaired by James M. Inhofe, R-Okla., taking the lead. Although Inhofe made it clear that he favored higher spending, his committee complied with a leadership directive to keep the price tag below $283.9 billion. Majority Leader Bill Frist, R-Tenn., said if the bill exceeded that limit, he would not allow it onto the Senate floor. However, the chairmen of the four committees indicated that once the bill reached the floor, all bets would be off.

Highway programs. The Environment and Public Works Committee approved the core highway provisions by a vote of 17–1 on March 16 (S 732—S Rept 109-53). The bill called for $191 billion in contract authority for highway programs in fiscal 2005 through 2009—$227 billion when fiscal 2004 spending was counted. The provisions, with minor exceptions, were similar to those in the Senate's 2004 highway bill. The bill proposed an "equity bonus" program to guarantee each state at least a 92 percent rate of return in fiscal 2005 through 2009 and to ensure that each state received at least 10 percent more funding over the life of the bill than it got under the 1988 law. The bill did not propose changing the scope of the program.

Public transit. The Banking, Housing and Urban Affairs Committee, chaired by Richard C. Shelby, R-Ala., approved $51.6 billion for public transit programs, an 18 percent share of total transportation funding. The provisions were approved by voice vote March 17. Transit advocates had fought for a 20 percent share, up from 18.8 percent in the 1998 law. But lobbyists said Inhofe used his position as de facto lead committee chairman on transportation issues to snare an additional $900 million for highways, leaving less for transit.

Safety. The Commerce, Science and Transportation Committee, which was responsible for safety provisions, approved its piece of the bill by voice vote April 14. The

HIGHLIGHTS OF 2005 SURFACE TRANSPORTATION LAW

Out of the $286.5 billion authorization in the bill, $227.5 billion was allocated to the Federal Highway Administration, $52.6 billion to the Federal Transit Administration, $3.4 billion to the National Highway Traffic Safety Administration (NHTSA), and $2.9 billion to the Federal Motor Carrier Administration.

The following are some of the major components of the new law:

Highway programs. Limited to $189.5 billion obligational, or contract, authority for federal-aid highway programs in fiscal 2005 through 2009, but made available additional funding that was exempt from those obligation limits. Each state was allocated a specific amount of contract authority, which it could use to sign contracts for highway projects. The state would draw the money from the Highway Trust Fund when it was time to actually pay for the work.

Minimum guarantee. Established a new "equity bonus" program to ensure that each state received at least a 92 percent rate of return on its contribution to the trust fund by fiscal 2008, up from 90.5 percent under the 1998 law. All states would get more from the trust fund than they received over the life of the 1998 law. Each state's allocation was calculated based on a formula that took into account population, traffic, and other factors, plus the equity bonus.

Members' projects. Included more than 5,000 earmarks for highway and public transportation projects. Most were in the High Priority Projects program in the highway title and counted as part of the formula allocation for that state.

Projects of regional and national significance. Included $1.8 billion for a new competitive grant program for projects that would have a significant impact on the movement of goods and people beyond an immediate area.

Toll roads. Gave states authority to charge tolls on newly constructed roads and on some existing roads as part of a demonstration project. States could allow reduced tolls or exemptions for vehicles such as gas-electric hybrids.

State project financing. Continued a so-called innovative financing program to help states raise funds, often using unconventional means, for certain highway projects. The law also expanded a State Infrastructure Bank program that made loans for transportation projects, making it easier for states to collaborate with private entities to build and operate highways or public transportation lines.

Safety. Provided $5.6 billion for safety programs, including $3.1 billion for programs operated by the NHTSA and $2.5 billion for programs administered by the Federal Motor Carrier Safety Administration, which focused on large trucks and buses. The law included incentive grants for states to crack down on drivers who were caught not using seat belts and on repeat drunken driving offenders. The NHTSA was given tighter deadlines for issuing rules or reports on several pending safety issues, including vehicle rollover prevention and side-impact protection.

Environment. Created a new, consolidated planning process for highway and public transportation projects in metropolitan areas and states. The law for the first time designated the Transportation Department as the lead agency in conducting environmental impact reviews of transportation projects. It set new procedures aimed at expediting the review process, including a requirement that claims against a permit, license, or approval be filed within 180 days of the issuance.

Public transportation. Provided $45.3 billion over five years to aid mass transit and public transportation programs. The law expanded a program that helped localities build light-rail and subway systems to include bus rapid transit lines. Private transit operators were eligible for grants. Funding for transit in rural areas was expanded, and a "New Freedom Program" targeted funding for elderly and disabled populations.

Revenue. Extended through 2011 the six taxes that funded the Highway Trust Fund. The bill authorized the expenditure of money from the trust fund through fiscal 2009. The main funding source was the 18.4 cent per gallon federal tax on gasoline, of which 18.3 cents went to the trust fund. (The other 0.1 cent went to the Leaking Underground Storage Tank fund.) The other five taxes were excise taxes on diesel fuel and kerosene; an excise tax on special motor fuels; a retail sales tax on heavy highway vehicles; a manufacturers' excise tax on heavy vehicle tires; and an annual use tax on heavy vehicles.

A new provision to combat fuel fraud was projected to increase revenue available in the Highway Trust Fund by almost $2 billion through 2009. It achieved this by taxing aviation-grade kerosene at the higher diesel fuel rate and crediting the initial tax receipts to the Highway Trust Fund, rather than to the Airport and Airway Trust Fund as in prior law.

The bill authorized $15 billion in tax-exempt bonds for highway projects or facilities to transfer freight between trucks and rail. It also included a series of unrelated special interest tax breaks, for groups such as liquor wholesalers and retailers.

provisions included grants for a White House–backed program to reward states for passing "primary" seat belt laws that allowed police to pull drivers over for not wearing their seat belts even if the police observed no other violations. Alternatively, states could get the grants if 90 percent of their drivers buckled up for two straight years.

Revenue. The Finance Committee approved revenue provisions by voice vote April 19 that would pay for a $283.9 billion, six-year surface transportation bill. Chairman Charles E. Grassley, R-Iowa, said he was keeping his commitment to hold to $283.9 billion as the upper limit for the bill, but he told the committee he would seek additional revenue for the Highway Trust Fund once the bill reached the floor. The provisions reauthorized the Highway Trust Fund through fiscal 2009 and extended the taxes that went into it through fiscal 2011.

SENATE FLOOR ACTION

The Senate passed a $295 billion version of the bill by a vote of 89–11 on May 17. The "nay" votes came from a small core of fiscal conservatives and from members who believed their states were being seriously shortchanged.

Inhofe had added $11.1 billion to the authorization as part of a substitute amendment that was adopted by voice vote before the bill was passed. The increase allowed an additional $8.9 billion for highway programs and an extra $2.2 billion for transit. That brought the bill's authorization levels to $199.7 billion for highway programs and $46.5 billion for public transit. The amendment also included new revenue for the Highway Trust Fund that supporters said would make the increased spending "revenue neutral."

The revised bill posed a direct challenge to the White House, which had issued a statement of administration policy April 26 warning that if Congress broke the $283.9 billion mark, Bush's "senior advisers would recommend he veto the bill."

But without the extra funds, Inhofe could not come up with a formula for distributing highway money that could win majority support. The increase enabled him to raise the minimum rate of return for each state to 91 percent in fiscal 2006 and 92 percent by 2009. States that received more than they contributed to the trust fund would be guaranteed a 15 percent increase in funding over what they received under the 1998 law.

The revenue provisions, which were incorporated into the amendment with Inhofe's enthusiastic support, were written by Grassley and Max Baucus of Montana, the ranking Democrat on the Finance Committee. The provisions included a proposed crackdown on fuel tax evasion schemes that would place more tax money in the Highway Trust Fund. Another provision would temporarily put revenue from a "gas guzzler" tax on cars getting less than 22.5 miles per gallon into the highway fund instead of the general treasury.

The largest revenue raiser was a proposal to tighten the tax treatment of financial transactions that were deemed to lack "economic substance"—meaning they were conducted primarily for the purpose of reducing taxes. The House had rejected the provision several times.

During the lengthy debate on the bill, the Senate:

- Adopted by voice vote May 10 an amendment by Kay Bailey Hutchison, R-Texas, to end a pilot program from the 1998 bill that allowed a select group of states to levy tolls on existing interstate highways.
- Rejected an attempt by New Jersey senators Jon Corzine and Frank R. Lautenberg, both Democrats, to add language similar to the House amendment limiting the ability of contractors seeking highway contracts to make campaign contributions to state lawmakers. The amendment was tabled, 57–40, on May 11.

CONFERENCE, FINAL ACTION

A ninety-three-member conference committee held its first and only public meeting June 9, a few days after approving a thirty-day extension of the 1998 surface transportation law. It was not until two and a half months later, with the August recess looming, that the conferees finished.

The House adopted the conference report (H Rept 109-203) by a **key vote of 412–8 (R 217–8; D 194–0; I 1–0)** on July 29. The Senate cleared the bill by a **key vote of 91–4 (R 48–4; D 42–0; I 1–0)**, later the same day. *(2005 key votes, p. 915)*

Two stopgap extensions of the 1988 law expired while conferees worked through June and July to resolve their differences. With the month-long August recess approaching, members and staff held marathon sessions to draft language, but frustrating snags seemed to pop up at every turn. One of the last delays was insistence by House GOP leaders that the conferees not file their report until after the House voted to approve the Central American Free Trade Agreement, feeding speculation that they were using projects in the highway measure to drum up support for the pact. The conference report was filed July 28, about nineteen hours after the House passed the trade bill. *(Trade agreement, p. 202)*

The following are among the hundreds of decisions made by the conferees:

Equity bonus. The bill created a new program, similar to that proposed by the Senate, to ensure that states received at least 92 percent of the money they contributed to the Highway Trust Fund by 2008. The guaranteed rate of return was 91.5 percent in fiscal 2007, and 92 percent in fiscal 2008 and 2009. States would receive an average of 17 percent more in fiscal 2006 than they did under the previous highway bill, rising to 21 percent in 2009. Conferees dropped the House re-opener clause. In a key concession to donor states, funds for members' projects were included in the pot of money that would be distributed by formula.

Members' projects. The agreement authorized a total of $14.8 billion through fiscal 2009 for High Priority Projects, those earmarked by members. The conference agreement listed more than 5,000 individual highway projects and more than 1,000 projects in other categories of transportation funding, a record level of earmarking. Conferees agreed to provide 60 percent of the earmarks to the House and 40 percent to the Senate.

Toll and HOV lanes. The agreement allowed states to establish high-occupancy toll (HOT) lane systems in which otherwise ineligible vehicles could use high-occupancy vehicle (HOV) lanes by paying a toll. States could reduce tolls, including charging no toll at all, for certain low-emission and energy-efficient vehicles, such as hybrid, gas/electric cars. The bill also authorized a pilot program to allow states to charge tolls for the use of interstate highways to manage congestion, reduce emissions in areas with air pollution, or expand the highway to reduce congestion.

Safety. Using elements of both bills, conferees agreed on one-time grants to states that had primary seat belt laws or that could show at least 85 percent seat belt use for two consecutive years. The final bill also included a House provision to authorize penalties and grants to encourage states to enact a 0.08 blood alcohol standard. The National Highway and Traffic Safety Administration (NHTSA) was given deadlines for establishing standards to reduce deaths and injuries associated with vehicle rollovers, side-impact crashes, and vehicles backing up. The bill required safety switches on power windows and required rollover testing for fifteen-passenger vans.

Hours-of-service regulations. The measure exempted certain drivers—including the operators of utility service vehicles, vehicles transmitting agricultural commodities, and vehicles transporting equipment for the motion picture industry—from the maximum hours of service rules. The 2003 rules had been thrown out by a federal court in 2004, but Congress extended them through Sept. 30, 2005, by one of the short-term highway law extensions to allow additional time to develop new rules. Conferees rejected an administration request to incorporate the 2003 rules into the conference agreement.

Tax provisions. In addition to renewing through 2009 the six taxes that supported the Highway Trust Fund, the final bill included a number of the tax provisions added by the Senate. The Joint Committee on Taxation estimated these changes would increase revenue in the Highway Account of the Highway Trust Fund by a total of $1.8 billion in fiscal 2005 through 2009 and reduce revenue to the general treasury by $886 million. The main addition to the trust fund was the change in the taxation of aviation-grade kerosene, which contributed $1.7 billion. The provision was projected to reduce funds in the Airport and Airway Account by $1.8 billion in that period.

Other Provisions

- Conferees dropped the House provision that would have allowed states to enact anticorruption laws curbing the practice of "pay-to-play" contracting without losing their federal-aid highway dollar.
- The bill included an $8.5 billion rescission of prior contract authority that would become available at the end of fiscal 2009, boosting the available contract authority at that point to $295 billion.
- The measure set tougher licensing standards for haulers of hazardous cargo.
- Negotiators stripped from the bill a House provision that would have added a fuel surcharge to the prices charged by motor carriers, brokers, and freight forwarders when the price of fuel rose above a benchmark per gallon price. The surcharge requirement was sought by independent truckers competing against large carriers who could better absorb or avoid spikes in fuel prices.

While some fiscal conservatives and taxpayer watchdog groups denounced the final bill as a political grab-bag, lawmakers supporting it generally made no apology for fighting for their share of the funds.

The loudest protest arose over a pair of costly bridges in Alaska, inserted into the bill by Young, and dubbed "bridges to nowhere" because they connected to small, remote communities. When the appropriations bill that funded transportation projects came to the Senate floor in October, freshman Tom Coburn, R-Okla., a staunch fiscal conservative, proposed taking the $454 million for the bridges and spending it instead to reconstruct a Mississippi River bridge in New Orleans damaged by Hurricane Katrina. "People are fed up," Coburn told his colleagues. "All across the country, Americans are rising up against government overspending." Sen. Ted Stevens, R-Alaska, former chairman of the Senate Appropriations Committee, was incensed at this challenge to the earmark system. "This amendment is an offense to me," Stevens thundered. "It is not only an offense to me, it is a threat to every person in my state.... It is wrong to do this to any state." Most senators agreed, and Coburn's amendment was defeated on a **key vote of 15–82 (R 11–43; D 4–38; I 0–1).** *(2005 key votes, p. 915)*

Conferees on the appropriations bill quietly removed the specific funding for the two bridges, redirecting the money to a general fund that the state of Alaska could spend on transportation projects at its discretion—including on the two bridges, if it chose.

MAJOR PROVISIONS

As signed into law, HR 3 (PL 109-59) included the following major provisions.

Highway Programs

PL 109-59 provided $189.5 billion in guaranteed spending for federal-aid highway programs in fiscal 2005 through 2009. The obligation limits were set at $34.4 billion for

BRIDGES TO NOWHERE

The $286.5 billion surface transportation bill that became law in 2005 was loaded with more than 5,000 projects that were "earmarked" by lawmakers for their districts and states. But no earmark drew as much public attention, and derision, as $454 million for the construction of two "bridges to nowhere" in Alaska that had been championed by the state's key legislators. Widespread news coverage of the earmark became an acute embarrassment to the Senate, and by extension the House, although this unfavorable coverage was not enough to threaten the congressional tradition of members earmarking federal projects and programs for their states.

Rep. Don Young, R-Alaska, included bridge projects at Ketchikan and Anchorage in a highway authorization bill (PL 109-59) moving through Congress in 2005 even though the structures would connect to lightly settled areas. One bridge would connect the town of Ketchikan, with a population of about 8,900, with Gravina Island, which had about fifty residents and Ketchikan's airport; the town and island were currently served by a ferry. A second bridge, known as the Knik Arm bridge, would cross a portion of Cook Inlet, north of Anchorage, to a sparsely populated area. The two soon were known as bridges to nowhere.

In the Senate, Republican Tom Coburn of Oklahoma, a staunch fiscal conservative, decided to take action when the fiscal 2006 Transportation-Treasury-Housing appropriations bill came to the Senate floor. "What I am here to tell you is that the rumble against spending is getting louder. People are fed up," Coburn told his colleagues. "All across the country, Americans are rising up against government overspending." Coburn proposed removing the $454 million for the bridges and spending some of the money instead to reconstruct a Mississippi River bridge in New Orleans damaged in 2005 by Hurricane Katrina.

Alaska Republican Ted Stevens, former chairman of the Senate Appropriations Committee, was incensed at this challenge to the earmark system. "This amendment is an offense to me," Stevens thundered. "It is not only an offense to me, it is a threat to every person in my state.... It is wrong to do this to any state."

If Coburn's amendment were adopted, Stevens said, then Congress might shift earmark money from one state to another at will. "I will put the Senate on notice--and I don't kid people," Stevens said later. "If the Senate decides to discriminate against our state and take money only from our state, I will resign from this body. This is not the Senate I came to. This is not the Senate I devoted thirty-seven years to. If one senator can decide he will take all the money from one state to solve a problem of another, that is not a union. That is not equality and is not treating my state the way I have seen it treated for thirty-seven years."

The Senate agreed. On Oct. 20, 2005, it rejected Coburn's amendment on a **key vote of 15–82 (R 11–43; D 4–38; I 0–1.** *(2005 key votes, p. 915)*

Although the amendment was defeated, it had at least in part the effect Coburn wanted. Media attention to the Alaska bridges increased the pressure on Congress to do something about the earmark. Conferees on the appropriations bill quietly removed the specific funding for the two bridges as part of the final agreement. Instead, the conference report redirected the money to a general fund that the state of Alaska could spend on transportation projects at its discretion, including the bridges. Coburn achieved a public relations coup, while Alaska still got the money that Young and Stevens sought.

The issue arose again during the 2008 presidential context when Sen. John McCain, the prospective Republican presidential nominee who was a long-time opponent of federal pork-barrel spending, chose for a running mate Alaska governor Sarah Palin, who actively had sought congressional earmarks for her state. In addition, Palin in 2006 had campaigned for governor on a platform that included building the Ketchikan airport bridge. When announced as McCain's vice presidential choice in August 2008, Palin ignored her earlier support of the bridge and said that she as governor in 2007 had said no to Congress's bridges to nowhere. But critics pointed out that Congress had scuttled the specific earmark in 2005 before she was governor, and while she directed Alaska's general transportation fund to other projects in 2007, this was partly because there was not enough money left in the fund to build the bridges.

fiscal 2005, $36 billion for fiscal 2006, $38.2 billion for fiscal 2007, $39.6 billion for fiscal 2008, and $41.2 billion for fiscal 2009. The agreement provided certain exemptions from these limits similar to those that were in the 1998 surface transportation law, which it replaced. As a result, the total amount available was expected to exceed $189.5 billion.

Core Highway Programs

Most federal-aid highway funds were for six activities, known as core programs, that were apportioned to the states under specified formulas. The 2005 law authorized:

Interstate maintenance program. $25.2 billion for maintenance of the Interstate Highway System, including $500 million for a maintenance discretionary program.

National highway system. $30.5 billion for the nation's systems of interstate highways, major arterial routes, and routes important to the national defense, plus an increase in the annual amount set aside for the Alaska Highway to $30 million.

Surface transportation program. $32.5 billion to provide states with flexible funding for projects on any federally funded highway. Continued a requirement that states allocate a portion of their funds to urban areas with populations greater than 200,000, and allowed funds for projects on intersections with high accident rates or congestion.

Bridge program. $21.6 billion over five years for the bridge replacement and rehabilitation. Required that $100 million be set aside each year in fiscal 2006 through 2009 for designated projects, including $18.8 million annually for a bridge in Alaska and $12.5 million annually for the Golden Gate Bridge.

Air quality. $8.6 billion for state and local government use on transportation projects that help meet Clean Air Act goals.

Highway safety. Established a new, $5.1 billion program to reduce traffic fatalities and injuries on public roads, replacing an existing requirement that states set aside at least 10 percent of their funding for safety purposes. Set aside annual amounts for installation of protective devices at railway-highway crossings and work on rural roads at high risk.

Other Highway Grant Programs

PL 109-59 authorized amounts for the remaining nonapportioned programs:

Appalachian highways. $2.4 billion for the construction of Appalachian corridor highways in thirteen states to complete the system. Prohibited use of toll revenue to meet matching state and local fund requirements.

Recreational trails. $370 million to provide and maintain recreational trails for motorists, bicyclists, and other users.

Federal lands. $4.5 billion for public roads and transit facilities on federally owned and Indian lands.

National corridor infrastructure. $1.9 billion for highway construction projects in corridors of national significance, such as routes with heavy interstate shipping traffic.

National scenic byways. $175 million for a network of scenic roads, also called All-American Roads or America's Byways.

Ferries. $285 million for construction of ferry boats and facilities.

Puerto Rico highways. $665 million for commonwealth highway programs.

Earmaked projects. $1.8 billion for a new program to finance transportation projects that address critical national economic and transportation needs and cost at least $500 million, or 75 percent of a state's highway apportionment in the fiscal year prior to the state's application. Earmarked twenty-five projects for funding under this program. $14.8 billion for more than 5,100 specific projects designated by members, of which about 3,600 originated in the House and the remainder in the Senate.

School routes. $612 million for a new Safe Routes to School program aimed at making biking and walking to school safer and more appealing.

Maglev trains. $90 million for two magnetic levitation (MAGLEV) transportation projects (fixed guideway systems allowing speeds in excess of 240 miles per hour) with one project located in Las Vegas, the second in an undetermined eastern location.

Equity Bonus: Highway Tax Payments to States

Equity Bonus program. Created an Equity Bonus program, in place of the previous Minimum Guarantee program, to set the rate of return for each state on the money it contributes to the highway account of the Highway Trust Fund through gasoline taxes. Based the calculation on funding for fourteen programs: the six core programs, the High Priority Projects program, the Equity Bonus program, the Appalachian Development Highway System program, the Recreational Trails program, the Safe Routes to School Program, the Metropolitan Planning Program, the Railway-Highway Crossings program, and the Coordinated Border Infrastructure Program. Excluded the Regional and National Significance program.

Minimum rate of return. Increased the minimum rate of return from 90.5 percent in existing law to 91.5 percent in fiscal 2007 and 92 percent in fiscal 2008 and 2009. Set benchmarks for each year to ensure that states get more from the trust fund than they received during the life of the previous reauthorization measure. Specified states were to receive 117 percent in fiscal 2005, 118 percent in 2006, 119 percent in 2007, 120 percent in 2008, and 121 percent in 2009.

Budget and Contract Authority

Budget authority. Extended through fiscal 2009 revenue-aligned budget authority, or RABA, a mechanism under which budget authority available for highway programs is adjusted upward or downward based on revenues in the Highway Trust Fund. Changed the basis for calculating available budget authority to a two-year rather than a one-year period to avoid significant fluctuations in funding levels.

Unobligated balances. Required that $8.5 billion of the unobligated balances that have been apportioned to states for specified highway programs be rescinded Sept. 30, 2009, to ensure that the net total contract authority does not exceed the bill's total funding level of $286.5 billion.

Tolls and Innovative Financing

HOT lanes. Allowed states to establish high-occupancy toll (HOT) lanes to allow otherwise ineligible vehicles to use high-occupancy vehicle (HOV) lanes by paying a toll. Required systems to automatically collect tolls and adjust the toll amount to manage demand and to enforce violations.

HOV restrictions. Permitted states to change HOV lane restrictions for low-emission and energy-efficient vehicles. Specified that vehicles deemed "inherently low-emission" under existing regulations can use the lanes if a state develops procedures for their use. Allowed other low-emission and energy-efficient vehicles, certified under EPA regulations, to use HOV lanes by paying tolls; allowed states to charge lower tolls than those applicable to other vehicles, or to waive tolls entirely.

Tolls for new roads. Established a new pilot program, called EXPRESS Lanes, for fifteen demonstration projects to collect tolls to finance additional interstate highway lanes to manage high levels of congestion to reduce emissions in areas designated as a "nonattainment" or "maintenance" under the Clean Air Act.

TIFIA program. Authorized $610 million for programs under the 1998 Transportation Infrastructure Finance and Innovation Act, which provided federal credit assistance for major investments in transportation. Modified the programs, including extending eligibility for assistance to private rail facilities that serve a public benefit for highway users, and lowered to $50 million, from $100 million, the minimum cost for an eligible project and lowered to $15 million the minimum cost for an eligible intelligent transportation systems (ITS) project.

State infrastructure banks. Codified the existing State Infrastructure Bank program, which allowed the Federal Highway Administration and states to enter into agreements to establish state infrastructure banks that make loans and provide other forms of credit assistance.

Highway Safety Programs

- Provided a total of $3.1 billion through fiscal 2009 from the Highway Trust Fund for highway safety programs operated by the NHTSA.
- Provided $1.1 billion for grants to state and local governments for highway safety programs including efforts to combat aggressive, fatigued, and distracted drivers.
- Provided $502 million for studies on topics such as the causes of traffic accidents, the impact of distracted and inattentive drivers, the effectiveness of various safety initiatives, pedestrian safety, the frequency that intoxication tests were refused, impaired motorcycle driving, and the effectiveness of advanced alcohol-detection technology to reduce alcohol-related crashes and fatalities.
- Provided $120 million in grants to help states enforce use of seat belts and child safety seats, including laws that allow drivers to be stopped and fined for not wearing a seat belt even if no other traffic violation occurred.
- Provided $498 million for grants to states that have either enacted a primary safety belt law since Dec. 31, 2002, or have a seat belt use rate after Dec. 31, 2005, of 85 percent or more for each of the two fiscal years prior to the year of the grant. Allowed the grants to be used for safety purposes or for projects that correct road hazards or highway safety issues.
- Provided $555 million over five years for incentive grants to states that implement programs to deter drunk driving. Directed the Transportation Department, in a separate provision in the federal aid highways title, to withhold a portion of highway funds from states that have not enacted or enforced a 0.08 blood alcohol content law and authorized $110 million in incentive grants in fiscal 2004 and 2005 for states that have enacted such laws.
- Provided $25 million for a motorcycle safety incentive grant program for states that adopt and implement effective programs to reduce the number of crashes involving motorcycles.
- Provided $25 million for a new grant program for states that have enacted a law requiring children in passenger vehicles to be secured in child safety seats or child booster seats that meet certain requirements in existing law.

Public Transportation

- Authorized $45.3 billion through fiscal 2009 for the Federal Transit Administration (FTA) to assist public transportation activities, an amount that represented about 18.6 percent of the total surface transportation funding for fiscal 2005 through 2009—a slightly higher percentage than under existing law. Of this amount, up to $37.2 billion (82 percent) was to be derived from the mass transit account of the Highway Trust Fund; the remaining $8.1 billion was to come from the general fund. The law discarded the phrase "mass transit" in favor of "public transportation" to refer to rural and other nontraditional service areas as well as typical bus and light-rail systems.

Transportation Planning

- Required that FTA grants meet new state and metropolitan planning requirements, and required the FTA to certify that planning organizations are carrying out their duties.
- Required states and metropolitan planning organizations, representing areas of at least 50,000 people, to develop long-range transportation plans and transportation improvement programs for their service areas.
- Required metropolitan planning organizations to consider proposals that meet several transportation

and community objectives, such as improved mobility, promoting economic activity, and increasing safety, over a twenty-year forecast period. Protected the organizations from being sued for the failure to consider a project in light of one or more of those objectives, and specified that decisions made by the Transportation Department regarding the suitability of a transportation plan or an improvement program is not challengeable as a federal action under the National Environmental Policy Act.

Capital Investment Grants

New starts. Authorized $8 billion over five years for major capital investment grants—better known as "new starts" grants—of $75 million or more for new, fixed-guideway transit systems or extensions to existing transit systems. Allowed grants under the new starts program to cover 80 percent of the net cost of the project.

Small starts. Created a new "small starts" program for capital investment grants of under $75 million for projects having a total cost under $250 million. Allowed projects that do not involve fixed guideways, such as bus rapid transit lines, to get funds through the program. Provided $200 million every year from new starts funding in 2007 through 2009 for small starts grants.

Rail modernization. Authorized $7.3 billion over the five-year period for grants to modernize existing fixed guideway systems, such as subways and light-rail systems.

Buses and bus facilities. Authorized $4.3 billion over six years for grants to assist in procuring buses, or constructing or modernizing bus facilities. Earmarked funding from fiscal 2006 through 2009 for 665 specified projects, with sixteen projects funded through the Clean Fuels Grants program.

Other Discretionary Grant Programs

Clean fuels grants. Authorized $238 million over five years for grants to cities of more than 200,000 people, or to the states for smaller areas, that are in "nonattainment" or "maintenance" under the Clean Air Act for purchasing buses that use natural gas, biodiesel, alcohol-based fuels, or fuel cells, or are hybrid gas-electric vehicles, to construct or lease facilities for such buses, or to construct or improve public-transportation facilities to accommodate the buses.

Transportation in national parks. Created a new program, administered by the Transportation Department, for alternative transportation in national parks and on public lands, in consultation with the Interior Department, including clean-fuel buses, rail, "innovative technologies or methods," and facilities for pedestrians, bicycles or nonmotorized watercraft. Provided $97 million over four years for the program, which covered national parks, the National Wildlife Refuge System, recreational areas managed by the Bureau of Land Management, and national forests.

Motor Carrier Safety Programs

Authorized $2.5 billion through fiscal 2009 for safety programs administered by the Federal Motor Carrier Safety Administration with responsibility for large trucks and buses.

Vehicle towing. Allowed states to require tow truck operators to have written authorization from a property owner to tow vehicles from the property, and to require the owner or a designee to be on the property at the time the vehicle is being towed. (The provision was designed to curb "predatory" tow truck operators.)

Motor carrier safety grants. Reauthorized the Motor Carrier Safety Assistance Program and provided $984 million for it through fiscal 2009. Added new requirements to a state's annual safety plan to tighten reporting, enforcement, and oversight responsibilities. Expanded a recipient's ability to use grants to enforce vehicle size and weight limitations other than at fixed weight facilities, to detect unlawful substances in commercial vehicles, or to enforce state traffic laws and regulations related to commercial vehicles.

Maximum hours of service. Exempted from hours-of-service regulations that limit the number of hours that truck drivers and commercial vehicle operators may drive for utility-truck operators, operators transporting agricultural commodities and farm supplies, operators of vehicles transporting groundwater well-drilling rigs, and drivers who operate vehicles for the motion picture industry. Provided exemptions for harvest-time drivers transporting grapes in parts of New York and for drivers responding to propane fuel or pipeline emergencies.

Household Goods Movers

Responded to increased complaints against interstate movers received by the Federal Motor Carrier Safety Administration (FMCSA), including reports from consumers whose goods were held hostage pending payment of unexpected expenses, with the following provisions:

Releasing goods. Codified existing regulations that require movers to relinquish possession of household goods when the shipper pays 100 percent of a binding estimate or 110 percent of a nonbinding estimate.

Brokers. Required a household-goods broker to provide prospective shippers with information about the motor carriers that the broker uses, the broker's Transportation Department identification number and a statement that it is not a motor carrier. Required household-goods carriers to offer shippers arbitration on matters of loss or damage as well as over disputes about charges, with the threshold for binding arbitration raised to $10,000 from $5,000. Required movers to give consumers written estimates as well as educational materials including Department of Transportation information pamphlets.

Federal-state cooperation. Allowed state agencies to enforce consumer protection laws and authorized state attorneys general to file civil suits in behalf of their residents to compel a motor carrier to relinquish possession of a household goods shipment or to pay civil penalties.

Research

- Authorized $2.3 billion over five years for transportation research, education, and technology deployment programs, and set an annual obligation limit of $411 million per year.
- Established three bridge research programs, including a 20-year, long-term bridge performance program and a program to demonstrate and evaluate the use of innovative designs, materials, and construction methods.
- Established several technology deployment initiatives in areas such as new pavement materials, safety-related technology uses, wood composite materials, asphalt reclamation, and the prevention of alkali silica reactivity.

Planning, Environmental Review

- Designated the Transportation Department as the lead agency in the environmental review process for any highway, transit, or multimodal project that required the department's approval, and permitted a state or local government agency sponsoring a project to serve as joint lead agency and share in decision making about the environmental review process.
- Allowed other agencies that have an interest in the project to be invited to serve as "participating agencies."
- Required the project sponsor to submit a notice to the department detailing the scope and location of the project, as well as a statement of the federal approvals that are believed necessary.
- Specified that the lead agency, through consultation with the other participating agencies and the public, was responsible for defining the purpose and goals of the project and developing potential alternatives. (The conference report on the bill specifies that the lead agency's definitions are "not binding on other agencies that have independent [environmental] responsibilities," but it says "other agencies shall show substantial deference to the purpose and need as defined by the lead agency.")
- Required federal agencies to carry out concurrent reviews to the maximum extent practicable.
- Required the lead agency to establish a plan for public and agency participation in the environmental review process.
- Specified that participating agencies and the public have a maximum of sixty days to review a draft environmental-impact statement and thirty days for other documents. Allowed both deadlines to be extended, and made clear the provisions were not meant to reduce the time period provided under existing federal laws for public comments.
- Required lead and participating agencies to work cooperatively to identify and resolve issues that could delay the process or result in a denial of the necessary approvals. Provided that, if no resolution is reached within thirty days, and the lead agency determines that all needed information has been obtained, then the agency will provide notification to all participating parties and to Congress.
- Established a 180-day period for filing any lawsuit challenging a permit, license, or approval issued by a federal agency for a highway or transit project, unless another law allows a shorter period, with the period starting when the lead agency gives public notice that a final decision has been issued.
- Allowed transportation projects to go forward as long as they have minimal impact on protected parks, recreation areas, refuges, and historic sites, and as long as the department has the concurrence of appropriate state or tribal officials.

Hazardous Materials

- Authorized $114 million from fiscal 2005 through 2008 for hazardous materials activities of the Pipeline and Hazardous Materials Safety Administration, and provided for the release of $111 million from the Hazardous Materials Emergency Preparedness Fund.
- Updated terminology used to describe hazardous materials and required the Health and Human Services Department (HHS) to recommend any chemical and biological agents that should be regulated as hazardous materials.
- Permitted the FMCSA to engage in international activities to implement the North American Free Trade Agreement (NAFTA), and it subjected Canadian and Mexican drivers transporting hazardous materials to the same background checks as U.S. drivers.
- Allowed the department to require all persons who design or inspect packaging for the transporting of hazardous materials to register.
- Increased the maximum civil penalty in a hazardous materials accident to $50,000, from $27,500, and allowed the fine to be increased to $100,000 if the incident results in death, serious illness, or severe injury.
- Allowed criminal penalties of up to five years in cases where an individual knowingly, recklessly or willingly violates the law with an increase to ten years if an infraction results in death or bodily injury.

Rail Transportation

- Reauthorized existing law provisions for the acquisition of track, signals, rail rolling stock, and locomotives, and authorized $100 million annually in fiscal

2006 through 2013: $70 million for high-speed rail corridor development and $30 million for technology deployment.

- Authorized $350 million annually from fiscal 2006 through 2009 for a grant program to provide financial assistance for local rail-line relocation and improvement.
- Authorized unspecified amounts for grants to the Alaska Railroad for capital rehabilitation and improvements for its passenger operations.

Highway Trust Fund, Taxes

- Extended the authority to expend funds from the Highway Trust Fund through fiscal 2009 and extended the excise taxes used to finance that fund though fiscal 2011, including motor fuel taxes, such as the 18.3 cents-per-gallon tax on gasoline, the 24.3 cents-per-gallon tax on diesel fuels, and three other excise taxes imposed on heavy highway vehicles or tires. (An additional 0.1 cent tax is also collected on those fuels and placed in the Leaking Underground Storage Tank trust fund.)

(The Joint Committee on Taxation estimated that the tax provisions would reduce revenue to the federal government by $1.3 billion over eleven years, although provisions to reduce fuel fraud would increase the revenue available in the Highway Trust Fund by nearly $2 billion over the same period.)

Transportation Excise Taxes

Limousine tax. Repealed the so-called gas-guzzler tax on limousines that have an unloaded vehicle weight of more than 6,000 pounds. (Revenue loss: $46 million over eleven years.)

Heavy-vehicle highway use tax. Specified that a 12 percent excise tax on the first retail sale of heavy trucks and trailers that are used chiefly for highway transportation in combination with a trailer or semi-trailer will not apply to tractor-trailer trucks sold after Sept. 30, 2005. (Revenue loss: $31 million over eleven years.)

Commercial cargo tax. Repealed a tax on the value of most commercial cargo exported from U.S. ports, which was ruled unconstitutional by the U.S. Supreme Court.

Excise tax on jet fuel. Continued an excise tax of 19.4 cents per gallon on aviation gasoline and a tax of 21.9 cents per gallon on jet fuel, all but 0.1 cent of which is dedicated to the Airport and Airways Trust Fund.

Miscellaneous Provisions

- Required the development of a comprehensive plan by the Transportation and Homeland Security departments for evacuating Gulf coastal areas during catastrophic hurricanes.
- Eliminated so-called vicarious liability under state law for motor vehicle rental and leasing companies, provided there is no negligence or criminal wrongdoing by the company. (Vicarious liability laws impose unlimited liability on car and truck rental and leasing companies for injury and property damage caused by a vehicle solely because the company owns the vehicle, even if it had no involvement in the accident. Under the new law, the rental or leasing company must comply with state financial responsibility and insurance standards for each vehicle in the state law where the vehicle is registered.)

Digital TV Conversion

The 109th Congress set a firm deadline of Feb. 17, 2009, for broadcast television stations to fully convert to digital broadcasts and return their analog frequencies to the federal government. Some of the frequencies made available by the requirement were to be allocated to emergency responders. The rest were to be auctioned off for an estimated $10 billion in government revenue. The law directed $2.6 billion of the proceeds to other uses, leaving $7.4 billion over five years for deficit reduction.

The legislation cleared Feb. 1, 2006, as part of the 2005 budget reconciliation bill. President George W. Bush signed the bill into law Feb. 8, 2006 (S 1932—PL 109-171).

To prepare for a transition from analog to digital television, the Federal Communications Commission (FCC) in 1997 allocated television stations an additional bank of electromagnetic spectrum in which to begin broadcasting a digital signal. Stations were expected to continue analog broadcasts while they made the transition. Congress codified many of the FCC's deadlines for this transition in the 1997 Balanced Budget Act (PL 105-33), including a final requirement that all stations broadcast digital signals by the end of 2006. At that point, broadcasters would be required to discontinue their analog broadcasts and return that spectrum to the FCC for reassignment to other users. *(Congress and the Nation Vol. X, p. 325; earlier action, Congress and the Nation Vol. IX, p. 396)*

The conversion to digital TV broadcasts was repeatedly delayed in the following years, and even the Feb. 17 deadline slipped further when Congress in early 2009 authorized a four-month delay to June 12, when analog broadcasting did finally come to an end.

Enactment of the 2009 deadline marked a rare defeat for the powerful broadcasting lobby, which had fended off similar proposals for nearly a decade, and a victory for the wireless communications industry, which wanted access to the new frequencies for a variety of innovative technologies. The switch to digital was repeatedly delayed under intense pressure from the National Association of Broadcasters. In setting the 2006 deadline Congress included a crucial caveat: stations were allowed to keep their analog frequencies until 85 percent of their market had equipment capable of viewing digital programming—a threshold that essentially allowed broadcasters to hang on to their old frequencies indefinitely.

By 2005 pressure to free up the TV spectrum for new uses was enough to overpower the broadcasters' protests. The communications industry was a leading voice for action because it wanted access to the frequencies to allow new wireless services. Signals on those frequencies, which were in the 700 MHz band, can pass through walls easily and travel long distances, making the spectrum perfect for a variety of wireless broadband services.

Congress, meanwhile, looked to the billions of dollars the federal government might reap by auctioning off the returned spectrum to help trim the budget deficit. In 2005, Hurricane Katrina, which left the Gulf Coast devastated in late August, highlighted weaknesses in emergency communications systems that prevented first-responders from being able to talk with one another, a problem that also had hampered life-saving efforts after the Sept. 11, 2001, terrorist attacks.

Lawmakers were sensitive to warnings, mainly from the broadcast industry, that setting a hard deadline for conversion to digital signals could leave millions of Americans without access to television. The Government Accountability Office (GAO) said about 21 million Americans, many in low-income households, relied on over-the-air analog programming. Congress's answer was to use part of the proceeds from auctioning the analog spectrum to subsidize set-top boxes that would convert digital signals to analog to keep old television sets working.

PROVISIONS

In the section on digital TV conversion, the budget reconciliation bill (S 1932—PL 109-171) addressed the following areas:

Reclaiming spectrum. Set Feb. 17, 2009, as the deadline for full-power television stations to return to the FCC the frequencies used for analog broadcasts.

Spectrum auctions. Required the FCC to begin auctioning off the reclaimed spectrum to wireless carriers and others by Jan. 28, 2008. The auction proceeds were to be deposited in a newly created fund, the Digital Television Transition and Public Safety Fund. Specified that on Sept. 30, 2009, $7.4 billion from the proceeds would be transferred to the Treasury and treated as offsetting receipts.

Converter box subsidies. Set aside up to $1.5 billion of the proceeds to subsidize digital-to-analog converter boxes for those who still relied on over-the-air television broadcasts who would otherwise not receive a useable television signal after the transition.

Public safety systems. Set aside up to $1 billion to help public safety agencies purchase and deploy interoperable communications systems. Allocated up to $156 million to build a unified national emergency alert and tsunami warning system and $44 million to upgrade 911 emergency phone systems.

Other uses of proceeds. Allocated up to $65 million to help eligible low-power television stations purchase equipment to upgrade from analog to digital operations, $44 million to upgrade 911 emergency phone systems, and $10 million to help eligible low-power television stations purchase digital-to-analog conversion devices to convert incoming digital signals to analog format.

Other. Allocated $30 million in fiscal 2007 and 2008 for a temporary digital television broadcast system to serve New York City until a permanent facility could be built atop the planned Freedom Tower. Provided an additional $30 million for the Essential Air Service Program, which subsidized commercial airline service in remote places, if funds appropriated to operate the program equaled or exceeded $110 million for that fiscal year.

SENATE COMMITTEE ACTION

The fiscal 2006 budget resolution (H Con Res 95) instructed specific authorizing committees in the House and Senate to prepare legislation that would contribute to an overall goal of reducing mandatory spending by $34.7 billion over five years. To reach their targets, the Senate Commerce, Science and Transportation Committee and the House Energy and Commerce Committee proposed requiring broadcasters to return analog spectrum, which the government would auction for an estimated $10 billion. Both committees proposed that part of the proceeds go to other uses.

The Senate Commerce, Science and Transportation Committee approved its spectrum provisions, 19–3, on Oct. 20. The committee proposed to:

- Set an April 7, 2009, deadline for TV broadcasters to relinquish analog spectrum.
- Set aside $3 billion of the proceeds for converter boxes, though the committee did not spell out how that money would be distributed other than to say it would be managed by the Commerce Department.
- Dedicate at least $5 billion from the spectrum auction to deficit reduction.
- Direct the FCC to collect $10 million in fees for licenses in 2006 to be used as offsetting receipts.
- Dedicate $1 billion to interoperable first-responder communications. An additional $250 million would be used to implement a national alert system, including a tsunami warning program.
- Allocate funds for other purposes, including $200 million to convert low-power television stations from analog to digital, $250 million for a program to upgrade emergency 911 phone systems, and $250 million for hurricane relief. The bill listed a number of other uses for any funds that were left over.

The committee rejected, 5–17, an attempt by John McCain, R-Ariz., to advance the transition by two years to April 7, 2007, with the auction of recovered analog spectrum to begin Jan. 28, 2006, two years earlier than proposed in the bill. Senators worried that the earlier deadline might prevent millions of television viewers from watching the New Year's bowl games and holiday festivities, creating a political embarrassment.

The Senate Budget Committee packaged the spectrum provisions with those of seven other committees and approved the resulting budget reconciliation bill (S 1932), 12–10, on Oct. 26.

HOUSE COMMITTEE ACTION

The House Energy and Commerce Committee approved its spectrum proposal, 33–17, on Oct. 26. The provisions would:

- Set a Dec. 31, 2008, deadline for broadcasters to relinquish the spectrum.
- Devote $990 million to subsidize converter boxes. The committee proposed providing up to two coupons worth $40 each to households that requested them.
- Provide $500 million for first-responder communication efforts.
- Provide $30 million for New York transition and $3 million to aid low-power stations in converting digital to analog signals.
- Deposit the remainder of the proceeds from the spectrum auctions in the treasury.
- Allow cable and satellite operators to convert digital broadcasts into an analog-viewable format to avoid disrupting service.
- Require TV manufacturers to label analog sets with warnings that the equipment would not work after the digital switch.

The committee rejected, 21–28, an amendment by John D. Dingell, D-Mich., that would have delayed the hard deadline for digital conversion to April 7, 2009, and spent as much of the money from the spectrum sale as needed on consumer subsidies. Democrats estimated it would cost between $3.5 billion and $4 billion to ensure that no televisions went dark. The amendment would have dedicated $5.8 billion to increase interoperability among emergency responders.

The House Budget Committee combined the provisions with those of six other committees and approved its reconciliation bill (HR 4241—H Rept 109-276), 21–17, on Nov. 3.

HOUSE AND SENATE FLOOR ACTION

The Senate passed its budget reconciliation bill, 52–47, on Nov. 3. During the floor debate, senators rejected, 30–69, an attempt by McCain to accelerate digital TV conversion by another year to April 7, 2008, to speed the availability of the spectrum for public safety radios.

The House passed its version of the bill, 217–215, on Nov. 18, 2005.

CONFERENCE AND FINAL ACTION

The House adopted the conference report on the reconciliation bill (H Rept 109-362), by a **key vote of 212–206 (R 212–9; D 0–196; I 0–1)** on Dec. 19, 2005. The Senate approved an amended version of S 1932 on a **key vote of 51–50 (50–5; D 0–44; I 0–1)** on Dec. 21—with Vice President Dick Cheney casting a "yea" tie-breaking vote—but refused to approve the conference report, sending it back to the House. The House cleared the bill by voice vote Feb. 1, 2006. *(2005 key votes, p. 915)*

The conference report set the deadline for returning analog spectrum in February 2009, about halfway between the House and Senate proposals. Conferees agreed on a $1.5 billion subsidy for converter boxes, $500 million more than the House wanted but $1.5 billion less than the Senate proposed. They adopted the $40 coupon proposal passed by the House. The $1 billion for first-responder interoperable emergency communications systems came after the Senate plan and was $500 million above the House figure.

To avoid running afoul of Senate rules barring items in reconciliation bills that do not affect government revenue, the conferees dropped several provisions from the House version, among them was language sought by the cable television industry to let cable providers convert high-definition digital signals to other formats. Also dropped were provisions aimed at preparing consumers for the digital transition, including the requirement that analog TV sets bear a notice that they would no longer work after the transition. Conferees provided $5 million for consumer education, but did not say how the money should be spent.

Broadcasting Indecency Penalties

Congress in 2006 increased fines tenfold for television broadcasters that aired lewd, violent, or other objectionable programming. The key provision increased the maximum fine to $325,000, from $32,500, for each violation. The legislation had been simmering in Congress for a number of years as television programming—especially from cable and satellite outlets—increasingly presented shows with substantial violent and sexual content.

However, the legislators did not act on related proposals to extend broadcast-decency rules to cable and satellite operators or to require such companies to sell programming on a per-channel—or "a la carte"—basis. The per-channel issue was not directly tied to controversy over show content but had become a rising issue as an increasing number of watchers complained they were paying ever higher fees for cable and satellite channels they did not want and never watched.

President George W. Bush signed the legislation (S 193—PL 109-235) into law on June 15, 2006. The bill was sponsored by Sen. Sam Brownback, R-Kan. The legislation that became law focused only on financial penalties. But other, more expansive, bills were introduced in both chambers.

Ted Stevens, R-Alaska, who chaired the Senate Commerce, Science and Transportation Committee, favored the creation of a "family friendly" tier of programming on cable, as did several other senators. Sen. Ron Wyden, D-Ore., in 2005 introduced a bill to that effect, but Stevens said he would prefer that the industry police itself. Others wanted to mandate "a la carte" programming, which would allow consumers to pick and pay for only the channels they wanted, and still others favored applying FCC regulations to cable and satellite operators.

Hoping to avoid mandatory regulation, the National Cable and Telecommunications Association in April 2005 announced a $250 million campaign to educate consumers about the channel-blocking tools built into many cable set-top boxes. In late November, the Senate Commerce Committee held a widely publicized forum on indecency at which FCC chairman Kevin J. Martin announced his support for a la carte programming and family tiers, reversing his agency's previous position.

With pressure from regulators and lawmakers growing, several major cable companies, including Comcast Corp. and Time Warner Inc., announced plans to offer family tiers. That was enough to keep the Senate from acting on indecency legislation before the end of 2005.

BACKGROUND

The broadcast-decency controversy became headline news after entertainer Janet Jackson's breast was briefly exposed during the 2004 Super Bowl halftime show in what Justin Timberlake, with whom she had shared the stage, called a "wardrobe malfunction." Jackson and Timberlake issued apologies in the weeks that followed, as did CBS that broadcast the event. Many networks began using time delays for live programming to catch and remove potentially offensive content. *(Congress and the Nation Vol. XI, p. 394)*

But Congress was under increasing pressure to crack down on programming that many watchers considered indecent, particularly by self-proclaimed "family values" groups, an important Republican constituency. The Jackson episode and the ensuing uproar also led the Federal Communications Commission (FCC) to crack down on objectionable programming, which spurred legal battles as broadcasters went to court to challenge indecency fines levied by the agency.

In 2004, the House overwhelmingly passed a standalone measure that would have raised the maximum fine for indecent broadcasting to $500,000, but it also contained a contentious provision that would have allowed the FCC to fine individual artists who acted in an indecent manner during broadcast programs.

That same year, the Senate voted to add language to its version of a defense authorization bill (PL 108-375) that would have raised the cap to $275,000. The bill also included a controversial provision to block an FCC proposal to ease media ownership restrictions. Many lawmakers blamed increasing media consolidation for a proliferation of indecent broadcasts. But during the conference on the defense measure, the decency language was dropped because the White House and House GOP leadership supported the FCC's proposed ownership rules.

HOUSE ACTION

The House in 2005 passed a much broader bill than became law one year later. But the Senate was unable to act on that bill and turned instead to a narrower proposal that simply increased penalties. In February 2005, the House overwhelmingly passed a bill (HR 310) introduced by Fred Upton, R-Mich., that would have increased the top penalty to $500,000 and made performers liable for their actions. It also would have required the FCC to consider revoking the license of a broadcaster with three or more violations.

The House Energy and Commerce Committee Feb. 9, 2005, approved HR 310 (H Rept 109-5) by a vote of 46–2. "For those broadcasters who continue to act irresponsibly, the FCC needs adequate authority to enforce the law, and this bill would deliver that," Upton said.

The bill, which mirrored the measure the House passed in 2004, included provisions to:

- Increase to $500,000 the ceiling on FCC fines for broadcasting indecent, obscene, or profane material on radio or television programs, with no limit for repeat violations.
- Apply the same penalties to individuals who uttered obscene, indecent, or profane material during a radio or television broadcast. Under existing law, artists could be fined only $11,000 under a process that had yet to be used.
- Require the FCC to consider whether the objectionable material was part of a live or recorded program and was scripted or unscripted; whether the broadcaster used a time delay to block objectionable material; whether there was reasonable opportunity to review the program or to believe that it might contain objectionable material; the size of the viewing audience; and whether the programming was part of a children's television program. Network affiliates would not be liable for objectionable material in a network broadcast if they did not have the opportunity to review its content or did not have a reasonable basis to believe that the program would contain objectionable material.
- Require the FCC to consider revoking a station's broadcast license after three violations, known as the three-strikes provision.
- Instruct the FCC to consider violations and fines assessed against a broadcaster during license-renewal proceedings.

The House Feb. 16 passed the bill, 389–38. The White House issued a statement the day of the vote expressing strong support for the measure. The House gave voice vote approval to a manager's amendment by Upton to clarify that the FCC could punish performers only if they intentionally violated indecency standards and knew the material would be broadcast. It also required the FCC to consider whether an individual was able to pay the fine.

SENATE ACTION

In 2006, Senate Majority Leader Bill Frist, R-Tenn., decided to bring decency legislation directly to the floor in May. Frist first tried to call up Upton's bill, but several unidentified senators had placed holds on it. He then turned to Brownback's proposal and worked behind the scenes to secure passage. The Senate passed Brownback's bill (S 193) by voice vote May 18, and the House cleared it 379–35 on June 7.

MAJOR PROVISIONS

As enacted, S 193 (PL 109-235) contained the following major provisions.

- Increased to $325,000, from $32,500, the maximum fine the FCC could assess for each violation, or for each day of a continuing violation, for the broadcasting of indecent, obscene, or profane language.
- Set a maximum penalty of $3 million for continuing violations.
- Specified that the penalties applied to radio or television operators with a broadcast license or permit, as well as to applicants seeking a license, permit, or other FCC authorization. The penalties did not apply to cable or satellite operators.

Internet Gambling

After years of trying, opponents of Internet gambling in 2006 won enactment of legislation to curb wagering on the Internet, which had grown to an estimated $12 billion-per-year industry spread across about 2,500 Web sites. Conservatives said Internet gambling created a host of social ills, from addictive behavior to criminal activity, including money laundering, and that minors could too easily gain access to gambling Web sites. The effort had the support of Christian groups and sports leagues, including the National Football League and Major League Baseball, who wanted to stop the betting on games.

The legislation was finally slipped through a maze of controversies by attaching the provisions to the conference report on a port security bill. The measure was signed into law by President George W. Bush on Oct. 13, 2006 (HR 4954—PL 109-347). *(Port security, p. 237)*

The legislation met with substantial opposition from gaming companies that wanted to set up shop online. Banking companies—especially smaller banks—argued that compliance would be almost impossible because of the detailed monitoring required. Many financial institutions also disliked the idea of policing how their customers spent their money.

In 2006, proponents offered their legislation as an antidote to the scandals related to former lobbyist Jack Abramoff, who had helped sink the 2000 Internet gambling bill on behalf of a client. Abramoff was sentenced to five years and ten months in prison, after pleading guilty Jan. 4 to conspiracy and fraud stemming from the 2000 purchase of a gambling-boat fleet. He also was under investigation for alleged improper lobbying methods for eLottery, the Connecticut-based gambling company that wanted the 2000 bill stopped. *(Abramoff, p. 809)*

BACKGROUND

Gambling opponents had tried for years to curtail the growing online versions, arguing that unregulated, offshore, and sometimes fraudulent Internet casinos hurt American consumers. Some critics also linked online casinos to money laundering and said they were a potential source of cash for terrorists.

Internet gambling was considered illegal under the 1961 Interstate Wire Act (PL 87-216), which barred gambling businesses from using a "wire communication facility" to transmit "bets or wagers on any sporting event or contest" over state or international lines, which at the time meant telephone lines. Although the Justice Department said the law made Internet gambling illegal in the United States, doubt remained if that assertion was enforceable since many consumers never used the telephone to access the Internet.

Actually restricting the industry was difficult because almost all online casinos were outside the United States and beyond the reach of U.S. law, often in the Caribbean and Europe. As a result, lawmakers sought to strangle the industry financially by blocking Internet wagers, thereby cutting off the sources of money. While many major credit card companies prohibited customers from using credit cards for online wagering, electronic transfers from bank accounts remained largely unfettered.

The Senate had passed a bill in the 106th Congress to make Internet gambling illegal, but a companion House Judiciary Committee measure was rejected in the House in 2000 when it failed to obtain the necessary two-thirds vote for passage under suspension of the rules. An earlier effort died in 1998 when conferees on a bill could not reach agreement. *(Congress and the Nation Vol. X, pp. 328, 337)*

In the 107th Congress, the House passed a bill by voice vote that was intended to make it harder for illegal offshore Internet casinos to operate by prohibiting U.S. banks and credit card companies from processing payments for those businesses. The Senate did not act on that measure. *(Congress and the Nation Vol. XI, p. 391)*

HOUSE ACTION

The House in July 2006 passed a bill sponsored by Rep. Jim Leach, R-Iowa, after incorporating provisions from a second measure sponsored by Robert W. Goodlatte, R-Va. House GOP leaders tried to catch a ride for the measure on the must-pass fiscal 2007 defense authorization bill (HR 5122), but negotiators on that measure insisted on keeping it free of unrelated provisions.

"Congress is in certain disrepute," said Rep. Jim Leach, R-Iowa, who described his online gambling bill as "part and parcel of what I consider to be necessary to clean up the Congress."

The House Financial Services Committee and Judiciary Committee both marked up legislation to limit online gambling. The Financial Services Committee approved a bill by voice vote March 15 to prohibit banks and credit card companies from processing payments for online gambling bets. The measure (HR 4411—H Rept 109-412, Part 1), sponsored by Leach, would have required the Treasury Department and the Federal Reserve to establish policies and procedures to enable payment processors to identify and prevent online gaming transactions.

The Judiciary Committee approved Goodlatte's bill by a vote of 25–11 on May 25. The measure (HR 4777—H Rept 109-552) focused on modifying the 1961 Wire Act to clarify that its prohibitions applied to all forms of gambling, including Internet gambling—not just sports bets placed over telephone wires. The bill also sought to prohibit gambling businesses from accepting certain forms of noncash payment, including credit cards and electronic transfers, to transmit such bets and wagers.

The Judiciary Committee approved the bill after giving voice vote approval to a Goodlatte amendment that included language stating that the bill would not prohibit activities allowed under the 1978 Interstate Horseracing Act (PL 95-515), which allowed off-track betting facilities to accept interstate horse bets. The panel also approved Leach's bill by voice vote with only technical changes (H Rept 109-412, Part 2).

The House passed a version of HR 4411 on July 11 that also incorporated the major provisions from Goodlatte's bill. The vote was 317–93.

As passed, the bill included the provisions to bar banks and credit card companies from processing payments for online bets. It also modified the 1961 Wire Act to clarify that its prohibitions applied to all gambling by any technological means of communication. The bill retained the committee provision that stated explicitly the prohibitions did not apply to interstate online wagering on horse races, and it contained an exemption for certain online state lotteries and for fantasy sports leagues that offered cash prizes.

Much of the criticism focused on the provision excluding wagering on horses. The horse-racing industry and the Justice Department were locked in a battle over whether the 1978 law allowed online interstate horse betting. Goodlatte bristled at suggestions that the bill contained "carve-outs" for the horse-racing industry, arguing that it took no position in the fight over interpretation of the 1978 law. But some critics said that by remaining silent on the debate, the bill would have the effect of creating an exemption.

FINAL ACTION

Passage of the proposal, however, appeared unlikely in the Senate as that chamber was immersed in a range of more controversial issues as the session neared an end. Finally, Senate Majority Leader Bill Frist, R-Tenn., turned to the conference report on the port security bill to carry the provisions. Frist agreed to insert some of the Internet gambling language into the conference report on the port security bill (HR 4954—H Rept 109-711). The House adopted the conference report, 409–2, on Sept. 30, and the Senate cleared the bill by voice vote later the same day.

The gambling provisions were virtually the only add-on that Senate Republicans were willing to accept from House Speaker J. Dennis Hastert, R-Ill., who pushed to attach a number of House-passed bills to the must-pass ports legislation. The provisions were taken from Leach's bill and did not include Goodlatte's language on updating the Wire Act.

The final bill barred online gambling businesses from accepting credit cards or electronic transfers for the purpose of betting, except for wagers made on horse races. It also directed the Treasury Department and the Federal Reserve to issue procedures that financial institutions could use to identify and stop gambling-related transactions. Once the rules were promulgated, financial institutions would be required to use those procedures to block transactions intended for illegal online wagering.

Spyware Controls

Congress in 2005 again wrestled with and again did not complete action on legislation to control spyware computer programs. These were software programs that surreptitiously access hard drives to collect personal data, track an individual's behavior on the Web, gather sensitive personal information, and damage users' computers.

As in 2004 disagreements over balancing industry and consumer interests stalled the legislation. The House passed a pair of antispyware bills. In the Senate, a separate measure won committee approval but did not reach the floor. *(Congress and the Nation Vol. XI, p. 402)*

The House passed the two bills by lopsided votes in May after efforts to merge the proposals—one preventive, the other punitive—failed. The first bill (HR 29), sponsored by Rep. Mary Bono, R-Calif., required software companies to obtain the computer user's permission before installing programs that could collect personal information. Some technology companies opposed Bono's approach, saying it could restrict legitimate interactive software and result in consumers being deluged with consent notices.

The second bill (HR 744), sponsored by Robert W. Goodlatte, R-Va., was preferred by the software industry because it did not dictate specific technological requirements. Instead, it called for fines and prison sentences for individuals convicted of tapping into personal computers with the intent of committing fraud or damaging a machine.

A similar debate occurred in the Senate Commerce, Science and Transportation Committee. In November, the panel approved legislation (S 687) sponsored by Conrad Burns, R-Mont., that was similar to Bono's approach of asking consumer's permission before installing programs. A rival bill (S 1004) sponsored by George Allen, R-Va., followed Goodlatte's approach of stiffer punishment.

HOUSE ACTION

The House Energy and Commerce Committee approved Bono's bill 43–0 on March 9 (HR 29—H Rept 109-32). The panel's Subcommittee on Commerce, Trade, and Consumer Protection had approved it Feb. 16. The measure, which closely resembled Bono's 2004 bill, had bipartisan support and the backing of companies such as Microsoft Corp., Yahoo! Inc., and eBay Inc.

The bill included provisions to bar anyone from installing an information-collection program on a computer without the user's consent. It outlawed a list of specific practices, including keystroke logging, computer hijacking, and online advertisements that could not be closed. The Federal Trade Commission (FTC) was empowered to seek civil penalties of up to $3 million for violations. Subcommittee chairman Cliff Stearns, R-Fla., added language to the 2005 bill to increase enforcement against "phishing"—the use of fake or "evil-twin" Web sites that resembled a legitimate site but collect personal information fraudulently.

The subcommittee adopted an amendment by Stearns aimed at alleviating industry concerns that the bill was too broad. Among other things, the amendment clarified that the provisions would not apply to Internet "cookies," the strings of text saved in a browser when a computer user visited a Web site. Cookies were commonly used to store personal data, allowing companies to customize their Web sites for individual users. The amendment also stated that the bill was not meant to police computer users who voluntarily transmitted personal information to another party online.

But even with those changes, the measure ran into resistance from the Information Technology Association of America (ITAA). The trade group said the bill would impose excessive technical requirements on software developers, restrict interactive software programs, and constrain legitimate businesses that relied on "adware" programs to deliver targeted online advertising.

Committee chairman Joe L. Barton, R-Texas, said he would "put considerable pressure on the Senate to act this year." The House Judiciary Committee gave voice vote approval May 18 to Goodlatte's bill (HR 744—H Rept 109-33), which was backed by the ITAA.

Like the 2004 version, the bill sought to impose criminal penalties for accessing a computer to steal information or damage hardware. Goodlatte said he wanted to punish "bad actors" without stifling the growth of legitimate online businesses and new technologies.

The bill made it a crime to use spyware to break the law, commit fraud, or breach computer security. It called for fines or prison sentences of up to two years for intentionally gaining access to a computer without authorization and installing software to steal personal information with the intent to defraud, damage hardware, or impair a security program. Using spyware as part of another criminal offense would bring fines or sentences of up to five years. States would be preempted from creating civil remedies based on violations of the bill.

Lawmakers gave up trying to meld the bills into a single measure that would protect consumers and still satisfy technology companies wary of government regulation. Instead, the House passed both bills May 23. Members voted 395–1 in favor of Goodlatte's bill, then passed the Bono bill 393–4.

SENATE ACTION

The Commerce, Science and Transportation Committee approved Burns's bill (S 687) 14–8 on Nov. 17. Like the House Energy and Commerce measure, it sought to prohibit installation of software programs that automatically collected and transmitted personal information from computers without telling users.

The bill also would ban the installation of software that delivered online ads without identifying their source and would prohibit software that a user could not uninstall. Other provisions would outlaw "modem hijacking," which could leave victims saddled with unauthorized charges, and "denial of service" attacks, which could cripple Web sites by overloading them with traffic.

The committee rejected 9–13 an amendment by Allen, who tried to substitute language from his own bill (S 1004) aimed at increasing civil and criminal penalties for using spyware to commit fraud or other crimes. Allen's amendment also would have given the FTC more resources to enforce the law.

Committee chairman Ted Stevens, R-Alaska, said he was hopeful a compromise would be reached before a floor vote, but he set no specific timetable and the legislation never did go to the floor.

Dallas Airport Agreement

Congress in 2006 cleared a bill to resolve a decades-old local conflict over statutory restrictions imposed on Southwest Airlines' flights out of its Dallas Love Field headquarters. The measure, which President George W. Bush signed into law Oct. 13 (S 3661—PL 109-352), codified an agreement reached by local parties to lift most of the restrictions in eight years.

Southwest had been limited to short-haul flights to neighboring states out of Love Field since the Wright amendment—named for former House Speaker Jim Wright, D-Texas (1955–1989)—was enacted in 1980. The bill repealed the Wright amendment in eight years, allowing Southwest to fly national—but not international—routes to and from Love Field.

The Wright amendment was intended to allow Love Field to remain open, while limiting operations to ensure growth at the new Dallas-Fort Worth Airport (DFW), which was about twenty miles away. The new airport was supposed to replace existing facilities in the area, including Love Field, and a 1965 bond ordinance stipulated that passenger air service would be phased out at those airports. While most carriers moved to Dallas-Fort Worth, Southwest Airlines continued to offer service within Texas from Love Field, which led to several lawsuits.

Under the Wright amendment, direct flights from Love Field were limited to four states: Louisiana, Arkansas, Oklahoma, and New Mexico. The amendment prohibited direct international flights. Congress subsequently added Alabama, Kansas, Mississippi, and Missouri. But members of Congress and local participants urged a long-term solution to end the dispute.

On June 15, an agreement was reached between the mayors of Dallas and Fort Worth, the chief executive officer of DFW International Airport, and the heads of both Southwest Airlines and American Airlines. The agreement required that the number of gates at Love Field be reduced from thirty-two to twenty, with sixteen going to Southwest Airlines, two to American Airlines, and two to Continental Airlines. The agreement was incorporated into a contract, which would terminate unless Congress acted on it by Dec. 31.

Progress on the bill to codify the agreement was slowed by antitrust concerns. Members of the House Judiciary Committee argued that the gate reduction, together with a provision to protect the agreement from antitrust suits, would allow Southwest Airlines to have a near monopoly on Love Field gates. Proponents of the deal said that some antitrust protections were needed to prevent endless legal wrangling that would end up preserving the status quo for years. Lawmakers reached agreement on a final bill by watering down the antitrust language but keeping the gate cap.

The House Transportation and Infrastructure Committee approved a version of the bill (HR 5830—H Rept 109-600, Part 1) by voice vote July 19. The Senate Commerce, Science and Transportation Committee approved its bill (S 3661—S Rept 109–317) by a vote of 22–0, the same day. On Sept. 13, the House Judiciary Committee, concerned about the antitrust issues, approved an amended version of the bill (HR 5830—H Rept 109-600, Part 2) by voice vote. Negotiations in September led to compromise language intended to address antitrust concerns. The Senate passed the final bill (S 3661) by voice vote Sept. 29, after amending it to reflect the compromise. The House cleared the bill 386–22 later that night.

Telecommunications Overhaul

For the first time since the telephone industry was deregulated in 1996, Congress in 2006 began work on a major overhaul of telecommunications laws but the issues were too complex for lawmakers to resolve before the end of the year. With Democrats back in the majority in the 110th Congress (2007–2008), no action occurred then either.

Both chambers began 2006 with plans to overhaul the 1996 law (PL 104-104) and other outdated telecom laws to encourage the expansion of high-speed fiber-optic networks that could deliver voice, video, and broadband Internet services. A central goal was to streamline existing rules that required companies that wanted to offer video services to negotiate "franchising" deals with individual municipalities.

Changing that requirement was a top priority for the big phone companies, such as AT&T Inc. and Verizon Communications Inc., which were investing billions of dollars in new fiber-optic networks but said the video-franchising rules were a barrier to the market, slowing their efforts to offer video services.

The House passed a bill in June that would have allowed video operators to obtain a single national franchise from the Federal Communications Commission (FCC) instead of negotiating with each municipality in the areas they wanted to serve. Joe L. Barton, R-Texas, chairman of the Energy and Commerce Committee, sponsored the bill.

The Senate Commerce, Science and Transportation Committee approved a broader bill, sponsored by Chairman Ted Stevens, R-Alaska, in late June. Stevens's bill would have kept the basic local franchising framework but simplified the system and set limits on the terms that local governments could require in negotiating franchising contracts with video providers. It also included provisions to shore up the $7 billion-a-year Universal Service Fund, which helped subsidize phone service for rural and low-income customers.

Despite bipartisan support for updating the franchising system and broad agreement on the need to update the Universal Service Fund, both telecom bills became ensnared in a bitter battle over "network neutrality." The question was whether there should be rules to prevent the phone and cable giants from using their control over the broadband network to favor their own online traffic or that of companies that paid extra to ensure that consumers got fast access to their services.

The dispute pitted companies such as AT&T and Verizon that wanted to control the fiber-optic networks they were building, against Microsoft Corp., Google Inc., Yahoo!

Inc., and other Internet providers that wanted equal, nondiscriminatory access to the delivery systems.

Net neutrality proponents lost the battle in the House, which passed Barton's bill after defeating a key net neutrality amendment by Edward J. Markey, D-Mass. But Democrats fought to a draw in the Senate. Stevens's committee approved his bill in a largely party-line vote after a strong net neutrality amendment was defeated on a tie vote. The fight over that amendment led at least one Democrat to block floor action on the bill. Stevens was unable to secure the sixty votes needed to overcome a potential filibuster, and GOP leaders were unwilling to give the bill floor time unless he could.

BACKGROUND

The 1996 telecommunications law was heralded as an essential step to deregulate the industry and promote competition. It preempted state and local laws that blocked local phone competition, required phone companies to share their infrastructure with competitors, allowed regional Bell companies to offer long-distance service and enter additional markets, removed barriers to telephone companies offering TV services, and required the development of rules to ensure universal service. *(1996 law, Congress and the Nation Vol. IX, p. 387)*

But the new law was soon overtaken by a rapidly evolving industry as technology swiftly surpassed that available in 1996. Wireless phones and related communication devices, such as the popular iPhone and BlackBerry, were becoming widely available and quickly adopted. Partly because of the 1996 law, a single company could offer consumers phone, cable, and Internet services. People used high-speed broadband Internet access to make phone calls and watch TV shows.

Telecommunications companies, regulators, and members of Congress agreed on the need to overhaul the 1996 law but not on specifics. Debate focused on a number of issues, such as simplifying entry into the cable TV market, allowing local governments to create broadband networks that would compete with private firms, how to regulate telephone services over the Internet, and whether to overhaul the Universal Service Fund.

But the central issue in 2006 was network neutrality. A 2005 FCC policy statement set out four network neutrality principles. It stated that consumers were entitled to access legal Internet content of their choice; to run applications and services of their choice; to connect to legal devices of their choice as long as they did not harm the network; and to benefit from competition among network providers, service providers, and content providers.

The FCC said it did not need legislation to implement these standards, but others argued that legal language was needed, especially in light of FCC decisions exempting broadband service providers from having to share their networks with competitors. In 2005, the Supreme Court upheld an FCC decision, in *National Cable and Telecommunications Association v. Brand X Internet Services,* that cable companies did not have to open their high-speed networks to rival Internet service providers. The FCC subsequently exempted DSL providers as well. *(Supreme Court decision, p. 761)*

HOUSE COMMITTEE ACTION

The House Energy and Commerce Committee approved Barton's bill by a vote of 42–12 on April 26. Fifteen Democrats joined most of the committee's Republicans to vote for the measure (HR 5252—H Rept 109-470, Part 1), despite the panel's rejection of a series of Democratic amendments.

In its major provisions, the measure:

- Allowed, but did not require, telephone companies to obtain a national franchise to offer video service, rather than having to navigate the existing system.
- Required video providers to pay local franchising fees of up to 5 percent of their local revenue and provide support and channel capacity for public, educational, and governmental use.
- Codified the four network neutrality principles adopted by the FCC in 2005, and allowed penalties of up to $500,000 per violation.
- Required companies that offered Internet phone service to provide 911 emergency service to their customers and required phone companies that controlled the 911 infrastructure to grant Internet calling companies access to those systems.
- Prohibited broadband providers from requiring subscribers to buy other telecom services in order to purchase broadband access.

During the markup, the committee:

- Rejected 22–34 an amendment by Markey and other Democrats to require phone and cable companies to operate their high-speed networks in a nondiscriminatory manner and give equal treatment to similar types of Internet traffic.
- Rejected 22–33 an amendment by Hilda L. Solis, D-Calif., to require phone companies entering the video business under a national franchise to gradually "build out" service to every home in a given area. In exchange, the companies would get access to public rights of way.

In a direct challenge to Barton and the Energy and Commerce Committee, the House Judiciary Committee approved 20–13 on May 25 legislation that called for broadband providers to operate their networks in a nondiscriminatory manner and treat similar types of Internet traffic equally.

The bill (HR 5417—H Rept 109-541) was sponsored by Chairman F. James Sensenbrenner Jr., R-Wis., and supported by three high-ranking committee Democrats.

HOUSE FLOOR ACTION

In a victory for the big phone companies, the House passed Barton's bill by a vote of 321–101 on June 8, after rejecting an amendment by Markey that would have barred broadband providers from favoring or discriminating against Internet traffic.

During the floor debate, the House:

- Rejected on a **key vote of 152–269 (R 11–211; D 140–58; I 1–0)** Markey's amendment to add a net neutrality section to the bill. *(2006 key votes, p. 937)*
- Rejected 165–256 an effort by Solis to include the build-out requirement and expand the nondiscrimination requirements to include race, color, religion, national origin, and sex, in addition to income.

SENATE COMMITTEE ACTION

The Senate Commerce, Science and Transportation Committee approved Stevens's bill (HR 5252—S Rept 109-355) on June 28, after narrowly defeating a strong net neutrality amendment. But the largely partisan 15–7 vote, which came at the end of a three-day markup, did not bode well for the bill. With time running out on the 109th Congress and the midterm election looming, Stevens lacked the sixty votes necessary to overcome a Democratic filibuster if he wanted to convince GOP leaders to bring the measure to the floor.

In major provisions, the bill:

- Retained the existing local franchising framework, leaving it to municipalities to negotiate franchise agreements with video operators. But it proposed to simplify the process.
- Preserved local control over rights of way, required video operators to pay local franchising fees of up to 5 percent of gross revenue, and provide channels and financial support for public, educational, and governmental use.
- Required the FCC to develop a new contribution system for the Universal Service Fund, which helped underwrite phone service for rural and low-income underserved customers through a surcharge on long-distance bills.

Soon after the markup, Oregon Democrat Ron Wyden, a proponent of strong net neutrality requirements, placed a hold on the measure, and it never reached the Senate floor.

2007–2008

The 110th Congress (2007–2008), now fully under Democratic control after the 2006 elections, approved—and President George W. Bush signed—a number of significant bills affecting consumers, transportation, and the Internet. Taken together with legislative action in the 109th Congress, members produced a relatively solid record—significantly improving on the four years of Bush's first term.

Arguably the most important piece of legislation for Americans was a far-reaching revision of safety standards for toys and other consumer goods. The changes were made in connection with a five-year reauthorization of the Consumer Product Safety Commission, which had received little attention from the Bush administration that was more closely attuned to business interests. The action came in the wake of a series of product recalls that included many Chinese-made toys that occurred shortly before holiday shopping began. The national outrage was so strong that the House passed the safety legislation without a single dissenting vote.

Another unexpected action was a multiyear reauthorization of the national passenger railroad, Amtrak, for the first time in more than a decade. The bill included substantial new funding and an array of other provisions to improve rail safety throughout the nation.

In telecommunications policy, Congress once again extended an existing ban on taxing Internet commerce and passed legislation directing a number of federal agencies to create an extensive new database on broadband usage in the country. The bill also directed that information be gathered on similar broadband usage in other countries. The information was to be a baseline for future policy decisions on expanding high-speed broadband, especially in rural areas.

Near the end of the 110th Congress, legislators hurriedly poured $8 billion dollars from the U.S. Treasury general fund into the Highway Trust Fund, which normally was supported by gasoline and other taxes. The Bush administration had opposed this move until its Transportation Department officials discovered that the Highway Trust Fund would be out of money within weeks if no action were taken, thereby cutting off payments to states for highway and other projects. Legislators quickly approved the transfer of funds without dissenting votes.

Consumer Product, Toy Safety

A major rewrite of safety standards for toys and other consumer goods was enacted as part of a five-year reauthorization of the Consumer Product Safety Commission. Congress cleared the bill in July 2008 and President George W. Bush signed it into law Aug. 14 (HR 4040—PL 110-314).

The legislation authorized $626 million for the agency in fiscal 2010 through 2014, modified toy safety requirements, provided whistleblower protections to private workers, gave states more consumer protection authority, and increased damage awards in product safety cases. It also required the commission to review and adopt widely accepted international product safety standards or write its own similar standards if the international standards were deemed inadequate.

The House passed a three-year overhaul bill without a single dissenting vote in December 2007. The action was spurred by a number of product recalls that included Chinese-made toys pulled from shelves before the holiday shopping season because they contained dangerous levels of lead. The Senate passed a seven-year authorization bill the following March. The chief disagreement in the House-Senate conference on the bill concerned phthalates, a family of chemicals that make plastic soft and durable. The Senate-passed bill banned six phthalates in children's products, while the House version was silent on the issue. There was some evidence that children could ingest phthalates by putting toys in their mouths, causing problems related to reproduction, especially with boys. The final bill banned three permanently and three others temporarily while new studies were conducted.

HOUSE COMMITTEE ACTION

The House Energy and Commerce Committee approved a bill sponsored by chairman John D. Dingell, D-Mich., (HR 4040—H Rept 110-501) by a vote of 51–0 on Dec. 18, 2007, following a voice vote endorsement by the panel's Commerce, Trade and Consumer Protection Subcommittee on Nov. 15. The authorization called for $80 million in fiscal 2009, $90 million in fiscal 2010, and $100 million in fiscal 2011. Fiscal 2007 appropriations for the agency totaled $62.7 million.

The bill banned children's products with lead levels higher than 600 parts per million, dropped the level to 300 parts per million in two years, and to 100 parts per million in four years, unless that level was found to be unfeasible. The standard for paint was set at 90 parts per million.

It required third-party testing of toys by accredited labs and required tracking labels on toys for children age twelve or younger to help locate faulty products in a recall. The CPSC was given authority to quickly halt distribution of products that posed an imminent risk of severe injury or death. The agency did not gain new powers to stop unsafe imports at the border, but it would be required to conduct a study on whether that would be feasible.

Other provisions sought to overhaul the embattled agency, which was widely seen as understaffed and underfunded. It required a consumer database, set requirements for recalls, limited travel expenses, and authorized funding to renovate the CPSC testing laboratory.

The bill proposed a temporary increase in the maximum civil penalty for violations of the Consumer Product

Safety Act to $5 million, and a permanent increase to $10 million that would take effect 360 days after enactment.

HOUSE FLOOR ACTION

The House passed the bill 407–0 on Dec. 19. Lawmakers had hoped to send the measure to Bush's desk while the holiday shopping season was in full swing, but efforts to clear the bill on a voice vote in the Senate came up short in the hours before senators were sent home for the year.

SENATE COMMITTEE ACTION

The Senate Commerce, Science and Transportation Committee approved its seven-year bill (S 2045—S Rept 110-265) by voice vote Oct. 30, 2007. The measure:

- Authorized $80 million for the agency in fiscal 2009, with 10 percent increases annually until the authorization reached $141.7 million in fiscal 2015.
- Raised the agency's authorized staffing to 500 employees from 420.
- Increased civil penalties for violations of the Consumer Product Safety Act to $250,000 per violation, with a cap of $100 million; the cap under existing law was $1.3 million.
- Required the commission to enforce whistleblower protections for employees of manufacturers and importers, allowed state attorneys general to bring civil suits under the law, and prohibited retailers to sell recalled products.
- Banned toys and other children's products with a lead content that exceeded 400 parts per million; the existing standard of 600 parts per million did not have the force of law. The permissible lead content in paint used by consumers was reduced from 600 parts per million to 90 parts per million.
- Adopted amendments that added consumer safety provisions for a variety of products, including all-terrain vehicles and garage door openers. It also added whistleblower protections for commission employees.

SENATE FLOOR ACTION

The Senate passed HR 4040 by a vote of 79–13 on March 6, 2008, after inserting a manager's amendment based on a bill (S 2663) sponsored by Mark Pryor, D-Ark. Two days before passing the bill, senators voted, 57–39, to table (or kill) an attempt by Jim DeMint, R-S.C., to substitute the House version of the bill.

During several days of debate, the Senate also:

- Adopted by voice vote an amendment by Dianne Feinstein, D-Calif., to ban the use of three types of phthalates in all children's toys and three others from toys that children put in their mouths.
- Adopted 96–0 an amendment by Klobuchar to prohibit agency employees or commissioners from accepting payment or reimbursement for travel or lodging from anyone with interests before the commission. Instead, it proposed to authorize up to $1 million annually for travel and other expenses for employees to attend meetings and other functions.

CONFERENCE, FINAL ACTION

House and Senate negotiators announced July 28 that they had resolved the last of the issues that had mired negotiations on the bill. A breakthrough on restricting the use of phthalates cleared the way for a deal. A major holdout on the phthalates provision, Rep. Joe L. Barton, R-Texas, said conferees "reached a sensible compromise" that "every member of the conference committee can support."

The House adopted the conference report (H Rept 110-787) by a vote of 424–1 on July 30. The Senate cleared the measure 89–3 the next day.

Among the compromises:

- The agreement prohibited the sale of children's toys or child care articles that contained more than 0.1 percent of three phthalates. Items that contained more than 0.1 percent of three others were temporarily prohibited pending a report and a new rule.
- The restriction on lead in products intended for children age twelve and younger began at 0.06 percent of the item's weight, as opposed to the stricter 0.03 percent required in the Senate bill. After that, the threshold was reduced quicker than in the House bill, reaching 0.01 percent in three years, rather than four as specified in the House version.
- Conferees included a strengthened version of the Senate provision directing the commission to create an online database to allow people to search consumer reports and official accounts of product related injuries and risks.
- The compromise included the Senate's whistleblower protections; there were none in the House version.
- Conferees also sparred over mandatory toy safety standards. The final agreement went significantly further than the early House and Senate versions of the bill by adopting the ASTM International standards on an interim basis and directing the commission to make them the basis of its rules or to write tougher standards if necessary.

MAJOR PROVISIONS

As enacted, HR 4040 (PL 110-314) contained the following major provisions:

Authorization. Authorized $626 million for the commission over five fiscal years: $118 million in 2010, $116 million in 2011, $124 million in 2012, $132 million in 2013, and $136 million in 2014.

Toy standards. Required the commission to adopt widely recognized safety standards set by the nongovernmental ASTM International as interim product safety standards, pending an assessment. Required the commission, within two years, to issue new rules based on the international standards unless it found them inadequate, and if so to write more stringent standards. Required third-party testing of certain children's products and authorized the commission to inspect manufacturers' proprietary laboratories.

Plastics. Permanently outlawed use of three of the phthalates in children's toys and child care articles and temporarily banned three others pending further study and rulemaking.

Lead. Phased in restrictions aimed at reducing the permissible lead content in children's products to the lowest level that was technically feasible. Set the cap at 0.06 percent of the item's weight beginning 180 days after enactment, dropping to 0.03 percent after one year and to 0.01 percent or as close as feasible after three years. Reduced the lead level for paint from 600 parts per million to 90 parts per million one year after enactment.

Product identification. Required companies that manufactured children's products to place distinguishing marks on the product and the packaging to aid in identifying recalled items.

ATV safety. Required domestic and foreign manufacturers of all-terrain vehicles sold in the United States to meet U.S. safety standards. Included standards that effectively banned all three-wheel ATVs. (U.S. manufacturers already complied with voluntary standards, but critics said foreign manufacturers often skirted such precautions. Critics said three-wheel ATVs were more prone to rollovers than four-wheel models.)

Product safety database. Directed the commission to create a publicly available, searchable database on the safety of consumer products. Required the Government Accountability Office to study the general utility of the database and recommend steps to increase its use.

Penalties. Increased the maximum civil penalty for each violation of consumer product laws to $100,000 from $8,000. Increased the maximum for a series of related violations to $15 million from $1.8 million. Authorized the commission to seek asset forfeiture as a penalty for criminal violations. Removed a requirement in existing law that directors, officers, and agents of a company had to know about the company's violations to be subject to fines or penalties.

Whistleblower protections. Provided whistleblower protections for employees of private companies who reported violations of product safety rules.

State enforcement. Authorized state attorneys general to obtain appropriate injunctions against toy manufacturers that were allegedly in violation of the law. Required states to notify the commission prior to filing any action and to give the commission thirty days to respond to or assist with an action.

Travel and lodging. Barred agency employees or commissioners from accepting payment or reimbursement for travel or lodging from anyone with interests before the commission, and authorized additional funds for travel and other expenses for employees to attend meetings and other functions.

Amtrak Reauthorization, Rail Safety

For the first time in more than a decade, Congress in 2008 reauthorized Amtrak, the national passenger rail line. The legislation combined substantial increases in authorized passenger rail funding with new rail-safety measures. President George W. Bush signed the measure into law Oct. 16 (HR 2095—PL 110-432).

The law authorized $13 billion over five years for Amtrak programs and another $1.6 billion for rail safety. An additional $1.5 billion was authorized over ten years for grants for the Washington Metropolitan Area Transit Authority, which operated the Metro subway system.

The Bush administration sought minimal to zero funding for Amtrak each year, arguing the government should end federal subsidies for the system and move it toward privatization. While under Republican control during the Bush years, the House typically backed the proposed budget cuts, while the Senate supported more generous funding.

The last Amtrak authorization (PL 105-134), enacted in 1997, expired at the end of fiscal 2002. Congress continued to provide funding through the annual appropriations bills, but there was an ongoing tug of war between those who thought Amtrak should become a private enterprise and others who regarded rail as a federal responsibility. In the end, Amtrak usually received just enough to limp along.

In fiscal 2008, Amtrak asked for $1.7 billion; Bush had requested $900 million, including $100 million for intercity rail. Congress appropriated $1.3 billion for Amtrak (PL 110-161).

BACKGROUND

Amtrak was created in 1970 to relieve private railroads of money-losing passenger lines. Although continuing to lose riders in the following years, the system enjoyed strong political support in Congress from members—especially senators—who did not want to see service to their constituents reduced or even eliminated. Also, the system was enthusiastically backed by a well-organized group of railway buffs who argued not only for the romance of railroading but also for the public policy advantages of a balanced transportation policy that offered alternatives to auto and air travel. *(1970 act, Congress and the Nation Vol. III, p. 161; additional background, Congress and the Nation Vol. XI, pp. 379, 404; Vol. X, p. 320; Vol. IX, p. 369)*

LEGISLATIVE HISTORY

In 2007, during the first session of the 110th Congress, the Senate passed a six-year, $11.4 billion Amtrak reauthorization bill (S 294) that rejected privatization proposals. The House in June 2008 passed HR 6003 to authorize

$14.4 billion for Amtrak and related rail investments for five years, with limited private-sector competition on high-speed rail. A formal conference to meld the bills was blocked by Senate opponents. Instead, House and Senate negotiators reached an informal agreement on the $13 billion Amtrak reauthorization, including controversial privatization provisions, and folded them into a stalled rail-safety bill (HR 2095).

The House had passed that bill in October 2007, and the Senate passed an amended version in August 2008. The legislation gained new urgency after a Sept. 12, 2007, collision between a passenger train and a freight train in California that killed twenty-five people and injured dozens more.

The Bush White House threatened to veto the legislation because of its cost and because it did not seek to restructure Amtrak. The administration's proposal, issued in the 109th Congress, would have split Amtrak into three entities: a private company to provide infrastructure maintenance and operations for the Northeast Corridor between New York and Washington, a second company to operate the trains, and a government corporation to hold the Amtrak name and logo and the right of access to existing routes on lines owned by the freight railroads.

But the majorities that voted for the bill in both chambers in the 100th Congress were large enough to override a veto, and John L. Mica of Florida, the ranking Republican on the House Transportation and Infrastructure Committee, worked to persuade Bush to back the bill, saying that it would hold Amtrak more financially accountable than before and allow some small-scale privatization of high-speed rail lines.

SENATE COMMITTEE ACTION: AMTRAK

The Senate Commerce, Science and Transportation Committee approved its Amtrak bill (S 294—S Rept 110-67) by voice vote on April 25, 2007. The legislation was the product of a compromise brokered by New Jersey Democrat Frank R. Lautenberg and Mississippi Republican Trent Lott during the 109th Congress. It proposed mandating a strategic overhaul of Amtrak that supporters said was necessary to help rail travel become a realistic alternative to other forms of transportation.

The bill called for a total of $3.3 billion in operating subsidies and $4.9 billion for capital grants over six years, including $1.4 billion for states for intercity passenger rail upgrades. Like federal highway aid, the grants would require states to provide a 20 percent match for all federal funds. It also directed the federal government to refinance Amtrak's $3 billion debt.

The legislation contained provisions aimed at holding Amtrak more financially accountable, including requirements for a new accounting and reporting system, as well as a host of reports to Congress. It also proposed a pilot program to allow up to two routes to be considered for competitive bidding each year.

SENATE FLOOR ACTION: AMTRAK

The Senate passed the bill 70–22 on Oct. 30, 2007, after voting a few hours earlier to limit debate on the measure. Democratic leaders had hoped a cloture vote to limit debate would be unnecessary but changed their minds after John E. Sununu, R-N.H., briefly held up consideration of the bill the previous week with an amendment related to Internet taxes. Sununu withdrew that amendment when lawmakers decided instead to consider a stand-alone Internet tax bill. *(Internet tax moratorium, p. 434)*

The Senate rejected the White House goal of weaning Amtrak off federal subsidies by moving toward privatization. Lautenberg said no country in the world had been able to successfully operate a national passenger rail service without government subsidies, and he argued that the United States was no exception. "You cannot carry the obligations that are required with a passenger rail system. My colleagues will excuse me when I say this: It is kind of fallacious to even believe that it is possible. We tried it," he said.

HOUSE COMMITTEE ACTION: AMTRAK

The House Transportation and Infrastructure Committee May 22, 2008, approved by voice vote a $14.4 billion, five-year Amtrak reauthorization bill (HR 6003—H Rept 110-690). The panel's Subcommittee on Railroads, Pipelines and Hazardous Materials had approved it by voice vote two days earlier.

The bill was the result of a bipartisan agreement between committee chairman James L. Oberstar of Minnesota, who opposed privatization, and Mica, who previously supported significant budget cuts for Amtrak. Mica agreed to the higher funding level; Oberstar accepted Mica's proposal to allow private companies to bid on building a high-speed rail line in the Northeast Corridor. Mica was an ardent supporter of a high-speed rail line in the corridor that could compete with airline travel.

The $14.4 billion authorization included $6.7 billion for capital expenses ($4.2 billion in grants for Amtrak and $2.5 billion in grants to states to develop intercity rail service). The total also covered $3 billion for operations, including money to help Amtrak repay the millions of dollars it owed unionized workers for the nearly eight years they worked without a wage increase, and $1.8 billion for grants to develop high-speed rail corridors.

The bill included a requirement that the transportation secretary solicit bids to design, construct, and operate an initial high-speed rail system operating between Washington, D.C., and New York City, subject to review by a special commission. This allowed bids from private companies. After reporting to Congress on a successful bid for the Northeast Corridor, the secretary could consider private-sector proposals for other high-speed rail projects.

To alleviate tensions between freight and passenger rail lines, the bill proposed creating federal guidelines for negotiations over rights of way. Amtrak experienced significant delays when waiting for freight trains to pass, costing the passenger line millions of dollars. Although no members spoke in opposition to the bill, Mica acknowledged that some Republicans would balk at its cost.

HOUSE FLOOR ACTION: AMTRAK

Despite a presidential veto threat, the House passed the bill June 11 by a vote of 311–104. It was the first time the House had passed an Amtrak authorization bill in eleven years. The House adopted, 295–127, an amendment by Thomas M. Davis III, R-Va., to add to the total authorization $1.5 billion for the Washington Metropolitan Area Transit Authority to provide for capital needs on the Metro transit system.

HOUSE COMMITTEE ACTION: RAIL SAFETY

The House Transportation and Infrastructure Committee by voice vote June 14, 2007, approved HR 2095 (H Rept 110-336) on rail safety that was rewritten to balance the demands of industry management and labor unions. It was a priority of Oberstar, the committee's chairman.

The committee altered the bill to address industry concerns about hours-of-service limits for workers. Oberstar's original bill eliminated "limbo time," the on-duty hours in which workers are transported back to officially complete their shifts. Railroad employees cannot currently count limbo time against hours-of-service limits. The amended bill phased in restrictions on railroads' use of limbo time; two years after enactment, an employee's monthly limbo time would be limited to ten hours. The railroad industry argued the original bill would create significant scheduling problems.

The bill boosted the number of federal rail safety inspectors and renamed the Federal Railroad Administration the Federal Railroad Safety Administration.

HOUSE FLOOR ACTION: RAIL SAFETY

The House Oct. 17, 2007, passed HR 2095 to improve railroad safety by increasing inspections and reducing work hours. The vote was 377–38.

The measure almost doubled the number of rail safety inspection and enforcement personnel, required that employees have at least ten hours off per day, prohibited work shifts longer than twelve consecutive hours and imposed restrictions on "limbo time," such as when workers travel to a point of release after their shift ends.

In addition, HR 2095 reorganized the Federal Railroad Administration, renamed it the Federal Railroad Safety Administration and authorized $1.1 billion for its activities over four years. It provided a four-year authorization (fiscal 2008 through 2011) at $1.1 billion plus grant money.

The White House issued a statement of administration policy that called the hours-of-service requirements "overly prescriptive" and said some of the new rules were unnecessary but did not threaten a veto.

SENATE ACTION: RAIL SAFETY

The Senate by voice vote passed an amended version of HR 2095. It had been brought directly to the floor without committee action.

The measure proposed a six-year authorization of the Federal Railroad Administration (fiscal 2009 through 2014) and authorized $1.4 billion over that period, plus funds for grant programs.

Like the House version, the Senate bill included increases in the number of rail-safety inspection and enforcement personnel and steps toward implementing positive train control systems. Both also proposed modifying hours-of-service requirements for rail workers in an effort to limit worker fatigue and improve safety.

However, the Senate version proposed to cap rail workers' total on-duty and limbo time at 276 hours per month. It required time off for employees who were in limbo for more than twelve consecutive hours and limited to three hours the time a railroad employee could spend on a train after working a twelve-hour shift.

FINAL ACTION: AMTRAK AND RAIL SAFETY

The House took up the Senate-amended bill on Sept. 24, 2008, and replaced the text with a complete substitute worked out in informal House-Senate negotiations. The compromise was adopted by voice vote. The Senate cleared the combined bill, 74–24, on Oct. 1.

Lawmakers had been ready to hold a conference on the Amtrak bill (S 294), but Tom Coburn, R-Okla., blocked Senate leaders from appointing conferees. Coburn strongly opposed the House provision authorizing $1.5 billion for improvements to the Washington Metro subway system. "He thinks that's the mother of all earmarks," an aide said. "If there's money for D.C. Metro, the senator will object to it." Although Coburn continued to oppose the legislation, Senate Majority Leader Harry Reid, D-Nev., won a vote Sept. 29 to invoke cloture, which limited further debate on the bill and paved the way for final action. The vote was 69–17, well above the sixty votes needed for cloture.

Major compromises made during the negotiations include:

- The major sticking point in the Amtrak portion of the bill was the House proposal to allow private bids on a high-speed rail line in the Northeast Corridor. Mica said there was no room for compromise on the language. Lautenberg, one of Amtrak's staunchest allies, said he would fight to keep Mica's provision out of the final bill, although he stopped short of saying he would seek to kill the measure if he failed. The argument during informal meetings ended up being whether the Northeast Corridor, Amtrak's most profitable line, should be bid first. Some senators said it made more sense to allow private companies to invest in struggling corridors elsewhere. The compromise was to allow private companies to bid on any one of eleven corridors.

- The $13 billion, five-year Amtrak authorization was closer to the House provision. The $1.6 billion, five-year authorization for rail-safety programs was more than either chamber recommended.
- Like the Senate bill, the final measure capped the total on-duty and limbo time for rail workers at 276 hours per month. Like both measures, it limited shifts to twelve hours and required that workers receive at least ten consecutive hours off duty in a twenty-four-hour period. The measure gradually reduced the allowable limbo time from forty hours per month to thirty hours per month. The final bill also extended hours-of-service standards to contractors. It also gave the Transportation Department the authority to reduce the maximum hours of service or increase the minimum period of rest based on scientific and medical research.
- The increases in civil penalties for certain rail-safety violations were similar to those in the original House bill.

MAJOR PROVISIONS

As enacted, HR 2095 (PL 110-432) contained the following major provisions:

Passenger Rail

- Authorized $13 billion over five years (fiscal 2009 through 2013) for Amtrak and federal passenger rail programs, including $5.3 billion for capital grants to Amtrak, $2.9 billion for operating grants, and $1.4 billion to retire Amtrak's debt, with an additional $1.9 billion over five years for intercity passenger rail service grants.
- Directed the Transportation Department to solicit bids for the financing, design, construction, operation, and maintenance of a high-speed intercity rail system within one of eleven high-speed rail corridors that included the Northeast Corridor, and authorized $5 million for preliminary engineering. Specified that any proposal meeting criteria set in the bill would be subject to review and recommendation by a special commission before a contract was signed.
- Directed the department to create a pilot program under which a rail carrier that owned tracks used by Amtrak could bid on providing passenger services over that route in lieu of Amtrak for up to five years. Gave preference to bidders seeking to operate routes that were identified as among the five worst-performing Amtrak routes.
- Authorized $1.5 billion over five years for grants to states and Amtrak to develop high-speed rail lines that could accommodate speeds of 110 mph or more.
- Required a plan to restore Northeast Corridor infrastructure to good repair.
- Authorized $1.5 billion over ten years for capital and maintenance grants for the Washington Metropolitan Area Transit Authority.

Rail Safety

- Authorized $1.6 billion over five years (fiscal 2009 through 2013) for rail-safety programs, including $1.3 billion for the Federal Railroad Administration.
- Required each Class I railroad carrier, as well as intercity and passenger train companies, to submit plans to have positive train control systems in place by the end of 2015 that could sense impending collisions and stop the trains. It authorized $50 million per year to help implement the technology.
- Capped rail workers' on-duty and "limbo" time—the time during which workers traveled to the location where they officially completed their shifts or remained on a train after a shift ended—at 276 hours per month, barred shifts longer than twelve hours, and required that workers receive at least ten consecutive off-duty hours every twenty-four hours. Reduced total per-month limbo time from forty hours to thirty hours.
- Authorized $3 million annually for highway-rail grade-crossing safety grants and $5 million annually in grants for safety improvements to railroad infrastructure.
- Increased maximum civil penalties for certain rail-safety violations from $10,000 to $25,000, and from $20,000 to $100,000 for grossly negligent violations.

Internet Taxation

Congress in 2007 extended a moratorium on Internet access taxes for seven years. The legislation was signed into law by President George W. Bush on Oct. 31, hours before the previous version expired on Nov. 1 (HR 3678—PL 110-108).

The extension of the ban, which dated from 1998, showed again that legislators were unable to resolve conflicting interests of state and local governments seeking new sources of revenue and the technology industry and Internet users who sought to keep the rapidly expanding communications media free of taxation that they believed could cripple its future development. The ban had been extended before, most recently in 2001 and 2004. *(Background, previous extensions, Congress and the Nation Vol. XI, pp. 376, 400; Congress and the Nation Vol. X, p. 327)*

The 2007 legislation barred local, state, and federal taxes on services such as digital subscriber lines, cable modems, wireless connections, and dial-up plans. Features often bundled with Internet access, such as television and telephone service, could still be taxed. Some states that had long taxed Internet access could continue do so if they were actively collecting the tax.

Legislators interested in technology issues made the extension a priority at the outset of the 110th Congress, but it took months before they were able to send it to the president. Lawmakers fought over the length and scope of the extension, with industry and state governments weighing in. Technology and telecommunications firms generally supported a permanent ban on access taxes, but state and local government officials argued that any extension should be temporary so that Congress would have to revisit the tax laws governing the rapidly evolving sector.

The House passed a four-year extension in October. After the Senate Commerce, Science and Transportation Committee was unable to agree on a bill, Senate leaders brought the House bill to the floor and amended it with a seven-year extension, and the House cleared the measure.

LEGISLATIVE ACTION

The House Judiciary Committee approved a four-year extension (HR 3678—H Rept 110-372) by a vote of 38–0 on Oct. 10. The committee defeated 15–21 an attempt by Robert W. Goodlatte, R-Va., to make the ban permanent.

The House passed the bill by an overwhelming 405–2 vote Oct. 16, despite grumbling by lawmakers who were pushing for a permanent ban.

The Senate passed the House bill by voice vote Oct. 25 after first approving by voice vote an amendment by John E. Sununu, R-N.H., that lengthened the extension from four years to seven. Sununu's amendment also added language to clarify that the tax ban covered some services, including paid e-mail, instant messaging, and electronic storage. Also added was language to phase out "grandfather" provisions for states that were taxing Internet access before the nationwide moratorium was first imposed. For a state to continue to be grandfathered under the new bill, it had to be actively collecting the tax.

The House cleared the Senate-passed bill 402–0 on Oct. 30, and the president signed it the next day.

Broadband Access

Congress in 2008 completed action on legislation designed to produce an accurate and detailed picture of the structure and use of broadband communications in the United States. Supporters of the bill said the information was vital as Internet use continued to expand.

The legislation required several agencies, including the Federal Communications Commission (FCC), the Small Business Administration, and the Census Bureau, to revise or update existing broadband definitions, identify tiers of broadband service, and revise reporting requirements. The information gathered was expected to provide a base on which to provide expanded availability of broadband services nationwide, especially in rural areas.

It authorized a federal grant program to assist states in expanding and improving broadband services. It also instructed the Federal Trade Commission to launch a public awareness campaign focused on promoting best practices for Internet safety, national outreach, and education for children. A principal concern was protecting minors from pornography on the Internet.

The House passed a version of the bill (H 3919) in 2007, and a Senate committee approved a similar measure (S 1492). The Senate passed its version in September 2008 after adding provisions on Internet safety for children. The House accepted the Senate's bill, which President George W. Bush signed into law Oct. 10, 2008 (PL 110-385).

The Congressional Budget Office estimated the legislation would cost $29 million in 2009 and would total $217 million between 2009 and 2018, assuming it were fully funded in appropriations.

Democrats in the 110th Congress had made broadband access one of their top telecommunications priorities, stressing that the United States was falling behind in availability, speed, and price of access, a gap with serious implications for the nation's economic competitiveness. A report by the Organization for Economic Cooperation and Development (OECD) showed that by the end of 2006, the United States had slipped to fifteenth among thirty leading countries in broadband penetration, the measure of how many people subscribed to high-speed service. That was down from fourth place in 2001.

"Broadband is no longer a luxury item," said Sen. Daniel K. Inouye of Hawaii, chairman of the Commerce Committee that wrote the Senate bill. "It is an essential component of a strong America in an information age." An accurate, detailed broadband map, Inouye and other supporters said, could guide government efforts to boost the nation's declining international broadband access ranking.

The legislation had strong support from consumer groups and companies within the broadband industry. Consumers Union, the nonprofit testing and information organization that published Consumer Reports, said that existing FCC data on broadband use was "woefully inadequate." The cable industry as well as U.S. Telecom Association, which represented the phone industry, also said they favored at least some parts of the legislation.

BACKGROUND

The need to expand Internet access in the United States was widely accepted. In 2004, President Bush set a goal of "universal, affordable access for broadband technology by the year 2007" and called for ensuring that "as soon as possible thereafter, consumers have got plenty of choices when it comes to [their] broadband carrier."

With its three-to-two Republican majority, the FCC lifted rules that required telecommunications companies to share their lines and equipment with competitors. The Supreme Court affirmed that approach in 2005 when it upheld FCC rules classifying cable modem service as a lightly regulated "information service." That freed cable companies from obligations to share their networks with rival Internet service providers. The FCC adopted similar rules for the digital subscriber line (DSL) services offered by phone companies.

Republican regulators also tried to prod phone companies to deploy high-speed lines by making it easier for them to offer profitable video services as well as Internet access over those lines. The FCC video franchising order, which was adopted over the objection of the commission's two Democrats, came in 2006 after franchising legislation stalled in the Senate. *(Congress and the Nation Vol. XI, p. 373)*

Internet providers such as Verizon Communications Inc. said those policies were paying off, with phone companies spending billions of dollars to deploy fiber-optic lines that could deliver voice, video, and data, and cable companies upgrading their coaxial lines to keep up. While Republicans argued that their approach would spur competition and deliver more choices, many Democrats asserted that deregulation had put consumers at the mercy of big telephone and cable vendors who were delivering slow connection speeds at high prices.

In 2007, the Democrats were in a position to use their new majority on Capitol Hill after winning the 2006 midterm elections to open a debate about whether the federal government should do more to ensure universal access to high-speed connections at affordable rates. They were bolstered by several studies, including the OECD report, showing that the United States lagged behind other developed countries in broadband availability, speed, and price.

The problem of high-speed Internet access was most starkly evident in rural areas that often had too few customers to justify expensive network investments. As a result, many Americans in sparsely populated areas were lucky to have a choice of even one land-line broadband provider.

A survey by the Communications Workers of America found that median download speeds in the United States were 1.9 megabits per second, considerably slower than in other developed countries, particularly those in Asia and Scandinavia. Many Japanese consumers had access to 100-megabit fiber-optic service that was fifty times faster and permitted videoconferencing and movie downloads in minutes, not hours.

Although Verizon was testing similar speeds, most broadband customers of various U.S. services received five-megabit service. U.S. broadband service also was comparatively expensive when speed was taken into account. In Korea, 100-megabit Internet access cost the equivalent of about $45 per month; Verizon charged about $40 a month for five-megabit service.

Still, Democrats had the job of convincing their colleagues that intervention would help, not stifle, the Internet economy and that broadband was a necessity like telephone service and not just a way to surf the Web more quickly. The first step, proponents said, was getting a more accurate picture of the market. "To pave the way for a comprehensive broadband policy, first we must get better data," said Edward J. Markey, D-Mass. "The first stage has to be political education and recognition that there is a problem."

HOUSE ACTION

The Energy and Commerce Committee approved the bill (HR 3919—H Rept 110-443) by voice vote Oct. 30, 2007. Its major provisions focused on creating an annual inventory of existing broadband services:

- Required the FCC to complete an annual broadband assessment and report on the deployment of broadband service capability including the speed of service in the United States by tiers. The legislation also required an annual consumer survey to evaluate characteristics of consumers' broadband use, including the prices they paid, the speed they used and the reasons why some did not subscribe at all.
- Directed the Commerce Department to develop and maintain a broadband inventory map.
- Authorized grants to states to assess broadband services.
- Authorized $20 million per year for the program in fiscal 2008 through 2010, and $275 million for state grants over the three-year period.

The House passed the bill by voice vote Nov. 13, 2007, under suspension of the rules, an expedited procedure that allows no amendments and is commonly used for noncontroversial legislation. No member rose to oppose the bill.

SENATE COMMITTEE ACTION

The Senate Commerce, Science and Transportation Committee approved its bill (S 1492—S Rept 110-204) by voice vote July 19, 2007, emphasizing improving the quality of the data collected on broadband access. In major provisions, the bill:

- Required the FCC to reevaluate its definition of broadband, which was adopted in 1999 and was far slower than many cable-modem and DSL services available on the market.
- Required broadband providers to report which service tiers were capable of reliably delivering high-definition video.
- Revised rules that required broadband providers to report high-speed connections only by five-digit ZIP code, which Democrats and even many Republicans said contributed to the FCC overstating broadband availability. The new rules would have to provide a closer look at various populations by neighborhood or other area.
- Authorized a five-year, $200 million grant program to fund state-based, nonprofit, public-private partnerships to map broadband availability and identify barriers to broadband adoption.

SENATE FLOOR AND FINAL ACTION

The Senate passed S 1492 by voice vote on Sept. 26, 2008, after adopting some changes to the legislation. In one major addition, the Senate appended the provisions of another pending bill (S 1965) to increase protection for children from inappropriate content on the Internet, including pornography. The Senate deleted specific dollar authorizations for grants authorized in the bill. The House had authorized $335 million and the Senate, in the committee bill, $200 million. The final bill contained no specific number. The amended bill incorporated House provisions requiring the FCC to gather information that compared broadband service capability in seventy-five communities in at least twenty-five countries.

The House on Sept. 29 concurred with minor changes, which the Senate accepted Sept. 30, both by voice votes. Those action sent the bill to the president for his signature.

MAJOR PROVISIONS

As signed into law, S 1492 (PL 110-385) contained the following major provisions.

Broadband Survey and Grants

- Required the FCC to compile a list of geographical areas that are not served by any provider and provide the demographic data including population, population density, and average per capita income for each underserved area.
- Directed the FCC to require broadband providers to report which service packages are capable of reliably delivering high-definition video.
- Directed the Government Accountability Office to conduct a study on the average price of broadband, the average speed of broadband, and a comparison of the availability and quality of broadband in the United States compared to other countries.
- Directed the Small Business Administration office of advocacy to conduct a study evaluating the impact of broadband speed and price on small businesses.
- Authorized the commerce secretary to create a grant program to fund state-based, nonprofit, public-private partnerships to map broadband availability and identify barriers to broadband adoption. Specified that an entity would be eligible if it applied to the secretary, contributed at least 20 percent of the grant's total, and agreed to certain confidentiality requirements. Specified that a grant could be used to provide a baseline assessment of broadband service deployment in each state that would identify and track a number of items such as areas in each state that have low levels of broadband service deployment; the rate at which residential and business users use broadband services and other information-technology services; and possible suppliers of broadband services.
- Prohibited an eligible entity in a state from receiving a new grant if it has obtained prior grant awards in each of the previous four consecutive years.
- Directed the FCC to provide information comparing the extent of broadband service capability, including data transmission speeds and price for broadband service, in seventy-five communities in at least twenty-five countries. Specified that the communities had to resemble certain types of U.S. cities on such specification as population, topography, and demographics, and required each country's capital city be included.
- Required the FCC to conduct and make public, at least once a year, consumer surveys in urban, suburban, and rural markets to determine a number of things, including types of technology used to provide the broadband service capability; amounts consumers pay per month; data transmission speeds; and types of applications and services consumers use most frequently.

Internet Child Protection

- Directed the Federal Trade Commission to launch a national campaign to inform and educate the public about safe Internet use by children.
- Directed the Commerce Department to create an online safety and technology working group to encourage Internet safety for children and monitor the initiatives of the industry to comply.
- Amended the 1934 Communications Act (PL 73-416) to mandate that schools inform children of how to conduct themselves properly on the Internet.

FAA Reauthorization

The 110th Congress considered a wide-ranging reauthorization of the Federal Aviation Administration (FAA) but did not complete action. Rather, legislators approved short-term extensions of its authorities into 2009.

A bill to reauthorize the FAA passed the House, while companion legislation won approval from two Senate committees, all in 2007. The last FAA authorization (PL 108-176)) expired Sept. 30, 2007. Under the fiscal 2008 omnibus spending bill (PL 110-161), the agency's ability to collect certain taxes, including ticket and cargo taxes, and to spend the money through the Airport and Airway Trust Fund was extended through Feb. 29, 2008. These authorities then were extended, first to Sept. 30 and then into 2009, when Congress was expected to revisit a complete reauthorization of the agency. *(2003 reauthorization and FAA background, Congress and the Nation Vol. XI, p. 382)*

There was broad agreement that the nation's aging air traffic control system needed to be replaced with a system that could handle the projected growth in demand for air travel. However, there was no consensus on methods to pay for the changes.

Some congressional Republicans and the administration of President George W. Bush argued that the FAA needed a new revenue mechanism. They proposed replacing the existing fuel and ticket taxes with new usage fees, such as per-flight charges based on distance traveled. Such a major change was unpopular with many Democrats and appropriators, who disliked the idea of shifting most FAA funding off budget. They generally preferred tweaking the existing system, perhaps by raising federal gas taxes.

A lobbying war between the major passenger airlines and general aviation interests further complicated the debate. General aviation businesses—air traffic other than regularly scheduled commercial airline flights or military aviation—stood to pay more under most user fee proposals. They wanted to retain the existing funding scheme, arguing that the proposed user fees amounted to corporate welfare for the airlines. The airlines, on the other hand, argued that the existing system was unfair because it required them to pay more of the total cost of air traffic control than general aviation paid.

The Senate Commerce, Science and Transportation Committee approved a bill (S 1300) in May 2007 for fiscal 2008 through 2011 that tended to favor the airline industry, requiring general aviation to pay a new $25-per-flight surcharge.

General aviation groups preferred a version passed by the House in September, which proposed raising some fuel taxes on general aviation without altering the basic fee structure. The Senate Finance Committee approved a measure (S 2345), similar to the House bill, that would raise gas taxes on general aviation.

Further action on the Senate bill was delayed in part because of the disagreement between Commerce and Finance. The White House, meanwhile, threatened to veto the House bill because it would not make "critical reforms" for the air traffic control system.

HOUSE COMMITTEE ACTION

After a lengthy debate, the House Transportation and Infrastructure Committee gave voice vote approval June 28, 2007, to a four-year, $66 billion FAA reauthorization bill (HR 2881—H Rept 110-331).

Before approving the measure, the panel added a union-backed proposal aimed at jump-starting talks between air traffic controllers and the FAA. The amendment, adopted 53–16, called for a binding arbitration process for contract disputes. Under the proposal by Aviation Subcommittee Chairman Jerry F. Costello, D-Ill., the parties in a stalled labor dispute would have to go back to the bargaining table for forty-five days while the old contract remained in place. That would effectively have reopened a contract the FAA had imposed on its unionized controllers the previous summer.

"This is the showstopper," said ranking Republican John L. Mica of Florida, who described the amendment as a poison pill that would kill the bill. Transportation Secretary Mary E. Peters issued a statement saying that President Bush would veto "any reauthorization with language altering the existing controller contract or reopening negotiations."

Under a 1996 law that governed the way the FAA negotiated with its unions, the agency could impose its last contract offer if talks reached an impasse and Congress did not intervene. Unions had been pushing for a change in the law, and prolabor Democrats and some Republicans said it put workers at a disadvantage.

Lawmakers, the FAA, the White House, and the National Air Traffic Controllers Association had met numerous times in a futile effort to settle the dispute. Costello said the impasse left "only one course of action to take—and that is binding arbitration."

Committee chairman James L. Oberstar, D-Minn., said the language was "essentially a placeholder" designed to pressure the FAA and the controllers to negotiate a deal without congressional intervention.

The committee also adopted 51–18 an amendment by Oberstar that called for placing FedEx Corp. under the same collective-bargaining statute that applied to United Parcel Service Inc. and other competitors. Language in the 1996 law placed all of FedEx's operations under the auspices of the 1926 Railway Labor Act instead of the National Labor Relations Act, which typically governed trucking companies and allowed local units to unionize. The Railway Labor Act allowed unionization only on a national scale—a more difficult task.

Oberstar said the language would "ensure equal treatment of all truck delivery employees."

Despite fights over the two amendments, the underlying legislation drew broad bipartisan support. "We have 100 percent agreement on 98 percent of the bill and 100 percent disagreement—some of us—on 2 percent of this bill," Oberstar said.

The four-year authorization included:

- $37.2 billion for FAA operations.
- $15.8 billion for the Airport Improvement Program, a source of grants to update runways and other airport infrastructure.
- $13 billion for the FAA's facilities and equipment account.

It also included an increase in the cap on fees airports could levy for improvements, from $4.50 per leg of a flight to $7 per leg. The nation's airlines, which usually opposed any new fee or tax that raised the price of a plane ticket, argued that raising the cap would unfairly drive up costs for passengers.

HOUSE FLOOR ACTION

The House passed an expanded, $68 billion version of the bill by a vote of 267–151 on Sept. 20. A set of tax provisions, which the Ways and Means Committee had approved by voice vote Sept. 18, was added to the bill as part of the rule for floor debate. It included provisions to raise the commercial aviation fuel tax from 19.3 cents per gallon to 24.1 cents and to increase the general aviation fuel tax from 21.8 cents per gallon to 35.9 cents, with the new revenue dedicated to air traffic control modernization. Provisions also included a tax on certain previously held fuel that was in stock as of Jan. 1, 2008, to be paid by the end of April 2008.

The bill included passenger protection provisions, spurred by high-profile incidents earlier in the year when JetBlue and American Airlines passengers were stranded for hours in parked planes because of bad weather. Ways and Means Chairman Charles B. Rangel, D-N.Y., said he had expected a debate focused on money. Instead, his committee was inundated with complaints from airline passengers. "Rather than dealing with the question of revenue, I had to deal with the issue of outrage," Rangel said.

The original bill required that airlines provide food, water, restroom facilities, cabin ventilation, and access to medical treatment for passengers on board an aircraft sitting on the tarmac for an extended period of time without access to the terminal. The plan added a provision that passengers be allowed to leave the plane after excessive delays, though it did not specify what was excessive. The Transportation Department could impose civil penalties on airlines or airports that did not adhere to those rules.

SENATE COMMITTEE ACTION

The committee with jurisdiction over transportation issues in the Senate approved a broad FAA bill, while the Finance Committee marked up the tax provisions.

Transportation Committee. The Senate Commerce, Science and Transportation Committee gave voice vote approval May 16 to a four-year, $65 billion FAA bill (S 1300—S Rept 110-144), after reaffirming a provision to establish a new user fee.

The four-year authorization included: $36.6 billion for FAA operations; $15.8 billion for the Airport Improvement Program; $11.9 billion for facilities and equipment.

Finance Committee. Senate Finance voted, 13–0, on Sept. 21 to reauthorize the fuel and ticket taxes that helped fund FAA activities. The provisions (S 2345—S Rept 110-228) were expected to be folded into the FAA reauthorization measure when it reached the floor. With proxies, the unofficial vote was 16–5.

The bill proposed increasing the general aviation fuel tax to 36 cents per gallon, up from 21.8 cents, but leaving commercial-aviation fuel taxes unchanged. It also proposed adding $430 million annually to the Airport and Airway Trust Fund to support the satellite-based NextGen air traffic system.

FAA AUTHORIZATION EXTENSIONS

The Senate never voted on its bill in 2008. With no final resolution in sight, Congress turned to short-term extensions.

Congress in mid-2008 approved HR 6327 that extended the FAA authorization through Sept. 30, 2008 (PL 110-253). Then in September both chambers again passed an addition extension to March 31, 2009 (PL 110-330) Both bills were passed without dissent.

Pilot Retirement Act

Congress in 2007 raised the mandatory retirement age for commercial pilots to sixty-five from sixty. The House passed the bill (HR 4343) by a 390–0 vote Dec. 11 and the Senate by voice vote Dec. 12. President George W. Bush signed the bill on Dec. 13, 2007 (PL 110-135).

The retirement provision was included in the FAA reauthorization legislation that did not clear in the 110th Congress. *(See previous story.)*

Older pilots had lobbied for decades to require the FAA to boost the mandatory retirement age. The legislation was pushed in part to deter potential lawsuits over age discrimination. The final bill required that pilots older than sixty must fly with younger pilots on international flights, a standard adopted by the International Civil Aviation Organization in 2006.

The legislation allowed pilots who were forced to retire because of age to return to the cockpit but did not restore lost seniority, which translated into higher salaries and other benefits, including better routes on larger planes.

Highway Trust Fund

The federal Highway Trust Fund, which was nearing bankruptcy, was rescued when Congress in 2008 cleared legislation to transfer $8 billion from the Treasury's general fund into the highway account. President George W. Bush signed the bill into law Sept. 15 (HR 6532—PL 110-318).

The Bush administration had strongly opposed attempts by Congress to replenish the highway fund, which was projected to face a shortfall in 2009. When the House passed an $8 billion bill in July, the White House issued a veto threat, calling it a "gimmick and a dangerous precedent that shifts costs from users to taxpayers at large."

But the impending depletion of the trust fund, which seemed to take the administration by surprise, led officials in September to urge lawmakers to pass the legislation immediately. The highway fund was financed primarily by an 18.4-cents-a-gallon federal excise tax on gasoline. Revenues were declining as Americans drove less and switched to more fuel-efficient vehicles in response to increasing gas prices. The administration opposed using money from the Treasury to make up the shortfall, proposing instead that the highway fund borrow $3.2 billion from a separate mass transit account.

HOUSE ACTION

On July 23, the House passed a bill (HR 6532), sponsored by Ways and Means Committee Chairman Charles

B. Rangel, D-N.Y., to inject $8 billion from the general fund into the Highway Trust Fund. Despite a White House veto threat issued the day of the vote, lawmakers backed the bill by a vote of 387–37—substantially more than the two-thirds majority required to override the president.

A handful of fiscal conservatives voted against the measure, saying it would only add to the nation's deficit, but most supported it. "I wish, as one of the strongest conservatives in the House, to have some other alternative to bring you today, but I do not have that," said John L. Mica of Florida, ranking Republican on the House Transportation and Infrastructure Committee. Mica voted for the bill.

SENATE, FINAL ACTION

Efforts by Senate Finance Chairman Max Baucus, D-Mont., and others to push the highway fund replenishment through the Senate were blocked by fiscal conservatives who opposed adding to the deficit or using tax increases to offset the cost.

One major push came on a bill (HR 2881) to reauthorize the Federal Aviation Administration (FAA). Baucus and Charles E. Grassley of Iowa, the ranking Republican on the Finance Committee, tried to add provisions transferring $8 billion to the highway fund, offset primarily by a five-cent increase in an oil-spill tax. Republicans derailed the FAA bill on the Senate floor, complaining mainly about the trust fund proposal and the taxes used to offset it. An attempt to limit debate by invoking cloture failed May 6, and the FAA bill went no further. *(FAA bill action, p. 437)*

Baucus also tried unsuccessfully to add the Highway Trust Fund plan to a bill to renew popular expiring tax provisions. After seeing earlier attempts fail, Senate appropriators decided in July to include an $8 billion replenishment in a draft of the fiscal 2009 Transportation-Housing and Urban Development spending bill. House appropriators had opted in June not to include the fund, saying that fixing the trust fund was a job for authorizers and did not belong in a spending bill. The difference was not resolved because Congress did not finish any of the domestic appropriations bills. *(Details, pp. 121, 124)*

Senate action seemed uncertain until Sept. 5 when Transportation Secretary Mary E. Peters announced that the Highway Trust Fund would run dry by the end of the month, much sooner than expected, and urged Congress to act quickly to send the bill to Bush. "At current spending rates, we will start the new fiscal year on Oct. 1 with a zero balance in the trust fund, and will continue to spend more than we take in," Peters said. Peters said that because the trust fund was so close to zero, the Transportation Department would have to start within a week changing the way it reimbursed states by cutting checks less often or paying them on a pro rata basis.

Baucus said he was "encouraged that the administration is acknowledging the urgent need" for highway funds, and he urged "senators who have blocked this vital funding until now to get out of the way." Three days later, a handful of Senate Republicans blocked an attempt by Majority Leader Harry Reid, D-Nev., to clear the House passed bill by voice vote.

But the combined pressure from the White House, state governments, and powerful contracting and road-building lobbyists—and members concerned that highway dollars continued flowing to their areas—was too much to resist.

The Senate passed the bill by voice vote Sept. 10 with an amendment that released the funds as soon as the bill was signed. The House cleared the revised measure 376–29 the next day.

CHAPTER 7

Energy and Environment

Energy and Environment

For Republicans and Democrats alike, energy issues became a high priority during President George W. Bush's second term, as rising oil prices stoked debate over reducing U.S. dependence on imported oil. The GOP-led 109th Congress cleared a comprehensive overhaul of energy policy that aimed to encourage more production of traditional energy sources while providing incentives for renewable energy and conservation. Newly empowered Democrats, taking the majority in the 110th Congress, cleared a more targeted bill aimed at reducing energy use, which included a long-sought increase in vehicle fuel efficiency standards.

Lawmakers also turned to other legislative vehicles to pass energy priorities. The 2008 farm bill contained popular tax breaks for ethanol and other biofuels. A major tax bill in 2008 contained a number of incentives for renewable energy conservation that were offset with revenue increases on the oil and gas industry.

Both Republican leaders in the 109th Congress and Democratic leaders in the 110th Congress were forced to yield on key policy goals. During debate over the 2005 energy bill, Republicans had to jettison a plan to open the Arctic National Wildlife Refuge (ANWR) to drilling, even though that had been a central component of Bush's energy proposal. Democrats, to win passage of broader energy legislation in 2007, agreed to drop a requirement that utilities derive a minimum percentage of electricity from renewable sources. Perhaps most surprisingly, the Democrats in 2008 were forced to open up coastal areas to offshore drilling, as record-breaking fuel prices stirred public demand for more production.

Environmental issues settled down into something of a stalemate, as neither Republicans who wanted to relax federal regulations nor Democrats who wanted to respond to the threat of climate change could win passage of significant legislation. However, amid concerns about plummeting fish stocks in the world's oceans, lawmakers agreed to overhaul fishing regulations.

After failing to resolve differences over a water resources bill in the 109th Congress, lawmakers in the 110th Congress overrode a presidential veto to enact a $23.2 billion bill for nine hundred Army Corps of Engineers projects. But Congress failed to reauthorize the popular Clean Water State Revolving Fund because of disputes over a labor provision.

NEW ENERGY LAWS

By wide margins, lawmakers in both chambers passed a sweeping overhaul of the nation's energy policies in 2005. The bill, which built on an energy plan that President Bush had first proposed four years earlier, addressed nearly every sector of the energy industry. It provided incentives for the coal, nuclear power, oil and gas, and renewable energy industries, as well as for energy efficiency and electric utilities, and it contained a variety of additional provisions aimed at spurring new technologies, infrastructure, and energy production.

One of the original bill's most controversial goals, to open up the Arctic National Wildlife Refuge to oil and gas drilling, could not survive the determined opposition of Democrats and moderate Republicans. Drilling advocates tried to get ANWR language into the budget-reconciliation package instead, but they were defeated there as well. Backers of the energy bill also had to drop provisions to shield manufacturers of the fuel additive methyl tertiary butyl

REFERENCES

Discussion of environmental and energy policy for the years 1945–1964 may be found in *Congress and the Nation Vol. I*, pp. 771–1095; for the years 1965–1968, *Congress and the Nation Vol. II*, pp. 463–528; for the years 1969–1972, *Congress and the Nation Vol. III*, pp. 745–849; for the years 1973–1976, *Congress and the Nation Vol. IV*, pp. 201–320; for the years 1977–1980, *Congress and the Nation Vol. V*, pp. 451–530, 533–597; for the years 1981–1984, *Congress and the Nation Vol. VI*, pp. 333–400, 403–482; for the years 1985–1988, *Congress and the Nation Vol. VII*, pp. 417–495; for the years 1989–1992, *Congress and the Nation Vol. VIII*, pp. 467–532; for the years 1993–1996, *Congress and the Nation Vol. IX*, pp. 401–476; for the years 1997–2001, *Congress and the Nation Vol. X*, pp. 341–414; for the years 2001–2004, *Congress and the Nation Vol. XI*, pp. 409–444.

Outlays for Natural Resources and Environment

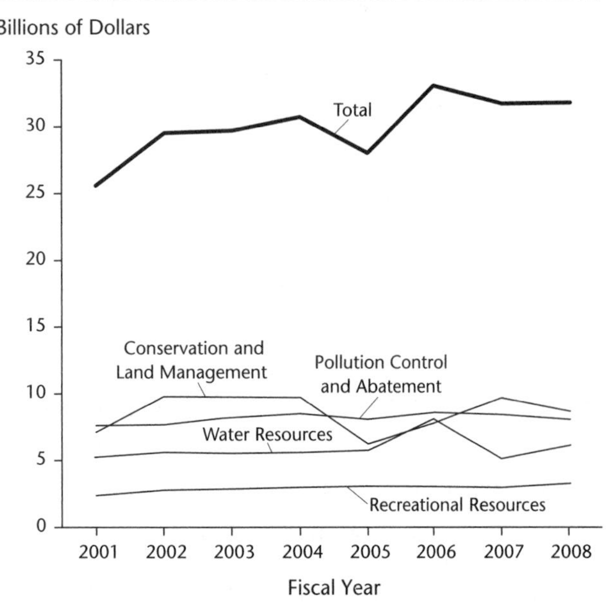

SOURCE: Office of Management and Budget, *Historical Tables, Budget of the United States Government: Fiscal Year 2010* (Washington, D.C.: U.S. Government Printing Office, 2009), Table 3.2.

NOTE: Total line includes some expenditures not shown separately.

ether (MTBE) from most product liability suits associated with groundwater contamination. The attempt to provide a liability waiver for MTBE had been a deal-killer in the 108th Congress. *(108th Congress action, Congress and the Nation Vol. XI, p. 525)*

For GOP leaders, the energy overhaul legislation struck a balance between traditional energy sources and new, "greener" alternatives such as renewable energy and conservation. Critics, however, contended that the new law would do little to help reduce the nation's appetite for fuel. Many Democrats worried that the measure did not set new vehicle fuel efficiency standards or take steps to reduce the threat of climate change.

When Democrats assumed the majority in the House and Senate in 2007, they vowed to put a greater focus on conservation. After nearly a year of debate, Congress cleared a major energy bill that set the first statutory increase in vehicle fuel efficiency standards in thirty-two years, mandated an increase in the use of ethanol and other biofuels, and called for a broad range of energy-use standards. But Democratic leaders dropped two initiatives from the bill to win Senate passage and avert a presidential veto: a package of tax incentives for alternative energy and a renewable electricity standard.

In 2008 Democrats succeeded in winning enactment of a $16.9 billion package of tax incentives for the production and use of alternative energy by attaching it to a larger tax package. Other provisions designed to spur the production of biofuels were added to the 2008 farm bill, with bipartisan support. But as public outrage grew over rising gasoline prices, Democrats faced unexpected pressure to lift a twenty-six-year-old moratorium on new offshore oil and gas drilling. With Republicans threatening to block passage of a continuing resolution to keep much of the government operating, Democrats bowed to election year pressure and agreed to end the moratorium.

ENVIRONMENTAL BATTLES

Apart from a rewrite of fisheries law in the 109th Congress, neither party could gain much traction on divisive environmental issues during Bush's second term. Republicans sought to add more flexibility to key environmental laws, while Democrats aimed at curbing industrial emissions blamed for climate change. But a consensus proved elusive.

In the 109th Congress, GOP leaders tried to advance an administration initiative, known as Clear Skies, that would have revamped the Clean Air Act by replacing industrial pollution regulatory structure with a market-based framework to curb power plant emissions of three pollutants—sulfur dioxide, nitrogen oxides, and mercury. The plan, backed by coal-fired utilities and other industries, aimed to reduce costly litigation, establish a stable regulatory environment, and allow power plants to curb pollution in a cost-effective way. But it ran into opposition from environmentalists because it would not regulate carbon dioxide, the greenhouse gas associated with climate change. The bill failed on a tie vote in the Senate Environment and Public Works Committee and was never revived.

The House in 2005 passed a bill that called for sweeping changes to the 1973 Endangered Species Act. It proposed to streamline the controversial law through such steps as ending the federal government's power to protect critical habitats, while compensating private property owners who faced restrictions because of endangered species on their land. But Democrats and lawmakers from more urban districts opposed the plan as providing a financial windfall for private interests and weakening environmental protections. The Senate never took it up.

Lawmakers, however, had more success when it came to reauthorizing the 1976 Magnuson-Stevens Act, which governed commercial and recreational fisheries. Faced with growing concerns about the impact of overfishing on ocean health and on profit margins in the fishing industry, Congress in 2006 cleared a bill regulating catch limits. In a debate that broke along regional, not partisan, lines, members battled over whether to force fisheries that exceeded their annual quotas to reduce the following year's catch by the same amount. In the end, lawmakers settled for a compromise that directed the nation's eight regional fishery councils to develop and begin implementing plans to end overfishing, while setting a ten-year time frame for rebuilding overfished stock.

Outlays for Energy

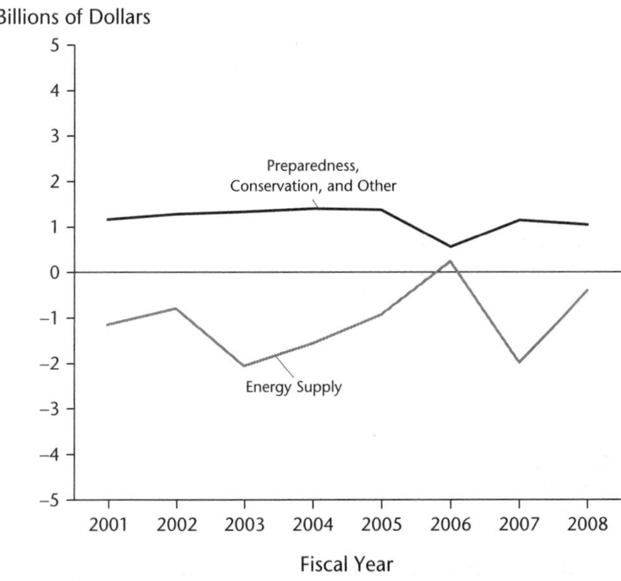

SOURCE: Office of Management and Budget, *Historical Tables, Budget of the United States Government: Fiscal Year 2010* (Washington, D.C.: U.S. Government Printing Office, 2009), Table 3.2.

Democrats in the 110th Congress took aim at the increasingly prominent issue of climate change, pursuing a far-reaching measure designed to cap U.S. emissions of carbon dioxide and other greenhouse gases blamed for warming the planet. Legislation, which sought to establish a comprehensive national policy to address global warming, would have redistributed trillions of dollars collected from polluters to industries, states, and electricity consumers over the following four decades. But the complexity of the issue and the opposition of key Republicans proved insurmountable. Although Senate Democrats won approval of the bill in committee, they pulled it from the floor in 2008 after Republicans succeeded in forcing a prolonged floor debate that had no apparent end. The House never took action on a companion bill.

CONFLICTS OVER INFRASTRUCTURE

Congress had mixed success on infrastructure projects related to the environment. A bill that would have authorized billions of dollars for popular water resources projects died at the end of the 109th Congress after House and Senate conferees were unable to agree on the size and scope of a final bill. Lawmakers also were at odds over provisions to impose stricter oversight of the Army Corps of Engineers, an issue that had gained traction after Hurricane Katrina in 2005, which destroyed levees in New Orleans that were administered by the agency. Taxpayer and environmental groups generally favored language to increase scrutiny to corps projects. Industries that relied on public works activities worried over adding new layers of bureaucracy that would slow infrastructure improvements.

The 110th Congress returned to the issue, passing a $23.2 billion water resources bill in 2007. When Bush vetoed the bill because of concerns over its costs and priorities, Congress overrode the veto—the first time a Bush veto was overridden. The legislation authorized funding for nine hundred Army Corps of Engineers navigation, flood control, and environmental restoration projects. Some of the costliest projects were on the Mississippi River, in the Florida Everglades, and along coastal Louisiana, with others scattered throughout the country. Democrats and Republicans alike, including a number of fiscal conservatives, defended the costly measure as vital for spurring infrastructure improvements around the country, especially in areas of the Gulf Coast ravaged in 2005 by Hurricanes Katrina and Rita.

Lawmakers in the 110th Congress also tried to reauthorize the popular Clean Water State Revolving Fund, the largest source of low-interest loans for constructing wastewater treatment facilities and other water pollution abatement projects. The House passed a bill in 2007, but it contained a controversial labor provision, backed by Democrats, requiring that workers on projects carried out with assistance from the revolving fund receive local prevailing wages and benefits. The White House threatened a veto over the language. The Senate never took up the bill despite bipartisan support for the revolving fund.

Chronology of Action on Energy and Environment

2005–2006

Amid concerns over rising oil prices, the 109th Congress put a spotlight on energy legislation. The Bush administration won a major victory in 2005 when lawmakers passed an overhaul of the nation's energy policies that, in key respects, hewed to the president's priorities—although environmentalists blocked efforts to open the Arctic National Wildlife Refuge to drilling. Congress also cleared legislation to allow new offshore drilling in the Gulf of Mexico and reauthorized a federal pipeline safety program.

The 2005 energy overhaul followed the general contours of measures that George W. Bush had proposed since 2001. The bill addressed virtually every sector of the energy industry, providing incentives for producers of traditional energy sources as well as for renewable energy, while calling for extensive research and development and enacting strategies aimed at spurring new technologies, infrastructure, and energy production. Supporters hailed the legislation as balancing incentives for renewable energy and conservation with the need to increase domestic production of traditional fuel sources. Critics, however, worried that the law put too great an emphasis on subsidies for producers of oil and natural gas and would do little to help reduce the nation's appetite for fuel.

An offshore drilling bill, cleared on the final day of the 109th Congress, represented a signature victory for Gulf Coast legislators. The measure, which opened 8.3 million acres south of the Florida Panhandle to drilling, was spurred by a series of spikes in oil and gasoline prices, related in part to damage caused by 2005 hurricanes. House GOP leaders pressed for a more ambitious measure that aimed to open most of the nation's coastline to drilling, but they could not overcome opposition in the Senate.

On a major environmental issue, Congress in 2006 rewrote the main federal law governing commercial and recreational fisheries. Lawmakers were driven by growing concerns about the impact of overfishing on ocean health and on profit margins in the fishing industry. Support for the measure broke down along regional, not partisan, lines, as lawmakers sought to support fishing interests in their areas.

Congress could not reach a consensus on other energy and environmental issues. House and Senate conferees failed to resolve differences over a bill to authorize billions of dollars for popular Army Corps of Engineers water projects. The legislation, known as the Water Resources Development Act, had broad support, but lawmakers differed over the size and scope of a final bill, as well as over provisions to impose stricter oversight of the corps. Congress also failed to advance GOP-backed measures to overhaul the Endangered Species Act and the Clean Air Act, with moderate Republicans siding with Democrats to successfully block the initiatives. Similarly, environmentalists blocked repeated efforts to open the Arctic National Wildlife Refuge to oil and gas drilling, even though the proposal was a central focus of the administration's energy agenda.

As in past years, lawmakers found themselves deeply divided over the issue of constructing a nuclear waste repository in Nevada. Controversy over the proposed site at Yucca Mountain helped snarl the fiscal 2007 energy-water appropriations bill, casting new doubt on whether Congress could agree on how to handle waste from nuclear power plants.

Energy Overhaul

President George W. Bush, who had called for a comprehensive overhaul of the nation's energy policies for more than four years, signed a sweeping new law on Aug. 8, 2005, that addressed nearly every sector of the energy industry. The bill (HR 6—PL 109-58) provided incentives for coal producers, nuclear power, oil and gas companies, renewable power, energy efficiency, and electric utilities. It called for extensive research and development (R&D) and streamlined permitting processes, along with tax breaks and other strategies aimed at spurring new technologies, infrastructure, and energy production.

Congressional Republicans, who had fallen short in attempts to clear comprehensive energy legislation earlier in the decade, hailed the bill as balancing incentives for new, "greener" alternatives, such as renewables and conservation, with the need to increase domestic production of more traditional resources, such as oil, nuclear power, and coal. Critics, however, argued that the new law mainly subsidized traditional producers of oil and natural gas and would do little to help reduce the nation's appetite for fuel. Many Democrats were particularly unhappy that the measure did not set new vehicle fuel efficiency standards or require reductions in greenhouse gas emissions, such as carbon dioxide, which scientists called a primary contributor to climate change.

The legislation followed the general contours of the energy proposals that Bush first outlined in 2001, with its emphasis on greater production of oil, gas, and coal. But a centerpiece of Bush's plan, and its most controversial proposal—drilling for oil in Alaska's Arctic National Wildlife Refuge (ANWR)—did not survive. *(ANWR, pp. 455, 474)*

The new law provided a package of tax breaks worth $14.6 billion over eleven years. Revenue-raising offsets were expected to reduce the net loss to the Treasury to $11.5 billion. The law also provided for $1.6 billion in new mandatory spending over ten years that was not subject to the appropriations process and authorized tens of billions more that would be up to appropriators to provide.

Republicans had written energy bills in the 107th and 108th Congresses, but disputes over issues such as fuel additives and oil exploration in Alaska prevented the massive proposals from becoming law. In 2003, the House adopted the conference report on an omnibus energy bill, but the measure collapsed in the Senate. *(Earlier action, Congress and the Nation Vol. XI, pp. 412, 425)*

Returning to the issue, the House passed a bill in April 2005 that closely followed the Bush administration's priorities and the 2003 conference report. The Senate moved slower in an effort to draw bipartisan support. In late June, the Senate passed a bill that differed substantially from the House measure, putting more emphasis on renewable fuels and technologies as well as dropping several of the House's most controversial provisions.

House and Senate conferees completed negotiations on a final bill with surprising speed, reaching agreement in less than two weeks. Lawmakers were eager to show they were taking action in the face of gasoline prices that had reached more than $2 per gallon. The president publicly called on Congress to send him a bill before leaving for the August recess. And top Republican energy negotiators—determined to avoid a repeat of their 2003 experience—were more willing to compromise.

Energy experts said the bill would have little or no effect on gas prices, which were governed by worldwide supply and demand. It also would not reduce U.S. dependence on imported oil, though that was the administration's rationale for the legislation in the first place. By the time the bill was finished, Republicans instead were emphasizing its broader economic effects. "This bill will create jobs, job security and clean energy," said Pete V. Domenici, R-N.M., chairman of the Senate Energy and Natural Resources Committee.

To get the bill to Bush's desk, House GOP leaders agreed to drop two of the most contentious items: the plan to allow drilling for oil and natural gas in ANWR, and provisions to shield manufacturers of the fuel additive methyl tertiary butyl ether (MTBE) from most product liability suits associated with groundwater contamination. The attempt to provide a liability waiver for MTBE producers had been a deal-killer in the 108th Congress. Like corn-based ethanol, MTBE was used to increase the oxygen content of gasoline so that it would burn more cleanly. But the additive also had been found to contaminate groundwater. House Majority Leader Tom DeLay, R-Texas, insisted that the waiver be included in the 2003 energy bill conference report. More than half the country's MTBE producers had operations in his state. But GOP senators from the Northeast, whose states did not want to be stuck picking up the costly tab for MTBE cleanups, rejected the liability waiver and joined a Democratic filibuster that prevented the conference report from reaching the Senate floor.

Drilling advocates agreed to drop the ANWR provisions from the energy bill. They assumed they would be able to get them into law as part of a separate budget-reconciliation package later in the year. However, drilling opponents were able to erect enough obstacles to defeat those plans as well.

BACKGROUND

Energy had been a top priority for the Bush administration since 2001, when escalating gasoline prices and an electricity shortage that produced rolling blackouts in California pushed energy issues onto the top of the national agenda. Congress had last passed a major energy bill in 1992 (PL 102-486) in the wake of high oil prices following Iraq's invasion of Kuwait. *(Congress and the Nation Vol. VIII, p. 500)*

Shortly after Bush took office, he established the National Energy Policy Development Group charged with putting together a national strategy. Chaired by Vice President Dick Cheney, the group issued more than one hundred recommendations and warned of "the most serious energy shortage since the oil embargoes of the 1970s." The recommendations emphasized increased production while also offering some proposals to reduce energy demand.

Bush subsequently sent Congress a plan for comprehensive energy legislation. But falling gasoline prices and the stabilization of electricity supplies on the West Coast reduced the sense of urgency, and old disputes stymied progress on the bill.

ENERGY, ENVIRONMENT LEADERSHIP

In his second term, President George W. Bush nominated well-regarded administrators or politicians for key energy and environment leadership posts, thereby steering clear of major confirmation battles. However, the administration's efforts to pare back provisions of environmental laws and its continued emphasis on expanded energy exploration led to heated conflicts with environmentalists.

Department of Energy. Samuel W. Bodman had already served as deputy commerce secretary and deputy Treasury secretary in the Bush administration when the president nominated him on Dec. 10, 2004, to succeed Spencer Abraham as secretary of energy. Although Bodman had little experience in the energy realm, he was seen as a status-quo nominee with hands-on management skills. Industry groups reacted favorably to a nominee with a business background, while environmental concerns were relatively muted because Bodman had not staked out any controversial energy positions. He received praise from senators in both parties.

At his Jan. 19, 2005, confirmation hearing before the Senate Energy and Natural Resources Committee, Bodman portrayed his role as that of an administrator, not a policy maker. He said he would help implement existing administration positions on Yucca Mountain, the Arctic National Wildlife Refuge, and incentives for energy exploration and production. While acknowledging that he was no expert on many of the specific fields he would oversee, he told lawmakers he would seek a "balanced" approach to meeting the country's energy needs with a mix of conservation, new technologies, and traditional resources such as oil, gas, and coal. The Senate confirmed his nomination by voice vote on Jan. 31.

Bodman had a busy and relatively controversy-free tenure. He helped shepherd a major energy bill (HR 6—PL 109-58) through Congress in 2005 that was a high priority for the Bush administration, and he worked with lawmakers to boost incentives for biofuels. But he ran into headwinds on Capitol Hill over some proposals that would expand the use of nuclear energy, including researching ways to safely recycle nuclear fuel employing technologies that would make the fuel difficult to use in nuclear weapons.

Department of the Interior. When Dirk Kempthorne was nominated by Bush on March 16, 2006, as secretary of the interior, he was already widely known in political circles. He had served as a Republican U.S. senator from Idaho from 1993 to 1999 and subsequently won two elections as the state's governor. His nomination to the Department of Interior post drew bipartisan praise, with lawmakers pleased to hear Kempthorne's pledges of stricter ethics policies and better cooperation with Congress after the often-controversial tenure of the previous secretary, Gale A. Norton. Environmentalists, however, worried that Kempthorne, who had a pro-development record, would push for more oil and gas drilling and seek to weaken such signature environmental laws as the Endangered Species Act. Despite such concerns, the Senate Energy and Natural Resources Committee approved Kempthorne's nomination by voice vote on May 10 and the full Senate confirmed his appointment by voice vote on May 26.

As secretary, Kempthorne worked to repair relations on Capitol Hill, and he generally enjoyed good relationships with key lawmakers. He pursued some policies with bipartisan appeal, including a proposal to provide billions in extra funding to the National Park Service over the following decade. But, like Norton, he often drew scathing criticism from environmentalists who accused him of favoring developers and energy interests at the expense of conserving public lands. Under Kempthorne's tenure, the Interior Department expanded drilling and mining on public lands, proposed allowing loaded guns in national parks, and pursued rule changes to make the Environmental Protection Act more flexible—policies that generally were backed by the energy industry and advocates of gun and private property rights but were denounced by many Democrats.

Trying to balance the competing demands for public lands proved extremely challenging. Kempthorne in 2008, for example, provoked the ire of both environmentalists and the oil and gas industry when he proposed placing the

Republicans contended that increasing domestic production of oil and gas was a national security priority, at a time when the United States was importing more than half its oil. Democrats countered that expanded energy independence lay in conservation, not more drilling. The different camps clashed fiercely over such issues as opening ANWR to drilling and raising corporate average fuel economy (CAFE) standards.

By the end of the 107th Congress, comprehensive energy legislation had collapsed with the GOP-led House focused on increasing energy production and the Democratic-led Senate giving emphasis to energy conservation.

Republicans returned to the fray in the 108th Congress, confident that their control of both chambers would enable them to pass a sweeping measure. But Republicans turned out to be anything but unified. They had to negotiate polar bear under the protection of the Environmental Protection Act. Environmentalists had pressed for the listing because warming temperatures were threatening the bear's habitat. They were disappointed, however, by Kempthorne's decision to add stipulations to allow oil and gas exploration and development to generally proceed in the Arctic. Despite such stipulations, the State of Alaska sued the Interior Department over the listing, saying it would cripple offshore oil and gas development.

Kempthorne placed a great emphasis on ethics. In an attempt to burnish the department's image, he proposed restrictions on meeting with lobbyists and stronger disciplinary procedures in an effort to transform it into what he termed "a model of an ethical workplace." Nevertheless, the department was embarrassed in 2008 when its inspector general found wrongdoing in the department's Minerals Management Service, with a dozen past and current employees accused of accepting gifts from energy companies and engaging in cocaine use and sexual misconduct.

Environmental Protection Agency. When Bush nominated Stephen L. Johnson to become administrator of the Environmental Protection Agency (EPA) on March 4, 2005, the selection was endorsed by both White House supporters and critics of the administration's environmental policies. Johnson, a biologist with expertise in pesticide regulation and a twenty-four-year veteran of the agency, had served as EPA's acting chief since late January, when Bush moved Michael O. Leavitt to head the Department of Health and Human Services. The nomination represented a shift from the well-known political figures who had led the agency in the past to a lower-profile, career employee with a scientific background.

But Johnson's road to confirmation faced a couple of obstacles. First, Democratic senators Barbara Boxer of California and Bill Nelson of Florida warned that they would hold up Johnson's nomination unless he canceled a program to pay parents to monitor the effects of pesticides on their children. Johnson agreed to end the program, but another Democrat, Thomas R. Carper of Delaware, threatened to block the nomination unless the EPA released an analysis of proposed administration changes to the Clean Air Act. In a 61–37 vote shortly after midnight April 29 (in the session that began April 28), Republicans—joined by seven Democrats—won a motion to cut off debate on the nomination. The Senate then immediately confirmed Johnson by voice vote.

During his tenure, Johnson was frequently buffeted by criticism from environmentalists and occasionally from industry. The EPA's proposal in 2007 to tighten standards for ozone, a key component of smog, drew fire from industry groups that felt it went too far as well as from environmentalists who worried it did not go far enough.

Environmentalists were particularly angered when Johnson overruled his own agency's legal and technical advisers by denying a Clean Air Act waiver to California that would have allowed it to set its own air quality standards for carbon dioxide and other greenhouse gases blamed for global warming. The decision drew a legal challenge from the Golden State and incensed Democratic lawmakers over allegations that Johnson allowed White House officials to influence the decision. House Oversight and Government Reform Committee chair Henry Waxman, D-Calif., told Johnson during a contentious hearing in May 2008, "You have essentially become a figurehead.... The president apparently insisted in his judgment and overrode the unanimous recommendations of EPA scientific and legal experts." Johnson, however, parried the criticism, saying he had consulted with the White House but made his own decisions.

Johnson also came under fire from environmental scientists, who accused him of putting politics over science in rejecting recommendations of experts on air pollutants, failing to regulate greenhouse gases, and delaying action on toxic chemicals. Labor unions representing most of the EPA's professional staff wrote an open letter to Johnson on Feb. 29, 2008, accusing him of failing to deal in good faith on issues such as scientific integrity and job evaluations. Industry groups, however, defended Johnson's efforts to take economic impacts into account when weighing new environmental regulations. Supporters of Johnson also praised him for managing the difficult task of incorporating scientific findings into public policy.

regional disagreements over federal electricity regulation and requirements for the use of ethanol—a corn-based additive for gasoline—as well as over tax provisions. However, the issue that most galvanized opposition was a liability waiver for producers of MTBE. That dispute, on top of the underlying divisions over the emphasis on increased production versus conservation, ultimately doomed the measure.

But, with Bush winning a second term and Republicans expanding their congressional majorities in the 2004 elections, GOP leaders again set their sights on a major energy bill. The issue gained traction throughout 2005, as gasoline prices, driven by sharply rising oil prices worldwide, increased from about $1.80 a gallon in early January to about $2.40 a gallon by early August, when Bush signed the legislation.

President Bush holds up the Energy Policy Act of 2005 after it was signed into law, with senator Peter Domenici, R-N.M., left, chairman of the Senate Energy Committee, senator Jeff Bingaman, D-N.M., center, and Energy Secretary Samuel Bodman, right, during a ceremony on Kirtland Air Force Base in Albuquerque on August 1, 2005.
Source: AP Photo/J. Scott Applewhite

HOUSE COMMITTEE ACTION

Four committees marked up portions of House legislation, completing their work April 13. The result largely mirrored the 2003 conference agreement, except that it included provisions to allow oil and gas production in ANWR. Research and development provisions—which the Science Committee had approved by voice vote Feb. 10 (HR 610) and reported July 29 (H Rept 109-216, Part I)—were also added.

The Energy and Commerce Committee approved the core of the bill (HR 6) by a vote of 39–16 at the end of a marathon, three-day markup. The bill was drafted largely by Chairman Joe L. Barton, R-Texas. Though Democrats lost virtually every attempt to change the bill, Edward J. Markey, D-Mass., paid tribute to Barton for conducting a fair markup that allowed Democrats to offer their amendments and make their arguments.

The Ways and Means Committee approved an $8.1 billion package of energy tax breaks (HR 1541) on a 26–11 vote and formally reported it (H Rept 109-45) on April 18. Chairman Bill Thomas, R-Calif., indicated that the measure was essentially a bargaining tool to take to conference. He said his strategy was to load the House package with provisions that he did not expect the Senate to include in its bill.

Nearly all of the tax incentives were for traditional energy sources such as oil, natural gas, coal, nuclear power, and electricity transmission. Only about 5 percent of the total was aimed at renewables and conservation. Democrats made two attempts to strike specific tax breaks for oil and coal, both of which failed. Several Republicans also voiced support for more incentives for renewables and energy conservation.

The Resources Committee gave voice-vote approval to sections of HR 6 related to public lands, following an eight-hour session in which Democratic amendments were similarly rebuffed. The bill included drilling in ANWR and provisions to reduce regulations and provide incentives to promote energy production on public lands. "Energy continues to be the foundation and lifeblood of America's economy," said Chairman Richard W. Pombo, R-Calif. "But we have grown complacent. Our federal policies have lost sight of this simple yet critical fact."

The Government Reform Committee approved HR 1533, a small piece of the overall energy bill, by voice vote April 13. The provisions dealt with energy efficiency and conservation in the federal government.

The resulting House energy bill included provisions to

ANWR. Authorize the Interior Department to grant leases for oil and gas exploration, development, and production on about 1.5 million acres of ANWR. Oil and gas exports from ANWR were barred.

The Resources Committee rejected 13–30 an attempt by Markey to strike the provision. "My people, my state, the people who live on the land, want to do this," said Don Young, R-Alaska.

The panel also rejected 16–31 an attempt by Raúl M. Grijalva, D-Ariz., to remove incentives for traditional oil and natural gas exploration on public lands. "These kickbacks are not needed," Grijalva said. "They are an insult to the American taxpayer."

MTBE. Provide a "safe harbor" to protect U.S. manufacturers of MTBE against product liability for groundwater contamination, retroactive to Sept. 5, 2003. MTBE would be phased out as a gasoline additive but would not be banned until 2015. The bill would authorize $250 million a year in fiscal 2005 through 2012 to help MTBE manufacturers convert their plants to produce other fuel additives.

The Energy and Commerce Committee rejected 20–31 an attempt by Lois Capps, D-Calif., to strike the MTBE liability waiver. It rejected 23–29 a Capps amendment to phase out the use of MTBE over four years and eliminate the transition assistance to MTBE manufacturers. Barton said he was holding "intense negotiations" on the MTBE dispute. "We will have the issue solved," he pledged, noting that the Republican majority in the Senate had grown. "We fully expect if there is a filibuster threat we'll have 60 votes for cloture."...

Tax provisions. Cut energy taxes by $8.1 billion over eleven years, with no revenue offsets. More than 90 percent of the tax breaks were aimed at domestic energy production and traditional energy sources such as oil, natural gas, and electricity transmission.

Ethanol. Require refiners to increase the amount of renewable fuels added to gasoline in the United States, starting with an annual average volume of 3.1 billion gallons in 2005, reaching 5 billion gallons in 2012. The requirement that reformulated gasoline contain 2 percent oxygen by weight would be eliminated.

Electricity. Repeal the 1935 Public Utility Holding Company Act (PUHCA), and give the Federal Energy Regulatory Commission (FERC) jurisdiction over reliability standards for electricity transmission networks. All mergers and all sales or leases of transmission facilities valued in excess of $10 million would have to be approved by FERC. FERC would have the authority to issue permits for the construction of new power lines to relieve congestion over the objections of states and could seek eminent domain right-of-way in federal court when necessary.

Republicans and some Democrats agreed that PUHCA was outdated and inhibited investment in the power industry, but many Democrats argued that the 1935 law should be replaced only if the FERC provided new oversight to protect consumers from price spikes resulting from bad business deals. Republicans countered that further regulation would slow investment in the sector and unnecessarily obstruct market forces that they said would ultimately benefit consumers.

The Energy and Commerce Committee rejected 22–27 an amendment by John D. Dingell of Michigan, ranking Democrat on the panel, to retain PUHCA and give FERC more power to punish fraud. The committee rejected 13–31 a separate amendment to strike the provisions giving FERC the power to site power transmission lines on private lands.

LNG terminals. Clarify that FERC, not state agencies, had final authority over the siting of liquefied natural gas (LNG) terminals. The question of whether FERC could override state objections to the sitings was the subject of a lawsuit by the State of California. Many localities had sought to block new LNG terminals over safety concerns, and opponents said the provision would allow FERC to ignore local objections.

Supporters argued that federal law already gave FERC the authority for siting and that the provision was needed to encourage a better investment climate for more natural gas import projects.

Markey failed 18–35 to strike the LNG siting provision during the Energy and Commerce markup.

Nuclear energy. Reauthorize through 2025 the Price-Anderson Act (PL 100-408), which limited nuclear power companies' liability for accidents. *(Nuclear insurance, Congress and the Nation Vol. VII, p. 479)*

Hydrogen. Authorize $4.1 billion over five years for Bush's initiative to develop hydrogen fuel cell cars.

Fuel efficiency. Require the National Highway Traffic Safety Administration (NHTSA) to study the "feasibility and effects" of significantly reducing auto fuel consumption by model year 2014. The study would include alternatives to the existing system of CAFE standards and the effects of new standards on the automobile industry, vehicle safety, and air quality. The NHTSA was responsible for setting corporate average fuel economy standards. The existing standards were 27.5 miles per gallon for passenger cars and 20.7 miles per gallon for light trucks and sport utility vehicles, aka SUVs (22.7 miles per gallon for model year 2007).

The bill would authorize $2 million a year in fiscal 2005 through 2010 for the NHTSA to carry out these studies.

The Energy and Commerce Committee rejected 10–36 an amendment by Markey to require that most cars get thirty-three miles to the gallon by 2014. "People want SUVs," countered Dingell. "This is a mandate with no incentives."

Daylight saving time. Extend daylight saving time by two months, from the first Sunday in March through the last Sunday in November.

HOUSE FLOOR ACTION

The House passed HR 6 on April 21 by a vote of 249–183, with the support of forty-one Democrats.

The House made a number of changes to the bill, but Republicans were able to defeat a handful of high-profile amendments on issues such as ANWR, fuel economy standards, and the siting of LNG terminals. In a move that took GOP leaders by surprise, Capps nearly succeeded in striking the MTBE liability protections.

Bush issued a statement praising the bill as "largely consistent with the key objectives of my comprehensive national energy policy." However, he criticized the tax package, saying he wanted more incentives for renewables and efficiency initiatives.

Democrats called the bill a windfall for the fossil fuel industry that would harm the environment and do little to lower consumer energy costs. They pointed in particular to the fact that the tax cuts were aimed almost entirely at traditional energy sectors and said the bill would shortchange alternative energy and conservation efforts, such as improved fuel efficiency, that were the cheapest and quickest ways to cut costs and reduce oil imports.

Among the dozens of amendments considered during the floor debate, the House:

- Rejected, by a narrow 213–219 vote on April 21, an amendment by Capps to strike the bill's liability protections for MTBE manufacturers. Capps read from a statement by the Congressional Budget Office (CBO) that concluded the waiver would impose an unfunded mandate on state and local governments by blocking them from suing MTBE makers to recover the costs of cleanup. Twenty-five Republicans backed the amendment. The rule for floor debate had denied Capps the right to offer an MTBE amendment, but it did not prohibit an amendment on unfunded mandates.
- Rejected 200–231 on April 20 an attempt by Markey to strike the ANWR drilling provisions.
- Rejected 194–237 on April 21 an amendment by Michael N. Castle, R-Del., to strike the provision giving FERC exclusive authority over the siting of LNG terminals.
- Adopted 259–172 on April 20an amendment by Mike Rogers, R-Mich., to require the Environmental Protection Agency (EPA) to update its test procedure for measuring fuel economy to reflect changed driving habits, such as higher speed limits, faster acceleration, differences between city and highway driving, and air conditioning.
- Rejected 177–254 on April 20 an amendment by Sherwood Boehlert, R-N.Y., to increase CAFE standards to thirty-three miles per gallon for cars manufactured by model year 2015.
- Adopted by voice vote on April 21 an amendment by Harold E. Ford Jr., D-Tenn., to require the EPA to set up a program to encourage the production of efficient hybrid and advanced diesel vehicles and to provide consumer incentives for buying the vehicles. The amendment authorized $300 million per year in fiscal 2006 through 2015 to carry out the program.

SENATE COMMITTEE ACTION

The Senate Energy and Natural Resources Committee gave bipartisan support May 26 to the bulk of the Senate energy bill (S 10), which was assembled by Domenici. The 21–1 vote came at the end of five days of markups over two weeks. The bill was formally reported (S Rept 109-78) on June 9.

The Environment and Public Works Committee had already given voice-vote approval March 16 to a bill (S 606) requiring an increase in renewable fuel production to 6 billion gallons by 2012. The bill also required a halt to the production of MTBE within four years. S 606 was reported (S Rept 109-74) on May 26.

The Finance Committee gave voice-vote approval June 16 to a package of energy tax incentives that focused heavily on renewable fuels, energy efficiency, and conservation. The tax breaks were projected to have a net cost of $14.1 billion over eleven years.

Many committee Democrats thanked Chairman Charles E. Grassley, R-Iowa, for allowing bipartisan input on the bill. "The House bill heavily favors conventional sources of energy, such as oil, gas and electricity," said the ranking Democrat, Max Baucus of Montana. By contrast, he said, the Finance bill provided "a more balanced approach. It provides tax incentives needed to support and develop renewable energy sources." Democrat Charles E. Schumer of New York praised Grassley for how "green" the legislation was, saying the House-passed bill "didn't even seem to be the palest shade of green."

The resulting Senate energy bill included provisions to

Tax provisions. Cut energy taxes by a net $14.1 billion over eleven years. The package included a $4.6 billion extension of a credit for electricity produced from renewable sources, $2.3 billion for a clean-coal tax credit, $3.8 billion for conservation and energy efficiency, $2.6 billion for alternative motor vehicles and fuels, and $2.8 billion for oil and gas producers.

Ethanol. Require refiners to increase the amount of renewable fuels added to gasoline, starting with an annual average volume of 4 billion gallons in 2005, reaching 8 billion gallons in 2012, compared with 5 billion in the House bill. The bill would eliminate the 2 percent oxygen requirement for reformulated gasoline.

Dianne Feinstein, D-Calif., won a 12–10 vote in the Energy and Natural Resources Committee to exempt California from a requirement to use ethanol-blended fuel all year long. The amendment would allow the state to use a different fuel during summer months. Feinstein said the emissions from ethanol could increase as the temperature increases making it less useful for improving air quality during hot weather.

MTBE. Phase out the use of MTBE in fuel within four years and authorize $250 million a year in 2005 through 2008 to help MTBE manufacturers convert their facilities to produce other fuel additives.

Electricity. Repeal PUHCA and replace it with language pushed by Democrats that would give FERC new authority over utility mergers. As in the House version, all mergers of electric utilities and all sales or leases valued in excess of $10 million would have to be approved by FERC. The Senate bill added the requirement that, when approving mergers, the commission consider cross-subsidization and whether it would be harmful to the consumer. In cross-subsidization, one company is charged higher prices so that a second company owned by the same parent company can get a lower rate.

Like the House bill, the measure gave FERC jurisdiction over reliability standards for electricity transmission networks, as well as the authority to issue permits for the construction of new power lines over the objections of states and to use eminent domain to obtain rights-of-way when necessary.

The much-heralded compromise on PUHCA, which had been reached in the Energy and Natural Resources Committee, did not please everyone. "This is an unbelievable expansion of FERC authority," said Richard M. Burr, R-N.C., who joined several other Republicans in urging senators to reconsider the language before a floor vote.

Outer Continental Shelf. Direct the Interior Department to conduct an inventory of oil and natural gas resources on the Outer Continental Shelf and report to Congress within six months of enactment.

After senators warned that any move to encourage offshore drilling could be a "poison pill," Domenici declined to offer an amendment in the Energy and Natural Resources Committee that would allow states to opt out of existing federal moratoriums on offshore drilling that covered most of the country's coastal areas. At the time, new leases were allowed only in parts of the Gulf Coast and off parts of Alaska.

LNG terminals. Give FERC exclusive authority over the siting of LNG terminals.

Hydrogen. Authorize $3.8 billion over five years for Bush's hydrogen initiative.

Nuclear energy. Reauthorize the Price-Anderson Act through 2025.

Energy efficiency. Call for the president to take steps to cut oil consumption by 1 million barrels per day from the 25 million barrels-per-day demand projected for 2015. Democrats applauded the title as stronger than past Republican proposals.

Fuel economy. Authorize $2 million per year in fiscal 2006 through 2010 for NHTSA rulemaking on fuel efficiency and require the agency to report to Congress within a year on the potential impact of significantly increasing fuel efficiency standards for new cars by 2012. The study would include the effects on gasoline supplies, vehicle safety, sales of U.S. vehicles, and air quality.

An amendment by Feinstein to require a 27.5 miles per gallon fuel economy standard by 2011 for light trucks and SUVs was rejected 7–15 in the Energy and Natural Resources Committee. Republicans said the markets were already imposing greater fuel efficiency, pointing to plummeting sales of SUVs in response to high gas prices. They also argued that mandating tougher standards would threaten jobs and force manufacturers to produce lighter vehicles that would be less safe. Democrats cited a federal study showing that in many cases stricter fuel efficiency standards could be achieved by improving transmissions, which would not alter vehicle weight. They also said domestic automakers had been slow to respond to gasoline prices and the need to reduce U.S. dependency on imported oil.

SENATE FLOOR ACTION

The Senate passed HR 6 by 85–12 on June 28, after completing work on it the week before. The bill had more bipartisan support than the House-passed version and was less friendly to oil, natural gas, and coal producers. Senators postponed the battles over ANWR and MTBE for the upcoming conference with the House.

The following were among the key amendments considered.

Renewable energy. The Senate adopted 52–48 on June 16 a proposal by Jeff Bingaman, D-N.M., to establish a "renewable portfolio standard" that would require utilities to generate at least 10 percent of their electricity from renewable energy sources by 2020. Bingaman and Domenici had agreed not to debate the issue in committee because the panel was so divided.

Climate change. Although the Senate cast a relatively strong vote against a detailed proposal to reduce greenhouse gases, the chamber went on record for the first time as recognizing that climate change was a significant problem and endorsing the need for mandatory emission limits.

The Senate also

- Defeated 38–60 on June 22 an amendment by Joseph I. Lieberman, D-Conn., and John McCain, R-Ariz., to cap greenhouse gas emissions at 2000 levels by 2010 using a market-based program to cap overall pollution while allowing businesses to buy and sell permits to meet their obligations. The loss was more decisive than a 43–55 vote in 2003 rejecting similar legislation. However, the 2005 amendment included nuclear energy as an energy source that emits no greenhouse gases. Though the sponsors hoped that would attract more votes, it backfired, angering environmentalists and losing the support of several liberal Democrats.
- Adopted by voice vote a nonbinding sense of the Senate amendment by Bingaman stating that climate change was a problem and endorsing mandatory, market-based measures to "slow, stop and reverse" emissions. The amendment gained support from some senators who said they were ready to acknowledge global warming as a problem but still could not sign on to the mandatory reductions sought by McCain and Lieberman. The amendment was adopted June 22 after a motion to table (kill) it failed on a **key vote of 44–53 (R 42–12; D 2–40; I 0–1).** *(2005 key votes, p. 915)*
- Adopted 66–29 on June 21 an amendment by Chuck Hagel, R-Neb., to create a program of economic incentives—including direct loans, loan guarantees, lines of credit, and production incentive payments—for businesses to reduce emissions of carbon dioxide and other greenhouse gases.
- Rejected 46–49 on June 22 an amendment by John Kerry, D-Mass., calling for the United States to engage actively in international climate change negotiations.

Fuel economy. On the issue of CAFE standards, the Senate

- Adopted 64–31 on June 23 an amendment by Christopher S. Bond, R-Mo., to add several factors to be used in determining CAFE standards, including whether higher standards would divert resources from developing advanced technologies. The amendment also increased the authorization for NHTSA rulemaking to $5 million a year in fiscal 2006 through 2010 and required the agency to issue new fuel economy standards for cars and light trucks within a few years.
- Rejected 28–67 on June 23 a proposal by Richard J. Durbin, D-Ill., to increase fuel economy standards for passenger vehicles to 40 miles per gallon by model year 2016 and for light trucks to 27.5 miles per gallon. The White House said Bush was likely to veto a bill that set specific new CAFE standards.

Energy efficiency. The Senate rejected 47–53 on June 16 an amendment by Maria Cantwell, D-Wash., calling on the president to develop and implement measures to reduce petroleum imports by 40 percent by 2025.

Offshore drilling. Like the House bill, the measure did not seek to lift an existing ban on new federal offshore leases outside parts of the Gulf of Mexico and Alaska. On related issues, the Senate

- Rejected 44–52 on June 21 an amendment by Republican Mel Martinez and Democrat Bill Nelson, both of Florida, to strike the provision authorizing an inventory of offshore oil and natural gas resources.
- Adopted an amendment by Democrat Mary L. Landrieu and Republican David Vitter, both of Louisiana, to direct $1 billion over four years in federal oil and natural gas royalties to six states that allowed drilling along qualifying parts of their coastlines. Budget Committee Chairman Judd Gregg, R-N.H., said the amendment would create an entitlement program, but the Senate voted 69–26 on June 23 to waive Gregg's budget point of order, then adopted the $1 billion coastal assistance program by voice vote.

LNG terminals. The Senate voted 52–45 on June 22 to table an amendment by Feinstein that would have given states more authority in decisions to site LNG import facilities along their coasts.

CONFERENCE, FINAL ACTION

The House-Senate conference on HR 6 began July 14 and concluded July 26. The House on July 28 adopted the conference report (H Rept 109-190) on a **key vote of 275–156 (R 200–31; D 75–124; I 0–1)**, and the Senate cleared the bill the next day on a **key vote of 74–26 (R 49–6; D 25–19; I 0–1)**. *(2005 key votes, p. 915)*

Negotiations before and during conference contrasted sharply with the bitter partisanship of years past, when Republican leaders such as Billy Tauzin of Louisiana, Barton's predecessor as chairman of the House committee, and Frank H. Murkowski of Alaska, who preceded Domenici at the helm of the Senate panel, tried to force the legislation through. When Democrats briefly regained control of the Senate in 2001, they tried to rewrite the bill to their liking.

The difference this time, said Michigan Democrat Bart Stupak, a House conferee, was that Republicans "didn't shut us out." A turning point came in a closed-door meeting in June among Barton, Dingell, Domenici, and Bingaman, where Barton pledged to have open discussions and allow input from Democrats. In exchange, the Democrats agreed not to stall the deliberations. Those promises of cooperation played out in a conference that involved intense, lengthy late-night trade-offs but featured an inclusiveness between the parties that had not existed in the 2003 conference. "It's hard to sit there and negotiate when you know you have the votes" to win without the support of Democrats, Barton said. "But if you do that, at the end when it comes to the floor, everybody has a stake in it."

The following were among the main issues resolved by the conferees:

MTBE. A chief obstacle to finishing the bill was removed when Barton and House GOP leaders gave up on the MTBE "safe harbor" provisions. Barton made one final try for a compromise that would have linked liability protection for the manufacturers with the creation of an $11.4 billion industry-government fund to pay to clean up MTBE-contaminated groundwater. But groups representing municipalities and water supplies, as well as senators from states with groundwater contamination, rejected the fund as inadequate. From the other side, the oil and natural gas industry balked at the cost.

Barton succeeded in winning a provision to allow future MTBE-related lawsuits to be moved to federal court. Business groups generally viewed federal courts as less sympathetic to plaintiffs than many state courts.

ANWR. House Republican leaders also agreed to drop the ANWR drilling provisions, which were unlikely to survive a filibuster in the Senate. Drilling supporters thought they had a better chance of winning enactment as part of the budget-reconciliation bill that would be assembled in the fall. Special rules prohibited filibusters on reconciliation bills, which meant the supporters would need only a majority, not the sixty votes required to limit debate. In the end, however, opponents succeeded in blocking the ANWR provisions on both the reconciliation bill (S 1932) and the defense appropriations bill (HR 2863). *(Reconciliation, p. 81; Appropriations, pp. 73, 400)*

Renewable energy. Conferees dropped the Senate's "renewable portfolio standards" that would have required utilities to generate at least 10 percent of their electricity from renewable energy sources.

Climate change. The final bill created a new cabinet-level advisory committee to develop a national climate change policy and promote technologies to reduce greenhouse gas emissions. Conferees dropped the Senate amendment that would have created specific incentives for technologies to reduce greenhouse gases. The sense-of-the-Senate resolution on climate change also was dropped.

Offshore drilling. The final bill retained the Senate's proposal for an inventory of oil and natural gas resources on the Outer Continental Shelf. The bill also authorized reduced royalty payments for deep gas wells leased in shallow waters in parts of the Gulf of Mexico. States that allowed offshore oil and gas production would share $1 billion in mandatory funding for conservation and restoration projects related to coastal drilling.

LNG. Efforts to give states more authority in siting LNG terminals failed. The final bill gave that power to FERC.

Fuel economy. The final bill authorized $3.5 million a year, halfway between the amounts in the House and Senate bills, for NHTSA rulemaking on fuel efficiency standards. It directed the NHTSA to study the potential effects of a significant increase in fuel efficiency standards by model year 2014 on the auto industry, the gasoline supply, and the environment. The study was to include the examination of alternatives to the existing system, as the House wanted. The bill also included the House provision on expanding the factors used in determining fuel efficiency.

Conferees dropped the Senate requirement that the NHTSA issue new car and light truck standards within a few years, as well as the Senate provision requiring that the United States reduce oil consumption by 1 million barrels a day by 2015.

Nuclear energy. Incentives for constructing new nuclear power plants included production tax credits, loan guarantees, insurance against regulatory delays, and extension of the Price-Anderson Act limiting liability. The bill authorized payments of up to $500 million for the first new reactor and up to $250 million for the next four if government delays in licensing caused cost overruns.

The bill directed the Energy Department to establish a Next Generation Nuclear Plant Project to design, build, and operate a nuclear power plant that would generate electricity, hydrogen, or both. The Idaho National Laboratory was named as the lead laboratory, and the bill authorized $1.3 billion for the project in fiscal 2006 through 2015. The House bill proposed $750 million in 2006 through 2010.

Taxes. The $14.6 billion tax package in the final bill provided $2.8 billion in tax benefits for producers of fossil fuels. It had scaled-back versions of several Senate provisions including the $2.7 billion extension of a credit for electricity produced from renewable sources; $1.6 billion in credits for investment in clean-coal facilities, mainly for producing electricity; $1.3 billion in tax breaks for conservation and energy efficiency; and $1.3 billion for alternative motor vehicles and fuels.

The final bill included a new tax credit for purchasing gas-electric hybrid and "lean-burn" diesel-powered cars. The size of the credit would depend on the weight and fuel economy of the specific vehicle. The full credit would be available on sixty thousand cars per manufacturer. The bill also established tax credits for investments in alternative fuel refueling stations and for manufacturers of energy-efficient dishwashers, washing machines, and refrigerators.

Although the tax credits for oil and gas production were significantly less than the House wanted, the industry won a $974 million provision allowing companies to amortize over two years the geological and geophysical costs of oil and gas exploration in the United States.

Most of the $3 billion in revenue that brought the net total for the tax package to $11.5 billion came from reinstating a 5-cents-per-barrel fee on crude oil to fund the Oil Spill Liability Trust Fund. That provision was expected to bring in $2.5 billion over eleven years.

Daylight saving time. The agreement extended daylight saving time by one month, instead of two as the House had wanted. Supporters said a longer extension would save energy and money and reduce crime. Farmers, airlines with international routes, and religious groups concerned about the effect on their prayer schedules objected, as did the National Parent Teacher Association (National PTA), which raised safety concerns about children walking to school in the dark.

PROVISIONS

Following are the main provisions of the energy policy overhaul law (HR 6—PL 109-58) as signed into law by President Bush on Aug. 8, 2005.

Energy Savings, Assistance

Federal energy consumption. The new law required reductions in energy consumed by federal buildings, starting in 2006. By fiscal 2015, agencies were to reduce consumption by 20 percent, relative to 2003 levels. When acquiring new equipment, agencies had to purchase products designated as energy efficient by the Energy Star program or the Federal Energy Management Program.

Energy efficiency standards for new federal buildings would be set by the Energy Department within one year of enactment. The goal was for new buildings to use 30 percent less energy than the current standards. The Interior, Commerce, and Agriculture Departments were required to use hybrid or other energy-efficient vehicles "to the extent practicable."

U.S. Capitol. The architect of the Capitol was required to develop, update, and implement a conservation and management plan for all congressional facilities to meet the same standards as federal buildings. The law authorized a total of $10 million in fiscal 2006 through 2010 for a study to evaluate the energy infrastructure of the Capitol.

Daylight saving time. Daylight saving time would be extended by one month beginning in 2007. The start date would move from the first Sunday in April to the second Sunday of March; the end date would be the first Sunday of November instead of the last Sunday in October. By allowing one more hour of daylight in the evening, lawmakers hoped to reduce energy needed for electric lighting.

The Energy Department was required to report to Congress within nine months on the impact on domestic energy consumption. After reviewing the report, Congress could reinstate daylight saving time to its current schedule.

Weatherization assistance. The law reauthorized the weatherization-assistance program, which provided grants to improve the energy efficiency of low-income homes. It authorized a total of $1.8 billion in fiscal 2006 through 2008 for the purpose.

Low-income home energy assistance program. The law reauthorized the Low-Income Home Energy Assistance Program, which helped low-income consumers pay their energy bills. It authorized a total of $15.3 billion for the program in fiscal 2005 through 2007.

State energy conservation programs. The law authorized a total of $325 million for state energy conservation programs in fiscal 2006 through 2008 and required that states receiving the aid set a goal of reducing energy consumption by 25 percent from 1990 levels by 2012. In addition, a total of $150 million was authorized in fiscal 2006 through 2010 for grants to states to design energy-efficient buildings.

State appliance rebate program. The law authorized a total of $250 million in fiscal 2006 through 2010 to provide matching grants to states that established or had programs to provide rebates to residential consumers for the purchase of Energy Star products.

Commercial products. The law included a number of provisions to increase the energy efficiency of commercial and industrial products, including establishing new standards for commercial refrigerators, freezers, and clothes washers and calling for studies of efficiency requirements for other products.

The General Services Administration was required to conduct a study on the use of intermittent escalators, which used sensors to stop when not in use, and specified procedures to test the energy efficiency of illuminated exit signs, traffic signals, and compact fluorescent lamps.

Energy reduction in public housing. The Department of Housing and Urban Development was directed to develop a strategy for reducing utility expenses through conservation and efficiency in the design and construction of public housing.

Renewable Energy

Resource assessment. The law authorized a total of $50 million in fiscal 2006 through 2010 for the Energy Department to assess domestically available renewable energy resources, such as geothermal, wind, and solar power.

Federal consumption. The government was required to purchase at least 3 percent of its electricity from renewable sources in fiscal 2007, 5 percent in fiscal 2010, and 7.5 percent in fiscal 2013 and beyond. Sources could include solar, wind, biomass, landfill gas, geothermal, municipal solid waste, or new hydroelectric generation capacity achieved from increased efficiency or additions of new capacity at an existing hydroelectric project.

Solar energy in public buildings. The law authorized a total of $250 million in fiscal 2006 through 2010 to enable federal officials to purchase and use solar electric systems in public buildings in an effort to accelerate the commercialization of the technology and reduce federal fossil fuel consumption. Separately, the law authorized $20 million for a solar electric system to be used in the Energy Department's Washington, D.C., headquarters and a total of $50 million in fiscal 2006 through 2010 to evaluate the program.

Consumer rebates. Consumers who installed renewable power energy systems in their homes or small businesses could qualify for a rebate of up to $3,000 per unit. The law authorized a total of $1 billion for the program from fiscal 2006 to 2010.

Sugar-cane ethanol. The law authorized $36 million for an EPA program to demonstrate the production of ethanol from sugar cane. The program was limited to producers in Florida, Louisiana, Texas, and Hawaii.

Biomass grants. The law authorized a total of $550 million in fiscal 2006 through 2016 for grants of up to $500,000 for the use of specific types of biomass materials for purposes such as electricity or fuel.

Geothermal leases. Several provisions in the law were aimed at making geothermal energy more competitive with fossil fuels. While this energy could refer to any form of naturally occurring heat from the ground, steam was currently the most practical and common source used for generating electricity.

The Interior Department was required to hold a competitive lease sale every two years for areas that may produce geothermal energy. If the department received no bids for a specific area, it could hold a noncompetitive lease sale.

Under prior law, the Interior Department could issue geothermal leases on Forest Service land only with the consent of the Agriculture Department. However, there was no common procedure for the Agriculture Department to process such requests. The new law directed the departments to develop coordinated procedures for processing lease applications. The departments also had to establish a program to reduce the backlog of applications for geothermal leases.

Hydroelectric licensing. Under prior law, all applications to operate a hydroelectric facility were reviewed by federal environmental agencies, which could require the applicant to provide specified protections for water and wildlife as a condition for approval. Under the new law, applicants and other interested parties, such as environmental groups or Indian tribes, could offer alternatives to those government conditions. The federal agency had to accept the alternative if it determined that it would provide adequate protection to water and wildlife and that it would cost less to implement than the initial proposed requirement or would result in improved operation of the project. Appeals could be heard by the Federal Energy Regulatory Commission.

Hydroelectric incentives. The law authorized a total of $100 million in fiscal 2006 through 2015 for incentive payments to hydroelectric facilities that began operation within ten years of enactment. Facilities were eligible for a sliding scale of payments, not to exceed $750,000 per year, based on their production.

In addition, a total of $100 million was authorized in fiscal 2006 through 2015 for incentives to existing hydroelectric facilities that improved their efficiency by at least 3 percent. The payments could not exceed 10 percent of the cost of the upgrade, or $750,000.

Oil and Gas

Strategic Petroleum Reserve. The law directed the Energy Department, as soon as practical, to acquire oil to fill the reserve to its full capacity of 1 billion barrels. The department was required to establish guidelines for acquiring crude oil that maximized domestic supply, increased cost-effectiveness, and protected national security.

Natural gas. FERC was given exclusive authority to approve the construction, expansion, or operation of liquefied natural gas terminals. LNG, a compressed form of natural gas, was being shipped increasingly from overseas as demand rose. FERC was directed to consult with state governments about the safety of sites for liquefaction or gasification facilities, but the new law clarified that the federal agency had final siting authority.

FERC could authorize a natural gas company to provide storage facilities for natural gas at market-based rates. The law also increased civil and criminal penalties to $1,000,000, from as low as $5,000, for individuals who knowingly violated laws regarding natural gas.

Hydraulic fracturing. Hydraulic fracturing was the practice of injecting fluids or other agents into the ground to crack open underground areas for oil and gas exploration. The law exempted the practice, which environmentalists maintained contaminated groundwater, from review under the federal Safe Drinking Water Act (PL 93-523). *(1974 law, Congress and the Nation Vol. IV, p. 293)*

In-kind payments. The Interior Department could require companies to pay royalties for drilling on federal lands in the form of oil or gas instead of cash. The department could then sell the oil or gas, transport it, or process it. The department was prohibited from using funds from the sale of in-kind payments for personnel, travel, or other administrative purposes. For each year of fiscal 2006 through 2015 in which the department received in-kind royalty payments, it would have to report to Congress on the methods and impact of taking such payments.

Royalty rate reductions. The law allowed oil and gas companies to pay lower royalty fees for marginal gas and oil wells, or those that produced no more than fifteen barrels per day of oil or gas. It also reduced royalty payments for deep gas wells leased in the shallow waters of the western and central areas of the Gulf of Mexico and for drilling in deep water—more than four hundred meters—of the Gulf. Companies also got royalty breaks for operations in which they injected captured carbon dioxide underground to help produce oil and gas. The practice was seen as a way to reduce emissions of the greenhouse gas.

Orphan wells. Orphan wells were abandoned or capped wells that had no identifiable entity legally responsible for them or financially able to reclaim them. The Interior Department, in cooperation with the Agriculture Department, was required to establish a program to remediate, reclaim, and close orphaned wells located on public lands. The Energy Department would provide technical and financial assistance to states to address orphan wells on state or private land. For the various orphan well provisions, the measure authorized a total of $125 million in fiscal 2006 through 2010, of which $25 million had to be dedicated to assisting those who leased federal land for remediating and closing orphan wells on the property.

Outer Continental Shelf. The Interior Department was authorized to conduct an inventory of oil and natural gas resources in the Outer Continental Shelf, a federally controlled area that in most states began three miles offshore. The bill did not authorize new oil or gas production in parts of the Outer Continental Shelf where such production was currently prohibited, such as off the California and Florida coasts.

Permits for federal lands. The law called for federal agencies to speed up and better coordinate the permitting process for oil and gas development on federal lands, in some cases setting specific deadlines by which decisions on applications must be made. It also called for agencies to designate corridors for infrastructure such as pipelines and electricity transmission lines.

Coastal impact assistance zones. States that allowed offshore production of oil and gas—a handful of Gulf states as well as Alaska—would share a total of $1 billion in fiscal 2007 through 2010 for conservation, protection, or restoration projects that addressed the impacts of coastal drilling. The money was not subject to appropriations.

Great Lakes and Finger Lakes. Oil or gas drilling was prohibited under any of the Great Lakes or Finger Lakes.

Refinery revitalization. In an effort to address the need for new U.S. refinery capacity, the law authorized the EPA, at the request of a governor, to establish a streamlined permit process that would coordinate state and federal processes.

National Petroleum Reserve. The law directed the Interior Department to begin oil and gas exploration in the National Petroleum Reserve, which covered more than 23 million acres of public land on Alaska's North Slope. The oil and gas leases, issued by means of competitive bidding, would be for ten years.

Coal

Clean-coal initiative. The clean-coal technology program, co-funded by the government and industry, was aimed at developing clean-coal technologies that reduced pollutants such as carbon dioxide, mercury, and sulfur dioxide by specified amounts. The law authorized a total of $1.8 billion in fiscal 2006 through 2014 for the project; 70 percent of the funding was to be used for gasification technology.

The law authorized funds for an experimental clean-coal plant, created grants to universities to establish clean-coal centers for excellence that would demonstrate new technologies for reducing pollution from coal, and authorized loan guarantees for projects to cleanly produce energy from coal. It authorized a demonstration project to produce energy from coal mined in the Western United States and a program to evaluate the potential of advanced technology to produce energy from Illinois basin coal.

Clean air coal program. A new program under the law was designed to encourage the production of power using clean-coal electric-generating equipment.

The law authorized a total of $2.5 billion in fiscal 2007 through 2013 for the Energy Department to provide financial assistance, not to exceed 50 percent of the cost of any project, to aid the production of coal-based power using clean-coal electric-generating equipment that improved energy efficiency or reduced pollution but was not yet competitive. Between 25 percent and 75 percent of these projects had to be for the sole purpose of generating electricity.

The law also authorized a total of $500 million from fiscal 2007 through 2011 for projects at existing coal-based electricity generation plants that used advanced air pollution control equipment and processes. The goal was to reduce air pollution by encouraging industry to voluntarily exceed existing standards.

Coal on federal lands. The law repealed the previous 160-acre cap on coal leases, allowed for advanced payment of royalties from coal mines, and required an assessment of coal resources on federal lands other than national parks.

Indian Tribal Energy Development

Indian energy office. A new Office of Indian Energy Policy and Programs within the Energy Department would coordinate the production of energy resources on Indian reservations.

Incentives. A new Indian energy resource development program to be created within the Interior Department would provide grants and low-interest loans to tribes to develop energy resources. The Energy Department was authorized to provide loan guarantees—not to exceed a total of $2 billion at any given time—to spur energy production on reservations. Federal agencies purchasing energy could give preference to Indian-produced resources, as long as the cost did not exceed the market price.

Development agreements, leases. The law established guidelines allowing tribes to enter into business agreements or grant leases or rights-of-way expressly for the purpose of energy development or transmission. Specifically, tribes could submit an application to the Interior Department to enter into an energy-resource agreement with a separate entity. If the agreement was approved, the tribe could negotiate leases or other business deals related to energy on tribal lands without federal approval. Tribes were also allowed to grant leases or rights-of-way without federal approval if the terms did not exceed thirty years.

Nuclear Power

The law extended until 2025 the Price-Anderson Act, which limited nuclear power companies' liability for accidents and required companies to purchase insurance coverage up to a certain amount—currently about $10 billion. The federal government would be responsible for damages in excess of the cap, which was adjusted periodically.

The extension applied to new plants; coverage for existing plants would have continued even if the law were allowed to expire. Federal protection was considered necessary to encourage new nuclear power.

Antitrust review. The law eliminated a previous requirement that a company's application to the Nuclear Regulatory Commission (NRC) to build or operate a nuclear plant be reviewed by the U.S. attorney general for antitrust concerns.

Whistleblowers. The law expanded whistleblower protections to federal contractors and subcontractors who worked in nuclear energy.

Export of uranium for medical purposes. Under certain conditions, the legislation allowed the export of highly enriched uranium to Canada, Belgium, France, Germany, and the Netherlands for the production of medical isotopes.

Export controls. The law barred the sale, export, or transfer of nuclear materials and "sensitive nuclear technology" to any nation the State Department identified as a state sponsor of terrorist activities. The president could waive the ban if such a sale was vital to national security or if the State Department certified that the country had not encouraged international proliferation of nuclear weapons within the previous twelve months.

Hydrogen production at nuclear plants. The law authorized $100 million for the Energy Department to establish two projects to demonstrate commercial production of hydrogen at nuclear plants.

Federal insurance for permitting delays. A company that built a new advanced nuclear reactor would be reimbursed for costs resulting from delays—for example, if the NRC missed schedules or deadlines or if litigation postponed completion of a project. The first two advanced reactors starting construction would be eligible for full reimbursement of such costs, up to $500 million each, and the next four would be covered for 50 percent of the costs, up to $250 million each.

Next Generation nuclear plant project. The law authorized $1.25 billion through 2015 and unspecified sums from fiscal 2016 through 2021 to develop a prototype Next Generation nuclear power plant by Sept. 30, 2021. The program was to be administered by the Energy Department.

Radiation source protection. The law imposed new restrictions on the import and export of radioactive materials and called on the NRC to establish a new tracking system for shipments of radioactive materials in the United States. It also called for a task force that would report to Congress periodically with recommendations for new regulations or legislation regarding radioactive materials.

Reactor security. The law called for the NRC at least every three years to evaluate the security procedures at nuclear plants and the ability of their private security forces to defend against threats. The NRC also was instructed to study and possibly revise regulations regarding threats to nuclear plants, taking into account suicide attacks, water- and air-based threats, and the potential for attacks on spent fuel shipments.

Before issuing a license for a nuclear power plant, the NRC must consult with the Department of Homeland Security regarding the vulnerability of the proposed location to terrorist attack. Nuclear power companies were required to fingerprint and conduct more extensive background checks on employees who have access to sensitive areas. The law also clarified that security forces at nuclear facilities could carry certain firearms regardless of state laws restricting the firearms that could be used by private security forces.

Vehicles and Fuels

Hybrid vehicles. The Energy Department was directed to create a program to encourage domestic production and sales of efficient hybrid and advanced diesel vehicles and was authorized to make grants to domestic automakers for this purpose.

The law also authorized $40 million for a new grant program to encourage the development of technologies for commercially viable hybrid or flexible fuel-cell vehicles. These cars would need to have a range of at least 250 miles, consume greatly reduced amounts of petroleum, and have commercial sales potential within five years.

State and local programs. A pilot program, to be administered through the Energy Department's Clean Cities Program, was to provide up to thirty geographically dispersed grants to states, local governments, or metropolitan transport authorities to acquire alternative-fueled passenger vehicles, motorized two-wheel bicycles, buses, delivery vehicles, and airport ground-support vehicles. Along with purchasing vehicles, the money could be used for infrastructure, operations, and maintenance costs. The law authorized $200 million for the program, with the restriction that the federal money could make up no more than 50 percent of a specific project's cost. Individual applicants were limited to a maximum grant of $15 million.

Fuel-cell transit bus initiative. The Energy and Transportation Departments were directed to create a demonstration program that would award competitive grants to five local projects involving the use of up to twenty-five fuel-cell buses. The law authorized a total of $50 million in fiscal 2006 through 2010 for the program.

Clean School Bus grants. The EPA and the Energy Department were directed to establish a Clean School Bus program to help replace school buses manufactured prior to 1977 with alternative-fueled school buses—those using natural gas, hydrogen, propane, methanol, ethanol, or ultra-low-sulfur diesel. The grants could also be used to retrofit buses manufactured before 1991 with new, more efficient fuel technology. The program would pay up to 50 percent of the cost of a new bus or up to 100 percent of the cost of a retrofit. The law authorized a total of $110 million in fiscal 2006 and 2007 and unspecified sums through 2010 for the program.

The legislation also authorized a total of $25 million in fiscal 2006 through 2009 for the Energy Department to cooperate with school bus companies in developing fuel-cell buses.

Diesel trucks. The EPA and Energy Department were directed to create a similar program of grants to public agencies for retrofitting and modernizing diesel truck fleets, with the goal of reducing emissions. A total of $100 million was authorized in fiscal 2006 through 2008.

Railroad efficiency. The law called for a partnership among the Energy and Transportation Departments, the EPA, the railroad industry, and locomotive manufacturers to develop train technologies that increased fuel economy, reduced emissions, and lowered costs. It authorized a total of $65 million in fiscal 2006 through 2008 for the program.

Aviation fuel and emissions. The Energy Department and the National Aeronautics and Space Administration (NASA) were directed to enter into a partnership to develop "ultra-efficient" engine technology for aircraft. The law authorized a total of $250 million in fiscal 2006 through 2010 for the project.

Promoting bicycling. The law authorized $6.2 million for a new Conserve by Bicycling program that would involve ten geographically diverse pilot projects designed to encourage bicycling to reduce the use of fuels.

Automobile fuel efficiency. The law authorized $17.5 million annually in fiscal 2006 through 2010 for the National Highway Traffic Safety Administration to enforce existing corporate average fuel economy standards. Existing law required automobile manufacturers to produce a product line with an average fuel economy of 27.5 miles per gallon for cars and a 20.7 miles per gallon average for light trucks. The measure did not require an increase in vehicle fuel economy.

The NHTSA was required to study the feasibility and potential effects of reducing fuel consumption for the model year 2014. The study, to be completed within one year, was to include consideration of alternatives to current CAFE standards, safety effects of greater efficiency, and the impact on the automobile industry.

Federal procurement of fuel-cell technology. Federal departments were required to begin using fuel-cell technologies within specific time frames. The law authorized a total of $105 million from fiscal 2008 through 2010, and unspecified sums through 2015, for the purchase of fuel-cell vehicles or hydrogen energy systems by 2010. It also authorized a total of $345 million in fiscal 2006 through 2010, and unspecified sums through 2015, for the purchase of stationary, portable, or microfuel cells for electricity generation by 2006.

Diesel emissions. The law authorized a total of $1 billion in fiscal 2007 through 2011 for an EPA program aimed at reducing diesel emissions. The money would go toward grants and low-interest loans to government agencies and nonprofit organizations for new engine configurations in truck fleets.

Hydrogen

Several provisions were aimed at developing technologies for producing hydrogen to be used as fuel with a goal of getting a commitment from automakers to offer hydrogen fuel-cell vehicles no later than 2015.

To ensure hydrogen production, storage, and distribution, the law authorized a total of $1.1 billion in fiscal 2006 through 2010 and unspecified sums through 2020.

To fund a limited number of Energy Department demonstration projects using hydrogen, the law authorized a total of $1.3 billion in fiscal 2006 through 2010 and unspecified sums through 2020.

It also directed the Energy Department to provide grants or enter into contracts to develop safety codes and standards for fuel-cell vehicles and other hydrogen energy systems.

Research and Development

The law authorized billions of dollars for research and development programs to be administered by the Energy Department. The stated goal was to increase energy efficiency in all sectors, diversify energy supplies, reduce U.S. dependence on foreign energy sources, improve U.S. energy security, and reduce the environmental impact of energy production. The authorizations included

Energy efficiency. A total of $2.8 billion in fiscal 2007 through 2013 for research on a range of topics, such as improved lighting and building efficiency.

Distributed energy and electric energy systems. A total of $768 million in fiscal 2007 through 2009 for research in fields such as reliable electricity transmission and the efficient cooling of electronics.

Renewable energy. A total of $2.2 billion in fiscal 2007 through 2009 for research on renewable energy technologies such as wind, solar, and geothermal power.

Agricultural biomass. A total of $2 billion in fiscal 2006 through 2015 for research on biofuels made from organic matter such as plants and agricultural byproducts, with additional authorizations for specific programs.

Nuclear power. A total of $2.3 billion in fiscal 2007 through 2009 for new technologies and programs to encourage the expansion of nuclear power—such as the Bush administration's Nuclear Power 2010 program, which aimed to build a new U.S. nuclear power plant by 2010.

Fossil energy. A total of nearly $1.9 billion in fiscal 2007 through 2009 for research activities involving fossil fuels. Much of the money was for coal research, including methods for improving existing plants and new technologies such as gasification and sequestration, in which coal is converted into a gas and carbon is removed. Oil and gas development technologies, including methods for maximizing production from low-volume wells, were also to get a significant share of the funds. An additional $155 million was authorized for methane hydrate research and development. The Office of Arctic Energy was to get extended funding of $25 million per year in 2010 through 2012.

Science. A total of $14 billion in fiscal 2007 through 2009 for energy-related research in fields such as physics, biology, and environmental science, with additional funds for specific projects such as the rare isotope accelerator and the Spallation Neutron Source project.

International cooperation. A total of $6 million in fiscal 2007 through 2010 for international energy training and outreach. The law also authorized a total of $39 million in 2007 through 2009 to promote international cooperation on energy issues, with university participation. A sense-of-Congress clause urged cooperation with Israel.

Ultra-deep-water oil and gas. A total of $550 million in direct spending in fiscal 2007 through 2017 for grants to encourage unconventional and new technologies in oil and gas exploration, such as ultra-deep-water drilling. The grants would be awarded to a private consortium selected by the Energy Department. In addition, the law authorized the appropriation of a total of $1 billion in fiscal 2007 to 2016.

Energy Department Management, Training

To improve Energy Department management, the law called for a new technology transfer coordinator to advise the department in transferring its work to the private sector and included a sense of Congress clause directing the department to develop more stringent procurement and inventory controls.

The law authorized a total of $60 million in fiscal 2006 through 2008 for the department to monitor workforce trends and establish training programs as necessary. It also called for the department to establish educational programs in science and math, including programs to promote professional development for teachers.

Electricity

Reliability standards. The law called for new mandatory reliability standards for electricity transmission networks and gave FERC jurisdiction to oversee and enforce them. FERC would certify electric reliability organizations (EROs) and grant them authority to create and enforce the standards. EROs would have to file reliability standards and any other changes with FERC, which could then approve or disapprove the standards.

All operators of bulk-electric power-generating systems were required to comply with the standards, which were to be designed to limit instability and cascading failures. EROs would have the authority to enforce penalties on any bulk-power operators that violate the standards. The measure also allowed FERC to impose penalties if it found violations.

Alaska and Hawaii were exempted from the provision.

Transmission facility siting. The Energy Department was directed to study congestion in the nation's electricity transmission system and designate troubled areas as "national interest" corridors. FERC would have new "backstop" authority to issue construction permits for transmission facilities in such corridors under certain conditions—for example, if FERC determined that the facility was in the public interest but a state commission withheld approval.

Under certain conditions, electric companies could petition in district court for eminent domain to acquire right-of-way property for transmission facilities.

When the proposed power line was to be on federal property, the Energy Department would be designated as the lead agency in coordinating all related federal authorizations. The department was responsible for producing a single environmental review to be used in all federal proceedings. In most cases, final permitting decisions must be made within one year, and federal agencies were required to communicate with applicants within sixty days on the likelihood of approval and key issues of concern.

If a permit was denied, the applicant had the right to appeal to the White House, which could overturn agency decisions.

The measure authorized an internal review of existing rights-of-way on federal lands, including specifics about the status and time frame for individual applications. It also directed federal agencies involved in permitting transmission facilities to agree within one year to take steps to ensure "timely and coordinated" reviews of applications.

Transmission rates and incentives. The Energy Department was authorized to establish an Advanced Power System Technology Incentive Program to provide incentive payments for utilities to employ new technologies to ensure reliability and efficiency and thereby reduce the cost of power. A total of $70 million was authorized in fiscal 2006 through 2012 for the payments, which were to be based on kilowatt-hours generated.

FERC was directed to establish incentive-based rates for interstate electricity transmission by public utilities within one year of enactment. This provision was intended to promote investment in electric transmission networks and technologies to ensure reliability. Additional incentives would be provided for participation in regional transmission organizations.

FERC could require any utility company that transmitted electricity in multiple states to provide transmission services at rates comparable to the rates the utility company charged itself. FERC could exempt companies that sold fewer than four million megawatt hours of electricity per year or did not operate a large-scale transmission system.

Electricity metering. The law required utilities to provide "net-metering" upon request to customers that used their own on-site power sources, such as solar panels or wind turbines. The metering would allow the electricity to be better accounted for on the customers' bills.

The electric utilities must provide customers, at their request, with "smart-metering" service, giving customers a real-time schedule showing how the rates vary by the time of day, according to changes in wholesale power costs. The intent of the provision, which would take effect within eighteen months of enactment, was to enable customers to manage energy use and cost by reducing demand during peak times.

The Energy Department was directed to educate consumers about the availability and benefits of advanced metering and to work with states and energy companies to develop the smart-metering technologies.

PUHCA repeal. The law repealed the 1935 Public Utility Holding Company Act, which restricted the ownership and operations of power companies and their ability to control energy prices. It replaced PUHCA with provisions designed to provide disclosure of power company finances. Specifically, it gave FERC—and, to a lesser extent, state authorities—the power to examine all relevant books, records, accounts, and memorandums belonging to a company that owned or partly owned a power facility to ensure that costs were allocated fairly to public utilities.

All sales or leases of facilities valued in excess of $10 million and all mergers must be approved by FERC.

Market transparency rules. FERC was to establish rules to provide the public and the government with information to facilitate price transparency and participation in electricity markets. The rules must provide for the distribution of timely information about wholesale electric energy prices and transmission. The information was to be available to federal agencies, buyers and sellers of wholesale electricity, and the public. FERC must ensure that the disclosure of information would not harm the energy market or consumers.

The law also dramatically increased criminal penalties for market manipulation.

Energy Independence

United States Commission on North American Energy Freedom. The law established a commission of sixteen members appointed by the president to develop a comprehensive national policy for achieving North American energy independence by 2025. The law authorized

$10 million over two years for the commission, which was scheduled to be appointed within sixty days of the bill's enactment and to submit its report within one year.

Ethanol and Motor Fuels

Renewable fuels mandate. Fuel refiners were required to roughly double the amount of biofuels used in the United States by 2012. The provision was most likely to result in the production of corn-based ethanol but also could include fuels derived from sewage waste, landfill, or other organic matter. The annual average volume of renewable fuel was to increase incrementally, starting at 4 billion gallons in 2006 and reaching 7.5 billion gallons in 2012.

The EPA, in consultation with the Energy and Agriculture Departments, could reduce or waive the requirement for a state, upon request. The requirement could be waived if it was determined that the mandate would have a significant adverse economic or environmental impact on the state or region or that the renewable fuel supply or distribution capacity was inadequate to meet the requirement. Any waiver granted would last one year but would be renewable. The Energy Department also could waive the requirement if it determined that the mandate would impose an economic hardship on a refinery.

The Federal Trade Commission was required to conduct an analysis within 180 days of enactment of the market concentration of ethanol and determine whether enough industry competition existed to avoid price-setting or other anticompetitive behavior.

Methyl tertiary butyl ether. MTBE was an oxygenate additive that produced cleaner-burning gasoline but had contaminated drinking water in communities across the country. A provision that would have provided limited liability protection to producers of MTBE was dropped, but the law allowed any future lawsuits to be moved to federal district court.

Oxygenate requirement. The law eliminated a 1990 requirement that reformulated gasoline contain at least 2 percent oxygen by weight, while calling for the EPA to establish standards to reduce toxic air pollutants from gasoline with fuel additives. It also required the EPA to study the public health and environmental impacts of potential MTBE substitutes, including ethanol. Refiners had met the requirement by using more oxygenates, primarily MTBE but also ethanol, and MTBE producers had cited the requirement in defending themselves against lawsuits.

Market study. The law called for the EPA and Energy Department to conduct a study of the wide variety of federal, state, and local fuel requirements, including their effect on market supply, consumer prices, environmental goals, and industry practices.

Incentives. The law authorized various grants and loan guarantees aimed at encouraging demonstration projects for the production of alternative fuels from sources such as biomass or sugar cane. Authorizations included

- A total of $650 million in fiscal 2006 and 2007 to provide grants for the construction of plants that produce cellulosic biomass ethanol from agricultural residues or municipal solid waste.
- A total of $750 million in fiscal 2006 through 2008 for the production of ethanol and other renewable fuels derived from agricultural residues, wood residues, municipal solid waste, or agricultural byproducts.
- A total of $550 million in fiscal 2005 through 2009 for the EPA to fund demonstration projects of advanced biofuel technologies.

Underground storage tanks. The Leaking Underground Storage Tank (LUST) Trust Fund was a federal program created by Congress in 1986 (PL 99-499) to finance the cleanup of sites where underground storage tanks had leaked petroleum or other hazardous substances. The fund was financed through a 0.1-cent-per-gallon tax on motor vehicle fuel sold in the United States. *(1986 law, Congress and the Nation Vol. VII, p. 421)*

The law required the EPA to distribute at least 80 percent of the available funds each year to participating states for cleanup of hazardous sites or for enforcement activities. The remaining money—up to 20 percent of available funds—could be used to enforce regulations related to leaking storage tanks.

The measure required extra leak-containment standards for underground tanks that were installed or replaced within 1,000 feet of a community drinking water system or a potable drinking water well. It required manufacturers and installers of underground storage tanks to maintain evidence of financial responsibility to cover the costs of faulty manufacture or installation, and it required more frequent inspections.

The law authorized a total of $3 billion in fiscal 2005 through 2009 for the LUST fund and related activities.

Boutique fuels. The EPA could waive individual state fuel-blending requirements for up to twenty days in "extreme and unusual" supply circumstances. The law also capped the number of special fuel blends, known as boutique fuels, that states could require at the number that existed on Sept. 1, 2004.

Climate Change

Advisory committee. The law created a new Climate Change Technology Advisory Committee to coordinate federal activities and studies related to climate change to develop a national strategy to promote technologies for reducing greenhouse gas emissions. The law did not mandate specific reductions in such emissions.

The president was to appoint at least seven members to the committee, including the secretaries of commerce, agriculture, and transportation and the EPA administrator. Within eighteen months of enactment, the committee was to submit to the president and Congress a plan to reduce greenhouse gas emissions through commercial technologies.

Federal coordination. A new Climate Change Technology Program would assist the committee by coordinating federal research and development efforts. The Energy Department could authorize demonstration projects relating to emissions-reducing technology.

Foreign policy. The law directed the State Department to devise a policy to help developing countries reduce their greenhouse gas emissions. The department was required to report to Congress within 180 days of enactment on twenty-five developing countries that emit such gases. The department was to provide assistance in the form of bilateral agreements, private investments, or the export of technologies that reduced greenhouse gases.

Incentives for Innovative Technologies

Loan guarantees. Under a new Energy Department program, the federal government was authorized to provide loan guarantees for up to 80 percent of the cost of approved energy facilities. Projects eligible for the loan guarantees included renewable energy, advanced fossil energy, hydrogen fuel cells, advanced nuclear, carbon capture and sequestration, efficient electricity generation and distribution, production facilities for fuel-efficient vehicles, pollution control equipment, and refineries.

Studies

The law called for federal agencies to study a variety of energy-related issues and submit reports to Congress. Topics included oil and natural gas storage capacity and inventory, energy efficiency standards, telecommuting, the Low-Income Home Energy Assistance Program, oil bypass filtration technology, total integrated thermal systems, energy integration with Latin America, low-volume gas reservoir, gasoline markets and prices, progress on the Alaska natural gas pipeline, coal-bed methane, backup fuel capacity for industrial and power-generation facilities, Indian land rights-of-way, mobility of federal science and technology personnel, competition in the wholesale and retail electricity markets, rapid electrical grid restoration, distributed generation of electricity, natural gas supply shortage, hydrogen participation and employment, best management practices for the Energy Department, effect of electrical contaminant on energy production, alternative fuels, excessive charges for electricity, fuel-cell and hydrogen technology, links between energy security and increases in vehicle-miles traveled, cumulative impacts of offshore liquefied natural gas facilities, energy- and water-saving measures in congressional buildings, availability of skilled workers for energy and mineral security, impacts of the Energy Policy Act of 1992, benefits of utilities' economic dispatch, renewable energy on federal land, increased hydroelectric generation at existing federal facilities, split-estate federal oil and gas leasing and development practices, federal resource development conflicts in the Powder River Basin, national security review of international energy requirements, used oil refining, transmission system monitoring, and potential hydropower facilities.

Federal Revenue Impact

Congress's Joint Committee on Taxation estimated that the new law would provide $14.6 billion in tax reductions and $3 billion in revenue increases, for a net reduction in federal revenues of $11.5 billion over the eleven-year period of fiscal 2005 through 2015. All cost and revenue estimates were according to the committee.

Production and Supply Incentives

Clean-coal technology credit. The law provided a 20 percent tax credit for the use of integrated gasification combined cycle (IGCC) generation technologies. It provided a 15 percent tax credit for other advanced clean-coal projects producing electricity and a 15 percent credit for certain industrial gasification projects that converted coal, petroleum residue, biomass, or other materials recovered for their energy or feedstock value into a gas composed primarily of carbon monoxide and hydrogen for direct use or subsequent chemical or physical conversion. The Treasury secretary was directed to allocate up to $800 million in credits to IGCC projects, up to $500 million in credits for other advanced clean-coal projects, and up to $350 million in credits to industrial gasification projects. (Cost: $1.6 billion over eleven years)

Depreciation of electricity transmission property. The law reduced the depreciation period for property used in the transmission of electricity for sale and related land improvements from twenty years to fifteen years. The provision was effective for property placed in service after April 11, 2005. (Cost: $1.2 billion over eleven years)

Production credit for wind energy and biomass electricity. The tax credit allowed for the production of electricity from renewable resources was extended for two years and modified for certain facilities. Specifically, the placed-in-service date was extended through 2007 for "closed-loop" biomass produced from plants grown specifically to produce electricity, "open-loop" biomass (including agricultural livestock waste nutrients) facilities, geothermal energy facilities, small irrigation power facilities, landfill gas facilities, and trash-combustion facilities. The placed-in-service dates for solar energy facilities, which were to expire Dec. 31, 2005, and refined coal facilities, which were to expire Dec. 31, 2008, were not extended.

Eligibility for the tax credit was to include electricity from hydropower and Indian coal. The credit was extended for ten years for all renewable electricity sources under this provision, except Indian coal. The credit for Indian coal was available for seven years, beginning in 2006.

The credit was indexed for inflation and for 2005 was 0.9 cents per kilowatt-hour for open-loop biomass, small irrigation power facilities, landfill gas facilities, and trash-combustion facilities and 1.9 cents per kilowatt-hour for all other qualified renewable electricity.

The credit for wind and closed-loop biomass facilities placed in service by the end of 2005 was available for a ten-year period. The amount of the credit that may be claimed was phased out as the market price of electricity exceeded certain threshold levels. The credit was available for five years for the remaining facilities. The credit for refined coal in 2005 was $5.481 per ton and was available for ten years.

The agreement also permitted agricultural cooperatives to pass any portion of the credit through to their members.

Amortization for pollution control facilities in older plants. Electric generation plants opened after 1975 could write off the cost of certified air pollution control facilities—but not water pollution control facilities—over a five-year period. The law provided a seven-year amortization period for air pollution control facilities used in connection with electric generation plants that were primarily coal-fired and placed in service after 1975.

Until the passage of the law, the only electricity generation plants that could amortize the cost of certain air pollution control facilities over a five-year period were those placed in service before Jan. 1, 1976. A "certified pollution control facility" was defined as a treatment facility that controls water or air pollution and that did not lead to a significant increase in output or capacity, to an extension of the useful life, to a reduction in total operating costs for the plant, or to an alteration in the nature of the manufacturing production process. (Cost: $1.1 billion over eleven years)

Nuclear decommissioning costs. The law modified the tax rules governing the cost of decommissioning nuclear power plants. It repealed a "cost of service" requirement that previously limited the deductibility of contributions made by nuclear power plant owners to independent trust funds for the decommissioning of nuclear plants when they are retired. Under the law, regulated and unregulated contributors would qualify for the deduction.

A rule that prohibited these trust funds from accumulating more reserves than were needed to pay for decommissioning costs incurred after 1984 was also repealed. The law allowed the trust funds to accumulate amounts sufficient to cover the present value of 100 percent of the estimated decommissioning costs. The provisions would be effective beginning in 2006. (Cost: $1.3 billion over eleven years)

Clean renewable energy bonds. The law allowed a tax credit to holders of Clean Renewable Energy Bonds for bonds purchased before Dec. 31, 2007. (Cost: $411 million over eleven years)

Income for rural electric cooperatives. The law made permanent recent changes designed to allow rural electric cooperatives to earn income from certain transactions with nonmembers of the cooperative tax-free. Cooperatives had been exempt from federal taxes as long as 85 percent of their annual income came from members of the cooperative. (Cost: $277 million over eleven years)

Credit for production from advanced nuclear power facilities. A tax credit was created for electricity produced at advanced nuclear power facilities. A credit of 1.8 cents per kilowatt-hour would be allowed during the eight-year period beginning on the date the facility was placed in service. An advanced nuclear facility was defined as such if the reactor design was approved by the Nuclear Regulatory Commission after 1993 and placed in service by 2021. The total credit that could be claimed was subject to certain limitations. (Cost: $278 million over eleven years)

Operating loss carryover for certain electric utility companies. The law extended for five years the net operating loss (NOL) carryback period for taxable years 2003 through 2005 for certain electric utility companies. In general, the NOL—the amount by which a taxpayer's allowable deductions exceeded gross income—could be carried back two years, or carried forward 20 years, to offset taxable income in those years.

Under the extension, refunds could be claimed only through 2008, and the amount of the NOL was limited to 20 percent of combined qualifying investment in transmission and pollution control equipment.

Domestic Fossil Fuel

Nonconventional fuel production credit. The law made the credit for producing fuel from an unconventional source—such as oil produced from shale and tar sands—part of the general business credit. The credit was equal to $3 per barrel, or British thermal unit (BTU) oil barrel equivalent, adjusted for inflation. Unused credits could be carried back one year or carried forward up to twenty years. The provision was effective beginning in 2006, but no carryback of unused credits was permitted for taxes paid prior to 2006. The credit is set to expire in 2007. The law also allowed a production credit for facilities that produce coke or coke gas. (Cost: $101 million over eleven years)

Expensing equipment for refining liquid fuels. Certain businesses were allowed to deduct 50 percent of the cost of liquid fuel refining equipment in the year the equipment was bought. The other 50 percent of the cost could be written off over a ten-year period, as was the case for all such costs before enactment. The new deduction applied to equipment placed in use after enactment and before 2012. (Cost: $406 million over eleven years)

Depreciation of natural gas pipelines. The law decreased the recovery, or depreciation, period for natural gas distribution pipelines from twenty years to fifteen years. The provision applied to gas lines placed in service after April 11, 2005, and expired at the end of 2010. A seven-year depreciation period was allowed for natural gas-gathering lines. The allowable amount of depreciation could not be reduced by the alternative minimum tax. (Cost: $1 billion over eleven years)

Natural gas prepayment exempt from arbitrage rules. The measure exempted from arbitrage rules certain bond-financed prepayments by public utilities for natural gas, by creating an exception to the general rule that tax-exempt, bond-financed prepayments violate the arbitrage restrictions. (Cost: $53 million over eleven years)

Geological and geophysical expenses. Companies could amortize geological and geophysical costs incurred in connection with oil and gas exploration in the United States over two years. Previously, geological and geophysical costs were not deductible as ordinary business expenses in the year they occurred. (Cost: $974 million over eleven years)

Small oil and gas producers. The law allowed more small oil and gas producers to take advantage of special tax breaks by changing the definition of "independent producer" from a producer that refines no more than 50,000 barrels a day to one that produces no more than 75,000 barrels a day. It allowed the limit to be calculated on a yearly average basis, instead of on a daily basis as under prior law. (Cost: $158 million over eleven years)

Conservation and Other Provisions

Deduction for energy-efficient commercial buildings. The measure created a deduction for energy-efficient commercial buildings that met a 50 percent energy reduction standard. The maximum deduction was $1.80 per square foot of the building. The law also allowed a 60-cents-per-square-foot deduction for building subsystems. The provision was effective beginning in 2006 and applied to property placed in service before 2008. (Cost: $243 million over eleven years)

Business credit for construction of energy-efficient homes. As part of the business tax credit, the law established a credit to contractors for the construction of new energy-efficient homes. Contractors could claim a $1,000 credit for construction that reduced energy consumption by 30 percent for manufactured homes or $2,000 for homes with construction that reduced energy consumption by 50 percent. The provision applied to homes whose construction was "substantially" completed after 2005 and which were purchased prior to 2008. (Cost: $28 million over eleven years)

Credit for improving energy efficiency. The law established a 10 percent tax credit for the cost of certain energy-efficient improvements to existing homes, including improvements to insulation. It created credits of up to $50 for the purchase of advanced main air-circulating fans and up to $150 for natural gas, propane, or oil furnaces or hot water boilers. The credit applied to improvements made in 2006 and 2007. (Cost: $556 million over three years)

Credit for energy-efficient appliances. A manufacturer tax credit was allowed for certain energy-efficient clothes washers, dishwashers, and refrigerators. The amount of the credit depended on the appliance and its energy efficiency. The provision applied to appliances produced in 2006 and 2007. The manufacturer could not claim credits in excess of $75 million for all taxable years. (Cost: $180 million over two years)

Credit for energy-efficient equipment. The law established a nonrefundable 30 percent tax credit for the purchase of certain solar water-heating equipment, photovoltaic devices, and fuel-cell equipment used exclusively for purposes other than heating swimming pools and hot tubs. The credit applied to purchases made in 2006 and 2007. The maximum credit for each of these systems was $2,000. (Cost: $31 million in fiscal 2006 through 2008)

Business fuel-cell investment credit. The law created a 30 percent tax credit for the installation of qualified fuel cells and a 10 percent credit for the purchase of stationary microturbine power plants. The credit was available for 2006 and 2007. (Cost: $222 million over eleven years)

R&D energy research credit. The measure modified the research and development tax credit and made expenditures to certain research consortia for energy-related research eligible for the credit. (Cost: $92 million over eleven years)

Alternative Motor Vehicle and Fuels Incentives

Alternative power motor vehicle credit. Under the law, tax credits would be allowed for the purchase of hybrid, fuel-cell, advanced "lean-burn" technology and other alternative-power vehicles. The amount of the credit would vary based on the rated fuel economy of the vehicle and its estimated lifetime fuel savings. The credit ranged from $400 to $3,400 for hybrid cars and trucks; from $4,000 to $44,000 for fuel-cell vehicles; and from $4,000 to $32,000 for alternative fuel vehicles. The credits were available for vehicles purchased in 2006 through 2014 for fuel-cell vehicles; before 2011 for hybrid cars, light trucks, advanced lean-burn technology vehicles, and alternative fuel motor vehicles; and before 2010 for hybrid medium and heavy trucks. The tax credit declined for hybrid vehicles in the quarter after a manufacturer's hybrid vehicle sales exceeded 60,000. (Cost: $874 million over eleven years)

Credit for installation of alternative fueling stations. The law allowed a 30 percent tax credit in the first year for the cost of equipment for refueling vehicles with alternative fuels, either at a business or a residence. To qualify, the fuels must be at least 85 percent ethanol, natural gas, liquefied natural gas, liquefied petroleum gas, or hydrogen or any mixture of diesel and biodiesel fuel containing at least 20 percent biodiesel. In the case of retail clean-fuel refueling equipment, the allowable maximum was $30,000. The maximum credit for residential use was $1,000. The credit was effective for equipment placed in service in 2006 and 2007. (Cost: $71 million over eleven years)

Extension of income and excise tax credits for biodiesel fuel. The law extended, from 2006 through 2008, the income tax credit and excise tax credit for biodiesel and biodiesel mixtures, and it provided a similar income and excise tax credit for renewable diesel fuel. (Cost: $194 million over three years)

Small business agri-biodiesel producer credit. The biodiesel fuels credit was expanded by the addition of a 10-cents-per-gallon credit for agri-biodiesel produced by small producers. The credit was available on the date of enactment and expired at the end of 2008. The limits on production capacity for small ethanol producers eligible for the credit were increased from 30 million to 60 million gallons. (Cost: $181 million over eleven years)

Oil Spill Liability Trust Fund. The law reinstated, through 2014, the 5-cents-per-barrel Oil Spill Liability Trust Fund tax beginning in April 2006 or on the last day of any calendar quarter for which the Treasury Department estimated that the unobligated balance of the fund was less than $2 billion.

The tax, which was credited to the Oil Spill Liability Trust Fund, would be suspended during a quarter if the department estimated that the unobligated balance exceeded $2.7 billion.

The tax was imposed between 1990 and 1994 on imported petroleum products and crude oil received at a U.S. refinery and any domestically produced crude oil exported from the United States if the crude oil had not been taxed before exportation. Taxes received were credited to the Oil Spill Liability Trust Fund. (Revenue: $2.5 billion over eleven years)

Extend LUST tax. Under the law, the LUST tax was extended through Sept. 30, 2011. In addition, the tax was applied to dyed fuel. (Revenue: $349 million over eleven years)

Modify recapture rules for amortization of intangible assets. The law made changes to the recapture rules for amortizing the cost of Section 197 intangibles, such as information base, licenses, or permits issued by a government agency or a franchise, trademark, or trade name. (Revenue: $171 million over 11 years)

Fisheries Overhaul

Faced with growing concerns about the impact of overfishing on ocean health and on profit margins in the fishing industry, Congress in 2006 cleared a bill to overhaul the main federal law governing commercial and recreational fisheries. The House-Senate compromise reached shortly before adjournment settled a months-long impasse over penalties for overfishing. President George W. Bush signed the bill into law Jan. 12, 2007 (HR 5946—PL 109-479).

BACKGROUND

The 1976 Magnuson-Stevens Act (PL 94-265) had last been reauthorized in a 1996 law known as the Sustainable Fisheries Act (PL 104-297). At that time, concern was widespread that some fish stocks had been so depleted by persistent overfishing as to threaten the health of the oceans and the economic prosperity of the seafood industry. In response, Congress amended the 1976 law to require fisheries and regional managers to rebuild overfished stock in ten years or less, unless the life span of the fish or other factors made it impossible to do so. *(1996 law, Congress and the Nation Vol. IX, p. 452)*

A decade later, fishing industry analysts said the changes had failed to rebuild some major fish populations, threatening the long-term viability of the seafood industry. Officials at both ends of Pennsylvania Avenue thus had serious interest in reauthorizing the Magnuson-Stevens law. "Overfishing is harmful. It's harmful to our country, and it's harmful to the world," President Bush said in a 2006 address calling on Congress to rewrite the law.

But lawmakers struggled to find consensus on how to curtail overfishing and rebuild depleted stocks. Some in Congress said strict rules were needed to restore certain species and guarantee the viability of the industry. Others said making the rules too tough would bankrupt fishermen.

The difference in views on Capitol Hill stemmed from the regional nature of both the law and the industry. Magnuson-Stevens established the United States' exclusive right to harvest fishery resources from three miles to two hundred miles from shore. The 1976 law authorized eight regional fishery councils, overseen by the Department of Commerce's National Oceanic and Atmospheric Administration (NOAA), that were charged with developing management plans for specific fish stocks to ensure they were not overfished and with taking steps to rebuild fish populations and protect their habitats. Each council governed a specific section of the U.S. coastline. As a result, the rules varied considerably from region to region—depending on the fish species, the state of the local fishing economy, the health of the fish stock, and the state of the habitat, among other issues—as did the profits of fishermen. The council that managed Alaskan catches, for instance, imposed some rules that were far stricter than those set by the New England council.

A variety of stakeholders also weighed in, including the fishing and fish-processing industries, recreational fishermen, and consumers. And the stakes were high. U.S. consumers in 2004 ate 4.8 billion pounds of seafood, averaging 16.6 pounds per person annually, the third largest total in the world, according to a Senate report. In the same year, the United States industry caught more than 9.6 billion pounds of fish and shellfish and generated $61.9 billion in sales.

"It seems clear that society and industry would all benefit from rebuilt fisheries," said Galen Tromble, chief of the domestic division in the sustainable fisheries office at the National Marine Fisheries Service. "But the difficulty is the transition"—the steps involved in forcing fisheries to rebuild depleted stock.

The battle in the 109th Congress mirrored the debate over fisheries legislation in 1996. In that case, Congress enacted mandates forcing fisheries and regional managers to rebuild overfished stock within ten years in most cases. Yet numerous studies since then, including a 2004 report by the U.S. Commission on Ocean Policy, said that overfishing remained a problem.

In a 2006 report to Congress, the National Marine Fisheries Service found that 26 percent of the nation's fish stocks were overfished, including seventeen types of fish in the Northeast, twenty-one in the Southeast, one in the Pacific Islands, and two in the Alaska region. The agency considered a species to be overfished if the amount of "biomass" for that stock was lower than the threshold set by the regional fisheries management plan.

Lawmakers in the 109th Congress debated whether to impose stricter rules to force immediate rebuilding or whether regional councils and fishers needed more leeway to figure out alternative measures to reduce overfishing.

Sen. Ted Stevens, R-Alaska, chair of the Commerce, Science, and Transportation Committee and cosponsor with the panel's ranking Democrat, Daniel K. Inouye of Hawaii, of S 2012, wanted to impose nationwide mandates similar to the rules that were already being implemented in Alaska, where fisheries had some of the most robust stocks in the country. His plan would force fisheries that went beyond their annual limits to reduce the following year's catch by the exceeded amount. Every regional council would have to enforce catch limits for individual fisheries.

Proponents of such strict rules pointed to the Northeast in arguing that the flexibility fought for by some major fisheries in that region had contributed to widespread overfishing and poor profit margins.

An October 2005 study by a University of British Columbia researcher said seventeen overfished stocks that were being rebuilt had an estimated value triple those of stocks not being rebuilt to healthy levels.

"There are political pressures not to restrict fishermen," said Andrew Rosenberg, a professor at the University of New Hampshire. "Unfortunately, you need to take very direct and rapid steps to begin rebuilding, not whittle around the edges." Some powerful House lawmakers, however, countered that further tightening of overfishing rules could provide a major blow to some fisheries. "In Alaska, the fisheries are healthy, and they have done a lot of things right over the years. In the Northeast, they've done some things wrong, and we do need to rebuild those stocks," said Resources Committee Chairman Richard W. Pombo, R-Calif., sponsor of HR 5018. "But they need the flexibility in rebuilding those fisheries so they don't put all the fishermen out of business in the process. What good does it do to have a healthy fishery if you put all the fishermen out of business?"

HOUSE COMMITTEE ACTION

The House Resources Committee approved Pombo's bill (HR 5018) by a vote of 26–15 on May 17. Four Democrats joined all twenty-two Republicans in voting for the bill, which was cosponsored by Don Young, R-Alaska, and Barney Frank, D-Mass. The panel formally reported the bill (H Rept 109-567) on July 17.

The five-year reauthorization bill would require each of the eight regional councils to set an annual "total allowable catch" based on scientific information. The allowable catch could not exceed the "acceptable biological catch" for fisheries set by each council's Scientific Committee and Statistical Committee. A "maximum sustainable yield" would also have to be determined.

The councils would use various management tools to reduce the following year's catch if a fishery exceeded the limit. But the bill did not require the councils to limit the following year's quota.

The bill included waivers from the existing ten-year time frame for rebuilding overfished stocks in certain cases, such as when a stock was part of a multispecies fishery or an international agreement, or when the cause of overfishing was outside a council's jurisdiction.

It also allowed the councils to avoid National Environmental Policy Act (NEPA) requirements if the commerce secretary found that the review process they used was "substantially equivalent."

During the markup, the committee adopted by voice vote an amendment by H. James Saxton, R-N.J., to strike a provision that would have made marine sanctuaries subject to fishing regulations under the act. Pombo agreed to pull the provision on the understanding that the issue would be revisited during reauthorization of the National Marine Sanctuaries Act.

The fourteen marine protected areas in the sanctuary system encompassed more than 150,000 square miles of marine and Great Lakes areas. Sanctuaries protected a variety of resources, including humpback-whale calving grounds, coral reefs, kelp forests, deep sea canyons, and underwater archeological sites. Pombo's substitute would have exempted two sanctuaries off the Hawaii coast.

Pombo said sanctuary managers should not be able to ignore Magnuson rules, but Saxton said Pombo's language would keep only a few, small "no take" areas in the sanctuary system off-limits to fishing. Saxton said that, as a child learning to squirrel hunt, he was taught "you should not shoot squirrels in their nests."

The committee also

- Rejected, 17–18, an amendment by Saxton to strike the language allowing exemptions to the ten-year deadline for rebuilding depleted fish populations. Saxton said allowing exemptions "unduly undermines the intent of the law." Pombo said the provision was intended to provide flexibility.
- Rejected, 18–22, an attempt by Wayne T. Gilchrest, R-Md., chairman of the House Resources Committee's Fisheries and Oceans Subcommittee, to mandate the development of a plan that would integrate the requirements for environmental analysis in the NEPA and the Magnuson law. Pombo argued that satisfying both laws was expensive and time-consuming and that Gilchrest's proposal would take years to implement.
- Rejected by voice vote a proposal by Nick J. Rahall II, D-W.Va., to delete the provision that would allow the commerce secretary to waive NEPA requirements if the councils were using a substantially equivalent review process.

The bill drew criticism from environmental groups and their supporters on Capitol Hill. The National Environmental Trust pointed to the lack of enforcement provisions for maintaining and rebuilding fish populations and said the bill would "reverse more than a decade of significant conservation gains in fishery management."

Pombo negotiated additional changes to the bill with Gilchrest and Saxton in July, at the behest of Majority Leader John A. Boehner, R-Ohio, who wanted to limit fights within the Republican caucus before bringing the bill to the floor. The changes included a two-year statutory deadline to end overfishing, revised language on rebuilding depleted fish stocks, and a rewrite of how the bill would apply the NEPA to fishery management plans. But they did not deal with the question of enforcing catch limits, and they did not allay concerns from those on either side of Pombo who wanted more, or fewer, strict rules. As a result, the bill did not reach the House floor.

SENATE ACTION

Legislation (S 2012) to strengthen regulation of the offshore fishing industry was approved by the Senate Commerce, Science, and Transportation Committee on Dec. 15, 2005, by voice vote. But the committee agreed to the bill only after adoption of a manager's amendment that would relax enforcement of annual catch limits for each fishery.

The full Senate passed the committee-approved bill, without any changes, on June 19, 2006, also by voice vote. The measure had been reported (S Rept 109-229) on April 4.

S 2012 had bipartisan support and was generally endorsed by both environmental and industry groups. However, environmentalists criticized the committee's decision to soften the annual fishing quotas in response to pressure from New England fishermen.

The bill required the eight regional councils to establish total annual quotas for each fishery. If a fishery exceeded the quota, it would have to reduce the following year's catch by the same amount, though its quota would not be reduced. It would be up to the council to determine what management tools to use to achieve that reduction.

Under the original bill by Stevens, a fishery that exceeded the limit would have had its quota cut the following year. The tough approach mirrored the regulatory program employed by Alaska fisheries, but it was not embraced by other regions, most notably the Northeast. The New England council used other restrictions—such as limiting how many days fishermen could be at sea, prohibiting certain gear, restricting gear in certain areas or at certain times, or limiting the poundage each boat could land—instead of setting a lower catch limit.

Giving the councils flexibility to address overfishing by reducing the number of fishing days or instituting area closures "should ultimately allow us to accomplish the same goal," said Olympia J. Snowe, R-Maine.

Environmental groups and others, however, maintained that reliance on those historical practices led in the first place to the overfishing that threatens the industry's long-term viability.

Stevens negotiated the changes on annual fishing quotas with Northeastern lawmakers, including Snowe, Democrat John Kerry of Massachusetts, and Republican John E. Sununu of New Hampshire.

The bill would bolster the use of biological assessments in fisheries management and align the planning process with requirements for environmental analysis under the National Environmental Policy Act. However, the commerce secretary would be allowed to waive the NEPA rules for fisheries plans.

The bill also increased technical training for council members, who may be fishermen, government employees, or representatives of environmental and recreational advocacy groups.

New language in the bill established a research program focused on deep-sea coral and authorized the councils to designate coral protection zones.

The amended legislation also authorized $17.5 million over six years for a disaster assistance program benefiting the shrimp industries along the Gulf Coast and required the Commerce Department to produce reports on the effect of Hurricanes Katrina and Rita on commercial and recreational fisheries and fishery habitats.

The legislation retained the existing requirement for fisheries to rebuild depleted stock in ten years.

FINAL ACTION

A week of intense negotiations between the Senate Commerce and House Resources led by Stevens resulted in a compromise bill (HR 5946). A motion to suspend the rules and pass the measure had been agreed to by voice vote in the House on Sept. 27. The Senate passed an amended version by voice vote Dec. 7. The House, by agreeing to suspend the rules and accept the Senate amendment, cleared it two days later, also by voice vote.

The bill was less stringent than measures 2012, but it required new efforts to shut down overfishing. It required the eight regional councils—based on advice from their Science and Statistical Committees—to devise ways to specify annual catch limits to prevent overfishing. The plans had to be in place within four years for fisheries that were subject to overfishing and in five years for the rest.

The bill included a provision similar to Senate-passed language that required NOAA, in consultation with the Council on Environmental Quality and the regional councils, to develop environmental review procedures specific to fishery management that would satisfy the requirements of the NEPA.

The compromise also set new training and conflict-of-interest disclosure requirements for council members and members of the Science and Statistical Committees, and it authorized a peer review process for scientific information used by each council.

Unlike HR 5018, the compromise retained the ten-year time frame to rebuild overfished stock. But after heavy lobbying by lawmakers from mid-Atlantic states, it exempted summer flounder from the rule.

MAJOR PROVISIONS

As enacted, HR 5946 (PL 109-479) contained the following major provisions.

Authorization. Reauthorized the Magnuson-Stevens Act through fiscal 2013. The bill authorized $338 million in fiscal 2007 and a total of $2.6 billion over seven years to carry out the programs in the bill.

Fishing limits. Required the regional fishing councils to devise a way to specify annual catch limits that would prevent overfishing. The limits had to be set by 2010 for fisheries that were subject to overfishing and by 2011 for all other fisheries.

Science. Increased the role of the scientific committees that advised the councils and required the councils to base their catch limits on peer-reviewed information submitted by the committees.

Training. Directed the federal government to develop a new training program that would be required for all new members of the regional councils but also would be available to existing members. The training course was to cover fish species and habitat management, as well as public policy making.

Limited access programs. Established national guidelines for Limited Access Privilege Programs that assigned specific shares of the annual harvest quota in overfished areas to individuals, fishing communities, and regional fishery associations. The programs were required to encourage the restoration of species of fish and their habitats, promote safe fishing practices, and include a system to monitor the status of the fishing area. Fishermen would have to apply to regional councils and meet specific criteria set by the councils to be able to fish through the limited access programs. While the quota shares could not be treated as a property right, they could be transferred. The quotas had to be reviewed at least every ten years.

Environmental review. Required the development of new environmental review procedures specific to fishery management that would allow the review, analysis, and public participation required under the National Environmental Policy Act along timelines appropriate for fishery management decisions.

International fishing. Directed the Commerce Department to set up an international fisheries monitoring program to address illegal, unreported, and unregulated fishing on the high seas. The bill also included implementing language for several fishing agreements and reauthorized several fisheries conservation and management statutes.

Army Corps of Engineers

Legislation (S 728, HR 2864) to authorize billions of dollars for popular Army Corps of Engineers water projects died at the end of the 109th Congress after House and Senate conferees were unable to resolve a range of differences. Although the legislation, known as the Water Resources Development Act, had broad support, House and Senate negotiators could not agree on its size and scope. They also were at odds over provisions to impose stricter oversight of the corps, an issue that had gained traction after Hurricane Katrina in 2005, which destroyed levees in New Orleans that were administered by the agency.

One of the main differences between the two chambers was over the number and types of projects to fund. The House-passed bill included more than seven hundred projects dealing with shoreline protection, flood control, inland navigation, and environmental restoration. The Congressional Budget Office (CBO) put the cost at $10 billion over fifteen years. The Senate-passed version covered two hundred projects but was more expensive. CBO said it would cost about $14 billion over the same period. Both price tags drew strong objections from the White House.

In addition, under S 728, corps projects costing more than $40 million would have been subject to external reviews. A state governor, federal agency, or the Army secretary also could request a review of any project. HR 2864 would have subjected projects costing $50 million or more to peer review, but the corps would have had discretion to exempt certain projects. Taxpayer and environmental groups said the Senate language would add much-needed scrutiny to corps projects, while industries that relied on public works activities said it would add new layers of bureaucracy that would slow badly needed infrastructure improvements.

BACKGROUND

A civilian-run agency of the Pentagon, the Army Corps of Engineers had the responsibility for managing and often transforming the nation's waterways for societal uses. The corps constructed dams and flood control projects, dredged navigable channels, and operated hydropower plants. Since it began overseeing engineering projects in the early nineteenth century, the corps' massive public works projects had spurred economic growth across much of the nation.

Because the agency's massive projects were highly visible and were credited with generating numerous jobs, they tended to be popular with local lawmakers. Congress generally passed a corps water resources bill every two years. But members had not been able to agree on a new legislation since 2000 because of disagreements over how to improve the management of corps projects. In the 108th Congress, the House overwhelmingly passed a reauthorization bill, but the Senate never acted on it. *(108th Congress action, Congress and the Nation Vol. XI, p. 438)*

With reauthorizing bills stalled, lawmakers turned to annual appropriations bills that funded the corps, adding instructions about project management and specifying hundreds of water projects to be carried out. The corps during this time faced increasing scrutiny as fiscal conservatives and environmentalists criticized many of the projects as overly costly and damaging to native ecosystems. The dams and other structures interfered with the natural ebb and flow of thousands of miles of rivers, threatening numerous plant and animal species. In some cases, the agency's attempts to reroute rivers appeared to exacerbate flooding while spurring little barge traffic or other economic benefits. The criticism reached a crescendo after levies that the corps had constructed failed to stop floodwaters in the wake of Hurricane Katrina.

Farmers and other industries that depended on the nation's rivers to ship goods were particularly eager for the corps to get started on new projects, such as the replacement of locks and dams along the upper Mississippi and Illinois rivers. A coalition of environmental and taxpayer-watchdog groups wanted projects to undergo more stringent reviews and meet strict environmental restoration requirements. But lobbyists for shipbuilders, port authorities, and others who benefited from the projects warned that new federal requirements would simply add to government waste by bogging down the system.

The proposed legislation in the 109th Congress would reauthorize the Water Resources Development Act (PL 106-541), which gave the Army Corps of Engineers the authority to carry out civilian water projects. *(PL 106-541, Congress and the Nation Vol. X, p. 372)*

HOUSE ACTION

The House passed its water projects bill (HR 2864) by a vote of 406–14 on July 14, 2005. The Transportation and Infrastructure Committee had given voice-vote approval to the measure on June 22 and reported it (H Rept 109-154) on June 24. Supporters of the bill said it would do more to improve corps operations than any previous legislation. But a White House statement of administration policy said the measure still "does not include much-needed policy and program reforms and has a significant overall cost."

Sponsored by committee chairman Don Young, R-Alaska, the bill provided for the corps to undertake nearly seven hundred projects and studies. John J. "Jimmy" Duncan Jr., R-Tenn., chairman of the Water Resources and Environment Subcommittee, said the lengthy list of projects reflected pent-up demand caused by Congress's inability to clear a water development bill since 2000.

Under the bill, water projects costing $50 million or more would be subject to an independent peer review process. Smaller projects also would undergo peer review if they were considered controversial. Peer review panels would be established by the National Academy of Sciences or a similar independent scientific organization.

For improvements to the Upper Mississippi River-Illinois Waterway System, the bill authorized $235 million for short-term navigation improvements, $1.8 billion for seven new locks, and $1.6 billion for environmental restoration. That proposal survived an effort by Jeff Flake, R-Ariz., and Earl Blumenauer, D-Ore., to make the authorization contingent on an increase in barge traffic through the existing locks to an annual average of more than 35 million tons a year per lock for 2007 to 2009. According to the corps, the average was 28.8 million tons per lock in 2004. Kenny Hulshof, R-Mo., said the reason for declining traffic passing through the Depression-era locks was precisely because of "the declining conditions of these locks and dams."

The bill also authorized about $1 billion each for the Louisiana coastal and Everglades projects.

Senate Action

The Senate Environment and Public Works Committee approved its water projects bill (S 728) by voice vote April 13, 2005, but not before some committee members raised long-standing concerns that many corps projects were unnecessary and environmentally harmful.

The panel's ranking minority member, James M. Jeffords, I-Vt., said the measure retreated from a compromise worked out by committee members in 2004 that required the corps to perform more rigorous environmental reviews. "The simple fact is that we will only get a bill passed on the Senate floor and sent to the president if we aim for the center," responded the bill's sponsor, Christopher S. Bond, R-Mo. He said the bill failed to come to a vote in the Senate in 2004 because of industry opposition to the compromise language. "If we do what we did last year with policy issues, we will end up where we did last year, with no bill."

The bill required "major engineering, scientific and technical work products" related to corps projects to undergo a peer review, as long as the review did not delay the project or increase its cost. It also would give the corps the option of purchasing credits from a mitigation or conservation bank in lieu of taking action when it concluded that environmental restoration on a site would be too difficult.

The 2003 bill had required peer review for a broader range of projects and provided for creation of a commission to investigate corps management and environmental practices and to submit a report to Congress.

During the markup, the committee

- Rejected by voice vote an amendment by Jeffords that would have required peer review of corps projects and established a Water Resources Planning Council to advise the corps on changing its planning process. Bond said the amendment would impose "significant, if not insurmountable, burdens" on corps projects.

- Adopted 12–6 an amendment by David Vitter, R-La., to clarify the limits of corps jurisdiction over obstructions to maritime traffic on private property. Vitter and Bond said the corps had used a clause in the existing law to order changes on privately owned wetlands that, as Bond put it, "nobody in their right mind would want to navigate."

S 728 was formally reported (S Rept 109-61) on April 26.

The Senate passed HR 2864 by voice vote July 19, 2006, after inserting the text of S 728. Responding to criticism that the corps had done an inadequate job of maintaining the New Orleans levees, the Senate voted to increase oversight of the agency. But it rejected efforts to force the corps to prioritize the $58 billion in backlogged projects and the billions of dollars the measure would authorize for new projects.

Senate bill sponsors Bond and James M. Inhofe, R-Okla., defended the hefty price tag, saying the bill was expensive because Congress had not enacted a water projects authorization bill since 2000. Inhofe also defended the measure against charges that it was filled with pet projects targeted for lawmakers' home states. "As one of the most fiscally conservative members of this body, I have long argued that the two most important functions of the federal government is to provide for the national defense and public infrastructure," Inhofe said.

The main topic in the Senate debate, however, was overhauling the corps, which had faced increased scrutiny after Hurricane Katrina exposed design flaws in the New Orleans levees. During the floor debate, the Senate

- Adopted 54–46 on July 19 an amendment to establish external reviews of all corps projects that cost more than $40 million. A governor, a federal agency, or the secretary of the Army also could request a review of any project, and an independent board of experts would review all flood control projects. The amendment was offered by Russ Feingold, D-Wis., and John McCain, R-Ariz.

Bond and Inhofe strongly opposed the amendment, saying it would stifle much-needed projects and create unnecessary delays and bureaucracy. They agreed that corps operations should be overhauled, but they said the McCain-Feingold plan would go too far.

- Rejected 49–51 on July 19 a competing amendment by Bond and Inhofe to require reviews on projects that cost more than $100 million.
- Rejected 19–80 on July 19 another McCain-Feingold amendment that would have established an interagency panel to recommend priorities for the corps. Proponents said it was necessary after Katrina's aftermath raised questions about whether the corps was spending its resources wisely. But critics said the plan would be a delegation of Congress's responsibilities to the executive branch.
- Rejected 43–56 on July 19 a competing Bond-Inhofe amendment that would have required the corps to report annually to Congress on how well its projects were meeting national needs.
- Adopted 63–36 on July 18 an amendment by Arlen Specter, R-Pa., and Thomas R. Carper, D-Del., to block the retirement of a dredging vessel operated by the corps primarily along the Delaware River. Specter said the vessel, the *McFarland*, was needed to respond immediately to emergency blockages at the Defense Department's military seaports. "At a time when terrorism is a major threat in this country, it is hard to understand why we would want to give up the only dredger which is available on the East Coast and on the Gulf Coast," Specter said.

Offshore Drilling

Lawmakers agreed to allow new offshore drilling in the Gulf of Mexico as part of a tax and trade package cleared on the final day of the 109th Congress. The measure, which opened 8.3 million acres south of the Florida Panhandle to drilling, was the only significant energy bill to survive after months of debate spurred by a series of spikes in oil and gasoline prices. President George W. Bush signed it into law Dec. 20, 2006 (HR 6111—PL 109-432). *(Tax and trade, p. 105)*

The bill was a landmark achievement for Gulf Coast lawmakers whose states could reap hundreds of millions of dollars from royalties that otherwise would have gone to the Treasury. At the same time, it created drilling-free buffer zones to protect the west coast of Florida.

Offshore drilling for oil and natural gas had been generally prohibited except in the western Gulf of Mexico and along parts of Alaska's coast. Energy companies had long sought to drill in an area known as Lease Area 181, south of the Florida Panhandle, because of its reserves and proximity to existing infrastructure. The Clinton administration proposed opening the area to exploration in 1997, but the region had remained closed due to opposition from Florida, which feared the potential impact on its tourism industry.

Support for drilling increased in 2005 when energy prices shot up after Hurricanes Katrina and Rita knocked out offshore platforms and other energy infrastructure in the Gulf. Prices increased again in the spring of 2006.

SENATE COMMITTEE ACTION

The Senate Energy and Natural Resources Committee gave bipartisan support March 8, 2006, to a narrow bill (S 2253) assembled by Republican chairman Pete V. Domenici and ranking Democrat Jeff Bingaman, both of New Mexico. The bill, approved 16–5 and reported (S Rept 109-240) on April 20, proposed to open up about 3 million acres in Lease Area 181 to oil and gas drilling, while protecting the area within one hundred miles of the Florida coast. It also allowed for leasing east of the Military Mission Line but only with the consent of the secretary of defense.

Despite the solidly bipartisan vote, the bill's fate was uncertain, and Domenici and Bingaman were under pressure from disparate interests to make significant concessions. Florida lawmakers wanted stronger protections for their beaches. Louisiana Democrat Mary L. Landrieu insisted that hurricane-battered Gulf Coast states get revenue generated from oil and gas leasing off their shores. Meanwhile, many pro-environment and coastal state lawmakers were expected to oppose any effort to expand offshore drilling. "We in New Jersey and I believe other coastal states have a real concern about the creep that begins," said Democrat Robert Menendez, who was among the five on the panel who voted against the bill. "The ocean has no borders, and God forbid if a spill takes place, it doesn't respect any lines."

Shortly after the markup, Landrieu and five Gulf Republicans introduced a bill (S 2384) to give Louisiana, Alabama, and Mississippi 50 percent of the leasing revenue under S 2253.

HOUSE COMMITTEE ACTION

The House Resources Committee voted June 21 to repeal a quarter-century ban on most offshore oil and gas exploration. The panel approved the bill (HR 4761) by a vote of 29–9, after giving voice-vote approval to a substitute amendment by Chairman Richard W. Pombo, R-Calif. Ten Democrats voted for the bill, which was formally reported (H Rept 109-531) on June 26.

The committee-approved bill included the following provisions.

Leases for drilling. The Interior Department was directed to offer leases for offshore oil and gas drilling for 75 percent of available offshore locations on the Outer Continental Shelf. The department would have to consult with other federal agencies and governors of affected states.

Opt out. States had the power to opt out of the drilling program. One year after enactment, the department would begin to issue leases for natural gas development in areas between fifty and one hundred miles from the coastline, unless a state petitioned the department by that date for a ban on drilling off its coast. Starting in July 2009, the department could grant leases for offshore oil development in these areas, unless a state petitioned for a ban.

Distance from coastline. The measure allowed the federal government to offer leases on areas that were more than one hundred miles beyond the coastline.

Prohibited areas. Drilling would be prohibited in areas less than fifty miles from the shore unless a state specifically requested drilling there. A state could petition the department to lease any area that was at least twenty-five miles away from the coastline of a neighboring state for natural gas drilling or fifty miles away for oil drilling. States could set certain conditions on offshore drilling within twenty-five miles of their coastline, such as limits on the total number of production platforms.

Ninety-day requirement. The department was required to approve a state's petition to permit drilling within ninety days unless it determined that the drilling was likely to cause serious harm to the environment. If the department did not act within ninety days, the state could consider its petition approved.

Revenue sharing. The measure would give participating coastal states a share of the revenue from both current and future production. The share to the states would increase gradually until it reached what the White House said would be as much as 64 percent of revenue from drilling in waters three miles to twelve miles off the coast.

During the markup, the committee

- Rejected, by voice vote, an amendment by Mark Udall, D-Colo., that would have replaced the entire bill with legislation based on the bipartisan Senate measure. "I think it makes more sense to start with simple and straightforward legislation that is based on sound science and that has some strong support," Udall said. Pombo opposed the amendment but credited Udall for taking "a step in the right direction" by recognizing a need to produce energy.
- Rejected, 7–23, an amendment by Edward J. Markey, D-Mass., to strike everything in the bill except a provision that would impose a new fee on oil companies that were not paying royalties on deep-water production in the Gulf because of a glitch in leases that were issued in the late 1990s.

HOUSE FLOOR ACTION

The House passed HR 4761 by 232–187 on June 29. The measure aimed to open most of the nation's coastline to drilling. Sponsors said their goal was to break U.S. dependency on foreign sources of oil by increasing domestic production. To that end, HR 4761 would allow states to permit energy exploration in waters out to one hundred miles from the coast and encouraged them to do so by giving them a share of the revenue generated. The bill made other changes to reduce the cost from what the Congressional Budget Office (CBO) initially projected as $11 billion over ten years. One significant concession to Florida lawmakers, made as part of a manger's amendment, prohibited leasing east of the Military Mission Line, thereby protecting what C. W. Bill Young, R-Fla., said would be a 235-mile zone off his state's west coast.

In passing the bill, GOP leaders had to overcome staunch opposition to the revenue-sharing provisions from the administration and from many Democrats. "This is about a raid on the federal Treasury," said Markey. Markey's argument was bolstered by a White House statement of administration policy that registered strong opposition to language it said would redirect "several hundred billion dollars" in federal revenue to the states. Administration officials had said they were open to sharing revenue from future leases but opposed altering the formula for existing royalties, which already were included in future budgets.

Pombo said it was only fair to give states some of the offshore drilling revenue, because states with energy production on land collected 50 percent of royalties. The funds also were expected to serve as an incentive to promote drilling.

During the debate, the House

- Rejected 170–249 on June 29 another attempt by Markey to strike everything in the bill except provisions aimed at getting money from oil companies whose leases did not require them to pay royalties on deep-water production in the Gulf.
- Rejected 65–353 on June 29 an attempt by Michael Bilirakis, R-Fla., to bar leases for oil or natural gas development within 125 miles of a state's coast unless the state chose to "opt in."

SENATE FLOOR ACTION

A revised version of Domenici's bill (S 3711) sailed through the Senate by a vote of 71–25 on Aug. 1, with eighteen Democrats joining fifty-three Republicans in support of the measure. Olympia J. Snowe of Maine was the only Republican to vote against it.

Passage followed weeks of negotiations led by Domenici, who worked with Floridians and other Gulf Coast lawmakers to produce a bill that could garner the sixty votes needed to withstand a filibuster. The agreement, announced July 12, proposed to open about 8.3 million acres in the eastern Gulf, including about 2.5 million acres within Lease Area 181. It included a ban on exploration within 125 miles of the Florida Panhandle until at least 2022, as sought by the Florida delegation. And it included provisions to direct a portion of the revenue from new leases to coastal states and to the Land and Water Conservation Fund. The White House issued a statement saying it supported Senate passage. The statement expressed concern about the rate of revenue sharing with the states but welcomed the $500 million annual cap.

Majority Leader Bill Frist, R-Tenn., deployed a parliamentary technique known as "filling the amendment tree" to block unwanted amendments to the bill, rejecting Democratic calls for an open debate. "It's clear to me," Domenici said, "that anything that changes this very much won't pass the Senate."

One of the biggest holdups on the bill was the fear by many senators that passage would lead to a conference in which House Republicans would prevail with their much more sweeping bill. "I give high honors to the House," Domenici said, "but I will do everything within my power to ... bring back a bill that can pass the Senate."

Minority Leader Harry Reid, D-Nev., allayed some of the fears by saying he would join a Democratic filibuster to block the bill if the House did not yield to the Senate-passed language. That, along with an assurance by Frist that Florida would be protected in any potential compromise between the two chambers, won over Bill Nelson, D-Fla. Nelson had often led the fight against drilling to protect his state's beaches, and many Democrats fell in line once he decided to vote for the bill.

Bingaman opposed the revised bill, arguing that it would lock up far more oil and natural gas than would be produced in the area to be opened for exploration. He said the bill was bad fiscal policy because it would give too much revenue to Gulf states.

Although Bingaman had partnered with Domenici on the committee-approved bill, he opposed the revision as "bad energy supply policy" because it would create a sixteen-year moratorium hundreds of miles off Florida's coast, while Cuba could drill within fifty miles. The bill might make an additional 2.76 trillion cubic feet of natural gas available, he said, but it would cut off access to some 21 trillion cubic feet.

FINAL ACTION

Backers of S 3711 argued that it represented a delicate balance between competing interests that would collapse if the House tried to amend it. Numerous trade groups representing the agriculture, petrochemical, and utilities industries as well as oil and gas interests wanted the House leaders to accept the Senate bill, arguing that it was the best deal they could get. Gulf Coast lawmakers and organizations also pushed for the Senate bill because it promised their states a portion of the drilling revenue for coastal restoration efforts.

House negotiators held out for months, saying the Senate version would accomplish little more than what the Bush administration already wanted to do administratively. The White House had proposed offering leases on about 2 million acres within Lease Area 181 as early as 2007. House leaders did not give up until Dec. 1 when they agreed to bring S 3711 to the floor without changes. With natural gas prices rising again and uncertain prospects for expanding offshore drilling in the incoming Democratic-controlled 110th Congress, they were under pressure from trade groups representing the oil and gas industry, as well as natural gas consumers and electric utilities, to clear the Senate bill.

The offshore drilling language was inserted into legislation (HR 6111) dealing with taxes and trade with Vietnam, which both chambers were rushing to finish. The House passed the bill 367–45 on Dec. 8, after narrowly rejecting, 205–207, an attempt by Markey to bar energy companies with royalty-free offshore leases from drilling in the newly opened area. GOP leaders conceded that Markey's amendment had Republican support, but they were able to defeat it by arguing that it would kill the tax package in the Senate. Republicans held the vote open for more than fifteen minutes while pressing members to switch their votes.

The Senate cleared the bill 79–9 on Dec. 9. CBO estimated that the leases would generate a net $926 million in federal revenue in fiscal 2007 through 2016.

Environmental groups said both the House and Senate bills were gifts to industry that ignored broader conservation and efficiency goals that would ultimately be necessary to address energy demand. For his part, Domenici was quick to suggest that he would be back for more in the future.

MAJOR PROVISIONS

The following were the main offshore drilling provisions in HR 6111.

New leases. The Interior Department was directed to offer leases for oil and natural gas drilling in about 8.3 million acres of the eastern Gulf of Mexico, including 2.5 million acres within Lease Area 181. The leases were to be offered as soon as possible but no later than one year after the bill was enacted.

Buffer zone. The bill barred new oil and gas leases until June 30, 2022, in areas within 125 miles of Florida's coast and in any areas in Lease Area 181 that were within 100 miles of Florida's coast.

It also prohibited new leases east of the Military Mission Line, an area used by the Air Force and Navy as a test range for weapons. That area extended from the Florida Panhandle to the southern Florida coast in waters about two hundred miles west of the coast. Energy companies that held leases to drill in those areas prior to enactment could exchange their leases for bonuses or royalty credits to be used on other drilling operations in the Gulf of Mexico.

Revenue from new leases. Half of all revenue from new oil and gas leases authorized under the bill—including lease bids and royalties—would go to the Treasury. Up to $500 million per year of the remaining income would be split, with 75 percent going to the Gulf Coast states of Alabama, Louisiana, Mississippi, and Texas and 25 percent going to the Land and Water Conservation Fund, which provided grants to states to develop public outdoor recreation areas.

Anything more than $500 million per year in fiscal years 2016 through 2055 would go to the federal Treasury.

State distribution formula. The Interior Department was required to develop a formula under which each state's share of income from oil and gas leasing was allocated based on the proximity of its coastline to offshore facilities. Those closest to the drilling would get the most money, although no state could receive less than 10 percent of the total revenue available to all states.

Beginning in fiscal 2017, the formula would apply to all offshore energy leases granted between 2002 and 2007, not just those authorized in the bill.

Uses for state funds. The bill stipulated that states could use revenue from offshore drilling only for coastal protection or conservation projects, restoration of wildlife or natural resources, federally approved marine or coastal conservation plans, or projects to reduce the environmental impact of offshore energy production. A small amount could be used for administrative costs.

Arctic National Wildlife Refuge

Republican leaders in the 109th Congress believed they had the best chance in years to win enactment of a law opening Alaska's Arctic National Wildlife Refuge (ANWR) to energy exploration. The GOP gains in the November 2004 elections seemed to put them within striking distance of achieving what had been the centerpiece of President George W. Bush's energy policy since 2001. But, in the end, they came away empty-handed. It was the second time during the Bush presidency that a GOP-controlled Congress failed to muster the necessary votes for an ANWR drilling proposal, and the defeat showed the enduring strength of environmentalists to defend one of the nation's most storied wilderness areas.

BACKGROUND

For a quarter-century, ANWR had been the subject of a bitter tug-of-war in Congress between environmentalists and supporters of the oil and gas industry. Few energy issues stirred as much passion as the question of whether to drill in ANWR, a spectacular landscape that was home to millions of migrating birds, elk, wolves, and bears and that covered vast reserves of oil.

Congress established the refuge in 1960 and expanded it in 1980 under the Alaska National Interest Lands Conservation Act (PL 96-487). Under that act, the refuge's 1.5-million acre coastal plain was reserved for potential energy development. The Reagan administration first proposed opening the federal wildlife preserve for drilling in 1987. However, the 1980 law required a separate act of Congress to allow energy exploration, and the only such measure to pass both houses of Congress was vetoed by President Bill Clinton in 1995. (*1980 law, Congress and the Nation Vol. V, p. 577; 1995 action, Congress and the Nation Vol. IX, p. 472*)

The U.S. Geological Survey estimated that the refuge could produce between 500,000 and 1.4 million barrels of crude oil a day at peak production. By comparison, the United States consumed some 20.4 million barrels a day, according to the Department of Energy.

Drilling advocates argued that the development of ANWR would reduce U.S. dependence on foreign oil, reduce gas prices, and result in hundreds of thousands of new jobs. They said drilling and production would not harm wildlife, citing Alaska's nearby Prudhoe Bay as an example in which oil development and wildlife coexisted and flourished. New, advanced technology, supporters said, made it easier to reap the maximum amount of fuel on less land and with fewer adverse effects on the environment.

Environmentalists argued that the area was unique and ecologically fragile and that drilling would lay waste to vast areas of the tundra, its water sources, and its wildlife. They noted that the amount of recoverable oil in ANWR was unknown and that it could take decades for production to be realized. Drilling in ANWR, they said, would have no immediate effect on energy supplies or price.

ENERGY OVERHAUL

The House version of the energy policy overhaul bill (HR 6), which passed 249–183 on April 21, 2005, included a section authorizing the Interior Department to grant leases for oil and gas exploration, development, and production in 1.5 million acres of ANWR. The measure barred the export of oil or gas products from ANWR.

The bill included provisions requiring the department to ensure that drilling and production in ANWR would have "no significant adverse effect" on fish and wildlife and their habitats and would ban above-ground surface occupancy by oil and gas producers in special areas. It required seasonal limits on oil and gas activities when necessary to avoid adverse effects during periods of concentrated fish and wildlife breeding, nesting, and migration. The bill provided for expedited judicial review of any actions taken in ANWR by the Interior Department.

Companies would pay royalties of at least 12.5 percent of the value of the oil or gas they removed. Half of the money would go to Alaska and half to the federal government.

The House on April 20 rejected 200–231 an attempt by Edward J. Markey, D-Mass., to strike the ANWR drilling provisions.

The Senate version of HR 6 did not include ANWR provisions. Knowing the proposal would trigger a filibuster, the two bill managers—Republican Pete V. Domenici and Democrat Jeff Bingaman, both of New Mexico—left the issue out. Bingaman was the ranking member on the Energy and Natural Resources Committee.

When the bill went to conference, House leaders agreed to drop the section on ANWR, because supporters did not have the sixty votes to stop a filibuster. Their hopes lay instead with a budget-reconciliation bill.

BUDGET RESOLUTION AND RECONCILIATION

The first step toward including the ANWR provisions in the 2005 reconciliation bill (S 1932—PL 109-171) came in April 2005, when both chambers adopted a fiscal 2006 budget resolution (H Con Res 95) that assumed the federal government would generate $2.4 billion by leasing the drilling rights. That arcane step was crucial: Including an estimate of revenues was the only way the ANWR proposal could be part of the filibuster-proof budget-reconciliation package. *(S 1932, p. 81)*

The decisive vote came in the Senate on March 16, when GOP leaders succeeded in blocking a Democratic attempt to strike the drilling provisions from the budget resolution. The gain of four GOP seats in November provided the winning margin, allowing for the defeat of the amendment by Maria Cantwell of Washington, 49–51. Seven Republicans voted to drop the ANWR provision, while three Democrats voted to keep the language.

Two years before, the Senate had voted 52–48 to remove the provision from a budget resolution, a step that was the death knell for ANWR legislation for that session.

When Congress began assembling the budget-reconciliation bill in the fall, the Senate went first. The Energy and Natural Resources Committee approved language Oct. 19 to authorize the Interior Department to hold two lease sales for oil and gas drilling in ANWR by 2010. It said the leases would produce $2.5 billion in revenue over five years.

The Senate passed the bill 52–47 on Nov. 3, after again defeating an attempt by Cantwell to strip out the ANWR provision. Cantwell's amendment was rejected 48–51. The Senate on Nov. 3 also adopted 83–16 an amendment by Ron Wyden, D-Ore., and Jim Talent, R-Mo., to ban the export of oil or gas from ANWR. The proposal was consistent with House language, and Ted Stevens, R-Alaska, said he backed it partly to boost ANWR leasing prospects in the other chamber.

The House Resources Committee approved similar ANWR provisions Oct. 26 by a vote of 24–16, as part of the House budget-reconciliation bill (HR 4241). But House leadership was having difficulty balancing the demands of moderates and conservatives in their caucus to win floor support for the overall budget-reconciliation bill. On Nov. 8, twenty-six GOP lawmakers signed a letter urging leaders to drop ANWR drilling from the bill. The next day, following a meeting with House moderates, acting majority leader Roy Blunt, R-Mo., agreed to do so. With all House Democrats prepared to vote against the measure anyway—even a handful who in the past had supported ANWR drilling—GOP leaders had to get their moderates on board.

The House passed HR 4241, without the ANWR provisions, by a narrow vote of 217–215 on Nov. 18.

For a number of GOP senators, including Stevens, Domenici, and Lisa Murkowski of Alaska, ANWR drilling was by far the most important provision in the bill. Leaving it out also was a blow to the White House. But House leaders said they could not get the conference report through their chamber if it contained the provisions. Stevens, who chaired the Senate Defense Appropriations Subcommittee, agreed to move the proposal to the conference report on the defense spending bill (HR 2863), where House leaders predicted it would have a better chance. *(Appropriations, p. 73)*

The House adopted the reconciliation conference report (H Rept 109-362) by 212–206 on Dec. 19, but the Senate raised other objections, forcing the House to vote again. The House cleared S 1932 by 216–214 on Feb. 1, 2006.

DEFENSE APPROPRIATIONS

By the time House and Senate conferees on the fiscal 2006 defense spending bill met Dec. 18, the legislation had been selected to carry the ANWR drilling plan. In a bid to sweeten the deal, Stevens earmarked part of the future profits from ANWR drilling leases for additional aid to the Gulf Coast, which was suffering in the aftermath of Hurricanes Katrina and Rita, as well as for border security.

HR 2863 had to clear before lawmakers left for the holidays, especially because it included $50 billion in emergency funds that the Pentagon said were urgently needed to support operations in Iraq and Afghanistan. The House overwhelmingly adopted the conference report (H Rept 109-359) Dec. 19 (in the session that began Dec. 18), with the ANWR provisions included. The vote was 308–106.

But the ANWR add-on sparked a bitter dispute in the Senate. Stevens argued that the drilling was related to national security because it would reduce reliance on foreign oil supplies. Democrats accused Republicans of stretching Senate rules and playing politics with funding for the troops. Ranking Appropriations Democrat Robert C. Byrd of West Virginia, a longtime friend of Stevens, said, "I love this man, but I love the Senate more!" An attempt to cut off the debate failed Dec. 21 on a **key vote of 56–44 (R 52–3; D 4–40; I 0–1),** four votes short of the number needed. *(2005 key votes, p. 915)*

Because most House members had already left for the year, Senate GOP leaders used an enrolling resolution (S Con Res 74) to get rid of the ANWR provisions. The Senate Dec. 21 adopted the resolution 48–45 then cleared the defense spending bill, 93–0. The House adopted the enrolling resolution by voice vote Dec. 22.

2006 ACTION

After their repeated failures to open ANWR to drilling in 2005, Republican lawmakers followed up with comparatively feeble attempts in the second session.

As in 2005, Senate supporters tried to pursue drilling in ANWR through the budget-reconciliation process, which would have made the provisions immune to a filibuster. On March 16, 2006, the Senate voted 51–49 to adopt a fiscal 2007 budget resolution (S Con Res 83) that assumed the government would collect a total of $3 billion in revenue from ANWR leases through fiscal 2011. The resolution directed the Energy and Natural Resources Committee to draft a separate budget-reconciliation bill authorizing the government to lease oil- and gas-drilling rights in a portion of ANWR to meet that goal.

The leadership won the extra vote needed to adopt the resolution by agreeing to a request by Mary L. Landrieu, D-La., to set aside some of the ANWR revenue, along with some other funds, to help rebuild the hurricane-battered Gulf Coast. Landrieu was the sole Democratic senator to support the budget resolution, sparing Vice President Dick Cheney the need to break a tie.

The effort stalled, however, because the two chambers never adopted a joint budget resolution, which was a necessary precondition to introducing a budget-reconciliation bill.

In the House, Republicans passed a symbolic bill (HR 5429) to authorize energy exploration in ANWR, knowing that such a straightforward effort did not stand a chance in the Senate. The bill, which would have authorized the interior secretary to begin selling oil- and gas-drilling leases in a portion of ANWR along Alaska's northern coast, passed 225–201 on May 25. It was brought to the floor without a committee vote.

GOP backers knew the bill could not get through the Senate because it was not protected from a filibuster. The Senate did not take up the measure.

Yucca Mountain Funding

The planned nuclear waste dump at Yucca Mountain in Nevada sparked appropriations battles over both fiscal 2006 and 2007 spending bills, casting new doubt over whether lawmakers could agree on how to handle the spent fuel rods piling up at commercial nuclear reactors around the country.

In the first session, the 109th Congress cleared a $30.5 billion energy-water spending bill for fiscal 2006 that provided far less than requested for Yucca Mountain. The lower funding level was a reflection, in part, of the fact that construction was far behind schedule. President George W. Bush signed the bill into law on Nov. 19, 2005 (HR 2419—PL 109-103).

In the second session, House and Senate appropriators could not reach agreement on energy-water legislation, largely because of differences over the nuclear waste issue. Lawmakers were split between concentrating resources on Yucca Mountain or spending $250 million on a controversial administration proposal to reprocess spent fuel for reuse in a new generation of nuclear reactors. The House passed a $30.5 billion version of the fiscal 2007 spending bill (HR 5427) but the full Senate never considered its version.

Instead, Republican leaders in November 2006 decided to forward all the unfinished spending bills to the 110th Congress. A stopgap spending bill signed Dec. 9 (H J Res 102—PL 109-383) funded energy and water programs through Feb. 15, 2007, at the lower of the House-passed or fiscal 2006 levels.

The issue of storing highly radioactive waste from the nation's nuclear power plants had generated fierce debate in Congress since the 1970s. Lawmakers in 1987 designated Yucca Mountain, a 6,000-foot-high ridge about one hundred miles northwest of Las Vegas, as the best potential site for an underground repository. Nevada's small congressional delegation objected strenuously, and many also worried about the consequences of trucking tons of nuclear waste across the country every year and storing it in a potentially unsafe place. The nuclear power industry, however, contended that it could be handled safely. *(1987 action, Congress and the Nation Vol. VII, p. 483)*

The federal government had a statutory mandate to take charge of the nuclear waste and put it into a permanent repository. But the Energy Department did not expect the repository—planned for Yucca Mountain in Nevada—to open before 2017. Lawmakers were divided over both the wisdom of continuing to plan for Yucca Mountain and questions over what to do with spent fuel rods until it, or another repository, could be opened.

2005 ACTION

The fiscal 2006 energy-water bill (HR 2419) provoked disputes over money management at the corps and research funding for a new breed of nuclear weapon, as well as over the future of the planned storage site at Yucca Mountain.

Most of the funding in the final bill—$24.3 billion—went for Energy Department defense and nuclear activities, energy research, and renewable energy and conservation programs. The annual appropriations bill also provided money for civil works projects by the Army Corps of Engineers, Interior Department water projects, and the Nuclear Regulatory Commission (NRC).

House Action. The House Appropriations Subcommittee on Energy and Water Development and Related Agencies approved HR 2419 by voice vote May 12, 2005. The full Appropriations Committee approved it May 18, also by voice vote, and reported it (H Rept 109-86) the same day. The House passed the measure 416–13 on May 24.

The bill included $651 million for the Yucca Mountain site, as requested. But because the administration had announced that the site would not open before 2012, David L. Hobson, R-Ohio, chairman of the House Appropriations Subcommittee on Energy and Water Development, added another $10 million for the department to provide interim storage for waste that was accumulating at nuclear facilities across the country. The report directed the department "to take action in fiscal year 2006 to begin accepting spent commercial fuel from the nuclear utilities and placing it in centralized interim storage at one or more [Energy Department] sites."

The measure also set aside $5.5 million for an integrated spent fuel recycling initiative. The report directed the department to select a spent fuel reprocessing technology by the end of fiscal 2007 and to begin planning fuel reprocessing sites and facilities to handle part of the accumulating nuclear waste. The United States had not reprocessed radioactive fuel since 1977 because of proliferation worries.

During the debate on the floor, the House on May 24 rejected, 110–312, an amendment by Edward J. Markey, D-Mass., to reduce nuclear waste disposal funding by $15.5 million and spend it on energy efficiency and conservation.

Senate Action. The Senate Appropriations Committee approved, by 28–0, and reported on June 16 a $31.2 billion version of HR 2419 (S Rept 109-84). Its bill included $577 million for Yucca Mountain, the same as in fiscal 2005 and $84 million less in than in the House bill. The committee did not include funds for temporary waste storage.

Minority Leader Harry Reid of Nevada, a staunch opponent of Yucca Mountain and ranking Democrat on the subcommittee, said, "A far more serious effort than the half-baked approach taken by the House is required to address the mounting failures of the Yucca Mountain program."

The Senate passed the bill 92–3 on July 1.

Conference, Final Action. House and Senate conferees reached agreement Nov. 7 on a $30.5 billion energy-water bill. The House adopted the conference report (H Rept 109-275) by a vote of 399–17 on Nov. 9. The Senate adopted it 84–4 on Nov. 14, completing congressional action on the bill.

Conferees agreed to provide $450 million for Yucca Mountain—$100 million from the industry-funded Nuclear Waste Fund and $350 million for defense-related nuclear disposal. That figure was only a third of what the Energy Department had said in the past that it needed each year to keep the project on track. It represented a 21 percent cut from fiscal 2005 spending. Even the repository's most ardent supporters, however, accepted the reduced funding without much opposition because the facility was mired in delays, including a court battle over safety requirements.

The bill also included $50 million in new funding for the Energy Department to plan a facility for recycling nuclear waste, with construction to begin in fiscal 2010. The conference report directed the energy secretary to submit a detailed plan to the Appropriations Committees by March 31, 2006, and to initiate a site selection competition by June 30, 2006.

The measure included $3.6 billion, less than 1 percent above 2005 funding but about 5 percent more than Bush requested, for research in areas such as high energy physics, nuclear physics, and basic energy sciences. Much of the funding was earmarked for specific institutions.

Republican leaders in both chambers insisted the reduced funding did not mean that Congress was backing away from plans for a permanent waste dump at Yucca Mountain. The agreement did not include the House provision that would have directed the department to begin consolidating the interim storage of nuclear waste starting in 2006.

2006 ACTION

Both a House-passed fiscal 2007 energy-water appropriations bill (HR 5427) and a Senate Appropriations Committee-approved version of the measure would have provided more than the $30 billion that President Bush requested for fiscal 2007. The biggest difference between the two chambers was over nuclear energy programs. House and Senate appropriators disagreed sharply over how to handle the spent fuel rods piling up at commercial nuclear reactors around the country.

The White House requested $250 million for a new program intended to reduce the volume of waste by reprocessing spent fuel for reuse in a new generation of nuclear reactors. The plan, the Global Nuclear Energy Partnership (GNEP), was billed as a way to promote nuclear power internationally and to mitigate problems with nuclear waste.

The proposal ran into problems in the House, where key supporters of nuclear power argued that the initiative was too risky and could divert resources from building a permanent repository at Yucca Mountain—the top priority for the nuclear power industry. At the behest of Hobson, the House agreed to fully fund the president's request for Yucca Mountain but cut the reprocessing budget to $120 million.

Hobson's counterpart in the Senate, the Appropriations Committee's Energy and Water Subcommittee chair Pete V. Domenici, R-N.M., backed the reprocessing program and insisted on providing the full amount requested. Domenici also included a provision in the Senate bill requiring the Energy Department to establish interim facilities for storing spent nuclear fuel rods.

The decision to finish the fiscal 2007 appropriations in the 110th Congress meant the administration's reprocessing program would be put in the hands of Democrats, who were expected to follow Hobson's lead in scaling back the program.

House Subcommittee Action. House Energy and Water Appropriations Subcommittee gave voice-vote approval May 11 to a draft of the bill written by Hobson. In a victory for advocates of nuclear energy, the measure recommended full funding for the Yucca Mountain nuclear waste depository for the first time in several years. However, Hobson included less than half the amount requested for the GNEP, Bush's ambitious initiative to develop new technologies to reprocess spent nuclear fuel.

The bill included

- $545 million, as requested, for Yucca Mountain, a 10 percent increase over fiscal 2006. It also included $30 million for interim waste storage, if such storage were authorized. Supporters of nuclear energy argued that a renaissance of the industry depended on opening the permanent repository in the Nevada desert.
- $150 million, $100 million less than requested, for the GNEP. "I have serious policy, technical and financial reservations about the GNEP proposal," Hobson said. Hobson was relatively skeptical of new technological initiatives, preferring to focus on Yucca Mountain and ways to meet the federal government's commitment to take title to spent nuclear fuel piling up at reactors around the country. He and Joe L. Barton, R-Texas, who chaired the Energy and Commerce Committee, had expressed concern that the GNEP could divert resources from Yucca Mountain.

Overall, most of the funding in the bill—$24.4 billion—would fund the Energy Department.

House Committee Action. The full Appropriations Committee approved the $30.5 billion bill (HR 5427) by voice vote May 17, after further trimming funds for the GNEP. The measure was reported (H Rept 109-474) on May 19.

The committee agreed by voice vote to cut $30 million from the $150 million that had been approved by the subcommittee for the nuclear energy partnership. The amendment, by the subcommittee's ranking Democrat, Peter J. Visclosky of Indiana, specified that the $30 million would go to energy conservation and weatherization activities instead.

House Floor Action. The House passed HR 5427 by a vote of 404–20 on May 24. Among other actions on May 24, the House

- Adopted by voice vote an amendment by Barton to block the use of any money in the $18 billion Nuclear Waste Fund—underwritten by a surcharge on ratepayers to pay for a permanent nuclear waste repository—for the GNEP.
- Rejected 128–295 an attempt by Edward J. Markey, D-Mass., to slash an additional $40 million from the GNEP. Markey described the program as a subsidy for nuclear energy companies that would bring nuclear waste from other nations to the United States for reprocessing—an idea that the administration had promoted as a check on potential proliferation of weapons-grade materials.

Science Committee chairman Sherwood Boehlert, R-N.Y., endorsed the reprocessing program but said it was not ready for the kind of large-scale demonstration programs the administration envisioned.

The White House issued a statement endorsing the bill but opposing the cuts to the GNEP, as well as several other provisions in the measure.

Senate Committee Action. The Senate Appropriations panel approved a $31.2 billion version of HR 5427, 28–0, on June 29 and reported it (S Rept 109-274) the same day. The total for the measure was $1.3 billion above Bush's request and about $710 million more than in the House-passed version. The panel's Energy and Water Subcommittee, which wrote the bill, approved it by voice vote June 27.

For nuclear waste disposal, the committee provided $495 million for Yucca Mountain, $50 million less than in the House bill or Bush's budget. But the appropriators included $250 million for the GNEP, the full amount requested.

Domenici also included a provision requiring the Energy Department to designate interim storage sites for spent fuel in states that were home to nuclear reactors, with an initial down payment of $10 million to get the program off the ground. The House had previously included money for the government to take responsibility for interim radioactive waste storage, but Domenici had left it out of the Senate bill.

Domenici had the support of Senate minority leader Reid, the ranking Democrat on his panel, who had led the fight against Yucca Mountain. "This bill acknowledges something I've said for years—that no geological repository will be operational for decades, and the proposed Yucca Mountain nuclear waste dump is so riddled with problems that it will never open," Reid said.

But Domenici said the interim storage initiative was not a vote of no confidence in Yucca and that short- and long-term waste disposal programs had to move in concert.

The committee's report on the bill said that completion of the interim storage requirements would provide "sufficient and independent grounds" for the Nuclear Regulatory Commission to certify that nuclear waste from future reactors could be handled properly. Such a finding, known as the "waste confidence" rule, was necessary before the NRC could license new nuclear reactors.

Pipeline Safety

Four months after pipeline corrosion prompted the shutdown of the nation's largest oil field, Congress cleared a bill in 2006 intended to help prevent similar occurrences. President George W. Bush signed the measure into law Dec. 29, 2006 (HR 5782—PL 109-468).

Energy giant BP Plc announced Aug. 6 that widespread corrosion would force a temporary suspension of production at its Prudhoe Bay facility on Alaska's North Slope. Lawmakers with responsibility for energy programs called for swift action to preclude such incidents from recurring, but it took House and Senate committees until the end of the session to reconcile different versions of the legislation.

One of the central issues in the reauthorization debate was the regulation of "low-stress" pipelines. These smaller pipelines operate at lower stress or pressure levels, below 20 percent of their normal capacity, and are used to feed liquids into larger pipelines. The pipelines where BP found corrosion were low-stress lines that fed oil to the Trans-Alaska pipeline.

On Aug. 31, the Pipeline and Hazardous Materials Safety Administration, which was responsible for the oversight of pipeline safety, announced that it was developing regulations for low-stress pipelines in certain environmentally sensitive areas. Critics said the plan would leave too many pipelines unregulated. Both the House Energy and Commerce Committee and the Senate Commerce, Science, and Transportation Committee versions of the bill required that regulations be developed to cover all low-stress pipelines. The House Transportation and Infrastructure Committee bill would have limited the regulation to pipelines in unusually sensitive areas.

The last authorization for federal pipeline safety programs (PL 107-355) expired Sept. 30, 2006. *(Earlier action, Congress and the Nation Vol. XI, p. 424)*

LEGISLATIVE ACTION

The House Transportation and Infrastructure Committee approved a limited version of HR 5782 that would have given the safety administration new oversight over low-stress pipelines, but only in especially environmentally sensitive areas. The bill, sponsored by Chairman Don Young, R-Alaska, would have authorized about $340 million over four years. The committee approved it by voice vote on July 19, 2006, and formally reported it (H Rept 109-717, Part I) on Dec. 5.

The House Energy and Commerce Committee approved an amended version of HR 5782 by voice vote on Sept. 27 and reported it (H Rept 109-717, Part II) on Dec. 5. The bill proposed to bring regulation of low-stress pipelines up to the standards applied to larger ones and to authorize $331 million through 2010, $8 million less than in the Transportation bill.

The Senate Commerce, Science, and Transportation Committee approved its own bill (S 3961) Nov. 16 without holding a formal markup. Like the Energy and Commerce bill, it called for subjecting low-stress pipelines to the same standards and regulations as other hazardous-liquid pipelines. It would have authorized $353 million through 2010. Chairman Ted Stevens, R-Alaska, the bill's sponsor, said he hoped that the Senate would pass the measure that evening by voice vote, but the leadership did not call it up.

After negotiations among the three committees, the House passed a compromise version of HR 5782 by voice vote Dec. 6. The rule for floor debate substituted the amended bill. The Senate passed, and thus cleared, the bill by voice vote Dec. 7.

MAJOR PROVISIONS

Following are the major provisions of HR 5782, as enacted.

- Reauthorized the Transportation Department's pipeline safety programs for four years, through fiscal 2010.
- Authorized a total of $353 million over that period for activities relating to gas and hazardous liquid pipelines, as well as additional amounts for other pipeline safety programs. The total included $276 million from accounts funded by fees paid by operators and $77 million from the Oil Spill Liability Trust Fund.
- Required that nearly all low-stress pipelines be subject to the "same standards and regulations as other hazardous liquid pipelines." The Transportation Department was directed to issue regulations by Dec. 31, 2007, to accomplish this.
- Established civil penalties for excavators who did not follow requirements. Contractors were barred from digging without contacting available one-call systems.

Such systems notified local utilities so that they could come out to the site of a project and mark the location of underground pipes or facilities that could be damaged. Excavators also were prohibited from disregarding markers of underground facilities made by a pipeline operator.

- Directed the Transportation Department to issue regulations by June 1, 2008, aimed at combating fatigue in pipeline control rooms. Operators of pipeline facilities were required to develop plans for control room operators that included maximum hours of service.
- Required the Transportation Department, by Dec. 31, 2007, to issue minimum standards for managing distribution pipelines.
- Authorized grants to state pipeline authorities and municipalities to improve the quality and effectiveness of their pipeline damage prevention programs.

Clean Air Act

A Bush administration push for a major rewrite of the Clean Air Act, known as Clear Skies, made little headway in the 109th Congress. The legislation (S 131) stalled in the first session when the Senate Environment and Public Works Committee rejected it on a tie vote, dashing White House hopes to move one of its highest environmental priorities.

The White House plan, first outlined in 2002, would replace the Clean Air Act's industrial pollution regulatory structure with a market-based framework to curb power plant emissions of three pollutants—sulfur dioxide, nitrogen oxides, and mercury. Under a "cap and trade" system, power plants that exceeded federal standards for pollutants could buy credits from companies that reduced their emission levels below the federal standards. *(108th Congress action, Congress and the Nation Vol. XI, p. 437)*

Sponsors said S 131, backed by coal-fired utilities and other industries, would short-circuit costly litigation, establish a stable regulatory environment, and allow power plants to curb pollution in a cost-effective way. Environmentalists and many Democrats opposed the plan largely because it would not regulate a fourth pollutant—carbon dioxide, the greenhouse gas associated with climate change. Without carbon dioxide as part of the measure, Lincoln Chafee, R-R.I., joined all the Democrats and James M. Jeffords, I-Vt., on the Environment and Public Works Committee to defeat the bill in a 9–9 vote March 9.

Chafee and two Democrats, Max Baucus of Montana and Barack Obama of Illinois, said they were willing to negotiate on legislation that would regulate carbon dioxide but without imposing a strict cap on emissions. But committee chairman James M. Inhofe, R-Okla., was unyielding on the carbon dioxide issue, and the plan died.

Both sides blamed the other for the defeat. Inhofe said the bill "has been killed by environmental extremists who care more about continuing the litigation-friendly status quo and making a political statement on carbon dioxide than they do about reducing air pollution."

Regulation of carbon dioxide emissions, which many scientists saw as a major contributor to global warming, had been the biggest sticking point in debate over the bill. Several Democrats said they would accept language that would address the carbon dioxide issue without placing mandatory caps on the emissions, but committee members could not agree on exactly what the carbon dioxide language should be.

Inhofe had repeatedly called global warming a "hoax" and was reluctant to support any significant action on carbon dioxide emissions. Several opponents of the legislation said the current Clean Air Act was preferable to the Clear Skies legislation.

Democrats complained that the process was much more partisan than in 1990, the last time the Clean Air Act was revised. That law (PL 101-549) imposed new federal standards on urban smog, automobile exhaust, toxic air pollution, and acid rain. *(1990 action, Congress and the Nation Vol. VIII, p. 473)*

The rejected S 131 would prohibit power plants from emitting any pollutant in excess of the allowance it currently held. The EPA administrator would create a monitoring and recording system to ensure that utilities were not exceeding their prescribed allowances. A penalty would be charged to owners or operators of facilities that exceeded their emission requirements. Allocations would be based on how much fuel a utility used to operate. In addition, facilities would be required to submit a permit application that laid out a plan to meet the emission allowance requirements.

The bill would permit a one-year waiver of emissions limits to be obtained by utilities through a petition to the Energy Department. The owner of the unit would have to prove that compliance with the bill's regulations would threaten the unit's reliability in providing power or its prospects for staying in business.

It would establish a ceiling price for those units of plant emissions allowances that could be sold. If the emission trading market reached the price ceiling, then the amounts stipulated in the bill would take effect: $2,000 per ton of sulfur dioxide, $4,000 per ton of nitrogen oxides, and $2,187 for each unit of mercury. The ceiling prices would be annually adjusted to inflation. Once the safety prices were reached, no limit was placed on how many emission allowances a utility could purchase.

Some clean-coal technology projects were exempted from new source performance standards and new source review. The bill also would allow overall exceptions to new source review, which required some new or expanded power plants and factories to install new antipollution equipment. Other units that would not be required to participate in the program could opt into the emissions program if they chose.

The bill set separate standards for Western states. The collection of Western states known as the Western Regional Air Partnership (WRAP) was made up of Arizona, California, Colorado, Idaho, Nevada, New Mexico, Oregon, Utah, and Wyoming. WRAP would be allowed to emit 271,000 tons of sulfur dioxide per year.

Endangered Species

The House passed a bill (HR 3824) in 2005 that called for sweeping changes to the 1973 Endangered Species Act. But the Senate took no action on the measure.

HR 3824—written by House Resources Committee Chairman Richard W. Pombo, R-Calif.—proposed to revise scientific standards used in developing endangered species policies, end the federal government's power to protect critical habitats, and compensate affected private property owners.

Pombo and his supporters said the bill would streamline the environmental law and enlist the help of landowners instead of penalizing them for having threatened or endangered species on their property. But Democrats and lawmakers from more urban districts opposed Pombo's approach as providing a financial windfall for private interests and stripping away the environmental protections that were essential to restoring endangered species.

Lincoln Chafee, R-R.I., who chaired the Senate Environment and Public Works subcommittee with jurisdiction over endangered species, did not bring the bill up in the 109th Congress. Instead, Chafee and other senators requested a study of the critical habitat issue.

BACKGROUND

The 1973 Endangered Species Law (PL 93-205) was enacted with little opposition to protect wildlife at risk of extinction because of human development and pollution. It allowed the Fish and Wildlife Service and the National Marine Fisheries Service to designate species as endangered or threatened and to issue regulations protecting their habitats to increase their numbers. The law's last reauthorization effort failed in 1992, but Congress had continued to appropriate money for the agencies to issue and enforce regulations. *(1973 law, Congress and the Nation Vol. IV, p. 289; 1992 action, Congress and the Nation Vol. VIII, p. 521)*

Over time, the act had become among the most controversial and powerful of the nation's environmental laws. Unlike many major environmental measures that sought to protect human health or enhance outdoor recreation, the Endangered Species Act aimed to protect rare species of plants and animals. Developers and property owners worried that it put the interests of obscure flowers or insects over the construction of commercial or residential projects. Environmentalists successfully used the law to block work on highways, dams, and other projects, forcing the government to designate and preserve critical habitats that were home to endangered species.

Since the law's enactment, the government had listed nearly thirteen hundred domestic species as threatened or endangered. The law had helped spur the recover of a few high-profile species, such as the bald eagle and the grizzly bear. But just seventeen species had increased their populations enough to be removed from endangered lists since the law's enactment, and the federal government faced numerous lawsuits over the status of critical habitat land.

For years, lawmakers of both parties, ranchers, and environmental groups had contended that the law needed to be updated in light of new challenges. But sharp disagreement existed over what should be done. Private property rights advocates and developers generally felt that the government should provide incentives for landowners to voluntarily conserve species on their land, instead of imposing mandatory restrictions. Environmentalists worried that the government spent years listing a species as endangered and taking the necessary steps to begin to protect it.

LEGISLATIVE ACTION

As chairman of the House Resources Committee, Pombo negotiated with committee Democrats for several months before releasing a detailed bill. The bipartisan effort paid off Sept. 22, 2005, when eight committee Democrats joined all but two Republicans to approve HR 3824 by 26–12. The measure was reported (H Rept 109-237) on Sept. 27.

A group of twenty-three moderate Republican House members urged Majority Leader Tom DeLay, R-Texas, not to rush the bill to the floor, saying it contained "perhaps the most profound changes to environmental law since the Clean Air Act Amendments of 1990." Nevertheless, the House on Sept. 29 passed HR 3824 on a **key vote of 229–193 (R 193–34; D 36–158; I 0–1).** Pombo succeeded in offsetting the Republican votes he lost with support from thirty-six Democrats, many from Western and Midwestern states. *(2005 key votes, p. 915)*

Supporters said the bill would replace a broken law with a more inclusive program that enlisted landowners in a coordinated species recovery effort. But environmentalists and many Democrats said the changes would go too far and would primarily benefit private interests, to the detriment of plants and animals in need of protection. They also raised concerns about the bill's potential cost.

Before passing HR 3824, the House Sept. 29 narrowly rejected 206–216 a Democratic substitute amendment offered by George Miller, D-Calif., which won support from twenty-nine Republicans. The substitute was designed to eliminate the "critical habitat" designation and rely instead on recovery plans. It also would have offered new financial incentives and legal protections to landowners to save species and require greater state involvement in decision making.

MAJOR PROVISIONS

The House-passed bill would have

- Reauthorized the Endangered Species Act through 2010.
- Eliminated the ability of federal officials to protect plant and animal species in danger of extinction by designating areas of critical habitat and placing restrictions on use of the land or water.
- Replaced the critical habitat designation with a much-expanded recovery program to increase the populations of endangered species. Each recovery plan would have to contain measurable steps and identify areas of "special value" to the conservation of the species. These special value areas would replace the critical habitat designation for any species whose recovery plan was being developed shortly before the bill's enactment. The bill did not specify whether recovery plans would be legally binding.
- Authorized the Interior Department to enter into species recovery agreements with private landowners, in which the landowner would develop and carry out conservation plans and the government would provide grants to pay the costs of implementation. The grant money would have to be used to conserve a species by increasing its numbers.
- Required the federal government to compensate property owners who were adversely affected by a decision about an endangered species. The property owner would be reimbursed for the fair market value of the land use if no compromise could be reached to permit otherwise legal development.
- Changed the standard for making decisions about endangered species to the "best available scientific data," defined as the best information available to the Interior Department at the time of a decision to protect a species. The information would have to come from peer-reviewed sources. The existing standard was the "best scientific and commercial data available."
- Expanded the Interior Department's ability to enter into conservation agreements with states to protect species at risk of being threatened or endangered. Existing law allowed such agreements only for species already listed as endangered or threatened.

Oil Refineries

House GOP leaders won passage of an energy bill in 2005 (HR 3893) intended to spur construction of oil refineries. But Democrats and moderate Republicans lambasted the legislation, calling it a giveaway to the industry. The Senate Environment and Public Works Committee rejected a similar bill (S 1772).

Joe L. Barton, R-Texas, chairman of the House Energy and Commerce Committee, promoted the legislation as a way to alleviate distribution bottlenecks of the kind that occurred in the Gulf Coast after Hurricanes Katrina and Rita in 2005. The storms devastated much of the energy infrastructure in the Gulf of Mexico region, which contained 47 percent of the nation's oil refining capacity and 19 percent of the natural gas production. The national retail price for gasoline increased by 46 cents to $3.07 per gallon in the week after Hurricane Katrina.

Supporters stressed that no U.S. refineries had been built since 1976 and that the number of operating facilities had dropped by more than half since 1981. The bill sought to put the Energy Department in charge of the permit process for new refineries, expedite court challenges, and allow companies to petition the government for economic damages if their refinery projects were unnecessarily delayed. The number of specialty gasoline and diesel fuel blends that had to be produced to meet regional air pollution rules would be limited to six.

HR 3893 called for the president to designate potential new refinery sites on federal lands, including three on closed military bases.

In response to soaring gas prices, the measure specified that it was illegal for gasoline or diesel fuel vendors to engage in price-gouging in any region that had been declared a major disaster area. It also required the Federal Trade Commission (FTC) to investigate and report to Congress on possible price-gouging after Katrina and Rita.

The Congressional Budget Office calculated that the bill would increase direct spending by $3 billion over ten years.

The bill drew sharp criticism from environmental groups. "Unfortunately, this appears to be a cynical attempt to exploit the recent hurricanes for political gain—and the gain of well-connected special-interest polluters," said Frank O'Donnell, president of the environmental advocacy group Clean Air Watch. Most Democrats and a group of moderate Republicans said the legislation would undermine environmental safeguards to help an already profitable industry.

Before the floor debate, Barton dropped a contentious White House-backed provision that would have clarified for the courts an Environmental Protection Agency (EPA) rule designed to make it easier for power plants to upgrade their facilities without installing new equipment to reduce smokestack pollutants.

HOUSE COMMITTEE ACTION

The House Energy and Commerce Committee approved Barton's bill (HR 3893) by voice vote Sept. 29, 2005, at the end of a sixteen-hour markup. The bill was formally reported (H Rept 109-244, Part I) on Oct. 6.

Much of the committee debate was over a White House-backed provision to amend new source review language in the Clean Air Act that required industries upgrading their facilities to install modern antipollution controls unless the improvements were routine maintenance.

The bill proposed to codify a regulation issued by the Bush administration changing the definition of routine maintenance. That regulation was being challenged in court. Barton included the provision, which would shield the administration from such court challenges, at the administration's request.

During the markup, the committee

- Rejected 16–24 an attempt to limit the new source review provision to oil and gas facilities.

Agreed by voice vote to add language directing the FTC to crack down on alleged price-gouging by gasoline and diesel fuel sellers, with penalties of up to $11,000 per day for violators.

- Defeated 23–27 a Democratic substitute amendment that would have charged the Energy Department with constructing and operating a "strategic refining reserve" similar in concept to the Strategic Petroleum Reserve, the nation's crude oil stockpile. It also called for steeper fines and broader federal authority to investigate price-gouging throughout petroleum markets.

HOUSE FLOOR ACTION

House Republican leaders eked out a 212–210 win for the bill Oct. 7, after holding the balloting open an extra forty minutes while they persuaded two Republicans to change their "nay" votes to "yea." Democrats chanted, "Shame! Shame! Shame!" when the gavel finally fell.

The night before the vote, Barton dropped the new source review provisions at the request of the House leadership and the White House. The provisions had become a lightning rod for most Democrats and some moderate Republicans, who said the plan was the latest example of House GOP leaders using the hurricanes in the Gulf Coast as an excuse to try to get rid of environmental rules unpopular with energy companies. Barton said Speaker J. Dennis Hastert, R-Ill., and White House chief of staff Andrew H. Card Jr. decided late Oct. 6 that it would be wise to remove the provision from the bill, hold hearings, and move it later as separate legislation. That did not go far enough to satisfy bill critics, including a small band of moderate Republicans, who said the bill was fatally flawed because it would compromise too many existing environmental laws.

Democrats again offered their substitute, but the amendment was rejected 199–222 on Oct. 7.

At one point, sponsors had hoped to attach another bill that would have allowed energy leasing in protected coastal waters and the Arctic National Wildlife Refuge (ANWR). But Resources chairman Richard W. Pombo, R-Calif., decided to hold off on that plan after the measure drew sharp criticism from Florida lawmakers and the state's Republican governor, Jeb Bush.

Pombo's original bill would have let coastal states choose to opt out of a federal moratorium on energy leasing on the Outer Continental Shelf—already a tough sell in the Senate and with Florida lawmakers. But in marking up the bill, the Resources Committee went further, adopting an amendment to lift the moratorium outright for natural gas development, leaving states at the mercy of the federal government.

SENATE COMMITTEE ACTION

The Senate Environment and Public Works Committee rejected a narrower refinery bill (S 1772—no written report) by a 9–9 vote, after moderate Republican Lincoln Chafee of Rhode Island joined Democrats in voting against the measure. Chafee said Congress should be addressing gasoline consumption as well as demand.

The measure, sponsored by Chairman James M. Inhofe, R-Okla., included provisions to reduce the number of "boutique" fuels used to meet air-quality regulations, allow states to opt into a new program streamlining the permitting process for new refinery projects, encourage the siting of new refineries on former military bases, and authorize federal funding for state and local organizations working to redevelop those sites.

Opponents argued that the bill would lower environmental standards and authorize monetary aid for oil refiners that were already profiting from gasoline prices.

The committee rejected, 8–10, a Democratic substitute that would have directed the EPA to establish and run refineries as part of a Strategic Refinery Reserve similar to the Strategic Petroleum Reserve.

2007–2008

Lawmakers in the 110th Congress continued to focus on energy issues. Environmentalists achieved a key priority in 2007 when Congress agreed to increase fuel efficiency standards as part of a wide-ranging energy bill. The measure also called for an increase in the use of ethanol and other biofuels and stipulated that the incandescent light bulb would be replaced by more energy-efficient alternatives. To win enactment, however, Democrats agreed to drop controversial provisions, including a renewable fuels mandate for electricity companies.

One year later, Republicans won an unexpected victory by ending a moratorium on new offshore oil and gas drilling. Amid public angst over the high price of gasoline, they skillfully forced Democratic leaders to agree to lift the twenty-six-year ban, which had prohibited expanded drilling off the Atlantic and Pacific coasts to prevent potentially damaging oil spills. Republicans contended that offshore production would help bring down prices and reduce dependence on foreign oil without jeopardizing the environment, and they were boosted by polls showing rising public sentiment for offshore drilling.

Lawmakers in both parties supported tax breaks to increase renewable energy. Some of these tax incentives made their way into a 2008 package of popular tax cuts, while those that focused on biofuels were added to the 2008 farm bill.

On a key environmental issue, Democrats failed to schedule a floor vote on a climate change bill that would have capped emissions of greenhouse gases, blamed for causing global warming. Although climate change was a priority for Democratic leaders, the complexity of the issue and the opposition of key Republicans prevented action on the matter.

Congress also considered two major infrastructure bills. Lawmakers overrode a presidential veto to enact a \$23.2 billion water resources bill, authorizing funding for nine hundred Army Corps of Engineers navigation, flood control, and environmental restoration projects. Differences over a labor provision, however, prevented lawmakers from agreeing on a reauthorization of the popular Clean Water State Revolving Fund, the largest source of low-interest loans for constructing wastewater treatment facilities and other water pollution abatement projects.

Energy Policy

Just two years after passing comprehensive energy legislation, Congress in 2007 cleared another significant energy bill (HR 6), which President George W. Bush signed into law Dec. 19 (PL 110-140).

The new law focused on conservation and alternative energy sources. It set the first statutory increase in vehicle fuel efficiency standards in thirty-two years, mandated the use of at least 36 billion gallons of ethanol and other biofuels annually by 2022, and spelled the end of the incandescent light bulb in favor of energy-efficient lighting.

The measure cleared after nearly a year of negotiations, partisan bickering, and White House veto threats. Late in the first session, Democratic leaders dropped two initiatives from the bill to win Senate passage and avert a presidential veto: a package of tax incentives for alternative energy and a renewable electricity standard.

Democrats had set energy and climate issues as a legislative priority when they took control of the new Congress in January. Although forced to pare back some of the more ambitious provisions to overcome Republican filibuster threats in the Senate, the Democratic leadership called the final product a down payment on weaning the United States off foreign sources of oil and reducing emissions.

BACKGROUND

Faced with rising oil prices and concerns over energy supplies, Congress had passed a sweeping energy bill in 2005. The law (HR 6—PL 109-58) addressed nearly every sector of the energy industry, providing incentives for coal producers, nuclear power, oil and gas companies, renewable power, energy efficiency, and electric utilities. *(Energy overhaul, p. 447)*

GOP leaders praised the measure as striking a balance among traditional energy sources, such as oil, coal, and nuclear power; alternatives such as renewable energy; and conservation. But Democrats were unhappy that the measure failed to set new vehicle fuel efficiency standards or require reductions in greenhouse gas emissions, such as carbon dioxide, that scientists called a primary contributor to climate change. They also worried that the new law mainly subsidized traditional producers of oil and natural gas and would do little to help reduce the nation's appetite for fuel.

When Democrats took control of both chambers at the beginning of the 110th Congress, they intended to pursue an aggressive reexamination of the way the government encouraged energy production. In particular, some wanted oil and gas companies to pay for having profited handsomely throughout an energy crunch.

Their immediate focus was on the Gulf of Mexico, where Exxon Mobil Corp. and other large energy companies drilled in government waters without paying royalties to the Treasury, the result of a drafting error in more than 1,000 leases. Democratic leaders wanted to recoup the lost royalties and funnel the money toward alternative fuel development and conservation measures.

Royalties aside, Democrats were concerned that higher energy prices were stoking economic anxiety and, in fact, hurting middle- and working-class families. They blamed the Bush administration and Republican-controlled Congresses for creating a regulatory atmosphere conducive to profiteering. As Rep. Edward J. Markey, D-Mass., liked to say, "Subsidizing an oil company to drill is like subsidizing a fish to swim"

Many Democrats were determined to advance a number of energy initiatives, such as increasing fuel efficiency standards for passenger cars and mandating the expanded use of ethanol and other alternative fuels. They had in mind a restructuring of the nation's approach to energy with an eye toward reducing oil dependence and fostering more environmentally friendly sources of energy.

For the powerful oil and gas industry, this represented a jarring turn of events. The administration and Congress had worked hard, especially after the Sept. 11, 2001, terrorist attacks, to encourage more domestic oil and gas production, arguing that such moves would over time make the United States less vulnerable to supply shocks triggered by political instability around the globe.

Although concerned by the political landscape, supporters of the oil and gas industry could point to examples over the past thirty years when ambitious proposals to transform energy policy had been scaled back in the name of political expediency. In 1978, for example, Congress scuttled President Jimmy Carter's plan to raise gasoline taxes—part of a larger effort to eliminate industry incentives and reduce domestic energy consumption—after Democrats fragmented because of fears that raising gasoline prices would alienate voters.

The industry characterized attempts to roll back the tax breaks and incentives as misguided policy on a par with the windfall tax on oil industry profits that Congress imposed on oil companies in 1980. That tax, which was repealed in 1988 as the government dismantled its price controls for oil, essentially imposed an excise tax of up to 70 percent on the difference between the market price of oil and a predetermined base price. *(Windfall profits tax, Congress and the Nation Vol. V, p. 503; Repeal, Congress and the Nation Vol. VII, p. 491)*

HOUSE PASSAGE OF HR 6

On Jan. 18, 2007, the House passed a narrow bill (HR 6) that proposed to cancel $14 billion in tax breaks and other subsidies for oil and gas companies and deposit the resulting revenue into a fund to promote alternatives to fossil fuels. The measure passed 264–163 after a contentious daylong debate on both the substance of the measure and the fact that Democratic leaders did not send it through the regular committee process or allow floor amendments.

The main provisions of the House-passed bill were as follows.

- Created a new Strategic Energy Efficiency and Renewables Reserve account, funded by any new federal royalties and taxes collected as a result of the bill. The account would support projects to accelerate the use of domestic renewable energy resources and alternative fuels; promote the use of energy-efficient products; and increase research, development, and deployment of clean, renewable energy and efficiency technologies.
- Required oil companies holding flawed offshore drilling leases issued in 1998 and 1999 to renegotiate the deals or pay a "conservation of resources fee" as compensation before they could bid on more drilling leases. (Revenue: $4.45 billion over ten years)

Under a 1995 law (PL 104-58), oil companies were granted waivers from paying production royalties as an incentive to drill in deep Gulf of Mexico waters when energy prices were low. However, in a drafting error, some 1998 and 1999 leases did not include a threshold price above which companies would have to pay royalties to the Treasury. Bipartisan anger erupted over reports in 2006 that many companies were extracting oil and gas royalty-free while running up record profits. *(1995 law, Congress and the Nation Vol. IX, p. 471)*

However, many Republicans joined the White House and the oil industry in arguing that the legislation violated the sanctity of contracts by retroactively imposing new legal conditions.

- Imposed a similar fee on all nonproducing oil and gas leases in the gulf. (Revenue: $1.75 billion over ten years)
- Eliminated a tax credit for oil and gas companies that was extended to those industries in 2004 (PL 108-357). (Revenue: $7.6 billion over ten years) *(2004 law, Congress and the Nation Vol. XI, p. 115)*
- Increased the period over which major oil companies could deduct geological and geophysical expenses to seven years from five. (Revenue: $104 million over ten years)

Republicans argued that the bill would increase dependence on foreign oil and cause gas prices to rise by reducing incentives for domestic production. But Democrats said the price of oil was incentive enough for oil companies to do what they did best, which was to produce more crude.

SENATE REWRITE OF HR 6

The Senate on June 21 passed a complete rewrite of HR 6, based largely on a bill (S 1321) that the Energy and Natural Resources Committee had approved 20–3 on May 2 and formally reported (S Rept 110-65) on May 7. HR 6, which the Senate passed 65–27, included an increase in fuel efficiency requirements for cars and trucks, but senators rejected a package of tax incentives for renewable energy and a plan to require that utilities generate more power from cleaner fuels.

Passage came shortly before midnight, after a delay of several hours during which Democratic leaders called senators back to the Capitol to fend off a last-minute challenge by the auto industry and to invoke cloture to end debate.

The bill contained provisions to

Renewable fuels mandate. Require the use of 36 billion gallons of renewable fuels annually by 2022. Use would have to increase to 15 billion gallons of biofuels annually, largely corn ethanol, by 2015. Beginning in 2016, the bill would require an annual increase of 3 billion gallons from advanced biofuels such as cellulosic ethanol, which could be made from switchgrass, agricultural waste, or wood chips.

Fuel economy standards. Increase corporate average fuel economy (CAFE) standards for all passenger cars and light trucks by roughly 40 percent by 2020, to a fleetwide average of thirty-five miles per gallon.

Energy efficiency. Codify pending efficiency standards for various household appliances; require the federal government to purchase 15 percent of its electricity from renewable sources by 2015; and promote energy-savings programs in public buildings.

International partnerships. Direct the secretary of state to pursue "strategic energy partnerships" with major energy-producing and energy-consuming nations to increase international energy security.

Carbon sequestration research. Promote research and development into technologies that could capture carbon dioxide from power plants and other industrial facilities and then sequester the greenhouse gas underground.

Price-gouging. Make price-gouging in petroleum markets a federal crime during a presidentially declared "national energy emergency."

OPEC. Make the Organization of Petroleum Exporting Countries subject to U.S. antitrust laws.

The last two provisions drew veto threats from the White House.

The bill was the object of intense lobbying by oil and gas companies, environmental groups, and especially automakers, which ran print and broadcast ads touting a less stringent proposal for increased CAFE standards. Domestic auto manufacturers had beaten back attempts to raise CAFE standards as recently as 2005 by arguing that higher standards threatened U.S. manufacturing jobs and ignored the safety advantages of sport utility vehicles (SUVs), pickups, and minivans, which were treated as light trucks.

But the Democratic takeover of Congress and widespread concern over climate change altered the calculus in 2007. The matter was decided in surprisingly swift fashion on the Senate floor after Ted Stevens, R-Alaska, offered a compromise to drop the distinction between cars and trucks and raise the standards by roughly 40 percent by 2020, to a fleetwide average of thirty-five miles per gallon. As part of the compromise, proponents of tough CAFE standards dropped a proposal to raise standards 4 percent annually after 2020.

Stevens praised the deal at a news conference, then proceeded to the Senate floor, where it was adopted by voice vote as an amendment. The quick resolution to an issue that had stymied the chamber for more than a decade caught some negotiators by surprise.

Tax package. During the floor debate, the Senate rejected a $32.1 billion tax package that would have raised taxes on oil and gas production to fund initiatives for renewable energy and new technologies. Senators on June 21 rejected 57–36 a motion to cut off debate on the tax proposals, which the Finance Committee had approved 15–5 on June 19. The cost reflected in the committee draft had more than doubled during the markup—in part because many of the proposed tax benefits for renewable energy were changed to five years from the two years in the original bill.

Republicans objected mainly to the majority's way of paying for new and extended tax breaks by prohibiting the major oil companies from claiming a deduction that was used by domestic manufacturers and adding a new tax on oil and gas extracted from the gulf to penalize the companies that signed royalty-free leases.

Electricity. Democrats surrendered on another top priority when Majority Leader Harry Reid, D-Nev., declined to file a petition to shut off debate on a proposal to require investor-owned utilities to produce 15 percent of their electricity from renewable fuels by 2020. The amendment was offered by New Mexico Democrat Jeff Bingaman, chairman of the Energy and Natural Resources Committee. It was widely opposed by senators from the Southeast, who said their region did not have sufficient wind power—the most economically competitive form of renewable energy—to meet the proposed standard.

Under the amendment, utilities that reduced power consumption by up to 4 percent through efficiency measures could count that amount toward the 15 percent mandate or use it to buy efficiency credits from other utilities. That drew strenuous objection from Pete V. Domenici of New Mexico, the ranking Republican on Energy and Natural Resources, who branded the mandate a poison pill for the entire bill.

Although Democrats insisted they had sixty votes to adopt Bingaman's proposal, Reid never filed the petition that was a precondition for the vote—a decision he later said he regretted.

Coal-to-liquid fuels. Senators turned back two amendments that would have encouraged the development of coal-to-liquid fuels. Both were opposed by a coalition of environmental groups—including Friends of the Earth, the Sierra Club, Greenpeace, and the U.S. Public Interest Research Group—which expressed concerns that the proposals would increase greenhouse gas emissions and exacerbate global warming.

The Senate on June 19 rejected, 39–55, an amendment by Jim Bunning, R-Ky., and Domenici to require an increase in production of coal-to-liquid fuels to six billion gallons by 2022. The proposal also would have required that liquefied coal emit 20 percent less greenhouse gases than gasoline, the same standard applied in the bill for cellulosic ethanol.

"Coal-to-liquid process could one day produce a fuel that is carbon-neutral," Bunning said. "This is not pie in the sky."

The Senate also rejected 33–61 on June 19 an amendment by Jon Tester, D-Mont., to provide federal loans for coal-to-liquid plants that captured and stored 75 percent of carbon dioxide emissions. Tester's amendment prompted letters of support from Dow Chemical Co. and labor unions, including the AFL-CIO and the United Mine Workers of America.

OPEC. Ignoring Bush's veto threat, the Senate adopted 70–23 on June 19 an amendment by Herb Kohl, D-Wis., to make it illegal under U.S. antitrust laws for any foreign state, including OPEC members, to limit production or set the prices of oil and other petroleum products. Kohl maintained that decisions by OPEC nations to fix prices were commercial in nature, not governmental, and should not be shielded by sovereign immunity.

HOUSE PASSAGE OF HR 3221

The House passed a comprehensive energy bill (HR 3221) by a vote of 241–172 on Aug. 4 that drew on measures approved by the Energy and Commerce Committee in June, along with contributions from several other panels.

A $16.1 billion tax package reported by the Ways and Means Committee (HR 2776—H Rept 110-214) was automatically incorporated into HR 3221 under the rule for floor debate, after the House passed the tax proposals 221–189 on Aug. 4.

Minority Leader John A. Boehner, R-Ohio, charged that the bill was written "at the behest of radical environmentalists" and that Democrats opted for legislation "that cuts the lifeblood of our economy off at the knees by increasing taxes to pay for 'green' pork projects and imposing new regulations that discourage American exploration."

The combined House bill differed in major ways from the Senate-passed HR 6. Conspicuously absent were proposals for new vehicle fuel economy standards and requirements for the use of renewable fuel, both of which were in the Senate-passed bill.

At the same time, HR 3221 included sections not in the Senate measure, such as tax incentives to promote alternative fuels, a requirement for electricity companies to use renewable fuels, and a cutback in tax breaks for oil companies that had royalty-free leases in the gulf.

Fuel economy standards. The fact that the bill omitted new fuel economy standards—a priority for top Democrats in both chambers—was a victory for auto manufacturers that had waged an unsuccessful battle to keep the issue off the table when the Senate considered energy legislation.

Some congressional aides said the industry failed to appreciate new political forces driven by mounting concerns about global warming, the security of foreign oil supplies, and higher energy prices. House Energy and Commerce Committee chair John D. Dingell, D-Mich., said tough fuel economy standards would "seriously threaten" his support for the bill, adding that he would fight "most emphatically" in conference to put off the issue until it could be considered as part of a separate climate change bill in the fall. Few observers expected such a measure to be enacted before the 2008 election.

Republicans had tried during the Energy and Commerce Committee markup to increase the CAFE standards, but their amendment was rejected 26–31. The Bush administration also weighed in with a letter to Speaker Nancy Pelosi, D-Calif., urging her to address both CAFE standards and biofuels at the time, instead of in the fall as Dingell wanted. The letter was signed by the secretaries of energy, transportation, interior, and Treasury, as well as the Environmental Protection Agency (EPA) administrator.

Alternative fuels. Also absent from the House energy package was a requirement for increased use of ethanol and other alternative transportation fuels. The White House had made an alternative fuels mandate a centerpiece of its plan to reduce gasoline consumption by 20 percent in a decade. The Senate energy bill included the required use of thirty-six billion gallons a year of renewable fuels by 2022.

Pelosi said she supported a renewable fuels mandate in principle but noted concerns raised by a variety of interests, including environmental and agricultural groups, about potential increases in air and water pollution as well as habitat destruction from increased agricultural production.

Electricity standard. Despite opposition from some leading Democrats, the House voted 220–190 on Aug. 4, largely along regional lines, to adopt an amendment by Tom Udall, D-N.M., requiring that utilities produce 15 percent of their power from renewable sources by 2020.

Opponents of Udall's amendment included several committee chairmen, three of whom spearheaded the bulk of the energy legislation: Dingell, Science and Technology's Bart Gordon of Tennessee, and Natural Resources' Nick J. Rahall II of West Virginia. As in the Senate, the amendment presented a particular problem for Southern Democrats. The dispute extended into the leadership ranks: Majority Whip James E. Clyburn, D-S.C., voted against the amendment.

Gulf oil leases. The bill included the provisions requiring companies holding royalty-free deep-water leases in the gulf to renegotiate the leases. Otherwise, they would have to pay a conservation-of-resources fee on production and be unable to acquire new leases. The Congressional Budget Office said that would bring in $5.8 billion over ten years. Imposition of the fee on all nonproducing oil and gas leases in the gulf would bring in an additional $1.65 billion in that period.

Tax package. The tax package, introduced by Ways and Means chairman Charles B. Rangel, D-N.Y., and added by the rule, consisted of $13.6 billion in revenue-losing tax incentives and $15.2 billion in revenue-raising provisions over ten years, according to the Joint Committee on Taxation. The net effect would be an increase to the Treasury of $1.6 billion over that period. The committee had approved HR 2776, 24–16, along party lines June 20. The proposals applied the same philosophy that the Senate

Finance Committee followed: Take money from the oil and gas industry and use it to spur alternative fuels.

The main provisions of HR 2776 were as follows.

- A modification and extension of the main tax credit for companies that produced electricity from sources such as wind and solar energy. The credit was due to expire for property added after 2008. (Cost: $6.6 billion over ten years)
- A series of tax breaks to encourage energy conservation, such as a credit for plug-in hybrid vehicles. (Cost: $5.8 billion over ten years)
- The denial to oil and gas companies of a deduction for domestic manufacturing activities. (Revenue: $11.4 billion over ten years)
- A change in the way companies were required to calculate their foreign earnings. (Revenue: $3.6 billion over ten years)

Oil-state Democrats, led by Gene Green of Texas, joined Republicans who opposed the tax provisions. Pelosi discussed the issue with Green and his colleagues, often in one-on-one conversations on the House floor, but flatly refused to make any concessions. Eleven Democrats voted against the tax package.

Republicans offered an alternative tax proposal, in the form of a motion to recommit the bill, that included $5 billion in increases, shorter extensions of tax breaks than in the Democrats' version, and a focus on conventional energy sources, including fossil fuels and nuclear power. It was defeated 65–346 on Aug. 4.

Many Republicans voted "yea," then changed their votes to avoid being listed as backing a tax increase. As they flocked to the well, they were greeted by a smiling Rangel, who eagerly handed out the red cards members use to change their votes.

Energy efficiency. The House followed the Senate's lead in several areas dealing with energy efficiency. Like the Senate bill, the House measure targeted billions of dollars for energy research, including studies into carbon dioxide sequestration efforts necessary to promote clean-burning coal. It also included subsidies for research into plug-in hybrid cars, along with a tax credit for buying such vehicles.

HOUSE PASSAGE OF DEMOCRATIC COMPROMISE

The House agreed 235–181 on Dec. 6 to a compromise version of HR 6 that was the result of four months of negotiations by Democratic leaders in both chambers. The agreement, which Dingell endorsed, combined the Senate-passed CAFE standards and alternative fuels mandate with the House-passed tax package and electricity standard.

The main provisions of the revamped bill were as follows.

Renewable electricity. Require utilities to generate 15 percent of their electricity from renewable sources such as wind, biomass, solar, geothermal, and ocean tides by 2020. Utilities could use energy efficiency to meet up to 4 percentage points of the mandate.

Fuel economy standards. Increase fleetwide CAFE standards for all new cars and light trucks to thirty-five miles per gallon by 2020.

Renewable fuels. Require 36 billion gallons of ethanol and other biofuels to be produced and used domestically as motor fuel by 2022, and provide incentives to boost production of biofuels and vehicles that could run on renewable fuels.

Energy efficiency. Mandate the production of more energy-efficient home appliances, such as washing machines, dishwashers, and refrigerators, and require the Energy Department to expedite the approval of new efficiency standards. Federal and commercial buildings would have to become more energy efficient.

Hybrid incentives. Establish a tax credit for individuals buying plug-in hybrid vehicles and encourage domestic development and production of such vehicles.

Taxes. Enact a $21.5 billion tax package that was a compromise between the $16.1 billion package in HR 3221 and a $32.1 billion package approved by the Senate Finance Committee. The compromise did not include new taxes or royalties on oil extraction in the gulf.

Of the $21.5 billion, $13 billion would be offset through the repeal of oil and gas industry tax breaks.

The main tax breaks would

- Extend and modify the renewable energy production tax credit. (Cost: $6.6 billion over ten years)
- Expand and modify tax credits for coal gasification projects that demonstrated carbon capture and sequestration technology. (Cost: $1.8 billion over ten years)
- Establish a tax credit for plug-in electric-drive vehicles. (Cost: $992 million over ten years)
- Provide New York City and the State of New York with tax credits for transportation infrastructure projects. (Cost: $1.1 billion over ten years)
- Allow electric utilities to depreciate smart meters over seven years. (Cost: $1.2 billion over ten years)

The chief revenue-raising provisions would

- Exclude much of the revenue earned by oil and gas companies from a tax deduction for domestic manufacturing activities. HR 3221 would have eliminated the deduction completely for the companies. (Revenue: $10 billion over ten years)
- Alter the way oil and gas companies were required to calculate their foreign earnings. (Revenue: $3.2 billion over ten years)
- Require brokers to report to the Internal Revenue Service (IRS) the cost basis for transactions involving stock, commodities, derivatives, and other publicly traded securities. The provision was expected to increase taxpayers' compliance in reporting capital

gains—the difference between the original cost and a higher sales price—on their tax returns. (Revenue: $4.1 billion over ten years)

- Extend for one year a temporary surtax added to the federal unemployment tax paid by employers. (Revenue: $1.4 billion over ten years)

The White House cited the tax increases in issuing a veto threat, saying it was unfair to single out a particular industry for higher taxes. The administration also said the renewables standard would not account for regional differences in the availability of alternative energy sources such as wind and solar power.

SENATE FILIBUSTER

The compromise version of HR 6 quickly collapsed in the Senate in the face of strong GOP opposition. Two attempts to avert a filibuster fell short of the sixty votes needed to invoke cloture.

On Dec. 7, the Senate rejected an attempt to end debate on the bill by a vote of 53–42. Republicans criticized the tax package and the renewable electricity mandate and said that, before Democrats added those provisions, there was bipartisan backing for the increase in fuel economy standards and other parts of the bill.

Domenici, who led the charge to block the cloture attempt, said the House-passed HR 6 would do little to encourage the development of biofuels beyond ethanol because it would allow the EPA to opt out of the mandate. He also criticized a requirement in the bill that workers on tax-subsidized projects receive prevailing wages under the Davis-Bacon law (PL 88-349).

Democratic leaders made one last try Dec. 12, after tweaking the bill in an effort to sway swing votes. The details of the proposal had been released jointly by Max Baucus, D-Mont., chairman of the Finance Committee, and the panel's ranking Republican, Charles E. Grassley of Iowa, who had voted against debating the House-passed version of the bill because he objected to portions of the tax package. Among the chief changes, the negotiators

- Dropped the renewable electricity mandate for electric utilities.
- Reworked the package of tax incentives for renewable energy, although the bill still banked on $12.7 billion in offsets from rolling back tax breaks on the oil and gas industry. Grassley's concerns were assuaged by a two-year extension of the tax credit for facilities that produced renewable energy, along with removal of a 35 percent cap on costs eligible for the credit.
- Dropped the language requiring that workers on tax-subsidized projects be covered by the Davis-Bacon law.

But the strategy fell one vote short, ending efforts to include tax incentives for energy efficiency and renewable fuels in HR 6. The Senate vote to limit debate on the plan failed on Dec. 13 on a **key vote of 59–40 (R 9–39; D 48–1; I 2–0).** Among the Democrats, only Mary L. Landrieu of Louisiana joined thirty-nine Republicans in voting "nay." *(2007 key votes, p. 955)*

FINAL ACTION ON HR 6

Forced to abandon the tax package, Senate Democrats agreed to a pared-down bill, which easily passed by a vote of 86–8 on Dec. 13. Forty Republicans and the two independents joined forty-four Democrats in support of the bill.

The House easily cleared HR 6 on Dec. 18 on a **key vote of 314–100 (R 95–96; D 219–4).** Bush signed the bill the next day. *(2007 key votes, p. 955)*

The core of the legislation remained the same: the increase in CAFE standards for cars and light trucks to thirty-five miles per gallon by 2020, and the requirement that 36 billion gallons of ethanol and other biofuels to be used annually by 2022.

Gone were the two chief obstacles for Senate Republicans and the White House: the Democrats' tax package and the electricity requirements. To comply with pay-as-you-go rules, negotiators kept about $2.1 billion in tax increases to pay for the loss in gasoline tax revenue expected to result from the change in CAFE standards.

Domenici reiterated that passing the broader bill would have been futile because of the veto threat. Senators addressed a Bush administration concern by clarifying—without changing the bill's language—that the Transportation Department would retain its lead role in setting fuel economy standards. The U.S. Supreme Court decided in April 2007, in *Massachusetts v. Environmental Protection Agency,* that the EPA had authority to regulate tailpipe emissions of carbon dioxide. Some senators and the White House worried that this could lead the EPA to set separate standards that conflicted with Transportation Department thresholds. *(Court case, p. 760)*

Dianne Feinstein, D-Calif., the original sponsor of the higher fuel economy standards, said on the Senate floor that the intent of the bill was that EPA regulations should be consistent with the CAFE standards in the bill and with regulations issued by the Transportation Department.

MAJOR PROVISIONS

The following are major provisions of HR 6, as enacted.

Vehicle Efficiency and Motor Fuels

Fuel efficiency standards. The law mandated the first statutory increase in corporate average fuel economy standards since 1975. By 2020, automobiles sold in the United States that had a gross vehicle weight of less than 8,500 pounds—including sport utility vehicles—would need to meet a minimum fleetwide fuel economy average of thirty-five miles per gallon, a 40 percent increase over current standards.

The law required the Energy Department to set different standards for work trucks (between 8,500 and 10,000 pounds gross weight) and heavy-duty trucks (more than

10,000 pounds gross weight). It also permitted the Transportation Department to establish a fuel economy credit-trading program, which would allow manufacturers to earn credits when they exceeded CAFE standards and sold them to manufacturers who could use them to comply with fuel economy targets. Credits could also be used within the same company to compensate for CAFE deficiencies in different car classes produced by the same manufacturer.

The law also temporarily extended and expanded a flex-fuel credit. Through 2014, manufacturers that produced flexible-fuel vehicles capable of running on regular gasoline and E-85 (a blend of 85 percent ethanol and 15 percent gasoline) could fall 1.2 miles per gallon short of meeting the standard. The flex-fuel credit tapered off by 0.2 miles per gallon per year until model year 2020, when it expired.

By increasing fuel efficiency, the new standards were expected to reduce fuel usage, consequently cutting federal gasoline tax revenue by $2.1 billion over ten years.

Hybrid vehicles. Under the law, the Energy Department was authorized to provide loan guarantees for the construction of domestic advanced vehicle-battery manufacturing facilities. The aim was to increase the use of hybrid vehicles, which use both gasoline and electric battery power to operate.

Electric transportation. A new Energy Department grant program would assist states to encourage the use of plug-in electric vehicles, as well as a revolving-loan program to help states with electric transportation projects, such as electricity at truck stops for refrigerated trucks, electric ground support equipment at airports, and electric or dual-mode freight trains. The law authorized $95 million annually for the loan program from fiscal 2008 to 2013. It also directed the department to develop a national electric drive transportation education program.

Federal fleets. Federal agencies were prohibited from acquiring passenger vehicles that were not "low greenhouse gas emitting" vehicles. The EPA would provide guidelines on which vehicles met the requirement. The law also barred agencies from procuring alternative fuels unless the contract specified that the emissions from the fuel were equal to or lower than those from conventional fuels.

By Jan. 1, 2010, each federal agency was required to install at least one renewable fuel pump at most of its fleet-fueling centers in the United States. Beginning in fiscal 2010, federal vehicle fleets were required to reduce annual petroleum consumption and increase alternative fuel consumption. By fiscal 2015, each federal agency's petroleum consumption had to be down by 20 percent and its alternative fuel consumption up by 10 percent.

BIOFUEL STANDARDS

Renewable fuels standards. The law set new standards for the use of biofuels, energy sources that were derived from organic matter. By 2022, a total of 36 billion gallons of biofuels had to be made available for domestic use, a fivefold increase over current law. No more than 15 billion gallons of the biofuel could be corn-based ethanol. The remaining 21 billion gallons had to be advanced biofuels derived from feedstocks other than corn, including cellulose (16 billion gallons is required by 2022), sugar, starch, and landfill and sewage waste gases. By 2012, at least 1 billion gallons of the biofuel had to be biomass-based diesel.

Life cycle greenhouse gas emissions. Biofuels produced at facilities built a year or more after the law's enactment had to generate less greenhouse gases over their life cycles than do conventional fuels. The requirement applied to all three types of biofuels—corn-based ethanol, advanced biofuels, and biomass-derived diesel. The fuel's life cycle was defined as going from feedstock generation through the distribution, delivery, and use of the finished fuel by the consumer.

Corn-based ethanol had to produce 20 percent less global warming gases than conventional gasoline produces. Advanced biofuels had to produce 50 percent less; biomass-based diesel, 60 percent. The law allowed the EPA to adjust these reductions if they are not "commercially feasible." However, if the agency did adjust them, it was required to conduct a review in five years.

Impact assessments. The secretary of energy, in consultation with the secretary of agriculture and the EPA administrator, was to arrange for the National Academy of Sciences to assess the impact of the requirements on producers of feed grains, livestock, food, forest products, and energy. The report was due no later than eighteen months after enactment.

No later than three years after enactment and every three years after that, the EPA, in consultation with the Agriculture and Energy Departments, was required to assess the impact of the new standards on the environment and resource conservation—including air quality; effects on pesticides, sediment, nutrient, and pathogen levels in waters; soil conservation; water availability; and ecosystem health and biodiversity, including impacts on forests, grasslands, and wetlands.

BIOFUEL INFRASTRUCTURE

Gasoline stations. No new or renewed franchise agreement could restrict the installation or conversion of pumps or tanks for renewable fuels or restrict the franchisee from selling or advertising renewable fuels that are purchased from another company. A franchise agreement that required the station to sell three grades of gasoline could not prevent the franchisee from selling a renewable fuel in lieu of one of the grades of conventional gasoline.

Studies. The Energy Department was required to report annually on the penetration of flexible-fuel vehicles within various regions of the country. Within two years of enactment, the Energy Department was required to report to Congress on the feasibility of requiring motor fuel retailers to install pumps compatible with E-85 in areas where flexible fuels make up 15 percent of the market.

The department was also directed to study the feasibility of constructing pipelines dedicated to the transportation of ethanol. Existing petroleum pipelines were not compatible with biofuels, which could cause corrosion and clogging.

Grants. The law authorized a total of $1.4 billion in fiscal 2008 through 2014 for a new grant program to assist retail and wholesale dealers in installing, replacing, or converting pumps and storage tanks to be used exclusively for renewable fuel blends. The aim is to ensure that such blends were available nationwide.

Bioenergy research. The law authorized increased funding for bioenergy research: $377 million in fiscal 2008, $398 million in 2009, and $419 million in 2010. Prior law authorized $251 million in fiscal 2008 and $274 million in fiscal 2009 for bioenergy research.

The law created several research programs aimed at developing new biofuel infrastructure and technology as well as grants to research biofuels production. The Energy Department was directed to establish a research and development program to improve energy efficiency at biofuel-refining facilities. The department also would research infrastructure to transport and deliver biofuels and, in consultation with the National Institute of Standards and Technology, develop standards for biofuel dispenser systems. The measure also required the Energy Department to study the effect of different blends of biodiesel on engine durability and performance and to research whether the use of E-85 would increase the fuel efficiency of flexible-fuel vehicles.

The bill authorized the department to grant $25 million annually in fiscal 2008 through 2010 to states with low rates of ethanol production.

Small business programs. The law required the creation of a Renewable Fuel Capital Investment Pilot Program to be run by the Small Business Administration. It authorized $15 million per year for loan guarantees and grants to newly created companies or subsidiaries whose primary business is investing in the research, production, and development of renewable fuels. Companies receiving the funds would have to raise at least $3 million in capital or capital commitments.

ENERGY EFFICIENCY

Lighting. The law effectively phased out the incandescent light bulb, invented by Thomas Edison, in the United States by setting new energy efficiency standards for all common household lamps. It required the Energy Department to set progressively more stringent standards and mandated that lamps produce at least forty-five lumens per watt by 2020. (A lumen is a measurement of light output.) Specialty lights, such as those used for medical procedures, public safety, or historical purposes, were exempt from the new standard.

The law authorized $10 million annually in fiscal 2008 through 2013 for the Energy Department to conduct lighting technology research and to assist lighting manufacturers in meeting the new standards. The department also was required to submit two reports to Congress, in consultation with the National Academy of Sciences, on the status of advanced solid-state lighting research, the impact of the new standard on the types of lighting available to consumers, and the time frame for possible commercialization of lighting that could replace current incandescent and halogen technology. The first report was due by Dec. 31, 2013, and the second by July 31, 2015.

Appliances. The Energy Department was required to set new energy-use standards for appliances, electric motors, walk-in refrigerators and freezers, air conditioners, and residential boilers. By July 2010, the department had to develop standards for limiting the amount of energy used by consumer and industrial products when they were in "standby" or "sleep" modes.

The department was required to review appliance energy efficiency standards six years after they took effect to determine whether new standards were needed. If new standards were necessary, the department had to finalize them within two years of the review. If the department concluded that new standards were not needed, it must reconsider that determination after three years. The Energy Department also could use an expedited process to change water or energy efficiency standards if manufacturers, state governments, and environmental groups agreed that they needed to be adjusted.

Consumer electronic equipment. Using the Energy Star program, the Energy Department and the EPA were required to establish labeling requirements that described the energy usage of consumer electronic equipment such as televisions, personal computers, cable and satellite converter boxes, and digital recorder boxes.

Electricity grid. The law stated that it was U.S. policy to develop an electricity transmission and distribution system that was characterized as a "smart grid." The term referred to modernizing electricity infrastructure to increase reliability and security, using technology that could respond to changing conditions in the electricity market and to the addition of renewable energy. The aim of the program was to develop technologies to reduce peak power usage and increase energy efficiency. The law authorized expenditures as may be necessary to develop and implement the program from fiscal 2008 through 2012.

The Energy Department was required to establish and maintain a research and development program for smart-grid technology. The department was also directed to establish a smart-grid residential initiative to demonstrate power grid sensing, communications, analysis, and electric power flow control. The law restricted the federal share to 50 percent of the cost of the project and authorized $100 million annually in fiscal 2008 through 2012.

In addition, the Energy Department was directed to create a new grant program to provide 20 percent of the cost of smart-grid technology projects. Technologies eligible for funding included new appliances, new monitors for electricity use, and technology that communicated electricity use remotely. The grants could not be used for electricity-generation projects, physical connections for generators, or customer operations of energy providers. The law authorized the necessary sums to implement the program.

Residential buildings. The Energy Department would issue new energy efficiency standards for residential buildings, allowing for regional differences based on climate. The law authorized a total of $5.3 billion for fiscal 2008 through 2012 for weatherization grants to help the elderly and those with low incomes to insulate their homes. The authorization was $750 million in fiscal 2008, $900 million in fiscal 2009, $1.1 billion in fiscal 2010, $1.2 billion in fiscal 2011, and $1.4 billion in fiscal 2012.

Commercial and federal buildings. The law created two new offices within the Energy Department: an Office of Energy Efficiency and Renewable Energy and an Office of Commercial High-Performance Green Buildings. The offices were charged with working to reduce commercial-building energy use, with all new commercial and federal buildings using a minimal amount of energy by 2050. To implement the building efficiency goals, the law authorized $20 million in fiscal 2008, $50 million in each of fiscal years 2009 and 2010, $100 million in each of fiscal years 2011 and 2012, and $200 million annually in fiscal years 2013 through 2018.

Federal buildings had to gradually reduce their energy use, reaching a 30 percent reduction by 2015. Each federal agency was required to designate managers to conduct periodic analyses of energy and water usage for each building and recommend ways to conserve energy. Within two years, the managers could recommend energy-saving techniques and must ensure that any steps taken were effective. The General Services Administration was required to install solar panels at the Energy Department headquarters in Washington, D.C.

Three years after enactment, all federal agencies could lease space only in buildings that had earned an Energy Star rating in the most recent year. The requirement did not apply when an agency used historically or architecturally significant places, when an agency wanted to remain in a space it had previously occupied, or when no other space was available to meet the agency's needs. Agencies developing or redeveloping a federal facility with a footprint of more than 5,000 feet had to use planning, design, and construction to maintain or restore the water circulation as it existed before development. The law authorized $4 million annually in fiscal 2008 through 2012 to implement federal energy efficiency requirements.

Industrial facilities. The EPA was directed to create a Recoverable Waste Energy Inventory Program, in cooperation with the states, to continually survey large commercial combustion sources to determine whether there was excess energy that could be used elsewhere. The EPA would create a public registry of sites that were found to be wasting recoverable excess energy. The law authorized $1 million per year in fiscal 2008 through 2012 to establish and maintain the registry, $2 million in fiscal 2008 through 2012 to assist site owners in determining the feasibility of cost-saving projects, and $5 million for state efforts for the program.

U.S. Capitol. The architect of the Capitol was required to take the following steps to improve energy efficiency: perform a feasibility study on the construction of a photovoltaic roof for the Rayburn House Office Building, install technologies that capture and then store or use carbon dioxide at the Capitol power plant, construct a fuel tanking and pumping system for E-85, and consider energy efficiency, climate change mitigation, and other environmental measures in its master plan.

State and local programs. The law authorized $2 billion annually in fiscal 2008 through 2012 for a new Energy Efficiency and Conservation Block Grant Program. The grants were to be awarded to cities with populations of at least 35,000 and counties with populations of at least 200,000 to reduce fossil fuel emissions and energy use and to improve energy efficiency.

Small business programs. The law authorized grants of $100,000 to $300,000 to small business development centers for developing, marketing, or investing in energy efficiency technology.

REVENUE-RAISING PROVISIONS

The law contained two tax provisions, which the Joint Committee on Taxation estimated would raise $1.5 billion over ten years. Together, the tax provisions and various other savings in the bill were expected to offset the $2.1 billion decline in federal gas tax revenue that was expected to result from greater fuel efficiency in cars and trucks under the new CAFE standards.

Federal Unemployment Tax Act surtax. The legislation extended for one year, through 2008, a temporary 0.2 percent surtax under the Federal Unemployment Tax Act (FUTA) to raise an estimated $1.4 billion over ten years. The current FUTA tax had an effective rate of 0.8 percent, which applied to the first $7,000 in wages paid by certain employers for a maximum of $56 per employee per year. That rate included a permanent 0.6 percent tax plus a 0.2 percent "surtax" that would have expired at the end of 2007. The maximum amount paid under the surtax was $14 per employee.

Amortization period for oil and gas exploration. The law extended from five years to seven years the period over which major integrated oil companies could deduct geological and geophysical expenditures associated with oil and gas exploration in the United States. The provision was expected to raise approximately $103 million through fiscal 2017.

POOL AND SPA SAFETY

The law incorporated the provisions of the Pool and Spa Safety Act (HR 1721), which the House Energy and Commerce Committee approved (H Rept 110-365) on Sept. 27, 2007, and the full House passed on Oct. 9. The provisions required pool and spa drain covers to conform to "entrapment protection standards." The requirement took effect Dec. 19, 2008, and would be considered an official rule by the Consumer Product Safety Commission. The law also established new grants to states to hire and train enforcement personnel and to educate pool owners, construction and service companies, and operators. To be eligible, states had to require the drain entrapment prevention devices on all pools and spas, as well as the enclosure of residential pools.

MISCELLANEOUS

School buildings. The Energy Department was permitted to provide grants to states to develop and implement environmental and health standards for school facilities. The EPA, the Education Department, and the Health and Human Services Department had to issue voluntary guidelines. The law authorized $1 million in fiscal 2009 and $1.5 million annually in fiscal 2010 through 2013 for the program.

Carbon sequestration. The law expanded the Energy Department's current carbon sequestration program by requiring the agency to conduct large-volume tests of carbon sequestration—a process by which carbon was captured from large industrial polluters and stored underground—to examine its costs and feasibility.

Green jobs. The Labor Department was authorized to spend $125 million each year to administer a new grant program to train workers in the renewable energy and energy efficiency sectors. The program had to be created within six months of enactment and target workers who needed updated training related to the energy industry, as well as veterans, the unemployed, formerly incarcerated nonviolent offenders, and at-risk youth. The measure also established a national research program in the Bureau of Labor Statistics to track market data and identify workforce trends in the renewable energy sector.

Alternative Energy

The massive, five-year farm bill (HR 6124—PL 110-246) that became law in 2008 contained significant provisions for alternative energy sources, especially biofuels. *(Farm bill, p. 514)*

The market for biofuels, which were liquid fuels derived from plant materials, had boomed in recent years, driven by rising oil prices, the need for increased energy security, and concerns over the impacts of traditional fuels such as oil and coal on global warming. Further stoking the demand for biofuels, especially ethanol, were federal incentives, including a 51-cents-per-gallon tax credit for ethanol and a 2005 renewable fuels standard. At the same time, gasoline producers moved away from the fuel additive methyl tertiary butyl ether (MTBE) over concerns about water contamination, and they started mixing their product with ethanol.

As a result, farmers saw ethanol production as a way to ensure crop sales and create jobs. They looked to the farm bill to win further incentives for ethanol, which was largely derived from corn.

Biofuel advocates garnered the support of lawmakers who wanted to tackle high energy prices, reduce America's reliance on foreign oil, and open new markets to farmers. Corn and cellulosic ethanol producers found powerful friends in the chairmen of the House and Senate Agriculture Committees, as well as House Speaker Nancy Pelosi, D-Calif., who viewed alternative energy as a top priority.

The overall farm bill sparked an intense, eighteen-month debate in Congress in 2007 and 2008. Lawmakers had to override a veto by President George W. Bush to enact HR 6124 into law. But most of the differences focused on the overall cost of the bill, including subsidies for farmers. Lawmakers were generally supportive of the provisions to spur biofuel production. *(Veto message, p. 1073)*

The key energy provisions of HR 6124 included the following.

Rural Energy for America Program. A new program authorized grants and loan guarantees to farmers and rural small businesses to purchase renewable fuel systems and make energy efficiency improvements to their operations. The program was to get $250 million in mandatory funding over four years, part of which would go to grants for energy experts to help farmers and businesses do energy audits.

Biorefinery assistance. The farm bill authorized grants and loan guarantees for the construction and retrofitting of biorefineries to produce advanced biofuels—non-corn-based biofuels such as those from cellulose, sugar, and waste products. It authorized grants for up to 30 percent of the cost of pilot biorefineries and loan guarantees to support 90 percent of the principal and interest on loans to develop and construct commercial-scale biorefineries. The aim of the program was to accelerate commercial production of advanced biofuels.

Biomass research and development. The law provided about $120 million over four years in mandatory spending for a program that provided competitive funding for research projects on biofuels and biobased chemicals and products. It authorized an additional $1 billion in discretionary funds for the program over four years.

Bioenergy Program. About $300 million was authorized for the Bioenergy Program, which provided incentives to expand production of advanced biofuels made from farm and forestry waste and manure, among other things.

Biomass crop assistance. The law established a program to provide financial assistance to promote the development of new biofuels made from cellulosic products. The program included contracts with farmers and forestry companies to grow cellulosic crops and incentives to harvest, store, and transport those crops to production facilities.

Biobased markets program. A new voluntary program was created to recognize agencies, contractors, and farmers that used significant amounts of biobased products. The purpose was to help farmers label biobased products as "USDA Certified Biobased Product" and help the federal government establish procurement preferences for those products.

Forest and wood fuels. The law authorized $60 million over four years for a competitive research and development program to encourage use of forest biomass for energy. Another $20 million was authorized for a new program of grants to state and local governments to develop ways to use wood scraps for energy.

Biofuels infrastructure assessment. The U.S. Department of Agriculture (USDA) was directed to work with the Environmental Protection Agency and the Department of Energy on a study to determine how best to expand the production, transport, and distribution of biofuels.

Sugar ethanol program. A new program was established to allow the government to buy U.S. sugar equal to any excess in imports to maintain market prices above support levels. The sugar then would be sold to be turned into ethanol. The change was meant to address a provision in the North American Free Trade Agreement that eliminated tariffs on Mexican sugar.

Energy-Related Tax Incentives

Democrats in 2008 turned to a major tax bill to win enactment of a $16.9 billion package of tax incentives for the production and use of alternative energy. The provisions, similar to revenue proposals that were dropped from a 2007 energy bill, were successfully added to a $107 billion tax bill (HR 1424—PL 110-343) that cleared after a series of skirmishes in both chambers.

The energy tax provisions included extensions of expiring benefits, such as a tax credit for producing electricity from wind and solar power and a tax benefit for purchasing energy-efficient appliances. Other proposals were new, such as assistance for state energy conservation projects and a tax credit for plug-in hybrid cars. The total cost of $16.9 billion was fully offset with a variety of revenue-raisers, many of which targeted the oil and gas industry.

The tax incentives were a high priority for Democrats, who wanted to reduce the nation's dependence on traditional energy sources. But Republicans and oil-state Democrats successfully resisted similar provisions in the 2007 energy measure (HR 6—PL 110-140), concerned that they would disadvantage traditional energy companies. *(Energy policy, pp. 447, 484)*

Lawmakers renewed the debate early in 2008, launching a months-long struggle against the backdrop of soaring oil prices. The House moved first, passing a bill (HR 5351) on Feb. 27 that contained $17.6 billion in tax breaks for renewable energy, fully offset by changes in tax breaks targeted at oil and gas companies. The vote was 236–182, with all but seventeen Republicans voting "nay." But the administration threatened to veto it, saying such a "targeted tax increase" was unfair to the oil and gas industry.

The Senate then took up the ball, voting in April to attach an $8.3 billion package of energy tax breaks to a high-profile mortgage bill (HR 3221). But House Democrats, who had previously pledged to offset any new taxes, stripped out the energy provisions. *(Mortgage finance overhaul, pp. 153, 630)*

Two weeks later, the House combined the energy tax breaks with an extension of other expired or expiring tax breaks into a $54.1 billion bill (HR 6049—H Rept 110-658) that was fully offset. The measure passed 263–160 on May 21. Thirty-five Republicans supported the bill, but Senate Republicans declared it "dead on arrival." After fashioning compromise language, the Senate overwhelmingly passed HR 6049, a bipartisan tax package that included energy incentives, by 93–2 on Sept. 23.

After the House on Sept. 26 passed yet another version (HR 7060), with offsets that prompted another White House veto threat, the stalemate was unexpectedly broken when the crisis in the financial services industry forced lawmakers to take action. Senate leaders added the language of the Senate's version of HR 6049 to a financial services bailout bill (HR 1424). Both chambers swiftly passed it, and President George W. Bush signed the measure into law on Oct. 3. In addition to the energy provisions, the $107 billion tax package extended popular tax breaks and included a one-year fix for the alternative minimum tax. *(Financial services bailout, p. 154)*

Although advocates of renewable energy could claim a victory, the final product was not exactly what they had wanted. The provisions included incentives for coal and a new tax break for oil-shale refining.

Highlights of the energy provisions are as follows.

Production tax credit. Extended the main tax incentive for generating electricity from wind, refined coal, geothermal power, hydropower, and trash combustion. Made energy generated from tides and waves eligible for the tax credit.

Solar energy. Extended a 30 percent investment tax credit for solar energy and certain fuel cells. Applied it also to residential wind turbines and geothermal pumps.

Coal production. Provided $1.5 billion in tax credits for projects that produced electricity from coal and met certain conditions. Created a tax credit for capturing carbon dioxide. Provided a new credit to producers of coal used to make coke for steel production.

Fuels. Extended credits for production of biodiesel and for fueling station pumps that dispensed natural gas or ethanol. Expanded the credit to cover electric-recharging stations. Allowed certain investments in many cellulosic biofuels, not just ethanol, to qualify for a 50 percent write-off.

Bond authority. Allocated $800 million in Clean Renewable Energy Bonds, to provide tax-advantaged financing for facilities that produced electricity from renewable sources. Created a category of tax-advantaged bonds, setting aside $800 million for state and local governments to use for projects designed to reduce greenhouse gas emissions.

Refineries. Extended a tax deduction for refinery owners that undertook capital improvements to increase refinery capacity or allow certain nonconventional fuels to be processed. Added oil shale and tar sands to the fuels eligible for the refining credit.

Energy efficiency. Provided a series of provisions to encourage energy efficiency and conservation, including extensions of tax credits for energy-efficient improvements to existing homes and commercial buildings, energy-efficient appliances through 2010, and energy-efficient new homes.

Smart meters. Allowed utility companies wanting to deploy electric meters that provided more detailed information about consumption to depreciate the meters more quickly.

Recycling. Permitted companies that bought equipment for collecting and processing certain recyclable materials an accelerated depreciation.

Plug-in vehicles. Created a new tax credit for plug-in vehicles that typically ranged from $2,500 to $7,500.

Oil and gas offsets. Offset most of the cost of the energy tax breaks by revenue increases targeting the oil and gas industry, including freezing a manufacturing deduction that had been scheduled to increase, increasing the oil spill liability tax, and altering the treatment of oil companies' foreign income in a way that would force higher taxes on income earned from transporting and refining oil.

Climate Change

Although Democratic leaders in both chambers viewed the issue of climate change as a priority, lawmakers in the 110th Congress made little headway on it. The complexity of the issue and the opposition of key Republicans prevented passage of legislation designed to cap U.S. emissions of carbon dioxide and other greenhouse gases blamed for warming the planet.

Environmentalists had become increasingly focused on the issue, worrying that greenhouse gas emissions, if left unchecked, could have devastating worldwide impacts. If temperatures were to rise by several degrees during the twenty-first century, they warned that the consequences could include melting Arctic ice sheets, rising sea levels, more powerful storms, and a growing number of deadly heat waves and droughts.

Their concerns were buttressed in 2007 by a report of the Intergovernmental Panel on Climate Change, a worldwide organization of scientists operating under the auspices of the United Nations. The report found that climate change was affecting weather patterns worldwide and concluded that human activities were "very likely" to blame for global warming.

But powerful industry organizations, such as the American Petroleum Institute, said the potential impacts of global warming were being exaggerated. Many Republicans felt that the science needed to be fleshed out further before the government took steps that, while targeting greenhouse gases, might inadvertently undermine the U.S. economy. They also worried that a cap on greenhouse gas emissions in the United States would be of little benefit to the environment if other nations, such as China and India, did not take similar steps.

The climate change legislation in the 110th Congress aimed to establish a comprehensive national policy to address global warming. It would have capped emissions of greenhouse gases and set up a market-based trading program for businesses to meet the cap. It would have redistributed trillions of dollars collected from polluters to industries, states, and electricity consumers over the following four decades.

While the environmental community pushed hard for the measure, even supporters acknowledged that it was an uphill battle to secure Senate passage. The scope of the bill was vast, and opponents argued it would raise the price of energy during a summer of record-high gas prices. Still, sponsors at least wanted to get the Senate on the record on several amendments that could help shape a climate change bill in the 111th Congress.

But Republicans were able to prevent the Senate from even taking up amendments, much less voting on them. As a result, the Senate never addressed issues that could be critical to any future legislation, such as the role of nuclear power or whether to preempt more stringent action at the state level.

Climate change was a comparatively minor issue among appropriators. The fiscal 2008 omnibus spending bill (HR 2764—PL 110-161) contained language expressing the sense of Congress favoring mandatory limits on greenhouse gas emissions, and it provided new funding for research on global warming and wildlife by the U.S. Geological Survey. But appropriators dropped a provision that would have provided $50 million for a new commission on climate change mitigation and adaptation. *(Appropriations, pp. 111, 112)*

2007 ACTION

The Senate Environment and Public Works Committee approved a bill (S 2191)—sponsored by Joseph I. Lieberman, I-Conn., and John W. Warner, R-Va.—by a vote of 11–8 on Dec. 5, 2007. The vote fell largely along party lines, with Warner the only Republican voting in favor. The partisan divide was expected to be just as strong when the bill reached the floor. The committee formally reported the measure (S Rept 110-337) on May 20, 1008.

The bill proposed to cap nationwide emissions of greenhouse gases from power plants, manufacturers, petroleum refiners, and other sectors of the economy. It aimed to reduce emissions by 18 percent to 25 percent below 2005 levels by 2020, and by 62 percent to 66 percent by 2050, according to an analysis by the World Resources Institute and the Natural Resources Defense Council.

A market-based emissions-trading program would be established to help companies meet the cap. A coal-burning power company that was unable to meet its emissions targets, for example, could purchase allowances on the open market. The government would hand out some of the initial credits for free; the rest would be sold through an auction. The free allowances would be phased out in 2031.

Democrats fended off a host of GOP amendments reflecting concerns that S 2191 would hurt the economy and cost jobs and that it would do little to help the environment if countries such as China and India did not also reduce their emissions. Many GOP lawmakers also wanted explicit language to promote the construction of nuclear power plants, which do not emit greenhouse gases. Republicans vowed to block the bill from coming up at least until the Environmental Protection Agency and the Energy Information Administration released analyses of its economic impact.

Some Democrats on the committee argued that the bill should impose more stringent emissions limits and that the government should not be so generous in providing emissions credits.

Among the many amendments considered during the markup, the committee

- Rejected 6–13 a proposal by Bernard Sanders, I-Vt., and Hillary Rodham Clinton, D-N.Y., to eliminate free allowances to most industries that emitted greenhouse gases. The allowances would still be available to other entities, including states, electricity consumers, farmers, and foresters.

The question of how far the government should go in providing such incentives was one of the most contentious issues for Democrats. Environmental groups, for example, wanted all of the allowances to be auctioned, with the proceeds used to fund clean-energy technologies, help low-income consumers with their energy bills, and fund wildlife adaptation programs.

"I believe we should not be giving these companies windfall profits," Sanders said. But Lieberman said the amendment was a poison pill that would destroy any industry support for the bill.

- Rejected 7–11 an amendment by Sanders, Clinton, and other Democrats to require 80 percent reductions from 1990 levels by 2050. Sponsors said it would make the bill much more difficult to pass.
- Approved 13–6 an amendment by Lamar Alexander, R-Tenn., to impose a low-carbon fuel performance standard. Oil used for transportation would have to meet a standard of 5 percent less carbon per unit of energy in 2015 and 10 percent less in 2020. This standard would be in addition to the bill's caps on emissions from petroleum refiners.
- Rejected 8–11 an amendment by Larry E. Craig, R-Idaho, to sunset the bill if China and India did not adopt similar measures within ten years.
- Rejected several GOP amendments aimed at encouraging nuclear energy generation. However, sponsors of the bill promised to work on the floor to determine how the legislation could be adjusted to benefit nuclear power plants.

The House moved at a slower pace, in part because the Energy and Commerce Committee was tied up until the end of the year in negotiations over the comprehensive energy bill (HR 6—PL 110-140). *(Energy policy, pp. 447, 484)*

Early in 2007, House Speaker Nancy Pelosi, D-Calif., set up a House Select Committee on Energy Independence and Global Warming. The panel had no authority to take up legislation, but Chairman Edward J. Markey, D-Mass., held regular hearings to keep up the pressure for Congress to pass a bill.

2008 ACTION

Senate Democrats abandoned efforts to hold a floor vote on a revamped bill (S 3036) in the face of a Republican filibuster.

The Senate on June 2 voted 74–14 to bring up S 3036 and started what promised to be the most serious congressional debate yet on how to respond to climate change.

But hopes for that debate evaporated June 4, when Majority Leader Harry Reid, D-Nev., offered a substitute amendment by Barbara Boxer, D-Calif., that was to serve as the base legislation. Minority Leader Mitch McConnell, R-Ky., quickly objected to a routine motion to dispense with reading the measure, forcing clerks to read the entire five hundred-page amendment aloud. McConnell said he was protesting the majority party's handling of the unrelated confirmation process for appellate court nominees.

When the clerks had finished more than eight hours later, an angry Reid complained about GOP delaying tactics and demanded a live quorum call, asking the sergeant at arms to compel senators to appear in the chamber. The request was rejected 27–28 on June 4.

Reid and McConnell could not agree on how many amendments to allow. Reid proposed five amendments per side, with action completed by the end of the week. Republicans disagreed. "We shouldn't get off this bill until the July recess because of the tremendous impact it has on our country," said Bob Corker, R-Tenn. "I hope we have 40 or 50 amendments. I hope we have hundreds and hundreds of hours of debate."

Republicans particularly disliked the idea of collecting and redistributing trillions of dollars in fees from polluters, saying it would increase energy prices for Americans. The White House threatened a veto, listing dozens of objections.

Supporters said the critics were ignoring provisions designed to ease the sting of higher costs for consumers and to invest in new technologies that could drive down energy costs. "This bill, in fact, will lead us to a strong economy, with the creation of millions of new jobs," Boxer said.

When Reid attempted on June 6 to limit the debate on Boxer's amendment itself, the motion to invoke cloture was rejected on a **key vote of 48–36 (R 7–32; D 39–4; I 2–0)**—a dozen votes short of the sixty needed. Neither Barack Obama, D-Ill., nor John McCain, R-Ariz., the prospective 2008 presidential nominees for their parties, was present for the cloture vote, but each issued statements saying he would have voted in favor of limiting debate. Similar statements were issued by Clinton and a few others who missed the vote. *(2008 key votes, p. 972)*

Boxer noted that the absent senators who had declared their intentions would have brought the total vote to fifty-four—a solid majority, but still well short of the sixty votes needed to invoke cloture.

Reid pulled the bill from floor consideration, and the Senate went on to other issues. McConnell sought to put the onus on the Democrats. "The majority says climate change is the most important issue facing the planet," he said. "Yet they've rushed the debate on that topic and brought the bill to a premature end."

HIGHLIGHTS

Following were highlights of the plan laid out in S 3036.

Greenhouse gas emission cap. Utilities, factories, natural gas producers, petroleum refiners, producers of hydrofluorocarbons, and similar facilities would have to reduce their levels of greenhouse gas emissions by 19 percent by 2020 and by 71 percent by 2050. Greenhouse gas producers would have to directly reduce their own emissions or purchase allowances from other producers that exceeded requirements. Gas producers could meet a portion of their required reduction through domestic and international offset credits, such as for planting trees. Violations would be treated as if they were violations of the Clean Air Act.

Trading mechanism. A trading market for greenhouse gas allowances would be created, with oversight and regulatory boards. The market would include an automatic mechanism to reduce costs by releasing additional allowances when prices rose to unexpected levels.

Revenue. The Congressional Budget Office calculated that the bill would raise $901.1 billion in revenue over ten years from auctioning emission allowances.

Hardship assistance and mitigation. An estimated $800 billion in tax benefits would be provided for consumers "in need of assistance related to energy costs." In addition, revenue from the cap-and-trade system would be used to provide almost $575 billion to industries for adjustment assistance and $190 billion for worker training and assistance programs.

- States, localities, and Indian tribes would be eligible for an estimated $911 billion to reduce the impact of emission limits, $254 billion for adjustment assistance, and $171 billion for mass transit.
- States would also be eligible for an estimated $566 billion for early action activities, $253 billion for natural resources programs, and $237 billion for wildlife adaptation.
- Federal programs to alleviate the impact of climate change on natural resources would be allocated an estimated $288 billion.

Immediate action. A tracking system for significant emissions from across the country would be created, with rewards to companies that took early action to reduce emissions and use renewable energy technologies. Money would be provided for research and development of new technologies.

Offshore Drilling

Republicans in 2008 scored an unexpected victory on one of their energy priorities: ending a moratorium on new offshore oil and gas drilling. Bolstered by growing public outrage over the high price of gasoline, they succeeded in forcing Democrats to lift the twenty-year-old ban, which prohibited expanded drilling off the Atlantic and Pacific coasts.

The moratorium had been included in the Interior Department appropriations bill every year since 1982. Supporters, including coastal lawmakers from both parties, said it was essential to protecting the coast from the risk of a catastrophic oil spill. Those who wanted to lift the ban argued that expanding domestic supplies of oil and gas was critical to bringing down prices and reducing a dangerous dependence on foreign oil. They also said that improved drilling techniques had greatly minimized the risk of a major oil spill.

Democrats had focused on promoting the production and use of renewable fuels and encouraging conservation and energy efficiency. They worked through the spring and summer to produce a set of tax incentives aimed at achieving those goals, and in the fall they were able to clear a $16.9 billion energy tax package by attaching it to a massive financial services rescue bill (HR 1424—PL 110-343). *(Financial services bailout, p. 154)*

But the Democrats were caught off guard by the swift change in public sentiment on domestic drilling driven by record gasoline prices. By July, a Pew Research Center poll found that 60 percent of voters said developing new energy sources was a higher priority than protecting the environment.

Surprised at having to play defense, Senate Majority Leader Harry Reid of Nevada, House Speaker Nancy Pelosi of California, and others concentrated on preventing votes that would put their rank and file on the spot in advance of the November 2008 elections—even when it meant derailing major legislation such as the annual spending bills and the defense authorization act. They cast their opponents as shills for the big oil companies, which strongly supported open drilling, and tried to redirect the debate with bills to curb energy speculation and help low-income families with heating bills.

Republicans, meanwhile, spent much of the summer hammering the Democrats, gaining traction on what they hoped would be a potent campaign issue. Day after day, GOP senators went to the floor to speak about drilling, outline amendments they wanted to offer, and demand votes that would put Democrats in an uncomfortable position.

"Why is this so hard?" Christopher S. Bond, R-Mo., asked in a speech similar to many others. "Why are Democrats so desperate to deny the relief the American people need and are demanding?"

When Congress left for the August recess, Republicans staged daily protests on the House floor, as various members flew back to Washington, D.C., to demand that Pelosi return the House to session and have an up-or-down vote on offshore drilling.

Pressure for action intensified when GOP presidential nominee John McCain endorsed offshore drilling. Democratic nominee Barack Obama said in early August that he would accept it as part of a larger package. A number of Democratic congressional candidates followed suit. At the Republican National Convention, delegates erupted into a chant of "Drill, baby, drill!" as their vice presidential nominee, Alaska governor Sarah Palin, extolled the advantages of domestic oil production.

Finally, in September, Republicans used their trump card. Before lawmakers could adjourn to campaign for the election, they had to pass a continuing resolution, or CR, to keep federal domestic agencies and foreign aid going into the new year. Nine of the twelve fiscal 2009 spending bills had fallen by the wayside. Republicans threatened to block passage of a CR unless the drilling moratorium in the interior-environment section was dropped. At that point, Democrats saw no alternative. In addition to omitting the moratorium, the continuing resolution (HR 2638—PL 110-329) allowed the expiration of a ban on drilling for oil shale in the Rocky Mountain West. *(Appropriations, p. 124)*

HOUSE APPROPRIATIONS ACTION

The fiscal 2009 appropriations process effectively broke down in June 2008, when House Democrats halted action instead of allowing Republicans on the Appropriations Committee to force votes on drilling.

At a June 26 committee markup, Jerry Lewis of California, the panel's senior Republican, pressed Chairman David R. Obey, D-Wis., to promise that he would bring up the interior-environment spending bill immediately after the July Fourth recess. "If the gentleman wants to set the agenda of the committee, he needs to go out and get thirty Republicans elected," Obey responded.

Lewis next tried to insert the interior bill into the measure that was scheduled for consideration—the spending bill for the Departments of Labor, Health and Human Services, and Education. Republicans planned to offer several energy amendments, including proposals to expand offshore drilling, open the Arctic National Wildlife Refuge (ANWR) to drilling, and allow a leasing program for oil shale in Western states.

Obey called off the markup. "I'll see them in September on a CR," he said, referring to a continuing resolution. Republicans said Democrats were acting out of fear that the GOP amendments might be adopted, not an unrealistic outcome given voters' growing concern about high gas prices.

Acting with Pelosi's support, Obey held no further appropriations markups. Congress ultimately cleared just three fiscal 2009 spending bills, for defense, homeland security, and military construction-veterans affairs. To fund the remaining departments, Congress would need to pass a continuing resolution.

ENERGY-RELATED BILLS

In response to persistent GOP calls for legislation to open public lands and offshore areas to new drilling, House leaders brought a series of energy-related bills to the floor in June and July.

The most contentious was what was dubbed "use it or lose it" legislation requiring that oil and gas companies with leases on federal lands drill or risk losing their leases. Democrats said oil companies already had leases on 68 million acres of government land and waters that they were not exploiting. Before talking about opening new areas, they argued, the companies should be required to use the leases they held.

In a strategy that infuriated Republicans, Pelosi brought two versions of the legislation (HR 6251, HR 6515) to the floor under suspension of the rules. The expedited procedure required a two-thirds vote and barred amendments, which meant Republicans could not offer drilling proposals. Both bills won a majority, but the votes fell short of the two-thirds threshold and the bills were rejected.

HR 6251 would have required the annual sale of oil and natural gas leases on public lands, but those who held such leases would have to proceed with exploration and drilling or relinquish their leases and be barred from getting more. The measure fell 223–195 on June 26, fifty-six votes short.

Democrats tried again the following month with HR 6515, adding several provisions to pick up more support. They included the annual sale of oil and gas leases in the National Petroleum Reserve, a 23-million-acre territory on Alaska's North Slope where oil exploration was permitted. Other provisions would have sped up construction of oil pipelines from drilling sites in the reserve to the existing Trans-Alaska Pipeline System and prohibited the export of Alaskan oil. The bill was rejected 244–173 on July 17, thirty-four votes short of the necessary two-thirds.

The White House threatened to veto both versions. It issued a statement of administration policy in response to HR 6251, saying, "It is incredible that Congress is considering legislation that would reduce domestic oil supply. Congress should instead remove barriers to domestic production of oil."

The House rejected another Democratic energy bill (HR 6346), brought to the floor under suspension of the rules June 24. The measure, which was aimed at retail gasoline price-gouging, was defeated 276–146. It would have authorized the Federal Trade Commission to impose fines and other punishments on anyone who charged "unconscionably excessive" prices for motor fuels during a presidentially declared "energy emergency." The White House issued a veto threat against this measure as well.

Two Democratic energy bills passed June 26. HR 6052, passed 322–98, would have provided transit agencies with grants to expand services and subsidize fares. HR 6377, passed 402–19 under suspension of the rules, would have directed federal regulators to take action to tighten oversight of trading in the oil futures market. Later, on Sept. 18, the House passed a similar bill (HR 6604) by a vote of 283–133.

SENATE STALEMATE

The Senate did not take up any of the House offshore drilling measures.

In the weeks before the August recess, the skirmishing over expanded drilling produced a stalemate on the Senate floor that stalled a number of bills, most notably the fiscal 2009 defense authorization measure (S 3001). The standoff also prevented Democrats from bringing up several other major bills that they had hoped to pass before the break. *(Defense authorization, p. 390)*

Energy futures speculation. A bill (HR 3268) aimed at curbing oil speculation became the focal point of the GOP campaign to get a prolonged floor debate on offshore drilling.

The measure would have increased staffing at the Commodity Futures Trading Commission and limited the number of futures contracts an investor could own. Democrats presented it as a first step toward bringing down gasoline prices. But Republicans said the legislation addressed only a tiny part of the problem, and they insisted on a chance to offer multiple amendments aimed at increasing domestic energy supplies.

Reid used a procedure known as "filling the amendment tree," offering a string of amendments that left no room for Republicans to offer their own. He then moved to invoke cloture, a step that would have ended the GOP filibuster. The cloture motion failed 50–43 on July 25, well short of the sixty votes that were required. GOP leaders vowed to use every procedural opportunity to keep debating the bill.

Low-income heating assistance. On July 26, Republicans turned back a cloture motion on another Democratic energy bill (S 3186), this one aimed at boosting assistance for low-income families struggling with energy costs. The measure would have nearly doubled fiscal 2008 funding for the Low Income Home Energy Assistance Program, or LIHEAP, with an infusion of $2.5 billion.

Republicans insisted that the focus should remain on amending the futures speculation bill. The motion on proceeding to the bill failed 50–35, ten votes short of the number needed to invoke cloture.

Defense authorization. The biggest casualty of the partisan skirmishing in advance of the August recess was the fiscal 2009 defense authorization bill (S 3001). While members on both sides considered it must-pass legislation, the battle over oil drilling amendments pushed action into September.

Carl Levin, D-Mich., chairman of the Armed Services Committee, worked behind the scenes to seek agreement to limit amendments. He argued that it was important to pass the defense bill early, given the busy floor schedule anticipated in September and the lack of any certainty that there would be a lame-duck session. He was supported by John W. Warner of Virginia, who was standing in as ranking Republican on the panel while McCain was out campaigning.

Reid asked for a unanimous consent agreement July 26 to allow the defense bill to come to the floor and limit amendments to those considered germane. But Minority Leader Mitch McConnell, R-Ky., objected and pledged not to consent to any agreement on the bill until his demands on votes on energy legislation were addressed.

On July 31, the Senate rejected a cloture motion to proceed to the bill. The vote was 51–39. However, by the time lawmakers returned in September, partisan sparring had shifted to the earmarks issue, and the Senate cleared S 3001 (PL 110-417) on Sept. 27.

DEMOCRATS' DRILLING BILL

After resisting for months, House Democratic leaders responded in September 2008 by passing a bill to authorize coastal states to permit oil and gas drilling fifty miles offshore. It was a major concession designed to prevent defections by moderate members of their own caucus. The House passed the bill (HR 6899) by a vote of 236–189 on Sept. 16, with just fifteen Republicans supporting it.

The Senate was not expected to take up the bill, but the vote allowed House Democrats, particularly those in tight election races, to go on record in support of drilling. At the same time, the measure included Democratic priorities such as incentives for renewable energy and energy-efficient buildings, similar to those offered in a Senate tax bill.

Most Republicans said the measure was a sham because the revenue would be devoted entirely to alternative energy. They said states would be unlikely to allow drilling near their shores if they did not get any of the royalties. Lewis called it a "backdoor disincentive." The White House threatened a veto.

The bill, which Democrats described as a compromise, included provisions to

- Allow oil and natural gas drilling in areas of the Outer Continental Shelf that were one hundred miles or more from the coast.
- Permit leases for drilling fifty to one hundred miles offshore on the Outer Continental Shelf if a state chose to allow it.
- Require energy companies to explore their existing oil and gas leases or lose them.
- Expedite oil and gas production in Alaska's National Petroleum Reserve.
- Keep certain areas off-limits to petroleum companies, including the eastern Gulf of Mexico off the coast of Florida and the historic Georges Bank fishery in New England.
- Lift a moratorium—perpetuated in the Interior Department spending bill—on an oil shale leasing program for Colorado, Utah, and Wyoming, but only if each state decided to move ahead with its leases.
- Require utilities to generate 15 percent of their energy from renewable sources by 2020.
- Use the new oil and gas royalties to pay for incentives designed to promote energy efficiency, renewable energy, or carbon capture and sequestration.

The bill included a variety of tax credits for renewables such as wind and solar energy, as well as new tax breaks for coal projects that captured carbon, fueling stations for natural gas vehicles, and energy conservation.

By a vote of 191–226, the House on Sept. 16 rejected a GOP effort to delay the bill by recommitting it to the Natural Resources Committee with instructions to substitute language repealing the moratorium on drilling in the Pacific, Atlantic, and the eastern Gulf of Mexico, while allowing states to restrict drilling twenty-five to fifty miles offshore.

Nick J. Rahall II, D-W.Va., chairman of the House Natural Resources Committee, sought to reassure pro-environmentalist Democrats that lifting the moratorium would not allow oil companies to start drilling at will because the leasing process contained "built-in environmental safeguards." Rahall said, "Unlike what [the Republicans] may lead us to believe, lifting the moratoria does not immediately mean there's going to be drilling and certainly no immediate relief at the pump for taxpayers."

GOP DECLARES VICTORY

Democratic leaders acknowledged after the August recess that they did not have the votes to clear a resolution to keep the federal government running after Oct. 1 without dropping the moratorium language. Republicans vowed to fight any spending package that extended the drilling ban, and those in the Senate had demonstrated they had the votes to do so.

Democrats had floated the idea of including provisions from the House-passed HR 6899, but they dropped that idea and decided instead to simply eliminate the language that had imposed the ban, thereby allowing drilling as close as three miles from shore. The ban on developing oil shale deposits in the Rocky Mountains was also allowed to expire.

"Thank you to the American people for getting it right down to the point: 'Drill, drill, drill,' said they," said Sen. Pete V. Domenici, N.M. "And that's why we're here today, because that was finally heard by the majority party."

The House passed the continuing resolution (HR 2638) on Sept. 24 when it agreed by a vote of 370–58, with one member voting present, to an Obey motion to concur in the Senate amendment with an additional change. The Senate cleared the measure 78–12 on Sept. 27.

Policy experts and moderate Democrats said that once the ban had been lifted, it would be difficult to entirely reinstate it, even under a Democratic Congress and president. Rahall said the "sea change" by Democrats reflected the reality of future high energy prices, relentless campaigning by the GOP, and, most of all, pressure from constituents.

The Interior Department's Minerals Management Service, whose job was to lease and manage offshore energy production, said the process of completing environmental reviews, holding lease sales, conducting geologic studies, and building new infrastructure could take five to ten years before any new offshore drilling could begin.

Some lawmakers said that would give the next Congress and the new administration a chance to work out some restrictions and barriers to drilling in the newly opened waters, including strict permitting processes and environmental reviews.

District Water Projects

Congress in 2007 overrode President George W. Bush's veto of a $23.2 billion water resources bill packed with projects in districts across the country. It was Bush's fifth veto since taking office and the first time that Congress enacted a law over his objections. The bill became law on Nov. 9, 2007 (HR 1495—PL 110-114).

The legislation authorized funding for nine hundred Army Corps of Engineers navigation, flood control, and environmental restoration projects. Some of the costliest projects were on the Mississippi River, in the Florida Everglades, and along coastal Louisiana, with others scattered throughout the country.

Bush vetoed the measure Nov. 2, citing its cost and contending that it did not give priority to the most urgent corps projects. "It is fiscally irresponsible," said White House spokeswoman Emily Lawrimore. "It falls outside of the scope of the Army Corps' mission and is filled with hundreds of projects that lack any sense of merit in terms of how and why they are proposed and prioritized by Congress." *(Veto message, p. 1064)*

Lawmakers of both parties said the reauthorization of the Water Resources Development Act was necessary to spur infrastructure improvements around the country, especially in areas of the Gulf Coast ravaged in 2005 by Hurricanes Katrina and Rita. Even some fiscal conservatives who counted themselves among Bush's staunchest allies rejected the White House argument that the bill was too expensive. Several of them also pointed out that the bill was an authorization for spending and did not appropriate any money. "This bill does not spend a dime," stressed Sen. James M. Inhofe of Oklahoma, ranking Republican on the Environment and Public Works Committee.

The Water Resources Development Act had not been reauthorized since 2000 (PL 106-541), mainly because of disputes about oversight of the corps. Supporters said the new law would help address a backlog of overdue infrastructure projects. In response to demands for greater oversight, the bill established an independent review process for most projects costing $45 million or more. *(2000 action, Congress and the Nation Vol. X, p. 372)*

BACKGROUND

Congress had formerly passed a corps water resources bill every two years. But lawmakers had been unable to agree on a renewal since 2000, as corps projects faced increasing scrutiny over their costs and impacts on the environment. In the 109th Congress, the House and Senate both passed versions of a reauthorization bill, but conferees could not agree on the size and scope of the package or on how strictly to set requirements for independent peer reviews. *(109th Congress action, p. 469)*

Instead, the annual appropriations bills that funded the corps included instructions about project management and specified hundreds of water projects to be carried out. That means of authorization became a problem in fiscal 2007, however, because the energy-water spending bill became part of a long-term continuing resolution enacted in February 2007 (H J Res 20—PL 110-5), and the resolution did not contain any authorization provisions. It provided funding for the corps but specified that prior law or language in accompanying reports earmarking money for individual water projects would not apply to fiscal 2007 funds. *(Appropriations, pp. 107, 285)*

In recent years, many lawmakers had expressed concern about the corps' management of project funding. Going back to 2002, the Government Accountability Office, the National Academy of Sciences, and media outlets issued reports questioning the corps' oversight of its projects. The damage from Hurricane Katrina heightened the controversy over the corps' efficiency and ability to conduct necessary repairs to water infrastructure.

Some former corps officials said the hurricane damage was intensified by lack of funding for upkeep of levees and pumping stations in New Orleans. Officials still at the corps said that the intensity of the storm would have overwhelmed even the newest systems. The corps had received billions of dollars in supplemental spending to restore flood control infrastructure and repair other water facilities.

Environmentalists and fiscal conservatives, in an unusual alliance, wanted projects to undergo more stringent reviews and meet strict environmental restoration requirements. But those who benefited from the projects, including farmers and the shipping industry, were eager for lawmakers to fund new projects.

HOUSE ACTION

The House Transportation and Infrastructure Committee approved a version of the bill (HR 1495) by voice vote March 15, 2007, that authorized more than seven hundred projects. The bill was formally reported (H Rept 110-80) on March 29. Chairman James L. Oberstar, D-Minn., said the legislation, which was nearly identical to a bill the House passed in 2005, would address "pent-up demand" for project authorizations. The Congressional Budget Office (CBO) estimated the cost of the committee-approved measure at $13.2 billion over fifteen years. It included

- $4.8 billion for restoration and hurricane prevention projects in coastal Louisiana and Florida's Everglades.
- $3.6 billion for navigational improvements and ecosystem restoration in the Upper Mississippi River-Illinois waterway.
- $3 billion for Gulf Coast hurricane-recovery efforts.
- Independent peer review of corps projects costing $50 million or more, with discretion for the corps chief of engineers to add or exempt certain projects.

At Republicans' request, the committee adopted a manager's amendment, by Eddie Bernice Johnson, D-Texas, chairwoman of the Water Resources and Environment Subcommittee, that added several projects to the bill. The panel also adopted an amendment by Jerry F. Costello, D-Ill., to require the corps to give contracting preference, in most instances, to companies that employed at least half their workers from the local area. Both amendments were adopted by voice vote.

The House passed HR 1495 by a vote of 394–25 on April 19, over the objections of the Bush administration and a handful of fiscally conservative lawmakers.

During the debate on April 19, the House

- Adopted by voice vote a manager's amendment that added almost ninety more projects to the bill, bringing the total authorization to $14.9 billion.
- Adopted by voice vote a proposal by Democrats Earl Blumenauer of Oregon and Peter Welch of Vermont to require the corps to update guidelines for evaluating and implementing water resources projects.

> Blumenauer said the proposal would "help bridge the gap" between the House and Senate versions of the bill.

The White House expressed strong opposition to the bill's price tag but did not issue an explicit veto threat.

SENATE ACTION

The Senate Environment and Public Works Committee approved its version of the bill (S 1248) by voice vote March 29 and reported the measure (S Rept 110-58) the next day. CBO estimated that the bipartisan bill, which mirrored a 2006 Senate-passed bill, would authorize $15 billion over fifteen years for more than six hundred projects.

Subsequently, however, the CBO said that language in the committee bill to expedite projects in storm-battered Louisiana could cost more than $15 billion. Under the provisions, the Senate Environment and Public Works Committee and the House Transportation and Infrastructure Committee could authorize projects to protect against the most severe, Category 5 storms without further congressional action.

The bill also authorized

- Nearly $1.9 billion for sixteen coastal restoration projects in Louisiana, and about $3.6 billion for flood control and storm-protection projects for areas damaged by Katrina and Rita.
- $3.4 billion for navigational improvements and ecosystem restoration on the Upper Mississippi River-Illinois Waterway.
- Independent review by a board of experts for projects costing more than $40 million. The bill also called for an interagency review committee to recommend revisions to planning principles and guidelines used in undertaking water resources projects.

Senators agreed to withhold amendments after Chairwoman Barbara Boxer, D-Calif., and ranking member Inhofe said they would resolve members' concerns when the bill reached the floor.

The Senate passed HR 1495 on May 16 by a vote of 91–4, after substituting the text of S 1248. But first, sponsors had to mollify the Louisiana senators and fiscal conservatives. Bill sponsors dropped the provisions for expedited hurricane-protection projects in the face of CBO's cost estimates. Louisiana's senators, Republican David Vitter and Democrat Mary L. Landrieu, disputed CBO's projection and wanted the provisions restored.

To assuage them, Boxer and Inhofe agreed to an expedited procedure under which the White House would recommend hurricane-protection projects based on a corps report due by the end of the year. The Senate Environment and Public Works Committee and the House Transportation and Infrastructure Committee would have to mark up the authorizing legislation within forty-five days or the bill could go directly to the floor. Debate in the Senate would be limited to twenty hours, and nongermane amendments would be barred.

As passed, the bill authorized about $14 billion worth of projects, including more than one hundred environmental infrastructure projects, such as wastewater treatment plants, that were not in the committee-approved bill. Previous efforts by the House to win backing for similar projects had faced Senate resistance. Including the projects in the bill carried added significance because the House was operating under new rules that barred conferees from adding projects not in the bills passed by either chamber.

The White House strongly objected to the bill's cost but did not threaten to veto it.

Negotiations off the Senate floor also focused on resolving concerns of two fiscal conservatives. As part of the negotiation, Boxer and Inhofe added at least seventeen provisions and projects. Tom Coburn, R-Okla., objected to projects in Hawaii, Iowa, Massachusetts, and New York, but those projects remained in the bill. Coburn and fellow conservative Jim DeMint, R-S.C., did win the addition of language aimed at reducing the estimated $58 billion backlog of corps water projects. The provision required annual reports from the corps on project funding, and projects that did not receive construction funding would be deauthorized after nine years. Coburn and DeMint still voted against passage.

To appease Democrats upset over having to give up antiwar language in the war supplemental spending bill (HR 2206), Senate leaders arranged a series of votes on Iraq-related amendments to the water resources bill, all of which were defeated.

CONFERENCE, FINAL ACTION

House and Senate negotiators on July 31 filed a conference report (H Rept 110-280) on HR 1495 that combined projects from the earlier House and Senate versions. The House adopted the conference report 381–40 on Aug. 1, and the Senate adopted the conference report, thus clearing the bill, 81–12 on Sept. 24. Both vote tallies exceeded the two-thirds majority needed to override a veto.

A CBO report released Sept. 24 said the measure would authorize $11.2 billion between 2008 and 2012 and an additional $12 billion over the following ten years, for a total of $23.2 billion. The final bill authorized nine hundred projects and studies, including many sought by Republicans. John L. Mica of Florida, the ranking Republican on the House Transportation and Infrastructure Committee, said GOP lawmakers would have a strong incentive to override a presidential veto. "With the backlog of members' projects and not having [an authorization] bill since 2000, I think it would be difficult to sustain [Bush's] veto," Mica said.

In a letter Aug. 1, the White House warned committee leaders that the bill's overall cost, as well as provisions that would shift the cost of some projects from nonfederal entities to taxpayers, would result in a veto. The administration also said the measure would authorize some projects outside the legislation's scope, such as abandoned mine reclamation and wastewater and drinking water infrastructure.

In the floor debate, senators said the bill's potential cost simply reflected the fact that Congress had not passed water resources legislation in nearly seven years. Also, they noted the bill would authorize funding, not appropriate any money. "Please know this is a respectful request to join with us," Boxer said of the president. "You don't have to fight on every single thing."

However, others, including DeMint, complained about the addition of projects to the bill during conference. DeMint tried to invoke a new Senate rule that made items added in conference subject to a point of order, but his effort was shot down when leaders told him the rule was meant for appropriations bills, not authorizations.

VETO OVERRIDE

Bush vetoed HR 1495 on Nov. 2, citing its cost and contending that it did not give priority to the most urgent corps projects. Both the House and Senate quickly voted to enact the bill anyway. The House on Nov. 6 overrode the veto on a **key vote of 361–54 (R 138–54; D 223–0).** The Senate followed suit two days later, enacting the bill on a **key vote of 79–14 (R 34–12; D 43–2; I 2–0).** Both tallies comfortably surpassed the two-thirds majority required. *(2007 key votes, p. 955)*

"It is very difficult for me to do, because I love our president," said Inhofe, who described himself as the Senate's most conservative member. Mica said, "I'm disappointed the president has decided to veto this legislation that includes many critically needed infrastructure and restoration projects." Republican senator Mel Martinez of Florida said he agreed with Bush that the final legislation lacked fiscal discipline. But he said he had concluded that the need to speed restoration of the Florida Everglades outweighed any reservations about the legislation's potential fiscal impact.

Some backers of the bill said the destruction of New Orleans after Hurricane Katrina underscored the dangers of neglecting flood control infrastructure. "This water bill is absolutely crucial for our entire country, and nowhere more so than my state of Louisiana," Vitter said. He said the bill would help jump-start coastal restoration and other major projects to guard against the sort of devastation wreaked by Katrina in 2005.

Senate minority whip Trent Lott, R-Miss., said he would support Bush on virtually all other vetoes but could not back him on this one. "We still have people in my state that don't have safe drinking water—in 2007," he said.

MAJOR PROVISIONS

The following are highlights of HR 1495, as enacted.

Water projects. The largest projects authorized under the bill included

- $1.9 billion for restoration of the hurricane-damaged Louisiana coastal area. It directed the Army Corps of Engineers to expedite planning, design, and construction for projects to reduce flood damage in areas that, within the past five years, had been subject to severe flooding and were declared a major disaster by the president. Within five years, the corps was required to report on a comprehensive, long-term plan to restore the area's water ecosystem.

The bill also deauthorized and called for the physical closure of the Mississippi River Gulf Outlet near New Orleans, which area residents called the "hurricane highway." They had lobbied for closure of the seventy-six-mile ship channel, which had resulted in the destruction of wetlands that had provided some flood protection.

- $3.7 billion for a system of new locks and dams and environmental restoration on the upper Mississippi River (from southern Illinois to the Minneapolis-St. Paul area) and on the Illinois Waterway (from its confluence with the Mississippi River in southern Illinois to Chicago). The total included $1.9 billion for new locks and $1.7 billion for ecosystem restoration projects, including construction of fish passages, floodplain restoration, and water level management.
- $1.4 billion for ecosystem restoration in the Florida Everglades, with the federal government paying half the amount. The bill also authorized the first projects in a sweeping restoration plan for the Everglades.

Peer review. The bill required an independent peer review process for projects with an estimated cost of $45 million or more. Alternatively, the governor of an affected state could request such a review. Peer review was also required for any project, regardless of cost, if the corps' chief of engineers determined that it was controversial. The chief of engineers also could exempt a project from the review process if he determined that it would have a negligible effect on environmental and other resources. The peer review panels had to be established by the National Academy of Sciences or a similar independent scientific technical-advisory organization. The studies had to be available to the public and to Congress.

Levees. The law created a new National Levee Safety Program and required the corps to establish a public database of all levees in the United States, with information about the population and structures that would be at risk if a levee failed. The corps was required to inspect all federally constructed levees.

Emergency projects. The Senate could expedite the approval of projects proposed by the president to prevent the loss of life and property in a hurricane or storm. The Environment and Public Works Committee would have forty-five days to report such legislation or the measure could come directly to the floor.

Streamlining. The corps was required to take dozens of specific steps to streamline water projects, such as developing a coordinated review process with simultaneous environmental review, analysis, and licensing completed within a specific time frame. The bill also allowed expedited planning, design, and construction of flood projects in areas that had been declared a national disaster in the preceding five years.

Environmental provisions. The bill required the corps to provide mitigation plans to assist ecological recovery in areas that had lost fish and wildlife as a result of corps projects. It extended for ten years the corps' National Shoreline Erosion Control Development Program. It allowed the corps to conduct projects to transport and place sediment dislodged during water projects in new locations that would benefit another project.

Clean Water

Lawmakers failed to resolve a dispute over wages in a measure (HR 720) to reauthorize the popular Clean Water State Revolving Fund, the largest source of low-interest loans for constructing wastewater treatment facilities and other water pollution abatement projects. The White House threatened a veto over the provision in the House-passed version of the bill that would apply federal wage rules to projects funded by the loans. The Senate did not consider similar legislation.

Congress also failed to clear a smaller measure to provide grants to replace aging sewer systems.

State and local governments were pressing Congress to reauthorize the revolving fund, established as part of the 1987 Clean Water Act amendments (PL 100-4). The 1987 act had been part of an effort to reduce nonpoint source pollution—that is, runoff from a variety of sources that swept pollutants into waterways. Under the amendments, the federal government provided seed money to the states, which then made low-interest loans to local communities to help construct or renovate sewage treatment plants and related facilities. *(1987 act, Congress and the Nation Vol. VII, p. 454)*

The last authorization had expired in 1994. Although appropriators continued to fund the program, federal contributions had declined significantly in recent years.

The bill's supporters cited Environmental Protection Agency estimates that the nation's wastewater infrastructure would face a funding shortfall of $300 billion to $400 billion over the following twenty years.

But congressional Republicans and the White House objected to language in the bill requiring that projects carried out with assistance from the revolving fund meet standards set in the Davis-Bacon Act (PL 88-349). This act required that workers on federal construction projects would receive local prevailing wages and benefits.

Many Republicans objected that the proposed measure would go beyond the original clean water amendments by subjecting state matching funds, as well as the federal seed money, to Davis-Bacon requirements. They warned this would hurt small businesses, especially in the eighteen states that did not have state-level prevailing wage laws. Although labor leaders endorsed the language, businesses generally opposed it.

HOUSE ACTION

The House Transportation and Infrastructure Committee approved HR 720 by a vote of 55–13 on Feb. 7, 2007, and reported it (H Rept 110-30) on March 5. The panel's Water Resources and Environment Subcommittee had approved the measure by voice vote Jan. 31. The legislation, sponsored by James L. Oberstar, D-Minn., chairman of the full committee, proposed to authorize $20 billion over five years for the revolving fund.

The committee's ranking Republican, John L. Mica of Florida, opposed the Davis-Bacon provision, saying it would "ensure that more states will have guaranteed cost increases—and will get less for paying more." He said the measure would especially hurt communities that were small and disadvantaged.

The committee rejected by voice vote a Republican amendment that would have required the Government Accountability Office to study the impact of applying Davis-Bacon to wastewater projects. Oberstar said the question had been studied before.

The committee returned to the legislation a month later after a preliminary analysis by the Congressional Budget Office (CBO) suggested that it did not comply with pay-as-you-go budget rules. The rules, adopted at the start of the 110th Congress, required that new entitlements or revenue reductions be offset so that they did not add to the deficit. The CBO said the bill was expected to reduce revenue because it would prompt states to issue additional tax-exempt bonds for wastewater improvement projects. The potential loss of revenue would have exposed the measure to a point of order on the House floor. To solve the problem, the committee gave voice-vote approval to an amendment to offset the lost federal revenue by increasing tonnage fees levied on ships that entered the United States from foreign waters. The substitute also reduced the bill's cost by $6 billion by shortening the authorization period by one year. As amended by the committee, the bill would authorize $14 billion in loans through 2011.

The full House passed HR 720 by 303–108 on March 9, despite a White House veto threat that was issued the previous day.

Although the overall bill garnered strong bipartisan support, Republicans continued to protest the inclusion of the Davis-Bacon language. After a contentious, partisan floor debate, lawmakers rejected, 140–280 on March 9, an amendment by Republicans Richard H. Baker of Louisiana and Steve King of Iowa that would have taken out the Davis-Bacon provision. Mica said the strong showing of GOP support for the amendment indicated that Democrats would not be able to achieve the two-thirds vote needed to override a veto.

Oberstar and other Democrats defended the Davis-Bacon language. Majority Leader Steny H. Hoyer of Maryland said he and other Democratic leaders were "absolutely committed" to protecting it. Unions also aggressively battled attempts to remove the language. Terence M. O'Sullivan, president of the Laborers' International Union, said lawmakers should reject what he described as "backdoor, piecemeal attempts to dismantle this family-supporting law."

Business groups lobbied against the provision. A coalition that included the U.S. Chamber of Commerce and various construction and contracting groups sent a letter to House leaders urging them to drop the language "to obtain the highest construction value for the taxpayers' dollar."

The House adopted several amendments by voice vote on March 9, including

- A proposal by Bart Stupak, D-Mich., aimed at encouraging greater cooperation between Canada and the United States to clean up sewage discharges in the Great Lakes.
- An amendment by John Hall, D-N.Y., and Earl Blumenauer, D-Ore., to require states to give priority to repairing existing wastewater infrastructure over building new facilities.
- A proposal by Todd R. Platts, R-Pa., to ensure that small contractors were given equal opportunity to secure contracts for wastewater projects.

In an unusual tactic that House Republicans had been using to amend or block bills, Eric Cantor, R-Va., won on a motion to recommit the bill to committee, in this case to the Transportation and Infrastructure Committee to add language barring convicted felons from using a transportation worker identification card to board a ship. The March 9 vote was 359–56. However, Oberstar accepted the amendment and the House adopted it by voice vote, eliminating the need to return the bill to the committee.

AGING SEWER SYSTEMS

The House on March 7, 2007, passed by 367–58 a smaller bill (HR 569) to authorize $1.7 billion over five years for grants to replace aging sewer systems. The House Transportation and Infrastructure Committee had approved the measure by voice vote on Feb. 7 and reported it (H Rept 110-16) on Feb. 16. The Senate took no action on the bill.

The legislation aimed to help local governments fund the repair and replacement of "combined sewer overflows"—outmoded sewer systems designed to carry both domestic sewage and industrial wastewater. Supporters said such sewer systems, which still existed in more than seven hundred communities nationwide, posed a risk to public health and the environment.

The White House and fiscal conservatives in Congress raised concerns over the bill's costs. In a concession to conservatives, Oberstar agreed to accept a King amendment that would cut the bill's authorization level by 5 percent—to $1.7 billion—from the original $1.8 billion. King's amendment was adopted by voice vote on March 7.

CHAPTER 8

Agriculture

Agriculture

In agriculture policy the four years of President George W. Bush's second term of office paralleled his first term, but with the important difference that the major farm legislation of the period was written after Democrats took control of Congress in 2007. This meant that groups, businesses, and individuals interested in agricultural laws had more room to maneuver in putting into place programs and spending backed by their members—and in the case of senators and representatives, backed by their voting constituents.

The president, critical of the cost of overall farm spending, pressed for reductions in crop subsidies and other outlays and threatened to veto legislation that he said would be too costly. He wound up in 2008 doing just that by vetoing the major omnibus farm legislation of the period. But the Democratic-led Congress had no problem overriding the president with bipartisan support, demonstrating—as in the past—that farm politics in Congress easily crossed political boundaries.

Other than the 2008 omnibus bill, neither the 109th nor the 110th Congress enacted major farm legislation. The 2008 omnibus legislation was in many ways a continuation of the last major agricultural bill, which was passed—with the president's approval—in 2002. *(Congress and the Nation Vol. XI, p. 447)*

That legislation was passed in the wake of a train of natural disasters, including drought, floods, and hurricanes, and a failed experiment enacted in 1996 to change the basic agricultural policy of the nation.

In 2002, the primary farm law, which was scheduled to expire that year, was crafted to take account of changed realities since the law was last revised in 1996 when Republicans—who had recently regained control of Congress—sought to move farmers away from the farm policy of subsidies that stretched back to New Deal days a half century earlier. The GOP sought to encourage farmers to base production decisions on market forces, not government supports. But the plan was undermined by a series of international financial crises, particularly in Asia, that dramatically undercut commodity prices. Congress in response passed a series of emergency farm aid packages between 1998 and 2001 but still faced the question of whether the 1996 law would work in the agricultural world of the new

Outlays for Agriculture

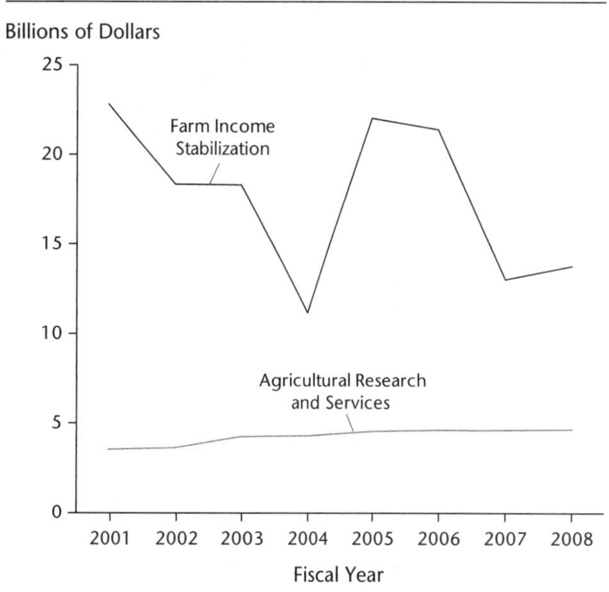

SOURCE: Office of Management and Budget, *Historical Tables, Budget of the United States Government: Fiscal Year 2010* (Washington, D.C.: U.S. Government Printing Office, 2009), Table 3.2.

REFERENCES

Discussion of agricultural policy for the years 1945–1964 may be found in *Congress and the Nation Vol. I*, pp. 665–767; for the years 1965–1968, *Congress and the Nation Vol. II*, pp. 555–597; for the years 1969–1972, *Congress and the Nation Vol. III*, pp. 331–352; for the years 1973–1976, *Congress and the Nation Vol. IV*, pp. 717–740; for the years 1977–1980, *Congress and the Nation Vol. V*, pp. 365–395; for the years 1981–1984, *Congress and the Nation Vol. VI*, pp. 485–516; for the years 1985–1988, *Congress and the Nation Vol. VII*, pp. 499–539; for the years 1989–1992, *Congress and the Nation Vol. VIII*, pp. 535–557; for the years 1993–1996, *Congress and the Nation Vol. IX*, pp. 479–505; for the years 1997–2000, *Congress and the Nation Vol. X*, pp. 417–431; for the years 2001–2004, *Congress and the Nation Vol. XI*, pp. 447–468.

U.S. senator and chairman of the Agriculture Committee Saxby Chambliss, R-Ga., left, Rep. Randy Neugebauer, R-Lubbock, center, and Rep. Mike Conaway, R-Midland, listen to testimony during a Senate hearing on the Farm Bill on September 8, 2006, in Lubbock, Texas.
Source: AP Photo/Lubbock Avalanche Journal, Jim Watkins

century. The decision, in the 2002 omnibus farm bill, the major agricultural legislation of the period, was to reestablish farm subsidies abolished in 1996 but also to retain a fixed payment scheme that was put in place at that time to wean farmers off subsidies.

The 2008 bill that passed did not try to return to the Republican approach of the 1990s—in part because the Democrats, then in the minority, never fully accepted the market approach favored by the GOP, and because the natural disasters and economic troubles of farmers that followed left both parties more comfortable with the traditional approach to farm support.

The final bill significantly boosted spending on nutrition programs, preserved the existing approach to crop subsidies, and expanded conservation programs. The legislation did, however, limit eligibility for farming subsidies, although less than the president and some members of Congress wanted. The legislation also set up a permanent disaster fund to help farmers hit by floods and droughts more quickly than through separation legislation, the approach used in response to past natural disasters.

The nutrition titles were particularly important to urban and hunger groups that lobbied aggressive to push through more than $10 billion in new funding for these programs. The minimum benefit for the food stamp program was raised for the first time in more than thirty years. The program, widely acclaimed as one of the nation's most effective antipoverty activities, was renamed the Supplemental Nutrition Assistance Program.

Chronology of Action on Agriculture

2005–2006

The 109th Congress, 2005 through 2006, was not an important period for agriculture legislation. Congress completed the regular appropriations for farm supports and, in a reconciliation bill, made changes to agriculture and rural development programs that were expected to yield net savings of $2.7 billion over five years. These savings were part of a much larger effort to cut program spending by nearly $39 billion, the first significant reductions in mandatory spending since 1997. *(Reconciliation bill, p. 81)*

Both chambers tried to reauthorize the Commodity Futures Trading Commission but ran out of time at the end of 2006. The agency was continued on an interim basis and fully reauthorized in the omnibus farm bill in 2008. *(Details, p. 514)*

Commodity Futures

The 109th Congress considered but did not finish action on legislation to reauthorize the Commodity Futures Trading Commission (CFTC) and the Commodity Exchange Act through 2010. The legislation broadened and clarified the CFTC's antifraud powers and jurisdiction over foreign currency exchanges and natural gas markets.

The House passed the relatively noncontroversial bill (HR 4473) on Dec. 14, 2005. The Senate passed a similar bill (S 1566) on Aug. 1, 2006, but the two versions were never reconciled before Congress adjourned. (Similar legislation was included in the omnibus farm bill passed in 2008.) *(Details, p. 514)*

The legislation reauthorized the CFTC for five years, through 2010, expanded its jurisdiction to include foreign currency exchanges, and clarified the legal definitions of futures transactions. It also clarified that the CFTC has jurisdiction over all foreign currency transactions not made on a national securities exchange offered to people who are not brokers or associated with registered futures commission merchants, insurance companies, or investment banks.

As amended in the House Agriculture Committee, HR 4473 expanded the CFTC's authority to include jurisdiction over natural gas contract trading, and required the commission to conduct automatic investigations into price manipulation whenever certain "triggers" take place, such as highly unusual changes in the price of natural gas or large futures and option market transactions in natural gas. Civil penalties for violations (including manipulation of natural gas prices) were increased to the greater of $1 million or three times the amount that a person profited from the violation. Previously, the maximum fine was $500,000. The bill also doubled the jail time maximum for any criminal violations to ten years from five years.

BACKGROUND

The CFTC was created in 1974 to protect market users and the public from fraud, manipulation, and abusive practices related to the sale of commodity and financial futures and options. In fiscal 2004 the CFTC had regulation authority over more than 1.5 billion futures and options contracts in ten different exchanges, and the commission watched over the activities of more than 2,500 businesses and 50,000 individuals.

The CFTC in 2005 reported it had brought seventy-nine retail foreign currency fraud enforcement actions over the previous four years, winning some $267 million in restitution and civil penalties on behalf of 23,000 victims who invested about $350 million.

However, President George W. Bush's administration was not supportive of the changes dealing with gas contracts. Less than a week after the House Committee approved the measure in December, the Bush administration and Federal Reserve Chairman Alan Greenspan expressed concerns about the natural gas language. "The case for such a broad expansion of the commission's mandate has not been made," Greenspan said in a Dec. 12, 2005, letter to Michael G. Oxley, R-Ohio, chairman of the House Financial Services Committee. Greenspan blamed natural gas price spikes on a shortage of liquefied natural

AGRICULTURE LEADERSHIP

President George W. Bush appointed two more secretaries to head the Agriculture Department during his second term in office. His first secretary, Ann M. Veneman, served throughout his first term, leaving to become head of UNICEF, the United Nations International Children's Emergency Fund.

Veneman left on Jan. 20, 2005, and Bush replaced her with Mike Johanns, who was sworn in as Bush was inaugurated for his second term. Johanns, who was halfway through his second four-year term as governor of Nebraska, remained as secretary until resigning in late 2007 to run for an open Senate seat from his state, which he won without difficulty. He was replaced by another midwesterner from a farm state, Ed Schafer, who served as North Dakota's Republican governor from 1992 to 2000.

Both men were widely praised by Democrats and Republicans alike and each won Senate confirmation with little difficulty, Johanns by voice vote on Jan. 4, 2005, and Schafer by unanimous consent on Jan. 28, 2008.

Johanns, with a reputation as a strong conservative and a careful politician who was first elected Nebraska governor in 1998, grew up on a dairy farm in Iowa operated by his father. He later said the experience made everything else in life seem easy. As governor, he traveled on a number of agricultural trade missions. Bush cited this experience in nominating him as the United States faced increasingly complex agricultural international trade issues with other nations.

As secretary, Johanns was in office when each party held control of Congress—Republicans during the 109th and Democrats during the 110th. However, it was during the latter, 2007–2008, that legislators drafted and passed the sweeping farm reauthorization legislation that extended and in many ways expanded the basic 2002 farm bill that was done during Veneman's term. Most of the legislative work was done during 2007, with Johanns still in office and voicing administration concerns about the cost of the bill.

Schafer took over as Agriculture secretary as conferees started to reconcile differences in the two versions of the bill, which both chambers passed in spring 2008. Bush's new agriculture secretary once again held the position that the bill was too expensive, and when the farm reauthorization legislation reached the president' desk, Bush vetoed it. However, Congress overrode his veto with bipartisan support.

Schafer's ties to the farming community were evident in Senate hearings on his nomination. Although receiving a warm reception, members questioned whether he could be able to balance the needs of the farming community, which was behind the expansive new farm bill, or aggressively back the administration's position on the legislation on issues such as Bush's opposition to a new disaster fund for farmers. Schafer had long represented farmers who supported the existing mix of subsidies and lobbied for a disaster trust fund. But Schafer conceded that he could not push a policy position at odds with the administration in which he served, even though previously he had backed the disaster fund as governor. After his term in office, Schafer served as president of a company his father began and at the time of his appointment was chief executive of Extend America, a startup wireless communications company.

Farming interests were surprised by the appointment and had expected that the acting secretary—a deputy to Johanns—would serve out the remaining year of the term. These interests, however, endorsed Schafer's appointment. Ranchers, for example, lauded Schafer's trade experience, pointing to his role in a 2000 trade mission to China to open new beef markets.

gas imports and production facilities, and said the bill does not affect those "market fundamentals" and "will not lower natural gas prices or reduce price volatility."

Industry groups also objected to the legislation. The Bond Market Association, Futures Industry Association, and the Securities Industry Association asked the committee to delay consideration of the measure, arguing that the natural gas amendment includes "expansive new provisions" that would "expand the CFTC's authority far beyond the commission's traditional authority."

Food Uniformity

The House on May 8, 2005, passed legislation (HR 4167) amending the Federal Food, Drug, and Cosmetic Act of 1938 to create uniform national food safety and labeling standards. The bill, formally known as the National Uniformity for Food Act of 2005, was vigorously opposed by consumer advocates and many state agriculture agencies.

The House action came on a vote of 283–139. The Senate did not act on related legislation before adjournment of the 109th Congress.

The legislation, sponsored by Rep. Mike Rogers, R-Mich., gave the Food and Drug Administration (FDA) the authority to establish national food and safety warning requirements. For example, the agency would be authorized to set uniform rules for labeling food products with warnings about carcinogenic ingredients.

Under the legislation, states were required to comply with uniform federal food safety and labeling guidelines.

States could petition the FDA to add food labeling and safety requirements. If the FDA had not set a standard for a particular item, states would be permitted to set and enforce state standards but had to petition the FDA to adopt the requirement, or to exempt it from the uniformity requirement.

Supporters of the bill said that varying food notification requirements created unnecessary bottlenecks and disruptions to interstate commerce. Differences in state labeling standards increased costs of production for manufacturers and distributors and ultimately increased the costs of the products consumers will purchase, they argued.

Supporters claimed that uniform standards would improve the safety of the nation's food supply. House sponsor Rogers said: "It is incredibly important that we have a national standard." Sylvia Warner, spokeswoman for Rogers, said uniform federal legislation would clean up the patchwork of state laws.

"The manufacture and distribution of food is now a national business," said Energy and Commerce Chairman Joe L. Barton, R-Texas. "Many believe that it is just common sense for these types of food manufacturers and distributors to have one labeling standard for the country, not fifty standards, one for each of the fifty states."

Democrats charged that national standards would override stricter state laws. Critics, such as the Consumers Union and U.S. Public Interest Research Group, said the law would eviscerate more restrictive state laws while allowing for a lenient federal law that does little to protect consumers. These opponents said the legislation's intent is not primarily to protect consumers from unsafe food, but rather to benefit the food industry by offering lower costs of production and less restrictive consumer protection laws. Rep. Henry A. Waxman, D-Calif., said the bill would preempt eighty food standard and labeling laws in thirty-seven states. Also weighing in against the bill were California governor Arnold Schwarzenegger, a Republican, and state attorney general Bill Lockyer, a Democrat.

In a letter to Rogers, Lockyer expressed concern that the legislation would preempt California's Proposition 65, a law that requires warnings on consumer products containing chemicals that may cause cancer or birth defects. Lockyer said California has acted under the 1986 law to reduce toxic chemicals in food products, in some cases years ahead of the FDA. He cited the state's efforts to reduce levels of lead in ceramic tableware, foil wine bottle caps, and calcium supplements. The Association of Food and Drug Officials said the bill's scope extended well beyond labeling and might preempt state action in case, for example, of an anthrax attack on the food supply.

The bill was approved by the Energy and Commerce Committee 30–18 on Dec. 15, 2005, and had attracted 226 cosponsors as of March 8, 2006, including fifty-nine Democrats. No hearings were held on the legislation.

The Energy and Commerce Committee approved a similar bill in 2004, but the legislation never made it to the floor for consideration. The Senate never took up similar legislation during this period.

Horse Protection

The House on Sept. 7, 2006, passed legislation (HR 503) to prohibit slaughter of horses and other equines for human consumption. The bill would have amended the Horse Protection Act (PL 91-540). The vote was 263–146. The Senate did not act on a companion bill (S 1915) before the 109th Congress adjourned.

Around 90,000 horses are slaughtered each year in America for foreign food markets—mainly in Europe. The controversy surrounding the practice pitted the image of the horse as an American symbol and companion against what advocates in Congress called a legitimate business that employed many American workers and contributed more than $40 billion to the U.S. economy annually. They also contended that a ban would cost hundreds of millions of dollars per year in the care of unwanted and abandoned horses.

Opponents of the practice argued that horse slaughter was neither humane nor necessary. They said house slaughter encouraged horse owners not to care for their animals before bringing them in for slaughter. They also said there was sufficient sanctuary for unwanted horses.

This conflict did not break down along partisan lines in Congress. Although 133 of the House bill's 201 cosponsors were Democrats as of Sept. 1, 2006, the main backers of the legislation—John E. Sweeney of New York and Edward Whitfield of Kentucky in the House and Sen. John Ensign of Nevada, sponsor of Senate companion bill S 1915—were all Republicans. Sweeney represented Saratoga Springs, home to the famous race track and several major horse breeders. Whitfield's wife, Connie Harriman Whitfield, was a lobbyist for the Kentucky Racing Authority. Thoroughbred horse breeders and racing associations tend to oppose slaughter.

HR 503 was sponsor Sweeney's second attempt to guide a stand-alone bill outlawing horse slaughter through the House. In the 108th Congress he sponsored a bill that would have directly outlawed the slaughter of equines, rather than activities associated with the practice. It was never reported to the full House.

2007–2008

The inactivity of Congress on agriculture legislation in the 109th Congress was—as expected—reversed in the 110th as both chambers approved a sweeping revision and extension of the primary farm laws for an additional five years. The last major revision was done in 2002, which extended the laws to 2008. Congress did most of its work on the new extension in 2007, with both chambers passing legislation. But time ran out in 2007, requiring conference negotiations to spill over into early 2008. Agreement was reached by spring, but President George W. Bush vetoed the legislation on the grounds that it was too expensive. Congress, as everyone expected, quickly overrode the veto to enact the legislation into law.

The massive bill covered fifteen titles. It reauthorized basic crop support programs dating from the 2002 legislation. The bill also expanded many activities including the widely popular food stamp program, and included an energy section that sought to develop more extensive use of biofuels from nonconventional sources such as switch grass. In response to continuing criticism that the farm programs were paying rich farmers who had little need for supports, the legislation set a $500,000 limit on nonfarm income for all commodity benefits and a $750,000 cap on farm income for those receiving direct payments. Previously, the limit for benefits was $2.5 million for those who got less than 75 percent of their income from farming.

The bill also resolved a long-simmering dispute about labeling of certain foods by country of origin. Existing law required all meat have a country-of-origin label beginning in September 2008. Meat labeling was originally mandated in the 2002 farm law, but Congress had twice delayed its implementation except in the case of fish, which was already being labeled.

Omnibus Farm Bill

Congress in 2008 enacted—over two presidential vetoes—a massive bill that extended and expanded the nation's basic agricultural laws for an additional five years, from 2008 through 2012.

The legislation (HR 6124—PL 110-246) covered fifteen titles and hundreds of provisions. It covered a vast array of subjects from reauthorizing basic farm laws, expanding nutrition programs, and encouraging biofuels development to more mundane matters such as protecting historic barns and ordering the government not to close certain farm offices for two years.

The legislators reauthorized crop support programs included in an equally sprawling 2002 farm bill, struggled to find an acceptable formula to limit payments to the richest farmers but in the end tightened income eligibility limits for farm payments, reauthorized countercyclical programs and created a new one, expanded the food stamp program (and renamed it), authorized an array of conservation programs, included an extensive energy section that emphasized development of new biofuels, extended or implemented several trade agreements, and reaffirmed an existing requirement that all meats show the country of origin on its label starting in September 2008. *(Major provisions, p. 522; Bill highlights, p. 516)*

President George W. Bush objected to the cost of the measure and pushed for sharp reductions in farm subsidies, arguing that generous aid to farmers was not needed at a time of high crop prices and farm revenue. Support in both chambers for a less-stringent bill, however, was strong enough to rebuff him.

A clerical error that omitted a section on international trade from the first version sent to the White House forced Congress and Bush to repeat the process. The first bill was enacted over Bush's veto May 22 (HR 2419—PL 110-234). Although that version became law, the complete bill was enacted June 18 (HR 6124—PL 110-246).

PAYING FOR THE FARM PROGRAMS

Although the massive bill moved through Congress with considerable bipartisan support, finding revenue to pay for the programs remained a constant challenge. The measure was expected to result in a net $289 billion in outlays over five years for farm, nutrition, conservation, and other related programs. At least two-thirds of the funding was for nutrition activities such as food stamps and school lunches for low-income children.

The bill's price tag—specifically its cost compared with a March 2007 baseline from the Congressional Budget Office (CBO)—was the source of nearly every hurdle, stalemate, and fight along the way. The fiscal 2008 budget resolution (S Con Res 21) instructed the House and Senate agriculture committees to stay within the five- and ten-year CBO baseline limits when they wrote the new farm bill. Committees could add up to $20 billion, but the extra spending would have to be offset by cuts in other mandatory programs or by tax increases. *(Budget resolution, p. 108)*

Under S Con Res 21, the agriculture committees could obligate a total of $280.3 billion for mandatory programs over five years. The number came from the CBO "baseline" calculations of the costs of existing programs over the following five years without any changes. The total included $59.8 billion over five years for crop supports, conservation, and agriculture export incentives—$16.4 billion less than was actually spent under the 2002 law (after adjusting it to cover five years instead of six). The committees could add up to $20 billion more over five years, but only if it was offset by revenue increases or cuts in other programs.

The reduction from spending over the past five years was the result of a decline projected by CBO in the cost of farm programs because of an expected increase in market prices for major commodity crops such as corn and soybeans. Higher prices reduced the subsidies available to farmers.

By contrast, mandatory spending on food stamps was expected to increase by $29.9 billion to total $186 billion over five years. Other programs in the bill covered areas such as rural development, some research and conservation programs, and forestry. The House-passed bill exceeded CBO's baseline by $5.7 billion, mainly to boost nutrition programs. The extra funding was offset by a proposed new tax on some foreign companies working in the United States and increased revenue from offshore oil drilling. The Senate bill was $5.3 billion above the baseline, offset by proposals to limit corporate tax shelters. These did not survive conference committee actions in 2008.

These calculations ensured an extended fight over spending levels and acceptable offsets that forced lawmakers to make tough choices about programs to cut back or increase and how to pay for the added costs. After months of negotiations, House and Senate conferees on May 7, 2008, reached agreement on most provisions of the multiyear bill. As negotiators released details the following day, Agriculture Secretary Ed Schafer reiterated the administration's veto threat, saying farm subsidies in the bill were still much too generous. It took conferees another five days to complete their work and file the conference report. Among the last issues resolved were choices to pay for the extra spending and the extent of limiting farm payments.

Disaster aid, nutrition, conservation, and alternative energy topped the list of programs that benefited from increased spending in the bill. Some of the extra costs were offset by cutting other programs below the CBO baseline. The largest reductions were in crop insurance ($3.9 billion over five years and $5.6 billion over ten years) and commodity supports ($1.7 billion over both five and ten years). Much of the reduction in crop insurance was achieved through shifts in timing for receipts and expenditures. The cuts in commodity programs also came in part from timing shifts, as well as from reducing the percentage of a farmer's acreage that was eligible for direct payments.

Even with the reductions, CBO calculated the cost of the final bill as exceeding the baseline by about $5 billion over five years and $10 billion over ten years. The conferees used an accounting maneuver to cover the five-year cost. Congress offset the ten-year cost by extending customs user fees. Some Republicans sharply opposed the tax increases, and Bush cited them in his veto message.

BACKGROUND

Multiyear farm bills were enacted every five or six years to authorize and shape major federal farm, nutrition assistance, rural development, agricultural trade, and forestry programs. Nearly 90 percent of the authorization in the 2008 legislation was for mandatory programs, and the funds were distributed automatically based on formulas in the legislation or in other laws. The remaining 10 percent was for discretionary programs and was only available when it was appropriated in a separate bill.

The previous, six-year farm bill (PL 107-171), enacted in 2002, expired Sept. 30, 2007. It was kept alive by six short-term extensions from Congress. Pending the new legislations, lawmakers last used an omnibus appropriations bill enacted in December 2007 (PL 110-161) to extend farm programs through March 15, 2009. *(Congress and the Nation Vol. XI, p. 449)*

The 2008 farm bill followed several earlier attempts to reshape farm programs and reduce their costs. The 1996 Freedom to Farm Act (PL 104-127) sought to wean farmers off crop subsidies, which were based on market prices, and replace them with annual fixed, but declining, payments. The effort was unsuccessful, as evidenced in the $30.5 billion in supplemental aid to farmers provided in fiscal 1998 through fiscal 2002. *(Major farm laws, Congress and the Nation Vol. XI, p. 451)*

The 2002 farm act (PL 107-171) again sought to reconfigure subsidy payments, this time by creating a new countercyclical program. However, the readjustments again did not stem the flow of additional farm payments: Congress had provided agriculture disaster aid every year since 2002, totaling more than $30 billion.

The main farm programs in the 2002 law included:

Direct payments. Fixed but declining annual payments to producers of major crops.

Marketing assistance loans and loan-deficiency payments. Marketing loans that allowed producers of major crops to borrow money from the government so they could pay their bills until they sold their harvested crops. Farmers used their crops as collateral, with loan rates set by statute. If a crop sold for less than the price established in the loan program, farmers could forfeit the crop to the government as full payment. Loan deficiency payments were direct payments to producers for the difference between the going rate for their crop and the marketing assistance loan rate.

Countercyclical payments. A new program to aid producers of major crops and soybeans when market prices dropped below a target price defined in the law. The government made up the difference between the average market price, plus the fixed payment, and the target price.

Payment limits. A cap of $2.5 million in adjusted gross income on farmers eligible for farm payments, unless 75 percent of their income came from farming. The law set a combined cap on annual payments to individual farmers of $360,000, down from $460,000 under the 1996 farm law. Fixed payments were limited to $40,000 per person, marketing loans and loan deficiency payments to $75,000 per person, and countercyclical payments to $65,000 per person. Allowances for additional farms effectively doubled those amounts.

HIGHLIGHTS OF 2008 FARM BILL

Farm program reauthorization. The law reauthorized crop support programs included in the last major farm legislation, enacted in 2002, including:

- Direct, or fixed, payments based on the farmers' acreage and the type of crops grown.
- Countercyclical payments, which went to farmers of major crops when the market price for their crops fell below a target price defined in the law.
- Marketing loans, which allowed producers to borrow from the government using their crops as collateral until they sold their harvests.
- Loan-deficiency payments, which allowed farmers to forgo the marketing loan when market prices fell below loan prices and to receive payments equal to the difference between the loan and the market price.

Farm income limits. The legislation set a $500,000 limit on nonfarm income for all commodity benefits and a $750,000 cap on farm income for those receiving direct payments. Previously, the limit for benefits was $2.5 million for those who got less than 75 percent of their income from farming.

Payment limits. The law made no change to the previous limits of $40,000 in direct payments and $65,000 in countercyclical payments to qualified farmers. However, the overall cost was expected to drop by about $300 million because of a provision that reduced the portion of farmed acreage on which a farmer could collect direct payments from 85 percent to 83.3 percent.

The final bill retained provisions in the 2002 law that allowed farmers to double the limits on direct and countercyclical payments if their spouses also farmed. The bill contained no limit on marketing loans, which were capped under the 2002 law at $75,000 ($150,000 for a couple farming the same land). The law eliminated the so-called three-entity rule, which had allowed farmers to collect full payments on one farm plus 50 percent of the payment limit on two more farms. That rule was replaced by a "direct attribution" requirement that did not restrict the number of farms in which a producer could have a share but specified that the total amount of direct and countercyclical payments that the individual received could not exceed the caps.

Countercyclical payments. In addition to reauthorizing the existing price-based countercyclical program, the law created a new, optional countercyclical program based on revenue. The new ACRE program tied payments to producers to a state's revenue level for a crop. Participants had their rates for direct payments and marketing loans reduced, and they had to remain in the program for the duration of the farm bill.

Dairy assistance. Two milk price support programs—the Milk Income Loss Contract Program and the Dairy Export Incentive Program—were extended through fiscal 2012.

Nutrition programs. The bill authorized $188.9 billion for domestic nutrition programs over five years, a net increase of $2.9 billion in outlays above the Congressional Budget Office (CBO) baseline. (The baseline number came from CBO's "baseline" calculations of the costs of existing programs over the following five years without any changes.) Most of the increase went to expanding food stamp benefits and easing the eligibility rules. Other significant increases went to providing emergency food aid and fresh fruit and vegetables for schools.

Conservation programs. The legislation authorized $24.1 billion for conservation programs, a $2.7 billion increase over the baseline, not counting related revenue increases and offsets. The bill reauthorized most programs from the 2002 law, including the conservation reserve, wetlands and grasslands program, and the Environmental Quality Incentives Program. It prohibited farmers with

LEGISLATIVE HISTORY

A new five-year farm bill began to take shape in 2007, but budget constraints and competing partisan and regional priorities combined to prolong the process. The House and Senate each passed versions of the legislation, which covered fiscal 2008 through fiscal 2012, but a conference to resolve the many differences between the two chambers was put off until 2008.

Work on the House farm bill moved relatively quickly. The House Agriculture Committee spent a few weeks debating and amending each title of the bill before approving it with significant bipartisan support. The House passed the bill in July 2007, after committee members fended off efforts to cut subsidies, including an amendment that would have set tight caps on traditional crop supports and shifted the money to conservation programs, rural development, and nutrition.

By contrast, debate in the Senate dragged on for months while the Agriculture Committee wrote its version. Once the measure was scheduled for floor time, Republicans and Democrats bickered over a long list of proposed amendments, several of which were unrelated to the underlying bill. Senators finally worked out a deal limiting debate to adjusted gross incomes of more than $1 million from receiving conservation payments.

Disaster aid. A total of $3.8 billion was provided for new agriculture disaster programs in fiscal 2008 through 2012, mainly for crop and livestock losses. The Senate had proposed a permanent trust fund for agriculture disaster aid, with $5.1 billion authorized over five years. The House bill had no comparable proposal.

Country-of-origin meat labeling. The legislation reaffirmed an existing law that required that all meat have a country-of-origin label beginning in September 2008. The label had to specify whether the product was from U.S.-raised and -slaughtered animals, was of completely foreign origin, or contained meat from more than one country, such as in some ground beef. Meat labeling was originally mandated in the 2002 farm law, but Congress had twice delayed its implementation except in the case of fish, which was already being labeled.

Energy. The legislation put a major focus on developing advance biofuels made from stock such as switch grass. It authorized $1 billion for new research, development, loan, and incentive programs, including about $320 million in loan guarantees for biorefineries for advanced biofuels and $35 million to help ethanol facilities reduce their use of fossil fuels. It also authorized $1 billion in discretionary funds, subject to the regular annual appropriations process.

Farm bill offsets. Nearly all of the ten-year cost of the law was offset by an extension of customs user fees through Sept. 20, 2015. This method of raising revenue was favored by the Bush administration but had not been in either chamber's version of the bill. But that money was not due to start coming in until 2015, after the existing customs authorization expired. Under the budget resolution, Congress had to pay for increases over the CBO baseline in both the five-year and ten-year periods. To overcome the five-year shortfall, conferees required corporations with assets of at least $1 billion to shift some of their estimated tax payments from fiscal 2013 to the last quarter of fiscal 2012. That was expected to boost revenue by $4.5 billion in the 2008–2012 period but reduce it by a similar amount after that.

Tax package. The farm bill became a vehicle for a package of tax reductions, mainly to encourage conservation and alternative energy, that totaled $1.7 billion over ten years. The tax breaks were accompanied by other provisions designed to bring in $2 billion over the same period, more than offsetting the cost of the reductions. The surplus was used to pay for a small number of trade provisions.

The most expensive tax breaks included a new credit for producing cellulosic biofuel (at a ten-year cost of $403 million), authorization for tax-exempt bonds to finance forest conservation ($250 million over ten years) and a deduction for expenses related to the Endangered Species Act ($283 million over ten years). The main method of raising revenue was a reduction in the existing federal tax credit for ethanol, which was expected to generate $1.2 billion in revenue over ten years. Beginning in 2009, the credit was slated to drop from 51 cents per gallon to 45 cents per gallon. Also, a 54-cents-per-gallon duty on imported ethanol was extended for two years.

A provision that prohibited farmers who received commodity payments from using more than $300,000 in farm losses to reduce other income for tax purposes was expected to bring in about $480 million over ten years.

Trade. The extra funds from the revenue-raisers paid for the cost of several trade provisions, including extending the Caribbean Basin Initiative, with expanded preferences for Haiti. The trade section also included language to comply with a 2005 World Trade Organization (WTO) decision that a U.S. cotton program violated trade rules. However, the WTO ruled June 2, 2008, that U.S. subsidies for cotton producers still failed to comply with trade obligations.

twenty amendments on each side, and the bill passed almost five months after the House vote.

In addition to the partisan and regional fighting, the debate was complicated by budget limits that made it difficult for the both the House and Senate to maintain funding for established programs, let alone new ones.

Before the House and Senate began working on the 2007 bill, the administration outlined sixty-five proposals to make farm programs "more equitable, predictable and better able to withstand challenge." The proposals included barring farmers who made more than $200,000 in annual adjusted gross income from receiving federal subsidies; providing more equitable support for specialty crops; providing new funding for renewable-energy research, development and production; and increasing funding for and consolidation of conservation programs.

HOUSE COMMITTEE ACTION

After three days of debate, the House Agriculture Committee gave voice vote approval July 19 to an initial version of the farm bill (HR 2419–H Rept 110-256, Part 1) after adopting a key amendment to require that mandatory country-of-origin labeling for meat begin in September 2008.

Chairman Collin C. Peterson, D-Minn., was squeezed by budget constraints and pressure from Democratic leaders to revamp farm policies without alienating rural constituents. He joked that the bill would "make everybody equally angry." Peterson wrote the bill using draft language from several weeks of subcommittee markups and negotiations with lawmakers and interest groups. He offered it as a comprehensive substitute, which the committee adopted by voice vote at the beginning of its deliberations.

Peterson faced a growing restiveness in the days leading up to the markup as he struggled to meet conflicting regional and other demands. At the last minute, Peterson was able to make concessions that appeased most committee members, including a total of $1.6 billion for fruit and vegetable grants and marketing programs.

Some of the main provisions of the bill proposed to:

- Continue the main farm programs—direct payments, countercyclical payments, and crop loan programs—with some modifications, but eliminate advance payments beginning with the 2012 crop year. This would reduce costs by $1.1 billion over ten years, but increase them by the same amount after 2017. Also, producers would get a one-time choice between the existing program of price-based countercyclical payments and a new countercyclical program based on the difference between a national average revenue and a specified revenue per acre.
- Bar producers who made more than $1 million a year in adjusted gross income from collecting government subsidies, and eliminate payments to those who earned more than $500,000 if less than 67 percent of their income came from farming. Peterson said the changes would save $226 million over five years, helping the bill comply with House budget rules.
- Increase the limit on direct payments to individual farmers to $60,000 a year from $40,000. If a husband and wife both farmed the same land and both were eligible, they could collect up to $120,000 a year. In addition, they could continue to get up to $65,000 in countercyclical payments.
- Eliminate the so-called three-entity rule, which allowed individuals to double their payments if they owned more than one farm.
- Remove a $75,000 limit on marketing assistance loans, a concession that aides said won support from Southern lawmakers who worried that otherwise the bill would hurt cotton and rice growers.
- Increase conservation funding by $2.8 billion over five years and by $3.7 billion over ten years, including more funds for the Environmental Quality Incentives Program. The proposal would expand the acreage that could be enrolled in the Wetland Reserve and Grassland Reserve programs, but it would also reduce funding for the Conservation Security Program by about $700 million over five years and $4.8 billion over ten years.

Producers would be limited to a maximum of $60,000 for a single program and $125 million for multiple programs. That worried environmentalists. "Prohibiting and limiting large commercial farmers, in particular, from participating in conservation programs makes no sense," said Scott Faber, director of Environmental Defense's farm policy campaign. "Large commercial farmers are more likely to participate in conservation programs and manage a disproportionately large share of the landscape."

During the markup, the committee also:

- Adopted by voice vote the amendment on country-of-origin labeling for beef, pork, and poultry, after Peterson negotiated a deal between livestock producers and processors. The labeling was to specify whether meat was raised and slaughtered in the United States; was of completely foreign origin, including the country it came from; or might contain meat from more than one country, as in ground beef.
- Adopted, 26–17, an amendment by Mike D. Rogers, R-Ala., to require the establishment of standards for mandatory arbitration clauses in livestock contracts. The language overturned a provision added in subcommittee by Leonard L. Boswell, D-Iowa, that would have allowed arbitration clauses only when farmers and buyers agreed. Livestock farmers complained that they were often forced into arbitration contracts with companies that purchased their meat, which barred them from suing a buyer if they had a complaint. Because arbitration could cost more than a lawsuit, livestock producers often dropped their complaints.
- Adopted, 14–10, an amendment by Bob Etheridge, D-N.C., to make federal dollars available to expand foreign markets for tobacco. The panel adopted the amendment, with Peterson's support. Robin Hayes, R-N.C., warned that without the assistance for U.S. growers, Chinese growers would dominate the tobacco industry.

HOUSE FLOOR ACTION

The House passed the bill, 231–191, on July 27, 2007, after adding $7.5 billion in revenue-raisers—mainly from a tax that targeted foreign-owned companies. The CBO said provisions aimed at increasing royalties from oil drilling would offset $5.8 billion over ten years. The CBO estimated the total cost of the bill at $286 billion over five years, but the combined offsets brought the net total to about $282 billion.

The tax provision, which was incorporated into the bill as part of the rule for floor debate, sparked strong objections from Republican members and drew a White House veto threat against the bill. Minority Whip Roy Blunt, R-Mo., said it had killed GOP support for a package that could "easily have been a huge bipartisan victory." The rule (H Res 574) was adopted 222–202.

Realizing that he could no longer count on Republican support, Peterson focused the night before the vote on cutting deals with the undecided Democrats, many of whom were pressing regional issues. Only fourteen Democrats voted against passage. Nineteen Republicans voted for the bill, most of them from rural districts.

The tax change was one of several substantive amendments added by the rule, which was written by the leadership-controlled Rules Committee. The amendments included:

Taxes. The chief tax provision, a proposal aimed at ending a practice known as "earnings stripping" in which foreign companies took advantage of tax treaties to shift income out of the United States, reducing the tax liability of their U.S. subsidiaries. The provision, by Lloyd Doggett, D-Texas, was projected to raise $3.2 billion over five years and $7.5 billion over ten years.

Doggett and other Democrats said the change would close a loophole that put U.S.-based companies at a disadvantage. But business groups rebelled and joined the Bush administration in complaining that the proposal would discourage foreign companies from investing in the United States, abrogate tax treaties that benefited U.S. corporations, and unfairly affect legitimate transactions not designed to avoid taxes.

Another amendment proposed shifting some corporate estimated tax payments from fiscal 2013 to 2012, increasing revenue by $465 million in the five-year time period but having no net effect over ten years.

Nutrition. Additional nutrition provisions offset by some of the tax revenue. They included an increase in the minimum value of food stamps that a recipient could receive. The amendment also proposed to increase the monthly standard deduction for food stamp recipients to $145 from $134, and eliminate a dependent care cap used in calculating recipients' income. The changes were expected to increase the number of people eligible for food stamp assistance.

Oil and gas. Provisions aimed at recouping billions of dollars lost on a series of royalty-free leases in the Gulf of Mexico. Congress had granted royalty relief in the late 1990s (PL 104-58) to spur deep-water production at a time when energy prices were low, but more than 1,000 leases issued in 1998 and 1999 did not require the companies to resume paying royalties if prices were to rise, as they had in recent years. The GAO estimated the loss to the federal Treasury at $7 billion to $11 billion.

Under the amended bill, oil companies that did not revise those leases would have to pay a "conservation of resources fee." Other provisions sought to repeal several portions of the 2005 energy law (PL 109-58), eliminating certain incentives and royalty relief for oil and gas production in the Gulf and allowing the federal government to collect fees on drilling permits. The Interior Department would be authorized to change oil and gas leases in the National Petroleum Reserve in Alaska. *(Energy legislation, p. 447)*

The increased royalties and fees, which the Joint Committee on Taxation said would raise $2.2 billion over five years and $6.1 billion over ten years, were used to help pay for energy provisions, including incentives for biofuel research and development, energy efficiency programs and renewable-energy projects.

During the floor debate, the House:

- Rejected, 117–309, a substitute amendment by Democrat Ron Kind of Wisconsin and Republican Jeff Flake of Arizona to cut crop subsidies and invest the money in conservation, nutrition, rural development, and deficit reduction. Among other things, it would have prohibited farmers who made more than $250,000 per year in adjusted gross income from receiving federal subsidies, and replaced the existing price-based countercyclical program with a revenue-based program.

Kind's amendment, which appealed both to fiscal conservatives who viewed farm subsidies as wasteful and to liberals who wanted to allocate money to different priorities, was seen as a threat to the committee-approved measure. Peterson had tried to preempt Kind's effort by amending the bill in committee with language to bar the nation's richest farmers from getting subsidy payments.

The amendment was a slimmed-down version of an alternative farm bill (HR 2720) that Kind and Flake had introduced with Earl Blumenauer, D-Ore., and Paul D. Ryan, R-Wis., earlier in the year. None of the four were on the Agriculture Committee, and their opposition reflected the divide between members of the committee—many of whom represented rural districts that relied on subsidies—and nonmembers who viewed the payment system as wasteful and wanted to put the money into other priorities.

The Bush administration said the approach would save money and be more compliant with international trade rules. Critics said the alternative bill would leave farmers vulnerable, and House leaders worried that it could alienate members of the Democratic Caucus who represented farming districts. Democratic leaders also feared that if the amendment were adopted, it would stall action on the farm bill for good and give the Republicans a political victory.

- Rejected, 182–245, an amendment by Charles B. Rangel, D-N.Y., to make it easier for Cuba to buy U.S. crops. Ileana Ros-Lehtinen, R-Fla., a leader of the anti-Castro bloc in Congress, called it an effort to "support state-sponsored terrorism." Rangel argued, "If we really want to win the hearts and minds of Cubans, we should make it abundantly clear... we'll make nutrition available to them."
- Rejected, 153–271, an amendment by John A. Boehner, R-Ohio, to prevent farmers from locking in artificially high payments.
- Rejected, 175–252, an amendment by Adam H. Putnam, R-Fla., that would have permitted payments to farmers making more than $1 million annually as long as 75 percent of their income came from farming.

SENATE COMMITTEE ACTION

The Senate Agriculture, Nutrition and Forestry Committee approved its version of the bill (S 2302–S Rept 110-220) by voice vote Oct. 25, 2007. Approval came after two days of debate that focused mainly on a proposed new subsidy option called the Average Crop Revenue Program.

Farm payments. The bill continued the main farm programs—direct payments, countercyclical payments, and loan programs—with some modifications. Like the House bill, it proposed to eliminate advance payments beginning with the 2012 crop year. But the Senate bill also allowed farmers to make a one-time choice between the traditional federal farm subsidy programs and the Average Crop Revenue Program. Under the new program, farmers would get a fixed payment of $15 per acre. In addition, they would get a per-acre payment when the actual average revenue per acre in their state was less than a revenue target set in law. The idea was developed by Richard J. Durbin, D-Ill., and Sherrod Brown, D-Ohio, with help from some farm groups.

Committee chairman Tom Harkin, D-Iowa, said the new program would offer farmers in some regions better protection against the risks inherent in farming, which in turn would result in lower crop insurance premiums. Because the government partially subsidized the premiums, that would mean an overall savings. Harkin said the money would go to other portions of the bill, including nutrition programs and conservation programs popular in his home state.

But the plan drew fire from some farm groups and the crop insurance industry, which said it would be prohibitive for some farmers and would take business from insurers. To mollify opponents, the committee adopted by voice vote an amendment by Pat Roberts, R-Kan., to reduce the number of acres on which farmers could collect payments and keep insurance premium rates unchanged, meaning crop insurers would preserve their bottom line. Farmers opting into the new program would have to continue participating for the life of the farm bill.

Some of the most vocal opponents of Roberts's amendment were corn growers, who helped Harkin design the program and who were facing increasingly expensive insurance policies as more acres of corn were planted. They said the amendment would nullify the new subsidy's benefits.

Payment limits. The Senate bill proposed to:

- Retain the existing annual limit for receiving farm payments in 2008. The limit would be reduced to $1 million in 2009, unless the farmer got more than 67 percent of his income from farming, and would drop to $750,000 in 2010 though 2012.
- Eliminate the three-entity rule.
- Lower the limit on traditional countercyclical payments from $65,000 to $60,000.
- Eliminate the $75,000 limit on the marketing loan program.

Country-of-origin. Like the House bill, the Senate measure required that the Agriculture Department implement the program on schedule.

Conservation. The bill reauthorized existing programs but with a number of changes that were different from those in the House bill. Unlike the House measure, it did not propose payment limits for conservation programs.

Nutrition programs. The standard deduction for food stamp recipients was increased to $145 per month and the cap on deductions for dependent care was eliminated.

During the markup, the committee:

- Adopted by voice vote an en bloc amendment, which included a proposal to allow fruits and vegetables meant for canning to be grown on farms that collected subsidies for other commodities. The language was a compromise for fruit and vegetable growers, who opposed changing existing law that barred growers who collected federal dollars, including corn and wheat farmers, from planting fruit and vegetables on subsidized land. Harkin had proposed lifting those planting restrictions, which kept produce prices high, on land enrolled in the Average Crop Revenue Program. Meat processors were also barred from owning livestock until shortly before slaughter under the en bloc amendment, a victory for ranchers who said processors forced them into unfair contracts.
- Adopted by voice vote an amendment by Ben Nelson, D-Neb., to require the Agriculture Department to confer with an outside consultant when rerating crop insurance premiums.
- Rejected by voice vote an amendment by Bob Casey, D-Pa., to block the use of eminent domain to build a new electricity transmission corridor. The 2005 Energy Policy Act (PL 109-58) authorized the Energy Department to designate the corridors to expedite construction of electric transmission lines. Under the law, federal regulators could overrule state and federal siting decisions in those corridors. Critics said the mandate could have a negative impact on rural farmland and infringe on property rights. Electric utilities lobbied heavily against the amendment. *(Energy legislation, p. 447)*
- Adopted by voice vote another Casey amendment to guarantee a profit margin for dairy producers based on their input costs.
- Adopted by voice vote an amendment by John Thune, R-S.D., and Max Baucus, D-Mont., to prevent the closing of some Farm Services Agency offices. Tight funding had forced the Agriculture Department to shut many regional offices.

SENATE FLOOR ACTION

After weeks of stalemate, the Senate substituted its own amended bill for the text of the House measure and passed it by a vote of 79–14 on Dec. 14, 2007. Senators had been debating the bill on and off since early November, slogging through a seemingly endless list of amendments.

But with the session coming to an end, Majority Leader Harry Reid, D-Nev., made a last-minute decision to invoke cloture, bringing the debate to a close. "The time has come that we stop this. We need the farm bill," he said. "We don't have time for 26 more amendments." The motion to limit debate succeeded 78–12 on Dec. 13.

As passed, the five-year farm bill totaled $285.6 billion, $5.3 billion above the CBO baseline. The substitute incorporated many changes, from a bill (S 2242–H Rept 110-206) that the tax-writing Finance Committee had approved in October, including the addition of tax increases, various tax benefits and farm disaster assistance. CBO said the net effect was to provide $5 billion in offsets.

During the floor debate, the Senate:

- Rejected an amendment by Byron L. Dorgan, D-N.D., and Charles E. Grassley of Iowa, ranking Republican on the Finance Committee, to cap annual farm payments at $250,000 per couple, down from $360,000 in the bill. The amendment, which required a sixty-vote majority for adoption, was rejected Dec 13 on a **key vote of 56–43 (R 17–31; D 38–11; I 1–1).** *(2007 key votes, p. 955)*

The vote was a victory for Southern senators, who had warned that the proposal would lead to the demise of cotton and rice farms in their region. Dorgan said the fifty-six votes showed that "most members of the Senate want real subsidy reform."

- Rejected, 48–47, a bid to bar subsidies to full-time farmers making more than $750,000 a year and part-time farmers making more than $250,000 annually. The proposal, by Amy Klobuchar, D-Minn., also required sixty votes for adoption. Like Grassley and Dorgan, Klobuchar argued that too many taxpayer dollars went to people who farmed very little, or not at all.
- Adopted by voice vote a Harkin amendment to reauthorize the Commodity Futures Trading Commission through 2013 and give it more powers to fight fraud.
- Rejected, 32–63, a proposal by Brown and John E. Sununu, R-N.H., to cut more than $2 billion from the federal crop insurance program and use the savings for improvements to conservation and nutrition programs.
- Rejected, 37–58, an attempt to make deep cuts to federal subsidies and expand crop insurance. Under the proposal, by Richard G. Lugar, R-Ind., and Frank R. Lautenberg, D-N.J., traditional farm subsidies would have been phased out and replaced by crop insurance that would cover either 85 percent of a farmer's expected crop revenue or 80 percent of a farm's five-year average adjusted gross revenue. About $2 billion saved from the subsidy cuts was to be reinvested in various nutrition programs, with another $1 billion shifted to conservation programs and other farm-related initiatives.

Peterson said the debate over payment limits was not over yet. He said he wanted the eventual conference committee on the farm bill to work out a provision that would ensure that subsidies went only to people who made their entire living from agriculture.

CONFERENCE, FINAL ACTION

After nearly a year and a half of debate, Congress in May 2008 cleared the five-year farm bill and overrode a presidential veto to enact the legislation into law. After months of negotiations, House and Senate conferees reached agreement on most provisions of the multiyear bill May 7, 2008. As negotiators released details the following day, Agriculture Secretary Schafer reiterated the administration's veto threat, saying farm subsidies in the bill were still far too generous. It took conferees another five days to complete their work and file the conference report. Among the last issues resolved were choices to pay for the extra spending and the extent of limiting farm payments.

Conferees struggled to set an adjusted gross income eligibility level that could get through Congress but still satisfy President Bush. The president had threatened to veto the bill unless Congress prohibited anyone making more than $200,000 a year from getting crop subsidies. White House aides said a compromise cap of $500,000 was part of the discussion at one point, but conferees ultimately went for a more complicated formula that distinguished between farm and nonfarm income and set limits based on a three-year average.

The result was a $500,000 limit on nonfarm income for all commodity benefits and a $750,000 cap on farm income for those receiving direct payments. Previously, the limit for benefits was $2.5 million for those who got less than 75 percent of their income from farming. The House proposed changing that to a $500,000 limit for those who received less than 67 percent of their income from farming, with an absolute limit of $1 million. The Senate would have started with a $2.5 million cap, declining to $750,000 by the end of the five-year period. Although the final deal did not satisfy Bush, it represented a major compromise between southern lawmakers, who tended to represent larger farming operations, and midwestern lawmakers, who largely spoke for farmers with much smaller incomes.

Conferees retained existing provisions that allowed farmers to double the limits on direct and countercyclical payments if their spouses also farmed. Conferees also paid for the bill's costs by an extension of customs user fees through Sept. 20, 2015, an approach favored by the Bush administration but not originally approved by either chamber. Because that revenue was not due until 2015, after the existing customs authorization expired, conferees required corporations with assets of at least $1 billion to shift some of their estimated tax payments from fiscal 2013 to the last quarter of fiscal 2012. That was expected to boost revenue by $4.5 billion in the 2008–2012 period but reduce it by a similar amount after that.

Both chambers had to abandon some of their biggest revenue proposals. The Senate could not get House support for a plan to raise $10 billion over ten years by codifying the "economic substance" doctrine, a judicial precedent that disallowed shelters that did not result in real economic benefit but merely provided tax savings. The House had to give up a plan to raise $7.5 billion over ten years by barring so-called earnings stripping, a practice by which foreign-owned companies that operated subsidiaries in the United States reduced their tax liability by shifting U.S. income to a country with lower tax rates. Lawmakers also gave up on a plan to require stockbrokers and mutual funds to report the cost basis of securities sold to their customers, after the White House warned that Bush would veto the measure if it included the provision. The proposal was estimated to raise about $6 billion over ten years by improving taxpayers' compliance in reporting their capital gains.

VETO OVERRIDES

Brushing aside the veto threats, the House May 14, 2008, adopted the conference report on the bill (HR 2419—H Rept 100-667) by a vote a of 318–106, and the Senate May 15 cleared the bill by a **key vote of 81–15 (R 35–13; D 44–2; I 2–0)**. One hundred Republicans in the House voted for the bill. *(2008 key votes, p. 972)*

First Veto Override

The president returned the measure to Congress without his signature May 21, saying in a statement that it "continues subsidies for the wealthy and increases farm bill spending by more than $20 billion, while using budget gimmicks to hide much of the increase." Later the same day, the House on a **key vote of 316–108 (R 100–94; D 216–14)** to override the veto. The Senate agreed, 82–13, on May 22. With more than two-thirds voting in favor, the bill was enacted over the president's veto. *(2008 key votes, p. 972)*

Second Veto Override.

The bill's eighteen-month saga was not quite over, however. Because of a clerical mistake, Congress had to repeat the process, clearing a new bill (HR 6124) and overriding a second veto. *(Veto messages, p. 1073)*

The problem stemmed from an error by a House enrollment clerk, who dropped one of the bill's fifteen titles—covering trade and international food assistance—before sending the bill to the White House. Democrats initially considered passing a stand-alone bill with just the missing title, but Republicans protested that Congress would be inviting a constitutional challenge to the fourteen titles already enacted because that bill was incomplete. Democratic leaders agreed, although some of them insisted publicly that the GOP was making too much of the situation.

The House passed the new bill, HR 6124, that was identical to the fifteen-title, $289 billion version that cleared May 15. The 306–110 vote came on May 22, shortly before lawmakers recessed for Memorial Day. The measure was passed under suspension of the rules, a procedure prohibiting amendments. An attempt by Minority Leader John A. Boehner, R-Ohio, to force an ethics committee investigation into the way the bill was handled was tabled, or killed, 220–188. Republicans were particularly annoyed that the bill managers in the House—Agriculture chairman Collin C. Peterson, D-Minn., and ranking Republican Robert W. Goodlatte of Virginia—had discovered the omitted title hours before they went to the House floor for the veto override vote without telling members about it.

Senate action was stalled for a time by Republicans Tom Coburn of Oklahoma and Jim DeMint of South Carolina, who objected to the cost and to the inclusion of provisions unrelated to agriculture. But the logjam was broken with an agreement allowing them floor time to express their concerns, and the Senate cleared the bill, 77–15, on June 5.

The president reprised his role June 18, saying in his veto message that Congress should have taken the opportunity to modify "certain objectionable, onerous and fiscally imprudent provisions." Later the same day, the House voted, 317–109, to override the veto, and the Senate followed, 80–14. Once again, the votes in both chambers exceeded the needed two-thirds majority, and the bill was enacted into law over the president's veto.

The action was the third successful veto override during the Bush presidency and the second for the farm bill. In 2007 Congress enacted a water projects bill over the president's veto (PL 110-114). *(Water projects, p. 500)*

MAJOR PROVISIONS

Following are major provisions of the five-year farm bill HR 2419—H Rept 100-667 (PL 110-246) enacted over the President Bush's veto on June 18, 2008.

Commodity Programs

Fixed payments. Reauthorized through 2012 direct payments, which farmers received regardless of actual crop prices.

Market loans. Renewed marketing loans and deficiency payments for major commodity crops, including soybeans, corn, cotton, rice and wheat, for the 2008 through 2012 crop years. Adjusted the price levels at which farmers become eligible for such loans if the market prices of their crops fall below levels specified in the bill. Allowed farmers to use their crops as collateral for federal loans to cover crop production costs; if the crop sold for less than the loan rate, farmers could repay the government at the lower rate. Deficiency payments covered the difference between the going rate for the crop and the assistance loan rate.

Countercyclical payments. Extended the countercyclical program, which paid farmers when the price of their crop dropped below a statutory target price, through the 2012 crop year. Increased the target prices for several crops, including grain sorghum, barley, oats, soybeans and other oil seeds, beginning in 2010.

State-based countercyclical payments. Gave farmers the option, beginning in the 2009 crop year, of choosing a new program, dubbed ACRE for Adjusted Crop Revenue Election, as an alternative to the countercyclical program, but required farmers who did so to remain in the program through 2012, and to forgo 20 percent of the direct payment rate and 30 percent of the marketing assistance loan rate for the crops. Allowed participants to receive a government payment when revenue for the crop fell below a target based on 90 percent of the five-year state average yield (excluding the years with the highest and lowest yields) times the two-year national average price for the crop. Allowed ACRE revenue payments on 85 percent of the acreage planted with the covered commodity or with peanuts. Allowed payments for the 2009, 2010, and 2011 crop years, on 83.3 percent of the planted acres.

Repealed the "three entity" rule. Prohibited farmers from collecting subsidies on more than one property, rather than on up to three properties as previously allowed, but permitted the limits to be doubled if the farmer had a spouse who also farmed.

Sugar programs. Increased the loan rate for sugar growers by a quarter cent a year for three years, raising the loan rate for cane sugar to 18.75 cents and for beet sugar to 24 cents. Continued the marketing allotment program that allowed some sugar imports every year but ensured that most of the sugar used by U.S. consumers came from domestic sugar cane and beet producers.

Payment limits. Ended direct payments for farmers making more than a three-year average of $750,000 a year in gross adjusted farm income. Ended subsidies for farmers making more than a three-year average of $500,000 in nonfarm-related income. Allowed a farmer who fell within both categories to make up to $1.3 million a year and collect the full array of government supports.

Payment amounts. Continued provisions under the 2002 agriculture legislation that prohibited direct payments to an individual farmer of more than $40,000 per year and more than $65,000 in countercyclical amounts. Allowed a couple to collect up to double the combined amount, or $210,000, if both spouses were actively engaged in farming. Ended previous limits on marketing loan benefits.

Dairy programs. Extended through 2012 the milk income loss contract program, which paid farmers when dairy prices dropped below a government-set target. Continued the government purchase of cheese, butter and nonfat dry milk. Reestablished a program that allowed dairy farmers to voluntarily enter into forward contracts with milk handlers that allowed sale of a quantity of milk at a certain price for an agreed upon period of time, allowing milk producers to lock in prices early.

Fruit and vegetables. Continued prohibitions under existing law that barred farmers from growing fruit and vegetables on land that was enrolled in commodity crop programs to help farmers of these crops keep produce prices relatively high and limit competition in the market. Established a pilot program to allow farmers in seven states to grow certain fruits or vegetables meant for processing on enrolled land.

Direct attribution of farm payments. Required that all agricultural subsidies be directly attributed to the person who receives them in order to bring more transparency to the system and ensure that owners were not receiving multiple payments.

Conservation Programs

Conservation Reserve Program. Reduced enrollment in the reserve program, which allowed participants to receive government payments for taking highly erodible and sensitive land out of production, to 32 million acres through 2012. Established a new program to allow use of a portion of the enrolled acreage for grazing or crop production if the land was being given to a new or socially disadvantaged farmer or rancher. Prohibited a farmer from receiving more than $200,000 over five years for all contracts.

Wetlands Reserve Program. Extended the voluntary program, which paid farmers for preserving wetlands, through 2012, and increased the maximum enrollment to more than three million acres. Provided new payment schedules for easements valued at less than $500,000 a year to be paid out over a period of up to thirty years and easements valued at more than $500,000 to be paid out between five and thirty years. Allowed the Agriculture Department to grant waivers to give lump sum payments on easements over $500,000.

Environmental Quality Incentives Program (EQIP). Increased funding by $3.4 billion for the EQIP program, which paid ranchers to improve water and soil quality on their land. Allowed farmers using conservation practices related to organic certification to become eligible for payments. Improved the evaluation process for applications and established a program to help ranchers improve water quality. Allowed participating farmers a maximum of $300,000 in EQIP payments over six years, but permitted the Agriculture Department to grant waivers up to $450,000 over the same period.

Conservation Security Program. Increased funding for the program by about $1.1 billion, allowing enrollment of about 13 million acres a year, and added private forests to land eligible for the program. Restructured the program, which provided government subsidies to participants using soil-saving and habitat-conservation techniques on working lands, to encourage producers to implement additional conservation practices.

Grassland Reserve Program. Reauthorized the program through 2012 and allowed the enrollment of an additional 1.2 million acres. Under the program, created in the 2002 farm law, ranchers and other private grassland owners entered ten-, fifteen-, and twenty-year contracts that barred development of the land and preserved grassland ecosystems.

Other conservation funding. Authorized $438 million in new funding for the Chesapeake Bay region. Created a $50 million Open Fields Program to help state governments and Native American tribes open private land to public hunting and fishing, and doubled the authorization for the Farm Protection Program to $773 million.

Payment limits. Prohibited farmers collecting more than $1 million in nonfarm income from receiving conservation payments, but allowed the Agriculture Department to waive the rule in cases where it would prevent the protection of particularly environmentally sensitive land.

Trade Programs

Local purchase pilot program. Created a pilot program to allow the government to use about $60 million to purchase in-country food for hungry people abroad.

McGovern-Dole international food program. Reauthorized the McGovern-Dole program and provided about $84 million in mandatory funding to subsidize school lunches for hungry children abroad.

Market Access Program. Authorized $200 million a year for the program, which helped U.S. farmers and exporters promote their products in other countries. Dedicated part of the funds—about $37 million over five years—to helping fruit and vegetable growers overcome sanitation issues that kept them from exporting their produce.

Global Crop Diversity Trust. Authorized the U.S. Agency for International Development to contribute funds to the Global Crop Diversity Trust, an organization that collected and stored seeds in case of a major natural disaster.

Softwood Lumber Act. Required lumber importers to declare that their imports met the terms of international agreements and set penalties for importers who violated the new rules, among other things.

Caribbean trade. Extended for two years, through fiscal 2010, trade preferences under the Caribbean Basin Initiative. *(Congress and the Nation Vol. X, pp. 157, 167; Congress and the Nation Vol. XI, p. 158)*

Haiti trade. Expanded the scope of trade preferences for Haiti by making it easier for Haitian apparel to qualify for duty-free access to the United States.

Nutrition Programs

Food stamps. Increased to $144 from $134 per month the minimum amount households were allowed to deduct from their annual gross income in determining their benefits, the first increase in years, and provided inflation adjustments in subsequent years. Excluded from the cap retirement and education savings in addition to special combat pay. The bill also:

- Increased the asset limits for individual food stamp recipients by indexing them to inflation.
- Increased the minimum benefit for food stamp recipients, expected to be of particular help to senior citizens.
- Renamed the food stamp program the Supplemental Nutrition Assistance Program.
- Provided new authority for the Agriculture Department to combat fraud in the program.
- Ended the use of food stamp coupons in favor of Electronic Benefit Transfer cards, which could also be used at some farmers' markets.

Emergency Food Assistance Program. Increased funding for the program, which provided states with food and other resources to stock food banks, by $1.3 billion.

Support for child and senior nutrition. Extended the Commodity Supplemental Food Program for seniors who needed additional assistance; increased funding for a snack program for school children by $1 billion and expanded it to all fifty states; and reauthorized the Women, Infants and Children Program, which was funded through annual discretionary appropriations.

Farm Credit

Loans for farmers. Authorized an increase of about $400 million, to $4.2 billion, for direct and guaranteed loans to help farmers make down payments and to operate their farms and increased the limit for the loans to $300,000 from $200,000. Set the interest rate at 1.5 percent or at 4 percent below regular rates, whichever was greater. Reduced the borrower down payment to 5 percent from 10 percent, and increased the Agriculture Department's portion of a loan to 45 percent from 40 percent.

Conservation loans. Established a conservation loan and loan guarantee program for farmers who carried out qualified conservation projects. Set the government guarantee at 75 percent of the principal loan amount, with a priority given to young and socially disadvantaged farmers.

Beginning farmer program. Expanded and made permanent a pilot program that guaranteed loans made by a private seller of a farm or ranch to qualified beginning farmers or ranchers. Increased to three years from two years the limit on payment guarantees under the program. Gave the seller the option of taking the three-year guarantee or a standard 90 percent guarantee. Expanded the program nationwide and broadened it to include socially disadvantaged buyers. Set the maximum purchase price for the farm or ranch at $500,000.

Other programs for socially disadvantaged and beginning farmers. Increased the number of loans that could be given to young and disadvantaged farmers and fixed the interest rate for those loans at 1.5 percent or at 4 percent below regular rates, whichever was greater. Allowed farmers to get a down payment requirement as low as 5 percent.

Rural Development

Water and wastewater programs. Authorized about $120 million to fund pending applications for rural infrastructure programs, including Waste Disposal Grants and Rural Water and Wastewater Circuit Rider programs, which helped lower water and waste disposal operating costs in small towns, and the Emergency and Imminent Community Water Assistance Grants program, which helped towns improve the quality of their drinking water.

Rural health care programs. Reauthorized the Rural Firefighters and Emergency Medical Service Assistance Program, which supported emergency services in rural areas, and expanded a 911 access program for small towns.

Rural broadband, telephone and energy. Limited large companies from getting broadband loans and grants under the Rural Electrification Act to better target rural and underserved areas. Required the loan to provide serve to an area where at least 25 percent of the households could only get service from one provider. Provided for bond guarantees for telephone or electrification purposes, and grants to bring alternative energy to small towns. Directed the Federal Communications Commission and the Agriculture Department to develop a comprehensive broadband strategy for rural areas and authorized $25 million annually through fiscal 2012 for a new National Center for Rural Telecommunications.

Rural employment and business development. Created a new, $15 million rural micro-enterprise program to provide grants for training and marketing, and other activities. Authorized about $10 million in grants to help disabled people get jobs in rural areas. Authorized through 2012 the Rural Business Investment Program, which provided grants for rural business investment companies, and set the authorization funding at $50 million. Established a new investment program to allow multicommunity regions to invest in rural development projects.

Research Programs

National Institute of Food and Agriculture. Reorganized offices in charge of applied research, extension, and education programs at the institute and created new offices to develop new programs and track ongoing agriculture research.

Agriculture and food research. Created a new research program, the Agriculture and Food Initiative, to support fundamental and applied research and research that supported entrepreneurship and business development. Authorized $700 million annually in 2008 through 2012 to provide grants to colleges and universities, agriculture experiment stations, and other organizations doing farm-related research.

Energy research. Authorized $50 million in each of fiscal years 2008 through 2012 to establish a new bioenergy and biobased products research initiative to award competitive grants for on-farm biomass crop research and dissemination of results. Directed the Agriculture secretary to establish a best-practices database on the production, harvest, transport, and storage of various biomass crops. Authorized competitive grants for on-farm energy efficiency research and extension projects aimed at improving the energy efficiency of agricultural operations.

Minority researchers. Made historically black and Native American universities a priority for research funding, expanded funding to Hispanic colleges and universities, created an endowment fund for Hispanic universities, and made Hispanic universities eligible for research programs.

Specialty crops. Provided $230 million for research grants on fruits and vegetables, $25 million for produce safety grants, and $78 million for organic produce research. Targeted about $23 million for fighting food-borne illnesses.

Forestry

Healthy Forests Reserve Program. Authorized $39 million over four years for the program, which helped property owners preserve endangered species.

Training for minorities. Established a new grant program to help train Hispanics and other underserved groups in forestry careers.

Emergency Forestry Conservation Reserve Program. Extended the program, which helped land owners restore forests after a natural disaster.

Community forest and open space conservation program. Established a new program to provide communities with grants to buy forest and park land for public use.

Energy Programs

Rural Energy for America Program. Authorized a new program of grants and loan guarantees to farmers and rural small businesses to purchase renewable fuel systems and make energy efficiency improvements to their operations. Established $250 million in mandatory funding over four years, part of which would go to grants for energy experts to help farmers and businesses do energy audits.

Biorefinery assistance. Authorized grants and loan guarantees for the construction and retrofitting of biorefineries to produce advanced biofuels—noncorn-based biofuels such as those from cellulose, sugar, and waste products—to accelerate commercial production of advanced biofuels. Authorized grants up to 30 percent of the cost of pilot biorefineries and loan guarantees to support 90 percent of the principal and interest on loans to develop and construct commercial-scale biorefineries.

Biomass research and development. Provided about $120 million over four years in mandatory spending for a program that provided competitive funding for research projects on biofuels and biobased chemicals and products. Authorized an additional $1 billion in discretionary funds for the program over four years.

Bioenergy program. Authorized about $300 million for the Bioenergy Program, which provided incentives to expand production of advanced biofuels made from farm and forestry waste and manure, among other things.

Biomass crop assistance. Established a program to provide financial assistance to promote the development of new biofuels made from cellulosic products including contracts with farmers and forestry companies to grow cellulosic crops and incentives to harvest, store, and transport those crops to production facilities.

Biobased markets program. Created a new voluntary program to recognize agencies, contractors, and farmers that used significant amounts of biobased products in order to help farmers label biobased products as "USDA Certified Biobased Products" and to help the federal government establish procurement preferences for those products.

Forest and wood fuels. Authorized $60 million over four years for a competitive research and development program to encourage use of forest biomass for energy. Authorized an additional $20 million for a new program of grants to state and local governments to develop ways to use wood scraps for energy.

Biofuels infrastructure assessment. Directed the Agriculture Department to work with the EPA and the Energy Department on a study to determine how best to expand the production, transport and distribution of biofuels.

Sugar ethanol program. Established a new program to allow the government to buy U.S. sugar equal to any excess in imports to maintain market prices above support levels and to sell the sugar to be turned into ethanol. The change was meant to address a provision in the North American Free Trade Agreement (NAFTA) eliminated tariffs on Mexican sugar.

Horticulture and Organic Agriculture

Farmers' market promotion. Expanded the use of food stamps at farmers' markets and provided $33 million in grants for market advertising and for the expansion of markets, roadside stands and other community farm programs. Included $3 million to bring produce to underserved urban areas.

Pest and disease management. Authorized $377 million for pest and disease control and directed collaboration between federal and state governments to do a better job of detecting plant pests and disease earlier, as well as mandating an audit-based certification system between growers and the government.

Honey bees. Extended a marketing loan program for beekeepers that provided income support if the market price of honey fell below 69 cents per pound. Dedicated $10 million a year to research on colony collapse, which was threatening honey bees.

National Clean Plant Network. Provided $20 million in new funding for a strategy to keep plants free from pests and diseases.

Miscellaneous provisions. Provided $22 million for a Agriculture Department cost-sharing program to mitigate the costs farmers incurred while seeking organic certification. Provided $5 million for organic marketing data collection and publication. Made fruit and vegetable growers eligible for $466 million in grant money for marketing, research, disease management, and food safety. Required the Agriculture Department, in the future, to include produce in its census of agriculture and directed the department to conduct a feasibility study on whether to establish a federal marketing order for Haas avocados. Allowed asparagus growers who lost money between 2004 and 2007 from competing imports to collect part of $15 million in government funding.

Livestock

Country-of-origin labeling. Kept in place a requirement that all meat be labeled by Sept. 30, 2008, to indicate the country where the animal was raised. Permitted meat to be labeled as originating in the United States only if the animal was born here or was in the country before July 15, 2008. Added goat meat and chicken to the list of meat that had to be labeled and added macadamia nuts and peanuts to the list of products that had to be labeled.

Livestock contracts. Allowed persons who raised livestock or poultry to decline mandatory arbitration before entering into contracts with meat processors. (Livestock producers said they were being put out of business by costly arbitration and often did not have enough money to take their case to court.) Required the department to develop criteria to decide whether there was market discrimination against smaller poultry and pig operations.

Packers and Stockyards Act. Directed the Agriculture Department to compile an annual report detailing investigations and potential violations of the act.

Interstate shipment of meat. Allowed some meat inspection facilities participating in state meat and poultry inspection programs to receive federal inspection from state inspectors and ship products across state lines.

Miscellaneous livestock provisions. Authorized $10 million for the National Sheep Industry Improvement Center, created a voluntary trichinae certification program, authorized cooperative agreements to carry out aquatic animal health plans to detect and control disease in aquaculture species, and required a study to evaluate animal manure as a source of fertilizer and the potential impact on consumers.

Crop Insurance

Cost and revenue. Cut sections of the crop insurance program, which insures against weather losses and falling prices, to provide savings for other parts of the farm bill, and provided "timing shifts," such as requiring farmers to pay premiums earlier, starting in 2012.

Administrative and operating subsidies. Reduced by 2.3 percent the reimbursements to private crop insurance companies for administrative and operating expenses, saving about $929 million. Allowed a 50 percent restoration in states where the loss ratio is greater than 1:2.

Investigating fraud and abuse. Authorized new funding for a Agriculture Department investigation into crop insurance records to identify fraud.

Organic crop insurance. Required the Agriculture Department to compare production risks for conventional and organic crops and to reduce premium surcharges on organic crops if the analysis demonstrated no difference. Directed the study to examine organic produce prices in the marketplace to incorporate those prices in the crop insurance options available for organic crops.

Standard Reinsurance Agreement. Authorized the Department of Agriculture to conduct periodic renegotiations of its Standard Reinsurance Agreement, which required the government to share in any program losses experienced by the private insurers that administered the federal crop insurance program. Required the agreements be renegotiated every five years beginning in 2011. (The purpose of the reinsurance was to make it viable for the companies to offer crop insurance in all regions of the country, including high-risk areas.)

Commodity Futures

CFTC authorization. Reauthorized the Commodity Futures Trading Commission (CFTC) through 2013 and strengthened the agency's oversight of commodity derivatives and futures trading.

Foreign currency transactions. Clarified that the CFTC had authority to regulate foreign currency transactions and combat fraud. Required retail foreign exchange dealers to register with the CFTC and comply with its rules. Strengthened the qualifications and capital requirements for futures merchants and foreign-exchanges dealers.

Energy speculation. Established record-keeping requirements for electronic energy traders and required them to provide an audit trail, to guard against speculation in energy markets. Established monitoring aimed at detecting market manipulation and increased financial penalties for such manipulation and excessive speculation.

Market manipulation. Provided that traders violating CFTC rules would face higher penalties in some cases and would face felony charges if they failed to comply with cease-and-desist orders. (Previously, noncompliance was subject to a misdemeanor charge.)

Tax Provisions

Customs user fees. Extended Customs user fees through fiscal 2017, to raise an estimated $10 billion over ten years.

Ethanol tax credits. Reduced the tax credit for manufacturers of ethanol fuel to 45 cents from 51 cents per gallon starting in 2009, increasing tax revenue by $1.2 billion over five years. Approved other ethanol provisions that were expected to bring in a total of $206 million over five years and $211 million over ten years but offset these increases to a degree by including a new credit of $1.01 per gallon for producing ethanol from cellulosic feedstocks that would cost $348 million over five years and $403 million over ten years.

Limitation of farming losses claimed on tax returns. Limited the farming losses that could be used to offset nonfarm business income to the greater of $300,000 or the net farm income the taxpayer had received over the previous five years. (The provision was expected to bring in $206 million over five years and $479 million over ten years.)

Endangered species. Approved a tax deduction for property owners who took steps to preserve endangered species on their land at an estimated cost of $72 million over five years and $283 million over ten years.

Conservation Reserve Program payments. Excluded Conservation Reserve Program payments from self-employment taxes for retired or disabled individuals, costing $84 million over five years and $192 million over ten years.

Taxation of qualified timber gain and timber REIT provisions. Provided an alternative minimum tax rate of 15 percent for gains on some timber harvests. (Previously, timber sales were eligible for capital gains treatment.) Modernized timber real estate investment trusts by clarifying that gains from timber sales held for less than one year qualified as income, and changed safe harbors for timber property sales. (The expected cost was $184 million over five years and $221 million over ten years.)

Forest conservation bonds. Established a new program to allow the issuance of $500 million in timber conservation bonds to allow nonprofits to buy forest land for conservation, at a cost of $250 million over five years.

Other Provisions

Socially disadvantaged farmers. Set aside $75 million in mandatory funding for programs to educate and support poor farmers. Required the Agriculture Department to seek to bring more disadvantaged producers into their programs and provide an annual report to Congress on its progress. Required the department to establish an Office of Advocacy and Outreach to develop diversity in the farming industry, and charged the office with providing a liaison to groups that represented low-income migrant and seasonal workers to ensure that farm workers were treated well on the job and that their needs were met during disasters and emergencies. Established an advisory committee to conduct civil rights activities and ensure that minority farmers and ranchers were participating in farm programs.

Farm Service Agency offices. Prohibited any agency office from being closed or relocated within two years of the legislation's enactment.

Office of Homeland Security. Created a new Agriculture Department office to develop interagency emergency response plans and coordinate with the Homeland Security Department. Established a new communications center to prepare for emergencies such as animal disease outbreaks or agro-terrorism.

Animal welfare. Increased animal fighting penalties and penalties under the Animal Welfare Act. Prohibited dogs younger than six months from being imported from other countries.

Disaster aid. Provided for a four-year, $3.8 billion disaster trust fund for farmers who lost crops or livestock to flood, fire, drought, and other natural disasters. (Ranchers and farmers had to have crop insurance to participate.)

CHAPTER 9

Health and Human Services

Health and Human Services

When it came to health care, President George W. Bush in his first term managed to beat Democrats at their own game—with largely GOP backing—by enacting a Medicare prescription drug benefit that had long been a Democratic party priority, albeit with a decidedly free-market bent. With that singular accomplishment behind him, health and human services once again became a somewhat second-tier issue for the president during his second term. A handful of important measures did become law, mainly during the 110th Congress, when Democrats regained control of the House and Senate for the first time in more than a decade. But domestic policy became more a source of partisan finger-pointing rather than policy making.

The major GOP accomplishment on the health and human services front in President Bush's second term was passage of the 2005 Deficit Reduction Act, the fiscal 2006 budget-reconciliation bill. The legislation made major changes to the Medicaid health program for the poor, although it did not go as far as many Republicans and President Bush himself had wanted. The bill also reauthorized the 1996 welfare overhaul law, something Congress had been trying without success to do since 2002.

Congress and Bush were unable to come to terms, however, on renewal of another key program created during the 1990s: the State Children's Health Insurance Program, or CHIP. Democrats passed a major expansion of the program twice in 2007, and the president vetoed both versions, claiming they were too expensive and represented too large a federal intrusion into the nation's health care system.

Although abortion specifically played a less central role in health policy in President Bush's second term than it had during his first, several abortion-related fights played out during the 109th and 110th Congresses. One was over whether to relax the president's restrictions on federal funding of research using cell lines derived from human embryos. Scientists said such research held promise for treating or curing dozens of dread diseases. Bush and other right-to-life forces decried the need to destroy human embryos to obtain the cells. Bush vetoed two bills in two succeeding Congresses; neither was overridden.

In 2005 Congress also involved itself in the controversy over whether the comatose Florida woman Terri Schiavo should be taken off life support. In the end Schiavo died before the court relief granted by Congress could be used by her parents to have her feeding tube restored.

But while partisan bickering may have been the rule, there were several bipartisan exceptions. After years of work, Congress during Bush's second term managed to complete work on bills to create programs to reduce medical errors, to require parity between health insurance benefits for mental health and all other ailments, to substantially boost the regulatory powers of the Food and Drug Administration, and to streamline the organizational structure of the National Institutes of Health.

Medical and Deficit Reduction

Since budget-reconciliation procedures began to be used as a tool of health policy in the 1980s, Medicare had been a major target. In 2006, for the first time, lawmakers used the budget process to try to remake the Medicaid health program for the poor.

Over the vehement objections of most Democrats, the $38.8 billion budget-reconciliation bill that President Bush

REFERENCES

Discussion of health policy for the years 1945–1964 may be found in *Congress and the Nation Vol. I*, pp. 1122–1194; for the years 1965–1968, *Congress and the Nation Vol. II*, pp. 665–707; for the years 1969–1972, *Congress and the Nation Vol. III*, pp. 551–580; for the years 1973–1976, *Congress and the Nation Vol. IV*, pp. 323–375; for the years 1977–1980, *Congress and the Nation Vol. V*, pp. 601–653; for the years 1981–1984, *Congress and the Nation Vol. VI*, pp. 521–556; for the years 1985–1988, *Congress and the Nation Vol. VII*, pp. 547–606; for the years 1989–1992, *Congress and the Nation Vol.* VIII, pp. 561–610; for the years 1993–1996, *Congress and the Nation Vol. IX*, pp. 513–569; for the years 1997–2001, *Congress and the Nation Vol. X*, pp. 429–503; for the years 2001–2004, *Congress and the Nation Vol. XI*, pp. 471–519.

Outlays for Medicare and Medicaid

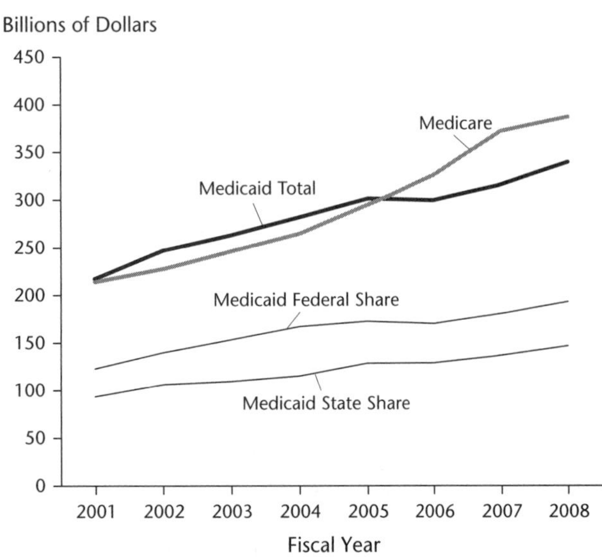

SOURCE: Medicare: Office of Management and Budget, *Historical Tables, Budget of the United States Government: Fiscal Year 2010* (Washington, D.C.: U.S. Government Printing Office, 2009), Table 8.5. Medicaid: Centers for Medicare and Medicaid Services, *2008 Actuarial Report on the Financial Outlook for Medicaid* (Washington, D.C., Department of Health and Human Services, www.cms.hhs.gov/ActuarialStudies/downloads/MedicaidReport2008.pdf, October 17, 2008)

signed into law Feb. 8, 2006 (S 1932—PL 109-171) included a net $4.7 billion in Medicaid savings over five years. That was only a fraction of the amount conservatives in Congress had hoped for, but far more than most Democrats and a group of Republican moderates wanted.

But it was less the money than the policy changes that made Democrats fear for the future of the program that served an estimated fifty million low-income women, children, seniors, and disabled individuals each year. Among those policy shifts were new rules that made it more difficult for seniors who transferred their assets at less than fair market value to qualify for Medicaid nursing home care, new rules that allowed states to charge premiums and require higher cost-sharing by Medicaid beneficiaries with incomes at or above the poverty level, and the ability for states to offer plans with fewer benefits than had been previously allowed.

CHIP

The State Children's Health Insurance Program was created in 1997 as a bipartisan compromise. It was a way to help provide health insurance to children in families with incomes too high to qualify for Medicaid, but still too low to afford private coverage. Democrats liked the fact that it would cover an estimated five million more children who would otherwise remain without health insurance. Republicans liked the idea that states would be given substantial flexibility to determine eligibility thresholds and benefit packages.

But a decade later, even with the program an unqualified success according to nearly all concerned, efforts to renew it divided along partisan lines. Fresh from taking over Congress for the first time in twelve years, Democrats in 2007 attempted to dramatically expand the program by more than doubling its funding. President Bush offered up an increase so small that it would not have kept up with inflation and would have required some states to drop children already in the program. Republicans accused Democrats of using the CHIP expansion as a first step toward a government takeover of the entire health care system.

The two sides fought to a draw. Democrats passed two separate bills, both of which the president vetoed. The bills did gain considerable bipartisan support. CHIP was, after all, popular both with the public and with state governments. But neither bill was able to muster the required two-thirds supermajority needed to override a presidential veto. Congress ended up simply extending the existing program until after the next presidential election.

Stem Cells

One of the most divisive fights of President Bush's second term did not break down along party lines. It concerned an ethical issue—whether to relax restrictions the president imposed in 2001 on federal funding of stem cell lines derived from human embryos.

The fight mostly split along the same lines as the abortion debate. Many abortion opponents, including the president, said that because embryos had to be destroyed to obtain the medically promising embryonic stem cells, they were ethically tainted.

But some abortion opponents, including such notable foes as Sen. Orrin Hatch, R-Utah, insisted that embryonic stem cell research was different from abortion. "As I evaluate these factors, I concluded that this research is consistent with bedrock pro-life, pro-family values," Hatch had written in a widely quoted analysis of the subject.

Congress in both 2006 and 2007 passed bills to loosen the restrictions imposed by the president. The bills would have allowed expanded federal research funding, although only on stem cell lines derived from embryos left over and no longer needed for in vitro fertilization treatment. In both cases, however, despite broad bipartisan support in the House and Senate, in neither the 109th nor the 110th Congress was the tally large enough to override President Bush's veto of the measure.

Food and Drug Administration

Concerns about the safety of the nation's prescription drug approval and oversight process led Congress in 2007 to pass the most sweeping expansion of the Food and Drug

Surrounded by House and Senate supporters of the bill, President Bush signs the Deficit Reduction Act of 2005 in the White House in Washington, D.C., on February 8, 2006. *Source: AP Photo/Gerald Herbert*

Administration's regulatory authority in more than ten years. The legislation was prompted in large part by a series of highly publicized problems with prescription drugs after they had been available for several years, most notably the withdrawal from the market of the popular arthritis drugs Vioxx and Celebrex, which were linked to serious cardiovascular risks.

The bill gave the agency vast new powers to regulate the labeling, advertising, and other types of promotion of prescription drugs. It also called for the creation of a new database to provide consumers with information about the results of clinical trials of drugs.

Mental Health Parity

Another bill that became law after more than a decade of effort required health insurance plans that offered mental health or substance abuse benefits to offer them to the same extent they offered all other benefits. The Mental Health Parity measure first passed the Senate in 1996. But it would take a dozen years, the death of its lead sponsor, and final negotiations between a senator father and his representative son to finally get a bill to the president's desk to be signed.

The issue was a fairly simple one. For years, health insurance companies frequently offered mental health benefits, but with higher co-payments or lesser benefits than for comparable physical ailments. For example, policies in many cases covered only a limited number of visits or inpatient hospital days for mental health but offered unlimited coverage for physical ailments. Legislation originally passed in 1996 and renewed thereafter banned health plans from offering unequal annual or lifetime dollar limits for mental and physical ailments. But many plans evaded that law by simply offering unequal day or visit limits instead.

The final bill was ultimately negotiated by Sen. Edward Kennedy, D-Mass., the chairman of the Senate Health, Education, Labor, and Pensions Committee, and his son, Rep. Patrick Kennedy, D-R.I., the lead sponsor of the House version of the bill. The younger Kennedy had struggled publicly with his own substance abuse problems.

Human Services

The policy area of human services saw relatively little action in Bush's second term. But Congress did manage to accomplish, although in somewhat limited form, the two priorities that did not get completed from his first term: renewal of the 1996 welfare overhaul law and reauthorization of the Head Start preschool program.

On welfare, Congress extended the Temporary Assistance for Needy Families Program through 2010 as part of the 2006 budget-reconciliation bill. But disputes over work requirements for adult recipients of government aid and child care subsidies prevented the bill from making more than minor changes to the program that had ended welfare as an entitlement a decade earlier.

Meanwhile, disputes over whether to allow faith-based providers to take religion into account in hiring slowed renewal of the popular Head Start program. But a five-year reauthorization finally became law in 2007. It expanded eligibility for the program that got its start during President Lyndon B. Johnson's War on Poverty in the 1960s, ended a controversial standardized testing program, and set higher education standards for Head Start teachers.

Veterans

Veterans' issues took on increased urgency during President Bush's second term, as the wars in Iraq and Afghanistan began to produce increased numbers of veterans.

Health issues were paramount, particularly as advances in medical care saved many soldiers who in previous conflicts would not have survived their injuries. But such seriously wounded servicemen and -women put increased strain on both the military's medical system and the Department of Veterans Affairs (VA) medical system and, in particular, the system by which individuals were handed off between those two systems.

It would take a Pulitzer Prize–winning investigation by the *Washington Post* uncovering serious neglect at Walter Reed Army Medical Center to prompt Congress to act to ensure better care for some of the most seriously "wounded warriors." Also, pressure increased for additional funds for the VA's health system.

Congress updated the GI Bill, the post–World War II legislation that helped a generation of returning military personnel go to college, buy houses, start businesses, and generally readjust to civilian life. Over the years, the value of the GI Bill's education benefits had dwindled to the point that they no longer could pay for a full college education, even at most public colleges.

Chronology of Action on Health

2005–2006

Growing rifts between moderate and conservative Republicans limited the ability of the 109th Congress to make much headway on health issues.

The biggest achievement by far was the health provisions included in the fiscal 2006 budget-reconciliation bill (S 1932—PL 109-171). The measure included major changes to the Medicaid program for the poor and some lesser changes to Medicare and the State Children's Health Insurance Program. Moderate Republican resistance, however, prevented the Medicaid alterations from going as far as President George W. Bush and many conservatives would have preferred.

Moderate Republicans also joined with Democrats to prompt the first veto of the Bush presidency in 2006. The bill would have loosened the restrictions the president imposed in 2001 on federal funding of research on embryonic stem cell lines. Scientists had been complaining for some time that the policy was holding back potentially lifesaving research. But opponents remained adamant that the research was unethical, because the stem cell lines could not be created without the destruction of human embryos.

Congress, however, did manage to resolve several longstanding health issues. It reauthorized and overhauled the management of the National Institutes of Health for the first time since 1993. It renewed the Ryan White acquired immune deficiency syndrome (AIDS) programs, despite an ugly regional dispute about how funding should be distributed, and it finally finished work on a bill to create a system aimed at reducing medical errors.

Medicare, Medicaid, Children's Insurance

Congress agreed to cut the growth of spending on Medicaid as part of the $38.8 billion budget-reconciliation bill that President George W. Bush signed into law Feb. 8, 2006 (S 1932—PL 109-171). The Medicaid savings—a net $4.7 billion over five years—was only a fraction of the amount conservatives in Congress had hoped for, but far more than most Democrats and a group of Republican moderates wanted. *(Reconciliation, p. 81)*

Bush and his congressional allies had begun 2005 with bold plans to overhaul Medicaid, the jointly administered federal-state health care entitlement program for the poor, to significantly slow the program's soaring costs and give states more flexibility. Medicaid spending had surged 63 percent over the previous five years and totaled more than $300 billion annually. The president called for $60 billion in savings from the program over ten years as part of a broader drive to get control of entitlement spending, which consumed about 54 percent of the federal budget and continued to increase as if on autopilot. After putting $15 billion back into Medicaid and the State Children's Health Insurance Program (CHIP), the net savings in Bush's plan came to $45 billion.

Bush called for reducing overpayments for prescription drugs, tightening restrictions on seniors who transferred their assets to qualify for Medicaid-paid nursing home care, and eliminating overpayments to the states. In a proposal that particularly alarmed his critics, Bush also wanted to give states more flexibility to tailor their Medicaid programs, which some saw as opening the door to setting spending caps.

The selection of Michael O. Leavitt, confirmed in January to head the Department of Health and Human Services (HHS), seemed to signal plans for big changes in the program. As governor of Utah, Leavitt had won permission from the U.S. government to finance an expansion of Medicaid coverage in his state by reducing benefits for some patients and increasing cost-sharing for low-income beneficiaries.

But moderate Republicans in both chambers managed to scale back Bush's plan, reducing the total cuts to Medicaid and instead getting a substantial share of the mandated entitlement savings from Medicare, the federal health care program for the elderly and disabled.

Still, many of the Medicaid provisions that made it into the budget-reconciliation bill reflected ideas championed

Outlays for Health

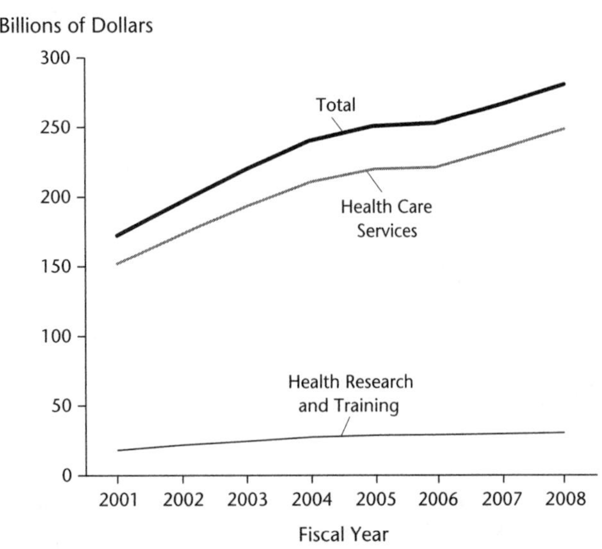

SOURCE: Office of Management and Budget, *Historical Tables, Budget of the United States Government: Fiscal Year 2010* (Washington, D.C.: U.S. Government Printing Office, 2009), Table 3.2.

NOTE: Total line includes some expenditures not shown separately.

by conservatives, such as increased co-payments and cost-sharing by Medicaid beneficiaries and flexibility for states to reduce benefits to some participants.

The final bill also preserved a stabilization fund that was created by the 2003 Medicare drug law (PL 108-173) to entice preferred provider organizations to offer coverage in underserved regions. The Senate proposed eliminating it for a savings of $5.4 billion over five years. The fund had been a key to gaining support for the 2003 bill from House conservatives, who saw it as a way to encourage more private sector involvement. The White House had warned that Bush was likely to veto a bill that killed the fund. *(Medicare drug law, Congress and the Nation Vol. XI, p. 496)*

Republicans had tried to overhaul Medicaid twice in the previous decade. In 1995 the GOP sought to cut program spending by $163 billion over seven years, but the move was thwarted by President Bill Clinton, who said the cuts would force states to make untenable choices. President Bush made a more limited attempt in 2003, proposing to give states more flexibility in running the program in return for a capped allotment of money for optional Medicaid populations, which included some nursing home patients and certain low-income pregnant women and children in households with incomes not low enough for mandatory coverage. That proposal also went nowhere in Congress. *(1995 Medicaid action, Congress and the Nation Vol. IX, p. 559)*

HIGHLIGHTS

The following are among the main components of the Medicaid and Medicare sections of S 1932.

Medicaid

As calculated by the Congressional Budget Office, the Medicaid changes were expected to reduce mandatory spending by a net $4.7 billion over five years, after paying for $3.6 billion in new Medicaid spending and $2.1 billion in hurricane-related health care. The new law

Asset transfers. Increased penalties and tightened restrictions on individuals who transferred their assets at less than fair market value to qualify for Medicaid nursing home care. Individuals with more than $500,000 in home equity were ineligible for Medicaid nursing home benefits. (Savings: $2.4 billion over five years)

Prescription drugs. Reduced payments for certain outpatient prescription drugs, mainly by reducing Medicaid reimbursements to pharmacies. (Savings: $3.9 billion over five years)

Cost-sharing and premiums. Allowed states to charge premiums and require cost-sharing by beneficiaries at or above the poverty level, with some restrictions. Under prior law, premiums and enrollment fees generally were prohibited and nominal cost-sharing was limited to $3. The new law also allowed states to require cost-sharing by enrollees for certain prescription drugs. (Savings: $1.9 billion over five years)

State financing. Altered some rules on state financing of Medicaid programs that affected federal payments to the states. Changes included barring states from levying special taxes on Medicaid managed care organizations and using the proceeds to help pay the state's share of Medicaid. The organizations got the money back in the form of increased Medicaid payments, which also generated federal matching funds that the states often kept. (Savings: $1.2 billion over five years)

Alternative benefit packages. Allowed states to replace the traditional Medicaid benefits package with a reduced-benefit, or "benchmark," plan for certain groups. The plans had to provide basic services, such as physician and hospital coverage. Certain beneficiaries could not be required to participate in these plans. (Savings: $1.3 billion over five years)

Fraud, waste, and abuse. Saved money through steps such as requiring states to do more to find parties responsible for paying outstanding claims instead of relying on Medicaid as the payer of last resort. (Savings: $822 million over five years, $528 million of which was to be spent on education and other steps to improve program integrity)

Family Opportunity Act. Extended eligibility for Medicaid benefits to certain low-income children with disabilities whose families earned too much for them to otherwise qualify for the program, beginning in 2008, if families paid premiums for that coverage. (Cost: $1.4 billion over five years)

Home and community-based care. Allowed up to ten states to participate in a five-year demonstration project to provide home and community-based services to children who would otherwise require hospital care. (Cost: $766 million over five years)

HEALTH AND HUMAN SERVICES LEADERSHIP

Michael O. Leavitt was confirmed by voice vote Jan. 26, 2005, as the successor to Tommy G. Thompson as secretary of health and human services (HHS). Leavitt, fifty-four, had spent the previous fourteen months as the administrator of the Environmental Protection Agency after the departure of Christine Todd Whitman. Leavitt was hailed in both parties as having the political and administrative skills to implement the new Medicare prescription drug benefit, a huge undertaking.

As governor of Utah for a decade before joining the administration, he raised some Democratic eyebrows by winning permission from the federal government to revamp the state's Medicaid program of medical coverage for the poor in a manner that increased the number of people covered but reduced some benefits. As HHS secretary, Leavitt pursued legislation to ease the way for other states to make similar changes but was ultimately unsuccessful in getting Congress to pass it.

Leavitt did leave the department with a long list of accomplishments, however, including a nationwide plan to deal with a flu pandemic, a foundation laid to move the nation's health system toward electronic medical records, and an expansion of inspections of both food and drug products by the Food and Drug Administration to sites in other countries.

Katrina relief. Appropriated funds to help with health care costs for residents of states evacuated because of Hurricane Katrina. (Cost: $2.1 billion)

Citizenship documentation. Required individuals applying for Medicaid to use original documents (birth certificates or passports) to prove their citizenship and identity, to prevent illegal immigrants from gaining access to the program. Previously, applicants needed only to "attest" under oath that they were citizens. (Savings: $220 million over five years)

Medicare

Changes to Medicare were projected to achieve $6.4 billion in net savings over five years. The law

Payments for home health services. Eliminated a scheduled 2.8 percent increase in home health care payments for 2006, although it provided for a one-year 5 percent additional payment to rural home health care providers. Starting in 2007, payments to home health care providers would be reduced by 2 percentage points if they did not report required health care quality data to HHS. (Savings: $2 billion over five years)

Risk adjustment. Altered payments to Medicare Advantage plans starting in 2006, to take into account the health status of the beneficiaries served. (Savings: $6.5 billion over five years)

Imaging services. Reduced the reimbursement rate for imaging services. (Savings: $2.8 billion over five years)

Physician payments. Froze Medicare payments to physicians at the 2005 level for 2006. Under prior law, the payments would have fallen by 4.4 percent as of January 2006. (Cost: $7.3 billion over five years)

LEGISLATIVE ACTION

The first round in the fight over Medicaid cuts took place when the House and Senate put together the fiscal 2006 budget resolution (H Con Res 95). The budget was important because it set the terms of the later budget-reconciliation bill.

The House adopted a budget resolution that instructed the Energy and Commerce Committee—the House panel with jurisdiction over Medicaid—to find a total of $20 billion in savings over five years. Leaders expected about $14 billion of that to come from Medicaid.

The Senate took up a version of the budget resolution (S Con Res 18) that called on the Finance Committee to find $15 billion in savings, with $14 billion expected to come from Medicaid.

But Republican senator Gordon H. Smith of Oregon upset the leadership plans with an amendment that stripped out the Finance Committee instructions and called instead for a commission to analyze the efficiency and effectiveness of the Medicaid program. Despite furious lobbying by GOP leaders, seven Republicans broke ranks in favor of their states and cast the deciding votes. Smith's amendment was adopted 52–48 on March 17, 2005.

The vote stung Budget Committee chairman Judd Gregg, R-N.H., who had made Medicaid cuts the centerpiece of his budget, and exasperated House Republicans. But it forced conferees on the budget resolution to walk a fine line between finding enough spending reductions to satisfy House conservatives and still reassuring just enough Senate GOP moderates that Medicaid would not take too big of a hit.

In talks with the White House and Senate GOP leaders over several weeks, Smith agreed to accept $10 billion in Medicaid cuts if a presidential study commission was created to recommend ways to wring savings from the program without hurting beneficiaries. None of the Medicaid savings would occur in the first year to give the commission time to report. But Smith said he would support the bill only if the conferees gave up plans to require the Finance Committee to produce an additional $6 billion in cuts from other programs for the poor.

Senate leaders, who needed Smith's vote and those of two or three moderates expected to vote with him, agreed to drop the extra $6 billion in cuts. House leaders accepted the decision, saying that taking the first steps to cut mandatory spending was more important than the exact amount.

The final budget resolution instructed the House Energy and Commerce Committee to save $14.7 billion.

Senate Action

Republican leaders put off the task of finding the savings until the fall. By the time the authorizing committees started working on budget-reconciliation legislation in October, the mood had changed considerably. Now they faced both the enormous costs of recovering from Hurricanes Katrina and Rita, which devastated New Orleans and the Gulf Coast, and the new sympathy for the poor and displaced that grew out of the tragedy.

For fiscal conservatives, the priority was finding more savings to offset the billions already appropriated for relief and recovery efforts. For Democrats and GOP moderates, it was preserving programs that helped the least fortunate. Both sides dug in.

Senate Finance voted 11–9 along party lines Oct. 25, 2005, to approve a package of cuts that promised to save a net $9.9 billion. To secure the votes of GOP moderates Smith and Olympia J. Snowe of Maine, Chairman Charles E. Grassley, R-Iowa, split the cuts between Medicaid and Medicare. The panel proposed to save a net $4.3 billion from Medicaid and $5.7 billion from Medicare.

The panel rejected a series of Democratic amendments that included attempts to expand Medicaid eligibility to victims of Hurricane Katrina. The panel did insert $1.8 billion to reimburse states for providing health care services to those in the path of the storm.

On the floor, senators added billions in new spending, including some changes to Medicaid and Medicare, before passing the reconciliation bill 52–47 on Nov. 3. The changes reduced the net savings to $35 billion from the $39.1 billion proposed by the Budget Committee. Savings from the Finance Committee Medicare and Medicaid provisions fell to $9.2 billion over five years.

House Action

House Republicans took a sharply different tack Oct. 28, 2005, by focusing exclusively on cuts to Medicaid and recommending no changes to Medicare. The Energy and Commerce Committee voted 28–22 along party lines to approve a $9.5 billion package of cuts to Medicaid. The proposal included

- $1.2 billion in savings over five years from changing the way Medicaid paid for prescription drugs, including changing the formula for determining the cost of drugs to take into account factors such as bulk discounts.
- $2.7 billion in savings over five years by allowing states to increase some Medicaid beneficiaries' cost-sharing over a three-year period from $3 to $5 and allowing states to collect co-payments at emergency rooms. Conservatives, backed by Bush, argued that beneficiaries would take more control of their health care if they had a financial stake in it.
- $2.5 billion in savings over five years by putting in place stricter guidelines for seniors who transferred assets to qualify for Medicaid coverage.
- $2 billion in savings over five years from giving states the flexibility to structure their Medicaid coverage more like private health plans, including allowing co-payments on drugs for pregnant women and children.
- $2.5 billion for health care related to hurricane relief.

After making a number of concessions to win over reluctant party moderates, GOP leaders eked out a narrow 217–215 victory on the bill (HR 4241) in the early morning hours of Nov. 18, in the session that began Nov. 17. The changes, made as part of the rule (H Res 560) that governed floor debate on the bill, included significant changes in the Medicaid provisions.

The revised provisions

- Allowed seniors to retain up to $750,000 in home equity—up from $500,000 in the committee version—and still be entitled to Medicaid coverage for nursing home care.
- Dropped the attempt to increase from $3 to $5 the cap on Medicaid co-payments for individuals with incomes below the poverty line.
- Permitted HHS to delay a reduction in reimbursements for prescription drugs required in the committee version if the average prices pharmacies paid for the drugs were higher than the new amounts that HHS would pay.

Conference, Final Action

Deciding how much to cut Medicaid and whether and how much to cut Medicare were among the biggest issues that faced conferees on the overall budget-reconciliation bill.

Under persistent pressure from moderate Republicans in both chambers, GOP leaders pared back the Medicaid cuts to an amount relatively close to the Senate figure, making up the difference with Medicare cuts that conservatives had not planned to include in the reconciliation bill. The legislation that emerged from conference cut a net $4.7 billion from Medicaid over five years—about 12 percent or $500 million more than the Senate had approved, but 50 percent or $4.7 billion less than the House wanted. Net Medicare cuts totaled $6.4 billion, about $1.4 billion more than in the Senate-passed bill. The House wanted no Medicare cuts at all.

At the last minute, after the conferees thought they were finished, House Speaker J. Dennis Hastert, R-Ill., and Senate negotiators had to give up $1.9 billion in anticipated cuts to secure the votes of Ohio lawmakers. The Ohioans threatened to scuttle the overall deal unless providers of home oxygen equipment, including a major Ohio company, were protected from planned cuts to Medicare.

Although the size of the Medicaid savings was reduced, conservatives prevailed on many of the decisions about how to cut the program. While the Senate would have gotten the lion's share of the savings from pharmacies and the pharmaceutical industry, the final bill looked as much to cost-sharing, reducing benefit packages, and cracking down on seniors who disposed of assets to qualify for Medicaid nursing care.

The final bill got $3.6 billion in savings from Medicaid prescription drug programs, compared with $6.3 billion in the Senate bill and $1.9 billion in the House version. Conferees dropped the Senate plan to increase the rebates pharmaceutical companies paid to states under Medicaid. Instead, they got virtually all of the savings by changing the way pharmacists were reimbursed to more accurately reflect the actual costs pharmacists paid to acquire the drugs.

House conservatives also prevailed on the issue of tightening restrictions on seniors who transferred their assets to qualify for Medicaid, saving $2.4 billion over five years. The final bill limited home equity for individuals qualifying for nursing home care to $500,000, though states could change that to $750,000. The House had recommended $750,000. Prior law did not set a limit on home equity. The Senate bill would have made only minor changes to the asset-transfer rules.

Like the House bill, the final version allowed states to require co-payments and premiums for Medicaid recipients, saving $1.9 billion over five years. The House would have saved $2.7 billion; the Senate bill had no such provisions. States also got some flexibility in designing Medicaid benefit packages, a top conservative demand. The House would have saved $2 billion (the final bill, $1.3 billion) from allowing states to offer reduced benefits.

Like the Senate bill, the conference report blocked the scheduled 4.4 percent cut in physicians' reimbursements, though it froze the existing rates instead of increasing them by 1 percent as the Senate wanted.

Like the Senate bill, the final measure saved $6.5 billion over five years by implementing a White House plan to give higher Medicare payments to insurers that covered sicker patients and lower payments to plans that enrolled healthier people. Conferees dropped the Senate plan to save $5.4 billion by eliminating the Medicare stabilization fund. Some House Republicans had said that eliminating the fund was a "no-brainer" because of the amount it would save. But conservatives and the White House rejected a move they said would erode provisions in the law designed to increase competition and private sector involvement in the Medicare program.

The House adopted the conference report on S 1932 (H Rept 109-362) on a **key vote of 212–206 (R 212–9; D 0–196; I 0–1)** on Dec. 19, in the session that began Dec. 18. The Senate on Dec. 21 rejected the conference report on procedural grounds and then approved a slightly amended version of S 1932, on a **key vote of 50–50 (R 50–5; D 0–44; I 0–1)**, with Vice President Dick Cheney breaking the tie. That sent the bill back to the House, which by then had adjourned for the year. It subsequently cleared the bill 216–214 on Feb. 1, 2006. *(2005 key votes, p. 915)*

MAJOR PROVISIONS

Following are the major provisions affecting Medicare, Medicaid, and the State Children's Health Insurance Program in the 2005 budget-reconciliation law.

Medicare Part A

Hospital quality improvement. Hospitals that did not submit required quality data would get a lower increase in payments beginning in fiscal 2007. Their increase would drop by 2.0 percent, instead of 0.4 percent under previous law. (Savings: $300 million over five years)

Disproportionate share hospitals. Inpatient hospital stays for patients who were covered by Medicaid for other services, but not for hospital inpatient services, would not count as Medicaid days for the purposes of calculating the additional payments Medicare made to hospitals that served a large number of low-income patients. (Savings: $1.2 billion over five years.)

Skilled nursing facilities. Medicare was to reduce the percentage of its payments to skilled nursing facilities for uncollected debts from 100 percent to 70 percent. Unpaid debts incurred by beneficiaries eligible for both Medicare and Medicaid would be paid at 100 percent.

Inpatient rehabilitation facilities. The "75 percent rule"—which requires that 75 percent of patients in a hospital classified as an "inpatient rehabilitation facility" have specified medical conditions—would begin in July 2008, instead of July 2007. In July 2006, a 60 percent threshold would be in place. In July 2007, it would increase to 65 percent. (Savings: $100 million over five years)

Gain-sharing demonstration. Up to six demonstration programs would be created to evaluate gain-sharing agreements between hospitals and other providers beginning on Jan. 1, 2007. The practice allowed doctors and hospitals to share the savings from treating patients more efficiently.

Specialty hospitals. A moratorium on the enrollment of specialty hospitals in Medicare was extended for six months from the date of enactment or until the health and human services secretary issued a report containing a strategic plan on how to handle the issue of physicians' investments in such hospitals and how such hospitals would care for low-income patients. If the secretary did not issue the report within six months, the suspension would be extended two more months.

Medicare Part B

Durable medical equipment. Beneficiaries would be required to assume ownership of rental durable medical goods (excluding oxygen equipment) after thirteen months of rental. For oxygen equipment, ownership would be required after thirty-six months. Medicaid could pay for service and maintenance if it was determined necessary. (Savings: $700 million over five years)

Imaging services. The law reduced the reimbursement rate for imaging services by $2.8 billion over four years. Reimbursement rates for imaging services conducted in a physician's office could not be greater than the rate paid to hospitals for the same service. Savings from reduced rates for multiple images of contiguous body parts in 2006 and 2007 could be used to reduce overall spending. (Savings: $2.8 billion over five years)

Ambulatory surgical centers. The law reduced Medicare payments to ambulatory care surgical centers to the rate Medicare paid to hospitals, if the hospital payment rates were lower. (Savings: $300 million over five years)

Physician payments. The law froze Medicare payments to physicians at the 2005 level for 2006. Without the change, the payments would have fallen by 4.4 percent as of January 2006. (Cost: $7.3 billion over five years)

Dialysis services. The reimbursement rate for facilities providing end-stage renal disease services was increased by 1.6 percent in 2006. (Cost: $500 million over five years)

Part B premiums for individuals with higher incomes. The law accelerated the phase-in of a scheduled increase in Medicare Part B premiums for beneficiaries with incomes above certain levels. The phase-in was to begin in 2007 and be completed by 2009, instead of 2011. (Savings: $1.6 billion over five years)

Preventive screenings. Screenings to detect abdominal aortic aneurysms would be covered as part of the physical exam for new Medicare beneficiaries who were at risk. The deductible in the Part B program would not apply to screenings for colorectal cancer. (Cost: $200 million over five years)

Provisions Related to Parts A and B

Home health payments. The law eliminated a scheduled 2.8 percent increase in home health care payments for 2006, although it provided for a one-year 5 percent additional payment to rural home health care providers in 2006. Starting in 2007, home health care providers would have their payments reduced by 2 percentage points if they did not report required health care quality data to HHS.

Risk adjustment. Starting in 2007, payments to Medicare Advantage plans would be altered to take into account the health status of the beneficiaries served in each plan, paying higher amounts for care of sicker patients. (Savings: $6.5 billion over five years)

Medicaid Asset Transfers

The law was projected to save $2.4 billion over five years by increasing the penalties on people who transferred their house or other assets for less than fair market value to qualify for Medicaid-funded nursing home care.

Five-year "look back." States would look back five years, instead of three, when determining whether a senior applying for Medicaid-funded nursing home care had transferred assets below fair value to qualify for Medicaid.

Penalty. Beneficiaries who made improper transfers would be penalized with a period of ineligibility for certain long-term care services beginning the month following the date of the asset transfer or the date the senior became eligible for Medicaid long-term care services, whichever was later.

Hardship waiver. If the ineligibility period deprived an individual of medical care that would endanger his health or life, or deprive him of food or shelter, he could apply for a waiver of the penalty because of undue hardship.

Home equity. The law excluded individuals with more than $500,000 in home equity from eligibility for nursing home or other long-term care coverage paid for by Medicaid. States could raise the limit to $750,000. Starting in 2011 the amount would increase each year based on the consumer price index.

Prescription Drugs

Changes to payments for prescription drugs, mainly lowering Medicaid reimbursements to pharmacies, were expected to reduce spending by $3.9 billion over five years.

Limit on pharmacy reimbursement. Medicaid would reimburse pharmacies for purchasing and dispensing multisource prescription drugs for up to 250 percent of the average sales price, known as the average manufacturers price (AMP). The AMP reimbursement rate takes into account the discounts and other savings that could be negotiated with manufacturers. Formerly, pharmacies were reimbursed for up to 150 percent of the average manufacturers' published price, known as average wholesale price. A multisource drug was defined as a drug that had at least one other drug on the market that was therapeutically equivalent.

Disclosure of AMP. The HHS secretary was required to give states access to monthly AMP data, which were previously confidential.

Fraud, Waste, and Abuse

Provisions to reduce fraud, waste, and abuse were expected to save $822 million over five years; $528 million of that was to be spent on education and other steps to improve the integrity of the program.

Third party recovery. The law required states to do more to find a party responsible for paying outstanding claims instead of relying on Medicaid as the payer of last resort.

State False Claims Act. States with laws that met certain requirements for handling false claims were allowed to reduce by 10 percentage points the amount that they had to pay back to the federal government once the false claim was discovered.

Education. States had to provide written explanations of fraud and whistleblower policies to providers that received more that $5 million a year from Medicaid.

Proof of citizenship. The government would not reimburse states for a beneficiary who had not given a state proof of U.S. citizenship, using original documents. Immigrants who were eligible for benefits were exempt from this provision.

Medicaid Integrity Program. The HHS secretary could contract out duties such as reviewing audits, identifying overpayments, and providing education on proper payments.

Cost-Sharing and Benefit Reductions

Allowing states to set higher premiums and cost-sharing payments and to offer limited benefits for some in Medicaid was projected to reduce outlays by $3.2 billion over five years

Premiums and cost-sharing. The law permitted states to charge premiums and require cost-sharing by beneficiaries at or above the poverty level, with some restrictions. Under prior law, premiums and enrollment fees were generally prohibited and nominal cost-sharing was limited to $3.

Under the new law, beneficiaries with incomes between 100 percent and 150 percent of the federal poverty line could not be charged a premium. Cost-sharing could not exceed 10 percent of the cost of the service for families with incomes between 100 percent and 150 percent of the poverty level, and 20 percent for families with incomes above 150 percent. Total payments for the year could not exceed 5 percent of the family income.

Certain groups could not be subject to cost-sharing for some services, such as pregnancy-related care and preventive care for children under age eighteen.

Enforcement. States could allow providers to refuse to offer service or dispense a drug if cost-sharing payments were not made at the time of service. If a beneficiary failed to pay premiums for sixty days, a state could terminate coverage.

Prescription drugs. States were allowed to waive or lower co-payments for "preferred drugs" and could not require cost-sharing from beneficiaries who otherwise were exempt from cost-sharing. For drugs not designated as preferred drugs on a state's formulary, a state could set higher cost-sharing and co-payments and could impose cost-sharing on any beneficiary, even those who were otherwise exempt from cost-sharing in the program. For beneficiaries with family incomes below 150 percent of poverty, cost-sharing could not exceed a set nominal amount. For beneficiaries with family incomes above 150 percent of poverty, cost-sharing could not exceed 20 percent of the cost of the drug.

Indexing. The nominal rate for cost-sharing, previously $3, would be indexed to the medical cost component of the Consumer Price Index.

Emergency room. States were allowed to increase cost-sharing for certain beneficiaries who used the emergency room for nonurgent care. The law provided $50 million in mandatory funds for payments over four years to states to make nonemergency health services available and accessible.

Alternative benefit packages. The law allowed states to replace the traditional Medicaid benefits package with a reduced-benefit, or "benchmark," plan for certain populations. The plans had to provide basic services, such as physician and hospital coverage, and be actuarially equivalent to one of the following benchmarks: standard Blue Cross/Blue Shield plan offered in the Federal Employees Health Benefit Plan, health coverage offered to state employees, coverage offered by the largest commercial health maintenance organization in the state, or a different coverage plan approved by HHS. States could not require certain beneficiaries to participate in the benchmark plans, including seniors who were poor enough to qualify for Medicaid and who qualified for Medicare because they were over sixty-five. Other exempted groups included pregnant women who had to be covered by state Medicaid programs, patients in Medicaid-funded hospice facilities or receiving long-term care, some children in foster care, and blind or otherwise disabled individuals.

State Financing

Changes to the rules for state financing of Medicaid programs, which affected the amount of federal grants, were estimated to save $1.2 billion over five years.

Restrictions on provider taxes. The law required states that levied taxes on Medicaid managed care organizations and used the proceeds to help pay the state's share of Medicaid spending to apply the tax to all managed care organizations, not just those that served Medicaid recipients. Generally, the organizations that paid the taxes got the money back in the form of increased Medicaid payments. But the increased payments also generated increased federal matching funds, and the states often kept the difference. The change was expected to save $435 million over five years and $2.9 billion over ten years, as states came under pressure to eliminate the taxes.

Case management costs. States would be able to charge Medicaid only for case management services that were not covered under other programs such as foster care, saving a net $760 million over five years.

Spending Increases

The law included a number of provisions that were projected to increase spending under Medicaid by a combined total of $3.6 billion over five years.

Family Opportunity Act. Children with disabilities whose families earned more than the cut-off for Supplemental Social Security Income, but less than 300 percent of the poverty level, would be eligible for Medicaid benefits beginning in 2008. States choosing to offer these benefits were allowed to charge a premium, and parents would be required to enroll in any available employer-sponsored coverage for themselves while the child was on Medicaid. (Cost: $1.4 billion over five years)

Home and community-based care. Up to ten states could participate in a five-year demonstration project to provide home and community-based services to children who would be hospitalized otherwise. (Cost: $766 million over five years)

Health information centers. The law increased funding for health information centers that assisted families of children with special needs by a total of $22 million over five years.

"Money follows the person" demonstration. The law authorized a demonstration project under which the federal government would pay a higher share of costs than under existing law for the first twelve months of long-term care services provided in the home or community for a person who was formerly in a nursing home. (Cost: $340 million over five years)

Health Opportunity Accounts. Up to ten states were allowed to participate in a demonstration program to set up Health Opportunity Accounts that could be used by Medicaid beneficiaries who volunteered for the program to pay for medical treatment. Once a deductible was reached, beneficiaries would be covered under the state Medicaid program. States could not set a deductible that was higher than 110 percent of the state contribution to the account. States could contribute up to $2,500 for each adult and $1,000 for each child into a family's account. The programs had to disclose the cost of the care, encourage prevention, and discourage overuse of health services. If beneficiaries became ineligible for Medicaid, they could keep the accounts for future health care costs. States could also choose to allow the beneficiaries to use the accounts to pay for job training.

Medicaid transformation grants. The HHS secretary could provide extra funding to state Medicaid programs that adopted innovative methods for reducing medical errors; improving collection of payments and reducing fraud, waste, and abuse; increasing the use of generic drugs; implementing a medication risk management program for beneficiaries who use a number of prescription drugs; and increasing the use of university-based hospitals and clinics by the uninsured.

Katrina Relief. The law appropriated $2.1 billion to be used by the HHS secretary to help with health care costs for residents of states evacuated because of Hurricane Katrina.

CHIP. The law provided an additional $283 million in funds under the State Children's Health Insurance Program for states that faced funding shortfalls in 2006. No additional states were allowed to use CHIP funds to cover adults without children.

Stem Cell Research

Congress and President George W. Bush sparred repeatedly over whether to increase federal funding for embryonic stem cell research in 2005 and 2006. It was an issue over which Republicans were deeply divided and resulted in the first veto of the Bush presidency. In the end, policy remained unchanged, as Congress lacked the votes for an override.

"This bill would support the taking of innocent human life in the hope of finding medical benefits for others. It crosses a moral boundary that our decent society needs to respect," Bush said in announcing his veto of the bill in a White House ceremony July 19, 2006, flanked by adopted children produced from frozen embryos. "These boys and girls are not spare parts," Bush said to vigorous applause from his supporters. *(Veto message, p. 1056)*

In a planned sequence of events, the House came back a few hours later and voted to sustain the veto, putting the issue to rest for the Congress.

The vetoed bill (HR 810) would have allowed the use of federal funds for research on embryonic stem cells, regardless of when they were obtained, as long as the following requirements were met: The stem cells were derived from human embryos that were donated from in vitro fertilization clinics where they had been created for the purpose of fertility treatment. The embryos were in excess of the clinical needs of those seeking treatment and would otherwise be destroyed. And the donors would have had to give informed, written consent that the excess embryos could be used for research without any financial payment or other inducement to make the donation.

An executive order signed by Bush on Aug. 9, 2001, allowed some federally funded research for embryonic stem cell research, but it was restricted to the seventy-eight stem cell lines that already existed on that date. Critics said those lines were not diverse enough and that some were contaminated. The National Institutes of Health said that only twenty-two of those lines were viable for human research.

Leading scientists said embryonic stem cells—which could turn into almost any type of cell in the body—had the potential to offer cures for illnesses such as diabetes, Parkinson's disease, some cancers, and possibly Alzheimer's. The prospects for such medical breakthroughs won many converts for expanded research, even among members of Congress who identified with the antiabortion movement.

But many conservatives remained adamantly opposed to such research because it involved the destruction of an embryo. They equated it with abortion and said it amounted to taking a human life. Conservatives advocated alternative avenues of research, such as the use of cells from umbilical cord blood. The use of stem cells from the umbilical cord, which was usually discarded following the birth of a baby, did not carry the same sorts of ethical problems. Like donated bone marrow, umbilical cord blood could be used to treat various genetic disorders. Congress cleared a separate bill (HR 2520—PL 109-129) in 2005 to provide federal funding for cord blood research. *(Umbilical cord blood, p. 544)*

2005 HOUSE ACTION

Pressed by constituents and buoyed by support from celebrities such as actor Michael J. Fox, who has Parkinson's disease, and former first lady Nancy Reagan, whose husband, President Ronald Reagan, had Alzheimer's disease in the latter years of his life, supporters of expanding embryonic stem cell research built enough momentum in Congress to secure promises from the leadership in March 2005 that they would get a floor vote on the issue.

On May 24, the House on a **key vote of 238–194 (R 50–180; D 187–14; I 1–0),** passed HR 810, allowing federal funding of research on embryonic stem cell lines derived from surplus embryos at in vitro fertilization clinics that would otherwise be discarded. Donors would have to give consent for the research and could not accept payment. The Department of Health and Human Services (HHS) would have to issue ethical guidelines for federally funded researchers within sixty days of enactment. *(2005 key votes, p. 915)*

The bill—sponsored by Michael N. Castle, R-Del., and Diana DeGette, D-Colo.—had more than two hundred cosponsors. It was much narrower than other measures aimed at expanding stem cell research, a strategy backers hoped would garner support from members who might be uncomfortable voting for a broader bill.

House leaders tried to cast the cord blood bill as an alternative, but backers of the Castle-DeGette measure disputed that argument, saying more options should be available for scientific investigation.

The floor debate was emotional, with many of the fifty Republicans who supported the bill citing personal experiences—or those of close relatives—with illnesses such as diabetes, cancer, and Parkinson's disease. Joe L. Barton, R-Texas, who noted that his antiabortion voting record previously stood at 100 percent, said he backed the bill because of his father, who had diabetes, and a brother, who had liver cancer. "Maybe the breakthrough will come in adult stem cells. I hope it does," said Barton, chairman of the House Energy and Commerce Committee. "But maybe, just maybe, it's going to come because of embryonic stem cells. Let's look at all avenues."

Jim Langevin, an antiabortion Democrat from Rhode Island who was paralyzed as a teenager, also broke ranks. "What could be more life-affirming than using what would otherwise be discarded to save, extend and improve lives?" he said.

But abortion opponents maintained that destroying an embryo is akin to murder. "I believe that life begins at conception and that a human embryo is human life," said Mike Pence, R-Ind. "I believe it is morally wrong to take the tax dollars of millions of pro-life Americans, who believe that human life is sacred, and use it to fund the destruction of human embryos for research."

Bush reiterated his threat to veto an embryonic stem cell bill the day the measure passed. "This bill would take us across a critical ethical line by creating new incentives for the ongoing destruction of emerging human life," he said. "Crossing this line would be a great mistake."

The 238 votes in favor of the bill fell short of the 290 votes that would be needed to override a veto if all members of the House were present and voting, and House GOP leaders vowed to fight an override attempt if the bill landed back in their chamber. But supporters still were eager to see the Senate take up the bill.

SENATE ACTION

Majority Leader Bill Frist, R-Tenn., pledged to hold a Senate vote on the issue, but he spent much of July 2005 trying to figure out how to bring a series of bills to the floor to allow votes on a number of options. Arlen Specter, R-Pa., and Tom Harkin, D-Iowa, who had introduced a Senate version of the House bill (S 471), saw this as a strategy to siphon votes away from their legislation, and Frist could not get unanimous consent for his plan.

Then on July 29, the final day before the August recess, Frist unexpectedly went to the Senate floor and threw his support behind the House embryonic stem cell bill. "I believe the president's policy should be modified," Frist said. "We should expand federal funding . . . carefully and thoughtfully staying within ethical bounds." Before entering politics Frist was a physician and surgeon.

Frist said he had several problems with the House bill, including the potential for donors to be wooed by financial incentives for their embryos, but he said it was "fundamentally consistent" with his views. Supporters of the House bill said Frist's concerns easily could be addressed during the process of drawing up regulations and that the bill would not need to be amended.

Specter, a leading proponent of broader federal funding for embryonic stem cell research, called Frist's speech "an earthquake" and said, "The majority leader has given cover to the entire Senate" to vote for the bill despite the veto threat.

Although Specter and others hoped Frist's support would add momentum to the bill, Frist continued to insist on bringing it to the floor in concert with other measures that addressed all sides of the debate. Democrats refused to agree, leading to a stalemate. Specter threatened to attach his measure to the Labor-HHS-Education spending bill if he did not get a separate floor vote. But given the tight Senate schedule after Hurricane Katrina and the pressure to finish the appropriations bills, Frist and Specter agreed to table the issue until 2006.

The Senate ultimately took up and passed HR 810 on July 18, 2006, on a **key vote of 63–37 (R 19–36; D 43–1; I 1–0)**, completing congressional action. The tally was four votes short of the two-thirds majority needed to override the promised veto. *(2006 key votes, p. 937)*

The vote followed Senate passage of two other stem cell bills (S 3504, S 2754) designed to offer alternatives to those who opposed the House measure. Both of those bills passed 100–0 on July 18, 2006. By agreement, no amendments could be offered and sixty votes were required to pass each of the three bills. S 3504—cosponsored by anti-abortion conservatives Rick Santorum, R-Pa., and Sam Brownback, R-Kan.—made it illegal to perform research on embryos from "fetal farms," where embryos could be created for the purpose of research. No one opposed the measure, and sponsors acknowledged that no such facilities existed. S 2754, cosponsored by Santorum and Specter, encouraged research on ways to obtain stem cells with the same properties as embryonic stem cells without destroying embryos.

2006 HOUSE ACTION

The House passed, and thus cleared, S 3504 later on July 18 by a vote of 425–0, under an expedited process that required a two-thirds majority. Bush signed it into law July 19 (PL 109-242).

But GOP leaders met with surprise defeat when they tried to bring up S 2754 under the same rules. The vote on July 18 was 273–154, twelve votes short of the necessary two-thirds. House backers of HR 810 said they thought the "alternatives" bill was an effort to give opponents of embryonic stem cell research political cover and so they voted against it.

The leadership could have brought the bill back to the floor with a rule, which would have enabled it to pass with a simple majority. But under House rules, that would have given Democrats a parliamentary opportunity to revive the embryonic stem cell bill, muddling the message of Bush's impending veto. Instead, the bill died at the end of the session.

VETO OVERRIDE VOTE

An attempt to override Bush's veto failed July 19 in the House, on a **key vote of 235–193 (R 51–179; D 183–14; I 1-0)**. Bill supporters needed two-thirds of those present and voting—286 in this case—to override the veto.

Before the vote, Majority Leader John A. Boehner, R-Ohio, urged lawmakers to support Bush. "No just society should condone the destruction of innocent life, even in the name of medical research," he said. Thomas M. Davis III of Virginia, one of fifty-one House Republicans who went against their leaders in the override vote, said those seeking reelection would have to defend their decision to constituents. *(2006 key votes, p. 937)*

Umbilical Cord Blood

Congress in 2005 cleared legislation to fund research on umbilical cord blood cells. The measure had broad support in both chambers, and President George W. Bush signed it into law Dec. 20 (HR 2520—PL 109-129).

Supporters of cord blood use as a source of stem cells contended that the cells could be used to reproduce human tissue for use in research. Some leading stem cell researchers, however, believed that embryonic stem cells were more capable of reproducing any type of human tissue for research purposes and that cord blood stem cells, like adult stem cells, were of more limited use in research.

The cord blood bill included provisions to

Cord blood stem cell inventory. Establish a new federal program to collect and store 150,000 units of human cord blood. The cord blood would be made available for transplantation or, if not appropriate for clinical use, for peer-reviewed research. The cord blood could be acquired only with the informed consent of the donor. The law authorized $79 million for fiscal 2007 through 2010 for the inventory.

Bone marrow program. Authorize $158 million over five years for the National Bone Marrow Registry and expand it to deal with both bone marrow and cord blood transplants. The expanded program was renamed the C. W. Bill Young Cell Transplantation Program.

Single access point. Require the health and human services secretary to establish an electronic database to give health care professionals and patients a single access point to search for cord blood and bone marrow matches.

House leaders scheduled a vote on the cord blood bill for May 24 as an alternative to the embryonic stem cell measure (HR 810) being considered the same day. The House easily passed HR 2520 by 431–1. Sponsored by Christopher H. Smith, R-N.J., the bill authorized funding for the less controversial practice of collecting and storing stem cells from umbilical cord blood. It also called for establishing a database to help physicians and researchers access the cells and bone marrow to use in treatment and research. *(Stem cell research, pp. 542, 573)*

On June 29, the Senate Health, Education, Labor, and Pensions Committee gave voice-vote approval to a similar bill (S 1317), after adopting a substitute amendment that incorporated language from the House measure on improvements in the bone marrow program. Sponsor Orrin G. Hatch, R-Utah, said the language was negotiated with the House and no conference would be needed. A report on the bill (S Rept 109-129) was filed on Aug. 31.

Supporters of Specter's S 471 were reluctant to pass the cord blood measure unless it was paired with the more divisive embryonic stem cell legislation. But, on Dec. 16, they relented and the Senate passed an amended version of HR 2520 by voice vote. The House cleared the measure 413–0 the next day.

National Institutes of Health

Congress in 2006 cleared legislation (HR 6164) reauthorizing the National Institutes of Health (NIH) for the first time in thirteen years, with the goal of promoting multidisciplinary research, increasing the budget, and modernizing the structure and management of the sprawling agency. Before the bill cleared, the Senate added provisions to help states pay for health insurance for children under the State Children's Health Insurance Program (CHIP). President George W. Bush signed HR 6164 into law Jan. 15, 2007 (PL 109-482).

The National Institutes of Health, the most important medical research institution in the country, had a budget approaching $30 billion in fiscal 2007, making it by far the largest source of discretionary spending by the Department of Health and Human Services (HHS). The agency had not been reauthorized since 1993 (PL 104-43). In the absence of such legislation, Congress made a commitment to double the NIH budget over five years, beginning in fiscal 1999. *(1993 action, Congress and the Nation Vol. IX, p. 525)*

Although the NIH had broad support in Congress, lawmakers said it should do a better job of monitoring the research it funded at universities and research labs across the country and questioned whether it had become too big to manage effectively. The NIH had grown from seventeen research institutes and centers in 1984 to twenty-seven in 2006. Lawmakers also heeded recommendations from experts who noted that scientific research no longer fit into the neat silos into which NIH's institutes were divided, necessitating a change in the agency's structure.

HIGHLIGHTS

The law reauthorized the NIH for three years, through fiscal 2009.

Authorization. Authorized $30.3 billion in fiscal 2007, $32.8 billion in fiscal 2008, and unspecified sums in fiscal 2009 for the NIH. No specific authorizations were included for any of the component institutes.

Common Fund. Established a Common Fund to promote research cutting across disciplines and institutes. Authorized the NIH director to allocate money from the fund for research that reflected emerging scientific opportunities, rising public health challenges, or existing knowledge gaps that deserved special emphasis and that involved two or more NIH institutes or centers. Required the director to consistently reserve a certain percentage of appropriated funds for the Common Fund, although it did not specify the percentage.

Tracking system. Required the NIH to establish an electronic system to uniformly track the research grants and programs of all its institutes and centers. Required the system to be searchable by criteria such as the type of research grant, who was managing the grant, and what areas of public health were involved.

Restructuring. Established a formal public process to review the agency's structural organization every seven years. Required a "scientific management review" group composed of institute and center directors and other scientific experts to evaluate the existing structure and recommend any necessary changes. Specified a series of public meetings and reports to Congress that were required as a follow-up to the restructuring recommendations.

CHIP. Reallocated unused CHIP funds from fiscal 2004 and 2005 to state programs that faced funding shortfalls in fiscal 2007. Set guidelines for how HHS would determine a state funding shortfall and how the money would be distributed to states. CHIP insured children from low- and moderate-income families who did not qualify for Medicaid.

LEGISLATIVE ACTION

The House Energy and Commerce Committee approved HR 6164, sponsored by Chairman Joe L. Barton, R-Texas, by 42–1 on Sept. 20 and formally reported the measure (H Rept 109-687) on Sept. 26. A key element of the legislation was the effort to encourage research that involved cooperation among the agency's many disease-based centers.

Most of Barton's bill was reflected in the version that became law. It proposed to freeze the number of institutes and centers at twenty-seven, require the creation of an electronic system to keep track of research and activities across institutes, and create a panel to study reorganizing the agency as a way to streamline its operations. The NIH director was to be given greater authority to reorganize, consolidate, or eliminate institutes. The bill clarified that the director was responsible for program coordination, strategic planning, and priority setting for all research activities. The director would be allowed to create a Common Fund to finance research that cut across the specialties of multiple centers and to use some of the money to finance research in new medical subjects or neglected areas.

The proposed total authorization for the NIH was somewhat smaller than in the final bill: $29.7 billion in fiscal 2007, $31.2 billion in 2008, and $32.8 billion in 2009. Under the committee measure, 5 percent of the NIH's annual appropriations would be devoted to the Common Fund. Barton said the NIH's fiscal 2006 budget was about $28.5 billion, which was only about 1.5 percent more than its fiscal 2003 budget.

During the markup, the committee

- Rejected 15–28 an amendment by Edward J. Markey, D-Mass., to raise the authorization to $30.8 billion in fiscal 2007, with further increases in fiscal 2008 and 2009. Barton said he supported increased spending on the NIH, but he said Markey's amendment would set an unrealistic goal, reducing the committee's influence with appropriators.

- Rejected 17–26 a second Markey amendment to adjust the authorization for inflation for fiscal 2008 and each subsequent year.
- Rejected 17–22 an amendment by Lois Capps, D-Calif., to prohibit the NIH director from eliminating any institutes or centers in the agency that were created by an act of Congress.
- Rejected 20–23 a second Capps amendment to order the NIH to fund research into links between breast cancer and environmental factors.

The House passed HR 6164 by a vote of 414–2 on Sept. 26 with broad support from the scientific and medical community. The only opposition came from Democrats who wanted to authorize more spending. Barton said he was sympathetic to that position but thought it unrealistic.

The Senate Health, Education, Labor, and Pensions Committee had jurisdiction over the NIH in the Senate, but the panel had not considered similar legislation. Although Chairman Michael B. Enzi, R-Wyo., generally supported the goals of Barton's bill, a spokesman said, committee members and other senators were expected to want considerable time to review it.

Unhappy that the Senate had not acted on the bill, Barton persuaded House GOP leaders not to schedule a vote on another priority—a bill (HR 6143) to reauthorize Ryan White acquired immune deficiency syndrome (AIDS) programs—for final action. Publicly, Barton said it would be "much easier" for him to "accommodate" House action on the AIDS bill if the Senate first passed his NIH measure. Barton also held up a popular Senate bioterrorism preparedness measure (S 3678). *(AIDS bill, below; bioterrorism law , p. 226)*

Enzi responded by surrendering his committee's jurisdiction over the NIH bill and asking Senate GOP leaders to "hotline" it, or try to pass it quickly by consensus. At that point, Senate Democrats also saw an opportunity to act on a projected financial shortfall faced by several state CHIP programs. The Congressional Research Service projected that as many as twenty-two states faced a combined shortfall totaling from $456 million to $1.1 billion in fiscal 2007. Democrats insisted on adding the redistribution of funds within CHIP, as well as increasing the authorized spending for the NIH.

After an all-night negotiating session, the lawmakers reached a compromise late Dec. 8. The Senate amended and passed HR 6164 by voice vote Dec. 8. In the early morning hours of Dec. 9, the House cleared the NIH bill by voice vote, followed by the bioterrorism bill and the AIDS measure.

Ryan White AIDS Reauthorization

Shortly before the 109th Congress adjourned, lawmakers in 2006 renewed the primary federal programs for low-income HIV (human immunodeficiency virus) and AIDS (acquired immune deficiency syndrome) patients. Named for Ryan White, a young AIDS activist who died from the disease in 1990, the programs are a last resort for assistance to those who cannot get treatment help from other sources, including Medicaid. President Bush signed the bill into law Dec. 19 (HR 6143—PL 109-415).

Although the programs enjoyed broad support in Congress, efforts to reauthorize the law exposed geographic disparities that had developed in tracking and treating AIDS and HIV. It pitted urban lawmakers from the Northeast and California against their counterparts from rural areas and the South, who said their regions were not getting a fair share of the funding. The dispute prevented the bill from clearing until the final day of the Congress.

The 1990 Ryan White Comprehensive AIDS Resources Emergency (CARE) Act (PL 101-381) had last been reauthorized in 2000 (PL 106-345). Congress had been appropriating about $2 billion a year for the programs since 2003. *(1990 law, Congress and the Nation Vol. VIII, p. 588; 2000 action, Congress and the Nation Vol. X, p. 483)*

The funds were distributed to states according to a formula based on their respective number of AIDS cases, which meant that the largest share went to places such as New York and San Francisco that had been the epicenter of the epidemic for years. In more recent times, however, HIV had spread rapidly through states such as Alabama and Arkansas, but those states received a proportionately smaller share of Ryan White funds because they had far fewer patients with full-blown AIDS. As a result, spending per patient varied widely throughout the country. While low-income New Yorkers with HIV and AIDS faced no wait to receive government-subsidized AIDS drugs and had access to a range of support services offered under the law, South Carolina had a waiting list for the life-saving drugs.

The fight was not only about where the money should go. It was also about whether the government should continue to spend most of its resources on those who already had developed AIDS, most of whom were in the large cities, or on helping those who tested positive for the virus to enable them to avoid developing full-blown AIDS. Until fiscal 2007, the formulas for distributing grants ignored people who were HIV-positive but had not developed AIDS.

The 2000 reauthorization required HIV cases to be included in the formula starting in fiscal 2007. States were required to report the names of HIV-infected people to the government so cases could be tracked across state lines to avoid duplicate counts. That highlighted another complication: Seventeen states and the District of Columbia reported HIV cases to the federal government using anonymous codes, not names, to identify those infected because of privacy concerns. As a result, they were about to lose millions of dollars in Ryan White funds.

Hoping to find a remedy, Sen. Michael B. Enzi, R-Wyo., and Rep. Joe L. Barton, R-Texas—the chairmen of the

Senate Health, Education, Labor, and Pensions (HELP) Committee and the House Energy and Commerce Committee, respectively—and Edward M. Kennedy, the senior Democrat on HELP, worked out a compromise reauthorization bill (HR 6143). The bill changed funding formulas to direct more money to states with growing populations of HIV patients at the expense of places with large, established populations of people with AIDS. It also included provisions to give states more time to begin reporting the names of HIV patients to the federal government.

The House passed the bill in September, but it was blocked in the Senate by Democrats from New York and New Jersey who complained that the compromise would divert too much money from their states. That led to yet another compromise, which guaranteed that no state would lose more than 5 percent of the money it received under the law in fiscal 2006. It also reduced the reauthorization to three years instead of five.

That version cleared Dec. 9, but only after a dustup over other health-related legislation had been resolved. Rep. Barton essentially held the AIDS bill hostage to force the Senate to pass a reauthorization bill for the National Institutes of Health (HR 6164). In the end Barton's gambit was successful. Both the NIH and AIDS bills became law at the tail end of the 109th Congress *(NIH reauthorization, p. 545)*

HIGHLIGHTS

HR 6143 reauthorized the Ryan White HIV/AIDS programs—including emergency relief, comprehensive care, and early intervention programs—for three years, through fiscal 2009.

Emergency relief. The bill authorized $1.9 billion ($604 million in fiscal 2007, $626 million in fiscal 2008, and $649.5 million in fiscal 2009) for the Ryan White Emergency Relief program. The program provided grants to metropolitan areas with very high numbers of AIDS cases for outpatient health care and support services, including home health care, hospice care, housing, transportation, and nutrition services. The following were among the changes made in the program:

The allocation formula was modified to include the number of people living with HIV or AIDS. Previously, formula grants were awarded to local governments in metropolitan areas that had a population of at least fifty thousand and had at least five hundred AIDS cases.

States that did not have accurate name-based records of HIV patients had until April 1, 2008, to create such a database.

At least 75 percent of the grant funds had to be used for primary care and other core medical services. The remaining 25 percent could be used for support services.

A "hold harmless" mechanism ensured that states would get at least 95 percent of the money they received under the law in fiscal 2006 for each of the three years covered by the bill.

Comprehensive care. The bill authorized $3.7 billion ($1.2 billion each in fiscal 2007 and 2008, and $1.3 billion in fiscal 2009) for the comprehensive care program. Grants under the program were used for home and community-based health care and support services, as well as for subsidized AIDS drugs.

Early intervention. The bill authorized $681 million ($219 million in fiscal 2007, $227 million in fiscal 2008, and $235 million in fiscal 2009) for grants to fund community-based programs that provided comprehensive primary care services to prevent or reduce HIV-related deaths. The recipients of the grants had to provide counseling and information about hepatitis A, B, and C and to develop an electronic information system to improve their ability to report data.

Pediatric program. The bill authorized $72 million per year in each of fiscal 2007 through 2009 for grants to improve and expand primary care and support services for women, infants, and children with HIV/AIDS and for their families.

Minority AIDS initiative. The bill authorized $405 million over three years to evaluate and address the disproportionate impact of HIV/AIDS on racial and ethnic minorities and the disparities in access to treatment and care.

LEGISLATIVE HISTORY

The House Energy and Commerce Committee approved a five-year reauthorization of the Ryan White program (HR 6143) by a vote of 38–10 on Sept. 20 and reported the measure (H Rept 109-695) on Sept. 28.

The bill, sponsored by Mary Bono, R-Calif., revised the allocation formula to provide more funds to rural areas with rising numbers of AIDS and HIV cases. But the bill authorized only 3.7 percent annual increases in spending from 2008 to 2011, so the change in formula meant taking money away from larger urban areas.

The bill, championed by Barton, included a hold harmless provision for fiscal 2007, 2008, and 2009. It would have guaranteed that, in each of those years, states would get at least 95 percent of what they had gotten the previous year. That did not satisfy urban lawmakers, particularly from New York and New Jersey. "This bill is designed to have clear winners and losers in funding, and there should be none," said Eliot L. Engel, D-N.Y. He said the entire New York House delegation was opposed to Barton's bill. But Nathan Deal, R-Ga., said the existing distribution of money was based on outdated counts of AIDS patients and that more money should be directed to southern states, where HIV was now spreading faster than in any other region.

The bill required that 75 percent of the money be used for "core medical services" and that the rest be used for services related to medical care, such as transporting patients to doctors' offices.

An amendment by Edolphus Towns, D-N.Y., to extend the hold harmless period to five years was narrowly rejected, 21–22. Frank Pallone Jr., D-N.J., offered an amendment that would have replaced Barton's bill with a simple one-year extension of Ryan White programs, so that Congress could spend more time working on the funding formulas. It was also rejected, 21–23.

The House passed HR 6143 by 325–98 on Sept. 28, after an often emotional debate.

"I came to this floor intending to support this bill," Maxine Waters, D-Calif., said. "But I'm not going to do it. We have a piece of legislation that is pitting us against each other instead of funding what needs to be done for AIDS." Waters spoke after several Democrats from New York and New Jersey denounced the bill for shifting AIDS money from their states to rural areas. "There's no question other states have mounting epidemics and absolutely are entitled to increased Ryan White funding," said Engel. "A good bill would make sure there was adequate funds to meet every state's needs." Engel said New York would lose about $78 million over four years under the bill.

Barton argued that the bill would correct many inequities in the existing law. At times, he said, dead people were included in counts of AIDS patients that were used to calculate funding, and in many states, much of the money was used for services unrelated to medical treatment.

House minority leader Nancy Pelosi, D-Calif., agreed that there were "a number of good provisions in this bill, including the recognition of emerging communities and the use of actual living AIDS counts rather than estimated living AIDS cases [to calculate funding]." But Pelosi said she could not support the bill because San Francisco, her home, would lose about $30 million over five years. Congress's first priority, she said, should be to "do no harm."

Action on the legislation in the Senate was delayed for months by a quarrel between Northeast Senate Democrats and lawmakers from rural and southern states, followed by a last-minute power play by Barton.

Democratic senators Hillary Rodham Clinton and Charles E. Schumer of New York and Frank R. Lautenberg and Robert Menendez of New Jersey blocked Senate consideration of the House bill, forcing Enzi to negotiate with them. It took until nearly the end of the Congress to reach a compromise.

Enzi agreed to limit financial losses for New York and New Jersey by including stronger hold harmless provisions. He reduced the length of the reauthorization from five years to three—lopping off the last two years of the House bill, when the losses would have been steepest for New York and New Jersey. And he agreed to explicitly repeal the Ryan White law after three years, forcing Congress to overhaul the program before fiscal 2010.

The Senate passed the revised HR 6143 by voice vote Dec. 6, sending it back to the House where it stalled once again. Barton did not like the Senate's changes, and he also was unhappy that the Senate had declined to clear a separate bill that he had sponsored (HR 6164) to restructure the NIH. He persuaded House GOP leaders not to schedule the AIDS bill for final action, though he said publicly that he could more easily pave the way for House consideration of HR 6143 if the Senate first acted on HR 6164.

Lawmakers reached a compromise late Dec. 8. The Senate amended and passed the NIH bill by voice vote Dec. 9. The House then cleared the NIH bill, followed by the Ryan White measure, both by voice vote.

Medical Errors

After years of laborious negotiations, the House in 2005 cleared legislation intended to reduce the number of injuries and fatalities from medical errors. The aim was to spot trends and patterns to help health care providers learn from mistakes without fear of liability. President George W. Bush signed the bill into law July 29 (S 544—PL 109-41).

The bill established a framework for voluntary, confidential reporting of medical errors, with feedback for health professionals and a national database to allow the identification of regional and national trends.

Enactment was the culmination of six years of effort in both chambers that began in 1999, when the Institute of Medicine, the health sciences arm of the National Academy of Sciences, issued a study on medical errors. The institute cited estimates that as many as 98,000 patients died each year as a result of mistakes by health care professionals, making medical errors the eighth-leading cause of death in the United States. Many thousands more were injured, driving up health care costs, the report said. The authors offered several recommendations, including legislation to provide for the confidential reporting of medical errors and a subsequent analysis of the data to devise ways to improve patient safety. *(1999–2000 action, Congress and the Nation Vol. X, p. 478)*

Under the new law,

- The Department of Health and Human Services (HHS) would certify "patient safety organizations" based on criteria to be established by the department. The organizations were required to have appropriately qualified staff, including licensed or certified medical professionals. The patient safety organizations, to be run by private, state, and local entities, would receive information on medical errors voluntarily reported by doctors and other health care providers. The organizations would analyze the information and then report back to providers on ways to improve patient safety and health care quality.
- All information reported to the organizations had to be kept confidential and could not identify any specific patient, health care provider, or other person. Anyone who disclosed the information would be subject to a fine of $10,000 per violation. The data could not be used in malpractice suits, although the law did not shield information already available to lawyers for use in court cases.

- Employers were barred from taking any retaliatory job action against an employee who reported patient safety information.
- HHS was required to establish a network of patient safety databases to collect reported, nonidentifiable information concerning patient safety and analyze national and regional statistics on health care errors.

LEGISLATIVE ACTION

The House and Senate had passed separate bills dealing with medical errors in the 108th Congress, but the House never formally appointed conferees and the differences were not settled. During informal discussions, negotiators could not agree on how to reconcile the need for information on medical errors with the health care providers' fear of liability.

The Senate Health, Education, Labor, and Pensions (HELP) Committee approved a bill (S 544—no written report) by voice vote March 9 that was identical to the chamber's 2004 measure.

The House Energy and Commerce Committee by voice vote July 20, 2005, approved a companion bill (HR 3205), which was reported (H Rept 109-197) on July 27. Supporters said the legislation would encourage health care providers to report medical errors by ensuring the data could not be used against them in liability cases. Chairman Joe L. Barton, R-Texas, said the bill language had been negotiated with Senate HELP chairman Michael B. Enzi, R-Wyo., and Sen. Edward M. Kennedy, D-Mass., and would pass in both chambers.

With a compromise finally achieved, the Senate passed S 544 by voice vote July 21. The House passed, and thus cleared, the bill under suspension of the rules by a vote of 428–3 on July 27.

Kennedy, who had expressed concern that the bill not allow the concealment of criminal activity, voiced his satisfaction on the floor. "The bill is intended to make medical professionals feel secure in reporting errors without fear of punishment, and it is right to do so," Kennedy said. "But the bill tries to do so carefully, so that it does not accidentally shield persons who have negligently or intentionally caused harm to patients. The legislation also upholds existing state laws on reporting patient safety information."

Abortion

Social conservatives appeared poised during the summer of 2006 to finally enact a bill to make it a crime to transport a minor across state lines for an abortion. They had been trying since 1998 to get the measure made law.

But once again it was not to be. The bill (S 403) the Senate passed in July 2006 was similar, but not identical, to the one (HR 748) passed by the House in 2005. Although Democrats in the Senate were unable to block the bill, which passed by a filibuster-proof margin, they were able to erect a procedural roadblock to prevent a conference with the House.

With the midterm elections approaching and the Senate seemingly stuck, House Republican leaders took up the Senate bill and substituted a modified version of their own measure, including the section included in the House bill, but not the Senate measure, requiring doctors to provide twenty-four hours' notice to a teen's parent, either in person or in writing, before performing an abortion, even if the state in which the doctor was performing the abortion did not have such a parental notification law. The twenty-four-hour waiting period was required even if the parent accompanied the teen across state lines to obtain the abortion. The House passed the bill in late September.

Senate majority leader Bill Frist, R-Tenn., tried to get the Senate to agree to the changes, but he could not get the sixty votes necessary to prevent a filibuster.

Republicans said they were trying to protect girls from men who were abusive or exerted undue influence. Democrats said they, too, were trying to protect minors from abusive parents or situations of rape or incest and that laws should not prevent girls from turning to trusted adults when they needed help.

BACKGROUND

The legislation was part of a strategy by antiabortion lawmakers to pass a series of narrow bills to limit abortions, instead of pushing for a federal law or constitutional amendment outlawing the procedure. Narrowly tailored antiabortion measures that had been enacted in recent years included a 2003 law (PL 108-105) that criminalized a specific abortion procedure that opponents labeled "partial-birth" abortion. The law had not yet taken effect because of legal challenges in federal courts. Another law enacted in 2004 (PL 108-212) made it a separate offense to harm a fetus during the commission of a federal crime against a pregnant woman, thereby giving federal legal status to a fetus for the first time. Also in 2004, Congress included language in the fiscal 2005 omnibus spending bill (PL 108-447) that denied federal aid to states and localities that required health care providers, facilities, or insurance companies to provide, fund, or refer abortion services. *(2003–2004 action, Congress and the Nation Vol. XI, pp. 510, 513)*

Just prior to the end of the 109th Congress, following the 2006 elections, as Republicans were about to give up the power they had held since 1995, GOP members tried and failed to pass one more abortion-limiting law. It was a bill (HR 6099) called the Unborn Child Pain Awareness Act. It would have required women obtaining an abortion after twenty weeks' gestation to be told that their fetuses could feel pain and to offer them fetal anesthesia. Although the bill won a majority of votes in the House on Dec. 6, 2006, on a 250–162 tally, it was brought to the floor under a fast-track procedure that required a two-thirds supermajority to pass, a threshold it failed to reach.

LEGISLATIVE ACTION

The Senate held the key to the teen abortion bill, formally known as the Child Custody Protection Act. The House had passed similar bills three times in previous Congresses; the Senate had not taken up any of them. Supporters were hopeful that they would be more successful in the 109th Congress because several abortion opponents had won Senate seats in the 2004 elections.

House Bill

House Republican leaders easily won passage of a bill (HR 748) by 270–157 on April 27, 2005, that would have made it illegal to take a minor across state lines for an abortion to avoid her home state's requirement for parental notification. But sponsors added the new section targeting doctors, which made the bill less palatable in the Senate. It required that a doctor notify the parents—in person or by certified mail—of an out-of-state minor's request for an abortion. Parents or guardians of the minor could sue doctors who did not comply.

The House Judiciary Committee had reported HR 748 (H Rept 109-51) on April 21.

The House-passed bill would

Transporting a minor. Make it a federal crime—punishable by a fine of up to $100,000 and up to one year in prison, or both—to knowingly take a minor across state lines with the intent that the minor have an abortion, if the minor lived in a state that had a parental notification law and no parental consent or notification was obtained.

The bill included an exception if the abortion was necessary to save the minor's life, but not if it was to protect the pregnant minor's health. The minor and her parents would be exempt from prosecution.

Individuals accused of violating this provision could defend themselves against civil and criminal actions by showing that they "reasonably believed" that parental consent or notification had been obtained, or they were presented with documents showing that a court in the minor's home state had waived any parental notification required under that state's laws.

Performing an abortion. Make it a federal crime—punishable by a fine of up to $100,000 or a year in prison, or both—for a doctor to perform an abortion on a minor from another state in violation of the minor's home-state parental notification laws.

A physician would be required to provide at least twenty-four hours' notice directly to the minor's parent—either in writing or in person—before performing an abortion on a minor who was a resident of another state. Even if the parent accompanied the minor and consented to the abortion, there would still be a twenty-four-hour waiting period. If such notice was not possible after a reasonable effort had been made, the physician would have to provide a twenty-four-hour notice by certified mail, with return receipt requested. The notice would be considered delivered forty-eight hours from noon on the day after it was mailed.

A doctor would be exempt from the bill's notification requirements if the abortion was necessary to save the minor's life; if it was performed in a state that had a law requiring parental notification or involvement and the doctor complied with that law; if the doctor was given documents showing with a reasonable degree of certainty that a court in the minor's home state waived any parental notification requirement; or if the minor declared in a signed, written statement that she was the victim of sexual abuse, neglect, or physical abuse by a parent. In the last case, the doctor would have to notify the authorities in the minor's home state to receive any reports of abuse or neglect before performing the abortion.

Senate Bill

The Senate passed its bill (S 403) by a vote of 65–34 on July 25, 2006. Four Republicans and Independent James M. Jeffords of Vermont voted against the bill; fourteen Democrats, including Minority Leader Harry Reid of Nevada, voted for it.

Before passing the bill, the Senate:

- Adopted 98–0 on July 25 a compromise amendment on incest worked out between Nevada Republican John Ensign and California Democrat Barbara Boxer. In addition to stopping a father who raped his daughter from suing adults who helped the girl end the pregnancy, as Ensign's original amendment would have done, the compromise included language by Boxer to stop fathers or other family members who committed incest from transporting a pregnant minor across state lines for an abortion. Boxer said the compromise amendment was "an improvement" but noted that, unlike her original proposal, the compromise still would not bar fathers who impregnated their daughters from exercising their parental consent rights or block criminal prosecution against adults who helped incest victims.
- Rejected 48–51 on July 25 an amendment by Frank R. Lautenberg, D-N.J., to direct the Department of Health and Human Services to make grants to state and local governments as well as nonprofit groups to provide sex education about abstinence and contraception.

As passed by the Senate, S 403 contained provisions to

- Make it a federal crime—punishable by a fine, up to one year in prison, or both—to knowingly take a minor across state lines to have an abortion in violation of parental notification laws in the girl's home state.
- Provide an exception if the abortion was necessary to save the pregnant minor's life, but not if it was to protect her health. The minor and her parents would be exempt from prosecution.

- Allow an affirmative defense for individuals prosecuted under these provisions who could show they "reasonably believed" that parental consent or notification had been obtained or that they were presented with documents showing that a court in the minor's home state had waived any parental notification requirements.
- Bar a family member who committed incest from transporting a minor across state lines for an abortion, and prohibit a parent who was guilty of incest from suing adults who helped end the resulting pregnancy.

Minority Whip Richard J. Durbin, D-Ill., objected to taking the procedural step necessary to begin a House-Senate conference. GOP leaders had bypassed the Judiciary Committee, bringing the bill straight to the floor, because Judiciary chairman Arlen Specter, R-Pa., strongly opposed the legislation. Frist said at a news conference the day after the vote that Durbin's move was "very offensive" to him. He said that he had the sixty-vote supermajority needed to overcome the procedural hurdles and that he intended to start the conference before the Senate recessed in October for the midterm election. Bill sponsor Ensign said he knew that the subject of abortion rights was divisive, but that lawmakers should be able to agree on his bill.

Democrats assailed the legislation as a politically motivated attempt to appease the Republican Party's base of socially conservative voters in advance of the November 2006 elections. Durbin said the Senate action was a "make-good vote" for antiabortion rights Republicans who had voted the week before to clear a House bill (HR 810) expanding federal funding of embryonic stem cell research. President George W. Bush vetoed the bill. *(Stem cell research, pp. 542, 573)*

The opponents gambled that Frist would not want to devote precious Senate floor time after the August recess to jumping procedural hurdles.

REVISED BILL

With conference blocked, the House passed an amended version of the Senate bill on a **key vote of 264–153 (R 215–9; D 49–143; I 0–1),** on Sept. 26, 2006. The measure was virtually identical to the 2005 House-passed bill, but it also included the Boxer-Ensign language on incest, an exclusion for ectopic pregnancies, and language stating that the provisions would apply when a minor was transported to a foreign country as well as to another state. *(2006 key votes, p. 937)*

Democratic opponents argued that GOP leaders were passing the bill again to mobilize their base of socially conservative voters in advance of the November election. Republicans supporters argued that it was a "common sense" bill that protected parental rights and had broad public support.

On Sept. 27, Robert F. Bennett, R-Utah, speaking on Frist's behalf, asked the Senate to concur in the House amendment, a step that would have cleared the bill for the White House. But on Sept. 29, the Senate rejected an attempt by Frist to invoke cloture, which would have limited the debate and averted a potential filibuster. Eight Democrats who had supported Ensign's bill two months earlier balked at the added provisions and voted against cloture. The motion failed, on a **key vote of 57–42 (R 51–4; D 6–37; I 0-1),** three votes short of the sixty-vote threshold, ending efforts on the bill for the year.

Ken Salazar, D-Colo., who voted for Ensign's bill in July but against cloture, decried what he said was a "political stunt" by the House. Salazar said the House "decided to play these last-minute political games" instead of simply clearing the Senate bill.

Terri Schiavo Case

Republican leaders spent a frantic week in March 2005 trying to intervene in the case of Terri Schiavo, a forty-one-year-old severely brain-damaged woman whose husband and parents had been battling since 1998 over whether to keep her alive through artificial means.

Schiavo had suffered severe brain damage in 1990 when her heart stopped for several minutes. Court-appointed doctors said she was in a persistent vegetative state. Her husband, Michael Schiavo, said she had told him she would not want to be kept alive artificially. Her parents, Bob and Mary Schindler, disputed that and insisted that she could get better with rehabilitative therapy. A Florida court had ruled that her feeding tube be removed March 18 in accordance with her husband's wishes.

According to a Florida appellate court, much of Terri Schiavo's cerebral cortex was gone. The court concluded that "unless an act of God, a true miracle, were to recreate her brain, [Schiavo] will always remain in an unconscious, reflexive state, totally dependent upon others to feed her and care for her most private needs."

The effort to save Schiavo was championed by Republican leaders and their conservative religious supporters. It prompted a national debate about end-of-life medical care and raised questions about the meaning of conservatism in national politics. Public opinion polls showed a majority of Americans opposed congressional intervention in the case.

COMPETING BILLS

On Wednesday, March 16, the House passed a broadly worded bill (HR 1332) to authorize the transfer to federal courts—within thirty days after all state remedies were exhausted—of cases such as Schiavo's, involving incapacitated people who had not executed an advance directive authorizing the withholding of sustenance. The bill, drafted by Judiciary Committee chairman F. James Sensenbrenner Jr., R-Wis., and Dave Weldon, R-Fla., passed by voice vote.

There was some disagreement on the floor. Alcee L. Hastings, D-Fla., said the decision to continue his mother's life support was one of the most difficult of his life. "There are certain things perhaps we ought not to legislate," he said. Jerrold Nadler, D-N.Y., called the bill "a dangerous, reckless way to deal with very serious issues."

In the Senate, Florida Republican Mel Martinez introduced a narrow private relief bill (S 653), and the Senate passed it by voice vote on Thursday, March 17.

House Republican leaders were preparing to leave Washington, D.C., for a two-week spring recess, and they refused to take up the Senate bill, insisting that the Senate consider their broader measure instead. Sensenbrenner issued a statement after the Senate vote saying, "The House has completed its business and has adjourned." He said the Senate could pass the House bill "to ensure Terri Schiavo's civil rights are protected or it can allow Ms. Schiavo to starve to death."

House GOP leaders blamed Senate Democrats for the impasse, particularly Ron Wyden, D-Ore., who had indicated he would oppose any broader bill that might affect his state's assisted-suicide law. "As Terri Schiavo lays helpless in Florida, one day away from the unthinkable and unforgivable, the Senate Democrats refused to join Republicans to act on her behalf," House Speaker J. Dennis Hastert, R-Ill., and Majority Leader Tom DeLay, R-Texas, said in a joint statement.

That analysis was disputed, however, by the bill's strongest Republican supporters in both chambers, who said House GOP leaders were to blame. "There was broad opposition on both sides of the aisle" in the Senate to the House bill, said Rick Santorum of Pennsylvania, the chairman of the Senate Republican Conference.

Majority Leader Bill Frist, R-Tenn., a well-known heart surgeon before he joined the Senate, went to the floor late Thursday night for the second time in twelve hours to argue that Florida doctors had erred in saying Terri Schiavo was in a persistent vegetative state. "I question it based on a review of the video footage, which I spent an hour or so looking at last night in my office," Frist said. "She certainly seems to respond to visual stimuli." Critics said that in relying on family videotapes to challenge the diagnosis of doctors who had examined Schiavo, Frist was pandering to social conservatives rather than following his medical training.

SUBPOENAS ISSUED, SPRING RECESS DELAYED

On Friday, March 18, the House and Senate delayed the start of their spring recess for one last effort to reach agreement on a bill.

"This act of barbarism must be prevented," DeLay told reporters. DeLay said lawmakers would work through the weekend to try to reconcile the competing House and Senate bills, but he assailed the Senate for refusing to accept the House approach. "All wisdom is not in the Senate," DeLay said.

House GOP leaders said the Senate bill would not guarantee that Schiavo's parents would be able to get a federal judge to hear their case. House supporters also insisted their broader approach was better because it would apply to all incapacitated people, not just Schiavo.

But Senate Republicans and Democrats were concerned the House bill would establish a dangerous precedent and clog courts with an untold number of such cases. They also feared it could interfere with state laws, such as Oregon's assisted-suicide statute. Privately, Senate Republicans also were seething that DeLay sent House lawmakers out of town March 17 before the Senate passed its bill.

In a last-ditch attempt to block removal of Schiavo's feeding tube, Thomas M. Davis III, R-Va., chairman of the House Government Reform Committee, subpoenaed Schiavo and her husband, Michael, to attend a March 25 hearing at the Florida hospice where Schiavo lived. The panel also subpoenaed two doctors treating Schiavo, as well as the hospice director. The committee instructed Michael Schiavo, the doctors, and the hospice director to bring all the medical equipment used to provide nutrition and hydration to Schiavo in its "current and continuing state of operations"—language designed to prevent the removal of the feeding tube.

Henry A. Waxman of California, the ranking committee Democrat, denounced the subpoenas. "Congress has no authority to use subpoenas to tell doctors what treatment they can and cannot provide to any individual under their care," Waxman said. "These subpoenas were issued unilaterally by Tom Davis, acting at the request of the Republican leadership. There was no vote and no opportunity to debate the issue in committee."

Senate Republican leaders took a different approach, summoning Terri and Michael Schiavo to a March 28 Senate Health, Education, Labor, and Pensions Committee hearing in Washington. They invoked federal criminal law that prohibited any attempt "to obstruct or impede" the attendance or testimony of a witness, which carried a penalty of up to five years in prison and a $100,000 fine, according to Senate Republican aides. They said the protection would extend to Terri Schiavo, even if her husband declined to appear, and even if Mrs. Schiavo did not appear.

Social conservatives praised the aggressive congressional moves. "Congress, and the Florida Legislature, must not let this travesty stand," said James C. Dobson, chairman of the advocacy group Focus on the Family. "They must continue to work to ensure that the weakest among us, who cannot speak for themselves, have the same legal rights and protections that even the most heinous criminals are afforded."

Some legal scholars were critical. "For Congress to reach out in a country of 300 million and intervene in a single case raises very disturbing questions of legitimacy," said Jonathan Turley, a George Washington University law professor.

A lawyer for the House of Representatives also filed a motion in a Florida state court to intervene in the case and modify a Florida judge's order that Schiavo's feeding tube be removed at 1 p.m. But Florida Circuit Judge George Greer refused the request. "I have had no cogent reason why the [congressional] committee should intervene," Greer told attorneys in a conference call, adding that last-minute action by Congress did not invalidate years of court rulings.

REPUBLICANS REACH AN AGREEMENT

Frist and Hastert agreed Saturday, March 19, on a narrow proposal to give Schiavo's parents the right to file a lawsuit in the U.S. District Court for the Middle District of Florida, alleging that Schiavo's rights had been violated under the U.S. Constitution or federal law. The federal judge would be required to consider the Schindlers' allegations de novo, that is, without taking into account any of the various Florida state court decisions that led to the removal of Schiavo's feeding tube. However, the law was silent on whether a federal judge should issue a temporary restraining order to force doctors to reinsert the feeding tube.

As part of the compromise, the new bill included a provision specifying that it did not "confer additional jurisdiction" on federal courts to hear any case related to a state law on assisted suicide. It also included a sense of Congress provision urging the 109th Congress to consider broader legislation dealing with similar cases.

On Sunday, March 20, the Senate passed the bill (S 686) by voice vote. The House, on a **key vote of 203–58 (R 156–5; D 47–53; I 1–0)**, early Monday, in the session that began March 20, cleared the legislation under suspension of the rules. Bush signed the bill into law less than an hour later, and an attorney for Schiavo's parents quickly went to the federal district court in Tampa to file a request for an emergency injunction. *(2005 key votes, p. 915)*

Republicans expressed confidence that a federal judge would immediately order doctors to reinsert Schiavo's feeding tube. "I can't imagine that a judge that would legitimately take a case [under the bill] would allow the subject matter of the case to die," said Santorum, a driving force behind the bill. "That would be an irresponsible abuse of that judge's authority."

"She's not a vegetable. She's just handicapped, mentally challenged," DeLay said of Schiavo at a Sunday news conference.

FEDERAL APPEALS DENIED

The Schindlers, however, had no more success with federal judges than they had had in the Florida courts. They met with a succession of rejections.

- March 22. U.S. District Judge James D. Whittemore denied the Schindlers' motion for a temporary restraining order to force doctors to reinsert Schiavo's feeding tube because the Schindlers did not meet the legal burden of proving they had a substantial likelihood of succeeding at trial.
- March 23. A three-judge panel of the U.S. Court of Appeals for the Eleventh Circuit affirmed Whittemore's decision. The two-to-one ruling expressed sympathy with the Schindlers but concluded that the law did not support any of the parents' legal arguments. The full Eleventh Circuit declined to review the decision.
- March 24. The U.S. Supreme Court declined to hear the Schindlers' appeal. House GOP leaders had filed a friend-of-the-court brief arguing that Congress intended for a federal court to order doctors to reinsert Schiavo's feeding tube. DeLay and Sensenbrenner issued a joint statement after the Court refused to hear the case, saying they "strongly believe that the court erred in reaching its conclusion and that once again they have chosen to ignore the clear intent of Congress."
- March 25. Whittemore rejected another motion by the Schindlers for a temporary restraining order, and a three-judge panel on the Eleventh Circuit affirmed that decision.
- March 30. The Eleventh Circuit denied the Schindlers' emergency petition for a rehearing by the full court. The U.S. Supreme Court once again refused to order Schiavo's feeding tube reinserted. It was the sixth time the high court had declined to intervene.
- March 31. Terri Schiavo died

AFTERWARD

In the immediate aftermath, angry Republican congressional leaders vowed to rein in the federal judiciary. In comments that generated widespread criticism, DeLay said after Schiavo's death that "this loss happened because our legal system did not protect the people who need protection most, and that will change. The time will come for the men responsible for this to answer for their behavior, but not today."

DeLay later apologized, saying April 13, "I said something in an inartful way. And I shouldn't have said it that way. And I apologize for saying it that way." But he said the judges' handling of the case still should be investigated.

Autopsy results, announced at a June 15 news conference in Largo, Fla., showed that Schiavo had massive and irreversible brain damage and was blind. The report said her brain was discolored and scarred, shriveled to half its normal size, and damaged in nearly all its regions, including the one responsible for vision. The autopsy could not determine what caused the original damage.

Medicare Physician Payments

Congress acted at the end of 2006 to prevent cuts in Medicare reimbursement to doctors in 2007. Without the legislation, physicians would have taken a 5.1 percent reduction in their pay from Medicare, starting Jan. 1, 2007. The negotiated package avoided the cut, keeping physician pay rates at their 2006 levels. Physicians who submitted data to the government on a set of quality-of-care measurements that had previously been part of a voluntary pilot program would get a 1.5 percent increase in payments.

The provisions were enacted as part of a tax and trade bill cleared on the day the 109th Congress adjourned. The House passed the package, 367–45, on Dec. 8. The Senate cleared the bill 79–9 on Dec. 9, in the session that began Dec. 8, and President George W. Bush signed it into law Dec. 20 (HR 6111—PL 109-432). *(Tax package, p. 105)*

The biggest sticking point was over how to pay for the pay cut's cancellation. Ways and Means chairman Bill Thomas, R-Calif., who led the House side of the negotiations and was retiring from Congress, wanted to make a larger cut to physician pay in 2008 to offset the cuts scheduled for 2007. But Senate Finance chairman Charles E. Grassley, R-Iowa, and ranking committee Democrat Max Baucus of Montana argued against it. They did not want to deal with the issue in 2007. They were backed by fiscal conservatives such as Sen. Judd Gregg, R-N.H., and prevailed.

Instead, they agreed to pay for the freeze by taking $6.5 billion from the Medicare stabilization fund that was created in 2003 (PL 108-173) to entice preferred provider organizations to offer coverage in underserved regions. Additional funds would come from capping state taxes on Medicaid providers at 5.5 percent, down from the previous cap of 6 percent. Reducing the state tax lowered the required federal match. The remaining funds were to come from attempting to reduce fraud and waste in the Medicare program. *(2003 action, Congress and the Nation Vol. XI, p. 496; 2008 action, p. 571)*

In addition to physician payments, other health provisions in the year-end tax and trade bill included increased payments for rural providers, a priority for Grassley; more money for dialysis providers; extra funds to uncover fraud and waste in the Medicare program; and changes to promote the use of health savings accounts. *(Health savings accounts, below)*

Health Savings Accounts

An expansion of health savings accounts, one of President George W. Bush's top health care priorities, became law as part of one of the last bills to clear the 109th Congress. Bush had called repeatedly for expanding the accounts, including the request in his 2006 State of the Union address. But it appeared that Congress would take no action until lawmakers managed to insert the language into the tax, trade, and health package (HR 6111) that Bush signed into law (PL 109-432) on Dec. 20, 2006. *(2006 State of the Union, text, p. 1052)*

Created as part of the 2003 Medicare prescription drug law (PL 108-173), health savings accounts allowed people with high-deductible insurance plans to put aside tax-free income to cover health care expenses. Together, the savings account and insurance plan were seen by advocates as creating a "consumer-driven" health care system in which individuals would have incentives to make more informed and cost-effective decisions. *(2003 law, Congress and the Nation Vol. XI, p. 496)*

Many Democrats in both chambers opposed the proposals, arguing that the program could discourage patients from seeking preventive treatment or other needed medical care, and expressing concern over the paucity of information about the accounts to date. They also warned that the wealthy could use the accounts as tax shelters.

The House Ways and Means Committee approved the provisions as a stand-alone bill (HR 6134) by a vote of 24–14 on Sept. 27 and reported the legislation (H Rept 109-704) on Sept. 29. The measure, which faced strong opposition from Democrats, did not make it to the floor of either chamber. Senate Finance chairman Charles E. Grassley, R-Iowa, indicated that without a filibuster-proof majority of sixty votes it would go nowhere.

However, in the final hours of the 109th Congress, Ways and Means chairman Bill Thomas, R-Calif., attached the language to a popular package of tax "extenders," which became the vehicle for trade and other health provisions. The Joint Committee on Taxation put the cost of the provisions at $1 billion over ten years. *(Tax package, p. 131)*

The health savings accounts portions of HR 6111 included provisions to

- Repeal the limit on annual tax-deductible contributions to the accounts, raising the ceiling to $2,850 for an individual and $5,650 for a family. Previously, the contributions could not be larger than the annual deductible in an employee's high-deductible insurance plan.
- Allow a one-time rollover from a flexible spending account or health reimbursement account into a health savings account.
- Permit a one-time transfer from an individual retirement account (IRA) to a health savings account without the 10 percent tax penalty usually applied to early withdrawals from IRAs.

The House passed HR 6111 by 367–45 on Dec. 8, and the Senate cleared it 79–9 on Dec. 9, in the session that began Dec. 8.

Medical Malpractice

A Medical liability bill that Republicans called an antidote to rising health care costs won House passage in 2005 but went no further. The measure was part of GOP efforts to restrict lawsuits and cap jury awards, sometimes referred to as tort reform. Democrats decried the bill as a gift to the insurance and drug industries.

It was the eighth time since 1995 the House had passed legislation to limit medical malpractice liability awards, but supporters had not been able to get enough support to get a vote in the Senate.

The House passed the bill (HR 5) by a vote of 230–194 on July 28.

The measure proposed to cap noneconomic damages awarded in medical malpractice suits for pain and suffering at $250,000 and to limit punitive damages to two times the economic damages or $250,000, whichever is greater. It also would have limited attorney fees.

In their effort to defeat the bill, opponents targeted a provision that would have shielded drug and medical device companies from most punitive damages if their products were approved by the Food and Drug Administration (FDA). The FDA approval process had come into question the previous two years after popular painkillers such as Vioxx and Celebrex were found to increase the risk of heart attacks and strokes, and some antidepressants were shown to increase the risk of suicide in children.

Sponsors of a Senate medical malpractice bill (S 354) removed the drug and device-maker liability provision from the legislation they introduced in 2005.

Republicans argued that soaring malpractice awards were driving up health care costs and that physicians' malpractice insurance premiums were increasing to the point that some doctors were being forced to change specialties, move to different states, or stop practicing medicine. Democrats countered that capping noneconomic damages was unfair to injured plaintiffs, who, by definition, had already proved their case. They contended that malpractice insurance companies were raising premiums to recoup investment losses, not because of increased litigation costs.

Capping malpractice damage awards was a prominent part of President George W. Bush's health care platform, and he strongly supported the House bill.

Senate majority leader Bill Frist, R-Tenn., a physician himself, tried to get two separate variations of the medical malpractice bill to the Senate floor in 2006. Not only did the bills fail to win the sixty votes needed to pass the first threshold for a full debate, but they also did not even win a majority.

Health Information Technology

Legislation to spur the use of information technology (IT) in health care had strong Republican support but was left unfinished at the end of the 109th Congress.

The issue was a priority for President George W. Bush, who called for most Americans to have electronic medical records within a decade, and for Senate majority leader Bill Frist, R-Tenn. They said greater use of electronic records would reduce medical errors and cut costs. The Department of Health and Human Services (HHS) estimated that about $140 billion a year could be saved. Many Democrats, however, were concerned about the implications for privacy.

The House passed a health information technology bill in July 2006 that was similar to a measure passed by the Senate in 2005. Both measures had provisions to establish the Office of the National Coordinator for Health Information Technology in statute and authorize it to oversee a process of developing interoperability guidelines for the many competing health information technologies. A major hurdle for a national health IT system was the lack of a uniform standard for the technologies, despite efforts by numerous outside study groups.

But the legislation was sidelined by other priorities before the midterm election, and conferees were never appointed to resolve the differences.

Although the legislation died when the 109th Congress adjourned, Bush signed an executive order on Aug. 22, 2006, calling for the government to use its purchasing power to encourage the use of electronic medical records. The order directed government agencies to use health IT to develop quality and efficiency standards. It also called on them to share pricing information and encourage pricing transparency, under which hospitals and physicians would have to disclose publicly how much they charged for care.

LEGISLATIVE ACTION

The Senate passed a bipartisan bill (S 1418) by voice vote Nov. 18, 2005. It included the provision to codify the Office of the National Coordinator for Health Information Technology, which was created by executive order in 2004, within HHS.

The bill proposed to authorize $116 million in fiscal 2006 and $141 million in fiscal 2007 for three new grant programs aimed at promoting the use of health information technology and encouraging interoperable systems. In an effort to answer privacy concerns, the bill explicitly applied existing health privacy rules to any health information stored or transmitted electronically.

The Senate Health, Education, Labor, and Pensions (HELP) Committee had approved S 1418 by voice vote July 20 and reported it (S Rept 109-111) July 27.

On June 15, 2006, the House Energy and Commerce Committee approved a health information technology bill (HR 4157—H Rept 109-601, Part I) by a vote of 28–14. The Ways and Means Committee approved a somewhat different version of the measure (H Rept 109-601, Part II) by a vote of 23–17 the same day. The panels formally reported the legislation on July 26. Both versions were designed to speed up the adoption of national standards for data storage and the sharing of medical information. Like the Senate bill, both proposed to codify the Office of the National Coordinator for Health Information Technology within HHS.

However, several significant differences existed among the bills. The Ways and Means version included provisions—not in the Energy and Commerce–approved measure or Senate-passed bill—to increase the number of diagnosis and procedure codes used in medical reports from 24,000 to more than 200,000. Insurers and providers used the codes for billing, and proponents said a larger number of codes would permit improved tracking of coverage trends and medical outcomes. But many insurers opposed the proposal, particularly a 2009 deadline for having the codes in place, which they said would not give them enough time to adjust to the new system. The Energy and Commerce bill originally had similar provisions, but they were stripped when the panel's Health Subcommittee marked up the measure.

Ways and Means also included a provision not in the other bills to allow federal privacy regulations to preempt state laws. That provision, too, had been removed from the Energy and Commerce version in subcommittee.

The House bills included small grants for programs serving uninsured and underserved groups, but they did not propose broader grants to encourage the use of interoperable IT systems as the Senate bill did.

The House passed a version of the bill (HR 4157) on July 27 that combined elements of both committee measures. The vote was 270–148. The measure included the requirement for increasing the number of billing codes but extended the deadline to 2011. The preemption of state laws was dropped.

House GOP leaders had hoped to include a provision to encourage pricing transparency, but they removed the language to smooth the bill's passage after other lawmakers and industry groups strongly objected.

Prescription Drug Imports

Advocates of allowing citizens to import prescription drugs continued their battle, winning a small victory: language in the fiscal 2007 Homeland Security appropriations bill that permitted Americans to bring in small amounts of such drugs for personal use. But legislation to broaden that option by letting U.S. residents order drugs from foreign pharmacies by direct mail or over the Internet did not come up for a vote in either chamber in 2005 or 2006.

The language in the Homeland Security spending law (HR 5441—PL 109-295) allowed individuals to bring in a ninety-day supply of drugs bought in Canada without fear of confiscation during fiscal 2007. It prohibited U.S. Customs and Border Protection officials from using funds to stop such individual imports. *(Appropriations, p. 102)*

Similar provisions had been included in both the House- and Senate-passed versions of the bill. In the House, the language was added by Jo Ann Emerson, R-Mo., during the Homeland Security Appropriations Subcommittee markup in May. The Senate provision was added on the floor. The amendment, by David Vitter, R-La., was adopted 68–32 on July 11.

The House Appropriations Committee added a broader exemption as an amendment to the fiscal 2007 Agriculture Department spending bill (HR 5384). The amendment, by Anne M. Northup, R-Ky., was adopted by voice vote. It would have barred the use of funds in the bill to prevent individuals, pharmacists, or wholesalers from importing prescription drugs approved by the Food and Drug Administration.

The Senate version did not include a similar provision, and the Agriculture spending bill was left unfinished at the end of the Congress.

The White House repeatedly threatened to veto bills containing drug import language, and similar provisions had been dropped from the Agriculture bill in conference in previous years. The pharmaceutical industry also continued to lobby heavily against all drug importation legislation, concerned that an international buyers' market would drive down its prices and profits. As it had in the past, the industry also warned that there was no way to confirm the safety or authenticity of drugs from foreign pharmacies. Drug import advocates argued that Canada and the European Union had similar drug safety systems to that of the United States with good track records.

Emergency Flu Funding

Concern about the spread of a new strain of flu virus led Congress to appropriate $3.8 billion in emergency fiscal 2006 funds for programs to prepare for and respond to a potential flu pandemic. The funds cleared as part of the Defense Department appropriations bill (HR 2863—PL 109-148), which President George W. Bush signed Dec. 30, 2005. The provisions also gave liability protection to vaccine manufacturers. *(Appropriations, pp. 73, 400)*

Of the total, $3.3 billion went to the Department of Health and Human Services (HHS), with $350 million provided to help state and local governments and $267 million for international activities and surveillance.

The legislation barred lawsuits against drug manufacturers that supplied drugs or vaccines needed to cope with a disease that HHS had designated as a public health emergency. Instead, the department could create a compensation schedule for individuals who suffered serious injury or death because of the product. Manufacturers could be sued in cases of public epidemics only on grounds of willful misconduct related to drugs or vaccines. The liability language was added to the conference report by Senate majority leader Bill Frist, R-Tenn.

The new virus—known as the H5N1 virus, or avian flu—had been found in birds in Asia and had shown that it could jump to humans, with sometimes deadly results. Public health officials said that if the virus were to adopt so that it could spread from one human to another, it could very well result in the next human pandemic.

The Senate took action Sept. 29, 2005, adopting by voice vote a proposal by Tom Harkin, D-Iowa, to add $3.9 billion in emergency flu funds to the defense spending bill. Harkin took up the cause again when the Senate considered the Labor-HHS-Education appropriations bill (HR 3010). He won voice-vote approval Oct. 27 to add $8 billion for preparation to combat avian flu.

Supporters said the amendment was necessary because the Bush administration had not released any plans to combat a possible flu pandemic. Bush subsequently sent a proposal to Congress asking for $7.1 billion in emergency funding to prepare for a possible avian flu pandemic. The Nov. 1 request included $251 million to detect and contain flu outbreaks before they spread around the world; $2.8 billion to accelerate development of cell-culture technology; $800 million to develop new treatments and vaccines; $1.5 billion for HHS and the Pentagon to purchase influenza vaccines; $1 billion to stockpile antiviral medications for first responders and high-risk populations; and $644 million to coordinate preparedness and response plans at the federal, state, and local levels. The plan also included government subsidies to help states buy antiviral medications.

Republican leaders considered several possibilities but settled on the defense bill to carry the flu money. The $3.8 billion was $3.3 billion below Bush's request. The House Appropriations Committee said it would fund roughly the fiscal 2006 portion of the White House request.

2007–2008

Democrats retook control of Congress in 2007 for the first time since 1995. They immediately made health care one of their top priorities, attempting to draw distinctions between their view of what the public consistently said was one of its top domestic priorities and what President George W. Bush's direction had been for the preceding six years. But lacking the votes to override a veto or even to break a Republican filibuster in the Senate, Democrats were limited in their ability to get many bills enacted into law.

By far the biggest health fight of Congress came of the renewal of the State Children's Health Insurance Program, better known as CHIP. The Democratic-led House and Senate in 2008 sent the president two separate bills to dramatically expand the popular program that provided health insurance to children in families who earned too much to qualify for Medicaid, but not enough to afford private coverage. President Bush vetoed both, arguing that the measures would have represented too big a government intrusion into the nation's health care system.

Bush also vetoed, for the second consecutive Congress, legislation to relax his restrictions on federal funding of biomedical research using stem cells derived from human embryos. Scientists argued that the cells, with their ability to turn into any cell in the human body, represented the potential to treat or cure a myriad of dread diseases and ailments, including diabetes, spinal cord injuries, and Alzheimer's disease. But the research was opposed by individuals and groups who objected to the fact that acquiring the cells required the destruction of human embryos, even those left over from in vitro fertilization attempts that would have been destroyed in any case.

But there were also significant bipartisan accomplishments on the health front. One was enactment in 2007 of the most sweeping rewrite of the Food and Drug Administration's regulatory powers in more than a decade. The bill was promoted in large part by several scandals, including reports of tainted food and drug products from China and the discovery that many popular and broadly advertised prescription drugs, including the painkillers Vioxx and Celebrex, were linked to serious cardiovascular side effects.

In addition, Congress in 2008 approved legislation in the works for more than a dozen years to require the health insurance companies to provide equal benefits for mental and physical ailments. The "mental health parity" legislation finally became law despite the death of its original Senate sponsor, Paul Wellstone, D-Minn., in a 2002 plane crash. It was also one of the last major health bills sponsored by Sen. Edward Kennedy, D-Mass., chairman of the Senate Health, Education, Labor, and Pensions Committee, who negotiated the final version with his son, Rep. Patrick Kennedy, D-R.I., who was the lead sponsor of the House version of the bill. The younger Kennedy had struggled publicly with substance abuse issues.

CHIP Reauthorization

Fresh from taking over Congress for the first time in twelve years, Democrats attempted an ambitious expansion of the State Children's Health Insurance Program (CHIP) in 2007, sparking the most contentious health care debate of the year. President George W. Bush fought them every step of the way, vetoing one bill (HR 976) in October and another (HR 3963) in December. Democrats lacked the votes to override the vetoes, and in the end they settled for a long-term extension.

CHIP was established in 1997 (PL 105-33) to provide health care to low-income children whose parents could not afford private insurance but were not poor enough to qualify for Medicaid. The federal government provided grants while the states administered the program and matched a portion of the grant money. *(1997 law, Congress and the Nation Vol. X, p. 432)*

States had considerable flexibility to create their own eligibility requirements for the program. According to the Congressional Budget Office (CBO), about half the states set their eligibility thresholds at 200 percent of the poverty level in 2006, fifteen states set the threshold above 200 percent, and nine states set it below that level. About 6.6 million children were covered by CHIP during some portion of 2006.

Democratic leaders made expanding CHIP a top priority in the 110th Congress. They argued that an additional six million uninsured children beyond those already being served were eligible for CHIP or Medicaid but were not enrolled in either program. By expanding income eligibility and authorizing more funding for the program, they hoped to take a significant step toward their goal of insuring all children whose parents could not afford private health insurance.

Bush and congressional Republicans warned that the campaign was an effort to move the country toward a government-run health care system. They cited efforts to cover adults, as well as children of families earning three times the poverty level, as evidence that the Democratic majority wanted to expand the program far beyond the goal of insuring low-income children.

In his fiscal 2008 budget, Bush called for increasing CHIP funding by $5 billion over five years, to $30 billion, a proposal that Democrats and the CBO said would not even keep up with inflation and would result in some children losing coverage. Democrats made room in their budget resolution (S Con Res 21) for a $50 billion expansion that would bring total spending on CHIP to $75 billion over five years.

The House and Senate each passed CHIP legislation in August. The Senate bill, which passed with eighteen Republicans voting "yea," was a relatively narrow measure that called for a $35 billion expansion of the program over five years, paid for mainly with a 61 cents-a-pack boost in the federal tax on cigarettes.

The House voted largely along party lines in favor of a far broader bill that combined a $47.8 billion CHIP expansion with substantial cuts to Medicare Advantage, a program created under the 2003 Medicare prescription drug law (PL 108-173) in which private insurers, not the government, provided benefits to seniors. The savings were used mainly to pay for reversing a scheduled reduction in Medicare reimbursement rates for physicians, which doctors and their powerful trade association, the American Medical Association, lobbied for annually. The bill also included a smaller, 45 cents-a-pack increase in the cigarette tax. *(2003 law, Congress and the Nation Vol. XI, p. 496)*

Tobacco companies, led by Altria Group, mounted a broad grass-roots lobbying effort against the bills, urging smokers to call their representative to complain about the financing mechanism, even though the original CHIP law was also paid for with a tobacco tax increase.

Lawmakers sent Bush a version of the bill in September that reflected the Senate measure, and he promptly vetoed it. After an override attempt in the House failed, Democrats made a second try. In November they sent Bush a revised bill they hoped would garner enough additional GOP support to produce the necessary override supermajority. But when Bush vetoed the second bill, Democrats put off a vote until 2008, when they came no closer to an override.

LEGISLATIVE ACTION: FIRST BILL

House Committee Action

House Democratic leaders wrote their bill without Republican input. Energy and Commerce chairman John D. Dingell, D-Mich., said he was not inclined to work with Republicans on the legislation after House GOP leaders said they would back a presidential veto. Frustrated at being shut out of negotiations, Republicans on July 26, 2007, forced clerks in both the Energy and Commerce Committee and the Ways and Means Committee to read the enormous bill aloud for hours. The tactic slowed action but did not derail the legislation, which Ways and Means managed to send to the floor.

Energy and Commerce. The committee worked late into the evening on July 26 and for almost eight hours the next day, but it never got beyond the reading of the 495-page bill and a massive substitute amendment. Dingell finally ended the deadlock by adjourning, leaving panel members to raise any issues they may have in the Rules Committee and on the House floor. Lawmakers and staff stood to applaud the committee clerk who undertook the marathon reading chore.

Ways and Means. The Ways and Means Committee approved the bill (HR 3162) on a 24–17 party-line vote early on the morning of July 27, 2007, and formally reported it (H Rept 110-284, Part I) on Aug. 1.

The main elements of the bill included the following.

- An expansion of CHIP that was estimated to cost $47.8 billion over five years and $159.9 billion over ten years.
- A reversal of cuts in Medicare physician reimbursement rates that were scheduled to take effect Jan. 1, 2008. The cost was $20.1 billion over five years and $101 billion over ten years. The bill also included new Medicare subsidies for low-income seniors.
- A 45 cents-a-pack increase in the federal tax on cigarettes, bringing the tax to 84 cents per pack. Together with some small changes in other taxes, the revenue was estimated at $28.9 billion over five years and $59.7 billion over ten years.
- Cuts in spending for Medicare Advantage, a program championed by Republicans but criticized by many Democrats. CBO said the private health plans were paid about 12 percent more per beneficiary than traditional Medicare would have cost to provide the same services. The Medicare Advantage cuts were estimated to save $50.2 billion over five years and $157 billion over ten years.

Together with the tobacco tax increase, the cuts were enough to pay for both the CHIP expansion and the reversal of the scheduled cuts in Medicare reimbursements for doctors at least over the first years. CBO said the plan would reduce deficits by $1.4 billion in the five-year period but increase them by $72.9 billion over ten years.

Ranking Republican Jim McCrery of Louisiana complained that the GOP had few opportunities to make meaningful contributions to the bill. Committee Republicans objected to waiving the bill's reading, so committee staff read aloud the first 152 pages for more than two hours. Once the panel finally began considering amendments, GOP efforts to alter the bill piece by piece were defeated wholesale.

The committee

- Rejected by voice vote an amendment by Jim Ramstad, R-Minn., to redefine Medicare Chronic Care Special Needs Plans, a program used by very sick patients with certain conditions.
- Rejected on a 14–21 party-line vote an amendment aimed at sparing Medicare Advantage plans from payment cuts. The proposal, by Phil English, R-Pa., would have allowed the Department of Health and Human Services to set county-by-county payment levels for Medicare Advantage plans.
- Rejected 16–23 a proposal by Ron Lewis, R-Ky., to strip out the proposed tobacco tax increase. He pleaded with Democrats not to hurt his district's tobacco industry.

Sam Johnson, R-Texas, tried to strike a provision banning physicians from referring patients to hospitals they owned, effectively a ban on specialty hospitals. Pete Stark, D-Calif., attacked the amendment, and Johnson withdrew it.

House Floor Action

The House passed a modified version of HR 3162 by a party-line vote of 225–204 on Aug. 1. Five Republicans voted for the bill; ten Democrats opposed it, primarily because of the tobacco tax.

Democratic leaders brought the bill to the floor under a rule that automatically made several changes to meet pay-as-you-go requirements to keep the measure deficit-neutral. The budget rules, which Democrats put in place at the start of the 110th Congress, required that any expansion of mandatory programs be fully offset over both five years and ten years. CBO said the revised bill met the requirement and would reduce the deficit by $2.5 billion over five years and $100 million over ten years.

Among the changes, Democrats shaved $20.4 billion off the ten-year cost by eliminating bonus payments to states for enrolling more children in CHIP after five years. Together with some smaller reductions, that brought the cost of the expansion to $127.8 billion. They saved an additional $35.7 billion over ten years by reducing Medicare physician payments, money that was likely to be restored later. The bill sought an increase in physician payments over the following two years.

Other offsets came from minor changes to CHIP, including the imposition of new age limits that would save $3.6 billion. Democrats also added a provision that would bar CHIP payments to illegal immigrants.

Before the vote on passage, Republicans offered a motion to recommit the bill that would have scrapped the provisions and replaced them with a one-year extension of the existing program. The House defeated the motion 202–226 on Aug. 1.

Senate Committee Action

The Senate Finance Committee endorsed a narrower, bipartisan bill (S 1893—no written report) by a vote of 17–4 on July 19. The legislation was negotiated by a small group of committee members who met privately for months trying to determine how large an expansion they could agree on and how to pay for it. Finance chairman Max Baucus, D-Mont., was finally able to produce a consensus bill, cosponsored by Republicans Charles E. Grassley of Iowa and Orrin G. Hatch of Utah.

The bill limited the CHIP expansion, capped eligibility at three times the federal poverty level, and phased out coverage of most adults, a practice increasingly allowed by the Bush administration but criticized by Grassley and other Republicans. The expansion was expected to cost $35.2 billion over five years and $71 billion over ten years, paid for by a larger boost in the tobacco tax than the House wanted. The tax, which would go up by 61 cents to $1 per pack, was expected to generate $35.7 billion over five years and $71.7 billion over ten years.

"It's obscene that millions of kids go to bed at night without decent health care," said Democrat Ron Wyden of Oregon. "These aren't poor kids that go to bed without health coverage," responded Republican Jon Kyl of Arizona, who noted that families earning up to about $82,000 a year could be covered under CHIP, which was true in New York State, which had proposed an income eligibility threshold of 400 percent of poverty level.

Senior Finance Republicans, including Grassley, criticized the administration's veto threat, saying at a news conference after the markup that the White House should recognize that the committee's bill "is good policy."

Senate Floor Action

To get around the requirement that tax bills originate in the House, Senate leaders used a House-passed small-business tax measure (HR 976) as a shell and inserted the language of S 1893. The Senate passed HR 976 by 68–31 on Aug. 2. CBO said the budget effects were the same as for the committee version.

Grassley said he planned to ask for a meeting with Bush to try to persuade him not to veto the bill. Many Republicans feared a political backlash for opposing a CHIP expansion but also were upset that the program had been used in some states to cover adults and children in families with incomes three or four times the federal poverty level. Senate minority whip Trent Lott, R-Miss., acknowledged that a veto override was possible but only if negotiators accepted the lower spending total in the Senate bill.

Democrats dispensed with several GOP attempts to modify the Finance Committee bill. During the floor debate, the Senate

- Rejected 32–64 on Aug. 1 an amendment by Elizabeth Dole, R-N.C., to create a new budget point of order, requiring sixty votes to overcome, against increases in excise taxes such as those on tobacco.
- Rejected 35–61 on Aug. 1 an alternative CHIP reauthorization by Lott and Minority Leader Mitch McConnell, R-Ky. It expanded CHIP to nearly $35 billion over five years, which they said would allow about 1.3 million more children to be covered by the program. Costs were offset by reducing federal reimbursements for administration expenses in the program and by health insurance proposals, including a long-debated proposal to allow small businesses to band together across state lines to purchase health insurance plans.
- Rejected 39–60 on Aug. 2 an amendment by Lindsey Graham, R-S.C., to sunset the tax increase on tobacco products on Sept. 30, 2012.
- Rejected 43–55 on Aug. 2 an amendment by John Ensign, R-Nev., to prohibit a state from using CHIP funds for nonpregnant adults until it enrolled at least 95 percent of low-income children.

- Rejected 37–62 on Aug. 2 an amendment by Kyl to prohibit the legislation from taking effect until the Congressional Budget Office certified that the bill would not reduce private health insurance coverage by more than 20 percent.
- Rejected 37–62 on Aug. 2 an amendment by Tom Coburn, R-Okla., to require states to charge a premium subsidy for children and pregnant women whose family incomes exceeded 200 percent of the poverty line and who had access to cost-effective employer-sponsored coverage.
- Rejected 35–64 on Aug. 2 an amendment by David Vitter, R-La., to make individuals with employer-sponsored health coverage ineligible for CHIP.
- Rejected 21–78 on Aug. 2 an amendment by Kay Bailey Hutchison, R-Texas, to limit the proposed expansion of eligibility in high-cost areas to those whose family income did not exceed 200 percent of the poverty line as based on cost-of-living adjustments for the state. It also would have allowed the health and human services secretary to adjust the poverty line on a county-by-county basis.

Final Action

Senate Republicans prevented a formal conference on the measure out of concern that Medicare changes might remain in the conference report. In informal negotiations, House Democrats agreed to accept legislation substantially similar to the Finance Committee bill, with a 61 cents-a-pack cigarette tax increase and no Medicare provisions.

On Sept. 25, the House took up HR 976 as amended by the Senate and agreed 265–159 to substitute the negotiated compromise. The Senate cleared the measure 67–29 on Sept. 27. While the Senate tally was sufficient to override Bush's promised veto, the House vote was nineteen votes shy of the two-thirds majority that was required.

CBO said the proposed expansion of CHIP would cost $36.3 billion over five years, bringing the total cost for the program to $55.9 billion. The expansion would cost $72.8 billion over ten years, bringing the overall cost of the program to $83.4 billion. The cigarette tax more than paid for the expansion, leaving surpluses of $1.4 billion over five years and $1.3 billion over ten years.

Dropped from the bill were the House-passed provisions on physicians' payments, Medicaid and Medicare revisions, and the substantial cuts proposed for Medicare Advantage. The final bill also did not include an option in the House bill for states to provide coverage under Medicaid and CHIP for the children of legal immigrants.

"I think it's basically a very good bill," said Hatch, who helped negotiate the compromise. But agreeing to what was essentially a Senate bill represented a major concession for House Democrats, and many of them were not pleased. Ways and Means chairman Charles B. Rangel, D-N.Y., said Senate Republicans controlled the outcome because of the sixty votes needed to stop a filibuster.

At a Sept. 21 news conference, the day before the agreement was announced, Bush blasted the compromise and again vowed to veto the measure. He said that it would "move millions of American children who now have private health insurance into government-run health care" and would raise taxes on "working people." The plan, he said, would turn a program meant to help poor children into "one that covers children in households with incomes of up to $83,000 a year." Bush called the CHIP expansion "a step toward federalization of health care," and he accused members of Congress of "putting health coverage for poor children at risk so they can score political points in Washington."

Republicans who supported the compromise reacted angrily. "The president has been served wrong information about what our bill would do," said Grassley, one of the negotiators. Grassley noted in particular the statement that families earning up to $83,000 would be able to enroll their children in CHIP, a claim the negotiators said was not true. Under existing law, the president could authorize states to use CHIP to cover families earning $83,000, but Bush had declined to do so. The bill did not change that procedure and sought to discourage states from expanding CHIP to families making three times the federal poverty level or more, $61,950 for a family of four.

Presidential Veto

As he had threatened to do for months, Bush vetoed HR 976 on Oct. 3, 2007. House Democratic leaders delayed an override vote in an effort to allow interest groups to build pressure on Republicans to support the bill. But the lobbying push, featuring television ads criticizing GOP members considered vulnerable in 2008, did not work. On Oct. 18, the House rejected the attempt to override the veto on a **key vote of 273–156 (R 44–154; D 229–2).** A two-thirds majority of those present and voting (286 in this case) is required to override a veto. *(2007 key votes, p. 955; Veto message, p. 1064)*

LEGISLATIVE ACTION: SECOND TRY

House Floor Action

House and Senate Democrats drew up a second bill (HR 3963—no written report), with changes intended to draw enough new GOP votes in the House to override a veto. But Democrats did not consult with House Republican leaders on the new bill, and it ultimately drew less GOP support than the first one. The Oct. 25 vote on passage was 265–142.

Bush said he would veto the rewrite. A White House statement said the new bill "has not addressed in a meaningful way the objections that caused the president to veto" the earlier legislation. Democrats insisted they had addressed all major GOP complaints about the vetoed version of the bill: that it could allow wealthy families, illegal immigrants, and adults to enroll in a program intended for poor children. "Those who vote against today's legislation can only be voting against the government providing health care to poor children who have no other means of obtaining medical care," said Stark, the chairman of the Ways and Means Health Subcommittee. "That's the only reason left to vote against this."

In most areas, HR 976 and HR 3963 were nearly identical. The revised bill provided for a five-year, $35.4 billion expansion of CHIP ($71.5 billion over ten years). It was financed mainly by a 61 cents-a-pack boost in the cigarette tax, for total revenue of $36.3 billion over five years ($72.8 billion over ten years). CBO said the bill would reduce the deficit by $900 million over five years ($1.3 billion over ten years).

In the most substantive change, the new bill limited CHIP eligibility to families earning at or less than three times the federal poverty level, about $62,000 for a family of four. But Republicans said that states would be able to evade that cap by disregarding some income, such as money parents spent on housing or transportation, for the purpose of calculating eligibility.

The new bill also was expected to result in slightly fewer children enrolling in CHIP and slightly more enrolling in Medicaid. That was because it would limit the bonus payments that states could have earned under the vetoed bill for increasing enrollment in CHIP and Medicaid. Under the new bill, states would receive the bonuses only for enrolling more children in Medicaid. The change was a response to the GOP criticism that the earlier bill did not focus on poor children.

Other changes in the revised bill were largely cosmetic, one reason that it did not attract more Republicans. The measure had no substantive new provisions to prevent families from dropping private insurance to enroll in CHIP. Instead, it offered states an incentive to help low-income people with private insurance pay their premiums. If they did, the states might collect bonuses from the government. CBO estimated that both bills would lead about two million families to drop or forgo private insurance to enroll in public programs.

Republicans complained about the haste with which Democrats brought the bill to the floor. It was introduced the evening before it came to the floor and immediately sent to the Rules Committee, which allowed no amendments. Democrats said they had to hurry passage because a temporary extension of CHIP (H J Res 52—PL 110-92) that provided funding in the first weeks of fiscal 2008 was due to expire Nov. 16, 2007.

Senate Floor Action

The Senate passed HR 3963 by a vote of 64–30 on Nov. 1, completing congressional action. Before the vote, Majority Leader Harry Reid, D-Nev., said there would be no rush on an override vote, and Baucus agreed. Baucus and other Senate leaders, including Grassley, still believed they could force a slightly modified bill into law by reaching a deal with House Republicans. Both sides had been working toward a deal when McConnell objected to allowing more time for the talks. That forced an end to debate and led to a vote on the existing bill. Reid told the negotiators that he still wanted a piece of legislation, no matter what happened to HR 3963, and that House Speaker Nancy Pelosi, D-Calif., had indicated the House would take up a bill if a deal were reached.

Bush vetoed HR 3963 on Dec. 12, citing the price tag and reiterating that the proposal would "move children who already have private health insurance to government coverage." He also opposed raising tobacco taxes to pay for the expansion.

Instead of holding an override vote immediately, the House voted Dec. 12 to postpone it until Jan. 23, 2008. The motion was agreed to 211–180 although House GOP leaders condemned the move.

In the meantime, CHIP had been operating under a temporary authorization, which was set to expire Dec. 14, 2007. Congress extended it for another week under a new continuing resolution (H J Res 69—PL 110-137) that was good through Dec. 21.

Democrats and their Senate Republican allies had been in intense negotiations with House Republicans for more than a month in an effort to create a third CHIP bill that might draw a dozen or so new House Republican votes, the margin Democrats thought they needed to override Bush's veto. Republicans said they would not support an expansion unless it focused on enrolling children from families earning less than twice the federal poverty level, or about $41,000 for a family of four, and included strong prohibitions against enrolling any adults or illegal immigrants in the program.

The earlier bill did not cap eligibility, but it allowed states to serve children from families earning more than three times the poverty level if the state met certain conditions to make sure that poorer children were being served. States and child advocates wanted any long-term extension to include extra money to help states facing shortfalls. There were twenty-one such states, according to the Congressional Research Service (CRS), and they were going to start running out of money in March 2008. They faced shortfalls totaling $1.6 billion in fiscal 2008, CRS said.

Temporary Fix

Congress dispensed with two contentious health care issues before adjournment, extending CHIP funding through March 31, 2009, and blocking the scheduled Medicare reduction for physicians. The bare-bones measure (S 2499—PL 110-173) passed the Senate by voice vote Dec. 18. The House passed it under suspension of the rules by 411–3 the next day, completing congressional action. Bush signed HR 2499 into law Dec. 29.

Written by leaders of the Senate Finance Committee, the bill was designed to be narrow and noncontroversial to secure the president's signature. The committee said the measure would provide enough for states to continue serving their existing enrollment levels, about six million people. The bill also provided a temporary patch to prevent a scheduled 10 percent cut in pay to Medicare doctors in 2008. Instead, physicians received a 0.5 percent increase in their Medicare reimbursements for six months.

Spending in the package totaled $5.3 billion over five years, according to CBO. The cost was offset by cuts to other Medicare programs, including $1.5 billion from a stabilization fund for privately run Medicare plans and $1.4 billion in payments to hospitals for inpatient rehabilitation services. An additional $1 billion came from reducing payments for drugs administered directly by doctors instead of taken at home by patients.

POSTSCRIPT

The House waited until 2008 to hold an override vote on HR 3963. As expected, the attempt failed 260–152 on Jan. 23, fifteen votes short of the two-thirds majority required.

Most Republicans opposed the bill, as they had HR 976. They argued variously that the legislation would be too costly, that it would raise tobacco taxes too much, that it would draw too many middle-income families out of private insurance, that it would allow CHIP to continue covering adults, and that it would allow illegal immigrants to enroll in the program. A statement from the White House called the legislation "misguided," saying it "would have expanded CHIP to higher-income households while increasing taxes."

FDA Overhaul

Congress in 2007 cleared the largest expansion of Food and Drug Administration (FDA) regulatory powers in a decade, with the goal of bolstering the agency's monitoring of prescription drugs and medical devices. President George W. Bush signed the measure into law Sept. 27 (HR 3580—PL 110-85). *(1997 FDA overhaul, Congress and the Nation Vol. X, p. 444)*

The bill expanded labeling, tightened the regulation of drug advertising, and gave consumers access to information on clinical trials of drugs and medical devices. It allowed the FDA to require re-labeling and even new clinical trials for drugs after they had gone on the market if new safety issues arose. Enactment marked a success for the Democratic majority, which had been pressing all summer to complete action on the measure.

The cornerstone of the legislation was a five-year reauthorization of the 1992 Prescription Drug User Fee Act (PL 102-571), which required drug companies to pay fees to the FDA to expedite the agency's review of new pharmaceutical products. Under HR 3580, the FDA was authorized to collect $393 million in fees per year from fiscal 2008 through 2012. The funding was needed to pay for staff and science resources for the drug review process. The bill was considered must-pass legislation by the drug industry, which relied on the agency's ability to expedite the review process to get products to market faster. The previous reauthorization (PL 107-188) expired Sept. 30, 2007, and if a new law had not been in place, the FDA would have had to lay off about two thousand employees. The bill also reauthorized a 2002 user fee that paid to speed the approval of medical devices (PL 107-250); that law also expired Sept. 30. *(PL 102-571, Congress and the Nation Vol. VIII, p. 603; PL 107-188, Congress and the Nation Vol. XI, p. 477; PL 107-250, Congress and the Nation Vol. XI, p. 482)*

Responding to several drug-related scandals, principally over the popular prescription painkiller Vioxx and its accompanying heart risks, Democrats also used the legislation to draft new regulations that enabled the FDA to monitor the safety of drugs after they came to market and to subject some newly approved medicines to follow-up studies and further analysis.

HIGHLIGHTS

The following are highlights of HR 3580, as enacted.

Prescription drug approval fees. The bill reauthorized the Prescription Drug User Fee Act through 2012, allowing the FDA to charge at least $393 million per year for expedited review of drug-approval applications. It authorized an additional $225 million over five years in user fees to monitor the safety of drugs after they had gone on the market. A newly created program authorized the FDA to collect fees for voluntary agency review of prescription drug direct-to-consumer television advertisements.

Medical device approval fees. The bill reauthorized a parallel program for medical devices, created by the Medical Device and User Fee Act. The FDA was authorized to collect $185 million in pre-market application fees in 2008, increasing annually until the amount reached $256 million in 2012. The bill also authorized $7 million a year for five years to review the safety of devices after they had been approved and marketed, with annual increases for inflation. A unique identifier number had to be assigned to all medical devices to help the FDA track individual devices for malfunctions.

Risk evaluation and mitigation. The FDA was given the authority to require drug companies seeking approval for new drugs to submit a tailored plan, called a risk evaluation and mitigation strategy, for determining and addressing the risks of a product, including possible steps after a drug was on the market. The FDA would have to approve the plan. The agency also could require a company to carry out a risk evaluation and mitigation plan for a previously approved drug if necessary to reduce safety risks. Among other things, the agency could require changes in product labels.

The bill set fines of up to $250,000 per violation or $1 million for several violations. A company that ignored a warning would be subject to higher fines.

Direct-to-consumer drug ads. The FDA was authorized to pre-review direct-to-consumer drug advertisements. False or misleading ads could lead to fines of up to $500,000.

Print ads for the drugs had to contain a toll-free phone number for consumers to report harmful side effects.

Clinical trials database. The bill required the creation of a public database, accessible over the Internet, where the results of clinical trials of approved products would be posted. For products in development, the company had to register information about the ongoing trial. The FDA could require additional data posting, and drug companies that did not comply could be fined.

Conflicts of interest. Experts serving on FDA advisory panels were required to disclose all financial interests that could pose a conflict. The health and human services (HHS) secretary was required to reduce the number of conflict-of-interest waivers by 5 percent per year from 2008 through 2012.

Food safety. Food producers were required to report contamination of their products to the FDA within twenty-four hours of discovering it, and the agency was directed to create a Reportable Food Registry to post safety alerts on food affecting humans or pets.

Pediatric products. The bill reauthorized the Pediatric Research Equity Act (PL 108-155), which required manufacturers of drugs and other biological products to submit assessments for pediatric use along with applications for new drugs or new uses for existing drugs. It also reauthorized the Best Pharmaceuticals for Children Act (PL 107-109), which allowed the FDA to give drug manufacturers who found new pediatric uses for a medication six additional months of marketing exclusivity for the drug, as an incentive to research new treatments for children. The bill also created new incentives for makers of medical devices to develop pediatric products. *(Pediatric drug exclusivity, Congress and the Nation Vol. XI, p. 489)*

SENATE COMMITTEE ACTION

The Senate Health, Education, Labor, and Pensions (HELP) Committee approved S 1082 (no written report), sponsored by Chairman Edward M. Kennedy, D-Mass., by a vote of 15–5 on April 18. All of the committee's Democrats supported the bill, but Republicans were split, with half of them opposing the legislation on the grounds that it would have "unintended consequences," such as delays in drug development and loss of access to drugs for patients. The bill proposed to reauthorize the prescription drug user fee at $393 million a year and to add new fees for companies that voluntarily sought review of advertisements before they were released.

The most contentious section of Kennedy's drug safety provisions was the proposed post-market evaluation, which would require FDA-approved labeling and periodic reviews of a drug's safety record after it was marketed. The bill initially would have required manufacturers to use the process for all new drugs. The version approved by the committee allowed the FDA to decide when the process would be required. It also proposed to dedicate $50 million in user fee revenue to drug safety programs, down from $70 million in previous versions.

The FDA had drawn some criticism for using the pharmaceutical industry fees to pay for a substantial part of its drug safety budget. Drug safety and consumer advocates were concerned that by relying so heavily on industry funds, the FDA created the appearance of being beholden to the manufacturers. Kennedy acknowledged a desire to reduce the FDA's reliance on industry money, but for the time being, he said, the fees were a fact of life. HHS secretary Michael O. Leavitt said developing new procedures would be a burden for the FDA and drug companies and would duplicate work the agency already did.

During the markup, the committee

- Adopted by voice vote a proposal by Sherrod Brown, D-Ohio, to require the FDA to assist the Federal Trade Commission with an investigation into so-called authorized generics, drugs licensed by brand-name drug companies to compete with generic versions of their products. (The provision was included in the final bill.)
- Adopted by voice vote a proposal by Richard M. Burr, R-N.C., to set deadlines for negotiations between the FDA and drug companies over labeling changes for drugs. Burr said his provision would ensure that a label change would take no longer than four months after problems were detected.
- Adopted 11–9 an amendment by Tom Coburn, R-Okla., to subject medical marijuana to FDA approval, including a review of its safety and efficacy. (The language was not included in the final bill.)
- Rejected on a 10–11 party-line vote an amendment by Pat Roberts, R-Kan., aimed at loosening the bill's restrictions on direct-to-consumer ads by drug companies. The bill required that all such ads be submitted for pre-review at least forty-five days before their release and allowed the HHS secretary to impose a two-year moratorium on an ad if the disclosure of the drug's risks was not adequate to ensure public safety. The amendment would have required companies to submit direct-to-consumer ads to the FDA at least forty-five days before their broadcasting. It would not have required FDA approval, but it proposed civil penalties if an ad was found to be misleading or false.

Roberts threatened to oppose the bill on the floor unless Kennedy changed the language. Opponents of the ads argued that they artificially drove up demand for drugs and interfered with the doctor-patient relationship. Foes of giving the FDA this authority said it was a First Amendment issue.

SENATE FLOOR ACTION

The Senate passed S 1082 by 93–1 on May 9 with Bernard Sanders, I-Vt., casting the only "no" vote. The issue of prescription drug imports dominated much of the debate. The White House issued a statement of administration policy threatening to veto the bill if it permitted drug importation.

The Senate May 7 adopted by voice vote an amendment by Byron L. Dorgan, D-N.D., to allow individuals, distributors, and pharmacies to import drugs from Canada, much of the European Union, New Zealand, Japan, and a handful of other countries with drug safety systems similar to that of the FDA. But a second-degree amendment by Thad Cochran, R-Miss., made Dorgan's language effectively meaningless. Cochran's amendment, adopted May 7 by a vote of 49–40, required HHS to certify the safety and cost savings of any drug imports. The Bush administration had said repeatedly that it could not do that. Vice President Dick Cheney was on hand in case he was needed to cast a tie-breaking vote on the Cochran amendment.

During the debate, the Senate also

- Adopted 94–0 on May 2 an amendment by Richard J. Durbin, D-Ill., to address food-safety concerns after contaminated pet food was found responsible for sickening and killing hundreds of cats and dogs. It proposed giving the FDA the authority to impose fines on food producers, including those that made pet food, if they failed to report food contamination promptly. It also required companies to keep food-safety records that were accessible by the FDA but did not try to give the FDA mandatory recall power over food products, which would have generated strong opposition from food producers.
- Rejected 41–53 on May 2 an amendment by Wayne Allard, R-Colo., to strike a provision that would shorten the exclusive sales agreements for pharmaceutical companies that found new pediatric uses for existing drugs. Under the bill, if a drug already had $1 billion in sales, the exclusivity limit on pediatric uses would be three months, instead of six months, as under existing law.
- Adopted fifteen amendments by voice vote May 8, the result of closed-door talks aimed at moving the bill to a vote. They included language written to appease Roberts and others who objected to the two-year moratorium on ads for certain drugs and the potential for requiring warnings on some ads. Roberts agreed to new language that would limit FDA authority to impose a maximum $150,000 fine for false or misleading ads. The FDA could fine companies $300,000 for additional violations.
- Adopted 64–30 on May 9 an amendment by Republican Charles E. Grassley of Iowa to allow increased fines against drug companies that did not comply with FDA requests to take safety steps, such as changing labels or undertaking additional studies on drugs they were selling. The minimum fine under the bill rose from $15,000 to $250,000, and the maximum fine, from $1 million to $2 million. As chairman of the Senate Finance Committee when the GOP controlled the Senate, Grassley conducted a number of investigations into the FDA's approval of drugs, including Vioxx.
- Rejected 46–47 on May 9 a Grassley amendment to give the FDA's Office of Surveillance and Epidemiology, which was responsible for monitoring drug safety, a more even footing with the Office of New Drugs, which could approve drugs and order safety restrictions once a drug was on sale.
- Rejected 47–47 on May 9 an amendment by Durbin that would have tightened conflict-of-interest rules to allow only one waiver for any advisory committee meeting. The Senate bill did not limit the number of waivers.

HOUSE SUBCOMMITTEE ACTION

The House legislation began as nine separate draft measures approved by the Energy and Commerce Health Subcommittee on June 19.

During the markup, Edolphus Towns, D-N.Y., led a rebellion against Chairman Frank Pallone Jr., D-N.J., gutting tough restrictions on direct-to-consumer prescription drug advertising. The subcommittee adopted 23–9 a Towns amendment that relied on fines and voluntary ad reviews by the FDA.

The original provisions would have given the FDA the discretion to ban a direct-to-consumer ad for up to three years. The Towns amendment struck that language and instead allowed the FDA to review an advertisement in question and make a determination about its truthfulness. If the agency found the ad to be "false or misleading," it could impose a penalty of up to $250,000 for the first offense and $500,000 for each repeated violation within three years.

Towns was joined by fellow New York Democrats Anthony Weiner and Eliot L. Engel in leading the split from Pallone and California Democrat Henry A. Waxman, the author of much of the ad provision. The New Yorkers and six other Democrats voted with Republicans.

Much of the rhetoric centered on First Amendment concerns, but the New Yorkers also stressed the importance of the issue to their state's economy. "The networks are all located in New York; the advertisers are all located in New York," said Engel. "It's a big hometown industry."

The amendment was one of the few substantial changes approved during the daylong markup.

Risk evaluation and mitigation strategies. Like the Senate bill, the measure proposed a new program that would give the FDA the authority to require expanded risk-management plans for drugs. Newly approved drugs could be subject to follow-up studies after they went to market, and the FDA would be required to revisit the drugs several years later for further analysis. Exceptions would be made in the case of a public health emergency.

Drug manufacturers could be fined $20 million for a single violation of the requirements, up to a $100 million maximum. The drug safety programs would be funded largely by $225 million in new user fees assessed to drug manufacturers.

The panel rejected 13–17 an attempt by ranking Republican Nathan Deal of Georgia to reduce the proposed penalties for companies that failed to abide by approved risk evaluation and mitigation strategies. Deal said the "exorbitant" penalties were unprecedented and unfair. Waxman defended the provision, saying if the fines were too low, drug manufacturers would view them as a cost of doing business.

Prescription drug user fees. The fees would be reauthorized through fiscal 2012 and increased to $393 million per year. The bill also authorized $225 million in new fees over five years to pay for post-market studies of drug safety. The subcommittee

- Rejected by voice vote an attempt by Michael C. Burgess, R-Texas, to eliminate the $225 million in new fees.
- Rejected 14–18 an attempt by Deal to cut the amount from $225 million to $112.5 million over five years. Republicans wanted Congress to appropriate funds for the new drug safety program instead of collecting fees. "There is no reason to believe that in the budget process we would ever get the appropriation," Pallone responded.

Conflicts of interest. Under the bill, each advisory committee was allowed one conflict-of-interest waiver. The panel rejected by voice vote an attempt by Burgess to eliminate the restriction. Republicans and the FDA argued that the FDA needed the freedom to bring in experts, who often conducted research for the companies whose products were being considered, and that disclosure of the conflicts went far enough.

Other issues. The subcommittee also gave voice-vote approval to draft bills to reauthorize and increase user fees for review of medical devices, create a clinical trials database for drugs and medical devices, reauthorize incentives for development of pediatric medical devices, extend the FDA's authority to give drug manufacturers six months of sales exclusivity for new pediatric uses of drugs, and make permanent the requirement that drug manufacturers submit pediatric assessments when seeking approval of new drugs or new uses for existing drugs.

HOUSE COMMITTEE ACTION

On June 29, the full Energy and Commerce Committee voted 30–9 to combine the bills into a single package (HR 2900) and send it to the floor. The measure was formally reported (H Rept 110-115) on July 11. Before approving the bill, the committee

- Adopted by voice vote an amendment by Deal aimed at reducing the FDA's reliance on drug companies for the money to pay for the safety surveillance of drugs already on the market. The bipartisan amendment that Deal offered proposed to cut the $225 million by an amount equal to whatever appropriators provided. "Practically speaking, and I hate to be a cynic, but there aren't going to be any appropriations," said Edward J. Markey, D-Mass., who added that he still supported the amendment.
- Adopted by voice vote an amendment by Pallone to lower the proposed fines for violating a risk evaluation and mitigation strategy. In place of the maximum $20 million fine for a single violation and the $100 million fine for several violations approved by the subcommittee, the amendment set maximum fines of $250,000 per violation, or $1 million for several violations. If the company had been notified of its violation and yet continued, the fines could rise to $10 million for one violation or $50 million for several.
- Adopted by voice vote an amendment by Jay Inslee, D-Wash., to strike language limiting the number of times the same private inspector could be hired by a medical device company, a safeguard that Pallone said would prevent inspectors from returning positive inspections to get repeat business.
- Adopted by voice vote a manager's amendment, including a provision to require a unique identifier number for all medical devices, allowing the FDA and health care providers to better track individual devices for malfunctions and safety.

HOUSE FLOOR ACTION

The House by 403–16 on July 11 passed HR 2900, which was sponsored by John D. Dingell, D-Mich. Democratic leaders put the bill on the floor under suspension of the rules, which meant it could not be amended and needed a two-thirds majority to pass. The House-passed measure had more far-reaching drug safety provisions and stiffer fines for violators. It also had tougher conflict-of-interest rules for members of FDA advisory panels.

FINAL ACTION

With the Sept. 30 expiration date close at hand and efforts to hold a conference blocked, House and Senate negotiators agreed to a compromise and introduced the FDA overhaul legislation as a new bill (HR 3580). Joe L. Barton of Texas, the ranking Republican on the House Energy and Commerce Committee, emphasized that it was a bipartisan deal.

The House passed the measure 405–7 under suspension of the rules Sept. 19. Senate majority leader Harry Reid, D-Nev., attempted to pass it by voice vote the same day but was blocked by several Republicans who wanted more time to study the 422-page measure. The Senate cleared the bill by voice vote Sept. 20.

Staff from the Senate HELP panel and the House Energy and Commerce Committee had been working to reach a compromise before the August recess. But a spokesman for Michael B. Enzi of Wyoming, the ranking Republican on HELP, said Waxman was pushing to include the database of drug manufacturers' clinical trials and their results, and that this and other demands had stalled negotiations.

At the same time, Senate lawmakers were pushing for inclusion of language (S 1695) that would create a pathway for the approval of generic biotech drugs, also known as "biogenerics" or "follow-on biologics." The HELP Committee had approved the biotech bill June 27, with tepid support from the industry. House Democrats, led by Dingell, had planned to hold hearings on their own legislation in the fall and were not inclined to include it in the conference report.

Among the compromises in the final bill were the following.

Penalties. The final measure mirrored both bills in setting fines for companies that violated the new drug safety regulations at $250,000 per violation or $1 million for several violations. Companies that continued the violation despite notification faced maximum fines of $1 million for a single prolonged violation or $10 million for several violations. The Senate had no higher fines after notification; the House bill called for maximums of $10 million and $50 million.

Direct-to-consumer ads. The FDA could review drug ads and fine companies for false or misleading ads but could not ban them, even temporarily. The final bill included the stiffer House fines of $250,000 for the first violation, with fines for subsequent violations not to exceed $500,000 each. The Senate bill would have authorized fines of up to $150,000 for a first violation and up to $300,000 for subsequent violations.

Conflicts of interest. The House bill had a limit of one waiver for each advisory committee meeting. The Senate bill largely would have preserved existing law, which did not limit waivers. Instead of specifying the number of allowable waivers, the final bill required the FDA to reduce gradually the percentage of waivers, compared with a baseline of 2007.

Clinical trial database. House Democrats won inclusion of the provision sought by Waxman to create a public, searchable database of clinical trials for drugs and medical devices. It was to include information on safety risks and would be administered by the National Institutes of Health.

Exclusivity for pediatric drugs. Drug manufacturers that conducted studies on new pediatric uses of drugs were granted six additional months of market exclusivity. In the Senate version, so-called blockbuster drugs would have been given only three months of exclusivity. A similar provision was struck from the House bill in subcommittee.

Drug company liability. The measure did not include language in the Senate bill that would have made it more difficult for consumers to sue drug companies for failure to provide timely safety alerts on marketed drugs. The Senate version would have required the FDA to approve any such safety alerts, thereby removing the drug companies as a focus of such suits.

Even the bill's strongest advocates in the Senate were not entirely happy. "This is not a perfect bill, and compromises were made to assure its passage," Kennedy said. "But after so many recent instances in which Americans have been harmed by unsafe prescription drugs and contaminated food," he added, "America cannot afford inaction on this important measure."

MAJOR PROVISIONS

Following are major provisions of the overhaul of the Food and Drug Administration that President Bush signed into law (HR 3580—PL 110-85) on Sept. 27, 2007.

Drug and Device Fees

Drug approval user fees. The bill reauthorized the Prescription Drug User Fee Act, which allowed the FDA to charge drug companies user fees in exchange for expedited reviews of new products. The bill authorized $393 million annually in fees in fiscal 2008 through 2012. The previous reauthorization expired Sept. 30, 2007.

Under existing patent law, a new drug or device's patent life begins when it is invented and subsequently patented, not when the FDA approves it. Faster FDA approval meant the company gained several months of exclusive sales before the patent ran out and generics manufacturers drove down prices. As a result, drug companies were willing to pay the fees even though they added to drug development costs.

Medical device approval user fees. Device companies operated under a similar law, the Medical Device User Fee and Modernization Act, which also expired Sept. 30, 2007, and was reauthorized under the bill. Manufacturers were required to pay $185,000 per application in 2008, increasing annually to $256,000 per application in 2012.

Drug safety fees. Drug and device companies were required to pay a new user fee to finance FDA drug and device safety operations. Drug companies were required to pay a total of $225 million in fiscal 2008 through 2012. Device makers were required to pay a total of $35 million over the same period. The new fees were to be used to study drugs once they were on the market and being taken by far larger numbers of patients than in the pre-approval clinical trials typically conducted by drug manufacturers.

Drug and Device Regulations

Post-approval studies. In addition to conducting its own drug safety activities, the FDA was authorized to require pharmaceutical companies to conduct post-approval safety studies on new medications, including those already on the market. The post-market studies were designed to test for risks that become evident only after large numbers of patients had taken a drug for an extended period of time and that may not have been found in earlier clinical trials. The health and human services secretary may also require additional clinical trials, but only after finding that the studies were not sufficient to assess serious potential risks.

Risk evaluation and mitigation strategies. Under the bill, the FDA could require drug companies seeking approval of a new drug to submit a plan, known as a risk evaluation and mitigation strategy, for continued review of what the agency considered higher-risk drugs after they are on the market. Drug manufacturers could be required to conduct post-market studies and engage in enhanced communication with doctors about drug effects. Doctors and pharmacists could be required to have special training before prescribing or dispensing the drug.

Drug-labeling changes. The FDA was given new authority to require labeling changes to drugs if important new safety information becomes available. Previously, labeling changes were up to the discretion of the drug company.

Penalties. Drug manufacturers that failed to comply with the new regulations could be fined up to $250,000 per violation, or $1 million for several violations adjudicated at one time. A company notified of its violations and continues them could be fined up to $250,000 for the first thirty-day period. The fine could then be doubled for every additional thirty-day period that the violations continue, up to a maximum of $1 million for a single violation or $10 million for several violations adjudicated during a single disciplinary proceeding.

Medical device identifiers. The bill required the FDA to create a unique identifier number for all medical devices to better track individual devices for malfunctions.

Clinical trials database. The FDA is directed to keep a publicly available registry of clinical trials being conducted by drug and device makers, with information detailing the purpose, methods, and results of each trial. The data would be publicly searchable and would include information about "adverse events," that is, serious drug or device actions that resulted in patient harm during the trial.

Advertising

Direct-to-consumer ads. The FDA was authorized to pre-review drug companies' direct-to-consumer ads, which had become increasingly common on television and radio and in print. The agency could suggest changes to the ads but could not require those changes. Companies and advertisers responsible for "false or misleading" ads would be subject to fines.

Penalties. The agency was authorized to assess fines of up to $250,000 for the first violation in a three-year period and up to $500,000 for each subsequent violation during the same period. Each day an ad was run counted as a single violation. In the case of weekly or monthly print publications, each issue of the publication would count as a single violation.

New fees. The FDA was authorized to charge fees for reviewing direct-to-consumer television ads sufficient to generate $6.2 million per year in fiscal 2008 through 2012, with adjustments for inflation. The fee for a single ad could not exceed $83,000 in fiscal 2008, with the amount adjusted for inflation each year after that.

Print ads. Direct-to-consumer print ads were required to feature a toll-free number to report drug side effects to the FDA. The FDA was required to issue a report within six months on whether the number should be included in television advertisements and, if so, to issue regulations requiring it.

Conflicts of Interest

Disclosure. An individual under consideration for an appointment to an advisory committee was required to disclose all financial interests related to any drug or medical product the committee might review.

Prohibitions. Advisory committee members were prohibited from participating in committee meetings if they had financial interests that could be affected by the outcome of the meetings.

Waivers. An advisory committee member whose expertise was needed could be given a waiver to participate in the meeting. However, the FDA was required to decrease the number of conflict-of-interest waivers by 5 percent each year from fiscal 2008 through 2012, using as a base the number of waivers allowed in 2007. Waivers were required to be made public at least fifteen days before the meeting of the advisory committee and to be posted on the Internet.

Pediatric Drugs and Devices

Pediatric drug research. The bill reauthorized the Pediatric Research Equity Act through 2012. The act required drug manufacturers that submit applications to market a new active ingredient, dosage, or usage to also submit a pediatric assessment. The assessments were required to contain information on how the drug could be used in pediatric populations, along with any safety and efficacy issues. In some cases, drug companies could request a waiver for those requirements.

Pediatric drug incentives. To encourage drug companies to develop new pediatric uses for drugs, the FDA was authorized to grant six months of market exclusivity to new drugs or existing drugs that were newly approved for pediatric use.

Medical devices. The bill authorized grants to encourage medical device manufacturers to develop pediatric equipment.

Food Safety

Pet food. Within two years of enactment, pet food makers would be subject to new standards for ingredients, processing, and labeling. Within one year, the FDA was required to establish an early warning and notification system for adulterated pet food.

Food registry. The FDA was required to create a Reportable Food Registry to issue alerts to the public about contaminated human or pet food. Food producers were required to report any cases of contamination to the agency within twenty-four hours.

Other Provisions

Reagan-Udall Foundation. The law established a foundation to further the FDA's mission of improving the safety of medical devices, cosmetics, and food and to explore unmet needs in the development, manufacture, and evaluation of medical products, including diagnostics, drugs, and biologics. The not-for-profit foundation was to be funded with FDA money as well as private grants.

Mental Health Parity

After more than a decade of effort, Congress in 2008 cleared a bill requiring that mental health and addiction benefits be equal in cost and scope to traditional medical benefits. The measure, which became the vehicle for the financial sector rescue package, was signed into law Oct. 3 (HR 1424—PL 110-343). *(Financial bailout, p. 154)*

Some, but not all, insurers offered equal benefits for mental health, and mental health advocates argued that patients needing treatment often had to pay higher co-payments and face stricter treatment limits and restrictions on out-of-network coverage. HR 1424 did not require health plans to offer mental health benefits. It applied only to plans that offered both those benefits and traditional health services.

The bill was named after Sens. Paul Wellstone, D-Minn., and Pete V. Domenici, R-N.M., early advocates of mental health parity legislation. In 1996 they won enactment of the Mental Health Parity Act, which was folded into the fiscal 1997 Veterans Affairs–Housing and Urban Development appropriations law (PL 104-204). That legislation prohibited group health plans and health insurance issuers from imposing annual and lifetime dollar limits on mental health coverage that were more restrictive than limits imposed on medical and surgical coverage. *(1996 action, Congress and the Nation Vol. IX, p. 565)*

The original law, however, did not apply to substance abuse and did not bar group health plans from limiting the number of inpatient treatment days, visits to doctors' offices, or charging higher co-payments for those benefits. After Wellstone died in 2002, Domenici—joined by Sen. Edward M. Kennedy, D-Mass.—continued trying to expand the parity requirements.

On the House side, the campaign was led by Patrick J. Kennedy, D-R.I., the senator's son, and Jim Ramstad, R-Minn. Both Kennedy and Ramstad were recovering addiction patients.

Throughout much of the 110th Congress, supporters of parity legislation were locked in disagreement over how specific to be in setting requirements for insurers.

The Senate passed a mental health parity bill (S 558) in September 2007 that was the result of almost two years of meetings and negotiations led by Domenici and Kennedy that involved senators, insurance and business groups, and mental health advocates. The parties found common ground in part by not trying to specify precisely which mental illnesses would be covered under the bill.

Kennedy and his Senate colleagues argued that they had put together the only package that could win the endorsement of these powerful lobbies and that the House should back it. Kennedy's son disagreed. Years of struggle with his own personal issues had convinced him that mental health and addiction patients needed stronger protections than the Senate bill afforded. The younger Kennedy also won the backing of the late senator Wellstone's son, David, who became a tireless lobbyist for the bill.

Patrick Kennedy and Ramstad worked persistently to bring a bill (HR 1424) to the House floor that would require insurers offering mental health benefits to cover a specific list of disorders outlined by the American Psychiatric Association. Business and health insurance lobbyists opposed the bill, arguing that it would impose heavy mandates on health plans, add to their costs, and discourage them from offering mental health and substance abuse benefits at all. A number of senators also were adamantly opposed to it.

Nevertheless, Kennedy in 2007 guided the measure through a legislative gauntlet of subcommittee and committee markups. At each step, he and his supporters fended off GOP attempts to replace the text of the bill with the Senate version. In March 2008, Kennedy won easy House passage for the bill, forcing senators to reconsider their unwillingness to negotiate.

Over the next several months, the two sides negotiated a compromise, even while the elder Kennedy began undergoing treatment for brain cancer. Patrick Kennedy had to give up on requiring that specific conditions be covered, but the compromise set up studies to make sure certain conditions were not left out. Unlike the Senate bill, it did not preclude more stringent state parity laws.

With the policy compromise in place, supporters turned to finding a vehicle that would carry the plan into law. In September the House passed a new version of the bill (HR 6983) that encompassed the compromises. The Senate added the language to a tax package (HR 6049), which it passed the same day. In the end, the Senate used HR 1424 as a vehicle for a financial sector bailout package that also included the tax provisions and the mental health language.

MAJOR PROVISIONS

The following are major provisions of the parity law.

Financial requirements. Prohibited group health plans that offered medical and surgical benefits from imposing more restrictive financial requirements, such as deductibles, co-payments, and out-of-pocket expenses, for mental health and addiction care than for other services.

Treatment limitations. Specified that limits set by insurers on the scope or duration of coverage for mental health and drug addiction could not be more restrictive than those for other care, and there could not be separate treatment limits, including limits on the frequency of treatment, the number of visits, and the number of days of treatment covered.

Covered conditions. Required the Government Accountability Office to send Congress two follow-up studies analyzing how insurers were covering mental health and substance abuse services, whether they were excluding coverage for specific diagnoses, and whether the new law affected trends in mental health and drug abuse benefits. (The law did not specify what conditions insurers that offered mental health or drug addiction benefits had to cover. As before, those decisions were left to insurers.)

Out-of-network coverage. Required insurance plans that provided coverage for medical or surgical services from out-of-network providers to provide the same coverage for out-of-network mental health and substance abuse services. Required the benefits for those conditions to be just as generous as the medical and surgical benefits, without higher co-pays or cost-sharing.

Notification. Specified that the beneficiary had the right to be notified of the reason for being denied mental health or substance abuse benefits.

Small business exemption. Exempted from the rules group health plans for companies with no more than fifty employees.

Cost exemption. Exempted a group health plan if implementing the parity requirements would increase the combined one-year cost of coverage for traditional and mental health and substance abuse services by more than 2 percent in the first year and 1 percent in the second year. Specified that the exemption would occur in the year after the cost increase. Required the increase to be determined and certified by a licensed actuary, and authorized the Department of Health and Human Services (HHS) to audit the books of a health plan claiming the exemption.

No state preemption. Did not preempt stricter state mental health parity laws.

Compliance. Required the HHS secretary to report to Congress every two years starting in 2012 on health plans' compliance with the law.

Cost. The Joint Committee on Taxation estimated that the act would result in a loss of $3.9 billion in federal income and payroll taxes over ten years because employees would get more of their compensation in the form of nontaxable employer-paid premiums.

HOUSE FLOOR ACTION

The House passed Patrick Kennedy's bill (HR 1424) by a vote of 268–148 on March 5, 2008. The measure was an amalgam of the versions approved by three separate committees in 2007 and was inserted into the bill by the rule for floor debate. The House Education and Labor Committee approved the bill 33–9 on July 18 and reported it (H Rept 110-374, Part I) on Oct. 15. The House Ways and Means Committee approved the measure 27–13 on Sept. 26 and reported it (H Rept 110-374, Part II) on Oct. 15. The Energy and Commerce Committee approved HR 1424 by 32–13 on Oct. 16 and reported it (H Rept 110-374, Parat II) on March 3, 2008.

Critics in both chambers argued that Kennedy's hard line in support of his legislation endangered chances of getting a mental health parity bill into law. But many members strongly supported the measure.

House Republicans, who objected to the specific mental health coverage requirements as well as the cost offsets, offered a motion to recommit the bill. The motion, which would have substituted the Senate text, failed 196–221 on March 5.

The House-passed HR 1424 provided for the following.

Parity requirements. Health plans could not set more restrictive financial requirements or treatment limits than those for medical and surgical benefits. The requirements applied only to health plans that offered mental health or substance abuse benefits.

Benefits for out-of-network mental health treatment had to be subject to the same financial requirements and treatment limitations as other out-of-network benefits.

Minimum coverage. Health plans that provided mental health and substance abuse benefits would have to cover "any mental health condition or substance-related disorder included in the most recent edition of the Diagnostic and Statistical Manual (DSM) of Mental Disorders published by the American Psychiatric Association."

Exemptions. Exemptions were similar to those in the final bill for small businesses and for plans that experienced significant cost increases because of the requirements in the act.

Offsets. To offset at least part of the estimated $3.9 billion cost of the bill, the measure included provisions to

- Increase the Medicaid drug rebate, or discount, that pharmaceutical companies paid to state Medicaid programs from 15.1 percent to 20.1 percent. The change would cut the cost of what state programs paid for beneficiaries' drugs, in turn reducing the matching payments that the federal government made to the states.

- Limit the expansion of "specialty hospitals," which typically specialized in one or more surgical procedures, such as heart surgery or orthopedics, and were owned at least in part by physician investors. Physicians also would be prohibited from referring patients to hospitals in which they had an ownership interest, although existing physician-owned hospitals could be exempted from the restrictions. The change was expected to reduce the number of medical procedures and result in Medicaid savings.

Genetic discrimination. The rule also attached a bill (HR 493) sponsored by Louise M. Slaughter, D-N.Y., aimed at prohibiting insurers and employers from discriminating or making business decisions using data from genetic tests. *(Genetic discrimination, p. 717)*

The White House issued a statement March 5 saying the administration opposed any bill that would expand mental health parity benefits beyond those laid out in the Senate legislation.

HOUSE-SENATE COMPROMISE

On Sept. 23, the House passed a new version of the mental health parity bill (HR 6983) that was the product of three months of negotiation with the Senate. The bipartisan measure passed by on a **key vote of 376–47 (R 143–47; D 233–0).** The bill was considered under suspension of the rules, thereby requiring a two-thirds majority of those present and voting (282 in this case) for passage. *(2008 key votes, p. 972)*

Instead of passing the compromise as a separate bill, the Senate incorporated the provisions into a package containing energy incentives, tax extenders, and an exemption from the alternative minimum tax. The bill (HR 6049) passed 93–2 also on Sept. 23. *(Tax bill, p. 131; HR 6049, p. 132)*

Following are among the chief differences between the compromise and the earlier House- and Senate-passed bills.

Minimum coverage. Unlike the earlier House bill, the compromise did not specify which services had to be covered by a plan that offered such mental health or substance abuse benefits. Instead, it simply required that they cover such services as defined under the terms of the plan and relevant state laws.

Preemption. Unlike the original Senate bill, the compromise did not preempt state mental health parity laws.

Offsets. The new Senate version did not include direct cost offsets. Instead, the mental health parity provisions were offset as part of the larger tax package. Under House rules, however, the cost of the legislation still had to be offset. The House bill proposed to delay, until 2013, a provision of the 2004 corporate tax overhaul (PL 108-357) that allowed companies to use a modified "worldwide interest allocation" rule for allocating their interest expenses between U.S. and foreign sources when determining their foreign tax credit limitation. In the first year that the allocation rules took effect, the amount that a business would have to attribute to U.S. sources would increase from 30 percent to 85 percent. *(Corporate tax changes, Congress and the Nation Vol. XI, p. 115)*

FINAL BILL

The Senate Oct. 1 passed what had become the financial industry bailout bill (HR 1424), including the parity provisions, as well as the tax provisions from its earlier measure. The vote for the package was 74–25. The House cleared it 263–171 on Oct. 3.

The Senate assembled the package, using the mental health parity bill as the vehicle, after the House had stunned the stock markets and others by rejecting a slightly different version of the rescue provisions. Like HR 6049, the bill offset the parity provisions as part of the tax package. The measure also included the genetic discrimination bill.

Medicare Physician Payments

Congress in 2008 canceled a scheduled 10.6 percent cut in payments to physicians who treated Medicare patients, overriding President George W. Bush's veto to do it. The bill froze the existing payment rates and allowed a 1.1 percent increase in 2009. The cost was offset mainly by reducing payments to private plans known as Medicare Advantage. President Bush objected to the financing mechanism. The measure became law without his signature on July 15 (HR 6331—PL 110-275).

Payments to physicians who treated Medicare patients were subject to a cost control formula enacted in 1997 as part of that year's Balanced Budget Act (PL 105-33). The rates were based on a preset spending cap that required cuts if the cost of the health care program for the elderly and disabled exceeded the limit. Since 2002 the formula had required reductions in doctors' rates, but Congress regularly stepped in to avert the cuts. *(PL 105-33, Congress and the Nation Vol. X, p. 432)*

In late 2007, lawmakers voted to delay for six months a 10 percent rate cut that was scheduled to go into effect Jan. 1, 2008, and to give physicians a 0.5 percent increase during that time (S 2499—PL 110-173). That gave Congress until July 1, 2008, to decide how to address what would have been a 10.6 percent cut. Doctors said the reduction was so large that if it took effect it might mean they would begin refusing new Medicare patients. The prospect of physicians turning away seniors on Medicare made the issue one of paramount importance to Congress.

While eliminating the pay cut had broad, bipartisan support, Republicans opposed paying for it through cuts to Medicare Advantage. The program, created by Republicans in the 2003 Medicare overhaul (PL 108-173), encouraged private managed-care plans to provide benefits to seniors in place of the government. *(2003 overhaul, Congress and the Nation Vol. XI, p. 496)*

The Government Accountability Office, Congressional Budget Office (CBO), and Medicare Payment Advisory Commission had all said that Medicare Advantage plans were overpaid compared with traditional Medicare, making the plans a target for Democrats.

However, the Bush administration and many Republicans regarded the private plans as the future of Medicare. The higher payments enabled the plans to offer additional benefits and, thus, attract more beneficiaries to the Medicare Advantage program. Republicans hoped that over time the plans would begin to perform more cost-effectively than the traditional, government-run program.

Democrats tried to cut payments to the Medicare Advantage plans in 2007, but they were thwarted by Bush's veto threat and by his GOP allies in the Senate. In 2008 House Democrats opted to see what their Senate colleagues could get through that chamber.

MAJOR PROVISIONS

The following are the main provisions of HR 6331 as enacted, with costs and offsets estimated by CBO.

Medicare physician payments. Canceled the 10.6 percent cut in payments to physicians treating Medicare patients scheduled to take effect July 1, 2008. The measure froze existing payment rates for eighteen months and provided for a 1.1 percent increase in 2009. CBO said the change would cost $94 billion over both six years (fiscal 2008 through 2013) and eleven years (fiscal 2008 through 2018). After 2009 the rates would revert to the levels in prior law, requiring physicians' fees to be reduced by 21 percent in 2010.

Preventive and mental health services. Expanded the coverage of preventive services for some beneficiaries and reduced the 50 percent co-payment for mental health services to 20 percent, which was the usual co-payment rate for regular medical services such as doctor visits. The combined cost was estimated at $1.9 billion over six years and $8.7 billion over eleven years.

Low-income beneficiaries. Allowed more beneficiaries to qualify for low-income assistance by adjusting asset requirements. For example, the measure excluded life insurance from the asset test applied to beneficiaries. CBO estimated the cost at $2.2 billion over six years and $7.8 billion over eleven years.

Medicare Improvement Fund. Created a new fund available to the health and human services secretary to make improvements to Medicare Part A and Part B benefits. The fund replaced an earlier fund. CBO estimated that it would save $3.1 billion in 2013 but increase costs by a total of $18.9 billion over eleven years.

Medical suppliers. Postponed for eighteen months a Bush administration plan to require providers of home medical equipment to competitively bid for Medicare business. The program was expected to save $1 billion a year when fully implemented. But many lawmakers were concerned about the bidding process because suppliers of the equipment—known as durable medical equipment—had complained that they were unfairly prevented from bidding or that companies unfamiliar with the business won bids. Some seniors said they worried that the confusing process could result in them losing access to needed medical equipment such as oxygen, walkers, and hospital beds. The change was not expected to affect the budget.

Medicare Advantage. Offset the cost of the bill primarily by reductions to Medicare Advantage. The legislation phased out "indirect medical education" payments, which went to Medicare Advantage plans that had teaching hospitals in their service area. It also required private fee-for-service plans—a subset of Medicare Advantage—to establish networks of health care providers. Previously, the fee-for-service plans were not required to have provider networks, and doctors could choose to accept or reject plan payment at the point of service. CBO estimated that the changes would reduce spending by $13.6 billion over six years and $48.7 billion over eleven years.

Welfare. Extended the Temporary Assistance for Needy Families supplemental grant program through fiscal 2009. CBO estimated the extension would cost $300 million over both six years and eleven years.

SENATE ACTION STALLED

Senate Democrats tried June 12 to bring to the floor S 3101, sponsored by Finance Committee chair Max Baucus, D-Mont., but Republicans denied them the sixty-vote majority needed to limit debate on a motion to begin considering the legislation. The vote was 54–39. Democrats were closer than they seemed, however. Five Democrats missed the vote, and Baucus switched his vote to "no" at the last minute in a parliamentary move to be able to reconsider the vote at a later time. The Republicans' main objection was Baucus's plan to use cuts to Medicare Advantage to pay for most of the bill.

The bill would have canceled the pay cut and instead given doctors a 1.1 percent pay increase in 2009. The bill also proposed to extend many expiring Medicare provisions, expand Medicare's coverage of preventive services, and modify the rules governing eligibility for the Medicare Savings Program, which provided benefits to low-income seniors.

Before the vote, Senate majority leader Harry Reid, D-Nev., rejected a GOP request for a cloture vote on an alternative Medicare bill written by the senior Republican on the Finance Committee, Charles E. Grassley of Iowa. Grassley's bill would have provided doctors the same pay increase as S 3101, but without changes to the Medicare Advantage private fee-for-service plans.

With the failure of the Baucus bill, Baucus and Grassley were widely expected to restart stalled negotiations on a compromise bill.

HOUSE FLOOR ACTION

Although House Democrats expected that the final bill would come from the Senate, they lost faith that Senate negotiators would send them a bill before the July Fourth recess. The House June 24 passed its bill (HR 6331), on a **key vote of 355–59 (R 129–59; D 226–0),** a tally that was more than enough to overcome a presidential veto. *(2008 key votes, p. 972)*

Although the GOP leadership urged Republicans to vote against the bill, at least a dozen of them changed their votes from "nay" to "yea." Lawmakers from both sides were hoping to go home during the recess and tell physicians and patients that they did something to keep doctors from leaving Medicare. "This overwhelming vote should send a strong signal to the Senate," Majority Leader Steny H. Hoyer, D-Md., said in a statement.

SENATE ACTION DELAYED

Two days after the House vote, Reid tried to bring up HR 6331, but the Senate refused to invoke cloture to proceed to the legislation. The June 26 vote was 58–40, just shy of the sixty votes needed.

Minority Leader Mitch McConnell, R-Ky., offered a motion to extend the existing physician payment rates for thirty days, but Reid objected. Republicans were upset at having only one option to vote, in the form of a House bill, instead of getting a chance to support a tentative compromise that Baucus and Grassley had worked out earlier in the week. McConnell said that Grassley would lead negotiations to produce a new Senate bill that more Republicans would support.

Congress then left for the July Fourth recess, missing the July 1 deadline when the cuts were supposed to take effect. The administration, however, announced it would not apply the cut immediately, instead holding doctors' Medicare claims for ten business days—until July 15—to give Congress more time to pass a bill. Over the recess, bill supporters, including the American Medical Association (AMA), launched a flurry of political ads aimed at swaying politically vulnerable Republican lawmakers.

SENATE CLEARS BILL

Reid tried again when Congress reconvened July 9. The debate was filled with partisan rhetoric, and Democrats appeared to be one vote short of the sixty votes they needed—until Edward M. Kennedy, D-Mass., who had surgery June 2 for a malignant brain tumor, made a surprise return to cast his first vote in more than six weeks. In one of the most dramatic moments of the 110th Congress, Kennedy's presence electrified the chamber. Sen. Barack Obama of Illinois, then the presumed 2008 Democratic presidential nominee, entered with him, an arm around his shoulder. As they walked through the door, stunned fellow senators, aides, and gallery watchers broke into lengthy applause.

Once Kennedy voted, nine Republicans joined him, providing a wide enough margin to invoke cloture and to override a threatened veto of the bill, with votes to spare. The Senate on a **key vote of 69–30 (R 18–30; D 49–0; I 2–0)** on July 9 easily achieved cloture on the bill. Cloture required a three-fifths vote of the total Senate. The Senate then cleared the bill by voice vote.

Republicans seemed philosophical. "We've had a very dramatic moment in the room here," said Kay Bailey Hutchison of Texas. "I voted for the bill. It's not the way I would have written it." John Cornyn, R-Texas, who continued to criticize the bill but who had also been hammered at home by the AMA over the break, explained his vote for it. "It reversed the cut. That's the commitment I made to the physicians in my state," he said.

VETO OVERRIDE

Bush vetoed the bill July 15, and his veto was overridden by both chambers the same day. The House vote, taken July 15, was 383–41, surpassing the two-thirds majority required by one hundred votes. The Senate the same day followed suit with a 70–26 vote that enacted the bill into law. *(Veto message, p. 1074)*

Stem Cell Research

For the second year in a row, Congress in 2007 cleared a bill to expand federal funding of embryonic stem cell research, and for the second time lawmakers were unable to override President George W. Bush's veto of the legislation. Knowing they were short of the necessary votes, Democrats did not even attempt an override.

The bill (S 5) that Congress sent to President Bush on June 7 was much the same as the measure he vetoed in 2006. It would have lifted some restrictions on funding that Bush put in place in 2001 and allowed federal funding for research on stem cells from surplus embryos discarded by fertility clinics. The 2007 version had an additional section that would have supported efforts to develop stem cells derived from sources other than human embryos. *(2006 action, p. 542)*

Bush vetoed S 5 on June 20, stating in a message to Congress that "[c]ompelling American taxpayers to support the deliberate destruction of human embryos would be a grave mistake. I will not allow our nation to cross this moral line." *(Veto message, p. 1063)*

Unlike the Republicans who controlled the 109th Congress, the new Democratic majority sought to make the veto and the surrounding debate as politically painful as possible for Bush and congressional Republicans who opposed the legislation. Republicans in 2006 used a carefully sequenced series of events, sending Bush the stem cell bill the day after it passed. He vetoed it the next day, and hours later the House tried and failed to override him. The story was quickly off the front pages. This time, the Democrats sent Bush a bill that originated not in the House, where there were not nearly enough votes for an override, but in the Senate. A vetoed bill first returns for an override vote to the chamber where it was introduced, and supporters of the bill believed they were only one or two votes away in the Senate from the two-thirds majority required to override a veto. They hoped a success in one chamber would show progress on the issue for supporters.

Instead of scheduling an override vote immediately after the veto, Senate Democratic leaders chose to wait, allowing interest groups time to continue to pressure vulnerable Republicans to change their position on the issue. A favorite target was John E. Sununu of New Hampshire, who had said that he would sustain Bush's veto, but who nonetheless came under regular fire from left-leaning groups such as Americans United that believed the issue could resonate in his 2008 reelection campaign. Sununu subsequently lost that contest to former New Hampshire Democratic governor Jeanne Shaheen.

In the end, Democrats decided to save the override vote until just before the 2008 elections in hopes of making the mostly GOP opponents look bad. But still lacking the votes, that vote was never called.

The fight had been going on since 2001, when Bush issued an order that allowed federal funding for embryonic stem cell research only on cell lines created before Aug. 9 of that year. Critics said the order did not allow the number or diversity of cell lines needed for research. According to the National Institutes of Health (NIH), of the seventy-eight stem cell lines declared eligible for federal funding in 2001, only about twenty-two lines were available for distribution to researchers, and some of those lines were contaminated.

Stem cells are the building blocks of the body—blank cellular templates that have the ability to develop into many different organs or tissue. Supporters of embryonic stem cell research saw it as holding the potential for treatment of diseases such as diabetes, Alzheimer's, and Parkinson's. The cells can divide indefinitely and can either grow into more stem cells or develop into specialized matter, such as nerve cells, organs, or blood cells. That led scientists to believe that stem cells could be used to replace tissue lost to degenerative and other diseases, most notably nerve damage that causes paralysis or brain disorders.

The president and other social conservatives likened embryonic stem cell research to abortion because embryos are destroyed in the process. The administration argued that other scientific methods for extracting stem cells—deriving them from adult tissue, umbilical cords, amniotic fluid, or other sources—provided the only morally acceptable approach. Opponents insisted that those cells had not been shown to have the flexibility and promise of embryonic stem cells.

The day after the veto, the Senate Appropriations Committee included a provision in the fiscal 2008 Labor–Health and Human Services (HHS)–Education funding bill to extend Bush's 2001 deadline to June 15, 2007. The language drew one of several veto threats against the spending bill, and sponsors removed it before the Senate passed the measure.

HIGHLIGHTS

The vetoed bill included the following provisions.

Embryonic stem cell research. The bill authorized the Health and Human Services Department to conduct and support research involving human embryonic stem cells, regardless of when they were obtained, as long as the following criteria were met.

- The stem cells were derived from human embryos that were donated from in vitro fertilization clinics where they were created for the purpose of fertility treatment.
- The embryos would not have been used and would otherwise have been discarded.
- The individuals seeking fertility treatment donated the embryos with informed written consent and without any financial payment or other inducement to make the donation.

Within sixty days of enactment, HHS, in consultation with NIH, would have been required to issue final guidelines to carry out those requirements.

Pluripotent stem cell research. The bill required HHS to conduct and support research involving stem cells not derived from human embryos. The measure authorized funding as needed in fiscal 2008 through 2010 for such research.

Within ninety days of enactment, HHS, in consultation with NIH, was required to issue final guidelines to carry out those requirements.

HOUSE FLOOR ACTION

As part of their "first 100 hours" agenda in the new Congress, House Democrats passed an embryonic stem cell bill (HR 3) on Jan. 11 that was identical to the vetoed 2006 measure. The vote was 253–174, well short of the two-thirds majority needed to override the president, but supporters said they were gaining momentum.

Opening the floor debate, Energy and Commerce chairman John D. Dingell, D-Mich., quoted from Bush's 2001 speech noting the great promise of embryonic stem cells to develop into almost any tissue in the body and cure many ailments. "It is time the House listened to the president's words and disregarded his veto," Dingell said.

The White House issued a statement the day of the vote calling the bill "seriously flawed legislation that would undo essential ethical protections, and slow the development of new techniques that avoid bio-ethical concerns."

SENATE FLOOR ACTION

The Senate passed its own stem cell bill (S 5) by a vote of 63–34 on April 11. Three Democratic supporters missed the vote: Christopher J. Dodd of Connecticut, Mary L. Landrieu of Louisiana, and Tim Johnson of South Dakota. Johnson was absent in the first part of the 110th Congress while recovering from a brain hemorrhage. Without Johnson, supporters needed sixty-six votes, rather than sixty-seven. Either way, they were one vote shy of a two-thirds majority.

The Senate bill included the same provisions on embryonic stem cell research found in the House measure. But unlike the House bill, it included language from a bill (S 2754)—passed by the Senate but rejected by the House in 2006—that provided for research on stem cells not derived from human embryos.

Senate supporters began the week with the expectation that they might be able to reach sixty-seven votes. After gaining four new Democratic supporters in the 2006 election and losing one Republican backer, they were only a vote shy. Speculation swirled around senators such as Sununu and Democrat Bob Casey of Pennsylvania, who were seen as potential swing votes. In the end, however, bill supporters were not able to pick up the additional vote.

Because both Democrats who voted against the measure—Casey and Ben Nelson of Nebraska—said they would not switch on a veto override, supporters were left looking for a Republican. Despite strong public support for stem cell research, it was especially difficult to persuade a GOP senator to switch when the House clearly was not going to override Bush.

After the bill passed, Republican Sen. Orrin G. Hatch of Utah, an abortion rights opponent but a backer of embryonic stem cell research, emphasized patience. "Every year we go up more," Hatch said. "It's just a matter of time until we win."

Also on April 11, the Senate passed a competing bill (S 30) to promote research on stem cells that did not involve "the destruction or discarding of, or risk of injury to, a human embryo or embryos other than those that are naturally dead." The vote was 70–28.

Supporters of embryonic stem cell research saw S 30, sponsored by Norm Coleman, R-Minn., as political cover for those who wanted to support research that could lead to medical advances but who were opposed to using human embryos. Coleman said he offered the bill as a way of getting new federal support for stem cell research without crossing moral boundaries. Tom Harkin, D-Iowa, a strong supporter of the embryonic stem cell bill, said Coleman's bill would have little effect on research.

During the floor debate, senators frequently invoked testimony from Dr. Elias Zerhouni, the NIH director. Zerhouni, a Bush appointee, broke with administration policy and told the Senate Labor, Health and Human Services, and Education Appropriations Subcommittee on March 19 that science and the nation would be better served by reversing Bush's 2001 order.

Harkin and Arlen Specter, R-Pa., an ardent supporter of embryonic stem cell research, expressed hope that Bush would change his mind and sign the bill.

HOUSE FLOOR ACTION

The House passed S 5 on June 7 by a vote of 247–176, completing congressional action.

During the debate, bill opponents stressed new reports that scientists had reprogrammed adult mouse skin cells back to an embryonic state. If replicated successfully in humans, the experiment offered the potential of bypassing controversial research using embryonic cells.

Bush alluded to the news reports in renewing his veto threat soon after the House vote. "Recent scientific developments have reinforced my conviction that stem cell science can progress in ethical ways," Bush said. "Researchers have been investigating innovative techniques that could allow doctors and scientists to produce stem cells just as versatile as those derived from human embryos, but without harming life."

Reid countered that scientists were just "treading water" with the new developments, and House supporters scoffed at the notion that the new research might change supporters' minds about the bill.

The House June 7 rejected 180–242 a GOP motion to recommit the bill to the Energy and Commerce Committee with instructions to replace the text with provisions limited to funding for research on stem cells derived from sources other than human embryos.

FDA Tobacco Regulation

A bill (HR 1108) to give the Food and Drug Administration (FDA) the authority to regulate tobacco products passed in the House in 2008. But a companion measure (S 625) approved by a Senate committee never reached the floor, and the legislation died at the end of the Congress.

Democrats had promised a strong push in the 110th Congress to give the FDA sweeping new powers to regulate tobacco products, including nicotine levels, packaging, sales, and marketing. While both bills would have allowed the FDA to regulate tobacco and nicotine levels, they would not have empowered the agency to ban cigarettes or to force the elimination of nicotine from tobacco products. Still, public health groups supported the bill, with the expectation that it would decrease smoking rates and reduce tobacco-related illnesses and deaths.

Market leader Philip Morris USA, maker of Marlboro cigarettes, supported the legislation, saying FDA regulation "would bring predictability and clear standards to the tobacco industry in the United States." But second-level tobacco companies such as Lorillard and R.J. Reynolds fiercely opposed the legislation, saying it would enable Philip Morris to gain a near monopoly because the larger company could more easily afford regulation and essentially lock in its share of sales.

Although almost all lawmakers had come to agree that tobacco was a dangerous product and hardly any of them publicly defended the industry, opponents said it was inappropriate to have the FDA regulate the substance because the agency could never certify a tobacco product as safe.

BACKGROUND

Efforts to allow the FDA to regulate tobacco went back more than a decade. The FDA first tried to assert control over tobacco products as part of a broad effort under the Clinton administration to curb teen smoking. The agency issued regulations in 1996 to prohibit the sale of tobacco products to people younger than eighteen and strictly limit tobacco advertising. But, in 2000, the U.S. Supreme Court in *Food and Drug Administration v. Brown & Williamson Tobacco Corp.* prohibited the FDA from enforcing the requirements, ruling that Congress had not granted the agency such power. The decision was widely viewed by antitobacco lawmakers as an invitation for Congress to act. *(2000 case, Congress and the Nation Vol. X, p. 712)*

In 2004 the Senate endorsed a compromise plan that paired FDA regulation of tobacco with a multibillion-dollar buyout aimed at gradually easing farmers out of the tobacco business. Supporters said that combining the two proposals, which had very different constituencies, was the only way to get either through the Senate. Senators adopted the combined plan as an amendment to a corporate tax bill. But House opponents, led by Majority Leader Tom DeLay, R-Texas, dropped the FDA regulations from the final bill, while including the bailout for farmers (PL 108-357). *(2004 action, Congress and the Nation Vol. XI, p. 516)*

2007 SENATE COMMITTEE ACTION

The Senate Health, Education, Labor, and Pensions (HELP) Committee on Aug. 1, 2007, approved S 625 by 13–8. Bill sponsor Edward M. Kennedy, D-Mass., said he hoped it would reach the floor sometime after that year's August recess.

S 625 gave the FDA authority over most tobacco advertising and over many ingredients in cigarettes, as well as the ability to regulate, or at least disclose, the ingredients of cigarettes. It subjected to scrutiny industry claims about "light" and "low tar" cigarettes and limited or eliminated advertising targeted toward children. It required the agency to hire a much larger staff. The costs would have been paid for with a user fee on tobacco companies amounting to about 2.5 cents per pack of cigarettes.

Opposition from tobacco-state senators and from Michael B. Enzi of Wyoming, the panel's ranking Republican, had stalled two previously scheduled markups. Opponents Richard M. Burr of North Carolina and Tom Coburn of Oklahoma argued that the FDA was not the best agency for the job, given the bill's focus on advertising and marketing. Coburn said the Federal Trade Commission (FTC) might be better suited to regulate the industry's advertising claims.

The committee agreed to add language by Enzi to put new, bold health warnings on tobacco packaging that featured color pictures and graphics akin to warnings on cigarette packs in Canada and the Netherlands. Enzi also won an amendment to bar the use of cloves, which appealed particularly to young people, in tobacco products marketed in the United States.

The panel defeated several attempts by Burr, a former House member whose Winston-Salem–based district was home to employees of R.J. Reynolds, to strip some regulatory powers from the legislation.

2008 LEGISLATIVE ACTION

The House Energy and Commerce Health Subcommittee approved HR 1108, sponsored by Henry A. Waxman, D-Calif., in a tumultuous session March 11, 2008.

The bill proposed to authorize the FDA to regulate tobacco companies' marketing practices, evaluate their product claims, control nicotine levels in products, and dictate warning labels. Like S 625, it required tobacco companies to pay user fees to cover the cost of regulating their products, as drug companies did. And it did not seek to allow the FDA to ban tobacco.

Chairman Frank Pallone Jr., D-N.J., had been forced to abandon an earlier markup, in part because of fierce GOP opposition to a provision that would have allowed the Congressional Budget Office to set an annual percentage increase in the tobacco user fee, with the extra funds going to the Treasury. Democrats said the provision was necessary to meet pay-as-you-go rules and make the bill budget-neutral, but Republicans argued that the fees amounted to a tax and, therefore, fell outside the committee's jurisdiction.

The subcommittee approved two GOP amendments by voice vote. Ranking member Nathan Deal of Georgia won approval for a requirement that all regulations stemming from the bill undergo the usual rule-making process. Deal was concerned the legislation might allow for an expedited regulatory process. Michael C. Burgess of Texas added a requirement that tobacco regulation be funded entirely from user fees and that the FDA be barred from shifting money from other areas if user fees were insufficient.

But all GOP attempts to make major changes to the bill or delay the proposed regulations were rejected.

The full Energy and Commerce Committee approved a revised version of the bill (HR 1108) by a vote of 38–12 on April 2 and reported it (H Rept 110-672) on July 17.

Chairman John D. Dingell, D-Mich., made a number of changes that diffused some of the GOP hostility to the bill and made it a more bipartisan measure. Panel Republicans complimented Dingell for negotiating with them, and eleven of them supported the bill. Dingell's revisions, made in a manager's amendment that was adopted by voice vote, also persuaded several small tobacco companies and the National Association of Convenience Stores to drop their opposition.

Twelve Republicans still voted against the bill, however. Some of them cited the measure's potential effect on the

FDA itself. "It is incongruous that the FDA would be able to regulate a product that is as inherently dangerous as tobacco," said Burgess, who voted against approval. "If we're going to regulate tobacco, I think it should be done at the Federal Trade Commission and not as a health issue at the Food and Drug Administration," said Joe L. Barton of Texas, the ranking Republican on the committee.

The committee-approved HR 1108 provided for the following.

- The user fees would be assessed by the Health and Human Services Department (HHS) and would be dedicated only to the FDA's tobacco activities.
- The FDA would have more time to comply with the bill. HHS would be required to issue a rule implementing the law six months after it was enacted. The original bill required a rule within thirty days.
- Convenience stores won provisions requiring the regulation of tobacco sales beyond over-the-counter transactions—putting them on the same footing as Internet and mail order retailers.
- Before prohibiting stores from selling tobacco products or issuing fines for violations, the government would have to consider whether those retailers had programs in place to prevent sales of tobacco products to minors and whether they had been subject to state fines.
- Tobacco companies employing fewer than 350 people won provisions giving them more time to comply with product-testing and reporting requirements in the bill and allowing them to jointly purchase laboratory testing services.
- Growers won provisions requiring that foreign-produced tobacco be subject to the same limits on pesticides and other chemicals and meet the same standards the FDA applied to domestic tobacco.
- Tobacco opponents won language to ensure that tobacco companies would not be able to claim that "smoke-free" or similarly labeled products had lower health risks.

The committee rejected nine GOP amendments, including one by Burgess that would have allowed the FDA to ban tobacco outright.

Steve Buyer of Indiana and Mike Rogers of Michigan offered five amendments to delay implementation of the bill for up to ten years after its enactment, saying the delay was needed to give the FDA time to improve its regulation of food, drugs, medical devices, and overseas factories. The agency had been beleaguered in recent years by reports that it could not adequately fulfill its existing responsibilities. Democrats largely agreed but said the answer was to fix the agency's problems, not to abandon giving it authority over tobacco products.

The committee adopted by voice vote three Republican amendments, which removed language that critics said might have allowed the FDA to award no-bid research grants; required the FTC to study whether the tobacco industry would become more concentrated and less competitive should the bill become law; and required the government to study the health effects of "cross-border trade in tobacco products," including smuggled and counterfeit products.

HOUSE FLOOR ACTION

The House passed HR 1108 by a **key vote of 326–102 (R 96–99; D 230–3)** on July 30, 2008, under suspension of the rules, a procedure that barred amendments and required a two-thirds vote for passage. The margin was large enough to override a threatened presidential veto. *(2008 key votes, p. 972)*

Democratic infighting had tied up the bill for months, with the Ways and Means Committee and the Natural Resources Committee making claims on tax and tribal government provisions, respectively.

The gridlock was broken in late July, just as Congress was preparing to recess. Waxman found a new $300 million offset for the bill by attaching an unrelated piece of legislation (HR 6500) that he had introduced regarding the Federal Thrift Savings Plan. That satisfied Ways and Means chairman Charles B. Rangel, D-N.Y. Waxman and Dingell also removed or altered the Indian affairs provisions.

The House debate on HR 1108 grew heated at times, especially after Minority Leader John A. Boehner, R-Ohio, weighed in. "Most people who smoke in America probably don't need the federal government to tell them that smoking isn't good for their health," Boehner, a cigarette smoker, argued. "This is a bone-headed idea! A bone-headed idea! How much government do we need?"

Dingell quickly fired back in unusually personal terms. "This legislation is on the floor because people are killing themselves smoking these evil cigarettes! And the distinguished gentleman, the minority leader, is going to be amongst the next to die!" Dingell yelled. "I am trying to save him, as the rest of us are, because he is committing suicide every time he puffs on one of those," Dingell concluded, refusing to yield to Boehner for a response.

The White House issued its veto threat the day the House voted. It said the bill would "undermine one of the nation's premier public health and regulatory institutions and potentially lead the public to mistakenly conclude some tobacco products are safe." The administration argued that the bill would divert the FDA from its primary responsibilities, such as reviewing new pharmaceutical drugs and overseeing food safety. The White House also objected to the proposed user fees on cigarettes, calling them "a new tax that would be paid disproportionately by low-income individuals."

Industry lobbyists fighting the bill counted—accurately, as it turned out—on opponents in the Senate and the brief time left on the legislative schedule to kill the bill.

Prescription Drug Imports

Backers of rules to make it easier for Americans to import lower-cost prescription drugs from other industrialized countries that impose price controls in 2007 were once again successful in getting language into agriculture appropriations legislation. But that language eventually was dropped and did not become law.

The agriculture spending bill was long the vehicle of choice for advocates of so-called drug reimportations because that bill also included annual funding for the Food and Drug Administration (FDA). But the FDA opposed the idea of allowing Americans to bring drugs into the country from outside the closed supply chain for safety reasons. The powerful drug industry opposed it for fear of losing considerable profits and for years had thwarted bipartisan efforts to loosen restrictions on citizens, pharmacies, and drug wholesalers purchasing drugs from outside the United States.

In 2007 the fiscal 2008 agriculture bill that came before the House Appropriations Committee (HR 3161—H Report 110-258) for markup July 19 already included a provision to lift the ban on the importation of prescription drugs. Rep. Rodney Frelinghuysen, R-N.J., attempted to keep the ban in place and proposed that individuals be allowed instead to bring in a ninety-day supply from Canada for personal use. His amendment was rejected by voice vote.

The issue came up again during floor consideration of HR 3161 on Aug. 2. The House rejected 146–283 an amendment by Jack Kingston of Georgia, ranking Republican on the Agriculture Appropriations Subcommittee, to strike the importation language in the bill. Somewhat confusingly, Kingston favored allowing the reimportation of prescription medications and voted against his own amendment. He said he wanted to put a House majority on record as favoring drug reimportation because the Bush administration had threatened to veto the spending bill over the provision.

Kingston's gambit, however, was for naught. The full Senate never formally debated HR 3161. When the bill was folded into an omnibus (HR 2764—PL 110-161) with ten other appropriations measures, the contentious importation language was dropped, as it had been in several previous years.

Chronology of Action on Human Services

2005–2006

Although the 109th Congress did renew, for the first time, the landmark 1996 rewrite of the nation's major welfare law, disputes over child care funding and work requirements prevented the five-year extension from making more than minor changes to the program that had ended welfare as an entitlement for low-income mothers and children a decade earlier.

Lawmakers also renewed for five years the Older Americans Act, a popular group of programs, first enacted as part of the Great Society under President Lyndon B. Johnson, that provided social services and job opportunities for senior citizens.

But they proved unable to reach agreement on another popular Johnson-era program, the Head Start education and social service program for preschool children. Lawmakers could not settle disputes over teacher salaries and whether religious-based Head Start programs should be able to make hiring decisions based on faith.

Welfare Extension

Unable to agree on a major rewrite of the 1996 welfare overhaul, Congress opted to extend the law through fiscal 2010 with relatively modest changes. The reauthorization was part of the 2005 budget-reconciliation bill that President George W. Bush signed into law Feb. 8, 2006 (S 1932—PL 109-171). *(Reconciliation, p. 81)*

The landmark 1996 law (PL 104-193), which ended more than sixty years of guaranteed cash assistance to welfare beneficiaries, required adult recipients to work in exchange for benefits and gave states new flexibility to operate their programs. States received federal aid in the form of Temporary Assistance for Needy Families (TANF) block grants. The law originally was slated to expire in October 2002, but lawmakers temporarily extended the program twelve times while they tried to reach agreement on a broader bill. *(1996 law, Congress and the Nation Vol. IX, p. 578; reauthorizations, Congress and the Nation Vol. XI, p. 525)*

The chief issues that separated the House and Senate concerned work rules for adult recipients and the level of funding for child care. The final bill did not change the individual work requirements, but most states had to ensure that more of their welfare recipients were meeting the law's work requirements.

Democrats and moderate Republicans said the bill imposed new requirements on states without providing additional money to meet them and that it did not include sufficient funds for government-subsidized child care programs that were essential to moving people into the workforce. House Republicans and the White House contended that tougher work requirements and programs promoting marriage were the best ways to help the two million families who relied on welfare assistance to escape poverty.

Supporters of the bill also said it would fix an accounting problem under the 1996 law. The 1996 law required states to make sure that at least 50 percent of their adult welfare recipients spent at least thirty hours a week

REFERENCES

Discussion of human services policy for the years 1945–1964 may be found in *Congress and the Nation Vol. I*, pp. 1225–1331; for the years 1965–1968, *Congress and the Nation Vol. II*, pp. 745–778; for the years 1969–1972, *Congress and the Nation Vol. III*, pp. 605–633; for the years 1973–1976, *Congress and the Nation Vol. IV*, pp. 403–432; for the years 1977–1980, *Congress and the Nation Vol. V*, pp. 679–712; for the years 1981–1984, *Congress and the Nation Vol. VI*, pp. 581–612; for the years 1985–1988, *Congress and the Nation Vol. VII*, pp. 607–632; for the years 1989–1992, *Congress and the Nation Vol. VIII*, pp. 611–624; for the years 1993–1996, *Congress and the Nation Vol. IX*, pp. 571–596; for the years 1997–2001, *Congress and the Nation Vol. X*, pp. 486–496; for the years 2001–2004, *Congress and the Nation Vol. XI*, pp. 520–529.

Outlays for Income Security

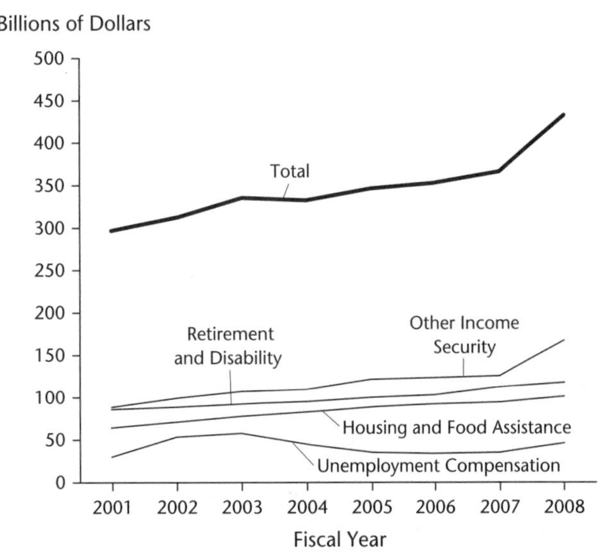

SOURCE: Office of Management and Budget, *Historical Tables, Budget of the United States Government: Fiscal Year 2010* (Washington, D.C.: U.S. Government Printing Office, 2009), Table 3.2.

engaged in activities considered "work." But the requirement came with an exception: the work-participation rate was reduced by 1 percentage point for every 1 percent that a state reduced its welfare caseloads. By 2004, welfare caseloads had decreased by 56 percent nationwide, according to the Congressional Research Service. As a result, many states were not required to make any of their welfare recipients work at all. The rewrite in the budget bill revised the caseload reduction credit.

HIGHLIGHTS

The welfare section of the budget-reconciliation law included these major provisions.

Authorization. Reauthorized TANF block grants for five years, through fiscal 2010, at the existing level of about $16.5 billion a year.

Work requirements. Left the individual work requirement at thirty hours per week for adults receiving TANF funds. However, states were required to have 50 percent of their recipients engaged in work, and starting in fiscal 2007, states could count only reductions since fiscal 2005.

State bonuses. Eliminated two annual state bonuses—the $200 million "high performance" bonus and one of up to $100 million for the five states with the greatest percentage decrease in out-of-wedlock births and a decline from 1995 levels in abortion rates.

Child care. Provided $2.9 billion per year in mandatory funding for child care subsidies—an increase of $1 billion over five years, or $200 million a year.

Marriage promotion. Provided about $100 million a year over five years for grants to encourage "healthy marriage." Up to another $50 million per year was set aside for "responsible fatherhood" initiatives.

SENATE COMMITTEE ACTION

The Senate Finance Committee gave voice-vote approval March 9, 2005, to a five-year reauthorization bill (S 667) sponsored by Finance Committee chairman Charles E. Grassley, R-Iowa. The bill, formally reported (S Rept 109-51) March 30, required welfare recipients to work thirty-four hours a week, up from thirty hours under the 1996 law, with ten hours of those hours permitted to be used for education and training. It retained a provision from existing law that allowed recipients to count vocational education and training as a core work activity for up to twelve months.

States would have to increase the proportion of their welfare recipients engaged in work from 50 percent in 2006 to 70 percent in 2010.

The bill eliminated the bonus for reducing out-of-wedlock births and created a $100 million-a-year mandatory program to provide matching grants to states and Indian tribes to promote healthy marriage and fatherhood. In addition, it included $50 million a year in mandatory grants to promote responsible fatherhood, another $26 million a year in discretionary funds for the same purpose, and $100 million a year in research funds, 80 percent of which was to promote healthy marriage.

At the urging of Rick Santorum of Pennsylvania, chairman of the Senate Republican Conference, the bill authorized an increase of $1 billion over five years for the Social Services Block Grant program, paid for by tightening eligibility standards for Supplemental Security Income beneficiaries. The existing block grant was funded at $1.7 billion annually.

Senate moderates, particularly Republican Olympia J. Snowe of Maine, played a major role in shaping the legislation. At Snowe's insistence, the bill called for increasing mandatory child care subsidies by a total of $6 billion over five years. Snowe and panel Democrats said a lack of affordable child care remained a major stumbling block to employment for many welfare recipients. Snowe said only one in seven children eligible for subsidized child care received such aid.

Santorum voiced "serious concerns" about the $6 billion increase. He said the funds to encourage marriage and responsible fatherhood would do more to help children. However, he supported the Snowe provision because it would be funded by changing the eligibility standards for the earned income tax credit (EITC), a refundable tax credit for poor families whose wage earners made too little to owe income taxes. Jeff Bingaman, D-N.M., opposed the offset, saying it would end the rights of some legal immigrant families to receive the EITC.

Grassley hoped to move the bill early in the year with Democratic support so it would not get caught up in other partisan squabbles. But fiscal conservatives objected to the bill's cost. The Congressional Budget Offices said it would add about $10.8 billion in mandatory spending over five years. With the funding dispute unresolved, Senate GOP leaders did not try to bring the bill to the floor.

HOUSE COMMITTEE ACTION

The Ways and Means Committee folded a GOP-backed welfare reauthorization bill (HR 240) into the House budget-reconciliation package (HR 4241). The committee approved the provisions 22–17 on Oct. 26. The panel's Human Resources Subcommittee had approved HR 240 by a vote of 7–4 on March 15.

The House Education and the Workforce Committee also approved the bill (no written report) by 23–20 on Oct. 20. The measure, sponsored by Deborah Pryce, R-Ohio, had the support of the Bush administration. It called for adult recipients to work forty hours a week, with sixteen hours of that allowed for education and training. The other twenty-four hours had to be devoted to direct work activities such as private or public employment, on-the-job training, or supervised community service. The bill proposed to increase federal child care subsidies by $1 billion over five years. The portion of recipients engaged in work would have to increase to 70 percent, as under the Senate bill.

The measure included proposals to promote healthy marriage similar to those in the Senate bill and provided for a $20-million-a-year discretionary program to encourage responsible fatherhood.

FINAL ACTION

The House provisions were largely included in the conference report (H Rept 109-362) on the budget-reconciliation bill (S 1932). The House adopted the conference report 212–206 on Dec. 19, in the session that began Dec. 18.

The Senate voted 50–50 on Dec. 21, with Vice President Dick Cheney casting a "yea" vote to break the tie, to approve the budget bill with three provisions unrelated to the welfare reauthorization stricken from the conference report, sending the bill back to the House for final action. The House had by then adjourned for the year. So it did not agree to the amended version until Feb. 1, 2006, clearing the bill by voice vote.

MAJOR PROVISIONS

Following are the major changes in welfare law, child support, and child welfare provisions in S 1932, which were estimated to create a net savings of $1.5 billion over five years.

Welfare

The law reauthorized the 1996 Temporary Assistance for Needy Families law (PL 104-193) at a projected cost of $374 million over five years. Viewed over a ten-year period, however, the changes were projected to save $344 million.

TANF block grant. The main TANF block grant to states was reauthorized through fiscal 2010 at the existing level of $16.5 billion per year. Supplemental grants were reauthorized through fiscal 2008 at $319 million per year.

Work requirements. The law retained a thirty-hour-per-week work requirement for individuals, but it altered what was known as the caseload reduction credit so that states would have to ensure that at least 50 percent of their welfare recipients were engaged in work. For the first time, the law applied work participation rules to state welfare programs that were funded entirely with state dollars, such as programs for people with disabilities or drug addictions and two-parent families.

Marriage promotion. The law authorized grants of $150 million per year to states through fiscal 2010 for activities to promote "healthy marriage" and "responsible fatherhood."

Child care. The law extended grants to states to provide child care subsidies to low-income families through 2010 and increased funding by a total of $1 billion over five years, for total funding of $2.9 billion per year.

Child Support

Changes to child support enforcement were expected to save a net $1.5 billion over five years.

Federal matching payments. The law barred states from using federal incentive payments to receive matching child support enforcement funds, beginning in 2008. States were still required to spend the incentive awards on child support services, but they could not also count the money as a match for additional federal funds. (Savings: a net $1.6 billion over five years.)

Distribution of child support payments. The law provided incentives to encourage states to give families receiving TANF more of the child support payments collected on their behalf. Previously, families that applied for TANF had to allow the state to collect their child support payments. The money was divided between the state and federal government as partial repayment for the welfare assistance. The new law allowed states to pay up to $100 a month ($200 for families with two or more children) of the child support collections to the TANF family. The federal government would compensate states for part of the funds they lost as a result. The law also simplified an existing requirement that states distribute to former TANF families child support arrearages from before and after the family was in the TANF program. (Combined cost: $423 million over five years.)

New enforcement rules. To increase collections, parents would be denied passports if they owed more than $2,500 in past-due child support payments, down from $5,000 under prior law. A triennial update of child support orders was required, and insurance payment data could be used as ammunition against noncustodial parents who owed child support.

Annual fee. States were required to collect a new $25 annual fee from families that had never been on TANF but had received at least $500 in child support services in a year. The states could retain part of the money.

Paternity tests. The federal share of the cost for paternity tests dropped from 90 percent to 66 percent.

CHILD WELFARE

Changes to child welfare programs were projected to save a net $320 million over five years. However, the law increased spending on two programs—funding for family courts and a program intended to keep troubled families together or, if that was impossible, to promote adoption of abused and neglected children.

Limitation of matching funds. The law limited states' claims to matching funds for administrative costs related to placing abused and neglected children in unlicensed foster homes. States had to license the home within twelve months of the placement. (Savings: $174 million over five years.)

Eligibility for foster care aid. The law limited eligibility for foster care and adoption assistance for about four thousand children each month in nine western states who would be subject to a Ninth Circuit Court of Appeals ruling. The court had broadened those states' latitude to determine eligibility for such assistance in cases in which children lived with a relative outside the home from which they were removed. (Savings: $380 million over five years.)

Mandatory spending increases. The law provided $20 million a year for new grants to improve the ability of state courts to track child abuse and neglect cases and train judges and other court personnel in child welfare law. Spending authority for the Safe and Stable Families program was increased. (Cost: $234 million over five years.)

SUPPLEMENTAL SECURITY INCOME

Disability reviews. The Social Security Administration was directed to review at least 20 percent of disability claims approved by state-level Disability Determination Service offices in fiscal 2006, rising to 40 percent in fiscal 2007 and 50 percent in fiscal 2008. (Savings: $287 million.)

Retroactive benefits. The threshold for paying retroactive benefits owed to the disabled because of delays in approval was lowered. Any lump sum greater than three times the maximum monthly benefit would be subject to payments in installments, except under certain conditions, such as terminal illness. (Savings: $425 million.)

Older Americans Act

Congress in 2006 cleared a five-year reauthorization of the law governing social services for seniors, after agreeing to modify an employment program for the elderly and alter the formula for distributing grants to states. President George W. Bush signed the bill into law Oct. 17 (HR 6197—PL 109-365).

Best known for the popular Meals on Wheels program for low-income, homebound seniors, the Older Americans Act (PL 89-73) also covered the activities of the Administration on Aging, which distributed about $1.2 billion in grants to states and local agencies for services including transportation and referrals to health care, legal aid, and nutrition programs for seniors. In addition, the law authorized the Senior Community Service Employee Program, which provided job training for low-income elderly people and placed them in community service positions at nonprofits and government agencies. The program was administered by nonprofits under contract to the Labor Department.

The Older Americans Act first became law in 1965 as part of President Lyndon B. Johnson's Great Society agenda. It had last been reauthorized in 2000 (PL 106-501) and technically expired at the end of fiscal 2005, although annual appropriations for the programs continued. Given the vocal and politically active constituency for the law, its renewal was one of the easiest and most bipartisan pieces of legislation the 109th Congress produced. Still, two disputes had to be resolved: how to allocate program grants among the states, and whether the Senior Community Service Employee Program should be required to move seniors into private sector jobs. *(1965 law, Congress and the Nation Vol. II, p. 762; 2000 reauthorization, Congress and the Nation Vol. X, p. 496)*

The first issue divided states with fast-growing elderly populations from those whose senior populations were declining. On the second issue, Democrats and advocates for nonprofits that provided the job-placement services for seniors wanted community service to remain a priority of the program. The Bush administration, meanwhile, wanted the program to focus on training seniors for higher-paying work in private firms that would not be subsidized by the government. Democrats said that goal was unrealistic. The Labor Department had already opened the job-training program to competitive bidding, angering some of the nonprofits.

The House passed a five-year reauthorization bill (HR 5293) in June, and the Senate Health, Education, Labor, and Pensions (HELP) Committee approved a related bill (S 3570) that same month. But the Senate left for the August recess without considering the measure. Instead of waiting for the Senate to act and then going to conference, House and Senate negotiators informally and drafted a compromise bill (HR 6197), which cleared at the end of September.

HR 6197 modified the method of distributing grants to give somewhat more money to states with rapidly expanding senior populations. Under the 2000 law, each state's share of total grant funding was based on the percentage of the nation's senior population living in that state, with a guaranteed minimum grant of one-half of 1 percent of the total amount appropriated. In addition, no state could receive less than it got in fiscal 2000 (known as the "hold harmless" provision), and every state was guaranteed a share of any increase in overall funding above the fiscal 2000 amount (known as "guaranteed growth").

The final bill substituted fiscal 2006 for fiscal 2000 and phased out the guaranteed growth provision over four years.

The compromise bill continued to define the mission of the Senior Community Service Employee Program in community service terms—a particular concern of many senators in both parties—but it also included the goal of increasing "the number of people who may enjoy the benefits of unsubsidized employment in both the public and private sectors." It required 25 percent of participants in the program to be in private sector jobs by 2011. At least 75 percent of a project's costs had to be used for wages and related expenses, as under prior law, but a group administering a project could request that be reduced to 65 percent.

LEGISLATIVE ACTION

The House passed a five-year reauthorization bill (HR 5293) by voice vote June 21 that would have required 30 percent of the participants in the job-training program to be placed in private employment within five years.

The Select Education Subcommittee of the House Education and the Workforce Committee had approved the bill by voice vote May 10. The full committee approved it May 17, also by voice vote, and reported it (H Rept 109-493) June 8. The subcommittee made several changes in the Senior Community Service Employee Program, including

- Reducing the portion of federal grant money that had to be used for wages and benefits for seniors employed through the program from 75 percent to 65 percent.
- Gradually increasing the percentage of participants placed in unsubsidized jobs from 20 percent to 30 percent in fiscal 2011. Also, seniors in the program would be allowed to work in for-profit companies. Under existing law, they could be placed only in public or nonprofit organizations.
- Imposing a four-year limit on participation in the program; there was no limit under existing law.

The subcommittee also gave voice-vote approval to an amendment by Chairman Pat Tiberi, R-Ohio, that reflected a compromise between panel Democrats who insisted that community service remain a prominent goal of the program and Republicans who wanted to reflect the administration's philosophy.

Under existing law, the Labor Department program was described simply as "an older American community-service employment program." The bill described it as a "community-service employment-based training program to foster and promote useful part-time public- and private-sector employment-based training opportunities ... and to provide vital social and human services to communities by providing work experience ... in public agencies, community-based and faith-based organizations."

The bill also proposed to make fiscal 2006, rather than 2000, the baseline for the hold harmless provision.

The Senate HELP Committee easily approved a bill (S 3570) by voice vote June 28, after adopting a substitute amendment by Chairman Michael B. Enzi, R-Wyo, also by voice vote. A report on the bill (S Rept 109-366) was filed Dec. 6.

The bill did not require any set percentage of participants in the senior employee program to find unsubsidized work. Enzi's substitute set a three-year limit on participation in the program, though it allowed for the nonprofits to waive the limit for 20 percent of their participants.

Jeff Bingaman, D-N.M., and other senators from states with fast-growing senior populations complained about the hold harmless provisions. "The effect of 'hold harmless' is to create a disparity in funding," he said. Bingaman also said he would try to reach a compromise before the bill reached the floor.

With members of both parties eager to renew services for seniors before the midterm election, the top Republicans and Democrats on the two committees bypassed a conference and worked out the terms of a compromise bill (HR 6197) that was introduced Sept. 27.

The negotiators were Enzi and Edward M. Kennedy of Massachusetts, the ranking Democrat on the HELP Committee, together with Howard P. "Buck" McKeon, R-Calif., chairman of the House Education and the Workforce Committee, and that panel's ranking Democrat, George Miller of California.

The House passed HR 6197 by voice vote Sept. 28, and the Senate passed, and thus cleared, it by voice vote as part of its pre-dawn wrap-up of business Sept. 30.

Head Start Reauthorization

Prospects for clearing a bill to revamp and reauthorize Head Start, the preschool program for low-income children, appeared to improve in 2005 after Republicans dropped a controversial White House proposal to let some states take greater control of the program. But the 109th Congress would expire without final action on the legislation (HR 2123, S 1107). *(110th Congress action, p. 586)*

BACKGROUND

The Head Start program, which began in 1965 as part of President Lyndon B. Johnson's War on Poverty (PL 89-253), was designed to help break the cycle of poverty by providing children between the ages of three and five from low-income families with a comprehensive preschool program intended to prepare them for school. From the beginning, Head Start provided not just educational services, but also health, nutritional, and other services to these children and their families. *(1965 law, Congress and the Nation Vol. II, p. 760)*

By 2005 Head Start had become a $6.8 billion federally funded program, operated locally by nonprofit organizations and faith-based groups and serving more than 900,000 low-income children. The last authorization, enacted in 1998 (PL 105-285), had expired at the end of fiscal 2003. The program had been extended by annual appropriations bills. *(1998 action, Congress and the Nation Vol. X, p. 491)*

President George W. Bush called for reshaping Head Start in early 2003 as part of his fiscal 2004 budget. He proposed giving states considerably more authority over the program and moving its administration from the Department of Health and Human Services (HHS) to the Department of Education as part of a plan to increase its emphasis on literacy. *(2003 action, Congress and the Nation Vol. XI, p. 527)*

The Bush administration and some congressional Republicans argued that allowing more state control of the federal-state program would ensure coordination with state school curricula. Democrats and the National Head Start Association, which represented 1,680 local operators, campaigned vigorously against the proposed change, arguing that it would eventually turn Head Start into a block grant program and erode its effectiveness in areas such as nutrition and health.

Anticipating stiff resistance to the plan, House Republicans introduced a five-year reauthorization bill in 2003 that dropped the idea of moving the program to the Education Department and replaced the shift of control to the states with a pilot program that would allow eight states to integrate their own preschool programs into Head Start. Head Start centers operated by church groups would have been allowed to hire staff on the basis of religious preferences.

A bill approved by the Senate Health, Education, Labor, and Pensions Committee in 2003 left out the pilot projects and the faith-based hiring language because of significant opposition from Republicans on the panel. Democrats blocked the bill from reaching the Senate floor in 2004, because they feared that they would be shut out of a GOP-controlled conference committee and would be unable to influence the final version.

HOUSE COMMITTEE ACTION

The House Education and the Workforce Committee approved a new, six-year Head Start reauthorization bill (HR 2123) by a vote of 48–0 on May 18 and reported it (H Rept 109-136) on June 16. The panel's Subcommittee on Education Reform approved the bill by voice vote May 11. Subcommittee chairman Michael N. Castle, R-Del., who had also written the 2003 bill, abandoned the controversial pilot projects. Instead, the bill required that Head Start operators work with local school districts to ensure that children entering kindergarten were well prepared for academic work and that their programs were in line with state academic standards. Castle said this was a less contentious route toward Bush's goal of ensuring that children were academically prepared for elementary school.

The bill also included changes to prevent financial abuse in local programs. A report in the spring by Congress's Government Accountability Office (GAO) had found that 76 percent of local Head Start operators surveyed in 2000 had some form of financial irregularity. Operators would be required to establish a local governance board to monitor all program activities. Operators with program deficiencies would have to compete for grants.

Democrats thanked Castle for reaching out to them and removing the administration-backed pilot project, but they said they would like the bill to contain more funding for Head Start teachers.

The bill authorized $6.9 billion for the program in fiscal 2006 and "such sums as are necessary" in fiscal 2007 through 2011. Castle said he was "a little reluctant" to establish specific authorization levels because appropriators were never able to meet them and they could become a major source of contention.

HOUSE FLOOR ACTION

The House passed HR 2123 on Sept. 22 on a largely party-line vote of 231–184.

The most fractious debate surrounded an amendment, adopted 220–196 on Sept. 22, to allow faith-based charities operating local programs to hire staff based on their religious preference. John A. Boehner, R-Ohio, chairman of the Education and the Workforce Committee, offered the amendment. He argued that religious groups already had the authority to hire employees based on their religious beliefs under the 1964 Civil Rights Act (PL 88-352). But, he said, "Too often, the federal government has ignored or impeded the efforts of faith-based organizations willing to lend a helping hand in providing critical services to the neediest in our communities."

Opponents said the amendment was unnecessary because more than one hundred Head Start programs were already being run by faith-based providers without any problems.

"Faith-based organizations sponsor Head Start programs now. They have and they will continue to. My own church hosted a Head Start program," said Democrat Robert C. Scott of Virginia. "We are talking just about [hiring] discrimination."

The House also on Sept. 22

- Adopted by voice vote an amendment by Ron Kind, D-Wis., to suspend the Head Start National Reporting System, a new standardized test developed by the Bush administration that measured the skills and progress of more than 400,000 children ages four and five years old. A GAO study in May found that HHS had not demonstrated that the test would accurately measure the progress of Head Start children. Some program advocates were concerned that the testing would later be used to shut down operators whose students did not score well. Under the Kind amendment, the National Academy of Sciences would review the test and make recommendations.

- Adopted by voice vote an amendment by John L. Mica, R-Fla., to require HHS to use an outside consulting firm to help overhaul its management of Head Start.
- Rejected 153–266 an amendment by Mark Souder, R-Ind., to retain the existing governance structure for Head Start and give councils of parents some authority over how local programs were operated. Castle's bill gave parent councils only an advisory role.
- Rejected 175–241 a proposal by Marilyn Musgrave, R-Colo., to allow for-profit providers participating in Head Start to make a profit.

SENATE COMMITTEE ACTION

The Senate Health, Education, Labor, and Pensions Committee took less than half an hour May 25 to give voice-vote approval to a five-year reauthorization bill (S 1107) that did not include the faith-based language. The bill was reported (S Rept 109-131) on Aug. 31.

The Senate bill called for a $300 million increase in authorized funding for each of the following three fiscal years, for a total of $7.2 billion in 2006, $7.5 billion in 2007, and $7.8 billion in 2008. Fiscal 2009 and 2010 would be funded with "such sums as necessary."

Some Democrats expressed concern about funding levels for teacher salaries. Under the bill, at least half of all Head Start teachers would have to have a bachelor's degree by 2011. Under existing law, half of all Head Start teachers had to have an associate's degree. Teachers were paid an average of $25,000 annually. Democrats said that, with a college degree, those educators could easily earn more teaching elementary school.

Sen. Patty Murray, D-Wash., a former preschool teacher, said she wanted a "trigger" that would delay the teacher qualification requirements unless Congress appropriated $7.2 billion annually for the program, but she agreed to work with Chairman Michael B. Enzi, R-Wyo., on a compromise before the bill reached the floor.

Senate Democrats also said that they would like stronger safeguards in the bill to monitor the Bush administration's new standardized test for preschool children. The Senate bill required that the National Academy of Sciences review all of the tests used in Head Start and within a year report its recommendations to improve the assessments.

S 1107 included two provisions to help the program reach more needy children. Head Start income eligibility requirements for families would be increased from 100 percent of the federal poverty level—nearly $19,000 annually for a family of four—to 130 percent. The legislation also would increase the funding for Early Head Start, which served families with children age three and younger, from 10 percent of Head Start's $6.8 billion overall funding to 18 percent by 2010.

Enzi also included more stringent standards for local operators applying to renew their grants, including allowing HHS to terminate a grant if a program was found to have multiple and recurring deficiencies. Enzi noted that under existing law some failing programs could operate almost two years before all appeals were exhausted.

2007–2008

The 110th Congress was fairly quiet on the human services front, save for a resolution of the Head Start fight that had prevented the program from being reauthorized since President George W. Bush took office.

Head Start Reauthorization

For the first time in nearly a decade, Congress in 2007 cleared legislation renewing and updating the policy guidelines for Head Start, the nation's principal child development program for low-income preschoolers. President George W. Bush signed the five-year authorization into law Dec. 12 (HR 1429—PL 110-134). *(109th Congress action, p. 107)*

The bill increased authorized spending for Head Start—a federally funded but locally operated program—starting at $7.35 billion in fiscal 2008. It also expanded eligibility, ended a much-criticized system of standardized testing for children four and five years old, and set higher education standards for Head Start teachers.

The bill did not include controversial language backed by Bush that would have allowed faith-based Head Start providers to take religion into account when hiring employees for the program. Partisan disputes over that issue, as well as over proposals by the Bush administration to give states more control over Head Start programs, had for years stalled efforts to renew the program.

Begun in 1965 as part of President Lyndon B. Johnson's War on Poverty, Head Start served low-income children up to age five, with the regular Head Start program serving children ages three to five and the Early Head Start program serving infants and toddlers up to age three. More than 900,000 children were enrolled in fiscal 2006, the last year for which data were available.

The program combined education activities with comprehensive social services, such as health and nutrition, and emphasized parental involvement. It was intended to help children from poor families catch up to their more affluent peers in preparation for elementary school and beyond.

The last Head Start authorization, enacted in 1998 (PL 105-285), expired at the end of fiscal 2003. The program had been kept alive since then through annual appropriations bills, receiving $6.9 billion under the fiscal 2007 omnibus spending law (PL 110-5). *(1998 action, Congress and the Nation Vol. X, p. 491; Fiscal 2007 appropriations, p. 107)*

HIGHLIGHTS

The following are highlights of the conference agreement on HR 1429.

Funding. The bill authorized $7.4 billion for Head Start in fiscal 2008, $7.7 billion in fiscal 2009, $8 billion in fiscal 2010, and unspecified amounts in fiscal 2011 and 2012.

Expanded eligibility. Head Start programs were given the flexibility to increase the income threshold for eligible families from 100 percent of the federal poverty level for a family of four, or $20,560 in 2007, to 130 percent, or $26,728. To expand eligibility, a program had to demonstrate a community need for such a change and continue its outreach to children and families at or below the poverty level. Homeless children were deemed eligible for Head Start.

Quality improvements. At least 30 percent of any increase in fiscal 2008 appropriations for Head Start over the previous year had to be used for quality improvements, such as professional development and higher salaries for Head Start teachers. At least 40 percent of any increase in fiscal 2009 through 2012 had to be used to improve quality.

By 2013, at least 50 percent of Head Start teachers nationwide—up from 37 percent—had to have at least a bachelor's degree in early childhood education or a related field. Teaching assistants had to have at least a child development associate credential and be enrolled in a program leading to a degree.

Accountability. The Department of Health and Human Services (HHS) was given two years to develop and put in place a new application review system to determine whether each local Head Start program was providing high-quality comprehensive early childhood services. HHS could de-fund seriously underperforming programs more quickly. People with conflicts of interest were barred from serving on Head Start governing boards. In a new program, HHS was directed to identify up to two hundred exemplary Head Start agencies as "centers of excellence" that would receive bonus grants.

National testing. The bill terminated any further use of the National Reporting System, a controversial test that had been given twice a year to all four- and five-year-olds in the Head Start program. It directed HHS to use the results of a forthcoming National Academy of Sciences study as guidance on the appropriate use of assessments in early childhood education programs.

Assessments. Any assessments used in the Head Start program had to be developmentally, linguistically, and culturally appropriate and consistent with nationally recognized professional and technical standards on assessing young children. The assessments had to be administered by individuals who were adequately trained, and accommodations had to be made for children with disabilities or limited English proficiency. The assessments could not be used to exclude children.

Early learning standards. HHS was required to consult with experts in reevaluating and updating early learning standards, based on the best available scientific findings.

Limited English. The measure required improved outreach to families of children with limited English proficiency, set standards for communicating with such parents, and targeted training resources to meet the needs of communities that experienced a rapid increase in children with limited English proficiency.

HOUSE ACTION

The House Education and Labor Committee approved a Head Start reauthorization bill (HR 1429) by a vote of 42–1 on March 14, after a five-hour markup that focused primarily on faith-based hiring practices. The bill was reported (H Rept 110-67) on March 23.

The bill included provisions to

- Authorize $7.4 billion for Head Start in fiscal 2008 and such amounts as might be necessary in fiscal 2009 through 2012. Supporters said the increase would allow up to ten thousand additional children to participate in the program.
- Require that by 2013 at least 50 percent of Head Start teachers nationally have a bachelor's degree. All teachers would have to have an associate's degree by 2009.
- Require that, in fiscal 2008 through 2012, 60 percent of the increase appropriated for Head Start over the prior year's level be used for quality improvements.
- Suspend the use of the standardized national testing program for preschoolers.
- Increase the amount set aside for Early Head Start from 10 percent of Head Start funding to 12 percent in fiscal 2008, rising annually until it reached 20 percent in fiscal 2012.

During the markup, the committee

- Rejected 19–26 an amendment by Luis Fortuño, Puerto Rico's Republican resident commissioner, that would have allowed faith-based providers to take religion into account when hiring. Republicans said the amendment was critical to the future of the program because it would allow more faith-based groups to become providers. Bill sponsor Dale E. Kildee of Michigan and other panel Democrats countered that the amendment would allow religious groups to discriminate while receiving federal funds.
- Rejected 18–27 an amendment to allow a pilot program in which eight states would take over their local Head Start programs. The same pilot program drew significant opposition in 2003 when Republicans included it in a Head Start bill. The Bush administration and GOP supporters said more state control would ensure coordination with state school curricula. Democrats and the National Head Start Association said it would lead to Head Start being turned into a block grant with decreased emphasis on health and nutrition.
- Adopted by voice vote an amendment by Chairman George Miller, D-Calif., that included provisions to increase the annual income level at which families would become eligible for Head Start from 100 percent of the federal poverty level for a family of four to 130 percent. It also required that 25 percent of the 60 percent set aside for quality improvements go toward increasing teachers' salaries.

The full House passed HR 1429 by a vote of 365–48 on May 2, 2007, after another emotionally charged debate about religious preference in hiring.

A majority of Republicans ultimately supported the measure, but only after protesting a decision by Democratic leaders not to allow a faith-based hiring amendment. Republicans offered a motion to recommit the bill with instructions to add the faith-based provision. The motion was rejected May 2 on a **key vote of 195–222 (R 191–2; D 4–220).** *(2007 key votes, p. 955)*

Instead, the House voted 229–195 on May 2 to amend the bill with language noting the history and importance of allowing faith-based and community-based organizations to participate in Head Start programs and explicitly stating that they would continue to be eligible to participate on the same basis as other organizations.

The House on May 2 also rejected 165–254 an amendment by Tom Price, R-Ga., to allow the eight-state pilot program.

SENATE ACTION

The Senate Health, Education, Labor, and Pensions Committee had gotten started on Head Start legislation first, giving voice-vote approval Feb. 14 to a bipartisan measure (S 556) written by Chairman Edward M. Kennedy, D-Mass., and ranking Republican Michael B. Enzi of Wyoming. The bill was reported (S Rept 110-49) on April 10.

The provisions were similar to those in the House bill, with some exceptions. For example, the Senate version included provisions to

- Increase authorized funding for Head Start to $7.4 billion in fiscal 2008, as in the House bill, but also specified amounts for the following two years. It called for $7.7 billion in 2009, $8 billion in 2010, and "such sums as necessary" through fiscal 2012.
- Place no cap on the number of children from families with incomes between 100 percent and 130 percent of the poverty level that could participate in the program.
- Require that 30 percent of any funding increase for Head Start in fiscal 2008 go to improving quality. In fiscal 2009 through 2012, the portion would be 40 percent.
- Authorize $100 million for a new state incentive grant program for Head Start agencies identified as "centers of excellence." The proposal was a priority for Kennedy, who said the bill aimed to create a "seamless web" between Head Start and other

education programs by dedicating 1 percent of funding for programs that aligned Head Start with state early learning standards. It also included literacy training for Head Start teachers to develop children's reading skills. Like the House version, the bill did not include GOP proposals to give states more control over the program or to allow faith-based hiring.

The Senate easily passed HR 1429 by voice vote June 19, after substituting the text of S 556.

CONFERENCE, FINAL ACTION

After months of informal negotiations, House and Senate conferees Nov. 8 reached agreement on HR 1429. The House adopted the conference report (H Rept 110-439) by a vote of 381–36 on Nov. 14. Hours later, the Senate cleared the measure 95–0.

Among their decisions, the conferees

- Adopted the Senate's specific authorization amounts for fiscal 2009 and 2010.
- Did not include the House's cap on the number of children above 100 percent of the poverty level who could participate in Head Start. However, the conference report stated that funds should go first to serving children living below the poverty line.
- Required, as did the Senate bill, that 30 percent of any funding increase for Head Start in fiscal 2008 be set aside for quality improvement, rising to 40 percent in fiscal 2009 through 2012.
- Did not reserve a specific amount for Early Head Start.

Chronology of Action on Veterans Affairs

Veterans issues began demanding more attention from lawmakers during the 109th Congress, as the number of retiring servicemen and -women from the wars in Iraq and Afghanistan suddenly began to balloon. Funding issues were paramount. As Congress was quick to spend for the conflicts themselves, finding the additional money to care for injured soldiers upon their return home proved somewhat more difficult. Although the Department of Veterans Affairs health system was known for having one of the nation's most advanced electronic health records systems, it, too, was not immune to problem of identity theft. That led to corrective legislation in 2006.

Outlays for Veterans

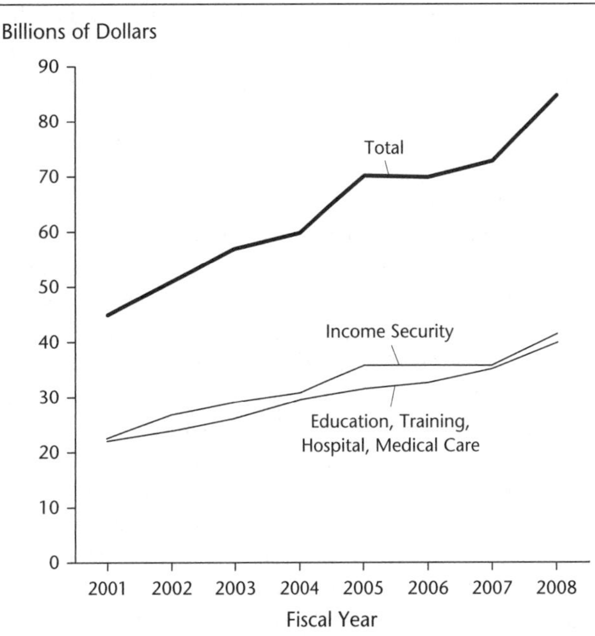

SOURCE: Office of Management and Budget, *Historical Tables, Budget of the United States Government: Fiscal Year 2010* (Washington, D.C.: U.S. Government Printing Office, 2009), Table 3.2.

NOTE: Total line includes expenditures not shown separately.

REFERENCES

Discussion of veterans' programs for the years 1945–1964 may be found in *Congress and the Nation Vol. I*, pp. 1335–1373; for the years 1965–1968, *Congress and the Nation Vol. II*, pp. 453–460; for the years 1969–1972, *Congress and the Nation Vol. III*, pp. 537–548; for the years 1973–1976, *Congress and the Nation Vol. IV*, pp. 158–181; for the years 1977–1980, *Congress and the Nation Vol. V*, pp. 177–191; for the years 1981–1984, *Congress and the Nation Vol. VI*, pp. 613–625; for the years 1985–1988, *Congress and the Nation Vol. VII*, p. 633–644; for the years 1989–1992, *Congress and the Nation Vol. VIII*, pp. 625–637; for the years 1993–1996, *Congress and the Nation Vol. IX*, pp. 597–603; for the years 1997–2001, *Congress and the Nation Vol. X*, pp. 497–503; for the years 2001–2004, *Congress and the Nation Vol. XI*, pp. 530–534.

2005–2006

Identity Theft Protections

Congress cleared legislation in 2006 to protect veterans from data losses at the Department of Veterans Affairs (VA). The provisions were enacted as part of a broader veterans package signed into law Dec. 22 (S 3421—PL 109-461). *(Identify theft, p. 701)*

The push for legislation to protect veterans from data theft grew out of the theft in May 2006 of a VA laptop computer containing the personal information of 26.5 million veterans and their families. The computer was later recovered, and authorities said they had found no evidence that the data had been accessed. But the VA's information technology operation had drawn sharp criticism for years, and the incident sparked outrage in Congress.

The House passed a bill (HR 5835—H Rept 109-651) by voice vote Sept. 26, 2006, to revamp information technology operations at the VA and offer credit monitoring to those affected in the event of a data breach. The measure, sponsored by Veterans' Affairs chairman Steve Buyer, R-Ind., had been approved in committee by voice vote on July 20 and reported (H Rept 109-651, Part I) on Sept. 13. Among other provisions, it called for the creation of an undersecretary for information services with three deputy undersecretaries reporting to the new officer.

On Dec. 8, with the 109th Congress about to adjourn, Buyer proposed that the House add data protection provisions, along with language from other House-passed veterans bills, to a Senate-passed bill (S 3421) on VA medical facilities. The House agreed by voice vote, and the Senate accepted the changes, also by voice vote, on Dec. 9, the last day of the session.

The bill set up a program in the VA to monitor and improve the department's data security, though it did not elevate the position of the chief information officer to undersecretary. If a data breach occurred, the department was required to determine whether there was "a reasonable risk . . . for the potential misuse of sensitive personal information." If so, the department was required to notify those affected and provide free credit protection services. The VA also had to notify law enforcement and certain congressional committees when a data breach was discovered.

Veterans Health Spending

Before departing for the 2005 August recess, Congress appropriated $1.5 billion in supplemental spending to make up an unexpected shortfall in fiscal 2005 funding for veterans' health care programs. The emergency money was attached to the fiscal 2006 Interior-environment spending bill, which President George W. Bush signed into law Aug. 2 (HR 2361—PL 109-54). *(Appropriations, pp. 77, 78)*

Six weeks earlier, Veterans Affairs Department (VA) officials had told stunned lawmakers that the VA faced shortages of $1 billion in fiscal 2005 and an unknown amount in fiscal 2006 because of faulty health care cost projections. Agency officials told the House Veterans' Affairs Committee June 23 that their original spending requests for fiscal 2005 were based on a financial model that predated the 2003 invasion of Iraq. Spending growth had jumped from an expected 2.5 percent to 5 percent since then, and the number of patients had grown significantly because of the war. The officials said they had known about the mistake for two months.

House members were furious they had not been told about the shortfall before they passed their fiscal 2006 spending bill (HR 2528) for the Veterans Affairs Department and military construction in May. California Republican Jerry Lewis, chairman of the Appropriations Committee, said it "borders on stupidity" for the VA not to have come forward sooner.

Democrats, who had attempted earlier in the year to add billions in veterans funding as part of an Iraq war supplemental (PL 109-13), crowed. "We hate to say, 'I told you so,'" Bob Filner of California said at a news conference with fellow Democrats, "but, 'I told you so.'"

Eager to act, the Senate voted 96–0 on June 29 to attach $1.5 billion in fiscal 2005 funds for VA medical services to the Interior-environment spending bill, figuring the funds could spill over into fiscal 2006 if needed. The measure passed later that day.

House leaders took a different route, waiting for the administration to submit a request. On June 30, the White House asked Congress for a $975 million fiscal 2005 supplemental. The House passed a stand-alone bill (HR 3130) for that amount by a vote of 419–0 the same day.

Senators dug in, saying they would accept nothing less than $1.5 billion, which they said would cover the immediate funding gap and give the VA a cushion for fiscal 2006 when the shortfall could amount to $2.7 billion. House Republicans, however, wanted to stick to the president's request. "They're making up numbers over in the Senate," said Steve Buyer, R-Ind., chairman of the House Veterans' Affairs Committee. "We're not going to make up numbers over here in the House."

The standoff delayed what lawmakers had hoped would be a quick solution, forcing them to go home for the July Fourth recess empty-handed.

After returning to Washington, D.C., senators reaffirmed their strong support for the $1.5 billion in emergency fiscal 2005 funding, voting 95–0 on July 12 to add the money to the fiscal 2006 Homeland Security spending bill (HR 2360) as well.

On July 14, the White House acknowledged that more funding would be needed. It said the VA would need

$2 billion more for health care in fiscal 2006 than Bush had assumed when he sent his budget to Capitol Hill in February. The revised request included $300 million to replace fiscal 2005 VA funds the administration had assumed would be available in fiscal 2006. The $300 million for fiscal 2005 was a surprise, but it helped convince the House to agree to the Senate's $1.5 billion figure.

Lawmakers' desire to get the veterans funding approved before the August recess in turn helped make the Interior-environment bill the first of the fiscal 2006 measures to clear. The House adopted the conference report (H Rept 109-188) 410–10 on July 28. The Senate cleared the bill 99–1 on July 29.

To make up the shortfall for fiscal 2006, Congress subsequently approved an extra $1.2 billion in emergency funds for VA health programs as part of the appropriations bill for military construction and Veterans Affairs.

Veteran Fee Hikes

Reflecting the strong public support for the nation's troops in wartime, both chambers voted to significantly increase the size of the military construction and the Department of Veterans Affairs (VA) spending bill for fiscal 2007 (HR 5385). They rejected proposals by the George W. Bush administration to increase fees and other out-of-pocket health costs for both veterans and military retirees.

But final action on the bill in 2006 was blocked in the post-election lame-duck session by Senate conservatives who feared that the conference report could be used as a vehicle for a costly year-end spending package. As a result, the bill was one of nine unfinished fiscal 2007 spending measures left for the Democratic-controlled 110th Congress. Programs covered by the legislation were funded through Feb. 15, 2007, under a stopgap spending law signed Dec. 9, 2006 (H J Res 102—PL 109-383). Democrats said they would clear a year-long joint resolution for all nine bills when they took over the leadership of the new Congress.

The House Appropriations Committee approved HR 5385 by voice vote May 10 and reported it (H Rept 109-464) May 15. A supplemental report (H Rept 109-464, Part II) was filed May 16. The $136.1 billion bill included $94.7 billion in discretionary funding—an 11 percent increase over fiscal 2006. The bill was drafted by the panel's Military Quality of Life and Veterans Affairs' Subcommittee, which approved it by voice vote May 4.

The subcommittee rejected Bush's request to increase fees for some veterans and retirees. Appropriators said in their report on the bill that the increases had not been authorized and were not included by the Congressional Budget Office in estimating the cost of Bush's request.

The administration had proposed requiring a $250 annual enrollment fee and increasing prescription drug co-payments from $8 to $15 for veterans who made more than $26,902 a year and were not disabled. The VA estimated that the changes would reduce its costs by $765 million in fiscal 2007. The administration also proposed increased enrollment fees, deductibles, and pharmacy co-payments for military retirees under age sixty-five who were eligible for TRICARE, the military health insurance system.

The appropriators said they were able to make up for the proposed veterans offsets, but they could not find the money to replace the $735 million that Bush would have

VETERANS LEADERSHIP

James B. Peake was confirmed by voice vote Dec. 14, 2007, to be the third head of the Veterans Affairs Department (VA) under President George W. Bush. The Senate Veterans' Affairs Committee had endorsed his nomination 15–0 the day before. Jim Nicholson resigned as VA head on Oct. 1, 2007, after a sometimes-tumultuous two-and-a-half-year tenure. Nicholson had succeeded Anthony Principi. *(Nicholson background, Principi service, Congress and the Nation Vol. XI, p. 926)*

Nicholson, who had previously served as head of the Republican National Committee, presided over a particularly difficult period for the department, including the 2006 theft of an unsecured laptop computer that contained personal information on more than 26 million veterans and service members. The VA was also feeling the strain of thousands of returning troops from Iraq and Afghanistan, without commensurate funding increases to serve them.

Peake, sixty-three, was the Army surgeon general from 2000 until 2004, when he retired as a lieutenant general. He then became chief operating officer of QTC Management Inc., which provided medical examination and electronic medical records services to government clients, including the VA.

Peake arrived at the VA at a time of unprecedented demand for health services from aging veterans of World War II, Korea, and Vietnam, as well as a new wave of Iraq and Afghanistan veterans with traumatic brain injury, post-traumatic stress disorder, and other illnesses. Congress was also plainly annoyed at the VA's handling of a disability claims backlog.

In addition, it fell to Peake to handle implementation of legislation (HR 1585) to ease the transition of wounded soldiers from the Pentagon's health care system to the VA. The measure was written at the urging of a presidential commission chaired by former senator Bob Dole, R-Kan. (1969–1996), and former health and human services secretary Donna E. Shalala. The commission was created after reports surfaced about dilapidated facilities and poorly managed care at Walter Reed Army Medical Center in Washington, D.C.

gotten from the increased TRICARE fees. James T. Walsh, R-N.Y., chairman of the subcommittee, said the TRICARE funding gap probably would be addressed in conference.

Like their House counterparts, Senate appropriators rejected White House proposals for an annual enrollment fee and higher prescription drug co-payments for some veterans. Military Construction-Veterans Affairs Subcommittee chairwoman Kay Bailey Hutchison, R-Texas, suggested that a compromise on the proposed income threshold for higher fees was possible. Dianne Feinstein of California, ranking Democrat on the subcommittee, criticized the administration's proposal as "another back-door fee scheme embedded in the appropriations process to balance the VA's books without going through the proper policy channels."

In its report on the bill, the GOP-controlled Senate Appropriations Committee criticized the administration for relying on un-enacted fees instead of requesting enough money to pay for the veterans' health programs, thereby putting the onus on Congress to "either enact the fees, shortchange veterans healthcare, or make up the difference." The appropriators said this was "not responsible budgeting. It is not a practice that the Congress should tolerate."

2007–2008

Thanks to new medical advances, many wounded troops who in previous conflicts would have succumbed to their injuries instead survived, though with disabilities, which placed new strains on both the military's medical system and the Department of Veterans Affairs (VA) medical system. The sudden influx of seriously injured soldiers highlighted the difficulty in handing patients off between the military and VA medical systems. The problem was painfully brought to public view in a Pulitzer Prize–winning series published by the *Washington Post* in 2007. That, in turn, led to legislation passed as part of the fiscal 2008 defense authorization bill to better care for so-called wounded warriors.

Lawmakers also successfully managed to enact a major update of the GI Bill, the post–World War II legislation that helped returning veterans of that conflict obtain a college education, buy their first homes, and start businesses, helping spur the nation's economic growth in the 1950s.

Wounded Warrior Act

The defense authorization bill cleared by Congress in 2007 included provisions of the House and Senate versions of legislation referred to as the Wounded Warrior Act. President George W. Bush signed the measure into law Jan. 28, 2008 (HR 4986—PL 110-181). It was the largest defense authorization bill since World War II in real terms, and the first since Sept. 11, 2001, to authorize emergency funding for an entire fiscal year of operations in Iraq and Afghanistan. *(Defense authorization, p. 373)*

President Bush unexpectedly vetoed the first version of the bill over a single provision opposed by the Iraqi government. Congress sent him a revised bill in January 2008 that allowed him to waive application of the provision to Iraq, paving the way for a 3.5 percent pay raise for U.S. troops along with major improvements in their medical care and other benefits. *(Veto message, p. 1066)*

The "wounded warriors" provisions came in response to problems at the Walter Reed Army Medical Center disclosed by the *Washington Post* in a Pulitzer Prize–winning series published in February 2007. The newspaper highlighted problems of neglect at Walter Reed in Washington, D.C., sparking a public outcry and the resignations of the center's commanding general, the army's chief medical officer, and the secretary of the army. Revelations of poor patient care throughout the military's health care system, including problems experienced in navigating the military's medical bureaucracy, subsequently came to light. To improve patient care and service, the bill

- Created the Wounded Warrior Resource Center to serve as a single point of contact for service members, their families, and their primary caregivers to help them get needed care and to navigate the military's health care bureaucracy.
- Required semiannual inspections of housing facilities for recovering service members.
- Required the Defense Department and the VA to jointly develop a comprehensive policy on the care and management of members of the armed forces, including the creation of fully interoperable electronic health records.
- Mandated the establishment of new Defense Department standards for processing medical evaluations and for training and qualifying staff to perform the evaluations. This included assigning independent medical advisers to assist recovering service members and their families.
- Mandated the establishment of new department standards for processing disability evaluations to reduce discrepancies between the Defense Department assessments and those conducted by the VA and to ensure consistent decisions among the military departments.
- Required a comprehensive policy to address traumatic brain injury, post-traumatic stress disorder, other mental health conditions, and military eye injuries, as well as the creation of centers of excellence focused on those conditions.

GI Bill Expansion

GI education benefits were significantly increased for the first time in nearly twenty-five years as part of an emergency war supplemental spending bill that President George W. Bush signed June 30, 2008 (HR 2642—PL 110-252).

The provisions created a permanent entitlement program that expanded education benefits for veterans who had served since Sept. 11, 2001. The measure was based on a bill written by Virginia Democratic senator Jim Webb, a former marine and Vietnam War veteran who served as secretary of the navy in the Reagan administration (1981–1989). The program was expected to cost as much as $62 billion over ten years.

The Servicemen's Readjustment Act of 1944 (PL 78-346), as the first GI Bill was formally known, was written to provide money for college or vocational education, as well as cheap loans to buy homes and start businesses, for returning World War II veterans. The program was reworked in 1984 under the Montgomery GI Bill (PL 98-525), named for Rep. G.V. "Sonny" Montgomery, D-Miss. (1967–1997), the longtime chairman of the House Veterans' Affairs Committee. *(1984 law, Congress and the Nation Vol. VI, p. 621)*

Veterans said the money they received was inadequate to pay for their college educations. Active-duty service members who became full-time students received up to $1,101 per month for a maximum of thirty-six months—a fraction of the total cost of tuition, books, and room and board at most colleges and universities.

Webb introduced his bill in 2007 on his first day in office, but the measure stagnated. In February 2008, he joined with John W. Warner, R-Va., also a former navy secretary as well as a previous chairman of the Senate Armed Services Committee, to revise the bill and make it more palatable to Senate fiscal conservatives.

The White House and the Pentagon said repeatedly that Webb's plan to overhaul the GI Bill would hurt Pentagon efforts to retain members of the armed services and would work against the government's ability to maintain an all-volunteer military. Webb called such reasoning "absurd." He said, "It is going to expand their recruiting base, and I think it would improve the active-duty military."

In a statement of administration policy released May 15, the White House said the president wanted to work with Democrats on the issue but repeated concerns about retention and complained that the bill would not allow veterans to transfer unused education benefits to family members.

In addition, "Blue Dog" Democrats, a forty-nine-member House coalition of fiscal conservatives, opposed providing the expensive benefits without paying for them through increased tax revenues or reduced spending elsewhere in the budget.

Democratic leaders in the House and Senate were ultimately able to sway Republicans by using the war supplemental as leverage and by agreeing to allow veterans to transfer their education benefits to family members. The Blue Dogs were brought along despite the lack of offsets, which were not acceptable to Senate Republicans.

HIGHLIGHTS

The following were the main provisions of the GI Bill expansion.

Education benefits. Eligible veterans were entitled to receive tuition assistance. Depending on their length of service, the amount could equal what in-state residents paid at the costliest public educational institution in the veteran's home state. Benefits were scaled back for veterans with shorter time on active duty.

Other benefits included a monthly stipend to cover housing expenses, based on average housing prices in the area, and stipends for books and other required educational expenses. An additional payment of $100 per month was available for tutorial assistance, expiring after twelve months or until a total of $1,200 had been used. The bill also allowed payment for one licensing or certification test, not to exceed the lesser of $2,000 or the exam fee.

Eligibility and terms. To qualify for the increased education benefits, a veteran had to have served between three months and three years of active duty after Sept. 11, 2001. National Guard and reserve members were fully eligible for the assistance. The assistance covered thirty-six months, equal to four academic years. The entitlement was protected if the veteran's education was interrupted by deployment or transfer, and veterans had fifteen years to use the benefits. Service members could transfer education benefits to their spouses and dependents.

Benefit levels. Payment for tuition and stipends ranged from 40 percent to 100 percent of total costs, based on how long the veteran had served on active duty. A veteran who served three months was eligible for 40 percent of the maximum award. Six months earned 50 percent. The benefit topped out at 100 percent for those who served a thirty-six-month tour on active duty.

Public-private contributions. The measure created a program under which the federal government would provide a dollar-for-dollar match to contributions made by private colleges and universities that were more expensive.

LEGISLATIVE ACTION

Democrats in both chambers appended similar education benefits to their versions of the supplemental spending bill (HR 2642). The provisions were part of a domestic spending section of the bill that also included items such as extended unemployment benefits.

The House approved the portion of the bill devoted to the GI benefits and numerous other domestic provisions by a vote of 256–166 on May 15, 2008. The veterans' benefits were virtually the same as those included in the final bill, with one major exception. To win the support of the Blue Dogs, a group of fiscally conservative House Democrats, the leadership included a 0.47 percent surtax on modified adjusted gross incomes above $500,000 ($1 million for joint filers) to pay for the expansion. The Blue Dogs had delayed action on the bill and threatened to defect if it included the new benefits without offsets.

The Senate sent a revised version of the domestic spending package back to the House by a vote of 75–22 on May 22. The only significant difference in the GI Bill provisions was the omission of the surtax, which Republicans rejected as a part of their general opposition to tax increases.

Senate Republicans had offered a competing version of the GI benefits bill cosponsored by John McCain of Arizona and Lindsey Graham of South Carolina. It would have increased the monthly education benefit by $400 to $1,500, with a maximum of $2,000 per month after twelve years of service. The benefit could have been transferred to family members. The senators offered the plan May 14 as an amendment to an unrelated collective-bargaining bill (HR 980), but the Senate voted 55–42 to table the proposal, thus killing it.

The final version of the supplemental was worked out by House leaders and the White House. The House adopted the domestic spending portion 416–12 on June 19. The Senate cleared the bill 92–6 on June 26.

The negotiators dropped the House plan to offset the cost of the veterans provisions with a surtax on wealthy taxpayers, a decision that did not go over well with the House Blue Dogs. Not only was the offset removed, but Democrats also agreed to a White House proposal to allow veterans to transfer the benefit to family members, which was likely to add $10 billion to its cost.

But most of the Blue Dogs chose to express their opposition to the decision by voting against the rule (H Res 1284) that governed the floor debate, and not against the supplemental itself. Forty Democrats voted against the rule, which was adopted by a vote of 342–83 on June 19, but only three cast "nay" votes on the domestic spending amendment, which included the veterans' education benefit.

CHAPTER 10

Education

Education

The ideological divide between Democrats and Republicans came into sharp focus in the 109th and 110th Congresses through members' efforts to shape and direct the federally financed student loan system. Meanwhile, turmoil in the national credit markets put a new spin on the debate.

SLOW DECLINE

The system of private federally guaranteed student loans predated the government-run direct loan program. President Bill Clinton and a Democratic Congress in 1993 overhauled the student loan system (PL 103-66), establishing parallel programs of both private and direct lending. For a brief time, direct loans were in the ascendancy—at one point accounting for more than 30 percent of all lending. If Clinton had gotten his way, private loans would have been abandoned. Instead, Republicans, who ruled Capitol Hill from the mid-1990s to the mid-2000s, along with the succeeding George W. Bush administration, maintained a decidedly antagonistic view of government-issued loans. As a result, the course was reversed.

In incremental steps, during a time when the cost of obtaining a college degree soared, Republicans chipped away at direct loans and gave advantage after advantage to private lenders. For instance, lawmakers imposed tighter caps on the market share permitted to direct loans, and they shielded private lenders from the risk inherent in borrowing at one rate and earning interest at a lower rate. In 1997, Congress took away the $10 per loan payment to colleges that participated in the direct loan program.

Bush in early 2006 signed into law a budget-cutting bill (PL 109-171) designed to save the government $39 billion over five years. Of that, $14 billion in savings came mostly from cutting the federal subsidies paid to banks that made college loans. In the same measure, Congress trimmed loan fees and increased the amounts that students could borrow. But even as lawmakers reduced the subsidies for banks, buried in the legislation were provisions restricting the business of their main competitor in offering student loans: the federal government.

In PL 109-171, Congress weakened two features unique to the government loan program that helped students manage their debts. One change ended a process known as in-school consolidation, which allowed borrowers to lump together multiple student loans from different lenders under a single direct loan while still in school. That prevented many borrowers from changing lenders by consolidation—a procedure akin to mortgage refinancing. The other change limited the ability of borrowers with private loans to obtain an income-contingent repayment plan from the direct loan program. Income-contingent repayment allowed low-income borrowers to repay as they were able and forgave any remaining debt after twenty-five years. Some critics contended that the changes appeared intended to make private lending look more attractive to colleges.

The law also changed the financing of the Department of Education office that supervised student loan programs. No longer would administrative costs be a mandatory expense, relatively immune from the congressional appropriations process. Instead, appropriators would be able—if they chose—to cut the budget. That change was more important for direct loans, because most administrative costs for private loans were borne by lenders. Supporters maintained that it promoted accountability of the student loan office.

REFERENCES

Discussion of education policy for the years 1945–1964 may be found in *Congress and the Nation Vol. I,* pp. 1195–1215; for the years 1965–1968, *Congress and the Nation Vol. II,* pp. 709–733; for the years 1969–1972, *Congress and the Nation Vol. III,* pp. 581–604; for the years 1973–1976, *Congress and the Nation Vol. IV,* pp. 377–402; for the years 1977–1980, *Congress and the Nation Vol. V,* pp. 655–677; for the years 1981–1984, *Congress and the Nation Vol. VI,* pp. 555–580; for the years 1985–1988, *Congress and the Nation Vol. VII,* pp. 647–663; for the years 1989–1992, *Congress and the Nation Vol. VIII,* pp. 641–660; for the years 1993–1996, *Congress and the Nation Vol. IX,* pp. 607–634; for the years 1997–2001, *Congress and the Nation Vol. X,* pp. 507–549; for the years 2001–2004, *Congress and the Nation Vol. XI,* pp. 537–552.

Outlays for Education

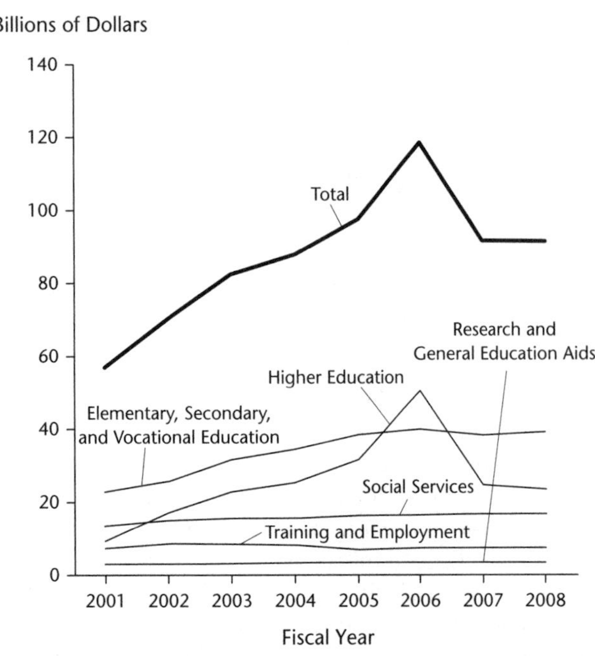

SOURCE: Office of Management and Budget, *Historical Tables, Budget of the United States Government: Fiscal Year 2010* (Washington, D.C.: U.S. Government Printing Office, 2009), Table 3.2.

NOTE: Total line includes expenditures not shown separately

Direct loan system advocates said most of the changes in the 2006 law were designed to make private loans more desirable to the people who decided which types of loans would be available to students: college administrators. Meanwhile, banks and other lenders lured colleges away from direct lending by offering discounts to borrowers that generally were not available to the government-run program. These discounts included a reduction in the amount of the loan principal after a borrower had made several years of on-time payments. Lenders also made their loans easier to administer than the government program's loans. And lenders sometimes formed partnerships that allowed schools to earn money by making loans themselves to their graduate students.

Proponents of the shift toward private lending said it was driven by the notion that a market-based system of loans was superior to one run by the government, just as they said was the case with health care, energy generation, and other kinds of regulated industries. But with the student loan business, it was hard to say whether the advantages of the marketplace benefited the student or the taxpayer. Both the Congressional Budget Office and the White House Office of Management and Budget said that, by their calculations, the government's direct lending program was cheaper for taxpayers than the guaranteed loan program run by banks. In fact, experts noted, the private lending system was hardly market-based at all. Private college loan providers do not compete on price because, except for some optional discounts, the government sets the terms for all student loans. And private lenders bear almost none of the risk usually associated with free-market business because federal law guarantees that as much as 100 percent of a student's loan would be repaid and, at the same time, promised a minimum return on every dollar borrowed. Experts said that the ability of the banks to gain market share had less to do with inherent advantages of a private system than with Congress's drive to get the government out of the loan business.

NEW LIFE

By the time the Democrats took over the majority in the 110th Congress, banks and other private lenders accounted for 80 percent of all government-backed loans, drawing on federal guarantees and subsidies to make a profit. Democrats, however, were determined to make good on their 2006 campaign promise to make college more affordable. Direct loan supporters had long insisted that the government-run direct loan system was a cheaper and more efficient way to help students and their parents cope with rising tuitions and fees. Most Democrats were convinced that the student loan system, by GOP design, had been tailored to benefit big private lenders. Moreover, they suspected that some lenders were gaming the system, citing the practices of Nelnet, a large student loan company that Education Department auditors in 2006 accused of overbilling the government for hundreds of millions of dollars.

Direct loan advocates had faced an uphill battle, with many lawmakers and lending advocates saying that students might not get the same services or benefits from the Department of Education that they did from private companies. In 2007 New York attorney general Andrew M. Cuomo showed that some private lenders were paying schools for their endorsements. That scandal helped the direct-lending cause, leading to Congress cutting the federal subsidy for lenders by more than $20 billion. That, in turn, lowered the companies' guaranteed profit and led credit agencies to downgrade their ratings, making borrowing more expensive.

By early 2008, the widening global credit crunch began making it much harder for private lenders to get the capital they needed to make loans. Essentially, the collapse of subprime mortgage lending also upended the financial route used by student loan companies. The market for securities backed by all sorts of loans, including those issued to students and mortgages, was frozen. And the value of securities backed by student loans began to decline.

As a result, a growing number of student lenders started to bail. In addition, some lenders, financial aid administrators, and lawmakers wanted the federal government to consider putting cash into the private loan market to keep it functioning. The idea was to give money to lenders in the

President George W. Bush signs the bill "Ensuring Continued Access to Student Loans Act of 2008" into law on May 7, 2008, during a ceremony in the Oval Office. Supporters looking on include Senator Ted Kennedy, D-Mass.; Representative Rubén Hinojosa, D-Tex. Representative George Miller, D-Calif. Representative Buck McKeon, R-Calif. Senator Mike Enzi, R-Wyo.; Secretary of the Treasury Hank Paulson; Representative Rick Keller R-Fla.; and Secretary of Education Margaret Spellings.
Source: AP Photo/White House, Chris Greenberg

same way the Federal Reserve floated loans to rescue investment bank Bear Stearns Companies.

For colleges, the key concern was whether their students would have access to loans. Those in the direct lending program, which relied on government capital and was not affected by the credit crunch, did not have any worries. But schools that relied on private lenders started to wonder if enough would stay in the program.

Chronology of Action on Education

2005–2006

Congress made limited progress in tackling reauthorization of the Higher Education Act, the nation's main federal college aid program. In a rebuke to the White House, Congress renewed two vocational education programs for high school students, which, by providing career and technical training, many lawmakers believed helped to strengthen the economy. Reforms in education-related policies were prompted by the devastating 2005 Gulf Coast hurricanes, including, for example, allowing the waiving of financial rules for campus-based aid programs at colleges affected by natural disasters.

Higher Education

Congress in 2006 revised and reauthorized for eight years, under budget reconciliation legislation (S 1932—PL 109-171), the sections of the Higher Education Act that covered the two largest federal student loan programs. Congress also cleared a nine-month extension (HR 6138—PL 109-292) of the main federal law governing higher education programs, through June 30, 2007. *(Reconciliation, p. 81)*

The 1965 Higher Education Act (PL 89-329) had not been fully reauthorized since 1998 (PL 105-244). It covered all federal aid to students and colleges, including direct and guaranteed loans, Pell grants, and campus-based aid such as low-interest Perkins loans and work-study programs. A series of temporary extensions had kept the law in effect since the end of fiscal 2003, when it was originally set to expire. *(PL 89-329, Congress and the Nation Vol. II, p. 716; PL 105-244, Congress and the Nation Vol. X, p. 509; previous extension, Congress and the Nation Vol. XI, p. 550; campus-based aid programs, p. 607)*

Congress cleared a major overhaul of the higher education law in 2008. *(110th Congress action, p. 611)*

2005 ACTION ON REAUTHORIZATION BILLS

The 21st Century Competitiveness Subcommittee of the House Education and the Workforce Committee approved, 18–15, a higher education reauthorization (HR 609) on July 14, 2005. During markup, the subcommittee adopted by voice vote a Michael N. Castle, R-Del., amendment to restore a rule requiring that at least 10 percent of a for-profit college's revenue be from sources other than federal aid and that the rule be applied to all colleges. Under Castle's proposal, students would not be immediately penalized with a loss of federal aid if their for-profit college violated the rule. The amendment was meant to be a placeholder to give lawmakers more time to work on a compromise. The subcommittee adopted, 22–10, an amendment by Del. Luis Fortuño, R-Puerto Rico, to prohibit for-profit colleges from receiving funding for programs specifically designated for historically black colleges and Hispanic-serving institutions. The panel also adopted, by voice vote, a Virginia Foxx, R-N.C., amendment to prohibit the Department of Education from creating a database to compile college students' personal information.

The full committee approved HR 609 by 27–20 on July 22, following a three-day markup. The bill, sponsored by committee chair John A. Boehner, R-Ohio, and reported (H Rept 109-231) on Sept. 22, was expected to produce net savings of $8.7 billion from student loan entitlement programs in fiscal 2006 through 2010, mainly by increasing the interest rates and fees paid by students and reducing subsidies to lenders.

The committee-approved bill would eliminate a 6.8 percent fixed rate for student loans that was scheduled to start in July 2006 under a 2002 law (PL 107-139). Instead, HR 609 would keep the existing variable rate, which was capped at 8.25 percent. The government paid the interest on subsidized loans while the student was in school. Democrats complained that Republicans should have used the anticipated savings for additional student aid. The measure also would allow borrowers who wanted to consolidate their student loans to choose between a variable or a fixed rate, both capped at 8.25 percent. Under existing law, consolidated loans had a low fixed rate for up to thirty years, capped at 8.25 percent. HR 609 would require those choosing the fixed rate to pay a new 1 percent loan origination fee.

EDUCATION LEADERSHIP

By voice vote on Jan. 20, 2005, the Senate confirmed Margaret Spellings as secretary of education, succeeding Rod Paige. Spellings was George W. Bush's education adviser when he was governor of Texas, and she served as the top domestic policy adviser in the Bush White House. *(Paige background, Congress and the Nation, Vol. XI, p. 922)*

Paige was known as being among the most loyal members of the Bush cabinet. He oversaw implementation of No Child Left Behind, a cornerstone of the administration's first-term domestic policy agenda. Paige vigorously promoted the law throughout his tenure. Controversy arose in February 2004 when he called the National Education Association, the nation's largest teachers union, a "terrorist organization" for opposing No Child Left Behind. He subsequently apologized to teachers, but not to the union.

Observers across the political spectrum recognized the limits placed on Paige in his position. Chester E. Finn Jr., president of the Thomas B. Fordham Foundation, a conservative think tank, in a *National Review* comment, wrote that Paige "didn't always have the leeway he should have had to lead [the Education Department] to the best of his ability.... Paige had limited authority to pick his team, and even less to pick his policy targets." Jack Jennings, president of the Center on Education Policy and a former Democratic congressional staffer, was quoted in the *New York Times* as saying Paige "was a good salesman for Bush. But, in terms of having influence on policy, he was a nonentity."

Spellings was seen as the real power behind education policy during Bush's first term and was one of the authors of No Child Left Behind. Her nomination signaled to conservatives that the administration was not planning any major new education initiatives in his second term, such as a serious push for more charter schools and vouchers. That proved to be true.

During Spellings's tenure, questionable practices in the federal student loan programs came to light. Democrats accused the Education Department of mismanagement and complacency in failing to address the problems. Spellings came under fire from members of Congress as well as advocates for students and nonprofit groups for allowing large lender Nelnet to keep $278 million in illegal subsidy payments that it billed the agency. The Education Department later proposed new regulations for the student loan industry.

Spellings used her executive powers to issue new rules regarding implementation of No Child Left Behind, such as establishment of a standard formula for calculating high school dropout rates. Bruce Hunter, a lobbyist for the American Association of School Administrators, in the *New York Times* said she was "trying to rewrite the law without benefit of Congressional action." Senate Health, Education, Labor, and Pensions Committee chairman Edward M. Kennedy, D-Mass., however, characterized the proposals as offering "important improvements." Congress failed to reconsider the legislation before Bush left office.

The committee bill would require lenders to rebate to the government income generated when the interest rate they charged to students was higher than what lenders were guaranteed to receive by the federal government. The measure would eliminate a provision in existing law that allowed some lenders to receive interest payment totaling 9.5 percent on their federally backed loans, with the Education Department picking up the difference between that figure and the students' variable rate. HR 609 also would make it easier for private for-profit colleges to compete for federal aid by redefining the term "institute of higher education" to include accredited for-profit colleges. Public and nonprofit universities argued that taxpayers should not be asked to subsidize for-profit schools. But Republicans said for-profit schools, which offered degree-granting courses in business, nursing, and other specialty fields, were increasingly important for nontraditional students, especially those changing careers.

Education and the Workforce adopted, 26–20, a Tom Petri, R-Wis., amendment to allow graduates who wanted to consolidate their federally subsidized student loans to choose between a variable or a fixed rate, both capped at 8.25 percent. It rejected, 17–26, a competing proposal by George Miller, D-Calif., the panel's ranking member, to cap the variable or fixed rate on consolidated loans at 6.8 percent. The amendment also would have increased the maximum Pell grant award by $500 over five years, to an overall total of $4,550. (Pell grants provided assistance to undergraduates based on financial need.) The committee adopted, by voice vote, a Castle amendment to permit for-profit colleges to compete for campus-based aid programs, but not for federal funding outside the bill's jurisdiction, such as grants from the National Science Foundation or the Department of Energy.

The Senate Health, Education, Labor, and Pensions Committee, by 20–0 on Sept. 8, 2005, approved a five-year reauthorization bill (S 1614). The legislation was a bipartisan effort led by committee chair Michael B. Enzi, R-Wyo., and ranking Democrat Edward M. Kennedy of Massachusetts. As a result, no amendments were offered during the markup. A report (S Rept 109-218) was filed Feb. 28, 2006.

The committee-approved S 1614 was projected to reduce spending on mandatory student loan programs by a net $7 billion over five years as part of the panel's effort to comply with instructions in the fiscal 2006 budget resolution (H Con Res 95). But S 1614 also called for $8 billion in new money for student aid programs. The bill would retain the scheduled change to a 6.8 percent fixed rate for student loans, saving students money if interest rates continued to rise. It would require lenders to rebate to the government income generated when interest rates charged to students were higher than the guaranteed rate for lenders. S 1614 would limit but not eliminate the ability of some lenders to charge a 9.5 percent interest rate. It set aside $4.5 billion over five years for a new entitlement program to give grants to low-income students to supplement Pell grant awards and $1 billion over five years for a new scholarship program for low-income students who majored in math and science fields.

BUDGET RECONCILIATION

Late in the first session of the 109th Congress, authorizing committees in both chambers began working on a budget reconciliation package (S 1932) aimed at reducing the automatic annual growth in entitlement spending. The House and Senate committees sent their provisions to their respective Budget committees, which packaged them and took them to the floor.

The House Education and the Workforce Committee agreed Oct. 26, 2005, to send the House Budget Committee a package of cuts to mandatory student loan programs drawn from HR 609. The proposal, adopted 22–19 along party lines, would save an estimated $14.3 billion over five years, according to the Congressional Budget Office (CBO). Boehner said none of the provisions would cost students directly, except one that would change the interest rate structure for graduates who consolidated their loans. He said most of the cuts would be borne by lenders, who would see decreases in federal subsidies. Democrats argued that lenders would cover their losses by passing the financial burden on to students.

The committee rejected, 20–27, a Miller proposal to end the subsidy that allowed some lenders to earn a 9.5 percent return and use the savings to expand the Pell grant program.

The bill would increase the maximum amount of subsidized loans that students could borrow to $3,500 from $2,625 for first-year students and to $4,500 from $3,500 for second-year students. The limit for unsubsidized loans for each year of graduate school would rise to $12,000 from $10,000. These changes were estimated to increase federal spending by $1.6 billion in fiscal 2007 through 2010.

The legislation also included relief for student loan borrowers and institutions of higher education that were adversely affected by Hurricanes Katrina and Rita. CBO said those provisions would cost $210 million in fiscal 2006, with no costs after that. Boehner originally included a $2.5 billion education relief proposal that would have provided parents displaced by Hurricane Katrina with up to $6,700 per child to send their children to a public, private, or religious school for one year. However, critics described it as a voucher plan that would use public funds to educate children in private schools. The committee rejected it, 21–26, with four Republicans joining the Democrats to defeat the amendment.

The Senate Health, Education, Labor, and Pensions Committee on Oct. 18 approved, 15–5, a package that CBO said would cut mandatory spending on student loan programs by a net $8.5 billion over five years. The panel adopted by voice vote a substitute by Enzi changing some of the provisions taken from S 1614. It increased the proposed low-income grant program from $4.5 billion to $6 billion, and it increased the math and science grants from $1 billion to $2.3 billion. It proposed to reduce borrower origination fees on federally subsidized loans from 3 percent to 2.5 percent and to add $1.5 billion for financial relief to students affected by Hurricane Katrina.

During floor consideration of S 1932, the Senate by voice vote on Nov. 3 adopted an Enzi amendment to provide $1.2 billion in financial assistance for students displaced by Hurricane Katrina attending public, private, or religious schools and $450 million in grants to schools in the Gulf Coast region. The grants could be used for items such as curriculum development, textbooks, and computers. The amendment would also provide $900 million to reduce loan origination fees for college students from 3 percent to 2 percent.

Enzi worked with Kennedy in an attempt to avoid the contentious issue of school vouchers. Under Enzi's proposal, federal money would go to local school districts based on the number of displaced children attending school, public or private, in the area. The districts would then deposit the money into accounts for displaced students—up to $6,000 per child and $7,500 for each disabled student—in public, private, or religious schools.

John Ensign, R-Nev., tried to amend the Enzi language to allow the federal funds to flow to the states, which would have sent checks to public, private, and religious schools that received Hurricane Katrina evacuees. Nonpublic schools would have had to take the additional step of obtaining permission from parents of displaced children attending them before they could use the government money. Ensign argued that the Enzi amendment would be too restrictive on parochial schools because the funds could not be used for religious purposes. The Ensign motion failed, 31–68 on Nov. 3.

The student loan provisions in the final budget reconciliation bill were expected to save a net $11.9 billion over five years, according to CBO. That was roughly halfway between the House and Senate proposals. The House adopted the conference report on S 1932 (H Rept 109-362) by a vote of 212–206 on Dec. 19. But a successful procedural challenge in the Senate forced the House to vote again in 2006. On Feb. 1, the House agreed to a Senate change in the final bill, clearing the measure for the president.

The major elements of the student loan sections of S 1932 are as follows:

Student loan reauthorization. The law reauthorized the government's two college loan programs through 2012. The Federal Family Education Loan program provided government guarantees for loans made by private lenders. The William D. Ford Direct Loan Program provided government loans to students and their families. Consolidation loans, which enabled students to lock in prior-year interest rates and combine multiple loans into a single payment, were reauthorized through 2012.

Parent loan rate increase. The fixed interest rate charged for guaranteed loans made to parents was changed to 8.5 percent starting in July 2006, instead of 7.9 percent under prior law.

Excess interest. Lenders earning more than the fair market return on student loans were required to rebate the excess interest paid by students and parents to the federal government. Prior law allowed the lender to receive the higher of the market rate or the amount paid by the borrower. (Combined savings under this and the parent loan rate provision: $14.3 billion over five years)

9.5 percent loans. The law eliminated a provision of prior law that allowed lenders making loans backed by certain tax-exempt bonds to receive up to a 9.5 percent return from the government. An exception allowed nonprofit lenders with less than $100 million in outstanding 9.5 percent loans to make new loans under the system for five years. (Savings: $1.8 billion over five years)

Administrative costs. The law eliminated mandatory funding for the costs of administering student loan programs beginning in fiscal 2007. After that, administrative costs would have to be paid through discretionary appropriations. (Savings: $2.2 billion over five years)

Guaranty agency fees. Loan guaranty agencies were required to pay the government a 1 percent default insurance premium on guaranteed loans, which they could charge to student and parent borrowers. Previously, guaranty agencies had the option of charging such a fee, but they often waived it. (Savings: $1.5 billion over five years)

Federal lender insurance. The law reduced the portion of a defaulted loan for which the lender was reimbursed to 97 percent from 98 percent for most lenders and to 99 percent from 100 percent for "exceptional" lenders. (Savings: $505 million over five years)

Consolidation loans. Borrowers would be able to get a direct loan from the government to consolidate existing loans only if the purpose was to enter into an income-contingent repayment plan. Also, the loan had to be submitted to a guaranty agency that counseled the borrower on rehabilitating the loan instead of defaulting. The government had to offer a direct consolidation loan to any borrower who defaulted or was rejected by a private lender. In-school consolidation was eliminated by prohibiting students from requesting early repayment of their loans. Married couples were prohibited from jointly consolidating their separate student loans. The government was required to establish regulations to preclude consolidation loans from being "an excessive proportion" of defaulted loans for which the government was required to reimburse guaranty agencies.

Guaranty agencies. As of Oct. 1, 2006, the collection cost a guaranty agency could charge a borrower for including a defaulted loan in a consolidation loan was limited to 18.5 percent of the outstanding principle and interest of the defaulted loan. The guaranty agency was required to remit part of the collection charges to the government immediately and remit the full amount of the charges by Oct. 1, 2009, if its proceeds from consolidating defaulted loans exceeded 45 percent of the agency's total collection of defaulted loans in a fiscal year.

Schools as lenders. Colleges were prohibited from lending to undergraduates or to people who were not their students and were limited to the loans they could make to their graduate students. Schools had to award contracts for financing, servicing, or administering their loans on a competitive basis. Schools were required to offer lower interest rates or lower origination fees, or both, than those offered by either private lenders or the government. The permissible default rate for a lending school was reduced to 10 percent from 15 percent. Annual audits had to be submitted to the government. Schools were required to use proceeds from interest paid by borrowers, subsidies from the government, or sales of loans to increase need-based student grants. They were forbidden to use those proceeds to supplant federal grant money.

Increased loan limits. The maximum amount of subsidized loans was increased to $3,500 from $2,625 for first-year students and to $4,500 from $3,500 for second-year students, beginning in fiscal 2007. The limit for each year of graduate school was increased to $12,000 from $10,000. (Cost: $1.5 billion over five years)

Origination fees. The 3 percent origination fee for Stafford loans would be phased out by 2010 for guaranteed loans and reduced to 1 percent by 2010 for direct loans. (Cost: $4 billion over five years)

New grant programs. The law created two new mandatory grant programs for college students who were eligible for Pell grants. The first was available to first- and second-year college students who had completed a "rigorous" high school education. The second program aided third- and fourth-year students who were pursing degrees in the physical, life, or computer sciences, math, technology, engineering, or one of several foreign languages considered critical for national security. The grants were $750 for a first-year student, $1,300 for a second-year student, and $4,000 for third- and fourth-year students. The law appropriated $790 million in fiscal 2006 for the grants, a sum rising to $1 billion in fiscal 2010. (Cost: $3.7 billion over five years)

Teacher loan forgiveness. The law reauthorized an existing provision that allowed the government to forgive up to $5,000 in loans to highly qualified teachers of math, science, or special education. Private school teachers who were exempt from state certification requirements could benefit from the provision in some cases.

NINE-MONTH EXTENSION

Unable to agree on legislation to renew the Higher Education Act, Congress acted to extend the existing law for nine months, through June 30, 2007.

The House passed HR 609, 221–199, on March 30, 2006. For a time, it appeared that the House might produce a bipartisan bill as a result of negotiations among members of the House Education and the Workforce Committee. When the talks broke down, Republicans charged that the minority party had decided it would be more profitable to use the bill as a campaign issue. Democrats said Republicans never made a serious effort to compromise.

Miller offered a substitute amendment that was rejected, 200–220, on March 30. It was distinguished from the GOP bill chiefly by proposing to cut interest rates on student loans by half for one year. Members made several changes to the bill, some of them in response to complaints from colleges and universities.

The House adopted, 418–2 on March 30, a Louie Gohmert, R-Texas, amendment stripping language that would have allowed states to create college accreditation agencies. Republicans wanted to provide more competition to private accreditors, but colleges saw it as a threat to their independence. Also on March 30, the House adopted by voice vote an amendment offered by Mark Souder, R-Ind., and Timothy H. Bishop, D-N.Y., dropping provisions that would have prohibited colleges from refusing to accept transfers of academic credits based solely on the accreditation of the student's former school. The amendment retained provisions that required schools to publicly disclose their credit transfer policies. It also required schools to disclose any policy that would deny transfer of credit based solely on the accreditation of the institution where the credit was earned.

The House also modified the language aimed at setting up a system to track tuition increases at colleges, which the schools saw as a price control mechanism. The requirement that colleges submit a report on their costs originally applied to the 25 percent of colleges that had the steepest increases. That was reduced to the top 5 percent, partially through a manager's amendment by Howard P. "Buck" McKeon, R-Calif., that was adopted by voice vote on March 29. The House rejected a Dan Burton, R-Ind., amendment, 120–306 on March 29, that would require colleges and universities that received federal education funds to disclose contributions and gifts in a publicly searchable database.

The House-passed bill included provisions to:

Aid to for-profit colleges. Make it easier for private, for-profit colleges to compete for federal aid by redefining the term "institute of higher education" to include accredited for-profit colleges.

Tuition increases. Require the Department of Education to assign an "affordability index" to every college that used federal financial aid programs. Colleges with track records of large tuition increases were required to analyze their costs and submit a report to the government.

Pell grants. Authorize an increase in the maximum Pell grant to $6,000 from $5,800. However, the actual funding for Pell grants was determined by annual appropriations legislation. Under the fiscal 2006 law (PL 109-149), the maximum grant was $4,050, but the authorized amount was $5,800. The bill also authorized year-round Pell grants so students could use them for summer classes, as well as bonus grants of up to $1,000 for the first two years of school for high-achieving students. It eliminated the "tuition sensitivity"provision of the existing law that limited Pell grants for students attending very inexpensive colleges. The bill also limited Pell grant eligibility to eighteen semesters or twenty-seven quarters.

Loan consolidation. Repeal the "single-holder rule"—long supported by the SLM Corporation, or Sallie Mae, the largest college student loan company in the United States—which required student and parent borrowers to consolidate, or refinance, their loans with the lender that originally made them, even if they could obtain lower interest rates elsewhere.

Transferring credits. Require that schools disclose their policies on transfers of academic credit. Colleges successfully lobbied against a related provision that would have forbidden them to deny transfers based solely on the accreditation of a student's former school.

Ideological nondiscrimination. Create a nonbinding "academic bill of rights" to discourage colleges from discriminating against students based on "personal political views or ideological beliefs." Republicans included the language at the behest of conservative activists who argued that a liberal political climate at many universities resulted in harassment of students with conservative views, a contention that the American Federation of Teachers and other education groups strongly disputed.

The Senate version of the reauthorization legislation (S 1614) reportedly was being held up in hopes of repealing some of the student loan reductions made in the budget reconciliation law. With the bill stalled in the Senate, Congress cleared the fifth in a series of short-term extensions enacted in the 109th Congress. In addition to extending authorizations for existing programs through June 30, 2007, HR 6138 canceled the student loan debt of the spouses of public servants, such as police and firefighters, who died in the Sept. 11, 2001, terrorist attacks. The bill also canceled student loans made to other Sept. 11 victims whose spouses or parents were repaying the loans and changed the rules for federal grants to colleges with large populations of Hispanic students.

The House passed HR 6138 by voice vote under suspension of the rules on Sept. 27. The Senate passed the bill by voice vote on Sept. 30, completing congressional action. The president signed the measure on Sept. 30.

Vocational Education

Congress in 2006 cleared legislation (S 250) to reauthorize a pair of popular vocational and technical education programs that the George W. Bush administration wanted to eliminate. The president signed the measure into law (PL 109-270) without formal comment on Aug. 12.

The two programs—Carl D. Perkins grants and Tech Prep—totaled about $1.3 billion and had broad support in Congress. Bush requested that the programs be eliminated and that the money used to extend the testing and standards required by the 2002 No Child Left Behind (PL 107-110) education law into high schools. *(PL 107-110, Congress and the Nation Vol. XI, p. 540)*

BACKGROUND

The federal law funding vocational education, which dated to the early 1900s, had been rewritten and renamed many times. The most recent version was the 1998 Carl D. Perkins Vocational and Technical Education Act (PL 105-332), named for the former Kentucky Democratic representative (1949–1984). S 250 reauthorized that act and made a number of changes designed to improve accountability and academic achievement. *(PL 105-332, Congress and the Nation Vol. X, p. 513)*

Perkins grants, by far the largest program under the act, provided formula grants to states to support coursework in high schools and community colleges in fields such as welding, business services, and nursing that did not require four-year degrees. Congress appropriated $1.2 billion for the program in fiscal 2006.

Tech Prep, the second-largest federal vocational education program, was created under the Perkins Act in 1990 (PL 101-392) in an effort to prepare students for highly skilled technical occupations. Tech Prep combined the last two years of high school with two years of postsecondary education, and it included both academic and technical coursework. Graduates received an associate's degree or a certificate in a specific career field. The program received $105 million in fiscal 2006. *(PL 101-392, Congress and the Nation Vol. VIII, p. 644)*

LEGISLATIVE ACTION

The Senate Health, Education, Labor, and Pensions Committee approved S 250 by voice vote on March 9, 2005. Sen. Edward M. Kennedy of Massachusetts, the ranking Democrat on the committee, cosponsored the measure with Michael B. Enzi, R-Wyo, the committee chair. The Senate passed S 250 by 99–0 on March 10. A written report on the bill (S Rept 109-65) was filed on May 10.

The House Education and the Workforce Committee approved a companion measure (HR 366) by voice vote on March 9, 2005, and reported it (H Rept 109-25) on March 17. The House passed HR 366 by a vote of 416–9 on May 4.

Both the Senate-passed S 250 and the House-passed HR 366 would authorize federal grants to states for supplemental programs, such as courses in emerging technologies, and sought to increase access to coursework for women and minorities. The Senate bill would keep funding streams separate for the main Perkins grant program and the smaller Tech Prep program. The House bill, sponsored by Michael N. Castle, R-Del., proposed to merge the two.

During floor consideration May 4, the House by voice vote adopted a Castle amendment that would require states to fund Tech Prep activities at fiscal 2005 levels ($107 million). It was an attempt to quell Democratic concerns that Tech Prep would erode if the two programs were consolidated.

Under existing law, states could reserve up to 10 percent of Perkins grants for professional development and 5 percent for administrative activities. HR 366 restricted states to using no more than 2 percent for administration. S 250 offered states more freedom to transfer funds between training and administrative accounts and proposed removing spending caps on nontraditional programs, such as prisoner training.

The House passed S 250 by voice vote on July 12, 2006, after substituting the language of HR 366.

The conference agreement on S 250 kept the Perkins grants and Tech Prep separate but allowed states to use Tech Prep money to broaden the Perkins program if they chose. Some argued that states were unlikely to do so, however. Tech Prep money was controlled by governors, who decided how to divide it among high schools. Perkins grants were divided among high schools according to funding formulas. Governors probably would want to continue to have a say in the allocation of the Tech Prep funds.

The conference agreement also changed the name of the law to the Carl D. Perkins Career and Technical Education Improvement Act to reflect the focus on preparing students for the jobs of the future.

The Senate adopted the conference report (H Rept 109-597) by voice vote on July 26. The House acted, 399–1, on July 29, clearing the measure.

Student Loans

Congress in 2005 cleared legislation (HR 2132) to give the education secretary authority to waive student loan and aid regulations during a war or national emergency. The bill, sponsored by John Kline, R-Minn., would extend for two years a provision in a 2003 law (PL 108-136) that authorized the Education Department to waive or modify any requirement or regulation applicable to federal student financial assistance program for students called to active duty. *(2003 law, Congress and the Nation Vol. XI, p. 337)*

The House agreed by voice vote on Sept. 20 to a Kline motion to suspend the rules and pass HR 2132. The Senate passed the bill by voice vote on Sept. 27, completing congressional action. The president signed HR 2132 into law (PL 109-78) on Sept. 30.

Campus-Based Aid Programs

Continuing its effort to aid victims of Hurricanes Katrina and Rita, Congress in 2005 cleared legislation (HR 3863) to authorize the education secretary to waive financial rules for campus-based aid programs at colleges affected by natural disasters. Bobby Jindal, R-La., sponsored HR 3853.

Under the bill, higher education institutions in hurricane disaster areas would not have to match federal funds provided to campus-based student aid programs such as Supplemental Educational Opportunity Grants, federal work-study, and the Perkins loan program.

Democrats did not oppose the bill but did complain that pending legislation to reauthorize the Higher Education Act (HR 609) would harm campus-based aid programs for some of the schools in the affected Gulf Coast region. HR 609 would change the formula used to provide campus-based aid to colleges through programs such as work-study and Perkins loans. The existing formula rewarded colleges that had been in the program the longest, guaranteeing the same share of funding. Under HR 609, funds would be allocated to campuses based on the financial need of their student populations. *(Higher education, pp. 602, 611)*

The House agreed by voice vote on Sept. 27 to a Jindal motion to suspend the rules and pass HR 3863. The Senate passed the bill by voice vote on Sept. 30, completing congressional action. The president signed the measure into law (PL 109-86) on Oct. 7.

Displaced Student Aid

Congress in 2005 cleared legislation (HR 3668, HR 3169) that would waive repayment requirements for displaced college students who received aid.

HR 3668 was directed at students receiving campus-based aid. The House on Sept. 8 agreed by 414–0 to a Charles Boustany Jr., R-La., motion to suspend the rules and pass the bill. The Senate passed the measure on Sept. 15 by voice vote, completing congressional action. HR 3668 was signed into law (PL 109-67) on Sept. 21.

HR 3169 was for those receiving Pell grants. The House agreed, by 412–0 on Sept. 7, to a Ric Keller, R-Fla., motion to suspend the rules and pass the measure. The Senate passed HR 3169 by voice vote on Sept. 15, clearing the legislation. The bill was signed into law (PL 109-66) on Sept. 21.

Technology Instruction at Minority Colleges

The Senate by voice vote on July 1, 2005, passed S 432, authorizing $1.25 billion—$250 million annually—from fiscal 2006 through fiscal 2010 to fund technology and telecommunications upgrades and to expand technology instruction at minority colleges and universities. The bill would create a program within the National Science Foundation to award grants to qualifying institutions for software, hardware, and network equipment, technical assistance, faculty development, and teacher training. Money also would be available to promote research and instruction in science, math, technology, and engineering.

The Senate Commerce, Science, and Transportation Committee had approved S 432 by voice vote April 14 and formally reported it (S Rept 109-94) on June 27.

The House Science Committee by voice vote approved a companion measure (HR 921) on May 4, 2005, and formally reported it (H Rept 109-211, Part I) on July 28. HR 921 would locate the technology grant program inside the Commerce Department.

Restrictions on School Districts

The House agreed by voice vote on Nov. 16, 2005, to a Bobby Jindal, R-La., motion to suspend the rules and pass HR 3975 to provide regulatory relief for states and school districts affected by Hurricanes Katrina and Rita, including the authority to consider as "highly qualified" displaced teachers working in schools outside their home states if they served a large number of evacuees. Under the 2002 No Child Left Behind Act (PL 107-110), states were required to have a "highly qualified" teacher in every classroom by the end of the 2005–2006 school year. *(No Child Left Behind, Congress and the Nation Vol. XI, p. 540)*

HR 3975 also would permit schools in the disaster area to delay reporting requirements for special education students, make Gulf Coast states eligible to participate in a new pilot program that would reduce paperwork requirements for special-needs students, require colleges and universities to adjust financial aid award formulas if a student's family suffered financial problems because of the hurricanes, and provide student borrowers in the region a six-month moratorium on the accrual of interest on their loans.

Teachers and School Supplies

The Senate by voice vote on Sept. 22, 2005, passed S 1764, which would transfer funds from the Federal Emergency Management Agency to the Department of Education to pay for new teachers and extra supplies in school systems that had taken in students after Hurricane Katrina. Kay Bailey Hutchison, R-Texas, sponsored the bill.

Behavior-Modifying Medication

The House on Nov. 16, 2005, agreed, by 407–12, to a John Kline, R-Minn., motion to suspend the rules and pass HR 1790, which was intended to discourage schools from requiring students to take psychotropic drugs such as antidepressants.

Under the bill, sponsored by Kline, states would have to establish policies preventing schools from requiring students to take any drug that alters "perception, emotion or behavior" as a condition for attending class. Federal education money would be cut off from states that did not comply with the legislation within one year.

Some experts said that children with behavioral problems were overmedicated and that schools sometimes coerced parents into seeking prescriptions for children with psychiatric issues by threatening to bar them from classrooms unless they took the drugs. The extent of the problem remained unclear, however.

The 2004 reauthorization of the Individuals with Disabilities Education Act (PL 108-446), which governed the education of disabled children, included a provision preventing schools from requiring disabled children to be medicated to attend class. *(2004 law, Congress and the Nation Vol. XI, p. 547)*

College Grant Reauthorization

The House Select Education Subcommittee of the Education and the Workforce Committee by voice vote on June 16, 2005, approved two bills (HR 509, HR 510) that would reauthorize grants to colleges and universities for graduate and international students.

HR 509 would reauthorize grants to establish and strengthen international affairs and foreign language programs and to provide internships and opportunities for study abroad. Congress provided $94 million for such programs in the fiscal 2005 appropriations law (PL 108-447). The legislation would authorize grants to provide coordination between international affairs and foreign language studies programs. It also would create an advisory board for such international programs. Some professors expressed their concern that the board would impose an ideological litmus test on scholars who specialize in the Middle East or Arab affairs or who criticize U.S. foreign policy. Subcommittee chair, and sponsor of both HR 509 and HR 510, Pat Tiberi, R-Ohio, said that the board would only advise Congress and the Education Department and that it would have no authority beyond that role. *(PL 108-447, Congress and the Nation Vol. XI, p. 81)*

HR 510 would reauthorize grants for graduate programs, which had received $209 million in fiscal 2005. The bill would prioritize grants to graduates who planned to teach math, science, and special education.

Math, Science Competitiveness

The House Science Committee on June 7, 2006, approved by voice vote two bills (HR 5356, HR 5358) designed to improve math and science education. The Senate Commerce, Science, and Transportation Committee had approved similar legislation (S 2802) by voice vote on May 18, 2006.

The committee-approved HR 5356 would expand a National Science Foundation program that awarded grants for "pathbreaking" scientific research by early career scientists and engineers at institutions of higher learning. A related bill (HR 5357) that also dealt with research was merged into the legislation.

HR 5358 would direct the science foundation to implement a teacher training partnership between higher education institutions and grade school science and math teachers. The bill was aimed at increasing the pool of qualified primary and secondary school math and science teachers and would expand the Robert Noyce Teacher Scholarship Program, which helped finance the tuition of math and science education majors in exchange for a commitment to teach two years for each year of financial aid received.

Both HR 5356 (H Rept 109-525) and HR 5358 (H Rept 109-524) were reported on June 22.

S 2802, reported (S Rept 109-285) on July 19, would authorize $47.7 billion, while the House bills together authorized $450 million through 2011.

In his 2006 State of the Union address, President George W. Bush proposed a ten-year, $136 billion government-wide investment in research and development, science and math education, and programs to encourage entrepreneurship and innovation. The White House disliked both chambers' initiatives, saying they would authorize too much money for the wrong programs.

Congress's actions were partly a response to a National Academy of Sciences report released in October 2005 warning that the United States was losing its competitive edge in the sciences, math, and applied sciences.

The 110th Congress cleared competitiveness legislation. *(110th Congress action, p. 617)*

Tuition for D.C. Students

The House Government Reform Committee on July 11, 2006, reported a bill (HR 4855—H Rept 109-553) to authorize for five years, through 2012, the D.C. Tuition Assistance Grant Program (TAG), which was created in 1999 (PL 106-98) and was scheduled to expire at the end of fiscal 2007. The panel had approved the legislation by voice vote March 9. *(1999 law, Congress and the Nation Vol. X, p. 547; 2004 extension, Congress and the Nation Vol. XI, p. 551; 110th Congress action, p. 616)*

The program enabled students from Washington, D.C., to attend public colleges throughout the United States at in-state tuition rates or receive $2,500 annually to help with tuition at certain private universities in the region or historically black colleges nationwide. Students pay the in-state tuition rate at their public college, and the grant pays the difference between that amount and the out-of-state tuition, up to $10,000 a year.

Advocates of TAG said it was one of the city's best programs for developing a workforce that could meet the high education requirements for jobs in the region. It addressed the District's lack of a state university system and sought to deter families from moving to surrounding states for their in-state tuition rates.

D.C. mayor Anthony Williams credited the program with a 35 percent increase in college attendance among District residents.

D.C. School Vouchers

The Senate Appropriations Committee on July 13, 2006, by 27–0 approved a stand-alone fiscal 2007 appropriations bill for the District of Columbia (S 3660), which provided $40 million to improve the District's schools, including $13 million each to fund school vouchers, charter schools, and the public schools. S 3660 was formally reported (S Rept 109-281) the same day. *(Creation of the D.C. voucher program, Congress and the Nation Vol. XI, p. 549)*

Over objections from locally elected officials, Senate appropriators endorsed changes to the District's school voucher system that would allow families already in the program to earn more and still qualify.

The Senate panel gave voice-vote approval to a Richard J. Durbin, D-Ill., amendment to order a Government Accountability Office study of the District's public school operation.

The provisions of S 3660 were expected to be incorporated into the larger fiscal 2007 funding bill for the Departments of Transportation, Treasury, and Housing and Urban Development (HR 5576). However, Congress adjourned without completing action on HR 5576, and funding for the programs covered by the legislation was extended through Feb. 15, 2007, under a stopgap spending law (PL 109-383). *(Fiscal 2007 appropriations, p. 105)*

2007–2008

The Higher Education Act got its long overdue makeover, including an extensive list of new requirements aimed at keeping down the cost of college while authorizing increases in federal financial aid programs. Congress also enacted the most sweeping changes to federal student aid programs in nearly fifteen years. The biggest no-starter was reauthorization of the 2002 No Child Left Behind education law. A draft proposal—roundly criticized by the administration, congressional Republicans and Democrats, business lobbyists, and the largest teachers union—fizzled out and was put on hold indefinitely.

Higher Education

For the first time in a decade, Congress in 2008 cleared a major overhaul of the law governing federal aid to higher education.

The measure (HR 4137—PL 110-315) reauthorized the Higher Education Act through fiscal 2012. It authorized increases in federal financial aid programs such as Pell grants, required schools and lenders to provide more information to students, and barred lenders from giving schools financial perks to get on a "preferred lender list." It penalized states that cut funding for institutions of higher education and reauthorized teacher education programs and aid to historically minority colleges and universities.

The original Higher Education Act (PL 89-329), signed into law in 1965 as part of President Lyndon B. Johnson's Great Society program, was aimed at helping students from low-income families afford a college education. It had last been reauthorized in 1998 (PL 105-244). Sections of the law were revised and reauthorized in 2006. *(PL 89-329, Congress and the Nation Vol. II, p. 716; PL 105-244, Congress and the Nation Vol. X, p. 509; 109th Congress action, p. 602)*

LEGISLATIVE ACTION

The House passed HR 4137 by a vote of 354–58 on Feb. 7, 2008. The House Education and Labor Committee had approved the measure, 45–0, on Nov. 15, 2007, and formally reported it (H Rept 110-500, Part I) on Dec. 19. The bill proposed maximum Pell grants of $9,000 per year through the 2013–2014 academic year. It also called for withholding some grants to states that cut funding for higher education below the average spent in the previous five years.

During the floor debate, Republicans attempted to eliminate language reauthorizing the Fund for the Improvement of Postsecondary Education, which made grants to colleges and universities to improve the quality of higher education. For many years, lawmakers had used the program to target funds to favored higher education institutions. Mike Ferguson, R-N.J., offered a motion to recommit the bill that would have redirected the funds to the Pell grant program. It was rejected, 194–216, on Feb. 7.

Disappointing student groups and the Project on Student Debt, members rejected, 179–236 on Feb. 7, a bid by Danny K. Davis, D-Ill., to make it easier for borrowers to discharge private student loans through bankruptcy. Lenders lobbied vigorously against Davis's amendment. Howard P. "Buck" McKeon of California, the ranking Republican on the Education and Labor Committee, said it would have added "uncertainty and additional risk" to lending.

The Senate passed HR 4137 by voice vote July 29, 2008, after substituting the text of a bill (S 1642) that had passed, 95–0, on July 24, 2007. The Senate Health, Education, Labor, and Pensions Committee filed a report on S 1642 (S Rept 110-231) on Nov. 15, 2007.

The Senate-passed HR 4137 proposed a smaller increase in the maximum Pell grant, raising it to $5,400 for academic year 2008–2009, $5,700 for 2009–2010, $6,000 for 2010–2011, and $6,300 for 2011–2012. It did not include penalties for states that reduced their funding for higher education.

House and Senate negotiators reached agreement on HR 4137 on July 30, 2008. The House adopted the conference report (H Rept 110-803) by a vote of 380–49 the next day; hours later, the Senate cleared the bill by a vote of 83–8.

The two main obstacles to reaching a deal were the dispute over penalties for states that reduced education funding and questions about the distribution of funds for historically black colleges. Senate conferees accepted a modified version of the House's state penalties provision, after rejecting an attempt by Sen. Lamar Alexander, R-Tenn., to put it on hold until the federal funding for state special education programs met the 40 percent goal set in law. Many state governors and legislators joined Alexander in opposing the penalties.

Rep. John F. Tierney, D-Mass., made one important concession in the version he presented to the conferees. Instead of affecting states' access to the well-established Leveraging Educational Assistance Partnership grants that were awarded to students with exceptional financial need, the amendment targeted the newer College Access Challenge Grants program, which was set to expire in fiscal 2009. Those grants were available to state-sanctioned non-profit lenders for projects helping to improve college access for low-income students.

The other snag in the talks was a lower-profile disagreement over a Senate provision making four new types of graduate programs (in the physical and natural sciences, mathematics, technology, and nursing) eligible for funding at historically black graduate institutions. Several members of the Congressional Black Caucus—along with the National Association for Equal Opportunity in Higher Education and the United Negro College Fund—worried that, with no promise to increase overall funding for historically black schools, the provision would result in less money for existing programs.

The final bill created a new grant program for predominantly black institutions and authorized $75 million for it in fiscal 2009. In supporting the bill, Davis also noted that it increased authorized funding for historically black colleges to $375 million, an amount he said was almost three times the amount set in the previous law, and provided $125 million for historically black graduate institutions.

Although President George W. Bush raised numerous objections to the bill as it made its way through Congress, he signed it into law, without issuing a statement, on Aug. 14.

HIGHLIGHTS

The main elements of the new law included the following:

Pell grants. A gradual increase in the maximum Pell grant, to $8,000 per year by the 2014–2015 academic year from the previous level of $5,800. The grants could be used year-round and would be accessible to part-time students.

State spending penalties. A requirement that states provide at least as much for higher education in any academic year beginning after July 1, 2008, as the average amount provided over the previous five years. Capital investments were not included. States that violated this "maintenance of effort" requirement would lose access to federal funding for College Access Challenge Grants for low-income students until they showed progress in meeting the funding goal. Grants for students with exceptional financial need were not subject to the reduction.

Consumer information. A variety of online tools to help students and parents calculate net average annual costs at different colleges, which factored in student aid. The data to be posted included:

- A sortable and searchable list on the Education Department's Web site of all institutions eligible for federal aid and loans. The list was to include information such as tuition and fees, the average net price for students receiving federal student financial aid, the total amount of need- and merit-based federal, state, and institutional aid to students, and the total number of students receiving aid.
- Listings on the department Web site of the 5 percent of institutions of higher education that had the highest costs, with and without student aid; the 5 percent with the largest percentage increase in those costs over three years; and the 10 percent with the lowest costs. The top 5 percent of colleges with the greatest cost increases were required to submit detailed reports to the education secretary explaining why their costs had risen and what they would do to hold them down in the future.
- A net price calculator on the Web sites of all institutions of higher learning that received federal funds. The calculator, to be based on a model that the Education Department would develop, would show the average annual price charged to first-time, full-time undergraduate students, after subtracting their student aid.

Lenders' ties to schools. Tighter regulations aimed at preventing private lenders from offering inducements to schools to advertise their loans. The bill banned gifts, revenue sharing, and the co-branding of loans. Students would have thirty days after a loan was approved to accept the terms and interest rates and up to three days to back out after signing a loan agreement. Students would have to obtain as much federal aid as possible before they took out private loans.

Lobbying ban. Language specifying that colleges and universities could not use federal higher education funds to lobby employees of any agency, members of Congress, or congressional staff in an effort to influence federal contracts, grants, or loans. Schools also could not use federal aid funding to hire a registered lobbyist or pay any person or entity for securing an earmark.

Simplified aid application. A new, two-page "EZ-FAFSA"—the Free Application for Federal Student Aid—in place of the existing seven-page version.

For-profit schools. A two-year reprieve to private schools from having to count a $2,000 increase in federal loan limits enacted in 2008 toward a requirement that they get at least 10 percent of revenue from sources other than federal loans and other aid.

Armed forces benefits. A requirement that schools readmit members of the armed forces who were called away to duty assignments elsewhere. The bill also provided interest-free deferrals on student loans for service members on active duty and in-state tuition rates for service members, their spouses, or dependent children when they moved to a new state because of military service. Children and family members of service members who had died since Sept. 11, 2001, were exempted from the family contribution requirement for Pell grant eligibility.

Federal Student Loan Programs

Congress in 2007 cleared the most sweeping changes to federal student aid programs in nearly fifteen years as part of fiscal 2008 budget reconciliation legislation (HR 2669—PL 110-84).

The legislative action represented a significant victory for the Democrats, who had made college affordability a key plank in their 2006 campaign to retake Congress. The crux of their plan was to reduce the subsidies that the government paid to private lenders for offering student loans and redirect the money to students through Pell grants and other forms of direct federal aid. If private lenders dropped out, the government-run direct lending program could pick up the extra business at a lower cost to taxpayers.

BACKGROUND

Democrats laid the groundwork for the legislation early in 2007, when the House and Senate adopted a fiscal 2008 budget resolution (S Con Res 21) that called for a reconciliation bill to achieve savings in education programs. The reconciliation process, originally created to expedite deficit reduction legislation, included special rules that protected the bill from a filibuster in the Senate. *(Fiscal 2008 budget resolution, p. 108)*

The budget resolution instructed the House Education and Labor Committee and the Senate Health, Education, Labor, and Pensions Committee to find $750 million in savings over five years (through fiscal 2012). The Congressional Budget Office said the final bill would save $13.8 billion in mandatory outlays over that period, while costing $13 billion and producing a net savings of $752 million ($3.6 billion over eleven years) to be used for deficit reduction.

As the 110th Congress began, Rep. George Miller, D-Calif., and Sen. Edward M. Kennedy, D-Mass., who shepherded the legislative changes, received some unexpected help in their bid to alter the loan programs. An investigation by New York attorney general Andrew M. Cuomo found that private lenders had given kickbacks—including stock options, trips, and a percentage of a lender's profits—to colleges and aid administrators across the country in return for directing student borrowers to the lender. Then, in February 2007, President George W. Bush outlined a plan in his fiscal 2008 budget to cut nearly $20 billion from lender subsidies to pay for higher awards under the Pell grant program, which helped low-income students attend college.

Both developments made it politically difficult for Republicans to stand in the way of the Miller and Kennedy plans. Once Democrats succeeded in getting the legislation protected under the budget resolution, opponents became essentially powerless to stop the cuts.

HOUSE ACTION

The House Education and Labor Committee approved HR 2669, 30–16, on June 13, 2007, and reported it (H Rept 110-210) on June 25. The committee-approved bill promised to cut more than $18 billion from lender subsidies over five years and redirect virtually all of the money to aid for college students and institutions.

The measure would gradually cut interest rates on subsidized student loans to 3.4 percent by July 2013; cap loan repayments at 15 percent of discretionary income; increase the federally backed loan limit by $7,500, to $30,500 over the course of an undergraduate's career; add mandatory funds to the Pell program to bring the maximum Pell grant award to $5,200 in 2012; require a study to select the best method for auctioning loans and direct the Education Department to create a pilot program based on the study; and create nine new entitlement programs, including grants for students who became public school teachers, loan forgiveness for certain public sector employees, income-contingent loan repayment, grants for certain institutions that served minorities, and matching grants for companies' philanthropic efforts to improve college access and retention.

During markup, the committee rejected, 21–27, an attempt by ranking Republican Howard P. "Buck" McKeon of California to direct $12 billion of the savings in the bill toward Pell grants. It also rejected, 20–27, attempts by Tom Price, R-Ga., to eliminate the TEACH grants, and by Mark Souder, R-Ind., to strike the income-contingent repayment and debt-forgiveness programs. The panel adopted, by voice vote, an amendment directing $500 million over five years to the Perkins need-based loan program, which was zeroed out in the president's budget. A manager's package, adopted by voice vote, directed $500 million over five years to schools that served large numbers of minorities.

The floor debate on HR 2669 was heated and partisan. Republicans blasted the use of reconciliation procedures for a measure that would create new entitlement programs and maintained that the bill betrayed the intent of federal student aid by directing roughly two-thirds of its funding to institutions or people no longer in school.

The House rejected, 189–231 on July 11, a McKeon substitute amendment to eliminate all the new mandatory programs and instead direct $9.4 billion to Pell grants (nearly double the amount in the original bill), channel $5.7 billion toward deficit reduction, and reduce the lender subsidy cuts to $15.3 billion. Also rejected on July 11, 199–223, was a Peter Roskam, R-Ill., motion to recommit the bill to committee to add language that would have barred full-time elected officials and lobbyists from using the loan-forgiveness provisions.

The bill included a new fee for private agencies that guaranteed government-backed student loans and added school counselors to the list of those eligible for debt forgiveness. The changes, made part of the rule for floor debate (H Res 531), which was adopted 222–197 on July 11, also eliminated a section that would have penalized states that cut higher education funding to a level below the average funding for the preceding five years.

The House passed HR 2669 by a vote of 273–149 on July 11.

SENATE ACTION

The Senate Health, Education, Labor, and Pensions Committee approved a draft bill, later introduced as S 1762, by 17–3 on June 20. Like HR 2669, the Senate version proposed to cut more than $18 billion in lender subsidies and redirect most of the money to student aid. However, it did not include the interest rate cut that was central to the House bill.

The Senate committee-approved measure would increase the maximum Pell grant by $700, to $5,400, by 2011; create a new Promise grant program for the neediest Pell recipients, a provision not included in HR 2669; offer loan forgiveness for certain public sector employees; and authorize a pilot program to auction the rights to offer federally backed PLUS loans for parents.

In a statement, Kennedy pointed out that twenty years before the maximum Pell grant covered 55 percent of the cost of attending a public college. In 2007 it paid for less than a third, he said. Although offering large Pell grants was popular in Congress, Republicans said paying for them by cutting lender subsidies would drive small private lenders out of business and reduce competition by pushing more students into government-run direct lending.

The Senate passed HR 2669 by a vote of 78–18 on July 20 (in the session that began July 19), after substituting the text of its own bill. The measure reflected a bipartisan agreement between Kennedy and the ranking Republican on Health, Education, Labor, and Pensions, Michael B. Enzi of Wyoming.

The main challenge to supporters had been getting the cuts through the Senate, where Democrats held a slimmer majority and support was broad for sustaining the federally backed private lending program. The bill survived a major test when the Senate rejected, 35–62 on July 19, a Richard M. Burr, R-N.C., and Ben Nelson, D-Neb., amendment to eliminate $2.4 billion of the more than $18 billion in proposed cuts in lender subsidies. Kennedy winningly argued that adoption of the amendment would mean a reduction in the funding available to increase Pell grants for the neediest college students.

The Senate rejected, 42–55 on July 19, an amendment offered by Jeff Sessions, R-Ala., to eliminate the debt-forgiveness programs for public sector employees.

FINAL ACTION

House and Senate negotiators reached agreement on a final version of the bill on Sept. 5. The Senate adopted the conference report (H Rept 110-317) by a vote of 79–12 on Sept. 7, and the House cleared the bill, 292–97, hours later.

The final bill included the House proposal to cut interest rates from 6.8 percent to 3.4 percent, despite Republican complaints that it was expensive and poorly targeted. Conferees also included the House's repayment cap of 15 percent of discretionary spending as well as the stronger Senate provision creating a pilot program for auctioning PLUS loans. Republicans warned that sunsets included in the measure to meet budgetary requirements for offsets of new spending masked the true long-term costs of the legislation.

As signed into law Sept. 27, HR 2669 would:

Interest rates. Cut interest rates in half for students with subsidized student loans. The interest rate would fall from 6.8 percent to 6 percent on July 1, 2008; 5.6 percent on July 1, 2009; 4.5 percent on July 1, 2010; and 3.4 percent on July 1, 2011.

Pell grants. Increase the maximum Pell grant award by $1,090 over five years, to $5,400. The increases would be phased in, beginning with a jump from $4,310 under previous law to $4,800 in the 2008–2009 and 2009–2010 academic years; $5,000 in the 2010–2011 and 2011–2012 academic years; and $5,400 in the 2012–2013 academic year.

The measure also relaxed eligibility requirements for Pell grants by raising the income threshold to $30,000 from $20,000. Families with incomes below the threshold automatically qualified for the grants.

The bill gradually increased the amount of a student's discretionary income that was exempt from use in making loan repayments. The conference agreement raised, by the 2012–2013 academic year, the protected income to $6,000 for dependent students; $9,330 for independent students who were single, separated, or married to a spouse who also was enrolled; and $14,690 for independent students without dependents other than a spouse, who were married, and whose spouse was not enrolled.

Loan auction. Create a pilot program to develop a mechanism for auctioning the rights to offer federally backed PLUS loans to parents of dependent students. The education secretary was required to administer one auction for each state, in which eligible lenders would compete to originate all eligible PLUS loans at institutions of higher education in that state.

Loan repayment. Cap loan repayments at 15 percent of the borrower's discretionary income and offer loan forgiveness after twenty years for borrowers with adjusted gross incomes up to 150 percent of the poverty line. The bill also created a debt-forgiveness program for many public sector employees with loans from the Education Department's direct loan program, including public school teachers, law enforcement and emergency management professionals, social workers, librarians, prosecutors and public defenders, public health doctors and nurses, and child care workers.

Grants. Create the TEACH grant program to provide prepaid tuition grants of $4,000 per year to promising students who agreed to teach in highly demanded fields in high-poverty schools for four years. It also created a $510 million grant program to help improve graduation rates at schools that served minorities. It provided $66 million per year in fiscal 2008 and 2009 for College Access Challenge Grants to assist states in carrying out activities to increase college access for low-income students. The federal share of the matching grant was two-thirds; the state had to pay one-third.

The bill allocated an additional $228 million for Upward Bound, a program to help prepare low-income students, or students whose parents did not go to college, for higher education.

Special allowance payments. Reduce the special allowance payment—the subsidy the government paid lenders to offer student loans—by fifty-five basis points for for-profit lenders, such as Sallie Mae and Citibank, and forty basis points for nonprofit lenders. Bush had called for a fifty-basis-point cut for all lenders. The White House said it opposed a different rate for nonprofit lenders out of fear that for-profit lenders could use that as a way to game the system.

Insurance. Reduce lender insurance rates (the percentage of a loan the government paid the lender when a student or parent defaulted) from 97 percent to 95 percent.

Exceptional performers. Eliminate a program that required the Education Department to designate lenders as "exceptional performers" if they were in "substantial compliance" with loan-servicing requirements. The federal government reimbursed such lenders at a rate of 99 percent for loans that went into default, 2 percentage points higher than the general rate.

Loan origination fees. Increase to 1 percent from 0.5 percent the loan origination fee that lenders had to pay the government on each new student loan.

Collection agencies. Reduce from 23 percent to 16 percent the share of recovered money that private guaranty agencies contracted by the government to collect loans could keep. An administrative fee paid to those agencies by the government for collecting loans was reduced.

Federal Student Loan Access

Congress in 2008 cleared a bill (HR 5715) to ensure that the widening credit crunch and growing crisis in the economy did not prevent college students from getting the loans they needed to finance their education. President George W. Bush signed the bill, which affected the 2008–2009 academic year, on May 7 (PL 110-227).

A second bill (HR 6889), which extended the provisions for the 2009–2010 year, was signed into law Oct. 7 (PL 110-350).

The legislation covered both loans offered directly by the federal government and those offered by private lenders with federal guarantees under the Federal Family Education Loan program. The bill increased the total amount that students and parents could borrow under the federal loan program and authorized the Education Department to purchase student loans from private lenders to ensure that the lenders had capital for more loans.

No eligible student had been denied a loan, but the freezing up of the credit markets and the dropping out of dozens of lenders from the program frightened lawmakers, students, and aid administrators.

LEGISLATIVE ACTION ON HR 5715

The House passed HR 5715 by a vote of 383–27 on April 17, 2008. The Education and Labor Committee had approved the measure by voice vote on April 9 and formally reported it (H Rept 110-583) on April 14. The panel's chairman, George Miller, D-Calif., was the sponsor.

Education Department officials said the law needed to be in place by July, when the high season for student borrowing began. The vote came a day after Sallie Mae, the nation's largest student lender, announced it lost $104 million in the first quarter and that almost all its new loans would be made at a loss. JPMorgan Chase & Co. and Citigroup had said they would be more selective in the schools to which they loaned money, which was interpreted as meaning they would back away from schools with high default rates—most frequently community colleges, schools that historically served minorities, and others that educated many people from low-income backgrounds.

Fifty-seven lenders had already dropped out of the Federal Family Education Loan program in 2008, driven away by the credit crunch. Before approving the measure, the committee rejected, 16–21, an amendment by Tom Price, R-Ga., to include language saying that the bill would not take effect if it would result in new costs to the government without offsets.

The Senate passed an amended version of the bill by voice vote on April 30, and the House cleared it the following day, 388–21, on a Miller motion to suspend the rule and agree to the Senate changes.

The revisions included language to:

- Sunset the Education Department's authority to designate institutions as lenders of last resort at the end of the 2008–2009 academic year.
- Require that lenders operating under the lender-of-last-resort program be subject to the same conflict-of-interest requirements as private lenders operating under the guaranteed loan program.
- Clarify that the delinquency period on a mortgage payment would not disqualify a parent from accessing a PLUS loan.
- Require that any savings generated by the bill be used for grants to low-income math and science students with good grades.

HIGHLIGHTS OF HR 5715

As enacted, HR 5715 included the following major provisions:

Federal loan caps. The measure increased the annual limit on direct federal college loans by $2,000 for all students and raised the aggregate loan limit (spanning the entire course of a student's education) to $31,000 from $23,000 for dependent undergraduates and to $57,500 from $46,000 for independent undergraduates.

PLUS loans. Parents who had fallen up to 180 days behind in mortgage payments or medical bills would still be able to take out PLUS loans to help finance their children's education. Under prior law, being delinquent on those bills would have made them ineligible. Also under the bill, parent borrowers could defer repayment until six months after their children left school. The federally sponsored Parent PLUS loan was a low-interest student loan for parents of undergraduate, dependent students. Parents could borrow up to the total cost of education through the loans, after subtracting any aid they had already received.

Guaranteed private loans. The bill gave the Education Department temporary authority to purchase existing loans that lenders were unable to sell to inject liquidity into the market. It also codified the "lender of last resort" program, which allowed the government to advance funds to state guarantee agencies so the agencies could make loans if more lenders drop out of the student loan program.

ONE-YEAR EXTENSION

The House passed a one-year extension (HR 6889) of the provisions of HR 5715 by a vote of 368–4, under suspension of the rules, on Sept. 15, 2008. The Senate passed the measure by voice Sept. 17, completing congressional action.

Antitrust Exemption for Financial Aid

Congress in 2008 cleared legislation (HR 1777) to extend for seven years an exemption from antitrust law allowing colleges and universities to make collective decisions about financial aid. The bill would allow two or more schools to agree on a common aid offer for accepted students.

Congress first enacted the exemption in 1992, after the Justice Department had sued nine colleges and universities (dubbed the "overlap group") in 1991, alleging that they had restrained competition by making collective financial aid determinations for students accepted to more than one of them. Lawmakers renewed the exemptions three times since then, and their most recent exemption would have expired Sept. 30, 2008. The exemption applied only to institutional financial aid, not federal funding, and only to schools that admitted students regardless of their ability to pay.

A September 2006 Government Accountability Office report requested by Congress showed virtually no difference in the amounts students and their families were expected to pay between schools using the exemption and similar schools that did not use it. In addition, collaboration between groups reduced costs for some students. The practice also helped some groups, such as middle-income Asian and Hispanic students, receive higher grant aid.

The House Judiciary Committee approved HR 1777 by voice vote on April 2, 2008, and reported it (H Rept 110-577) on April 10. The House on April 30 agreed by voice vote to a Bill Delahunt, D-Mass., motion to suspend the rules and pass the bill. The Senate passed an amended version by voice vote on Sept. 25. The House on Sept. 27 agreed by voice vote to a Zoe Lofgren, D-Calif., motion to suspend the rules and accept the Senate changes, completing congressional action. The president signed the bill into law (PL 110-327) on Sept. 30.

Tuition for D.C. Students

A bill (HR 1124) extending for five years a program (PL 106-98) that gave District of Columbia high school graduates tuition assistance to attend colleges nationwide was signed into law (PL 110-97) on Oct. 24, 2007. *(1999 law, Congress and the Nation Vol. X, p. 547; 109th Congress action, p. 609)*

Under the program, D.C. students could receive grants of up to $10,000 per year to attend public schools at or near in-state tuition rates. A lifetime limit was set of $50,000 per student. Students also could receive $2,500 annually to attend certain private colleges within the Washington, D.C., area or private historically black colleges and universities. A lifetime limit of $12,500 per student was set for those grants.

The House Oversight and Government Reform Committee approved HR 1124 by voice vote on March 29, 2007, and formally reported it (H Rept 110-112) on April 30. The House agreed, 268–100 on May 14, to a Danny K. Davis, D-Ill., motion to suspend the rules and pass the bill. During floor consideration of the legislation, the Senate on Sept. 18 by voice vote adopted a Tom Coburn, R-Okla., amendment to limit the assistance to students from families with incomes of less than $1 million. The House by voice vote agreed to the Senate changes on Oct. 9, clearing the measure.

A Senate companion bill (S 343) was reported by the Senate Homeland Security and Governmental Affairs Committee (S Rept 110-52) on April 11, 2007.

D.C. School System Control

Congress in 2007 cleared legislation (HR 2080) allowing the mayor to take control of the budget and administrative functions of the 55,000-student school system in the District of Columbia.

The bill also would give the mayor control over a proposed ten-year, $2.3 billion bid to upgrade and improve school facilities. The mayor would be given the line-item veto until 2010 and would allow the school board, which would still be elected, to set academic standards and teacher certification requirements. The D.C. City Council could revoke the mayor's control if the changes did not produce "sufficient progress in education" within five years. Under the changes, the school superintendent, to be known as the chancellor, would be nominated by the mayor and approved by the council and would report to the mayor.

The House Oversight and Government Reform Committee on May 1 approved the bill by voice vote (no written report). The full House agreed by voice vote on May 8 to a Danny K. Davis, D-Ill., motion to suspend the rules and pass HR 2080.

Del. Eleanor Holmes Norton, D-D.C., said in a statement May 11 that Sen. Benjamin L. Cardin, D-Md., had agreed to lift a hold on the bill after he reached a deal on a separate issue. Cardin had blocked the measure over a dispute involving the District's plan for a youth detention center in Maryland. However, during the week of May 14, Sen. Mary L. Landrieu, D-La., placed a hold on the bill at the request of Robert C. Bobb, the president of the District's Board of Education. The board would lose power under the plan, and Bobb had complained to Landrieu that D.C. mayor Adrian M. Fenty had stopped returning his phone calls to request a different system of checks and balances. Landrieu's hold spurred Fenty to return Bobb's calls, and the two subsequently reached an agreement. Landrieu lifted her hold on May 22. Then, Sen. Carl Levin, D-Mich., placed another hold, over concerns about the District's cab commission. Norton persuaded Levin to relent by assuring him that Fenty would call him, too.

The Senate passed the measure by voice vote on May 22, completing congressional action. The bill was signed into law (PL 110-33) on June 1.

The city council had approved the plan, 9–2, on April 19, 2007. Under the Home Rule Charter that governs the District, Congress had to sign off on the change. HR 2080 would amend the charter to allow the changes to take place. Norton said that the various holdups highlighted the negative impact of congressional review of the city's legislative actions.

Math, Science Competitiveness

Congress in 2007 cleared a bill (HR 2272) aimed at significantly bolstering federal funding for math and science research and education.

The legislation, an amalgamation of several similar measures (S 761, passed by the Senate, 88–8, on April 25, 2007; HR 362, reported (H Rept 110-85) by the House Science and Technology Committee on April 16, 2007, and passed by the House, 389–22, on April 24; HR 363, reported (H Rept 110-39) by the House Science and Technology Committee on March 8, 2007, and passed by the House, 397–20, on April 24; HR 1068, reported (H Rept 110-40) by the House Science and Technology Committee on March 8, 2007, and passed by the House by voice vote under suspension of the rules on March 12; HR 1867, reported (H Rept 110-114) by the House Science and Technology Committee on April 30, 2007, and passed by the House, 399–17, on May 2; and HR 1868, reported (H Rept 110-115) by the House Science and Technology Committee on April 30, 2007, and passed by the House, 385–23, on May 3), was partially a response to a 2005 National Academy of Sciences report predicting that the United States would lose technology jobs to other nations if it did not increase spending for and attention to math and science research and education.

HR 2272 would reauthorize the National Science Foundation at $22 billion from fiscal 2008 to 2010, spread over several grant programs intended to encourage more students to teach math and science, as well as grants for college and graduate student science research. The National Institute of Standards and Technology (NIST) would be authorized at $2.7 billion from fiscal 2008 through 2010, including funding for NIST's laboratories. The bill would establish the Technology Innovation Program and authorize $372 million from fiscal 2008 through 2010 for the program, which was intended to help turn cutting-edge research into commercially viable products. The Energy Department would receive almost $17 billion from fiscal 2008 through 2010, and a new cutting-edge energy research agency would be established, the Advanced Research Projects Agency for Energy.

The House agreed by voice vote on May 21, 2007, to a David Wu, D-Ore., motion to suspend the rules and pass HR 2272. The Senate passed the bill by voice vote July 19, after substituting the text of S 761. The House adopted the conference report (H Rept 110-289) by a vote of 367–57 on Aug. 2. The Senate adopted the conference report by voice vote the same day, completing congressional action. The president signed the bill into law (PL 110-69) on Aug. 9.

Student Borrower Interest Rate

The House on Jan. 17, 2007, by 356–71 passed HR 5, which would cut in half federal interest rates for college students whose families qualified for subsidized loans. More than 60 percent of the Republican caucus joined Democrats in favor of the legislation. President George W. Bush issued a statement opposing the bill, but he did not threaten to veto it.

The measure would phase in cuts to interest rates on subsidized student loans over a five-year schedule based on the date a loan was first handed out. The current rate was 6.8 percent and under the bill would fall to 3.4 percent by 2011. The first cut would be made on loans distributed from July 2007 to July 2008, and subsequent reductions would go into effect with each July-to-July loan period. For individual students, however, the interest rate they were charged when they first got the loan would be the rate they would pay throughout the life of the loan. On Jan. 12, 2012—after the bill's schedule expired—the rate would return to 6.8 percent.

Because the government guaranteed lenders certain yields on federal student loans, reducing borrowers' payments would shift costs to the federal government. Those costs would be recouped by cutting the rate guaranteed to lenders, boosting origination fees paid by banks, and ending an incentive program for certain lenders.

Democrats decided to phase in the reduction to reduce the overall cost of the rate cuts. Through 2012, the $7.1 billion cost of reducing the rate was fully offset. However, because the offsets would continue to bring in revenue through 2017, the bill would generate an extra $7.1 billion in savings over the entire period, according to the Congressional Budget Office.

Republicans said HR 5 would do little to increase college access. Howard P. "Buck" McKeon of California, the ranking Republican on the House Education and Labor Committee, made a bid to recommit the bill with a motion that would have applied the subsidized interest rate reductions only to graduates who earned less than $65,000 annually and to active-duty military personnel. It also would have directed the panel to use the additional savings for deficit reduction or for an increase in Pell grants, which went to the neediest students and did not need to be repaid. McKeon's motion was rejected, 186–241, on Jan. 17.

Pell Grant Limit

The House on Feb. 27, 2007, agreed by voice vote to a George Miller, D-Calif., motion to suspend the rules and pass HR 990, which would eliminate a limit on the amount of Pell grant funds available to students attending the least-expensive schools in the United States.

The bill would repeal the so-called tuition sensitivity provision that effectively lowered the maximum Pell grant award available to students at schools where tuition and fees were less than $675 a year. Under the provision, the government calculates the amount of Pell funds that students at very-low-cost schools could receive using a different formula than that used for students at costlier schools.

HR 990 would be in effect for one year.

The 109th Congress included a similar repeal in legislation to reauthorize portions of the Higher Education Act. *(109th Congress action, p. 602)*

Student Loan Subsidies

By 414–3 on May 9, 2007, the House agreed to a George Miller, D-Calif., motion to suspend the rules and pass HR 890, which would curb abuses in preferred-lender lists for students.

As passed, the legislation was tougher than the initial measure, requiring colleges and universities to adopt codes of conduct governing their relationships with private lenders and banning outright revenue-sharing between lenders and students. The extent of loan industry problems had not come to light when the measure was introduced by House Education and Labor Committee chair Miller.

The House-passed version combined provisions from Miller's original proposal with those of a bill (HR 1994) introduced by Howard P. "Buck" McKeon, R-Calif. The compromise measure would require schools to disclose all relationships with lenders, ban lender staffing of school financial aid offices or help lines, and require schools to conduct annual audits. Ostensibly, the lists helped students identify private lenders with the lowest interest rates and the best services.

New York attorney general Andrew M. Cuomo's investigation into the $85 billion-per-year industry uncovered dozens of cases in which schools accepted kickbacks from lenders eager for a spot on the list. On May 9, a Miller probe uncovered a lender that employed college officials who were still on their schools' payroll. The lender sponsored a $74,000 New York harbor cruise for financial aid officers who served on its advisory board. Miller's bill would bar aid administrators from serving on bank boards and would ratchet up disclosures required by schools and lenders alike.

Green Schools

The House on June 4, 2008, passed, by 250–164, a bill (HR 3021) aimed at bolstering environmentally friendly school construction and repair. The House Education and Labor Committee approved the bill, 28–19, on April 30, 2008, and reported it (H Rept 110-623) on May 8.

The bill would authorize $6.4 billion in fiscal 2009 to build environmentally friendly public schools and an additional $500 million over five years to help rebuild and renovate public schools damaged by Gulf Coast hurricanes in 2005. All schools receiving authorized funds would have to be built according to "green" standards, such as those set by the government's Energy Star rating system. The standards often involved use of recycled construction materials as well as designs that minimized energy costs and maximized use of energy sources such as solar and wind. HR 3021, sponsored by Ben Chandler, D-Ky., also included a "maintenance of effort" provision that would require the education secretary to award grants only to states that maintain spending on public schools.

Democrats said the bill, by funding school repairs, would improve learning. Republicans opposed the measure, saying it would divert money from education priorities, weaken state funding efforts, and infringe on local control.

During House floor consideration, Cathy McMorris Rodgers, R-Wash., offered a motion to recommit the bill "promptly," which would have sent it back to committee, preventing immediate reconsideration and adding language allowing schools with significant energy cost increases to spend the money on maintenance. That effort failed, 187–230, on June 4.

Environmental Education

By 293–109, the House on Sept. 18, 2008, passed a bill (HR 3036) to promote environmental education through a new national grant program that supporters said would not only help get kids outdoors but also would develop their interest in environmental protection. The measure was dubbed the "No Child Left Inside Act."

The House Education and Labor Committee approved the bill, 37–8, on June 18, 2008, and reported it (H Rept 110-754) on July 10.

During floor consideration Sept. 18, the House adopted three amendments to the bill. A John Sarbanes, D-Md., amendment, adopted 383–23, would ensure that environmental education programs would also include discussion of drilling for oil and natural gas, as well as nuclear power and new coal technologies. By voice vote, the House adopted a Peter Welch, D-Vt., amendment to allow municipalities to be eligible and a Joe Courtney, D-Conn., amendment to allow applicants to describe how they intended to partner with local recreation departments. A Tom Price, R-Ga., motion to recommit the bill with instructions was rejected, 172–230, on Sept. 18.

CHAPTER 11

Housing and Urban Aid

Housing and Urban Aid

Owning a home has long been considered essential to attaining the American dream. For many, that dream went bust in the mid- to late 2000s and along with it went the housing boom that pushed the number of homeowners in the United States to an all-time high of almost 70 percent. The housing market was battered by a collapse in the market for subprime mortgages, which in turn threatened broader economic consequences, by sparking a crunch in credit markets. *(Troubled asset relief program, p. 154)*

SUBPRIME MORTGAGE MARKET

From 1994 to 2005, the subprime market expanded from \$35 billion to \$665 billion. The growth stemmed in part from federal measures aimed at increasing access to credit. The 1974 Equal Credit Opportunity Act (PL 93-495, PL 94-239) and the 1975 Home Mortgage Disclosure Act (PL 94-200), combined with new products and technologies, made credit available to many more borrowers. That was largely viewed as beneficial. Buying a home is the biggest investment most Americans make, and homeownership was shown to provide financial and social security. The rise of the subprime market, therefore, represented the "democratization of credit." *(Credit discrimination, Congress and the Nation Vol. IV, pp. 438, 448; disclosure, Congress and the Nation Vol. IV, p. 490)*

However, during the housing boom, low interest rates, rising home prices, and new products allowed lenders to qualify marginal borrowers. Brokers eager to close loans while the market was hot enticed riskier borrowers with ever more exotic loan products. Adjustable-rate mortgages had low monthly payments in the early years of the thirty-year loan after which the loan resets, triggering significantly higher interest rates. Many lenders made no effort to determine if borrowers could afford the higher payments once the loan reset.

MARKET RISK

Banking regulators and other experts said that one idea—the absence of market risk—was at the heart of the collapse of the subprime mortgage market. A basic principle of financial market regulation is that attaching risk to an investment venture would make those who were putting up the money pay closer attention to the threat of adverse consequences, and their attention could help apply the brakes to bad decisions.

Investors are supposed to be smart enough to put a price on a particular risk and create financial instruments that allow them to profit. In turn, the pricing mechanism is supposed to act as a check against excessive risky behavior. But innovations in the way mortgage loans were made, and then packaged for sale to investors, minimized the risks, even while these same changes were being applauded for helping borrowers with poor credit histories and limited incomes buy houses and push the rate of U.S. homeownership to record levels.

Mortgage loans used to be relatively simple instruments. Someone who wanted to buy a house would go to the local bank or credit union and apply for a loan, typically a thirty-year fixed-rate mortgage. After collecting extensive information, the bank would decide whether to provide the money and then would collect the monthly payments of loan interest and principal. If a borrower fell behind on those payments, the bank would have the option of working with the borrower to find a solution that benefited both sides or, in extreme cases, foreclosing on the property. Because bad loans would hurt the bank's bottom

REFERENCES

Discussion of housing and urban aid action for the years 1945–1964 may be found in *Congress and the Nation Vol. I*, pp. 459–515; for the years 1965–1968, *Congress and the Nation Vol. II*, pp. 183–226; for the years 1969–1972, *Congress and the Nation Vol. III*, pp. 635–657; for the years 1973–1976, *Congress and the Nation Vol. IV*, pp. 471–502; for the years 1977–1980, *Congress and the Nation Vol. V*, pp. 429–448; for the years 1981–1984, *Congress and the Nation Vol. VI*, pp. 629–639; for the years 1985–1988, *Congress and the Nation Vol. VII*, pp. 667–684; for the years 1989–1992, *Congress and the Nation Vol. VIII*, pp. 663–700; for the years 1993–1996, *Congress and the Nation Vol. IX*, pp. 637–650; for the years 1997–2000, *Congress and the Nation Vol. X*, pp. 553–567; for the years 2001–2004, *Congress and the Nation Vol. XI*, pp. 555–560.

Outlays for Community and Regional Development

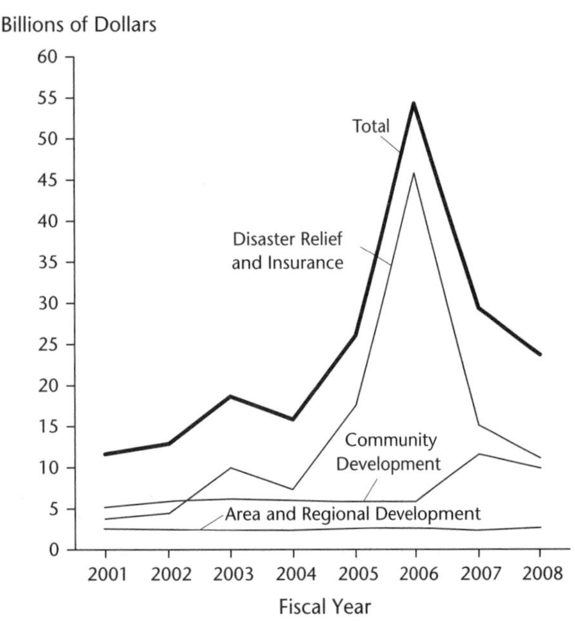

SOURCE: Office of Management and Budget, *Historical Tables, Budget of the United States Government: Fiscal Year 2010* (Washington, D.C.: U.S. Government Printing Office, 2009), Table 3.2.

line, loan officers and their institutions had an incentive to make sure the mortgages they lent out were made on terms that the borrowers could meet.

During the housing boom, homebuyers or people who wanted to refinance their homes typically applied through a mortgage broker, who served as an intermediary between borrowers and lenders in return for a fee paid for closing the deal. Banks used to hold on to the loan, but mortgages came to be sold in blocks to issuers, who packaged them in various combinations into securities that were backed by the interest payments or the principal amounts of the loans or both. These securities were sold to investors—many of whom were outside the United States—and the payments were passed along to them. The homeowner had no idea who owned the loan, and the investor who put up the money had no real idea who the borrower was. Because the risk was so widely spread, it was a terrific way to increase the amount of capital available for home loans and for keeping down interest rates.

For a long time, most mortgage-backed securities were sold through the Federal National Mortgage Association (Fannie Mae) and Federal Home Loan Mortgage Corporation (Freddie Mac), the two large government-created companies that financed a huge share of U.S. mortgages. The two government-backed lenders tended to package into securities the "plain vanilla" loans, mortgages that had similar characteristics and whose risks were relatively easily assessed by investors.

Things began to change when new financial companies came into the mortgage-backed securities market and became sophisticated at packaging riskier subprime mortgages with more stable fixed-rate loans. Issuers quickly realized that they could slice and dice combinations of hundreds of different mortgages with varying risk profiles to suit the appetites of investors, who would be mostly protected from problems that could arise with an individual mortgage because so many loans, of so many different types, undergirded the security they purchased.

This system flourished in the early 2000s, when low interest rates and rapidly rising home price appreciation drove the market. But as issuers and investors became used to steady profits, concern about risk diminished. Mortgage brokers who got paid to write loans needed to keep the process churning, and they increasingly offered special deals to nontraditional borrowers with blemished credit scores. The market pushed borrowers into riskier and riskier loans to keep the profits coming in. Those individuals, meanwhile, had to repay the loan or face foreclosure.

HIGH PRICE OF FORECLOSURE

Foreclosure—essentially the process of a lender taking possession of a home on which the borrower could no longer make mortgage payments—has an obvious and immediate impact on homeowners, who must deal with the financial and emotional consequences associated with giving up perhaps their most valuable asset. Those consequences included losing any equity value that might have been built up in the property from a down payment, the amount of the principal paid each month on the mortgage, and any market appreciation.

Homeowners also must bear a direct financial cost of foreclosure, which includes charges from lawyers and other professionals as well as administrative fees. The tally can run into thousands of dollars. Because people facing foreclosure frequently are already in financial trouble, they likely pay many of the foreclosure costs with credit cards, digging themselves further into debt. Struggling homeowners often skip payments due on credit cards and other loans, adding to their woes. The result is a cascade of trouble that is likely to ruin a foreclosed homeowner's credit for some time.

But the costs of foreclosure extend well beyond the homeowners themselves to their neighborhoods and subdivisions. That effect can be compounded in areas where a single mortgage broker or lender had concentrated its business and where deteriorating economic conditions have extensive impact. Property values are driven down, and sale prices of homes drop.

Supply-and-demand forces play a role in this price decline. A foreclosure means that yet another house is on the market competing for a buyer, often at a fire-sale price

HOUSING LEADERSHIP

President George W. Bush began his second term with a holdover at the head of the Department of Housing and Urban Development (HUD), Alphonso R. Jackson, who had been serving as HUD secretary since March 2004. After Jackson resigned on April 18, 2008, Steven C. Preston filled out the reminder of the term. *(Jackson background, Congress and the Nation Vol. XI, p. 924)*

In his four-year tenure at HUD, Jackson attracted both critics and supporters. After the 2005 hurricane season devastated the Gulf Coast, members of Congress questioned HUD's oversight of millions of dollars in rebuilding grants in the region. Some critics demanded Jackson's resignation for not responding to their inquiries. In 2007 HUD was at the crux of the Bush administration's plans to address the subprime mortgage mess that rippled through the economy and left millions with ruined credit and no homes. Some Senate leaders, including Joint Economic Committee chairman Charles E. Schumer, D-N.Y., praised Jackson for his work to keep Americans in their homes. In April 2008, however, while under investigation for allegations of cronyism, corruption, and political favoritism at several public housing agencies, including those in Philadelphia and New Orleans, Jackson resigned.

Upon Jackson's resignation, President Bush nominated Preston, who had been serving as head of the Small Business Administration (SBA) since July 2006, to be HUD secretary. Senate Banking, Housing, and Urban Affairs Committee chairman Christopher J. Dodd, D-Conn., said in a statement that Preston's apparent lack of background in housing "raises questions" and indicated that he would press for details on the SBA director's qualifications. President Bush said that, with the looming housing crisis, he needed someone heading HUD who had a background in finance. The Senate, by voice vote, confirmed Preston as HUD secretary June 5, 2008. During Preston's short tenure, profound changes took place in housing policy, including a massive bailout of the financial services industry and an overhaul of the mortgage finance system.

or at auction. Studies also have shown a correlation between a rise in foreclosures and an increase in violent crime. A foreclosure typically results for a time in an abandoned house, which imposes social and economic stigmas on the surrounding neighborhoods.

Some municipalities have taken on significant expenses to maintain abandoned and foreclosed properties, including utility costs, grass mowing, and general repairs, plus stepped-up police presence to prevent squatting and vandalism. Those costs rise even as the municipality's tax base erodes because of the decline in home values.

CONGRESSIONAL ACTION

With Republican George W. Bush in the White House, the GOP-controlled 109th Congress accomplished little in the way of new housing legislation. Although the House passed several bills, including measures to overhaul the struggling government-sponsored mortgage giants Fannie Mae and Freddie Mac, to improve the effectiveness of the Federal Housing Administration (FHA), to reauthorize the HOPE VI program, and to recodify the "brownfields" cleanup program, the Senate did not act. The two chambers found agreement, however, on two bills that provided funding for the Section 8 Voucher Program and for the Low Income Home Energy Assistance Program (LIHEAP).

After Democrats regained control of both the House and the Senate, the 110th Congress proceeded on a different note. With the housing market and the U.S. economy worsening, Congress passed legislation overhauling Fannie Mae and Freddie Mac. The legislation signed into law by President Bush created a new agency, the Federal Housing Finance Agency (FHFA), which was given broad oversight over Fannie Mae and Freddie Mac and the twelve Federal Home Loan banks. The measure also authorized the Treasury Department to purchase Fannie Mae and Freddie Mac securities in order to keep the two mortgage lenders from going under. The law also attempted to boost the housing market by providing incentives and tax credits for prospective home buyers.

Chronology of Action on Housing and Urban Aid

2005–2006

While the Republican-led 109th Congress passed few housing bills, two measures that President George W. Bush signed into law expanded funding for the Low Income Home Energy Assistance Program (LIHEAP) and the Section 8 Voucher Program. LIHEAP provided federal grants to help low-income people with their heating and cooling costs; the Section 8 Voucher Program allowed disabled students to stay in government-subsidized housing. Other measures passed by the House, notably an overhaul of the struggling government-backed mortgage lenders Fannie Mae and Freddie Mac, floundered in the Senate.

Mortgage Regulation

In October 2005 the House passed legislation (HR 1461) to overhaul regulation of government-sponsored enterprises, including the Federal National Mortgage Association (Fannie Mae), the Federal Home Loan Mortgage Corporation (Freddie Mac), and the twelve Federal Home Loan banks. The Senate Banking, Housing, and Urban Affairs Committee had approved a companion bill (S 190) in July 2005. Neither measure went any further. Efforts to strengthen oversight of Fannie Mae and Freddie Mac had also stalled in the 108th Congress. *(Earlier action, Congress and the Nation Vol. XI, p. 559)*

Fannie Mae and Freddie Mac provide capital and liquidity in the financial markets, buying mortgages from lenders, packaging the mortgages into securities, and then selling off those securities. The push to tighten regulation of the two companies followed the revelation of multibillion-dollar accounting scandals at the firms, which lead to the ouster of a number of executives. Questionable accounting practices raised concerns in Congress and the White House that oversight was insufficient to regulate the two lending giants.

Both HR 1461 and S 190 called for a new regulator for Fannie Mae and Freddie Mac, as well as the twelve Federal Home Loan banks. Lawmakers agreed that the new regulator would be independent of existing agencies, function outside of the appropriations process, and have broader authority to oversee the firms than the existing regulator, the Office of Federal Housing Enterprise Oversight. The chambers differed, however, on how to regulate the firms' trillion-dollar investment portfolios and whether to require them to set aside a percentage of their profits to create an affordable housing fund. While the House and Senate did not come to agreement on legislation in the 109th Congress, the issue was taken up again in the 110th. *(110th Congress action, mortgage regulation, p. 641; Mortgage relief, p. 630)*

HOUSE ACTION

The House Financial Services Committee approved HR 1461 on a 65–5 vote May 25, 2005. The bill was formally reported (H Rept 109-171, Part I) July 14.

Chairman Michael G. Oxley, R-Ohio, was at odds with the Bush administration over how best to rein in the massive investment portfolios held by Fannie Mae and Freddie Mac, which combined totaled about $1.5 trillion. The White House on May 19, 2005, sent lawmakers a proposal urging them to insert language in the bill greatly limiting the types of assets the two firms could purchase for their portfolios, with the aim of reducing the size of the portfolios. Critics of the mortgage finance companies said their huge portfolios were not essential to their mission of increasing home ownership and instead served to enrich executives and shareholders.

Company supporters said the holdings provided liquidity to the mortgage market, allowing lenders to offer more loans at lower interest rates. Oxley resisted pressure to add the administration provisions, choosing instead to retain language in the bill that would give the new regulator discretion to restrict the portfolios if that were found necessary for reasons of fiscal safety and soundness.

The key to Democratic support for the measure was a provision that Oxley included to beef up the affordable housing responsibilities of the two firms. Fannie Mae and Freddie Mac would be required to donate 5 percent of their after-tax profits to an affordable housing fund to be used for community and economic development programs.

The committee rejected, 53–17, an attempt by Ed Royce, R-Calif., to strike the provision, which he called "an experiment in socialism." Bill sponsor Richard H. Baker, R-La., who rarely differed from Oxley on financial matters, said he was concerned that there was no cap on the size of the funds and not enough guidance on how the money would be disbursed. But Democrats, joined by a number of Republicans, praised the provision as appropriate to the firms' housing mission.

The panel adopted several other amendments, including one to require the companies to disclose charitable contributions to nonprofit organizations and another to require them to review interest rate disparities on mortgages offered to minority borrowers. The committee also adopted amendments authorizing studies into alternatives to Fannie Mae and Freddie Mac, affordable housing opportunities for long-term care facilities, and loan guarantee fees charged to lenders.

Opposition by conservatives to the affordable housing fund delayed House floor action for months. Despite bill language specifically aimed at preventing the fund from being used for partisan purposes, the conservative Republican Study Committee (RSC) said liberal lobbying groups could use the money to defeat GOP candidates and interests. The RSC relented only when Oxley agreed to add language restricting the groups that could receive grants.

Before voting on HR 1461 on Oct. 26, 2005, the House adopted a managers' amendment by Oxley by a 210–205 vote that contained language specifying that groups would be deemed ineligible for affordable housing fund grants if they had been involved in any political activity in the previous year, including nonpartisan voter registration and get-out-the-vote programs. The amendment also reduced contributions to the fund to 3.5 percent of after-tax profits in the first two years and required the program to end after five years. Critics, including civil rights groups and faith-based charities, said the restrictions ran afoul of the First Amendment, as well as the 1993 "motor voter" law (PL 103-31) that required many nonprofits to get involved in registering voters. *("Motor voter" law, Congress and the Nation Vol. IX, p. 807)*

The same day, the House rejected, 200–220, a motion by Barney Frank, D-Mass., to send the bill back to committee with instructions to add language clarifying that housing must be among a nonprofit organization's primary purposes and that recipients of money from the affordable housing fund could participate in any voter registration or get-out-the-vote activity conducted on a nonpartisan basis. Frank noted that the RSC language would affect only nonprofit groups. For-profit companies still could receive funds, regardless of their political activities and donations.

Four other amendments went down in defeat on the House floor Oct. 26. An amendment offered by Royce, to authorize the new regulator to reduce the size of the portfolios if they posed a "systemic risk" to the economy, lost by 73–346. An amendment offered by Jim Leach, R-Iowa, to allow the new regulator to establish a minimum capital level for Fannie Mae, Freddie Mac, or any Federal Home Loan bank if it is needed for the long-term viability of any of the institutions, lost by 36–378. An amendment offered by Ron Paul, R-Texas, to eliminate the ability of Fannie Mae, Freddie Mac, and the Federal Home Loan Bank Board to borrow from the U.S. Treasury, lost 47–371. An amendment by Scott Garrett, R-N.J., to strike language in the bill to increase by 50 percent the maximum mortgages Fannie Mae and Freddie Mac can buy in areas with high home prices, lost 57–358.

After voting on the amendments, the House on Oct. 26 turned to voting on the measure itself, passing HR 1461 on a 331–90 vote. The White House issued a statement stating its opposition to the bill because it would not restrict the mortgage giants' portfolios.

SENATE ACTION

A companion measure to HR 1461, S 190 was debated in the Senate Banking, Housing, and Urban Affairs Committee in summer 2005. Adhering more closely to the administration's wishes than HR 1461, the Senate bill, championed by committee chairman Richard C. Shelby, R-Ala., proposed restrictions on the firms' portfolios and avoided creation of an affordable housing fund.

The major sticking point was a provision, opposed by Democrats, giving the new regulator authority to limit the types of assets the two companies could hold in their portfolios. Charles E. Schumer, D-N.Y., said requiring the companies to have smaller portfolios would reduce the nation's overall commitment to housing. He said the winners would be the private banks. Unlike Fannie Mae and Freddie Mac, which were chartered by Congress to further the nation's housing goals, Schumer said, banks were not required to help provide affordable housing.

Some GOP panel members also expressed concern. Robert F. Bennett of Utah said he disagreed with claims that the companies posed a systemic risk to the economy. However, he said he would vote for the bill to get it through committee.

Democrats also were unhappy that the bill did not contain the affordable housing fund. A amendment offered by ranking Democrat Paul S. Sarbanes of Maryland that included the affordable housing proposal was rejected, 9–11. The Senate Banking, Housing, and Urban Affairs Committee then approved S 190 by 11–9 July 28, 2005, with no Democrats voting in favor. The measure went no further in the Senate that year.

FHA Competitiveness

The House on July 25, 2006, agreed, 415–7, to a motion by Bob Ney, R-Ohio, to suspend the rules and pass HR 5121, which was intended to keep the Federal Housing Administration (FHA) competitive with private mortgage financiers. The House Financial Services Committee had formally reported the bill (H Rept 109-589) July 20.

HR 5121 would change many of the ways that FHA functioned to help it reclaim market share in the mortgage insurance business. The bill would raise loan limits for FHA-backed loans, allow the FHA to reduce its fees for buyers with strong credit histories, and allow the agency to insure loans made with low or no down payments.

The measure would eliminate the FHA's long-standing requirement for a 3 percent down payment on loans it insures and allow the agency to vary the premiums it charges borrowers. It also would allow the FHA to expand its reverse-mortgage business, which it dominated. Reverse mortgages allow homeowners age sixty-two and older to take equity out of their homes by taking out a loan that is not due until they die or the house is sold.

In other FHA-related action, the House by a 412–4 vote agreed July 25 to a motion by Paul E. Gillmor, R-Ohio, to suspend the rules and pass HR 4804, making it easier for the FHA to insure loans for mobile homes. HR 4804 would require the FHA to insure 90 percent of an individual's loan for the purchase and improvement of manufactured housing. It also would increase the loan limits for insuring a manufactured home to $68,040 in 2008 and require that the limits be indexed for inflation annually. The Senate did not take up HR 5121 or HR 4804.

Section 8 Voucher Program

In 2006 Congress passed a measure (HR 5117) to allow disabled students to stay in government-subsidized housing. The bill was meant to correct an oversight in fiscal 2006 appropriations legislation for the Department of Housing and Urban Development (PL 109-115), which included language forbidding most college students from using the rent voucher program known as Section 8. *(110th Congress action, Section 8, p. 644)*

The House Financial Services Committee approved HR 5117 by voice vote May 24, 2006, and formally reported it (H Rept 109-500) June 13. The House agreed by voice vote June 13 to a Deborah Pryce, R-Ohio, motion to suspend the rules and pass the bill. The Senate, also by voice vote, passed HR 5117 on July 18 without amendment, clearing the measure. President George W. Bush signed the measure into law July 27, 2006 (HR 5117—PL 109-249).

The committee also by voice vote June 14, 2006, approved HR 5443 (no written report), to make Section 8 easier for local housing authorities to administer. It would simplify rules for calculating the cost of apartments in the program and how much tenants should pay. It also would expand the Moving to Work program, which allowed housing authorities to help tenants find better-paying jobs so they could leave Section 8. Under existing law, twenty-five agencies participated in the program; under HR 5443, that number would grow to forty.

The committee by voice vote rejected three amendments offered by Gary G. Miller, R-Calif. The first would have expanded the Moving to Work program to one hundred housing authorities. The second amendment would have provided housing authorities a set grant each year, which the authorities themselves would allocate to vouchers. The third amendment would have eliminated a 30 percent cap on the amount of income families could be required to pay toward rent. The panel by voice vote, however, adopted a Miller amendment to prevent people who owned a home from also collecting rent vouchers. HR 5443 saw no further congressional action.

In another Section 8–related move, the House, 418–0, agreed Oct. 6, 2005, to a motion by Richard H. Baker, R-La., to suspend the rules and pass HR 3894, to waive several limitations on Section 8 to assist displaced hurricane victims. Under the bill, HUD would be prevented from canceling contracts with government-subsidized apartment complexes that were damaged or destroyed by Hurricane Katrina or Rita, and federal agencies would be required to compile an inventory of government property that could be used as emergency housing. The Senate took no action.

HOPE IV Reauthorization

In 2006 the House considered legislation to reauthorize the HOPE VI program, which demolishes and rebuilds dilapidated public housing complexes. The bill, HR 5347, sponsored by Christopher Shays, R-Conn., would renew the program for five years but did not specify spending levels or make any other program changes. *(110th Congress action, p. 644)*

HOPE VI provides funds to demolish run-down housing projects and replace them with affordable housing and to place dislocated residents into mixed-income communities. By moving low-income residents into more economically diverse neighborhoods, the program aims to expose lower-income families to better employment and educational opportunities.

The program was created as an offshoot of the Homeownership and Opportunity for People Everywhere (HOPE) initiative, which was designed to sell off public housing projects to tenants. The original HOPE project was part of the 1990 landmark Cranston-Gonzalez National Affordable Housing Act (PL 101-625). *(1990 act, Congress and the Nation Vol. VIII, p. 665)*

The House Financial Services Committee first approved HR 5347 by voice vote May 24, 2006, and formally reported it (H Rept 109-605) on July 27. The House agreed Sept. 27, 2006, by voice vote to a Michael G. Oxley, R-Ohio, motion to suspend the rules and pass HR 5347. The Senate did not take up the legislation.

The administration of George W. Bush had sought to kill the housing program since fiscal 2004. For fiscal 2007, the president went even further, proposing to rescind $99 million that Congress appropriated for the program in 2006.

During consideration of the fiscal 2007 Transportation-Treasury-Housing appropriations bill (HR 5576) in 2006, the House Appropriations Committee zeroed out funding for HOPE VI. The panel rejected, 25–31, a John W. Olver, D-Mass., amendment to provide more money to public housing agencies and to fund the HOPE VI program. On the House floor, however, members adopted, 262–162, on June 13, 2006, an amendment offered by Artur Davis, D-Ala., to include $30 million for the program, to be offset by a cut in the General Services Administration Federal Buildings Fund. The Senate Appropriations Committee included $100 million for HOPE VI in HR 5576. The measure subsequently stalled.

Home Energy Aid

The 109th Congress provided fiscal 2006 and fiscal 2007 funding for the Low Income Home Energy Assistance Program (LIHEAP). LIHEAP offered federal grants to states to help low-income people pay their heating and cooling bills and to weatherize their homes. The program was established in 1981 budget reconciliation legislation (PL 97-35) and is administered by the Department of Health and Human Services (HHS). *(1981 reconciliation, Congress and the Nation Vol. VI, pp. 40, 631)*

Conferees on HR 3010, the fiscal 2006 appropriations bill for the Departments of Labor, HHS, and Education (PL 109-149), agreed to $2.2 billion for LIHEAP, as recommended by the Senate. House appropriators rejected a Sen. Arlen Specter, R-Pa., proposal to designate the funding as emergency spending not subject to discretionary budget caps, which would have freed up money for earmarks and other programs. A group of Senate GOP moderates from the Snow Belt won a last-minute promise from Majority Leader Bill Frist, R-Tenn., for a floor vote in the following year on additional funds for home heating subsidies.

During Senate floor consideration of HR 3010 on Oct. 26, 2005, Jack Reed, D-R.I., failed, 54–43, in a motion to waive the budget act with respect to a Michael D. Crapo, R-Idaho, point of order against a Reed amendment to provide an additional $2.9 billion in emergency funding for LIHEAP. (A three-fifths majority vote—sixty—of the total Senate is required to waive the budget act.) The chair subsequently upheld the point of order, and the amendment fell. The Senate also rejected, 46–53, on Oct. 26 an amendment to HR 3010 by Judd Gregg, R-N.H., that would provide an additional $1.3 billion for LIHEAP, offset with a 0.92 percent across-the-board cut in budget authority in the bill.

Earlier, on Oct. 5, during floor consideration of the fiscal 2006 Defense appropriations bill (HR 2863—PL 109-148), the Senate rejected a John Kerry, D-Mass., motion to waive the budget act with respect to a Ted Stevens, R-Alaska, point of order against the emergency designation of a Kerry amendment to appropriate $3.1 billion for LIHEAP and designate it as emergency spending. The 50–49 vote fell short of the three-fifths majority vote required. The chair upheld the point of order and struck the emergency designation. The Kerry amendment subsequently fell on a second budget point of order.

In a similar vein, the Senate, on Oct. 20, 2005, during consideration of the fiscal 2006 appropriations bill for the Departments of Transportation, Treasury, and Housing and Urban Development (HR 3058—PL 109-115), rejected a Reed motion to waive the budget act with respect to a Christopher S. Bond, R-Mo., point of order against a Reed amendment to provide an additional $3.1 billion in emergency funding for LIHEAP. The 53–46 vote fell short of the needed three-fifths majority vote of the total Senate membership. The chair upheld the point of order, and the amendment was rejected.

Congress in 2006 completed action on budget reconciliation legislation (S 1932—PL 109-171), which added $1 billion in fiscal 2007 to LIHEAP. Of that amount, $750 million was reserved for emergency needs. *(Budget reconciliation, p. 81)*

The fiscal 2007 funds were made available in S 2320 (PL 109-204). On March 7, 2006, the Senate proceeded to consideration of the bill after agreeing to a motion to invoke cloture, 75–25, and then adopted, 68–31, an amendment by Olympia J. Snowe, R-Maine, to a substitute amendment by Jon Kyl, R-Ariz. The Snowe amendment would require that half the $1 billion provided in the substitute be distributed under the formula set in the Low Income Home Energy Assistance Program Act of 1981 (PL 97-35) and half be put into a contingency fund to be distributed by the administration. The same day, by voice vote, the Senate adopted the Kyl amendment and passed S 2320. The House agreed, 287–128, to a motion to suspend the rules and pass the bill on March 16, clearing the measure. President George W. Bush signed the measure into law on March 20, 2006. *(PL 97-35, Congress and the Nation Vol. VI, p. 588)*

Fiscal 2007 Labor-HHS-Education appropriations legislation (HR 5647, S 3708) gained committee approval in both chambers but then stalled. The House Appropriations Committee bill provided $2.1 billion for LIHEAP; the Senate panel version, $2.2 billion. The administration had requested $1.8 billion. A short-term continuing resolution (H J Res 102—PL 109-383) provided funding at fiscal 2006 levels for the departments and agencies covered by the spending legislation through Feb. 15, 2007.

The House rejected March 16, 2006, by a 76–342 vote, an amendment by K. Michael Conaway, R-Texas, to a fiscal 2006 supplemental appropriations bill (HR 4939—PL

109-234) to strike the section of the legislation that makes $750 million in fiscal 2007 emergency funding for LIHEAP in existing law available in fiscal 2006 as well as fiscal 2007. Conferees subsequently decided not to include the House proposal to shift the LIHEAP funds to fiscal 2006.

Rental Assistance

By 335–81 on Oct. 6, 2005, the House agreed to a Richard H. Baker, R-La., motion to suspend the rules and pass HR 3895, allowing the Agriculture Department to redirect money used to subsidize rural public housing that was damaged or destroyed by Hurricane Katrina to rental assistance for tenants. The Senate took no action.

Brownfields

The House by voice vote on Dec. 13, 2005, agreed to a Michael G. Oxley, R-Ohio, motion to suspend the rules and pass a bill (HR 280) to codify the Department of Housing and Urban Development (HUD) program that provided grants to help communities clean up sites, known as "brownfields," contaminated by pollutants or hazardous substances.

The Brownfields Economic Development Initiative grant program, started in 1998 as part of HUD's Economic Development Initiative, helped communities convert contaminated property into useful land. HUD said the money was to be used as a stimulus for local governments and private parties to begin redevelopment or continue phased redevelopment efforts of a site and not for remediation or land acquisition purposes alone.

Under current law, communities must apply for a HUD loan and use some of the Community Development Block Grant money as collateral to qualify for the grant. HR 280, sponsored by Gary G. Miller, R-Calif., would eliminate that requirement. The bill also would expand HUD's definition of brownfields to allow the popular program to be used in rural areas where abandoned mines, or "blackfields," posed problems for communities.

The House Financial Services Committee had approved HR 280 by voice vote March 16 and formally reported the measure (H Rept 109-138) on June 16. A Senate companion bill (S 3620), sponsored by Carl Levin, D-Mich., was referred to the Senate Banking, Housing, and Urban Affairs Committee but saw no further action.

In 2002 the House had passed similar legislation on brownfields, and Congress cleared a measure (PL 107-118) to provide liability protection for those who buy affected sites. *(Previous action, Congress and the Nation Vol. XI, pp. 418, 557)*

Small Housing Authorities

The House agreed on a 387–2 vote Dec. 13, 2005, to suspend the rules and pass HR 3422, which would exempt qualified small public housing authorities from the requirement of preparing an annual housing agency plan. The measure, sponsored by Randy Neugebauer, R-Texas, had been formally reported (H Rept 109-342) from the House Financial Services Committee earlier the same day. *(108th Congress action, Congress and the Nation Vol. XI, p. 559)*

A Senate companion bill (S 2707), introduced by John E. Sununu, R-N.H., was referred to the Senate Banking, Housing, and Urban Affairs Committee but saw no further action.

2007–2008

The Democratic-led 110th Congress was able to accomplish a major housing goal that eluded the previous Congress: it passed legislation to overhaul the struggling government-backed mortgage lenders Fannie Mae and Freddie Mac. The legislation created a new regulatory agency, the Federal Housing Finance Agency (FHFA), to oversee the two mortgage lenders as well as the twelve Federal Home Loan banks. The measure also gave the Treasury Department temporary authority to purchase securities issued by Fannie Mae and Freddie Mac, in order to keep the two solvent. The legislation also addressed the deteriorating housing market by providing tax credits and incentives to homebuyers.

As with the 109th Congress, the House during 2007–2008 passed many other housing bills that were ignored or shelved by the Senate. House-passed bills to overhaul the regulation of mortgage lenders, to increase the availability of mortgages to low- and middle-income homebuyers, to reauthorize the HOPE VI program, and to deal with disaster public housing and other housing issues did not advance in the Senate. The two chambers, however, were able to pass a mortgage forgiveness tax measure, signed into law by President Bush.

Mortgage Relief

Motivated by the need to protect overall market stability, Congress in 2008 cleared housing finance legislation (HR 3221) that included two of the White House's top priorities: providing a backstop for the Federal National Mortgage Association (Fannie Mae) and the Federal Home Loan Mortgage Corporation (Freddie Mac) and establishing a new regulator for the two mortgage giants. The bill also contained provisions to help borrowers get out from under loans they could not afford, offered a one-time tax credit to first-time homebuyers, and provided grants for local governments to acquire foreclosed properties.

Under the legislation, signed into law (PL 110-289) on July 30, the Treasury Department could buy assets from Fannie Mae and Freddie Mac, essentially expanding their existing line of credit with the government, or buy stock in the companies to keep them capitalized and boost the confidence of their private investors. On Sept. 7, 2008, barely five weeks after the bill's enactment, the Treasury announced that it has put both Fannie Mae and Freddie Mac into conservatorships and would funnel as much as $200 billion into the companies to keep them functioning.

BACKGROUND

Lawmakers had tried repeatedly to impose new rules on Fannie Mae and Freddie Mac, but disagreements over creating a new federal regulator and limiting the firms' portfolios—combined with Fannie Mae's and Freddie Mac's legendary lobbying clout—had stymied every effort. The two companies paid a critical role in creating a secondary housing market. They purchased mortgages from banks, giving them the money to make new loans at lower rates than might otherwise be available. It was a role that had led Democrats to support the firms for many years. Fannie Mae and Freddie Mac bundled the mortgages into packages that became the basis for mortgage-backed securities. Over time they had become involved in more complicated transactions, buying and selling complex, unregulated financial instruments such as derivatives to hedge against risks. The management of the companies also was a problem. In 2003 and 2004, multibillion-dollar accounting scandals led to the ouster of top executives in both companies.

Members of Congress worried about the complex portfolios and about the inability of the existing regulator, the tiny Office of Federal Housing Enterprise Oversight, to police the mortgage finance giants. Although Fannie Mae and Freddie Mac were public corporations, they originally were chartered by Congress as government-sponsored enterprises (GSEs), a status that created an implied guarantee of federal support. The thought that taxpayers might be on the hook, in the event the GSEs failed, was a major motivator for Congress to act.

In October 2003 a bill to split oversight of the companies between the Department of Housing and Urban Development (HUD) and a new Treasury agency stalled in the House Financial Services Committee, after the White House came out against it, saying it did not go far enough. In April 2004 the Senate Banking, Housing, and Urban Affairs Committee approved a bill to create a new safety and soundness regulator that could raise minimum capital requirements for the GSEs. The measure, however, was derailed by partisan tensions, lobbying, and disagreement over how to regulate the two companies. *(Oversight, Congress and the Nation Vol. XI, p. 559; regulator, Congress and the Nation Vol. XI, p. 143)*

In 2005 the House passed a GSE regulation bill (HR 1461) and Senate Banking, Housing, and Urban Affairs approved a similar measure (S 190). Both proposed creating an independent regulator, but disagreements arose over a House provision to require the companies to contribute 5 percent a year to a new affordable housing fund and a Senate plan to allow the regulator to restrict Fannie Mae's and Freddie Mac's portfolios. The measures went no further. *(109th Congress action, mortgage regulation, p. 625)*

HOUSE ACTION

The House passed HR 3221 by a 241–172 vote Aug. 4, 2007, as an energy bill. A subsequent House-Senate compromise led to the enactment of a revamped energy bill (HR 6—PL 110-140). *(Energy overhaul, p. 484)*

Financial company executives, including WMC Mortgage chief executive officer Laurent Bossard and Countrywide Financial executive managing director Sandy Samuels, testify on Capitol Hill on March 22, 2007, before the Senate Banking, Housing, and Urban Affairs Committee hearing on subprime mortgages.
Source: AP Photo/Dennis Cook

SENATE ACTION

The Senate rejected a motion, offered by Majority Leader Harry Reid, D-Nev., to invoke cloture and take up HR 3221, which was intended to become the vehicle for Senate mortgage legislation (S 2636). The 48–46 vote, taken Feb. 28, 2008, fell short of the three-fifths (sixty) of the entire Senate required.

Republicans aligned with the administration of President George W. Bush and the lending industry to oppose a provision that would allow bankruptcy court judges to alter the terms of a homeowner's mortgage. Under existing law, bankruptcy judges could modify mortgages on vacation homes but not on principal residences. Consumer advocates and many Democrats said that allowing judges to reduce loan balances or restructure loans could help hundreds of thousands of struggling homeowners stave off foreclosure. Opponents said the bankruptcy law change would lead to higher interest rates for all borrowers, because lenders would raise their rates to offset the chance that a loan could be modified in the future. The White House on Feb. 26 had threatened to veto the measure.

In its mortgage legislation, the Senate included a provision, avidly sought by homebuilders, to allow businesses with net operating losses in 2006, 2007, or 2008 to use them to offset profits from five prior years and receive applicable tax refunds. The existing loss carry-back limit was two years. Another provision called for an extra $10 billion of tax-exempt, private-activity bond authority that could be used to refinance subprime loans or provide mortgages for first-time homebuyers. Both provisions had been included in the Senate Finance Committee's version of an economic stimulus bill (HR 5140—PL 110-185) but dropped in final negotiations. The House Judiciary Committee approved similar bankruptcy language in 2007, as part of HR 3609. *(Subprime mortgage relief, p. 640)*

With the U.S. housing market and other economic indicators dropping, senators returned from their spring 2008 recess having settled their differences over mortgage relief legislation. The Senate on April 1 voted, 94–1, to agree to a Reid motion to invoke cloture and proceed to debate on HR 3221. Before the vote, Senate leaders sought to make the legislation more bipartisan to improve its chances of advancing. Negotiators reached what they called an "agreement in principle" on the package. Tax breaks for homeowners and builders and a major overhaul of the Federal Housing Administration (FHA) mortgage insurance program were included in the legislation. The bankruptcy provision was removed, with an agreement that Majority Whip Richard J. Durbin, D-Ill., would try to add it on the floor.

Senate Banking, Housing, and Urban Affairs Committee chairman Christopher J. Dodd, D-Conn., and the panel's ranking Republican, Richard C. Shelby of Alabama, wrote a bipartisan substitute for the Democratic housing bill S 2636. Because the legislation included tax language, which must originate in the House, the Senate used HR 3221, an energy bill, as its vehicle. The energy language would be stripped and the Senate mortgage package substituted into that bill.

To ensure passage of HR 3221, Democrats walked away from their pet provision—and the most contentious in the package—to allow bankruptcy judges to modify subprime and nontraditional mortgages, including reducing the outstanding principal on the mortgage. Lawmakers on April 3 voted, 58–36, to table (thus kill) a Durbin amendment to add the bankruptcy language to the measure. In a move illustrating the priority being placed on the legislation, Durbin made the motion to table his own amendment.

The Senate passed an amended HR 3221 on a 84–12 vote April 10. The measure was a bipartisan package built around tax incentives designed to spur the purchase of homes in foreclosure and to grant relief to struggling homebuilders and other businesses in the red.

Under the Senate-passed HR 3221, people who purchased homes in the foreclosure process would receive a $7,500 tax credit, spread over two years. Home buyers would not have to repay the money. In addition, taxpayers who did not itemize their deductions but paid property taxes would receive a $500 additional standard deduction ($1,000 for married couples) in 2008. Taxpayers would not be eligible for the deduction if their local governments raised the property tax rate in 2008.

The Senate-approved measure would make available an additional $10 billion in mortgage revenue bonds and allow those tax-exempt bonds to be used to refinance some subprime loans. It also included an $8.3 billion package of extensions of expiring tax breaks for producing renewable energy and energy efficiency.

A centerpiece of the measure was language incorporated from HR 1852 and its companion (S 2338) to overhaul the FHA mortgage insurance program, to enable the agency to help more borrowers refinance their mortgages into FHA-backed loans, which typically carry lower interest rates. The bills were passed by their respective chambers in 2007 but saw no further action. *(Affordable housing, p. 642)*

The Senate dropped a contested bankruptcy provision that supporters said would have provided an incentive for lenders to work out new loans with borrowers who could not afford their mortgages. The amendment, offered by Durbin, would have allowed judges to modify subprime and nontraditional mortgages, including reducing outstanding principal.

Included in the Senate-passed HR 3221 was language to allow businesses to use net operating losses in 2008 and 2009 to offset profits from four prior years and receive tax refunds. The bill also provided $4 billion in Community Development Block Grants to purchase and rehabilitate foreclosed properties in the hardest-hit areas.

HOUSE COMMITTEE ACTION

On April 9, 2008, the House Ways and Means Committee had approved, 35–5, an estimated $11.1 billion tax bill (HR 5720) to encourage home purchases and aid low-income renters. Committee chairman and bill sponsor Charles B. Rangel, D-N.Y., described the panel's strategy as consumer-friendly, taking a thinly veiled shot at the Senate-passed HR 3221, which would primarily help money-losing businesses. HR 5720 did not include an expansion of net operating loss carry-back.

The largest provision in HR 5720 was essentially a zero-interest, fifteen-year loan for first-time homebuyers, providing them up to $7,000 for a home purchase over the next year. The proposal was broader than the similar element in the Senate plan, but the Senate version would apply only to foreclosed properties, though it did not require the credit to be repaid.

Like the Senate-passed measure, the House Ways and Means bill would help homeowners who paid property taxes but did not itemize deductions on their federal income tax returns, although HR 5720 was less generous. It would provide a one-time $350 deduction ($700 for married couples) in 2008. The bill also would increase temporarily the volume cap for the low-income housing tax credit, allowing states to allocate more credits to developers of low-cost housing. Under the bill, both that credit and the rehabilitation tax credit could be applied against the alternative minimum tax, a change designed to give investors an additional incentive. The committee by voice vote adopted an amendment by Kenny Hulshof, R-Mo., designed to encourage more low-income housing tax credits to be used in poor rural areas.

The Ways and Means Committee formally reported HR 5720 (H Rept 110-606) on April 24. The bill saw no further action.

Meanwhile House Financial Services Committee chairman Barney Frank, D-Mass., put together a proposal to overhaul the FHA, allow the agency to insure trouble mortgages, increase the cap for mortgage revenue bonds, and provide money for low-income housing. The White House put forth a plan April 9 that was similar to Frank's but narrower in scope. The administration's plan would allow the FHA to insure refinancing mortgages if lenders agreed to cut the outstanding principal on the loan to reflect the property's reduced value. The plan would help an estimated 500,000 homeowners by expanding eligibility for a current program, while Frank's proposal would aid between one and two million homeowners by putting more federal money into the program. Under the White House plan, lenders would be encouraged, but not required, to write down the outstanding principal of loans to obtain FHA insurance. They could make other arrangements instead to meet the FHA's standards, such as bringing in new subordinate liens.

HOUSE ACTION

On May 8, 2008, the House in effect repassed HR 3221 by agreeing to three motions to concur on amendments to the Senate-passed version. A Frank amendment, by a 266–154 vote, provided for an independent agency, the Federal Housing Finance Agency (FHFA), to regulate Fannie Mae, Freddie Mac, and the Federal Home Loan Bank System with the power to place these entities into conservatorship or receivership in the event of a financial crisis. The amendment also would raise the GSEs' conforming loan limit for homes in high-cost areas. It created an affordable housing fund financed from Fannie Mae's and Freddie Mac's portfolios. Only very low-income families would be eligible for assistance from the fund. The amendment included increases in the loan limits for FHA-backed loans, with a further increase for homes in high-cost areas. It also provided for an expanded FHA program to help borrowers threatened with foreclosure on their primary residence refinance to new, affordable, fixed-rate, government-backed mortgages. The House Financial Services Committee had approved this language as a separate bill (HR 5830) by a 46–21 vote May 1. The bill, formally reported (H Rept 110-619) May 5, included a $300 billion authorization for the new loan guarantees and required both the lenders' and the borrowers' voluntary participation and agreement to take losses.

The Senate had not been able to pass an overhaul of Fannie Mae and Freddie Mac or FHA expansion language. The Bush administration opposed the FHA rescue plan, arguing that it would bail out real estate speculators and the lenders who made bad loans in the first place.

Based on expectations for future foreclosures and potential participation from borrowers, mortgage holders, and second lien holders, the Congressional Budget Office (CBO) estimated about 500,000 borrowers would refinance under the refashioned FHA program. The total price tag, which included the cost of new mortgages that go bad, would be about $2.7 billion over the 2008–2013 period.

The House agreed, 322–94, to a motion to concur on an amendment, taken from HR 5720, designed to relieve tax burdens on new and struggling homeowners. The amendment would establish a refundable tax credit of up to $7,500 for first-time homebuyers that would serve as an interest-free, fifteen-year loan and would provide an additional standard deduction in 2008 for nonitemizers who paid property taxes of up to $350 for individuals and $700 for couples. It included authority for $10 billion in tax-exempt bonds that would be used to refinance subprime loans, finance the construction of low-income rental housing, and support loans to first-time homebuyers. Revenue-raisers provided in the amendment offset the cost of the tax provisions, mainly by requiring that brokers report their customers' basis, or purchase cost, for securities transactions and by a one-year delay in new rules allocating interest expenses between foreign and domestic sources.

The House also agreed, 256–160, to an amendment offered by Brad Miller, D-N.C., and Steven C. LaTourette, R-Ohio, to prevent any provisions in the bill or either of the two major federal banking statutes, the Home Owner's Loan Act and the National Bank Act, from preempting state laws dealing with residential foreclosures. The financial services industry strongly opposed the amendment, arguing that it could interfere with federal banking regulators. Supporters promised to modify the provision to answer industry concerns.

In separate action May 8, the House passed a bill (HR 5818) by a 239–188 vote that aimed at easing the foreclosure burden on cities and states. Sponsored by Maxine Waters, D-Calif., the measure would establish a $15 billion loan and grant program to help states purchase and rehabilitate owner-occupied foreclosure properties. The House Committee on Financial Services formally reported the bill (H Rept 110-616) on May 1.

SENATE ACTION

The Senate took up HR 3221, as amended by the House, in mid-June. It agreed, 79–16, June 25 to replace most of the text with a comprehensive substitute written by Dodd and Shelby. The Senate then voted, 76–10, July 7 to concur in the House decision to strip out the Senate energy tax language. The chamber July 11 voted, 63–5, to reject the House tax amendment and the provision on state law.

The bipartisan substitute combined provisions of HR 3221 as passed by the Senate with a draft bill that the Senate Banking, Housing, and Urban Affairs Committee approved May 20. The draft measure created a new regulator for Fannie Mae, Freddie Mac, and the FHA, with authority similar to that in the House version. The regulator would have to consider the broader effect on markets in the event of a GSE failure when setting limits on the companies huge portfolios. The bill also provided for an increase in Fannie Mae's and Freddie Mac's conforming loan limits in high-cost housing markets, a new affordable housing fund financed from Fannie Mae's and Freddie Mac's portfolios, and the HOPE for Homeowners program to help borrowers avoid foreclosure. Unlike the House-passed bill, the Senate version proposed that the $300 billion authorized for the program come from the affordable housing fund. The draft measure included about $12 billion in revenue-raisers over ten years.

During the floor debate June 19, the Senate rejected two amendments by Christopher S. Bond, R-Mo., aimed at the heart of the legislation. The first amendment, rejected 11–77, would have prevented the use of funds from Fannie Mae and Freddie Mac for the affordable housing fund. The second, which would have eliminated the HOPE for Homeowners program, was rejected on a procedural vote, 21–69.

The House and Senate versions of the legislation were similar in many respects, but they also had significant differences. The House proposed delaying the start date of the new GSE regulator for six months after enactment, when a new president would be in the White House. The Senate made the effective date immediate. The House favored higher conforming loan limits for Fannie Mae and Freddie Mac—the lesser of 125 percent of the median home price in a local market or $729,750. The Senate proposed to decrease the limit to $625,000 in high-cost areas. The Senate, but not the House, included the $3.9 billion in Community Development Block Grants to assist localities in buying and rehabilitating foreclosed homes. This was one of the provisions that drew a White House veto threat. The House included a fully offset package of roughly $11 billion in housing-focused tax breaks. The Senate included $14.5 billion in tax breaks; all but $2.4 billion were offset.

The debate was suddenly transformed on Sunday, July 13, when Treasury secretary Henry M. Paulson Jr. asked Congress for largely unfettered authority to provide Fannie Mae and Freddie Mac with capital and potentially to take them over. The two firms had taken a financial beating the week before, as investors lost confidence in the housing market and in the companies' ability to repay $1.5 trillion in loans. Given Fannie Mae's and Freddie Mac's unique size and structure and their fundamental involvement in the U.S. and global economies, the Treasury and the Federal Reserve said they had little choice but to take action. Lawmakers expressed trepidation at giving the Treasury such broad authority so quickly, but most thought the alternatives were more perilous.

FINAL ACTION

Congress and the White House reached a compromise in late July. Lawmakers agreed to the administration's insistence that no dollar limit be placed on the Treasury's lending or equity purchases. However, all agreed to make any spending subject to the statutory debt limit and to increase that limit by $800 billion to cover the cost of the bailout. The compromise gave the Federal Reserve a "consultative" role to a new regulator for Fannie Mae and Freddie Mac, but that provision would expire at the end of 2009. The administration plan would not have sunset the Fed's role. The cap on the size of mortgages that Fannie Mae and Freddie Mac could buy and package as securities was set at the lesser of 115 percent of the median home price or $625,000 in certain high-cost areas, with language aimed at allowing more homes to qualify for the programs. House members also made some changes to the package of housing-focused tax breaks. The compromise version totaled about $15.1 billion. The measure included about $18.5 billion in offsets, which covered the cost of the housing tax breaks as well as most of the cost of grants to states and localities to buy and rehabilitate foreclosed properties.

The legislation gained momentum when the administration dropped its final objections to the bill July 23. Just two days earlier, the White House had renewed its veto threat, singling out the $3.9 billion in grants to state and local governments. Administration officials said grant-financed purchases of homes in foreclosure would simply benefit lenders, not individuals. However, White House deputy press secretary Tony Fratto said Treasury secretary Paulson recommended the president sign the bill because of the regulatory overhaul of Fannie Mae and Freddie Mac long sought by the administration as well as Paulson's plan to backstop the troubled mortgage finance giants to calm the jittery financial markets.

The House on July 23 inserted the compromise language into HR 3221 on a **key vote of 272–152 (R 45–149; D 227–3)**. The Senate voted 80–13 on July 25 to invoke cloture (thus limiting debate) on the House amendment. The next day, the Senate cleared the bill, on a **key vote of 72–13 (R 27–13; D 43–0; I 2–0)**. *(2008 key votes, p. 972)*

MAJOR PROVISIONS

Following are the major provisions of the mortgage finance bill, which President Bush signed into law July 30, 2008 (HR 3221—PL 110-289).

Federal Backstop

Stock purchase. The Treasury Department was given temporary emergency authority to purchase securities issued by Fannie Mae and Freddie Mac, including stock, if the purchase was expected to provide stability to the financial markets, prevent disruptions in the availability of mortgage finances, and protect taxpayers. The Treasury secretary was required to consider protections for the government's investment, such as limitations on existing stock dividends or executive compensation.

Debt limit. The law raised the statutory limit on the federal debt to $10.6 trillion, up from $9.8 trillion. The increase set the limit for Treasury's purchase of stock.

Sunset. The authority would expire on Dec. 31, 2009.

Regulation of GSEs

New regulatory agency. The law established a new, independent federal regulator, the Federal Housing Finance Agency, with broad oversight over three government-sponsored enterprises: the mortgage finance giants Fannie Mae and Freddie Mac and the twelve Federal Home Loan banks.

The new agency replaced the Office of Federal Home Enterprise Oversight (OFHEO), which was responsible for regulating Fannie Mae and Freddie Mac. It also replaced the Federal Housing Finance Board, which oversaw the Federal Home Loan Bank System. The OFHEO and the Federal Housing Finance Board were abolished one year after enactment.

Funding. Funding for the Federal Housing Finance Agency was to come through assessments on the three GSEs; it did not need an annual appropriation. The Treasury Department could invest excess funds from the assessments in government securities.

Agency structure. The director of the Federal Housing Finance Agency was responsible for overseeing the financial health and soundness of the three GSEs. The director was to be appointed by the president and confirmed by the Senate for a five-year term. The agency had three divisions, each headed by a deputy director: the Division of Enterprise Regulation, with oversight of Fannie Mae and Freddie Mac; the Division of Federal Home Loan Bank Regulation, with oversight of the Federal Home Loan banks; and Housing Mission and Goals, which would oversee the housing missions of the three GSEs.

Duties. The director's principal duties included ensuring that each GSE maintained adequate capital and internal controls, fostered a healthy national housing finance market that minimized the cost of housing financing, and complied with all applicable regulations. The director could review and reject any acquisition or transfer of a controlling interest in one of the GSEs.

Oversight board. The law created a five-member Housing Finance Oversight Board to advise the director on overall strategy and policies. It was to be chaired by the director and include the secretaries of HUD and the Treasury and two members appointed by the president and confirmed by the Senate. Board members served four-year terms, and no more than three members could be from the same political party.

Regulatory powers. The director was responsible for issuing new regulations to govern the mortgage portfolios of Fannie Mae and Freddie Mac, which together totaled about $1.5 trillion. The purpose of the regulations was to ensure that the mortgage portfolios were backed by sufficient capital, were consistent with the GSEs' mission, and allowed for safe and sound operations. The director also had to take into account the ability of the enterprises to provide a liquid secondary market through securitization activities and the portfolio holdings in relation to the overall mortgage market, among other factors.

The FHFA had the authority to approve or modify executive compensation at the GSEs.

Any new financial products offered by the GSEs had to be reviewed and approved by the regulatory agency, taking into consideration whether the product was in the public interest and whether it would interfere with the safety and soundness of the companies or the broader financial system. After a new product request had been made, there would be a thirty-day period for public comment, at the end of which the director would be required to make a decision.

Capital requirements. The FHFA was required to issue regulations setting risk-based capital requirements to ensure that the GSEs operated in a safe and sound manner. It also was responsible for setting minimum capital levels and could raise the levels temporarily or permanently, if needed, to preserve the safe and sound operation of Fannie Mae and Freddie Mac.

Rating system. The GSEs were to be rated under a system similar to that used by other federal banking regulators, with four classifications: adequately capitalized, undercapitalized, significantly undercapitalized, and critically undercapitalized.

Classification. An undercapitalized GSE would be monitored to ensure compliance with capital restoration plans, among other requirements. The FHFA could restrict the GSE's asset growth, including the expansion of its mortgage portfolios. An undercapitalized GSE could not acquire a stake in other companies or expand new business activities without the regulator's approval.

If a GSE was found to be significantly undercapitalized, the FHFA had to take actions that could include removing the board of directors and electing a new board, dismissing directors or executives, or requiring the GSE to hire qualified management. A GSE found to be significantly undercapitalized would be barred from paying bonuses or increased salaries to its executives unless approved by the FHFA.

If a GSE was rated critically undercapitalized, the FHFA could be appointed conservator or receiver to reorganize, rehabilitate, or close it. However, the regulator could not revoke the GSE's charter.

Enforcement. The law set three tiers of civil monetary penalties for violations. The first tier—for violating the new law and the authorizing statutes or engaging in unsafe and unsound practices—carried penalties of up to $10,000 per day. The second tier—for violations involving "reckless engagement in unsound business practices" and breaches of trust in sound business—carried penalties of up to $50,000 per day. The third tier—covering violations committed by an employee who engaged in unsound business practices and knowingly caused a substantial loss or substantial gain by breaking laws or regulations—brought a maximum penalty of $2 million per day.

Federal Reserve consultation. The FHFA director was required to consult with the Federal Reserve chair about risks to the financial system posed by the GSEs prior to issuing any regulation, order, or guidelines on prudent management, safety and soundness, or capital requirements, and portfolio standards. This requirement expired on Dec. 31, 2009.

Other GSE Changes

Conforming loan limits. The law permanently raised the GSEs' conforming loan limits, which governed the size of the mortgages that the companies could purchase, in areas where the median home price exceeded the general conforming loan limit of $417,000. The size of individual mortgage loans that Fannie Mae and Freddie Mac could buy was increased to the lesser of 115 percent of an area's median price or $625,000. The economic stimulus law (HR 5140—PL 110-185) included this increase for loans originated between July 1, 2007, and Dec. 31, 2008. *(Stimulus bill, p. 151)*

Underserved markets. Under previous law, the GSEs were supposed to purchase mortgages for households representing three income levels as measured by an area's median income (AMI): moderate income (100 percent AMI), low income (80 percent AMI), and very low income (60 percent AMI or less).

The new law redefined low-income families as those with 50 percent AMI or less and very low-income families as those with incomes of 30 percent AMI or less.

The GSEs were required to meet new goals established by the FHFA for purchasing single-family and multifamily home mortgages for households in these categories, based on Home Mortgage Disclosure Act data by using three-year averages to determine the market. The goals were to be set annually but could be set for a multiyear period.

The GSEs also were directed to include mortgages in central cities, rural areas, and other underserved housing areas, as well as loans for manufactured housing and the preservation of affordable housing.

Affordable Housing Fund

Fund creation. The law created a new, permanent Affordable Housing Trust Fund administered by HUD and funded by proceeds from Fannie Mae and Freddie Mac. The fund's purpose was to support homeownership among low-income and very low-income families, increase investment in economically distressed areas, and increase the supply of rental and owner-occupied housing for those families.

GSE assessments. Fannie Mae and Freddie Mac were required each year to divert 0.42 percent of the total value of newly purchased mortgages to pay for the trust fund.

However, the funding stream was to be diverted in the first few years to pay for a new program created under the bill to help borrowers avoid foreclosure. To reimburse the government for administrative expenses associated with the borrower rescue program, known as HOPE for Homeowners, 25 percent of the funds would be set aside. In fiscal 2009, the remaining 75 percent would go to offset the rescue program, declining to 50 percent in fiscal 2010 and 25 percent in fiscal 2011. Beginning in fiscal 2012, 75 percent of the GSE assessments would be allocated to the Affordable Housing Trust Fund.

Distribution formula. HUD was responsible for devising the formula for dispersing money from the trust fund, which had to be published in the *Federal Register.* Grants were to be awarded to state housing agencies, housing and community development agencies, and tribally designated housing entities. None of the affordable housing funds could be used for political activities, advocacy, lobbying, counseling, travel expenses, or preparation or advice on tax returns. No more than 10 percent of the funds could be used for grantee administrative costs or expenses. The CBO estimated that outlays for the trust fund would total $1.6 billion in fiscal 2008 through 2013.

Federal Home Loan Banks

The FHFA's responsibilities included regulatory control over the Federal Home Loan Bank System. The new law reduced the number of directors on the Federal Home Loan Bank Board to thirteen from fourteen. Two or more banks were allowed to establish a joint office to perform banking functions that each was individually authorized to perform. The FHFA was required to create regulations to ensure that the Federal Home Loan banks had access to the information they needed to determine joint liability. Individual Federal Home Loan banks could merge, subject to approval from the new regulator and each of the bank's boards. The cap on director compensation was lifted, and the term was lengthened to four years from three.

Mortgage Licensing

New licensing system. The law set out standards for a nationwide licensing and registration system for mortgage brokers and for bank loan officers who dealt with real estate loans. The states were encouraged to administer the system on their own, in accordance with the standards set out under the law. But if HUD found that a state-run system was deficient, the federal government was required to put a backstop licensing system in place.

Licensing standards. Under the new law, a broker had to be licensed and registered by the Nationwide Mortgage Licensing System and Registry (NMLSR) to be a loan originator. Anyone applying for licensing and registry had to provide fingerprints, personal history, and relevant experience. The applicant had to meet minimum standards to receive a license, including not having his or her loan originator license revoked in the previous five years, no felony conviction in the previous seven years, demonstration of financial responsibility, complete prelicensing education, and correctly answering 75 percent of a written test developed and administered by the NMLSR.

Federal banking regulators were required to jointly develop systems for registering employees of banks as registered loan originators within one year of enactment. The bank regulators, through the Federal Financial Institutions Examination Council, were directed to coordinate with the new broker-licensing agency to establish a unique identifier for all registered loan originators. The Justice Department was authorized to provide access to criminal history records to states for background checks on state-licensed loan originators.

Federal backup. HUD was required to create a backup licensing system for states that failed to meet the minimum standards established by law or did not participate in the licensing system.

Fees. Federal banking agencies, along with the new licensing agency, could charge fees to cover the costs of the program, provided the fees were not passed on to consumers.

Immunity. State or HUD officials acting in good faith while administering the program were afforded civil liability protection within the scope of their office or employment.

FHA Overhaul

The new law updated and modernized several elements of the FHA, a Depression-era agency that insured mortgages made by qualified lenders to low- and moderate-income families to purchase or refinance a home. The program provided mortgage insurance to protect lenders against the risk of default on mortgages to qualified buyers, enabling the lenders to provide better terms.

Loan limit. The FHA's loan limit—the maximum loan amount that the agency could insure—was permanently increased to $417,000 from $362,790. The minimum loan was raised to $271,050 from $200,160. For high-cost residential areas, the loan limit was increased to the lesser of 115 percent of an area's median home price or $625,000.

Premiums. The FHA could charge upfront premiums of up to 3 percent of the original insured principal obligation and 2.75 percent for first-time homebuyers who completed a counseling program.

Down payment. Down payment requirements for getting an FHA-backed loan were increased to 3.5 percent from 3 percent. Borrowers getting FHA-backed loans could not get down payment assistance from the seller. The law also set a one-year moratorium on risk-based pricing for FHA insurance products, effective Oct. 1, 2008.

Loan-to-value limit. The law set the loan-to-value limit—the ratio of the fair market value of a house to the value of the loan that would finance the purchase—for FHA single-family loans at 97.75 percent of the appraised value, plus the upfront FHA mortgage premium.

The FHA could increase single-family loan limits up to 100 percent of the appraised value of a home, plus closing costs for thirty-six months, in a presidentially declared disaster area.

Mutual Mortgage Insurance Fund. The bill made changes to the Mutual Mortgage Insurance Fund, through which the FHA insured mortgage loans on one- to four-family residential housing. The program was self-funding, taking in premiums from mortgagors and paying claims from lenders on losses from mortgage defaults.

Under the bill, the FHA was allowed to change the premiums or underwriting standards if the fund was at risk of becoming financially unsound. The law also added four types of government-backed mortgages to the fund's responsibilities: mortgages used in conjunction with the Homeownership Voucher program, reverse mortgages insured by FHA, Hawaiian Home Lands insured mortgages, and single-family mortgages insured on Native American reservations.

Reverse mortgages. The law removed the limit on the number of reverse mortgages (previously set at 275,000) that the FHA could insure. Reverse mortgages allowed homeowners age sixty-two and older to convert their home equity into a monthly stream of income and a line of credit to be repaid when they no longer occupied the house. The law created a uniform nationwide cap of $417,000 on reverse mortgage loans. The FHA was required to set limits on the origination fee that could be charged for such loans. Reverse mortgage loans were permitted in co-op units.

Borrower ID. Borrowers were required to provide personal identification to receive an FHA-insured loan. Acceptable forms of identification included a Social Security card along with a photo ID issued by the federal or state government, a driver's license or ID card issued by a state in accordance with the REAL ID Act, a passport, or a U.S. Citizenship and Immigration Services photo ID card.

Help for Borrowers

HOPE for Homeowners. The law established a temporary FHA-administered program to help borrowers who could not afford their mortgage payments to avoid foreclosure. Under the program, which was authorized from Oct. 1, 2008, until Sept. 30, 2011, certain borrowers could refinance into new, FHA-insured mortgages if the lender agreed to reduce the mortgage debt. Participation in the program was voluntary and required agreement from both the borrower and the holder of the mortgage. Costs of the program were to be paid for by funds diverted from Fannie Mae and Freddie Mac.

Insurance limit. The FHA was authorized to insure up to $300 billion worth of newly refinanced mortgages through fiscal 2011.

Procedure for getting insurance. The process began with an applicant contacting an FHA-approved lender to refinance the applicant's current mortgage. The lender would determine the loan size that would meet the program's requirements, including a requirement that the borrower be able to repay the new loan. If the borrower's existing lender agreed to take a write-down on the existing loan to a level that was affordable for the borrower, the FHA lender would then pay off the discounted existing mortgage.

Eligibility. Borrowers and lenders had to meet eligibility requirements to participate in the program. Only owner-occupied principal residences were eligible, and borrowers had to certify that they owned no other homes. Borrowers could not have a mortgage-debt-to-income ratio of more than 31 percent as of March 1, 2008. Borrowers also had to certify that they had not intentionally defaulted on existing mortgages and had not obtained the existing loan fraudulently.

Lenders had to agree to waive any existing penalties or fees on the existing mortgage and to accept the proceeds from the new loan as payment in full. Holders of secondary liens—such as a home equity line—on the property also had to relinquish any claims, and borrowers could not take such loans for at least five years.

Other loan requirements. If all those requirements were met, the existing lender would agree to reduce the outstanding principal on the loan. To participate in the program, the lender would have to pay the FHA a 3 percent upfront premium and would have to write down the value of the existing mortgage to no greater than 90 percent of the property's appraised value. After refinancing a mortgage, the borrower would be required to pay annual insurance premiums to the FHA that would be equal to 1.5 percent of the principal. The new loan would have a fixed interest rate and a maturity of not less than thirty years.

Equity share. The borrower getting an insured loan had to agree to share a portion of the house's future appreciation with the government, both to help lower the program's cost and to prevent borrowers from unfairly profiting from the federal program.

A borrower who sold a home or refinanced the loan within five years had to share equity with the government according to the following formula: 100 percent in year one, 90 percent in year two, 80 percent in year three, 70 percent in year four, 60 percent in year five, and 50 percent through the rest of the loan. A borrower who sold a home was required to share a flat 50 percent of the home's appreciated value with the government.

Board of directors. The law established a new board to oversee the program, made up of the Treasury and HUD secretaries and the chairs of the Federal Reserve and the Federal Deposit Insurance Corporation (FDIC). The board is directed to issue regulations setting a "reasonable" limit on origination fees for the new loans and to establish rules to ensure that the interest rate was comparable to similar market rates.

Other Foreclosure-Related Provisions

Mortgage disclosure. The law required more disclosure from lenders on the terms of mortgages, particularly adjustable-rate mortgages. A lender was required to state clearly and conspicuously that an adjustable-rate mortgage would have an interest rate that varies over time and to disclose the maximum possible payment on the mortgage.

Protection for servicemembers. The law temporarily expanded a provision of the Servicemembers Civil Relief Act (PL 108-189) that required lenders to wait ninety days before they could begin foreclosure proceedings against a returning servicemember. The new law lengthened the grace period to nine months. The change applied to sales, foreclosures, or seizures of property made on or after the law's enactment. A lender or loan servicer had to provide a written financial disclosure to a servicemember who failed to make a mortgage payment for two consecutive months. The expansion expires on Dec. 31, 2010. *(Civil relief act, Congress and the Nation Vol. XI, p. 534)*

Veterans. The Department of Veterans Affairs was authorized to make improvements and structural alterations to the homes of servicemembers who had a permanent disability that required a discharge as a result of injury in the line of duty.

Abandoned and foreclosed homes. The law appropriated $3.9 billion for grants to states and local governments to purchase and rehabilitate abandoned and foreclosed homes. HUD was directed to develop a formula for distributing the grants. Recipients had to use the funds within eighteen months to purchase and redevelop the property. At least 25 percent of the money had to be used on properties that would house individuals or families whose incomes were below 50 percent of the area median income. Homes purchased with the funds had to be sold at a price equal to or less than the cost of buying and rehabilitating the house. Any excess revenue generated during the first five years of the program though resale, rental, or redevelopment of the property had to be reinvested in rehabilitating other homes. After the five-year period, excess revenue would be deposited in the U.S. Treasury.

Homeowner counseling. The law provided a total of $180 million for counseling services for homeowners facing foreclosure, $80 million was set aside for preforeclosure counseling, and $100 million was allocated for the Neighborhood Reinvestment Corporation until Dec. 31, 2008, for foreclosure mitigation efforts and outreach to borrowers at risk of losing their homes.

Housing Incentives

First-time homebuyer credit. Under the law, first-time homebuyers would receive a refundable tax credit of up to $7,500 for purchases made between April 8, 2008, and July 1, 2009. The credit would effectively function as an interest-free loan, covering 10 percent of the purchase price of the house, up to $7,500. The credit also was "refundable," meaning that it could be claimed even if it was worth more than the taxes owed by the homebuyer. The credit was phased out for higher-income buyers, beginning at $75,000 in modified adjusted gross income for individuals ($150,000 for joint filers).

The credit had to be repaid over fifteen years, meaning a participating homebuyer's taxes would increase each year by 6.67 percent of the total amount of the credit. The credit would not be available if the house qualified for the Washington, D.C., homebuyer credit, the residence was financed by a tax-exempt mortgage bond, the taxpayer was a nonresident alien, or the taxpayer disposed of the house before the end of the taxable year.

The expected cost, calculated by the Joint Tax Committee, was $4.5 billion over eleven years.

Property tax deduction. The law created an additional standard deduction in 2008 for state and local property taxes. Taxpayers who did not itemize could deduct up to $500 for individuals ($1,000 for joint filers) for those taxes. If the property taxes were less than the standard deduction amount, the taxpayer would claim the amount of taxes paid. The additional deduction was expected to cost $1.5 billion over eleven years.

Low-income-housing tax credit. The limit on state allocations of low-income-housing tax credits was increased by 20 cents for 2008 and 2009, thus providing a limit of $2.20 per resident for those years. The program provides tax credits that can be claimed over a ten-year period for the costs of building or rehabilitating certain rental housing occupied by low-income tenants. The dollar amount used to determine credits for states with smaller populations was increased by 10 percent. These and other tax incentives for multifamily low-income housing were expected to cost $1.9 billion over eleven years.

Tax-exempt housing bonds. The law authorized $11 billion in additional state-issued tax-exempt private activity bonds in 2008 for housing-related financing, and it changed certain rules regarding the bonds. The bonds are officially issued by state and local governments, but the proceeds are used by private entities and the payment of the bonds comes from private entities. The types of private-activity bonds eligible for tax-exempt treatment included qualified mortgage bonds, qualified veterans' mortgage bonds, and bonds used to finance certain residential rental projects.

The new bonds had to be used to finance new mortgages or certain residential rental properties that met low-income eligibility requirements. Some mortgage bonds also could be used to refinance adjustable-rate single-family mortgages that originated between 2002 and 2007, if a bond issuer determined that refinancing would be "reasonably likely" to cause financial hardship to the borrower. Increasing the tax-exempt bond cap in this way was expected to cost about $1.5 billion over eleven years.

AMT provisions. Certain housing-related tax incentives were not covered by the alternative minimum tax (AMT). Specifically, the law allowed certain low-income-housing tax credits to be used to offset tax liability under the AMT, allowed the rehabilitation credit to be used to offset tax liability when calculating the AMT, and prevented interest earned on tax-exempt housing bonds issued after the enactment date from being treated as taxable income under AMT. The estimated cost was $2.1 billion under eleven years.

Revenue Provisions

AMT credits. Corporations were allowed to accelerate the use of certain tax credits in lieu of the bonus depreciation for certain equipment purchases. The available tax credits that could be swapped out included stored-up historic credits under the AMT, as well as research and development credits. The amount that could be obtained was capped at $30 million or 6 percent of the shored-up credits, whichever was less. The estimated cost was $996 million over eleven years.

Hurricane losses. The law modified the statutory rules for the Gulf Opportunity Zone, or GO Zone, which covered the area affected by the 2005 Hurricanes Katrina, Rita, and Wilma. Taxpayers could file an amended tax return if they received a grant authorized under certain federal laws that reimbursed them for hurricane-related casualty losses for their primary residence after they had previously claimed a deduction for those losses on a tax return. Generally, when taxpayers were reimbursed for casualty losses in a subsequent year, they took those reimbursements into account on the return for the year in which they were received. The estimated cost was $1.3 billion over eleven years.

Revenue Offsets

Credit card reporting. "Payment settlement" companies, which process transactions for debit and credit cards, were required to provide certain information to the Internal Revenue Service (IRS) and to the merchant or seller that accepted payments processed by those companies. The provision amounted to a tax compliance measure to prevent merchants from successfully avoiding taxes by underreporting their income from credit card, debit card, or third-party transactions. It was expected to raise $9.5 billion over eleven years.

Exclusion of gain on home sales. The law placed a new condition on the amount of gain or profits from the sale of a home that a taxpayer could exclude from taxation. Under previous law, individual taxpayers could exclude $250,000 and couples could exclude $500,000, as long as they occupied the home as a primary residence for at least two of the previous five years. The new law specified that the taxpayer could only exclude the portion of the gain that was attributed to the period during which the home was used as a primary residence, as opposed to a second residence or a rental property. The provision, which affected sales and exchanges after Dec. 31, 2008, was expected to raise $1.4 billion over eleven years.

Worldwide interest allocation rules. The act delayed for two years the effective date for a provision of the 2004 corporate tax overhaul (PL 108-357) that allowed companies to use a modified rule for allocating their interest expenses between U.S. and foreign sources when determining their foreign tax credit limitation. Implementation would take effect for taxable years beginning in 2011, instead of 2009, increasing revenue by an estimated $7.6 billion over eleven years. *(Corporate tax overhaul, Congress and the Nation Vol. XI, p. 115)*

Mortgage Forgiveness

Congress in 2007 cleared legislation (HR 3648) to amend the Internal Revenue Code of 1986 to exclude discharges, prior to Jan. 1, 2010, of indebtedness on principal residences from gross income. The excludable amount was limited to $2 million. The chairman of the House Ways and Means Committee, Charles B. Rangel, D-N.Y., sponsored the bill.

The Ways and Means Committee formally reported the measure (H Rept 110-356) on Oct. 1, 2007. The full House passed HR 3648 by 386–27 Oct. 4. The Senate by voice vote Dec. 14 passed an amended version of the bill. The House cleared the legislation Dec. 18, after agreeing by voice vote to a motion to suspend the rules and accept the Senate changes. President George W. Bush signed the bill into law (HR 3648—PL 110-142) on Dec. 20, 2007.

As described by the Congressional Research Service, the legislation also provided for an extension of the tax deduction for mortgage insurance premiums through 2010; offered additional tests for qualifying as a cooperative housing corporation for tax deduction purposes; permitted members of qualified volunteer emergency response organizations an exclusion from gross income for state and local tax benefits until after 2010; allowed certain full-time, single-parent students and their children to live in units eligible for the low-income housing tax credit; provided under stipulated circumstances that a surviving spouse could exclude from gross income up to $500,000 of a gain from the sale or exchange of a principal residence owned jointly with the deceased spouse; increased the penalty for failing to file a partnership tax return; set an additional penalty on S corporations for failing to file required tax returns; and increased the estimated tax payment due in

President Bush signs the Mortgage Forgiveness Debt Relief Act of 2007 on December 20, 2007, surrounded by Sen. Debbie Stabenow, D-Mich., Rep. Rob Andrews, D-Ohio, Rep. Jim McCrey, R-La., Sen. Max Baucus, D-Mont., Treasury Secretary Henry Paulson, Sen. George Voinovich, R-Ohio, Housing Secretary Alphonso Jackson, and Rep. Stephanie Tubbs Jones, D-Ohio.
Source: AP Photo/Ron Edmonds

the third quarter of 2012 for corporations with at least $1 billion in assets.

Subprime Mortgage Relief

The House Judiciary Committee Dec. 12, 2007, approved a bill (HR 3609) on a 17–15 vote to provide relief to borrowers who had taken out adjustable-rate subprime loans and were facing steep monthly payment increases as the loans reset. HR 3609, sponsored by Brad Miller, D-N.C., aimed to let bankruptcy judges modify the terms of some home mortgages or write down the value of a mortgage to reflect a home's existing value during bankruptcy proceedings.

Bankruptcy judges were not allowed under existing law to change the terms of a mortgage for a primary residence, although they could make changes to mortgages for vacation homes and investment properties.

The panel had adopted, by voice vote, a compromise amendment that narrowed the bill's scope. The compromise, worked out by committee chairman John Conyers Jr., D-Mich., and Steve Chabot, R-Ohio, limited the measure's coverage to subprime or nontraditional mortgages made between Jan. 1, 2000, and the legislation's date of enactment. It also provided for some of the key provisions to expire in seven years.

Supporters said the bill was one of the few congressional efforts that would help borrowers already in trouble. Much of the lending industry strongly opposed the legislation, saying that it would drive up borrowing costs because banks would charge higher interest rates to guard against the risk that the loans could be changed sometime in the future. The industry favored a Bush administration plan to allow loan services to freeze interest rates for five years on some adjustable-rate subprime mortgages. Some saw that agreement, which was worked out among regulators, loan servicers, and investors, as an attempt to blunt momentum behind potentially more decisive congressional actions, such as the bankruptcy changes. The bill did not reach the House floor.

In related action, the House on Dec. 5, 2007, had agreed by voice vote to a Barney Frank, D-Mass., motion to suspend the rules and pass a bill (HR 3526) that would give new powers to federal regulators to write rules prohibiting deceptive financial practices. The measure would add the Office of the Comptroller of the Currency and the Federal Deposit Insurance Corporation to the agencies that could write such rules. Only the Federal Reserve Board (Fed), the Office of Thrift Supervision, and the National Credit Union Administration had that power.

Lawmakers criticized federal regulators, particularly the Fed, for not acting quickly enough to curtail overly aggressive lending practices in the subprime mortgage markets. The measure would give the additional agencies an opportunity to act to curb deceptive lending practices, although it extends beyond mortgage lending to the broader credit market.

The House Financial Services Committee had approved the bill by voice vote on Sept. 18 and formally reported it (H Rept 110-472, Part I) on Dec. 5. The House Energy and Commerce Committee had approved the measure by voice vote on Oct. 30 and reported it (H Rept 110-472, Part II) on Dec. 5. The measure did not go further.

Mortgage Lender Regulation

In response to a mortgage crisis that began reverberating through the economy in 2007, the House passed a bill (HR 3915) to reform the regulation of mortgage lenders. The measure was referred to the Senate Banking, Housing and Urban Affairs Committee but saw no further action.

The catalyst for the legislation was the collapse of the subprime mortgage market. Subprime mortgages enable borrowers with spotty credit histories to get adjustable-rate loans at low "teaser" interest rates. Hundreds of thousands of those borrowers faced the loss of their homes as their payments jumped to levels they could not afford when the introductory rate expired.

Industry critics said the lenders, including mortgage brokers, helped stoke the crisis by pushing unqualified borrowers into subprime loans, which carried higher-than-average interest rates because of the extra risk, without ensuring that the borrowers knew what they were getting into. The lenders could unload the risk by selling the mortgages to companies that pooled the loans into mortgage-backed securities or bonds. As the subprime market expanded, Wall Street began to invest in the securities, which had potential for higher returns because of the extra risk.

Many critics including some Democrats argued that the growing demand from investors encouraged subprime lenders to abandon reasonable qualifying standards, to loosen standard documentation requirements, and to ignore whether borrowers could afford the loan. But many Republicans argued that excessive regulation would dry up the market for subprime mortgages, forcing homebuyers with poor credit histories out of the market.

HOUSE ACTION

On Nov. 6, 2007, by 45–19, the House Financial Services Committee approved HR 3915. The bill was formally reported (H Rept 110-441) on Nov. 9.

Before the markup, committee chairman Barney Frank, D-Mass., consulted with consumer groups, the lending industry, and GOP lawmakers to revise the measure and broaden support for it. Changes included making liability standards for mortgage scrutinizers national, thus preempting state laws. Also, the amount of time a borrower would have to bring a liability claim against a scrutinizer or lender would be narrowed. And federal regulators would have the power to revise some of the safe-harbor provisions dealing with minimum standards for mortgages.

The committee-approved bill would:

- Require all mortgage providers, including brokers, to be registered and licensed under state or federal laws that included certain standards for verifying the credibility of the lender.
- Direct the states, through the Conference of State Bank Supervisors and the American Association of Residential Mortgage Regulators, to create a new Nationwide Mortgage Licensing System and Registry to license and register mortgage providers, including bank employees. The Department of Housing and Urban Development (HUD) would set up the system if the states did not do so. The department would also establish a backup licensing system for states that chose not to participate in the registry or that had programs that did not meet minimum federal standards.
- Set out minimum standards for all residential mortgages, including a requirement that lenders make a good-faith effort to determine in advance that the borrower had a reasonable ability to repay the loan.
- Provide for the development of regulations against steering borrowers to subprime mortgages.
- Make mortgage lenders, and the scrutinizers that bundled the loans into mortgage-backed securities, liable if loans did not meet the minimum standards. The bill also included liability protection for those companies if they met certain due-diligence requirements.
- Preempt state laws on the liability and penalties for securitizers but not for lenders. States would be allowed to pass laws or strengthen penalties for lenders.
- Direct HUD to create an Office of Housing Counseling to set standards and provide assistance to states for counseling on homeownerhip, mortgage loans, and rental housing.

Lenders wanted the legislation to preempt all state regulation so they would not have to deal with a patchwork of laws. The industry saw federal preemption of state securitizer liability laws as a minimum requirement. However, the National Governors Association, along with several other state organizations, opposed any effort to preempt state liability laws.

The committee rejected, 22–42, an amendment by John Campbell, R-Calif., to remove the language establishing liability for mortgage securitizers. The panel also defeated, by voice vote, an amendment by Richard H. Baker, R-La., to preempt states on all related laws for seven years.

The House passed HR 3915 on a **key vote of 291–127 (R 64–127; D 227–0)** on Nov. 15. A majority of Republicans from states such as Ohio and Michigan, which were hit hard by mortgage troubles, voted in favor of the bill. Still, the industry, along with some Republicans and the administration, remained concerned that tightening mortgage regulations could make it harder for potential homebuyers to get loans. The White House on Nov. 14 released a statement of administration policy that objected to certain provisions but stopped short of threatening a veto. *(2007 key votes, p. 955)*

On the floor Nov. 15, the House:

- Adopted by voice vote a manager's amendment that clarified provisions dealing with liability for the companies that bundled home loans into securities sold on the secondary market.
- Adopted, by voice vote, an amendment by Paul E. Kanjorski, D-Pa., to require escrow accounts for risky loan applicants and establish federal standards for appraisers. The amendment contained provisions from a separate bill (HR 3837), which was ordered reported from the House Financial Services Committee on Nov. 7, 2007 (no written report).
- Adopted, by voice vote, an amendment by Ginny Brown-Waite, R-Fla., to exclude loans insured by the Federal Housing Administration from the bill.
- Rejected, 169–250, an amendment by Melvin Watt, D-N.C., to allow for actual damages in the bill's liability section. Critics said the proposal could prevent lenders from being able to calculate potential liability costs when issuing them.
- Rejected, 188–231, an amendment by Marsha Blackburn, R-Tenn., to recommit the bill to the committee with instructions to add language prohibiting lenders from extending mortgage loans without verifying the identity and legal immigration status of the potential borrowers by means of a secure identification.

SENATE ACTION

Like the House bill, S 2452, introduced by Senate Banking, Housing, and Urban Development Committee chairman Christopher J. Dodd, D-Conn., proposed a series of minimum standards for subprime mortgages, including a requirement for lenders to demonstrate that prospective borrowers had the ability to repay loans.

However, the Senate legislation sought to establish liability for the investors who bought the mortgage-backed securities, while HR 3915 placed liability on the companies that packaged the securities. The House bill proposed to preempt potentially tougher state measures on securitizer liability; the Senate measure did not. No further action occurred on either measure.

Mortgage Regulation

The House in 2007 passed a bill (HR 1427) to establish an independent regulator with broad oversight authority over the Federal National Mortgage Association (Fannie Mae), the Federal Home Loan Mortgage Corporation (Freddie Mac), and the twelve Federal Home Loan banks. The legislation died upon adjournment. *(109th Congress action, p. 625)*

Critics of Fannie Mae and Freddie Mac began the first session of the 110th Congress anticipating a breakthrough on long-stalled legislation aimed at reining in the two mortgage-financing giants. Working with the Treasury Department, the new Democratic majority seemed poised to significantly tighten regulation of the firms, which critics said posed a systemic risk to the economy because of their vast size and scope.

However, over the year, the momentum shifted, and many members of Congress wanted the two government-sponsored enterprises to increase their role in the real estate markets. The chief cause for the reversal was the subprime mortgage crisis. Fannie Mae and Freddie Mac were newly regarded as potential heroes with the ability to provide financing that could help struggling homeowners refinance debt and avert foreclosure.

The House Financial Services Committee approved HR 1427, 45–19, March 29, 2007, and formally reported the measure (H Rept 110-142) on May 9. The measure reflected a compromise agreement committee chairman Barney Frank, D-Mass., had reached through extensive negotiations with the Treasury Department in 2006.

In addition to providing for an independent regulator, the bill included the creation of a new affordable housing fund financed by a percentage of the two firms' portfolios. Under the committee-approved HR 1427, the fund would distribute an estimated $500 million a year to states for housing programs for the disadvantaged, with all of the money in the first year targeted to rebuild Gulf Coast communities devastated in 2005 by Hurricanes Katrina and Rita.

The biggest target of GOP criticism was the affordable housing fund. The bill included language aimed at addressing previous GOP complaints that the program would benefit housing groups aligned with Democrats by giving the firms regulatory authority over the fund. However, not all Republicans were mollified, and deregulation-minded Republicans warned that tighter mortgage regulations could make it harder for potential homebuyers to get loans.

The House passed HR 1427 by a 313–104 vote May 22, but changes made on the floor threatened to unravel the compromise put together by Frank and the George W. Bush administration. The amendment that threw a wrench into the works added language limiting the ability of the new regulator to assess the risk posed to Fannie Mae and Freddie Mac by their large investment portfolios. The proposal, offered by a group that included Randy Neugebauer, R-Texas, went against the approach sought by many Fannie Mae and Freddie Mac critics, including the administration. The amendment was adopted, 383–36, May 22.

The affordable housing fund proved the most contentious issue in the floor debate. The House May 17 on a 148–269 vote rejected an amendment by Spencer Bachus, R-Ala., to strike the fund. The same day the House rejected an amendment by Jeb Hensarling, R-Texas, to suspend the companies' contribution to the housing fund if the payments contributed to an increase in mortgage costs, 164–253.

Adopted May 22 were an amendment by John T. Doolittle, R-Calif., 217–205, to prohibit Fannie Mae, Freddie Mac, and the Federal Home Loan banks from obtaining primary residential mortgages that were granted to individuals lacking a valid Social Security number, and an amendment by Tom Price, R-Ga., 235–188, to require all owners or renters of housing built with money from the fund to prove legal residency.

The bill was referred to the Senate Banking, Housing, and Urban Affairs Committee but saw no further action.

Mortgage Fraud Coordinator

On Sept. 22, 2008, the House agreed, 350–23, to a Betty Sutton, D-Ohio, motion to suspend the rules and pass the bill (HR 6853) that would establish a Federal Bureau of Investigation (FBI) national mortgage fraud coordinator with regional task forces that include federal, state, and local participation. The coordinator would provide training, collect data, and recommend efforts to combat mortgage fraud. The measure saw no further congressional action.

Affordable Housing

Both chambers in 2007 passed legislation (HR 1852, S 2338) to overhaul the mortgage-lending practices of the Federal Housing Administration (FHA). The measures sought to increase the availability of mortgages to low- and middle-income homebuyers in the midst of the mortgage crisis brought on by the collapse of the subprime market. Neither bill completed congressional action.

The House in 2007 also passed a bill (HR 2895) to create a national affordable housing fund that would be financed by a small portion of the profits from the Federal Housing Administration and mortgage-financing giants Fannie Mae (Federal National Mortgage Association) and Freddie Mac (Federal Home Loan Mortgage Corporation). The measure died upon adjournment.

The FHA was created during the Great Depression of the 1930s to protect lenders against losses if a homeowner defaulted on a mortgage loan. By reducing the risks of default, the insurance enabled FHA-approved lenders to offer lower interest rates and require lower down payments. The result had been to allow lower-income Americans to borrow money to buy a home that they could not otherwise afford. The agency was the largest insurer of mortgages in the world.

HR 1852 and S 2338 were initially drafted to modernize the FHA, which had lost market share to subprime and other private mortgage providers because of its outdated loan limits and stringent credit requirements. But as the scope of the crisis spread from the subprime market to other lenders, Congress began looking to the FHA to help borrowers holding risky loans refinance their mortgages and to give more homebuyers an alternative to such loans.

HOUSE ACTION

The House Financial Services Committee approved HR 1852, 45–19, May 3, 2007. The measure, sponsored by Maxine Waters, D-Calif., was formally reported (H Rept 110-217) on June 28. A supplemental report (H Rept 110-217, Part II) was filed Sept. 17.

The full House passed HR 1852 by 348–72 Sept. 18. The bill would raise FHA-backed loan limits, allow higher loan limits in high-cost areas, and permit the agency to vary the premiums it charged borrowers. It also proposed authorizing the use of some FHA surpluses to help finance a National Affordable Housing Trust Fund that was a key element of a plan by House Financial Services Committee chairman Barney Frank, D-Mass., to increase the nation's affordable housing stock. The fund would be created under separate legislation (HR 2895).

The House-passed HR 1852 would:

- Raise the dollar limit on the single-family mortgages that the FHA could ensure to 100 percent of the conforming loan limit—the size of loans that government-sponsored enterprises Fannie Mae and Freddie Mac could purchase. That limit was $417,000, compared with the maximum limit for FHA-insured loans of $362,790, far below what borrowers needed in states such as New York, New Jersey, Connecticut, and California. The loan floor would be raised to $271,050 from $200,160.
- Simplify the calculation of the down payment for an FHA-insured loan, while retaining the minimum of 3 percent of the appraised value of the house. However, under certain circumstances, the FHA could offer higher premiums for loans with zero down payments.
- Allow a special dispensation for high-cost areas, raising the size of single-family mortgages the FHA could insure to 125 percent of the median area home price or 175 percent of the Fannie Mae conforming loan limit, whichever was lower.
- Give the Housing and Urban Development (HUD) secretary the authority to raise the limit by as much as another $100,000 "if market conditions warrant." Loans larger than $417,000, known as "jumbos," were becoming harder to obtain and more expensive as the secondary market shunned mortgages not backed by Fannie Mae and Freddie Mac.
- Authorize, with some restrictions, the use of some FHA profits for the affordable housing fund.

The dispensation for high-cost areas and for jumbo loans was added by voice vote in a floor amendment offered by Dennis Cardoza, D-Calif.

The administration and House Republicans said the bill went too far and could overextend the FHA. Frank and others said the higher limit was needed to allow low- and middle-income homebuyers in high-cost housing markets to use FHA programs.

During floor consideration of HR 1852, the House on Sept. 18 rejected, 148–280, an amendment offered by Jeb Hensarling, R-Texas, to remove the funding mechanism for the affordable housing fund. Also rejected that same day, 209–216, was a motion by Tom Price, R-Ga., to recommit the bill to add language requiring those who received trust fund money to prove legal residency in the United States.

SENATE ACTION

The Senate passed its version of the FHA legislation (S 2338) by a 93–1 vote Dec. 14, 2007. The Senate Banking, Housing, and Urban Affairs Committee had approved the bill 20–1 on Sept. 19 and formally reported it (S Rept 110-227) on Nov. 13. The measure, sponsored by committee chairman Christopher J. Dodd, D-Conn., did not include the affordable housing fund and had the support of the Bush administration.

As passed, S 2338 would allow the FHA to insure loans of up to 100 percent of the conforming loan limit of $417,000 and would reduce the minimum down payment for an FHA-insured loan and simplify its calculation, requiring a flat 1.5 percent of the appraised value of the home. Borrowers who put down less than 3 percent would have to complete a counseling program.

The Senate by voice vote Dec. 14 rejected a Tom Coburn, R-Okla., effort to strip a provision removing a cap on the number of reverse mortgages that the FHA could insure until a study of the plan, already required by the bill, was completed. The House bill contained a similar provision. Reverse mortgages allowed homeowners age sixty-two or older to borrow from the equity in their homes. Coburn said that there was no crisis in reverse mortgages and that removing the cap would increase government risks.

No further action of S 2338 or HR 1852 occurred.

HOUSE ACTION

The House Financial Services Committee July 31 approved, 45–23, HR 2895, to establish a National Affordable Housing Trust Fund. The measure was formally reported (H Rept 110-362) on Oct. 2.

The purpose of the fund was to distribute grants to state and local governments to finance low-income housing units or help low-income homebuyers make a down payment on a first home. It was intended to help build, refurbish, or maintain 1.5 million affordable housing units over ten years. The funding would be categorized as mandatory spending, which meant it would flow automatically and not be subject to the vagaries of the appropriations process, although the legislation also would authorize any discretionary budget authority that Congress might decide to appropriate.

The trust fund would be financed by diverting some of the income paid to the FHA, as well as the portfolios of Fannie Mae and Freddie Mac. Authorization for those funding streams was included in the House-passed versions of the FHA bill (HR 1852) and a bill (HR 1427) to overhaul Fannie Mae and Freddie Mac. *(Affordable housing, p. 642; Mortgage regulation, p. 625)*

During the floor debate on Oct. 10, the House rejected, 163–257, an amendment offered by Randy Neugebauer, R-Texas, to merge the trust fund into HUD's HOME program, which helped state and local governments build, buy, and rehabilitate affordable housing. The amendment also would eliminate funding from the FHA, Fannie Mae, and Freddie Mac. The same day the House rejected, 199–218, a motion by Marilyn Musgrave, R-Colo., to send the bill back to committee with instructions to add work requirements from the 1996 welfare law (PL 104-193) as a prerequisite for adults to live in housing financed by the trust fund. *(1996 welfare law, Congress and the Nation Vol. IX, p. 578)*

Opponents of the trust fund, including ranking Republican on the Financial Services Committee Spencer Bachus of Alabama, said that it would be duplicative and inefficient and that it would threaten other HUD programs by diverting money away from them. The administration also called the proposed fund "redundant" and "duplicative," and the White House warned that the president's advisers would recommend a veto.

The National Association of Homebuilders, the National Association of Realtors, and the U.S. Conference of Mayors supported the trust fund proposal. The Senate did not take up the measure.

HOPE VI Reauthorization

The House Jan. 17, 2008, on a 271–130 vote, passed HR 3524, authorizing $800 million per year in fiscal 2008 through 2015 for the HOPE VI public housing program. The George W. Bush administration had sought to kill HOPE VI, asserting that the program was inefficient and obsolete. *(109th Congress action, p. 627)*

The House Financial Services Committee had approved HR 3524 by voice vote Sept. 26, 2007, and formally reported it (H Rept 110-507) on Jan. 3, 2008. Among the changes to the program in the panel's bill were new tenant protections and a one-for-one replacement requirement for all public housing units proposed for demolition. The bill would require public housing agencies to create mixed-income housing on the sites of demolished low-income housing. The legislation also would prohibit authorities from creating strict reentry requirements, such as credit checks, for returning residents, and it would require public housing agencies to develop relocation plans that provide comparable housing for all relocated residents.

The panel adopted a manager's amendment by bill sponsor Maxine Waters, D-Calif., and an amendment offered by Emanuel Cleaver II, D-Mo., both by voice vote. The

Waters package would require public housing authorities to coordinate projects with the school calendar, so displaced children would not have to transfer schools, and would strengthen the relocation benefits and services given to displaced residents. The Cleaver amendment would allow displaced tenants to receive Section 8 tenant–based vouchers, which allow low-income tenants to receive government help in paying rent for residences that are not public housing.

During House floor consideration of HR 3524 on Jan. 17, members adopted, 388–20, a manager's amendment by Waters and House Financial Services Committee chairman Barney Frank, D-Mass., that applied the one-for-one replacement requirement to all units in existence as of Jan. 1, 2005—a bid to help New Orleans public housing residents driven from their homes by Hurricane Katrina in August 2005. The amendment also would allow a limited waiver of the one-for-one replacement requirement, extend from one year to four and a half years the amount of time developers have to replace demolished units, and clarify that existing rules deny financial assistance to illegal immigrants.

Democratic critics had complained that funds provided through the program too often had been used to demolish run-down public housing without building new units. HR 3524 would require public housing agencies to create mixed-income housing on the sites of demolished low-income housing. In addition, other units developed to replace demolished public housing would have to be built in areas with low concentrations of poverty in an effort to avoid concentrating public housing in low-income neighborhoods.

The House also adopted, by voice vote on Jan. 17, an amendment by Barbara Lee, D-Calif., that would safeguard elderly and disabled HOPE VI tenants from eviction. The Senate did not act on the legislation.

Section 8 Voucher Program

In the 110th Congress, the House acted on two measures (HR 1851, HR 3965) that would affect the Section 8 voucher program, which accounts for more than 60 percent of the Department of Housing and Urban Development (HUD) budget. The Senate, however, did not take up either measure. *(109th Congress action, p. 627)*

The House July 12, 2007, passed, 333–83, HR 1851, which would authorize 100,000 new vouchers over five years and direct HUD, at least through 2012, to allocate voucher money based on housing data from the previous twelve months instead of on older statistics. Democrats and housing advocates contended that the older data formula had resulted in the loss of about 150,000 vouchers nationally since it was implemented in 2004.

The administration of President George W. Bush opposed passage of HR 1851, saying the bill would cause "unsustainable" cost increases, but the White House stopped short of threatening a veto. House Financial Services Committee chair Barney Frank, D-Mass., said the Congressional Budget Office estimated that the bill would save the government $20 billion over five years.

Three GOP amendments were defeated July 12 on the House floor. An attempt by Steve Chabot, R-Ohio, to eliminate the new vouchers failed, 144–277. A proposal by Chabot and Gary G. Miller, R-Calif., to impose a seven-year time limit on participation in the Section 8 program, with exceptions for the elderly and disabled, was rejected, 151–267. Chabot and Jeb Hensarling, R-Texas, offered an amendment to require all adults in a household receiving Section 8 tenant assistance for more than seven consecutive years to perform twenty hours per week of approved work activities, with exemptions for senior citizens, the disabled, and single parents with children younger than six. It failed, 197–222.

The House on July 12 agreed, 233–186, to a motion by Shelley Moore Capito, R-W.Va., to recommit the bill to the House Financial Services Committee with instructions to report it back with language requiring all adult occupants of Section 8 housing to establish proof of legal residency with a Social Security card in conjunction with a state or federal photo identification card, a U.S. passport, a driver's license, or a U.S. Citizenship and Immigration Services photo identification card.

During markup of HR 1851, Financial Services rejected by voice vote a Miller amendment to limit to seven years the time families can receive Section 8 vouchers. It also defeated, 27–34, an amendment by Ed Royce, R-Calif., to eliminate a rule requiring landlords to issue rental documents in a language tenants can understand. The panel adopted, by voice votes, an amendment to authorize 100,000 new vouchers over five years and another to increase the number of public housing agencies—from forty to sixty—that could run a pilot program called "moving-to-work." Renamed the "housing innovation program" by the bill, it gives HUD and public housing authorities more flexibility in testing ways to promote tenant self-sufficiency. The committee also adopted, 52–9, an amendment offered by bill sponsor Maxine Waters, D-Calif., to withhold payments to landlords until housing unit repairs were made in compliance with predetermined quality standards. The amendment also would allow public housing authorities to use withheld funds to contract for repairs, and it would prohibit landlords from terminating leases in substandard properties.

The committee approved HR 1851 by 52–9 on May 25 and formally reported it (H Rept 110-216) on June 28.

The House Financial Services Committee by voice vote Oct. 31, 2007, approved HR 3965, which would overhaul HUD's program for project-based Section 8 housing vouchers. The bill was formally reported (H Rept 110-579) on April 10, 2008.

The vouchers are given to landlords who rehabilitate or build low-income housing units or who agree to set aside a portion of units for low-income tenants. Enacted in 1998, the program uses the "market to market" accounting approach to ensure that the rents they charge reflect market value. Landlords who charge above-market rents receive lower Section 8 subsidies. Also, for those properties where rents are kept low, mortgages are restructured.

According to committee staff, the Bush administration requested the overhaul in part because it expected that by Dec. 30, 2007, the program would reach the 5 percent portfolio cap on properties that charged rents above the market, defined as 120 percent of the fair market rent. The bill would increase that cap to 9 percent.

It also would expand the program to include developments with below-market rents, would allow higher rents for disaster-damaged properties, and would extend the period of debt forgiveness for properties acquired by a tenant or nonprofit organization. The bill would extend the program through 2012.

Public Housing Regulations

By voice vote on July 9, 2008, the House agreed to a motion by Barney Frank, D-Mass., to suspend the rules and pass legislation (HR 6216) that would allow some housing authorities to manage their developments separately, instead of managing their entire portfolios on an agency-wide basis. The Department of Housing and Urban Development (HUD) required agencies administering more than 250 public housing units to adopt asset-based management, which meant retraining their personnel, reorganizing physical assets, and restructuring the organizations. HR 6216 would increase to five hundred the number of units that public housing agencies could manage before they were required to manage their housing portfolios using the asset management system.

The House Financial Services Committee approved the bill by voice vote on June 25 (no written report). HR 6216 was the third incarnation of legislation considered by the 110th Congress that was designed to loosen the regulatory burden on local housing authorities. Two earlier versions (HR 3521, HR 5829) stalled over language concerning gun ownership by residents.

HR 3521 was relatively noncontroversial until President George W. Bush issued a policy statement on Feb. 12, 2008, outlining strong opposition to it. The administration said the bill would exempt 88 percent of housing agencies from the requirement to convert to an asset management system.

After debating and amending HR 3521 on Feb. 26, Republicans offered a motion to recommit the bill to committee with instructions to amend it to prohibit public housing authorities from banning guns in their buildings. The motion, which called for the bill to be returned to the floor "promptly," instead of the customary "forthwith," would have had the effect of taking the bill off the floor and sending it to the House Financial Services Committee. That essentially would have killed it. Because most Republicans and many Democrats supported gun ownership rights, leaders did not want to force a vote on the issue if the bill would be sent back to committee.

The House Financial Services Committee approved the legislation by voice vote Sept. 25, 2007, and formally reported it (H Rept 110-521) on Jan. 29, 2008.

HR 5829 would allow local housing authorities to bar possession of firearms or require their registration only if required by local law. The committee held a markup on the bill on April 24, 2008, but the measure moved no further.

HR 6216 contained compromise language that permitted gun possession by residents but allowed public housing authorities to terminate the lease of any tenant found illegally using a firearm.

Hurricane Housing

The House March 21, 2007, passed, 302–125, a bill (HR 1227) that aimed at helping low-income Gulf Coast hurricane victims return home. The legislation would require one-for-one rebuilding of any demolished public housing units and grant displaced public housing tenants an absolute right of return.

The House Financial Services Committee approved HR 1227 by 50–16 on March 7 and formally reported it (H Rept 110-51, Part I) on March 16. The committee-approved measure would block demolition of damaged public housing units in New Orleans, Louisiana, until the federal government had a plan to replace them and grant displaced public housing tenants an absolute right of return. The bill also would require New Orleans to reopen enough housing—at least three thousand units—to accommodate the tenants by Aug. 1, 2007.

Committee Republicans put forth a spirited effort to amend the bill, but they were beat back. The panel adopted nineteen amendments on March 6, including many that contained more stringent requirements aimed at ensuring that all former tenants could return. Among those adopted was a provision to bar for two years the transfer of public housing units in hurricane-affected areas to private groups. Critics complained that the government was essentially using the displacement of residents to demolish or convert low-income housing into private developments. An amendment that would require all voucher recipients to work at least twenty hours per week was rejected, 18–47. Also rejected, 30–35, was an amendment to set a limit of $755 million instead of "such sums as necessary" to repair and rebuild New Orleans public housing.

The full House rejected, 185–247, on March 21 an amendment offered by Randy Neugebauer, R-Texas, to delete language in the bill providing that families who were receiving temporary disaster vouchers distributed by the Department of Housing and Urban Development (HUD) would be moved to the permanent Section 8 housing program after the other vouchers expired and if they met income eligibility requirements. HR 1227 also would extend the HUD disaster voucher program to January

2008. The program was serving an estimated 27,000 to 30,000 families.

The House also adopted, 242–184, on March 21 an amendment by Al Green, D-Texas, to extend another voucher program, run by the Federal Emergency Management Agency (FEMA). The provision also would transfer those families who were eligible from the FEMA program to the Section 8 voucher system, which helped low-income families pay rent. According to housing advocates, 37,000 families received FEMA vouchers.

A dispute over the bill's provision to allow cities and states receiving federal disaster aid to use other government grants to meet matching requirements caused Republicans to invoke a rarely used rule to try to remove a Democrat from the debate. Tom Price, R-Ga., offered an amendment to remove the language, saying it would have ensured "that local and state individuals have a responsibility, have an incentive to make sure these programs are sound." Price's reasoning led to an angry rebuke by Gene Taylor, D-Miss. He told Price he should "have the decency" to visit Mississippi "before you hold them to a standard that you would never hold your own people to and you failed to hold the Bush administration to."

Price asked the chair that Taylor's words "be taken down." The chair ruled that Taylor had impugned Price's character by questioning his decency and struck his words from the record. Because House rules restrict members whose words were struck from participating in floor debate for the rest of the day, members had to vote on whether to allow Taylor to stay in the debate on HR 1277. With thirty-six Republicans joining Democrats, the chamber decided, 265–160, on March 21 to allow Taylor to participate. Price's amendment, which had been rejected during House Financial Services Committee markup of the bill, subsequently was rejected, 98–333, on March 21.

Republicans were successful in amending the legislation through a motion to recommit, offered by Bobby Jindal, R-La. The parliamentary maneuver added language that would bar some people, including convicted drug dealers, sex offenders, and domestic violence offenders, from occupying rebuilt public housing in New Orleans. Jindal said the language would make New Orleans's public housing safer. The motion was agreed to, 249–176, on March 21.

In related action, the House on March 27, 2007, agreed by voice vote to a Charles B. Rangel, D-N.Y., motion to suspend the rules and pass HR 1562, a $237 million extension of tax incentives for low-income housing in areas damaged by Hurricane Katrina. Jim McCrery of Louisiana, the panel's ranking Republican, said the bill was needed to help builders and investors deal with construction delays. The panel by voice vote adopted a manager's amendment that added two revenue-raising offsets to pay for the bill. The first would raise $241 million over ten years by allowing the Internal Revenue Service (IRS) to seize assets of delinquent taxpayers in certain cases and exempting it from a requirement to provide a collection due-process hearing in advance. The second would institute a bookkeeping change to help the measure comply with House pay-as-you-go rules. It would require corporations with more than $1 billion in assets to pay slightly more in estimated taxes in July and September 2012. That provision would raise $107 million in 2012 but could carry no net cost over ten years.

The House Ways and Means Committee had approved HR 1562 by voice vote on March 21 and formally reported it (H Rept 110-66) on March 23. The measure went no further.

Disaster-Damaged Public Housing

The House on June 18, 2008, agreed by voice vote to a Don Cazayoux, D-La., motion to suspend the rules and pass HR 6276, which made clear that the Federal Emergency Management Agency (FEMA) must foot the bill for repairs to disaster-damaged public housing. The legislation would eliminate a section added in 1998 (PL 105-276) to the U.S. Housing Act of 1937 that authorized the Department of Housing and Urban Development (HUD) to pay for the repairs to disaster-damaged public housing. The administration of George W. Bush had requested no funding for that section for fiscal 2009 and had proposed its elimination. *(PL 105-276, Congress and the Nation Vol. X, p. 555)*

During a June 4 joint hearing held by subcommittees of the House Financial Services and Homeland Security panels, FEMA official Carlos J. Castillo cited the HUD provision as the reason FEMA refused to pay for repairs to public housing after natural disasters, such as Hurricanes Katrina and Rita in 2005. According to Homeland Security chair Bennie Thompson, D-Miss., because of the FEMA refusals, public housing authorities in the Gulf Coast received only a fraction of the dollars needed for repairs since the hurricanes.

Rural Multifamily Housing

The House on Jan. 23, 2008, agreed by voice vote to a Paul W. Hodes, D-N.H., motion to suspend the rules and pass a bill (HR 3873) to change the process by which the Agriculture Department allows Section 515 rural multifamily housing projects to be transferred from one owner to another. The measure would require a review of the department's procedure for rural housing projects involving low-income housing tax credits.

In addition, HR 3873 would send unprocessed applications for transfer of ownership to the federal level after a certain number of days of inaction at the state level. In doing so, the bill would set guidelines for the federal government to intervene in the processing of applications.

The House Financial Services Committee had approved HR 3873 by voice vote Oct. 31, 2007. The measure was formally reported (H Rept 110-464) on Dec. 4. The bill did not reach the House floor.

Rural Housing and Economic Development Authorization

The House agreed, 350–49, July 16, 2007, to a Rubén Hinojosa, D-Texas, motion to suspend the rules and pass HR 1982, which would authorize $30 million for the Department of Housing and Urban Development Rural Housing and Economic Development program in fiscal 2008 and $40 million each year in fiscal 2009 through 2013.

The House Financial Services Committee approved the bill by voice vote on May 23. HR 1982 (H Rept 110-205) was formally reported on June 21.

In the Senate, the measure was referred to the Banking, Housing, and Urban Affairs Committee. It saw no further congressional action and died upon adjournment.

Mobile Home Mortgages

The House by voice vote on June 25, 2007, agreed to a Joe Donnelly, D-Ind., motion to suspend the rules and pass HR 2139, which sought to help middle- and low-income families by expanding the government's ability to back mortgages for mobile homes.

The House Financial Services Committee had approved the bill by voice vote on May 23 and formally reported it (H Rept 110-206) on June 21. The measure died upon adjournment.

Housing Assistance Council Authorization

The House on July 16, 2007, agreed to a motion, offered by Rubén Hinojosa, D-Texas, to suspend the rules and pass HR 1980, which would authorize the Department of Housing and Urban Development to provide $10 million in fiscal 2008 and $15 million each year in fiscal 2009 through 2014 to the Housing Assistance Council. The vote was 350–49.

The House Financial Services Committee approved the bill by voice vote on May 23 and formally reported it (H Rept 110-204) on June 21.

HR 1980, as well as a companion measure (S 1450), was referred to the Senate Banking, Housing, and Urban Affairs Committee but saw no further action. The panel on Aug. 1, 2007, reported S 1923 (no written report), which included an authorization for appropriations for the Housing Assistance Council, among other things. The measure died upon adjournment.

Seller-Financed Down Payments

The House Financial Services Committee by voice vote Sept. 16, 2008, approved a bill (HR 6694) that would allow home sellers to provide down payment assistance to buyers whose mortgages were backed by the Federal Housing Administration (FHA). The measure also added new standards for the borrowers' creditworthiness and penalties for appraisal fraud. The bill was formally reported (H Rept 110-905) on Oct. 2. The bill did not reach the House floor, however.

The 2008 housing finance law (HR 3221—PL 110-289) prohibited the FHA from insuring mortgages if the seller aided the borrower in making the down payment. HR 6694 would have reinstated that program. *(Mortgage relief, p. 630)*

Many Republicans and President George W. Bush's administration argued that borrowers who needed down payment assistance were much more likely to default than those who could make the down payment on their own. HR 6694 would require that participants in the program have credit scores higher than 680. Those with scores above 620 could participate but would have to pay a risk-based mortgage insurance premium to cover possible defaults.

The committee amended the bill by voice vote to impose civil penalties for attempting to influence an appraisal for a loan. Low-income-housing advocates said the program was essential to help working people who could afford a mortgage payment but not a down payment and that eliminating it would disproportionately hurt minorities.

Homeless Assistance

The House Financial Services Committee by voice vote July 31, 2008, approved HR 840, to renew and overhaul the 1987 McKinney-Vento Homeless Assistance Act (PL 100-77) for five years. The bill, sponsored by Julia Carson, D-Ind., would expand the definition of "homeless" in determining eligibility for Department of Housing and Urban Development (HUD) assistance. *(1987 act, Congress and the Nation Vol. VII, p. 677)*

The panel adopted, by voice vote, a modified manager's amendment by Gwen Moore, D-Wis., and Maxine Waters, D-Calif., which narrowed the original bill's definition of homeless individuals who qualify for HUD assistance to cover people temporarily in institutional care who would lack homes when they leave, those about to lose their housing who lack resources to find a replacement home, those who face eviction within fourteen days, people living in a motel or doubled up with another family and who either lack the resources to stay for more then fourteen days or must leave within fourteen days, and those fleeing domestic violence. The amendment also would allocate 30 percent of funding under the bill for new permanent housing for families and individuals with a disability.

The overall bill would authorize $2.2 billion for fiscal 2010 and "such sums as necessary" for fiscal years 2011 through 2013. The measure also would streamline several competitive grant programs. HR 840 was formally reported (H Rept 110-906) on Oct. 2.

In related action, the House agreed Oct. 2, 2008, to a Moore motion to suspend the rules and pass HR 7221, by 355–61. The bill would consolidate HUD's homeless assistance competitive grant programs into a single program and authorize $2.2 billion in fiscal 2009 for grants for emergency shelter needs of the homeless. The measures died upon adjournment.

Hawaiian Housing

On March 28, 2007, the House passed, by a 272–150 vote, HR 835 to authorize through fiscal 2012 the Native Hawaiian Housing Block Grant and Native Hawaiian Housing Loan Guarantee programs, which provided grants for affordable housing for low-income Native Hawaiians and guaranteed loans to families residing on land dedicated for homesteading Native Hawaiians.

A week earlier, on March 21, the House had rejected, 262–162, a Maxine Waters, D-Calif., motion to suspend the rules and pass HR 835. (A two-thirds majority of those present is required under suspension of the rules.) The House Financial Services Committee had reported the measure (H Rept 110-50) on March 15.

The Senate Banking, Housing, and Urban Affairs Committee reported HR 835 (no written report) on Sept. 26. The bill saw no further action.

During consideration of the fiscal 2008 appropriations bill for the Departments of Transportation and Housing and Urban Development (HR 3074) on July 24, 2007, the House rejected, 116–307, an amendment by Lynn Westmoreland, R-Ga., to eliminate the $9 million provided in the bill for the Native Hawaiian Housing Block Grant program.

Starrett City Housing

The House on May 7, 2008, agreed to a Gregory W. Meeks, D-N.Y., motion to suspend the rules and pass HR 5937, to allow any new owner of the Starrett City housing project in Brooklyn, N.Y., to request from the Department of Housing and Urban Development (HUD) that two subsidy contracts be converted into a new housing assistance contract. The vote was 345–73. The Senate took no action.

CHAPTER 12

Labor and Pensions

Labor and Pensions

Although labor legislation was never a high priority in the second term of Republican president George W. Bush, several important bills did become law between 2005 and 2009. The national minimum wage was increased for the first time in nearly ten years, which affected mainly lower-wage earners. For all workers, Congress approved a far-reaching reform of pension security laws. In addition, legislators approved significant changes in mine safety regulations after a series of fatal accidents in early 2006. As the Bush term was winding down in 2008, Congress twice extended unemployment compensation benefits for workers who had exhausted their normal payments. The extensions reflected the downward spiral of the national and world economy as a housing bubble burst, Wall Street and banks teetered on failure, and unemployment rates skyrocketed.

Labor advocates, however, did not win approval of several bills to outlaw wage, gender, and sexual discrimination in the workplace. Organized labor also faced serious continuing problems as union membership continued to decline, until 2008, as it had for decades. Membership had increased by a tiny percentage in 2007, but economists said it was too small to be significant. That changed in 2008 when union members accounted for 12.4 percent of employed workers, up from 12.1 percent a year earlier.

Organized labor was thwarted in the closely divided Congress and by a Republican in the White House in its effort to enact top legislative priority: passage of the union check card bill that would allow a company to be organized simply by a majority of workers signing a card. Business vehemently opposed this, saying the traditional secret ballot for certifying a union was essential to retain.

Historically, labor has been a key constituent of Democrats and never fared well under Republican administrations or congressional majorities. During Bush's eight years in office, organized labor focused on blocking GOP proposals they saw as favoring business interests at the expense of workers. Much of this warfare went on in legal and administrative areas as labor sought to prevent the Labor Department, under GOP control, from regulations and other actions unions saw as harmful to their members. Labor efforts were a continuation of their activity during

Outlays for Social Security

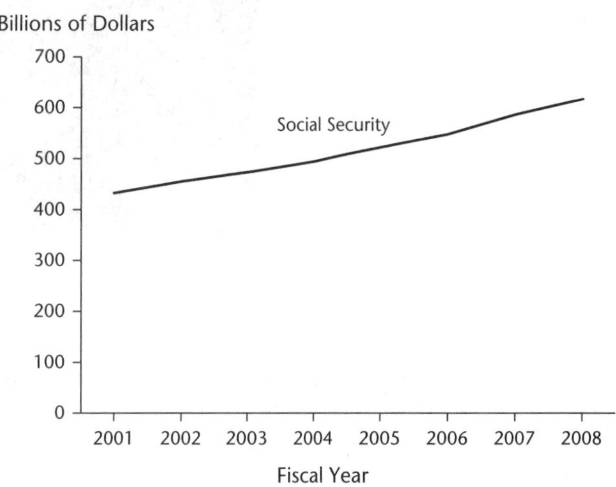

SOURCE: Office of Management and Budget, *Historical Tables, Budget of the United States Government: Fiscal Year 2010* (Washington, D.C.: U.S. Government Printing Office, 2009), Table 3.2.

REFERENCES

Discussion of labor and pension policy for the years 1945–1964 may be found in *Congress and the Nation Vol. I,* pp. 565–657, 1220–1272, 1289–1320; for the years 1965–1968, *Congress and the Nation Vol. II,* pp. 601–622, 734–743, 745–778; for the years 1969–1972, *Congress and the Nation Vol. III,* pp. 605–621, 703–742; for the years 1973–1976, *Congress and the Nation Vol. IV,* pp. 403–432, 681–713; for the years 1977–1980, *Congress and the Nation Vol. V,* pp. 231–251, 399–425; for the years 1981–1984, *Congress and the Nation Vol. VI,* pp. 643–672; for the years 1985–1988, *Congress and the Nation Vol. VII,* pp. 687–709; for the years 1989–1992, *Congress and the Nation Vol. VIII,* pp. 703–738; for the years 1993–1996, *Congress and the Nation Vol. IX,* pp. 653–675; for the years 1997–2000, *Congress and the Nation Vol. X,* pp. 571–585; for the years 2001–2004, *Congress and the Nation Vol. XI,* pp. 563–578.

Senate majority leader Harry Reid of Nevada, left, listens as Sen. Edward Kennedy, D-Mass., speaks on raising the minimum wage on January 26, 2007, on Capitol Hill in Washington. *Source: AP Photo/Susan Walsh*

Bush's first term. *(Labor overview 2001–2005, Congress and the Nation Vol. XI, p. 563)*

In the context of this ongoing adversarial relationship, some observers were surprised that the two centerpiece bills of the period—minimum wage and pension security—became law. Others were less surprised because their enactment played to the interests of at least some constituencies in both parties.

Minimum wage legislation had usually been supported by Democrats and labor supporters and opposed by Republicans and business interests, especially small business. But by 2007 even some Republicans were feeling the heat of constituents in the lower-income categories who were still working for the $5.15 an hour level established in 1997; at this hourly rate a person working a forty-hour week would earn about $10,700 annually. An important push for an increase came from Republicans in House districts that were being aggressively challenged by Democrats and who wanted to see a more flexible approach from party leaders. In the end, Republicans relented on their traditional opposition but in doing so won Democratic acceptance of combining a higher minimum wage with tax cuts for small businesses.

Pension security had been a brewing issue for some years as an increasing number of companies discarded traditional pensions, known as defined-benefit plans in which the employer promises a set payment for an employee's life, and adopted a new model that left fundamental decisions to the worker. These plans were known as defined-contribution systems in which an employee, and often the employer, made contributions to investment funds—frequently a selection of mutual funds offered by the employer. This required the employee to, first, participate in the plan and, second, to make wise investment choices. The frailty of the pension system became increasingly a concern of voters of all political stripes—and therefore both parties—as some high-profile bankruptcies including, in the early 2000s, energy trader Enron and communications giant WorldCom collapsed, wiping out retirement funds for employees. Later other bankruptcies either ended pension plans or transferred obligations, often at a reduced level, to a government agency, the Pension Benefit Guaranty Corporation (PBGC), that itself was threatened with insolvency because of the company failures plus the decision of healthier firms to end pension plans and let the agency take them over.

In this environment, Congress—after failing to enact changes in Bush's first term—passed legislation to shore up the finances of the PBGC. This law required pension plans to be more fully funded and made other changes to protect workers' retirement savings.

In light of the growing national concern about retirement income, it was an interesting irony that one of Bush's top legislative priorities in his second term went nowhere. This was the president's proposal to revamp the nation's primary retirement system, Social Security, by allowing younger workers to invest some of their contributions in individual retirement accounts that would be invested in financial markets rather than in the Social Security system's trust fund that was devoted to paying benefits to already retired workers.

Bush argued that over a long time period, private investment accounts would provide more retirement money and better security than a government program. Democrats and senior citizen advocacy groups, however, said the plan was nothing more than a lightly disguised effort to undermine a program that was seen by most progressives as the crowning achievement of the New Deal programs that came out of the Great Depression in the 1930s. His proposal gained no traction with Democrats and was viewed skeptically by many Republicans who feared most voters did not want to make huge changes in the Social Security system. Members of both parties acknowledged that important changes were needed with Social Security to protect its long-term financial viability, but—as in the past—no active proposals to do so were put forth in Congress.

Chronology of Action on Labor and Pensions

2005–2006

The most important congressional action on labor and pension issues in the 109th Congress was passage of legislation to shore up the finances of the Pension Benefit Guaranty Corporation (PBGC) and to provide new legal requirements to protect retirement benefits for American workers. The issue had ballooned as the PBGC had to take over increasing numbers of pension plans that were either jettisoned by financially strapped companies or were wiped out in bankruptcies. The urgency of threatened retirement security for millions of workers brought Republicans and Democrats together after years of wrestling with the issue.

The two-year Congress from 2005 to 2007, at the beginning of George W. Bush's second term in office and with Republicans still in control of both houses, was also noted for passing a much strengthened mine safety bill after a series of accidents claiming several lives. But Bush's signature new proposal—to enact far-reaching changes to the Social Security system—received little attention and went nowhere.

Pension Security: 2005

Congress in 2005 began work on legislation to protect retirement funds of employees from company actions that threatened to limit, or even wipe out, pension commitments made to workers. Both chambers passed bills to require private companies to better fund their pension plans and shore up the finances of the Pension Benefit Guaranty Corporation (PBGC), the federal agency that insured traditional pension plans. Final action was delayed until 2006 when a compromise bill became law. *(2006 action, p. 658)*

Concern about the sanctity of pension promises, which had been growing for years, increased following the massive bankruptcies in 2001 and 2002 of Enron, a giant energy trading company, and WorldCom, a major player in telecommunications. Later in the decade a series of high-profile bankruptcy filings by companies in the airline, steel, and auto parts industries further increased concern over the health of the private pension system and the impact on the PBGC.

In May 2005, for example, a bankruptcy court allowed United Airlines to terminate its four pension plans, which were underfunded by about $9.8 billion, causing the PBGC to assume about $6.6 billion in liabilities for the plans. On Nov. 15, the agency reported that its fiscal 2005 deficit was $22.8 billion. For lawmakers, the PBGC's problems raised the specter of a taxpayer bailout of the agency.

Legislation to deal with pension security died at the end of the 107th Congress in 2002 and did not come up again during President George W. Bush's first term in office. *(Congress and the Nation Vol. XI, p. 569)*

BACKGROUND

Historically, companies that provided worker pensions typically offered defined-benefit plans under which the employers contributed annually to a pension trust fund and the employee was guaranteed a set yearly benefit after retiring. A trustee or fiduciary appointed by the employer decided how to invest the funds in the pension plan. Under the 1974 Employee Retirement Income Security Act (PL 93-406), known as ERISA, the fiduciary was required to act solely in the best interests of those covered by the plan. *(Congress and the Nation Vol. IV, p. 690)*

The number of workers in such plans fell from 30 million in 1983 to 22.3 million in 2000. Increasing numbers of workers instead participated in defined-contribution plans, such as 401(k) retirement savings accounts, first authorized by Congress in 1978 (PL 95-600).

Under these plans employees made pretax contributions to their retirement accounts and employers often matched some of those savings in cash or company stock. Distributions were taxed on withdrawal, but the accounts continued to grow tax free until then. Employees had to

LABOR LEADERSHIP

President George W. Bush's labor secretary during his first term, Elaine L. Chao, remained with the president throughout his second term. Chao was the only cabinet member to serve the full eight years with Bush. *(Chao nomination background, Congress and the Nation Vol. XI, p. 566)*

Most of the years of Chao's tenure were during complete Republican control of the government, with Bush in the White House and the GOP in the majority in both houses of Congress (Democrats controlled the Senate for a period between 2001–2003). That changed dramatically in the last two years of Bush's second term, when Democrats won back full congressional control and challenged the president on a variety of fronts, including worker rights, labor protections, and other labor interests.

Chao and the Labor Department benefited during Bush's two terms from a relatively low profile compared to other departments—particularly Defense and Treasury where major issues of the period played out. Nevertheless, labor issues remained controversial as organized labor and its allies in Congress charged Chao and the Labor Department with neglecting worker rights and safety concerns while constantly siding with business interests. The department historically was seen as a lightening rod for deep philosophical differences between business interests and organized labor, with Republicans usually supporting business on labor issues, while Democrats mostly supported the union point of view.

Chao spent many of her last days in office in late 2008 granting newspaper interviews to defend her eight-year tenure. She argued that occupational deaths and workplace injuries declined to record lows during her time in office and said the Labor Department won record amounts of pay back for discrimination against workers. She defended her department's enforcement actions as an "education outreach" rather than a traditional regulatory approach that emphasized workers knowing their rights and employers their responsibilities.

Her adversaries in organized labor saw her record quite differently, arguing that the department abandoned significant enforcement action, making workers vulnerable to workplace dangers and without adequate protection from employers who exploit their staffs. Labor unions also charged that the Labor Department during Bush's tenure established much more detailed union reporting requirements, which they called onerous. Chao and other officials said the information was needed to inform union members how their dues were being spent.

Critics of the Bush Labor Department received some support from government investigative agencies. In July 2008 the Government Accountability Office (GAO) reported, after an extensive investigation, that the Labor Department did not adequately probe complaints of low-wage workers about such matters as overtime pay or meeting the minimum wage. Another GAO report found inconsistencies in the department's handling of worker complaints. Department officials disputed both reports. In November 2008 the GAO also reported that the department had given Congress inaccurate and unreliable numbers that understated the cost of contracting work to outside companies. Finally, the Labor Department's own inspector general found that mine safety regulators failed to conduct mandated inspections at more than 14 percent of the nations underground coal mines in 2006.

make their own investment decisions, usually choosing from a range of alternatives selected by the employer or the fiduciary. The value of the retirement benefit depended on the balance in the account: the sum of all contributions, plus interest, dividends, and capital gains or losses. The PBGC, established by ERISA, insured only defined-benefit plans, not defined-contribution plans. Companies originally were given broad leeway to run their 401(k) programs in the hope of encouraging more of them to participate.

The drive to assert more control over defined-contribution plans began in early 2002 after revelations that thousands of employees at Enron had lost much of their retirement nest eggs because Enron's contributions to its 401(k) plans were almost entirely in the form of company stock, which became worthless. Workers at WorldCom Inc., which was driven toward insolvency in June by nearly $4 billion in accounting wrongdoing, also had invested heavily in company stock.

LEGISLATIVE ACTION

Solutions to the pension issues were not easily found. To strengthen the PBGC, lawmakers agreed that increased premiums were needed. Pension experts also contended that the health of private pension plans required tighter accounting rules and more disclosure. Such changes, however, could prompt companies to walk away from existing pension plans and transfer their obligations to the PBGC.

Efforts on a broad overhaul of the pension system began in January 2005 when Labor Secretary Elaine L. Chao outlined the Bush administration's plan to simplify the pension contribution process and increase incentives for companies that adequately funded their plans. The proposal applied only to single-employer defined-benefit pension plans that paid employees a set amount after retirement. The plan called for the annual premium rate, last changed in 1991, to rise to $30 per worker from $19; after that, the rate would be indexed to increases in workers' wages. Companies with credit ratings below investment grade or with underfunded plans would pay an additional risk-adjusted premium.

The plan changed the benchmark for measuring a company's pension liabilities, using a yield curve pegged to corporate bond rates instead of the interest rate on thirty-year Treasury bonds. A temporary change enacted in 2004 (PL 108-218) used a corporate bond rate, but it was good only until the end of 2005.

Lawmakers used the White House proposal as a starting point but made some provisions less stringent. Business and labor groups wanted a phase-in of changes that increased their costs. Business groups—including the U.S. Chamber of Commerce, the ERISA Industry Committee, and the American Benefits Council—cautioned against sweeping changes, arguing that pension problems involved a handful of troubled companies. They called for generous phase-in periods for new rules to avoid encouraging more firms to default on their obligations.

The Senate passed a pension overhaul bill (S 1783) in November, based on legislation approved by two of its committees: the Health, Education, Labor and Pensions (HELP) Committee and the Finance Committee.

Two House committees—Education and the Workforce, and Ways and Means—drafted a pension bill (HR 2830), but that measure stalled because of objections from the United Auto Workers. With time in the first session of the 109th Congress running out, bill sponsors secured a last-minute endorsement from the powerful union, a step that won some Democratic support and enabled them to pass the bill in mid-December.

Both bills proposed to increase the PBGC premium to $30 per employee and require companies to fund 100 percent of the benefits they had pledged to employees, though the full-funding requirements would be phased in over different periods, depending on the health of companies.

The biggest differences included provisions in the Senate bill, but not the House version, to give special treatment to airlines and to use a company's credit rating as a factor in determining how well it had funded its pension plans. The White House opposed industry-specific language and said the president's advisers would recommend a veto if the legislation weakened existing funding requirements for pension plans.

One provision, the PBGC premium increases, was included in the budget reconciliation bill that the House cleared Feb. 1, 2006. Language in the reconciliation bill

PENSION PLAN PREMIUMS

In drafting budget reconciliation legislation, Congress included provisions to increase premiums to support the Pension Benefit Guaranty Corporation (PBGC), the federal agency that insured worker retirement plans, while legislators worked on a bill to overhaul pension security laws. Final action on the reconciliation measure, which was debated in 2005, was delayed until 2006 when it was signed into law (S 1932—PL 109-171) on Feb. 8 by President George W. Bush. *(Reconciliation action, p. 81)*

The broader measures being drafted in separate committees increased the premiums and contained other provisions to shore up the threatened financial stability of the PBGC, which was facing increasing claims as companies jettisoned their pension obligations. The PBGC was created to protect workers from losing all of their pension claims if companies went bankrupt or unilaterally canceled benefit plans.

However, with wide disagreements in Congress about major pension security legislation, legislators decided to move the urgent financial section to the high-priority reconciliation bill. In its major provisions the PBGC section increased the premiums that companies paid to the corporation by an estimated $3.6 billion over five years.

Single-employer plans. Payments to the PBGC by individual corporations that offered their workers defined-benefit pension plans—which pay retirees a set amount, usually based on years of service and earnings—were set at $30 per employee starting in 2006, an increase from $19. Future premium levels were indexed to account for increases in average wages. (Receipts: $2.3 billion over five years)

Multi-employer plans. Premiums paid to cover pension plans that applied to multiple employers were set at $8 per year for each participant, up from $2.60, beginning in 2006. After 2006 the premiums were increased to account for gains in average wages. (Receipts: $300 million over five years)

Termination premium. Companies that attempted to terminate their pension plans while in bankruptcy between the end of 2005 and the start of 2011 would have to pay a special annual premium of $1,250 per participant for three years after the termination of the plan. The special premium also applied to cases in which the PBGC moved to terminate a plan. If a company was assessed the premium while in bankruptcy, it would not have to make the payment until after it exited from bankruptcy protection. The provision did not apply to companies that started bankruptcy proceedings prior to Oct. 18, 2005. (Receipts: $1 billion over five years) increased the annual premium per plan participant to $30. Companies that terminated their plans while under bankruptcy protections would have to pay additional premiums once they left bankruptcy. *(Reconciliation bill premium increase, PL 109-171, pp. 82, 89; box, p. 656)*

HOUSE COMMITTEE ACTION

The House Education and the Workforce Committee on June 30, 2005, approved 27–0 HR 2830 (H Rept 109-232, Part 1) introduced by Chairman John A. Boehner, R-Ohio. All the votes came from Republicans voting; twenty-two Democrats voted "present" to protest what they said was the quick pace of the legislation.

The bill included provisions to raise PBGC premiums to $30 per employee, change the benchmark for measuring pension liabilities to be similar to that in Bush's plan, and force companies to fully fund their plans over time.

The committee adopted a number of amendments during the two-day markup, including a substitute offered by Boehner that would give legal certainty to so-called cash-balance plans, and a five-year phase-in period for companies to increase funding of their plans to 100 percent. Existing law generally allowed 90 percent funding.

The House Ways and Means Committee approved its version of HR 2830 (H Rept 109-232, Part 2) on a mostly party-line 23–17 vote Nov. 9.

Republican leaders had considered a broader retirement package that included an overhaul of the Social Security system, as called for by Bush. But with little support for Social Security changes, Ways and Means chairman Bill Thomas, R-Calif., settled for attaching some modest retirement provisions to the pension bill.

The panel gave voice vote approval to an amendment by Thomas that added a number of provisions dealing with defined-contribution plans, such as 401(k)s. The provisions would make it easier to contribute to Individual Retirement Accounts (IRAs) and make permanent a tax credit for low-income people who contributed to qualified retirement plans.

HOUSE FLOOR ACTION

The House passed HR 2830 by a vote of 294–132 on Dec. 15. The rule for floor debate substituted a version that combined provisions from the two committees, with a modification that secured the support of the International Union, United Automobile, Aerospace and Agricultural Implement Workers of America (UAW).

The measure won support from both sides of the aisle, with seventy Democrats voting for it even though party leaders urged members to vote against it. The Democratic support was due in part to a change in the UAW position. Boehner and Thomas won the union's endorsement for the bill Dec. 13 after agreeing to modify certain provisions.

They agreed to a five-year phase-in of a provision that would prohibit plans that were less than 80 percent funded from increasing pension benefits, unless the benefits were immediately paid for by increased contributions. Another element of the agreement permitted plans that were at least 80 percent funded to use pension assets to pay plant shutdown benefits.

Opponents said the bill would do more harm than good. Calling it an "assault" on the retirement security of American workers, Rep. George Miller, D-Calif., said it would cause more companies to freeze traditional plans or dump them on the PBGC. Democrat David Scott of Georgia, who voted for the bill, said he hoped language helping the airline industry would be added during conference talks.

SENATE COMMITTEE ACTION

The Senate Finance Committee gave voice vote approval July 26 to a bipartisan bill (S 1953—S Rept 109-174) sponsored by Chairman Charles E. Grassley, R-Iowa, and ranking Democrat Max Baucus of Montana. The Grassley-Baucus bill required companies to fully fund their pension plans and use a bond curve to more accurately estimate their pension liabilities. It would increase the PBGC premium to $30 per worker and eliminate "smoothing," an accounting technique that critics said masked deterioration in plan assets.

Like the House bill, the measure would offer greater legal certainty to cash-balance, or hybrid, benefit plans. Left in legal limbo by a 2003 court decision, the plans combined aspects of pension and defined-contribution plans. The bill set age-discrimination standards and parameters for companies to convert a pension plan to a cash-balance system.

The Senate HELP Committee voted 18–2 on Sept. 8 to approve a bill offered jointly by the chairman of the committee, Republican Michael B. Enzi of Wyoming, and the ranking minority member, Democrat Edward M. Kennedy of Massachusetts.

Like the other bills, the legislation established new rules to calculate companies' pension liabilities, required companies to fully fund their pension plans, and increased PBGC premiums to $30 per worker. But the bill also included a number of provisions considered more business-friendly than those in either the Senate Finance or House measures. Under the HELP bill, companies would have ten years to make up for any underfunding of a plan, compared with five years in the House bill and seven years in the Senate Finance legislation.

The bill included airline-industry-specific language that allowed certain "legacy carriers" to make up any funding requirements over fourteen years, rather than ten. Other provisions adjusted the funding rules for multi-employer pension plans and postponed certain payment and funding deadlines for companies with plans that were affected by Hurricane Katrina. *(Hurricane Katrina, p. 787)*

SENATE FLOOR ACTION

The Senate passed a version of the bill negotiated by Grassley and Enzi (S 1783) by a vote of 97–2 on Nov. 16.

The only two "no" votes came from Michigan Democrats Carl Levin and Debbie Stabenow, who expressed concern about the legislation's effect on manufacturing jobs in their state. The Senate compromise was more lenient in treating distressed firms than either the House proposal or the earlier Finance Committee bill.

The new Senate bill required companies to use a modified yield curve to determine their plans' funding status and to fund 100 percent of their pension obligations. Companies with underfunded plans had seven years to reach 100 percent and could not offer additional pension benefits if their plans were less than 80 percent funded. The bill included the premium increase to $30 per year. Employers were required to provide more detailed information to pensioners about the funding status of their plans.

During floor debate, the Senate adopted two amendments, both of which addressed pension issues in the airline industry. The first, by Johnny Isakson, R-Ga., gave airlines twenty years to make up any underfunding in their pension plans. The companies then had seven years to phase in the more stringent funding requirements included in the legislation. As originally written, airlines had fourteen years before the new rules would take effect. It was adopted by voice vote. The second, by Daniel K. Akaka, D-Hawaii, lowered to sixty the age at which pilots could receive maximum pension benefits allowed by the PBGC, resolving a discrepancy in federal law that required pilots to retire at age sixty but did not allow them to draw maximum benefits unless they retired at sixty-five. The amendment was adopted 58–41.

Pension Security: 2006

Congress in 2006 completed action to revamp the nation's private pension system, overcoming concerns about the treatment of certain financially troubled airlines, as well as GOP infighting and delays that had held up the legislation for months. The Senate cleared the legislation Aug. 3. President George W. Bush signed it (HR 4—PL 109-280) at a public ceremony Aug. 17.

The measure required private companies to fully fund their pension plans and to do more to shore up the finances of the Pension Benefit Guaranty Corporation (PBGC), the federal agency responsible for insuring private plans. It also included steps to boost participation in company-sponsored 401(k) retirement savings plans.

Conference negotiators had been trying for almost five months to resolve House-Senate differences on a similar pension bill (HR 2830). Those talks had deadlocked repeatedly, and just before the August recess they broke down over efforts to add a set of tax provisions to the conference report. *(2005 action, p. 654)*

Republican leaders abandoned the negotiations, instead bringing up a clean pension bill that reflected most of the decisions made in conference. They moved the popular tax cut extensions to a separate bill (HR 5970) that also included a permanent reduction in the estate tax and an increase in the minimum wage. The decision angered a number of lawmakers on both sides of the aisle, and the Senate defeated an attempt to bring up the tax bill *(Tax legislation, pp. 96, 97)*

Passage of the pension bill then became the last vote taken by the Senate prior to adjourning for the rest of August. The House had already passed the bill, and after a scant twenty-minute debate, the Senate followed suit, clearing the bill for the president.

Enactment was the culmination of years of work by lawmakers concerned about record deficits at the PBGC and chronic underfunding in a number of company pension plans. Although the PBGC was financed entirely through premiums paid by private companies, lawmakers worried that the agency could be overwhelmed if it had to take over too many terminated plans, requiring taxpayers to bail out the agency.

The new law affected both defined-benefit and defined-contribution plans. Under a defined-benefit plan, the company contributes annually to a pension trust fund and the employee is guaranteed a set yearly benefit after retiring. In a defined-contribution plan, the employer contributes a set amount to a 401(k) or other retirement account, to which the employee can also contribute pretax dollars. The employee decides how the funds are invested, usually choosing from a range of options, and the retirement benefit depends on how the investments perform.

The law required companies with underfunded pension plans—those whose liabilities exceeded their commitments—to pay extra premiums, with some airlines getting extra time to achieve full funding. It extended a requirement that companies terminating their pension plans pay an additional premium to the PBGC and provided a new system for companies to compute their pension plan obligations more accurately. The legislation also included some provisions dealing with the treatment of charities, including tax incentives for charitable giving.

Lawmakers had to walk a fine line in writing the provisions. They wanted to ensure that companies met the pension promises made to employees. At the same time, however, business groups warned that overly restrictive legislation could cause more companies to abrogate their pension plans. Financially troubled airlines were especially vocal, threatening to dump their plans on the PBGC unless they were given specific relief as part of pension overhaul legislation.

LEGISLATIVE ACTION

The House and Senate each passed versions of a pension overhaul bill in late 2005. Both bills proposed to increase the premiums that employers paid to the PBGC from $19 per plan participant to $30, and to require that companies fund 100 percent of the benefits they had pledged to employees, though they had different phase-in periods.

The Senate measure (S 1783), passed Nov. 16, was a compromise between versions approved separately by the Finance Committee and the Health, Education, Labor and Pensions Committee. It proposed that companies be given seven years to reach 100 percent funding of their pension plans. Plans that were less than 80 percent funded would not be able to offer additional benefits. The Senate adopted a floor amendment to give airlines twenty years to make up any underfunding of their plans and another seven years to phase in other bill requirements.

The House bill (HR 2830), passed Dec. 15, combined provisions from two committees—Education and the Workforce, and Ways and Means—and included modifications that won the support of the United Auto Workers. Earlier opposition from the union had delayed House action. The bill gave companies whose plans were more than 80 percent funded five years to reach 100 percent; firms with more serious underfunding would have three years. It also phased in over five years a provision barring plans that were less than 80 percent funded from offering new benefits that were not paid for by new contributions.

CONFERENCE ACTION

Conference negotiations were expected to move swiftly, but got off to a slow start. The Senate did not name conferees until March because of a partisan dispute over how many negotiators to appoint.

For months, a conference agreement seemed nearly within reach. But each time negotiators said they were close, the many complex issues combined to resist a final resolution, leading lawmakers to miss several self-imposed deadlines.

Among the biggest differences was the Senate's inclusion of special pension relief for the airlines. The White House opposed such industry-specific language and threatened to veto the final bill if it weakened existing funding requirements for pension plans. Other differences included a Senate proposal to use a company's credit rating as a factor in determining how well it had funded its pension plans and Senate language to protect older workers during a conversion from a defined-benefit to a cash-balance pension plan. Also, the House included a provision not in the Senate bill to allow financial firms that administered pension plans to give investment advice to plan participants on investment products for which the advisers' firm received fees or other commissions.

The final deadlock was over whether the conference report should serve as a vehicle to extend a number of popular tax credits, including the expired research and development tax credit for businesses and the tax credit for college tuition. Senate negotiators, led by Finance chairman Charles E. Grassley, R-Iowa, insisted on including the extenders. Grassley said he had agreed to drop the provisions from the big tax reconciliation package that cleared in May (PL 109-222) because he was given assurances by his House counterpart—Bill Thomas, R-Calif., chairman of the Ways and Means Committee—that they would be attached to other legislation, probably the pension bill.

But with the August recess approaching and the conference dragging on, Republican leaders decided to use the tax extenders instead to help win support for an indefinite reduction to the estate tax, a GOP priority in an election year. The bill they had in mind also included a third element, an increase in the minimum wage. Grassley and his supporters said prospects for the estate tax bill in the Senate were so shaky that it could pull down the tax cut extensions with it.

The dispute led to a showdown late July 27 when House Republicans boycotted a pension bill conference meeting that was scheduled to vote on whether to keep the tax cut extensions in the conference report. A furious Grassley wondered out loud why they "wouldn't have the guts to come forward and vote." Grassley said stripping out the tax provisions broke his agreement with Thomas. "When my credibility is abused and used, I resent it," he yelled. "I will still continue to keep my word even if I am stabbed in the back."

FINAL ACTION

On July 28, Republican House leaders introduced a quickly drafted replacement pension bill (HR 4) that mainly reflected agreements reached by the conference but without the tax extenders that were a priority for Senate conferees. They were put into a second measure (HR 5970) that also included the permanent reduction in the estate tax and the minimum wage increase.

The House passed the new pension bill on a **key vote of 279–131 (R 203–16; D 76–114; I 0–1)** later that day. A bipartisan group of Senate pension negotiators fiercely opposed the strategy and called on their House counterparts to sign a conference agreement on the original bill. But the House departed as planned for the August recess. By the time the Senate took up the bill Aug. 3, tempers had cooled and the measure passed 93–5, clearing it for the president. *(2006 key votes, p. 937)*

MAJOR PROVISIONS

As enacted HR 4 (PL 109-280) contained the following major provisions.

Defined-benefit plan funding requirements. Changed the rules for the method companies used to calculate pension liabilities to accurately measure liabilities as they became due. Required companies to fund 100 percent of their pension liabilities, up from 90 percent under existing law. Allowed companies seven years to make up funding shortfalls. Allowed financially distressed airlines additional time to make up pension underfunding: seventeen years, expected to help Northwest and Delta, or ten years, expected to benefit American and Continental.

Termination premium. Indefinitely extended an existing provision requiring companies that terminated their pension plans on an involuntary or distressed-termination basis to pay a special annual premium of $1,250 per plan participant to the PBGC for three years. Specified that, if the employer were in bankruptcy, the premium would be assessed after the firm emerged from bankruptcy.

Benefit restrictions. Prohibited defined-benefit plans that were less than 80 percent funded from increasing their benefits unless the added benefits were paid for immediately through increased contributions.

Multi-employer plans. Required multi-employer plans that were less than 80 percent funded to improve their financial health by one-third within ten years. Prohibited plans that were less than 65 percent funded from increasing benefits.

IRA rules. Extended indefinitely several individual retirement account (IRA) and pension provisions first enacted in 2001 (PL 107-16) that were scheduled to expire in 2010, including an increase in annual contribution limits for IRAs and additional "catch-up" contributions for persons age fifty or older.

Professional investment advice. Allowed financial advisers to offer guidance to retirement plan participants without running afoul of conflict-of-interest restrictions. Required advisers for 401(k)s and other employer-sponsored plans to base their recommendations on a computer model certified by a third party.

Allowed companies to enroll workers automatically in 401(k) and other defined-contribution plans but permitted employees to opt out if they chose. (Under exiting law, the employee had to elect to participate in such plans.)

Hybrids. Clarified the legality of hybrid plans that incorporated elements of both defined-benefit and defined-contribution pensions, including imposition of nondiscrimination rules on hybrid plans. (Hybrids had been in legal limbo since a 2003 court decision found that they discriminated against older workers.)

Saver's credit. Indefinitely extended the saver's credit, a nonrefundable credit to taxpayers with incomes below certain levels who made contributions to 401(k)s or IRAs.

Tariffs. Created or extended special tariff treatment of several hundred imported items for which there was generally no domestic supply. (Many of the provisions were taken from a trade bill [HR 4944] the House passed in March.) *(Trade action, p. 197)*

Charities. Included provisions to end tax abuses by charities and private foundations, coupled with certain incentives intended to increase charitable giving.

Mine Safety

Several fatal mine accidents in early 2006 led Congress to enact the first significant overhaul of mine safety laws in twenty-eight years. President George W. Bush signed the legislation (S 2803—PL 109-236) into law June 15.

The bill established new federal safety regulations for coal mines, requiring owners to install wireless communications equipment and tracking devices within three years and to arrange for faster public notification and quicker responses when accidents occur. It also raised maximum fines for accidents and gave the government the power to shut down mines when operators failed to pay fines.

Deaths in the coal industry had been on a steady decline since the early 1980s, when more than 100 miners died every year. Coal mine fatalities reached an all-time low of twenty-two in 2005. However, a spate of mining tragedies in 2006—beginning with an explosion and fire at the Sago Mine in West Virginia on Jan. 2, which led to the deaths of twelve miners—convinced lawmakers and the mining industry that new legislation was needed.

Eight days after the Sago tragedy, a miner died in Kentucky. On Jan. 19, two miners died in a fire in another West Virginia mine. By the end of the month, the industry had experienced as many deaths as had occurred during the first eleven months of 2005.

In the House, Democrats blamed the government's Mine Safety and Health Administration (MSHA) for lax enforcement of mine safety laws, which they said contributed to the accidents. Republicans, however, resisted holding hearings or writing legislation until all the facts from the mine investigations had been compiled.

In the Senate, the Health, Education, Labor and Pensions (HELP) Committee approved a bipartisan mine safety bill in May, and the Senate passed it within less than a week, after yet another mine explosion.

After holding hearings in March, the House Education and the Workforce Committee was preparing to mark up its own bill. But GOP leaders, spurred by continuing accidents, agreed to take up the Senate-passed bill, sending it to the president June 7.

LEGISLATIVE ACTION

With more than two dozen coal-mining deaths already recorded for the year, the Senate HELP Committee approved a bipartisan bill (S 2803—S Rept 109-365) by a vote of 20–0 on May 17. The chairman of the committee, Republican Michael B. Enzi of Wyoming, and the panel's ranking Democrat, Edward M. Kennedy of Massachusetts, drafted the bill after months of negotiations among Republicans, Democrats, miners, and mine companies.

Mine owners and miners said they were pleased with the bill. "It's fair to say that virtually everyone ... in the coal-mining community was fairly stunned by the quick succession of accidents," said Luke Popovich, a spokesperson for the National Mining Association. "There was a distinct desire among our leadership to address this through legislation, to be sure that rules and laws emerging in various states, and that would inevitably pop up here in Washington, would embody principles that we believe would actually improve mine safety."

The Senate passed the bill by voice vote May 24, four days after yet another mine explosion, which killed five miners in Harlan County, Ky. The latest tragedy brought the year's death toll in coal mines to more than thirty.

The House cleared the Senate bill by a vote of 381–37 on June 7. GOP leaders decided to forgo writing their own legislation after the May 20 Kentucky coal mine deaths increased the pressure for swift action.

Under prodding by Republican Shelley Moore Capito of West Virginia, where mining was an important industry, the leadership had been prepared to quickly clear the Enzi-Kennedy bill the day after the Senate vote. But it ran into an unexpected roadblock: Rep. George Miller of California, the senior Democrat on the House Education and the Workforce Committee, which had jurisdiction over worker safety issues.

Miller wanted the bill strengthened by requiring mine owners to store forty-eight hours of oxygen in underground mines for trapped miners; installing wireless communications devices within fifteen months, instead of three years; and requiring MSHA to conduct more frequent and random inspections of emergency breathing devices. Miller's suggested changes were opposed by the mining industry.

When no agreement could be reached on considering the amendments, Miller refused to allow the measure to be cleared by voice vote. With no time before the Memorial Day recess, GOP leaders scheduled a roll-call vote for June 7. Capito blasted Miller, saying, "It is outrageous that personal posturing has blocked the passage of this important mine safety legislation."

During the June 7 debate, Miller argued that the Senate bill "fails to make the reforms that go to the very heart of what happened in the Sago mine disaster." Recalling that eleven of the twelve miners at Sago did not die from the initial explosion, Miller said, "They died because they did not have communication tools to lead them to safety; they died because they did not have an oxygen supply to last the forty hours that they were trapped."

Democrat Nick J. Rahall II of West Virginia praised Miller for working for decades to improve mine safety, but he said the Senate bill was the best Congress could do at that time. "To delay, no matter how noble the intentions, is to gamble recklessly with the lives of our nation's coal miners," he said. Coal-mining incidents in West Virginia had already claimed nineteen lives since the start of the year, more than in any other state.

Miller was one of thirty-three Democrats who voted against the bill.

MAJOR PROVISIONS

The following are the main provisions of S 2803 (PL 109-236).

Emergency response plans. Required underground coal mines to develop new emergency response plans that were regularly reviewed, updated, and recertified by MSHA, including plans to provide for emergency supplies of breathable air for miners trapped underground "for a sustained period of time."

Communications. Required coal mine owners to install wireless two-way communications systems as well as electronic tracking equipment within three years.

Rescue teams. Directed the Labor Department to issue regulations within eighteen months to require coal mine operators to have two certified rescue teams that could reach the mine within one hour.

Seals. Required the Labor Department to issue stronger regulations within eighteen months for the seals that cut off abandoned areas of mines. (Seals had failed in both the Sago explosion and a later explosion that killed five miners in Kentucky.)

Notification. Required mine operators to notify MSHA within fifteen minutes of becoming aware of any incidents or accidents that posed a reasonable risk of death. Subjected mine operators who failed to do so to civil penalties of between $5,000 and $60,000.

Penalties. Established fines of up to $250,000 or one year in prison, or both, for mine operators who willfully violated mandatory health or safety standards, and allowed fines of to $500,000 or five years in prison, or both, for repeat offenders. Provided civil penalties of up to $220,000 for flagrant violations. Authorized MSHA to request an injunction to shut down a mine if the operator refused to pay a fine issued under a final order.

Other provisions. Authorized new mine safety technology grants, education and training grants, and a scholarship program for future miners and mine inspectors.

Minimum Wage

Congressional supporters of an higher national minimum wage tried in three different ways in 2006 to increase the pay mandate, which had remained at $5.15 an hour since 1996. All failed in the face of adamant opposition from Republican leaders and small business lobbyists, as in recent congressional sessions. In addition, in 2006 the effort was complicated by Democratic maneuvering to entwine the issue with efforts to force President George W. Bush to wind down the war in Iraq. *(Iraq war funding, p. 383)*

However, the 2006 efforts helped lay the groundwork for passage the following year, with Democrats back in a majority in both chambers, of a $2.10 an hour increase phased in over two years. *(2007 action, p. 664; 108th Congress action, Congress and the Nation Vol. XI, p. 575)*

Raising the minimum wage was a signature issue for Democrats as they planned for the midterm election that fall. Even a growing number of moderate Republicans supported a vote as the campaign season approached, although the GOP leadership and the Bush White House remained opposed unless an increase was combined with tax law changes that were anathema to Democrats. Republicans tried to combine the two in legislation that tied a wage increase to tax breaks for businesses and a permanent reduction of the estate tax. This maneuver was met with a Democratic filibuster in the Senate, which killed the bill for the year.

HOUSE ACTION

With support from some GOP moderates, Democrats on the House Appropriations Committee succeeded in adding a federal minimum wage increase to the fiscal 2007 spending bill for the Labor, Health and Human Services (HHS), and Education Department, (HR 5647).

Minority Whip Steny H. Hoyer, D-Md., offered the amendment, which would have raised the wage to $7.25 over two years, during the committee markup of the bill. It was adopted 32–27 on June 13.

Moderate Republicans who faced closely contested reelection races in November said they would not vote for the bill if the wage increase was dropped. But conservatives who were already unhappy with the cost of the bill said the wage boost was a job killer and warned that they would not support the bill if the amendment remained. As a result, Majority Leader John A. Boehner, R-Ohio, kept the bill off the House floor. *(HHS appropriations, p. 104)*

SENATE ACTION

On June 21, Edward M. Kennedy, D-Mass., won majority support in the Senate for an amendment to the defense authorization bill (S 2766) to boost the minimum wage in stages to $7.25 an hour. The vote was 52–46, but the amendment failed under a unanimous consent agreement that required a majority of sixty for adoption. Kennedy said his proposal picked up eight more Republican votes than a similar amendment that failed in October 2005.

Michael B. Enzi, R-Wyo., offered an alternative that would have raised the wage in stages to $6.25 an hour one year after enactment, exempted businesses with gross annual sales of under $1 million, and permitted private-sector workers to participate in biweekly flex-hour programs. Enzi's amendment was rejected 45–53.

SENATE FILIBUSTER

House Republican leaders came under pressure in July from a growing group of party moderates who worried they would be vulnerable to a barrage of Democratic attack ads during the August recess if the leadership did not schedule a minimum wage vote.

House Speaker J. Dennis Hastert, R-Ill., and Boehner were reluctant to do so. They sided with conservatives who believed that the wage increase would raise costs for small businesses and lead to fewer jobs. "I've had every rotten job there ever was, and I'm glad I had every one of them," Boehner told reporters July 13. "And if we'd had a high minimum wage, I wouldn't have had the opportunity to have some of those jobs." In addition, Hastert said he did not like the idea of being forced, even by members of his own party, to take up a bill he did not like.

But Republican moderates, such as Ray LaHood of Illinois, Frank A. LoBiondo of New Jersey, Steven C. LaTourette of Ohio, and Sherwood Boehlert of New York, stepped up their demands, threatening to block the House from adjourning for the August recess if they did not get a vote. "A minimum of thirty members need that vote so they don't get skewered and barbecued over the summer break," said LaHood. "They know the thirty-second commercials have already been cut."

Hastert and Boehner also were hearing from rank-and-file conservatives who did not want to allow any vote on the minimum wage. At the very least, these Republican House members wanted to balance a wage increase with measures they thought would cushion the blow to businesses. "Any proposal containing a minimum wage increase should be jobs-neutral," said Mike Pence of Indiana, chairman of the conservative Republican Study Committee. "If the federal government increases costs for businesses with one hand, it is only right that it reduce costs for businesses with the other."

Republican leaders decided to combine a minimum wage increase with a permanent reduction in the estate tax, a favorite goal of conservatives, and extensions of tax breaks that were important to business. The legislation (HR 5970) was designed with the expectation that most lawmakers would find something appealing in it. The bill proposed to boost the wage in three steps: to $5.85 an hour on Jan. 1, 2007; to $6.55 an hour on June 1, 2008; and to $7.25 an hour on June 1, 2009. The House passed the three-part bill by a vote of 230–180 on July 29.

In the Senate, where more than a simple majority was required for most controversial legislation, the House approach went nowhere with most Democrats and two Republicans, Lincoln Chafee of Rhode Island and George V. Voinovich of Ohio, who viewed the estate tax cut as too high a price to pay for the rest of the package.

"This is not a good minimum wage bill. This is not even a fairly good minimum wage bill. This is an awful minimum wage bill," said Minority Leader Harry Reid, D-Nev. On Aug. 3, the Senate voted 65–42 against ending a filibuster led by Reid. The vote was four short of the sixty needed to invoke cloture. That ended the 2006 minimum wage debate although the tax extenders cleared separately *(Tax details, p. 131)*

Social Security Changes

President George W. Bush began his second term with a major push to make major changes in the country's preeminent retirement program, the government-run Social Security system. After much public debate in 2005, Bush's plan to reshape Social Security and add individual investment accounts to the government pension system never found a place on the congressional agenda. With strong opposition by Democrats to the concept of individual accounts, Bush's top legislative priority for the 109th Congress was unceremoniously dropped later that year and was not taken up in the 110th Congress.

Even before he was inaugurated in 2005 for his second term, Bush began urging a broad overhaul of Social Security, the first in twenty-two years. At the core of his plan was a proposal to permit younger workers to divert some of their Social Security payroll tax payments into individual investment accounts. A bipartisan commission appointed by Bush in May 2001 late that same year recommended three options, all centered on his proposal to allow workers to invest some Social Security contributions in private markets. *(Details, Congress and the Nation Vol. XI, p. 568)*

Some Republican leaders vigorously backed Bush. Senate majority leader Bill Frist, R-Tenn., announced that an overhaul bill he expected the Finance Committee to write would carry the symbolic designation S 1. But almost from the beginning Bush had trouble selling the "fiscal crisis" element of his plan to Democrats, some Republicans, and the public. Even Frist, in early 2005, began to say an overhaul might not make it through the Senate.

Democrats uniformly rejected individual accounts and future benefit cuts that also were part of Bush's concept. Many conservatives who believed the entire Social Security retirement system could be replaced by individual accounts also balked at Bush's benefit cuts.

By June, congressional interest rebounded somewhat, and House and Senate Republicans offered bills that they hoped would stimulate debate on the stalled issue. It was never clear, however, how much support the Republican proposals would get from the two members of Congress most responsible for overseeing a Social Security overhaul: Sen. Charles E. Grassley, R-Iowa, the chairman of the Senate Finance Committee; and Bill Thomas, R-Calif., the chairman of the House Ways and Means Committee. By the end of 2005, no action had been taken on any measure, and in 2006 the issue was shoved aside as lawmakers focused on an agenda they hoped would play well during the midterm election campaign that fall.

In his 2006 State of the Union address, Bush called for a bipartisan commission to study the government's costliest entitlement programs: Social Security, Medicare, and Medicaid. No such commission was appointed, however.

2007–2008

The most significant action taken by the 110th Congress, which had returned to Democratic control as a result of the 2006 midterm elections, was a $2.10 increase in the national minimum wage, the first in nearly a decade. Even many Republicans were at least open if not enthusiastic about an increase. House Republicans in swing districts that were actively contested by Democrats were especially receptive and urged their party leaders—who had strongly opposed a change in recent years—to allow action, lest they face defeat in the face of sharp political attacks by Democrats and allies in labor unions.

Congress also extended unemployment benefits, in 2008, in the face of the financial crisis that sent unemployment rates toward 10 percent. Many workers who lost jobs were not finding new work and quickly used up their existing twenty-six weeks of unemployment benefits.

Although the benefits extension was a high priority for unions, organized labor had no success in other legislation important to workers. Several attempts to enact new employment discrimination laws all failed, and unions could not push through a bill to expand union membership through a new system that did not require a secret ballot to certify a union at a company. The proposed system was called a check card authority. Workers could create a union at a firm by having a majority of employees sign a card. Employers adamantly opposed the concept, arguing that doing away with a secret ballot was undemocratic and allowed union representatives to coerce workers to sign the cards. Unions replied that management typically did the same by pressuring workers not to vote for a union where an organizing effort was underway.

Minimum Wage

Congress in 2007 increased the federal minimum wage by $2.10 over two years, from $5.15 an hour to $7.25 an hour. It was the first increase in nearly ten years. The provisions, which were paired with tax breaks for small businesses, were attached to a supplemental spending bill for the wars in Iraq and Afghanistan. President George W. Bush signed it into law (HR 2206—PL 110-28) May 25.

The tax breaks totaled $7.1 billion over six years and $4.8 billion if the period was extended to eleven years. As required by House rules adopted at the start of the Congress, the costs were fully offset. *(Tax bill provisions, p. 120)*

Democrats had pledged in the 2006 midterm election campaign that a minimum wage increase would be a top priority if the party won control of the 110th Congress, which they did in November. House Democrats moved quickly in 2007 by passing a stand-alone minimum wage bill (HR 2) as the second item on the Democrats' "first 100 hours" agenda. But the legislation followed a twisted path to enactment. *(2006 action, p. 661)*

In the Senate, where Democrats held the slimmest of majorities—51–49—and needed GOP votes to pass controversial legislation, Democratic leaders paired the wage increase with an $8.3 billion tax break package to benefit small businesses. The Senate passed the amended bill Feb. 1. The House Ways and Means Committee responded with a smaller $1.3 billion tax break package (HR 976), which the House passed Feb. 16.

With the two chambers far apart on the tax proposals, the House tried an alternative route, inserting minimum wage and tax cut provisions into its version of the fiscal 2007 supplemental spending bill for the wars in Iraq and Afghanistan. From that point on, the fate of the minimum wage provisions was tied up in the fight between congressional Democrats and the White House over setting a timetable to pull U.S. troops out of Iraq. *(Iraq war funding, pp. 314, 350, 383, 387)*

Bush vetoed the first supplemental (HR 1591) over the war provisions and nondefense spending. Democrats subsequently backed away from the war demands, and Bush signed the bill, carrying the minimum wage and tax proposals to enactment.

BACKGROUND

Congress first established a nationwide uniform minimum wage, 25 cents an hour, in the Fair Labor Standards Act of 1938 (PL 75-718). The level was increased periodically in subsequent decades. *(Congress and the Nation Vol. I, pp. 1119, 1228)*

The 2007 increase was the first since Sept. 1, 1997. That increase had been approved by Congress in 1996 legislation (PL 104-188) signed by President Bill Clinton on Aug. 20 that year. The 1997 hike was the second of a two-step increase. *(Congress and the Nation Vol. IX, p. 666)* An effort to further increase the minimum by a dollar failed in 2000. *(Congress and the Nation Vol. X, p. 579)*

A full-time minimum wage worker in 2006 earned $10,712, which was $5,888 less than the poverty level for a family of three. Most states had state minimum wage laws, a majority of which exceeded the uniform federal minimum. When state and federal minimum wage rates were different, the higher rate prevailed.

Democrats argued that nearly 13 million Americans would benefit from a minimum wage increase—5.6 million directly and 7.4 million indirectly—and that the vast majority were adults. They said the purchasing power of the minimum wage was at its lowest level in fifty-one years.

Democrats also argued that past increases had not hurt the economy, pointing out that in the four years after the last minimum wage increase, the economy enjoyed its strongest growth in more than three decades, adding nearly 11 million new jobs. Small business employment grew more in states with higher minimum wage rates than in federal minimum wage states: 9.4 percent versus 6.6 percent.

Many Republicans opposed an increase, arguing that it would force employers to reduce the number of jobs, especially entry-level jobs that were important to those joining the workforce. Republicans said that minimum-wage workers typically were not the sole wage-earners in the family but were teenagers or second-wage earners, and that there were more efficient ways to target assistance to low-income workers, such as expanding the earned-income tax credit.

The White House supported increasing the minimum wage, but only if Congress also included tax preferences to aid small businesses that could be hurt by paying higher wages.

In the 109th Congress, Democrats tried repeatedly to force a vote on a minimum wage hike. Even with the support of GOP moderates, fearful of voter discontent in the fall, the then-Republican-controlled Congress did not complete a bill. *(2006 action, p. 661)*

HOUSE FLOOR ACTION

The House passed its stand-alone bill (HR 2) by a **key vote of 315–116 (R 82–116; D 233–0)** Jan. 10, 2007. The rule for floor debate, adopted as part of the leadership's rules package, barred amendments. Republicans lost on a motion to recommit the bill with instructions to add a provision exempting employers from the wage increase if they provided employee health coverage. That vote was 144–287. *(2007 key votes, p. 955)*

In a statement of administration policy, the White House Office of Management and Budget (OMB) said it strongly supported adding tax and regulatory relief provisions to the bill.

SENATE COMMITTEE ACTION

The Senate Finance Committee gave voice vote approval Jan. 17 to a package of small business tax incentives that Joint Tax said would cost $8.6 billion over five years and $8.3 billion over ten. The draft also included business-related revenue-raisers to pay for them. *(Senate tax provisions, p. 120)*

The provisions were negotiated by the Democratic chairman of the Finance Committee, Max Baucus of Montana, and the ranking Republican, Charles E. Grassley of Iowa. Majority Leader Harry Reid of Nevada and his Republican counterpart, Minority Leader Mitch McConnell of Kentucky, said they would add the package to the House-passed minimum wage bill when it was considered on the Senate floor.

That set up a public conflict between House and Senate Democratic leaders. Speaker Nancy Pelosi, D-Calif., and her allies strongly opposed efforts to incorporate the tax breaks into the minimum wage bill because they hoped to avoid potentially difficult votes on the revenue-raising offsets that would be required. Under the new House rules adopted in January, any new tax cuts had to be offset by tax increases or cuts in entitlement programs. Democrat Charles B. Rangel of New York, chairman of the House Ways and Means Committee, even threatened to make a "blue slip" objection to a combined Senate tax and minimum wage bill, invoking the constitutional requirement that revenue measures originate in the House.

But Reid and Baucus said the tax proposals were the only way they could get enough support for the minimum wage provisions to avert a Senate filibuster. "It is a little different world," Senate majority whip Richard J. Durbin, D-Ill., said of his chamber, noting his party's slim 51–49 majority that included two independents.

The dispute between Rangel and Baucus mirrored their different constituencies. Baucus, who was running for reelection in 2008, had a reputation for bucking party leaders on tax and trade issues. He referred to Montana as a "small business state" and made passage of tax breaks for small businesses and farmers a legislative priority.

In contrast, Rangel said he would consider including small business tax provisions in a broader measure incorporating changes to the alternative minimum tax and eliminating certain tax deductions for businesses and individuals.

SENATE FLOOR ACTION

Capping two weeks of floor debate, the Senate on Feb. 1 passed a version of HR 2 that combined the minimum wage provisions with the $8.3 billion package of small business tax cuts. The bill passed on an overwhelming, bipartisan **key vote of 94–3 (R 45–3; D 47–0; I 2–0)**. *(2007 key votes, p. 955)*

Pelosi's and Rangel's vehement opposition to some of the tax provisions led Reid to hold the bill at the desk, rather than sending it to conference, while he continued to negotiate with House leaders. By agreeing to include the tax incentives, Reid brought all but three of his chamber's Republicans on board for the wage increase. A Senate vote the previous week proved his point that he could not do it without the tax cuts. On Jan. 24, the Senate rejected a motion to limit debate on the House-passed stand-alone minimum wage bill. The 54–43 tally was six votes short of the sixty required to invoke cloture and curtail a filibuster.

The deal still made many Senate Democrats unhappy. Edward M. Kennedy, D-Mass., a longtime advocate for raising the minimum wage, vehemently opposed including the tax package. Barack Obama, D-Ill., said at a news conference after the vote: "This should not be loaded up. This should not be complicated.... The notion that we are still using this as a bargaining chip or dickering for various other tax breaks makes no sense. It's time to get this done." Even Baucus said he wished the Senate could pass a stand-alone minimum wage bill.

After cloture on the House-passed bill failed, Baucus offered a substitute that included the tax package. The proposals had been carefully negotiated with Republicans

Grassley, McConnell, and Michael B. Enzi of Wyoming, and the three made good on their promise to deliver GOP support to move the legislation along. On Jan. 30, the Senate agreed 87–10 to limit debate on Baucus's substitute, with thirty-eight Republicans voting with the majority.

Despite the overwhelming show of support, Republicans drew out the time in order to forestall the next order of business on the Senate agenda: a highly anticipated debate on Bush's Iraq strategy. For the most part, Democrats fended off GOP amendments. One notable exception came from Sen. Jeff Sessions of Alabama, who succeeded in associating the explosive immigration issue with the plight of low-wage U.S. workers. His amendment—to bar companies from receiving lucrative government contracts if they were caught hiring illegal immigrants—was adopted 94–0. Democrats refused to call up another Sessions amendment that would have raised fines for all companies caught hiring illegal workers.

The Senate defeated 28–69 an amendment by Sen. Wayne Allard, R-Colo., that would have undercut the federal minimum wage increase by exempting states that had a lower rate.

HOUSE ACTION

With HR 2 being held at the Senate desk, House leaders looked for a way to push the minimum wage increase forward. On Feb. 12, the House Ways and Means Committee gave voice vote approval to its own, much smaller package of small business tax breaks (HR 976—H Rept 110-14). The bill, written by Rangel and ranking Ways and Means Republican Jim McCrery of Louisiana, was estimated to cost $4.6 billion over six years and $1.3 billion over 11 years.

The White House issued a statement Feb. 13 giving tepid support to the bill, calling it a step toward increasing the minimum wage but saying that the tax breaks should be larger to mitigate potential job losses and that offsets were unnecessary. Business lobbyists backed the bill because it did not contain the large offsets needed to pay for the heftier Senate measure. They especially opposed the Senate proposals to cap deductions for deferred compensation for business executives and end business deductions for punitive damages and cash settlements from lawsuits.

The House passed the $1.3 billion Ways and Means Committee tax package 360–45 on Feb. 16. The bill was considered under suspension of the rules, which limited debate, prohibited amendments, and required a two-thirds majority for passage. Republicans, including David Dreier of California, the ranking minority member on the House Rules panel, complained that they were prevented from offering a motion aimed at enlarging the tax cuts.

SUPPLEMENTAL APPROPRIATIONS

In a shift of strategy, House Speaker Pelosi decided in March to attach a minimum wage–tax package to the fiscal 2007 supplemental appropriations bill for the war. Top aides said the move was intended to break the stalemate with the Senate and win quick enactment for the minimum wage increase. They also held out the hope of picking up votes from liberals who were otherwise inclined to vote against war funding.

The initial House version of the supplemental (HR 1591—H Rept 110-60), which passed 218–212 on March 23, included the House-passed minimum wage and small business tax provisions.

The Senate passed its version of the supplemental 51–47 on March 29, after agreeing by voice vote to an amendment by Kennedy that added the minimum wage increase and what the Joint Tax Committee said was a $12.6 billion package of tax breaks through 2017, with offsetting revenue increases. The cost of the tax package had grown by about $4.3 billion since the Senate passed it as part of HR 2 in February.

CONFERENCE ACTION AND VETO

The House adopted a conference report (H Rept 110-107) on the first supplemental by a vote of 218–208 on April 25. The Senate cleared the bill 51–46 the next day. Bush vetoed the measure May 1, citing the bill's timeline for troop withdrawals from Iraq and billions in unrequested spending. The House was unable to override the veto. *(Veto message, p. 1063)*

The conference's agreement included the basic minimum wage proposal and a compromise $4.8 billion package of tax cuts over eleven years. The tax package was more than three times as large as the one the House had passed, but it was still less than half the size of the Senate-passed plan.

FINAL ACTION

After one more attempt by the House to set dates for withdrawal from Iraq, Democrats ultimately dropped the timeline and sent Bush a revised Iraq supplemental spending bill (HR 2206) that he was ready to sign. The enacted bill carried the minimum wage and the package of tax breaks from the earlier conference report.

The House separated the compromise into two amendments, both of which were adopted May 24. The amendment that included the minimum wage and tax provisions was adopted 348–73. Under the rule, the bill was then sent back to the Senate, which cleared it 80–14 the same day.

MAJOR PROVISIONS

The following are the main provisions of HR 2206 (PL 110-28) that pertained to minimum wage and small business. *(Additional tax provision details, p. 120)*

Minimum wage. Increased the minimum wage floor by $2.10 an hour in three increments of 70 cents each: sixty days after enactment, the $5.15 hourly rate would rise to $5.85; one year later it would rise to $6.55; two years later it would increase to $7.25. Applied the federal minimum wage to the Northern Mariana Islands and to American Samoa.

Work opportunity tax credit. Extended for forty-four months through Aug. 31, 2011, the credit for businesses that hired certain low-income workers, including food stamp recipients, those on welfare, and some high-risk youth.

Small business expensing. Extended for one year through 2010 provisions that allowed small business owners to deduct an extra amount in the first year for purchases of depreciable assets.

Tip credit. Permitted businesses to use the old $5.15 minimum wage as the basis for calculating their "tip credit"—a credit for Social Security taxes that they paid on tips that brought an employee's pay above the minimum wage.

AMT credits. Allowed individual and business taxpayers to claim the work opportunity tax credit and the tip credit against their liability under the alternative minimum tax (AMT).

Unemployment Benefits

Congress in 2008 twice extended emergency unemployment benefits in the face of the nation's growing economic crisis. The first extension was enacted June 30 as part of a supplemental spending bill for the wars in Iraq and Afghanistan (HR 2642—PL 110-252). The second, a stand-alone bill, was cleared during the lame-duck session following the fall elections and became law Nov. 21.

The bills provided additional compensation to unemployed workers who had already exhausted their regular twenty-six weeks of benefits. The regular unemployment program was funded through federal and state payroll taxes and administered by the states. The additional compensation provided under the bills came from the federal government.

FIRST EXTENSION

Lawmakers made several failed attempts to enact the first extension of unemployment benefits before successfully adding it to the 2008 supplemental spending bill.

Stimulus bill. The Senate Finance Committee included a thirteen-week extension of federal unemployment benefits, with an additional thirteen weeks in hard-hit areas, in a draft economic stimulus bill that it approved Jan. 30. The provision was one of many that made the Senate measure far more expensive than a relatively narrow stimulus bill passed by the House. After days of partisan maneuvering, the Senate rejected the Finance Committee draft by voting down an attempt to limit debate on it. On Feb. 7, the Senate passed a version of the bill (HR 5140) that omitted the unemployment benefits and many other committee provisions. The House cleared the measure the same day. *(Stimulus legislation, p. 151)*

Stand-alone House bill. With the stimulus bill no longer available, Democrats planned to add the unemployment compensation provisions to a fiscal 2009 supplemental war spending bill that appropriators were writing. When work on the supplemental stalled and the Bureau of Labor Statistics reported that the May unemployment rate had risen to 5.5 percent from 5 percent the previous month, House leaders decided to bring a narrow benefits extension bill to the floor. That measure (HR 5749—H Rept 110-607) passed 274–137 on June 12.

The legislation, similar to the Senate Finance Committee plan, called for thirteen weeks of federal unemployment benefits for workers whose twenty-six weeks of regular benefits had run out. An additional thirteen weeks would be available in states with unemployment rates of 6 percent or higher. The House Ways and Means Committee had approved the bill 23–13 on April 16. While both parties agreed on the need for some type of extension, Republicans argued that the Democrats' plan was too broad. They endorsed a more limited approach that targeted states with unemployment rates of 5 percent or higher and states where unemployment rates had grown by more than 20 percent in the previous year. They said their plan would apply to twenty-two states.

Senate leaders preferred to keep the unemployment extension as part of the supplemental bill. But House leaders were concerned that because President George W. Bush had threatened to veto the unemployment provisions including them could provoke a veto fight that would slow the supplemental at a time when the Pentagon was urging quick action.

Supplemental spending bill. Although it took longer than Democratic leaders hoped, the supplemental spending bill became the vehicle for enacting the extension of jobless benefits into law. The House attached a large package of domestic provisions to the supplemental that included a thirteen-week extension of unemployment benefits in all states, plus an additional thirteen weeks in states where the jobless rate was 6 percent or higher. The House adopted the amendment on domestic programs 256–166 on May 15. The Senate revised other parts of the amendment but left the unemployment provisions unchanged before adopting it 75–22 on May 22. *(HR 2642 details, p. 387)*

After weeks of negotiations, House Democrats reached agreement on the overall bill with the White House and the chamber's GOP leadership. The House agreed to the compromise on June 19 in the form of two amendments. The portion on domestic programs, including the extended unemployment benefits, was adopted 416–12. The Senate agreed to the House amendment 92–6 on June 26, clearing the entire supplemental for the president.

The unemployment provisions were less generous than either chamber had proposed. They did not include extra compensation for the hardest-hit states, and the bill required twenty weeks of work before an unemployed worker could collect the extended federal benefit, a restriction that House Republicans had fought to include.

SECOND EXTENSION

On Sept. 26, House Democrats passed a new $61 billion stimulus bill (HR 7110) that included an additional seven weeks of federal unemployment benefits, plus another thirteen weeks in states with high jobless rates. The vote was 264–158. Republicans blocked the Senate from taking up the measure.

Shortly before adjourning for the election campaign, House leaders put the unemployment provisions into a separate bill (HR 6867), which the House passed 368–28 on Oct. 3. "Unemployment insurance does not simply help those struggling through tough times," said Majority Leader Steny H. Hoyer, D-Md. "Economists consider it one of the best ways to stimulate our economy." Again, Senate Republicans held up the measure, putting the issue off until the lame-duck session after the elections.

When Congress returned, it was against the backdrop of a deepening economic crisis and an unemployment rate that had reached 6.6 percent in October. Republicans were ready to go along with the temporary extension, and the Senate cleared the House bill by voice vote Nov. 20, after agreeing 89–6 to invoke cloture and proceed to the measure.

Sen. Edward M. Kennedy of Massachusetts reiterated the Democrats' argument that the bill would help stimulate the economy. "Each dollar of unemployment benefits," he said, "generates $1.64 in economic growth. I urge my colleagues to join me in supporting this critical extension of unemployment assistance."

"This dramatic downturn in the economy and surge in unemployment convinced me to support this extension of unemployment coverage," said Republican whip Jon Kyl of Arizona. But Kyl made it clear that he did not buy the argument that the bill would have broader effects. "I do not believe an extension or expansion of federal unemployment benefits stimulates the economy," he said.

President Bush signed the measure into law (PL 110-449) Nov. 21.

MAJOR PROVISIONS

June extension. The 2008 supplemental appropriations legislation (HR 2642—PL 110-252) established a temporary program for individuals who had exhausted their regular twenty-six weeks of compensation by March 28, 2009. The emergency program, which became effective July 6, 2008, provided up to thirteen weeks of federal benefits equal to the amount the person had received under the regular state-run program. To qualify, the person had to have worked for twenty weeks prior to being laid off. Those who had not completed their thirteen weeks of extended benefits by the March 28, 2009, cutoff were able to receive the remaining compensation. President Bush signed the bill June 30.

October extension. The stand-alone bill (HR 6867—PL 110-449) added seven weeks of benefits to the thirteen-week compensation provided in the earlier law. The emergency benefits still applied only to workers who had used up their regular twenty-six weeks by March 28, 2009. Unlike the earlier law, the measure provided an extra thirteen weeks of compensation to people who had worked in states with unemployment rates of 6 percent or higher. President Bush signed the bill Nov. 21.

Union Check Card

Democrats in 2007 won House passage of legislation to make unionizing a workplace almost as simple as circulating a petition, but the measure was blocked by Senate opponents who denied Democrats the sixty votes needed to prevent a filibuster. The legislation did not proceed in 2008 either, leaving it a top priority of organized labor, a traditionally important Democratic Party constituency. But it was vehemently opposed by business groups, which opposed eliminating the right of employers to demand a secret-ballot election before a union could be certified.

Under the legislation (HR 800), sponsored by Rep. George Miller, D-Calif., chairman of the House Education and Labor Committee, employers would no longer be able to insist on a secret-ballot election if a majority of employees signed cards certifying the union, a process known as a card check. A secret ballot would still be available, but only if a majority of workers requested one.

Under existing law, after organizers gathered a majority of the employees' signatures in favor of a union, the employer could insist on a vote by secret ballot. Employers did not always choose to have an election, but if they did, the balloting had to be held before the union could be certified as a bargaining agent for the employees.

Once an election date was set, employers were free to campaign against the union, and many did so actively. Labor groups, led by the AFL-CIO, said the election period gave management an opportunity to coerce workers into opposing the union. Business groups said the opposite was true: Without a secret-ballot election, labor organizers would be able to intimidate workers into backing a union.

The bill also proposed giving the employer and the union the option of moving toward mediation on the first contract if they could not agree within ninety days. If mediation failed to produce a result after thirty days, the parties would go to arbitration, and the results would be binding for two years. Under existing law, the sides had a duty to bargain in good faith but were under no obligation to reach an agreement.

Also, the National Labor Relations Board (NLRB) would have the authority to seek a federal court injunction against an employer if there was "reasonable cause" to believe that the employer had discharged or discriminated against employees, threatened to discharge or discriminate against employees, or engaged in conduct that "significantly interferes" with the rights of employees while organizing. Employers found to have "willfully or repeatedly" violated these employee rights could face civil fines of up to $20,000.

HOUSE ACTION

In a lengthy markup, the House Education and Labor Committee approved HR 800 (H Rept 110-23) by a vote of 26–19 on Feb. 14, 2007. Speaking to the National Association of Manufacturers the same day, Vice President Dick Cheney said President George W. Bush would veto the bill if it cleared Congress. "Our administration rejects any attempt to short-circuit the rights of workers," Cheney said. "We will defend their right to vote 'yes' or 'no' by secret ballot and their right to fair bargaining."

Republican attempts to change the bill during the markup all failed. Thirteen GOP amendments were rejected, including a proposal by Rep. John Kline, R-Minn., to allow workers to use the card-check system to decertify a union, defeated 19–28, and an amendment by Charles Boustany Jr., R-La., to require that cards be signed in the presence of a NLRB representative, rejected 19–28.

The House passed HR 800 by a vote of 241–185 March 1, but the margin was well short of the two-thirds majority needed to override a veto. In a statement of administration policy released the day before the vote, the White House said Bush would veto the bill if Congress sent it to him. "It is a fundamental tenet of democracy that individuals are able to vote their conscience, privately, free from the threat of reprisal," the White House said. "Substituting a 'card-check' mechanism for private ballots would turn back the clock sixty years and return us to a failed system."

SENATE ACTION

The Senate June 26 rejected a motion to limit debate on the bill, effectively killing it for the year. The vote was 51–48, well short of the sixty votes needed to invoke cloture. The outcome was no surprise. "This vote, we all know, is really going to be pro forma," said Arlen Specter, R-Pa., before the roll call. "We have the partisanship lined up to the extreme." Specter was the only Republican supporting the effort to proceed to the bill.

Interest groups reacted swiftly and predictably to the vote: business advocates hailed the action, and prolabor groups assailed it. "We hope this is the last time Congress brings forward a bill that would take away a worker's right to a federally supervised, private-ballot election," said Kirk Pickerel, president and chief executive officer of Associated Builders and Contractors. The pro-union group Americans United for Change said Senate Republicans had "denied middle-class workers a real opportunity to get ahead in a system."

Employment Wage-Gender Discrimination

The House in 2008 passed two bills targeting wage discrimination, but the Senate did not approve either of them. Although the measures died at the end of the closing session of the 109th Congress, Democrats, who were the driving force behind the legislation, promised to try again in 2009 when their majority in both chambers would be larger.

The first bill sought to extend the period of time during which an employee could file a wage discrimination suit. That made it easier for women whose pay was below that of their male counterparts to sue their employers and receive compensation.

LEGISLATIVE ACTION: WAGE DISCRIMINATION

House Democrats passed a bill (HR 2831) in July 2007 that was intended to reverse a Supreme Court decision in a wage-discrimination case. The vote was 225–195. All but two Republicans voted against the bill, and all but six Democrats supported it. The legislation was known as the Ledbetter bill after the name of a person who lost a high-profile discrimination case in the Supreme Court.

The Supreme Court on May 29, 2007, had ruled 5–4, in *Ledbetter v. Goodyear Tire & Rubber Co.,* that under the Civil Rights Act of 1964 (PL 88-352) a worker claiming pay discrimination had to file a suit within 180 days of the date of the alleged discrimination. *(Supreme Court cases, p. 738).*

The case grew out of a complaint filed in 1998 by Lilly Ledbetter, who alleged that during her nineteen-year career at a Goodyear Tire plant in Alabama, her supervisors conspired to pay her less than men doing substantially identical work. A federal jury awarded her back pay, but an appeals court reversed the decision. The Supreme Court ruled that Ledbetter's complaint was "untimely." HR 2831 would have amended the Civil Rights Act to make the 180-day statute of limitations begin anew with each discriminatory paycheck.

Backers of the Ledbetter bill argued that the court decision made it too difficult for many employees to bring legitimate pay-discrimination claims and that it permanently shielded employers from liability once the initial 180-day period had elapsed.

In April 2008 Senate majority leader Harry Reid, D-Nev., planned to bring the measure up for a vote in that chamber. Barbara A. Mikulski, D-Md., the most senior woman in the Senate, sought to rally support. "Women of America: Put your lipstick on; square those shoulders. We've got a hell of a fight," she said. The bill drew strong support from several other women in the Senate, including Republicans Olympia J. Snowe and Susan Collins of Maine.

Republican opponents argued that the bill was not an antidiscrimination measure but an attempt to upend congressional intent behind the Civil Rights Act, which envisioned a statute of limitations for claims of discrimination. They said the measure would open corporations to endless lawsuits.

On April 23, Reid scheduled Senate debate on the bill until 5 p.m., to ensure that Democratic presidential candidates Barack Obama of Illinois and Hillary Rodham Clinton of New York could deliver comments of support on the floor. Democratic senators, however, were unable to rally enough GOP moderates to achieve the sixty-vote majority needed to avert a filibuster and proceed to the bill. The cloture motion was rejected 56–42 on April 23.

The White House issued a statement the day before the cloture vote warning that the president would veto the bill. It said the measure would effectively eliminate any statute of limitations, allowing employees "to bring a claim of pay or other employment-related discrimination years or even decades after the alleged discrimination occurred."

LEGISLATIVE ACTION: GENDER DISCRIMINATION

The House passed the second bill on pay discrimination by a vote of 247–178 on July 31, 2008. However, the margin of support was not enough to overcome a threatened veto. The measure would have shifted the burden of proof in wage discrimination suits from the employee—who was required under existing law to prove that the employer's pay discrepancy was intentional—to the employer, who would have to prove it was not.

The House Education and Labor Committee had approved the bill (HR 1338—H Rept 110-783) 26–17 on July 24. Under the Equal Pay Act (PL 88-38) employers taken to court for paying women less than men for the same job could raise "any factor other than sex" to justify the disparity, regardless of whether the factor was related to the employee's job or to the business. The House-passed bill required that the employer demonstrate that the disparity was based on a factor other than gender, such as education, training, or experience, that was not the result of a gender-based difference and that it was required by "business necessity." That defense would not apply if the employee could prove that an alternative employment practice existed that would serve the same business purpose without producing the pay difference and that the employer refused to adopt the alternative.

According to census data cited by bill supporters, women in 2006 made about 77 cents for every dollar earned by men, a difference that could amount to $2 million over a lifetime of earnings, retirement pay, and Social Security benefits. Opponents said the disparities could be accounted for by other causes, such as women leaving the workforce to have children.

Under the bill, employees could sue for discrimination if they learned that they earned lower wages than similar workers within the same company, even if the employees worked at different locations of a business but in the same country.

Workers who won wage discrimination cases could collect compensatory and punitive damages, not just back pay and liquidity damages, and employers would be barred from retaliating against employees who discussed their pay with one another.

Republicans criticized the bill as duplicative of existing antidiscrimination standards and fodder for frivolous lawsuits. "This bill will make it easier for trial lawyers to cash in, and taxpayers should be outraged that their money is being put to such use," said Rep. Virginia Foxx, R-N.C.

The White House said the changes would "encourage discrimination claims to be made based on factors unrelated to actual pay discrimination." Supporters said the bill would close the loophole in the Equal Pay Act. Rep. George Miller, D-Calif., the House Education and Labor chairman, said the measure was needed to avoid discrimination like that cited in the Ledbetter case. The Senate did not take up the measure in 2008.

Employment Sexual Orientation Discrimination

The House in 2007 passed legislation (HR 3685) to protect gays and lesbians from employment discrimination, but a White House veto threat kept the measure from advancing further in the 110th Congress. Expanding workplace protections was a top priority for House Democrats after the party retook control of Congress in the 2006 elections. Democrats vowed to pass legislation to protect gay, lesbian, bisexual, and transgendered people from workplace discrimination. The House in 2008 also approved two separate bills aimed at wage discrimination, but neither of them made it through the Senate. *(2008 action, p. 669)*

HR 3685 made illegal a refusal to hire or to dismiss an individual, or to otherwise discriminate, based on "actual or perceived sexual orientation." The bill defined sexual orientation as "homosexuality, heterosexuality, or bisexuality." The prohibitions applied to employers, employment agencies, labor organizations, training programs, or associations. An individual alleging discrimination had to demonstrate that the discrimination was intentional. Religious organizations and the armed forces were exempt.

Rep. Barney Frank, D-Mass., introduced broad antidiscrimination legislation (HR 2015) in April that focused on sexual orientation and gender identity. His bill stalled because of a provision to extend the job protections to the transgendered, or people who have had sex changes. Supporting that controversial bill was considered a politically risky move for some Democrats, especially freshmen from Republican-leaning districts. Democrats decided in late September 2007 to put aside the contentious language, which was removed from the new bill, HR 3685, that Frank introduced. HR 3685 also added a broader exemption to ensure churches and religious groups did not have to follow the employment policy.

The move to narrow the effort infuriated human rights groups, who criticized Democrats for backing down on a promise to pass broad legislation. House Speaker Nancy Pelosi, D-Calif., attempted to mitigate the damage by delaying the markup. Frank, who twenty years earlier became the first member of Congress to voluntarily come out as gay, regretted taking out the language. But he warned that pushing the gender identity issue when the support was not there risked future attempts to enact those protections.

Ultimately the House Education and Labor Committee approved the narrower bill 27–21 on Oct. 18, with four Republicans joining a solid majority of Democrats to vote in favor. Four Democrats, angered by the decision to drop the transgender language, voted against it, along with seventeen Republicans.

When the bill reached the House floor, Rep. Tammy Baldwin, D-Wis., tried to revive the gender identity debate, insisting that the bill include protection for transsexuals and cross-dressers. Democratic leaders delayed bringing the bill to the floor for two weeks, using the time to gauge support for an amendment adding Baldwin's categories. On Nov. 7, Baldwin was allowed to offer her amendment but she withdrew it to thwart a GOP attempt to force a recorded vote. The chamber then passed the narrower bill on a **key vote of 235–184 (R 35–159; D 200–25).** *(2007 key votes, p. 955)*

In the Senate, Edward M. Kennedy, D-Mass., indicated he would like to bring the broader issue up in the Senate. But a veto threat raised the threshold for votes—from the sixty needed to end debate—to the sixty-seven that would be required to override a veto. Facing almost certain defeat, Kennedy decided to hold off until the second session of the 110th Congress. But no Senate action occurred in the session either.

CHAPTER 13

Law and Justice

Law and Law Enforcement

Law and justice issues featured a curious dynamic during President George W. Bush's second term: Lawmakers clashed predictably along party lines over politically charged issues, but they formed unusual bipartisan alliances on a number of high-profile initiatives. On one of the top goals of the Bush administration—a sweeping overhaul of immigration law—the emergence of a partnership between Democratic and Republican leaders in the Senate failed to overcome resistance by conservative members. Instead, lawmakers settled for measures to tighten border security despite strong Democratic objections. On several other issues, including genetic discrimination and civil rights legislation, Democratic and Republican leaders worked successfully with each other and the White House.

Enjoying sizable majorities in both chambers in the 109th Congress, Republicans cleared two long-standing conservative priorities: placing restrictions on class action lawsuits and protecting firearms manufacturers and dealers from liability. Both bills enjoyed the support of numerous Democrats. Congress also passed a landmark reauthorization of the 1965 Civil Rights Act, with the White House and congressional leaders in both parties overcoming resistance by a small group of southern Republicans.

But conservatives fell short in other areas, including constitutional amendments to ban flag desecration and same-sex marriage. The setbacks, which were particularly disappointing to their backers given the large Republican majorities, left such issues in limbo. Conservatives also failed to pass legislation that would have provided property owners with streamlined access to federal courts.

Several bills in the 109th Congress resisted resolution because of competing priorities among business groups, and the fierce lobbying sometimes left Republicans divided. Lawmakers could not agree on legislation to crack down on identity theft and fraud, as well as to create a $140 billion trust fund to compensate people sickened by asbestos exposure.

The Democratic-led 110th Congress was defined largely by bitter clashes between Congress and the Justice Department. Democrats and many Republicans assailed the administration's abrupt firings of several U.S. attorneys, with Attorney General Alberto R. Gonzales coming under harsh and often skeptical questioning from lawmakers. His effectiveness greatly diminished, Gonzales announced his resignation in August 2007. Less than three months later, the Senate approved Michael B. Mukasey as attorney general despite considerable Democratic misgivings. Relations between congressional Democrats and the Justice Department remained strained for the remainder of the Bush administration.

Despite such distractions, the 110th Congress cleared two significant pieces of legislation with strong bipartisan support. Lawmakers in 2007, with the backing of the White House, expanded the reach of the 1990 Americans with Disabilities Act. One year later, they agreed to a compromise bill to bar employers and health insurers from discriminating on the basis of genetic information, clearing the legislation overwhelmingly despite objections by some in the business community.

IMMIGRATION

Bush began his second term by focusing on immigration policy. He envisioned a broad and balanced approach that would combine tougher enforcement to reduce illegal immigration with a new guest worker program that would,

REFERENCES

Discussion of law enforcement policy for the years 1945–1964 may be found in *Congress and the Nation Vol. I*, pp. 1671–1676; for the years 1965–1968, *Congress and the Nation Vol. II*, pp. 309–334; for the years 1969–1972, *Congress and the Nation Vol. III*, pp. 255–286; for the years 1973–1976, *Congress and the Nation Vol. IV*, pp. 559–618; for the years 1977–1980, *Congress and the Nation Vol. V*, pp. 715–753; for the years 1981–1984, *Congress and the Nation Vol. VI*, pp. 675–709; for the years 1985–1988, *Congress and the Nation Vol. VII*, pp. 713–784; for the years 1989–1992, *Congress and the Nation Vol. VIII*, pp. 741–799; for the years 1993–1996, *Congress and the Nation Vol. IX*, pp. 679–758; for the years 1997–2001, *Congress and the Nation Vol. X*, pp. 589–683; for the years 2001–2004, *Congress and the Nation Vol. XI*, pp. 581–629.

Outlays for Law Enforcement

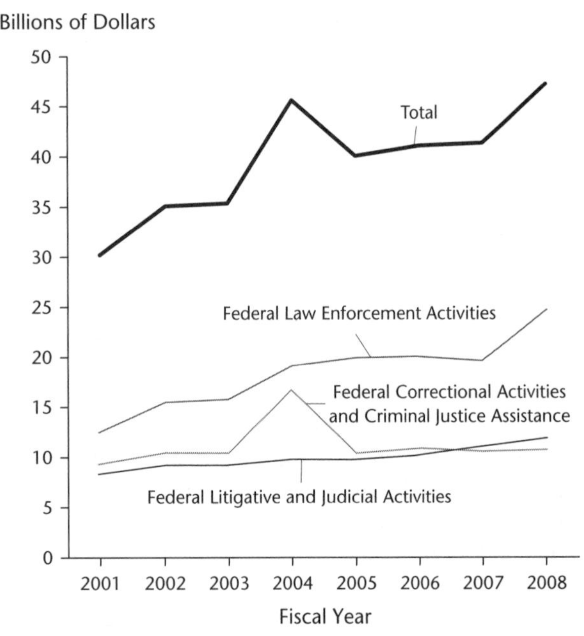

SOURCE: Office of Management and Budget, *Historical Tables, Budget of the United States Government: Fiscal Year 2010* (Washington, D.C.: U.S. Government Printing Office, 2009), Table 3.2.

over time, give illegal immigrants already living in the United States a potential path to citizenship. For three years, from 2005 into 2007, the White House worked with key lawmakers on both sides of the aisle in an effort to clear a comprehensive measure, but immigration politics in both the Republican-led 109th and the Democratic-led 110th Congresses ultimately proved too treacherous.

Political battle lines had been hardening for years over the increasingly charged issue of immigration. By the beginning of 2005, an estimated twelve million illegal aliens were living in the United States and hundreds of thousands of more people each year were illegally crossing the border from Mexico. Anti-immigration sentiment was on the rise amid concerns that the influx was creating competition for jobs, as well as for services such as health care and education. Conservatives such as Rep. Tom Tancredo, R-Colo., wanted to take all possible steps to cut down on illegal immigration, including establishing jail terms for employers who hired illegal immigrants. Meanwhile, many businesses and consumers benefited from the supply of cheap labor, and Latinos—a fast-growing voting bloc—worried about anti-immigration initiatives.

The House in 2005 moved quickly on the issue of border security, which it linked to the need to safeguard the nation against terrorist attacks. At the urging of Judiciary Committee chairman F. James Sensenbrenner Jr., R-Wis., Republicans passed a bill to make it harder for illegal immigrants to seek asylum or get driver's licenses, while removing obstacles to the construction of a fence and other barriers along portions of the U.S.-Mexico border. Despite resistance in the Senate, most of the provisions became law as part of an $82 billion supplemental spending bill for operations in Iraq and Afghanistan.

Lawmakers then spent much of the rest of the 109th Congress battling over a broader bill. Bush made a nationally televised speech to advocate a major overhaul of immigration law that would simultaneously crack down on illegal immigration and allow aliens to enter the country temporarily in a guest worker program that would establish a path to citizenship. But many rank-and-file Republicans, particularly in the House, denounced the Bush plan as amounting to amnesty for illegal immigrants.

The House in 2005 instead passed legislation that emphasized border security and stepped-up enforcement of immigration laws, making it a felony to be in the United States without a visa, establishing a mandatory employee verification system, and requiring tamper-proof identification cards for all workers. In the Senate, however, a number of Republicans sided with Democrats to support the broader concept proposed by Bush. After considerable debate, senators in 2006 passed a comprehensive bill that tracked with Bush's vision of combining border security and work-site enforcement with a guest worker program and a path to citizenship for most of the illegal immigrants in the country. Instead of going to conference, however, House leaders passed a series of narrow bills aimed at border enforcement. Most died at the end of the Congress, but lawmakers cleared a bill authorizing the construction of fencing along the southwestern border with Mexico.

The Democratic takeover in the aftermath of the 2006 elections did little to change the underlying dynamics of immigration politics. Many moderate and conservative Democrats, like their Republican counterparts, thought that a path to citizenship for illegal immigrants was anathema—even if that meant defying their leaders and opposing immigration legislation. The White House early in the 110th Congress worked closely with a bipartisan group of senators to fashion a bill that would pick up the necessary votes from each party, but the legislation ultimately collapsed in 2007 amid a series of failed cloture votes. With the House on the sidelines, reluctant to take up immigration unless the Senate reached consensus, the issue died upon adjournment of Congress.

MIXED RECORD FOR CONSERVATIVES

For conservatives, the 109th Congress provided not only a pair of significant victories but also several disappointing losses. Republicans began by successfully advancing long-sought legislation to limit class action lawsuits. After failing to pass similar legislation in each of the previous three Congresses, GOP leaders took advantage of their increased majorities to clear the measure within weeks, and it was promptly signed into law by Bush. The legislation aimed to move more consumer protection cases into federal courts, which were often perceived as less friendly to plaintiffs. Business interests, led by the U.S. Chamber of

Chief Justice John Roberts reaches out to shake Justice Samuel Alito's hand after swearing him into office on February 1, 2006. Alito was confirmed Tuesday by the Senate on a 58–42 vote.
Source: AP Photo/Ron Edmonds

Commerce, had spent six years and tens of millions of dollars lobbying for the bill's enactment, which ultimately won the backing of several Democrats after supporters agreed to alter and soften some of the provisions.

Later in the year, Congress cleared a top priority of the National Rifle Association: limiting the legal liability of firearms makers and dealers. Lawsuits were posing a threat to the firearms industry, with cities attempting to sue handgun manufacturers over the cost of urban violence. Gun control advocates, frustrated by the pro-gun tilt of lawmakers, viewed such lawsuits as a potential route toward curbing the easy availability of firearms. The legislation, backed by Republicans and a number of rural Democrats, barred civil lawsuits against the firearms industry except in certain cases in which laws were violated, guns were sold with the knowledge they would be used in crimes, or the firearm was defective and resulted in injury.

But conservatives suffered defeats that were particularly stinging given the size of the Republican majorities in Congress. The Senate's failure, by a single vote, to pass a proposed constitutional amendment in 2006 to criminalize desecration of the American flag raised questions about whether that conservative priority would win congressional approval in the foreseeable future. Similarly, supporters of a constitutional amendment to ban gay marriage failed to muster even a simple majority in a 2006 Senate vote. Conservatives also were disappointed when legislation to strengthen the rights of property owners failed to gain traction in the Senate.

A major priority for conservatives throughout the second Bush administration was winning Senate confirmation of judicial nominees. With Senate majority leader Bill Frist, R-Tenn., threatening to take steps in 2005 to end filibusters against proposed judgeships, a group of seven Republicans and seven Democrats—known as the "Gang of 14"—worked out an agreement to vote against filibusters of judicial nominees except in extraordinary circumstances. This opened the way for approval of several appellate court nominees as well as U.S. Supreme Court nominees John G. Roberts Jr. and Samuel A. Alito Jr. But the compromise also ended the confirmation prospects for Bush's most controversial nominees. *(Filibuster change, p. 820; Judicial nominations, box, p. 712; Supreme Court confirmations, box, pp. 728, 729)*

BIPARTISAN VICTORIES

In both the 109th and the 110th Congresses, legislative leaders worked closely with the administration to produce an impressive string of bipartisan victories. Lawmakers in both parties banded together to advance the rights of the disadvantaged and guard against discrimination in certain cases.

Congress in 2006 cleared a reauthorization of the 1965 Voting Rights Act, extending the landmark civil rights law for twenty-five years while clarifying and strengthening certain provisions. The debate brought together legislative leaders from both parties who worked to overcome the objections of a group of mostly southern Republicans. The following year, Congress voted to strengthen protections in the 1990 Americans with Disabilities Act, expanding the category of those classified as disabled and adding protections to the bill. The legislation was a response, in part, to a series of Supreme Court decisions that appeared to narrow the protections in the original law.

Lawmakers in the 110th Congress cleared legislation to bar employers and health insurers from discriminating on the basis of genetic information, breaking a decade-long deadlock over the issue. Business leaders worried that the bill was unnecessary and could lead to frivolous lawsuits, but lawmakers reached a bipartisan compromise that passed each chamber overwhelmingly. The measure, which gained Bush's support, prohibited employers from using genetic screening results in hiring, assignment, or promotion decisions, and it barred insurers from requiring genetic testing or making decisions on enrollment, coverage, or premiums based on the results of such tests.

On other measures, however, conflicting interests prevented lawmakers from reaching consensus even on issues that cut across party lines. In the 109th Congress, Congress failed to coalesce behind a bill to create a $140 billion trust fund to compensate people sickened by asbestos exposure, with lawmakers on both sides of the aisle uneasy about the potential scope of the measure. Members also could not agree over competing proposals aimed at protecting U.S. citizens from identity theft and other types of fraud, with partisan bickering, committee turf wars, and fierce lobbying preventing passage in either chamber. In the 110th Congress, lawmakers who wanted to make changes to patent rules found themselves stymied by the competing interests of powerful industries.

CLASHES WITH THE JUSTICE DEPARTMENT

Almost as soon as the Democrats took control of Congress in 2007, they moved to confront the Justice Department over the abrupt firings of nine U.S. attorneys across the country. The House and Senate Judiciary Committees launched probes that soon escalated into a high-profile clash between the White House and lawmakers who wanted to reassert their oversight prerogatives. During several months of hearings, Gonzales angered lawmakers of both parties by appearing to be evasive while testifying. Some of his statements were contradicted by other officials. Gonzales, who also faced criticism for the handling of a classified surveillance program, announced his resignation in August 2007.

Bush's nomination of Mukasey to succeed Gonzales was initially hailed by Democrats. But Mukasey, a former federal prosecutor and district judge, drew criticism during his Senate Judiciary confirmation hearings when he declined to say whether he considered the interrogation technique of simulated drowning, known as waterboarding, to be torture. Democrats also worried that Mukasey shared the president's robust views of executive power and prerogatives. The Senate approved the nomination in November, but Mukasey won the lowest level of support in a recorded vote for an attorney general nominee since 1952. During his tenure, which continued for the remainder of the administration, he clashed frequently with Democrats who viewed him as putting loyalty to the president above independent judgment.

To prevent a repeat of the scandal over the firing of the U.S. attorneys, lawmakers cleared a bill that repealed a little-noticed provision, passed in 2006, that had allowed the attorney general to appoint permanent interim U.S. attorneys without Senate confirmation. The new bill, supported by Bush, restored a previous limit of 120 days on such appointments.

Chronology of Action on Law Enforcement

2005–2006

GOP leaders in the 109th Congress successfully brought to fruition several long-standing legislative priorities, such as tightening border security, placing new restrictions on class action lawsuits, and protecting gun manufacturers from liability. But they failed to reach a consensus on the politically charged issue of immigration, despite the prodding of President Bush.

Although most contentious issues broke across party lines, immigration left Republicans sharply divided and created unusual alliances across the aisle. Bush and many senators in both parties favored creating a guest worker program that provided illegal immigrants with a path to citizenship. Guided by a rare partnership between Majority Leader Bill Frist, R-Tenn., and Minority Leader Harry Reid, D-Nevada, the Senate passed a bill that combined a guest worker program with stricter border security. Conservatives, however, denounced the guest worker provisions as amounting to amnesty for illegal immigrants. The House took a more hard-line approach, passing legislation that sharply toughened enforcement of immigration laws, especially in the workplace.

The gaps within the Republican Party proved too wide for lawmakers to bridge. Instead, Congress focused on reducing the flow of illegal immigrants from Mexico. With the House taking the lead, lawmakers cleared legislation early in 2005 to made it harder for illegal immigrants to seek asylum or get driver's licenses. Shortly before the 2006 elections, lawmakers authorized the construction of hundreds of miles of fencing along the southwestern border.

With comfortable majorities in both chambers, Republicans generally united behind bills that reflected traditional conservative priorities. They scored a major victory by clearing legislation to limit class action lawsuits. The new law, strongly backed by the U.S. Chamber of Commerce and supported by a number of Democratic lawmakers, aimed to move more consumer protection cases into federal courts, often considered less friendly to plaintiffs. Republicans also handed the National Rifle Association a key win with legislation that limited lawsuits against firearms manufacturers and dealers. The bill, which drew support from some Democrats, was spurred by concerns that the lawsuits could otherwise pose a major threat to the firearms industry.

Republican and Democratic leaders joined forces in the second session to clear a reauthorization of the 1965 Voting Rights Act, overcoming the objections of a group of mostly southern Republicans. Symbolizing the bipartisan nature of the reauthorization bill, more than two dozen lawmakers from both parties and both chambers descended the Capitol steps to announce the introduction of identical versions of the legislation—a sharp contrast with the law's initial enactment, which generated vigorous dissent from segregationist southern Democrats in Congress.

A number of other issues, however, resisted resolution. Despite efforts throughout the 109th Congress to enact legislation aimed at protecting U.S. citizens from identity theft and other types of fraud, the combination of partisan bickering, a turf war among committee chairs, and fierce lobbying prevented passage in either chamber. Efforts to establish a $140 billion trust fund to compensate people sickened by asbestos exposure died in the face of a filibuster, partly over conservative concerns that taxpayers could end up footing the bill. Conservatives fell short in an effort to provide property owners with streamlined access to federal courts, and they failed to muster the needed two-thirds majorities to pass constitutional amendments on such politically charged issues as same-sex marriage and flag desecration.

Border Security

At the start of the first session of the 109th Congress, House Republicans won quick enactment of legislation to crack down on illegal immigrants and tighten U.S. border security. The House passed the provisions in February 2005 as a separate bill (HR 418), most of which became law as part of an $82 billion supplemental spending bill for operations in Iraq and Afghanistan. President George W. Bush

JUSTICE LEADERSHIP

Attorney General Alberto Gonzales announces his resignation during a press conference at the Department of Justice on August 27, 2007. *Source: AP Photo/Pablo Martinez Monsivais*

Leadership of the Justice Department changed hands twice during President George W. Bush's second term, while the department was awash in controversy over interrogation techniques used on prisoners, firing of a group of U.S. attorneys, intelligence surveillance methods, and other issues.

Alberto R. Gonzales

Bush in 2005 chose Alberto R. Gonzales to replace John Ashcroft, who served as attorney general during the president's first term. Gonzales had been part of Bush's inner circle of advisers since Bush was governor of Texas in the 1990s. He was Bush's gubernatorial counsel for three years before Bush tapped him to be Texas secretary of state and then a Texas Supreme Court justice. Gonzales was White House counsel during Bush's first term. *(Department leadership, 2001–2005, Congress and the Nation Vol. XI, p. 586)*

The Senate confirmed Gonzales as attorney general on Feb. 3, 2005, by a vote of 60–36. It was the most votes cast against any of Bush's second-term cabinet nominees to that time.

Upon convening of the Democratic-led 110th Congress in 2007, the Senate Judiciary Committee opened an investigation into the Justice Department's 2006 dismissal of nine U.S. attorneys. Although the president had the authority to dismiss U.S. attorneys, critics charged that the department's actions were politically motivated with the goal of either punishing prosecutors for taking steps that could damage the Republican Party or installing prosecutors who were more reliably loyal to the administration. Most of the fired attorneys had received positive performance reviews at the Department of Justice.

In testimony at congressional hearings and in news conferences, Gonzales made conflicting statements and appeared to be unaware of some of the basic workings of his department. Lawmakers accused him of deliberately misleading Congress and charged that the administration had politicized the quasi-independent department to serve its own ends.

Gonzales's insistence that none of the dismissals were political was contradicted by congressional testimony from other administration officials and from several of the fired prosecutors. E-mail messages on the issue released by the Justice Department, and the administration's shifting rationale for the firings, added to growing calls for Gonzales to resign or be fired.

During a Senate Judiciary hearing in April, Gonzales said he had no intention of leaving his post. He apologized for the handling of the firings but stood by the decision to replace the prosecutors. He took responsibility but repeatedly painted the target list of U.S. attorneys as wholly the work of other department officials. His inability to recall several details about the firings left committee members from both parties incredulous.

The turning point for many came in May over the separate issue of intelligence surveillance. The attorney general had testified before the Senate Judiciary Committee in February 2006 that no serious disagreement existed among Justice Department officials about the legality of a presidentially confirmed National Security Agency (NSA) program of warrantless surveillance that the administration dubbed the "Terrorist Surveillance Program."

But on May 15, former deputy attorney general James Comey appeared to contradict the attorney general's assertion. Comey vividly described a 2004 showdown between the Justice Department and the White House over renewal of a classified surveillance program at the intensive-care-unit bedside of then–Attorney General Ashcroft. Comey recounted how he ordered his security detail to turn on the sirens so he could race to George Washington University Hospital the night of March 10, 2004, after he learned that Gonzales and Andrew H. Card Jr. were en route there to try to persuade Ashcroft to sign papers renewing the program. Gonzales was White House counsel at the time, and Card was Bush's chief of staff. Comey testified that although his boss was clearly ailing, he raised his head long enough to express his refusal to do so "in very strong terms." Ashcroft was suffering from acute pancreatitis and had formally turned over the running of Justice to Comey, who had balked at approving the renewal.

The administration, Comey said, went ahead with the program without Justice's approval, which was required under procedures set up by the White House. Comey testified that he decided he had to resign and that a mass resignation was averted only after Bush intervened and gave Comey and Federal Bureau of Investigation director Robert S. Mueller III the authority to force changes to the program.

At a contentious Senate Judiciary hearing July 24, Democrats, along with ranking Republican Arlen Specter of Pennsylvania, questioned Gonzales about the hospital trip, the firings of the U.S. attorneys, and other matters. Gonzales testified that he went to Ashcroft's hospital room with Card after an "emergency meeting" in the White House Situation Room earlier that day among senior administration officials, congressional leaders, and the top members of the House and Senate Intelligence Committees. He said the visit "was about other intelligence activities." He said, "It was not about the Terrorist Surveillance Program that the president announced to the American people." A Justice Department spokesman backed up Gonzales, saying that the disagreement at the hospital concerned "intelligence activities that have not been publicly disclosed and that remain highly classified."

Two days after Gonzales's testimony, Mueller, who arrived at the hospital and spoke with Ashcroft after Gonzales and Card had left, said the discussion the two officials had with Ashcroft "was on . . . an NSA program that has been much discussed, yes."

Four Senate committee Democrats—Dianne Feinstein of California, Charles E. Schumer of New York, Russ Feingold of Wisconsin, and Sheldon Whitehouse of Rhode Island—asked the Justice Department to appoint a special counsel to investigate whether Gonzales had lied under oath to Congress. Feinstein, Feingold, and Whitehouse also served on the Senate Intelligence Committee.

On June 11, the Senate rejected 53–38 a procedural motion on a sense-of-the-Senate resolution (S J Res 14) stating that Gonzales "no longer holds the confidence of the Senate and of the American people." Although a majority supported cloture, the tally was seven votes short of the sixty needed, killing the resolution.

But the attorney general's lack of credibility with lawmakers was starkly apparent in July when the White House was pushing for a rewrite of a federal law on intelligence surveillance. Lawmakers balked because the administration's proposal gave the attorney general a significant role in authorizing electronic surveillance for counterterrorism purposes. However, they ultimately cleared a six-month bill (S 1927—PL 110-55) shortly before the August recess. *(Intelligence legislation, p. 249)*

Gonzales steadfastly defied bipartisan calls for his resignation. Then, on Aug. 27, he announced that he had told Bush the day before that he would leave his post Sept. 17. Bush said Gonzales was "impeded from doing important work because his good name was dragged through the mud for political reasons." Most Democrats and some Republicans saw it differently. "Alberto Gonzales was never the right man for this job. He lacked independence; he lacked judgment; and he lacked the spine to say no to top White house officials," said Senate majority leader Harry Reid, D-Nev.

Michael B. Mukasey

To replace Gonzales, Bush on Sept. 17, 2007, announced his choice of Michael B. Mukasey, who had been a federal prosecutor and a district court judge in New York before returning to private practice in 2006.

From the outset, Senate Judiciary Committee members seemed relieved to be in the process of replacing Gonzales. However, Democrats knew that Mukasey did not agree with them on the substance of many policy questions. Lawmakers sought to measure whether the nominee could distance himself from controversial administration policies and whether he would be willing to stand up to the White House.

The panel approved Mukasey's nomination by 11–8 on Nov. 6. During the committee hearing held Oct. 17 and Oct. 18, Mukasey sought to allay any concerns that he would be beholden to the White House or unwilling to cooperate with Congress. He said he would not tolerate politicization of the Justice Department, and he said he would resign if he could not persuade the president not to pursue a policy that Mukasey saw as unconstitutional. But the nominee also made it clear that the days of Democrats clashing with the Bush Justice Department were not necessarily over, especially on issues related to executive power. Mukasey indicated that he might agree with the administration's stance that Bush had the authority to withhold information from Congress, skirt federal statutes, and authorize harsh interrogation techniques.

The full Senate confirmed Mukasey Nov. 8 as the eighty-first attorney general of the United States on a **key vote of 53–40 (R 46–0; D 6–39; I 1–1).** He garnered the lowest level of support in a recorded vote for an attorney general nominee since 1952. All but one of the "no" votes were from Democrats, with Independent Bernard Sanders of Vermont joining them. *(2007 key votes, p. 955)*

Democratic discontent with Mukasey became more pronounced during his tenure. When he appeared before the Senate Judiciary Committee on Jan. 30, 2008, Democrats applauded some of his steps at the Justice Department, such as limiting the department's contacts with the White House and launching a criminal probe into the destruction of Central Intelligence Agency interrogation tapes. However, the substance of his firm defense of presidential prerogatives against inquiries by both Republicans and Democrats seemed little different from that of Gonzales. For instance, Mukasey flatly refused to say whether waterboarding amounted to torture and maintained that it could be appropriate in some scenarios.

As attorney general, Mukasey took additional stands that angered Democrats. He argued that Congress should grant retroactive immunity to communications companies for cooperating with the administration's warrantless surveillance of Americans for more than five years after Sept. 11, 2001. He stymied congressional attempts to uncover the role played by senior White House aides in the firings of U.S. attorneys, although he appointed a special prosecutor in October 2008 to probe the firings after the Justice Department's inspector general and its Office of Professional Responsibility released a joint report that called the process surrounding the firings "fundamentally flawed."

Mukasey also seconded administration policy in its widespread application of the state secrets privilege. The Bush White House invoked the privilege in reacting to lawsuits challenging its surveillance and detention policies, saying it should not have to turn over evidence, if it became public, that could harm national security. Judges had generally sided with the administration when it has invoked such a privilege. Democrats proposed legislation that would narrow the privilege and instruct judges how to apply it. But Mukasey argued that the privilege, which was endorsed by the Supreme Court during the cold war, was rooted in the U.S. Constitution.

Democrats came to view Mukasey as little more than a caretaker, guarding administration interests as the Bush presidency came to an end. Despite the disagreements, tensions between congressional Democrats and Mukasey did not reach the level of the tensions with Gonzales. Mukasey showed enough threads of independence from the White House to tamp down criticism and proved more agile in managing relations with Congress.

signed that bill (HR 1268—PL 109-13) on May 11. *(Supplemental appropriations, pp. 78, 276, 281, 348)*

The driving force behind the legislation was House Judiciary Committee chairman F. James Sensenbrenner Jr., R-Wis., who said his intent was to "prevent another 9/11-type terrorist attack by disrupting terrorist travel." The bill made it harder for illegal immigrants to seek asylum or get driver's licenses and removed some obstacles to the construction of physical barriers along portions of the U.S.-Mexico border.

Most of the provisions had been included in the 2004 intelligence overhaul bill (PL 108-458), but House Republican leaders agreed to drop them as the price of getting the measure through the Senate. To placate an infuriated Sensenbrenner, they promised that the provisions would be included in the first must-move piece of legislation in 2005. *(Intelligence overhaul, Congress and the Nation Vol. XI, p. 263)*

BACKGROUND

Immigration loomed as a contentious issue as the 109th Congress convened, pitting Republicans against one another. Lawmakers such as Sensenbrenner believed Congress and the administration should make a priority of securing the borders and deporting illegal aliens already in the United States. But President Bush and many others within the GOP wanted to make it easier for immigrants to enter the country and take lower-skilled jobs that Americans would not fill.

As chairman of the House panel with jurisdiction over immigration, Sensenbrenner had the power to broker or block immigration legislation and could derail an administration initiative to create a class of guest worker visas. Sensenbrenner had demonstrated at the end of the 108th Congress that he was not afraid to raise a ruckus about illegal immigration, even when it meant threatening a top Bush administration priority to make his point. The Wisconsin conservative blocked a vote on a conference agreement to legislation overhauling the nation's intelligence agencies (PL 108-458) because it did not include a series of House-passed immigration restrictions, including language that would make it easier to deport illegal immigrants without judicial review. Sensenbrenner backed down only after winning assurances from House leaders that some of the provisions would be revived early in the 109th Congress and attached to the first must-pass bill of the year, such as a supplemental spending bill for military operations in Iraq and Afghanistan or a similar measure to provide aid to tsunami-stricken countries in South Asia. He indicated that he might not work to advance other immigration proposals, such as Bush's guest worker initiative, unless his provisions were enacted.

With the promise of House leaders that the bill would be quickly moved to the floor, Sensenbrenner bypassed the Judiciary Committee. He focused on three provisions: preventing illegal immigrants from obtaining driver's licenses, making it more difficult for foreigners to claim political asylum in the United States, and closing a three-mile gap in a fence on the California-Mexico border. Sensenbrenner opted not to revive a more incendiary provision allowing deportation without judicial review.

The Judiciary chairman described his bill as aimed at "terrorist travel," not illegal immigrants. His proposals had their roots in recommendations by the National Commission on Terrorist Attacks Upon the United States (Sept. 11 commission). For example, the legislation would require people applying for, or seeking renewal of, state-issued driver's licenses and identification (ID) cards to prove their "lawful presence" in the United States. According to the Sept. 11 commission, the nineteen terrorists who carried out the 2001 attacks had a total of thirteen driver's licenses and twenty-one ID cards. *(Sept. 11 commission, Congress and the Nation Vol. XI, p. 275; action on recommendations, p. 245)*

Under Sensenbrenner, the House Judiciary Committee had become a key center of support for proposals to tighten immigration restrictions. Sensenbrenner and many senior Republicans on the committee, as well as some members of the House GOP leadership, believed the government should spend more resources on preventing illegal immigrants from entering the country and deporting those already in the country. But immigrant advocacy groups contended that strengthening the border was not the only solution for what all sides described as a crisis of illegal immigration.

In the Senate, Judiciary chairman John Cornyn R-Texas, took a more moderate approach, supporting Bush's guest worker proposal. Some other Senate Republicans and most Senate Democrats favored even more liberalized immigration policies. Backed by immigrant advocacy interest groups, as well as the influential business lobby the U.S. Chamber of Commerce, they advocated sweeping measures that would cover workers in other industries or allow all law-abiding illegal immigrants to stay in the country.

Sensenbrenner wanted his enforcement bill to move separately from any measures that would liberalize immigration. By attaching his bill to a must-pass appropriations measure, Sensenbrenner hoped to avoid seeing it come back from the Senate carrying a guest worker program or other provisions to liberalize immigration. But Senate majority leader Bill Frist, R-Tenn., aimed to keep the immigration language out of the supplemental in his chamber for fear it would cause major delays.

HOUSE ACTION

The House wasted no time on Sensenbrenner's bill (HR 418), which he dubbed the "Real ID Act." After easily defeating several Democratic amendments aimed at scaling it back, lawmakers passed the bill on Feb. 10, 2005, on a **key vote of 261–161 (R 219–8; D 42–152; I 0–1)** in one of their first major legislative actions of the year. House GOP leaders planned to attach the provisions to an anticipated supplemental spending bill for

Iraq and Afghanistan as soon as Bush requested the funds. *(2005 key votes, p. 915)*

Despite the quick approval, a number of the bill's provisions attracted considerable controversy.

Asylum. The White House issued a statement the day before the vote saying it "strongly" supported the Sensenbrenner asylum bill. Bush was promoting a policy that stressed border security and a guest worker visa program that would allow immigrants to fill low-skill jobs. His support for the legislation was seen as part of his effort to woo reluctant Republicans who opposed any initiatives they saw as giving "amnesty" to lawbreakers.

Under the bill, applicants for asylum would be required to prove that race, religion, nationality, membership in a particular social group, or political opinion was, or would be, a "central reason" for their persecution. In some cases, immigration judges could require applicants to provide corroborating evidence to back up their claims. There would be "no presumption of credibility" on the part of an asylum applicant, meaning the burden of proof would be on the person seeking asylum.

The legislation also would give immigration judges broader authority to weigh the credibility of people seeking asylum in the United States. Judges could determine credibility based on demeanor or the consistency of an applicant's written or oral statements, including those not made under oath.

Critics said the language would impose an unfairly high barrier for refugees seeking asylum, who might be forced to seek corroborating evidence from their persecutors. Religious organizations and human rights groups said that judges might question an applicant's credibility based on cultural differences. For instance, an applicant might cast his or her eyes down and avoid eye contact as a sign of respect—an action that could lead a judge to question the refugee's honesty. Supporters responded that the bill would simply give immigration judges the discretion that judges in other civil and criminal proceedings already had.

The House on Feb. 10 rejected 185–236 an attempt by Jerrold Nadler, D-N.Y., and Kendrick B. Meek, D-Fla., to strike the asylum provisions.

Driver's licenses. The National Conference of State Legislatures opposed the driver's license provisions, saying they would be costly and burdensome for states to implement. But many lawmakers, particularly those from states that would not see dramatic changes under the legislation, said the language made sense. Ten states did not require people to show they had a lawful presence in the United States before issuing them driver's licenses. An eleventh state, Tennessee, issued separate driver's licenses and certificates for those who could prove legal residency and for those who could not.

Border fence. Under the bill, the secretary of homeland security could waive all laws that impeded the construction of physical barriers and roads designed to curb illegal border crossings. Judicial review of the decision would not be allowed. The provision was designed to spur the completion of a fence on the border near San Diego, which had a three-mile gap near a canyon called "Smuggler's Gulch." The project had been delayed because of environmental concerns.

Critics said that while they did not necessarily object to completing the fence, the provisions were too broad. Under the language, any local, state, or federal laws—whether governing child labor, competition for federal contracts, or environmental protection—could be overruled to expedite physical barriers to curb illegal border crossings. Jane Harman, D-Calif., said it would set a "dangerous precedent" by placing the secretary of homeland security "above all laws."

The House on Feb. 10 rejected 179–243 an attempt by Sam Farr, D-Calif., to delete the border fence provisions.

With widespread criticism of the fence and asylum provisions, it appeared that the most likely part of the bill to make its way into law would be keeping illegal immigrants from getting driver's licenses.

A month after the House passed Sensenbrenner's bill, GOP leaders added the provisions from HR 418 to the supplemental (HR 1268) as part of the rule for floor debate (H Res 151). The rule was adopted by voice vote on March 15. The House passed the supplemental 388–43 on March 16. *(Driver's license restrictions, p. 685)*

Despite Frist's statements that he preferred to handle the crackdown on illegal immigrants in a separate bill, House Republicans said they were confident that the provisions would eventually be included in the supplemental sent to the president.

SENATE ACTION

Senate appropriators pointedly excluded immigration provisions from their version of the supplemental (HR 1268—S Rept 109-52). But senators immediately began offering amendments once the bill reached the floor. The debate sidetracked action on the spending bill for nearly a week, but in the end the only major amendment adopted was a proposal to allow more seasonal workers into the country.

The amendment, by Barbara A. Mikulski, D-Md., exempted seasonal workers who had worked in the United States in previous years from a cap on the number of so-called H-2B visas issued nationwide. Amendment backers said the cap of 66,000 had been reached early in the fiscal year, leaving an insufficient workforce for the summer tourism and seafood-harvesting seasons. Hotels, restaurants, and the crab and lobster industries were particularly dependent on temporary immigrants. The amendment, adopted 94–6 on April 19, was not expected to complicate negotiations with House Republicans.

A separate amendment by Jon Kyl, R-Ariz., requiring the Department of Homeland Security to certify that the visa recipients were returning workers was adopted by voice vote on April 19. The Senate also gave voice-vote approval on April 19 and April 21, respectively, to proposals to redirect unused visas toward foreign nurses and increase the number of visas available for highly skilled Australian workers.

The Senate was able to vote on Mikulski's amendment because supporters secured the sixty votes needed to cut off debate. Senators refused to limit debate on competing amendments addressing the legal status of temporary agricultural workers.

An amendment by Saxby Chambliss, R-Ga., would have created a temporary guest worker program for farm laborers. Eligible workers could work in the United States for up to nine years, but they could not obtain permanent resident status without returning home for at least a year and waiting in line with other applicants for green cards. A cloture motion on the amendment failed 21–77 on April 19.

Larry E. Craig, R-Idaho, and Edward M. Kennedy, D-Mass., offered a competing amendment that would have created a two-step process for agricultural workers to apply for temporary and then permanent legal residency status. A cloture motion failed 53–45 on April 19.

The two guest worker amendments, and another by Dianne Feinstein, D-Calif., that would have expressed the sense of the Senate that immigration provisions should not be included in the final bill, were all ruled nongermane and thrown out after the Senate voted 100–0 on April 10 to cut off debate on the underlying bill. The Senate passed the supplemental 99–0 on April 21.

CONFERENCE AND FINAL ACTION

The conference agreement on the supplemental spending bill kept the House immigration provisions largely intact. Sensenbrenner credited the White House with ensuring that the language was included in the final bill. The House adopted the conference report (H Rept 109-72) by a vote of 368–58 on May 5. The Senate cleared the bill 100–0 on May 10.

Senate conferees won a few concessions that softened some House language, but sponsors and opponents agreed they made changes only at the margins. "Democrats were shut out of all negotiations in conference, and none of our concerns were addressed," said John Conyers Jr. of Michigan, the ranking Democrat on House Judiciary.

In the main changes, conferees agreed to

- Remove language that would have allowed deportation of asylum applicants while their cases were pending in federal court.
- Modify the grounds for seeking asylum to state that the applicant had to establish that race, religion, nationality, membership in a particular social group, or political opinion was or would be "at least one central reason" for his or her persecution. Critics of the original asylum language credited Sen. Sam Brownback, R-Kan., a conferee on the bill, for incorporating the changes.
- Allow federal district courts to hear claims that actions by the homeland security secretary in waiving existing laws to build the border fence were unconstitutional.
- Allow states to issue two tiers of driving documents: one for federal purposes, and a lower-tier document that would authorize driving for one year without proof of legal residency. The latter had to state that it was not acceptable by federal agencies and must have a unique design or color to alert federal agencies to that fact.

MAJOR PROVISIONS

Following are the major asylum and border security provisions included in the supplemental legislation, which President Bush signed into law (HR 1268—PL 109-13) on May 11, 2005. *(Supplemental, pp. 78, 276, 281, 348)*

Asylum

Central reasons. Required applicants for refugee status to establish that race, religion, nationality, membership in a particular social group, or political opinion was, or would be, at least one "central reason" for their persecution.

Corroboration. Specified that the applicant's testimony alone without corroboration could be sufficient to satisfy this requirement if his or her testimony was credible, was persuasive, and referred to specific facts that demonstrated that he or she was a refugee.

Credibility. In reviewing the application, allowed the judge to weigh the credibility of the testimony along with other evidence. Among other factors, a judge could base his or her determination of credibility on the demeanor, candor, or responsiveness of the applicant or witness, as well as the plausibility of the testimony and the consistency between written and oral statements. If the judge did make an adverse determination of credibility, there was a presumption of credibility upon appeal. (Similar standards for credibility applied to immigrants seeking a stay of their deportation order.)

Application. Made provisions related to conditions for granting asylum effective on the date of enactment and applicable only to individuals who applied on or after that date. Made provisions regarding standards of review for reversing determinations applicable on the date of enactment and applicable retroactively to all final deportation orders issued before or after that date.

Cap lifted. Lifted a cap that limited the number of people granted asylum in the United States who could have their status adjusted to permanent resident each year (ten thousand in 2005) and removed a separate one entirely that limited the number of applicants who could be admitted for escaping coercive population control methods.

Exclusion and removal

Inadmissibility. Expanded the terrorism-related justifications for denying admission to the United States under the Immigration and Nationality Act (INA). Barred admission of any person who had engaged in or incited terrorist activity, was a representative of a terrorist organization or group that espoused terrorist activity, or endorsed or espoused terrorist activity or persuaded others to do so. Denied admission to persons who had received military-type training from terrorist organizations, and the spouse and children of someone deemed inadmissible if the activity serving as the basis for the denial occurred within the five years prior to application.

Engaging in terrorist activities. Expanded the definition of terrorist activities to include gathering information on potential targets; soliciting funds for terrorist activities and organizations; soliciting individuals to engage in conduct or membership in terrorist organizations; and providing material support, including safe houses, transportation, communications, funds, false documents, weapons, or training. Narrowed an exception that previously protected those who did not know their actions would further a terrorist organization's goals so that it protected only those who could demonstrate that they did not know and should not reasonably have known that it was a terrorist organization.

Terrorist organization. Expanded the definition of a terrorist organization to include groups of two or more people, whether organized or not, who engaged in the terrorist activities, even if the group had not been designated by the State Department as a terrorist organization.

Waiver. Gave the secretary of state, in consultation with the attorney general and homeland security secretary, sole authority to waive the inadmissibility of people who represented political, social, or other groups that endorsed or espoused terrorist activity, those who endorsed or espoused terrorist activity or persuaded others to do so, or those who provided material support to organizations engaging in terrorist activities.

Made the waiver authority unavailable if removal proceedings had already been started against the person. Required the secretaries of state and homeland security to provide Congress a report identifying individual recipients of the waiver within ninety days of the fiscal year and within a week of waiving inadmissibility of a group.

Removal. Provided that any immigrant considered inadmissible would also be deportable on the same grounds as detailed above, thereby erasing the previous distinction that made it easier to deny entry to those outside the country than remove those already in the United States legally.

Judicial review. Aligned restrictions on judicial review of orders of removal with the Immigration and Nationality Act so that statutory and nonstatutory habeas corpus review was barred wherever it was barred in the INA. Allowed an exception for judicial review of "constitutional claims or questions of law," but such cases could be brought only in a U.S. court of appeals, not in lower federal district courts. Transferred to circuit courts all cases challenging removal orders that were pending in district courts the day the law was enacted.

U.S.-Mexico Border Fence

Waiver. Gave the homeland security secretary the authority to waive all legal requirements to build barriers and roads.

Judicial review. Required legal challenges to the homeland security secretary's waiver decision to allege constitutional violations and filed only in U.S. district courts. Allowed only the U.S. Supreme Court to hear appeals, thereby excluding the appeals courts from review.

Driver's Licenses

Federal use. Prohibited driver's licenses that did not meet the requirements set out in the law from being used by federal agencies for any official purpose, beginning three years after enactment. Required a state-issued driver's license or identification card that did not satisfy the requirements to state on its face that it was not acceptable for federal identification or other purposes. Required such licenses to use a unique design or color to indicate that they were not acceptable for federal purposes. (The law did not set a time for states to comply with the new requirements, other than the three-year deadline.)

License physical features. Required licenses to include the driver's full legal name, date of birth, gender, driver's license or identification card number, digital photo, address of principal residence, and signature. Required the licenses to have "physical security features" designed to prevent anyone from changing or duplicating them and to use a common machine-readable technology.

Issuance requirements. Required an applicant for a license to present, and states to verify the authenticity of, a photo identity document, documentation showing the applicant's date of birth, proof of a Social Security number, and documentation showing the applicant's name and address of principal residence.

Required applicants to provide valid documentary evidence that they were lawfully in the United States as citizens; that they were immigrants lawfully admitted for permanent or temporary residency; that they were recipients of or applicants for conditional permanent status, asylum, or refugee status; or that they had a valid unexpired nonimmigrant visa.

Permitted applicants who had a pending asylum application or pending approval for temporary protected status, had approved deferred action status, or had a pending application for adjustment of status to permanent residency to be issued only a temporary driver's license or temporary identification card.

Specified that temporary licenses and identification cards were valid only during the time the applicant was authorized to stay in the United States, or for one year in instances in which the period was indefinite. Allowed these licenses to be renewed only if the applicant's stay was extended by the Department of Homeland Security. Licenses that were not temporary could not be valid for more than eight years.

Document verification. Required states, before issuing a license or identification card, to verify the validity and completeness of all documents with the agencies that issued them. Prohibited states from accepting any foreign documents other than official passports. Required states, by Sept. 11, 2005, to agree to routinely use an automated system, the Systematic Alien Verification for Entitlements, maintained by the Department of Homeland Security, to verify the legal presence of persons other than U.S. citizens. Required applicants' Social Security numbers to be confirmed with the Social Security Administration.

Record maintenance and access. Required states to retain digital copies of documents presented by applicants and take digital pictures of them, and to retain the digital copies for ten years, or paper copies for seven years. Required states to provide other states with electronic access to their motor vehicle data base that contained all the data printed on the driver's licenses or identification cards as well as the license holders' histories of violations and suspensions.

Counterfeits. Made it unlawful to traffic in either false or actual authentication features used in false documents. Provided that information about persons convicted of using false driver's licenses at airports be included in aviation security screening data bases.

Funding. Authorized the homeland security secretary to make grants to help states conform to the new driver's license standards, and authorized "such sums as may be necessary to carry out this title."

Border Infrastructure

Threat assessment. Directed the Homeland Security Department to study "the technology, equipment, and personnel needed to address security vulnerabilities within the United States" for all Bureau of Customs and Border Protection field offices that had responsibility for border regions, and required follow-up studies, with findings, conclusions, and legislative recommendations, to Congress at least every five years.

Ground surveillance technologies. Directed the Homeland Security and Defense Departments to begin work on a pilot program within six months of enactment that would use ground surveillance technologies such as video cameras, sensors, and motion detectors along the border, and report the results to Congress.

Information sharing. Directed the Homeland Security Department to begin work on a plan within six months of enactment to integrate communications among federal, state, and local government agencies and Indian tribal agencies regarding border security, and report the results to Congress.

Worker Visas

Seasonal workers. Lifted the annual cap (66,000 in 2005) on the number of H-2B visas issued annually to people who had held temporary jobs in the United States for one of the three previous years.

Australia. Increased the number of visas available for highly skilled Australian workers to 10,500.

Nurses. Directed up to 50,000 visas that were unused for other purposes between 2001 and 2004 to foreign nurses.

Immigration

A concerted push by President George W. Bush for a new immigration policy was not enough to overcome deep divisions among Republicans, particularly over the question of creating a guest worker program. Bush used news conferences, meetings with lawmakers, and a nationally televised speech to call for what he termed "comprehensive immigration reform" in legislation that would crack down on illegal immigrants while also allowing aliens to enter the country temporarily to work.

The same fate awaited immigration reform in the 110th Congress. *(110th Congress action, p. 711)*

But memories of Sept. 11, 2001, terrorists who exploited immigration laws and the reality of twelve million illegal immigrants living in the United States prompted many rank-and-file House Republicans, in particular, to demand that Congress concentrate on securing the border and cracking down on illegal aliens. As a result, even though the 109th Congress began with passage of a border security bill (HR 1268—PL 109-13) and ended with legislation on constructing a border fence (HR 6061—PL 109-367), lawmakers failed to agree on broader immigration policy. *(Border security, p. 679; Border fence, p. 694)*

The House passed a bill (HR 4437) in December 2005 that focused on border security and tough enforcement of immigration laws, especially in the workplace. The centerpiece of the legislation was a mandatory employee verification system and tamper-proof identification cards for all workers. The bill, sponsored by Judiciary Committee chairman F. James Sensenbrenner, R-Wis., would have made it a felony to be in the United States without a visa and would have punished those found aiding illegal immigrants, including humanitarian workers and clergy.

The legislation drew praise from the most vocal opponents of illegal immigration, but business groups, religious leaders, and immigrants' rights advocates complained that it would make felons out of illegal immigrants caught working in the United States, ignoring the fact that these immigrants provided a vital labor pool for some industries. Anger over the bill, especially among Latinos, led during the spring to huge protests in some of the nation's largest cities.

The Senate took a different approach, with a sizable group of Republicans joining Democrats in supporting the broader concept proposed by Bush. After six Judiciary Committee markups and two weeks of floor debate, the Senate passed a bill (S 2611) in May 2006 that combined border security and work-site enforcement with a guest worker program and a path to citizenship for most of the illegal immigrants in the country. The legislation, sponsored by

Judiciary chairman Arlen Specter, R-Pa., survived because of a unique partnership between John McCain, R-Ariz., and Edward M. Kennedy, D-Mass., who shepherded the bill through the Senate. It produced a rare moment when Majority Leader Bill Frist, R-Tenn., stood with Minority Leader Harry Reid, D-Nev., to cheer the bill's passage.

But the legislative euphoria was short-lived. House Republicans dismissed the Senate measure as "amnesty" for illegal immigrants and the work of Democrats. They refused to convene a conference to negotiate a final bill and instead held two dozen field hearings around the country during the August recess. When they returned to Washington, D.C., it was to proclaim what was for all intents and purposes already known: They would not accept core elements of the Senate bill.

BACKGROUND

The nation's population of illegal immigrants was estimated at about twelve million, with several hundred thousand additional people crossing the Mexican border illegally each year. Illegal immigration was supposed to have at least slowed down after Congress passed the Immigration Reform and Control Act (PL 99-603) in 1986. That law granted amnesty to 2.7 million people living in the country illegally while imposing tough sanctions on employers who hired undocumented workers. But the law had never been strictly enforced. *(1986 act, Congress and the Nation. Vol. VII, p. 717)*

The unspoken fact was that there were many beneficiaries of the status quo, including businesses and families that employed illegal labor, as well as the immigrants themselves, who wanted any job they could get. Consumers also benefited from the lower-priced goods and services that resulted from immigrant labor. As a report published in 2005 by the investment banking and securities firm Bear, Stearns & Co. Inc. concluded, "The United States is simply hooked on cheap, illegal workers and deferring the costs of providing public services to these quasi-Americans."

Immigration experts said the only thing that would halt illegal immigration was decreasing the supply of jobs, so-called interior enforcement. But by the late 1990s, the Immigration and Naturalization Service, at the urging of Congress, had all but given up on interior enforcement and the accompanying workplace raids, shifting its emphasis to catching smugglers and reinforcing the border.

The Border Patrol nearly tripled its force of agents and built new barriers along the most heavily traveled urban stretches of the border in Arizona, California, and Texas. Those high-profile moves were popular with politicians and the public. But instead of stopping the flow, it simply pushed it out of public view toward isolated sections of Arizona. Entry became more expensive as fees to smugglers went up, and more deadly for immigrants who could not survive the heat of the Sonoran Desert. The border enforcement also increased the number of undocumented immigrants who stayed in the United States instead of going back and forth to their home countries.

Once they passed through checkpoints on the roads leading out of the border region, illegal immigrants had little fear of getting caught and numerous job opportunities awaiting them. Though the 1986 law outlawed hiring illegal immigrants, employers satisfied their legal obligation as long as they saw identification that looked real. In fact, employers had an incentive not to ask too many questions, as denying someone a job could prompt a discrimination lawsuit. This led to a burgeoning industry in fake documents that could satisfy the government requirements.

Immigration advocates argued that new arrivals filled the types of jobs Americans did not want or would be unable to fill as the workforce aged. However, some studies suggested that illegal immigration suppressed the wages of the least-skilled Americans.

A mismatch also existed between the costs and benefits of immigration at various levels of government. The federal government collected income and payroll taxes from the 50 percent to 60 percent of illegal immigrants whose work was reported by businesses and individuals. Because illegal immigrants used fake Social Security numbers, their payroll taxes piled up in a fund for mismatched and invalid Social Security numbers that contained $463 billion as of 2002, according to the *Economic Report of the President.* The money served to offset other federal spending. Meanwhile, state and local governments were footing most of the bill for health care, education, and other services for illegal immigrants. They wanted the federal government to either reduce the flow of illegal immigration or help defray the costs. Though this still was an issue that mainly concerned border communities, the cost of illegal immigration was being felt in the Midwest and South as well.

States had long sought relief from the federal government, but that assistance was slow in coming. The 1996 Immigration Reform Act (PL 104-193), which reduced government benefits for noncitizens, authorized reimbursements to hospitals for emergency care and ambulance services provided to illegals injured during border crossings. But neither program had been funded. The 2003 Medicare drug law (PL 108-173) included $250 million in annual payments to local hospitals for such expenses. Border senators, however, complained in early 2005 that the money had not been paid out. *(1996 act, Congress and the Nation Vol. IX, p. 717; 2003 act, Congress and the Nation Vol. XI, p. 496)*

President Bush, as well as the U.S. Chamber of Commerce and Hispanic advocacy groups, called on Congress to create a guest worker program that would allow illegal immigrants to become legal residents and eventually citizens. "We should not be content with laws that punish hard-working people who want only to provide for their families and deny businesses willing workers," Bush said Feb. 2, 2005, in his State of the Union address. *(2005 State of the Union address, text, p. 1044)*

Mexican president Vicente Fox wanted the president to use his political capital to get the guest worker program enacted. But Bush faced significant opposition from many lawmakers in his own party, especially conservatives in the

House. They viewed such a plan as a form of amnesty for people who broke the law by entering the country illegally. Some lawmakers, such as Rep. Tom Tancredo, R-Colo., would even go so far as to establish jail terms for employers who hired illegal immigrants.

Nationally, a poll in February 2005 by Westhill Partners Inc. suggested that the public was growing uneasy with what it saw as too many immigrants getting away with breaking the law. In focus groups, people of all ethnic backgrounds expressed concerns about losing jobs to illegal immigrants or even having to wait too long at hospital emergency rooms because of people they believe were in the United States illegally. Concern was highest among lower-income households, who faced the greatest competition from immigrants.

2005 ACTION

In the hectic final days of the first session of the 109th Congress, the House passed a bill (HR 4437) to tighten border security and stiffen criminal penalties on illegal immigration. The bill, a late addition to the schedule, was the subject of a raucous floor debate and displayed deep divisions among Republicans on immigration. House passage represented a win for the Immigration Reform Caucus, a group of more than ninety House conservatives led by Tancredo.

But the bill did not address an issue that many in both parties said was crucial to the debate: how to provide a pathway to legal residency for the millions of undocumented immigrants who were living and working in the United States, often in low-skilled, low-wage jobs. Senate leaders promised to take up immigration in 2006, and any Senate bill was likely to include some kind of guest worker visa program for illegal immigrants already in the country, a proposal that Tancredo's caucus said was unacceptable.

The most controversial elements of the House-passed bill were provisions that would make it a crime to be in the United States illegally, require all employers to use a government system to check the immigration status of employees including those already working for them, and punish those who helped illegal aliens, not only through smuggling, but also by assisting those already in the country.

House Committee Action

Facing escalating pressure from Tancredo and others in the Republican Party to crack down on illegal immigrants, the House Judiciary Committee approved HR 4437 on a 23–15 party-line vote Dec. 8 and formally reported it (H Rept 109-345, Part I) on Dec. 13. Chairman Sensenbrenner, who sponsored the bill, included most of the language from a border security bill (HR 4312) that the House Homeland Security Committee had approved in November. He added new provisions aimed at reducing incentives for people to migrate illegally to the United States.

Sensenbrenner's chief provision was the requirement that employers use the Basic Pilot Employment Verification Program, a system run by the Department of Homeland Security (DHS), to screen employees' Social Security and foreign identification numbers. Groups favoring reduced immigration said the program, which was voluntary, had worked well in trials. The U.S. Chamber of Commerce opposed making its use mandatory, saying it produced "false positive" results. The bill also, for the first time, would designate illegal immigration as a criminal, instead of a civil, offense. It would increase penalties for a variety of immigration-related crimes.

The border security bill (HR 4312—H Rept 109-329, Part I) that Sensenbrenner drew on required the government to create a comprehensive strategy for guarding the borders. It called for adding police and surveillance equipment at the borders, particularly the porous boundary with Mexico. Democrats supported the border security bill, sponsored by Peter T. King, R-N.Y., but they harshly criticized Sensenbrenner's version.

An amendment by Howard L. Berman, D-Calif., to add a guest worker visa program was defeated 13–22. Republican Jeff Flake of Arizona, whose legislation was the model for Berman's amendment, voted "present" as a "gesture of appreciation" to the Democrat. But Flake said Berman's amendment did not include an important provision of his bill that would reduce a backlog of visa applications that forced many families to wait years for foreign relatives to receive permission to enter the United States.

Tancredo was not entirely satisfied with Sensenbrenner's bill. He and more than twenty members of his caucus sent a letter to House GOP leaders Dec. 5 asking them to allow votes on a series of floor amendments that would make the bill more restrictive. Among them was a proposal to end "birthright" citizenship, the constitutional guarantee that all children born on American soil, regardless of the immigration status of their parents, were citizens.

House Floor Action

The House passed HR 4437 by a vote of 239–182 on Dec. 16, after adopting two dozen amendments. Members had proposed about 128 amendments to the bill, evidence of the divisions over immigration and border security in the chamber and within the Republican Party itself. To the delight of Tancredo and his allies, the rule for floor debate did not allow a guest worker program amendment or even nonbinding language proposed by Flake to express support for the principle behind guest worker proposals.

Democrats opposed to the bill looked to the Senate to temper or strike many of the provisions—an expectation shared by many Republicans. Arizona Republican Jim Kolbe told reporters Dec. 15 that he would bet $100 the House immigration bill would never go to a conference committee with the Senate.

Lawmakers from Tancredo's caucus won two of their long-term goals: amendments to drop the diversity visa and to put pressure on local law enforcement to aid in cracking down on illegal immigrants. But they did not get a vote on an amendment to end birthright citizenship. Some in the caucus believed the children of illegal immigrants should not automatically be granted citizenship, calling them "anchor babies" that enabled whole families to immigrate to the United States.

For a time on Dec. 15 it appeared the legislation might not reach the floor. The day was marked by an emotional clash between rank-and-file Republicans and their leaders over the way the leadership planned to bring the bill to the floor and what amendments would be allowed. GOP leaders corralled their members for a private meeting in the basement of the Capitol in the early afternoon, where they explained a confusing set of rules governing debate and listened to several dozen lawmakers vent their concerns.

During the debate, the House

- Adopted 273–148 on Dec. 16 an amendment by Robert W. Goodlatte, R-Va., to eliminate the visa diversity lottery. Many Republicans and some Democrats considered the lottery a security risk, susceptible to fraud and discriminatory toward others who had to claim work or family ties to the United States to qualify for immigration.
- Adopted 237–180 on Dec. 16 an amendment by Charlie Norwood, R-Ga., to encourage local police to help catch illegal immigrants. Federal money would be withheld from state and local governments that enacted policies forbidding their police to ask people about their immigration status or otherwise preventing them from assisting in apprehending illegal immigrants. State and local officials and police had long protested such proposals, saying illegal immigrants would avoid reporting crimes to police if they believed they might be arrested for being in the country.
- Rejected 164–257 on Dec. 16 an amendment by Sensenbrenner to reduce the bill's criminal penalties for illegal immigrants found either crossing the border or living in the country from 366 days in prison to six months. Sensenbrenner said the White House requested the change because the penalties in the bill would give the crimes felony status, entailing indictments and jury trials and discouraging prosecution. But many Republicans preferred the tougher penalties, and most Democrats were not going to help Sensenbrenner correct his bill or be seen as voting for any criminal penalty for illegal immigrants. Most Democrats said it should not be a crime to reside in the country illegally, something considered only a civil violation under existing law.
- Adopted 247–170 on Dec. 16 an amendment by Lynn Westmoreland, R-Ga., to cap penalties for companies caught hiring illegal immigrants. The amendment also would allow a company, on a first offense, to escape fines by claiming that it had made a good-faith effort to verify legality and would exempt companies from fines for hiring by their subcontractors.
- Adopted 260–159 on Dec. 15 an amendment by Duncan Hunter, R-Calif., to authorize extensive new fencing on the Mexican border.
- Adopted by voice vote on Dec. 15 an amendment by Rick Renzi, R-Ariz., to require that Border Patrol uniforms be made in the United States. Renzi said the uniforms were being made in Mexico, presenting a security risk because people might steal them and sneak into the country posing as border agents.

Highlights

The House-passed HR 4437 included provisions to

Border security. Require the Department of Homeland Security to increase its "operational control" over U.S. borders within eighteen months of enactment. The bill required the construction of a double security fence—along with access roads, lighting, cameras, and sensors—across several portions of the U.S.-Mexico border. Fences would be built from Calexico, Calif., along most of the Arizona border; around Tecate, Calif., and El Paso, Texas; from Del Rio, Texas, to Eagle Pass, Texas; and from Laredo, Texas, to Brownsville, Texas. A study into the feasibility of a fence along the northern border with Canada also would be required.

Mandatory detention. End a policy critics called "catch and release" that allowed apprehended illegals to be released with a promise to show up for a deportation hearing. Under the bill, all such illegals would be detained until they were deported or admitted into the country.

Expedited removal. Allow non-Mexican aliens to be deported based on an order from an immigration official instead of an immigration judge. The expedited removal would apply to illegal aliens who had not been admitted or paroled and who had been apprehended within fourteen days of entry and within one hundred miles of an international border.

Cargo screening. Require that radiation detectors be installed at all points of entry and that all cargo bound for the United States be screened for nuclear or radiological materials within one year of enactment.

Mandatory employee verification. Require employers to use the Basic Pilot Employment Verification Program, a system run by the DHS, to screen employees' Social Security and foreign identification numbers. The mandatory system would be implemented in phases starting two years after enactment, when all employers would have to use the system for newly hired employees. Within three years, federal, state, and local governments and certain other private employers would have to use the system to check the eligibility of all of their employees—both new hires and the existing workforce. Within six years of enactment, all other employers would have to do so for all of their workforce.

Employers who hired individuals who were ineligible to work in the United States would face minimum civil penalties ranging from $5,000 for a first offense to $25,000 to $40,000 per illegal employee for anything beyond the second offense. The existing range was $250 to $2,000 for a first offense and $3,000 to $10,000 per employee for a third offense.

Assisting illegal aliens. Make it a crime to assist, encourage, direct, or induce people to enter or remain in the country "knowing or in reckless disregard" of the fact that they were illegal immigrants. It would be a crime to transport such people into or within the country or conceal them from authorities.

Illegal presence. Make it a criminal, not civil, violation to enter or reside in the country illegally, punishable by 366 days in prison.

Visa diversity. Eliminate the visa diversity lottery, which provided about 50,000 permanent residency visas a year to people selected randomly from countries considered to be underrepresented in the U.S. immigrant flow.

Local law enforcement. Encourage local police to help enforce immigration law and withhold federal money from state and local governments that maintained policies preventing their police from reporting illegal immigrants to federal authorities or assisting in enforcement.

Terrorists and gangs. Make it easier to deport illegal immigrants identified as terrorists and explicitly bar them from becoming citizens. The DHS could designate groups as criminal gangs, making it easier for their members to be detained and deported.

2006 ACTION

At Bush's prodding, senators overcame procedural delays to pass a broad immigration bill (S 2611) that had bipartisan backing. The bill aimed to both crack down on illegal immigration and create a guest worker program. Republican and Democratic supporters came together in an unusual alliance to fend off hostile amendments, overcoming the partisan rancor that marked many other pieces of major legislation.

Like the House bill, the Senate measure emphasized enforcement by increasing the number of border agents, funding construction of a border fence, and placing new requirements on companies to try to prevent the hiring of illegal immigrants. It would also allow illegal immigrants who met certain requirements to begin the process toward becoming citizens.

House GOP leaders refused to go to conference with the Senate because of provisions that they regarded as amnesty for illegal immigrants. The House instead broke up its proposal into smaller bills that had political appeal. Congress cleared one of those bills, mandating the construction of a fence along seven hundred miles of the U.S.-Mexico border (HR 6061).

Senate Committee Action

It took six markup sessions stretching over three weeks for Specter to put together a bill that could win majority support in the Judiciary Committee. When the panel finally approved the resulting draft, 12–6, on March 27, Specter ceremoniously brought down his gavel, and lawmakers and staff broke into applause. All eight committee Democrats and four of the ten Republicans—Sam Brownback of Kansas, Lindsey Graham of South Carolina, Mike DeWine of Ohio, and Specter—supported the measure.

March 27 was the deadline Frist had set for floor action. He said if the committee did not have a bill ready by that date, he would bring his own enforcement-only bill (S 2454) up for a vote instead.

Like the House-passed bill, the draft that came out of the Senate Judiciary Committee included provisions to strengthen border security and immigration enforcement. The chief difference was that it also included a guest worker program and a path to earned citizenship for people already in the country illegally. The draft contained major portions of bipartisan legislation (S 1033) cosponsored by McCain and Kennedy. The path to citizenship was the most difficult part.

Path to citizenship. The draft included what supporters called a series of "gates" that illegal immigrants would have to pass through before they could qualify for citizenship.

Illegal immigrants would first have to apply for a six-year, conditional nonimmigrant visa. At the end of the six years, they could apply for legal permanent residence—a green card—if they paid $2,000 in fines, paid all back taxes, passed a criminal background check, stayed employed, and demonstrated an effort to learn English and civics.

Because a green-card holder had to wait five years to apply for citizenship, illegal workers would be eligible for citizenship eleven years after applying for the visa. However, they would have to get in line behind those already waiting legally, which meant it could take longer.

The language was offered by Graham and adopted 12–5 as one of the last actions before the committee voted to report the measure.

Guest workers. The committee agreed 11–6 to a proposal by Kennedy to create a new temporary work visa for people entering the United States to work, at least initially, in industries that were not high skilled or agricultural in nature. The three-year visa could be extended for one additional three-year period. After four years, those admitted with the visa could petition for a green card if they were sponsored by an employer, and they could become eligible for citizenship five years later. The number of guest worker visas would be capped at 400,000 in the first year.

Kennedy's amendment was adopted after Specter gave up on a protracted effort to combine elements of Kennedy's plan with provisions from a bill (S 1438) sponsored by Jon Kyl, R-Ariz., and John Cornyn, R-Texas, that called for illegal immigrants to return home before being allowed to participate in a temporary work program for a limited time.

Agricultural workers. Undocumented agricultural workers could apply for a "blue card" if they had worked in U.S. agriculture for at least 150 work days within the previous two years before Dec. 31, 2005. After another 150 work days per year for three years, or 100 work days per year for five years, they would be eligible for a green card. The program would be capped at 1.5 million blue cards and would sunset after five years. Employment would not be limited to agriculture so long as the worker satisfied the 100 or 150 workdays each year. Illegal immigrants participating in the program would have to pay a $500 fine, be current on their taxes, and show they had not been convicted of a serious crime. The proposal, by Dianne Feinstein, D-Calif., was adopted 11–5.

Border security. The bill proposed to increase the number of Border Patrol agents by twelve thousand, authorizing twenty-four hundred new agents per year in fiscal 2007 through 2011. It called for the creation along the U.S. southern border of a "virtual fence" with cameras, unmanned aerial vehicles, and other technology; proposed construction of a 150-mile vehicle barrier and all-weather roads in the Tucson sector and a fifty-mile vehicle barrier and all-weather roads in the Yuma sector of the Arizona border; and would have made it a crime to construct or finance a tunnel beneath the border. It also included mandatory detention and removal of anyone from countries other than Mexico who tried to enter the United States illegally.

Enforcement. Specter's original Senate draft would have increased the penalty for illegal immigrants caught in the United States to a criminal misdemeanor and imposed new penalties on those caught helping illegals. But those provisions were stripped at the March 27 markup. An amendment by Richard J. Durbin, D-Ill., adopted 11–6, preserved the existing civil violation for illegal presence. Another Durbin amendment, adopted 10–7, removed the proposed penalties against those who aided illegal immigrants.

The House-passed bill would have made it a felony, punishable by up to a year and one day in prison, to be in the United States illegally. The House bill also had come under widespread criticism for proposing new penalties for those caught aiding illegal immigrants.

House Republican leaders defended their bill at a news conference March 29. Speaker J. Dennis Hastert, R-Ill., noted that an attempt on the floor to change the proposed crime of illegal presence from a felony to a misdemeanor had been derailed, 164–257, on Dec. 16, 2005. Republican J. D. Hayworth of Arizona, who described the flow of illegal immigration as "an invasion," suggested that the House refuse to go to conference on the Senate bill.

SENATE FLOOR ACTION

The Senate passed a modified version of the bill (S 2611) by a **key vote of 62–36 (R 23–32; D 38–4; I 1–0)** on May 25. During the two weeks of debate that preceded the vote, a bipartisan coalition led by McCain and Kennedy defeated every amendment that might have dragged the bill down to defeat. Amendments that were adopted tended to tweak the bill at the margins. Many of them were intended to toughen the measure enough to satisfy some worried conservatives. *(2006 key votes, p. 937)*

Chuck Hagel, R-Neb., brokered a compromise with Mel Martinez, R-Fla., which brought more Republicans on board. Meanwhile, Frist and Reid stood together with a dozen senators, all pointing to a debate that featured an unusual spate of up-or-down votes on a wide range of amendments from both parties. No one attempted a filibuster. Republicans and Democrats paired up on the floor. Coalitions shifted, but the main bloc of backers held together.

All the comity, however, came after a rocky start. The prospects for a bill nearly collapsed in April over procedural differences and were revived only after Bush brought a bipartisan group to the White House for a pep talk and followed up with a prime-time televised address calling for Congress to act.

Specter began March 30 by offering the Judiciary Committee draft as a substitute to Frist's bill (S 2454), but Reid brought the debate to a standstill by refusing to allow votes on a string of GOP amendments. On April 6, Republicans resoundingly defeated a Democratic attempt to invoke cloture on the committee substitute, a step that would have limited the debate and led to a vote. The cloture motion was rejected 39–60, twenty-one votes short of the sixty needed to prevail. That brought floor action on the bill to a halt.

Shortly afterward, Frist and Reid declared a "huge breakthrough": a revised bill put together by Hagel and Martinez. But the deal crumbled just as quickly when the two leaders could not agree on amendments and Frist bristled at a demand by Reid to know who would represent the Senate in conference. Democrats feared that GOP leaders would appoint opponents of the Judiciary Committee approach, who would agree to a bill more along the lines of the House measure. On April 7, the Senate rejected cloture on both the Hagel-Martinez compromise and the underlying bill.

Two weeks later, on April 25, Bush called a White House meeting with a bipartisan group of senators led by Frist and Reid. With the president clearly behind them, the two leaders worked the week of May 8 to patch up the political and procedural differences that were holding up the bill.

Frist agreed that twelve out of twenty-six conferees on the bill would be Democrats. In exchange, Reid agreed to allow unlimited amendments. But Kennedy also warned opponents that any attempt to "filibuster by amendment" would be halted by leaders of both parties. Conservatives such as Jeff Sessions, R-Ala., felt they had been cut out. Sessions was among those who opposed any move to permit illegal immigrants to remain in the country and legalize their status.

In a speech to the nation the evening of May 15, Bush explained his preference for the Senate's broader approach over the enforcement-only tack in the House version. "An immigration-reform bill needs to be comprehensive, because all elements of this problem must be addressed together, or none of them will be solved at all," he said.

Bush reiterated his goal for a guest worker program. "To secure the border effectively, we must reduce the numbers of people trying to sneak across," he said. "Therefore, I support a temporary worker program that would create a legal path for foreign workers to enter our country in an orderly way, for a limited period of time."

For those most concerned about border security, Bush also announced a plan to deploy up to six thousand National Guard troops to the U.S.-Mexico border in June to help the Border Patrol with missions such as intelligence gathering, fence building, and training.

The next day, the Senate voted down a potential deal breaker—an amendment by Johnny Isakson, R-Ga., that would have required Homeland Security to certify that U.S. borders were secure and new detention facilities were fully operational before the guest worker and legalization programs could take effect. The amendment, which effectively would have gutted the bill, was rejected 40–55 on May 16, with eighteen Republicans joining thirty-six Democrats and the chamber's one independent in voting against it.

After defeating the Isakson amendment, the Senate on May 16 adopted 79–16 a proposal by Ken Salazar, D-Colo., to allow the president to trigger implementation of the guest worker and legalization provisions by certifying they would strengthen the national security of the United States.

From that point on, supporters of the bill seemed to have the upper hand. In the first week, the Senate voted to table, or kill, three amendments that threatened coalition support of the bill, including a proposal by Kyl to strike the provisions allowing guest workers to apply for legal resident status, which was tabled 58–35 on May 18. The Senate also rebuffed on May 17 by 33–66 an attempt by David Vitter, R-La., to strike the guest worker and agricultural worker provisions.

Although critics were able to narrow the provisions, especially on guest workers, no amendments that could have dismantled the plan were adopted.

Guest workers. Senators agreed to

- Cap the number of H-2C guest workers at 200,000 per year. The bill would have permitted 325,000 in the first year and adjusted the number annually. The amendment, by Jeff Bingaman, D-N.M., was adopted by voice vote after an attempt to table it was defeated 18–79 on May 16.
- Reject, but only narrowly, a proposal by Byron L. Dorgan, D-N.D., to sunset the guest worker program after five years. The May 24 vote was 48–49.

Permanent legal residents. The Senate agreed to

- Narrow the path to permanent residence for guest workers. Under the bill, guest workers would have been allowed to sponsor their own petitions for legal permanent residence after four years. An amendment by Cornyn, adopted 50–48 on May 17, struck that provision and required that to petition for permanent resident status, a person who had been employed for four years as a guest worker had to have an employer to sponsor him or her and documentation showing that no American was available to fill the position.
- Restructure the allocation of employment-based green cards to allow 650,000 per fiscal year, including spouses and children. The underlying bill would have capped the number at 450,000, without including spouses and children. The amendment, by Bingaman, was adopted 51–47 on May 25.
- Bar convicted felons, repeat misdemeanor offenders, and illegal immigrants who ignored deportation orders from earning legal U.S. residence. The amendment by Cornyn and Kyl, adopted, 99–0 on May 17, was one that Reid had blocked in April. It was rewritten to give the homeland security secretary discretion to make certain exceptions for "humanitarian" reasons.

Border security. The Senate agreed to

- Require the construction of more than 370 miles of triple-layered fencing and 500 miles of vehicle barriers along the U.S.-Mexican border. The proposal, by Sessions, was adopted 83–16 on May 17.
- Authorize state governors, with approval from the secretary of defense, to order their National Guard units to devote their annual training to border security duties along the border with Mexico. The amendment by John Ensign, R-Nev., was adopted 83–10 on May 22.

Other amendments. The Senate also

- Adopted 50–47 on May 25 an amendment by Ensign to bar illegal immigrants from collecting tax refunds or filing claims for the earned income tax credit or other benefits for tax years prior to 2006.
- Adopted on May 18 a pair of rival amendments by James M. Inhofe, R-Okla., and Salazar that addressed the role of the English language. Inhofe's amendment, after being modified, stated that English was the national language and required that immigrants seeking to become permanent legal residents prove they had learned the language. Salazar's alternative described English as "the common and unifying language of the United States" and made no other changes to the bill or existing law. Inhofe's amendment was adopted 62–35, and then Salazar's amendment was adopted 58–39, leaving the issue of which version to use up to conferees.
- Adopted 59–39 on May 23 a proposal by Charles E. Grassley, R-Iowa, to replace the employment verification system required in the bill with an electronic verification system that would allow employers to

verify the legal status of workers within three days. If a worker's status could not be verified, the employer would have to discharge the worker. Workers wrongly discharged because of a verification system error could be compensated for lost wages.

Highlights

The following are major elements of the Senate bill (S 2611), with comparisons to the House-passed HR 4437. The Senate bill contained provisions to

Border agents. Authorize a net of four thousand additional border agents and at least twenty-five hundred port-of-entry inspectors. The House bill authorized hiring at least 250 port-of-entry inspectors in each of the following four fiscal years.

Border fence. Authorize the Homeland Security Department to build a "virtual fence" consisting of unmanned aircraft, cameras, sensors, and other technology. The House bill called for construction of a double security fence—accompanied by access roads, cameras, and sensors—across several portions of the Mexican border. Fences would be built from Calexico, Calif., along most of the Arizona border; around Tecate, Calif., and El Paso, Texas; from Del Rio, Texas, to Eagle Pass, Texas; and from Laredo, Texas, to Brownsville, Texas.

Employee verification. Phase in a program under which all employers would have to check Social Security numbers of new hires against a federal data base developed by the Homeland Security Department and based on an employment eligibility verification system known as Basic Pilot. To enforce the stiffer employment regulations, the bill would authorize hiring ten thousand agents. The House bill expanded use of Basic Pilot. All employers had to participate within six years.

Guest workers. Create a guest worker program to allow up to 200,000 people outside the country to enter and fill vacant nonagricultural jobs during the first year. Workers could get a three-year H-2C visa, renewable for one three-year period. After holding a visa for four years, an individual could apply for permanent residence. The House bill had no guest worker provisions.

Agricultural workers. Make an additional 1.5 million agricultural workers eligible for permanent legal residence if they proved they had worked in agriculture in the United States before enactment of the bill and if they worked three to five more years in agriculture after enactment. The House bill had no similar provisions.

Permanent residency. Allow illegal immigrants who had been in the United States since April 5, 2001, and had worked for at least three years to apply for an "earned adjustment" to legal status. They would have to work in the United States for six years after the bill's enactment, pass a background check, pay back taxes, learn civics and English, and pay a $2,000 fine. No cap would be placed on green cards issued under these rules.

Illegal immigrants who had been in the United States working for two to five years as of January 2006 could apply for deferred mandatory departure and remain in the United States for up to three years. They could apply for permanent resident status while in the United States. After clearing a background check and meeting other requirements, they would qualify for legal permanent residence status. However, they would have to leave the United States and return to receive the new status.

STALEMATE, SUBSEQUENT ACTION

The House and Senate remained locked in a stalemate over the two contrasting bills, and election-year politics left no room for compromise.

Republicans such as Sensenbrenner, who would have led House representatives in any conference, adamantly opposed the Senate approach. Rep. Lamar Smith, R-Texas, an influential Judiciary member, during the summer expressed the views of his allies. "It's hard to justify legislation that would reward millions of lawbreakers, attract more illegal immigrants and depress American workers' wages," he said. "The Senate bill may be good for other countries and foreign workers, but it's not good for America and American workers."

House Republicans hoped to build their case against the Senate bill by convening more than twenty hearings across the country during the August congressional recess. The hearings generated considerable local news coverage but did not set off the groundswell against illegal immigration that planners had hoped for. Instead, Republicans found themselves speaking mostly to those who already supported them.

Back in Washington, House GOP leaders were under growing pressure from the rank and file for new votes in advance of the midterm elections to show they were getting tough on illegal immigration. House leaders in September decided to break off popular pieces of their immigration enforcement bill (HR 4437) and pass them separately.

Only one of the bills—requiring construction of seven hundred miles of border fence along portions of the border with Mexico—became law (HR 6061—PL 109-367). Hastert tried to attach others to the fiscal 2007 Homeland Security appropriations bill and the defense authorization bill, but Senate Republicans rebuffed most efforts. The remaining bills died at the end of the Congress.

In addition to the border fence bill, the House passed the following measures.

Tunneling. A bill (HR 4830) to criminalize tunneling under the nation's borders passed, 422-0, on Sept. 21. Similar provisions were in the Senate version of the Homeland Security appropriations bill, and they were included in the final bill (PL 109-295).

Gangs. A bill (HR 6094) to make it easier to deny entry into the United States for legal or illegal immigrants who were gang members or to deport them if they were found in the country. It passed 328–95 on Sept. 21. Hastert tried to add the provisions to the fiscal 2007 defense authorization measure (HR 5122), but he backed off after John W. Warner, R-Va., who chaired the Senate Armed Services Committee, warned that such an action would provoke a bipartisan revolt in the Senate.

Enforcement. A measure (HR 6095) to clarify that local police could enforce federal immigration law—but were not required to do so. It also would have required expedited consideration of lawsuits against the federal government over enforcement of immigration laws. The bill passed 277–140 on Sept. 21.

Border Patrol. A bill (HR 6160) to allow the U.S. Border Patrol to rehire retired agents for up to five years and offer recruitment and retention bonuses. It passed by voice vote Sept. 26.

Border security contracts. A bill (HR 6162) to allow the Homeland Security Department's inspector general to review and report on any contract or task order relating to the Secure Border Initiative that was valued at more than $20 million. It passed by voice vote Sept. 28. The Senate included a similar requirement in its version of the Homeland Security spending bill, and it was retained in the conference report.

Border Fence

Two weeks before the 2006 midterm elections, President George W. Bush signed a bill (HR 6061—PL 109-367) authorizing the construction of seven hundred miles of fencing along the southwestern border with Mexico as well as a "virtual fence" of cameras, sensors, unmanned aerial vehicles, and other surveillance technology along the entire U.S.-Mexican border.

The relatively narrow bill was the only significant piece of legislation to clear in 2006 after nine months of intense debate over the direction of U.S. immigration policy. Republican leaders pushed for its enactment after splits within the party made it impossible to agree on broader immigration overhaul legislation. *(Immigration, pp. 679, 711)*

HR 6061 did not authorize funding to construct the fence, which some estimates said would cost at least $2 billion. However, the fiscal 2007 Homeland Security appropriations law (PL 109-295) included $1.2 billion in emergency funding for the fence and barriers. *(Appropriations, p. 102)*

LEGISLATIVE ACTION

The House passed HR 6061 on a **key vote of 283–138 (R 219–6; D 64–131; I 0–1),** on Sept. 14, just minutes before Hastert held a news conference to announce plans to pass a list of narrow bills, pushing broader immigration questions until after the election. *(2006 key votes, p. 937)*

Some House Democrats criticized the border fence bill as nothing more than political gamesmanship as midterm elections loomed.

The piecemeal approach was designed to gain widespread support of select security initiatives before the election. More contentious items, such as the mandatory employee screening, were not included. House leaders said they hoped to pass the individual bills in two or three packages, then negotiate to include them in the conference report for the Homeland Security appropriations bill.

While acknowledging the chamber's desire for a broader immigration bill, Senate GOP leaders agreed to go along with the House on the border fence during the rush of votes before adjourning for the campaign. The Senate passed HR 6061 unamended by 80–19 on Sept. 29, clearing the measure.

Democrats were torn between supporting legislation that many considered inadequate or voting against it and potentially being attacked as opposing border security. In the end, they decided not to make opposition to the bill a test of party loyalty. Eighteen Democrats voted for cloture and twenty-six voted for the bill.

Several Republicans said that by giving in to the House on items cherry-picked from that chamber's enforcement-oriented bill, the Senate would eliminate any pressure the House might feel to negotiate a broader measure with the Senate. But Majority Leader Bill Frist, R-Tenn., who voted for the Senate's immigration bill, said that passing legislation to secure the southern border was a better option than doing nothing before the November election. Bush said Sept. 20 that he would sign the fence bill into law, giving many Republicans who backed the Senate overhaul the political cover to vote for it.

Although Frist used a procedural tactic called "filling the amendment tree" to block any amendments, he agreed to allow minor changes offered by Kay Bailey Hutchison, R-Texas, who was concerned that the amount of fencing and the locations were being determined by Congress without giving local authorities or the department enough input. Any changes would have sent the bill back to the House for another vote, however, and in the end House leaders pledged to work with Hutchison after the elections.

Bush signed the bill at a White House ceremony Oct. 26, saying, "We have a responsibility to enforce our laws. We have a responsibility to secure our borders. We take this responsibility seriously." But he emphasized that the measure had not satisfied his call for Congress to pass a broader overhaul of immigration policy.

MAJOR PROVISIONS

The following are the major provisions of the border fence bill.

"Operational control." Required the Homeland Security Department, within eighteen months of enactment, to take all actions necessary to maintain "operational control" over all U.S. land and maritime borders, which was defined as preventing the entry of terrorists, other unlawful aliens, instruments of terrorism, narcotics, and other contraband. Included in the plan was systematic surveillance of the borders using means such as unmanned aerial vehicles, ground-based sensors, satellites, radar coverage, and cameras. Required physical infrastructure to prevent unlawful entry and to facilitate access by Customs and Border Protection, such as checkpoints, all-weather access roads, and vehicle barriers.

Southwest border fencing. Directed the department to construct at least two layers of reinforced fencing and to install additional physical barriers, roads, lighting cameras, and sensors along about seven hundred miles of the U.S.-Mexican border, but allowed the department to use other means to secure areas with elevation grades greater than 10 percent.

Designated five specific areas along the border for the construction. Set a May 30, 2007, deadline for installing cameras and a May 30, 2008, deadline for completing fencing along a 361-mile section of the border from Calexico, Calif., to Douglas, Ariz., and a Dec. 31, 2008, deadline to complete fencing from fifteen miles northwest of, to fifteen miles southeast of, the Laredo, Texas, port of entry.

Northern border. Directed the department to study the feasibility of a state-of-the-art infrastructure security system along the U.S. border with Canada and report within one year of enactment to the House and Senate Homeland Security Committees.

Fleeing vehicles. Required the department to evaluate the ability of Customs and Border Protection personnel to stop vehicles that entered the country illegally and refused to stop.

Class Action Lawsuits

Congress cleared legislation (S 5) in 2005 aimed at limiting class action lawsuits that bring together the often small claims of a number of individual plaintiffs. The bill was a top priority for congressional Republicans and for President George W. Bush, who signed the measure into law (PL 109-2) on Feb. 18, less than twenty-four hours after Congress completed action on it.

The new law gave federal courts jurisdiction over class action lawsuits when the total amount in dispute exceeded $5 million and the defendant and a large portion of the plaintiffs lived in different states. This meant that federal courts for the first time were expected to hear large numbers of consumer protection cases. Federal judges would use state consumer protection laws, but the cases would move forward using federal procedural law, often considered less friendly to plaintiffs.

Under previous law, class action suits could be heard in federal court only if each plaintiff stood to receive at least $75,000 and all the plaintiffs lived in different states from the defendants. As a result, most class action cases were heard in state courts, and the standards used to determine whether a suit qualified as a class action varied from one state to another.

Business interests, led by the U.S. Chamber of Commerce, spent six years and tens of millions of dollars lobbying for the bill's enactment. Supporters said the new law would help prevent "forum shopping," in which attorneys tried to file their lawsuits in jurisdictions that were known for giving plaintiffs large awards, as well as "coupon settlements," which they said tended to benefit lawyers, not aggrieved consumers.

Enactment was a significant defeat for consumer, civil rights, and public-interest groups, which said the measure would deprive seriously injured plaintiffs—ranging from mistreated foster children to drivers left paralyzed in accidents—of their day in court by shifting cases to the already overworked federal courts. Another loser was the Association of Trial Lawyers of America, which represented plaintiffs' attorneys who sent most of their political donations to Democrats.

The House had approved similar class action bills in each of the previous three Congresses, most recently in June 2003. After failing to get the sixty votes needed to limit debate on the bill in 2003, Senate supporters agreed to several compromises that won additional Democratic support. For example, they agreed to raise the threshold for federal court jurisdiction to $5 million, compared with $2 million in an earlier version of the legislation. Compromise legislation also left out a provision that would bar "bounties," or disproportionate payments to the plaintiff that represented the class. The bill stalled again in 2004, however, when members in both parties tried to attach unrelated amendments on issues ranging from a minimum wage increase to global warming and immigration. *(Previous action, Congress and the Nation Vol. XI, pp. 591, 608)*

The GOP's increased majority in the Senate, where Republicans held fifty-five seats as a result of the 2004 elections, made the difference in 2005, enabling supporters to fight off five Democratic amendments and send the House a clean bill that it easily cleared.

SENATE ACTION

The Senate Judiciary Committee approved S 5 on Feb. 3 by a 13–5 vote. A report (S Rept 109-14) on the bill was filed Feb. 28. Three Democrats—Dianne Feinstein of California, Herb Kohl of Wisconsin, and Charles E. Schumer of New York—joined all ten Republicans in voting for the measure.

The bill reflected the 2003 Senate compromise that brought several Democrats into the fold. Supporters said keeping the bill free of amendments was key to retaining the support of those Democrats and ensuring passage in the House, where GOP leaders said they were willing to take up the Senate version only if it remained clean.

The committee rejected 5–13 an amendment by ranking Democrat Patrick J. Leahy of Vermont that would have increased federal judges' salaries by 16.5 percent. Several Republicans said they supported the pay raise but considered the class action bill to be the wrong vehicle.

Adding to the pressure for a clean bill, John Cornyn, R-Texas, indicated that if changes were made, he might introduce several proposals he said could make the bill stronger. Aides said Cornyn probably would not introduce the amendments unless Democrats pressed on with their additions.

The full Senate passed the bill without amendments Feb. 10. Supporters prevailed on a **key vote of 72–26 (R 53–0; D 18–26; I 1–0).** *(2005 key votes, p. 915)*

During a week of floor debate, supporters defeated five Democratic amendments that might have complicated passage in the House. Democratic and GOP backers insisted any tinkering would push the House to consider an even stricter version. The House had its own class action legislation (HR 516), which included provisions that were eliminated in the Senate bill, among them a ban on so-called bounty payments—disproportionate payments to named plaintiffs who actually testified and had their names appear on the class action suit.

The Senate

- Rejected 40–59 on Feb. 9 a proposal by Edward M. Kennedy, D-Mass., to exempt wage-and-hour and civil rights suits from the class action bill.
- Rejected 38–61 on Feb. 9 an amendment by Feinstein and Jeff Bingaman, D-N.M., to give federal judges more flexibility about which state consumer laws to apply in class action suits when plaintiffs were from multiple states.
- Rejected 37–61 on Feb. 10 a proposal by Russ Feingold, D-Wis., to place a sixty-day limit on the amount of time federal judges would have to consider whether to send a class action case back to state court.
- Agreed 60–39 on Feb. 9 to table (kill) an amendment by Mark Pryor, D-Ark., to exempt suits brought by state attorneys.

Feinstein and Bingaman ultimately voted for the final bill.

HOUSE ACTION

One week later, on Feb. 17, the House passed the bill 279–149, completing congressional action. Fifty Democrats joined GOP colleagues in supporting the bill. Only one Republican, John T. Doolittle of California, voted against it.

During floor debate on Feb. 17, the House

- Rejected 175–249 a motion by Sherrod Brown, D-Ohio, to commit the bill to House Judiciary Committee with instructions to add an exemption for class action cases involving the arthritis drug Vioxx. The drug had been withdrawn from the market because of heart attack risks. On Feb. 18, a Food and Drug Administration panel ruled it suitable for sale, saying its benefits might outweigh the risks.
- Rejected 178–247 a substitute by John Conyers Jr. of Michigan, the Judiciary Committee's ranking Democrat, that incorporated amendments rejected or withdrawn in the Senate Feb. 10. The substitute included exemptions for civil rights and wage-and-hour lawsuits; suits initiated by state attorneys general; and "mass torts" involving physical injuries to a large number of people within a state, among other things.

MAJOR PROVISIONS

As cleared, S 5 contained the following major provisions.

Federal jurisdiction. Gave federal district courts jurisdiction over class action suits in which the amount in dispute exceeded $5 million, the class included one hundred or more plaintiffs, and two-thirds or more of the plaintiffs lived in states other than that of the defendant.

Home state jurisdiction. Retained state court jurisdiction if two-thirds or more of the plaintiffs lived in the main defendant's home state. Provided that a federal district court judge would make the decision if between one-third and two-thirds of the defendants were citizens of the main defendant's home state.

Plaintiff protection. Allowed a federal judge to approve a settlement that gave class members noncash benefits, such as coupons for goods or services, after a hearing and a written finding that the terms were reasonable and fair to the plaintiffs. Required attorney fees to be proportional to the value of the coupons that plaintiffs redeemed, and specified that they could not result in a net loss to the plaintiffs unless the judge determined that the plaintiffs' loss was outweighed by other, nonmonetary benefits. Barred a class action settlement from giving more to some plaintiffs just because they were geographically close to the court.

Voting Rights Act

After overcoming the objections of a group of mostly southern Republicans, Congress in 2006 cleared a reauthorization of the 1965 Voting Rights Act, extending the landmark civil rights law for twenty-five years. President George W. Bush signed the bill into law July 27 (HR 9—PL 109-246) at a ceremony on the South Lawn of the White House, where he recalled the bloody voting rights march in Selma, Ala., in March 1965 that led to passage of the act later that year.

Plans to extend expiring provisions of the 1965 law began as a rare bipartisan, bicameral effort—a contrast with the law's initial enactment, which generated vigorous dissent from segregationist southern Democrats in Congress. Symbolizing the shift, more than two dozen lawmakers from both parties and both chambers descended the Capitol steps together May 2 to attend an afternoon ceremony announcing the introduction of identical versions of the reauthorization bill in both chambers.

Although the provisions were not set to expire until August 2007, Republican leaders hoped to win enactment before the 2006 midterm elections. House Judiciary Committee chairman F. James Sensenbrenner Jr., R-Wis., and his Senate counterpart, Arlen Specter, R-Pa., made it clear that they hoped to move the legislation through both chambers quickly and with no changes.

Despite that auspicious start, action on the bill quickly broke down in the House, where southern Republicans and opponents of bilingual voter assistance repeatedly forced GOP leaders to delay floor consideration. The leadership finally decided to bring the bill to a vote after agreeing to allow four amendments that supporters of the legislation said could kill the measure. None of the changes were adopted, although some fell only because of Democratic opposition.

Determined not to repeat the House's experience, GOP leaders in the Senate propelled the legislation through that chamber in little more than a day, clearing the bill July 20 and ensuring that it would be enacted before Congress left for its August recess.

BACKGROUND

The 1965 Voting Rights Act (PL 89-110) was explicitly intended to enforce the Fifteenth Amendment to the Constitution, ratified after the Civil War to guarantee African Americans the right to vote. President Lyndon B. Johnson guided the bill to enactment at a time when civil rights workers in the South were being beaten and in some cases killed for trying to register African Americans to vote. *(Voting rights, Congress and the Nation Vol. I, p. 1635; Congress and the Nation Vol. II, p. 356)*

The law barred the use of any mechanism or prequalification—such as literacy requirements or poll taxes—to deny U.S. citizens the right to vote because of their race or color. Electoral jurisdictions with a history of discriminatory voting practices, generally southern states, were required to get advance permission from the federal government before making any changes to their voting procedures. The law also allowed the Justice Department to send federal agents to register voters in the South and to monitor elections to ensure fairness.

The U.S. Supreme Court upheld the law's constitutionality in 1966, ruling in *South Carolina v. Katzenback* that although the Voting Rights Act was an "uncommon exercise of congressional power," the "exceptional conditions" of racism justified Congress's authority to enact legislation to remedy voting discrimination.

The law was credited with enabling more African Americans to vote, and to exert significant political clout, in previously segregated southern states. The provisions were meant to be temporary, but Congress extended them four times—in 1970, 1975, 1982, and 1992—concluding each time that, though progress had been made, minority citizens continued to need protection to guarantee their right to vote. *(1970 action, Congress and the Nation Vol. III, p. 498; 1975 action, Congress and the Nation Vol. IV, p. 668; 1982 action, Congress and the Nation Vol. VI, p. 680; 1992 action, Congress and the Nation Vol. VIII, p. 793)*

When reauthorizing the law in 1975 (PL 94-73), Congress added a requirement that a jurisdiction provide bilingual ballots and offer bilingual assistance at polling places if at least 5 percent of its citizens belonged to a language minority and its English illiteracy rate exceeded the national average. Seven years later, in 1982, Congress agreed to reauthorize the law for twenty-five years (PL 97-205) and added language to clarify that a voting requirement or procedure was illegal under the act if the effect was to discriminate against minority voters, regardless of whether that was the intent. The provision essentially overrode the Supreme Court's 1980 decision in *City of Mobile v. Bolden*, which held that a plaintiff had to show that a voting procedure was specifically designed to discriminate against nonwhites. *(Court decision, Congress and the Nation Vol. V, p. 777)*

In 1992 Congress reauthorized the requirement for bilingual assistance through 2007 (PL 102-344) and expanded its reach to cover areas that had at least ten thousand non-English-speaking voters, even if they did not constitute 5 percent of the population. The law also specified that both bilingual election materials and bilingual voting assistance were required.

Two recent Supreme Court cases loosened the restrictions on jurisdictions that had to obtain advance permission, or "pre-clearance," before changing their voting laws. In *Reno v. Bossier Parish School Board*, the Court ruled 5–4 in 2000 that the Voting Rights Act did not prohibit the Justice Department from pre-approving a redistricting plan that was enacted "with a discriminatory but non-retrogressive purpose"—meaning that nonwhite voters fared no worse under the new plan than under the previous one. In a 2003 case, *Georgia v. Ashcroft*, the high court ruled 5–4 that Georgia's redistricting plan satisfied the "nonretrogressive" standard because it did not diminish overall minority influence. The plan spread black voters across several districts instead of concentrating them in a select few. Critics said the ruling meant jurisdictions were in compliance with the law as long as blacks could "influence" the elections of white candidates, even if they could not elect the candidates they preferred, including candidates of their own race. *(2000 case, Congress and the Nation Vol. X, p. 710; 2003 case, Congress and the Nation Vol. XI, p. 658)*

HOUSE ACTION

The House Judiciary Committee approved the reauthorization bill (HR 9) by a vote of 33–1 on May 10, 2006, and reported it (H Rept 109-478) on May 22. The lone dissenter was Steve King, R-Iowa, who opposed the section extending the assistance for bilingual voters.

The committee said in its report on the bill that despite the successes of the previous forty years, the temporary provisions of the Voting Rights Act were still needed. "Discrimination today is more subtle than the visible methods used in 1965," the report stated. "However, the effect and results are the same, namely a diminishing of the minority community's ability to fully participate in the electoral process."

During the markup, the committee

- Rejected 9–26 a proposal by King to allow the bilingual program to expire as scheduled in 2007. Nine Republicans voted for King's amendment; eleven others joined all fifteen Democrats present in voting against it.

- Rejected 10–24 a proposal by King to shorten the extension of the bilingual program to six years. Republicans split 10–9; all fifteen Democrats voted "no." Sensenbrenner and Melvin Watt, D-N.C., his counterpart in the negotiations that produced the bipartisan bill, stressed that any changes could jeopardize quick passage in both chambers.

Lamar Smith, R-Texas, who was expected to succeed Sensenbrenner if Republicans retained the House, supported King. King said he would try to bring the amendment up on the floor even though GOP leaders hoped to avoid another vote that could risk alienating Latinos in an election year so soon after their support of immigration legislation (HR 4437) that was viewed as harsh by many minority voters. *(Immigration bill, pp. 679, 711)*

The House passed HR 9 by 390–33 on July 13, after Republican leaders yielded to rebellious members of their caucus and allowed votes on the four amendments by bill opponents. Sensenbrenner led the opposition to each of the amendments and prevailed on all four.

Minority Leader Nancy Pelosi, D-Calif., warned that Democrats would vote against the bill if any of the changes were adopted. A majority of Republicans, including Whip Roy Blunt of Missouri, voted for three of the amendments against the wishes of GOP leaders. The solid Democratic opposition made the difference on those votes.

Reflecting the historic significance of the bill, a large contingent of Congressional Black Caucus members sat in the chamber throughout the debate, and civil rights leader Jesse Jackson sat in a gallery above, flashing thumbs-up signs to several Democrats.

After debating the amendments, the House:

- Rejected July 13 on a **key vote of 185–238 (R 181–44; D 4–193; I 0–1)** King's proposal to allow the bilingual voter assistance requirement to expire in 2007. An attempt to cut off funding needed to enforce the bilingual language requirement had been rejected 167–254 on June 28 during consideration of the fiscal 2007 Science, State, Justice, and Commerce spending bill (HR 5672). The amendment was offered by Cliff Stearns, R-Fla. *(2006 key votes, p. 937)*
- Rejected 96–318 on July 13 an amendment by Charlie Norwood, R-Ga., to revise the formula used to determine which voting jurisdictions had to get pre-clearance before they could change voting policies or procedures. Norwood's amendment made the requirement applicable to state or local jurisdictions that had a discriminatory policy or test in place, or where voter turnout or registration rates were less than 50 percent in any of the three most recent presidential elections. Republicans opposed Norwood's amendment 95–124.
- Rejected 118–302 on July 13 an amendment by Lynn Westmoreland, R-Ga., to require the Justice Department to compile an annual list of jurisdictions subject to the pre-clearance requirement that had met the standards in the law and could therefore be removed, and to approve those jurisdictions' requests for removal. Republicans supported the amendment 117–105.
- Rejected 134–288 on July 13 an amendment by Louie Gohmert, R-Texas, to extend the 1965 law by ten years instead of twenty-five years. Republicans supported Gohmert 132–92.

GOP leaders had pulled the bill from the floor schedule June 21 after a closed-door conference meeting where rank-and-file Republicans rebelled. Some conservatives objected to the requirement for bilingual voter assistance, calling it an unfunded mandate and contrary to the goal of assimilating immigrants. A group of southern Republicans, particularly those from Georgia and Texas, wanted to modify the requirement to get advanced permission for changes in their election laws. They said the provision was outdated and did not take into account strides their states had made since 1965 in eliminating racial discrimination.

The rebellion was fueled by a sense that Sensenbrenner and other leaders were attempting to push the bill through with Democratic support, without accommodating views within their own party. By July 11, GOP leaders were still negotiating with King and the Georgia and Texas Republicans. Majority Leader John A. Boehner, R-Ohio, told the caucus July 12 that he intended to press ahead with the bill on the floor the next day. The leadership helped to quell the rebellion by allowing King to offer his amendment—something it had been resisting.

Sensenbrenner declared victory after the bill passed, though it was a somewhat lonely endeavor on the Republican side of the aisle.

SENATE ACTION

The Senate Judiciary Committee gave unanimous support to a companion bill (S 2703-) on July 19, approving it 18–0 after thirty minutes of debate. A report on the measure (S Rept 109-295) was filed July 26. Chairman Specter said he wanted the committee to mark up its own version of the bill to ensure a full record in case of court challenges later. After the GOP rebellion that delayed action in the House, Senate Republicans with similar concerns decided to avoid any foot-dragging that might alienate minority voters in an election year.

Most of the audience seats at the markup were filled by members of the National Association for the Advancement of Colored People (NAACP), which was holding its annual convention in Washington, D.C. They gave the panel a standing ovation after the vote.

The committee rejected by voice vote an amendment by Tom Coburn, R-Okla., to narrow the requirement for bilingual language assistance to citizens who were unable to speak English very well. The panel agreed by voice vote to add the name of Cesar Chavez, the Mexican American labor leader, to the title of the Senate bill, though it did not carry over to the final version.

The Senate passed HR 9 by 98–0 on July 20, clearing the measure. Adding to the sense of urgency was a speech given by Bush the previous day at the NAACP convention, the first such appearance of his presidency. "I look forward to the Senate passing this bill promptly without amendment so I can sign it into law," he said to loud applause.

The sudden pressure for quick action was an abrupt shift for the White House, which had been largely unresponsive to the attempts in the House to add amendments opposed by the bill's sponsors. Democrats were quick to attribute the new GOP urgency to the venue of the NAACP convention.

Much of the nearly seven hours of Senate floor debate was filled with laudatory speeches urging the law's renewal. Edward M. Kennedy, D-Mass., recalled watching President Johnson sign the act in the Capitol. He called it "a momentous piece of legislation, which marks the continuation of this nation being a true democracy." Kennedy was joined on the floor during the vote by Rep. John Lewis, D-Ga., a veteran of the 1960s civil rights movement who was severely beaten in March 1965, while leading the first of three voting rights marches in Selma.

MAJOR PROVISIONS

The twenty-five-year reauthorization enacted in 2006 was named after Fannie Lou Hamer, Rosa Parks, and Coretta Scott King, three southern women who were giants of the civil rights movement in the 1960s.

The following are its major provisions.

Pre-clearance. Reauthorized Section 5 of the Voting Rights Act, which required certain jurisdictions to obtain pre-approval from the Justice Department before they could complete a redistricting plan or make any changes to their election laws. The rule originally applied to states or counties that imposed a discriminatory "test or device" and had less than 50 percent participation by residents of voting age in the 1964 presidential elections. That was later amended to include the 1968 and 1972 presidential contests. The requirement covered eight states in their entirety: Alabama, Alaska, Arizona, Georgia, Louisiana, Mississippi, South Carolina, and Texas. Eight other states were partially covered: California, Florida, Michigan, New Hampshire, New York, North Carolina, South Dakota, and Virginia.

Congressional intent. Included a statement of findings that said the Supreme Court had "significantly weakened" the effectiveness of the Voting Rights Act in its rulings in *Reno v. Bossier Parish School Board* and *Georgia v. Ashcroft*, which "misconstrued Congress' original intent . . . and narrowed the protections afforded by Section 5."

Stated that a change in voting laws could not be preapproved if the intention was to discriminate and that the purpose of the requirement was to protect the ability of minority citizens to elect a candidate they preferred, including a minority candidate.

Bilingual voting assistance. Reauthorized the requirement that jurisdictions provide bilingual voting materials in areas where 5 percent or ten thousand of the citizens of voting age had limited English skills and spoke a single minority language.

Census data. Specified that the bilingual language assistance requirements were to be triggered by data in the American Community Survey, not the decennial longform census, which had been discontinued.

Election examiners. Eliminated the role of federal election examiners, who had registered minority voters at one time. (The provision had not been used for many years and had been supplanted by other laws, such as "motor voter" statutes, designed to ease registration. The Justice Department could still deploy election observers in polling places during elections.)

Expert fees. Allowed parties who won lawsuits under the law to recover fees for expert witnesses. Previously, only attorney fees were authorized.

Gun Liability

Republicans in 2005 cleared legislation limiting the legal liability of firearms makers and dealers. Enactment was a victory for the National Rifle Association (NRA) and advocates of overhauling the civil justice system, who easily overcame Democratic resistance. President George W. Bush strongly supported the bill and signed it into law Oct. 26 (S 397—PL 109-92).

The debate over lawsuits against the firearms industry went back to 1998, when New Orleans led several cities in an effort to sue handgun manufacturers to pay for the cost of urban violence. Gun control advocates viewed such lawsuits as a potential avenue toward ultimately curbing widespread access to arms, much as antismoking advocates turned to liability suits in an effort to weaken cigarette manufacturers. To counter this threat, gun rights lobbyists led by the NRA succeeded in enacting protections for the industry at the state level. But their efforts to change federal law took much longer because of resistance by Senate Democrats.

A federal gun liability law had been the top legislative priority of the NRA for years. Supporters of the legislation said allowing lawsuits against gun makers was like taking car manufacturers to court when people drive drunk. They said the liability suits were often filed by anti-gun critics hoping to force manufacturers out of business with exorbitant legal fees. House Judiciary Committee chairman F. James Sensenbrenner Jr., R-Wis., said such litigation threatened to "bankrupt the national firearms industry and deny all Americans their fundamental, constitutionally guaranteed right to bear arms."

Opponents said the law also would shield gun dealers who sold weapons to criminals, although the statute did not preclude lawsuits against those who sold firearms that they knew would be used for a crime or when the firearm was defective.

In the 108th Congress, Senate gun control advocates halted action on legislation to protect the firearms industry by attaching three amendments opposed by the bill's backers, including a renewal of the assault weapons ban (PL 103-322). As a result, Republicans, at the urging of the NRA, voted down their own bill. *(Weapons ban, Congress and the Nation Vol. XI, p. 615)*

In 2005, Senate majority leader Bill Frist, R-Tenn., turned the tables on Democrats, using procedural maneuvers to control the amendments that could be offered. As a result, only three relatively noncontroversial provisions were added.

The wide margins by which both chambers passed the bill in 2005, with many Democrats joining Republicans in support, reflected the changing politics of gun control. Both chambers appeared staunchly supportive of the rights of gun owners. The votes also reflected the increasing desire of many lawmakers, especially conservatives, to revamp the nation's tort law system.

LEGISLATIVE ACTION

The Senate passed the gun liability bill (S 397), which was sponsored by Larry E. Craig, R-Idaho, on a **key vote of 65–31 (R 50–2; D 14–29; I 1–0)** on July 29. *(2005 key votes, p. 915)*

Determined to avoid a replay of 2004, Frist took control of the debate from the beginning. On July 22 he filed a cloture motion to limit debate and bar nongermane amendments. He then filed a succession of amendments—a legislative procedure known as "filling the amendment tree"—that allowed him to control amendments that would be brought for debate. He allowed only those proposals he thought were harmless or easy to defeat, thus thwarting any potential Democratic efforts to add gun control language.

The Senate agreed to Frist's cloture motion 66–32 on July 26. The maneuvers gave Republicans tight control of the floor debate and enabled bill supporters to direct the substance of the debate.

Republicans then easily defeated Democratic amendments to allow individuals, but not municipalities, to sue gun makers; preserved the right of police officers or minors injured by firearms to sue for damages; and blocked the sale of so-called cop-killer bullets.

Passage was a victory for GOP leaders, who had promised to push the legislation through before Congress began its August recess. The fourteen Democrats who voted for the bill were all from states with large rural areas where hunting was popular. Independent James M. Jeffords of Vermont also voted for the legislation, while two Republicans—Lincoln Chafee of Rhode Island and Mike DeWine of Ohio—voted against it.

During the floor debate, the Senate

- Adopted 70–30 on July 28 a proposal by Herb Kohl, D-Wis., to require that child safety locks be sold with all handguns. The safety locks proposal was noncontroversial and received the same number of votes that it garnered when it was added to the 2004 bill.
- Adopted 72–26 on July 29 an amendment by Craig to clarify that individuals under age seventeen could recover damages authorized under federal and state law in a civil suit that met the existing exceptions in the bill.
- Adopted 87–11 on July 29 a Craig amendment requiring the attorney general to commission a study to determine whether a uniform standard for the testing of projectiles against body armor was feasible. The amendment also increased to fifteen years in prison the minimum penalty for violent or drug trafficking crimes in which the perpetrator used or possessed armor-piercing ammunition. If use of such ammunition resulted in death, the person could face life in prison or the death penalty.

The House passed S 397 by a vote of 283–144 on Oct. 20, completing congressional action.

The House Judiciary Committee had approved its version of the legislation (HR 800) by a vote of 22–12 on May 25 and reported it (H Rept 109-124) on June 14. But leaders decided to bypass that measure and clear the Senate bill instead. The rule for floor debate, approved by the Republican-controlled Rules Committee, barred any amendments.

MAJOR PROVISIONS

As enacted, the gun liability law included provisions that

Lawsuits. Prohibited civil liability actions from being brought in any state or federal court against manufacturers, distributors, dealers, or importers of firearms and ammunition. Trade groups also were protected, and all pending legal action against gun makers was dismissed.

Exceptions. Exempted from liability protection anyone who sold or transferred a firearm knowing it was intended to be used for a crime of violence or drug trafficking, or anyone who knowingly violated state or federal laws applicable to the marketing or sale of firearms, when the violation resulted in harm.

Exempted cases in which proper use resulted in physical injury, death, or property damage because of a defect in the firearm.

Gun safety. Required importers, manufacturers, and dealers to provide a secure gun storage or safety device for each handgun sold, delivered, or transferred to any individual. Exempted firearms sold to U.S. agencies, law enforcement officials, and rail police officers from the requirement. Provided that violators could have their licenses revoked or suspended for up to six months and could be subject to a $2,500 fine.

Armor-piercing bullets. Prohibited the manufacture or sale of armor-piercing ammunition, unless it was for use by the federal or state government, was for export only, or had been approved by the Justice Department for testing and experimentation uses.

Criminal penalties. Increased penalties for individuals who used or carried armor-piercing ammunition in a violent or drug trafficking crime. In addition to any sentences for the crime, required a minimum prison sentence of fifteen years or, if the crime resulted in death, a sentence of execution or life imprisonment.

Projectile testing. Required the attorney general to conduct a study to determine whether a uniform standard for projectile testing against body armor was feasible and submit a report to Congress two years after enactment.

Identity Theft

News of several high-profile data breaches prompted efforts throughout the 109th Congress to clear legislation aimed at protecting U.S. citizens from identity theft and other types of fraud. But jurisdictional conflicts among committee chairs, partisan bickering over the scope of each bill, and fierce lobbying prevented any of those measures from passing in either chamber.

Congress did clear legislation to protect veterans from data losses at the Department of Veterans Affairs (VA). The provisions were enacted as part of a broader veterans package (S 3421—PL 109-461) signed into law Dec. 22, 2006. *(Details, pp. 590, 703)*

The 108th Congress in 2004 had cleared legislation to deter identity theft. PL 108-275 increased criminal penalties for identity theft and eased the job of prosecutors in court cases. In 2003 legislators as part of a broad financial services law (PL 108-159) added identify theft provisions, including one that prohibited more than the last five digits of a credit card number from appearing on a sales or restaurant receipt. *(108th Congress action, Congress and the Nation Vol. XI, pp. 140, 622)*

Nevertheless, the safety of consumers' personal information continued as a high-profile bipartisan concern after repeated disclosures of breaches at financial services companies and at less-well-known data brokers such as ChoicePoint Inc. and LexisNexis that collected, collated, and resold dossiers of personal information. A Justice Department study released in April 2006 showed that about 3.6 million American households, or roughly 3 percent of the population, had been the victims of at least one type of identity theft during a six-month period in 2004. A congressional committee reported that in 2005 there were more than one hundred data security breaches involving sensitive information relating to more than fifty million consumers.

The high level of interest in the legislation, however, was its undoing in the 109th Congress. At least five different committees—two in the Senate and three in the House—approved legislation designed to ensure the security of consumer data and prevent identity theft. Several scrambled to assert primary jurisdiction over the subject. In the House, the Energy and Commerce and the Financial Services Committees marked up competing bills in 2006, then called up the other panel's measure and substituted its own version.

Instead of compromising, Energy and Commerce Committee chairman Joe L. Barton, R-Texas, told reporters that he would do everything possible to ensure that his panel's bill was the measure sent to the House floor, saying that the other committees' bills were weaker. Financial Services Committee chairman Michael G. Oxley, R-Ohio, said his bill's version (HR 3997) was broader.

The House Judiciary Committee also approved an identity theft bill (HR 5318) in 2006, while the Senate Commerce, Science, and Transportation Committee (S 1408) and the Senate Judiciary Committee (S 1789) approved bills in 2005. None of the measures went to the floor in either chamber.

Consumer groups such as Consumers Union and the U.S. Public Interest Research Group favored S 1789 and HR 4127. Industry groups, however, favored HR 3997, which included the broadest preemption of state law and the highest threshold for notification. It did not authorize consumers to lock their consumer credit reports from being used to obtain new credit.

The American Bankers Association and the National Retail Federation lobbied for a high threshold for the type of security breaches that would trigger notification, arguing that consumers would start ignoring notices if they received them too frequently.

SENATE COMMITTEE ACTION

Two Senate committees approved competing measures in 2005.

Commerce, Science, and Transportation. The Commerce Committee bill (S 1408), sponsored by Gordon H. Smith, R-Ore., was approved by voice vote July 28, 2005, and reported (S Rept 109-203) on Dec. 8. It allowed companies to take into account whether unauthorized third parties could gain access to the lost data when determining whether there was a reasonable risk of identity theft.

The bill included provisions to

- Require companies to notify consumers of a loss of personal data unless there was "no reasonable risk of identity theft, fraud or other unlawful conduct." Companies could take into account whether unauthorized third parties could gain access to the lost data when determining whether there was a reasonable risk of identity theft.
- Allow consumers to place freezes on credit reports that would prevent the consumer reporting agencies from releasing the credit report to a third party without the consumer's prior authorization.
- Include provisions that could be interpreted to mean that most applicable state laws were to be preempted.
- Prohibit the sale, purchase, or display of Social Security numbers without consumers' consent.

Judiciary. The Judiciary Committee approved a bill (S 1789—no written report), sponsored by Chairman Arlen Specter, R-Pa., by a vote of 13–5 on Nov. 17. The bill, which was preferred by consumer groups, included provisions to

- Require brokers to disclose breaches to affected consumers when there was a significant risk of harm to an individual.
- Require companies that maintained personal information on more than ten thousand individuals to develop comprehensive data privacy programs.
- Require brokers to disclose to consumers "for a reasonable fee" all personal electronic records maintained for disclosure to third parties and to provide guidance on correcting inaccurate information. Brokers would have to correct inaccurate or incomplete information and provide written notice of changes.
- Preempt state regulations but allow state attorneys general to launch enforcement actions.

HOUSE COMMITTEE ACTION

Three House committees approved data security bills in 2006.

Financial Services. The Financial Services Committee approved its bill (HR 3997), sponsored by Steven C. LaTourette, R-Ohio, by a vote of 48–17 on March 16 and reported it (H Rept 109-454, Part I) on May 4. Later, on May 24, the committee gave voice-vote approval to HR 4127, after substituting the text of HR 3997. HR 4127 was reported (H Rept 109-453, Part III) on June 2.

The Financial Services bill included provisions to

- Require companies to investigate any data security breaches and notify affected customers if it was "reasonably likely" that the lost information would be misused.
- Allow consumers to obtain "credit freezes"—preventing their consumer credit reports from being used to obtain new credit—only in instances in which they had been the victims of identity theft.
- Preempt all applicable state laws, including those that allowed all consumers to freeze their data.

The measure provided the broadest preemption of state laws of any of the bills and the highest threshold for notifying people that their personal information might have been compromised. The business community favored the "reasonably likely" standard over requirements in more stringent state laws, such as a California law that had helped make public the information that thieves had gained access to the consumer data base of ChoicePoint Inc. in 2005.

Consumer and privacy groups said the bill would undermine more pro-consumer state laws under the guise of setting a national standard. Committee Democrats took up their case.

Republicans rebuffed Democratic attempts to give state governments a greater role in consumer notification, arguing that "rogue" state governments could abuse the law. They defeated a proposal by Luis V. Gutierrez of Illinois to allow state attorneys general to enforce the legislation with the approval of federal regulators. They also rejected amendments to bar preemption of state identity theft laws and to allow states to use the bill as a floor for standards but pass tougher legislation if they found it to be necessary.

Energy and Commerce. The House Energy and Commerce Committee approved its bill (HR 4127), sponsored by Cliff Stearns, R-Fla., by a vote of 41–0 on March 29 and reported it (H Rept 109-453, Part I) on May 4. The measure won praise from both sides of the aisle, although Sherrod Brown, D-Ohio, expressed concern that it would not allow consumers to freeze their information. The committee subsequently voted 42–0 on May 24 to approve the Financial Services bill, amended with the text of its own measure (HR 3997—H Rept 109-454, Part II).

The Energy and Commerce version included provisions to

- Require companies to notify consumers of breaches unless there was "no reasonable risk of identity theft, fraud or other unlawful conduct." The committee agreed by voice vote to lower the threshold from no "significant risk of identity theft." The use of encryption or other technologies could satisfy that requirement.
- Require information brokers, such as LexisNexis and ChoicePoint Inc., to verify the accuracy of the information they sold. Consumers would be able to access their information files each year and flag, change, or delete incorrect data.
- Allow state attorneys general to bring enforcement actions.
- Prohibit information brokers from obtaining information under false pretenses, a practice known as pretexting.

Judiciary. The Judiciary Committee on May 25 gave voice-vote approval to a narrower data privacy bill (HR 5318) that would have stiffened criminal penalties and required notification to law enforcement. The legislation was reported (H Rept 109-522) on June 22.

The bill included provisions to

- Broaden existing law by criminalizing computer activities "affecting" interstate or foreign commerce, instead of specifically requiring that the criminal act itself involve an interstate or foreign communication. It would have authorized $30 million annually through fiscal 2011 for the Secret Service, the Justice Department, and the Federal Bureau of Investigation (FBI) to investigate and prosecute those involved in breaching cybersecurity.
- Make it a crime for data base owners to fail to notify the FBI or Secret Service of a major security breach

that affected personal information of ten thousand or more individuals and carried a "significant risk of identity theft." Failure to inform authorities within two weeks of discovery could result in a maximum $1 million fine and five years in jail.

- Add computer crimes and data theft to the list of crimes that could be prosecuted under the Racketeer Influenced and Corrupt Organizations statute (PL 91-452). *(1970 law, Congress and the Nation Vol. III, p. 272)*

The committee approved the measure after agreeing by voice vote to a substitute amendment by bill sponsor and Judiciary Committee chairman F. James Sensenbrenner Jr., R-Wis. It clarified that the FBI and Secret Service would be required to notify the attorney general in each state affected by a security breach in certain circumstances. It also specified that the federal law enforcement notification requirements would supersede those under state law. It stated that nothing in the bill would affect any requirement to notify consumers of a security breach under state law.

VETERANS´ INFORMATION SECURITY

The push for legislation to protect veterans from data theft grew out of the theft in May 2006 of a Department of Veterans Affairs laptop computer containing the personal information of 26.5 million veterans and their families. The computer was later recovered, and authorities said they had found no evidence that the data had been accessed. But the VA's information technology operation had drawn sharp criticism for years, and the incident sparked outrage in Congress.

The House passed a bill (HR 5835—H Rept 109-651) by voice vote Sept. 26 to revamp information technology operations at the VA and offer credit monitoring to those affected in the event of a data breach. The measure was sponsored by Veterans' Affairs Committee chairman Steve Buyer, R-Ind. Among other provisions, it called for the creation of an undersecretary for information services with three deputy undersecretaries reporting to the new officer.

On Dec. 8, with the 109th Congress about to adjourn, Buyer proposed that the House add data protection provisions, along with language from other House-passed veterans' bills, to a Senate-passed bill (S 3421) on VA medical facilities. The House agreed to suspend the rules and pass the bill by voice vote, and the Senate accepted the changes, also by voice vote, the next day, Dec. 9. The president signed the measure on Dec. 22. *(Details, p. 590)*

The bill set up a program in the VA to monitor and improve the department's data security, though it did not elevate the position of the chief information officer to undersecretary. If a data breach occurred, the department was required to determine whether there was "a reasonable risk ... for the potential misuse of sensitive personal information." If so, the department was required to notify those affected and provide free credit protection services. The VA also had to notify law enforcement and certain congressional committees when a data breach was discovered.

Asbestos Fund

The Senate Judiciary Committee in 2005 approved a bill (S 852) to create a $140 billion trust fund to compensate people sickened by asbestos exposure. But the bill died in 2006 in the face of a filibuster.

Dozens of companies had been driven into bankruptcy because of lawsuits brought by people exposed to asbestos, a fire-resistant but cancer-causing substance that was used in products such as insulation and automobile brake linings. S 852, sponsored by Judiciary Committee chairman Arlen Specter, R-Penn., aimed to end the litigation and channel victims' claims through a government office that would use specific criteria set in the law to determine compensation.

Specter struggled to draft legislation that would be acceptable to a majority of the committee members, as well as to the defendant companies and insurers that would pay into the fund and be shielded from further liability. But senators on both sides of the aisle remained uneasy because no one knew how many claimants would qualify, which defendant companies and insurers would contribute to the fund, and how much each would owe. Perhaps the biggest challenge was easing conservatives' concerns that taxpayers could end up footing the bill if the trust fund was depleted before all the claims were paid. Conservatives also worried that defendant companies could pay billions into the fund and still end up with future lawsuits if the fund became insolvent.

Specter tried, unsuccessfully, to coax companies into revealing the extent of their liability, but the companies were unwilling to provide information that might make them targets for additional lawsuits if a trust fund were not created.

The Congressional Budget Office (CBO) issued an analysis that showed a wide range of uncertainty about the costs of such a fund. CBO estimated the trust fund would collect a maximum of $140 billion but would face claims of $120 billion to $150 billion. A study released by Bates White, a Washington, D.C., national economics consulting firm, concluded the fund could quickly be overwhelmed by claims and run out of money.

Significant differences also remained among the companies and insurers that would pay into the trust fund. Smaller companies complained that larger ones would contribute less than their share based on potential liability. In addition, organized labor and trial lawyers, two major Democratic constituencies, attacked the trust fund's size as inadequate to compensate claimants fairly.

The most vocal supporters were coalitions of large companies that were defendants in asbestos suits, as well as the National Association of Manufacturers. Some veterans' organizations and unions also endorsed the bill.

In the House, fiscal conservatives preferred a much more limited approach that would keep asbestos cases in the court system and require plaintiffs to meet specific medical criteria.

BACKGROUND

Specter had taken on the job of trying to reconcile the needs of the various stakeholders when he became Judiciary chairman at the beginning of the year. Specter introduced his bill in April 2005, and by trying to please as many sides as possible, he eventually attracted six cosponsors on his committee, including his predecessor as chairman, Orrin G. Hatch, R-Utah.

Hatch had managed to usher asbestos legislation through the committee in 2003. But Senate majority leader Bill Frist, R-Tenn., who later introduced a revised version of the bill on the floor, could not get the sixty votes needed to cut off debate in April 2004. *(108th Congress action, Congress and the Nation Vol. XI, p. 611)*

In the months of negotiations that followed, Frist and Minority Leader Tom Daschle, D-S.D., managed to narrow their differences over the size of the fund but could not reach a deal before the November 2004 elections.

SENATE COMMITTEE ACTION

After months of starts and stops, the Senate Judiciary Committee approved S 852 by a vote of 13–5 on May 26 and reported it (S Rept 109-97) on June 30. However, three Republicans who voted for the bill made it clear they were only trying to advance the bill out of committee and that significant changes would have to be made during Senate floor consideration before they would vote to pass the legislation. All five "no" votes were cast by Democrats. Democrats Dianne Feinstein of California, Herb Kohl of Wisconsin, and Patrick J. Leahy of Vermont, the ranking member on the committee, voted for the bill.

During six markup sessions spanning four weeks, the panel debated dozens of amendments, many of them offered by Specter as he continued to tweak the bill to gain more support. As approved by the committee, the bill included provisions to

- Establish an Office of Asbestos Disease Compensation in the Labor Department to handle victims' claims and awarding damages.
- Establish an Asbestos Injury Claims Resolution Fund to pay for the awards. Companies that had been sued for asbestos-related injuries and the companies that insured them would be required to contribute a combined total of about $140 billion to the fund—up to $90 billion from the companies and $46 billion from their insurers.
- Move virtually all pending asbestos claims from the courts to the compensation office.
- Base awards on the seriousness of a person's asbestos-related disease or condition and his or her exposure to asbestos. The bill set criteria for nine levels of compensation. Awards would range from medical monitoring for someone with a nonmalignant disease to $1.1 million for a person with mesothelioma, a deadly form of lung cancer.
- Require that claims be filed within five years of getting the medical diagnosis. For those who had claims pending in court, the period would be five years from enactment of the bill.
- Specify that if the fund ran out of money, it would sunset and any further claims would be handled in court.
- Require a general prohibition on the manufacturing or distribution of asbestos products, with an exception for uses considered critical to the Pentagon.

In the course of the markups, the committee

- Adopted a Specter amendment to allow insurers that covered a shortfall in the companies' contributions during the first five years to receive credits to reduce their later liability by an equal amount. Insurers had worried they could be stuck paying their share and part of the industry's. To allay concerns of another industry, Specter added language that would limit the financial obligations of wholesalers that were only conduits for products containing asbestos.
- Adopted by voice vote an amendment by Feinstein to give mesothelioma victims one lump-sum payment within thirty days from the date the claim was approved or six months from when the claim was filed, whichever was shorter. Feinstein had indicated that failure to guarantee that the sickest claimants would be paid first would be a "deal breaker" for her.
- Adopted by voice vote an amendment by Specter to exempt the Pentagon from the bill's ban on the sale and distribution of asbestos. Jon Kyl, R-Ariz., had worried the bill would be a burden on the Defense Department, which used asbestos in military hardware.

Other amendments in Specter's manager's package included one to allow for additional hardship adjustments for companies whose payments into the system might force them into bankruptcy, and another, requested by Sam Brownback, R-Kan., to ease the financial burden on smaller companies.

- Rejected 5–12 an amendment by Edward M. Kennedy, D-Mass., that would have granted payment to smokers exposed to asbestos who did not show signs of asbestos-related disease, if an Institute of Medicine study showed such a link existed. Specter had excluded claims by smokers who showed no signs of asbestos-related disease in response to Republican concerns.
- Rejected an amendment by Lindsey Graham, R-S.C., and Kennedy that would have treated claimants living near other affected areas the same as residents near Libby, Mont., which was singled out for special treatment in the bill as it was where the contaminated ore was mined. Instead, the committee adopted a proposal by Specter and Leahy that called for a study of other potential exposure sites.

Specter acknowledged that he left some issues unresolved to move the bill out of committee before the Memorial Day recess in hopes of getting it to the floor during the summer.

One area of persistent disagreement was what would happen if the trust fund's administrators determined that it was running out of money. Kyl said he wanted concrete intermediate steps before the fund could sunset and claimants could return to the courts. The text of the bill remained vague about exactly how the administrators' recommendations for the fund would be considered by Congress. Another sticking point was how to treat residents of areas near mines and processing plants that emitted asbestos fibers into the atmosphere.

Considerable resistance also remained from stakeholders who for years had taken the lead in negotiating the trust fund. The AFL-CIO wrote in a May 24 letter to Specter and Leahy that it had "grave concerns" about many of the amendments to the bill that were adopted in earlier markups. Similarly, the American Insurance Association said in a statement after the committee's vote that it could not support the bill in its existing form.

SENATE FLOOR ACTION

Efforts to advance the legislation in the second session collapsed when supporters were unable to get the sixty votes they needed to overcome procedural roadblocks in the Senate. Frist refused to bring an asbestos bill to the floor again unless supporters had the votes to get past such hurdles, a threshold that backers were unable to meet.

Frist set aside two weeks of floor time for the bill in February, fulfilling a pledge made to Specter at the end of the previous session that the asbestos bill would be the first new piece of legislation the Senate considered in 2006.

Specter easily won the first round, preventing a filibuster on whether to take up the bill. The cloture motion was agreed to 98–1 on Feb. 7, with even the strongest Democratic opponents, such as Minority Leader Harry Reid of Nevada and Minority Whip Richard J. Durbin of Illinois voting in favor after it was clear the bill had enough support to advance.

In hopes of building support, Specter introduced a revised version of the bill Feb. 9 with more than forty changes. The revisions did not satisfy John Cornyn, R-Texas, who offered an amendment to drop the $140 billion trust fund and instead require plaintiffs to meet stricter medical criteria than was required under existing law to bring asbestos-related injury claims in court. It would have required a person to be physically impaired at the time of a claim, with asbestos exposure a substantial factor in his or her illness. It would have suspended the statute of limitations for claimants who were exposed to asbestos but were not yet impaired so that they could pursue a claim later if they did become impaired. The amendment also would have banned asbestos class action suits.

Specter rejected Cornyn's amendment as insufficient. He succeeded in tabling, or killing, the amendment by a vote of 70–27 on Feb. 9. But twenty-six Republicans, joined by Democrat Kent Conrad of North Dakota, had gone on record as opposing the trust fund concept.

Waiting to offer what bill supporters said was a killer amendment was Graham, who planned to try to greatly increase the number of people eligible for the fund. His amendment would have opened the trust fund to claims from people who lived near dozens of plants that processed ore containing asbestos. It would have put them on an equal basis under the bill as people residing near Libby, Mont. Under Specter's bill, all nonoccupational applicants to the trust fund beyond Libby would first be required to prove to a panel of medical experts that asbestos exposure from those plants was the source of their sickness.

Graham did not get a chance to offer his amendment, however, because the bill was brought down on a budget point of order. Raised by John Ensign, R-Nev., the point of order was based on a prohibition of legislation that would authorize more than $5 billion in spending during any ten-year period starting in 2016. Ensign said he doubted the legislation could be changed enough "to make sure that the taxpayers in the future aren't ending up holding a huge mess that includes a great deal of debt for future generations."

GOP leaders backed Specter, who argued that the budget concern was a mere technicality because no public money would be required. Even some GOP critics of the bill who backed the medical criteria amendment, including Cornyn and Tom Coburn of Oklahoma, indicated they were willing to waive the point of order.

However, senators who backed Specter's bill fell one short of the sixty required to waive the budget point of order. The supporters failed on Feb. 14 on a **key vote of 58–41 (R 44–11; D 13–30; I 1–0)**. Frist had switched his vote to "no" so that he could move to reconsider the motion. *(2006 key votes, p. 937)*

In May, Specter and Leahy introduced a new bill (S 3274) that made slight changes to the earlier version. It would have tightened requirements for claimants seeking compensation from the $140 billion trust fund and recalculated the contributions required from small and midsize companies with insurance coverage. It never saw action.

Eminent Domain

The House passed a bill (HR 4128) in 2005 aimed at limiting the effects of a controversial U.S. Supreme Court ruling on eminent domain. The bill proposed to bar states and local communities that received federal development funds from using eminent domain to seize private property for economic development. Although the Senate did not take up the bill, senators indicated their opposition to the court ruling by voting to bar such use of eminent domain in transportation or housing projects funded in fiscal 2006.

Lawmakers' ire was touched off by a 5–4 Supreme Court ruling on June 23 that found that New London, Conn., was allowed under state law to use its power of eminent domain to require several homeowners to vacate their properties to make way for commercial development. Writing for the majority in *Kelo v. City of New London*, Justice John Paul Stevens said, "Promoting economic development is a traditional and long-accepted function of government." *(Court decision, p. 774)*

Many lawmakers from both parties said the ruling was contrary to the U.S. Constitution's prohibition on government "takings" other than "for public use, with just compensation." The House adopted a resolution (H Res 340) expressing its disapproval of the decision by an overwhelming vote of 365–33 on June 30.

HR 4128 was introduced by Judiciary Committee chairman F. James Sensenbrenner Jr., R-Wis., and backed by the panel's ranking Democrat, John Conyers Jr. of Michigan. Its supporters ran the gamut from conservative Republican Tom DeLay of Texas to liberal Democrat Maxine Waters of California. Opponents of the *Kelo* decision in both parties said it meant economically disadvantaged homeowners could be preyed upon by any state or local government that wanted to generate more revenue by transferring their property to commercial developers.

The Senate added language to the fiscal 2006 Transportation, Treasury, and Housing appropriations bill (HR 3058) that barred use of funds in the bill to support "any federal, state, or local projects that seek to use the power of eminent domain" for anything other than a public use. The amendment, by Christopher S. Bond, R-Mo., also directed the Government Accountability Office to send Congress a study within twelve months on the nationwide use of eminent domain and its impact. The Senate adopted Bond's amendment by voice vote, and conferees retained it in the final bill (PL 109-115). *(HR 3058, p. 78)*

However, it was not clear if Congress could have much impact in seeking to counteract the Supreme Court decision. Many smaller eminent domain condemnations involved local funding and would not be directly affected by legislation involving federal dollars. States appeared to be in a stronger position to regulate eminent domain, and state legislatures began weighing steps to place various restrictions on the use of eminent domain for economic development.

HOUSE COMMITTEE ACTION

The House Judiciary Committee approved the Sensenbrenner bill (HR 4128) by a vote of 27–3 on Oct. 27 and reported it (H Rept 109-262, Part I) on Oct. 31. A supplemental report (H Rept 109-262, Part II) was filed Nov. 3. Under the terms of the committee-approved bill,

- State and local governments that received federal economic development funds would be barred from using eminent domain to seize private land that was to be used for private economic development—or was subsequently used for such development. The bill defined "economic development" as private projects carried out for profit or to increase tax revenue, the tax base, or jobs.
- State and local governments that violated the restrictions would be ineligible to receive federal economic development funds for two years.
- Any private property owner who suffered injury as a result of a state or local government violating these restrictions could bring a lawsuit against the government or seek a temporary restraining order or a preliminary injunction.
- The federal government would be similarly barred from using eminent domain to seize land for economic development.
- The prohibitions would not apply to the transfer of private property that had been abandoned or was considered an immediate threat to public health and safety, or that was going to be used for public-use roads or hospitals, or for military bases.

The bill also contained a nonbinding sense-of-Congress provision stating that it was "the policy of the United States to encourage, support, and promote the private ownership of property and to ensure that the constitutional and other legal rights of private property owners are protected by the federal government."

During the markup, the committee

- Adopted by voice vote an amendment by Chris Cannon, R-Utah, to clarify that the bill's provisions should be construed as favoring broad protection of private property rights.
- Rejected by voice vote an amendment by Waters to prohibit the seizure of private property for any private use.
- Adopted by voice vote two Cannon amendments specifying that taking private property for use by a public utility was not prohibited.

HOUSE FLOOR ACTION

The House passed HR 4128 by 376–38 on Nov. 3. Two Republicans and thirty-six Democrats voted "no." Republicans allowed ten amendments to be offered, an unusually high number that reflected GOP leaders' confidence that the legislation would sail through the chamber. During debate on Nov. 3, the House

- Rejected 63–355 a proposal by Jerrold Nadler, D-N.Y., to allow a property owner to go to court to challenge the use of eminent domain to seize his or her property before any property was taken. The amendment would have dropped the two-year penalty on governments that violated restrictions in the bill.
- Rejected 49–368 a proposal by James P. Moran, D-Va., to narrow the definition of economic development to cover development undertaken for profit or where the primary purpose was to increase tax revenue, the

tax base, jobs, or economic development. Moran said that, as written, the definition was so broad as to include virtually every use of condemned property. Moran also proposed to remove the reference to future use of the property and to limit the time in which a suit could be filed to seven years from the time the property was finally condemned. Under the bill, it was seven years after the economic development was completed.

- Rejected 44–371 an amendment by Melvin Watt, D-N.C., to strike the text of the bill and retain only a provision expressing the sense of Congress recognizing the importance of property rights and stating that the *Kelo* decision could lead to abuses of eminent domain power.

Pledge of Allegiance

The House in 2006 passed a bill (HR 2389) to bar most federal courts, including the U.S. Supreme Court, from hearing constitutional challenges to the Pledge of Allegiance. The legislation, sponsored by Todd Akin, R-Mo., was aimed at preventing federal judges from ruling that the phrase "under God" in the pledge was unconstitutional. But the bill went no further and died at the end of the session.

In 2002 the U.S. Court of Appeals for the Ninth Circuit ruled that the phrase "under God," which Congress inserted in the pledge in 1954 (PL 83-396), amounted to an unconstitutional establishment of religion. The Supreme Court reversed the Ninth Circuit in June 2004 on technical, not constitutional, grounds.

The high court ruled that Michael A. Newdow, the father of a girl who attended school in a California district that required daily recitation of the pledge, did not have legal standing to sue in her behalf. The child's mother had legal custody and did not support the father's lawsuit. Bill supporters said the technical ruling left them fearful that the Supreme Court eventually would rule that the phrasing of the pledge was unconstitutional.

The House passed the bill by 260–167 on July 19, after the Judiciary Committee deadlocked 15–15 over sending the measure to the floor (no written report). Bob Inglis, R-S.C., who joined fourteen committee Democrats in opposing the bill, said he was concerned it would leave the fate of the pledge in the hands of state judges who might be more liberal than their federal counterparts. He also said a future, Democratic-controlled Congress could strip courts of jurisdiction over other issues.

Supporters contended that the phrase "under God" was central to the nation's heritage and traditions and should be protected from court decisions. But Democrats who opposed the bill said it would undercut the independence of the judicial branch and set a dangerous precedent.

Before passing the bill, the House on July 19 rejected by 183–241 an amendment by Democrat Melvin Watt of North Carolina that would have allowed the Supreme Court to retain authority to hear constitutional challenges to the pledge.

The Senate, which was reluctant to consider legislation to strip federal courts of jurisdiction over other such divisive issues, did not consider the bill.

Property Rights

An attempt in 2006 to provide property owners with streamlined access to federal courts when challenging state and local land-use regulations succeeded in the House over Democratic opposition. The legislation gained no traction in the Senate and died at the end of the Congress.

The bill (HR 4772) allowed private landowners challenging the government over the use of their land to file claims directly in federal court. It also barred governments from imposing conditions on developers that were out of proportion to the effects of the development on a surrounding community.

Under existing law, private landowners who wanted to challenge government regulation of their land had to do so in state courts and could not file a challenge directly with a federal court. In a 2005 case, *San Remo Hotel LP v. City and County of San Francisco*, the U.S. Supreme Court ruled 9–0 that a property owner could not bring a claim alleging an uncompensated "taking" of property in federal court after a state court had ruled on the claim. The case, which started in a California state court, involved a San Francisco hotel that was seeking to avoid paying a fee aimed at limiting the conversion of residential units to tourist units. *(Court decision, p. 774)*

Advocates for private property rights maintained that this unfairly denied landowners access to federal courts. Defenders of the existing system argued that it was necessary to prevent wealthy developers from engaging in "forum shopping" among state and federal courts when they sued the government.

The bill would have allowed challengers to quickly take their suits to federal court instead of first going through the state court system. Sponsor Steve Chabot, R-Ohio, and his allies contended that this would enable homeowners to avoid lengthy legal battles that otherwise would be financially ruinous. They also said it would hold the government accountable if it took actions that violated private property rights. But Democrats and some Republicans worried that it would make it more difficult for local governments to enforce zoning and land-use restrictions against developers.

The House Judiciary Committee approved HR 4772 by voice vote on July 12 and reported it (H Rept 109-658) on Sept. 14. An amendment by Jeff Flake, R-Ariz., adopted by voice vote, added language to allow developers to challenge federal agencies in federal court over conditions they imposed.

House GOP leaders took up the bill Sept. 25 under suspension of the rules, a procedure that allows for limited debate, bars amendments, and requires two-thirds support for passage. Chabot said that the *San Remo* decision meant property owners were "effectively shut out of federal court[,] . . . setting them unfairly apart from those asserting any other federal right." John Conyers Jr. of Michigan, ranking Democrat on the Judiciary Committee, responded that the bill "does little more than single out developers and corporations for a special fast track into the federal courts."

The vote on passage the next day was 234–172, nearly forty votes short of the 271 needed to prevail.

Majority Leader John A. Boehner, R-Ohio, promised to reschedule the bill under rules requiring a simple majority for passage. On Sept. 29, 2006, House Republican leaders brought the measure back to the floor under a rule that allowed no amendments. This time, the House passed the bill on a **key vote of 231–181 (R 194–25; D 37–155; I 0–1).** *(2006 key votes, p. 937)*

Gay Marriage

Supporters of a constitutional amendment aimed at banning gay marriage in June 2006 fell eleven votes short of the number needed to overcome a procedural hurdle in the Senate, failing to muster even a simple majority. The House rejected a companion measure the following month. The votes represented a setback for conservatives who had hoped that a stronger showing would eventually lead the way toward passage of the controversial amendment.

The proposed constitutional amendment would have defined marriage as "the union of a man and a woman." It would have prohibited states from recognizing same-sex marriages. The issue of same-sex marriage had become a political flashpoint after the Massachusetts Supreme Court ordered the state in 2003 to begin permitting marriages between two men or two women. The overwhelming majority of other states prohibited same-sex marriage, either with constitutional amendments or with statutes.

To win ratification, the constitutional amendment would need two-thirds support in the Senate and House as well as ratification by three-quarters of state legislatures. Both chambers had voted on the issue in the 108th Congress, with supporters falling well short of the needed votes. *(Earlier action, Congress and the Nation Vol. XI, p. 613)*

In 2006 Senate proponents could not muster the three-fifths majority required to limit debate on a motion to take up the resolution (S J Res 1) by Sen. Wayne Allard, R-Colo. The vote on June 7 was 49–48. Seven Republicans voted against invoking cloture, or limiting debate; two Democrats voted in favor of doing so. Proponents made a net pickup of just one vote from the last time the chamber had held a procedural vote on the issue, in 2004, even though Republicans had picked up an additional four seats.

The vote was a setback for social conservatives who had hoped to muster more than fifty votes for cloture. They vowed to pursue the issue in the future, contending the amendment was needed to protect traditional family values and to uphold the right of states to prohibit same-sex marriage. But many senators expressed reluctance to amend the U.S. Constitution, including Republicans who doubted that the nation was threatened by same-sex marriage. Sen. Judd Gregg, R-N.H., had supported the measure in 2004, but he voted against it in 2006, saying the Massachusetts court decision permitting same-sex marriage had not undermined efforts in other states to prohibit such unions.

Despite the defeat of the measure in the Senate, House Republican leaders put their chamber's resolution—(H J Res 88), sponsored by Marilyn Musgrave, R-Colo.—to a vote in July as part of the GOP's American "values" agenda. The measure was brought up under an expedited procedure that allowed no amendments but required a two-thirds vote. It was rejected 236–187 on July 18, falling forty-six votes short of the threshold for passage.

Steroids in Sports

Amid mounting concern over the issue of steroid use in professional sports, the House Government Reform Committee in 2005 held a series of high-profile hearings featuring testimony from Major League Baseball stars. After the hearings, lawmakers in both chambers introduced legislation (HR 2565, HR 3084, S 1960) to require sports leagues to follow rigid testing regimens and impose tough penalties on players who use steroids and other performance-enhancing drugs.

Even though many lawmakers at the forefront of the effort said they preferred that the sports leagues police themselves, two House bills won approval in committee. But Congress backed off after Major League Baseball announced on Nov. 15 a tentative agreement with its players on a three-strikes-and-out policy for offenders.

HOUSE HEARINGS

The Government Reform Committee launched its highly publicized hearings in March on the prevalence of steroids in sports. Medical experts had been warning that anabolic steroids were linked to an array of physical and mental ailments along with the extraordinary muscle growth that makes them appealing to athletes. At a March 17 hearing, three of the game's top players—sluggers Sammy Sosa and Rafael Palmeiro and pitcher Curt Schilling—testified that they never used steroids. A fourth star, Mark McGwire, declined to say whether he had ever used the illegal drugs. "I'm not here to discuss the past," he said.

One of the most vivid scenes was the firm declaration before the panel by Palmeiro, the Baltimore Orioles first baseman, that "I have never used steroids, period." In August Major League Baseball announced that the slugger had tested positive for a performance-enhancing drug and was being suspended for ten days. In November the committee decided against seeking a perjury charge against

Palmeiro, ruling that the circumstances surrounding the positive test were too murky.

Commissioner Bud Selig and Donald Fehr, the executive director of the players association, came under withering criticism for what lawmakers described as three decades of looking the other way while more and more pharmaceutically bulked-up millionaires set a dangerous example for young athletes.

Lawmakers bluntly warned that they would take action if Major League Baseball failed to crack down on steroid use. Rep. Thomas M. Davis III, R-Va., chairman of the Government Reform Committee, held open the possibility at the hearing that legislation could be written to regulate the behavior of professional athletes to an unprecedented degree. He added, however, that "we always prefer not to legislate."

Critics suggested that Congress was overreaching for the sake of easy headlines and had tested the bounds of its subpoena powers by compelling the testimony of a half-dozen prominent players. But many members of the committee, in both parties, suggested that baseball's unique place in American culture—which means the players set examples, good or bad, for the nation's youth—creates for Congress an obligation to protect the public trust.

COMMITTEE ACTION

The Government Reform Committee on May 26 approved by voice vote a bill (HR 2565—no written report) to require the National Football League, the National Basketball Association, Major League Baseball, and the National Hockey League to test players randomly five times each year for performance-enhancing drugs. The bill would also require the leagues to adhere to the same list of banned substances and to adopt the same penalties as those implemented by the International Olympic Committee: a two-year suspension for first-time offenders and a lifetime ban for those caught again.

Keeping up the pressure, the committee on June 16 added provisions of HR 2565 to a bill (HR 2829) reauthorizing the Office of National Drug Control Policy. Committee members then passed the reauthorization measure by voice vote. HR 2829 was formally reported (H Rept 109-315, Part I) on Nov. 18.

The House Energy and Commerce Committee approved its own bill 38–2 on June 29 to create uniform drug-testing standards for professional sports. The bill (HR 3084) required six professional sports leagues—the National Football League, the National Basketball Association, Major League Baseball, the National Hockey League, Major League Soccer, and the Arena Football League—to test players for illegal drugs five times a year. It would give the Department of Commerce the power to oversee steroid regulation in sports. HR 3084 was formally reported (H Rept 109-210, Part I) on July 28.

Tests would be conducted without advance notice at random intervals throughout the year, both during and after each sport's season. A first offense would lead to a half-season suspension, and a second violation would bring a full season's suspension. Any third violation would result in a permanent ban from the sport.

On Nov. 15, as the Senate prepared to take up its version of the legislation (S 1960), baseball team owners announced an agreement with players to give first-time offenders a fifty-game suspension and a lifetime suspension for a third offense. Lawmakers agreed to hold off on pursuing additional measures.

Flag Desecration

The 109th Congress came within a single vote of passing a proposed constitutional amendment to allow lawmakers to criminalize desecration of the American flag. The House passed the measure by the required two-thirds vote in 2005. But Senate supporters fell just short of a two-thirds majority when voting on virtually identical legislation in 2006.

The battle over flag burning had become a staple of congressional debate for more than a decade. The most recent action came in 2003 when the House, but not the Senate, approved a constitutional amendment. *(Background, earlier action, Congress and the Nation Vol. XI, p. 620)*

Conservatives had been trying to win such a constitutional change since 1990, when the U.S. Supreme Court in *United States v. Eichman* struck down a federal law (PL 101-131) that banned flag desecration. That law had been enacted after the high court ruled in 1989 in *Texas v. Johnson* that a conviction under a Texas state law for desecration of the flag violated the First Amendment. *(1990 and 1989 cases, Congress and the Nation Vol. VIII, p. 836; PL 101-131, Congress and the Nation Vol. VIII, p. 761)*

Supporters said the amendment was needed to protect a revered symbol of American values, as well as to wrest control of the Constitution from unelected judges. Critics said it would violate a critical U.S. value: freedom of expression. The mainly Democratic opponents also decried the debate as politically motivated. Although the president has no formal role in the process, the White House issued a supportive statement calling the flag "a cherished symbol of national unity."

If passed by a two-thirds vote in each chamber of Congress, a proposed constitutional amendment would have to be ratified by three-quarters (thirty-eight) of the states within seven years to become part of the Constitution.

If Congress had passed the resolution, it would have been the first constitutional amendment to go to the states since 1978, when Congress passed a proposed amendment to give the District of Columbia the full voting rights of a state. That amendment was not ratified by the requisite number of states. *(D.C. representation, Congress and the Nation Vol. V, p. 838)*

LEGISLATIVE ACTION

The House passed the resolution (H J Res 10) by a vote of 286–130 on June 22, 2005, after rejecting 129–279 a substitute by Melvin Watt, D-N.C., to require Congress to act in a manner consistent with the First Amendment. The House Judiciary Committee had approved the resolution 17–9 on May 25 and reported it (H Rept 109-131) on June 14. On the floor, Gene Taylor, D-Miss., made two motions to recommit the resolution to the House Judiciary Committee with instructions to add language proposing a balanced budget amendment and the segregation of the Social Security trust fund from the federal budget. House Republicans employed parliamentary tactics to turn aside Taylor's motions.

This was the sixth time since 1995 that the necessary two-thirds of those present and voting in the House supported the constitutional change. But the tally in 2005 showed the lowest level of support yet for the amendment. In 2003 three hundred members had supported it.

The Senate took up its version of the resolution (S J Res 12) on June 27, 2006. It was worded almost identically to the House version.

Senators had not voted on a flag-burning amendment since 2000, when the measure fell four votes short. Though the 2006 resolution attracted the largest number of "yeas" yet in the Senate, the **key vote of 66–34 (R 52–3; D 14–30; I 0–1)** was not enough. *(2000 action, Congress and the Nation Vol. X, p. 666; 2006 key votes, p. 937)*

Three Republican senators, including Majority Whip Mitch McConnell of Kentucky, voted against the resolution. Fourteen Democrats, including Minority Leader Harry Reid of Nevada, voted in favor.

For weeks, supporters and opponents alike had been counting no more than sixty-six votes in favor. Nevertheless, Senate Republicans, who presented the resolution as a necessary strike against an unelected Supreme Court, scheduled the vote anyway. "This amendment is, pure and simple, a restoration of the Constitution to what it was before unelected jurists changed it in a 5–4 decision," said Orrin G. Hatch, R-Utah, who sponsored the legislation.

Opponents of the resolution, however, said that Majority Leader Bill Frist, R-Tenn., had scheduled the chamber's vote for an entirely different reason: to appeal to the Republican Party's conservative core of supporters in advance of the November midterm election.

Before voting on the resolution, the Senate on June 27 rejected 36–64 a substitute by Richard J. Durbin, D-Ill., to make it a crime to desecrate a U.S. flag under certain circumstances, including inciting imminent violence or threatening another person. Durbin included language that would also have set new restrictions on demonstrations conducted at the funerals of military service members. In May, legislation had been enacted (HR 5037—PL 109-228) to restrict political demonstrations at military funerals at federally controlled cemeteries.

Human Trafficking

Congress in 2005 cleared a bill (HR 972—PL 109-164) to allow the United States to prosecute federal employees and federal contractors working overseas for violating laws against human trafficking. The House on Dec. 14 by a vote of 426–0 agreed to a motion by sponsor Christopher H. Smith, R-N.J., to suspend the rules and pass the measure. The Senate passed the House bill on Dec. 22 by voice vote, completing congressional action. President George W. Bush signed the legislation on Jan. 10, 2006.

The measure extended for two years a 2000 anti-trafficking law (PL 106-386) and authorized $188 million in fiscal 2006 and $173 million in fiscal 2007 for programs overseen by the departments of State, Health and Human Services, and Defense. *(2000 law, Congress and the Nation Vol. X, p. 629)*

The legislation toughened anti-trafficking measures by allowing prosecutors to bring federal contractors and government employees who work overseas, as well as members of their households, back to the United States to face charges of violating human trafficking laws.

It also sought to combat trafficking and sexual exploitation by international peacekeepers. Before endorsing any peacekeeping mission, the secretary of state would have to report to Congress on the safeguards implemented by the United Nations, or other international organizations responsible for a post-conflict mission, to prevent and punish trafficking or sexual abuse.

The bill authorized an additional $18 million in each of the next two fiscal years for the Department of Homeland Security to investigate trafficking and enforce the laws against it.

An amendment by Wisconsin Republican F. James Sensenbrenner Jr., chairman of the House Judiciary Committee, also directed the attorney general to conduct studies about "severe forms of human trafficking." The amendment authorized $10 million in fiscal 2006 and another $10 million in 2007 to help immigrants who have been the victims of sexual trafficking.

According to U.S. government statistics, between 600,000 and 800,000 people, some 80 percent of whom were women or girls, were trafficked across international borders each year and exploited as forced labor or sex industry workers. An estimated 14,500 to 17,500 were trafficked into the United States each year.

The House International Relations Committee had approved HR 972 by voice vote on March 10. A report on the bill (H Rept 109-317, Part I) was filed on Nov. 18. The House Judiciary Committee approved the legislation, also by voice vote, Dec. 8 and reported it (H Rept 109-317, Part II) the same day.

2007–2008

With Democrats taking control of both chambers in the 110th Congress, clashes with the administration of President George W. Bush intensified. Attorney General Alberto R. Gonzales resigned amid intense criticism of his leadership of the Justice Department, including the abrupt firings of several U.S. attorneys. His successor, Michael B. Mukasey, also sparred frequently with lawmakers. However, Democratic leaders worked with President Bush in an unsuccessful effort to clear immigration legislation, and they succeeded in passing bipartisan bills to expand the American with Disabilities Act and bar genetic discrimination.

While much in Congress changed with the 2006 elections, the issue of immigration remained as difficult as ever to resolve. A proposed overhaul of immigration law died in 2007 despite bipartisan negotiations and Bush's strong support. As in the 109th Congress, lawmakers could not reach a compromise over whether immigration law should focus exclusively on law enforcement or combine a crackdown on illegal immigrants with temporary visas for guest workers and a path to citizenship for some immigrants.

The issue proved difficult for both parties, dividing liberals and inflaming grassroots conservatives. Many moderate and conservative Democrats thought that providing illegal immigrants with a path to citizenship sounded like amnesty, and they were willing to defy their leaders and oppose such legislation—just as their Republican counterparts had in the 109th Congress. So contentious was the issue that House and Senate leaders did not attempt to revisit it in the election year of 2008.

Lawmakers, however, found common ground on a pair of politically popular bills to protect Americans from discrimination. Congress in 2007 cleared legislation, backed by the White House, to expand the reach of the 1990 Americans with Disabilities Act and ensure that those who met the act's standards were not denied protection. The bill was a response to a series of U.S. Supreme Court decisions over the previous decade that appeared to narrow the scope of the protection available under the 1990 law.

The following year, Congress broke a years-long logjam and cleared legislation to bar employers and health insurers from discriminating on the basis of genetic information. Business lobbyists opposed key provisions, but both chambers voted for the bill overwhelmingly after reaching compromise language, which was supported by the administration.

Lawmakers also reached bipartisan consensus on overhauling the Freedom of Information Act. However, attempts to change patents laws stalled amid infighting among business groups.

Immigration

A sweeping overhaul of immigration law died in the 110th Congress despite the strong support of President George W. Bush and months of fruitful bipartisan negotiations. Refusal by the Senate to limit debate on legislation (S 1348, S 1639) in 2007 brought an end to Bush's long effort to win a comprehensive overhaul of immigration policy. It showed that lawmakers remained deeply divided over whether immigration law should focus exclusively on law enforcement or combine a crackdown on illegal immigrants with temporary visas for guest workers and a path to citizenship for some immigrants.

The issue was one that divided liberals and inflamed grassroots conservatives who constituted a core GOP constituency. The same splits sank attempts to clear a comprehensive immigration bill in the 109th Congress. Even though control of both chambers changed to the Democrats in the 110th Congress, the divisions remained intact. Many moderate and conservative Democrats, like their Republican counterparts, believed that a path to citizenship sounded like amnesty, and they were willing to defy their leaders and oppose such legislation. *(109th Congress action, p. 686)*

To escape the dilemma, both Bush and the Democratic leadership had to devise a package that could attract sufficient support that both parties could afford to lose substantial numbers of their members. Some strategists looked to the No Child Left Behind education law in 2001 (PL 107-110) as a strategic model. That bill had enough tradeoffs and bragging rights for both parties that it won wide support and lost only a handful of votes from both ends of the ideological spectrum. *(Education law, Congress and the Nation Vol. XI, p. 540)*

As the new Congress convened in 2007, such an approach looked viable, aided by Bush's commitment to help broker a deal and an unusual alliance between Senate Republicans and Democrats. Homeland Security Secretary Michael Chertoff and Commerce Secretary Carlos Gutierrez convened daily closed-door meetings on Capitol Hill, attended by a core group of senators who called themselves the "grand bargainers." The effort gained momentum when Republican Jon Kyl of Arizona, a vocal critic of the comprehensive approach favored by the White House, joined the negotiations and forged a partnership with Democrat Edward M. Kennedy of Massachusetts.

The group produced a bipartisan bill (S 1348) that combined border security and enforcement measures with a temporary-worker program and a plan to allow the estimated twelve million illegal immigrants to remain and work in the United States. Under the bill, the illegal population would be eligible to take steps toward earned citizenship after eight years and if they paid fines, passed an English and civics exam, made a return trip to their native country, and remained employed and in good legal standing. The measure also sought to change the future distribution of green cards by moving away from the existing system, which rewarded family ties, and toward a merit point system based on the nation's economic needs.

JUDICIAL NOMINATIONS

Senate Democrats, still smarting from the GOP blockade of many of President Bill Clinton's judicial nominees during his presidency (1993–2001), were in no mood to be charitable as President George W. Bush's final term wound down. The Senate confirmed ten appeals court nominees in 2007, two-thirds the number that the GOP-controlled Senate approved in the last two years of Clinton's presidency and five fewer than Minority Leader Mitch McConnell, R-Ky., demanded. *(2001–2005 judicial nomination controversies, Congress and the Nation Vol. XI, pp. 595, 623)*

The Senate also confirmed fifty-eight district court judges.

By the end of his presidency, Bush succeeded in placing sixty-one appellate court judges and 216 district court judges. In contrast, among the two previous two-term presidents, Clinton successfully named sixty-two appellate court judges and 306 district court judges, and Ronald Reagan successfully named seventy-eight appellate court judges and 292 district court judges.

Bush made many nominations without consulting home-state senators, virtually guaranteeing they would not be confirmed. Judiciary Committee chairman Patrick J. Leahy, D-Vt., revived the Senate's "blue slip" tradition that barred nominations from advancing without the approval of both home-state senators.

At the end of the 110th Congress, there were twelve vacancies on appeals courts. Bush had submitted nominations for ten of the vacancies. Some of the seats had been open for years because Bush nominated candidates whom Democrats filibustered or whom Republicans simply chose not to advance when they were in the majority in the Senate.

2005 Action

One of the most controversial judicial nominees by Bush was Texas Supreme Court justice Priscilla Owen, who was among the first the president nominated for the federal bench in 2001. Her nomination to the U.S. Court of Appeals for the Fifth Circuit languished for four years before winning approval immediately in the wake of the threat by the Senate GOP leader to change Senate rules to prevent filibusters on judicial nominations, and the successful effort by a group of fourteen senators to reach a compromise. *(Filibuster change, p. 820)*

Owen was perhaps the most ideologically controversial of the ten appellate court nominations whom Democrats filibustered. Her opponents charged she would be hostile to abortion rights.

The showdown came in 2005 when a new filibuster was mounted against Owen. The GOP leader, Sen. Bill Frist, R-Tenn., said that if a cloture vote failed he would use a procedural device to stop this and all future filibusters on judicial nominations. Before that happened the fourteen senators, seven from each party, reached an agreement that pledged members not to filibuster nominations except in "exceptional circumstances," which was not defined.

The cloture vote on Owen came on May 24, 2005. It easily carried on a **key vote of 81–18 (R 55–0; D 26–17; I 0–1).** She was then confirmed 55–43. *(2005 key votes, p. 915)*

2006 Action

The Senate confirmed twenty-nine of Bush's nominees in 2006 for lifetime seats on federal district and appellate courts. But Frist did not try to force floor votes on three of the president's most controversial choices: William G. Myers III and Norman Randy Smith, both for the U.S. Court of Appeals for the Ninth Circuit, and Terrence W. Boyle for the U.S. Court of Appeals for the Fourth Circuit.

Under Senate rules, all nominations pending at the start of a recess that lasts more than thirty days are returned to the president. Democrats took advantage of that to have five nominations sent back to Bush at the beginning of the August recess. The Senate Judiciary Committee had not acted on two of the nominations, those of William J. Haynes II for the Fourth Circuit and Michael Wallace for the Fifth

But the goodwill that existed behind the scenes never caught on beyond the bargaining table, and politics dominated congressional reaction the moment the nearly eight-hundred-page bill was made public on May 17, 2007. Republicans continued a familiar complaint: that the earned citizenship was on par with offering "amnesty" to those who had broken the law. Democrats, joined by organized-labor groups and civil rights organizations, opposed replacing family ties with a point system and criticized the guest worker plan for not offering a path to citizenship.

The bargainers tried to win over their colleagues on the Senate floor, but the tension was exacerbated by a Memorial Day deadline that Majority Leader Harry Reid, D-Nev., set for holding a final vote. Reid ultimately extended the debate into June, giving in to GOP demands for more time to debate amendments. But the extra time only made matters worse. When Reid filed a motion to cut off debate, the legislation collapsed amid three failed cloture votes on June 7.

A new compromise surfaced when the president and bill backers offered a revised measure (S 1639) on June 18 that included $4.4 billion in mandatory spending for border security and enforcement. But that was as close as they came to success. Again, the Senate fell short of the sixty votes needed to invoke cloture.

Circuit. Bush resubmitted all five nominations in September, but the Senate again returned them when the chamber recessed for the midterm elections. Bush resubmitted the nominations again in November, but the Senate did not act on them.

Bush withdrew two other appellate nominations, those of Henry W. Saad for the Sixth Circuit and James H. Payne for the Tenth Circuit.

Democrats signaled their desire to avoid another high-stakes confrontation in May, when twelve of their number joined all fifty-five Republicans in voting 67–30 to limit debate on the nomination of Bush's staff secretary, Brett M. Kavanaugh, to the U.S. Court of Appeals for the D.C. Circuit. Bush first selected Kavanaugh for the D.C. court in 2003, but the nomination languished. Kavanaugh had served as associate White House counsel and associate counsel to independent counsel Kenneth W. Starr, and some considered him too partisan and too inexperienced for the D.C. Circuit, which is regarded as the most important federal appeals court. Upon Kavanaugh's renomination in the 109th Congress, he was confirmed on a 57–36 vote May 26.

2007 Action

All but one of the nominations approved on a roll call vote in 2007 won by an overwhelming majority, usually without a single dissenter.

The exception was Leslie Southwick, who was nominated to the U.S. Court of Appeals for the Fifth Circuit. Mississippi's two Republican senators, Thad Cochran and Trent Lott, backed Southwick, a former appeals court judge in the state. The Congressional Black Caucus and other liberal activists opposed him, focusing on a 1998 case in which he joined an opinion that upheld the reinstatement of a social worker who had used a racial epithet to describe a colleague. His critics also said his record on the state bench showed he was hostile to African Americans and the disadvantaged and was overly sympathetic toward business.

Supporters said Southwick was a highly qualified nominee whom liberals attacked unfairly. The Senate Judiciary Committee narrowly approved the nomination Aug. 2. Democrat Dianne Feinstein of California joined all nine Republicans on the committee in voting for the nomination.

The Senate confirmed Southwick 59–38 on Oct. 24, after voting 62–35 to invoke cloture on the nomination, thereby heading off a potential Democratic filibuster.

2008 Action

The Senate confirmed another five appellate court judges in 2008, along with twenty-seven district court judges.

The most heated confirmation battle broke out over Helene N. White, nominated to the U.S. Court of Appeals for the Sixth Circuit. On the Judiciary Committee, Orrin G. Hatch of Utah was the only Republican to join Democrats in support of her. Republicans said the panel should have first acted on nominees whom President Bush selected earlier, including candidates for seats on the Fourth and District of Columbia circuits.

But Judiciary chairman Leahy made a higher priority of the nomination of White, who was favored by Michigan's two Democratic senators, Carl Levin and Debbie Stabenow. President Clinton originally nominated White, but Senate Republicans blocked her nomination for four years. Bush nominated her in April at the behest of Levin and Stabenow.

Although Republicans questioned whether White was qualified for a federal appellate judgeship, the Senate confirmed her 63–32 on June 24.

McConnell vowed to wage a retaliatory campaign against Democrats unless at least five more appellate court judges were confirmed. At times, he made some parliamentary strikes, mostly by invoking a Senate rule that prevented committees from calling a meeting more than two hours after the start of a Senate floor session.

The leaders made faint promises to revisit smaller pieces of the bill later in the session. But an attempt in October to do just that—in a bill to allow some children of illegal immigrants to adjust their status—failed to win enough support to open the debate. Advocates of the so-called DREAM Act (S 2205) mustered fifty-two votes, eight short of the sixty required.

Instead of wrestling with the divisive issue, House Democratic leaders warily watched the Senate debate. Speaker Nancy Pelosi, D-Calif., made it clear that she was in no hurry to take up an issue that could split the Democratic Caucus and lose a substantial number of votes from her side.

Neither chamber took up comprehensive immigration reform in the second session.

FIRST COMPROMISE REJECTED

The Senate began debate soon after the bipartisan compromise was reached in May 2007. The compromise plan was presented May 21 as a substitute amendment to an immigration bill (S 1348) that was already on the floor. The plan survived a tough first week, including four days of floor debate and a flurry of amendments from both sides.

As lawmakers prepared to leave for the Memorial Day break, the seven senators that had led the negotiations—Democrats Kennedy, Ken Salazar of Colorado, and Dianne Feinstein of California, and Republicans Kyl, Lindsey Graham of South Carolina, Arlen Specter of Pennsylvania, and Mel Martinez of Florida—stood together at a news conference amid fleeting signs of victory.

Although they accepted compromises on the floor, they warded off amendments that threatened to gut core elements of the agreement. For example, they agreed to a Democratic amendment that cut the size of the bill's temporary guest worker program by at least half, but they defeated two attempts to scrap the program altogether.

During the first week of debate, the Senate

- Adopted 74–24 on May 23, with the help of twenty-seven Republicans, an amendment by Democrat Jeff Bingaman of New Mexico to reduce the number of work visas allowed under the program from at least 400,000 a year to 200,000. The amendment also eliminated an escalator clause that would have adjusted the cap to match demand for foreign workers.

Altering the guest worker program was a top priority for some Democrats, who severely criticized it for lacking any direct path to citizenship. As written, the bill would allow low-skilled immigrants to work in the country for two-year stints, renewable twice but only if they returned home for one year in between. Allies such as unions and Hispanic advocacy groups echoed the criticism.

- Rejected 31–64 on May 22 an amendment by Democrat Byron L. Dorgan of North Dakota to eliminate the guest worker provision from the bill.
- Rejected 48–49 on May 24 an amendment by Dorgan to terminate the guest worker program after five years.
- Rejected 48–49 on May 24 an amendment by Republican Norm Coleman of Minnesota to allow federal, state, or local government officials to question individuals about their immigration status if the officials had probable cause to believe they lacked legal status.
- Adopted by voice vote on May 23 an amendment by Republican Judd Gregg of New Hampshire to boost the border security and enforcement "triggers" that would have to be reached under the bill before the temporary-worker program could be put in place. Under Gregg's amendment, the triggers would require twenty thousand Border Patrol agents instead of eighteen thousand; three hundred miles of vehicle barriers along the border instead of two hundred; and 31,500 detention beds instead of 27,500.

Kennedy initially opposed the higher triggers and moved to table the amendment, citing assurances by the homeland security secretary that the border security provisions in the bill were sufficient. But the two reached an accommodation, with Gregg agreeing to consider further adjustments to the numbers when the bill went to conference.

- Adopted 59–35 on May 24 an amendment by Vermont Independent Bernard Sanders to assess companies that hired technology industry workers through the H-1B visa program a $3,500 surcharge on top of other fees. The money would go to a scholarship fund that would award up to $15,000 a year to various American students.
- Adopted by voice vote on May 23 a Graham proposal to establish new mandatory minimum sentences for individuals caught trying to reenter the United States after being deported.
- Adopted by voice vote on May 23 an amendment by Feinstein to establish procedures and standards to protect thousands of undocumented children who were in the country unaccompanied.
- Adopted by voice vote on May 24 a proposal by Republican John McCain of Arizona to require applicants for Z visas, which would grant probationary status to undocumented workers, to pay state and federal taxes, including penalties and interest, owed for certain periods of employment in the United States.
- Rejected 29–66 on May 24 an attempt by David Vitter, R-La., to strip what immigration hard-liners viewed as the bill's most offensive provision: the legalization of millions of illegal immigrants. Twenty-six Republicans voted against Vitter.

Senators returned from the Memorial Day recess prepared to complete work on the bill and spent most of the week addressing proposed changes to it. They held roll call votes on twenty-one amendments, adopting ten of them. The extra week for amendments was made possible after Reid agreed to extend the debate, with a goal of wrapping up deliberations by June 8.

But the momentum started to reverse course after two amendments were adopted:

- A proposal by Republican John Cornyn of Texas, adopted 57–39 on June 6, to remove confidentiality protections in the bill for illegal immigrants who were denied a Z visa. Under the new Z visa, illegal immigrants already in the country would be on a path to citizenship. Kennedy called it a "report to deport" plan and said it would deter illegal immigrants from coming forward. But eleven Democrats and several GOP negotiators supported the proposal.
- Another effort by Dorgan, adopted 49–48 on June 7, in the session that began June 6, to terminate the bill's core temporary-worker program after five years. Dorgan had narrowed his amendment from the version that had been rejected in May by exempting an agricultural worker visa program. Kennedy tried in vain to persuade his colleagues not to support Dorgan's revised amendment.

Republicans who helped write the compromise regarded the guest worker provisions as essential. Feinstein pointed to both the Dorgan and the Cornyn amendments as potential deal-breakers for the bill.

The bipartisan group of senators who wrote the bill huddled, trying to figure out how to undo the damage. But by then the effort was in serious doubt, with Republicans blocking efforts to limit the debate and Reid vowing to pull the bill if a cloture motion were rejected.

In a series of votes held June 7 to test each side's resolve, Republicans—even those supporting the bill—stuck together. The Senate

- Defeated 33–63 the first cloture vote of the day, on the substitute amendment to the bill.
- Defeated 34–61 a cloture vote on the bill itself.
- Defeated 45–50 a motion to reconsider the cloture vote on the substitute. The final vote was a bit closer, with some Democrats and a few GOP supporters returning to the fold, but it still came up short. Eleven Democrats and Sanders joined thirty-eight Republicans to oppose cloture in the final vote.

Republicans had asked Reid to delay the last cloture vote until the next day, June 8, so they could continue working on a short list of amendments. But Reid felt they had had enough time to whittle the list of amendments.

SENATE: SECOND BILL REJECTED

On June 12, Bush went to Capitol Hill to make his case for a comprehensive bill to the Senate Republican Conference at its regular Tuesday lunch meeting.

Two weeks later, the Senate began debate on a revised bill (S 1639) that included a more extensive section on border security, among other changes. It included $4.4 billion in mandatory spending for border security and enforcement. But in a vote that spelled the end of the road for the legislation, a majority of senators turned down a motion to invoke cloture and limit debate on the bill. The vote, on June 28, was 46–53. Bush expressed disappointment at the outcome. "The American people understand the status quo is unacceptable when it comes to our immigration laws," he said. "A lot of us worked hard to see if we couldn't find a common ground—it didn't work."

In an attempt to prevent opponents from dragging out the debate, Reid had used a rare procedural tactic to structure amendments, known as a "clay pigeon." Instead of holding an up-or-down vote on each amendment, senators cast votes on tabling the individual amendments. If a component was tabled, which required at least fifty votes, it was killed. If a component was not tabled, senators could not dispense with it without unanimous consent. At the end of thirty hours of post-cloture debate, senators were expected to cast up-or-down votes on any components not tabled.

The plan only seemed to fan the partisan bickering. Combined with a deluge of phone calls to Senate offices on the morning of the decisive cloture vote, the plan left Reid unable to gain even a majority on the amendments. Five of the amendments were tabled June 27, and another was withdrawn. But the process came to a halt when the chamber refused 45–52 to table a seventh amendment that would have dropped all references in the bill to requirements for issuing secure driver's licenses and identification cards under a 2005 law (PL 109-13). *(Border security, p. 679)*

Vitter, who had been a leading critic of the compromise and an advocate for focusing on enforcement, hailed the bill's collapse. Supporters said determining exactly when and why the momentum slipped away could be difficult, but they began to sense trouble early on June 28 when Senate switchboards lit up. Hours before the cloture vote spelled the demise of the complex and highly contentious bill, a deluge of phone calls from constituents, mostly clamoring for the measure's defeat, tied up the lines to several Senate offices. Yet even before the telephones rang off the hook, both backers and critics pointed to a number of factors that converged early that day and convinced enough senators that Congress was not ready to pass Bush's vision of an immigration overhaul. Senate GOP aides said the tipping point came when Alaska Republicans Lisa Murkowski and Ted Stevens cast "no" votes together. Shortly after that, Sam Brownback, R-Kan., who had cast an early "yea," switched his vote.

SENATE: CHILDREN'S STATUS

An attempt to break out a provision of the larger immigration bill that would allow some children of illegal immigrants to change their status in the United States met a similar fate. On Oct. 24, the Senate rejected cloture on a motion to proceed to the bill (S 2205) by a vote of 52–44, eight short of the sixty needed.

The measure would have allowed the children of illegal immigrants who entered the United States before age sixteen and lived in the country at least five years to gain conditional legal status and eventual citizenship if they attended college or joined the military for at least two years. Only those who were thirty or younger on the date of enactment would be eligible.

Although a dozen Republicans voted to consider the bill, thirty-six voted "no." Most of them remained clearly opposed to even limited efforts to legalize the status of illegal immigrants. Graham said the bill would "stiff the will" of the American people who oppose any form of "amnesty" for illegal immigrants and would put 1.3 million people on a path to citizenship ahead of those who entered the country legally.

Supporters suffered a blow an hour before the vote, when the White House released a statement of administration policy opposing the bill. "By creating a special path to citizenship that is unavailable to other prospective immigrants—including young people whose parents respected the nation's immigration laws—[the bill] falls short," the statement read.

Americans with Disabilities

President George W. Bush signed legislation (S 3406—PL 110-325) on Sept. 25, 2008, that expanded the category of those classified as disabled and included provisions to ensure that protections under the 1990 Americans with Disabilities Act (ADA) were not withheld from anyone meeting those standards. The bill was the result of parallel efforts from the White House and Capitol Hill in response to a series of U.S. Supreme Court decisions over the previous decade that lawmakers said had narrowed the scope of the protection available under the 1990 law (PL 101-336).

The original act was intended to make it easier for people with disabilities to work and use services available to the nondisabled by requiring businesses to make accommodations, such as wheelchair ramps and wider doors and stalls in restrooms. *(ADA, Congress and the Nation Vol. VIII, p. 743)*

The Court had ruled that disabled individuals who corrected or mitigated the effect of their disability—for example, through the use of medication or medical devices such as hearing aids—should not be considered disabled for the purpose of decisions relating to hiring, firing, or job performance. Advocates for the disabled argued that the Court's decisions created a situation in which people attempting to treat their disabilities could lose legal protections against discrimination. They said the decisions were contrary to the law's intent.

An unusual coalition of business groups and advocates for the disabled worked behind the scenes for the better part of the 110th Congress to amend the original act. The first product of their efforts was a bill (HR 3195) introduced in 2007 by House majority leader Steny H. Hoyer, D-Md., and ranking Judiciary Committee Republican F. James Sensenbrenner Jr. of Wisconsin. The bill, which passed by a sizable margin in June 2008, would have specified in statute the categories of physical and mental ailments that could be considered disabilities for the purposes of the ADA and revised the definition of "disabled" in the original law. The bill would have changed the definition from a condition that "substantially limits" a bodily function to something that "materially restricts" such a function.

The White House was eager for the Senate to clear the measure in time for Bush to sign it July 26—eighteen years after his father signed the original law. But efforts slowed in the Senate, where lawmakers disagreed over whether to include the House's new definition of "disabled." That sent the coalition of business groups and advocates for the disabled back to the drawing board. In September the Senate passed a new bill (S 3406), sponsored by Tom Harkin, D-Iowa, that did not revise the definition of "disabled" but stated that the ability to mitigate the effects of the disability through means such as medication, prosthetics, or hearing aids did not affect the person's qualification under the ADA. The House cleared the Senate's bill a week later.

BACKGROUND

The following were key Supreme Court rulings cited by lawmakers as narrowing the categories of people who qualified under the ADA.

Bragdon v. Abbott (1998). When Randon Bragdon, a dentist, found a cavity in patient Sidney Abbott's gumline, he told Abbott that because she was HIV-positive, filling the cavity in his office would be dangerous and offered to complete the procedure in a hospital. Abbott insisted the ADA entitled her to office treatment, and her lawsuit against Bragdon made it to the Supreme Court as both its first ADA- and AIDS (acquired immune deficiency syndrome)-related case. Although the Court agreed that having HIV (human immunodeficiency virus) met the ADA's definition of a physical impairment impacting numerous life activities, it said it did not have enough evidence to rule on the risk of her condition to Bragdon's office and sent the case back to the lower courts. *(Court case, Congress and the Nation Vol. X, p. 719)*

Sutton v. United Air Lines Inc. (1999). In 1992 Karen Sutton and Kimberly Hinton were rejected for pilot positions with United Air Lines because they did not meet the company's vision standard for pilots. The twin sisters were severely myopic, but with corrective measures, both functioned identically to individuals without similar impairments. They were pilots for regional carriers and claimed they were discriminated against on the basis of their vision. The Supreme Court, however, stated that the ADA's definition of disability did not include correctable physical impairments that did not substantially limit a major life activity. *(Court case, Congress and the Nation Vol. X, p. 720)*

Murphy v. United Parcel Service Inc. (1999). This case, reviewed with *Sutton v. United Air Lines Inc.*, concerned Vaughn Murphy, a United Parcel Service mechanic who was fired when tests showed that his blood pressure exceeded the government's limit of what it considered safe for truck drivers. The high court ruled against Murphy, citing the same argument used in its *Sutton* decision. *(Court case, Congress and the Nation Vol. X, p. 720)*

Albertson's Inc. v. Kirkingburg (1999). In a second case reviewed with *Sutton*, Oregon truck driver Hallie Kirkingburg sued his company, which fired him for failing to meet basic vision standards and refused to rehire him after he received a waiver under an experimental government program. The high court ruled that the ADA did not require a company to waive safety regulations for individual cases. *(Court case, Congress and the Nation Vol. X, p. 720)*

Toyota Motor Manufacturing, Kentucky, Inc. v. Williams (2002). After Ella Williams, an assembly-line worker for Toyota, was diagnosed with carpal tunnel syndrome and reassigned tasks, disputes with the company eventually led to her dismissal. Williams sued, claiming that Toyota refused to accommodate her worsening condition. The Supreme Court decided she did not prove that her physical problems prevented her from performing tasks pertinent to daily life activities. *(Court case, Congress and the Nation Vol. XI, p. 672)*

LEGISLATIVE ACTION

Two House committees approved identical versions of Hoyer's bill (HR 3195) on June 18, 2006, and reported them on June 23. The Education and Labor Committee approved the measure 43–1 (H Rept 110-730, Part I). The Judiciary Committee approved it 27–0 (H Rept 110-730, Part II).

Hoyer's bill gained support earlier in the year, after a series of hearings in the House and Senate considered the issue of whether the Supreme Court was trampling on the rights of the disabled. Experts and lawmakers wondered whether legislation to broaden and restore the reach of the ADA to persons whose disabilities were less evident on the job would be doing a disservice to the most severely disabled. Or, they asked, would it set an unprecedented standard in the realm of equal opportunity employment by shifting the burden of proving that a worker is able or unable to do the job at hand from the employee to the employer?

The bill, a compromise measure shaped by lawmakers and lobbyists, explicitly rejected the relevant Supreme Court rulings. It expanded the definition of the term "disabled," which the original law described as meaning "a physical or mental impairment that substantially limits one or more of the major life activities." Hoyer's bill stated that "substantially limits" in the law meant "materially restricts." It also provided several examples of major life activities such as caring for oneself, eating, sleeping, breathing, and walking. It authorized the Equal Employment Opportunity Commission, the attorney general, and the secretary of transportation to issue regulations implementing the new definitions.

The bill reiterated protections for people with disabilities not immediately evident in the workplace—such as those involving the immune, digestive, and neurological systems. It also stated that the effects of "mitigating measures," such as hearing aids and prosthetics, could not be used in weighing whether a person's disability substantially affected his or her life activities. In response to concerns that the changes might be abused by those with minor disabilities, the bill exempted anyone with disabilities that were minor or were expected to last less than six months, as well as those whose disability could be corrected through contact lenses or eyeglasses.

The measure was hailed from both sides of the aisle as a vital piece of civil rights legislation. The day before the two markups, the Bush administration announced a series of proposed new ADA regulations that included several specific infrastructure rules and changes, such as mandating the construction of wheelchair ramps to and from court witness stands, setting height regulations for light switches, and clarifying the types of animals that could be used in service for the disabled. The Justice Department said the changes, which had been in the planning stages for the better part of four years, would cost as much as $23 billion, a price that brought protests from businesses. Advocates for the disabled said they wanted language put into statute, adding there was a huge difference between that and regulation.

Reflecting the strong bipartisan support for HR 3195, the House passed the measure June 25 by a vote of 402–17.

The Senate passed Harkin's version of the bill (S 3406) by voice vote Sept. 11, 2008. The House passed the bill by voice vote under suspension of the rules Sept. 17, completing congressional action. Much of the language was identical to that in the House-passed HR 3195. Unlike the House version, however, it did not include a change in the definition of "disability." But it directed the courts to broadly construe the definition of "disability" and to adjudicate the merits of a disability claim and not the severity of the disability when hearing cases involving clinically certified disabled people. House leaders said they were comfortable with that change.

Genetic Discrimination

After more than a decade of debate, Congress cleared legislation to bar employers and health insurers from discriminating on the basis of genetic information. President George W. Bush signed the bill into law May 21, 2008 (HR 493—PL 110-233), after insisting on a handful of minor modifications.

The legislation prohibited employers from using genetic screening results—data about cancer or heart disease risk, for example—in hiring, assignment, or promotion decisions. It also prohibited training programs run by employers or labor unions from discriminating on the basis of genetic information. The measure barred insurers from requiring genetic testing or making decisions on enrollment, coverage, or premiums based on the results of such tests. The law applied to group health plans, individual health plans, and Medicare supplementary policies. It also extended the prohibitions to include genetic information on the fetus of a pregnant woman.

Bill sponsor Louise M. Slaughter, D-N.Y., had first introduced antidiscrimination legislation in 1995, inspired by reports that people were avoiding tests for dangerous genetic conditions out of fear that the data would be used against them. The Senate had passed an identical bill twice, in 2003 and 2005. But the House did not vote on genetic discrimination legislation until April 25, 2007, when it passed Slaughter's bill overwhelmingly. *(2003 action, Congress and the Nation Vol. XI, p. 606)*

During the previous twelve years, when the House was under Republican control, the influential U.S. Chamber of Commerce had successfully lobbied the leadership to keep the bill bottled up. Business leaders argued that the bill was unnecessary and could lead to frivolous lawsuits against businesses. They said that they should not be barred from simply collecting genetic information. They also argued that businesses had been punished in court in documented cases of genetic discrimination.

Actual cases of genetic discrimination were rare, but supporters of the bill argued that the mere threat of discrimination stymied the field of genetic medicine, in which doctors targeted treatments to patients' specific genetic code. Enactment of legislation, they said, would reassure people that the results of genetic tests could not be used against them, and more tests could mean more opportunities to advance genetic medicine.

The Senate Health, Education, Labor, and Pensions Committee approved its own version of the bill (S 358) in 2007. The measure was sponsored by Olympia J. Snowe, R-Maine, with the support of ranking committee Republican Michael B. Enzi of Wyoming. The measure languished for more than a year, however, because of a hold placed on it by Tom Coburn, R-Okla., who said it would expose employers and insurers to undue risk of lawsuits. Coburn ultimately lifted his hold in April 2008 after reaching a compromise with the bill's sponsors, and the Senate passed the bill by an overwhelming majority.

The House cleared the amended bill, but at the last minute the White House demanded another change affecting the military's ability to collect genetic information. That language was adopted as a separate resolution, and the bill was signed.

BACKGROUND

When the mapping of the human genome was completed in 2003, there was widespread excitement about the possibility that genetic medicine could lead to better diagnoses and treatments, and even cures for diseases such as diabetes and cancer. But the advances also raised concerns that employers and insurers could discriminate against people who might be genetically predisposed to certain conditions and that the fear of such discrimination might discourage people from undergoing genetic testing or participating in clinical studies.

Two major court cases were often cited as pointing out the potential for such discrimination. In 1998 the U.S. Court of Appeals for the Ninth Circuit ruled unconstitutional the practice of testing certain employees for diseases related to their genetic makeup. In this case, the Lawrence Berkeley National Laboratory in California secretly tested black employees for sickle cell anemia.

In a second case, the Equal Employment Opportunity Commission (EEOC) sued Burlington Northern Santa Fe Railroad on behalf of employees who claimed they had been forced to undergo genetic tests after complaining of carpal tunnel syndrome, which in rare cases could be attributed to a chromosome. The railroad settled with the EEOC and the employees in 2002, paying them $2.2 million.

Existing law provided some protection against discrimination on the basis of an individual's genetic information. The Health Insurance Portability and Accountability Act (PL 104-191) prohibited group health plans from establishing eligibility rules for individual enrollment based on genetic information and prohibited group health plans from requiring individuals to pay higher premiums based on such data. *(PL 104-191, Congress and the Nation Vol. IX, p. 547)*

In addition, under an executive order issued Feb. 10, 2000, federal employees could not be dismissed or subjected to restrictions in employment or benefits on the basis of their genetic information. The executive order also barred improper collection and unauthorized disclosure of federal employees' genetic data.

2007 ACTION

The Senate Health, Education, Labor, and Pensions Committee approved S 358 by 19–2 on Jan. 31, 2007. It prohibited insurers and employers from requiring people to submit to genetic testing or from using genetic information to deny people insurance coverage, raise insurance premiums, or hire and fire workers. A report on the bill (S Rept 110-48) was filed April 10.

Snowe said it would help reassure people who were concerned that data from genetic tests for hereditary diseases could be used against them. She noted that research showed many women declined tests to possibly reveal a gene alteration that had been linked to breast cancer, fearing a positive test would lead to cancellation of health insurance.

Republicans Coburn and Richard M. Burr of North Carolina voted against the bill. Coburn said the measure could have unintended consequences for doctors, hospitals, police, and others. The U.S. Chamber of Commerce said it was too broad because it sought to punish employers not only for discrimination using genetic information, but also for collecting the data in the first place. Most states outlawed genetic discrimination, according to the chamber, and businesses feared new federal law would simply mean another layer of regulation to contend with, as well as new opportunities for lawsuits. The Snowe-Enzi bill did not preempt state laws.

In the House, the Education and Labor Committee approved its version of the bill (HR 493) by voice vote on Feb. 14, 2007, and reported it (H Rept 110-28, Part I) on March 5. The bill, by Slaughter, prohibited employers and insurers from collecting genetic data about their employees or patients or from using the information in business decisions such as hiring and firing or setting insurance premiums. The panel rejected 20–27 an amendment by Tim Walberg, R-Mich., to extend the bill's protections to fetuses.

The Ways and Means Committee approved the bill by voice vote on March 21 and reported it (H Rept 110-28, Part II) on March 26. The Energy and Commerce Committee approved it by voice vote on March 23 and reported it (H Rept 110-28, Part III) on March 29. The committee filed a supplemental report (H Rept 110-28, Part IV) on April 19. During the Energy and Commerce markup,

Republicans argued that the language was too broad. Some of their concerns resulted in changes such as a provision to include fetuses and embryos in the protections while not giving them new rights regarding abortion.

The House passed HR 493 under suspension of the rules by a 420–3 vote April 25.

With the bill stalled in the Senate because of Coburn's hold, Majority Leader Harry Reid, D-Nev., considered attaching it to an omnibus appropriations measure (PL 110-161) that was headed for certain enactment. The gamble almost paid off. But days before the session's end, a senior administration official from the Office of Management and Budget called Reid's office with a threat: The president would veto the spending measure, which contained the appropriations for nearly the entire federal government, if the genetic discrimination measure was included. With little choice, Reid dropped the genetics language from the omnibus, and the bill was held over to 2008. *(Appropriations, p. 111)*

2008 ACTION

The Senate passed a revised version of HR 493 on a **key vote of 95–0 (R 46–0; D 47–0; I 2–0)** on April 24, after agreeing by voice vote to a compromise that assuaged concerns raised by Coburn and the White House. On May 1, the House cleared the amended bill 414–1. *(2008 key votes, p. 972)*

The compromise was the result of two weeks of intense negotiations among aides to Snowe, Coburn, Democratic senator Edward M. Kennedy of Massachusetts, and other members, as well as representatives from the departments of Labor and Health and Human Services.

Coburn's office, backed by nine other GOP senators and the White House, insisted on changing the bill language to clarify a stronger "firewall" to protect companies from excess legal jeopardy. Among other changes, the sponsors added language providing that an employer who was also acting as an insurer could not be sued twice. Coburn also wanted to include a broad "business necessity" provision that would let employers collect and use genetic information in cases in which it was "job related and consistent with business necessity." But that proposal was unacceptable to bill sponsors, and Coburn's office agreed to drop it.

Lawmakers signed off on the deal on April 22, and Coburn dropped his hold. Administration officials gave assurances that the stronger "firewall" provisions met their needs, and the bill passed with Coburn voting in favor.

But proponents still had to overcome one more White House concern. The administration wanted language that would allow the military to collect genetic information to identify human remains. After clearing the bill on May 1, the House adopted a resolution (H Con Res 340) by voice vote to amend the measure by adding the language requested by the White House. The Senate adopted the resolution that night, also by voice vote.

Patent Rewrite

A bipartisan group of lawmakers began the 110th Congress hoping to end a multi-year logjam that had blocked efforts to overhaul the nation's patent laws. The House passed a patent bill (HR 1908) in the first session, but a surge of opposition from industry and labor groups critical of the legislation prevented Senate floor action and blocked the bill for the remainder of the Congress.

Sponsors said the legislation would help ensure the quality of patents issued by the U.S. Patent and Trademark Office, align the U.S. system more closely with those in other countries, and curb disruptive lawsuits challenging patent validity.

High-technology companies had long sought changes to the patent system to speed up the approval of patents and provide some protection from infringement lawsuits. The biotechnology and pharmaceutical industries, meanwhile, favored the existing system and were concerned that changes in the law, such as creating a new administrative avenue for challenging patents outside court, might imperil their businesses.

The House and Senate Judiciary Committees approved similar bills in July, and the House passed its measure by a comfortable majority in September. But the high-tech lobby's success in getting the bipartisan package through the House alarmed a new group—manufacturers, research universities, inventors, and unions—that had not paid as much attention to the issue of patents while it remained on Congress's back burner.

The result was an intense, unexpected lobbying effort by the AFL-CIO, the National Association of Manufacturers (NAM), and other groups to slow action in the hope that the legislation would be derailed. NAM, for example, opposed provisions to alter the way damages were awarded and to create a new procedure for post-grant challenges to patents. A coalition of unions wrote members of Congress arguing that the legislation would weaken patent protections, increase the likelihood of U.S. inventions being stolen by foreign interests, and undermine U.S. competitiveness.

Their efforts were successful. Senate majority leader Harry Reid, D-Nev., never scheduled the highly complex measure for the floor, where it might have taken weeks of time, in part because there was no guarantee it would get the sixty votes needed to block a filibuster.

BACKGROUND

All sides of the patent debate considered patents vital for protecting American innovation. Widespread concern existed that many of the patents issued by the overburdened Patent and Trademark Office were not justified. An often-cited example was a company that tried to patent a crustless peanut butter and jelly sandwich. But that was where the agreement ended, because businesses differed dramatically in how much they depended on and used patents.

Technology companies such as Microsoft, Apple, and Oracle wanted an accelerated patent approval process to match the speed of their industry's evolution, along with some protection from the endless gnawing of legal fees and expensive judgments from patent infringement lawsuits. Features of the current patent system that especially annoyed technology companies, however, were treasured by other industries, principally the pharmaceutical and biotechnology trade groups that had fought the technology lobby to a near standstill year after year. Their products had far fewer patents and longer shelf lives than cell phone ring tones or computer software. These companies were concerned that changes in the law, such as an administrative avenue to challenge patents outside court, might imperil their businesses.

Big technology companies, which frequently released updated versions of their products, were typically less dependent on any individual patent because their products might contain hundreds or thousands of different patented components. They relied on cross-licensing agreements that allowed them to share technology with other companies.

These tech companies—as well as some financial services companies, such as Goldman Sachs and Citigroup, which sought patents for some of their business methods—said the current system allowed people to threaten them with lawsuits based on overly broad patents. These companies said it was less expensive to settle such lawsuits than risk subjecting themselves to lengthy litigation that could result in huge damage awards.

The legislation considered in the 110th Congress made it easier to challenge granted patents through the Patent and Trademark Office instead of the courts, in what was called a post-grant review process. The change gave companies a weapon to use against what they considered were low-quality patents that, once awarded, were used to challenge other product patents in court. The bill also based damage awards for infringement on the fraction that the patented invention contributed to the overall value of the product, not the value of the entire product. Damage for infringement on a patented feature of a major software program, for instance, would not be based on the sales of the whole program.

Another fundamental shift in patent policy proposed by the tech industry would award patents to the first to file, not to the first to invent. That would harmonize U.S. patent law with the rest of the world and, the industry argued, reduce lengthy litigation about the origin of ideas.

Smaller companies and inventors were concerned that a first-to-file shift in patent law sought by the tech industry would put them at a disadvantage against bigger competitors that could afford to send a stream of applications to the patent office. Newer companies that relied on private financing and some research universities argued that creating new procedures for reviewing patents would scare off venture capital that invests in startups. They argued that investors would be reluctant to put their money into a company with a valuable patent under a post-grant review process that left patents vulnerable to open-ended challenges for years.

Opponents to the patent proposals in the 110th Congress coalesced around the argument that the proposed changes would leave American companies and workers more vulnerable to foreign competitors. They said that foreign competitors could exploit the new process to challenge the patents of U.S. competitors and that provisions to limit damage awards would make it less expensive for foreigners to infringe.

LEGISLATION HIGHLIGHTS

Both House and Senate bills included common provisions.

Patent filing order. Changed the system to award patents from the first-to-invent to a modified version of a first-to-file system. Under the first-to-invent system, used exclusively in the United States, conflicting claims were resolved by determining who made the invention first. The more efficient first-to-file approach, used by all other patent-issuing nations, awarded a patent to the first inventor to file an application.

Authors of the legislation said they were drawing on the best aspects of both systems to create a new first-inventor-to-file system. The plan retained the one-year grace period in existing law that allowed an inventor to secure a place in the application-filing queue if the invention was described in a publication or was in public use or on sale before another application was filed, so long as the inventor submitted the patent application within one year. A new administrative process called a derivation proceeding was created to ensure that the first person to file the application was the true inventor and not someone who misappropriated the invention.

Challenges. Created a new process for challenging the issuance of a patent that moved many such appeals out of the courts to the Patent Trial and Appeal Board, a new version of the existing Board of Patent Appeals and Interferences.

Post-grant review. Established a new post-grant review process that allowed a petitioner to seek to have an existing patent canceled, as long as the petition was filed within twelve months of the patent being issued. The Patent Trial and Appeal Board would not start from a presumption that the patent was valid.

Patent invalidating standard. Relaxed the standard for invalidating patents in some cases to the "preponderance of evidence" from the previous "clear and convincing evidence."

Challenge venues. Limited the venue where suits could be filed for patent infringement to the judicial district where the defendant's principal place of business was located or where the infringement took place.

Damages. Provided guidance to the courts in determining damages. Under existing law, the court was supposed to award damages adequate to compensate the patent-holder for the infringement, but those damages could in no event be less than a reasonable royalty for the use that was made of the invention by the infringer. In calculating a reasonable royalty, the bills directed the court to consider only the portion of a product or process that was attributable to the invention.

Under existing law the courts often calculated lost royalties based on the overall value of the product that included the patent, a standard that critics said tended to inflate the damages collected by patent-holders. The bills did not seek to eliminate that possibility, but they offered alternatives such as the value of the patent's contributions over prior patents, its impact on supply and demand for a product or process that incorporated the patented invention, and the patent's effects on other products or processes, such as cost savings and increased efficiency. The effect would be to lower damage awards in cases in which the judge found that the value of the patent was not equal to the overall value of the product that used the invention.

HOUSE ACTION

The House Judiciary Committee approved its bill (HR 1908) by voice vote July 18, 2007, after adopting several amendments, and reported it (H Rept 110-314) on Sept. 4.

One amendment, approved by voice vote, eliminated a provision to create a "second window" for challenging patents more than a year after they were granted. Instead, the bill proposed to strengthen the existing reexamination process. Critics complained that the new post-grant review procedure would open patent-holders to constant challenges. The amendment was backed by the bill's chief sponsors: Howard L. Berman, D-Calif., chairman of the Subcommittee on Courts, the Internet, and Intellectual Property; and Lamar Smith of Texas, the ranking Republican on the full committee.

Another amendment adopted by voice vote, offered by Hank Johnson, D-Ga., would give judges more discretion in apportioning damages in patent infringement suits.

Rejecting pleas by manufacturing and technology lobbyists, the House passed HR 1908 by 220–175 on Sept. 7. Supporters hailed the measure as important for U.S. competitiveness. Opponents, however, circulated a list of dozens of organizations with concerns about the bill, including manufacturers such as 3M and DuPont and research universities such as Cornell and Michigan State.

House minority leader John A. Boehner, R-Ohio, and Minority Whip Roy Blunt, R-Mo., sent Speaker Nancy Pelosi, D-Calif., a letter Aug. 30 urging her to delay consideration of the bill. But Berman and Smith said they were the ones with momentum, after accommodating major stakeholders over the course of three years of hearings, meetings, and negotiations.

The most important concerns of critics centered on provisions to expand post-grant challenges and apportion damages according to an invention's contribution to the value of a product or process.

The House Judiciary Committee had removed the "second window" provision, but critics said the twelve-month window would still leave too much opportunity to challenge patents after they had been issued. Proponents of a more robust review process argued that it would help eliminate patents of questionable validity.

Berman said that the most controversial remaining issue concerned the provisions addressing how to award damages in patent infringement cases. The bill emphasized apportioning damages according to the patent's contribution to an invention. Critics complained that the emphasis on apportionment, instead of other factors considered by judges, would make it difficult to determine damages and would probably result in lower royalty rates for their patents.

Berman said he was willing to compromise on apportionment but would prefer to negotiate that during a conference with the Senate. Berman persuaded two organizations that had opposed the bill, the University of California and the AFL-CIO, to step back from their criticisms. Both released letters saying they favored moving ahead despite lingering reservations.

In a statement of administration policy released Sept. 6, the White House opposed the bill because of the apportionment provision. "Making this change to a reasonably well-functioning patent legal system is unwarranted and risks reducing the rewards from innovation—a result that would undercut the other useful reforms in this bill," the statement said.

SENATE COMMITTEE ACTION

The Senate Judiciary Committee approved its version of the bill (S 1145) by 13–5 on July 19, 2007, after three days of markup interrupted intermittently because of a lack of quorum. The measure was formally reported (S Rept 110-259) on Jan. 14, 2008. Chairman Patrick J. Leahy, D-Vt., succeeded in defeating the most substantial efforts to change his bill, aided by the support of lead GOP sponsor Orrin G. Hatch of Utah. Jon Kyl, R-Ariz., offered amendments addressing the chief concerns of the bill's critics: the post-grant review process and the proposal to apportion damages according to the patent's contribution to the overall value of the product.

The committee

- Rejected 7–11 Kyl's proposal to eliminate the bill's post-grant review provisions. The Senate bill included a petition filed within twelve months of the patent, but it also included a "second window" that would allow some challenges throughout the life of the patent. The provision had been removed in the House version.
- Rejected 7–10 Kyl's attempt to strike the apportionment provisions.

Fired U.S. Attorneys

The new Democratic majority in Congress in 2007 moved quickly to confront the George W. Bush administration over the abrupt firings in 2006 of several United States attorneys across the country. The House and Senate Judiciary Committees conducted probes that quickly grew into a high-profile clash between the White House and a Congress eager to reassert its oversight prerogatives that were seldom used in the first six years of Bush's term in office, when Republicans held the majority on Capitol Hill.

The firings grew from a complaint into a full-blown political scandal that led not only to the restoration of limits on interim appointments but also to the resignation under fire of Attorney General Alberto R. Gonzales. *(Justice Department leadership, box, p. 680)*

Lawmakers cleared a bill (S 214) in May that repealed a provision in law that had allowed the attorney general to appoint interim U.S. attorneys without Senate confirmation. The bill restored a previous limit of 120 days on such appointments. President Bush signed the measure into law June 14 (PL 110-34).

The dispute arose out of an unusual move in December 2006 when the Bush administration ousted seven federal prosecutors in a single day: David C. Iglesias of Albuquerque, N.M.; Daniel C. Bogden of Las Vegas; Paul K. Charlton of Phoenix; Carol S. Lam of San Diego; John McKay of Seattle; Margaret Chiara of Grand Rapids, Mich.; and Kevin V. Ryan of San Francisco. Two others had been dismissed earlier in the year: H.E. "Bud" Cummins III of Arkansas, whose firing made way for a protégé of senior presidential adviser Karl Rove, and Todd Graves of Kansas City, Mo., who was replaced with a department official who had drawn fire for his work in the Civil Rights Division.

Led by Dianne Feinstein, D-Calif., senators questioned whether the administration had fired the attorneys for political reasons to replace them with Bush loyalists who did not have to undergo Senate confirmation. U.S. attorneys serve at the pleasure of the president for four-year terms after Senate confirmation. They are responsible for prosecuting federal criminal and civil cases and for defending the federal government in civil cases heard in their districts. But a little-noticed provision enacted in 2006 allowed the president to appoint an interim attorney to fill a vacancy until the Senate confirmed a replacement, without setting limits on how long the appointee could serve. The language, contained in the reauthorization of the anti-terrorism law known as the Patriot Act (PL 109-177), had not been part of either chamber's versions of the legislation but was added by conferees and included in the conference report. *(USA Patriot Act, p. 222)*

During several months of hearings, the Senate and House Judiciary Committees heard from a number of the ousted prosecutors, as well as Justice Department officials and others in the executive branch. Gonzales, who angered lawmakers of both parties by appearing to be evasive while testifying, and whose testimony was contradicted by other officials, resigned in August. Bush subsequently nominated Michael B. Mukasey to the post of attorney general, and the Senate confirmed the nomination on Nov. 8.

HEARINGS AND SUBPOENAS

Gonzales told the Senate Judiciary Committee on Jan. 18 that politics had played no role in the dismissal of the attorneys. But in a Feb. 6 hearing before the same committee, Deputy Attorney General Paul J. McNulty testified that one prosecutor—Cummins—had been dismissed so that a former aide to Rove could be appointed to the slot. He said the other U.S. attorneys had been asked to resign because of "performance-related" problems. That angered the former prosecutors, some of whom began speaking to media outlets in defense of their records.

Several of the fired U.S. attorneys testified under subpoena March 6 at hearings held by the House and Senate panels. The most explosive testimony was from Iglesias, who told of telephone calls from two New Mexico Republicans—Sen. Pete V. Domenici and Rep. Heather A. Wilson. Iglesias said Wilson called in mid-October 2006 to ask whether he had any sealed indictments related to public corruption cases involving New Mexico Democrats. At the time, Wilson was in the midst of a tight reelection race. Iglesias said he declined to answer Wilson's inquiry. Iglesias said Domenici called him at home about two weeks later to ask about public corruption investigations and the timing of indictments. "He said, 'Are these going to be filed before November?' And I said I didn't think so, to which he replied, 'I'm very sorry to hear that,'" Iglesias said. "And then the line went dead."

Both lawmakers issued statements before the hearings. Wilson said she contacted Iglesias after a constituent complained that he was slow-walking public corruption prosecutions. Iglesias said Wilson did not discuss such an allegation. Domenici apologized for the call and maintained that he never pressured Iglesias. But the former federal prosecutor said he "felt pressured to get these matters moving."

Other fired prosecutors told of being contacted by administration officials and by members' staffs. Cummins said that a Justice Department official called and warned him that the administration might have to disparage the former prosecutors if they kept talking to the news media or decided to cooperate with Congress.

In a closed-door meeting March 8, Gonzales told senators that the administration would not oppose legislation restoring the 120-day limit on interim appointments. He also said the Senate Judiciary Committee would be allowed to question five Justice Department officials identified as being involved in the firings, after committee chairman Patrick J. Leahy, D-Vt., threatened to subpoena them as part of the widening probe.

House Judiciary Committee chairman John Conyers Jr., D-Mich., and Judiciary Commercial and Administrative Law Subcommittee chairwoman Linda T. Sánchez, D-Calif., soon requested access to the same five officials, as well as McNulty, relevant documents, and the names of any lawmakers informed in advance about the firings.

As the investigation widened, Gonzales repeatedly told the committees and the press that he took responsibility for department mistakes in handling the dismissals, but that he could not recall or was unaware of many conversations and events related to the firings.

Justice Department documents released to the committees showed close coordination between the department and the White House on the firings. Candid e-mail exchanges among administration officials showed that the former prosecutors were carefully chosen for removal after then-White House counsel Harriet Miers suggested firing all of those whose original four-year terms had expired. The administration executed a coordinated plan, including a series of phone calls to GOP senators, to fire the seven in December and braced for fallout from lawmakers.

D. Kyle Sampson, who had resigned as Gonzales's chief of staff, told the Senate Judiciary Committee on March 29, "I don't think the attorney general's statement that he was not involved in any discussions about U.S. attorney removals is accurate." Sampson also made clear that Gonzales and Miers had made the final decision about whom to fire.

Bush offered to make his aides available for private, nontranscribed interviews. He also offered to give Democrats copies of communications about the issue between the White House and the Justice Department or third parties, but not internal White House communications. Democrats rejected the offer. In the weeks that followed, the two Judiciary Committees subpoenaed documents and testimony from the administration. Although they received some cooperation from the Justice Department, Bush asserted executive privilege regarding White House documents and top officials.

On July 25, the House Judiciary Committee voted 22–17 to recommend that the full House cite Miers and White House chief of staff Joshua B. Bolten for contempt of Congress for refusing to comply with subpoenas. The Senate committee voted 12–7 on Dec. 13 to seek contempt citations against Bolten and Rove. Two Republicans, ranking member Arlen Specter of Pennsylvania and Charles E. Grassley of Iowa, joined all ten Democrats in voting in favor of the resolutions.

Neither chamber voted on the contempt citations before the end of the session. If a contempt citation passes in either chamber, federal law requires the "appropriate United States attorney" to take the matter to a grand jury.

SENATE ACTION

As the first hearings on the firings were getting under way, the Senate Judiciary Committee voted Feb. 8 to approve a bill (S 214—no written report) reinstituting the 120-day limit on interim U.S. attorney appointments. The legislation, sponsored by Feinstein, was approved by a vote of 13–6.

As introduced, the bill would have authorized federal judges, instead of the attorney general, to make interim appointments, which was the practice until 1986. But Feinstein revised it after negotiations with Specter. As rewritten, the bill authorized the attorney general to make appointments of up to 120 days. If the Senate did not confirm a permanent replacement by then, the chief federal judge in the district could appoint a temporary replacement to serve until the Senate acted, as was the practice between 1986 and 2006. The bill applied to anyone who was appointed by the attorney general under existing law and was serving as a U.S. attorney on the day before the bill's enactment.

During the markup, the committee rejected two GOP amendments designed to limit the involvement of federal judges. Jon Kyl of Arizona warned that Republicans might complicate passage unless Democrats negotiated on the judges language.

The Senate passed Feinstein's bill on a **key vote of 94–2 (R 46–2; D 46–0; I 2–0)** on March 20, 2007. *(2007 key votes, p. 955)*

Before passage, the Senate on March 20

- Rejected 40–56 an amendment by Kyl to eliminate the ability to make interim appointments, whether exercised by the attorney general or by a judge. It required the president to nominate a replacement within 120 days and the Senate to act on the nomination within 120 days.
- Rejected 47–50 an amendment by Jeff Sessions, R-Ala., a former U.S. attorney, specifying that judges could appoint only Justice Department officials or federal law enforcement officers to temporarily fill a U.S. attorney post. Sessions's proposal also barred judges from appointing temporary replacements who were under investigation or who had been sanctioned by the Justice Department or another federal agency.

Republicans Christopher S. Bond of Missouri and Chuck Hagel of Nebraska voted against the bill because they opposed allowing judges to appoint temporary U.S. attorneys. Both cited concerns about separation of powers.

HOUSE AND FINAL ACTION

The House passed a companion bill (HR 580) by a vote of 329–78 on March 26.

The House Judiciary Committee had approved the measure by voice vote March 15 and reported it (H Rept 110-58) on March 20. Like the Senate measure, the House bill proposed to limit to 120 days the tenure of U.S. attorneys appointed on an interim basis. If the 120 days expired, the district court for that district could appoint a U.S. attorney to serve until a replacement had been confirmed. Howard L. Berman, D-Calif., sponsored the measure.

The main difference between the two bills was that the House version included a provision mandating that the process delineated in the legislation be "the exclusive means for appointing a person to temporarily perform the functions of a United States attorney." Sánchez added that language in the committee, along with a provision making the 120-day limit applicable to interim U.S. attorneys who were already serving.

On May 22, the House brought up the Senate-passed S 214 and passed it under suspension of the rules by a vote of 306–114, completing congressional action.

Berman said the House voted on the Senate bill because Senate Republicans had blocked consideration of the House-passed measure. Berman said that as the Judiciary Committee pored over e-mail messages and other materials, it had become clear that "whether or not it was the original intent of the administration," officials at the White House and the Justice Department "quickly figured out that the provision [in the 2006 law] created the possibility of circumventing the Senate and decided to exploit that authority."

Freedom of Information

Shortly before adjourning at the end of the first session of the 110th Congress, lawmakers sent President George W. Bush a compromise bill to overhaul the Freedom of Information Act (FOIA), the federal statute governing public access to government records. Bush signed the measure into law on Dec. 31, 2007 (S 2488—PL 110-175).

The legislation made it more difficult for the government to deny or delay the release of government documents under the act (PL 85-619). The Senate Judiciary Committee reported that a study by the nongovernmental National Security Archive found that some FOIA requests had been pending since 1989.

The measure included provisions to

- Require government agencies to set up new tracking systems for those FOIA requests that were expected to take more than ten days to process and required agencies to publish information about their ten oldest active requests.
- Allow complainants who were litigating FOIA requests to recover attorney fees if the pursuit of a nonfrivolous claim in court resulted in a government decision to comply with the request before the court ordered it to do so. The provision was written in response to the 2001 U.S. Supreme Court decision in *Buckhannon Board and Care Home, Inc. v. West Virginia Department of Health and Human Resources*, which called into question the ability to recover fees under such circumstances. *(Court case, Congress and the Nation Vol. XI, p. 643)*

The House passed an initial version of the bill (HR 1309) by a vote of 308–117 on March 14, despite opposition from conservative Republicans who said that, with no offsets, it would cost $63 million over ten years. Democrats said the bill was modified so it could not be implemented until offsets were found, a last-minute maneuver they said complied with pay-as-you-go rules. The White House objected to some provisions in the House bill, saying they would place additional "administrative and financial burdens on the executive branch," but it did not threaten a veto.

The House Oversight and Government Reform Committee had approved HR 1309 by voice vote on March 6 and reported it (H Rept 110-45) on March 12.

The House-passed legislation would have required agencies to respond to FOIA requests within twenty business days and to establish a publicly available tracking system for requests. Those who were denied requests by an agency and subsequently won a court judgment would have been eligible to recover legal fees from the agency.

The Senate passed its version (S 849) by voice vote Aug. 3, after lawmakers broke a months-long impasse.

The initial version of S 849 won approval by voice vote in the Judiciary Committee on April 12 and was reported (S Rept 110-59) on April 30. Sponsored by Judiciary chairman Patrick J. Leahy, D-Vt., and John Cornyn, R-Texas, it would require agencies to respond to a FOIA request within twenty days or lose the ability to claim several exemptions under existing law, such as for information that is privileged in a court case or that could identify a confidential source. It also would create hot-line services for the public to track requests by telephone or on the Internet, and it would authorize the Office of Special Counsel to take disciplinary action against government officials who refused to release information.

Leahy worked out a compromise with Jon Kyl, R-Ariz., who blocked floor action after committee approval. The compromise eliminated the twenty-day provision. Instead, the new version made a waiver of search fees the penalty for an agency's noncompliance.

Instead of negotiating in a formal conference, Congress cleared a compromise bill (S 2488) that included House pay-as-you-go language, as well as a House provision requiring government agencies to describe the FOIA exemptions upon which they relied to redact material. The Senate passed the bill by voice vote Dec. 14, and the House passed it Dec. 18, also by voice vote, completing congressional action.

Guantánamo Bay Detainees

Congress did not act in 2007 on habeas corpus rights for enemy combatants and other detainees held at Guantánamo Bay, Cuba. Many Democrats had wanted to reinstate the right of habeas corpus for detainees who either were designated as enemy combatants or were awaiting such determination. Congressional jurisdiction over the issue was removed when the U.S. Supreme Court ruled in June 2008 that terrorism suspects in Guantánamo had a right to seek their release in federal court. The Court's 5–4 ruling in *Boumediene v. Bush* meant that about 270 remaining detainees in Guantánamo would be able to challenge their detentions in civilian courts. *(2008 case, p. 764)*

BACKGROUND

President George W. Bush issued an executive order on Nov. 13, 2001, providing for the creation of military commissions to try noncitizens charged with belonging to al Qaeda or having participated in terrorist activities directed against the United States.

In 2004 the Supreme Court ruled in *Rasul v. Bush* that federal courts had jurisdiction to hear habeas corpus petitions from detainees held at Guantánamo Bay, Cuba, who were seeking a determination of whether they were lawfully incarcerated. The following year, Congress cleared legislation (HR 2863—PL 109-148; HR 1815—PL 109-163), known as the Detainee Treatment Act, that included language intended to eliminate statutory habeas jurisdiction. However, the high court ruled in June 2006 in *Hamdan v. Rumsfeld* that it had jurisdiction to hear pending habeas challenges. *(2004 case, Congress and the Nation Vol. XI, p. 665; 2006 case, p. 764)*

The Court held in *Hamdan* that the military commission lacked the power to proceed because its structure and procedures violated the Uniform Code of Military Justice (UCMJ) and the Geneva Conventions. It rejected the government's argument that Congress had specifically authorized the military commissions as established by Bush in either the Authorization to Use Military Force (PL 107-40) or in the Detainee Treatment Act. The president's authority thus depended on the UCMJ, which (in Article 21) described the jurisdiction of commissions as extending to "offenses or offenders" defined "by statute or by the law of war." The conspiracy charge against Salim Ahmed Hamdan was improper because it was not recognized in U.S. practice or in international law as a violation of the law of war. *(2001 use of force resolution, Congress and the Nation Vol. XI, p. 234)*

In September 2006, Congress cleared legislation (S 3930—PL 109-366) authorizing military commissions for detainees that included new provisions stripping habeas corpus rights from the detainees. The Military Commissions Act (MCA) was upheld in February 2007 by a three-judge panel of the U.S. Court of Appeals for the District of Columbia Circuit. The appellate panel ruled that the habeas language in the 2006 law did not violate the suspension clause, the constitutional mandate that habeas rights not be suspended except during invasions or rebellions. "Precedent in this court and the Supreme Court holds that the Constitution does not confer rights on aliens without property or presence in the United States," Judge A. Raymond Randolph wrote in the majority opinion. *(Military commissions, p. 366)*

But opponents of the law noted that the Supreme Court had yet to weigh in on the issue. House Armed Services Committee chairman Ike Skelton, D-Mo., and Senate Armed Services Committee chairman Carl Levin, D-Mich., said they would review the 2006 law.

Two military commissions in June 2007 dismissed charges against two detainees because neither had been found to be an "unlawful enemy combatant" as prescribed by the military commissions law. One of those detainees was Hamdan, whose petitions for habeas and mandamus resulted in the Supreme Court's 2006 decision to invalidate a military commission system that the Bush administration had unilaterally constructed. Congress enacted the 2006 legislation in response to the high court's ruling. A military commission granted Hamdan's motion to dismiss all charges for lack of jurisdiction because Hamdan had not been designated an "unlawful enemy combatant" as required by the 2006 law.

In *Boumediene,* the Court in 2008 held the MCA unconstitutional, ruling that habeas jurisdiction extended to Guantánamo and that the act's procedures were not an adequate substitute for habeas corpus.

LEGISLATIVE ACTION

The same week that the two military commissions dismissed charges, the Senate Judiciary Committee on June 7, 2007, approved 11–8 a measure (S 185) by Arlen Specter, R-Pa., to repeal the relevant language in all three laws. The bill, reported (S Rept 110-90) on June 26, faced staunch GOP opposition. Every Republican except Specter voted against the measure. In the committee report, five of the panel's GOP members said the legislation could force the government to choose between revealing secret intelligence sources and methods and releasing committed terrorists.

Committee chairman Patrick J. Leahy, D-Vt., said the rollback of habeas corpus rights was a "historic error in judgment" that the Senate should correct. Other critics said that the 2006 law could also be used to deny habeas corpus rights to an estimated twelve million permanent residents in the United States, should the president decide that any of them might be enemy combatants.

Specter ultimately turned his measure into an amendment to the fiscal 2008 defense authorization bill (HR 1585), which the Senate considered in July. But Majority Leader Harry Reid, D-Nev., pulled the bill from the floor after Republicans filibustered another amendment related to military operations in Iraq.

Reid called up the authorization measure again in September, but a cloture vote on the Specter amendment failed. The Senate Sept. 19 on a **key vote of 56–43 (R 6–42; D 49–0; I 1–1)** rejected a motion to invoke cloture on the habeas corpus amendment. *(2007 key votes, p. 955)*

Five bills on the subject were introduced in the House. None advanced, except legislation (HR 2826) by Skelton. The House Judiciary Constitution, Civil Rights, and Civil Liberties Subcommittee voted along party lines 7–4 on Sept. 6 to approve that bill, which would have restored habeas rights for Guantánamo detainees. Republicans vehemently opposed the measure.

Gun Trace Data

Allies of the gun industry in 2007 defeated efforts to allow the Bureau of Alcohol, Tobacco, Firearms, and Explosives (ATF) to release gun trace data more widely. Language restricting the release had been part of annual appropriations legislation since 2003, but some Democrats had hoped to leave it out this time. Instead, Congress adopted modified language to soften the prohibition in some respects but also make it permanent.

Law enforcement officials used trace data from ATF for investigations of firearm-related crimes. They provided ATF with certain information about a particular firearm, such as the manufacturer, model, caliber, and serial number. ATF specialists then searched through transfer documents showing the movement of the firearm from the manufacturer or importer to the wholesaler or distributor and then to the retailer. These records often led investigators to the initial purchaser of the firearm, which could help generate leads to solve a crime.

The issue of trace data became controversial as cities began trying to use the data in lawsuits against the gun industry. Congressional appropriators each year, beginning in 2003, adopted language known as the Tiahrt amendment to prevent that practice. Named for its sponsor, Rep. Todd Tiahrt, R-Kan., the amendment restricted the ATF from disclosing trace data unless such data were requested as part of a criminal investigation. As a result, cities and firearms critics could not use the data to help with civil lawsuits against gun manufacturers and dealers in civil lawsuits.

LEGISLATIVE ACTION

The House Appropriations Committee approved a $55.2 billion version of a stand-alone appropriations bill for the departments of Commerce, Justice, and State (HR 3093—H Rept 110-240) by voice vote July 12. *(Appropriations action, p. 113)*

The issue that drew the most attention concerned the Tiahrt amendment. Appropriations Committee chairman David R. Obey, D-Wis., who sought to avoid policy fights with Republicans, agreed to keep it in the measure. The committee rejected by voice vote an attempt by James P. Moran, D-Va., to strip the language.

Opponents of the restrictions said that they hampered local law enforcement officials from battling crimes involving illegal guns. They cited statistics showing that approximately 1 percent of gun dealers were responsible for most of the illegal firearms in circulation. But supporters of the restrictions cast the issue as a Second Amendment question. Tiahrt said the effort to strip his language from the bill was "an attack on legal ownership of firearms in America."

Tiahrt's provision was backed by the National Rifle Association and the Fraternal Order of Police. A coalition of 225 mayors, led by Independent Michael R. Bloomberg of New York, along with other law enforcement groups, sought to remove Tiahrt's language from the legislation.

The House passed the bill by a vote of 281–142 on July 26 after two days of low-key debate. The issue of releasing gun trace data was not raised on the floor

The Senate Appropriations Committee approved a $56 billion version of the bill (S 1745—S Rept 110-124) by a 28–1 vote on June 28. In a defeat for Sen. Barbara Mikulski, D-Md., chair of the appropriations subcommittee handling the bill, the full committee agreed to keep the language restricting access to federal gun trace data. Mikulski had vowed to keep the provision out of the bill.

The committee adopted 19–10 an amendment by ranking subcommittee Republican Richard C. Shelby of Alabama to allow the release of the bureau's gun trace data to local law enforcement only for "bona fide criminal investigations." Mikulski said the provision limited the ability of police departments to track gun dealers who knowingly sold weapons to criminals. The gun data amendment attracted four Democratic supporters: Byron L. Dorgan of North Dakota, Mary L. Landrieu of Louisiana, Ben Nelson of Nebraska, and, by proxy, Tim Johnson of South Dakota.

In the final version of the bill, lawmakers modified the language to state that it did not prevent

- Disclosure of statistical information concerning total production, importation, and exportation of firearms.
- Exchange of such information among law enforcement agencies, prosecutors, and national security officials.
- Publication of annual statistical reports on the total production, importation, and exportation of firearms or aggregate data regarding firearms traffickers or firearms misuse.

The language continued to prohibit the release of firearm trace data for the purposes of suing gun manufacturers and dealers. Moreover, the provision included the phrase "in fiscal year 2008 and thereafter," thereby making the limitation permanent law.

The Supreme Court

The U.S. Supreme Court's first vacancies in eleven years gave President George W. Bush in 2005 the opportunity to make two appointments to the high court, including a new chief justice of the United States. The Republican chief executive relied heavily on conservative interest groups in making his selections, and his appointees—Chief Justice John G. Roberts Jr. and Justice Samuel A. Alito Jr.—fulfilled their supporters' hopes by casting consistently conservative votes during their first three terms on the Court.

Roberts and Alito cast decisive votes in closely divided conservative rulings on issues ranging from abortion and school integration to campaign finance and separation of church and state. Nevertheless, the Court followed its 2004 decisions rejecting Bush's aggressive legal posture on antiterrorism issues with two more rulings upsetting the administration's plans to try suspected enemy combatants held at the U.S. naval base at Guantánamo Bay, Cuba, in truncated military proceedings with only limited review in federal courts. *(Terrorism cases, Congress and the Nation Vol. XI, p. 632; box, p. 730)*

Roberts succeeded Chief Justice William H. Rehnquist, who died on Sept. 3, 2005, after a yearlong fight against thyroid cancer. As chief justice, Roberts became the leader of a conservative bloc that included Justices Antonin Scalia and Clarence Thomas and Bush's other appointee, Alito.

Alito succeeded Justice Sandra Day O'Connor, who continued in her final sixteen months in office to cast pivotal votes in many cases that divided the Court's conservative and liberal blocs. O'Connor's retirement left that role to another moderate conservative, Justice Anthony M. Kennedy. He gave conservatives critical votes in many cases, but he also sided with liberal justices in some other decisions, including the two rulings in 2006 and 2008 guaranteeing habeas corpus rights to Guantánamo detainees.

As the Court's senior justice, John Paul Stevens led a bloc of four moderate liberals that included David H. Souter and President Bill Clinton's two appointees, Ruth Bader Ginsburg and Stephen G. Breyer. Stevens, who turned eighty-eight on April 20, 2008, surpassed nineteenth-century chief justice Roger B. Taney to become the Court's second oldest member ever. He appeared to be in good health and showed no sign of contemplating retirement. Some observers speculated that Stevens hoped to serve until February 2011, when he would surpass Oliver Wendell Holmes Jr. to become the Court's oldest justice ever.

Roberts and Alito both came of age as legal conservatives in the 1970s, held Justice Department positions under President Ronald Reagan during the 1980s, and displayed generally conservative orientations on federal appeals courts before Bush elevated them to the Supreme Court. They won confirmation in the Republican-controlled Senate—Alito more narrowly than Roberts—in the face of opposition from liberal interest groups and Democratic senators.

With the appointment of two justices in their fifties—Roberts, at age fifty, was the youngest chief justice since John Marshall assumed the post at age forty-five—Bush appeared to have solidified the Court's general conservative orientation for the immediate future. The election of Democrat Barack Obama as president in November 2008 stirred hopes among liberal interest groups that he would fill any vacancies during the next four years with left-leaning justices. But with liberals Stevens and Ginsburg as

REFERENCES

Discussion of the Supreme Court for the years 1945–1964 may be found in *Congress and the Nation Vol. I,* pp. 1141–1454; for the years 1965–1968, *Congress and the Nation Vol. II,* pp. 335–340; for the years 1969–1972, *Congress and the Nation Vol. III,* pp. 289–327; for the years 1973–1976, *Congress and the Nation Vol. IV,* pp. 619–659; for the years 1977–1980, *Congress and the Nation Vol. V,* pp. 755–791; for the years 1981–1984, *Congress and the Nation Vol. VI,* pp. 711–768; for the years 1985–1988, *Congress and the Nation Vol. VII,* pp. 785–840; for the years 1989–1992, *Congress and the Nation Vol. VIII,* pp. 801–851; for the years 1993–1996, *Congress and the Nation Vol. IX,* pp. 759–799; for the years 1997–2001, *Congress and the Nation Vol. X,* pp. 684–729; for the years 2001–2004, *Congress and the Nation Vol. XI* pp. 630–680.

SUPREME COURT CONFIRMATIONS

President George W. Bush in 2005 nominated two conservative federal appeals court judges, John G. Roberts Jr. and Samuel A. Alito Jr., to fill U.S. Supreme Court vacancies. Despite opposition from liberal groups and some Democratic senators, Roberts and Alito won confirmation in the Republican-controlled Senate on the strength of impressive resumes and pledges not to pursue ideological agendas on the Court.

The vacancies created by the retirement of Justice Sandra Day O'Connor and the death of Chief Justice William H. Rehnquist came after an eleven-year period with no changes in the Court's membership—the longest interval between vacancies since the early nineteenth century.

O'Connor touched off the sequence of events by announcing her plans to retire on July 1, 2005, after the Court ended its 2004–2005 term. Bush deliberated for a little over two weeks before choosing Roberts, then a judge on the U.S. Court of Appeals for the District of Columbia Circuit, as O'Connor's successor.

Roberts, then fifty, had a nearly unmatchable legal resume. He had been a star student at Harvard College and Harvard Law School. He went on to judicial clerkships with an influential federal appeals court judge and with then-Justice Rehnquist. Roberts served during the Reagan administration as special assistant to the attorney general and as associate White House counsel and later as deputy U.S. solicitor general during the George H. W. Bush administration. He gained a reputation as an outstanding Supreme Court advocate in ten years in private practice before being appointed to the D.C. Circuit in 2003.

Roberts was awaiting Senate hearings on his nomination when Rehnquist died on Sept. 3, after a nearly year-long fight against thyroid cancer. Two days later, Bush announced that he would nominate Roberts as Rehnquist's successor. With an additional week to prepare, Roberts appeared before the Senate Judiciary Committee on Sept. 12 with no notes and a memorized opening statement in which he said he had "no platform" except "the rule of law." Republican senators praised Roberts's qualifications, while Democrats pressed Roberts unsuccessfully for views on major legal issues.

Roberts skirted the most divisive issue—abortion—by promising to treat precedent as important but not sacrosanct. Other questions Roberts parried with a combination of encyclopedic knowledge and noncommittal analysis. Some Democratic senators asked for more specifics, but in the end half of the Democrats joined all of the Republicans on a **key vote of 78–22 (R 55–0; D 22–22; I 1–0)** to confirm Roberts as chief justice of the United States on Sept. 29. He presided over the Court's opening session on Oct. 3, with O'Connor still on the bench awaiting confirmation of her successor. *(2005 key votes, p. 915)*

Bush had stunned supporters and critics alike earlier that morning by choosing Harriet Miers, his White House counsel, to succeed O'Connor. Miers had earlier been Bush's counsel when he was governor of Texas. Conservative groups that had played a leading role in Roberts's nomination and confirmation criticized Miers for her limited experience and lack of constitutional law background. With Miers gaining little support from Republican senators, Bush agreed on Oct. 27 to her request to withdraw the nomination.

Like Roberts, Alito moved from an Ivy League education—Princeton University and Yale Law School—to positions in the Justice Department and solicitor general's office during the Regan administration. Alito served three years as U.S. attorney for New Jersey before President George H. W. Bush appointed him to the U.S. Court of Appeals for the Third Circuit in 1990. Alito had been on the White House's short list for O'Connor's vacancy in the summer and was interviewed for the position before Bush chose Roberts.

Conservative groups praised Alito. Liberal groups mobilized to oppose his confirmation, fearing that, as O'Connor's successor, he would tilt the balance of power on the Court decisively to the right.

In a four-day confirmation hearing that began on Jan. 9, 2006, Democrats sharply questioned Alito about conservative views he had expressed as Justice Department attorney—including opposition to abortion rights—and an appeals court record that opponents saw as favoring government and business over individual rights. Alito followed Roberts's example in disavowing any "agenda." On abortion, Alito promised to approach the issue "with an open mind."

With Democrats still dissatisfied, the Judiciary Committee approved the nomination on Jan. 24 on a 10–8 party-line vote. The Senate voted 72–25 on Jan. 30 to cut off a threatened filibuster and then confirmed Alito's nomination the next day by a **key vote of 58–42 (R 54–1; D 4–40; I 0–1).** The tally was the second closest vote for a confirmed nominee since 1900. Four Democrats voted for Alito; Lincoln Chafee of Rhode Island was the lone Republican to vote "no," as did Vermont independent James M. Jeffords. *(2006 key votes, p. 937)*.

Alito was sworn in later that day and sat with the Court for the first time in February. As the term continued, three cases that had been argued with O'Connor on the bench were scheduled for reargument, indicating that the remaining eight justices were evenly divided and giving Alito the decisive vote in each.

Roberts and Alito are both Roman Catholics. Along with Justices Antonin Scalia, Anthony M. Kennedy, and Clarence Thomas, they formed the first-ever Catholic majority on the Court.

THE COURT OF 2005–2008

The members of the U.S. Supreme Court in 2005–2008:

- Chief Justice of the United States William H. Rehnquist, born in 1924, appointed to the Court by President Richard M. Nixon in 1971; promoted to chief justice by President Ronald Regan in 1986; died Sept. 3, 2005.
- Chief Justice John G. Roberts, born in 1955, appointed chief justice in 2005 by President George W. Bush, succeeding Rehnquist.
- Justice John Paul Stevens, born in 1920, appointed by President Gerald R. Ford in 1975.
- Justice Sandra Day O'Connor, born in 1930, appointed by President Ronald Reagan in 1981; announced in 2005 her intention to retire from the Court; retired in 2006 on confirmation of her successor, Samuel A. Alito Jr.
- Justice Antonin Scalia, born in 1937, appointed by President Ronald Reagan in 1986.
- Justice Anthony M. Kennedy, born in 1936, appointed by President Ronald Reagan in 1987; began service in 1988.
- Justice David H. Souter, born in 1939, appointed by President George H. W. Bush in 1990.
- Justice Clarence Thomas, born in 1948, appointed by President George H. W. Bush in 1991.
- Justice Ruth Bader Ginsburg, born in 1933, appointed by President Bill Clinton in 1993.
- Justice Stephen G. Breyer, born in 1938, appointed by President Bill Clinton in 1994.
- Justice Samuel A. Alito Jr., born in 1950, appointed by President George W. Bush in 2005; began service in 2006.

the Court's oldest two members, the most likely retirements seemed unlikely to give Obama the chance to change the balance of power on a Court that remained closely divided on many issues.

Statistically, the Court's output continued to decline despite Chief Justice Roberts's statement during his confirmation hearing that he thought the Court should be deciding more cases. The Court issued fewer than seventy decisions in each of Roberts's three terms as chief justice. With sixty-seven decisions in the 2006–2007 term, the number fell to its lowest since the early 1950s.

The decline, which had begun early in Chief Justice Rehnquist's tenure, continued despite a historically high number of cases brought to the Court. The Court's docket reached a record high 10,296 cases in the 2006–2007 term, a 20 percent increase over Rehnquist's final term. The number fell to 9,600 cases at the end of the 2007–2008 term.

In his confirmation hearing and in later speeches, Roberts also expressed a preference for unanimous or nearly unanimous decisions whenever possible. Nevertheless, the 2006–2007 term witnessed the highest percentage of one-vote decisions in the Court's history. Out of sixty-eight signed decisions, twenty-four—or 35 percent—were by 5–4 votes.

INDIVIDUAL RIGHTS

The Roberts Court flexed its conservative muscles most dramatically in a trio of 5–4 rulings that recognized an individual right to possession of firearms, limited racial balance policies by school districts, and upheld a federal law banning a controversial abortion procedure. Each of the decisions—issued over a two-year period—significantly departed from prior cases and drew pointed rebukes from the four liberal dissenters.

The gun rights ruling, *District of Columbia v. Heller* (2008), established for the first time an individual right under the Second Amendment to own and possess guns. For the majority, Scalia rejected the Court's previous interpretation in a 1939 decision that the amendment protected gun rights only in the context of state militias.

In immediate effect, the ruling struck down a thirty-year-old Washington, D.C., ordinance that banned handguns and required other weapons stored in homes to be trigger-locked or disassembled. Scalia said handguns were "the quintessential self-defense weapon" and the home-storage restrictions rendered them useless for that purpose. But he stressed that the ruling left untouched other restrictions, including laws against carrying concealed weapons or prohibiting gun ownership by felons, juveniles, or people with mental illness.

Gun rights advocates hailed the ruling as a historic victory. For the dissenters, Stevens warned the ruling would drag the courts into the "political thicket" of gun control.

The school integration decision *Parents Involved in Community Schools v. Seattle School District No. 1* (2007) struck down pupil assignment policies used by the Seattle, Wash., and Louisville, Ky., school systems to try to achieve racial and ethnic diversity in individual schools. In the main opinion, Roberts said the school systems' use of race to assign pupils was not "narrowly tailored" as needed to satisfy the "strict scrutiny" constitutional standard.

Speaking for four justices, Roberts also found the school's claimed interest in racial diversity to be illegitimate. In a pivotal concurrence, however, Kennedy recognized racial diversity to be a "compelling" government interest and refused to rule out race-conscious policies to promote the goal. Nevertheless, Breyer warned in a seventy-seven-page dissent that the ruling—which he said contradicted prior decisions—would hamper efforts to prevent resegregation of public schools.

TERRORISM CASES

In the aftermath of the Sept. 11, 2001, attacks on the United States, President George W. Bush claimed broad powers to detain suspected "enemy combatants" for indefinite periods and to try them, if at all, in specially established military tribunals. The detainees included more than eight hundred foreigners rounded up in the war in Afghanistan or from other countries and taken to the U.S. naval base at Guantánamo Bay, Cuba.

Many of the detainees, supported by civil liberties and human rights groups, challenged Bush's expansive claims of executive power. In a series of cases beginning in 2004, the U.S. Supreme Court ruled that Bush's policies went beyond his powers as commander in chief and violated U.S. law and international treaties regarding treatment of wartime captives.

In the first of the decisions, *Hamdi v. Rumsfeld* (2004), the Court held that the president can detain as an enemy combatant a U.S. citizen captured on the battlefield, but that the government must afford the detainee some hearing before a "neutral decisionmaker." In a second decision, *Rasul v. Bush* (2004), the Court ruled that the Guantánamo detainees could use habeas corpus to challenge their detentions in federal courts even though they were outside U.S. borders. *(2004 cases, Congress and the Nation Vol. XI, p. 632)*

At Bush's urging, Congress responded by enacting the Detainee Treatment Act, which denied federal courts jurisdiction over habeas corpus petitions by Guantánamo detainees. Meanwhile, the Pentagon had adopted plans to try the detainees before specially created "military commissions" operating with rules affording the accused fewer procedural rights than recognized in regular courts-martial or civilian courts.

The Supreme Court agreed to consider the legality of the military commissions in a habeas corpus case filed by Salim Ahmed Hamdan, a Yemeni who was accused of being a driver for Osama Bin Laden, the leader of the anti-American organization responsible for the Sept. 11 attacks, al Qaeda. Hamdan claimed that the military commissions did not comply with either the Uniform Code of Military Justice (UCMJ) or the Geneva Conventions, the international treaties governing treatment of wartime captives. When the justices agreed to hear Hamdan's case, the government argued that the Detainee Treatment Act barred his habeas corpus petition altogether. Alternatively, the administration's lawyers argued that the military commissions did not need to comply with the detailed provisions of either the UCMJ or the Geneva Conventions.

By a 5–3 vote, the Supreme Court rejected both of the administration's arguments. (Chief Justice John G. Roberts Jr. recused himself because he was on the federal appeals court panel that heard the case.) Writing for the majority in *Hamdan v. Rumsfeld* (2006), Justice John Paul Stevens preliminarily concluded that the Detainee Treatment Act's "court-stripping" provision did not apply to cases such as Hamdan's pending case when the law was enacted.

Stevens went on to find the creation of the military tribunals invalid because the president had not demonstrated any need to depart from regular court-martial procedures. He also said they violated the Geneva Conventions' requirement that detainees be tried by a "regularly constituted court." Justice Anthony M. Kennedy cast the pivotal vote in the case, joining Stevens and the three other liberal justices: David H. Souter, Ruth Bader Ginsburg, and Stephen G. Breyer. Conservative justices Antonin Scalia, Clarence Thomas, and Samuel A. Alito Jr. dissented.

Within three months, Congress responded—again at Bush's urging—by passing a new law, the Military Commissions Act (PL 109-366), which unambiguously denied federal courts jurisdiction over any habeas corpus petitions by Guantánamo detainees. Ruling in a pair of consolidated cases brought by groups of Guantánamo detainees, the U.S. Court of Appeals for the District of Columbia Circuit upheld the act as a constitutional exercise of Congress's power to suspend habeas corpus and ordered the detainees' cases dismissed. *(Military commissions, p. 366)*

Rejecting the administration's position once again, the Court ruled the act unconstitutional. "We hold that petitioners may invoke the fundamental procedural protections of *habeas corpus,*" Kennedy wrote for the 5–4 majority in *Boumediene v. Bush* (2008). Federal courts had jurisdiction, Kennedy explained, because the United States exercised effective control over the Guantánamo base.

After establishing jurisdiction, Kennedy went on to hold the procedures for the military commissions defective because the accused was not guaranteed the opportunity to present favorable evidence. The courts' role "cannot be circumscribed in this manner," Kennedy said. Noting that some of the detainees had been held for more than six years, Kennedy called for "prompt" hearings in their cases. He stressed, however, that the decision did not require release of any of the detainees.

Despite that concession, dissenting justices warned that the ruling would necessarily result in release of some enemy combatants who would resume fighting against the United States. The result "will almost certainly cause more Americans to be killed," Justice Antonin Scalia wrote in a dissent joined by Roberts, Thomas, and Alito.

The abortion decision *Gonzales v. Carhart* (2007) upheld a federal law that banned a procedure that doctors called dilation and extraction (D&X) and that opponents termed a "partial-birth abortion." The rarely used procedure entailed pulling the fetus into the vagina and then piercing the skull to complete its removal through the cervix.

With O'Connor in the majority, the Court in 2000 had voted 5–4 to strike down a Nebraska law banning the procedure, in part because it did not allow an exception to protect the woman's health. In passing the federal ban, Congress refused to include a health exception. But with Alito on the bench, the Court upheld the federal law.

For the majority, Kennedy said no health exception was needed because medical experts disagreed whether the procedure was ever necessary. For the dissenters, Ginsburg called the ruling an "alarming" departure from prior decisions.

Besides the terrorism rulings, conservative groups suffered their greatest disappointment on individual rights issues with a decision in the Rehnquist Court's final term that upheld the government's power to take private property for economic development by private companies. The 5–4 ruling in *Kelo v. City of New London* (2005) upheld a plan by an economically depressed Connecticut city to take parts of a working-class neighborhood for private companies to use for a hotel and commercial center.

For the majority, Stevens said economic development qualifies as a "public use" under the takings clause. Kennedy joined the opinion but wrote separately to warn against the use of eminent domain for "pretextual" or "incidental" public benefits.

O'Connor led four dissenters in saying that the ruling effectively eliminated the public use requirement. The ruling was widely criticized and prompted many state legislatures to pass laws limiting what property rights advocates called "eminent domain abuse." Because Rehnquist and O'Connor both dissented, the ruling would likely have been the same had Roberts and Alito been on the bench.

Under Roberts, the Court issued a series of rulings limiting private damage suits against companies and mixed decisions in job discrimination suits under federal civil rights laws. The Roberts Court also displayed what many observers saw as its aversion to litigation in several decisions that limited individual claims against governmental officials or entities.

In *Scott v. Harris* (2007), for example, the Court rejected a suit by a Georgia man left paralyzed after a deputy sheriff rammed his car off the road to end a high-speed chase. With only Stevens dissenting, the justices said that police can use deadly force if necessary to protect pedestrians or other motorists.

The same year, the Court rejected a Wyoming ranch owner's effort to hold federal officials liable for an alleged campaign of intimidation and harassment aimed at persuading him to grant the government an easement over part of his land. The ranch owner had other remedies, the 7–2 majority said. A year later, the Court ruled, 6–3, that a government employee cannot sue for damages under the equal protection clause to challenge a personnel decision affecting only himself or herself as arbitrary or capricious. Allowing so-called class of one claims could turn any number of personnel decisions into federal constitutional suits, Roberts wrote for the 6–3 majority.

In immigration cases, the Court in *Dada v. Mukasey* (2008) voted 5–4 to make it easier for aliens facing deportation to remain in the United States while challenging a removal order. Earlier, the Rehnquist Court had reached opposite results in a pair of decisions on the government's deportation powers. In *Clark v. Martinez* (2005), the Court said that the government cannot indefinitely detain aliens who have been ordered deported if their home country—Cuba, in this case—refuses to take them back. But in *Jama v. Immigration and Customs Enforcement* (2005), the Court held that the government could deport a Somali man even though his home country had no functioning government.

ELECTION LAW

The Roberts Court displayed its conservative leaning with decisions striking down or narrowing laws regulating campaign finance, upholding a stringent voter identification (ID) law, and rejecting a closely watched challenge to partisan gerrymandering of congressional districts.

Along with Roberts, Alito provided a critical vote in shifting the court's stance on campaign finance regulation. The Court in 2003 had voted 5–4 to uphold the major parts of a law, the Bipartisan Campaign Reform Act (BCRA), aimed in part at restricting corporate and union financing of thinly veiled campaign advertising on TV. The law permitted corporations or unions to pay for election-time TV ads referring to a candidate for federal office only from a separate political action committee, not from their own treasuries. O'Connor had cast a pivotal vote in upholding the law, also known as the McCain-Feingold Act, after its principal Senate cosponsors, John McCain, R-Ariz., and Russell D. Feingold, D-Wis.

As O'Connor's successor, Alito joined a 5–4 majority in a decision, *Federal Election Commission v. Wisconsin Right to Life, Inc.* (2007), that significantly narrowed BCRA's restriction on so-called electioneering communications. Writing the controlling opinion for himself and Alito, Roberts said the law could be constitutionally applied only to TV ads that unmistakably advocated the election or defeat of a particular candidate. Three justices—Scalia, Kennedy, and Thomas—went further and called for the provision to be invalidated in its entirety. The four dissenters said the ruling effectively overturned the earlier decision upholding the law.

A year later, Alito wrote for the same conservative majority in a decision, *Davis v. Federal Election Commission*, that struck down BCRA's so-called millionaire's amendment. The provision allowed a candidate for federal office to raise more money from contributors if he or she was significantly outspent by an opponent running a largely self-financed campaign. Alito said that the law infringed on the self-financing candidate's First Amendment rights and that its stated purpose of "leveling the playing field" for nonwealthy candidates was illegitimate.

Earlier, both Roberts and Alito had also joined a decision striking down a Vermont law that limited total spending by candidates for state offices and also imposed very low limits on contributions to state candidates. Breyer wrote the main opinion in the 6–3 decision, *Randall v. Sorrell* (2006). He said the contribution limits imposed "disproportionately severe" burdens on political rights of candidates and contributors, while the spending limits contradicted the court's previous decision holding spending caps at any level to be unconstitutional.

The voter ID decision, *Crawford v. Marion County Election Board* (2008), upheld an Indiana statute that was the strictest of several newly enacted state laws that Republicans claimed were needed to prevent election fraud. Democrats generally opposed the laws as unnecessary to prevent fraud and likely to reduce turnout by poor or less educated voters. Indiana's statute required voters to show a government-issued photo identification at the polls but allowed them to cast a provisional vote subject to submitting the required ID within ten days after an election. Stevens helped give conservatives a 6–3 majority in rejecting a facial challenge to the law on the ground that the challengers had failed to demonstrate an impermissible burden on voting rights. The ruling left the door open to future challenges, but supporters of the laws said the decision effectively settled the issue.

The redistricting decision *League of United Latin American Citizens v. Perry* (2006) upheld a congressional remap written by a Republican-controlled legislature that helped the GOP win a 21–11 edge over Democrats in the Texas congressional delegation in the 2004 election. In the main opinion, Kennedy found no impermissible use of partisan classifications in the legislature's decision to substitute its plan for a court-ordered districting map. Kennedy also had the controlling vote in rulings on individual district maps challenged by minority groups. He led the conservative bloc in breaking up a Dallas-Fort Worth area district where African Americans and Latinos together had comprised nearly a majority of the population. But Kennedy spoke for a liberal majority in finding that the breakup of a Latino-majority district in South Texas had impermissibly diluted minority voting strength.

In state election cases, the Court in 2005 said states could adopt a "semi-closed" primary system that allowed independents to cast ballots in a party primary but barred voters registered in a different party. Oklahoma's Libertarian Party had challenged the system as a violation of voters' rights. Three years later, the Court upheld Washington State's distinctive "top two" primary system, which allowed candidates to make known their own party preference in an initial open primary and then advanced the top two vote getters to the general election ballot regardless of party. The state's Republican and Democratic parties had challenged the system—established by a voter initiative—as an infringement of their right to control the listing of partisan affiliations.

FIRST AMENDMENT

The Court's few direct rulings on First Amendment issues showed a general conservative orientation by strengthening protection for political speech but supporting government restrictions on speech rights in other contexts. On church-state issues, the Court limited without completely prohibiting the display of the Ten Commandments on government property. Separately, the Court made it harder for taxpayers to challenge church-related organizations as an improper establishment of religion.

In two rulings on the Bipartisan Campaign Reform Act, Roberts and Alito helped shift the Court away from the deference toward campaign finance regulation shown in the 2003 ruling upholding the law. Writing the main opinion in the first of the decisions, *Federal Election Commission v. Wisconsin Right to Life, Inc.* (2007), Roberts memorably wrote: "Where the First Amendment is implicated, the tie goes to the speaker, not the censor." On the very same day, however, Roberts led a 5–4 majority in limiting free speech rights of high school students. The ruling in *Frederick v. Morse* (2007) upheld the power of school authorities to punish students for speech reasonably interpreted as advocating or promoting use of illegal drugs. "The First Amendment does not require schools to tolerate at school events student expression that contributes to [the] dangers" of drug use, Roberts wrote.

Several other rulings favored governmental policies challenged on First Amendment grounds. A coalition of law schools and law professors failed to invalidate a federal law penalizing colleges or universities that limited campus access by military recruiters because of opposition to the "don't ask, don't tell" policy against homosexuals. Roberts wrote the unanimous decision in *Rumsfeld v. Forum for Academic and Institutional Rights, Inc. (FAIR)* (2007) that found no violation of freedom of speech or freedom of association.

In the same year, the Court ruled 5–4 that government employees can be disciplined for speech made pursuant to their official duties. Alito cast the decisive vote in the case, *Garcetti v. Ceballos*, which had been argued with O'Connor on the bench and was then reargued after Alito's appointment.

Earlier, some dissident beef producers had failed in their effort to invalidate a government tax used to pay for the generic advertising campaign built around the slogan "Beef. It's What's for Dinner." The 6–3 ruling in *Johanns v. Livestock Marketing Association* (2005) said the tax was a valid industry-specific levy used to convey government speech.

In a criminal case, the Court in *United States v. Williams* (2008) rejected a First Amendment challenge to a recently enacted federal anti-pandering statute that made it a crime to offer or solicit child pornography even if the materials being offered or solicited do not exist. The Court in 2006 also upheld a Pennsylvania prison policy that denied a small group of disruptive inmates any access to newspapers, magazines, or personal photographs.

The Ten Commandments issue reached the Court in separate cases challenging a monument erected on the grounds of the Texas state capitol in 1961 and displays of the Decalogue in two county courthouses in Kentucky. With Breyer casting the pivotal votes in a pair of 5–4 decisions, the Court ruled the courthouse displays an improper establishment of religion but allowed the Texas monument to stand.

Writing for the majority in *McCreary County, Kentucky v. American Civil Liberties Union of Kentucky* (2005), Souter stressed evidence that county officials in both cases had the "predominant purpose of advancing religion." In the Texas case, *Van Orden v. Perry* (2005), Breyer wrote a controlling concurrence that stressed the secular purpose—preventing juvenile delinquency—in the erection of the monument. Religious advocacy groups speculated that the rulings, the final decisions in what would be Chief Justice Rehnquist's last court session, would generally allow most existing displays of the Ten Commandments to stand but could limit future displays.

Religious advocacy groups hoped that Roberts and Alito would fortify a trend begun under Rehnquist toward greater discretion for government aid to religion. The two justices did provide the critical votes in the decision *Hein v. Freedom From Religion Foundation, Inc.* (2007), limiting taxpayer suits under the establishment clause. The ruling rejected a challenge to President Bush's so-called faith-based initiatives, which provided federal social service funding to organizations with explicitly religious programs.

Alito wrote the pivotal opinion that barred taxpayer suits challenging federal spending on religious establishment grounds unless Congress had expressly authorized the funding. Roberts joined Alito's opinion. Three other conservative justices went further and called for barring such taxpayer suits altogether.

BUSINESS LAW

Business groups won a series of significant victories limiting legal remedies for investors, consumers, workers, rival companies, and the general public in suits against business defendants. The Court also cheered business groups with rulings backing federal preemption of state laws in areas subject to federal regulation.

Two important decisions continued the Court's nearly twenty-year trend of increased scrutiny of punitive damage awards. In one high-profile ruling, the Court voted 5–3 to slash to $500 million from $2.5 billion the punitive award that Alaskan plaintiffs had won for damages to their business from the 1989 *Exxon Valdez* oil spill. The ruling in *Exxon Shipping Co. v. Baker* (2008) held that punitive damages in federal maritime cases should generally be no greater than the compensatory award.

Business groups hoped that the same one-to-one ratio—based on the Court's supervisory authority over maritime cases—might be extended generally to state court cases, too. In the meantime, however, they were counting as a partial victory a 2007 ruling that somewhat limited state juries' discretion in imposing punitive damages. The decision in *Philip Morris USA v. Williams* held that juries cannot base damages on harm to anyone other than the individual plaintiffs before the court. But the ruling also allowed juries to consider harm to others in assessing a defendant's "reprehensibility"—one of the factors permitted in calculating punitive damages.

The Court also displayed skepticism toward securities fraud suits by investors. In the most important ruling, the justices voted 5–3 to limit suits by defrauded investors against companies not directly involved in the alleged fraud. The ruling in *Stoneridge Investment Partners, LLC v. Scientific-Atlanta Inc.* (2008) effectively ended a suit against two electronics manufacturers who were accused by investors of helping a big company doctor its books to maintain its stock price. The Court held that investors cannot sue a company's suppliers or customers for participating in a securities fraud unless they relied on misstatements from those companies.

Two rulings a year earlier also raised hurdles for investors in securities fraud suits. In one, the Court required plaintiffs to be more specific in allegations of securities fraud. The other blocked investors from using antitrust laws, with their potent treble damage remedy, in suits against investment bankers for joint marketing techniques used in initial public offerings.

The Court cheered business groups with a ruling that blocked on federal preemption grounds suits against manufacturers of medical devices subject to premarket approval by the Food and Drug Administration (FDA). The 8–1 decision in *Riegel v. Medtronic, Inc.* (2008) blocked a suit in New York state courts by the widow of a man seriously injured by the rupture of a balloon catheter manufactured by Medtronic that had been inserted into his coronary artery during an operation. The Court held that federal law preempts any state common law claims challenging the safety or effectiveness of a medical device marketed in a form approved by the FDA.

In the same term, a tie vote in a case with one justice recused left unsettled the broader question of preemption under federal drug safety laws. But the Court agreed to hear a case raising that issue early in the 2008–2009 term.

The Court continued a trend of narrowing remedies under federal antitrust law. The most important decision overturned a century-old precedent that had treated a manufacturer's minimum-price requirement for retailers as a per se antitrust violation. The 5–4 ruling in *Leegin*

Creative Leather Products, Inc. v. PSKS, Inc. (2007) required plaintiffs instead to prove that the anti-competitive effects of resale price maintenance policies outweigh any benefits to manufacturers, retailers, or consumers.

Two other antitrust decisions the same year required plaintiffs to be more specific in alleging illegal agreements between competitors and set a high standard for liability in so-called predatory pricing suits—suits blaming competitive injury on a rival's below-market pricing.

The Court favored employers with a 5–4 decision in *Ledbetter v. Goodyear Tire & Rubber Co., Inc.* (2007) that limited workers' ability to recover damages under federal civil rights laws for past discrimination on pay. Other rulings helped employees, however. The Court held in *Smith v. City of Jackson* (2005) that employers could be held liable under the Age Discrimination in Employment Act for policies that have a "disparate impact" on older workers even if they are not shown to be intentionally discriminatory. A ruling three years later held that employers, not employees, had the burden of proof in age discrimination cases to show that a challenged policy was legal because it was based on reasonable factors other than age.

The Court also made it easier for workers to seek damages for retaliation by employers after raising discrimination claims. A unanimous decision in *Burlington Northern and Santa Fe Railway Company v. White* (2006) allowed employees to recover under the anti-retaliation provision of Title VII of the Civil Rights Act of 1964 for any action that might have dissuaded a reasonable employee from complaining about bias on the job. Two years later, the Court also ruled that employees could bring an anti-retaliation suit under the Reconstruction-era civil rights statute guaranteeing equal contract rights. The ruling was significant because the earlier statute provided a longer time period to bring suits and no limit on damages.

In non-litigation settings, the Court favored business interests by striking down several state regulatory laws on federal preemption grounds. The Court voted 5–3 in *Watters v. Wachovia Bank, N.A* (2007) that national banks' mortgage lending subsidiaries are subject only to federal regulation and exempt from state oversight. A year later, the Court unanimously struck down as preempted a Maine law requiring trucking companies or other delivery firms to verify the age of recipients of tobacco products. A 7–2 decision the same year also invalidated a California law that prohibited employers receiving state funds from using any of the moneys in opposing unionization drives.

The Court also struck down as unconstitutional interference with interstate commerce state laws discriminating against out-of-state wineries. The 5–4 ruling in *Granholm v. Heald* (2005) struck down Michigan and New York laws that allowed direct shipments to customers by in-state but not by out-of-state wineries.

In a major intellectual property case, the Court backed the right of movie and recording companies to hold software companies liable for promoting illegal downloading of copyrighted materials. The unanimous ruling in *Metro-Goldwyn-Mayer Studios Inc. v. Grokster, Ltd.* (2005) held that companies that developed and marketed "file-sharing" technologies could be held liable if found to have taken "affirmative steps" to foster copyright infringement.

The Court issued several rulings, however, that limited intellectual property rights for patent holders. In the most important, *eBay Inc. v. MercExchange, L.L.C.* (2006), the Court weakened the ability of patent holders to obtain injunctions, instead of money damages, in infringement cases. The ruling favored the giant Internet auction site in a suit by a company that claimed a patent on a process used in matching winning bidders with sellers. In a second important decision, *KSR International Co. v. Teleflex, Inc.* (2007), the Court made it easier for a defendant in a patent infringement case to challenge a claimed invention as "obvious" and therefore not entitled to patent protection.

ENVIRONMENTAL LAW

With Justice Kennedy casting decisive votes, the Court gave environmentalists a clear victory by upholding the authority of the Environmental Protection Agency (EPA) to regulate greenhouse gases and a partial win by backing some expansive federal regulation of wetlands.

The greenhouse gas ruling, *Massachusetts v. EPA* (2007), rejected the Bush administration's position that the agency had no authority to regulate the greenhouse gases in automobile emissions or that the agency had adequate grounds for refusing to do so. The EPA decided in 2003 that carbon dioxide did not constitute an "air pollutant" under the Clean Air Act. The agency said that it would decline to regulate the CO_2 content of auto emissions anyway because of a lack of evidence linking greenhouse gases to global warming.

Massachusetts and nine other states joined environmentalist plaintiffs in challenging the EPA's decision. In a 5–4 ruling, the Court rejected the EPA's stance on both issues. Stevens said carbon dioxide fell within what he called the Clean Air Act's "sweeping definition" of air pollutant as any "physical" or "chemical" substance emitted into "the ambient air." And he said the agency had offered "no reasoned explanation" for refusing to regulate greenhouse gas emissions from new vehicles. Dissenting justices argued that the buildup of greenhouse gases in the upper atmosphere did not amount to air pollution.

A year earlier, the Court issued a murkier decision on the contentious issue of federal regulation of wetlands. In immediate effect, the decision in *Rapanos v. United States* (2006) backed two Michigan developers in setting aside a federal appeals court ruling supporting the U.S. Army Corps of Engineers' authority to regulate wetlands remote from recognized waterways. Writing for a plurality of four justices, Scalia said that the corps had gone beyond its statutory authority under the Clean Water Act. He proposed that the corps could regulate wetlands only if they had a continuous connection to a continuously flowing waterway.

Four dissenters led by Stevens argued that Scalia's test was too narrow. In a pivotal concurrence, Kennedy agreed with Scalia that the corps had gone beyond its statutory authority, but he rejected Scalia's test as too strict. Instead, Kennedy said wetlands were subject to federal regulation if they significantly affected the chemical, physical, or biological integrity of recognized waterways. Initially disappointed, environmentalists later said that Kennedy's controlling opinion endorsed their principal arguments for protecting wetlands from development.

Kennedy also cast a pivotal vote in a 5–4 ruling, *National Association of Home Builders v. Defenders of Wildlife* (2007), that represented a setback for environmentalists on endangered species issues. In an opinion joined by the four conservatives, Kennedy upheld the EPA's authority to transfer water pollution permitting authority to a state without consulting with the federal agency—the Fish and Wildlife Service (FWS)—responsible for enforcing the Endangered Species Act. Dissenting justices said the ruling contradicted the act's provision requiring federal agencies to consult with FWS on any "action" that could affect a threatened or endangered species.

FEDERAL, STATE, AND LOCAL GOVERNMENTS

The Rehnquist Court's use of federalism principles to protect states' prerogatives vis-à-vis the federal government came to a crashing halt in Rehnquist's final term with a decision invoking federal drug law to strike down California's medical marijuana initiative. Then the federalism revolution lay dormant in the Roberts Court's first three terms.

The 6–3 decision in *Gonzales v. Raich* (2005) struck down a California law that exempted from criminal prosecution patients or primary caregivers who possessed or cultivated marijuana for medicinal purposes as recommended or approved by a physician. Federal drug law included no such exemption, but two California women who used marijuana to relieve pain associated with chronic illnesses challenged enforcement of the federal ban. One of the women grew her own marijuana; the other got hers free from caregivers.

In striking down the law, however, the Court said it ran afoul of Congress's power to regulate interstate commerce. Allowing the exemption, Stevens wrote for the majority, would necessarily affect the interstate market for what he called "this extraordinarily popular substance" and create a "gaping hole" in the federal regulatory scheme. Dissenting, O'Connor said evidence was lacking that the medical marijuana laws, which were on the books then in ten states, would weaken the federal ban. Rehnquist and Thomas were the other dissenters.

In the same year, the Court also upheld federal power in a challenge to a law, the Religious Land Use and Institutionalized Persons Act, requiring state prison authorities to make accommodations for inmates' religious practices. Ohio officials challenged the law, among other grounds, as an unconstitutional establishment of religion. The Court in *Cutter v. Wilkinson* unanimously rejected the argument but also said that restrictions on prisoners could often be justified by security concerns.

The federalism revolution remained at a standstill with a pair of rulings in Roberts' first term. In *Central Virginia Community College v. Katz* (2006), the Court ruled that states cannot invoke sovereign immunity to prevent a bankruptcy trustee from seeking to recover funds that a debtor improperly transferred to a state agency before filing for bankruptcy. O'Connor, in one of her final cases, gave the liberal bloc the critical fifth vote in the 5–4 decision; Roberts dissented.

Two weeks earlier, the Court had opened the door slightly to damage suits by prison inmates under the federal Americans with Disabilities Act (ADA). The unanimous decision allowed suits against state governments under the ADA, but only if the prison conditions amounted to cruel and unusual punishment. Later that year, the Court ruled, also unanimously, that county governments cannot rely on states' sovereign immunity to protect themselves from private damage suits.

State governments did win several significant decisions on tax policies. In the most important, the Court upheld the states' universal practice of giving a tax exemption to interest paid on bonds issued by the state or local governments within the state but not to interest paid to state residents on bonds from other states. Writing for the 7–2 majority in *Department of Revenue of Kentucky v. Davis* (2008), Souter said the policy was motivated by "legitimate objectives," not by "simple economic protectionism."

Two years earlier, the Court had turned aside a taxpayer challenge to states' common practice of extending tax breaks to companies to locate new facilities within their borders. Ohio taxpayers had challenged a tax break for Daimler Chrysler as improper discrimination against out-of-state manufacturers, but the Court dismissed the case, saying the taxpayers lacked legal standing to bring the suit in federal court.

States also won two rulings in tax disputes with Indian tribes. In 2006 the Court upheld imposition of a state motor fuel tax on off-reservation distributors even though the gasoline was delivered to Indian-owned service stations located on tribal reservations. A year earlier, the Court had also upheld the power of state and local governments to tax previously tribal lands that had passed into private hands and were then later repurchased by tribal members.

CRIMINAL LAW AND PROCEDURE

The Rehnquist Court in its final term and the Roberts Court in its first three generally favored law enforcement in criminal cases, according to lawyers, academics, and other experts on both sides of the criminal law divide. In capital punishment cases, however, the Court barred the death penalty for juvenile offenders and child rapists and set aside death sentences in several other cases because of constitutional errors at trial. The Court also set the stage for possibly lower sentences in federal court by eliminating the mandatory effect of guidelines that had often forced judges to impose longer prison terms than might ordinarily have been imposed.

Kennedy wrote and provided the critical fifth vote in the two 5–4 rulings excluding juvenile offenders and child rapists from the death penalty. In *Roper v. Simmons* (2005), Kennedy cited the infrequency of execution of juvenile offenders and juveniles' "diminished culpability" in finding a "national consensus" against subjecting them to the death penalty. In *Kennedy v. Louisiana* (2008), Justice Kennedy noted that only five states permitted the death penalty in child rape cases and only two defendants—both from Louisiana—had received a death sentence. Conservative justices sharply criticized both rulings in dissent.

Several other capital cases found Kennedy in the pivotal position between conservative and liberal blocs. He wrote the 5–3 decision in 2006 giving a Tennessee death row inmate a new chance to prove his innocence on the basis of newly available DNA (deoxyribonucleic acid) evidence. In 2007 he joined five-justice majorities in three cases reinstating death penalty challenges that lower courts had thrown out. But Kennedy also wrote an important 5–4 decision, *Uttecht v. Brown* (2007), giving trial judges broad discretion to exclude potential jurors who voiced doubts about the death penalty. Kennedy also led four dissenters in the 2005 decision, *Rompilla v. Beard,* that gave a Pennsylvania inmate a new sentencing hearing because his appointed counsel had failed to investigate his history of child abuse and mental illness that jurors might have considered as mitigating evidence. O'Connor joined the four liberal justices in the majority.

In 2008 the Roberts Court shut the door on two challenges that could have upset death sentences in many states. In *Baze v. Rees* (2008), the Court rejected, by a 7–2 vote, challenges by two Kentucky inmates to the state's three-drug protocol for lethal injection executions. The inmates, supported by death penalty opponents and critics, claimed the sequence of drugs—an anesthetic followed by a paralytic agent and then a heart-stopping drug—caused unnecessary pain for the condemned.

For the majority, Roberts said the inmates had failed to prove their case. He went on to say that a method of execution was unconstitutional only if a readily implemented alternative in fact significantly reduced the risk of severe pain. Death penalty supporters said the ruling was likely to end broad challenges to lethal injection.

In a second decision, the Court voted 6–3 to reject a Mexican national's effort to overturn his conviction and death sentence because Texas authorities had failed to afford him a treaty-guaranteed right to consult with diplomatic representatives after his arrest. Again writing for the majority in *Medellin v. Texas* (2008), Roberts said Texas courts were justified in ruling that the inmate had raised the claim belatedly even though both the International Court of Justice and President Bush had said the claim should be considered. A contrary ruling might have benefited some fifty other Mexican nationals on death rows in the United States.

The federal sentencing rulings stemmed from an intricate decision in the Rehnquist Court's final term, *United States v. Booker* (2005). A five-justice majority said the federal sentencing guidelines improperly gave judges instead of juries the power to make factual findings needed to raise a defendant's sentence. But with Ginsburg switching sides, a different majority went on to rule that the guidelines could still be used if judges treated them as advisory instead of mandatory.

In its first post-*Booker* ruling on the guidelines, the Court decided in *Rita v. United States* (2007) that appellate courts could treat the guidelines as presumptively reasonable. The ruling represented a setback for defendants seeking to challenge trial judges' use of the sometimes harsh guideline-range sentences. Later that year, however, the Court favored defendants by ruling in *Gall v. United States* that trial judges had discretion to depart downward from the ranges prescribed by the guidelines. On the same day, the Court ruled in *Kimbrough v. United States* that judges were free to disregard guidelines that imposed disproportionately harsh sentences in crack-cocaine cases compared with those prescribed for use or sale of powdered cocaine.

Most rulings on search and seizure issues upheld challenged police procedures. In the most significant, the Court voted 5–4 in *Hudson v. Michigan* (2006) to allow use of evidence found in a home search even though police did not comply with the requirement to "knock and announce" before entering. Scalia's opinion for the majority openly questioned the deterrent value of the exclusionary rule—prompting Breyer in dissent to call the decision "deeply troubling."

In another divided ruling, the justices voted 6–2 in 2005 to allow police to use drug-sniffing dogs to search a car after a traffic stop even if there was no suspicion of drug trafficking. The Court in 2008 also said that state courts need not exclude evidence found in an automobile search after a custodial arrest not authorized by state law. A year earlier, however, the Court had ruled for the first time that a passenger has standing to challenge a car search after a traffic stop.

In the only divided search ruling favoring defendants, the Court held that a co-occupant of a home can deny police permission to search even if the other resident agrees. The 5–3 ruling in *Georgia v. Randolph* (2006) barred admission of drugs found in a home after the defendant's estranged wife had allowed police access.

The Court issued mixed rulings on trial and appellate procedures challenged by defendants. In one of the most important, the Court held in *Davis v. Washington* (2006) that courts can allow the use of some statements given to police even if the witness is unavailable to testify at trial.

The statements are admissible, Scalia wrote, if given during an emergency, but not if made later.

Women's rights groups had feared that an absolute restriction would have hampered domestic violence prosecutions because victims were susceptible to intimidation after filing complaints with police. In a later ruling, however, the Court refused to allow use of statements made to police by a woman who was later killed by her estranged husband. Writing for the 6–3 majority in *Giles v. California* (2008), Scalia said the statements were not admissible because the defendant had not been shown to have killed the victim specifically to prevent her from testifying.

Both under Rehnquist and under Roberts, the Court made it easier for defendants to challenge prosecutors for using peremptory challenges to exclude potential jurors on racial grounds. In 2005 the Court said that defendants need present only a "reasonable inference" of racial motivation to raise the issue. In the same year, the Court ordered a new trial for a Texas death row inmate after finding that Dallas prosecutors had improperly excluded blacks from the jury. Three years later, the Court held in a capital case from Louisiana that appellate courts can overturn a trial judge's decision to allow prosecutors to exclude jurors if claimed race-neutral explanations are "implausible."

In a closely divided ruling, the Court held in *Clark v. Arizona* (2006) that states may prevent a defendant from using mental illness to show he could not form the intent to commit a crime. The decision also allowed states to restrict the insanity defense to an inability to tell right from wrong.

In 2008 the Court ruled, 7–2, that states can deny a mentally ill defendant the right to represent himself at trial. In dissent, Scalia said the ruling violated the defendant's right to counsel. Scalia also took a strict view of the right to counsel in writing a 5–4 decision in 2006 holding that a defendant denied his choice of counsel is entitled to a retrial without showing evidence of prejudice.

The Court in 2005 found a defendant's right to a fair trial improperly prejudiced by visibly shackling him during the trial. A year later, the Court unanimously found no unreasonable prejudice in allowing spectators to wear buttons with the victim's picture during the trial. In separate opinions, however, three justices questioned the practice.

The Court favored defendants in two rulings on state post-trial procedures. In *Danforth v. Minnesota* (2008), the Court held 7–2 that states can use new constitutional rulings to benefit defendants even if federal habeas courts would not apply the rulings retroactively. Three years earlier, the Court said that states must provide indigent defendants appointed counsel for appeals even if the appeal is discretionary.

In federal habeas corpus cases, the Court generally rejected inmates' challenges to state convictions or sentences, often by tightly enforcing statutory time limits or requiring lower federal courts to defer to state court rulings. In one notable case, the Court in *Bowles v. Russell* (2007) dismissed an Ohio inmate's habeas corpus petition because he had filed an appeal too late even though he filed it within the time limit given to him, erroneously, by the trial judge.

Supreme Court Decisions November 2004–June 2008

Business Law

ANTITRUST

Texaco, Inc. v. Dagher (547 U.S. 1), decided by an 8–0 vote, Feb. 28, 2006; Thomas wrote the opinion; Alito did not participate.

A joint venture between competing companies can set a common price for products sold by the new entity without violating the anti–price-fixing provisions of federal antitrust law. The ruling rejected a suit brought by service stations against a joint venture established by Texaco and Shell to consolidate their refining, distribution, and marketing of gasoline in the western United States.

Illinois Tool Works, Inc. v. Independent Ink, Inc. (547 U.S. 47), decided by an 8–0 vote, March 1, 2006; Stevens wrote the opinion; Alito did not participate.

Courts will not presume, for antitrust purposes, that a company has market power by simply holding a patent on a product that it ties to the sales of another, unpatented product.

Weyerhaeuser Co. v. Ross-Simmons Hardwood Lumber Co. (549 U.S. 312), decided by a 9–0 vote, Feb. 20, 2007; Thomas wrote the opinion.

A company accusing another of illegal predatory bidding in violation of federal antitrust laws must meet the same rigorous legal standard as companies accusing others of illegal predatory pricing.

Bell Atlantic Corp. v. Twombly (550 U.S. 544), decided by a 7–2 vote, May 21, 2007; Souter wrote the opinion; Stevens and Ginsburg dissented.

An antitrust complaint charging a conspiracy to restrain trade must include specific allegations of fact to show an agreement, not merely an allegation, of parallel conduct and an assertion of a conspiracy.

Credit Suisse Securities (USA) LLC v. Billing (551 U.S. 264), decided by a 7–1 vote, June 18, 2007; Breyer wrote the opinion; Thomas dissented; Kennedy did not participate.

Federal antitrust laws do not apply to the marketing techniques used by bank underwriters in initial public offerings (IPOs). Instead, the Securities and Exchange Commission is solely responsible for enforcing securities laws related to IPOs. The ruling dismissed an antitrust suit brought against ten leading investment banks by sixty investors who lost billions of dollars after the technology bubble burst in 2001.

Leegin Creative Leather Products, Inc. v. PSKS, Inc. (551 U.S. 877), decided by a 5–4 vote, June 28, 2007; Kennedy wrote the opinion; Breyer, Stevens, Souter, and Ginsburg dissented.

Manufacturers are not automatically prohibited under federal antitrust law from dictating a minimum price that retailers can charge for their products, but the policies may be illegal if the anticompetitive effects outweigh pro-competitive benefits. The ruling overturned a nearly century-old precedent holding that minimum-pricing agreements—in legal parlance, vertical price restraints—are a per se violation of Section 1 of the Sherman Act, which prohibits any "contract, combination . . . or conspiracy . . . in restraint of trade or commerce." Instead, the ruling said that minimum-pricing agreements are to be judged by the so-called rule of reason, which weighs anticompetitive effects against pro-competitive benefits.

BANKRUPTCY

Rousey v. Jacoway (544 U.S. 320), decided by a 9–0 vote, April 4, 2005; Thomas wrote the opinion.

The Bankruptcy Code permits debtors to exempt assets held in an Individual Retirement Account (IRA) from the bankruptcy estate and, thus, from the reach of creditors. The ruling extended the reach of bankruptcy protection—which exempts other tax-deferred retirement accounts—to increasingly popular and federally endorsed IRAs, preventing older Americans from having to choose between seeking the protections of bankruptcy and safeguarding their retirement.

Howard Delivery Service, Inc. v. Zurich American Insurance Co. (547 U.S. 651), decided by a 6–3 vote, June 15,

2006; Ginsburg wrote the opinion; Kennedy, Souter, and Alito dissented.

An insurance provider is not entitled to priority status over other unsecured creditors in a claim for unpaid workers' compensation premiums owed by an employer in a Chapter 11 bankruptcy proceeding.

Marrama v. Citizens Bank of Massachusetts (549 U.S. 365), decided by a 5–4 vote, Feb. 21, 2007; Stevens wrote the opinion; Alito, Roberts, Scalia, and Thomas dissented.

A debtor in a bankruptcy case who engages in bad-faith conduct by concealing assets forfeits the statutory right to change the proceeding from a reorganization plan administered by a trustee to one with the estate under the individual's control. The ruling was a victory for banks and other creditors.

Travelers Casualty and Surety Company of America v. Pacific Gas and Electric Co. (549 U.S. 443), decided by a 9–0 vote, March 20, 2007; Alito wrote the opinion.

Federal bankruptcy does not prohibit the recovery of attorney fees when that right is recognized by contract. The ruling, which resolved a conflict between federal courts of appeals, paved the way for Travelers to collect attorney fees from Pacific Gas & Electric Co. from litigation in bankruptcy court.

Watters, Commissioner, Michigan Office of Insurance and Financial Services v. Wachovia Bank, N.A. (550 U.S. 1), decided by a 5–3 vote, April 17, 2007; Ginsburg wrote the opinion; Stevens, Roberts, and Scalia dissented; Thomas did not participate.

National banks' mortgage lending subsidiaries are subject only to federal regulation and are exempt from state oversight. The ruling, broadly interpreting the preemptive effect of the National Bank Act, restored Wachovia Mortgage's ability to engage in lending in Michigan without being subject to the state's registration and investigation requirements.

CLASS ACTIONS

Buckeye Check Cashing, Inc. v. Cardegna (546 U.S. 440), decided by a 7–1 vote, Feb. 21, 2006; Scalia wrote the opinion; Thomas dissented; Alito did not participate.

A challenge to the validity of a contract containing an arbitration provision aimed at the contract as a whole and not specifically to the arbitration clause must go to an arbitrator, not to a court.

COPYRIGHT

Metro-Goldwyn-Mayer Studios Inc. v. Grokster, Ltd. (545 U.S. 913), decided by a 9–0 vote, June 27, 2005; Souter wrote the opinion.

Companies that produce file-sharing software for the primary purpose of infringing copyright-protected works are liable for resulting acts of infringement by third parties. The decision reversed and remanded a 2004 ruling by the Ninth U.S. Circuit Court of Appeals that rejected copyright-infringement suits against two California-based companies, Grokster, Ltd., and StreamCast Networks, Inc., for distribution of so-called person-to-person (P2P) software. The Court reversed lower courts' rulings for Grokster and StreamCast by holding that the two companies could be held liable because of evidence that they induced users to engage in copyright infringement. The Court wrote that the lower courts had ignored evidence "replete" in the record that Grokster and StreamCast had "acted with a purpose to cause copyright violations by use of software suitable for illegal use." "Mere knowledge" of illegal use would not result in liability, the Court stated, but a company "that distributes a device with the object of promoting its use to infringe copyright . . . is liable for the resulting acts of infringement regardless of the device's lawful uses."

FALSE CLAIMS

Graham County Soil and Water Conservation District v. United States ex rel. Wilson (545 U.S. 409), decided by a 7–2 vote, June 20, 2005; Thomas wrote the opinion; Breyer and Ginsburg dissented.

An employee who sues her employer for retaliatory discharge under the federal False Claims Act is bound by the statute of limitations provided by the most closely analogous state law.

INSURANCE

Sereboff v. Mid Atlantic Medical Services, Inc. (547 U.S. 356), decided by a 9–0 vote, May 15, 2006; Roberts wrote the opinion.

The administrator of an employee health insurance plan can enforce a term requiring reimbursement from any recovery received by the employee from a third party for the employee's injuries or condition.

MARITIME LAW

Norfolk Southern Railway Co. v. James N. Kirby, Pty. Ltd. (543 U.S. 14), decided by a 9–0 vote, Nov. 9, 2004; O'Connor wrote the opinion.

A U.S. railroad was allowed under federal maritime law to limit its liability for freight damaged in a derailment according to the terms of a shipping contract negotiated between an Australian manufacturer and an international cargo shipping company.

Stewart v. Dutra Construction Co. (543 U.S. 481), decided by an 8–0 vote, Feb. 22, 2005; Thomas wrote the opinion; Rehnquist did not participate.

A dredge is considered a "vessel" under the federal law that authorizes covered employees to sue a vessel's owner for negligence. The ruling allowed Willard Stewart, a marine engineer, to file a court suit instead of a workers' compensation claim against the Dutra Construction Co. for injuries sustained while working on a giant dredge floating in the Boston Harbor. The Longshore and Harbor Workers Compensation Act of 1927 allowed a sea-based maritime worker to sue the owner of a vessel for injuries but limited land-based maritime workers to scheduled compensation.

PATENTS

Merck KGaA v. Integra Lifesciences I, Ltd. (545 U.S. 193), decided by a 9–0 vote, June 13, 2005; Scalia wrote the opinion.

A pharmaceutical company that uses patented chemical compounds in the early stages of research does not commit patent infringement if its research is "reasonably related" to developing drugs that could later be approved by the Food and Drug Administration. The ruling expanded the reach of a statutory "safe harbor" that Congress enacted in 1984 to speed up the marketing and distribution of generic drugs.

The Court read the statute as providing "a wide berth for the use of patented drugs in activities related to the federal regulatory process." That process requires drug companies to submit applications both to conduct testing on humans and to market a drug, but the Court found no reason to read the safe harbor as protecting only the research that would appear directly in those applications.

eBay Inc. v. MercExchange, L.L.C. (547 U.S. 388), decided by a 9–0 vote, May 15, 2006; Thomas wrote the opinion.

Courts should issue injunctions in patent infringement cases according to the ordinary rules governing injunctions instead of a presumptive rule either favoring or disfavoring injunctions in such suits. The ruling left it up to a lower federal court to decide whether the popular Internet auction site eBay would face a potentially disruptive injunction or only a big damage award for infringing a patent held by a Virginia-based firm, MercExchange.

MedImmune, Inc. v. Genentech, Inc. (549 U.S. 118), decided by an 8–1 vote, Jan. 9, 2007; Scalia wrote the opinion; Thomas dissented.

A company with a license agreement to use a patent can challenge the validity of the patent without first breaking the contract by refusing to pay agreed upon royalties. The ruling, significantly easing challenges to questionable patents, reinstated a suit by the Maryland-based biotech company MedImmune seeking to invalidate a patent on a genetic engineering technology held by the industry giant Genentech.

KSR International Co. v. Teleflex, Inc. (550 U.S. 398), decided by a 9–0 vote, April 30, 2007; Kennedy wrote the opinion.

The federal appeals court that handles patent cases adopted an overly strict rule to determine whether a claimed invention is obvious and therefore not entitled to patent protection. The ruling represented a significant setback for patent holders on an issue that often arises in infringement suits.

Microsoft Corp. v. AT&T Corp. (550 U.S. 437), decided by a 7–1 vote, April 30, 2007; Ginsburg wrote the opinion; Stevens dissented; Roberts did not participate.

Software manufacturers are not liable for patent infringement in the United States for shipping another party's patented software abroad to be copied and installed on computers to be sold abroad.

Quanta Computer, Inc. v. LG Electronics, Inc. (553 U.S. _), decided by a 9–0 vote, June 9, 2008; Thomas wrote the opinion.

A patent holder that has authorized a licensee to sell patented products cannot assert patent rights against manufacturers of downstream products that substantially embody the patents. The ruling strictly applied the well-established "patent exhaustion" doctrine to prevent LG Electronics (LGE), a South Korean computer maker, from collecting royalties from Taiwanese companies that manufactured computers containing LGE-patented components.

PRICE DISCRIMINATION

Volvo Trucks North America, Inc. v. Reeder-Simco GMC, Inc. (546 U.S. 164), decided by a 7–2 vote, Jan. 10, 2006; Ginsburg wrote the opinion; Stevens and Thomas dissented.

Manufacturers are not liable for price discrimination under the Robinson-Patman Act (also known as the Anti-Price Discrimination Act of 1936) unless the discrimination is between dealers in competition for the same retail customer.

SECURITIES LAW

Dura Pharmaceuticals, Inc. v. Broudo (544 U.S. 336), decided by a 9–0 vote, April 19, 2005; Breyer wrote the opinion.

Disgruntled investors must prove a clear connection between a company's misrepresentations and a subsequent loss in stock price before they can recover in securities fraud cases. The ruling made it easier for companies to resist claims by shareholders seeking financial compensation for stock market losses by overturning a federal appeals court holding that a plaintiff could prevail merely by showing the stock price was inflated at the time of purchase because of the company's misrepresentations.

Stoneridge Investment Partners, L.L.C. v. Scientific-Atlanta, Inc. (552 U.S. 148), decided by a 5–3 vote, Jan. 16, 2008; Kennedy wrote the opinion; Stevens dissented; Breyer did not participate.

Investors cannot sue a company's suppliers and customers for fraud under federal securities law if the investors did not rely upon misstatements from the suppliers and customers. The ruling, a major victory for business groups, rejected a suit by investors in Charter Communications against two of its suppliers for their alleged role in helping Charter to fraudulently manipulate its financial reports.

Tellabs, Inc. v. Makor Issues & Rights, Ltd. (551 U.S. 308), decided by an 8–1 vote, June 21, 2007; Ginsburg wrote the opinion; Stevens dissented.

Plaintiffs in private securities fraud suits must allege facts that lead to an inference of fraudulent intent that is at least as strong as innocent explanations. The ruling tightened somewhat a central provision in the Private Securities and Litigation Reform Act, which Congress cleared in 1995 in an effort to curb abusive shareholder lawsuits.

STATE LAW

Exxon Mobil Corp. v. Saudi Basic Industries Corp. (544 U.S. 280), decided by a 9–0 vote, March 30, 2005; Ginsburg wrote the opinion.

The judicially created "Rooker-Feldman doctrine" does not prevent a party from filing suit in federal court as an "insurance policy" against an unfavorable outcome in a pending state court lawsuit. The ruling resolved a persistent conflict in the federal courts of appeals regarding the scope of the doctrine, which prohibits the lower federal courts from hearing what are in essence "appeals" by parties who lost in state court. The Court held that application of the Rooker-Feldman doctrine is limited to situations in which the losing party in a state court proceeding "invites" a federal district court to review and reject the state court judgment.

Bates v. Dow AgroSciences LLC (544 U.S. 431), decided by a 7–2 vote, April 27, 2005; Stevens wrote the opinion; Thomas and Scalia dissented in part.

The federal law that regulates the labeling, sale, and use of pesticides and herbicides does not protect the manufacturers of those products from all state law–based tort suits. The ruling reinstated some state law claims by a group of west Texas peanut farmers against the agrichemical firm Dow AgroSciences for alleged damage to their crops stemming from the use of Dow's newly marketed herbicide Strongarm. The U.S. Supreme Court held that the herbicide's defective design and manufacturing, negligent testing, and breach of express warranty claims were not premised on labeling or packaging requirements under the Federal Insecticide, Fungicide, and Rodenticide Act (FIFRA) and thus were not preempted. The Court explained that only state law labeling requirements that are "in addition to or different from" those imposed by FIFRA are prohibited.

TAXATION

Commissioner of Internal Revenue v. Banks (543 U.S. 426), decided by an 8–0 vote, Jan. 24, 2005; Kennedy wrote the opinion; Rehnquist did not participate.

When a plaintiff recovers money through a court judgment or settlement, the money paid to an attorney under a contingency fee arrangement must be included as part of the plaintiff's taxable gross income. The ruling reversed the judgments of two federal appeals courts that had concluded that contingency fees paid to attorneys did not constitute taxable income.

Ballard v. Commissioner of Internal Revenue (544 U.S. 40), decided by a 7–2 vote, March 7, 2005; Ginsburg wrote the opinion; Rehnquist and Thomas dissented.

The U.S. Tax Court cannot exclude from the record on appeal the trial reports prepared by special trial judges that the regular Tax Court judge must defer to in making a final adjudication. The ruling overturned the Tax Court's practice since 1984 of keeping the reports of special trial judges out of the official record and thus permitted the contents of the reports to be used for purposes of appealing the Tax Court's ultimate decision to the authorized U.S. Court of Appeals.

Grable & Sons Metal Products, Inc. v. Darue Engineering & Manufacturing (545 U.S. 308), decided by a 9–0 vote, June 13, 2005; Souter wrote the opinion.

A title action between two private parties in the same state may be removed to federal court when the action turns on a substantial question of federal tax law.

EC Term of Years Trust v. United States (550 U.S. 429), decided by a 9–0 vote, April 30, 2007; Souter wrote the opinion.

A taxpayer who misses the nine-month deadline for challenging a levy by the Internal Revenue Service cannot bring the challenge as a tax-refund claim with its longer filing period. The Court held that challenges to levies wrongfully issued against third parties must be brought within the nine-month period and may not later be brought as tax refund claims. The Court said that the specific statute governing levy claims preempted the more general provision providing tax remedies.

Hinck v. United States (550 U.S. 501), decided by a 9–0 vote, May 21, 2007; Roberts wrote the opinion.

The U.S. Tax Court has exclusive jurisdiction over lawsuits challenging the Internal Revenue Service's refusal to forgive all or part of the interest owed for unpaid taxes based on unreasonable errors or delay by the agency.

Knight v. Commissioner of Internal Revenue (552 U.S. 181), decided by a 9–0 vote, Jan. 16, 2008; Roberts wrote the opinion.

Investment advisory fees incurred by a trust are generally deductible for federal income tax purposes only to the extent that they exceed 2 percent of adjusted gross income.

Boulware v. United States (552 U.S. 421), decided by a 9–0 vote, March 3, 2008; Souter wrote the opinion.

A defendant in a federal criminal tax case does not need to show a contemporaneous intent to treat diversions of property from a company as returns of capital to demonstrate that no taxes are owed.

United States v. Clintwood Elkhorn Mining Co.(553 U.S. _), decided by a 9–0 vote, April 15, 2008; Roberts wrote the opinion.

A federal taxpayer seeking a refund of a tax assessed in violation of the export clause of the U.S. Constitution must first file a timely claim with the Internal Revenue Service. The ruling frustrated the attempt by three coal companies to receive refunds totaling slightly over $1 million of an unconstitutional tax paid in the years 1994 through 1996.

Florida Department of Revenue v. Piccadilly Cafeterias, Inc. (554 U.S. _), decided by a 7–2 vote, June 16, 2008; Thomas wrote the opinion; Breyer and Stevens dissented.

An exemption from state transfer taxes when a business reorganizes after a bankruptcy is available only if the transfer of assets occurs after the court approves the plan of reorganization.

TRADEMARK LAW

KP Permanent Make-Up, Inc. v. Lasting Impressions I, Inc. (543 U.S. 111), decided by a 9–0 vote, Dec. 8, 2004; Souter wrote the opinion.

The defendant in a trademark infringement case can claim a "fair use" defense without first proving that there was no possibility of consumer confusion between its product and that of a rival company. The ruling—resolving an important trademark law issue—came in a dispute between two manufacturers of permanent makeup over use of some version of the term "micro color" in marketing and selling their respective products.

TRUTH IN LENDING

Koons Buick Pontiac GMC, Inc. v. Nigh (543 U.S. 50), decided by 8–1 vote, Nov. 30, 2004; Ginsburg wrote the opinion; Scalia dissented.

Congress retained the $1,000 cap on the amount consumers can collect from creditors for violating the federal Truth in Lending Act when it later adopted ambiguously drafted provisions raising the limit for mortgage loan violations.

Courts and Judicial Procedure

APPEALS

Unitherm Food Systems, Inc. v. Swift-Eckrich, Inc. (546 U.S. 394), decided by a 7–2 vote, Jan. 23, 2006; Thomas wrote the opinion; Stevens and Kennedy dissented.

Federal appeals courts have no power to order a new trial or issue a directed verdict if the losing party fails to file a post-verdict motion under the Federal Rules of Civil Procedure.

Whitman v. Department of Transportation (547 U.S. 512), decided by an 8–0 vote, June 5, 2006; per curiam opinion; Alito did not participate.

The Court instructed a federal appeals court to reconsider whether a federal employee can sue the agency for which he works for allegedly violating his constitutional rights by subjecting him to nonrandom drug testing. The ruling appeared to invite the Ninth U.S. Circuit Court of Appeals to decide the suit brought by Federal Aviation Administration employee Terry Whitman on limited or procedural grounds to allow the justices to avoid the question they took the case to consider.

APPOINTMENT OF COUNSEL

Kowalski, Judge 26th Judicial Circuit Court of Michigan v. Tesmer (543 U.S. 125), decided by a 6–3 vote, Dec. 13, 2004; Rehnquist wrote the opinion; Ginsburg, Stevens, and Souter dissented.

Defense lawyers had no standing to challenge a state law denying appointed counsel for indigent defendants to appeal a plea of guilty or no contest except under special circumstances. The decision reversed an appeals court ruling that had called into question the validity of Michigan's recently codified practice of denying appellate counsel to most indigent criminal defendants.

The Court rejected the lawyers' argument that they had third party standing, or the legal right to sue in federal court on behalf of another party. Although the Court had previously permitted suits on behalf of third parties, particularly in the context of lawyer-client relations, these lawyers did not satisfy the Court's two-part standard. The lawyers could not demonstrate a "close relationship" with potential clients with whom they currently have "no relationship at all," the Court said. The lawyers also failed to show that indigent defendants faced a "hindrance" in advancing their own cause, the Court said, pointing to a series of challenges to Michigan's practice brought in state court without the help of appointed counsel.

ARBITRATION

Preston v. Ferrer (552 U.S. 346), decided by an 8–1 vote, Feb. 20, 2008; Ginsburg wrote the decision; Thomas dissented.

A contract providing for arbitration of all questions relating to the contract supersedes any state laws giving jurisdiction to judicial or administrative decision makers. The ruling strengthened the Federal Arbitration Act by clarifying that its provisions confirming the enforceability of arbitration agreements take precedence over any state laws giving jurisdiction over contract disputes to administrative agencies or, as previously held, to courts.

Hall Street Associates, L.L.C. v. Mattel, Inc. (552 U.S. 576), decided by a 6–3 vote, March 25, 2008; Souter wrote the opinion; Stevens, Kennedy, and Breyer dissented.

The Federal Arbitration Act does not permit parties to an arbitration agreement to provide for a court to review an arbitrator's decision for legal error other than the serious grounds listed in the act. The ruling strictly interpreted the terms of a 1925 law intended to encourage arbitration in a way that a small business group warned would make arbitration less attractive to some businesses. The Court held that the Federal Arbitration Act's grounds for setting aside or modifying an arbitrator's award are exclusive and cannot be enlarged by an agreement by the parties to the arbitration.

ATTORNEY FEES

Martin v. Franklin Capital Corp. (546 U.S. 132), decided by a 9–0 vote, Dec. 7, 2005; Roberts wrote the opinion.

Federal district courts should not award attorneys' fees for an unsuccessful attempt to remove a case from state to federal court if the removing party has an objectively reasonable basis for seeking removal. The ruling blocked a New Mexico couple, Gerald and Juana Martin, from collecting attorneys' fees from Franklin Capital Corp. and Century-National Insurance Co. for the companies' unsuccessful effort to remove the Martins' class action suit from state to federal court.

Sole, Secretary, Florida Department of Environmental Protection v. Wyner (551 U.S. 74), decided by a 9–0 vote, June 4, 2007; Ginsburg wrote the opinion.

A plaintiff who gains a preliminary injunction in a federal civil rights suit but ultimately loses the case on the merits is not entitled to receive attorneys' fees available to prevailing parties in such actions. The Court said: "Prevailing party status does not attend achievement of a preliminary injunction that is reversed, resolved, or otherwise undone by the final decision in the same case."

Richlin Security Service Co. v. Chertoff, Secretary of Homeland Security (553 U.S. _), decided by a 9–0 vote, June 2, 2008; Alito wrote the opinion.

A private party that prevails in a lawsuit against the federal government may recover paralegal fees from the government at the prevailing market rate for paralegal services, not just the law firm's cost of the services. The ruling rejected the government's effort to narrow reimbursement for paralegal services under the provision in the Equal Access to Justice Act allowing for the award of "fees and other expenses" incurred by a party in a successful suit against the government.

CLAIMS

Sprint Communications Co., L.P. v. APCC Services, Inc. (554 U.S. _), decided by a 5–4 vote, June 23, 2008; Breyer wrote the opinion; Roberts, Scalia, Thomas, and Alito dissented.

An assignee that is granted a right to collect on a claim has standing to pursue the claim in a lawsuit in federal court even if it agrees to remit all proceeds to the assignor. The ruling permitted pay phone operators to continue a practice of assigning their claims for the collection of legally required calling fees from long-distance carriers to "aggregators" that promised to turn over to the pay phone companies all moneys received through court suits. Under industry practice and federal communications law, long-distance carriers collect fees from pay phone customers for 1-800 or access code calls and then are required to compensate the pay phone operator for connecting the call to the carrier in the first place. Federal law permitted the pay phone operators to sue in federal court if a carrier failed to pay compensation. Given the small amounts involved, pay phone operators adopted the practice of assigning their collection rights in these "dial-around claims" to aggregators, which agreed to pursue the claims for a fee and to remit proceeds of lawsuits to the pay phone operators.

CLASS ACTIONS

Merrill Lynch, Pierce, Fenner & Smith, Inc. v. Dabit (547 U.S. 71), decided by an 8–0 vote, March 21, 2006; Stevens wrote the opinion; Alito did not participate.

Investors who claim that they were fraudulently induced to hold on to overvalued securities cannot use state law to file large class action suits in state or federal court. The ruling extended the reach of the Securities Litigation Uniform Standards Act (SLUSA) to limit securities-related class actions.

Congress in 1995 had passed the Private Securities Litigation Reform Act, which established an array of substantive and procedural limitations on securities-related class actions under federal law. Many plaintiffs' attorneys sought to circumvent the law by filing such suits under state investor-protection laws. Congress responded in 1998 by passing SLUSA, which prohibited the use of state law in any class action on behalf of more than fifty people alleging "a misrepresentation or omission of a material fact in connection with the purchase or sale of a [nationally traded] security."

DIVERSITY

Lincoln Property Co. v. Roche (546 U.S. 81), decided by a 9–0 vote, Nov. 29, 2005; Ginsburg wrote the opinion.

Defendants in federal court under diversity jurisdiction need not prove the nonexistence of potential in-state defendants whose presence in the suit would destroy the federal courts' diversity jurisdiction. The ruling reversed a federal appeals court decision that defendant corporations must identify additional nondiverse parties that could have an interest in the cause of action. Federal law allows defendants sued in state court to remove the case to a federal district court if the plaintiffs reside in different states from all defendants and the amount is greater than $75,000.

Wachovia Bank, National Association v. Schmidt (546 U.S. 303), decided by an 8–0 vote, Jan. 17, 2006; Ginsburg wrote the opinion; Thomas did not participate.

National banks are citizens of the states where their main offices are located for purposes of establishing diversity jurisdiction to bring suit in federal court. The ruling reinstated a federal court suit by the North Carolina–headquartered Wachovia Bank seeking to require arbitration of a consumer complaint brought by customers of the bank's South Carolina branches in a South Carolina state court.

FEDERAL COURTS

Rice, Warden v. Collins (546 U.S. 333), decided by a 9–0 vote, Jan. 18, 2006; Kennedy wrote the opinion.

Federal courts reviewing state court convictions in habeas corpus cases may not replace a state court's reasonable determinations of fact with their own determinations of fact. The ruling reversed a federal appeals court decision that a California prosecutor improperly removed a woman from a jury based on race.

Attorneys generally can remove any potential juror with a peremptory challenge, but the U.S. Supreme Court had ruled that no juror can be removed on account of race or gender. Collins's lawyer objected to the juror's removal, charging that it was based on her race. The prosecutor, in response, cited her demeanor, gender, youth, likely tolerance of drug use, and lack of ties to the community as reasons for her dismissal. On appeal, courts determined the prosecutor credible and the race-neutral reasons for rejecting the juror sufficient. The Ninth U.S. Circuit Court of Appeals reversed, holding that the state trial court had been unreasonable to accept the prosecutor's explanation for striking the juror.

The Court rebuked the Ninth Circuit for relying on its independent determination that the prosecutor was not credible instead of the state court's determination of the prosecutor's credibility.

Kircher v. Putnam Funds Trust (547 U.S. 633), decided by a 9–0 vote, June 15, 2006; Souter wrote the opinion.

Federal appeals courts cannot review a federal district court's decision to remand to state court for lack of jurisdiction a class action by investors challenged under a law aimed at limiting securities litigation. The procedurally complex ruling reaffirmed in the context of securities litigation the law that bans most appeals of a federal court's decision to send back to state court a case originally filed in state court and then "removed" to federal court.

FOREIGN IMMUNITY

Powerex Corp. v. Reliant Energy Services, Inc. (551 U.S. 224), decided by a 7–2 vote, June 18, 2007; Scalia wrote the opinion; Breyer and Stevens dissented.

A federal court of appeals may not review a federal district court's decision to remand a case to state court for lack of subject matter jurisdiction. The ruling defeated an effort by a British Columbia utility and its subsidiary, Powerex, to remove from state to federal court an indemnification dispute stemming from allegations of price-fixing during California's energy crisis in the late 1990s.

INCONVENIENT FORUM

Sinochem International Co. Ltd. v. Malaysia International Shipping Corp. (549 U.S. 422), decided by a 9–0 vote, March 5, 2007; Ginsburg wrote the opinion.

A federal court has discretion to dismiss a suit on the ground that the case belongs in a foreign tribunal without first determining whether it has jurisdiction over the case. The ruling ended an effort by a foreign shipper, Malaysia International Shipping Corp., to bring a factually complex maritime lawsuit against Sinochem International Co., a state-owned Chinese importer, in U.S. courts instead of in Chinese courts.

INMATES RIGHTS

Beard, Secretary, Pennsylvania Department of Corrections v. Banks (548 U.S. 521), decided by a 6–2 vote, June 28, 2006; Breyer wrote a plurality opinion; Thomas and Scalia concurred in the judgment; Stevens and Ginsburg dissented; Alito did not participate.

Pennsylvania prison officials presented sufficient justification to uphold against an inmate's First Amendment challenge a policy denying newspapers, magazines, or personal photographs to a small segregated group of dangerous prisoners. The ruling reinstated a policy applicable to about forty inmates housed in Pennsylvania's long-term segregation unit. Pennsylvania officials said the facility was reserved for "the most incorrigible, recalcitrant inmates," prisoners with histories of dangerous behavior in prison and prisoners who failed to respond to other disciplinary sanctions. Along with severe limits on visitation, time outside their cells, and other privileges, the inmates were allowed no access to newspapers, magazines, or personal photographs. The rules did allow access, however, to legal and personal correspondence, religious and legal materials, two library books, and writing paper. Ronald Banks, a prisoner in the unit, filed a federal court class action suit in 2001 contending that the policy violated the First Amendment because it had no reasonable relation to any legitimate penological objective. In a motion for summary judgment, prison officials argued that the policy was aimed at motivating better behavior on the inmates' parts; minimizing the amount of property in their cells; and assuring prison safety by, for example, diminishing the amount of material that might be used to start a cell fire.

JURY SELECTION

Gonzalez v. United States (553 U.S. _), decided by an 8–1 vote, May 12, 2008; Kennedy wrote the opinion; Thomas dissented.

A felony defendant in a federal criminal trial need not give personal consent to a magistrate judge, instead of a district court judge, presiding over jury selection if the attorney agrees to the procedure. The ruling resolved a conflict among federal appeals courts on the procedure for allowing jury selection in federal felony trials to be presided over by magistrate judges, who are appointed for a fixed term by federal district court judges and take on specified duties under the district court judges' supervision.

PROBABLE CAUSE

Hartman v. Moore (547 U.S. 250), decided by a 5–2 vote, April 26, 2006; Souter wrote the opinion; Ginsburg and Breyer dissented; Roberts and Alito did not participate.

A plaintiff suing a government official for retaliatory prosecution must prove the absence of probable cause to support the underlying criminal charges. The ruling represented a potentially fatal setback for a Dallas businessman's damages suit against five postal inspectors for allegedly instigating a bribery-conspiracy prosecution against him in retaliation for his aggressive efforts to win a lucrative U.S. Postal Service contract for optical address-reading machinery.

REMOVAL

Watson v. Philip Morris Co. (551 U.S. 142), decided by a 9–0 vote, June 11, 2007; Breyer wrote the opinion.

Federal regulation is insufficient to allow cigarette manufacturers to remove lawsuits filed against them from state to federal court under the "federal officer removal statute." The ruling sent Philip Morris Co. back to an Arkansas state court to defend against a deceptive and unfair business practices claim filed by smokers of two brands of its "light" cigarettes.

STATE COURTS

Marshall v. Marshall (547 U.S. 293), decided by a 9–0 vote, May 1, 2006; Ginsburg wrote the opinion.

The probate exception to federal jurisdiction does not prevent a federal court from hearing a tort claim simply because it is related to the administration of an estate being probated in state court. The ruling reinstated a lawsuit filed by the celebrity model Vickie Lynn Marshall (professionally known as Anna Nicole Smith) against her adult stepson claiming that he had engaged in fraud and forgery to deprive her of a trust worth millions of dollars allegedly created for her by her husband.

Empire HealthChoice Assurance, Inc. v. McVeigh (547 U.S. 677), decided by a 5–4 vote, June 15, 2006; Ginsburg wrote the opinion; Breyer, Kennedy, Souter, and Alito dissented.

Federal courts do not have jurisdiction to adjudicate reimbursement claims brought by health plan carriers against federal employee beneficiaries whose medical bills have been paid by the carrier but who subsequently recover damages for the same injuries from a third party. The ruling resolved in favor of state courts a jurisdictional issue over insurance reimbursement claims against federal employees that had divided federal appeals courts.

STATUTE OF LIMITATIONS

BP America Production Co. v. Burton, Acting Assistant Secretary, Land and Minerals Management, Department of the Interior (549 U.S. 84), decided by a 7–0 vote, Dec. 11, 2006; Alito wrote the opinion; Roberts and Breyer did not participate.

The six-year statute of limitations in federal law for actions for contractual money damages brought by the United States applies only to court actions and not to administrative payment orders. The ruling upheld an order from the Interior Department's Mineral Management Service that BP America pay additional royalties owed on federal gas leases.

John R. Sand & Gravel Co. v. United States (552 U.S. 130), decided by a 7–2 vote, Jan. 8, 2008; Breyer wrote the opinion; Stevens and Ginsburg dissented.

The Court of Federal Claims must consider whether a claim is filed within the six-year statute of limitations even if the government does not raise untimeliness as a defense.

VIRTUAL REPRESENTATION THEORY

Taylor v. Sturgell, Acting Administrator, Federal Aviation Administration (553 U.S. _), decided by a 9–0 vote, June 12, 2008; Ginsburg wrote the opinion.

A plaintiff cannot be precluded from bringing a suit on a theory of "virtual representation" simply because someone with identical interests has already litigated the same issue. The ruling disapproved a theory adopted by several federal appeals courts to preclude nonparties to prior suits from litigating the same issue.

Criminal Law and Procedure

APPEALS

Erickson v. Pardus (551 U.S. 89), decided by a 7–2 vote, June 4, 2007; per curiam opinion; Thomas dissented; Scalia voted to deny certiorari.

A federal appeals court made a mistake in dismissing a Colorado inmate's federal civil rights suit claiming that prison officials denied him medication for a life-threatening disease.

Bowles v. Russell, Warden (551 U.S. 205), decided by a 5–4 vote, June 14, 2007; Thomas wrote the opinion; Souter, Stevens, Ginsburg, and Breyer dissented.

DUE PROCESS, EQUAL PROTECTION

. . . Nor shall any state deprive any person of life, liberty, or property, without due process of law; nor deny to any person within its jurisdiction the equal projection of the laws.

Fourteenth Amendment, U.S. Constitution

Untimely filing of a notice of an appeal in a civil case in federal court bars appellate court jurisdiction even if the appellant filed the appeal within the time allowed by a district court order.

ARRESTS

Devenpeck v. Alford (543 U.S. 146), decided by an 8–0 vote, Dec. 13, 2004; Scalia wrote the opinion; Rehnquist did not participate.

An arrest is lawful if an officer has probable cause to believe the suspect has committed some offense even if the charge ultimately filed is for a different crime. The ruling underscored previous decisions holding that an officer's subjective state of mind is largely irrelevant as long as the officer has objective probable cause that the suspect has committed a crime.

Brigham City, Utah v. Stuart (547 U.S. 398), decided by a 9–0 vote, May 22, 2006; Roberts wrote the opinion.

Police may enter a home without a warrant when they have an objectively reasonable basis for believing that an occupant is seriously injured or imminently threatened with such injury. The Court held that the officers' entry was "plainly reasonable" to help an injured adult and prevent further violence. "Nothing in the Fourth Amendment required them to wait until another blow rendered someone 'unconscious' or 'semi-conscious' or worse before entering," the Court wrote.

CAPITAL PUNISHMENT

Smith v. Texas (543 U.S. 37), decided by a 7–2 vote, Nov. 15, 2004; per curiam decision; Scalia and Thomas dissented.

The Court threw out a Texas inmate's death sentence because the trial judge's instructions did not allow jurors to consider the defendant's learning disability and other personal background as mitigating factors.

Roper, Superintendent, Potosi Correctional Center v. Simmons (543 U.S. 551), decided by a 5–4 vote, March 1, 2005; Kennedy wrote the opinion; Scalia, Rehnquist, O'Connor, and Thomas dissented.

The U.S. Supreme Court abolished the death penalty for persons who commit capital crimes as juveniles, ruling that the practice amounted to cruel and unusual punishment under the Eighth Amendment. The decision barred the executions of a total of seventy-three inmates in thirteen states, including Christopher Simmons, who had been convicted and sentenced to death for the 1993 kidnapping and drowning of an elderly Missouri woman. Simmons was seventeen at the time of the crime. The ruling effectively overturned the Court's decision in *Stanford v. Kentucky* (1989), which had allowed the execution of sixteen- and seventeen-year-old offenders. In that decision, the Court held that without a "settled consensus" against execution of juvenile offenders, the Eighth Amendment did not bar the practice.

The context of the issue changed with the Court's 2002 decision in *Atkins v. Virginia,* which barred the execution of mentally retarded offenders largely because of what the majority said was a "national consensus" against the practice. Simmons cited *Atkins* in a new petition for postconviction relief that he filed in Missouri courts.

The Court held that the death penalty is a "disproportionate" punishment for juveniles. The opinion cited "objective indicia of consensus" against the practice and "the Court's own determination" of "the diminished culpability of juveniles" compared with adult offenders.

Bell, Warden v. Thompson (545 U.S. 794), decided by a 5–4 vote, June 27, 2005; Kennedy wrote the opinion; Breyer, Stevens, Souter, and Ginsburg dissented.

A federal appeals court abused its discretion in a state death penalty case when, after a judge discovered previously overlooked evidence, it waited five months following a final decision to overturn its previous ruling. The ruling in this complex procedural dispute reversed a federal appeals court's decision to withdraw its previous ruling and order reconsideration of the death sentence imposed on Gregory Thompson for the 1985 murder of a Tennessee woman after abducting her from a department store parking lot.

Schriro, Director, Arizona Department of Corrections v. Smith (546 U.S. 6), decided by a 9–0 vote, Oct. 17, 2005; per curiam opinion.

The Court upheld, for the time being, states' discretion not to use jury trials to determine whether a defendant in a capital case is mentally retarded and on that basis ineligible for the death penalty. The ruling threw out a federal appeals court decision ordering a jury trial on a mental retardation claim by an Arizona death row inmate, Robert Douglas Smith, who had been convicted in 1982 of first-degree murder and other offenses. The Count noted, however, that states' procedures might be subject to constitutional challenge later.

Bradshaw, Warden v. Richey (546 U.S. 74), decided by a 9–0 vote, Nov. 28, 2005; per curiam opinion.

An Ohio man was properly sentenced to death for starting a fire that killed a two-year-old child though he started the fire to kill his ex-girlfriend and her companion, not the infant victim. The ruling set aside a federal appeals court decision to grant habeas corpus relief to Kenneth Richey based on its conclusion that Ohio law did not allow the use of "transferred intent" to sustain a conviction for aggravated murder.

Brown, Warden v. Sanders (546 U.S. 212), decided by a 5–4 vote, Jan. 11, 2006; Scalia wrote the opinion; Stevens, Souter, Ginsburg, and Breyer dissented.

A death sentence based upon an invalid sentencing factor may be upheld if another factor exists that gives aggravating weight to the same aspects of the crime. The ruling, reinstating a California inmate's death sentence, represented a victory for law enforcement as well as a simplification of the Court's death penalty decisions. It abolished a distinction that the Court had established between so-called weighing and nonweighing states in determining the impact of the use of an invalid sentencing factor in capital cases.

Kansas v. Marsh (548 U.S. 163), decided by a 5–4 vote, June 26, 2006; Thomas wrote the opinion; Souter, Stevens, Ginsburg, and Breyer dissented.

A Kansas statute does not violate the U.S. Constitution in requiring the imposition of the death penalty when the capital sentencing jury unanimously determines that aggravating circumstances are not outweighed by mitigating circumstances. The ruling reversed the Kansas Supreme Court's decision to strike down the state's death penalty law as violating the Eighth and Fourteenth Amendments by mandating a death sentence if the jury found aggravating and mitigating factors "in equipoise."

Ayers, Acting Warden v. Belmontes (549 U.S. 7), decided by a 5–4 vote, Nov. 13, 2006; Kennedy wrote the opinion; Stevens, Souter, Ginsburg, and Breyer dissented.

A California death row inmate failed in an effort to overturn his death sentence on the ground that the jury instruction used in his 1982 trial improperly limited jurors from considering post-crime mitigating evidence. The ruling represented the Court's third rejection of challenges to a later-discarded California jury instruction known as "factor k," which directed jurors to consider certain specific aggravating and mitigating factors along with "any other circumstance which extenuates the gravity of the crime even though it is not a legal excuse for the crime."

Abdul-Kabir v. Quarterman, Director, Texas Department of Criminal Justice, Correctional Institutions Division (550 U.S. 233), decided by a 5–4 vote, April 25, 2007; Stevens wrote the opinion; Roberts, Scalia, Thomas, and Alito dissented.

The Court reinstated a Texas inmate's challenge to his death sentence, holding that state courts had misapplied U.S. Supreme Court precedent in rejecting his plea that jurors had been improperly prevented from considering mitigating evidence. The ruling revived a federal habeas corpus challenge brought by Jalil Abdul-Kabir, who—under his birth name, Ted Calvin Cole—had been sentenced to death for his part in the December 1987 strangulation of his sister-in-law's grandfather during a robbery that netted $20.

Smith v. Texas (550 U.S. 297), decided by a 5–4 vote, April 25, 2007; Kennedy wrote the opinion; Alito, Roberts, Scalia, and Thomas dissented.

The Court threw out a Texas inmate's death sentence for the second time, saying that a state appellate court had misapplied federal law in concluding that the inmate had failed to preserve a challenge to an erroneous jury instruction. The ruling ordered the Texas Court of Criminal Appeals to reconsider a challenge by LaRoyce Lathair Smith to his death sentence for the 1991 murder of a former coworker at a fast-food restaurant in Dallas during a robbery.

Baze v. Rees, Director, Kentucky Department of Corrections (553 U.S. _), decided by a 7–2 vote, April 16, 2008; Roberts wrote the main opinion; Stevens, Scalia, Thomas, and Breyer concurred in the judgment; Ginsburg and Souter dissented.

The three-drug protocol commonly used in executions by lethal injection does not violate the U.S. Constitution's ban on cruel and unusual punishment. The ruling ended a de facto ban on executions in the United States.

The method of execution used by Kentucky, along with the federal government and at least twenty-nine of the thirty-five other states that use capital punishment, consisted of the administration of drugs. The first drug, sodium thiopental, induces unconsciousness and, properly administered, prevents the individual from feeling any pain; the second drug, pancuronium bromide, stops muscle movement and breathing; and the final drug, potassium chloride, induces cardiac arrest. All parties in the case agreed that the administration of the drugs would cause a humane death if properly administered.

Kennedy v. Louisiana (554 U.S. _), decided by a 5–4 vote, June 25, 2008; Kennedy wrote the opinion; Alito, Roberts, Scalia, and Thomas dissented.

The death penalty cannot be imposed for the crime of child rape or for any nonhomicide crime committed against an individual person. The ruling struck down capital child rape laws in Louisiana and five other states on the ground that the death penalty would amount to cruel and unusual punishment for the offense under the Eighth Amendment. The Court held—on the basis of a "national consensus" and its own "independent judgment"—that the Eighth Amendment's cruel and unusual punishment clause prohibits the death penalty for raping a child.

CIVIL RIGHTS

Jones v. Bock, Warden (549 U.S. 199), decided by a 9–0 vote, Jan. 22, 2007; Roberts wrote the opinion.

Prisoners filing federal civil rights claims against prison officials do not have to show in their initial complaint that they have exhausted administrative remedies and can include defendants not named in administrative grievances. In addition, an entire action need not be dismissed if it is found to include some claims that the prisoner did not pursue first through administrative channels. The ruling, allowing three Michigan inmates to refile federal civil rights suits against state prison officials, rejected one federal appeals court's strict interpretation of procedural requirements under the Prison Litigation Reform Act of 1995. The act aimed to reduce prison litigation by, among other things, requiring that inmates filing suit under the federal civil rights statute known as Section 1983 exhaust all remedies within the institutions before bringing claims in federal court.

COMPETENCY

Indiana v. Edwards (554 U.S. _), decided by a 7–2 vote, June 19, 2008; Breyer wrote the opinion; Scalia and Thomas dissented.

A state court may find a criminal defendant competent to stand trial but incompetent to represent him- or herself and, in such a case, may appoint counsel for the defendant against his or her will. The ruling reinstated the attempted murder and battery convictions of Ahmad Edwards that Indiana appellate courts had set aside on the ground that he had been denied a constitutional right to represent himself at trial. Edwards was arrested in July 1999 after allegedly attempting to steal a pair of shoes from a department store.

CONSENT

Florida v. Nixon (543 U.S. 175), decided by an 8–0 vote, Dec. 13, 2004; Ginsburg wrote the opinion; Rehnquist did not participate.

A defense lawyer in a capital case need not obtain a defendant's express consent to a strategic decision to concede guilt at trial and concentrate instead on presenting mitigating evidence during the penalty phase.

CONSTITUTIONAL ERROR

Fry v. Pliler, Warden (551 U.S. 112), decided by a 5–4 vote, June 11, 2007; Scalia wrote the opinion; Stevens, Souter, Ginsburg, and Breyer dissented in part.

Federal courts may not throw out a state court conviction because of a constitutional error unless the error had a "substantial and injurious effect" on the verdict. The ruling rejected an effort by a California inmate, John Fry, to extend to federal habeas corpus cases a stricter "harmless beyond a reasonable doubt" standard for constitutional errors used when state convictions are on direct appeal. Fry had been convicted of murder in a third state court trial after juries in the first two trials deadlocked. He appealed his conviction on the ground that the judge's refusal to allow testimony by a defense witness violated his constitutional right.

> **DOUBLE JEOPARDY, SELF-INCRIMINATION**
>
> . . . Nor shall any person be subject for the same offense to be twice put in jeopardy of life or limb nor shall be compelled in any criminal case to be a witness against himself, nor be deprived of life, liberty, or property, without due process of law . . .
>
> *Fifth Amendment, U.S. Constitution*

DOUBLE JEOPARDY

Smith v. Massachusetts (543 U.S. 462), decided by a 5–4 vote, Feb. 22, 2005; Scalia wrote the opinion; Ginsburg, Rehnquist, Kennedy, and Breyer dissented.

Trial judges are barred by the U.S. Constitution's double jeopardy clause from reversing a mid-trial decision to acquit a defendant of a criminal charge unless a preexisting rule explicitly permits them to do so. The narrow decision voided Melvin Smith's conviction for unlawful possession of a firearm under Massachusetts law. Smith was convicted by a jury of three charges related to the shooting of his girlfriend's cousin, among them unlawful possession of a firearm. The shooting victim later died.

EVIDENCE

Holmes v. South Carolina (547 U.S. 319), decided by a 9–0 vote, May 1, 2006; Alito wrote the opinion.

A defendant cannot be prevented from introducing evidence that someone else committed the crime that he or she is accused of committing merely because of the strength of the prosecution's case. The ruling breathed new life into an effort by a South Carolina man, Bobby Lee Holmes, to overturn his first-degree murder conviction and death sentence for the 1989 rape and murder of an elderly woman during a residential break-in. In a retrial following reversal of an earlier conviction in the case, prosecutors relied heavily on forensic evidence linking Holmes to the killing. In defense, Holmes sought to introduce testimony from four witnesses showing that another man had either described Holmes as innocent or acknowledged committing the crime himself.

Hudson v. Michigan (547 U.S. 586), decided by a 5–4 vote, June 15, 2006; Scalia wrote the opinion; Breyer, Stevens, Souter, and Ginsburg dissented.

Police violation of the "knock-and-announce" rule requiring officers to knock and wait before entering a private home does not require suppression of evidence obtained in the subsequent search. The ruling upheld the drug conviction of a Detroit man, Booker Hudson, even though police officers executing a search warrant violated the knock-and-announce rule by waiting only a few seconds after announcing their presence before entering his home.

The Court said that the costs of applying the exclusionary rule to knock-and-announce violations in terms of releasing criminals and inviting additional litigation would outweigh any benefits in terms of protecting privacy or deterring police misbehavior. The ruling eliminated any federal constitutional basis for suppressing evidence for knock-and-announce violations but left states free to exclude evidence under their own constitutions or laws. Michigan had been the only state to allow the use of evidence that police obtained without complying with the rule.

Davis v. Washington and *Hammon v. Indiana* (547 U.S. 813), decided by 9–0 and 8–1 votes, June 19, 2006; Scalia wrote the opinion; Thomas dissented in part.

Crime victim statements or other eyewitness statements made to help police meet an ongoing emergency may be used as evidence in a criminal trial even if the witness refuses or is unavailable to testify. Statements made to police after an emergency has ended, however, may not be introduced. The ruling involved a pair of closely watched domestic violence cases. It upheld a Washington State man's conviction based in part on the use of the contents of a 911 call placed by his estranged girlfriend, but it overturned an Indiana man's conviction because of the use of an interview with his wife after officers had separated the couple. Neither of the women testified at trial. The defendants in both cases claimed that the use of the out-of-court statements violated their rights under the Sixth Amendment's confrontation clause, which guarantees a defendant the right "to be confronted with the witnesses against him."

Sanchez-Llamas v. Oregon (548 U.S. 331), decided by a 6–3 vote, June 28, 2006; Roberts wrote the opinion; Breyer, Stevens, and Souter dissented.

Foreign nationals deprived of the treaty-protected right to consular notification and access after an arrest may not use the treaty violation to suppress evidence obtained in police interrogation or belatedly raise legal challenges after trial. The ruling rejected decisions by the International Court of Justice that foreign nationals be given remedies in U.S. courts for violations of the Vienna Convention on Consular Relations requiring notice and access to consular representatives after an arrest or detention.

Whorton, Director, Nevada Department of Corrections v. Bockting (549 U.S. 406), decided by a 9–0 vote, Feb. 28, 2007; Alito wrote the opinion.

The U.S. Supreme Court's ruling in 2004 excluding out-of-court statements by witnesses unavailable for cross-examination does not apply retroactively. The ruling reversed a Ninth U.S. Circuit Court of Appeals decision to bar from evidence a six-year-old's description to a detective of sexual assault by her stepfather, Marvin Bockting.

Giles v. California (554 U.S. _), decided by a 6–3 vote, June 25, 2008; Scalia wrote the opinion; Breyer, Stevens, and Kennedy dissented.

Testimonial statements by a witness who is unavailable at trial because of a defendant's actions can be admitted as evidence only if the defendant's actions were designed to prevent the witness from testifying. The ruling—strictly applying the Sixth Amendment's right to confront witnesses—vacated the murder conviction of a California man, Dwayne Giles, for the shooting death of his ex-girlfriend, Brenda Avie. At trial, Giles claimed he killed Avie in self-defense after she charged at him with something in her hand. To refute the testimony, prosecutors succeeded in admitting into evidence several statements that Avie had made to a police officer responding to a domestic violence report only three weeks before the shooting. The trial court allowed these statements into evidence based on a state law that permits admission of out-of-court statements that describe the infliction or threat of physical violence on a declarant when the declarant is unavailable to testify at trial.

EXPLOSIVES

United States v. Ressam (553 U.S. _), decided by an 8–1 vote, May 19, 2008; Stevens wrote the opinion; Breyer dissented.

An individual who carries explosives during the commission of a felony can be charged with a second felony under the Organized Crime Control Act, even if the initial felony is unrelated to carrying the explosives.

FAIR TRIAL

Carey, Warden v. Musladin (549 U.S. 70), decided by a 9–0 vote, Dec. 11, 2006; Thomas wrote the opinion.

A state appellate court did not unreasonably apply federal law when it concluded that allowing a victim's family to wear buttons displaying his image at trial did not violate the defendant's right to a fair trial. The ruling came after a California state trial court denied Mathew Musladin's motion to prevent the victim's family members from wearing the buttons during his trial.

FIREARMS

Small v. United States (544 U.S. 385), decided by a 5–3 vote, April 26, 2005; Breyer wrote the opinion; Thomas, Scalia, and Kennedy dissented; Rehnquist did not participate.

The federal law making it a crime for a convicted criminal to possess a firearm applies to convictions in domestic courts solely, not to those in foreign courts. The ruling overturned the federal firearms conviction of a Pennsylvania man, Gary Small, for buying a small-caliber pistol from a Pennsylvania gun dealer in 1998 shortly after he had completed a prison sentence in Japan for having tried to smuggle firearms and ammunition into that country.

Dixon v. United States (548 U.S. 1), decided by a 7–2 vote, June 22, 2006; Stevens wrote the opinion; Breyer and Souter dissented.

Defendants claiming duress as a defense to federal firearms violations under a 1968 gun control law have the burden of proving that defense by a preponderance of the evidence. The ruling rejected the view of most federal appeals courts to have considered the question that once a defendant raises the issue, the government must prove the absence of duress beyond a reasonable doubt. In immediate effect, the ruling upheld the firearms-related convictions of a Texas woman, Keisha Dixon, who said she provided false information to buy weapons at gun shows because her boyfriend had threatened to kill her or hurt her daughters if she did not buy the guns for him.

Watson v. United States (522 U.S. 74), decided by a 9–0 vote, Dec. 10, 2007; Souter wrote the opinion.

The mandatory minimum sentence provisions of federal law for using a firearm in a drug trafficking offense do not apply to a person who receives a firearm in trade for drugs.

GUILTY PLEAS

Bradshaw, Warden v. Stumpf (545 U.S. 175), decided by a 9–0 vote, June 13, 2005; O'Connor wrote the opinion.

A guilty plea is voluntary if the charge's elements and nature were explained to the defense lawyer or defendant even if the defendant did not understand all of the plea's implications. The fact-bound ruling reinstated the death sentence of an Ohio man, John David Stumpf, who pleaded guilty to murder in the 1984 shooting death of a woman during a home burglary but blamed the shooting on an accomplice.

HABEAS CORPUS

Bell, Warden v. Cone (543 U.S. 447), decided by a 9–0 vote, Jan. 24, 2005; per curiam opinion.

A federal appeals court erred in granting a convicted murderer a writ of habeas corpus on the ground that a factor the jury had to find to sentence him to death was impermissibly vague. The ruling reversed a decision by a federal appeals court invalidating the death sentence of Gary Bradford Cone, who was convicted in 1982 of the murders of an elderly couple in Memphis, Tenn.

Brown, Warden v. Payton (544 U.S. 133), decided by a 5–3 vote, March 22, 2005; Kennedy wrote the opinion; Souter, Stevens, and Ginsburg dissented; Rehnquist did not participate.

A California death row inmate was not entitled to federal habeas corpus relief to overturn his death sentence despite the prosecutor's misstatements appearing to limit jurors' consideration of post-crime evidence as mitigation and the trial judge's failure to correct these misstatements in the jury instructions. The ruling—based on the deferential standard toward state court decisions established by the 1996 rewrite of federal habeas corpus law—reinstated the 1982 death sentence for William Payton for the rape-murder of a fellow boarder at a boarding house in Garden Grove, Calif. At issue was the state's catch-all mitigation instruction, which required the jury to give general consideration to extenuating circumstances in deciding whether to impose the death penalty.

Rhines v. Weber, Warden (544 U.S. 269), decided by a 9–0 vote, March 30, 2005; O'Connor wrote the opinion.

A federal court has discretion to hold a state prisoner's federal habeas corpus petition in abeyance so that the inmate can ask state courts to rule on any claims not yet considered there. The ruling resolved a significant conflict in the federal courts as to whether the 1996 Antiterrorism and Effective Death Penalty Act barred federal district courts from adopting a so-called stay-and-abeyance procedure to "mixed petitions" for habeas corpus—petitions with some claims reviewed by state courts and some presented for the first time.

Gonzalez v. Crosby, Secretary, Florida Department of Corrections (545 U.S. 524), decided by a 7–2 vote, June 23, 2005; Scalia wrote the opinion; Stevens and Souter dissented.

A motion seeking relief from judgment is not necessarily a second or "successive" petition for federal habeas corpus relief and is available in some suits challenging a state conviction in federal court. The ruling resolved a conflict in the federal courts of appeals concerning whether the 1996 federal law governing petitions for writs of habeas corpus categorically barred motions for "relief from judgment" under Rule 60(b) of the Federal Rules of Civil Procedure.

Mayle, Warden v. Felix (545 U.S. 644), decided by a 7–2 vote, June 23, 2005; Ginsburg wrote the opinion; Souter and Stevens dissented.

An amendment to a federal habeas corpus petition does not "relate back" to the original filing date for purposes of the statute of limitations if it asserts a new ground for relief based on different facts. The ruling overturned a federal appeals court's decision permitting a California inmate, Jacoby Lee Felix, to use a provision of the Federal Rules of Civil Procedure to amend his habeas corpus petition outside the one-year statute of limitations imposed by the Antiterrorism and Effective Death Penalty Act, the 1996 law governing federal habeas corpus.

Dye v. Hofbauer Warden (546 U.S. 1), decided by a 9–0 vote, Oct. 11, 2005; per curiam opinion.

The Court allowed a Michigan man to use federal habeas corpus to challenge his two murder convictions on the ground that a federal appeals court improperly dismissed the petition. The ruling reinstated the habeas corpus petition filed by Paul Allen Dye challenging his 1990 conviction for the shooting deaths of two women outside a nightclub near Detroit. Dye had filed the habeas corpus petition claiming various federal constitutional errors.

Kane, Warden v. Garcia Espitia (546 U.S. 9), decided by a 9–0 vote, Oct. 31, 2005; per curiam opinion.

A federal appeals court was wrong to throw out a California inmate's criminal conviction because he had not been provided pretrial access to a law library while representing himself. The ruling reversed a decision by the Ninth U.S. Circuit Court of Appeals granting habeas corpus relief to Jose Garcia Espitia after his conviction in a California state court for carjacking and other offenses.

Evans, Acting Warden v. Chavis (546 U.S. 189), decided by a 9–0 vote, Jan. 10, 2006; Breyer wrote the opinion.

In the absence of clear direction from the state court, federal appellate courts must examine each case to determine whether a prisoner's delay in filing a state court appeal renders the prisoner ineligible for federal habeas corpus relief. The ruling stemmed from a provision in the Antiterrorism and Effective Death Penalty Act of 1996, which gives prisoners convicted in state court only one year to seek federal habeas corpus relief.

Day v. McDonough, Interim Secretary, Florida Department of Corrections (547 U.S. 198), decided by a 5–4 vote, April 25, 2006; Ginsburg wrote the opinion; Scalia, Thomas, and Breyer dissented on the main issue; Stevens and Breyer dissented on a procedural issue.

A federal judge can act on his or her own to correct a clear computation error in determining whether a habeas corpus petition should be dismissed because it was filed past the one-year deadline. The ruling upheld the dismissal of a habeas corpus petition by a Florida prison inmate, Patrick Day, despite the state's failure to object that Day had filed it past the one-year statute of limitations Congress established in revising habeas corpus law in 1996.

Hill v. McDonough, Interim Secretary, Florida Department of Corrections (547 U.S. 573), decided by a 9–0 vote, June 12, 2006; Kennedy wrote the opinion.

A death row inmate may use federal civil rights law instead of habeas corpus to challenge the particular means of administering a lethal injection if the success of the inmate's suit would not necessarily bar the execution. The ruling—benefitting death row inmates in several states—reinstated a claim by a Florida prisoner, Clarence Hill, that the three-drug combination used by the state for lethal injection could cause him severe pain in violation of the Eighth Amendment's prohibition of cruel and unusual punishment. Hill's challenge paralleled claims being made by death row inmates in other states that the first drug injected, the anesthetic sodium pentothal, would not render painless the administration of the second and third drugs, pancuronium bromide and potassium chloride. On that basis, Hill alleged that he might remain conscious and suffer severe pain as the other drugs first paralyzed his lungs and then caused a fatal heart attack. Florida had adopted lethal injection as the presumptive method of execution in 2000, but the law did not specify the drug protocol to be used.

Lawrence v. Florida (549 U.S. 327), decided by a 5–4 vote, Feb. 20, 2007; Thomas wrote the opinion; Ginsburg, Stevens, Souter, and Breyer dissented.

The one-year time limit for seeking federal habeas relief from a state court judgment is not put on hold while a petition for review is pending in the U.S. Supreme Court. The ruling strictly interpreted the one-year statute of limitations established in the 1996 overhaul of federal habeas corpus law in rejecting a bid by a Florida death row inmate, Gary Lawrence, to set aside his 1995 conviction for first-degree murder in the beating death of his wife's lover.

Schriro, Director, Arizona Department of Corrections v. Landrigan (550 U.S. 465), decided by a 5–4 vote, May 14, 2007; Thomas wrote the opinion; Stevens, Souter, Ginsburg, and Breyer dissented.

A federal court may deny a state prison inmate an evidentiary hearing in a habeas corpus case if the inmate cannot present enough evidence to show the state courts' decisions were unreasonable. The ruling barred a hearing for an Arizona death row inmate, Jeffrey Landrigan, on a claim of ineffective assistance of counsel based on his trial lawyer's failure to investigate or present mitigating evidence on his behalf.

Uttecht, Superintendent, Washington State Penitentiary v. Brown (551 U.S. 1), decided by a 5–4 vote, June 4, 2007; Kennedy wrote the opinion; Stevens, Souter, Ginsburg, and Breyer dissented.

Federal judges hearing habeas corpus challenges by death row inmates should give state trial judges great leeway in disqualifying potential jurors in capital cases for expressing doubts about capital punishment. The ruling rejected a habeas corpus challenge by a Washington State death row inmate, Cal Coburn Brown, who was convicted in 1991 for capital murder of a young woman whom he robbed, raped, and left for dead in a motel after abducting her from a car.

Panetti v. Quarterman, Director, Texas Department of Criminal Justice, Correctional Institutions Division (551 U.S. 930), decided by a 5–4 vote, June 28, 2007; Kennedy wrote the opinion; Thomas, Roberts, Scalia, and Alito dissented.

Courts must consider delusional disorders that prevent a prisoner from understanding the reason for his pending execution in determining whether the prisoner is incompetent to be executed. The ruling in a procedurally complex federal habeas corpus case gave a Texas death row inmate, Scott Louis Panetti, a new chance to block his execution on insanity grounds for the 1992 killings of the parents of his estranged wife. Despite suffering from delusions and hallucinations, Panetti was found competent to stand trial in a Texas court, where he was convicted and sentenced to death in 1995 after representing himself. While Panetti understood the reason that the state gave for his execution, he was under the delusion that he was being executed to prevent him from preaching.

Wright, Sheriff, Shawano County, Wisconsin v. Van Patten (552 U.S. 120), decided by a 9–0 vote, Jan. 7, 2008; per curiam opinion.

A Wisconsin inmate was denied a new trial even though his lawyer participated in a plea hearing by speakerphone instead of in person. The ruling rejected a federal habeas corpus petition filed by Joseph Van Patten, who was sentenced in a Wisconsin court in 1995 to twenty-five years in prison after pleading no contest to the reduced charge of first-degree reckless homicide in a fatal shooting.

Munaf v. Geren, Secretary of the Army (553 U.S. _), decided by a 9–0 vote, June 12, 2008; Roberts wrote the opinion.

U.S. citizens held by the U.S. military operating as part of the Multinational Force in Iraq on charges of violating Iraqi law may not use habeas corpus to win their release or prevent their transfer to Iraqi authorities. The ruling ordered the dismissal of habeas corpus petitions filed in federal court in Washington, D.C., on behalf of two U.S. citizens, Mohammad Munaf and Shawqi Omar, after their arrest by U.S. military forces in Iraq. Munaf, a dual citizen of Iraq and the United States, was charged with orchestrating the kidnapping of Romanian journalists. Omar, an American Jordanian citizen, was charged with supporting insurgent activities by the group al Qaeda in Iraq. Munaf initially confessed to the crime and then recanted the confession. He was convicted, but an Iraqi court vacated the conviction for further investigation. Omar was detained after a U.S. military tribunal determined he was a security threat to Iraq.

INSANITY DEFENSE

Clark v. Arizona (548 U.S. 735), decided by 6–3 and 5–4 votes, June 29, 2006; Souter wrote the opinion; Kennedy, Stevens, and Ginsburg dissented; Breyer dissented in part.

States may prevent a defendant from using mental illness to show he could not form the intent to commit a crime and may restrict the insanity defense to an inability to tell right from wrong. The ruling rejected an effort by an Arizona man, Eric Clark, to reverse his first-degree murder conviction on grounds that application of state law had improperly prevented him from using his mental illness—paranoid schizophrenia—as a defense.

JURY SELECTION

Miller-El v. Dretke, Director, Texas Department of Criminal Justice, Correctional Institutions Division (545 U.S. 231), decided by a 6–3 vote, June 13, 2005; Souter wrote the opinion; Thomas, Rehnquist, and Scalia dissented.

The Court ordered a new trial for a black Texas death row inmate because prosecutors were guilty of racial discrimination in using peremptory challenges to excuse African Americans from the trial jury. The ruling in favor of Thomas Joe Miller-El marked the second time the Court had reversed decisions by the Fifth U.S. Circuit Court of Appeals rejecting his challenge to his conviction and death sentence in the 1985 robbery-murder of a Dallas hotel employee. During the trial, prosecutors from the Dallas County District Attorney's Office used peremptory challenges to excuse ten black members of the jury pool.

Snyder v. Louisiana (552 U.S. 472), decided by a 7–2 vote, March 19, 2008; Alito wrote the opinion; Thomas and Scalia dissented.

Appellate courts can overturn trial courts' determinations that peremptory jury strikes were not discriminatory if the trial court fails to explain its ruling and the race-neutral reasons for striking the juror are implausible. The ruling expanded the ability of criminal defendants to challenge prosecutors for alleged racial discrimination in using peremptory challenges to strike potential jurors.

MONEY LAUNDERING

Whitfield v. United States (543 U.S. 209), decided by a 9–0 vote, Jan. 11, 2005; O'Connor wrote the opinion.

The federal offense of conspiring to commit money laundering does not require proof of an overt act in furtherance of the conspiracy. The ruling upheld the convictions of two men, David Whitefield and Don Hall, for their roles as board members of a phony nationwide investment fund operating under the name Greater Ministries International Church. Congress in 1992 added a conspiracy provision to the Money Laundering Control Act of 1986 that, unlike some other conspiracy statutes, did not include proof of an overt act for a conviction.

Regalado Cuellar v. United States (553 U.S. _), decided by a 9–0 vote, June 2, 2008; Thomas wrote the opinion.

A prosecution for the federal money laundering offense of taking proceeds of an unlawful activity outside the

United States requires proof that the purpose of the transportation was to conceal the nature or source of the funds.

United States v. Santos (553 U.S. _), decided by a 5–4 vote, June 2, 2008; Scalia wrote the main opinion; Stevens concurred in the judgment; Alito, Roberts, Kennedy, and Breyer dissented.

A person involved in an illegal gambling business can be convicted of money laundering only for using the profits from that business for illegal purposes, not just the monetary receipts of the business. The ruling significantly narrowed use of the federal money laundering statute in gambling cases, but the splintered decision left uncertain the impact in other areas.

PAROLE

Wilkinson, Director, Ohio Department of Rehabilitation and Correction v. Dotson (544 U.S. 74), decided by an 8–1 vote, March 7, 2005; Breyer wrote the opinion; Kennedy dissented.

State prisoners may invoke the federal civil rights statute to challenge the constitutionality of state parole procedures and are not required to seek relief under federal habeas corpus law. The ruling allowed two Ohio prison inmates, William Dotson and Rogerico Johnson, to continue using the civil rights statute to challenge the state parole board's use of guidelines adopted after the beginning of their sentences to deny them parole. The inmates said use of the 1998 guidelines violated the U.S. Constitution's ex post facto and due process clauses.

PORNOGRAPHY

United States v. Williams (553 U.S. _), decided by a 7–2 vote, May 19, 2008; Scalia wrote the opinion; Souter and Ginsburg dissented.

A federal law that prohibits individuals from offering to provide, or requesting to receive, child pornography does not violate the First Amendment, even when the underlying pornography does not exist. The ruling upheld the conviction of Michael Williams under one challenged provision of the 2003 anti–child pornography PROTECT Act (Prosecutorial Remedies and Other Tools to End the Exploitation of Children Today Act). The law was aimed at circumventing the U.S. Supreme Court's decision in *Free Speech Coalition v. Ashcroft* (2002) that ruled unconstitutional a 1996 law prohibiting possession of, or trafficking in, "virtual" child pornography, material presented as child pornography but without the use of real children. The new law made it a crime for anyone to knowingly pander or solicit material containing actual child pornography or material intended to cause another person to believe that it contains actual child pornography.

POSTCONVICTION PROCEDURES

Pace v. DiGuglielmo, Superintendent, State Correctional Institution at Graterford (544 U.S. 408), decided by a 5–4 vote, April 27, 2005; Rehnquist wrote the opinion; Stevens, Souter, Ginsburg, and Breyer dissented.

A state prisoner who applies for postconviction relief in state court before filing in federal court can take advantage of an extended federal limitations period only if the state court accepts his application as "properly filed." The ruling affirmed a federal appeals court's decision denying as untimely John Pace's petition for a writ of habeas corpus.

Eberhart v. United States (546 U.S. 12), decided by a 9–0 vote, Oct. 31, 2005; per curiam opinion.

A defendant's failure to meet the deadlines in the Federal Rules of Criminal Procedure for filing a motion for a new trial does not prevent a court from considering the motion unless the government objects on a timely basis.

Allen, Commissioner, Alabama Department of Corrections v. Siebert (552 U.S. 3), decided by a 7–2 vote, Nov. 5, 2007; per curiam opinion; Stevens and Ginsburg dissented.

A petition for postconviction relief in state court does not extend the time for filing a federal habeas corpus petition if the state court dismisses the petition as untimely. The ruling dismissed a federal habeas corpus petition filed by Daniel Siebert challenging his Alabama state court murder conviction and death sentence.

Danforth v. Minnesota (552 U.S. 264), decided by a 7–2 vote, Feb. 20, 2008; Stevens wrote the opinion; Roberts and Kennedy dissented.

State courts may apply a new constitutional rule from the U.S. Supreme Court in postconviction challenges even if the Court rules that retroactive application is not required by federal law. The ruling opened a potential avenue of relief for Stephen Danforth, a disbarred attorney convicted in Minnesota in 1996 of first-degree criminal sexual conduct with a minor.

PRISONS AND JAILS

Garrison S. Johnson v. California (543 U.S. 499), decided by a 5–3 vote, Feb. 23, 2005; O'Connor wrote the opinion; Stevens, Thomas, and Scalia dissented; Rehnquist did not participate.

California's policy of racially segregating prisoners for up to sixty days upon their arrival at a new facility is subject to the same demanding constitutional standard of strict scrutiny that applies to other race-based classifications. At issue was the policy of segregating new prisoners, on their arrival, in a "reception center," while prison officials reviewed the record to determine appropriate permanent housing for the inmates.

Wilkinson, Director, Ohio Department of Rehabilitation and Correction v. Austin (545 U.S. 209), decided by a 9–0 vote, June 13, 2005; Kennedy wrote the opinion.

Ohio's process for assigning inmates to a special maximum-security facility sufficiently protects inmates' liberty interest in avoiding the additional hardships of maximum-security confinement. The ruling rejected a constitutional challenge to the policy that Ohio had adopted in 2002 for classifying violent offenders and assigning them to its highest security prison, the Ohio State Penitentiary.

Woodford v. Ngo (548 U.S. 81), decided by a 6–3 vote, June 22, 2006; Alito wrote the opinion; Stevens, Souter, and Ginsburg dissented.

The Prison Litigation Reform Act requires prisoners to properly exhaust all administrative remedies, including meeting any prescribed deadlines, before challenging prison conditions in federal court. The ruling upheld the dismissal of a federal court suit by a California inmate, Viet Mike Ngo, for failing to meet the deadline for challenging his exclusion from religious activities because of prior misconduct.

QUALIFIED IMMUNITY

Brosseau v. Haugen (543 U.S. 194), decided by an 8–1 vote, Dec. 13, 2004; per curiam opinion; Stevens dissented.

A federal appeals court was wrong to deny a police officer qualified immunity from civil suit for shooting a suspect while he attempted to flee in his vehicle. The ruling reinstated qualified immunity from civil suit for Rochelle Brosseau, a police officer in Washington State who shot suspect Kenneth Haugen in the back in 1999 while Haugen was attempting to flee in a Jeep Cherokee. Haugen was wanted on drug charges and had been accused of theft by a former criminal associate when Brosseau responded to a scuffle between Haugen and that associate.

RIGHT TO COUNSEL, EFFECTIVE COUNSEL

Rompilla v. Beard, Secretary, Pennsylvania Department of Corrections (545 U.S. 374), decided by a 5–4 vote, June 20, 2005; Souter wrote the opinion; Kennedy, Rehnquist, Scalia, and Thomas dissented.

A Pennsylvania death row inmate had been denied effective assistance of counsel because his lawyer failed to investigate evidence of child abuse and mental illness that might have persuaded the jury to spare his life. The U.S. Supreme Court ruled for Ronald Rompilla by finding that his lawyers had been "deficient" in failing to examine the court file on Rompilla's prior convictions.

Halbert v. Michigan (545 U.S. 605), decided by a 6–3 vote, June 23, 2005; Ginsburg wrote the opinion; Thomas, Rehnquist, and Scalia dissented.

Indigent criminal defendants who plead guilty or no contest must be provided appointed counsel for an initial appeal even if appellate court review is discretionary and not a matter of right.

SEARCH AND SEIZURE

> The right of the people to be secure in their person, houses, papers and effects, against unreasonable searches and seizures, shall not be violated, and no warrants shall issue but upon probable cause, supported by oath or affirmation and particularly describing the place to be searched, and the persons or things to be seized.
>
> *Fourth Amendment, U.S. Constitution*

United States v. Gonzalez-Lopez (548 U.S. 140), decided by a 5–4 vote, June 26, 2006; Scalia wrote the opinion; Alito, Roberts, Kennedy, and Thomas dissented.

A defendant who is improperly denied his choice of counsel is entitled to a reversal of a conviction without having to show he was prejudiced as a result. The ruling upheld a federal appeals court's decision granting a new trial to Cuahtemoc Gonzalez-Lopez, who was convicted in federal court in Missouri in 2003 of conspiracy to distribute more than one hundred kilograms of marijuana.

SEARCH AND SEIZURE

Illinois v. Caballes (543 U.S. 405), decided by a 6–2 vote, Jan. 24, 2005; Stevens wrote the opinion; Souter and Ginsburg dissented; Rehnquist did not participate.

Police use of a drug-sniffing dog during an otherwise lawful traffic stop does not constitute an unlawful search under the Fourth Amendment, even if there is no reason to believe that the driver is transporting drugs. The ruling provided police departments with broad authority to employ highly trained drug-sniffing dogs to detect illegal drugs transported in cars.

Muehler v. Mena (544 U.S. 93), decided by a 9–0 vote, March 22, 2005; Rehnquist wrote the opinion.

An extended handcuffed detention by police during a lawful search and the subsequent suspicionless questioning of a resident's immigration status do not violate the Fourth Amendment. The ruling bolstered the view that concerns about officers' safety give police broad authority to handcuff, detain, and question even innocent occupants of a home during a proper search.

United States v. Grubbs (547 U.S. 90), decided by an 8–0 vote, March 21, 2006; Scalia wrote the opinion; Alito did not participate.

The Fourth Amendment does not require the triggering condition for an anticipatory search warrant to be set forth in the warrant itself. The ruling upheld the conviction of a California man, Jeffrey Grubbs, for receiving child pornography. Grubbs purchased a videotape containing child pornography from an undercover postal inspector. The inspector obtained a so-called anticipatory warrant, a warrant based upon an affidavit showing probable cause that at some future time certain evidence of crime will be located at a specified place. Most anticipatory warrants require a triggering condition before they can be executed. In Grubbs's case, a postal inspector submitted an affidavit stating that the warrant would not be executed until the parcel containing the videotape had been received and taken into Grubbs's residence. After the package was delivered and the search began, Grubbs was given a copy of the warrant, which described the residence and the items to be seized but did not include the affidavit. Following his indictment, Grubbs moved to suppress the seized evidence, arguing that the warrant was invalid because it failed to list the triggering condition set forth in the affidavit.

Georgia v. Randolph (547 U.S. 103), decided by a 5–3 vote, March 22, 2006; Souter wrote the opinion; Roberts, Scalia, and Thomas dissented; Alito did not participate.

A warrantless search is unreasonable and invalid under the Fourth Amendment when a co-occupant of a home is physically present and refuses to permit a police search of the premises, despite the consent of another co-occupant. The ruling upheld the suppression of cocaine discovered during a police search of the marital home of Scott Randolph in Americus, Ga., based on the consent of his estranged wife, Janet, and over his express refusal.

Samson v. California (547 U.S. 843), decided by a 6–3 vote, June 19, 2006; Thomas wrote the opinion; Stevens, Souter, and Breyer dissented.

Police officers can search parolees without a warrant or individualized suspicion of wrongdoing. The ruling upheld the drug conviction of a California man, Donald Samson, who was found with a plastic baggie containing methamphetamine after a suspicionless search on the street by a San Bruno police officer in September 2002. A California statute required parolees to agree to police searches "at any time" during their parole even if the officer lacked any cause to search. Before trial, Samson moved to suppress the drugs on the ground that the officer's search was unreasonable under the Fourth Amendment. The Court extended a prior decision to permit suspicionless searches of parolees.

Brendlin v. California (551 U.S. 249), decided by a 9–0 vote, June 18, 2007; Souter wrote the opinion.

A passenger in a car stopped by police may challenge the constitutionality of the stop and any subsequent search. The ruling reinstated an attempt by a California man, Bruce Brendlin, to suppress evidence taken from him while a passenger in a car stopped by Yuba City police in November 2001 because of a suspected registration violation. The Court held that, just like the driver, a passenger in a car is seized for constitutional purposes when the police make a traffic stop. The ruling sent the case back to California to determine whether suppression of the evidence turned on any other issue.

Virginia v. Moore (553 U.S. _), decided by a 9–0 vote, April 23, 2008; Scalia wrote the opinion.

A police officer does not violate the Fourth Amendment by making a search incident to an arrest when the arrest is prohibited by state law. The ruling upheld the constitutionality of a search of motorist David Lee Moore by two Portsmouth, Va., police officers in February 2003 after they had stopped and arrested him for driving with a suspended license. Virginia law permits only a citation, not an arrest, for that offense. The subsequent search revealed that Moore possessed sixteen grams of crack cocaine. Moore unsuccessfully sought to suppress the admission of the cocaine evidence at trial by arguing that the Fourth Amendment does not permit the seizure of evidence after an arrest in prohibition of state law.

SENTENCING

United States v. Booker (543 U.S. 220), decided by separate 5–4 votes, Jan. 12, 2005; Stevens wrote the opinion on the main legal issue; Breyer, Rehnquist, O'Connor, and Kennedy dissented; Breyer wrote the opinion on the remedy; Stevens, Scalia, Souter, and Thomas dissented.

The Court ruled the federal sentencing guidelines unconstitutional because they allowed judges instead of juries to determine factual issues used to raise a defendant's maximum sentence. However, the Court softened the impact of the decision by ruling the guidelines to be advisory instead of mandatory for lower federal courts, subject to appellate review on a middle-ground standard of reasonableness.

Shepard v. United States (544 U.S. 13), decided by a 5–3 vote, March 7, 2005; Souter wrote the opinion; O'Connor, Kennedy, and Breyer dissented; Rehnquist did not participate.

In deciding whether a criminal defendant who pleads guilty qualifies as a repeat violent offender under federal law, judges can examine only official court documents to determine the details of previous criminal convictions. The ruling overturned a fifteen-year mandatory minimum sentence that a federal appeals court had imposed on Reginald Shepard for selling a gun to an undercover agent.

Johnson v. United States (544 U.S. 295), decided by a 5–4 vote, April 4, 2005; Souter wrote the opinion; Kennedy, Stevens, Scalia, and Ginsburg dissented.

A federal prisoner challenging a sentence increased because of prior state criminal convictions must act with "due diligence" to overturn those convictions to take advantage of a more favorable statute of limitations. The narrow ruling left in place an enhanced sentence imposed upon Robert Johnson Jr. after pleading guilty in federal court in 1994 to a charge of distributing cocaine.

Deck v. Missouri (544 U.S. 622), decided by a 7–2 vote, May 23, 2005; Breyer wrote the opinion; Thomas and Scalia dissented.

The due process clauses of the Fifth and Fourteenth Amendments of the U.S. Constitution prohibit the visible shackling of a criminal defendant during a trial or during the sentencing phase of a capital trial unless justified by an essential state interest particular to the defendant. The ruling overturned the death sentence of a Missouri inmate who, after being convicted of a double murder, was ordered by the trial judge to appear before the jury with visible leg irons and a belly chain throughout his sentencing proceeding. On appeal, Deck argued that the visible shackling violated his right to a fair trial by prejudicing the jury against him.

Oregon v. Guzek (546 U.S. 517), decided by an 8–0 vote, Feb. 22, 2006; Breyer wrote the opinion; Alito did not participate.

States can limit innocence-related evidence in a sentencing proceeding of a capital defendant to the evidence introduced at the original trial. The ruling rejected a decision by the Oregon Supreme Court recognizing a constitutional right for capital defendants following a guilty verdict to introduce so-called residual doubt evidence in a sentencing proceeding.

Salinas v. United States (547 U.S. 188), decided by a 9–0 vote, April 24, 2006; per curiam opinion.

The Court ordered a federal appeals court to reconsider a Texas man's sentence for bank robbery because it mistakenly counted a conviction for simple drug possession as making him eligible for sentencing as a career offender under federal guidelines. The summary ruling, issued after the solicitor general's office acknowledged the error by the Fifth U.S. Circuit Court of Appeals, sent the case against Jeffrey Jerome Salinas back to the appeals court for further proceedings.

Washington v. Recuenco (548 U.S. 212), decided by a 7–2 vote, June 26, 2006; Thomas wrote the opinion; Ginsburg and Stevens dissented.

A judge's error in failing to submit a sentencing factor for a jury to decide may be excused as harmless instead of requiring automatic reversal. The ruling limited the impact of the Court's decision in *Blakely v. Washington* (2004) requiring that juries instead of judges find any facts necessary to raise a defendant's sentence above the normal statutory range.

Cunningham v. California (549 U.S. 270), decided by a 6–3 vote, Jan. 22, 2007; Ginsburg wrote the opinion; Alito, Kennedy, and Breyer dissented.

A California sentencing law that authorizes judges to find facts for elevating jail sentences violates defendants' right to a jury trial. The ruling reversed a California trial court judge's decision to sentence John Cunningham to six additional years in prison for child sex abuse based on his finding six aggravating factors.

James v. United States (550 U.S. 192), decided by a 5–4 vote, April 18, 2007; Alito wrote the opinion; Scalia, Stevens, Thomas, and Ginsburg dissented.

Attempted burglary qualifies as a violent felony to trigger a mandatory fifteen-year prison sentence under the federal Armed Career Criminal Act for a three-time offender convicted of possessing a firearm after a felony conviction. The ruling upheld the fifteen-year prison sentence imposed in March 2006 on a Fort Myers, Fla., man, Alphonso James, after a traffic stop for a defective headlight resulted in his arrest for possession of a handgun. James had three prior state felony convictions—two for drug offenses and one for attempted burglary of a dwelling.

Rita v. United States (551 U.S. 338), decided by an 8–1 vote, June 21, 2007; Breyer wrote the opinion; Souter dissented.

A federal appeals court may treat as presumptively reasonable a sentence within the range established by the federal sentencing guidelines. The ruling represented a setback for criminal defendants by safeguarding lower courts' use of the sometimes severe sentence ranges prescribed by the federal guidelines.

Logan v. United States (552 U.S. 23), decided by a 9–0 vote, Dec. 4, 2007; Ginsburg wrote the opinion.

A state conviction that does not entail the loss of civil rights may be counted under the sentence-enhancing provisions of the federal Armed Career Criminal Act despite an exemption for convictions for which civil rights are restored. The ruling upheld the mandatory fifteen-year prison sentence that James Logan received after pleading guilty in federal court in Wisconsin to being a felon in possession of a firearm. Because of his three prior state convictions for battery, Logan was sentenced under the Armed Career Criminal Act, which provides for a fifteen-year mandatory minimum sentence when the defendant has three prior convictions for certain violent crimes.

Kimbrough v. United States (552 U.S. 85), decided by a 7–2 vote, Dec. 10, 2007; Ginsburg wrote the opinion; Thomas and Alito dissented.

Federal judges do not have to follow provisions of the sentencing guidelines prescribing substantially longer sentences for crack cocaine offenses than for offenses involving the same quantities of powdered cocaine. The ruling represented a substantial victory for civil rights, civil liberties, and drug law reform groups that had long complained about disparate sentences for crack and powdered cocaine. The critics charged that the disparity was illogical and also racially discriminatory against African Americans, who comprised the vast majority of crack cocaine offenders. Under the federal sentencing guidelines, one gram of crack cocaine was treated as the equivalent of one hundred grams of powdered cocaine. The disparity yielded sentences three to six times longer for crack cocaine than for the equivalent amount of powdered cocaine.

Gall v. United States (552 U.S. 38), decided by a 7–2 vote, Dec. 10, 2007; Stevens wrote the opinion; Alito and Thomas dissented.

Appeals courts must review all federal sentences under a deferential abuse of discretion standard whether or not the sentencing court followed the federal sentencing guidelines.

Begay v. United States (553 U.S. _), decided by a 6–3 vote, April 16, 2008; Breyer wrote the opinion; Alito, Souter, and Thomas dissented.

Drunk driving does not count as a "violent felony" for purposes of triggering a mandatory fifteen-year prison sentence under the federal Armed Career Criminal Act for a felon convicted of possessing a firearm. The ruling reversed a 188-month sentence that had been imposed on Larry Begay, who pleaded guilty in 2004 to possessing a firearm while being a felon.

Burgess v. United States (553 U.S. _), decided by a 9–0 vote, April 16, 2008; Ginsburg wrote the opinion.

A state drug offense punishable by more than one year qualifies as a "felony drug offense" under the federal Controlled Substances Act for purposes of doubling the mandatory minimum sentence for specified offenses. The ruling rejected a legal challenge by a South Carolina man, Keith Burgess, to the 156-month prison term he received after pleading guilty in federal court to conspiracy to possess with intent to distribute fifty grams or more of cocaine. Under the Controlled Substances Act, a conspiracy conviction usually carries a minimum sentence of ten years, but the minimum is doubled if the defendant had a prior conviction for a felony drug offense.

United States v. Rodriguez (553 U.S. _), decided by a 6–3 vote, May 19, 2008; Alito wrote the opinion; Souter, Stevens, and Ginsburg dissented.

A state drug offense punishable by more than ten years' imprisonment for repeat offenders counts as a "serious drug offense" for triggering the mandatory fifteen-year sentence under federal law for a felon in possession of a firearm. The ruling upheld a fifteen-year prison sentence imposed on a Washington State man, Gino Rodriguez, after he was convicted under the federal Armed Career Criminal Act of being a convicted felon in possession of a firearm.

Irizarry v. United States (553 U.S. _), decided by a 5–4 vote, June 12, 2008; Stevens wrote the opinion; Breyer, Kennedy, Souter, and Ginsburg dissented.

Judges are not required to give prior notice to the parties when imposing a sentence outside the range recommended by the federal sentencing guidelines for a reason not identified in the presentence report or the prehearing submission. The ruling affirmed the sixty-month sentence imposed on an Alabama man, Richard Irizarry, for making a threatening interstate communication. In 2003 Irizarry sent an e-mail to his ex-wife in which he threatened to kill her and her new husband.

Greenlaw v. United States (554 U.S. _), decided by a 7–2 vote, June 23, 2008; Ginsburg wrote the opinion; Alito and Stevens dissented.

A federal appeals court may not act on its own to increase a criminal defendant's sentence absent a cross-appeal by the government. The ruling effectively vacated the fifteen additional years of imprisonment that the Eighth U.S. Circuit Court of Appeals had given to Michael Greenlaw, a member of a gun-toting gang that had controlled the sale of crack cocaine on the south side of Minneapolis for years.

SPEEDY TRIAL ACT

Zedner v. United States (547 U.S. 489), decided by a 9–0 vote, June 5, 2006; Alito wrote the opinion.

A defendant can assert rights under the Speedy Trial Act even after signing a prospective waiver, and courts cannot invoke procedural or harmless error rules to disregard trial delays in violation of the act. The ruling, strictly enforcing the 1974 law, required dismissal of fraud charges against a New York man, Jacob Zedner, for attempting to cash $10 million in counterfeit U.S. bonds in March 1996.

STATUTE OF LIMITATIONS

Dodd v. United States (545 U.S. 353), decided by a 5–4 vote, June 20, 2005; O'Connor wrote the opinion; Stevens, Souter, Ginsburg, and Breyer dissented.

Federal prisoners challenging their convictions based on a U.S. Supreme Court ruling issued after their convictions must seek relief within one year of the date on which the Court "initially recognized" the right they assert. The ruling resolved a conflict in the federal appellate courts concerning the proper interpretation of a statute of limitations provision in the Antiterrorism and Effective Death Penalty Act, the 1996 law governing federal habeas corpus.

Election Law

CAMPAIGN FINANCE

Davis v. Federal Election Commission (554 U.S. _), decided by a 5–4 vote, June 26, 2008; Alito wrote the opinion; Stevens, Souter, Ginsburg, and Breyer dissented.

A law that allows a candidate for federal office to raise more money from contributors when a wealthy opponent runs a largely self-financed campaign violates the opponent's First Amendment rights. The ruling struck down the "millionaire's amendment" that Congress included in the

Bipartisan Campaign Reform Act of 2002—known as the McCain-Feingold Act, after its main Senate sponsors—to level the playing field for candidates for federal office who run against self-financed candidates.

Jack Davis, a candidate for the U.S. House of Representatives from western New York in 2004 and 2006, challenged the law. Davis spent more than $3 million of his own money to fund those campaigns. He filed the suit in May 2006, two months after announcing his candidacy against the incumbent, Thomas Reynolds, and one month after the Federal Election Commission had preliminarily found he had violated the act's disclosure provisions in 2004. A three-judge federal district court for the District of Columbia rejected Davis's challenge and upheld the constitutionality of the millionaire's amendment. The case was directly appealed to the U.S. Supreme Court.

CONGRESSIONAL REDISTRICTING

League of United Latin American Citizens v. Perry, Governor of Texas (548 U.S. 399), decided by 7–2, 6–3, and 5–4 votes, June 28, 2006; Kennedy wrote the main opinion; Stevens and Breyer dissented on the broadest ruling; Souter, Stevens, and Ginsburg dissented on one ruling; Roberts, Scalia, Thomas, and Alito dissented on one ruling.

The Court largely upheld against a political gerrymandering challenge a Republican-drawn congressional redistricting plan for Texas that replaced a court-ordered map created two years earlier. The Court held, however, that the dismantling of one "Latino opportunity" district improperly diluted minority voting strength in violation of the federal Voting Rights Act. The ruling required the drawing of a third map in six years for the state's thirty-two congressional districts but appeared likely to preserve the gains Republicans made in the 2004 elections under a plan drawn by the GOP-controlled state legislature. The justices' splintered voting and multiple opinions demonstrated the Court's continuing inability to forge a majority position on what standard, if any, to use in determining whether a politically drawn redistricting plan violates constitutional requirements.

On the broadest issue, the ruling rejected arguments by the Democratic challengers that the redistricting plan amounted to an unconstitutional political gerrymander because it was enacted mid-decade and was solely motivated by partisan objectives. In reaching that conclusion, the Court said that the GOP-written plan was "fairer" than either the court-drawn plan or the Democratic-drawn maps of the 1990s because it "more closely reflects the distribution of state party power."

Lance v. Coffman, Colorado Secretary of State (549 U.S. 437), decided by a 9–0 vote, March 5, 2007; per curiam opinion.

Citizens have no standing to challenge a court-ordered congressional redistricting plan on the ground that it violates the constitutional provision giving state legislatures power to determine the procedures for electing members of Congress. The ruling, a legally significant interpretation of the U.S. Constitution's elections clause, appeared to end efforts by Colorado Republicans to substitute a GOP-backed congressional redistricting plan for a map drawn by a state court. Under the court-drawn map, Democrats won five of the state's nine congressional seats in the 2002 elections. The court drew its plan after the state legislature deadlocked. In 2003, however, a GOP-controlled legislature and Republican governor approved a new districting plan and, along with the Republican secretary of state, defended the plan in court after the Democratic attorney general sued to block it. The Colorado Supreme Court blocked the legislature's plan, citing a provision in the state constitution limiting legislative or congressional redistricting to one time per decade.

Four Colorado voters brought a new suit in federal court seeking to throw out the court-ordered redistricting plan on the ground that it violated the Constitution's elections clause, which states that the "manner of holding elections for senators and representatives shall be prescribed in each state by the legislature thereof" subject to regulation by Congress. A three-judge federal court ruled that the voters had standing to bring the suit but dismissed it on the ground that they had been on the same side as the secretary of state and legislature—in legal terms, "in privity with" the officials—in the earlier suit.

The Court held instead that the voters had no legal standing to bring the suit under the elections clause because they had "no particularized stake" in the litigation. "The only injury plaintiffs allege is that the law—specifically the Elections Clause—has not been followed," the unsigned opinion read. Those allegations amounted to an "undifferentiated, generalized grievance," the Court said, different from the kinds of injuries alleged in other voting rights cases in which legal standing had been recognized.

ELECTIONEERING COMMUNICATIONS

Wisconsin Right to Life, Inc. v. Federal Election Commission (546 U.S. 410), decided by a 9–0 vote, Jan. 23, 2006; per curiam opinion.

The Court opened the door to case-by-case constitutional challenges to the newly enacted federal law barring unions or corporations from financing election-time, campaign-related advertising on radio or television except through separate political action committees. The ruling—a setback for supporters of the Bipartisan Campaign Reform Act of 2002—directed a three-judge federal district court in Washington, D.C., to reconsider a so-called as-applied challenge to the act's restriction on "electioneering communications" brought by a state antiabortion group, Wisconsin Right to Life, Inc. The Court held that a previous decision upholding restrictions on electioneering communications did not preclude individual challenges to application of the law.

Federal Election Commission v. Wisconsin Right to Life, Inc. (551 U.S. 449), decided by a 5–4 vote, June 25, 2007; Roberts wrote the main opinion; Scalia, Kennedy, and Thomas concurred in the judgment; Souter, Stevens, Ginsburg, and Breyer dissented.

Labor unions and corporations can buy issue advertising on television shortly before federal elections as long as the ads do not unmistakably advocate the election or defeat of a particular candidate. The ruling significantly weakened a major provision of the Bipartisan Campaign Reform Act of 2002 in an effort to curtail the spread of thinly veiled campaign-related television advertising by labor unions, business corporations, and advocacy groups. The McCain-Feingold Act, as the law was commonly known, prohibited unions and corporations from paying for "electioneering communications" except through separately organized political action committees.

The Court ruled that the electioneering communications provision was unconstitutional as applied to the Wisconsin Right to Life ads. The decision stated that the provision can be applied only if an ad "is susceptible of no reasonable interpretation other than as an appeal to vote for or against a specific candidate."

JUDICIAL ELECTIONS

New York State Board of Election v. López Torres (552 U.S. 196), decided by a 9–0 vote, Jan. 16, 2008; Scalia wrote the opinion.

States may require political parties to use nominating conventions—and not primary elections—to choose the parties' nominees in local trial court elections. The ruling rejected a First Amendment challenge brought by a former Brooklyn civil court judge, Margarita López Torres, to a convention system established under a New York State judicial elections law.

LEGISLATIVE DISTRICTING

Lance v. Dennis, Colorado Secretary of State (546 U.S. 459), decided by an 8–1 vote, Feb. 21, 2006; per curiam opinion; Stevens dissented.

A federal district court was wrong to dismiss a lawsuit by Colorado voters challenging a judicially drawn congressional redistricting plan on the ground that it was an improper attempt to overturn a ruling by state courts on the issue. The ruling reinstated a Republican-backed suit seeking to substitute a congressional map drawn in 2003 by the GOP-controlled legislature for a plan drawn by a state court in 2002 after a previous legislature deadlocked. The Colorado Supreme Court blocked the use of the later plan on the ground that the state's constitution prohibited more than one congressional redistricting in a decade. Following that ruling, four voters—three Republicans and one Democrat—filed a new suit in federal court, contending that the state legislature had the power to enact the redistricting plan under the elections clause of the U.S. Constitution. The federal court dismissed the suit on the basis of the so-called Rooker-Feldman doctrine, which generally prohibits losers in state court cases from bringing new suits in federal court to challenge a state court decision. The court said the doctrine barred the voters' suit because they were "in privity with" the state officials who had been named as defendants in the state court case. The Court held that the lower court had misapplied the Rooker-Feldman doctrine in dismissing the voters' suit because they were not parties to the earlier case. The ruling specified, however, that the federal court should decide whether the legal doctrine known as preclusion would require dismissal of the voters' suit.

PRIMARY ELECTIONS

Clingman, Secretary, Oklahoma Election Board v. Beaver (544 U.S. 581), decided by a 6–3 vote, May 23, 2005; Thomas wrote the opinion; Stevens, Souter, and Ginsburg dissented.

A state election law that permits a political party to invite only its own members and registered independent voters to participate in its partisan primary is valid under the First Amendment. The ruling struck down a challenge to Oklahoma's semi-closed primary election law brought by the state's Libertarian Party. The law, which barred any political party from inviting registered voters from other parties to participate in its partisan primary election, was invoked by the Oklahoma State Board of Elections in denying the Libertarian Party permission to open its primary to all registered voters.

The Court ruled that the state statute was subject to the less stringent "rational basis" standard of review and was justified by the state's interest in preserving political parties and preventing "party raiding." The ruling said the law furthered at least three legitimate state interests: The law preserves political parties as "viable and identifiable interest groups," "enhances parties' electioneering and party-building efforts," and "guards against party raiding and 'sore loser' candidacies by spurned party contenders."

Washington State Grange v. Washington Republican Party (552 U.S. 442), decided by a 7–2 vote, March 18, 2008; Thomas wrote the opinion; Scalia and Kennedy dissented.

States may create a "top two" primary voting system that allows candidates to state their own party preference and advances the top two vote-getters to the general election ballot regardless of party. The ruling reinstated a primary system approved by Washington State voters in 2004 that was challenged by political parties as an unconstitutional interference with their freedom of association under the First Amendment. Under the top two system, all candidates for "partisan" offices may declare their own party preference on the primary ballot with no opportunity for the party to prevent the listing. Voters in the primary election can vote for any candidate regardless of the voters' or the candidate's party affiliations. The candidates with the two highest vote totals from the primary, regardless of party, advance to the general election, where they will again be listed according to their self-described party affiliation.

The system replaced the state's so-called blanket primary, which listed candidates from all parties on a single ballot, allowed voters to choose a candidate from any party, and placed the plurality vote-getter from each party on the general election ballot as the party's nominee. The Ninth U.S. Circuit Court of Appeals ruled in 2003 that the blanket primary was an unconstitutional interference with parties' freedom of association. In response, the Washington State Grange, a nonpartisan reform group, proposed Initiative 872, a top two primary system, that won approval from 60 percent of the voters in 2004. The Republican, Democratic, and Libertarian parties in Washington immediately challenged the initiative before it could be put into effect, alleging that the system violated their associational rights to nominate their own candidates and forced them to be affiliated with candidates they did not endorse.

SPECIAL ELECTIONS

Riley, Governor of Alabama v. Kennedy (553 U.S. _), decided by a 7–2 vote, May 27, 2008; Ginsburg wrote the opinion; Stevens and Souter dissented.

Alabama did not have to obtain preclearance under the Voting Rights Act to reinstate an election practice that was in place prior to the enactment of a law that was immediately challenged and then invalidated by a state court. The ruling—carefully limited to what the Court called an "extraordinary circumstance"—effectively allowed Alabama governor Bob Riley to appoint a new official to a seat on the Mobile County Commission that had become vacant midterm.

VOTER IDENTIFICATION

Purcell, Maricopa County Recorder v. Gonzalez (549 U.S. 1), decided by a 9–0 vote, Oct. 20, 2006; per curiam opinion.

A federal appeals court was wrong to issue a preliminary injunction blocking an Arizona law requiring voters to present identification on election day from taking effect before the November 2006 election. The ruling came in a challenge by Arizona voters, Indian tribes, and community organizations to Proposition 200, a statewide ballot measure approved in 2004 that requires voters to present proof of citizenship when they register and to present identification when they vote.

Crawford v. Marion County Election Board (553 U.S. _), decided by a 6–3 vote, April 28, 2008; Stevens wrote the main opinion; Scalia, Thomas, and Alito concurred in the judgment; Souter, Ginsburg, and Breyer dissented.

States can require voters to present a government-issued photo identification (ID) at the polls, at least if they provide the identification for free and allow voters without the identification to cast a provisional ballot subject to later verification. The ruling upheld a 2005 Indiana law that was the strictest of a flurry of voter ID laws that states adopted for the stated purpose of deterring in-person voter fraud.

Environmental Law

AIR POLLUTION

Environmental Defense v. Duke Energy Corp. (549 U.S. 561), decided by a 9–0 vote, April 2, 2007; Souter wrote the opinion.

Power plants must obtain new operating permits from the Environmental Protection Agency (EPA) when renovations increase total emissions, even if the total hourly rate of emissions is not increased. The ruling gave environmentalists a temporary victory in a dispute over the EPA's interpretation of regulations under overlapping pollution control programs requiring a power plant or other stationary source of air pollution to obtain a permit for any "major modification" to the facility.

Massachusetts v. Environmental Protection Agency (549 U.S. 497), decided by a 5–4 vote, April 2, 2007; Stevens wrote the opinion; Roberts, Scalia, Thomas, and Alito dissented.

The Environmental Protection Agency (EPA) has authority to regulate emissions from new vehicles contributing to climate change, and individual states have standing to challenge the agency's exercise of that authority. The ruling—a major victory for environmentalists—reversed EPA's denial of a rulemaking petition filed in 1999 by nineteen private organizations seeking to require the agency to regulate new motor vehicles' emission of carbon dioxide and other so-called greenhouse gases that contribute to global warming.

The Court held that Massachusetts had standing to challenge the EPA's refusal to issue the rule, that the EPA had authority to regulate the emissions, and that the EPA's decision not to regulate was unreasonable. On the statutory issue, the Court said the EPA has authority to regulate greenhouse gas emissions because they fall within the Clean Air Act's "sweeping definition" of air pollutant as any "physical" or "chemical" substance emitted into "the ambient air." The decision not to regulate greenhouse gases, the ruling continued, was arbitrary and capricious. The decision stopped short, however, of requiring EPA to find that greenhouse gas emissions endangered the public health or welfare.

FEDERAL LICENSING

S. D. Warren Co. v. Maine Board of Environmental Protection (547 U.S. 370), decided by a 9–0 vote, May 15, 2006; Souter wrote the opinion.

Operators of hydroelectric dams must meet state water quality requirements to qualify for a federal license. The ruling upheld state court decisions requiring the S. D. Warren Company to obtain approval from Maine's Department of Environmental Protection to renew federal licenses for five hydropower dams on the Presumpscot River used to generate electricity for its paper mill. For a corporation to receive or renew a federal license, the Clean Water Act, in Section 401, requires it to obtain state certification that water protection law will not be violated if its activities "may result in any discharge into the navigable waters of the United States." The company argued that the term "discharge" referred only to the addition of pollutants and that the act was therefore inapplicable because the dams did not add pollutants to the water. The Court held that the flow of water over a dam or through a turbine constitutes a "discharge" for purposes of triggering the Clean Water Act's federal licensing requirement.

SUBMERGED LANDS

Alaska v. United States (545 U.S. 75), decided by 9–0 and 6–3 votes, June 6, 2005; Kennedy wrote the opinion; Scalia, Rehnquist, and Thomas dissented in part.

The United States retains title to submerged lands in two ecologically sensitive areas of southeastern Alaska. The decision overruled Alaska's objections to a special master's 327-page report rejecting the state's efforts to obtain title to submerged lands beneath the Alexander Archipelago and Glacier Bay National Park. In 2000 Alaska invoked the Court's original jurisdiction to quiet title—that is, to establish its ownership—to the submerged lands. The state relied on the equal footing doctrine, which provides that each new state obtains the United States' title to submerged lands on "equal footing" with the original thirteen colonies, as well as the federal Submerged Lands Act of 1953. Read together, these provisions create a presumption that states possess title to submerged lands beneath inland navigable waters within their boundaries and beneath territorial waters within three nautical miles of their coasts. The United States, however, can rebut this presumption by taking steps, before statehood, to set aside the lands and demonstrate clear intent to retain title to them.

SUPERFUND LAW

Cooper Industries, Inc. v. Aviall Services, Inc. (53 U.S. 157), decided by a 7–2 vote, Dec. 13, 2004; Thomas wrote the opinion; Ginsburg and Stevens dissented.

The Court barred one legal route under the federal Superfund law for a company that voluntarily cleans up a contaminated site to recover part of its costs from other concerns responsible for the contamination. It left unresolved, however, the issue whether a separate provision of the law would allow recovery.

WETLANDS

Rapanos v. United States (547 U.S. 715), decided by a 5–4 vote, June 19, 2006; Scalia wrote the opinion; Kennedy concurred in the judgment; Stevens, Souter, Ginsburg, and Breyer dissented.

Two Michigan developers won a splintered, interim ruling in their challenge to broad federal power to protect wetlands remote from recognized waterways, but the controlling opinion could let the government preserve much of its regulatory authority. The ruling, involving a pair of closely watched environmental cases, produced a sharp debate among the justices over the government's power under the Clean Water Act to require developers to obtain a permit from the Army Corps of Engineers before filling covered wetlands. Kennedy's solitary concurrence appeared to establish a rule for future cases that wetlands are subject to federal regulation if they have "a significant nexus" to waters traditionally regarded as navigable.

Federal Government

FEDERAL EMPLOYEES

Osborn v. Haley (549 U.S. 225), decided by a 6–3 vote, Jan. 22, 2007; Ginsburg wrote the opinion; Souter agreed with the main holding but dissented on a jurisdictional issue; Breyer dissented on the main holding; Scalia and Thomas dissented.

A private damage suit against a federal worker must be removed from state to federal court if the attorney general certifies the conduct was within the scope of employment even if the government denies the alleged events occurred. The ruling interpreted favorably for federal workers a provision of the Federal Employees Liability Reform and Tort Compensation Act of 1988, commonly known as the Westfall Act.

FEDERAL REGULATION

National Cable & Telecommunications Association v. Brand X Internet Services (545 U.S. 967), decided by a 6–3 vote, June 27, 2005; Thomas wrote the opinion; Scalia, Souter, and Ginsburg dissented.

The Federal Communications Commission properly exercised its discretion in deciding not to require cable companies that offer high-speed "broadband" Internet service to open their networks to competitors. The ruling represented a major victory for the cable industry, a setback for telephone companies offering competitive high-speed Internet services, and a defeat for smaller Internet service providers needing connections to cable systems to reach customers. The dispute turned on whether Internet connection constituted "telecommunications services" subject to mandatory, common-carrier regulation under federal communications law or "information services" that did not need to be regulated. Common-carrier regulation entailed, among other provisions, a requirement that companies allow other carriers to interconnect with their communications networks.

Rockwell International Co. v. United States (549 U.S. 457), decided by a 6–2 vote, March 27, 2007; Scalia wrote the opinion; Stevens and Ginsburg dissented; Breyer did not take part in the decision.

A government contractor whistleblower cannot maintain a suit under the federal False Claims Act if he or she is the original source of information used in allegations included in the initial complaint but later dropped. The ruling defeated a fraudulent payments claim brought by James Stone against his former employer, Rockwell International, which ran a nuclear weapons plant in Colorado under a contract with the federal government. After leaking to the press his predictions that Rockwell's waste removal system would fail, Stone filed suit under the False Claims Act. The Civil War–era statute allows a whistleblower with knowledge of fraud against the government to initiate a so-called qui tam suit brought in the government's name and to be awarded a portion of any damages recovered as a result of the suit.

Global Crossing Telecommunications, Inc. v. Metrophones Telecommunications, Inc. (550 U.S. 45), decided by a 7–2 vote, April 17, 2007; Breyer wrote the opinion; Scalia and Thomas dissented.

A company operating pay phones can file suit in federal court against a long-distance carrier under Section 201 of the Communications Act for failing to pay compensation required by the Federal Communications Commission.

Zuni Public School District No. 89 v. Department of Education (550 U.S. 81), decided by a 5–4 vote, April 17, 2007; Breyer wrote the opinion; Scalia, Roberts, Souter, and Thomas dissented.

The secretary of education used a permissible method of applying a federal law that allows a state in some circumstances to reduce aid to local school districts to offset federal "impact aid" received because of the presence of federal facilities. The ruling turned on a technical question of statistics but produced a sharp dissent from four justices who complained that the majority had essentially ignored the text of the law. In immediate effect, the ruling rejected an effort by two New Mexico school districts to reverse the Education Department's long-standing interpretation of the law. Under that interpretation, the state had reduced its aid to the districts because of federal funds they were receiving under the Impact Aid Act.

Safeco Insurance Co. of America v. Burr (551 U.S. 47), decided by a 9–0 vote, June 4, 2007; Souter wrote the opinion.

Insurance companies can be held liable for recklessly disregarding the federal obligation to notify applicants who, after review of their credit reports, are offered higher rates than they would have received without a credit review by the insurers. The ruling, in immediate effect, rejected proposed class actions in two consolidated cases against Safeco and GEICO insurance companies under the Fair Credit Reporting Act.

United States v. Atlantic Research Corp. (551 U.S. 128), decided by a 9–0 vote, June 11, 2007; Thomas wrote the opinion.

A private party may sue the federal government to recover costs incurred while undertaking a voluntary cleanup of a polluted Superfund site. The ruling allowed Atlantic Research Corp. to seek partial reimbursement from the federal government for the $2.5 million it spent to decontaminate a naval ammunition storage facility in Camden, Ark.

National Association of Home Builders v. Defenders of Wildlife (551 U.S. 644), decided by a 5–4 vote, June 25, 2007; Alito wrote the opinion; Stevens, Souter, Ginsburg, and Breyer dissented.

The Environmental Protection Agency (EPA) can transfer water pollution permitting authority to a state under the Clean Water Act without consulting with the federal agency responsible for enforcing the Endangered Species Act. The ruling settled an apparent conflict between the two landmark environmental laws by interpreting the Endangered Species Act's consultation requirement to apply only to discretionary actions taken by federal agencies. In immediate effect, it removed an obstacle to the EPA's plan to transfer to Arizona responsibility for administering the federal water pollution control program, the National Pollution Discharge Elimination System. The Clean Water Act specifies that the government "shall" transfer authority to a state if it meets nine listed criteria. The Endangered Species Act's key provision (Section 7) specifies that each federal agency "shall, in consultation with [one of two agencies responsible for enforcing the law], insure that any action authorized, funded, or carried out by such agency . . . is not likely to jeopardize" an endangered or threatened species.

Riegel v. Medtronic, Inc. (552 U.S. 312), decided by an 8–1 vote, Feb. 20, 2008; Scalia wrote the opinion; Ginsburg dissented.

Individuals cannot sue the makers of medical devices under state law for personal injuries caused by the device if the Food and Drug Administration approved the device and it meets the agency's specifications. The ruling seriously limited the ability of individuals injured by medical devices to recover damages from the manufacturers.

Rowe, Attorney General of Maine v. New Hampshire Motor Transport Association (552 U.S. 364), decided by a 9–0 vote, Feb. 20, 2008; Breyer wrote the opinion.

A federal law deregulating the trucking industry prevents states from passing laws that regulate the manner in which tobacco products are transported within the state. The ruling upheld lower federal courts' interpretation of a broad preemption provision that the Federal Aviation Administration Authorization Act of 1994 added to the landmark trucking deregulation law, the Motor Carrier Act of 1980.

Warner-Lambert Co. v. Kent (552 U.S. 440), decided by a 4–4 vote, March 3, 2008; per curiam opinion; Roberts did not participate.

An evenly divided Court allowed a lawsuit against a drug maker to go forward even though the lawsuit contained a claim that the manufacturer committed fraud against the federal Food and Drug Administration (FDA). The decision failed to resolve whether individuals in certain circumstances can sue manufacturers under state law when they committed fraud in obtaining the FDA's approval for their products. In 2001 the Court held in *Buckman v. Plaintiffs' Legal Committee* that the federal Food, Drug, and Cosmetic Act preempted lawsuits under state law that claimed that the manufacturer committed fraud against the FDA.

Allison Engine Co., Inc. v. United States ex rel. Sanders (553 U.S. _), decided by a 9–0 vote, June 9, 2008; Alito wrote the opinion.

A whistleblower law intended to combat fraud against the federal government can be applied against subcontractors only if the subcontractor intends a false claim to be material to the government's payment of the claim. The ruling narrowed a lawsuit brought under the Civil War–era False Claims Act by two employees of a government subcontractor, General Tool Company, that built electrical generators for a U.S. Navy destroyer.

Morgan Stanley Capital Group Inc. v. Public Utility District 1 of Snohomish County (554 U.S. _), decided by a 5–2 vote, June 26, 2008; Scalia wrote the opinion; Stevens and Souter dissented; Roberts and Breyer did not participate.

The Federal Energy Regulatory Commission (FERC) may not modify utility rates set by a contract between electricity sellers and utilities absent a finding that the rates "harm the public interest." The decision gave electricity wholesalers a legal victory but allowed several western utilities a second chance to challenge high-priced contracts negotiated during the 2000–2001 energy crisis. The contractual rates, filed with but not requiring approval by FERC, were higher than historic rates but substantially lower than then-existing market rates. After energy prices abated to normal levels, the utilities complained of the contractual rates, which by then were substantially higher than settled market prices. The utilities asked the FERC to modify the contracts, claiming that the high rates "violated the public interest."

FEDERAL TORT CLAIMS ACT

United States v. Olson (546 U.S. 43), decided by a 9–0 vote, Nov. 8, 2005; Breyer wrote the opinion.

A federal appeals court misinterpreted the Federal Tort Claims Act (FTCA) to allow the U.S. government to be sued by miners for injuries from an accident that they blamed on negligent safety inspections. The Court's ruling, however, opened the door to allowing the miners' suit on an alternate ground rejected by the appeals court. The ruling sent back to the Ninth U.S. Circuit Court of Appeals a case brought under the FTCA by Joseph Olson and Javier Vargas for injuries suffered in a January 2000 accident at the Arizona copper mine where they worked. The FTCA waives the government's sovereign immunity in certain circumstances.

Will v. Hallock (546 U.S. 345), decided by a 9–0 vote, Jan. 18, 2006; Souter wrote the opinion.

The Court made it more difficult for federal employees sued for deprivation of an individual's constitutional rights to avoid trial after the government has won dismissal of a claim arising from the same conduct. The ruling dismissed on jurisdictional grounds a pretrial appeal by U.S. Customs Service agents seeking to throw out a suit by an upstate New York woman stemming from damage to computers seized in 2002 in what proved to be an unwarranted child pornography investigation.

Dolan v. United States Postal Service (546 U.S. 481), decided by a 7–1 vote, Feb. 22, 2006; Kennedy wrote the opinion; Thomas dissented; Alito did not participate.

The United States Postal Service can be sued in federal court for slip-and-fall accidents caused by negligent placement of mail at a delivery point. The ruling allowed Barbara Dolan, a postal patron in suburban Philadelphia, to go forward with a suit seeking $200,000 for injuries sustained when she fell over mail left on her porch by her letter carrier.

Ali v. Federal Bureau of Prisons (552 U.S. 214), decided by a 5–4 vote, Jan. 22, 2008; Thomas wrote the opinion; Kennedy, Stevens, Souter, and Breyer dissented.

All federal law enforcement officers are immune from claims under the Federal Tort Claims Act arising from injury to or loss of property that they have detained. The ruling prevented Abdus-Shahid M.S. Ali, a federal prisoner, from pursuing a claim under the act against prison officials for the loss of $177 worth of personal property while he was being transferred from a penitentiary in Atlanta to a facility in Kentucky.

GUANTÁNAMO CASES

Hamdan v. Rumsfeld, Secretary of Defense (548 U.S. 557), decided by a 5–3 vote, June 29, 2006; Stevens wrote the opinion; Scalia, Thomas, and Alito dissented; Roberts did not participate.

The military commissions established by President George W. Bush to try enemy combatants held at the Guantánamo Bay naval base were improperly constituted because the president failed to justify departures from procedures required by U.S. military law and the Geneva Conventions. The ruling—a clear if carefully limited rebuke to Bush's post–Sept. 11 antiterrorism policies—had the immediate effect of requiring new procedures and possibly a new charge in the case of a Yemeni national, Salim Ahmed Hamdan, who had been bodyguard and driver for al Qaeda leader Osama bin Laden.

More broadly, the Court ruled that one part of the Geneva Conventions, the so-called Common Article 3, applies to the U.S. conflict with al Qaeda. The administration had contended that the Geneva Conventions applied only to wars between countries, not to a conflict with a nonstate actor, such as a terrorist organization. The article specifies, however, that signatory countries must provide some minimal safeguards for combatants even in nontraditional conflicts.

Boumediene v. Bush, President of the United States (553 U.S. _), decided by a 5–4 vote, June 12, 2008; Kennedy wrote the opinion; Roberts, Scalia, Thomas, and Alito dissented.

The Military Commissions Act unconstitutionally restricted the right of detainees held at Guantánamo Bay to file habeas corpus petitions in federal court. The ruling effectively rebuked both President George W. Bush and Congress regarding the rules for legal challenges by hundreds of foreigners held as suspected enemy combatants at the U.S. naval base at Guantánamo Bay, Cuba, following the September 11, 2001, terrorist attacks in the United States and the ensuing war in Afghanistan. The detainees—most but not all of them captured in Afghanistan—were brought to Guantánamo Bay on the Bush administration's assumption that they would be outside the jurisdiction of federal courts. But in *Rasul v. Bush* (2004) the U.S. Supreme Court ruled that the detainees had a statutory right to file habeas corpus petitions. At Bush's urging, Congress responded in 2005 by clearing the Detainee Treatment Act, which purported to bar pending habeas corpus petitions. Instead, the law provided the detainees a procedurally limited review before newly created military panels called Combatant Status Review Tribunals with limited review of the tribunals' rulings in the U.S. Court of Appeals for the District of Columbia Circuit. In 2006 the Court ruled in *Hamdan v. Rumsfeld* that the law did not affect habeas corpus petitions pending when the law was signed.

Congress, again at Bush's urging, subsequently cleared the Military Commissions Act, which unambiguously denied habeas corpus rights to any Guantánamo detainee "determined" to be an enemy combatant or "awaiting such a determination." The D.C. circuit court upheld the act in two consolidated challenges—*Boumediene v. Bush* and *Al Odah v. United States*—originally brought in behalf of more than sixty detainees, all of whom denied membership in the al Qaeda terrorist network. (Lakhdar Boumediene was one of six Algerians arrested in Bosnia by Bosnian authorities in 2001 on suspicion of plotting to bomb the U.S. embassy in Sarajevo and then turned over to the United States.) In dismissing the petitions, the D.C. circuit court ruled that the act was consistent with the U.S. Constitution's suspension clause, which provides that habeas corpus cannot be suspended except "in cases of rebellion or invasion." The court said that as aliens outside the United States, the detainees had no habeas corpus rights. After declining to review the decision in April 2007, the U.S. Supreme Court changed its mind in June and agreed to hear the detainees' appeal. By then, many of these detainees had been released, but thirty-seven remained when the Court heard arguments in December.

MEDICAID SETTLEMENTS

Arkansas Department of Health and Human Services v. Ahlborn (547 U.S. 268), decided by a 9–0 vote, May 1, 2006; Stevens wrote the opinion.

State Medicaid administrators may not place a lien on a patient's settlement or award proceeds greater than the amount allocated for medical costs. The ruling favored an Arkansas woman, Heidi Ahlborn, in a dispute over the state's effort to recover $215,645.30 in Medicaid payments for her medical treatment following a 1996 automobile accident out of the proceeds of Ahlborn's subsequent lawsuit against the driver of the vehicle. Under Arkansas law, the state sought to recover the entire amount Ahlborn obtained in her lawsuit even though it was more than twice the actual medical costs.

NATIVE AMERICANS

Cherokee Nation of Oklahoma v. Leavitt, Secretary of Health and Human Services (543 U.S. 631), decided by an 8–0 vote, March 1, 2005; Breyer wrote the opinion; Rehnquist did not participate.

The U.S. government is legally bound to pay Indian tribes for the administrative expenses they incur while performing services usually provided by a federal agency. The ruling resolved a conflict between two federal appellate courts concerning the government's obligations under multimillion-dollar contracts with the Shoshone-Pauite Tribe and the Cherokee Nation.

City of Sherrill, New York v. Oneida Indian Nation of New York (544 U.S. 197), decided by an 8–1 vote, March 29, 2005; Ginsburg wrote the opinion; Stevens dissented.

Native American tribes that repurchase aboriginal lands on the open market may not revive tribal sovereignty over the lands and thus claim immunity from local property taxes. The ruling forced the Oneida Indian Nation of New York to pay property taxes on recently purchased lands that once were a part of the tribe's original reservation even though the U.S. Supreme Court in two previous decisions had recognized the Oneidas' right to compensatory damages because of past violations of the tribe's treaty-based rights.

Plains Commerce Bank v. Long Family Land and Cattle Company, Inc. (554 U.S. _), decided by a 5–4 vote, June 25, 2008; Roberts wrote the opinion; Ginsburg, Stevens, Souter, and Breyer dissented.

Tribal courts do not have jurisdiction to hear claims arising out of the sale of land located within the reservation if the sale is between parties who are not members of the tribe. The ruling dismissed a discrimination claim brought by members of the Cheyenne River Sioux Indian tribe against a non–Indian-owned bank located on non-Indian land bounded by the Cheyenne River reservation in central South Dakota.

STUDENT LOAN RECOVERY

Lockhart v. United States (546 U.S. 142), decided by a 9–0 vote, Dec. 7, 2005; O'Connor wrote the opinion.

The federal government may withhold an individual's Social Security benefits to collect on a federally insured student loan debt that has been outstanding for more than ten years. The ruling allowed the government to continue withholding a portion of James Lockhart's Social Security disability benefits as an offset for student loans that Lockhart had incurred between 1984 and 1989 under the Guaranteed Student Loan Program.

The Court held that the Debt Collection Improvement Act of 1996 made Social Security benefits subject to offset for unpaid loans and that the Higher Education Technical Amendments of 1991 repealed the ten-year statute of limitations under the Debt Collection Act of 1982. The Court wrote that the 1996 law "clearly makes Social Security benefits subject to offset" and that it was also "clear" that the 1991 amendments removed the ten-year statute of limitations.

U.S. TERRITORIES

Limtiaco, Attorney General of Guam v. Camacho, Governor of Guam (549 U.S. 483), decided by a 5–4 vote, March 27, 2007; Thomas wrote the opinion; Souter, Stevens, Ginsburg, and Alito dissented.

Guam's debt limitation must be calculated according to the assessed value of property in the territory, not the appraised value. The ruling, interpreting an ambiguous provision in Guam's territorial constitution, prevented the governor of Guam from issuing $400 million in revenue-raising bonds authorized by the territorial legislature in April 2003. Guam's attorney general had refused to approve the bonds on the ground that their issuance would violate the provision in Guam's Organic Act prohibiting debt "in excess of 10 per centum of the aggregate tax valuation of the property in Guam." (The act, approved by Congress in 1950, serves as Guam's constitution.) The governor argued that the debt limitation provision referred to the appraised valuation of property, which was 65 percent more than the assessed value used by the attorney general.

First Amendment

CHURCH AND STATE

Cutter v. Wilkinson, Director, Ohio Department of Rehabilitation and Correction (544 U.S. 709), decided by a 9–0 vote, May 31, 2005; Ginsburg wrote the opinion.

A federal law requiring state prison officials to accommodate the religious beliefs of inmates is not an unconstitutional establishment of religion. The ruling upheld against First Amendment challenge one of the principal sections of the Religious Land Use and Institutionalized Persons Act of 2000, the most recent in a series of congressional attempts to protect religious exercise from government-imposed burdens.

McCreary County, Kentucky v. American Civil Liberties Union of Kentucky (545 U.S. 844), decided by a 5–4 vote, June 27, 2005; Souter wrote the opinion; Scalia, Rehnquist, Kennedy, and Thomas dissented.

Displays of the Ten Commandments in two Kentucky county courthouses violated the establishment clause because the counties had a predominantly religious purpose in mounting the exhibits. The ruling came in one of two closely watched cases challenging government displays of the Ten Commandments as amounting to improper endorsement of religion. While a five-justice majority ruled the displays in the McCreary County and Pulaski County courthouses as unconstitutional, a different five-justice majority in *Van Orden v. Perry* voted to allow a six-foot granite monument displaying the Ten Commandments to remain on the grounds of the Texas State Capitol in Austin.

Van Orden v. Perry, Governor of Texas (545 U.S. 677), decided by a 5–4 vote, June 27, 2005; Rehnquist wrote the plurality opinion; Breyer concurred in the judgment; Stevens, O'Connor, Souter, and Ginsburg dissented.

A monument on the grounds of the Texas State Capitol bearing the text of the Ten Commandments did not violate the establishment clause because the passive display among other historical markers did not convey an improper religious message. The ruling came in one of two closely watched cases challenging government displays of the Ten Commandments as unconstitutional endorsement of religion. While a fractured, five-justice majority ruled the placement of the six-foot granite monument to be constitutional, a different five-justice majority in *McCreary County, Kentucky v. American Civil Liberties Union of Kentucky* voted to bar displays of the Ten Commandments in two local courthouses in Kentucky.

Gonzales, Attorney General v. O Centro Espírita Beneficente União Do Vegetal (546 U.S. 418), decided by an 8–0 vote, Feb. 21, 2006; Roberts wrote the opinion; Alito did not participate.

A small religious sect can import a sacramental tea that contains a banned hallucinogenic substance because the government failed to show a compelling interest in burdening the group's free exercise of religion. The ruling upheld a preliminary injunction preventing the government from seizing hoasca, a sacramental tea imported by U.S. members of O Centro Espírita Beneficente Uniãao Do Vegetal, a Brazilian-based Christian spiritist sect known as UDV. Members of the sect—numbering about 130 in the United States—receive communion through drinking hoasca, which is brewed from two plants indigenous to the Brazilian

RELIGION, SPEECH, AND PRESS

Congress shall make no law respecting an establishment of religion, or prohibiting the free exercise thereof; or abridging the freedom of speech, or of the press; or the right of the people peaceably to assemble, and to petition the Government for a redress of grievances.

First Amendment, U.S. Constitution

rainforest. One of the plants contains dimethyltryptamine (DMT), a substance listed in Schedule I of the federal Controlled Substances Act.

FREEDOM OF SPEECH

Tory v. Cochran (544 U.S. 734), decided by a 7–2 vote, May 31, 2005; Breyer wrote the opinion; Thomas and Scalia dissented.

A disgruntled former client of celebrity defense lawyer Johnny Cochran won a limited ruling that lifted an injunction barring him from any public comments about his former attorney. The ruling vacated an injunction obtained by Cochran in a libel suit against the former client, Ulysses Tory.

Rumsfeld, Secretary of Defense v. Forum for Academic and Institutional Rights, Inc. (547 U.S. 47), decided by an 8–0 vote, March 6, 2006; Roberts wrote the opinion; Alito did not participate.

The Court rejected a First Amendment challenge to a law denying federal funds to any college or university that limited campus access for military recruiters because of the "don't ask, don't tell" policy on homosexuals in the armed services. The ruling reversed a federal appeals court decision that the so-called Solomon Amendment violated law schools' freedoms of speech and association. The law—named after its original sponsor, Rep. Gerald Solomon, R-N.Y. (1979–1999)—was aimed at law schools that limited assistance to military recruiters on the ground that the armed services' policy on homosexuals violated the schools' antidiscrimination standards for legal employers. The policy, adopted by Congress in 1993, barred gay men or lesbians from serving in the military if they engaged in homosexual acts or publicly disclosed their homosexuality.

Garcetti v. Ceballos (547 U.S. 410), decided by a 5–4 vote, May 30, 2006; Kennedy wrote the opinion; Souter, Stevens, Ginsburg, and Breyer dissented.

The First Amendment does not protect government employees from discipline for speech made pursuant to their official duties. The ruling rejected claims made by a Los Angeles prosecutor, Richard Ceballos, that the Los Angeles County district attorney's office violated his free speech rights by taking retaliatory employment actions after he complained about possible police misconduct in a case he was handling.

Tennessee Secondary School Athletic Association v. Brentwood Academy (551 U.S. 291), decided by a 9–0 vote, June 21, 2007; Stevens wrote the opinion.

A high school athletic association deemed to be a "state actor" can penalize a voluntary member school for violating anti-recruiting rules without infringing the school's freedom of speech. The ruling rejected a challenge by the private Brentwood Academy in Tennessee to penalties that the Tennessee Secondary School Athletic Association imposed after the school's football coach sent a recruiting letter to prospective students in April 1997. The school challenged the penalties as an infringement of its freedom of speech.

Morse v. Frederick (551 U.S. 393), decided by a 5–4 vote, June 25, 2007; Roberts wrote the opinion; Breyer dissented in part; Stevens, Souter, and Ginsburg dissented.

Public school students can be disciplined for speech on school grounds or at school events that can reasonably be interpreted as advocating or celebrating illegal drug use. The ruling upheld the decision of Deborah Morse, a Juneau, Alaska, high school principal, to discipline then-student Joseph Frederick for displaying a banner reading "BONG HiTS 4 JESUS" at a school event.

GOVERNMENT SPEECH

Johanns, Secretary of Agriculture v. Livestock Marketing Association (544 U.S. 550), decided by a 6–3 vote, May 23, 2005; Scalia wrote the opinion; Souter, Stevens, and Kennedy dissented.

A government program that imposes an assessment on cattle sales to fund a pro-beef advertising campaign is "government speech" immune from a direct First Amendment challenge. The ruling marked the third time in eight years that the Court had evaluated the constitutionality of federal programs to fund advertising campaigns promoting agricultural products. In immediate effect, the ruling upheld against First Amendment challenge the twenty-year-old federal program that created and disseminated the well-known slogan "Beef. It's What's for Dinner."

OBSCENITY AND INDECENCY

City of San Diego v. Roe (543 U.S. 77), decided by a 9–0 vote, Dec. 6, 2004; per curiam decision.

A municipality's decision to fire an employee who sold indecent videos of himself over the Internet did not violate the First Amendment because the videos neither related to his employment nor were a matter of public concern. The ruling affirmed the City of San Diego's discharge of police officer "John Roe," who produced and sold explicit custom videos of himself masturbating in a police uniform on the Internet auction site eBay. A supervisor discovered the material while searching for other merchandise for sale by Roe, linked to his auction of an official San Diego Police uniform. The police department instructed him to remove the items and cease his online presence and, upon Roe's failure to fully comply, fired him. Roe subsequently sued, claiming that the city violated his right to free speech.

Immigration Law

ASYLUM

Gonzales, Attorney General v. Thomas (547 U.S. 183), decided by a 9–0 vote, April 17, 2006; per curiam opinion.

A federal appeals court should have let immigration judges rule whether a white South African family was entitled to asylum because of their kinship with a racist company foreman in their native country. The ruling summarily reversed a decision by the Ninth U.S. Circuit Court of Appeals backing an asylum claim by Michelle Thomas and members of her immediate family. Thomas claimed that she and her family had been threatened and attacked in South Africa because they are related to a racist company foreman known as "Boss Ronnie."

DEPORTATION

Leocal v. Ashcroft, Attorney General (543 U.S. 1), decided by a 9–0 vote, Nov. 9, 2004; Rehnquist wrote the opinion.

A drunken driving conviction ordinarily does not constitute a "crime of violence" that can be used as a basis for deporting a criminal alien under federal immigration law. The ruling reinstated an appeal by a Haitian immigrant, Josue Leocal, who was ordered deported in 2002 after serving two years in a Florida prison for a state driving under the influence conviction.

Clark, Field Office Director, Seattle, Immigration and Customs Enforcement v. Martinez (543 U.S. 371), decided by a 7–2 vote, Jan. 12, 2005; Scalia wrote the opinion; Thomas and Rehnquist dissented in part.

The United States cannot indefinitely detain aliens who, though once permitted to reside in the country, have been ordered deported but are also refused permission to return home by their countries of origin. The decision raised the possibility that seven hundred Cubans who arrived during the 1980 Mariel boatlift and who had since served prison time for felony convictions would be released from government custody.

Fernandez-Vargas v. Gonzales, Attorney General (548 U.S. 30), decided by an 8–1 vote, June 22, 2006; Souter wrote the opinion; Stevens dissented.

A 1996 law easing the deportation of aliens who reenter the United States illegally after an earlier deportation order applies to aliens whose reentry occurred before the effective date of the law. The ruling, extending the reach of the Illegal Immigration Reform and Immigrant Responsibility Act of 1996, upheld the reinstatement of a deportation order against a Mexican citizen, Humberto Fernandez-Vargas, who had lived in the United States for more than twenty years after his last illegal entry in 1982.

Lopez v. Gonzales, Attorney General (549 U.S. 47), decided by an 8–1 vote, Dec. 5, 2006; Souter wrote the opinion; Thomas dissented.

An immigrant convicted of a crime classified as a felony under state law but as a misdemeanor under federal law may contest his deportation from the United States. The ruling paved the way for reopening the government's decision to deport Jose Antonio Lopez to his native Mexico after he had completed a sentence for a state drug offense in South Dakota.

Gonzales, Attorney General v. Duenas-Alvarez (549 U.S. 183), decided by an 8–1 vote, Jan. 17, 2007; Breyer wrote the opinion; Stevens dissented in part.

An alien convicted of aiding and abetting a theft is subject to deportation under the Immigration and Nationality Act. The ruling ended Luis Alexander Duenas-Alvarez's quest to stave off deportation after being convicted of aiding and abetting a car theft in California in 2002.

Dada v. Mukasey, Attorney General (554 U.S. _), decided by a 5–4 vote, June 16, 2008; Kennedy wrote the opinion; Scalia, Roberts, Thomas, and Alito dissented.

An alien who agrees to a voluntary departure can renounce that agreement before the departure period expires. The decision opened the door for Samson Taiwo Dada, a Nigerian citizen living in the United States since 1998 on a temporary visa, to challenge a decision requiring him to leave the country.

Individual Rights

ABORTION RIGHTS

Ayotte, Attorney General of New Hampshire v. Planned Parenthood of Northern New England (546 U.S. 320), decided by a 9–0 vote, Jan. 18, 2006; O'Connor wrote the opinion.

An abortion statute need not be invalidated in its entirety if enforcement of one of its provisions would be unconstitutional in medical emergencies. Instead, a court may issue a narrower ruling providing declaratory or injunctive relief. The ruling partly deflected a closely watched challenge to a New Hampshire law requiring parental notification prior to a minor obtaining an abortion.

Gonzales, Attorney General v. Carhart (550 U.S. 124), decided by a 5–4 vote, April 18, 2007; Kennedy wrote the opinion; Ginsburg, Stevens, Souter, and Breyer dissented.

The federal law banning so-called partial birth abortions is constitutional and need not include an exception permitting the procedure if necessary to protect a woman's health. The ruling—a major victory for opponents of abortion—upheld a law Congress passed in 2003, three years after the U.S. Supreme Court had invalidated a similar Nebraska law.

AGE DISCRIMINATION

Smith v. City of Jackson, Mississippi (544 U.S. 228), decided by a 5–3 vote on the legal issue and an 8–0 vote on the result, March 30, 2005; Stevens wrote the main opinion; Scalia concurred in the judgment; O'Connor, Kennedy, and Thomas disagreed on the legal issue but concurred in the judgment; Rehnquist did not participate.

The federal age discrimination law prohibits employment practices that disadvantage older workers whether intentionally or not unless they are based on reasonable factors other than age. By permitting "disparate impact" suits under the Age Discrimination in Employment Act, the ruling scuttled the requirement previously imposed by a number of lower federal courts that the plaintiff in an age bias suit meet the high threshold of providing evidence of an actual intent to discriminate.

Sprint/United Management Company v. Mendelsohn (552 U.S. 379), decided by a 9–0 vote, Feb. 26, 2008; Thomas wrote the opinion.

Trial judges should decide on a case-by-case basis whether to admit "me too" evidence offered by a plaintiff in an age discrimination suit from coworkers who claim discrimination by other supervisors in the company. The ruling shed only a little light on a major controversy between employers and employees in federal job discrimination suits under either the Age Discrimination in Employment Act or Title VII of the Civil Rights Act of 1964. Employers had urged the Court either to bar or set a high standard for admitting "me too" evidence, while civil rights groups wanted the Court to adopt a rule easing the use of such evidence.

Federal Express Corp. v. Holowecki (552 U.S. 389), decided by a 7–2 vote, Feb. 27, 2008; Kennedy wrote the opinion; Thomas and Scalia dissented.

A "charge" of age discrimination under the Age Discrimination in Employment Act is sufficient if it contains an allegation of age discrimination and the name of the charged party and can be reasonably construed as a request for the Equal Employment Opportunity Commission to act.

Gomez-Perez v. Potter, Postmaster General (553 U.S. _), decided by a 6–3 vote, May 27, 2008; Alito wrote the opinion; Roberts, Scalia, and Thomas dissented.

A federal employee may sue for retaliation under the 1967 Age Discrimination in Employment Act. The ruling reinstated a suit by a former United States Postal Service employee, Myrna Gomez-Perez, who claimed that she was subjected to various forms of retaliation, including false accusations by her supervisors and coworkers and a drastic reduction of hours, after she filed an equal opportunity age discrimination complaint against the postal service for converting her position to part time.

Kentucky Retirement Systems v. Equal Employment Opportunity Commission (554 U.S. _), decided by a 5–4 vote, June 19, 2008; Breyer wrote the opinion; Kennedy, Scalia, Ginsburg, and Alito dissented.

A state pension plan that gives workers who become disabled before reaching retirement age more generous benefits than those who become disabled after reaching retirement age does not discriminate on the basis of age.

Meacham v. Knolls Atomic Power Laboratory (554 U.S. _), decided by a 7–1 vote, June 19, 2008; Souter wrote the opinion; Thomas dissented in part; Breyer did not participate.

An employer accused of discriminating against workers because of age bears the burden of proving the defense recognized in federal law that the challenged practice was based on factors other than age. The ruling favored older workers fired as part of a reduction in force at the private, New York–based defense contractor Knolls Atomic Power Laboratory, which designed nuclear reactors for the U.S. Navy's nuclear-powered warships.

DAMAGE SUITS

Scott v. Harris (550 U.S. 372), decided by an 8–1 vote, April 30, 2007; Scalia wrote the opinion; Stevens dissented.

Police can use force to terminate a high-speed vehicular chase that threatens innocent bystanders even if the action places the fleeing suspect at risk of serious injury or death. The ruling rejected a federal civil rights suit by a Georgia man, Victor Harris, who was left permanently paralyzed in March 2001 after a Coweta County deputy sheriff, Timothy Scott, rammed Harris's car off the road to bring a ten-minute high-speed chase to an end.

Los Angeles County v. Rettele (550 U.S. 609), decided by an 8–1 vote, May 21, 2007; per curiam opinion; Souter voted not to hear the case.

Police officers need not call off a search after entering a home with a valid search warrant and finding occupants of a different race than the named suspects. The ruling rejected a federal civil rights suit by two white individuals rousted from their bed in California in December 2001 by Los Angeles County sheriff's deputies executing a drug investigation search warrant. The warrant named four African American suspects, one of whom was said to own a gun.

DISABILITY RIGHTS

Spector v. Norwegian Cruise Line Ltd. (545 U.S. 119), decided by a 6–3 vote, June 6, 2005; Kennedy wrote the opinion; Scalia, Rehnquist, and O'Connor dissented.

Provisions of the federal law that guarantee equal access for disabled persons apply to foreign-flagged cruise ships that call at U.S. ports but may not require removal of all structural barriers for the disabled. The Court held that the ships are subject to the Americans with Disability Act but left it for lower courts to determine how far the law could go in requiring structural changes on vessels.

Schaffer v. Weast, Superintendent, Montgomery County Public Schools (546 U.S. 49), decided by a 6–2 vote, Nov. 14, 2005; O'Connor wrote the opinion; Ginsburg and Breyer dissented; Roberts did not participate.

A student with a disability, not the school district of the student, has the burden of persuasion when the student challenges the efficacy of an Individualized Education Program required under federal law. The ruling rejected an effort by Jocelyn and Martin Schaffer under the federal Individuals with Disabilities Education Act to recover from their local school system the costs of private tuition for their son Brian, who suffered from learning disabilities and speech-language impairments.

United States v. Georgia (546 U.S. 151), decided by a 9–0 vote, Jan. 10, 2006; Scalia wrote the opinion.

Prison inmates can sue the state for money damages under the Americans with Disabilities Act (ADA) for conduct by prison officials that violates both the act and the constitutional prohibition against cruel and unusual punishment. The ruling reversed a federal appeals court holding that state sovereign immunity bars money damage suits by inmates for violations of the ADA's provisions barring discrimination in government services and facilities.

Arlington Central School District Board of Education v. Murphy (548 U.S. 291), decided by a 6–3 vote, June 26, 2006; Alito wrote the opinion; Breyer, Stevens, and Souter dissented.

The federal law providing funding for education for students with disabilities does not authorize recovery for the services of expert witnesses during proceedings. The ruling blocked a New York family from recovering from its local school board any part of the $29,350 in fees paid to an educational consultant who assisted in proceedings under the Individuals with Disabilities Education Act.

Winkelman v. Parma City School District (550 U.S. 516), decided by a 7–2 vote, May 21, 2007; Kennedy wrote the opinion; Scalia and Thomas dissented.

Parents have an independent right to free appropriate public education for their children under the Individuals with Disabilities Education Act and can sue to enforce their rights in federal court without a lawyer. The ruling represented a setback for school systems seeking to limit federal court litigation over education for children with disabilities.

Board of Education of City of New York v. Tom F. (552 U.S. 1), decided by a 4–4 vote, Oct. 10, 2007; per curiam opinion; Kennedy did not participate.

An evenly divided Court upheld a New York City parent's right under federal law to receive private school tuition reimbursement for his learning disabled son without first having sent the boy to a public school. The split vote left unresolved an important legal issue for families of children with disabilities and for school districts facing the cost of private special education for many of those children.

FALSE ARREST

Wallace v. Kato (549 U.S. 384), decided by a 7–2 vote, Feb. 21, 2007; Scalia wrote the opinion; Breyer and Ginsburg dissented.

The time limit for filing a federal civil rights suit for false arrest in violation of the Fourth Amendment starts to run as soon as the suspect is arraigned in court or bound over for trial. The ruling upheld the dismissal of a federal civil rights suit filed by a Chicago man, Andre Wallace, who was arrested on a murder charge in January 1994 but won a reversal of his conviction after a state appeals court ruled the arrest unlawful in 2001. Wallace filed a suit in 2003 against the city of Chicago and several police officers. The U.S. Supreme Court agreed with a federal district court and the Seventh U.S. Circuit Court of Appeals that the two-year period to bring the suit began at the time of his arrest and not when his conviction was later set aside.

GUN OWNERSHIP

District of Columbia v. Heller (554 U.S. _), decided by a 5–4 vote, June 26, 2008; Scalia wrote the opinion; Stevens, Souter, Ginsburg, and Breyer dissented.

The Second Amendment guarantees an individual right to own or possess guns, which at the least protects the right to keep a lawful firearm in an immediately operable condition in one's home for self-defense. The ruling struck down a strict District of Columbia law that essentially banned privately owned handguns and required other weapons when stored in homes to be either trigger-locked or disassembled. It opened the door to challenges to other gun control laws by viewing the Second Amendment as an individual right instead of as a protection for state militias. At the same time, the ruling listed several categories of laws likely to be upheld, including bans on the carrying of concealed weapons and prohibitions on possession by, among others, felons.

The Court held that an absolute prohibition on handguns held and used for self-defense in the home violates the Second Amendment's individual right to "keep and bear arms." The decision noted that the handgun ban prohibited what people consider to be "the quintessential self-defense weapon" because of the ease of storing, aiming, or using a handgun when needed. The requirement to render weapons stored in the home inoperable was deemed invalid because it "makes it impossible for citizens to use them for the core lawful purpose of self-defense."

JOB DISCRIMINATION

Ledbetter v. Goodyear Tire & Rubber Co., Inc. (550 U.S. 618), decided by a 5–4 vote, May 29, 2007; Alito wrote the opinion; Ginsburg, Stevens, Souter, and Breyer dissented.

Workers may not sue their employer for pay discrimination unless they file a complaint with the Equal Employment Opportunity Commission (EEOC) within a specified time period, typically 180 days following the employer's intentional discriminatory action. Later paychecks that reflect the initial discrimination do not extend the statute of limitations. The ruling represented an important victory for employers and a significant hurdle for workers seeking to sue for adverse pay decisions under Title VII of the Civil Rights Act of 1964, the major federal job discrimination statute.

The Court ruled Ledbetter's claim untimely, holding that later effects of past discrimination do not restart the time for filing a charge with the EEOC. The Court said the decision was dictated by the text of Title VII and previous U.S. Supreme Court rulings applying the deadline in the act. The "short deadline" for filing suit under Title VII "reflects Congress's strong preference for the prompt resolution of employment discrimination allegations through voluntary conciliation and cooperation."

CBOCS West, Inc. v. Humphries (553 U.S. _), decided by a 7–2 vote, May 27, 2008; Breyer wrote the opinion; Thomas and Scalia dissented.

A former employee can use the Reconstruction-era civil rights law guaranteeing equal contract rights to sue his former employer for firing him in retaliation for having complained about mistreatment of a coworker. The ruling allowed Hedrick G. Humphries, formerly an assistant manager of a Cracker Barrel restaurant, to sue the corporate owner for firing him after he complained that an African American employee had been discharged because of his race.

PHYSICIAN-ASSISTED SUICIDE

Gonzales, Attorney General v. Oregon (546 U.S. 243), decided by a 6–3 vote, Jan. 17, 2006; Kennedy wrote the opinion; Scalia, Roberts, and Thomas dissented.

The attorney general has no authority under the federal Controlled Substances Act to penalize doctors for prescribing drugs to a terminally ill patient to end his or her life as permitted by Oregon's physician-assisted suicide law. The ruling, a setback for social conservatives, nullified an "interpretive rule" issued by Attorney General John Ashcroft in November 2001 aimed at overriding Oregon's landmark assisted-suicide law. The Death with Dignity Act, an initiative enacted by Oregon voters in 1994, allows physicians to prescribe lethal drugs to patients suffering from an incurable, irreversible disease expected to result in death within six months.

PROPERTY RIGHTS

Jones v. Flowers (547 U.S. 220), decided by a 5–3 vote, April 26, 2006; Roberts wrote the opinion; Thomas, Scalia, and Kennedy dissented; Alito did not participate.

A state must take reasonable additional steps to notify property owners of an impending tax sale if notice by certified mail is returned unclaimed. The ruling backed a Little Rock man, Gary Jones, in a dispute with the Arkansas commissioner of state lands over seizure and sale of his former residence for failure to pay state property taxes.

Wilkie v. Robbins (551 U.S. 537), decided by a 7–2 vote, June 25, 2007; Souter wrote the opinion; Ginsburg and Stevens dissented.

A landowner cannot bring a constitutional tort suit against federal officials for retaliating against the exercise of his property rights when other means for obtaining legal relief exist. The ruling rejected a damage suit brought by a Wyoming landowner, Frank Robbins, against officials of the U.S. Bureau of Land Management for an alleged campaign of intimidation and harassment aimed at getting him to grant the government an easement over part of his property.

RACIAL DISCRIMINATION

Johnson v. California (543 U.S. 499), decided by an 8–1 vote, June 13, 2005; Stevens wrote the opinion; Thomas dissented.

A defendant who challenges a prosecutor's use of peremptory challenges as racially motivated need only present evidence raising a "reasonable inference" of discriminatory intent before the prosecutor is required to respond to the accusation. The ruling reinstated a racial discrimination challenge by an African American defendant, Jay Shawn Johnson, who was accused of killing his former girlfriend's white, nineteen-month-old daughter. The charge arose when the prosecutor decided to strike all three black prospective jurors during Johnson's state murder trial in California.

Domino's Pizza, Inc. v. McDonald (546 U.S. 470), decided by an 8–0 vote, Feb. 22, 2006; Scalia wrote the opinion; Alito did not participate.

The post–Civil War statute prohibiting racial discrimination in contracts does not allow the owner of a corporation to recover damages personally for another party's breach of contract with the corporation. The ruling rejected an effort by the owner of a bankrupt construction company to recover damages in his own name for failed contracts to build four restaurants for Domino's Pizza in the Las Vegas area.

Parents Involved in Community Schools v. Seattle School District No. 1 (551 U.S. 701), decided by a 5–4 vote, June 28, 2007; Roberts wrote the opinion; Kennedy wrote a partial concurrence; Breyer, Stevens, Souter, and Ginsburg dissented.

School districts generally cannot use race as the determinative factor in assigning individual students to schools but may be able to adopt general policies aimed at promoting a compelling interest in racial diversity. The ruling had the immediate effect of striking down plans voluntarily adopted by school boards in Seattle, Wash., and metropolitan Louisville, Ky., aimed at keeping the racial mix at individual schools within specified ranges. The decision in the two consolidated cases—*Parents Involved* and *Meredith v. Jefferson County Board of Education*—involved pupil assignment plans that were adopted within two years of each other but had somewhat different origins.

RESTRAINING ORDERS

Town of Castle Rock, Colorado v. Gonzales (545 U.S. 748), decided by a 7–2 vote, June 27, 2005; Scalia wrote the opinion; Stevens and Ginsburg dissented.

Local police officers did not deprive a woman of a constitutionally protected property interest when they failed to enforce a state-issued restraining order against the woman's estranged husband. The ruling barred a federal civil rights suit by a Colorado woman against the town of Castle Rock for the police department's failure to enforce a state court–issued restraining order against her estranged husband. The suit arose from an episode that ended with the death of the couple's three young daughters at the husband's hands and his own death in an ensuing police shootout.

RIGHT TO COUNSEL

Rothgery v. Gillespie County (554 U.S. _), decided by an 8–1 vote, June 23, 2008; Souter wrote the opinion; Thomas dissented.

An individual's right to counsel attaches at an initial appearance before a magistrate to conduct a probable cause determination and set bail. The carefully limited ruling rejected the practice of a few states that did not recognize a right to counsel attaching at an accused person's initial appearance, but it stopped short of requiring appointment of counsel for indigents at that point.

SEXUAL DISCRIMINATION

Jackson v. Birmingham Board of Education (544 U.S. 167), decided by a 5–4 vote, March 29, 2005; O'Connor wrote the opinion; Thomas, Rehnquist, Scalia, and Kennedy dissented.

The federal law prohibiting sex-based discrimination in schools and colleges permits lawsuits by whistleblowers retaliated against for complaining about sex discrimination against another person. The ruling reinstated a lawsuit against an Alabama school board brought by Roderick Jackson, a teacher and coach at a Birmingham public high school. Jackson, a physical education teacher in Birmingham since 1993, was hired as the coach of a high school girls' basketball team in 1999. He claimed that he made a series of complaints about the unequal treatment of the girls' team but that the school board took no action to remedy the situation. Instead, it gave him negative work evaluations and then terminated his coaching position in 2001, allowing him to remain only as a teacher.

TAXPAYER RIGHTS

Hein, Director, White House Office of Faith-Based and Community Initiatives v. Freedom From Religion Foundation, Inc. (551 U.S. 587), decided by a 5–4 vote, June 25, 2007; Alito wrote the main opinion; Scalia and Thomas concurred in the judgment; Souter, Stevens, Ginsburg, and Breyer dissented.

Taxpayers have no general legal standing to challenge federal spending to promote religion as a violation of the establishment clause unless Congress has specifically authorized or mandated the expenditure. The ruling represented a victory for the George W. Bush administration's program to provide federal funds to religious organizations that offer social services in their communities. The program, centered in the White House Office of Faith-Based and Community Initiatives and with branches in several federal agencies, was created by an executive order signed by Bush to ensure that faith-based groups could compete with other community groups for federal funds. The Freedom From Religion Foundation, a nonprofit organization that advocated for the separation of church and state, along with three of its members, brought suit against the directors of the Office of Faith-Based and Community Initiatives for violating the establishment clause by holding conferences that the group alleged promoted religious community groups over secular ones. The conferences were paid for with funds generally appropriated by Congress to the executive branch and not specifically designated for such use.

WORKPLACE HARASSMENT

Engquist v. Oregon Department of Agriculture (553 U.S. _), decided by a 6–3 vote, June 9, 2008; Roberts wrote the opinion; Stevens, Souter, and Ginsburg dissented.

A public employee cannot use the equal protection clause to challenge a personnel decision affecting only the employee as arbitrary or irrational. The ruling ended a "class of one" claim brought by Anup Engquist under the equal protection clause challenging her dismissal from a position with the Oregon Department of Agriculture.

WRONGFUL TERMINATION

Office of Senator Mark Dayton v. Hanson (550 U.S. 511), decided by an 8–0 vote, May 21, 2007; Stevens wrote the opinion; Roberts did not participate.

A former aide to former Minnesota Democratic senator Mark Dayton (2001–2007) was allowed to proceed with a wrongful discharge suit against Dayton but without a definitive U.S. Supreme Court ruling on the constitutionality of the lawsuit. The ruling left undecided whether the suit, brought under the Congressional Accountability Act of 1995, would be prohibited under the speech or debate clause, which generally protects members of Congress from criminal prosecution or civil suit for their official actions.

International Law

CONSULAR ASSISTANCE

Medellín v. Dretke, Director, Texas Department of Criminal Justice, Correctional Institutions Division (544 U.S. 660), decided by a 5–4 vote, May 23, 2005; per curiam opinion; O'Connor, Stevens, Souter, and Breyer dissented.

The Court dismissed an effort by a Mexican national to overturn his murder conviction and death sentence because of Texas officials' failure to provide him access to consular assistance as required by international treaty. The action, in a closely watched and procedurally complex test of international law, had the effect of shifting José Ernesto Medellín's request for postconviction relief from federal to Texas state courts.

Medellín v. Texas (552 U.S. 491), decided by a 6–3 vote, March 25, 2008; Roberts wrote the opinion; Breyer, Souter, and Ginsburg dissented.

A Mexican national lost his attempt to belatedly challenge his murder conviction and death sentence in Texas on the ground that police failed to tell him of his right under an international treaty to confer with Mexican diplomats after his arrest. The ruling limited the authority of either the International Court of Justice or the president to establish binding obligations of international law on the states. In immediate effect, it rejected an effort by José Ernesto Medellín to challenge his conviction and death sentence for the 1993 gang-related rape-murder of two Houston teenagers. Medellín, a Mexican national who had spent most of his life in the United States, signed a written confession to the crime after being advised of his rights under U.S. law. But Houston police failed to tell him of his right under the Vienna Convention on Consular Relations, a treaty ratified by the United States in 1969, to confer with the Mexican consulate about his detention.

FOREIGN SOVEREIGN IMMUNITY

Ministry of Defense and Support for the Armed Forces of the Islamic Republic of Iran v. Elahi (546 U.S. 450), decided by a 9–0 vote, Feb. 21, 2006; per curiam opinion.

A federal appeals court was wrong to rely on an opposing party's view in ruling that Iran's Ministry of Defense was not entitled to protection from seizure of property in U.S. courts under the Foreign Sovereign Immunities Act. The ruling blocked an effort by a U.S. citizen, Dariush Elahi, to collect a portion of a $300 million default judgment awarded him in federal court in 2000 against the Iranian government for the alleged murder of his brother.

Republic of the Philippines v. Pimentel (553 U.S. _), decided by a 7–2 vote, June 12, 2008; Kennedy wrote the opinion; Stevens and Souter dissented in part.

A lawsuit in which a foreign sovereign is an interested party may not proceed when the sovereign is excused from appearing before the court on the basis of foreign sovereign immunity. The ruling further delayed payment of money from the estate of former Philippine president Ferdinand Marcos to victims of his human rights abuses.

FOREIGN TAX ENFORCEMENT

Pasquantino v. United States (544 U.S. 349), decided by a 5–4 vote, April 26, 2005; Thomas wrote the opinion; Ginsburg, Scalia, Souter, and Breyer dissented.

A common law rule preventing one country from enforcing the tax laws of another does not bar the United States from prosecuting U.S. citizens for a scheme to defraud Canada of tax revenue. The ruling resolved a conflict among the federal courts of appeals concerning whether the "common law revenue rule" limited the reach of the broadly worded federal wire fraud statute.

Permanent Mission of India to the United Nations v. City of New York (551 U.S. 193), decided by a 7–2 vote, June 14, 2007; Thomas wrote the opinion; Stevens and Breyer dissented.

Foreign governments can be sued to determine the validity of tax liens placed on buildings in the United States used as residences for lower-level diplomatic employees. The ruling upheld an effort by New York City to collect property taxes on buildings used by foreign countries to house their diplomatic missions to the United Nations. The city exempted property used for offices or ambassadors' residences, but not for housing for lower-level diplomatic personnel.

Labor Law

PENSIONS

LaRue v. DeWolff, Boberg & Associates, Inc. (552 U.S. 248), decided by a 9–0 vote, Feb. 20, 2008; Stevens wrote the opinion.

Workers can sue their employers or pension plan administrators under federal law for losses resulting from mismanagement of their 401(k) retirement accounts. The ruling represented a major expansion of liability under the Employee Retirement Income Security Act of 1974, the federal law regulating employer-provided pensions and benefits.

Beck v. PACE International Union (551 U.S. 96), decided by a 9–0 vote, June 11, 2007; Scalia wrote the opinion.

A company terminating an employee pension plan as part of a bankruptcy cannot merge the plan's assets with a multiemployer plan administered by a union that represents workers for that company and others. The ruling rejected an effort by PACE International Union to require Crown Paper Company to consider merging the assets of its pension plan with the plan the union administered for its members employed by Crown and other companies.

Metropolitan Life Insurance Co. v. Glenn (554 U.S. _), decided by a 6–3 vote, June 19, 2008; Breyer wrote the opinion; Scalia and Thomas dissented; Kennedy dissented in part.

Courts reviewing an employee's denial of benefits under an employee benefit plan must consider the conflict of interest created when the plan administrator determines both eligibility for benefits and pays them. The ruling gave many employees who have been denied benefits a better chance to challenge the denial in court.

PROTECTED ACTIVITIES

IBP, Inc. v. Alvarez (546 U.S. 21), decided by a 9–0 vote, Nov. 8, 2005; Stevens wrote the opinion.

Employees required to wear protective clothing are entitled to be paid for the time spent walking between changing rooms and production areas, but not for the time spent waiting to put on protective gear. The ruling settled a financially significant split between federal appeals courts on how to apply a 1947 law, the Portal-to-Portal Act, which eliminated any employer obligation to pay workers for the time spent traveling to their principal workplace or engaging in "activities ... preliminary to or postliminary to" their "principal activity or activities."

TITLE VII DISCRIMINATION

Ash v. Tyson Foods, Inc. (546 U.S. 454), decided by a 9–0 vote, Feb. 21, 2006; per curiam opinion.

The use of the term "boy" may be discriminatory, even in the absence of any racial modifier, while an employer's allegedly discriminatory hiring decision need not "jump off the page" to be considered pretextual. The decision breathed new life into a discrimination suit brought in 1995 by two African American men against their former employer, Tyson Foods.

Arbaugh v. Y&H Corp. (546 U.S. 500), decided by an 8–0 vote, Feb. 22, 2006; Ginsburg wrote the opinion; Alito did not participate.

Federal district courts have subject-matter jurisdiction to hear claims brought under Title VII of the Civil Rights Act of 1964 against businesses that employ fewer than fifteen employees. The ruling resolved a split among federal appeals courts concerning whether Title VII's employee-numerosity threshold was a requirement for federal jurisdiction or only an element of the federal claim.

Burlington Northern and Santa Fe Railway Company v. White (548 U.S. 53), decided by a 9–0 vote, June 22, 2006; Breyer wrote the opinion.

The federal civil rights law's anti-retaliatory provision prohibits an employer from taking any action against an employee at or outside the workplace that might have deterred a reasonable person from having complained of the alleged discrimination. The ruling, resolving a conflict among federal courts of appeals, endorsed a relatively broad interpretation of the anti-retaliation provision found in Title VII of the Civil Rights Act of 1964.

UNIONS

Davenport v. Washington Education Association (551 U.S. 177), decided by a 9–0 vote, June 14, 2007; Scalia wrote the opinion.

Public employee unions can be required to obtain affirmative consent from contributing nonmembers before spending a portion of their dues on election-related purposes. The ruling upheld a Washington State law invalidated on First Amendment grounds by the state supreme court in a challenge brought by the state teachers union.

Chamber of Commerce of the United States v. Brown, Attorney General of California (554 U.S. _), decided by a 7–2 vote, June 19, 2008; Stevens wrote the opinion; Breyer and Ginsburg dissented.

A state cannot prohibit employers that receive state funds from using the funds in connection with unionization drives. The ruling struck down on federal preemption grounds a California law passed in 2000 that prohibited employers that receive state funds from using any of the funds "to assist, promote, or deter union organizing." The labor-backed statute—comparable to laws in nine other states—required employers to maintain sufficient records to demonstrate that no state funds were spent in connection with union drives.

WAGES

Long Island Care at Home, Ltd. v. Coke (551 U.S. 158), decided by a 9–0 vote, June 11, 2007; Breyer wrote the opinion.

The Court upheld a Labor Department regulation that denies federally mandated minimum wage or overtime pay to home health care workers. The ruling—a setback for the more than one million home health care workers—rejected a labor union–financed suit brought by Evelyn Coke, a New York woman who had worked in the field for two decades before retiring. Coke sued her former employer, Long Island Care at Home, in 2002, claiming that she was entitled to minimum wage and overtime pay under the

Fair Labor Standards Act, the landmark federal wage and hours law.

WITNESS TAMPERING

Arthur Andersen LLP v. United States (544 U.S. 696), decided by a 9–0 vote, May 31, 2005; Rehnquist wrote the opinion.

The accounting firm of Arthur Andersen LLP was improperly convicted of having violated the federal witness-tampering statute by encouraging its employees to destroy documents related to its audits of the Enron Corporation. The ruling overturned the criminal conviction that sealed the fate of the once-venerable accounting firm. The Enron Corporation's controversial collapse in late 2001 captured international headlines as well as the attention of the Securities and Exchange Commission.

Property Law

TAKINGS

Lingle, Governor of Hawaii v. Chevron U.S.A. Inc. (544 U.S. 528), decided by a 9–0 vote, May 23, 2005; O'Connor wrote the opinion.

The Court relaxed the standard for determining whether a government regulation amounts to an unconstitutional taking of property. The ruling had the immediate effect of setting aside decisions by two lower federal courts to strike down a Hawaii law limiting the rent that oil companies could charge independent service station franchisees. More broadly, the ruling scrapped a test set out in a 1980 decision that a government regulation affecting property rights amounted to an unconstitutional taking if it failed to "substantially advance legitimate state interests."

San Remo Hotel, L.P. v. City and County of San Francisco (545 U.S. 323), decided by a 9–0 vote, June 20, 2005; Stevens wrote the opinion.

A property owner cannot bring a claim of uncompensated taking of property in federal court after state courts have ruled on the claim. The ruling represented a sharp setback for property rights advocates in an important but procedurally complex case.

Kelo v. City of New London (545 U.S. 469), decided by a 5–4 vote, June 23, 2005; Stevens wrote the opinion; O'Connor, Rehnquist, Scalia, and Thomas dissented.

Economic development qualifies as a "public use" needed to authorize taking of private property even if the property is transferred to a private company and is not required by law to be open to use by the public. The ruling in a closely watched case from New London, Conn., represented a major victory for municipal governments and a disappointing defeat for property rights advocates. In immediate effect, the decision rejected a constitutional challenge by a number of homeowners in New London's Fort Trumbull neighborhood to acquisition of their property for planned commercial, residential, and recreational development. The city—suffering from a loss of jobs and population—authorized the private, city-chartered New London Development Corporation in 1998 to devise a development plan that would provide jobs, increase municipal revenue, and attract tourists. The corporation acquired most of the properties through voluntary purchases but brought condemnation actions against nine homeowners who refused to sell. They in turn challenged the acquisitions in state court, contending in part that economic development did not constitute a public use as needed to justify a governmental taking under the Fifth Amendment's takings clause. The Court cited precedents dating from the late nineteenth century upholding taking of private property for economic purposes.

State and Local Governments

ANTI-RACKETEERING

Anza v. Ideal Steel Supply Corp. (547 U.S. 451), decided by a 7–2 vote, June 5, 2006; Kennedy wrote the opinion; Thomas dissented in part; Breyer dissented in part.

A company suing a rival firm under the federal anti-racketeering law must prove that the defendant's conduct directly caused the plaintiff's injury, not merely that it placed the plaintiff at a competitive disadvantage.

BANKRUPTCY

Central Virginia Community College v. Katz (546 U.S. 356), decided by a 5–4 vote, Jan. 23, 2006; Stevens wrote the opinion; Thomas, Roberts, Scalia, and Kennedy dissented.

A state cannot use sovereign immunity to bar a bankruptcy trustee's proceeding to recover funds that a debtor improperly transferred to state agencies before filing for bankruptcy. The Court held that a bankruptcy trustee's proceeding to set aside the debtor's preferential transfers to state agencies is not barred by sovereign immunity.

BORDER DISPUTES

New Jersey v. Delaware (552 U.S. 597), decided by a 6–2 vote, March 31, 2008; Ginsburg wrote the opinion; Scalia and Alito dissented; Breyer did not participate.

Delaware can exercise concurrent jurisdiction with New Jersey over "extraordinary" structures that originate on the New Jersey shore but extend into the Delaware River, the border between the two states. The ruling effectively blocked a proposal by British Petroleum to construct on the New Jersey shore a liquefied natural gas (LNG) terminal that the Delaware Department of Natural Resources and Environmental Control determined would violate the state's coastal management act.

COMMERCE CLAUSE

Granholm, Governor of Michigan v. Heald (544 U.S. 460), decided by a 5–4 vote, May 16, 2005; Kennedy wrote the opinion; Thomas, Rehnquist, Stevens, and O'Connor dissented.

State laws that permit in-state but not out-of-state wineries to make direct sales to consumers violate the commerce clause and are not authorized by the Twenty-first Amendment. The ruling—in separate cases from Michigan and New York—resolved a conflict in the federal courts of appeals as to whether, in the area of alcohol sales, the Twenty-first Amendment overrides the general principle that a state may not discriminate against out-of-state products. The Twenty-first Amendment formally ended federal Prohibition in 1933 and conferred on the states broad powers to regulate the production and sale of alcoholic beverages. In one of the cases, Michigan residents and out-of-state wineries challenged a Michigan law that gave only in-state wineries permission to bypass the state's three-tier liquor sale system and sell directly to consumers via other outlets, principally the Internet. In the second case, Virginia and California winemakers joined with consumers to challenge a New York law that allowed out-of-state wineries to sell directly to New Yorkers only if they established a physical branch in the state.

The Court held both states' laws unconstitutional. The Court first found that both the Michigan and New York laws discriminated against out-of-state wineries—the former through a complete ban on direct shipment, and the latter by offering only the prohibitively expensive physical branch option, which "not a single out-of-state winery" had been able to choose. The two states' schemes, the Court wrote, were part of a "patchwork of laws" in an "ongoing low-level trade war" that the U.S. Constitution and the commerce clause "were designed to avoid." The ruling rejected the states' reliance on the Twenty-first Amendment, finding that the amendment did nothing more than restore to the states the regulatory powers they possessed before Prohibition. Finally, the state laws did not survive commerce clause scrutiny because the states' legitimate local interests in controlling liquor sales to minors and avoiding tax evasion could be served by "reasonable nondiscriminatory alternatives."

Gonzales, Attorney General v. Raich (545 U.S. 1), decided by a 6–3 vote, June 6, 2005; Stevens wrote the opinion; O'Connor, Rehnquist, and Thomas dissented.

Congress's power to regulate interstate commerce includes the power to prohibit possession of marijuana even when state law permits medical use and the substance is grown and used locally and noncommercially. The ruling—limiting the force of medical marijuana laws passed in California and nine other states—validated a broad construction of Congress's commerce clause power in a closely watched constitutional challenge brought by two California women who used marijuana to relieve pain associated with serious and chronic illnesses. The Court held that Congress's commerce clause power extended to intrastate, noncommercial possession or cultivation of marijuana because of the potential impact of medical use of marijuana on the national market for the product.

American Trucking Associations, Inc. v. Michigan Public Service Commission (545 U.S. 429), decided by a 9–0 vote, June 20, 2005; Breyer wrote the opinion.

A $100 per truck annual fee that Michigan charges trucking companies engaged in intrastate commercial hauling does not violate the dormant commerce clause, which generally bars state and local governments from discriminating against out-of-state business or excessively burdening interstate commerce. The ruling rejected a constitutional challenge to the fee assessed under Michigan's Motor Carrier Act.

United Haulers Association, Inc. v. Oneida-Herkimer Solid Waste Management Authority (550 U.S. 330), decided by a 6–3 vote, April 30, 2007; Roberts wrote the opinion; Alito, Stevens, and Kennedy dissented.

State and local governments can enact laws requiring private haulers to deliver solid waste to publicly owned waste processing facilities without improperly discriminating against interstate commerce.

COMMUNICATIONS LAW

City of Ranchos Palos Verdes v. Abrams (544 U.S. 113), decided by a 9–0 vote, March 22, 2005; Scalia wrote the opinion.

A local government's refusal to permit a resident to operate a wireless communications tower may be redressed only under a 1996 federal communications law and not under the broader provisions of the general federal civil rights statute. The ruling prevents individuals and companies that seek to operate cell phone towers from suing local governments for money damages and attorneys' fees over denials of operating permits.

IMMUNITY

Northern Insurance Company of New York v. Chatham County, Georgia (547 U.S. 189), decided by a 9–0 vote, April 25, 2006; Thomas wrote the opinion.

Local governments do not share state governments' sovereign immunity from private damage suits merely because they are exercising power delegated from the state. The Court held that a state's sovereign immunity does not extend to a political subdivision unless it qualifies as an arm of the state.

PROPERTY VALUATION

CSX Transportation, Inc. v. Georgia State Board of Equalization (552 U.S. 9), decided by a 9–0 vote, Dec. 4, 2007; Roberts wrote the opinion.

Railroads may use a federal law to challenge in federal court a state's methods for determining the value of railroad property for property tax purposes.

STATE FEES

Mid-Con Freight Systems, Inc. v. Michigan Public Service Commission (545 U.S. 440), decided by a 6–3 vote, June 20, 2005; Breyer wrote the opinion; Kennedy, Rehnquist, and O'Connor dissented.

A federal law regulating interstate trucking does not preempt a Michigan law imposing a $100 fee on trucks that are registered in the state but that engage exclusively in interstate commerce.

TAXATION

Wagnon, Secretary, Kansas Department of Revenue v. Prairie Band Potawatomi Nation (546 U.S. 95), decided by a 7–2 vote, Dec. 6, 2005; Thomas wrote the opinion; Ginsburg and Kennedy dissented.

States may tax motor fuel received by non–Indian distributors located off tribal reservations even if the fuel is delivered to a gas station owned by an Indian tribe and located on its reservation.

DaimlerChrysler Corp. v. Cuno (547 U.S. 332), decided by a 9–0 vote, May 15, 2006; Roberts wrote the opinion.

State taxpayers do not have standing in federal court to sue their state about taxing and spending decisions. The ruling dismissed a case brought by Ohio taxpayers to stop Ohio from giving large tax breaks to DaimlerChrysler. The Court emphasized that Article III of the U.S. Constitution limits the federal courts' jurisdiction to concrete cases in which the plaintiff's injury is caused by the defendant and the desired relief will adequately redress the injury. State taxpayers—like federal taxpayers—lack standing to challenge taxing and spending decisions in federal court because the harm is "indeterminable." The ruling left the state taxpayers the option of refiling their case in state court.

MeadWestvaco Corp. v. Illinois Department of Revenue (553 U.S. _), decided by a 9–0 vote, April 15, 2008; Alito wrote the opinion.

A state may tax a multistate enterprise on the sale of assets only if the assets are part of a "unitary business," even if the assets serve an "operational purpose" for the parent enterprise.

Department of Revenue of Kentucky v. Davis (553 U.S. _), decided by a 7–2 vote, May 19, 2008; Souter wrote the opinion; Kennedy and Alito dissented.

States may exempt from taxation the interest earned from bonds issued by the state or its political subdivisions while taxing interest earned from bonds issued by other states or their political subdivisions. The ruling upheld tax preferences that Kentucky and forty other states provided for their own state or municipal bonds.

WATER RIGHTS

Kansas v. Colorado (543 U.S. 86), decided by 9–0 and 8–1 votes, Dec. 7, 2004; Breyer wrote the opinion; Stevens dissented in part.

In an ongoing dispute regarding the Arkansas River, the state of Kansas was entitled to collect prejudgment interest from Colorado based on damages suffered only between 1985 and 1994. The six-part ruling answered some of the questions left unresolved by the Court's 1995 and 2001 decisions in the same matter. The case involved Kansas's accusations that Colorado improperly diverted water from the Arkansas River in violation of a 1949 regional compact.

Orff v. United States (545 U.S. 596), decided by a 9–0 vote, June 23, 2005; Thomas wrote the opinion.

Farmers who purchase water for irrigation from water districts supplied under contract with the U.S. Bureau of Reclamation cannot sue the government in court for water delivery reductions imposed during the term of the contract.

Tort Law

NEGLIGENCE

Norfolk Southern Railway Co. v. Sorrell (549 U.S. 158), decided by a 9–0 vote, Jan. 10, 2007; Roberts wrote the opinion.

The federal law governing suits by injured railroad workers uses the same standard to determine whether an injury was caused by negligence on the railway's part or by contributory negligence by the employee. The ruling rejected a jury instruction unique to the state of Missouri making it easier for an injured worker to show that a railroad's negligence caused the injury than for the railroad to show that the worker's negligence contributed.

PUNITIVE DAMAGES

Philip Morris USA v. Williams (549 U.S. 346), decided by a 5–4 vote, Feb. 20, 2007; Breyer wrote the opinion; Ginsburg, Stevens, Scalia, and Thomas dissented.

Punitive damages cannot be imposed on defendants on the basis of harm caused to others who are not before the court. The ruling—representing a significant victory for big business in personal injury cases—set aside a $79.5 million punitive damage award won by the Oregon widow of a long-time smoker who died from lung cancer in 1997. In her state court suit against Philip Morris—which manufactured her husband's favorite brand, Marlboro—Jesse

Williams claimed that the tobacco company had deceived her husband and other smokers in the state by depicting cigarettes as safe.

The Court held that the due process clause of the Fourteenth Amendment prohibits a state from using punitive damages to punish a defendant for injury upon nonparties to the litigation. The court said that plaintiffs may use harm to others to show that a defendant's conduct "posed a substantial risk of harm to the general public, and so was particularly reprehensible." But, "a jury may not go further than this and use a punitive damages verdict to punish a defendant directly on account of harms it is alleged to have visited on nonparties."

Exxon Shipping Co. v. Baker (554 U.S. _), decided by a 5–3 vote, June 25, 2008; Souter wrote the opinion; Stevens, Ginsburg, and Breyer dissented; Alito did not participate.

The Court reduced from $2.5 billion to about $500 million the punitive damages won by Alaskan plaintiffs for the Exxon Valdez oil spill in 1989, holding that punitive awards in maritime cases should ordinarily be no greater than the compensatory award. The ruling brought an end to a fourteen-year-old class action filed in 1994 on behalf of around 32,000 plaintiffs who claimed that the massive oil spill, the worst in U.S. history, damaged the fishing economy in and around Prince William Sound on Alaska's south coast. They sought to hold Exxon Shipping, a wholly owned subsidiary of Exxon Mobil, liable for the March 24, 1989, disaster on the ground that the company was reckless in allowing Captain Joseph Hazelwood, a relapsed alcoholic, to command the supertanker with its cargo of 53 million gallons of oil. Hazelwood, who had been observed drinking heavily on the evening before the ship set sail from the port of Valdez, left the bridge with a third mate at the helm shortly before the vessel ran aground on a reef. Approximately eleven million gallons of oil spilled into the sound, fouling the waters and beaches over a six-hundred-mile area.

In a three-phase trial, a federal court jury initially found Exxon liable, then awarded compensatory damages of $287 million, and finally voted a punitive damage award of $5,000 against Hazelwood and $5 billion against Exxon.

RACKETEERING

Bridge v. Phoenix Bond & Indemnity Co. (553 U.S. _), decided by a 9–0 vote, June 9, 2008; Thomas wrote the opinion.

A plaintiff in a federal racketeering suit based on mail fraud does not have to prove that it relied on the defendant's allegedly fraudulent misrepresentations.

CHAPTER 14

General Government

General Government

Some general government issues facing the 109th and 110th Congresses raised serious questions: What level of competence should be expected from government in a time of crisis? How much does the public need to know about White House activities? How do Congress and the president reconcile budgetary realities with rival policy goals?

GOVERNMENT´S RESPONSE VERSUS PUBLIC´S FAITH

Hurricane Katrina's 140 mph winds swept away towns from western Florida to eastern Louisiana in August 2005. Widespread flooding in New Orleans, as a result of the failure of the levees, left thousands of stranded residents in need of rescue and sustenance and made refugees out of those who left the city. In the immediate aftermath of the storm, mounting chaos and despair consumed the area. As the days progressed, the region's distress turned to pointed anger over how long it took for federal, state, and local agencies to aid survivors who were injured, displaced, and without food and water. While the president and lawmakers were charged with handling recovery efforts in the wake of a devastating disaster, they subsequently were presented with a separate challenge: trying to repair the public's faith in the government's willingness and ability to care for its citizens in times of crisis.

Four years later, the American public's confidence in its federal government had not been fully restored. According to figures released in 2009 by the Greater New Orleans Community Data Center and the Metropolitan Policy Program at the Brookings Institution, New Orleans had not fully recovered. For instance, nearly 66,000 residences were unoccupied; less than 49 percent of the people in the largely African American and working-class Lower Ninth Ward were receiving mail; and just 58 percent of the $7.8 billion the Federal Emergency Management Agency (FEMA) had obligated for infrastructure repairs in Louisiana since Katrina had been paid out to localities. Moreover, it remained unknown how vulnerable the city was to future storm-related flooding or how the federal government's retooled emergency preparedness would perform in another natural disaster or terrorist act.

SECURITY VERSUS TRANSPARENCY

The reluctance of the administration of President George W. Bush to share information became the rule rather than the exception, a phenomenon that lawmakers, journalists, public interest groups, and even ordinary Americans said interfered with their ability to participate in government and to hold it accountable for its actions.

The Bush administration classified a record amount of government information—an estimated 15.6 million documents and other records in fiscal 2004 alone, according to the Information Security Oversight Office of the National Archives and Records Administration. The administration also made easier applying official secrecy to a wider range of materials. It created and expanded categories of documents that were kept secret yet were not classified, hiding them under such labels as "sensitive but unclassified" that had fewer requirements than the official classification system.

In some instances, top administration officials withheld information that had already been released in other places. Officials delayed giving information to Congress or simply withheld it, forcing lawmakers to threaten to issue

REFERENCES

Discussion of general government action for the years 1945–1964 may be found in *Congress and the Nation Vol. I,* pp. 1455–1516; for the years 1965–1968, *Congress and the Nation Vol. II,* pp. 655–660; for the years 1969–1972, *Congress and the Nation Vol. III,* pp. 435–468; for the years 1973–1976, *Congress and the Nation Vol. IV,* pp. 795–826; for the years 1977–1980, *Congress and the Nation Vol. V,* pp. 817–870; for the years 1981–1984, *Congress and the Nation Vol. VI,* pp. 771–793; for the years 1985–1988, *Congress and the Nation Vol. VII,* pp. 843–867; for the years 1989–1992, *Congress and the Nation Vol. VIII,* pp. 855–909; for the years 1993–1996, *Congress and the Nation Vol. IX,* pp. 803–858; for the years 1997–2000, *Congress and the Nation Vol. X,* pp. 733–754; for the years 2001–2004, *Congress and the Nation Vol. XI,* pp. 683–701.

Outlays for Science, Space, and General Government

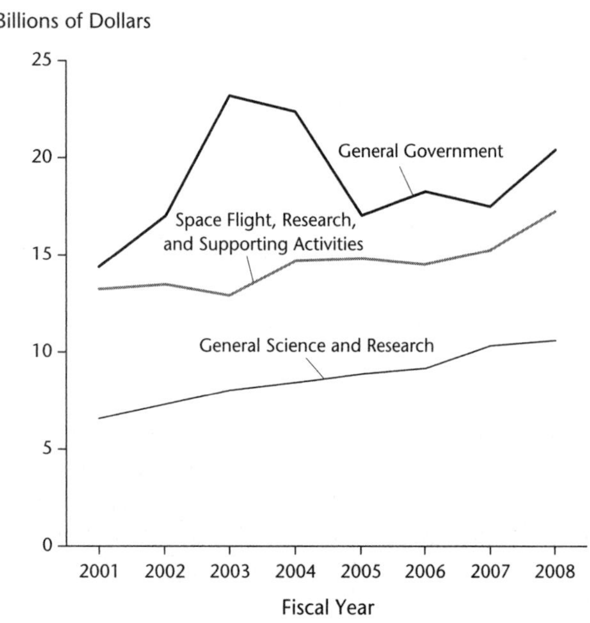

SOURCE: Office of Management and Budget, *Historical Tables, Budget of the United States Government: Fiscal Year 2010* (Washington, D.C.: U.S. Government Printing Office, 2009), Table 3.2.

subpoenas to get material that in the past would have been routinely supplied. Watchdog and journalism groups also claimed that the administration gave agencies instructions that effectively discouraged them from releasing materials under the Freedom of Information Act.

Some critics argued that such automatic secrecy was pointless because positive information got swept up along with the negative. The White House said it was seeking a balance between running the government "as openly as possible" while protecting information that could be dangerous if it were disclosed. This stance could be seen as a natural response to the Sept. 11, 2001, terrorist attacks. However, some of the documents that the Bush administration withheld seemed to have little to do with the so-called war on terrorism and much to do with keeping embarrassing information from the public.

While other presidents fought battles to prevent disclosure of information, critics contended that the Bush administration regarded secrecy as a guiding philosophy of government and that it sought no oversight for its actions. In 2008 the House passed a bill to set stricter standards for the capture, maintenance, and preservation of White House and federal agency e-mail records. Past investigations by the House Oversight and Government Reform Committee had been stymied by lost administration e-mail records. In 2007 the House passed a measure that would in effect reverse the 2001 executive order that limited access to presidential and vice-presidential papers. Both pieces of legislation died upon adjournment. Incoming president Barack Obama issued an executive order Jan. 21, 2009, revoking Bush's order regarding the disclosure of presidential papers. A future president could reverse Obama's action, however.

MOON VERSUS SCIENCE

When President Bush in 2004 announced that he wanted the National Aeronautics and Space Administration (NASA) to send astronauts back to the moon and eventually to Mars, most of the space community rallied around him, eager to have a sweeping vision for exploration after decades of space shuttle missions close to Earth. However, Bush did not call for spending significantly more money to help NASA reach its goal, instead relying on shrinking other areas of the agency's budget to make up the difference. What some considered vital scientific research programs underwent cuts, including satellites that monitored weather and climate change.

The budget trade-offs caused scientists across numerous disciplines, from earth science to aeronautics, to worry that NASA could not deliver scientific research and a moon mission. In January 2007 the National Research Council, a part of the National Academies, released a report that said NASA was "being asked to accomplish too much with too little" and called on Congress and the White House to "seriously examine the mismatch between the tasks assigned to NASA and the resources that the agency has been provided to accomplish them."

While the administration denied neglecting science, a clear gap emerged between Bush's mission and NASA's means. According to the council's report, when the administration plan was announced, science programs were estimated to grow from $5.5 billion in 2004 to about $7 billion in 2008. That did not happen. Between 2000 and 2007, according to the report, NASA's earth science budget had fallen 30 percent. Meanwhile, although lawmakers involved in science issues mostly supported the exploration plans, the new focus failed to resonate with the majority of rank-and-file members. Even the plan's strongest advocates in Congress had serious concerns about the drastic cuts to NASA's science budgets required to pay for the moon and Mars missions. These sentiments could explain Congress's action in trying to ensure, in NASA reauthorization legislation cleared in 2008, that science and aeronautics were not sacrificed for the sake of the agency's exploration goals.

Of particular concern to some scientists was the expectation that, in the short term, returning to the moon as a staging ground for a trip to Mars would result in little tangible new science data, compared with the amount of research data that would be lost from other programs that were cut. NASA disagreed, compiling a list of about 200 scientific research objectives to be achieved.

Many scientists who complained about the cuts to science were not completely dissatisfied with NASA's new exploration focus, which in many ways reinvigorated the agency's morale and provided a stirring sense of purpose for NASA. Cited as a significant benefit was retiring the costly and aging space shuttles in favor of a new vehicle able to travel beyond low Earth orbit. However, some equated the proposed permanent moon base with a form of corporate welfare for construction companies that would build it with government contract money.

Chronology of Action on General Government

2005–2006

Postal Service Overhaul

The aim of HR 6407 (PL 109-435), which President George W. bush signed into law Dec. 20, 2006, was to ensure the future solvency of the U.S. Postal Service by streamlining its operations, reducing its costs, and increasing its ability to compete. Enactment of the bill marked the first comprehensive change in the Postal Service since it was created from the former Post Office Department in 1970. The agency had been in financial decline for years in the face of competition from private carriers, increased use of e-mail, and the rising cost of employee benefits. *(1970 action, Congress and the Nation Vol. III, p. 441)*

A small cadre of lawmakers, led by Rep. John M. McHugh, R-N.Y., had pushed for more than ten years to overhaul the Postal Service's operations. These members of Congress warned that the Postal Service was falling into a "death spiral" in which declining business led to higher rates and the higher rates hurt business, particularly as cheaper forms of communication gained traction. McHugh, who represented one of the most rural districts east of the Mississippi River, saw the effort as a way to preserve "universal service" to every corner of the United States, one of the central concepts of Postal Service operations. *(108th Congress action, Congress and the Nation Vol. XI, p. 691)*

HOUSE COMMITTEE ACTION

The House Government Reform Committee by 39–0 approved the McHugh-sponsored HR 22 April 13, 2005. The legislation was formally reported (H Rept 109-66, Part I) April 28.

Before passage the panel by voice vote adopted an amendment by Steven C. LaTourette, R-Ohio, to remove a section of the bill opposed by the airlines. This part of the bill would have allowed the Postal Service to contract with foreign airlines at prices negotiated by the service. Existing law required the Transportation Department to handle such negotiations. As amended, the legislation called for the Government Accountability Office (GAO) to conduct a one-year study of the effects of changing the procedure for using foreign airlines to transport U.S. mail.

The amendment also would give the Postal Service more flexibility to award bonuses to employees and require the service to file the same public financial statements and reports required of private companies.

To give the Postal Service more flexibility, the bill would allow the service to go to an eleven-member board of governors when it wanted to propose a rate increase. The board would be able to act immediately. However, the increase could not exceed the annual change in the consumer price index, a provision intended to ensure rate stability and predictability for consumers. Under existing law, the service had to get permission for a postage rate increase from the Postal Rate Commission—a process that could take more than a year.

HR 22 also would reconstitute that commission as the Postal Regulatory Commission with power to ensure that postal rates were properly set and that the Postal Service engaged in fair competition and thorough disclosure. The regulatory commission would have the authority to issue subpoenas and fines.

The measure introduced the concept of "pay for performance" into the Postal Service, which under existing law could not pay its top officials more than the government-capped salary for cabinet secretaries. The committee-approved HR 22 would allow the Postal Service to hire executives with salaries above that cap.

To help the Postal Service compete with the private sector, the legislation would allow it to give discounts to businesses that helped move bulk mail.

HOUSE FLOOR ACTION

The full House passed HR 22 by a 410–20 vote July 26. The same day, the White House threatened to veto the bill over two provisions it said would have an adverse effect on the federal budget. The first would eliminate a requirement that the Postal Service set aside $3 billion a year in an escrow account to cover retiree health benefits. The legislation would allow the agency to use part of the money for operations, thereby avoiding the need to raise the price of postage in the short term to help cover day-to-day expenses. The second would make the Treasury, instead of the Postal Service, responsible for a $27 billion liability for benefits to military retirees who were Postal Service employees. The liability had been transferred from Treasury to the Postal Service in 2003 (PL 108-18). Leaving the pension responsibility with the Postal Service had the added effect of keeping the expenses off-budget and thus not counting them toward the deficit.

On July 26, the House rejected by voice vote an attempt by Jeb Hensarling, R-Texas, to remove the provisions that were opposed by the White House. His amendment would require that all of the $3 billion in escrow be used to cover the Postal Service's unfunded health care liability. The amendment also would strike the language permitting the Postal Service to shift $27 billion in pension benefits to the Treasury. The same day the House rejected, 82–345, an amendment offered by Mike Pence, R-Ind., to strike a provision that would alter the composition of the board of governors. The existing board was made up of nine presidential appointees, the postmaster general, and the deputy postmaster general. The bill would substitute a labor union representative for one of the appointees. The House also on July 26 rejected an amendment offered by Jeff Flake, R-Ariz., 51–379, to create pilot programs for up to twenty communities to determine the feasibility of alternative mail delivery services.

SENATE COMMITTEE ACTION

The Senate Homeland Security and Governmental Affairs Committee had approved S 662 by 15–1 on June 22 (no written report). The bill would streamline the process for setting postal rates, linking them to the consumer price index to allow the Postal Service to respond more quickly to changes in the market. It would grant a new Postal Regulatory Commission the power to institute emergency price increases in the event of "unexpected and extraordinary circumstances," such as the 2001 anthrax attacks.

The panel gave voice approval to an amendment, offered by committee chair Susan Collins, R-Maine, to strike the foreign airline provisions that were dropped from HR 22.

FINAL ACTION

The bill did not reach the Senate floor until early in the next year. The Senate passed HR 22 by voice vote Feb. 9, 2006, after substituting the language of S 662. As the end of the 109th Congress approached, it seemed likely that the legislation would meet a fate similar to past efforts. However, McHugh, together with a bipartisan group of members from both chambers, managed to reconcile House and Senate differences and, more important, to reach an agreement with the White House that allowed the overhaul to move forward.

House Government Reform Committee chairman Thomas M. Davis III, R-Va., introduced a compromise bill (HR 6407) Dec. 7. The next day the House agreed by voice vote to a Davis motion to suspend the rules and pass the bill. The Senate acted by voice vote Dec. 9, clearing the measure for the president's signature.

MAJOR PROVISIONS

Postal Regulatory Commission. HR 6407 created a new Postal Regulatory Commission with much broader regulatory and oversight authority than the existing Postal Rate Commission, including the ability to set rates for mail and prices for Postal Service products that competed with those offered by private delivery companies such as FedEx Corp. and United Parcel Service.

The new commission also had the authority to issue subpoenas, develop and implement rules and regulations, and set its own budget. It was to consist of five members appointed by the president to six-year terms, subject to Senate confirmation.

Regulating rates. The bill established separate systems for market-dominated products and competitive products.

The commission was given eighteen months to design a new system of rate regulation in areas in which the Postal Service had a monopoly or clearly dominated the market. The market-dominated products, such as first-class mail, periodicals, and standard mail, accounted for about 90 percent of the Postal Service's revenue. The goals of the new system included fostering efficiency, maintaining high standards of service, covering costs, and not allowing rates to increase faster than the rate of inflation.

Within eighteen months, the commission was to issue regulations to ensure that competitive products, such as express and priority mail, expedited mail, and bulk international mail, were not subsidized by revenue from market-dominated products and that each product covered its own costs. Once the commission issued its regulations, the Postal Service would have pricing flexibility somewhat comparable to that exercised by private competitors.

Work-share discounts. The legislation allowed discounts to private mailers that did part of the work by presorting, pre–bar-coding, handling, or transporting mail.

Pension benefits. The Treasury Department was required to resume responsibility for paying the costs of benefits for military retirees who were Postal Service employees. The bill eliminated the requirement that the Postal Service place its retirement fund savings in an escrow account.

Health care benefits. The bill created a Postal Service Retiree Health Benefits Fund and required that, beginning in 2006, the Postal Service pay into the fund the projected retirement health care costs for its current employees. Previously, it had paid a portion of health care premiums for retirees who participated in the Federal Employee Health Benefits Program. The Postal Service was to pay for retirees' health benefits from the fund as soon as enough money had accrued. Also, any excess funds remaining in the Postal Service's escrow account would be transferred to the health benefit fund.

Business model. The measure directed the comptroller general to appoint an "expert research organization" to evaluate which business model would best enable efficiency, reliability, and innovation in the Postal Service and to report to the president and Congress within fifteen months of enactment. The report was to assess the costs, benefits, and options both of maintaining the Postal Service in its existing form and of transforming it into a corporation that was wholly or partly owned by private shareholders.

NASA Reauthorization

Congress in 2005 cleared a bill (S 1281—PL 109-155) reauthorizing $17.9 billion in fiscal 2007 and $18.7 billion in fiscal 2008 for the National Aeronautics and Space Administration (NASA). *(110th Congress action, p. 797)*

Lawmakers had not enacted NASA reauthorization legislation since 2000 (PL 106-391), relying instead on authorizing language in annual appropriations bills. Authorizers sought to pass a stand-alone bill in light of the many challenges facing NASA, perhaps most significantly the debate about how and when to retire the decades-old space shuttle fleet. NASA also had to contend with budget cuts while trying to complete expensive infrastructure repairs. *(2000 action, Congress and the Nation Vol. X, p. 752)*

The Senate bill (S 1281) endorsed President George W. Bush's plan to send astronauts back to the moon and to Mars, directed NASA to continue work on the International Space Station, urged a shuttle mission to repair the Hubble Space Telescope if it could be conducted safely, and required NASA to dedicate 15 percent of its funding for space station research to subjects not related to human space exploration.

Bush's plan to return astronauts to the moon in preparation for a mission to Mars called for the space shuttle fleet to be retired in 2010 and for a new vehicle to be operational by 2014. The four-year gap in U.S. ability to send humans into space was partly responsible for scuttling a NASA authorization bill in the 108th Congress. Many lawmakers were loath to rely on Russia to get U.S. astronauts to and from the International Space Station. *(108th Congress action, Congress and the Nation Vol. VI, p. 694)*

HOUSE ACTION

The House Science Committee on July 14, 2005, approved HR 3070, which recommended $33.4 billion for NASA for fiscal 2006 and fiscal 2007. The bill was formally reported July 18 (H Rept 109-173). It encouraged, but did not require, a new space vehicle to be operational as close as possible to the shuttle fleet's scheduled retirement in 2010. Democrats were unsuccessful in winning language to prohibit NASA from grounding the shuttle fleet until a new spacecraft was ready to launch.

However, they were able to win a two-year authorization in place of the one-year, $16.5 billion reauthorization approved by the panel's Space and Aeronautics Subcommittee. That panel had approved its draft, 10–0, June 29. Full committee action came as part of an amendment, offered by Chairman Sherwood Boehlert, R-N.Y., that was adopted by voice vote.

The committee rejected, 18–18, an amendment by Jerry F. Costello, D-Ill., to strike language allowing NASA to outsource certain federal jobs. Instead, the committee gave voice approval to an amendment that would require NASA to report on contracts performed overseas and on the purchases NASA made from foreign entities.

HR 3070 required that several policies and strategies be included with NASA's budget requests for fiscal 2007, including a national aeronautics policy and a science policy to direct programs through 2020. The bill called for NASA to set a schedule for a shuttle mission to fix the ailing Hubble Space Telescope.

Lawmakers avoided addressing the problem of how the United States would pay Russia in the event that American astronauts had to hitch rides on its spacecraft past 2006. The Iran Nonproliferation Act (PL 106-178) banned U.S. payments to Russia in connection with the International Space Station, creating logistical problems for NASA. *(Space travel, p. 787)*

The full House passed HR 3070 by a 383–15 vote July 22, 2005, after adopting an amendment requested by the White House to boost the bill's space exploration funding by at least $1.3 billion. The House also gave voice approval to a manager's amendment to increase the exploration systems account to $8.4 billion—a move that Boehlert said was necessary to garner administration support for the legislation. The extra money brought the bill's total to about $34.7 billion.

SENATE ACTION

The Senate Commerce, Science, and Transportation Committee by voice vote June 23, 2005, approved S 1281, an $87.7 billion, five-year NASA authorization bill. The legislation, which was formally reported (S Rept 109-108) July 26, authorized $16.6 billion in fiscal 2006, rising to $18.5 billion in fiscal 2010.

The panel tacitly accepted Bush's plan to retire the space shuttle, but not before another vehicle was ready to replace it. The committee report said it was the intent of Congress "that there be no gap in the nation's ability to transport humans into space."

The committee also differed with the White House on the types of research that would be performed on the space shuttle. Bush wanted to restrict space station research to projects that supported space exploration. S 1281 proposed to retain that emphasis but designate the space station as a national laboratory, which would expand the types of research that could be conducted on board. Like the House-passed HR 3070, the Senate measure required that the agency set a schedule for a shuttle mission to repair the Hubble Space Telescope.

The full Senate passed S 1281 by voice vote Sept. 28, after adopting, also by voice vote, a manager's amendment that included language modifying the directive on retiring the space shuttle to encourage, but not require, NASA to keep it going until a new vehicle to carry astronauts into space was operational.

The manager's amendment, offered by Kay Bailey Hutchison, R-Texas, chair of the Senate Commerce Committee's Science and Space Subcommittee, required NASA to keep Congress informed on its progress and to give lawmakers a one-year notice if a replacement vehicle would not be ready before the final shuttle flight. NASA would have to report on the strategic risks associated with the gap, the estimated length of time during which the United States would not have independent human access to space, the steps that would be taken to shorten that length of time, and what other means would be used to allow human access to space during that period.

FINAL ACTION

In preparation for conference, the House passed S 1281 by voice vote Nov. 18, after substituting the text of HR 3070. The House-Senate conference was relatively smooth, and a conference agreement was reached Dec. 15 with bipartisan support. The House agreed to a Boehlert motion to suspend the rules and adopt the conference report on S 1281 (H Rept 109-354) by voice vote Dec. 17. The Senate adopted the conference report by voice vote Dec. 22, completing congressional action. While largely endorsing Bush's blueprint for manned space exploration, the conference report included a number of directives requiring NASA to report to Congress on its progress toward meeting its space exploration goals.

The president signed S 1281 (PL 109-155) into law Dec. 30, 2005. While the law did not set a specific date for retiring the shuttle fleet, it encouraged NASA to wait until a new vehicle that could transport humans was functional. NASA would have to report to Congress on any gap in the time the shuttle program retired and a new vehicle was ready. NASA had said it planned to have a new space vehicle operational by 2012, reducing to two years the gap in the ability to launch humans into space.

The new law also directed NASA to send Congress a schedule for dispatching a crew to repair the Hubble Space Telescope, providing the mission could be carried out safely. Without repairs, the telescope would fail when its gyroscopes and batteries wore out. The law stated the sense of Congress that the Hubble Space Telescope "is an extraordinary instrument that has provided, and should continue to provide, answers to profound scientific questions."

Space Travel

Congress in 2005 cleared legislation (S 1713) to allow the United States to pay Russia for ferrying U.S. astronauts to the International Space Station, solving a major problem for the National Aeronautics and Space Administration (NASA). It also served as a vehicle to broaden sanctions against Iran and apply them to Syria as well.

The 2000 Iran Nonproliferation Act (PL 106-178) barred U.S. payments to Russia in connection with the International Space Station unless the president certified that Moscow was not helping Iran gain access to nuclear materials or other weapons of mass destruction. But the United States needed transportation on the Russian *Soyuz* to get to and from the space station, especially after 2010. NASA was planning to retire the space shuttle fleet in that year, but it did not expect to have a new vehicle ready for use before 2012.

S 1713 essentially allowed NASA to ignore the Iran Nonproliferation Act for the purpose of sending astronauts to the space station until 2012.

The Senate passed S 1713 by voice vote Sept. 21, 2005. The House agreed to suspend the rules and pass the measure by voice vote Oct. 26, after adding a section that expanded the sanctions in the Iran Nonproliferation Act. The sanctions originally applied to countries or companies that supplied materials, technology, or services that helped Iran develop weapons of mass destruction. The amendment extended the sanctions to Syria and applied them to imports as well as exports of goods and services related to weapons of mass destruction. *(Sanctions legislation, p. 301)*

The Senate accepted the House changes Nov. 8, clearing the bill. The president signed S 1713 (PL 109-112) into law Nov. 22, 2005.

Hurricane Response Inquiries

Both chambers conducted inquiries into the government's response to Hurricane Katrina. *(Legislative action, box, p. 788; lessons learned, box, p. 790)*

HOUSE INVESTIGATION

A select Republican-dominated House committee, chaired by Thomas M. Davis III, R-Va., issued a report Feb. 15, 2006, assessing blame at the local, state, and federal levels.

The panel concluded that the White House should have realized Aug. 29, 2005, the day the storm made landfall, that the levees had broken, causing flooding that did the majority of the damage. Instead, the Bush administration discounted some of the information it received. The committee said the administration was hampered in assessing the response of the president and top aides with him at the time at his ranch in Crawford, Texas, because the White

SWIRL OF LEGISLATIVE ACTIVITY IN THE AFTERMATH OF GULF COAST HURRICANES

The hurricanes that battered the Gulf Coast region in 2005 prompted Congress to enact a range of disaster-related legislation.

109th Congress

Relief and cleanup. In the aftermath of Hurricane Katrina, Congress cleared a pair of emergency supplemental appropriations bills (HR 3645—PL 109-61; HR 3673—PL 109-62) totaling $62.3 billion to begin paying for relief and cleanup. *(Supplementals, p. 79)*

FEMA borrowing authority. As signed into law in 2005, HR 3669 (PL 109-65) granted an additional $2 billion in borrowing authority to the Federal Emergency Management Agency (FEMA) so that the agency could pay for the flood insurance claims expected from Katrina.

Student aid. Two bills (HR 3169—PL 109-66; HR 3668—PL 109-67), signed into law in 2005, waived repayment requirements for displaced college students who received aid. *(Details, p. 608)*

Welfare assistance. Enacted in 2005, HR 3672 (PL 109-68) was intended to make it easier for hurricane survivors to obtain cash assistance grants through the Temporary Assistance for Needy Families program.

Temporary work and training. HR 3761, enacted in 2005 (PL 109-72), made changes to the Labor Department's National Emergency Grants program, which provided disaster relief and training for up to six months to those who took part in projects assisting disaster victims. The program was authorized for employment projects located outside an area designated as a natural disaster area.

Tax relief. Congress in 2005 cleared two bills providing tax relief to the victims of hurricanes Katrina, Rita, and Wilma. HR 3768 (PL 109-73) was a $6.1 billion package of tax breaks aimed at individuals and corporations in the hurricane-ravaged Gulf Coast region. HR 4440 (PL 109-135) provided $7.8 billion in tax incentives to encourage investment in the hurricane disaster areas. *(Details, p. 80)*

Student loans. Congress in 2005 cleared HR 2132 (PL 109-78), to authorize the secretary of education to waive student loan and aid regulations during a war or national emergency. *(Details, p. 607)*

Vocational rehabilitation services. Enacted in 2005, HR 3864 (PL 109-82) gave preferences to hurricane-affected states in receiving additional funds from the Rehabilitation Services Administration.

Campus-based aid. Enacted in 2005, HR 3863 (PL 109-86) provided that the secretary of education could waive financial rules for campus-based aid programs at colleges in areas of natural disasters. *(Details, p. 607)*

Community disaster loans. Congress in 2005 cleared S 1858 (PL 109-88), providing $750 million for a program to loan money to local governments to maintain services such as police and fire protection in the aftermath of hurricanes Katrina and Rita.

Coast Guard's Deepwater. The Coast Guard's well-regarded performance during Katrina search-and-rescue operations persuaded lawmakers to include $933 million in the fiscal 2006 Homeland Security appropriations bill (HR 2360—PL 109-90) for Deepwater, the Coast Guard program to replace its aging ships, aircraft, and communications systems. Conferees on HR 2360 added language requiring the administration to detail credit card expenditures, contracting agreements, and other Katrina-related costs not previously required in its weekly reports to Congress.

Local projects. HR 2419 (PL 109-103), the fiscal 2006 appropriations bill for energy and water development, provided $5.4 billion for the Army Corps of Engineers, including hundreds of millions of dollars in earmarks for popular local projects such as river restoration and flood protection.

Business, housing, and development aid. During consideration of the fiscal 2006 appropriations measure for Commerce, Justice, and State (HR 2862—PL 109-108), the Senate adopted an amendment offered by Olympia J. Snowe, R-Maine, to supply $595 million in emergency disaster aid to Hurricane Katrina victims through modified Small Business Administration programs for business owners, homeowners, and renters. The chamber adopted an amendment offered by Paul S. Sarbanes, D-Md., to make federal rent assistance available to Katrina evacuees. HR 2862 appropriated $3.5 billion for the program. The government would cover all of the housing costs—including utilities, relocation, and security deposits—for families until their income was restored. The Senate also adopted an amendment offered by Max Baucus, D-Mont., to allow spending totaling $210 million for economic development activity in areas affected by the hurricane. *(Fiscal 2006 appropriations, pp. 76, 352)*

Micropurchase charges. During consideration of HR 3058 (PL 109-115), fiscal 2006 appropriations for Transportation, Treasury, and Housing and Urban Development, the Senate adopted an amendment by Susan Collins, R-Maine, to repeal a provision in hurricane supplemental appropriations legislation (HR 3673) that increased the amount federal employees could charge on government credit cards for micropurchases from $2,500 to $250,000. The Office of Management and Budget already had instructed federal employees to ignore the controversial increase and keep the previous $2,500 cap.

Emergency disaster assistance. Fiscal 2006 Defense appropriations legislation (HR 2863—PL 109-148) provided $29 billion in emergency supplemental spending for disaster assistance to areas along the Gulf Coast affected by hurricanes Katrina and Rita. The emergency funding included $11.5 billion for Community Development Block Grants, $2.9 billion for the Army Corps of Engineers, $4.4 billion for the Defense Department, and $2.8 billion for emergency repairs to highways, roads, and bridges.

Medicaid. In the 2005 budget reconciliation bill (S 1932—PL 109-171), Congress appropriated $2.1 billion to be used by the secretary of health and human services to help with health care costs for residents of states evacuated because of Hurricane Katrina. *(Details, p. 535)*

Digital TV conversion. In 2005 budget reconciliation legislation (S 1932—PL 109-171), Congress set a deadline for broadcast television to convert to digital broadcasts and required some of the freed-up analog frequencies to be allocated to emergency responders. Katrina had highlighted weaknesses in emergency communications systems that prevented first-responders from talking with one another. *(Details, p. 419)*

Higher education relief. Contained in 2005 budget reconciliation legislation (S 1932—PL 109-171) was relief for student loan borrowers and institutions of higher education that were adversely affected by hurricanes Katrina and Rita. *(Details, pp. 81, 602)*

Unemployment benefits. S 1777, cleared in 2006 (PL 109-176), extended the limit on disaster unemployment benefits and lengthened the period in which jobless workers could apply for assistance. The measure would help small business owners who would not typically need unemployment insurance but for losing their businesses in the hurricanes. *(Details, p. 667)*

Hurricane recovery. A fiscal 2006 wartime supplemental appropriations bill (HR 4939—PL 109-234) providing an infusion of money for military operations in Iraq and Afghanistan included additional funds for hurricane recovery in the Gulf Coast region. The final bill provided $6 billion for the FEMA disaster relief fund; $5.2 billion for Community Development Block Grants for the region; $3.7 billion for levee repair and flood control; $1.2 billion to pay for hurricane damage to Defense Department facilities and equipment; $542 million for assistance to small businesses; $285 million for education assistance; $775 million for hurricane-related damage to shipbuilding programs; and $118 million for cleanup and restoration of Gulf Coast fisheries.

Coast Guard reauthorization. The fiscal 2006 Coast Guard reauthorization bill (HR 889—PL 109-241) included $300 million in supplemental funding for operations and fuel costs associated with Hurricane Katrina, preserved annual leave for employees involved in Katrina response, and temporarily extended the expiration date of merchant marine licenses and vessel inspection certifications that were lost or damaged during Katrina and Rita. *(Details, p. 228)*

FEMA restructuring. The fiscal 2007 Homeland Security appropriations bill (HR 5441—PL 109-295) included language restructuring FEMA while keeping it within the Department of Homeland Security. The Senate adopted a Collins amendment to restore FEMA's role in preparing for disasters and give it more autonomy within Homeland Security. The amendment's language reflected many of the changes proposed in a stand-alone measure (S 3595) introduced by Collins and Trent Lott, R-Miss., which drew on the recommendations of a report issued by the Collins-chaired Homeland Security and Governmental Affairs Committee. *(Details, pp. 102, 236)*

During consideration of HR 5441, the Senate also adopted an amendment by David Vitter, R-La., to bar law enforcement agencies from using funds in the legislation to seize lawfully owned firearms during a state of emergency. More than 1,000 firearms had been confiscated in the aftermath of Katrina.

Waterway navigation and flood control. The House-passed HR 5427, the fiscal 2007 Department of Energy water resources appropriations measure, provided $5 billion, and the Senate Appropriations Committee–approved version offered $5.1 billion for waterway navigation and flood control projects carried out by the Army Corps of Engineers. The provisions were folded into a stopgap funding measure (H J Res 102—PL 109-383), which made funding available through Feb. 15, 2007, at the lower of the House-passed or fiscal 2006 levels. *(Fiscal 2007 appropriations, p. 105)*

Bioterrorism. The inadequate and chaotic local, state, and federal responses to Hurricane Katrina served, in part, to prompt action in 2006 on legislation (S 3678—PL 109-417) to strengthen the nation's capacity to prepare for potential bioterrorism attacks and pandemic diseases. *(Details, p. 226)*

Offshore drilling. Support for new offshore drilling increased following sharp hikes in energy prices in 2005 after hurricanes Katrina and Rita knocked out energy infrastructure in the Gulf Coast, and again in spring 2006. A tax and trade package (HR 6111), enacted in 2006 (PL 109-432), opened 8.3 million acres south of the Florida panhandle in the Gulf of Mexico to drilling. *(Details, pp. 105, 471)*

110th Congress

Recovery programs. A fiscal 2007 emergency appropriations bill (HR 2206—PL 110-28) for the wars in Iraq and Afghanistan included $6.3 billion for hurricane recovery programs in the Gulf Coast area. HR 2206 also provided an extension of low-income housing credits, special small business expensing rules, and other tax relief for Gulf Coast areas affected by 2005 hurricanes. *(Supplemental, pp. 117, 383)*

Water resources. Congress in 2007 overrode President George W. Bush's veto of a water resources bill (HR 1495—PL 110-114), which contained an authorization of $1.9 billion for restoration of the hurricane-damaged Louisiana coastal area. *(Details, p. 500)*

Housing assistance. Tucked into the fiscal 2008 Defense appropriations bill (HR 3222—PL 110-116) was a fiscal 2007 continuing resolution funding the government through Dec. 14, 2007. It provided emergency appropriations of $3 billion to assist housing for victims of hurricanes Katrina and Rita and $2.9 billion for FEMA. *(Continuing resolution, pp. 116, 380)*

Acting FEMA director David Paulison appears before the Senate Homeland Security and Governmental Affairs Committee on October 6, 2005, to study the disaster relief and response efforts following Hurricane Katrina. Left to right are Paulison, Sen. Carl Levin, D-Mich., Sen. Joseph Lieberman, D-Conn., and Sen. Susan Collins, R-Maine.
Source: AP Photo/Dennis Cook

House refused to turn over e-mails and other data the panel had requested.

The panel said that the secretary of the Homeland Security Department, Michael Chertoff, should have declared Katrina an "incident of national significance" at least two days prior to landfall, when the National Weather Service predicted a Category 4 or 5 hurricane would strike New Orleans. Doing so would have sped the deployment of federal resources to the region. The committee also said Chertoff should not have sent Federal Emergency Management Agency (FEMA) director Michael D. Brown to serve as the "principal federal official" at the disaster scene. Instead, he should have picked someone who had undergone the required training. Before landfall, Chertoff should have convened an interagency group to examine the potential consequences of Katrina. He lacked the disaster experience to provide "adequate advice and counsel" to the White House, the report concluded.

The panel also pointed out that a slow exodus of senior FEMA employees had left the agency and the Homeland Security Department without "adequate trained and experienced staff for the Katrina response." The lack of readiness of the agency's national emergency teams hindered the federal response, the committee said.

The panel found that local and state officials failed in aspects of the hurricane response. While the evacuation of the general population went well, later mandatory evacuations by local officials led to unnecessary deaths. Overhyped proclamations by local officials about the extent of the disaster and the chaos in New Orleans, widely publicized by the media, delayed the arrival of relief teams because of fears for their safety, according to the report.

Democrats had boycotted the House panel, pressing instead for an independent investigation. After the report's release, the Democrats again expressed their desire for an independent investigation because, they said, the panel failed to gain possession of important White House documents. They also called on Chertoff to step down as head of Homeland Security.

SENATE INQUIRY

The Senate Homeland Security and Governmental Affairs Committee, chaired by Susan Collins, R-Maine, conducted a seven-month investigation into the government's response to Hurricane Katrina. The panel released its list of eighty-six recommendations on April 27, 2006.

At the top of that list was the creation of a National Preparedness and Response Authority within the Department of Homeland Security to replace FEMA. The proposed new structure would reunite emergency preparedness and response functions. Homeland Security head Chertoff in 2005 had split the two functions in a departmental reorganization.

The panel did not advocate taking FEMA out of the department. Collins and Joseph I. Lieberman of Connecticut, ranking Democrat on the panel, said they thought an independent FEMA would create overlapping and redundant response agencies, because most proposals for removing FEMA would limit its authority to natural disasters and leave terrorism incidents to the Department of Homeland Security.

In addressing the issue of preparedness, the panel also called for the enhancement of regional operations to provide better coordination between federal agencies and states; the establishment of regional strike teams; the creation of a National Operations Center to communicate with and coordinate various government agencies before, during, and in the wake of a disaster; the provision of enough resources and funding to ensure that the new

LESSONS LEARNED FROM HURRICANE KATRINA

On Feb. 23, 2006, the administration of President George W. Bush issued a 228-page report outlining lessons learned from Hurricane Katrina and making recommendations for governmental change. The president's homeland security adviser Frances Fragos Townsend had led the internal administrative review, which largely did not seek to assign blame for hurricane response problems.

Some recommendations would require legislation, new agency offices or positions, or additional funding. Included in the report were proposals to:

- Amend the Robert T. Stafford Disaster Relief and Emergency Assistance Act (PL 93-288) to require states to meet certain basic standards, such as having mass evacuation plans, to receive federal reimbursement. *(PL 93-288, Congress and the Nation Vol. IV, p. 147)*
- Authorize the Federal Emergency Management Agency (FEMA) to reimburse certain rental fees, such as security deposits, utilities, and repairs, to existing federal housing.
- Transfer the National Disaster Medical System from the Department of Homeland Security back to the Department of Health and Human Services, reversing a shift ordered when the Department of Homeland Security was established in 2002 (PL 107-296). *(PL 107-296, Congress and the Nation Vol. XI, p. 176)*
- Create new positions and offices within the Department of Homeland Security to improve emergency preparedness.
- Create a single National Operations Center within the Department of Homeland Security that would consolidate existing emergency centers.
- Issue to each state, beginning in fiscal 2007, a report card that would track how well homeland security dollars were being spent. If states were not using the money effectively, the grants would be reduced or eliminated.

response agency, and other federal agencies with disaster-related responsibilities, could be effective; and the development of clear operational plans and training programs and the requirement that the Department of Homeland Security work with federal and regional agencies and states to ensure that they are aware of the plans and are well trained in their details and execution.

HURRICANE RESPONSE OVERSIGHT

In related action, on Sept. 15, 2005, the House approved, 224–188, H Res 437 (H Rept 109-220, Part I), to establish the Select Bipartisan Committee to Investigate the Preparation for and Response to Hurricane Katrina. The resolution saw no further action.

Demands by Democrats for an independent investigation into the federal government's widely criticized response to the catastrophe that followed Hurricane Katrina in New Orleans and along the Gulf Coast went nowhere in the face of opposition from congressional Republicans and the White House.

National Flood Insurance

Legislation to overhaul the federal flood insurance program passed in the House (HR 4973) and was reported from the Senate Banking, Housing, and Urban Affairs Committee (S 3589) in 2006 but could not overcome the opposition of Louisiana's two senators, who saw it as onerous for flood-prone regions and blocked action in their chamber. Efforts to pass flood insurance program legislation also failed in the 110th Congress. *(110th Congress action, p. 797)*

The National Flood Insurance Program, created by Congress in 1968 (PL 90-448), offered government-backed insurance to about 5.1 million homeowners, renters, and businesses. To be eligible, the property had to be in one of the more than 20,000 communities that participated in the program by agreeing to enforce regulations for land use and new construction in high-risk flood zones. The program carried about $950 billion in risk exposure. Liability was capped at $250,000 for residential property and $500,000 for commercial property. Congress had reauthorized the program through fiscal 2008 under 2004 legislation (PL 108-264). *(1968 act, Congress and the Nation Vol. II, p. 968; 2004 act, Congress and the Nation Vol. XI, p. 693)*

The National Flood Insurance Program was designed to be funded by premiums, but the program had to borrow billions of dollars from the Treasury to pay the record claims stemming from the 2005 Gulf Coast hurricanes. Officials estimated that when all the claims from those storms and subsequent floods were tallied, the program's shortfall would be as much as $25 billion—more than the total claims since the program was established.

The catastrophic losses led Congress to increase the program's statutory borrowing limits three times, from $1.5 billion before Hurricane Katrina to a temporary level of $3.5 billion, then to $18.5 billion, and finally to $20.8 billion in March 2006 (PL 108-208).

HOUSE ACTION

The House Financial Services Committee approved a flood insurance bill (HR 4973) by voice vote March 16, 2006. As formally reported (H Rept 109-410) April 6, the measure, sponsored by Richard H. Baker, R-La., would:

- Phase out subsidized insurance premiums for vacation homes, second homes, and commercial properties. Subsidies on primary residences would be phased out when the homes were sold.
- Allow premiums to rise by as much as 15 percent a year until they reflected the risk of flooding for covered properties.
- Increase the program's borrowing authority to $25 billion, the amount needed to fully pay claims from hurricanes Katrina, Rita, and Wilma and to cover related expenses.
- Introduce new categories of optional coverage, such as business interruption and additional living expenses.
- Increase maximum coverage limits for residential properties to $335,000 from $250,000 and for commercial properties to $670,000 from $500,000.

The committee rejected, 10–45, an amendment offered by Jeb Hensarling, R-Texas, to require the immediate elimination of all subsidies in the program. Hensarling, a leader of the conservative Republican Study Committee, urged Congress to reduce the potential risk to taxpayers that he said the program posed.

On June 27, before passing HR 4973 by 416–4, the full House rejected, 76–347, an amendment by Steve Pearce, R-N.M., to speed up the ending of subsidies for nonprimary residences and commercial properties. The House also adopted, by voice vote, an amendment by Scott Garrett, R-N.J., to add primary residences to the subsidy phase-out list when they were sold and an amendment by Gene Taylor, D-Miss., to require the Department of Homeland Security's inspector general to investigate whether private insurers who administered the program had improperly attributed damage to flooding, which the federal government covered, instead of to wind, which insurers would have covered.

SENATE ACTION

On May 25, 2006, the Senate Banking, Housing, and Urban Affairs Committee, by a 20—0 vote, had approved S 3589, sponsored by Chairman Richard C. Shelby, R-Ala. The bill was formally reported (S Rept 109-271) June 28. The measure would:

- Phase out subsidies on second homes, businesses, and properties that had been flooded repeatedly or severely.
- Direct the Federal Emergency Management Agency, which administered the program, to update flood maps.
- Create a reserve fund to help the program survive catastrophic years such as 2005.
- Direct state-regulated financial institutions to require mortgage holders in flood zones to buy flood insurance by 2009. Under existing law, that requirement applied only to federally chartered institutions.
- Forgive the programs existing debt and allow it to borrow additional funds to cover costs from the 2005 hurricanes.

Experts said S 3589 would have moved the program more quickly toward actuarial soundness by mandating more accurate flood maps and ensuring that premiums reflected the risk of catastrophic years. Home builders and mortgage lenders preferred HR 4973's approach, which would have increased coverage limits and added lines of coverage at actuarial rates. They said the Senate bill might make coverage too costly for people living in flood-prone areas, a concern shared by Louisiana's senators, Democrat Mary L. Landrieu and Republican David Vitter, who placed formal holds that prevented the legislation from reaching the Senate floor. No further action was taken on either the House or Senate measure.

Flood Insurance Grants

In June 2004 the Internal Revenue Service (IRS) ruled that Federal Emergency Management Agency (FEMA) disaster mitigation grants not tied to a specific natural disaster must be reported as income for tax purposes. The IRS ruling was directed at grants for property improvements to prevent future or repetitive damage from floods, hurricanes, tornadoes, and other natural disasters. According to critics, however, the IRS ruling created an unintended consequence—causing some grant recipients to lose eligibility for means-tested programs, such as food stamps and Medicaid.

Republican Richard H. Baker sponsored HR 804 to provide that National Flood Insurance Program grants could not be considered as income by federal agencies other than the IRS. Baker, who represented a flood-prone district in Louisiana, sought to clarify flood insurance legislation (PL 108-264) that was intended to reduce the number of homeowners filing repetitive claims. *(2004 law, Congress and the Nation Vol. XI, p. 693)*

The House Financial Services Committee approved HR 804 by voice vote March 16 and formally reported it (H Rept 109-44) April 14. The full House by voice vote July 12 agreed to a Baker motion to suspend the rules and pass the bill. The Senate Banking, Housing, and Urban Affairs Committee reported an unamended version (no written report) of HR 804 on July 29, and the Senate passed the measure by voice vote Sept. 8, completing congressional action. President George W. Bush signed HR 804 (PL 109-64) into law Sept. 20, 2005.

Bush, in time for the tax-filing deadline, also signed separate legislation (HR 1134—PL 109-7) April 15, 2005, to prevent disaster mitigation payments for floods and other natural disasters from being counted as income by the IRS.

Flood Insurance Funding

Congress in 2005 cleared legislation (HR 4133) to increase the borrowing authority for the National Flood Insurance Program, which had used up its funds paying off hurricane-related claims. The House Financial Services Committee approved HR 4133 by voice vote Oct. 28 and formally reported it (H Rept 109-274) Nov. 7. The House Nov. 16 agreed by voice vote to a motion by Bob Ney, R-Ohio, to suspend the rules and pass the bill. The Senate passed the measure by voice vote Nov. 18, and the House accepted the Senate changes the same day. President George W. Bush signed the bill into law (PL 109-106) Nov. 21.

HR 4133 would increase to $18.5 billion from $3.5 billion the money available to the Federal Emergency Management Agency (FEMA) to borrow from the Treasury to pay flood insurance claims. Congressional action came after FEMA was forced to stop paying claims to homeowners because its flood insurance fund ran out of money following the huge damages of hurricanes Katrina, Rita, and Wilma.

Congress had given FEMA a small boost to its borrowing authority in HR 3669 (PL 109-65), which increased to $3.5 billion from $1.5 billion the amount it could borrow to pay flood claims. The House had agreed, 416–0, Sept. 8, 2005, to a Ney motion to suspend the rules and pass the bill. The Senate passed HR 3669 without amendment by voice vote Sept. 12. The president signed the measure Sept. 20. According to FEMA, the money represented only a small percentage of the $23 billion in claims that the agency expected from the three hurricanes.

The House Financial Services Committee Nov. 16 approved a bill (HR 4320) that would increase FEMA's borrowing authority to $22 billion. The measure also would increase coverage limits for flood insurance and make other changes intended to boost protections for the flood program. HR 4320 was formally reported (H Rept 109-370) Feb. 1, 2006, but saw no further action.

"Leave Bank" Program

The 109th Congress passed legislation (S 1736) that allows judicial branch employees to participate in a "leave bank" program, which assisted government workers struck by a disaster. The measure, sponsored by Susan Collins, R-Maine, allows employees to donate unused annual leave to a pool that could be tapped by employees who must miss work because of a disaster.

The Senate Homeland Security and Governmental Affairs Committee approved the bill by voice vote Sept. 22, 2005. The Senate passed the bill by voice vote Oct. 19. A written report (S Rept 109-158) was filed the next day. The House Government Reform Committee approved S 1736 by voice vote March 9, 2006, and formally reported it (H Rept 109-449) May 2. The House, by voice vote May 22, agreed to a motion by Christopher Shays, R-Conn., to suspend the rules and pass the bill. President George W. Bush signed S 1736 (PL 109-229) into law May 31, 2006.

Animal Evacuation

A bill (HR 3858) requiring states and municipalities to create plan as to evacuate pets and service animals, such as seeing-eye dogs, in disasters was signed into law (PL 109-308) Oct. 6, 2006.

Sponsor Tom Lantos, D-Calif., was prompted to write the legislation as a result of Hurricane Katrina. Hundreds of New Orleans residents refused to leave during the storm because they were not allowed to take their pets, and thousands of abandoned animals were rescued in the aftermath.

The House Transportation and Infrastructure Committee approved HR 3858 (no written report) by voice vote April 5, 2006. The House May 22 agreed, 349–24, to a motion by Bill Shuster, R-Pa., to suspend the rules and pass the bill. The Senate Homeland Security and Governmental Affairs Committee approved the measure (no written report) by voice vote July 27. The Senate passed an amended version by voice vote Aug. 4. The House by voice vote Sept. 20 agreed to a Shuster motion to suspend the rules and accept the Senate changes, thus completing congressional action.

Disaster Assistance

The House Transportation and Infrastructure Committee in 2005 acted on two bills (HR 3208, HR 2338) regarding disaster assistance. HR 3208, approved by voice vote by the Economic Development, Public Buildings, and Emergency Management Subcommittee on July 14, 2005, would amend the definition of "private nonprofit facility" under the Stafford Disaster Relief Act (PL 93-288) to make clear to regulators that all educational nonprofit religious institutions were eligible for Federal Emergency Management Agency (FEMA) aid. *(1974 disaster relief law, Congress and the Nation Vol. IV, p. 147)*

FEMA in 2001 denied earthquake aid to the Seattle Hebrew Academy because the agency said the institution did not meet the criteria for assistance under existing law. In 2002, after the Justice Department disagreed with the White House's interpretation, the policy was changed and the school received aid. Lawmakers said they wanted to make sure religious nonprofit organizations got the money that was coming to them.

The bill also would require the president to ensure that FEMA's relief assistance process be accomplished without discrimination on the grounds of race, color, religion, nationality, sex, age, or economic status.

HR 2338, which the subcommittee also approved by voice vote July 14, would create a small-state advocate at FEMA for rural communities. The legislation would require a report to Congress within 180 days of enactment on the extent to which disaster declaration regulations serve the needs of states with smaller populations. The panel adopted by voice vote an amendment that would increase the small-state population requirement in the bill to include those states with fewer than 1.5 million people. No further action was taken on either bill.

NOAA Reorganization

The House by voice vote on Sept. 20, 2006, agreed to a motion by Vernon J. Ehlers, R-Mich., to suspend the rules and pass HR 5450, which codified the existence of the National Oceanic and Atmospheric Administration (NOAA) as a single entity within the Department of Commerce. The bill, sponsored by Ehlers, wrote into law for the first time NOAA's role and responsibilities. NOAA had been created by executive order in 1970 and had been authorized under several separate laws.

The House Science Committee reported (H Rept 109-545, Part I) June 29. Lawmakers also had considered the issue of NOAA's reorganization in the 108th Congress. *(Earlier action, Congress and the Nation Vol. XI, p. 693)*

The restructuring was largely modeled on 2005 suggestions by the U.S. Commission on Ocean Policy, which Congress created in 2000 (PL 106-256). The commission found that fragmenting the agency had hampered efforts to protect coastal waters from overfishing, pollution, and other threats. *(Commission creation, Congress and the Nation Vol. X, p. 392)*

In June 2006, a bipartisan group of senators released a report by the Joint Ocean Commission Initiative that listed NOAA codification as one of at least ten actions Congress should take to restore and protect the health of the oceans.

A similar NOAA authorization bill (HR 50—no written report) was approved by voice on May 17, 2005, by the House Science Committee. HR 50 would restructure the agency around four areas: the National Weather Service, Research and Education, Operations and Services, and Resources Management. The jobs of chief operating officer, to manage day-to-day operations, and deputy assistant secretary for science and technology, to coordinate science activities across the agency, also would be created by the bill. The panel approved the measure after adopting a substitute amendment, offered by Ehlers, emphasizing NOAA's role in forecasting tsunamis and requiring the agency to notify Congress when it started new satellite programs.

HR 50 subsequently stalled because the House Transportation and Infrastructure Committee, which shared jurisdiction, raised concerns that it would create new regulatory authority for the agency. Compromise language was worked out in HR 5450 that would provide no new regulatory authority to NOAA.

NOAA reorganization legislation ultimately suffered delays and inaction due to Congress's need to first streamline the number of committees with jurisdiction over ocean issues and the lack of consensus among members of Congress as to the best way to reorganize the agency.

Government Online Database

A bill (S 2590) that would require the federal government to create a searchable database of every recipient of federal contracts and grants was signed into law (PL 109-282) Sept. 26, 2006. The legislation was sponsored by two freshmen senators, Tom Coburn, R-Okla., and Barack Obama, D-Ill., who said they believed it would bring more transparency to who gets what amount of money from the federal government.

Users of the Web site, to be named "expectmore.gov," would type in key words that would bring up exactly how much money any particular recipient had received. Approximately thirty thousand entities each year received federal grants worth more than $25,000, and that information would appear in the database. All contracts worth more than $25,000 also would be entered into the database. The free site would not include classified information or figures and would be running by Jan. 1, 2008.

S 2590 had widespread support in the Senate and became something of a cause célèbre in the "blogosphere," where liberal and conservative bloggers united in trying to figure out which senator had placed an anonymous hold blocking the legislation. The role Web activists played in bringing publicity to the legislation was indicative of the newfound influence of bloggers in public life.

The Senate Homeland Security and Governmental Affairs Committee approved S 2590 by voice vote July 27, 2006. The bill was formally reported Aug. 2, and a written report (S Rept 109-329) was filed Sept. 8. The Senate passed S 2590 by voice vote Sept. 7.

The House agreed by voice vote Sept. 13 to a Thomas M. Davis III, R-Va., motion to suspend the rules and pass S 2590. Before the bill went to the president, the Senate and House adopted changes (S Con Res 114) so that the database would have separate search engines for grants and contracts instead of a combination search engine.

The House June 21, 2006, had agreed by voice vote to a Davis motion to suspend the rules and pass its own version, HR 5060. The bill provided for a database that would not include searches of government contracts.

Federal Outsourcing

Bowing to White House veto threats and to aid passage of the fiscal 2006 appropriations bill (HR 3058—PL 109-115) for the Departments of Transportation, Treasury, and Housing and Urban Development, Congress in 2005 dropped language in the measure aimed at limiting the administration's policy of seeking private bids for certain federal jobs. *(Appropriations bill, p. 78)*

During floor consideration of HR 3058 June 30, the House adopted, 222–203, an amendment by Chris Van Hollen, D-Md., to prohibit the administration from enforcing a 2003 Office of Management and Budget rule allowing hundreds of thousands of federal jobs to be contracted out to private companies. Van Hollen argued that the rule gave unfair advantages to private companies over federal employees competing for the jobs and that it did not do enough to ensure cost savings. Similar language added to the spending legislation the previous two years had been removed or watered down in conference.

Also on June 30, the House adopted, 238–177, an amendment by Bernard Sanders, I-Vt., to nullify a Federal Aviation Administration (FAA) contract with the Lockheed Martin Corp. that shut thirty-eight of sixty-one flight service stations and privatized all but three of the rest. The stations provided general aviation pilots with weather, terrain, route, and other flight information. The White House threatened to veto the bill over this provision, saying that canceling the contract would cost the FAA more than $300 million.

Conferees on HR 3058 dropped the provisions that would block changes to the rules for outsourcing government jobs, but they included modified Senate language to prevent the government from contracting out government jobs performed by more than ten employees unless the change would save 10 percent or $10 million, whichever was less.

The House amendment to block the privatization of flight service stations also was dropped. The conference agreement (H Rept 109-307) generally prevented federal agencies funded under the measure from contracting with expatriate companies that located overseas.

Whistleblower Protection

The House Government Reform Committee approved, 34–1, on Sept. 29, 2005, legislation (HR 1317) that would reinforce job protections for government employees who disclosed malfeasance in federal programs. The panel formally reported the measure (H Rept 109-544, Part I) June 29, 2006.

HR 1317 contained language that would undo a 1999 federal court ruling that raised the standard federal workers must meet to receive protection under the existing whistleblower statute (PL 101-12). That ruling said an employee must have irrefutable evidence of waste, fraud, or abuse in a federal program to receive whistleblower protection. Government watchdog groups said the ruling had made it virtually impossible for employees to win retaliation cases in federal court. The committee-approved language would provide whistleblower protection to an employee who "reasonably believes" evidence of malfeasance existed. *(2007 action, p. 801)*

A Senate version of whistleblower protection legislation had been reported (S 494—S Rept 109-72) from the Senate Homeland Security and Governmental Affairs Committee May 25, 2005. The bill, however, went no further that year.

Presidential Succession

The Senate on July 26, 2005, gave voice approval to a bill (S 442) that would give the secretary of the Department of Homeland Security the eighth place in the succession line in the event that the president would have to be replaced.

The custom had been for the heads of new cabinet offices to go to the back of the line of succession. But given the significance and size of the new department, lawmakers sought to move it up on the list. *(2002 creation of the department, Congress and the Nation Vol. XI, p. 176)*

According to S 442, the order of presidential succession would begin with the vice president (which was already constitutionally ordained) before tapping the Speaker of the House, president pro tempore of the Senate, secretary of state, secretary of the Treasury, secretary of defense, attorney general, and then the newly elevated secretary of homeland security.

The House Government Reform Committee by voice vote Oct. 20, 2005, approved a companion measure (HR 1455—no written report). Similar legislation was introduced in the House in the 108th Congress. HR 1455, however, did not go further in the House. *(Earlier action, Congress and the Nation Vol. XI, p. 692)*

Presidential Dollar Coin

Legislation providing for the U.S. minting of a series of $1 coins to commemorate the nation's presidents, beginning in 2007, was signed into law by President George W. Bush (S 1047—PL 109-145) Dec. 22, 2005.

Under the law, four coins a year would be issued, each bearing the image of a president according to chronological order. They would not include sitting presidents, living ex-presidents, and those who had been dead for less than two years. The legislation also authorized production of $10 coins burnished with images of the first ladies. Those were to be made of 99.99 percent pure gold and aimed at collectors.

One-third of the $1 coins minted each year were required to be Sacagawea coins, the existing design. Sacagawea was the Native American guide for Meriwether Lewis and William Clark. Furthermore, the penny, which carries the image of President Abraham Lincoln, would be redesigned to honor the two hundredth anniversary of his birth, in 2009. The new penny would have four designs representing different aspects of Lincoln's life.

In an attempt to boost use of the $1 coins, the law required federal officials to consult with vending machine operators, municipal parking officials, and other agencies and businesses that depended on the availability of certain coins.

The Senate Banking, Housing, and Urban Affairs Committee approved S 1047, sponsored by John E. Sununu, R-N.H., by voice vote July 28, 2005 (no written report). The full Senate passed S 1047 by voice vote Nov. 18. The House agreed, 291–113, Dec. 13 to a motion by Michael G. Oxley, R-Ohio, to suspend the rules and pass the bill, completing congressional action.

Companion legislation (HR 902), sponsored by Michael N. Castle, R-Del., had been reported (H Rept 109-39) by the House Financial Services Committee April 13. The House, 422–6, April 27 agreed to a Castle motion to suspend the rules and pass the bill. Castle had been the primary advocate of the popular state quarters program (PL 105-124). Backers of the $1 presidential coin initiative hoped it would attract the interest of historians and numismatists. Because of collectors, the state quarters program raised almost $5 billion in the first six years. *(State quarters, Congress and the Nation Vol. X, p. 129)*

Castle had introduced similar legislation in the 108th Congress. *(Earlier action, Congress and the Nation Vol. XI, p. 697)*

D.C. Marriage Promotion

The fiscal 2006 funding measure for the departments of Transportation, Treasury, and Housing and Urban Development (HR 3058—PL 109-115), which also covered the District of Columbia, established a $3 million pilot program in the District to create "marriage development accounts" aimed at encouraging low-income people to get married and raise children in two-parent households.

The language had been offered to a stand-alone D.C. spending bill (S 1446) by Senate D.C. Appropriations Subcommittee chairman Sam Brownback, R-Kan. The Senate Appropriations Committee approved that measure on a 28–0 vote July 21, 2005, and formally reported it (S Rept 109-106) the same day. The bill was added by voice vote Oct. 18 to HR 3058 as an amendment. *(Fiscal 2006 appropriations, p. 76)*

The first-of-its-kind pilot project to encourage marriage in the District provided a three-to-one match for married couples who saved money for several specific purposes, such as buying a house or starting a small business. Social conservative lawmakers had been eager to enact programs that would counter the high percentage of children born to single mothers, which in the District was 57 percent. The city's single House delegate, Democrat Eleanor Holmes Norton, endorsed the proposal.

D.C. Gun Law

During consideration of the fiscal 2006 appropriations bill for the departments of Transportation, Treasury, and Housing and Urban Development (HR 3058—PL 109-115), which included funding for the District of Columbia, the House on June 30, 2005, adopted, 259–161, an amendment by Mark Souder, R-Ind., to bar use of any funds in the bill, including both federal and local city funds, to enforce the district's 1976 gun control law. *(Fiscal 2006 appropriations, p. 76; D.C. gun-related action, 110th Congress, p. 803)*

The D.C. law allowed residents to own firearms legally as long as the guns were kept disassembled and unloaded. However, handguns were prohibited from being kept in the home unless they were purchased prior to the 1976 law. The law allowed registered gun owners to keep loaded firearms at their place of business for self-defense.

Souder maintained that "the constitutional right to bear arms supersedes local authority" and said that his proposal was "about self-protection in your home." D.C. officials opposed his amendment. Senate appropriators did not include the House gun ownership language in its version of the funding measure, and the provision was not in the final bill.

National Indian Gaming Commission

Federal regulators gained financial flexibility to keep pace with the booming tribal gambling industry under legislation (HR 3351—PL 109-221) signed into law May 12, 2006.

The measure increased funding for the National Indian Gaming Commission by capping fees assessed on Native American gambling operations at 0.080 percent of gross gaming revenues. The fees had been capped at a fixed $12 million nationwide. Native American gaming operations in 2004 took in an estimated $18.5 billion from more than four hundred bingo halls and casinos in twenty-eight states, up from $105 million twenty years earlier, according to tribal organizations.

The commission was charged with keeping organized crime out of Native American casinos and ensuring that games were played fairly and that the revenue benefited tribes. The additional funds were expected to be used to hire more auditors and staff.

The House Resources Committee reported HR 3351 (H Rept 109-298, Part I) Nov. 16, 2005. The House agreed by voice vote the same day to a motion by Rick Renzi, R-Ariz., to suspend the rules and pass the bill. The Senate passed an amended version by voice vote April 7, 2006, and the House by voice vote May 2 agreed to a Steve Pearce, R-N.M., motion to suspend the rules and accept the changes, thus clearing the measure.

The Senate Indian Affairs Committee had reported similar legislation (S 1295—S Rept 109-122) Aug. 31, 2005, and the Senate had passed the bill by voice vote Dec. 12.

Tribal Gaming

The House on Sept. 13, 2006, rejected a motion by Richard W. Pombo, R-Calif., to suspend the rules and pass HR 4893, which sought to tighten restrictions on the development of Native American casinos on off-reservation sites. The 247–171 vote fell short of the two-thirds of those present (in this case, 279) required under suspension of the rules.

The 1988 Indian Gaming Regulatory Act (PL 100-497) prohibited Native American tribes from constructing a casino outside reservation lands, but the law contained exceptions for tribes that gained federal recognition after the measure was enacted and therefore had no land. It also included exceptions such as allowing a tribe to build an off-reservation gaming hall if the interior secretary and state governor agreed that the casino was in the best interest of the tribe and host community. *(1988 law, Congress and the Nation Vol. VII, p. 864)*

HR 4893 would allow a tribe to propose a casino only on lands where it had its primary historical, geographical, social, or cultural ties and would bar off-reservation casinos outside a tribe's home state. Tribes that had filed petitions before the bill's introduction date (March 7, 2006) would proceed under old rules. The measure would involve affected communities in the decision process, mandating that the tribe and host municipality enter into an agreement that spelled out the tribe's responsibility to pay costs associated with a casino's effect on such services and infrastructure as roads and public safety. The state and the Interior Department would have to approve the deal.

Some tribes opposed the bill, arguing that it could prevent tribes pushed off their lands years ago from eventually opening casinos in areas where they have ancestral claims. Some lawmakers complained that the measure would erode tribes' sovereignty by requiring certain new tribal casinos to win local governments' approval.

The House Resources Committee had approved HR 4893 by 27–9 on July 26, 2006. The bill was formally reported (H Rept 109-650) on Sept. 13. The measure went no further.

2007–2008

NASA Reauthorization

Congress took up HR 6063, which reauthorized the National Aeronautics and Space Administration (NASA) for one year at a funding level of $20.2 billion, endorsed President George W. Bush's plan to send astronauts to the moon in preparation for missions to Mars, and designated $1 billion for accelerated development of a spacecraft to replace the existing shuttle fleet. The legislation sought to ensure that NASA did not neglect science and aeronautics for the sake of its exploration goals. The agency would have to establish a long-term technology research and development program "not tied to specific flight goals." That program would receive no less than 10 percent of the total exploration systems budget. *(109th Congress action, p. 786)*

The House Science and Technology Committee approved HR 6063 by voice vote June 4, 2008, and reported it (H Rept 110-702) June 9. The panel tabled (killed), 22–15, an amendment by Phil Gingrey, R-Ga., that would have deleted language from the 2007 energy law (PL 110-140) that prohibited federal agencies from buying alternative fuels unless the substances produce less greenhouse gases than conventional fuel sources. A second Gingrey amendment that would have given the NASA administrator the ability to waive the biofuels statute for the space agency was also tabled, 22–15. *(Energy law, p. 484)*

Before passing HR 6063 on June 18 by a vote of 409–15, the House adopted, 429–1, an amendment by Nick Lampson, D-Texas, to allow NASA to buy fuel that contained small amounts of alternative fuels. During earlier floor consideration, twelve amendments—mostly small programmatic changes or nonbinding provisions—were adopted by voice vote. In some cases, the bill would put specific limitations on how NASA could spend its money. For example, it would mandate a new space shuttle flight that the Bush administration opposed.

The Senate by voice vote on Sept. 25 passed an amended version. The House accepted the changes Sept. 27, completing congressional action. President Bush signed HR 6063 (PL 110-422) into law Oct. 15, 2008.

National Flood Insurance

After hurricanes Wilma, Katrina, and Rita devastated the Gulf Coast in 2005 and put the National Flood Insurance Program into the red, many in Congress believed that an overhaul of the federal program was needed. Conferees were appointed in 2008 to consider legislation (HR 3121) to overhaul and reauthorize the insurance program, but differences were not resolved before Congress adjourned and the measure died. The 109th Congress also was unable to produce flood insurance legislation. *(Background, 109th Congress action, p. 791)*

The House Financial Services Committee approved HR 3121 by 38–29 on July 26, 2007, and formally reported it (H Rept 110-340) on Sept. 24. The legislation, sponsored by Maxine Waters, D-Calif., combined two bills: HR 1682, to overhaul the National Flood Insurance Program; and HR 920, sponsored by Gene Taylor, D-Miss., to add wind damage to the program's coverage.

Proponents of the wind coverage, including some Gulf Coast Republicans, castigated the insurance industry for refusing to pay thousands of claims from Katrina by maintaining that the damages were caused by water from storm surges and levee breaches, not wind. Taylor, whose home was destroyed by Katrina, sued his insurer for denying his wind damage claim.

A approved by the committee, HR 3121 would:

- Reauthorize the program for five years, from fiscal 2009 through fiscal 2013, and increase its temporary borrowing authority to $21.5 billion.
- Increase coverage limits, which had not been raised since 1994, for residential properties to $335,000, from $250,000; for residential contents to $135,000, from $100,000; and for nonresidential properties to $670,000, from $500,000.
- Allow the Federal Emergency Management Agency (FEMA), which administered the program, to increase premium rates by 15 percent a year, up from 10 percent under existing law.
- Phase out subsidized premium rates on commercial properties and second homes built before 1974, when flood insurance rate maps went into effect and homes already in flood zones began receiving subsidies. About 25 percent of all insured properties still had subsidized premiums.
- Allow an optional multiperil policy to cover both wind and flood risk. Wind coverage would be available only to property owners who also had flood policies. Premiums would have to be adequate to cover claims. The maximum combined coverage for residences would be $500,000 for the structure and $150,000 for contents and loss of use. For nonresidential properties, the maximum would be $1 million for the structure and $750,000 for contents and business interruption. The policies would be restricted to areas where local governments agreed to adopt and enforce building codes and standards designed to minimize wind damage.
- Increase civil penalties from $350 to $2,000 per violation for lenders who did not ensure that owners of properties required to have flood coverage purchased such coverage.

The full House passed HR 3121 by 263–146 on Sept. 27. The day before, the White House issued a statement warning that President George W. Bush's senior advisers would recommend a veto if the bill included wind coverage. The statement said that shifting liabilities for windstorm damage from the private sector to the flood insurance program would be "fiscally irresponsible" and would "displace insurance that is already provided in the private sector."

During the floor debate Sept. 27, the House adopted 268–143 a Taylor amendment to make apartments eligible for both flood and wind policies up to the maximum coverage limits for each individual unit. Among the twelve amendments adopted the same day by voice vote were those offered by:

- Dennis Cardoza, D-Calif., to provide that people forced to purchase flood insurance as a result of a new map, who live in an area where the levees previously were certified and subsequently were decertified, would receive a grace period of five years in which they would be entitled to a 50 percent reduction in their flood insurance premium.
- Kathy Castor, D-Fla., to require the Government Accountability Office to conduct a study to identify and analyze factors affecting enrollment in the multiperil insurance program.
- Castor, to instruct the FEMA director to consider natural protective sand dunes and wetlands when developing criteria for multiperil insurance.
- Earl Blumenauer, D-Ore., to require FEMA to take into consideration the impact of global warming, currently and in the future, when updating and maintaining flood insurance program rate maps.
- Patrick J. Murphy, D-Pa., to provide for the creation of the position of national flood insurance advocate, who would be required to report to Congress with analysis of the major problems facing the program.
- Taylor, to prohibit a company that sells and services flood insurance policies from including language in its windstorm policies that would exclude coverage of wind damage solely because flooding also contributed to the damage and to require an insurance company and the National Flood Insurance Program to state that the company has a fiduciary responsibility to federal taxpayers and would act in the best interests of the federal insurance program.
- Jerry F. Costello, D-Ill., to provide that FEMA would not be able to adjust premium rates or require the purchase of flood insurance until all remapping had been completed for an entire district of the Corps of Engineers affected by the remapping.
- Gene Green, D-Texas, to provide a five-year phase-in of flood insurance premiums for low-income homeowners or renters whose primary residence was placed within a flood plain through an updating of the flood insurance program maps.
- Tim Walz, D-Minn., to require FEMA to make information available about the risk of flooding that might occur if a flood control measure other than a dam or levee would fail.

The Senate Banking, Housing, and Urban Affairs Committee approved a companion version (S 2284) by 21–0 on Oct. 17, 2007, and formally reported it (S Rept 110-214) on Nov. 1. The committee bill would:

- Reauthorize the National Flood Insurance Program from fiscal 2009 through fiscal 2013.
- Allow multifamily residential buildings—those with four or more units—to purchase flood insurance up to the commercial coverage limits, $500,000 for the structure at the time.
- Allow FEMA to increase premiums by 15 percent a year.
- Phase out premium subsidies over four years for second homes, commercial property, and property with major repeat losses or where flood losses had exceeded the property value. No subsidies could be offered on any new policy for property not already covered by a flood insurance policy.
- Increase civil penalties from $350 to $2,000 per violation for lenders who did not ensure that property owners required to have flood coverage purchased such coverage.
- Eliminate the National Flood Insurance Program's debt to the Treasury from the 2005 hurricane season.
- Reduce the borrowing authority for the program from $20.8 billion to $1.5 billion, the amount in effect prior to the 2005 storm season.

Sen. David Vitter, R-La., subsequently said he would place a hold on S 2284 because it did not propose to expand coverage or raise maximum coverage levels. He also opposed the bill because it did not include the wind damage coverage. Gulf Coast lawmakers favored expanding the program, whereas many Senate Republicans, the White House, and the insurance industry opposed doing so. The critics, including disparate interest groups such as the National Wildlife Federation and the Consumer Federation of America, argued variously that the provisions could expose taxpayers to massive losses, interfere with private insurance markets, and derail the flood overhaul effort.

The House Financial Services Committee on Oct. 31, 2007, gave voice approval to HR 3959, which would phase out the flood insurance subsidies for homes built before 1974. The bill, formally reported (H Rept 110-510) on Jan. 16, 2008, was sponsored by Barney Frank, D-Mass., and Scott Garrett, R-N.J., and enjoyed broad bipartisan support.

The committee-approved HR 3959 also provided that people who bought homes for at least $600,000 would have to begin paying the market-based rates paid by owners of more recently built properties. The higher rates would be phased in.

HR 3959 originally was intended as an amendment to the broader flood insurance bill, but the Democratic-controlled Rules Committee did not allow it to be considered. The full House by voice vote agreed to a Frank motion to suspend the rules and pass the bill on Jan. 23.

The bill was referred to the Senate Banking, Housing, and Urban Affairs Committee but saw no further action.

The full Senate took up consideration of S 2284 after voting, 90–1, May 6, 2008, to invoke cloture on a motion to proceed to the bill. It rejected, 19–74, May 7 an amendment by Roger Wicker, R-Miss., to expand the federal program to include coverage for damage caused by wind. The Senate May 8 defeated a budget-related point of order. Tom Coburn, R-Okla., objected to a provision in the substitute amendment offered by Christopher J. Dodd, D-Conn., chairman of the Senate Banking, Housing, and Urban Affairs Committee, that would forgive the program's $17.5 billion debt without offsetting the cost. The same day, the Senate voted 70–26 to waive the pay-as-you-go budget rules, which required such offsets.

The Senate passed HR 3121 on May 13 by 92–6 after incorporating the text of S 2284. The measure would forgive the $17.5 billion debt to the Treasury that the program incurred after the 2005 hurricane season and would authorize the program for five years. The House-passed version would not forgive the debt. Also unlike the House-passed bill, the Senate version would not expand the program to cover damage caused by wind.

The Senate-approved bill included a new requirement that residents in areas behind levees and dams buy flood insurance. The Senate defeated an effort by Mary L. Landrieu, D-La., to strike that requirement from the bill in favor of language that would require a study to assess the risk for properties protected by such structures. The bill also would update the nation's flood maps through the establishment of a thirteen-member Technical Mapping Advisory Council and by authorizing $2 billion for the mapping.

The legislation would phase out subsidized premium rates on vacation homes and allow premiums in general to increase by as much as 15 percent, up from 10 percent. The bill included language from S 2286, which would require a panel to study the federal role in providing broader catastrophic insurance. Dodd agreed to add a provision sponsored by Landrieu that would boost oversight of insurance companies as they determine whether storm damage is caused by privately covered wind damage or federally covered water damage.

The House agreed 385–26 on July 10, 2008, to a Randy Neugebauer, R-Texas, motion to instruct the conferees on HR 3121 to include in the conference report a section of the Senate-passed bill that would phase out premium subsidies more quickly and for more types of properties. The motion also called for conferees to provide that some premium subsidies be eliminated ninety days after enactment. HR 3121 did not go any further, however, and died at the end of the Congress.

Inspectors General Tenure

A measure (HR 928—PL 110-409) that set seven-year terms for inspectors general and restricted the circumstances under which they could be fired was signed into law by President George W. Bush Oct. 14, 2008. The legislation was designed to insulate the federal government's internal watchdogs from political influence.

The House Oversight and Government Reform Committee by voice vote approved HR 928 on Aug. 2, 2007. The measure was reported (H Rept 110-354) on Sept. 27. The full House passed the bill, 404–11, on Oct. 3. The Senate passed an amended version by voice vote on Sept. 24, 2008. The House cleared the bill Sept. 27, when it voted, 414–0, on a motion by Edolphus Towns, D-N.Y., to suspend the rules and agree to the Senate changes.

The Senate had passed a companion version (S 2324) by voice vote April 23, 2008. The Senate Homeland Security and Governmental Affairs Committee had reported S 2324 (S Rept 110-262) Feb. 22, 2008.

Surplus Food Donations

Legislation (S 2420) to promote the donation of surplus food by federal agencies and contractors was signed into law (PL 110-247) on June 20, 2008. Sponsored by Charles E. Schumer, D-N.Y., the measure would require all government food contracts valued at more than $25,000 to include a clause encouraging the donation of edible leftover food to soup kitchens or shelters.

The Senate Homeland Security and Governmental Affairs Committee approved S 2420 by voice vote on April 10, 2008, and reported it (S Rept 110-338) on May 22. The Senate passed the bill by voice vote on May 22. The House on June 3 agreed by voice vote to a motion by William Lacy Clay, D-Mo., to suspend the rules and pass the bill, completing congressional action.

The House had agreed by voice vote on Dec. 17, 2007, to suspend the rules and pass HR 4220, similar to S 2420. Both bills would protect donors from liability for tainted food under a 1996 law (PL 104-210), which shields from legal liability the donors of "apparently wholesome food" donated in good faith.

The nonpartisan antipoverty organization Rock and Wrap It Up, which arranged the pickup of surplus food from rock concerts, sporting contests, and other events, conceived the legislation.

Ocean Exploration Programs

The Senate Commerce, Science, and Transportation Committee by voice vote Feb. 13, 2007, approved a bill (S 39) to expand the ocean exploration programs of the National Oceanic and Atmospheric Administration (NOAA). The panel reported S 39 (S Rept 110-39) on March 27.

The measure, sponsored by Ted Stevens, R-Alaska, would authorize NOAA to spend $486 million over ten years on a coordinated program to explore little-known areas of the marine environment. The National Science Foundation also would participate in the program.

The committee by voice vote adopted an amendment by Kay Bailey Hutchison, R-Texas, to require NOAA to study and evaluate U.S. coastal resources, with a focus on wave, current, tidal, and biological resources in the coastal areas. The measure subsequently stalled.

No-Bid Contracts

The House in 2007 passed a bill (HR 1362) aimed at curbing no-bid contracts, which Democrats said had been abused by firms providing goods and services in Iraq and on the hurricane-ravaged Gulf Coast. The House Oversight and Government Reform Committee reported HR 1362 (H Rept 110-47, Part I) on March 12, and the House Armed Services Committee reported it (H Rept 110-47, Part II) on March 14.

The measure passed the full House, 347–73, on March 15, after Republicans succeeded in amending it through a procedural maneuver that was rarely successful when Democrats were in the minority. The GOP amendment would prohibit the federal government from contracting with colleges that allowed private employers to recruit on campus while denying the same access to U.S. military recruiters. The amendment was added after a motion by Thomas M. Davis III, R-Va., to recommit the bill to the Oversight and Government Reform Committee was agreed to, 309–114.

HR 1362 would put a one-year limit on no-bid contracts of $1 million or more, unless the head of an agency determined that an extension was necessary. It also would require agencies that awarded $1 billion in contracts in the previous year to devise plans for minimizing no-bid contracts and maximizing fixed-price contracts. Agencies would be required to publicize the justifications for sole-source contracts. The bill would prohibit federal procurement officers from dealing with contracts involving their former private sector employers for one year. The Senate took no action.

Federal Contracts to Small Businesses

The House by 409–13 on May 10, 2007, passed a bill (HR 1873) to increase the federal government's small business procurement goal to 30 percent from 23 percent. The legislation, sponsored by Bruce Braley, D-Iowa, would clarify the definition of "contract bundling." The legislation also would limit the ability of federal agencies to bundle smaller projects into larger contracts, a practice that bill supporters said barred small businesses from bidding competitively on federal contracts.

The House Small Business Committee approved HR 1873 by voice vote on April 24 and reported it (H Rept 110-111, Part I) on April 26. The House Oversight and Government Reform Committee approved the measure by voice vote May 1 and reported it (H Rept 110-111, Part II) May 3. The same panel filed a supplemental report (H Rept 110-111, Part III) May 8.

Lawmakers adopted eight amendments before voting for final passage and rejected a Phil English, R-Pa., motion to recommit the bill with instructions. One amendment—offered by Melissa Bean, D-Ill., and the Small Business Committee ranking Republican Steve Chabot of Ohio and adopted 371–55 on May 10—changed the procurement goal to 30 percent. The House Oversight panel had set a 25 percent goal.

An amendment offered by Heath Shuler, D-N.C., was adopted, 398–29, May 10 to extend small business contracting goals to overseas contracts, a provision that the Oversight and Government Reform Committee removed from the Small Business Committee-approved version of the bill. The House also adopted, 423–0 on May 10, an amendment offered by Joe Sestak, D-Pa., to exempt general contracts of less than $1.5 million from the measure's provisions that would require more detailed analysis of bundled contracts and their effects on small businesses as well as savings to taxpayers. The Senate did not take up the legislation.

Contractor Fraud

The House agreed by voice vote on April 23, 2008, to a motion by Edolphus Towns, D-N.Y., to suspend the rules and pass HR 5712, requiring contractors to report fraud by their employees. The bill covered contracts worth more than $5 million and lasting more than 120 days. The contractor fraud language subsequently was included in supplemental appropriations legislation (HR 2642—PL 110-252). *(Supplemental, pp. 129, 387)*

Existing law contained a so-called fraud loophole that exempted commercial and overseas contractors from notifying the government if an employee broke a criminal law in obtaining or carrying out a contract or if an employee was significantly overcompensated. George W. Bush administration officials called the loophole a "bureaucratic mistake."

The House Oversight and Government Reform approved HR 5712 by voice vote on April 16, 2008, and reported it (H Rept 110-599) on April 22. The measure saw no further congressional action.

Contractors in Debt

The House agreed to a motion by Bruce Braley, D-Iowa, to suspend the rules and pass HR 4881, prohibiting companies with significant tax debts from getting federal contracts, by voice vote on April 14, 2008. The House Oversight and Government Reform Committee had approved the bill by voice vote on March 13, 2008, and reported it (H Rept 110-578) on April 10. The Senate did not take up the bill.

The bill would require potential contractors to certify in writing that they did not have seriously deficient tax debts. It would authorize federal tax officials to disclose information confirming or refuting that claim to the agency awarding the contract. The measure defined a significant tax debt as one in which a notice of a lien had been filed in public records and taxes were not being paid under an agreement with the Internal Revenue Service or being handled in certain administrative hearings.

The House Oversight and Government Reform Subcommittee on Government Management, Organization, and Procurement on May 9, 2007, had approved by voice vote a similar bill (HR 1870). Among the contested issues surrounding the bill was how to set the threshold that defined a delinquent taxpayer. HR 1870 defined a delinquent debt as one that had not been paid within 180 days of an assessment of taxes, penalties, or interest.

HR 4881 used the filing of a tax lien as the trigger. The change was designed to ensure that only significant cases would be used to prevent companies from getting contracts. It also was made to give federal contracting officers a simpler way to check whether a company was eligible for a contract.

Whistleblower Protections

On March 14, 2007, the House passed, on a 331–94 vote, legislation (HR 985) designed to give government whistleblowers expanded protections. The bill would allow national security workers to disclose information to authorized members of Congress and executive branch officials and prohibit retribution, including the revocation of security clearance, for such disclosures. The White House threatened to veto the measure, saying it would promote frivolous complaints. *(2006 action, p. 795)*

During floor consideration on March 14, the House adopted several amendments, including one executed by a successful GOP motion to recommit. That motion, by Lynn Westmoreland of Georgia, added language to prevent retaliation against workers for religious expression and exercise in the workplace. It was agreed to, 426–0. A proposal by Bart Stupak, D-Mich., adopted 252–173, would bar those supervising federally funded researchers from retaliating against them if they published nonproprietary information in peer-reviewed journals or discussed it with professional associations. By voice vote, the House adopted an amendment to limit the number of members of Congress to whom a national security whistleblower could legally give information and another amendment pertaining to the application of burdens of proof in the administrative adjudication of whistleblower cases.

The House Oversight and Government Reform Committee had approved HR 985 by 28–0 on Feb. 14, 2007, and formally reported it (H Rept 110-42, Part I) on March 9. The panel filed a supplemental report (H Rept 110-42, Part II) on March 12. The Senate did not act on the bill and it died at the end of Congress.

Foreign Service Pay

The House Foreign Affairs Committee on July 16, 2008, by voice vote approved and on Sept. 24 formally reported a bill (HR 3202—H Rept 110-877, Part I) aimed at eliminating a pay disparity between Foreign Service employees serving in Washington, D.C., and those operating overseas.

The measure would change a law that gave Foreign Service officers a de facto pay cut of up to 20 percent at two-thirds of overseas posts. Most members of the State Department and the U.S. Agency for International Development who worked in Washington, along with many other federal employees, were paid 21 percent more than what they would otherwise receive to bring their salaries closer to those in similar private-sector jobs. Overseas postings did not get the premium pay, which Foreign Service officers said hurt recruitment and retention at a time when demand for such personnel was increasing. HR 3202 would phase in the Washington pay rate for overseas personnel over three years. The Senate, however, did not take up the bill.

Community Service Programs

House Republicans in 2008 managed to stop two bills (HR 2857; HR 5563) that would renew and expand community service programs. House Democratic leaders March 6 pulled HR 2857 to reauthorize the Corporation for National and Community Service, best known for its AmeriCorps program, in the face of a GOP move to force a politically difficult vote. Republicans sought to highlight their anger at being shut out of negotiations on an unrelated electronic surveillance bill (HR 3773). *(Intelligence surveillance legislation, pp. 249, 251)*

The five-year reauthorization of the national service programs (PL 101-610), which placed young people in community service jobs, had broad bipartisan support. However, after a harmonious morning of debate March 6, 2008, during which members adopted ten amendments, Republicans offered a motion to recommit the bill and add language requiring that organizations receiving program grants to run criminal background checks on volunteers. The motion called for the bill to be returned to the floor "promptly," an arcane move that would have taken the bill off the floor and sent it to committee—in this case, the House Education and Labor Committee. The more common motion to return the bill "forthwith" would have returned the amended bill to the floor immediately. *(PL 101-610, Congress and the Nation Vol. VIII, p. 616)*

Committee chairman George Miller, D-Calif., said the law already required such background checks. However, voting against the motion would be difficult for Democrats to explain to voters. He subsequently pulled HR 2857 from the floor indefinitely.

House Education and Labor had approved the bill 44–0 on June 27, 2007, and reported it (H Rept 110-420) on Nov. 1.

The House rejected HR 5563 on March 12 by a vote of 277–140, one vote shy of the two-thirds majority required under suspension of the rules, a procedure meant to expedite noncontroversial legislation. The bill would reauthorize the Corporation for National and Community Service for five years.

All votes cast against the measure came from the GOP. Some fiscally conservative Republicans complained about the program's concept of paying people to volunteer. HR 5563 incorporated the ten amendments to HR 2857 that were adopted on the floor, including the creation of new service initiatives such as a "Silver Scholarship" program for people fifty-five and older who performed six hundred hours of service. Another called for the creation of an Energy Conservation Corps.

2010 Census

Fiscal 2009 spending legislation for the Department of Commerce, the Department of Justice, the National Aeronautics and Space Administration, and several other agencies (HR 7322, S 3182) stalled in 2008. As a result, funding for programs was extended at fiscal 2008 levels through March 6, 2009, under a continuing resolution (HR 2638—PL 110-329). While the measure largely froze funding levels until lawmakers could agree on a full-year bill, it did provide a handful of increases. The Census Bureau, which was part of the Commerce Department, was funded at an annual level of $2.9 billion—about $1.7 billion above fiscal 2008 funding—to help it prepare for the 2010 census. The administration of President George W. Bush initially requested $1.2 billion, or double the amount the bureau received in fiscal 2008.

On June 9, 2008, the president asked for an additional $546 million. Census takers were going to use paper questionnaires, not handheld computers as originally planned, to gather information from residents who did not mail back the form. The change increased expected costs for the census by as much as $3 billion. Both the Senate and House Appropriations Committees said they received the request too late to include in their spending bills.

The Senate Appropriations Committee included $3.2 billion for the Census Bureau in S 3182, approved 29–0 on June 19. The legislation was formally reported (S Rept 110-397) on June 23. The House Appropriations Committee provided the bureau with $2.6 billion in HR 7322, approved by voice vote June 25. The measure was formally reported (H Rept 110-919) on Dec. 10. The measures did not go further in the 110th Congress.

Coin Composition

The House agreed by voice vote on May 8, 2008, to a motion offered by Luis V. Gutierrez, D-Ill., to suspend the rules and pass HR 5512, which would change the composition of pennies and nickels and address dramatic rises in metal prices that made the coins more expensive to produce than their face value.

According to the U.S. Mint, it cost about 1.3 cents to make a penny and 7.7 cents make a nickel. HR 5512, sponsored by Zack Space, D-Ohio, estimated that reducing the cost of penny production to face value would save approximately $500 million over ten years, while similar changes to nickel production would save $60 million annually. The measure would allow for the minting of pennies made primarily of steel but coated with a copper-colored dye so they would appear similar to the current zinc-copper alloy. It also would require the production of five-cent coins made primarily of steel, with a coating of nickel, in place of the nickel-copper composition originally authorized in 1866. The last time the penny and the nickel were produced at face value was fiscal year 2005, according to the Mint.

The U.S. Mint opposed the bill, raising concerns about the timeframe it set for the production of steel-based pennies. The legislation would require changes to the metallic composition of pennies nine months after enactment. The Mint preferred eighteen to twenty-four months, allowing for more public comment. The Senate did not take up the legislation.

Access to Presidential Records

Despite a veto threat, the House on March 14, 2007, agreed, 333–93, to a motion by William Lacy Clay, D-Mo., to suspend the rules and pass HR 1255, to revoke restrictions imposed on access to presidential records. The House Oversight and Government Reform Committee had approved the bill by voice vote on March 8 and had reported it (H Rept 110-44) on March 9. The Senate Homeland Security and Governmental Affairs Committee by voice vote approved a companion measure (S 886) on June 13, 2007, and reported it (no written report) on June 20.

Executive Order 13233 issued in 2001 by President George W. Bush effectively allowed former presidents and former vice presidents to determine which of their records could be released to the public. HR 1255 would repeal that executive order and allow the archivist of the United States to reassume control of access to presidential records and information.

Those who sought release of President Ronald Reagan's records noted that they could shed light on whether the nation's top executives, including Bush's father, George H.W. Bush, who was Reagan's vice president, played a role in the Iran-contra scandal in the mid-1980s. *(Iran-contra affair, Congress and the Nation Vol. VII, p. 253)*

President Barack Obama on Jan. 21, 2009, issued Executive Order 13489, which revoked Bush's order. Without congressional action, however, any future president can reinstate Bush's order.

Presidential Library Donations

The House agreed, 390–34 on March 14, 2007, to a motion offered by Christopher S. Murphy, D-Conn., to suspend the rules and pass HR 1254, requiring the disclosure of the identities of big-dollar donors to presidential library funds. Organizations that raise money for libraries would have to file quarterly reports during the president's term and for four years thereafter, detailing the donors who gave $200 or more. The National Archives and Records Administration would be ordered to make the reports available to the public.

The House Oversight and Government Reform Committee had approved the bill by voice vote on March 8 and formally reported it (H Rept 110-43) on March 9.

The Senate Homeland Security and Governmental Affairs Committee approved HR 1254 by voice vote on Aug. 1 and formally reported it (S Rept 110-202) on Oct. 22. Action by the Senate panel had been delayed because committee member Ted Stevens, R-Alaska, objected to the bill because he thought it would unfairly force President George W. Bush to disclose donors for his presidential library while he was in the middle of the fundraising process. Stevens argued that the legislation should apply either to only future presidents or to all presidential libraries, past and present. The measure saw no further congressional action.

E-Mail Records Protection

Defying a veto threat, the House by 286–137 on July 9, 2008, passed a bill (HR 5811) that would stiffen the standards for tracking White House and federal agency e-mail messages. The House Oversight and Government Reform Committee approved the measure by voice vote on May 1, 2008, and formally reported it (H Rept 110-709) on June 11.

Lawmakers passed HR 5811 after adopting language to protect classified records at the National Archives from destruction or unauthorized removal. The new language was introduced in the form of a motion to recommit the bill to the House Oversight and Government Reform Committee by the panel's ranking Republican, Thomas M. Davis III of Virginia. Chairman Henry A. Waxman, D-Calif., the bill's author, supported the addition and raised it on the House floor, where it was adopted by voice vote on July 9.

The bill would direct the archivist of the United States to set new standards for tracking federal e-mail records and to certify that the White House met those standards. It also would require the National Archives and Records Administration to more aggressively oversee e-mail policies at federal agencies.

HR 5811 was a response to senior George W. Bush administration officials' use of Republican National Committee e-mail accounts for official business, as well as the White House's loss of hundreds, if not thousands, of e-mail messages. The Senate did not act on the bill.

D.C. Gun Law

The House passed, 266–152 on Sept. 17, 2008, a bill (HR 6842) to broadly roll back the District of Columbia's weapons regulations in the wake of a landmark U.S. Supreme Court ruling—*District of Columbia v. Heller,* issued June 26, 2008—that voided the city's handgun ban. *(Court ruling, p. 769)*

The original HR 6842, sponsored by Eleanor Holmes Norton, D-D.C., would have required the District simply to revise its laws "as necessary to comply" with the Court's ruling. The high court agreed 5–4 to void the city's strongest-in-the-nation ban on handgun possession, as well as its requirement that handguns in the home be either locked or disassembled. For the first time, the Court declared that the Second Amendment protected an individual's right to bear arms. Norton introduced HR 6842 as a defensive move against a push by the National Rifle Association (NRA) for a House vote on broader legislation. Norton's language was not strong enough to satisfy the NRA, however.

Democratic leaders, hoping to protect conservative Democrats in close reelection contests in 2008, allowed Mississippi Democrat Travis W. Childers to offer a substitute amendment, drawn from his own bill (HR 6691), which would repeal a ban on semiautomatic weapons, prohibit registration requirements for most guns, and drop criminal penalties for possessing an unregistered firearm. The House adopted, 260–160, the Childers amendment Sept. 17. The amended Norton bill was subsequently passed.

The D.C. City Council enacted new temporary handgun regulations in July 2008, and the city began allowing residents to register handguns. The council promulgated another set of temporary laws in September 2008. However, gun rights advocates said the new regulations continued to improperly constrain gun ownership in light of the Court ruling.

Senate majority whip Richard J. Durbin, D-Ill., objected to a unanimous consent request put forth by Kay Bailey Hutchison, R-Texas, to bring up HR 6842, calling it an attempt to "take away the authority" of the city to write its own gun laws. Hutchison said it was "the prerogative of Congress" to make laws affecting the District. The bill did not advance. *(D.C. gun-related action, 109th Congress, p. 796)*

D.C. Needle-Exchange Program

The Financial Services and General Government section of the fiscal 2008 omnibus appropriations bill (HR 2764—PL 110-161) retained a policy change opposed by the administration of President George W. Bush that allowed the District of Columbia to use local dollars to fund a needle-exchange program to combat the spread of HIV (human immunodeficiency virus), which causes AIDS (acquired immunodeficiency syndrome). Approximately one in twenty D.C. residents was HIV-positive. *(Omnibus appropriations, p. 111)*

The House Appropriations Committee approved by voice vote on June 11, 2007, the fiscal 2008 Financial Services and General Government appropriations measure (HR 2829—H Rept 110-207). The Financial Services and General Government Subcommittee, which drafted the legislation, had approved it by voice vote June 5. Democrats pushed to lift restrictions, enacted when Congress was under GOP control, that prohibited the District from spending local money for a needle-exchange program.

The White House June 26 issued a statement saying that it strongly opposed the language allowing the District to use its funds to operate a needle-exchange program. The administration said such programs abetted illegal drug use.

Before passing HR 2829 by 240–179 on June 28, the House rejected, 208–216, an amendment by Mark Souder, R-Ind., that would bar the District from using its own tax receipts to run a needle-exchange program. During the debate, Rep. José E. Serrano, D-N.Y., objected to the federal government dictating how D.C. should conduct its affairs.

D.C. Autonomy

The House Oversight and Government Reform Subcommittee on the Federal Workforce, Postal Service, and District of Columbia by voice vote June 21, 2007, approved two bills (HR 733; HR 1054) designed to give the District independence from its congressional overseers on matters that involved local tax revenue and laws.

HR 733 would remove the federal mandate that Congress approve the District's budget each year. It would give the District full autonomy over revenue raised annually through local taxes. Congress would still determine federal funding for the District. The subcommittee by voice vote adopted an amendment by delegate Eleanor Holmes Norton, D-D.C., to allow Congress to maintain oversight of multiyear District government contracts and those in excess of $1 million.

HR 1054 would remove the mandatory congressional review of the District's local laws and would end Congress's power to revoke D.C. laws by adopting a resolution of disapproval. Neither measure was taken up by the Senate.

D.C. Partners Benefits

To ease passage of an omnibus fiscal 2008 spending bill (HR 2764—PL 110-161), Congress stripped some of the more controversial provisions in the Financial Services and General Government appropriations bill (HR 2829). Appropriators dropped language that would allow the District of Columbia to use federal funds to register unmarried, cohabitating couples in the District and to extend to them unemployment benefits similar to those enjoyed by legally married couples; the city could still use its own funds for that purpose. *(Omnibus appropriations, p. 111)*

The White House cited the partners benefit provision, among others, in its June 26, 2007, statement threatening to veto HR 2829. The Senate did not act on the measure.

Native American Housing

Legislation (HR 2786) to reauthorize several programs offering housing assistance to Native Americans, provided under the 1996 Native American Housing Assistance and Self-Determination Act (PL 104-330), and to authorize fiscal 2009 through 2013 funding for the Native American Housing Block Grant program was signed into law (PL 110-411) on Oct. 14, 2008.

The House Financial Services Committee approved HR 2786 by voice vote on June 26, 2007, and formally reported it (H Rept 110-295) on Aug. 3. On Sept. 6, before passing the legislation, 333–75, the House acted on a number of amendments. It adopted, 263–146, an amendment by Steve King, R-Iowa, to bar funding in the bill from being used to employ illegal immigrants. Financial Services Committee chairman Barney Frank, D-Mass., opposed the language, calling it unnecessary.

By voice vote, the House adopted an amendment by Melvin Watt, D-N.C., to deny the Cherokee Nation of Oklahoma funding unless it recognized descendants of former African American slaves as citizens. Tribal members had voted in 2007 to revoke the citizenship of descendants of former slaves who could not also prove Cherokee ancestry. Also adopted by voice vote was a second-degree amendment by Dan Boren, D-Okla., to give the tribe access to the funds while the case was under appeal and would revoke access only if the courts did not rule in favor of recognizing the former slaves' tribal membership. The House adopted an amendment by Steve Pearce, R-N.M., to create a grant program for infrastructure needs, such as plumbing and wiring.

On Sept. 6, the House rejected a bid by Tom Price, R-Ga., to require that all authorized spending be offset by the pay-as-you-go rule, 184–228, and a proposal by Lynn Westmoreland, R-Ga., to strike language to provide housing assistance for native Hawaiians, 112–298.

The Senate passed, by voice vote on Sept. 25, 2008, an amended version of HR 2786. Two days later, the House agreed to the Senate changes under suspension of the rules, completing congressional action. The president signed the bill (HR 2786— PL 110-411) into law Oct. 14, 2008.

Indian Health Service

The Senate Feb. 26, 2008, passed, 83–10, the first overhaul of Native American health care programs since 1992 (PL 102-573). The bill (S 1200) would authorize new money and services for 1.8 million Native Americans and Alaska Natives on reservations. *(1992 action, Congress and the Nation Vol. VIII, p. 905)*

S 1200 would renew through fiscal 2017 the Indian Health Service, the agency that administered the health care programs and directed Native American patients to services such as Medicare, Medicaid, and the State Children's Health Insurance Program. Spending for the programs in fiscal 2008 was expected to total about $3 billion. The Congressional Budget Office estimated that the bill would cost $35 billion over ten years.

A lack of agreement on amendments and a veto threat issued Jan. 22, 2008, by President George W. Bush had impeded efforts to advance the bill. Bill sponsor Byron L. Dorgan, D-N.D., drafted a package of changes as a substitute amendment to the legislation, intended in part to avert a veto. Majority Leader Harry Reid, D-Nev., filed a cloture motion on Dorgan's substitute amendment and on the bill to end filibusters.

The Bush administration's main concern was a provision to expand federal prevailing wage requirements to projects funded under the bill. The administration also took issue with what it said were the bill's lax citizenship documentation requirements for enrolling patients in Medicaid and other government programs. A Dorgan amendment to his substitute amendment, adopted 95–0 on Feb. 14, would return the prevailing wage language to current law and would tighten requirements for Indians applying for health benefits to prove their citizenship.

The Senate also adopted, by voice vote Feb. 14, an amendment designed to block the administration from implementing a new Medicaid regulation that states said was too costly. The new regulation, set to take effect on March 3, 2008, would limit Medicaid reimbursement for ancillary services, such as help finding housing and jobs, that states offered to beneficiaries under case management plans. The administration considered the services, many of them nonmedical in nature, outside the scope of Medicaid. The amendment—offered by Barbara A. Mikulski, D-Md., Norm Coleman, R-Minn., and Amy Klobuchar, D-Minn.—would prevent the Centers for Medicare and Medicaid Services (CMS) from implementing the new rule before April 1, 2009, when a new president was in the White House. CMS said the regulation would save Medicaid about $1.3 billion over five years. But state officials complained that the states would have to pick up the costs of the services or eliminate them, hurting Medicaid's beneficiaries.

The way was cleared for debate on Feb. 25, when the Senate agreed, 85–2, to invoke cloture (thus limiting debate) on the Dorgan substitute. The Senate adopted, 78–11 on Feb. 25, an amendment by Jim DeMint, R-S.C., to ban any funds authorized under the bill from being used to decrease gun ownership. The Senate adopted, 52–42 on Feb. 26, language, offered by David Vitter, R-La., requested by the White House that would bar funding authorized under the bill from being used to provide abortions, expect in cases of rape or incest. Also on Feb. 26, the Senate adopted 56–38, an amendment by Gordon H. Smith, R-Ore., to redistribute authorized funds for construction of health facilities.

The Senate adopted, by voice vote Feb. 26, the Dorgan substitute amendment, to which all subsequent amendments had been attached. The chamber then passed S 1200.

The Senate Indian Affairs Committee had approved S 1200 by voice vote on May 10, 2007, and reported it (S Rept 110-197) on Oct. 16. The House Natural Resources Committee by voice vote on April 25, 2007, had approved a similar measure (HR 1328), which was reported (H Rept 110-564, Part I) on April 4, 2008. The bill, however, went no further in the House.

Native American Land Deal

In 2008 the House considered a land swap bill (HR 2176) that would have allowed two Native American tribes in Michigan to open casinos far from their reservations. Some Michigan lawmakers supported the legislation, saying it would help the state's economy. Opponents, including other Michigan members, said the bill would set a dangerous precedent encouraging other tribes to pursue casinos away from their own lands. The bill would have allowed the Native American tribes to swap their claims to 110 acres of land in Michigan's Upper Peninsula for property close to Detroit and its suburbs. The land would be put in trust held by the federal government.

Sponsored by Bart Stupak, D-Mich., HR 2176 would have given the Bay Mills Indian Community land rights in Port Huron. It incorporated another measure (HR 4115—H Rept 110-542, Parts I and II), sponsored by John D. Dingell, D-Mich., that would have given the Sault Ste. Marie Tribe of Chippewa Indians land in either Flint or Romulus. In 2002 both tribes entered into agreement with the state to own land in southeast Michigan. Congressional action was necessary to make the swap official.

The House Natural Resources Committee had approved the measure, 21–5, on Feb. 13, 2008, and reported it (H Rept 110-541, Part I) on March 6. The House Judiciary Committee by a 29–0 vote April 2, however, ordered that HR 2176 be reported unfavorably, and the bill was reported adversely (H Rept 110-541, Part II) April 4. The House rejected, 121–298, the legislation June 25, 2008, ending congressional action.

CHAPTER 15

Inside Congress

Inside Congress

Well-connected lobbyist Jack Abramoff on Jan. 3, 2006, pleaded guilty to conspiracy, mail fraud, and tax evasion in connection with a fraudulent casino deal in Florida. He agreed to greatly reduced jail time of nearly six years in exchange for telling federal investigators everything he knew about what one Justice Department official called a "very extensive" scheme of trading favors for legislative action on behalf of American Indian tribes and casinos he represented. Within hours of his court appearance, the trickle of formerly close Abramoff friends in Congress who had moved to distance themselves from his activities and his money turned into a stampede. By week's end, seventy-seven lawmakers—including House Speaker J. Dennis Hastert, R-Ill., and Rep. Tom Delay, R-Texas—had announced that they were returning or donating to charity campaign contributions that Abramoff steered their way. Even President George W. Bush sent back money.

Two-and-a-half years later, on Sept. 4, 2008, Abramoff was sentenced to four years in federal prison—on top of the Florida sentence—for defrauding some of his clients, predominantly several Indian tribes, and for bribing public officials in Washington, D.C., including Rep. Bob Ney, R-Ohio, who had been released from prison just the month before, having served time after pleading guilty to making false statements and conspiracy to commit fraud. Abramoff offered gifts, including meals, drinks, and tickets to sporting events and concerts, in exchange for official acts on behalf of him and his clients. He provided some officials with higher-ticket items, such as trips to Scotland and to the Super Bowl.

LOBBYING REFORM

In 2007, between Abramoff's two appointments in court for sentencing, Congress cleared major reform legislation to further regulate transactions between lobbyists and the lobbied. Members' actions came in part as an effort to repair their own images. They were terrified of a voter backlash over the Abramoff scandal, and they became wary of taking on anything that could look like a special interest favor or midnight fix.

But those involved in the legislative process said that the integrity of the system would always rest on the daily judgment of those who worked within it. Lobbyists would still find members willing to take on their causes. The difference could be that lawmakers more than ever would want policy arguments that withstood inspection in the light of day. Lobbying practices based largely or solely on relationships with specific members of Congress likely would wane. The emphasis was expected to shift from less on "who you know" and to more on "what you know"—the political and policy expertise that lobbyists said the vast majority in their profession rely on anyway. A great deal of institutional knowledge rested in the lobbying shops around Washington, which were populated by former congressional staff and lawmakers. With the pace and complexity of the business on Capitol Hill, the information they provided—from the potential consequences of a policy change to where the votes were on a particular bill—would continue to be valuable coin that assured lobbyists access to congressional offices.

Lobbyists have something else politicians need at least as much as information: money. Lawmakers view lobbyists as important contributors and fund-raisers. Although the Abramoff scandal could make lobbyists more cautious about the timing of fund-raisers, they would continue to

REFERENCES

Discussion of congressional action for the years 1945–1964 may be found in *Congress and the Nation Vol. I*, pp. 1407–1431; for the years 1965–1968, *Congress and the Nation Vol. II*, pp. 893–924; for the years 1969–1972, *Congress and the Nation Vol. III*, pp. 353–433; for the years 1973–1976, *Congress and the Nation Vol. IV*, pp. 743–794; for the years 1977–1980, *Congress and the Nation Vol. V*, pp. 873–953; for the years 1981–1984, *Congress and the Nation Vol. VI*, pp. 797–840; for the years 1985–1988, *Congress and the Nation Vol. VII*, pp. 871–910; for the years 1989–1992, *Congress and the Nation Vol. VIII*, pp. 913–988; for the years 1993–1996, *Congress and the Nation Vol. IX*, pp. 861–925; for the years 1997–2001, *Congress and the Nation Vol. X*, pp. 757–794; for the years 2001–2004, *Congress and the Nation Vol. XI*, pp. 705–742.

Senate Democratic leader Harry Reid calls for lawmakers to clean up the tainted relationship between lawmakers and lobbyists in the wake of the scandal involving former lobbyist Jack Abramoff on January 18, 2006. From left to right are: Sen. Dick Durbin, D-Ill., Sen. Barack Obama, D-Ill., Senate Democratic leader Harry Reid of Nevada, House Democratic leader Nancy Pelosi of California, Rep. James E. Clyburn, D-S.C., and Rep. Louise Slaughter, N.Y.
Source: AP Photo/J. Scott Applewhite

feel intense pressure to contribute money. In 2004 election cycle, for example, 171 of the lobbyists who gave the most to campaigns contributed $12 million, according to an analysis by Public Citizen. That did not include the money that lobbyists raised from their clients and others on behalf of members.

DELAY AND HOUSE ETHICS

Abramoff described himself as one of DeLay's closest friends. Since Republicans took over Capitol Hill in the mid-1990s, the Texas Republican, who would rise to become the House majority leader, derived his near mythical power from his self-anointed role as the House GOP's fund-raiser in chief and from a network of loyal former aides who set up shop on K Street, the location of many of Washington's most influential lobbying firms. His ability to leverage that power by working his will on policy was a modern political marvel. But his fund-raising and close ties to donors and lobbyists also were at the root of the ethics scandal within which he would find himself mired.

In 2004, DeLay had been admonished three times by the bipartisan House Committee on Standards of Official Conduct, in one instance for holding a fund-raiser on a golf course with energy officials at the same time he was working out the details of major energy legislation. Bolstered by their victories in the November 2004 elections and angered by the ethic panel's disciplinary actions against DeLay, the majority House Republicans opened the 109th Congress in 2005 by pushing through a set of rules changes that affected how the committee conducted its business, that is, by making it harder to bring and prosecute ethics cases. Some proposed rule changes, such as permitting a Republican lawmaker under criminal indictment to remain in the leadership, were clearly meant to protect DeLay, who at the time was under investigation in Texas.

In another move widely viewed as punishment for the actions against DeLay, Speaker Hastert replaced the ethic committee chair as well as two other Republicans on the panel. All five of the GOP members of the refashioned panel had received campaign contributions from DeLay's political organization. Two of the new members, Lamar Smith of Texas and Tom Cole of Oklahoma, gave generous donations to DeLay's legal defense fund. The new chair, Doc Hastings, R-Wash., began to fire the committee's staff. A dispute arose over his effort to install his chief aide as the committee's staff director, which Democrats said violated established practice and a rule requiring ethics staff to be nonpartisan.

Taken together, the changes set off a firestorm of criticism and led to the virtual shutdown of the committee. Led by ranking member Alan B. Mollohan of West Virginia, the panel's five Democrats blocked approval of the committee's operating rules, making it impossible for the ten-member, evenly divided panel to function. The panel could accomplish only simple administrative duties, while well-publicized cases of potential misconduct went unchecked.

In April 2005, the House reversed the rules changes, which meant that the committee in effect reverted to the same standards it had operated under in previous Congresses. Even with that vote, though, the panel remained dormant because Mollohan and Hastings disagreed over who should be hired for chief counsel. They resolved that disagreement in June, but the committee did little for the rest of the year. The predicament the House ethics panel faced renewed the long-standing debate about whether Congress was capable of policing itself or whether the job should be taken over by an outside commission or group.

In September 2005, a Texas grand jury handed down an indictment accusing DeLay of conspiring with his top fund-raisers to use corporate political contributions in state house races in 2002, something that was illegal in Texas. In the wake of the indictment, DeLay relinquished his post as majority leader. He denied any wrongdoing and vowed to reclaim his leadership role. In 2006, however, four days after Abramoff pleaded guilty to three felony charges, DeLay announced that he would give up his pursuit of the majority leader position. DeLay had came under fire because of revelations that Abramoff either directly or indirectly picked up the tab for some of his all-expenses paid excursions. DeLay subsequently resigned his House seat.

Chronology of Action on Congress: Members and Procedures

2005–2006

Republicans retained their majority status in both houses of Congress. Senate Democrats had to deal with the repercussions of their leader having faced electoral defeat in November 2004, while House Republicans watched their majority leader be indicted and eventually resign his seat. A group of Republican and Democratic senators joined forces to thwart a potential crisis involving the filibuster. Congress succeeded in making contingency plans for its continuity in case of an emergency. The House and Senate could not bridge the gap between their differing visions of lobbying reform, leaving the issue for the next Congress to tackle.

Organization: 109th Congress

Upon the opening of the 109th Congress on Jan. 4, 2005, Republicans were buoyed by their 2004 election victories, which increased their majorities in both chambers.

SENATE

Senate Republicans and Democrats began organizing for the new Congress during the 2004 lame duck session. The defeat at the polls of Minority Leader Tom Daschle of South Dakota set off a scramble to reorganize the Senate Democratic leadership, producing an almost entirely new slate of leaders.

Majority Leadership

The Republican leadership contained many familiar faces. Continuing in their posts were Bill Frist of Tennessee as majority leader, Mitch McConnell of Kentucky as majority whip, Rick Santorum of Pennsylvania as Republican Conference chair, and Jon Kyl of Arizona as Republican Policy Committee chair. Elizabeth Dole of North Carolina succeeded George Allen of Virginia as National Republican Senatorial Committee chair.

Ted Stevens of Alaska remained as president pro tempore.

Minority Leadership

Minority Whip Harry Reid of Nevada was elected the new minority leader without any contest. He succeeded Daschle, who had lost his reelection bid. Richard J. Durbin of Illinois took Reid's place as minority whip, warding off a challenge from Byron L. Dorgan of North Dakota, who remained as Senate Democratic Policy Committee chair at Reid's request.

Barbara A. Mikulski of Maryland stepped down as secretary of the Democratic Conference, the No. 3 elected position in the Democratic leadership. She was succeeded by Debbie Stabenow of Michigan. Hillary Rodham Clinton of New York kept her post as chair of the Steering and Outreach Committee, which was renamed from the Steering and Coordination Committee. Charles E. Schumer of New York succeeded Jon Corzine of New Jersey as Democratic Senatorial Campaign Committee chair.

Committees

Senate committees for the first time felt the impact of GOP-imposed term limits for chairmanships. Adding to the musical chairs was the agreement among Senate Republicans, reached in their party caucus, to dilute the traditional power of seniority in selecting committee chairs.

Because of the term limits, Alaska's Ted Stevens on Appropriations, Arizona's John McCain on Commerce, Science, and Transportation, Utah's Orrin G. Hatch on Judiciary, and Pennsylvania's Arlen Specter on Veterans' Affairs had to give up their positions. Stevens took over at Commerce and was succeeded on Appropriations by Thad Cochran, R-Miss. McCain assumed the top spot at Indian Affairs, succeeding Ben Nighthorse Campbell, R-Colo. Specter became chair at Judiciary, following Orrin G. Hatch, R-Utah.

There were more changes. Saxby Chambliss of Georgia took the helm at Agriculture, Nutrition, and Forestry, succeeding Cochran. Judd Gregg of New Hampshire succeeded

Don Nickles, R-Okla., on Budget. Larry E. Craig of Idaho headed Veterans' Affairs, after Specter.

Retaining their chairs were John W. Warner of Virginia at Armed Services, Richard C. Shelby of Alabama at Banking, Housing, and Urban Affairs, Pete V. Domenici of New Mexico at Energy and Natural Resources, James M. Inhofe of Oklahoma at Environment and Public Works, George V. Voinovich of Ohio at the Select Committee on Ethics, Charles E. Grassley of Iowa at Finance, Richard G. Lugar at Foreign Relations, Michael B. Enzi of Wyoming at Health, Education, Labor, and Pensions, Susan Collins of Maine at Homeland Security and Governmental Affairs, Pat Roberts of Kansas at the Select Committee on Intelligence, Trent Lott of Mississippi at Rules, and Olympia J. Snowe of Maine at Small Business and Entrepreneurship.

Democrats keeping their spots as ranking members were Tom Harkin of Iowa at Agriculture, Robert C. Byrd of West Virginia at Appropriations, Carl Levin of Michigan at Armed Services, Paul S. Sarbanes of Maryland at Banking, Kent Conrad of North Dakota at Budget, Jeff Bingaman of New Mexico at Energy, Max Baucus of Montana at Finance, Joseph R. Biden Jr. of Delaware at Foreign Relations, Edward M. Kennedy of Massachusetts at Health, John D. Rockefeller IV of West Virginia at Intelligence, Patrick J. Leahy of Vermont at Judiciary, Christopher J. Dodd of Connecticut at Rules, and John Kerry of Massachusetts at Small Business. Independent James M. Jeffords of Vermont remained as ranking member at Environment, and Independent Joseph I. Lieberman of Connecticut kept his ranking member position at Homeland Security and Governmental Affairs.

Daniel K. Inouye of Hawaii became ranking member on Commerce, succeeding Ernest F. Hollings, D-S.C., who retired from Congress. Tim Johnson of South Dakota took over the vice chair slot from Harry Reid on Ethics. Byron Dorgan succeeded Inouye as ranking member on Indian Affairs. Daniel K. Akaka of Hawaii took the ranking slot on Veterans' Affairs, following Bob Graham, D-Fla., who retired from Congress.

Rules

The GOP caucus voted 27–26 by secret ballot on Nov. 17, 2004, to adopt a proposal by Lott that allowed the majority leader to appoint half of all open seats on the most coveted panels, known as "A" committees. Other seats on those committees would continue to be filled based on seniority. Lott praised the vote as an attempt to fix "a hide-bound, muscle-bound, dysfunctional institution" by giving the majority leader more weapons to prevent Republican senators from going their own way. The change, meanwhile, left defenders of the seniority system—moderates, senators from swing states, and senior members—sputtering in anger over the jab at their independence.

HOUSE

Ethics troubles prompted changes by the majority GOP, whose leadership sought to protect its own and to punish those party members who defied its wishes.

Majority Leadership

By 226–199 on Jan. 4, 2005, J. Dennis Hastert, R-Ill., was reelected Speaker over Nancy Pelosi, D-Calif.

Tom DeLay of Texas retained his post as majority leader. However, he was required by GOP Conference rules to vacate the position after his Sept. 28, 2005, indictment in Texas on campaign finance charges. Hastert named Roy Blunt of Missouri, who had been majority whip since 2003, to act as majority leader for the remainder of the first session of the 109th Congress. DeLay hoped to resume his job as majority leader after being exonerated of the Texas charges. However, he announced on Jan. 7, 2006, that he would not try to regain his leadership post in the wake of public disclosures of his close association with disgraced lobbyist Jack Abramoff.

On Feb. 2, John A. Boehner of Ohio scored an upset victory in a second-ballot runoff against Blunt, who had been the frontrunner to replace DeLay. The rank and file seemed to see Boehner as offering more of a break from the DeLay era. He won 122–109, backed by a loose coalition of disaffected conservatives and moderates, including a number of committee chairs and longtime allies. A third candidate, John Shadegg of Arizona, was dropped after the first ballot, when he drew 40 votes, to 79 for Boehner and 110 for Blunt. Shadegg had been a late entry, backed by conservatives who said neither Blunt nor Boehner offered a true break from the past. To run for majority leader, Shadegg had given up his role as Republican Policy Committee chair, which he had assumed at the beginning of the 109th Congress, succeeding Christopher Cox of California. Shadegg was replaced as panel chair by Adam H. Putnam of Florida, and Blunt resumed his position as majority whip.

Deborah Pryce of Ohio was unchallenged to continue as House Republican Conference chair, and Thomas M. Reynolds of New York remained as National Republican Congressional Committee chair.

Minority Leadership

Pelosi continued as minority leader, a post she first assumed at the beginning of the 108th Congress two years earlier. Also retained were Steny H. Hoyer of Maryland as minority whip and Robert Menendez of New Jersey as Democratic Caucus chair. James E. Clyburn of South Carolina became caucus chair in 2006, after Menendez was appointed to fill the Senate seat vacated by Jon Corzine, who had been elected governor of New Jersey. Rahm Emanuel of Illinois became Democratic Congressional Campaign Committee chair, succeeding Robert T. Matsui of California, who died Jan. 1, 2005. Matsui had been expected to relinquish the post at the beginning of the 109th Congress.

ROSA PARKS LYING IN REPOSE

By voice votes, the Senate on Oct. 27, 2005, and the House the next day adopted a resolution (S Con Res 61) allowing the casket of Rosa Parks to be placed in the Capitol Rotunda on Oct. 30 so that visitors could pay their respects. Parks helped usher in the civil rights movement by refusing to move to the back of a segregated bus. She had died on Oct. 24 at the age of ninety-two.

Assistant Senate Historian Betty K. Koed said the honor of lying in repose in the rotunda was traditionally reserved for government officials and some members of the U.S. military, but Congress had made exceptions twice before. For one day in 1998, the caskets of two officers gunned down at the Capitol, Jacob J. Chestnut and John M. Gibson, rested in the rotunda. Eighty-nine years earlier, Congress made the same accommodation before the reinterment of Pierre L'Enfant, who created the city plan for Washington, D.C.

The death of another civil rights leader, the Rev. Dr. Martin Luther King Jr., sparked interest for allowing his body to lie in honor in the Capitol, but Koed said Congress in 1968 stopped short of passing legislation to do so. Instead, Congress adopted a resolution expressing sympathy to his family.

Committees

House GOP leaders made it clear that they would punish party members who were not sufficiently loyal.

Christopher H. Smith of New Jersey was removed as chair of the Veterans' Affairs Committee on the first day of the new Congress, replaced by Steve Buyer of Indiana. Smith had frequently clashed with GOP leaders in his bid to increase funding levels for veterans' programs. It was the first time since Republicans took power a decade earlier that they deposed a sitting chair.

Joel Hefley of Colorado was replaced as chair of the House Committee on Standards of Official Conduct (ethics committee) by Doc Hastings of Washington. The move was punishment for the panel's admonishments of DeLay for ethical lapses in 2004. *(2004 action, Congress and the Nation Vol. XI, p. 721)*

Jerry Lewis of California took the helm of the House Appropriations Committee, succeeding C.W. Bill Young of Florida, who stepped down due to GOP-imposed term limits. David Dreier of California was the beneficiary of the majority's power, keeping his spot as Rules Committee chair by receiving a waiver from Hastert to extend his chairmanship despite the customary six-year term limit.

When Porter J. Goss of Florida left the chairmanship of the Intelligence Committee in August 2004 to become director of central intelligence, Hastert tapped Peter Hoekstra of Michigan to take over, bypassing four more-senior members. Hoekstra retained the top spot in the 109th Congress. Also keeping their chairs were Robert W. Goodlatte of Virginia at Agriculture, Duncan Hunter of California at Armed Services, Jim Nussle of Iowa at Budget, Michael G. Oxley of Ohio at Financial Services, Henry J. Hyde of Illinois at International Relations, F. James Sensenbrenner Jr. of Wisconsin at Judiciary, Richard W. Pombo of California at Resources, Thomas M. Davis III at Government Reform, Sherwood Boehlert of New York at Science, Donald Manzullo of Illinois at Small Business, Don Young of Alaska at Transportation and Infrastructure, and Bill Thomas of California at Ways and Means.

Joe L. Barton of Texas succeeded W. J. "Billy" Tauzin of Louisiana as Energy and Commerce chair. John A. Boehner of Ohio headed Education and the Workforce until early 2006, when he became majority leader, succeeding Tom DeLay. Howard P. "Buck" McKeon of California took over at Education. Peter T. King of New York became head of Homeland Security, which had been a select committee from 2002 to 2005. He succeeded Christopher Cox of California. House Administration continued to be steered by Bob Ney of Ohio. However, he stepped down in January 2006 in the wake of being implicated in the Justice Department investigation of lobbyist Jack Abramoff. Vernon J. Ehlers of Michigan assumed the post.

Democrats staying put in their ranking member slots were David R. Obey of Wisconsin at Appropriations, Ike Skelton of Missouri at Armed Services, John M. Spratt Jr. of South Carolina at Budget, George Miller of California at Education and the Workforce, John D. Dingell of Michigan at Energy and Commerce, Barney Frank of Massachusetts at Financial Services, Tom Lantos of California at International Relations, Jane Harman of California at Intelligence, John Conyers Jr. at Judiciary, Nick J. Rahall II of West Virginia at Resources, Henry A. Waxman of California at Government Reform, Nydia M. Velázquez of New York at Small Business, Alan B. Mollohan of West Virginia at Standards of Official Conduct, James L. Oberstar of Minnesota at Transportation and Infrastructure, Lane Evans of Illinois at Veterans' Affairs, and Charles B. Rangel of New York at Ways and Means. Democrat Ralph M. Hall of Texas, who was the ranking member of Science at the start of the 108th Congress, switched to the Republican Party in January 2004. Taking over as ranking member was Bart Gordon of Tennessee, who retained the post in the 109th Congress.

Collin C. Peterson of Minnesota succeeded Charles W. Stenholm, D-Texas, who was defeated for reelection in 2004, as ranking member on Agriculture. Bennie Thompson of Mississippi became ranking member on Homeland Security, succeeding Jim Turner, D-Texas. Juanita

Millender-McDonald of California took over as ranking member at House Administration, following John B. Larson of Connecticut. Louise M. Slaughter of New York succeeded Martin Frost, D-Texas, as ranking member at Rules. Frost was defeated in his 2004 reelection bid.

Rules

The leadership rules package (H Res 5) was adopted on a 220–195 party-line vote on Jan. 4, 2005. Democrats were particularly angered by a rule change that would effectively kill an ethics complaint unless the Committee on Standards of Official Conduct (ethics committee) chair and ranking member found within forty-five days that it had merit. Under previous rules, if the forty-five days went by without action, the case automatically passed to an investigative subcommittee. The new rules also gave targeted members a right to respond to the ethics panel's conclusions before a decision was made final or made public.

Under pressure from their own members, Republican leaders abandoned plans for a proposed change that would have significantly curtailed the power of the ethics committee by prohibiting admonishments except when the behavior at issue violated a specific law or House rule. They also agreed to reverse a Nov. 17, 2004, decision by the House Republican Conference to alter its caucus rules in a way that would allow a member to keep his leadership job even if he were indicted. The intention was to protect Minority Leader DeLay, who was the subject of an ethics committee investigation. The panel in 2004 had admonished DeLay, but in none of the issues raised was a written ethics or House rule violated. *(DeLay ethics probe, p. 822)*

Previously, House Republican caucus rules required that a party leader or committee chair indicted on a felony charge step aside until the case was resolved. Although the rule was never invoked, DeLay contended that it made Republican leaders vulnerable to politically motivated criminal investigations. The rule approved in November 2004 would have let the caucus decide if one of its leaders should step down if indicted. It would have given the Republican Steering Committee, an arm of the leadership, thirty days to review a case and make a recommendation on which the full conference would vote. A leader who was convicted of a felony had to be removed immediately. Democrats and congressional watchdog groups had vigorously criticized the proposed change, and individual Republicans had gotten an earful from constituents who were displeased with the rule.

On a **key vote of 406–20 (R 208–20; D 197–0; I 1–0)**, the House on April 27, 2005, adopted a resolution (H Res 241) governing floor debate on another resolution (H Res 240) that rolled back three rules changes instituted at the start of the new Congress: that any complaint against a House member would die after forty-five days unless the House Committee on Standards of Official Conduct had voted by then to proceed with an investigation; that members who were the object of an investigation had the right to respond to the ethic panel's conclusions before a decision was made final or publicly announced; and that codified what had been an occasional practice of permitting one attorney to represent multiple members involved in an ethics case. *(2005 key votes, p. 915)*

H Res 5 also provided for the creation of a permanent Homeland Security Committee with jurisdiction over the Transportation Security Administration, some border security functions, and port security. However, it left much of the jurisdiction subject to interpretation and failed to solve all the turf battles that hobbled the Homeland Security panel during the 108th Congress, when it was a select committee. A series of "legislative history" provisions were written to accompany the House rules package. The language would enable ten other chairs besides the Homeland Security chair to claim for their committees jurisdiction over legislation that would affect various agencies and policies of the Department of Homeland Security.

By 379–50 on Feb. 1, 2006, the House agreed to suspend the rules and pass H Res 648, which revoked the floor and gymnasium privileges of former members who were lobbyists. The House Rules Committee had reported the resolution (H Rept 109-369, Part I) on Jan. 31. The GOP membership went along with the leadership in allowing the rules change but rejected a larger proposal that was slated to be introduced that would have banned privately funded travel for lawmakers, lowered the gift limit, and increased disclosure for lobbyists and members.

The House on Sept. 14, 2006, adopted 245–171 a narrow change in House rules (H Res 1000) requiring that earmarks and their sponsors be identified in future appropriations, tax, and authorizing legislation. If the earmarks were not disclosed, the legislation would be subject to a point of order. *(Lobbying reform, p. 816)*

The rule change was not retroactive, and the House had already passed all but one of its fiscal 2007 appropriations bills. Nevertheless, Republican appropriators fought the resolution before it came to the floor, arguing that it did not apply equally to tax and authorizing bills. Although the rule did apply to "tax earmarks," it defined them narrowly as revenue-losing provisions that provided a tax break to a single beneficiary. Congress's Joint Committee on Taxation would determine which provisions qualified.

Appropriators said the threshold should be set at one hundred beneficiaries and expressed skepticism that the joint committee would fairly identify earmarks that its members had written. In an effort to round up votes for the resolution, Hastert sent GOP appropriators a letter seeking their support and assuring them that if problems with the rule arose, they would be corrected in the future.

Twenty-two of the twenty-four Republicans who voted against the rule were appropriators. Their numbers were more than offset by forty-five Democrats who voted for the measure. The Speaker, who typically did not vote, cast a "yea" vote for the rules change.

Lobbying Reform

The House and Senate in 2006 passed lobbying reform legislation (S 2349), but lawmakers were so far apart that they never held a conference to reconcile their differences and the bill died upon adjournment. The House did make a narrow rule change, requiring members to identify the earmarks—the special interest provisions directing federal dollars to particular organizations, businesses, or projects—they inserted into legislation. *(House rules changes, p. 815)*

The 110th Congress was successful in enacting a lobbying reform overhaul measure. *(Lobbying reform, p. 830)*

SENATE COMMITTEE ACTION

The Senate Rules and Administration Committee and the Senate Homeland Security and Governmental Affairs Committee drafted lobbying reform bills, which were subsequently combined for floor consideration.

Rules and Administration on Feb. 28, 2006, voted 18–0 to approve a measure, introduced by Chairman Trent Lott, R-Miss., to ban lobbyist-paid travel and gifts. Lobbyists still could buy meals and drinks for senators and their staffs as long as senators disclosed the gifts. The legislation also required that all Senate bills and conference reports include a list of earmarks with the names of the senators who proposed them. To curtail senators' ability to insert earmarks late in the life cycle of legislation—at the conference committee stage—any earmark that originated in conference would be subject to a point of order. The conference committee section was written to apply to all kinds of legislation, not just appropriations bills. Conference reports would have to be posted online twenty-four hours before a Senate floor vote.

During the markup, the panel:

- Adopted by voice vote a Dianne Feinstein, D-Calif., amendment to require sixty votes to overcome a point of order against an earmark added in conference. Lott proposed a simple majority.
- Adopted by voice vote a Daniel K. Inouye, D-Hawaii, amendment to strike proposed new disclosure requirements for Indian tribes.
- Adopted 17–0 a Richard J. Durbin, D-Ill., amendment intended to end the K Street Project, through which congressional Republicans had pressed lobbying shops to hire GOP staff members. It would bar senators from using their elected positions to persuade "any private entity" to hire or refuse to hire a particular employee based on political affiliation.
- Adopted by voice vote a Rick Santorum, R-Pa., amendment to bar a senator's spouse or family members from lobbying the senator's staff.

Homeland Security and Governmental Affairs on March 2 by 12–1 approved S 2128, sponsored by John McCain, R-Ariz. The bill called for more frequent, in-depth, and user-friendly disclosure of how much lobbyists spent on lobbying and campaign contributions. It also would require quarterly reports, instead of semiannual disclosure as under existing law, and the information would be made available electronically so the public could learn what firms were lobbying on what bills, how much they were spending, and which congressional offices were being lobbied. Furthermore, the legislation said members of Congress and high-level executive branch officials would have to wait two years, instead of one, before they could lobby their former colleagues.

During markup, the committee:

- Rejected 11–5 an amendment offered by committee chair Susan Collins, R-Maine, to create an independent Office of Public Integrity within the legislative branch. Members of the Select Ethics Committee opposed the provision, which would have created a powerful office with subpoena and investigative powers. Meanwhile, groups such as Common Cause and Public Citizen said that not establishing the office crippled the bill, arguing that the focus would be on disclosing corruption instead of deterring it.
- Adopted 10–6 a Joseph I. Lieberman, D-Conn., and Carl Levin, D-Mich., amendment to require groups that spent more than $25,000 per quarter or $100,000 per year on grassroots operations to disclose their expenditures and activities. Groups such as the Grover Norquist–led Americans for Tax Reform argued against any new lobbing disclosure rules for grassroots activities. Some committee Republicans expressed concern that local organizations that rallied constituents to write or call Congress could be ensnared by such lobbying disclosure rules. But Lieberman said the goal was to expose groups that received money from lobbying firms to advocate for legislation without revealing their tie to corporate lobbyists.

SENATE FLOOR ACTION

The Senate, after incorporating the provisions of S 2128, passed S 2349 by 90–8 on March 29. McCain and Barack Obama, D-Ill., two of the original sponsors, voted against the bill, objecting that it lacked any enforcement mechanism to truly change the culture in Washington, D.C.

Floor debate began March 6 but was derailed March 8, when Charles E. Schumer, D-N.Y., caught the leadership off guard by offering an unrelated amendment to block a Dubai-based company from taking over operations at six U.S. port facilities. When a motion to invoke cloture, and thereby limit debate and block nongermane amendments, fell nine votes short of the sixty needed, Majority Leader Bill Frist, R-Tenn., moved on to other legislation. The cloture vote failed 51–47 on March 9.

Lott, who led the Senate effort to enact lobbying reform legislation, labored for two weeks to tamp down amendments and win support for cloture. When Frist allowed the bill back on the floor March 28, the Senate voted 81–16 to invoke cloture, a step that also killed off several potential amendments without forcing members to go on the record in an election year as opposing reform efforts.

During the floor debate, the Senate rejected 30–67 on March 28 a Collins amendment to create an independent Office of Public Integrity to investigate possible violations of the Senate rules. The same day it adopted 84–13 a Ron Wyden, D-Ore., and Charles E. Grassley, R-Iowa, amendment to put an end to "secret holds" in the Senate. The two had tried unsuccessfully for years to force a vote to make members be candid when blocking legislation. The amendment would require senators to declare in writing to the Senate leadership when they objected to bringing up a bill or nomination. They would have three days to resolve their concerns privately before being required to declare publicly that they were holding up the measure or nominee.

The Senate voted 68–30 on March 29 to table (kill) a Russ Feingold, D-Wis., amendment to broaden the definition of "lobbyist," so that the underlying bill's ban on gifts could not be circumvented by having another corporate representative pick up the tab for a senator. Also on March 29, the Senate voted 57–41 to table a John Ensign, R-Nev., amendment to expand the earmark disclosure requirement to include money designated for federal programs.

The Senate-passed S 2349 contained the following provisions.

Earmarks. Bills, amendments, and conference reports could not come to the floor unless the lawmaker responsible for each earmark was identified. Earmarks added to appropriations bills in conference would be subject to a sixty-vote point of order on the floor. Conference reports had to be posted on the Internet at least forty-eight hours before a Senate vote.

Travel. Senators would have to submit itineraries for privately funded travel and get approval from the Ethics Committee before taking the trip. Lobbyists would be barred from such trips. A detailed report on the trip would be required within thirty days of the lawmaker's return and would be posted on the senator's Web site.

Gifts, meals, drinks. Senators and aides could not accept gifts, including meals and drinks, from registered lobbyists, although they still could accept meals valued at up to $50 from others as long as they disclosed them on their official Web site within fifteen days. Lobbyists would be barred from making gifts, including travel, in violation of House or Senate rules.

Disclosure by lobbyists. Registered lobbyists would have to file quarterly reports on their activities. The reports would be filed electronically and would be available to the public online. They would include campaign contributions and lobbyists' past congressional and executive branch employment.

Penalties. Penalties for violating the 1995 Lobbying Disclosure Act (PL 104-65) would be increased to $100,000 from $50,000. *(1995 act, Congress and the Nation Vol. IX, p. 834)*

Revolving door. The bill would double to two years the period during which senators and very senior executive branch officials were barred from lobbying their colleagues after leaving office. Top congressional aides would have to wait a year before doing any congressional lobbying. Under existing law, the one-year period applied only to lobbying their former office. Senior Senate staff members who became lobbyists could not lobby any member or office for one year. The Senate also adopted a nonbinding sense of the Senate amendment that the lobbying employment restrictions should also apply to the executive and judicial branches.

Secret holds. Senators would not be able to secretly block floor consideration of bills or nominees for more than three days.

Floor access. Senate floor privileges would be revoked for former senators, Speakers of the House, secretaries of the Senate, and Senate sergeants at arms who were registered lobbyists.

Grassroots lobbying. Nonprofit advocacy groups that spent more than $100,000 a year or $25,000 per quarter on lobbying activities would have to disclose how much money they raised, how much they spent, and whether they were affiliated with lobbying firms.

Relatives. Members of a senator's staff could not have "official contact" with the family members of the senator who were lobbyists.

Ethics training. The Senate Ethics Committee would be required to conduct ethics training for Senate personnel and for new senators and staff.

K Street Project. Senators would be barred from using their positions to pressure any private entity to hire or refuse to hire a particular employee based on political affiliation.

Pay raise. Lawmakers who voted to block Congress's automatic annual cost-of-living pay increase would not receive the raise if it took effect.

Audits. The comptroller general would have to annually audit lobbying disclosure reports. Complaints had been made that too many reports were filed late, were incomplete, or contained inaccurate information.

HOUSE COMMITTEE ACTION

Speaker J. Dennis Hastert, R-Ill., asked the chairs of five committees with jurisdiction over the House's lobbying bill (HR 4975) to try to complete their markups the week after the Senate vote. In the meantime, the leadership won narrow passage of a bill (HR 513) restricting the activities of 527 organizations. *(Campaign finance, p. 844)*

The leadership-backed HR 4975 progressed largely intact through all five panels. Democrats contended that some of the changes were designed more to insulate the party from retribution for ethics scandals than to make a difference in the way Congress worked. A few in the Republican rank and file said the leadership was overreacting.

The Judiciary Committee approved HR 4975 18–16 on April 5 and formally reported it (H Rept 109-439, Part I) on April 25. The Rules Committee approved the bill by voice vote on April 5 and reported it (H Rept 109-439, Part III) on April 25. The House Administration Committee approved the measure 5–2 on April 6 and reported it (H Rept 109-439, Part II) on April 25. The Government Reform Committee approved HR 4975 by voice vote on April 6 and reported it (H Rept 109-439, Part IV) on April 25. The Committee on Standards of Official Conduct (ethics committee) approved the legislation in closed session April 6 with no vote tally made public.

Democrats in several of the committees tried to get features of a bill (HR 4682), introduced by Democratic leaders, written into HR 4975, but to no avail. HR 4682 included provisions to extend the revolving door prohibition to two years and ban gifts and meals from lobbyists. It also included earmark restrictions.

Some of the committee action on HR 4975 made provisions drafted by the leadership tougher. For example, the Judiciary Committee amended the bill to permit prison sentences of up to five years for lobbyists and members of Congress who failed to disclose gifts and free lunches. The Rules Committee adopted an amendment to allow staff salaries to be withheld from those who failed to participate in ethics training. It also defined "earmarks" to include not only funds dedicated to specific projects but also any allocation of funds "outside of the normal formula-driven or competitive bidding process" and directed to "an identifiable person, specific state or congressional district." The Government Reform Committee expanded a provision that would deny pension benefits to members convicted of crimes related to their government positions to all congressional employees and to all political appointees of the executive branch. The committee also extended a requirement that lobbyists disclose contacts with lawmakers to include staff members. The Government Reform Committee–added language was inspired by the prosecution of former representative Randy "Duke" Cunningham, R-Calif. (1991–2005), who pleaded guilty to taking antiques, a yacht, and other bribes from defense contractors for whom he arranged legislative earmarks. *(Ethics probes, p. 822)*

The House Government Reform Committee voted 32–0 on April 6 to approve HR 5112, which would tighten the rules governing executive branch lobbying. The measure was formally reported (H Rept 109-445) on April 27 but saw no further action.

HOUSE FLOOR ACTION

A rebellion of Republican appropriators, who were furious at being singled out in the earmark language, almost derailed HR 4975 before it got to the floor. Led by House Appropriations Committee chairman Jerry Lewis, R-Calif., the appropriators threatened to defeat the rule for floor debate unless the earmark language was changed. Hastert and Majority Leader John A. Boehner, R-Ohio, quelled the uprising and avoided an embarrassing defeat, but only by promising not to accept a conference report on the legislation unless it included the broader Senate language, which applied the earmark disclosure to authorization and tax legislation, as well as appropriations bills.

In addition to controlling the floor debate, the rule (H Res 783) automatically incorporated HR 513, aimed at cracking down on 527 groups. HR 4975 originally included the 527 provisions, but they were taken out to avoid generating additional opposition to the lobbying measure. Before bringing HR 4975 to the floor, the leadership made some changes. Provisions dealing with lobbying disclosure reports remained the same, but the bill omitted some changes made by the committees during markup.

Opponents said the measure would do little to clean up what they said was an ethics swamp of sleazy and illegal behavior, that it would be better to defeat it and start over. But enough members viewed the bill as at least a starting point in the cleanup process.

HR 4975, as passed by the House on May 3 on a **key vote of 217–213 (R 209–20; D 8–192; I 0–1),** contained the following provisions. *(2006 key votes, p. 937)*

Earmarks. Appropriations bills could not come to the floor unless the committee report listed and identified the sponsor of each earmark. Appropriations conference reports could not come to the floor without a similar list of any earmarks added in conference. The rule would be enforced by a point of order.

Travel. Originally, the House bill would have suspended privately funded travel through the end of 2006 while the ethics committee rewrote travel and gift rules. But a Dan Lungren, R-Calif., amendment, adopted by voice vote on May 3, established a process for the ethics panel to approve trips and set a June 15 deadline for new travel guidelines.

Gifts. Rules limiting the value of a gift that a member could receive to less than $50 would remain unchanged, but the ethics committee would review the gift rules and make recommendations. Lobbyists would be prohibited from making gifts or providing travel to a member if they knew it was in violation of House or Senate rules.

Disclosure by lobbyists. Lobbyists would be required to file quarterly reports to be posted on the Internet in a searchable database. Lobbyists would have to report congressional and executive branch employment in the previous seven years and whether they had solicited money or done work for candidates or political action committees.

Penalties. Penalties for violating the Lobbying Disclosure Act would be increased to $100,000.

Revolving door. The bill did not alter the one-year ban against departing members and staff accepting jobs related to their legislative work. Members would have to report salary discussions with prospective employers to the ethics committee and refrain from votes that would affect those employers.

Pensions. The bill would prohibit former members of Congress convicted of corruption while in office from receiving their government pensions. The leadership dropped language added by the Government Reform Committee that would have extended the provision to congressional staff and executive branch political appointees.

Grassroots lobbying. Requirements were similar to those in the Senate bill.

Ethics training. The House ethics committee was required to provide ethics training to House employees. As amended, the bill also required registered lobbyists to complete eight hours of ethics training during each Congress. Another amendment added a voluntary ethics training program for members. The names of members choosing not to participate within one hundred days of being sworn in would be posted on the Web and published in the *Congressional Record.*

The House-passed bill also would hold lobbyists liable for giving members gifts that violated the House limit of $50, with civil fines of up to $50,000. Furthermore, the measure clarified that it was illegal for public officials to demand, seek, or accept anything of value in return for any official action relating to a funding earmark.

The House passed S 2349 by voice vote May 23 after inserting the text of HR 4975.

Contingency Plans for Congress

The need for a plan to ensure that the legislative branch would live on even if most of its members were killed or incapacitated was a pressing concern for Congress since the Sept. 11, 2001, terrorist attacks on the World Trade Center and the Pentagon. The fiscal 2006 legislative branch appropriations bill (HR 2985—PL 109-55) established a process for states to hold special elections if more than one hundred House members could no longer perform their duties. *(Legislative branch appropriations, p. 77)*

The House had passed the provisions as a stand-alone bill (HR 841) by 329–68 on March 3, 2005. That bill had been formally reported (H Rept 109-8, Part I) from the House Committee on House Administration on Feb. 24.

The House Appropriations Committee added the provisions of HR 841 to HR 2985 before approving that measure on June 16. The amendment was offered by Chairman Jerry Lewis, R-Calif., as a way of prodding the Senate to approve the language. The House had passed a separate "continuity of Congress" bill in 2004, but the Senate never took it up. *(2004 action, Congress and the Nation Vol. XI, p. 719)*

In the Senate, Robert C. Byrd of West Virginia, the ranking Democrat on the Appropriations Committee, struck the language from that chamber's version of the legislative branch spending bill. The long-standing tradition of allowing each chamber to decide its own fate prevailed when the measure went to a House-Senate conference. The House adopted the conference report on the bill (H Rept 109-189), 305–122, on July 28, and the Senate followed suit, 96–4, on July 29.

As cleared, HR 2985 provided that:

- States were required to hold special elections within forty-nine days following an announcement by the Speaker of the House that more than one hundred vacancies existed in the House. If a state had a regularly scheduled election to fill the seat within seventy-five days of the Speaker's announcement, it would not have to hold the special election.
- Candidates for the special elections had to be nominated no later than ten days after the Speaker announced that the vacancies existed. The nomination could be made by the parties authorized by state law to nominate candidates or by any method the state determined was appropriate, including holding primary elections, as long as the method ensured that the special election would be held before the required deadline.
- Delegates from the District of Columbia and the territories as well as the resident commissioner from Puerto Rico were subject to the special election provisions of the bill. However, vacancies in those offices would not count toward the one hundred vacancies threshold.
- States were required to ensure, to the greatest extent practicable, that absentee ballots for special elections were transmitted to military voters and overseas voters within fifteen days of the Speaker's announcement. States had to accept and process otherwise valid ballots from such voters as long as they were received by the state election official no later than forty-five days after the ballot was transmitted to the voter.
- Any challenge to the Speaker's announcement had to be filed within two days of the announcement in the federal district court with jurisdiction over that congressional district and heard by a three-judge panel that would have to issue a final decision within three days of the filing. The governor of the state would have the right to intervene in support of, or in opposition to, the challenge. The decision of this three-judge panel was subject to further judicial review.

Previously, states decided how to fill vacancies, though lawmakers did make some rules changes regarding continuity at the beginning of the 108th Congress. For example, the House and Senate were allowed to convene outside Washington, D.C., and the Speaker could declare an emergency recess at any time. The Speaker also regularly filed a secret list of temporary successors should he be incapacitated. A small cadre of members would go to a secure location whenever the president addressed a joint session of

Congress. *(Earlier rules changes, Congress and the Nation, Vol. XI, p. 719)*

Sen. John Cornyn, R-Texas, pushed for a constitutional amendment (S J Res 6) that would require any procedures established in response to a widespread loss of lawmakers to expire after 120 days. However, it would permit 120-day extensions as long as one-fourth of the seats in either chamber remained vacant. The joint resolution was referred to the Senate Judiciary Committee but saw no further action.

D.C. Representation

The House Government Reform Committee on May 18, 2006, voted 29–4 to approve HR 5388, giving the nation's capital a vote on the House floor. The measure was formally reported (H Rept 109-593, Part I) on July 24. *(110th Congress action, p. 836)*

Washington, D.C., which had about 550,000 residents, had voting representation in the House on only two occasions: once during the 103rd Congress when a rules change allowed the D.C. delegate and four other nonvoting delegates to vote on some measures as long as their decisions did not alter the final outcome; and from 1790 to 1801, when District residents could vote as residents of either Maryland or Virginia and the District's boundaries included what is now Arlington County, Va. *(Delegate voting privileges, Congress and the Nation Vol. IX, p. 881)*

HR 5388 would allow that the District "shall be considered a congressional district for the purposes of representation in the House of Representatives." It also would grant an additional member to a state based on the results of the 2000 census. Utah would be entitled to that member based on its population. The new lawmaker would serve at-large until the state's next redistricting. The District was overwhelmingly Democratic and Utah was heavily Republican, so the political effect on the House was expected to be neutral.

Opponents raised concerns that the bill would violate the vision of the U.S. Constitution's framers of a federal district that, as the home of Congress, must be treated differently from a state.

Filibuster Change

A showdown over President George W. Bush's judicial nominations was averted in the 109th Congress by seven Republican and seven Democratic senators—who became known as the "Gang of 14"—when they seized control of the process and struck a deal among themselves.

Senate majority leader Bill Frist, R-Tenn., went to the floor hours after the start of the session to warn that he would not hesitate to execute an arcane parliamentary move, dubbed the "nuclear option," to end minority filibusters of Bush's appellate court nominees. Democrats had filibustered ten of the president's nominees in the 108th Congress and threatened to block several more. *(Earlier action, Congress and the Nation Vol. XI, p. 719)*

Emboldened by the four-seat increase in the Republican Senate majority as a result of the 2004 elections, Frist said that if Democrats mounted another filibuster, he would use the nuclear option. In February 2005, Bush renominated seven of the ten previously filibustered candidates, along with several others whom Democrats had threatened to block.

Among the possible sequence of moves, Frist was expected to break a filibuster by making a point of order that further debate on a nomination would be dilatory—in other words, intended only to indefinitely delay a vote. The presiding officer, probably Vice President Dick Cheney, would sustain Frist's point of order. That decision could be appealed, but if it were, Frist probably would move to table (kill) the appeal, a nondebatable motion that would require a simple majority of those present and voting to succeed.

Frist needed the support of forty-nine of his fifty-four fellow Republicans, assuming that all one hundred senators were present and voting and that no one on the other side of the aisle joined the Republicans. Cheney would be on hand to break a tie. On April 22, Cheney announced he would back Frist from the presiding officer's chair if necessary. Senate Democrats said they would retaliate by selectively hamstringing Senate business.

After Frist and Minority Leader Harry Reid, D-Nev., traded compromise proposals to no avail, Frist scheduled the showdown for May 24, during consideration of the nomination of Priscilla Owen to the U.S. Court of Appeals for the Fifth Circuit. On the evening of May 23, the fourteen senators emerged from a meeting with a "memorandum of understanding" that diffused the crisis.

The seven Democrats in the group—Robert C. Byrd of West Virginia, Daniel K. Inouye of Hawaii, Mary L. Landrieu of Louisiana, Joseph I. Lieberman of Connecticut, Mark Pryor of Arkansas, and Ken Salazar of Colorado—agreed to vote to invoke cloture on three previously filibustered nominations but made no specific commitments on four others. The Democrats also agreed that judicial nominees should be filibustered only under "extraordinary circumstances," although the definition of that term was left to each senator to decide.

In return, the seven Republicans—Lincoln Chafee of Rhode Island, Susan Collins of Maine, Mike DeWine of Ohio, Lindsay Graham of South Carolina, John McCain of Arizona, Ben Nelson of Nebraska, Olympia J. Snowe of Maine, and John W. Warner of Virginia—agreed to oppose any change in Senate rules or procedures that would eliminate filibusters of judicial nominees. The Republicans retained the right to back Frist in the nuclear option if Democrats mounted a filibuster in what Republicans considered less than "extraordinary circumstances."

In the three weeks following the agreement, the Senate confirmed five of the seven previously filibustered judicial nominees: Owen, 55–34 on May 25; Janice Rogers Brown, to the U.S. Court of Appeals for the D.C. Circuit, 56–43 on June 8; William H. Pryor Jr., to the U.S. Court of Appeals for the Eleventh Circuit, 53–45 on June 9; Richard A. Griffin, to the U.S. Court of Appeals for the Sixth Circuit, 95–0 on June 9; and David W. McKeague, to the U.S. Court of Appeals for the Sixth Circuit, 96–0 on June 9.

The members of the Gang of 14 said they intended to continue to act in unison on judicial nominees for as long as necessary. However, the group's agreement never had to be put to the test.

An attempt to weaken the filibuster failed in the 108th Congress. *(Previous effort, Congress and the Nation Vol. XI, p. 719)*

Congressional Gold Medal

The House on Jan. 26, 2005, passed a bill (HR 54) to make the Congressional Gold Medal harder to get—and therefore more valuable. The vote was 231–173.

The legislation, sponsored by Michael N. Castle, R-Del., would limit to two the number of gold medals Congress could award each year. In addition, the medals could be awarded only to individuals, no longer to groups or couples or for events. Posthumous medals could be awarded only during a twenty-year period beginning five years after a person's death.

Before passing the bill, the House on Jan. 26 rejected two amendments offered by Joseph Crowley, D-N.Y. The first, defeated 189–212, would allow six gold medals to be awarded in a two-year Congress. The second, rejected 182–211, would require that sponsorship of medals be divided equally between the two parties.

Supporters of HR 54 said Congress needed to restrict the rules for awarding medals to maintain the prestige of the honor. Critics pointed out that the legislation would have prevented Congress from awarding a joint medal, which it did in 2000, to former president Ronald Reagan and his wife, Nancy, as well as past group recipients such as the Navajo Code Talkers, who had helped the U.S. military confound Japanese intelligence during World War II. Some believed that groups would be more properly honored with commemorative coins.

The Senate had in place strict requirements for consideration of medal nominee proposals. Two-thirds of the membership, or sixty-seven senators, must cosponsor any medal or commemorative coin bill or resolution before the Senate Banking, Housing, and Urban Affairs Committee would consider it.

Capitol Visitor Center

The fiscal 2006 legislative branch appropriations bill (HR 2985—PL 109-55) included funding for the U.S. Capitol Visitor Center, which was plagued by soaring costs and slipping schedules. *(Legislative branch appropriations, p. 77; earlier action, Congress and the Nation Vol. XI, p. 725)*

The underground facility was originally budgeted at $265 million, but the Government Accountability Office (GAO) said the final cost would reach $522 million, plus an additional $37 million to cover "risks and uncertainties." Although the center was scheduled to be finished in September 2006, GAO director Bernard L. Ungar said that a more realistic date was somewhere between December 2006 and March 2007.

Congress had provided no construction funds in fiscal 2005 but allowed $10 million to be transferred from the Capitol building account to cover anticipated funding gaps. The fiscal 2006 bill included $44 million. That amount, however, did not reflect the 1 percent across-the-board cut in most nonemergency discretionary appropriations enacted as part of the fiscal 2006 defense spending bill (HR 2863—PL 109-148). *(Defense appropriations, pp. 73, 400)*

The House Appropriations Committee–approved version of HR 2985 (H Rept 109-139) provided $37 million for the visitor center, far less than the $72 million requested by the architect of the Capitol. Appropriators also called for a governing board for the center that would include members of the House and Senate leadership, along with the chairs and ranking members of the Senate Rules and Administration and the House Administration Committees.

On the House floor, members by 180–232 on June 22, 2005, rejected a David R. Obey, D-Wis., motion to recommit the bill to the House Appropriations Committee. Among other things, he complained about the visitor center, which he said was out of control.

The House passed HR 2985, 330–82, on June 22.

The Senate Appropriations Committee included in its version of the bill (S Rept 109-89) $44 million for the center. The panel also proposed an executive director position to help get the center in order. The full Senate passed the measure with little debate by voice vote June 30.

The House adopted the conference report (H Rept 109-189) 305–122 on July 28. The Senate followed suit 96–4 the next day. The president signed the bill on Aug. 2.

The fiscal 2007 legislative appropriations measure (HR 5521) stalled. The House-passed version (H Rept 109-485) included $46 million for the visitor center, as well as language offered by Obey that essentially would have removed the man in charge of the project, Architect of the Capitol Alan M. Hantman, three months before his ten-year term was due to expire in January 2007. Earlier in 2006 the Office of Compliance, which monitored worker safety and employment concerns in the Capitol complex, issued a complaint against the architect's office, alleging that hazardous conditions in utility tunnels had not been addressed and were endangering workers' lives. Hantman announced in August 2006 that he would not seek reappointment to the office. The architect's responsibilities were to be transferred to the GAO until a successor was confirmed. The bill also included the establishment of an inspector general to audit and report semi-annually on management and operations issues related to the architect's office.

The Senate Appropriations Committee–approved HR 5521 (S Rept 109-267) provided $40 million for the center. The measure did not include the Obey provision on the architect, but the Senate appropriators agreed with the House on establishing an inspector general to keep closer tabs on the architect's office.

Ethics Probes

Tom DeLay, R-Texas, was the most visible, but not the only, member of Congress under criminal investigation in the 109th Congress. The House Committee on Standards of Official Conduct (ethics committee) was not involved and conducted no investigations in 2005 because of partisan disputes over the rules and over who should work on the committee's staff.

REP. TOM DELAY

Dogged by ethical problems, Texas Republican representative and former House majority leader Tom DeLay resigned from Congress on June 9, 2006. DeLay had had a history of ethical troubles while serving in Congress. The House Committee on Standards of Official Conduct in 2004 had admonished DeLay for exceeding the bounds of acceptable behavior in promoting his political and legislative agenda. The panel in 1999 had found that the then-majority whip DeLay had improperly threatened to retaliate against a trade association for hiring a Democrat as its president. *(2004 action, Congress and the Nation Vol. XI, p. 721; 1999 action, Congress and the Nation Vol. X, p. 773)*

When the 109th Congress convened, the Republican Conference, the group of all House Republicans, was faced with deciding how to handle several rules changes the conference had agreed to in November 2004 at DeLay's insistence. Members particularly complained of being tarred in local newspapers and on talk radio for an internal conference decision to keep members of the GOP leadership in power even if they were indicted. The plan was meant to protect DeLay if he were indicted in Texas as part of a political fund-raising investigation being led by Ronnie Earle, the district attorney of Travis County. DeLay agreed in early January 2005 to drop the plan because it was giving Democrats too much ammunition. Although Republican leaders pushed through several changes to House rules that affected the ethics committee, they also backed away from plans for a controversial change that would have prohibited the committee from admonishing members for behavior that was unbecoming but did not violate specific written rules. *(109th Congress organization, p. 812)*

In the months that followed, Republicans endured a steady diet of negative revelations about DeLay, some tying him to the shady practices of prominent GOP lobbyist Jack Abramoff and others raising questions about his fund-raising machine in Texas. A series of press reports in March and April described expensive trips DeLay had taken to golf resorts in Scotland and other places with lobbyist friends who had close ties to the organizations paying for the trips. Lawmakers were prohibited under House rules from accepting free trips from lobbyists. In some cases, it appeared that DeLay's expenses were ultimately paid by Abramoff, who was under investigation for fraud in connection with a casino in Florida and multimillion-dollar contracts with Indian tribes on whose behalf he lobbied Congress. DeLay denied knowing his expenses were covered by the lobbyist. The *New York Times* also reported that DeLay's wife and daughter had been paid $500,000 from his political action committee since 2001. DeLay countered that the travel was tied to his work in Congress and his fight for important causes, such as building the conservative movement in Great Britain.

The criticism grew more serious when it started to bubble up from quarters usually friendly toward DeLay, such as the conservative editorial page of the *Wall Street Journal,* and politically vulnerable Republicans, including two senators. DeLay, in response, made an unusual appeal to GOP senators at a private luncheon April 12, asking them to hold their fire and give him a chance to make his case. He said publicly that he found the travel rules of the House "confusing" and suggested that the House ethics committee draft a more cogent policy for all members.

DeLay had jumped into the controversy over Terry Schiavo, a severely brain-damaged Florida woman whose fate was the subject of an intense debate over the right to die. In late March, he led a movement in Congress to intervene in the case, though ultimately a state court's decision to allow the woman's husband to remove her feeding tube prevailed. After Schiavo died March 31, DeLay said, "The time will come for the men responsible for this to answer for their behavior." A few days later, he apologized for "inartful" remarks, which many perceived as a threat of retaliation against liberal judges. In late April, DeLay complained about how an unnamed "left-wing syndicate" that was out to destroy his career.

By late spring, House Republicans were ready for a less visible majority leader. DeLay began spending less time in front of the camera, letting Speaker J. Dennis Hastert, R-Ill., and others in the top leadership speak for congressional Republicans at news conferences. But he remained a force behind the scenes, scheduling bills for floor action and mapping strategy to endure their passage. In May the leaders of several prominent conservative groups hosted a formal dinner party for the majority leader to give him a highly visible showing of support. In remarks to the crowd, DeLay again blamed Democrats for his predicament.

Meanwhile, trouble awaited DeLay in Texas. On May 26, state district judge Joseph Hart ruled in a civil case that Texans for a Republican Majority (TRMPAC) had failed to report $613,000 in contributions and $685,000 in expenditures as required by state law. DeLay was not named in the lawsuit, which was brought by Democrats, but three of his close associates who ran the committee were named in either the civil suit or a concurrent criminal case.

On Sept. 28, a Texas grand jury indicted DeLay in the fund-raising scandal. He was charged with conspiracy to violate the state's campaign finance laws. Prosecutors alleged that he had a role in an arrangement that passed at least $155,000 in corporate contributions from TRMPAC to the Republican National Committee, which then used the money to finance Republican state candidates. Under Texas law, corporate money could not be spent to influence state elections. A violation would be a third-degree felony, punishable by two to ten years in jail and a fine of up to $10,000.

In keeping with GOP rules, DeLay temporarily stepped aside as majority leader the day he was indicted. DeLay called the charges baseless, saying that while he had been on the board of directors of the political action committee, he left the day-to-day operations to others. DeLay's indictment followed that of three close associates, who had set up TRMPAC at his direction: Jim Ellis, his long-time chief fund-raiser; John Colyandro, executive director of TRMPAC; and Warren RoBold, a fund-raiser for the committee.

Many House Republicans believed, as DeLay asserted, that the investigation was politically motivated, and they rallied to his defense. At a private meeting on Sept. 28, the GOP conference chose Republican whip Roy Blunt of Missouri to act as the temporary majority leader while DeLay fought the charges.

On Oct. 3, another round of more serious charges was brought against DeLay as well as Ellis and Colyandro. A Travis County grand jury added charges of money laundering and conspiracy to launder money to the original indictment for conspiracy to violate the Texas election code. On Dec. 5, the campaign finance conspiracy charge against DeLay was dismissed.

With Hastert behind him, DeLay kept a substantial informal role in the leadership, continuing to be a force in decisions and strategy. The lobbyist community along Washington, D.C.'s K Street corridor also was reluctant to abandon DeLay, fearing that he would freeze out anyone who did not stick with him should he eventually recover all of his previous power. Still, DeLay's absence from the formal post had an immediate impact on the majority's productivity. Without his ability to bend the GOP conference and individual members to his will—attributes that had earned him the nickname "the Hammer"—Republicans began to lose their cohesion.

In the closing weeks of the first session of the 109th Congress, DeLay retained a devoted following among Republicans, but change seemed to be in the offing. A few members privately encouraged Hastert to talk with DeLay to try to persuade him to give up his quest to return to power. Some even suggested that the Speaker call for new leadership elections to select a permanent replacement.

Although DeLay insisted that he would be exonerated of the charges against him and would be ready to resume his leadership role in 2006, he announced Jan. 7, 2006, that he would not try to reclaim the post of majority leader. Four days earlier, Abramoff had pleaded guilty to federal charges of conspiracy, mail fraud, and tax evasion and had promised to cooperate with the investigation into lobbying-legislative relationships.

On March 31, Tony Rudy, a former deputy chief of staff to DeLay, pleaded guilty to a conspiracy charge in the Abramoff scandal. DeLay was not implicated in any wrongdoing in the Rudy court documents, but prosecutors described him as "Representative No. 2," who, at Rudy's urging, took official actions that helped some of Abramoff's clients. Rudy at the time was still working for DeLay but was taking money and other considerations from Abramoff, for whom he later went to work.

With the lobbying scandal creeping closer to him and faced with poll numbers showing he had only a 50–50 chance of winning reelection in November, DeLay on April 4 announced that he would resign his House seat and not seek reelection to a twelfth term.

As of January 2010, the Texas case against DeLay was still pending.

REP. RANDY "DUKE" CUNNINGHAM

Randy "Duke" Cunningham, R-Calif., resigned on Dec. 1, 2005, after pleading guilty to one count of bribery and one count of tax evasion. He admitted accepting at least $2.4 million in bribes, including about $1 million in cash as well as rugs, antiques, furniture, yacht club fees, boat repairs, moving costs, and vacation expenses, in exchange for using his seat on the House Appropriations Committee to obtain earmarks on behalf of defense contractors.

Among the evidence prosecutors used was a "bribe menu" written on Cunningham's office stationery that sketched out for a contractor how much of a bribe he wanted based on the dollar value of earmarks the contractor sought in an appropriations bill. The prosecutors' statements made apparent, and lawyers in the case confirmed, that the defense contractors were Brent Wilkes, head of the California-based ADCS Inc., which made software for digitizing documents and had won about $80 million in federal contracts since 1999; and Mitchell J. Wade, a founder of Washington, D.C.–based MZM Inc., which had won $163 million in federal intelligence-gathering and analysis contracts in the previous three years. What first drew investigators' attention was Wade's purchase of Cunningham's home in Del Mar, Calif., for almost $1.7 million, and its subsequent sale at a $700,000 loss, as well as a forty-two-foot yacht, which Wade named the *Duke-Stir,* made available rent-free as Cunningham's D.C. home.

Lawyers in the case said the other co-conspirators were Thomas Kontogiannis, a Long Island developer who sought Cunningham's help in trying to get a presidential pardon for a 2002 bribery conviction, and John T. Michael, a nephew of Kontogiannis's wife, who ran a mortgage company that financed Cunningham's purchase of a condominium in Arlington, Va., and a home in Rancho Santa Fe, Calif.

Cunningham was sentenced March 3, 2006, to eight years and four months in prison and was ordered to pay $1.8 million in restitution.

The ethics panel in 2006 opened a preliminary inquiry into whether other House members and aides might have been involved in the bribery scandal that ended Cunningham's career.

REP. BOB NEY, R-OHIO

Rep. Bob Ney, R-Ohio, pleaded guilty on Oct. 13, 2006, to two felony counts of conspiracy and making false statements to Congress. He resigned from Congress on Nov. 3.

Ney in 2005 had been implicated in a far-reaching Justice Department investigation of lobbyist Jack Abramoff, who gained notoriety from the more than $80 million he and his associates charged Indian tribes for their services. One of those associates, Michael Scanlon, a former press secretary for House majority leader Tom DeLay, R-Texas, pleaded guilty Nov. 21, 2005, to conspiring to bribe Ney, identified in court documents as "Representative No. 1."

At that time, Ney insisted there was never any quid pro quo in his dealings with Abramoff. In 2002 Ney had tried to insert into an elections overhaul bill language that would have benefited an Indian gambling casino operated by an Abramoff client. Ney said he was duped by Abramoff. Ney also placed statements in the *Congressional Record* in support of an Abramoff effort to buy a Florida gambling boat company. Ney and DeLay received golf trips to Scotland that were paid for by Abramoff, though the source of the financing was reported as being a charity founded by Abramoff.

Upon the urging of House Speaker J. Dennis Hastert, R-Ill., Ney stepped down as chairman of the House Administration Committee on Jan. 15, 2006. However, he maintained his innocence. Then, in a deal announced Sept. 15, Ney did an abrupt about-face and agreed to plead guilty to two felony counts. In documents detailing the agreement, Ney admitted to receiving gifts, including expensive meals and trips worth more than $170,000, from Abramoff and his lobbying associates during the previous five years in exchange for trying to shape legislation and inserting statements in the *Congressional Record* for the benefit of Abramoff's clients. He also admitted to making false statements to Congress by not reporting his gifts from Abramoff and an unidentified "foreign businessman" in his travel and financial disclosure statements.

The House Committee on Standards of Official Conduct had voted on May 17, 2006, to open an ethics inquiry into Ney's involvement in the Abramoff scandal, but the panel dropped the case after Ney resigned because it does not have jurisdiction to investigate former members.

On Jan. 19, 2007, Ney was sentenced to thirty months in prison, a $6,000 fine, and two hundred hours of community service.

REP. MARK FOLEY

The House Committee on Standards of Official Conduct in 2006 undertook one of the most intense and politically charged investigations in its history—over whether the Republican majority leadership had mishandled allegations of inappropriate behavior by Rep. Mark Foley, R-Fla., toward teenage boys who served as House pages.

The Foley case centered on inappropriate e-mails and instant messages the lawmaker sent over several years to both serving and former teenage male pages. Foley resigned abruptly on Sept. 29, after some of the sexually explicit communications he sent to pages became public. Because he was no longer a member of Congress, the committee could not investigate his actions. However, on Oct. 5, the ethics committee announced that it had formed a four-member investigative subcommittee to determine whether House Republican leaders and officials had acted expeditiously to curb Foley's behavior or had ignored signs that he had been acting inappropriately toward the pages.

The subcommittee consisted of ethics chairman Doc Hastings, R-Wash., ranking Democrat Howard J. Berman of California, Judy Biggert, R-Ill., and Stephanie Tubbs Jones, D-Ohio. They worked almost daily for nine weeks, interviewing dozens of witnesses, including House Speaker J. Dennis Hastert, R-Ill.

The ethics panel on Dec. 8 issued a bipartisan report saying Hastert, other lawmakers, and Capitol Hill aides had violated no laws or House rules in the way they handled the allegations against Foley. At the same time, the committee took Hastert, other members, and officials to task for not doing all they could to protect pages from what some lawmakers said appeared to be homosexual advances by Foley.

The eighty-nine-page report said Hastert and others "failed to exercise appropriate diligence and oversight" of Foley's contact with pages. "Rather than addressing the issue fully, some . . . did far too little, while attempting to pass the responsibility for acting to others. Some relied on unreasonably fine distinctions regarding their defined responsibilities. Almost no one followed up adequately on the limited actions they did take," the report said. The panel recommended that no further action be taken in the case.

Incoming House Speaker Nancy Pelosi, D-Calif., said Dec. 11 that she planned to make the House Page Board bipartisan. The board had been composed of two House members from the majority and one from the minority, the House sergeant at arms, and the House clerk. Pelosi said she planned to require "regular meetings of the Page Board" and wanted to expand the panel to include the parents of a current and a former page and perhaps others. She also wanted a full review of the functions of the board, as recommended in the ethics report. *(110th Congress action, House Page Board, p. 837)*

REP. WILLIAM J. JEFFERSON

Rep. William J. Jefferson, D-La., was the subject of House ethics committee and Justice Department investigations regarding whether he demanded and accepted bribes in exchange for helping to arrange contracts between a U.S. telecommunications company, iGate Inc., and Nigerian officials. Despite his ethics troubles, Jefferson in 2006 won a ninth term representing New Orleans. However, he lost his reelection bid in 2008. The probes were ongoing as the 110th Congress convened. *(110th Congress action, p. 841)*

In 2005 two of Jefferson's former associates pleaded guilty to bribing the lawmaker, and on Aug. 3 federal agents raided Jefferson's homes in New Orleans and Washington, D.C. Agents also searched offices of iGate. According to a Federal Bureau of Investigation (FBI) affidavit, the agents found $90,000 in marked bills in a freezer in Jefferson's Capitol Hill home.

The FBI followed up on May 20, 2006, with a weekend raid of Jefferson's Rayburn Building office, provoking outcries from both political parties. House lawyers filed a brief in court stating that the raid was a "blatant constitutional violation," and Jefferson launched a series of court challenges to recover documents and computer files taken in the search. The challenges remained unresolved when the 109th Congress adjourned.

In an emotional session June 15, 2006, Minority Leader Nancy Pelosi, D-Calif., won the support of the Democratic Caucus to remove Jefferson from his seat on the powerful Ways and Means Committee. The next day, the full House gave voice-vote approval to a resolution (H Res 872) ousting Jefferson from the panel.

REP. CURT WELDON

The House ethics committee in 2006 dropped an informal inquiry begun by Chairman Doc Hastings, R-Wash., and ranking Democrat Howard L. Berman of California into the actions of Rep. Curt Weldon, R-Pa., who was accused of using his office to help his daughter's lobbying firm. Weldon in 2004 had requested that the panel investigate the allegations. *(Background, Congress and the Nation Vol. XI, p. 724)*

The allegations included praising Russia-based natural gas company Itera International Energy Corp. during a House floor speech and hosting a dinner to honor the company's chairman shortly before Itera signed a $500,000-per-year contract with Solutions North America, a company co-owned by Weldon's daughter, Karen.

In April 2004, Citizens for Responsibility and Ethics in Washington (CREW) asked the Justice Department to investigate those actions and examine how Karen Weldon won a $240,000-a-year contract with two Serbian brothers after her father had urged the State Department to reverse its decision to deny visas for the brothers, who had been linked to former Serbian president Slobodan Milosevic. CREW also sought an inquiry into Curt Weldon's actions in urging the navy to buy a flying drone made by a Russian manufacturer that was paying his daughter $20,000 a month. On Oct. 16, 2006, the Federal Bureau of Investigation searched Solutions North America offices as well as the homes of Weldon's daughter and of her business partner, Charles Sexton.

Weldon, who denied any wrongdoing, lost his reelection bid in 2006. The Justice Department investigation continued.

REP. JERRY LEWIS

The Justice Department in 2006 opened an investigation into the relationship among House Appropriations Committee chair Jerry Lewis, R-Calif., former representative Bill Lowery (R-Calif., 1981–1993), and Lowery's lobbying firm, Copeland Lowery Jacquez Denton & White, which specialized in seeking earmarks. The watchdog group Citizens for Responsibility and Ethics in Washington had filed a complaint with the Justice Department in January 2006.

Lowery and his firm and clients had been eager contributors to Lewis's campaign committee, donating 37 percent of the $1.3 million the committee received from 2000 to 2005, according to a *San Diego Union-Tribune* tally. The *Union-Tribune* also reported in December 2005 that Lewis helped Lowery clients—among them one of the defense contractors cited in California Republican representative Randy "Duke" Cunningham's plea agreement in bribery charges—secure millions in earmarked funding. Most of the beneficiaries, however, were local California governments and universities, and most of the funding went to fairly mundane projects, such as a solar energy project in Yucca Valley, California.

Lowery and Lewis also kept a revolving door going between their offices. Lewis's Appropriations Committee deputy staff director Jeffrey Shockey used to work for Lowery; Shockey's wife, Alexandra Heslop Shockey, took a subcontracting job with the firm in 2005; and former Lewis staffer Letitia White went to work for Lowery in 2003.

Both Lewis and Lowery denied any wrongdoing.

REP. PATRICK J. KENNEDY

Rep. Patrick J. Kennedy, D-R.I., was stopped by police at 2:45 a.m. on May 4, 2006, after hitting a concrete barrier head-on with his Ford Mustang at the heavily patrolled corner of 1st and C Streets Southeast, near the Capitol. Police supervisors were called to the scene and ordered officers to drive Kennedy home.

On June 13, the representative, son of Sen. Edward M. Kennedy, D-Mass., was ordered to begin a year of probation after pleading guilty to driving under the influence of prescription drugs. In addition to receiving probation, Kennedy was ordered to attend weekly Alcoholics Anonymous meetings, submit to random drug tests, complete fifty hours of community service, and donate $100 to the city's Victims of Crimes Fund and $250 to the Boys and Girls Club of Greater Washington. Rep. Jim Ramstad, R-Minn., would be Kennedy's sponsor in his recovery efforts.

Prosecutors dropped charges of reckless driving and failure to exhibit a driving permit. Kennedy said after the incident that he was coping with an addiction to prescription drugs, which made him disoriented. He checked into a drug treatment program at the Mayo Clinic in Minnesota, where he stayed for twenty-eight days.

REP. CYNTHIA A. MCKINNEY

A federal grand jury on June 16, 2006, declined to indict Rep. Cynthia A. McKinney, D-Ga., for her actions during an altercation with a Capitol Police officer outside the Longworth House Office Building on March 29.

McKinney had been stopped by police officer Paul McKenna after she went around a metal detector at the House office building. She was not wearing her congressional pin at the time, and the officer apparently did not recognize her. She had a hairstyle significantly different from the braided style in her official photo. When the officer placed a hand on McKinney, she struck him in the chest with her cell phone. She and her lawyers suggested that his actions may have been racially motivated and threatened a lawsuit.

McKinney released a statement the next day saying that she regretted the incident but then held a rally-style event at Howard University with cameo appearances by actor-activists Harry Belafonte and Danny Glover. McKinney on April 6 apologized on the House floor for hitting the officer after many of her colleagues, including members of the Congressional Black Caucus, criticized her actions. She called the incident a "misunderstanding."

In its statement, the U.S. attorney's office said the grand jury, after a nearly two-and-a-half month investigation, found no probable cause for an indictment.

SEN. RICHARD C. SHELBY

The Senate Ethics Committee in 2005 cleared Richard C. Shelby, R-Ala., of wrongdoing in connection with an investigation into whether he leaked classified information to the media about what U.S. intelligence agencies knew about the Sept. 11, 2001, terrorist attacks.

The panel had been looking into whether Shelby was the source who leaked information regarding how the National Security Agency (NSA) handled intercepted communications before the attacks occurred. Several news organizations reported in 2002 that the NSA had intercepted messages on Sept. 10, 2001, that hinted an attack was going to take place the next day, but the intercepts were not translated until after the attacks. A report aired by CNN at the time said that the messages were "Tomorrow is zero hour" and "the match begins tomorrow." *(108th Congress action, Congress and the Nation Vol. XI, p. 724)*

Vice President Dick Cheney complained about the leak, and Intelligence Committee leaders called on the Justice Department to find the source. The department investigated and dropped the case in 2004, referring it to the Ethics Committee. The panel focused on Shelby, who was vice chairman of the Senate Intelligence Committee at the time of the leak. The information about the pre-attack intelligence apparently came from closed-door testimony by then–NSA director Gen. Michael V. Hayden during a joint hearing of the House and Senate Intelligence panels in June 2002—on the same day as the CNN report.

Ethics chair George V. Voinovich, R-Ohio, and ranking Democrat Tim Johnson of South Dakota in a Nov. 11 letter told Shelby that the case had been dismissed and that the committee "considers this matter to be closed." The letter went on to say the Justice Department had "produced evidence and information concerning your conduct in connection with the disclosure" about the NSA intercepts, but the panel found no evidence that Shelby had done anything wrong.

SEN. HARRY REID

Senate minority leader Harry Reid, D-Nev., announced on Oct. 16, 2006, that he would file amended disclosure forms that went beyond what lawmakers were required to provide about their financial affairs in an effort to combat news reports that he hid details of a highly profitable land transaction. Reid said he would not wait for the Senate Ethics Committee to respond to his request for guidance on what additional information to file because he did not want Republicans to be able to raise the issue in the 2006 elections as an ethical lapse by Democrats.

Reid also said he would reimburse his political campaign $3,300 for contributions it made to the staff holiday fund at the Ritz-Carlton condominiums, where he resided when in Washington, D.C.

The Associated Press reported on Oct. 11 that Reid had not disclosed that he held a partnership in a limited liability corporation (LLC) that bought a parcel of land from him for $400,000 and sold it in 2004 for $1.1 million. In his annual financial disclosure form, Reid failed to mention the existence of the corporation, which left the impression that he still owned the land directly.

Reid also planned to file amendments to clarify two additional land deals: the sale of a small tract of land in his hometown, Searchlight, Nev., for $12,000, and the appreciation of another piece of land beyond the $1,000 reporting threshold. The land reportedly was worth $4,300.

SEN. BILL FRIST

In 2005 Senate majority leader Bill Frist's sale of his shares in a family-owned hospital company drew the attention of federal prosecutors and the Securities and Exchange Commission (SEC). In a letter to his financial managers dated June 13, the Tennessee Republican ordered all shares of HCA Inc. held by his personal and family trusts to be sold. At the time, the shares were selling for about $55 each. A month later, the price fell 9 percent after the company announced that its second-quarter earnings would be lower than expected.

Although Frist said insider knowledge did not influence the timing of the sale, news of the sale prompted calls from watchdog groups for a Senate ethics inquiry into possible conflict of interest issues regarding the GOP leader's relationship with his brother, Thomas Frist Jr., who was a director of HCA.

HCA announced Sept. 23 that it received a subpoena from the office of the U.S. Attorney for the Southern District of New York, and the SEC contacted Frist's office about the sale after the Foundation for Taxpayer and Consumer Rights asked it to examine whether Frist got improper information from his brother. The private watchdog group previously had charged in an ethics complaint that Frist had a conflict of interest in supporting medical malpractice lawsuit limits that could benefit HCA and its malpractice insurance subsidiary, Health Care Indemnity (HCI). In April 2004, the Senate Ethics Committee dismissed the complaint, noting that Frist had "non-controlling financial interests in HCA and HCI."

The Federal Election Commission (FEC) in 2006 ruled that Frist's congressional campaign committee violated campaign laws by not properly reporting a loan. Citizens for Responsibility and Ethics in Washington, which had filed a complaint against Frist's 2000 Senate campaign, released documents June 1 showing the FEC's findings. According to the documents, Frist's campaign committee, Frist 2000 Inc., and its treasurer, Dawn Perkerson, agreed in April to pay an $11,000 fine.

The FEC agreed with the watchdog group that Frist's 2000 campaign should have disclosed a $1.4 million loan, which it took out jointly with Frist's 1994 campaign committee. The FEC also found that the campaign should have reported the loan's repayment in 2001. The 1994 committee did disclose the loan.

Frist retired from the Senate at the end of the 109th Congress. He announced April 27, 2007, that he had been informed that parallel insider trading inquiries by the SEC and the Justice Department had ended without any charges.

2007–2008

The wheel of fortune turned, and Democrats found themselves in the majority in both chambers. The House made history by electing the first woman Speaker. The time finally proved right for major lobbying reform legislation to clear. And, as usual, some members faced ethics investigations and criminal prosecutions.

Organization: 110th Congress

The 110th Congress convened at noon on Jan. 4, 2007, with Democrats in control of both the House and Senate for the first time in twelve years. In organizing for the new Congress, rank-and-file members in both chambers showed that they wanted proven leadership teams made up of veteran members who had a record of being able to cut deals and who brought their own strong political bases.

SENATE

Eking out a razor-thin margin of control, Democrats recaptured the majority.

Majority Leadership

The leadership for the Senate Democrats looked much as it did when they were in the minority. Harry Reid of Nevada and Richard J. Durbin of Illinois continued to lead the party, but as majority leader and majority whip, respectively. Byron L. Dorgan of North Dakota remained Democratic Policy Committee chair, and Charles E. Schumer of New York agreed to an encore as Democratic Senatorial Campaign Committee chair. Schumer also gained a new title as vice chair of the Democratic Caucus.

Patty Murray of Washington was the only new face on the five-member elected team. She was chosen to replace Debbie Stabenow of Michigan as Democratic Conference secretary. Stabenow became Steering and Outreach Committee chair.

Robert C. Byrd of West Virginia was president pro tempore. Byrd on June 12, 2006, had become the longest-serving senator in U.S. history. On Nov. 18, 2009, he became the longest-serving member in congressional history.

Minority Leadership

New minority leader Mitch McConnell of Kentucky was unopposed in his bid to succeed retiring majority leader Bill Frist of Tennessee. McConnell had served as majority whip for four years.

Senate Republicans elected former majority leader Trent Lott of Mississippi as minority whip for the 110th Congress. Lott's public career had been derailed after the 2002 elections, when, just weeks after GOP members voted to return him to the post of majority leader, he was pressured out of the job after suggesting that the country would have been better off had Sen. Strom Thurmond, R-S.C. (1954–2003) won the presidency in 1948 running on his segregationist Dixiecrat platform. Lott prevailed over Lamar Alexander of Tennessee by a single vote, 25–24.

Jon Kyl of Arizona succeeded Rick Santorum of Pennsylvania as Republican Conference chair. Kay Bailey Hutchison of Texas succeeded Kyl as Republican Policy Committee chair. John Ensign of Nevada succeeded Elizabeth Dole of North Carolina as National Republican Senatorial Committee chair.

Committees

Many Democrats who sat as the ranking member in the 109th Congress took the committee chair in the 110th Congress: Tom Harkin of Iowa at Agriculture, Nutrition, and Forestry, Robert C. Byrd of West Virginia at Appropriations, Carl Levin of Michigan at Armed Services, Kent Conrad of North Dakota at Budget, Daniel K. Inouye of Hawaii at Commerce, Science, and Transportation, Jeff Bingaman of New Mexico at Energy and Natural Resources, Tim Johnson of South Dakota at the Select Committee on Ethics, Max Baucus of Montana at Finance, Joseph R. Biden Jr. of Delaware at Foreign Relations, Edward M. Kennedy of Massachusetts at Health, Education, Labor, and Pensions, Byron L. Dorgan of North Dakota at Indian Affairs, John D. Rockefeller IV of West Virginia at the Select Committee on Intelligence, Patrick J. Leahy of Vermont at Judiciary, John Kerry of Massachusetts at Small Business and Entrepreneurship, and Daniel K. Akaka of Hawaii at Veterans' Affairs. Former ranking member and Independent Joseph I. Lieberman of Connecticut became chair of Homeland Security and Governmental Affairs.

Christopher J. Dodd of Connecticut assumed the top slot at Banking, Housing, and Urban Affairs; Barbara Boxer of California, at Environment and Public Works; and Dianne Feinstein of California, at Rules and Administration.

Many Republicans who held the committee chair in the previous Congress became the ranking member: Saxby Chambliss of Georgia at Agriculture, Thad Cochran of Mississippi at Appropriations, Richard C. Shelby of Alabama at Banking, Judd Gregg of New Hampshire at Budget, Ted Stevens of Alaska at Commerce, Pete V. Domenici of New Mexico at Energy and Natural Resources, James M. Inhofe of Oklahoma at Environment and Public Works, Charles E. Grassley of Iowa at Finance, Richard G. Lugar of Indiana at Foreign Relations, Michael B. Enzi of Wyoming at Health, Education, Labor, and Pensions, Susan Collins of Maine at Homeland Security and Governmental Affairs, Arlen Specter of Pennsylvania at Judiciary, Olympia J. Snowe of Maine at Small Business and Entrepreneurship, and Larry Craig of Idaho at Veterans' Affairs. After becoming the focus of an Ethics Committee investigation following his arrest for lewd conduct and his guilty plea to disorderly conduct, Craig relinquished the ranking member position on Veterans' Affairs. Richard M. Burr of North Carolina succeeded him in the post. *(Craig ethics probe, p. 839)*

John McCain of Arizona became ranking member on Armed Services; John Cornyn of Texas, Ethics; Christopher S. Bond of Missouri, Intelligence; and Robert F. Bennett of Utah, Rules and Administration. Craig Thomas of Wyoming, ranking member on Indian Affairs, died on June 4, 2007. Lisa Murkowski of Alaska assumed the post.

Rules

A package of ethics, lobbying, and earmark overhaul proposals affecting senators and their staffs was enacted in 2007 (S 1—PL 110-81). *(Lobbying reform, p. 830)*

HOUSE

History was made in the 110th Congress with the election of the first female Speaker of the House.

Majority Leadership

Democrat Nancy Pelosi of California became the first woman Speaker, besting Republican John A. Boehner of Ohio by 233–202 on Jan. 4, 2007. Pelosi had received a unanimous thumbs-up from the Democratic Caucus on Nov. 16, 2006.

The caucus elected Steny H. Hoyer of Maryland 149–86 over John P. Murtha of Pennsylvania to be majority leader. Pelosi had endorsed and vigorously lobbied for Murtha. The caucus also unanimously elected James E. Clyburn of South Carolina as majority whip and Rahm Emanuel of Illinois as Democratic Caucus chair. Clyburn became the second African American to serve as Democratic whip, after William H. Gray III of Pennsylvania.

Succeeding Emanuel as Democratic Congressional Campaign Committee chair was Chris Van Hollen of Maryland.

Minority Leadership

House Republicans rejected by wide margins candidates for leadership posts from the party's conservative faction. They kept in place as majority leader Boehner, who defeated Mike Pence of Indiana 168–27, and as minority whip Roy Blunt of Missouri, who defeated John Shadegg of Arizona 137–57.

Four members sought the post of House Republican Conference chair: Dan Lungren of California, Marsha Blackburn of Tennessee, Jack Kingston of Georgia, and Adam H. Putnam of Florida. Putnam, the only non–Republican Study Committee candidate, was the winner on the third ballot, defeating Kingston 100–91. Thaddeus McCotter of Michigan bested Darrell Issa of California 132–63 for the position of Republican Policy Committee chair. Tom Cole of Oklahoma defeated Pete Sessions of Texas, 102–81 on the second ballot, for the National Republican Congressional Committee chair. Phil English of Pennsylvania was eliminated in the first round.

Committees

With the new Democratic majority, all committee chairs changed hands. Many had served as ranking members in the 109th Congress: Collin C. Peterson of Minnesota at Agriculture, David R. Obey of Wisconsin at Appropriations, Ike Skelton of Missouri at Armed Services, John M. Spratt Jr. of South Carolina at Budget, George Miller of California at Education and Labor (formerly Education and the Workforce), John D. Dingell of Michigan at Energy and Commerce, Barney Frank of Massachusetts at Financial Services, Tom Lantos of California at International Relations, Bennie Thompson of Mississippi at Homeland Security, Juanita Millender-McDonald of California at House Administration, John Conyers Jr. of Michigan at Judiciary, Nick J. Rahall II of West Virginia at Natural Resources (formerly Resources), Henry A. Waxman of California at Oversight and Government Reform (formerly Government Reform), Louise M. Slaughter of New York at Rules, Bart Gordon of Tennessee at Science and Technology (formerly Science), Nydia M. Velázquez of New York at Small Business, James L. Oberstar of Minnesota at Transportation and Infrastructure, and Charles B. Rangel of New York at Ways and Means. Millender-McDonald died on April 22, 2007. Robert A. Brady of Pennsylvania subsequently took the top spot at House Administration. Lantos died on Feb. 11, 2008. Howard L. Berman assumed the chair of International Relations.

Silvestre Reyes of Texas became chair of the Permanent Select Committee on Intelligence; Stephanie Tubbs Jones of Ohio, Standards of Official Conduct; and Bob Filner of California, Veterans' Affairs. Edward J. Markey of Massachusetts helmed the newly established Select Committee on Energy Independence and Global Warming.

Taking over ranking member spots in many instances were Republicans who had been chairs: Robert W. Goodlatte of Virginia at Agriculture, Jerry Lewis of California at Appropriations, Duncan Hunter of California at Armed Services, Howard P. "Buck" McKeon of California at Education and Labor, Joe L. Barton of Texas at Energy and Commerce, Peter T. King of New York at Homeland Security, Vernon J. Ehlers of Michigan at House Administration, Peter Hoekstra of Michigan at Intelligence, Thomas M. Davis III of Virginia at Oversight and Government Reform, David Dreier of California at Rules, Doc Hastings of Washington at Standards of Official Conduct, and Steve Buyer of Indiana at Veterans' Affairs.

Paul D. Ryan of Wisconsin became ranking member on Budget; F. James Sensenbrenner Jr. of Wisconsin, Energy Independence and Global Warming; Spencer Bachus of Alabama, Financial Services; Ileana Ros-Lehtinen of Florida, International Relations; Lamar Smith of Texas, Judiciary; Don Young of Alaska, Natural Resources; Ralph M. Hall of Texas, Science and Technology; Steve Chabot of Ohio, Small Business; John L. Mica of Florida, Transportation and Infrastructure; and Jim McCrery of Louisiana, Ways and Means.

Rules

H Res 6 established the rules of the House of Representatives for the 110th Congress. New rules affecting House members and their staffs also were included in lobbying reform legislation (S 1—PL 110-81). *(Lobbying reform, this page)*

The House adopted Title II of H Res 6 (lobbying) 430–1 and Title III (votes and conference committees) 430–0 on Jan. 4, 2007. It adopted Title V (setting rules for debate on upcoming bills) 232–200 on Jan. 5.

Under Title II:

- Members and staff would not be able to accept any gifts or meals from lobbyists. Under the old rules, there was a $50 limit.
- Lobbyists could not pay for travel, and members must get pre-approval for trips funded by private entities or nonprofits.
- Official, personal, or campaign funds could not be spent on noncommercial, private jets for travel.
- House employees had to participate in annual ethics training.

Title III of the package set rules for recorded votes and House-Senate conferences. Votes could not be held open for longer than the fifteen-minute minimum just to reverse an outcome—a highly criticized practice employed from time to time when Republicans were in charge. (The Select Committee to Investigate the Voting Irregularities of August 2, 2007, voted 6–0 on Sept. 25, 2008, to recommend that the House do away with this rule. A dispute over procedures used during a floor vote as part of the consideration of the fiscal 2008 agriculture appropriations bill (HR 3161) triggered the creation of the special committee, which had a budget of $450,000 with which to investigate and write the report. The vote at one point showed that Republicans had won, but their victory was erased because Democrats kept the tally open long enough for some of their members to change their votes.) *(Agriculture appropriations omnibus bill, pp. 111, 112, 113)*

Also, in another effort to prevent former GOP methods from returning to the new Congress, the rule required conference committees to be open to all conferees.

Title V allowed the Democrats to forgo a recorded vote in the Rules Committee.

The House adopted Title IV, the budget-related section of H Res 6, by 280–152 on Jan. 5. The pay-as-you-go budget rule would require offsets for any new entitlement spending or tax cuts. However, the House could waive a point of order against a measure that violated the requirement.

The new rules also required the disclosure of earmarks and their sponsors. Requests for earmarks, members' pet projects, would have to include justifications and certification that the provisions would not benefit lawmakers or their spouses. Leaders could not promise earmarks in exchange for votes on legislation.

By 226–191 on Jan. 27, 2007, the House adopted H Res 78, allowing the delegates representing the District of Columbia, the Virgin Islands, Guam, and American Samoa and the resident commissioner of Puerto Rico to cast votes and preside when the chamber meets as the Committee of the Whole, which it does when debating and voting on amendments to legislation. Any time their votes provided the winning margin, an automatic revote would occur from which the delegates would be excluded. The delegates also would be unable to cast votes on final passage. Delegates were given similar voting limitation in 1993, a change that survived a federal court challenge only to be reversed in 1995, when Republicans took control of the House. *(Delegate voting privileges, Congress and the Nation Vol. IX, p. 881)*

Lobbying Reform

Signed into law on Sept. 14, 2007, S 1 (PL 110-81) was meant to give the public more information about the work of lobbyists and their political fund-raising efforts, while slowing the revolving door from Capitol Hill to K Street.

Efforts to fashion lobbying reform legislation had failed in the 109th Congress. *(Lobbying reform, p. 816)*

SENATE ACTION

The Senate passed S 1 by 96–2 on Jan. 18, 2007.

The legislation was a product of an agreement between Majority Leader Harry Reid, D-Nev., and Minority Leader Mitch McConnell, R-Ky. At several points during the lengthy floor debate, however, the legislation seemed about to collapse in the face of partisan wrangling. In each case, after passionately fighting for his position, Reid relented and managed to negotiate his way past the obstacles.

Reid suffered his first setback on Jan. 11, when the leadership lost on a 46–51 vote to table, or kill, a Jim DeMint, R-S.C., amendment to expand the definition of earmarks subject to the bill's disclosure rules. DeMint wanted to include federal projects. Customarily, once a motion to table is rejected, the amendment in question is adopted by voice vote. Reid angered Republicans, however, when he instructed the sergeant at arms to round up senators for a roll call, a procedure that Republicans had used in 2006. Still unable to switch enough votes to defeat the amendment, Reid subsequently offered an olive branch and agreed to embrace DeMint's amendment with some minor modifications. It was adopted 98–0 on Jan. 16.

The Republican minority staged a filibuster in support of a Judd Gregg, R-N.H., amendment that would have allowed the president to propose line-item rescissions of previously enacted spending or tax provisions and give those proposals expedited consideration in Congress. Gregg's chief opponent was Appropriations Committee chairman Robert C. Byrd, D-W.Va., who had fought against a previous effort by Congress to create a line-item veto (PL 104-130). The U.S. Supreme Court struck down that law as unconstitutional in 1998. Gregg argued that his plan was different enough to pass constitutional muster. (*Line-item law, Congress and the Nation Vol. IX, p. 78; Supreme Court ruling, Congress and the Nation Vol. X, p. 714)*

Reid tried Jan. 17 to invoke cloture and thus limit debate on the bill. Gregg's proposal then would have been prohibited because it was not germane to the bill. But Reid was eight votes short of the sixty required. Reid voted against his own motion, to preserve his right to press for reconsideration, resulting in a 51–46 tally. Gregg finally backed down after Reid agreed to allow a vote on the amendment during a debate the following week on a minimum wage increase (HR 2). Gregg lost that vote. *(Minimum wage, pp. 661, 664)*

In other action on S 1, the Senate:

- Adopted 89–5 on Jan. 17 a Russ Feingold, D-Wis., amendment to prohibit lobbyists from sponsoring lavish parties at national party conventions.
- Adopted 51–46 on Jan. 17 a Robert F. Bennett, R-Utah, amendment to allow nonprofit 501(c)3 organizations to continue paying for congressional trips.
- Adopted 55–43 on Jan. 18 a Bennett amendment to language subjecting grassroots lobbying groups to disclosure requirements.
- Rejected 27–71 on Jan. 1 a Joseph I. Lieberman, I-Conn., amendment to create an independent Office of Public Integrity with the power to investigate ethics complaints and make recommendations to the Senate Select Ethics Committee.
- Adopted 88–9 on Jan. 17 a Reid amendment to require senators to reimburse private aircraft owners at the full charter rate for seats, not at the much cheaper first-class rate, as they did under existing rules. The amendment was opposed by senators from some large states, such as Republican Ted Stevens of Alaska, who argued that a state like his, with far-flung population centers, forced travel by private airplanes and that reimbursing at a higher rate would add significantly to the cost of doing the people's business.
- Adopted by voice vote on Jan. 18 a Tom Coburn, R-Okla., amendment to prevent lawmakers' families from being the beneficiaries of earmarks.
- Adopted by voice vote on Jan. 18 a David Vitter, R-La., amendment to prohibit the husbands and wives of senators from lobbying the Senate unless they were employed as lobbyists for at least one year before their spouse's election.

The Senate-passed S 1 included rules changes to:

- Prohibit senators and their staff from accepting gifts or trips funded by lobbyists or organizations that employed lobbyists. Senators could fly on corporate aircraft, but they would have to pay at the full charter rate.
- Prohibit former senior staff from lobbying the chamber where they worked for one year after their departure.
- Prohibit senators from negotiating for a private sector job until their successor had been elected, unless they filed a publicly available statement with the secretary of the Senate within three days of beginning the negotiations. Senior Senate staff would have to notify the Senate Select Ethics Committee within three days of starting negotiations for a private sector job and would have to recuse themselves from congressional matters that might involve a conflict of interest.
- Require senators to prohibit their staff from having official contact with any member of the senator's immediate family who was a registered lobbyist. Staff also could not have official contact with any senator's spouse who was a lobbyist, unless the spouse was a registered lobbyist at least one year before the senator's last election or one year before their marriage.
- Allow a point of order against floor consideration of any bill or conference report unless a list of spending earmarks and limited tax and trade benefits, including the sponsors' names, was posted publicly on the Internet at least forty-eight hours beforehand. Senators also would have to certify that they had no financial interest in the projects.
- Permit a point of order against an item or earmark added in conference that was not in either chamber's version of the legislation. The provision could be stricken without rejecting the conference report. A sixty-vote majority would be required to waive the point of order.

S 1 also contained statutory changes to:

- Extend to two years the cooling-off period during which senators would be prohibited from lobbying Congress after leaving office.
- Require lobbyists to file quarterly, instead of semi-annual, disclosure reports.
- Require lobbyists to disclose bundled contributions that they collected and forwarded to federal candidates, party committees, and leaders political action committees (PACs).
- Increase the maximum fine for failing to comply with disclosure rules to $200,000 from $50,000.

HOUSE ACTION

On May 17, 2007, the House Judiciary Committee gave voice-vote approval to a broad lobbying disclosure bill (HR 2316) and a measure on bundled campaign contributions (HR 2317). HR 2316 (H Rept 110-161, Part I) and HR 2317 (H Rept 110-162) were formally reported on May 21.

Democrats were forced to scale back the scope of HR 2316 in the face of near rebellion by rank-and-file members in a closed-door meeting the week of May 14. Members were particularly unhappy with a leadership plan to extend to two years the ban on lobbying by former House members and senior staff. The proposal was part of the Honest Leadership and Open Government Act touted by Democrats as they campaigned in 2006. Getting rid of the provision had the full support of committee chairman John Conyers Jr., D-Mich., and the panel's top Republican, Lamar Smith of Texas, both of whom said it was excessive and likely to make it harder to hire qualified congressional staff. House Speaker Nancy Pelosi, D-Calif., backed the extension but, according to Democrats, would agree to drop it as the price of winning support for the bill.

The change was made in a manager's amendment that also altered the original bill to allow members to negotiate for an outside job in secret, notifying only the House Committee on Standards of Official Conduct (ethics committee) of their search. Under the original language, members would have had to notify the House clerk's office, which would have made the notification a matter of public record. The amendment also exempted nonprofit organizations from having to disclose funding and membership in political coalitions that lobbied Congress.

During markup of HR 2316, the committee also rejected, by voice vote, a Martin T. Meehan, D-Mass., amendment to tighten restrictions on grassroots lobbying firms and rejected 5–27 another Meehan amendment to bar lobbyists from sponsoring lavish parties at presidential nomination conventions. The panel by voice vote adopted a Darrell Issa, R-Calif., amendment to require lobbyists to report contributions to 527 groups and a Chris Cannon, R-Utah, amendment to prohibit law firms or lawyers under temporary contract with congressional offices from lobbying.

The committee-approved HR 2316 would:

- Add a new House rule barring members from negotiating over private sector employment until their successor had been elected, unless they notified the House ethics committee within three days of starting the negotiations. Senior staff also would have to notify the committee within three days of starting negotiations for a private sector job. Members and senior staff would be required to recuse themselves from official activity that could be seen as a conflict of interest.
- Require a member to prohibit his staff from having official contact with the member's spouse if the spouse was a registered lobbyist.
- Prohibit members and senior staff from influencing employment decisions of private firms for partisan political gain.
- Require lobbyists to provide publicly available quarterly electronic disclosure reports. The reports would have to include the amount provided to 527 organizations, which were not treated as PACs under existing law.
- Bar lobbyists from providing gifts or travel to members if they knew it could be in violation of House or Senate rules. Lobbyists would have to certify in their reports that they had not provided any such gifts or travel.
- Increase the penalty for violating the 1995 Lobbying Disclosure Act (PL 104-65) to $100,000 from $50,000 and impose a criminal penalty of up to five years for knowing and corrupt failure to comply with the act. *(1995 act, Congress and the Nation Vol. IX, p. 834)*

HR 2317 proposed for the first time to require lobbyists to file disclosure reports on the contributions that they collected and bundled for delivery to individual candidates. Registered lobbyists would have to provide quarterly reports to Congress on bundled contributions totaling more than $5,000.

Democratic leaders overcame weeks of internal strife, conceded several parliamentary maneuvers to Republicans, and jettisoned some of the most controversial provisions before they succeeded in passing the lobbying legislation May 24. The House voted on the two bills separately, passing the proposal on bundled contributions 382–37, then passing the lobbying disclosure measure, 396–22. Under the rule for floor debate, the bills were automatically combined as HR 2316.

Republicans won motions to recommit both bills with instructions—the instructions being GOP amendments, some of which Democrats had resisted during Judiciary Committee consideration of the legislation. On May 24, the motion to recommit HR 2317 was agreed to 228–192; the motion to recommit HR 2316, 346–71. The modified bills were then immediately reported back to the floor.

The provisions added by Republicans included language to remove an exemption under the gifts rules for state and local governments, thus requiring lobbyists for state and local governments, including government entities such as universities, to comply with gift rules; require lobbyists to include in their disclosure forms information on the congressional earmarks for which they lobbied; and prohibit lobbyists who became congressional staff members from having official contact with their former employer for one year.

FINAL ACTION

Final action on the legislation was stalled for months as a result of DeMint's repeated objections to appointing Senate conferees. DeMint, who had been arguing for the disclosure of individual member projects in bills, demanded advance guarantees that Senate language he had written making it far easier to identify and challenge such earmarks would be in the conference version of the legislation. Democratic leaders eventually worked around him by informally negotiating a compromise. The House leadership then called up S 1, used the rule for floor debate to substitute the compromise language, and then suspended the rules and passed the revised bill 411–8 on July 31, sending it to the Senate for final action.

The Senate cleared the bill on Aug. 2 when it agreed to a Reid motion to concur in the House amendment to the measure on a **key vote of 83–14 (R 34–14; D 47–0; I 2–0).** A critical vote came beforehand when the senators agreed, 80–17, to limit debate. Because the bill included changes to Senate rules, Reid had to secure the votes of two-thirds of those present and voting (sixty-five votes in this case) to invoke cloture. *(2007 key votes, p. 955)*

The main opposition to the bill in the House came from members of the conservative Republican Study Committee, who complained that it did not do enough to expedite challenges to earmarks on the floor. Republicans also complained that they had no chance to offer amendments because the bill was considered under suspension of the rules, which barred amendments and required a two-thirds vote for passage. Majority Leader Steny H. Hoyer, D-Md., responded that it was a Republican who blocked Senate Democrats from setting up a House-Senate conference on the bill.

The following were among the issues resolved in the informal negotiations.

Revolving door. Because neither chamber would give up its stance, the final bill extended the cooling-off period for senators to two years but left the one-year rule unchanged in the House.

Convention parties. The Senate proposal to forbid lawmakers in most cases from attending lobbyist-sponsored parties in their honor at national conventions was retained.

Bundled contributions. The final bill required campaign committees to report to the Federal Election Commission (FEC) on any donor that provided at least $15,000 in bundled contributions in a six-month period. The FEC was required to provide access to the information in the new schedule on bundled contributions in a form that could be sorted, searched, and downloaded.

Job negotiations. The House kept its requirement that members notify the ethics committee, instead of the clerk, thereby allowing the member to keep his or her job hunt secret. The Senate retained its requirement that senators file a publicly available statement with the secretary of the Senate.

Penalties. The maximum penalty for violating disclosure rules was set at $200,000, as under the Senate bill, not $100,000, as in the House version.

Earmarks. Republicans complained that the final version allowed the majority leader to declare whether a bill or conference report complied with the earmark disclosure requirement. As first passed by the Senate, the bill required that all earmarks be listed in the committee or conference report and that the relevant committee publish them on its Web site.

MAJOR PROVISIONS

Following are the major provisions of the bill to overhaul lobbying and ethics restrictions (S 1—PL 110-81).

Lobbying Disclosure

Quarterly reports. Lobbyists must file quarterly reports with the secretary of the Senate and the clerk of the House, instead of semi-annual ones as under previous law. The reports were due twenty days after the periods ending on the first days of January, April, July, and October. The reports must be filed electronically and be made available on the Internet in a searchable, sortable, and downloadable manner "as soon as technically practicable."

The law also cut the reporting threshold in half, so that lobbyists must report when organizations or coalitions pay at least $5,000 per quarter. Within coalitions, lobbyists must identify each member that contributes at least $2,500. These requirements take effect Jan. 1, 2008.

Penalties. Civil penalties for failure to comply with lobbyist disclosure requirements were increased to $200,000, from the previous $50,000. The law created new criminal penalties for those who "knowingly and corruptly" fail to comply with any provision of the Lobbying Disclosure Act: fines and up to five years in prison.

Bundling. The new law required campaign committees—including a candidate's campaign committee, a party committee, or a leadership political action committee (PAC)—to provide reports to the Federal Election Commission two times a year on the bundled campaign contributions they received from a lobbyist or a committee established or controlled by a lobbyist in excess of $15,000 over six months.

Bundled contributions include those forwarded to the committee by the lobbyist and credited to the lobbyist through records, designations, or other means of recognition. The required report must include the name, address, and employer of each lobbyist "reasonably known" to have provided two or more bundled contributions, as well as the total amount of contributions provided by that lobbyist.

The $15,000 threshold did not include contributions from the lobbyist or the lobbyist's spouse and would be indexed for inflation.

FEC requirements. The FEC had six months from enactment to develop regulations for the reports, including guidance on determining whether it was "reasonable" to know that a contributor was a lobbyist. The information must be disclosed on the FEC's Web site in a searchable, sortable, and downloadable format and linked to the Web sites of the secretary of the Senate and the clerk of the House. The reports must be filed beginning three months after the regulations took effect.

Semi-annual reports to Congress. Registered lobbyists were required to file semi-annual reports with the secretary of the Senate and the clerk of the House, disclosing any political committees they controlled and any candidate, PAC, or party committee to which they contributed at least $200 in a six-month period. The reports must also disclose how much the lobbyist contributed in excess of $200 to honor an official in the legislative or executive branch, to presidential library foundations, or to inaugural committees.

Lobbying by spouses. The law changed House rules to require a member to prohibit his or her staff, whether in the member's personal, committee, or leadership office, from having "lobbying contact" with the member's spouse if that spouse was a registered lobbyist or was employed or retained by a lobbyist. The spouse could continue to have lobbying contacts with other members and their staff, however.

The legislation also amended Senate rules to prohibit a senator's staff from having contact with any senator's spouse or immediate family member who was a registered lobbyist. The rule exempted spouses who served as lobbyists at least one year before the senator's last election or before their marriage to a senator, although a senator's own staff could not have contact with that senator's lobbyist spouse.

Lobbyist-sponsored events at conventions. The law barred a lawmaker from participating in an event at a national convention that honored the lawmaker, other than in a capacity as a candidate for president or vice president, if the event was paid for by a registered lobbyist.

Lobbyists for foreign governments. The law required lobbyists for foreign governments to file their registration statements and supplements with the Justice Department in electronic form. It also required the Justice Department to maintain and make publicly available an electronic database containing the registration statements and updates of those lobbyists. The Justice Department started making registrations available online while the bill was under consideration.

Gifts and travel. The law changed Senate rules to bar members from accepting gifts or travel from lobbyists. Nonprofit organizations were exempted. Also, private entities that employed lobbyists could reimburse a senator, staff member, or committee for transportation and lodging for one-day trips with an overnight stay that were preapproved by the Select Ethics Committee. The committee could permit a two-night stay. Senators and staffers also could accept travel for a home-state conference that was not attended by lobbyists and where meals cost less than $50. The expenses must be reported to the secretary of the Senate, who must establish a searchable Web site by Jan. 1, 2008, that publishes and retains the travel information for four years.

Senate and presidential candidates who used private planes for their campaigns were required to reimburse the owners at a charter rate, which was substantially more expensive than the reimbursement requirement of first-class travel rates. There was an exception for planes owned or leased by candidates or their immediate family members.

The House rules package (H Res 6) adopted in January 2007 barred members from accepting gifts or travel from lobbyists or organizations that employed lobbyists. It also banned the use of official or campaign funds for travel on corporate jets. There was an exception for one-day trips with an overnight stay or trips paid for by universities. Members must obtain pre-approval of trips from the ethics committee, which could approve a two-night stay. The legislation also provided exceptions for planes owned or leased by a candidate or immediate family member. (The House by voice vote on May 2, 2007, adopted H Res 363, amending rules on official conduct to include several exceptions to make private air travel more permissible. For example, if lawmakers or their family members own or lease a plane, they now could travel on it. In addition, anyone now could allow a member the use of a plane "on the basis of personal friendship.") *(House rules, p. 830)*

The new law added a requirement that the House clerk must post on the Internet the advance authorizations, certifications, and disclosures related to travel by members, officers, or employees of the House, as well as the personal financial disclosure reports required of House members. The Web site must be created by Aug. 1, 2008, in a searchable, sortable, and downloadable format. Members were allowed to omit personally identifiable information that was not required to be disclosed, such as home addresses and telephone numbers, Social Security numbers, bank account information, and children's names. Information must be posted for six years.

Revolving door restrictions. The law set different cooling-off periods in the House and Senate. The period during which former senators were prohibited from lobbying members or employees of either chamber was doubled to two years. Former Senate officers, as well as former staff members who made 75 percent of the salary of a senator for at least sixty days of their last year of employment, were barred for a year from lobbying the entire Senate, instead of just the office where they worked.

The House kept its one-year cooling-off period. Restrictions on members applied to communications with members, staff, and officers of either chamber, while the limit on elected officers of the House applied to communications only with House members, officers, and employees.

The law also extended to two years, from one year, the cooling-off period for very senior personnel in executive branch offices and independent agencies, including the vice president, from lobbying their former department or agency.

These restrictions took effect after the sine die adjournment of the first session of the 110th Congress or Dec. 31, 2007, whichever came first.

Notification requirements. The law required the House clerk, in consultation with the House ethics committee, as well as the secretary of the Senate to inform members, officers, and employees of their respective chambers about the beginning and end dates of the period during which they were restricted from lobbying. It also required that the information be placed on the Internet in a searchable, sortable, and downloadable format to the extent possible. The notification requirements must be posted by Jan. 1, 2008.

Post-congressional job negotiations. The law prohibited lawmakers from negotiating for a job in the private sector until a successor was elected, unless the member filed a statement with either the secretary of the Senate or the House Committee on Standards of Official Conduct, within three days of beginning negotiations. Staffers earning at least 75 percent of a member's salary also had to disclose negotiations within three days to the ethics committee in whichever chamber they served.

A House rules change in the law also required members, officers, and employees to recuse themselves from matters in which there was a conflict of interest or the appearance of a conflict of interest. The member, officer, or employee must notify the ethics committee of such a recusal and provide a statement of disclosure and notification to the House clerk for public disclosure. The rule, which was effective on the date of enactment, applied to negotiations or agreements after the date of enactment.

Pensions. The federal government could not contribute to the pension of a member of Congress who was convicted of certain felonies committed after the date of enactment. The financial penalty applied to both the Federal Employee Retirement System and the Civil Service Retirement System. Members could still receive payments that they made into the system. The Office of Personnel Management must develop regulations to consider continuing payments to spouses and children of convicted members, depending on the crime and whether the relatives were involved.

The pension prohibition applied to the following felonies: bribery of public officials and witnesses; offenses related to officers or employees acting as agents of foreign principals; fraud using wire, radio, or television, including as part of a scheme to deprive citizens of honest services; prohibited foreign trade practices; engaging in monetary transactions in property derived from unlawful activity; tampering with a witness or victim; and racketeering or other organized crime. It also covered conspiracy to commit such offenses, perjury committed in falsely denying such offenses, or the subornation of perjury.

K Street Project. The law created penalties for members or congressional employees who took or withheld official actions with the intent of influencing private sector hiring based on partisan political affiliation. Violators could be fined and imprisoned for up to fifteen years and be disqualified from holding any office of honor, trust, or profit.

Legislating

Earmarks. The law changed Senate rules to bar the Senate from voting on a motion to proceed to consideration of a bill or joint resolution unless a list, chart, or other means with information about each "congressionally directed spending item," targeted tax benefit, or limited trade benefit—including the names of requesting members—is made available in searchable format on the Internet forty-eight hours before the vote.

The relevant committee chair or the majority leader must certify that the information was available. A three-fifths majority was required to waive a point of order based on the rule, with one hour of debate allowed.

Votes on adoption of a conference report were subject to a similar point of order, which could be waived through a three-fifths vote or through the joint agreement of the majority and minority leaders if necessary because of a significant disruption to Senate facilities or the availability of the Internet.

The law also amended Senate rules to require requesting members to provide to the chair and ranking member of the committee of jurisdiction a written statement listing their name and the beneficiaries of an earmark, with the certification that neither the member nor the member's immediate family had a monetary interest in the provision. These certifications must be posted on the Internet. The law prohibited members from using their position to advance an earmark that would further their monetary interest.

The House rules package adopted in January 2007 allowed points of order against committee or conference reports that failed to list the names of lawmakers who requested the included earmarks, targeted tax benefits, or targeted tariff benefits. Chairs also could certify that a bill contained no earmarks.

"Dead of night" items in conference reports. The legislation allowed senators to raise a point of order against one or more provisions of a conference report if the provisions constituted new direct spending that was not in either the House or Senate versions of the bill. If a point of order were sustained against one or more provisions, the language would be stricken from the conference report, and the Senate would then vote on whether to send the bill, minus those items, to the House as a Senate amendment to the measure sent to conference. The point of order could be waived through a three-fifths majority vote after one hour of debate.

Holds. Senators were required to explain their holds on legislation or nominations. When a senator raised an objection to a request for unanimous consent to proceed to a matter, the objecting senator had six session days to either submit the reason in writing or withdraw the objection. The reason need not be submitted if the objection were withdrawn.

Privileges. The legislation eliminated Senate floor privileges for former members, officers, and Speakers of the House who were lobbyists or sought to influence passage or rejection of legislation. It also barred the use of the Senate gym and members-only parking spaces by former senators who were lobbyists. The House rules package revoked gym and floor privileges for former members who became lobbyists.

Penalties. The new penalty for knowingly failing to comply with the ethics requirements was a year in prison and a $50,000 fine, up from $10,000.

D.C. Representation

Efforts (HR 1905, S 1257) to give the District of Columbia full voting representation in the House of Representatives, coupled with an additional seat for Utah, collapsed in the Senate in 2007. Because the District was heavily Democratic and Utah was largely Republican, the seats would not have affected party ratios in the House. *(109th Congress action, p. 836)*

Under existing rules, the District's one House delegate could vote in committees and in the House when it was sitting as the Committee of the Whole. Any time a delegate's vote was decisive in the outcome, however, the vote was automatically retaken in the full House, where delegates could not vote. *(House rules, p. 830)*

The administration and most Republicans opposed the legislation on constitutional grounds. The White House argued that the proposal would violate a section of the U.S. Constitution stating that House members shall be elected "by people of the several states." The District was not a state. To give D.C. a vote in Congress, the administration said, would require a constitutional amendment.

Supporters countered that the Constitution's District clause allowed Congress to decide all matters related to the District of Columbia, including voting representation. Senate majority leader Harry Reid, D-Nev., and other advocates raised the issue of fairness, arguing that District residents paid taxes, served in the armed forces, and sat on federal juries, yet they had only a delegate in Congress, not a real voting member.

In 1978 the 95th Congress passed a constitutional amendment to grant the District full membership in both the House and Senate. The amendment carried a seven-year limit for ratification by three-fourths of the states (thirty-eight), but only sixteen had ratified it by the time the deadline arrived. *(1978 action, Congress and the Nation Vol. V, p. 838)*

The House passed HR 1905 by 241–177 on April 19, 2007. As passed, HR 1905 would:

- Treat the District of Columbia as a congressional district with one voting representative, beginning with the 110th Congress. The District would also retain its delegate, but it could not receive additional seats through reapportionment, even if its population justified it.
- Increase the voting membership of the House from 435 to 437 to accommodate one representative from the District of Columbia and another state, presumably Utah. Utah's population was almost large enough to add another representative in the previous decennial reapportionment.
- Give Utah a fourth House seat to be elected at-large until after the 2010 census, which was expected to show enough population growth to merit the additional seat.
- Give Utah another vote in the electoral college, bringing the total number of presidential electors from 538 to 539. (The District had three electoral votes under the Twenty-third Amendment and would not receive any additional members as a result of the bill.)

During the floor debate, Rep. Robert W. Goodlatte, R-Va., argued that superimposing an at-large seat atop three Utah districts would allow the state's voters to cast two votes for Congress.

To comply with pay-as-you-go budget rules, the House passed a small tax bill to cover the estimated $400,000 a year that would be required for salaries and benefits for the two new members. The bill (HR 1906), which passed 216–203 on April 19, proposed a slight boost to the estimated tax payments required for individuals earning more than $5 million a year. The measure was automatically appended to the District bill after passage.

Republicans had derailed Democrats' attempts to pass an earlier version of D.C. voting representation legislation (HR 1433) with a procedural motion that would have sent the measure back to committee, instructing the panel to add language repealing the District's ban on semiautomatic weapons and prohibiting the local government from passing new gun control measures. The strategy forced Democrats into an uncomfortable box, because a portion of the caucus backed gun-ownership rights. If the motion had succeeded, however, the bill would have been sent back to committee, where it would have died. As a result, the leadership pulled HR 1433.

The Senate Homeland Security and Governmental Affairs Committee approved a companion bill (S 1257) by 9–1 on June 13 and formally reported it (S Rept 110-123) on June 28. The provisions of S 1257 were largely the same as in HR 1905, except the Senate bill specified that the new members would not be seated until the 111th Congress and that the additional representative from Utah would be elected according to a redistricting plan enacted by the State of Utah. S 1257 also stated that any legal challenge should be expedited and that any appeal would have to be made directly to the U.S. Supreme Court.

During markup, the committee:

- Adopted by voice vote a Susan Collins, R-Maine, amendment to emphasize that the District should not be considered a state and therefore could not have representation in the Senate.
- Adopted, 15–1, a Collins amendment to allow for expedited judicial review of the bill to test its constitutionality. A special three-judge panel would be the first stop for any constitutional challenge, followed by a direct appeal to the Supreme Court.

On Sept. 18, the Senate fell three votes short of the sixty needed to agree to a motion to invoke cloture (thus limiting debate). The **key vote was 57–42 (R 8–41; D 47–1;**

I 2–0). It was a fatal blow to the legislation. *(2007 key votes, p. 955)*

House Page Board

Congress in 2007 cleared legislation (HR 475—PL 110-2) retooling the House Page Board in an effort to prevent future scandals involving the teen workers and the lawmakers they served.

The bill expanded the House Page Board from five to eight members, adding one member from the minority party for partisan balance, a former page, and a parent of a current page. The enlarged board was intended to give pages with complaints additional avenues through which to have their concerns heard.

The House employed approximately seventy pages, usually sixteen-year-olds, from all over the country, who spend a school year running errands for lawmakers and House officials after attending early-morning classes.

The House passed HR 475 by 41–0 on Jan. 19. The Senate passed the measure by voice vote on Jan. 23, completing congressional action. The president signed the bill into law on Feb. 2.

The overhaul of the page program was prompted by the 2006 scandal involving Rep. Mark Foley, R-Fla. *(Foley ethics probe, p. 824)*

Capitol Visitor Center

The fiscal 2008 legislative branch appropriations legislation (HR 2764—PL 110-161) provided $414 million for the architect of the Capitol, including $29 million for the Capitol Visitor Center, which had been dogged by delays and cost overruns. Lawmakers, who repeatedly had expressed frustration about the architect's managing of the construction of the visitor center, used the bill to create an inspector general for the architect's office. *(Legislative branch appropriations, pp. 112, 115; 109th Congress action, p. 821)*

During House Appropriations Committee consideration of HR 2764, a lengthy debate took place over what to call the large hall in the unfinished visitor center. Committee members overruled both the chair of the Legislative Branch Subcommittee, Debbie Wasserman-Schultz, D-Fla., and the full committee chair, David R. Obey, D-Wis., voting to replace $250,000 worth of signs for the Capitol Visitor Center's "Great Hall" with new ones for "Emancipation Hall."

Democrat Jessie L. Jackson Jr. of Illinois teamed with Republican Zach Wamp of Tennessee to convince appropriators to change the name of the center's main room. Wamp had argued unsuccessfully for the change in the subcommittee, saying the original name would be confusing because the Library of Congress already had a well-known, ornate "Great Hall." Obey and Wasserman-Schultz argued that other committees should weigh in and that an official process should be created before giving a permanent name to such an important element of the visitor center. They had Democrat John Lewis of Georgia, a civil rights pioneer, in their corner. Lewis asked the committee in a letter to hold off on renaming the Hall. However, Jackson and Wamp prevailed.

The provision for renaming the large hall was not part of the final version of HR 2764. However, Jackson and Wamp introduced a stand-alone measure (HR 3315) renaming the hall. The House Committee on Transportation and Infrastructure reported it (H Rept 110-436) on Nov. 8, 2007. The full House agreed 398–6 on Nov. 13 to an Eleanor Holmes Norton, D-D.C., motion to suspend the rules and pass the bill. The Senate passed the legislation unamended by voice vote on Dec. 6, completing congressional action. The bill was signed into law (PL 110-139) on Dec. 18, 2007.

The House Legislative Branch Appropriations Subcommittee in 2008, during consideration of draft legislation for fiscal 2009 legislative branch appropriations, put off a decision on whether Congress should foot the cost of visitors' bus rides between Union Station and entrance of the new U.S. Capitol Visitor Center, leaving the matter for the full committee. The distance was only a few blocks to the Capitol, making it an easy walk for the physically fit, but not for everyone.

Because the draft bill was not approved by the full committee, the legislation was not formally introduced and no report was filed. The subcommittee approved the draft version by voice vote June 23.

Office of Congressional Ethics

The House on March 11, 2008, voted 229–182 to create an independent Office of Congressional Ethics (H Res 895) to review ethics complaints from outside individuals or groups against members, delegates, officers, and employees of the House.

The Speaker and the minority leader were responsible for jointly appointing a six-member board composed of people who were not members of Congress at the time and were not registered lobbyists. The board was meant to supplement the work of the House Committee on Standards of Official Conduct (ethics committee), which still would handle complaints filed by members of the House. The office did not affect Senate ethics procedures.

H Res 895 established a two-stage review process to be initiated at the joint request of two board members who were from different political parties. If three members voted to continue the matter after the initial review, the board would conduct a second-phase review, after which it would refer the matter to the ethics committee, recommending dismissal or further review.

A task force created by Speaker Nancy Pelosi, D-Calif., and headed by Michael E. Capuano, D-Mass., proposed the plan. The purpose was to make good on a 2006 House Democratic campaign promise to "drain the swamp of corruption" in Washington, D.C.

In late July, Pelosi and Minority Leader John A. Boehner, R-Ohio, appointed former representative David Skaggs (D-Colo., 1987–1999) to chair the six-member group, with former representative Porter Goss (R-Fla., 1981–1987, 1989–2004) serving as co-chair. The other panel members were former Democratic representatives Yvonne B. Burke of California (1973–1979) and Karan English of Arizona (1993–1995); former House chief administrative officer Jay Eagen; and assistant professor Allison Hayward of George Mason University School of Law. The group met for the first time on Sept. 26, 2008.

On Jan. 23, 2009, the board approved its rules and code of conduct, allowing it to begin taking complaints.

The Senate in 2006 during consideration of lobbying reform legislation (S 2349) rejected an amendment to establish an independent Office of Public Integrity to investigate alleged violations of Senate rules. *(Lobby reform, pp. 816, 830)*

Ethics Probes

The House Committee on Standards of Official Conduct (ethics committee) and the Senate Select Ethics Committee were spared having to wrestle with major ethics investigations, as high-profile cases—such as those against Rep. William J. Jefferson, D-La., and Sen. Ted Stevens, R-Alaska—were making their way through the criminal justice system.

SEN. TED STEVENS

Alaska Republican Ted Stevens was convicted on Oct. 27, 2008, on seven felony counts of lying on his Senate financial disclosure forms by omitting sizable gifts he received from Alaska business interests. Throughout the process, Stevens steadfastly maintained his innocence. The conviction was overturned in 2009 because of prosecutors' mistakes.

Stevens was indicted on July 27, 2008, by a federal grand jury in Washington, D.C., on seven counts of filing false financial disclosures from 2000 through 2006. As required by the Senate Republican Conference rules he stepped down from posts as the top Republican on the Commerce, Science, and Transportation Committee; the Defense Appropriations Subcommittee; and the Home Security and Governmental Affairs Subcommittee on Disaster Recovery.

The first count in the indictment concerned his alleged failure to report gifts that he received from oil services company VECO Corp. and its former chief executive, Bill Allen—most notably labor and supplies for the renovation and improvement of Stevens's Girdwood, Alaska, home. The project added a new first floor, a garage, a second-story deck, a Jacuzzi, and other amenities. The Federal Bureau of Investigation (FBI) and the Internal Revenue Service (IRS), which was reportedly investigating whether VECO had covered Stevens's home renovation costs, had searched the senator's home on July 30, 2007. The charge stated that Stevens was aware of the project on his home and who was doing the work.

The indictment also alleged that Stevens used his Senate position to aid VECO at the request of Allen and other company employees. It said the solicitations included "funding requests and other assistance with certain international VECO projects and partnerships, including those in Pakistan and Russia; requests for multiple federal grants and contracts to benefit VECO . . . including grants from the National Science Foundation to a VECO subsidiary; and assistance on both federal and state issues in connection with the effort to construct a natural gas pipeline from Alaska's North Slope Region."

In addition, the count alleged, Stevens and Allen arranged for Allen to transfer a new 1999 Land Rover Discovery, purchased for $44,000, to a child of Stevens in exchange for Stevens's 1964 Ford Mustang and $5,000. The Mustang was worth less than $20,000, according to the indictment. In failing to report the gifts, the count charged that Stevens "knowingly and intentionally sought to conceal and cover up his receipt of things of value."

The other six counts alleged that Stevens essentially amplified the violation listed in the first count in his annual Senate financial disclosure forms for the years 2001 through 2006.

Allen and former VECO vice president Richard L. Smith had pled guilty in May 2007 to providing more than $400,000 in payments to Alaska public officials. A lobbyist, a former chief of staff to Alaska's then-governor, and three Alaska state lawmakers were also convicted in the scandal.

Stevens's trial opened in Washington, D.C., on Sept. 25, 2008, after the defense failed to have the proceedings moved to Alaska. Allen appeared as the prosecution's star witness. He testified that he never sent Stevens a bill for the work, despite a written request from the senator in 2002, because he thought Stevens only asked for the invoice as legal cover. He said a Stevens confidant told him that Stevens did not really want to get the bill.

Stevens testified that he believed that all the disclosure forms he filed with the Senate were accurate, that he never intended to file false forms, and that he never tried to conceal gifts. He told the jury that his wife received and paid the bills for the renovation. Defense lawyers said their client was unaware of any renovations to his Alaska home that he did not pay for personally and that, in fact, Stevens provided more than $160,000 to cover the cost of home improvements. Prosecutors contended that VECO, not Stevens, paid nearly all the renovation's costs and that, at minimum, the senator was required to disclose the gifts.

Stevens and his lawyers repeatedly accused prosecutors in the case of gross misconduct. During the trial, the presiding U.S. district court judge, Emmet G. Sullivan, on Sept. 29 scolded prosecutors for sending a witness back to Alaska, a move that defense lawyers asserted was intended to hide exculpatory evidence. On Oct. 2, he admonished the Justice Department and its Public Integrity Section for redacting information favorable to Stevens from FBI notes turned over to defense lawyers before the trial started.

After the verdict was rendered, Sullivan postponed sentencing indefinitely while the Justice Department probed allegations of misconduct lodged by FBI special agent Chad Joy and David Anderson, a former VECO employee who facilitated improvements to Stevens's home and testified at the trial. Joy complained that another FBI agent on the case, Mary Beth Kepner, had an inappropriate relationship with Allen. Joy also said prosecutors hid information from the defense that could have helped prove Stevens's innocence.

On Feb. 13, 2009, Sullivan cited William M. Welch II, chief of the Public Integrity Section, and his deputy Brenda Morris, who argued the case against Stevens, for contempt for failing to turn over documents to the defense, as they had been ordered to do on Jan. 21. The judge called their failure to release the documents to defense lawyers "outrageous." The lawyers turned over the documents later that day. On Feb. 16, the Justice Department announced that it had removed the legal team that prosecuted Stevens from further post-trial proceedings.

In the new Obama administration, Attorney General Eric H. Holder Jr. on April 1, 2009, asked Sullivan to throw out Stevens's conviction. The Justice Department's five-page motion to dismiss the charges said defense attorneys should have been provided notes from an interview that authorities had with Allen on April 15, 2008. The motion said prosecutors discovered their notes from the meeting only in recent weeks and turned them over to defense attorneys. Two prosecutors who participated in the interview said Allen was asked about a note to him from Stevens dated Oct. 6, 2002. The notes from the April 15 interview indicated that Allen did not recall talking to a key prosecution witness, Bob Persons, about billing the defendant for the home improvements. But that statement was inconsistent with Allen's recollections at trial, where he described a conversation with Persons about billing Stevens. Allen estimated his work had a fair-market value of $80,000, according to the April 15 notes. The information could have been used by the defense in cross-examining Allen.

On April 7, Sullivan set aside the conviction. In response, the Alaska Republican Party called on Democrat Mark Begich, who defeated Stevens at the polls in November 2008, to resign to allow for a special election. Begich did not resign his seat.

SEN. LARRY E. CRAIG

The Senate Select Ethics Committee on Feb. 13, 2008, admonished Sen. Larry E. Craig, R-Idaho, saying he brought discredit on the Senate through his actions in 2007 in an airport rest room, his attempt to withdraw a guilty plea, and his unapproved use of campaign funds to pay lawyers.

Craig was arrested in a bathroom at the Minneapolis-St. Paul International Airport by a police officer investigating reports that the restroom had become a rendezvous point for men seeking gay sex. Initially accused of lewd behavior in the June 11, 2007, incident, Craig pleaded guilty on Aug. 1 to the lesser charge of disorderly conduct and paid a $500 fine.

Republican leaders abandoned their support for Craig within days of the case becoming public on Aug. 27. In a statement the next day, Craig said his guilty plea had been a panicky response to what he called a "witch hunt" by the media. (The *Idaho Statesman* had been working for almost a year on a story exploring reports that Craig was homosexual.) Craig said he had consulted no one—family, lawyer, or political aides—before deciding to enter the plea, and he announced that he would fight in court to withdraw the plea.

At issue was Craig's behavior in the airport men's room. He denied that he was trying to proposition the undercover airport police investigator from an adjacent men's room stall, as alleged in a police incident report. The report by Sgt. Dave Karsnia described his being in a bathroom stall and seeing Craig peer through a crack, "'fidget' with his fingers," and make a series of motions with his foot that the officer interpreted as a proposition. "At 12:16 hours, Craig tapped his right foot. I recognized this as a signal used by persons wishing to engage in lewd conduct," Karsnia wrote. "Craig tapped his toes several times and moved his foot closer to my foot. I moved my foot up and down slowly.... The presence of others did not seem to deter Craig as he moved his right foot so that it touched the side of my left foot, which was within my small area," Karsnia wrote. The report continued: "At 12:17 hours, I saw Craig swipe his hand under the stall divider for a few seconds. The swipe went in the direction from the front [door side] of the stall back towards the back wall. His palm was facing towards the ceiling as he guided it." According to Karsnia's report, Craig denied that he was trying to proposition the officer and maintained that he used "a wide stance when going to the bathroom and that his foot may have touched mine" and asserted that he "reached down with his right hand to pick up a piece of paper that was on the floor."

The GOP leadership was furious at Craig's apparent lack of remorse and was concerned that the incident could harm the party in the 2008 elections. Republican leaders on Aug. 28 called for a Select Ethics Committee investigation into the circumstances surrounding his guilty plea. On Aug. 29, Craig agreed to temporarily step down as ranking Republican on the Senate Veterans' Affairs Committee as well as the Appropriations Subcommittee on the Interior and the Energy and Natural Resources Subcommittee on Public Lands and Forests.

On Sept. 1, Craig announced plans to resign from the Senate on Sept. 30 and said he would fight to clear his name after he left public life. Four days later, however, he called Minority Leader Mitch McConnell, R-Ky., to say he might decide to stay longer if his effort to reverse his guilty plea was still pending. Craig changed his mind altogether on

Oct. 4, announcing he would serve out the rest of his term but would not seek a fourth term in 2008. He said he concluded that he could remain an effective senator and needed to stay in office to try and clear his name before the Ethics Committee. He made the announcement the same day District Court Judge Charles A. Porter Jr. in Minneapolis denied the senator's request to withdraw his guilty plea.

The six-member Ethics panel, in a letter to Craig, said, "We consider your attempt to withdraw your guilty plea to be an attempt to evade the legal consequences of an action freely undertaken by you—that is, pleading guilty." The committee wrote, "In our view, you committed the offense to which you pled guilty and you entered your plea knowingly, voluntarily and intelligently. Even if an attempt to withdraw a guilty plea under the circumstances present in this case is a course that a defendant in the state of Minnesota may take . . . it is a course that a United States senator should not take."

The panel also chided Craig for using more than $213,000 in campaign funds to pay legal and public relations fees without approval from the Ethics panel or the Federal Election Commission. Craig later set up a legal expense fund to help defray his legal fees.

Craig did not seek reelection in 2008.

SEN. PETE V. DOMENICI

The Senate ethics panel in 2008 concluded that Pete V. Domenici, R-N.M., did not try to influence a probe involving the construction of an Albuquerque courthouse but said the senator should have known better than to contact a prosecutor on a matter related to corruption, especially during an election year. A call by Domenici in 2006 to U.S. Attorney David C. Iglesias "created an appearance of impropriety that reflected unfavorably on the Senate," the committee said in an April 24 "letter of qualified admonition." There was no additional punishment.

The Justice Department fired Iglesias after the 2006 elections, when Republicans lost control of Congress. Iglesias on March 6, 2007, told the Senate Judiciary Committee that a few days before the elections Domenici called to inquire about the status of an investigation into a courthouse construction contract in Albuquerque that might have been illegally influenced by prominent Democrats. Iglesias testified he believed the senator was seeking to pressure him to return indictments, although Domenici did not say so explicitly. The incident was linked to a larger scandal in 2007 that involved the Justice Department's firing of several U.S. attorneys and contributed to the resignation of Attorney General Alberto R. Gonzales.

The Select Ethics Committee launched its inquiry in March 2007, after Citizens for Responsibility and Ethics in Washington, a public corruption interest group, filed a complaint alleging that Domenici had violated Senate rules, including a rule that barred lawmakers from contacting agencies for political reasons. Domenici publicly apologized for contacting Iglesias but insisted that he had "never pressured him nor threatened him in any way."

Domenici did not seek reelection in 2008.

SEN. DAVID VITTER

The Senate Select Ethics Committee on May 8, 2008, closed a probe of Louisiana Republican David Vitter's ties to a Washington, D.C., prostitution ring. A watchdog group, Citizens for Responsibility and Ethics in Washington, had filed a complaint alleging that Vitter's actions violated rules requiring conduct that reflected well on the Senate. The committee dismissed the complaint, but panel members said in a letter to Vitter that the case could be reopened "should new allegations or evidence" surface.

Vitter acknowledged in July 2007 that his telephone number appeared in the records for Pamela Martin and Associates, a since-defunct escort service run by "D.C. Madam" Deborah Palfrey that catered to an upscale Washington clientele. Vitter indicated that he had contacted the escort service before his 2004 Senate campaign.

The Senate committee said it opted not to launch an investigation because Vitter's conduct occurred while he was a member of the House, he was never charged with a crime, and his behavior "did not involve use of public office or status for improper purposes."

SENS. KENT CONRAD AND CHRISTOPHER J. DODD

Citizens for Responsibility and Ethics in Washington on June 13, 2008, filed a complaint with the Senate Ethics Committee after an article in *Condé Nast's Portfolio* magazine said Democrats Kent Conrad of North Dakota and Christopher J. Dodd of Connecticut benefited from a special loan program at Countrywide Financial Corp. in which certain points, fees, and borrowing rules were waived for officials. Both Conrad and Dodd said they did not know they were given special interest rates and loan terms because they were senators, as suggested by an e-mail obtained by *Portfolio.*

Conrad, chair of the Senate Budget Committee, told the Ethics Committee about the article just before it was published June 12. Conrad said he gave $10,700—the value of the benefit he said he received—to the charity Habitat for Humanity. He said he paid off the $32,000 left on the mortgage on a Bismarck, N.D., apartment house. Dodd, chair of the Senate Banking, Housing, and Urban Affairs Committee, said he had no reason to think being in Countrywide's "VIP" program would get him special treatment, adding that he would have rejected the loan if he had thought that was the case.

In letters to Conrad and Dodd dated Aug. 7, 2009, the Ethics Committee dismissed the complaint against the two senators, saying that while it found "no substantial credible evidence" that their actions violated Senate rules, they "should have exercised more vigilance in [their] dealings with Countrywide to avoid the appearance" that they received "preferential treatment" because they were in the Senate.

REP. WILLIAM J. JEFFERSON

A federal grand jury on June 4, 2007, handed up a sixteen-count indictment against Rep. William J. Jefferson, D-La., alleging bribe-taking, money laundering, misuse of office, and racketeering. It also alleged that Jefferson sought to bribe a Nigerian official—the first time, according to the Justice Department, that a federal official had been charged under the Foreign Corrupt Practices Act (PL 105-366). Jefferson pleaded not guilty on June 8 at an arraignment at the federal courthouse in Alexandria, Va. He was convicted on eleven of the sixteen counts on Aug. 5, 2009, and was sentenced to thirteen years in prison on Nov. 13, 2009.

The House voted 273–26 on June 5, 2007, for a resolution (H Res 452) calling for the House Committee on Standards of Official Conduct to determine whether Jefferson should be expelled. Three days later, the ethics panel announced it would relaunch a subcommittee probe into Jefferson's conduct. The inquiry was originally authorized in the 109th Congress. In August, the investigative panel suspended its work pending the outcome of the criminal case, saying it was acting at the Justice Department's request. *(109th Congress action, p. 825)*

Meanwhile, a legal battle was ongoing over some of the evidence against Jefferson, which was seized during a Federal Bureau of Investigation (FBI) raid on his suite in the Rayburn House Office Building in 2006. On Aug. 3, 2007, the U.S. Court of Appeals for the D.C. Circuit ruled that much of the material the FBI seized was taken in violation of the U.S. Constitution's speech or debate clause. Jefferson sought to toss out nearly all of the corruption and bribery charges on the grounds that the evidence violated the constitutional protections afforded to legislators. A three-judge panel rejected the request, saying that the grand jury that indicted Jefferson had not seen any protected material. In December 2008, the Fourth U.S. Circuit Court of Appeals in Richmond, Va., refused to reconsider the panel's ruling, paving the way for Jefferson's trial.

Jefferson was accused of using his position as co-chair of the caucuses on Nigeria and African trade to influence business deals between iGate Inc., a Kentucky telecommunications firm, and Nigerian officials. He was charged with soliciting and accepting more than $400,000 in bribes from iGate and ten other companies in return for promoting telecommunications, oil, sugar, and recycling deals in Nigeria, Ghana, Equatorial Guinea, Botswana, and the Congo. He was also accused of using his office to engage in "a pattern of racketeering activity" from roughly August 2000 to August 2005 that included taxpayer-funded trips abroad, arranged to promote deals that might benefit him financially, and using his congressional aides, e-mail, and stationery to promote those business ventures.

Jefferson lost his 2008 reelection bid.

REP. JIM MCDERMOTT

Ending a legal battle that began a decade earlier, the District of Columbia Circuit Court of Appeals ruled in a 5–4 decision on May 1, 2007, that Rep. Jim McDermott, D-Wash., was liable for $60,000 in damages and more than $850,000 in legal fees in a lawsuit brought against him by Rep. John A. Boehner, R-Ohio. The U.S. Supreme Court decided Dec. 3 to let that decision stand.

The appeals court held that McDermott was not protected by the First Amendment when he accepted a copy of an illegally taped conversation in December 2006—among Boehner, other GOP leaders at the time, and Speaker Newt Gingrich of Georgia—and passed it along to two reporters. The topic of discussion was the ethical allegations that Gingrich was facing.

When the incident took place, McDermott was the ranking Democrat on the House Committee on Standards of Official Conduct, which ruled in 2006 that he broke panel rules when he leaked the secretly recorded information. McDermott argued that he was exercising his free speech rights when he gave the tape to the press. *(Earlier action, Congress and the Nation Vol. XI, p. 723; Congress and the Nation Vol. X, pp. 765, 774)*

McDermott in 2008 paid his bill with money from his legal defense fund and his campaign. He refused to apologize, saying the public had a right to know what the Republican leaders said.

REP. RICK RENZI

Rep. Rick Renzi, R-Ariz., on March 4, 2008, pleaded not guilty to federal conspiracy, fraud, extortion, and money laundering charges related to a land-swap deal in his home state.

A thirty-five-count indictment unsealed on Feb. 22 accused Renzi of conspiring with James W. Sandlin in a land-swap scheme and with Andrew Beardall to commit insurance fraud. Prosecutors said that Renzi, as a member of what was then called the Resources Committee, in 2005 and 2006 conditioned his support for approval of a federal lands exchange on whether the deal would include property that Sandlin owned in Cochise County, Ariz. When a company seeking Renzi's support failed to purchase Sandlin's property, Renzi allegedly told the company, "No Sandlin property, no bill."

Renzi was charged with directing a second group of investors to purchase the property and include it in their land-exchange proposal, resulting in a $733,000 payment to Renzi from Sandlin in 2005, according to the indictment. Renzi, a father of twelve, was facing financial troubles in 2005 and needed a "substantial infusion of funds" to keep his insurance business afloat and "maintain his personal lifestyle," according to the indictment.

The Justice Department also charged that Renzi and Beardall embezzled more than $400,000 in insurance premiums from the trust account of the Patriot Insurance

Agency Inc., a Renzi family-owned business, and said the money helped fund Renzi's first congressional campaign. Renzi was accused of concealing illegal profits from Congress and the public.

Renzi had agreed to resign from the House Select Intelligence Committee after announcing April 19, 2005, that the Federal Bureau of Investigation had raided the offices of Patriot Insurance Agency Inc. Federal prosecutors in Phoenix, Ariz., had begun investigating Renzi's business practices in 2006.

The House Committee on Standards of Official Conduct on Feb. 28, 2008, in compliance with House rules, formed an investigative subcommittee to look into the case. The panel in May decided to delay its inquiry at the request of the Justice Department. Renzi lost his 2008 reelection bid, making the issue moot.

Prosecutors in 2009 added new corruption charges to the original indictment against Renzi. As of January 2010 the case was still pending.

REP. TOM FEENEY

By paying the Treasury $5,643 to symbolically cover some of his expenses while on a golf trip to Scotland as a guest of lobbyist Jack Abramoff, Rep. Tom Feeney, R-Fla., in January 2007 ended the House ethics committee investigation into his activities. Feeney said he was unaware that the trip's bills were being paid for by a registered lobbyist, in violation of House rules.

The Justice Department in July 2009 dropped its investigation, ongoing for more than two years, into Feeney and his involvement with Abramoff.

REP. JOHN T. DOOLITTLE

Under pressure from Republican leaders, Rep. John T. Doolittle, R-Calif., resigned from the House Appropriations Committee after the Federal Bureau of Investigation raided his home in suburban Virginia on April 13, 2007. Doolittle said agents were seeking records connected to Sierra Dominion Financial Solutions, a firm run by his wife, Julie. It had raised money to promote events for Republican lobbyist Jack Abramoff, who was sent to federal prison in 2006 after pleading guilty to fraud and trying to bribe public officials. In September Doolittle and six of his aides were subpoenaed by a federal grand jury in Washington, D.C.

Doolittle on Jan. 10, 2008, announced that he would not seek reelection. As of January 2010, the investigation was ongoing.

REP. JOHN P. MURTHA

The House on May 22, 2007, voted 219–189 to table (kill) a resolution (H Res 428) to reprimand Democratic representative John P. Murtha, chair of the Defense Appropriations Subcommittee, for allegedly threatening on the floor May 17 to deny earmarks to Rep. Mike Rogers, R-Mich., "now and forever" in retaliation for Rogers' unsuccessful effort May 11 to strip a Murtha earmark from the fiscal 2008 intelligence authorization bill (HR 2082). The House had defeated 181–241 a Rogers procedural motion to transfer $23 million from the National Drug Intelligence Center (NDIC) in Murtha's district to the Central Intelligence Agency's human intelligence budget and required the inspector general of the Department of Justice to investigate the NDIC. In a written statement May 18, Murtha declined to confirm or deny any remarks he made to Rogers. *(Intelligence authorization, pp. 320, 322)*

Rogers contended that Murtha threatened him in a way "clearly designed for intimidation." Democratic leaders did not take the claim seriously, in part, some said, because Murtha was known for his brusque manner.

REP. PETE STARK

By a 196–173 vote on Oct. 23, 2007, the House tabled, and thus killed, a privileged resolution (H Res 767) offered by Minority Leader John A. Boehner, R-Ohio, seeking to censure Rep. Pete Stark, D-Calif., for what the GOP leader called "personally abusive language" aimed at President George W. Bush and his supporters in the House.

During debate Oct. 18 on the House's unsuccessful attempt to override Bush's veto of an expansion of the State Children's Health Insurance Program (HR 976), Stark said, "You don't have money to fund the war or children. But you're going to spend it to blow up innocent people if we can get enough kids to grow old enough for you to send to Iraq to get their heads blown off for the president's amusement." Boehner said he wanted Stark formally rebuked for his "reprehensible attacks" because they had "dishonored our soldiers, their families and our commander in chief." *(Children's health insurance, p. 558)*

After the censure attempt failed, Stark apologized for his remarks, saying he did not want them to divert attention from the "serious issues" he had been trying to spotlight. Stark had faced pressure to apologize from party leaders.

REP. BOB FILNER

A House Committee on Standards of Official Conduct subcommittee was impaneled on Sept. 18, 2007, to investigate the conduct of House Veterans' Affairs Committee chairman Bob Filner, D-Calif. Filner on Aug. 19, 2007, had been charged with misdemeanor assault and battery for allegedly pushing a United Airlines baggage employee at Dulles International Airport. On Nov. 26, he pleaded guilty to a lesser trespassing charge and paid $166 in fines and court costs.

On Dec. 19, 2007, the subcommittee unanimously found that Filner "demonstrated poor judgment" in the airport incident and was "responsible for creating a situation that implicated the reputation of the House of Representatives." No further action was taken against him by the panel.

REP. CHARLES B. RANGEL

The House Committee on Standards of Official Conduct agreed on Sept. 24, 2008, to form a subcommittee to launch an investigation into allegations against Charles B. Rangel, D-N.Y., chairman of the House Ways and Means Committee. Rangel, who denied any wrongdoing, asked for the probe to clear himself of allegations that he had violated House rules.

Rangel sought the formal investigation after reports during the summer questioned lapses on his financial disclosure forms, his lease on four rent-controlled apartments in New York City, the use of his official parking spot in a House garage for long-term storage of a car with expired tags, and the use of his official letterhead to set up meetings with potential donors to the Charles B. Rangel Center for Public Service established at the City College of New York. The *New York Times* subsequently reported that Rangel had failed to report and pay taxes on more than $75,000 in rental income from a villa he had owned in the Dominican Republic since 1988. Rangel denied all allegations, although he paid the back taxes in September.

An attempt by Minority Leader John A. Boehner, R-Ohio, to censure Rangel failed July 31, on a 254–138 vote to table (kill) the resolution (H Res 1396). Boehner tried again Sept. 18 with a resolution (H Res 1460) that would have required Rangel to step down as chair of the tax-writing committee. The House voted 226–176 to table the measure.

On Dec. 9, acting ethics panel chair Gene Green, D-Texas, and ranking Republican Doc Hastings of Washington announced that, responding to a formal request from Rangel, the subcommittee would expand the investigation to include newspaper reports that in 2007 Rangel preserved tax breaks for an oil drilling company the same day he solicited donations from the firm for his public service center.

The investigation was ongoing as of January 2010.

REP. TIM MAHONEY

House Speaker Nancy Pelosi, D-Calif., in 2008 called for an ethics investigation into allegations that Florida Democrat Tim Mahoney paid a former employee and mistress $121,000 not to file suit against him. Mahoney said Oct. 14 that he broke no laws, and he apologized for his family's "embarrassment and heartache." Mahoney was defeated in his 2008 reelection bid, making the issue moot.

Chronology of Action on Congress: Election Issues

2005–2006

Nothing came of efforts to make changes in the 2002 campaign finance law. Also among the stalled legislation were measures to require that voters in federal elections show photo identification and to exempt Internet speech from campaign finance laws.

Campaign Finance

The 109th Congress failed in its attempts to rewrite or rollback parts of the 2002 campaign finance law (PL 107-155), in both stand-alone legislation (HR 1316, HR 513, S 271, S 1053) and as part of lobbying reform (HR 4975, S 2349). *(2002 law, Congress and the Nation Vol. XI, p. 730; 109th Congress, lobbying reform, pp. 816, 830)*

The effort to revise campaign rules was driven mainly by Republicans who wanted to rein in so-called 527 organizations, tax-exempt groups that had spent more than $400 million in soft or unregulated money trying to influence the 2004 elections. Unlike political campaigns or political action committees (PACs), these groups, named for the section of the tax code under which they operated, were able to accept unlimited contributions from wealthy individuals, unions, and corporations. Among the most frequently cited of these organizations were Moveon.org and Swift Boat Veterans for Truth. While a substantial portion of the groups financed GOP attack ads, Democrats were seen as the main beneficiaries of 527 fund-raising.

Some Republicans, meanwhile, were interested less in writing new rules for 527s than in relaxing existing campaign finance restrictions. The 2002 law banned previously unlimited soft money contributions to political parties and imposed curbs on the financing and placement of broadcast issue advertisements within thirty days of a primary or sixty days of a general election. Critics claimed the law trampled the free speech rights of individuals and associations.

Democratic party leaders said that they wanted to give the 2002 law more time to work without interference and that 527 groups were deliberately left unrestricted by that law to allow other avenues for election spending.

HOUSE ACTION

The House on April 5, 2006, passed HR 513 by 218–209, despite opposition from a majority of Democrats and a sizable faction of conservative Republicans.

The bill, sponsored by Christopher Shays, R-Conn., and Martin T. Meehan, D-Mass., two architects of PL 107-155, had been sent to the floor without recommendation, on a June 29, 2005, vote of 5–3 by the House Administration Committee. The legislation was formally reported June 22 (H Rept 109-181, Part I), and a supplemental report (H Rept 109-181, Part II) was filed Sept. 22. During the somewhat acrimonious committee markup, panel Democrats—led by ranking member Juanita Millender-McDonald of California—strongly opposed the legislation, saying it would lower voter turnout, impede voter registration activities, and violate independent groups' right to free speech. The panel's GOP majority blasted committee Democrats for their support of the 2002 campaign finance law criticized by its detractors for ultimately failing to halt the flow of soft money in federal elections.

The House-passed HR 513 would:

- Treat independent 527 organizations like other political committees. They would be required to register with and report to the Federal Election Commission (FEC), effectively barring large, unlimited soft money contributions.
- Exempt groups with annual receipts of less than $25,000 that worked exclusively on state or local elections.
- Require that any public communications and get-out-the-vote activities related only to federal campaigns be

financed entirely with hard money, which was subject to reporting requirements. If both federal and state or local candidates were involved, at least 50 percent of the groups' spending had to come from hard money. The 50 percent requirement would also apply to administrative expenses and fund-raising activities that involved both federal and nonfederal funds.
- Repeal the limits on expenditures by party committees that were coordinated with candidates' campaigns. Existing law limited only the coordinated expenditures. Political parties could make unlimited independent expenditures on behalf of Senate and House candidates as long as they were not coordinated with the campaigns.
- Require constitutional challenges to the bill to be filed in the U.S. District Court in the District of Columbia and be heard by a three-judge panel. Any appeal to the U.S. Supreme Court would have to be filed within ten days of an initial decision. The provisions would be effective through the end of 2008.

Language in the House-passed HR 513 calling for the repeal of an existing cap on the amount of money political parties could spend in coordination with a candidate's campaign was incorporated from competing legislation (HR 1316, sponsored by Mike Pence, R-Ind., and Albert R. Wynn, D-Md.). Despite the addition of the provision, Pence, who was chair of the conservative Republican Study Committee (RSC), opposed HR 513 and urged RSC members to vote against it. He argued that by regulating 527s Congress would invite organizations to find other ways—perhaps by tax-exempt 501(c)(4) groups—to raise money. Pence argued instead that fund-raising restrictions on state and local parties should be lifted.

Minority Leader Nancy Pelosi, D-Calif., said HR 513 was unfair and hypocritical because of its narrow target.

The House Administration Committee, by 6–3 on June 8, 2005, had approved HR 1316, aimed at strengthening the role of political parties and repealing sections of the 2002 campaign finance law and the Watergate-era laws that preceded it. Panel Democrats unanimously opposed the measure, saying it would roll back progress made by the 2002 campaign finance law and invoke the pre-Watergate days of scandal and corruption. HR 1316 was formally reported (H Rept 109-146) on June 22.

Sponsors Pence and Wynn said that reducing the regulation of hard and soft money would put other groups more on par with 527 organizations. The panel adopted, 6–3, a substitute amendment offered by Chairman Bob Ney, R-Ohio, that added a provision requiring 527 groups to abide by FEC disclosure requirements. It also prohibited the FEC from regulating online communication and allowed federal candidates to endorse state and local candidates without the endorsements being considered as coordinated contributions that had to be paid for with hard dollars.

The committee-approved HR 1316 would:

- Remove the aggregate $101,400 limit on contributions an individual could make to candidates and party committees in each two-year election cycle.
- Remove a cap on the amount party committees could spend on coordinated expenditures.
- Allow unlimited transfers from leadership PACs to party committees.
- Require 527 groups to file the same FEC reports as federal political committees.
- Allow state and local parties to spend nonfederal dollars for voter registration and sample ballots.
- Exempt Internet communications from the definition of "public communications" regulated by the FEC, thereby settling an ongoing debate over FEC regulation of the political postings of bloggers, Web writers, and other Internet-publishing partisans.

SENATE ACTION

The Senate Rules and Administration Committee gave voice-vote approval April 27, 2005, to a campaign finance bill (S 271) introduced by John McCain, R-Ariz., and Russ Feingold, D-Wis.—the two main Senate sponsors of the 2002 law—and by Chairman Trent Lott, R-Miss. The bill was intended as a companion to HR 513, but the committee made a number of changes during the markup. Afterward, Lott introduced it as a clean bill (S 1053).

The initial S 271 would:

- Require all 527s to register as political committees and comply with FEC rules unless they raised and spent money only for nonfederal candidate elections, state or local ballot initiatives, or the nomination or confirmation of individuals to nonfederal offices.
- Require that at least 50 percent of funds spent on voter registration activities affecting both federal and nonfederal elections be hard money.
- Require that 527s maintaining a nonfederal account accept no more than $25,000 per year per donor for that account. Corporations and labor unions could not contribute to those accounts.

During the markup, the committee:

- Adopted by voice vote a substitute by Lott that, among other things, exempted nonprofits that filed under section 501(c) of the tax code from the FEC restrictions. Also, 527 groups that received less than $25,000 a year would be exempt.
- Adopted a number of amendments by Robert F. Bennett, R-Utah, that would prevent the FEC from regulating the Internet, allow trade associations to solicit campaign funds from member companies without prior written approval, raise the amounts PACs could

receive and contribute to other PACs from $5,000 to $7,500, and allow unlimited transfers from leadership PACs to national parties.

- Adopted a Charles E. Schumer, D-N.Y., amendment to exempt 527s that funded only non-broadcast voter registration and get-out-the-vote drives.
- Adopted a Richard J. Durbin, D-Ill., amendment to require radio and television stations to sell advertising to candidates at the lowest rate available throughout the election cycle.

LOBBYING REFORM LEGISLATION

When House GOP leaders began to address lobbying reform in early 2006, they decided to incorporate HR 513 into a lobby regulation overhaul bill (HR 4975) and address the two issues at the same time. But some Republicans wanted a separate vote on the campaign finance provisions, so the leadership pulled them out and passed HR 513 as a stand-alone measure. Subsequently, the same provisions were reattached to the lobbying bill through the rule for floor debate. The House passed HR 4975 by 217–213 on May 3. No final agreement was reached on a lobbying bill, however, largely because the Senate refused to accept the 527 provisions as part of the legislation and House Republicans would not budge without them.

Voter Photo Identification

The House passed HR 4844, by 228–196 on Sept. 20, 2006, to require voters in federal elections to show photo identification and prove they are U.S. citizens. The House Administration Committee approved the bill 4–3 on Sept. 14 and reported it (H Rept 109-666) on Sept. 19.

The measure, sponsored by Henry J. Hyde, R-Ill., would require all election officials to check voters' photo ID starting with the November 2008 election. By November 2010, they could accept only identification that showed proof of citizenship. The bill required states to provide identification cards to eligible voters who could not pay for them and authorized funds to reimburse the states.

Democrats strongly opposed the measure and said it would make it harder for many people to vote. They said elderly and minority voters often do not have picture identification, access to birth certificates, or the money to pay for passports or other documents that prove citizenship.

HR 4844 was viewed as an immigration-targeted measure. In passing the bill, the House was following in the footsteps of a number of states that had acted to require voters to show proof of citizenship. In September 2006, a Georgia superior court judge struck down a similar state law, saying it disenfranchised otherwise-qualified voters and added unconstitutional conditions to voting.

The Senate did not act on the bill.

Voting Equipment

The Senate by voice vote on Feb. 9, 2006, passed a bill (S 2166) to allow the Election Assistance Commission to give grants to states to replace election equipment or paperwork destroyed by Hurricanes Katrina and Rita. The bill authorized up to $50 million in grants in fiscal 2006 to help polling places or local election commissions buy supplies or technology. The grants would be administered under the 2002 Help America Vote Act (PL 107-252). *(2002 law, Congress and the Nation Vol. XI, p. 726)*

Internet Speech

The House Administration Committee on March 13, 2006, reported a bill (HR 1606—H Rept 109-389) to exempt blogs, e-mail, and other Internet speech from campaign finance laws. The vote came as the Federal Election Commission (FEC) was preparing to rule on how those laws applied to online communications.

The bill, sponsored by Jeb Hensarling, R-Texas, had been defeated on Nov. 2, 2005, when the House rejected a motion 225–182 to suspend the rules and pass the measure. Suspension of the rules requires a two-thirds vote.

HR 1606 became a flashpoint in the debate over how campaign finance laws, including the 2002 overhaul (PL 107-252), should be extended to the Internet. The 2002 law aimed to limit the influence of big money in politics by imposing restrictions and disclosure requirements on campaign spending, donations, and political speech. *(2002 election overhaul, Congress and the Nation Vol. XI, p. 726)*

Supporters argued that regulating online political speech would stifle the very type of grass-roots democratic activity that the campaign finance laws were intended to encourage. Opponents said it would open up new loopholes that would allow corporations, unions, wealthy individuals, and political parties to skirt restrictions on campaign spending and contributions and to fund political advertising on the Internet.

Floor action on HR 1606 was indefinitely postponed after the FEC voted unanimously on March 27, 2006, to regulate online political advertising but to exempt individual online political speech, including blogs, to avoid choking off grass-roots activity on the Web. The FEC vote came after two authors of the 2002 law—Reps. Martin T. Meehan, D-Mass., and Christopher Shays, D-Conn.—sued in federal court, arguing that the commission had been too lax in enforcing the law. The judge in the case ruled in 2005 that the FEC could not completely exempt the Internet from the statute.

A substitute measure (HR 4900), which would codify the new FEC rules and exempt most individual online communications from campaign finance laws, was referred to the House Administration Committee but saw no further action.

2007–2008

Elections-related issued considered by the 110th Congress included requiring states and localities to have paper ballots, providing a paper trail for electronic voting, and establishing protections for voters against intimidation and deception.

Paper Ballots

The House on July 15, 2008, defeated a bill (HR 5803) to authorize up to $75 million to pay for backup paper ballots in the November elections. The measure, sponsored by Zoe Lofgren, D-Calif., was brought up under suspension of the rules, which requires a two-thirds vote for passage. The vote of 248–170 fell short of that.

The measure was an attempt to reimburse states and localities that opted to purchase pre-printed paper ballots to have at the ready should electronic voting machines fail on election day.

The House Administration Committee approved HR 5803 by 5–3 on May 7 and reported the bill (H Rept 110-637) on May 15. Committee Republicans argued that the measure was too expensive and not necessary.

The House on April 15, 2008, had rejected a motion to suspend the rules and pass another paper ballot bill (HR 5036) by 239–178. The House Administration Committee had approved the measure by voice vote on April 2 and reported it (H Rept 110-582, Part I) on April 14.

Electronic Voting

The House Administration Committee by 6–3 on May 8, 2007, approved HR 811, to require states to use voting machines that produce a paper trail. The bill also required states to perform random audits of voting results and make voting-machine software available for inspection. It authorized the federal government to spend up to $1 billion to help states replace their old machines. Though the intent of the measure was to put a paper trail in place for the 2008 elections, it also provided for waivers to give states using older voting technology more time.

The committee reported HR 811 (H Rept 110-154) on May 16. The bill would add the requirements to a 2002 law (PL 107-252) enacted in the wake of Florida's contested 2000 presidential election results. *(2000 presidential election, Congress and the Nation Vol. X, p. 21)*

HR 811 was strongly opposed by the National Association of Counties and other organizations that wanted states to be granted either more time or guaranteed funding to implement paper-ballot technology. It also was opposed by the American Association of People with Disabilities and groups representing people who speak English as a second language. The legislation had the backing of government watchdog groups, such as Common Cause.

Voting Machines Challenge

The House by voice vote on Feb. 25, 2008, adopted a resolution (H Res 989) closing the books on a bitterly contested congressional race that led Florida to ban touch-screen voting machines.

Republican Vern Buchanan had been certified the winner, by 369 votes, of the Sarasota-based Thirteenth District seat in the November 2006 election. More than eighteen thousand ballots were recorded as having no choice made in that race. Democratic challenger Christine Jennings said she was certain that machine problems were responsible for at least some of those no-vote ballots.

After an automatic machine recount and a manual recount, a state-run audit found no evidence that the machines had contributed to an inaccurate vote count. On May 2, 2007, a three-member House Administration Committee task force agreed by voice vote to embark on a formal investigation. The task force, also by voice vote, agreed to use Government Accountability Office (GAO) experts to design a method to test the reliability of the voting machines.

The task force on Feb. 8, 2008, recommended that the House Administration Committee dismiss the challenge. In its report, the GAO said there was no way to completely rule out an election night glitch. But based on the evidence, examined under video cameras, the GAO said its experts saw no need for further examination of the Florida machines.

Campaign Pay to Spouses

The House by voice vote under suspension of the rules on July 23, 2007, passed a bill (HR 2630) to prohibit candidates from paying their spouses to work on their campaigns. The measure, sponsored by Adam B. Schiff, D-Calif., also required that candidates file a separate disclosure to the Federal Election Commission detailing all campaign payments made to immediate family members. Campaigns would not be allowed to reimburse family members for penalties incurred because of violation of the legislation.

Some Republicans objected that HR 2630 would do little to raise the ethical bar in Washington, D.C., or to prevent recent ethics scandals from recurring, as the measure's supporters claimed.

The watchdog group Citizens for Responsibility and Ethics in Washington said it studied campaign reports covering three dozen election cycles and found dozens of examples of lawmakers' campaigns paying family members. Members of both political parties paid their spouses for campaign work.

"MILLIONAIRE'S AMENDMENT" STRUCK DOWN

The U.S. Supreme Court, in a 5–4 decision on June 26, 2008, rejected the so-called millionaire's amendment in the 2002 Bipartisan Campaign Reform Act (PL 107-155), which allowed congressional candidates to collect more than the normal contributions per donor when they ran against wealthy, self-financing opponents. Justice Samuel A. Alito Jr., who wrote the decision in *Davis v. Federal Election Commission,* said that the provision was "at war" with rulings such as the 1976 decision in *Buckley v. Valeo,* which equated money with political speech. *(Court decision, p. 758; 2002 law, Congress and the Nation Vol. XI, p. 730; 1976 case, Congress and the Nation Vol. IV, pp. 639, 995)*

The majority attacked the provision's strategy of raising contribution limits for challengers, an attempt by Congress to level the fund-raising playing field. The millionaire's amendment allowed a House candidate whose opponent spent at least $350,000 of his or her own money to collect contributions at triple the standard limit of $2,300 per donor per election. Senate candidates also were able to increase their per-donor contribution limits under a formula based on state population.

Electronic Filing

The Senate Rules and Administration Committee by voice vote on March 28, 2007, approved a bill (S 223) that would force members of the Senate to file campaign finance records with the Federal Election Commission (FEC) electronically, which would shorten the process of making the filings available to the public by about a month. The bill was formally reported the same day (no written report).

S 223 would have virtually no impact on Senate offices themselves. They would continue to use computer software to fill out the same disclosure forms designed to make campaign finance data available to the public. Instead of having those forms printed and hand-delivered to a vendor in Fredericksburg, Va., which then inputted the data and transmitted them to the FEC at a cost of $250,000, the Senate offices would simply transmit the forms electronically to the secretary of the Senate. The secretary's office would then transmit the reports directly to the FEC.

The committee gave voice-vote approval to an amendment that would delay the new rules until January 2008, to give the Senate secretary's office time to prepare its computer servers to handle the influx of new traffic.

House candidates filed their campaign finance information directly with the FEC.

Voter Intimidation, Deception

By voice vote on June 25, 2007, the House agreed to a John Conyers Jr., D-Mich., motion to suspend the rules and pass HR 1281 to punish anyone who attempted to deceive or intimidate voters. The measure was a response to civil rights groups' complaints of efforts to mislead voters in predominantly minority neighborhoods.

The House Judiciary Committee had approved HR 1281 by voice vote on March 29 and reported it (H Rept 110-101) on April 18.

Since 2000 civil rights groups have documented cases of voters receiving phone calls and flyers with false information about endorsements or the location of polling places, or warnings that immigrants who voted could go to prison.

The two political parties traded charges of voting irregularities. Democrats alleged efforts to suppress minority votes through deception or intimidation. Republicans focused on voter fraud by people not qualified to vote. Under HR 1281, people who knowingly communicate false information about the time, place, or manner of an election or about voter eligibility would be punished with fines or prison sentences up to five years.

As introduced, the bill would have dealt only with those who mislead or intimidate voters in the sixty days preceding a federal election. But the Judiciary panel adopted an amendment by ranking member Lamar Smith, R-Texas, to make the actions punishable year-round. The bill also would require the attorney general to establish a Voting Integrity Task Force to "undertake all effective measures necessary to provide correct information to voters" and refer matters to the Justice Department's Civil Rights Division for prosecution.

The Senate Judiciary Committee by voice vote on Sept. 6, 2007, approved a substitute version of a bill (S 453) that would create penalties for voter intimidation. The substitute stripped language from the original bill, introduced by Barack Obama, D-Ill., allowing private parties to bring lawsuits to block deceptive voting practices. Without that language, S 453 was more closely aligned with HR 1281. In place of that broader right of action, private parties would only be able to obtain injunctions against the Justice Department to force compliance with the legislation's requirements.

Chronology of Action on Congress: Pay and Benefits

2005–2006

Congressional salaries continued to inch up with annual pay increases.

Congressional Pay

As signed into law Nov. 30, 2005 (HR 3058—PL 109-115), the fiscal 2006 appropriations bill for the departments of Transportation, Treasury, and Housing and Urban Development (HUD) included a 1.9 percent pay increase for members of Congress in 2006, bringing their annual compensation to $165,200, up from $162,100. The leadership in the House and Senate gets a higher salary. The Speaker in 2006 received $212,100, up from $208,100 in 2005; the majority and minority leaders of both chambers and the Senate president pro tempore, $183,500, up from $180,100. The 2005 amounts had been set in 2004 (PL 108-447), when members opted not to fight the automatic annual salary adjustment. *(Fiscal 2006 Transportation, Treasury, HUD appropriations, p. 78; 2004 action, Congress and the Nation Vol. XI, p. 741)*

HR 3058 also included a 3.1 percent pay raise for federal civilian employees, equal to that for military personnel. The administration had proposed a 2.3 percent increase for civilian personnel.

Members were put on course for the pay raise when the House, 263–152 on June 28, agreed to a procedural motion to "order the previous question," which foreclosed the possibility of an amendment being offered to HR 3058 that would nullify the pay increase.

The House Appropriations Committee, during the markup of the legislation, gave voice-vote approval to an amendment, offered by Minority Whip Steny H. Hoyer, D-Md., to ensure that federal civilian employees received annual pay raises equal to those of the Defense Department.

In a nod to the growing expense of reconstruction efforts following Hurricanes Katrina and Rita, the Senate on Oct. 18, during floor consideration of the funding bill, adopted 92–6 a Jon Kyl, R-Ariz., amendment to save about $2 million by forgoing the automatic cost-of-living adjustment (COLA) for members of Congress. House leaders of both parties said they favored the COLA, which was worth $3,100. Conferees subsequently dropped the Senate provision that would have rejected the automatic COLA for lawmakers.

During consideration of the fiscal 2007 Transportation, Treasury, and HUD funding bill (HR 5576), the House voted 249–167 on June 13, 2006, to order the previous question, effectively quashing debate on the issue of raising the annual pay of members. Thus, they were scheduled to receive a 2 percent increase, bringing their annual salaries to $168,500, with House and Senate leaders receiving more. In fiscal 2007 continuing appropriations legislation (H J Res 102—PL 109-383), which cleared on Dec. 8, Congress delayed the pay raise until Feb. 16, 2007. However, lawmakers in 2007 blocked the pay increase. *(Fiscal 2007 Transportation, Treasury, HUD appropriations, p. 105; fiscal 2007 continuing appropriations, p. 105; 2007–2008 congressional pay, p. 849)*

Franking Privilege

The House on April 27, 2005, agreed by voice vote to suspend the rules and pass H Res 224, putting new limits on the mass mailings by committees. The resolution, approved by the House Administration Committee by voice vote on April 21 and reported (H Rept 109-54) on April 26, provided that committees during the 109th Congress would not be allowed to spend more than $5,000 on mailings in each session, and new rules would limit the content.

The restrictions followed a partisan dust-up in 2004 in which Democrats accused House Resources Committee chair Richard W. Pombo, R-Calif., of abusing his panel's franking privilege by sending favorable newsletters to the districts of Republicans in close races.

2007–2008

Members denied themselves a pay raise in the first session of the 110th Congress but were back on track in the second.

Congressional Pay

Lawmakers, in a fiscal 2007 continuing resolution (H J Res 20—PL 110-5) signed into law Feb. 15, 2007, blocked a scheduled cost-of-living adjustment (COLA) congressional pay raise from taking effect. That action kept the annual salary for representatives and senators at $165,200 in 2007, unchanged from 2006. The higher compensation for the leadership also was frozen at $212,100 for the Speaker of the House and $183,500 for the majority and minority leaders of the House and Senate as well as the Senate president pro tempore. In 2006 Congress had delayed the pay increase until Feb. 16, 2007. *(2005–2006 congressional pay, p. 849)*

Under the procedure for determining the annual COLA established by the Ethics Reform Act of 1989 (PL 101-194), members were due to receive a 2.7 percent salary increase in January 2008. However, the increase was revised to 2.5 percent, thus matching the salary boost in the base pay of General Schedule employees. Thus, in 2008 representatives and senators received $169,300; the Speaker, $217,400; and the majority and minority leaders of the House and Senate and the Senate president pro tempore, $188,100. *(Ethics law, Congress and the Nation Vol. VIII, p. 920)*

The House on June 27, 2007, during consideration of the fiscal 2008 financial services appropriations bill (HR 2829) did consider the issue of the 2008 congressional salary increase, in a procedural vote that would prevent members from offering an amendment to block the next scheduled pay increase. A coalition of politically safe Democrats and Republicans voted 244–181 in favor of the previous question, a roll call on whether to hold a vote on the rule (H Res 517) governing debate for the bill. The raises thus were never truly endangered.

In January 2009, a pay adjustment of 2.8 percent kicked in, bringing members' salary to $174,000; the Speaker, $223,500; and the House and Senate majority and minority leaders and the Senate president pro tempore, $193,400.

Congressional Pensions

The House on Jan. 23, 2007, by 431–0 agreed to a motion by Juanita Millender-McDonald, D-Calif., to suspend the rules and pass HR 476, to force members of Congress convicted of crimes related to their official duties to give up their retirement benefits. The bill would strip the pensions accrued by members convicted of certain felonies, including bribery, defrauding the government, and perjury involving "falsely denying commission of an act."

Democrats added a provision under which pensions would be denied to members convicted of coercing others to lie in their behalf. Making that change and trying to alter the bill's effective date triggered a small GOP uprising on the floor Jan. 22. Rank-and-file Republicans said HR 476 should have included more crimes, such as tax evasion, and they objected to having to deal with last-minute changes just before being asked to vote. The changes were part of an effort to align the measure with Senate-passed language in a broad lobbying and ethics bill (S 1), which included a congressional pension forfeiture provision that would not take effect until January 2009. *(Lobbying reform, pp. 816, 830)*

That enactment date was chosen to comport with the U.S. Constitution's Twenty-seventh Amendment banning mid-Congress changes in lawmakers' compensation. But, prodded by Republicans, the House agreed to keep forfeiture effective immediately despite the constitutional concern.

The bill would not be retroactive.

CHAPTER 16

The Bush Presidency

The Bush Presidency

Rarely in American history has a presidency imploded as thoroughly as it did in George W. Bush's second term from 2005 to 2009. The same man who once scored a 90 percent approval rating in the Gallup opinion polls a few weeks after the Sept. 11, 2001, terrorist attacks in New York City and just outside Washington, D.C.- the highest rating in the history of the Gallup poll, which started when Franklin D. Roosevelt was president—had plummeted to a 25 percent approval rating by October 2008. Only two presidents, Harry S Truman and Richard M. Nixon, received lower Gallup scores at the height of their unpopularity.

It was a stunning turn of events, coming so quickly after Bush had defeated Democratic senator John Kerry of Massachusetts in his 2004 re-election bid. The broad storyline of the Iraq war, the event that Bush knew would determine the fate of his presidency, was already clear: The nation had gone to war over weapons of mass destruction that were never found, and American troops and Iraqi civilians were dying in a seemingly endless barrage of insurgent attacks. Yet Bush had prevailed, and there was every reason to believe that if Bush could win re-election in that environment, he would maintain enough influence with Congress and hold onto just enough public confidence to achieve a successful second term.

Instead, the Bush presidency unraveled as a series of disasters and misjudgments made it impossible to rewrite the narrative of his years in office. The elements of the popular perception were already set: the Iraq war, even after the violence began to subside, increasingly was seen as the war that did not have to happen and was going on too long. Hurricane Katrina, which hit the U.S. Gulf Coast in August 2005, turned the Bush administration into a portrait of incompetence (even though the disaster planning at the local levels was not much better). Various scandals, from the public identification of an undercover CIA agent to the firing of several U.S. attorneys, depicted a level of political vindictiveness within the administration that seemed unusual even by Washington standards. The financial crisis that dominated Bush's final two years in office seemed to be just another catastrophe that happened on his watch.

Through it all, Bush gained the reputation of a president who was not especially curious, lacked self-awareness, refused to second-guess his strategies even when new strategies were called for, treated Congress like an annoyance rather than a co-equal branch of government, and made the nation's political polarization worse rather than better. By the end of his presidency, only 37 percent of Americans in a CNN/Opinion Research Corporation poll said they found him "honest and trustworthy."

President Bush comments on the commission on weapons of mass destruction report that found failures throughout U.S. spy agencies that led to botched estimates of the threat posed by Saddam Hussein. Left to right are commission co-chairmen Senator Chuck Robb, D-Va., and Judge Laurence Silberman.
Source: AP Photo/Gerald Herbert

Most of that implosion could be tied directly to the decisions and events of Bush's first term. Before he had been in office even a year, Bush was faced with the national trauma of the destruction of New York's World Trade Center and the attack on the Pentagon in northern Virginia on Sept. 11, 2001. He responded with a new doctrine that would lead down roads that could not have been predicted at the time. Any state that gives aid and comfort to terrorists, he declared on the night of the attacks, would be considered just as guilty as the terrorists themselves. That policy led to the U.S. attack on Afghanistan that ousted the Taliban from power—depriving al Qaeda, the organization behind the 2001 attacks, and its leader, Osama bin Laden, of the state sponsor that gave his terrorist forces so much power.

But U.S. forces failed to catch bin Laden himself, leaving the nation with an agonizing lack of closure after the deaths of more than 3,000 Americans in the 2001 attacks. In just over a year, the attention of U.S. military forces shifted elsewhere: to a new war in Iraq, aimed at toppling the nation's dictator, Saddam Hussein. The Bush administration vaguely linked the Iraq war to the Sept. 11 attacks, partly by noting that Saddam supported other terrorist organizations, which was true, but also by implying that there were links between Saddam and al Qaeda, which was not true. Most of all, though, the administration argued that Saddam might pass his weapons of mass destruction to terrorists, making another attack like Sept. 11 many times worse. Saddam, however, had no weapons of mass destruction. He had been thoroughly defeated in the 1991 Gulf War, which occurred after he invaded neighboring Kuwait, and his entire rationale for not cooperating with international arms inspectors turned out to be a ruse to make his Middle East rivals think he was stronger than he actually was.

Moreover, Bush set in motion a series of antiterrorism policies that were intended to stop future attacks. He opened a detention facility at Guantanamo Bay, Cuba, to hold suspected terrorists. Many of the inmates truly were dangerous, but there were also, it turned out, a large number of people who may simply have been in the wrong place at the wrong time. He authorized a warrantless eavesdropping program to monitor suspected terrorists' communications. He created military commissions to try suspected terrorists outside of the regular court system, without asking for approval from Congress, but the Supreme Court struck down the system and forced his administration to ask for congressional authorization in 2006. In a series of legal opinions later released by his successor as president, Barack Obama, the Office of Legal Counsel, a little-known but powerful arm of the Department of Justice, authorized interrogators to use a series of brutal techniques in questioning prisoners that most outside legal experts considered torture.

Historians may revise this portrait of Bush's presidency, depending on events in the coming years. Bush and his defenders often pointed out that the United States was not attacked again after Sept. 11, 2001. Vice president Richard B. Cheney, in particular, insisted that that was no accident, but rather a function of the tough antiterrorism policies the Bush administration put in place, particularly the harsh interrogation techniques used on suspected terrorists, which increasingly came to be seen as torture as more details became known. If independent evidence were to emerge that the Bush administration's policies did prevent other terrorist attacks from taking place, or if a future attack could be linked to the reversal of Bush policies by later administrations, it is possible that Bush's place in history will be more respected than it was immediately after his presidency ended. It also was plausible that a reinvented and stable Iraq, with Western-style free and fair elections, would help justify Bush's decision to overthrow Saddam.

There was also a reasonable argument that, with more historical perspective on the economic meltdown of fall 2008, Bush will get credit for pushing for a financial bailout package—against stiff resistance in his own party, and against his own resistance to government involvement in the free market—that might have helped to avoid a vast economic collapse, not just in the United States but globally. Short of that, however, there appeared, in the year after he left office, to be few opportunities for Bush to rehabilitate a record that made him one of history's least popular presidents by the time he left office.

BUSH CLAIMS ELECTION MANDATE

Bush started his second term convinced that he had won vindication for his policies in fighting the war on terrorism, as well as a popular mandate for an ambitious agenda that included giving people more control over their health care plans, an overhaul of the tax code to make it simpler, and a rewrite of Social Security to include, for the first time, private savings accounts. He gave these initiatives a name: ownership society.

At a press conference in November 2004, just after his re-election, Bush told reporters he had talked about his agenda so often on the campaign trail that his election victory was a clear endorsement of his policies. His message to Congress, he said, was "that I made it clear what I intend to do as the president and the people made it clear what they wanted, now let's work together." The bottom line, he said, was this: "I earned capital in the campaign, political capital, and now I intend to spend it."

In terms of pure political muscle, Bush should have been in a good position to do just that. In Congress, the Republicans had just expanded their majorities in both chambers. At the beginning of 2005, they held 55 seats in the Senate and 231 seats in the House, their biggest margins of control since they took over Congress from the Democrats in 1995. Clearly, the voters had spoken, and they had given Bush the freedom to move forward on his agenda. Even from the beginning, though, Bush was overstating the strength of his mandate. His top political advisers, like Karl Rove, made much of the fact that Bush won 51 percent of the popular vote—the first president to win an outright majority of the popular vote in the past four elections. Yet 51 percent was still more of an indicator of a closely divided nation than a decidedly unified one. Moreover, Bush's victory over Kerry in the electoral college, 286 votes to 252, was clear but hardly overwhelming.

Still, the first signs were encouraging. In the first half of 2005, Congress gave Bush early victories by clearing legislation to limit class-action lawsuits and make it more difficult for people to declare bankruptcy without making arrangements to pay off their debts. Both measures were part of the GOP's "tort reform" agenda that had stalled in previous years. Bush also won congressional approval of an energy policy overhaul he had been seeking since 2001, with incentives to increase domestic production of oil, gas, and coal. In Iraq, the first legislative elections in January 2005—with the widely televised images of Iraqi citizens proudly displaying the dyed-purple thumbs that proved they had voted—briefly made even Bush's critics wonder if his goal of bringing democracy to Iraq just might take hold. But those hopes faded quickly as sectarian violence continued to increase, raising the threat that the unstable country would simply plunge into civil war.

Then, on Aug. 29, 2005, Hurricane Katrina made landfall in southern Louisiana. It killed nearly 2,000 people, caused more than $80 billion in damage, and gave the Bush administration an image of incompetence from which it never fully recovered. Images of storm survivors stranded in their flooded homes, on rooftops, or in the Louisiana Superdome—begging for help after New Orleans' levees failed—were televised around the world. They depicted a federal government that could not handle one of its most basic responsibilities: protecting its citizens in the event of a natural disaster.

Bush did not help his case by appearing out of touch with the scope of the disaster. His comment to Federal Emergency Management Agency director Michael Brown—"You're doing a heck of a job, Brownie"—became the butt of jokes when Brown was widely blamed for the agency's lack of preparedness. But Brown later insisted he had been made a scapegoat, and indeed, evidence later emerged that undermined Bush's claim that the damage could not have been expected. In a television interview on Sept. 1, Bush said, "I don't think anyone anticipated the breach of the levees." But in March 2006, transcripts from video conferences among top federal and state government officials, including Bush, showed that some officials warned that widespread flooding was a possibility because the storm might at least push water over the levee walls.

SCANDALS PROLIFERATE

Just as the Bush administration was getting battered with criticism over Katrina, another scandal erupted that had been simmering since Bush's first term. In October 2005, a federal grand jury indicted I. Lewis "Scooter" Libby, Cheney's chief of staff, for his role in the public identification of covert Central Intelligence Agency operative Valerie Plame after her husband, diplomat Joseph Wilson, challenged the credibility of some of the intelligence the Bush administration used to go to war with Iraq. Libby resigned after his indictment on one count of obstruction of justice, two counts of perjury, and two counts of making false statements. He was later convicted on one count of obstruction, two counts of perjury, and one count of lying to the FBI, and was sentenced to thirty months in prison and a $250,000 fine, plus two years of supervised release including 400 hours of community service. On July 2, 2007, Bush commuted the prison sentence while leaving the other portions of the sentence unchanged.

Libby's fall helped create an image of the Bush White House as vindictive and bent on revenge toward its political enemies. Libby was not actually the source of the leak of Plame's identity that became public in a column by conservative pundit Robert Novak; Richard L. Armitage, a deputy secretary of state during Bush's first term, later admitted he was Novak's source. But a lengthy investigation by special prosecutor Patrick Fitzgerald revealed that Libby had talked about Plame with several reporters, and Fitzgerald accused him of lying about those conversations. Moreover, although he never faced legal charges, Bush's top political adviser, Karl Rove, confirmed Plame's identity to Novak and discussed her with other reporters, giving Bush's opponents even more ammunition to depict his White House as scheming and overly political.

At the same time, a series of ethics scandals created an unrelenting drumbeat of bad news that threatened Bush's main leverage for his agenda: the strong Republican majority in Congress. In September 2005, Tom DeLay, the arm-twisting and highly effective House majority leader, stepped down from his leadership post after a Texas grand jury indicted him on charges of violating campaign finance laws. It was only supposed to be a temporary move, but as the legal proceedings dragged on with no end in sight, DeLay made his departure from the leadership permanent and resigned his House seat in June 2006.

That was only the beginning of the Republicans' ethics troubles. Jack Abramoff, an influential Republican lobbyist, pleaded guilty in January 2006 to charges of conspiracy, mail fraud, and income tax evasion in a case that revealed how he and his associates had defrauded his clients—mainly Native American tribes—of tens of millions of dollars. Some of DeLay's associates were swept up in the case, and in October 2006, Rep. Bob Ney of Ohio, once the chairman of the House Administration Committee, pleaded guilty to accepting gifts in exchange for helping Abramoff's clients. He resigned before Congress could expel him, as the embarrassed House Republican leadership had threatened to do.

Then, on Sept. 29, 2006, Rep. Mark Foley of Florida, a deputy whip, resigned abruptly after media reports revealed he had sent sexually explicit computer messages to former House pages. The leadership, notably Speaker J. Dennis Hastert of Illinois, faced tough questions about whether they had paid enough attention to allegations about Foley's conduct. The House ethics committee investigated, and concluded that while Hastert and other GOP officials did not break any laws or House rules, neither did they look into Foley's behavior as aggressively as they should have.

The ethics scandals, combined with public discontent over the Iraq war and growing doubts over Bush's performance, gave Democrats the clearest opening they had had in a dozen years to knock the Republicans out of power. They campaigned on promises to end the Iraq war, make health care and student loans more affordable, revamp the nation's energy policies, and generally keep the Bush administration in check by providing the aggressive oversight they said the Republicans had never provided.

On Nov. 7, 2006, the Democrats won a net gain of thirty seats in the House and six in the Senate, winning a solid House majority with 233 seats and the slimmest possible one in the Senate. They only controlled the upper chamber because two independents, Joseph I. Lieberman of Connecticut and Bernard Sanders of Vermont, agreed to caucus with the Democrats, giving them effective control of fifty-one seats. For his last two years in office, Bush would have to contend not with a like-minded Republican majority, but a hostile Democratic one that had vowed to oppose almost everything he stood for.

BUSH SEEKS NEW COURSE

At first, following the 2006 midterm elections, Bush said he had received the voters' message and sent signals that he would change gears to adjust to the new political environment. He fired his defense secretary, Donald H. Rumsfeld, the abrasive Cheney ally who had become the main target of public criticism for the planning of the Iraq war that many observers later considered inadequate. He also expressed hope that he and the Democrats could work together on issues where they shared goals, such as raising the minimum wage, rewriting the nation's immigration laws, and reauthorizing the No Child Left Behind education law that was one of the few genuinely bipartisan accomplishments of his first term.

But there was only so much he could expect to accomplish with the congressional leadership that had come to power. The new House Speaker, Nancy Pelosi of California, once accused Bush of "incompetence" in his leadership of the Iraq war. The new Senate majority leader, Harry Reid, was blunt to a fault and once had to apologize for calling Bush "a loser" to a group of Las Vegas high school students. He did not apologize, however, for calling Bush a "liar" in 2002 after the president decided to store nuclear waste at Nevada's Yucca Mountain.

Besides, Bush was not about to agree to the main thing Democrats wanted: a timeline for withdrawing troops from Iraq. Like most Republicans, Bush thought it made no sense to advertise to insurgents how long they would have to hold out before U.S. troops would be gone. Indeed, he went in the opposite direction on Iraq war strategy, listening to critics who said the real problem in Iraq was his failure to commit enough troops to make security gains permanent. One of them was Sen. John McCain of Arizona, his old presidential rival, who was preparing his second run for the White House and would become the Republican nominee to succeed Bush.

On Jan. 10, 2007, Bush announced he planned to send an additional 21,500 troops to Iraq. His decision touched off a firestorm of criticism from Democrats and even some Republicans, and Democrats vowed to use their new congressional muscle to force an end to the war. The political reality, though, was that they had overpromised how much they could actually do on that front because on military matters, even a weakened Bush had the upper hand. As commander in chief, he could send troops to Iraq before Democrats could mobilize to stop the deployment. Once the troops were there, Democrats needed far more votes to force a troop pullout than they could ever hope to win.

Bush's victory was only temporary, though. Even as Democrats continued to fail with other attempts to force him to withdraw troops, the repeated failures gave ammunition to the party's presidential candidates, allowing them to energize their voters as they called for an end to the war. That was particularly true for Obama, then a charismatic freshman senator from Illinois with a skillful campaign team that used the Iraq war and other issues to mobilize volunteers and register thousands of new voters. Bush also alienated Democrats and independent voters with unpopular domestic policy vetoes, including a bill to lift his restrictions on federal funding for embryonic stem cell research and a measure to reauthorize and expand the State Children's Health Insurance Program (he vetoed both bills twice). Both measures had broad bipartisan support.

Other administration scandals continued to erode the public's support for Bush. The revelation that nine U.S. attorneys had been fired in 2006 created a picture of a politicized Department of Justice and raised questions about the leadership of Attorney General Alberto R. Gonzales, who had been part of Bush's inner circle since his days as Texas governor. Gonzales gradually lost the confidence of congressional Democrats, and their questioning of him at committee hearings grew increasingly contentious, particularly as he repeatedly claimed he could not recall key incidents related to the attorneys' firings. They also became suspicious of him after FBI director Robert S. Mueller III appeared to contradict his testimony about a 2004 visit to then–Attorney General John Ashcroft in a hospital bed to get him to authorize a secret intelligence program.

Four Senate Judiciary Committee Democrats called for the appointment of a special counsel to investigate whether Gonzales lied under oath. Many Democrats and even a few Republicans called for Gonzales to resign, and Senate Democrats even scheduled a "no confidence" vote in him (it failed after the Democrats could not round up the sixty votes needed to end debate). On Aug. 27, Gonzales bowed to the pressure and announced his resignation. Bush accepted it reluctantly, telling reporters, "It's sad that we live in a time when a talented and honorable person like Alberto Gonzales is impeded from doing important work because his good name was dragged through the mud for political reasons."

FINAL CRISIS: FINANCIAL

By 2008 Bush was firmly in lame-duck status and overshadowed by the campaign to replace him. In his final State of the Union address that year, he called on Congress to rewrite the nation's immigration laws, make his 2001 and 2003 tax cuts permanent, provide tax breaks for health insurance obtained outside the workplace, overhaul Fannie Mae and Freddie Mac, and reauthorize the No Child Left Behind education law he had steered to passage in his first year in office. But he was so unpopular that he was unable to advance much of anything in Congress; by then, his approval ratings were stuck in the thirty-percent range. The immigration initiative stalled in the Senate and never even came to a vote in the House, and most of the other initiatives did not advance at all. Congressional Democrats, tired of negotiating with Bush over the domestic spending limits he wanted, refused to send most of the annual appropriations bills to the White House until Bush left office, betting—correctly—that they would be able to deal with a Democratic president in 2009 who would be more sympathetic to their priorities.

Instead, Bush began to travel more. In January he visited Israel and the West Bank for the first time as president, meeting with Israeli prime minister Ehud Olmert and Palestinian president Mahmoud Abbas to try to jump-start their stalled peace talks, and met with leaders in Kuwait, Bahrain, the United Arab Emirates, Saudi Arabia, and Egypt to ask for their help in reining in Iran. But his trip produced no breakthroughs, which was hardly a surprise, since most international leaders had little interest in making commitments to a president who was about to leave office.

Then, in September 2008, Bush was tested with one more crisis: a global financial meltdown that threatened to become the biggest economic calamity since the Great Depression. The deepening crisis—caused by widespread sales of mortgage-backed securities that became worthless because of a wave of foreclosures, as well as the threat of mass defaults on subprime home loans—forced Treasury secretary Henry M. Paulson Jr. and Federal Reserve chairman Ben S. Bernanke to ask Congress for a $700 billion bailout of Wall Street. At the height of election season, Congress was in no mood to spend so much of the taxpayers' money to rescue irresponsible financial institutions. After the House rejected the package, however, stocks plummeted and raised fears of a total economic collapse. Grudgingly, the Senate approved a slightly modified bailout, and the House followed. But the bailout only became more unpopular with the public over time, and regardless of how closely the economic collapse could be tied to any one political leader, it further soured Americans' mood over the events of the Bush years.

As the presidential campaign progressed, Bush's record became a prime recruiting tool for the Democratic candidates and a liability for the GOP candidates. The Republican Party already had been split over two of the biggest accomplishments of his first term, the No Child Left Behind law and the creation of the Medicare prescription drug program, as many small-government conservatives saw them as an unwelcome expansion of the role of the federal government. Now, their nominee, McCain, campaigned on a promise to restore the party's traditional conservative principles, implying that the party had not adhered to them over the last eight years.

Unfortunately for McCain—who had actually fought Bush more frequently than most Republicans—Obama campaigned against him by painting him as a Bush clone, arguing that he sided with Bush on virtually all of the issues that mattered, from economic policy to foreign affairs. He constantly reminded voters that McCain had voted in support of Bush's policies 90 percent of the time during Bush's eight years. (That was true, according to Congressional Quarterly's annual vote studies, but it hardly made McCain a Bush clone, since his score was somewhere in the middle of the rankings of all Senate Republicans.) In the final presidential debate, McCain was reduced to telling Obama, "I am not President Bush. If you wanted to run against President Bush, you should have run four years ago."

But Obama's argument was effective enough that McCain, and many of the Republicans running for re-election to Congress that year, never stood a chance. Obama won the presidency with 53 percent of the popular vote—the first Democrat to win an outright majority since Jimmy Carter in 1976—and 365 electoral votes to McCain's 173. Congressional Democrats strengthened the majorities they had won just two years earlier, with House Democrats winning control of 257 seats—a net gain of twenty-one—and Senate Democrats gaining effective control of fifty-nine seats, a net gain of eight and just one short of the number they needed to keep Republicans from filibustering their agenda. (They later gained the sixtieth seat when Republican senator Arlen Specter of Pennsylvania switched parties in early 2009.) With Democrats on the winning end of two "wave" elections in a row, it was hard to read the results as anything other than a solid rejection of Bush's policies, especially with independent voters largely siding with the Democrats.

Throughout much of his presidency, Bush never showed much of a reflective side. That became evident at a press conference during his first term, when a reporter asked what he considered the biggest mistake of his presidency and he could not think of any. At his final press conference, however, Bush admitted to being "discouraged" and "disappointed" when no weapons of mass destruction were found in Iraq. As president, he acknowledged, "you don't get to do do-overs."

For the most part, though, Bush left office projecting confidence in the decisions he had made, even the ones that had drawn the harshest criticism during his last years in the White House. "People will look back and put this administration in perspective to those that have come before me and those that will come after me," Bush told CNN's Larry King just before leaving Washington. "And they will analyze whether or not decisions I made the country safer and, you know, more secure. And I am comfortable that I have given every decision a good hard look and that I have given it my all and that I put my country first."

Bush Foreign Policy

The irony of Bush's second term was that public dissatisfaction with his foreign policy peaked just as his administration was turning to a more pragmatic view of the world, as foreign policy realists gained ascendancy over the neoconservatives who had dominated in his first term.

Administration critics said the damage they believed had been inflicted in his early years could not be undone. No foreign policy shifts would undo the fact that he had launched a costly war of choice against Iraq, based on the belief that Iraqi leader Saddam Hussein possessed and might use weapons of mass destruction against the United States or its allies, especially Israel. That belief turned out to be unfounded when no weapons of mass destruction were located. Moreover, nothing in Bush's later foreign policy record would change the fact that his administration allowed, and even encouraged, a perception that Saddam was involved in the Sept. 11, 2001, terrorist attacks in New York City and just outside Washington, D.C., when he had no role at all. Cheney, for example, claimed that Sept.11 hijacker Mohammed Atta had met with an Iraqi intelligence official in Prague before the attacks, which was not true, and continued to claim for years that there was "a link" between Saddam and al Qaeda. Congressional investigators disagreed. The Senate Intelligence Committee concluded that, in fact, Saddam and Osama bin Laden hated each other.

By the end of Bush's years in the White House, there remained little doubt that Bush's conduct of the war was instrumental in returning control of Congress to the Democrats. His resistance to withdrawing troops or even changing the military strategy in Iraq helped the Democrats win back both houses in 2006, the first time since 1994. His decision to send more U.S. troops to Iraq in 2007, an action known as the "surge," in seeming defiance of the message of the 2006 election, further mobilized Democrats to channel their energy into helping Obama win the White House in 2008, even though the surge was a significant factor in the reduction of violence that made Iraq a less prominent issue by election day.

Still, Bush's foreign policy by the end of his second term was more nuanced and realistic than the signature events of his first term. His administration reached out to the Sunnis in Iraq, dropping its initial tendency to see all Sunnis as the enemy, which helped bring sectarian violence under control. The administration backed away from its resistance to talks with North Korea, took that nation off the list of state sponsors of terrorism in October 2008, and even began a low-level dialogue with Iran. John R. Bolton, who briefly served as Bush's bellicose ambassador to the United Nations, slammed the Bush administration's North Korea policy as a "surrender," adding that "the only upside is that the Bush administration may not have time to concede anything more to Pyongyang before it limps into history." Bolton's sharp comments were important because he often was a public face of the administration's dogmatic attitude on foreign policy during the earlier days of staunchly conservative and hard-line attitudes in the government. This criticism by one-time administration allies drew attention from analysts at the end of Bush's presidency, such as foreign policy writer Fareed Zakaria, who cited the hardliners' backlash as evidence that "the foreign policies in place now are more sensible, moderate and mainstream" and that "in many cases the next president should follow rather than reverse them."

Even Bush's most idealistic view of foreign policy—that the key to preventing the root causes of terrorism was to promote democracy and freedom in the Middle East—had survived the most turbulent years of the Iraq war and was expected to be at least a general guiding principle for future presidents. The initial hopes raised by the Iraqi parliamentary elections of 2005 faded as sectarian violence continued, and most of the public did not view the new Iraq as a success story. But even Obama, while criticizing much of Bush's foreign policy legacy as a presidential candidate, echoed Bush's theme that the United States should provide moral leadership and take an interest in the freedom of other nations. "America's forty-third president may go down as one of the most criticized in American history," foreign policy scholar Amy Zegart of UCLA's School of Public Affairs wrote in the journal *National Interest* near the end of Bush's presidency, "but his grand strategy will undoubtedly set the course of American foreign policy for the next administration, and possibly the next generation."

EVOLVING STRATEGY IN IRAQ

Bush's second inaugural address in 2005 was full of hope for the power of spreading democracy and freedom throughout the world, with the clear implication that Iraq would be the testing grounds for attacking terrorism at its supposed source. In Bush's view, people who lived under tyrannical governments were vulnerable to conditions that encouraged hateful ideologies and violence. "The survival of liberty in our land increasingly depends on the success of liberty in other lands," he told the nation. "It is the policy of the United States to seek and support the growth of democratic movements and institutions in every nation and culture with the ultimate goal of ending tyranny in our world."

There were some hopes for that approach when Iraqis turned out for parliamentary elections in December 2005, the first since the downfall of Saddam's government. The images of smiling Iraqi voters with purple-stained fingers, signaling that they had cast their ballots, were shown around the world and became symbolic of the possibilities of a democratic Iraq. Even Sunni Arabs, who had resented the Shiite-dominated transitional government, turned out in large numbers to vote, although the election resulted in another Shiite-dominated government. Still, many foreign policy experts were skeptical, noting that the grievances between the Shiites and the Sunnis were centuries old, undermining the chances for a stable democratic government, and that there were simply too many entrenched powers in the Middle East to expect democracy to spread.

Nevertheless, throughout the year Americans had increasingly lost patience with the U.S. military presence in Iraq, as insurgent attacks continued to kill U.S. troops and bloody sectarian violence made the prospect of a stable Iraq look distant. In November 2005, the Republican-controlled Senate added a provision to a defense bill requiring quarterly reports on progress in the Iraq war and calling for 2006 to be a year of "significant transition" to Iraqi sovereignty. Two days after that vote, Rep. John P. Murtha of Pennsylvania, the ranking Democrat on the Defense Appropriations Subcommittee and a decorated ex-marine who had voted for the Iraq war, called for a withdrawal of troops from Iraq over the next six months. Six out of ten Americans disapproved of Bush's handling of the war in several polls taken at the time, and in an NBC News-*Wall Street Journal* poll in November 2005, 57 percent said the United States should withdraw troops now that the Iraqis had approved a constitution.

The political landscape of the Iraq war was changing, but Bush and congressional Republicans continued to resist Democrats' calls for a timetable to withdraw troops. House Speaker J. Dennis Hastert of Illinois said he was "saddened" that Murtha and other Democrats "want us to wave the white flag of surrender to the terrorists of the world." In Iraq, though, the sectarian violence escalated throughout 2006. And members of Congress criticized Prime Minister Nouri al-Maliki for not doing more to get the situation under control, as well as for running a corrupt government.

After the Republicans lost control of Congress in November 2006, Bush's ouster of Rumsfeld was taken as a signal that he was finally ready to consider changes in the military strategy in Iraq. The new defense secretary, Robert Gates, was a pragmatist who admitted during his Senate confirmation hearing that the United States was not winning the war. Some Republicans said the changes were long overdue. "It's not encouraging to those of us who have heard time after time that things are, quote, progressing well, that we're making progress, et cetera, because we're hearing from many other sources that that's not the case," McCain, who was preparing to run for president, told General John P. Abizaid, the commander of U.S. forces in the Middle East, at a hearing a week after the election. "And I'm, of course, disappointed that basically you're advocating the status quo here today, which I think the American people in the last election said that is not an acceptable condition."

But in January 2007, Bush announced a strategy seemingly at odds with the message of the election. He planned to send 21,500 additional troops to Iraq, in a "surge" designed to help U.S. commanders boost security and secure the gains they had made. "Our military commanders and I have carefully weighed the options. We discussed every possible approach. In the end, I chose this course of action because it provides the best chance for success," Bush told the nation in his State of the Union address later that month. "Whatever you voted for, you did not vote for failure. Our country is pursuing a new strategy in Iraq, and I ask you to give it a chance to work."

Most Democrats rejected the "surge" approach, saying it was clear that only a political accommodation between the rival Iraqi factions—not a military strategy—could bring peace to the country. They pressed ahead with efforts to force Bush to end the war, as they had promised during the campaign. But in foreign policy, the president has the upper hand over Congress, and the Iraq war was no exception.

In April the Democrats sent Bush a supplemental funding bill for the Iraq and Afghanistan wars that required him to withdraw most U.S. troops from Iraq by the end of March 2008. Bush vetoed the bill, and the House could not assemble the two-thirds majority the Democrats needed to override him. Only two Republicans in the House and two in the Senate sided with the Democrats. The only alternative would have been not to fund the war, effectively ending it by cutting off funds for military operations, but most Democrats were not about to do that because voters would punish them for abandoning troops in the middle of a war. Later in May, Congress sent Bush a war funding bill that abandoned all requirements to withdraw U.S. troops. Instead, it simply set eighteen benchmarks for progress that the Iraqi government would have to meet in order to qualify for more reconstruction aid. Bush signed the bill into law, but the episode demoralized much of the Democrats' most outspoken core constituency, as supporters thought the party had sold out its commitment to end the war.

Soon, though, the violence in Iraq began to subside, which allowed Republicans to conclude that, in fact, the surge had worked. Some independent foreign policy experts agreed; Peter Beinart, a senior fellow at the Council on Foreign Relations, concluded that Bush "endured an avalanche of scorn, and now he has been vindicated. He was not only right; he was courageous." In reality, the surge most likely was a major factor in the reduction of violence, but only in combination with another factor that started before the surge. The Anbar Awakening, named for a region in Iraq in which Sunni tribal leaders turned against al Qaeda in their area, began in September 2006, well before Bush announced the surge plan.

Still, the two developments probably reinforced each other. Gen. David H. Petraeus, the top U.S. military commander in Iraq, told a House committee that the Anbar Awakening "started before the surge, but then was very much enabled by the surge, because that enabled us to clear areas over time." Moreover, the U.S. ambassador to Iraq,

Zalmay Khalilzad, pushed hard to reach a reconciliation between the United States and Sunni insurgents, arguing that Iraq would never become stable until the minority Sunnis were brought into the political process.

As he prepared to leave the presidency, Bush said the image of Iraqis with ink-stained fingers, voting for the first time, would always stay with him. As for the unpopularity of the surge, "I guess I could have taken the popular way out and retreated," Bush said in December 2008, "but I felt strongly that defeat in Iraq would be terrible for the security of the country, it would be terrible for the morale of the military, and would be really hard for me, the Commander-in-Chief, to face a mother who lost a son in combat." Bush's presidency will always be defined significantly by the Iraq war, and that the conflict was justified by reasons that did not hold up. But the decisions he and his administration made in his final years might prove critical to the future stability of Iraq —and they showed an approach that did evolve over time.

The evolving approach was seen late in Bush's term as violence declined and economic activity began to return in Iraq. These trends were pronounced enough that by the summer of 2008 Bush, who had battled every Democratic attempt to set a timetable for withdrawal, accepted in principle an Iraqi proposal that most combat forces would be pulled out of cities and villages by the summer of 2009 and out of the country by the end of 2011. That agreement on U.S. withdrawal was formalized in a security agreement signed by the U.S. ambassador and the Iraqi foreign minister in November 2008, several weeks after the American electorate had chosen war opponent Barack Obama as their next president. Bush signed the agreement again in December during a visit to Baghdad.

FROM HARD-LINE TO PRACTICAL VOICES

Bush's second term was not entirely free of the hard-line foreign policy influences of his first term, but personnel changes showed the growing strength of more practical voices than those who dominated earlier in his presidency. Condoleezza Rice, who had been outmaneuvered by Cheney and Rumsfeld during her days as national security adviser, gained leverage when she became secretary of state in 2005, and particularly after Rumsfeld was ousted to make room for Gates. Foreign policy realists such as R. Nicholas Burns, the undersecretary of state for political affairs who took charge of administration policy on Iran, became moderating influences as well.

Bush's choices for ambassador to the United Nations also illustrated how his thinking changed over the course of his second term, although in this case he did not have much of a choice. In 2005 his nomination of Bolton was roundly criticized by Democrats, who said his abrasive personality and preference for unilateral American action was inimical to productive diplomacy. Bush, however, said his blunt style was the best way to confront the United Nations about longstanding weaknesses that needed to be overhauled. Senate Democrats blocked his nomination twice, but in August 2005 Bush prevailed by installing Bolton through a "recess appointment," a way to get around the Senate by waiting until it's no longer in session. The move cost Bush and Bolton much goodwill, however, and made it virtually certain that Bolton would not win Senate confirmation to make his temporary appointment permanent, especially after the Democrats won control of the Senate. Bolton resigned in December 2006, and Bush replaced him with Khalilzad, the pragmatist who had spearheaded the United States' outreach to the Sunnis as the U.S. ambassador to Iraq.

In his first term, Bush had described Iraq, Iran, and North Korea as an "axis of evil." But the disastrous consequences of the war with the first country seemed to have taught the administration to take a more cautious approach with the other two. Hardliners such as Cheney still favored a tough approach to resolving conflicts, particularly in Iran, which was believed to be enriching uranium that could be used for nuclear weapons. In February 2007, Cheney declared that "all options are still on the table," a remark Democrats took as an indication that the Bush administration might be considering military action even though the nation's armed forces were already overextended in Iraq and Afghanistan. Even at the State Department, officials declared that they would only talk to Iran if that nation stopped trying to build nuclear weapons. (Later that year, an intelligence report concluded that Iran had actually halted its nuclear weapons program years ago.)

Ultimately, though, it became clear that Cheney and the hardliners were no longer setting the policies. "For the umpteenth time," Defense Secretary Robert M. Gates told reporters in February 2007, "we are not looking for an excuse to go to war with Iran." Indeed, State Department pragmatists like Burns had gained the upper hand. "It's my judgment that diplomacy is the best course of action in blocking and containing the Iranian regime," Burns told the House Foreign Affairs Committee in March 2007. "I do not believe a military confrontation with Iran is either inevitable or desirable." Later, at the height of the 2008 presidential election, Burns wrote a guest column for *Newsweek* magazine criticizing McCain for suggesting the next president should not hold talks with Iran, citing the famous quote from the late Israeli prime minister Yitzhak Rabin: "You don't make peace with friends, you make peace with very unsavory enemies."

By July 2008, the Bush administration even allowed Burns's successor—William J. Burns, no relation—to participate in international talks with Iran's nuclear negotiator, a sign that the administration had abandoned its condition that Iran had to suspend its uranium enrichment activities first. The move enraged neoconservatives like Bolton, who said that "this is further evidence of the administration's complete intellectual collapse." But that development also highlighted the fact that, until then, even the pragmatists' hands had been tied compared to what they wanted to do. "To illustrate how far we have isolated ourselves," Nicholas Burns wrote in *Newsweek*, "think about this: I served as the Bush administration's point person on Iran for three years but was never permitted to meet an Iranian."

The Bush administration's dealings with North Korea saw an even sharper turnaround. When he first took office, Bush rejected President Bill Clinton's approach of dealing directly with the regime. But in 2003 the administration eventually backed down and agreed to participate in six-party, multilateral talks, which included Russia, China, South Korea, and Japan, that were supposed to lead to the end of North Korea's nuclear program. In October 2008, the Bush administration removed North Korea from the list of state sponsors of terrorism—a status that limited the availability of foreign aid and defense exports and sales—after North Korea agreed to several measures to allow monitoring of its nuclear program. The multilateral talks had worked, Rice declared, because North Korea had shut down its nuclear reactor in 2005 and because "they can't just make this a bilateral problem with the United States" when the other nations are involved in the talks too.

Conservative critics said the administration had acted prematurely, arguing that there were important gaps in the documents North Korea had turned over concerning its nuclear program earlier that year. Rice admitted as much, arguing that the administration was still trying to negotiate "the last 20 percent" of the verification agreement. "Of course we didn't trust them," Rice said in December 2008. "What we are negotiating is a verification protocol because nobody does trust them." But, in fact, North Korea quit the six-party talks in 2009 and began testing nuclear weapons again—proving that the unpredictable regime can be a headache whether the United States talks to them or not.

AMERICA AND THE WORLD: 2008

As George W. Bush was preparing to leave office in 2008, America's role and reputation in the world was seen, fairly or not, as diminished, especially compared to the outpouring of sympathy after the Sept. 11, 2001, terrorist attacks and the opportunity for global leadership presented at the time.

The Bush administration's unilateral view of the world, which characterized its earlier years and was replaced with a more nuanced approach only late in Bush's time in office, was a muscular foreign policy often with a patina of moral righteousness but always with an American view of the world at the center. Many nations saw Bush's internationalism as a fall-in-line diplomacy, and it did not sit well with much of the world. The administration's unpopularity was made worse by the global economic crisis that began in 2007 and was seen as originating in exotic financial activity in the United States, even though the roots of the near-depression collapse were in private sector rather than the halls of government.

The Middle East was at the center of the administration's outlook, with Iraq and the war begun there in 2003 the focal point. Although the U.S. military was headed out as Bush departed, Iraq remained unsettled as conditions in Afghanistan, the location of the original American response to the Sept. 11 attacks, worsened. Iran too remained an unsettled problem even though the international response to its nuclear ambitions was far more unified than had been the situation with Iraq. North Korea remained an unpredictable enigma, but possessing nuclear capacity already.

The intense attention given to these nations obscured other dimensions of international affairs, including the endless tensions between Israel and most of its neighbors but especially the Palestinians seeking a state of their own, a conflict that appeared no nearer resolution at the end than at the beginning of Bush's presidency.

Relations with much of Europe also had soured in the face of America's sometimes shrill admonitions that American foreign policy was the wave of the future.

In South Asia, tensions between Pakistan and India rose and fell with the United States trying to comfortably straddle its interests in the growing economic dynamics of India, a fully democratic nation, and the strategic importance of the unstable Pakistan.

India, however, provided Bush one of his more successful foreign policy undertakings when his administration negotiated a nuclear cooperation agreement with that nation.

The White House saw this agreement as a means of forging an important partnership with a country that was both the world's largest democracy and a key counterweight to China. It was seen as a way of bringing the South Asian nuclear power into the global nonproliferation framework and providing it with energy security.

However, to proceed with the pact the president needed legislation that would waive provisions of the 1954 Atomic Energy Act (PL 83-703) in order to permit exports of nuclear materials, equipment, and technology. Along with the waivers, the White House proposal would have allowed the agreement to take affect after ninety days unless both chambers of Congress opposed it. Congress granted the approval, but only after winning a more significant role for itself. The waiver bill members passed required that Bush submit the agreement to Congress for an up-or-down vote before it could take effect. It also required the administration to report to Congress on the final negotiations and on India's nuclear programs. Passage of the bill in 2006 was a major foreign policy victory for the White House. It was for the 109th Congress, too.

The 110th Congress approved the final agreement, but again with provisions for greater safeguards and congressional oversight.

Bush Domestic Policy

As his second term began, Bush seemed to have a sweeping framework for the domestic policy changes he wanted to make and a memorable name for it: the ownership society. Under his model, more individuals would have a chance to own homes, businesses, health care plans, and retirement benefits. They would have more freedom to do so, and as they became owners, they would have a greater incentive to make wise choices and take care of everything they owned. On the campaign trail in 2004, Bush regularly explained his vision by noting that "no one ever washes a rental car."

Bush talked about the ownership society as a way of setting up an ambitious second-term agenda he shared with the Republicans in Congress. He wanted a rewrite of the tax code, laws to curtail lawsuits, tax credits and expanded tax-free savings accounts to help Americans pay for their own health coverage, and a more business-friendly environment with less regulation and looser overtime laws. Nothing, however, illustrated his vision for the ownership society better than his plans for overhauling Social Security. He wanted to allow younger workers to redirect some of their payroll taxes into private savings accounts, a change he said would strengthen Social Security's long-term solvency and ease the strain as baby boomers started to retire and receive benefits.

"We want more people owning their own home. We want people owning their own business. We want people owning their own farm," Bush said in a February 2005 speech in Great Falls, Mont. "We want people owning and managing their own health care accounts. And I think it makes sense to have people owning and managing their own retirement account." In doing so, Bush said, Social Security will become more solvent because younger workers would more easily earn their promised benefits: "We're talking about a better rate of return on your money, something you own that cannot be taken away, and something you can pass on from one generation to the next."

But the proposal also illustrated how fundamentally Bush wanted to rewrite the social contract of the New Deal and the Great Society, both of which were based on the idea of using government to strengthen the social safety net. In Bush's view, the new role of government was to "help people improve their lives, not try to run their lives." By the end of his second term, though, not only had Congress rejected the centerpiece Social Security proposal without even bringing it to a vote, but Bush had to ask Congress for a massive, taxpayer-funded bailout—the ultimate government intervention—to keep the imploding financial markets from bringing the entire economy down with them.

At first, Bush scored a series of domestic policy accomplishments as a strengthened Republican majority in Congress passed a backlog of legislation that had stalled in his first term. He signed into law two major initiatives restricting lawsuits: a bill that limited class action lawsuits by moving the biggest ones to the federal courts, and a separate measure that made it more difficult for people to file for bankruptcy as a way to avoid paying their debts. Because both bills drew significant opposition from Democrats, broad GOP majorities in both chambers were required to steer them to passage.

In July 2005, Congress finally sent to Bush's desk the energy legislation he had been proposing since 2001. It included $14.6 billion in tax breaks to encourage more energy production, reduced regulation, and included incentives to encourage, but not require, energy conservation. It did not, however, include the centerpiece of Bush's 2001 energy proposal: opening Alaska's Arctic National Wildlife Refuge (ANWR) to oil and gas exploration. That idea had become too controversial to include in the energy package, and its supporters failed when they tried to attach it to other legislative vehicles.

Bush also won a victory on trade policy in July 2005, when Congress approved the Central American Free Trade Agreement (CAFTA)—free trade pacts with Costa Rica, El Salvador, Guatemala, Honduras and Nicaragua—and a closely linked agreement with the Dominican Republic. The struggle Republican leaders faced in finding enough votes to approve it, however, underscored the growing unpopularity of free-trade agreements as GOP lawmakers began to worry about the impact on jobs in their districts. Since nearly all Democrats were opposed to the agreements, administration officials had to help the leadership win votes from Republicans lawmakers from textile- and sugar-producing states by promising to take steps to control imports of sugar and protect U.S. textile and manufacturing jobs.

SOCIAL SECURITY, SCHIAVO, IMMIGRATION

None of those initiatives, however, spoke to the philosophy of the ownership society in the way that Bush's Social Security proposal did. But that proposal sank quickly as Democrats united against it and polls showed the public disapproved of the president's idea of carving out individual savings accounts from the program. Bush and Cheney campaigned for the overhaul in a "60 Stops in 60 Days" tour of the country, but they made no noticeable headway. It soon was clear that Bush's re-election did not mean that the public had endorsed everything on his agenda.

There were brief flashes of interest among Republicans in both the House and Senate, but neither chamber actually got a proposal moving. In the House, Ways and Means Committee chairman Bill Thomas of California endorsed a private savings accounts proposal and suggested it might become part of a broader retirement package he planned to draft, but his time quickly became consumed by other issues. His Senate counterpart, Finance Committee chairman Charles E. Grassley of Iowa, showed little interest in a similar bill sponsored by a group of conservative Senate Republicans. Democrats, meanwhile, refused to negotiate until Bush dropped his insistence on including private savings accounts in any Social Security overhaul. "If the first thing you do, in trying to find some common ground, is unravel the safety net, it makes it pretty difficult," said Democratic senator Ron Wyden of Oregon, a member of the Finance Committee.

That spring, Bush and Congress also got unwisely entangled in a drama that convinced many Americans that government was too involved in personal decisions of life and death. That issue was over a person named Terri Schiavo, a woman who had been in a persistent vegetative state after her heart stopped for several minutes in 1990. Lawmakers passed a bill to allow her parents to ask federal courts to stop the scheduled removal of her feeding tube. The move allowed the parents to bypass a state judge who had ordered the removal of the tube—and to continue their legal fight with Schiavo's husband, who insisted she had told him she never would have wanted to be kept alive artificially.

Bush supported the congressional action, flying back from Texas to Washington to sign the bill into law. But polls showed that more than seven out of ten Americans thought Congress should have stayed out of the matter. The episode also demonstrated how strong a force social conservatives had become in the Republican Party: they were the main voting bloc that thought the congressional action was a good idea. House majority leader Tom DeLay of Texas, who supported many of the social conservatives' goals, even attacked Schiavo's husband, Michael Schiavo, for saying his wife would have wanted the feeding tube taken out. "What kind of man is he?" DeLay demanded. Ultimately, the federal courts declined to reverse the state judge's decision, the tube was removed, and Terri Schiavo died. An autopsy later showed her brain had shriveled to half its original size and most of it had suffered irreversible damage.

In 2006 Bush encountered strong resistance from his own party to an issue he thought was vital to the Republican Party's fortunes: overhauling the nation's immigration system. Bush wanted to create a guest worker program to allow some leniency for illegal immigrants who were already in the country. Many Republicans, under pressure from the party's base, considered his plan an ill-advised change that would reward people who had broken the law. Bush had a different perspective. As the former governor of Texas, he had a border-state perspective that made him sensitive to the economic importance of immigrants—and to the need for tolerance.

The immigration issue was one of the most politically complicated issues Bush could have taken on because it was driven by forces that divided political coalitions in unpredictable ways. Business groups, which sided with Republicans on many issues, were reluctant to embrace hard-line border security strategies because they needed the labor that immigrants provided. For the same reason, labor unions, normally allies of the Democrats, were wary of being undercut by the cheap labor that guest workers could provide—especially if employers did not check their citizenship status. Some Democrats in conservative districts were just as adamant as most Republicans that no bill should reward lawbreakers. In addition, there were some Republicans—notably McCain—who insisted, just as most Democrats did, that it was impractical to expect the United States to return 12 million illegal immigrants to their countries.

The Senate passed a bill that was based on the guest worker proposal, but also included elements of border security and worksite enforcement, and would have created a "path to citizenship" for immigrants who agreed to take a series of steps to earn legal status. The bill featured a unique collaboration between McCain, who already was taking early steps to prepare for his run for the White House, and Democratic senator Edward M. Kennedy of Massachusetts. McCain told his audiences that it was unrealistic to think the United States would ever be able to deport all of the immigrants who were living in the country illegally, and insisted that "we can't just have the status quo."

Still, House Republicans, facing a backlash from their constituents, rejected the bill and called it "amnesty" for lawbreakers. They repeatedly called it "the Kennedy bill," implicitly dismissing the idea that either Bush or McCain had anything to do with it. By the end of the year, the only step both chambers could agree to take was the passage of a bill to build 700 miles of fence along the border with Mexico, along with a "virtual fence" of cameras, sensors, unmanned aerial vehicles and other surveillance technology to cover the rest of the border.

DOMESTIC GOALS AFTER 2006 ELECTION

After the Democratic victory in the 2006 congressional elections, Bush was no longer able to set the domestic agenda in the same way that he could with Republican majorities. But he laid out a series of domestic policy goals that, while less ambitious than his talk of an ownership society, suggested concrete ways in which he hoped to work with Democrats to advance his own priorities.

In his 2007 State of the Union address, he called on Congress to eliminate the deficit over the next five years; reauthorize the No Child Left Behind education law that was the signature domestic achievement of his first year in office; expand health coverage by creating a standard tax deduction for health insurance and providing federal aid to states that make basic health insurance available to all residents; limit medical malpractice lawsuits; reduce gasoline usage by 20 percent over ten years; and try once more to pass the immigration overhaul package that had failed the year before. "We are not the first to come here with government divided and uncertainty in the air. Like many before us, we can work through our differences and we can achieve big things for the American people," said Bush.

The Democrats, however, had campaigned on their own list of priorities: the "Six for '06" agenda, which called for increasing the minimum wage, implementing most of the recommendations of a bipartisan commission created to examine the Sept. 11 terror attacks, repealing the Bush administration's restrictions on federal funding for embryonic stem-cell research, using the purchasing power of the federal government to negotiate lower Medicare drug prices, cutting student loan rates, and encouraging energy-efficient technologies and alternative sources of energy. The message of their "retirement security" platform could not have been clearer: "Stop any plan to privatize Social Security, in whole or in part."

As a result, Bush had to find ways to adjust to the Democratic agenda and find common ground where possible. He signed a minimum wage increase into law in May 2007, raising it from $5.15 to $7.25 over two years—the first time it had been increased in more than a decade. That development was almost lost in the debate over the broader legislative vehicle that carried it: the supplemental spending bill for the Iraq and Afghanistan wars, in which the Democrats bowed to Bush's demands to fund the military operations without including a deadline for him to withdraw U.S. troops from Iraq.

That summer, Bush signed into law a bill implementing many, though not all, of the Sept. 11 commission recommendations. The legislation changed the funding formula for anti-terrorism aid to state and local governments to send more money to the highest-risk areas, and it expanded the screening of cargo for nuclear devices or other dangerous materials. But Bush was still able to win concessions from Democrats through the use of veto threats; they took out a provision from the Senate version, for example, that would have given collective bargaining rights to airport screeners, a provision that would have made the legislation unacceptable to Bush.

He had less power, however, to stop the Democratic initiative to make college more affordable by cutting subsidies to private lenders that offer federally backed student loans. The centerpiece of the legislation, championed by Kennedy and House Education and Labor Committee chairman George Miller of California, was a provision cutting the interest rate on subsidized student loans in half over four years. Their goal was to give the money to students in other ways, such as through Pell grants and other forms of aid. Since Bush, in his budget proposal that year, had proposed increasing Pell grants by cutting funds to lenders, it was hard for him to put up any resistance—especially after the House and Senate passed their versions of the bills with veto-proof majorities. After some early veto threats, Bush signed the bill into law in September 2007.

LOSING CONTROL OF DOMESTIC POLICY

By the end of the year, Bush had signed a new energy bill requiring an increase in fuel efficiency standards and boosting production of biofuels. He was able to force changes, though, such as making the Democrats give up a provision that would have rolled back subsidies for oil and gas companies and a separate section that would have required utilities to produce more of their electricity from alternative sources. Bush and his Republican allies in the Senate had opposed both provisions.

Even with a Democratic majority to work with, however, Bush was unable to convince Congress to pass an immigration bill—which had been one of his best hopes for working across the aisle. For all of the grassroots Republican opposition, Democrats had their own members who were wary of rewarding people who had broken the law. So House leaders decided to let the Senate go first, hoping that a clear Senate vote for a bill would create enough momentum to pass it in the House later. Instead, the Senate effort collapsed as Republican opponents offered a slew of amendments and Democrats were unable to end the debate. Many Republicans were still convinced that the new bill would have provided "amnesty" to illegal immigrants, just like the 2006 bill. But some Democrats also criticized a proposed merit-based point system that would have been used to award green cards, and they said the guest worker provision in the new bill would not have offered a path to citizenship.

Still, Bush was able to use the leverage of his veto power to exert some control over the agenda. He insisted on capping the year's annual appropriations at $933 billion, and Democrats were forced to go along with it after he vetoed the spending bill for labor, health, and education programs because it cost too much. Bush also was able to block two top Democratic health care priorities—though both were widely popular and his opposition handed the Democrats two potent campaign issues for the 2008 election. Bush vetoed a bill that would have expanded funding for embryonic stem cell research, lifting restrictions he had put in place in an August 2001 executive order; he had also rejected a similar measure in 2006 that had passed Congress while Republicans were still in control. He also vetoed two versions of a bill to expand the State Children's Health Insurance Program, a Democratic priority intended to make the coverage available to some middle-class families as well as low-income Americans. Such a change, Bush said, would have encouraged many Americans to leave private insurance and forced taxpayers to pick up the tab.

By 2008 Bush had lost much of his remaining influence over domestic policy. With the presidential campaign in full swing—and Democratic candidates hammering Bush's record on the trail every day—he became less relevant to the day-to-day business of Congress. Lawmakers were even able to enact some priorities over Bush's opposition. In June they overrode his veto of a farm bill providing expenditures of $289 billion over five years; Bush said the bill was too expensive and did too little to rein in crop subsidies. In July they overrode his veto of a bill preventing a cut in payments to physicians who treat Medicare patients.

In perhaps the ultimate sign of Democratic weariness with Bush, Congress did not even bother to send him most of the annual spending bills, preferring to wrap them into a stopgap omnibus spending measure in the hopes that they could negotiate the real appropriations bills with a Democratic president the next year. The decision was a direct consequence of Bush's victory in 2007 in blocking spending bills that were more expensive than he wanted.

Still, with the economy starting to falter, his administration did negotiate a $151.7 billion stimulus package early in the year with House leaders. In a rare example of true bipartisanship, Treasury secretary Henry M. Paulson Jr. worked out the package in January with House Speaker Nancy Pelosi of California and Minority Leader John A. Boehner of Ohio. It included rebate checks of up to $600 for individuals and $1,200 for married couples, encouraged businesses to buy new equipment by allowing them to write off the purchases, and tried to stabilize the housing market by allowing Fannie Mae and Freddie Mac to buy more expensive mortgages. The Senate tried to add several provisions that could have jeopardized the bipartisan support, but lawmakers threw most of them out before clearing the bill for Bush's signature in February.

Nevertheless, the economy continued to deteriorate through a wave of home foreclosures as a collapse of the market for subprime loans caused a broader credit crisis. Congress tried to address the problem in July with a bill that set up a $300 billion trust fund to allow the Federal Housing Administration to help homeowners refinance from unaffordable loans into new mortgages backed by the government. It also gave Paulson the authority to bail out the struggling Fannie Mae and Freddie Mac, the price Democrats had to pay to get the administration to drop its opposition to the mortgage relief measures.

FINANCIAL CRISIS

The ultimate sign of how much the political environment had changed, however, came with the bailout of the financial markets in fall 2008. Faced with the extraordinary global economic collapse, Bush put aside all pretense of an ownership society and let his Treasury secretary beg Congress for the authority to turn the government into a different kind of social safety net—a force for reducing the most severe effects of the worst economic disaster since the Depression.

In September Paulson and Federal Reserve chairman Ben S. Bernanke went to Capitol Hill and asked lawmakers to give the Bush administration unprecedented authority to take troubled assets off the hands of struggling banks and investment firms. All of the hundreds of billions of dollars in mortgage-backed securities held by those financial institutions were now basically worthless, thanks to all of the home foreclosures and the likelihood of others failing in the subprime mortgage market. Moreover, the credit markets were now frozen as banks refused to lend money. The ever-expressive Democratic senator Charles E. Schumer of New York said afterwards, "I gulped when I heard Paulson's description of what could happen if we didn't act."

Until that point, the Treasury Department and the Federal Reserve had acted unpredictably, bailing out the Bear Stearns Cos. investment house but letting its larger rival, Lehman Brothers Holdings Inc., go bankrupt. But as the threat of financial collapses mounted, the Federal Reserve loaned $85 billion to prevent the implosion of the nation's largest insurance company, American International Group Inc. (AIG); other big-name financial institutions were in deep trouble as well. Finally, Paulson told Congress it was time to attack what he saw as the root of the problem: the troubled assets dragging the firms down. "What began as a subprime lending problem has spread to other, less-risky mortgages and contributed to excess home inventories that have pushed down home prices for responsible homeowners" and threatened the stability of financial institutions, Paulson said at a press conference after the meeting with lawmakers. "As a result, Americans' personal savings are threatened, and the ability of consumers and businesses to borrow and finance spending, investment and job creation has been disrupted."

The amount of aid Paulson proposed, however, was staggering: $700 billion. The scale of the proposed bailout created a critical mass of opposition from both ends of the political spectrum, as conservative Republicans questioned the wisdom of involving the federal government so deeply in the financial markets and liberal Democrats balked at helping Wall Street without similar aid to people about to lose their homes.

Bush made a personal appeal to Congress to approve the bailout, declaring that even he, a conservative wary of big government, thought it was the right thing to do. "I know that an economic rescue package will present a tough vote for many members of Congress," he said in a prime time broadcast address. But "the government's top economic experts warn that, without immediate action by Congress, America could slip into a financial panic, and a distressing scenario would unfold. More banks could fail, including some in your community. The stock market would drop even more, which would reduce the value of your retirement account. The value of your home could plummet. Foreclosures would rise dramatically. And if you own a business or a farm, you would find it harder and more expensive to get credit. More businesses would close their doors, and millions of Americans could lose their jobs."

But many lawmakers remained unconvinced, and the bailout talks soon became entangled in a presidential campaign sideshow as the two nominees—both still senators—left the campaign trail. McCain, who had staked much of his candidacy on his ability to broker bipartisan deals on difficult issues, announced he was suspending his campaign and returning to Washington to help with the talks. Obama declined to join him at first, saying he thought the candidates' presence would hurt more than help, but he reluctantly flew back to Washington after Bush invited him to a White House meeting with McCain and congressional leaders. That meeting nearly sank the entire effort, though, as House Republicans—who complained that they had not been consulted in the negotiations—offered an alternative plan to offer insurance to holders of risky mortgage-backed securities. The move infuriated Democratic leaders, and as they left, Paulson chased after them and—half-jokingly—got down on one knee and begged them not to give up on the original plan.

Eventually, the negotiators struck an agreement in which Congress would give the administration the money in installments: $250 billion at first, another $100 billion if Bush certified that the money was needed, and another $350 billion if the president asked for it and Congress agreed. But House members were hearing loud complaints from their constituents. When they were asked to approve the legislation in late September, conservative Republicans and liberal Democrats joined forces to defeat the bill, with 95 House Democrats and 133 Republicans voting against the deal. The stock markets went into a near-panic in response; the Dow Jones industrial average fell 777 points, the largest one-day point drop in history.

Stunned by the market reaction and fearful of even worse consequences, the Senate stepped in to rescue the bill. Senators added a package of sweeteners, mostly extensions of popular tax breaks that were about to expire. Once again, Obama and McCain flew back from the campaign trail, with Obama taking the more vocal role this time as he urged his Senate colleagues to approve the unpopular deal. "It is conceivable, it is possible, that if we did nothing, everything would turn out okay," Obama said in a floor speech to a crowded Senate chamber. "And there is no doubt there may be other plans out there that, had we had two or three or six months to develop, might be even more refined and might serve our purposes better. But we don't have that kind of time, and we can't afford to take that risk that the economy of the United States of America—and, as a consequence, the worldwide economy—could be plunged into a very deep hole. So to Democrats and Republicans who have opposed this plan, I say: Step up to the plate. Let's do what is right for the country at this time, because the time to act is now."

The Senate put its concerns aside and passed the modified bailout bill on Oct. 1, and the House did the same two days later. Bush gave one final defense of such an extraordinary action by an administration that was supposed to be about small government: "As a strong supporter of free enterprise, I believe government intervention should occur only when necessary. In this situation, action is clearly necessary." With that, the about-face from the vision he had at the beginning of his second term was complete.

Bush and Congress

On rare occasions, Bush engaged in active, bipartisan give-and-take with Congress during his presidency. He dealt directly with key Republicans and Democrats during the negotiation of the No Child Left Behind education law in 2001, and he pushed successfully for the creation of the Medicare prescription drug benefit in 2003 that won support from lawmakers of both parties. In his final year in office, he invited congressional leaders and other key lawmakers to the White House to hear their views on the financial bailout package that was needed to head off a global economic meltdown.

For the most part, though, Bush had a CEO's view of Congress: he viewed lawmakers largely as subordinates, to be dealt with when necessary, but mostly to be given tasks that they were expected to perform without complaint. That attitude created tensions with Republicans when they were in the majority, although they mostly shared enough priorities with the president to make the relationship work. But by the time the Democrats took control of Congress during the final two years, Bush paid a price for his approach, as the new majority seemed determined to prove that Congress was a separate branch of government that would follow its own agenda.

During his years working with a Republican majority, Bush took relatively few positions on legislative battles, a strategy that helped to minimize his defeats. He was also helped by cooperation from Republican leaders such as House Speaker J. Dennis Hastert of Illinois, who tried to keep disagreements with Bush behind closed doors and did not put bills on the floor if they were likely to draw veto threats. During most of those years, the House was able to deliver the crucial votes to Bush largely because of the efforts of House majority leader Tom DeLay of Texas, a fiercely ideological man who was not afraid to use power to achieve his ends and strong-armed rank-and-file Republicans to keep them from straying from the party line.

As a result, Congress sided with Bush on 78 percent of the roll calls votes in which he took a position in 2005, and on 81 percent of the votes in 2006, a track record much like his first term, in which he generally had the highest support levels from Congress since Lyndon B. Johnson in the mid-1960s. After the Democrats gained control, Bush's success rate plummeted; he won on only 38 percent of the roll call votes in which he took a clear position in 2007, and on just 48 percent in 2008, according to Congressional Quarterly's annual studies of lawmakers' support for the president's policies.

But legislative victories are only one dimension of a president's relationship with Congress. During Bush's first six years in office, lawmakers did not push back much against his priorities and rarely performed oversight on controversial issues. That was partly because lawmakers had little interest in aggressively challenging his national security and antiterrorism policies in the first few years after the Sept. 11 terrorist attacks, and partly because active oversight rarely happens when one party controls the White House and Congress. In this case, Republicans' interest in staying in power trumped any desire to use congressional muscle to keep the executive branch in check. "Our party controls the levers of government. We're not about to go out and look beneath a bunch of rocks to try to cause heartburn," said Republican representative Ray LaHood of Illinois, who in 2009 became President Obama's Transportation secretary. "Unless they really screw up, we're not going to go after them."

Perhaps the ultimate example of that attitude came early in Bush's second term, when the Senate came to the brink of a showdown over Bush's judicial nominees that could have brought all work in that chamber to a halt. Furious over Democrats' repeated filibusters over judicial nominees they considered too ideologically extreme, Republican leaders considered triggering a confrontation in which they would have asked the Senate parliamentarian for a ruling that, in effect, would have barred the minority party from engaging in any more filibusters of judicial nominees. Republicans called the planned maneuver the "constitutional option," but Democrats referred to it as the "nuclear option," because if the minority party lost its traditional right to block confirmation of presidential nominees they found objectionable, they would have retaliated by using all procedures in their power to shut down practically all Senate business.

In May 2005, Senate majority leader Bill Frist of Tennessee called up the nomination of Priscilla R. Owen for the U.S. Court of Appeals for the Fifth Circuit, the Bush nominee who would have been the subject of the parliamentary ruling if Democrats refused to vote to end the debate. "Vote for the nominee, vote against the nominee, confirm the nominee, reject the nominee," Frist said. "But in the end, vote." Frist and Minority Leader Harry Reid of Nevada had been negotiating for ways to defuse the upcoming confrontation, but neither would budge.

The Republican leaders' plan, however, actually resulted in a memorable show of Senate independence. Once it became clear that the leaders would not solve the problem, a bipartisan group of senators led by McCain, a Republican, and Democratic senator Ben Nelson of Nebraska negotiated an agreement among themselves to block any changes to Senate filibuster rules—as long as Democrats swore off future judicial filibusters in all but extraordinary cases. In doing so, the "Gang of 14," as they called themselves, made it easier for the Senate to confirm a few Bush nominees who might have been blocked otherwise (including Owen). But they also upheld the Senate's tradition as an independent body whose "advice and consent" role included the power to deny confirmation to an objectionable nominee. "The one unanswered question that guided me all the way through is...what would happen to the Senate if the nuclear option were done?" said Republican senator John W. Warner of Virginia, a member of the group. "No one was able to answer that to my satisfaction."

McCain also forced Bush, through the power of broad majorities in Congress, to accept a ban on torture and abuse of prisoners in the war on terrorism. McCain, a former prisoner of war in Vietnam, got ninety senators to vote for his amendment to the annual defense spending bill in 2005, and it was later added to a separate defense authorization measure that became the final vehicle for it. Bush said the language would tie his hands in fighting terrorism, and Cheney urged McCain to exempt the Central Intelligence Agency from its provisions. But McCain refused, and ultimately Bush backed down and accepted the language. Torture, McCain said, ultimately makes the war on terrorism less effective because it leads the prisoner to say anything to interrogators, including giving false information, just to stop the pain.

In 2006 Bush paid a price for his refusal, in his first term, to ask Congress to authorize the use of military tribunals to try suspected terrorists. The Supreme Court ruled that the military tribunals at Guantanamo Bay, Cuba, violated U.S. and international law, and that they could not be used unless Congress signed off on them. Bush then asked lawmakers to give him the legal authority to use them. Once again, he encountered resistance from McCain—not to the general idea of military tribunals, but to a provision within the proposal that would have reinterpreted U.S. obligations under the Geneva Conventions. McCain and two Republican colleagues, Warner of Virginia and Lindsey Graham of South Carolina, said such a change would have put future U.S. prisoners of war in jeopardy because it would have given other countries an excuse to reinterpret the conventions as well.

The three worked out a compromise with the Bush administration that dropped the Geneva language and listed offenses that would be considered "grave breaches" of the Geneva Conventions, such as biological experiments, mutilation, serious bodily injury, and rape or sexual assault. But it gave Bush the authority to issue an executive order addressing techniques that fell short of those breaches. It also created controversy because it did not allow prisoners to challenge their detention in federal courts, a provision that the Supreme Court declared in June 2008 "operates as an unconstitutional suspension of the writ" of *habeas corpus.* Fortunately for Bush, though, the bill was before Congress in September of an election year, when most lawmakers, particularly Republicans, were only willing to go so far in challenging legislation aimed at keeping Americans safe. Congress passed the bill and Bush had his legal framework for the military tribunals.

With a new Democratic majority in place in 2007, Congress had a much greater interest in providing oversight of the Bush administration. The most prominent action was their investigation into the firings of nine U.S. attorneys in 2006. The House and Senate Judiciary committees uncovered evidence that the dismissals were part of a pattern of politically motivated decisions in the Department of Justice. But they were frustrated in their attempts to get high-ranking administration officials to testify about who made those decisions. In 2008 the House voted to hold White House chief of staff Joshua B. Bolten and former White House counsel Harriet Miers in contempt for refusing to provide subpoenaed documents and, in Miers's case, for refusing to testify before the House Judiciary Committee. But a lawsuit filed by House lawyers, after Attorney General Michael B. Mukasey refused to refer the contempt citations to a federal grand jury, had not been resolved by the end of the Bush presidency. The Senate Judiciary added its own contempt charge against Bolten and aimed another one at former White House deputy chief of staff Karl Rove, but the full Senate never acted on the charges.

Congressional committees also became more active in routine oversight, particularly of the Iraq war. The House Oversight and Government Reform Committee, chaired by Henry A. Waxman of California, looked into corruption in the Iraqi government and waste and fraud in the reconstruction of Iraq, while the House Armed Services Committee, chaired by Ike Skelton of Missouri, probed the readiness of military forces strained by continuing deployments in Iraq. Numerous committees held hearings on the Iraq war and the impact of Bush's troop "surge."

In addition, Waxman's committee found out about a PowerPoint presentation that one of Rove's deputies had delivered to General Services Administration officials about the 2008 elections, leading to a broader probe of political briefings at agencies in possible violation of the Hatch Act, which restricts the political activities of federal employees. Waxman's committee also uncovered evidence that Blackwater USA, a private military contractor in Iraq, had been involved in numerous shooting incidents—including one in which a drunken contractor killed the guard of one of the Iraqi vice presidents—and questioned the State Department's oversight of Blackwater's actions. He opened a separate investigation into White House officials' use of Republican National Committee e-mail accounts, suggesting that the practice could have violated the federal law that requires the preservation of presidential records.

The Democrats' oversight efforts did bring some results, notably the resignation of Gonzales, who quit under pressure after congressional investigations undermined his credibility in his accounts of the U.S. attorney firings and key decisions about the National Security Agency's warrantless wiretapping program. However, there were limits to how far Congress would go in challenging the president himself. Some liberal Democrats, notably House Judiciary Committee chairman John Conyers Jr. of Michigan, wanted to open impeachment proceedings against Bush, alleging various abuses of power and deception in presenting his case for the Iraq war. But Democratic leaders shut down all such talk, insisting—as did many rank-and-file Democrats who had won seats formerly held by Republicans—that impeachment efforts would be a divisive waste of time and that it was better to look forward.

Democratic representative Dennis Kucinich of Ohio, a presidential candidate in 2004 and 2008, tried to bypass his leadership by bringing articles of impeachment straight to the House floor—against Cheney in November 2007, and then against Bush in June 2008. He introduced both as privileged resolutions, which the House is required to act on within two days; he accused Bush of abusing his power "to manufacture a false case for war against Iraq," and Cheney of misrepresenting intelligence on Iraq and Iran. In both cases, though, Republicans simply treated Kucinich as a joke, voting with him solely to allow him more floor time at the expense of Democrats who wanted to bury his resolutions. Voting mostly along party lines, the House voted to refer both resolutions to the Judiciary Committee, where they were never heard from again.

Even when Bush and Congress worked together, the administration sometimes took liberties with the authority Congress had given it. The financial industry bailout legislation, for example, was supposed to allow the administration to buy troubled assets from banks, relieving them of the worthless mortgage-backed securities that were seen as the cause of the worsening credit crunch. That was the argument Treasury secretary Paulson made to members of Congress in asking for the $700 billion bailout initiative, which even carried the name "Troubled Assets Relief Program." Yet after Congress reluctantly approved the money, Paulson used most of the first installment to make direct capital injections into banks by buying their stock, rather than to take the troubled assets off of their books.

Bush and Executive Power

A major factor complicating Bush's relationship with Congress was his expansive view of the powers of the presidency. In most issues, but particularly in his approaches to foreign policy and the war on terrorism, his concept of executive power gave Congress only a limited role in second-guessing his decisions, even when lawmakers were inclined to do so. Some of Bush's policies set precedents for a lasting expansion of presidential authority. His successor, Barack Obama, embraced certain Bush antiterrorism policies, such as claiming a president has the right to detain some suspected terrorists indefinitely. In picking so many fights with Congress, however, some presidential scholars argued by the end of Bush's term that he may have weakened presidential power more than he enhanced it because his administration's actions will increase public scrutiny of future presidential policies and activities.

Bush never showed any signs of fully formed views of executive power when he first ran for the presidency in 2000. Instead, his approach appeared to be mostly shaped by Cheney and his top advisers, particularly David Addington, who was Cheney's counsel during Bush's first term and then became the vice president's chief of staff after the resignation of I. Lewis "Scooter" Libby in 2005. Cheney had strongly held views about the powers of the presidency, which he believed had been weakened by Congress during the presidency of Gerald R. Ford, when Cheney had served as White House chief of staff. In 2006 Cheney told reporters that Congress had overreached by passing the War Powers Act—which required Congress to authorize the president to keep troops in battle longer than sixty days and was never been fully recognized as constitutional by any president—and by narrowing presidential powers in other ways, such as limiting the president's ability to impound funds.

"I clearly do believe and have spoken directly about the importance of a strong presidency, and that I think there have been times in the past, oftentimes in response to events such as Watergate or the war in Vietnam, where Congress has begun to encroach upon the powers and responsibilities of the president; that it was important to go back and try to restore that balance," Cheney told reporters in June 2006. "I think if you look at things like the War Powers Act, for example, adopted in the aftermath of the Vietnam conflict, that that was an infringement on the president's ability to deploy troops. It's never really been tested. I think it's probably unconstitutional. There are a series of events like that that we believed needed to have the balance righted, if you will. And I think we've done that successfully."

But in trying to swing the pendulum back to a strong presidency, Bush and Cheney created a backlash among lawmakers, constitutional scholars, civil liberties groups, and the media, as critics concluded the president and vice president simply were not interested in checks and balances. Those critics focused on a litany of controversial decisions made without consulting Congress or in direct defiance of lawmakers' demands. For example, the Bush team launched a secret warrantless surveillance program that, according to the critics, operated outside the law. The administration declared that a president, as commander in chief, could singlehandedly decide how long to detain suspected terrorists and which interrogations techniques to use. They set up military tribunals without asking Congress to authorize them, until the Supreme Court made them do so. They declared that a president could pull the United States out of treaties, as Bush did in 2001 when he abandoned the 1972 Anti-Ballistic Missile Treaty. They declared that because of executive privilege, administration officials could refuse to testify before Congress or provide documents even after lawmakers had issued subpoenas.

In addition, Bush raised the concept of signing statements—usually routine declarations issued after a president signs a bill into law—to a new level, turning the statements into warnings to Congress that he would treat certain provisions as optional if he thought they intruded on his presidential prerogatives. According to political scientist Christopher S. Kelley of Miami University in Ohio, Bush used the statements to challenge 1,168 provisions of bills he had signed into law—more than twice as many as Presidents Ronald Reagan, George H.W. Bush, George W. Bush's father, and Bill Clinton combined. The statements, many of which were written by Addington, often declared that the executive branch would interpret a provision "in a manner consistent with the constitutional authority of the President to supervise the unitary executive branch." That was a reference to the unitary executive theory, a view promoted by Bush's and Cheney's legal teams, which declared that the president had the sole power to control the executive branch without interference from Congress or the judiciary.

In his book *The Terror Presidency*, Jack Goldsmith, a former head of the Office of Legal Counsel during Bush's first term, wrote that Addington drove an especially hard line against consulting Congress on national security matters. "Addington would always ask two simple questions," Goldsmith wrote, "whenever someone proposed that the White House work with Congress to clear away a legal restriction or to get the legislature on board: 'Do we have the legal power to do it ourselves?' (meaning the President's sole authority), and 'Might Congress limit our options in ways that jeopardize American lives?' "

CHECKS AND BALANCES

While many of Bush's executive power policies originated in his first term, two developments toward the end of 2005 put them under harsher scrutiny than they had received before. The first, in December 2005, was the *New York Times* report that disclosed the existence of a warrantless surveillance program run by the National Security Agency to look for signs of terrorist activity within the United States. The program operated outside the boundaries of the Foreign Intelligence Surveillance Act (FISA), the 1978 law that governs surveillance; under the law, the government could only conduct surveillance of phone calls and e-mails within the United States by obtaining a warrant from the Foreign Intelligence Surveillance Court, a secretive panel that rarely rejects such requests.

Although the administration had urged the *Times* not to publish the story, saying the disclosure of the program could damage national security, Bush issued a full-throated defense once the story was out. "We know that a two-minute phone conversation between somebody linked to Al Qaida here and an operative overseas could lead directly to the loss of thousands of lives," Bush said. "We've got to be fast on our feet, quick to detect and prevent." But the disclosure of the program tripped up an effort in the Senate to reauthorize the antiterrorism law known as the Patriot Act, already in trouble as a handful of senators raised civil liberties concerns, and it took until the next year before Congress reauthorized the law with minor changes. Senate Judiciary Committee chairman Arlen Specter of Pennsylvania called the decision to bypass the courts "categorically wrong," and Sen. Patrick J. Leahy of Vermont, the ranking Democrat on the committee, said the program raised questions about "how to reconcile two shared and fundamental goals—assuring the safety of the American people and protecting their liberty by a system of checks and balances."

The second development was the signing statement Bush issued after he reluctantly signed McCain torture ban into law. The statement, issued on Dec. 30, 2005, implied that Bush might simply ignore the new statute, saying the executive branch would construe the ban "in a manner consistent with the constitutional authority of the President to supervise the unitary executive branch and as Commander in Chief and consistent with the constitutional limitations on the judicial power, which will assist in achieving the shared objective of the Congress and the President . . . of protecting the American people from further terrorist attacks."

That signing statement drew significant media attention and led to broader examinations of how many times Bush had used the practice. An American Bar Association task force on presidential signing statements declared that declining to enforce provisions of newly signed legislation was "contrary to the rule of law and our constitutional system of separation of powers." The task force urged presidents to discuss any constitutional concerns with Congress before bills are passed, and said Congress should pass legislation allowing the courts to review any such disputes after a bill has been signed into law.

In 2006 the Supreme Court ruled that Bush had overstepped his authority by creating the military tribunals at Guantanamo Bay, Cuba, through executive order. Bush asked Congress to approve the tribunals, saying that "as soon as Congress acts on this bill, the men our intelligence believed helped orchestrate the 9/11 attacks can face justice." He also suggested that the Central Intelligence Agency's interrogation program was at stake as well, arguing that it could not continue without specific direction from lawmakers. "So Congress has got a decision to make: You want the program to go forward or not?" Bush said at a September 2006 press conference. The final bill, however, did not allow prisoners to challenge their detention in federal courts. Specter tried to amend the bill to allow the appeals, but the amendment failed, as most Republicans argued that the appropriate model to use was the laws of war, not the criminal justice system. "Habeas corpus applies to citizens," said Republican senator Jeff Sessions of Alabama. The Founding Fathers, he said, "didn't mean for it to apply to those attacking America." In 2008, however, the Supreme Court disagreed, ruling that the language was an unconstitutional suspension of a fundamental right.

INTELLIGENCE SURVEILLANCE, EXECUTIVE PRIVILEGE

Bush also asked Congress to rewrite the 1978 FISA law to allow the administration to continue its surveillance of suspected terrorists. In 2007 Democrats tried to put together a bill to fix the main problem that had been identified by Director of National Intelligence Michael McConnell: by having to go through the secret FISA court, the government was limited in its ability to monitor overseas communications that happened to be routed through the U.S. fiber-optic cable network. But the Democratic bills failed in the House and Senate, so lawmakers instead approved a short-term bill, written by the Republicans, to let the surveillance continue for six months.

The next year, Congress approved a long-term overhaul of the law after a bitter debate over whether to give immunity to telecommunications companies that had cooperated in Bush's surveillance program. The final bill authorized warrantless eavesdropping on foreign targets communicating with people in the United States, as long as the government is not specifically trying to monitor U.S. citizens, and required courts to dismiss lawsuits against telecommunications companies if there was "substantial evidence" they had been assured the program was legal and authorized by the president. Most Democrats did not like the measure, but they also did not want to be exposed to election-year charges that they were leaving the United States vulnerable to terrorist attacks. Even Obama, who had staked his 2008 presidential candidacy on balancing his antiterrorism policies with civil liberties concerns, voted for the bill, arguing that it re-established judicial oversight and called for agency inspectors general to review past conduct. "It is not all that I would want," Obama said. "But given the legitimate threats we face, providing effective intelligence collection tools with appropriate safeguards is too important to delay."

When the House and Senate Judiciary committees issued subpoenas in 2007 for documents and testimony about the firing of nine U.S. attorneys, the Bush administration took a broad view of executive privilege, arguing that White House officials should be given blanket immunity from questioning by congressional committees. "For the presidency to operate consistent with the Constitution's design, presidents must be able to depend upon their advisers and other executive branch officials speaking candidly and without inhibition while deliberating and working to advise the president," White House counsel Fred F. Fielding wrote in a letter to the House and Senate Judiciary Committee chairmen. Both committees had subpoenaed documents from White House chief of staff Joshua Bolten, and the House panel had issued a subpoena for testimony and documents from Fielding's predecessor, Harriet Miers, as well. Later in 2007, the Senate Judiciary committee also subpoenaed Karl Rove, Bush's top political strategist, in its investigation. In 2008 the House Judiciary committee subpoenaed Rove for testimony in a probe of whether the administration had targeted Democratic officials, including former Alabama governor Donald Siegelman, for prosecution.

When all refused to testify, the House voted in February 2008 to hold Bolten and Miers in contempt of Congress. But in doing so, lawmakers exposed their own inability to enforce contempt citations when the executive branch is determined to put up a fight. The Justice Department, under Attorney General Michael B. Mukasey, took the position that the contempt statute did not apply when an executive branch official claims executive privilege. Therefore, Mukasey refused to allow the U.S. attorney for the

District of Columbia to take the contempt citations to a federal grand jury. The House sued, and in July 2008, U.S. district court judge John D. Bates ordered Bolten and Miers to comply with the subpoenas. But a federal appeals court issued a stay of the order in September, ensuring a drawn-out legal battle that would drag on long after the Bush presidency ended—and after the subpoenas expired.

Perhaps the ultimate dilemma in the reach of executive power—what's permissible in interrogating suspected terrorists—remained the subject of furious debate. In a May 2009 speech at the National Archives, Obama made it clear that he thought harsh interrogation techniques violated America's core values. "We do not torture," Obama said, and "we will vigorously protect our people while forge a strong and durable framework that allows us to fight terrorism while abiding by the rule of law." But Cheney, in a speech the same day, dismissed the criticisms of the Bush administration and said no president can afford the luxury of agonizing over how to stop the next terrorist attack—providing a unique insight into the thinking that went into the executive power decisions that helped shape Bush's presidency.

"You cannot keep just some nuclear-armed terrorists out of the United States; you must keep every nuclear-armed terrorist out of the United States," Cheney said in his speech at the American Enterprise Institute. "Triangulation is a political strategy, not a national security strategy. When just a single clue that goes unlearned or one lead that goes unpursued can bring on catastrophe, it's no time for splitting differences. There is never a good time to compromise when the lives and safety of the American people hang in the balance."

Bush Nominations

Bush began his second term by moving more loyalists into top positions, a pattern consistent with his view that he had won a mandate to continue and strengthen his policies. Condoleezza Rice, his first-term national security adviser with an unusually close relationship with the president, became the new secretary of state—replacing Colin Powell, the popular former army general who had clashed with Vice President Cheney and Defense Secretary Rumsfeld in the lead-up to the Iraq war. Henry M. Paulson Jr. stepped in as Treasury secretary after two predecessors—John Snow and Paul O'Neill—showed an inability to fit in with the personalities and policies of the Bush team.

Later on, though, Bush showed a more pragmatic streak, replacing troubled Cabinet secretaries with outsiders who could broaden his public appeal and establish a better working relationship with the new Democratic majority in Congress. He also got a chance to fill two Supreme Court seats, nominating justices who could turn the tide toward a more solidly conservative majority—exactly the kind of majority his political base called for while the Republicans were still in charge.

JUSTICE DEPARTMENT

No nominee represented the trend toward Bush loyalists in the cabinet more than Alberto R. Gonzales, Bush's choice to become the second-term attorney general. At first, Republicans and Democrats welcomed the choice. They hoped Gonzales—who had served as White House counsel during Bush's first term and had been in his inner circle since Texas days—would be more cooperative with Congress than Bush's first attorney general, John Ashcroft. Lawmakers viewed Ashcroft as reluctant to testify and work with Congress despite his previous role as a senator from Missouri. Moreover, Ashcroft had earned a popular image as a champion of antiterrorism policies with questionable civil liberties protections—notably the "Patriot Act"—and a new attorney general offered Bush a chance to have one less lightning rod in the cabinet.

But the tone of Gonzales' confirmation process changed quickly in January 2005, when Senate Judiciary Committee Democrats focused on his role as White House counsel in developing the administration's legal strategy for dealing with terrorists, particularly his views on what constitutes torture. In a January 2002 memo to Bush, Gonzales advised the president that the Geneva Conventions on the treatment of prisoners of war do not apply to members of al Qaeda or the Taliban. Gonzales wrote that the "war against terrorism is a new kind of war" that effectively "renders obsolete Geneva's strict limitations on questioning of enemy prisoners and renders quaint some of its provisions."

Democrats also wanted to know whether Gonzales consulted on memos by the Justice Department's Office of Legal Counsel that defined torture narrowly. One memo concluded that for an interrogation tactic to count as torture, it must have the "precise objective" of inflicting severe pain. But Sens. Edward M. Kennedy, D-Mass., and Dianne Feinstein, D-Calif., were frustrated by Gonzales' written responses to questions, in which he said he could not discuss "deliberative material" or classified information. "To say this is classified, when he knows we have access to classified information...doesn't portend well for the oversight responsibilities of this committee," Feinstein said.

On Jan. 26, 2005, the Senate Judiciary Committee endorsed Gonzales' nomination on a party-line vote of 10–8. That action set the stage for his narrow confirmation by the Senate Feb. 3 on a 60–36 vote, with only six Democrats voting with all of the Republicans to approve him for the job. Even Judiciary Committee chairman Arlen Specter, R-Pa., who voted to confirm Gonzales, warned the new attorney general that he expected him to testify before the Judiciary Committee at least twice a year—a way of keeping a close eye on him.

In his two and a half years in office, Gonzales' political standing deteriorated rapidly, weakened by rocky relations with the Democrats and mounting questions over the truthfulness of his congressional testimony. He lost credibility in 2007 during the congressional investigations of

BUSH ADMINISTRATION CABINET

Following is a list of cabinet officers who served in the administration of President George W. Bush during his four years in office between Jan. 20, 2005, and Jan. 20, 2009. Dates given are for actual service in office, beginning with the cabinet officers' swearing-in date, which often varies from date of confirmation by the Senate. Offices that have been designed cabinet-level are not included. *(For cabinet members during President Bush's first term, see Congress and the Nation Vol. XI, p. 920)*

	Dates of Service
Secretary of State	
Colin L. Powell	Jan. 20, 2001–Jan. 26, 2005
Condoleezza Rice	Jan 26, 2005–Jan. 20, 2009
Secretary of the Treasury	
John W. Snow	Feb. 3, 2003–June 28, 2006
Henry M. Paulson Jr.	July 10, 2006–Jan. 20, 2009
Secretary of Defense	
Donald H. Rumsfeld	Jan. 20, 2001–Dec. 18, 2006
Robert M. Gates	Dec. 18, 2006[1]
Attorney General	
John Ashcroft	Feb. 1, 2001–Feb. 3, 2005
Alberto Gonzales	Feb. 14, 2005–Sept. 17, 2007
Michael Mukasey	Nov. 19, 2007–Jan. 20, 2009
Secretary of the Interior	
Gale A. Norton	Jan. 31, 2001–March 31, 2006
Dick Kempthorne	June 7, 2006–Jan. 20, 2009
Secretary of Agriculture	
Mike Johanns	Jan. 21, 2005–Sept. 20, 2007
Edward Schafer	Jan. 28, 2008–Jan. 20, 2009
Secretary of Commerce	
Donald L. Evans	Jan. 20, 2001–Feb. 7, 2005
Carlos M. Gutierrez	Feb. 7, 2005–Jan. 20, 2009
Secretary of Labor	
Elaine L. Chao	Jan. 31, 2001–Jan. 20, 2009

	Dates of Service
Secretary of Health and Human Services	
Tommy G. Thompson	Feb. 2, 2001–Jan 26, 2005
Michael O. Leavitt	Jan. 26, 2005–Jan. 20, 2009
Secretary of Education	
Margaret Spellings	Jan. 20, 2005–Jan. 20, 2009
Secretary of Housing and Urban Development	
Alphonso R. Jackson	April 1, 2004–April 18, 2008
Steven Preston	June 5, 2008–Jan. 20, 2009
Secretary of Transportation	
Norman Y. Mineta	Jan. 25, 2001–July 7, 2006
Mary Peters	Oct. 17, 2006–Jan. 20, 2009
Secretary of Energy	
Spencer Abraham	Jan. 20, 2001–Feb. 1, 2005
Samuel W. Bodman	Feb. 1, 2005–Jan. 20, 2009
Secretary of Veterans Affairs	
Anthony J. Principi	Jan. 24, 2001–Jan, 26, 2005
Jim Nicholson	Jan. 26, 2005–Oct. 1, 2007
James Peake	Dec. 20, 2007–Jan. 20, 2009
Secretary of Homeland Security	
Tom Ridge	Jan. 24, 2003–Feb. 1, 2005
Michael Chertoff	Feb. 15, 2005–Jan. 21, 2009[2]

[1] President Barack Obama retained Gates as defense secretary when his administration began in January 2009. Gates did not require re-confirmation by the Senate.

[2] Chertoff remained in office until the day after Bush was inaugurated to expedite transition to the new administration.

the firing of nine U.S. attorneys during the 2006 election season, which the Democrats, now in the majority, suspected were politically motivated. Gonzales made conflicting statements during his testimony and seemed to be plagued by memory loss when asked for details.

The final straw, however, took place when Gonzales testified in July 2006 that a much-publicized visit he made to the hospital bedside of then–Attorney General Ashcroft in March 2004 "was not about the terrorist surveillance program that the president announced to the American people." In fact, two days later, FBI director Robert S. Mueller III suggested in separate testimony that was exactly the purpose of the visit. Four Senate Democrats asked the Justice Department to appoint a special counsel to investigate whether Gonzales lied under oath to Congress. In late August, Gonzales bowed to the pressure and stepped down.

Lawmakers were optimistic about the chances for a fresh start when Bush nominated Michael B. Mukasey, a former federal judge, to replace Gonzales. Mukasey had served eighteen years as a federal trial court judge in New York, earning a reputation as an independent-minded legal voice—just the kind of person who might be able to re-establish the proper distance between the Department of Justice and the White House. But Democrats soured on him when he refused, during his confirmation, to call waterboarding torture. "To me, it is not a hard call," Judiciary Committee chairman Patrick J. Leahy of Vermont said in a floor speech opposing Mukasey's nomination. "Nothing is more fundamental to our constitutional democracy than our basic notion that no one is above the law. This administration has undercut that precept time after time. They are now trying to do it again."

When the Senate confirmed Mukasey on Nov. 8, 2007, the vote was 53–40—an even thinner margin than Gonzales received. By the end of Bush's term, Mukasey had hardly improved relations with Congress at all. He fought the House's efforts to force senior administration officials to comply with subpoenas in its investigation of the U.S. attorney firings, refused to investigate the administration's interrogation tactics, and generally upheld its expansive views of executive power. Bruce Fein, who served in President Ronald Reagan's Justice Department and became a critic of Bush's executive power views, concluded that Mukasey was just "Alberto Gonzales with slightly more brains."

DEFENSE DEPARTMENT

Rumsfeld was the most immediate and prominent casualty of the Democratic victory in the 2006 congressional elections. Bush announced his departure as defense secretary the day after Democrats won control of Congress, saying "the timing is right for new leadership at the Pentagon."

Rumsfeld, who had also served as defense secretary under President Gerald R. Ford in the 1970s, had become the swaggering face of U.S. policy in Iraq to much of the public: confident to the point of cockiness, and dismissive of criticisms that often turned out to be valid. Privately, Republicans were furious at Bush for not getting rid of Rumsfeld sooner; if he had announced his decision in the last couple of weeks of the campaign, some GOP lawmakers thought, they might have narrowly held onto control of Congress.

By contrast, Robert M. Gates, the president of Texas A&M University and a former director of the Central Intelligence Agency, won a warm reception from lawmakers from both sides of the aisle. At his confirmation hearing before the Armed Services Committee in December 2006, they praised him for being candid and for promising to cooperate with their inquiries—in short, for not being Rumsfeld. At one point, when Carl Levin of Michigan, the top Democrat on the committee, asked Gates if he thought the United States was winning the Iraq war, Gates answered simply, "No, sir."

Gates's favorite phrase was that he was "open" to a lot of ideas, and that "all options are on the table" in changing the strategy in Iraq. He said he had learned the importance of "consultations, the importance of a lack of surprises [and] the importance of treating people's views with respect" from his experience working with Congress as director of the Central Intelligence Agency under Bush's father. On Dec. 6, 2006, the Senate confirmed him 95–2.

STATE DEPARTMENT

Rice was well known as one of Bush's closest advisers when the Senate confirmed her in Jan. 26, 2005, on an 85–13 vote, as his second-term secretary of state—seemingly a strong endorsement of her promises to restore international diplomacy as a top priority of the administration. But Rice, Bush's national security adviser during his first term, also suffered a grilling from Democrats during her confirmation hearing in the Foreign Relations Committee. Democrats used the hearing to examine the conduct of the Iraq war and the administration's decision to go to war in the first place.

Sen. John Kerry, D-Mass., who had just returned to Capitol Hill after his unsuccessful campaign to unseat Bush, told Rice that he had "reservations" about voting for her nomination. When she said she thought current U.S. troop levels were high enough to defeat the Iraqi insurgency, Kerry said her statement was "contrary to the most thoughtful people who have been analyzing this.... You need to be more precise about what you intend to do to change the dynamics." When Sen. Barbara Boxer, D-Calif., noted apparent contradictions in Rice's past statements about weapons of mass destruction in Iraq, Rice bristled: "We can have this discussion in any way that you would like, but I really hope that you will refrain from impugning my integrity. I really hope that you will not imply that I take the truth lightly."

But Rice also made it clear she would pursue a foreign policy based on more international cooperation and less unilateralism than some of Bush's top advisers had promoted during his first term. "Our interaction with the rest of the world must be a conversation, not a monologue," she said. "Public diplomacy will be a top priority for me."

HOMELAND SECURITY DEPARTMENT

Michael Chertoff, a former head of the Justice Department criminal division, left a lifetime appointment as a federal judge to become the new homeland security secretary, winning Senate confirmation Feb. 15, 2005, on a 98–0 vote. He replaced Tom Ridge, the moderate former governor from Pennsylvania who presided over the creation of the department in Bush's first term but never fully managed to make the different bureaucracies mesh together. Chertoff gained a reputation for candor—acknowledging that it is impossible to protect against every conceivable risk—but he did not earn praise for his managerial competence, particularly after he was unable to take charge of the federal government's response to Hurricane Katrina.

EDUCATION DEPARTMENT

Margaret Spellings, who had been one of Bush's top domestic policy advisers during his first term and had advised him on education policy when he was Texas governor, took over as education secretary during his second term. She replaced Rod Paige, the former superintendent of Houston schools who earned a strong reputation there but was seen as largely irrelevant during the passage of No Child Left Behind, the education overhaul law that was one of Bush's top domestic policy achievements. Spellings, by contrast, was heavily involved in the writing of that law, and as education secretary she worked with state and local education officials to refine it.

HEALTH AND HUMAN SERVICES DEPARTMENT

Michael O. Leavitt, a former governor of Utah who had headed the Environmental Protection Agency during Bush's first term, won easy confirmation by voice vote as the new health and human services secretary on Jan. 16, 2005. He replaced Tommy Thompson, the former Wisconsin governor who later ran a brief campaign for the 2008 presidential nomination.

ENERGY DEPARTMENT

Samuel W. Bodman, who served stints as deputy Treasury secretary and deputy commerce secretary in Bush's first term, became the new energy secretary in Jan. 31, 2005, winning Senate approval unanimously. He replaced Spencer Abraham, the former Michigan senator who held the post throughout Bush's first term.

TREASURY DEPARTMENT

On June 28, 2006, Paulson, the chief executive of the investment bank Goldman Sachs, won easy confirmation by voice vote as the new Treasury secretary. He replaced Snow, who had been outside Bush's inner circle for a while because Republicans thought he was not a particularly vocal advocate for the administration's economic policies. Paulson championed tax cuts as the key to sound fiscal policy, telling the Finance Committee it would be a "big mistake" not to extend Bush's 2001 tax cuts after 2010, when they were set to expire. He told the committee that tax cuts do not pay for themselves "as a general rule," but he insisted that "tax cuts do change behavior; there is no doubt." Paulson in 2008 was to become the leading cabinet member in the administration's multi-billion effort to halt the rapidly accelerating recession from turning into a full-scale depression.

COMMERCE DEPARTMENT

Carlos Gutierrez, previously the chairman of the board of the Kellogg Company, won quick, unanimous Senate confirmation as the new commerce secretary on Jan. 24, 2005. Gutierrez was a native of Cuba who escaped with his family to Florida when he was six years old. He replaced one of Bush's longtime friends, Donald L. Evans, who had been in Bush's inner circle since his Midland, Texas, days and had served as chairman of Bush's 2000 presidential campaign.

HOUSING AND URBAN DEVELOPMENT DEPARTMENT

Former Small Business Administration (SBA) chief Steven C. Preston became the housing and urban development secretary on June 29, 2008, replacing Alphonso R. Jackson, who had resigned in March 18, 2008, as he faced a criminal investigation for allegations of cronyism, corruption, and political favoritism.

AGRICULTURE DEPARTMENT

Mike Johanns, a former governor of Nebraska, easily won Senate confirmation by voice vote as the new agriculture secretary on Jan. 4, 2005. He replaced Ann M. Veneman, who held the job during Bush's first term and had been a top agriculture official under Bush's father. In September 2007, Johanns resigned to pursue a successful campaign for Nebraska's open U.S. Senate seat. He was replaced by former North Dakota governor Ed Schafer, a surprise choice who had represented farmers who opposed the administration's efforts to cut farm subsidies. He won Senate confirmation by voice vote on Jan. 28, 2008.

INTERIOR DEPARTMENT

Dirk Kempthorne, Idaho's governor and a former senator, replaced Gale Norton as Bush's interior secretary on May 26, 2006 after Norton resigned. Norton had been a controversial figure as she opened up Western lands to oil and gas drilling, and one of her former deputies was under investigation for possible links to the Jack Abramoff lobbying scandal.

Kempthorne's confirmation was delayed while two Democratic senators placed holds on his nomination to press their concerns over offshore oil drilling. Mary L. Landrieu of Louisiana wanted her state and other Gulf Coast states to earn a greater share of the royalties, while Bill Nelson of Florida wanted guarantees that his state's beaches would be protected from drilling. But the Senate cut off debate decisively, on an 85–8 vote, and then confirmed Kempthorne by voice vote.

TRANSPORTATION DEPARTMENT

In September 2006, Mary E. Peters, a former Federal Highway Administration chief, replaced Norman Y. Mineta as Bush's transportation secretary. Mineta, who had resigned on July 7, 2006, had served as the only Democratic member of the cabinet since the beginning of Bush's first term, and famously gave the order to ground all civilian flights in the United States during the Sept. 11 attacks. Peters also had headed the Arizona Department of Transportation and had been a vocal advocate of tapping private money for public roads. She was confirmed by the Senate Sept. 26 by voice vote.

VETERANS' AFFAIRS DEPARTMENT

Jim Nicholson, who had been the U.S. ambassador to the Vatican and previously had chaired the Republican National Committee, was confirmed by voice vote as the new veterans' affairs secretary on Jan. 26, 2005. He replaced Anthony J. Principi, who had served as acting secretary and deputy secretary of the department under Bush's father.

In December 2007, retired general James B. Peake stepped into the job after Nicholson resigned, having experienced a rocky tenure that included chronic underfunding and the theft of a laptop computer from an employee's home that contained the personal data of millions of navy and National Guard veterans. Peake, who had served as army surgeon general, was the first general and first medical doctor to head the VA. He was confirmed by the Senate Dec. 14 by voice vote.

SUPREME COURT

Bush named two Supreme Court justices, Chief Justice John G. Roberts Jr. and Justice Samuel A. Alito Jr., both of whom were expected to be leading conservative voices on the nation's highest court. Many observers believe that their appointment could be among Bush's most significant actions in his two terms in office. In their initial service the two new justices moved the court's balance to the right, unsettling the rough balance that had been provided by Sandra Day O'Connor, the swing-vote justice whose retirement had provided the openings.

O'Connor gave Bush his first opportunity to reshape the court when she announced her retirement in July 2005. Bush nominated Roberts, 50, to replace her, ensuring that a judge with solid conservative credentials would take the place of the more moderate O'Connor. Roberts, a former associate counsel to President Ronald Reagan and deputy solicitor general under Bush's father, was affable and well-regarded by senators from both parties, and the initial feedback suggested that he could be one of Bush's rare chances to please conservative activists without picking a major fight with liberal Democrats. Two months later, when Chief Justice William Rehnquist died, Bush used that opportunity to leave an even more significant legacy by moving Roberts to Rehnquist's position, nominating him for chief justice.

Roberts's confirmation went smoothly, and the Senate approved him on a 78–22 vote on Sept. 29, 2005. Bush's effort to find a new nominee for O'Connor's seat, however, was anything but smooth. For reasons that his own Republican allies in the Senate never quite understood, Bush nominated his own White House counsel, Harriet Miers, to take O'Connor's place on the high court. Miers was a loyal underling to Bush, but she had no credible experience on constitutional issues to recommend her, and she struck conservative activists as a blank slate on crucial issues rather than a respected jurist who could change the balance on the court. Many Senate Republicans regarded her nomination as a show of arrogance—a sign that Bush expected them to rubber-stamp anyone he wanted. Under withering fire, Miers withdrew her nomination and returned quietly to her White House counsel job.

Bush's next choice was Alito, 55, a federal appeals court judge and former Justice Department lawyer under Reagan with a track record much more reassuring to conservatives. But he was also a lightning rod to Democrats, who saw him as hostile to their values on abortion, civil rights, and workers' rights and too eager to side with government and business in disputes with individuals. They also noted his vocal support for the "unitary executive" theory, a doctrine pushed by Cheney and his advisers—and adopted by Bush—that suggested that Congress has no right to interfere with the president's control of the executive branch.

Kennedy and Kerry even tried to filibuster his nomination on the Senate floor—an effort that did not get far, as the Senate voted 72–25 to end the debate, well above the sixty votes Alito's supporters needed. But his actual confirmation vote was closer: 58–42, the closest vote in modern times since Clarence Thomas squeaked through the Senate in 1991 by a 52–48 margin.

Appendix

Glossary of Congressional Terms

AA—*(See Administrative Assistant.)*

Absence of a Quorum—Absence of the required number of members to conduct business in a house or a committee. When a quorum call or roll-call vote in a house establishes that a quorum is not present, no debate or other business is permitted except a motion to adjourn or motions to request or compel the attendance of absent members, if necessary by arresting them.

Absolute Majority—A vote requiring approval by a majority of all members of a chamber rather than a majority of members present and voting. Also referred to as constitutional majority.

Account—Organizational units used in the federal budget primarily for recording spending and revenue transactions.

Act—(1) A bill passed in identical form by the House and Senate and signed into law by the president or enacted over the president's veto. A bill also becomes an act without the president's signature if it is unsigned but not returned to Congress within ten days (Sundays excepted) and if Congress has not adjourned within that period. (2) Also, the technical term for a bill passed by at least one house and engrossed.

Ad Hoc Select Committee—A temporary committee formed for a special purpose or to deal with a specific subject. Conference committees are ad hoc joint committees. A House rule adopted in 1975 authorizes the Speaker to refer measures to special ad hoc committees, appointed by the Speaker with the approval of the House.

Adjourn—A motion to adjourn is a formal motion to end a day's session or meeting of a house or a committee. A motion to adjourn usually has no conditions attached to it, but it sometimes may specify the day or time for reconvening or make reconvening subject to the call of the chamber's presiding officer or the committee's chairman. In both houses, a motion to adjourn is of the highest privilege, takes precedence over all other motions, is not debatable, and must be put to an immediate vote. Adjournment of a house ends its legislative day. For this reason, the House or Senate sometimes adjourns for only one minute, or some other brief period of time, during the course of a day's session. The House does not permit a motion to adjourn after it has resolved into the Committee of the Whole or when the previous question has been ordered on a measure to final passage without an intervening motion.

Adjourn for More Than Three Days—Under Article I, Section 5 of the Constitution, neither house may adjourn for more than three days without the approval of the other. The necessary approval is given in a concurrent resolution to which both houses have agreed.

Adjournment *Sine Die*—Final adjournment of an annual or two-year session of Congress; literally, adjournment without a day. The two houses must agree to a privileged concurrent resolution for such an adjournment. A *sine die* adjournment precludes Congress from meeting again until the next constitutionally fixed date of a session (Jan. 3 of the following year) unless Congress determines otherwise by law or the president calls it into special session. Article II, Section 3 of the Constitution authorizes the president to adjourn both houses until such time as the president thinks proper when the two houses cannot agree to a time of adjournment. No president, however, has ever exercised this authority.

Adjournment to a Day (and Time) Certain—An adjournment that fixes the next date and time of meeting for one or both houses. It does not end an annual session of Congress.

Administration Bill—A bill drafted in the executive office of the president or in an executive department or agency to implement part of the president's program. An administration bill is introduced in Congress by a member who supports it or as a courtesy to the administration.

Administrative Assistant (AA)—The title usually given to a member's chief aide, political advisor, and head of office staff. The administrative assistant often represents the member at meetings with visitors or officials when the member is unable (or unwilling) to attend.

Adoption—The usual parliamentary term for approval of a conference report. It is also commonly applied to amendments.

Advance Appropriation—In an appropriation act for a particular fiscal year, an appropriation that does not become available for spending or obligation until a subsequent fiscal year. The amount of the advance appropriation is counted as part of the budget for the fiscal year in which it becomes available for obligation.

Advance Funding—A mechanism whereby statutory language may allow budget authority for a fiscal year to be increased, and obligations to be incurred, with an offsetting decrease in the budget authority available in the succeeding fiscal year. If not used, the budget authority remains available for obligation in the succeeding fiscal year. Advance funding is sometimes used to provide contingency funding of a few benefit programs.

Adverse Report—A committee report recommending against approval of a measure or some other matter. Committees usually pigeonhole measures they oppose instead of reporting them adversely, but they may be required to report them by a statutory rule or an instruction from their parent body.

Advice and Consent—The Senate's constitutional role in consenting to or rejecting the president's nominations to executive branch and judicial offices and treaties with other nations. Confirmation of nominees requires a simple majority vote of senators present and voting. Treaties must be approved by a two-thirds majority of those present and voting.

Aisle—The center aisle of each chamber. When facing the presiding officer, Republicans usually sit to the right of the aisle, Democrats to the left. When members speak of "my side of the aisle" or "this side," they are referring to their party.

Amendment—A formal proposal to alter the text of a bill, resolution, amendment, motion, treaty, or some other text. Technically, it is a motion. An amendment may strike out (eliminate) part of a text, insert new text, or strike out and insert—that is, replace all or part of the text with new text. The texts of amendments considered on the floor are printed in full in the *Congressional Record.*

Amendment in the Nature of a Substitute—Usually, an amendment to replace the entire text of a measure. It strikes out everything after the enacting clause and inserts a version that may be somewhat, substantially, or entirely different. When a committee adopts extensive amendments to a measure, the panel often incorporates them into such an amendment. Occasionally, the term is applied to an amendment that replaces a major portion of a measure's text.

Amendment Tree—A diagram showing the number and types of amendments that the rules and practices of a house permit to be offered to a measure before any of the amendments is voted on. It shows the relationship of one amendment to the others, and it may also indicate the degree of each amendment, whether it is a perfecting or substitute amendment, the order in which amendments may be offered, and the order in which they are put to a vote. The same type of diagram can be used to display an actual amendment situation.

Amendments between the Houses—This is a method for reconciling differences between the House and Senate versions of a measure by passing the measure back and forth between the two chambers until both have agreed to identical language.

Annual Authorization—Legislation that authorizes appropriations for a single fiscal year and usually for a specific amount. Under the rules of the authorization-appropriation process, an annually authorized agency or program must be reauthorized each year if it is to receive appropriations for that year. Sometimes Congress fails to enact the reauthorization (or authorization) but nevertheless provides appropriations to continue (or fund) the program, circumventing the rules by one means or another.

Appeal—A member's formal challenge of a ruling or decision by the presiding officer or committee chair. On appeal, a house or a committee may overturn the ruling by majority vote. The right of appeal ensures the body against arbitrary control by the chair. Appeals are rarely made in the House and are even more rarely successful. Rulings are more frequently appealed in the Senate and occasionally overturned, in part because its presiding officer is not the majority party's leader, as in the House.

Apportionment—The action, after each decennial census, of allocating the number of members in the House of Representatives to each state. By law, the total number of House members (not counting delegates and a resident commissioner) is fixed at 435. The number allotted to each state is based approximately on its proportion of the nation's total population. Because the Constitution guarantees each state one representative no matter how small its population, exact proportional distribution is virtually impossible. The mathematical formula currently used to determine the apportionment is called the Method of Equal Proportions. *(See Method of Equal Proportions.)*

Appropriated Entitlement—An entitlement program, such as veterans' pensions, that is funded through annual appropriations rather than by a permanent appropriation. Because such an entitlement law requires the government to provide eligible recipients the benefits to which they are entitled, whatever the cost, Congress must appropriate the necessary funds.

Appropriation—(1) Legislative language that permits a federal agency to incur obligations and make payments from the Treasury for specified purposes, usually during a specified period of time. (2) The specific amount of money made available by such language. The Constitution prohibits payments from the Treasury except "in Consequence of Appropriations made by Law." With some exceptions, the rules of both houses forbid consideration of appropriations for purposes that are unauthorized in law or of appropriation amounts larger than those authorized in law. The House of Representatives claims the exclusive right to originate appropriation bills—a claim the Senate denies in theory but accepts in practice.

At-Large—Elected by and representing an entire state instead of a district within a state. The term usually refers to a representative rather than to a senator. *(See Apportionment; Congressional District; Redistricting.)*

August Adjournment—A congressional adjournment during the month of August in odd-numbered years, required by the Legislative Reorganization Act of 1970. The law instructs the two houses to adjourn for a period of at least thirty days before the second day after Labor Day, unless Congress provides otherwise or if, on July 31, a state of war exists by congressional declaration.

Authorization—(1) A statutory provision that establishes or continues a federal agency, activity, or program for a fixed or indefinite period of time. It may also establish policies and restrictions and deal with organizational and administrative matters. (2) A statutory provision, as described in (1), may also, explicitly or implicitly, authorize congressional action to provide appropriations for an agency, activity, or program. The appropriations may be authorized for one year, several years, or an indefinite period of time, and the authorization may be for a specific amount of money or an indefinite amount ("such sums as may be necessary"). Authorizations of specific amounts are construed as ceilings on the amounts that subsequently may be appropriated in an appropriation bill, but not as minimums; either house may appropriate lesser amounts or nothing at all.

Authorization-Appropriation Process—The two-stage procedural system that the rules of each house require for establishing and funding federal agencies and programs: first, enactment of authorizing legislation that creates or continues an agency or program; second, enactment of appropriations legislation that provides funds for the authorized agency or program.

Automatic Roll Call—Under a House rule, the automatic ordering of the yeas and nays when a quorum is not present on a voice or division vote and a member objects to the vote on that ground. It is not permitted in the Committee of the Whole.

Backdoor Spending Authority—Authority to incur obligations that evades the normal congressional appropriations process because it is provided in legislation other than appropriation acts. The most common forms are borrowing authority, contract authority, and entitlement authority.

Baseline—A projection of the levels of federal spending, revenues, and the resulting budgetary surpluses or deficits for the upcoming and subsequent fiscal years, taking into account laws enacted to date and assuming no new policy decisions. It provides a benchmark for measuring the budgetary effects of proposed changes in federal revenues or spending, assuming certain economic conditions.

Bells—A system of electric signals and lights that informs members of activities in each chamber. The type of activity taking place is indicated by the number of signals and the interval between them. When the signals are sounded, a corresponding number of lights are lit around the perimeter of many clocks in House or Senate offices.

Bicameral—Consisting of two houses or chambers. Congress is a bicameral legislature whose two houses have an equal role in enacting legislation. In most other national bicameral legislatures, one house is significantly more powerful than the other.

Bigger Bite Amendment—An amendment that substantively changes a portion of a text including language that had previously been amended. Normally, language that has been amended may not be amended again. However, a part of a sentence that has been changed by amendment, for example, may be changed again by an amendment that amends a "bigger bite" of the text—that is, by an amendment that also substantively changes the unamended parts of the sentence or the entire section or title in which the previously amended language appears. The biggest possible bite is an amendment in the nature of a substitute that amends the entire text of a measure. Once adopted, therefore, such an amendment ends the amending process.

Bill—The term for the chief vehicle Congress uses for enacting laws. Bills that originate in the House of Representatives are designated as HR, those in the Senate are designated as S, followed by a number assigned in the order in which they are introduced during a two-year Congress. A bill becomes a law if passed in identical language by both houses and signed by the president, or passed over the president's veto, or if the president fails to sign it within ten days after receiving it while Congress is in session.

Bill of Attainder—An act of a legislature finding a person guilty of treason or a felony. The Constitution prohibits the passage of such a bill by the U.S. Congress or any state legislature.

Bills and Resolutions Introduced—Members formally present measures to their respective houses by delivering them to a clerk in the chamber when their house is in session. Both houses permit any number of members to join in introducing a bill or resolution. The first member listed on the measure is the sponsor; the other members listed are its cosponsors.

Bills and Resolutions Referred—After a bill or resolution is introduced, it is normally sent to one or more committees that have jurisdiction over its subject, as defined by House and Senate rules and precedents. A Senate measure is usually referred to the committee with jurisdiction over the predominant subject of its text, but it may be sent to two or more committees by unanimous consent or on a motion offered jointly by the majority and minority leaders. In the House, a rule requires the Speaker to refer a measure to the committee that has primary jurisdiction. The Speaker is also authorized to refer measures sequentially to additional committees and to impose time limits on such referrals.

Bipartisan Committee—A committee with an equal number of members from each political party. The House Committee on Standards of Official Conduct and the Senate Select Committee on Ethics are the only bipartisan, permanent full committees.

Borrowing Authority—Statutory authority permitting a federal agency, such as the Export-Import Bank, to borrow money from the public or the Treasury to finance its operations. It is a form of backdoor spending. To bring such spending under the control of the congressional appropriation process, the Congressional Budget Act requires that new borrowing authority shall be effective only to the extent and in such amounts as are provided in appropriations acts.

Budget—A detailed statement of actual or anticipated revenues and expenditures during an accounting period. For the national government, the period is the federal fiscal year (Oct. 1 to Sept. 30). The budget usually refers to the president's budget submission to Congress early each calendar year. The president's budget estimates federal government income and spending for the upcoming fiscal year and contains detailed recommendations for appropriation, revenue, and other legislation. Congress is not required to accept or even vote directly on the president's proposals, and it often revises the president's budget extensively. *(See Fiscal Year.)*

Budget Act—Common name for the Congressional Budget and Impoundment Control Act of 1974, which established the basic procedures of the current congressional budget process; created the House and Senate Budget Committees; and enacted procedures for reconciliation, deferrals, and rescissions. *(See Budget Process; Deferral; Impoundment; Reconciliation; Rescission. See also Gramm-Rudman-Hollings Act of 1985.)*

Budget and Accounting Act of 1921—The law that, for the first time, authorized the president to submit to Congress an annual budget for the entire federal government. Before passage of the act, most federal agencies sent their budget requests to the appropriate congressional committees without review by the president.

Budget Authority—Generally, the amount of money that may be spent or obligated by a government agency or for a government program or activity. Technically, it is statutory authority to enter into obligations that normally result in outlays. The main forms of budget authority are appropriations, borrowing authority, and contract authority. It also includes authority to obligate and expend the proceeds of offsetting receipts and collections. Congress may make budget authority available for only one year, several years, or an indefinite period, and it may specify definite or indefinite amounts.

Budget Enforcement Act of 1990—An act that revised the sequestration process established by the Gramm-Rudman-Hollings Act of 1985, replaced the earlier act's fixed deficit targets with adjustable ones, established discretionary spending limits for fiscal years 1991 through 1995, instituted pay-as-you-go rules to enforce deficit neutrality on revenue and mandatory spending legislation, and reformed the budget and accounting rules for federal credit activities. Unlike the Gramm-Rudman-Hollings Act, the 1990 act emphasized restraints on legislated changes in taxes and spending instead of fixed deficit limits.

Budget Enforcement Act of 1997—An act that revised and updated the provisions of the Budget Enforcement Act of 1990, including by extending the discretionary spending caps and pay-as-you-go rules through 2002.

Budget Process—(1) In Congress, the procedural system it uses (a) to approve an annual concurrent resolution on the budget that sets goals for aggregate and functional categories of federal expenditures, revenues, and the surplus or deficit for an upcoming fiscal year; and (b) to implement those goals in spending, revenue, and, if necessary, reconciliation and debt-limit legislation. (2) In the executive branch, the process of formulating the president's annual budget, submitting it to Congress, defending it before congressional committees, implementing subsequent budget-related legislation, impounding or sequestering expenditures as permitted by law, auditing and evaluating programs, and compiling final budget data. The Budget and Accounting Act of 1921 and the Congressional Budget and Impoundment Control Act of 1974 established the basic elements of the current budget process. Major revisions were enacted in the Gramm-Rudman-Hollings Act of 1985, the Budget Enforcement Act of 1990, and the Budget Enforcement Act of 1997.

Budget Resolution—A concurrent resolution in which Congress establishes or revises its version of the federal budget's broad financial features for the upcoming fiscal year and several additional fiscal years. As with other concurrent resolutions, it does not have the force of law, but it provides the framework within which Congress subsequently considers revenue, spending, and other budget-implementing legislation. The framework consists of two basic elements: (1) aggregate budget amounts (total revenues, new budget authority, outlays, loan obligations and loan guarantee commitments, deficit or surplus, and debt limit); and (2) subdivisions of the relevant aggregate amounts among the functional categories of the budget. Although it does not allocate funds to specific programs or accounts, the budget committees' reports accompanying the resolution often discuss the major program assumptions underlying its functional amounts. Unlike those amounts, however, the assumptions are not binding on Congress.

By Request—A designation indicating that a member has introduced a measure on behalf of the president, an executive agency, or a private individual or organization. Members often introduce such measures as a courtesy because neither the president nor any person other than a member of Congress can do so. The term, which appears next to the sponsor's name, implies that the member who introduced the measure does not necessarily endorse it. A House rule dealing with by-request introductions dates from 1888, but the practice goes back to the earliest history of Congress.

Byrd Rule—The popular name of an amendment to the Congressional Budget Act that bars the inclusion of extraneous matter in any reconciliation legislation considered in the Senate. The ban is enforced by points of order that the presiding officer sustains. The provision defines different categories of extraneous matter, but it also permits certain exceptions. Its chief sponsor was Sen. Robert C. Byrd, D-W.Va.

Calendar—A list of measures or other matters (most of them favorably reported by committees) that are eligible for floor consideration. The House has four calendars; the Senate has two. A place on a calendar does not guarantee consideration. Each house decides which measures and matters it will take up, when, and in what order, in accordance with its rules and practices.

Calendar Wednesday—A House procedure that on Wednesdays permits its committees to bring up for floor consideration nonprivileged measures they have reported. The procedure is so cumbersome and susceptible to dilatory tactics, however, that it is rarely used.

Call Up—To bring a measure or report to the floor for immediate consideration.

Casework—Assistance to constituents who seek assistance in dealing with federal and local government agencies. Constituent service is a high priority in most members' offices.

Caucus—(1) A common term for the official organization of each party in each house. (2) The official title of the organization of House Democrats. House and Senate Republicans and Senate Democrats call their organizations "conferences." (3) A term for an informal group of members who share legislative interests, such as the Black Caucus, Hispanic Caucus, and Children's Caucus.

Censure—The strongest formal condemnation of a member for misconduct short of expulsion. A house usually adopts a resolution of censure to express its condemnation, after which the presiding officer reads its rebuke aloud to the member in the presence of his or her colleagues.

Chairman—The presiding officer of a committee, a subcommittee, or a task force. At meetings, the chairman preserves order, enforces the rules, recognizes members to speak or offer motions, and puts questions to a vote. The chairman of a committee or subcommittee usually appoints its staff and sets its agenda, subject to the panel's veto.

Chamber—The Capitol room in which a house of Congress normally holds its sessions. The chamber of the House of Representatives, officially called the Hall of the House, is considerably larger than that of the Senate because it must accommodate 435 representatives, five delegates, and one resident commissioner. Unlike the Senate chamber, members have no desks or assigned seats. In both chambers, the floor slopes downward to the well in front of the presiding officer's raised desk. A chamber is often referred to as "the floor," as when members are said to be on or going to the floor. Those expressions usually imply that the member's house is in session.

Christmas Tree Bill—Jargon for a bill adorned with amendments, many of them unrelated to the bill's subject, that provide benefits for interest groups, specific states, congressional districts, companies, and individuals.

Classes of Senators—A class consists of the thirty-three or thirty-four senators elected to a six-year term in the same general election. Because the terms of approximately one-third of the senators expire every two years, there are three classes.

Clean Bill—After a House committee extensively amends a bill, it often assembles its amendments and what is left of the bill into a new measure that one or more of its members introduce as a "clean bill." The revised measure is assigned a new number.

Clerk of the House—An officer of the House of Representatives responsible principally for administrative support of the legislative process in the House. The clerk is invariably the candidate of the majority party.

Cloakrooms—Two rooms with access to the rear of each chamber's floor, one for each party's members, where members may confer privately, sit quietly, or have a snack. The presiding officer sometimes urges members who are conversing too loudly on the floor to retire to their cloakrooms.

Closed Hearing—A hearing closed to the public and the media. A House committee may close a hearing only if it determines that disclosure of the testimony to be taken would endanger national security, violate any law, or tend to defame, degrade, or incriminate any person. The Senate has a similar rule. Both houses require roll-call votes in open session to close a hearing.

Closed Rule—A special rule reported from the House Rules Committee that prohibits amendments to a measure or that only permits amendments offered by the reporting committee.

Cloture—A Senate procedure that limits further consideration of a pending proposal to thirty hours to end a filibuster. Sixteen senators must first sign and submit a cloture petition to the presiding officer. One hour after the Senate meets on the second calendar day thereafter, the chair puts the motion to a yea-and-nay vote following a live quorum call. If three-fifths of all senators (sixty if there are no vacancies) vote for the motion, the Senate must take final action on the cloture proposal by the end of the thirty hours of consideration and may consider no other business until it takes that action. Cloture on a proposal to amend the Senate's standing rules requires approval by two-thirds of the senators present and voting.

Code of Official Conduct—A House rule that bans certain actions by House members, officers, and employees; requires them to conduct themselves in ways that "reflect creditably" on the House; and orders them to adhere to the spirit and the letter of House rules and those of its committees. The code's provisions govern the receipt of outside compensation, gifts, and honoraria, and the use of campaign funds; prohibit members from using their clerk-hire allowance to pay anyone who does not perform duties commensurate with that pay; forbid discrimination in members' hiring or treatment of employees on the grounds of race, color, religion, sex, disability, age, or national origin; restrict members convicted of a crime who might be punished by imprisonment of two or more years from participating in committee business or voting on the floor until exonerated or reelected; and restrict employees' contact with federal agencies on matters in which they have a significant financial interest. The Senate's rules contain some similar prohibitions.

College of Cardinals—A popular term for the subcommittee chairmen of the appropriations committees, reflecting their influence over appropriation measures. The chairmen of the full appropriations committees are sometimes referred to as popes.

Colloquy—A discussion between members to put a mutual understanding about the intent of a measure or amendment on the record. The discussion usually is scripted in advance.

Comity—The practice of maintaining mutual courtesy and civility between the two houses in their dealings with each other and in members' speeches on the floor. Although the practice is largely governed by long-established customs, a House rule explicitly cautions its members not to characterize any Senate action or inaction, refer to individual senators except under certain circumstances, or quote from Senate proceedings except to make legislative history on a measure. The Senate has no rule on the subject but references to the House have been held out of order on several occasions. Generally the houses do not interfere with each other's appropriations although minor conflicts sometimes occur. A refusal to receive a message from the other house has also been held to violate the practice of comity.

Committee—A panel of members elected or appointed to perform some service or function for its parent body. Congress has four types of committees: standing, special or select, joint, and, in the House, a Committee of the Whole. Committees conduct investigations, make studies, issue reports and recommendations, and, in the case of standing committees, review and prepare measures on their assigned subjects for action by their respective houses. Most committees divide their work among several subcommittees. With rare exceptions, the majority party in a house holds a majority of the seats on its committees, and their chairmen are also from that party.

Committee Jurisdiction—The legislative subjects and other functions assigned to a committee by rule, precedent, resolution, or statute. A committee's title usually indicates the general scope of its jurisdiction but often fails to mention other significant subjects assigned to it.

Committee of the Whole—Common name of the Committee of the Whole House on the State of the Union, a committee consisting of all members of the House of Representatives. Measures from the union calendar must be considered in the Committee of the Whole before the House officially completes action on them; the committee often considers other major bills as well. A quorum of the committee is 100, and it meets in the House chamber under a chairman appointed by the Speaker. Procedures in the Committee of the Whole expedite consideration of legislation because of its smaller quorum requirement, its ban on certain motions, and its five-minute rule for debate on amendments. The Senate no longer uses a Committee of the Whole.

Committee Ratios—The ratios of majority to minority party members on committees. By custom, the ratios of most committees reflect party strength in their respective houses as closely as possible.

Committee Report on a Measure—A document submitted by a committee to report a measure to its parent chamber. Customarily, the report explains the measure's purpose, describes provisions and any amendments recommended by the committee, and presents arguments for its approval.

Committee Veto—A procedure that requires an executive department or agency to submit certain proposed policies, programs, or action to designated committees for review before implementing them. Before 1983, when the Supreme Court declared that a legislative veto was unconstitutional, these provisions permitted committees to veto the proposals. Committees no longer conduct this type of policy review, and the term is now something of a misnomer. Nevertheless, agencies usually take the pragmatic approach of trying to reach a consensus with the committees before carrying out their proposals, especially when an appropriations committee is involved.

Concur—To agree to an amendment of the other house, either by adopting a motion to concur in that amendment or a motion to concur with an amendment to that amendment. After both houses have agreed to the same version of an amendment, neither house may amend it further, nor may any subsequent conference change it or delete it from the measure. Concurrence by one house in all amendments of the other house completes action on the measure; no vote is then necessary on the measure as a whole because both houses previously passed it.

Concurrent Resolution—A resolution that requires approval by both houses but does not need the president's signature and therefore cannot have the force of law. Concurrent resolutions deal with the prerogatives or internal affairs of Congress as a whole. Designated H Con Res in the House and S Con Res in the Senate, they are numbered consecutively in each house in their order of introduction during a two-year Congress.

Conferees—A common title for managers, the members from each house appointed to a conference committee. The Senate usually authorizes its presiding officer to appoint its conferees. The Speaker appoints House conferees and under a rule adopted in 1993 can remove conferees "at any time after an original appointment" and also appoint additional conferees at any time. Conferees are expected to support the positions of their houses despite their personal views, but in practice this is not always the case. The party ratios of conferees generally reflect the ratios in their houses. Each house may appoint as many conferees as it pleases. House conferees often outnumber their Senate colleagues; however, each house has only one vote in a conference, so the size of its delegation is immaterial.

Conference—(1) A formal meeting or series of meetings between members representing each house to reconcile House and Senate differences on a measure (occasionally several measures). Because one house cannot require the other to agree to its proposals, the conference usually reaches agreement by compromise. When a conference completes action on a measure, or as much action as appears possible, it sends its recommendations to both houses in the form of a conference report, accompanied by an explanatory statement. (2) The official title of the organization of all Democrats or Republicans in the Senate and of all Republicans in the House of Representatives. *(See Party Caucus.)*

Conference Committee—A temporary joint committee formed for the purpose of resolving differences between the houses on a measure. Major and controversial legislation usually requires conference committee action. Voting in a conference committee is not by individuals but within the House and Senate delegations. Consequently, a conference committee report requires the support of a majority of the conferees from each house. Both houses require that conference committees open their meetings to the public. The Senate's rule permits the committee to close its meetings if a majority of conferees in each delegation agree by a roll-call vote. The House rule permits closed meetings only if the House authorizes them to do so on a roll-call vote. Otherwise, there are no congressional rules governing the organization of, or procedure in, a conference committee. The committee chooses its chairman, but on measures that go to conference annually, such as general appropriation bills, the chairmanship traditionally rotates between the houses.

Conference Report—A document submitted to both houses that contains a conference committee's agreements for resolving their differences on a measure. It must be signed by a majority of the conferees from each house separately and must be accompanied by an explanatory statement. Both houses prohibit amendments to a conference report and require it to be accepted or rejected in its entirety.

Congress—(1) The national legislature of the United States, consisting of the House of Representatives and the Senate. (2) The national legislature in office during a two-year period. Congresses are numbered sequentially; thus, the 1st Congress of 1789–1791 and the 106th Congress of 1999–2001. Before 1935, the two-year period began on the first Monday in December of odd-numbered years. Since then it has extended from January of an odd-numbered year through noon on Jan. 3 of the next odd-numbered year. A Congress usually holds two annual sessions, but some have had three sessions and the 67th Congress had four. When a Congress expires, measures die if they have not yet been enacted.

Congressional Accountability Act of 1995 (CAA)—An act applying eleven labor, workplace, and civil rights laws to the legislative branch and establishing procedures and remedies for legislative branch employees with grievances in violation of these laws. The following laws are covered by the CAA: Fair Labor Standards Act of 1938; Title VII of the Civil Rights Act of 1964; Americans with Disabilities Act of 1990; Age Discrimination in Employment Act of 1967; Family and Medical Leave Act of 1993; Occupational Safety and Health Act of 1970; Chapter 71 of Title 5, *U.S. Code* (relating to federal service labor-management relations); Employee Polygraph Protection Act of 1988; Worker Adjustment and Retraining Notification Act; Rehabilitation Act of 1973; and Chapter 43 of Title 38, *U.S. Code* (relating to veterans' employment and reemployment).

Congressional Budget and Impoundment Control Act of 1974—The law that established the basic elements of the congressional budget process, the House and Senate budget committees, the Congressional Budget Office, and the procedures for congressional review of impoundments in the form of rescissions and deferrals proposed by the president. The budget process consists of procedures for coordinating congressional revenue and spending decisions made in separate tax, appropriations, and legislative measures. The impoundment provisions were intended to give Congress greater control over executive branch actions that delay or prevent the spending of funds provided by Congress.

Congressional Budget Office (CBO)—A congressional support agency created by the Congressional Budget and Impoundment Control Act of 1974 to provide nonpartisan budgetary information and analysis to Congress and its committees. CBO acts as a scorekeeper when Congress is voting on the federal budget, tracking bills to ensure they comply with overall budget goals. The agency also estimates what proposed legislation would cost over a five-year period. CBO works most closely with the House and Senate Budget committees.

Congressional Directory—The official who's who of Congress, usually published during the first session of a two-year Congress.

Congressional District—The geographical area represented by a single member of the House of Representatives. For states with only one representative, the entire state is a congressional district. After the reapportionment from the 2000 census, seven states had only one representative each: Alaska, Delaware, Montana, North Dakota, South Dakota, Vermont, and Wyoming.

Congressional Record—The daily, printed, and substantially verbatim account of proceedings in both the House and Senate chambers. Extraneous materials submitted by members appear in a section titled "Extensions of Remarks." A "Daily Digest" appendix contains highlights of the day's floor and committee action plus a list of committee meetings and floor agendas for the next day's session.

Although the official reporters of each house take down every word spoken during the proceedings, members are permitted to edit and "revise and extend" their remarks before they are printed. In the Senate section, all speeches, articles, and other material submitted by senators but not actually spoken or read on the floor are set off by large black dots, called bullets. However, bullets do not appear when a senator reads part of a speech and inserts the rest. In the House section, undelivered speeches and materials are printed in a distinctive typeface. The term "permanent *Record*" refers to the bound volumes of the daily *Records* of an entire session of Congress.

Congressional Research Service (CRS)—Established in 1917, a department of the Library of Congress whose staff provide nonpartisan, objective analysis and information on virtually any subject to committees, members, and staff of Congress. Originally the Legislative Reference Service, it is the oldest congressional support agency.

Congressional Support Agencies—A term often applied to three agencies in the legislative branch that provide nonpartisan information and analysis to committees and members of Congress: the Congressional Budget Office (CBO), the Congressional Research Service (CRS) of the Library of Congress, and the Government Accountability Office (GAO)—previously called the General Accounting Office.

Congressional Terms of Office—A term normally begins on Jan. 3 of the year following a general election and runs two years for representatives and six years for senators. A representative chosen in a special election to fill a vacancy is sworn in for the remainder of the predecessor's term. An individual appointed to fill a Senate vacancy usually serves until the next general election or until the end of the predecessor's term, whichever comes first. Some states, however, require their governors to call a special election to fill a Senate vacancy shortly after an appointment has been made.

Constitutional Option—*(See Nuclear Option.)*

Constitutional Rules—Constitutional provisions that prescribe procedures for Congress. In addition to certain types of votes required in particular situations, these provisions include the following: (1) the House chooses its Speaker, the Senate its president pro tempore, and both houses their officers; (2) each house requires a majority quorum to conduct business; (3) less than a majority may adjourn from day to day and compel the attendance of absent members; (4) neither house may adjourn for more than three days without the consent of the other; (5) each house must keep a journal; (6) the yeas and nays are ordered when supported by one-fifth of the members present; (7) all revenue-raising bills must originate in the House, but the Senate may propose amendments to them. The Constitution also sets out the procedure in the House for electing a president, the procedure in the Senate for electing a vice president, the procedure for filling a vacancy in the office of vice president, and the procedure for overriding a presidential veto.

Constitutional Votes—Constitutional provisions that require certain votes or voting methods in specific situations. They include (1) the yeas and nays at the desire of one-fifth of the members present; (2) a two-thirds vote by the yeas and nays to override a veto; (3) a two-thirds vote by one house to expel one of its members and by both houses to propose a constitutional amendment; (4) a two-thirds vote of senators present to convict someone whom the House has impeached and to consent to ratification of treaties; (5) a two-thirds vote in each house to remove political disabilities from persons who have engaged in insurrection or rebellion or given aid or comfort to the enemies of the United States; (6) a majority vote in each house to fill a vacancy in the office of vice president; (7) a majority vote of all states to elect a president in the House of Representatives when no candidate receives a majority of the electoral votes; (8) a majority vote of all senators when the Senate elects a vice president under the same circumstances; and (9) the casting vote of the vice president in case of tie votes in the Senate.

Contempt of Congress—Willful obstruction of the proper functions of Congress. Most frequently, it is a refusal to obey a subpoena to appear and testify before a committee or to produce documents demanded by it. Such obstruction is a misdemeanor and persons cited for contempt are subject to prosecution in federal courts. A house cites an individual for contempt by agreeing to a privileged resolution to that effect reported by a committee. The presiding officer then refers the matter to a U.S. attorney for prosecution.

Continuing Body—A characterization of the Senate on the theory that it continues from Congress to Congress and has existed continuously since it first convened in 1789. The rationale for the theory is that under the system of staggered six-year terms for senators, the terms of only about one-third of them expire after each Congress and, therefore, a quorum of the Senate is always in office. Consequently, under this theory, the Senate, unlike the House, does not have to adopt its rules at the beginning of each Congress because those rules continue from one Congress to the next. This makes it extremely difficult for the Senate to change its rules against the opposition of a determined minority because those rules require a two-thirds vote of the senators present and voting to invoke cloture on a proposed rules change.

Continuing Resolution (CR)—A joint resolution that provides funds to continue the operation of federal agencies and programs at the beginning of a new fiscal year if their annual appropriation bills have not yet been enacted; also called continuing appropriations. Continuing resolutions are enacted shortly before or after the new fiscal year begins and usually make funds available for a specified period. Additional resolutions are often needed after the first expires. Some continuing resolutions have provided appropriations for an entire fiscal year. Continuing resolutions for specific periods customarily fix a rate at which agencies may incur obligations based either on the previous year's appropriations, the president's budget request, or the amount as specified in the agency's regular annual appropriation bill if that bill has already been passed by one or both houses. In the House, continuing resolutions are privileged after Sept. 15.

Contract Authority—Statutory authority permitting an agency to enter into contracts or incur other obligations even though it has not received an appropriation to pay for them. Congress must eventually fund them because the government is legally liable for such payments. The Congressional Budget Act of 1974 requires, with a few exceptions, that new contract authority may not be used unless provided for in advance by an appropriation act.

Cordon Rule—A Senate rule that requires a committee report to show changes the reported measure would make in current law. The rule is named after its sponsor, Sen. Guy Cordon, R-Ore. The House's analogous rule is called the Ramseyer rule. *(See Ramseyer Rule.)*

Correcting Recorded Votes—The rules of both houses prohibit members from changing their votes after a vote result has been announced. Nevertheless, the Senate permits its members to withdraw or change their votes, by unanimous consent, immediately after the announcement. In rare instances, senators have been granted unanimous consent to change their votes several days or weeks after the announcement. Votes tallied by the electronic voting system in the House may not be changed. But when a vote actually given is not recorded during an oral call of the roll, a member may demand a correction as a matter of right. On all other alleged errors in a recorded vote, the Speaker determines whether the circumstances justify a change. Occasionally, members merely announce that they were incorrectly recorded; announcements can occur hours, days, or even months after the vote and appear in the *Congressional Record.*

Cosponsor—A member who has joined one or more other members to sponsor a measure. Joining on the day of introduction qualifies the member as an original sponsor.

Credit Authority—Authority granted to an agency to incur direct loan obligations or to make loan guarantee commitments. The Congressional Budget Act of 1974 bans congressional consideration of credit authority legislation unless the extent of that authority is made subject to provisions in appropriation acts.

C-SPAN—Cable-Satellite Public Affairs Network, which provides live, gavel-to-gavel coverage of Senate floor proceedings on one cable television channel and coverage of House floor proceedings on another channel. C-SPAN also televises important committee hearings in both houses. Each house also transmits its televised proceedings directly to congressional offices.

Current Services Estimates—Executive branch estimates of the anticipated costs of federal programs and operations for the next and future fiscal years at existing levels of service and assuming no new initiatives or changes in existing law. The president submits these estimates to Congress with the annual budget and includes an explanation of the underlying economic and policy assumptions on which they are based, such as anticipated rates of inflation, real economic growth, and unemployment, plus program caseloads and pay increases.

Custody of the Papers—Possession of an engrossed measure and certain related basic documents that the two houses produce as they try to resolve their differences over the measure.

Dance of the Swans and the Ducks—A whimsical description of the gestures some members use in connection with a request for a recorded vote, especially in the House. When members want their colleagues to stand in support of the request, they move their hands and arms in a gentle upward motion resembling the beginning flight of a graceful swan. When they want their colleagues to remain seated to avoid such a vote, they move their hands and arms in a vigorous downward motion resembling a diving duck.

Dean—Within a state's delegation in the House of Representatives, the member with the longest continuous service; also the longest-serving member of the House.

Debate—In congressional parlance, speeches delivered during consideration of a measure, motion, or other matter, as distinguished from speeches in other parliamentary situations, such as one-minute and special order speeches when no business is pending. Virtually all debate in the House of Representatives is under some kind of time limitation. Most debate in the Senate is unlimited; that is, a senator, once recognized, may speak for as long as he or she chooses, unless the Senate invokes cloture.

Debt Limit—The maximum amount of outstanding federal public debt permitted by law. The limit (or ceiling) covers virtually all debt incurred by the government except agency debt. Each congressional budget resolution sets forth the new debt limit that may be required under its provisions.

Deferral—An impoundment of funds for a specific period of time that may not extend beyond the fiscal year in which it is proposed. Under the Impoundment Control Act of 1974, the president must notify Congress that he is deferring the spending or obligation of funds provided by law for a project or activity. Congress can disapprove the deferral by legislation.

Deficit—The amount by which the government's outlays exceed its budget receipts for a given fiscal year. Both the president's budget and the annual congressional budget resolution provide estimates of the deficit or surplus for the upcoming and several future fiscal years.

Degrees of Amendment—Designations that indicate the relationships of amendments to the text of a measure and to each other. In general, an amendment offered directly to the text of a measure is an amendment in the first degree, and an amendment to that amendment is an amendment in the second degree. Both houses normally prohibit amendments in the third degree—that is, an amendment to an amendment to an amendment.

Delegate—A nonvoting member of the House of Representatives elected to a two-year term from the District of Columbia, the territory of Guam, the territory of the Virgin Islands, the territory of American Samoa, or the territory of the Northern Marianas. By law, delegates may not vote in the full House but they may participate in debate, offer motions (except to reconsider), and serve and vote on standing and select committees. On their committees, delegates possess the same powers and privileges as other members and the Speaker may appoint them to appropriate conference committees and select committees.

Denounce—A formal action that condemns a member for misbehavior; considered by some experts to be equivalent to censure. *(See Censure.)*

Dilatory Tactics—Procedural actions intended to delay or prevent action by a house or a committee. They include, among others, offering numerous motions, demanding quorum calls and recorded votes at every opportunity, making numerous points of order and parliamentary inquiries, and speaking as long as the applicable rules permit. The Senate rules permit a battery of dilatory tactics, especially lengthy speeches, except under cloture. In the House, possible dilatory tactics are more limited. Speeches are always subject to time limits and debate-ending motions. Moreover, a House rule instructs the Speaker not to entertain dilatory motions and lets the Speaker decide whether a motion is dilatory. However, the Speaker may not override the constitutional right of a member to demand the yeas and nays and in practice usually waits for a point of order before exercising that authority. *(See Cloture.)*

Discharge a Committee—Remove a measure from a committee to which it has been referred in order to make it available for floor consideration. Noncontroversial measures are often discharged by unanimous consent. However, because congressional committees have no obligation to report measures referred to them, each house has procedures to extract controversial measures from recalcitrant committees.

District Office—Representatives maintain one or more offices in their districts for the purpose of assisting and communicating with constituents. The costs of maintaining these offices are paid from members' official allowances. Senators can use the official expense allowance to rent offices in their home state, subject to a funding formula based on their state's population and other factors.

District Work Period—The House term for a scheduled congressional recess during which members may visit their districts and conduct constituency business.

Division Vote—A vote in which the chair first counts those in favor of a proposition and then those opposed to it, with no record made of how each member votes. In the Senate, the chair may count raised hands or ask senators to stand, whereas the House requires members to stand; hence, often called a standing vote. Committees in both houses ordinarily use a show of hands. A division usually occurs after a voice vote and may be demanded by any member or ordered by the chair if there is any doubt about the outcome of the voice vote. The demand for a division can also come before a voice vote. In the Senate, the demand must come before the result of a voice vote is announced. It may be made after a voice vote announcement in the House, but only if no intervening business has transpired and only if the member was standing and seeking recognition at the time of the announcement. A demand for the yeas and nays or, in the House, for a recorded vote takes precedence over a division vote.

Earmark—A set-aside within an appropriations measure for a specific purpose.

Effective Dates—Provisions of an act that specify when the entire act or individual provisions in it become effective as law. Most acts become effective on the date of enactment, but it is sometimes necessary or prudent to delay the effective dates of some provisions.

Electronic Voting—Since 1973 the House has used an electronic voting system to record the yeas and nays and to conduct recorded votes. Members vote by inserting their voting cards in one of the boxes at several locations in the chamber. They are given at least fifteen minutes to vote. When several votes occur immediately after each other, the Speaker may reduce the voting time to five minutes on the second and subsequent votes. The Speaker may allow additional time on each vote but may also close a vote at any time after the minimum time has expired. Members can change their votes at any time before the Speaker announces the result. The House also uses the electronic system for quorum calls. While a vote is in progress, a large panel above the Speaker's desk displays how each member has voted. Smaller panels on either side of the chamber display running totals of the votes and the time remaining. The Senate does not have electronic voting.

Enacting Clause—The opening language of each bill, beginning "Be it enacted by the Senate and House of Representatives of the United States of America in Congress assembled. . . ." This language gives legal force to measures approved by Congress and signed by the president or enacted over the president's veto. A successful motion to strike it from a bill kills the entire measure.

Engrossed Bill—The official copy of a bill or joint resolution as passed by one chamber, including the text as amended by floor action, and certified by the clerk of the House or the secretary of the Senate (as appropriate). Amendments by one house to a measure or amendments of the other also are engrossed. House engrossed documents are printed on blue paper; the Senate's are printed on white paper.

Enrolled Bill—The final official copy of a bill or joint resolution passed in identical form by both houses. An enrolled bill usually is printed on parchment. After it is certified by the chief officer of the house in which it originated and signed by the House Speaker and the Senate president pro tempore, the measure is sent to the White House for the president's signature.

Entitlement Program—A federal program under which individuals, businesses, or units of government that meet the requirements or qualifications established by law are entitled to receive certain payments if they seek such payments. Major examples include Social Security, Medicare, Medicaid, unemployment insurance, and military and federal civilian pensions. Congress cannot control their expenditures by refusing to appropriate the sums necessary to fund them because the government is legally obligated to pay eligible recipients the amounts to which the law entitles them.

Equality of the Houses—A component of the Constitution's emphasis on checks and balances under which each house is given essentially equal status in the enactment of legislation and in the relations and negotiations between the two houses. Although the House of Representatives initiates revenue and appropriation measures, the Senate has the right to amend them. Either house may initiate any other type of legislation, and neither can force the other to agree to, or even act on, its measures. Moreover, each house has a potential veto over the other because legislation requires agreement by both. Similarly, in a conference to resolve their differences on a measure, each house casts one vote, as determined by a majority of its conferees. In most other national bicameral legislatures, the powers of one house are markedly greater than those of the other.

Ethics Rules—Several rules or standing orders in each house that mandate certain standards of conduct for members and congressional employees in finance, employment, franking, and other areas. The Senate Select Committee on Ethics and the House Committee on Standards of Official Conduct investigate alleged violations of conduct and recommend appropriate actions to their respective houses.

Exclusive Committee—(1) Under the rules of the Republican Conference and House Democratic Caucus, a standing committee whose members usually cannot serve on any other standing committee. As of 2010 the Appropriations, Energy and Commerce (for Democrats beginning service in the 105th Congress), Financial Services (for Democrats beginning in the 109th Congress), Ways and Means, and Rules committees were designated as exclusive committees. (2) Under the rules of the two-party conferences in the Senate, a standing committee whose members may not simultaneously serve on any other exclusive committee.

Executive Calendar—The Senate's calendar for executive business, namely treaties and nominations. The calendar numbers indicate the order in which items were referred to the calendar but have no bearing on when or if the Senate will consider them. The Senate, by motion or unanimous consent, resolves itself into executive session to consider them.

Executive Document—A document, usually a treaty, sent by the president to the Senate for approval. It is referred to a committee in the same manner as other measures. Resolutions to ratify treaties have their own "treaty document" numbers. For example, the first treaty submitted in the 106th Congress would be "Treaty Doc 106-1."

Executive Order—A unilateral proclamation by the president that has a policy-making or legislative impact. Members of Congress have challenged some executive orders on the grounds that they usurped the authority of the legislative branch. Although the Supreme Court has ruled that a particular order exceeded the president's authority, it has upheld others as falling within the president's general constitutional powers.

Executive Privilege—The assertion that presidents have the right to withhold certain information from Congress. Presidents have based their claim on (1) the constitutional separation of powers; (2) the need for secrecy in military and diplomatic affairs; (3) the need to protect individuals from unfavorable publicity; (4) the need to safeguard the confidential exchange of ideas in the executive branch; and (5) the need to protect individuals who provide confidential advice to the president.

Executive Session—(1) A Senate meeting devoted to the consideration of treaties or nominations. Normally, the Senate meets in legislative session; it resolves itself into executive session, by motion or by unanimous consent, to deal with its executive business. It also keeps a separate *Journal* for executive sessions. Executive sessions are usually open to the public, but the Senate may choose to close them.

Expulsion—A member's removal from office by a two-thirds vote of his or her chamber; the supermajority is required by the Constitution. It is the most severe and most rarely used sanction a house can invoke against a member. Although the Constitution provides no explicit grounds for expulsion, the courts have ruled that it may be applied only for misconduct during a member's term of office, not for conduct before the member's election. Generally, neither house will consider expulsion of a member convicted of a crime until the judicial processes have been exhausted. At that stage, members sometimes resign rather than face expulsion. In 1977 the House adopted a rule urging members convicted of certain crimes to voluntarily abstain from voting or participating in other legislative business.

Extensions of Remarks—An appendix to the daily *Congressional Record* that consists primarily of miscellaneous extraneous material submitted by members. It often includes members' statements not delivered on the floor, newspaper articles and editorials, praise for a member's constituents, and noteworthy letters received by a member, among other material. Representatives supply the bulk of this material; senators submit little. "Extensions of Remarks" pages are separately numbered, and each number is preceded by the letter "E." Materials may be placed in the Extensions of Remarks section only by unanimous consent. Usually, one member of each party makes the request each day on behalf of his or her party colleagues after the House has completed its legislative business of the day.

Fast Track—This is a procedure that circumvents or speeds up all or part of the legislative process. Some rulemaking statutes prescribe expedited procedures for certain measures, such as trade agreements.

Federal Debt—The total amount of monies borrowed and not yet repaid by the federal government. Federal debt consists of public debt and agency debt. Public debt is the portion of the federal debt borrowed by the Treasury or the Federal Financing Bank directly from the public or from another federal fund or account. For example, the Treasury regularly borrows money from the Social Security trust fund. Public debt accounts for about 99 percent of the federal debt. Agency debt refers to the debt incurred by federal agencies such as the Export-Import Bank but excluding the Treasury and the Federal Financing Bank, which are authorized by law to borrow funds from the public or from another government fund or account.

Filibuster—The use of time-consuming parliamentary tactics by one member or a minority of members to delay, modify, or defeat proposed legislation or rules changes. Filibusters are also sometimes used to delay urgently needed measures to force the body to accept other legislation. The Senate's rules permitting unlimited debate and the extraordinary majority it requires to impose cloture make filibustering particularly effective in that chamber. Under the stricter rules of the House, filibusters in that body are short-lived and therefore ineffective and rarely attempted.

Fiscal Year—The federal government's annual accounting period. It begins Oct. 1 and ends on the following Sept. 30. A fiscal year is designated by the calendar year in which it ends and is often referred to as FY. Thus, fiscal year 2009 began Oct. 1, 2008, ended Sept. 30, 2009, and is called FY09. In theory, Congress is supposed to complete action on all budgetary measures applying to a fiscal year before that year begins. It rarely does so.

Five-Minute Rule—(1) A House rule that limits debate on an amendment offered in the Committee of the Whole to five minutes for its sponsor and five minutes for an opponent. In practice, the committee routinely permits longer debate by three devices: offering pro forma amendments, each debatable for five minutes; unanimous consent for a member to speak longer than five minutes; and special rule. Consequently, debate on an amendment sometimes continues for hours. At any time after the first ten minutes, however, the committee may shut off debate immediately or by a specified time, either by unanimous consent or by majority vote on a nondebatable motion. The motion, which dates from 1847, is also used in the House as in Committee of the Whole, where debate also may be shut off by a motion for the previous question.

Floor—The ground level of the House or Senate chamber where members sit and the houses conduct their business. When members are attending a meeting of their house they are said to be on the floor. Floor action refers to the procedural actions taken during floor consideration such as deciding on motions, taking up measures, amending them, and voting.

Floor Manager—A majority party member responsible for guiding a measure through its floor consideration in a house and for devising the political and procedural strategies that might be required to get it passed. The presiding officer gives the floor manager priority recognition to debate, offer amendments, oppose amendments, and make crucial procedural motions. The minority party member is referred to as the minority floor manager.

Frank—Informally, members' legal right to send official mail postage free under their signatures; often called the franking privilege. Technically, it is the autographic or facsimile signature used on envelopes instead of stamps that permits members and certain congressional officers to send their official mail free of charge. The franking privilege has been authorized by law since the first Congress, except for a few months in 1873. Congress reimburses the U.S. Postal Service for the franked mail it handles.

Function *or* **Functional Category**—A broad category of national need and spending of budgetary significance. A category provides an accounting method for allocating and keeping track of budgetary resources and expenditures for that function because it includes all budget accounts related to the function's subject or purpose such as agriculture, administration of justice, commerce and housing, and energy. Functions do not necessarily correspond with appropriations acts or with the budgets of individual agencies. As of 2010 there were twenty functional categories, each divided into a number of subfunctions.

Gag Rule—A pejorative term for any type of special rule reported by the House Rules Committee that proposes to prohibit amendments to a measure or only permits amendments offered by the reporting committee.

Galleries—The balconies overlooking each chamber from which the public, news media, staff, and others may observe floor proceedings.

General Appropriation Bill—A term applied to each of the annual bills that provide funds for most federal agencies and programs and also to the supplemental appropriation bills that contain appropriations for more than one agency or program.

Germaneness—The requirement that an amendment be closely related—in terms of subject or purpose, for example—to the text it proposes to amend. A House rule requires that all amendments be germane. In the Senate, only amendments offered to general appropriation bills and budget measures or proposed under cloture must be germane. Germaneness rules can be waived by suspension of the rules in both houses, by unanimous consent agreements in the Senate, and by special rules from the Rules Committee in the House. Moreover, presiding officers usually do not enforce germaneness rules on their own initiative; therefore, a nongermane amendment can be adopted if no member raises a point of order against it. Under cloture in the Senate, however, the chair may take the initiative to rule amendments out of order as not being germane, without a point of order being made. All House debate must be germane except during general debate in the Committee of the Whole, but special rules invariably require that such debate be "confined to the bill." The Senate requires germane debate only during the first three hours of each daily session. Under the precedents of both houses, an amendment can be relevant but not necessarily germane. A crucial factor in determining germaneness in the House is how the subject of a measure or matter is defined. For example, the subject of a measure authorizing construction of a naval vessel is defined as being the construction of a single vessel; therefore, an amendment to authorize an additional vessel is not germane.

Gerrymandering—The manipulation of legislative district boundaries to benefit a particular party, politician, or minority group. The term originated in 1812 when the Massachusetts legislature redrew the lines of state legislative districts to favor the party of Gov. Elbridge Gerry, and some critics said one district resembled a salamander. *(See also Congressional District; Redistricting.)*

Government Accountability Office (GAO)—A congressional support agency, often referred to as the investigative arm of Congress. It evaluates and audits federal agencies and programs in the United States and abroad on its initiative or at the request of congressional committees or members. The office, created in 1921, was called the General Accounting Office until 2004.

Gramm-Rudman-Hollings Act of 1985—Common name for the Balanced Budget and Emergency Deficit Control Act of 1985, which established new budget procedures intended to balance the federal budget by fiscal year 1991. (The timetable subsequently was extended and then deleted.) The act's chief sponsors were senators Phil Gramm, R-Texas, Warren Rudman, R-N.H., and Ernest Hollings, D-S.C.

Grandfather Clause—A provision in a measure, law, or rule that exempts an individual, entity, or a defined category of individuals or entities from complying with a new policy or restriction. For example, a bill that would raise taxes on persons who reach the age of sixty-five after a certain date inherently grandfathers out those who are sixty-five before that date. Similarly, a Senate rule limiting senators to two major committee assignments also grandfathers some senators who were sitting on a third major committee before a specified date.

Grants-in-Aid—Payments by the federal government to state and local governments to help provide for assistance programs or public services.

Hearing—Committee or subcommittee meetings to receive testimony on proposed legislation during investigations or for oversight purposes. Relatively few bills are important enough to justify formal hearings. Witnesses often include experts, government officials, spokespersons for interested groups, officials of the Government Accountability Office, and members of Congress.

Hold—A senator's request that his or her party leaders delay or halt floor consideration of certain legislation or presidential nominations. The majority leader usually honors a hold for a reasonable period of time, especially if its purpose is to assure the senator that the matter will not be called up during his or her absence or to give the senator time to gather necessary information.

Hold (or Have) the Floor—A member's right to speak without interruption, unless he or she violates a rule, after recognition by the presiding officer. At the member's discretion, he or she may yield to another member for a question in the Senate or for a question or statement in the House, but may reclaim the floor at any time.

Hold-Harmless Clause—In legislation providing a new formula for allocating federal funds, a clause to ensure that recipients of those funds do not receive less in a future year than they did in the current year if the new formula would result in a reduction for them. Similar to a grandfather clause, it has been used most frequently to soften the impact of sudden reductions in federal grants. *(See Grandfather Clause.)*

Hopper—A box on the clerk's desk in the House chamber into which members deposit bills and resolutions to introduce them. In House jargon, to drop a bill in the hopper is to introduce it.

Hour Rule—A House rule that permits members, when recognized, to hold the floor in debate for no more than one hour each. The majority party member customarily yields one-half the time to a minority member. Although the hour rule applies to general debate in the Committee of the Whole as well as in the House, special rules routinely vary the length of time for such debate and its control to fit the circumstances of particular measures.

House as in Committee of the Whole—A hybrid combination of procedures from the general rules of the House and from the rules of the Committee of the Whole, sometimes used to expedite consideration of a measure on the floor.

House Calendar—The calendar reserved for all public bills and resolutions that do not raise revenue or directly or indirectly appropriate money or property when they are favorably reported by House committees.

House Manual—A commonly used title for the handbook of the rules of the House of Representatives, published in each Congress. Its official title is *Constitution, Jefferson's Manual, and Rules of the House of Representatives.*

House of Representatives—The house of Congress in which states are represented roughly in proportion to their populations, but every state is guaranteed at least one representative. By law, the number of voting representatives is fixed at 435. Five delegates and one resident commissioner also serve in the House; they may vote in their committees but not on the House floor. Although the House and Senate have equal legislative power, the Constitution gives the House sole authority to originate revenue measures. The House also claims the right to originate appropriation measures, a claim the Senate disputes in theory but concedes in practice. The House has the sole power to impeach (only the Senate convicts, however) and elects the president when no candidate has received a majority of the electoral votes. The House is sometimes referred to as the lower body.

Immunity (1) Members' constitutional protection from lawsuits and arrest in connection with their legislative duties. They may not be tried for libel or slander for anything they say on the floor of a house or in committee. Nor may they be arrested while attending sessions of their houses or when traveling to or from sessions of Congress, except when charged with treason, a felony, or a breach of the peace. (2) In the case of a witness before a committee, a grant of protection from prosecution based on that person's testimony to the committee. It is used to compel witnesses to testify who would otherwise refuse to do so on the constitutional ground of possible self-incrimination. Under such a grant, none of a witness's testimony may be used against him or her in a court proceeding except in a prosecution for perjury or for giving a false statement to Congress. *(See also Contempt of Congress.)*

Impeachment—The first step to remove the president, the vice president, Supreme Court justices, or other federal civil officers from office and to disqualify them from any future federal office "of honor, Trust or Profit." An impeachment is a formal charge of treason, bribery, or "other high Crimes and Misdemeanors." The House has the sole power of impeachment and the Senate the sole power of trying the charges and convicting. The House impeaches by a simple majority vote; conviction requires a two-thirds vote of all senators present.

Impeachment Trial, Removal, and Disqualification—The Senate conducts an impeachment trial under a separate set of twenty-six rules that appears in the *Senate Manual.* Under the Constitution, the chief justice of the Supreme Court presides over trials of the president, but the vice president, the president pro tempore, or any other senator may preside over the impeachment trial of another official.

The Constitution requires senators to take an oath for an impeachment trial. During the trial, senators may not engage in colloquies or participate in arguments, but they may submit questions in writing to House managers or defense counsel. After the trial concludes, the Senate votes separately on each article of impeachment without debate unless the Senate orders the doors closed for private discussions. During deliberations senators may speak no more than once on a question, not for more than ten minutes on an interlocutory question and not more than fifteen minutes on the final question. These rules may be set aside by unanimous consent or suspended on motion by a two-thirds vote.

The Senate's impeachment trial of President Bill Clinton in 1999 was only the second such trial involving a president. It continued for five weeks, with the Senate voting not to convict on the two impeachment articles.

Senate impeachment rules allow the Senate, at its discretion, to name a committee to hear evidence and conduct the trial, with all senators thereafter voting on the charges. The impeachment trials of three federal judges were conducted this way, and the Supreme Court upheld the validity of these rules in *Nixon v. United States,* 506 U.S. 224, 1993.

An official convicted on impeachment charges is removed from office immediately. However, the convicted official is not barred from holding a federal office in the future unless the Senate, after its conviction vote, also approves a resolution disqualifying the convicted official from future office. For example, federal judge Alcee L. Hastings was impeached and convicted in 1989, but the Senate did not vote to bar him from office in the future. In 1992 Hastings was elected to the House of Representatives, and no challenge was raised against seating him when he took the oath of office in 1993.

Impoundment—An executive branch action or inaction that delays or withholds the expenditure or obligation of budget authority provided by law. The Impoundment Control Act of 1974 classifies impoundments as either deferrals or rescissions, requires the president to notify Congress about all such actions, and gives Congress authority to approve or reject them.

Inspector General in the House of Representatives—A position established with the passage of the House Administrative Reform Resolution of 1992. The duties of the office have been revised several times and are now contained in House Rule II. The inspector general (IG), who is subject to the policy direction and oversight of the Committee on House Administration, is appointed for a Congress jointly by the Speaker and the majority and minority leaders of the House. The IG communicates the results of audits to the House officers or officials who were the subjects of the audits and suggests appropriate corrective measures. The IG submits a report of each audit to the Speaker, the majority and minority leaders, and the chairman and ranking minority member of the House Administration Committee; notifies these five members in the case of any financial irregularity discovered; and reports to the Committee on Standards of Official Conduct on possible violations of House rules or any applicable law by any House member, officer, or employee. The IG's office also has certain duties to audit various financial operations of the House that had previously been performed by the Government Accountability Office.

Instruct Conferees—A formal action by a house urging its conferees to uphold a particular position on a measure in conference. The instruction may be to insist on certain provisions in the measure as passed by that house or to accept a provision in the version passed by the other house. Instructions to conferees are not binding because the primary responsibility of conferees is to reach agreement on a measure and neither house can compel the other to accept particular provisions or positions.

Investigative Power—The authority of Congress and its committees to pursue investigations, upheld by the Supreme Court but limited to matters related to, and in furtherance of, a legitimate task of the Congress. Standing committees in both houses are permanently authorized to investigate matters within their jurisdictions. Major investigations are sometimes conducted by temporary select, special, or joint committees established by resolutions for that purpose.

Some rules of the House provide certain safeguards for witnesses and others during investigative hearings. These permit counsel to accompany witnesses, require that each witness receive a copy of the committee's rules, and order the committee to go into closed session if it believes the testimony to be heard might defame, degrade, or incriminate any person. The committee may subsequently decide to hear such testimony in open session. The Senate has no rules of this kind.

Item Veto—Item veto authority, which is available to most state governors, allows governors to eliminate or reduce items in legislative measures presented for their signature without vetoing the entire measure, and sign the rest into law. A similar authority was briefly granted to the U.S. president under the Line Item Veto Act of 1996. According to the majority opinion of the Supreme Court in its 1998 decision overturning that law, a constitutional amendment would be necessary to give the president item such veto authority.

Jefferson's Manual—Short title of *Jefferson's Manual of Parliamentary Practice,* prepared by Thomas Jefferson for his guidance when he was president of the Senate from 1797 to 1801. Although it reflects English parliamentary practice in his day, many procedures in both houses of Congress are still rooted in its basic precepts. Under a House rule adopted in 1837, the manual's provisions govern House procedures when applicable and when they are not inconsistent with its standing rules and orders. The Senate, however, has never officially acknowledged it as a direct authority for its legislative procedure.

Johnson Rule—A policy instituted in 1953 under which all Democratic senators are assigned to one major committee before any Democrat is assigned to two. The Johnson Rule is named after its author, Sen. Lyndon B. Johnson, D-Texas, then the Senate's Democratic leader. Senate Republicans adopted a similar policy soon thereafter.

Joint Committee—A committee composed of members selected from each house. The functions of most joint committees involve investigation, research, or oversight of agencies closely related to Congress. Permanent joint committees, created by statute, are sometimes called standing joint committees. Once quite numerous, only four joint committees remained as of 2010: Joint Economic, Joint Taxation, Joint Library, and Joint Printing. None has authority to report legislation.

Joint Explanatory Statement—This is a statement appended to a conference report that explains in plain English the conference agreement and the intent of the conferees.

Joint Resolution—A legislative measure that Congress uses for purposes other than general legislation. Similar to a bill, it has the force of law when passed by both houses and either approved by the president or passed over the president's veto. Unlike a bill, a joint resolution enacted into law is not called an act; it retains its original title. Most often, joint resolutions deal with such relatively limited matters as the correction of errors in existing law, continuing appropriations, a single appropriation, or the establishment of permanent joint committees. Unlike bills, however, joint resolutions also are used to propose constitutional amendments; these do not require the president's signature and become effective only when ratified by three-fourths of the states. The House designates joint resolutions as H J Res, the Senate as S J Res. Each house numbers its joint resolutions consecutively in the order of introduction during a two-year Congress.

Joint Session—Informally, any combined meeting of the Senate and the House. Technically, a joint session is a combined meeting to count the electoral votes for president and vice president or to hear a presidential address, such as the State of the Union message; any other formal combined gathering of both houses is a joint meeting. Joint sessions are authorized by concurrent resolutions and are held in the House chamber, because of its larger seating capacity. Although the president of the Senate and the Speaker sit side by side at the Speaker's desk during combined meetings, the former presides over the electoral count and the latter presides on all other occasions and introduces the president or other guest speaker. The president and other guests may address a joint session or meeting only by invitation.

Joint Sponsorship—Two or more members sponsoring the same measure.

Journal—The official record of House or Senate actions, including every motion offered, every vote cast, amendments agreed to, quorum calls, and so forth. Unlike the *Congressional Record,* it does not provide reports of speeches, debates, statements, and other items. The Constitution requires each house to maintain a *Journal* and to publish it periodically.

Junket—A member's trip at government expense, especially abroad, ostensibly on official business but, it is often alleged, for pleasure.

Killer Amendment—An amendment that, if agreed to, might lead to the defeat of the measure it amends, either in the house in which the amendment is offered or at some later stage of the legislative process. Members sometimes deliberately offer or vote for such an amendment in the expectation that it will undermine support for the measure in Congress or increase the likelihood that the president will veto it.

King of the Mountain (or Hill Rule)—*(See Queen of the Hill Rule.)*

LA—*(See Legislative Assistant.)*

Lame Duck—Jargon for a member who has not been reelected, or did not seek reelection, and is serving the balance of his or her term.

Lame Duck Session—A session of a Congress held after the election for the succeeding Congress, so-called after the lame duck members still serving.

Last Train Out—Colloquial name for last must-pass bill of a session of Congress.

Law—An act of Congress that has been signed by the president, passed over the president's veto, or allowed to become law without the president's signature.

Lay on the Table—A motion to dispose of a pending proposition immediately, finally, and adversely; that is, to kill it without a direct vote on its substance. Often simply called a motion to table, it is not debatable and is adopted by majority vote or without objection. It is a highly privileged motion, taking precedence over all others except the motion to adjourn in the House and all but three additional motions in the Senate. It can kill a bill or resolution, an amendment, another motion, an appeal, or virtually any other matter.

Tabling an amendment also tables the measure to which the amendment is pending in the House, but not in the Senate. The House does not allow the motion against the motion to recommit, in the Committee of the Whole, and in some other situations. In the Senate it is the only permissible motion that immediately ends debate on a proposition, but only to kill it.

(The) Leadership—Usually, a reference to the majority and minority leaders of the Senate or to the Speaker and minority leader of the House. The term sometimes includes the majority leader in the House and the majority and minority whips in each house and, at other times, other party officials as well.

Legislation—(1) A synonym for legislative measures: bills and joint resolutions. (2) Provisions in such measures or in substantive amendments offered to them. (3) In some contexts, provisions that change existing substantive or authorizing law, rather than provisions that make appropriations.

Legislation on an Appropriation Bill—A common reference to provisions changing existing law that appear in, or are offered as amendments to, a general appropriation bill. A House rule prohibits the inclusion of such provisions in general appropriation bills unless they retrench expenditures. An analogous Senate rule permits points of order against amendments to a general appropriation bill that propose general legislation.

Legislative Assistant (LA)—A member's staff person responsible for monitoring and preparing legislation on particular subjects and for advising the member on them; commonly referred to as an LA.

Legislative Day—The day that begins when a house meets after an adjournment and ends when it next adjourns. Because the House of Representatives normally adjourns at the end of a daily session, its legislative and calendar days usually coincide. The Senate, however, frequently recesses at the end of a daily session, and its legislative day may extend over several calendar days, weeks, or months. Among other uses, this technicality permits the Senate to save time by circumventing its morning hour, a procedure required at the beginning of every legislative day.

Legislative History—(1) A chronological list of actions taken on a measure during its progress through the legislative process. (2) The official documents relating to a measure, the entries in the *Journals* of the two houses on that measure, and the *Congressional Record* text of its consideration in both houses. The documents include all committee reports and the conference report and joint explanatory statement, if any. Courts and affected federal agencies study a measure's legislative history for congressional intent about its purpose and interpretation.

Legislative Process—(1) Narrowly, the stages in the enactment of a law from introduction to final disposition. An introduced measure that becomes law typically travels through reference to committee; committee and subcommittee consideration; report to the chamber; floor consideration; amendment; passage; engrossment; messaging to the other house; similar steps in that house, including floor amendment of the measure; return of the measure to the first house; consideration of amendments between the houses or a conference to resolve their differences; approval of the conference report by both houses; enrollment; approval by the president or override of the president's veto; and deposit with the Archivist of the United States. (2) Broadly, the political, lobbying, and other factors that affect or influence the process of enacting laws.

Legislative Veto—A procedure, declared unconstitutional in 1983, that allowed Congress or one of its houses to nullify certain actions of the president, executive branch agencies, or independent agencies. Sometimes called congressional vetoes or congressional disapprovals. Following the Supreme Court's 1983 decision, Congress amended several legislative veto statutes to require enactment of joint resolutions, which are subject to presidential veto, for nullifying executive branch actions.

Limitation on a General Appropriation Bill—Language that prohibits expenditures for part of an authorized purpose from funds provided in a general appropriation bill. Precedents require that the language be phrased in the negative: that none of the funds provided in a pending appropriation bill shall be used for a specified authorized activity. Limitations in general appropriation bills are permitted on the grounds that Congress can refuse to fund authorized programs and, therefore, can refuse to fund any part of them as long as the prohibition does not change existing law. House precedents have established that a limitation does not change existing law if it does not impose additional duties or burdens on executive branch officials, interfere with their discretionary authority, or require them to make judgments or determinations not required by existing law. The proliferation of limitation amendments in the 1970s and early 1980s prompted the House to adopt a rule in 1983 making it more difficult for members to offer them. The rule bans such amendments during the reading of an appropriation bill for amendments, unless they are specifically authorized in existing law. Other limitations may be offered after the reading, but the Committee of the Whole can foreclose them by adopting a motion to rise and report the bill back to the House. In 1995 the rule was amended to allow the motion to rise and report to be made only by the majority leader or his or her designee. The House Appropriations Committee, however, can include limitation provisions in the bills it reports.

Line Item—An amount in an appropriation measure. It can refer to a single appropriation account or to separate amounts within the account. In the congressional budget process, the term usually refers to assumptions about the funding of particular programs or accounts that underlie the broad functional amounts in a budget resolution. These assumptions are discussed in the reports accompanying each resolution and are not binding.

Line-Item Veto—*(See Item Veto; Line Item Veto Act of 1996.)*

Line Item Veto Act of 1996—A law, in effect only from January 1997 until June 1998, that granted the president authority intended to be functionally equivalent to an item veto, by amending the Impoundment Control Act to incorporate an approach known as enhanced rescission. Key provisions established a new procedure that permitted the president to cancel amounts of new discretionary appropriations (budget authority), new items of direct spending (entitlements), or certain limited tax benefits. It also required the president to notify Congress of the cancellation in a special message within five calendar days after signing the measure. The cancellation would become permanent unless legislation disapproving it was enacted within thirty days. On June 25, 1998, in *Clinton v. City of New York* the Supreme Court held the Line Item Veto Act unconstitutional, on the grounds that its cancellation provisions violated the presentment clause in Article I, clause 7, of the Constitution.

Live Pair—A voluntary and informal agreement between two members on opposite sides of an issue, one of whom is absent for a recorded vote, under which the member who is present withholds or withdraws his or her vote to offset the failure to vote by the member who is absent. Usually the member in attendance announces that he or she has a live pair, states how each would have voted, and votes "present." In the House, under a rules change enacted in the 106th Congress, a live pair is only permitted on the rare occasions when electronic voting is not used.

Live Quorum—In the Senate, a quorum call to which senators are expected to respond. Senators usually suggest the absence of a quorum, not to force a quorum to appear, but to provide a pause in the proceedings during which senators can engage in private discussions or wait for a senator to come to the floor. A senator desiring a live quorum usually announces his or her intention, giving fair warning that there will be an objection to any unanimous consent request that the quorum call be dispensed with before it is completed.

Loan Guarantee—A statutory commitment by the federal government to pay part or all of a loan's principal and interest to a lender or the holder of a security in case the borrower defaults.

Lobby—To try to persuade members of Congress to propose, pass, modify, or defeat proposed legislation or to change or repeal existing laws. Lobbyists attempt to promote their preferences or those of a group, organization, or industry. Originally the term referred to persons frequenting the lobbies or corridors of legislative chambers in order to speak to lawmakers. In a general sense, lobbying includes not only direct contact with members but also indirect attempts to influence them, such as writing to them or persuading others to write or visit them, attempting to mold public opinion toward a desired legislative goal by various means, and contributing or arranging for contributions to members election campaigns. The right to lobby stems from the First Amendment to the Constitution, which bans laws that abridge the right of the people to petition the government for a redress of grievances.

Lobbying Disclosure Act of 1995—The principal statute requiring disclosure of—and also, to a degree, circumscribing—the activities of lobbyists. In general, it requires lobbyists who spend more than 20 percent of their time on lobbying activities to register and make semiannual reports of their activities to the clerk of the House and the secretary of the Senate, although the law provides for a number of exemptions. Among the statute's prohibitions, lobbyists are not allowed to make contributions to the legal defense fund of a member or high government official or to reimburse for official travel. Civil penalties for failure to comply may include fines of up to $50,000. The act does not include grassroots lobbying in its definition of lobbying activities.

The act amended several other lobby laws, notably the Foreign Agents Registration Act (FARA), so that lobbyists can submit a single filing. Since the measure was enacted, the number of lobby registrations has risen from about 12,000 to more than 20,000. In 1998 expenditures on federal lobbying, as disclosed under the Lobbying Disclosure Act, totaled $1.42 billion. The 1995 act supersedes the 1946 Federal Regulation of Lobbying Act, which was repealed in Section 11 of the 1995 Act.

Logrolling—Jargon for a legislative tactic or bargaining strategy in which members try to build support for their legislation by promising to support legislation desired by other members or by accepting amendments they hope will induce their colleagues to vote for their bill.

Lower Body—A way to refer to the House of Representatives, which is considered pejorative by House members.

Mace—The symbol of the office of the House sergeant at arms. Under the direction of the Speaker, the sergeant at arms is responsible for preserving order on the House floor by holding up the mace in front of an unruly member, or by carrying the mace up and down the aisles to quell boisterous behavior. When the House is in session, the mace sits on a pedestal at the Speaker's right; when the House is in Committee of the Whole, it is moved to a lower pedestal. The mace is forty-six inches high and consists of thirteen ebony rods bound in silver and topped by a silver globe with a silver eagle, wings outstretched, perched on it.

Majority Leader—The majority party's chief floor spokesperson, elected by that party's caucus—sometimes called floor leader. In the Senate, the majority leader also develops the party's political and procedural strategy, usually in collaboration with other party officials and committee chairmen. The majority leader negotiates the Senate's agenda and committee ratios with the minority leader and usually calls up measures for floor action. The chamber traditionally concedes to the majority leader the right to determine the days on which it will meet and the hours at which it will convene and adjourn. In the House, the majority leader is the Speaker's deputy and heir apparent and helps plan the floor agenda and the party's legislative strategy and often speaks for the party leadership in debate.

Managers—(1) The official title of members appointed to a conference committee, commonly called conferees. The ranking majority and minority managers for each house also manage floor consideration of the committee's conference report. (2) The members who manage the initial floor consideration of a measure. (3) The official title of House members appointed to present impeachment articles to the Senate and to act as prosecutors on behalf of the House during the Senate trial of the impeached person.

Mandatory Appropriations—Amounts that Congress must appropriate annually because it has no discretion over them unless it first amends existing substantive law. Certain entitlement programs, for example, require annual appropriations.

Markup—A meeting or series of meetings by a committee or subcommittee during which members mark up a measure by offering, debating, and voting on amendments to it.

Means-Tested Programs—Programs that provide benefits or services to low-income individuals who meet a test of need. Most are entitlement programs, such as Medicaid, food stamps, and Supplementary Security Income. A few—for example, subsidized housing and various social services—are funded through discretionary appropriations.

Members' Allowances—Official expenses that are paid for or for which members are reimbursed by their houses. Among these are the costs of office space in congressional buildings and in their home states or districts; office equipment and supplies; postage-free mailings (the franking privilege); a set number of trips to and from home states or districts, as well as travel elsewhere on official business; telephone and other telecommunications services; and staff salaries.

Member's Staff—The personal staff to which a member is entitled. The House sets a maximum number of staff and a monetary allowance for each representative. The Senate does not set a maximum staff level, but it does set a monetary allowance for each senator. In each house, the staff allowance is included with office expenses allowances and official mail allowances in a consolidated allowance. Representatives and senators can spend as much money in their consolidated allowances for staff, office expenses, or official mail, as long as they do not exceed the monetary value of the three allowances combined. This provides members with flexibility in operating their offices.

Method of Equal Proportions—The mathematical formula used since 1950 to determine how the 435 seats in the House of Representatives should be distributed among the fifty states in the apportionment following each decennial census. It minimizes as much as possible the proportional difference between the average district population in any two states. Because the Constitution guarantees each state at least one representative, fifty seats are automatically apportioned. The formula calculates priority numbers for each state, assigns the first of the 385 remaining seats to the state with the highest priority number, the second to the state with the next highest number, and so on until all seats are distributed. *(See Apportionment.)*

Midterm Election—The general election for members of Congress that occurs in November of the second year in a presidential term.

Minority Leader—The minority party's leader and chief floor spokesperson, elected by the party caucus; sometimes called minority floor leader. With the assistance of other party officials and the ranking minority members of committees, the minority leader devises the party's political and procedural strategy.

Minority Staff—Employees who assist the minority party members of a committee. Most committees hire separate majority and minority party staffs, but they also may hire nonpartisan staff. Senate rules state that a committee's staff must reflect the relative number of its majority and minority party committee members, and the rules guarantee the minority at least one-third of the funds available for hiring partisan staff. In the House, each committee is authorized thirty professional staff, and the minority members of most committees may select up to ten of these staff (subject to full committee approval). Under House rules, the minority party is to be "treated fairly" in the apportionment of additional staff resources. Each House committee determines the portion of its additional staff it allocates to the minority; some committees allocate one-third; and others allot less.

Modified Rule—A special rule from the House Rules Committee that permits only certain amendments to be offered to a measure during its floor consideration or that bans certain specified amendments or amendments on certain subjects.

Morning Business—In the Senate, routine business that is to be transacted at the beginning of the morning hour. The business consists, first, of laying before the Senate, and referring to committees, matters such as messages from the president and the House, federal agency reports, and unreferred petitions, memorials, bills, and joint resolutions. Next, senators may present additional petitions and memorials. Then committees may present their reports, after which senators may introduce bills and resolutions. Finally, resolutions coming over from a previous day are taken up for consideration. In practice, the Senate adopts standing orders that permit senators to introduce measures and file reports at any time, but only if there has been a morning business period on that day. Because the Senate often remains in the same legislative day for several days, weeks, or months at a time, it orders a morning business period almost every calendar day for the convenience of senators who wish to introduce measures or make reports.

Morning Hour—A two-hour period at the beginning of a new legislative day during which the Senate is supposed to conduct routine business, call the calendar on Mondays, and deal with other matters described in a Senate rule. In practice, the morning hour rarely, if ever, occurs, in part because the Senate frequently recesses, rather than adjourns, at the end of a daily session. Therefore the rule does not apply when the Senate next meets. The Senate's rules reserve the first hour of the morning for morning business. After the completion of morning business, or at the end of the first hour, the rules permit a motion to proceed to the consideration of a measure on the calendar out of its regular order (except on Mondays). Because that normally debatable motion is not debatable if offered during the morning hour, the majority leader may, but rarely does, use this procedure in anticipating a filibuster on the motion to proceed. If the Senate agrees to the motion, it can consider the measure until the end of the morning hour, and if there is no unfinished business from the previous day the Senate can continue considering it after the morning hour. But if there is unfinished business, a motion to continue consideration is necessary, and that motion is debatable.

Motion—A formal proposal for a procedural action, such as to consider, to amend, to lay on the table, to reconsider, to recess, or to adjourn. It has been estimated that at least eighty-five motions are possible under various circumstances in the House of Representatives, somewhat fewer in the Senate. Not all motions are created equal; some are privileged or preferential and enjoy priority over others. Some motions are debatable, amendable, or divisible, while others are not.

Multiple and Sequential Referrals—The practice of referring a measure to two or more committees for concurrent consideration (multiple referral) or successively to several committees in sequence (sequential referral). A measure may also be divided into several parts, with each referred to a different committee or to several committees sequentially (split referral). In theory this gives all committees that have jurisdiction over parts of a measure the opportunity to consider and report on them.

Before 1975, House precedents banned such referrals. A 1975 rule required the Speaker to make concurrent and sequential referrals "to the maximum extent feasible." On sequential referrals, the

Speaker could set deadlines for reporting the measure. The Speaker ruled that this provision authorized him to discharge a committee from further consideration of a measure and place it on the appropriate calendar of the House if the committee fails to meet the Speaker's deadline. The Speaker also used combinations of concurrent and sequential referrals. In 1995 joint referrals were prohibited. Measures are referred to a primary committee and also may be referred, either concurrently or sequentially, to one or more other committees, but usually only for consideration of portions of the measure that fall within the jurisdiction of each of those other committees. In 2003 the Speaker was authorized to not designate a primary committee under "extraordinary circumstances."

In the Senate, before 1977 concurrent and sequential referrals were permitted only by unanimous consent. In that year, a rule authorized a privileged motion for such a referral if offered jointly by the majority and minority leaders. Debate on the motion and all amendments to it is limited to two hours. The motion may set deadlines for reporting and provide for discharging the committees involved if they fail to meet the deadlines. To date, this procedure has never been invoked; multiple referrals in the Senate continue to be made by unanimous consent.

Multiyear Appropriation—An appropriation that remains available for spending or obligation for more than one fiscal year; the exact period of time is specified in the act making the appropriation.

Multiyear Authorization—(1) Legislation that authorizes the existence or continuation of an agency, program, or activity for more than one fiscal year. (2) Legislation that authorizes appropriations for an agency, program, or activity for more than one fiscal year.

Nomination—A proposed presidential appointment to a federal office submitted to the Senate for confirmation. Approval is by majority vote. The Constitution explicitly requires confirmation for ambassadors, consuls, "public Ministers" (department heads), and Supreme Court justices. By law, other federal judges, all military promotions of officers, and many high-level civilian officials must be confirmed.

Nuclear Option—A common name for a parliamentary maneuver that changes Senate rules to prevent filibusters on judicial nominations to force a floor vote. Also referred to as the constitutional option.

Oath of Office—On taking office, members of Congress must swear or affirm that they will "support and defend the Constitution . . . against all enemies, foreign and domestic," that they will "bear true faith and allegiance" to the Constitution, that they take the obligation "freely, without any mental reservation or purpose of evasion," and that they will "well and faithfully discharge the duties" of their office. The oath is required by the Constitution, and the wording is prescribed by a statute. All House members must take the oath at the beginning of each new Congress. Usually, the member with the longest continuous service in the House swears in the Speaker, who then swears in the other members. The president of the Senate or a surrogate administers the oath to newly elected or reelected senators.

Obligation—A binding agreement by a government agency to pay for goods, products, services, studies, and so on, either immediately or in the future. When an agency enters into such an agreement, it incurs an obligation. As the agency makes the required payments, it liquidates the obligation. Appropriation laws usually make funds available for obligation for one or more fiscal years but do not require agencies to spend their funds during those specific years. The actual outlays can occur years after the appropriation is obligated, as with a contract for construction of a submarine may provide for payment to be made when it is delivered in the future. Such obligated funds are often said to be "in the pipeline." Under these circumstances, an agency's outlays in a particular year can come from appropriations obligated in previous years as well as from its current-year appropriation. Consequently, the money Congress appropriates for a fiscal year does not equal the total amount of appropriated money the government will actually spend in that year.

Off-Budget Entities—Specific federal entities whose budget authority, outlays, and receipts are excluded by law from the calculation of budget totals, although they are part of government spending and income. As of 2005 these included the Social Security trust funds (Federal Old-Age and Survivors Insurance Fund and the Federal Disability Insurance Trust Fund) and the Postal Service. Government-sponsored enterprises are also excluded from the budget because they are considered private rather than public organizations.

Office of Management and Budget (OMB)—A unit in the Executive Office of the President, reconstituted in 1990 from the former Bureau of the Budget. The Office of Management and Budget (OMB) assists the president in preparing the budget and in formulating the government's fiscal program. The OMB also plays a central role in supervising and controlling implementation of the budget, pursuant to provisions in appropriations laws, the Budget Enforcement Act, and other statutes. In addition to these budgetary functions, the OMB has various management duties, including those performed through its three statutory offices: Federal Financial Management, Federal Procurement Policy, and Information and Regulatory Affairs.

Officers of Congress—The Constitution refers to the Speaker of the House and the president of the Senate as officers and declares that each house "shall chuse" its "other Officers," but it does not name them or indicate how they should be selected. A House rule refers to its clerk, sergeant at arms, and chaplain as officers. Officers are not named in the Senate's rules, but *Riddick's Senate Procedure* lists the president pro tempore, secretary of the Senate, sergeant at arms, chaplain, and the secretaries for the majority and minority parties as officers. A few appointed officials are sometimes referred to as officers, including the parliamentarians and the legislative counsels. The House elects its officers by resolution at the beginning of each Congress. The Senate also elects its officers, but once elected, Senate officers serve from Congress to Congress until their successors are chosen.

Official Objectors—House members who screen measures on the Private Calendar and decide whether or not to object to the consideration of any one or more of them.

Omnibus Bill—A measure that combines the provisions of several disparate subjects into a single and often lengthy bill.

One-Minute Speeches—Addresses by House members that can be on any subject but are limited to one minute. They are usually permitted at the beginning of a daily session after the chaplain's prayer, the pledge of allegiance, and approval of the *Journal.* They are a customary practice, not a right granted by rule. Consequently, recognition for one-minute speeches requires unanimous consent and is entirely within the Speaker's discretion. The Speaker sometimes refuses to permit them when the House has a heavy legislative schedule or limits or postpones them until a later time of the day.

Open Rule—A special rule from the House Rules Committee that permits members to offer as many floor amendments as they wish as long as the amendments are germane and do not violate other House rules.

Order of Business (House)—The sequence of events prescribed by a House rule during the meeting of the House on a new legislative day that is supposed to take place, also called the general order of business. The sequence consists of (1) the chaplain's prayer; (2) reading and approval of the *Journal;* (3) the pledge of allegiance; (4) correction of the reference of public bills to committee; (5) disposal of business on the Speaker's table; (6) unfinished business; (7) the morning hour call of committees and consideration of their bills; (8) motions to go into Committee of the Whole; and (9) orders of the day. In practice, the House never fully complies with this rule. Instead, the items of business that follow the pledge of allegiance are supplanted by any special orders of business that are in order on that day (for example, conference reports; the corrections, discharge, or private calendars; or motions to suspend the rules) and by other privileged business (for example, general appropriation bills and special rules) or measures made in order by special rules or unanimous consent. The regular order of business is also modified by unanimous consent practices and orders that govern recognition for one-minute speeches (which date from 1937) and for morning-hour debates, begun in 1994. By this combination of an order of business with privileged interruptions, the House gives precedence to certain categories of important legislation, brings to the floor other major legislation from its calendars in any order it chooses, and provides expeditious processing for minor and noncontroversial measures.

Order of Business (Senate)—The sequence of events at the beginning of a new legislative day, as prescribed by Senate rules and standing orders. The sequence consists of (1) the chaplain's prayer; (2) the pledge of allegiance; (3) the designation of a temporary presiding officer if any; (4) *Journal* reading and approval; (5) recognition of the majority and minority leaders or their designees under the standing order; (6) morning business in the morning hour; (7) call of the calendar during the morning hour (largely obsolete); and (8) unfinished business from the previous session day.

Organization of Congress—The actions each house takes at the beginning of a Congress that are necessary to its operations. These include swearing in newly elected members, notifying the president that a quorum of each house is present, making committee assignments, and fixing the hour for daily meetings. Because the House of Representatives is not a continuing body, it must also elect its Speaker and other officers and adopt its rules.

Original Bill—(1) A measure drafted by a committee and introduced by its chairman or another designated member when the committee reports the measure to its house. Unlike a clean bill, it is not referred back to the committee after introduction. The Senate permits all its legislative committees to report original bills. In the House, this authority is referred to in the rules as the "right to report at any time," and five committees (Appropriations, Budget, House Administration, Rules, and Standards of Official Conduct) have such authority under circumstances specified in House Rule XIII, clause 5.

(2) In the House, special rules reported by the Rules Committee often propose that an amendment in the nature of a substitute be considered as an original bill for purposes of amendment, meaning that the substitute, as with a bill, may be amended in two degrees. Without that requirement, the substitute may only be amended in one further degree. In the Senate, an amendment in the nature of a substitute automatically is open to two degrees of amendment, as is the original text of the bill, if the substitute is offered when no other amendment is pending.

Original Jurisdiction—The authority of certain committees to originate a measure and report it to the chamber. For example, general appropriation bills reported by the House Appropriations Committee are original bills, and special rules reported by the House Rules Committee are original resolutions.

Other Body—A commonly used reference to a chamber by a member of the other chamber. Congressional comity discourages members from directly naming the other chamber during debate.

Outlays—Amounts of government spending. They consist of payments, usually by check or in cash, to liquidate obligations incurred in prior fiscal years as well as in the current year, including the net lending of funds under budget authority. In federal budget accounting, net outlays are calculated by subtracting the amounts of refunds and various kinds of reimbursements to the government from actual spending.

Override a Veto—Congressional enactment of a measure over the president's veto. A veto override requires a recorded two-thirds vote of those voting in each house, a quorum being present. Because the president must return the vetoed measure to its house of origin, that house votes first, but neither house is required to attempt an override, whether immediately or at all. If an override attempt fails in the house of origin, the veto stands and the measure dies.

Oversight—Congressional review of the way in which federal agencies implement laws to ensure that they are carrying out the intent of Congress and to inquire into the efficiency of the implementation and the effectiveness of the law. The Legislative Reorganization Act of 1946 defined oversight as the function of exercising continuous watchfulness over the execution of the laws by the executive branch.

Oxford-Style Debate—The House held three Oxford-style debates in 1994, modeled after the famous debating format favored by the Oxford Union in Great Britain. Neither chamber has held Oxford-style debates since then. The Oxford-style debates aired nationally over C-SPAN television and National Public Radio. The organized event featured eight participants divided evenly into two teams, one team representing the Democrats (then holding the majority in the chamber) and the other the Republicans. Both teams argued a single question chosen well ahead of the event. A moderator regulated the debate and began it by stating the resolution at issue. The order of the speakers alternated by team, with a debater for the affirmative speaking first and a debater for the opposing team offering a rebuttal. The rest of the speakers alternated in kind until all gained the chance to speak.

Parliamentarian—The official advisor to the presiding officer in each house on questions of procedure. The parliamentarian and his or her assistants also answer procedural questions from members and congressional staff, refer measures to committees on behalf of the presiding officer, and maintain compilations of the precedents. The House parliamentarian revises the House Manual at the beginning of every Congress and usually reviews special rules before the Rules Committee reports them to the House. Either a parliamentarian or an assistant is always present and near the podium during sessions of each house.

Party Caucus—Generic term for each party's official organization in each house. Only House Democrats officially call their organization a caucus. House and Senate Republicans and Senate Democrats call their organizations conferences. The party caucuses elect their leaders, approve committee assignments and chairmanships (or ranking minority members, if the party is in the minority), establish party committees and study groups, and discuss party and legislative policies. On rare occasions, they have stripped members of committee seniority or expelled them from the caucus for party disloyalty.

Pay-as-You-Go (PAYGO)—A provision first instituted under the Budget Enforcement Act of 1990 that applies to legislation enacted before Oct. 1, 2002. It requires that the cumulative effect of legislation concerning either revenues or direct spending should not result in a net negative impact on the budget. If legislation does provide for an increase in spending or decrease in revenues, that effect is supposed to be offset by legislated spending reductions or revenue increases. If Congress fails to enact the appropriate offsets, the act requires presidential sequestration of sufficient offsetting amounts in specific direct spending accounts. Congress and the president can circumvent this requirement if both agree that an emergency requires a particular action or if a law is enacted declaring that deteriorated economic circumstances make it necessary to suspend the requirement.

Permanent Appropriation—An appropriation that remains continuously available, without current action or renewal by Congress, under the terms of a previously enacted authorization or appropriation law. One such appropriation provides for payment of interest on the public debt and another the salaries of members of Congress.

Permanent Authorization—An authorization without a time limit. It usually does not specify any limit on the funds that may be appropriated for the agency, program, or activity that it authorizes, leaving such amounts to the discretion of the appropriations committees and the two houses.

Permanent Staff—Term used formerly for committee staff authorized by law, who were funded through a permanent authorization and also called statutory staff. Most committees were authorized thirty permanent staff members. Most committees also were permitted additional staff, often called investigative staff, who were authorized by annual or biennial funding resolutions. The Senate eliminated the primary distinction between statutory and investigative staff in 1981. The House eliminated the distinction in 1995 by requiring that funding resolutions authorize money to hire both types of staff.

Personally Obnoxious (or Objectionable)—A characterization a senator sometimes applies to a president's nominee for a federal office in that senator's state to justify his or her opposition to the nomination.

Pocket Veto—The indirect veto of a bill as a result of the president withholding approval of it until after Congress has adjourned *sine die.* A bill the president does not sign but does not formally veto while Congress is in session automatically becomes a law ten days (excluding Sundays) after it is received. But if Congress adjourns its annual session during that ten-day period the measure dies even if the president does not formally veto it.

Point of Order—A parliamentary term used in committee and on the floor to object to an alleged violation of a rule and to demand that the chair enforce the rule. The point of order immediately halts the proceedings until the chair decides whether the contention is valid.

Pork or Pork Barrel Legislation—Pejorative terms for federal appropriations, bills, or policies that provide funds to benefit a legislator's district or state, with the implication that the legislator presses for enactment of such benefits to ingratiate himself or herself with constituents rather than on the basis of an impartial, objective assessment of need or merit. The terms are often applied to such benefits as new parks, federal offices, dams, canals, bridges, roads, water projects, sewage treatment plants, and public works of any kind, as well as demonstration projects, research grants, and relocation of government facilities. Funds released by the president for various kinds of benefits or government contracts approved by him allegedly for political purposes are also sometimes referred to as pork.

Postcloture Filibuster—A filibuster conducted after the Senate invokes cloture. It employs an array of procedural tactics rather than lengthy speeches to delay final action. The Senate curtailed the postcloture filibuster's effectiveness by closing a variety of loopholes in the cloture rule in 1979 and 1986.

Power of the Purse—A reference to the constitutional power Congress has over legislation to raise revenue and appropriate monies from the Treasury. Article I, Section 8 states that Congress "shall have Power To lay and collect Taxes, Duties, Imposts and Excises, [and] to pay the Debts." Section 9 declares: "No Money shall be drawn from the Treasury, but in Consequence of Appropriations made by Law."

Preamble—Introductory language describing the reasons for and intent of a measure, sometimes called a whereas clause. It occasionally appears in joint, concurrent, and simple resolutions but rarely in bills.

Precedent—A previous ruling on a parliamentary matter or a long-standing practice or custom of a house. Precedents serve to control arbitrary rulings and serve as the common law of a house.

President of the Senate—One constitutional role of the vice president is serving as the presiding officer of the Senate, or president of the Senate. The Constitution permits the vice president to cast a vote in the Senate only to break a tie, but the vice president is not required to do so.

President Pro Tempore—Under the Constitution, an officer elected by the Senate to preside over it during the absence of the vice president of the United States. Often referred to as the "pro tem," this senator is usually a member of the majority party with the longest continuous service in the chamber and also, by virtue of seniority, a committee chairman. When attending to committee and other duties the president pro tempore appoints other senators to preside.

Presiding Officer—In a formal meeting, the individual authorized to maintain order and decorum, recognize members to speak or offer motions, and apply and interpret the chamber's rules, precedents, and practices. The Speaker of the House and the president of the Senate are the chief presiding officers in their respective houses.

Previous Question—A nondebatable motion that, when agreed to by majority vote, usually cuts off further debate, prevents the offering of additional amendments, and brings the pending matter to an immediate vote. It is a major debate-limiting device in the House; it is not permitted in the Committee of the Whole in the House or in the Senate.

Private Bill—A bill that applies to one or more specified persons, corporations, institutions, or other entities, usually to grant relief when no other legal remedy is available to them. Many private bills deal with claims against the federal government, immigration and naturalization cases, and land titles.

Private Calendar—Commonly used title for a calendar in the House reserved for private bills and resolutions favorably reported by committees. The private calendar is officially called the Calendar of the Committee of the Whole House.

Private Law—A private bill enacted into law. Private laws are numbered in the same fashion as public laws.

Privilege—An attribute of a motion, measure, report, question, or proposition that gives it priority status for consideration. Privileged motions and motions to bring up privileged questions are not debatable.

Privilege of the Floor—In addition to the members of a house, certain individuals are admitted to its floor while it is in session. The rules of the two houses differ somewhat but both extend the privilege to the president and vice president, Supreme Court justices, cabinet members, state governors, former members of that house, members of the other house, certain officers and officials of Congress, certain staff of that house in the discharge of official duties, and the chamber's former parliamentarians. They also allow access to a limited number of committee and members' staff when their presence is necessary.

Pro Forma Amendment—In the House, an amendment that ostensibly proposes to change a measure or another amendment by moving "to strike the last word" or "to strike the requisite number of words." A member offers it not to make any actual change in the measure or amendment but only to obtain time for debate.

Pro Tem—A common reference to the president pro tempore of the Senate or, occasionally, to a Speaker pro tempore. *(See President Pro Tempore; Speaker Pro Tempore.)*

Procedures—The methods of conducting business in a deliberative body. The procedures of each house are governed first by applicable provisions of the Constitution, and then by its standing rules and orders, precedents, traditional practices, and any statutory rules that apply to it. The authority of the houses to adopt rules in addition to those specified in the Constitution is derived from Article I, Section 5, clause 2 of the Constitution, which states: "Each House may determine the Rules of its Proceedings. . . ." By rule, the House of Representatives also follows the procedures in *Jefferson's Manual* that are not inconsistent with its standing rules and orders. Many Senate procedures also conform with Jefferson's provisions, but by practice rather than by rule. At the beginning of each Congress, the House uses procedures in general parliamentary law until it adopts its standing rules.

Proxy Voting—The practice of permitting a member to cast the vote of an absent colleague in addition to his or her own vote. Proxy voting is prohibited on the floors of the House and Senate, but the Senate permits its committees to authorize proxy voting, and most do. In 1995, House rules were changed to prohibit proxy voting in committee.

Public Bill—A bill dealing with general legislative matters having national applicability or applying to the federal government or to a class of persons, groups, or organizations.

Public Debt—Federal government debt incurred by the Treasury or the Federal Financing Bank by the sale of securities to the public or borrowings from a federal fund or account.

Public Law—A public bill or joint resolution enacted into law. It is cited by the letters "PL" followed by a hyphenated number. The digits before the hyphen indicate the number of the Congress in which it was enacted; the digits after the hyphen indicate its position in the numerical sequence of public measures that became law during that Congress. For example, the Budget Enforcement Act of 1990 became PL 101-508 because it was the 508th measure in that sequence for the 101st Congress. *(See also Private Law.)*

Qualification (of Members)—The Constitution requires members of the House of Representatives to be twenty-five years of age at the time their terms begin. They must have been citizens of the United States for seven years before that date and, when elected, must be "Inhabitant[s]" of the state from which they were elected. There is no constitutional requirement that they reside in the districts they represent. Senators are required to be thirty years of age at the time their terms begin. They must have been citizens of the United States for nine years before that date and, when elected, must be "Inhabitant[s]" of the states in which they were elected. The "Inhabitant" qualification is broadly interpreted, and in modern times a candidate's declaration of state residence has generally been accepted as meeting the constitutional requirement.

Queen of the Hill Rule—A special rule from the House Rules Committee that permits votes on a series of amendments, especially complete substitutes for a measure, in a specified order, but directs that the amendment receiving the greatest number of votes shall be the winning one. This kind of rule permits the House to vote directly on a variety of alternatives to a measure. In doing so, it sets aside the precedent that once an amendment has been adopted, no further amendments may be offered to the text it has amended. Under an earlier practice, the Rules Committee reported "king of the hill" rules under which there also could be votes on a series of amendments, again in a specified order. If more than one of the amendments was adopted under this kind of rule, it was the last amendment to receive a majority vote that was considered as having been finally adopted, whether or not it had received the greatest number of votes.

Quorum—The minimum number of members required to be present for the transaction of business. Under the Constitution, a quorum in each house is a majority of its members: 218 in the House and 51 in the Senate when there are no vacancies. By House rule, a quorum in the Committee of the Whole is 100. In practice, both houses usually assume a quorum is present even if it is not, unless a member makes a point of no quorum in the House or suggests the absence of a quorum in the Senate. Consequently, each house transacts much of its business, and even passes bills, when only a few members are present. For House and Senate committees, chamber rules allow a minimum quorum of one-third of a committee's members to conduct most types of business.

Quorum Call—A procedure for determining whether a quorum is present in a chamber. In the Senate, a clerk calls the roll (roster) of senators. The House usually employs its electronic voting system.

Ramseyer Rule—A House rule that requires a committee's report on a bill or joint resolution to show the changes the measure, and any committee amendments to it, would make in existing law. The rule requires the report to present the text of any statutory provision that would be repealed and a comparative print showing, through typographical devices such as stricken-through type or italics, other changes that would be made in existing law. The rule, adopted in 1929, is named after its sponsor, Rep. Christian W. Ramseyer, R-Iowa. The Senate's analogous rule is called the Cordon Rule. *(See Cordon Rule.)*

Rank or Ranking—A member's position on the list of his or her party's members on a committee or subcommittee. When first assigned to a committee, a member is usually placed at the bottom of the list, then moves up as those above leave the committee. On subcommittees, however, a member's rank may not have anything to do with the length of his or her service on it.

Ranking Member—(1) Most often a reference to the minority member with the highest ranking on a committee or subcommittee. (2) A reference to the majority member next in rank to the chairman or to the highest ranking majority member present at a committee or subcommittee meeting.

Ratification—(1) The president's formal act of promulgating a treaty after the Senate has approved it. The resolution of ratification agreed to by the Senate is the procedural vehicle by which the Senate gives its consent to ratification. (2) A state legislature's act in approving a proposed constitutional amendment. Such an amendment becomes effective when ratified by three-fourths of the states.

Reapportionment—*(See Apportionment.)*

Recess—(1) A temporary interruption or suspension of a meeting of a chamber or committee. Unlike an adjournment, a recess does not end a legislative day. Because the Senate often recesses from one calendar day to another, its legislative day may extend over several calendar days, weeks, or even months. (2) A period of adjournment for more than three days to a day certain, especially over a holiday or in August during odd-numbered years.

Recess Appointment—A presidential appointment to a vacant federal position made after the Senate has adjourned *sine die* or has adjourned or recessed for more than thirty days. If the president submits the recess appointee's nomination during the next session of the Senate, that individual can continue to serve until the end of the session even though the Senate might have rejected the nomination. When appointed to a vacancy that existed thirty days before the end of the last Senate session, a recess appointee is not paid until confirmed.

Recommit—To send a measure back to the committee that reported it; sometimes called a straight motion to recommit to distinguish it from a motion to recommit with instructions. A successful motion to recommit kills the measure unless it is accompanied by instructions.

Recommit a Conference Report—To return a conference report to the conference committee for renegotiation of some or all of its agreements. A motion to recommit may be offered with or without instructions.

Recommit with Instructions—To send a measure back to a committee with instructions to take some action on it. Invariably in the House and often in the Senate, when the motion recommits to a standing committee, the instructions require the committee to report the measure "forthwith" with specified amendments.

Reconsider—A practice that gives a chamber an opportunity to review its action on any proposition. Any member who voted on the prevailing side can ask to reconsider the vote, creating, in effect, another vote on the same proposition. Usually this procedure creates the anomalous situation of an opponent of a measure changing his or her "no" vote to a "yea" vote to force a new vote.

Reconciliation—A procedure for changing existing revenue and spending laws to bring total federal revenues and spending within the limits established in a budget resolution. Congress has applied reconciliation chiefly to revenues and mandatory spending programs, especially entitlements. Discretionary spending is controlled through annual appropriation bills.

Recorded Vote—(1) Generally, any vote in which members are recorded by name for or against a measure; also called a record vote or roll-call vote. The only recorded vote in the Senate is a vote by the yeas and nays and is commonly called a roll-call vote. (2) Technically, a recorded vote is one demanded in the House of Representatives and supported by at least one-fifth of a quorum (forty-four members) in the House sitting as the House or at least twenty-five members in the Committee of the Whole.

Recorded Vote by Clerks—A voting procedure in the House where members pass through the appropriate "aye" or "no" aisle in the chamber and cast their votes by depositing a signed green (yea) or red (no) card in a ballot box. These votes are tabulated by clerks and reported to the chair. The electronic voting system is much more convenient and has largely supplanted this procedure. *(See Committee of the Whole; Recorded Vote; Teller Vote.)*

Redistricting—The redrawing of congressional district boundaries within a state after a decennial census. Redistricting may be required to equalize district populations or to accommodate an increase or decrease in the number of a state's House seats that might have resulted from the decennial apportionment. The state governments determine the district lines, but by 2010 some states were turning to outside entities, such as a panel of judges, as an option to conduct the redistricting. *(See Apportionment; Congressional District; Gerrymandering.)*

Referral—The assignment of a measure to committee for consideration. Under a House rule, the Speaker can refuse to refer a measure if the Speaker believes it is "of an obscene or insulting character."

Report—(1) As a verb, a committee is said to report when it submits a measure or other document to its parent chamber. (2) A clerk is said to report when he or she reads a measure's title, text, or the text of an amendment to the body at the direction of the chair. (3) As a noun, a committee document that accompanies a reported measure. It describes the measure, the committee's views on it, its costs, and the changes it proposes to make in existing law; it also includes certain impact statements. (4) A committee document submitted to its parent chamber that describes the results of an investigation or other study or provides information it is required to provide by rule or law.

Representative—An elected and duly sworn member of the House of Representatives who is entitled to vote in the chamber. The Constitution requires that a representative be at least twenty-five years old, a citizen of the United States for at least seven years, and an inhabitant of the state from which he or she is elected. Customarily, members reside in the districts they represent. Representatives are elected in even-numbered years to two-year terms that begin the following January.

Reprimand—A formal condemnation of a member for misbehavior, considered a milder reproof than censure. The House of Representatives first used it in 1976. The Senate first used it in 1991. *(See also Censure; Code of Official Conduct; Denounce; Ethics Rules; Expulsion; Seniority Loss.)*

Rescission—A provision of law that repeals previously enacted budget authority in whole or in part. Under the Impoundment Control Act of 1974, the president can impound such funds by sending a message to Congress requesting one or more rescissions and the reasons for doing so. If Congress does not pass a rescission bill for the programs requested by the president within forty-five days of continuous session after receiving the message, the president must make the funds available for obligation and expenditure. If the president does not, the comptroller general of the United States is authorized to bring suit to compel the release of those funds. A rescission bill may rescind all, part, or none of an amount proposed by the president, and may rescind funds the president has not impounded.

Reserving the Right to Object—Members' declaration that at some indefinite future time they may object to a unanimous consent request. It is an attempt to circumvent the requirement that members may prevent such an action only by objecting immediately after it is proposed.

Resident Commissioner from Puerto Rico—A nonvoting member of the House of Representatives, elected to a four-year term. The resident commissioner has the same status and privileges as delegates. As with the delegates, the resident commissioner may not vote in the House or Committee of the Whole.

Resolution—(1) A simple resolution; that is, a nonlegislative measure effective only in the house in which it is proposed and not requiring concurrence by the other chamber or approval by the president. Simple resolutions are designated H Res in the House and S Res in the Senate. Simple resolutions express nonbinding opinions on policies or issues or deal with the internal affairs or prerogatives of a house. (2) Any type of resolution: simple, concurrent, or joint. *(See Concurrent Resolution; Joint Resolution.)*

Resolution of Inquiry—A resolution usually simple rather than concurrent calling on the president or the head of an executive agency to provide specific information or papers to one or both houses.

Resolution of Ratification—The Senate vehicle for agreeing to a treaty. The constitutionally mandated vote of two-thirds of the senators present and voting applies to the adoption of this resolution. However, it may also contain amendments, reservations, declarations, or understandings that the Senate had previously added to it by majority vote.

Revenue Legislation—Measures that levy new taxes or tariffs or change existing ones. Under Article I, Section 7, clause 1 of the Constitution, the House of Representatives originates federal revenue measures, but the Senate can propose amendments to them. The House Ways and Means Committee and the Senate Finance Committee have jurisdiction over such measures, with a few minor exceptions.

Revise and Extend One's Remarks—A unanimous consent request to publish in the *Congressional Record* a statement a member did not deliver on the floor, a longer statement than the one made on the floor, or miscellaneous extraneous material.

Revolving Fund—A trust fund or account whose income remains available to finance its continuing operations without any fiscal year limitation.

Rider—Congressional slang for an amendment unrelated or extraneous to the subject matter of the measure to which it is attached. Riders often contain proposals that are less likely to become law on their own merits as separate bills, either because of opposition in the committee of jurisdiction, resistance in the other house, or the probability of a presidential veto. Riders are more common in the Senate.

Roll Call—A call of the roll to determine whether a quorum is present, to establish a quorum, or to vote on a question. Usually, the House uses its electronic voting system for a roll call. The Senate does not have an electronic voting system; its roll is always called by a clerk.

Rule—(1) A permanent regulation that a house adopts to govern its conduct of business, its procedures, its internal organization, behavior of its members, regulation of its facilities, duties of an officer, or some other subject it chooses to govern in that form. (2) In the House, a privileged simple resolution reported by the Rules Committee that provides methods and conditions for floor consideration of a measure or, rarely, several measures.

Rule Twenty-Two—A common reference to the Senate's cloture rule. *(See Cloture.)*

Second-Degree Amendment—An amendment to an amendment in the first degree. It is usually a perfecting amendment.

Section—A subdivision of a bill or statute. By law, a section must be numbered and, as nearly as possible, contain "a single proposition of enactment."

Select or Special Committee—A committee established by a resolution in either house for a special purpose and, usually, for a limited time. Most select and special committees are assigned specific investigations or studies but are not authorized to report measures to their chambers.

Secretary of the Senate—The chief financial, administrative, and legislative officer of the Senate. Elected by resolution or order of the Senate, the secretary is invariably the candidate of the majority party and usually chosen by the majority leader. In the absence of the vice president and pending the election of a president pro tempore, the secretary presides over the Senate. The secretary is subject to policy direction and oversight by the Senate Committee on Rules and Administration. The secretary manages a wide range of functions that support the administrative operations of the Senate as an organization as well as those functions necessary to its legislative process, including record keeping, document management, certifications, housekeeping services, administration of oaths, and lobbyist registrations. The secretary is responsible for accounting for all funds appropriated to the Senate and conducts audits of Senate financial activities. On a semiannual basis the secretary issues the Report of the Secretary of the Senate, a compilation of Senate expenditures.

Senate—The house of Congress in which each state is represented by two senators; each senator has one vote. Article V of the Constitution declares that "No State, without its Consent, shall be deprived of its equal Suffrage in the Senate." The Constitution also gives the Senate equal legislative power with the House of Representatives. Although the Senate is prohibited from originating revenue measures, and as a matter of practice it does not originate appropriation measures, it can amend both. Only the Senate can give or withhold consent to treaties and nominations from the president. It also acts as a court to try impeachments by the House and elects the vice president when no candidate receives a majority of the electoral votes. It is often referred to as "the upper body," but not by members of the House.

Senate Manual—The handbook of the Senate's standing rules and orders and the laws and other regulations that apply to the Senate, usually published once each Congress.

Senator—A duly sworn elected or appointed member of the Senate. The Constitution requires that a senator be at least thirty years old, a citizen of the United States for at least nine years, and an inhabitant of the state from which he or she is elected. Senators are usually elected in even-numbered years to six-year terms that begin the following January. When a vacancy occurs before the end of a term, the state governor can appoint a replacement to fill the position until a successor is chosen at the state's next general election or, if specified under state law, the next feasible date for such an election, to serve the remainder of the term. Until the Seventeenth Amendment was ratified in 1913, senators were chosen by their state legislatures.

Senatorial Courtesy—The Senate's practice of declining to confirm a presidential nominee for an office in the state of a senator of the president's party unless that senator approves.

Seniority—The priority, precedence, or status accorded members according to the length of their continuous service in a house or on a committee.

Seniority Loss—A type of punishment that reduces a member's seniority on his or her committees, including the loss of chairmanships. Party caucuses in both houses have occasionally imposed such punishment on their members, for example, for publicly supporting candidates of the other party.

Seniority Rule—The customary practice, rather than a rule, of assigning the chairmanship of a committee to the majority party member who has served on the committee for the longest continuous period of time.

Seniority System—A collection of long-standing customary practices under which members with longer continuous service than their colleagues in their house or on their committees receive various kinds of preferential treatment. Although some of the practices are no longer as rigidly observed as in the past, they still pervade the organization and procedures of Congress.

Sequestration—A procedure for canceling budgetary resources—that is, money available for obligation or spending—to enforce budget limitations established in law. Sequestered funds are no longer available for obligation or expenditure.

Sergeant at Arms—The officer in each house responsible for maintaining order, security, and decorum in its wing of the Capitol, including the chamber and its galleries. Although elected by their respective houses, both sergeants at arms are invariably the candidates of the majority party.

Session—(1) The annual series of meetings of a Congress. Under the Constitution, Congress must assemble at least once a year at noon on Jan. 3 unless it appoints a different day by law. (2) The special meetings of Congress or of one house convened by the president, called a special session. (3) A house is said to be in session during the period of a day when it is meeting.

Severability (or Separability) Clause—Language stating that if any particular provisions of a measure are declared invalid by the courts the remaining provisions shall remain in effect.

Sine Die—Without fixing a day for a future meeting. An adjournment *sine die* signifies the end of an annual or special session of Congress.

Slip Law—The first official publication of a measure that has become law. It is published separately in unbound, single-sheet form or pamphlet form. A slip law usually is available two or three days after the date of the law's enactment.

Speaker—The presiding officer of the House of Representatives and the leader of its majority party. The Speaker is selected by the majority party and formally elected by the House at the beginning of each Congress. Although the Constitution does not require the Speaker to be a member of the House, in fact, all Speakers have been members.

Speaker Pro Tempore—A member of the House who is designated as the temporary presiding officer by the Speaker or elected by the House to that position during the Speaker's absence.

Speaker's Vote—The Speaker is not required to vote, and the Speaker's name is not called on a roll-call vote unless so requested. Usually, the Speaker votes either to create a tie vote, and thereby defeat a proposal, or to break a tie in favor of a proposal. Occasionally, the Speaker also votes to emphasize the importance of a matter.

Special Session—A session of Congress convened by the president, under his constitutional authority, after Congress has adjourned *sine die* at the end of a regular session. *(See Adjournment* Sine Die; *Session.)*

Spending Authority—The technical term for backdoor spending. The Congressional Budget Act of 1974 defines it as borrowing authority, contract authority, and entitlement authority for which appropriation acts do not provide budget authority in advance. Under the Budget Act, legislation that provides new spending authority may not be considered unless it provides that the authority shall be effective only to the extent or in such amounts as provided in an appropriation act.

Spending Cap—The statutory limit for a fiscal year on the amount of new budget authority and outlays allowed for discretionary spending. The Budget Enforcement Act of 1997 requires a sequester if the cap is exceeded.

Split Referral—A measure divided into two or more parts, with each part referred to a different committee.

Sponsor—The principal proponent and introducer of a measure or an amendment.

Staff Director—The most frequently used title for the head of staff of a committee or subcommittee. On some committees, that person is called chief of staff, clerk, chief clerk, chief counsel, general counsel, or executive director. The head of a committee's minority staff is usually called minority staff director.

Standing Committee—A permanent committee established by a House or Senate standing rule or standing order. The rule also describes the subject areas on which the committee may report bills and resolutions and conduct oversight. Most introduced measures must be referred to one or more standing committees according to their jurisdictions.

Standing Order—A continuing regulation or directive that has the force and effect of a rule but is not incorporated into the standing rules. The Senate's numerous standing orders, such as its standing rules, continue from Congress to Congress unless changed or the order states otherwise. The House uses relatively few standing orders, and those it adopts expire at the end of a session of Congress.

Standing Rules—The rules of the Senate that continue from one Congress to the next and the rules of the House of Representatives that it adopts at the beginning of each new Congress.

Standing Vote—An alternative and informal term for a division vote, during which members in favor of a proposal and then members opposed stand and are counted by the chair.

Star Print—A reprint of a bill, resolution, amendment, or committee report correcting technical or substantive errors in a previous printing; so called because of the small black star that appears on the front page or cover.

State of the Union Message—A presidential message to Congress under the constitutional directive that the president shall "from time to time give to the Congress Information of the State of the Union, and recommend to their Consideration such Measures as he shall judge necessary and expedient." Customarily, the president sends an annual State of the Union message to Congress, usually late in January.

Statutes at Large—A chronological arrangement of the laws enacted in each session of Congress. Though indexed, the laws are not arranged by subject matter, nor is there an indication of how they affect or change previously enacted laws. The volumes are numbered by Congress, and the laws are cited by their volume and page number. The Gramm-Rudman-Hollings Act, for example, appears as 99 Stat. 1037.

Straw Vote Prohibition—Under a House precedent, a member who has the floor during debate may not conduct a straw vote or otherwise ask for a show of support for a proposition. Only the chair may put a question to a vote.

Strike from the *Record*—Expunge objectionable remarks from the *Congressional Record,* after a member's words have been taken down on a point of order.

Strike the Last Word—*(See Pro Forma Amendment.)*

Subcommittee—A panel of committee members assigned a portion of the committee's jurisdiction or other functions. On legislative committees, subcommittees hold hearings, mark up legislation, and report measures to their full committee for further action; they cannot report directly to the chamber. A subcommittee's party composition usually reflects the ratio on its parent committee.

Subpoena Power—The authority granted to committees by the rules of their respective houses to issue legal orders requiring individuals to appear and testify, or to produce documents pertinent to the committee's functions, or both. Persons who do not comply with subpoenas can be cited for contempt of Congress and prosecuted.

Subsidy—Generally, a payment or benefit made by the federal government for which no current repayment is required. Subsidy payments may be designed to support the conduct of an economic enterprise or activity, such as ship operations, or to support certain market prices, as in the case of farm subsidies.

Sunset Legislation—A term sometimes applied to laws authorizing the existence of agencies or programs that expire annually or at the end of some other specified period of time. One of the purposes of setting specific expiration dates for agencies and programs is to encourage the committees with jurisdiction over them to determine whether they should be continued or terminated.

Sunshine Rules—Rules requiring open committee hearings and business meetings, including markup sessions, in both houses, and also open conference committee meetings. However, all may be closed under certain circumstances and using certain procedures required by the rules.

Supermajority—A term sometimes used for a vote on a matter that requires approval by more than a simple majority of those members present and voting; also referred to as extraordinary majority.

Supplemental Appropriation Bill—A measure providing appropriations for use in the current fiscal year, in addition to those already provided in annual general appropriation bills. Supplemental appropriations are often for unforeseen emergencies.

Suspension of the Rules (House)—An expeditious procedure for passing relatively noncontroversial or emergency measures by a two-thirds vote of those members voting, a quorum being present.

Suspension of the Rules (Senate)—A procedure to set aside one or more of the Senate's rules; it is used infrequently, and then most often to suspend the rule banning legislative amendments to appropriation bills.

Task Force—A title sometimes given to a panel of members assigned to a special project, study, or investigation. Ordinarily, these groups do not have authority to report measures to their respective houses.

Tax Expenditure—Loosely, a tax exemption or advantage, sometimes called an incentive or loophole; technically, a loss of governmental tax revenue attributable to some provision of federal tax laws that allows a special exclusion, exemption, or deduction from gross income or that provides a special credit, preferential tax rate, or deferral of tax liability.

Televised Proceedings—Television and radio coverage of the floor proceedings of the House of Representatives have been available since 1979 and of the Senate since 1986. They are broadcast over a coaxial cable system to all congressional offices and to some congressional agencies on channels reserved for that purpose. Coverage is also available free of charge to commercial and public television and radio broadcasters. C-SPAN carries gavel-to-gavel coverage of both houses. *(See C-SPAN.)*

Teller Vote—A voting procedure, formerly used in the House, in which members cast their votes by passing through the center aisle to be counted, but not recorded by name, by a member from each party appointed by the chair. The House deleted the procedure from its rules in 1993, but during floor discussion of the deletion a leading member stated that a teller vote would still be available in the event of a breakdown of the electronic voting system.

Third-Degree Amendment—An amendment to a second-degree amendment. Both houses prohibit such amendments.

Third Reading—A required reading to a chamber of a bill or joint resolution by title only before the vote on passage. In modern practice, it has merely become a pro forma step.

Three-Day Rule—(1) In the House, a measure cannot be considered until the third calendar day on which the committee report has been available. (2) In the House, a conference report cannot be considered until the third calendar day on which its text has been available in the *Congressional Record.* (3) In the House, a general appropriation bill cannot be considered until the third calendar day on which printed hearings on the bill have been available. (4) In the Senate, when a committee votes to report a measure, a committee member is entitled to three calendar days within which to submit separate views for inclusion in the committee report. (In House committees, a member is entitled to two calendar days for this purpose, after the day on which the committee votes to report.) (5) In both houses, a majority of a committee's members may call a special meeting of the committee if its chairman fails to do so within three calendar days after three or more of the members, acting jointly, formally request such a meeting. In calculating such periods, the House omits holiday and weekend days on which it does not meet. The Senate makes no such exclusion.

Tie Vote—When the votes for and against a proposition are equal, it loses. The president of the Senate—the constitutional role of the vice president—may cast a vote only to break a tie. Because the Speaker is invariably a member of the House, the Speaker is entitled to vote but usually does not. The Speaker may choose to do so to break, or create, a tie vote.

Title—(1) A major subdivision of a bill or act, designated by a roman numeral and usually containing legislative provisions on the same general subject. Titles are sometimes divided into subtitles as well as sections. (2) The official name of a bill or act, also called a caption or long title. (3) Some bills also have short titles that appear in the sentence immediately following the enacting clause. (4) Popular titles are the unofficial names given to some bills or acts by common usage. For example, the Balanced Budget and Emergency Deficit Control Act of 1985 (short title) is almost invariably referred to as Gramm-Rudman (popular title). In other cases, significant legislation is popularly referred to by its title number *(see definition (1) above)*. For example, the federal legislation that requires equality of funding for women's and men's sports in educational institutions that receive federal funds is popularly called Title IX.

Track System—An occasional Senate practice that expedites legislation by dividing a day's session into two or more specific time periods, commonly called tracks, each reserved for consideration of a different measure.

Transfer Payment—A federal government payment to which individuals or organizations are entitled under law and for which no goods or services are required in return. Payments include welfare and Social Security benefits, unemployment insurance, government pensions, and veterans benefits.

Treaty—A formal document containing an agreement between two or more sovereign nations. The Constitution authorizes the president to make treaties, but the president must submit them to the Senate for its approval by a two-thirds vote of the senators present. Under the Senate's rules, that vote actually occurs on a resolution of ratification. Although the Constitution does not give the House a direct role in approving treaties, that body has sometimes insisted that a revenue treaty is an invasion of its prerogatives. In any case, the House may significantly affect the application of a treaty by its equal role in enacting legislation to implement the treaty.

Trust Funds—Special accounts in the Treasury that receive earmarked taxes or other kinds of revenue collections, such as user fees, and from which payments are made for special purposes or to recipients who meet the requirements of the trust funds as established by law. Of the more than 150 federal government trust funds, several finance major entitlement programs, such as Social Security, Medicare, and retired federal employees' pensions. Others fund infrastructure construction and improvements, such as highways and airports.

Unanimous Consent—Without an objection by any member. A unanimous consent request asks permission, explicitly or implicitly, to set aside one or more rules. Both houses and their committees frequently use such requests to expedite their proceedings.

Uncontrollable Expenditures—A frequently used term for federal expenditures that are mandatory under existing law and therefore cannot be controlled by the president or Congress without a change in the existing law. Uncontrollable expenditures include spending required under entitlement programs and also fixed costs, such as interest on the public debt and outlays to pay for prior-year obligations. In recent years, uncontrollables have accounted for approximately three-quarters of federal spending in each fiscal year.

Unfunded Mandate—Generally, any provision in federal law or regulation that imposes a duty or obligation on a state or local government or private sector entity without providing the necessary funds to comply. The Unfunded Mandates Reform Act of 1995 amended the Congressional Budget Act of 1974 to provide a mechanism for the control of new unfunded mandates.

Union Calendar—A calendar of the House of Representatives for bills and resolutions favorably reported by committees that raise revenue or directly or indirectly appropriate money or property. In addition to appropriation bills, measures that authorize expenditures are also placed on this calendar. The calendar's full title is the Calendar of the Committee of the Whole House on the State of the Union.

Upper Body—A common reference to the Senate, but not used by members of the House.

U.S. Code—Popular title for the *United States Code: Containing the General and Permanent Laws of the United States in Force on* ... It is a consolidation and partial codification of the general and permanent laws of the United States arranged by subject under fifty titles. The first six titles deal with general or political subjects, the other forty-four with subjects ranging from agriculture to war, alphabetically arranged. A supplement is published after each session of Congress, and the entire *Code* is revised every six years.

User Fee—A fee charged to users of goods or services provided by the federal government. When Congress levies or authorizes such fees, it determines whether the revenues should go into the general collections of the Treasury or be available for expenditure by the agency that provides the goods or services.

Veto—The president's disapproval of a legislative measure passed by Congress. The president returns the measure to the house in which it originated without his signature but with a veto message stating his objections to it. When Congress is in session, the president must veto a bill within ten days, excluding Sundays, after the president has received it; otherwise it becomes law without his signature. The ten-day clock begins to run at midnight following his receipt of the bill. *(See also Committee Veto; Item Veto; Line Item Veto Act of 1996; Override a Veto; Pocket Veto.)*

Voice Vote—A method of voting in which members who favor a question answer aye in chorus, after which those opposed answer no in chorus, and the chair decides which position prevails.

Voting—Members vote in three ways on the floor: (1) by shouting "aye" or "no" on voice votes; (2) by standing for or against on division votes; and (3) on recorded votes (including the yeas and nays), by answering "aye" or "no" when their names are called or, in the House, by recording their votes through the electronic voting system.

War Powers Resolution of 1973—An act that requires the president "in every possible instance" to consult Congress before committing U.S. forces to ongoing or imminent hostilities. If the president commits forces to a combat situation without congressional consultation, the president must notify Congress within forty-eight hours. Unless Congress declares war or otherwise authorizes the operation to continue, the forces must be withdrawn within sixty or ninety days, depending on certain conditions. No president has ever acknowledged the constitutionality of the resolution.

Well—The sunken, level, open space between members' seats and the podium at the front of each chamber. House members usually address their chamber from their party's lectern in the well on its side of the aisle. Senators usually speak at their assigned desks.

Whip—The majority or minority party member in each house who acts as assistant leader, helps plan and marshal support for party strategies, encourages party discipline, and advises his or her leader on how colleagues intend to vote on the floor.

Yeas and Nays—A vote in which members usually respond "aye" or "no" (despite the official title of the vote) on a question when their names are called in alphabetical order. The Constitution requires the yeas and nays when a demand for it is supported by one-fifth of the members present, and it also requires an automatic yea-and-nay vote on overriding a veto. Senate precedents require the support of at least one-fifth of a quorum, a minimum of eleven members with the present membership of 100.

The Legislative Process in Brief

Note: *Parliamentary terms used below are defined in the glossary.*

INTRODUCTION OF BILLS

A House member (including the resident commissioner of Puerto Rico and nonvoting delegates of the District of Columbia, Guam, the Virgin Islands, and American Samoa) may introduce any one of several types of bills and resolutions at any time the House is in session by handing it to the clerk of the House or placing it in a box called the hopper. A senator usually introduces a measure by presenting it, along with a formal statement, to a clerk at the presiding officer's desk.

As the usual next step in either the House or Senate, the bill is numbered, referred to the appropriate committee, labeled with the sponsor's name and sent to the Government Printing Office (GPO) so that copies can be made for subsequent study and action. House and Senate bills may be jointly sponsored and carry several lawmakers' names. Print and electronic versions of the bill are available to the public. A bill written in the executive branch and proposed as an administration measure usually is introduced by the chairman of the congressional committee that has jurisdiction, as a courtesy to the White House.

Bills—Prefixed with HR in the House, S in the Senate, followed by a number. Used as the form for most legislation, whether general or special, public or private.

Joint Resolutions—Designated H J Res or S J Res. Subject to the same procedure as bills, with the exception of a joint resolution proposing an amendment to the Constitution. The latter must be approved by two-thirds of both houses and is thereupon sent directly to the administrator of general services for submission to the states for ratification instead of being presented to the president for his approval.

Concurrent Resolutions—Designated H Con Res or S Con Res. Used for matters affecting the operations of both houses. These resolutions do not become law.

Resolutions—Designated H Res or S Res. Used for a matter concerning the operation of either house alone and adopted only by the chamber in which it originates.

COMMITTEE ACTION

With few exceptions, bills are referred to the appropriate standing committees. The job of referral formally is the responsibility of the Speaker of the House and the presiding officer of the Senate, but this task usually is carried out on their behalf by the parliamentarians of the House and Senate. Precedent, statute and the jurisdictional mandates of the committees as set forth in the rules of the House and Senate determine which committees receive what kinds of bills. Bills are technically considered "read for the first time" when referred to House committees.

When a bill reaches a committee it is placed on the committee's calendar. Failure of a committee to act on a bill is equivalent to killing it and most fall by the legislative roadside. The measure can be withdrawn from the committee's purview by a discharge petition signed by a majority of the House membership on House bills, or, for example, by adoption of a special resolution in the Senate. Discharge attempts rarely succeed and the Senate procedure is rarely used.

The first committee action taken on a bill may be a request for comment on it by interested agencies of the government. The committee chairman may assign the bill to a subcommittee for study and hearings, or it may be considered by the full committee. Hearings may be public, closed (executive session), or both. A subcommittee, after considering a bill, reports to the full committee its recommendations for action and any proposed amendments.

The full committee then votes on its recommendation to the House or Senate. This procedure is called "ordering a bill reported." Occasionally a committee may order a bill reported unfavorably; most of the time a report, submitted by the chairman of the committee to the House or Senate, calls for favorable action on the measure since the committee can effectively "kill" a bill by simply failing to take any action.

After the bill is reported, the committee chairman instructs the staff to prepare a written report. The report describes the purposes and scope of the bill, explains the committee revisions, notes proposed changes in existing law and, usually, includes the views of the executive branch agencies consulted. Often committee members opposing a measure issue dissenting minority statements that are included in the report.

Usually, the committee "marks up" or proposes amendments to the bill. If they are substantial and the measure is complicated, the committee may order a "clean bill" introduced, which will embody the proposed amendments. The original bill then is put aside and the clean bill, with a new number, is reported to the floor.

The chamber must approve, alter or reject the committee amendments before the bill itself can be put to a vote.

FLOOR ACTION

After a bill is reported back to the house where it originated, it is placed on the calendar.

There are four legislative calendars in the House, issued in one cumulative calendar titled *Calendars of the United States House of Representatives and History of Legislation.* The House calendars are:

The Union Calendar to which are referred bills raising revenues, general appropriations bills, and any measures directly or indirectly appropriating money or property. It is the Calendar of the Committee of the Whole House on the State of the Union.

The House Calendar to which are referred bills of public character not raising revenue or appropriating money.

The Private Calendar to which are referred bills for relief in the nature of claims against the United States or private immigration bills that are passed without debate when the Private Calendar is called the first and third Tuesdays of each month.

The Discharge Calendar to which are referred motions to discharge committees when the necessary signatures are signed to a discharge petition.

There is only one legislative calendar in the Senate and one "executive calendar" for treaties and nominations submitted to the Senate.

Debate

A bill is brought to debate by varying procedures. In the Senate the majority leader, in consultation with the minority leader and others, schedules the bills that will be taken up for debate. If it is urgent or important it can be taken up in the Senate either by unanimous consent or by a motion agreed to by majority vote.

In the House, precedence is granted if a special rule is obtained from the Rules Committee. A request for a special rule usually is made by the chairman of the committee that favorably reported the bill. The request is considered by the Rules Committee in the same fashion that other committees consider legislative measures. The committee proposes a resolution providing for the consideration of the bill. The Rules Committee reports the resolution to the House where it is debated and voted on in the same fashion as regular bills.

The resolutions providing special rules are important because they specify how long the bill may be debated and whether it may be amended from the floor. If floor amendments are banned, the bill is considered under a "closed rule."

When a bill is debated under an "open rule," germane amendments may be offered from the floor. Committee amendments always are taken up first but may be changed, as may all amendments up to the second degree; that is, an amendment to an amendment to an amendment is not in order.

Duration of debate in the House depends on whether the bill is under discussion by the House proper or before the House when it is sitting as the Committee of the Whole House on the State of the Union. In the former, the amount of time for debate occurs under the one-hour rule, which allows members to hold the floor for one hour each. In practice, the members first recognized to speak move the previous question after an hour, which the House almost always approves and which ends further debate. In the Committee of the Whole the amount of time specified in the special rule for general debate is equally divided between proponents and opponents. At the end of general debate, the bill is often read section by section for amendment if it is considered under an open rule. Debate on an amendment is limited to five minutes for each side; this is called the "five-minute rule." In practice, amendments regularly are debated more than ten minutes, with members gaining the floor by offering pro forma amendments or obtaining unanimous consent to speak longer than five minutes.

Senate debate usually is unlimited. It can be halted or limited only by unanimous consent, by certain laws, by adoption of a motion to table, or by "cloture," which requires a three-fifths majority of the entire Senate except for proposed changes in the Senate rules. The latter requires a two-thirds vote.

The House considers almost all important bills within a parliamentary framework known as the Committee of the Whole. It is not a committee as the word usually is understood; it is the full House meeting under another name for the purpose of speeding action on legislation. Technically, the House sits as the Committee of the Whole when it considers any tax measure or bill dealing with public appropriations. Upon adoption of a special rule, the Speaker declares the House resolved into the Committee of the Whole and appoints a member of the majority party to serve as the chairman. Instead of the required quorum of 218 for the House, the rules of that chamber permit the Committee of the Whole to meet when a quorum of 100 members is present on the floor and to amend and act on bills. When the Committee of the Whole has concluded consideration of a bill for amendment, it "rises," the Speaker returns as the presiding officer of the House and the member appointed chairman of the Committee of the Whole reports the action of the committee and its recommendations. The Committee of the Whole cannot pass a bill; instead it reports the measure to the full House with whatever amendment it has adopted. The full House then may pass or reject the bill—or, on occasion, recommit the bill to committee. Amendments adopted in the Committee of the Whole may be put to a second vote in the full House.

Votes

Voting on bills may occur repeatedly before they are finally approved or rejected. The House votes on the rule for the bill and on various amendments to the bill. Voting on amendments often is a more illuminating test of a bill's support than is the final tally. Sometimes members approve final passage of bills after vigorously supporting amendments that, if adopted, would have scuttled the legislation.

The Senate has three different methods of voting: an untabulated voice vote, a standing vote (called a division), and a recorded roll call to which members answer "yea" or "nay" when their names are called. The House also employs voice and standing votes, but since January 1973 yeas and nays have been recorded by an electronic voting device, eliminating the need for time-consuming roll calls.

After amendments to a bill have been voted on, it is "read for the third time." Then a vote may be taken on a motion to recommit the bill or joint resolution to committee. If carried, which rarely occurs, this vote is usually a death blow to the bill. Rejection of the motion to recommit is followed by a vote on final passage of the bill. The final vote is followed by a pro forma motion to reconsider, which is automatically laid on the table. With that, the bill has been formally passed by the chamber.

ACTION IN SECOND CHAMBER

After a bill is passed it is sent to the other chamber. This body may then take one of several steps. It may pass the bill as is—accepting the other chamber's language. It may send the bill to committee for scrutiny or alteration, or reject the entire bill, advising the other house of its actions. Or it simply may ignore the bill submitted while it continues work on its own version of the proposed legislation. Frequently, one chamber may approve a version of a bill that is greatly at variance with the version already passed by the other house, and then substitute its contents for the language of the other, retaining only the latter's bill number.

Often the second chamber makes only minor changes. If these are readily agreed to by the other house, the bill then is routed to the president. However, if the opposite chamber significantly alters the bill submitted to it, the measure usually is "sent to conference." The chamber that has possession of the "papers" (engrossed bill, engrossed amendments, messages of transmittal) requests a conference, and the other chamber may agree to it. If the second chamber does not agree, the bill dies, unless other parliamentary actions take place. For example, a senator could reoffer the rejected bill as a nonrelevant amendment to another measure. If both chambers agreed to the nonrelevant amendment, the president could sign the legislative package into law.

CONFERENCE ACTION

A conference works out conflicting House and Senate versions of a legislative bill. The conferees usually are senior members from the committees that managed the legislation who are appointed by the presiding officers of the two houses. Under this arrangement the conferees of one house have the duty of trying to maintain their chamber's position in the face of amending actions by the conferees (also referred to as "managers") of the other house.

How a Bill Becomes Law

This graphic shows the most typical way in which proposed legislation is enacted into law. There are more complicated, as well as simpler, routes, and most bills never become law. The process is illustrated with two hypothetical bills, House bill No. 1 (HR 1) and Senate bill No. 2 (S 2). Bills must be passed by both houses in identical form before they can be sent to the president. The path of HR 1 is traced by a black line, that of S 2 by a gray line. In practice, most bills begin as similar proposals in both houses.

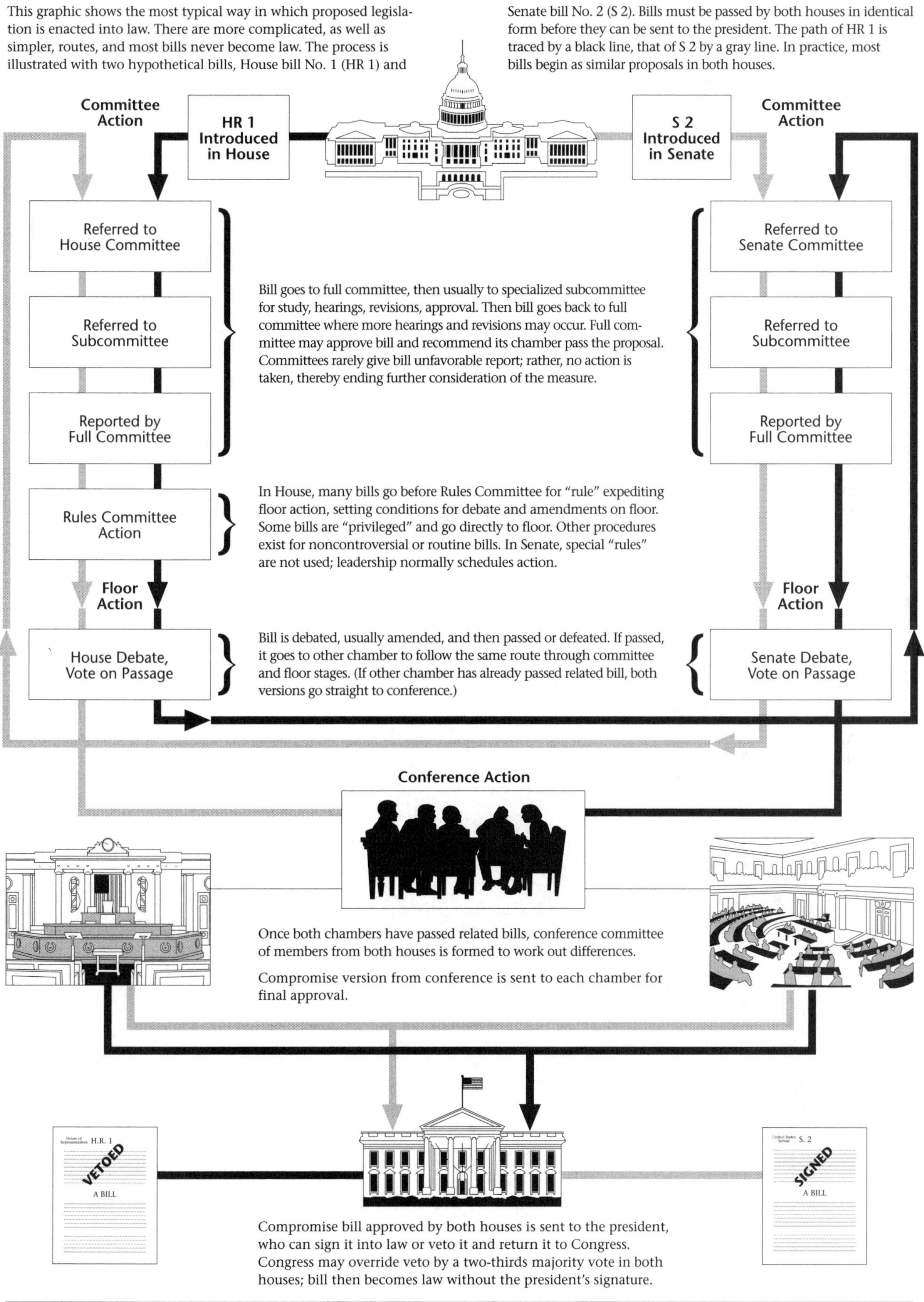

Examples of Legislative Documents
Calendar No. 35
S. CON. RES. 17
CONCURRENT RESOLUTION
Union Calendar No. 180
H. R. 1411
A BILL
S. J. RES. 33
JOINT RESOLUTION
Calendar No. 277
S. 845
A BILL
S. RES. 54
RESOLUTION
H. CON. RES. 90
CONCURRENT RESOLUTION
S. J. RES. 33
JOINT RESOLUTION
H. R. 668
Calendar No. 19
AN ACT

The number of conferees from each chamber may vary from single to double or even triple digits depending on the length or complexity of the bill and the number of committees involved. But a majority vote controls the action of each group so that a large representation does not give one chamber a voting advantage over the other chamber's conferees.

Theoretically, conferees are not allowed to write new legislation in reconciling the two versions before them, but this curb sometimes is bypassed. Many bills have been put into acceptable compromise form only after new language was provided by the conferees. Frequently the ironing out of difficulties takes days or even weeks. Conferences on complex and controversial bills sometimes are particularly drawn out.

As a conference proceeds, conferees reconcile differences between the versions, but generally they grant concessions only insofar as they remain sure that the chamber they represent will accept the compromises. Occasionally, uncertainty over how either house will react, or the positive refusal of a chamber to back down on a disputed amendment, results in an impasse, and the bills die in conference even though each was approved by its sponsoring chamber.

When the conferees have reached agreement, they prepare a conference report embodying their recommendations (compromises) and a joint explanatory statement. The report, in document form, must be submitted to each house. The conference report must be approved by each house. Consequently, approval of the report is approval of the compromise bill. In the order of voting on conference reports, the chamber that asked for a conference yields to the other chamber the opportunity to vote first.

FINAL ACTION

After a bill has been passed by both the House and Senate in identical form, all of the original papers are sent to the enrolling clerk of the chamber in which the bill originated. He then prepares an enrolled bill, which is printed on parchment paper.

When this bill has been certified as correct by the secretary of the Senate or the clerk of the House, depending on which chamber originated the bill, it is signed first (no matter whether it originated in the Senate or House) by the Speaker of the House and then by the president of the Senate. It is next sent to the White House to await action.

If the president approves the bill, he signs it, dates it and usually writes the word "approved" on the document. If he does not sign it within 10 days (Sundays excepted) and Congress is in session, the bill becomes law without his signature.

If Congress adjourns *sine die* at the end of the second session the president can pocket veto a bill and it dies without Congress having the opportunity to override.

A president vetoes a bill by refusing to sign it and, before the 10-day period expires, returning it to Congress with a message stating his reasons. The message is sent to the chamber that originated the bill. If no action is taken on the message, the bill dies. Congress, however, can attempt to override the president's veto and enact the bill, "the objections of the president to the contrary notwithstanding." Overriding a veto requires a two-thirds vote of those present in each chamber, who must number a quorum and vote by roll call.

If the president's veto is overridden by a two-thirds vote in both houses, the bill becomes law. Otherwise it is dead.

When bills are passed finally and signed, or passed over a veto, they are given law numbers in numerical order as they become law. There are two series of numbers, one for public and one for private laws, starting at the number "1" for each two-year term of Congress. They are then identified by law number and by Congress—for example, Private Law 10, 109th Congress; Public Law 33, 109th Congress (or PL 109-33).

Key Votes

Each year Congressional Quarterly editors select a series of key votes on major issues, and CQ Press reproduces those votes here with permission. An issue is judged by the extent to which it represents one or more of the following:

- A matter of major controversy.
- A test of presidential or political power.
- A decision of potentially great impact on the nation and lives of Americans.

For each series of related votes on an issue only one key vote is usually chosen. This vote is the roll call in the House or Senate that in the opinion of Congressional Quarterly editors was the most important in determining the outcome.

Senate

1. CLASS ACTION SUITS

For six years, business interests lobbied for restrictions on class action lawsuits, only to be thwarted by opponents in the Senate. But the 2004 elections, which increased the number of Republicans in that chamber from fifty-one to fifty-five, showed that elections matter and can change public policy. *(Story, p. 695)*

When the new Congress convened in 2005, GOP leaders moved quickly to a class action bill to give federal courts jurisdiction over cases involving at least 100 plaintiffs if at least $5 million was at stake and two-thirds of the plaintiffs lived in different states.

Majority Leader Bill Frist, R-Tenn., who was contemplating running for president in 2008, wanted an early victory to demonstrate his political influence and leadership. He had pulled the class action bill from the Senate floor in 2004 when a cloture motion fell sixteen votes short of cutting off debate. Frist had help from enough Democrats to prevent opponents from filibustering or using parliamentary delays to stop passage of the bill, as they had before.

Five Democratic amendments to the bill were defeated by wide margins. Supporters argued that adopting any of the amendments would derail the Senate compromise on the bill and complicate House passage. Democratic leaders were resigned to passage of the bill, but contended it would be the "high-water mark" for Republican efforts to limit certain types of lawsuits, such as establishing an asbestos trust fund and limiting damage awards in medical malpractice suits. Those two bills did not get enough support to reach the Senate floor, but legislation to shield gun manufacturers and dealers from being sued when third parties misuse their products was cleared by Congress later in the year.

Without strong opposition from their leadership, eighteen Democrats voted for the class action measure. No Republican voted against it. The bill was passed Feb. 10, 72–26: R 53–0; D 18–26; I 1–0. The House easily cleared the measure the next week, giving President George W. Bush his first major legislative accomplishment of his second term. *(Vote, p. 923)*

Democratic supporters included Sen. Blanche Lincoln of Arkansas, home of retail giant Wal-Mart Stores Inc., which has been the defendant in major class action suits. Another key supporter was Christopher Dodd, D-Conn., whose home state is headquarters to many insurance companies.

In the aftermath of the vote, the Association of Trial Lawyers of America, a vocal opponent of the measure and a major source of campaign funds for Democratic candidates, increased its outreach efforts to Republican lawmakers.

2. BANKRUPTCY LAW OVERHAUL

With an increased majority in the Senate and several Democratic defections, Senate Republican leaders were able to defeat a controversial amendment that had become the critical obstacle to enacting a bankruptcy overhaul bill. The defeat of the amendment by Democrat Charles E. Schumer of New York, which would have prevented violent protesters from avoiding fines by filing for bankruptcy protection, all but guaranteed a victory for the banking and credit card industries and their congressional supporters, who had pushed for eight years to revamp the bankruptcy code.

The Senate passed the bill, 74–25, on March 10. The House followed on April 14 by a 302–126 vote. *(Story, p. 142)*

Approval was not expected if Schumer had prevailed. House Republican leaders had made clear they would not take up the Senate-passed bankruptcy bill if it included the amendment. In earlier versions, the amendment had specifically targeted anti-abortion protesters. In 2002 negotiations between Schumer and a group of House Republicans resulted in the language being changed to include all violent protesters, but the amendment was still anathema to conservative Republicans.

The belief of bankruptcy reform advocates that the Schumer amendment could stop the legislation was not unfounded. During the 106th Congress, President Bill Clinton pocket vetoed a bankruptcy overhaul measure after the Schumer language was dropped from the bill. The amendment continued to plague overhaul advocates in the 107th and 108th Congresses. In 2004 Senate GOP leaders refused to bring the bill to the floor rather than risk having the language adopted.

Aware of the potential implications, Senate GOP leaders aggressively pressured their members to vote against the amendment. This time, Senate Republicans had more factors working in their favor. The most important was control of fifty-five seats in the chamber. That gave them greater leeway to allow some moderate caucus members to vote for the amendment while still ensuring its defeat.

Republicans also could rely on the support of conservative Democrats who opposed abortion rights and did not want to vote for a provision aimed at punishing abortion protesters. Finally, the influence of the credit card and finance industries was substantial. Industry groups reported donating $29.5 million to federal candidates during the eight years it took to enact the bankruptcy overhaul.

Schumer called on the Senate not to "protect those who use violence," telling his colleagues that a vote against his proposal was a vote "against the rule of law." He stressed that the language would apply to any violent protester, not just those who oppose abortion rights. "If violent atheists burn down a church, it would apply to them," Schumer told his colleagues.

Senate Republicans said the amendment was unnecessary and, more immediately, that it would once again prevent Congress from overhauling federal bankruptcy laws.

Jeff Sessions, R-Ala., characterized the amendment as the "most perfect example of a poison pill" he had ever seen. Orrin G. Hatch, R-Utah, argued that bankruptcy courts made clear they would not allow debtors to escape fines and judgments for willful, violent actions.

Republican efforts were enough to kill the amendment. The Senate March 8 voted against it 46–53: R 4–51; D 41–2; I 1–0. *(Vote, p. 923)*

3. CONFIRMATION OF JUDGE PRISCILLA OWEN

Texas Supreme Court justice Priscilla Owen was among the first candidates for the federal bench that President George W.

Bush submitted in 2001, but her nomination languished for more than four years before the Senate voted to confirm her in May 2005.

Owen was perhaps the most ideologically controversial of the ten appellate court nominees whom Democrats filibustered in the Republican-controlled Senate in the 108th Congress. Her opponents argued that she would be hostile to abortion rights as a federal judge. Bush renominated Owen and six of the other previously filibustered candidates in February. Still, the Senate Democratic caucus opposed an up-or-down vote until a group of senators—seven Republicans and seven Democrats—brokered a deal on judicial nominations in May, agreeing not to oppose cloture on the nomination. *(Story, pp. 712, 820)*

A potential showdown over judicial nominations escalated in January, when Majority Leader Bill Frist, R-Tenn., went to the Senate floor on the first day of the 109th Congress to warn that he would not tolerate further Democratic filibusters of appellate court nominees. For the first few months of the year, Frist repeatedly threatened to execute an esoteric procedural gambit, dubbed the "nuclear option," to end minority filibusters of judicial nominees.

Frist and Minority Leader Harry Reid, D-Nev., exchanged half-hearted proposals and rhetorical potshots, to no avail. Finally, Frist scheduled a vote on cloture, which would cut off debate and lead to a vote on Owen's nomination, for May 24.

Frist went before a battery of cameras outside the chamber May 23 to announce that if the cloture vote fell short of the sixty-vote threshold for the motion to succeed, Vice President Dick Cheney would preside over the Senate while Frist made a point of order that there should be a finite amount of debate time for an appellate or a Supreme Court nominee. If Cheney upheld Frist's point of order and Democrats challenged the ruling, a simple majority was all Republicans would need to sustain Cheney's ruling.

Later that day, the group that became known as the "gang of 14" emerged from the Capitol Hill office of Arizona Republican John McCain with the deal that thwarted Frist, but also guaranteed the confirmation of Owen and several other contentious nominees. The fourteen senators also agreed that judicial nominees should be filibustered only under "extraordinary circumstances," a term that was left to each group member to define.

The cloture vote on Owen the next day demonstrated that the fourteen senators had defused what had promised to be a dramatic parliamentary showdown on judicial nominations, effectively taking control of the issue away from Senate leaders. The Senate agreed to the motion to invoke cloture on an 81–18 vote, which easily exceeded the sixty votes needed: R 55–0; D 26–17; I 0–1. *(Vote, p. 923)*

Owen was confirmed the next day with the support of only two Democrats. But the fact that more than half the Democrats had voted to limit debate was a sign of their relief that the "gang of 14" had given the Senate a way to back away from a showdown over rules that could have fundamentally undermined the power of the minority party in the chamber.

4. CONFIRMATION OF JOHN R. BOLTON AS U.N. AMBASSADOR

John R. Bolton's nomination was in trouble from the moment President George W. Bush announced him as his pick for the top job at the United Nations. Viewed as abrasive, confrontational, and willing to run roughshod over his peers at the State Department while he was an undersecretary of state, Bolton faced serious opposition from Democrats and some moderate Republicans. *(Story, p. 280)*

Several former colleagues testified against Bolton during his confirmation hearings. In public testimony, former State Department official Carl Ford Jr. provided the Senate Foreign Relations Committee with a damaging portrait of the nominee, describing him as a "quintessential kiss-up, kick down sort of guy." Bolton's nomination emerged from the committee in May "without recommendation"—not an outright rejection, but a cautionary message that the nominee would have trouble winning approval from the full Senate.

Democrats threatened to filibuster the Bolton nomination as it headed to the Senate floor. In public and private testimony, Bolton's critics accused him of verbally abusing subordinates and trying to manipulate intelligence appraised by State Department analysts regarding Iraq's weapons of mass destruction programs. In an attempt to end debate, Majority Leader Bill Frist, R-Tenn., made a motion to invoke cloture, which requires sixty votes.

But on May 26 the Senate rejected the motion 56–42: R 53–1; D 3–40; I 0–1. That was a major setback for the Bush administration and a blow to Bolton, who had routinely criticized the United Nations and vowed to push for changes at the institution. *(Vote, p. 923)*

The cloture vote showed that Democrats were prepared to obstruct Bush's nominees and reflected the tenuous hold Republicans had on their majority in the Senate. Several moderate Republicans, such as Lincoln Chafee of Rhode Island, George V. Voinovich of Ohio, and Chuck Hagel of Nebraska, remained undecided on Bolton throughout the nomination process, making it that much harder for Frist to bring home a victory for Bush on the controversial nomination.

Democrats contended that Bolton was unworthy of going to the United Nations to represent the U.S. government. They said they would allow a vote only if the White House released a series of intelligence documents showing how Bolton had handled information regarding Syria's weapons programs. Bolton was also accused of requesting National Security Agency intercepts so he could snoop on subordinates at the State Department.

The White House was not forthcoming with the documents, and Democrats refused to budge. The Senate held a second cloture vote June 20, but the result was so apparent that many senators skipped the vote, and cloture failed by even more votes than it did the first time, 54–38.

None of the Senate's parliamentary delays ended up mattering in the end. Bush bypassed the Senate and installed Bolton at the United Nations with a recess appointment on the first day of the August recess. Bolton has been working at the United Nations for five months. His recess appointment expired at the end of the 109th Congress in January. Bush, acknowledging the depth of opposition, did not renominate Bolton at the beginning of the new Congress.

5. GLOBAL WARMING POLICY

From 1997, when the Senate voted 95–0 to condemn the international global warming agreement signed in Kyoto, Japan, through 2004 Congress resisted every effort to set mandatory limits on emissions of carbon dioxide and other gases that were widely blamed for contributing to worldwide climate change.

The Bush administration and, for the most part, Congress argued that the Kyoto accord would damage the U.S. economy while not requiring similar pollution controls from developing nations that were projected to emit more greenhouse gases than the United States. There also remained a core of lawmakers who rejected the premise of global warming, led by Senate Environment and Public Works Committee chairman James M. Inhofe, R-Okla., who called climate change theories "phony science" and a "hoax."

An attempt in 2005 by Sens. John McCain, R-Ariz., and Joseph I. Lieberman, D-Conn., to mandate a reduction in greenhouse gas emissions to 2000 levels by 2010 actually lost ground, winning just thirty-eight votes in favor, down from forty-three votes in 2003. *(Story, p. 495)*

In a change from past practice, however, the Senate went on record for the first time ever as recognizing that climate change was a significant problem and endorsing the need for mandatory emission limits. While largely symbolic, the action, in support of a resolution offered by Jeff Bingaman, D-N.M., signaled a shift in political attitudes.

McCain and Lieberman offered their proposal in June to a comprehensive energy bill (HR 6). Their plan, which they had promoted for several years, would establish a domestic cap-and-trade model similar to the Kyoto approach. Such market-based programs cap overall pollution while allowing businesses to buy and sell permits in order to meet their obligations.

In a bid to attract more votes in 2005, senators embraced nuclear energy as an energy source that emitted no greenhouse gases. The tactic backfired, angering environmentalists and losing the support of several liberal Democrats who had supported the legislation in 2003. The Senate did approve 66–29 a separate amendment by Chuck Hagel, R-Neb., to offer economic incentives for businesses to reduce emissions of carbon dioxide and other greenhouse gases. The voluntary approach appealed to many Republicans, but critics derided it as inadequate.

Bingaman sought to bridge the gap between the McCain-Lieberman proposal to mandate a reduction in emissions and the laissez-faire model advanced by Hagel. He proposed tying emissions caps to economic growth and allowing the government to sell more permits to companies that failed to meet the targets once the market price for credits reached a certain level. This "safety valve" would give businesses economic certainty, but would allow emissions to rise in the future, albeit at a slower rate.

As the ranking Democrat on the Energy and Natural Resources Committee, Bingaman had a cooperative relationship with the panel's GOP chairman, fellow New Mexican Pete V. Domenici, and the two discussed the idea of jointly offering Bingaman's plan as an amendment to the energy bill. Domenici eventually backed off, saying he feared splitting Republicans, alienating the White House, and jeopardizing the energy bill's prospects. But Domenici agreed to hold hearings on the idea and to support an amendment expressing the sense of the Senate that climate change is a problem and endorsing mandatory, market-based measures to "slow, stop, and reverse" emissions.

Inhofe moved to table Bingaman's resolution, thereby presenting the fundamental question of whether global warming was true and illustrating the shifting sentiments on the issue among some Republican senators.

"Climate change is here," said Mike DeWine, R-Ohio, who voted against the McCain-Lieberman amendment. "I am confident that we can draft a bill that will own up to our obligations to our children and our grandchildren and at the same time have dates that are practical." Domenici, who also had voted against McCain-Lieberman, expressed his conviction that the science showed that global warming was occurring and must be addressed.

Bingaman's resolution was adopted by voice vote June 22, after the Senate rejected Inhofe's motion to table the proposal 44–53; R 42–12; D 2–40; I 0–1. *(Vote, p. 923)*

In addition to the six Republicans who had voted for McCain-Lieberman, six more Republicans voted against the attempt to kill Bingaman's resolution. With that vote, fifty-three became a magic number in the Senate's global warming debate, offering a new baseline for potential support and a list of lawmakers who would, in principle, support climate change legislation. It also laid the groundwork for Bingaman, backed by Domenici, to pursue an alternative to the McCain-Lieberman plan in 2006.

6. CENTRAL AMERICAN TRADE LIBERALIZATION

President W. Bush made expansion of trade with Western Hemisphere countries a hallmark of his administration from his first election in 2000. In 2004, after several fits and starts, his administration secured an agreement to relax trade barriers between the United States and Costa Rica, El Salvador, Guatemala, Honduras, and Nicaragua. A parallel agreement was reached with the Dominican Republic. *(Story, p. 202)*

The Constitution gives Congress explicit authority for trade pacts, but for several decades lawmakers allowed the president to negotiate agreements that are then sent to Congress for approval on up-or-down votes. Because no amendments are allowed in committee or on the floor, the White House often had to make side promises to lawmakers to win their votes on trade agreements.

That was the case with the Central American agreement, also known as CAFTA, in 2005. The name evoked echoes the 1993 North American Free-Trade Agreement (NAFTA) with Mexico and Canada, which many members of the House and Senate thought had not been as beneficial for the United States as promised.

Following NAFTA, trade agreements became an increasingly tough sell on Capitol Hill, and CAFTA was the first in more than a decade with low-wage countries that interest groups, especially organized labor, believed were taking U.S. jobs. As a result, supporters of the Central American pact decided to press for a vote first in the Senate, where its prospects were considered better than the House. Because House Republican leaders were uncertain they had the votes to win in that chamber, it was hoped that a Senate vote to pass a bill implementing the agreement would give the House an incentive to do the same.

Trade votes are generally easier in the Senate because senators have more diverse constituencies and the luxury of a six-year term to explain an unpopular vote. But even the Senate was reluctant to pass the CAFTA implementing bill (S 1307) and agreed to do so only after several weeks of administration efforts to address senators' concerns about sugar imports, labor rights in Central America, and general uneasiness about the effects of globalization. When the Senate finally voted late in the evening of June 30, as Congress was trying to stop work for its July Fourth recess, the agreement was approved by the close tally of 54–45: R 43–12; D 10–33; I 1–0. *(Vote, p. 923)*

The closeness of the vote illustrated a shift in sentiment among lawmakers of both parties on trade issues, especially among Democrats.

The Senate vote had the desired effect of pushing the House to approve the pact, although that chamber came close to rejecting it also. The Senate had to vote again to clear the separate House-passed bill (HR 3045). The July 28 vote was almost identical to the early tally—55–45.

7. ENERGY POLICY OVERHAUL

In the culmination of a four-year debate on energy policy, the Senate in 2005 agreed to compromise legislation (HR 6) that followed the outlines of the energy plan President George W. Bush proposed not long after taking office in 2001 but without the centerpiece of his proposal: drilling for oil and gas in Alaska's Arctic National Wildlife Refuge (ANWR). That proved too difficult for Republican leaders to force through.

Negotiators also dropped from the final bill liability protection for companies that make the fuel additive methyl tertiary butyl ether (MTBE), an issue that prevented passage for two consecutive years. *(Story, p. 447)*

The vote showed the broad support for energy legislation once ANWR and MTBE were set aside. More than half of the Senate's Democrats supported the final conference version, with only six Republicans opposed to it. The Senate easily cleared the measure July 29, 74–26: R 49–6; D 25–19; I 0–1. *(Vote, p. 923)*

The bill was a mixed success for the Bush administration and GOP leaders who were intent on increasing domestic production of oil, gas, and nuclear power to reduce U.S. dependence on foreign fuels. Opening the coastal plain of ANWR to energy exploration had been the main feature of Bush's energy plan but a rallying point for environmentalists trying to protect one of the nation's most pristine and remote wilderness areas. Dropping the provision was a GOP defeat.

Under pressure to deliver a bill, Republican leaders—particularly in the House—also had to give up on a contentious liability waiver for MTBE makers that had blocked final action on the bill in the Senate for two years.

The chemical, used at low levels since 1979, became more prevalent when refiners had to meet fuel standards established under the 1990 Clean Air Act amendments to reduce smog. But the additive had since been found to contaminate groundwater in some areas, including the Northeast and West Coast. Lawmakers from those areas worried that giving liability protection for manufacturers might leave states responsible for cleaning up MTBE in the ground.

The new energy law included tax incentives for both traditional and alternative energy producers. It authorized $14.6 billion in tax breaks and credits between 2005 and 2015, including $2.8 billion for fossil fuel production; $2.7 billion to extend the renewable electricity production credit; $1.6 billion for investments in plants designed to use cleaner-burning coal; $1.3 billion for conservation and energy efficiency; and $1.3 billion for alternative-fuel motor vehicles and fuels.

The legislation also made important changes in the regulation of electricity markets, including repeal of the 1935 Public Utility Holding Company Act that restricted some large power companies to certain geographic areas and lines of business. Lawmakers decided that the Federal Energy Regulatory Commission would be better able to examine electric utility books and to block mergers.

8. GUN INDUSTRY LIABILITY SHIELD

A top priority of the National Rifle Association (NRA) was legislation to protect gun makers and dealers from being sued for death and injuries from use of firearms. The NRA was backed by business groups seeking to limit liability lawsuits for their own products. The legislation had stalled in the Senate because of Democratic opposition.

In 2005 Majority Leader Bill Frist, R-Tenn., wanted to avoid a replay of a similar bill's fate in 2004 when Republicans halted action on the entire measure rather than allow it to pass with three amendments attached by Democrats, including renewal of a ban on assault weapons.

When the new bill (S 397) reached the floor in July, Frist filed a succession of amendments—a legislative procedure known as "filling the amendment tree"—that allowed him to control amendments that could be brought up for debate. He allowed consideration only of those proposals he thought were harmless or easy to defeat on the floor, thus thwarting Democratic efforts to add gun control language. *(Story, p. 699)*

Republicans easily defeated Democratic amendments to allow individuals, but not municipalities, to sue gun makers; preserved the right of police officers or minors injured by firearms to sue for damages; and blocked the sale of so-called cop-killer bullets. Instead, the Senate adopted a Republican alternative amendment requiring a study of a uniform standard for testing projectiles against body armor and increasing the penalties for violent or drug-trafficking crimes in which the perpetrator uses or possesses armor-piercing ammunition.

The Senate adopted only one Democratic amendment, by Herb Kohl of Wisconsin, to require that child safety locks be sold with all handguns.

The final vote on July 29 was a victory for GOP leaders, who had promised to pass the legislation before the August recess, and showed the power of the gun rights lobby led by the NRA. The vote was 65–31: R 50–2; D 14–29; I 1–0. *(Vote, p. 923)*

The fourteen Democrats who voted for the bill were all from states with large rural areas where hunting was popular. Independent James M. Jeffords of Vermont also voted for the legislation, while two Republicans—Lincoln Chafee of Rhode Island and Mike DeWine of Ohio—voted against it.

The House cleared the bill 283–144 in October.

9. SURFACE TRANSPORTATION SPENDING

For the second straight year, Majority Leader Bill Frist, R-Tenn., in 2005 had to contain open defiance within his caucus at the administration's transportation spending policy. Even fiscal conservatives such as James M. Inhofe of Oklahoma, chairman of the Environment and Public Works Committee, and Charles E. Grassley of Iowa, who chaired the Finance Committee, wanted to spend more on highway programs than was acceptable to the administration. *(Story, p. 407)*

The long impasse and the vote accepting the eventual compromise showed the enduring power of public works projects for members of Congress, irrespective of their party. Frist was able to claim a victory of sorts for fiscal responsibility because the final conference version of the bill (HR 3) exceeded the administration's request by just $2.5 billion. But the administration had made the task easier at the beginning of 2005 by increasing its request from $256 billion to $284 billion. Also, the bill included an $8.5 billion rescission of prior contract authority that was to become available at the end of fiscal 2009, boosting the available total contract authority at that point and increasing the cost of the bill to $295 billion. The authorization was good through fiscal 2009 and was retroactive to fiscal 2004.

Frist attempted to set the parameters early by saying that he stood by the administration's $284 billion request and threatening to bar anything more expensive from coming to the floor. But Inhofe said the nation's legitimate transportation needs required far more money and that transportation was one of the few areas where he, as a conservative, felt increased federal spending was justified. His committee sent to the floor a $284 billion package, but supported amending it to increase the authorization to $295 billion.

Grassley put together a package of tax changes and measures designed to crack down on fuel fraud that supporters claimed fully paid for the additional spending, a proposal quickly attacked by fiscal conservatives as insufficient. Grassley's proposals also drew a veto threat from the White House and warnings from House Republican leaders that they would not survive conference negotiations.

Those negotiations were predictably difficult. The Senate took a different approach from the House in determining how much highway money each state would receive and in resolving long-standing complaints from the states that collect significantly more in gasoline taxes than they receive back from the government for transportation projects. The final bill was nearly the same as the Senate approach, guaranteeing each state a bonus to ensure by fiscal 2008 a return of at least 92 cents on each dollar contributed to the Highway Trust Fund.

The House adopted the conference report 412–8 on July 29 and sent it to the Senate. A little more than an hour later, the Senate cleared the measure 91–4: R 48–4; D 42–0; I 1–0. *(Vote, p. 923)*

10. CONFIRMATION OF JOHN G. ROBERTS JR. AS CHIEF JUSTICE

After President George W. Bush took office in 2001, conservative and liberal activists alike braced for a major Senate battle over his first Supreme Court nominee. But by the time the nomination of John G. Roberts Jr. to succeed William H. Rehnquist as chief justice reached the Senate floor in September 2005, there was no suspense about the outcome. *(Stories, pp. 727, 728, 729)*

Roberts, an accomplished appellate lawyer and federal appeals court judge, was originally nominated to replace centrist Justice Sandra Day O'Connor, who announced her retirement July 1 contingent on her successor's confirmation. After Rehnquist died Sept. 3, Bush instead nominated Roberts to succeed the chief justice.

Roberts performed brilliantly in his Senate Judiciary Committee confirmation hearing. Given that, and the fact that he was to replace the conservative Rehnquist, many Democrats chose not to heed the urging of liberal activists to vote against him.

The vote on Roberts marked a turning point in the judicial nomination war that had raged in the Senate since 2003. The filibuster-proof tally was a clear sign that many Senate Democrats lacked the appetite to oppose Bush's pick for the high court for ideological reasons.

Still, the Sept. 29 vote was historic, infused with more than a little sense of drama. It was the first Senate action on a chief justice nominee since 1986. Many senators had never voted on a Supreme Court nominee; the last high court vacancy occurred in 1994. In recognition of the rarity of the moment, senators voted from their desks as the roll was called, rather than by their usual method of casting their votes in the well. Jane Roberts, the nominee's wife, watched from the gallery.

Twenty-two Democrats and Independent James M. Jeffords of Vermont joined all Republicans to support Roberts. The vote was 78–22: R 55–0; D 22–22; I 1–0. *(Vote, p. 923)*

11. TREATMENT OF MILITARY DETAINEES

No proposal caused more waves in Congress in the fall of 2005 than legislation championed by John McCain, R-Ariz., to regulate the treatment of enemy combatants captured and detained by U.S. military forces or law enforcement officers. The proposal resulted in the delay of two major defense bills, a veto threat, and frequent personal visits and phone calls to key lawmakers by Vice President Dick Cheney. The White House repeatedly told lawmakers they must not pass any legislation that would tie the president's hands in the war on terror. *(Story, pp. 366, 724, 764.)*

The Republican-controlled Senate responded, but not with the outcome the White House wanted. On Oct. 5, the Senate adopted McCain's amendment 90–9: R 46–9; D 43–0; I 1–0. *(Vote, p. 923)*

With such strong bipartisan support, the vote was the most direct slap to the administration on the moral conduct of the war on terrorism since it began four years ago. After a string of prison abuse scandals and questions over the legal rights of detainees, lawmakers agreed with McCain that the policy on handling military detainees should be decided by Congress.

McCain's amendment, adopted as part of the fiscal 2006 defense appropriations bill (HR 2863), banned cruel, inhuman, or degrading treatment of detainees. It also required military interrogators to use an Army field manual when trying to extract intelligence from suspects. The field manual, under revision at the time of the vote, outlined specific interrogation techniques that complied with the Geneva Conventions. President George W. Bush has argued that the Geneva standards applied to state-sponsored, uniformed soldiers, but not to terrorists.

McCain, who as a Navy flier during the Vietnam War was shot down, captured, and tortured for five and a half years, told his colleagues that banning the abuse of suspected terrorists was necessary. "They don't deserve our sympathy. But this isn't about who they are. This is about who we are. These are the values that distinguish us from our enemies." Terrorists do not adhere to anti-torture treaties, McCain said, "but "we're better than them, and we are the stronger for our faith."

A member of the Armed Services Committee, McCain initially proposed the language as an amendment to the fiscal 2006 defense authorization bill (S 1042), which was on the Senate floor in July. But Majority Leader Bill Frist, R-Tenn., pulled the authorization bill, citing more than 200 pending amendments. Frist said debate would take too long, and the Senate turned its attention to legislation that would shield gun makers from liability lawsuits. McCain, however, insisted that his proposal was the primary reason the bill was pulled.

In October, McCain sought to attach the detainee requirements to the must-pass defense appropriations bill. Frist was among the Republicans who voted in favor of the antiabuse proposal. McCain subsequently won voice vote approval to add the language to the defense authorization bill as well.

After the House expressed strong support for the amendment in mid-December, Bush backed away from his veto threat. The amendment, with a relatively minor change, was cleared as part of both defense bills.

12. REDIRECTION OF LAWMAKERS' EARMARKS

The Senate was embarrassed in 2005 by news coverage of its multimillion-dollar appropriations for "bridges to nowhere" on the coast of Alaska, but not enough to threaten the congressional tradition of members earmarking federal projects and programs for their own states. Not long after Rep. Don Young, R-Alaska, included the bridge projects at Ketchikan and Anchorage in a highway authorization bill someone noticed that they would connect to lightly settled areas—the Ketchikan bridge would link the town to an island with fifty residents and Ketchikan's airport—and dubbed them bridges to nowhere. *(Story, pp. 74, 414.)*

Freshman Republican Tom Coburn of Oklahoma, a staunch fiscal conservative, decided to take action when the fiscal 2006 Transportation-Treasury-Housing appropriations bill came to the Senate floor. "What I am here to tell you is that the rumble against spending is getting louder. People are fed up," Coburn told his colleagues. "All across the country, Americans are rising up against government overspending." Coburn proposed removing the $454 million for the bridges and spending it instead to reconstruct a Mississippi River bridge in New Orleans damaged by Hurricane Katrina.

Alaska Republican Ted Stevens, former chairman of the Senate Appropriations Committee, was incensed at this challenge to the earmark system. "This amendment is an offense to me," Stevens thundered. "It is not only an offense to me, it is a threat to every person in my state.... It is wrong to do this to any state."

If Coburn's amendment were adopted, then money might be shifted from one state to another at will. "I will put the Senate on notice—and I don't kid people," Stevens said later. "If the Senate decides to discriminate against our state and take money only from our state, I will resign from this body. This is not the Senate I came to. This is not the Senate I devoted thirty-seven years to. If one senator can decide he will take all the money from one state to solve a problem of another, that is not a union. That is not equality and is not treating my state the way I have seen it treated for thirty-seven years."

The Senate agreed, and the Oct. 20 vote was a lopsided 15–82: R 11–43; D 4–38; I 0–1. *(Vote, p. 923)*

Although the amendment was defeated, it had at least in part the effect Coburn wanted. Media attention to the Alaska bridges increased the pressure on Congress to do something about them. Conferees on the appropriations bill quietly removed the specific funding for the two bridges as part of the final agreement. Instead, the conference report redirected the money to a general fund that the state of Alaska could spend on transportation projects at its discretion.

This achieved two goals: enabling Coburn and those who campaigned against such projects to declare a victory, while also allowing Stevens and his Alaskan colleagues to save face by keeping the money in their state.

But there was nothing in the final bill that would prevent the state from simply deciding to allocate money to the two bridges.

13. CONDUCT OF THE WAR IN IRAQ

More than any legislation passed since the invasion of Iraq in 2003, the Senate vote Nov. 15, 2005, sent a strong message to President George W. Bush that Republicans were losing patience with his "stay the course" argument and were watching the decline in public support for the war with increasing wariness as the 2006 midterm elections approached. The vote also represented Congress' most forceful assertion since the war began that it has authority equal to the administration's in overseeing the conduct of the conflict.

The vote was on an amendment to the fiscal 2006 defense authorization bill (S 1042), offered by Majority Leader Bill Frist, R-Tenn., and John W. Warner, R-Va., chairman of the Armed Services Committee. Its stated purpose was "to clarify and recommend changes to the policy of the United States on Iraq and to require reports on certain matters related to Iraq." *(Story, pp. 270, 303.)*

The amendment, which was included in the final bill, required the Bush administration to set a schedule for meeting preconditions for a pullout of U.S. troops from Iraq, such as the training of Iraqi security forces. It required quarterly reports to Congress, in which the administration would define the criteria for success in Iraq, including details on the number of Iraqi battalions that must be able to fight independently before U.S. troops can withdraw.

In addition, in nonbinding "sense of the Senate" language, the amendment declared 2006 as the year that Iraqis should take the lead on their security. It called on the administration to tell Iraqi leaders to make the compromises necessary for political progress, and to explain to the American people what the president has called his "strategy for success." The Senate adopted the amendment 79–19: R 41–13; D 37–6; I 1–0. *(Vote, p. 923)*

Previous legislation had required the administration to provide Congress with reports on its progress in Iraq. The 2005 action required the White House to describe—in unclassified reports available to the public—how conditions in Iraq related to goals for withdrawing U.S. troops. The measure also required classified reports for lawmakers.

The GOP proposal was nearly identical to a Democratic plan sponsored by Carl Levin of Michigan, ranking member on Armed Services. The only significant difference was that Republicans rejected Democratic language that called for "estimated dates for the phased redeployment of the United States Armed Forces from Iraq." On Nov. 15, Republicans defeated Levin's version of the amendment 40–58.

14. USA PATRIOT ACT REAUTHORIZATION

Throughout 2005 a small band of Senate Republicans worked closely with their Democratic colleagues to increase restrictions on surveillance powers granted to the executive branch under the 2001 antiterrorism law known at the Patriot Act. But when it became clear that GOP leaders in the House and Senate, working with the White House, would not go far enough to satisfy critics' concerns about civil liberties protections, a nearly unanimous bloc of Democrats stuck with the small group of Republicans and refused to end a filibuster of the conference report on a bill (HR 3199) to reauthorize sixteen provisions of the law that were set to expire Dec. 31. *(Story, p. 222)*

On Dec. 16, two days after the House adopted the conference report on HR 3199, the Senate defeated a motion to invoke cloture, or limit debate, on the report. The action forced President George W. Bush and GOP leaders to do something they vowed they would never do: accept a short-term extension of the law to give negotiators more time to resolve their differences.

The vote illustrated that four years after the Sept. 11, 2001, terrorist attacks, the mood of lawmakers had shifted toward recognizing public concerns about civil liberties and the extent of police powers exercised in the fight against terrorism. The vote was taken on the same day *The New York Times* reported that Bush had authorized warrantless monitoring of international phone calls placed by U.S. citizens.

The motion to invoke cloture and limit debate on the conference report fell eight votes short of the sixty required for it to succeed. The vote was 52–47: R 50–5; D 2–41; I 0–1. Majority Leader Bill Frist, R-Tenn., switched his vote to "no" in a procedural tactic so he could move to reconsider the vote later. *(Vote, p. 923)*

Republicans John E. Sununu of New Hampshire, Larry E. Craig of Idaho, Lisa Murkowski of Alaska, and Chuck Hagel of Nebraska joined forty-one Democrats and the Senate's single independent, James M. Jeffords of Vermont, in voting against cloture. Two Democrats—Ben Nelson of Nebraska and Tim Johnson of South Dakota—voted with the Republicans.

15. CUTS IN MANDATORY SPENDING

Clearing the $38.8 billion budget reconciliation package (S 1932) for fiscal 2006 was a top priority for President George W. Bush and Republican leaders of both chambers in late 2005. The only obstacle as the Senate entered the final day of the session was adoption of the conference report. The spending-cut measure survived, more or less intact, when Vice President Dick Cheney cut short a trip to the Middle East to cast a tie-breaking vote.

But Democrats spoiled Republican hopes for a pre-adjournment victory on a package of savings from entitlement programs such as Medicare, Medicaid, and student loans, the first since 1997. The measure was sent back to the House where final action was put off until 2006. *(Story, pp. 81, 535.)*

The key vote came on a motion by Judd Gregg, R-N.H., to concur in House amendments on the conference report with a Senate amendment of its own to change programs that would result in a net savings of $38.8 billion over five years. Compared to the original conference agreement, the Senate amendment removed two reporting requirements and a third dealing with Medicaid liability treatment for hospitals. The Senate adopted a motion to concur in the House version of the bill, with its own amendment that amounted to the original conference agreement minus the three stricken provisions. The motion was agreed to with Cheney casting a "yea" vote to break a tie vote of 50–50: R 50–5; D 0–44; I 0–1. *(Vote, p. 923)*

The three provisions were deleted before the final Senate vote on the measure Dec. 21 when Kent Conrad, D-N.D., invoked the so-called Byrd Rule, named after Sen. Robert C. Byrd, D-W.Va. That rule prohibited the inclusion of items in a reconciliation bill that have only an incidental budgetary effect, and sixty votes were required to override the rule. An attempt by Gregg, chairman of the Budget Committee, to waive the rule—and preserve the conference agreement without change—failed on a 52–48 vote.

But more important, once the Byrd Rule was invoked, the conference report was no longer valid for floor action, and the Senate therefore had to amend the bill and return it to the House, which would then have to accept the Senate's changes in order to clear the measure for the president. Of the three provisions the one that was controversial would have granted hospitals immunity from malpractice lawsuits if they chose not to treat Medicaid recipients who could not afford co-payments. Two other provisions were technical ones.

Although the language of the conference agreement was largely unchanged when it got over to the House, Minority Leader Nancy Pelosi, D-Calif., insisted on a roll-call vote. Because most House members had already headed home for the holidays, Republican leaders had little choice but to put off the vote on the slightly altered package until early 2006.

16. OIL DRILLING IN ALASKA

Legislation enacted in 1980, PL 96-487, left it up to Congress, not the White House, to decide whether to open part of the Arctic National Wildlife Refuge (ANWR) to oil and gas development. Lawmakers rejected ANWR drilling measures over the next several years, until a Republican-led Congress included a provision in a 1995 budget-saving measure to allow energy development in the area. President Bill Clinton vetoed the bill, and a decade later the fight over developing ANWR—fueled by record gasoline prices—was as fierce as ever. *(Story, p. 474)*

In recent years leading up to 2005, the Senate consistently blocked ANWR drilling efforts. But Republican gains in the November 2004 election provided additional votes needed to keep an ANWR provision in the fiscal 2006 budget resolution (H Con Res 95). A Democratic attempt to delete it was defeated 49–51 in March. That allowed Republicans to include ANWR drilling in a budget savings bill (S 1932) that was subject to special rules in the Senate. Those rules protected a budget reconciliation bill from a filibuster, which means supporters need only fifty votes to prevail, rather than the sixty needed to overcome a filibuster.

But in 2005, ANWR supporters ran into difficulty in the House where moderates insisted the language be stripped out of that chamber's version of the reconciliation bill. House GOP leaders said they could not get enough votes for the conference report on the bill if the ANWR provision were included.

As a result, Sen. Ted Stevens, R-Alaska, who had been promoting ANWR drilling for decades, agreed to include the provision in the separate conference report on the fiscal 2006 defense spending bill (HR 2863). That measure, which provided $453.5 billion for military spending, including $50 billion for operations in Iraq and Afghanistan, was considered legislation Congress had to clear before adjourning for the year.

In a bid to ensure that the ANWR provision would stick, Stevens tied billions of dollars in expected revenue from ANWR to additional hurricane relief and homeland security programs. He dared Democrats, in effect, to vote against funding for the troops and other popular spending items. The House adopted the conference report 308–106 on Dec. 19.

Many senators, though, were furious with the treatment given the appropriations bill in conference, where it gained not only the ANWR language but a number of other provisions as well. Because it was no longer protected by Senate budget rules, the ANWR language was now vulnerable to a filibuster and Democrats made it clear they would not accept it. Facing this opposition, Majority Leader Bill Frist, R-Tenn., scheduled a vote to invoke cloture, or limit debate, on the measure.

The motion came up four votes short of the sixty required for it to succeed. The Dec. 21 vote was 56–44: R 52–3; D 4–40; I 0–1. *(Vote, p. 923)*

All but four Democrats—Hawaiians Daniel K. Akaka and Daniel K. Inouye, Mary L. Landrieu of Louisiana, and Ben Nelson of Nebraska—voted against cloture. They were joined by Republicans Lincoln Chafee of Rhode Island and Mike DeWine of Ohio, as well as Frist, who changed his vote to "no" at the last minute to preserve the option of seeking reconsideration of the vote.

After an hours-long quorum call, during which leaders worked off the floor to come up with a way to complete work on the defense bill, Frist announced a deal in which the Senate would clear the measure, but would also pass a separate enrolling resolution (S Con Res 74) under which the ANWR language would be removed from the bill. After adopting the resolution 48–45 the Senate cleared the spending bill 93–0 on Dec. 21. President George W. Bush signed the appropriations bill—without ANWR leasing language—Dec. 30.

1. **S 5. Class Action Overhaul/Passage.** Passage of the bill to give federal courts jurisdiction over class action cases involving at least 100 plaintiffs if at least $5 million was at stake and two-thirds of the plaintiffs lived in different states. The bill required judges to review all noncash settlements, such as coupons for goods and services, and limit attorney's fees paid in such settlements. Passed 72–26: R 53–0; D 18–26; I 1–0. A "yea" was a vote in support of the president's position. Feb. 10, 2005.

2. **S 256. Bankruptcy Overhaul/Violent Protesters.** Schumer, D-N.Y., amendment to prohibit violent protesters, such as antiabortion activists, from escaping court-ordered fines or judgments by filing for bankruptcy protection. The amendment barred such debtors from discharging debts, such as damages, court fines, penalties, citations or attorney fees, incurred from acts of violence or potential acts of violence. Rejected 46–53: R 4–51; D 41–2; I 1–0. March 8, 2005.

3. **Owen Nomination/Cloture.** Motion to invoke cloture (thus limiting debate) on President George W. Bush's nomination of Priscilla R. Owen of Texas to be a judge for the U.S. Court of Appeals for the Fifth Circuit. Motion agreed to 81–18: R 55–0; D 26–17; I 0–1. Three-fifths of the total Senate (sixty) was required to invoke cloture. May 24, 2005.

4. **Bolton Nomination/Cloture.** Motion to invoke cloture (thus limiting debate) on President George W. Bush's nomination of John R. Bolton of Maryland to be the permanent U.S. representative to the United Nations. Motion rejected 56–42: R 53–1; D 3–40; I 0–1. Three-fifths of the total Senate (sixty) was required to invoke cloture. A "yea" was a vote in support of the president's position. May 26, 2005.

5. **HR 6. Energy Policy/Climate Change.** Inhofe, R-Okla., motion to table (kill) the Bingaman, D-N.M., amendment to express the sense of the Senate that Congress should enact a national program of mandatory, market-based limits and incentives on greenhouse gas emissions that slow, stop, and reverse their growth at a rate that would not harm the economy, and would encourage comparable action by other nations. Motion rejected 44–53: R 42–12; D 2–40; I 0–1. (Subsequently, the amendment was adopted by voice vote.) A "yea" was a vote in support of the president's position. June 22, 2005.

6. **S 1307. Central American Free-Trade Agreement/Passage.** Passage of the bill to implement a free-trade agreement between the United States and Costa Rica, El Salvador, Guatemala, Honduras, Nicaragua, and a separate pact with the Dominican Republic. S 1307 eliminated customs duties on all originating goods traded among the participating nations within ten days. Passed 54–45: R 43–12; D 10–33; I 1–0. A "yea" was a vote in support of the president's position. June 30, 2005.

7. **HR 6. Energy Policy/Conference Report.** Adoption of the conference report on the bill to overhaul the nation's energy policy and provide for $14.6 billion in energy-related tax incentives. It allowed lawsuits involving the gasoline additive methyl tertiary butyl ether (MTBE) to be moved to a federal district court and required refiners to annually use 7.5 billion gallons of renewable fuels by 2012. Adopted 74–26: R 49–6; D 25–19; I 0–1. A "yea" was a vote in support of the president's position. July 29, 2005.

8. **S 397. Gun Liability/Passage.** Passage of the bill to bar certain civil lawsuits against manufacturers, distributors, dealers, and importers of firearms and ammunition; principally those lawsuits aimed at making them liable for gun violence. The bill also protected trade groups and dismissed all legal action against gun makers. Passed 65–31: R 50–2; D 14–29; I 1–0. A "yea" was a vote in support of the president's position. July 29, 2005.

9. **HR3 Surface Transportation Conference Report.** Adoption of the conference report on the bill to bring the total authorization for federal highway, mass transit, safety, and research programs, including fiscal 2004 funding, to $286.5 billion through 2009. The bill increased the rate of return to states on their Highway Trust Fund contributions to 92 percent by fiscal 2008. It made the Transportation Department the lead agency in the environmental review process for transportation projects. Adopted 91–4: R 48–4; D 42–0; I 1–0. July 29, 2005.

10. **Roberts Nomination to Supreme Court.** Confirmation of President George W. Bush's nomination of John G. Roberts Jr. of Maryland to be chief justice of the United States. Confirmed 78–22: R 55–0; D 22–22; I 1–0. A "yea" was a vote in support of the president's position. Sept. 29, 2005.

11. **Interrogation Techniques, Torture.** McCain, R-Ariz., amendment to establish the U.S. Army Field Manual on Intelligence Interrogation as the uniform standard for interrogating persons detained by the Department of Defense and to prohibit cruel, inhuman, or degrading treatment of any prisoner detained by the U.S. government. Adopted 90–9: R 46–9; D 43–0; I 1–0. A "nay" was a vote in support of the president's position. Oct. 5, 2005.

12. **HR 3058. Bridge Funding.** Coburn, R-Okla., amendment to the fiscal 2006 transportation spending bill to transfer $125 million in funding from the Ketchikan-Gravina and Knik Arm bridge projects in Alaska to the reconstruction of the Twin Spans Bridge connecting New Orleans and Slidell, La. It placed remaining Alaska bridge funds into a general highway fund for Alaska. Rejected 15–82: R 11–43; D 4–38; I 0–1. Oct. 20, 2005.

13. **S 1042. Iraq Withdrawal.** Warner, R-Va., amendment to require the president to submit an unclassified report to Congress ninety days after enactment of the fiscal 2006 defense authorization bill (S 1042) and every three months thereafter on U.S. policy and operations in Iraq. It also states that 2006 should be a period of significant transition to Iraqi sovereignty; that U.S. forces should not remain in Iraq any longer than necessary; and that the administration needs to explain to Congress and the American public the strategy for the completion of the Iraq mission. Adopted 79–19: R 41–13; D 37–6; I 1–0. Nov. 15, 2005.

14. **HR 3199. Patriot Act Reauthorization/Cloture.** Motion to invoke cloture (thus limiting debate) on the conference report on the bill to reauthorize the law known as the Patriot Act, and make permanent fourteen of the sixteen provisions of the act set to expire at the end of the year, and extend for four years the two provisions on access to business and other records and "roving" wiretaps. Motion rejected 52–47: R 50–5; D 2–41; I 0–1. Three- fifths of the total Senate (sixty votes) was required to invoke cloture. A "yea" was a vote in support of the president's position. Dec. 16, 2005.

15. **S 1932. Budget Reconciliation.** Gregg, R-N.H., motion to concur in the House amendment with a Senate amendment on the bill that would make changes to various programs for a net savings of $38.8 billion over five years. The Senate amendment removed two reporting requirements and language that granted hospitals immunity from malpractice lawsuits if they chose not to treat Medicaid recipients who could not afford co-payments. Motion agreed to 50–50: R 50–5; D 0–44; I 0–1. Vice President Dick Cheney cast a "yea" vote to break the tie A "yea" was a vote in support of the president's position. Dec. 21, 2005.

16. **HR 2863. Defense Appropriations Cloture, ANWR Drilling.** Motion to invoke cloture (thus limiting debate) on the conference report on the bill to appropriate $453.5 billion for defense spending in fiscal 2006, including $50 billion for operations in Iraq and Afghanistan. It also allowed oil and gas leasing in the Arctic National Wildlife Refuge. Motion rejected 56–44: R 52–3; D 4–40; I 0–1. Sixty votes were required to invoke cloture. A "yea" was a vote in support of the president's position. Dec. 21, 2005.

KEY

Democrat — *Republican* — **Independent**

Y	Voted for (yea)	–	Announced against
#	Paired for	P	Voted "present"
+	Announced for	C	Voted "present" to avoid possible conflict of interest
N	Voted against (nay)	?	Did not vote or otherwise make a position known
X	Paired against		

Senate Key Votes	1	2	3	4	5	6	8	9	10	11	12	13	14	15	16
ALABAMA															
Shelby	Y	N	Y	Y	Y	N	Y	Y	Y	Y	N	Y	Y	Y	Y
Sessions	Y	N	Y	Y	Y	Y	Y	Y	Y	N	Y	N	Y	Y	Y
ALASKA															
Stevens	Y	N	Y	Y	Y	Y	Y	Y	Y	N	N	Y	Y	Y	Y
Murkowski	Y	N	Y	Y	Y	Y	Y	Y	Y	Y	N	Y	N	Y	Y
ARIZONA															
McCain	Y	N	Y	Y	N	Y	Y	N	Y	Y	?	N	Y	Y	Y
Kyl	Y	N	Y	Y	Y	Y	Y	N	Y	Y	Y	N	Y	Y	Y
ARKANSAS															
Lincoln	Y	Y	N	N	N	Y	Y	Y	Y	Y	N	Y	N	N	N
Pryor	N	Y	Y	Y	N	Y	Y	Y	Y	Y	N	Y	N	N	N
CALIFORNIA															
Feinstein	Y	Y	Y	N	N	Y	–	+	N	Y	N	Y	N	N	N
Boxer	N	Y	N	N	N	N	N	+	N	Y	N	Y	N	N	N
COLORADO															
Allard	Y	N	Y	Y	Y	Y	Y	Y	Y	N	Y	Y	Y	Y	Y
Salazar	Y	Y	Y	N	N	N	Y	Y	Y	Y	N	Y	N	N	N
CONNECTICUT															
Dodd	Y	Y	N	N	N	N	N	Y	Y	Y	N	Y	?	N	N
Lieberman	Y	Y	Y	N	N	?	N	Y	Y	Y	N	Y	N	N	N
DELAWARE															
Biden	N	Y	N	N	N	N	N	Y	N	Y	N	Y	N	N	N
Carper	Y	Y	Y	N	N	Y	N	Y	Y	Y	N	Y	N	N	N
FLORIDA															
Nelson	N	Y	Y	N	N	Y	Y	Y	Y	Y	N	Y	N	N	N
Martinez	Y	N	Y	Y	Y	Y	Y	Y	Y	Y	N	Y	Y	Y	Y
GEORGIA															
Chambliss	Y	N	Y	Y	Y	Y	Y	Y	Y	Y	N	N	Y	Y	Y
Isakson	Y	N	Y	Y	Y	Y	Y	Y	Y	Y	N	N	Y	Y	Y
HAWAII															
Inouye	N	Y	?	?	N	N	N	Y	N	Y	N	Y	N	N	Y
Akaka	N	Y	Y	N	N	N	N	Y	N	Y	N	Y	N	N	Y
IDAHO															
Craig	Y	N	Y	Y	Y	N	Y	Y	Y	Y	N	Y	N	Y	Y
Crapo	Y	N	Y	Y	Y	N	Y	Y	Y	Y	N	Y	Y	Y	Y
ILLINOIS															
Durbin	N	Y	Y	N	N	N	N	Y	N	Y	N	Y	N	N	N
Obama	Y	Y	Y	N	N	N	N	Y	N	Y	N	Y	N	N	N
INDIANA															
Lugar	Y	N	Y	Y	N	Y	Y	Y	Y	Y	N	Y	Y	Y	Y
Bayh	Y	Y	Y	N	N	N	N	Y	N	Y	Y	Y	N	N	N
IOWA															
Grassley	Y	N	Y	Y	Y	Y	Y	Y	Y	Y	N	Y	Y	Y	Y
Harkin	N	Y	Y	N	N	N	N	Y	N	Y	N	N	N	N	N
KANSAS															
Brownback	Y	N	Y	Y	Y	Y	Y	Y	Y	Y	N	Y	Y	Y	Y
Roberts	Y	N	Y	Y	Y	Y	+	+	Y	N	N	Y	Y	Y	Y
KENTUCKY															
McConnell	Y	N	Y	Y	Y	Y	Y	Y	Y	Y	N	Y	Y	Y	Y
Bunning	Y	N	Y	Y	Y	Y	Y	Y	Y	Y	N	N	Y	Y	Y
LOUISIANA															
Landrieu	Y	Y	Y	Y	N	N	Y	Y	Y	Y	Y	Y	N	N	Y
Vitter	Y	N	Y	Y	Y	N	Y	Y	Y	Y	Y	N	Y	Y	Y
MAINE															
Snowe	Y	Y	Y	Y	N	N	Y	Y	Y	Y	N	Y	Y	N	Y
Collins	Y	Y	Y	Y	N	N	Y	Y	Y	Y	N	Y	Y	N	Y
MARYLAND															
Sarbanes	N	Y	N	N	N	N	N	Y	N	Y	N	Y	N	N	N
Mikulski	N	Y	Y	N	N	N	N	Y	N	Y	N	Y	N	N	N
MASSACHUSETTS															
Kennedy	N	Y	N	N	N	N	N	Y	N	Y	N	N	N	N	N
Kerry	N	Y	N	N	N	N	N	Y	N	Y	N	N	N	N	N
MICHIGAN															
Levin	N	Y	N	N	N	N	N	Y	Y	Y	N	Y	N	N	N
Stabenow	N	Y	N	N	N	N	N	Y	N	Y	N	Y	N	N	N
MINNESOTA															
Dayton	N	Y	N	N	N	N	N	Y	N	Y	N	Y	N	N	N
Coleman	Y	N	Y	Y	–	Y	Y	Y	Y	Y	N	Y	Y	Y	Y
MISSISSIPPI															
Cochran	Y	N	Y	Y	Y	Y	Y	Y	Y	N	N	Y	Y	Y	Y
Lott	Y	N	Y	Y	Y	Y	Y	Y	Y	Y	N	Y	Y	Y	Y
MISSOURI															
Bond	Y	N	Y	Y	Y	Y	Y	Y	Y	N	N	Y	Y	Y	Y
Talent	Y	N	Y	Y	Y	Y	Y	Y	Y	Y	N	Y	Y	Y	Y
MONTANA															
Baucus	N	Y	Y	N	Y	N	Y	Y	Y	Y	N	Y	N	N	N
Burns	Y	N	Y	Y	Y	N	Y	Y	Y	Y	N	Y	Y	Y	Y
NEBRASKA															
Hagel	Y	N	Y	Y	Y	Y	Y	Y	Y	Y	N	Y	N	Y	Y
Nelson	Y	N	Y	Y	Y	Y	Y	Y	Y	Y	N	Y	Y	N	Y
NEVADA															
Reid	N	Y	Y	N	N	N	Y	Y	N	Y	N	Y	N	N	N
Ensign	Y	N	Y	Y	Y	Y	Y	Y	Y	Y	N	Y	Y	Y	Y
NEW HAMPSHIRE															
Gregg	Y	N	Y	Y	N	Y	Y	N	Y	Y	N	Y	Y	Y	Y
Sununu	?	N	Y	Y	Y	Y	?	?	Y	Y	Y	Y	N	Y	Y
NEW JERSEY															
Corzine	N	?	N	N	N	N	N	Y	N	?	?	?	N	N	N
Lautenberg	N	Y	N	N	N	N	N	Y	N	Y	N	Y	N	N	N
NEW MEXICO															
Domenici	Y	N	Y	Y	N	Y	Y	Y	Y	Y	N	Y	Y	Y	Y
Bingaman	Y	Y	Y	N	N	Y	N	Y	Y	Y	N	Y	N	N	N
NEW YORK															
Schumer	Y	Y	Y	N	N	N	N	Y	N	Y	?	Y	N	N	N
Clinton	N	Y	Y	N	N	N	N	Y	N	Y	N	Y	N	N	N
NORTH CAROLINA															
Dole	Y	N	Y	Y	Y	Y	Y	Y	Y	Y	N	Y	Y	Y	Y
Burr	Y	N	Y	Y	Y	Y	Y	Y	Y	Y	Y	N	Y	Y	Y
NORTH DAKOTA															
Conrad	Y	Y	Y	N	?	N	Y	Y	Y	Y	Y	N	N	N	N
Dorgan	N	Y	N	N	?	N	Y	Y	Y	Y	N	Y	N	N	N
OHIO															
DeWine	Y	N	Y	Y	N	Y	N	Y	Y	Y	Y	Y	Y	N	N
Voinovich	Y	N	Y	Y	Y	Y	Y	Y	Y	Y	N	Y	Y	Y	Y
OKLAHOMA															
Inhofe	Y	N	Y	Y	Y	Y	Y	Y	Y	N	N	N	Y	Y	Y
Coburn	Y	N	Y	Y	Y	Y	Y	Y	Y	N	Y	N	Y	Y	Y
OREGON															
Wyden	N	Y	Y	N	N	Y	N	Y	Y	Y	N	Y	N	N	N
Smith	Y	N	Y	Y	Y	Y	+	+	Y	Y	N	Y	Y	N	Y
PENNSYLVANIA															
Specter	Y	Y	Y	?	N	N	Y	Y	Y	Y	N	Y	Y	Y	Y
Santorum	?	N	Y	Y	Y	Y	Y	Y	Y	Y	N	Y	Y	Y	Y
RHODE ISLAND															
Reed	Y	Y	N	N	N	N	N	Y	N	Y	N	Y	N	N	N
Chafee	Y	Y	Y	Y	N	Y	N	Y	Y	Y	N	Y	Y	N	N

Senate Key Votes	1	2	3	4	5	6	8	9	10	11	12	13	14	15	16
SOUTH CAROLINA															
Graham	Y	N	Y	Y	N	N	Y	Y	Y	Y	Y	N	Y	Y	Y
DeMint	Y	N	Y	Y	Y	Y	Y	Y	Y	Y	Y	N	Y	Y	Y
SOUTH DAKOTA															
Johnson	Y	Y	Y	N	N	N	Y	Y	Y	Y	N	Y	Y	N	N
Thune	Y	N	Y	Y	Y	N	Y	Y	Y	Y	N	N	Y	Y	Y
TENNESSEE															
Frist	Y	N	Y	N	Y	Y	Y	Y	Y	Y	N	Y	N	Y	N
Alexander	Y	N	Y	Y	N	Y	Y	Y	Y	Y	N	+	Y	Y	Y
TEXAS															
Hutchison	Y	N	Y	Y	Y	Y	Y	Y	Y	Y	N	Y	Y	Y	Y
Cornyn	Y	N	Y	Y	Y	Y	Y	N	Y	N	N	Y	Y	Y	Y
UTAH															
Hatch	Y	N	Y	Y	Y	Y	Y	Y	Y	Y	N	Y	Y	Y	Y
Bennett	Y	N	Y	Y	Y	Y	Y	Y	Y	Y	N	Y	Y	Y	Y
VERMONT															
Leahy	N	Y	Y	N	N	N	N	Y	Y	Y	N	N	N	N	N
Jeffords	Y	Y	N	N	N	Y	Y	Y	Y	Y	N	Y	N	N	N

Senate Key Votes	1	2	3	4	5	6	8	9	10	11	12	13	14	15	16
VIRGINIA															
Warner	Y	N	Y	Y	N	Y	Y	Y	Y	Y	N	Y	Y	Y	Y
Allen	Y	N	Y	Y	Y	Y	Y	Y	Y	Y	Y	Y	Y	Y	Y
WASHINGTON															
Murray	N	Y	N	N	N	Y	N	Y	Y	Y	N	Y	N	N	N
Cantwell	Y	Y	N	N	N	Y	N	Y	N	Y	N	Y	N	N	N
WEST VIRGINIA															
Byrd	N	N	Y	N	N	N	Y	Y	Y	Y	N	N	N	N	N
Rockefeller	Y	Y	Y	N	N	N	Y	Y	Y	Y	N	Y	N	N	N
WISCONSIN															
Kohl	Y	Y	Y	N	N	N	Y	Y	Y	Y	N	Y	N	N	N
Feingold	N	Y	N	N	N	N	N	Y	Y	Y	Y	Y	N	N	N
WYOMING															
Thomas	Y	N	Y	Y	Y	N	Y	Y	Y	Y	N	Y	Y	Y	Y
Enzi	Y	N	Y	Y	Y	N	Y	Y	Y	Y	N	Y	Y	Y	Y

House

1. IMMIGRATION POLICY CHANGES

Immigration emerged early in 2005 as one of the year's biggest issues. Supporters of tighter borders won an early victory when House Judiciary Committee chairman F. James Sensenbrenner Jr., R-Wis., revived provisions dropped from intelligence overhaul legislation at the end of the 108th Congress and pushed them through to enactment.

Forty-two House Democrats backed the measure, which showed that even with Republicans split on some aspects of the immigration debate the goal of securing the border was attractive to both parties. *(Story, pp. 686, 711.)*

To pass the bill (HR 418), which included new requirements for persons seeking driver's licenses and state ID cards, Republicans set aside issues of states' rights in favor of the higher priority of homeland security.

The driver's license and other provisions were included in intelligence overhaul legislation in the 108th Congress but were dropped in conference. Sensenbrenner was the only House conferee not to sign the conference agreement. He won assurances that the provisions would be among the first items of business in the 109th Congress, either as a stand-alone bill or attached to another measure.

The immigration bill included language giving the secretary of homeland security the power to preempt state and federal laws if necessary to construct physical barriers and roads to curb illegal border crossings. The provision was intended to push completion of a fence along the U.S.-Mexican border near San Diego.

Critics said the provision was wildly out of proportion to the problem. The preemption applied to any local, state, or federal laws—whether governing child labor, competition for federal contracts, or environmental protection—that would impede physical barriers to curb illegal border crossings. An attempt by Sam Farr, D-Calif., to remove the provision was rejected 179–243.

Some members, echoing the concerns of state governors, argued that the driver's license requirement was an unfunded mandate and would draw states into the expensive role of enforcing immigration laws.

But concerns for national security and anger over the leaky southern border prevailed. The House Feb. 10 passed Sensenbrenner's bill 261–161: R 219–8; D 42–152; I 0–1. Most of the measure was subsequently incorporated into the fiscal 2005 emergency supplemental appropriations bill, which President George W. Bush signed into law in May. *(Vote, p. 932)*

2. TERRI SCHIAVO LITIGATION

Three days into Congress's spring recess in 2005, House Speaker J. Dennis Hastert, R-Ill., summoned members back to Washington for a vote that would become symbolic in the continuing struggle between social conservatives and liberals and libertarians. It also stoked public dissatisfaction with Congress.

In 1990 a Florida woman, Terri Schiavo, suffered severe brain damage after her heart briefly stopped. Doctors declared her to be in a persistent vegetative state, and her husband, Michael Schiavo, tried to stop life support, saying it was in accordance with her wishes.

But Terri Schiavo did not have a living will, a document outlining her treatment preferences. A legal battle ensued between Michael Schiavo and his wife's parents, Robert and Mary Schindler, who believed she might recover. After various Florida courts considered and rejected the Schindlers' arguments over a seven-year span, Terri Schiavo's feeding tube was removed March 18. *(Stories, pp. 551, 862.)*

But the case had become a cause célèbre for social conservatives. They argued that Schiavo, much like a fetus, was a person with a "right to life" but incapable of speaking for herself and deserving of the government's protection. Republicans, seeing an opportunity to support an important part of the party's base, brought Congress into the controversy. As Schiavo's condition began to deteriorate after removal of her feeding tube, the Senate passed a bill (S 686) to give the Schindlers access to federal courts for a final consideration of their daughter's case. The Senate passed the bill by voice vote March 20.

A handful of House Democrats, opposed to congressional intervention in matters they believed were family concerns, objected to a voice vote on the bill in that chamber. Republican leaders called members back to town for a roll call vote the morning of March 21.

President George W. Bush, expecting that the House would clear the bill, returned to Washington from his ranch in Crawford, Texas, to sign it, bringing public attention to the controversy.

As the vote neared its conclusion, Republican members clapped when the tally reached 218—a quorum, that ensured enough members were present to pass the bill. The bill was considered under suspension of the rules, which required a two-thirds majority (174) for approval. The final tally was 203–58: R 156–5; D 47–53; I 0–0. Many Democrats, wary of the 2004 elections in which social issues such as gay marriage were perceived to have played an important role, voted for the bill while expressing discomfort with the precedent it set. *(Vote, p. 932)*

Bush signed the bill into law an hour later, but the Republicans' effort came to naught. Schiavo's case quickly went to the Supreme Court, which on March 24 declined to hear the appeal. She died a week later.

GOP leaders faced an unexpected political backlash. Senate majority leader Bill Frist, R-Tenn., had questioned Schiavo's diagnosis on the Senate floor after watching a videotape of her apparently responding to "visual stimuli" such as a floating balloon, but an autopsy confirmed that she was not only severely brain-damaged but also blind.

Various polls showed that most Americans, including a majority of Republicans, disapproved of Congress's action in the case.

3. HOUSE ETHICS REGULATIONS

In an unusual retreat in the face of Democratic criticism, House Republicans on April 27, 2005, voted to reverse three changes in ethics rules they had pushed through on the opening day of the session. The changes had been made to help lawmakers such as Majority Leader Tom DeLay, R-Texas, who had been admonished three times by the ethics committee in the previous Congress. But it was the growing number of questions about DeLay's conduct, and the political damage it might cause his party, that led Republicans to reverse their decision. *(Story, p. 815)*

The short-lived rules changes specified that any complaint against a House member would die after forty-five days unless the committee had voted by then to proceed with an investigation. Previously, the ethics panel, known formally as the Committee on

Standards of Official Conduct, had to make a decision on a complaint for it to either expire or proceed.

The House in January also gave members who were the object of an investigation the right to respond to the committee's conclusions before a decision was made final or publicly announced. Republicans said they devised this change to prevent the ethics committee from catching a member off-guard with an admonishment or other punishment.

A third change codified what had been an occasional practice of permitting one attorney to represent multiple members involved in an ethics case. Democrats on the committee wanted to prohibit such a move, saying it allowed the subject of a complaint to collaborate with witnesses via a single attorney and made it impossible for the panel to properly investigate a charge.

Democrats condemned the changes as soon as they were made in January, but Republicans largely ignored their objections. Then, in March, Democrats on the evenly divided ethics committee refused to vote for a proposed set of procedural rules for the 109th Congress, leaving the panel in procedural limbo and unable to conduct investigations.

The committee's ranking Democrat, Alan B. Mollohan of West Virginia, had meanwhile gathered 208 co-sponsors, including three Republicans, for a resolution (H Res 131) to reverse the three ethics rule changes. Mollohan threatened to file a discharge petition that, if he could get 218 signatures, would bring his resolution directly to the floor.

At that point, Republican leaders decided the ethics impasse and bad publicity were not worth the fight. At a conference meeting with rank-and-file members the morning of April 27, House Speaker J. Dennis Hastert, R-Ill., defended the rules changes as "fair for all members," but said, "We need to move the ethics process forward." Republicans leaving the conference said Hastert told them the best course of action would be to reverse the rules changes.

Almost all of them ultimately agreed. Many said they simply followed the direction of Hastert, who told them it was time to end the stalemate. Other Republicans said they had come to oppose some or all of the rules changes.

The House adopted the rules changes by a vote of 406–20: R 208–20; D 197–0; I 1–0. *(Vote, p. 932)*

The vote was one of the first of a series of strategic victories for Democrats. On June 30, they forced Republicans on the ethics committee to retreat once again on disputed staffing issues. Democrats prevailed in an effort to hire only nonpartisan professionals to work on the committee.

4. FEDERAL STEM CELL RESEARCH

Republican moderates in 2005 held House majority leader Tom DeLay, R-Texas, to a promise that he would hold a vote before summer on a bill (HR 810) by Michael N. Castle, R-Del., to expand the number of stem cell lines available to federally funded researchers by allowing them to work on lines derived from surplus embryos at in vitro fertilization clinics. *(Story, p. 542)*

An executive order issued by President George W. Bush on Aug. 21, 2001, allowed federally funded scientists to conduct research only on stem cell lines that existed before that date. The National Institutes of Health estimated twenty-two such lines were viable for research, though they were contaminated and probably would not be usable for medical treatments.

Supporters of the bill campaigned among their colleagues, stressing that days-old embryos, which have the ability to morph into almost any other kind of cell in the body, showed much promise to cure diseases such as Parkinson's and some cancers.

In an effort to derail the legislation, GOP leaders and conservatives who opposed the research because it required the destruction of an embryo, backed an alternative bill (HR 2520) by Christopher H. Smith, R-N.J. Smith's bill encouraged the use of stem cells, sometimes referred to as "adult stem cells," taken from umbilical cords after birth. Stem cells found in umbilical cord blood were less elastic because they come from specific tissue and were used mainly in treating blood disorders. House leaders hoped Smith's bill would enable members who faced pressure from their constituents to cast a "pro–stem cell" vote without relaxing Bush's restrictions on research using embryos.

Supporters of Castle's bill said they did not oppose Smith's measure, but contended that it did not address the need for funding research on embryonic cells. The moderate Republican Main Street Partnership launched a multimillion-dollar advertising campaign in support of Castle's bill that highlighted former first lady Nancy Reagan's support for embryonic research.

The floor debate May 24 demonstrated the emotion and personal experiences that influenced members' votes and led many Republicans to disregard their leadership to support Castle's bill.

Joe L. Barton, R-Texas, noted that his antiabortion voting record stood at 100 percent until 2005, but said he backed the embryonic stem cell bill because of his father, who has diabetes, and a brother, who had liver cancer. Antiabortion Democrat Jim Langevin of Rhode Island, who was paralyzed as a teenager, and Lane Evans, D-Ill., who had Parkinson's disease, made personal pleas to allow federal funding for embryonic research.

Opponents made equally emotional appeals. Twenty-one children were escorted around the Capitol to illustrate the use of surplus embryos to help infertile couples. The youths were born to mothers from surplus frozen embryos donated by other couples. "The best one can say about embryonic stem cell research is it is a scientific exploration into the potential benefits of killing human beings," said DeLay, who along with the rest of the House GOP leadership voted against Castle's bill.

Although Bush had reiterated his veto threat, Majority Whip Roy Blunt, R-Mo., said leaders wanted members to vote their consciences. When the vote was finished, fifty Republicans had broken with their leadership. The House passed Castle's bill 238–194: R 50–180; D 187–14; I 1–0. *(Vote, p. 932)*

The tally fell short of the 290 votes that would be needed to override a veto if all members of the House were present and voting, but supporters expressed hope that a compromise could be reached. Although the Senate did not take up the Castle bill in the first session, the cord blood bill was subsequently cleared.

5. LIMITS ON FEDERAL SEARCH POWERS

Weeks before the House took up legislation in 2005 to reauthorize expiring provisions of the Patriot Act, a group of Republicans joined every House Democrat save one in making a bold—though ultimately symbolic—gesture toward limiting one of the law's most contentious provisions. Section 215 of the Patriot Act allowed FBI investigators to seize "any tangible things (including books, records, papers, documents and other items)" as part of a terrorism investigation once they get a warrant from a top-secret court established under the Foreign Intelligence Surveillance Act (FISA). *(Story, p. 236)*

The section was one of sixteen provisions of the antiterrorism law that were scheduled to expire at the end of 2005. The White House pressed Congress to make all sixteen permanent as part of a bill reauthorizing the act.

Civil liberties advocates, the American Conservative Union, librarians, doctors, business groups, gun rights advocates, and former Georgia GOP Rep. Bob Barr (1995–2003) spent much of the year lobbying hard to keep the provision out of the Patriot Act reauthorization or, short of that, to exempt certain records and minimize access.

On June 15, the administration's effort suffered a bipartisan blow during House debate on the fiscal 2006 Commerce-Justice-Science appropriations bill (HR 2862). Not waiting for the Patriot Act debate, Vermont independent Bernard Sanders offered an amendment to bar use of money in the bill to seek a FISA court order to seize library circulation records, library patron lists, book sales records, or bookseller customer lists.

Defying a White House veto threat, 38 Republicans and 199 Democrats supported Sanders, pushing his amendment to approval by a vote of 238–187: R 38–186; D 199–1; I 1–0. Dan Boren of Oklahoma was the only Democrat to vote against the amendment. *(Vote, p. 932)*

Sanders won more votes than he had with a similar amendment the previous year, when he lost 210–210. He noted that the 2004 amendment had drawn some opposition from members who did not like the fact that it would have barred FBI access to library Internet records. Sanders dropped that provision in the 2005 version.

The vote was perceived as a snub to the White House and a small victory for those arguing for more balance between the need to find terrorists and the desire to protect civil liberties. "A number of conservatives voted conservatively today, and 'conservative' means limited government," said Sanders, one of the most liberal members of the House, who pumped his arm in the air to applause as he left the chamber.

The provision was short-lived. When the House passed a bill (HR 3199) in July to renew the sixteen expiring Patriotic Act provisions, the power to seize library and bookstore records was intact. It survived in conference, though the provision was one of two that were accorded a four-year extension; the rest were made permanent.

Nevertheless, the vote on Sanders' amendment suggested that reauthorizing the Patriot Act would be controversial.

6. MILITARY SALES TO CHINA

The intense, last-minute lobbying around legislation than start as a noncontroversial bill to tighten sanctions on illegal arms sales to China highlighted Congress' continued dilemma on China policy: how to punish the Asian nation's anticompetitive business practices and arms trade while not jeopardizing U.S. commerce with it.

The bill (HR 3100) was designed to discourage European countries from lifting their embargoes on military trade with China. "The bill is not intended to be punitive; its primary purpose is deterrence," said Henry J. Hyde, R-Ill., chairman of the International Relations Committee and the bill's sponsor. It required the administration to annually report the names of countries that permit trade in military material with China and required an export license before any U.S. company could send military goods to such countries. The president could apply a range of sanctions against countries selling arms to China, including denying licenses for "dual use" goods—those that have both civilian and potential military applications—barring their participation in research projects or prohibiting them from owning U.S. defense companies.

Both Republicans and Democrats initially supported the legislation, and House leaders brought it to the floor under a suspension of the rules, a procedure used for noncontroversial bills that required a two-thirds vote for passage. Just two weeks earlier, the House had overwhelmingly adopted an amendment and a resolution expressing concern that the China National Offshore Oil Corp. Ltd. was trying to buy Unocal, a U.S. oil company, for $18.5 billion. *(Sales to China, p. 296; Unocal, p. 241)*

But House leaders underestimated the opposition from the defense industry, which had companies and manufacturing plants in many congressional districts. Defense manufacturers said the bill punished companies for selling dual-use products to China. Defense contractors such as Boeing Co. did not want to be punished for selling aircraft parts to commercial companies in China if those parts ended up on military jets.

When the roll call began July 14, the bill appeared headed for easy passage. But Donald Manzullo, R-Ill., the chairman of the Small Business Committee, was at work on the floor, trying to persuade his colleagues to change their votes.

Manzullo, whose district includes aircraft and machine parts manufacturers, worked both sides of the aisle, telling members that the legislation was a bad deal. He circulated a flyer drawn up by defense contractors saying "passage of this bill means that Boeing and other aircraft manufacturers will sell fewer planes overseas."

In rapid sequence, dozens of lawmakers, worried that the bill could unintentionally punish defense contractors who do business with European companies that in turn sell to China, began to change their votes. What had been scheduled as a five-minute vote was held open for twenty-three minutes, but the measure failed to get the necessary two-thirds majority. The vote was 215–203: R 118–106; D 96–97; 1–0. *(Vote, p. 932)*

A revised version of the measure was later attached to the State Department authorization bill (HR 2601) passed by the House in July. The amended version would still monitor European governments or companies that sell military hardware or technology to China, but would punish U.S. companies only if they knew their products would ultimately be used for military purposes. The bill went no further.

7. CENTRAL AMERICAN TRADE LIBERALIZATION

Hours before leaving for a month-long recess in August 2005, the House voted to pass a bill implementing a free-trade accord between the United States and Costa Rica, El Salvador, Guatemala, Honduras, and Nicaragua, plus a parallel agreement with the Dominican Republic. *(Story, p. 202)*

The vote on the Central American accord, or CAFTA, was a referendum on U.S. trade policy, and a test both of President George W. Bush's power and GOP party loyalty amid growing congressional partisanship and skepticism on trade.

Although the bill (HR 3045) was a marquee piece for the president's trade agenda, it took all of the wiles of then–Majority Leader Tom DeLay, R-Texas, to twist enough arms to eke out a two-vote victory margin. The close vote suggested that GOP members were increasingly wary about trade pacts, carefully weighing the potential impact on their districts with the goals and desires of the president. Bush even made a rare appearance before the House Republican Conference the morning of the vote, and several members of the cabinet spent part of the day on Capitol Hill helping to convince reluctant lawmakers.

Democratic support for CAFTA was almost nonexistent. Analysts saw that as evidence of a backlash Democrats felt after a large number from their party supported NAFTA, the North American Free-Trade Agreement, in 1993.

The Senate acted first to give momentum to the House, but even there the vote was a relatively close 54–45. *(Senate key vote, p. 917)*

The voting began in the House shortly after 11 p.m. on July 27 and did not end until well after midnight when the bill passed 217–215: R 202–27; D 15–187; I 0–1. *(Vote, p. 932)*

Almost until the end, a small but vital bloc of Republicans remained concerned that beleaguered domestic textile and apparel makers would be wiped out by imports of Chinese-made goods that they said could slip into the United States duty-free under CAFTA.

The administration had argued vigorously that, if anything, CAFTA would strengthen the bond between U.S. textile mills and Central American apparel factories. Just the same, U.S. Trade Representative Rob Portman promised to go back into the accord later to amend three textile provisions to prevent circumvention by the Chinese, winning over a handful of textile state members just days before the vote.

Additional maneuvering was required even as debate got under way. Robert B. Aderholt, R-Ala., received a letter from Portman and Commerce Secretary Carlos Gutierrez pledging administration help to protect sock makers from import surges possible under CAFTA and other trade pacts, support for an application by the Hosiery Technology Center for a Commerce Department export grant, and a commitment to work with the Pentagon to encourage purchase of U.S.-made socks only.

Another trouble spot was the concern that a modest increase in sugar imports permitted by CAFTA would undermine domestic producers and cost U.S. jobs. An administration proposal to use commodity swaps to contain additional sugar imports for the remaining two years of the current farm bill and to undertake a study of government initiatives to spur production of ethanol made from sugar helped win the votes of Dave Camp, R-Mich., Adam H. Putnam, R-Fla., and Mark Kennedy, R-Minn., among others. But Mark Foley, R-Fla., and several Louisiana lawmakers remained skeptical. Foley called his eventual decision to vote for the CAFTA bill a "gut wrencher."

One final issue involved demonstrating more resolve in countering unfair trade practices by China. Phil English, R-Pa., pressed for floor action on a bill (HR 3283) to strengthen U.S. enforcement of trade rules against China. He estimated that as many as ten Republicans agreed to vote for CAFTA after the House passed the China bill earlier in the day.

A half-hour after the nominal fifteen-minute roll call vote on the CAFTA bill began, the count froze at 214–211 in favor. Eight Republicans who had either expressed opposition to CAFTA or said they were reluctant to support it had not cast their votes. About midnight, DeLay and GOP leaders persuaded Robin Hayes of North Carolina to switch his vote from no to yes. DeLay then persuaded two of the hesitant Republicans to vote for the trade agreement and allowed the rest to cast last-minute votes against it.

Only 15 Democrats voted yes, a sharp contrast to the 102 Democrats who had supported President Bill Clinton on the 1993 NAFTA vote. Democrats' opposition was based in part on their concerns that the CAFTA agreement was a lost opportunity to improve on the NAFTA model and raise labor and environmental standards in developing countries. But Republicans claimed that those "no" votes were simply a partisan effort to weaken Bush.

8. ENERGY POLICY CONFERENCE REPORT

It took four years, but record fuel prices gave Congress the motivation in 2005 to pass energy legislation similar to proposals from President George W. Bush in 2001. The final bill (HR 6) emphasized greater production of domestic energy, a central element of the Bush proposal. But to get the bill through the Senate, the White House had to forgo the centerpiece of its energy plan, drilling for oil and natural gas in Alaska's Arctic National Wildlife Refuge (ANWR). In addition, House Republican leaders gave up one of their top priorities: liability protection for the oil companies that made the fuel additive MTBE (methyl tertiary butyl ether), which has been found to contaminate some groundwater. *(Story, p. 447)*

For two years running, MTBE liability had blocked final action on an energy bill as House members from oil-producing states, led by then–Majority Leader Tom DeLay, R-Texas, demanded that it be included, while a coalition of Democrats and moderate Republicans demanded that it be dropped.

Although the administration lost on energy exploration in the Alaska wilderness, it was successful in reducing the cost of tax breaks and other incentives in the legislation to about half those sought by GOP congressional leaders in past years.

In one of the most significant energy votes in decades, the House adopted the conference report on the omnibus energy bill July 28 by a vote of 275–156: R 200–31; D 75–124; I 0–1. *(Vote, p. 932; Senate key vote on energy, p. 918)*

The House had passed other energy bills several times dating back to 2001 only to see them bog down in the Senate, where sponsors had trouble winning the sixty votes necessary to beat filibuster threats from senators upset by what they considered a bias in the legislation toward energy companies.

But in 2005 DeLay and fellow Texas Republican Joe L. Barton, the chairman of the Energy and Commerce Committee, dropped their insistence that the bill include liability relief for the makers of MTBE, which has been used since the 1970s but became more prevalent after federal clean fuel requirements in the early 1990s. Like ethanol, MTBE was used to make gasoline burn more completely, helping to lower harmful tailpipe emissions. But it also has been found to contaminate groundwater where it has leaked from storage tanks. Some lawmakers, including northeastern Republicans, worried that the liability protection would leave their states to pay for the cleanup.

Unlike previous years, House leaders also won support for the measure by holding down the cost of its tax incentives, which in past years had exceeded $30 billion. That had been a point of criticism from fiscal conservatives and the White House in 2005. The conference agreement provided $14.6 billion in tax breaks and credits between 2005 and 2015.

To help deliver the bill, House Republicans agreed to drop language to open ANWR to energy exploration. GOP leaders shifted the provision to other legislation, first a spending-cut package (S 1932) and later a Defense appropriations bill (HR 2863), but those maneuvers also failed.

9. SURFACE TRANSPORTATION SPENDING

It took more than two years and four congressional sessions, but the House on July 29, 2005, adopted the conference report on a bill (HR 3) reauthorizing the nation's highway and public transit programs. The House and Senate had reached the conference stage on a six-year reauthorization bill in 2004, but the negotiators could not get beyond disputes among members over how to divide up highway money, and with the White House over the total cost of the bill *(Story, p. 407)*.

In 2005 Congress finally settled for less money than it wanted; the Bush administration settled for more. The agreement gave a larger share of highway funds to fast-growing states, mainly in the South and Southwest, that argued they had been shortchanged by the previous highway law. In another victory for those states, the House agreed to deduct from each state's formula highway funds any money it received for earmarked projects—a blow to influential lawmakers, such as Don Young, R-Alaska, the chairman of the Transportation and Infrastructure Committee, who were adroit at getting such projects for their states.

The final $286.5 billion bill contained more than 5,100 earmarks, reflecting the perennial popularity of highway spending among lawmakers. While the overwhelming majority were for road projects, some were for museums and other amenities not related to traffic. Watchdog groups and fiscal conservatives used the bill and the vote as symbols of the inability of either Republicans or Democrats to exercise self-restraint when it came to home-state public works projects.

President Bush had for two years demanded that Congress authorize no more than $256 billion for surface transportation programs, while lawmakers were thinking more in the range of $319 billion to as much as $375 billion. The administration made a more realistic deal early in 2005 when it lifted its bottom-line demand to $284 billion—close to the compromise amount conferees had been negotiating in 2004 and just $2.5 billion away from the final figure.

Befitting the tortuous path the legislation had followed since the previous surface transportation law expired in September 2003, the final days of negotiations featured marathon sessions to draft language and frustrating snags that developed each time the bill drew close to final action.

Only eight dissidents were prepared to vote against the conference report when it reached the House floor July 29. Six of them were members of the Republican Study Committee, a group of fiscal and social conservatives frustrated with GOP leaders and the White House over spending issues. The House adopted the conference report and sent it to the Senate by a vote of 412–8: R 217–8; D 194–0; I 1–0. *(Vote, p. 932)*

10. ENDANGERED SPECIES POLICY REWRITE

Congress in 2005 attempted to resolve long-simmering controversy over the application and reach of the Endangered Species Act, which environmentalists had championed for years and land owners had continually attacked. A bill to revise the act was passed in the House, but went no further. *(Story, p. 481)*

Rep. Richard W. Pombo, R-Calif., had been fighting environmentalists for years over the law, arguing that it harmed private property owners while doing little to aid the recovery of threatened animal and plant species. In 2005 Pombo changed course somewhat and found a new, albeit limited, source of support among Democrats, many of them from western states where the endangered species program had faced considerable opposition. As a result, Pombo persuaded the House to pass the most extensive changes to the species protection program since the law was last reauthorized in 1988.

As chairman of the House Resources Committee, Pombo spent several months negotiating with committee Democrats before releasing a detailed bill (HR 3824) in September. The bipartisan effort paid off Sept. 22, when eight Democrats joined all but two Republicans to approve the bill in committee.

The bill required the use of peer-reviewed science in federal regulatory decisions and required compensation for landowners affected by federal conservation efforts. It also eliminated a requirement that the government designate and protect critical habitat within a year of listing a species as endangered. Instead, the government would have to come up with a recovery plan, keeping in mind habitat and cost.

Opponents of the bill argued that the recovery plans might not be enforceable on private landowners or other government agencies. Environmental groups, which for years have sued the government for failing to designate critical habitat as required under existing law, said habitat protection was a critical component of any long-term recovery plan. They declared the bill a frontal assault on a landmark law that, despite its problems, has kept alive most of the species it aimed to protect.

Democrats attracted some bipartisan support for a substitute amendment that emphasized recovery planning on federal lands, while promoting technical assistance and grants for private property owners who cooperate on federal conservation programs. Twenty-nine Republicans joined Democrats on the vote but the amendment failed 206–216.

Pombo succeeded in offsetting the Republican votes he lost with support by thirty-six Democrats, many from western and midwestern states. The bill passed Sept. 29, 229–193: R 193–34; D 36–158; I 0–1. *(Vote, p. 932)*

The bill did not advance in the Senate. It was sent to an Environment and Public Works subcommittee chaired by Lincoln Chafee, a Rhode Island Republican who often sides with Democrats on environmental issues.

11. TREATMENT OF MILITARY DETAINEES

In an overwhelming vote Dec. 14, 2005, the House demonstrated its support for a proposal by Sen. John McCain, R-Ariz., to ban the use of torture on prisoners held in U.S. custody. The timing of the vote and the compelling margin of victory appeared to force President George W. Bush to back away from his months-long opposition to McCain's initiative. *(Story, pp. 336, 724, 764)*

The president's compromise with McCain ended an internecine battle in Republican ranks over how to respond to reports of abuse that had tarnished America's image and complicated efforts to win the war of ideas against radical Islamic terrorists. The political conflict in Washington pitted the president against lawmakers who ordinarily stood with him, including McCain, who was a victim of torture in Vietnam and the man Bush had defeated for the Republican nomination in the hard-fought primaries of 2000.

McCain's amendment banned "cruel, inhuman or degrading" treatment of detainees, and made an Army field manual on interrogations the standard for Defense Department handling of prisoners. McCain had won a 90–9 vote in early October to attach the language to the Senate version of the spending bill. For good measure, the Senate agreed by voice vote in early November to add it to the defense authorization bill (HR 1815) as well. *(Senate key vote, p. 919)*

The House was voting on a "motion to instruct" its conferees on the fiscal 2006 defense appropriations bill (HR 2863) to retain McCain's provision. Such motions are not binding, but the force of this one was undeniable. In a House where Republicans typically move in lockstep, more than 100 of them defied the president on the torture vote. The motion was agreed to 308–122: R 107–121; D 200–1; I 1–0. *(Vote, p. 932)*

Bush was so opposed to the amendment that he threatened to veto the two military bills in the middle of a war. Bush dispatched Vice President Dick Cheney to try to persuade McCain to create an exemption for the CIA, but the lobbying campaign backfired. It created the impression that the administration was in favor of torture, or at least opposed to Congress passing a law against it.

National Security Adviser Stephen J. Hadley soon replaced Cheney in the talks with McCain, and Bush spoke with the senator about the amendment on several occasions. Meanwhile, McCain negotiated with Duncan Hunter, R-Calif., chairman of the House Armed Services Committee, who sided with the administration and had his own ideas on changes he thought could improve McCain's amendment in the defense authorization bill.

With all of those talks, described by one aide as "a three-ring circus," going nowhere, the two massive defense bills were stalled going into December. On Dec. 14, House Republican leaders finally named conferees on the appropriations bill, clearing the way for John P. Murtha, D-Pa., to offer his motion to instruct the conferees.

The day after the highly publicized House vote, Bush invited McCain and Sen. John W. Warner, R-Va., to the White House to announce a compromise on the detainee amendment. McCain had not budged on his provision, but he agreed to additional language allowing U.S. interrogators—whether they work for the Defense Department, the CIA, the FBI, or a contractor—to have the same legal protections that U.S. military personnel are accorded.

The language was cleared as part of both the defense spending and defense authorization bills.

12. CUTS IN MANDATORY SPENDING

At the start of 2005, Republican leaders vowed to slow the growth of mandatory entitlement programs such as Medicare, Medicaid, and student loans for the first time since 1997, and the House brought them close to achieving their goal. Despite having no Democratic support, they put themselves in position to clear a $38.8 billion savings package (S 1932) in early 2006. *(Story, pp. 81, 535)*

The effort was hanging in the balance in the pre-dawn hours of Dec. 19. House and Senate negotiators had labored into the night to reconcile a $35 billion Senate plan and a far different $50 billion House package. A deal was announced, then altered, as new objections arose and leaders sought to ensure they had enough support before a final vote.

Negotiations had been stalled for days because of an impasse over efforts to open Alaska's Arctic National Wildlife Refuge (ANWR) to drilling. House Republican moderates vowed to oppose any bill with the ANWR provision, and Sen. Ted Stevens, R-Alaska, a member of the conference committee, vowed to oppose any bill without it.

Stevens relented during a final weekend of negotiations once House and Senate leaders agreed to try to enact the ANWR provisions by attaching them to the fiscal 2006 defense appropriations bill (HR 2863) instead, a plan that ultimately failed. On the evening of Dec. 18, House Speaker J. Dennis Hastert, R-Ill., announced that conferees had agreed on a $41.6 billion budget savings package. But after midnight, Hastert and Senate negotiators had to shrink the package to $38.8 billion to secure the votes of Ohio lawmakers who threatened to scuttle the overall deal unless oxygen tank manufacturers, including a major Ohio company, were protected from planned cuts to Medicare. The 774-page conference report was filed well after midnight. The vote came shortly after 6 a.m. on Dec. 19, with a number of lawmakers in both parties already having left town for the winter recess.

But with the backing of enough moderates, GOP leaders managed a 212–206 victory: R 212–9; D 0–196; I 0–1. The vote turned out to be largely devoid of suspense, even though all of the Democrats who showed up voted no. *(Vote, p. 932)*

House leaders had won a narrower 217–215 vote shortly before 2 a.m. Nov. 18 on their original package, which contained deeper cuts and fewer spending plums.

The final vote was a triumph for the House leadership team, which overcame months of doubt about its ability to deliver votes for the budget package in the face of the criminal indictment of former majority leader Tom DeLay, R-Texas, low poll ratings, carping by some moderates, and unusually united Democratic opposition.

Yet the victory came at a cost, with House leaders unable to deliver on the $45 billion savings goal they had announced for the conference report. House and Senate moderates had forced leaders to abandon plans to cut off 250,000 recipients from food stamps and to shrink cuts planned for child support enforcement and welfare. Meanwhile, House leaders refused to go along with a Senate plan to eliminate a $10 billion subsidy for companies included as part of the new Medicare drug benefit. The Senate cut had prompted a veto threat.

Alongside the budget cuts came a number of sweeteners to win votes, including $7.3 billion to prevent doctors from receiving a 4.4 percent Medicare pay cut, $2.1 billion to extend Medicaid to hurricane victims, $1 billion to continue a milk subsidy for two years, $1 billion in home heating subsidies for the poor, and $1.5 billion for digital television converters for analog televisions.

The bill did not clear, however. A procedural maneuver by Senate Democrats required an additional vote in the House. House minority leader Nancy Pelosi, D-Calif., refused a quick voice vote before the holidays, saying she wanted to force a vote "in the light of day."

Democrats and their allies vowed to renew pressure on House GOP moderates who supported the conference report to change their minds. Still, after a long night of waiting and deal making, GOP leaders declared victory.

1. **HR 418. Immigration Bill Passage.** Passage of the bill to tighten national standards for state driver's licenses and identity cards, make it more difficult for foreign nationals to claim asylum, and authorize the completion of a security fence along the U.S.-Mexico border. Passed 261–161: R 219–8; D 42–152; I 0–1. A "yea" was a vote in support of the president's position. Feb. 10, 2005.

2. **S 686. Schiavo Medical Care Passage.** Sensenbrenner, R-Wis., motion to suspend the rules and pass the bill to give the parents of Theresa Marie Schiavo, a severely brain-damaged Florida woman, the right to file a lawsuit in the U.S. District Court for the Middle District of Florida alleging that Schiavo's rights related to life-sustaining medical treatment had been violated under the Constitution or federal law. Motion agreed to, thus clearing the bill for the president, 203–58: R 156–5; D 47–53; I 0–0. A two-thirds majority of those present and voting (174 in this case) was required for passage under suspension of the rules. March 21, 2005.

3. **H Res 240. House Rules Changes.** Approval of a resolution repealing three changes to House rules, made at the beginning of the 109th Congress in January, dealing with ethics committee procedures, including a rule that allowed the automatic dismissal of an ethics complaint that is not disposed of by the committee within forty-five days. Adopted 406–20: R 208–20; D 197–0; I 1–0. April 27, 2005.

4. **HR 810. Stem Cell Research.** Passage of the bill to allow the use of federal funds in research on embryonic stem cell lines derived from surplus embryos at in vitro fertilization clinics if donors give their consent and are not paid for the embryos. The bill authorized the Health and Human Services Department to conduct and support research involving human embryonic stem cells that meet certain criteria, regardless of when the stem cells were derived from a human embryo. Passed 238–194: R 50–180; D 187–14; I 1–0. A "nay" was a vote in support of the president's position. May 24, 2005.

5. **HR 2862. Surveillance of Library Records.** Sanders, I-Vt., amendment to the fiscal 2006 Commerce-Justice-Science appropriations bill to prohibit the use of funds to make an application under the Foreign Intelligence Surveillance Act to acquire library circulation records, library patron lists, bookseller sales records, or bookseller customer lists. Adopted 238–187: R 38–186; D 199–1; I 1–0. A "nay" was a vote in support of the president's position. June 15, 2005.

6. **HR 3100. Military Sales to China.** Hyde, R-Ill., motion to suspend the rules and pass the bill to require the president to report to Congress 180 days after the bill's enactment, and yearly thereafter, identifying European or other entities that have exported any arms or dual-use technology to China for military use since Jan. 1, 2005. Motion rejected 215–203: R 118–106; D 96–97; I 1–0. A two-thirds majority of those present and voting (279 in this case) was required for passage under suspension of the rules. July 14, 2005.

7. **HR 3045.Central American Free-Trade Agreement.** Passage of the bill to implement a free-trade agreement between the United States and Costa Rica, El Salvador, Guatemala, Honduras, and Nicaragua and a separate pact with the Dominican Republic. HR 3045 also eliminated customs duties on all originating goods traded among the participating nations within ten days. Passed 217–215: R 202–27; D 15–187; I 0–1. A "yea" was a vote in support of the president's position. July 28, 2005.

8. **HR6. Energy Policy Conference Report.** Adoption of the conference report on legislation to overhaul the nation's energy policy and provide for $14.6 billion in energy-related tax incentives. Included were provisions allowing lawsuits involving the gasoline additive methyl tertiary butyl ether to be moved to a federal district court, requiring refiners to annually use 7.5 billion gallons of renewable fuels by 2012, granting the Federal Energy Regulatory Commission (FERC) jurisdiction over reliability standards for electricity transmission networks, and extending daylight-saving time by one month. Adopted 275–156: R 200–31; D 75–124; I 0–1. A "yea" was a vote in support of the president's position. July 28, 2005.

9. **HR 3. Surface Transportation Reauthorization Conference Report.** Adoption of the conference report on legislation to bring total authorization for federal highway, mass transit, safety, and research programs, including fiscal 2004 funding, to $286.5 billion through 2009. The bill increased the rate of return to states on their Highway Trust Fund contributions to 92 percent by fiscal 2008 and made the Transportation Department the lead agency in the environmental review process for transportation projects. Adopted 412–8: R 217–8; D 194–0; I 1–0. July 29, 2005.

10. **HR 3824. Endangered Species Act Overhaul Passage.** Passage of the bill to overhaul and reauthorize the Endangered Species Act through 2010. The legislation replaced the critical habitat designation with expanded authority to develop recovery plans for species. It also required the Interior Department to reimburse landowners who were not allowed to develop their land because of protections for endangered species, and it authorized grants for private landowners to protect endangered species. Passed 229–193: R 193–34; D 36–158; I 0–1. Sept. 29, 2005.

11. **HR 2863. Intelligence Interrogation Methods.** Murtha, D-Pa., motion to instruct House conferees on the fiscal 2006 defense appropriations bill to include Senate-passed language to establish the U.S. Army Field Manual on Intelligence Interrogation as the uniform standard for interrogating persons detained by the Department of Defense, and prohibit cruel, inhuman, or degrading treatment of any prisoner detained by the U.S. government. Motion agreed to 308–122: R 107–121; D 200–1; I 1–0. A "nay" was a vote in support of the president's position. Dec. 14, 2005.

12. **S 1932. Budget Reconciliation Conference Report.** Adoption of the conference report on the bill to make changes to programs for a net savings of $38.8 billion over five years. The total included savings of roughly $12.7 billion from the student loan program, $1.5 billion from aid to states to enforce child support payments, and $4.8 billion from Medicaid. The bill provided $2.1 billion in hurricane assistance, authorized an additional $1 billion for low-income energy assistance, and provided $7.3 billion to avoid a scheduled Medicare reimbursement cut to physicians. Adopted 212–206: R 212–9; D 0–196; I 0–1. A "yea" was a vote in support of the president's position. Dec. 19, 2005.

KEY

	Democrat		*Republican*	**Independent**
Y	Voted for (yea)	–	Announced against	
#	Paired for	P	Voted "present"	
+	Announced for	C	Voted "present" to avoid possible conflict of interest	
N	Voted against (nay)	?	Did not vote or otherwise make a position known	
X	Paired against			

House Key Votes	1	2	3	4	5	6	7	8	9	10	11	12
ALABAMA												
1 *Bonner*	Y	Y	Y	N	N	N	Y	N	Y	Y	N	Y
2 *Everett*	Y	?	Y	N	N	N	Y	Y	Y	Y	N	Y
3 *Rogers*	Y	Y	Y	N	N	Y	Y	Y	Y	Y	N	Y
4 *Aderholt*	Y	Y	Y	N	N	Y	Y	Y	Y	Y	N	Y
5 Cramer	Y	Y	Y	Y	Y	N	N	Y	Y	Y	Y	N
6 *Bachus*	Y	Y	Y	N	N	Y	Y	Y	Y	Y	Y	Y
7 Davis	Y	?	Y	Y	Y	Y	N	Y	Y	Y	Y	N
ALASKA												
AL *Young*	N	?	Y	Y	Y	N	Y	Y	Y	Y	N	Y
ARIZONA												
1 *Renzi*	Y	Y	Y	N	N	N	Y	Y	Y	Y	N	Y
2 *Franks*	Y	Y	Y	N	N	Y	Y	Y	Y	Y	N	Y
3 *Shadegg*	Y	?	Y	N	N	Y	Y	Y	N	Y	N	Y
4 Pastor	N	?	Y	Y	Y	N	N	N	Y	N	Y	N
5 *Hayworth*	Y	Y	Y	N	N	Y	Y	Y	Y	Y	N	Y
6 *Flake*	Y	?	Y	N	Y	N	Y	N	N	Y	Y	Y
7 Grijalva	N	?	Y	Y	Y	Y	N	N	Y	N	Y	N
8 *Kolbe*	Y	?	Y	Y	N	N	Y	Y	Y	Y	Y	?
ARKANSAS												
1 Berry	Y	Y	Y	Y	Y	N	N	Y	Y	Y	Y	N
2 Snyder	N	Y	Y	Y	Y	N	Y	Y	Y	N	Y	N
3 *Boozman*	Y	?	Y	N	Y	Y	Y	Y	Y	Y	Y	Y
4 Ross	Y	Y	Y	Y	Y	Y	N	Y	Y	Y	Y	N
CALIFORNIA												
1 Thompson	N	?	Y	Y	Y	N	N	N	Y	N	Y	N
2 *Herger*	Y	?	Y	N	N	Y	Y	Y	Y	Y	N	Y
3 *Lungren*	Y	?	Y	N	N	Y	Y	Y	Y	Y	N	Y
4 *Doolittle*	Y	Y	Y	N	N	Y	Y	Y	Y	Y	N	Y
5 Matsui[1]		N	Y	Y	Y	Y	N	N	Y	N	Y	N
6 Woolsey	N	?	Y	Y	Y	N	N	N	Y	N	Y	N
7 Miller, George	N	?	Y	Y	Y	N	N	N	?	N	Y	N
8 Pelosi	N	?	Y	Y	Y	Y	N	N	Y	N	Y	N
9 Lee	N	?	?	Y	Y	N	N	N	Y	–	Y	N
10 Tauscher	N	?	Y	Y	Y	N	N	N	Y	N	Y	N
11 *Pombo*	N	?	Y	N	N	Y	Y	Y	+	Y	Y	Y
12 Lantos	N	?	Y	Y	Y	Y	N	N	Y	N	Y	N
13 Stark	N	?	Y	Y	Y	N	N	N	?	N	Y	N
14 Eshoo	?	?	Y	Y	Y	N	N	N	Y	N	Y	N
15 Honda	–	?	Y	Y	Y	N	N	N	Y	N	Y	N
16 Lofgren	N	?	Y	Y	Y	N	N	N	Y	N	Y	N
17 Farr	N	?	Y	Y	Y	Y	N	N	Y	N	Y	N
18 Cardoza	Y	?	Y	Y	Y	Y	N	Y	Y	Y	Y	N
19 *Radanovich*	Y	?	Y	N	N	Y	Y	Y	Y	Y	N	?
20 Costa	Y	?	Y	Y	Y	Y	N	Y	Y	Y	+	N
21 *Nunes*	Y	?	Y	N	N	N	Y	Y	Y	Y	N	Y
22 *Thomas*	Y	?	Y	Y	N	N	Y	Y	Y	Y	Y	Y
23 Capps	N	?	Y	Y	Y	+	N	N	+	N	Y	N
24 *Gallegly*	Y	?	Y	N	N	+	Y	Y	Y	Y	N	Y
25 *McKeon*	Y	?	Y	Y	N	N	Y	Y	Y	Y	N	Y
26 *Dreier*	Y	Y	Y	Y	N	N	Y	Y	Y	Y	N	Y
27 Sherman	N	?	Y	Y	Y	Y	N	N	Y	N	Y	N
28 Berman	N	?	Y	Y	Y	N	N	N	Y	N	Y	N
29 Schiff	N	N	Y	Y	Y	Y	N	N	Y	N	Y	N
30 Waxman	N	?	?	Y	Y	N	N	N	Y	N	Y	N
31 Becerra	N	–	Y	Y	Y	N	N	N	Y	N	Y	N
32 Solis	N	?	Y	Y	Y	Y	N	N	Y	N	Y	N
33 Watson	N	?	Y	Y	Y	Y	N	N	Y	N	Y	N
34 Roybal-Allard	N	?	Y	Y	Y	Y	N	N	Y	N	Y	?
35 Waters	N	?	Y	Y	Y	N	N	N	Y	N	Y	N
36 Harman	N	?	Y	Y	Y	N	N	N	Y	–	Y	?
37 Millender-McD.	N	?	Y	?	Y	N	N	N	Y	N	Y	N
38 Napolitano	N	?	Y	Y	Y	N	N	Y	Y	N	Y	N
39 Sánchez, Linda	N	?	Y	Y	Y	Y	N	N	Y	N	Y	N
40 *Royce*	Y	?	Y	N	N	Y	Y	N	N	Y	N	Y
41 *Lewis*	Y	Y	Y	Y	N	N	Y	Y	Y	Y	N	Y
42 *Miller, Gary*	Y	?	Y	N	N	Y	Y	Y	Y	Y	N	?
43 Baca	N	Y	Y	Y	Y	N	N	Y	Y	Y	Y	?
44 *Calvert*	Y	Y	Y	Y	N	N	Y	Y	Y	Y	N	Y
45 *Bono*	Y	?	Y	Y	?	Y	Y	Y	Y	Y	N	Y
46 *Rohrabacher*	Y	?	Y	Y	N	Y	Y	N	Y	Y	N	Y
47 Sanchez, Loretta	?	?	Y	Y	Y	N	N	N	Y	N	Y	N
48 *Cox*[2]	Y	Y	Y	N	N	Y	Y	Y				
48 *Campbell*[2]											N	Y
49 *Issa*	Y	+	Y	Y	N	N	Y	Y	Y	Y	Y	Y
50 *Cunningham*[3]	Y	?	Y	Y	N	?	Y	Y	Y	Y		
51 Filner	N	?	Y	Y	Y	Y	N	N	Y	N	Y	N
52 *Hunter*	Y	?	Y	N	N	Y	N	Y	Y	Y	N	Y
53 Davis	N	?	Y	Y	Y	N	N	N	Y	N	Y	N
COLORADO												
1 DeGette	N	?	Y	Y	Y	Y	N	N	Y	N	Y	N
2 Udall	N	?	Y	Y	Y	N	N	N	Y	N	Y	N
3 Salazar	Y	?	Y	Y	Y	Y	N	Y	Y	Y	Y	N
4 *Musgrave*	Y	Y	Y	N	Y	Y	Y	Y	Y	Y	N	Y
5 *Hefley*	Y	Y	Y	N	N	Y	Y	Y	Y	Y	N	Y
6 *Tancredo*	Y	Y	Y	N	N	N	N	Y	Y	Y	Y	Y
7 *Beauprez*	Y	Y	Y	N	N	N	Y	Y	Y	Y	Y	Y
CONNECTICUT												
1 Larson	N	N	Y	Y	Y	Y	N	N	Y	N	Y	N
2 *Simmons*	Y	?	Y	Y	N	?	N	Y	Y	N	Y	Y
3 DeLauro	N	?	Y	Y	Y	Y	N	N	Y	N	Y	N
4 *Shays*	Y	N	Y	Y	N	N	Y	N	Y	N	Y	Y
5 *Johnson*	Y	?	Y	Y	N	N	Y	Y	Y	N	Y	Y
DELAWARE												
AL *Castle*	Y	N	Y	Y	Y	Y	Y	N	Y	N	Y	Y
FLORIDA												
1 *Miller*	Y	Y	Y	N	Y	+	Y	N	Y	Y	N	Y
2 Boyd	Y	?	Y	Y	Y	Y	N	N	Y	Y	Y	N
3 Brown	N	?	?	Y	Y	Y	N	N	Y	N	Y	N
4 *Crenshaw*	Y	Y	Y	N	N	N	Y	N	Y	Y	N	Y
5 *Brown-Waite*	Y	N	Y	Y	N	Y	Y	N	Y	Y	Y	Y
6 *Stearns*	Y	?	Y	N	N	Y	Y	Y	Y	Y	N	Y
7 *Mica*	Y	?	Y	N	N	N	Y	Y	?	Y	N	Y
8 *Keller*	Y	?	Y	N	N	Y	Y	N	Y	Y	Y	Y
9 *Bilirakis*	Y	Y	Y	N	N	Y	Y	Y	Y	Y	N	Y
10 *Young*	Y	?	Y	Y	N	?	Y	N	Y	Y	N	Y
11 Davis	Y	N	Y	Y	Y	Y	N	N	Y	?	Y	N
12 *Putnam*	Y	Y	Y	N	N	Y	Y	N	Y	Y	N	Y
13 *Harris*	Y	Y	Y	N	Y	N	Y	N	Y	Y	Y	Y
14 *Mack*	Y	Y	Y	Y	N	Y	N	N	Y	Y	Y	Y
15 *Weldon*	Y	Y	N	N	N	Y	Y	N	Y	Y	N	Y
16 *Foley*	Y	Y	Y	Y	N	Y	Y	N	Y	N	Y	Y
17 Meek	N	Y	Y	Y	Y	N	N	N	Y	N	Y	N
18 *Ros-Lehtinen*	N	Y	Y	N	N	Y	Y	N	Y	Y	Y	Y
19 Wexler	N	N	Y	Y	Y	N	N	N	?	N	Y	N
20 Wasserman-Schultz	N	N	Y	Y	Y	Y	N	N	Y	N	Y	N
21 *Diaz-Balart, L.*	N	Y	Y	N	N	Y	Y	N	Y	Y	Y	Y
22 *Shaw*	Y	?	Y	Y	N	Y	Y	N	Y	N	Y	Y
23 Hastings	N	N	Y	Y	Y	N	N	N	Y	N	Y	N
24 *Feeney*	?	Y	Y	N	N	Y	Y	N	Y	Y	N	Y
25 *Diaz-Balart, M.*	N	Y	Y	N	N	Y	Y	N	Y	Y	+	Y
GEORGIA												
1 *Kingston*	Y	Y	Y	N	Y	N	Y	Y	Y	Y	N	Y
2 Bishop	Y	Y	Y	Y	Y	Y	N	Y	Y	Y	Y	N
3 Marshall	Y	Y	Y	N	Y	N	N	Y	Y	Y	N	N
4 McKinney	N	N	Y	Y	Y	N	N	N	Y	N	Y	N
5 Lewis	N	N	Y	Y	Y	N	N	N	Y	N	Y	N
6 *Price*	Y	Y	N	N	N	N	Y	Y	Y	Y	N	Y
7 *Linder*	Y	Y	Y	N	N	Y	Y	Y	Y	Y	N	Y
8 *Westmoreland*	Y	Y	–	N	N	N	Y	Y	Y	Y	N	Y
9 *Norwood*	Y	?	Y	N	N	Y	N	Y	Y	Y	N	Y
10 *Deal*	Y	?	Y	N	N	Y	Y	Y	Y	Y	N	Y
11 *Gingrey*	Y	Y	Y	N	N	Y	Y	Y	Y	Y	N	Y

[1]Rep. Doris Matsui, D-Calif., was sworn in March 10, 2005.

[2]Rep. John Campbell, R-Calif., was sworn in Dec. 7, 2005, to replace Republican Christopher Cox, who resigned effective Aug. 2.

[3]Rep. Randy "Duke" Cunningham, R-Calif., resigned effective Dec. 1, 2005.

KEY

Democrat   *Republican*   **Independent**

Y	Voted for (yea)	–	Announced against
#	Paired for	P	Voted "present"
+	Announced for	C	Voted "present" to avoid possible conflict of interest
N	Voted against (nay)		
X	Paired against	?	Did not vote or otherwise make a position known

House Key Votes	1	2	3	4	5	6	7	8	9	10	11	12
12 Barrow	Y	Y	Y	Y	Y	Y	N	Y	Y	Y	Y	N
13 Scott	Y	Y	Y	Y	Y	Y	N	Y	Y	Y	Y	N
HAWAII												
1 Abercrombie	N	?	Y	Y	Y	Y	N	Y	Y	Y	Y	N
2 Case	Y	?	Y	Y	Y	Y	N	N	Y	N	Y	N
IDAHO												
1 *Otter*	Y	Y	N	N	Y	N	N	Y	Y	Y	Y	Y
2 *Simpson*	Y	Y	N	N	N	N	N	Y	Y	Y	N	Y
ILLINOIS												
1 Rush	N	?	Y	Y	Y	N	N	Y	Y	N	Y	N
2 Jackson	N	Y	Y	Y	Y	N	N	N	Y	N	Y	N
3 Lipinski	Y	Y	Y	N	Y	N	N	Y	Y	N	Y	N
4 Gutierrez	N	N	Y	Y	Y	+	N	N	Y	–	Y	?
5 Emanuel	N	?	Y	Y	Y	N	N	N	Y	N	Y	?
6 *Hyde*	Y	?	Y	N	–	Y	Y	Y	Y	Y	+	?
7 Davis	N	?	Y	Y	Y	N	N	N	Y	N	Y	N
8 Bean	Y	Y	Y	Y	Y	N	Y	Y	Y	N	Y	N
9 Schakowsky	N	?	Y	Y	Y	N	N	?	?	N	Y	N
10 *Kirk*	Y	Y	Y	Y	Y	N	Y	Y	Y	N	Y	Y
11 *Weller*	Y	?	Y	N	N	N	Y	Y	Y	Y	Y	Y
12 Costello	Y	Y	Y	N	Y	N	N	Y	Y	Y	Y	N
13 *Biggert*	Y	Y	Y	Y	N	N	Y	Y	Y	N	Y	Y
14 *Hastert*[4]		Y		N			Y	Y	Y			Y
15 *Johnson*	Y	Y	Y	N	Y	Y	Y	Y	Y	N	Y	N
16 *Manzullo*	Y	Y	Y	N	Y	N	Y	Y	Y	Y	Y	Y
17 Evans	N	N	Y	Y	Y	Y	N	Y	Y	N	Y	N
18 *LaHood*	Y	Y	Y	N	Y	N	Y	Y	Y	N	N	Y
19 *Shimkus*	Y	?	Y	N	N	N	Y	Y	Y	Y	Y	Y
INDIANA												
1 Visclosky	N	N	Y	Y	Y	N	N	Y	Y	N	Y	N
2 *Chocola*	Y	Y	Y	N	N	Y	Y	Y	Y	Y	Y	Y
3 *Souder*	Y	Y	P	N	N	Y	Y	Y	Y	Y	N	Y
4 *Buyer*	Y	Y	N	N	N	Y	Y	Y	Y	Y	N	N
5 *Burton*	Y	Y	N	N	N	Y	Y	Y	Y	Y	N	Y
6 *Pence*	Y	Y	N	N	N	Y	Y	Y	Y	Y	N	Y
7 Carson	N	N	Y	Y	Y	?	N	Y	Y	N	Y	N
8 *Hostettler*	Y	?	Y	N	N	Y	N	Y	Y	Y	N	?
9 *Sodrel*	Y	Y	Y	N	N	N	Y	Y	Y	Y	Y	Y
IOWA												
1 *Nussle*	Y	Y	Y	N	N	N	Y	Y	Y	Y	Y	Y
2 *Leach*	Y	Y	Y	Y	Y	N	Y	Y	Y	N	Y	N
3 Boswell	N	?	Y	Y	Y	N	N	Y	Y	?	Y	N
4 *Latham*	Y	Y	Y	N	N	N	Y	Y	Y	Y	Y	Y
5 *King*	Y	Y	N	N	N	N	Y	Y	Y	Y	N	Y
KANSAS												
1 *Moran*	Y	?	Y	N	Y	N	Y	Y	Y	Y	Y	Y
2 *Ryun*	Y	Y	Y	N	N	N	Y	Y	Y	Y	N	Y
3 Moore	N	–	Y	Y	Y	N	Y	Y	Y	N	Y	N
4 *Tiahrt*	Y	Y	N	N	N	N	Y	Y	Y	Y	N	Y
KENTUCKY												
1 *Whitfield*	Y	Y	Y	N	Y	N	Y	Y	Y	Y	Y	Y
2 *Lewis*	Y	Y	Y	N	N	N	Y	Y	Y	Y	N	Y
3 *Northup*	Y	Y	Y	N	N	Y	Y	Y	Y	Y	Y	Y
4 *Davis*	Y	Y	Y	N	N	N	Y	Y	Y	Y	Y	Y
5 *Rogers*	Y	?	Y	N	N	Y	Y	Y	Y	Y	N	Y
6 Chandler	Y	Y	Y	Y	Y	Y	N	N	Y	N	Y	N

House Key Votes	1	2	3	4	5	6	7	8	9	10	11	12
LOUISIANA												
1 *Jindal*	Y	Y	Y	N	N	Y	N	Y	Y	Y	N	Y
2 Jefferson	N	?	Y	Y	Y	N	Y	Y	Y	N	Y	N
3 Melancon	Y	Y	Y	Y	Y	Y	N	Y	Y	Y	Y	N
4 *McCrery*	Y	?	Y	N	N	N	Y	Y	Y	Y	Y	Y
5 *Alexander*	Y	Y	Y	N	N	Y	Y	Y	Y	Y	Y	Y
6 *Baker*	Y	Y	Y	N	N	N	Y	Y	Y	Y	N	Y
7 *Boustany*	Y	?	Y	N	N	N	N	Y	Y	Y	Y	Y
MAINE												
1 Allen	N	?	Y	Y	Y	Y	N	N	Y	N	Y	N
2 Michaud	N	Y	Y	Y	Y	Y	N	N	Y	N	Y	N
MARYLAND												
1 *Gilchrest*	Y	Y	Y	Y	N	N	Y	Y	Y	N	Y	Y
2 Ruppersberger	N	?	Y	Y	Y	N	N	Y	Y	N	Y	N
3 Cardin	N	N	Y	Y	Y	?	N	N	Y	N	Y	N
4 Wynn	N	Y	Y	Y	Y	N	N	Y	Y	Y	Y	N
5 Hoyer	N	N	Y	Y	Y	N	N	Y	Y	N	Y	N
6 *Bartlett*	?	Y	Y	N	Y	N	Y	N	Y	Y	Y	Y
7 Cummings	N	Y	Y	Y	Y	Y	N	N	Y	N	Y	N
8 Van Hollen	N	N	Y	Y	Y	N	N	N	Y	N	Y	N
MASSACHUSETTS												
1 Olver	N	N	Y	Y	Y	N	N	N	Y	N	Y	N
2 Neal	N	?	Y	Y	Y	Y	N	N	Y	N	Y	N
3 McGovern	N	?	Y	Y	Y	N	N	N	Y	N	Y	N
4 Frank	N	N	Y	Y	Y	Y	N	N	Y	N	Y	N
5 Meehan	N	?	Y	Y	Y	N	N	N	Y	N	Y	N
6 Tierney	N	?	Y	Y	Y	Y	N	N	Y	N	Y	N
7 Markey	N	?	Y	Y	Y	Y	N	N	Y	N	Y	N
8 Capuano	N	N	Y	Y	Y	N	N	N	Y	N	Y	N
9 Lynch	N	Y	Y	Y	Y	N	N	N	Y	N	Y	N
10 Delahunt	N	?	Y	Y	Y	N	N	N	?	N	Y	N
MICHIGAN												
1 Stupak	?	Y	Y	N	Y	Y	N	Y	Y	N	Y	N
2 *Hoekstra*	Y	?	Y	N	N	N	Y	Y	Y	Y	N	Y
3 *Ehlers*	Y	Y	Y	N	Y	N	Y	Y	Y	N	Y	Y
4 *Camp*	Y	Y	Y	N	N	N	Y	Y	Y	Y	Y	Y
5 Kildee	N	Y	Y	N	Y	Y	N	N	Y	N	Y	N
6 *Upton*	Y	Y	Y	Y	N	N	Y	Y	Y	N	Y	Y
7 *Schwarz*	Y	Y	Y	Y	Y	Y	Y	Y	?	N	Y	Y
8 *Rogers*	Y	?	Y	N	N	Y	Y	Y	Y	Y	N	Y
9 *Knollenberg*	Y	?	Y	N	N	Y	Y	Y	Y	Y	Y	Y
10 *Miller*	Y	Y	Y	N	N	Y	N	Y	Y	Y	Y	Y
11 *McCotter*	Y	Y	Y	N	N	Y	N	Y	Y	Y	Y	Y
12 Levin	N	N	Y	Y	Y	N	N	Y	Y	N	Y	N
13 Kilpatrick	N	?	Y	Y	Y	+	N	N	Y	N	Y	N
14 Conyers	N	N	Y	Y	Y	Y	N	N	Y	N	Y	N
15 Dingell	N	?	Y	Y	Y	Y	N	Y	Y	N	Y	N
MINNESOTA												
1 *Gutknecht*	Y	?	Y	N	N	N	N	Y	Y	Y	Y	Y
2 *Kline*	Y	Y	Y	N	N	N	Y	Y	Y	Y	Y	Y
3 *Ramstad*	Y	Y	Y	Y	N	Y	Y	Y	Y	N	Y	Y
4 McCollum	N	?	Y	Y	Y	N	N	N	Y	N	Y	N
5 Sabo	N	?	Y	Y	Y	N	N	N	Y	N	Y	N
6 *Kennedy*	Y	Y	Y	N	N	N	Y	Y	Y	Y	Y	Y
7 Peterson	Y	?	Y	N	Y	Y	N	Y	Y	Y	Y	N
8 Oberstar	N	Y	Y	N	+	?	N	Y	Y	N	Y	N
MISSISSIPPI												
1 *Wicker*	Y	+	?	N	N	Y	Y	Y	Y	Y	N	Y
2 Thompson	N	N	Y	Y	Y	Y	N	Y	Y	Y	Y	N
3 *Pickering*	Y	Y	Y	N	N	Y	Y	Y	Y	Y	Y	Y
4 Taylor	Y	?	Y	N	Y	Y	N	N	Y	Y	Y	N
MISSOURI												
1 Clay	N	N	Y	Y	Y	N	N	N	Y	N	Y	N
2 *Akin*	Y	Y	Y	N	N	Y	Y	Y	Y	Y	N	Y
3 Carnahan	N	N	Y	Y	Y	Y	N	N	Y	N	Y	N
4 Skelton	Y	Y	Y	Y	Y	N	Y	Y	Y	Y	Y	N
5 Cleaver	N	N	Y	Y	Y	Y	N	N	Y	N	Y	N
6 *Graves*	Y	Y	Y	N	N	Y	Y	Y	Y	Y	N	Y
7 *Blunt*	Y	Y	Y	N	N	Y	Y	Y	Y	Y	N	Y
8 *Emerson*	Y	Y	Y	Y	Y	Y	Y	Y	Y	Y	Y	Y
9 *Hulshof*	Y	Y	Y	N	N	N	Y	Y	Y	Y	Y	Y

[4]The Speaker votes only at his discretion, usually to break a tie or to emphasize the importance of a matter.

House Key Votes	1	2	3	4	5	6	7	8	9	10	11	12
MONTANA												
AL *Rehberg*	Y	Y	Y	N	Y	N	N	Y	Y	Y	N	Y
NEBRASKA												
1 *Fortenberry*	Y	Y	Y	N	N	Y	Y	Y	Y	Y	Y	Y
2 *Terry*	Y	Y	Y	N	N	Y	Y	Y	Y	Y	N	Y
3 *Osborne*	Y	?	Y	N	N	Y	Y	Y	Y	Y	Y	Y
NEVADA												
1 Berkley	N	N	Y	Y	Y	Y	N	N	Y	N	Y	N
2 *Gibbons*	Y	?	Y	Y	N	N	Y	Y	Y	Y	Y	Y
3 *Porter*	Y	Y	Y	Y	Y	Y	Y	Y	Y	Y	Y	Y
NEW HAMPSHIRE												
1 *Bradley*	Y	?	Y	Y	N	Y	Y	N	Y	N	Y	Y
2 *Bass*	Y	Y	Y	Y	N	N	Y	Y	Y	N	Y	Y
NEW JERSEY												
1 Andrews	N	?	Y	Y	Y	Y	N	N	Y	N	Y	N
2 *LoBiondo*	Y	Y	Y	N	N	N	N	N	Y	N	Y	Y
3 *Saxton*	Y	Y	Y	N	N	N	Y	N	Y	N	Y	Y
4 *Smith*	N	Y	Y	N	N	Y	N	N	Y	N	Y	N
5 *Garrett*	Y	Y	Y	N	–	N	N	Y	Y	Y	N	Y
6 Pallone	N	N	Y	Y	Y	N	N	N	Y	N	Y	N
7 *Ferguson*	+	Y	Y	N	N	N	Y	Y	Y	N	Y	Y
8 Pascrell	N	N	Y	Y	Y	Y	N	N	Y	N	Y	N
9 Rothman	N	N	?	Y	Y	Y	N	N	Y	N	Y	N
10 Payne	N	N	Y	Y	Y	N	N	?	Y	?	Y	N
11 *Frelinghuysen*	Y	?	Y	Y	N	N	Y	Y	Y	N	N	Y
12 Holt	N	N	Y	Y	Y	N	N	N	Y	N	Y	N
13 Menendez	N	?	Y	Y	Y	N	N	N	Y	N	Y	N
NEW MEXICO												
1 *Wilson*	N	?	Y	Y	N	N	Y	Y	Y	Y	Y	N
2 *Pearce*	Y	Y	Y	N	N	Y	Y	Y	Y	Y	N	Y
3 Udall	N	?	Y	Y	Y	N	N	Y	Y	N	Y	N
NEW YORK												
1 Bishop	N	N	Y	Y	Y	Y	N	N	Y	N	Y	N
2 Israel	N	N	Y	Y	Y	N	N	N	Y	N	Y	N
3 *King*	Y	?	Y	N	N	Y	Y	Y	Y	Y	N	Y
4 McCarthy	N	?	Y	Y	Y	N	N	N	Y	N	Y	N
5 Ackerman	N	?	Y	Y	Y	Y	N	N	Y	N	Y	N
6 Meeks	N	?	Y	Y	Y	N	Y	Y	Y	N	Y	N
7 Crowley	N	?	Y	Y	Y	Y	N	N	Y	N	Y	N
8 Nadler	N	N	Y	Y	Y	Y	N	N	Y	N	Y	N
9 Weiner	N	N	Y	Y	Y	?	N	N	Y	N	Y	N
10 Towns	N	?	Y	Y	Y	Y	Y	Y	Y	?	Y	N
11 Owens	N	?	Y	Y	Y	Y	N	N	Y	N	Y	N
12 Velázquez	N	?	Y	Y	Y	N	N	N	Y	N	Y	N
13 *Fossella*	Y	Y	Y	Y	N	N	Y	Y	Y	Y	N	Y
14 Maloney	N	?	Y	Y	Y	Y	N	N	Y	N	Y	N
15 Rangel	N	?	Y	Y	Y	N	N	N	Y	N	Y	N
16 Serrano	N	Y	Y	Y	Y	Y	N	N	Y	N	Y	N
17 Engel	N	Y	Y	Y	Y	Y	N	N	Y	N	Y	N
18 Lowey	N	?	Y	Y	Y	Y	N	N	Y	N	Y	N
19 *Kelly*	Y	Y	Y	Y	N	Y	Y	N	Y	N	Y	Y
20 *Sweeney*	Y	?	Y	Y	N	N	Y	Y	Y	Y	Y	Y
21 McNulty	Y	Y	Y	Y	Y	Y	N	N	Y	N	Y	N
22 Hinchey	?	?	Y	Y	Y	N	N	N	Y	N	Y	N
23 *McHugh*	Y	Y	Y	N	N	N	N	Y	Y	Y	Y	N
24 *Boehlert*	Y	?	Y	Y	Y	N	Y	N	Y	N	Y	Y
25 *Walsh*	Y	Y	Y	N	N	Y	Y	Y	Y	N	Y	Y
26 *Reynolds*	Y	?	Y	N	N	Y	Y	Y	Y	Y	Y	Y
27 Higgins	N	Y	Y	Y	Y	Y	N	N	Y	N	Y	N
28 Slaughter	N	?	Y	Y	Y	N	N	Y	Y	N	Y	N
29 *Kuhl*	Y	Y	Y	N	N	N	Y	Y	Y	Y	Y	Y
NORTH CAROLINA												
1 Butterfield	Y	N	Y	Y	Y	Y	N	Y	Y	N	Y	N
2 Etheridge	N	Y	Y	Y	Y	N	N	Y	Y	N	Y	N
3 *Jones*	Y	Y	Y	N	Y	Y	N	N	N	Y	Y	?
4 Price	N	N	Y	Y	Y	N	N	N	Y	N	Y	N
5 *Foxx*	Y	Y	Y	N	N	Y	N	Y	Y	Y	N	Y
6 *Coble*	Y	+	Y	Y	N	N	N	Y	Y	Y	N	Y
7 McIntyre	Y	Y	Y	N	Y	?	N	Y	Y	Y	Y	N
8 *Hayes*	Y	Y	Y	N	N	Y	Y	Y	Y	Y	N	Y
9 *Myrick*	Y	Y	Y	N	N	Y	Y	Y	Y	Y	N	?
10 *McHenry*	Y	Y	N	N	N	Y	N	Y	Y	Y	N	Y
11 *Taylor*	Y	Y	Y	N	Y	Y	–	Y	Y	Y	N	Y
12 Watt	N	N	Y	Y	Y	N	N	N	Y	N	Y	N
13 Miller	N	N	Y	Y	Y	N	N	N	Y	N	Y	N

House Key Votes	1	2	3	4	5	6	7	8	9	10	11	12
NORTH DAKOTA												
AL Pomeroy	N	Y	Y	Y	Y	N	N	Y	Y	Y	Y	N
OHIO												
1 *Chabot*	Y	Y	Y	N	N	Y	Y	Y	Y	Y	N	Y
2 *Portman*[5]	Y	Y	Y									
2 *Schmidt*[5]										Y	N	Y
3 *Turner*	Y	Y	Y	N	N	N	Y	Y	Y	Y	N	Y
4 *Oxley*	Y	?	Y	N	N	Y	Y	Y	Y	Y	N	Y
5 *Gillmor*	Y	Y	N	N	Y	Y	Y	Y	Y	Y	N	Y
6 Strickland	Y	N	Y	Y	Y	Y	N	Y	Y	N	Y	N
7 *Hobson*	Y	Y	Y	N	N	N	Y	Y	Y	?	N	Y
8 *Boehner*	Y	Y	Y	N	N	N	Y	Y	N	Y	N	Y
9 Kaptur	N	N	Y	N	Y	Y	N	N	Y	N	Y	N
10 Kucinich	N	?	Y	Y	Y	Y	N	N	Y	N	Y	N
11 Jones	N	?	Y	Y	Y	N	N	N	Y	N	Y	N
12 *Tiberi*	Y	Y	Y	N	N	N	Y	Y	Y	Y	Y	Y
13 Brown	N	?	Y	Y	Y	Y	N	N	Y	N	Y	N
14 *LaTourette*	Y	?	Y	Y	Y	N	Y	Y	Y	N	Y	N
15 *Pryce*	Y	Y	Y	Y	N	N	Y	Y	Y	Y	Y	Y
16 *Regula*	Y	Y	Y	Y	N	N	Y	Y	Y	Y	Y	Y
17 Ryan	Y	?	Y	Y	Y	Y	N	Y	Y	N	Y	N
18 *Ney*	Y	Y	Y	N	Y	Y	N	Y	Y	Y	N	N
OKLAHOMA												
1 *Sullivan*	Y	Y	Y	N	?	N	Y	Y	Y	Y	N	Y
2 Boren	Y	Y	Y	Y	N	N	N	Y	Y	Y	Y	N
3 *Lucas*	Y	Y	Y	N	N	Y	Y	Y	Y	Y	N	Y
4 *Cole*	Y	Y	Y	N	N	Y	Y	Y	Y	Y	N	Y
5 *Istook*	Y	Y	Y	N	N	Y	Y	Y	Y	Y	N	?
OREGON												
1 Wu	N	N	Y	Y	Y	Y	N	N	Y	N	Y	N
2 *Walden*	Y	?	Y	Y	Y	Y	Y	Y	Y	Y	Y	Y
3 Blumenauer	N	?	Y	Y	Y	N	N	N	Y	N	Y	N
4 DeFazio	Y	?	Y	Y	Y	Y	N	N	Y	N	Y	N
5 Hooley	Y	?	Y	Y	Y	N	N	N	Y	N	Y	N
PENNSYLVANIA												
1 Brady	N	Y	Y	Y	Y	Y	N	?	?	N	Y	N
2 Fattah	N	Y	Y	Y	Y	Y	N	N	?	–	Y	N
3 *English*	Y	Y	Y	N	N	N	Y	Y	Y	Y	Y	Y
4 *Hart*	Y	Y	Y	N	N	N	Y	Y	Y	Y	N	Y
5 *Peterson*	Y	Y	Y	N	Y	Y	Y	Y	Y	Y	N	Y
6 *Gerlach*	Y	?	Y	Y	N	Y	Y	Y	Y	N	Y	Y
7 *Weldon*	Y	Y	Y	N	?	Y	Y	Y	Y	N	Y	Y
8 *Fitzpatrick*	Y	Y	Y	N	Y	Y	Y	N	Y	N	Y	Y
9 *Shuster*	Y	?	Y	N	N	N	Y	Y	Y	Y	N	Y
10 *Sherwood*	Y	Y	Y	N	N	Y	Y	Y	Y	Y	Y	Y
11 Kanjorski	Y	Y	Y	Y	Y	Y	N	Y	Y	N	Y	N
12 Murtha	N	N	Y	Y	Y	N	N	Y	Y	Y	Y	N
13 Schwartz	N	N	Y	Y	Y	Y	N	N	Y	N	Y	N
14 Doyle	N	N	Y	Y	Y	Y	N	Y	Y	N	Y	N
15 *Dent*	Y	N	Y	Y	N	Y	Y	Y	Y	Y	Y	Y
16 *Pitts*	Y	Y	Y	N	N	Y	Y	Y	?	Y	Y	Y
17 Holden	Y	Y	Y	N	Y	Y	N	Y	Y	Y	Y	N
18 *Murphy*	Y	Y	Y	N	N	N	Y	Y	Y	Y	Y	Y
19 *Platts*	Y	Y	Y	Y	N	Y	Y	Y	Y	N	Y	Y
RHODE ISLAND												
1 Kennedy	N	N	Y	Y	Y	Y	N	N	Y	N	Y	N
2 Langevin	N	Y	Y	Y	Y	Y	N	N	Y	N	Y	N
SOUTH CAROLINA												
1 *Brown*	Y	?	Y	N	N	N	Y	Y	Y	Y	N	Y
2 *Wilson*	Y	Y	Y	N	N	Y	Y	Y	Y	Y	N	Y
3 *Barrett*	Y	Y	Y	N	N	Y	Y	Y	Y	Y	N	Y
4 *Inglis*	Y	Y	Y	N	N	Y	Y	Y	Y	Y	Y	Y
5 Spratt	N	N	Y	Y	Y	Y	N	Y	Y	N	Y	N
6 Clyburn	N	N	Y	Y	Y	N	N	Y	Y	N	Y	N
SOUTH DAKOTA												
AL Herseth	Y	Y	Y	Y	Y	N	N	Y	Y	Y	Y	N
TENNESSEE												
1 *Jenkins*	Y	Y	Y	N	N	N	Y	Y	Y	Y	Y	Y
2 *Duncan*	Y	Y	Y	N	Y	Y	Y	Y	Y	Y	Y	Y
3 *Wamp*	Y	Y	Y	N	N	Y	Y	Y	Y	Y	Y	Y
4 Davis	Y	Y	Y	N	Y	Y	N	Y	Y	Y	Y	N
5 Cooper	Y	?	Y	Y	Y	Y	Y	N	Y	N	Y	N
6 Gordon	Y	?	Y	Y	Y	N	N	Y	Y	N	Y	N
7 *Blackburn*	Y	Y	N	N	N	Y	Y	Y	Y	Y	N	Y

[5]Rep. Jean Schmidt, R-Ohio, was sworn in Sept. 6, 2005, to replace Republican Rob Portman, who resigned effective April 29.

KEY

Democrat | *Republican* | **Independent**

Y	Voted for (yea)	–	Announced against
#	Paired for	P	Voted "present"
+	Announced for	C	Voted "present" to avoid possible conflict of interest
N	Voted against (nay)		
X	Paired against	?	Did not vote or otherwise make a position known

House Key Votes	1	2	3	4	5	6	7	8	9	10	11	12
8 Tanner	Y	Y	Y	Y	Y	Y	Y	Y	Y	Y	Y	N
9 Ford	Y	Y	Y	Y	Y	Y	N	Y	Y	Y	Y	N
TEXAS												
1 *Gohmert*	Y	Y	N	N	N	N	Y	Y	Y	Y	N	Y
2 *Poe*	Y	Y	N	N	Y	N	Y	Y	Y	Y	N	Y
3 *Johnson, Sam*	Y	?	Y	N	N	Y	Y	Y	?	Y	N	?
4 *Hall, R.*	Y	Y	Y	N	N	N	Y	Y	Y	Y	N	Y
5 *Hensarling*	Y	Y	Y	N	N	N	Y	Y	N	Y	N	Y
6 *Barton*	Y	?	N	Y	N	Y	Y	Y	Y	Y	N	Y
7 *Culberson*	Y	Y	N	N	N	Y	Y	Y	Y	?	N	Y
8 *Brady*	Y	?	Y	N	N	N	Y	Y	Y	Y	N	Y
9 Green, A.	N	Y	Y	Y	Y	Y	N	Y	Y	N	Y	N
10 *McCaul*	Y	Y	Y	N	N	Y	Y	Y	Y	Y	Y	Y
11 *Conaway*	Y	Y	Y	N	N	N	Y	Y	Y	Y	N	Y
12 *Granger*	Y	?	Y	Y	N	Y	Y	Y	Y	Y	N	Y
13 *Thornberry*	Y	Y	N	N	N	N	Y	Y	N	Y	N	Y
14 *Paul*	N	?	Y	N	Y	N	N	N	?	?	Y	N
15 Hinojosa	–	?	Y	Y	Y	Y	Y	Y	Y	Y	Y	N
16 Reyes	N	?	Y	Y	Y	N	N	Y	Y	N	Y	?
17 Edwards	Y	Y	Y	Y	Y	Y	N	Y	Y	Y	Y	N
18 Jackson-Lee	N	?	Y	Y	Y	Y	N	Y	Y	N	Y	N
19 *Neugebauer*	Y	Y	Y	N	N	N	Y	Y	Y	Y	N	Y
20 Gonzalez	N	?	Y	Y	Y	N	N	Y	Y	N	Y	N
21 *Smith*	Y	Y	Y	N	N	N	Y	Y	Y	Y	N	Y
22 *DeLay*	Y	Y	Y	N	N	Y	Y	Y	Y	Y	N	Y
23 *Bonilla*	Y	?	Y	N	N	N	Y	Y	Y	Y	N	Y
24 *Marchant*	Y	Y	Y	N	N	N	Y	Y	Y	Y	N	Y
25 Doggett	N	?	Y	Y	Y	Y	N	N	Y	N	Y	N
26 *Burgess*	Y	Y	N	N	Y	N	Y	Y	Y	Y	N	Y
27 Ortiz	N	?	Y	Y	Y	N	Y	Y	Y	Y	Y	N
28 Cuellar	Y	Y	Y	Y	?	N	Y	Y	Y	Y	Y	N
29 Green, G.	?	?	Y	Y	Y	Y	N	Y	Y	N	Y	N
30 Johnson, E.B.	N	?	Y	Y	Y	Y	N	Y	Y	N	Y	N

House Key Votes	1	2	3	4	5	6	7	8	9	10	11	12
31 *Carter*	+	Y	N	N	N	N	Y	Y	Y	Y	N	Y
32 *Sessions*	Y	?	Y	N	?	N	Y	Y	Y	Y	N	Y
UTAH												
1 *Bishop*	Y	?	Y	N	Y	Y	Y	Y	Y	Y	N	Y
2 Matheson	Y	Y	Y	Y	Y	Y	Y	Y	Y	Y	Y	N
3 *Cannon*	Y	Y	Y	N	N	N	Y	Y	Y	Y	N	Y
VERMONT												
AL **Sanders**	N	?	Y	Y	Y	Y	N	N	Y	N	Y	N
VIRGINIA												
1 *Davis, Jo Ann*	Y	Y	Y	N	N	Y	–	Y	Y	Y	Y	?
2 *Drake*	Y	Y	Y	N	N	Y	Y	Y	Y	Y	N	Y
3 Scott	N	N	Y	Y	Y	N	N	Y	Y	N	Y	N
4 *Forbes*	Y	Y	Y	N	N	Y	Y	Y	Y	Y	Y	Y
5 *Goode*	Y	Y	Y	N	N	Y	N	Y	Y	Y	N	Y
6 *Goodlatte*	Y	Y	Y	N	N	N	Y	Y	Y	Y	Y	Y
7 *Cantor*	Y	Y	Y	N	N	Y	Y	Y	Y	Y	N	Y
8 Moran	N	N	Y	Y	Y	N	Y	N	Y	N	Y	N
9 Boucher	Y	?	?	Y	Y	N	N	Y	Y	N	Y	N
10 *Wolf*	Y	?	Y	N	N	Y	Y	Y	Y	N	Y	Y
11 *Davis, T.*	Y	Y	Y	Y	N	N	Y	Y	Y	N	Y	Y
WASHINGTON												
1 Inslee	N	?	Y	Y	Y	N	N	N	Y	N	Y	N
2 Larsen	N	?	Y	Y	Y	N	N	Y	Y	N	Y	N
3 Baird	N	Y	Y	Y	Y	N	N	N	Y	N	Y	N
4 *Hastings*	Y	Y	Y	?	N	Y	Y	Y	Y	Y	N	Y
5 *McMorris*	Y	?	Y	N	N	Y	Y	Y	Y	Y	Y	Y
6 Dicks	N	N	Y	Y	Y	N	Y	Y	Y	N	Y	N
7 McDermott	N	N	Y	Y	Y	N	N	N	Y	N	Y	N
8 *Reichert*	Y	N	Y	N	N	N	Y	Y	Y	N	Y	Y
9 Smith	N	?	Y	Y	Y	N	N	N	Y	N	Y	N
WEST VIRGINIA												
1 Mollohan	N	Y	Y	N	Y	Y	N	Y	Y	Y	Y	N
2 *Capito*	Y	Y	Y	Y	N	Y	N	Y	Y	Y	Y	Y
3 Rahall	N	?	Y	N	Y	N	N	Y	Y	N	Y	N
WISCONSIN												
1 *Ryan*	Y	Y	Y	N	N	N	Y	Y	Y	Y	Y	Y
2 Baldwin	N	N	Y	Y	Y	Y	N	N	Y	N	Y	N
3 Kind	N	?	Y	Y	Y	N	N	N	Y	N	Y	N
4 Moore	N	?	Y	Y	Y	Y	N	N	Y	N	Y	N
5 *Sensenbrenner*	Y	Y	Y	N	N	N	Y	Y	N	Y	Y	Y
6 *Petri*	Y	?	Y	N	Y	N	Y	Y	Y	Y	Y	Y
7 Obey	N	?	Y	Y	Y	?	N	N	Y	N	Y	N
8 *Green*	Y	Y	Y	N	N	Y	Y	Y	Y	Y	Y	Y
WYOMING												
AL *Cubin*	Y	?	N	N	Y	?	N	Y	Y	Y	N	Y

Senate

1. CONFIRMATION OF SAMUEL A. ALITO JR. TO SUPREME COURT

Federal appeals court judge Samuel A. Alito Jr. was President George W. Bush's third choice to succeed Sandra Day O'Connor on the Supreme Court. He also was the nominee who drew the most opposition from liberal activists. *(Story, pp. 727, 728, 729)*

Bush nominated Alito on Oct. 31, 2005, to replace O'Connor, who was retiring. John G. Roberts Jr. had been Bush's original choice to succeed her, but after Chief Justice William H. Rehnquist died in September 2005, the president nominated Roberts to fill that seat. Bush withdrew his second choice, White House counsel Harriet Miers, after his socially conservative supporters protested that they could not be sure her rulings coincide with their views.

Although the White House wanted a vote on Alito in 2005, Senate Judiciary Committee chairman Arlen Specter, R-Pa., did not schedule confirmation hearings until Jan. 9, 2006. Democrats challenged the nomination on numerous fronts during Alito's five-day hearing, but he carefully avoided giving opponents grounds they could use to derail his nomination.

Republicans wanted the committee vote on Alito in time to schedule a floor vote on the nomination by Bush's State of the Union address Jan. 31. But Democratic resistance delayed the panel's vote until Jan. 24. On that day, the Judiciary Committee approved Alito 10–8, an unusually close outcome for a Supreme Court nomination.

As Democrats began lining up against Alito, Republicans warned that they would remember that opposition the next time a Democratic president nominated a Supreme Court justice. Majority Leader Bill Frist, R-Tenn., tried to schedule a confirmation vote Jan. 27. But Massachusetts Democrats John Kerry and Edward M. Kennedy mounted a futile last-minute bid to filibuster the nomination. On Jan. 26, Frist filed a cloture petition. On Jan. 30, the Senate voted 72–25 to invoke cloture, easily surpassing the sixty-vote threshold needed to limit debate. Nineteen Democrats voted against the attempted filibuster.

The next day, senators sat at their desks for the confirmation vote, rising one by one as their names were called rather than milling around the chamber as they normally do during votes. Alito was confirmed by a vote of 58–42: R 54–1; D 4–40; I 0–1. *(Vote, p. 943)*

Alito was confirmed by the second-closest margin in modern times. Only four of the Senate's forty-four Democrats voted for Alito. Rhode Island senator Lincoln Chafee was the one Republican to vote against him. Vermont Independent James M. Jeffords also voted no.

2. ASBESTOS COMPENSATION FUND

For years, legislation to create a $140 billion trust fund to compensate victims of asbestos exposure faced strong opposition on both sides of the aisle and from a variety of competing special-interest groups.

Nonetheless, Majority Leader Bill Frist, R-Tenn., agreed to bring the measure (S 852) to the Senate floor in February and set aside two weeks for its consideration as a favor to Pennsylvania Republican Arlen Specter, the Senate Judiciary Committee chairman who had made its passage a personal priority.

But even Specter's perseverance could not overcome the concerns of senators in both parties. Many Democrats and labor unions complained that the fund was not large enough to compensate victims adequately. Many conservative lawmakers feared that taxpayers would ultimately foot the bill if the fund became insolvent. One of those uneasy conservatives, Nevada Republican John Ensign, raised the budget point of order based on a prohibition against legislation that would authorize more than $5 billion in spending during any ten-year period starting in 2016, which the asbestos bill would have done *(Story, p. 703)*.

Specter struggled to persuade senators to waive the point of order. "The fact is, there's no federal money, so there's no substantive merit to the point of order," he said in a floor speech before the vote. "Give us the benefit of the doubt."

But ten GOP senators, including Budget Committee chairman Judd Gregg of New Hampshire, joined thirty Democrats in voting against waiving the point of order. Several other Republicans who voted to waive it, including Judiciary Committee members John Cornyn of Texas and Jon Kyl of Arizona, made clear that they still had deep misgivings about the underlying legislation.

As a result, senators who backed Specter's bill fell one vote short of the sixty required to waive the point of order. The final vote was 58–41: R 44–11; D 13–30; I 1–0. Frist initially voted for the bill but switched to "no" so that he could move to reconsider the motion. Daniel K. Inouye, D-Hawaii, missed the vote because his wife was undergoing medical treatment. *(Vote, p. 943)*

After the vote, Frist pulled the measure from the Senate floor, effectively ending its chances of being enacted in the 109th Congress. Frist later said the bill would not return to the Senate floor unless backers of the bill lined up enough supporters to overcome budget points of order or filibuster attempts.

3. ANTITERRORISM LAW REAUTHORIZATION

In October 2001, just weeks after terrorists flew hijacked commercial airliners into the World Trade Center, the Pentagon, and a Pennsylvania field, Congress rallied behind President George W. Bush and passed a law commonly known as the USA PATRIOT Act that gave the Justice Department extraordinary surveillance powers.

Four years later, when the time came to renew sixteen provisions of the law that were set to expire Dec. 31, 2005, the bipartisan spirit of 2001 had faded. For some members, the priority had become recalibrating the balance between the pursuit of terrorists and preserving the basic civil liberties guaranteed to all citizens.

In the House, the markup and subsequent passage of legislation to extend the sixteen provisions (HR 3199) turned partisan, with Judiciary chairman F. James Sensenbrenner Jr., R-Wis., instructing Republicans to vote down most Democratic efforts to change the bill.

In the Senate, a handful of Republicans shared concerns raised by Democrats and an unusual band of civil liberties advocates on the left and right, who were aligned with business groups, medical practitioners, gun rights advocates, and librarians. Consequently, Senate Judiciary chairman Arlen Specter,

R-Pa., presided over a more cordial markup and produced a bipartisan bill (S 1389).

Both bills proposed making fourteen provisions permanent, but they disagreed on the two most contentious provisions. One, often referred to as the "library provision," gave the FBI access to business records; the other allows law enforcement to attach wiretaps to multiple devices. The House version included ten-year sunsets for both; the Senate bill had four-year limits. When the conference began, Sensenbrenner pressed Senate Republicans to accept a deal favored by the Justice Department to extend the two provisions for seven years.

Despite some concerns, Specter tentatively agreed, and the bill seemed headed for completion in late November. But a bipartisan group of six senators threatened to block action unless several changes were made to increase civil liberties protection. A decision to accept four-year sunsets for the two provisions did not mollify them.

Although the House adopted the conference report in December 2005, the six senators—Republicans Larry E. Craig of Idaho, John E. Sununu of New Hampshire, and Lisa Murkowski of Alaska, and Democrats Russ Feingold of Wisconsin, Ken Salazar of Colorado, and Richard J. Durbin of Illinois—led a filibuster that prevented the Senate from clearing the bill.

Sununu subsequently met with White House and Justice Department officials and in February won support for three changes to provisions dealing with records seizures. The changes allowed recipients of a business records request to challenge a gag order under relatively restricted circumstances; removed a requirement that recipients of national security letters, which do not require court approval, disclose the name of their attorneys; and included a clarification that libraries operating in traditional roles and not as Internet service providers are not subject to national security letters *(Story, p. 222)*.

The majority of senators seemed satisfied, and the reauthorization cleared March 2 by a vote of 89–10: R 55–0; D 34–9; I 0–1. The House cleared Sununu's changes in a separate measure, and Bush signed the reauthorization and Sununu's bill a week later. *(Vote, p. 943)*

4. TAX CUT RECONCILIATION

Extending tax breaks on dividends and capital gains originally enacted in 2003 was a priority for President George W. Bush and Republican leaders in both chambers. GOP leaders intended to pass the extensions as part of a reconciliation bill, which would be protected from a filibuster under Senate rules.

Although the House passed a two-year extension of the investment breaks as the centerpiece of its tax reconciliation bill in 2005, the Senate version did not include either provision. It was built instead around provisions aimed at shielding some 20 million middle-class taxpayers from the alternative minimum tax (AMT), tax provisions intended to ensure that wealthy individuals could not escape tax liability. Senate Finance chairman Charles E. Grassley, R-Iowa, supported lower rates on capital gains and dividends, but he could not overcome the opposition of Democrats and GOP moderates on the panel. *(Story, p. 89)*

Once the bill reached conference, the tax writers were confronted with the problem of combining the costly House and Senate priorities into a single bill without exceeding a ceiling of $70 billion set by the fiscal 2006 budget resolution (H Con Res 95). The capital gains and dividends provisions were estimated to cost $20.6 billion over five years, but $50.8 billion over ten years. The AMT "patch" was expected to cost $33.9 billion over five years, with no additional cost over ten years.

For House Ways and Means chairman Bill Thomas, R-Calif., the simplest solution was to put the AMT patch in a separate bill on the assumption that it was popular enough that it would pass in the Senate without reconciliation protection. But Grassley warned that he could not get fifty-one votes in the Senate for the investment tax breaks unless the package also carried the AMT provision.

The conferees managed to fit both into the final bill (HR 4297), but Grassley had to give up one of his main priorities: Senate provisions to extend a variety of popular expiring tax breaks, such as the research credit and deductions for education expenses. Grassley agreed only after securing a promise from Thomas that the so-called extenders would be enacted separately.

To help keep the net cost within the $70 billion limit, the conferees also agreed to eliminate in 2010 the income cap on taxpayers who could convert standard individual retirement accounts (IRAs) into Roth IRAs. That provision was expected to increase federal revenue in the short run, but cut it by a potentially much larger amount in years beyond the ten-year window when the same taxpayers take tax-free withdrawals from their Roth IRAs.

All but three Democrats voted against the conference report, which they attacked as fiscally irresponsible and of benefit primarily to the rich. GOP leaders lost three of their own caucus, but without the ability to filibuster, the opponents were easily defeated. The vote on May 11 was 55–44: R 51–3; D 3–40; I 0–1. *(Vote, p. 943)*

Grassley worked doggedly for the remainder of the session to clear the package of tax extensions that he had had to drop from the reconciliation bill, succeeding only on the final day of the session, when Congress cleared the tax breaks as part of a tax and trade package (HR 6111).

5. IMMIGRATION POLICY CHANGES

Few issues divided Republicans in the 109th Congress more than efforts to change the nation's immigration policies. House Republicans favored an enforcement-first policy and passed legislation in 2005 focusing on that approach. But a sizable group of Senate Republicans, along with most Democrats, sided with President George W. Bush in favoring a broader effort that combined some aspects of the House enforcement and security bill with an economic plan that included legalizing millions of illegal immigrants and opening new channels for guest workers. *(Story, pp. 686, 711)*

The Senate Judiciary Committee held six markups in March 2006 before sending a bill (S 2611) to Majority Leader Bill Frist, R-Tenn., that contained core elements of bipartisan legislation (S 1033) sponsored by Sens. John McCain, R-Ariz., and Edward M. Kennedy, D-Mass. Some Senate Republicans, however, including Frist, remained uneasy about a provision that would offer a path to citizenship for an estimated 12 million illegal immigrants. A solution came from Republican senators Mel Martinez of Florida and Chuck Hagel of Nebraska, who brokered a compromise that limited "earned citizenship" to those who could demonstrate that they had been in the country for at least two years.

Frist was optimistic that in early April his chamber could debate, amend, and pass the Judiciary bill, sponsored by Chairman Arlen Specter, R-Pa. Frist and Minority Leader Harry Reid, D-Nev., stood together with a large bipartisan group to declare a "huge breakthrough" April 6. But in the days that followed, the two leaders could not reach agreement on amendments, and the Senate adjourned for the two-week spring recess with nothing to show for its efforts.

Even so, the immigration debate resonated outside Washington, occupying hours on talk radio and cable television programs and prompting mass demonstrations in several major cities. Bush, who had kept a low profile on the issue during the early part of the year, summoned a bipartisan group of senators to the White House on April 25 to try to break the impasse. The president pressed for a compromise in a May 15 prime-time address from the Oval Office, and McCain and other prominent Republicans pledged to join Democrats in defeating amendments that would alter the scope of Specter's bill.

McCain delivered as promised, starting May 16, when a bipartisan group voted down an amendment by Georgia Republican Johnny Isakson to delay the guest worker program and path to citizenship until the secretary of homeland security certified in writing that the borders were secure and new detention facilities were operational. That was followed by a rare spectacle of up-or-down votes on a wide range of amendments from senators of both parties, and an old-fashioned, freewheeling debate that culminated May 25 with passage of the bill 62–36: R 23–32; D 38–4; I 1–0. *(Vote, p. 943)*

The vote was a victory for the president, but it turned out to be his only win on an issue he had turned into a personal mission. Despite the willingness of most Senate Republicans to follow Bush's lead on immigration overhaul, the House GOP held steadfast against it and even organized nationwide forums to lobby against the Senate bill.

6. PERMANENT REPEAL OF ESTATE TAX

Majority Leader Bill Frist, R-Tenn., had promised a vote in spring 2006 on a top priority for the Republicans' conservative base: a permanent repeal of the estate tax. The House easily passed a repeal bill (HR 8) in April 2005, as it had done several times before. But Frist held off bringing the measure to the Senate floor for more than a year, unable to line up the sixty votes needed to avert a filibuster. All of the earlier House bills had died in the Senate, where they came under fire from most Democrats.

The estate tax was declining annually under 2001 tax law changes enacted in 2001 at the behest of President George W. Bush. It was scheduled to be completely eliminated in 2010, but after that one year, it would revert to pre-2001 law, with rates up to 55 percent on assets in excess of $1 million if nothing was changed. The reversion occurred because of parliamentary procedures Congress used in 2001 that precluded a permanent elimination of the levy.

Acting on appeals from conservatives, Frist scheduled a vote for early June on a motion to limit debate and proceed to the repeal bill. The cloture motion, held June 8, fell three votes short. The tally was 57–41: R 53–2; D 4–38; I 0–1. The two Republican opponents were Lincoln Chafee of Rhode Island and George V. Voinovich of Ohio. Four Democrats—ranking Finance Committee member Max Baucus of Montana, Blanche Lincoln of Arkansas, Ben Nelson of Nebraska, and Bill Nelson of Florida—voted for cloture. *(Story, p. 96; vote, p. 943)*

Before the vote, Republican allies insisted that the leadership not allow Democrats a political escape route by permitting compromise language to reach the floor. But lawmakers were already talking about alternatives. Sen. Jon Kyl, R-Ariz., was negotiating with Baucus on a compromise to raise exemption limits to $5 million per individual and $10 million per couple after 2010 and reduce the tax rates on remaining assets to 15 percent, the same rate applicable to capital gains.

Frist kept trying, but he was never able to get more than 57 votes for cloture. He first tried to build support for a House-passed compromise (HR 5638) that would have permanently scaled back the tax. Lacking the votes, he did not bring it to the floor.

Then he worked with House leaders to combine a permanent reduction with other provisions, including a package of popular tax break extensions, an increase in the minimum wage, and some sweeteners aimed at potential swing votes. Democrats did not take the bait. An Aug. 3 vote on a motion to proceed to the new bill (HR 5970) was defeated by the same margin as on June 8. Frist then changed his vote, producing a 56–42 tally, to reserve the right to resurrect it once again. He never did.

7. CONDUCT OF THE WAR IN IRAQ

The Senate in 2006 considered an amendment containing nonbinding language urging President George W. Bush to start withdrawing some U.S. troops from Iraq by the end of the year; how to proceed thereafter was left open. The amendment was drafted by Democrats Carl Levin of Michigan and Jack Reed of Rhode Island. It attracted the support of most Democrats and one Republican: moderate Lincoln Chafee of Rhode Island. But it was rejected with the help of six Democratic senators, including Joseph I. Lieberman of Connecticut. The tally on June 22 was 39–60: R 1–54; D 37–6; I 1–0. *(Story, pp. 270, 303; vote, p. 943)*

"Beginning the phased redeployment of American troops in 2006 would send a clear message to Iraqis," Levin said. "You, the Iraqis, must now decide whether you want a civil war or a nation."

The Levin-Reed proposal was seen as a more palatable version of a proposal by John Kerry, D-Mass., that would have mandated the withdrawal of most U.S. forces from Iraq by July 2007, with the exception of those needed to train Iraqi troops, protect Americans, and target terrorists. Kerry's plan was rejected 13–86. Taken together, however, the two amendments marked the first time since the war began in 2003 that congressional critics dared to challenge administration policy in Iraq, a reflection of the public's growing disenchantment with the war and the way it was being run.

Democrats played down the party divisions that the votes exposed, saying the two amendments were written to send essentially the same message to three important audiences. To the Iraqis, they said, the message was that the U.S. military commitment to their country was not open-ended and that they had to stand up for themselves faster. To insurgents and terrorists in Iraq, the Democratic signal was that their main reason for fighting—the presence of U.S. forces—would soon be gone. To voters back home, the message was that Democrats cared about the war's toll and had a solution.

Republicans assailed the Democrats, charging that the amendments would tell allies and foes alike that America lacked the resolve to see the war through and prevent Iraq from descending further into chaos. Senate majority whip Mitch McConnell, R-Ky., branded Democrats as the party of "cut and run" or, in the case of the Levin-Reed measure, "cut and jog."

Senate Republicans also warned that any requirement for withdrawal would embolden America's enemies in Iraq and elsewhere. "I cannot imagine saying that America will not have the stamina to stand up and fight and win a war at all costs for the freedom of future generations," said Kay Bailey Hutchison of Texas. "That is the message we would send to our enemies."

They also argued that the Iraqi security forces were not ready to hold the society together without U.S. help. "I believe such a move would be a significant step on the road to disaster," said John McCain of Arizona, a senior member of the Senate Armed Services Committee.

Several Democratic senators eyeing White House runs in 2008 backed the Levin-Reed proposal, including Kerry, Hillary Rodham Clinton of New York, Evan Bayh of Indiana, and Barack Obama of Illinois.

8. FLAG-BURNING CONSTITUTIONAL AMENDMENT

Six years after last considering a similar measure, the Senate in June 2006 took up a proposed constitutional amendment to prevent physical desecration to the American flag, with supporters and opponents both expecting it to receive 66 votes. The problem for supporters was that a constitutional amendment requires 67 backers, two-thirds of those present, provided that all 100 senators show up. *(Story, p. 709)*

The House had passed a companion measure (H J Res 10) by a vote of 286–130 in 2005. But two-thirds of both chambers must support an amendment before it can go to the states for ratification.

The chief sponsor of the Senate resolution, Orrin G. Hatch, R-Utah, said he was confident that he could pick up the necessary votes. "This amendment is, pure and simple, a restoration of the Constitution to what it was before unelected jurists changed it in a 5–4 decision," Hatch said.

The amendment was prompted by a pair of 5–4 Supreme Court rulings in 1989 and 1990 that found flag burning to be a form of speech protected by the First Amendment. Supporters of the resolution said it was necessary to send a message to the judiciary that the Supreme Court decisions usurped the will of the American people and Congress when it comes to treatment of the flag.

But Majority Whip Mitch McConnell of Kentucky made clear that he opposed the measure out of concern for its potential impact on freedom of expression.

On the Democratic side, McConnell's counterpart, Richard J. Durbin of Illinois, led the opposition, because Minority Leader Harry Reid of Nevada supported the proposed amendment. Still, Reid said, the Senate should be focusing on "more important issues," such as health care and gas prices. Other Democrats decried Senate consideration of the resolution as a political ploy in advance of the November midterm election.

When the amendment reached the floor shortly before the Fourth of July, the predictions on the vote count proved correct. The amendment fell one vote short of the sixty-seven needed. It was rejected 66–34: R 52–3; D 14–30; I 0–1. *(Vote, p. 943)*

Hatch took some solace in the fact that the amendment attracted more supporters than in 2000, when it fell four votes short.

9. FEDERAL EMERGENCY MANAGEMENT AGENCY RESTRUCTURING

The future of the Federal Emergency Management Agency (FEMA) was extensively debated in Congress and elsewhere after Hurricane Katrina devastated the Gulf Coast in late August 2005. The agency's response to the hurricane, immediately after it hit and in the months that followed, was roundly criticized as too little, too late. Many lawmakers called for revamping the structure and responsibilities of the agency. A split developed in both chambers between those who wanted to keep it in the Homeland Security Department and those who wanted to move it. *(Story, p. 236)*

The Senate Homeland Security and Governmental Affairs Committee, in a report in spring 2006, recommended that the agency be replaced with a new entity responsible for preparedness as well as response to disasters. But the panel did not recommend that the agency's responsibilities be removed from Homeland Security.

Committee chairwoman Susan Collins, R-Maine, offered an amendment in July to the $32.8 billion fiscal 2007 Homeland Security appropriations bill (HR 5441) that followed the recommendations of her panel's report. The amendment, which contained provisions from a bill (S 3595) that Collins had introduced in June, called for adding preparedness functions to the agency's mission and renaming it the U.S. Emergency Management Authority.

Democrats Hillary Rodham Clinton of New York and Daniel K. Akaka of Hawaii strongly opposed the Collins measure in floor debate and offered an alternative amendment to give FEMA independent, cabinet-level status, with the agency director reporting directly to the president. The proposal was rejected 32–66.

The Senate on July 11 adopted the Collins amendment 87–11: R 51–2; D 36–8; I 0–1. *(Vote, p. 943)*

The vote in effect endorsed retaining emergency and disaster responsibilities in the Homeland Security Department, ending the debate not only in the Senate but also in the House, which approved the conference report on the spending bill with the Collins amendment largely intact.

10. STEM CELL RESEARCH FUNDING

Ever since President George W. Bush issued restrictions confining federal spending on embryonic research to stem cell lines known to exist before Aug. 9, 2001, there had been pressure for Congress to reverse the policy. Scientists said embryonic stem cells showed promise for curing many diseases, but they also argued there were not enough stem cell lines eligible for funding under Bush's policy and that some of them were contaminated and unusable. *(Story, p. 542)*

Many conservatives opposed such research because it resulted in the destruction of the embryos from which the cells are derived, an action they considered tantamount to abortion. However, even some antiabortion Republicans, such as Sens. Orrin G. Hatch of Utah and Gordon H. Smith of Oregon, support the research because of its potential to save lives.

A showdown in the Senate on embryonic research had been looming for a year before the vote.

The House passed a bill (HR 810) to lift Bush's restrictions in May 2005, after moderate Republicans pressured their leaders to allow a vote. The Senate did not immediately consider the legislation because at the time Senate majority leader Bill Frist, R-Tenn., supported Bush's policy.

But on July 29, 2005, Frist publicly broke with Bush on the issue, announcing that his position had shifted and that he believed "the president's policy should be modified." His change of mind cleared the way for the vote, which became three votes, a year later.

Along with the contentious measure that was at the heart of the debate, Frist brought to the floor a pair of bills intended to shield opponents of embryonic stem cell research from political fallout. One (S 2754) encouraged research into ways to obtain stem cells that did not destroy embryos. The other (S 3504) prohibited so-called fetal farms, hypothetical institutions—both sides agreed none existed—that might create embryos strictly for research purposes. The bill also barred the collection of embryos from pregnancies intended only for research.

The fetal farm bill later cleared the House and became law. The bill encouraging research that did not destroy embryos was defeated in the House.

Under an agreement Frist made with Democrats, all three bills required sixty votes for passage and could not be amended. The bill to lift Bush's restrictions passed on July 18 by 63–37: R 19–36; D 43–1; I 1–0. Ben Nelson of Nebraska was the only Democrat opposed. *(Vote, p. 943)*

The bill did not pass in the Senate with the sixty-seven votes required to override a Bush veto, which came the next day. In addition, a House vote to override it fell short by fifty-one votes.

11. ESTABLISHMENT OF MILITARY TRIBUNALS

The Supreme Court's decision in June 2006 that President George W. Bush had overstepped his authority by setting up military tribunals to try terrorism suspects led to a debate in Congress over the framework for such trials and the legal rights of those detained by the government in Guantánamo Bay, Cuba. Subsequent negotiations would have far-reaching implications for civil liberties and for efforts to combat terrorism.

Bush wanted as much leeway as possible from Congress to pursue suspected terrorists. He asked for legislation to authorize the tribunals, broaden the definition of people who could be detained as enemy combatants, and allow him to define how the United States would treat prisoners under the Geneva Conventions. Bush also wanted to deny noncitizens held at Guantánamo any right to challenge their detentions through writs of *habeas corpus*, an issue the administration thought had been settled but the Supreme Court did not. *(Story, pp. 364, 366)*

Although Bush's popularity was sinking because of the Iraq war and he was losing his leverage with Congress, even some opposition Democrats were reluctant to challenge such counterterrorism legislation. The most effective opposition came instead from a trio of senior Republicans in the Senate—John W. Warner of Virginia, John McCain of Arizona, and Lindsey Graham of South Carolina—upset by Bush's plan to change prisoner treatment under the Geneva Conventions.

An eventual compromise bill (S 3930) limited Bush's ability to define prisoner treatment and dropped the use of secret evidence by military tribunals. But Bush got most of what he wanted, including authority for the tribunals themselves, an expanded definition of enemy combatants, and a denial of *habeas corpus* for detainees.

Before the vote on Sept. 28, Bush met with Senate Republicans on Capitol Hill to solidify their support. In fact, only one deserted him: Lincoln Chafee of Rhode Island, who was running for reelection in a heavily Democratic state and later lost his seat in the voting.

Bush and his GOP allies were able to win, and avoid a filibuster, because a dozen Democrats supported the compromise bill. Some, such as New Jersey's Robert Menendez, said they thought it was better to pass imperfect legislation than to allow terrorism suspects to go free.

Six of the twelve, including Menendez, were running for reelection, and all six won. After defeating amendments that would have denied Bush some authority, the Senate on Sept. 28 passed the measure 65–34: R 53–1; D 12–32; I 0–1. *(Vote, p. 943)*

The House cleared the bill 270–150 the next day, showing the continuing power of the terrorism issue, regardless of Bush's troubles.

12. PARENTAL NOTIFICATION OF ABORTION

After the Senate passed its version of parental notification legislation (S 403) in late July 2006 by a filibuster-proof sixty-five-vote majority, it appeared opponents of abortion rights would score another victory in their campaign to incrementally restrict access to abortion services. *(Story, p. 549)*

But although Democratic opponents of the bill could not muster forty-one votes for a filibuster, they could—and did—use a procedural roadblock to a conference with the House. Senate majority leader Bill Frist, R-Tenn., vowed to overcome the obstacle to a conference when the Senate returned from its August recess, but he decided to spend September on national security issues instead.

The House responded by taking up the Senate-passed bill in late September. Rather than clearing it, the House substituted modified text of its own, a broader measure (HR 748) regarding parental notification requirements for abortion providers. It retained the Senate language on incest victims.

The House-passed version also changed the definition of abortions covered under the legislation to exclude ectopic pregnancies, in which a fertilized egg attaches itself in a place other than inside the uterus. The amended version applied to people transporting minors across state lines to another country or an American Indian reservation.

On Sept. 27, the day after the House passed the modified Senate bill, Sen. Robert F. Bennett, R-Utah, engineered a procedural vote on Frist's behalf. Bennett called up the modified Senate bill and filed two inconsequential amendments to "fill the amendment tree" to prevent other lawmakers from proposing changes. Bennett then filed a petition to invoke cloture, or limit debate, on a motion to concur with the House amendment.

Activists on both sides of the issue swung into action to try to round up enough lawmakers for their side. Neither the sponsor of the bill, Republican John Ensign of Nevada, nor one of its leading opponents, Democrat Barbara Boxer of California, could predict whether cloture would be invoked.

The Sept. 29 cloture question was the decisive vote in determining whether Congress would send the legislation to President George W. Bush. Ultimately, the changes made by the House—particularly its provisions on parental notification by abortion providers, which were not in the original Senate bill—were enough to cause eight of the fourteen Democrats who in July voted for Ensign's bill to vote in September against limiting debate. The motion did not garner the required three-fifths of the total Senate, sixty votes, and was rejected 57–42: R 51–4; D 6–37; I 0–1. *(Vote, p. 943)*

1. **Alito Nomination Confirmation.** Confirmation of President George W. Bush's nomination of Samuel A. Alito Jr. of New Jersey to be an associate justice of the U.S. Supreme Court. Confirmed 58–42: R 54–1; D 4–40; I 0–1. A "yea" was a vote in support of the president's position. Jan. 31, 2006.

2. **S 852. Asbestos Trust Fund.** Specter, R-Pa., motion to waive the Budget Act with respect to the Ensign, R-Nev., point of order against the bill to establish a $140 billion trust fund to compensate victims of asbestos exposure. Motion rejected 58–41: R 44–11; D 13–30; I 1–0. A three-fifths majority vote (sixty) of the total Senate is required to waive the Budget Act. (Subsequently, the chair upheld the point of order, and the bill was recommitted to the Judiciary Committee.) Feb. 14, 2006.

3. **HR 3199. "USA Patriot Act" Reauthorization Conference Report.** Adoption of the conference report on the bill to make permanent fourteen of the sixteen provisions of the 2001 antiterrorism law known as the Patriot Act, set to expire March 10, and extend for four years the provisions on access to business and other records and on "roving" wiretaps. Adopted 89–10: R 55–0; D 34–9; I 0–1. A "yea" was a vote in support of the president's position. March 2, 2006.

4. **HR4297. Tax Reconciliation Conference Report.** Adoption of the conference report on the bill to extend about $70 billion in tax cuts over a five-year period. Reduced tax rates on capital gains and dividends would be extended through 2010. The bill extended through 2009 a tax provision that allowed small businesses to write off up to $100,000 in depreciable assets in the year they are made. It extended and increased alternative minimum tax exemption amounts for 2006. Adopted 54–44: R 51–3; D 3–40; I 0–1. A "yea" was a vote in support of the president's position. May 11, 2006.

5. **S 2611. Immigration Overhaul.** Passage of the bill to overhaul U.S. immigration policies and offer a path to citizenship for most illegal immigrants in the country. In major provisions, the bill required persons in the United States less than two years to return to their native countries and go through normal channels if they wanted to return; created a guest worker program to accommodate an additional 200,000 immigrants a year; and authorized increased border security and enforcement provisions, including a requirement that businesses verify documents of all prospective employees through an electronic system managed by the Department of Homeland Security. Passed 62–36: R 23–32; D 38–4; I 1–0. A "yea" was a vote in support of the president's position. May 25, 2006.

6. **HR 8. Estate Tax Permanent Repeal Cloture.** Motion to invoke cloture (thus limiting debate) on the motion to proceed to a bill that would permanently repeal the estate tax. Motion rejected 57–41: R 53–2; D 4–38; I 0–1. Three-fifths of the total Senate (sixty) votes were required to invoke cloture. A "yea" was a vote in support of the president's position. June 8, 2006.

7. **S 2766. Iraq Troop Withdrawal.** Levin, D-Mich., amendment to express the sense of Congress that the president should begin phased redeployment of U.S. troops from Iraq starting in 2006 and should submit to Congress by the end of 2006 a plan with estimated dates for continued phased withdrawal. Rejected 39–60: R 1–54; D 37–6; I 1–0. June 22, 2006.

8. **S J Res 12. Flag Desecration Constitutional Amendment.** Passage of the joint resolution to propose a constitutional amendment that would grant Congress the power to prohibit the physical desecration of the U.S. flag. Rejected 66–34: R 52–3; D 14–30; I 0–1. A two-thirds majority vote of those present and voting (sixty-seven in this case) is required to pass a joint resolution proposing a constitutional amendment. A "yea" was a vote in support of the president's position. June 27, 2006.

9. **HR 5441. FEMA Overhaul.** Collins, R-Maine, amendment to amend the 2002 Homeland Security Act to replace the Federal Emergency Management Agency with a new U.S. Emergency Management Authority within the Homeland Security Department. The amendment required the agency administrator to have at least five years of executive and management experience with significant experience in crisis management or a related field and specified that the person would report directly to the Homeland Security secretary and be the president's principal adviser on emergency preparedness and response. Adopted 87–11: R 51–2; D 36–8; I 0–1. July 11, 2006.

10. **HR 810. Embryonic Stem Cell Research Passage.** Passage of the bill to allow the use of federal funds in research on embryonic stem cell lines derived from surplus embryos at in vitro fertilization clinics, but only if donors give their consent and are not paid for the embryos. The bill required HHS to conduct and support research involving human embryonic stem cells that met certain criteria, regardless of when stem cells were derived from a human embryo. Passed 63–37: R 19–36; D 43–1; I 1–0. A "nay" was a vote in support of the president's position. July 18, 2006.

11. **S 3930. Military Tribunals Passage.** Passage of the bill to authorize military tribunals to try detainees designated as alien unlawful enemy combatants. Cases in which the accused was found guilty would be reviewed by a new Court of Military Commission Review. The bill barred *habeas corpus* appeals for detainees retroactive to Sept. 11, 2001. The bill also barred the use of evidence obtained through torture; it allowed the use of some coerced testimony and evidence seized without a warrant. Classified evidence would not be disclosed if it would be detrimental to national security. Passed 65–34: R 53–1; D 12–32; I 0–1. A "yea" was a vote in support of the president's position. Sept. 28, 2006.

12. **S 403. Parental Notification Cloture.** Motion to invoke cloture (thus limiting debate) on the motion to concur in the House amendment on the bill to make it a federal crime to take a minor across state lines to obtain an abortion in order to circumvent state parental notification and consent laws. Motion rejected 57–42: R 51–4; D 6–37; I 0–1. Three-fifths of the total Senate (sixty) was required to invoke cloture. A "yea" was a vote in support of the president's position. Sept. 29, 2006.

KEY

Democrat *Republican* **Independent**

- Y Voted for (yea)
- \# Paired for
- \+ Announced for
- N Voted against (nay)
- X Paired against
- – Announced against
- P Voted "present"
- C Voted "present" to avoid possible conflict of interest
- ? Did not vote or otherwise make a position known

Senate Key Votes	1	2	3	4	5	6	8	9	10	11	12
ALABAMA											
Shelby	Y	Y	Y	Y	N	Y	Y	Y	N	Y	Y
Sessions	Y	Y	Y	Y	N	Y	Y	Y	N	Y	Y
ALASKA											
Stevens	Y	Y	Y	Y	Y	Y	Y	Y	Y	Y	Y
Murkowski	Y	Y	Y	Y	Y	Y	Y	Y	Y	Y	Y
ARIZONA											
McCain	Y	N	Y	Y	Y	Y	Y	Y	Y	Y	Y
Kyl	Y	Y	Y	Y	N	Y	Y	Y	N	Y	Y
ARKANSAS											
Lincoln	N	Y	Y	N	Y	Y	Y	Y	Y	N	N
Pryor	N	N	Y	Y	Y	N	N	N	Y	Y	Y
CALIFORNIA											
Feinstein	N	Y	Y	N	Y	N	Y	Y	Y	N	N
Boxer	N	N	Y	N	Y	N	N	N	Y	N	N
COLORADO											
Allard	Y	Y	Y	Y	N	Y	Y	Y	N	Y	Y
Salazar	N	N	Y	N	+	N	Y	Y	Y	Y	N
CONNECTICUT											
Dodd	N	Y	Y	N	Y	N	N	Y	Y	N	N
Lieberman	N	Y	Y	N	Y	N	N	Y	Y	Y	N
DELAWARE											
Biden	N	N	Y	N	Y	N	N	Y	Y	N	N
Carper	N	Y	Y	N	Y	N	N	Y	Y	Y	N
FLORIDA											
Nelson	N	N	Y	Y	Y	Y	Y	Y	Y	Y	N
Martinez	Y	Y	Y	Y	Y	Y	Y	Y	N	Y	Y
GEORGIA											
Chambliss	Y	Y	Y	Y	N	Y	Y	Y	N	Y	Y
Isakson	Y	Y	Y	Y	N	Y	Y	Y	N	Y	Y
HAWAII											
Inouye	N	?	?	N	Y	N	N	Y	Y	N	N
Akaka	N	N	N	N	Y	N	N	N	Y	N	N
IDAHO											
Craig	Y	Y	Y	Y	Y	Y	Y	Y	N	Y	Y
Crapo	Y	N	Y	Y	N	Y	Y	Y	N	Y	Y
ILLINOIS											
Durbin	N	N	Y	N	Y	N	N	Y	Y	N	N
Obama	N	N	Y	N	Y	N	N	Y	Y	N	N
INDIANA											
Lugar	Y	Y	Y	Y	Y	Y	Y	Y	Y	Y	Y
Bayh	N	Y	Y	N	Y	N	Y	Y	Y	N	N
IOWA											
Grassley	Y	Y	Y	Y	N	Y	Y	Y	N	Y	Y
Harkin	N	Y	N	N	Y	N	N	Y	Y	N	N
KANSAS											
Brownback	Y	Y	Y	Y	Y	Y	Y	Y	N	Y	Y
Roberts	Y	Y	Y	Y	N	Y	Y	Y	N	Y	Y
KENTUCKY											
McConnell	Y	Y	Y	Y	Y	Y	N	Y	N	Y	Y
Bunning	Y	N	Y	Y	N	Y	Y	N	N	Y	Y
LOUISIANA											
Landrieu	N	Y	Y	N	Y	N	Y	Y	Y	Y	Y
Vitter	Y	Y	Y	Y	N	Y	Y	Y	N	Y	Y
MAINE											
Snowe	Y	Y	Y	N	Y	Y	Y	Y	Y	+	N
Collins	Y	Y	Y	Y	Y	Y	Y	Y	Y	Y	N
MARYLAND											
Sarbanes	N	N	Y	N	Y	N	N	Y	Y	N	N
Mikulski	N	N	Y	N	Y	N	N	Y	Y	N	N
MASSACHUSETTS											
Kennedy	N	N	Y	N	Y	N	N	Y	Y	N	–
Kerry	N	N	Y	N	Y	N	N	N	Y	N	N
MICHIGAN											
Levin	N	Y	N	N	Y	N	N	Y	Y	N	N
Stabenow	N	Y	Y	N	N	N	Y	Y	Y	Y	N
MINNESOTA											
Dayton	N	N	Y	N	Y	N	Y	Y	Y	N	N
Coleman	Y	Y	Y	Y	Y	Y	Y	Y	N	Y	Y
MISSISSIPPI											
Cochran	Y	Y	Y	Y	N	Y	Y	Y	Y	Y	Y
Lott	Y	Y	Y	Y	N	Y	Y	Y	Y	Y	Y
MISSOURI											
Bond	Y	Y	Y	Y	N	Y	Y	Y	N	Y	Y
Talent	Y	Y	Y	Y	N	Y	Y	Y	N	Y	Y
MONTANA											
Baucus	N	Y	Y	N	Y	Y	Y	Y	Y	N	N
Burns	Y	Y	Y	Y	N	Y	Y	Y	N	Y	Y
NEBRASKA											
Hagel	Y	Y	Y	Y	Y	Y	Y	Y	N	Y	Y
Nelson	Y	N	Y	Y	N	Y	Y	Y	N	Y	Y
NEVADA											
Reid	N	N	Y	N	Y	N	Y	Y	Y	N	Y
Ensign	Y	N	Y	Y	N	Y	Y	?	N	Y	Y
NEW HAMPSHIRE											
Gregg	Y	N	Y	Y	Y	Y	Y	Y	Y	Y	Y
Sununu	Y	N	Y	Y	N	Y	Y	Y	N	Y	Y
NEW JERSEY											
Lautenberg	N	N	Y	N	Y	N	N	N	Y	Y	N
Menendez	N	N	Y	N	Y	N	Y	Y	Y	Y	N
NEW MEXICO											
Domenici	Y	Y	Y	Y	Y	Y	Y	Y	N	Y	Y
Bingaman	N	N	N	N	Y	N	N	Y	Y	N	N
NEW YORK											
Schumer	N	N	Y	N	Y	?	N	N	Y	N	N
Clinton	N	N	Y	N	Y	N	N	N	Y	N	N
NORTH CAROLINA											
Dole	Y	Y	Y	Y	N	Y	Y	Y	N	Y	Y
Burr	Y	Y	Y	Y	N	Y	Y	Y	Y	Y	Y
NORTH DAKOTA											
Conrad	Y	N	Y	N	Y	N	N	Y	Y	N	N
Dorgan	N	N	Y	N	N	N	N	Y	Y	N	N
OHIO											
DeWine	Y	Y	Y	Y	Y	Y	Y	Y	N	Y	Y
Voinovich	Y	Y	Y	N	Y	N	Y	Y	N	Y	Y
OKLAHOMA											
Inhofe	Y	N	Y	Y	N	Y	Y	N	N	Y	Y
Coburn	Y	Y	Y	Y	N	Y	Y	Y	N	Y	Y
OREGON											
Wyden	N	N	N	N	Y	N	N	Y	Y	N	N
Smith	Y	Y	Y	Y	Y	Y	Y	Y	Y	Y	Y
PENNSYLVANIA											
Specter	Y	Y	Y	?	Y	Y	Y	Y	Y	Y	N
Santorum	Y	Y	Y	Y	N	Y	Y	?	N	Y	Y

Senate Key Votes	1	2	3	4	5	6	8	9	10	11	12
RHODE ISLAND											
Reed	N	N	Y	N	Y	N	N	Y	Y	N	N
Chafee	N	Y	Y	N	Y	N	N	Y	Y	N	N
SOUTH CAROLINA											
Graham	Y	N	Y	Y	Y	Y	Y	Y	N	Y	Y
DeMint	Y	N	Y	Y	N	Y	Y	Y	N	Y	Y
SOUTH DAKOTA											
Johnson	Y	N	Y	N	Y	N	Y	Y	Y	Y	Y
Thune	Y	N	Y	Y	N	Y	Y	Y	N	Y	Y
TENNESSEE											
Frist	Y	N	Y	Y	Y	Y	Y	Y	Y	Y	Y
Alexander	Y	Y	Y	Y	N	Y	Y	Y	Y	Y	Y
TEXAS											
Hutchison	Y	Y	Y	Y	N	Y	Y	Y	Y	Y	Y
Cornyn	Y	Y	Y	Y	N	Y	Y	Y	N	Y	Y
UTAH											
Hatch	Y	Y	Y	Y	N	Y	Y	Y	Y	Y	Y
Bennett	Y	Y	Y	Y	Y	Y	N	Y	Y	Y	Y
VERMONT											
Leahy	N	Y	N	N	Y	N	N	N	Y	N	N
Jeffords	N	Y	N	N	Y	N	N	N	Y	N	N
VIRGINIA											
Warner	Y	Y	Y	Y	Y	Y	Y	Y	Y	Y	Y
Allen	Y	Y	Y	Y	N	Y	Y	Y	N	Y	Y
WASHINGTON											
Murray	N	N	N	N	Y	N	N	Y	Y	N	N
Cantwell	N	N	Y	N	Y	N	N	Y	Y	N	N
WEST VIRGINIA											
Byrd	Y	N	N	N	N	N	N	Y	Y	N	Y
Rockefeller	N	N	Y	?	?	?	Y	Y	Y	Y	N
WISCONSIN											
Kohl	N	Y	Y	N	Y	N	N	Y	Y	N	N
Feingold	N	N	N	N	Y	N	N	Y	Y	N	N
WYOMING											
Thomas	Y	Y	Y	Y	N	Y	Y	Y	N	Y	Y
Enzi	Y	Y	Y	Y	N	Y	Y	Y	N	Y	Y

House

1. LOBBYING RULES

A year of bribery and lobbying scandals forced reluctant Republican House leaders to take up a lobbying bill in 2006 that critics say fell short of cracking down on the abuses that led to the lobbyist Jack Abramoff and other scandals. *(Story, pp. 816, 830)*

The key vote in the debate over lobbying reform came May 3, as the House passed a package of ethics and lobbying disclosure changes (HR 4975) on a 217–213 vote: R 209–20; D 8–192; I 0–1. *(Vote, p. 950)*

The roll call came as one disgraced Republican, former representative Randy "Duke" Cunningham of California, sat in prison after pleading guilty to accepting bribes and another GOP House member, Bob Ney of Ohio, was under criminal investigation for his affiliation with Abramoff. Ney would eventually plead guilty to federal conspiracy charges and resign from the House, but the scaled-down lobbying bill sparked by Abramoff's illegal activities went nowhere after the House passed it.

The May 3 vote was emblematic of the slow reaction of House leaders to a variety of scandals that endangered the GOP's control of Congress. The vote also showed fractures in both caucuses, as twenty mostly moderate Republicans voted against the legislation because they believed that it was not tough enough, while eight mostly southern, moderate Democrats voted for the bill, angering Minority Leader Nancy Pelosi, D-Calif., who wanted desperately to pin a loss on the struggling GOP majority.

The struggle by Speaker J. Dennis Hastert, R-Ill., to keep his caucus unified on a major political corruption issue may have been a portent of things to come, as Republicans later took a beating in the November election. But even Pelosi ran into trouble, as moderates in her caucus showed that they were willing to break ranks with the liberal leadership even if it cost the party a legislative victory. The bill would not have passed without the eight Democratic supporters.

The lobbying overhaul bill was widely criticized by government watchdog groups because it did not suspend privately funded travel and did not bar lawmakers from accepting meals from lobbyists. The legislation contained a campaign finance provision that would have essentially killed "527" advocacy groups such as MoveOn.org and the Club for Growth—regulated under Section 527 of the IRS code—because it would have barred them from spending unlimited sums of money on individual campaigns. Democrats said the amendment was designed to make the bill unpalatable, and it was the main reason the legislation never made it to a conference with the Senate.

In a separate vote Sept. 14, the House passed a resolution (H Res 1000) that ended up being the only formal response to the lobbying scandals. The resolution would require disclosure of the sponsors of earmarks in appropriations bills, a move designed to bring more transparency to the spending process.

2. TAX CUT RECONCILIATION

After months of stop-and-go negotiations, Republicans in 2006 agreed on a compromise package of tax benefits that satisfied the priorities of both chambers and gave President George W. Bush a long-sought victory. The reconciliation bill promised to reduce taxes by a net $70 billion over five years, mainly by extending tax breaks enacted in Bush's 2001 and 2003 tax laws. *(Story, p. 89)*

The two chambers passed significantly different versions of the measure in late 2005. The House bill had as its centerpiece an extension through 2010 of the capital gains and dividends tax cuts that were part of the 2003 tax cut law. It did not include a priority for many Democrats: short-term provisions to shield millions of middle-class taxpayers from the alternative minimum tax (AMT), which was designed to focus on the wealthy.

Because the AMT "patch" had bipartisan support, it did not need the special protection reserved for reconciliation bills, which are not subject to filibuster in the Senate. House Ways and Means chairman Bill Thomas, R-Calif., preferred to use the reconciliation process for more controversial provisions, such as the capital gains and dividends reductions.

The Senate version contained a one-year extension of the AMT patch and a substantial list of extensions for expiring provisions. In conference, Senate Finance chairman Charles E. Grassley, R-Iowa, said he could not obtain fifty-one votes in his chamber for a bill with the investment tax breaks unless it also carried the AMT provisions.

Thomas agreed to include the AMT provision in the final bill (HR 4297); to ensure that the resulting package did not exceed the $70 billion five-year cost cap set in the fiscal 2005 budget resolution (H Con Res 95), Grassley had to give up most of the so-called tax extenders.

With Bush and House Republicans' top priority—the capital gains and dividends provisions—secured, the House adopted the conference report May 10 on a largely party-line vote of 244–185: R 229–2; D 15–182; I 0–1. Only fifteen Democrats voted for the measure; only two Republicans voted against it. *(Vote, p. 950)*

3. BROADBAND NETWORK NEUTRALITY

The House vote June 8, 2006, on an amendment by Massachusetts Democrat Edward J. Markey to prevent broadband providers from giving priority to selected Internet traffic was the culmination of months of wrangling over the most contentious element of legislation intended to update the Telecommunications Act of 1996. The House firmly rejected the effort to enact strong "net neutrality" protections that would require broadband providers to treat similar types of Internet traffic equally. The battle over Markey's amendment also complicated the outlook for the Senate's companion telecom bill, which ultimately stalled amid a similar fight. *(Story, p. 435)*

The House vote was a significant victory for the big phone and cable companies, which were seeking more control over the traffic flowing across their high-speed lines. It was a defeat for Internet giants such as Microsoft, Google, and Yahoo, which argued that strong net neutrality protections were needed to prevent broadband operators from abusing their monopoly power.

The push for strong net neutrality rules grew out of fears that phone and cable companies such as Verizon Communications and Comcast would use their control over the nation's broadband networks to discriminate against content that did not originate from their Web sites.

Those fears escalated when executives at SBC Communications (which later became AT&T) and BellSouth began talking about charging Internet companies—particularly those that provide online video, games, and other services that require a lot of bandwidth—a premium for reliable access by customers. Internet companies called it a shakedown; the broadband companies said they needed the flexibility to control traffic and keep networks running smoothly.

In August 2005 the Federal Communications Commission (FCC) established four network neutrality principles that allowed consumers to access all lawful Internet content and services. Those principles became the heart of net neutrality language in the House telecom bill (HR 5252) sponsored by Energy and Commerce Committee chairman Joe L. Barton, R-Texas. But the Republican proposal ran into opposition from committee Democrats because it did not bar broadband providers from favoring their own online traffic or striking business deals with Internet companies to guarantee fast, reliable access to customers.

Led by Markey, the ranking member of the Subcommittee on Telecommunications and the Internet, Democrats pushed for stronger net neutrality protections that would require broadband providers to give similar treatment to similar types of Internet traffic, including competitors' traffic. They said such protections would safeguard the open, egalitarian nature of the Internet, preserve free speech in cyberspace and prevent phone and cable companies from picking winners and losers online. As Barton's bill moved through committee, the fight for stronger net neutrality protections became the rallying cry for an unlikely alliance of consumer watchdogs, big Internet companies, and advocacy groups ranging from MoveOn.org on the left to the Christian Coalition on the right.

But Barton and other Republicans beat back those efforts with the support of the phone and cable companies. Beyond arguing for more power over Internet traffic, they warned that strong net neutrality rules would amount to unnecessary regulation, leaving the broadband industry with little incentive to invest in new high-speed lines. That reasoning prevailed in the Energy and Commerce Committee, leading to the defeat of net neutrality amendments by Markey and other Democrats during subcommittee and committee markups.

Net neutrality proponents got a boost in May, when Judiciary Committee chairman F. James Sensenbrenner Jr., R-Wis., crossed party lines to move a measure similar to Markey's proposal through his own panel after losing a bid to mark up Barton's bill. Sensenbrenner, who insisted that net neutrality legislation fit under his panel's jurisdiction—as an antitrust and competition issue—wanted to offer his measure as an amendment to the broader telecom bill when it went to the House floor in June.

Faced with two very similar proposals—Markey's measure and Sensenbrenner's version—the Rules Committee allowed a vote only on Markey's. It also limited debate on the entire topic of net neutrality to under an hour. On June 8, the House defeated Markey's amendment 152–269: R 11–211; D 140–58; I 1–0. *(Vote, p. 950)*

The House then passed Barton's bill 321–101.

4. CONDUCT OF THE WAR IN IRAQ

On June 16, 2006, as Democrats grew more vocal in their criticism of the administration's policy in Iraq and debate continued over whether to set dates for U.S. troop withdrawals, the House adopted a resolution that Republicans had introduced as a test of loyalty to the war. *(Story, pp. 270, 303)*

The nonbinding resolution (H Res 861) honored Americans killed, wounded, or engaged in the war on terrorism at home and abroad, including first responders and service members, as well as coalition partners, naming Iraqis and Afghans in particular. The resolution also declared that setting an "arbitrary date" to withdraw troops from or redeploy them to Iraq was "not in the national security interest" and expressed commitment to completing the mission, described as a "sovereign, free, secure, and united Iraq." It concluded by declaring the United States' determination to prevail in "the Global War on Terror, the noble struggle to protect freedom from the terrorist adversary."

The House adopted the resolution 256–153 with the support of forty-two Democrats: R 214–3; D 42–149; I 0–1. *(Vote, p. 950)*

At the time, Republicans saw the vote as a successful response to calls for withdrawal, although the issue came back to haunt them in November when the public's increasingly negative view of the war helped to deny Republicans control of both chambers. The vote on the resolution came to be seen more as a rejection of the idea of a timed pull-out than a vote in favor of the war.

Democrats complained vigorously that the House rule for the vote barred them from offering amendments, and they objected to the fact that the document linked Iraq to the war on terrorism. But they did not introduce a competing version, prompting Republicans to charge them with papering over their intraparty differences on the war.

Only three Republicans opposed the resolution: John J. "Jimmy" Duncan Jr. of Tennessee, Jim Leach of Iowa, and Ron Paul of Texas. Leach, the moderate of the group, lost his seat in November. Ed Case of Hawaii was the only Democrat to vote. He, too, did not return to Congress when he unsuccessfully challenged fellow incumbent Democrat Daniel K. Akaka for one of the state's Senate seats.

5. BILINGUAL ASSISTANCE

Leaders in both parties expected smooth enactment of a bill to extend expiring provisions of the landmark 1965 Voting Rights Act when they gathered on the steps of the Capitol to introduce the measure (HR 9) in spring 2006.

But passage proved difficult in the House, where rank-and-file Republicans were unhappy over indications that their leaders planned to hold a vote on renewing the law without giving them a chance to offer amendments. A group of southern Republicans wanted to modify a requirement that jurisdictions with a history of discrimination get advanced permission, or preclearance, from the Justice Department before adopting any changes in their election laws. The group's members said the provision was outdated and did not reflect the strides that their states had made since 1965.

What sparked the greatest unease, however, was a requirement added in 1975 for bilingual ballots and other assistance in jurisdictions that have significant numbers of voters with limited English-language skills. According to the American Civil Liberties Union, 466 jurisdictions in thirty-one states were required to provide such assistance. The first hint of trouble occurred at the House Judiciary Committee markup of the bill in May, when nine Republicans broke with Chairman F. James Sensenbrenner Jr., R-Wis., and voted in favor of an amendment by Steve King, R-Iowa, to sunset the bilingual language assistance requirement. The amendment was defeated, but King said he would offer it on the House floor. *(Story, p. 696)*

In an election year, Republican leaders wanted to avoid another vote that could risk alienating Latinos so soon after GOP support of border control and asylum restrictions (HR 4437) that many minority voters considered harsh. GOP leaders repeatedly delayed floor action on the bill in hopes of sidestepping votes on the amendments.

Finally, however, they gave in and agreed to allow votes on amendments to let the bilingual requirements expire, revise the formula for requiring preclearance, provide a mechanism for states to get off the preclearance list, and sunset the provisions after ten years instead of twenty-five. The House rejected King's proposal July 13 by a vote of 185–238: R 181–44; D 4–193; I 0–1. *(Vote, p. 950)*

The vote represented the high-water mark of GOP opposition to extending the Voting Rights Act: None of the other three amendments received as many votes. It also was the strongest rebuke for Sensenbrenner, who in the waning months of his six-year tenure as chairman had to watch as seventeen of the twenty-two Republicans on his committee voted for the King amendment and against his position. The House passed the bill 390–33. Seeing the House amendments' fate, Senate critics of the law did not try to make changes to the bill. President George W. Bush signed the measure into law on July 27.

6. STEM CELL RESEARCH FUNDING

On Aug. 9, 2001, President George W. Bush announced that the federal government would fund research using stem cells only from lines that had existed before that date. It was an attempt to balance demands for expanded federal research into embryonic stem cells, which were believed to hold promise as a cure for many diseases, with the antiabortion concerns of conservatives who form the base of the Republican Party.

The National Institutes of Health estimated that twenty-two lines were viable for research, although they probably were not usable for medical treatment. For the next five years, lawmakers tried to pass legislation to expand the number of stem cell lines available to federally funded researchers by allowing them to work on lines derived from surplus embryos at in vitro fertilization clinics. The debate carried ethical implications: because such research involves the destruction of embryos, some conservatives consider it tantamount to abortion.

In May 2005, the House passed a bill (HR 810) that would have lifted the restrictions on federal funding for the research. More than a year later, an impasse in the Senate had been broken and the bill had enough support to clear. *(Senate stem cell vote, p. 940)*

But Bush had long made clear that he would veto the bill if it arrived on his desk. Knowing this, the Senate cleared the House bill July 18. The next day, Bush vetoed the bill and, in a vote hours later, a House attempt to override the veto was defeated. *(Story, p. 940)*

It was the first time that Bush used the veto in the five years and six months of his presidency. He said he exercised that power with this particular bill to protect a "moral boundary" for society. *(Veto message text, p. 1056)*

The House override vote showed that few lawmakers had changed their opinions on the issue in the year since the bill had passed. The 2005 vote was 238–194, with some abortion opponents supporting it. The vote to override Bush's veto, which required two-thirds of lawmakers present and voting in both chambers, fell to 235–193: R 51–179; D 183–14; I 1–0. Supporters needed 286 votes to set up a vote in the Senate. *(Vote, p. 950)*

Three Republicans voted differently for the override than they did for the original bill: Dave Reichert of Washington and Curt Weldon of Pennsylvania voted against the bill but then voted to override Bush's veto, and C.W. Bill Young of Florida voted for the bill but against the override. No Democrats changed their positions, although four who had voted for the bill were absent for the override vote.

7. U.S.-INDIAN NUCLEAR ENERGY PACT

On the Iraq War and other foreign policies dealing with the war on terrorism, the 109th Congress largely deferred to President George W. Bush. But on Bush's 2006 legislative proposal to permit the U.S. sale of civilian nuclear technology to India, lawmakers were not so quick to acquiesce. Although many lawmakers approved of the historic deal with India, Republicans and Democrats in the House insisted on a number of changes in the legislation to give Congress a bigger role. *(Story, pp. 277, 311)*

Republican Henry J. Hyde of Illinois, the chairman of the House International Relations Committee, instructed aides to amass as big a majority as possible for this crucial piece of legislation, which represented a matter of presidential power. Most Democrats signed on, agreeing that the opportunity to build a strategic alliance with India as a counterweight to China trumped India's development of nuclear weapons outside the framework of the Nuclear Non-Proliferation Treaty.

But the inclination to support the agreement did not prevent Hyde and the committee's ranking Democrat, Tom Lantos of California, from criticizing the executive branch's efforts to cut Congress out of a final deal with India. The pair rewrote the legislation to add extensive congressional oversight, including a congressional vote on any subsequent treaty. Bush wanted the deal so badly that he did not stand in their way.

An overwhelming majority in the House supported the measure (HR 5682) on the vote, giving Bush a major foreign policy victory at a time when the public was losing confidence in his leadership because of the war in Iraq. The vote was 359–68: R 219–9; D 140–58; I 0–1. *(Vote, p. 950)*

The split in the Democratic vote reflected divisions between those who agreed with Bush on the strategic importance of the agreement and those who saw it as a dangerous precedent. Edward J. Markey, D-Mass., who co-chaired the House Bipartisan Task Force on Nonproliferation, was one of the most vehement opponents of the legislation, which he saw as an invitation to countries such as Iran to ignore international calls to halt their nuclear programs.

The legislation followed a similar path in the Senate, where it passed Nov. 16 by a margin of 85–12, with all of the "nays" coming from Democrats. On Dec. 8, the House overwhelmingly adopted the conference report on the bill; the Senate cleared it the next day.

8. PENSION LAW CHANGES

Struggling to achieve a legislative victory on a long-stalled but important issue during an election year, Republican leaders in 2006 decided that going back to the basics was the only way to pass a pension overhaul. The result was the introduction and passage on the same day of a bill hastily cobbled together from the wreckage of months of negotiations aimed at strengthening the nation's pension laws. The bill restructured the way that companies fund their pension plans, measure their liabilities, and pay a federal agency to assume ultimate responsibility for the plans. *(Story, pp. 654, 658)*

Buoyed by seventy-six Democrats who defied fierce lobbying by their leadership to vote against the bill, the GOP plan succeeded in the hours before the House left for its August recess. Less than a week later, the Senate cleared it.

The last-minute maneuvering underscored the tumultuous nature of the pension debate. Lawmakers had been walking a fine line, seeking to ensure that companies meet their retirement promises to workers without creating rules so onerous that companies would subsequently dump their plans. Also, they needed to shore up funding for the Pension Benefit Guaranty Corporation (PBGC), the federal agency that insured private pension plans. The PBGC had reported large deficits in recent years amid a number of sizable bankruptcy filings in the airline, steel, and auto-parts industries.

The House and Senate each had passed overhaul bills in late 2005 (HR 2830, S 1783), but conference negotiations got off to a rocky start in 2006 and stalled. The legislation was a target of intense lobbying from corporations, led by the airline industry. Negotiations over industry-specific relief for the airlines slowed the process. But the final deadlock was over whether to attach some extensions of popular tax breaks. Matters came to a focus the evening of July 27, when House Republicans refused to attend a meeting with their Senate counterparts to sign a conference report that included some of the tax break extensions.

House GOP leaders preferred to use the tax provisions to win support for a separate bill to reduce the estate tax. As a result, together with their Senate counterparts they agreed to put most of the pension conference agreement into a separate bill (HR 4).

With a combination of incentives and punishments, the bill required companies to fully fund their pension plans but gave them a number of years to make up for underfunding. It permanently raised the premium that companies pay to the PBGC, and it instituted a penalty fee if a company dumped its plan on the agency while operating under bankruptcy protection and then emerged from financial difficulties.

Democrats were angered at being excluded. Their leadership urged the caucus to oppose the legislation, saying it favored corporate over employee interests.

Lawmakers from Texas, home to American Airlines and Continental Airlines, also criticized language in the bill giving rivals Delta and Northwest more time to make up for plan underfunding and a more favorable interest rate to calculate plan liabilities.

But those concerns were not enough to derail HR 4 when it came to the House floor. Just before midnight on July 28, the bill passed, 279–131: R 203–16; D 76–114; I 0–1. Of the sixteen Republicans who voted against the bill, fifteen were from Texas. *(Vote, p. 950)*

The Senate vote, less than a week later, was a formality. After just twenty minutes of debate, the chamber voted 93–5 to clear the legislation.

9. BORDER SECURITY

The House and Senate appeared deadlocked on a broad new immigration policy during the 109th Congress. By May 2006, both chambers had passed contrasting bills (HR 4437, S 2611), and House Republicans—who had focused solely on enforcement and border security—dismissed major portions of the bipartisan Senate legislation as being too lenient toward millions of illegal immigrants. Rather than go to conference and work on a compromise, House GOP leaders embarked on a summer of field hearings throughout the nation and derided the Senate bill as the work of Democrats—even though it was the approach President George W. Bush favored.

When Congress returned for a final legislative month just weeks before the midterm election, House Speaker J. Dennis Hastert, R-Ill., announced that he would seek a handful of targeted security measures that would resonate with Republican voters. The first came on Sept. 13, when Homeland Security Committee chairman Peter T. King, R-N.Y., presented a border security fence bill (HR 6061). In addition to a physical barrier, the measure also called for a "virtual fence" of sensors, cameras, unmanned aerial vehicles, and other surveillance technology. The bill passed the next day 283–138: R 219–6; D 64–131; I 0–1. *(Story, p. 679; Vote, p. 950)*

The process was far from smooth in the other chamber. A sizable group of Senate Republicans and most Democrats continued to push for the broader policy that included a guest worker program and a path to citizenship for millions of illegal immigrants. Bush met privately at the Capitol with House Republicans to say he would sign the fence bill but still wanted a "comprehensive" solution similar to the measure the Senate passed.

But with election day near, many Senate Republicans who voted for the comprehensive bill acknowledged the need to demonstrate that they were serious about border security. Majority Leader Bill Frist, R-Tenn., took the House fence bill to the Senate floor the week of Sept. 18. It became entangled with a wide range of other security authorization and spending measures in play during the final weeks of September, and Senate Democrats criticized the measure as a political vehicle. But in the final hours before adjourning for the midterm election, senators voted Sept. 28 to invoke cloture, or cut off debate by a vote of 71–28 and cleared the measure 80–19 the next day.

10. PARENTAL NOTIFICATION OF ABORTION

When Senate Democrats in late July 2006 put up a procedural roadblock to a conference on parental notification legislation (S 403, HR 748), House Republican leaders were left to decide its fate. The legislation made it a federal crime to take a minor across state lines to obtain an abortion in order to circumvent state parental notification and consent laws. It provided an exception when an abortion was necessary to save the life of the minor. Physicians who perform an abortion on an out-of-state minor were required to provide at least twenty-four hours' notice to the minor's parents. *(Story, p. 549)*

Senate Republicans devoted all of September to national security issues, leaving them no time to force a conference with a series of procedural votes. The Senate-passed bill tracked the House measure's provisions on criminalizing the transportation of minors across state lines, but it did not include a House section on parental notification to provide for criminal and civil penalties for doctors who did not comply with its requirements.

After the Senate passed its version in July on a 65–34 vote and Democrats blocked a conference, the House could have cleared the Senate bill for President George W. Bush's signature and codified several new restrictions on access to abortion services.

Instead, House Republicans decided to send a message. They called up the Senate bill Sept. 26 under a rule that allowed them to substitute modified text from the House bill on the parental notification requirements for abortion providers. House GOP leaders retained Senate-passed language related to incest victims. They also revised the bill so it would apply to transporting minors across state lines to another country or a Native American reservation. No other amendments could be offered on the House floor.

The House action was significant because it determined the fate of the legislation. By changing the Senate bill in a way that made it unacceptable to several Senate Democratic allies, backers of the bill ensured that it would not be enacted into law.

GOP supporters of the bill said it was necessary to create a safeguard for minors. "As a mother of two young ladies, I want to know what is going on with my girls on something as significant and as medically life-altering as an abortion," said Republican Ileana Ros-Lehtinen of Florida, sponsor of the House bill.

Democrats argued against not only the legislation but against the GOP decision to engineer a floor debate that did not allow for other amendments. "This is a bad bill, and it is a bad process under which it is coming to the floor," said Massachusetts Democrat Jim McGovern. "I don't care what you believe on the issue of choice."

House lawmakers passed the amended Senate bill Sept. 26 on a 264–153 vote: R 215–9; D 49–143; I 0–1. *(Vote, p. 950)*

Later the same week, proponents of the bill failed to obtain the required sixty votes in the Senate to limit debate on a motion to concur in the House amendment.

11. SURVEILLANCE OVERSIGHT

Lawmakers in both parties in 2006 searched for a legislative response after the *New York Times* revealed in December 2005 that President George W. Bush had authorized the National Security Agency (NSA) to conduct warrantless surveillance of communications between U.S. citizens and terrorist suspects abroad. The program operated outside a 1978 law, known as the Foreign Intelligence Surveillance Act (FISA), that required intelligence agencies to seek a warrant from a special court before they could eavesdrop on communications involving U.S. citizens or residents. *(Story, pp. 231, 249, 251)*

The most visible effort came in the Senate, where Judiciary chairman Arlen Specter, R-Pa., held high-profile hearings and negotiated with the White House to develop a bill that would provide a legal framework for the NSA program.

However, the only bill to reach the floor in either chamber was a House measure sponsored by Heather A. Wilson, R-N.M. House Republican leaders decided to bring the bill to a vote in September, a month they had dedicated to national security issues as a way of highlighting political differences with Democrats in advance of the midterm election. Supporters got a further impetus to push for speedy passage when a federal judge in August ruled that the NSA program was unconstitutional.

Although Bush asserted that he had authority as commander in chief to conduct such surveillance, he, too, was pushing Congress to give a stamp of approval to his program.

The bill would have authorized expanded warrantless surveillance for fixed, renewable periods both before an "imminent attack"—a proviso added to accommodate administration concerns—and after an attack. The president would have been required to notify the congressional Intelligence committees and the secret federal court established under FISA; the chairmen of the House and Senate Intelligence committees would have been allowed to share the substance of the administration's reports on electronic surveillance with all members of the committees.

The bill pitted most Democrats and some libertarian Republicans against most Republicans and some moderate Democrats. A bipartisan team of opponents—Adam B. Schiff, D-Calif.; Jeff Flake, R-Ariz.; Jane Harman, D-Calif.; and Bob Inglis, R-S.C.—drafted a substitute amendment that would have required a FISA court order for domestic surveillance of Americans and streamlined the process for seeking such warrants. They argued that by operating outside FISA, the NSA program jeopardized the civil liberties of average citizens who might be subjected to warrantless surveillance.

But GOP leaders blocked all amendments from floor consideration. Supporters of Wilson's bill argued that it included safeguards for civil liberties because it required additional congressional notification about how the program was being used. The measure passed 232–191: R 214–13; D 18–177; I 0–1. *(Vote, p. 950)*

A motion by Schiff, Flake, Harman, and Inglis to return the bill to committee and substitute their version was defeated 221–202. The Senate never took up NSA legislation, which died at the end of the 109th Congress.

12. PROPERTY RIGHTS LEGAL CHALLENGES

A bill to streamline access to federal courts for property owners challenging land-use regulations by state and local governments passed the House in September 2006 but was not acted on by the Senate. The bill, which allowed plaintiffs to take their lawsuits directly to federal court rather than to first go through the state court system, was a priority for developers. House Republican leaders scheduled the measure (HR 4772) for floor action in September in the wake of two 2005 Supreme Court decisions, *Kelo v. City of New London* and *San Remo Hotel LP v. City and County of San Francisco*, both of which addressed property rights issues. *(Story, p. 707)*

The House passed the bill Sept. 29 by 231–181: R 194–25; D 37–155; I 0–1. *(Vote, p. 950)*

Although the Senate did not act on the measure, the House vote showed that conservative GOP congressional leaders were willing to confront the Supreme Court on some issues, even though over the previous year two conservative justices took seats for a net gain of one in the Court's philosophical division. One of the new justices replaced an equally conservative member, but the other replaced a moderate who often voted with more liberal members.

House Republicans seized on the publicity surrounding the *Kelo* case, involving Connecticut's power of eminent domain, to build momentum for the land-use bill sponsored by Ohio Republican Steve Chabot. But the bill was aimed squarely at *San Remo*, and at another Court decision, from 1985. In *San Remo*, the Court ruled 9–0 that property owners cannot bring a claim alleging an uncompensated taking of property in federal court after state courts have ruled on the claim. In the 1985 case, *Williamson Planning Commission v. Hamilton Bank*, the Court ruled that property owners had to pursue such claims in state courts before going to a federal court. *(*Kelo *and* San Remo *decisions, p. 774)*

Chabot's bill would have allowed private landowners who wished to challenge a state's or local government's taking of their land to file a claim directly with a federal court only when a violation of a federal constitutional right was alleged.

House Republican leaders initially scheduled the measure for consideration Sept. 26 under suspension of the rules, a procedure that bars amendments, limits debate, and requires a two-thirds majority. But the motion to suspend the rules and pass the bill was rejected 234–172. The tally was thirty-seven votes short of the threshold for passage. House majority leader John A. Boehner, R-Ohio, promptly engineered floor consideration later that week, under a rule that did not allow for amendments.

1. **HR 4975. Lobbying and Ethics Overhaul Passage.** Passage of the bill to revise lobbying and ethics rules for lobbyists and members of Congress. The bill prohibited privately funded travel by House members and their staff for the rest of the 109th Congress unless the ethics committee certified that a proposed trip complied with House rules and standards; denied pension benefits to House members convicted after enactment of crimes related to their official positions; barred the House from considering an appropriations bill unless the accompanying report listed the earmarks in the bill or report along with the name of the member requesting the earmark; required lobbyists to file quarterly reports. Passed 217–213: R 209–20; D 8–192; I 0–1. May 3, 2006.

2. **HR4297. Tax Reconciliation Conference Report.** Adoption of the conference report on the bill to extend about $70 billion in tax cuts over a five-year period, including extending reduced tax rates on capital gains and dividends through 2010; extending through 2009 a tax provision that allowed small businesses to write off up to $100,000 in depreciable assets in the year they are made; and extending and increasing alternative minimum tax exemption amounts for 2006. Adopted 244–185: R 229–2; D 15–182; I 0–1. A "yea" was a vote in support of the president's position. May 10, 2006.

3. **HR 5252. Network Neutrality.** Markey, D-Mass., amendment to establish network neutrality requirements for broadband providers, including the duty to not block, impair, degrade, or discriminate against lawful content, applications, or services; to operate its network in a non-discriminatory manner; and to offer equal prioritization to all data of a particular type if it offers priority to one provider. Rejected 152–269: R 11–211; D 140–58; I 1–0. A "nay" was a vote in support of the president's position. June 8, 2006.

4. **H Res 861. Iraq War Resolution.** Adoption of the resolution to declare that it was not in the national security interest of the United States to set an arbitrary date for withdrawal or redeployment of U.S. armed forces from Iraq and that affirmed the U.S. commitment to establishing democracy in Iraq. Adopted 256–153: R 214–3; D 42–149; I 0–1. A "yea" was a vote in support of the president's position. June 16, 2006.

5. **HR 9. Voting Rights Act Bilingual Voting Assistance.** King, R-Iowa, amendment to strike a provision in the bill to reauthorize, for twenty-five years, the requirement that states provide bilingual voting assistance as well as the use of American Community Survey census data. Rejected 185–238: R 181–44; D 4–193; I 0–1. July 13, 2006.

6. **HR 810. Embryonic Stem Cell Research Veto Override.** Passage, over President George W. Bush's July 19, 2006, veto, of the bill to allow the use of federal funds in research on embryonic stem cell lines derived from surplus embryos at in vitro fertilization clinics, but only if donors give their consent and are not paid for the embryos. Rejected 235–193: R 51–179; D 183–14; I 1–0. A two-thirds majority of those present and voting (286 in the House) was required to override a veto. A "nay" was a vote in support of the president's position. July 19, 2006.

7. **HR 5682. United States-India Nuclear Agreements Passage.** Passage of the bill to permit the president to waive certain provisions of the Atomic Energy Act of 1954 to seek congressional approval for civilian nuclear cooperation agreements with India if the president makes certain determinations, including that India would provide the United States and the International Atomic Energy Agency with a plan to separate civilian and military nuclear facilities and programs. The bill required a joint resolution of approval by Congress for a nuclear cooperation agreement with India to enforce the agreement. Passed 359–68: R 219–9; D 140–58; I 0–1. A "yea" was a vote in favor of the president's position. July 26, 2006.

8. **HR 4. Pension Overhaul Passage.** Passage of the bill to rewrite federal pension requirements, including establishing a new premium that employers that terminate their plans pay the Pension Benefit Guaranty Corporation; changing the formula for determining whether a pension plan is fully funded; and requiring employers to meet a 100 percent funding target. Passed 279–131: R 203–16; D 76–114; I 0–1. July 28, 2006.

9. **HR 6061. Border Fencing Passage.** Passage of the bill to authorize the construction of about 700 miles of fencing along the U.S.-Mexican border. The bill required a study of implementing security systems along the U.S.-Canadian border and directed the agency to evaluate the ability of personnel to stop fleeing vehicles at the border. Passed 283–138: R 219–6; D 64–131; I 0–1. Sept. 14, 2006.

10. **S 403. Parental Notification/Passage.** Passage of the bill to make it a federal crime to take a minor across state lines to obtain an abortion in order to circumvent state parental notification and consent laws. It provided an exception when an abortion is necessary to save the life of the minor. Physicians who perform an abortion on an out-of-state minor were required to provide at least twenty-four hours' notice to the minor's parents. Passed 264–153: R 215–9; D 49–143; I 0–1. A "yea" was a vote in support of the president's position. Sept. 26, 2006.

11. **HR 5825. Warrantless Electronic Surveillance Passage.** Passage of the bill to authorize electronic surveillance of communications by suspected terrorists for specified periods without first obtaining approval from the secret FISA court, allowing warrantless surveillance for up to ninety days if an armed or terrorist attack against the United States has occurred or if there is an "imminent threat." Passed 232–191: R 214–13; D 18–177; I 0–1. A "yea" was a vote in support of the president's position. Sept. 28, 2006.

12. **HR 4772. Eminent Domain Passage.** Passage of the bill to ensure access to federal courts for those who are challenging government attempts to take their property under eminent domain. It allowed private landowners who want to challenge a state's or local government's "taking" of their land to file a claim directly with a federal court when only federal claims are alleged. Passed 231–181: R 194–25; D 37–155; I 0–1. Sept. 29, 2006.

KEY

Democrat	*Republican*	**Independent**

Y	Voted for (yea)	–	Announced against
#	Paired for	P	Voted "present"
+	Announced for	C	Voted "present" to avoid possible conflict of interest
N	Voted against (nay)	?	Did not vote or otherwise make a position known
X	Paired against		

House Key Votes	1	2	3	4	5	6	7	8	9	10	11	12
ALABAMA												
1 *Bonner*	Y	Y	N	Y	Y	N	Y	Y	Y	Y	Y	Y
2 *Everett*	Y	Y	N	Y	Y	N	Y	Y	Y	Y	Y	Y
3 *Rogers*	Y	Y	N	Y	Y	N	Y	Y	Y	Y	Y	Y
4 *Aderholt*	Y	Y	N	Y	Y	N	Y	Y	Y	Y	Y	Y
5 Cramer	N	Y	N	Y	N	Y	Y	Y	Y	Y	Y	Y
6 *Bachus*	Y	Y	N	+	Y	N	Y	Y	Y	Y	Y	Y
7 Davis	N	N	N	N	N	Y	Y	Y	Y	Y	N	Y
ALASKA												
AL *Young*	Y	Y	N	Y	N	Y	Y	Y	N	Y	N	Y
ARIZONA												
1 *Renzi*	Y	Y	N	Y	N	N	Y	Y	Y	Y	Y	Y
2 *Franks*	Y	Y	N	Y	Y	N	Y	Y	Y	Y	Y	Y
3 *Shadegg*	Y	Y	N	Y	N	N	Y	Y	Y	Y	Y	Y
4 Pastor	N	N	N	N	N	Y	N	N	N	N	N	N
5 *Hayworth*	Y	Y	N	Y	Y	N	Y	Y	Y	Y	Y	Y
6 *Flake*	Y	Y	N	Y	N	N	Y	N	Y	Y	N	Y
7 Grijalva	N	N	Y	N	N	Y	N	N	N	N	N	N
8 *Kolbe*	Y	Y	N	Y	N	Y	Y	Y	N	Y	Y	Y
ARKANSAS												
1 Berry	N	N	N	Y	N	Y	Y	Y	Y	Y	Y	Y
2 Snyder	N	N	Y	Y	N	Y	Y	N	N	Y	N	N
3 *Boozman*	Y	Y	N	Y	Y	N	Y	Y	Y	Y	Y	Y
4 Ross	N	N	Y	Y	N	Y	Y	Y	Y	Y	N	Y
CALIFORNIA												
1 Thompson	N	N	Y	N	N	Y	N	Y	N	N	N	N
2 *Herger*	Y	Y	N	Y	Y	N	Y	Y	Y	Y	Y	Y
3 *Lungren*	Y	Y	N	Y	Y	N	Y	Y	Y	Y	Y	Y
4 *Doolittle*	Y	Y	N	Y	Y	N	Y	Y	Y	Y	Y	Y
5 Matsui,D.	N	N	Y	N	D.	N	Y	N	N	N	N	N
6 Woolsey	N	N	Y	N	N	Y	N	N	N	N	N	N
7 Miller, George	N	N	Y	N	N	Y	N	N	N	N	N	N
8 Pelosi	N	N	Y	N	N	Y	Y	N	N	N	N	N
9 Lee	N	N	Y	N	N	Y	N	N	N	N	N	N
10 Tauscher	N	N	Y	N	N	Y	N	Y	N	N	N	N
11 *Pombo*	Y	Y	N	Y	Y	N	Y	Y	Y	?	Y	Y
12 Lantos	N	N	Y	N	N	Y	Y	N	N	N	N	N
13 Stark	N	N	Y	N	N	Y	N	?	N	N	N	N
14 Eshoo	N	N	Y	N	N	Y	Y	N	N	N	N	N
15 Honda	N	N	Y	N	N	Y	Y	N	N	N	N	N
16 Lofgren	N	N	Y	N	N	Y	Y	N	N	N	N	N
17 Farr	N	N	Y	N	N	Y	N	N	N	N	N	N
18 Cardoza	N	?	N	Y	N	Y	Y	Y	Y	Y	N	Y
19 *Radanovich*	Y	Y	N	Y	Y	N	Y	Y	Y	Y	Y	Y
20 Costa	N	N	N	Y	N	Y	Y	Y	Y	Y	N	Y
21 *Nunes*	Y	Y	N	Y	Y	N	Y	Y	Y	Y	Y	Y
22 *Thomas*	Y	Y	N	Y	Y	Y	Y	Y	Y	Y	Y	Y
23 Capps	N	N	Y	N	N	Y	N	N	N	N	N	N
24 *Gallegly*	Y	Y	N	Y	Y	N	Y	Y	Y	Y	Y	Y
25 *McKeon*	Y	Y	N	Y	Y	Y	Y	Y	Y	Y	Y	Y
26 *Dreier*	Y	Y	N	Y	Y	Y	Y	Y	Y	Y	Y	Y
27 Sherman	N	N	Y	P	N	Y	Y	N	N	N	N	N
28 Berman	N	N	Y	Y	N	Y	Y	N	N	N	N	N
29 Schiff	N	N	Y	N	N	Y	Y	N	N	N	N	N
30 Waxman	N	N	Y	?	N	Y	N	N	N	N	N	N
31 Becerra	N	N	Y	N	N	Y	N	N	N	N	N	N
32 Solis	N	N	Y	N	N	Y	N	N	N	N	N	N
33 Watson	N	N	Y	N	N	Y	N	N	N	N	N	N
34 Roybal-Allard	N	N	Y	N	N	Y	Y	N	N	N	N	N
35 Waters	N	N	Y	N	N	Y	N	N	N	N	N	N
36 Harman	N	N	Y	N	N	Y	N	Y	N	N	N	N
37 Millender-McD.	N	N	N	N	N	Y	Y	N	N	?	N	N
38 Napolitano	N	N	Y	N	N	Y	Y	N	N	N	N	N
39 Sánchez, Linda	N	N	Y	N	N	Y	Y	N	N	N	N	N
40 *Royce*	Y	Y	N	Y	Y	N	Y	Y	Y	Y	Y	Y
41 *Lewis*	Y	Y	N	?	N	Y	Y	Y	Y	Y	Y	Y
42 *Miller, Gary*	Y	Y	N	Y	Y	N	Y	Y	Y	Y	Y	Y
43 Baca	N	N	N	N	N	Y	Y	?	N	N	N	Y
44 *Calvert*	Y	Y	N	Y	Y	Y	Y	Y	Y	Y	Y	Y
45 *Bono*	Y	Y	?	Y	N	Y	Y	Y	Y	Y	Y	Y
46 *Rohrabacher*	Y	Y	N	Y	Y	Y	Y	Y	Y	Y	Y	Y
47 Sanchez, Loretta	N	N	N	N	N	Y	Y	N	N	N	N	N
48 *Campbell*	Y	Y	N	Y	Y	N	Y	Y	Y	Y	Y	Y
49 *Issa*	Y	Y	N	Y	Y	Y	Y	Y	Y	Y	Y	Y
50 *Bilbray*[1]				Y	Y	Y	Y	Y	Y	Y	Y	Y
51 Filner	N	N	Y	N	N	Y	Y	N	N	N	N	Y
52 *Hunter*	Y	Y	N	Y	Y	N	Y	Y	Y	Y	Y	Y
53 Davis	N	N	Y	N	N	Y	Y	N	N	N	N	N
COLORADO												
1 DeGette	N	N	Y	N	N	Y	Y	N	N	N	N	N
2 Udall	N	N	Y	N	N	Y	Y	Y	N	N	N	N
3 Salazar	N	Y	Y	Y	N	Y	Y	?	N	Y	N	Y
4 *Musgrave*	Y	Y	N	Y	Y	N	Y	Y	Y	Y	Y	Y
5 *Hefley*	N	Y	N	Y	Y	N	N	Y	Y	Y	Y	Y
6 *Tancredo*	Y	Y	N	Y	Y	N	Y	Y	Y	Y	Y	Y
7 *Beauprez*	Y	Y	N	Y	Y	N	Y	Y	Y	Y	Y	Y
CONNECTICUT												
1 Larson	N	N	Y	N	N	Y	Y	N	N	N	N	N
2 *Simmons*	N	Y	N	Y	N	Y	Y	Y	Y	N	Y	Y
3 DeLauro	N	N	Y	N	N	Y	N	N	N	N	N	N
4 *Shays*	N	Y	Y	Y	N	Y	Y	Y	Y	N	N	N
5 *Johnson*	N	Y	N	Y	Y	Y	Y	Y	Y	N	Y	N
DELAWARE												
AL *Castle*	Y	Y	N	Y	N	Y	Y	Y	Y	–	?	?
FLORIDA												
1 *Miller*	Y	Y	N	Y	Y	N	Y	Y	Y	Y	Y	Y
2 Boyd	N	N	N	P	N	Y	Y	Y	Y	Y	N	Y
3 Brown	N	N	N	N	N	Y	Y	N	Y	N	N	N
4 *Crenshaw*	Y	Y	N	Y	Y	N	Y	Y	Y	Y	Y	Y
5 *Brown-Waite*	Y	Y	N	Y	Y	Y	Y	Y	Y	Y	Y	Y
6 *Stearns*	Y	Y	N	Y	Y	N	Y	Y	Y	Y	Y	Y
7 *Mica*	Y	Y	N	Y	Y	N	Y	Y	Y	Y	Y	Y
8 *Keller*	Y	Y	N	Y	Y	N	Y	Y	+	Y	Y	Y
9 *Bilirakis*	Y	Y	N	Y	Y	N	Y	+	Y	Y	Y	Y
10 *Young*	Y	Y	N	Y	Y	N	Y	Y	Y	Y	Y	Y
11 Davis	N	N	?	N	N	Y	Y	N	?	?	N	N
12 *Putnam*	Y	Y	N	Y	Y	N	Y	Y	Y	Y	Y	Y
13 *Harris*	Y	Y	N	Y	Y	N	Y	Y	Y	Y	Y	Y
14 *Mack*	N	Y	N	Y	Y	Y	Y	Y	Y	Y	N	Y
15 *Weldon*	Y	Y	N	Y	Y	N	Y	Y	Y	Y	Y	Y
16 *Foley*	Y	Y	N	Y	N	Y	Y	Y	Y	Y	Y	?
17 Meek	N	N	N	N	N	Y	Y	Y	N	N	N	?
18 *Ros-Lehtinen*	Y	Y	N	Y	N	N	Y	Y	N	Y	Y	Y
19 Wexler	N	N	Y	N	N	Y	?	N	Y	N	N	N
20 Wasserman-Schultz	N	N	Y	N	N	Y	Y	N	N	N	N	N
21 *Diaz-Balart, L.*	Y	Y	N	Y	N	N	Y	Y	N	Y	Y	Y
22 *Shaw*	Y	Y	N	Y	N	Y	Y	Y	Y	Y	Y	Y
23 Hastings	N	N	N	N	N	Y	Y	N	N	N	N	N
24 *Feeney*	Y	Y	N	Y	Y	N	Y	Y	Y	Y	Y	Y
25 *Diaz-Balart, M.*	Y	Y	N	Y	N	N	Y	Y	N	Y	Y	Y
GEORGIA												
1 *Kingston*	Y	Y	?	Y	Y	N	Y	Y	Y	Y	Y	Y
2 Bishop	N	N	N	Y	N	Y	Y	Y	Y	Y	N	Y
3 Marshall	Y	Y	Y	Y	N	N	N	Y	Y	Y	Y	Y
4 McKinney	N	N	Y	N	N	?	?	?	N	N	N	N
5 Lewis	N	N	Y	N	N	?	N	?	N	–	–	–
6 *Price*	Y	Y	N	Y	Y	N	Y	Y	Y	Y	Y	Y
7 *Linder*	Y	Y	N	Y	Y	N	Y	+	Y	Y	Y	Y
8 *Westmoreland*	Y	Y	N	Y	Y	N	Y	Y	Y	Y	Y	Y
9 *Norwood*	Y	Y	N	Y	Y	N	Y	Y	Y	Y	Y	Y
10 *Deal*	Y	Y	N	Y	Y	N	?	?	Y	Y	Y	Y
11 *Gingrey*	Y	Y	N	Y	Y	N	Y	Y	Y	Y	Y	Y

[1]Rep. Brian P. Bilbray, R-Calif., was sworn in June 13, 2006, to replace Republican Randy "Duke" Cunningham, who resigned, effective Dec. 1, 2005.

KEY

Democrat	*Republican*	**Independent**

Y	Voted for (yea)	–	Announced against
#	Paired for	P	Voted "present"
+	Announced for	C	Voted "present" to avoid possible conflict of interest
N	Voted against (nay)	?	Did not vote or otherwise make a position known
X	Paired against		

House Key Votes	1	2	3	4	5	6	7	8	9	10	11	12
12 Barrow	Y	Y	N	Y	Y	Y	Y	Y	Y	Y	Y	Y
13 Scott	N	N	N	N	N	Y	Y	Y	N	N	N	Y
HAWAII												
1 Abercrombie	N	N	Y	N	N	Y	N	N	N	N	N	N
2 Case	N	Y	Y	Y	N	Y	Y	Y	?	N	N	?
IDAHO												
1 *Otter*	Y	Y	N	Y	Y	N	Y	Y	Y	Y	N	Y
2 *Simpson*	Y	Y	N	Y	Y	N	Y	Y	Y	Y	Y	Y
ILLINOIS												
1 Rush	N	N	N	N	N	Y	Y	Y	N	N	N	N
2 Jackson	N	N	Y	N	N	Y	Y	N	N	N	N	N
3 Lipinski	N	N	Y	Y	N	N	Y	Y	Y	Y	N	N
4 Gutierrez	N	N	Y	?	N	+	Y	N	N	N	?	N
5 Emanuel	N	N	Y	N	N	Y	Y	Y	N	N	N	N
6 *Hyde*	Y	Y	N	Y	Y	N	Y	Y	Y	Y	Y	Y
7 Davis	N	N	N	N	N	Y	Y	N	N	N	N	N
8 Bean	N	Y	Y	Y	N	Y	Y	Y	Y	N	Y	Y
9 Schakowsky	N	N	Y	N	N	Y	Y	N	N	N	N	N
10 *Kirk*	Y	Y	N	Y	N	Y	Y	Y	Y	N	Y	N
11 *Weller*	Y	Y	N	Y	Y	N	Y	Y	Y	Y	Y	Y
12 Costello	N	N	Y	Y	N	N	N	N	Y	Y	N	N
13 *Biggert*	Y	Y	N	Y	N	Y	Y	Y	Y	N	Y	N
14 *Hastert*[2]	Y	Y		Y		N	Y	Y				
15 *Johnson*	Y	Y	N	Y	Y	N	Y	Y	Y	Y	N	Y
16 *Manzullo*	Y	Y	?	Y	Y	N	Y	Y	Y	Y	Y	Y
17 Evans	?	?	?	?	?	?	?	?	?	?	?	?
18 *LaHood*	Y	Y	N	Y	Y	N	Y	Y	Y	Y	Y	Y
19 *Shimkus*	Y	Y	N	Y	Y	N	Y	Y	Y	Y	Y	Y
INDIANA												
1 Visclosky	N	N	Y	N	N	Y	Y	N	N	N	N	N
2 *Chocola*	Y	Y	N	Y	Y	N	Y	Y	Y	Y	Y	Y
3 *Souder*	Y	Y	N	Y	Y	N	Y	Y	Y	Y	Y	Y
4 *Buyer*	?	Y	N	Y	Y	N	Y	?	Y	Y	Y	Y
5 *Burton*	N	Y	Y	+	Y	N	Y	Y	Y	Y	Y	?
6 *Pence*	Y	Y	N	Y	N	N	Y	Y	Y	Y	Y	Y
7 Carson	N	N	Y	N	–	Y	Y	–	N	N	N	N
8 *Hostettler*	Y	Y	N	Y	Y	N	Y	Y	Y	Y	N	Y
9 *Sodrel*	Y	Y	N	Y	Y	N	Y	Y	Y	Y	Y	Y
IOWA												
1 *Nussle*	Y	Y	?	?	Y	N	Y	Y	Y	?	Y	Y
2 *Leach*	N	N	Y	N	N	Y	N	Y	Y	Y	N	N
3 Boswell	Y	N	N	Y	N	Y	Y	Y	Y	Y	Y	Y
4 *Latham*	Y	Y	N	Y	Y	N	Y	Y	Y	Y	Y	Y
5 *King*	N	Y	N	Y	Y	N	Y	Y	Y	Y	Y	Y
KANSAS												
1 *Moran*	Y	Y	N	Y	Y	N	N	Y	Y	Y	N	Y
2 *Ryun*	Y	Y	N	Y	Y	N	Y	Y	Y	Y	Y	Y
3 Moore	N	N	N	Y	N	Y	Y	Y	Y	N	N	N
4 *Tiahrt*	Y	Y	N	Y	?	N	Y	Y	Y	Y	Y	Y
KENTUCKY												
1 *Whitfield*	Y	Y	N	Y	Y	N	Y	Y	Y	Y	Y	N
2 *Lewis*	Y	Y	N	Y	Y	N	Y	Y	Y	Y	Y	Y
3 *Northup*	Y	Y	N	Y	?	?	Y	?	Y	Y	Y	Y
4 *Davis*	Y	Y	N	Y	Y	N	Y	Y	Y	Y	Y	Y

[2]The Speaker votes only at his discretion, usually to break a tie or to emphasize the importance of a matter.

House Key Votes	1	2	3	4	5	6	7	8	9	10	11	12
5 *Rogers*	Y	Y	N	Y	Y	N	Y	Y	Y	Y	Y	Y
6 Chandler	N	N	Y	Y	N	Y	Y	Y	Y	Y	N	N
LOUISIANA												
1 *Jindal*	Y	Y	N	Y	Y	N	Y	Y	Y	Y	Y	Y
2 Jefferson	N	N	N	N	N	Y	Y	Y	N	?	N	Y
3 Melancon	Y	Y	N	Y	N	Y	Y	Y	Y	Y	Y	Y
4 *McCrery*	Y	Y	N	Y	Y	N	Y	Y	Y	Y	Y	Y
5 *Alexander*	Y	Y	N	Y	Y	N	Y	Y	Y	Y	Y	Y
6 *Baker*	Y	Y	N	Y	Y	N	Y	Y	Y	Y	Y	Y
7 *Boustany*	Y	Y	N	Y	Y	N	Y	Y	Y	Y	Y	Y
MAINE												
1 Allen	N	N	Y	N	N	Y	Y	N	N	N	N	N
2 Michaud	N	N	N	N	N	Y	Y	N	N	N	N	N
MARYLAND												
1 *Gilchrest*	Y	Y	N	Y	N	Y	Y	Y	Y	N	Y	N
2 Ruppersberger	N	N	N	N	N	Y	Y	Y	Y	N	N	N
3 Cardin	N	N	Y	N	N	Y	Y	N	N	N	N	N
4 Wynn	N	N	N	N	N	Y	Y	Y	N	N	N	N
5 Hoyer	N	N	Y	N	N	Y	Y	N	N	N	N	N
6 *Bartlett*	Y	Y	N	Y	Y	N	Y	Y	Y	Y	Y	Y
7 Cummings	N	N	N	N	N	Y	N	N	N	N	N	N
8 Van Hollen	N	N	Y	N	N	Y	Y	N	N	N	N	N
MASSACHUSETTS												
1 Olver	N	N	Y	N	N	Y	Y	N	N	N	N	N
2 Neal	N	N	Y	N	N	Y	Y	N	N	N	N	N
3 McGovern	N	N	Y	N	N	Y	Y	N	N	N	N	N
4 Frank	N	N	Y	N	N	Y	Y	N	Y	N	N	N
5 Meehan	N	N	Y	N	N	Y	Y	?	N	?	?	?
6 Tierney	N	N	Y	N	N	Y	Y	N	N	N	N	N
7 Markey	N	N	Y	N	N	Y	N	N	N	N	N	N
8 Capuano	N	N	Y	N	N	Y	Y	N	Y	N	N	N
9 Lynch	N	N	Y	Y	N	Y	N	Y	Y	Y	N	N
10 Delahunt	N	N	Y	N	N	Y	Y	Y	Y	N	N	N
MICHIGAN												
1 Stupak	N	N	Y	N	N	N	Y	Y	Y	Y	?	N
2 *Hoekstra*	Y	Y	N	Y	Y	N	Y	Y	Y	Y	Y	Y
3 *Ehlers*	Y	Y	N	Y	N	N	Y	Y	Y	Y	Y	N
4 *Camp*	Y	Y	N	Y	Y	N	Y	Y	Y	Y	Y	Y
5 Kildee	N	N	Y	N	N	N	N	Y	Y	Y	N	N
6 *Upton*	Y	Y	N	Y	Y	Y	Y	Y	Y	Y	Y	Y
7 *Schwarz*	Y	Y	N	Y	N	Y	Y	Y	Y	Y	Y	N
8 *Rogers*	Y	Y	N	Y	Y	N	Y	Y	Y	Y	Y	Y
9 *Knollenberg*	Y	Y	N	Y	Y	N	Y	Y	Y	Y	Y	Y
10 *Miller*	Y	Y	N	Y	Y	N	Y	Y	Y	Y	Y	Y
11 *McCotter*	Y	Y	N	P	Y	N	Y	Y	Y	Y	Y	Y
12 Levin	N	N	Y	N	N	Y	Y	Y	N	N	N	N
13 Kilpatrick	N	N	Y	–	N	Y	N	Y	N	N	N	N
14 Conyers	N	N	Y	N	N	Y	N	Y	N	N	N	N
15 Dingell	N	N	Y	?	N	Y	N	Y	N	N	N	N
MINNESOTA												
1 *Gutknecht*	Y	Y	N	Y	Y	N	Y	Y	Y	Y	Y	Y
2 *Kline*	Y	Y	N	Y	Y	N	Y	Y	Y	Y	Y	Y
3 *Ramstad*	N	Y	N	Y	N	Y	Y	Y	Y	Y	Y	Y
4 McCollum	N	N	Y	N	N	Y	Y	Y	N	N	N	N
5 Sabo	N	N	Y	N	N	Y	Y	Y	N	N	N	?
6 *Kennedy*	Y	Y	N	Y	Y	N	Y	Y	Y	Y	Y	Y
7 Peterson	N	Y	Y	Y	Y	N	N	Y	Y	Y	Y	Y
8 Oberstar	N	N	Y	N	N	N	N	Y	N	Y	N	N
MISSISSIPPI												
1 *Wicker*	Y	Y	N	Y	Y	N	Y	Y	Y	Y	Y	Y
2 Thompson	N	N	Y	Y	N	Y	Y	Y	N	N	N	Y
3 *Pickering*	Y	Y	N	Y	Y	N	Y	Y	Y	Y	Y	Y
4 Taylor	Y	N	Y	Y	Y	N	N	N	Y	Y	Y	Y
MISSOURI												
1 Clay	N	N	N	N	N	Y	Y	Y	N	N	N	N
2 *Akin*	Y	Y	N	Y	Y	N	Y	Y	Y	Y	Y	Y
3 Carnahan	N	N	N	N	N	Y	Y	N	N	N	N	N
4 Skelton	N	N	N	N	N	Y	Y	Y	Y	Y	N	N
5 Cleaver	N	N	N	–	N	Y	Y	Y	?	N	N	N
6 *Graves*	Y	Y	N	Y	+	N	Y	Y	Y	Y	Y	Y
7 *Blunt*	Y	Y	N	Y	Y	N	Y	Y	Y	Y	Y	Y
8 *Emerson*	Y	Y	N	Y	Y	Y	Y	Y	Y	Y	Y	Y
9 *Hulshof*	N	Y	N	Y	Y	N	Y	Y	Y	Y	Y	Y
MONTANA												
AL *Rehberg*	Y	Y	N	Y	Y	N	Y	Y	Y	Y	Y	Y

House Key Votes	1	2	3	4	5	6	7	8	9	10	11	12
NEBRASKA												
1 *Fortenberry*	Y	Y	N	Y	Y	N	Y	Y	Y	Y	Y	Y
2 *Terry*	Y	Y	N	Y	Y	N	Y	Y	Y	Y	Y	Y
3 *Osborne*	+	Y	N	Y	N	N	Y	Y	Y	Y	Y	Y
NEVADA												
1 Berkley	N	N	Y	N	N	Y	Y	N	Y	N	N	N
2 *Gibbons*	Y	Y	?	Y	Y	Y	Y	Y	Y	Y	Y	Y
3 *Porter*	Y	Y	N	Y	Y	Y	Y	Y	Y	Y	Y	Y
NEW HAMPSHIRE												
1 *Bradley*	N	Y	N	Y	Y	Y	Y	Y	Y	Y	Y	Y
2 *Bass*	N	Y	N	Y	Y	Y	Y	Y	Y	N	Y	N
NEW JERSEY												
1 Andrews	N	N	Y	N	N	Y	Y	N	Y	N	N	N
2 *LoBiondo*	Y	Y	N	Y	N	N	Y	Y	Y	Y	Y	N
3 *Saxton*	Y	Y	N	Y	N	N	Y	Y	Y	Y	Y	N
4 *Smith*	Y	Y	N	Y	N	N	N	Y	Y	Y	Y	Y
5 *Garrett*	Y	Y	N	Y	Y	N	Y	Y	Y	Y	N	Y
6 Pallone	N	N	Y	N	N	Y	Y	N	N	N	N	N
7 *Ferguson*	Y	Y	N	Y	N	N	Y	Y	Y	Y	Y	N
8 Pascrell	N	N	Y	N	N	Y	N	N	Y	N	N	N
9 Rothman	N	N	Y	N	N	Y	N	Y	N	N	N	N
10 Payne	N	N	Y	N	N	Y	N	?	N	N	N	N
11 *Frelinghuysen*	Y	Y	N	Y	N	Y	Y	Y	Y	Y	Y	N
12 Holt	N	N	Y	N	N	Y	N	N	N	N	N	N
13 Vacant[3]												
NEW MEXICO												
1 *Wilson*	N	Y	Y	?	N	Y	Y	Y	Y	Y	Y	Y
2 *Pearce*	Y	Y	N	Y	N	N	Y	Y	Y	Y	Y	Y
3 Udall	N	N	Y	N	N	Y	N	N	N	N	N	N
NEW YORK												
1 Bishop	N	N	Y	–	N	Y	Y	N	Y	N	N	N
2 Israel	N	N	Y	N	N	Y	Y	Y	Y	N	N	N
3 *King*	Y	Y	N	Y	Y	N	Y	Y	Y	Y	Y	Y
4 McCarthy	N	N	Y	Y	N	Y	Y	Y	Y	N	N	N
5 Ackerman	N	N	N	N	N	Y	Y	Y	N	N	N	N
6 Meeks	N	N	N	N	N	Y	Y	Y	N	N	N	N
7 Crowley	N	N	N	N	N	Y	Y	Y	N	N	N	N
8 Nadler	N	N	Y	N	N	Y	N	N	N	N	N	N
9 Weiner	N	N	Y	N	N	Y	Y	N	Y	N	N	N
10 Towns	N	N	N	N	N	Y	Y	Y	N	N	N	N
11 Owens	N	N	Y	N	N	Y	N	N	N	N	N	N
12 Velázquez	N	N	Y	N	N	Y	N	Y	N	N	N	N
13 *Fossella*	Y	Y	N	Y	Y	Y	Y	Y	Y	Y	Y	?
14 Maloney	N	N	Y	N	N	Y	Y	N	Y	N	N	N
15 Rangel	N	N	Y	N	N	Y	Y	N	N	N	N	N
16 Serrano	N	N	Y	N	N	Y	N	N	N	N	N	N
17 Engel	N	N	Y	N	N	Y	Y	Y	N	N	N	N
18 Lowey	N	N	Y	N	N	Y	Y	N	N	N	N	N
19 *Kelly*	Y	Y	N	Y	Y	Y	Y	Y	Y	Y	Y	N
20 *Sweeney*	Y	Y	N	Y	Y	Y	Y	Y	Y	Y	Y	Y
21 McNulty	N	N	Y	N	?	Y	N	N	N	Y	N	N
22 Hinchey	N	N	Y	N	N	Y	N	N	N	N	N	N
23 *McHugh*	Y	Y	?	Y	Y	N	Y	Y	Y	Y	Y	Y
24 *Boehlert*	Y	N	N	Y	N	Y	Y	?	Y	N	Y	N
25 *Walsh*	Y	Y	N	Y	N	N	Y	Y	Y	Y	Y	N
26 *Reynolds*	Y	Y	N	Y	Y	N	Y	Y	Y	Y	Y	Y
27 Higgins	N	N	Y	Y	N	Y	Y	Y	N	N	N	N
28 Slaughter	N	N	Y	N	?	Y	N	N	N	N	N	N
29 *Kuhl*	Y	Y	N	Y	Y	N	Y	Y	Y	Y	Y	Y
NORTH CAROLINA												
1 Butterfield	N	N	N	N	N	Y	Y	Y	N	N	N	N
2 Etheridge	N	N	N	Y	N	Y	Y	N	Y	Y	N	Y
3 *Jones*	N	Y	Y	P	Y	N	N	?	Y	Y	N	+
4 Price	N	N	Y	N	N	Y	Y	N	N	N	N	N
5 *Foxx*	Y	Y	N	Y	Y	N	Y	Y	Y	Y	Y	Y
6 *Coble*	Y	Y	N	Y	Y	Y	Y	?	Y	Y	Y	Y
7 McIntyre	N	Y	N	Y	N	N	Y	Y	Y	Y	N	Y
8 *Hayes*	Y	Y	N	Y	Y	N	Y	Y	Y	Y	Y	Y
9 *Myrick*	Y	Y	N	Y	Y	N	Y	Y	Y	Y	Y	Y
10 *McHenry*	Y	Y	N	Y	Y	N	Y	Y	Y	Y	Y	Y
11 *Taylor*	Y	Y	N	Y	Y	N	N	Y	Y	Y	Y	Y
12 Watt	N	N	Y	N	N	Y	Y	N	N	N	N	N
13 Miller	N	N	Y	P	N	Y	Y	N	Y	N	N	N
NORTH DAKOTA												
AL Pomeroy	N	N	Y	N	N	Y	Y	N	Y	Y	N	?

House Key Votes	1	2	3	4	5	6	7	8	9	10	11	12
OHIO												
1 *Chabot*	Y	Y	N	Y	N	N	Y	Y	Y	Y	?	Y
2 *Schmidt*	Y	Y	N	Y	Y	N	Y	Y	Y	Y	Y	Y
3 *Turner*	Y	Y	N	Y	Y	N	Y	Y	Y	Y	Y	Y
4 *Oxley*	Y	Y	N	Y	Y	N	Y	?	Y	Y	Y	?
5 *Gillmor*	Y	Y	N	Y	Y	N	Y	Y	Y	Y	Y	Y
6 Strickland	N	N	Y	N	N	Y	Y	Y	?	?	?	?
7 *Hobson*	Y	Y	N	Y	Y	N	Y	Y	Y	Y	Y	Y
8 *Boehner*	Y	Y	N	Y	N	N	Y	Y	Y	Y	Y	?
9 Kaptur	N	N	Y	N	N	N	N	Y	P	N	N	Y
10 Kucinich	N	N	Y	N	N	Y	N	N	N	N	N	N
11 Jones	N	N	Y	N	N	Y	Y	N	N	N	N	N
12 *Tiberi*	Y	Y	N	Y	Y	N	Y	Y	Y	Y	Y	Y
13 Brown	N	N	Y	N	N	Y	Y	N	Y	?	N	N
14 *LaTourette*	Y	Y	N	Y	Y	Y	Y	Y	Y	Y	Y	Y
15 *Pryce*	Y	Y	N	Y	Y	Y	Y	Y	Y	Y	Y	Y
16 *Regula*	Y	Y	Y	Y	Y	Y	Y	Y	Y	Y	Y	N
17 Ryan	N	N	Y	N	N	Y	Y	N	Y	Y	N	N
18 *Ney*[4]	Y	Y	N	Y	Y	N	Y	Y	?	?	?	?
OKLAHOMA												
1 *Sullivan*	Y	Y	N	Y	Y	N	Y	Y	Y	Y	Y	Y
2 Boren	Y	Y	N	Y	N	Y	Y	Y	Y	Y	Y	Y
3 *Lucas*	Y	Y	N	Y	Y	N	Y	Y	Y	Y	Y	Y
4 *Cole*	Y	Y	N	Y	Y	N	Y	Y	Y	Y	Y	Y
5 *Istook*	Y	Y	N	Y	Y	N	?	?	Y	?	Y	Y
OREGON												
1 Wu	N	N	Y	N	N	Y	N	Y	N	N	N	N
2 *Walden*	Y	Y	N	Y	Y	Y	Y	Y	Y	Y	Y	Y
3 Blumenauer	N	N	Y	N	N	Y	N	Y	N	N	N	N
4 DeFazio	N	N	Y	N	N	Y	N	Y	Y	N	N	N
5 Hooley	N	N	Y	N	N	Y	N	Y	Y	N	N	N
PENNSYLVANIA												
1 Brady	N	N	N	N	N	Y	Y	N	N	N	N	N
2 Fattah	N	N	N	N	N	Y	Y	N	N	N	N	N
3 *English*	Y	Y	N	Y	N	N	Y	Y	Y	Y	Y	Y
4 *Hart*	Y	Y	N	Y	Y	N	Y	Y	Y	Y	Y	Y
5 *Peterson*	Y	Y	?	Y	Y	N	Y	Y	Y	Y	Y	Y
6 *Gerlach*	Y	Y	N	Y	N	Y	Y	Y	Y	Y	Y	N
7 *Weldon*	Y	Y	N	Y	Y	Y	N	Y	Y	Y	Y	N
8 *Fitzpatrick*	Y	Y	Y	Y	N	N	Y	Y	Y	Y	Y	N
9 *Shuster*	Y	Y	N	Y	Y	N	Y	Y	Y	Y	Y	Y
10 *Sherwood*	Y	Y	N	Y	Y	N	Y	Y	Y	Y	Y	Y
11 Kanjorski	N	N	Y	N	N	Y	Y	N	Y	Y	N	N
12 Murtha	N	N	Y	N	N	Y	Y	N	N	Y	N	N
13 Schwartz	N	N	N	N	N	Y	N	N	N	N	N	N
14 Doyle	N	N	Y	N	N	Y	Y	N	N	Y	N	N
15 *Dent*	Y	Y	N	Y	N	Y	Y	Y	Y	Y	Y	Y
16 *Pitts*	Y	Y	N	Y	Y	N	Y	Y	Y	Y	Y	Y
17 Holden	N	N	N	Y	Y	N	Y	N	Y	Y	N	Y
18 *Murphy*	Y	Y	N	Y	Y	N	Y	Y	Y	Y	Y	Y
19 *Platts*	N	Y	N	Y	Y	Y	Y	Y	Y	Y	Y	N
RHODE ISLAND												
1 Kennedy	N	?	Y	N	N	Y	N	N	N	N	N	N
2 Langevin	N	N	Y	N	N	Y	N	N	N	Y	N	N
SOUTH CAROLINA												
1 *Brown*	Y	Y	N	Y	Y	N	Y	Y	Y	Y	Y	Y
2 *Wilson*	Y	Y	N	Y	Y	N	Y	Y	Y	Y	Y	?
3 *Barrett*	Y	Y	N	Y	Y	N	Y	Y	Y	Y	Y	Y
4 *Inglis*	Y	Y	N	Y	Y	N	Y	Y	Y	Y	N	Y
5 Spratt	N	N	N	Y	N	Y	Y	N	Y	Y	Y	N
6 Clyburn	N	N	N	N	N	Y	Y	Y	N	N	N	N
SOUTH DAKOTA												
AL Herseth	N	N	Y	Y	N	Y	Y	Y	Y	N	Y	Y
TENNESSEE												
1 *Jenkins*	Y	Y	N	Y	Y	N	Y	Y	Y	Y	Y	Y
2 *Duncan*	Y	Y	N	N	Y	N	Y	Y	Y	Y	Y	Y
3 *Wamp*	Y	Y	N	Y	Y	N	Y	Y	Y	Y	Y	Y
4 Davis	N	Y	N	Y	N	N	Y	Y	Y	Y	Y	Y
5 Cooper	N	N	Y	Y	N	Y	Y	Y	Y	Y	N	N
6 Gordon	N	Y	Y	Y	N	Y	Y	?	Y	Y	Y	Y
7 *Blackburn*	Y	Y	N	Y	Y	N	Y	Y	Y	Y	Y	Y

[3]Rep. Bob Menendez, D-N.J., resigned, effective Jan. 16, 2006.

[4]Rep. Bob Ney, R-Ohio, resigned, effective Nov. 3, 2006.

KEY

Democrat	*Republican*	**Independent**

Y	Voted for (yea)	–	Announced against
#	Paired for	P	Voted "present"
+	Announced for	C	Voted "present" to avoid possible conflict of interest
N	Voted against (nay)		
X	Paired against	?	Did not vote or otherwise make a position known

House Key Votes	1	2	3	4	5	6	7	8	9	10	11	12
8 Tanner	N	N	N	N	N	Y	Y	Y	Y	Y	N	Y
9 Ford	N	Y	Y	N	N	Y	Y	Y	Y	?	Y	?
TEXAS												
1 *Gohmert*	Y	Y	N	Y	Y	N	Y	?	Y	Y	Y	Y
2 *Poe*	Y	Y	N	Y	Y	N	Y	N	Y	Y	Y	Y
3 *Johnson, Sam*	Y	Y	N	?	Y	N	Y	N	?	Y	Y	Y
4 *Hall*	Y	Y	N	Y	Y	N	Y	N	Y	Y	Y	Y
5 *Hensarling*	Y	Y	N	Y	Y	N	Y	N	Y	Y	Y	Y
6 *Barton*	Y	Y	N	Y	Y	Y	Y	N	Y	Y	Y	Y
7 *Culberson*	Y	Y	N	Y	Y	N	Y	N	?	Y	Y	Y
8 *Brady*	Y	Y	N	Y	Y	N	Y	N	Y	Y	Y	Y
9 Green, A.	N	N	N	N	A.	N	Y	Y	N	N	N	N
10 *McCaul*	Y	Y	N	Y	Y	N	Y	N	Y	Y	Y	?
11 *Conaway*	Y	Y	N	Y	Y	N	Y	N	N	Y	Y	Y
12 *Granger*	Y	Y	N	Y	Y	Y	Y	Y	Y	Y	Y	Y
13 *Thornberry*	Y	Y	N	Y	Y	N	Y	N	Y	Y	Y	Y
14 *Paul*	N	Y	N	N	Y	N	N	N	Y	N	N	Y
15 Hinojosa	N	N	N	N	N	Y	Y	N	N	Y	N	Y
16 Reyes	N	N	?	N	N	Y	Y	N	N	Y	N	Y
17 Edwards	N	N	N	Y	N	Y	Y	N	Y	Y	Y	Y
18 Jackson-Lee	N	N	N	N	N	Y	Y	N	N	N	N	N
19 *Neugebauer*	Y	Y	N	Y	Y	N	Y	N	Y	Y	Y	Y
20 Gonzalez	N	N	N	N	N	Y	Y	N	N	N	N	N
21 *Smith*	Y	Y	N	Y	Y	N	Y	Y	Y	Y	Y	Y
22 *DeLay*[5]	Y	Y	?									
23 *Bonilla*	N	Y	N	Y	Y	N	Y	N	Y	Y	Y	Y
24 *Marchant*	Y	Y	N	Y	Y	N	Y	Y	Y	Y	Y	Y
25 Doggett	N	N	Y	N	N	Y	N	N	N	N	N	N
26 *Burgess*	Y	Y	N	Y	Y	N	Y	N	Y	Y	Y	?
27 Ortiz	N	N	N	N	N	Y	Y	N	N	Y	N	Y
28 Cuellar	Y	Y	N	Y	N	Y	Y	Y	N	Y	Y	Y
29 Green G.,	G.	N	N	N	N	Y	Y	N	N	N	N	N
30 Johnson, E.	N	N	N	N	N	Y	Y	N	N	N	N	N
31 *Carter*	Y	Y	N	+	Y	N	Y	N	Y	Y	Y	Y
32 *Sessions*	Y	Y	N	?	?	N	Y	Y	Y	Y	Y	Y
UTAH												
1 *Bishop*	Y	Y	N	?	Y	N	Y	Y	Y	Y	Y	Y
2 Matheson	Y	Y	Y	Y	N	Y	Y	Y	Y	Y	Y	Y
3 *Cannon*	Y	Y	N	?	N	N	Y	Y	Y	Y	Y	Y
VERMONT												
AL **Sanders**	N	N	Y	N	N	Y	N	N	N	N	N	N
VIRGINIA												
1 *Davis, Jo Ann*	Y	Y	N	Y	?	N	?	?	Y	Y	Y	Y
2 *Drake*	Y	Y	N	Y	Y	N	Y	Y	Y	Y	Y	Y
3 Scott	N	N	Y	N	N	Y	Y	N	N	N	N	N
4 *Forbes*	Y	Y	N	Y	Y	N	Y	Y	+	Y	Y	Y
5 *Goode*	Y	Y	N	Y	Y	N	N	Y	Y	Y	Y	Y
6 *Goodlatte*	Y	Y	N	Y	Y	N	Y	Y	Y	Y	Y	Y
7 *Cantor*	Y	Y	N	Y	Y	N	Y	Y	Y	Y	Y	Y
8 Moran	N	N	Y	N	N	Y	Y	N	Y	N	N	N
9 Boucher	N	N	Y	Y	N	Y	Y	Y	Y	N	N	N
10 *Wolf*	N	Y	Y	Y	Y	N	Y	Y	Y	Y	Y	N
11 *Davis, T.*	Y	Y	Y	Y	N	Y	Y	Y	Y	Y	Y	N
WASHINGTON												
1 Inslee	N	N	Y	N	N	Y	Y	N	N	N	N	N
2 Larsen	N	N	N	Y	N	Y	Y	N	N	N	N	N
3 Baird	N	N	Y	N	N	Y	Y	P	Y	N	N	N
4 *Hastings*	Y	Y	N	Y	Y	N	Y	Y	Y	Y	Y	Y
5 *McMorris*	Y	Y	N	Y	Y	N	Y	Y	Y	Y	Y	Y
6 Dicks	N	N	Y	N	N	Y	Y	Y	N	N	N	N
7 McDermott	N	N	Y	N	N	Y	N	N	N	N	N	N
8 *Reichert*	Y	Y	Y	+	N	Y	Y	Y	Y	Y	Y	N
9 Smith	N	?	Y	Y	N	Y	Y	N	Y	N	N	N
WEST VIRGINIA												
1 Mollohan	N	N	N	N	N	N	Y	N	Y	Y	N	N
2 *Capito*	Y	Y	N	Y	Y	Y	Y	Y	Y	Y	Y	Y
3 Rahall	N	N	N	N	N	N	Y	Y	Y	Y	N	Y
WISCONSIN												
1 *Ryan*	Y	Y	N	Y	Y	N	Y	Y	Y	Y	Y	Y
2 Baldwin	N	N	Y	N	N	Y	N	N	N	N	N	N
3 Kind	N	N	Y	Y	N	Y	Y	Y	Y	N	N	N
4 Moore	N	N	Y	N	N	Y	N	N	N	N	N	N
5 *Sensenbrenner*	N	Y	Y	?	N	N	Y	Y	Y	Y	Y	Y
6 *Petri*	Y	Y	N	Y	Y	N	Y	Y	Y	Y	Y	Y
7 Obey	N	N	Y	N	N	Y	N	N	N	Y	N	N
8 *Green*	N	Y	N	Y	N	N	Y	Y	Y	+	Y	Y
WYOMING												
AL *Cubin*	Y	Y	N	Y	Y	N	Y	Y	Y	Y	Y	Y

[5]Rep. Tom DeLay, R-Texas, resigned, effective June 9, 2006.

Senate

1. MINIMUM WAGE INCREASE

The Senate in early 2007 overwhelmingly passed a bill (HR 2) to raise the minimum wage to $7.25 per hour over two years and provide $8.3 billion in small-business tax incentives. Although the House was first to pass a minimum wage increase, it was this Senate vote that paved the way for the plan to become law. *(Story, pp. 661, 664)*

The House voted on a wage-only bill, and Speaker Nancy Pelosi, D-Calif., urged the Senate to do the same. But the Democrats' majority in the Senate was too slim for the leadership to follow the House's lead. Because getting the sixty votes necessary to overcome an expected Republican filibuster would be impossible without some kind of accompanying tax-incentive package, Finance chairman Max Baucus, D-Mont., put together $8.3 billion in small-business tax breaks that could be added to the House's wage bill. Backed by Majority Leader Harry Reid, D-Nev., the strategy worked, bringing all but three Republicans on board for the first increase in the minimum wage in a decade.

At that point, House Ways and Means chairman Charles B. Rangel, D-N.Y., went to work on his own, smaller tax package, acknowledging that one would be necessary for the wage increase to be cleared. Almost four months later, Congress included the wage increase, along with $4.9 billion in tax breaks aimed at reducing its effect on businesses, in the war supplemental that President George W. Bush signed into law.

The Senate passed HR 2 on Feb. 1 by a vote of 94–3: R 45–3; D 47–0; I 2–0. *(Vote, p. 959)*

2. U.S. ATTORNEY APPOINTMENTS

By a convincing 94–2 margin, the Senate in March 2006 passed legislation that repealed the authority of the U.S. attorney general to make indefinite interim appointments of U.S. attorneys and reinstated a 120-day limit on the tenure of appointed attorneys.

The purpose of this bill was to roll back a provision that had been included in the antiterrorism law (PL 109-177) the Republican-led Congress wrote in 2005 and cleared in 2006. The provision had allowed the attorney general to appoint U.S. attorneys who could serve indefinitely without Senate action. By the start of the 110th Congress, it had become the center of controversy over the Justice Department's dismissal of eight U.S. attorneys in 2006 and the role White House officials played in the firings. *(Story, p. 721)*

The 94–2 vote showed not only a broad, bipartisan consensus in the Senate that the provision should be overturned but also a unified dissatisfaction over the way the Justice Department handled the hiring and firing of federal prosecutors and over the leadership in general of Attorney General Alberto R. Gonzales.

The House, following the Senate's lead, voted 306–114 to send the bill to President George W. Bush, who signed it June 14. In August, after months of acrimonious interaction with the Senate over the attorney firings and other issues that came to light, Gonzales announced that he would resign as attorney general. He left Sept. 17. The Senate approval on the key vote came March 20 by a vote of 94–2: R 46–2; D 46–0; I 2–0. *(Vote, p. 959)*

3. IMMIGRATION OVERHAUL

The Senate's refusal on June 28, 2007, to stop a filibuster on legislation to overhaul U.S. immigration laws brought an end to President George W. Bush's long effort to win a comprehensive overhaul of immigration policy. The legislation provided for a temporary guest worker program and instituted new border security measures. *(Story, pp. 686, 711)*

The cloture failure on S 1639, which did not even get a simple majority, demonstrated that lawmakers remained deeply divided over whether immigration law should focus exclusively on law enforcement or combine a crackdown on illegal immigrants with temporary visas for guest workers and a path to citizenship for some immigrants.

The issue divided liberals and aroused grassroots conservatives who were a core GOP constituency. The same splits blocked attempts to clear a comprehensive immigration bill in the 109th Congress.

The June 28 vote was the fourth time in less than a month that backers of the immigration legislation were unable to muster the sixty votes needed to surmount opposition from conservative Republicans and a mixed group of liberals and Democrats from GOP-leaning states. The effort had picked up only one new vote since June 7, when three attempts to limit debate on an earlier version of the bill (S 1348) were rejected.

Going into the June 28 vote, supporters thought they were only a handful of votes away from sixty and that they had a couple of potential backers that would give them the total needed. But that proved a vain hope when Alaska Republicans Lisa Murkowski and Ted Stevens cast "no" votes together. Shortly after that, Kansas Republican Sam Brownback, who had cast an early "yes," switched his vote. From there, it was clearly a lopsided vote. The Senate rejected the motion to invoke cloture by a vote of 46–53: R 12–37; D 33–15; I 1–1, well under the sixty votes needed. *(Vote, p. 959)*

The legislation was the product of a "grand bargain" involving the White House and about a dozen senators from both parties. It would have allowed millions of illegal immigrants to stay in the country, receive legal status, and ultimately earn citizenship. It also provided $4.4 billion in mandatory spending for border security and enforcement and created a temporary guest worker program. But the fragile compromise suited almost no one entirely, and in the end it was overwhelmed by doubts from all sides. Sixteen of the senators who voted against cloture—ten Republicans and six Democrats—had supported a broad immigration bill in the 109th Congress.

4. LOBBY AND ETHICS OVERHAUL

Senate Democrats in August 2007 cleared a bill overhauling congressional lobbying and ethics rules for members and their staffs and changing some Senate rules, thereby making good on a campaign promise to change what they called the "culture of corruption" on Capitol Hill under the Republican majority.

Democrats had symbolically given the measure the designation of S 1, to emphasize its political importance in winning the 2006 elections. The vote took place nineteen months after former lobbyist Jack Abramoff pleaded guilty to corruption charges that had ignited a call for improvements in the legislative process. *(Story, p. 830)*

The measure was designed primarily to give the public more information about the work of lobbyists and their political fundraising efforts, while limiting the ability of members and staff to move between congressional positions and Washington lobbying jobs. Embedded in it were some Senate rules changes, which meant it would need a two-thirds majority to break a filibuster.

The Senate originally passed the bill in January, but progress halted as Jim DeMint, R-S.C., blocked efforts by Senate majority leader Harry Reid, D-Nev., to set up a House-Senate conference. DeMint wanted guarantees that language he had written making it easier to identify and challenge member earmarks would be in the conference version of the bill. To circumvent DeMint's opposition, Reid and House Speaker Nancy Pelosi, D-Calif., decided in late July to use a different procedure to finish the package. They worked out a compromise version informally and then had the House call up and pass an amended version of the measure, which the Senate cleared Aug. 2 by agreeing to a motion to concur in the House amendment 83–14: R 34–14; D 47–0; I 2–0. A two-thirds majority vote of those present and voting (sixty-five in this case) was required to adopt a motion proposing a change in Senate rules. *(Vote, p. 959)*

5. FOREIGN SURVEILLANCE POLICY

With a vote on Aug. 3, 2007, senators sent a signal to House Democrats that they should join them in going along, at least temporarily, with a White House plan to fill gaps in the law governing terrorist surveillance and that they should try to address a broader bill later in the year. The vote also foreshadowed problems Democrats would have in coming up with a unified position on the issue. *(Story, p. 249)*

At issue was passage of a six-month bill (S 1927) to amend the Foreign Intelligence Surveillance Act of 1978 (FISA) to expand the authority of the U.S. attorney general and the director of national intelligence to conduct warrantless surveillance of foreign targets, whether or not the target was in communication with someone in the United States.

Senate Republicans introduced this bill Aug. 1—five days before the scheduled start of the summer recess—in response to intensifying pressure by the administration to quickly pass a change to the Foreign Intelligence Surveillance Act, PL 95-511. The White House and Director of National Intelligence Michael McConnell said they were limited under the 1978 law in their ability to monitor some suspect communications. They hinted at the potential for terrorism activity during the summer recess if Congress did not produce an immediate revision to the law.

Democrats spent days trying to negotiate changes to the plan being advanced by the White House, but in the end they were able to secure only the promise that it could be kept short-term, with an expiration date six months from enactment.

Sixteen Senate Democrats, and one independent who usually caucused with them, voted in favor of this Republican bill, mostly out of discontent over their own party leaders' attempt to come up with a viable solution to the problems with the FISA bill. Some Democrats voted for both the Republican bill and a measure (S 2011) sponsored by Carl Levin, D-Mich., the chairman of the Armed Services Committee, with the hope that one would reach a sixty-vote threshold. The Levin bill was defeated 43–45 just after the Senate had passed the GOP measure, which barely achieved the required majority of sixty votes that had been set by leaders.

Unable to pass their own FISA bill, House Democrats reluctantly agreed to take up and clear the Senate's bill. The temporary law was due to expire in February 2008. The Senate passed S 1927 on Aug. 3 by a vote of 60–28: R 43–0; D 16–27; I 1–1. By unanimous consent, the Senate agreed to raise the majority requirement for passage of the bill to sixty votes. *(Vote, p. 959)*

6. DISTRICT OF COLUMBIA REPRESENTATION

The District of Columbia once again lost a bid to have full voting representation in the House of Representatives when the Senate in September refused to invoke cloture on a bill (S 1257) to increase House membership to 437 by granting a seat to the District and an additional seat to Utah. *(Story, pp. 820, 836)*

The Senate's refusal to allow this bill to proceed, despite passage in the House, killed the measure for the year and for the rest of the 110th Congress. The one member who was absent for the vote, Democrat Robert C. Byrd of West Virginia, issued a statement opposing the measure because of constitutional concerns, which meant supporters were even further from success than the vote total suggested. The vote on cloture, on Sept. 18, was 57–42: R 8–41; D 47–1; I 2–0. Three-fifths of the total Senate (sixty) was required to invoke cloture. *(Vote, p. 959)*

7. HABEAS CORPUS FOR DETAINEES

An amendment to the fiscal 2008 defense authorization bill (HR 1585) to restore *habeas corpus* rights to enemy combatants under U.S. detention, as well as to those awaiting military reviews to determine their legal status, failed when the Senate in September refused to invoke cloture on a filibuster. *(Story, pp. 399, 400)*

By refusing to limit debate on the amendment, the Senate avoided having to vote on whether suspected terrorists held at Guantánamo Bay, Cuba, had the right to contest their incarceration in U.S. courts. The effect was to leave to the Supreme Court a determination of the legality of language in a 2006 law on military commissions (PL 109-366) that denied detainees such rights.

Under the 2006 law, no court could consider an application for a writ of *habeas corpus*—essentially a legal challenge to imprisonment—from any detainee who was regarded as an enemy combatant or who was awaiting such a determination. The amendment, offered by Arlen Specter of Pennsylvania, the ranking Republican on the Judiciary Committee, would have repealed that provision.

Supporters, including Specter and Judiciary chairman Patrick J. Leahy, D-Vt., claimed an increased number of senators for their side; Specter got forty-eight votes when he tried to keep the language out of the military detainee act in 2006. But the need to get sixty votes to invoke cloture still proved an insurmountable obstacle.

During its next term, the Supreme Court was to consider a case that questioned whether Congress exceeded its constitutional limits in denying the courts the right to hear petitions for *habeas corpus* from military detainees. *(Court decision, p. 730)*

The Senate's action rejecting cloture on Specter's amendment came on Sept. 19 by a vote of 56–43: R 6–42; D 49–0; I 1–1. Three-fifths of the total Senate (sixty) was required to invoke cloture. *(Vote, p. 959)*

8. TROOP DEPLOYMENT IN IRAQ

Attempts by Senate Democrats to put constraints on President George W. Bush's conduct of the war in Iraq repeatedly fell short of the sixty votes needed to overcome a filibuster. But after lawmakers returned from their August 2007 recess, opponents of the war thought they had a chance with an amendment to the annual defense authorization bill (HR 1585) sponsored by Virginia Democrat Jim Webb that was designed to be supportive of the troops and disruptive of the war effort. *(Story, pp. 303, 309)*

A former marine and a Navy secretary under President Ronald Reagan, Webb proposed requiring that active-duty troops be given as much time outside a war zone as they had in Iraq or Afghanistan. National Guard forces would get three years between deployments. Both supporters and critics of the proposal said it could reduce the number of troops available to fight in either country.

Webb had offered a similar amendment in July that was rejected, winning fifty-six of the needed sixty votes. However, the equation changed when South Dakota Democrat Tim Johnson returned to the chamber following an eight-month absence due to illness. In addition, several Republicans were considered potential supporters of the amendment in September to supplement the handful that had joined Webb before the recess. But supporters were disappointed when none of the potential additional GOP votes materialized and when Republican John W. Warner of Virginia—also a former Navy secretary—switched from supporting the amendment to opposing it.

Webb's amendment again won only fifty-six votes; its rejection was the high-water mark for Iraq War opponents in the Senate and their efforts to alter the administration's military policies. The Senate rejected Webb's amendment on Sept. 19 56–44: R 6–43; D 49–0; I 1–1. By unanimous consent, the Senate agreed to raise the majority requirement for adoption of the amendment to sixty votes. *(Vote, p. 959)*

9. WATER PROJECTS AUTHORIZATION

Overriding a presidential veto in Congress is difficult under most circumstances. One exception to that general rule came in 2007 when the legislators rejected President George W. Bush's Nov. 2 veto of a bill to authorize $23.2 billion for flood control, navigation, and environmental restoration projects and studies by the Army Corps of Engineers. *(Story, p. 500)*

The bill (HRS 1495) authorized more than 900 water-related projects. It demonstrated that, on both sides of the aisle, the politics of approving funds for home districts outweighed the politics of supporting the president. Supporters of the bill easily managed the two-thirds majority needed to pass it, and most of the "no" votes came from typically anti-earmark senators. The override vote came on Nov. 8, 2007, and easily surpassed the two-thirds majority needed, sixty-two in this case: 79–14: R 34–12; D 43–2; I 2–0. The Senate vote enacted the bill into law. *(Vote, p. 959)*

10. MUKASEY NOMINATION

By a relatively narrow vote of 53–40 the Senate Nov. 8, 2007, confirmed President George W. Bush's nomination of Michael Mukasey of New York to be U.S. attorney general. *(Story, pp. 680, 871)*

That vote put Mukasey, a former federal judge, at the helm of the Justice Department, replacing Alberto R. Gonzales. But the margin was the lowest level of support in a recorded vote for an attorney general nominee since 1952. Even Gonzales, whose relationship with the Senate was contentious from the start, received a slightly stronger endorsement when he was confirmed in 2005. Sixty senators backed Gonzales's confirmation; fifty-three voted for Mukasey.

Moreover, the Mukasey vote, with the support of only six Democrats, also foreshadowed a continuation of the skepticism that Gonzales faced from the Senate. Of the ten Democrats on the Judiciary Committee, eight voted against confirmation. The Nov. 8 vote was 53–40: R 46–0; D 6–39; I 1–1. *(Vote, p. 959)*

11. FARM ASSISTANCE REAUTHORIZATION

The Senate in late 2007 rejected an amendment to the vast farm bill that would have set lower limits than written in the legislation on the amount of government aid farms could receive. The defeat of this amendment, made easier because leaders required a higher threshold than a simple majority for its adoption, ended any effort to redraw the government's policy regarding subsidies to farmers, especially large corporate producers. *(Story, p. 514)*

The amendment sparked the most intense regional battle during debate over the Senate's farm bill, drawing stiff opposition from southern senators, who said it would wreak havoc on cotton and rice operations that relied heavily on subsidies to support the high cost of producing those crops. About a dozen members worked behind the scenes to build opposition to the amendment. Because Senate leaders set a sixty-vote requirement for the amendment to succeed, the opposition from the South was enough to keep supporters from reaching that target. Leaders delayed the vote so the members who were running for president could return to Washington for it. All but one, John McCain, R-Ariz., made it back, and they all voted for the amendment.

But it was not enough. Eleven Democrats joined thirty-one Republicans and Independent Joseph I. Lieberman of Connecticut in voting against it.

Amendment sponsor Byron L. Dorgan, D-N.D., decried the decision to set a sixty-vote majority: "We got fifty-six votes," Dorgan said. "That shows most members of the Senate want real subsidy reform." His amendment to HR 2419 was rejected on Dec. 13: 56–43: R 17–31; D 38–11; I 1–1. By unanimous consent, the Senate agreed to raise the majority requirement for adoption of the amendment to sixty votes. *(Vote, p. 959)*

12. ENERGY POLICY OVERHAUL

In another of many votes in 2007 requiring a supermajority for approval, the Senate in December refused—by one vote—to halt a filibuster on a bill (HR 6) to overhaul federal energy programs with an emphasis on fuel conservation that included a $21.8 billion package of tax incentives, offset in part by eliminating or reducing $13 billion in subsidies for major oil and gas companies. *(Story, p. 484)*

The issue of cutting subsidies for oil and gas companies had divided Republicans and Democrats all year, culminating in the especially close December vote, which favored the GOP's preferences. Despite persistent wooing and attempts at deal-making by bill writers, Republicans held firm and ensured that the president would not be sent an energy policy bill that contained a tax package he opposed.

After coming just short of success, 59–40, sponsors removed the tax package from the bill, which the Senate then passed 86–8 and the House soon cleared.

The first key vote on the energy tax package came in June, on a cloture motion on adding a $32.1 billion plan to the overall bill. The official tally was 57–36, as ten Republicans joined all Democrats, except Mary L. Landrieu of oil- and gas-rich Louisiana, in supporting cloture.

At one point during the summer, Finance chairman Max Baucus, D-Mont., said he had as many as sixty-four votes for another energy tax measure, but the bill did not come back to the floor until Dec. 7. That cloture vote failed 53–42. But that total was misleading, because the measure included a renewable-electricity standard opposed even by some Democrats, such as Robert C. Byrd of West Virginia.

In the Dec. 13 vote, the pressure was on Baucus and his supporters to find enough Republican support. They tried offering inducements, such as an expansion of the tax credit for energy-efficient residential heaters to include wood pellet stoves, aimed at Republicans John E. Sununu and Judd Gregg of New Hampshire, and John Thune of South Dakota.

Thune did vote for the measure, but Sununu and Gregg cast the votes that ensured that supporters would not get a majority of sixty. "That happened to be a provision that I supported," Sununu said of the wood-stove credit. "But something like that, you know, you've got to look at an entire piece of legislation, and I think getting something that's bipartisan, that can get signed into law this year, is extremely, extremely important." The Dec. 13 vote was 59–40: R 9–39; D 48–1; I 2–0. Three-fifths of the total Senate (sixty) is required to invoke cloture. *(Vote, p. 959)*

13. IRAQ WAR FUNDING

In a lopsided vote in December 2007, the Senate—including nearly all Republicans and many Democrats—flatly rejected the demand of a majority of House Democrats that Congress refuse to provide money to conduct military activities in Iraq. The decision involved an amendment to the fiscal 2008 omnibus spending bill that replaced $31 billion in funding for the war in Afghanistan with $70 billion to fund the war in Iraq as well as in Afghanistan. *(Story, pp. 303, 308)*

An unsuccessful, yearlong effort by the new congressional Democratic majority to bring the Iraq War to an end came down to the final days of the session. Democratic leaders knew they were unlikely to prevail, but they decided to force a vote. As part of an omnibus spending bill that financed all aspects of the federal government, except for routine activities of the Defense Department, the House voted to allocate $31 billion for military activities in Afghanistan and to bar use of that money in Iraq.

An overwhelming majority of the Senate refused to follow the House's lead and voted to substitute a $70 billion unrestricted appropriation for Iraq and Afghanistan. All but one Republican and twenty-one of forty-four Democrats who participated in the vote supported the substitute amendment. The Senate's action became the last word on Iraq funding for the calendar year because the House voted to go along the following day. But the $70 billion was barely a third of the amount sought by President George W. Bush for the Iraq and Afghanistan wars for fiscal 2008, which meant the issue would return in 2008.

The Senate rejection of the House's approach came on Dec. 18 on HR 2764, an omnibus appropriations bill, by a vote of 70–25: R 48–1; D 21–23; I 1–1. By unanimous consent, the Senate agreed to raise the majority requirement for the motion to concur to sixty votes. *(Vote, p. 959)*

1. **HR 2. Minimum Wage Increase Passage.** Passage of the bill to raise the minimum wage to $7.25 per hour over two years and provide $8.3 billion in small-business tax incentives, including extending the work opportunity tax credit for five years and the small-business expensing deduction through 2010. Passed 94–3: R 45–3; D 47–0; I 2–0. A "yea" was a vote in support of the president's position. Feb. 1, 2007.

2. **S 214. U.S. Attorney Appointments Passage.** Passage of the bill to repeal the authority of the U.S. attorney general to make indefinite interim appointments of U.S. attorneys and to reinstate a 120-day limit on the tenure of appointed attorneys. If the post remained vacant after that, the chief judge of the relevant federal district court would have the authority to appoint a temporary attorney until the vacancy was filled. Passed 94–2: R 46–2; D 46–0 ; I 2–0. March 20, 2007.

3. **S 1639. Immigration Overhaul Cloture.** Motion to invoke cloture (thus limiting debate) on the bill to overhaul U.S. immigration policies, provide for a temporary guest worker program, and institute new border security measures, including an electronic verification system. Motion rejected 46–53: R 12–37; D 33–15; I 1–1. Three-fifths of the total Senate (sixty) is required to invoke cloture. A "yea" was a vote in support of the president's position. June 28, 2007.

4. **S 1. Ethics and Lobbying Overhaul.** Reid, D-Nev., motion to concur in the House amendment to the bill to overhaul congressional lobbying and ethics rules for members and their staffs and require the disclosure of "bundled" campaign contributions that exceed $15,000 in a six-month period, require former senators to wait two years before becoming lobbyists, require quarterly disclosure reports on lobbying activities, and restrict members' and candidates' travel on private planes. Motion agreed to (thus clearing the bill for the president) 83–14: R 34–14; D 47–0; I 2–0. Aug. 2, 2007.

5. **S 1927. Foreign Intelligence Surveillance Revisions Passage.** Passage of the bill to amend the Foreign Intelligence Surveillance Act (FISA) of 1978 to expand the authority of the U.S. attorney general and the director of national intelligence to conduct surveillance of suspected foreign terrorists without a court warrant. The bill required the administration within 120 days of enactment to provide the FISA court with a description of the procedures used to determine whether the intelligence acquisition being conducted without a warrant was directed at foreign targets overseas. As amended, the legislation would expire after six months. Passed 60–28: R 43–0; D 16–27; I 1–1. (By unanimous consent, the Senate agreed to raise the majority requirement for passage of the bill to sixty votes.) A "yea" was a vote in support of the president's position. Aug. 3, 2007.

6. **S 1257. District of Columbia Voting Rights Cloture.** Motion to invoke cloture (thus limiting debate) on the Reid, D-Nev., motion to proceed to the bill to increase the membership of the House of Representatives to 437, by granting a seat to the District of Columbia and an additional seat to Utah. Motion rejected 57–42: R 8–41; D 47–1; I 2–0. Three-fifths of the total Senate (sixty) was required to invoke cloture. A "nay" was a vote in support of the president's position. Sept. 18, 2007.

7. **HR 1585. Fiscal 2008 Defense Authorization Cloture.** Motion to invoke cloture (thus limiting debate) on the Specter, R-Pa., amendment to the Levin, D-Mich., substitute. The Specter amendment would restore *habeas corpus* rights to enemy combatants under U.S. detention, as well as to those awaiting military reviews to determine their legal status. Motion rejected 56–43: R 6–42; D 49–0; I 1–1. Three-fifths of the total Senate (sixty) was required to invoke cloture. A "nay" was a vote in support of the president's position. Sept. 19, 2007.

8. **HR 1585. Fiscal 2008 Defense Authorization Troop Deployments.** Webb, D-Va., amendment to require active-duty forces to be guaranteed as much time at home as they served while deployed. National Guard and reservists would be guaranteed three years at home between deployments. Rejected 56–44: R 6–43; D 49–0; I 1–1. (By unanimous consent, the Senate agreed to raise the majority requirement for adoption of the amendment to sixty votes.) A "nay" was a vote in support of the president's position. Sept. 19, 2007.

9. **HR 1495. Water Resources Development Veto Override.** Passage, over President George W. Bush's Nov. 2, 2007, veto, of the bill to authorize $23.2 billion for more than 900 water resource development projects and studies by the Army Corps of Engineers for flood control, navigation, beach erosion control, and environmental restoration. Passed (thus enacted into law) 79–14: R 34–12; D 43–2; I 2–0. A two-thirds majority of those present and voting (sixty-two for the Senate) of both chambers was required to override a veto. A "nay" was a vote in support of the president's position. Nov. 8, 2007.

10. **Mukasey Confirmation as Attorney General.** Confirmation of President George W. Bush's nomination of Michael Mukasey of New York to be U.S. attorney general. Confirmed 53–40: R 46–0; D 6–39; I 1–1. A "yea" was a vote in support of the president's position. Nov. 8, 2007.

11. **HR 2419. Farm Bill Reauthorization Commodity Payments.** Dorgan, D-N.D., amendment to cap annual farm payments that any one individual or entity may receive at $250,000 per year, and to limit the amount that farms could receive during any crop year under specific programs to $40,000 for direct and fixed payments, $60,000 for countercyclical and average crop revenue payments, and $150,000 for marketing loan gains and loan deficiency payments. Rejected 56–43: R 17–31; D 38–11; I 1–1. (By unanimous consent, the Senate agreed to raise the majority requirement for adoption to sixty votes. The Dorgan amendment was later withdrawn.) Dec. 13, 2007.

12. **HR 6. Energy Policy Cloture.** Motion to invoke cloture (thus limiting debate) on the Reid, D-Nev., motion to concur in the House amendment to the Senate amendment with an additional amendment to the bill to require new Corporate Average Fuel Economy standards of 35 miles per gallon for cars and light trucks, and require the production and use of 36 billion gallons of biofuels by 2022. It directed the Energy Department to set new energy efficiency standards. The additional amendment increased to $21.8 billion a package of tax incentives that would be offset in part by eliminating or reducing $13 billion in subsidies for major oil and gas companies. Motion rejected 59–40: R 9–39; D 48–1; I 2–0. Three-fifths of the total Senate (sixty) is required to invoke cloture. Dec. 13, 2007.

13. **HR 2764. Fiscal 2008 Omnibus Appropriations.** McConnell, R-Ky., motion to concur in the House amendment to the Senate amendment to the bill with an amendment that would replace the $31 billion in funding for the war in Afghanistan, as approved in the House version, with $70 billion that the Defense Department could use to conduct the wars in Afghanistan and Iraq without restrictions. Motion agreed to 70–25: R 48–1; D 21–23; I 1–1. (By unanimous consent, the Senate agreed to raise the majority requirement for the motion to concur to sixty votes.) Dec. 18, 2007.

KEY

Democrat | *Republican* | **Independent**

Y	Voted for (yea)	–	Announced against
#	Paired for	P	Voted "present"
+	Announced for	C	Voted "present" to avoid possible conflict of interest
N	Voted against (nay)	?	Did not vote or otherwise make a position known
X	Paired against		

Senate Key Votes	1	2	3	4	5	6	7	8	9	10	11	12	13
ALABAMA													
Shelby	Y	Y	N	Y	Y	N	N	N	Y	Y	N	N	Y
Sessions	Y	Y	N	Y	Y	N	N	N	N	Y	N	N	Y
ALASKA													
Stevens	Y	Y	N	Y	Y	N	N	N	Y	Y	Y	N	Y
Murkowski	Y	Y	N	Y	Y	N	N	N	Y	Y	Y	Y	Y
ARIZONA													
McCain	Y	?	Y	N	?	N	N	N	?	?	?	?	Y
Kyl	N	Y	Y	N	Y	N	N	N	N	Y	N	N	Y
ARKANSAS													
Lincoln	Y	Y	Y	Y	Y	Y	Y	Y	Y	N	N	Y	Y
Pryor	Y	Y	N	Y	Y	Y	Y	Y	Y	N	N	Y	Y
CALIFORNIA													
Feinstein	Y	Y	Y	Y	Y	Y	Y	Y	Y	Y	Y	Y	?
Boxer	Y	Y	Y	Y	?	Y	Y	Y	Y	N	Y	Y	N
COLORADO													
Allard	Y	Y	N	Y	Y	N	N	N	N	Y	Y	N	Y
Salazar	Y	Y	Y	Y	Y	Y	Y	Y	Y	N	N	Y	Y
CONNECTICUT													
Dodd	Y	Y	Y	Y	N	Y	Y	Y	?	?	Y	Y	?
Lieberman	Y	Y	Y	Y	Y	Y	N	N	Y	Y	N	Y	Y
DELAWARE													
Biden	Y	?	Y	Y	N	Y	Y	Y	?	–	Y	Y	?
Carper	Y	Y	Y	Y	Y	Y	Y	Y	Y	Y	Y	Y	Y
FLORIDA													
Nelson	Y	Y	Y	Y	Y	Y	Y	Y	Y	N	Y	Y	Y
Martinez	Y	Y	Y	Y	Y	N	N	N	Y	Y	N	N	Y
GEORGIA													
Chambliss	Y	Y	N	Y	Y	N	?	N	Y	Y	N	N	Y
Isakson	Y	Y	N	Y	Y	N	N	N	Y	Y	N	N	Y
HAWAII													
Inouye	Y	Y	Y	Y	Y	Y	Y	Y	Y	N	N	Y	Y
Akaka	Y	Y	Y	Y	N	Y	Y	Y	Y	N	Y	Y	Y
IDAHO													
Craig	Y	Y	Y	N	Y	N	N	N	Y	Y	N	N	Y
Crapo	Y	Y	N	N	Y	N	N	N	Y	Y	N	N	Y
ILLINOIS													
Durbin	Y	Y	Y	Y	N	Y	Y	Y	Y	N	Y	Y	N
Obama	Y	Y	Y	Y	N	Y	Y	Y	?	?	Y	Y	?
INDIANA													
Lugar	Y	Y	Y	Y	?	Y	Y	N	Y	Y	Y	Y	Y
Bayh	Y	Y	N	Y	Y	Y	Y	Y	Y	Y	Y	Y	Y
IOWA													
Grassley	Y	Y	N	Y	Y	N	N	N	Y	Y	Y	Y	Y
Harkin	Y	Y	N	Y	–	Y	Y	Y	Y	N	Y	Y	N
KANSAS													
Brownback	Y	Y	N	Y	Y	N	N	N	N	Y	Y	N	Y
Roberts	Y	Y	N	Y	Y	N	N	N	Y	Y	N	N	Y
KENTUCKY													
McConnell	Y	Y	N	Y	Y	N	N	N	N	Y	N	N	Y
Bunning	Y	Y	N	Y	+	N	N	N	+	Y	N	N	Y

Senate Key Votes	1	2	3	4	5	6	7	8	9	10	11	12	13
LOUISIANA													
Landrieu	Y	Y	N	Y	Y	Y	Y	Y	Y	Y	N	N	Y
Vitter	Y	Y	N	Y	Y	N	N	N	Y	Y	N	N	Y
MAINE													
Snowe	Y	Y	Y	Y	Y	Y	Y	Y	Y	Y	N	Y	Y
Collins	Y	Y	N	Y	Y	Y	N	Y	Y	Y	Y	Y	Y
MARYLAND													
Mikulski	Y	+	Y	Y	Y	Y	Y	Y	Y	N	Y	Y	Y
Cardin	Y	Y	Y	Y	N	Y	Y	Y	Y	N	Y	Y	N
MASSACHUSETTS													
Kennedy	Y	Y	Y	Y	N	Y	Y	Y	Y	N	Y	Y	N
Kerry	Y	Y	Y	Y	?	Y	Y	Y	Y	N	Y	Y	N
MICHIGAN													
Levin	Y	Y	Y	Y	N	Y	Y	Y	Y	N	Y	Y	Y
Stabenow	Y	Y	N	Y	N	Y	Y	Y	Y	N	N	Y	N
MINNESOTA													
Coleman	Y	Y	N	+	Y	Y	N	Y	Y	Y	N	Y	Y
Klobuchar	Y	Y	Y	+	Y	Y	Y	Y	Y	N	Y	Y	N
MISSISSIPPI													
Cochran	Y	Y	N	N	Y	N	N	N	Y	Y	N	N	Y
Lott	Y	Y	Y	N	?	N	N	N	Y	Y	N	N	Y
MISSOURI													
Bond	Y	N	N	Y	Y	N	N	N	Y	Y	N	N	Y
McCaskill	Y	Y	N	Y	Y	Y	Y	Y	N	N	N	Y	Y
MONTANA													
Baucus	Y	Y	N	Y	N	N	Y	Y	Y	N	N	Y	Y
Tester	Y	Y	N	Y	N	Y	Y	Y	Y	N	Y	Y	Y
NEBRASKA													
Hagel	Y	N	Y	Y	Y	N	Y	Y	Y	Y	Y	N	Y
Nelson	Y	Y	N	Y	Y	Y	Y	Y	Y	Y	Y	Y	Y
NEVADA													
Reid	Y	Y	Y	Y	N	Y	Y	Y	Y	N	Y	Y	N
Ensign	Y	Y	N	N	Y	N	N	N	N	Y	Y	N	Y
NEW HAMPSHIRE													
Gregg	Y	Y	Y	Y	?	N	N	N	N	Y	N	N	Y
Sununu	Y	Y	N	Y	Y	N	Y	Y	N	Y	Y	N	Y
NEW JERSEY													
Lautenberg	Y	Y	Y	Y	N	Y	Y	Y	Y	N	Y	Y	N
Menendez	Y	Y	Y	Y	N	Y	Y	Y	Y	N	Y	Y	N
NEW MEXICO													
Domenici	Y	Y	N	Y	Y	N	N	N	Y	Y	N	N	Y
Bingaman	Y	Y	N	Y	N	Y	Y	Y	Y	N	Y	Y	N
NEW YORK													
Schumer	?	Y	Y	Y	N	Y	Y	Y	Y	Y	Y	Y	N
Clinton	Y	Y	Y	Y	N	Y	Y	Y	?	?	Y	Y	?
NORTH CAROLINA													
Dole	Y	Y	N	Y	Y	N	N	N	Y	Y	N	N	Y
Burr	Y	Y	N	N	Y	N	N	N	N	Y	N	N	Y
NORTH DAKOTA													
Conrad	Y	Y	Y	Y	Y	Y	Y	Y	Y	N	N	Y	Y
Dorgan	Y	Y	N	Y	?	Y	Y	Y	Y	N	Y	Y	Y
OHIO													
Voinovich	Y	Y	N	Y	Y	Y	N	N	Y	Y	N	N	Y
Brown	Y	Y	N	Y	N	Y	Y	Y	Y	N	Y	Y	N
OKLAHOMA													
Inhofe	–	Y	N	N	Y	N	N	N	Y	Y	N	N	Y
Coburn	N	Y	N	N	Y	N	N	N	N	Y	N	N	Y
OREGON													
Wyden	Y	Y	Y	Y	N	Y	Y	Y	Y	N	Y	Y	N
Smith	Y	Y	N	Y	Y	N	Y	Y	Y	Y	Y	Y	N
PENNSYLVANIA													
Specter	Y	Y	Y	Y	Y	Y	Y	N	Y	Y	Y	N	Y
Casey	Y	Y	Y	Y	Y	Y	Y	Y	Y	N	Y	Y	Y
RHODE ISLAND													
Reed	Y	Y	Y	Y	N	Y	Y	Y	Y	N	Y	Y	N
Whitehouse	Y	Y	Y	Y	N	Y	Y	Y	Y	N	Y	Y	N

Senate Key Votes	1	2	3	4	5	6	7	8	9	10	11	12	13
SOUTH CAROLINA													
Graham	Y	Y	Y	N	Y	N	N	N	Y	Y	N	N	Y
DeMint	N	Y	N	N	Y	N	N	N	N	Y	N	N	Y
SOUTHDAKOTA													
Johnson	?	?	?	?	?	Y	Y	Y	Y	N	Y	Y	Y
Thune	Y	Y	N	Y	Y	N	N	N	Y	Y	Y	Y	Y
TENNESSEE													
Alexander	Y	Y	N	Y	+	N	N	N	Y	+	N	N	Y
Corker	Y	Y	N	Y	Y	N	N	N	Y	Y	N	N	Y
TEXAS													
Hutchison	Y	Y	N	Y	Y	N	N	N	Y	Y	N	N	Y
Cornyn	Y	Y	N	N	Y	N	N	N	+	+	N	N	Y
UTAH													
Hatch	Y	Y	N	Y	Y	Y	N	N	Y	Y	Y	Y	Y
Bennett	Y	Y	Y	N	Y	Y	N	N	Y	Y	N	N	Y
VERMONT													
Leahy	Y	Y	Y	Y	N	Y	Y	Y	Y	N	N	Y	N
Sanders	Y	Y	N	Y	N	Y	Y	Y	Y	N	Y	Y	N
VIRGINIA													
Warner	Y	Y	N	Y	Y	N	N	N	Y	Y	Y	N	Y
Webb	Y	Y	N	Y	Y	Y	Y	Y	Y	N	Y	Y	Y
WASHINGTON													
Murray	Y	Y	Y	Y	?	Y	Y	Y	Y	N	Y	Y	N
Cantwell	Y	Y	Y	Y	N	Y	Y	Y	Y	N	Y	Y	N
WEST VIRGINIA													
Byrd	Y	Y	N	Y	N	?	Y	Y	Y	N	Y	Y	N
Rockefeller	Y	Y	N	Y	N	Y	Y	Y	Y	N	N	Y	Y
WISCONSIN													
Kohl	Y	Y	Y	Y	N	Y	Y	Y	Y	N	Y	Y	N
Feingold	Y	Y	Y	Y	N	Y	Y	Y	N	N	Y	Y	N
WYOMING													
Enzi	Y	Y	N	Y	Y	N	N	N	N	Y	Y	N	Y
Thomas[1]	Y	Y											
Barrasso[1]			N	Y	Y	N	N	N	Y	Y	Y	N	Y

[1]Sen. John A. Barrasso, R-Wyo., was sworn in June 25, 2007, to replace Republican Craig Thomas, who died June 4.

House

1. BUDGET PROCESS RULES CHANGES

As one of its first pieces of business in the new year, the House approved pay-as-you-go rules requiring offsets to any new entitlement spending or tax cuts, and requiring legislation and conference reports to be accompanied by a list of earmarks and targeted tax or trade benefits and their sponsors. *(Story, p. 118)*

The vote, by a substantial margin and including considerable Republican support, was held on the second day of the 110th Congress. The action represented the new Democratic majority's intent to distinguish itself from Republican predecessors by promoting fiscal discipline and responsibility. It set in motion House rules that dictated much of the legislative process throughout the year. Because of the pay-as-you-go provisions, writers of legislation on issues such as energy policy, farm subsidies, and federal student loans were forced to add revenue-raising offsets, often in the form of targeted tax increases, to their bills.

However, when it came to efforts to block an expansion of the alternative minimum tax (AMT), which threatened to reach an additional 21 million middle-class taxpayers, House Democrats acceded to political reality, abandoning their pay-as-you-go principle and accepting an AMT "patch," with its addition of $50 billion to the budget deficit.

The new rules on earmarks added an unprecedented level of transparency to the appropriations process—and to the workloads of appropriators and their staffs—but in the end had little effect on the amount of money specified for special projects. The House vote on the requirement (H Res 6) on Jan. 5 was 280–152: R 48–152; D 232–0. *(Vote, p. 966)*

2. MINIMUM WAGE INCREASE

The House, newly under Democratic control at the beginning of the 110th Congress in 2007, moved swiftly to pass a signature goal of the party: an increase in the minimum wage by $2.10 an hour over two years, from $5.15 an hour to $7.25. *(Story, p. 664)*

This was the first House vote on a "clean" minimum wage bill—one that addressed only that issue—since the last time the hourly wage was increased in 1996. Passing a minimum wage increase was one of the Democrats' campaign promises, and leaders included the vote in their "first 100 hours agenda." To quickly pass their priority bills at the opening of the 110th Congress, Democrats barred amendments. Even so, eighty-two Republicans joined in support of this bill.

In the end, though, Senate Democrats added a large package of tax incentives to the bill to gain enough Republican support in that chamber. That stalled the legislation until spring, when it was enacted as part of an emergency war spending bill, although that bill was vetoed. *(See next key vote on war appropriations.)*

The House passed HR 2 on Jan. 10 by a vote of 315–116: R 82–116; D 233–0. *(Vote, p. 966)*

3. WAR APPROPRIATIONS AND TROOP WITHDRAWAL

The House in April 2007 adopted the conference report on a bill to provide $124.2 billion in fiscal 2007 emergency funding for military operations as well as set a goal for redeployment of most U.S. combat troops in Iraq by the end of March 2008 if the president could certify that the Iraq government was meeting benchmarks and by the end of 2007 if he could not. *(Story, pp. 303, 308)*

The vote showed clearly that House Democrats would not be able to override any veto of legislation that included language dictating a change in Iraq War policy. The conference report on the supplemental bill was the result of negotiation with Senate leaders who knew they would be unable to get enough Republican support to clear a tougher version passed by the House. As a result, under the conference report the bill contained a nonbinding "goal" for troop redeployment—softer language than the binding targets for withdrawal in the original House measure. Conferees also added to the bill a $2.10 increase in the hourly minimum wage that had been approved separately. *(House key vote 2 and Senate key vote 1)*

Nonetheless, leaders gained no support among Republicans, with Wayne T. Gilchrest of Maryland and Walter B. Jones of North Carolina—both of whom voted for the original bill—as the only two GOP "yes" votes. Only one Democrat moved from the "no" column to "yes" on the conference report. That was Diane Watson of California, a liberal from Los Angeles, who said she cast the vote in honor of her friend Rep. Juanita Millender-McDonald, D-Calif., who had died of cancer the previous weekend. Millender-McDonald "would have cast her vote yes," Watson said.

It was Watson's vote that gave the Democrats the 218 needed to guarantee adoption of the conference report, but an insurmountable gap still remained between that tally and the 284 that was needed to override the veto when that vote was taken May 2. On the override vote, Democratic leaders gained the support of seven antiwar liberals from their party, but Gilchrest and Jones continued to be the only GOP "yes" votes. By the end of the year, the most votes the Democrats had mustered in favor of legislation to change Iraq War policy was 223, on a stand-alone bill (HR 2956) that passed July 12. The House vote on the conference report on HR 1591 on April 25 was 218–208: R 2–195; D 216–13. *(Vote, p. 966)*

4. FAITH-BASED HIRING IN HEAD START

An effort by House Republicans to add faith-based language to a Head Start reauthorization bill failed in May 2007 in the face of nearly unanimous Democratic opposition. The central element of the GOP proposal was language to permit faith-based providers to take religion into account when hiring. *(Story, p. 586)*

This vote against the GOP move not only paved the way for the first reauthorization of Head Start since 1998, it also demonstrated that the new Democratic majority would not allow social conservatism to dictate their approach to legislation.

In the 108th and 109th Congresses, Republican bills to reauthorize Head Start contained provisions to allow faith-based providers of the early-childhood program to take religion into account when hiring workers. But strong Democratic opposition to that plan, on the grounds that it was discriminatory, stalled the legislation. With Democrats in the majority in the Congress, bill writers produced an authorization measure that did not include such language. Luis Fortuño, Puerto Rico's Republican resident commissioner, wanted to offer an amendment to add a faith-based hiring provision, but Democrats wrote a rule for debate that did not allow it. As a result, Republicans instead called for a motion to recommit the bill to the Education and Labor Committee with instructions to add the language, a procedural device that sometimes worked for the minority in lieu of amendments. But the House rejected it, and the issue, for the first time in five years, was put to rest. The key vote on May 2 rejecting the recommittal was 195–222: R 191–2; D 4–220. *(Vote, p. 966)*

5. 2008 BUDGET RESOLUTION

For the first time since 1994, Democrats in May 2007 were able to put their party's mark on spending levels. That came through adoption of a conference report on a fiscal 2008 budget resolution that allowed up to $954.1 billion in discretionary spending for fiscal 2008, plus $145.2 billion in emergency spending for defense operations in Iraq and Afghanistan. It called for $21.3 billion more in spending than President George W. Bush had requested. By voting to accept this level, House Democrats (no Republicans voted for the conference report) also voted to start a budgetary tug-of-war with the White House that continued for the rest of the year. At the same time, the discretionary cap agreed to by House and Senate negotiators was slightly smaller than in the original House budget resolution, signaling some realization among Democrats that they would need to be cautious when it came to spending. The House adopted the conference report on S Con Res 21 on May 17, 214–209: R 0–196; D 214–13. *(Story, p. 108; Vote, p. 966)*

6. MEXICO CITY POLICY ON ABORTION

The House in June 2007 rejected an amendment to eliminate from the fiscal 2008 State-foreign operations appropriations bill a provision to modify the 1984 "Mexico City" policy on abortion by allowing the United States to provide contraceptives, but no monetary assistance, for family planning groups to distribute in developing countries. *(Story, p. 314)*

The House Appropriations Subcommittee on State and Foreign Operations had added the provision, sponsored by Nita M. Lowey, D-N.Y., during its markup of the bill, but by the time the bill reached the floor, abortion opponents had stirred up strong opposition to it. The Mexico City policy—created by President Ronald Reagan, rescinded by President Bill Clinton, and reinstituted by President George W. Bush—barred the federal government from providing funds to international family planning groups that performed or promoted abortion. Antiabortion groups protested that the Lowey language would violate the policy by aiding these organizations; Lowey and Democratic leaders insisted that it would provide only contraceptives, such as condoms, but no financial aid.

Some of those concerned about the language were antiabortion Democrats, such as Jim Langevin of Rhode Island and Henry Cuellar of Texas. To mollify those party members and ensure that the provision stayed in the bill, Lowey offered an amendment to clarify that the provision would not provide funds to family planning groups normally barred from receiving money under the Mexico City policy. Her amendment was adopted 223–201 with twenty-four Democrats voting against it. A number of undecided Democrats backed the amendment, including Langevin and Cuellar.

Adoption of the Lowey amendment made it more palatable for conservative Democrats to vote against an amendment by Christopher H. Smith, R-N.J., and Bart Stupak, D-Mich., to strike the subcommittee language from the bill. The tally on the Smith-Stupak amendment was 205–218—a mirror of the previous vote.

Not since Bush became president in 2001 had Democrats had a chance to address the issue of aiding international family planning groups, and the ability to send a message of change was important to House leaders.

However, the vote also showed how careful the new Democratic leadership, with an eye toward retaining its majority in 2008, wanted to be in handling the broad issue of abortion. The Lowey amendment opened the door ever so slightly to reducing the impact of the twenty-four-year-old Mexico City policy, but it did not come close to reversing it, as some members preferred and as the Senate did in its legislation.

In the end, with a veto threat hanging over the provision, appropriators decided to drop any reference to changing abortion policy when they cleared the State–foreign operations measure as part of an omnibus spending package. The key vote to reject the Smith amendment to HR 2764 came on June 21, 205–218: R 180–12; D 25–206. *(Vote, p. 966)*

7. FOREIGN SURVEILLANCE POLICY

A House vote in August 2007 to clear of a six-month bill amending the Foreign Intelligence Surveillance Act (FISA) of 1978 showed the limits Democrats faced in trying to fight President George W. Bush on issues of national security. The legislation expanded the authority of the attorney general and the director of national intelligence to conduct warrantless surveillance of foreign targets, whether or not the target was communicating with someone in the United States. *(Story, p. 249)*

Just a few days before the House and Senate were scheduled to recess for the August break, President Bush, Attorney General Alberto R. Gonzales, and Director of National Intelligence Michael McConnell suddenly altered their demand for an expansion of the executive branch's authority to eavesdrop without a warrant on foreign targets, whether or not the target was communicating with someone in the United States. They said the change was necessary to prevent a possibly imminent terrorist attack from occurring. During discussion of the bill, House minority leader John A. Boehner, R-Ohio, revealed in July that a FISA court ruling had limited the government's ability to spy on foreign-to-foreign communications that were routed through the United States.

In response to the president's urgent call for action, House Democrats tried to pass a narrower expansion of the White House's powers of surveillance. That bill did not pass, and with their legislative time dwindling and the pressure from Bush intensifying, Democrats reluctantly agreed to give the president the changes he had sought. The key vote on the bill, S 1926, on Aug. 4 was 227–183: R 186–2; D 41–181. *(Vote, p. 966)*

8. CHILDREN'S HEALTH INSURANCE

The House failed in October 2007 to override President George W. Bush's veto of a bill to reauthorize the State Children's Health Insurance Program (CHIP) at nearly $60 billion over five years, expanding the program by $35 billion. To offset the cost of the expansion, the legislation (HR 976) increased the tax on cigarettes by 61 cents, to $1 per pack, and raised taxes on other tobacco products. *(Story, pp. 558, 561)*

This vote showed that Democrats would not be able to enact such an expansion of CHIP under President Bush. The House passed the bill Sept. 25 with the support of 265 members, but Democrats were never able to persuade enough Republicans to join them to reach the number necessary to override Bush's veto. By the end of the year, Democrats had given up on expanding the program and instead passed an extension of CHIP, with enough money to maintain only current enrollment. The extension was set to expire at the end of March 2009, two months after the next president was inaugurated. The key vote to override, which failed, came on Oct. 18: 273–156: R 44–154; D 229–2. A two-thirds majority of those present and voting (286 in this case) of both chambers was required to override a veto. *(Vote, p. 966)*

9. WATER PROJECTS AUTHORIZATION

In contrast to the failed veto override of the children's health bill *(see key vote 8)* the House had no qualms about rejecting President George W. Bush's veto of a bill to authorize $23.2 billion for more than 900 flood control, navigation, and environmental restoration projects and studies by the Army Corps of Engineers. *(Story, p. 500)*

The vote to pass a measure authorizing billions of dollars for home-state water projects over Bush's veto showed the power of federal spending to House members of both parties. It was the first successful veto override of Bush's presidency to that time. Bush objected that the measure was fiscally irresponsible and overly broad in scope, but with large majorities in both parties agreeing to override, the vote served as proof that local concerns outweighed GOP efforts to remain loyal to the president and Democratic concerns over budget policy. The vote came on Nov. 6, 361–54: R 138–54; D 223–0. A two-thirds majority of those present and voting (277 in this case) was required to override a veto. *(Vote, p. 966)*

10. JOB DISCRIMINATION POLICY

Despite Republican opposition, the House in November 2007 easily passed a bill (HR 3685) to prohibit job discrimination on the basis of an individual's actual or perceived sexual orientation. In approving the legislation, House Democrats agreed to expand the reach of federal civil rights protections to include homosexuality, heterosexuality, and bisexuality. *(Story, p. 670)*

GOP members objected to the bill as unnecessary and too broad, but the measure had the support of a widespread coalition of business interests, many of which were already implementing similar protections in their workplaces. At the same time, the vote demonstrated that Democratic leaders were reluctant to take a traditionally liberal issue too far.

With Republicans ready to pounce on the issue in floor debate, leaders gave Tammy Baldwin, D-Wis., the option of dropping her amendment to add members of the transgender community to the list of protected individuals. That move drew the rage of the gay and lesbian community, but leaders—including openly gay Democrat Barney Frank of Massachusetts—worried that those opposed to the underlying legislation could use the transgender issue as "a weapon to defeat the whole bill." Baldwin opted to withdraw the amendment, losing the votes of some Democrats who insisted that the bill cover all aspects of sexual orientation but ensuring passage of the legislation itself. The Senate did not take up the bill. The House vote on passage on Nov. 7 was 235–184: R 35–159; D 200–25. *(Vote, p. 966)*

11. PERU FREE-TRADE AGREEMENT

Both parties came together in 2007 to easily pass a bill to implement a free-trade agreement (HR 3688) between the United States and Peru that was designed to reduce most tariffs on trade between the two countries and require Peru to strengthen its labor and environmental protection standards. *(Story, p. 209)*

Soon after Democrats took control of the 110th Congress, Charles B. Rangel of New York and other House leaders told the Bush administration they would consider several pending trade agreements only if the administration required significant new labor and environmental protections as integral elements of the accords. The White House agreed and heralded a new era of bipartisan cooperation on trade.

The Peru accord was one of four negotiated during 2007 under so-called fast-track rules, which required expedited consideration of the agreements in Congress. Those rules expired June 30. House passage of the implementing legislation was evidence that the administration's position was widely acceptable, at least in this one case. Among Democrats, 109 out of 225 voted to pass the implementing bill. The vote Nov. 8 was 285–132: R 176–16; D 109–116. *(Vote, p. 966)*

12. MORTGAGE INDUSTRY OVERHAUL

Without a dissenting vote, Democrats pushed through legislation in November 2007 to rewrite the nation's mortgage lending laws by bringing mortgage brokers under a nationwide licensing registry, establishing minimum standards for home loans, and prohibiting brokers from steering consumers into mortgages they were unlikely to be able to repay. They were joined by sixty-four Republicans to easily pass the bill, HR 3915, 291–127: R 64–127; D 227–0. *(Story, p. 640; Vote, p. 966)*

With this vote, House Democrats took the first major legislative step in response to the crisis in the subprime mortgage market that devastated the housing industry and the economy in 2007.

13. FISCAL 2008 LABOR-HHS-EDUCATION APPROPRIATIONS

Barely a week after overriding President George W. Bush's veto of a water projects bill (see key vote 9) the House was unable to muster the two-thirds margin needed to reverse the president's rejection of legislation to appropriate $150.7 billion in fiscal 2008 for the departments of Labor, Health and Human Services, and Education, as well as related agencies. The vote came on Nov. 15. *(Story, pp. 112, 114)*

Although the attempt to override the president's veto was only two votes short of the needed two-thirds majority, it had become clear that the Democrats could not win their battle with Bush over adding $21.3 billion to his requested limit of $932.8 billion in discretionary appropriations for fiscal 2008. After this vote, some discussion of a compromise with the White House ensued, but in the end House Democrats conceded defeat and gave the president the bottom line he had sought from the beginning.

The key vote was 277–141: R 51–141; D 226–0. A two-thirds majority of those present and voting (279 in this case) was required to override a veto. *(Vote, p. 966)*

14. ENERGY POLICY OVERHAUL

Late in the session, on Dec. 18, the House cleared a bill that overhauled federal energy programs with an emphasis on fuel conservation. It required new Corporate Average Fuel Economy (CAFE) standards of 35 miles per gallon for cars and light trucks by 2020 and required that 36 billion gallons of biofuels be used in the United States by 2022. *(Story, p. 484)*

This vote culminated an arduous year-long battle by sending to President George W. Bush the first statutory increase in CAFE standards in thirty-two years. The key vote was 314–100: R 95–96; D 219–4. *(Vote, p. 967)*

15. ALTERNATIVE MINIMUM TAX ADJUSTMENT

House Democrats in December 2007 reluctantly accepted a reality they had been trying to avoid all year: the only way to prevent the alternative minimum tax (AMT) from hitting millions of additional middle-income taxpayers was to abandon the pay-as-you-go budget rules they adopted at the beginning of the year. To do so the chamber cleared legislation (HR 3996) to provide a one-year adjustment to exempt an additional 21 million taxpayers from paying the ATM on income from 2007. *(Story, pp. 91, 118)*

At the same time, they accepted the narrowest of tax measures possible, acknowledging that they would have to put off a broad overhaul of the AMT, as well as the extension of billions of dollars in popular tax breaks for businesses and individuals that expired on Dec. 31.

But by clearing the Senate's version of a one-year fix, lawmakers were able to go back to their districts and boast that they prevented some millions of constituents from paying higher taxes on their 2007 incomes. Many of those likely to have been hit lived in Democratic-leaning states such as New York, California, and Massachusetts.

Even so, the vote was politically and ideologically painful for many Democrats. Throughout the year, on issues from energy policy to farm programs, they had worked diligently to find offsets for new spending. But this time the amount—about $50 billion—was too large, and resistance in the Senate was too great, and House Democrats had to walk away from that fight.

The vote was especially difficult for members of the fiscally conservative Blue Dog Coalition, who had made pay-as-you-go budget rules a top priority. They were pitted against representatives from high-tax states, who were hard-pressed to vote against the patch. It also was a tough vote for members of the Democratic leadership team, most of whom voted against the bill.

The House voted Dec. 19 to clear HR 3996 by agreeing to accept the Senate's version of the legislation 352–64: R 195–0; D 157–64. The bill was considered under suspension of the rules, which required a two-thirds majority of those present and voting (278 in this case) for passage. *(Vote, p. 967)*

16. FISCAL 2008 OMNIBUS SPENDING BILL

As its last major act of 2007 the House Dec. 19 cleared an omnibus appropriations bill for fiscal 2008 bill that provided $473.5 billion in discretionary spending, not counting emergency appropriations, for all federal departments and agencies for which regular spending bills had not been enacted. The measure incorporated eleven appropriations bills: agriculture; Commerce-Justice-science; energy-water; financial services; Homeland Security; Interior-environment; labor-HHS-Education; the legislative branch; military construction-VA; State–foreign operations; and Transportation-HUD. The bill also contained $11.2 billion in emergency funding for veterans programs, border security, nutrition aid, and drought relief, and $70 billion for military operations in Afghanistan and Iraq. *(Story, pp. 111, 112, 314)*

The vote sent to President George W. Bush the omnibus spending measure that financed all aspects of the federal government, except for routine activities of the Defense Department. The $70 billion for military operations in Iraq and Afghanistan was just a portion of the almost $200 billion the president wanted in war funding, but was still far more than House Democrats wanted to allocate. A previous House-passed version of the omnibus had included $31 billion only for operations in Afghanistan, and barred use of that money in Iraq.

The Senate—Republicans in particular—balked at the House approach, however, and voted 70–25 on Dec. 18 to replace the $31 billion appropriation with $70 billion that was designated without restriction for Iraq and Afghanistan. That put House Democrats in the untenable position of insisting on their approach—risking ending the session without providing full-year appropriations for most federal activities and limiting their ability to influence spending priorities for nondefense programs—or allowing the Senate, House Republicans, and the president to prevail. In the final roll call of the year, the House cleared the bill as amended by the Senate, with almost all Republicans and a third of the Democrats voting "yes." The vote was 272–142: R 194–1; D 78–141. *(Vote, p. 967)*

1. **H Res 6. House Rules Adoption.** Adoption of Title IV of the resolution that would set the rules for the 110th Congress. The title would require legislation and conference reports to be accompanied by a list of earmarks and targeted tax or trade benefits, and their sponsors. Members would have to provide information about the recipient and purpose of an earmark. It would create new budget points of order, including pay-as-you-go rules, which would require offsets to any new entitlement spending or tax cuts. Adopted 280–152: R 48–152; D 232–0. Jan. 5, 2007.

2. **HR 2. Minimum Wage Increase Passage.** Passage of the bill to increase the federal minimum wage by $2.10 over two years to $7.25 an hour. The bill also would extend federal minimum wage requirements to the Commonwealth of the Northern Mariana Islands. Passed 315–116: R 82–116; D 233–0. A "nay" was a vote in support of the president's position. Jan. 10, 2007.

3. **HR1591. War Appropriations and Troop Withdrawal.** Adoption of the fiscal 2007 supplemental appropriations conference report on the bill to provide $124.2 billion in fiscal 2007 emergency funding, as well as set a goal of redeploying most U.S. combat troops in Iraq by the end of March 2008, if the president can certify the Iraq government is meeting benchmarks, and by the end of 2007 if he cannot. The measure provided $95.5 billion for military operations in Iraq and Afghanistan, $6.8 billion for hurricane recovery and relief, $3.5 billion in crop and livestock disaster assistance, and $2.25 billion for homeland security antiterrorism programs. It also raised the minimum wage to $7.25 per hour over two years and provided $4.8 billion in small business tax incentives. Adopted 218–208: R 2–195; D 216–13. A "nay" was a vote in support of the president's position. April 25, 2007.

4. **HR 1429. Head Start Reauthorization** McKeon, R-Calif., motion to recommit the bill to the Education and Labor Committee with instructions that it be immediately reported back with language to permit faith-based Head Start providers to take religion into account when hiring employees for their Head Start program. It also clarified that faith-based organizations would not have to remove "religious art, icons, scripture or other symbols" in order to be eligible for Head Start programs. Motion rejected 195–222: R 191–2; D 4–220. A "yea" was a vote in support of the president's position. May 2, 2007.

5. **S Con Res 21. Fiscal 2008 Budget Resolution Conference Report.** Adoption of the conference report on the concurrent resolution to allow up to $954.1 billion in discretionary spending in fiscal 2008, plus $145.2 billion for operations in Iraq and Afghanistan. The discretionary total included $503.8 billion for defense, not counting the war money. Nondefense programs received $450.8 billion, plus $2 billion in advanced fiscal 2009 funding. The resolution assumed $1.8 trillion in mandatory outlays and included reconciliation instructions to cut $750 million from mandatory programs in 2007 through 2012. It reinstated pay-as-you-go rules in the Senate and established a "trigger" mechanism in the House that could block tax cuts if a projected fiscal 2012 surplus did not materialize. Adopted 214–209: R 0–196; D 214–13. May 17, 2007

6. **HR 2764. Mexico City Policy—Donated Contraceptives.** Smith, R-N.J., amendment to strike language in the bill to clarify that no contract or grant to provide donated contraceptives in developing countries would be denied to any nongovernmental organization solely on the basis of the Mexico City policy, which barred U.S. aid to international family planning organizations that performed or promoted abortions, even if they use their own funds to do so. Rejected 205–218: R 180–12; D 25–206 (ND 18–158, SD 7–48). A "yea" was a vote in support of the president's position. June 21, 2007

7. **S 1927. Foreign Intelligence Surveillance Revisions Passage.** Passage of the bill to amend the Foreign Intelligence Surveillance Act of 1978 (FISA) to expand the authority of the attorney general and the director of national intelligence to conduct surveillance of suspected foreign terrorists without a court warrant. Within 120 days of enactment, the administration was required to provide the FISA court with a description of the procedures it used to determine whether the intelligence acquisition being conducted without a warrant was directed at foreign targets overseas. The bill specified the authority would terminate after six months. Passed 227–183: R 186–2; D 41–181. A "yea" was a vote in support of the president's position. Aug. 4, 2007.

8. **HR 976. Children's Health Insurance Veto Override.** Passage over President George W. Bush's Oct. 3, 2007, veto, of the bill to reauthorize the State Children's Health Insurance Program at nearly $60 billion over five years, expanding the program by $35 billion, and increasing the tax on cigarettes by 61 cents to $1 per pack and raising taxes on other tobacco products to offset the cost of the expansion. The bill provided coverage to pregnant women and dental coverage to children enrolled in the program. Rejected 273–156: R 44–154; D 229–2. A two-thirds majority of those present and voting (286 in this case) was required to override a veto. A "nay" was a vote in support of the president's position. Oct. 18, 2007.

9. **HR1495. Water Resources Development Veto Override.** Passage, over President George W. Bush's Nov. 2, 2007, veto, of the bill to authorize $23.2 billion for more than 900 water resource development projects and studies by the Army Corps of Engineers for flood control, navigation, beach erosion control, and environmental restoration. The bill required independent peer review for certain projects that exceed $45 million. Passed 361–54: R 138–54; D 223–0. A two-thirds majority of those present and voting (277 in this case) was required to override a veto. A "nay" was a vote in support of the president's position. Nov. 6, 2007.

10. **HR 3685. Employee Non-Discrimination Passage.** Passage of the bill to prohibit job discrimination on the basis of an individual's actual or perceived sexual orientation. It defined sexual orientation as heterosexuality, homosexuality, or bisexuality. The legislation exempted religious organizations and specified that the bill would not alter the federal definition of marriage as being between a man and woman. Passed 235–184: R 35–159; D 200–25 (ND 161–10, SD 39–15). A "nay" was a vote in support of the president's position. Nov. 7, 2007.

11. **HR 3688. U.S.-Peru Free Trade Agreement.** Passage of the bill to implement a free-trade agreement between the United States and Peru. The agreement would reduce most tariffs and duties on goods traded between the two countries, increase protections for intellectual property, and require Peru to take steps to strengthen its labor and environmental enforcement standards. Passed 285–132: R 176–16; D 109–116. A "yea" was a vote in support of the president's position. Nov. 8, 2007.

12. **HR 3915. Mortgage Lending Overhaul Passage.** Passage of the bill to create a nationwide system to require licensing and registration of individual mortgage brokers and bank employees who originate mortgages. It required the Housing and Urban Development Department to establish a backup licensing system for loan originators in states that do not have a system that meets the minimum standards set in the bill. It established minimum standards for home loans, expanded certain limits on high-cost mortgages, and prohibited brokers from steering consumers to mortgages they are unlikely to be able to repay. Passed 291–127: R 64–127; D 227–0. Nov. 15, 2007.

13. **HR 3043. Fiscal 2008 Labor-HHS-Education Appropriations Veto Override.** Passage, over President George W. Bush's Nov. 13, 2007, veto, of the bill to appropriate $150.7 billion in fiscal 2008 for the departments of Labor, Health and Human Services, and Education, and for related agencies. Rejected 277–141: R 51–141; D 226–0. A two-thirds majority of those present and voting (279 in this case) was required to override a veto. A "nay" was a vote in support of the president's position. Nov. 15, 2007.

14. **HR 6. Energy Policy.** Dingell, D-Mich., motion to concur in a Senate amendment to require new corporate average fuel economy (CAFE) standards of 35 miles per gallon for cars and light trucks and require 36 billion gallons of biofuels to be used by 2022. Motion agreed to 314–100: R 95–96; D 219–4. Dec. 18, 2007.

15. **HR 3996. Alternative Minimum Tax Adjustment Passage.** Rangel, D-N.Y., motion to suspend the rules and concur in the Senate amendment to the bill to provide a one-year adjustment to exempt an additional 21 million taxpayers from paying the alternative minimum tax on income from 2007. Motion agreed to 352–64: R 195–0; D 157–64. A two-thirds majority of those present and voting (278 in this case) was required for passage under suspension of the rules. Dec. 19, 2007.

16. **HR 2764. Fiscal 2008 Omnibus Appropriations Bill.** Obey, D-Wis., motion to concur in Senate amendments to provide $473.5 billion in discretionary spending in fiscal 2008 for all federal departments and agencies whose regular fiscal 2008 spending bills had not been enacted: Agriculture, Commerce-Justice-Science, Energy-Water, Financial Services, Homeland Security, Interior-Environment, Labor-HHS-Education, Legislative Branch, Military Construction-VA, State–Foreign Operations, and Transportation-HUD. The total included $11.2 billion in emergency funding for veterans programs and provided $70 billion for military operations in Afghanistan and Iraq. Motion agreed to 272–142: R 194–1; D 78–141. Dec. 19, 2007.

KEY

Democrat | *Republican* | **Independent**

Y	Voted for (yea)	–	Announced against
#	Paired for	P	Voted "present"
+	Announced for	C	Voted "present" to avoid possible conflict of interest
N	Voted against (nay)	?	Did not vote or otherwise make a position known
X	Paired against		

House Key Votes	1	2	3	4	5	6	7	8	9	10	11	12	13	14	15	16
ALABAMA																
1 *Bonner*	N	Y	N	Y	N	?	Y	N	Y	N	Y	Y	N	Y	Y	Y
2 *Everett*	N	Y	N	Y	N	Y	Y	N	Y	N	Y	?	?	Y	Y	Y
3 *Rogers*	N	Y	N	Y	N	Y	Y	N	Y	N	Y	Y	Y	Y	Y	Y
4 *Aderholt*	N	Y	N	Y	N	Y	Y	N	Y	N	N	N	N	Y	Y	Y
5 Cramer	Y	Y	Y	N	Y	?	Y	Y	Y	N	Y	Y	Y	Y	N	Y
6 *Bachus*	N	Y	N	Y	N	Y	Y	N	N	N	Y	Y	N	N	Y	Y
7 Davis	Y	Y	Y	N	Y	N	Y	Y	Y	N	Y	Y	Y	Y	Y	Y
ALASKA																
AL *Young*	N	Y	N	Y	N	Y	?	Y	Y	N	Y	N	Y	N	Y	Y
ARIZONA																
1 *Renzi*	N	Y	N	Y	N	Y	Y	Y	Y	N	Y	Y	N	Y	Y	Y
2 *Franks*	N	N	N	Y	N	Y	Y	N	N	N	Y	N	N	N	Y	Y
3 *Shadegg*	N	N	N	Y	N	Y	Y	N	N	N	Y	N	N	N	Y	Y
4 Pastor	Y	Y	Y	N	Y	N	N	Y	?	Y	N	Y	Y	?	?	?
5 Mitchell	Y	Y	Y	N	N	N	Y	Y	Y	Y	Y	Y	Y	Y	Y	Y
6 *Flake*	N	N	N	Y	N	Y	Y	N	N	Y	Y	N	N	N	Y	Y
7 Grijalva	Y	Y	Y	N	Y	N	N	Y	Y	Y	N	Y	Y	Y	Y	N
8 Giffords	Y	Y	Y	N	Y	N	N	Y	Y	+	+	Y	Y	Y	Y	Y
ARKANSAS																
1 Berry	Y	Y	Y	N	Y	N	N	Y	Y	N	Y	Y	Y	Y	N	Y
2 Snyder	Y	Y	Y	N	Y	N	Y	Y	Y	Y	Y	Y	Y	Y	Y	Y
3 *Boozman*	Y	Y	N	Y	N	Y	Y	N	Y	N	Y	N	N	Y	Y	Y
4 Ross	Y	Y	Y	N	Y	N	Y	Y	Y	N	Y	Y	Y	Y	N	Y
CALIFORNIA																
1 Thompson	Y	Y	Y	N	Y	N	N	Y	Y	Y	Y	Y	Y	+	–	–
2 *Herger*	N	N	N	Y	N	Y	Y	N	Y	N	Y	N	N	N	Y	Y
3 *Lungren*	N	N	N	Y	N	Y	Y	N	Y	N	?	Y	N	N	Y	Y
4 *Doolittle*	N	N	N	Y	N	Y	Y	N	Y	N	Y	N	N	N	Y	Y
5 Matsui	Y	Y	Y	N	Y	N	N	Y	Y	Y	Y	Y	Y	Y	Y	N
6 Woolsey	Y	Y	N	N	Y	N	N	Y	Y	Y	N	Y	Y	+	?	?
7 Miller, George	Y	Y	Y	N	Y	N	N	Y	Y	Y	N	Y	Y	Y	N	N
8 Pelosi[1]	Y	Y	Y	N	Y		N	Y		Y	Y		Y	Y	N	
9 Lee	Y	Y	N	N	Y	N	N	Y	Y	Y	N	Y	Y	Y	Y	N
10 Tauscher	Y	Y	Y	N	Y	N	N	Y	Y	Y	Y	Y	Y	Y	Y	N
11 McNerney	Y	Y	Y	N	Y	N	N	Y	Y	Y	N	Y	Y	Y	Y	N
12 Lantos	Y	Y	Y	N	Y	N	?	Y	Y	Y	?	Y	Y	Y	Y	N
13 Stark	Y	Y	P	N	?	N	N	Y	Y	Y	N	Y	?	Y	N	N
14 Eshoo	Y	Y	Y	N	Y	N	N	Y	Y	Y	Y	Y	Y	Y	Y	N
15 Honda	Y	Y	Y	N	Y	N	N	Y	Y	Y	Y	Y	Y	Y	Y	N
16 Lofgren	Y	Y	Y	N	Y	N	N	Y	Y	Y	Y	Y	Y	Y	Y	N
17 Farr	Y	Y	Y	N	Y	N	N	Y	Y	Y	Y	Y	Y	Y	Y	N
18 Cardoza	Y	Y	Y	N	Y	N	N	Y	Y	Y	Y	Y	Y	Y	N	N
19 *Radanovich*	N	N	N	Y	N	Y	Y	N	N	N	Y	N	N	N	Y	Y
20 Costa	Y	Y	+	N	Y	N	Y	Y	Y	Y	Y	Y	Y	Y	N	Y
21 *Nunes*	N	N	N	Y	N	Y	Y	N	N	N	Y	N	N	N	Y	Y
22 *McCarthy*	N	N	N	Y	N	Y	Y	N	Y	N	Y	N	N	N	Y	Y
23 Capps	Y	Y	Y	N	Y	N	N	Y	Y	Y	Y	Y	Y	Y	N	N
24 *Gallegly*	N	N	N	Y	N	Y	Y	N	Y	N	Y	Y	N	?	Y	Y
25 *McKeon*	N	N	N	Y	N	Y	Y	N	N	N	Y	Y	N	N	Y	Y
26 *Dreier*	N	N	N	Y	N	Y	Y	N	Y	Y	Y	Y	N	Y	Y	Y
27 Sherman	Y	Y	Y	N	Y	N	N	Y	Y	Y	N	Y	Y	Y	N	N
28 Berman	Y	Y	Y	N	Y	N	N	Y	Y	Y	Y	Y	Y	Y	Y	Y
29 Schiff	Y	Y	Y	N	Y	N	N	Y	Y	Y	Y	Y	Y	Y	Y	N
30 Waxman	Y	Y	Y	N	Y	N	N	Y	Y	Y	Y	Y	Y	Y	N	N
31 Becerra	Y	Y	Y	N	Y	N	?	Y	Y	Y	Y	Y	Y	Y	N	N
32 Solis	Y	Y	Y	N	Y	N	N	Y	Y	Y	N	Y	Y	Y	Y	N
33 Watson	Y	Y	Y	N	Y	N	N	Y	Y	Y	N	Y	Y	Y	Y	N
34 Roybal-Allard	Y	Y	Y	N	Y	N	N	Y	Y	Y	N	Y	Y	Y	Y	N
35 Waters	Y	Y	N	N	Y	N	N	Y	Y	Y	N	Y	Y	Y	Y	N
36 Harman	Y	Y	Y	N	?	N	N	Y	Y	Y	Y	Y	Y	Y	N	N
37 Millender-McD[2]	Y	Y														
37 Richardson[2]								Y	Y	Y	N	Y	Y	Y	Y	N
38 Napolitano	Y	Y	Y	N	Y	N	N	Y	Y	Y	N	Y	Y	Y	N	N
39 Sánchez, Linda	Y	Y	Y	N	Y	N	N	Y	N	N	Y	N	N	N	Y	Y
40 *Royce*	N	N	N	Y	N	Y	Y	N	N	N	Y	Y	N	N	Y	Y
41 *Lewis*	N	N	N	Y	N	Y	Y	N	Y	N	Y	Y	N	?	?	?
42 *Miller, Gary*	N	?	N	Y	N	Y	Y	N	Y	Y	N	Y	Y	Y	Y	N
43 Baca	Y	Y	Y	N	Y	N	N	Y	Y	N	Y	Y	N	Y	Y	Y
44 *Calvert*	N	N	N	Y	N	Y	Y	N	Y	Y	Y	?	?	Y	Y	Y
45 *Bono*	N	Y	N	Y	N	N	Y	Y	Y	N	Y	N	N	N	Y	Y
46 *Rohrabacher*	Y	N	N	Y	N	Y	Y	N	Y	Y	N	Y	Y	Y	N	N
47 Sanchez, Loretta	Y	Y	Y	N	Y	?	N	Y	N	Y	Y	N	N	Y	Y	Y
48 *Campbell*	N	N	N	Y	N	Y	Y	N	N	N	Y	N	N	Y	Y	Y
49 *Issa*	N	N	N	Y	N	Y	Y	N	N	N	Y	N	N	N	Y	Y
50 *Bilbray*	N	N	N	Y	N	Y	Y	N	Y	Y	N	Y	Y	Y	Y	N
51 Filner	Y	Y	Y	N	Y	N	N	Y	Y	N	?	N	N	N	Y	Y
52 *Hunter*	N	N	N	?	N	?	?	N	Y	Y	Y	Y	Y	Y	Y	Y
53 Davis	Y	Y	Y	N	Y	N	N	Y								
COLORADO																
1 DeGette	Y	Y	Y	N	Y	N	N	Y	Y	Y	Y	Y	Y	Y	Y	N
2 Udall	Y	Y	Y	–	Y	N	N	Y	Y	Y	Y	Y	Y	Y	Y	Y
3 Salazar	Y	Y	Y	N	Y	N	Y	Y	Y	Y	Y	?	Y	Y	N	Y
4 *Musgrave*	N	N	N	Y	N	Y	Y	N	Y	N	Y	N	N	N	Y	Y
5 *Lamborn*	N	N	N	Y	N	Y	Y	N	N	N	Y	N	N	N	Y	Y
6 *Tancredo*	N	N	N	?	N	Y	?	N	?	N	Y	N	N	N	Y	Y
7 Perlmutter	Y	Y	Y	N	Y	N	N	Y	Y	Y	Y	Y	Y	Y	Y	N
CONNECTICUT																
1 Larson	Y	Y	Y	N	Y	N	N	Y	Y	Y	Y	Y	Y	Y	N	N
2 Courtney	Y	Y	Y	N	Y	N	N	Y	Y	Y	N	Y	Y	Y	Y	N
3 DeLauro	Y	Y	Y	N	Y	N	N	Y	Y	Y	N	Y	Y	Y	Y	N
4 *Shays*	Y	Y	N	N	–	N	Y	Y	Y	Y	Y	Y	Y	Y	Y	Y
5 Murphy	Y	Y	Y	N	Y	N	N	Y	Y	Y	N	Y	Y	Y	Y	N
DELAWARE																
AL *Castle*	Y	Y	N	Y	N	N	Y	Y	Y	Y	Y	Y	Y	Y	Y	Y
FLORIDA																
1 *Miller*	N	N	N	Y	N	Y	Y	N	N	N	?	Y	N	Y	Y	Y
2 Boyd	Y	Y	Y	N	Y	N	Y	Y	Y	?	Y	Y	Y	Y	N	Y
3 Brown	Y	Y	Y	N	Y	N	N	Y	Y	Y	Y	Y	Y	Y	Y	Y
4 *Crenshaw*	N	Y	N	Y	N	Y	+	N	Y	N	Y	N	N	Y	Y	Y
5 *Brown-Waite*	Y	Y	N	Y	N	Y	Y	N	Y	N	Y	N	N	Y	Y	Y
6 *Stearns*	N	Y	N	Y	N	Y	Y	N	N	N	Y	Y	N	N	Y	Y
7 *Mica*	N	N	N	Y	N	Y	Y	N	Y	N	Y	N	N	N	Y	Y
8 *Keller*	Y	Y	N	Y	N	Y	Y	N	Y	N	Y	N	Y	Y	Y	Y
9 *Bilirakis*	Y	Y	N	Y	N	Y	Y	N	Y	N	Y	N	Y	Y	Y	Y
10 *Young*	Y	Y	N	Y	N	Y	Y	Y	N	N	Y	Y	Y	Y	Y	Y
11 Castor	Y	Y	Y	N	Y	N	N	Y	Y	Y	Y	Y	Y	Y	N	N
12 *Putnam*	N	N	N	Y	N	Y	Y	N	N	N	Y	N	N	Y	Y	Y
13 *Buchanan*	N	Y	N	Y	N	Y	Y	Y	Y	N	Y	Y	Y	Y	Y	Y
14 *Mack*	N	N	N	Y	N	Y	Y	N	Y	N	Y	?	?	N	Y	Y
15 *Weldon*	N	N	N	Y	N	Y	Y	N	Y	N	Y	Y	N	N	Y	Y
16 Mahoney	Y	Y	Y	N	Y	N	N	Y	Y	Y	Y	Y	Y	Y	Y	Y
17 Meek	Y	Y	Y	N	Y	N	N	Y	Y	Y	Y	Y	Y	Y	N	N
18 *Ros-Lehtinen*	N	Y	N	Y	N	Y	Y	N	Y	Y	Y	Y	Y	Y	Y	Y
19 Wexler	Y	Y	Y	N	Y	N	N	Y	Y	Y	N	Y	Y	?	?	?
20 Wasserman-Schultz	Y	Y	Y	N	Y	N	N	Y	Y	Y	Y	Y	Y	Y	Y	N
21 *Diaz-Balart, L.*	N	Y	N	Y	N	Y	Y	N	Y	Y	Y	Y	Y	Y	Y	Y
22 Klein	Y	Y	Y	N	Y	N	–	Y	Y	Y	Y	Y	Y	Y	Y	N
23 Hastings	Y	Y	Y	N	Y	N	N	Y	Y	Y	N	Y	Y	?	?	?
24 *Feeney*	N	N	N	Y	N	Y	Y	N	N	N	Y	N	N	N	Y	Y
25 *Diaz-Balart, M.*	N	Y	N	Y	N	Y	Y	N	Y	Y	Y	Y	Y	Y	Y	Y
GEORGIA																
1 *Kingston*	N	N	N	Y	N	Y	Y	N	N	N	Y	N	N	Y	Y	Y
2 Bishop	Y	Y	Y	N	Y	N	N	Y	Y	Y	Y	Y	Y	Y	Y	Y
3 *Westmoreland*	N	N	?	Y	N	Y	Y	N	?	?	Y	N	N	N	Y	Y
4 Johnson	Y	Y	Y	N	Y	N	N	Y	Y	Y	N	Y	Y	Y	Y	N
5 Lewis	Y	Y	N	N	Y	N	N	Y	Y	Y	Y	Y	Y	Y	Y	N
6 *Price*	N	N	N	Y	N	Y	Y	N	Y	N	Y	N	N	N	Y	Y
7 *Linder*	N	N	N	Y	N	Y	Y	N	N	N	Y	N	N	N	Y	Y
8 Marshall	Y	Y	N	Y	N	Y	Y	N	Y	N	N	Y	Y	Y	Y	Y
9 *Deal*	N	N	N	Y	N	Y	Y	N	N	N	Y	N	N	N	Y	Y
10 *Norwood*[3]	N	?					Y	N								
10 *Broun*[3]							Y	N	N	N	Y	N	N	N	Y	Y

[1]The Speaker votes only at her discretion.

[2]Rep. Laura Richardson, D-Calif., was sworn in Sept. 4, 2007, to fill the seat of Democrat Juanita Millender-McDonald, who died April 22.

[3]Rep. Paul Broun, R-Ga., was sworn in July 25, 2007, to fill the seat of Republican Charlie Norwood, who died Feb. 13.

House Key Votes	1	2	3	4	5	6	7	8	9	10	11	12	13	14	15	16
11 *Gingrey*	N	N	N	Y	N	Y	Y	N	N	N	Y	N	N	N	Y	Y
12 Barrow	Y	Y	N	N	N	N	Y	Y	Y	N	Y	Y	Y	Y	Y	Y
13 Scott	Y	Y	Y	N	Y	N	N	Y	Y	Y	N	Y	Y	Y	Y	Y
HAWAII																
1 Abercrombie	Y	Y	Y	N	Y	N	N	Y	Y	Y	N	Y	Y	Y	Y	N
2 Hirono	Y	Y	Y	N	Y	N	N	Y	Y	Y	N	Y	Y	Y	Y	N
IDAHO																
1 *Sali*	N	N	N	Y	N	Y	Y	N	Y	N	Y	N	N	N	Y	Y
2 *Simpson*	Y	Y	N	+	N	+	Y	Y	Y	N	Y	Y	Y	Y	Y	Y
ILLINOIS																
1 Rush	Y	Y	Y	N	Y	N	N	Y	Y	Y	N	Y	Y	Y	Y	Y
2 Jackson	Y	Y	Y	N	Y	N	N	Y	Y	Y	N	Y	Y	Y	Y	N
3 Lipinski	Y	Y	Y	N	Y	Y	Y	Y	Y	N	N	Y	Y	Y	Y	N
4 Gutierrez	Y	Y	Y	N	Y	N	N	Y	Y	Y	N	Y	Y	Y	N	N
5 Emanuel	Y	Y	Y	N	Y	N	N	Y	Y	Y	Y	Y	Y	Y	N	Y
6 *Roskam*	N	N	N	Y	N	Y	Y	N	Y	N	Y	N	N	Y	Y	Y
7 Davis	Y	Y	Y	N	Y	N	N	Y	Y	Y	N	Y	Y	?	Y	N
8 Bean	Y	Y	Y	N	N	N	Y	Y	Y	Y	Y	Y	Y	Y	Y	Y
9 Schakowsky	Y	Y	Y	N	Y	N	N	Y	Y	Y	N	Y	Y	Y	Y	N
10 *Kirk*	Y	Y	N	N	N	N	Y	Y	Y	Y	Y	N	Y	Y	Y	Y
11 *Weller*	Y	Y	N	Y	N	Y	Y	N	Y	N	Y	+	–	?	?	?
12 Costello	Y	Y	Y	N	Y	Y	N	Y	Y	Y	N	Y	Y	Y	N	N
13 *Biggert*	N	Y	N	Y	N	N	Y	N	Y	Y	Y	Y	Y	Y	Y	Y
14 *Hastert*	N	N	N	Y	N	Y	?	N	Y	N	Y	N				
15 *Johnson*	N	Y	N	Y	N	Y	N	N	Y	N	Y	Y	Y	Y	Y	Y
16 *Manzullo*	Y	N	N	Y	N	Y	Y	N	Y	N	Y	N	N	N	Y	Y
17 Hare	Y	Y	Y	N	Y	N	N	Y	Y	Y	N	Y	Y	Y	Y	N
18 *LaHood*	Y	Y	N	Y	N	Y	?	Y	Y	?	?	Y	?	Y	Y	Y
19 *Shimkus*	Y	Y	N	Y	N	Y	Y	N	Y	N	Y	N	N	Y	Y	Y
INDIANA																
1 Visclosky	Y	Y	Y	N	Y	N	N	Y	Y	Y	N	Y	Y	Y	Y	Y
2 Donnelly	Y	Y	Y	N	N	Y	Y	Y	Y	Y	N	Y	Y	Y	Y	Y
3 *Souder*	N	N	N	Y	N	Y	Y	N	Y	N	Y	Y	N	Y	Y	Y
4 *Buyer*	?	?	N	Y	N	Y	Y	N	?	?	?	?	N	Y	Y	Y
5 *Burton*	N	N	N	Y	N	Y	Y	N	N	N	Y	–	N	N	Y	Y
6 *Pence*	N	N	N	Y	N	Y	Y	N	N	N	Y	N	N	N	Y	Y
7 Carson[4]	Y	Y	Y	N	Y	N	N	?	?	?	?	?	?			
8 Ellsworth	Y	Y	Y	N	N	Y	Y	Y	Y	Y	Y	Y	Y	Y	Y	Y
9 Hill	Y	Y	Y	N	N	N	Y	Y	Y	Y	Y	Y	Y	Y	N	Y
IOWA																
1 Braley	Y	Y	Y	N	Y	N	N	Y	Y	?	?	Y	Y	Y	Y	N
2 Loebsack	Y	Y	Y	N	Y	N	N	Y	Y	Y	N	Y	Y	Y	Y	N
3 Boswell	Y	Y	Y	N	Y	N	Y	Y	Y	Y	Y	Y	Y	Y	Y	N
4 *Latham*	N	Y	N	Y	N	Y	Y	Y	Y	N	Y	Y	N	Y	Y	Y
5 *King*	N	N	N	Y	N	Y	Y	N	Y	N	Y	N	N	?	Y	Y
KANSAS																
1 *Moran*	Y	Y	N	Y	N	Y	Y	Y	Y	N	Y	N	N	Y	Y	Y
2 Boyda	Y	Y	Y	N	Y	N	N	Y	Y	Y	N	Y	Y	N	N	Y
3 Moore	Y	Y	Y	N	Y	N	N	Y	Y	Y	Y	Y	Y	Y	N	Y
4 *Tiahrt*	N	N	N	Y	N	Y	Y	N	Y	N	Y	N	N	Y	Y	Y
KENTUCKY																
1 *Whitfield*	Y	Y	N	Y	N	?	Y	N	Y	N	Y	Y	Y	Y	Y	Y
2 *Lewis*	N	N	N	Y	?	Y	Y	N	Y	N	Y	N	N	Y	Y	Y
3 Yarmuth	Y	Y	Y	N	Y	N	N	Y	?	Y	N	Y	Y	Y	Y	N
4 *Davis*	N	Y	N	Y	N	Y	Y	N	N	N	Y	N	N	N	Y	Y
5 *Rogers*	N	Y	N	Y	N	Y	Y	N	Y	N	Y	N	N	N	Y	Y
6 Chandler	Y	Y	Y	N	Y	N	Y	Y	?	Y	N	Y	Y	Y	N	Y
LOUISIANA																
1 *Jindal*	Y	Y	N	Y	N	Y	?	?	Y	?	?	?	?	?	?	?
2 Jefferson	Y	Y	Y	N	Y	N	N	Y	Y	?	N	Y	Y	Y	?	?
3 Melancon	Y	Y	Y	N	Y	Y	Y	Y	Y	N	Y	Y	Y	Y	N	Y
4 *McCrery*	N	N	N	Y	N	Y	Y	N	Y	Y	Y	N	N	N	Y	Y
5 *Alexander*	N	Y	N	Y	N	Y	Y	N	Y	N	Y	N	N	N	Y	Y
6 *Baker*	N	N	N	Y	N	Y	Y	N	Y	N	Y	N	N	N	Y	Y
7 *Boustany*	N	N	N	Y	N	Y	Y	N	Y	N	Y	N	N	N	Y	Y
MAINE																
1 Allen	Y	Y	Y	N	Y	N	N	Y	Y	Y	N	Y	Y	Y	Y	N
2 Michaud	Y	Y	N	N	Y	N	N	Y	Y	N	N	Y	Y	Y	N	N
MARYLAND																
1 *Gilchrest*	Y	Y	Y	Y	N	N	Y	Y	Y	Y	Y	Y	Y	?	?	?
2 Ruppersberger	Y	Y	Y	N	Y	N	N	Y	Y	Y	Y	Y	Y	Y	Y	Y
3 Sarbanes	Y	Y	Y	N	Y	N	N	Y	Y	Y	N	Y	Y	Y	Y	N
4 Wynn	Y	Y	Y	N	Y	N	N	Y	Y	Y	N	Y	Y	Y	Y	N

House Key Votes	1	2	3	4	5	6	7	8	9	10	11	12	13	14	15	16
5 Hoyer	Y	Y	Y	N	Y	N	N	Y	Y	Y	Y	Y	Y	Y	N	Y
6 *Bartlett*	N	N	N	Y	N	Y	Y	N	Y	N	Y	Y	N	N	Y	Y
7 Cummings	Y	Y	Y	N	Y	N	N	Y	Y	Y	N	Y	Y	Y	Y	N
8 Van Hollen	Y	Y	Y	N	Y	N	N	Y	Y	Y	Y	Y	?	Y	Y	N
MASSACHUSETTS																
1 Olver	Y	Y	Y	N	Y	N	N	Y	Y	?	N	Y	Y	Y	Y	N
2 Neal	?	Y	Y	N	Y	N	N	Y	Y	Y	Y	Y	Y	Y	Y	N
3 McGovern	Y	Y	Y	N	Y	N	N	Y	Y	Y	N	Y	Y	Y	Y	N
4 Frank	Y	Y	Y	N	Y	N	N	Y	Y	Y	Y	Y	Y	Y	Y	N
5 Meehan[5]	Y	Y	Y	N	Y	N										
5 Tsongas[5]								Y	Y	Y	N	Y	Y	Y	Y	N
6 Tierney	Y	Y	Y	N	Y	N	N	Y	Y	Y	N	Y	Y	Y	Y	N
7 Markey	Y	Y	Y	N	Y	N	N	Y	Y	Y	N	Y	Y	Y	Y	–
8 Capuano	Y	Y	Y	?	Y	N	N	Y	Y	Y	N	Y	Y	Y	N	N
9 Lynch	Y	Y	Y	N	Y	N	N	Y	Y	Y	Y	Y	?	Y	Y	Y
10 Delahunt	Y	Y	Y	N	Y	N	?	Y	Y	Y	N	Y	Y	Y	N	N
MICHIGAN																
1 Stupak	Y	Y	Y	N	Y	Y	N	Y	Y	Y	N	Y	Y	Y	N	N
2 *Hoekstra*	N	N	N	Y	N	Y	Y	N	Y	N	N	N	N	N	Y	Y
3 *Ehlers*	Y	Y	N	Y	N	Y	Y	Y	Y	N	Y	Y	Y	Y	Y	Y
4 *Camp*	N	N	N	Y	N	Y	Y	N	Y	N	Y	N	N	N	Y	Y
5 Kildee	Y	Y	Y	N	Y	Y	N	Y	Y	Y	N	Y	Y	Y	Y	Y
6 *Upton*	Y	Y	N	Y	N	Y	Y	Y	Y	N	Y	Y	Y	Y	Y	Y
7 *Walberg*	N	N	N	Y	N	Y	Y	N	Y	N	Y	N	N	N	Y	Y
8 *Rogers*	Y	N	N	Y	N	Y	Y	N	Y	N	Y	Y	N	N	Y	Y
9 *Knollenberg*	N	+	N	Y	N	Y	Y	N	Y	Y	Y	Y	N	Y	Y	Y
10 *Miller*	Y	Y	N	Y	N	Y	Y	Y	Y	Y	Y	Y	Y	N	Y	Y
11 *McCotter*	N	Y	N	Y	N	Y	Y	N	Y	Y	Y	Y	N	N	Y	Y
12 Levin	Y	Y	Y	N	Y	N	N	Y	Y	Y	Y	Y	Y	Y	Y	Y
13 Kilpatrick	Y	Y	Y	N	Y	N	?	Y	Y	Y	N	Y	Y	Y	Y	N
14 Conyers	Y	Y	Y	N	Y	N	N	Y	Y	Y	N	Y	Y	Y	Y	N
15 Dingell	Y	Y	Y	N	Y	N	N	Y	Y	Y	Y	Y	Y	Y	Y	Y
MINNESOTA																
1 Walz	Y	Y	Y	N	Y	N	Y	Y	Y	Y	N	Y	Y	Y	N	Y
2 *Kline*	N	N	N	Y	N	Y	Y	N	Y	N	Y	Y	N	N	Y	Y
3 *Ramstad*	Y	Y	N	Y	N	N	Y	Y	Y	Y	Y	N	Y	Y	Y	Y
4 McCollum	Y	Y	Y	N	Y	N	N	Y	Y	Y	Y	Y	Y	Y	N	N
5 Ellison	Y	Y	Y	N	Y	N	N	Y	Y	Y	N	Y	Y	Y	Y	N
6 *Bachmann*	N	N	N	Y	N	Y	Y	N	Y	N	Y	N	N	N	Y	Y
7 Peterson	Y	Y	Y	N	Y	Y	Y	Y	Y	Y	N	Y	Y	Y	N	Y
8 Oberstar	Y	Y	Y	N	Y	Y	N	Y	?	?	?	?	?	Y	Y	N
MISSISSIPPI																
1 *Wicker*	N	N	N	Y	N	Y	Y	N	Y	N	Y	N	N	N	Y	Y
2 Thompson	Y	Y	Y	N	Y	N	N	Y	Y	Y	N	Y	Y	Y	Y	N
3 *Pickering*	N	N	N	Y	N	?	Y	N	Y	N	Y	N	Y	Y	Y	Y
4 Taylor	Y	Y	N	N	N	Y	Y	N	Y	N	N	Y	Y	Y	N	Y
MISSOURI																
1 Clay	Y	Y	Y	N	Y	N	?	Y	Y	Y	Y	Y	Y	Y	Y	N
2 *Akin*	N	N	N	Y	N	Y	Y	N	Y	N	Y	N	N	N	Y	Y
3 Carnahan	Y	Y	Y	N	Y	N	N	Y	Y	Y	N	Y	Y	Y	Y	N
4 Skelton	Y	Y	Y	N	Y	Y	?	Y	Y	N	Y	Y	Y	Y	Y	Y
5 Cleaver	Y	Y	Y	N	Y	N	N	Y	Y	Y	Y	Y	Y	Y	Y	N
6 *Graves*	N	N	N	?	N	Y	Y	N	Y	N	Y	Y	Y	Y	Y	Y
7 *Blunt*	N	N	N	Y	N	Y	Y	N	N	N	Y	N	N	Y	Y	Y
8 *Emerson*	Y	Y	P	Y	N	Y	Y	Y	Y	N	Y	Y	Y	Y	Y	Y
9 *Hulshof*	N	Y	N	Y	N	Y	Y	N	Y	N	Y	N	Y	Y	Y	Y
MONTANA																
AL *Rehberg*	Y	N	N	Y	N	Y	Y	Y	Y	N	Y	N	Y	Y	Y	Y
NEBRASKA																
1 *Fortenberry*	Y	N	N	Y	N	Y	Y	N	Y	N	Y	Y	Y	Y	Y	Y
2 *Terry*	N	N	N	Y	N	Y	Y	N	Y	N	Y	N	N	Y	Y	Y
3 *Smith*	N	N	N	Y	N	Y	Y	N	Y	N	Y	N	N	Y	Y	Y
NEVADA																
1 Berkley	Y	Y	Y	N	Y	N	N	Y	Y	Y	N	Y	Y	Y	Y	Y
2 *Heller*	N	N	N	Y	N	Y	Y	N	Y	N	Y	Y	N	N	Y	Y
3 *Porter*	Y	N	N	Y	N	Y	Y	Y	Y	Y	Y	Y	Y	Y	Y	Y
NEW HAMPSHIRE																
1 Shea-Porter	Y	Y	Y	N	Y	N	N	Y	Y	Y	N	Y	Y	Y	Y	N
2 Hodes	Y	Y	Y	N	Y	N	N	Y	Y	Y	N	Y	Y	Y	Y	N

[4]Rep. Julia Carson, D-Ind., died Dec. 15, 2007.

[5]Rep. Niki Tsongas, D-Mass., was sworn in Oct. 18, 2007, to fill the seat vacated by the resignation of Democrat Martin T. Meehan, who resigned effective July 1, 2007.

KEY

Democrat | *Republican* | **Independent**

Y	Voted for (yea)	–	Announced against
#	Paired for	P	Voted "present"
+	Announced for	C	Voted "present" to avoid possible conflict of interest
N	Voted against (nay)	?	Did not vote or otherwise make a position known
X	Paired against		

House Key Votes	1	2	3	4	5	6	7	8	9	10	11	12	13	14	15	16
NEW JERSEY																
1 Andrews	Y	Y	Y	N	Y	N	N	Y	Y	Y	N	Y	Y	Y	N	N
2 *LoBiondo*	Y	Y	N	Y	N	Y	Y	Y	Y	Y	N	Y	Y	Y	Y	Y
3 *Saxton*	N	Y	N	Y	N	Y	?	N	Y	Y	Y	N	N	Y	Y	Y
4 *Smith*	Y	Y	N	Y	N	Y	Y	Y	Y	N	N	Y	Y	Y	Y	Y
5 *Garrett*	N	N	N	Y	N	Y	Y	N	N	N	Y	N	N	N	Y	Y
6 Pallone	Y	Y	Y	N	Y	N	N	Y	Y	Y	N	Y	Y	Y	Y	N
7 *Ferguson*	Y	Y	N	Y	N	Y	Y	Y	?	N	Y	Y	Y	Y	Y	Y
8 Pascrell	Y	Y	Y	N	Y	N	N	Y	Y	Y	Y	Y	Y	Y	Y	N
9 Rothman	Y	Y	Y	N	Y	N	N	Y	Y	Y	?	Y	Y	Y	Y	N
10 Payne	Y	Y	Y	N	Y	N	N	Y	?	Y	N	Y	Y	Y	Y	N
11 *Frelinghuysen*	N	Y	N	Y	N	N	Y	N	Y	Y	Y	N	Y	Y	Y	Y
12 Holt	Y	Y	Y	N	Y	N	N	Y	Y	N	N	Y	Y	Y	Y	N
13 Sires	Y	Y	Y	N	Y	N	N	Y	Y	Y	Y	Y	Y	Y	Y	N
NEW MEXICO																
1 *Wilson*	Y	Y	N	Y	N	Y	Y	Y	Y	N	Y	Y	Y	Y	Y	Y
2 *Pearce*	N	N	N	Y	N	Y	Y	N	Y	N	Y	N	N	N	Y	Y
3 Udall	Y	Y	Y	N	Y	N	N	Y	Y	Y	N	Y	Y	Y	Y	N
NEW YORK																
1 Bishop	Y	Y	Y	N	Y	N	N	Y	Y	Y	Y	Y	Y	Y	Y	N
2 Israel	Y	Y	Y	N	Y	N	N	Y	Y	Y	Y	Y	Y	Y	Y	N
3 *King*	N	Y	N	Y	N	Y	Y	+	Y	N	Y	Y	N	Y	Y	Y
4 McCarthy	Y	Y	Y	N	Y	N	N	Y	Y	Y	Y	Y	Y	Y	Y	N
5 Ackerman	Y	Y	Y	N	Y	N	N	Y	Y	Y	Y	Y	Y	Y	Y	N
6 Meeks	Y	Y	Y	N	Y	N	N	Y	Y	Y	Y	Y	Y	Y	Y	N
7 Crowley	Y	Y	Y	N	Y	N	N	Y	Y	Y	Y	Y	Y	Y	Y	N
8 Nadler	Y	Y	Y	N	Y	N	N	Y	Y	N	N	Y	Y	Y	Y	N
9 Weiner	Y	Y	Y	N	Y	?	N	Y	Y	N	Y	Y	Y	Y	Y	N
10 Towns	Y	Y	Y	N	Y	N	N	Y	Y	N	Y	Y	Y	Y	Y	N
11 Clarke	Y	Y	Y	N	Y	N	?	Y	Y	N	Y	Y	Y	Y	Y	N
12 Velázquez	Y	Y	Y	N	Y	N	N	Y	Y	N	N	Y	Y	Y	Y	N
13 *Fossella*	N	Y	N	Y	N	Y	Y	Y	?	Y	Y	N	N	?	Y	Y
14 Maloney	Y	Y	Y	N	Y	N	N	Y	Y	Y	Y	Y	Y	Y	Y	N
15 Rangel	Y	Y	Y	N	Y	N	N	Y	Y	Y	Y	Y	Y	Y	Y	N
16 Serrano	Y	Y	Y	N	Y	N	N	Y	Y	Y	N	Y	Y	Y	Y	N
17 Engel	Y	Y	Y	?	?	N	N	Y	Y	Y	Y	Y	Y	Y	Y	N
18 Lowey	Y	Y	Y	N	Y	N	N	Y	Y	Y	Y	Y	Y	Y	Y	N
19 Hall	Y	Y	Y	N	Y	N	N	Y	Y	Y	N	Y	Y	Y	Y	N
20 Gillibrand	Y	Y	Y	N	Y	N	N	Y	Y	Y	Y	Y	Y	Y	Y	Y
21 McNulty	Y	Y	N	N	Y	N	N	Y	?	Y	N	Y	Y	Y	?	?
22 Hinchey	Y	Y	Y	N	Y	N	N	Y	Y	Y	N	Y	Y	Y	Y	N
23 *McHugh*	Y	Y	N	Y	N	Y	Y	Y	Y	Y	N	Y	Y	Y	Y	Y
24 Arcuri	Y	Y	Y	N	Y	N	N	Y	Y	Y	N	Y	Y	Y	Y	N
25 *Walsh*	Y	Y	N	Y	N	Y	Y	Y	N	N	Y	N	Y	Y	Y	Y
26 *Reynolds*	N	N	N	Y	N	Y	Y	N	Y	N	Y	N	Y	Y	Y	Y
27 Higgins	Y	Y	Y	N	Y	N	Y	Y	Y	Y	N	Y	Y	Y	Y	N
28 Slaughter	Y	Y	Y	N	Y	N	N	Y	Y	Y	N	Y	Y	Y	Y	N
29 *Kuhl*	N	Y	N	Y	N	Y	Y	N	Y	Y	Y	N	N	Y	Y	Y
NORTH CAROLINA																
1 Butterfield	Y	Y	Y	N	Y	N	N	Y	?	Y	Y	Y	Y	Y	N	N
2 Etheridge	Y	Y	Y	N	Y	N	Y	Y	Y	Y	Y	Y	Y	Y	Y	Y
3 *Jones*	Y	Y	Y	Y	N	Y	N	N	Y	N	N	Y	N	Y	Y	Y
4 Price	Y	Y	Y	N	Y	N	N	Y	Y	Y	Y	Y	Y	Y	N	N
5 *Foxx*	N	N	N	Y	N	Y	Y	N	N	N	Y	N	N	N	Y	Y
6 *Coble*	N	N	N	Y	N	Y	?	N	Y	N	Y	N	N	Y	Y	Y
7 McIntyre	Y	Y	Y	Y	Y	Y	Y	Y	Y	N	N	Y	Y	Y	Y	Y
8 *Hayes*	N	Y	N	Y	N	Y	?	N	Y	N	N	Y	Y	Y	Y	Y
9 *Myrick*	N	N	N	Y	N	Y	Y	N	N	N	Y	N	N	Y	Y	Y
10 *McHenry*	N	N	N	Y	N	Y	Y	N	N	N	Y	N	N	N	Y	Y

House Key Votes	1	2	3	4	5	6	7	8	9	10	11	12	13	14	15	16
11 Shuler	Y	Y	Y	Y	N	Y	Y	Y	Y	N	N	Y	Y	Y	N	Y
12 Watt	Y	Y	Y	N	Y	N	N	Y	Y	Y	Y	Y	Y	Y	N	N
13 Miller	Y	Y	Y	N	Y	N	N	Y	Y	Y	N	Y	Y	Y	Y	N
NORTH DAKOTA																
AL Pomeroy	Y	Y	Y	N	Y	N	Y	Y	Y	Y	Y	Y	Y	Y	Y	Y
OHIO																
1 *Chabot*	N	N	N	Y	N	Y	Y	N	N	N	Y	Y	N	N	Y	Y
2 *Schmidt*	N	Y	N	Y	N	Y	Y	N	Y	N	Y	N	N	Y	Y	Y
3 *Turner*	Y	Y	N	Y	N	Y	Y	Y	Y	N	Y	Y	Y	N	Y	Y
4 *Jordan*	N	N	N	Y	N	Y	Y	N	N	N	Y	N	N	N	Y	Y
5 *Gillmor*[6]	Y	Y	N	Y	N	Y	Y									
5 Latta														N	Y	Y
6 Wilson	Y	Y	Y	N	Y	Y	Y	Y	Y	Y	N	Y	Y	Y	Y	Y
7 *Hobson*	Y	N	N	Y	N	Y	Y	Y	N	Y	Y	Y	N	Y	Y	Y
8 *Boehner*	N	N	N	Y	N	Y	Y	N	N	N	Y	N	N	N	Y	Y
9 Kaptur	Y	Y	Y	N	Y	Y	N	Y	Y	Y	N	Y	Y	Y	Y	N
10 Kucinich	Y	Y	N	N	N	N	N	Y	Y	Y	N	?	?	Y	?	?
11 Jones	Y	Y	Y	N	?	N	N	Y	Y	Y	Y	Y	Y	Y	Y	N
12 *Tiberi*	Y	N	N	Y	N	Y	Y	Y	N	Y	Y	Y	N	Y	Y	Y
13 Sutton	Y	Y	Y	N	Y	N	N	Y	Y	Y	N	Y	Y	Y	Y	N
14 *LaTourette*	N	Y	N	Y	N	Y	Y	Y	Y	N	N	Y	Y	Y	Y	Y
15 *Pryce*	Y	Y	N	Y	N	N	Y	Y	?	Y	Y	Y	Y	?	Y	Y
16 *Regula*	N	Y	N	Y	N	Y	Y	Y	Y	N	Y	Y	Y	N	Y	Y
17 Ryan	Y	Y	Y	N	Y	N	N	Y	Y	Y	N	Y	Y	Y	Y	N
18 Space	Y	Y	Y	N	Y	N	Y	Y	Y	Y	N	Y	Y	Y	Y	Y
OKLAHOMA																
1 *Sullivan*	N	N	N	Y	N	+	Y	N	Y	N	Y	N	N	N	Y	Y
2 Boren	Y	Y	N	N	N	Y	Y	Y	Y	?	?	Y	Y	Y	Y	Y
3 *Lucas*	N	N	N	Y	N	Y	Y	N	Y	N	Y	N	N	N	Y	Y
4 *Cole*	N	N	N	Y	N	Y	Y	N	Y	N	Y	N	N	N	Y	Y
5 *Fallin*	N	N	N	Y	N	Y	Y	N	Y	N	Y	N	N	N	Y	Y
OREGON																
1 Wu	Y	Y	Y	N	Y	N	N	Y	Y	Y	N	Y	Y	Y	Y	N
2 *Walden*	N	Y	N	Y	N	N	Y	N	Y	Y	Y	N	Y	Y	Y	Y
3 Blumenauer	Y	Y	Y	N	Y	N	N	Y	Y	Y	Y	Y	Y	Y	Y	N
4 DeFazio	Y	Y	Y	N	Y	N	N	Y	Y	Y	N	Y	Y	N	N	N
5 Hooley	Y	Y	Y	N	Y	N	N	Y	Y	Y	Y	Y	Y	?	?	?
PENNSYLVANIA																
1 Brady	Y	Y	Y	?	Y	N	N	Y	?	Y	N	Y	Y	Y	Y	N
2 Fattah	Y	Y	Y	?	Y	N	N	Y	Y	Y	Y	Y	Y	Y	Y	N
3 *English*	N	Y	N	Y	N	Y	Y	Y	Y	Y	Y	Y	Y	Y	Y	Y
4 Altmire	Y	Y	Y	N	Y	Y	Y	Y	Y	Y	N	Y	Y	Y	Y	Y
5 *Peterson*	N	Y	N	Y	N	Y	Y	N	Y	N	Y	N	Y	Y	Y	Y
6 *Gerlach*	Y	Y	N	Y	N	Y	Y	Y	Y	Y	Y	Y	Y	Y	Y	Y
7 Sestak	Y	Y	Y	N	Y	N	N	Y	Y	Y	Y	Y	Y	Y	Y	Y
8 Murphy, P.	Y	Y	Y	N	N	N	N	Y	Y	Y	N	Y	Y	Y	N	N
9 *Shuster*	N	N	N	Y	N	Y	Y	N	Y	N	Y	N	N	Y	Y	Y
10 Carney	Y	Y	Y	N	Y	N	Y	Y	Y	Y	N	Y	Y	Y	Y	Y
11 Kanjorski	Y	Y	Y	N	Y	Y	N	Y	Y	Y	N	Y	Y	Y	N	Y
12 Murtha	Y	Y	Y	N	Y	Y	N	Y	Y	Y	Y	Y	Y	Y	Y	Y
13 Schwartz	Y	Y	Y	N	Y	N	N	Y	Y	Y	Y	Y	Y	Y	Y	Y
14 Doyle	Y	Y	Y	N	Y	N	N	Y	Y	Y	N	?	?	Y	Y	N
15 *Dent*	Y	Y	N	Y	N	N	Y	Y	Y	Y	Y	Y	Y	Y	Y	Y
16 *Pitts*	N	N	N	Y	N	Y	Y	N	N	N	Y	N	N	N	Y	Y
17 Holden	Y	Y	Y	N	Y	Y	N	Y	Y	Y	N	Y	Y	Y	Y	Y
18 *Murphy, T.*	Y	Y	N	Y	N	Y	Y	Y	Y	N	N	Y	Y	Y	Y	Y
19 *Platts*	Y	Y	N	Y	N	Y	Y	Y	N	Y	Y	N	Y	Y	Y	Y
RHODE ISLAND																
1 Kennedy	Y	Y	Y	N	Y	N	N	Y	Y	Y	N	Y	Y	Y	Y	N
2 Langevin	Y	Y	Y	N	Y	N	N	Y	Y	Y	N	Y	Y	Y	Y	N
SOUTH CAROLINA																
1 *Brown*	–	N	N	Y	N	Y	Y	N	Y	N	Y	N	N	Y	Y	Y
2 *Wilson*	N	N	N	Y	N	Y	Y	N	N	N	Y	N	N	Y	Y	Y
3 *Barrett*	N	N	N	Y	N	Y	Y	N	N	N	Y	N	N	N	Y	Y
4 *Inglis*	N	N	N	Y	N	Y	Y	N	N	N	Y	N	N	Y	Y	Y
5 Spratt	Y	Y	Y	N	Y	N	N	Y	Y	Y	N	Y	Y	Y	Y	Y
6 Clyburn	Y	Y	Y	N	Y	N	N	Y	Y	Y	Y	Y	Y	Y	N	Y
SOUTH DAKOTA																
AL Herseth-Sandlin	Y	Y	Y	N	Y	N	Y	Y	Y	Y	Y	Y	Y	Y	N	Y
TENNESSEE																
1 *Davis, D.*	N	N	N	Y	N	Y	Y	N	Y	N	Y	N	N	N	Y	Y
2 *Duncan*	N	Y	N	Y	N	Y	Y	N	Y	N	N	N	N	N	Y	N

[6] Rep. Paul E. Gillmor, R-Ohio, died Sept. 5, 2007. His seat was filled by Bob Latta, R,-Ohio, who was sworn in Dec. 13, 2007.

House Key Votes	1	2	3	4	5	6	7	8	9	10	11	12	13	14	15	16
3 *Wamp*	N	Y	N	Y	N	Y	Y	N	Y	N	Y	N	N	Y	Y	Y
4 Davis, L.	Y	Y	N	Y	Y	Y	Y	Y	Y	N	Y	Y	Y	Y	N	Y
5 Cooper	Y	Y	Y	N	Y	N	Y	Y	Y	Y	Y	Y	Y	Y	N	Y
6 Gordon	Y	Y	Y	N	Y	N	Y	Y	Y	N	Y	Y	Y	Y	N	Y
7 *Blackburn*	N	N	N	Y	N	Y	Y	N	N	N	Y	N	N	N	Y	Y
8 Tanner	Y	Y	Y	N	Y	N	Y	Y	Y	N	Y	Y	Y	Y	N	Y
9 Cohen	Y	Y	Y	N	Y	N	N	Y	Y	Y	N	Y	Y	Y	Y	N
TEXAS																
1 *Gohmert*	N	N	N	Y	N	Y	Y	N	N	N	Y	N	N	N	Y	Y
2 *Poe*	Y	Y	N	Y	N	Y	Y	N	Y	N	?	N	N	N	Y	Y
3 *Johnson, S.*	N	N	N	Y	N	Y	?	N	?	N	Y	N	N	N	Y	Y
4 *Hall*	N	N	N	Y	N	Y	Y	N	Y	N	Y	N	N	N	Y	Y
5 *Hensarling*	N	N	N	Y	N	Y	Y	N	N	N	Y	N	N	N	Y	Y
6 *Barton*	N	N	N	Y	N	Y	Y	N	Y	N	Y	N	N	N	Y	Y
7 *Culberson*	N	N	N	Y	N	Y	Y	N	Y	N	Y	N	N	N	Y	Y
8 *Brady*	N	N	N	Y	N	Y	Y	N	N	N	Y	N	N	N	Y	Y
9 Green, A.	Y	Y	Y	N	Y	N	N	Y	Y	Y	N	Y	Y	Y	Y	N
10 *McCaul*	N	N	N	Y	N	Y	Y	N	Y	N	Y	N	N	Y	Y	Y
11 *Conaway*	N	N	N	Y	N	Y	Y	N	Y	N	Y	N	N	N	Y	Y
12 *Granger*	N	N	N	Y	N	Y	Y	N	Y	N	Y	N	N	N	Y	Y
13 *Thornberry*	Y	N	N	Y	N	Y	Y	N	Y	N	Y	N	N	N	Y	Y
14 *Paul*	N	N	N	?	N	?	?	N	N	?	N	?	?	?	?	?
15 Hinojosa	Y	Y	Y	N	Y	N	?	Y	Y	Y	Y	Y	Y	Y	Y	Y
16 Reyes	Y	Y	Y	N	Y	N	N	Y	Y	Y	Y	Y	Y	Y	Y	Y
17 Edwards	Y	Y	Y	N	Y	N	Y	Y	Y	N	Y	Y	Y	Y	Y	Y
18 Jackson-Lee	Y	Y	Y	N	Y	N	N	Y	Y	Y	N	Y	Y	Y	Y	N
19 *Neugebauer*	N	N	N	Y	N	Y	Y	N	N	N	Y	N	N	N	Y	Y
20 Gonzalez	Y	Y	Y	N	Y	N	N	Y	Y	Y	Y	Y	Y	Y	Y	Y
21 *Smith*	N	Y	N	Y	N	Y	Y	N	Y	N	Y	N	N	Y	Y	Y
22 Lampson	Y	Y	?	?	Y	N	Y	Y	Y	N	Y	Y	Y	Y	Y	Y
23 Rodriguez	Y	Y	Y	N	Y	N	Y	Y	Y	Y	N	Y	Y	Y	Y	Y
24 *Marchant*	N	Y	N	Y	N	Y	Y	N	N	N	Y	N	N	N	Y	Y
25 Doggett	Y	Y	Y	N	Y	N	N	Y	Y	Y	Y	Y	Y	Y	N	N
26 *Burgess*	N	N	N	Y	N	Y	Y	N	Y	N	N	N	N	N	Y	Y
27 Ortiz	Y	Y	Y	?	Y	?	N	Y	Y	Y	Y	Y	Y	+	+	+
28 Cuellar	Y	Y	Y	N	Y	N	Y	Y	Y	Y	Y	Y	Y	Y	N	Y
29 Green, G.	Y	Y	Y	N	Y	N	N	Y	Y	Y	N	Y	Y	Y	N	Y
30 Johnson, E.	Y	Y	Y	?	Y	N	N	+	Y	Y	Y	Y	Y	+	+	+
31 *Carter*	N	N	N	Y	N	Y	Y	N	Y	N	Y	N	N	N	Y	Y
32 *Sessions*	N	N	N	Y	N	Y	Y	N	Y	N	Y	N	N	Y	Y	Y
UTAH																
1 *Bishop*	N	N	N	Y	N	Y	Y	N	Y	N	N	N	N	N	Y	Y
2 Matheson	Y	Y	N	N	N	N	Y	Y	Y	Y	Y	Y	Y	Y	N	Y
3 *Cannon*	N	N	N	Y	N	Y	Y	N	Y	N	Y	N	N	N	Y	Y

House Key Votes	1	2	3	4	5	6	7	8	9	10	11	12	13	14	15	16
VERMONT																
AL Welch	Y	Y	Y	N	Y	N	N	Y	Y	Y	N	Y	Y	Y	N	N
VIRGINIA																
1 *Davis, J.*[7]	N	Y	?	?	?	?	?									
1 Wittman[7]														N	Y	Y
2 *Drake*	N	N	N	Y	N	Y	Y	N	Y	N	Y	N	N	N	Y	Y
3 Scott	Y	Y	Y	N	Y	N	N	Y	Y	Y	N	Y	Y	Y	N	N
4 *Forbes*	N	Y	N	Y	N	Y	Y	N	Y	N	Y	N	N	Y	Y	Y
5 *Goode*	N	Y	N	Y	N	Y	?	N	N	N	N	N	N	Y	Y	Y
6 *Goodlatte*	N	Y	N	Y	N	Y	Y	N	N	N	Y	N	N	N	Y	Y
7 *Cantor*	N	N	N	Y	N	Y	Y	N	N	N	Y	N	N	N	Y	Y
8 Moran	Y	Y	Y	N	Y	N	N	Y	Y	Y	Y	Y	Y	Y	N	N
9 Boucher	Y	Y	Y	N	Y	N	N	Y	Y	Y	N	Y	Y	Y	Y	Y
10 *Wolf*	Y	Y	N	Y	N	Y	Y	Y	N	N	Y	Y	Y	Y	Y	Y
11 *Davis, T*	N	N	N	Y	N	N	Y	Y	Y	Y	Y	N	N	Y	Y	Y
WASHINGTON																
1 Inslee	Y	Y	Y	N	Y	N	N	Y	Y	Y	Y	Y	Y	Y	Y	N
2 Larsen	Y	Y	Y	N	Y	N	N	Y	Y	Y	Y	Y	Y	Y	N	Y
3 Baird	Y	Y	Y	N	?	N	N	Y	Y	Y	Y	Y	Y	Y	N	Y
4 *Hastings*	N	N	N	Y	N	Y	Y	N	Y	N	N	N	N	N	Y	Y
5 *Rodgers*	N	N	N	?	?	Y	Y	Y	Y	N	N	N	N	Y	Y	Y
6 Dicks	Y	Y	Y	N	Y	N	N	Y	Y	Y	Y	Y	Y	Y	Y	Y
7 McDermott	Y	Y	Y	N	Y	N	N	Y	Y	Y	Y	Y	Y	N	N	N
8 *Reichert*	N	Y	N	Y	N	Y	Y	Y	Y	Y	Y	Y	Y	Y	Y	Y
9 Smith	Y	Y	Y	N	Y	N	N	Y	Y	Y	Y	Y	Y	Y	N	N
WEST VIRGINIA																
1 Mollohan	Y	Y	Y	N	Y	Y	N	Y	Y	Y	N	Y	Y	Y	Y	Y
2 *Capito*	Y	Y	N	Y	N	Y	Y	Y	Y	N	Y	Y	Y	Y	Y	Y
3 Rahall	Y	Y	Y	N	Y	Y	N	Y	Y	N	N	Y	Y	N	Y	N
WISCONSIN																
1 *Ryan*	N	N	N	Y	N	Y	Y	N	Y	Y	Y	N	N	N	Y	Y
2 Baldwin	Y	Y	Y	N	Y	N	N	Y	Y	Y	N	Y	Y	Y	Y	N
3 Kind	Y	Y	Y	N	Y	N	N	Y	Y	Y	Y	Y	Y	Y	N	Y
4 Moore	Y	Y	Y	N	Y	N	N	Y	Y	Y	?	Y	Y	Y	Y	N
5 *Sensenbrenner*	N	N	N	Y	N	Y	Y	N	N	N	Y	N	N	N	Y	Y
6 *Petri*	Y	Y	N	Y	N	Y	Y	Y	Y	N	Y	N	N	Y	Y	Y
7 Obey	Y	Y	Y	N	Y	N	N	Y	Y	Y	N	Y	Y	Y	N	N
8 Kagen	Y	Y	Y	N	Y	N	N	Y	Y	Y	N	Y	Y	Y	Y	N
WYOMING																
AL *Cubin*	N	N	?	?	?	?	Y	N	?	?	?	?	?	?	?	?

[7]Rep. Rob Wittman, R-Va., was sworn in Dec. 13, 2007, to replace Republican Jo Ann Davis, who died Oct. 6.

Senate

1. ECONOMIC STIMULUS

Early in 2008, the Senate passed legislation to help stimulate the economy through a tax refund to most taxpayers of up to $600 for individuals and $1,200 for couples. This vote took place after a four-day standoff in the Senate about the reach and cost of the package. The week before, the Finance Committee had put together a measure that included not only the rebates at the core of the House-passed bill but also extended unemployment benefits and tax breaks for renewable-energy initiatives. *(Story, p. 151)*

The Senate at first rejected cloture on an amendment to substitute the Finance Committee language for the House measure. When that failed, the Senate moved on to pass a less sweeping measure the next day.

The final measure was a compromise between the two chambers and did include some provisions sought by the Finance panel, such as expanding eligibility for the rebates to include low-income senior citizens, disabled veterans, and survivors of veterans. Veterans' groups and the AARP lobbied heavily for those changes.

Republicans had initially opposed changing the House bill at all and had urged senators to coalesce behind the original language that Treasury Secretary Henry M. Paulson Jr. negotiated with House Speaker Nancy Pelosi, D-Calif., and house minority leader John A. Boehner, R-Ohio. But Senate minority leader Mitch McConnell, R-Ky., ultimately pushed for the expanded package. The Senate passed HR 5140 on Feb. 7 by a vote of 81–16: R 33–16; D 46–0; I 2–0. *(Vote, p. 975)*

Because the bill did not include the unemployment or renewable-energy provisions, which would have been opposed in the House and the White House, Senate passage pushed the legislation quickly to enactment. The House cleared it the same day, and the president signed it the next week.

2. GENETIC DISCRIMINATION BAN

The House had passed legislation to prohibit discrimination on the basis of genetic information by a wide margin in April 2007, but it languished for a year in the Senate, where leaders could not bring it up because of a hold on the measure by Tom Coburn, R-Okla. When a block of time unexpectedly opened up on the Senate floor in April 2008, leaders and bill sponsors—who had worked for thirteen years to ban the use of genetic-screening results in employment or insurance coverage decisions—began intense negotiations with Coburn and the White House.

They worked for a week, revising language on details in the bill that were causing concern, and on April 22, Coburn dropped his hold. Once the deal was reached, the Senate overwhelmingly voted to send the amended version back to the House, where it cleared a week later. *(Story, p. 717)*

The Senate passed HR 493 on April 24 by a vote of 95–0: R 46–0; D 47–0; I 2–0. *(Vote, p. 975)*

3. FARM BILL REAUTHORIZATION

In May the Senate cleared a massive agriculture bill that reauthorized federal farm and nutrition programs for five years. The vote completed an eighteen-month effort to extend the nation's farm programs, significantly increasing nutrition spending and continuing to preserve crop subsidies. The size of Senate support for the conference report on the bill, along with a similar level of backing in the House, showed a clear split with the White House when it came to the issue of agricultural assistance.

The Senate cleared the reauthorization on May 15 by adopting a conference report on the bill (HR 2419) by a vote of 81–15: R 35–13; D 44–2; I 2–0. *(Story, pp. 514, 522 Vote, p. 975)*

President George W. Bush said the bill did not do enough to trim subsidies, reduce the cost of farm programs, or address trade complaints by other nations about unfair U.S. agriculture subsidies. But Senate Republicans, by an almost three-to-one ratio, rejected the president's position, with thirty-five GOP members voting to clear the measure. When Bush vetoed the legislation, the same thirty-five Republicans voted to override, thus enacting HR 2419 into law a week later.

4. CLIMATE CHANGE

The Senate in June refused to invoke cloture on legislation (S 3036) to cap greenhouse gas emissions and set up a trading system for companies to buy and sell emissions allowances. With this vote, the Senate's long-touted debate on global warming fizzled before it got started, as partisan jousting over judicial nominations and other issues overtook the issue. *(Story, p. 495)*

The vote was on an amendment to a climate change bill offered by California Democrat Barbara Boxer that was to serve as the base legislation for the climate change debate. Although passage was never expected, supporters had hoped to get the Senate on the record on several amendments that could help shape a climate change bill in the next Congress. Instead, the Senate never addressed issues that were considered critical to any future legislation, such as the role of nuclear power or whether to preempt more stringent action at the state level.

The Senate opened the week by voting 74–14 to bring up the bill. But Majority Leader Harry Reid, D-Nev., and Minority Leader Mitch McConnell, R-Ky., were at odds all week over how to move forward with amendments to the bill. Reid had suggested that five amendments should be offered on each side; Republicans wanted dozens more. Also, McConnell said he was protesting the way the majority party had handled confirmation of appellate court nominees.

GOP senators filibustered to prevent the Senate from proceeding to Boxer's amendment. The vote to cut off debate fell so far short of the sixty needed that Reid did not keep open the option of reconsidering it, as he usually did when he intended to try again. The bill never came back to the floor.

The Senate on June 6 rejected a motion to invoke cloture on the Boxer amendment on S 3036. The vote was 48–36: R 7–32; D 39–4; I 2–0. Three-fifths of the total Senate (sixty) was required to invoke cloture. *(Vote, p. 975)*

5. FOREIGN INTELLIGENCE SURVEILLANCE

An attempt in July to allow lawsuits against companies that had participated in the National Security Agency's warrantless surveillance program fell flat by a huge margin of thirty-four votes when senators rejected an amendment to the Foreign Intelligence Surveillance Act reauthorization. *(Story, p. 251)*

The defeat of the amendment, offered by Christopher J. Dodd, D-Conn., as well as two subsequent efforts to amend the bill (HR 6304), was the final attempt in the 110th Congress to confront President George W. Bush over electronic surveillance laws. Democrats decided to drop the issue until a new administration took office.

Democrats voting in favor of the amendment included Barack Obama of Illinois, the party's presumed nominee for president, who earlier pledged to join a filibuster of any bill that provided retroactive legal immunity. But he also voted to clear the measure, noting compromises that had been made on the legislation as well as the need to ensure intelligence gathering. Senators opposing the amendment had decided that a commitment to electronic surveillance outweighed concern over granting legal immunity to the companies that had helped the government with its controversial spying program.

The Senate rejected Dodd's amendment to HR 6304 on July 9 by a vote of 32–66: R 0–48; D 31–17; I 1–1. *(Vote, p. 975)*

6. MEDICARE PHYSICIANS' PAY

The Senate by a comfortable margin invoked cloture and halted a filibuster on legislation (HR 6331) to prevent a scheduled 10.6 percent cut in pay rates for doctors who participated in Medicare. *(Story, p. 571)*

The vote in July cleared the way for a controversial Medicare bill to pass and showed there would be enough support to override an expected veto, sending President George W. Bush one of the strongest rebukes of his presidency.

The vote was on a motion to invoke cloture to proceed to the measure, the second such effort to move the bill in the Senate in fewer than two weeks. On the first attempt, on June 26, the motion fell just short of the sixty votes needed to succeed. In that instance, thirty-nine Republicans voted against the bill.

Congress left the next day for the July Fourth recess, during which the July 1 deadline for acting on the physician rate cut was due to pass. But the administration announced it would not apply the cut immediately, instead holding doctors' claims for 10 business days—until July 15—to give Congress more time to pass a bill. In the meantime, Senate Democrats hoped doctors' groups such as the American Medical Association could put enough pressure on vulnerable Republicans that the bill could pass when they returned from recess.

The second vote to invoke cloture came on July 9. It was successful 69–30: R 18–30; D 49–0; I 2–0, more than enough to override a veto. One vote in support came from Sen. Edward Kennedy, D-Mass., who missed the earlier vote while undergoing treatment for brain cancer. This time Kennedy returned to the chamber in a dramatic entrance, accompanied by his son, Rep. Patrick J. Kennedy, D-R.I., as well as John Kerry, his Democratic colleague from Massachusetts. *(Vote, p. 975)*

Nine Republicans who had voted against the June 26 cloture motion had changed their minds in the two weeks, including three—Lamar Alexander of Tennessee, Saxby Chambliss of Georgia, and John Cornyn of Texas—who were running for reelection

Immediately after the cloture motion succeeded, the Senate cleared the bill by voice vote. Six days later, Bush vetoed the legislation and both chambers voted to override it. The Senate vote to override was 70–26.

7. MORTGAGE RELIEF

In one of its major actions to combat the rapidly collapsing housing industry, the Senate in July cleared legislation (HR 3221) to let the Treasury Department extend new credit to and buy stock in mortgage giants Fannie Mae and Freddie Mac and to help homeowners with loans they could no longer afford. *(Story, p. 630)*

It was the second of three significant legislative efforts during the year to prevent an economic slowdown from becoming much worse, but the Senate had to overcome objections from conservatives. The legislation was intended to help homeowners facing foreclosure while also giving the administration authority to salvage mortgage giants Fannie Mae and Freddie Mac, which were facing bankruptcy.

The House and Senate had tried for months to agree on the bill to create a $300 billion trust fund in the Federal Housing Administration to help lenders refinance troubled mortgages, give money to local governments to rehabilitate foreclosed properties, and impose a new regulatory structure on Fannie and Freddie. As the two chambers got closer, however, the administration of President George W. Bush maintained its vigorous opposition to elements of the bill. In addition, for a time some Republican senators tried to use the measure to advance energy tax breaks.

A Senate vote to send the bill to the president became possible only after Treasury Secretary Henry M. Paulson Jr. decided that the survival of Fannie and Freddie was in doubt, as investors pushed down their share prices to improbably low levels. Paulson asked for authority to inject capital into the two companies and potentially to take them over, which eventually he was forced to do. He persuaded lawmakers to grant him the authority, and the administration dropped its veto threat over the mortgage relief provisions. After the House voted to pass the revised version of the measure, the Senate overwhelmingly went along during a rare Saturday session. That came on July 26 when the Senate cleared HR 3221 by a vote of 72–13: R 27–13; D 43–0; I 2–0. *(Vote, p. 975)*

8. U.S.-INDIA NUCLEAR AGREEMENT

The Senate on Oct. 1 cleared legislation (HR 7081) to approve the United States' nuclear cooperation agreement with India. This action gave President George W. Bush one of his most significant foreign policy victories of his two terms in office. *(Story, p. 311)*

The vote gave approval to a landmark agreement that allowed nuclear trade between India and the United States and brought India's civilian, but not military, reactors under international oversight. The deal was important because, as a country that had tested nuclear weapons but not signed the Nuclear Non-Proliferation Treaty, India had been gradually excluded from the global nuclear industry for more than three decades.

The Senate cleared HR 7081 on Oct. 1 by a vote of 86–13: R 49–0; D 36–12; I 1–1. *(Vote, p. 975)*

9. TROUBLED ASSET RELIEF PROGRAM (TARP)

In one of its most important votes of the 110th Congress, the Senate on Oct. 1 passed, by a wide margin, legislation authorizing the Troubled Asset Relief Program. TARP, as it was thereafter known, authorized $700 billion to buy a vast array of largely worthless mortgages—toxic assets as they were called—held by banks and other financial institutions that were at the center of the economic crises that began in 2007 and threatened to turn into a collapse as bad as the Great Depression of the 1930s. The law also authorized the government to provide guarantees for troubled assets in return for premiums paid by the companies involved, and authorized the government to take equity stakes in companies participating in the asset purchase program. *(Story, p. 154)*

The Oct. 1 passage vote on HR 1424 was 74–25: R 34–15; D 39–9; I 1–1. *(Vote, p. 975)*

After the House unexpectedly voted down the original version of the bill Sept. 29, in the face of outraged protests from constituents furious over a Wall Street bailout, an action that sent the stock market plunging to its worst one-day decline ever, Senate leaders took control of the issue, combining the core provisions of the financial industry bailout with a measure to extend expiring tax credits, create incentives for the use of renewable energy, and require parity from insurers in the handling of mental health benefits. They announced their decision Sept. 30 and scheduled the vote for the next evening.

Although Senate passage was expected, the event was filled with high drama seldom seen in Congress. Majority Leader Harry Reid, D-Nev., ordered the Senate to remain seated during the roll call. One by one, with the chamber otherwise silent, each member shouted out his or her vote. The only senator absent that nigh, and the only member of Congress to not vote on passage of the bill, was Edward M. Kennedy of Massachusetts, who was recovering from treatment for a brain tumor.

Eight Republican senators who were in tight races voted for the bill. Four of those—John E. Sununu of New Hampshire, Gordon H. Smith of Oregon, Ted Stevens of Alaska, and Norm Coleman of Minnesota—lost their seats. Of the nine Democrats who voted against the bill, only Mary L. Landrieu of Louisiana was in a tough fight back home, and she won reelection Nov. 4.

10. AUTO INDUSTRY BAILOUT

In one of its last acts in 2008, the Senate refused to come to the aid of the nation's three deeply ailing auto manufacturers: General Motors, Chrysler, and Ford Motor. On Dec. 11, senators refused to invoke cloture to end a filibuster against debating legislation allowing the Treasury Department to provide up to $14 billion in loans to domestic automakers, who, in return, would have been required to submit restructuring plans by March 31, 2009. *(Story, p. 159)*

The Senate vote that ended debate on an automaker rescue package showed that Republican lawmakers had reached a point of "bailout fatigue" after a year in which they were asked by the Bush administration and their congressional leaders to approve billions of dollars in aid for the mortgage industry and for financial services companies.

With at least two of the companies facing bankruptcy, President George W. Bush stepped in to provide funds from the Troubled Asset Relief Program (TARP) to keep the automakers afloat until the 111th Congress could consider legislation in 2009.

The Senate's action on Dec. 11 came when it rejected cloture on a bill (HR 7005) that was to be the vehicle for the auto industry bailout. The vote of was 52–35: R 10–31; D 40–4; I 2–0, eight votes short of the sixty needed. *(Vote, p. 975)*

1. **HR 5140. Economic Stimulus Passage.** Passage of the bill to provide tax refunds for most taxpayers of $300 to $600 for individuals and $600 to $1,200 for couples, with a phase-out for individuals with adjusted gross incomes above $75,000 and couples at $150,000. The bill also provided businesses a 50 percent depreciation for certain equipment purchased in 2008 and increased to $250,000 the amount small businesses could expense in the year items were purchased. It also raised the size of mortgage loans the Federal Housing Administration could insure and Fannie Mae and Freddie Mac could purchase. Passed 81–16: R 33–16; D 46–0; I 2–0. A "yea" was a vote in favor of the president's position. Feb. 7, 2008.

2. **HR 493. Genetic Information Discrimination Passage.** Passage of the bill to prohibit insurance companies, employers, employment agencies, and labor unions from discriminating on the basis of genetic information. It barred health plans from requiring genetic testing and from adjusting premiums or base enrollment decisions on genetic information. Passed 95–0: R 46–0; D 47–0; I 2–0. April 24, 2008.

3. **HR 2419. Farm Programs Reauthorization Conference Report.** Adoption of the conference report on the bill to reauthorize federal farm and nutrition programs for five years, including crop subsidies and food stamps, as well as conservation, rural development, and agricultural trade programs. HR 2419 authorized a $10.4 billion increase for nutrition programs and cut direct payment subsidies overall by $313 million. The bill also required country-of-origin labels for all meat by September 2008. Adopted 81–15: R 35–13; D 44–2; I 2–0. A "nay" was a vote in support of the president's position. May 15, 2008.

4. **S 3036. Climate Change Cloture.** Motion to invoke cloture (thus limiting debate) on the Boxer, D-Calif., substitute amendment to cap greenhouse gas emissions nationwide and set up a trading system for companies to buy and sell emission allowances. Motion rejected 48–36: R 7–32; D 39–4; I 2–0. Three-fifths of the total Senate (sixty) was required to invoke cloture. A "nay" was a vote in support of the president's position. June 6, 2008.

5. **HR 6304. Foreign Intelligence Surveillance Liability.** Dodd, D-Conn., amendment to delete provisions providing retroactive immunity from civil liability to telecommunications companies that participated in the Bush administration's warrantless surveillance program. Rejected 32–66: R 0–48; D 31–17; I 1–1. A "nay" was a vote in support of the president's position. July 9, 2008.

6. **HR 6331. Medicare Physician Payments Cloture.** Motion to invoke cloture (thus limiting debate) on legislation to prevent a 10.6 percent cut in Medicare physician payments scheduled to take effect July 1, 2008, by holding payments at current rates for eighteen months. HR 6331 gave doctors a 1.1 percent increase in 2009 and provided $16.6 billion over ten years for changes to Medicare beneficiary programs. Motion agreed to 69–30: R 18–30; D 49–0; I 2–0. Three-fifths of the total Senate (sixty) was required to invoke cloture. A "nay" was a vote in support of the president's position. July 9, 2008.

7. **HR 3221. Mortgage Relief.** Reid, D-Nev., motion to concur in House amendments to legislation to extend new credit and buy stock in Fannie Mae and Freddie Mac and create an independent regulator for the two mortgage giants and the Federal Home Loan Bank System. It also included a $7,500 tax credit for some first-time homebuyers, higher loan limits for FHA-backed loans, a standard tax deduction for property taxes, revenue-raisers to offset part of the costs; authorized $3.9 billion in grants to states and localities to purchase and rehabilitate foreclosed properties; and increased the federal debt limit to $10.6 trillion. Motion agreed to, clearing the bill for the president, 72–13: R 27–13; D 43–0; I 2–0. A "yea" was a vote in support of the president's position. July 26, 2008.

8. **HR 7081. U.S.-India Nuclear Agreement Passage.** Passage of the bill to grant congressional approval to the U.S.-India nuclear cooperation agreement. HR 7081 allowed the Nuclear Regulatory Commission to issue licenses for transfers of nuclear-related goods and services once the president determined and certified to Congress that certain actions had occurred, including that India had provided the International Atomic Energy Agency with a credible plan to separate civilian and military nuclear facilities, materials, and programs. Passed 86–13: R 49–0; D 36–12; I 1–1. A "yea" was a vote in support of the president's position. Oct. 1, 2008.

9. **HR 1424. Troubled Asset Relief Program (TARP) Passage.** Passage of the bill providing the Treasury Department with $700 billion to buy certain mortgage assets. The bill required the Treasury to create a program to insure mortgage assets, provided for congressional oversight, and limited compensation for executives of companies whose troubled assets were purchased. It also temporarily increased federal deposit insurance to $250,000 per bank account, extended dozens of expired or expiring tax provisions, provided a one-year adjustment to the alternative minimum tax, and required private insurance plans to put mental health benefits on par with other medical benefits. Passed 74–25: R 34–15; D 39–9; I 1–1. A "yea" was a vote in support of the president's position. Oct. 1, 2008.

10. **HR 7005. Automobile Industry Loan Program Cloture.** Motion to invoke cloture (thus limiting debate) on the motion to proceed to a bill on the alternative minimum tax, which was to serve as the vehicle for an emergency loan package for domestic automakers. Motion rejected 52–35: R 10–31; D 40–4; I 2–0. Three-fifths of the total Senate (sixty) was required to invoke cloture. A "yea" was a vote in support of the president's position. Dec. 11, 2008.

KEY

Democrat	*Republican*	**Independent**

Y	Voted for (yea)	–	Announced against
#	Paired for	P	Voted "present"
+	Announced for	C	Voted "present" to avoid possible conflict of interest
N	Voted against (nay)	?	Did not vote or otherwise make a position known
X	Paired against		

Senate Key Votes	1	2	3	4	5	6	7	8	9	10
ALABAMA										
Shelby	N	Y	Y	N	N	N	Y	Y	N	N
Sessions	N	Y	Y	N	N	N	Y	Y	N	N
ALASKA										
Stevens	Y	Y	Y	?	N	Y	Y	Y	Y	?
Murkowski	N	Y	N	?	N	Y	Y	Y	Y	N
ARIZONA										
McCain	Y	?	?	+	?	?	?	Y	Y	N
Kyl	N	Y	N	N	N	N	N	Y	Y	N
ARKANSAS										
Lincoln	Y	Y	Y	Y	N	Y	Y	Y	Y	N
Pryor	Y	Y	Y	Y	N	Y	Y	Y	Y	Y
CALIFORNIA										
Feinstein	Y	Y	Y	Y	N	Y	Y	Y	Y	Y
Boxer	Y	Y	Y	Y	Y	Y	Y	N	Y	Y
COLORADO										
Allard	N	Y	Y	N	N	N	?	Y	N	N
Salazar	Y	Y	Y	Y	N	Y	Y	Y	Y	Y
CONNECTICUT										
Dodd	Y	Y	Y	Y	Y	Y	Y	Y	Y	Y
Lieberman	Y	Y	Y	Y	N	Y	Y	Y	Y	Y
DELAWARE										
Biden	Y	Y	Y	+	Y	Y	Y	Y	Y	?
Carper	Y	Y	Y	Y	N	Y	+	Y	Y	Y
FLORIDA										
Nelson	Y	Y	Y	Y	N	Y	Y	Y	N	Y
Martinez	Y	Y	Y	Y	N	Y	Y	Y	Y	N
GEORGIA										
Chambliss	Y	Y	Y	N	N	Y	Y	Y	Y	N
Isakson	Y	Y	Y	N	N	Y	Y	Y	Y	N
HAWAII										
Inouye	Y	Y	Y	Y	N	Y	?	Y	Y	Y
Akaka	Y	Y	Y	Y	Y	Y	Y	N	Y	Y
IDAHO										
Craig	N	Y	Y	?	N	N	Y	Y	Y	?
Crapo	N	Y	Y	N	N	N	Y	Y	N	N
ILLINOIS										
Durbin	Y	Y	Y	Y	Y	Y	Y	Y	Y	Y
Obama[1]	?	?	?	+	Y	Y	?	Y	Y	
INDIANA										
Lugar	Y	Y	N	N	N	N	Y	Y	Y	Y
Bayh	Y	Y	Y	Y	N	Y	Y	Y	Y	Y
IOWA										
Grassley	Y	Y	Y	N	N	N	N	Y	Y	N
Harkin	Y	Y	Y	Y	Y	Y	?	N	Y	Y
KANSAS										
Brownback	Y	Y	Y	N	N	N	Y	Y	N	Y
Roberts	Y	Y	Y	N	N	Y	Y	Y	N	N
KENTUCKY										
McConnell	Y	Y	Y	N	N	N	Y	Y	Y	N
Bunning	Y	Y	Y	N	N	N	–	Y	N	N
LOUISIANA										
Landrieu	Y	Y	Y	N	N	Y	Y	Y	N	Y
Vitter	Y	Y	Y	N	N	N	N	Y	N	N
MAINE										
Snowe	Y	Y	Y	Y	N	Y	Y	Y	Y	Y
Collins	Y	Y	N	Y	N	Y	Y	Y	Y	Y
MARYLAND										
Mikulski	Y	Y	Y	Y	N	Y	Y	Y	Y	Y
Cardin	Y	Y	Y	Y	Y	Y	Y	Y	Y	Y
MASSACHUSETTS										
Kennedy	Y	Y	?	+	?	Y	?	?	?	?
Kerry	Y	Y	Y	Y	Y	Y	Y	Y	Y	+
MICHIGAN										
Levin	Y	Y	Y	Y	Y	Y	Y	Y	Y	Y
Stabenow	Y	Y	Y	Y	Y	Y	Y	Y	N	Y
MINNESOTA										
Coleman	Y	Y	Y	+	N	Y	Y	Y	Y	N
Klobuchar	Y	Y	Y	Y	Y	Y	Y	Y	Y	Y
MISSISSIPPI										
Cochran	Y	Y	Y	N	N	N	Y	Y	N	N
Wicker	Y	Y	Y	N	N	N	Y	Y	N	N
MISSOURI										
Bond	Y	Y	Y	N	N	N	?	Y	Y	Y
McCaskill	Y	Y	Y	Y	N	Y	Y	Y	Y	Y
MONTANA										
Baucus	Y	Y	Y	Y	Y	Y	Y	Y	Y	N
Tester	Y	Y	Y	Y	Y	Y	Y	Y	N	N
NEBRASKA										
Hagel	N	Y	N	N	N	N	Y	Y	Y	?
Nelson	+	Y	Y	Y	N	Y	Y	Y	Y	Y
NEVADA										
Reid	Y	Y	Y	Y	Y	Y	Y	Y	Y	N
Ensign	N	Y	N	N	N	N	N	Y	Y	N
NEW HAMPSHIRE										
Gregg	N	?	N	?	N	N	Y	Y	Y	N
Sununu	Y	Y	N	Y	N	N	Y	Y	Y	?
NEW JERSEY										
Lautenberg	Y	Y	Y	Y	Y	Y	Y	Y	Y	Y
Menendez	Y	Y	Y	Y	Y	Y	Y	Y	Y	Y
NEW MEXICO										
Domenici	Y	Y	N	N	N	N	Y	Y	Y	Y
Bingaman	Y	Y	Y	Y	Y	Y	Y	N	Y	Y
NEW YORK										
Schumer	Y	Y	Y	Y	Y	Y	Y	Y	Y	Y
Clinton	?	?	?	+	Y	Y	Y	Y	Y	Y
NORTH CAROLINA										
Dole	Y	Y	Y	Y	N	Y	?	Y	N	Y
Burr	Y	Y	Y	N	N	N	?	Y	Y	N
NORTH DAKOTA										
Conrad	Y	Y	Y	?	N	Y	Y	N	Y	Y
Dorgan	Y	Y	Y	N	Y	Y	Y	N	N	Y
OHIO										
Voinovich	Y	Y	N	N	N	Y	Y	Y	Y	Y
Brown	Y	Y	Y	N	Y	Y	Y	N	Y	Y
OKLAHOMA										
Inhofe	N	Y	Y	N	N	N	?	Y	N	N
Coburn	N	Y	N	N	N	N	N	Y	Y	N
OREGON										
Wyden	Y	Y	Y	Y	Y	Y	Y	Y	N	?
Smith	Y	Y	Y	Y	N	Y	Y	Y	Y	?
PENNSYLVANIA										
Specter	Y	Y	Y	?	N	Y	Y	Y	Y	Y
Casey	Y	Y	Y	Y	Y	Y	Y	Y	Y	Y

[1]Sen. Barack Obama, D-Ill., resigned Nov. 16, 2008, after winning the presidential election.

Senate Key Votes	1	2	3	4	5	6	7	8	9	10
RHODE ISLAND										
Reed	Y	Y	N	Y	Y	Y	Y	N	Y	Y
Whitehouse	Y	Y	N	Y	Y	Y	Y	N	Y	Y
SOUTH CAROLINA										
Graham	Y	Y	Y	?	N	N	?	Y	Y	?
DeMint	N	?	N	?	N	N	N	Y	N	N
SOUTH DAKOTA										
Johnson	Y	Y	Y	N	N	Y	Y	Y	N	Y
Thune	Y	Y	Y	N	N	N	N	Y	Y	N
TENNESSEE										
Alexander	Y	Y	Y	N	N	Y	Y	Y	Y	–
Corker	N	Y	Y	N	N	Y	N	Y	Y	N
TEXAS										
Hutchison	Y	Y	Y	N	N	Y	N	Y	Y	N
Cornyn	Y	Y	Y	?	N	Y	N	Y	Y	–
UTAH										
Hatch	Y	Y	Y	N	N	N	N	Y	Y	N
Bennett	Y	Y	N	N	N	N	Y	Y	Y	N

Senate Key Votes	1	2	3	4	5	6	7	8	9	10
VERMONT										
Leahy	Y	Y	Y	Y	Y	Y	Y	N	Y	Y
Sanders	Y	Y	Y	Y	Y	Y	Y	N	N	Y
VIRGINIA										
Warner	Y	Y	Y	Y	N	Y	?	Y	Y	Y
Webb	Y	Y	Y	Y	N	Y	Y	Y	Y	Y
WASHINGTON										
Murray	Y	Y	Y	Y	Y	Y	?	Y	Y	Y
Cantwell	Y	Y	Y	Y	Y	Y	Y	Y	N	Y
WEST VIRGINIA										
Byrd	Y	Y	Y	?	Y	Y	Y	N	Y	Y
Rockefeller	Y	Y	Y	Y	N	Y	Y	Y	Y	Y
WISCONSIN										
Kohl	Y	Y	Y	Y	N	Y	Y	Y	Y	Y
Feingold	Y	Y	Y	Y	Y	Y	Y	N	N	Y
WYOMING										
Enzi	N	Y	Y	N	N	N	N	Y	N	N
Barrasso	N	Y	Y	N	N	N	N	Y	N	N

House

1. ECONOMIC STIMULUS

In one of its earliest actions to counter the economic recession that was growing deeper by the month, the House in early February cleared a stimulus bill that authorized payments of $600 to $1,200 for most American taxpayers. The payments were designed as tax refunds. *(Story, p. 151)*

The vote to clear the bill, HR 5140, took place just two weeks after the announcement of a deal between House leaders and the administration of President George W. Bush to write the legislation. Senate Democrats had hoped to broaden the legislation to include unemployment benefits and energy tax incentives and did expand the tax refund to add low-income senior citizens and veterans, but the final bill was largely as it had been originally designed.

The fact that it moved so quickly through Congress, and that it was a rare example of accord between the two parties and between the legislative and executive branches, showed how seriously elected officials were starting to take the economic downturn that had begun with the popping of a housing bubble that had been expanding for much of the 2000s decade. The nation lost jobs in January for the first time in more than four years, and consumer spending slowed sharply in December, according to reports by the Labor and Commerce departments that had been released the week before the final House vote.

By the end of the year, the economy's slump dominated the nation's attention and was an important factor in the election of Barack Obama as president and the expansion of Democratic majorities in Congress. The House vote clearing the legislation came on Feb. 7 by a vote of 380–34: R 165–28; D 215–6. *(Vote, p. 982)*

2. COLOMBIA TRADE

House Democrats, with only negligible Republican support, changed the chambers rules in April to remove an existing requirement that trade deals with other nations be moved through under a fast-track procedure that assured an up-or-down vote quickly. The rules change applied to a trade agreement with Columbia that many Democrats adamantly opposed. In spite of warnings from House leaders, President George W. Bush sent the agreement to Congress, in effect daring the legislators to turn it down. *(Story, p. 211)*

This vote allowed House Democrats to sidestep a showdown with Bush over trade. The Columbia deal negotiated under fast-track procedures would have required Congress to vote within days of receiving the agreement and without possibility of amendment.

The fast-track procedure had been used repeatedly over the years for trade agreements both large and small, and Congress had never before rejected a trade pact. The opposition to the Colombia agreement was seen as sufficiently large that House leaders did not want to take the chance on the pact being rejected outright and sending a signal to the world that the United States was backing away from general support for opening trade between countries.

House Speaker Nancy Pelosi, D-Calif., asked President Bush to withhold sending Congress legislation to implement the agreement until changes could be made that would satisfy opponents. Many Democrats were concerned about the violence against labor union officials in Colombia, and they also wanted an expansion of benefits for U.S. workers who lost their jobs because of increasing international trade.

Bush, however, sent the implementing bill to Capitol Hill on April 8, which started the clock ticking on a potential vote. House Democratic leaders immediately introduced a resolution to change House rules and suspend fast-track procedures for the Colombia deal. That resolution was adopted on a near-party-line vote, putting action on the Colombia agreement on hold. House leaders declined for the rest of the year to say when they might restore the fast-track process or when the Colombia trade pact might be considered. The House vote to change its rules (H Res 1092) came on April 10 by a vote of 224–195: R 6–185; D 218–10. *(Vote, p. 982)*

3. IRAQ TROOP WITHDRAWAL

Congressional Democrats repeatedly tried—without success—to force President George W. Bush to end U.S. involvement in the Iraq war. One such attempt came in May 2008 on a proposal to amend a war supplemental appropriations bill with language to require a troop withdrawal from Iraq within thirty days of enactment. *(Story, pp. 387, 388)*

Just as they had done on several occasions in 2007, Democratic leaders decided to use a procedure that involved passing the supplemental through a series of votes on motions to concur that would allow lawmakers to tailor their votes on aspects of the measure without having to cast a single up-or-down vote on the bill. They planned votes on three amendments to the underlying measure, which in this case was the military construction appropriations bill that had been left over from 2007. One of the three amendments was for money to operate the wars in Iraq and Afghanistan; the second was to appropriate funds for domestic projects; and the third contained various conditions on U.S. war policy in Iraq, including a requirement that redeployment from Iraq begin within thirty days of enactment, with a "goal" of withdrawing most troops by December 2009. Splitting the measure into these three distinct parts allowed antiwar Democrats to vote against funding for military operations in Iraq and in favor of troop withdrawal. Conversely, it allowed Democrats from typically conservative districts to cast votes that were more in line with their constituents' viewpoints.

At the same time, House leaders and members casting those votes were well aware of the politics in the Senate, where the slim majority held by Democrats meant it would be unlikely that such troop withdrawal requirements could survive in a final bill.

Because efforts to dictate such terms in Iraq had failed repeatedly in the first session of the 110th Congress, and because other issues, such as the economy, were rising in priority, this was the only significant House vote on troop withdrawal in 2008. In fact, several of the Democrats' staunchest antiwar members—such as Maxine Waters and Lynn Woolsey, both of California—voted in favor of the troop withdrawal language, even though it was not as strong as they would have liked. They routinely voted against such language in 2007 because they wanted to see a more definitive deadline for withdrawal.

In this case the House on May 15 agreed to a motion to accept language ordering a troop draw-down and an end date for U.S. fighting. The amendment also included other provisions including one to prohibit interrogation techniques not authorized in the Army Field Manual. The language was added to HR 2642, the military construction bill, by a vote of 227–196: R 8–183; D 219–13. *(Vote, p. 982)*

4. FARM BILL REAUTHORIZATION

In one of the few instances of successfully challenging George W. Bush's use of the veto, Congress in May overrode the president's rejection of legislation to reauthorize federal farm and nutrition programs for five years. *(Story, pp. 514, 522)*

With this vote, the second veto override in the Bush presidency, lawmakers showed that the generations-old affinity for financial assistance for farmers continued, despite push-back from the White House. Among other complaints with the legislation, Bush wanted a much lower income cap on eligibility requirements for payments than the final bill provided.

Congress ended up double-stamping this sentiment with a second override less than a month later, after it turned out the first version of the bill Bush vetoed had been erroneously incomplete through a technical error. Lawmakers hastily put together a new measure (HR 6124) correcting the error, and Bush vetoed it June 18. Both chambers voted that same day to override the second veto, enacting the bill into law. This vote on the corrected measure was nearly identical to the first farm bill override: 317–109.

The 2008 key vote on the farm bill came on the first veto, which showed that Congress was determined to enact the legislation into law. On that vote, May 21, the House overrode Bush's veto of the first bill (HR 2419) by a vote of 316–108: R 100–94; D 216–14. A two-thirds majority of those present and voting (283 in this case) was required to override a veto. *(Vote, p. 982)*

5. AMTRAK REAUTHORIZATION

Congress in 2008 reauthorized the national rail passenger system, Amtrak, for five years. The legislation, always controversial, authorized $14.4 billion for Amtrak. *(Story, p. 431)*

House Democrats set the stage with a key vote in June that would lead to the biggest federal intervention in passenger rail since 1997. To win over enough Republicans to override a possible veto from President George W. Bush, House leaders agreed to insert language to promote private development of a high-speed rail line from New York to Washington—even though Democrats had long resisted such a move. That provision had the potential to stall the bill in the Senate, home to many Amtrak fans but few supporters of privatizing the railroad. However, the rising price of gasoline at the pump during the summer put pressure on lawmakers to reauthorize the only nationwide passenger rail line. The provisions from the House bill, for the most part, survived House-Senate negotiations. The president chose not to press his earlier veto threat, and a similar Amtrak reauthorization (HR 2095), with rail-safety provisions attached to it, cleared Congress on Oct. 1.

The House passage vote on HR 6003 came on June 11, 311–104: R 87–104; D 224–0. *(Vote, p. 982)*

6. FOREIGN INTELLIGENCE SURVEILLANCE

With a vote in June 2008, House Democrats essentially gave up a long-running and spirited fight against giving the administration of President George W. Bush unfettered power to spy on certain groups. This came on passage of a bill (HR 6304) to reauthorize the Foreign Intelligence Surveillance Act (FISA) to include warrantless spying on foreign targets who might be communicating with people in the United States and to provide for the likely dismissal of lawsuits against companies that assisted in the warrantless surveillance program. *(Story, p. 251)*

Democratic leaders had taken this battle to the brink in February by allowing provisions in a law enacted the previous August to expire. However, there were enough safety nets in place in that law to keep it effectively in force until August 2008.

But as that date drew closer—along with the November election—Democrats began to feel pressure from the White House and Republicans to move the legislation. House leaders drew up a new version of the bill that included some concessions to Democrats, such as a provision to strengthen the original law's statement that FISA was the only means by which the executive branch could conduct foreign intelligence-related surveillance.

Many Democrats, despite their initial opposition, decided to vote for the measure because of the growing political pressures associated with the issue. This was particularly true in the House, where opposition to retroactive legal immunity for the telecommunications companies and expanded spying authority for Bush was stronger than it had been in the Senate. The House had resisted the president on that issue previously.

When a group of House Democrats, the fiscally conservative Blue Dog Coalition who favored an earlier Senate bill, began to agitate for an end to the fight, leaders inched toward the administration's position. Some Democrats said privately that they feared election troubles if they did not pass something that the president would sign because Republicans could use the issue to attack them as weak on national security. Democratic party leaders, including Speaker Nancy Pelosi of California, voted for HR 6304 when it passed on June 20, 293–129: R 188–1; D 105–128. *(Vote, p. 982)*

7. MEDICARE PHYSICIANS´ PAY

With election-year considerations weighing heavily on their minds, two-thirds of the House Republicans bucked their leadership and supported legislation to prevent a scheduled 10.6 percent cut in pay rates for doctors who participated in Medicare, giving Democrats more than enough backing to ensure that a threatened presidential veto could be overcome. The lopsided vote in the House on the bill (HR 6331) suddenly and unexpectedly gave the measure impetus in the Senate, where it had languished in the face of steadfast opposition. *(Story, p. 571)*

Both parties had offered proposals to block the scheduled July 1 cut in Medicare payments to physicians. But Republicans and the White House objected to the offsetting cuts that House Democrats wanted to keep the legislation revenue-neutral.

House GOP leaders had urged their caucus to vote against the bill. Instead, at least a dozen Republicans changed their votes from "nay" to "yea" as the votes were tallied. The July Fourth recess was scheduled for the next week, and lawmakers wanted to be able to go home and tell physicians and patients that they did something to keep doctors from leaving Medicare.

The House passed HR 6331 on June 24, 355–59: R 129–59; D 226–0. *(Vote, p. 982)*

8. MORTGAGE RELIEF

A stalled effort to grant relief to homeowners facing foreclosure came to life in mid-July, when Treasury Secretary Henry M. Paulson Jr. abruptly asked Congress for the tools necessary to bail out Fannie Mae and Freddie Mac, the nation's two mortgage giants whose share prices were plummeting as investors feared that the entire home loan market would collapse. *(Story, p. 630)*

The administration of President George W. Bush had strongly objected to elements of the mortgage relief bill. But when the Fannie and Freddie bailout provisions were added to it, the White House reversed course and endorsed enactment. That gave congressional Democrats an opening, and with support from some Republicans, the House passed the measure.

The legislation (HR 3221), which allowed the Treasury Department to extend new credit to and buy stock in Fannie Mae and Freddie Mac and to help homeowners with loans they could not afford, was approved by the House July 23 on a vote of 272–152: R 45–149; D 227–3. *(Vote, p. 982)*

9. GLOBAL AIDS REAUTHORIZATION

Congress in 2008 authorized a significant expansion of efforts to improve health around the world when it cleared a bill to authorize $48 billion over five years for programs to fight AIDS, tuberculosis, and malaria overseas. The bill represented a bipartisan compromise started by Tom Lantos, D-Calif. (1981–2008), and completed in February by Howard L. Berman, also of California, who took over the Foreign Affairs Committee after Lantos died. *(Story, p. 312)*

Many Republicans, including President George W. Bush and some fiscal conservatives, signed on to the large funding boost ($18 billion more than the administration had sought), and in exchange bill writers largely avoided the social-policy debates that had surrounded the program since it was created in 2003. The House cleared the bill (HR 5501) on July 24 303–115: R 75–114; D 228–1. *(Vote, p. 982)*

10. REGULATION OF TOBACCO PRODUCTS

After more than a decade of trying, supporters of legislation to give the Food and Drug Administration power to regulate tobacco products not only managed to push a bill through the House but did so by a margin large enough to override a threatened presidential veto. However, because the House acted on the measure just before the August recess, the chances of getting it through the Senate before a planned adjournment in October were slim. As a result, supporters on that side of the Capitol did not bring it up for a vote, preferring to wait until the 111th Congress when Democrats hoped they would have larger majorities. The House passed the bill (HR 1108) on July 30 by a vote of 326–102: R 96–99; D 230–3. *(Story, p. 575; Vote, p. 982)*

11. MENTAL HEALTH PARITY

Congress in September passed legislation (HR 6983) to require insurers to treat mental illness the same as other medical issues, an action that showed a significant increase in support for mental health parity since a March vote on an earlier version (HR 1424). In that effort, 145 Republicans voted against the measure. After the March vote, supporters—led by Patrick J. Kennedy, D-R.I., and Jim Ramstad, R-Minn., in the House and Pete V. Domenici, R-N.M., and Edward M. Kennedy, D-Mass., in the Senate—spent the summer working out a compromise that could pass in both chambers and be signed by the president. *(Story, p. 569)*

Enactment was a priority for these four, two of whom (Ramstad and Domenici) were retiring, and one of whom (Edward Kennedy, the father of Patrick) was seriously ill. They all had confronted forms of mental illness or addiction themselves or with family members and had fought for such legislation for more than a decade. A 1997 parity law that was much more limited was scheduled to expire in December.

The compromise version (HR 6983) was less stringent on insurers than the previous House-passed measure and closer to a bill (S 558) the Senate had passed in 2007. Leaders brought the compromise to the floor as a free-standing bill in late September, and Republican support for it was triple that of the March vote. The degree of support garnered by the compromise encouraged congressional leaders to include the parity language in a broad financial markets bailout bill that needed help wherever backers could find it.

The House passed HR 6983 on Sept. 23 by a vote of 376–47: R 143–47; D 233–0. The bill was considered under suspension of the rules, thereby requiring a two–thirds majority of those present and voting (282 in this case) for passage. *(Vote, p. 982)*

12. TROUBLED ASSET RELIEF PROGRAM

In one of the most important financial votes of the 110th Congress, the House on Sept. 29 rejected legislation (HR 3997) to make available to the Treasury Department up to $700 billion to buy certain mortgage-related assets under a plan called the Troubled Asset Relief Program (TARP). The vote against the proposal was 205–228: R 65–133; D 140–95. It came in the midst of growing alarm over the meltdown in the housing market and the rapidly advancing worldwide recession. It sent the stock market plunging to a record one-day drop. *(Story, p. 154; Vote, p. 982)*

With this vote, most House members had to make a difficult choice between the wishes of their party leaders and the demands of their constituents. The election was five weeks away. Voters were objecting loudly and angrily to President George W. Bush's plan to buy up the toxic mortgage-related assets of a financial industry in deep trouble, calling it an unjustified Wall Street bailout while Main Street business and taxpayers were suffering. Two-thirds of the Republican caucus and 40 percent of Democrats voted against the measure, despite warnings from the Treasury secretary, the Federal Reserve chairman, and House leaders that the bailout, unprecedented in size and intent, was necessary to prevent the economy from falling into the worst slump since the Great Depression.

The vote was scheduled for the early afternoon of Sept. 29, about thirty-six hours after the deal producing the legislation was worked out between congressional leaders and the administration. While it was assumed that the vote would be close, leaders thought they could eke out passage.

But as the fifteen-minute clock on the vote wound down, it became clear that the numbers were not as solid as leaders had thought. Speaker Nancy Pelosi, D-Calif., begged members of the Congressional Black Caucus—who wanted the bill to more directly address the needs of poor people—to switch their votes. Minority Leader John A. Boehner's team had tried to persuade reluctant Republicans to fall in line with the leadership, but in the end, most GOP lawmakers voted against the bill. After holding the vote open for about thirty extra minutes, Pelosi conceded defeat and signaled the roll call to a close.

Usually, the effects of a House vote are not felt for months or even years, not until a law is enacted or until voters make known their own opinion of their representative's actions in the polling booth. The repercussions of this vote, however, were immediate. Stunned traders on the floor of the New York Stock Exchange watched the televised vote, and as the bill went down to defeat, the value of shares plummeted. The Dow Jones industrial average fell 777 points, the largest one-day point drop in the 112-year history of the stock index. Pelosi blamed Boehner, R-Ohio, for not coming through with the necessary GOP votes; Boehner said a prevote partisan speech by Pelosi riled members of his caucus and led them to allow the bill to fail.

After the House vote, and the stunned reaction of lawmakers to the stock market plunge sunk in, Senate leaders took control of the issue, quickly producing a new version of the measure that cleared by the end of the week.

A breakdown of the House vote showed broad and varied opposition to the legislation. Most members of the conservative Republican Study Committee voted against the bill and against the president. Members of specific Democratic groups—the fiscally conservative "Blue Dogs," the Hispanic and black caucuses, the Progressives, and New Democrats—split their votes almost evenly. Most members who were in highly competitive reelection races—nineteen Republicans and seventeen Democrats—voted against the bill. Members of the leadership in both parties held together and voted for the measure.

13. TROUBLED ASSET RELIEF PROGRAM.

Just four days after rejecting legislation to give the Treasury Department $700 billion to assist the ailing mortgage market, legislators turned around and approved essentially the same program. On Oct. 3 the House cleared HR 1424 by a vote of 263–171: R 91–108; D 172–63. *(See key vote 12, above)*

The October action came after the stock market plunged 777 points in a few hours following the House's Sept. 29 rejection of the bill to create the Troubled Asset Relief Program. The replacement legislation also allowed the Treasury to use up to $700 billion to buy troubled mortgage-related assets but in addition included the extension of expiring tax credits, a one-year patch to the alternative minimum tax, and a requirement that insurers treat mental health issues the same as other medical issues (which served as the underlying bill—HR 1424—that was used for the second mortgage bailout effort). *(Story, p. 151; Vote, p. 982)*

In clearing this bill the House gave the government unprecedented power to insert itself into the nation's financial markets in order to avert a credit crisis that had the potential to devastate the economy for months or years to come. For this vote, thirty-three Democrats and twenty-five Republicans who had opposed the earlier bill switched positions and voted in support.

Several members who switched cited the new elements in the Senate-revised package and fresh signs that the economy was under stress. Another fluid dynamic was public opinion. While most lawmakers reported hearing overwhelming opposition to the plan before the Sept. 29 vote, the stock market's plunge afterward appeared to rattle constituents worried about the effect the crisis was having on their retirement savings, particularly stock-based mutual funds and 401(k) plans. Business lobbyists also mobilized, warning that they had increasing difficulty getting credit to finance their day-to-day operations.

Four Republicans who voted to clear the bill—Joe Knollenberg of Michigan, John R. "Randy" Kuhl Jr. of New York, Jon Porter of Nevada, and Christopher Shays of Connecticut—were defeated Nov. 4. Knollenberg and Kuhl had voted against the original bill and had switched sides for the second vote. One Democratic supporter of the bill, Tim Mahoney of Florida, lost his reelection effort, but he had been embroiled in a sex scandal, which election analysts said hurt him at the polls.

14. AUTO INDUSTRY BAILOUT

The House, but not the Senate, in late 2008 passed legislation to allow the Treasury to provide up to $14 billion in loans to domestic automakers, which, in return, would be required to submit restructuring plans by March 31, 2009. *(Story, p. 159)*

For weeks before this vote, Democratic leaders and President George W. Bush were at odds over who would be responsible for a bailout package for the three major domestic automakers: General Motors, Ford Motor, and Chrysler. Democrats wanted the administration to use money from the $700 billion Troubled Asset Relief Program created in the financial services bailout law *(See key votes 12 and 13, above)*

Bush wanted Congress to use an existing Energy Department loan program that had been aimed at helping automakers shift to the production of more fuel-efficient vehicles.

Negotiations seemed at a standstill until Dec. 5, when, hours after the Labor Department announced that the economy had lost 553,000 jobs in November, House Speaker Nancy Pelosi, D-Calif., changed her mind and agreed to the administration's solution. In a scene that had already played out several times over the year, lawmakers and White House officials worked through the weekend to produce a bill, and the House passed it without much trouble Dec. 10. The House vote on the bill (HR 7321) was 237–170: R 32–150; D 205–20. *(Vote, p. 982)*

As with previous votes to help out certain sectors of the U.S. economy, Republicans were reluctant to go along with the plan, despite Bush's support of it, and it was GOP opposition that killed the effort in the Senate.

1. **HR 5140. Economic Stimulus.** Rangel, D-N.Y., motion to concur in the Senate amendment to provide tax refunds to most Americans as an economic stimulus to counteract the recession then underway. The amounts were to be $300 to $600 for individuals and $600 to $1,200 for couples. Families were to receive $300 for each child under seventeen. HR 5140 also provided businesses new depreciation benefits for equipment and raised the size of mortgage loans the Federal Housing Administration could insure and Fannie Mae and Freddie Mac could purchase. Motion agreed to (thus clearing the bill for the president) 380–34: R 165–28; D 215–6. A "yea" was a vote in support of the president's position. Feb. 7, 2008.

2. **H Res 1092. Colombia Trade.** Adoption of the resolution amending House rules to suspend "fast-track" requirements for considering a bill (HR 5724) to implement a U.S.-Colombia free-trade agreement. Adopted 224–195: R 6–185; D 218–10. April 10, 2008.

3. **HR 2642. Iraq Troop Withdrawal.** Require U.S. troop withdrawal from Iraq to begin within thirty days of the bill's enactment with a goal of completing the withdrawal of combat troops by December 2009, require Congress to authorize any agreement between the U.S. and the Iraqi government committing U.S. forces, prohibit any combat unit not assessed as fully mission-capable from deploying to Iraq, limit deployment time (subject to a presidential waiver), and prohibit interrogation techniques not authorized in the Army Field Manual. (The vote came on a motion by David Obey, D-Wis., to concur in the Senate amendments with a House amendment to the appropriations bill for military construction.) Motion agreed to 227–196: R 8–183; D 219–13. A "nay" was a vote in support of the president's position. May 15, 2008.

4. **HR 2419. Farm Bill Veto Override.** Passage, over President George W. Bush's May 21, 2008, veto, of legislation to reauthorize federal farm and nutrition programs for five years, including crop subsidies and food stamps, as well as conservation and rural development. HR 2419 authorized a $10.4 billion increase for nutrition programs, offset by extending customs user fees. It reduced payment subsidies overall by $313 million, in part by reducing the percentage of acres for which a farmer can collect payments. Passed 316–108: R 100–94; D 216–14. A two-thirds majority of those present and voting (283 in this case for the House) was required to override a veto. A "nay" was a vote in support of the president's position. May 21, 2008.

5. **HR 6003. Amtrak Reauthorization.** Passage of the bill to authorize $14.4 billion for Amtrak over five years, including $3 billion for operating assistance, $4.2 billion for capital grants, and $1.7 billion for Amtrak to pay down debts. The bill authorized grants for capital costs in certain high-congestion corridors and required changes in Amtrak's management, operations, and general policy regarding intercity passenger rail service. Passed 311–104: R 87–104; D 224–0. A "nay" was a vote in support of the president's position. June 11, 2008.

6. **HR 6304. Foreign Intelligence Surveillance.** Passage of the bill to overhaul the Foreign Intelligence Surveillance Act (FISA) governing electronic surveillance of foreign terrorism suspects. The bill allowed investigations of up to one year through surveillance of individuals who were not U.S. persons and who were reasonably believed to be outside the United States, subject to approval by the FISA court. Warrantless surveillance was allowed as long as it did not intentionally target U.S. persons or persons located within the United States. Passed 293–129: R 188–1; D 105–128. A "yea" was a vote in support of the president's position. June 20, 2008.

7. **HR 6331. Medicare Physician Payments.** Passage of the bill to prevent a 10.6 percent cut in payments to physicians treating Medicare patients, scheduled for July 1, and to provide an additional $16.6 billion over ten years for changes to Medicare beneficiary programs. Passed 355–59: R 129–59; D 226–0. A "nay" was a vote in support of the president's position. June 24, 2008.

8. **HR 3221. Mortgage Relief, Fannie Mae/Freddie Mac.** Frank, D-Mass., amendment to grant authority to the Treasury Department to extend new credit to and buy stock in housing mortgage companies Fannie Mae and Freddie Mac and to create an independent regulator for the companies and the Federal Home Loan Bank System. The amendment also overhauled the Federal Housing Administration (FHA) and allowed it to insure up to $300 billion worth of new, refinanced loans for struggling mortgage borrowers, and included a $7,500 tax credit for some first-time homebuyers, higher loan limits for FHA-backed loans, a standard tax deduction for property taxes, and revenue-raisers to offset part of the costs. Accepted 272–152: R 45–149; D 227–3. A "yea" was a vote in support of the president's position. July 23, 2008.

9. **HR 5501. Global HIV and AIDS Authorization.** Berman, D-Calif., motion to concur in the Senate amendment to the bill to authorize $48 billion from fiscal 2009 through 2013 for programs under the President's Emergency Plan for AIDS Relief used to fight AIDS, tuberculosis, and malaria overseas. The bill replaced existing requirements that one-third of all HIV prevention funding go to abstinence education with balanced funding for abstinence, fidelity, and condom programs, and also authorized $2 billion for Native American health and clean water and law enforcement programs. Motion agreed to (thus clearing the bill for the president) 303–115: R 75–114; D 228–1. A "yea" was a vote in support of the president's position. July 24, 2008.

10. **HR 1108. Tobacco Products Regulation.** Dingell, D-Mich., motion to suspend the rules and pass the bill to authorize the Food and Drug Administration (FDA) to regulate tobacco products. The FDA was authorized to restrict sales and distribution, including advertising and promotion, if it determined that it was necessary to protect public health. Motion agreed to 326–102: R 96–99; D 230–3. A two-thirds majority of those present and voting (286 in this case) was required for passage under suspension of the rules. A "nay" was a vote in support of the president's position. July 30, 2008.

11. **HR 6983. Mental Health Parity.** Pallone, D-N.J., motion to suspend the rules and pass the bill to require health insurers that cover mental illness to do so on a par with physical illness, including equal standards on co-payments, deductibles, number of doctor visits, days in the hospital and financial limits on coverage, but specified that the standards would not have to be upheld if they increase coverage costs by more than 2 percent during the first year of enactment and more than 1 percent in subsequent years. Employers with fewer than fifty employees were exempted. Motion agreed to 376–47: R 143–47; D 233–0. A two-thirds majority of those present and voting (282 in this case) was required for passage under suspension of the rules. Sept. 23, 2008.

12. **HR 3997 Troubled Asset Relief Program.** Frank, D-Mass., motion to concur, with changes, in Senate amendments to the bill to allow the Treasury to use up to $700 billion, in installments, to buy certain mortgage assets. Motion rejected 205–228: R 65–133; D 140–95. A "yea" was a vote in support of the president's position. Sept. 29, 2008.

13. **HR 1424. Troubled Asset Relief Program.** Frank, D-Mass., motion to concur in the Senate amendments to the bill to allow the Treasury Department to use up to $700 billion to buy certain mortgage assets believed to be of little or no value that threatened to bankrupt many of the nation's largest financial institution. The bill required the Treasury Department to create a program to insure mortgage assets, provided for congressional oversight, and limited compensation for executives of companies whose troubled assets were purchased. It temporarily increased federal deposit insurance to $250,000 per bank account. Motion agreed to (thus clearing the bill for the president) 263–171: R 91–108; D 172–63. A "yea" was a vote in support of the president's position. Oct. 3, 2008.

14. **HR 7321. Automobile Industry Loan Program.** Passage of the bill to allow up to $14 billion in loans to eligible domestic automakers and require presidentially appointed administrators to bring together auto companies, unions, creditors, and others to negotiate long-term restructuring plans by March 31, 2009. Passed 237–170: R 32–150; D 205–20. A "yea" was a vote in support of the president's position. Dec. 10, 2008.

KEY

Democrat	*Republican*	**Independent**

Y	Voted for (yea)	–	Announced against
#	Paired for	P	Voted "present"
+	Announced for	C	Voted "present" to avoid possible conflict of interest
N	Voted against (nay)	?	Did not vote or otherwise make a position known
X	Paired against		

House Key Votes	1	2	3	4	5	6	7	8	9	10	11	12	13	14
ALABAMA														
1 *Bonner*	Y	N	N	Y	N	Y	Y	N	Y	Y	N	Y	Y	N
2 *Everett*	?	N	N	Y	N	Y	Y	N	?	Y	Y	Y	Y	?
3 *Rogers*	Y	Y	N	Y	Y	Y	Y	Y	Y	Y	Y	Y	Y	N
4 *Aderholt*	Y	Y	N	Y	N	Y	Y	N	Y	N	Y	N	N	N
5 Cramer	?	N	Y	Y	Y	Y	Y	Y	Y	Y	Y	Y	Y	Y
6 *Bachus*	Y	N	N	Y	Y	Y	Y	N	Y	N	Y	Y	Y	N
7 Davis	Y	Y	Y	Y	Y	Y	Y	Y	Y	Y	Y	Y	Y	N
ALASKA														
AL *Young*	Y	N	N	Y	Y	Y	Y	N	N	Y	Y	N	N	Y
ARIZONA														
1 *Renzi*	Y	N	N	Y	Y	Y	N	N	Y	Y	Y	N	N	?
2 *Franks*	Y	N	N	N	N	Y	N	N	N	N	N	N	N	N
3 *Shadegg*	N	N	N	N	N	Y	N	N	N	N	N	N	Y	N
4 Pastor	Y	Y	Y	Y	Y	N	Y	Y	Y	Y	Y	N	Y	Y
5 Mitchell	Y	Y	Y	N	Y	Y	Y	Y	Y	Y	Y	N	Y	N
6 *Flake*	N	N	N	N	?	Y	N	N	N	N	N	N	N	N
7 Grijalva	Y	Y	Y	Y	Y	N	Y	Y	Y	Y	Y	N	N	Y
8 Giffords	Y	Y	Y	Y	Y	Y	Y	Y	Y	Y	Y	N	Y	N
ARKANSAS														
1 Berry	N	Y	Y	Y	Y	Y	Y	Y	Y	Y	Y	Y	Y	Y
2 Snyder	Y	Y	N	Y	Y	Y	Y	Y	Y	Y	Y	Y	Y	?
3 *Boozman*	Y	N	N	Y	Y	Y	Y	N	Y	Y	Y	Y	Y	N
4 Ross	Y	Y	Y	Y	Y	Y	Y	Y	Y	Y	Y	Y	Y	Y
CALIFORNIA														
1 Thompson	Y	Y	Y	Y	Y	N	Y	Y	Y	Y	Y	N	Y	Y
2 *Herger*	Y	N	N	Y	N	Y	N	N	N	N	–	Y	Y	N
3 *Lungren*	N	N	N	N	N	Y	N	Y	Y	N	Y	Y	Y	N
4 *Doolittle*	Y	N	N	Y	N	Y	N	N	N	N	N	N	N	?
5 Matsui	Y	Y	Y	Y	Y	N	Y	Y	Y	Y	Y	Y	Y	Y
6 Woolsey	+	Y	Y	Y	Y	N	Y	Y	Y	Y	Y	N	Y	Y
7 Miller, George	Y	Y	Y	Y	Y	N	+	Y	Y	Y	Y	Y	Y	Y
8 Pelosi[1]	Y	Y	Y	Y		Y		Y	Y			Y	Y	Y
9 Lee	Y	Y	Y	Y	Y	N	Y	Y	Y	Y	Y	N	Y	Y
10 Tauscher	Y	Y	Y	Y	Y	Y	Y	Y	Y	Y	Y	Y	Y	Y
11 McNerney	Y	Y	Y	Y	Y	Y	Y	Y	Y	Y	Y	Y	Y	Y
12 Lantos[2]	?													
12 Speier[2]		Y	Y	Y	Y	N	?	Y	Y	Y	Y	Y	Y	Y
13 Stark	Y	Y	Y	N	?	?	Y	Y	Y	Y	Y	N	N	N
14 Eshoo	Y	Y	Y	Y	Y	N	Y	Y	Y	Y	Y	Y	Y	Y
15 Honda	Y	Y	Y	Y	Y	N	Y	Y	Y	Y	Y	Y	Y	Y
16 Lofgren	Y	Y	Y	Y	Y	N	Y	Y	Y	Y	Y	Y	Y	Y
17 Farr	?	Y	Y	Y	Y	N	Y	Y	Y	Y	Y	Y	Y	Y
18 Cardoza	Y	Y	Y	Y	Y	Y	Y	Y	Y	Y	Y	Y	Y	N
19 *Radanovich*	Y	N	N	Y	N	Y	N	N	N	N	Y	Y	Y	N
20 Costa	Y	Y	N	Y	Y	Y	Y	Y	Y	Y	Y	Y	Y	?
21 *Nunes*	Y	N	N	N	N	Y	?	N	Y	N	Y	N	N	N
22 *McCarthy*	Y	N	N	N	N	Y	Y	N	N	Y	Y	N	N	N
23 Capps	Y	Y	Y	Y	Y	N	Y	Y	Y	Y	Y	Y	Y	Y
24 *Gallegly*	Y	N	N	Y	N	Y	Y	Y	N	Y	Y	N	N	N
25 *McKeon*	Y	N	N	N	N	Y	Y	Y	N	Y	Y	Y	Y	N
26 *Dreier*	Y	N	N	N	N	Y	Y	Y	Y	Y	Y	Y	Y	N
27 Sherman	Y	Y	Y	Y	Y	Y	Y	Y	Y	Y	Y	N	N	Y
28 Berman	Y	Y	Y	Y	Y	Y	Y	Y	Y	Y	Y	Y	Y	Y
29 Schiff	Y	Y	Y	Y	Y	Y	Y	Y	Y	Y	Y	N	Y	Y
30 Waxman	Y	Y	Y	N	Y	N	Y	Y	Y	Y	Y	Y	Y	Y
31 Becerra	Y	Y	Y	Y	Y	N	Y	Y	Y	Y	Y	N	N	Y
32 Solis	Y	Y	Y	Y	Y	N	Y	Y	Y	Y	Y	N	Y	Y
33 Watson	Y	Y	Y	Y	Y	N	Y	Y	Y	Y	Y	N	Y	?
34 Roybal-Allard	Y	Y	Y	Y	Y	N	Y	Y	Y	Y	Y	N	N	Y
35 Waters	Y	Y	Y	Y	Y	N	Y	Y	Y	Y	Y	Y	Y	Y
36 Harman	Y	Y	Y	N	Y	Y	Y	Y	Y	Y	Y	Y	Y	Y
37 Richardson	Y	Y	Y	Y	Y	Y	Y	Y	Y	Y	Y	Y	Y	Y
38 Napolitano	Y	Y	Y	Y	Y	N	Y	Y	Y	Y	Y	N	N	Y
39 Sánchez, Linda	Y	Y	Y	Y	Y	N	Y	Y	Y	Y	Y	N	N	Y
40 *Royce*	N	N	N	N	N	Y	N	N	N	N	N	N	N	N
41 *Lewis*	Y	N	N	N	N	Y	Y	Y	Y	N	Y	Y	Y	N
42 *Miller, Gary*	Y	N	N	N	N	Y	Y	Y	N	N	Y	Y	Y	?
43 Baca	Y	Y	Y	Y	Y	Y	Y	Y	Y	N	Y	N	Y	Y
44 *Calvert*	Y	N	N	N	N	Y	Y	Y	N	N	Y	Y	Y	N
45 *Bono Mack*	Y	N	?	Y	Y	Y	Y	Y	Y	Y	Y	Y	Y	N
46 *Rohrabacher*	N	N	N	N	N	Y	Y	N	N	N	N	N	N	?
47 Sanchez, Loretta	–	Y	Y	Y	Y	N	Y	Y	Y	Y	Y	N	N	Y
48 *Campbell*	N	N	?	N	N	Y	N	Y	N	N	N	Y	Y	P
49 *Issa*	Y	N	N	N	N	Y	Y	N	Y	N	N	N	N	N
50 *Bilbray*	Y	N	N	N	N	Y	Y	N	N	Y	Y	N	N	N
51 Filner	Y	Y	Y	Y	Y	N	Y	Y	Y	Y	Y	N	N	N
52 *Hunter*	N	N	N	N	N	Y	Y	Y	N	N	?	N	N	Y
53 Davis	Y	Y	Y	Y	Y	N	Y	Y	Y	Y	Y	Y	Y	Y
COLORADO														
1 DeGette	Y	Y	?	Y	Y	N	Y	Y	Y	Y	Y	Y	Y	Y
2 Udall	Y	Y	Y	Y	Y	Y	Y	Y	Y	Y	Y	N	N	Y
3 Salazar	Y	Y	Y	Y	Y	Y	Y	Y	?	Y	Y	N	N	Y
4 *Musgrave*	Y	N	N	Y	?	Y	Y	N	N	N	Y	N	N	N
5 *Lamborn*	Y	N	N	N	N	Y	N	N	N	N	N	N	N	N
6 *Tancredo*	N	N	N	N	?	Y	?	N	N	N	Y	Y	Y	?
7 Perlmutter	Y	Y	Y	Y	Y	Y	Y	Y	Y	Y	Y	Y	Y	Y
CONNECTICUT														
1 Larson	Y	+	Y	Y	Y	N	Y	Y	Y	Y	Y	Y	Y	Y
2 Courtney	Y	Y	Y	Y	Y	N	Y	Y	Y	Y	Y	N	N	Y
3 DeLauro	Y	Y	Y	Y	Y	N	Y	Y	Y	Y	Y	Y	Y	Y
4 *Shays*	Y	N	Y	N	Y	Y	Y	Y	Y	Y	Y	Y	Y	N
5 Murphy	Y	Y	Y	Y	Y	N	Y	Y	Y	Y	Y	Y	Y	Y
DELAWARE														
AL *Castle*	Y	N	Y	N	Y	Y	Y	Y	Y	Y	Y	Y	Y	Y
FLORIDA														
1 *Miller*	Y	N	N	N	N	Y	Y	N	N	N	N	N	N	N
2 Boyd	N	N	Y	Y	Y	Y	Y	Y	Y	Y	Y	Y	Y	N
3 Brown	Y	Y	Y	?	Y	Y	Y	Y	Y	Y	Y	Y	Y	Y
4 *Crenshaw*	Y	N	?	?	Y	Y	N	N	N	Y	Y	Y	Y	N
5 *Brown-Waite*	Y	N	N	Y	Y	?	Y	?	?	?	Y	N	N	N
6 *Stearns*	Y	N	N	N	N	Y	Y	N	N	N	Y	N	N	N
7 *Mica*	Y	N	N	N	Y	Y	N	N	N	N	Y	N	N	N
8 *Keller*	Y	N	N	N	Y	Y	Y	Y	N	N	Y	N	N	?
9 *Bilirakis*	Y	N	N	Y	N	Y	Y	N	Y	Y	Y	N	N	N
10 *Young*	Y	N	N	N	Y	Y	Y	N	Y	Y	Y	N	N	N
11 Castor	Y	Y	Y	+	Y	Y	Y	Y	Y	Y	Y	N	N	Y
12 *Putnam*	Y	N	N	Y	Y	Y	Y	Y	N	Y	Y	Y	Y	N
13 *Buchanan*	Y	N	N	Y	Y	Y	Y	Y	N	Y	Y	N	Y	N
14 *Mack*	Y	N	?	N	N	Y	Y	N	N	N	N	N	N	N
15 *Weldon*	Y	N	N	N	N	Y	Y	N	Y	N	N	Y	Y	?
16 Mahoney	Y	N	Y	Y	Y	Y	Y	Y	Y	Y	Y	Y	Y	Y
17 Meek	Y	Y	Y	Y	Y	N	Y	Y	Y	Y	Y	Y	Y	Y
18 *Ros-Lehtinen*	Y	N	N	Y	Y	Y	Y	Y	Y	Y	Y	N	Y	N
19 Wexler	Y	Y	Y	?	Y	N	Y	Y	Y	Y	Y	Y	Y	Y
20 Wasserman Schultz	Y	Y	Y	Y	Y	N	Y	Y	Y	Y	Y	Y	Y	Y
21 *Diaz-Balart, L.*	Y	N	N	Y	Y	Y	Y	Y	Y	N	Y	N	N	N
22 Klein	Y	Y	Y	Y	Y	Y	Y	Y	Y	Y	Y	Y	Y	Y
23 Hastings	Y	Y	Y	Y	Y	Y	Y	Y	Y	Y	Y	Y	Y	?
24 *Feeney*	Y	N	N	N	N	Y	Y	N	N	N	N	N	N	N
25 *Diaz-Balart, M.*	Y	N	N	Y	?	Y	Y	Y	Y	N	Y	N	N	N
GEORGIA														
1 *Kingston*	N	N	N	Y	N	Y	Y	N	N	N	N	N	N	N
2 Bishop	Y	Y	Y	Y	Y	Y	Y	+	Y	Y	Y	Y	Y	Y
3 *Westmoreland*	N	N	N	N	Y	Y	N	N	N	N	N	N	N	N
4 Johnson	Y	Y	Y	Y	Y	N	Y	Y	Y	Y	Y	N	N	Y
5 Lewis	Y	Y	Y	Y	Y	N	Y	Y	Y	Y	Y	N	Y	Y
6 *Price*	N	N	N	N	N	Y	Y	N	N	N	Y	N	N	N
7 *Linder*	N	N	N	N	N	Y	N	N	N	Y	N	N	N	N
8 Marshall	Y	Y	N	Y	Y	Y	Y	Y	Y	Y	Y	Y	Y	N

[1]The Speaker votes only at her discretion.

[2]Rep. Jackie Speier, D-Calif., was sworn in April 10, 2008, to fill the seat vacated by the death of Democrat Tom Lantos on Feb. 11.

KEY

Democrat *Republican* **Independent**

Y	Voted for (yea)	–	Announced against
#	Paired for	P	Voted "present"
+	Announced for	C	Voted "present" to avoid possible conflict of interest
N	Voted against (nay)	?	Did not vote or otherwise make a position known
X	Paired against		

House Key Votes	1	2	3	4	5	6	7	8	9	10	11	12	13	14
9 *Deal*	N	N	N	N	N	Y	Y	N	N	N	Y	N	N	N
10 *Broun*	N	N	N	N	N	Y	N	N	N	N	N	N	N	N
11 *Gingrey*	N	N	N	Y	N	Y	Y	N	N	N	Y	N	N	N
12 Barrow	Y	Y	N	Y	Y	Y	Y	Y	Y	Y	Y	N	N	Y
13 Scott	Y	Y	Y	Y	Y	Y	Y	Y	Y	Y	Y	N	Y	Y
HAWAII														
1 Abercrombie	Y	Y	Y	Y	Y	N	Y	Y	Y	Y	Y	N	Y	Y
2 Hirono	Y	Y	Y	Y	Y	N	Y	Y	Y	Y	Y	N	Y	Y
IDAHO														
1 *Sali*	Y	N	N	Y	N	Y	N	N	N	N	N	N	N	N
2 *Simpson*	N	N	N	Y	Y	Y	Y	N	N	Y	Y	Y	Y	N
ILLINOIS														
1 Rush	Y	+	+	+	+	–	+	+	+	Y	Y	N	Y	Y
2 Jackson	Y	Y	Y	Y	Y	N	Y	Y	Y	Y	Y	N	Y	Y
3 Lipinski	Y	Y	Y	Y	Y	Y	Y	Y	Y	Y	Y	N	N	Y
4 Gutierrez	Y	Y	Y	Y	?	Y	Y	Y	Y	Y	Y	Y	Y	?
5 Emanuel	Y	Y	Y	Y	Y	Y	Y	Y	Y	Y	Y	Y	Y	?
6 *Roskam*	Y	N	N	N	N	Y	N	N	N	Y	Y	N	N	N
7 Davis	Y	Y	Y	Y	Y	N	?	Y	Y	Y	Y	Y	Y	Y
8 Bean	Y	N	Y	N	Y	Y	Y	Y	Y	Y	Y	Y	Y	Y
9 Schakowsky	Y	Y	Y	Y	Y	N	Y	Y	Y	Y	Y	Y	Y	Y
10 *Kirk*	Y	N	N	N	Y	Y	Y	N	Y	Y	Y	Y	Y	N
11 *Weller*	Y	N	N	Y	Y	+	Y	Y	Y	Y	Y	?	Y	N
12 Costello	Y	Y	Y	Y	Y	N	Y	Y	Y	Y	Y	N	N	Y
13 *Biggert*	Y	N	N	N	Y	Y	Y	Y	Y	Y	Y	N	Y	N
14 Foster[3]		Y	Y	Y	Y	N	Y	Y	Y	Y	Y	Y	Y	Y
15 *Johnson*	Y	N	N	Y	Y	N	+	N	Y	Y	Y	N	N	N
16 *Manzullo*	Y	N	N	Y	Y	Y	Y	N	N	Y	Y	N	N	Y
17 Hare	Y	Y	Y	Y	Y	N	Y	+	Y	Y	Y	Y	Y	Y
18 *LaHood*	Y	N	N	Y	Y	Y	Y	Y	?	Y	Y	Y	Y	Y
19 *Shimkus*	Y	N	N	Y	Y	Y	N	N	Y	Y	Y	N	N	N
INDIANA														
1 Visclosky	Y	Y	Y	Y	Y	–	Y	Y	Y	Y	Y	N	N	Y
2 Donnelly	Y	Y	Y	Y	Y	Y	Y	Y	Y	Y	Y	Y	Y	Y
3 *Souder*	Y	N	N	Y	Y	Y	Y	N	N	N	Y	Y	Y	Y
4 *Buyer*	Y	?	N	Y	Y	Y	N	N	N	N	Y	N	N	Y
5 *Burton*	Y	N	N	N	N	Y	Y	N	N	Y	Y	N	N	N
6 *Pence*	Y	N	N	N	N	Y	?	N	Y	N	N	N	N	N
7 Carson[4]		Y	Y	Y	Y	N	Y	Y	Y	Y	Y	N	Y	Y
8 Ellsworth	Y	Y	Y	Y	Y	Y	Y	Y	Y	Y	Y	Y	Y	Y
9 Hill	Y	N	Y	Y	Y	N	Y	Y	Y	Y	Y	N	N	Y
IOWA														
1 Braley	Y	Y	Y	Y	+	N	Y	Y	Y	Y	Y	N	Y	Y
2 Loebsack	Y	Y	Y	Y	?	N	Y	Y	Y	Y	Y	Y	Y	Y
3 Boswell	Y	Y	Y	Y	Y	Y	Y	?	?	Y	Y	Y	Y	Y
4 *Latham*	Y	N	N	Y	Y	Y	Y	N	Y	N	Y	N	N	N
5 *King*	Y	N	N	Y	?	Y	N	N	N	N	N	N	N	N
KANSAS														
1 *Moran*	N	N	N	N	Y	Y	Y	N	Y	Y	Y	N	N	N
2 Boyda	Y	Y	Y	Y	Y	Y	Y	N	Y	Y	Y	N	N	Y
3 Moore	Y	Y	Y	Y	Y	Y	Y	Y	Y	Y	Y	Y	Y	Y
4 *Tiahrt*	Y	N	N	?	N	?	Y	N	Y	Y	Y	N	N	N
KENTUCKY														
1 *Whitfield*	Y	N	N	Y	Y	Y	Y	N	N	N	Y	N	N	N
2 *Lewis*	Y	N	?	Y	N	Y	N	N	N	N	N	Y	Y	Y
3 Yarmuth	Y	Y	Y	Y	Y	Y	Y	Y	Y	Y	Y	N	Y	Y
4 *Davis*	Y	N	N	Y	N	Y	Y	N	N	N	Y	N	N	N
5 *Rogers*	Y	N	N	Y	N	Y	Y	N	N	N	Y	Y	Y	N
6 Chandler	Y	Y	Y	Y	Y	Y	Y	Y	Y	Y	Y	N	N	Y
LOUISIANA														
1 *Scalise*[5]			N	N	N	Y	N	N	N	N	Y	N	N	N
2 Jefferson	Y	Y	Y	Y	Y	N	Y	Y	Y	Y	Y	N	N	Y
3 Melancon	Y	Y	Y	Y	Y	Y	Y	Y	Y	Y	Y	Y	Y	Y
4 *McCrery*	Y	N	N	N	?	Y	N	Y	Y	N	N	Y	Y	Y
5 *Alexander*	Y	N	N	Y	Y	Y	Y	N	Y	Y	Y	N	Y	N
6 Cazayoux[6]			Y	Y	Y	Y	Y	Y	Y	Y	Y	N	N	Y
7 *Boustany*	Y	N	N	Y	N	Y	N	Y	Y	N	Y	N	Y	N
MAINE														
1 Allen	Y	Y	N	Y	Y	N	Y	Y	Y	Y	Y	Y	Y	Y
2 Michaud	Y	Y	Y	Y	Y	N	Y	Y	Y	Y	Y	N	N	Y
MARYLAND														
1 *Gilchrest*	Y	N	Y	Y	Y	?	Y	Y	Y	Y	Y	Y	Y	?
2 Ruppersberger	?	Y	Y	Y	Y	Y	Y	Y	Y	Y	Y	Y	Y	Y
3 Sarbanes	Y	Y	Y	Y	Y	N	Y	Y	Y	Y	Y	Y	Y	Y
4 Wynn[7]	Y	Y	Y	Y										
4 Edwards[7]						N	Y	Y	Y	Y	Y	N	Y	Y
5 Hoyer	Y	Y	Y	Y	Y	Y	Y	Y	Y	Y	Y	Y	Y	Y
6 *Bartlett*	Y	N	N	Y	?	Y	N	N	N	Y	Y	N	N	N
7 Cummings	Y	Y	Y	Y	Y	N	Y	Y	Y	Y	Y	N	Y	Y
8 Van Hollen	Y	Y	Y	Y	Y	N	Y	Y	Y	Y	Y	Y	Y	Y
MASSACHUSETTS														
1 Olver	Y	Y	Y	Y	Y	N	Y	Y	Y	Y	Y	Y	Y	Y
2 Neal	Y	Y	Y	Y	Y	N	Y	Y	Y	Y	Y	Y	Y	Y
3 McGovern	Y	Y	Y	Y	Y	N	Y	Y	Y	Y	Y	Y	Y	Y
4 Frank	Y	Y	Y	Y	Y	N	Y	Y	Y	Y	Y	Y	Y	Y
5 Tsongas	Y	Y	Y	Y	Y	N	Y	Y	Y	Y	Y	Y	Y	Y
6 Tierney	Y	Y	Y	Y	Y	N	Y	Y	Y	Y	Y	N	Y	Y
7 Markey	Y	Y	Y	Y	Y	N	Y	Y	Y	Y	Y	Y	Y	Y
8 Capuano	Y	Y	Y	N	Y	N	Y	Y	Y	Y	Y	Y	Y	Y
9 Lynch	Y	Y	Y	Y	Y	N	Y	Y	Y	Y	Y	N	N	Y
10 Delahunt	Y	Y	Y	Y	Y	N	Y	Y	Y	Y	Y	N	N	?
MICHIGAN														
1 Stupak	Y	Y	Y	Y	Y	Y	Y	Y	Y	Y	Y	N	N	Y
2 *Hoekstra*	Y	N	N	Y	N	Y	Y	N	Y	Y	N	N	Y	Y
3 *Ehlers*	Y	N	N	N	Y	Y	Y	N	Y	Y	Y	Y	Y	Y
4 *Camp*	Y	N	N	Y	N	Y	N	N	N	Y	Y	Y	Y	Y
5 Kildee	Y	Y	Y	Y	Y	Y	Y	Y	Y	Y	Y	Y	Y	Y
6 *Upton*	Y	N	N	Y	Y	Y	Y	N	Y	Y	Y	Y	Y	Y
7 *Walberg*	Y	N	N	Y	N	Y	Y	N	Y	N	Y	N	N	?
8 *Rogers*	Y	N	N	Y	N	Y	N	N	N	Y	Y	N	N	Y
9 *Knollenberg*	Y	N	N	N	Y	Y	Y	Y	Y	Y	Y	N	Y	Y
10 *Miller*	Y	N	N	Y	Y	Y	Y	N	N	Y	Y	N	N	Y
11 *McCotter*	Y	N	N	Y	Y	Y	Y	N	Y	N	Y	N	N	Y
12 Levin	Y	Y	Y	Y	Y	N	Y	Y	Y	Y	Y	Y	Y	Y
13 Kilpatrick	Y	Y	Y	Y	Y	N	Y	Y	Y	Y	Y	N	Y	Y
14 Conyers	Y	Y	Y	Y	Y	N	Y	Y	Y	Y	Y	N	N	Y
15 Dingell	Y	Y	Y	Y	Y	N	Y	Y	Y	Y	Y	Y	Y	Y
MINNESOTA														
1 Walz	Y	Y	Y	Y	Y	N	Y	Y	Y	Y	Y	N	N	N
2 *Kline*	Y	N	N	Y	N	Y	Y	N	Y	N	Y	Y	Y	N
3 *Ramstad*	Y	?	N	N	N	Y	Y	N	Y	Y	Y	N	Y	Y
4 McCollum	Y	Y	Y	Y	Y	N	Y	Y	Y	Y	Y	Y	Y	Y
5 Ellison	Y	Y	Y	Y	Y	N	Y	Y	Y	Y	Y	Y	Y	?
6 *Bachmann*	Y	N	N	N	N	Y	N	N	N	N	N	N	N	N
7 Peterson	N	Y	Y	Y	Y	Y	Y	Y	Y	Y	Y	N	N	N
8 Oberstar	Y	Y	Y	Y	Y	N	Y	Y	Y	Y	Y	Y	Y	Y
MISSISSIPPI														
1 Childers[8]				Y	Y	Y	Y	Y	Y	Y	Y	N	N	N
2 Thompson	Y	Y	Y	Y	Y	Y	?	Y	Y	Y	Y	N	N	Y
3 *Pickering*	Y	N	N	Y	Y	Y	Y	Y	Y	Y	Y	Y	Y	N
4 Taylor	N	Y	N	Y	Y	Y	Y	Y	Y	Y	Y	N	N	Y

[3]Rep. Bill Foster, D-Ill., was sworn in March 11, 2008.

[4]Rep. André Carson, D-Ind., was sworn in March 13, 2008, to fill the seat vacated by the death of Democrat Julia Carson on Dec. 15, 2007.

[5]Rep. Steve Scalise, R-La., was sworn in May 7, 2008, to fill the seat vacated by Republican Bobby Jindal, who resigned Jan. 14 to become governor.

[6]Rep. Don Cazayoux, D-La., was sworn in May 6, 2008, to fill the seat vacated by Republican Richard H. Baker, who resigned Feb. 2.

[7]Rep. Donna Edwards, D-Md., was sworn in June 19, 2008, to fill the seat vacated by Democrat Albert R. Wynn, who resigned May 31.

[8]Rep. Travis W. Childers, D-Miss., was sworn in May 20, 2008.

House Key Votes	1	2	3	4	5	6	7	8	9	10	11	12	13	14
MISSOURI														
1 Clay	Y	Y	Y	Y	Y	N	Y	Y	Y	Y	Y	N	N	Y
2 *Akin*	Y	N	N	N	N	Y	N	N	N	N	N	N	N	N
3 Carnahan	Y	Y	Y	Y	Y	N	Y	Y	Y	Y	Y	Y	Y	Y
4 Skelton	Y	Y	Y	Y	Y	Y	Y	Y	Y	Y	Y	Y	Y	Y
5 Cleaver	Y	Y	Y	Y	Y	Y	Y	Y	Y	Y	Y	N	Y	Y
6 *Graves*	Y	N	N	Y	Y	Y	Y	N	N	Y	Y	N	N	N
7 *Blunt*	Y	N	N	Y	N	Y	N	N	N	?	?	Y	Y	N
8 *Emerson*	Y	N	N	Y	N	Y	Y	N	Y	Y	Y	Y	Y	Y
9 *Hulshof*	Y	?	?	Y	?	Y	N	?	?	?	Y	N	N	N
MONTANA														
AL *Rehberg*	Y	N	N	Y	Y	Y	Y	N	Y	Y	Y	N	N	N
NEBRASKA														
1 *Fortenberry*	+	N	N	Y	Y	Y	Y	N	Y	Y	Y	N	N	N
2 *Terry*	Y	N	N	N	N	Y	Y	N	N	Y	Y	N	Y	N
3 *Smith*	Y	N	N	Y	N	Y	Y	N	N	N	N	N	N	N
NEVADA														
1 Berkley	Y	Y	Y	Y	Y	Y	Y	Y	Y	Y	Y	N	Y	Y
2 *Heller*	Y	N	N	N	N	Y	Y	Y	N	N	Y	N	N	N
3 *Porter*	+	N	N	Y	N	Y	Y	Y	Y	Y	Y	Y	Y	Y
NEW HAMPSHIRE														
1 Shea-Porter	Y	Y	Y	Y	Y	N	Y	Y	Y	Y	Y	N	N	Y
2 Hodes	Y	Y	Y	Y	Y	N	Y	Y	Y	Y	Y	N	N	Y
NEW JERSEY														
1 Andrews	Y	?	Y	Y	Y	N	Y	Y	Y	Y	Y	Y	Y	Y
2 *LoBiondo*	Y	N	N	N	Y	Y	Y	N	N	Y	Y	N	N	N
3 *Saxton*	Y	N	N	N	Y	Y	?	N	?	Y	?	Y	Y	N
4 *Smith*	Y	N	N	N	Y	Y	N	Y	Y	Y	Y	N	N	Y
5 *Garrett*	N	N	N	N	Y	Y	N	N	N	N	N	N	N	N
6 Pallone	Y	Y	Y	Y	Y	N	Y	Y	Y	Y	Y	Y	Y	Y
7 *Ferguson*	Y	?	N	N	Y	Y	Y	Y	Y	Y	Y	Y	Y	N
8 Pascrell	Y	Y	Y	Y	Y	N	Y	Y	Y	Y	Y	N	Y	Y
9 Rothman	Y	Y	Y	Y	Y	N	Y	Y	Y	Y	Y	N	N	Y
10 Payne	Y	Y	Y	Y	Y	N	Y	Y	Y	Y	Y	N	N	Y
11 *Frelinghuysen*	Y	N	N	N	Y	Y	N	N	Y	Y	Y	N	Y	Y
12 Holt	Y	Y	Y	Y	Y	N	Y	Y	Y	Y	Y	Y	Y	Y
13 Sires	Y	?	Y	Y	Y	Y	Y	Y	Y	Y	Y	Y	Y	Y
NEW MEXICO														
1 *Wilson*	Y	N	N	N	N	Y	Y	N	Y	Y	Y	Y	Y	N
2 *Pearce*	Y	N	N	Y	N	Y	Y	N	Y	N	Y	N	N	N
3 Udall	Y	Y	Y	Y	Y	N	Y	Y	Y	Y	Y	N	N	Y
NEW YORK														
1 Bishop	Y	+	Y	Y	Y	Y	Y	Y	Y	Y	Y	Y	Y	Y
2 Israel	Y	Y	Y	Y	Y	N	Y	Y	Y	Y	Y	Y	Y	Y
3 *King*	Y	N	N	N	Y	Y	Y	Y	Y	Y	Y	Y	Y	Y
4 McCarthy	Y	Y	Y	Y	Y	Y	Y	Y	Y	Y	Y	Y	Y	Y
5 Ackerman	Y	Y	Y	Y	Y	Y	Y	Y	Y	Y	Y	Y	Y	Y
6 Meeks	Y	Y	Y	Y	Y	Y	Y	Y	Y	Y	Y	Y	Y	Y
7 Crowley	Y	Y	Y	Y	Y	Y	Y	Y	Y	Y	Y	Y	Y	Y
8 Nadler	Y	Y	Y	Y	Y	N	Y	Y	Y	Y	Y	Y	Y	Y
9 Weiner	Y	Y	Y	Y	Y	N	Y	Y	Y	Y	Y	Y	Y	Y
10 Towns	Y	Y	Y	Y	Y	N	Y	Y	?	Y	Y	Y	Y	Y
11 Clarke	Y	Y	Y	Y	Y	N	Y	Y	Y	Y	Y	Y	Y	Y
12 Velázquez	Y	Y	Y	Y	Y	N	Y	Y	Y	Y	Y	Y	Y	Y
13 *Fossella*	Y	N	N	?	Y	Y	Y	N	Y	Y	?	Y	Y	N
14 Maloney	Y	Y	Y	Y	Y	N	Y	Y	Y	?	Y	Y	Y	Y
15 Rangel	Y	Y	Y	Y	Y	N	Y	Y	Y	?	Y	Y	Y	Y
16 Serrano	Y	Y	Y	Y	Y	N	Y	Y	Y	Y	Y	N	N	Y
17 Engel	Y	Y	Y	Y	Y	Y	?	Y	Y	Y	Y	Y	Y	Y
18 Lowey	+	Y	Y	Y	Y	Y	Y	Y	Y	Y	Y	Y	Y	Y
19 Hall	Y	Y	Y	Y	Y	N	Y	Y	Y	Y	Y	Y	Y	Y
20 Gillibrand	Y	Y	?	?	?	Y	Y	Y	Y	Y	Y	N	N	Y
21 McNulty	Y	Y	Y	Y	Y	N	?	Y	Y	Y	Y	Y	Y	Y
22 Hinchey	Y	Y	Y	Y	Y	N	Y	Y	Y	Y	Y	N	N	Y
23 *McHugh*	Y	N	N	Y	Y	Y	Y	Y	Y	Y	Y	Y	Y	Y
24 Arcuri	Y	Y	Y	Y	Y	Y	Y	Y	Y	Y	Y	Y	Y	Y
25 *Walsh*	Y	N	Y	Y	Y	Y	Y	Y	Y	Y	Y	Y	Y	Y
26 *Reynolds*	Y	N	N	Y	Y	?	?	Y	Y	N	Y	Y	Y	N
27 Higgins	Y	Y	Y	Y	Y	Y	?	Y	Y	Y	Y	Y	Y	Y
28 Slaughter	Y	Y	Y	Y	Y	N	Y	Y	Y	Y	Y	Y	Y	Y
29 *Kuhl*	Y	N	N	Y	Y	Y	Y	N	Y	Y	Y	N	Y	?
NORTH CAROLINA														
1 Butterfield	Y	Y	Y	Y	+	Y	Y	Y	Y	Y	Y	N	N	N
2 Etheridge	Y	Y	Y	Y	Y	Y	Y	Y	Y	Y	Y	Y	Y	Y
3 *Jones*	Y	Y	Y	Y	Y	?	Y	N	N	N	Y	N	N	N
4 Price	Y	Y	Y	Y	Y	N	Y	Y	Y	Y	Y	Y	Y	Y

House Key Votes	1	2	3	4	5	6	7	8	9	10	11	12	13	14
5 *Foxx*	Y	N	N	N	N	Y	Y	N	N	N	N	N	N	N
6 *Coble*	N	N	Y	Y	N	Y	Y	N	N	N	Y	N	Y	N
7 McIntyre	Y	Y	Y	Y	Y	Y	Y	Y	N	Y	Y	N	N	N
8 *Hayes*	Y	Y	N	Y	Y	Y	Y	Y	N	N	Y	N	N	N
9 *Myrick*	Y	N	?	N	N	Y	Y	N	N	N	Y	N	Y	N
10 *McHenry*	Y	N	N	N	N	Y	N	N	N	N	N	N	N	N
11 Shuler	Y	Y	Y	Y	Y	Y	Y	Y	Y	N	Y	N	N	N
12 Watt	Y	Y	Y	Y	Y	N	Y	Y	Y	Y	Y	Y	Y	Y
13 Miller	Y	Y	Y	Y	Y	N	Y	Y	Y	Y	Y	Y	Y	Y
NORTH DAKOTA														
AL Pomeroy	Y	Y	Y	Y	Y	Y	Y	Y	Y	Y	Y	Y	Y	Y
OHIO														
1 *Chabot*	Y	N	N	N	N	Y	Y	N	N	Y	Y	N	N	N
2 *Schmidt*	Y	N	N	N	N	Y	Y	N	Y	N	Y	N	Y	N
3 *Turner*	Y	N	N	Y	Y	Y	Y	Y	Y	Y	Y	N	N	N
4 *Jordan*	Y	N	N	N	N	Y	N	N	N	N	N	N	N	N
5 *Latta*	Y	N	N	Y	N	Y	Y	N	N	N	N	N	N	N
6 Wilson	Y	Y	Y	Y	Y	Y	Y	Y	Y	Y	Y	Y	Y	Y
7 *Hobson*	Y	N	N	N	N	Y	Y	Y	?	Y	Y	Y	Y	N
8 *Boehner*	Y	N	N	N	N	Y	N	N	N	N	?	Y	Y	N
9 Kaptur	Y	Y	Y	Y	+	N	Y	N	Y	Y	Y	N	N	Y
10 Kucinich	Y	Y	N	Y	Y	N	Y	Y	Y	Y	Y	N	N	Y
11 Tubbs Jones[9]	Y	Y	Y	Y	Y	N	Y	Y	Y	Y				
11 Fudge[9]														Y
12 *Tiberi*	Y	N	N	N	Y	Y	Y	Y	N	Y	Y	N	Y	N
13 Sutton	Y	Y	Y	Y	Y	N	Y	Y	Y	Y	Y	N	Y	Y
14 *LaTourette*	Y	N	N	Y	Y	Y	Y	Y	Y	Y	Y	N	N	Y
15 *Pryce*	Y	N	N	N	Y	Y	?	Y	Y	Y	Y	Y	Y	?
16 *Regula*	Y	N	N	Y	Y	Y	Y	N	Y	Y	Y	Y	Y	Y
17 Ryan	Y	Y	Y	Y	Y	N	Y	Y	Y	Y	Y	Y	Y	Y
18 Space	Y	Y	Y	Y	Y	Y	Y	Y	Y	Y	Y	Y	Y	Y
OKLAHOMA														
1 *Sullivan*	Y	N	N	N	Y	Y	Y	N	N	N	Y	N	Y	N
2 Boren	Y	N	N	Y	Y	Y	Y	Y	Y	Y	Y	Y	Y	Y
3 *Lucas*	Y	N	N	Y	Y	Y	Y	N	N	N	Y	N	N	N
4 *Cole*	Y	N	N	Y	Y	Y	N	N	Y	N	Y	Y	Y	N
5 *Fallin*	Y	N	N	Y	Y	Y	Y	N	?	Y	Y	N	Y	N
OREGON														
1 Wu	Y	Y	Y	Y	Y	N	Y	Y	Y	Y	Y	N	Y	Y
2 *Walden*	Y	N	N	Y	Y	Y	Y	N	N	Y	Y	Y	Y	N
3 Blumenauer	Y	Y	Y	N	Y	N	Y	Y	Y	Y	Y	N	N	Y
4 DeFazio	Y	Y	Y	Y	Y	N	Y	N	Y	Y	Y	N	N	Y
5 Hooley	Y	Y	Y	Y	Y	N	Y	Y	?	Y	Y	Y	Y	?
PENNSYLVANIA														
1 Brady	Y	Y	Y	Y	Y	N	Y	Y	Y	Y	Y	Y	Y	Y
2 Fattah	Y	Y	Y	Y	Y	N	Y	Y	Y	Y	Y	Y	Y	Y
3 *English*	Y	N	Y	Y	Y	Y	Y	Y	Y	Y	Y	N	N	Y
4 Altmire	Y	Y	Y	Y	Y	Y	Y	Y	Y	Y	Y	N	N	Y
5 *Peterson*	Y	N	N	Y	N	?	?	?	N	Y	Y	Y	Y	?
6 *Gerlach*	Y	N	?	Y	Y	Y	Y	N	Y	Y	Y	N	Y	N
7 Sestak	Y	Y	Y	Y	Y	Y	Y	Y	Y	Y	Y	Y	Y	Y
8 Murphy, P.	Y	Y	Y	Y	Y	Y	Y	Y	Y	Y	Y	Y	Y	Y
9 *Shuster*	Y	N	N	Y	Y	Y	Y	N	N	Y	Y	N	Y	N
10 Carney	Y	Y	N	Y	Y	Y	Y	Y	Y	Y	Y	N	N	Y
11 Kanjorski	Y	Y	Y	Y	Y	Y	Y	Y	Y	Y	Y	Y	Y	Y
12 Murtha	Y	Y	Y	Y	Y	Y	Y	Y	Y	Y	Y	Y	Y	Y
13 Schwartz	Y	Y	Y	Y	Y	N	Y	Y	Y	Y	Y	Y	Y	Y
14 Doyle	Y	Y	Y	Y	Y	N	Y	Y	Y	Y	Y	Y	Y	Y
15 *Dent*	Y	N	N	N	Y	Y	Y	N	Y	Y	Y	N	Y	N
16 *Pitts*	?	N	N	N	N	Y	N	N	N	N	N	N	N	N
17 Holden	Y	Y	Y	Y	Y	Y	Y	Y	Y	Y	Y	N	N	Y
18 *Murphy, T.*	Y	N	N	Y	Y	Y	Y	Y	Y	Y	Y	N	N	Y
19 *Platts*	Y	N	N	Y	Y	Y	Y	N	Y	Y	Y	N	N	N
RHODE ISLAND														
1 Kennedy	Y	Y	Y	?	Y	N	Y	Y	Y	Y	Y	Y	Y	Y
2 Langevin	Y	Y	Y	Y	Y	Y	Y	Y	Y	Y	Y	Y	Y	Y
SOUTH CAROLINA														
1 *Brown*	Y	N	N	Y	Y	Y	Y	Y	N	Y	Y	Y	Y	N
2 *Wilson*	Y	N	N	N	N	Y	Y	N	Y	N	Y	Y	Y	N
3 *Barrett*	Y	N	N	N	N	Y	N	N	N	N	N	N	Y	N
4 *Inglis*	Y	N	N	N	N	Y	Y	N	Y	N	Y	Y	Y	N
5 Spratt	Y	Y	Y	Y	Y	Y	Y	Y	Y	Y	Y	Y	Y	Y
6 Clyburn	Y	Y	Y	Y	Y	Y	Y	Y	Y	Y	Y	Y	Y	Y

[9]Rep. Marcia L. Fudge, D-Ohio, was sworn in Nov. 19, 2008, to fill the seat vacated by the death of Democrat Stephanie Tubbs Jones on Aug. 20.

KEY

Democrat *Republican* **Independent**

Y	Voted for (yea)	–	Announced against
#	Paired for	P	Voted "present"
+	Announced for	C	Voted "present" to avoid possible conflict of interest
N	Voted against (nay)		
X	Paired against	?	Did not vote or otherwise make a position known

House Key Votes	1	2	3	4	5	6	7	8	9	10	11	12	13	14
SOUTH DAKOTA														
AL Herseth Sandlin	Y	Y	Y	Y	Y	Y	Y	Y	Y	Y	Y	N	N	N
TENNESSEE														
1 *Davis, D.*	Y	N	N	Y	N	Y	Y	N	N	N	Y	N	N	N
2 *Duncan*	N	N	Y	N	N	Y	N	N	N	Y	N	N	N	N
3 *Wamp*	Y	N	N	N	N	Y	Y	N	N	Y	Y	N	Y	N
4 Davis, L.	Y	Y	N	Y	Y	Y	Y	Y	Y	N	Y	N	N	Y
5 Cooper	N	N	Y	N	Y	Y	Y	Y	Y	Y	Y	Y	Y	N
6 Gordon	Y	Y	Y	Y	Y	Y	Y	Y	Y	Y	Y	Y	Y	?
7 *Blackburn*	Y	N	N	Y	N	Y	N	N	N	N	Y	N	N	N
8 Tanner	?	P	Y	Y	Y	Y	Y	Y	Y	Y	Y	Y	Y	Y
9 Cohen	Y	Y	Y	Y	Y	N	Y	Y	Y	Y	Y	Y	Y	Y
TEXAS														
1 *Gohmert*	N	N	N	Y	Y	?	?	?	N	N	Y	N	N	N
2 *Poe*	N	N	N	Y	Y	Y	Y	N	N	N	N	N	N	N
3 *Johnson, S.*	Y	N	N	N	N	Y	N	N	N	Y	N	N	N	N
4 *Hall*	Y	N	N	Y	N	Y	Y	N	N	Y	Y	N	N	N
5 *Hensarling*	Y	N	N	N	N	Y	N	N	N	N	N	N	N	N
6 *Barton*	Y	N	N	N	N	Y	N	N	N	N	Y	N	N	Y
7 *Culberson*	Y	N	N	N	N	Y	N	N	N	N	Y	N	N	N
8 *Brady*	Y	N	N	Y	N	Y	N	N	N	Y	N	Y	Y	N
9 Green, A.	Y	Y	Y	Y	+	Y	Y	Y	Y	Y	Y	N	Y	Y
10 *McCaul*	Y	N	N	Y	N	Y	Y	N	N	Y	Y	N	N	N
11 *Conaway*	Y	N	N	Y	N	Y	N	N	N	N	N	N	Y	N
12 *Granger*	Y	–	N	N	Y	Y	N	N	N	Y	Y	Y	Y	N
13 *Thornberry*	Y	N	N	Y	N	Y	N	N	N	N	N	N	Y	N
14 *Paul*	N	Y	N	N	N	?	N	N	N	N	N	N	N	N
15 Hinojosa	Y	Y	Y	Y	Y	Y	Y	Y	?	Y	Y	Y	Y	Y
16 Reyes	Y	Y	Y	Y	Y	Y	?	Y	Y	Y	?	Y	Y	Y
17 Edwards	Y	Y	Y	Y	Y	Y	Y	Y	Y	Y	Y	Y	Y	Y
18 Jackson Lee	Y	Y	Y	Y	Y	N	Y	Y	Y	Y	Y	N	Y	Y
19 *Neugebauer*	Y	N	N	Y	N	Y	N	N	N	N	N	N	N	N
20 Gonzalez	Y	Y	Y	Y	Y	N	Y	Y	Y	Y	Y	Y	Y	Y
21 *Smith*	Y	N	N	N	N	Y	Y	N	N	Y	Y	Y	Y	N
22 Lampson	Y	N	N	Y	Y	Y	Y	Y	Y	Y	Y	N	N	Y
23 Rodriguez	Y	Y	Y	Y	Y	Y	Y	Y	Y	Y	Y	N	N	N
24 *Marchant*	Y	N	N	N	N	Y	N	N	N	N	N	N	N	N
25 Doggett	Y	Y	Y	Y	Y	N	Y	Y	Y	Y	Y	N	N	Y
26 *Burgess*	N	?	N	N	N	Y	Y	N	N	N	Y	N	N	N
27 Ortiz	Y	Y	Y	Y	?	Y	Y	?	?	Y	Y	N	Y	Y
28 Cuellar	Y	N	Y	Y	Y	Y	Y	Y	Y	Y	Y	N	Y	Y
29 Green, G.	Y	Y	Y	Y	Y	Y	Y	+	Y	Y	Y	N	N	Y
30 Johnson, E.	Y	Y	Y	Y	Y	N	Y	Y	Y	Y	Y	Y	Y	?
31 *Carter*	Y	N	N	+	N	Y	N	N	N	N	N	N	N	N
32 *Sessions*	Y	N	N	N	N	Y	N	N	N	N	Y	Y	Y	N
UTAH														
1 *Bishop*	Y	?	N	?	Y	Y	?	?	?	N	?	N	N	N
2 Matheson	Y	N	N	N	Y	Y	Y	Y	Y	Y	Y	N	N	N
3 *Cannon*	Y	N	N	N	N	?	?	N	?	N	N	Y	Y	N
VERMONT														
AL Welch	Y	Y	Y	Y	Y	N	Y	Y	Y	Y	Y	N	Y	Y
VIRGINIA														
1 *Wittman*	Y	N	N	Y	N	Y	Y	N	N	Y	Y	N	N	N
2 *Drake*	Y	N	N	Y	Y	Y	Y	N	N	Y	Y	N	N	N
3 Scott	Y	Y	Y	Y	Y	N	Y	Y	Y	Y	Y	N	N	Y
4 *Forbes*	N	N	N	Y	N	Y	Y	N	Y	N	Y	N	N	N
5 *Goode*	N	Y	N	N	Y	Y	Y	N	N	N	Y	N	N	N
6 *Goodlatte*	Y	N	N	Y	Y	Y	Y	N	N	N	Y	N	N	N
7 *Cantor*	Y	N	N	N	Y	Y	N	N	N	Y	?	Y	Y	N
8 Moran	Y	Y	Y	Y	Y	N	Y	Y	Y	Y	Y	Y	Y	Y
9 Boucher	?	Y	Y	Y	Y	Y	Y	Y	Y	Y	Y	Y	Y	Y
10 *Wolf*	Y	N	N	N	Y	Y	Y	N	Y	Y	Y	Y	Y	N
11 *Davis, T.*[10]	?	N	N	N	Y	Y	Y	N	Y	Y	Y	Y	Y	
WASHINGTON														
1 Inslee	?	Y	Y	N	Y	N	Y	Y	Y	Y	Y	N	N	Y
2 Larsen	Y	Y	Y	Y	Y	N	Y	Y	Y	Y	Y	Y	Y	Y
3 Baird	N	Y	N	Y	Y	Y	Y	Y	Y	Y	Y	Y	Y	Y
4 *Hastings*	Y	N	N	Y	N	Y	Y	N	N	Y	N	N	N	N
5 *McMorris Rodgers*	Y	N	N	Y	Y	Y	Y	N	N	Y	Y	N	N	N
6 Dicks	Y	Y	Y	Y	Y	Y	Y	Y	Y	Y	Y	Y	Y	Y
7 McDermott	Y	Y	Y	N	Y	N	Y	Y	Y	Y	Y	Y	N	Y
8 *Reichert*	Y	N	N	N	Y	Y	Y	N	Y	Y	Y	N	N	N
9 Smith	–	Y	Y	N	Y	Y	Y	Y	Y	Y	Y	Y	Y	Y
WEST VIRGINIA														
1 Mollohan	Y	Y	Y	Y	Y	N	Y	Y	Y	Y	Y	Y	Y	Y
2 *Capito*	Y	N	N	Y	Y	Y	Y	Y	Y	Y	Y	N	N	Y
3 Rahall	Y	Y	Y	Y	Y	Y	Y	Y	Y	Y	Y	Y	Y	N
WISCONSIN														
1 *Ryan*	Y	N	N	N	N	Y	N	N	N	N	Y	Y	Y	Y
2 Baldwin	Y	Y	Y	Y	Y	N	Y	Y	Y	Y	Y	Y	Y	Y
3 Kind	Y	Y	Y	N	Y	Y	Y	Y	Y	Y	Y	Y	Y	Y
4 Moore	Y	Y	Y	N	Y	N	Y	Y	Y	Y	Y	Y	Y	Y
5 *Sensenbrenner*	N	N	N	N	N	Y	N	N	N	N	Y	N	N	?
6 *Petri*	Y	N	N	N	Y	Y	Y	N	N	N	Y	N	N	N
7 Obey	Y	Y	Y	Y	Y	N	Y	Y	Y	Y	Y	Y	Y	Y
8 Kagen	Y	Y	Y	Y	Y	N	Y	Y	Y	Y	Y	N	N	N
WYOMING														
AL *Cubin*	N	N	N	Y	N	Y	Y	N	?	?	?	Y	Y	?

[10]Rep. Thomas M. Davis III, R-Va., resigned Nov. 24, 2008.

Congress and Its Members

Senate Membership in the 109th Congress

Lineup as of Jan. 3, 2005: Republicans, 55; Democrats, 44; Independent, 1

Alabama
Richard C. Shelby (R)
Jeff Sessions (R)

Alaska
Ted Stevens (R)
Lisa Murkowski (R)

Arizona
John McCain (R)
Jon Kyl (R)

Arkansas
Blanche Lincoln (D)
Mark Pryor (D)

California
Dianne Feinstein (D)
Barbara Boxer (D)

Colorado
Wayne Allard (R)
Ken Salazar (D)

Connecticut
Christopher J. Dodd (D)
Joseph I. Lieberman (D)

Delaware
Joseph R. Biden Jr. (D)
Thomas R. Carper (D)

Florida
Bill Nelson (D)
Mel Martinez (R)

Georgia
Saxby Chambliss (R)
Johnny Isakson (R)

Hawaii
Daniel K. Inouye (D)
Daniel K. Akaka (D)

Idaho
Larry E. Craig (R)
Michael D. Crapo (R)

Illinois
Richard J. Durbin (D)
Barack Obama (D)

Indiana
Richard G. Lugar (R)
Evan Bayh (D)

Iowa
Charles E. Grassley (R)
Tom Harkin (D)

Kansas
Sam Brownback (R)
Pat Roberts (R)

Kentucky
Mitch McConnell (R)
Jim Bunning (R)

Louisiana
Mary L. Landrieu (D)
David Vitter (R)

Maine
Olympia J. Snowe (R)
Susan Collins (R)

Maryland
Paul S. Sarbanes (D)
Barbara A. Mikulski (D)

Massachusetts
Edward M. Kennedy (D)
John F. Kerry (D)

Michigan
Carl Levin (D)
Deborah Stabenow (D)

Minnesota
Mark Dayton (D)
Norm Coleman (R)

Mississippi
Thad Cochran (R)
Trent Lott (R)

Missouri
Christopher S. Bond (R)
Jim Talent (R)

Montana
Max Baucus (D)
Conrad Burns (R)

Nebraska
Chuck Hagel (R)
Ben Nelson (D)

Nevada
Harry Reid (D)
John Ensign (R)

New Hampshire
Judd Gregg (R)
John E. Sununu (R)

New Jersey
Frank R. Lautenberg (D)
Jon Corzine (D)

New Mexico
Pete V. Domenici (R)
Jeff Bingaman (D)

New York
Charles E. Schumer (D)
Hillary Rodham Clinton (D)

North Carolina
Elizabeth Dole (R)
Robert M. Burr (R)

North Dakota
Kent Conrad (D)
Byron L. Dorgan (D)

Ohio
Mike DeWine (R)
George V. Voinovich (R)

Oklahoma
James M. Inhofe (R)
Tom Coburn (R)

Oregon
Ron Wyden (D)
Gordon H. Smith (R)

Pennsylvania
Arlen Specter (R)
Rick Santorum (R)

Rhode Island
Jack Reed (D)
Lincoln Chafee (R)

South Carolina
Lindsey Graham (R)
Jim DeMint (R)

South Dakota
Tim Johnson (D)
John Thune (R)

Tennessee
Bill Frist (R)
Lamar Alexander (R)

Texas
Kay Bailey Hutchison (R)
John Cornyn (R)

Utah
Orrin G. Hatch (R)
Robert F. Bennett (R)

Vermont
Patrick J. Leahy (D)
James M. Jeffords (I)

Virginia
John W. Warner (R)
George F. Allen (R)

Washington
Patty Murray (D)
Maria Cantwell (D)

West Virginia
Robert C. Byrd (D)
John D. Rockefeller IV (D)

Wisconsin
Herb Kohl (D)
Russell D. Feingold (D)

Wyoming
Craig Thomas (R)
Michael B. Enzi (R)

House Membership in the 109th Congress

Lineup as of Jan. 3, 2005: Republicans, 232; Democrats, 201; Independent, 1, Vacancy, 1

Alabama

1. Jo Bonner (R)
2. Terry Everett (R)
3. Mike D. Rogers (R)
4. Robert B. Aderholt (R)
5. Robert E. "Bud" Cramer (D)
6. Spencer Bachus (R)
7. Artur Davis (D)

Alaska

AL Don Young (R)

Arizona

1. Rick Renzi (R)
2. Trent Franks (R)
3. John Shadegg (R)
4. Ed Pastor (D)
5. J.D. Hayworth (R)
6. Jeff Flake (R)
7. Raul M. Grijalva (D)
8. Jim Kolbe (R)

Arkansas

1. Marion Berry (D)
2. Vic Snyder (D)
3. John Boozman (R)
4. Mike Ross (D)

California

1. Mike Thompson (D)
2. Wally Herger (R)
3. Dan Lungren (R)
4. John T. Doolittle (R)
5. Robert T. Matsui (D)
   (died Jan. 1, 2005)
   Doris Matsui (D)
   (sworn in March 10, 2005)
6. Lynn Woolsey (D)
7. George Miller (D)
8. Nancy Pelosi (D)
9. Barbara Lee (D)
10. Ellen O. Tauscher (D)
11. Richard W. Pombo (R)
12. Tom Lantos (D)
13. Pete Stark (D)
14. Anna G. Eshoo (D)
15. Michael M. Honda (D)
16. Zoe Lofgren (D)
17. Sam Farr (D)
18. Dennis Cardoza (D)
19. George P. Radanovich (R)
20. Jim Costa (D)
21. Devin Nunes (R)
22. Bill Thomas (R)
23. Lois Capps (D)
24. Elton Gallegly (R)
25. Howard P. "Buck" McKeon (R)
26. David Dreier (R)
27. Brad Sherman (D)
28. Howard L. Berman (D)
29. Adam B. Schiff (D)
30. Henry A. Waxman (D)
31. Xavier Becerra (D)
32. Hilda L. Solis (D)
33. Diane Watson (D)
34. Lucille Roybal-Allard (D)
35. Maxine Waters (D)
36. Jane Harman (D)
37. Juanita Millender-McDonald (D)
38. Grace F. Napolitano (D)
39. Linda T. Sanchez (D)
40. Ed Royce (R)
41. Jerry Lewis (R)
42. Gary G. Miller (R)
43. Joe Baca (D)
44. Ken Calvert (R)
45. Mary Bono (R)
46. Dana Rohrabacher (R)
47. Loretta Sanchez (D)
48. Christopher Cox (R)
   (resigned Aug. 2, 2005)
   John Campbell (R)
   (sworn in Dec. 7, 2005)
49. Darrell Issa (R)
50. Randy "Duke" Cunningham (R)
   (resigned Dec. 1, 2005)
   Brian P. Bilbray (R)
   (sworn in June 13, 2006)
51. Bob Filner (D)
52. Duncan Hunter (R)
53. Susan A. Davis (D)

Colorado

1. Diana DeGette (D)
2. Mark Udall (D)
3. John Salazar (D)
4. Marilyn Musgrave (R)
5. Joel Hefley (R)
6. Tom Tancredo (R)
7. Bob Beauprez (R)

Connecticut

1. John B. Larson (D)
2. Rob Simmons (R)
3. Rosa DeLauro (D)
4. Christopher Shays (R)
5. Nancy L. Johnson (R)

Delaware

AL Michael Castle (R)

Florida

1. Jeff Miller (R)
2. Allen Boyd (D)
3. Corrine Brown (D)
4. Ander Crenshaw (R)
5. Ginny Brown-Waite (R)
6. Cliff Stearns (R)
7. John L. Mica (R)
8. Ric Keller (R)
9. Michael Bilirakis (R)
10. C.W. Bill Young (R)
11. Jim Davis (D)
12. Adam H. Putnam (R)
13. Katherine Harris (R)
14. Connie Mack (R)
15. Dave Weldon (R)
16. Mark Foley (R)
   (resigned Sept. 29, 2006)
17. Kendrick B. Meek (D)
18. Ileana Ros-Lehtinen (R)
19. Robert Wexler (D)
20. Debbie Wasserman-Schultz (D)
21. Lincoln Diaz-Balart (R)
22. E. Clay Shaw Jr. (R)
23. Alcee L. Hastings (D)
24. Tom Feeney (R)
25. Mario Diaz-Balart (R)

Georgia

1. Jack Kingston (R)
2. Sanford D. Bishop Jr. (D)
3. Jim Marshall (D)
4. Cynthia A. McKinney (D)
5. John Lewis (D)
6. Tom Price (R)
7. John Linder (R)
8. Lynn Westmoreland (R)
9. Charlie Norwood (R)
10. Nathan Deal (R)
11. Phil Gingrey (R)
12. John Barrow (R)
13. David Scott (D)

Hawaii

1. Neil Abercrombie (D)
2. Ed Case (D)

Idaho

1. C.L. "Butch" Otter (R)
2. Mike Simpson (R)

Illinois

1. Bobby L. Rush (D)
2. Jesse L. Jackson Jr. (D)
3. William O. Lipinski (D)
4. Luis V. Gutierrez (D)
5. Rahm Emanuel (D)
6. Henry J. Hyde (R)
7. Danny K. Davis (D)
8. Melissa Bean (D)
9. Jan Schakowsky (D)
10. Mark Steven Kirk (R)
11. Jerry Weller (R)
12. Jerry F. Costello (D)
13. Judy Biggert (R)
14. J. Dennis Hastert (R)
15. Timothy V. Johnson (R)
16. Donald Manzullo (R)
17. Lane Evans (D)
18. Ray LaHood (R)
19. John Shimkus (R)

Indiana

1. Peter J. Visclosky (D)
2. Chris Chocola (R)
3. Mark Souder (R)
4. Steve Buyer (R)
5. Dan Burton (R)
6. Mike Pence (R)
7. Julia Carson (D)
8. John Hostettler (R)
9. Mike Sodrel (R)

Iowa

1. Jim Nussle (R)
2. Jim Leach (R)
3. Leonard L. Boswell (D)
4. Tom Latham (R)
5. Steve King (R)

Kansas

1. Jerry Moran (R)
2. Jim Ryun (R)
3. Dennis Moore (D)
4. Todd Tiahrt (R)

Kentucky

1. Edward Whitfield (R)
2. Ron Lewis (R)
3. Anne M. Northup (R)
4. Geoff Davis (R)
5. Harold Rogers (R)
6. Ben Chandler (D)

Louisiana

1. Bobby Jindal (R)
2. William J. Jefferson (D)
3. Charlie Melancon (D)
4. Jim McCrery (R)
5. Rodney Alexander (D)
6. Richard H. Baker (R)
7. Charles Boustany Jr. (R)

Maine

1. Tom Allen (D)
2. Michael H. Michaud (D)

Maryland

1. Wayne T. Gilchrest (R)
2. C.A. Dutch Ruppersberger (D)
3. Benjamin L. Cardin (D)
4. Albert R. Wynn (D)
5. Steny H. Hoyer (D)
6. Roscoe G. Bartlett (R)
7. Elijah E. Cummings (D)
8. Chris Van Hollen (D)

Massachusetts

1. John W. Olver (D)
2. Richard E. Neal (D)
3. Jim McGovern (D)
4. Barney Frank (D)
5. Martin T. Meehan (D)
6. John F. Tierney (D)
7. Edward J. Markey (D)

8. Michael E. Capuano (D)
9. Stephen L. Lynch (D)
10. William Delahunt (D)

Michigan
1. Bart Stupak (D)
2. Peter Hoekstra (R)
3. Vernon J. Ehlers (R)
4. Dave Camp (R)
5. Dale E. Kildee (D)
6. Fred Upton (R)
7. Joe Schwarz (R)
8. Mike Rogers (R)
9. Joe Knollenberg (R)
10. Candice S. Miller (R)
11. Thaddeus McCotter (R)
12. Sander M. Levin (D)
13. Carolyn Cheeks Kilpatrick (D)
14. John Conyers Jr. (D)
15. John D. Dingell (D)

Minnesota
1. Gil Gutknecht (R)
2. John Kline (R)
3. Jim Ramstad (R)
4. Betty McCollum (D)
5. Martin Olav Sabo (D)
6. Mark Kennedy (R)
7. Collin C. Peterson (D)
8. James L. Oberstar (D)

Mississippi
1. Roger Wicker (R)
2. Bennie Thompson (D)
3. Charles W. "Chip" Pickering Jr. (R)
4. Gene Taylor (D)

Missouri
1. William Lacy Clay (D)
2. Todd Akin (R)
3. Russ Carnahan (D)
4. Ike Skelton (D)
5. Emanuel Cleaver II (D)
6. Sam Graves (R)
7. Roy Blunt (R)
8. Jo Ann Emerson (R)
9. Kenny Hulshof (R)

Montana
AL Denny Rehberg (R)

Nebraska
1. Jeff Fortenberry (R)
2. Lee Terry (R)
3. Tom Osborne (R)

Nevada
1. Shelley Berkley (D)
2. Jim Gibbons (R)
3. Jon Porter (R)

New Hampshire
1. Jeb Bradley (R)
2. Charles Bass (R)

New Jersey
1. Robert E. Andrews (D)
2. Frank A. LoBiondo (R)
3. H. James Saxton (R)
4. Christopher H. Smith (R)
5. Scott Garrett (R)
6. Frank Pallone Jr. (D)
7. Mike Ferguson (R)
8. Bill Pascrell Jr. (D)
9. Steven R. Rothman (D)
10. Donald M. Payne (D)
11. Rodney Frelinghuysen (R)
12. Rush D. Holt (D)
13. Robert Menendez (D) *(resigned Jan. 16, 2006)*
    Albio Sires (D) *(sworn in Nov. 13, 2006)*

New Mexico
1. Heather A. Wilson (R)
2. Steve Pearce (R)
3. Tom Udall (D)

New York
1. Timothy H. Bishop (D)
2. Steve Israel (D)
3. Peter T. King (R)
4. Carolyn McCarthy (D)
5. Gary L. Ackerman (D)
6. Gregory W. Meeks (D)
7. Joseph Crowley (D)
8. Jerrold Nadler (D)
9. Anthony Weiner (D)
10. Edolphus Towns (D)
11. Major R. Owens (D)
12. Nydia M. Velázquez (D)
13. Vito J. Fossella (R)
14. Carolyn B. Maloney (D)
15. Charles B. Rangel (D)
16. Jose E. Serrano (D)
17. Eliot L. Engel (D)
18. Nita M. Lowey (D)
19. Sue W. Kelly (R)
20. John E. Sweeney (R)
21. Michael R. McNulty (D)
22. Maurice D. Hinchey (D)
23. John M. McHugh (R)
24. Sherwood Boehlert (R)
25. James T. Walsh (R)
26. Thomas M. Reynolds (R)
27. Brian Higgins (D)
28. Louise M. Slaughter (D)
29. John R. "Randy" Kuhl Jr. (R)

North Carolina
1. G.K. Butterfield (D)
2. Bob Etheridge (D)
3. Walter B. Jones (R)
4. David E. Price (D)
5. Virginia Foxx (R)
6. Howard Coble (R)
7. Mike McIntyre (D)
8. Robin Hayes (R)
9. Sue Myrick (R)
10. Patrick T. McHenry (R)
11. Charles H. Taylor (R)
12. Melvin Watt (D)
13. Brad Miller (D)

North Dakota
AL Earl Pomeroy (D)

Ohio
1. Steve Chabot (R)
2. Rob Portman (R) *(resigned April 29, 2005)*
   Jean Schmidt (R) *(sworn in Sept. 6, 2005)*
3. Michael R. Turner (R)
4. Michael G. Oxley (R)
5. Paul E. Gillmor (R)
6. Ted Strickland (D)
7. David L. Hobson (R)
8. John A. Boehner (R)
9. Marcy Kaptur (D)
10. Dennis J. Kucinich (D)
11. Stephanie Tubbs Jones (D)
12. Pat Tiberi (R)
13. Sherrod Brown (D)
14. Steven C. LaTourette (R)
15. Deborah Pryce (R)
16. Ralph Regula (R)
17. Tim Ryan (D)
18. Bob Ney (R) *(resigned Nov. 3, 2006)*

Oklahoma
1. John Sullivan (R)
2. Dan Boren (D)
3. Frank D. Lucas (R)
4. Tom Cole (R)
5. Ernest Istook (R)

Oregon
1. David Wu (D)
2. Greg Walden (R)
3. Earl Blumenauer (D)
4. Peter A. DeFazio (D)
5. Darlene Hooley (D)

Pennsylvania
1. Robert A. Brady (D)
2. Chaka Fattah (D)
3. Phil English (R)
4. Melissa A. Hart (R)
5. John E. Peterson (R)
6. Jim Gerlach (R)
7. Curt Weldon (R)
8. Michael G. Fitzpatrick (R)
9. Bill Shuster (R)
10. Don Sherwood (R)
11. Paul E. Kanjorski (D)
12. John P. Murtha (D)
13. Allyson Y. Schwartz (D)
14. Mike Doyle (D)
15. Charlie Dent (R)
16. Joe Pitts (R)
17. Tim Holden (D)
18. Tim Murphy (R)
19. Todd R. Platts (R)

Rhode Island
1. Patrick J. Kennedy (D)
2. Jim Langevin (D)

South Carolina
1. Henry E. Brown Jr. (R)
2. Joe Wilson (R)
3. J. Gresham Barrett (R)
4. Bob Inglis (R)
5. John M. Spratt Jr. (D)
6. James E. Clyburn (D)

South Dakota
AL Stephanie Herseth (D)

Tennessee
1. William L. Jenkins (R)
2. John J. "Jimmy" Duncan Jr. (R)
3. Zach Wamp (R)
4. Lincoln Davis (D)
5. Jim Cooper (D)
6. Bart Gordon (D)
7. Marsha Blackburn (R)
8. John Tanner (D)
9. Harold E. Ford Jr. (D)

Texas
1. Louie Gohmert (R)
2. Ted Poe (R)
3. Sam Johnson (R)
4. Ralph M. Hall (R)
5. Jeb Hensarling (R)
6. Joe L. Barton (R)
7. John Culberson (R)
8. Kevin Brady (R)
9. Al Green (D)
10. Michael McCaul (R)
11. K. Michel Conway (R)
12. Kay Granger (R)
13. William M. "Mac" Thornberry (R)
14. Ron Paul (R)
15. Ruben Hinojosa (D)
16. Silvestre Reyes (D)
17. Chet Edwards (R)
18. Sheila Jackson-Lee (D)
19. Randy Neugebauer (R)
20. Charlie Gonzalez (D)
21. Lamar Smith (R)
22. Tom DeLay (R) *(resigned June 9, 2006)*
    Shelley Sekula-Gibbs (R) *(sworn in Nov. 13, 2006)*
23. Henry Bonilla (R)
24. Kenny Marchant (R)
25. Lloyd Doggett (D)
26. Michael C. Burgess (R)
27. Solomon P. Ortiz (D)
28. Henry Cuellar (D)
29. Gene Green (D)
30. Eddie Bernice Johnson (D)
31. John Carter (R)
32. Pete Sessions (R)

Utah
1. Rob Bishop (R)
2. Jim Matheson (D)
3. Christopher B. Cannon (R)

Vermont
AL Sanders Bernard (I)

Virginia
1. Jo Ann Davis (R)
2. Thelma Drake (R)

3. Robert C. Scott (D)
4. J. Randy Forbes (R)
5. Virgil H. Goode Jr. (R)
6. Robert W. Goodlatte (R)
7. Eric Cantor (R)
8. James P. Moran (D)
9. Rick C. Boucher (D)
10. Frank R. Wolf (R)
11. Thomas M. Davis III (R)

Washington

1. Jay Inslee (D)
2. Rick Larsen (D)
3. Brian Baird (D)
4. Richard "Doc" Hastings (R)
5. Cathy McMorris (R)
6. Norm Dicks (D)
7. Jim McDermott (D)
8. Dave Reichert (R)
9. Adam Smith (D)

West Virginia

1. Alan B. Mollohan (D)
2. Shelley Moore Capito (R)
3. Nick J. Rahall II (D)

Wisconsin

1. Paul D. Ryan (R)
2. Tammy Baldwin (D)
3. Ron Kind (D)
4. Gwen Moore (D)
5. F. James Sensenbrenner Jr. (R)
6. Tom Petri (R)
7. David R. Obey (D)
8. Mark Green (R)

Wyoming

AL Cubin Barbara (R)

NOTE: Changes that occurred during 2005 and 2006 are noted following the names of individuals who did not serve their full terms. Members of the 109th Congress also included delegates Eni F. H. Faleomavaega, D-American Samoa; Eleanor Holmes Norton, D-District of Columbia; Madeleine Z. Bordallo, D-Guam; Donna M. C. Christian, D-Virgin Islands; and resident commissioner Luis Fortuno, R-Puerto Rico.

Membership Changes, 109th and 110th Congresses

109th Congress

Member/party	*Died*	*Resigned*	*Switched Party*	*Successor*	*Elected*	*Sworn in*
Senate						
Jon Corzine, D-N.J.[1]		1/17/06		Robert Menendez, D		1/18/06
House						
Robert T. Matsui, D-Calif.	1/1/05			Doris Matsui, D	3/8/05	3/10/05
Rob Portman, R-Ohio[2]		4/29/05		Jean Schmidt, R	8/2/05	9/6/05
Christopher Cox, R-Calif.[3]		8/2/05		John Campbell, R	12/6/05	12/7/05
Randy "Duke" Cunningham, R-Calif.[4]		12/1/05		Brian P. Bilbray, R	6/6/06	6/13/06
Robert Menendez, D-N.J.[5]		1/16/06		Albio Sires, D	11/7/06	11/13/06
Tom DeLay, R-Texas[6]		6/9/06		Shelley Sekula-Gibbs, R	11/7/06	11/13/06
Mark Foley, R-Fla.[7]		9/29/06				
Bob Ney, R-Ohio[8]		11/3/06				

110th Congress

Member/party	*Died*	*Resigned*	*Switched Party*	*Successor*	*Elected*	*Sworn in*
Senate						
Craig Thomas, R-Wyo.	6/4/07			John A. Barrasso, R		6/25/07
Trent Lott, R-Miss.[9]		12/18/07		Roger Wicker, R		1/22/08
Barack Obama, D-Ill.[16]		11/16/08		Roland Burris, D		1/15/09
House						
Charlie Norwood, R-Ga.	2/13/07			Paul Broun, R	7/17/07	7/25/07
Juanita Millender-McDonald, D-Calif.	4/22/07			Laura Richardson, D	8/21/07	9/4/07
Martin T. Meehan, D-Mass.[10]		7/1/07		Niki Tsongas, D	10/16/07	10/18/07
Paul E. Gillmor, R-Ohio	9/5/07			Bob Latta, R	12/11/07	12/13/07
Jo Ann Davis, R-Va.	10/6/07			Rob Wittman, R	12/11/07	12/13/07
J. Dennis Hastert, R-Ill.[11]		11/26/07		Bill Foster, D	3/8/08	3/11/08
Julia Carson, D-Ind.	12/15/07			Andre Carson, D	3/11/08	3/13/08
Roger Wicker, R-Miss.[12]		12/31/07		Travis W. Childers, D	5/13/08	5/21/08
Bobby Jindal, R-La.[13]		1/14/08		Steve Scalise, R	5/3/08	5/7/08
Richard H. Baker, R-La.[14]		2/2/08		Don Cazayoux, D	5/3/08	5/6/08
Tom Lantos, D-Calif.	2/11/08			Jackie Speier, D	4/8/08	4/10/08
Albert Wynn, D-Md.[15]		5/31/08		Donna Edwards, D	6/17/08	6/19/08
Stephanie Tubbs Jones, D-Ohio	8/20/08			Marcia Fudge, D	11/18/08	11/19/08

1. Corzine resigned to run for governor. He appointed Menendez to succeed him. Menendez won a full six-year term in 2006.
2. Portman resigned to become U.S. trade representative.
3. Cox resigned to become chairman of the Securities and Exchange Commission.
4. Cunningham resigned after pleading guilty to tax evasion and taking at least $2.4 million in bribes from defense contractors.
5. Menendez was appointed to the Senate. See footnote 1.
6. DeLay resigned in the wake of a number of scandals that mostly affected House Republicans. His political fortunes rapidly declined in 2005 and early 2006 following an indictment in Texas on campaign finance charges and his close association with a lobbyist named Jack Abramoff who had pleaded guilty to federal charges of conspiracy, mail fraud, and tax evasion. The remainder of DeLay's term was filled in a special election by Sekula-Gibbs, but she lost in the general elections to a Democrat, Nick Lampson who had previously served four terms in the House.
7. Foley resigned after disclosure of inappropriate e-mails and instant messages he sent over several years to both serving and former teenage male pages. No special election was held to fill the seat for the remainder of his term in the 109th Congress.
8. Ney resigned after pleading guilty to two federal counts of conspiracy and false statements. He admitted receiving gifts including expense meals and trips worth more than $170,000 from Abramoff (see footnote 7) in return for trying to shape legislation to help lobbyist's clients. No special election was held to fill the remainder of his term in the 109th Congress.
9. Lott resigned to avoid lobbying restrictions that took effect for members beginning in January 2008. He subsequently joined former senator John Beraux, D-La, in a Washington lobbying firm.
10. Meehan resigned to become chancellor of the University of Massachusetts at Lowell.
11. Hastert, the House Speaker under Republican control until 2007, resigned to allow the Illinois governor to call a special election to fill the seat for the remainder of Hastert's 110th Congress term and to run for the seat in the 111th Congress. In May 2008 Hastert joined a Washington law and lobbying firm, Dickstein Shapiro, as a senior adviser. A spokesperson for the firm said Hastert would not be lobbying but would provide "strategic counseling" to clients.
12. Wicker resigned to accept appointment as Mississippi senator, replacing Trent Lott who resigned on Dec. 18, 2007.
13. Jindal resigned after being elected Louisiana governor on Oct. 20, 2007.
14. Baker resigned to take a lobbying position for the Managed Funds Association, a trade group for the hedge fund industry.
15. Wynn was defeated in a Feb. 12, 2008, primary by Democratic challenger Donna Edwards. He then resigned his seat, effective at the end of May, to join the law and lobbying firm of Dickstein Shapiro. Edwards later won a special June 17 election to fill out his term in the 110th Congress.
16. Barack Obama resigned Nov. 16, 2008, following his election as president of the United States.

Senate Membership in the 110th Congress

Lineup as of Jan. 3, 2007: Democrats, 49; Republicans, 49; Independents, 2

Alabama
Richard C. Shelby (R)
Jeff Sessions (R)

Alaska
Ted Stevens (R)
Lisa Murkowski (R)

Arizona
John McCain (R)
Jon Kyl (R)

Arkansas
Blanche Lincoln (D)
Mark Pryor (D)

California
Dianne Feinstein (D)
Barbara Boxer (D)

Colorado
Wayne Allard (R)
Ken Salazar (D)

Connecticut
Christopher J. Dodd (D)
Joseph I. Lieberman (I)

Delaware
Joseph R. Biden Jr. (D)
Thomas R. Carper (D)

Florida
Bill Nelson (D)
Mel Martinez (R)

Georgia
Saxby Chambliss (R)
Johnny Isakson (R)

Hawaii
Daniel K. Inouye (D)
Daniel K. Akaka (D)

Idaho
Larry E. Craig (R)
Michael D. Crapo (R)

Illinois
Richard J. Durbin (D)
Barack Obama (D)

Indiana
Richard G. Lugar (R)
Evan Bayh (D)

Iowa
Charles E. Grassley (R)
Tom Harkin (D)

Kansas
Sam Brownback (R)
Pat Roberts (R)

Kentucky
Mitch McConnell (R)
Jim Bunning (R)

Louisiana
Mary L. Landrieu (D)
David Vitter (R)

Maine
Olympia J. Snowe (R)
Susan Collins (R)

Maryland
Barbara A. Mikulski (D)
Benjamin L. Cardin (D)

Massachusetts
Edward M. Kennedy (D)
John F. Kerry (D)

Michigan
Carl Levin (D)
Deborah Stabenow (D)

Minnesota
Norm Coleman (R)
Amy Klobuchar (D)

Mississippi
Thad Cochran (R)
Trent Lott (R)

Missouri
Christopher S. Bond (R)
Claire McCaskill (D)

Montana
Max Baucus (D)
Jon Tester (D)

Nebraska
Chuck Hagel (R)
Ben Nelson (D)

Nevada
Harry Reid (D)
John Ensign (R)

New Hampshire
Judd Gregg (R)
John E. Sununu (R)

New Jersey
Frank R. Lautenberg (D)
Robert Menendez (D)

New Mexico
Pete V. Domenici (R)
Jeff Bingaman (D)

New York
Charles E. Schumer (D)
Hillary Rodham Clinton (D)

North Carolina
Elizabeth Dole (R)
Robert M. Burr (R)

North Dakota
Kent Conrad (D)
Byron L. Dorgan (D)

Ohio
George V. Voinovich (R)
Sherrod Brown (D)

Oklahoma
James M. Inhofe (R)
Tom Coburn (R)

Oregon
Ron Wyden (D)
Gordon H. Smith (R)

Pennsylvania
Arlen Specter (R)
Bob Casey (D)

Rhode Island
Jack Reed (D)
Sheldon Whitehouse (D)

South Carolina
Lindsey Graham (R)
Jim DeMint (R)

South Dakota
Tim Johnson (D)
John Thune (R)

Tennessee
Lamar Alexander (R)
Bob Corker (R)

Texas
Kay Bailey Hutchison (R)
John Cornyn (R)

Utah
Orrin G. Hatch (R)
Robert F. Bennett (R)

Vermont
Patrick J. Leahy (D)
Bernard Sanders (I)

Virginia
John W. Warner (R)
Jim Webb (D)

Washington
Patty Murray (D)
Maria Cantwell (D)

West Virginia
Robert C. Byrd (D)
John D. Rockefeller IV (D)

Wisconsin
Herb Kohl (D)
Russell D. Feingold (D)

Wyoming
Craig Thomas (R)
Michael B. Enzi (R)

House Membership in the 110th Congress

Lineup as of Jan. 3, 2007: Democrats, 233; Republicans, 202

Alabama

1. Jo Bonner (R)
2. Terry Everett (R)
3. Mike D. Rogers (R)
4. Robert B. Aderholt (R)
5. Robert E. "Bud" Cramer (D)
6. Spencer Bachus (R)
7. Artur Davis (D)

Alaska

AL Don Young (R)

Arizona

1. Rick Renzi (R)
2. Trent Franks (R)
3. John Shadegg (R)
4. Ed Pastor (D)
5. Harry E. Mitchell (D)
6. Jeff Flake (R)
7. Raul M. Grijalva (D)
8. Gabrielle Giffords (D)

Arkansas

1. Marion Berry (D)
2. Vic Snyder (D)
3. John Boozman (R)
4. Mike Ross (D)

California

1. Mike Thompson (D)
2. Wally Herger (R)
3. Dan Lungren (R)
4. John T. Doolittle (R)
5. Doris Matsui (D)
   (sworn in March 10, 2005)
6. Lynn Woolsey (D)
7. George Miller (D)
8. Nancy Pelosi (D)
9. Barbara Lee (D)
10. Ellen O. Tauscher (D)
11. Jerry McNerney (D)
12. Tom Lantos (D)
    (died Feb. 11, 2008)
    Jackie Speier (D)
    (sworn in April 10, 2008)
13. Pete Stark (D)
14. Anna G. Eshoo (D)
15. Michael M. Honda (D)
16. Zoe Lofgren (D)
17. Sam Farr (D)
18. Dennis Cardoza (D)
19. George P. Radanovich (R)
20. Jim Costa (D)
21. Devin Nunes (R)
22. Kevin McCarthy (R)
23. Lois Capps (D)
24. Elton Gallegly (R)
25. Howard P. "Buck" McKeon (R)
26. David Dreier (R)
27. Brad Sherman (D)
28. Howard L. Berman (D)
29. Adam B. Schiff (D)
30. Henry A. Waxman (D)
31. Xavier Becerra (D)
32. Hilda L. Solis (D)
33. Diane Watson (D)
34. Lucille Roybal-Allard (D)
35. Maxine Waters (D)
36. Jane Harman (D)
37. Juanita Millender-McDonald (D)
    (died April 22, 2007)
    Laura Richardson (D)
    (sworn in Sept. 4, 2007)
38. Grace F. Napolitano (D)
39. Linda T. Sanchez (D)
40. Ed Royce (R)
41. Jerry Lewis (R)
42. Gary G. Miller (R)
43. Joe Baca (D)
44. Ken Calvert (R)
45. Mary Bono (R)
46. Dana Rohrabacher (R)
47. Loretta Sanchez (D)
48. John Campbell (R)
49. Darrell Issa (R)
50. Brian P. Bilbray (R)
51. Bob Filner (D)
52. Duncan Hunter (R)
53. Susan A. Davis (D)

Colorado

1. Diana DeGette (D)
2. Mark Udall (D)
3. John Salazar (D)
4. Marilyn Musgrave (R)
5. Doug Lamborn (R)
6. Tom Tancredo (R)
7. Ed Perlmutter (D)

Connecticut

1. John B. Larson (D)
2. Joe Courtney (D)
3. Rosa DeLauro (D)
4. Christopher Shays (R)
5. Christopher S. Murphy (D)

Delaware

AL Michael Castle (R)

Florida

1. Jeff Miller (R)
2. Allen Boyd (D)
3. Corrine Brown (D)
4. Ander Crenshaw (R)
5. Ginny Brown-Waite (R)
6. Cliff Stearns (R)
7. John L. Mica (R)
8. Ric Keller (R)
9. Gus Bilirakis (R)
10. C.W. Bill Young (R)
11. Kathy Castor (D)
12. Adam H. Putnam (R)
13. Vern Buchanan (R)
14. Connie Mack (R)
15. Dave Weldon (R)
16. Tim Mahoney (D)
17. Kendrick B. Meek (D)
18. Ileana Ros-Lehtinen (R)
19. Robert Wexler (D)
20. Debbie Wasserman-Schultz (D)
21. Lincoln Diaz-Balart (R)
22. Ron Klein (D)
23. Alcee L. Hastings (D)
24. Tom Feeney (R)
25. Mario Diaz-Balart (R)

Georgia

1. Jack Kingston (R)
2. Sanford D. Bishop Jr. (D)
3. Lynn Westmoreland (R)
4. Hank Johnson (D)
5. John Lewis (D)
6. Tom Price (R)
7. John Linder (R)
8. Jim Marshall (R)
9. Nathan Deal (R)
10. Charlie Norwood (R)
    (died Feb. 13, 2007)
    Paul Broun (R)
    (sworn in July 25, 2007)
11. Phil Gingrey (R)
12. John Barrow (R)
13. David Scott (D)

Hawaii

1. Neil Abercrombie (D)
2. Mazie K. Hirono (D)

Idaho

1. Bill Sali (R)
2. Mike Simpson (R)

Illinois

1. Bobby L. Rush (D)
2. Jesse L. Jackson Jr. (D)
3. William O. Lipinski (D)
4. Luis V. Gutierrez (D)
5. Rahm Emanuel (D)
6. Peter Roskam (R)
7. Danny K. Davis (D)
8. Melissa Bean (D)
9. Jan Schakowsky (D)
10. Mark Steven Kirk (R)
11. Jerry Weller (R)
12. Jerry F. Costello (D)
13. Judy Biggert (R)
14. J. Dennis Hastert (R)
    (resigned Nov. 26, 2007)
    Bill Foster (D)
    (sworn in March 11, 2008)
15. Timothy V. Johnson (R)
16. Donald Manzullo (R)
17. Phil Hare (D)
18. Ray LaHood (R)
19. John Shimkus (R)

Indiana

1. Peter J. Visclosky (D)
2. Joe Donnelly (D)
3. Mark Souder (R)
4. Steve Buyer (R)
5. Dan Burton (R)
6. Mike Pence (R)
7. Julia Carson (D)
   (died Dec. 15, 2007)
   Andre Carson (R)
   (sworn in March 13, 2008)
8. Brad Ellsworth (D)
9. Baron P. Hill (D)

Iowa

1. Bruce Braley (D)
2. Dave Loebsack (D)
3. Leonard L. Boswell (D)
4. Tom Latham (R)
5. Steve King (R)

Kansas

1. Nancy Boyda (D)
2. Jerry Moran (R)
3. Dennis Moore (D)
4. Todd Tiahrt (R)

Kentucky

1. Edward Whitfield (R)
2. Ron Lewis (R)
3. John Yarmuth (D)
4. Geoff Davis (R)
5. Harold Rogers (R)
6. Ben Chandler (D)

Louisiana

1. Bobby Jindal (R)
   (resigned Jan. 14, 2008)
   Steve Scalise (R)
   (sworn in May 7, 2008)
2. William J. Jefferson (D)
3. Charlie Melancon (D)
4. Jim McCrery (R)
5. Rodney Alexander (D)
6. Richard H. Baker (R)
   (resigned Feb. 2, 2008)
   Don Cazayoux (D)
   (sworn in May 6, 2008)
7. Charles Boustany Jr. (R)

Maine

1. Tom Allen (D)
2. Michael H. Michaud (D)

Maryland

1. Wayne T. Gilchrest (R)
2. C.A. Dutch Ruppersberger (D)
3. John Sarbanes (D)

4. Albert R. Wynn (D)
   (resigned May 31, 2008)
   Donna Edwards (D)
   (sworn in June 19, 2008)
5. Steny H. Hoyer (D)
6. Roscoe G. Bartlett (R)
7. Elijah E. Cummings (D)
8. Chris Van Hollen (D)

Massachusetts

1. John W. Olver (D)
2. Richard E. Neal (D)
3. Jim McGovern (D)
4. Barney Frank (D)
5. Martin T. Meehan (D)
   (resigned July 1, 2007)
   Niki Tsongas (D)
   (sworn in Oct. 18, 2007)
6. John F. Tierney (D)
7. Edward J. Markey (D)
8. Michael E. Capuano (D)
9. Stephen L. Lynch (D)
10. William Delahunt (D)

Michigan

1. Bart Stupak (D)
2. Peter Hoekstra (R)
3. Vernon J. Ehlers (R)
4. Dave Camp (R)
5. Dale E. Kildee (D)
6. Fred Upton (R)
7. Tim Walberg (R)
8. Mike Rogers (R)
9. Joe Knollenberg (R)
10. Candice S. Miller (R)
11. Thaddeus McCotter (R)
12. Sander M. Levin (D)
13. Carolyn Cheeks Kilpatrick (D)
14. John Conyers Jr. (D)
15. John D. Dingell (D)

Minnesota

1. Tim Walz (D)
2. John Kline (R)
3. Jim Ramstad (R)
4. Betty McCollum (D)
5. Keith Ellison (D)
6. Michele Bachmann (R)
7. Collin C. Peterson (D)
8. James L. Oberstar (D)

Mississippi

1. Roger Wicker (R)
   (resigned Dec. 31, 2007)
   Travis W. Childers (D)
   (sworn in May 21, 2008)
2. Bennie Thompson (D)
3. Charles W. "Chip" Pickering Jr. (R)
4. Gene Taylor (D)

Missouri

1. William Lacy Clay (D)
2. Todd Akin (R)
3. Russ Carnahan (D)
4. Ike Skelton (D)
5. Emanuel Cleaver II (D)
6. Sam Graves (R)
7. Roy Blunt (R)
8. Jo Ann Emerson (R)
9. Kenny Hulshof (R)

Montana

AL Denny Rehberg (R)

Nebraska

1. Jeff Fortenberry (R)
2. Lee Terry (R)
3. Adrian Smith (R)

Nevada

1. Shelley Berkley (D)
2. Dean Heller (R)
3. Jon Porter (R)

New Hampshire

1. Carol Shea-Porter (D)
2. Paul W. Hodes (D)

New Jersey

1. Robert E. Andrews (D)
2. Frank A. LoBiondo (R)
3. H. James Saxton (R)
4. Christopher H. Smith (R)
5. Scott Garrett (R)
6. Frank Pallone Jr. (D)
7. Mike Ferguson (R)
8. Bill Pascrell Jr. (D)
9. Steven R. Rothman (D)
10. Donald M. Payne (D)
11. Rodney Frelinghuysen (R)
12. Rush D. Holt (D)
13. Albio Sires (D)

New Mexico

1. Heather A. Wilson (R)
2. Steve Pearce (R)
3. Tom Udall (D)

New York

1. Timothy H. Bishop (D)
2. Steve Israel (D)
3. Peter T. King (R)
4. Carolyn McCarthy (D)
5. Gary L. Ackerman (D)
6. Gregory W. Meeks (D)
7. Joseph Crowley (D)
8. Jerrold Nadler (D)
9. Anthony Weiner (D)
10. Edolphus Towns (D)
11. Yvette D. Clarke (D)
12. Nydia M. Velázquez (D)
13. Vito J. Fossella (R)
14. Carolyn B. Maloney (D)
15. Charles B. Rangel (D)
16. Jose E. Serrano (D)
17. Eliot L. Engel (D)
18. Nita M. Lowey (D)
19. John Hall
20. Kirsten Gillibrand (D)
21. Michael R. McNulty (D)
22. Maurice D. Hinchey (D)
23. John M. McHugh (R)
24. Michael Arcuri (D)
25. James T. Walsh (R)
26. Thomas M. Reynolds (R)
27. Brian Higgins (D)
28. Louise M. Slaughter (D)
29. John R. "Randy" Kuhl Jr. (R)

North Carolina

1. G.K. Butterfield (D)
2. Bob Etheridge (D)
3. Walter B. Jones (R)
4. David E. Price (D)
5. Virginia Foxx (R)
6. Howard Coble (R)
7. Mike McIntyre (D)
8. Robin Hayes (R)
9. Sue Myrick (R)
10. Patrick T. McHenry (R)
11. Heath Shuler (D)
12. Melvin Watt (D)
13. Brad Miller (D)

North Dakota

AL Earl Pomeroy (D)

Ohio

1. Steve Chabot (R)
2. Jean Schmidt (R)
3. Michael R. Turner (R)
4. Jim Jordan (R)
5. Paul E. Gillmor (R)
   (died Sept. 5, 2007)
   Bob Latta (R)
   (sworn in Dec. 13, 2007)
6. Charlie Wilson (D)
7. David L. Hobson (R)
8. John A. Boehner (R)
9. Marcy Kaptur (D)
10. Dennis J. Kucinich (D)
11. Stephanie Tubbs Jones (D)
    (died Aug. 20, 2008)
    Marcia Fudge (D)
    (sworn in Nov. 19, 2008)
12. Pat Tiberi (R)
13. Betty Sutton (D)
14. Steven C. LaTourette (R)
15. Deborah Pryce (R)
16. Ralph Regula (R)
17. Tim Ryan (D)
18. Zack Space (D)

Oklahoma

1. John Sullivan (R)
2. Dan Boren (D)
3. Frank D. Lucas (R)
4. Tom Cole (R)
5. Mary Fallin (R)

Oregon

1. David Wu (D)
2. Greg Walden (R)
3. Earl Blumenauer (D)
4. Peter A. DeFazio (D)
5. Darlene Hooley (D)

Pennsylvania

1. Robert A. Brady (D)
2. Chaka Fattah (D)
3. Phil English (R)
4. Jason Altmire (D)
5. John E. Peterson (R)
6. Jim Gerlach (R)
7. Joe Sestak (D)
8. Patrick J. Murphy (R)
9. Bill Shuster (R)
10. Christopher Carney (D)
11. Paul E. Kanjorski (D)
12. John P. Murtha (D)
13. Allyson Y. Schwartz (D)
14. Mike Doyle (D)
15. Charlie Dent (R)
16. Joe Pitts (R)
17. Tim Holden (D)
18. Tim Murphy (R)
19. Todd R. Platts (R)

Rhode Island

1. Patrick J. Kennedy (D)
2. Jim Langevin (D)

South Carolina

1. Henry E. Brown Jr. (R)
2. Joe Wilson (R)
3. J. Gresham Barrett (R)
4. Bob Inglis (R)
5. John M. Spratt Jr. (D)
6. James E. Clyburn (D)

South Dakota

AL Stephanie Herseth-Sandlin (D)

Tennessee

1. David Davis (R)
2. John J. "Jimmy" Duncan Jr. (R)
3. Zach Wamp (R)
4. Lincoln Davis (D)
5. Jim Cooper (D)
6. Bart Gordon (D)
7. Marsha Blackburn (R)
8. John Tanner (D)
9. Steve Cohen (D)

Texas

1. Louie Gohmert (R)
2. Ted Poe (R)
3. Sam Johnson (R)
4. Ralph M. Hall (R)
5. Jeb Hensarling (R)
6. Joe L. Barton (R)
7. John Culberson (R)
8. Kevin Brady (R)
9. Al Green (D)
10. Michael McCaul (R)
11. K. Michel Conway (R)
12. Kay Granger (R)
13. William M. "Mac" Thornberry (R)
14. Ron Paul (R)
15. Ruben Hinojosa (D)
16. Silvestre Reyes (D)
17. Chet Edwards (R)
18. Sheila Jackson-Lee (D)
19. Randy Neugebauer (R)
20. Charlie Gonzalez (D)
21. Lamar Smith (R)
22. Nick Lampson (D)
23. Ciro D. Rodriguez (D)
24. Kenny Marchant (R)
25. Lloyd Doggett (D)
26. Michael C. Burgess (R)
27. Solomon P. Ortiz (D)
28. Henry Cuellar (D)

29. Gene Green (D)
30. Eddie Bernice Johnson (D)
31. John Carter (R)
32. Pete Sessions (R)

Utah

1. Rob Bishop (R)
2. Jim Matheson (D)
3. Christopher B. Cannon (R)

Vermont

AL Peter Welch (D)

Virginia

1. Jo Ann Davis (R) *(died Oct. 6, 2007)*
   Rob Wittman (R) *(sworn in Dec. 13, 2007)*
2. Thelma Drake (R)
3. Robert C. Scott (D)
4. J. Randy Forbes (R)
5. Virgil H. Goode Jr. (R)
6. Robert W. Goodlatte (R)
7. Eric Cantor (R)
8. James P. Moran (D)
9. Rick C. Boucher (D)
10. Frank R. Wolf (R)
11. Thomas M. Davis III (R)

Washington

1. Jay Inslee (D)
2. Rick Larsen (D)
3. Brian Baird (D)
4. Richard "Doc" Hastings (R)
5. Cathy McMorris Rodgers (R)
6. Norm Dicks (D)
7. Jim McDermott (D)
8. Dave Reichert (R)
9. Adam Smith (D)

West Virginia

1. Alan B. Mollohan (D)
2. Shelley Moore Capito (R)
3. Nick J. Rahall II (D)

Wisconsin

1. Paul D. Ryan (R)
2. Tammy Baldwin (D)
3. Ron Kind (D)
4. Gwen Moore (D)
5. F. James Sensenbrenner Jr. (R)
6. Tom Petri (R)
7. David R. Obey (D)
8. Steve Kagen (D)

Wyoming

AL Barbara Cubin (R)

NOTES: Changes that occurred during 2007 and 2008 are noted following the names of individuals who did not serve their full terms. Members of the 110th Congress also included delegates Eni F. H. Faleomavaega, D-American Samoa; Eleanor Holmes Norton, D-District of Columbia; Madeleine Z. Bordallo, D-Guam; Donna M. C. Christian, D-Virgin Islands; and resident commissioner Luis Fortuno, R-Puerto Rico.

Members of Congress, 2005–2009

The names in this list include, alphabetically, all senators, representatives, resident commissioners, and territorial delegates who served in the 109th and 110th Congresses—from Jan. 3, 2005, to Jan. 3, 2009.

The material is organized as follows: name; relationship to other members and presidents and vice presidents (the political party and state of the relation are the same as the member unless noted otherwise); party, state (of service); date of birth; date of death (if applicable); congressional service; service as president, vice president, member of the cabinet or Supreme Court, governor, Speaker of the House, president pro tempore of the Senate, majority leader, minority leader, and chairman of the Democratic or Republican National Committee.

If the member changed parties during his or her congressional service, the party designation appearing after the member's name is that which applied at the end of such service and further information is included in the entry. Where the service date is left open, the member continued to serve in the 111th Congress (as of Jan. 4, 2009).

Dates of service are inclusive, starting in year of service and ending when service ends. Under the Constitution, terms of service since 1934 have been from Jan. 3 to Jan. 3. In actual practice, members have been sworn in on other dates at the beginning of a Congress. The exact date is shown (where available) if a member began or ended his or her service in midterm.

The major sources for the following list were *Congressional Quarterly's Biographical Directory of the American Congress 1774–1996*; *America Votes* series; the *CQ Almanac*; *American Political Leaders 1789–2005*; *CQ Weekly* magazine and online database.

In the list, D stands for Democrat; R, Republican; and I, Independent.

A

Abercrombie, Neil (D-Hawaii) June 26, 1938–; House Sept. 23, 1986–1987, 1991–.

Ackerman, Gary L. (D-N.Y.) Nov. 19, 1942–; House March 1, 1983–.

Aderholt, Robert (R-Ala.) July 22, 1965–; House 1997–.

Akaka, Daniel K. (D-Hawaii) Sept. 11, 1924–; House 1977–May 16, 1990; Senate May 16, 1990–.

Akin, Todd (R-Mo.) July 5, 1947–; House 2001–.

Alexander, Lamar (R-Tenn.) July 3, 1940–; Senate 2003–; Gov. 1979–1987.

Alexander, Rodney (R-La.) Dec. 5, 1946–; House 2003–(2003–Aug. 9, 2004 Democrat).

Allard, Wayne (R-Colo.) Dec. 2, 1943–; House 1991–1997; Senate 1997–2009.

Allen, George F. (R-Va.) March 18, 1952–; House 1991–1993; Senate 2001–2007; Gov. 1994–1998.

Allen, Thomas H. (D-Maine) April 18, 1945–; House 1997–2009.

Altmire, Jason (D-Pa.) March 7, 1968–; House 2007–.

Andrews, Robert E. (D-N.J.) Aug. 4, 1957–; House 1990–.

Arcuri, Michel (D-N.Y.) June 11, 1959–; House 2007–.

B

Baca, Joe (D-Calif.) Jan. 23, 1947–; House Nov. 16, 1999–.

Bachmann, Michele (R-Minn.) April 6, 1956–; House 2007–.

Bachus, Spencer (R-Ala.) Dec. 28, 1947–; House 1993–.

Baird, Brian (D-Wash.) March 7, 1956–; House 1999–.

Baker, Richard H. (R-La.) May 22, 1948–; House 1987–Feb. 2, 2008.

Baldwin, Tammy (D-Wis.) Feb. 11, 1962–; House 1999–.

Barrasso, John (R-Wyo.) July 21, 1952–; Senate June 25, 2007–.

Barrett, J. Gresham (R-S.C.) Feb. 14, 1961–; House 2003–.

Barrow, John (D-Ga.) Oct. 31 1955–; House 2005–.

Bartlett, Roscoe G. (R-Md.) June 3, 1926–; House 1993–.

Barton, Joe L. (R-Texas) Sept. 15, 1949–; House 1985–.

Bass, Charles (son of Perkins Bass) (R-N.H.) Jan. 8, 1952–; House 1995–2007.

Baucus, Max (D-Mont.) Dec. 11, 1941–; House 1975–Dec. 14, 1978; Senate Dec. 15, 1978–.

Bayh, Evan (son of Birch Bayh) (D-Ind.) Dec. 26, 1955–; Senate 1999–; Gov. 1989–1997.

Bean, Melissa (D-Ill.) Jan. 22, 1962–; House 2005–.

Beauprez, Bob (R-Colo.) Sept. 22, 1948–; House 2003–2007.

Becerra, Xavier (D-Calif.) Jan. 26, 1958–; House 1993–.

Bennett, Robert F. (R-Utah) (son of Wallace F. Bennett) Sept. 18, 1933–; Senate 1993–.

Berkley, Shelley (D-Nev.) Jan. 21, 1951–; House 1999–.

Berman, Howard L. (D-Calif.) April 15, 1941–; House 1983–.

Berry, Marion (D-Ark.) Aug. 27, 1942–; House 1997–.

Biden, Joseph R. Jr. (D-Del.) Nov. 20, 1942–; Senate 1973–.

Biggert, Judy (R-Ill.) Aug. 15, 1937–; House 1999–.

Bilbray, Brian P. (nephew of James Hubert Bilbray) (R-Calif.) Jan. 28, 1951–; House 1995–2001; June 13, 2006–.

Bilirakis, Gus (son of Michael Bilirakis) (R-Fla.) Feb. 8, 1963–; House 2007–.

Bilirakis, Michael (father of Gus Bilirakis) (R-Fla.) July 16, 1930–; House 1983–2007.

Bingaman, Jeff (D-N.M.) Oct. 3, 1943–; Senate 1983–.

Bishop, Rob (R-Utah) July 13, 1951–; House 2003–.

Bishop, Sanford D. Jr. (D-Ga.) Feb. 4, 1947–; House 1993–.

Bishop, Timothy H. (D-N.Y.) June 1, 1950–; House 2003–.

Blackburn, Marsha (R-Tenn.) June 6, 1952–; House 2003–.

Blumenauer, Earl (D-Ore.) Aug. 16, 1949–; House May 30, 1996–.

Blunt, Roy (R-Mo.) Jan. 10, 1950–; House 1997–.

Boehlert, Sherwood (R-N.Y.) Sept. 28, 1936–; House 1983–2007.

Boehner, John A. (R-Ohio) Nov. 17, 1949–; House 1991–; House majority leader 2006–2007; minority leader 2007–.

Bond, Christopher S. (R-Mo.) March 6, 1939–; Senate 1987–.

Bonilla, Henry (R-Texas) Jan. 2, 1954–; House 1993–2007.

Bonner, Jo (R-Ala.) Nov. 19, 1959–; House 2003–.

Bono-Mack, Mary (R-Calif.) (widow of Sonny Bono) Oct. 24, 1961; House April 21, 1998–.

Boozman, John (R-Ark.) Dec. 10, 1950–; House Nov. 29, 2001–.

Bordallo, Madeleine Z. (D-Guam) May 31, 1933–; House (Delegate) 2003–.

Boren, Dan (D-Okla.) (son of David L. Boren) Aug. 2, 1973–; House 2005–.

Boswell, Leonard L. (D-Iowa) Jan. 10, 1934–; House 1997–.

Boucher, Rick (D-Va.) Aug. 1, 1946–; House 1983–.

Boustany, Charles Jr. (R-La.) Feb. 21, 1956–; House 2005–.

Boxer, Barbara (D-Calif.) Nov. 11, 1940–; House 1983–1993; Senate 1993–.

Boyd, Allen (D-Fla.) June 6, 1945–; House 1997–.

Boyda, Nancy (D-Kan.) Aug. 2, 1955–; House 2007–2009.

Bradley, Jeb (R-N.H.) Oct. 20, 1952–; House 2003–2007.

Brady, Kevin (R-Texas) April 11, 1955–; House 1997–.

Brady, Robert A. (D-Pa.) April 7, 1945–; House May 28, 1998–.

Braley, Bruce (D-Iowa) Oct. 30, 1957–; House 2007–.

Broun, Paul (D-Ga.) May 14, 1946–; House July 25, 2007–.

Brown, Corrine (D-Fla.) Nov. 11, 1946–; House 1993–.

Brown, Henry E. Jr. (R-S.C.) Dec. 20, 1935–; House 2001–.

Brown, Sherrod (D-Ohio) Nov. 9, 1952–; House 1993–2007; Senate 2007–.

Brownback, Sam (R-Kan.) Sept. 12, 1956–; House 1995–Nov. 6, 1996; Senate Nov. 27, 1996–.

Brown-Waite, Ginny (R-Fla.) Oct. 5, 1943–; House 2003–.

Buchanan, Vern (R-Fla.) May 8, 1951–; House 2007–.

Bunning, Jim (R-Ky.) Oct. 23, 1931–; House 1987–1999; Senate 1999–.

Burgess, Michael (R-Texas) Dec. 23, 1950–; House 2003–.

Burns, Conrad (R-Mont.) Jan. 25, 1935–; Senate 1989–2007.

Burr, Richard M. (R-N.C.) Nov. 30, 1955–; House 1995–2005; Senate 2005–.

Burton, Dan (R-Ind.) June 21, 1938–; House 1983–.

Butterfield, G.K. (D-N.C.) April 27, 1947–; House July 21, 2004–.

Buyer, Steve (R-Ind.) Nov. 26, 1958–; House 1993–; Gov. 1971–1975.

Byrd, Robert C. (D-W.Va.) Nov. 20, 1917–; House 1953–1959; Senate 1959–; Senate minority leader, 1981–1987; Senate majority leader 1977–1981, 1987–1989; pres. pro tempore 1989–1995, June 6, 2001–2003, 2007–.

C

Calvert, Ken (R-Calif.) June 8, 1953–; House 1993–.

Camp, Dave (R-Mich.) July 9, 1953–; House 1991–.

Campbell, John (R-Calif.) July 19, 1955–; House Dec. 7, 2005–.

Cannon, Christopher B. (R-Utah) Oct. 20, 1950–; House 1997–.

Cantor, Eric I. (R-Va.) June 6, 1963–; House 2001–.

Cantwell, Maria (D-Wash.) Oct. 13, 1958–; House 1993–1994; Senate 2001–.

Capito, Shelley Moore (R-W.Va.) (daughter of Arch A. Moore Jr.) Nov. 26, 1953–; Houses 2001–.

Capps, Lois D. (D-Calif.) (widow of Rep. Walter Capps) Jan. 10, 1938–; House March 17, 1998–.

Capuano, Michael D. (D-Mass.) Jan. 9, 1952–; House 1999–.

Cardin, Benjamin L. (D-Md.) Oct. 5, 1943–; House 1987–2007; Senate 2007–.

Cardoza, Dennis (D-Calif.) March 31, 1959–; House 2003–.

Carnahan, Russ (D-Mo.) (son of Jean Carnahan; grandson of A. S. J. Carnahan) July 10, 1958–; House 2005–.

Carney, Christopher (D-Pa.) March 2, 1959–; House 2007–.

Carper, Thomas R. (D-Del.) Jan. 23, 1947–; House 1983–1993; Senate 2001–; Gov. 1993–2001.

Carson, Andre (D-Ind.) (grandson of Julia M. Carson) Oct. 16, 1974–; House March 13, 2008–.

Carson, Julia M. (D-Ind.) (grandmother of Andre Carson) July 8, 1938–Dec. 15, 2007; House 1997–Dec. 15, 2007.

Carter, John (R-Texas) Nov. 6, 1941–; House 2003–.

Case, Ed (D-Hawaii) Sept. 27, 1952–; House Nov. 30, 2002–2007.

Casey, Bob (D-Pa.) April 13, 1960–; Senate 2007–.

Castle, Michael N. (R-Del.) July 2, 1939–; House 1993–.

Castor, Kathy (D-Fla.) Aug. 20, 1966–; House 2007–.

Cazayoux, Don (D-La.) June 17, 1964–; House May 6, 2008–.

Chabot, Steve (R-Ohio) Jan. 22, 1953–; House 1995–.

Chafee, Lincoln (R-R.I.) (son of John H. Chafee) March 26, 1953–; Senate Nov. 4, 1999–2007.

Chambliss, Saxby (R-Ga.) Nov. 10, 1943–; House 1995–2003; Senate 2003–.

Chandler, Ben (D-Ky.) Sept. 12, 1959–; House Feb. 24, 2004–.

Childers, Travis W. (D-Miss.) March 29, 1958–; House May 21, 2008–.

Chocola, Chris (R-Ind.) Feb. 24, 1962–; House 2003–2007.

Christensen, Donna M.C. (D-Virgin Is.) Sept. 19, 1945–; House (Delegate) 1997–.

Clark, Yvette D. (D-N.Y.) Nov. 21, 1964–; House 2007–.

Clay, William Lacy Jr. (son of William L. Clay) (D-Mo.) July 27, 1956–; House 2001–.

Cleaver, Emanuel, II (D-Mo.) Oct. 26, 1944–; House 2005–.

Clinton, Hillary Rodham (D-N.Y.) (wife of President Bill Clinton) Oct. 26, 1947–; first lady 1993–2001; Senate 2001–2009.

Clyburn, James E. (D-S.C.) July 21, 1940–; House 1993–.

Coble, Howard (R-N.C.) March 18, 1931–; House 1985–.

Cochran, Thad (R-Miss.) Dec. 7, 1937–; House 1973–Dec. 26, 1978; Senate Dec. 27, 1978–.

Cohen, Steve (D-Tenn.) May 24, 1959–; House 2007–.

Cole, Tom (R-Okla.) April 28, 1949–; House 2003–.

Coleman, Norm (R-Minn.) Aug. 17, 1949–; Senate 2003–2009.

Collins, Susan (R-Maine) Dec. 7, 1952–; Senate 1997–.

Conrad, Kent (D-N.D.) March 12, 1948–; Senate 1987–Dec. 14, 1992, Dec. 14, 1992–.

Conway, K. Michael (R-Texas) June 11, 1948–; House 2005–.

Conyers, John Jr. (D-Mich.) May 16, 1929–; House 1965–.

Cooper, Jim (D-Tenn.) June 19, 1954–; House 1983–1995; 2003–.

Corker, Bob (R-Tenn.) Aug. 24, 1952–; Senate 2007–.

Cornyn, John (R-Texas) Feb. 2, 1952–; Senate Dec. 2, 2002–.

Corzine, Jon (D-N.J.) Jan. 1, 1947–; Senate 2001–Jan. 17, 2006; Gov. 2006–.

Costa, Jim (D-Calif.) April 13, 1952–; House 2005–.

Costello, Jerry F. (D-Ill.) Sept. 25, 1949–; House Aug. 11, 1988–.

Courtney, Joe (D-Conn.) April 6, 1953–; House 2007–.

Cox, Christopher (R-Calif.) Oct. 16, 1952–; House 1989–August 2, 2005.

Craig, Larry E. (R-Idaho) July 20, 1945–; House 1981–1991; Senate 1991–2009.

Cramer, Robert E. "Bud" (D-Ala.) Aug. 22, 1947–; House 1991–.

Crapo, Michael D. (R-Idaho) May 20, 1951–; House 1993–1999; Senate 1999–.

Crenshaw, Ander (R-Fla.) Sept. 1, 1944–; House 2001–.

Crowley, Joseph (D-N.Y.) March 16, 1962–; House 1999–.

Cubin, Barbara (R-Wyo.) Nov. 30, 1946–; House 1995–2009.

Cuellar, Henry (D-Texas) Sept. 19, 1955–; House 2005–.

Culberson, John (R-Texas) Aug. 24, 1956–; House 2001–.

Cummings, Elijah E. (D-Md.) Jan. 18, 1951–; House April 25, 1996–.

Cunningham, Randy "Duke" (R-Calif.) Dec. 8, 1941–; House 1991–Dec. 1, 2005.

D

Davis, Artur (D-Ala.) Oct, 9, 1957–; House 2003–.

Davis, Danny K. (D-Ill.) Sept. 6, 1941–; House 1997–.

Davis, David (R-Tenn.) Nov. 6, 1959–; House 2007–.

Davis, Geoff (R-Ky.) Oct. 26, 1958–; House 2005–.

Davis, Jim (D-Fla.) Oct. 11, 1957–; House 1997–2007.

Davis, Jo Ann (R-Va.) June 29, 1950–Oct. 6, 2007; House 2001–Oct. 6, 2007.

Davis, Lincoln (D-Tenn.) Sept. 13, 1943–; House 2003–.

Davis, Susan A. (D-Calif.) April 13, 1944–; House 2001–.

Davis, Thomas M. III (R-Va.) Jan. 5, 1949–; House 1995–2009.

Dayton, Mark (D-Minn.) Jan. 26, 1947–; Senate 2001–2007.

Deal, Nathan (R-Ga.) Aug. 25, 1942–; House 1993–(1993–April 10, 1995, Democrat).

DeFazio, Peter A. (D-Ore.) May 27, 1947–; House 1987–.

DeGette, Diana (D-Colo.) July 29, 1957–; House 1997–.

Delahunt, William (D-Mass.) July 18, 1941–; House 1997–.

DeLauro, Rosa (D-Conn.) March 2, 1943–; House 1991–.

DeLay, Tom (R-Texas) April 8, 1947–; House 1985–June 9, 2006.

DeMint, Jim (R-S.C.) Sept. 2, 1951–; House 1999–2005; Senate 2005–.

Dent, Charlie (R-Pa.) May 24, 1960–; House 2005–.

DeWine, Mike (R-Ohio) Jan. 5, 1947–; House 1983–1991; Senate 1995–2007.

Diaz-Balart, Lincoln (brother of Mario Diaz-Balart) (R-Fla.) Aug. 13, 1954–; House 1993–.

Diaz-Balart, Mario (brother of Lincoln Diaz-Balart) (R-Fla.) Sept. 25, 1961–; House 2003–.

Dicks, Norm (D-Wash.) Dec. 16, 1940–; House 1977–.

Dingell, John D. (son of John David Dingell Sr.) (D-Mich.) July 8, 1926–; House Dec. 13, 1955–.

Dodd, Christopher J. (son of Thomas Joseph Dodd) (D-Conn.) May 27, 1944–; House 1975–1981; Senate 1981–.

Doggett, Lloyd (D-Texas) Oct. 6, 1946–; House 1995–.

Dole, Elizabeth (wife of Robert "Bob" J. Dole, R-Kan.) (R-N.C.) July 29, 1936–; Senate 2003–.

Domenici, Pete V. (R-N.M.) May 7, 1932–; Senate 1973–2009.

Donnelly, Joe (D-Ind.) Sept. 29, 1959–; House 2007–.

Doolittle, John T. (R-Calif.) Oct. 30, 1950–; House 1991–2009.

Dorgan, Byron L. (D-N.D.) May 14, 1942–; House 1981–Dec. 14, 1992; Senate Dec. 15, 1992–.

Doyle, Mike (D-Pa.) Aug. 5, 1953–; House 1995–.

Drake, Thelma (R-Va.) Nov. 20, 1949–; House 2005–.

Dreier, David (R-Calif.) July 5, 1952–; House 1981–.

Duncan, John J. "Jimmy" Jr. (son of John J. Duncan) (R-Tenn.) July 21, 1947–; House 1988–.

Durbin, Richard J. (D-Ill.) Nov. 21, 1944–; House 1983–1997; Senate 1997–.

E

Edwards, Chet (D-Texas) Nov. 24, 1951–; House 1991–.

Edwards, Donna F. (D-Md.) June 28, 1958; House June 17, 2008

Ehlers, Vernon J. (R-Mich.) Feb. 6, 1934–; House Jan. 25, 1994–.

Ellison, Keith (D-Minn.) Feb. 6, 1984–; House 2007–.

Ellsworth, Brad (D-Ind.) Sept. 11, 1958–; House 2007–.

Emanuel, Rahm (D-Ill.) Nov. 29, 1959–; House 2003–.

Emerson, Jo Ann (R-Mo.) (widow of Bill Emerson) Sept. 16, 1950–; House Nov. 5, 1996–. (Elected as an Independent in a 1996 special election following the death of her husband because the filing date had passed but ran as a Republican in the general election and thereafter.)

Engel, Eliot L. (D-N.Y.) Feb. 18, 1947–; House 1989–.

English, Phil (R-Pa.) June 20, 1956–; House 1995–.

Ensign, John (R-Nev.) March 25, 1958–; House 1995–1999; Senate 2001–.

Enzi, Michael B. (R-Wyo.) Feb. 1, 1944–; Senate 1997–.

Eshoo, Anna G. (D-Calif.) Dec. 13, 1942–; House 1993–.

Etheridge, Bob (D-N.C.) Aug. 7, 1941–; House 1997–.

Evans, Lane (D-Ill.) Aug. 4, 1951–; House 1983–2007.

Everett, Terry (R-Ala.) Feb. 15, 1937–; House 1993–2009.

F

Faleomavaega, Eni F. H. (D-Am. Samoa) Aug. 15, 1943–; House (Delegate) 1989–.

Fallin, Mary (R-Okla.) Dec. 9, 1954–; House 2007–.

Farr, Sam (D-Calif.) July 4, 1941–; House June 16, 1993–.

Fattah, Chaka (D-Pa.) Nov. 21, 1956–; House 1995–.

Feeney, Tom (R-Fla.) May 21, 1958–; House 2003–.

Feingold, Russell D. (D-Wis.) March 2, 1953–; Senate 1993–.

Feinstein, Dianne (D-Calif.) June 22, 1933–; Senate Nov. 10, 1992–.

Ferguson, Mike (R-N.J.) July 22, 1970–; House 2001–2009.

Filner, Bob (D-Calif.) Sept. 4, 1942–; House 1993–.

Fitzpatrick, Michel G. (R-Pa.) June 28, 1963–; House 2005–2007.

Flake, Jeff (R-Ariz.) Dec. 31, 1962–; House 2001–.

Foley, Mark (R-Fla.) Sept. 8, 1954–; House 1995–Sept. 29, 2006.

Forbes, J. Randy (R-Va.) Feb. 17, 1952–; House June 26, 2001–.

Ford, Harold E. Jr. (son of Harold E. Ford) (D-Tenn.) May 11, 1970–; House 1997–2007.

Forenberry, Jeff (R-Neb.) Dec. 27, 1960–; House 2005–.

Fortuno, Luis (R-P.R.) Oct. 31, 1960–; House (Resident Commissioner) 2005–.

Fossella, Vito J. (R-N.Y.) March 9, 1965–; House Nov. 5, 1997–.

Foster, Bill (D-Ill.) March 7, 1955–; House March 11, 2008–.

Foxx, Virginia (R-N.C.) June 29, 1943–; House 2005–.

Frank, Barney (D-Mass.) March 31, 1940–; House 1981–.

Franks, Trent (R-Ariz.) June 19, 1957–; House 2003–.

Frelinghuysen, Rodney (son of Peter Hood Ballentine Frelinghuysen) (R-N.J.) April 29, 1946–; House 1995–.

Frist, Bill (R-Tenn.) Feb. 22, 1952–; Senate 1995–2007; Senate majority leader 2003–2007.

Fudge, Marcia L. (D-Ohio) Oct. 29, 1952; House 2008–.

G

Gallegly, Elton (R-Calif.) March 7, 1944–; House 1987–.

Garrett, Scott (R-N.J.) July 9, 1959–; House 2003–.

Gerlach, Jim (R-Pa.) Feb. 25, 1955–; House 2003–.

Gibbons, Jim (R-Nev.) Dec. 16, 1944–; House 1997–2007. Gov. 2007–.

Giffords, Gabrielle (D-Ariz.) June 8, 1970–; House 2007–.

Gilchrest, Wayne T. (R-Md.) April 15, 1946–; House 1991–.

Gillibrand, Kirsten (D-N.Y.) Dec. 9, 1966–; House 2007–.

Gillmor, Paul E. (R-Ohio) Feb. 1, 1939–Sept. 5, 2007; House 1989–Sept. 5, 2007.

Gingrey, Phil (R-Ga.) July 10, 1942–; House 2003–.

Gohmert, Louie (R-Texas) Aug. 18, 1953–; House 2005–.

Gonzalez, Charlie (son of Henry B. Gonzalez) (D-Texas) May 5, 1945–; House 1999–.

Goode, Virgil H. Jr. (R-Va.) (elected 1997 as a Democrat; announced in January 2000 he would seek reelection as an Independent; changed affiliation from Independent to Republican on Aug. 1, 2002) Oct. 17, 1946–; House 1997–.

Goodlatte, Robert W. (R-Va.) Sept. 22, 1952–; House 1993–.

Gordon, Bart (D-Tenn.) Jan. 24, 1949–; House 1985–.

Graham, Bob (D-Fla.) Nov. 9, 1936–; Senate 1987–2005.

Graham, Lindsey (R-S.C.) July 9, 1955–; House 1995–2003; Senate 2003–.

Granger, Kay (R-Texas) Jan. 18, 1943–; House 1997–.

Grassley, Charles E. (R-Iowa) Sept. 17, 1933–; House 1975–1981; Senate 1981–.

Graves, Sam (R-Mo.) Nov. 7, 1963–; House 2001–.

Green, Al (D-Texas) Sept. 1, 1947–; House 2005–.

Green, Gene (D-Texas) Oct. 17, 1947–; House 1993–.

Green, Mark (R-Wis.) June 1, 1960–; House 1999–2007.

Gregg, Judd (R-N.H.) Feb. 14, 1947–; Senate 1993–.

Grijalva, Raül M. (D-Ariz.) Feb. 19, 1948–; House 2003–.

Gutierrez, Luis V. (D-Ill.) Dec. 10, 1954–; House 1993–.

Gutknecht, Gil (R-Minn.) March 20, 1951–; House 1995–2007.

H

Hagel, Chuck (R-Neb.) Oct. 4, 1946–; Senate 1997–2009.

Hall, John (D-N.Y.) July 23, 1938–; House 2007–.

Hall, Ralph M. (R-Texas) May 3, 1923–; House 1981–(1981–Jan. 5, 2004 Democrat).

Hare, Phil (D-Ill.) Feb. 21, 1949–; House 2007–.

Harkin, Tom (D-Iowa) Nov. 19, 1939–; House 1975–1985; Senate 1985–.

Harman, Jane (D-Calif.) June 28, 1945–; House 1993–1999; 2001–.

Harris, Katherine (R-Fla.) April 5, 1957–; House 2003–2007.

Hart, Melissa (R-Pa.) April 4, 1962–; House 2001–2007.

Hastert, J. Dennis (R-Ill.) Jan. 2, 1942–; House 1987–Nov. 26, 2007. Speaker 1999–2007.

Hastings, Alcee L. (D-Fla.) Sept. 5, 1936–; House 1993–.

Hastings, Richard "Doc" (R-Wash.) Feb. 7, 1941–; House 1995–.

Hatch, Orrin G. (R-Utah) March 22, 1934–; Senate 1977–.

Hayes, Robin (R-N.C.) Aug. 14, 1945–; House 1999–.

Hayworth, J.D. (R-Ariz.) July 12, 1958–; House 1995–2007.

Hefley, Joel (R-Colo.) April 18, 1935–; House 1987–2007.

Heller, Dean (R-Nev.) May 10, 1960–; House 2007–.

Hensarling, Jeb (R-Texas) May 29, 1957–; House 2003–.

Herger, Wally (R-Calif.) May 20, 1945–; House 1987–.

Herseth, Stephanie (D-S.D.) Dec. 3, 1970–; House June 3, 2004–.

Hill, Baron P. (D-Ind.) June 23, 1953–; House 2007–.

Hinchey, Maurice D. (D-N.Y.) Oct. 27, 1938–; House 1993–.

Hinojosa, Ruben (D-Texas) Aug. 20, 1940–; House 1997–.

Hirono, Mazie K. (D-Hawaii) Nov. 3, 1947–; House 2007–.

Hobson, David L. (R-Ohio) Oct. 17, 1936–; House 1991–2009.

Hodes, Paul W. (D-N.H.) March 21, 1951–; House 2007–.

Hoekstra, Peter (R-Mich.) Oct. 30, 1953–; House 1993–.

Holden, Tim (D-Pa.) March 5, 1957–; House 1993–.

Holt, Rush D. (son of Rush Dew Holt, W.Va.) (D-N.J.) Oct. 15, 1948–; House 1999–.

Honda, Mike (D-Calif.) June 27, 1941–; House 2001–.

Hooley, Darlene (D-Ore.) April 4, 1939–; House 1997–2009.

Hostettler, John (R-Ind.) July 19, 1961–; House 1995–2007.

Hoyer, Steny H. (D-Md.) June 14, 1939–; House June 3, 1981–. House majority leader 2007–.

Hulshof, Kenny (R-Mo.) May 22, 1958–; House 1997–2009.

Hunter, Duncan L. (R-Calif.) May 31, 1948–; House 1981–2009.

Hutchison, Kay Bailey (R-Texas) July 22, 1943–; Senate June 14, 1993–.

Hyde, Henry J. (R-Ill.) April 18, 1924–Nov. 29, 2007; House 1975–2007.

I

Inglis, Bob (R-S.C.) Oct. 11, 1959–; House 1993–1999; 2005–.

Inhofe, James M. (R-Okla.) Nov. 17, 1934–; House 1987–Nov. 15, 1994; Senate Nov. 17, 1994–.

Inouye, Daniel K. (D-Hawaii) Sept. 7, 1924–; House Aug. 21, 1959–1963; Senate 1963–.

Inslee, Jay (D-Wash.) Feb. 9, 1951–; House 1993–1995; 1999–.

Isakson, Johnny (R-Ga.) Dec. 28, 1944–; House Feb. 25, 1999–2005; Senate 2005–.

Israel, Steven (D-N.Y.) May 30, 1958–; House 2001–.

Issa, Darrell (R-Calif.) Nov. 1, 1953–; House 2001–.

Istook, Ernest (R-Okla.) Feb. 11, 1950–; House 1993–2007.

J

Jackson, Jesse Jr. (D-Ill.) March 11, 1965–; House Dec. 14, 1995–.

Jackson-Lee, Sheila (D-Texas) Jan. 12, 1950–; House 1995–.

Jefferson, William J. (D-La.) March 14, 1947–; House 1991–.

Jeffords, James M. (I-Vt.) May 11, 1934–; House 1975–1989 (Republican); Senate 1989–2007 (1989–June 5, 2001 Republican; June 5, 2001–2007 Independent).

Jenkins, William L. (R-Tenn.) Nov. 29, 1936–; House 1997–2007.

Jindal, Bobby (R-La.) June 10, 1971–; House 2005–Jan. 14, 2008. Gov. 2008–.

Johnson, Eddie Bernice (D-Texas) Dec. 3, 1935–; House 1993–.

Johnson, Hank (D-Ga.) Oct. 2, 1954–; House 2007–.

Johnson, Nancy L. (R-Conn.) Jan. 5, 1935–; House 1983–2007.

Johnson, Sam (R-Texas) Oct. 11, 1930–; House May 22, 1991–.

Johnson, Tim (D-S.D.) Dec. 28, 1946–; House 1987–1997; Senate 1997–.

Johnson, Timothy V. (R-Ill.) July 23, 1946–; House 2001–.

Jones, Walter B. Jr. (son of Walter B. Jones Sr.) (R-N.C.) Feb. 10, 1943–; House 1995–.

Jordan, Jim (R-Ohio) Feb. 17, 1964–; House 2007–.

K

Kagen, Steve (D-Wis.) Dec. 12, 1949–; House 2007–.

Kanjorski, Paul E. (D-Pa.) April 2, 1937–; House 1985–.

Kaptur, Marcy (D-Ohio) June 17, 1946–; House 1983–.

Keller, Richard "Ric" (R-Fla.) Sept. 5, 1964–; House 2001–.

Kelly, Sue W. (R-N.Y.) Sept. 26, 1936–; House 1995–2007.

Kennedy, Edward M. (father of Patrick J. Kennedy, D-R.I.; brother of John Fitzgerald Kennedy, D-Mass., and Robert Francis Kennedy, D-N.Y.; grandson of John Francis Fitzgerald, D-Mass.; uncle of Joseph P. Kennedy II, D-Mass.) Feb. 22, 1932–Aug. 25, 2009; Senate Nov. 7, 1962–Aug. 25, 2009.

Kennedy, Mark (R-Minn.) April 11, 1957–; House 2001–2007.

Kennedy, Patrick J. (son of Edward M. Kennedy, D-Mass.; nephew of John Fitzgerald Kennedy, D-Mass., and Robert Francis Kennedy, D-N.Y.; cousin of Joseph P. Kennedy, D-Mass.; great grandson of John Francis Fitzgerald, D-Mass.) (D-R.I.) July 14, 1967–; House 1995–.

Kerry, John (D-Mass.) Dec. 11, 1943–; Senate 1985–.

Kildee, Dale E. (D-Mich.) Sept. 16, 1929–; House 1977–.

Kilpatrick, Carolyn Cheeks (D-Mich.) June 25, 1945–; House 1997–.

Kind, Ron (D-Wis.) March 16, 1963–; House 1997–.

King, Peter T. (R-N.Y.) April 5, 1944–; House 1993–.

King, Steve (R-Iowa) May 28, 1949–; House 2003–.

Kingston, Jack (R-Ga.) April 24, 1955–; House 1993–.

Kirk, Mark Steven (R-Ill.) Sept. 15, 1959–; House 2001–.

Klein, Ron (D-Fla.) July 10, 1957–; House 2007–.

Kline, John (R-Minn.) Sept. 6, 1947–; House 2003–.

Klobuchar, Amy (D-Minn.) May 25, 1960–; Senate 2007–.

Knollenberg, Joe (R-Mich.) Nov. 28, 1933–; House 1993–.

Kohl, Herb (D-Wis.) Feb. 7, 1935–; Senate 1989–.

Kolbe, Jim (R-Ariz.) June 28, 1942–; House 1985–2007.

Kucinich, Dennis J. (D-Ohio) Oct. 8, 1946–; House 1997–.

Kyl, Jon (son of John Henry Kyl, R-Iowa) (R-Ariz.) April 25, 1942–; House 1987–1995; Senate 1995–.

L

LaHood, Ray (R-Ill.) Dec. 6, 1945–; House 1995–2009.

Lamborn, Doug (R-Colo.) May 24, 1954–; House 2007–.

Lampson, Nick (D-Texas) Feb. 14, 1945–; House 1997–2005; 2007–.

Landrieu, Mary L. (D-La.) Nov. 23, 1955–; Senate 1997–.

Langevin, Jim (D-R.I.) April 22, 1964–; House 2001–.

Lantos, Tom (father-in-law of Dick Swett) (D-Calif.) Feb. 1, 1928–Feb. 11, 2008; House 1981–Feb. 11, 2008.

Larsen, Rick (D-Wash.) June 15, 1965–; House 2001–.

Larson, John B. (D-Conn.) July 22, 1948–; House 1999–.

Latham, Tom (R-Iowa) July 14, 1948–; House 1995–.

LaTourette, Steven C. (R-Ohio) July 22, 1954–; House 1995–.

Latta, Bob (son of Delbert L. Latta) (R-Ohio) April 18, 1956–; House Dec. 13, 2007–.

Lautenberg, Frank R. (D-N.J.) Jan. 23, 1924–; Senate Dec. 27, 1982–2001; 2003–.

Leach, Jim (R-Iowa) Oct. 15, 1942–; House 1977–2007.

Leahy, Patrick J. (D-Vt.) March 31, 1940–; Senate 1975–.

Lee, Barbara (D-Calif.) July 16, 1946–; House April 21, 1998–.

Levin, Carl (brother of Sander M. Levin) (D-Mich.) June 28, 1934–; Senate 1979–.

Levin, Sander M. (brother of Carl Levin) (D-Mich.) Sept. 6, 1931–; House 1983–.

Lewis, Jerry (R-Calif.) Oct. 21, 1934–; House 1979–.

Lewis, John (D-Ga.) Feb. 21, 1940–; House 1987–.

Lewis, Ron (R-Ky.) Sept. 14, 1946–; House May 26, 1994–2007.

Lieberman, Joseph I. (I-Conn.) Feb. 24, 1942–; Senate 1989–. (Democrat 1989–2006.)

Lincoln, Blanche Lambert (D-Ark.) Sept. 30, 1960–; House 1993–1997; Senate 1999–.

Linder, John (R-Ga.) Sept. 9, 1942–; House 1993–.

Lipinski, Dan (son of William O. Lipinski) (D-Ill.) July 15, 1966–; House 2005–.

LoBiondo, Frank A. (R-N.J.) May 12, 1946–; House 1995–.

Loebsack, Dave (D-Iowa) Dec. 23, 1952–; House 2007–.

Lofgren, Zoe (D-Calif.) Dec. 21, 1947–; House 1995–.

Lott, Trent (R-Miss.) Oct. 9, 1941–; House 1973–1989; Senate 1989–Dec. 18, 2007. Senate majority leader June 12, 1996–June 6, 2001; minority leader June 6, 2001–2003.

Lowey, Nita M. (D-N.Y.) July 5, 1937–; House 1989–.

Lucas, Frank D. (R-Okla.) Jan. 6, 1960–; House May 17, 1994–.

Lucas, Ken (D-Ky.) Aug. 22, 1933–; House 1999–2005.

Lugar, Richard G. (R-Ind.) April 4, 1932–; Senate 1977–.

Lungren, Dan (R-Calif.) Sept. 22, 1946–; House 1979–1989; 2005–.

Lynch, Stephen F. (D-Mass.) March 31, 1955–; House Oct. 23, 2001–.

M

Mack, Connie, IV (son of Connie Mack; husband of Mary Bono) (R-Fla.) Aug. 12, 1967–; House 2005–.

Mahoney, Tim (D-Fla.) Aug. 15, 1956–; House 2007–.

Maloney, Carolyn B. (D-N.Y.) Feb. 19, 1948–; House 1993–.

Manzullo, Donald (R-Ill.) March 24, 1944–; House 1993–.

Marchant, Kenny (R-Calif.) Feb. 23. 1951–; House 2005–.

Markey, Edward J. (D-Mass.) July 11, 1946–; House Nov. 2, 1976–.

Marshall, Jim (R-Ga.) March 31, 1948–; House 2003–.

Matheson, Jim (D-Utah) March 21, 1960–; House 2001–.

Matsui, Doris (widow of Robert T. Matsui) (D-Calif.) Sept. 25, 1944–; House March 10, 2005–.

McCain, John (R-Ariz.) Aug. 29, 1936–; House 1983–1987; Senate 1987–.

McCarthy, Carolyn (D-N.Y.) Jan. 5, 1944–; House 1997–.

McCarthy, Kevin (R-Calif.) Jan. 26, 1965–; House 2007–.

McCaskill, Claire (D-Mo.) July 24, 1953–; Senate 2007–.

McCaul, Michael (R-Texas) Jan. 14, 1962–; House 2005–.

McCollum, Betty (D-Minn.) July 12, 1954–; House 2001–.

McConnell, Mitch (R-Ky.) Feb. 20, 1942–; Senate 1985–.

McCotter, Thaddeus (R-Mich.) Aug. 22, 1965–; House 2003–.

McCrery, Jim (R-La.) Sept. 18, 1949–; House 1988–2009.

McDermott, Jim (D-Wash.) Dec. 28, 1936–; House 1989–.

McGovern, James (D-Mass.) Nov. 20, 1959–; House 1997–.

McHenry, Patrick T. (R-N.C.) Oct. 22, 1975–; House 2005–.

McHugh, John M. (R-N.Y.) Sept. 29, 1948–; House 1993–.

McIntyre, Mike (D-N.C.) Aug. 6, 1956–; House 1997–.

McKeon, Howard P. "Buck" (R-Calif.) Sept. 9, 1939–; House 1993–.

McKinney, Cynthia A. (D-Ga.) March 17, 1955–; House 1993–2003, 2005–2007.

McMorris, Cathy (R-Wash.) May 22, 1969–; House 2005–.

McNerney, Jerry (D-Calif.) June 18, 1951–; House 2007–.

McNulty, Michael R. (D-N.Y.) Sept. 16, 1947–; House 1989–2009.

Meehan, Martin T. (D-Mass.) Dec. 30, 1956–; House 1993–July 1, 2007.

Meek, Kendrick (son of Carrie P. Meek) (D-Fla.) Sept. 6, 1966–; House 2003–.

Meeks, Gregory W. (D-N.Y.) Sept. 25, 1953–; House Feb. 5, 1998–.

Melancon, Charlie (D-La.) Oct. 3, 1947–; House 2005–.

Menendez, Robert (D-N.J.) Jan. 1, 1954–; House 1993–Jan. 16, 2006; Senate Jan. 18, 2006–.

Mica, John L. (R-Fla.) Jan. 27, 1943–; House 1993–.

Michaud, Michael H. (D-Maine) Jan. 18, 1955–; House 2003–.

Mikulski, Barbara A. (D-Md.) July 20, 1936–; House 1977–1987; Senate 1987–.

Millender-McDonald, Juanita (D-Calif.) Sept. 7, 1938–April 22, 2007; House April 16, 1996–April 22, 2007.

Miller, Brad (D-N.C.) May 19, 1953–; House 2003–.

Miller, Candice S. (R-Mich.) May 7, 1954–; House 2003–.

Miller, Gary (R-Calif.) Oct. 16, 1948–; House 1999–.

Miller, George (D-Calif.) May 17, 1945–; House 1975–.

Miller, Jeff (R-Fla.) June 27, 1959–; House Oct. 23, 2001–.

Mitchell, Harry E. (D-Ariz.) July 18, 1940–; House 2007–.

Mollohan, Alan B. (son of Robert Homer Mollohan) (D-W.Va.) May 14, 1943–; House 1983–.

Moore, Dennis (D-Kan.) Nov. 8, 1945–; House 1999–.

Moore, Gwen (D-Wis.) April 18, 1951–; House 2005–.

Moran, James P. (D-Va.) May 16, 1945–; House 1991–.

Moran, Jerry (R-Kan.) May 29, 1954–; House 1997–.

Murkowski, Lisa (daughter of Frank H. Murkowski) (R-Alaska) May 22, 1957–; Senate Jan. 7, 2003–.

Murphy, Christopher S. (D-Conn.) April 20, 1947–; House 2007–.

Murphy, Patrick J. (D-Pa.) Oct. 19, 1973–; House 2007–.

Murphy, Tim (R-Pa.) Sept. 11, 1952–; House 2003–.

Murray, Patty (D-Wash.) Oct. 11, 1950–; Senate 1993–.

Murtha, John P. (D-Pa.) June 17, 1932–; House Feb. 5, 1974–.

Musgrave, Marilyn (R-Colo.) Jan. 27, 1949–; House 2003–.

Myrick, Sue (R-N.C.) Aug. 1, 1941–; House 1995–.

N

Nadler, Jerrold (D-N.Y.) June 13, 1947–; House Nov. 4, 1992–.

Napolitano, Grace Flores (D-Calif.) Dec. 4, 1936–; House 1999–.

Neal, Richard E. (D-Mass.) Feb. 14, 1949–; House 1989–.

Nelson, Ben (D-Neb.) May 17, 1941–; Senate 2001–; Gov. 1991–1999.

Nelson, Bill (D-Fla.) Sept. 29, 1942–; House 1979–1991; Senate 2001–.

Neugebauer, Randy (R-Texas) Dec. 24, 1949–; House June 5, 2003–.

Ney, Bob (R-Ohio) July 5, 1954–; House 1995–Nov. 3, 2006.

Northup, Anne E. (R-Ky.) July 22, 1948–; House 1997–2007.

Norton, Eleanor Holmes (D-D.C.) June 13, 1937–; House (Delegate) 1991–.

Norwood, Charlie (R-Ga.) July 27, 1941–Feb. 13, 2007; House 1995–Feb. 13, 2007.

Nunes, Devin (R-Calif.) Oct. 1, 1973–; House 2003–.

Nussle, Jim (R-Iowa) June 27, 1960–; House 1991–2007.

O

Obama, Barack (D-Ill.) Aug. 4, 1961–; Senate 2005-Nov. 16, 2008.

Oberstar, James L. (D-Minn.) Sept. 10, 1934–; House 1975–.

Obey, David R. (D-Wis.) Oct. 3, 1938–; House April 1, 1969–.

Olver, John W. (D-Mass.) Sept. 3, 1936–; House June 18, 1991–.

Ortiz, Solomon P. (D-Texas) June 3, 1937–; House 1983–.

Osborne, Tom (R-Neb.) Feb. 23, 1937–; House 2001–2007.

Otter, C.L. "Butch" (R-Idaho) May 3, 1942–; House 2001–2007. Gov. 2007–.

Owens, Major R. (D-N.Y.) June 28, 1936–; House 1983–2007.

Oxley, Michael G. (R-Ohio) Feb. 11, 1944–; House June 25, 1981–2007.

P

Pallone, Frank Jr. (D-N.J.) Oct. 30, 1951–; House Nov. 8, 1988–.

Pascrell, Bill Jr. (D-N.J.) Jan. 25, 1937–; House 1997–.

Pastor, Ed (D-Ariz.) June 28, 1943–; House Oct. 3, 1991–.

Paul, Ron (R-Texas) Aug. 20, 1935–; House 1976–1977; 1979–1985; 1997–.

Payne, Donald M. (D-N.J.) July 16, 1934–; House 1989–.

Pearce, Steve (R-N.M.) Aug. 23, 1947–; House 2003–2009.

Pelosi, Nancy (daughter of Thomas D'Allesandro Jr., D-Md.) (D-Calif.) March 26, 1940–; House June 9, 1987–; House minority leader 2003–2007; Speaker 2007–.

Pence, Mike (R-Ind.) June 7, 1959–; House 2001–.

Perlmutter, Ed (D-Colo.) May 1, 1953–; House 2007–.

Peterson, Collin C. (D-Minn.) June 29, 1944–; House 1991–.

Peterson, John E. (R-Pa.) Dec. 25, 1938–; House 1997–2009.

Petri, Thomas E. (R-Wis.) May 28, 1940–; House April 3, 1979–.

Pickering, Charles W. "Chip" Jr. (R-Miss.) Aug. 10, 1963–; House 1997–2009.

Pitts, Joseph R. (R-Pa.) Oct. 10, 1939–; House 1997–.

Platts, Todd (R-Pa.) March 5, 1962–; House 2001–.

Poe, Ted (R-Texas) Sept. 10, 1948–; House 2005–.

Pombo, Richard W. (R-Calif.) Jan. 8, 1961–; House 1993–2007.

Pomeroy, Earl (D-N.D.) Sept. 2, 1952–; House 1993–.

Porter, Jon (R-Nev.) May 16, 1955–; House 2003–.

Portman, Rob (R-Ohio) Dec. 19, 1955–; House May 5, 1993–April 29, 2005.

Price, David (D-N.C.) Aug. 17, 1940–; House 1987–1995, 1997–.

Pryce, Deborah (R-Ohio) July 29, 1951–; House 1993–2009.

Pryor, Mark (son of David Pryor) (D-Ark.) Jan. 10, 1963–; Senate 2003–.

Putnam, Adam (R-Fla.) July 31, 1974–; House 2001–.

R

Radanovich, George P. (R-Calif.) June 20, 1955–; House 1995–.

Rahall, Nick J. II (D-W.Va.) May 20, 1949–; House 1977–.

Ramstad, Jim (R-Minn.) May 6, 1946–; House 1991–2009.

Rangel, Charles B. (D-N.Y.) June 11, 1930–; House 1971–.

Reed, Jack (D-R.I.) Nov. 12, 1949–; House 1991–1997; Senate 1997–.

Regula, Ralph (R-Ohio) Dec. 3, 1924–; House 1973–2009.

Rehberg, Denny (R-Mont.) Oct. 5, 1955–; House 2001–.

Reichert, Dave (R-Wash.) Aug. 29, 1950–; House 2005–.

Reid, Harry (D-Nev.) Dec. 2, 1939–; House 1983–1987; Senate 1987–; Senate minority leader 2005–2007; majority leader 2007–.

Renzi, Rick (R-Ariz.) June 11, 1958–; House 2003–2009.

Reyes, Silvestre (D-Texas) Nov. 10, 1944–; House 1997–.

Reynolds, Thomas M. (R-N.Y.) Sept. 3, 1950–; House 1999–.

Richardson, Laura (D-Calif.) April 14, 1962–; House Sept. 4, 2007–.

Roberts, Pat (R-Kan.) April 20, 1936–; House 1981–1997; Senate 1997–.

Rockefeller, John D. IV (nephew of Vice President Nelson A. Rockefeller; and great grandson of Nelson Aldrich, R-R.I.) (D-W.Va.) June 18, 1937–; Senate Jan. 15, 1985–; Gov. 1977–1985.

Rodriguez, Ciro D. (D-Texas) Dec. 9, 1946–; House April 17, 1997–2005; 2007–.

Rogers, Harold (R-Ky.) Dec. 31, 1937–; House 1981–.

Rogers, Mike (R-Mich.) June 2, 1963–; House 2001–.

Rogers, Mike D. (R-Ala.) July 16, 1958–; House 2003–.

Rohrabacher, Dana (R-Calif.) June 21, 1947–; House 1989–.

Roskam, Peter (R-Ill.) Sept. 13, 1961–; House 2007–.

Ros-Lehtinen, Ileana (R-Fla.) July 15, 1952–; House 1989–.

Ross, Mike (D-Ark.) Aug. 2, 1961–; House 2001–.

Rothman, Steven R. (D-N.J.) Oct. 14, 1952–; House 1997–.

Roybal-Allard, Lucille (daughter of Edward R. Roybal) (D-Calif.) June 12, 1941–; House 1993–.

Royce, Ed (R-Calif.) Oct. 12, 1951–; House 1993–.

Ruppersberger, C.A. Dutch (D-Md.) Jan. 31, 1946–; House 2003–.

Rush, Bobby L. (D-Ill.) Nov. 23, 1946–; House 1993–.

Ryan, Paul D. (R-Wis.) Jan. 29, 1970–; House 1999–.

Ryan, Tim (D-Ohio) July 16, 1973–; House 2003–.

Ryun, Jim (R-Kan.) April 29, 1947–; House Nov. 27, 1996–2007.

S

Sabo, Martin Olav (D-Minn.) Feb. 28, 1938–; House 1979–2007.

Salazar, Ken (D-Colo.) March 2, 1955–; Senate 2007–.

Sali, Bill (R-Idaho) Feb. 17, 1954–; House 2007–.

Sanchez, Linda T. (sister of Loretta Sanchez) (D-Calif.) Jan. 28, 1969–; House 2003–.

Sanchez, Loretta (sister of Linda Sanchez) (D-Calif.) Jan. 7, 1960–; House 1997–.

Sanders, Bernard (I-Vt.) Sept. 8, 1941–; House 1991–2007; Senate 2007–.

Santorum, Rick (R-Pa.) May 10, 1958–; House 1991–1995; Senate 1995–2007.

Sarbanes, John (son of Paul Sarbanes) D-Md. May 22, 1961–; House 2007–.

Sarbanes, Paul S. (father of John Sarbanes) (D-Md.) Feb. 3, 1933–; House 1971–1977; Senate 1977–2007.

Saxton, H. James (R-N.J.) Jan. 22, 1943–; House 1984–2009.

Scalise, Steve (R-La.) Oct. 6, 1965–; House May 7, 2008–.

Schakowsky, Janice D. "Jan" (D-Ill.) May 26, 1944–; House 1999–.

Schiff, Adam (D-Calif.) June 22, 1960–; House 2001–.

Schmidt, Jean (R-Ohio) Nov. 29, 1951; House Sept. 6, 2005–.

Schuler, Heath (D-N.C.) Dec. 31, 1971–; House 2007–.

Schumer, Charles E. (D-N.Y.) Nov. 23, 1950–; House 1981–1999; Senate 1999–.

Schwartz, Allyson Y. (D-Pa.) Oct. 3, 1948–; House 2005–.

Schwarz, Joe (R-Mich.) Nov. 15, 1937–; House 2005–2007.

Scott, David (D-Ga.) June 27, 1946–; House 2003–.

Scott, Robert C. (D-Va.) April 30, 1947–; House 1993–.

Sekula-Gibbs, Shelley (R-Texas) June 22, 1953–; House Nov. 13, 2006–2007.

Sensenbrenner, F. James Jr. (R-Wis.) June 14, 1943–; House 1979–.

Serrano, Jose E. (D-N.Y.) Oct. 24, 1943–; House March 28, 1990–.

Sessions, Jeff (R-Ala.) Dec. 24, 1946–; Senate 1997–.

Sessions, Pete (R-Texas) March 22, 1955–; House 1997–.

Sestak, Joe (D-Pa.) Dec. 12, 1951–; House 2007–.

Shadegg, John (R-Ariz.) Oct. 22, 1949–; House 1995–2009.

Shaw, E. Clay Jr. (R-Fla.) April 19, 1939–; House 1981–2007.

Shays, Christopher (R-Conn.) Oct. 18, 1945–; House Sept. 9, 1987–.

Shea-Porter, Carol (D-N.H.) Dec. 2, 1952–; House 2007–.

Shelby, Richard C. (R-Ala.) May 6, 1934–; House 1979–1987; Senate 1987–(1979–Nov. 19, 1994, Democrat).

Sherman, Brad (D-Calif.) Oct. 24, 1954–; House 1997–.

Sherwood, Donald L. (R-Pa.) March 5, 1941–; House 1999–2007.

Shimkus, John M. (R-Ill.) Feb. 21, 1958–; House 1997–.

Shuster, Bill (son of E. G. "Bud" Shuster) (R-Pa.) Jan. 10, 1961–; House May 17, 2001–.

Simmons, Rob (R-Conn.) Feb. 11, 1943–; House 2001–2007.

Simpson, Mike (R-Idaho) Sept. 8, 1950–; House 1999–.

Sires, Albio (D-N.J.) Jan. 26, 1951–; House Nov. 13, 2006–.

Skelton, Ike (D-Mo.) Dec. 20, 1931–; House 1977–.

Slaughter, Louise M. (D-N.Y.) Aug. 14, 1929–; House 1987–.

Smith, Adam (D-Wash.) June 15, 1965–; House 1997–.

Smith, Adrian (R-Neb.) Dec. 19, 1970–; House 2007–.

Smith, Christopher H. (R-N.J.) March 4, 1953–; House 1981–.

Smith, Gordon H. (R-Ore.) Mary 25, 1952–; Senate 1997–.

Smith, Lamar (R-Texas) Nov. 19, 1947–; House 1987–.

Snowe, Olympia J. (wife of John R. McKernan Jr.) (R-Maine) Feb. 21, 1947–; House 1979–1995; Senate 1995–.

Snyder, Vic (D-Ark.) Sept. 27, 1947–; House 1997–.

Sodrel, Mike (R-Ind.) Dec. 17, 1945–; House 2005–2007.

Solis, Hilda (D-Calif.) Oct. 20, 1957–; House 2001–.

Souder, Mark (R-Ind.) July 18, 1950–; House 1995–.

Space, Zack (D-Ohio) Jan. 27, 1961–; House 2005–.

Specter, Arlen (R-Pa.) Feb. 12, 1930–; Senate 1981–.

Speier, Jackie (D-Calif.) May 14, 1950; House April 10, 2008–.

Spratt, John M. Jr. (D-S.C.) Nov. 1, 1942–; House 1983–.

Stabenow, Debbie (D-Mich.) April 29, 1950–; House 1997–2001; Senate 2001–.

Stark, Fortney "Pete" (D-Calif.) Nov. 11, 1931–; House 1973–.

Stearns, Clifford B. (R-Fla.) April 16, 1941–; House 1989–.

Stevens, Ted (R-Alaska) Nov. 18, 1923–; Senate Dec. 24, 1968–; pres. pro tempore 2003–2007.

Strickland, Ted (D-Ohio) Aug. 4, 1941–; House 1993–1995, 1997–2007. Gov. 2007–.

Stupak, Bart (D-Mich.) Feb. 29, 1952–; House 1993–.

Sullivan, John (R-Okla.) Jan. 1, 1965–; House Feb. 27, 2002–.

Sununu, John E. (R-N.H.) Sept. 10, 1964–; House 1997–2003; Senate 2003–.

Sutton, Betty (D-Ohio) July 31, 1963–; House 2007–.

Sweeney, John R. (R-N.Y.) Aug. 9, 1955–; House 1999–2007.

T

Talent, James M. (R-Mo.) Oct. 18, 1956–; House 1993–2001; Senate Nov. 25, 2002–2007.

Tancredo, Tom (R-Colo.) Dec. 20, 1945–; House 1999–2007.

Tanner, John (D-Tenn.) Sept. 22, 1944–; House 1989–.

Tauscher, Ellen O. (D-Calif.) Nov. 15, 1951–; House 1997–.

Taylor, Charles H. (R-N.C.) Jan. 23, 1941–; House 1991–2007.

Taylor, Gene (D-Miss.) Sept. 17, 1953–; House Oct. 24, 1989–.

Terry, Lee (R-Neb.) Jan. 29, 1962–; House 1999–.

Tester, Jon (D-Mont.) Aug. 21, 1956–; Senate 2007–.

Thomas, Craig (R-Wyo.) Feb. 17, 1933–June 4, 2007; House May 2, 1989–1995; Senate 1995–June 4, 2007.

Thomas, William (R-Calif.) Dec. 6, 1941–; House 1979–2005.

Thompson, Bennie (D-Miss.) Jan. 28, 1948–; House April 20, 1993–.

Thompson, Mike (D-Calif.) Jan. 24, 1951–; House 1999–.

Thornberry, William M. "Mac" (R-Texas) July 15, 1958–; House 1995–.

Thune, John (R-S.D.) Jan. 7, 1961–; House 1997–2003; Senate 2005–.

Tiahrt, Todd (R-Kan.) June 15, 1951–; House 1995–.

Tiberi, Pat (R-Ohio) Oct. 21, 1962–; House 2001–.

Tierney, John F. (D-Mass.) Sept. 18, 1951–; House 1997–.

Towns, Edolphus (D-N.Y.) July 21, 1934–; House 1983–.

Tsongas, Niki (D-Mass.) April 26, 1946–; House Oct. 18, 2007–.

Tubbs Jones, Stephanie (R-Ohio) Sept. 10, 1949–Aug. 20, 2008; House 1999–Aug. 20, 2008.

Turner, Michael R. (R-Ohio) Jan. 11, 1960–; House 2003–.

U

Udall, Mark (son of Morris K. Udall, D-Ariz.; cousin of Tom Udall, D-N.M.) (D-Colo.) July 18, 1950–; House 1999–2009.

Udall, Tom (son of Steward Udall, D-Colo.; cousin of Mark Udall, D-Colo.) (D-N.M.) May 18, 1948–; House 1999–2009.

Upton, Fred (R-Mich.) April 23, 1953–; House 1987–.

V

Van Hollen, Chris (D-Md.) Jan. 10, 1959–; House 2003–.

Velázquez, Nydia M. (D-N.Y.) March 22, 1953–; House 1993–.

Visclosky, Peter J. (D-Ind.) Aug. 13, 1949–; House 1985–.

Vitter, David (R-La.) May 3, 1961–; House June 8, 1999–2005; Senate 2005–.

Voinovich, George V. (R-Ohio) July 15, 1936–; Senate 1999–; Gov. 1991–1998.

W

Walberg, Tim (R-Mich.) April 12, 1951–; House 2007–.

Walden, Greg (R-Ore.) Jan. 10, 1957–; House 1999–.

Walsh, James T. (son of William F. Walsh) (R-N.Y.) June 19, 1947–; House 1989–2009.

Walz, Tim (D-Minn.) April 6, 1964–; House 2007–.

Wamp, Zach (R-Tenn.) Oct. 28, 1957–; House 1995–.

Warner, John W. (R-Va.) Feb. 18, 1927–; Senate Jan. 2, 1979–2009.

Wasserman-Schultz, Debbie (D-Fla.) Sept. 27, 1966–; House 2005–.

Waters, Maxine (D-Calif.) Aug. 15, 1938–; House 1991–.

Watson, Diane (D-Calif.) Nov. 12, 1933–; House June 7, 2001–.

Watt, Melvin (D-N.C.) Aug. 26, 1945–; House 1993–.

Waxman, Henry A. (D-Calif.) Sept. 12, 1939–; House 1975–.

Webb, Jim (D-Va.) Feb. 9, 1946–; Senate 2007–.

Weiner, Anthony (D-N.Y.) Sept. 4, 1964–; House 1999–.

Welch, Peter (D-Vt.) May 2, 1947–; House 2007–.

Weldon, Curt (R-Pa.) July 22, 1947–; House 1987–2007.

Weldon, Dave (R-Fla.) Aug. 31, 1953–; House 1995–2009.

Weller, Gerald C. (R-Ill.) July 7, 1957–; House 1995–2009.

Westmoreland, Lynn (R-Ga.) April 2, 1950–; House 2005–.

Wexler, Robert (D-Fla.) Jan. 2, 1961–; House 1997–.

Whitehouse, Sheldon (D-R.I.) Oct. 20, 1955–; Senate 2007–.

Whitfield, Edward (R-Ky.) May 25, 1943–; House 1995–.

Wicker, Roger (R-Miss.) July 5, 1951–; House 1995–Dec. 31, 2007; Senate Jan. 22, 2008–.

Wilson, Charlie (D-Ohio) Jan. 18, 1943–; House 2007–,

Wilson, Heather (R-N.M.) Dec. 30, 1960–; House June 25, 1998–2009.

Wilson, Joe (R-S.C.) July 31, 1947–; House Dec. 19, 2001–.

Wittman, Rob (R-Va.) Feb. 3, 1959–; House Dec. 13, 2007–.

Wolf, Frank R. (R-Va.) Jan. 30, 1939–; House 1981–.

Woolsey, Lynn (D-Calif.) Nov. 3, 1937–; House 1993–.

Wu, David (R-Ore.) April 8, 1955–; House 1999–.

Wyden, Ron (D-Ore.) May 3, 1949–; House 1981–Feb. 5, 1996; Senate Feb. 6, 1996–.

Wynn, Albert R. (D-Md.) Sept. 10, 1951–; House 1993–May 31, 2008.

Y

Yarmuth, John (D-Ky.) Nov 4, 1947–; House 2007–.

Young, C.W. "Bill" (R-Fla.) Dec. 16, 1930–; House 1971–.

Young, Don (R-Alaska) June 9, 1933–; House March 6, 1973–.

Congressional Committees, 109th and 110th Congresses

Following is a list of congressional committees and subcommittees for the 109th and 110th Congresses, 2005–2007 and 2007–2009.

Committee jurisdictions, party ratios, committee chairmen, ranking minority members (in italics), and subcommittee chairmen are included. Political and joint committees also are listed.

Senate Committees

AGRICULTURE, NUTRITION, AND FORESTRY

Agriculture in general; animal industry and diseases; crop insurance and soil conservation; farm credit and farm security; food from fresh waters; food stamp programs; forestry in general; home economics; human nutrition; inspection of livestock, meat, and agricultural products; pests and pesticides; plant industry, soils, and agricultural engineering; rural development, rural electrification, and watersheds; school nutrition programs.

R 11–D 9 *(109th Congress)*

Saxby Chambliss, Ga.
Tom Harkin, Iowa

Forestry, Conservation and Rural Revitalization—Michael D. Crapo, Idaho

Marketing, Inspection and Product Promotion—Jim Talent, Mo.

Production and Price Competitiveness—Mitch McConnell, Ky.

Research, Nutrition and General Legislation—Rick Santorum, Pa.

D 11–R 10 *(110th Congress)*

Tom Harkin, Iowa
Saxby Chambliss, Ga.

Domestic and Foreign Marketing, Inspection, and Plan and Animal Health—Max Baucus, Mont.

Energy, Science, and Technology—Ben Nelson, Neb.

Nutrition and Food Assistance, Sustainable and Organic Agriculture, and General Legislation—Patrick Leahy, Vt.

Production, Income Protection, and Price Support—Blanche Lincoln, Neb.

Rural Revitalization, Conservation, Forestry, and Credit—Debbie Stabenow, Mich.

APPROPRIATIONS

Appropriation of revenue; rescission of appropriations; new spending authority under the Congressional Budget Act.

R 15–D 13 *(109th Congress)*

Thad Cochran, Miss.
Robert C. Byrd, W.Va.

Agriculture, Rural Development and Related Agencies—Robert F. Bennett, Utah

Commerce, Justice, and Science—Richard C. Shelby, Ala.

Defense—Ted Stevens, Alaska

District of Columbia—Sam Brownback, Kan.

Energy and Water—Pete V. Domenici, N.M.

Homeland Security—Judd Gregg, N.H.

Interior and Related Agencies—Conrad Burns, Mont.

Labor, Health and Human Services, Education and Related Agencies—Arlen Specter, Pa.

Legislative Branch—Wayne Allard, Colo.

Military Construction and Veteran Affairs—Kay Bailey Hutchison, Texas

State, Foreign Operations and Related Programs—Mitch McConnell, Ky.

Transportation, Treasury, the Judiciary and HUD—Christopher S. Bond, Mo.

D 15–R 14 *(110th Congress)*

Robert C. Byrd, W.Va.
Thad Cochran, Miss.

Agriculture, Rural Development, FDA and Related Agencies—Herb Kohl, Wis.

Commerce, Justice, Science, and Related Agencies—Barbara A. Mikulski, Md.

Defense—Daniel K. Inouye, Hawaii

Energy and Water Development—Byron L. Dorgan, N.D.

Financial Services and General Government Richard J. Durbin, Ill.

Homeland Security—Robert C. Byrd, W.Va.

Interior, Environment, and Related Agencies—Dianne Feinstein, Calif.

Labor, Health and Human Services, Education, and Related Agencies—Tom Harkin, Iowa

Legislative Branch—Mary L. Landrieu, La.

Military Construction, Veterans Affairs, and Related Agencies—Tim Johnson, S.D.

State, Foreign Operations, and Related Programs—Patrick J. Leahy, Vt.

Transportation, Housing and Urban Development, and Related Agencies—Patty Murray, Wash.

ARMED SERVICES

Defense and defense policy generally; the Department of Defense and the Army, Navy, and Air Force, aeronautical and space activities peculiar to or primarily associated with the development of weapons systems or military operations; maintenance and operation of the Panama Canal, including the Canal Zone; military research and development; national security aspects of nuclear energy; naval petroleum reserves (except Alaska); armed forces generally; Selective Service System; strategic and critical materials.

R 13–D 11 *(109th Congress)*

John W. Warner, Va.
Carl Levin, Mich.

Airland—John McCain, Ariz.
Emerging Threats and Capabilities—John Cornyn, Texas
Personnel—Lindsey Graham, S.C.
Readiness and Management Support—John Ensign, Nev.
Seapower—Jim Talent, Mo.
Strategic Forces—Jeff Sessions, Ala.

D 13–R 12 *(110th Congress)*

Carl Levin, Mich.
John McCain, Ariz.

Airland—Joseph L. Lieberman
Emerging Threats and Capabilities—Jack Reed, R.I.
Personnel—Ben Nelson, Neb.
Readiness and Management Support—Daniel A. Akaka, Hawaii
Seapower—Edward M. Kennedy, Mass.
Strategic Forces—Bill Nelson, Fla.

BANKING, HOUSING, AND URBAN AFFAIRS

Banks, banking, and financial institutions; price controls; deposit insurance; economic stabilization; defense production; export and foreign trade promotion; export controls; federal monetary policy, including Federal Reserve System; financial aid to commerce and industry; issuance and redemption of notes; money and credit, including currency and coinage; nursing home construction; public and private housing, including veterans' housing; renegotiation of government contracts; urban development and mass transit; international economic policy.

R 11–D 9 *(109th Congress)*

Richard C. Shelby, Ala.
Paul S. Sarbanes, Md.

Economic Policy —Jim Bunning, Ky.
Financial Institutions—Robert F. Bennett, Utah
Housing and Transportation—Wayne Allard, Colo.
International Trade and Finance—Michael D. Crapo, Idaho
Securities and Investment—Chuck Hagel, Neb.

D 11–R 10 *(110th Congress)*

Christopher J. Dodd, Conn.
Richard C. Shelby, Ala.

Economic Policy—Thomas R. Carper, Del.
Financial Institutions—Tim Johnson, S.D.
Housing, Transportation, and Community Development—Charles E. Schumer, N.Y.
Securities, Insurance, and Investment—Jack Reed, R.I.
Security and International Trade and Finance—Evan Bayh, Ind.

BUDGET

Federal budget generally; concurrent budget resolutions; Congressional Budget Office.

R 12–D 10 *(109th Congress)*

Judd Gregg, N.H.
Kent Conrad, N.D.

D 12–R 11 *(110th Congress)*

Kent Conrad, N.D.
Judd Gregg, N.H.

No standing subcommittees.

COMMERCE, SCIENCE, AND TRANSPORTATION

Interstate commerce and transportation generally; Coast Guard; coastal zone management; communications; highway safety; inland waterways, except construction; marine fisheries; Merchant Marine and navigation; nonmilitary aeronautical and space sciences; oceans, weather, and atmospheric activities; interoceanic canals generally; regulation of consumer products and services; science, engineering, and technology research development and policy; sports; standards and measurement; transportation and commerce aspects of outer continental shelf lands.

R 12–D 10 *(109th Congress)*

Ted Stevens, Alaska
Daniel K. Inouye, Hawaii

Aviation—Conrad Burns, Mont.
Consumer Affairs, Product Safety, and Insurance—George Allen, Va.
Disaster Prevention and Prediction—Jim DeMint, S.C.
Fisheries and the Coast Guard—Olympia J. Snowe, Maine
Global Climate Change and Impacts—David Vitter, La.
Oceans Policy Study—John E. Sununu, N.H.
Science and Space—Kay Bailey Hutchison, Texas
Surface Transportation and Merchant Marine—Trent Lott, Miss.
Technology, Innovation, and Competitiveness—John Ensign, Nev.
Trade, Tourism, and Economic Development—Gordon H. Smith, Ore.

D 12–R 11 *(110th Congress)*

Daniel K. Inouye, Hawaii
Ted Stevens, Alaska

Aviation Operations, Safety, and Security—John D. Rockefeller IV, W.Va.

Consumer Affairs, Insurance, and Automotive Safety—Mark Pryor, Ark.

Interstate Commerce, Trade, and Tourism—Byron L. Dorgan, N.D.

Oceans, Atmosphere, Fisheries, and Coast Guard—Maria Cantwell, Wash.

Science, Technology and Innovation—John Kerry, Mass.

Space, Aeronautics, and Related Sciences—Bill Nelson, Fla.

Surface Transportation and Merchant Marine Infrastructure, Safety, and Security—Frank R. Lautenberg, N.J.

ENERGY AND NATURAL RESOURCES

Energy policy, regulation, conservation, research, and development; coal; energy-related aspects of deep-water ports; hydroelectric power, irrigation, and reclamation; mines, mining, and minerals generally; national parks, recreation areas, wilderness areas, wild and scenic rivers, historic sites, military parks, and battlefields; naval petroleum reserves in Alaska; nonmilitary development of nuclear energy; oil and gas production and distribution; public lands and forests; solar energy systems; territorial possessions of the United States.

R 12–D 10 *(109th Congress)*

Pete V. Domenici, N.M.
Jeff Bingaman, NW.

Energy—Lamar Alexander, Tenn.
National Parks—Craig Thomas, Wyo.
Public Lands and Forests—Larry E. Craig, Idaho
Water and Power—Frank H. Murkowski, Alaska

D 12–R 11 *(110th Congress)*

Jeff Bingaman, N.M.
Pete V. Domenici, N.M.

Energy—Byron L. Dorgan, N.D.
National Parks—Daniel K. Akaka, Hawaii
Public Lands and Forests—Ron Wyden, Ore.
Water and Power—Tim Johnson, S.D.

ENVIRONMENT AND PUBLIC WORKS

Environmental policy, research, and development; air, water, and noise pollution; construction and maintenance of highways; environmental aspects of outer continental shelf lands; environmental effects of toxic substances other than pesticides; fisheries and wildlife; flood control and improvements of rivers and harbors; nonmilitary environmental regulation and control of nuclear energy; ocean dumping; public buildings and grounds; public works, bridges, and dams; regional economic development; solid waste disposal and recycling; water resources.

R 10–D 8 *(109th Congress)*

James M. Inhofe, Okla.
James M. Jeffords, Vt.

Clean Air and Nuclear Safety—George V. Voinovich, Ohio
Fisheries, Wildlife, and Water—Lincoln Chafee, R.I.

Superfund, Waste Control, and Risk Assessment—John Thune, S.D.

Transportation and Infrastructure—Christopher S. Bond, Mo.

D 10–R 9 *(110th Congress)*

Barbara Boxer, Calif.
James M. Inhofe, Okla.

Clean Air and Nuclear Safety —Thomas R. Carper, Del.

Private Sector and Consumer Solutions to Global Warming and Wildlife Protection—Joseph I. Lieberman, Conn.

Public Sector Solutions to Global Warming, Oversight, and Children's Health Protection—Barbara Boxer, Calif.

Superfund and Environmental Health—Hillary Rodham Clinton, N.Y.

Transportation and Infrastructure—Max Baucus, Mont.

Transportation Safety, Infrastructure Security, and Water Quality—Frank R. Lautenberg, N.J.

FINANCE

Revenue measures generally; taxes; tariffs and import quotas; reciprocal trade agreements; customs; revenue sharing; federal debt limit; Social Security; health programs financed by taxes or trust funds.

R 11–D 9 *(109th Congress)*

Charles E. Grassley, Iowa
Max Baucus, Mont.

Health Care—Orrin G. Hatch, Utah
International Trade—Craig Thomas, Wyo.

Long-Term Growth, and Debt Reduction—Gordon H. Smith, Ore.

Social Security and Family Policy—Rick Santorum, Pa.
Taxation and IRS Oversight—Jon Kyl, Ariz.

D 11–R 10 *(110th Congress)*

Max Baucus, Mont.
Charles E. Grassley, Iowa

Energy, Natural Resources, and Infrastructure—Jeff Bingaman, N.M.

Health Care—John D. Rockefeller, IV, W.Va.

International Trade and Global Competitiveness—Blanche Lincoln, Ark.

Social Security, Pensions, and Family Policy—John Kerry, Mass.

Taxation and IRS Oversight and Long-Term Growth—Kent Conrad, N.D.

FOREIGN RELATIONS

Relations of the United States with foreign nations generally; treaties; foreign economic, military, technical, and humanitarian assistance; foreign loans; diplomatic service; International Red Cross; international aspects of nuclear energy; International Monetary Fund; intervention abroad and declarations of war; foreign trade; national security; oceans and international environmental and scientific affairs; protection of U.S. citizens abroad; United Nations; World Bank and other development assistance organizations.

R 10–D 8 *(109th Congress)*

Richard G. Lugar, Ind.
Joseph R. Biden Jr., Del.

African Affairs—Mel Martinez, Fla.
East Asian and Pacific Affairs—Lisa Murkowski, Alaska
European Affairs—George F. Allen, Va.
International Economic Policy, Export and Trade Promotion—Chuck Hagel, Neb.
International Operations and Terrorism—John E. Sununu, N.H.
Near Eastern and South Asian Affairs—Lincoln Chafee, R.I.
Western Hemisphere, Peace Corps, and Narcotics Affairs—Norm Coleman, Minn.

D 11–R 10 *(110th Congress)*

Joseph R. Biden Jr., Del.
Richard G. Lugar, Ind.

African Affairs—Russ Feingold, Wis.
East Asian and Pacific Affairs—Barbara Boxer, Calif.
European Affairs—Barack Obama, Ill.
International Development and Foreign Assistance, Economic Affairs, and International Environmental Protection—Robert Menendez, N.J.
International Operations and Organizations, Democracy and Human Rights—Bill Nelson, Fla.
Near Eastern and South and Central Asian Affairs—John Kerry, Mass.
Western Hemisphere, Peace Corps, and Narcotics Affairs—Christopher J. Dodd, Conn.

HEALTH, EDUCATION, LABOR, AND PENSIONS

Education, labor, health, and public welfare in general; aging; arts and humanities; biomedical research and development; child labor; convict labor; domestic activities of the Red Cross; equal employment opportunity; handicapped people; labor standards and statistics; mediation and arbitration of labor disputes; occupational safety and health; private pensions; public health; railway labor and retirement; regulation of foreign laborers; student loans; wages and hours; agricultural colleges; Gallaudet University; Howard University; St. Elizabeth's Hospital in Washington, D.C.

R 11–D 9 *(109th Congress)*

Michael B. Enzi, Wyo.
Edward M. Kennedy, Mass.

Bioterrorism and Public Health Preparedness—Richard M. Burr, N.C.
Education and Early Childhood Development—Lamar Alexander, Tenn.
Employment and Workplace Safety—Johnny Isakson, Ga.
Retirement Security and Aging—Mike DeWine, Ohio

D 11–R 10 *(110th Congress)*

Edward M. Kennedy, Mass.
Michael B. Enzi, Wyo.

Retirement and Aging—Barbara A. Mikulski, Md.
Children and Families—Christopher J. Dodd, Conn.
Employment and Workplace Safety—Patty Murray, Wash.

HOMELAND SECURITY AND GOVERNMENTAL AFFAIRS

Archives of the United States; budget and accounting measures; census and statistics; federal civil service; congressional organization; intergovernmental relations; government information; District of Columbia; organization and management of nuclear export policy; executive branch organization and reorganization; Postal Service; efficiency, economy, and effectiveness of government.

R 9–D 7 *(109th Congress)*

Susan Collins, Maine
Joseph I. Lieberman, Conn.

Federal Financial Management, Government Information, and International Security—Tom Coburn, Okla.
Permanent Subcommittee on Investigations—Norm Coleman, Minn.
Oversight of Government Management, the Federal Workforce, and the District of Columbia—George V. Voinovich, Ohio

D 9–R 8 *(110th Congress)*

Joseph I. Lieberman, Conn.
Susan Collins, Maine

Disaster Recovery—Mary L. Landrieu
Federal Financial Management, Government Information, Federal Services, and International Security—Thomas R. Carper, Del.
Oversight of Government Management, the Federal Workforce, and the District of Columbia—Daniel K. Akaka, Hawaii
Permanent Subcommittee on Investigations—Carl Levin, Mich.
State, Local, and Private Sector Preparedness and Integration—Mark Pryor, Ark.

INDIAN AFFAIRS

Problems and opportunities of Native Americans, including Native American land management and trust responsibilities, education, health, special services, loan programs, and claims against the United States.

R 8–D 6 *(109th Congress)*

John McCain, Ariz.
Byron L. Dorgan, N.D.

D 8–R 7 *(110th Congress)*

Byron L. Dorgan, N.D.
Craig Thomas, Wyo.

No standing subcommittees.

JUDICIARY

Civil and criminal judicial proceedings in general; national penitentiaries; bankruptcy, mutiny, espionage, and counterfeiting; civil liberties; constitutional amendments; apportionment of representatives; government information; immigration and naturalization; interstate compacts in general; claims against the United States; patents, copyrights, and trademarks; monopolies and unlawful restraints of trade; holidays and celebrations; revision and codification of the statutes of the United States; state and territorial boundary lines.

R 10–D 8 *(109th Congress)*

Arlen Specter, Pa.
Patrick J. Leahy, Vt.

Administrative Oversight and the Courts—Jeff Sessions, Ala.
Antitrust, Competition Policy, and Consumer Rights—Mike DeWine, Ohio
Constitution, Civil Rights, and Property Rights—Sam Brownback, Kan.
Corrections and Rehabilitation—Tom Coburn, Okla.
Crime and Drugs—Lindsey Graham, S.C.
Immigration, Border Security, and Citizenship—John Cornyn, Texas
Intellectual Property—Orrin G. Hatch, Utah
Terrorism, Technology, and Homeland Security—Jon Kyl, Ariz.

D 10–R 9 *(110th Congress)*

Patrick J. Leahy, Vt.
Arlen Specter, Pa.

Administrative Oversight and the Courts—Charles E. Schumer, N.Y.
Antitrust, Competition Policy, and Consumer Rights—Herb Kohl, Wis.
Constitution—Russ Feingold, Wis.
Crime and Drugs—Joseph R. Biden Jr., Del.
Human Rights and the Law—Richard J. Durbin, Ill.
Immigration, Refugees, and Border Security—Edward M. Kennedy, Mass.
Terrorism, Technology, and Homeland Security—Dianne Feinstein, Calif.

RULES AND ADMINISTRATION

Senate rules and regulations; Senate administration in general; corrupt practices; qualifications of senators; contested elections; federal elections in general; Government Printing Office; *Congressional Record*; meetings of Congress and attendance of members; presidential succession; the Capitol, congressional office buildings, the Library of Congress, the Smithsonian Institution, and the Botanic Garden; purchase of books and manuscripts and erection of monuments to the memory of individuals.

R 10–D 8 *(109th Congress)*

Trent Lott, Miss.
Christopher J. Dodd, Conn.

D 10–R 9 *(110th Congress)*

Dianne Feinstein, Calif.
Robert F. Bennett, Utah

No standing subcommittees.

SELECT ETHICS

Studies and investigates standards and conduct of Senate members and employees and may recommend remedial action.

R 3–D 3 *(109th Congress)*

George V. Voinovich, Ohio
Tim Johnson, S.D. (vice chairman)

D 3–R 3 *(110th Congress)*

Tim Johnson, S.D. (Barbara Boxer, Calif., acting chairwoman)
John Cornyn, Texas (vice chairman)

No standing subcommittees.

SELECT INTELLIGENCE

Legislative and budgetary authority over the Central Intelligence Agency, the Defense Intelligence Agency, the National Security Agency, and intelligence activities of the Federal Bureau of Investigation and other components of the federal intelligence community.

R 8–D 7 *(109th Congress)*

Pat Roberts, Kan.
John D. Rockefeller IV, W.Va.

D 8–R 7 *(110th Congress)*

John D. Rockefeller IV, W.Va.
Christopher S. Bond, Mo.

No standing subcommittees.

SMALL BUSINESS AND ENTREPRENEURSHIP

Problems of small business; Small Business Administration.

R 10–D 8 *(109th Congress)*

Olympia J. Snowe, Maine
John Kerry, Mass.

D 10–R 9 *(110th Congress)*

John Kerry, Mass.
Olympia J. Snowe, Maine

No standing subcommittees.

SPECIAL AGING

Problems and opportunities of older people including health, income, employment, housing, and care and assistance. Reports findings and makes recommendations to the Senate but cannot report legislation.

R 11–D 9 *(109th Congress)*

Gordon H. Smith, Ore.
Herb Kohl, Wis.

D 11–R 10 *(110th Congress)*

Herb Kohl, Wis.
Gordon H. Smith, Ore.

No standing subcommittees.

VETERANS´ AFFAIRS

Veterans' measures in general; compensation; life insurance issued by the government on account of service in the armed forces; national cemeteries; pensions; readjustment benefits; veterans' hospitals, medical care and treatment; vocational rehabilitation and education; soldiers' and sailors' civil relief.

R 8–D 6 *(109th Congress)*

Larry E. Craig, Idaho
Daniel K. Akaka, Hawaii

D 8–R 7 *(110th Congress)*

Daniel K. Akaka, Hawaii
Larry E. Craig, Idaho

POLITICAL COMMITTEES

Democratic Policy Committee (an arm of the Democratic Caucus that advises on legislative priorities)—Byron L. Dorgan, N.D., chairman (109th and 110th Congresses)

Democratic Senatorial Campaign Committee (campaign support committee for Democratic senatorial candidates)—Charles E. Schumer, chairman ((109th and 110th Congresses)

Democratic Steering and Outreach Committee (makes Democratic committee assignments)—Hillary Rodham Clinton, N.Y., chairwoman (109th Congress); Debbie Stabenow, Mich., chairwoman (110th Congress)

National Republican Senatorial Committee (campaign support committee for Republican senatorial candidates)—Elizabeth Dole, N.C., chairwoman (109th Congress); John Ensign, Nev., chairman (110th Congress)

Republican Policy Committee (advises on party action and policy)—Jon Kyl, Ariz., chairman (109th Congress); Kay Bailey Hutchison, Texas, chairwoman (110th Congress)

House Committees

AGRICULTURE

Agriculture generally; forestry in general, and forest reserves other than those created from the public domain; adulteration of seeds, insect pests, and protection of birds and animals in forest reserves; agricultural and industrial chemistry; agricultural colleges and experiment stations; agricultural economics and research; agricultural education extension services; agricultural production and marketing and stabilization of prices of agricultural products, and commodities (not including distribution outside the United States); animal industry and diseases of animals; commodities exchanges; crop insurance and soil conservation; dairy industry; entomology and plant quarantine; extension of farm credit and farm security; inspection of livestock, poultry, meat products, seafood and seafood products; human nutrition and home economics; plant industry, soils, and agricultural engineering; rural electrification; rural development; water conservation related to activities of the Department of Agriculture.

R 25–D 21 *(109th Congress)*

Robert W. Goodlatte, Va.
Collin C. Peterson, Minn.

Conservation, Credit, Rural Development, and Research—Frank D. Lucas, Okla.

Department Operations, Oversight, Nutrition, and Forestry—Gil Gutknecht, Minn.

General Farm Commodities and Risk Management—Jerry Moran, Kan.

Livestock and Horticulture—Robin Hayes, N.C.

Specialty Crops and Foreign Agriculture Programs—Bill Jenkins, Tenn.

D 25–R 21 *(110th Congress)*

Collin C. Peterson, Minn.
Robert W. Goodlatte, Va.

Conservation, Credit, Energy, and Research—Tim Holden, Pa.

General Farm Commodities and Risk Management —Bob Etheridge, N.C.

Horticulture and Organic Agriculture—Dennis Cardoza, Calif.

Livestock, Dairy, and Poultry—Leonard L. Boswell, Iowa

Operations, Oversight, Nutrition and Forestry—Joe Baca, Calif.

Specialty Crops, Rural Development, and Foreign Agriculture—Mike McIntyre, N.C.

APPROPRIATIONS

Appropriation of the revenue for the support of the government; rescissions of appropriations contained in appropriation acts; transfers of unexpended balances; new spending authority under the Congressional Budget Act.

R 37–D 29; I 1 *(109th Congress)*

Jerry Lewis, Calif.
David R. Obey, Wis.

Agriculture, Rural Development, FDA, and Related Agencies—Henry Bonilla, Texas

Defense—C. W. Bill Young, Fla.

Energy and Water Development, and Related Agencies—David L. Hobson, Ohio

Foreign Operations, Export Financing, and Related Agencies—Jim Kolbe, Ariz.

Homeland Security—Harold Rogers, Ky.

Interior, Environment, and Related Agencies—Charles H. Taylor, N.C.

Labor, Health and Human Services, Education, and Related Agencies—Ralph Regula, Ohio

Military Quality of Life and Veterans' Affairs, and Related Agencies—James T. Walsh, N.Y.

Science, State, Justice, Commerce, and Related Agencies—Frank R. Wolf, Va.

Transportation, Treasury, HUD, the Judiciary, and District of Columbia—Joe Knollenberg, Mich.

D 37–R 29 *(110th Congress)*

David R. Obey, Wis.
Jerry Lewis, Calif.

Agriculture, Rural Development, FDA, and Related Agencies—Rosa DeLauro, Conn.

Commerce, Justice, Science, and Related Agencies—Alan B. Mollohan, W.Va.

Defense—John P. Murtha, Pa.

Energy and Water Development—Peter J. Visclosky, Ind.

Financial Services and General Government—Jose E. Serrano, N.Y.

Homeland Security—David E. Price, N.C.

Interior, Environment, and Related Agencies—Norm Dicks, Wash.

Labor, Health and Human Services, Education, and Related Agencies—David R. Obey, Wis.

Legislative Branch—Debbie Wasserman-Schultz, Fla.

Military Construction, Veterans Affairs, and Related Agencies—Chet Edwards, Texas

State, Foreign Operations, and Related Programs—Nita M. Lowey, N.Y.

Transportation, Housing and Urban Development, and Related Agencies—John W. Olver, Mass.

Select Intelligence Oversight Panel—Rush D. Holt, D-N.J. (The panel's required designees from the Select Committee on Intelligence are Peter Hoekstra, R-Mich., Rush D. Hold, D-N.J., and Silvestre Reyes, D-Texas)

ARMED SERVICES

Ammunition depots; forts; arsenals; Army, Navy, and Air Force reservations and establishments; common defense generally; conservation, development, and use of naval petroleum and oil shale reserves; Department of Defense generally, including the Departments of the Army, Navy, and Air Force generally; interoceanic canals generally, including measures relating to the maintenance, operation, and administration of interoceanic canals; Merchant Marine Academy and state maritime academies; military applications of nuclear energy; tactical intelligence and intelligence-related activities of the Department of Defense; national security aspects of merchant marine, including financial assistance for the construction and operation of vessels, the maintenance of the U.S. shipbuilding and ship repair industrial base, cabotage, cargo preference, and merchant marine officers and seamen as these matters relate to the national security; pay, promotion, retirement, and other benefits and privileges of members of the armed forces; scientific research and development in support of the armed services; selective service; size and composition of the Army, Navy, Marine Corps, and Air Force; soldiers' and sailors' homes; strategic and critical materials necessary for the common defense.

R 34–D 28 *(109th Congress)*

Duncan Hunter, Calif.
Ike Skelton, Mo.

Military Personnel—John M. McHugh, N.Y.

Projection Forces—Roscoe G. Bartett, Md.

Readiness—Joel Hefley, Colo.

Strategic Forces—Terry Everett, Ala.

Tactical Air and Land Forces—Curt Weldon, Pa.

Terrorism, Unconventional Threats, and Capabilities—H. James Saxton, N.J.

D 34–R 28 *(110th Congress)*

Ike Skelton, Mo.
Duncan Hunter, Calif.

Air and Land Forces—Neil Abercrombie, Hawaii

Military Personnel—Vic Snyder, Ark.

Oversight and Investigations—Martin T. Meehan, Mass.

Readiness—Solomon P. Ortiz, Texas

Seapower and Expeditionary Forces—Gene Taylor, Miss.

Strategic Forces—Ellen O. Tauscher, Calif.

Terrorism, Unconventional Threats, and Capabilities—Adam Smith, Wash.

BUDGET

Congressional budget process generally; concurrent budget resolutions; measures relating to special controls over the federal budget; Congressional Budget Office.

R 22–D 17 *(109th Congress)*

Jim Nussle, Iowa
John M. Spratt Jr., S.C.

D 22–R 17 *(110th Congress)*

John M. Spratt Jr., S.C.
Paul D. Ryan, Wis.

No standing subcommittees.

EDUCATION AND THE WORKFORCE

Measures relating to education or labor generally; child labor; Columbia Institution for the Deaf, Dumb, and Blind; Howard University; Freedmen's Hospital; convict labor and the entry of goods made by convicts into interstate commerce; food programs for children in schools; labor standards and statistics; mediation and arbitration of labor disputes; regulation or prevention of importation of foreign laborers under contract; U.S. Employees' Compensation Commission; vocational rehabilitation; wages and hours of labor; welfare of miners; work incentive programs.

R 27–D 22 *(109th Congress)*

John A. Boehner, Ohio
George Miller, Calif.

21st Century Competitiveness—Howard P. "Buck" McKeon, Calif.
Education Reform—Michael N. Castle, Del.
Employer-Employee Relations—Sam Johnson, Texas
Select Education—Pat Tiberi, Ohio
Workforce Protections—Charlie Norwood, Ga.

D 27–R 22 *(110th Congress)*

George Miller, Calif.
Howard P. "Buck" McKeon, Calif.

Early Childhood, Elementary, and Secondary Education—Dale E. Kildee, Mich.
Health, Employment, Labor, and Pensions—Robert E. Andrews, N.J.
Healthy Families and Communities—Carolyn McCarthy, N.Y.
Higher Education, Lifelong Learning, and Competitiveness—Ruben Hinojosa, Texas
Workforce Protections—Lynn Woolsey, Calif.

ENERGY AND COMMERCE

Interstate and foreign commerce generally; biomedical research and development; consumer affairs and consumer protection; health and health facilities, except health care supported by payroll deductions; interstate energy compacts; measures relating to the exploration, production, storage, supply, marketing, pricing, and regulation of energy resources, including all fossil fuels, solar energy, and other unconventional or renewable energy resources; measures relating to the conservation of energy resources; measures relating to energy information generally; measures relating to (1) the generation and marketing of power (except by federally chartered or federal regional power marketing authorities), (2) the reliability and interstate transmission of, and ratemaking for, all power, and (3) the siting of generation facilities, except the installation of interconnections between government water power projects; measures relating to general management of the Department of Energy, and the management and all functions of the Federal Energy Regulatory Commission; national energy policy generally; public health and quarantine; regulation of the domestic nuclear energy industry, including regulation of research and development reactors and nuclear regulatory research; regulation of interstate and foreign communications; travel and tourism; nuclear and other energy.

R 31–D 26 *(109th Congress)*

Joe L. Barton, Texas
John D. Dingell, Mich.

Commerce, Trade, and Consumer Protection—Cliff Stearns, Fla.
Energy and Air Quality—Ralph M. Hall, Texas
Environment and Hazardous Materials—Paul E. Gillmor, Ohio
Health—Nathan Deal, Ga.
Oversight and Investigations—Edward Whitfield, Ky.
Telecommunications and the Internet—Fred Upton, Mich.

D 31–R 26 *(110th Congress)*

John D. Dingell, Mich.
Joe L. Barton, Texas

Commerce, Trade, and Consumer Protection—Bobby L. Rush, Ill.
Energy and Air Quality—Rick Boucher, Va.
Environment and Hazardous Materials—Albert R. Wynn, Md.
Health—Frank Pallone Jr., N.J.
Oversight and Investigations—Bart Stupak, Mich.
Telecommunications and the Internet—Edward J. Markey, Mass.

FINANCIAL SERVICES

Banks and banking, including deposit insurance and federal monetary policy; economic stabilization, defense production, renegotiation, and control of the price of commodities, rents, and services; financial aid to commerce and industry (other than transportation); insurance generally; international finance; international financial and monetary organizations; money and credit, including currency and the issuance of notes and redemption thereof; gold and silver, including the coinage thereof; valuation and revaluation of the dollar; public and private housing; securities and exchanges; and urban development

R 37–D 33 *(109th Congress)*

Michael G. Oxley, Ohio
Barney Frank, Mass.

Capital Markets, Insurance, and Government-Sponsored Enterprises—Richard H. Baker, La.
Domestic and International Monetary Policy, Trade, and Technology—Deborah Pryce, Ohio

Financial Institutions and Consumer Credit—Spencer Bachus, Ala.

Housing and Community Opportunity—Bob Ney, Ohio

`**Oversight and Investigations**—Sue W. Kelly, N.Y.

D 37–R 33 *(110th Congress)*

Barney Frank, Mass.
Spencer Bachus, Ala.

Capital Markets, Insurance, and Government-Sponsored Enterprises—Paul E. Kanjorski, Pa.

Domestic and International Monetary Policy, Trade, and Technology—Luis V. Gutierrez, Ill.

Financial Institutions and Consumer Credit—Carolyn B. Maloney, N.Y.

Housing and Community Opportunity—Maxine Waters, Calif.

Oversight and Investigations—Melvin Watt, N.C.

GOVERNMENT REFORM

Civil service, including intergovernmental personnel; the status of officers and employees of the United States, including their compensation, classification, and retirement; measures relating to the municipal affairs of the District of Columbia in general, other than appropriations; federal paperwork reduction; budget and accounting measures generally; holidays and celebrations; overall economy, efficiency, and management of government operations and activities, including federal procurement; National Archives; population and demography generally, including the census; Postal Service generally, including the transportation of mail; public information and records; relationship of the federal government to the states and municipalities generally; reorganizations in the executive branch of the government.

R 23–D 18–I 1 *(109th Congress)*

Thomas M. Davis III, Va.
Henry A. Waxman, Calif.

Criminal Justice, Drug Policy, and Human Resources—Mark Souder, Ind.

Energy and Resources—Darrell Issa, Calif.

Federal Workforce and Agency Organizations—Jon Porter, Nev.

Federalism and the Census—Michael R. Turner, Ohio

Government Management, Finance, and Accountability—Todd R. Platts, Pa.

National Security, Emerging Threats, and International Relations—Christopher Shays, Conn.

Regulatory Affairs—Candice S. Miller, Mich.

OVERSIGHT AND GOVERNMENT REFORM

D 23–R 18 *(110th Congress)*

Henry A. Waxman, Calif.
Thomas M. Davis III, Va.

Domestic Policy—Dennis J. Kucinich, Ohio

Federal Workforce, Postal Service, and the District of Columbia—Danny K. Davis, Ill.

Government Management, Organization, and Procurement—Edolphus Towns, N.Y.

Information Policy, Census, and National Archives—William Lacy Clay, Mo.

National Security and Foreign Affairs—John F. Tierney, Mass.

HOMELAND SECURITY

Overall homeland security policy; organization and administration of the Department of Homeland Security; functions of the Department of Homeland Security; border and port security (except immigration policy and nonborder enforcement); customs (except customs revenue); integration, analysis, and dissemination of homeland security information; domestic preparedness for and collective response to terrorism; research and development; transportation security

R 19–D 15 *(109th Congress)*

Christopher Cox, Calif.
Bennie Thompson, Miss.

Economic Security, Infrastructure Protection, and Cybersecurity—Dan Lungren, Calif.

Emergency Preparedness, Science and Technology—Peter T. King, N.Y.

Intelligence, Information Sharing, and Terrorism Risk Assessment—Rob Simmons, Conn.

Management, Integration, and Oversight—Mike D. Rogers, Ala.

Prevention of Nuclear and Biological Attach—John Linder, Ga.

D 19–R 15 *(110th Congress)*

Bennie Thompson, Miss.
Peter T. King, N.Y.

Border, Maritime, and Global Counterterrorism—Loretta Sanchez, Calif.

Emergency Communications, Preparedness, and Response—Henry Cuellar, Texas

Emerging Threats, Cybersecurity, and Science and Technology—Jim Langevin, R.I.

Intelligence, Information Sharing, and Terrorism Risk Assessment—Jane Harman, Calif.

Management, Investigations, and Oversight—Christopher Carney, Pa.

Transportation Security and Infrastructure Protection—Sheila Jackson-Lee, Texas

HOUSE ADMINISTRATION

Accounts of the House generally; assignment of office space for members and committees; disposition of useless executive papers; matters relating to the election of the president, vice president, or members of Congress; corrupt practices; contested elections; credentials and qualifications; federal elections generally; appropriations from accounts for committee salaries and expenses (except for the Committee on Appropriations), House Information Systems, and allowances and expenses of members, House officers, and administrative offices of the House; auditing and settling of all such accounts; expenditure of such accounts; employment of persons by the House, including clerks for members and committees, and reporters of debates; Library of Congress and the House Library; statuary and pictures; acceptance or purchase of works of art for the Capitol; the Botanic Garden; management of the Library of Congress; purchase of books and manuscripts; Smithsonian Institution and the incorporation of similar institutions; Franking Commission; printing and correction of the *Congressional Record*; services to the House, including the House restaurant, parking facilities, and administration of the House office buildings and of the House wing of the Capitol; travel of members of the House; raising, reporting, and use of campaign contributions for candidates for office of representative in the House of Representatives, of delegate, and of resident commissioner to the United States from Puerto Rico; compensation, retirement and other benefits of the members, officers, and employees of the Congress.

R 6–D 3 *(109th Congress)*

Bob Ney, Ohio
Juanita Millender-McDonald, Calif.

No standing subcommittees.

D 6–R 3 *(110th Congress)*

Juanita Millender-McDonald, Calif.
Vernon J. Ehlers, Mich.

Capitol Security—Robert A. Brady, Pa.
Elections—Zoe Lofgren, Calif.

INTERNATIONAL RELATIONS

Relations of the United States with foreign nations generally; acquisition of land and buildings for embassies and legations in foreign countries; establishment of boundary lines between the United States and foreign nations; export controls, including nonproliferation of nuclear technology and nuclear hardware; foreign loans; international commodity agreements (other than those involving sugar), including all agreements for cooperation in the export of nuclear technology and nuclear hardware; international conferences and congresses; international education; intervention abroad and declarations of war; measures relating to the diplomatic service; measures to foster commercial intercourse with foreign nations and to safeguard American business interests abroad; measures relating to international economic policy; neutrality; protection of American citizens abroad and expatriation; American National Red Cross; trading with the enemy; U.N. organizations.

R 27–D 23 *(109th Congress)*

Henry J. Hyde, Ill.
Tom Lantos, Calif.

Africa, Global Human Rights, and International Operations—Christopher H. Smith, N.J.
Asia and the Pacific—Jim Leach, Iowa
Europe and Emerging Threats—Elton Gallegly, Calif.
International Terrorism and Nonproliferation—Ed Royce, Calif.
Middle East and Central Asia—Ileana Ros-Lehtinen, Fla.
Oversight and Investigations—Dana Rohrabacher, Calif.
Western Hemisphere—Dan Burton, Ill.

FOREIGN AFFAIRS

D 27–R 23 *(110th Congress)*

Tom Lantos, Calif.
Ileana Ros-Lehtinen, Fla.

Africa and Global Health—Donald M. Payne, N.J.
Asia, the Pacific, and the Global Environment—Eni F.H. Faleomavaega, Am Samoa
Europe—Robert Wexler, Fla.
International Organizations, Human Rights, and Oversight—Bill Delahunt, Mass.
Middle East and South Asia—Gary Ackerman, N.Y.
Terrorism, Nonproliferation, and Trade—Brad Sherman, Calif.
Western Hemisphere—Eliot L. Engel, N.Y.

JUDICIARY

The judiciary and judicial proceedings, civil and criminal; administrative practice and procedure; apportionment of representatives; bankruptcy, mutiny, espionage, and counterfeiting; civil liberties; constitutional amendments; federal courts and judges, and local courts in the territories and possessions; immigration and naturalization; interstate compacts generally; measures relating to claims against the United States; meetings of Congress, attendance of members and their acceptance of incompatible offices; national penitentiaries; patents, the Patent Office, copyrights, and trademarks; presidential succession; protection of trade and commerce against unlawful restraints and monopolies; revision and codification of the Statutes of the United States; state and territorial boundaries; subversive activities affecting the internal security of the United States.

R 23–D 17 *(109th Congress)*

F. James Sensenbrenner Jr., Wis.
John Conyers Jr., Mich.

Commercial and Administrative Law—Chris Cannon, Utah
Constitution—Steve Chabot, Ohio
Courts, the Internet, and Intellectual Property—Lamar Smith, Texas
Crime, Terrorism, and Homeland Security—Howard Coble, N.C.
Immigration, Border Security, and Claims—John Hostettler, Ind.

D 21–R 16 *(110th Congress)*

John Conyers Jr., Mich.
Lamar Smith, Texas

Commercial and Administrative Law—Linda T. Sanchez, Calif.
Constitution, Civil Rights, and Civil Liberties—Jerrold Nadler, N.Y.
Courts, the Internet, and Intellectual Property—Howard L. Berman, Calif.
Crime, Terrorism, and Homeland Security—Robert C. Scott, Va.
Immigration, Citizenship, Refugees, Border Security, and International Law—Zoe Lofgren, Calif.
Anti-Trust Taskforce—John Conyers Jr., Mich.

RESOURCES

Public lands generally, including entry, easements, and grazing; mining interests generally; fisheries and wildlife, including research, restoration, refuges, and conservation; forest reserves and national parks created from the public domain; forfeiture of land grants and alien ownership, including alien ownership of mineral lands; Geological Survey; international fishing agreements; interstate compacts relating to apportionment of waters for irrigation purposes; irrigation and reclamation, including water supply for reclamation projects, and easements of public lands for irrigation projects, and acquisition of private lands when necessary to complete irrigation projects; measures relating to the care and management of Indians, including the care and allotment of Native American lands and general and special measures relating to claims which are paid out of Native American funds; measures relating generally to the insular possessions of the United States, except those affecting the revenue and appropriations; military parks and battlefields, national cemeteries administered by the secretary of the interior, parks within the District of Columbia, and the erection of monuments to the memory of individuals; mineral land laws and claims and entries thereunder; mineral resources of the public lands; mining schools and experimental stations; marine affairs (including coastal zone management), except for measures relating to oil and other pollution of navigable waters; oceanography; petroleum conservation on the public lands and conservation of the radium supply in the United States; preservation of prehistoric ruins and objects of interest on the public domain; relations of the United States with the Native Americans and Native American tribes; disposition of oil transported by the Trans-Alaska Oil Pipeline.

R 27–D 22 *(109th Congress)*

Richard W. Pombo, Calif.
Nick J. Rahall II, W.Va

Energy and Mineral Resources—Jim Gibbons, Nev.
Fisheries and Oceans—Wayne T. Gilchrest, Md.
Forests and Forest Health—Greg Walden, Ore.
National Parks—Devin Nunes, Calif.
Water and Power—George P. Radanovich, Calif.

NATURAL RESOURCES

D 27–R 22 *(110th Congress)*

Nick J. Rahall II, W.Va.
Don Young, Alaska

Energy and Mineral Resources—Jim Costa, Calif.
Fisheries, Wildlife, and Oceans—Madeleine Z. Bordallo, Guam
Insular Affairs—Donna M.C. Christensen, Virgin Is.
National Parks, Forests, and Public Lands—Raul M. Grijalva, Ariz.
Water and Power—Grace F. Napolitano, Calif.

RULES

Rules and joint rules (other than rules or joint rules relating to the Code of Official Conduct), and order of business of the House; recesses and final adjournments of Congress.

R 9–D 4 *(109th Congress)*

David Dreier, Calif.
Louise M. Slaughter, N.Y.

Legislative and Budget Process—Lincoln Diaz-Balart, Fla.
Rules and the Organization of the House—Doc Hastings, Wash.

D 9–R 4 *(110th Congress)*

Louise M. Slaughter, N.Y.
David Dreier, Calif.

Legislative and Budget Process—Alcee L. Hastings, Fla.
Rules and the Organization of the House—Jim McGovern, Mass.

SCIENCE

All energy research, development, and demonstration, and projects thereof, and all federally owned or operated nonmilitary energy laboratories; astronautical research and development, including resources, personnel, equipment, and facilities; civil aviation research and development; environmental research and development; marine research; measures relating to the commercial application of energy technology; National Institute of Standards and Technology, standardization of weights and measures and the metric system; National Aeronautics and Space Administration; National Space Council; National Science Foundation; National Weather Service; outer space, including exploration and control thereof; science scholarships; scientific research, development, and demonstration, and projects thereof.

R 24–D 20 *(109th Congress)*

Sherwood Boehlert, N.Y.
Bart Gordon, Tenn.

Energy—Judy Biggert, Ill.
Environment, Technology, and Standards—Vernon J. Ehlers, Mich.

Research—Bob Inglis, S.C.
Space and Aeronautics—Ken Calvert, Calif.

SCIENCE AND TECHNOLOGY

D 24–R 20 *(110th Congress)*

Bart Gordon, Tenn.
Ralph M. Hall, Texas

Energy and Environment—Nick Lampson, Texas
Investigations and Oversight—Brad Miller, N.C.
Research and Science Education—Brian Baird, Wash.
Space and Aeronautics—Mark Udall, Colo.
Technology and Innovation—David Wu, Ore.

SELECT INTELLIGENCE

Legislative and budgetary authority over the National Security Agency and the director of central intelligence, the Defense Intelligence Agency, the National Security Agency, intelligence activities of the Federal Bureau of Investigation and other components of the federal intelligence community.

R 12–D 9 *(109th Congress)*

Peter Hoekstra, Mich.
Jane Harman, Calif.

Intelligence Policy—Jo Ann Davis, Va.
Oversight—William M. "Mac" Thornberry, Texas
Technical and Tactical Intelligence—Heather A. Wilson, N.M.
Terrorism, Human Intelligence, Analysis, and Counterintelligence—Randy "Duke" Cunningham, Calif.

D 9–R 6 *(110th Congress)*

Silvestre Reyes, Texas
Peter Hoekstra, Mich.

Intelligence Community Management—Anna G. Eshoo, Calif.
Oversight and Investigations—Robert E. "Bud" Cramer, Ala.
Technical and Tactical Intelligence—C.A. Dutch Ruppersberger, Md.
Terrorism, Human Intelligence, Analysis, and Counterintelligence—Mike Thompson, Calif.

SELECT ENERGY INDEPENDENCE AND GLOBAL WARMING

Investigate, study, make findings, and develop recommendations on policies, strategies, technologies, and other innovations, intended to reduce the dependence of the United States on foreign sources of energy and achieve substantial and permanent reductions in emissions and other activities that contribute to climate change and global warming. The committee had no legislative jurisdiction or authority to take legislative action on any bill or resolution. Nine members were appointed by the Speaker, who also named the chair, and six by the minority leader.

D 9–R 6 *(110th Congress; committee did not exist in 109th Congress)*

Edward J. Markey, Mass.
F. James Sensenbrenner Jr., Wis.

No standing subcommittees.

SMALL BUSINESS

Assistance to and protection of small business, including financial aid, regulatory flexibility, and paperwork reduction; participation of small business enterprises in federal procurement and government contracts.

R 18–D 15 *(109th Congress)*

Donald Manzullo, Ill.
Nydia M. Velázquez, N.Y.

Regulatory Reform and Oversight—Todd Akin, Mo.
Rural Enterprises, Agriculture, and Technology —Sam Graves, Mo.
Tax, Finance, and Exports—Jeb Bradley, N.H.
Workforce, Empowerment, and Government Programs—Marilyn Musgrave, Colo.

D 18–R 15 *(110th Congress)*

Nydia M. Velázquez, N.Y.
Steve Chabot, Ohio

Contracting and Technology—Bruce Braley, Iowa
Finance and Tax—Melissa Bean, Ill.
Investigations and Oversight—Jason Altmire, Pa.
Regulations, Healthcare, and Trade—Charlie Gonzalez, Texas
Rural and Urban Entrepreneurship—Heath Shuler, N.C.

STANDARDS OF OFFICIAL CONDUCT

Measures relating to the Code of Official Conduct.

R 5–D 5 *(109th Congress)*

Doc Hastings, Wash.
Alan B. Mollohan, W.Va.

D 5–R 5 *(110th Congress)*

Stephanie Tubbs Jones, Ohio
Doc Hastings, Wash.

TRANSPORTATION AND INFRASTRUCTURE

Transportation, including civil aviation, railroads, water transportation, transportation safety (except automobile safety), transportation infrastructure, transportation labor, and railroad retirement and unemployment (except revenue measures); water power; the Coast Guard; federal management of emergencies and natural disasters; flood control and improvement of waterways; inspection of merchant marine vessels; navigation and related laws; rules and international arrangements to prevent collisions at sea; measures, other than appropriations, that relate to construction, maintenance, and safety of roads; buildings and grounds of the Botanic Gardens, the Library of Congress, and the Smithsonian Institution and other government buildings within the District of Columbia; post offices, customhouses, federal courthouses, and merchant marine, except for national security aspects; pollution of navigable waters; and bridges and dams and related transportation regulatory agencies.

R 41–D 34 *(109th Congress)*

Don Young, Alaska
James L. Oberstar, Minn.

Aviation—John L. Mica, Fla.
Coast Guard and Maritime Transportation—Frank A. LoBiondo, N.J.
Economic Development, Public Buildings, and Emergency Management—Bill Shuster, Pa.
Highways, Transit, and Pipelines—Tom Petri, Wis.
Railroads—Steven C. LaTourette, Ohio
Water Resources and Environment—John J. "Jimmy" Duncan Jr., Tenn.

D 41–R 34 *(110th Congress)*

James L. Oberstar, Minn.
John L. Mica, Fla.

Aviation—Jerry F. Costello, Ill.
Coast Guard and Maritime Transportation—Elijah E. Cummings, Md.
Economic Development, Public Buildings, and Emergency Management—Eleanor Holmes Norton, D.C.
Highways and Transit—Peter A. DeFazio, Ore.
Railroads, Pipelines, and Hazardous Materials—Corrine Brown, Fla.
Water Resources and Environment—Eddie Bernice Johnson, Texas

VETERANS' AFFAIRS

Veterans' measures generally; cemeteries of the United States in which veterans of any war or conflict are or may be buried, whether in the United States or abroad, except cemeteries administered by the secretary of the interior; compensation, vocational rehabilitation, and education of veterans; life insurance issued by the government on account of service in the armed forces; pensions of all the wars of the United States; readjustment of service personnel to civil life; soldiers' and sailors', civil relief; veterans' hospitals, medical care, and treatment of veterans.

R 16–D 12 *(109th Congress)*

Steve Buyer, Ind.
Lane Evans, Ill.

Disability Assistance and Memorial Affairs—Jeff Miller, Fla.
Economic Opportunity—John Boozman, Ark.
Health—Henry E. Brown Jr., S.C.
Oversight and Investigations—Michael Bilirakis, Fla.

D 16–R 13 *(110th Congress)*

Bob Filner, Calif.
Steve Buyer, Ind.

Disability Assistance and Memorial Affairs—John Hall, N.Y.
Economic Opportunity—Stephanie Herseth-Sandlin, S.D.
Health—Michael H. Michaud, Maine
Oversight and Investigations—Harry E. Mitchell, Ariz.

WAYS AND MEANS

Revenue measures generally; reciprocal trade agreements; customs, collection districts, and ports of entry and delivery; revenue measures relating to the insular possessions; bonded debt of the United States; deposit of public moneys; transportation of dutiable goods; tax-exempt foundations and charitable trusts; national Social Security, except (1) health care and facilities programs that are supported from general revenues as opposed to payroll deductions and (2) work incentive programs.

R 24–D 17 *(109th Congress)*

Bill Thomas, Calif.
Charles B. Rangel, N.Y.

Health—Nancy L. Johnson, Conn.
Human Resources—Wally Herger, Calif.
Oversight—Jim Ramstad, Minn.
Select Revenue Measures—Dave Camp, Mich.
Social Security—Jim McCrery, La.
Trade—E. Clay Shaw Jr., Fla.

D 24–R 27 *(110th Congress)*

Charles B. Rangel, N.Y.
Jim McCrery, La.

Health—Pete Stark, Calif.
Income Security and Family Support—Jim McDermott, Wash.

Oversight—John Lewis, Ga.
Select Revenue Measures—Richard E. Neal, Mass.
Social Security—Michael R. McNulty, N.Y.
Trade—Sander M. Levin, Mich.

POLITICAL COMMITTEES

Democratic Congressional Campaign Committee (provides campaign support for Democratic House candidates)—Rahm Emanuel, Ill., chairman (109th Congress); Chris Van Hollen, Md., chairman (110th Congress)

Democratic Steering and Policy Committee (makes Democratic committee assignments)—Rosa DeLauro, Conn., and George Miller, Calif., co-chairs (109th and 110th Congresses)

National Republican Congressional Committee (provides campaign support for Republican House candidates)—Thomas M. Reynolds, N.Y., chairman (109th Congress); Tom Cole, Okla., chairman (110th Congress)

Republican Policy Committee (advises on party action and policy)—John Shadegg, Ariz., chairman (109th Congress); Thaddeus McCotter, Mich., chairman (110th Congress)

Joint Committees

Joint committees are set up to examine specific questions and are established by public law. Membership is drawn from both chambers and both parties. When a senator serves as chairman, the vice chairman usually is a representative, and vice versa. The chairmanship traditionally rotates from one chamber to the other at the beginning of each Congress (except for the Committee on Taxation chairmanship, which rotates at the start of each session).

ECONOMIC

Studies and investigates all recommendations in the president's annual *Economic Report to Congress.* Reports findings and recommendations to the House and Senate.

Rep. H. James Saxton, N.J., chairman (109th Congress)

Sen. Robert F. Bennett, Utah, vice chairman (109th Congress)

Sen. Charles E. Schumer, N.Y., chairman (110th Congress)

Rep. Carolyn B. Maloney, N.Y., vice chairwoman (110th Congress)

No standing subcommittees.

LIBRARY

Management and expansion of the Library of Congress; receipt of gifts for the benefit of the library; development and maintenance of the Botanic Garden; placement of statues and other works of art in the Capitol.

Rep. Bob Ney, Ohio, chairman (109th Congress)

Sen. Ted Stevens, Alaska, vice chairman (109th Congress)

Sen. Dianne Feinstein, Calif. (110th Congress)

Rep. Juanita Millender-McDonald, Calif. (110th Congress)

No standing subcommittees.

PRINTING

Probes inefficiency and waste in the printing, binding, and distribution of federal government publications. Oversees arrangement and style of the *Congressional Record.*

Sen. Trent Lott, Miss., chairman (109th Congress)

Rep. Bob Ney Ohio, vice chairman (109th Congress)

Sen. Dianne Feinstein, Calif. (110th Congress)

Rep. Juanita Millender-McDonald, Calif. (110th Congress)

No standing subcommittees.

TAXATION

Operation, effects, and administration of the federal system of internal revenue taxes; measures and methods for simplification of taxes.

Rep Bill Thomas, Calif., chairman (109th Congress)

Sen. Charles E. Grassley, Iowa, vice chairman (109th Congress)

Rep. Charles B. Rangel, N.Y., chairman (110th Congress)

Sen. Max Baucus, Mont., vice chairman (110th Congress)

No standing subcommittees.

Postelection Sessions

A postelection session of Congress often is labeled a lame duck session. It takes place after an election for the next Congress but before the official end of the current Congress. As a result, members who participate in the lame duck session are from the existing, or current, Congress, not from the Congress that will convene as a result of the just-held elections.

Lame duck sessions in the modern sense began in 1935 after the Twentieth Amendment to the Constitution was ratified in 1933. This amendment specified that regular congressional sessions would begin on Jan. 3 of each year unless Congress passed a law designating a different date. Also, terms of members of Congress begin and end on Jan. 3 of odd-numbered years, regardless of the date that a Congress officially ends its session. Originally the Constitution specified much later starting dates in recognition of the difficulty of travel in the early years of the nation, but those dates meant that lame duck sessions occurred in the second session of every Congress. In the modern sense, post-1935, a lame duck session is any meeting of Congress after election day in even-numbered years but before the following Jan. 3.

Between 1935 and 2008, Congress held seventeen lame duck sessions.

1941. The 76th Congress actually had adjourned in 1939, but President Franklin D. Roosevelt called the legislators into special session—technically, the third session of that Congress—to deal with the threat of war in Europe. However, little of substance was accomplished during the lame duck session.

1942. By this year the United States was at war with Germany, Japan, and Italy, but little was done during the period as legislators decided to leave many major decisions to the next Congress. Congress did approve bills on overtime pay for government workers and to provide for the military draft of eighteen- and nineteen-year-old men.

1944. World War II was well along by this time, which meant Congress faced a host of exceptionally important issues, including postwar universal military training, continuing the war effort, Social Security taxes, a rivers and harbors bill, and various postwar reconstruction matters. But like the previous several lame duck sessions, legislators decided to postpone most actions until the new Congress convened in 1945.

1948. The 1948 postelection session of the 80th Congress lasted only two hours. Both chambers swore in new members, approved several minor resolutions, and received last-minute reports from committees. In addition to final floor action, several committees resumed work. The most active was the House Un-American Activities Committee, which continued its investigation of alleged communist espionage in the federal government.

1950. After the 1950 elections, President Harry S. Truman sent a "must" agenda to the lame duck session of the 81st Congress. The president's list included supplemental defense appropriations, an excess profits tax, aid to Yugoslavia, a three-month extension of federal rent controls, and statehood for Hawaii and Alaska. During a marathon session that lasted until only a few hours before its successor took over, the 81st Congress acted on all of the president's legislative items except the statehood bills, which were blocked by a Senate filibuster.

Congressional Lame Duck Sessions

Year	*Congress*	*Dates*
1941	76th	Adjourned Jan. 3, 1941*
1942	77th	Adjourned Dec. 16, 1942*
1944	78th	Nov. 14, 1944—Dec. 19, 1944
1948	80th	Dec. 31, 1948 (2-hour session)
1950	81st	Nov. 27, 1950—Jan. 2, 1951
1954	83rd	Nov. 8, 1954—Dec. 2, 1954 (Senate)
1970	91st	Nov. 16, 1970—Jan. 2, 1971
1974	93rd	Nov. 18, 1974—Dec. 20, 1974
1980	96th	Nov. 12, 1980—Dec. 16, 1980
1982	97th	Nov. 29, 1982—Dec. 23, 1982 (Senate)
		Nov. 29, 1982—Dec. 21, 1982 (House)
1994	103rd	Nov. 29, 1994 (House)
		Nov. 30, 1994—Dec. 1, 1994 (Senate)
1998	105th	Dec. 17, 1998—Dec. 19, 1998 (House)
2000	106th	Nov. 13, 2000—Dec. 15, 2000 (House)
		Nov. 14, 2000—Dec 15, 2000
2002	107th	Adjourned Nov. 20, 2002 (Senate)*
		Adjourned Nov. 22, 2002 (House)*
2004	108th	Nov. 16, 2004—Dec. 7, 2004 (House)
		Nov. 16, 2004—Dec. 8, 2004 (Senate)
2006	109th	Nov. 13, 2006—Dec. 8, 2006 (House)
		Nov. 13, 2006—Dec. 8, 2006 (Senate
2008	110th	Nov. 19, 2008—Dec. 10, 2008 (House)
		Nov. 17, 2008—Dec. 11, 2008 (Senate)

*Congress stayed in session.

1954. Only one chamber of the 83rd Congress convened after the 1954 elections. The Senate returned Nov. 8 to hold what has been called a "censure session," a continuing investigation into the conduct of Sen. Joseph R. McCarthy, R-Wis. (1947–1957). By a 67–22 roll call, the Senate Dec. 2 voted to "condemn" McCarthy for his behavior. In other postelection floor action, the Senate passed a series of miscellaneous and administrative resolutions and swore in new members.

1970. President Richard Nixon criticized the lame duck Congress as one that had "seemingly lost the capacity to decide and the will to act." Filibusters and intense controversy contributed to inaction on the president's request for trade legislation and welfare reform. Congress nevertheless claimed some substantive results during the session, which ended Jan. 2, 1971. Several major appropriations bills were cleared for presidential signature. Congress also approved foreign aid to Cambodia, provided interim funding for the supersonic transport (SST) plane, and repealed the Tonkin Gulf Resolution that had been used as a basis for American military involvement in Vietnam.

1974. In a session that ran from Nov. 18 to Dec. 20, 1974, the 93rd Congress cleared several important bills for presidential signature, including a mass transit bill, a Labor-Health, Education and Welfare appropriations bill and a foreign assistance package. A House-Senate conference committee reached agreement on a major strip-mining bill, but President Gerald R. Ford vetoed it. Congress approved the nomination of Nelson A. Rockefeller as vice president. It also overrode presidential vetoes of two bills—one broadening the Freedom of Information Act, a second authorizing educational benefits for Korean War and Vietnam-era veterans.

1980. The lame duck session of the 96th Congress was productive, at least until Dec. 5, the original adjournment date set by congressional leaders. By that date a budget had been approved, along with a budget reconciliation measure. Ten regular appropriations bills had cleared, though one subsequently was vetoed. Congress had approved two major environmental measures—an Alaskan lands bill and toxic waste "superfund" legislation—as well as a three-year extension of general revenue sharing.

After Dec. 5, however, the legislative pace slowed noticeably. Action on a continuing appropriations resolution for those departments and agencies whose regular funding had not been cleared was delayed, first by a filibuster on a fair housing bill and later by more than 100 "Christmas tree" amendments, including a $10,000-a-year pay raise for members. After the conference report failed in the Senate and twice was rewritten, the bill was shorn of virtually all its "ornaments" and finally cleared by both chambers on Dec. 16.

1982. Despite the reluctance of congressional leaders, President Ronald Reagan urged the convening of a postelection session at the end of the 97th Congress, principally to pass remaining appropriations bills. Rising unemployment—and Democratic election gains in the House—made job creation efforts the focus of the lame duck Congress, however. Overriding the objections of Republican conservatives, Congress passed Reagan-backed legislation raising the federal gasoline tax from 4 cents to 9 cents a gallon to pay for highway repairs and mass transit. Supporters said the legislation would help alleviate unemployment by creating 300,000 jobs.

Congress eventually cleared four additional appropriations bills, packaging the remaining six in a continuing appropriations resolution that also included a pay raise for House members. Conferees dropped funding for emergency jobs programs to avert a threatened veto of the resolution. The lame duck session also was highlighted by Congress's refusal to fund production and procurement of the first five MX intercontinental missiles. This was the first time in recent history that either house of Congress had denied a president's request to fund production of a strategic weapon.

1994. Congress reconvened to reconsider, and ultimately approve, the Uruguay Round pact strengthening the General Agreement on Tariffs and Trade (GATT). The bill had been submitted Sept. 27, 1994, by President Bill Clinton under fast-track rules for trade legislation, which allowed each chamber only an up-or-down vote on the bill without amendments. But the rules also allowed every chairman with jurisdiction to take up to forty-five days to review the bill. Sen. Ernest F. Hollings, D-S.C., demanded his forty-five days, forcing the Senate leadership to schedule a two-day lame duck session. Clinton asked the House to approve the bill before the October adjournment but the Democratic leadership delayed consideration. The House reconvened for a one-day session Nov. 29 and passed the GATT bill by a wide margin. Following a twenty-hour debate Nov. 30 and Dec. 1, the Senate gave overwhelming approval to the bill.

1998. The House reconvened in December for a remarkable and historic event: to vote on the impeachment of a president. After a tumultuous political year, House Republicans pushed through articles of impeachment for what they believe was President Clinton's lying under oath. The event was characterized by a year-long political chasm between House Republicans, who led the effort for impeachment, and Democrats in both chambers. It also was characterized by charges of sexual misconduct involving Clinton and release of a controversial and in places graphic report about sexual conduct of the president that Republicans defended as necessary to prove their case. The report was prepared by an independent prosecutor. In the short time the House was in session it voted—largely along party lines—in favor of impeachment charges, which would be tried—and rejected—by the Senate early in the following year.

2000. Congress returned after the 2000 elections largely to complete action of appropriations measures that had remained unfinished as President Clinton continued to wrestle with his Republican adversaries in Congress over spending priorities. Partisan fighting over spending and taxes had been one of the principal matters that divided the White House and Capitol Hill during the latter years of Clinton's presidency. The year 2000 was no exception as Congress was unable to avert its annual pileup of appropriations bills at the end of the session. The pileup was exacerbated in 2000 because of the controversial presidential elections that were not decided until a Supreme Court decision in December awarding contested Florida electoral votes to Republican George W. Bush. With the GOP about to reclaim the White House, party members in Congress suddenly had new leverage in the final bargaining over appropriations. The lame duck session lumbered into mid-December when an omnibus package was used to close the books on four spending bills and move other unrelated legislation.

2004. Congress came back after Republicans scored impressive gains in the fall elections that returned George W. Bush to the White House and increased GOP control of both chambers of Congress. The additional votes meant the GOP was strongly positioned to push Bush's legislative program in the 109th Congress. But before the could get there, important legislative matters remained for the 108th Congress. The most important was a sweeping overhaul of the U.S. intelligence community, Congress's last major act of the year. It came only at the prodding of the independent, bipartisan National Commission on Terrorist Attacks Upon the United States—better known as the 9/11 commission—and the powerful lobbying of some of the victims' families of those attacks. In addition, all but four of the appropriations bills had been left hanging when Congress went out of the elections break. Congress bundled the other nine into an omnibus bill during the lame duck session and cleared it on Nov. 20.

2006. Legislators returned after the 2006 midterm elections to a wholly new political playing field because Democrats had recaptured control of both chambers, although the Senate by a narrow one-vote margin. The principal agenda for the postelection session was completion of appropriations bills, only two of which—defense and homeland security—had been completed. A continuing resolution that kept the government operating was set to expire Nov. 17. Dealing with several expiring tax benefits also was on the list of actions needed. But much of the plan never got going as Democrats decided to fund the government until Feb. 15, 2007, through additional continuing resolutions, thereby leaving all the other regular appropriation bills to die. But some work was done. A package of tax benefits was completed in connection with a trade package. Perhaps most significant, Congress approved a bill allowing President Bush to negotiate a nuclear power agreement with India, one of the president's most significant foreign policy victories. The Senate also confirmed Robert M. Gates as defense secretary to replace the controversial Donald Rumsfeld.

2008. The main focus of attention in the postelection session was the continuing financial crisis in the United States and worldwide, but the elections, like those two years earlier, had put a new cast on events. In the elections, Democrats had improved their margin in the House and significantly increased it in the Senate, and they had won the presidential contest when Barack Obama defeated John McCain by a comfortable 53–47 percent margin. This meant that governmental activity to stave off an economic collapse that many economists thought would rival the Great Depression of the 1930s was left to coordination of action between the outgoing Bush administration and the new Obama administration. Congress, which had passed a $700 billion package of aid for the financial services industry before the election, was left with little to do. One major effort failed: with the nation's three principal auto manufacturers facing bankruptcy, Congress considered providing $14 billion in loans to the companies from an existing program. The House passed the bill, but the Senate did not go along. As a result, Bush later provided $13.4 billion in loans to the automakers from the funds previously approved to save the financial services industry.

Senate Cloture Votes, 1917–2008

The filibuster, identified by the public primarily as nonstop speech, has been an enshrined Senate tradition throughout the chamber's history but became a focus of increasing criticism in the twentieth century as a device to thwart majority decisions. It was not until 1917 that the Senate adopted a rule, known as cloture, that allowed a majority—albeit a supermajority—to end a filibuster and bring a measure to a vote. The number of votes required to invoke cloture has varied over the years, standing at sixty in 2005 if there are no Senate vacancies. (The actual rules required a three-fifths majority of members to invoke cloture; the Senate has 100 members.)

Even with the rule in place, however, the number of filibusters and attempts to invoke cloture were limited until the 92nd Congress in 1971–1973. From that time on, and especially after 2000, cloture attempts expanded greatly as the character of the Senate changed from what one scholar called "communitarian" and deliberative to individualistic, increasingly partisan, and media-driven. This pattern was seen during the 1990s also. In both decades, deep-seated partisan divisions in Congress led both parties to try whatever tools worked to block the initiatives or judicial or executive appointments of the other.

In the ten Congresses during the twenty years from 1971 to 1991 cloture was attempted no less than thirteen times in each two-year period, and on average twenty-five times each Congress. As dramatic as that growth was, it paled against the expansion in the following seven Congresses from 1991 through 2008. During the nine Congresses from the 102nd through the 110th cloture votes were taken an average of nearly forty-six times for each two-year period. *(Table, p. 1034)*

During President Bill Clinton's second term, a particularly partisan period from 1997 to 2001, a substantial number of cloture votes—more than 35 percent—were decided by a majority of 70 to 100 votes in favor. This higher success rate (than in previous decades) suggested that cloture was used less in connection with debates on far-reaching national issues—as was often the case in the past—and more for political and legislative maneuvering. The pattern in Clinton's second term occurred again in both President George W. Bush's terms, from 2001 to 2009.

CHANGES IN THE RULE

The Senate's ultimate check on the filibuster is the provision for cloture, or limitation of debate, contained in Rule 22 of its Standing Rules. The original Rule 22 was adopted in 1917 following a furor over the "talking to death" of a proposal by President Woodrow Wilson for arming American merchant ships before the United States entered World War I. The new cloture rule required the votes of two-thirds of all the senators present and voting to invoke cloture. In 1949, during a parliamentary skirmish preceding scheduled consideration of a Fair Employment Practices Commission bill, the requirement was raised to two-thirds of the entire Senate membership.

A revision of the rule in 1959 provided for limitation of debate by a vote of two-thirds of the senators present and voting, two days after a cloture petition was submitted by sixteen senators. If cloture was adopted by the Senate, further debate was limited to one hour for each senator on the bill itself and on all amendments affecting it. No new amendments could be offered except by unanimous consent. Amendments that were not germane to the pending business and dilatory motions were out of order. The rule applied both to regular legislation and to motions to change the Standing Rules.

Rule 22 was revised significantly in 1975 by lowering the vote needed for cloture to three-fifths of the Senate membership (sixty if there were no vacancies). That revision applied to any matter except proposed rules changes, for which the old requirement of a two-thirds majority of senators present and voting still applied.

In a further revision of the rule, the Senate in 1979 limited postcloture delaying tactics by providing that once cloture was invoked, a final vote had to be taken after no more than 100 hours of debate. All time spent on quorum calls, roll-call votes and other parliamentary procedures was to be included in the 100-hour limit.

When the Senate decided to televise its floor proceedings in 1986, it further tightened up the time on postcloture debate. Rule 22 was revised to reduce to thirty hours, from 100, the time allowed for debate, procedural moves and roll-call votes after the Senate had invoked cloture to end a filibuster.

Following is a list of the 819 cloture votes taken between 1917, when Senate Rule 22 was adopted, and the end of 2009; 331 of the votes (in **bold type**) were successful.

Issue	*Date*	*Vote*	*Yeas needed*
Versailles Treaty	Nov. 15, 1919	78–16	63
Emergency tariff	Feb. 2, 1921	36–35	48
Tariff bill	July 7, 1922	45–35	54
World Court	Jan. 25, 1926	68–26	63
Migratory birds	June 1, 1926	46–33	53
Branch banking	Feb. 15, 1927	65–18	56
Disabled officers	Feb. 26, 1927	51–36	58
Colorado River	Feb. 26, 1927	32–59	61
D.C. buildings	Feb. 28, 1927	52–31	56
Prohibition Bureau	Feb. 28, 1927	55–27	55
Banking Act	Jan. 19, 1933	58–30	59
Anti-lynching	Jan. 27, 1938	37–51	59
Anti-lynching	Feb. 16, 1938	42–46	59
Anti-poll tax	Nov. 23, 1942	37–41	52
Anti-poll tax	May 15, 1944	36–44	54
Fair Employment Practices Commission	Feb. 9, 1946	48–36	56
British loan	May 7, 1946	41–41	55
Labor disputes	May 25, 1946	3–77	54
Anti-poll tax	July 31, 1946	39–33	48
Fair Employment	May 19, 1950	52–32	64
Fair Employment	July 12, 1950	55–33	64

Issue	*Date*	*Vote*	*Yeas needed*
Atomic Energy Act	July 26, 1954	44–42	64
Civil Rights Act	March 10, 1960	42–53	64
Amend Rule 22	Sept. 19, 1961	37–43	54
Literacy tests	May 9, 1962	43–53	64
Literacy tests	May 14, 1962	42–52	63
Comsat Act	Aug. 14, 1962	63–27	60
Amend Rule 22	Feb. 7, 1963	54–42	64
Civil Rights Act	June 10, 1964	71–29	67
Legislative reapportionment	Sept. 10, 1964	30–63	62
Voting Rights Act	May 25, 1965	70–30	67
Right-to-work repeal	Oct. 11, 1965	45–47	62
Right-to-work repeal	Feb. 8, 1966	51–48	66
Right-to-work repeal	Feb. 10, 1966	50–49	66
Civil Rights Act	Sept. 14, 1966	54–42	64
Civil Rights Act	Sept. 19, 1966	52–41	62
D.C. Home Rule	Oct. 10, 1966	41–37	52
Amend Rule 22	Jan. 24, 1967	53–46	66
Open Housing	Feb. 20, 1968	55–37	62
Open Housing	Feb. 26, 1968	56–36	62
Open Housing	March 1, 1968	59–35	63
Open Housing	March 4, 1968	65–32	65
Fortas nomination	Oct. 1, 1968	45–43	59
Amend Rule 22	Jan. 16, 1969	51–47	66
Amend Rule 22	Jan. 28, 1969	50–42	62
Electoral College	Sept. 17, 1970	54–36	60
Electoral College	Sept. 29, 1970	53–34	58
Supersonic transport	Dec. 19, 1970	43–48	61
Supersonic transport	Dec. 22, 1970	42–44	58
Amend Rule 22	Feb. 18, 1971	48–37	57
Amend Rule 22	Feb. 23, 1971	50–36	58
Amend Rule 22	March 2, 1971	48–36	56
Amend Rule 22	March 9, 1971	55–39	63
Military Draft	June 23, 1971	65–27	62
Lockheed loan	July 26, 1971	42–47	60
Lockheed loan	July 28, 1971	59–39	66
Lockheed loan	July 30, 1971	53–37	60
Military Draft	Sept. 21, 1971	61–30	61
Rehnquist nomination	Dec. 10, 1971	52–42	63
Equal job opportunity	Feb. 1, 1972	48–37	57
Equal job opportunity	Feb. 3, 1972	53–35	59
Equal job opportunity	Feb. 22, 1972	71–23	63
U.S.-Soviet arms pact	Sept. 14, 1972	76–15	61
Consumer Agency	Sept. 29, 1972	47–29	51
Consumer Agency	Oct. 3, 1972	55–32	58
Consumer Agency	Oct. 5, 1972	52–30	55
School busing	Oct. 10, 1972	45–37	55
School busing	Oct. 11, 1972	49–39	59
School busing	Oct. 12, 1972	49–38	58
Voter registration	April 30, 1973	56–31	58
Voter registration	May 3, 1973	60–34	63
Voter registration	May 9, 1973	67–32	66
Public campaign financing	Dec. 2, 1973	47–33	54
Public campaign financing	Dec. 3, 1973	49–39	59
Rhodesian chrome ore	Dec. 11, 1973	59–35	63
Rhodesian chrome ore	Dec. 13, 1973	62–33	64
Legal services program	Dec. 13, 1973	60–36	64
Legal services program	Dec. 14, 1973	56–29	57
Rhodesian chrome ore	Dec. 18, 1973	63–26	60
Legal services program	Jan. 30, 1974	68–29	65
Genocide Treaty	Feb. 5, 1974	55–36	61
Genocide Treaty	Feb. 6, 1974	55–38	62
Government pay raise	March 6, 1974	67–31	66
Public campaign financing	April 4, 1974	60–36	64
Public campaign financing	April 9, 1974	64–30	63
Public debt ceiling	June 19, 1974	50–43	62
Public debt ceiling	June 19, 1974	45–48	62
Public debt ceiling	June 26, 1974	48–50	66
Consumer Agency	July 30, 1974	56–42	66
Consumer Agency	Aug. 1, 1974	59–39	66
Consumer Agency	Aug. 20, 1974	59–35	63
Consumer Agency	Sept. 19, 1974	64–34	66
Export-Import Bank	Dec. 3,1974	51–39	60
Export-Import Bank	Dec. 4, 1974	48–44	62
Trade reform	Dec. 13, 1974	71–19	60
Fiscal 1975 supplemental funds	Dec. 14, 1974	56–27	56
Export-Import Bank	Dec. 14, 1974	49–35	56
Export-Import Bank	Dec. 16, 1974	54–34	59
Social services programs	Dec. 17, 1974	70–23	62
Tax law changes	Dec. 17, 1974	67–25	62
Rail Reorganization Act	Feb. 26, 1975	86–8	63
Amend Rule 22	March 5, 1975	73–21	63
Amend Rule 22	March 7, 1975	73–21	63
Tax reduction	March 20, 1975	59–38	60
Tax reduction	March 21, 1975	83–13	60
Consumer Advocacy Agency	May 13, 1975	71–27	60
Senate staffing	June 11, 1975	77–19	64
New Hampshire Senate seat	June 24, 1975	57–39	60
New Hampshire Senate seat	June 25, 1975	56–41	60
New Hampshire Senate seat	June 26, 1975	54–40	60
New Hampshire Senate seat	July 8, 1975	57–38	60
New Hampshire Senate seat	July 9, 1975	57–38	60
New Hampshire Senate seat	July 10, 1975	54–38	60
Voting Rights Act	July 21, 1975	72–19	60
Voting Rights Act	July 23, 1975	76–20	60
Oil price decontrol	July 30, 1975	54–38	60
Anti-school busing amendments	Sept. 23, 1975	46–48	60
Anti-school busing amendments	Sept. 24, 1975	64–33	60
Common-site picketing	Nov. 11, 1975	66–30	60
Common-site picketing	Nov. 14, 1975	58–31	60
Common-site picketing	Nov. 18, 1975	62–37	60
Rail reorganization	Dec. 4, 1975	61–27	60
New York City aid	Dec. 5, 1975	70–27	60
Rice Production Act	Feb. 3, 1976	70–19	60
Antitrust amendments	June 3, 1976	67–22	60
Antitrust amendments	Aug. 31, 1976	63–27	60
Civil rights attorneys' fees	Sept. 23, 1976	63–26	60
Draft resisters pardons	Jan. 24, 1977	53–43	60
Campaign financing	July 29, 1977	49–45	60
Campaign financing	Aug. 1, 1977	47–46	60
Campaign financing	Aug. 2, 1977	52–46	60
Natural gas pricing	Sept. 26, 1977	77–17	60
Labor Law revision	June 7, 1978	42–47	60
Labor Law revision	June 8, 1978	49–41	60
Labor Law revision	June 13, 1978	54–43	60
Labor Law revision	June 14, 1978	58–41	60
Labor Law revision	June 15, 1978	58–39	60
Labor Law revision	June 22, 1978	53–45	60
Revenue Act of 1978	Oct. 9, 1978	62–28	60
energy taxes	Oct. 14, 1978	71–13	60
Windfall profits tax	Dec. 12, 1979	53–46	60
Windfall profits tax	Dec. 13, 1979	56–40	60
Windfall profits tax	Dec. 14, 1979	56–39	60
Windfall profits tax	Dec. 17, 1979	84–14	60
Lubbers nomination	April 21, 1980	46–60	60
Lubbers nomination	April 22, 1980	62–34	60

Issue	*Date*	*Vote*	*Yeas needed*
Rights of institutionalized	April 28, 1980	44–39	60
Rights of institutionalized	April 29, 1980	56–34	60
Rights of institutionalized	April 30, 1980	53–35	60
Rights of institutionalized	May 1, 1980	60–34	60
Bottlers' antitrust immunity	May 15, 1980	86–6	60
Draft registration funding	June 10, 1980	62–32	60
Zimmerman nomination	Aug. 1, 1980	51–35	60
Zimmerman nomination	Aug. 4, 1980	45–31	60
Zimmerman nomination	Aug. 5, 1980	63–31	60
Alaska lands	Aug. 18, 1980	63–25	60
Vessel tonnage/strip mining	Aug. 21, 1980	61–32	60
Fair Housing amendments	Dec. 3, 1980	51–39	60
Fair Housing amendments	Dec. 4, 1980	62–32	60
Fair Housing amendments	Dec. 9, 1980	54–43	60
Breyer nomination	Dec. 9, 1980	68–28	60
Justice Department authorization	July 10, 1981	38–48	60
Justice Department authorization	July 13, 1981	54–32	60
Justice Department authorization	July 29, 1981	59–37	60
Justice Department authorization	Sept. 10, 1981	57–33	60
Justice Department authorization	Sept. 16, 1981	61–36	60
Justice Department authorization	Dec. 10, 1981	64–35	60
State, Justice, Commerce, Judiciary funds	Dec. 11, 1981	59–35	60
Justice Department authorization	Feb. 9, 1982	63–33	60
Broadcast Senate proceedings	April 20, 1982	47–51	60
Criminal Code Reform Act	April 27, 1982	45–46	60
1982 supplemental funds	May 27, 1982	95–2	60
Voting Rights Act	June 15, 1982	86–8	60
Debt limit increase	Sept. 9, 1982	41–47	60
Debt limit increase	Sept. 13, 1982	45–35	60
Debt limit increase	Sept. 15, 1982	50–44	60
Debt limit increase	Sept. 20, 1982	50–39	60
Debt limit increase	Sept. 21, 1982	53–47	60
Debt limit increase	Sept. 22, 1982	54–46	60
Debt limit increase	Sept. 23, 1982	53–45	60
Antitrust Equal Enforcement Act	Dec. 2, 1982	38–58	60
Antitrust Equal Enforcement Act	Dec. 2, 1982	44–51	60
Transportation Assistance Act	Dec. 13, 1982	75–13	60
Transportation Assistance Act	Dec. 16, 1982	48–50	60
Transportation Assistance Act	Dec. 16, 1982	5–93	60
Transportation Assistance Act	Dec. 19, 1982	89–5	60
Transportation Assistance Act	Dec. 20, 1982	87–8	60
Transportation Assistance Act	Dec. 23, 1982	81–5	60
Jobs funding/interest withholding	March 16, 1983	50–48	60
Jobs funding/interest withholding	March 16, 1983	59–39	60
International trade/interest withholding	April 19, 1983	34–53	60
International trade /interest withholding	April 19, 1983	39–59	60
Defense authorizations, 1984	July 21, 1983	55–41	60
Radio broadcasting to Cuba	Aug. 3, 1983	62–33	60
National Gas Policy Act	Nov. 3, 1983	86–7	60
Capital punishment	Feb. 9, 1984	65–26	60
Hydroelectric power plants	July 30, 1984	60–28	60
Wilkinson nomination	July 31, 1984	57–39	60
Agriculture funds, fiscal 1985	Aug. 6, 1984	54–31	60
Agriculture funds, fiscal 1985	Aug. 8, 1984	68–30	60
Wilkinson nomination	Aug. 9, 1984	65–32	60
Financial Services Act	Sept. 10, 1984	89–3	60
Financial Services Act	Sept. 13, 1984	92–6	60
Broadcasting of Senate proceedings	Sept. 18, 1984	73–26	60
Broadcasting Senate proceedings	Sept. 21, 1984	37–44	60
Surface Transportation Act	Sept. 24, 1984	70–12	60
Continuing funds	Sept. 29, 1984	92–4	60
Anti-apartheid	July 10, 1985	88–8	60
Line-item veto	July 18, 1985	57–42	60
Line-item veto	July 23, 1985	57–41	60
Line-item veto	July 24, 1985	58–40	60
Anti-apartheid	Sept. 9, 1985	53–34	60
Anti-apartheid	Sept. 11, 1985	57–41	60
Anti-apartheid	Sept. 12, 1985	11–88	60
Debt limit/balanced budget	Oct. 6, 1985	57–38	64
Debt limit/balanced budget	Oct. 9, 1985[1]	53–39	62
Conrail sale	Jan. 23, 1986	90–7	60
Conrail sale	Jan. 30, 1986	70–27	60
Fitzwater nomination	March 18, 1986	64–33	60
Washington airports transfer	March 21, 1986	50–39	60
Washington airports transfer	March 25, 1986	66–32	60
Hobbs Act amendments	April 16, 1986	44–54	60
Defense authorization, fiscal 1987	Aug. 6, 1986	53–46	60
Aid to Nicaraguan contras	Aug. 13, 1986	59–40	60
South Africa sanctions	Aug. 13, 1986	89–11	60
Aid to Nicaraguan contras	Aug. 13, 1986	62–37	60
Rehnquist nomination	Sept. 17, 1986	68–31	60
Product liability reform	Sept. 25, 1986	97–1	60
Omnibus drug bill	Oct. 15, 1986	58–38	60
Immigration reform	Oct. 17, 1986	69–21	60
Contra aid moratorium	March 23, 1987	46–45	60
Contra aid moratorium	March 24, 1987	50–50	60
Contra aid moratorium	March 25, 1987	54–46	60
Relief for the homeless	April 9, 1987	68–29	60
Defense authorization, fiscal 1988	May 15, 1987	52–36	60
Defense authorization, fiscal 1988	May 19, 1987	58–41	60
Defense authorization, fiscal 1988	May 20, 1987	59–39	60
Campaign finance	June 9, 1987	52–47	60
Campaign finance	June 16, 1987	49–46	60
Campaign finance	June 17, 1987	51–47	60
Campaign finance	June 18, 1987	50–47	60
Campaign finance	June 19, 1987	45–43	60
Kuwaiti tanker reflagging	July 9, 1987	57–42	60
Kuwaiti tanker reflagging	July 14, 1987	53–40	60
Kuwaiti tanker reflagging	July 15, 1987	54–44	60
Wells nomination	Sept. 9, 1987	65–24	60
Campaign finance	Sept. 10, 1987	53–42	60
Campaign finance	Sept. 15, 1987	51–44	60
Kuwaiti tanker escort	Oct. 1, 1987	54–45	60
Defense authorization, fiscal 1988	Oct. 1, 1987	41–58	60
Verity nomination	Oct. 13, 1987	85–8	60
War powers compliance	Oct. 20, 1987	67–28	60
Nuclear waste depository	Nov. 10, 1987	87–0	60

Issue	*Date*	*Vote*	*Yeas needed*
Campaign finance	Feb. 26, 1988	53–41	60
Polygraph protection	March 3, 1988	77–19	60
Intelligence oversight	March 15, 1988	73–18	60
Risk notification	March 23, 1988	33–59	60
Risk notification	March 24, 1988	2–93	60
Risk notification	March 28, 1988	41–44	60
Risk notification	March 29, 1988	42–52	60
Campaign spending limitations	April 21, 1988	52–42	60
Campaign spending limitations	April 22, 1988	53–37	60
Immigration legalization program extension	April 28, 1988	40–56	60
Drug-Related killings death penalty	June 9, 1988	70–26	60
Great Smoky Mountain Wilderness Act	June 20, 1988	49–35	60
Great Smoky Mountain Wilderness Act	June 21, 1988	54–42	60
Plant-closing notification	June 29, 1988	58–39	60
Plant-closing notification	July 6, 1988	88–5	60
Textile import quotas	Sept. 7, 1988	68–29	60
Minimum wage restoration	Sept. 22, 1988	53–43	60
Minimum wage restoration	Sept. 23, 1988	56–35	60
Parental and medical leave	Oct. 3, 1988	85–6	60
Parental and medical leave	Oct. 7, 1988	50–46	60
Defense authorization, fiscal 1990	Aug. 2, 1989	84–13	60
Airline smoking ban	Sept. 14, 1989	77–21	60
Eastern Airlines strike commission	Oct. 3, 1989	61–36	60
Nicaraguan election aid	Oct. 13, 1989	52–42	60
Nicaraguan election aid	Oct. 17, 1989	74–25	60
Eastern Airlines strike commission	Oct. 26, 1989	62–38	60
Capital gains tax cut	Nov. 14, 1989	51–47	60
Capital gains tax cut	Nov. 15, 1989	51–47	60
Government pay-and-ethics package	Nov. 17, 1989	90–9	60
Armenian genocide day	Feb. 22, 1990	49–49	60
Armenian genocide day	Feb. 27, 1990	48–51	60
Hatch Act revisions	May 1, 1990	70–28	60
AIDS emergency relief	May 15, 1990	95–3	60
Chemical weapons sanctions	May 17, 1990	87–4	60
Omnibus crime package	June 5, 1990	54–37	60
Omnibus crime package	June 7, 1990	57–37	60
Air travel rights for the blind	June 12, 1990	56–44	60
Civil Rights Act of 1990	July 17, 1990	62–38	60
Defense authorization, fiscal1991	Aug. 3, 1990	58–41	60
Motor Vehicle Fuel Efficiency Act	Sept. 14, 1990	68–28	60
Motor Vehicle Fuel Efficiency Act	Sept. 25, 1990	57–42	60
Title X family planning amendments	Sept. 26, 1990	50–46	60
National motor-voter registration	Sept. 26, 1990	55–42	60
Foreign operations funds, fiscal 1991	Oct. 12, 1990	51–38	60
Vertical price fixing	May 7, 1991	61–37	60
Vertical price fixing	May 8, 1991	63–35	60
Crime bill	June 28, 1991	41–58	60
Crime bill	July 10, 1991	56–43	60
Crime bill	July 10, 1991	71–27	60
National motor-voter registration	July 18, 1991	57–41	60
VA-HUD funds, fiscal 1992	July 18, 1991	57–40	60
National motor-voter registration	July 18, 1991	59–40	60
Foreign aid authorization	July 24, 1991	87–10	60
Foreign aid authorization	July 25, 1991	52–44	60
Foreign aid authorization	July 25, 1991	63–33	60
Extended unemployment benefits	July 29, 1991	96–1	60
Defense authorization, fiscal 1992	Aug. 2, 1991	58–40	60
Interior funds, fiscal 1992	Sept. 19, 1991	55–41	60
Federal Facility Compliance Act	Oct. 17, 1991	85–14	60
Civil Rights Act	Oct. 22, 1991	93–4	60
National energy policy	Nov. 1, 1991	50–44	60
Banking reform	Nov. 13, 1991	76–19	60
Iranian hostage release investigation	Nov. 22, 1991	51–43	60
Crime conference report	Nov. 27, 1991	49–38	60
School improvement bill	Jan. 21, 1992	93–0	60
National energy strategy	Feb. 4, 1992	90–5	60
Joint ventures antitrust	Feb. 25, 1992	98–0	60
Lumbee Tribe recognition	Feb. 27, 1992	58–39	60
Public Broadcasting Corp.	March 3, 1992	87–7	60
Crime bill	March 19, 1992	54–43	60
Defense/domestic spending walls	March 26, 1992	50–48	60
Fetal tissue research	March 31, 1992	98–2	60
Motor-voter registration	May 7, 1992	61–38	60
Motor-voter registration	May 12, 1992	58–40	60
Drug abuse mental health	June 9, 1992	84–9	60
Striker replacement	June 11, 1992	55–41	60
Striker replacement	June 16, 1992	57–42	60
Balanced budget amendment	June 30, 1992	56–39	60
Balanced budget amendment	July 1, 1992	56–39	60
National energy strategy	July 23, 1992	58–33	60
National energy strategy	July 28, 1992	93–3	60
Carnes nomination	Sept. 9, 1992	66–30	60
Product liability	Sept. 10, 1992	57–39	60
Product liability	Sept. 10, 1992	58–38	60
School improvement bill	Sept. 15, 1992	85–6	60
Labor, HHS, education funds	Sept. 16, 1992	56–38	60
START treaty	Sept. 29, 1992	87–6	60
School improvement bill	Oct. 2, 1992	59–40	60
Crime bill	Oct. 2, 1992	55–43	60
Fetal tissue research	Oct. 2, 1992	85–12	60
National energy strategy	Oct. 8, 1992	84–8	60
Tax bill	Oct. 8, 1992	80–10	60
Motor-voter registration	March 5, 1993	52–36	60
Motor-voter registration	March 9, 1993	62–38	60
Motor-voter registration	March 16, 1993	59–41	60
Stimulus package	April 2, 1993	55–43	60
Stimulus package	April 3, 1993	52–37	60
Stimulus package	April 5, 1993	49–29	60
Stimulus package	April 21, 1993	56–43	60
Motor-voter registration	May 11, 1993	63–37	60
Campaign finance	June 10, 1993	53–41	60
Campaign finance	June 15, 1993	52–45	60
Campaign finance	June 16, 1993	62–37	60
National service	July 29, 1993	59–41	60
Dellinger nomination	Oct. 7, 1993	59–39	60

Issue	*Date*	*Vote*	*Yeas needed*
Interior funds	Oct. 21, 1993	53–41	60
Interior funds	Oct. 26, 1993	51–45	60
Interior funds	Oct. 28, 1993	54–44	60
State Department nominations	Nov. 3, 1993	58–42	60
Brady bill (gun controls)	Nov. 19, 1993	57–42	60
Napolitano nomination	Nov. 19, 1993	72–26	60
Brady bill (gun controls)	Nov. 19, 1993	57–41	60
Competitiveness bill	March 15, 1994	56–42	60
Federal worker retirement buyout	March 24, 1994	58–41	60
Federal worker retirement buyout	March 24, 1994	63–36	60
Education goals 2000	March 26, 1994	62–23	60
Shearer nomination	May 24, 1994	63–35	60
Brown nomination	May 24, 1994	54–44	60
Brown nomination	May 25, 1994	56–42	60
Product liability	June 28, 1994	54–44	60
Product liability	June 29, 1994	57–41	60
Striker replacement	July 12, 1994	53–47	60
Striker replacement	July 13, 1994	53–46	60
Crime bill	Aug. 25, 1994	61–38	60
Campaign finance	Sept. 22, 1994	96–2	60
California desert protection	Sept. 23, 1994	73–20	60
Campaign finance	Sept. 27, 1994	57–43	60
Campaign finance	Sept. 30, 1994	52–46	66[2]
Tigert nomination	Oct. 3, 1994	63–32	65[3]
Sarokin nomination	Oct. 4, 1994	85–12	60
Elementary and secondary education	Oct. 5, 1994	75–24	60
Lobbying disclosure/gift ban	Oct. 6, 1994	52–46	60
Lobbying disclosure/gift ban	Oct. 7, 1994	55–42	60
California desert protection	Oct. 8, 1994	68–23	60
Unfunded mandates	Jan. 19, 1995	54–44	60
Balanced-budget amendment	Feb. 16, 1995	57–42	60
Striker replacement	March 15, 1995	58–39	60
Health insurance tax deduction	April 3, 1995	83–0	60
Supplemental funds and rescissions	April 6, 1995	56–44	60
Product liability	May 4, 1995	46–53	60
Product liability	May 4, 1995	47–52	60
Product liability	May 8, 1995	43–49	60
Product liability	May 9, 1995	60–38	60
Interstate waste	May 12, 1995	50–47	60
Telecommunications	June 14, 1995	89–11	60
Foster nomination	June 21, 1995	57–43	60
Foster nomination	June 22, 1995	57–43	60
Regulatory overhaul	July 17, 1995	48–46	60
Regulatory overhaul	July 18, 1995	53–47	60
Regulatory overhaul	July 20, 1995	58–40	60
State Department authorization	Aug. 1, 1995	55–45	60
State Department authorization	Aug. 1, 1995	55–45	60
Cuba sanctions	Oct. 12, 1995	56–37	60
Cuba sanctions	Oct. 17, 1995	59–36	60
Cuba sanctions	Oct. 18, 1995	98–0	60
Farm bill	Feb. 1, 1996	53–45	60
Farm bill	Feb. 6, 1996	59–34	60
District of Columbia funds	Feb. 27, 1996	54–44	60
District of Columbia funds	Feb. 29, 1996	52–42	60
District of Columbia funds	March 5, 1996	53–43	60
District of Columbia funds	March 12, 1996	56–44	60
Whitewater committee extension	March 12, 1996	53–47	60
Whitewater committee extension	March 13, 1996	53–47	60
Whitewater committee extension	March 14, 1996	51–46	60
Product liability	March 20, 1996	60–40	60
Whitewater committee extension	March 20, 1996	53–47	60
Whitewater committee extension	March 21, 1996	52–46	60
Presidio Park management	March 27, 1996	51–49	60
Presidio Park management	March 28, 1996	55–45	60
Whitewater committee extension	April 16, 1996	51–46	60
Term limits constitutional amendment	April 23, 1996	58–42	60
Immigration revision	April 29, 1996	91–0	60
Immigration revision	May 2, 1996	100–0	60
White House Travel Office reimbursement	May 7, 1996	52–44	60
White House Travel Office reimbursement	May 8, 1996	53–45	60
White House Travel Office reimbursement	May 9, 1996	52–44	60
White House Travel Office reimbursement	May 14, 1996	54–43	60
Missile defense	June 4, 1996	53–46	60
Campaign finance overhaul	June 25, 1996	54–46	60
Defense authorization	June 26, 1996	52–46	60
Defense authorization	June 28, 1996	53–43	60
Right-to-work legislation	July 10, 1996	31–68	60
Nuclear waste storage	July 16, 1996	65–34	60
FAA reauthorization	Oct. 3, 1996	66–31	60
Volunteer liability limitation	April 29, 1997	53–46	60
Volunteer liability limitation	April 30, 1997	55–44	60
Supplemental funds	May 7, 1997	100–0	60
Compensatory time, flexible credit	May 15, 1997	53–47	60
Compensatory time, flexible credit	June 4, 1997	51–47	60
Defense authorization, fiscal 1998	July 8, 1997	46–45	60
Klein nomination	July 14, 1997	78–11	60
FDA overhaul	Sept. 5, 1997	89–5	60
FDA overhaul	Sept. 16, 1997	94–4	60
District of Columbia funds, fiscal 1998	Sept. 30, 1997	58–41	60
Campaign finance reform	Oct. 7, 1997	52–48	60
Campaign finance reform	Oct. 7, 1997	53–47	60
District of Columbia funds	Oct. 7, 1997	99–1	60
Campaign finance reform	Oct. 8, 1997	52–47	60
Campaign finance reform	Oct. 9, 1997	52–47	60
Campaign finance reform	Oct. 9, 1997	51–48	60
Highway and Transit reauthorization	Oct. 23, 1997	48–52	60
Highway and Transit reauthorization	Oct. 23, 1997	48–50	60
Highway and Transit reauthorization	Oct. 24, 1997	43–49	60
Highway and Transit reauthorization	Oct. 28, 1997	52–48	60
Education savings accounts	Oct. 31, 1997	56–41	60

Issue	*Date*	*Vote*	*Yeas needed*
Defense authorization, fiscal 1998	Oct. 31, 1997	93–2	60
Education savings accounts	Nov. 4, 1997	56–44	60
Fast track trade procedures	Nov. 4, 1997	69–31	60
Satcher confirmation	Feb. 10, 1998	75–23	60
Human cloning research ban	Feb. 11, 1998	42–54	60
Restrict political use of union dues	Feb. 26, 1998	51–48	60
Restrict political use of union dues	Feb 26, 1998	45–54	60
Highway and mass transit programs	March 11, 1998	96–3	60
Education savings accounts	March 17, 1998	74–24	60
Expand education savings accounts	March 19, 1998	55–44	60
Expand education savings accounts	March 26, 1998	58–42	60
U.S. anti-missile defense policy	May 13, 1998	59–41	60
Create nuclear waste storage in Nevada	June 2, 1998	56–39	60
Set federal policies to curb smoking	June 9, 1998	42–56	62
Set federal policies to curb smoking	June 10, 1998	43 –55	60
Set federal policies to curb smoking	June 11, 1998	43–56	60
Set federal policies to curb smoking	June 17, 1998	57–42	60
Limit product liability suits	July 7, 1998	71–24	60
Limit product liability punitive damages	July 9, 1998	51–47	60
U.S. court review, local zoning decisions	July 13, 1998	52–42	60
Legislative branch funds, fiscal 1999	July 21, 1998	83–16	60
U.S. missile defense policy	Sept. 9, 1998	59–41	60
Consumer bankruptcy laws	Sept. 9, 1998	99–1	60
Campaign finance reform	Sept. 10, 1998	52–48	60
Parental consent abortion bill	Sept. 11, 1998	97–0	60
Limit union organizing	Sept. 14, 1998	52–42	60
Evading parental consent abortion laws	Sept. 22, 1998	54–45	60
Limit presidential appointment powers	Sept. 24, 1998	96–1	60
Limit presidential appointment powers	Sept. 28, 1998	53–38	60
Ban Internet sales taxes	Sept. 29, 1998	89–6	60
Banking regulation revision	Oct. 5, 1998	93–0	60
Ban Internet sales taxes for two years	Oct. 7, 1998	94–4	60
Waive federal education spending rules	March 8, 1999	54–41	60
Waive federal education spending rules	March 9, 1999	55–39	60
Authorize $11.4 billion for new teacher hires	March 10, 1999	44–55	60
Special education funding	March 10, 1999	55–44	60
U.S. troops in Kosovo	March 23, 1999	55–44	60
Social Security "lockbox," debt limit	April 22, 1999	54–45	60
Y2K liability limits	April 26, 1999	94–0	60
Y2K liability limits	April 29, 1999	52–47	60
Social Security "lockbox." debt limit	April 30, 1999	49–44	60
Y2K liability limits	May 18, 1999	53–45	60
Social Security "lockbox," debt limit	June 15, 1999	53–46	60
Steel, oil, gas loan guarantee	June 15, 1999	70–29	60
Social Security "lockbox"	June 16, 1999	55–44	60
Steel import quotas	June 22, 1999	42–57	60
Agriculture funds, fiscal 2000	June 28, 1999	50–37	60
Transportation funds, fiscal 2000	June 28, 1999	49–40	60
Commerce, State, Justice funds, fiscal 2000	June 28, 1999	49–39	60
Foreign operations funds, fiscal 2000	June 28, 1999	49–41	60
Budget procedures	July 1, 1999	99–1	60
Social Security "lockbox," debt limit	July 16, 1999	52–43	60
Intelligence authorization, fiscal 2000	July 20, 1999	99–0	60
Juvenile justice programs	July 28, 1999	77–22	60
Agriculture funds/milk marketing, fiscal 2000	Aug. 4, 1999	53–47	60
Transportation funds, fiscal 2000	Sept. 9, 1999	49–49	60
Puerto Rican nationalists clemency	Sept. 13, 1999	93–0	60
Oil royalty valuation system	Sept. 13, 1999	54–40	60
Bankruptcy law revision	Sept. 21, 1999	53–45	60
Stewart nomination	Sept. 21, 1999	55–44	60
Oil royalty valuation system	Sept. 23, 1999	62–39	60
Agriculture funds, fiscal 2000	Oct. 12, 1999	79–20	60
Campaign finance soft money ban	Oct. 19, 1999	52–48	60
Campaign finance soft money, union dues	Oct. 19, 1999	53–47	60
Trade with Sub-Saharan Africa	Oct. 26, 1999	91–8	60
Sub-Saharan African, Caribbean trade	Oct. 29, 1999	45–46	60
Sub-Saharan African, Caribbean trade	Nov. 2, 1999	74–23	60
Omnibus funds, fiscal 2000	Nov. 19, 1999	87–9	60
Nuclear waste storage	Feb. 2, 2000	94–3	60
Berzon nomination	March 8, 2000	86–13	60
Paez nomination	March 8, 2000	85–14	60
Flag desecration constitutional amendment	March 29, 2000	100–0	60
Federal gas tax suspension	March 30, 2000	86–11	60
Federal gas tax suspension	April 11, 2000	43–56	60
Marriage penalty tax	April 13, 2000	53–45	60
Marriage penalty tax	April 13, 2000	53–45	60
Victims rights	April 25, 2000	82–12	60
Marriage penalty tax	April 27, 2000	51–44	60
African trade agreement	May 11, 2000	76–18	60
Estate tax repeal	July 11, 2000	99–1	60
Treasury funds, fiscal 2001	July 26, 2000	97–0	60
Intelligence authorization, fiscal 2001	July 26, 2000	96–1	60
Energy, water funds, fiscal 2001	July 27, 2000	100–0	60
Trade with China	July 27, 2000	86–12	60
High technology visas	Sept. 19, 2000	97–1	60
High technology visas	Sept. 26, 2000	94–3	60
High technology visas	Sept. 28, 2000	92–3	60

Issue	Date	Vote	Yeas needed
Interior funds, fiscal 2001	Oct. 5, 2000	89–8	60
Bankruptcy law revision	Nov. 1, 2000	53–30	60
Bankruptcy law revision	Dec. 5, 2000	67–31	60
Bankruptcy law revision	March 14, 2001	80–19	60
ESEA reauthorization	May 1, 2001	96–3	60
Bankruptcy law revision	July 12, 2001	88–10	60
Bankruptcy law revision	July 17, 2001	88–10	60
Mexican trucks access to U.S.	July 26, 2001	70–30	60
Transportation funds/Mexican trucks in U.S.	July 27, 2001	57–27	60
Supplemental farm funds	July 30, 2001	95–2	60
Transportation/Mexican trucks in U.S.	Aug. 2, 2001	100–0	60
Supplemental farm funds	Aug. 3, 2001	49–48	60
Defense/energy funds authorization	Oct. 2, 2001	100–0	60
Federal airport security	Oct. 9, 2001	97–0	60
Aviation workers assistance	Oct. 11, 2001	56–44	60
Foreign operations funds	Oct. 15, 2001	50–46	60
Foreign operations funds	Oct. 23, 2001	50–47	60
Safety officers collective bargaining rights	Nov. 6, 2001	56–44	60
Pension contribution limits	Nov. 29, 2001	96–4	60
Energy policies/human cloning	Dec. 3, 2001	1–94	60
Railroad retirement pension board	Dec. 3, 2001	81–15	60
Farm policy revisions	Dec. 5, 2001	73–26	60
Farm policy revisions	Dec. 13, 2001	53–45	60
Farm policy revisions	Dec. 18, 2001	54–43	60
Farm policy revisions	Dec. 19. 2001	54–43	60
Tax bill/unemployment benefits	Feb. 6, 2002	56–39	60
Business tax cut/ unemployment benefits	Feb. 6, 2002	48–47	60
Election procedures requirements	March 1, 2002	49–39	60
Election procedures requirements	March 4, 2002	51–44	60
Campaign finance revisions	March 20, 2002	68–32	60
Energy policy bill	April 10, 2002	48–50	60
Energy bill/ANWR drilling	April 18, 2002	36–64	60
Energy bill/ANWR drilling	April 18, 2002	46–54	60
Energy policy bill	April 23, 2002	86–13	60
Andean duty-free trade	April 29, 2002	69–21	60
Andean trade/steelworkers health insurance	May 21, 2002	56–40	60
Andean duty-free trade	May 22, 2002	68–29	60
Supplemental funds, fiscal 2002	June 6, 2002	87–10	60
Hate crimes definitions	June 11, 2002	54–43	60
Terrorism insurance	June 18, 2002	65–31	60
Defense authorization, fiscal 2003	June 26, 2002	98–0	60
Accounting industry reform	July 12, 2002	91–2	60
Smith appeals court nomination	July 15, 2002	94–3	60
Drug patents	July 17, 2002	99–0	60
Clifton appeals court nomination	July 18, 2002	97–1	60
Carmona surgeon general nomination	July 23, 2002	98–0	60
Gibbons appeals court nomination	July 26, 2002	89–0	60
Drug patents	July 31, 2002	66–33	60
Trade promotion authority	Aug. 1, 2002	64–32	60
Interior funds, fiscal 2002/ farm disaster aid	Sept. 17, 2002	50–49	60
Homeland security department	Sept. 19, 2002	50–49	60
Interior funds, fiscal 2002/ farm disaster aid	Sept. 23, 2002	49–46	60
Interior funds, fiscal 2002/ farm disaster aid	Sept. 25, 2002	51–47	60
Homeland security department	Sept. 25, 2002	49–49	60
Homeland security department	Sept. 26, 2002	50–49	60
Homeland security/worker union rights	Sept. 26, 2002	44–53	60
Homeland security/worker union rights	Oct. 1, 2002	45–52	60
Justice department reauthorization	Oct. 3, 2002	93–5	60
Use of force against Iraq	Oct. 3, 2002	95–1	60
Use of force against Iraq	Oct. 10, 2002	75–25	60
Homeland security/worker union rights	Nov. 13, 2002	89–8	60
Homeland security department	Nov. 15, 2002	65–29	60
Homeland security department	Nov. 19, 2002	83–16	60
Terrorism insurance	Nov. 19, 2002	85–12	60
Estrada appeals court nomination	March 6, 2003	55–44	60
Estrada appeals court nomination	March 13, 2003	55–42	60
Estrada appeals court nomination	March 18, 2003	55–45	60
Estrada appeals court nomination	April 2, 2003	55–44	60
Owen appeals court nomination	May 1, 2003	52–44	60
Estrada appeals court nomination	May 5, 2003	52–39	60
Estrada appeals court nomination	May 8, 2003	54–43	60
Owen appeals court nomination	May 8, 2003	52–45	60
Medical malpractice award caps	July 9, 2003	49–48	60
Owen appeals court nomination	July 29, 2003	53–43	60
Estrada appeals court nomination	July 30, 2003	55–43	60
Pryor appeals court nomination	July 31, 2003	53–44	60
Class action lawsuits	Oct. 22, 2003	59–39	60
Pickering appeals court nomination	Oct. 30, 2003	54–43	60
Pryor appeals court nomination	Nov. 6, 2003	51–43	60
Owen appeals court nomination	Nov. 14, 2003	53–42	60
Kuhl appeals court nomination	Nov. 14, 2003	53–43	60
Brown appeals court nomination	Nov. 14, 2003	53–43	60

Issue	*Date*	*Vote*	*Yeas needed*
Dorr agriculture undersecretary nomination	Nov. 18, 2003	57–39	60
Dorr Commodity Credit Corp. nomination	Nov. 18, 2003	57–39	60
Energy policy bill conference report	Nov. 21, 2003	57–40	60
Medicare prescription drug bill	Nov. 24, 2003	70–29	60
Omnibus appropriations, fiscal 2004	Jan. 20, 2004	48–45	60
Omnibus appropriations, fiscal 2004	Jan. 22, 2004	61–32	60
Highway funding	Feb. 2, 2004	75–11	60
Highway funding	Feb. 12, 2004	86–11	60
Medical malpractice lawsuit caps	Feb. 24, 2004	48–45	60
Gun liability lawsuits	Feb. 25, 2004	75–22	60
Corporate tax changes	March 24, 2004	51–47	60
Welfare reauthorization	April 1, 2004	51–47	60
Medical malpractice lawsuit caps	April 7, 2004	49–48	60
Corporate tax changes	April 7, 2004	50–47	60
Asbestos claims fund	April 22, 2004	50–47	60
Internet tax moratorium	April 26, 2004	74–11	60
Internet tax/ethanol	April 29, 2004	40–59	60
Internet tax/energy policy	April 29, 2004	55–43	60
Internet tax moratorium	April 29, 2004	64–34	60
Corporate tax changes	May 11, 2004	90–8	60
Class action lawsuits	July 8, 2004	44–43	60
Same-sex marriage amendment	July 14, 2004	48–50	60
Myers appeals court nomination	July 20, 2004	53–44	60
Saad appeals court nomination	July 22, 2004	52–46	60
Griffin appeals court nomination	Jul 22, 2004	54–44	60
McKeague appeals court nomination	July 22, 2004	53–44	60
Intelligence operations overhaul	Oct. 5, 2004	85–10	60
Senate intelligence oversight	Oct. 8, 2004	88–3	60
Corporate tax changes	Oct. 10, 2004	66–14	60
Tariffs and trade bill	Nov. 19, 2004	88–5	60
Bankruptcy overhaul	March 8, 2005	69–31	60
Foreign workers temporary U.S. status	April 19, 2005	21–77	60
Agricultural workers in U.S. illegally	April 19, 2005	53–45	60
Seasonal workers exemption	April 19, 2005	83–17	60
Iraq, Afghanistan war funding	April 19, 2005	100–0	60
Surface transportation reauthorization	April 26, 2005	94–6	60
Johnson EPA administrator nomination	April 28, 2005	61–37	60
Surface transportation reauthorization	May 12, 2005	92–7	60
Owen appeals court nomination	May 24, 2005	81–18	60
Bolton United Nations nomination	May 26, 2005	56–42	60
Brown appeals court nomination	June 7, 2005	65–32	60
Pryor appeals court nomination	June 8, 2005	67–32	60
Bolton United Nations nomination	June 20, 2005	54–38	60
Energy policy overhaul	June 23, 2005	92–4	60
Defense authorization	July 26, 2005	50–48	60
Gun liability limitations	July 26, 2005	66–32	60
Defense appropriations	Oct. 5, 2005	95–4	60
Labor-HHS-Education appropriations	Oct. 27, 2005	97–0	60
Patriot Act reauthorization	Dec. 16, 2005	52–47	60
Defense appropriations	Dec. 21,2005	56–44	60
Alito Supreme Court nomination	Jan. 30, 2006	72–25	60
Asbestos trust fund	Feb. 7, 2006	98–1	60
Patriot Act reauthorization	Feb. 16, 2006	96–3	60
Patriot Act reauthorization	Feb. 28, 2006	69–30	60
Patriot Act reauthorization	March 1, 2006	84–15	60
Low income home energy assistance	March 7, 2006	75–25	60
Lobbying overhaul	March 9, 2006	51–47	60
Lobbying overhaul	March 28, 2006	81–16	60
Immigration overhaul	April 6, 2006	39–60	60
Immigration overhaul	April 6, 2006	38–60	60
Flory Defense Department nomination	April 7, 2006	52–41	60
Iraq, Afghanistan war funding	May 2, 2006	92–4	60
Medical malpractice	May 8, 2006	48–42	60
Medical malpractice	May 8, 2006	49–44	60
Small business health plans	May 9, 2006	96–2	60
Small business health plans	May 11, 2006	55–43	60
Immigration overhaul	May 24, 2006	73–25	60
Kavanaugh appeals court nomination	May 25, 2006	67–30	60
Interior secretary nomination	May 26, 2006	85–8	60
Same-sex marriage ban amendment	June 7, 2006	49–48	60
Estate tax repeal	June 8, 2006	57–41	60
Native Hawaiians policy	June 8, 2006	56–41	60
Defense authorization	June 22, 2006	98–1	60
Gulf of Mexico offshore drilling	July 26, 2006	86–12	60
Gulf of Mexico offshore drilling	July 31, 2006	72–23	60
Tax package and minimum wage	Aug. 3, 2006	56–42	60
Port security overhaul	Sept. 14, 2006	98–0	60
U.S.-Mexican border fence	Sept. 20, 2006	94–0	60
U.S.-Mexican border fence	Sept. 28, 2006	71–28	60
Abortion parental notification	Sept. 29, 2006	57–42	60
FDA commissioner nomination	Dec. 7, 2006	89–6	60
Jordan appeals court nomination	Dec. 8, 2006	93–0	60
Tax and trade package	Dec. 9, 2006	78–10	60
Ethics and lobbying overhaul	Jan. 16 2007	92–2	60
Ethics and lobbying overhaul	Jan. 17, 2007	51–46	60
Minimum wage increase	Jan. 24, 2007	49–48	60
Minimum wage increase	Jan. 24, 2007	54–43	60
Minimum wage increase	Jan. 30, 2007	87–10	60
Minimum wage increase	Jan. 31,2007	88–8	60
U.S. troop levels in Iraq	Feb. 1, 2007	0–97	60

Issue	*Date*	*Vote*	*Yeas needed*
U.S. troop levels in Iraq	Feb. 5, 2007	49–47	60
Continuing appropriations FY 2007	Feb. 13, 2007	71–26	60
Iraq war troop surge	Feb. 17, 2007	56–34	60
Sept. 11 commission recommendations	Feb. 27, 2007	97–0	60
Sept. 11 commission recommendations	March 9, 2007	46–49	60
Sept. 11 commission recommendations	March 9, 2007	69–26	60
Iraq mission	March 14, 2007	89–9	60
FY 2007 supplemental appropriations	March 28, 2007	97–0	60
Intelligence authorization FY 2007	April 12, 2007	94–3	60
Intelligence authorization FY 2007	April 16, 2007	41–40	60
Intelligence authorization FY 2007	April 17, 2007	50–45	60
Medicare prescription drug negotiations	April 18, 2007	55–42	60
Court security	April 18, 2007	93–3	60
FDA overhaul	May 3, 2007	63–28	60
FDA overhaul	May 7, 2007	82–8	60
Water projects authorization	May 10, 2007	89–7	60
Iraq troop withdrawal by March 31, 2008	May 16, 2007	29–67	60
Economic aid for Iraq	May 16, 2007	52–44	60
Iraq aid sense of Senate	May 16, 2007	87–9	60
Iraq sense of Senate	May 17, 2007	94–1	60
Immigration overhaul	May 21, 2007	69–23	60
Immigration overhaul	June 7, 2007	33–63	60
Immigration overhaul	June 7, 2007	34–61	60
Immigration overhaul	June 7, 2007	45–50	60
No confidence in Attorney General Gonzales	June 11, 2007	53–38	60
Energy policy	June 11, 2007	91–0	60
Energy Policy	June 21, 2007	57–36	60
Energy Policy	June 21, 2007	61–32	60
Employee union formation	June 26, 2007	51–48	60
Immigration overhaul	June 26, 2007	64–35	60
Immigration overhaul	June 28, 2007	46–53	60
Defense authorization FY 2008	July 11, 2007	56–41	60
Defense authorization FY 2008	July 17, 2007	52–47	60
Small business tax breaks	July 30, 2007	80–0	60
Ethics and lobbying overhaul	Aug. 2, 2007	80–17	60
District of Columbia voting rights	Sept. 18, 2007	57–42	60
Defense authorization FY 2008	Sept. 19, 2007	56–43	60
Defense authorization FY 2008	Sept. 27, 2007	60–39	60
Children's Health Insurance	Sept. 27, 2007	69–30	60
Defense authorization FY 2008	Sept. 27, 2007	89–6	60
Southwick appeals court nomination	Oct. 24, 2007	62–35	60
Immigrant education	Oct. 24, 2007	52–44	60
Amtrak reauthorization	Oct. 30, 2007	79–13	60
Children's health insurance	Oct. 31, 2007	62–33	60
Children's health insurance	Nov. 1, 2007	65–30	60
Iraq war appropriations	Nov. 16, 2007	45–53	60
Iraq war appropriations/troop withdrawal	Nov. 16, 2007	53–45	60
Farm bill reauthorization	Nov. 16, 2007	55–42	60
Alternative minimum tax	Dec. 6, 2007	46–48	60
Energy policy	Dec. 7, 2007	53–42	60
Energy policy/CAFE standards	Dec. 13, 2007	59–40	60
Farm bill reauthorization	Dec. 13, 2007	78–12	60
Foreign intelligence surveillance	Dec. 17, 2007	76–10	60
Omnibus appropriations FY 2008	Dec. 18, 2007	44–51	60
Foreign intelligence surveillance	Jan. 28, 2008	48–45	60
Foreign intelligence surveillance	Jan. 28, 2008	48–45	60
Economic stimulus	Feb. 4, 2008	80–4	60
Economic stimulus	Feb. 6, 2008	58–41	60
Foreign intelligence surveillance	Feb. 12, 2008	69–29	60
Intelligence authorization FY 2008	Feb. 13, 2008	92–4	60
Indian health care reauthorization	Feb. 25, 2008	85–2	60
U.S. troop deployments in Iraq	Feb. 26, 2008	70–24	60
Report on al Qaeda	Feb. 27, 2008	89–3	60
Renewable energy	Feb. 28. 2008	48–46	60
Renewable energy	April 1, 2008	94–1	60
Renewable energy/mortgage relief	April 8, 2008	92–6	60
Surface transportation corrections	April 17, 2008	90–2	60
Veterans benefits expansion	April 22, 2008	94–0	60
Wage discrimination	April 23, 2008	56–42	60
FAA reauthorization	April 28, 2008	88–0	60
FAA reauthorization	May 6, 2008	49–42	60
National flood insurance	May 6, 2008	90–1	60
Public safety workers organizing rights	May 13, 2008	69–29	60
Climate change trading system	June 2, 2008	74–14	60
Climate change trading system	June 6, 2008	48–36	60
Energy and oil company taxes	June 10, 2008	51–43	60
Tax reduction extensions	June 10, 2008	50–44	60
Medicare physician payments	June 12, 2008	54–39	60
Tax reduction extensions	June 17, 2008	52–44	60
Mortgage relief	June 24, 2008	83–9	60
Foreign intelligence surveillance	June 25, 2008	80–15	60
Medicare physician payments	June 26, 2008	58–40	60
Mortgage relief	July 7, 2008	76–10	60
Foreign intelligence surveillance	July 9, 2008	72–26	60
Medicare physician payments	July 9, 2008	69–30	60
Mortgage relief	July 10, 2008	84–12	60
HIV/AIDS program reauthorization	July 11, 2008	65–3	60
Energy futures speculation	July 22, 2008	94–0	60
Energy futures speculation	July 25, 2008	50–43	60
Mortgage relief	July 25, 2008	80–13	60
Low-income energy assistance	July 26, 2008	50–35	60
Omnibus domestic and foreign policy bills	July 28, 2008	52–40	60
Tax reduction extensions	July 29, 2008	53–43	60
Media shield	July 30, 2008	51–43	60

Issue	*Date*	*Vote*	*Yeas needed*
Tax reduction extensions	July 30, 2008	51–43	60
Defense authorization FY 2009	July 31, 2008	51–39	60
Defense authorization FY 2009	Sept. 8, 2008	83–0	60
Defense authorization FY 2009	Sept. 16, 2008	61–32	60
Continuing appropriations	Sept. 27, 2008	83–12	60
Railroad safety/Amtrak authorization	Sept. 29, 2008	69–17	60
Unemployment benefits extension	Nov. 20, 2008	89–6	60
Automobile industry loans	Dec. 11, 2008	52–35	60

1. Vote was taken after midnight in the session that began Oct. 8, 1985.

2. Because the bill would have changed Senate rules, two-thirds of those present and voting were required to invoke cloture: 66 in this case instead of the usual 60.

3. Because the bill would have changed Senate rules, two-thirds of those present and voting were required to invoke cloture: 65 in this case instead of the usual 60.

Attempted and Successful Cloture Votes, 1919–2008

Congress		First Session		Second Session		Total	
		Attempted	*Successful*	*Attempted*	*Successful*	*Attempted*	*Successful*
66th	(1919–1921)	1	1	0	0	1	1
67th	(1921–1923)	1	0	1	0	2	0
68th	(1923–1925)	0	0	0	0	0	0
69th	(1925–1927)	2	1	5	2	7	3
70th	(1927–1929)	0	0	0	0	0	0
71st	(1929–1931)	0	0	0	0	0	0
72nd	(1931–1933)	1	0	0	0	1	0
73rd	(1933–1935)	0	0	0	0	0	0
74th	(1935–1937)	0	0	0	0	0	0
75th	(1937–1939)	0	0	2	0	2	0
76th	(1939–1941)	0	0	0	0	0	0
77th	(1941–1943)	0	0	1	0	1	0
78th	(1943–1945)	0	0	1	0	1	0
79th	(1945–1947)	0	0	4	0	4	0
80th	(1947–1949)	0	0	0	0	0	0
81st	(1949–1951)	0	0	2	0	2	0
82nd	(1951–1953)	0	0	0	0	0	0
83rd	(1953–1955)	0	0	1	0	1	0
84th	(1955–1957)	0	0	0	0	0	0
85th	(1957–1959)	0	0	0	0	0	0
86th	(1959–1961)	0	0	1	0	1	0
87th	(1961–1963)	1	0	3	1	4	1
88th	(1963–1965)	1	0	2	1	3	1
89th	(1965–1967)	2	1	5	0	7	1
90th	(1967–1969)	1	0	5	1	6	1
91st	(1969–1971)	2	0	4	0	6	0
92nd	(1971–1973)	10	2	10	2	20	4
93rd	(1973–1975)	10	2	21	7	31	9
94th	(1975–1977)	23	13	4	4	27	17
95th	(1977–1979)	5	1	8	2	13	3
96th	(1979–1981)	4	1	17	9	21	10
97th	(1981–1983)	7	2	20	7	27	9
98th	(1983–1985)	7	2	12	9	19	11
99th	(1985–1987)	9	1	14	9	23	10
100th	(1987–1989)	23	5	20	6	43	11
101st	(1989–1991)	9	6	15	5	24	11
102nd	(1991–1993)	20	9	28	14	48	23
103rd	(1993–1995)	20	4	22	10	42	14
104th	(1995–1997)	21	4	29	5	50	9
105th	(1997–1999)	24	7	29	11	53	18
106th	(1999–2001)	36	11	22	17	58	28
107th	(2001–2003)	22	11	39	22	61	33
108th	(2003–2005)	22	1	26	11	48	12
109th	(2005–2007)	20	13	33	21	53	34
110th	(2007–2009)	61	30	48	27	109	57
Totals		365	128	454	203	819	331

NOTES: The number of votes required to invoke cloture was changed March 7, 1975, from two-thirds of those present and voting, to three-fifths of the total Senate membership, as Rule XXII of the standing rules of the Senate was amended.

SOURCES: *Congress and the Nation*, selected volumes (Washington, D.C.: CQ Press, selected years); *CQ Almanac*, selected volumes (Washington, D.C.: Congressional Quarterly, selected years); Richard S. Beth, Congressional Research Service, Library of Congress.

House Discharge Petitions since 1931

The discharge petition is a little-used but dramatic House device that enables a majority of representatives to bring to the floor legislation blocked in committee. The following table shows the frequency with which the discharge petition has been used since the present discharge procedure was adopted in 1931 through 2008.

Although the procedure is rarely used and even more rarely successful, it may on occasion indirectly succeed by prompting a legislative committee, the Rules Committee, or the leadership to act on a measure and thereby avoid the discharge.

			Discharge motion			*Underlying measure*[3]	
Congress		*Discharge petitions filed*	*Entered*[1]	*Called up*[2]	*Committee Discharged*	*Passed House*	*Received final approval*[4]
72nd	(1931–1933)	12	5	5	1	1	–
73rd	(1933–1935)	31	6	1	1	1	–
74th	(1935–1937)	33	3	2	2	–	–
75th	(1937–1939)	43	4	4	3[5]	2	1
76th	(1939–1941)	37[5]	2	2	2	2	–
77th	(1941–1943)	15	1	1	1	1	–
78th	(1943–1945)	21	3	3	3	3	1[6]
79th	(1945–1947)	35	3	1	1	1	–
80th	(1947–1949)	20	1	1	1	1	–
81st	(1949–1951)	34	3[7]	1	1	1	–
82nd	(1951–1953)	14	–	–	–	–	–
83rd	(1953–1955)	10	1	1	1	1	–
84th	(1955–1957)	6	–	–	–	–	–
85th	(1957–1959)	7	1	1	1	1	–
86th	(1959–1961)	7	1	1	1	1	1
87th	(1961–1963)	6	–	–	–	–	–
88th	(1963–1965)	5	–	–	–	–	–
89th	(1965–1967)	6	1	1	1	1	–
90th	(1967–1969)	4	–	–	–	–	–
91st	(1969–1971)	12	1	1	1	1	–
92nd	(1971–1973)	15	1	1	1	–	–
93rd	(1973–1975)	10	–	–	–	–	–
94th	(1975–1977)	15	–	–	–	–	–
95th	(1977–1979)	11	–	–	–	–	–
96th	(1979–1981)	14	2	1	1	–	–
97th	(1981–1983)	24	1	–	–	–	–
98th	(1983–1985)	13	1	–	–	–	–
99th	(1985–1987)	10	1	–	–	–	–
100th	(1987–1989)	5[8]	–	–	–	–	–
101st	(1989–1991)	8	1	–	–	–	–
102nd	(1991–1993)	8	1[9]	1[9]	1[9]	–	–
103rd	(1993–1995)	26	2[9]	2[9]	2[9]	1	1[6]
104th	(1995–1997)	15	–	–	–	–	–
105th	(1997–1999)	8	–	–	–	–	–
106th	(1999–2001)	11	–	–	–	–	–
107th	(2001–2003)	12	1	–	–	–	–
108th	(2003–2005)	16	–	–	–	–	–
109th	(2005–2007)	18	–	–	–	–	–
110th	(2007–2009)	18	–	–	–	–	–
Totals		615	47	31	26	19	4

NOTE: As of the end of 2008.

1. A discharge motion is "entered" when the petition receives sufficient signatures for it to be entered on the Calendar of Motions to Discharge Committees. This number was 145 in the 72nd and 73rd Congresses, 219 in the 86th and 87th Congresses, and 218 for all other Congresses in the table.
2. A discharge motion may be offered on the floor on any second or fourth Monday falling at least seven legislative days after the discharge petition is entered. Each day on which the House convenes is usually a legislative day.
3. A discharge petition may be filed to bring to the floor either a substantive measure in committee or a "special rule" from the Committee on Rules providing for House consideration of such a measure that is either in committee or previously reported. The last two columns of this table reflect action on the underlying, substantive measure, not on the special rule, if any, on which discharge was directly sought.
4. Includes bills and joint resolutions becoming law; constitutional amendments submitted to the states for ratification; resolutions agreed to by the House; and concurrent resolutions finally agreed to by both chambers.
5. During this Congress, the Rules Committee was discharged from a special rule for consideration of one measure, and the measure was taken up but then recommitted. Subsequently, the Rules Committee was discharged from a second special rule for consideration of the measure. This measure accordingly appears twice under "Committee discharged" and earlier columns, but only once under "Passed House" and subsequently.
6. Resolution attempting to change House Rules.
7. Includes one petition entered with respect to a special rule on a measure and another on the same measure directly.
8. Includes one petition filed on a special rule for considering two measures.
9. Includes one measure in the 102nd Congress and two in the 103rd from which the committee was discharged, and which were brought to the floor, by unanimous consent after the discharge petition was entered.

SOURCE: Richard S. Beth, "The Discharge Rule in the House: Recent Use in Historical Context," Congressional Research Service, Library of Congress, September 15, 1997; update provided by CRS, September 1999, April 2000, December 2005. Clerk of the House, March 2010, http://clerk.house.gov/art_history/house_history/index.html.

Congressional Apportionment, 1789–2000

	Constitution (1789)[2]	*1790*	*1800*	*1810*	*1820*	*1830*	*1840*	*1850*	*1860*	*1870*	*1880*	*1890*	*1900*	*1910*	*1930*[3]	*1940*	*1950*	*1960*	*1970*	*1980*	*1990*	*2000*
											Year of census[1]											
Alabama				1[4]	3	5	7	7	6	8	8	9	9	10	9	9	9	8	7	7	7	7
Alaska																	1[4]	1	1	1	1	1
Arizona														1[4]	1	2	2	3	4	5	6	8
Arkansas						1[4]	1	2	3	4	5	6	7	7	7	7	6	4	4	4	4	4
California							2[4]	2	3	4	6	7	8	11	20	23	30	38	43	45	52	53
Colorado										1[4]	1	2	3	4	4	4	4	4	5	6	6	7
Connecticut	5	7	7	7	6	6	4	4	4	4	4	4	5	5	6	6	6	6	6	6	6	5
Delaware	1	1	1	2	1	1	1	1	1	1	1	1	1	1	1	1	1	1	1	1	1	1
Florida							1[4]	1	1	2	2	2	3	4	5	6	8	12	15	19	23	25
Georgia	3	2	4	6	7	9	8	8	7	9	10	11	11	12	10	10	10	10	10	10	11	13
Hawaii																	1[4]	2	2	2	2	2
Idaho											1[4]	1	1	2	2	2	2	2	2	2	2	2
Illinois				1[4]	1	3	7	9	14	19	20	22	25	27	27	26	25	24	24	22	20	19
Indiana				1[4]	3	7	10	11	11	13	13	13	13	13	12	11	11	11	11	10	10	9
Iowa							2[4]	2	6	9	11	11	11	11	9	8	8	7	6	6	5	5
Kansas									1	3	7	8	8	8	7	6	6	5	5	5	4	4
Kentucky		2	6	10	12	13	10	10	9	10	11	11	11	11	9	9	8	7	7	7	6	6
Louisiana				1[4]	3	3	4	4	5	6	6	6	7	8	8	8	8	8	8	8	7	7
Maine				7[4]	7	8	7	6	5	5	4	4	4	4	3	3	3	2	2	2	2	2
Maryland	6	8	9	9	9	8	6	6	5	6	6	6	6	6	6	6	7	8	8	8	8	8
Massachusetts	8	14	17	13[5]	13	12	10	11	10	11	12	13	14	16	15	14	14	12	12	11	10	10
Michigan						1[4]	3	4	6	9	11	12	12	13	17	17	18	19	19	18	16	15
Minnesota								2[4]	2	3	5	7	9	10	9	9	9	8	8	8	8	8
Mississippi				1[4]	1	2	4	5	5	6	7	7	8	8	7	7	6	5	5	5	5	4
Missouri					1	2	5	7	9	13	14	15	16	16	13	13	11	10	10	9	9	9
Montana											1[4]	1	1	2	2	2	2	2	2	2	1	1
Nebraska									1[4]	1	3	6	6	6	5	4	4	3	3	3	3	3
Nevada									1[4]	1	1	1	1	1	1	1	1	1	1	2	2	3
New Hampshire	3	4	5	6	6	5	4	3	3	3	2	2	2	2	2	2	2	2	2	2	2	2
New Jersey	4	5	6	6	6	6	5	5	5	7	7	8	10	12	14	14	14	15	15	14	13	13
New Mexico														1[4]	1	2	2	2	2	3	3	3
New York	6	10	17	27	34	40	34	33	31	33	34	34	37	43	45	45	43	41	39	34	31	29
North Carolina	5	10	12	13	13	13	9	8	7	8	9	9	10	10	11	12	12	11	11	11	12	13
North Dakota											1[4]	1	2	3	2	2	2	2	1	1	1	1
Ohio			1[4]	6	14	19	21	21	19	20	21	21	21	22	24	23	23	24	23	21	19	18
Oklahoma													5[4]	8	9	8	6	6	6	6	6	5
Oregon								1[4]	1	1	1	2	2	3	3	4	4	4	4	5	5	5
Pennsylvania	8	13	18	23	26	28	24	25	24	27	28	30	32	36	34	33	30	27	25	23	21	19
Rhode Island	1	2	2	2	2	2	2	2	2	2	2	2	2	3	2	2	2	2	2	2	2	2
South Carolina	5	6	8	9	9	9	7	6	4	5	7	7	7	7	6	6	6	6	6	6	6	6
South Dakota											2[4]	2	2	3	2	2	2	2	2	1	1	1
Tennessee		1[4]	3	6	9	13	11	10	8	10	10	10	10	10	9	10	9	9	8	9	9	9
Texas							2[4]	2	4	6	11	13	16	18	21	21	22	23	24	27	30	32
Utah												1[4]	1	2	2	2	2	2	2	3	3	3
Vermont		2	4	6	5	5	4	3	3	3	2	2	2	2	1	1	1	1	1	1	1	1
Virginia	10	19	22	23	22	21	15	13	11	9	10	10	10	10	9	9	10	10	10	10	11	11
Washington											1[4]	2	3	5	6	6	7	7	7	8	9	9
West Virginia										3	4	4	5	6	6	6	6	5	4	4	3	3
Wisconsin							2[4]	3	6	8	9	10	11	11	10	10	10	10	9	9	9	8
Wyoming											1[4]	1	1	1	1	1	1	1	1	1	1	1
Total	65	106	142	186	213	242	232	237	243	293	332	357	391	435	435	435	437[6]	435	435	435	435	435

1. Apportionment effective with congressional election two years after census.
2. Original apportionment made in Constitution, pending first census.
3. No apportionment was made in 1920.
4. These figures are not based on any census, but indicate the provisional representation accorded newly admitted states by Congress, pending the next census.
5. Twenty members were assigned to Massachusetts, but seven of these were credited to Maine when that area became a state.
6. Normally 435, but temporarily increased two seats by Congress when Alaska and Hawaii became states.

SOURCES: *Biographical Directory of the American Congress* and Bureau of the Census.

The Presidency

Presidential Vetoes, 2005–2008

President George W. Bush did not veto any legislation during his first four years in office, from 2001 through 2004. He was the first president since John Quincy Adams in the 1820s to complete a full term without issuing a veto. But in Bush's second term, from 2005 through 2008, he cast twelve vetoes, including three cases of two vetoes on the same subject, and in one of those cases—farm program reauthorization—nearly identical measures. In addition to the farm bill, Bush vetoed two reauthorizations of the State Children's Insurance Program and two bills that expanded stem cell availability for research. Other bills he vetoed involved Democratic efforts to change Bush's course on the Iraqi war. Of the twelve bills vetoed, Congress overrode four: the farm bill (twice), water projects legislation, and a bill to prevent a cut in Medicare reimbursements for doctors.

Bush was able to avoid first-term vetoes in part because his party controlled both houses throughout the 108th Congress and the first six months of the 107th before a disaffected Republican, James Jeffords of Vermont, became an independent and gave control of the Senate to the Democrats. The GOP, however, remained in firm control of the House. The Republican leadership was intent on avoiding presidential vetoes and willing to twist arms so that the president could score wins and conserve his political capital for essential battles. Bush threatened numerous vetoes to help shape legislation to his liking, a technique he used to considerable success to get legislation that he was able to sign.

Bush's first veto came in 2006 on a stem cell bill while the GOP still controlled Congress. But all the following vetoes came after Democrats recaptured control of both chambers in the 2006 election and took control of the 110th Congress beginning in 2007. Now in the majority for the first time since 1994, Democrats were eager to challenge Bush on a variety of issues, including the war in Iraq and domestic initiatives that carried high priority for their party. But on a few vetoes, including the farm and water projects bills, many Republicans joined Democrats to override, reflecting the parochial interests of sitting members. *(Veto messages, pp. 1043–1075)*

By contrast, all presidents from Dwight D. Eisenhower in 1953 issued many vetoes. Eisenhower, faced with a Democratic Congress throughout his eight years in the White House, issued many more than any of his successors. But only two were overridden.

Bush's predecessor, Bill Clinton, vetoed twenty bills during his second term in office. In his first four years, he vetoed seventeen, for a total thirty-seven during his two terms in office. The number is relatively low compared to veto totals of other presidents since 1953 who faced a Congress in the control of the opposition party. Democrats controlled Congress during only the first two years of Clinton's presidency. He did not cast any vetoes during that two-year period, making him the first president since 1853 to go an entire Congress without vetoing a single bill. The last president to do that was Millard Fillmore during the 32nd Congress (1851–1853).

Grover Cleveland issued the most vetoes in one term, 414. Franklin Roosevelt, who served as president for three full terms and into a fourth, vetoed the most measures, 635. Seven presidents before Bush vetoed no bills.

President	*Congress Vetoes*	*Regular Vetoes*	*Pocket Vetoes*	*Total*	*Overridden*
Dwight D. Eisenhower	83rd–86th	73	108	181	2
John F. Kennedy	87th–88th	12	9	21	0
Lyndon B. Johnson	88th–90th	16	14	30	0
Richard M. Nixon	91st–93rd	26	17	43	7
Gerald R. Ford	93rd–94th	48	18	66	12
Jimmy Carter	95th–96th	13	18	31	2
Ronald Reagan	97th–100th	39	39	78	9
George H.W. Bush[1]	101st–102nd	29	15	44	1
Bill Clinton[2]	103rd–106th	36	1	37	2
George W. Bush	107th–108th	12	0	12	4

1. President George H.W. Bush attempted to pocket veto two bills during recess periods. Congress considered the two bills enacted into law because of the President's failure to return the legislation. The bills are not counted as pocket vetoes in this table.

2. Does not include line-item vetoes, which were permitted under a 1996 law that was struck down by the Supreme Court.

Following is a list of bills vetoed by President George W. Bush during his second term, 2005–2009.

2006

1. HR 810 (Stem cell research expansion)
Vetoed: July 19, 2006
House sustained veto July 19, 2006: 235–19
(Story, p. 542; Message, p. 1056)

2007

1. HR 1591 (Funding for Iraq war and disaster relief)
Vetoed: May 1, 2007
House sustained veto May 2, 2007: 222–203
(Story, p. 308; Message, p. 1063)

2. S 5 (Stem cell research expansion)
Vetoed: June 20, 2007
No override attempt.
(Story, p. 573; Message, p.1063)

3. HR 976 (Reauthorize Children's Health Insurance Program)
Vetoed Oct. 3, 2007
House sustained veto Oct. 8, 2007: 273–156
(Story, p. 558; Message, p. 1064)

4. HR 1495 (Water projects authorization)
Vetoed Nov. 2, 2007
House overrode veto Nov. 6, 2007: 361–54
Senate overrode veto Nov. 8, 2007: 79–14
(Story, p. 500; Message p. 1064)

5. HR 3043 (Labor-HHS-Education appropriations
Vetoed Nov. 13, 2007
House sustained veto Nov. 15, 2007: 277–141
(Story, pp. 112, 114; Message, p. 1065)

6. HR 3963 (Reauthorize Children's Health Insurance Program
Vetoed Dec. 12, 2007
House sustained veto Jan. 23, 2008: 260–152
(Story, p. 558; Message, p. 1065)

7. HR 1585 (Defense authorization/Iraqi assets)
Vetoed Dec. 28, 2007
No override attempt
(Story, p. 373; Message, p. 1066)

2008

1. HR 2082 (Intelligence authorization)
House sustained veto March 11, 2008: 225–188
(Story, p. 320; Message, p. 1071)

2. HR 2419 (Farm program reauthorization)
Vetoed May 21, 2008
House overrode veto May 21, 2008: 316–108
Senate overrode veto May 22, 2008: 82–13
(Story, p. 514; Message, p. 1073)

3. HR 6124 (Farm program reauthorization)
Vetoed July 18, 2008
House overrode veto June 18, 2008: 317–109
Senate overrode veto June 18, 2008: 80–14
(Story, p. 514; Message, p. 1073)

4. HR 6331 (Medicare reimbursement to doctors)
Vetoed July 15, 2008
House overrode veto July 15, 2008: 383–41
Senate overrode veto July 15, 2008: 70–26
(Story, p. 571; Message, p. 571)

Selected Texts

Selected Texts on the Presidency

President Bush's Second Inaugural Address

Following is the second inaugural address of George W. Bush, the nation's forty-third president, delivered Jan. 20, 2005.

Vice President Cheney, Mr. Chief Justice, President Carter, President Bush, President Clinton, members of the United States Congress, Reverend, clergy, distinguished guests, fellow citizens:

On this day, prescribed by law and marked by ceremony, we celebrate the durable wisdom of our Constitution and recall the deep commitments that unite our country.

I am grateful for the honor of this hour, mindful of the consequential times in which we live and determined to fulfill the oath that I have sworn and you have witnessed.

At this second gathering, our duties are defined not by the words I use, but by the history we have seen together.

For a half a century, America defended our own freedom by standing watch on distant borders. After the shipwreck of communism came years of relative quiet, years of repose, years of sabbatical. And then there came a day of fire. We have seen our vulnerability and we have seen its deepest source.

For as long as whole regions of the world simmer in resentment and tyranny, prone to ideologies that feed hatred and excuse murder, violence will gather and multiply in destructive power and cross the most defended borders and raise a mortal threat.

There is only one force of history that can break the reign of hatred and resentment and expose the pretensions of tyrants and reward the hopes of the decent and tolerant, and that is the force of human freedom.

We are led, by events and common sense, to one conclusion: The survival of liberty in our land increasingly depends on the success of liberty in other lands. The best hope for peace in our world is the expansion of freedom in all the world.

America's vital interests and our deepest beliefs are now one. From the day of our founding, we have proclaimed that every man and woman on this earth has rights and dignity and matchless value, because they bear the image of the maker of heaven and Earth.

Across the generations, we have proclaimed the imperative of self-government, because no one is fit to be a master and no one deserves to be a slave.

ENDING TYRANNY

Fancying these ideals is the mission that created our nation. It is the honorable achievement of our fathers. Now it is the urgent requirement of our nation's security and the calling of our time.

So it is the policy of the United States to seek and support the growth of democratic movements and institutions in every nation and culture, with the ultimate goal of ending tyranny in our world. This is not primarily the task of arms, though we will defend ourselves and our friends by force of arms when necessary.

Freedom, by its nature, must be chosen and defended by citizens and sustained by the rule of law and the protection of minorities. And when the soul of a nation finally speaks, the institutions that arise may reflect customs and traditions very different from our own.

America will not impose our own style of government on the unwilling. Our goal, instead, is to help others find their own voice, attain their own freedom and make their own way.

The great objective of ending tyranny is the concentrated work of generations. The difficulty of the task is no excuse for avoiding it.

America's influence is not unlimited. But, fortunately for the oppressed, America's influence is considerable, and we will use it confidently in freedom's cause.

My most solemn duty is to protect this nation and its people from further attacks and emerging threats. Some have unwisely chosen to test America's resolve and have found it firm. We will persistently clarify the choice before every ruler and every nation: the moral choice between oppression, which is always wrong, and freedom, which is eternally right.

America will not pretend that jailed dissidents prefer their chains, or that women welcome humiliation and servitude, or that any human being aspires to live at the mercy of bullies. We will encourage reform in other governments by making clear that success in our relations will require the decent treatment of their own people.

America's belief in human dignity will guide our policies, yet rights must be more than the grudging concessions of dictators. They are secured by free dissent and the participation of the governed.

In the long run, there is no justice without freedom, and there can be no human rights without human liberty.

Some, I know, have questioned the global appeal of liberty—though this time in history, four decades defined by the swiftest advance of freedom ever seen, is an odd time for doubt.

Americans, of all people, should never be surprised by the power of our ideals.

Eventually, the call of freedom comes to every mind and every soul. We do not accept the existence of permanent tyranny because we do not accept the possibility of permanent slavery. Liberty will come to those who love it.

Today, America speaks anew to the peoples of the world. All who live in tyranny and hopelessness can know the United States will not ignore your oppression, or excuse your oppressors. When you stand for your liberty, we will stand with you.

Democratic reformers facing repression, prison or exile can know America sees you for who you are, the future leaders of your free country.

The rulers of outlaw regimes can know that we still believe as Abraham Lincoln did: "Those who deny freedom to others deserve it not for themselves; and, under the rule of a just God, cannot long retain it."

The leaders of governments with long habits of control need to know: To serve your people you must learn to trust them. Start on this journey of progress and justice, and America will walk at your side.

And all the allies of the United States can know: We honor your friendship, we rely on your counsel and we depend on your help.

Division among free nations is a primary goal of freedom's enemies. The concerted effort of free nations to promote democracy is a prelude to our enemies' defeat.

Today, I also speak anew to my fellow citizens. From all of you, I have asked patience in the hard task of securing America, which you have granted in good measure.

Our country has accepted obligations that are difficult to fulfill and would be dishonorable to abandon. Yet because we have acted in the great liberating tradition of this nation, tens of millions have achieved their freedom. And as hope kindles hope, millions more will find it.

By our efforts we have lit a fire as well—a fire in the minds of men. It warms those who feel its power. It burns those who fight its progress. And one day this untamed fire of freedom will reach the darkest corners of our world.

A few Americans have accepted the hardest duties in this cause. In the quiet work of intelligence and diplomacy, the idealistic work of helping raise up free governments, the dangerous and necessary work of fighting our enemies, some have shown their devotion to our country in deaths that honored their whole lives. And we will always honor their names and their sacrifice.

All Americans have witnessed this idealism, and some for the first time. I ask our youngest citizens to believe the evidence of your eyes.

You have seen duty and allegiance in the determined faces of our soldiers. You have seen that life is fragile, and evil is real, and courage triumphs. Make the choice to serve in a cause larger than your wants, larger than yourself, and in your days you will add not just to the wealth of our country, but to its character.

FREEDOM AT HOME

America has need of idealism and courage, because we have essential work at home: the unfinished work of American freedom.

In a world moving toward liberty, we are determined to show the meaning and promise of liberty.

In America's ideal of freedom, citizens find the dignity and security of economic independence, instead of laboring on the edge of subsistence. This is the broader definition of liberty that motivated the Homestead Act, the Social Security Act and the G.I. Bill of Rights.

And now we will extend this vision by reforming great institutions to serve the needs of our time.

To give every American a stake in the promise and future of our country, we will bring the highest standards to our schools and build an ownership society.

We will widen the ownership of homes and businesses, retirement savings and health insurance, preparing our people for the challenges of life in a free society.

By making every citizen an agent of his or her own destiny, we will give our fellow Americans greater freedom from want and fear, and make our society more prosperous and just and equal.

In America's ideal of freedom, the public interest depends on private character, on integrity, and tolerance toward others, and the rule of conscience in our own lives. Self-government relies, in the end, on the governing of the self.

That edifice of character is built in families, supported by communities with standards, and sustained in our national life by the truths of Sinai, the Sermon on the Mount, the words of the Koran, and the varied faiths of our people.

Americans move forward in every generation by reaffirming all that is good and true that came before: ideals of justice and conduct that are the same yesterday, today and forever.

In America's ideal of freedom, the exercise of rights is ennobled by service and mercy and a heart for the weak.

Liberty for all does not mean independence from one another. Our nation relies on men and women who look after a neighbor and surround the lost with love.

Americans at our best value the life we see in one another and must always remember that even the unwanted have worth.

And our country must abandon all the habits of racism because we cannot carry the message of freedom and the baggage of bigotry at the same time.

From the perspective of a single day, including this day of dedication, the issues and questions before our country are many.

From the viewpoint of centuries, the questions that come to us are narrowed and few. Did our generation advance the cause of freedom? And did our character bring credit to that cause?

These questions that judge us also unite us, because Americans of every party and background—Americans by choice and by birth—are bound to one another in the cause of freedom.

HEALING DIVISIONS

We have known divisions, which must be healed to move forward in great purposes. And I will strive in good faith to heal them. Yet those divisions do not define America.

We felt the unity and fellowship of our nation when freedom came under attack, and our response came like a single hand over a single heart. And we can feel that same unity and pride whenever America acts for good, and the victims of disaster are given hope, and the unjust encounter justice, and the captives are set free.

We go forward with complete confidence in the eventual triumph of freedom. Not because history runs on the wheels of inevitability; it is human choices that move events. Not because we consider ourselves a chosen nation; God moves and chooses as he wills.

We have confidence because freedom is the permanent hope of mankind, the hunger in dark places, the longing of the soul.

When our founders declared a new order of the ages, when soldiers died in wave upon wave for a union based on liberty, when citizens marched in peaceful outrage under the banner "Freedom Now," they were acting on an ancient hope that is meant to be fulfilled.

History has an ebb and flow of justice, but history also has a visible direction, set by liberty and the author of liberty.

When the Declaration of Independence was first read in public and the Liberty Bell was sounded in celebration, a witness said: "It rang as if it meant something." In our time it means something still.

America, in this young century, proclaims liberty throughout all the world and to all the inhabitants thereof. Renewed in our strength, tested but not weary, we are ready for the greatest achievements in the history of freedom.

May God bless you, and may he watch over the United States of America.

President Bush's 2005 State of the Union Address

Following is President Bush's State of the Union address delivered to a joint session of Congress Feb. 2, 2005.

Mr. Speaker, Vice President Cheney, members of Congress, fellow citizens: As a new Congress gathers, all of us in the elected branches of government share a great privilege: We've been placed in office by the votes of the people we serve. And tonight that is a privilege we share with newly elected leaders of Afghanistan, the Palestinian territories, Ukraine and a free and sovereign Iraq.

Two weeks ago, I stood on the steps of this Capitol and renewed the commitment of our nation to the guiding ideal of liberty for all. This evening I will set forth policies to advance that ideal at home and around the world.

Tonight, with a healthy, growing economy, with more Americans going back to work, with our nation an active force for good in the world, the state of our union is confident and strong.

Our generation has been blessed by the expansion of opportunity, by advances in medicine, by the security purchased by our parents' sacrifice. Now, as we see a little gray in the mirror—or a lot of gray—and we watch our children moving into adulthood, we ask the question: What will be the state of their union?

Members of Congress, the choices we make together will answer that question. Over the next several months, on issue after issue, let us do what Americans have always done and build a better world for our children and our grandchildren.

First, we must be good stewards of this economy and renew the great institutions on which millions of our fellow citizens rely.

America's economy is the fastest growing of any major industrialized nation. In the past four years, we have provided tax relief to every person who pays income taxes, overcome a recession, opened up new markets abroad, prosecuted corporate criminals, raised home ownership to its highest level in history. And in the last year alone, the United States has added 2.3 million new jobs. When action was needed, the Congress delivered, and the nation is grateful.

Now we must add to these achievements. By making our economy more flexible, more innovative and more competitive, we will keep America the economic leader of the world.

DOMESTIC POLICY

America's prosperity requires restraining the spending appetite of the federal government. I welcome the bipartisan enthusiasm for spending discipline. I will send you a budget that holds the growth of discretionary spending below inflation, makes tax relief permanent and stays on track to cut the deficit in half by 2009.

My budget substantially reduces or eliminates more than 150 government programs that are not getting results or duplicate current efforts or do not fulfill essential priorities. The principle here is clear: Taxpayer dollars must be spent wisely or not at all.

To make our economy stronger and more dynamic, we must prepare a rising generation to fill the jobs of the 21st century.

Under the No Child Left Behind Act, standards are higher, test scores are on the rise and we're closing the achievement gap for minority students. Now we must demand better results from our high schools so every high school diploma is a ticket to success.

We will help an additional 200,000 workers to get training for a better career by reforming our job-training system and strengthening America's community colleges. And we will make it easier for Americans to afford a college education by increasing the size of Pell Grants.

To make our economy stronger and more competitive, America must reward, not punish, the efforts and dreams of entrepreneurs. Small business is the path of advancement, especially for women and minorities. So we must free small businesses from needless regulation and protect honest job creators from junk lawsuits.

Justice is distorted and our economy is held back by irresponsible class actions and frivolous asbestos claims. And I urge Congress to pass legal reforms this year.

To make our economy stronger and more productive, we must make health care more affordable and give families greater access to good coverage and more control over their health decisions. I ask Congress to move forward on a comprehensive health care agenda with tax credits to help low-income workers buy insurance; a community health center in every poor county; improved information technology to prevent medical error and needless costs; association health plans for small businesses and their employees . . . expanded health savings accounts . . . and medical liability reform that will reduce health care costs and make sure patients have the doctors and care they need.

To keep our economy growing, we also need reliable supplies of affordable, environmentally responsible energy. Nearly four years ago, I submitted a comprehensive energy strategy that encourages conservation, alternative sources, a modernized electricity grid and more production here at home, including safe, clean nuclear energy. My "Clear Skies" legislation will cut power-plant pollution and improve the health of our citizens. And my budget provides strong funding for leading-edge technology, from hydrogen-fueled cars to clean coal to renewable sources such as ethanol. Four years of debate is enough. I urge Congress to pass legislation that makes America more secure and less dependent on foreign energy.

All these proposals are essential to expand this economy and add new jobs, but they are just the beginning of our duty. To build the prosperity of future generations, we must update institutions that were created to meet the needs of an earlier time.

Year after year, Americans are burdened by an archaic, incoherent federal tax code. I've appointed a bipartisan panel to examine the tax code from top to bottom. And when their recommendations are delivered, you and I will work together to give this nation a tax code that is pro-growth, easy to understand and fair to all.

America's immigration system is also outdated—unsuited to the needs of our economy and to the values of our country. We should not be content with laws that punish hardworking people who want only to provide for their families and deny businesses willing workers, and invite chaos at our border. It is time for an immigration policy that permits temporary guest workers to fill jobs Americans will not take, that rejects amnesty, that tells us who is entering and leaving our country, and that closes the border to drug dealers and terrorists.

SOCIAL SECURITY

One of America's most important institutions—a symbol of the trust between generations—is also in need of wise and effective reform. Social Security was a great moral success of the 20th century, and we must honor its great purposes in this new century. The system, however, on its current path, is headed toward bankruptcy. And so we must join together to strengthen and save Social Security.

Today, more than 45 million Americans receive Social Security benefits, and millions more are nearing retirement. And for them, the system is sound and fiscally strong. I have a message for every American who is 55 or older: Do not let anyone mislead you. For you, the Social Security system will not change in any way.

For younger workers, the Social Security system has serious problems that will grow worse with time. Social Security was created decades ago, for a very different era. In those days, people did not live as long, benefits were much lower than they are today, and a half-century ago, about 16 workers paid into the system for each person drawing benefits.

Our society has changed in ways the founders of Social Security could not have foreseen. In today's world, people are living longer and therefore drawing benefits longer. And those benefits are scheduled to rise dramatically over the next few decades. And instead of 16 workers paying in for every beneficiary, right now it's only about three workers. And over the next few decades, that number will fall to just two workers per beneficiary. With each passing year, fewer workers are paying ever-higher benefits to an ever-larger number of retirees.

So here is the result: Thirteen years from now, in 2018, Social Security will be paying out more than it takes in. And every year afterward will bring a new shortfall, bigger than the year before. For example, in the year 2027, the government will somehow have to come up with an extra $200 billion to keep the system afloat. And by 2033, the annual shortfall would be more than $300 billion. By the year 2042, the entire system would be exhausted and bankrupt.

If steps are not taken to avert that outcome, the only solutions would be dramatically higher taxes, massive new borrowing, or sudden and severe cuts in Social Security benefits or other government programs.

I recognize that 2018 and 2042 may seem a long way off. But those dates aren't so distant, as any parent will tell you. If you have a 5-year-old, you're already concerned about how you'll pay for college tuition 13 years down the road. If you've got children in their 20s, as some of us do, the idea of Social Security collapsing before they retire does not seem like a small matter. And it should not be a small matter to the United States Congress.

You and I share a responsibility. We must pass reforms that solve the financial problems of Social Security once and for all.

Fixing Social Security permanently will require an open, candid review of the options. Some have suggested limiting benefits for wealthy retirees. Former Congressman Tim Penny has raised the possibility of indexing benefits to prices rather than wages. During the 1990s, my predecessor, President Clinton, spoke of increasing the retirement age. Former Sen. John Breaux suggested discouraging early collection of Social Security benefits. The late Sen. Daniel Patrick Moynihan recommended changing the way benefits are calculated. All these ideas are on the table.

I know that none of these reforms would be easy. But we have to move ahead with courage and honesty, because our children's retirement security is more important than partisan politics. I will work with members of Congress to find the most effective combination of reforms. I will listen to anyone who has a good idea to offer.

We must, however, be guided by some basic principles: We must make Social Security permanently sound, not leave that task for another day. We must not jeopardize our economic strength by increasing payroll taxes. We must ensure that lower-income Americans get the help they need to have dignity and peace of mind in their retirement. We must guarantee that there is no change for those now retired or nearing retirement. And we must take care that any changes in the system are gradual, so younger workers have years to prepare and plan for their future.

As we fix Social Security, we also have the responsibility to make the system a better deal for younger workers. And the best way to reach that goal is through voluntary personal retirement accounts.

Here is how the idea works: Right now, a set portion of the money you earn is taken out of your paycheck to pay for the Social Security benefits of today's retirees. If you're a younger worker, I believe you should be able to set aside part of that money in your own retirement account, so you can build a nest egg for your own future.

Here is why the personal accounts are a better deal: Your money will grow, over time, at a greater rate than anything the current system can deliver. And your account will provide money for retirement over and above the check you will receive from Social Security. In addition, you'll be able to pass along the money that accumulates in your personal account, if you wish, to your children—or grandchildren. And best of all, the money in the account is yours, and the government can never take it away.

The goal here is greater security in retirement, so we will set careful guidelines for personal accounts: We'll make sure the money can only go into a conservative mix of bonds and stock funds. We'll make sure that your earnings are not eaten up by hidden Wall Street fees. We'll make sure there are good options to protect your investments from sudden market swings on the eve of your retirement. We'll make sure a personal account cannot be emptied out all at once, but rather paid out over time, as an addition to traditional Social Security benefits.

And we'll make sure this plan is fiscally responsible by starting personal retirement accounts gradually and raising the yearly limits on contributions over time, eventually permitting all workers to set aside 4 percentage points of their payroll taxes in their accounts.

Personal retirement accounts should be familiar to federal employees, because you already have something similar, called the Thrift Savings Plan, which lets workers deposit a portion of their paychecks into any of five different broadly based investment funds. It's time to extend the same security and choice and ownership to young Americans.

A FREE SOCIETY

Our second great responsibility to our children and grandchildren is to honor and to pass along the values that sustain a free society. So many of my generation, after a long journey, have come home to family and faith, and are determined to bring up responsible, moral children. Government is not the source of these values, but government should never undermine them.

Because marriage is a sacred institution and the foundation of society, it should not be redefined by activist judges. For the good of families, children and society, I support a constitutional amendment to protect the institution of marriage.

Because a society is measured by how it treats the weak and vulnerable, we must strive to build a culture of life. Medical research can help us reach that goal, by developing treatments and cures that save lives and help people overcome disabilities. And I thank the Congress for doubling the funding of the National Institutes of Health.

To build a culture of life, we must also ensure that scientific advances always serve human dignity, not take advantage of some lives for the benefit of others. We should all be able to agree on some clear standards. I will work with Congress to ensure that human embryos are not created for experimentation or grown for body parts and that human life is never bought or sold as a commodity.

America will continue to lead the world in medical research that is ambitious, aggressive and always ethical.

Because courts must always deliver impartial justice, judges have a duty to faithfully interpret the law, not legislate from the bench. As president, I have a constitutional responsibility to nominate men and women who understand the role of courts in our democracy and are well-qualified to serve on the bench, and I have done so. The Constitution also gives the Senate a responsibility: Every judicial nominee deserves an up-or-down vote.

Because one of the deepest values of our country is compassion, we must never turn away from any citizen who feels isolated from the opportunities of America. Our government will continue to support faith-based and community groups that bring hope to harsh places.

GANG VIOLENCE

Now we need to focus on giving young people, especially young men in our cities, better options than apathy or gangs or jail. Tonight I propose a three-year initiative to help organizations keep young people out of gangs and show young men an ideal of manhood that respects women and rejects violence.

Taking on gang life will be one part of a broader outreach to at-risk youth, which involves parents and pastors, coaches and community leaders, in programs ranging from literacy to sports. And I am proud that the leader of this nationwide effort will be our first lady, Laura Bush.

Because HIV/AIDS brings suffering and fear into so many lives, I ask you to reauthorize the Ryan White Act to encourage prevention and provide care and treatment to the victims of that disease. And as we update this important law, we must focus our efforts on fellow citizens with the highest rates of new cases: African American men and women.

Because one of the main sources of our national unity is our belief in equal justice, we need to make sure Americans of all races and backgrounds have confidence in the system that provides justice. In America we must make doubly sure no person is held to account for a crime he or she did not commit. So we are dramatically expanding the use of DNA evidence to prevent wrongful conviction. Soon I will send to Congress a proposal to fund special training for defense counsel in capital cases, because people on trial for their lives must have competent lawyers by their side.

NATIONAL SECURITY

Our third responsibility to future generations is to leave them an America that is safe from danger and protected by peace. We will pass along to our children all the freedoms we enjoy. And chief among them is freedom from fear.

In the three and a half years since September the 11th, 2001, we've taken unprecedented actions to protect Americans.

We've created a new department of government to defend our homeland, focused the FBI on preventing terrorism, begun to reform our intelligence agencies, broken up terror cells across the country, expanded research on defenses against biological and chemical attack, improved border security, and trained more than a half-million first responders.

Police and firefighters, air marshals, researchers and so many others are working every day to make our homeland safer—and we thank them all.

Our nation, working with allies and friends, has also confronted the enemy abroad with measures that are determined, successful and continuing.

The al Qaeda terror network that attacked our country still has leaders, but many of its top commanders have been removed. There are still governments that sponsor and harbor terrorists, but their number has declined. There are still regimes seeking weapons of mass destruction, but no longer without attention and without consequence.

Our country is still the target of terrorists who want to kill many and intimidate us all. And we will stay on the offensive against them until the fight is won.

Pursuing our enemies is a vital commitment of the war on terror. And I thank the Congress for providing our service men and women with the resources they have needed. During this time of war, we must continue to support our military and give them the tools for victory.

Other nations around the globe have stood with us. In Afghanistan, an international force is helping provide security. In Iraq, 28 countries have troops on the ground, the United Nations and the European Union provided technical assistance for the elections, and NATO is leading a mission to help train Iraqi officers. We're cooperating with 60 governments in the Proliferation Security Initiative to detect and stop the transit of dangerous materials. We're working closely with the governments in Asia to convince North Korea to abandon its nuclear ambitions. Pakistan, Saudi Arabia and nine other countries have captured or detained al Qaeda terrorists.

In the next four years, my administration will continue to build the coalitions that will defeat the dangers of our time.

In the long term, the peace we seek will only be achieved by eliminating the conditions that feed radicalism and ideologies of murder. If whole regions of the world remain in despair and grow in hatred, they will be the recruiting grounds for terror, and that terror will stalk America and other free nations for decades.

The only force powerful enough to stop the rise of tyranny and terror, and replace hatred with hope is the force of human freedom.

Our enemies know this, and that is why the terrorist Zarqawi recently declared war on what he called the "evil principle" of democracy. And we've declared our own intention: America will stand with the allies of freedom to support democratic movements in the Middle East and beyond, with the ultimate goal of ending tyranny in our world.

The United States has no right, no desire and no intention to impose our form of government on anyone else. That is one of the main differences between us and our enemies. They seek to impose and expand an empire of oppression, in which a tiny group of brutal, self-appointed rulers control every aspect of every life.

Our aim is to build and preserve a community of free and independent nations, with governments that answer to their citizens and reflect their own cultures. And because democracies respect their own people and their neighbors, the advance of freedom will lead to peace.

That advance has great momentum in our time, shown by women voting in Afghanistan, and Palestinians choosing a new direction, and the people of Ukraine asserting their democratic rights and electing a president. We are witnessing landmark events in the history of liberty. And in the coming years, we will add to that story.

THE MIDDLE EAST

The beginnings of reform and democracy in the Palestinian territories are now showing the power of freedom to break old patterns of violence and failure.

Tomorrow morning, Secretary of State Rice departs on a trip that will take her to Israel and the West Bank for meetings with Prime Minister Sharon and President Abbas. She will discuss with them how we and our friends can help the Palestinian people end terror and build the institutions of a peaceful, independent, democratic state.

To promote this democracy, I will ask Congress for $350 million to support Palestinian political, economic and security reforms. The goal of two democratic states, Israel and Palestine, living side by side in peace is within reach, and America will help them achieve that goal.

To promote peace and stability in the broader Middle East, the United States will work with our friends in the region to fight the common threat of terror, while we encourage a higher standard of freedom.

Hopeful reform is already taking hold in an arc from Morocco to Jordan to Bahrain. The government of Saudi Arabia can demonstrate its leadership in the region by expanding the role of its people in determining their future. And the great and proud nation of Egypt, which showed the way toward peace in the Middle East, can now show the way toward democracy in the Middle East.

To promote peace in the broader Middle East, we must confront regimes that continue to harbor terrorists and pursue weapons of mass murder.

Syria still allows its territory and parts of Lebanon to be used by terrorists who seek to destroy every chance of peace in the region. You have passed, and we are applying, the Syrian Accountability Act. And we expect the Syrian government to end all support for terror and open the door to freedom.

Today, Iran remains the world's primary state sponsor of terror—pursuing nuclear weapons while depriving its people of the freedom they seek and deserve. We are working with European allies to make clear to the Iranian regime that it must give up its uranium enrichment program and any plutonium reprocessing and end its support for terror. And to the Iranian people, I say tonight: As you stand for your own liberty, America stands with you.

IRAQ

Our generational commitment to the advance of freedom, especially in the Middle East, is now being tested and honored in Iraq. That country is a vital front in the war on terror, which is why the terrorists have chosen to make a stand there. Our men and women in uniform are fighting terrorists in Iraq so we do not have to face them here at home.

The victory of freedom in Iraq will strengthen a new ally in the war on terror, inspire democratic reformers from Damascus to Tehran, bring more hope and progress to a troubled region, and thereby lift a terrible threat from the lives of our children and grandchildren. We will succeed because the Iraqi people value their own liberty, as they showed the world last Sunday.

Across Iraq, often at great risk, millions of citizens went to the polls and elected 275 men and women to represent them in a new Transitional National Assembly.

A young woman in Baghdad told of waking to the sound of mortar fire on election day and wondering if it might be too dangerous to vote. She said, "Hearing those explosions, it occurred to me, the insurgents are weak, they are afraid of democracy, they are losing. So I got my husband, and I got my parents, and we all came out and voted together."

Americans recognize that spirit of liberty, because we share it. In any nation, casting your vote is an act of civic responsibility. For millions of Iraqis, it was also an act of personal courage, and they have earned the respect of us all.

One of Iraq's leading democracy and human rights advocates is Safia Taleb al-Suhail. She says of her country, "We were occupied for thirty-five years by Saddam Hussein. That was the real occupation. Thank you to the American people who paid the cost, but most of all to the soldiers."

Eleven years ago, Safia's father was assassinated by Saddam's intelligence service. Three days ago in Baghdad, Safia was finally able to vote for the leaders of her country. And we are honored that she is with us tonight.

The terrorists and insurgents are violently opposed to democracy and will continue to attack it. Yet the terrorists' most powerful myth is being destroyed. The whole world is seeing that the car bombers and assassins are not only fighting coalition forces, they are trying to destroy the hopes of Iraqis, expressed in free elections. And the whole world now knows that a small group of extremists will not overturn the will of the Iraqi people.

We will succeed in Iraq because Iraqis are determined to fight for their own freedom and to write their own history. As Prime Minister Allawi said in his speech to Congress last September, "Ordinary Iraqis are anxious to shoulder all the security burdens of our country as quickly as possible." That is the natural desire of an independent nation, and it also is the stated mission of our coalition in Iraq.

SUPPORT FOR IRAQIS

The new political situation in Iraq opens a new phase of our work in that country. At the recommendation of our commanders on the ground and in consultation with the Iraqi government, we will increasingly focus our efforts on helping prepare more capable Iraqi security forces—forces with skilled officers and an effective command structure.

As those forces become more self-reliant and take on greater security responsibilities, America and its coalition partners will increasingly be in a supporting role. In the end, Iraqis must be able to defend their own country, and we will help that proud, new nation secure its liberty.

Recently an Iraqi interpreter said to a reporter, "Tell America not to abandon us." He and all Iraqis can be certain: While our military strategy is adapting to circumstances, our commitment remains firm and unchanging. We are standing for the freedom of our Iraqi friends, and freedom in Iraq will make America safer for generations to come.

We will not set an artificial timetable for leaving Iraq, because that would embolden the terrorists and make them believe they can wait us out. We are in Iraq to achieve a result: a country that is democratic, representative of all its people, at peace with its neighbors and able to defend itself.

And when that result is achieved, our men and women serving in Iraq will return home with the honor they have earned.

Right now, Americans in uniform are serving at posts across the world, often taking great risks on my orders. We have given them training and equipment. And they have given us an example of idealism and character that makes every American proud. The volunteers of our military are unrelenting in battle, unwavering in loyalty, unmatched in honor and decency; and every day they are making our nation more secure.

Some of our service men and women have survived terrible injuries, and this grateful country will do everything we can to help them recover. And we have said farewell to some very good men and women who died for our freedom and whose memory this nation will honor forever.

One name we honor is Marine Corps Sgt. Byron Norwood of Pflugerville, Texas, who was killed during the assault on Fallujah. His mom, Janet, sent me a letter and told me how much Byron loved being a Marine and how proud he was to be on the front line against terror. She wrote, "When Byron was home the last time, I said that I wanted to protect him like I had since he was born. He just hugged me and said, 'You've done your job, Mom. Now it is my turn to protect you.' "

Ladies and gentlemen, with grateful hearts, we honor freedom's defenders and our military families, represented here this evening by Sgt. Norwood's mom and dad, Janet and Bill Norwood.

In these four years, Americans have seen the unfolding of large events. We have known times of sorrow and hours of uncertainty and days of victory. In all this history, even when we have disagreed, we have seen threads of purpose that unite us. The attack on freedom in our world has reaffirmed our confidence in freedom's power to change the world. We're all part of a great venture: to extend the promise of freedom in our country, to renew the values that sustain our liberty and to spread the peace that freedom brings.

As Franklin Roosevelt once reminded Americans, "Each age is a dream that is dying or one that is coming to birth."

And we live in the country where the biggest dreams are born. The abolition of slavery was only a dream—until it was fulfilled. The liberation of Europe from fascism was only a dream—until it was achieved. The fall of imperial communism was only a dream—until, one day, it was accomplished.

Our generation has dreams of its own, and we also go forward with confidence. The road of providence is uneven and unpredictable, yet we know where it leads: It leads to freedom.

Thank you. And may God bless America.

President Bush's Address following Hurricane Katrina

Following is the nationally televised address President Bush delivered from Jackson Square in New Orleans Sept. 15, 2005.

Good evening. I am speaking to you from the city of New Orleans—nearly empty, still partly under water, and waiting for life and hope to return.

Eastward from Lake Pontchartrain, across the Mississippi coast, to Alabama and into Florida, millions of lives were changed in a day by a cruel and wasteful storm. In the aftermath, we have seen fellow citizens left stunned and uprooted, searching for loved ones and grieving for the dead, and looking for meaning in a tragedy that seems so blind and random.

We have also witnessed the kind of desperation no citizen of this great and generous nation should ever have to know: fellow Americans calling out for food and water, vulnerable people left at the mercy of criminals who had no mercy, and the bodies of the dead lying uncovered and untended in the street.

These days of sorrow and outrage have also been marked by acts of courage and kindness that make all Americans proud.

Coast Guard and other personnel rescued tens of thousands of people from flooded neighborhoods. Religious congregations and families have welcomed strangers as brothers and sisters and neighbors. In the community of Chalmette, when two men tried to break into a home, the owner invited them to stay—and took in fifteen other people who had no place to go. At Tulane Hospital for Children, doctors and nurses did not eat for days so patients could have food, and eventually carried the patients on their backs up eight flights of stairs to helicopters.

Many first-responders were victims themselves—wounded healers, with a sense of duty greater than their own suffering. When I met Steve Scott of the Biloxi Fire Department, he and his colleagues were conducting a house-to-house search for survivors. Steve told me this: "I lost my house and I lost my cars, but I still got my family and I still got my spirit."

Across the Gulf Coast, among people who have lost much and suffered much and given to the limit of their power, we are seeing that same spirit: a core of strength that survives all hurt, a faith in God no storm can take away, and a powerful American determination to clear the ruins and build better than before.

RECOVERY AND REBUILDING

Tonight so many victims of the hurricane and the flood are far from home and friends and familiar things. You need to know that our whole nation cares about you, and in the journey ahead you are not alone.

To all who carry a burden of loss, I extend the deepest sympathy of our country. To every person who has served and sacrificed in this emergency, I offer the gratitude of our country.

And tonight I also offer this pledge of the American people: Throughout the area hit by the hurricane, we will do what it takes, we will stay as long as it takes, to help citizens rebuild their communities and their lives.

And all who question the future of the Crescent City need to know: There is no way to imagine America without New Orleans, and this great city will rise again.

The work of rescue is largely finished; the work of recovery is moving forward. In nearly all of Mississippi, electric power has been restored. Trade is starting to return to the port of New Orleans, and agricultural shipments are moving down the Mississippi River.

All major gasoline pipelines are now in operation, preventing the supply disruptions that many feared. The breaks in the levees have been closed, the pumps are running, and the water here in New Orleans is receding by the hour. Environmental officials are on the ground, taking water samples, identifying and dealing with hazardous debris, and working to get drinking water and wastewater treatment systems operating again. And some very sad duties are being carried out by professionals who gather the dead, treat them with respect, and prepare them for their rest.

In the task of recovery and rebuilding, some of the hardest work is still ahead. And it will require the creative skill and generosity of a united country.

MEETING THE NEED

Our first commitment is to meet the immediate needs of those who had to flee their homes and leave all their possessions behind. For these Americans, every night brings uncertainty, every day requires new courage and, in the months to come, will bring more than their fair share of struggles.

The Department of Homeland Security is registering evacuees who are now in shelters, churches or private homes—whether in the Gulf region or far away.

I have signed an order providing immediate assistance to people from the disaster area. As of today, more than 500,000 evacuee families have gotten emergency help to pay for food, clothing and other essentials.

Evacuees who have not yet registered should contact FEMA or the Red Cross. We need to know who you are, because many of you will be eligible for broader assistance in the future.

Many families were separated during the evacuation, and we are working to help you reunite. Please call this number: 1-877-568-3317. That's 1-877-568-3317. And we will work to bring your family back together and pay for your travel to reach them.

In addition, we are taking steps to ensure that evacuees do not have to travel great distances or navigate bureaucracies to get the benefits that are there for them.

The Department of Health and Human Services has sent more than 1,500 health professionals, along with over 50 tons of medical supplies—including vaccines, antibiotics and medicines for people with chronic conditions, such as diabetes. The Social Security Administration is delivering checks. The Department of Labor is helping displaced persons apply for temporary jobs and unemployment benefits. And the Postal Service is registering new addresses so that people can get their mail.

To carry out the first stages of the relief effort and begin rebuilding at once, I have asked for, and the Congress has provided, more than $60 billion. This is an unprecedented response to an unprecedented crisis, which demonstrates the compassion and resolve of our nation.

INFRASTRUCTURE

Our second commitment is to help the citizens of the Gulf Coast to overcome this disaster, put their lives back together and rebuild their communities.

Along this coast, for mile after mile, the wind and water swept the land clean. In Mississippi, many thousands of houses were damaged or destroyed. In New Orleans and surrounding parishes, more than a quarter-million houses are no longer safe to live in. Hundreds of thousands of people from across this region will need to find longer-term housing.

Our goal is to get people out of the shelters by the middle of October. So we are providing direct assistance to evacuees that allows them to rent apartments, and many are already moving into places of their own.

A number of states have taken in evacuees and shown them great compassion—admitting children to school and providing health care. So I will work with the Congress to ensure that states are reimbursed for these extra expenses.

In the disaster area and in cities that have received huge numbers of displaced people, we are beginning to bring in mobile homes and trailers for temporary use.

To relieve the burden on local health care facilities in the region, we are sending extra doctors and nurses to these areas. We're also providing money that can be used to cover overtime pay for police and fire departments while the cities and towns rebuild.

Near New Orleans, Biloxi and other cities, housing is urgently needed for police and firefighters, other service providers and the many workers who are going to rebuild these cities. Right now, many are sleeping on ships we have brought to the Port of New Orleans, and more ships are on their way to the region.

And we'll provide mobile homes and supply them with basic services, as close to construction areas as possible, so the rebuilding process can go forward as quickly as possible.

And the federal government will undertake a close partnership with the states of Louisiana and Mississippi, the city of New Orleans and other Gulf Coast cities, so they can rebuild in a sensible, well-planned way. Federal funds will cover the great majority of the costs of repairing public infrastructure in the disaster zone, from roads and bridges to schools and water systems.

Our goal is to get the work done quickly. And taxpayers expect this work to be done honestly and wisely. So we will have a team of inspectors general reviewing all expenditures.

In the rebuilding process, there will be many important decisions and many details to resolve. Yet we are moving forward according to some clear principles.

The federal government will be fully engaged in the mission, but Gov. [Haley] Barbour [of Mississippi], Gov. [Kathleen Babineaux] Blanco [of Louisiana], Mayor [C. Ray] Nagin [of New Orleans] and other state and local leaders will have the primary role in planning for their own future.

Clearly, communities will need to move decisively to change zoning laws and building codes, in order to avoid a repeat of what we have seen. And in the work of rebuilding, as many jobs as possible should go to the men and women who live in Louisiana, Mississippi and Alabama.

ANTI-POVERTY EFFORT

Our third commitment is this: When communities are rebuilt, they must be even better and stronger than before the storm.

Within the Gulf region are some of the most beautiful and historic places in America. As all of us saw on television, there is also some deep, persistent poverty in this region as well. That poverty has roots in a history of racial discrimination, which cut off generations from the opportunity of America. We have a duty to confront this poverty with bold action.

So let us restore all that we have cherished from yesterday, and let us rise above the legacy of inequality.

When the streets are rebuilt, there should be many new businesses, including minority-owned businesses, along those streets.

When the houses are rebuilt, more families should own, not rent, those houses.

When the regional economy revives, local people should be prepared for the jobs being created.

Americans want the Gulf Coast not just to survive, but to thrive; not just to cope, but to overcome. We want evacuees to come home, for the best of reasons—because they have a real chance at a better life in a place they love.

When one resident of this city who lost his home was asked by a reporter if he would relocate, he said, "No, I will rebuild, but I will build higher." That is our vision for the future in this city and beyond. We'll not just rebuild, we'll build higher and better.

To meet this goal, I will listen to good ideas from Congress and state and local officials and the private sector.

SAFETY AND SECURITY

I believe we should start with three initiatives that the Congress should pass.

Tonight, I propose the creation of a Gulf opportunity zone, encompassing the region of the disaster in Louisiana and Mississippi and Alabama.

Within this zone, we should provide immediate incentives for job-creating investment; tax relief for small businesses; incentives to companies that create jobs; and loans and loan guarantees for small businesses, including minority-owned enterprises, to get them up and running again. It is entrepreneurship that creates jobs and opportunity. It is entrepreneurship that helps break the cycle of poverty. And we will take the side of entrepreneurs as they lead the economic revival of the Gulf region.

I propose the creation of worker recovery accounts to help those evacuees who need extra help finding work. Under this plan, the federal government would provide accounts of up to $5,000, which these evacuees could draw upon for job training and education to help them get a good job and for child care expenses during their job search.

And to help lower-income citizens in the hurricane region build new and better lives, I also propose that Congress pass an Urban Homesteading Act.

Under this approach, we will identify property in the region owned by the federal government and provide building sites to low-income citizens free of charge, through a lottery. In return, they would pledge to build on the lot, with either a mortgage or help from a charitable organization like Habitat for Humanity.

Homeownership is one of the great strengths of any community, and it must be a central part of our vision for the revival of this region.

In the long run, the New Orleans area has a particular challenge, because much of the city lies below sea level. The people who call it home need to have reassurance that their lives will be safer in the years to come.

Protecting a city that sits lower than the water around it is not easy, but it can and has been done. City and parish officials in New Orleans and state officials in Louisiana will have a large part in the engineering decisions to come. And the Army Corps of Engineers will work at their side to make the flood-protection system stronger than it has ever been.

The work that has begun in the Gulf Coast region will be one of the largest reconstruction efforts the world has ever seen. When that job is done, all Americans will have something to be very proud of. And all Americans are needed in this common effort.

ARMIES OF COMPASSION

It is the armies of compassion—charities and houses of worship and idealistic men and women—that give our reconstruction effort its humanity. They offer to those who hurt a friendly face, an arm around the shoulder and the reassurance that, in hard times, they can count on someone who cares.

By land, by sea and by air, good people wanting to make a difference deployed to the Gulf Coast. And they have been working around the clock ever since.

The cash needed to support the armies of compassion is great, and Americans have given generously. For example, the private fundraising effort led by former Presidents [George] Bush and [Bill] Clinton has already received pledges of more than $100 million. Some of that money is going to the governors, to be used for immediate needs within their states. A portion will also be sent to local houses of worship, to help reimburse them for the expense of helping others.

This evening, the need is still urgent, and I ask the American people to continue donating to the Salvation Army, the Red Cross, other good charities and religious congregations in the region.

It is also essential for the many organizations of our country to reach out to your fellow citizens in the Gulf area. So I have asked USA Freedom Corps to create an information clearinghouse, available at usafreedomcorps.gov, so that families anywhere in the country can find opportunities to help families in the region or a school can support a school.

And I challenge existing organizations—churches and Scout troops or labor union locals—to get in touch with their counterparts in Mississippi, Louisiana or Alabama and learn what they can do to help.

In this great national enterprise, important work can be done by everyone, and everyone should find their role and do their part.

LEARNING THE LESSON

The government of this nation will do its part as well. Our cities must have clear and up-to-date plans for responding to natural disasters and disease outbreaks or a terrorist attack, for evacuating large numbers of people in an emergency, and for providing the food and water and security they would need.

In a time of terror threats and weapons of mass destruction, the danger to our citizens reaches much wider than a fault line or a flood plain. I consider detailed emergency planning to be a national security priority.

And therefore, I have ordered the Department of Homeland Security to undertake an immediate review, in cooperation with local counterparts, of emergency plans in every major city in America.

I also want to know all the facts about the government response to Hurricane Katrina. The storm involved a massive flood, a major supply and security operation, and an evacuation order affecting more than a million people.

It was not a normal hurricane, and the normal disaster relief system was not equal to it.

Many of the men and women of the Coast Guard, the Federal Emergency Management Agency, the United States military, the National Guard, Homeland Security, and state and local governments performed skillfully under the worst conditions. Yet the system, at every level of government, was not well-coordinated and was overwhelmed in the first few days.

It is now clear that a challenge on this scale requires greater federal authority and a broader role for the armed forces, the institution of our government most capable of massive logistical operations on a moment's notice.

Four years after the frightening experience of September the 11th, Americans have every right to expect a more effective response in a time of emergency.

When the federal government fails to meet such an obligation, I as president am responsible for the problem and for the solution. So I have ordered every Cabinet secretary to participate in a comprehensive review of the government response to the hurricane.

This government will learn the lessons of Hurricane Katrina. We're going to review every action and make necessary changes so that we are better prepared for any challenge of nature or act of evil men that could threaten our people.

The United States Congress also has an important oversight function to perform. Congress is preparing an investigation, and I will work with members of both parties to make sure this effort is thorough.

THE SECOND LINE

In the life of this nation, we have often been reminded that nature is an awesome force and that all life is fragile. We are the heirs of men and women who lived through those first terrible winters at Jamestown and Plymouth, who rebuilt Chicago after a great fire and San Francisco after a great earthquake, who reclaimed the prairie from the dust bowl of the 1930s.

Every time, the people of this land have come back from fire, flood and storm to build anew and to build better than what we had before. Americans have never left our destiny to the whims of nature, and we will not start now.

These trials have also reminded us that we are often stronger than we know—with the help of grace and one another. They remind us of a hope beyond all pain and death—a God who welcomes the lost to a house not made with hands. And they remind us that we are tied together in this life, in this nation, and that the despair of any touches us all.

I know that when you sit on the steps of a porch where a home once stood or sleep on a cot in a crowded shelter, it is hard to imagine a bright future. But that future will come.

The streets of Biloxi and Gulfport will again be filled with lovely homes and the sound of children playing. The churches of Alabama will have their broken steeples mended and their congregations whole. And here in New Orleans, the streetcars will once again rumble down St. Charles and the passionate soul of a great city will return.

In this place, there is a custom for the funerals of jazz musicians. The funeral procession parades slowly through the streets, followed by a band playing a mournful dirge as it moves to the cemetery. Once the casket has been laid in place, the band breaks into a joyful "second line," symbolizing the triumph of the spirit over death.

Tonight, the Gulf Coast is still coming through the dirge. Yet we will live to see the second line.

Thank you, and may God bless America.

President Bush's 2006 State of the Union Address

Following is President Bush's State of the Union address, delivered to a joint session of Congress Jan. 31, 2006.

Mr. Speaker, Vice President Cheney, members of Congress, members of the Supreme Court and diplomatic corps, distinguished guests, and fellow citizens: Today our nation lost a beloved, graceful, courageous woman who called America to its founding ideals and carried on a noble dream. Tonight we are comforted by the hope of a glad reunion with the husband who was taken so long ago, and we are grateful for the good life of Coretta Scott King.

Every time I'm invited to this rostrum, I am humbled by the privilege and mindful of the history we have seen together. We have gathered under this Capitol dome in moments of national mourning and national achievement. We have served America through one of the most consequential periods of our history. And it has been my honor to serve with you.

In a system of two parties, two chambers and two elected branches, there will always be differences and debate. But even tough debates can be conducted in a civil tone. And our differences cannot be allowed to harden into anger. To confront the great issues before us, we must act in a spirit of good will and respect for one another. And I will do my part.

Tonight the state of our union is strong, and together we will make it stronger.

In this decisive year, you and I will make choices that determine both the future and the character of our country. We will choose to act confidently in pursuing the enemies of freedom or retreat from our duties in the hope of an easier life. We will choose to build our prosperity by leading the world economy or shut ourselves off from trade and opportunity.

ADVANCING DEMOCRACY

In a complex and challenging time, the road of isolationism and protectionism may seem broad and inviting, yet it ends in danger and decline. The only way to protect our people, the only way to secure the peace, the only way to control our destiny is by our leadership.

So the United States of America will continue to lead. Abroad, our nation is committed to a historic, long-term goal: We seek the end of tyranny in our world. Some dismiss that goal as misguided idealism. In reality, the future security of America depends on it. On Sept. 11, 2001, we found that problems originating in a failed and oppressive state 7,000 miles away could bring murder and destruction to our country. Dictatorships shelter terrorists, and feed resentment and radicalism, and seek weapons of mass destruction.

Democracies replace resentment with hope, respect the rights of their citizens and their neighbors, and join the fight against terror. Every step toward freedom in the world makes our country safer, and so we will act boldly in freedom's cause. Far from being a hopeless dream, the advance of freedom is the great story of our time.

In 1945, there were about two dozen lonely democracies in the world. Today there are 122. And we are writing a new chapter in the story of self-government, with women lining up to vote in Afghanistan, and millions of Iraqis marking their liberty with purple ink, and men and women from Lebanon to Egypt debating the rights of individuals and the necessity of freedom. At the start of 2006, more than half the people of our world live in democratic nations. And we do not forget the other half—in places like Syria and Burma, Zimbabwe, North Korea and Iran—because the demands of justice and the peace of this world require their freedom as well.

NO RETREAT FROM TERRORISM

No one can deny the success of freedom, but some men rage and fight against it. And one of the main sources of reaction and opposition is radical Islam; the perversion by a few of a noble faith into an ideology of terror and death.

Terrorists like [Osama] bin Laden are serious about mass murder, and all of us must take their declared intentions seriously. They seek to impose a heartless system of totalitarian control throughout the Middle East and arm themselves with weapons of mass murder. Their aim is to seize power in Iraq and use it as a safe haven to launch attacks against America and the world. Lacking the military strength to challenge us directly, the terrorists have chosen the weapon of fear.

When they murder children at a school in Beslan or blow up commuters in London or behead a bound captive, the terrorists hope these horrors will break our will, allowing the violent to inherit the Earth. But they have miscalculated. We love our freedom, and we will fight to keep it.

In a time of testing, we cannot find security by abandoning our commitments and retreating within our borders. If we were to leave these vicious attackers alone, they would not leave us alone. They would simply move the battlefield to our own shores.

There is no peace in retreat. And there is no honor in retreat. By allowing radical Islam to work its will, by leaving an assaulted world to fend for itself, we would signal to all that we no longer believe in our own ideals or even in our own courage. But our enemies and our friends can be certain: The United States will not retreat from the world, and we will never surrender to evil.

America rejects the false comfort of isolationism. We are the nation that saved liberty in Europe, and liberated death camps, and helped raise up democracies and faced down an evil empire. Once again, we accept the call of history to deliver the oppressed and move this world toward peace.

PROGRESS IN IRAQ

We remain on the offensive against terror networks. We have killed or captured many of their leaders. And, for the others, their day will come. We remain on the offensive in Afghanistan, where a fine president and a national assembly are fighting terror while building the institutions of a new democracy.

We're on the offensive in Iraq, with a clear plan for victory. First, we are helping Iraqis build an inclusive government, so that old resentments will be eased and the insurgency will be marginalized. Second, we are continuing reconstruction efforts and helping the Iraqi government to fight corruption and build a modern economy, so all Iraqis can experience the benefits of freedom. Third, we are striking terrorist targets while we train Iraqi forces that are increasingly capable of defeating the enemy.

Iraqis are showing their courage every day, and we are proud to be their allies in the cause of freedom. Our work in Iraq is difficult, because our enemy is brutal. But that brutality has not stopped the dramatic progress of a new democracy. In less than three years, the nation has gone from dictatorship, to liberation, to sovereignty, to a constitution, to national elections.

At the same time, our coalition has been relentless in shutting off terrorist infiltration, clearing out insurgent strongholds and turning over territory to Iraqi security forces. I am confident in our plan for victory. I am confident in the will of the Iraqi people. I am confident in the skill and spirit of our military. Fellow citizens, we are in this fight to win, and we are winning. The road of victory is the road that will take our troops home.

As we make progress on the ground and Iraqi forces increasingly take the lead, we should be able to further decrease our troop levels. But those decisions will be made by our military commanders, not by politicians in Washington, D.C. Our coalition has learned from our experience in Iraq. We have adjusted our military tactics and changed our approach to reconstruction.

Along the way, we have benefited from responsible criticism and counsel offered by members of Congress of both parties. In the coming year, I will continue to reach out and seek your good advice. Yet there is a difference between responsible criticism that aims for success and defeatism that refuses to acknowledge anything but failure. Hindsight alone is not wisdom. And second-guessing is not a strategy.

STAYING THE COURSE

With so much in the balance, those of us in public office have a duty to speak with candor. A sudden withdrawal of our forces from Iraq would abandon our Iraqi allies to death and prison, would put men like bin Laden and [Abu Masab al-] Zarqawi in charge of a strategic country and show that a pledge from America means little. Members of Congress, however we feel about the decisions and debates of the past, our nation has only one option: We must keep our word, defeat our enemies and stand behind the American military in its vital mission.

Our men and women in uniform are making sacrifices and showing a sense of duty stronger than all fear. They know what it's like to fight house to house in a maze of streets, to wear heavy gear in the desert heat, to see a comrade killed by a roadside bomb. And those who know the costs also know the stakes.

Marine Staff Sgt. Dan Clay was killed last month fighting in Fabiani. He left behind a letter to his family, but his words could just as well be addressed to every American. Here is what Dan wrote: "I know what honor is. It has been an honor to protect and serve all of you. I faced death with the secure knowledge that you would not have to. Never falter. Don't hesitate to honor and support those of us who had the honor of protecting that which is worth protecting."

Staff Sgt. Dan Clay's wife, Lisa, and his mom and dad, Sara Jo and Bud, are with us this evening. Welcome. Our nation is grateful to the fallen who live in the memory of our country. We are grateful to all who volunteer to wear our nation's uniform. And as we honor our brave troops, let us never forget the sacrifices of America's military families.

HEARTS AND MINDS

Our offensive against terror involves more than military action. Ultimately, the only way to defeat the terrorists is to defeat their dark vision of hatred and fear by offering the hopeful alternative of political freedom and peaceful change. So the United States of America supports democratic reform across the broader Middle East. Elections are vital, but they are only the beginning. Raising up a democracy requires the rule of law, and protection of minorities, and strong, accountable institutions that last longer than a single vote.

The great people of Egypt have voted in a multiparty presidential election, and now their government should open paths of peaceful opposition that will reduce the appeal of radicalism. The Palestinian people have voted in elections. And now the leaders of Hamas must recognize Israel, disarm, reject terrorism and work for lasting peace. Saudi Arabia has taken the first steps of reform. Now it can offer its people a better future by pressing forward with those efforts.

Democracies in the Middle East will not look like our own, because they will reflect the traditions of their own citizens. Yet liberty is the future of every nation in the Middle East, because liberty is the right and hope of all humanity.

The same is true of Iran, a nation now held hostage by a small clerical elite that is isolating and repressing its people. The regime in that country sponsors terrorists in the Palestinian territories and in Lebanon, and that must come to an end. The Iranian government is defying the world with its nuclear ambitions, and the nations of the world must not permit the Iranian regime to gain nuclear weapons. America will continue to rally the world to confront these threats.

And, tonight, let me speak directly to the citizens of Iran: America respects you and we respect your country. We respect your right to choose your own future and win your own freedom. And our nation hopes one day to be the closest of friends with a free and democratic Iran.

To overcome dangers in our world, we must also take the offensive by encouraging economic progress and fighting disease and spreading hope in hopeless lands. Isolationism would not only tie our hands in fighting enemies; it would keep us from helping our friends in desperate need.

We show compassion abroad because Americans believe in the God-given dignity and worth of a villager with HIV/AIDS, or an infant with malaria, or a refugee fleeing genocide, or a young girl sold into slavery. We also show compassion abroad because regions overwhelmed by poverty, corruption and despair are sources of terrorism and organized crime and human trafficking and the drug trade.

In recent years, you and I have taken unprecedented action to fight AIDS and malaria, expand the education of girls, and reward developing nations that are moving forward with economic and political reform. For people everywhere, the United States is a partner for a better life. Shortchanging these efforts would increase the suffering and chaos of our world, undercut our long-term security and dull the conscience of our country. I urge members of Congress to serve the interests of America by showing the compassion of America.

STAYING VIGILANT

Our country must also remain on the offensive against terrorism here at home. The enemy has not lost the desire or capability to attack us.

Fortunately, this nation has superb professionals in law enforcement, intelligence, the military and homeland security. These men and women are dedicating their lives to protecting us all, and they deserve our support and our thanks. They also deserve the same tools they already use to fight drug trafficking and organized crime, so I ask you to reauthorize the Patriot Act.

It is said that prior to the attacks of Sept. 11, our government failed to connect the dots of the conspiracy. We now know that two of the hijackers in the United States placed telephone calls to al Qaeda operatives overseas. But we did not know about their plans until it was too late. So to prevent another attack—based on authority given to me by the Constitution and by statute—I have authorized a terrorist surveillance program to aggressively pursue the international communications of suspected al Qaeda operatives and affiliates to and from America.

Previous presidents have used the same constitutional authority I have, and federal courts have approved the use of that authority. Appropriate members of Congress have been kept informed. The terrorist surveillance program has helped prevent terrorist attacks. It remains essential to the security of America. If there are people inside our country who are talking with al Qaeda, we want to know about it, because we will not sit back and wait to be hit again.

In all these areas—from the disruption of terror networks, to victory in Iraq, to the spread of freedom and hope in troubled regions—we need the support of our friends and allies. To draw that support, we must always be clear in our principles and willing to act. The only alternative to American leadership is a dramatically more dangerous and anxious world.

Yet we also choose to lead because it is a privilege to serve the values that gave us birth. American leaders—from Roosevelt, to Truman, to Kennedy, to Reagan—rejected isolation and retreat because they knew that America is always more secure when freedom is on the march.

Our own generation is in a long war against a determined enemy, a war that will be fought by presidents of both parties who will need steady bipartisan support from the Congress. And tonight I ask for yours. Together, let us protect our country, support the men and women who defend us, and lead this world toward freedom.

ECONOMIC CHALLENGES

Here at home, America also has a great opportunity: We will build the prosperity of our country by strengthening our economic leadership in the world.

Our economy is healthy and vigorous, and growing faster than other major industrialized nations. In the last two-and-a-half years, America has created 4.6 million new jobs, more than Japan and the European Union combined. Even in the face of higher energy prices and natural disasters, the American people have turned in an economic performance that is the envy of the world.

The American economy is pre-eminent, but we cannot afford to be complacent. In a dynamic world economy, we are seeing new competitors like China and India. And this creates uncertainty, which makes it easier to feed people's fears. So we're seeing some old temptations return. Protectionists want to escape competition, pretending that we can keep our high standard of living while walling off our economy. Others say that the government needs to take a larger role in directing the economy, centralizing more power in Washington and increasing taxes. We hear claims that immigrants are somehow bad for the economy, even though this economy could not function without them.

All these are forms of economic retreat, and they lead in the same direction: toward a stagnant and second-rate economy.

TAX AGENDA

Tonight I will set out a better path: an agenda for a nation that competes with confidence, an agenda that will raise standards of living and generate new jobs. Americans should not fear our economic future, because we intend to shape it.

Keeping America competitive begins with keeping our economy growing. And our economy grows when Americans have more of their own money to spend, save and invest.

In the last five years, the tax relief you passed has left $880 billion in the hands of American workers, investors, small businesses and families. And they have used it to help produce more than four years of uninterrupted economic growth. Yet the tax relief is set to expire in the next few years. If we do nothing, American families will face a massive tax increase they do not expect and will not welcome. Because America needs more than a temporary expansion, we need more than temporary tax relief. I urge the Congress to act responsibly and make the tax cuts permanent. Keeping America competitive requires us to be good stewards of tax dollars.

Every year of my presidency, we've reduced the growth of non-security discretionary spending. And last year you passed bills that cut this spending. This year my budget will cut it again and reduce or eliminate more than 140 programs that are performing poorly or not fulfilling essential priorities. By passing these reforms, we will save the American taxpayer another $14 billion next year and stay on track to cut the deficit in half by 2009. I am pleased that the members of Congress are working on earmark reform, because the federal budget has too many special-interest projects. And we can tackle this problem together, if you pass the line-item veto.

EXAMINING ENTITLEMENTS

We must also confront the larger challenge of mandatory spending, or entitlements. This year, the first of about 78 million baby boomers turn 60, including two of my dad's favorite people: me and President [Bill] Clinton.

This milestone is more than a personal crisis. It is a national challenge. The retirement of the baby boom generation will put unprecedented strains on the federal government. By 2030, spending for Social Security, Medicare and Medicaid alone will be almost 60 percent of the entire federal budget. And that will present future Congresses with impossible choices: staggering tax increases, immense deficits or deep cuts in every category of spending.

Congress did not act last year on my proposal to save Social Security, yet the rising cost of entitlements is a problem that is not going away. And with every year we fail to act, the situation gets worse. So tonight I ask you to join me in creating a commission to examine the full impact of baby boom retirements on Social Security, Medicare and Medicaid. This commission should include members of Congress of both parties and offer bipartisan solutions. We need to put aside partisan politics and work together and get this problem solved.

Keeping America competitive requires us to open more markets for all that Americans make and grow. One out of every five factory jobs in America is related to global trade, and we want people everywhere to buy American. With open markets and a level playing field, no one can out-produce or out-compete the American worker.

Keeping America competitive requires an immigration system that upholds our laws, reflects our values and serves the interests of our economy. Our nation needs orderly and secure borders. To meet this goal, we must have stronger immigration enforcement and border protection. And we must have a rational, humane guest worker program that rejects amnesty, allows temporary jobs for people who seek them legally, and reduces smuggling and crime at the border.

Keeping America competitive requires affordable health care. Our government has a responsibility to help provide health care for the poor and the elderly, and we are meeting that responsibility. For all Americans—for all Americans—we must confront the rising cost of care, strengthen the doctor-patient relationship, and help people afford the insurance coverage they need.

We will make wider use of electronic records and other health information technology to help control costs and reduce dangerous medical errors. We will strengthen health savings accounts, making sure individuals and small-business employees can buy insurance with the same advantages that people working for big businesses now get. We will do more to make this coverage portable, so workers can switch jobs without having to worry about losing their health insurance. And because lawsuits are driving many good doctors out of practice—leaving women in nearly 1,500 American counties without a single ob-gyn—I ask the Congress to pass medical liability reform this year.

ENERGY AND EDUCATION

Keeping America competitive requires affordable energy. And here we have a serious problem: America is addicted to oil, which is often imported from unstable parts of the world.

The best way to break this addiction is through technology. Since 2001, we have spent nearly $10 billion to develop cleaner, cheaper and more reliable alternative energy sources. And we are on the threshold of incredible advances. So tonight I announce the Advanced Energy Initiative, a 22 percent increase in clean-energy research at the Department of Energy to push for breakthroughs in two vital areas. To change how we power our homes and offices, we will invest more in zero-emission coal-fired plants; revolutionary solar and wind technologies; and clean, safe nuclear energy. We must also change how we power our automobiles.

We will increase our research in better batteries for hybrid and electric cars and in pollution-free cars that run on hydrogen. We will also fund additional research in cutting-edge methods of producing ethanol, not just from corn but from wood chips and stalks or switch grass. Our goal is to make this new kind of ethanol practical and competitive within six years. Breakthroughs on this and other new technologies will help us reach another great goal: to replace more than 75 percent of our oil imports from the Middle East by 2025.

By applying the talent and technology of America, this country can dramatically improve our environment, move beyond a petroleum-based economy and make our dependence on Middle Eastern oil a thing of the past.

And to keep America competitive, one commitment is necessary above all: We must continue to lead the world in human talent and creativity. Our greatest advantage in the world has always been our educated, hard-working, ambitious people, and we are going to keep that edge.

Tonight I announce the American Competitiveness Initiative to encourage innovation throughout our economy and to give our nation's children a firm grounding in math and science. First, I propose to double the federal commitment to the most critical basic research programs in the physical sciences over the next 10 years. This funding will support the work of America's most creative minds as they explore promising areas such as nanotechnology, supercomputing and alternative energy sources.

Second, I propose to make permanent the research and development tax credit, to encourage bolder private-sector initiatives in technology. With more research in both the public and private sectors, we will improve our quality of life and ensure that America will lead the world in opportunity and innovation for decades to come.

Third, we need to encourage children to take more math and science, and to make sure those courses are rigorous enough to compete with other nations. We made a good start in the early grades with the No Child Left Behind Act, which is raising standards and lifting test scores across our country. Tonight I propose to train 70,000 high school teachers to lead advanced placement courses in math and science, bring 30,000 math and science professionals to teach in classrooms, and give early help to students who struggle with math so they have a better chance at good, high-wage jobs.

If we ensure that America's children succeed in life, they will ensure that America succeeds in the world. Preparing our nation to compete in the world is a goal that all of us can share. I urge you to support the American Competitiveness Initiative and, together, we will show the world what the American people can achieve.

CULTURE OF CHANGE

America is a great force for freedom and prosperity. Yet our greatness is not measured in power or luxuries, but by who we are and how we treat one another. So we strive to be a compassionate, decent, hopeful society.

In recent years, America has become a more hopeful nation. Violent crime rates have fallen to their lowest levels since the 1970s. Welfare cases have dropped by more than half over the past decade. Drug use among youth is down 19 percent since 2001. There are fewer abortions in America than at any point in the last three decades. And the number of children born to teenage mothers has been falling for a dozen years in a row.

These gains are evidence of a quiet transformation, a revolution of conscience in which a rising generation is finding that a life of personal responsibility is a life of fulfillment.

Government has played a role. Wise policies such as welfare reform, and drug education, and support for abstinence and adoption have made a difference in the character of our country. And everyone here tonight, Democrat and Republican, has a right to be proud of this record.

Yet many Americans, especially parents, still have deep concerns about the direction of our culture and the health of our most basic institutions. They are concerned about unethical conduct by public officials and discouraged by activist courts that try to redefine marriage. They worry about children in our society who need direction and love, and about fellow citizens still displaced by natural disaster, and about suffering caused by treatable diseases.

As we look at these challenges, we must never give in to the belief that America is in decline or that our culture is doomed to unravel. The American people know better than that. We have proven the pessimists wrong before, and we will do it again.

A hopeful society depends on courts that deliver equal justice under law.

The Supreme Court now has two superb new members—new members on its bench: Chief Justice John Roberts and Justice Sam Alito. I thank the Senate for confirming both of them. I will continue to nominate men and women who understand that judges must be servants of the law and not legislate from the bench.

Today marks the official retirement of a very special American. For 24 years of faithful service to our nation, the United States is grateful to Justice Sandra Day O'Connor.

A SOCIETY OF HOPE

A hopeful society has institutions of science and medicine that do not cut ethical corners and that recognize the matchless value of every life. Tonight I ask you to pass legislation to prohibit the most egregious abuses of medical research: human cloning in all its forms; creating or implanting embryos for experiments; creating human-animal hybrids; and buying, selling or patenting human embryos. Human life is a gift from our creator, and that gift should never be discarded, devalued or put up for sale.

A hopeful society expects elected officials to uphold the public trust. Honorable people in both parties are working on reforms to strengthen the ethical standards of Washington. I support your efforts. Each of us has made a pledge to be worthy of public responsibility, and that is a pledge we must never forget, never dismiss and never betray.

As we renew the promise of our institutions, let us also show the character of America in our compassion and care for one another.

A hopeful society gives special attention to children who lack direction and love. Through the Helping America's Youth Initiative, we are encouraging caring adults to get involved in the life of a child. And this good work is led by our first lady, Laura Bush. This year we will add resources to encourage young people to stay in school so more of America's youth can raise their sights and achieve their dreams.

A hopeful society comes to the aid of fellow citizens in times of suffering and emergency and stays at it until they're back on their feet. So far, the federal government has committed $85 billion to the people of the Gulf Coast and New Orleans. We are removing debris and repairing highways and rebuilding stronger levees. We're providing business loans and housing assistance.

Yet, as we meet these immediate needs, we must also address deeper challenges that existed before the storm arrived. In New Orleans and in other places, many of our fellow citizens have felt excluded from the promise of our country. The answer is not only temporary relief, but schools that teach every child, and job skills that bring upward mobility, and more opportunities to own a home and start a business. As we recover from a disaster, let us also work for the day when all Americans are protected by justice; equal in hope and rich in opportunity.

A hopeful society acts boldly to fight diseases like HIV/AIDS, which can be prevented and treated and defeated. More than a million Americans live with HIV, and half of all AIDS cases occur among African Americans. I ask Congress to reform and reauthorize the Ryan White Act and provide new funding to states so we end the waiting lists for AIDS medicines in America. We will also lead a nationwide effort, working closely with African American churches and faith-based groups, to deliver rapid HIV tests to millions, end the stigma of AIDS and come closer to the day when there are no new infections in America.

HISTORIC CHOICES

Fellow citizens, we have been called to leadership in a period of consequence. We have entered a great ideological conflict we did nothing to invite. We see great changes in science and commerce that will influence all our lives.

Sometimes it can seem that history is turning in a wide arc, toward an unknown shore. Yet the destination of history is determined by human action, and every great movement of history comes to a point of choosing.

Lincoln could have accepted peace at the cost of disunity and continued slavery. Martin Luther King could have stopped at Birmingham or at Selma and achieved only half a victory over segregation. The United States could have accepted the permanent division of Europe and been complicit in the oppression of others.

Today, having come far in our own historical journey, we must decide: Will we turn back or finish well? Before history is written down in books, it is written in courage. Like Americans before us, we will show that courage and we will finish well.

We will lead freedom's advance. We will compete and excel in the global economy. We will renew the defining moral commitments of this land. And so we move forward optimistic about our country, faithful to its cause and confident of the victories to come.

May God bless America.

President Bush's Veto of Stem Cell Legislation

Following is the text of President Bush's July 19, 2006, veto message on HR 810, broadening stem cell research opportunities. *(Story, p. 542)*

To the House of Representatives:

I am returning herewith without my approval H.R. 810, the "Stem Cell Research Enhancement Act of 2005."

Like all Americans, I believe our Nation must vigorously pursue the tremendous possibilities that science offers to cure disease and improve the lives of millions. Yet, as science brings us ever closer to unlocking the secrets of human biology, it also offers temptations to manipulate human life and violate human dignity. Our conscience and history as a Nation demand that we resist this temptation. With the right scientific techniques and the right policies, we can achieve scientific progress while living up to our ethical responsibilities.

In 2001, I set forth a new policy on stem cell research that struck a balance between the needs of science and the demands of conscience. When I took office, there was no Federal funding for human embryonic stem cell research. Under the policy I announced 5 years ago, my Administration became the first to make Federal funds available for this research, but only on embryonic stem cell lines derived from embryos that had already been destroyed. My Administration has made available more than $90 million for research of these lines. This policy has allowed important research to go forward and has allowed America to continue to lead the world in embryonic stem cell research without encouraging the further destruction of living human embryos.

H.R. 810 would overturn my Administration's balanced policy on embryonic stem cell research. If this bill were to become law, American taxpayers for the first time in our history would be compelled to fund the deliberate destruction of human embryos. Crossing this line would be a grave mistake and would needlessly encourage a conflict between science and ethics that can only do damage to both and harm our Nation as a whole.

Advances in research show that stem cell science can progress in an ethical way. Since I announced my policy in 2001, my Administration has expanded funding of research into stem cells that can be drawn from children, adults, and the blood in umbilical cords with no harm to the donor, and these stem cells are currently being used in medical treatments. Science also offers the hope that we may one day enjoy the potential benefits of embryonic stem cells without destroying human life. Researchers are investigating new techniques that might allow doctors and scientists to produce stem cells just as versatile as those derived from human embryos without harming life. We must continue to explore these hopeful alternatives, so we can advance the cause of scientific research while staying true to the ideals of a decent and humane society.

I hold to the principle that we can harness the promise of technology without becoming slaves to technology and ensure that science serves the cause of humanity. If we are to find the right ways to advance ethical medical research, we must also be willing when necessary to reject the wrong ways. For that reason, I must veto this bill

GEORGE W. BUSH.
THE WHITE HOUSE
July 19, 2006

National Intelligence Estimate

Following are the declassified key judgments of the National Intelligence Estimate titled "Trends in Global Terrorism: Implications for the United States," dated April 2006, which were released by the Office of the Director of National Intelligence at the direction of President Bush on Sept. 26, 2006.

United States-led counterterrorism efforts have seriously damaged the leadership of al Qaeda and disrupted its operations; however, we judge that al Qaeda will continue to pose the greatest threat to the Homeland and U.S. interests abroad by a single terrorist organization. We also assess that the global jihadist movement—which includes al Qaeda, affiliated and independent terrorist groups, and emerging networks and cells—is spreading and adapting to counterterrorism efforts.

- Although we cannot measure the extent of the spread with precision, a large body of all-source reporting indicates that activists identifying themselves as jihadists, although a small percentage of Muslims, are increasing in both number and geographic dispersion.
- If this trend continues, threats to U.S. interests at home and abroad will become more diverse, leading to increasing attacks worldwide.
- Greater pluralism and more responsive political systems in Muslim majority nations would alleviate some of the grievances jihadists exploit. Over time, such progress, together with sustained, multifaceted programs targeting the vulnerabilities of the jihadist movement and continued pressure on al Qaeda, could erode support for the jihadists. We assess that the global jihadist movement is decentralized, lacks a coherent global strategy, and is becoming more diffuse. New jihadist networks and cells, with anti-American agendas, are increasingly likely to emerge. The confluence of shared purpose and dispersed actors will make it harder to find and undermine jihadist groups.
- We assess that the operational threat from self-radicalized cells will grow in importance to U.S. counterterrorism efforts, particularly abroad but also in the Homeland.
- The jihadists regard Europe as an important venue for attacking Western interests. Extremist networks inside the extensive Muslim diasporas in Europe facilitate recruitment and staging for urban attacks, as illustrated by the 2004 Madrid and 2005 London bombings. We assess that the Iraq jihad is shaping a new generation of terrorist leaders and operatives; perceived jihadist success there would inspire more fighters to continue the struggle elsewhere.
- The Iraq conflict has become the "cause célèbre" for jihadists, breeding a deep resentment of U.S. involvement in the Muslim world and cultivating supporters for the global jihadist movement. Should jihadists leaving Iraq perceive themselves, and be perceived, to have failed, we judge fewer fighters will be inspired to carry on the fight. We assess that the underlying factors fueling the spread of the movement outweigh its vulnerabilities and are likely to do so for the duration of the timeframe of this estimate.
- Four underlying factors are fueling the spread of the jihadist movement:

(1) Entrenched grievances, such as corruption, injustice, and fear of Western domination, leading to anger, humiliation, and a sense of powerlessness;
(2) the Iraq "jihad";
(3) the slow pace of real and sustained economic, social, and political reforms in many Muslim majority nations; and
(4) pervasive anti-US sentiment among most Muslims—all of which jihadists exploit.

- Concomitant vulnerabilities in the jihadist movement have emerged that, if fully exposed and exploited, could begin to slow the spread of the movement. They include dependence on the continuation of Muslim-related conflicts, the limited appeal of the jihadists' radical ideology, the emergence of respected voices of moderation, and criticism of the violent tactics employed against mostly Muslim citizens.

- The jihadists' greatest vulnerability is that their ultimate political solution—an ultra-conservative interpretation of sharia-based governance spanning the Muslim world—is unpopular with the vast majority of Muslims. Exposing the religious and political straitjacket that is implied by the jihadists' propaganda would help to divide them from the audiences they seek to persuade.
- Recent condemnations of violence and extremist religious interpretations by a few notable Muslim clerics signal a trend that could facilitate the growth of a constructive alternative to jihadist ideology: peaceful political activism. This also could lead to the consistent and dynamic participation of broader Muslim communities in rejecting violence, reducing the ability of radicals to capitalize on passive community support. In this way, the Muslim mainstream emerges as the most powerful weapon in the war on terror.
- Countering the spread of the jihadist movement will require coordinated multilateral efforts that go well beyond operations to capture or kill terrorist leaders. If democratic reform efforts in Muslim majority nations progress over the next five years, political participation probably would drive a wedge between intransigent extremists and groups willing to use the political process to achieve their local objectives. Nonetheless, attendant reforms and potentially destabilizing transitions will create new opportunities for jihadists to exploit. Al Qaeda, now merged with Abu Musab al-Zarqawi's network, is exploiting the situation in Iraq to attract new recruits and donors and to maintain its leadership role.
- The loss of key leaders, particularly [Osama bin Laden], Ayman al-Zawahiri, and al-Zarqawi, in rapid succession, probably would cause the group to fracture into smaller groups. Although like-minded individuals would endeavor to carry on the mission, the loss of these key leaders would exacerbate strains and disagreements. We assess that the resulting splinter groups would, at least for a time, pose a less serious threat to U.S. interests than does al Qaeda.
- Should al-Zarqawi continue to evade capture and scale back attacks against Muslims, we assess he could broaden his popular appeal and present a global threat.
- The increased role of Iraqis in managing the operations of al Qaeda in Iraq might lead veteran foreign jihadists to focus their efforts on external operations. Other affiliated Sunni extremist organizations, such as Jemaah Islamiya, Ansar al-Sunnah, and several North African groups, unless countered, are likely to expand their reach and become more capable of multiple and/or mass-casualty attacks outside their traditional areas of operation.
- We assess that such groups pose less of a danger to the Homeland than does al Qaeda but will pose varying degrees of threat to our allies and to U.S. interests abroad. The focus of their attacks is likely to ebb and flow between local regime targets and regional or global ones. We judge that most jihadist groups—both well-known and newly formed—will use improvised explosive devices and suicide attacks focused primarily on soft targets to implement their asymmetric warfare strategy, and that they will attempt to conduct sustained terrorist attacks in urban environments. Fighters with experience in Iraq are a potential source of leadership for jihadists pursuing these tactics.
- CBRN [chemical, biological, radiological and nuclear weapons] capabilities will continue to be sought by jihadist groups. While Iran, and to a lesser extent Syria, remain the most active state sponsors of terrorism, many other states will be unable to prevent territory or resources from being exploited by terrorists. Anti-U.S. and anti-globalization sentiment is on the rise and fueling other radical ideologies. This could prompt some leftist, nationalist, or separatist groups to adopt terrorist methods to attack U.S. interests. The radicalization process is occurring more quickly, more widely, and more anonymously in the Internet age, raising the likelihood of surprise attacks by unknown groups whose members and supporters may be difficult to pinpoint.
- We judge that groups of all stripes will increasingly use the Internet to communicate, propagandize, recruit, train, and obtain logistical and financial support.

President Bush's 2007 State of the Union Address

Following is President Bush's State of the Union address delivered to a joint session of Congress on Jan. 23, 2007.

Thank you very much. And tonight, I have the high privilege and distinct honor of my own, as the first president to begin the State of the Union message with these words: "Madame Speaker."

In his day, the late Congressman Thomas D'Alesandro Jr., from Baltimore, Md., saw Presidents [Franklin D.] Roosevelt and [Harry S] Truman at this rostrum. But nothing could compare with the sight of his only daughter, Nancy, presiding tonight as Speaker of the House of Representatives. Congratulations, Madame Speaker.

Two members of the House and Senate are not with us tonight, and we pray for the recovery and speedy return of Sen. Tim Johnson and Congressman Charlie Norwood.

Madame Speaker, Vice President Cheney, members of Congress, distinguished guests and fellow citizens: The rite of custom brings us together at a defining hour, when decisions are hard and courage is needed. We enter the year 2007 with large endeavors under way, and others that are ours to begin. In all of this, much is asked of us. We must have the will to face difficult challenges and determined enemies, and the wisdom to face them together.

Some in this chamber are new to the House and the Senate, and I congratulate the Democrat majority. Congress has changed but not our responsibilities. Each of us is guided by our own convictions, and to these we must stay faithful. Yet we're all held to the same standards and called to serve the same good purposes: to extend this nation's prosperity; to spend the people's money wisely; to solve problems, not leave them to future generations; to guard America against all evil; and to keep faith with those we have sent forth to defend us.

We are not the first to come here with government divided and uncertainty in the air. Like many before us, we can work through our differences, and we can achieve big things for the American people. Our citizens don't much care which side of the aisle we sit on, as long as we are willing to cross that aisle when there is work to be done. Our job is to make life better for our fellow Americans, and to help them build a future of hope and opportunity. And this is the business before us tonight.

ECONOMIC PROPOSALS

A future of hope and opportunity begins with a growing economy, and that is what we have. We are now in the 41st month of uninterrupted job growth, a recovery that has created 7.2 million new jobs so far. Unemployment is low; inflation is low; wages are rising. This economy is on the move. And our job is to keep it that way—not with more government but with more enterprise.

Next week, I will deliver a full report on the state of our economy. Tonight, I want to discuss three economic reforms that deserve to be priorities for this Congress.

First, we must balance the federal budget. We can do so without raising taxes. What we need is spending discipline in Washington, D.C. We set a goal of cutting the deficit in half by 2009 and met that goal three years ahead of schedule.

Now let us take the next step. In the coming weeks, I will submit a budget that eliminates the federal deficit within the next five years. I ask you to make the same commitment. Together, we can restrain the spending appetite of the federal government, and we can balance the federal budget.

Next, there's the matter of earmarks. These special interest items are often slipped into bills at the last hour, when not even C-SPAN is watching. In 2005 alone, the number of earmarks grew to over 13,000 and totaled nearly $18 billion. Even worse, over 90 percent of the earmarks never make it to the floor of the House and the Senate; they're dropped into committee reports that are not even part of the bill that arrives on my desk. You didn't vote them into law. I didn't sign them into law. Yet they are treated as if they have the force of law.

The time has come to end this practice. So let us work together to reform the budget process, expose every earmark to the light of day and to a vote in Congress, and cut the number and cost of earmarks at least in half by the end of this session.

And, finally, to keep this economy strong, we must take on the challenge of entitlements. Social Security and Medicare and Medicaid are commitments of conscience, and so it is our duty to keep them permanently sound. Yet we're failing in that duty. And this failure will one day leave our children with three bad options: huge tax increases, huge deficits, or huge and immediate cuts in benefits.

Everyone in this chamber knows this to be true, yet somehow we have not found it in ourselves to act. So let us work together and do it now. With enough good sense and good will, you and I can fix Medicare and Medicaid, and save Social Security.

NO CHILD LEFT BEHIND

Spreading opportunity and hope in America also requires public schools that give children the knowledge and character they need in life.

Five years ago, we rose above partisan differences to pass the No Child Left Behind Act, preserving local control, raising standards in public schools and holding those schools accountable for results. And because we acted, students are performing better in reading and math, and minority students are closing the achievement gap.

Now the task is to build on this success, without watering down standards, without taking control from local communities, and without backsliding and calling it reform.

We can lift student achievement even higher by giving local leaders flexibility to turn around failing schools and by giving families with children stuck in failing schools the right to choose someplace better. We must increase funds for students who struggle and make sure these children get the special help they need. And we can make sure our children are prepared for the jobs of the future, and our country is more competitive, by strengthening math and science skills.

The No Child Left Behind Act has worked for America's children, and I ask Congress to reauthorize this good law.

HEALTH CARE DEDUCTION

A future of hope and opportunity requires that all our citizens have affordable and available health care.

When it comes to health care, government has an obligation to care for the elderly, the disabled and poor children. And we will meet those responsibilities.

For all other Americans, private health insurance is the best way to meet their needs. But many Americans cannot afford a health insurance policy. And so, tonight, I propose two new initiatives to help more Americans afford their own insurance.

First, I propose a standard tax deduction for health insurance that will be like the standard tax deduction for dependents. Families with health insurance will pay no income or payroll taxes on $15,000 of their income. Single Americans with health insurance will pay no income or payroll taxes on $7,500 of their income. With this reform, more than 100 million men, women and children who are now covered by employer-provided insurance will benefit from lower tax bills.

At the same time, this reform will level the playing field for those who do not get health insurance through their jobs. For Americans who now purchase health insurance on their own, this proposal would mean a substantial tax savings: $4,500 for a family of four making $60,000 a year. And for the millions of other Americans who have no health insurance at all, this deduction would help put a basic private health insurance plan within their reach.

Changing the tax code is a vital and necessary step to making health care affordable for more Americans.

My second proposal is to help the states that are coming up with innovative ways to cover the uninsured. States that make basic private health insurance available to all their citizens should receive federal funds to help them provide this coverage to the poor and the sick.

I have asked the secretary of Health and Human Services to work with Congress to take existing federal funds and use them to create "Affordable Choices" grants. These grants would give our nation's governors more money and more flexibility to get private health insurance to those most in need.

There are many other ways that Congress can help. We need to expand health savings accounts. We need to help small businesses through association health plans. We need to reduce costs and medical errors with better information technology. We will encourage price transparency. And to protect good doctors from junk lawsuits, we need to pass medical liability reform.

In all we do, we must remember that the best health care decisions are made not by government and insurance companies, but by patients and their doctors.

TEMPORARY WORKER PROGRAM

Extending hope and opportunity in our country requires an immigration system worthy of America, with laws that are fair and borders that are secure. When laws and borders are routinely violated, this harms the interests of our country.

To secure our border, we are doubling the size of the Border Patrol and funding new infrastructure and technology. Yet, even with all these steps, we cannot fully secure the border unless we take pressure off the border. And that requires a temporary worker program.

We should establish a legal and orderly path for foreign workers to enter our country to work on a temporary basis. As a result, they won't have to try to sneak in. And that will leave border agents free to chase down drug smugglers and criminals and terrorists. We will enforce our immigration laws at the work site and give employers the tools to verify the legal status of their workers so there is no excuse left for violating the law.

We need to uphold the great tradition of the melting pot that welcomes and assimilates new arrivals. We need to resolve the status of the illegal immigrants who are already in our country, without animosity and without amnesty.

Convictions run deep in this Capitol when it comes to immigration. Let us have a serious, civil and conclusive debate so that you can pass—and I can sign—comprehensive immigration reform into law.

ENERGY POLICY

Extending hope and opportunity depends on a stable supply of energy that keeps America's economy running and America's environment clean.

For too long, our nation has been dependent on foreign oil. And this dependence leaves us more vulnerable to hostile regimes and to terrorists who could cause huge disruptions of oil shipments and raise the price of oil, and do great harm to our economy.

It's in our vital interest to diversify America's energy supply, and the way forward is through technology.

We must continue changing the way America generates electric power by even greater use of clean-coal technology; solar and wind energy; and clean, safe nuclear power. We need to press on with battery research for plug-in and hybrid vehicles and expand the use of clean-diesel vehicles and biodiesel fuel. We must continue investing in new methods of producing ethanol using everything from wood chips to grasses to agricultural wastes.

We made a lot of progress, thanks to good policies here in Washington and the strong response of the market. And now, even more dramatic advances are within reach. Tonight, I ask Congress to join me in pursuing a great goal: Let us build on the work we've done and reduce gasoline usage in the United States by 20 percent in the next 10 years. When we do that, we will have cut our total imports by the equivalent of three-quarters of all the oil we now import from the Middle East.

To reach this goal, we must increase the supply of alternative fuels, by setting a mandatory fuels standard to require 35 billion gallons of renewable and alternative fuels in 2017. And that is nearly five times the current target.

At the same time, we need to reform and modernize fuel-economy standards for cars the way we did for light trucks, and conserve up to 8.5 billion more gallons of gasoline by 2017.

Achieving these ambitious goals will dramatically reduce our dependence on foreign oil, but it's not going to eliminate it. And so, as we continue to diversify our fuel supply, we must step up domestic oil production in environmentally sensitive ways.

And to further protect America against severe disruptions to our oil supply, I ask Congress to double the current capacity of the Strategic Petroleum Reserve.

America's on the verge of technological breakthroughs that will enable us to live our lives less dependent on oil. And these technologies will help us become better stewards of the environment, and they will help us to confront the serious challenge of global climate change.

JUDICIAL NOMINATIONS

A future of hope and opportunity requires a fair, impartial system of justice. The lives of our citizens across our nation are affected by the outcome of cases pending in our federal courts.

And we have a shared obligation to ensure that the federal courts have enough judges to hear those cases and deliver timely rulings.

As president, I have a duty to nominate qualified men and women to vacancies on the federal bench. And the United States Senate has a duty as well: to give those nominees a fair hearing and a prompt up-or-down vote on the Senate floor.

WAR ON TERROR

For all of us in this room, there's no higher responsibility than to protect the people of this country from danger.

Five years have come and gone since we saw the scenes and felt the sorrow that the terrorists can cause. We've had time to take stock of our situation. We've added many critical protections to guard the homeland. We know with certainty that the horrors of that September morning were just a glimpse of what the terrorists intend for us, unless we stop them. With the distance of time, we find ourselves debating the causes of conflict and the course we have followed. Such debates are essential when a great democracy faces great questions.

Yet one question has surely been settled—that, to win the war on terror, we must take the fight to the enemy.

From the start, America and our allies have protected our people by staying on the offense. The enemy knows that the days of comfortable sanctuary, easy movement, steady financing and free-flowing communications are long over. For the terrorists, life since 9/11 has never been the same.

Our success in this war is often measured by the things that did not happen. We cannot know the full extent of the attacks that we and our allies have prevented. But here is some of what we do know: We stopped an al Qaeda plot to fly a hijacked airplane into the tallest building on the West Coast. We broke up a Southeast Asian terrorist cell grooming operatives for attacks inside the United States. We uncovered an al Qaeda cell developing anthrax to be used in attacks against America. And, just last August, British authorities uncovered a plot to blow up passenger planes bound for America over the Atlantic Ocean. For each life saved, we owe a debt of gratitude to the brave public servants who devote their lives to finding the terrorists and stopping them.

Every success against the terrorists is a reminder of the shoreless ambitions of this enemy. The evil that inspired and rejoiced in 9/11 is still at work in the world. And, so long as that's the case, America is still a nation at war.

ISLAMIC EXTREMISM

In the mind of the terrorists, this war began well before September the 11th, and will not end until their radical vision is fulfilled. And these past five years have given us a much clearer view of the nature of this enemy.

Al Qaeda and its followers are Sunni extremists, possessed by hatred and commanded by a harsh and narrow ideology. Take almost any principle of civilization, and their goal is the opposite. They preach with threats, instruct with bullets and bombs, and promise paradise for the murder of the innocent.

Our enemies are quite explicit about their intentions. They want to overthrow moderate governments and establish safe havens from which to plan and carry out new attacks on our country. By killing and terrorizing Americans, they want to force our country to retreat from the world and abandon the cause of liberty. They would then be free to impose their will and spread their totalitarian ideology.

Listen to this warning from the late terrorist [al-]Zarqawi: "We will sacrifice our blood and bodies to put an end to your dreams, and what is coming is even worse."

Osama bin Laden declared: "Death is better than living on this earth with the unbelievers among us."

These men are not given to idle words, and they are just one camp in the Islamist radical movement. In recent times, it has also become clear that we face an escalating danger from Shiia extremists who are just as hostile to America, and are also determined to dominate the Middle East. Many are known to take direction from the regime in Iran, which is funding and arming terrorists like Hezbollah, a group second only to al Qaeda in the American lives it has taken.

The Shiia and Sunni extremists are different faces of the same totalitarian threat. But whatever slogans they chant, when they slaughter the innocent, they have the same wicked purposes: They want to kill Americans, kill democracy in the Middle East and gain the weapons to kill on an even more horrific scale.

MIDEAST VIOLENCE

In the sixth year since our nation was attacked, I wish I could report to you that the dangers have ended. They have not. And so it remains the policy of this government to use every lawful and proper tool of intelligence, diplomacy, law enforcement and military action to do our duty, to find these enemies and to protect the American people.

This war is more than a clash of arms. It is a decisive ideological struggle, and the security of our nation is in the balance. To prevail, we must remove the conditions that inspire blind hatred and drove nineteen men to get onto airplanes and to come and kill us.

What every terrorist fears most is human freedom—societies where men and women make their own choices, answer to their own conscience and live by their hopes instead of their resentments. Free people are not drawn to violent and malignant ideologies, and most will choose a better way when they're given a chance. So we advance our own security interests by helping moderates, reformers and brave voices for democracy.

The great question of our day is whether America will help men and women in the Middle East to build free societies and share in the rights of all humanity. And I say, for the sake of our own security: We must.

In the last two years, we've seen the desire for liberty in the broader Middle East, and we have been sobered by the enemy's fierce reaction. In 2005, the world watched as the citizens of Lebanon raised the banner of the Cedar Revolution and drove out the Syrian occupiers and chose new leaders in free elections. In 2005, the people of Afghanistan defied the terrorists and elected a democratic legislature.

And, in 2005, the Iraqi people held three national elections: choosing a transitional government; adopting the most progressive, democratic constitution in the Arab world; and then electing a government under that constitution. Despite endless threats from the killers in their midst, nearly 12 million Iraqi citizens came out to vote in a show of hope and solidarity that we should never forget.

A thinking enemy watched all of these scenes, adjusted their tactics, and, in 2006, they struck back. In Lebanon, assassins took the life of Pierre Gemayel, a prominent participant in the Cedar Revolution. Hezbollah terrorists, with support from Syria and Iran, sowed conflict in the region and are seeking to undermine Lebanon's legitimately elected government. In Afghanistan, Taliban and al Qaeda fighters tried to regain power by regrouping and engaging Afghan and NATO forces.

In Iraq, al Qaeda and other Sunni extremists blew up one of the most sacred places in Shiia Islam: the Golden Mosque of Samarra. This atrocity, directed at a Muslim house of prayer, was designed to provoke retaliation from Iraqi Shiia. And it succeeded. Radical Shiia elements, some of whom receive support from Iran, formed death squads. The result was a tragic escalation of sectarian rage and reprisal that continues to this day.

This is not the fight we entered in Iraq, but it is the fight we are in. Every one of us wishes this war were over and won. Yet it would not be like us to leave our promises unkept, our friends abandoned and our own security at risk. Ladies and gentlemen, on this day, at this hour, it is still within our power to shape the outcome of this battle. Let us find our resolve and turn events toward victory.

TROOP DEPLOYMENT

We're carrying out a new strategy in Iraq, a plan that demands more from Iraq's elected government and gives our forces in Iraq the reinforcements they need to complete their mission. Our goal is a democratic Iraq that upholds the rule of law, respects the rights of its people, provides them security and is an ally in the war on terror.

In order to make progress toward this goal, the Iraqi government must stop the sectarian violence in its capital. But the Iraqis are not yet ready to do this on their own. So we're deploying reinforcements of more than 20,000 additional soldiers and Marines to Iraq. The vast majority will go to Baghdad, where they will help Iraqi forces to clear and secure neighborhoods, and serve as advisers embedded in Iraqi army units.

With Iraqis in the lead, our forces will help secure the city by chasing down terrorists, insurgents and the roaming death squads. And, in Anbar province—where al Qaeda terrorists have gathered and local forces have begun showing a willingness to fight them—we are sending an additional 4,000 United States Marines, with orders to find the terrorists and clear them out. We didn't drive al Qaeda out of their safe haven in Afghanistan only to let them set up a new safe haven in a free Iraq.

The people of Iraq want to live in peace. And now it's time for their government to act. Iraq's leaders know that our commitment is not open-ended. They have promised to deploy more of their own troops to secure Baghdad, and they must do so. They pledged that they will confront violent radicals of any faction or political party. And they need to follow through and lift needless restrictions on Iraqi and coalition forces, so these troops can achieve their mission of bringing security to all of the people of Baghdad.

Iraq's leaders have committed themselves to a series of benchmarks to achieve reconciliation: to share oil revenues among all of Iraq's citizens, to put the wealth of Iraq into the rebuilding of Iraq, to allow more Iraqis to re-enter their nation's civic life, to hold local elections and to take responsibility for security in every Iraqi province.

But for all this to happen, Baghdad must be secure. And our plan will help the Iraqi government take back its capital and make good on its commitments.

NEW IRAQ STRATEGY

My fellow citizens, our military commanders and I have carefully weighed the options. We discussed every possible approach. In the end, I chose this course of action because it provides the best chance for success.

Many in this chamber understand that America must not fail in Iraq, because you understand that the consequences of failure would be grievous and far-reaching. If American forces step back before Baghdad is secure, the Iraqi government would be overrun by extremists on all sides. We could expect an epic battle between Shiia extremists backed by Iran, and Sunni extremists aided by al Qaeda and supporters of the old regime. A contagion of violence could spill out across the country. And, in time, the entire region could be drawn into the conflict.

For America, this is a nightmare scenario. For the enemy, this is the objective. Chaos is the greatest ally—their greatest ally—in this struggle. And out of chaos in Iraq would emerge an emboldened enemy with new safe havens, new recruits, new resources and an even greater determination to harm America. To allow this to happen would be to ignore the lessons of September the 11th and invite tragedy.

Ladies and gentlemen, nothing is more important at this moment in our history than for America to succeed in the Middle East, to succeed in Iraq and to spare the American people from this danger. This is where matters stand tonight, in the here and now.

I've spoken with many of you in person. I respect you and the arguments you've made. We went into this largely united in our assumptions and in our convictions. And whatever you voted for, you did not vote for failure. Our country is pursuing a new strategy in Iraq, and I ask you to give it a chance to work. And I ask you to support our troops in the field and those on their way.

"WAR AND DIPLOMACY"

The war on terror we fight today is a generational struggle that will continue long after you and I have turned our duties over to others. And that's why it's important to work together, so our nation can see this great effort through. Both parties and both branches should work in close consultation. That's why I've proposed to establish a special advisory council on the war on terror, made up of leaders in Congress from both political parties.

We will share ideas for how to position America to meet every challenge that confronts us. We'll show our enemies abroad that we're united in the goal of victory. And one of the first steps we can take together is to add to the ranks of our military, so that the American armed forces are ready for all of the challenges ahead. Tonight I ask the Congress to authorize an increase in the size of our active Army and Marine Corps by 92,000 in the next five years.

A second task we can take on together is to design and establish a volunteer civilian reserve corps. Such a corps would function much like our military reserve. It would ease the burden on the armed forces by allowing us to hire civilians with critical skills to serve on missions abroad when America needs them. It would give people across America who do not wear the uniform a chance to serve in the defining struggle of our time.

Americans can have confidence in the outcome of this struggle because we are not in this struggle alone. We have a diplomatic strategy that is rallying the world to join in the fight against extremism.

In Iraq, multinational forces are operating under a mandate from the United Nations. We're working with Jordan and Saudi Arabia and Egypt and the Gulf States to increase support for Iraq's government. The United Nations has imposed sanctions on Iran and made it clear that the world will not allow the regime in Tehran to acquire nuclear weapons.

With the other members of the quartet—the U.N., the European Union and Russia—we are pursuing diplomacy to help bring peace to the Holy Land and pursuing the establishment of a democratic Palestinian state living side-by-side with Israel in peace and security.

In Afghanistan, NATO has taken the lead in turning back the Taliban and al Qaeda offensive—the first time the alliance has deployed forces outside the North Atlantic area.

Together with our partners in China and Japan, Russia and South Korea, we are pursuing intensive diplomacy to achieve a Korean peninsula free of nuclear weapons.

We will continue to speak out for the cause of freedom in places like Cuba, Belarus and Burma, and continue to awaken the conscience of the world to save the people of Darfur.

GLOBAL INITIATIVES

American foreign policy is more than a matter of war and diplomacy. Our work in the world is also based on a timeless truth: To whom much is given, much is required. We hear the call to take on the challenges of hunger and poverty and disease. And that is precisely what America is doing. We must continue to fight HIV/AIDS, especially on the continent of Africa.

Because you funded the Emergency Plan for AIDS Relief, the number of people receiving life-saving drugs has grown from 50,000 to more than 800,000 in three short years. I ask you to continue funding our efforts to fight HIV/AIDS. And I ask you to provide $1.2 billion over five years so we can combat malaria in 15 African countries.

And I ask that you fund the Millennium Challenge Account, so that American aid reaches the people who need it, in nations where democracy is on the rise and corruption is in retreat.

And let us continue to support the expanded trade and debt relief that are the best hopes for lifting lives and eliminating poverty.

AMERICAN SPIRIT

When America serves others in this way, we show the strength and generosity of our country. These deeds reflect the character of our people. The greatest strength we have is the heroic kindness and courage and self-sacrifice of the American people. You see this spirit often if you know where to look. And tonight we need only look above to the gallery.

Dikembe Mutombo grew up in Africa, amid great poverty and disease. He came to Georgetown University on a scholarship to study medicine, but Coach John Thompson took a look at Dikembe and had a different idea. Dikembe became a star in the NBA and a citizen of the United States. But he never forgot the land of his birth or the duty to share his blessings with others. He built a brand-new hospital in his old hometown.

A friend has said of this good-hearted man, "Mutombo believes that God has given him this opportunity to do great things." And we are proud to call this son of the Congo a citizen of the United States of America.

After her daughter was born, Julie Aigner-Clark searched for ways to share her love of music and art with her child. So she borrowed some equipment and began filming children's videos in her basement. The Baby Einstein Co. was born. And, in just five years, her business grew to more than $20 million in sales. November 2001, Julie sold Baby Einstein to Walt Disney Co. and, with her help, Baby Einstein has grown into a $200 million business.

Julie represents the great enterprising spirit of America. And she's using her success to help others—producing child-safety videos with John Walsh of the National Center for Missing and Exploited Children. Julie says of her new project: "I believe it is the most important thing that I have ever done. I believe that children have the right to live in a world that is safe." And so, tonight, I—we are pleased to welcome this talented business entrepreneur and generous social entrepreneur, Julie Aigner-Clark.

Three weeks ago, Wesley Autrey was waiting at a Harlem subway station with his two little girls, when he saw a man fall into the path of a train. With seconds to act, Wesley jumped onto the tracks, pulled the man into the space between the rails and held him as the train passed right above their heads. He insists he's not a hero. He says: "We've got guys and girls overseas dying for us to have our freedoms. We have got to show each other some love." There is something wonderful about a country that produces a brave and humble man like Wesley Autrey.

Tommy Rieman was a teenager pumping gas in Independence, Ky., when he enlisted in the United States Army. In December 2003, he was on a reconnaissance mission in Iraq when his team came under heavy enemy fire. From his Humvee, Sgt. Rieman returned fire. He used his body as a shield to protect his gunner. He was shot in the chest and arm, and received shrapnel wounds to his legs, yet he refused medical attention and stayed in the fight. He helped to repel a second attack, firing grenades at the enemy's position.

For his exceptional courage, Sgt. Rieman was awarded the Silver Star. And like so many other Americans who have volunteered to defend us, he has earned the respect and the gratitude of our entire country.

In such courage and compassion, ladies and gentlemen, we see the spirit and character of America. And these qualities are not in short supply. This is a decent and honorable country—and resilient, too.

We have been through a lot together. We have met challenges and faced dangers, and we know that more lie ahead. Yet we can go forward with confidence because the State of our Union is strong, our cause in the world is right, and tonight that cause goes on. God bless.

President Bush's Veto of War Supplemental Legislation

Following is the text of President Bush's May 1, 2007, veto message on HR 1591, a supplemental spending measure for the war in Iraq and disaster relief. (Story, p. 308)

To the House of Representatives:

I am returning herewith without my approval HR 1591, the "U.S. Troop Readiness, Veterans' Care, Katrina Recovery, and Iraq Accountability Appropriations Act, 2007."

This legislation is objectionable because it would set an arbitrary date for beginning the withdrawal of American troops without regard to conditions on the ground; it would micromanage the commanders in the field by restricting their ability to direct the fight in Iraq; and it contains billions of dollars of spending and other provisions completely unrelated to the war.

Precipitous withdrawal from Iraq is not a plan to bring peace to the region or to make our people safer here at home. The mandated withdrawal in this bill could embolden our enemies—and confirm their belief that America will not stand behind its commitments. It could lead to a safe haven in Iraq for terrorism that could be used to attack America and freedom-loving people around the world, and is likely to unleash chaos in Iraq that could spread across the region. Ultimately, a precipitous withdrawal could increase the probability that American troops would have to one day return to Iraq—to confront an even more dangerous enemy.

The micromanagement in this legislation is unacceptable because it would create a series of requirements that do not provide the flexibility needed to conduct the war. It would constrict how and where our Armed Forces could engage the enemy and defend the national interest, and would provide confusing guidance on which of our enemies the military could engage. The result would be a marked advantage for our enemies and greater danger for our troops, as well as an unprecedented interference with the judgments of those who are charged with commanding the military.

Beyond its direction of the operation of the war, the legislation is also unacceptable for including billions of dollars in spending and other provisions that are unrelated to the war, are not an emergency, or are not justified. The Congress should not use an emergency war supplemental to add billions in spending to avoid its own rules for budget discipline and the normal budget process. War supplemental funding bills should remain focused on the war and the needs of our men and women in uniform who are risking their lives to defend our freedoms and preserve our nation's security.

Finally, this legislation is unconstitutional because it purports to direct the conduct of the operations of the war in a way that infringes upon the powers vested in the Presidency by the Constitution, including as Commander in Chief of the Armed Forces. For these reasons, I must veto this bill.

GEORGE W. BUSH
THE WHITE HOUSE,
May 1, 2007

President Bush's Veto of Stem Cell Research Legislation

Following is the text of President Bush's June 20, 2007, veto message on S 5, a bill to expand federal funding of embryonic stem cell research. (Story, p. 573)

To the Senate:

I am returning herewith without my approval S 5, the "Stem Cell Research Enhancement Act of 2007."

Once again, the Congress has sent me legislation that would compel American taxpayers, for the first time in our history, to support the deliberate destruction of human embryos.

In 2001, I announced a policy to advance stem cell research in a way that is ambitious, ethical, and effective. I became the first President to make Federal funds available for embryonic stem cell research, and my policy did this in ways that would not encourage the destruction of embryos. Since then, my Administration has made more than $130 million available for research on stem cell lines derived from embryos that had already been destroyed. We have also provided more than $3 billion for research on all forms of stem cells, including those from adult and other non-embryonic sources.

This careful approach is producing results. It has contributed to proven therapeutic treatments in thousands of patients with many different diseases. And it is opening the prospect of new discoveries that could transform lives. Researchers are now developing promising new techniques that offer the potential to produce pluripotent stem cells, without having to destroy human life—for example, by reprogramming adult cells to make them function like stem cells.

Technical innovation in this difficult area is opening up new possibilities for progress without conflict or ethical controversy. Researchers pursuing these kinds of ethically responsible advances deserve support, and there is legislation in the Congress to give them that support. Bills supporting alternative research methods achieved majority support last year in both the House and the Senate. Earlier this spring another bill supporting alternative research won overwhelming majority support in the Senate, and I call on House leaders to pass similar legislation that would authorize additional funds for ethical stem cell research. We cannot lose the opportunity to conduct research that would give hope to those suffering from terrible diseases and help move our Nation beyond the controversies over embryo destruction. I invite policymakers and scientists to come together to solve medical problems without compromising either the high aims of science or the sanctity of human life.

S 5, like the bill I vetoed last year, would overturn today's carefully balanced policy on stem cell research. Compelling American taxpayers to support the deliberate destruction of human embryos would be a grave mistake. I will not allow our Nation to cross this moral line. For that reason, I must veto this bill.

GEORGE W. BUSH
THE WHITE HOUSE,
June 20, 2007

President Bush's Veto of Children's Health Insurance Legislation

Following is the text of President Bush's Oct. 3, 2007, veto message on HR 976, a reauthorization and expansion of the State Children's Health Insurance Program. *(Story, p. 558)*

To the House of Representatives:

I am returning herewith without my approval HR 976, the "Children's Health Insurance Program Reauthorization Act of 2007," because this legislation would move health care in this country in the wrong direction.

The original purpose of the State Children's Health Insurance Program (CHIP) was to help children whose families cannot afford private health insurance, but do not qualify for Medicaid, to get the coverage they need. My administration strongly supports reauthorization of CHIP. That is why I proposed last February a 20 percent increase in funding for the program over five years.

This bill would shift CHIP away from its original purpose and turn it into a program that would cover children from some families of four earning almost $83,000 a year. In addition, under this bill, government coverage would displace private health insurance for many children. If this bill were enacted, one out of every three children moving onto government coverage would be moving from private coverage. The bill also does not fully fund all its new spending, obscuring the true cost of the bill's expansion of CHIP, and it raises taxes on working Americans.

Because the Congress has chosen to send me a bill that moves our health care system in the wrong direction, I must veto it. I hope we can now work together to produce a good bill that puts poorer children first, that moves adults out of a program meant for children, and that does not abandon the bipartisan tradition that marked the enactment of CHIP. Our goal should be to move children who have no health insurance to private coverage, not to move children who already have private health insurance to government coverage.

GEORGE W. BUSH
THE WHITE HOUSE,
Oct. 3, 2007

President Bush's Veto of Water Projects Legislation

Following is the text of President Bush's Nov. 2, 2007, veto message on HR 1495, a bill to reauthorize the Water Resources Development Act. Subsequently, lawmakers voted to override the veto. *(Story, p. 500)*

To the House of Representatives:

I am returning herewith without my approval HR 1495, the "Water Resources Development Act of 2007."

This bill lacks fiscal discipline. I fully support funding for water resources projects that will yield high economic and environmental returns to the Nation and each year my budget has proposed reasonable and responsible funding, including $4.9 billion for 2008, to support the Army Corps of Engineers' (Corps) main missions. However, this authorization bill makes promises to local communities that the Congress does not have a track record of keeping. The House of Representatives took a $15 billion bill into negotiations with a $14 billion bill from the Senate and instead of splitting the difference, emerged with a Washington compromise that costs over $23 billion. This is not fiscally responsible, particularly when local communities have been waiting for funding for projects already in the pipeline. The bill's excessive authorization for over 900 projects and programs exacerbates the massive backlog of ongoing Corps construction projects, which will require an additional $38 billion in future appropriations to complete.

This bill does not set priorities. The authorization and funding of federal water resources projects should be focused on those projects with the greatest merit that are also a federal responsibility. My administration has repeatedly urged the Congress to authorize only those projects and programs that provide a high return on investment and are within the three main missions of the Corps' civil works program: facilitating commercial navigation, reducing the risk of damage from floods and storms, and restoring aquatic ecosystems. This bill does not achieve that goal. This bill promises hundreds of earmarks and hinders the Corps' ability to fulfill the Nation's critical water resources needs—including hurricane protection for greater New Orleans, flood damage reduction for Sacramento, and restoration of the Everglades while diverting resources from the significant investments needed to maintain existing Federal water infrastructure. American taxpayers should not be asked to support a pork-barrel system of Federal authorization and funding where a project's merit is an afterthought.

I urge the Congress to send me a fiscally responsible bill that sets priorities. Americans sent us to Washington to achieve results and be good stewards of their hard-earned taxpayer dollars. This bill violates that fundamental commitment. For the reasons outlined above, I must veto HR 1495.

GEORGE W. BUSH
THE WHITE HOUSE,
Nov. 2, 2007

President Bush's Veto of Labor-HHS-Education Appropriations

Following is the text of President Bush's Nov. 13, 2007, veto message on HR 3043, a fiscal 2008 appropriations bill to fund the departments of Labor, Health and Human Services, and Education, and related agencies. (Story, pp. 112, 114)

To the House of Representatives:

I am returning herewith without my approval HR 3043, the "Departments of Labor, Health and Human Services, and Education, and Related Agencies Appropriations Act, 2008."

This bill spends too much. It exceeds the reasonable and responsible levels for discretionary spending that I proposed to balance the budget by 2012. The Congress is on a path to spend $205 billion more over the next five years than I requested. This puts a balanced budget in jeopardy and risks future tax increases. This year, the Congress plans to overspend my budget by $22 billion, of which $10 billion is for increases in this bill. Health care, education, job training, and other goals can be achieved without this excessive spending if the Congress sets priorities.

This bill continues to fund programs that are duplicative or ineffective. The Congress continues to fund 56 programs totaling more than $3.2 billion that I proposed to terminate because they are duplicative, narrowly focused, or not producing results.

This bill does not sufficiently fund programs that are delivering positive outcomes. For example, Reading First, a critical initiative that is demonstrating results, receives a 61 percent cut, even though low-income students enrolled in Reading First schools posted a more than 10-point improvement in reading proficiency from 2004 to 2006.

This bill has too many earmarks. I set out clear goals for the Congress to reform the earmarking process. The Congress chose not to put earmarks in bill text, instead including nearly all in report language, and they did not reach the goal of cutting the cost and number of earmarks by at least half. This bill contains more than 2,200 earmarks totaling nearly $1 billion. Congressional earmarks divert federal taxpayer funds to localities without the benefit of a merit-based process, resulting in fewer resources for national priorities or unnecessary spending above the requested level.

I urge the Congress to send me a fiscally responsible bill that sets priorities. Americans sent us to Washington to achieve results and be good stewards of their hard-earned tax dollars. Because the legislation violates that commitment, I must veto this bill.

GEORGE W. BUSH
THE WHITE HOUSE,
Nov. 13, 2007

President Bush's Second Veto of Children's Health Insurance Legislation

Following is the text of President Bush's Dec. 12, 2007, veto message on HR 3963, Congress's second attempt to reauthorize and expand the State Children's Health Insurance Program. (Story, p. 558)

To the House of Representatives:

I am returning herewith without my approval HR 3963, the "Children's Health Insurance Program Reauthorization Act of 2007." Like its predecessor, HR 976, this bill does not put poor children first and it moves our country's health care system in the wrong direction. Ultimately, our Nation's goal should be to move children who have no health insurance to private coverage—not to move children who already have private health insurance to government coverage. As a result, I cannot sign this legislation.

The purpose of the State Children's Health Insurance Program (CHIP) was to help low-income children whose families were struggling, but did not qualify for Medicaid, to get the health care coverage that they needed. My Administration strongly supports reauthorization of CHIP. That is why in February of this year I proposed a 5-year reauthorization of CHIP and a 20 percent increase in funding for the program.

Some in the Congress have sought to spend more on CHIP than my budget proposal. In response, I told the Congress that I was willing to work with its leadership to find any additional funds necessary to put poor children first, without raising taxes.

The leadership in the Congress has refused to meet with my Administration's representatives. Although they claim to have made "substantial changes" to the legislation, HR 3963 is essentially identical to the legislation that I vetoed in October. The legislation would still shift CHIP away from its original purpose by covering adults. It would still include coverage of many individuals with incomes higher than the median income in the United States. It would still result in government health care for approximately 2 million children who already have private health care coverage. The new bill, like the old bill, does not responsibly offset its new and unnecessary spending, and it still raises taxes on working Americans.

Because the Congress has chosen to send me an essentially identical bill that has the same problems as the flawed bill I previously vetoed, I must veto this legislation, too. I continue to stand ready to work with the leaders of the Congress, on a bipartisan basis, to reauthorize the CHIP program in a way that puts poor children first; moves adults out of a program meant for children; and does not abandon the bipartisan tradition that marked the original enactment of the CHIP program. In the interim, I call on the Congress to extend funding under the current program to ensure no disruption of services to needy children.

GEORGE W. BUSH
THE WHITE HOUSE
Dec. 12, 2007

President Bush's Veto of Defense Authorization Act and Iraqi Assets

Following is the text of President Bush's Dec. 28, 2007, veto message on HR 1585, a defense authorization bill. (Story, p. 373)

To the House of Representatives:

I am withholding my approval of H.R. 1585, the "National Defense Authorization Act for Fiscal Year 2008," because it would imperil billions of dollars of Iraqi assets at a crucial juncture in that nation's reconstruction efforts and because it would undermine the foreign policy and commercial interests of the United States.

The economic security and successful reconstruction of Iraq have been top priorities of the United States. Section 1083 of H.R. 1585 threatens those key objectives. Immediately upon enactment, section 1083 would risk the freezing of substantial Iraqi assets in the United States—including those of the Development Fund for Iraq (DFI), the Central Bank of Iraq (CBI), and commercial entities in the United States in which Iraq has an interest. Section 1083 also would expose Iraq to new liability of at least several billion dollars by undoing judgments favorable to Iraq, by foreclosing available defenses on which Iraq is relying in pending litigation, and by creating a new Federal cause of action backed by the prospect of punitive damages to support claims that may previously have been foreclosed. This new liability, in turn, will only increase the potential for immediate entanglement of Iraqi assets in the United States. The aggregate financial impact of these provisions on Iraq would be devastating.

While my Administration objected to an earlier version of this provision in previous communications about the bill, its full impact on Iraq and on our relationship with Iraq has become apparent only in recent days. Members of my Administration are working with Members of Congress to fix this flawed provision as soon as possible after the Congress returns.

Section 1083 would establish unprecedented legal burdens on the allocation of Iraq's funds to where they are most needed. Since the fall of Saddam Hussein, I have issued Executive Orders to shield from entanglement in lawsuits the assets of the DFI and the CBI. I have taken these steps both to uphold international legal obligations of the United States and to remove obstacles to the orderly reconstruction of Iraq. Section 1083 potentially would place these crucial protections of Iraq's core assets in immediate peril, by including a provision that might be misconstrued to supersede the protections I have put in place and to permit the judicial attachment of these funds. Iraq must not have its crucial reconstruction funds on judicial hold while lawyers argue and courts decide such legal assertions.

Moreover, section 1083 would permit plaintiffs to obtain liens on certain Iraqi property simply by filing a notice of pending action. Liens under section 1083 would be automatic upon filing a notice of a pending claim in a judicial district where Iraq's property is located, and they would reach property up to the amount of the judgment plaintiffs choose to demand in their complaints. Such pre-judgment liens, entered before claims are tested and cases are heard, are extraordinary and have never previously been available in suits in U.S. courts against foreign sovereigns. If permitted to become law, even for a short time, section 1083's attachment and lien provisions would impose grave—indeed, intolerable—consequences on Iraq.

Section 1083 also includes provisions that would expose Iraq to increased liability in lawsuits. Contrary to international legal norms and for the first time in U.S. history, a foreign sovereign would be liable for punitive damages under section 1083. Section 1083 removes defenses common for defendants in the United States—including *res judicata, collateral estoppel,* and statutes of limitation—upon which the Iraqi government has relied. And section 1083 would attempt to revive a $959 million judgment against the new democratic Government of Iraq based on the misdeeds of the Saddam Hussein regime.

Exposing Iraq to such significant financial burdens would weaken the close partnership between the United States and Iraq during this critical period in Iraq's history. If Iraq's assets are frozen, even temporarily, that could reduce confidence in the Iraqi dinar and undermine the success of Iraq's monetary policy. By potentially forcing a close U.S. ally to withdraw significant funds from the U.S. financial system, section 1083 would cast doubt on whether the United States remains a safe place to invest and to hold financial assets. Iraqi entities would be deterred from engaging in commercial partnerships with U.S. businesses for fear of entangling assets in lawsuits. Section 1083 would be viewed with alarm by the international community and would invite reciprocal action against United States assets abroad.

The adjournment of the Congress has prevented my return of H.R. 1585 within the meaning of Article I, section 7, clause 2 of the Constitution. Accordingly, my withholding of approval from the bill precludes its becoming law. The Pocket Veto Case, 279 U.S. 655 (1929). In addition to withholding my signature and thereby invoking my constitutional power to "pocket veto" bills during an adjournment of the Congress, I am also sending H.R. 1585 to the Clerk of the House of Representatives, along with this memorandum setting forth my objections, to avoid unnecessary litigation about the non-enactment of the bill that results from my withholding approval and to leave no doubt that the bill is being vetoed.

This legislation contains important authorities for the Department of Defense, including authority to provide certain additional pay and bonuses to service members. Although I continue to have serious objections to other provisions of this bill, including section 1079 relating to intelligence matters, I urge the Congress to address the flaw in section 1083 as quickly as possible so I may sign into law the National Defense Authorization Act for Fiscal Year 2008, as modified. I also urge the Congress to ensure that any provisions affecting service member pay and bonuses, as well as provisions extending expiring authorities, are retroactive to January 1, 2008.

GEORGE W. BUSH
THE WHITE HOUSE
DEC. 28, 2008

President Bush's 2008 State of the Union Address

Following is President Bush's State of the Union address, delivered to a joint session of Congress Jan. 28, 2008.

Madam Speaker, Vice President Cheney, members of Congress, distinguished guests and fellow citizens: Seven years have passed since I first stood before you at this rostrum. In that time, our country has been tested in ways none of us could have imagined. We faced hard decisions about peace and war, rising competition in the world economy, and the health and welfare of our citizens. These issues call for vigorous debate, and I think it's fair to say we've answered the call. Yet history will record that amid our differences, we acted with purpose. And together, we showed the world the power and resilience of American self-government.

All of us were sent to Washington to carry out the people's business. That is the purpose of this body. It is the meaning of our oath. It remains our charge to keep.

The actions of the 110th Congress will affect the security and prosperity of our nation long after this session has ended. In this election year, let us show our fellow Americans that we recognize our responsibilities and are determined to meet them. Let us show them that Republicans and Democrats can compete for votes and cooperate for results at the same time.

From expanding opportunity to protecting our country, we've made good progress. Yet we have unfinished business before us, and the American people expect us to get it done.

In the work ahead, we must be guided by the philosophy that made our nation great. As Americans, we believe in the power of individuals to determine their destiny and shape the course of history. We believe that the most reliable guide for our country is the collective wisdom of ordinary citizens. And so in all we do, we must trust in the ability of free peoples to make wise decisions and empower them to improve their lives for their futures.

ECONOMIC STIMULUS

To build a prosperous future, we must trust people with their own money and empower them to grow our economy. As we meet tonight, our economy is undergoing a period of uncertainty. America has added jobs for a record 52 straight months, but jobs are now growing at a slower pace. Wages are up, but so are prices for food and gas. Exports are rising, but the housing market has declined. At kitchen tables across our country, there is a concern about our economic future.

In the long run, Americans can be confident about our economic growth. But in the short run, we can all see that that growth is slowing. So last week, my administration reached agreement with Speaker Pelosi and Republican Leader Boehner on a robust growth package that includes tax relief for individuals and families and incentives for business investment. The temptation will be to load up the bill. That would delay it or derail it, and neither option is acceptable. This is a good agreement that will keep our economy growing and our people working. And this Congress must pass it as soon as possible.

TAX REFORM

We have other work to do on taxes. Unless Congress acts, most of the tax relief we've delivered over the past seven years will be taken away. Some in Washington argue that letting tax relief expire is not a tax increase. Try explaining that to 116 million American taxpayers who would see their taxes rise by an average of $1,800. Others have said they would personally be happy to pay higher taxes. I welcome their enthusiasm. I'm pleased to report that the IRS accepts both checks and money orders.

Most Americans think their taxes are high enough. With all the other pressures on their finances, American families should not have to worry about their federal government taking a bigger bite out of their paychecks. There's only one way to eliminate this uncertainty: Make the tax relief permanent. And members of Congress should know: If any bill that raises taxes reaches my desk, I will veto it.

Just as we trust Americans with their own money, we need to earn their trust by spending their tax dollars wisely. Next week, I'll send you a budget that terminates or substantially reduces 151 wasteful or bloated programs, totaling more than $18 billion. The budget that I will submit will keep America on track for a surplus in 2012. American families have to balance their budgets; so should their government.

CONGRESSIONAL EARMARKS

The people's trust in their government is undermined by congressional earmarks—special-interest projects that are often snuck in at the last minute, without discussion or debate. Last year, I asked you to voluntarily cut the number and cost of earmarks in half. I also asked you to stop slipping earmarks into committee reports that never even come to a vote. Unfortunately, neither goal was met. So this time, if you send me an appropriations bill that does not cut the number and cost of earmarks in half, I'll send it back to you with my veto.

And tomorrow, I will issue an executive order that directs federal agencies to ignore any future earmark that is not voted on by Congress. If these items are truly worth funding, Congress should debate them in the open and hold a public vote.

HOUSING AND HEALTH CARE

Our shared responsibilities extend beyond matters of taxes and spending. On housing, we must trust Americans with the responsibility of homeownership and empower them to weather turbulent times in the housing market. My administration brought together the HOPE NOW alliance, which is helping many struggling homeowners avoid foreclosure. And Congress can help even more. Tonight I ask you to pass legislation to reform Fannie Mae and Freddie Mac, modernize the Federal Housing Administration, and allow state housing agencies to issue tax-free bonds to help homeowners refinance their mortgages. These are difficult times for many American families, and by taking these steps, we can help more of them keep their homes.

To build a future of quality health care, we must trust patients and doctors to make medical decisions and empower them with better information and better options. We share a common goal: making health care more affordable and accessible for all Americans. The best way to achieve that goal is by expanding consumer choice, not government control. So I have proposed ending the bias in the tax code against those who do not get their health insurance through their employer. This one reform would put private coverage within reach for millions, and I call on the Congress to pass it this year.

The Congress must also expand health savings accounts, create Association Health Plans for small businesses, promote health information technology and confront the epidemic of junk medical lawsuits. With all these steps, we will help ensure that decisions about your medical care are made in the privacy of your doctor's office—not in the halls of Congress.

EDUCATION

On education, we must trust students to learn if given the chance and empower parents to demand results from our schools.

In neighborhoods across our country, there are boys and girls with dreams—and a decent education is their only hope of achieving them.

Six years ago, we came together to pass the No Child Left Behind Act, and today no one can deny its results. Last year, fourth- and eighth-graders achieved the highest math scores on record. Reading scores are on the rise. African American and Hispanic students posted all-time highs. Now we must work together to increase accountability, add flexibility for states and districts, reduce the number of high school dropouts, and provide extra help for struggling schools.

Members of Congress, the No Child Left Behind Act is a bipartisan achievement. It is succeeding. And we owe it to America's children, their parents and their teachers to strengthen this good law.

We must also do more to help children when their schools do not measure up. Thanks to the D.C. Opportunity Scholarships you approved, more than 2,600 of the poorest children in our nation's capital have found new hope at a faith-based or other non-public school. Sadly, these schools are disappearing at an alarming rate in many of America's inner cities. So I will convene a White House summit aimed at strengthening these lifelines of learning. And to open the doors of these schools to more children, I ask you to support a new $300 million program called Pell Grants for Kids. We have seen how Pell grants help low-income college students realize their full potential. Together, we've expanded the size and reach of these grants. Now let us apply that same spirit to help liberate poor children trapped in failing public schools.

TRADE AGREEMENTS

On trade, we must trust American workers to compete with anyone in the world and empower them by opening up new markets overseas. Today, our economic growth increasingly depends on our ability to sell American goods and crops and services all over the world. So we're working to break down barriers to trade and investment wherever we can. We're working for a successful Doha round of trade talks, and we must complete a good agreement this year. At the same time, we're pursuing opportunities to open up new markets by passing free-trade agreements.

I thank the Congress for approving a good agreement with Peru. And now I ask you to approve agreements with Colombia and Panama and South Korea. Many products from these nations now enter America duty-free, yet many of our products face steep tariffs in their markets. These agreements will level the playing field. They will give us better access to nearly 100 million customers. They will support good jobs for the finest workers in the world: those whose products say "Made in the USA."

These agreements also promote America's strategic interests. The first agreement that will come before you is with Colombia, a friend of America that is confronting violence and terror and fighting drug traffickers. If we fail to pass this agreement, we will embolden the purveyors of false populism in our hemisphere. So we must come together, pass this agreement and show our neighbors in the region that democracy leads to a better life.

Trade brings better jobs and better choices and better prices. Yet for some Americans, trade can mean losing a job, and the federal government has a responsibility to help. I ask Congress to reauthorize and reform trade adjustment assistance, so we can help these displaced workers learn new skills and find new jobs.

ENERGY POLICY

To build a future of energy security, we must trust in the creative genius of American researchers and entrepreneurs and empower them to pioneer a new generation of clean energy technology. Our security, our prosperity and our environment all require reducing our dependence on oil. Last year, I asked you to pass legislation to reduce oil consumption over the next decade, and you responded. Together we should take the next steps: Let us fund new technologies that can generate coal power while capturing carbon emissions. Let us increase the use of renewable power and emissions-free nuclear power. Let us continue investing in advanced battery technology and renewable fuels to power the cars and trucks of the future. Let us create a new international clean technology fund, which will help developing nations like India and China make greater use of clean energy sources. And let us complete an international agreement that has the potential to slow, stop and eventually reverse the growth of greenhouse gases.

This agreement will be effective only if it includes commitments by every major economy and gives none a free ride. The United States is committed to strengthening our energy security and confronting global climate change. And the best way to meet these goals is for America to continue leading the way toward the development of cleaner and more energy-efficient technology.

SCIENCE AND ETHICS

To keep America competitive into the future, we must trust in the skill of our scientists and engineers and empower them to pursue the breakthroughs of tomorrow. Last year, Congress passed legislation supporting the American Competitiveness Initiative but never followed through with the funding. This funding is essential to keeping our scientific edge. So I ask Congress to double federal support for critical basic research in the physical sciences and ensure America remains the most dynamic nation on Earth.

On matters of life and science, we must trust in the innovative spirit of medical researchers and empower them to discover new treatments while respecting moral boundaries. In November, we witnessed a landmark achievement when scientists discovered a way to reprogram adult skin cells to act like embryonic stem cells. This breakthrough has the potential to move us beyond the divisive debates of the past by extending the frontiers of medicine without the destruction of human life.

So we're expanding funding for this type of ethical medical research. And as we explore promising avenues of research, we must also ensure that all life is treated with the dignity it deserves. And so I call on Congress to pass legislation that bans unethical practices such as the buying, selling, patenting or cloning of human life.

JUDICIARY AND PUBLIC SERVICE

On matters of justice, we must trust in the wisdom of our founders and empower judges who understand that the Constitution means what it says. I've submitted judicial nominees who will rule by the letter of the law, not the whim of the gavel. Many of these nominees are being unfairly delayed. They are worthy of confirmation, and the Senate should give each of them a prompt up-or-down vote.

In communities across our land, we must trust in the good heart of the American people and empower them to serve their neighbors in need. Over the past seven years, more of our fellow citizens have discovered that the pursuit of happiness leads to the path of service. Americans have volunteered in record numbers. Charitable donations are higher than ever. Faith-based groups are bringing hope to pockets of despair, with newfound support from the federal government. And to help guarantee equal treatment of faith-based organizations when they compete for federal funds, I ask you to permanently extend Charitable Choice.

Tonight the armies of compassion continue the march to a new day in the Gulf Coast. America honors the strength and resilience of the people of this region. We reaffirm our pledge to help them build stronger and better than before. And tonight I'm pleased to announce that in April we will host this year's North American Summit of Canada, Mexico, and the United States in the great city of New Orleans.

SPENDING AND IMMIGRATION

There are two other pressing challenges that I've raised repeatedly before this body and that this body has failed to address: entitlement spending and immigration. Every member in this chamber knows that spending on entitlement programs like Social Security, Medicare and Medicaid is growing faster than we can afford. We all know the painful choices ahead if America stays on this path: massive tax increases, sudden and drastic cuts in benefits, or crippling deficits. I've laid out proposals to reform these programs. Now I ask members of Congress to offer your proposals and come up with a bipartisan solution to save these vital programs for our children and our grandchildren.

The other pressing challenge is immigration. America needs to secure our borders—and with your help, my administration is taking steps to do so. We're increasing work site enforcement, deploying fences and advanced technologies to stop illegal crossings. We've effectively ended the policy of "catch and release" at the border, and by the end of this year, we will have doubled the number of Border Patrol agents. Yet we also need to acknowledge that we will never fully secure our border until we create a lawful way for foreign workers to come here and support our economy. This will take pressure off the border and allow law enforcement to concentrate on those who mean us harm. We must also find a sensible and humane way to deal with people here illegally. Illegal immigration is complicated, but it can be resolved. And it must be resolved in a way that upholds both our laws and our highest ideals.

This is the business of our nation here at home. Yet building a prosperous future for our citizens also depends on confronting enemies abroad and advancing liberty in troubled regions of the world.

FOREIGN POLICY

Our foreign policy is based on a clear premise: We trust that people, when given the chance, will choose a future of freedom and peace. In the last seven years, we have witnessed stirring moments in the history of liberty. We've seen citizens in Georgia and Ukraine stand up for their right to free and fair elections. We've seen people in Lebanon take to the streets to demand their independence. We've seen Afghans emerge from the tyranny of the Taliban and choose a new president and a new parliament. We've seen jubilant Iraqis holding up ink-stained fingers and celebrating their freedom. These images of liberty have inspired us.

In the past seven years, we've also seen images that have sobered us. We've watched throngs of mourners in Lebanon and Pakistan carrying the caskets of beloved leaders taken by the assassin's hand. We've seen wedding guests in blood-soaked finery staggering from a hotel in Jordan, Afghans and Iraqis blown up in mosques and markets, and trains in London and Madrid ripped apart by bombs. On a clear September day, we saw thousands of our fellow citizens taken from us in an instant. These horrific images serve as a grim reminder: The advance of liberty is opposed by terrorists and extremists—evil men who despise freedom, despise America and aim to subject millions to their violent rule.

Since 9/11, we have taken the fight to these terrorists and extremists. We will stay on the offense, we will keep up the pressure and we will deliver justice to our enemies.

WAR ON TERRORISM

We are engaged in the defining ideological struggle of the 21st century. The terrorists oppose every principle of humanity and decency that we hold dear. Yet in this war on terror, there is one thing we and our enemies agree on: In the long run, men and women who are free to determine their own destinies will reject terror and refuse to live in tyranny. And that is why the terrorists are fighting to deny this choice to the people in Lebanon, Iraq, Afghanistan, Pakistan and the Palestinian territories. And that is why, for the security of America and the peace of the world, we are spreading the hope of freedom.

In Afghanistan, America, our 25 NATO allies and 15 partner nations are helping the Afghan people defend their freedom and rebuild their country. Thanks to the courage of these military and civilian personnel, a nation that was once a safe haven for al Qaeda is now a young democracy where boys and girls are going to school, new roads and hospitals are being built, and people are looking to the future with new hope. These successes must continue, so we're adding 3,200 Marines to our forces in Afghanistan, where they will fight the terrorists and train the Afghan army and police. Defeating the Taliban and al Qaeda is critical to our security, and I thank the Congress for supporting America's vital mission in Afghanistan.

IRAQ WAR

In Iraq, the terrorists and extremists are fighting to deny a proud people their liberty and fighting to establish safe havens for attacks across the world. One year ago, our enemies were succeeding in their efforts to plunge Iraq into chaos. So we reviewed our strategy and changed course. We launched a surge of American forces into Iraq. We gave our troops a new mission: Work with the Iraqi forces to protect the Iraqi people, pursue the enemy in its strongholds and deny the terrorists sanctuary anywhere in the country.

The Iraqi people quickly realized that something dramatic had happened. Those who had worried that America was preparing to abandon them instead saw tens of thousands of American forces flowing into their country. They saw our forces moving into neighborhoods, clearing out the terrorists and staying behind to ensure the enemy did not return. And they saw our troops, along with Provincial Reconstruction Teams that include Foreign Service officers and other skilled public servants, coming in to ensure that improved security was followed by improvements in daily life. Our military and civilians in Iraq are performing with courage and distinction, and they have the gratitude of our whole nation.

The Iraqis launched a surge of their own. In the fall of 2006, Sunni tribal leaders grew tired of al Qaeda's brutality and started a popular uprising called the Anbar Awakening. Over the past year, similar movements have spread across the country. And today, the grass-roots surge includes more than 80,000 Iraqi citizens who are fighting the terrorists. The government in Baghdad has stepped forward, as well—adding more than 100,000 new Iraqi soldiers and police during the past year.

While the enemy is still dangerous and more work remains, the American and Iraqi surges have achieved results few of us could have imagined just one year ago. When we met last year, many said that containing the violence was impossible. A year later, high-profile terrorist attacks are down, civilian deaths are down, sectarian killings are down.

When we met last year, militia extremists—some armed and trained by Iran—were wreaking havoc in large areas of Iraq. A year later, coalition and Iraqi forces have killed or captured hundreds of militia fighters. And Iraqis of all backgrounds increasingly realize that defeating these militia fighters is critical to the future of their country.

When we met last year, al Qaeda had sanctuaries in many areas of Iraq, and their leaders had just offered American forces safe passage out of the country. Today, it is al Qaeda that is searching for safe passage. They have been driven from many of the strongholds they once held, and over the past year, we've captured or killed thousands of extremists in Iraq, including hundreds of key al Qaeda leaders and operatives.

Last month, Osama bin Laden released a tape in which he railed against Iraqi tribal leaders who have turned on al Qaeda and admitted that coalition forces are growing stronger in Iraq. Ladies and gentlemen, some may deny the surge is working, but among the terrorists there is no doubt. Al Qaeda is on the run in Iraq, and this enemy will be defeated.

TROOP DRAWDOWNS

When we met last year, our troop levels in Iraq were on the rise. Today, because of the progress just described, we are implementing a policy of "return on success," and the surge forces we sent to Iraq are beginning to come home.

This progress is a credit to the valor of our troops and the brilliance of their commanders. This evening, I want to speak directly to our men and women on the front lines. Soldiers and sailors, airmen, Marines, and Coast Guardsmen: In the past year, you have done everything we've asked of you and more. Our nation is grateful for your courage. We are proud of your accomplishments. And tonight in this hallowed chamber, with the American people as our witness, we make you a solemn pledge: In the fight ahead, you will have all you need to protect our nation. And I ask Congress to meet its responsibilities to these brave men and women by fully funding our troops.

Our enemies in Iraq have been hit hard. They are not yet defeated, and we can still expect tough fighting ahead. Our objective in the coming year is to sustain and build on the gains we made in 2007, while transitioning to the next phase of our strategy. American troops are shifting from leading operations to partnering with Iraqi forces and, eventually, to a protective over-watch mission. As part of this transition, one Army brigade combat team and one Marine Expeditionary Unit have already come home and will not be replaced. In the coming months, four additional brigades and two Marine battalions will follow suit. Taken together, this means more than 20,000 of our troops are coming home.

Any further drawdown of U.S. troops will be based on conditions in Iraq and the recommendations of our commanders. Gen. Petraeus has warned that too fast a drawdown could result in the "disintegration of the Iraqi security forces, al Qaeda-Iraq regaining lost ground [and] a marked increase in violence." Members of Congress, having come so far and achieved so much, we must not allow this to happen.

In the coming year, we will work with Iraqi leaders as they build on the progress they're making toward political reconciliation. At the local level, Sunnis, Shia and Kurds are beginning to come together to reclaim their communities and rebuild their lives. Progress in the provinces must be matched by progress in Baghdad. We're seeing some encouraging signs. The national government is sharing oil revenues with the provinces. The parliament recently passed both a pension law and de-Baathification reform. They're now debating a provincial powers law. The Iraqis still have a distance to travel. But after decades of dictatorship and the pain of sectarian violence, reconciliation is taking place—and the Iraqi people are taking control of their future.

The mission in Iraq has been difficult and trying for our nation. But it is in the vital interest of the United States that we succeed. A free Iraq will deny al Qaeda a safe haven. A free Iraq will show millions across the Middle East that a future of liberty is possible. A free Iraq will be a friend of America, a partner in fighting terror and a source of stability in a dangerous part of the world.

By contrast, a failed Iraq would embolden the extremists, strengthen Iran and give terrorists a base from which to launch new attacks on our friends, our allies and our homeland. The enemy has made its intentions clear. At a time when the momentum seemed to favor them, al Qaeda's top commander in Iraq declared that they will not rest until they have attacked us here in Washington. My fellow Americans, we will not rest either. We will not rest until this enemy has been defeated. We must do the difficult work today, so that years from now people will look back and say that this generation rose to the moment, prevailed in a tough fight, and left behind a more hopeful region and a safer America.

MIDDLE EAST CONFLICT

We're also standing against the forces of extremism in the Holy Land, where we have new cause for hope. Palestinians have elected a president who recognizes that confronting terror is essential to achieving a state where his people can live in dignity and at peace with Israel. Israelis have leaders who recognize that a peaceful, democratic Palestinian state will be a source of lasting security. This month in Ramallah and Jerusalem, I assured leaders from both sides that America will do, and I will do, everything we can to help them achieve a peace agreement that defines a Palestinian state by the end of this year. The time has come for a Holy Land where a democratic Israel and a democratic Palestine live side by side in peace.

We're also standing against the forces of extremism embodied by the regime in Tehran. Iran's rulers oppress a good and talented people. And wherever freedom advances in the Middle East, it seems the Iranian regime is there to oppose it. Iran is funding and training militia groups in Iraq, supporting Hezbollah terrorists in Lebanon, and backing Hamas' efforts to undermine peace in the Holy Land. Tehran is also developing ballistic missiles of increasing range and continues to develop its capability to enrich uranium, which could be used to create a nuclear weapon.

Our message to the people of Iran is clear: We have no quarrel with you. We respect your traditions and your history. We look forward to the day when you have your freedom. Our message to the leaders of Iran is also clear: Verifiably suspend your nuclear enrichment, so negotiations can begin. And to rejoin the community of nations, come clean about your nuclear intentions and past actions, stop your oppression at home, cease your support for terror abroad. But above all, know this: America will confront those who threaten our troops. We will stand by our allies, and we will defend our vital interests in the Persian Gulf.

HOMELAND SECURITY

On the home front, we will continue to take every lawful and effective measure to protect our country. This is our most solemn duty. We are grateful that there has not been another attack on our soil since 9/11. This is not for the lack of desire or effort on the part of the enemy. In the past six years, we've stopped numerous attacks, including a plot to fly a plane into the tallest building in Los Angeles and another to blow up passenger jets bound for America over the Atlantic. Dedicated men and women in our government toil day and night to stop the terrorists from carrying out their plans. These good citizens are saving American lives, and everyone in this chamber owes them our thanks.

And we owe them something more: We owe them the tools they need to keep our people safe. And one of the most important tools we can give them is the ability to monitor terrorist communications. To protect America, we need to know who the terrorists are talking to, what they are saying and what they're planning. Last year, Congress passed legislation to help us do that. Unfortunately, Congress set the legislation to expire on Feb. 1. That means if you don't act by Friday, our ability to track terrorist threats would be weakened and our citizens will be in greater danger. Congress must ensure the flow of vital intelligence is not disrupted. Congress must pass liability protection for companies believed to have assisted in the efforts to defend America. We've had ample time for debate. The time to act is now.

FOREIGN AID

Protecting our nation from the dangers of a new century requires more than good intelligence and a strong military. It also requires changing the conditions that breed resentment and allow extremists to prey on despair. So America is using its influence to build a freer, more hopeful and more compassionate world. This is a reflection of our national interest; it is the calling of our conscience.

America opposes genocide in Sudan. We support freedom in countries from Cuba and Zimbabwe to Belarus and Burma.

America is leading the fight against global poverty with strong education initiatives and humanitarian assistance. We've also changed the way we deliver aid by launching the Millennium Challenge Account. This program strengthens democracy, transparency and the rule of law in developing nations, and I ask you to fully fund this important initiative.

America is leading the fight against global hunger. Today, more than half the world's food aid comes from the United States. And tonight, I ask Congress to support an innovative proposal to provide food assistance by purchasing crops directly from farmers in the developing world, so we can build up local agriculture and help break the cycle of famine.

America is leading the fight against disease. With your help, we're working to cut by half the number of malaria-related deaths in 15 African nations. And our Emergency Plan for AIDS Relief is treating 1.4 million people. We can bring healing and hope to many more. So I ask you to maintain the principles that have changed behavior and made this program a success. And I call on you to double our initial commitment to fighting HIV/AIDS by approving an additional $30 billion over the next five years.

VETERANS´ BENEFITS

America is a force for hope in the world because we are a compassionate people, and some of the most compassionate Americans are those who have stepped forward to protect us. We must keep faith with all who have risked life and limb so that we might live in freedom and peace. Over the past seven years, we've increased funding for veterans by more than 95 percent. And as we increase funding we must also reform our veterans' system to meet the needs of a new war and a new generation. I call on the Congress to enact the reforms recommended by Sen. Bob Dole and Secretary Donna Shalala, so we can improve the system of care for our wounded warriors and help them build lives of hope and promise and dignity.

Our military families also sacrifice for America. They endure sleepless nights and the daily struggle of providing for children while a loved one is serving far from home. We have a responsibility to provide for them. So I ask you to join me in expanding their access to child care, creating new hiring preferences for military spouses across the federal government, and allowing our troops to transfer their unused education benefits to their spouses or children. Our military families serve our nation, they inspire our nation and tonight our nation honors them.

The strength—the secret of our strength, the miracle of America—is that our greatness lies not in our government but in the spirit and determination of our people. When the Federal Convention met in Philadelphia in 1787, our nation was bound by the Articles of Confederation, which began with the words, "We the undersigned delegates." When Gouverneur Morris was asked to draft a preamble to our new Constitution, he offered an important revision and opened with words that changed the course of our nation and the history of the world: "We the people."

By trusting the people, our founders wagered that a great and noble nation could be built on the liberty that resides in the hearts of all men and women. By trusting the people, succeeding generations transformed our fragile young democracy into the most powerful nation on Earth and a beacon of hope for millions. And so long as we continue to trust the people, our nation will prosper, our liberty will be secure and the state of our union will remain strong.

So tonight, with confidence in freedom's power and trust in the people, let us set forth to do their business. God bless America.

President Bush's Veto of Fiscal Year 2008 Intelligence Legislation

Following is the text of President Bush's March 8, 2008, veto message on the intelligence authorization for fiscal year 2008 (HR 2082). *(Story, p. 320)*

To the House of Representatives:

I am returning herewith without my approval HR 2082, the "Intelligence Authorization Act for Fiscal Year 2008."

The bill would impede the United States government's efforts to protect the American people effectively from terrorist attacks and other threats because it imposes several unnecessary and unacceptable burdens on our intelligence community.

CONFIRMATIONS

Section 444 of the bill would impose additional Senate confirmation requirements on two national security positions—the director of the National Security Agency and the director of the National Reconnaissance Office. The National Commission on Terrorist Attacks Upon the United States (9/11 commission) observed that the effectiveness of the intelligence community suffers due to delays in the confirmation process; Section 444 would only aggravate those serious problems.

Senior intelligence officials need to assume their duties and responsibilities as quickly as possible to address the pressing requirements of national security. Instead of addressing the 9/11 commission's concern, the bill would subject two additional vital positions to a more protracted process of Senate confirmation. Apart from causing such potentially harmful delays, this unwarranted requirement for Senate confirmation would also risk injecting political pressure into these positions of technical expertise and public trust.

INSPECTORS GENERAL

Section 413 would create a new inspector general for the intelligence community. This new office is duplicative and unnecessary. Each intelligence community component already has an inspector general, and the inspector general of the Office of the Director of National Intelligence has been vested with all the legal powers of any inspector general to carry out investigations on matters under the jurisdiction of the director of national intelligence. There is no reason to commit taxpayer resources to an additional inspector general with competing jurisdiction over the same intelligence elements. Creating duplicative inspectors general, who may have inconsistent views on the handling of particular matters, has the potential to create conflicts and impede the intelligence community from efficiently resolving issues and carrying out its core mission. In addition, the creation of a new inspector general would add yet another position in the intelligence community subject to Senate confirmation, contrary to the 9/11 commission's recommendations.

INTERROGATION METHODS

Section 327 of the bill would harm our national security by requiring any element of the intelligence community to use only the interrogation methods authorized in the Army Field Manual on Interrogations. It is vitally important that the Central Intelligence Agency (CIA) be allowed to maintain a separate and classified interrogation program. The Army Field Manual is directed at guiding the actions of nearly 3 million active-duty and reserve military personnel in connection with the detention of lawful combatants during the course of traditional armed conflicts, but terrorists often are trained specifically to resist techniques prescribed in publicly available military regulations such as the manual.

The CIA's ability to conduct a separate and specialized interrogation program for terrorists who possess the most critical information in the war on terror has helped the United States prevent a number of attacks, including plots to fly passenger airplanes into the Library Tower in Los Angeles and into Heathrow Airport or buildings in downtown London.

While details of the current CIA program are classified, the attorney general has reviewed it and determined that it is lawful under existing domestic and international law, including Common Article 3 of the Geneva Conventions. I remain committed to an intelligence-gathering program that complies with our legal obligations and our basic values as a people. The United States opposes torture, and I remain committed to following international and domestic law regarding the humane treatment of people in its custody, including the "Detainee Treatment Act of 2005."

My disagreement over Section 327 is not over any particular interrogation technique; for instance, it is not over waterboarding, which is not part of the current CIA program. Rather, my concern is the need to maintain a separate CIA program that will shield from disclosure to al Qaeda and other terrorists the interrogation techniques they may face upon capture.

In accordance with a clear purpose of the "Military Commissions Act of 2006," my veto is intended to allow the continuation of a separate and classified CIA interrogation program that the Department of Justice has determined is lawful and that operates according to rules distinct from the more general rules applicable to the Department of Defense. While I will continue to work with the Congress on the implementation of laws passed in this area in recent years, I cannot sign into law a bill that would prevent me—and future presidents—from authorizing the CIA to conduct a separate, lawful intelligence program and from taking all lawful actions necessary to protect Americans from attack.

EXECUTIVE POWERS

Other provisions of the bill purport to require the executive branch to submit information to the Congress that may be constitutionally protected from disclosure, including information the disclosure of which could impair foreign relations, the national security, the deliberative processes of the executive, or the performance of the executive's constitutional duties.

Section 326, for example, would require that the executive branch report, on a very short deadline and in accordance with a rigid set of specific statutory requirements, the details of highly classified interrogation techniques and the confidential legal advice concerning them.

The executive branch voluntarily has provided much of this information to appropriate members of Congress, demonstrating that questions concerning access to such information are best addressed through the customary practices and arrangements between the executive and legislative branches on such matters, rather than through the enactment of legislation.

In addition, Section 406 would require a consolidated inventory of Special Access Programs (SAPs) to be submitted to the Congress. Special Access Programs concern the most sensitive information maintained by the government, and SAP materials are maintained separately precisely to avoid the existence of one document that can serve as a road map to our nation's most vital information. The executive branch must be permitted to present this information in a manner that does not jeopardize national security.

The executive branch will continue to keep the Congress appropriately informed of the matters to which the provisions relate in accordance with the accommodation principles the Constitution contemplates and the executive and legislative branches have long and successfully used to address information sharing on matters of national security.

GEORGE W. BUSH
THE WHITE HOUSE,
March 8, 2008

President Bush's First Veto of Farm Legislation

Following is the text of President Bush's May 21, 2008, veto message on HR 2419, a reauthorization of agriculture programs. Congress overrode the veto. (Story, p. 514)

To the House of Representatives:

I am returning herewith without my approval HR 2419, the "Food, Conservation and Energy Act of 2008."

For a year and a half, I have consistently asked that the Congress pass a good farm bill that I can sign. Regrettably, the Congress has failed to do so. At a time of high food prices and record farm income, this bill lacks program reform and fiscal discipline. It is our objective in international trade negotiations, to secure greater market access for American farmers and ranchers. It would needlessly expand the size and scope of government. Americans sent us to Washington to achieve results and be good stewards of their hard-earned taxpayer dollars. This bill violates that fundamental commitment.

In January 2007, my administration put forward a fiscally responsible farm bill proposal that would improve the safety net for farmers and move current programs toward more market-oriented policies. The bill before me today fails to achieve these important goals.

At a time when net farm income is projected to increase by more than $28 billion in one year, the American taxpayer should not be forced to subsidize that group of farmers who have adjusted gross incomes of up to $1.5 million. When commodity prices are at record highs, it is irresponsible to increase government subsidy rates for 15 crops, subsidize additional crops and provide payments that further distort markets. Instead of better targeting farm programs, this bill eliminates the existing payment limit on marketing loan subsidies.

Now is also not the time to create a new uncapped revenue guarantee that could cost billions of dollars more than advertised. This is on top of a farm bill that is anticipated to cost more than $600 billion over 10 years. In addition, this bill would force many businesses to prepay their taxes in order to finance the additional spending.

This legislation is also filled with earmarks and other ill-considered provisions. Most notably, HR 2419 provides: $175 million to address water issues for desert lakes; $250 million for a 400,000-acre land purchase from a private owner; funding and authority for the noncompetitive sale of National Forest land to a ski resort; and $382 million earmarked for a specific watershed. These earmarks, and the expansion of Davis-Bacon Act prevailing wage requirements, have no place in the farm bill. Rural and urban Americans alike are frustrated with excessive government spending and the funneling of taxpayer funds for pet projects. This bill will only add to that frustration.

The bill also contains a wide range of other objectionable provisions, including one that restricts our ability to redirect food aid dollars for emergency use at a time of great need globally. The bill does not include the requested authority to buy food in the developing world to save lives. Additionally, provisions in the bill raise serious constitutional concerns. For all the reasons outlined above, I must veto HR 2419, and I urge the Congress to extend current law for a year or more.

I veto this bill fully aware that it is rare for a stand-alone farm bill not to receive the president's signature, but my action today is not without precedent. In 1956, President Eisenhower stood firmly on principle, citing high crop subsidies and too much government control of farm programs among the reasons for his veto. President Eisenhower wrote in his veto message, "Bad as some provisions of this bill are, I would have signed it if in total it could be interpreted as sound and good for farmers and the nation." For similar reasons, I am vetoing the bill before me today.

GEORGE W. BUSH
THE WHITE HOUSE,
May 21, 2008

President Bush's Second Veto of Farm Legislation

Following is the text of President Bush's June 18, 2008, veto message on HR 6124, a reauthorization of agriculture programs. Congress overrode the veto. (Story, p. 514)

To the House of Representatives:

I am returning herewith without my approval HR 6124, the "Food, Conservation and Energy Act of 2008."

The bill that I vetoed on May 21, 2008, HR 2419, which became Public Law 110-234, did not include the Title III provisions that are in this bill. In passing HR 6124, the Congress had an opportunity to improve on HR 2419 by modifying certain objectionable, onerous and fiscally imprudent provisions. Unfortunately, the Congress chose to send me the same unacceptable farm bill provisions in HR 6124, merely adding Title III. I am returning this bill for the same reasons as stated in my veto message of May 21, 2008, on HR 2419.

For a year and a half, I have consistently asked that the Congress pass a good farm bill that I can sign. Regrettably, the Congress has failed to do so. At a time of high food prices and record farm income, this bill lacks program reform and fiscal discipline. It continues subsidies for the wealthy and increases farm bill spending by more than $20 billion, while using budget gimmicks to hide much of the increase. It is inconsistent with our objectives in international trade negotiations, which include securing greater market access for American farmers and ranchers. It would needlessly expand the size and scope of government. Americans sent us to Washington to achieve results and be good stewards of their hard-earned taxpayer dollars. This bill violates that fundamental commitment.

In January 2007, my administration put forward a fiscally responsible farm bill proposal that would improve the safety net for farmers and move current programs toward more market-oriented policies. The bill before me today fails to achieve these important goals.

At a time when net farm income is projected to increase by more than $28 billion in one year, the American taxpayer should not be forced to subsidize that group of farmers who have adjusted gross incomes of up to $1.5 million. When commodity prices are at record highs, it is irresponsible to increase government subsidy rates for 15 crops, subsidize additional crops and provide payments that further distort markets. Instead of better targeting farm programs, this bill eliminates the existing payment limit on marketing loan subsidies.

Now is also not the time to create a new uncapped revenue guarantee that could cost billions of dollars more than advertised. This is on top of a farm bill that is anticipated to cost more than

$600 billion over 10 years. In addition, this bill would force many businesses to prepay their taxes in order to finance the additional spending.

This legislation is also filled with earmarks and other ill-considered provisions. Most notably, HR 6124 provides: $175 million to address water issues for desert lakes; $250 million for a 400,000-acre land purchase from a private owner; funding and authority for the noncompetitive sale of National Forest land to a ski resort; and $382 million earmarked for a specific watershed. These earmarks, and the expansion of Davis-Bacon Act prevailing wage requirements, have no place in the farm bill. Rural and urban Americans alike are frustrated with excessive government spending and the funneling of taxpayer funds for pet projects. This bill will only add to that frustration.

The bill also contains a wide range of other objectionable provisions, including one that restricts our ability to redirect food aid dollars for emergency use at a time of great need globally. The bill does not include the requested authority to buy food in the developing world to save lives. Additionally, provisions in the bill raise serious constitutional concerns. For all the reasons outlined above, I must veto HR 6124.

I veto this bill fully aware that it is rare for a stand-alone farm bill not to receive the president's signature, but my action today is not without precedent. In 1956, President Eisenhower stood firmly on principle, citing high crop subsidies and too much government control of farm programs among the reasons for his veto. President Eisenhower wrote in his veto message, "Bad as some provisions of this bill are, I would have signed it if in total it could be interpreted as sound and good for farmers and the nation." For similar reasons, I am vetoing the bill before me today.

GEORGE W. BUSH
THE WHITE HOUSE,
June 18, 2008

President Bush's Veto of Medicare Services Reimbursement Legislation

Following is the text of President Bush's July 15, 2008, veto message on HR 6331, a bill to forestall a reduction in physician reimbursements for Medicare services. (Story, p. 571)

To the House of Representatives:

I am returning herewith without my approval HR 6331, the "Medicare Improvements for Patients and Providers Act of 2008." I support the primary objective of this legislation, to forestall reductions in physician payments. Yet taking choices away from seniors to pay physicians is wrong. This bill is objectionable, and I am vetoing it because:

- It would harm beneficiaries by taking private health plan options away from them. Already more than 9.6 million beneficiaries, many of whom are considered lower-income, have chosen to join a Medicare Advantage (MA) plan, and it is estimated that this bill would decrease MA enrollment by about 2.3 million individuals in 2013 relative to the program's current baseline.
- It would undermine the Medicare prescription drug program, which today is effectively providing coverage to 32 million beneficiaries directly through competitive private plans or through Medicare-subsidized retirement plans.
- And it is fiscally irresponsible, and it would imperil the long-term fiscal soundness of Medicare by using short-term budget gimmicks that do not solve the problem. The result would be a steep and unrealistic payment cut for physicians—roughly 20 percent in 2010—likely leading to yet another expensive temporary fix. And the bill would also perpetuate wasteful overpayments to medical equipment suppliers.

PRIVATE MEDICARE PLANS

In December 2003, when I signed the Medicare Prescription Drug, Improvement and Modernization Act (MMA) into law, I said that "when seniors have the ability to make choices, health care plans within Medicare will have to compete for their business by offering higher-quality service. For the seniors of America, more choices and more control will mean better health care." This is exactly what has happened with drug coverage and with Medicare Advantage.

Today, as a result of the changes in the MMA, 32 million seniors and Americans with disabilities have drug coverage through Medicare prescription drug plans or a Medicare-subsidized retirement plan, while some 9.6 million Medicare beneficiaries—more than 20 percent of all beneficiaries—have chosen to join a private MA plan. To protect the interests of these beneficiaries, I cannot accept the provisions of this legislation that would undermine Medicare Part D, reduce payments for MA plans and restructure the MA program in a way that would lead to limited beneficiary access, benefits and choices and lower-than-expected enrollment in Medicare Advantage.

Medicare beneficiaries need and benefit from having more options than just the one-size-fits-all approach of traditional Medicare fee-for-service. Medicare Advantage plan options include health maintenance organizations, preferred-provider organizations and private fee-for-service (PFFS) plans. Medicare Advantage plans are paid according to a formula established by the Congress in 2003 to ensure that seniors in all parts of the country—including rural areas—have access to private-plan options.

This bill would reduce these options for beneficiaries, particularly those in hard-to-serve rural areas. In particular, HR 6331 would make fundamental changes to the MA PFFS program. The Congressional Budget Office has estimated that HR 6331 would decrease MA enrollment by about 2.3 million individuals in 2013 relative to its current baseline, with the largest effects resulting from these PFFS restrictions.

While the MMA increased the availability of private plan options across the country, it is important to remember that a significant number of beneficiaries who have chosen these options earn lower incomes. The latest data show that 49 percent of beneficiaries enrolled in MA plans report incomes of $20,000 or less. These beneficiaries have made a decision to maximize their Medicare and supplemental benefits through the MA program, in part because of their economic situation. Cuts to MA plan payments required by this legislation would reduce benefits to millions of seniors, including lower-income seniors, who have chosen to join these plans.

PRESCRIPTION DRUG PRICES

The bill would constrain market forces and undermine the success that the Medicare prescription drug program has achieved in providing beneficiaries with robust, high-value coverage—including comprehensive formularies and access to network pharmacies—at lower-than-expected costs. In particular, the provisions that would enable the expansion of "protected classes" of drugs would effectively end meaningful price negotiations between Medicare prescription drug plans and pharmaceutical manufacturers for drugs in those classes. If, as is likely, implementation of this provision results in an increase in the number of protected drug classes, it will lead to increased beneficiary premiums and co-payments, higher drug prices, and lower drug rebates. These new requirements, together with provisions that interfere with the contractual relationships between Part D plans and pharmacies, are expected to increase Medicare spending and have a negative impact on the value and choices that beneficiaries have come to enjoy in the program.

The bill includes budget gimmicks that do not solve the payment problem for physicians, make the problem worse with an abrupt payment cut for physicians of roughly 20 percent in 2010, and add nearly $20 billion to the Medicare Improvement Fund, which would unnecessarily increase Medicare spending and contribute to the unsustainable growth in Medicare. In addition, HR 6331 would delay important reforms like the Durable Medical Equipment, Prosthetics, Orthotics and Supplies competitive bidding program, under which lower payment rates went into effect on July 1, 2008. This program will produce significant savings for Medicare and beneficiaries by obtaining lower prices through competitive bidding. The legislation would leave the Federal Supplementary Medical Insurance Trust Fund vulnerable to litigation because of the revocation of the awarded contracts. Changing policy in midstream is also confusing to beneficiaries who are receiving services from quality suppliers at lower prices. In order to slow the growth in Medicare spending, competition within the program should be expanded, not diminished.

For decades, we promised America's seniors we could do better, and we finally did. We should not turn the clock back to the days when our Medicare system offered outdated and inefficient benefits and imposed needless costs on its beneficiaries.

Because this bill would severely damage the Medicare program by undermining the Medicare Part D program and by reducing access, benefits and choices for all beneficiaries, particularly the approximately 9.6 million beneficiaries in MA, I must veto this bill.

I urge the Congress to send me a bill that reduces the growth in Medicare spending, increases competition and efficiency, implements principles of value-driven health care, and appropriately offsets increases in physician spending.

GEORGE W. BUSH
THE WHITE HOUSE,
July 15, 2008

Pelosi Accepts Speakership

Following are remarks of Democratic Rep. Nancy Pelosi of California delivered from the rostrum of the House of Representatives Jan. 4, 2007, after she was elected by the House as its fifty-second Speaker, the first woman to hold the position. She had been introduced by Rep. John A. Boehner of Ohio, the Republican nominee for the post.

Thank you, my colleagues. Thank you, Leader Boehner, Mr. Speaker.

I accept this gavel in the spirit of partnership, not partisanship, and I look forward to working with you, Mr. Boehner, and the Republicans in the Congress, for the good of the American people.

After giving this gavel away in the first two—in the last two Congresses, I'm glad someone else has the honor today.

In this House, we may be different parties, but we serve one country. And our pride and our prayers are united behind our men and women in uniform. They are working together to protect the American people. And in this Congress, we must work together to build a future worthy of their sacrifice.

In this hour, we need and pray for the character, courage and civility of a former member of this House: President [Gerald R.] Ford. He healed the country when it needed healing. This is another time, another war and another trial of our American will, imagination and spirit. Let us honor his memory not just in eulogy, but in dialogue and trust across the aisle. I want to join Leader Boehner in expressing our condolences and our appreciation to Mrs. Ford and to the entire Ford family for their decades of leadership and service to our country.

With today's convening of the 110th Congress, we begin anew. I congratulate all members of Congress on your election. I especially want to congratulate our new members of Congress.

The genius of our founders was that every two years, new members would bring to this House their spirit of renewal and hope for the American people. This Congress is reinvigorated, new members, by your optimism and your idealism, and your commitment to our country. Let us acknowledge your families, whose support has made your leadership possible today—to your families.

OF FAMILY AND SAINTS

Each of us brings to this Congress our shared values, our commitment to the Constitution and our personal experience.

My path to Congress and to the Speakership began in Baltimore, where my father was the mayor. I was raised in a large family that was devoutly Catholic, deeply patriotic, very proud of our Italian-American heritage, and staunchly Democratic. My parents taught us that public service was a noble calling, and that we had a responsibility to help those in need. I viewed them as working on the side of the angels, and now they are with them.

But I am so happy that my brother Tommy D'Alesandro, who was also a mayor of Baltimore, is here leading the D'Alesandro family from Baltimore today. He's sitting right up there with Tony Bennett.

Forty-three years ago, Paul Pelosi and I were married. We raised our five children in San Francisco, where Paul was born and raised. I want to thank Paul and our five children—Nancy Corinne, Christine, Jacqueline, Paul Jr. and Alexandra—and our magnificent grandchildren for their love, for their support and the confidence they gave me to go from the kitchen to the Congress.

And I thank my constituents in San Francisco, and the state of California, for the privilege of representing them in Congress. St. Francis of Assisi is our city's patron saint. And his "Song of St. Francis" is our city's anthem: "Lord, make me a channel of thy peace; where there is darkness may we bring light; where there is hatred, may we bring love; and where there is despair, may we bring hope."

Hope: That is what America is about. And it is in that spirit that I serve in the Congress of the United States.

And today, I thank my colleagues. By electing me Speaker, you have brought us closer to the ideal of equality that is America's heritage and America's hope. This is an historic moment. And I thank the leader for acknowledging it. Thank you, Mr. Boehner.

It's an historic moment for the Congress. It's an historic moment for the women of America. It is a moment for which we have waited over 200 years. Never losing faith, we waited through the many years of struggle to achieve our rights.

But women weren't just waiting; women were working. Never losing faith, we worked to redeem the promise of America, that all men and women are created equal.

For our daughters and our granddaughters, today we have broken the marble ceiling. For our daughters and our granddaughters now, the sky is the limit. Anything is possible for them.

DEFENDING THE COUNTRY

The election of 2006 was a call to change, not merely to change the control of Congress, but for a new direction for our country. Nowhere were the American people more clear about the need for a new direction than in the war in Iraq. The American people rejected an open-ended obligation to a war without end.

Shortly, President Bush will address the nation on the subject of Iraq. It is the responsibility of the president to articulate a new plan for Iraq that makes it clear to the Iraqis that they must defend their own streets and their own security, a plan that promotes stability in the region and a plan that allows us to responsibly redeploy our troops.

Let us work together to be the Congress that rebuilds our military to meet the national security challenges of the 21st century. Let us be the Congress that strongly honors our responsibility to protect the American people from terrorism. Let us be the Congress that never forgets our commitment to our veterans and our first-responders, always honoring them as the heroes that they are.

The American people also spoke clearly for a new direction here at home. They desire a new vision, a new America built on the values that have made our country great.

Our founders envisioned a new America driven by optimism, opportunity and strength. So confident were they in the America that they were advancing that they put on the seal, the Great Seal of the United States, *"novus ordo seclorum":* a new order for the centuries—centuries. They spoke of the centuries that they envisioned America as a just and good place, as a fair and efficient society, and as a source of opportunity for all.

This vision has sustained us for over 200 years, and it accounts for what is best in our great nation: liberty, opportunity and justice.

Now it is our responsibility to carry forth that vision of a new America into the 21st century. A new America that seizes the future and forges 21st century solutions through discovery, creativity and innovation, sustaining our economic leadership and ensuring our national security. A new America with a vibrant and strengthened middle class for whom college is affordable, health care is accessible and retirement reliable. A new America that declares our energy independence, promotes domestic sources of renewable energy and combats climate change. A new America that is strong, secure and a respected leader among the community of nations.

And the American people told us they expected us to work together for fiscal responsibility, with the highest ethical standard and with civility and bipartisanship. After years of historic deficits, this 110th Congress will commit itself to a higher standard: Pay as you go; no new deficit spending. Our new America will provide unlimited opportunity for future generations, not burden them with mountains of debt.

In order to achieve our new America for the 21st century, we must return this House to the American people. So our first order of business is passing the toughest congressional ethics reform in history. This new Congress doesn't have two years or 200 days. Let us join together in the first 100 hours to make this Congress the most honest and open Congress in history.

This openness requires respect for every voice in the Congress. As Thomas Jefferson said, every difference of opinion is not a difference of principle.

My colleagues elected me to be Speaker of the House—the entire House. Respectful of the vision of our founders, the expectations of our people and the great challenges that we face, we have an obligation to reach beyond partisanship to work for all America.

Let us stand together to move our country forward, seeking common ground for the common good.

We have made history. Now, let us make progress for the American people. May God bless our work, and may God bless America.

Obama 2008 Speech on Race

Following in the text of Barack Obama's speech on race delivered on March 18, 2008, in Philadelphia. The address followed controversy in the wake of remarks on race relations made by Obama's former pastor, the Rev. Jeremiah A. Wright Jr.

"We the people, in order to form a more perfect union."

Two hundred and twenty one years ago, in a hall that still stands across the street, a group of men gathered and, with these simple words, launched America's improbable experiment in democracy. Farmers and scholars; statesmen and patriots who had traveled across an ocean to escape tyranny and persecution finally made real their declaration of independence at a Philadelphia convention that lasted through the spring of 1787.

The document they produced was eventually signed but ultimately unfinished. It was stained by this nation's original sin of slavery, a question that divided the colonies and brought the convention to a stalemate until the founders chose to allow the slave trade to continue for at least twenty more years, and to leave any final resolution to future generations.

Of course, the answer to the slavery question was already embedded within our Constitution—a Constitution that had at is very core the ideal of equal citizenship under the law; a Constitution that promised its people liberty, and justice, and a union that could be and should be perfected over time.

And yet words on a parchment would not be enough to deliver slaves from bondage, or provide men and women of every color and creed their full rights and obligations as citizens of the United States. What would be needed were Americans in successive generations who were willing to do their part—through protests and struggle, on the streets and in the courts, through a civil war and civil disobedience and always at great risk—to narrow that gap between the promise of our ideals and the reality of their time.

This was one of the tasks we set forth at the beginning of this campaign—to continue the long march of those who came before us, a march for a more just, more equal, more free, more caring and more prosperous America. I chose to run for the presidency at this moment in history because I believe deeply that we cannot solve the challenges of our time unless we solve them together—unless we perfect our union by understanding that we may have different stories, but we hold common hopes; that we may not look the same and we may not have come from the same place, but we all want to move in the same direction—towards a better future for of children and our grandchildren.

This belief comes from my unyielding faith in the decency and generosity of the American people. But it also comes from my own American story.

I am the son of a black man from Kenya and a white woman from Kansas. I was raised with the help of a white grandfather who survived a Depression to serve in Patton's Army during World War II and a white grandmother who worked on a bomber assembly line at Fort Leavenworth while he was overseas. I've gone to some of the best schools in America and lived in one of the world's poorest nations. I am married to a black American who carries within her the blood of slaves and slave-owners—an inheritance we pass on to our two precious daughters. I have brothers, sisters, nieces, nephews, uncles and cousins, of every race and every hue, scattered across three continents, and for as long as I live, I will never forget that in no other country on Earth is my story even possible.

It's a story that hasn't made me the most conventional candidate. But it is a story that has seared into my genetic makeup the idea that this nation is more than the sum of its parts—that out of many, we are truly one.

Throughout the first year of this campaign, against all predictions to the contrary, we saw how hungry the American people were for this message of unity. Despite the temptation to view my candidacy through a purely racial lens, we won commanding victories in states with some of the whitest populations in the country. In South Carolina, where the Confederate Flag still flies, we built a powerful coalition of African Americans and white Americans.

This is not to say that race has not been an issue in the campaign. At various stages in the campaign, some commentators have deemed me either "too black" or "not black enough." We saw racial tensions bubble to the surface during the week before the South Carolina primary. The press has scoured every exit poll for the latest evidence of racial polarization, not just in terms of white and black, but black and brown as well.

And yet, it has only been in the last couple of weeks that the discussion of race in this campaign has taken a particularly divisive turn.

On one end of the spectrum, we've heard the implication that my candidacy is somehow an exercise in affirmative action; that it's based solely on the desire of wide-eyed liberals to purchase racial reconciliation on the cheap. On the other end, we've heard my former pastor, Reverend Jeremiah Wright, use incendiary language to express views that have the potential not only to widen the racial divide, but views that denigrate both the greatness and the goodness of our nation; that rightly offend white and black alike.

I have already condemned, in unequivocal terms, the statements of Reverend Wright that have caused such controversy. For some, nagging questions remain. Did I know him to be an occasionally fierce critic of American domestic and foreign policy? Of course. Did I ever hear him make remarks that could be considered controversial while I sat in church? Yes. Did I strongly disagree with many of his political views? Absolutely—just as I'm sure many of you have heard remarks from your pastors, priests, or rabbis with which you strongly disagreed.

But the remarks that have caused this recent firestorm weren't simply controversial. They weren't simply a religious leader's effort to speak out against perceived injustice. Instead, they expressed a profoundly distorted view of this country—a view that sees white racism as endemic, and that elevates what is wrong with America above all that we know is right with America; a view that sees the conflicts in the Middle East as rooted primarily in the actions of stalwart allies like Israel, instead of emanating from the perverse and hateful ideologies of radical Islam.

As such, Reverend Wright's comments were not only wrong but divisive, divisive at a time when we need unity; racially charged at a time when we need to come together to solve a set of monumental problems—two wars, a terrorist threat, a falling economy, a chronic health care crisis and potentially devastating climate change; problems that are neither black or white or Latino or Asian, but rather problems that confront us all.

Given my background, my politics, and my professed values and ideals, there will no doubt be those for whom my statements of condemnation are not enough. Why associate myself with Reverend Wright in the first place, they may ask? Why not join another church? And I confess that if all that I knew of Reverend Wright were the snippets of those sermons that have run in an endless loop on the television and You Tube, or if Trinity United Church of Christ conformed to the caricatures being peddled by some commentators, there is no doubt that I would react in much the same way

But the truth is, that isn't all that I know of the man. The man I met more than twenty years ago is a man who helped introduce me to my Christian faith, a man who spoke to me about our obligations to love one another; to care for the sick and lift up the poor. He is a man who served his country as a U.S. Marine; who has studied and lectured at some of the finest universities and seminaries in the country, and who for over thirty years led a church that serves the community by doing God's work here on Earth—by housing the homeless, ministering to the needy, providing day care services and scholarships and prison ministries, and reaching out to those suffering from HIV/AIDS.

In my first book, Dreams From My Father, I described the experience of my first service at Trinity:

"People began to shout, to rise from their seats and clap and cry out, a forceful wind carrying the reverend's voice up into the rafters....And in that single note—hope!—I heard something else; at the foot of that cross, inside the thousands of churches across the city, I imagined the stories of ordinary black people merging with the stories of David and Goliath, Moses and Pharaoh, the Christians in the lion's den, Ezekiel's field of dry bones. Those stories—of survival, and freedom, and hope—became our story, my story; the blood that had spilled was our blood, the tears our tears; until this black church, on this bright day, seemed once more a vessel carrying the story of a people into future generations and into a larger world. Our trials and triumphs became at once unique and universal, black and more than black; in chronicling our journey, the stories and songs gave us a means to reclaim memories that we didn't need to feel shame about ... memories that all people might study and cherish—and with which we could start to rebuild."

That has been my experience at Trinity. Like other predominantly black churches across the country, Trinity embodies the black community in its entirety—the doctor and the welfare mom, the model student and the former gang-banger. Like other black churches, Trinity's services are full of raucous laughter and sometimes bawdy humor. They are full of dancing, clapping, screaming and shouting that may seem jarring to the untrained ear. The church contains in full the kindness and cruelty, the fierce intelligence and the shocking ignorance, the struggles and successes, the love and yes, the bitterness and bias that make up the black experience in America.

And this helps explain, perhaps, my relationship with Reverend Wright. As imperfect as he may be, he has been like family to me. He strengthened my faith, officiated my wedding, and baptized my children. Not once in my conversations with him have I heard him talk about any ethnic group in derogatory terms, or treat whites with whom he interacted with anything but courtesy and respect. He contains within him the contradictions—the good and the bad—of the community that he has served diligently for so many years.

I can no more disown him than I can disown the black community. I can no more disown him than I can my white grandmother—a woman who helped raise me, a woman who sacrificed again and again for me, a woman who loves me as much as she loves anything in this world, but a woman who once confessed her fear of black men who passed by her on the street, and who on more than one occasion has uttered racial or ethnic stereotypes that made me cringe.

These people are a part of me. And they are a part of America, this country that I love.

Some will see this as an attempt to justify or excuse comments that are simply inexcusable. I can assure you it is not. I suppose the politically safe thing would be to move on from this episode and just hope that it fades into the woodwork. We can dismiss Reverend Wright as a crank or a demagogue, just as some have dismissed Geraldine Ferraro, in the aftermath of her recent statements, as harboring some deep-seated racial bias.

But race is an issue that I believe this nation cannot afford to ignore right now. We would be making the same mistake that Reverend Wright made in his offending sermons about America—to simplify and stereotype and amplify the negative to the point that it distorts reality.

The fact is that the comments that have been made and the issues that have surfaced over the last few weeks reflect the complexities of race in this country that we've never really worked through—a part of our union that we have yet to perfect. And if we walk away now, if we simply retreat into our respective corners, we will never be able to come together and solve challenges like health care, or education, or the need to find good jobs for every American.

Understanding this reality requires a reminder of how we arrived at this point. As William Faulkner once wrote, "The past isn't dead and buried. In fact, it isn't even past." We do not need to recite here the history of racial injustice in this country. But we do need to remind ourselves that so many of the disparities that exist in the African American community today can be directly traced to inequalities passed on from an earlier generation that suffered under the brutal legacy of slavery and Jim Crow.

Segregated schools were, and are, inferior schools; we still haven't fixed them, fifty years after Brown v. Board of Education, and the inferior education they provided, then and now, helps explain the pervasive achievement gap between today's black and white students.

Legalized discrimination—where blacks were prevented, often through violence, from owning property, or loans were not granted to African American business owners, or black homeowners could not access FHA mortgages, or blacks were excluded from unions, or the police force, or fire departments—meant that black families could not amass any meaningful wealth to bequeath to future generations. That history helps explain the wealth and income gap between black and white, and the concentrated pockets of poverty that persists in so many of today's urban and rural communities.

A lack of economic opportunity among black men, and the shame and frustration that came from not being able to provide for one's family, contributed to the erosion of black families—a problem that welfare policies for many years may have worsened. And the lack of basic services in so many urban black neighborhoods—parks for kids to play in, police walking the beat, regular garbage pick-up and building code enforcement—all helped create a cycle of violence, blight and neglect that continue to haunt us.

This is the reality in which Reverend Wright and other African Americans of his generation grew up. They came of age in the late fifties and early sixties, a time when segregation was still the law of the land and opportunity was systematically constricted. What's remarkable is not how many failed in the face of discrimination, but rather how many men and women overcame the odds; how many were able to make a way out of no way for those like me who would come after them.

But for all those who scratched and clawed their way to get a piece of the American Dream, there were many who didn't make it—those who were ultimately defeated, in one way or another, by discrimination. That legacy of defeat was passed on to future generations—those young men and increasingly young women who we see standing on street corners or languishing in our prisons, without hope or prospects for the future. Even for those blacks who did make it, questions of race, and racism, continue to define their worldview in fundamental ways. For the men and women of Reverend Wright's generation, the memories of humiliation and doubt and fear have not gone away; nor has the anger and the bitterness of those years. That anger may not get expressed in public, in front of white co-workers or white friends. But it does find voice in the barbershop or around the kitchen table. At times, that anger is exploited by politicians, to gin up votes along racial lines, or to make up for a politician's own failings.

And occasionally it finds voice in the church on Sunday morning, in the pulpit and in the pews. The fact that so many people are surprised to hear that anger in some of Reverend Wright's sermons simply reminds us of the old truism that the most segregated hour in American life occurs on Sunday morning. That anger is not always productive; indeed, all too often it distracts attention from solving real problems; it keeps us from squarely facing our own complicity in our condition, and prevents the African American community from forging the alliances it needs to bring about real change. But the anger is real; it is powerful; and to simply wish it away, to condemn it without understanding its roots, only serves to widen the chasm of misunderstanding that exists between the races.

In fact, a similar anger exists within segments of the white community. Most working- and middle-class white Americans don't feel that they have been particularly privileged by their race. Their experience is the immigrant experience—as far as they're concerned, no one's handed them anything, they've built it from scratch. They've worked hard all their lives, many times only to see their jobs shipped overseas or their pension dumped after a lifetime of labor. They are anxious about their futures, and feel their dreams slipping away; in an era of stagnant wages and global competition, opportunity comes to be seen as a zero sum game, in which your dreams come at my expense. So when they are told to bus their children to a school across town; when they hear that an African American is getting an advantage in landing a good job or a spot in a good college because of an injustice that they themselves never committed; when they're told that their fears about crime in urban neighborhoods are somehow prejudiced, resentment builds over time.

Like the anger within the black community, these resentments aren't always expressed in polite company. But they have helped shape the political landscape for at least a generation. Anger over welfare and affirmative action helped forge the Reagan Coalition. Politicians routinely exploited fears of crime for their own electoral ends. Talk show hosts and conservative commentators built entire careers unmasking bogus claims of racism while dismissing legitimate discussions of racial injustice and inequality as mere political correctness or reverse racism.

Just as black anger often proved counterproductive, so have these white resentments distracted attention from the real culprits of the middle class squeeze—a corporate culture rife with inside dealing, questionable accounting practices, and short-term greed; a Washington dominated by lobbyists and special interests; economic policies that favor the few over the many. And yet, to wish away the resentments of white Americans, to label them as misguided or even racist, without recognizing they are grounded in legitimate concerns—this too widens the racial divide, and blocks the path to understanding.

This is where we are right now. It's a racial stalemate we've been stuck in for years. Contrary to the claims of some of my critics, black and white, I have never been so naïve as to believe that we can get beyond our racial divisions in a single election cycle, or with a single candidacy—particularly a candidacy as imperfect as my own.

But I have asserted a firm conviction—a conviction rooted in my faith in God and my faith in the American people—that working together we can move beyond some of our old racial wounds, and that in fact we have no choice if we are to continue on the path of a more perfect union.

For the African American community, that path means embracing the burdens of our past without becoming victims of our past. It means continuing to insist on a full measure of justice in every aspect of American life. But it also means binding our particular grievances—for better health care, and better schools, and better jobs—to the larger aspirations of all Americans—the white woman struggling to break the glass ceiling, the white man who has been laid off, the immigrant trying to feed his family. And it means taking full responsibility for [our] own lives—by demanding more from our fathers, and spending more time with our children, and reading to them, and teaching them that while they may face challenges and discrimination in their own lives, they must never succumb to despair or cynicism; they must always believe that they can write their own destiny.

Ironically, this quintessentially American—and yes, conservative—notion of self-help found frequent expression in Reverend Wright's sermons. But what my former pastor too often failed to understand is that embarking on a program of self-help also requires a belief that society can change.

The profound mistake of Reverend Wright's sermons is not that he spoke about racism in our society. It's that he spoke as if our society was static; as if no progress has been made; as if this country—a country that has made it possible for one of his own members to run for the highest office in the land and build a coalition of white and black; Latino and Asian, rich and poor, young and old—is still irrevocably bound to a tragic past. But what we know—what we have seen—is that America can change. That is [the] true genius of this nation. What we have already achieved gives us hope—the audacity to hope—for what we can and must achieve tomorrow.

In the white community, the path to a more perfect union means acknowledging that what ails the African American community does not just exist in the minds of black people; that the legacy of discrimination—and current incidents of discrimination, while less overt than in the past—are real and must be addressed. Not just with words, but with deeds—by investing in our schools and our communities; by enforcing our civil rights laws and ensuring fairness in our criminal justice system; by providing this generation with ladders of opportunity that were unavailable for previous generations. It requires all Americans to realize that your dreams do not have to come at the expense of my dreams; that investing in the health, welfare, and education of black and brown and white children will ultimately help all of America prosper.

In the end, then, what is called for is nothing more, and nothing less, than what all the world's great religions demand—that we do unto others as we would have them do unto us. Let us be our brother's keeper, Scripture tells us. Let us be our sister's keeper. Let us find that common stake we all have in one another, and let our politics reflect that spirit as well.

For we have a choice in this country. We can accept a politics that breeds division, and conflict, and cynicism. We can tackle race only as spectacle—as we did in the OJ trial—or in the wake of tragedy, as we did in the aftermath of Katrina—or as fodder for the nightly news. We can play Reverend Wright's sermons on every channel, every day and talk about them from now until the election, and make the only question in this campaign whether or not the American people think that I somehow believe or sympathize with his most offensive words. We can pounce on some gaffe by a Hillary supporter as evidence that she's playing the race card, or we can speculate on whether white men will all flock to John McCain in the general election regardless of his policies.

We can do that.

But if we do, I can tell you that in the next election, we'll be talking about some other distraction. And then another one. And then another one. And nothing will change.

That is one option. Or, at this moment, in this election, we can come together and say, "Not this time." This time we want to talk about the crumbling schools that are stealing the future of black children and white children and Asian children and Hispanic children and Native American children. This time we want to reject the cynicism that tells us that these kids can't learn; that those kids who don't look like us are somebody else's problem. The children of America are not those kids, they are our kids, and we will not let them fall behind in a 21st century economy. Not this time.

This time we want to talk about how the lines in the Emergency Room are filled with whites and blacks and Hispanics who do not have health care; who don't have the power on their own to overcome the special interests in Washington, but who can take them on if we do it together.

This time we want to talk about the shuttered mills that once provided a decent life for men and women of every race, and the homes for sale that once belonged to Americans from every religion, every region, every walk of life. This time we want to talk about the fact that the real problem is not that someone who doesn't look like you might take your job; it's that the corporation you work for will ship it overseas for nothing more than a profit.

This time we want to talk about the men and women of every color and creed who serve together, and fight together, and bleed together under the same proud flag. We want to talk about how to bring them home from a war that never should've been authorized and never should've been waged, and we want to talk about how we'll show our patriotism by caring for them, and their families, and giving them the benefits they have earned.

I would not be running for President if I didn't believe with all my heart that this is what the vast majority of Americans want for this country. This union may never be perfect, but generation after generation has shown that it can always be perfected. And today, whenever I find myself feeling doubtful or cynical about this possibility, what gives me the most hope is the next generation—the young people whose attitudes and beliefs and openness to change have already made history in this election.

There is one story in particularly that I'd like to leave you with today—a story I told when I had the great honor of speaking on Dr. King's birthday at his home church, Ebenezer Baptist, in Atlanta.

There is a young, twenty-three year old white woman named Ashley Baia who organized for our campaign in Florence, South Carolina. She had been working to organize a mostly African American community since the beginning of this campaign, and one day she was at a roundtable discussion where everyone went around telling their story and why they were there.

And Ashley said that when she was nine years old, her mother got cancer. And because she had to miss days of work, she was let go and lost her health care. They had to file for bankruptcy, and that's when Ashley decided that she had to do something to help her mom.

She knew that food was one of their most expensive costs, and so Ashley convinced her mother that what she really liked and really wanted to eat more than anything else was mustard and relish sandwiches. Because that was the cheapest way to eat.

She did this for a year until her mom got better, and she told everyone at the roundtable that the reason she joined our campaign was so that she could help the millions of other children in the country who want and need to help their parents too.

Now Ashley might have made a different choice. Perhaps somebody told her along the way that the source of her mother's problems were blacks who were on welfare and too lazy to work, or Hispanics who were coming into the country illegally. But she didn't. She sought out allies in her fight against injustice.

Anyway, Ashley finishes her story and then goes around the room and asks everyone else why they're supporting the campaign. They all have different stories and reasons. Many bring up a specific issue. And finally they come to this elderly black man who's been sitting there quietly the entire time. And Ashley asks him why he's there. And he does not bring up a specific issue. He does not say health care or the economy. He does not say education or the war. He does not say that he was there because of Barack Obama. He simply says to everyone in the room, "I am here because of Ashley."

"I'm here because of Ashley." By itself, that single moment of recognition between that young white girl and that old black man is not enough. It is not enough to give health care to the sick, or jobs to the jobless, or education to our children.

But it is where we start. It is where our union grows stronger. And as so many generations have come to realize over the course of the two-hundred and twenty one years since a band of patriots signed that document in Philadelphia, that is where the perfection begins.

Obama Nomination Acceptance Speech

Following is the speech by Democratic presidential nominee Sen. Barack Obama of Illinois to the Democratic National Convention Aug. 28, 2008.

Thank you so much. Thank you very much. Thank you, everybody.

To Chairman Dean and my great friend Dick Durbin, and to all my fellow citizens of this great nation, with profound gratitude and great humility, I accept your nomination for [the] presidency of the United States.

Let me express my thanks to the historic slate of candidates who accompanied me on this journey, and especially the one who traveled the farthest, a champion for working Americans and an inspiration to my daughters and to yours, Hillary Rodham Clinton.

To President Clinton, to President Bill Clinton, who made last night the case for change as only he can make it—to Ted Kennedy, who embodies the spirit of service—and to the next vice president of the United States, Joe Biden, I thank you.

I am grateful to finish this journey with one of the finest statesmen of our time, a man at ease with everyone from world leaders to the conductors on the Amtrak train he still takes home every night.

To the love of my life, our next first lady, Michelle Obama—and to Malia and Sasha, I love you so much, and I am so proud of you.

Four years ago, I stood before you and told you my story, of the brief union between a young man from Kenya and a young woman from Kansas who weren't well-off or well-known, but shared a belief that in America their son could achieve whatever he put his mind to.

It is that promise that's always set this country apart, that through hard work and sacrifice each of us can pursue our individual dreams, but still come together as one American family, to ensure that the next generation can pursue their dreams, as well.

That's why I stand here tonight. Because for 232 years, at each moment when that promise was in jeopardy, ordinary men and women—students and soldiers, farmers and teachers, nurses and janitors—found the courage to keep it alive.

We meet at one of those defining moments, a moment when our nation is at war, our economy is in turmoil and the American promise has been threatened once more.

Tonight, more Americans are out of work and more are working harder for less. More of you have lost your homes and even more are watching your home values plummet. More of you have cars you can't afford to drive, credit card bills you can't afford to pay and tuition that's beyond your reach.

"BROKEN POLITICS"

These challenges are not all of government's making. But the failure to respond is a direct result of a broken politics in Washington and the failed policies of George W. Bush.

America, we are better than these last eight years. We are a better country than this.

This country is more decent than one where a woman in Ohio, on the brink of retirement, finds herself one illness away from disaster after a lifetime of hard work.

We're a better country than one where a man in Indiana has to pack up the equipment that he's worked on for 20 years and watch as it's shipped off to China, and then chokes up as he explains how he felt like a failure when he went home to tell his family the news.

We are more compassionate than a government that lets veterans sleep on our streets and families slide into poverty—that sits on its hands while a major American city drowns before our eyes.

Tonight, tonight, I say to the people of America, to Democrats and Republicans and independents across this great land: Enough.

This moment, this election is our chance to keep, in the 21st century, the American promise alive.

Because next week, in Minnesota, the same party that brought you two terms of George Bush and Dick Cheney will ask this country for a third.

And we are here because we love this country too much to let the next four years look just like the last eight.

On November 4th, we must stand up and say: Eight is enough.

Now, now, let me—let there be no doubt. The Republican nominee, John McCain, has worn the uniform of our country with bravery and distinction, and for that we owe him our gratitude and our respect.

And next week, we'll also hear about those occasions when he's broken with his party as evidence that he can deliver the change that we need. But the record's clear: John McCain has voted with George Bush 90 percent of the time.

Sen. McCain likes to talk about judgment, but, really, what does it say about your judgment when you think George Bush has been right more than 90 percent of the time?

I don't know about you, but I am not ready to take a 10 percent chance on change.

The truth is, on issue after issue that would make a difference in your lives—on health care, and education, and the economy—Sen. McCain has been anything but independent.

He said that our economy has made great progress under this president. He said that the fundamentals of the economy are strong.

And when one of his chief advisers, the man who wrote his economic plan, was talking about the anxieties that Americans are feeling, he said that we were just suffering from a mental recession and that we've become, and I quote, "a nation of whiners."

A nation of whiners? Tell that to the proud autoworkers at a Michigan plant who, after they found out it was closing, kept showing up every day and working as hard as ever, because they knew there were people who counted on the brakes that they made.

Tell that to the military families who shoulder their burdens silently as they watch their loved ones leave for their third, or fourth, or fifth tour of duty.

These are not whiners. They work hard, and they give back, and they keep going without complaint. These are the Americans I know.

Now, I don't believe that Sen. McCain doesn't care what's going on in the lives of Americans; I just think he doesn't know.

Why else would he define "middle class" as someone making under $5 million a year? How else could he propose hundreds of billions in tax breaks for big corporations and oil companies but not one penny of tax relief to more than 100 million Americans?

How else could he offer a health care plan that would actually tax people's benefits, or an education plan that would do nothing to help families pay for college, or a plan that would privatize Social Security and gamble your retirement?

It's not because John McCain doesn't care; it's because John McCain doesn't get it.

For over two decades—for over two decades—he's subscribed to that old, discredited Republican philosophy: Give more and more to those with the most and hope that prosperity trickles down to everyone else.

In Washington, they call this the "Ownership Society," but what it really means is that you're on your own. Out of work? Tough luck, you're on your own. No health care? The market will fix it. You're on your own. Born into poverty? Pull yourself up by your own bootstraps, even if you don't have boots. You are on your own.

Well, it's time for them to own their failure. It's time for us to change America. And that's why I'm running for president of the United States.

You see, we Democrats have a very different measure of what constitutes progress in this country.

We measure progress by how many people can find a job that pays the mortgage, whether you can put a little extra money away at the end of each month so you can someday watch your child receive her college diploma.

We measure progress in the 23 million new jobs that were created when Bill Clinton was president—when the average American family saw its income go up $7,500 instead of go down $2,000, like it has under George Bush.

We measure the strength of our economy not by the number of billionaires we have or the profits of the Fortune 500, but by whether someone with a good idea can take a risk and start a new business, or whether the waitress who lives on tips can take a day off and look after a sick kid without losing her job, an economy that honors the dignity of work.

The fundamentals we use to measure economic strength are whether we are living up to that fundamental promise that has made this country great, a promise that is the only reason I am standing here tonight.

Because, in the faces of those young veterans who come back from Iraq and Afghanistan, I see my grandfather, who signed up after Pearl Harbor, marched in Patton's army and was rewarded by a grateful nation with the chance to go to college on the G.I. Bill.

In the face of that young student, who sleeps just three hours before working the night shift, I think about my mom, who raised my sister and me on her own while she worked and earned her degree, who once turned to food stamps but was still able to send us to the best schools in the country with the help of student loans and scholarships.

When I listen to another worker tell me that his factory has shut down, I remember all those men and women on the South Side of Chicago who I stood by and fought for two decades ago after the local steel plant closed.

And when I hear a woman talk about the difficulties of starting her own business or making her way in the world, I think about my grandmother, who worked her way up from the secretarial pool to middle management, despite years of being passed over for promotions because she was a woman.

She's the one who taught me about hard work. She's the one who put off buying a new car or a new dress for herself so that I could have a better life. She poured everything she had into me. And although she can no longer travel, I know that she's watching tonight and that tonight is her night, as well.

Now, I don't know what kind of lives John McCain thinks that celebrities lead, but this has been mine.

These are my heroes; theirs are the stories that shaped my life. And it is on behalf of them that I intend to win this election and keep our promise alive as president of the United States.

THE AMERICAN PROMISE

What—what is that American promise? It's a promise that says each of us has the freedom to make of our own lives what we will, but that we also have obligations to treat each other with dignity and respect.

It's a promise that says the market should reward drive and innovation and generate growth but that businesses should live up to their responsibilities to create American jobs, to look out for American workers, and play by the rules of the road.

Ours is a promise that says government cannot solve all our problems, but what it should do is that which we cannot do for ourselves: protect us from harm and provide every child a decent education; keep our water clean and our toys safe; invest in new schools, and new roads, and science, and technology.

Our government should work for us, not against us. It should help us, not hurt us. It should ensure opportunity not just for those with the most money and influence, but for every American who's willing to work.

That's the promise of America, the idea that we are responsible for ourselves, but that we also rise or fall as one nation, the fundamental belief that I am my brother's keeper, I am my sister's keeper.

That's the promise we need to keep. That's the change we need right now.

So let me spell out exactly what that change would mean if I am president.

TAXES

Change means a tax code that doesn't reward the lobbyists who wrote it, but the American workers and small businesses who deserve it.

You know, unlike John McCain, I will stop giving tax breaks to companies that ship jobs overseas, and I will start giving them to companies that create good jobs right here in America.

I'll eliminate capital gains taxes for the small businesses and start-ups that will create the high-wage, high-tech jobs of tomorrow.

I will—listen now—I will cut taxes—cut taxes—for 95 percent of all working families, because, in an economy like this, the last thing we should do is raise taxes on the middle class.

ENERGY

And for the sake of our economy, our security and the future of our planet, I will set a clear goal as president: In 10 years, we will finally end our dependence on oil from the Middle East.

We will do this. Washington has been talking about our oil addiction for the last 30 years. And, by the way, John McCain has been there for 26 of them.

And in that time, he has said no to higher fuel efficiency standards for cars, no to investments in renewable energy, no to renewable fuels. And today, we import triple the amount of oil than we had on the day that Sen. McCain took office.

Now is the time to end this addiction and to understand that drilling is a stopgap measure, not a long-term solution, not even close. As president, I will tap our natural gas reserves, invest in clean-coal technology and find ways to safely harness nuclear power. I'll help our auto companies re-tool, so that the fuel efficient cars of the future are built right here in America.

I'll make it easier for the American people to afford these new cars.

And I'll invest $150 billion over the next decade in affordable, renewable sources of energy—wind power, and solar power, and the next generation of biofuels—an investment that will lead to new industries and 5 million new jobs that pay well and can't be outsourced.

EDUCATION

America, now is not the time for small plans. Now is the time to finally meet our moral obligation to provide every child a world-class education, because it will take nothing less to compete in the global economy.

You know, Michelle and I are only here tonight because we were given a chance at an education. And I will not settle for an America where some kids don't have that chance.

I'll invest in early childhood education. I'll recruit an army of new teachers, and pay them higher salaries, and give them more support. And in exchange, I'll ask for higher standards and more accountability.

And we will keep our promise to every young American: If you commit to serving your community or our country, we will make sure you can afford a college education.

HEALTH CARE AND FINANCES

Now is the time to finally keep the promise of affordable, accessible health care for every single American.

If you have health care, my plan will lower your premiums. If you don't, you'll be able to get the same kind of coverage that members of Congress give themselves.

And as someone who watched my mother argue with insurance companies while she lay in bed dying of cancer, I will make certain those companies stop discriminating against those who are sick and need care the most.

Now is the time to help families with paid sick days and better family leave, because nobody in America should have to choose between keeping their job and caring for a sick child or an ailing parent.

Now is the time to change our bankruptcy laws so that your pensions are protected ahead of CEO bonuses, and the time to protect Social Security for future generations.

And now is the time to keep the promise of equal pay for an equal day's work, because I want my daughters to have the exact same opportunities as your sons.

Now, many of these plans will cost money, which is why I've laid out how I'll pay for every dime: by closing corporate loopholes and tax havens that don't help America grow.

But I will also go through the federal budget line by line, eliminating programs that no longer work and making the ones we do need work better and cost less, because we cannot meet 21st century challenges with a 20th-century bureaucracy.

PERSONAL RESPONSIBILITY

And, Democrats, we must also admit that fulfilling America's promise will require more than just money. It will require a renewed sense of responsibility from each of us to recover what John F. Kennedy called our intellectual and moral strength.

Yes, government must lead on energy independence, but each of us must do our part to make our homes and businesses more efficient.

Yes, we must provide more ladders to success for young men who fall into lives of crime and despair. But we must also admit that programs alone can't replace parents, that government can't turn off the television and make a child do her homework, that fathers must take more responsibility to provide love and guidance to their children.

Individual responsibility and mutual responsibility—that's the essence of America's promise. And just as we keep our promise to the next generation here at home, so must we keep America's promise abroad.

If John McCain wants to have a debate about who has the temperament and judgment to serve as the next commander in chief, that's a debate I'm ready to have.

FOREIGN POLICY

For while Sen. McCain was turning his sights to Iraq just days after 9/11, I stood up and opposed this war, knowing that it would distract us from the real threats that we face.

When John McCain said we could just muddle through in Afghanistan, I argued for more resources and more troops to finish the fight against the terrorists who actually attacked us on 9/11, and made clear that we must take out Osama bin Laden and his lieutenants if we have them in our sights.

You know, John McCain likes to say that he'll follow bin Laden to the gates of hell, but he won't even follow him to the cave where he lives.

And today, today, as my call for a time frame to remove our troops from Iraq has been echoed by the Iraqi government and even the Bush administration, even after we learned that Iraq has $79 billion in surplus while we are wallowing in deficit, John McCain stands alone in his stubborn refusal to end a misguided war.

That's not the judgment we need; that won't keep America safe. We need a president who can face the threats of the future, not keep grasping at the ideas of the past.

You don't defeat a terrorist network that operates in 80 countries by occupying Iraq. You don't protect Israel and deter Iran just by talking tough in Washington. You can't truly stand up for Georgia when you've strained our oldest alliances.

If John McCain wants to follow George Bush with more tough talk and bad strategy, that is his choice, but that is not the change that America needs.

We are the party of Roosevelt. We are the party of Kennedy. So don't tell me that Democrats won't defend this country. Don't tell me that Democrats won't keep us safe.

The Bush-McCain foreign policy has squandered the legacy that generations of Americans, Democrats and Republicans, have built, and we are here to restore that legacy.

As commander in chief, I will never hesitate to defend this nation, but I will only send our troops into harm's way with a clear mission and a sacred commitment to give them the equipment they need in battle and the care and benefits they deserve when they come home.

I will end this war in Iraq responsibly and finish the fight against al Qaeda and the Taliban in Afghanistan.

I will rebuild our military to meet future conflicts, but I will also renew the tough, direct diplomacy that can prevent Iran from obtaining nuclear weapons and curb Russian aggression.

I will build new partnerships to defeat the threats of the 21st century: terrorism and nuclear proliferation, poverty and genocide, climate change and disease.

And I will restore our moral standing so that America is once again that last, best hope for all who are called to the cause of freedom, who long for lives of peace, and who yearn for a better future.

These are the policies I will pursue. And in the weeks ahead, I look forward to debating them with John McCain.

But what I will not do is suggest that the senator takes his positions for political purposes, because one of the things that we have to change in our politics is the idea that people cannot disagree without challenging each other's character and each other's patriotism.

The times are too serious, the stakes are too high for this same partisan playbook. So let us agree that patriotism has no party. I love this country, and so do you, and so does John McCain.

The men and women who serve in our battlefields may be Democrats and Republicans and independents, but they have fought together and bled together, and some died together under the same proud flag. They have not served a red America or a blue America; they have served the United States of America.

So I've got news for you, John McCain: We all put our country first.

America, our work will not be easy. The challenges we face require tough choices. And Democrats as well as Republicans will need to cast off the worn-out ideas and politics of the past, for part of what has been lost these past eight years can't just be measured by lost wages or bigger trade deficits. What has also been lost is our sense of common purpose, and that's what we have to restore.

We may not agree on abortion, but surely we can agree on reducing the number of unwanted pregnancies in this country.

The reality of gun ownership may be different for hunters in rural Ohio than they are for those plagued by gang violence in Cleveland, but don't tell me we can't uphold the Second Amendment while keeping AK-47s out of the hands of criminals.

I know there are differences on same-sex marriage, but surely we can agree that our gay and lesbian brothers and sisters deserve to visit the person they love in a hospital and to live lives free of discrimination.

You know, passions may fly on immigration, but I don't know anyone who benefits when a mother is separated from her infant child or an employer undercuts American wages by hiring illegal workers.

But this, too, is part of America's promise, the promise of a democracy where we can find the strength and grace to bridge divides and unite in common effort.

I know there are those who dismiss such beliefs as happy talk. They claim that our insistence on something larger, something firmer and more honest in our public life is just a Trojan horse for higher taxes and the abandonment of traditional values.

And that's to be expected, because if you don't have any fresh ideas, then you use stale tactics to scare voters.

If you don't have a record to run on, then you paint your opponent as someone people should run from. You make a big election about small things.

And you know what? It's worked before, because it feeds into the cynicism we all have about government. When Washington doesn't work, all its promises seem empty. If your hopes have been dashed again and again, then it's best to stop hoping and settle for what you already know.

I get it. I realize that I am not the likeliest candidate for this office. I don't fit the typical pedigree, and I haven't spent my career in the halls of Washington.

But I stand before you tonight because all across America something is stirring. What the naysayers don't understand is that this election has never been about me; it's about you.

It's about you.

For 18 long months, you have stood up, one by one, and said, "Enough," to the politics of the past. You understand that, in this election, the greatest risk we can take is to try the same old politics with the same old players and expect a different result.

"DEFINING MOMENTS"

You have shown what history teaches us, that at defining moments like this one, the change we need doesn't come from Washington. Change comes to Washington.

Change happens because the American people demand it, because they rise up and insist on new ideas and new leadership, a new politics for a new time.

America, this is one of those moments.

I believe that, as hard as it will be, the change we need is coming, because I've seen it, because I've lived it.

Because I've seen it in Illinois, when we provided health care to more children and moved more families from welfare to work.

I've seen it in Washington, where we worked across party lines to open up government and hold lobbyists more accountable, to give better care for our veterans and keep nuclear weapons out of the hands of terrorists.

And I've seen it in this campaign, in the young people who voted for the first time and the young at heart, those who got involved again after a very long time; in the Republicans who never thought they'd pick up a Democratic ballot but did.

I've seen it in the workers who would rather cut their hours back a day, even though they can't afford it, than see their friends lose their jobs; in the soldiers who re-enlist after losing a limb; in the good neighbors who take a stranger in when a hurricane strikes and the floodwaters rise.

You know, this country of ours has more wealth than any nation, but that's not what makes us rich. We have the most powerful military on Earth, but that's not what makes us strong. Our universities and our culture are the envy of the world, but that's not what keeps the world coming to our shores.

Instead, it is that American spirit, that American promise, that pushes us forward even when the path is uncertain; that binds us together in spite of our differences; that makes us fix our eye not on what is seen but what is unseen, that better place around the bend.

That promise is our greatest inheritance. It's a promise I make to my daughters when I tuck them in at night and a promise that you make to yours, a promise that has led immigrants to cross oceans and pioneers to travel west, a promise that led workers to picket lines and women to reach for the ballot.

And it is that promise that, forty-five years ago today, brought Americans from every corner of this land to stand together on a Mall in Washington, before Lincoln's Memorial, and hear a young preacher from Georgia speak of his dream.

The men and women who gathered there could've heard many things. They could've heard words of anger and discord. They could've been told to succumb to the fear and frustrations of so many dreams deferred.

But what the people heard instead—people of every creed and color, from every walk of life—is that, in America, our destiny is inextricably linked, that together our dreams can be one.

"We cannot walk alone," the preacher cried. "And as we walk, we must make the pledge that we shall always march ahead. We cannot turn back."

America, we cannot turn back. Not with so much work to be done; not with so many children to educate, and so many veterans to care for; not with an economy to fix, and cities to rebuild, and farms to save; not with so many families to protect and so many lives to mend.

America, we cannot turn back. We cannot walk alone.

At this moment, in this election, we must pledge once more to march into the future. Let us keep that promise, that American promise, and in the words of Scripture hold firmly, without wavering, to the hope that we confess.

Thank you. God bless you. And God bless the United States of America.

McCain Nomination Acceptance Speech

Following is the speech by Republican presidential nominee Sen. John McCain of Arizona to the Republican National Convention Sept. 4, 2008.

Thank you. Thank you all very much. Thank you.

Tonight, I have a privilege given few Americans: the privilege of accepting our party's nomination for president of the United States.

Thank you. Thanks. And I accept it with gratitude, humility and confidence.

In my life, no success has come without a good fight, and this nomination wasn't any different. That's a tribute to the candidates who opposed me and their supporters. They're leaders of great ability who love our country and wish to lead it to better days. Their support is an honor that I won't forget.

I'm grateful to the president of the United States for leading us in these dark days following the worst attack in American history—the worst attack on American soil in our history and keeping us safe from another attack that many thought was inevitable.

And to the first lady, Laura Bush, a model of grace and kindness in public and in private.

And I'm grateful to the 41st president and his bride of 63 years for their outstanding example of honorable service to our country.

As always, I'm indebted to my wife, Cindy, and my seven children. You know, the pleasures of family life can seem like a brief holiday from the crowded calendar of our nation's business. But I have treasured them all the more and can't imagine a life without the happiness that you've given me.

You know, Cindy said a lot of nice things about me tonight. But, in truth, she's more my inspiration than I am hers. Her concern for those less blessed than we are—victims of land mines, children born in poverty, with birth defects—shows the measure of her humanity. And I know that she will make a great first lady.

My friends, when I was growing up, my father was often at sea, and the job of raising my brother, sister and me would fall to my mother alone. Roberta McCain gave us her love of life, her deep interest in the world, her strength and her belief that we're all meant to use our opportunities to make ourselves useful to our country. I wouldn't be here tonight but for the strength of her character. And she doesn't want me to say this, but she's 96 years young.

My heartfelt thanks to all of you who helped me win this nomination and stood by me when the odds were long. I won't let you down. I won't let you down. I won't let you down.

To Americans who have yet to decide who to vote for, thank you for your consideration and the opportunity to win your trust. I intend to earn it.

And, finally, a word to Sen. Obama and his supporters: We'll go at it over the next two months—you know that's the nature of this business—and there are big differences between us. But you have my respect and my admiration. Despite our differences, much more unites us than divides us. We are fellow Americans, and that's an association that means more to me than any other. We're dedicated to the proposition that all people are created equal and endowed by our creator with inalienable rights. No country ever had a greater cause than that. And I wouldn't be an American worthy of the name if I didn't honor Sen. Obama and his supporters for their achievement.

"WE'RE GOING TO WIN"

But let there be no doubt, my friends: We're going to win this election. And after we've won, we're going to reach out our hand to any willing patriot, make this government start working for you again and get this country back on the road to prosperity and peace.

I know these are tough times for many of you. You're worried about . . . . [interrupted by crowd noise] Please, please, please. My friends, my dear friends, please. Please don't be diverted by the ground noise and the static. You know, I'm going to talk about it some more. But Americans want us to stop yelling at each other, OK?

These are tough times for many of you. You're worried about keeping your job or finding a new one, and you're struggling to put food on the table and stay in your home.

All you've ever asked of your government is to stand on your side and not in your way. And that's what I intend to do: stand on your side and fight for your future.

And I've found just the right partner to help me shake up Washington, Gov. Sarah Palin of the great state of Alaska.

And I want to thank everyone here and all over America for the tremendous, wonderful, warm reception you gave her last night. Thank you so much. She deserves it. What a great beginning.

You know, she has executive experience and a real record of accomplishment. She's tackled tough problems, like energy independence and corruption. She's balanced a budget, cut taxes, and she's taken on the special interests. She's reached across the aisle and asked Republicans, Democrats and independents to serve in her administration. She's the wonderful mother of five children. She's helped run a small business. She's worked with her hands and knows what it's like to worry about mortgage payments, and health care, and the cost of gasoline and groceries. She knows where she comes from, and she knows who she works for. She stands up for what's right, and she doesn't let anyone tell her to sit down. I'm very proud to have introduced our next vice president to the country, but I can't wait until I introduce her to Washington.

And let me just offer an advance warning to the old, big-spending, do-nothing, me-first, country-second crowd: Change is coming.

I'm not in the habit of breaking my promises to my country, and neither is Gov. Palin. And when we tell you we're going to change Washington and stop leaving our country's problems for some unluckier generation to fix, you can count on it.

And we've got a record of doing just that, and the strength, experience, judgment and backbone to keep our word to you.

THE MAVERICK

You well know I've been called a maverick, someone who marches to the beat of his own drum. Sometimes it's meant as a compliment; sometimes it's not. What it really means is I understand who I work for. I don't work for a party. I don't work for a special interest. I don't work for myself. I work for you.

I've fought corruption, and it didn't matter if the culprits were Democrats or Republicans. They violated their public trust, and they had to be held accountable.

I've fought the big spenders in both parties, who waste your money on things you neither need nor want, and the first big-spending, "pork barrel" earmark bill that comes across my desk, I will veto it. I will make them famous, and you will know their names. You will know their names.

We're not going to allow that while you struggle to buy groceries, fill your gas tank and make your mortgage payment. I've fought to get million-dollar checks out of our elections. I've fought lobbyists who stole from Indian tribes. I've fought crooked deals in the Pentagon. I've fought tobacco companies and trial lawyers, drug companies and union bosses. I've fought for the right strategy and more troops in Iraq when it wasn't the popular thing to do.

And when the pundits said my campaign was finished, I said I'd rather lose an election than see my country lose a war.

And thanks to the leadership of a brilliant general, David Petraeus, and the brave men and women he has the honor to command, that strategy succeeded, and it rescued us from a defeat that would have demoralized our military, risked a wider war and threatened the security of all Americans.

FIGHTING WORDS

I don't mind a good fight. For reasons known only to God, I've had quite a few tough ones in my life. But I learned an important lesson along the way: In the end, it matters less that you can fight. What you fight for is the real test.

I fight for Americans. I fight for you.

I fight for Bill and Sue Nebe from Farmington Hills, Mich., who lost their real estate investments in the bad housing market. Bill got a temporary job after he was out of work for seven months. Sue works three jobs to help pay the bills.

I fight for Jake and Toni Wimmer of Franklin County, Pa. Jake works on a loading dock, coaches Little League, and raises money for the mentally and physically disabled. Toni is a schoolteacher, working toward her master's degree. They have two sons. The youngest, Luke, has been diagnosed with autism. Their lives should matter to the people they elect to office. And they matter to me. And they matter to you.

I fight for the family of Matthew Stanley of Wolfeboro, N.H. Matthew died serving our country in Iraq. I wear his bracelet and think of him everyday. I intend to honor their sacrifice by making sure the country their son loved so well and never returned to remains safe from its enemies.

I fight to restore the pride and principles of our party. We were elected to change Washington, and we let Washington change us.

We lost the trust of the American people when some Republicans gave in to the temptations of corruption. We lost their trust when rather than reform government, both parties made it bigger. We lost their trust when instead of freeing ourselves from a dangerous dependence on foreign oil, both parties—and Sen. Obama—passed another corporate welfare bill for oil companies. We lost their trust when we valued our power over our principles.

We're going to change that.

We're going to recover the people's trust by standing up again to the values Americans admire. The party of Lincoln, Roosevelt and Reagan is going to get back to basics.

In this country, we believe everyone has something to contribute and deserves the opportunity to reach their God-given potential, from the boy whose descendents arrived on the Mayflower to the Latina daughter of migrant workers. We're all God's children, and we're all Americans.

We believe in low taxes, spending discipline and open markets. We believe in rewarding hard work and risk-takers and letting people keep the fruits of their labor.

We believe in a strong defense, work, faith, service, a culture of life, personal responsibility, the rule of law and judges who dispense justice impartially and don't legislate from the bench.

We believe in the values of families, neighborhoods and communities. We believe in a government that unleashes the creativity and initiative of Americans, government that doesn't make your choices for you but works to make sure you have more choices to make for yourself.

I will keep taxes low and cut them where I can. My opponent will raise them.

I will open new markets to our goods and services. My opponent will close them.

I will cut government spending. He will increase it.

My tax cuts will create jobs; his tax increases will eliminate them.

My health care plan will make it easier for more Americans to find and keep good health care insurance. His plan will force small businesses to cut jobs, reduce wages and force families into a government-run health care system where a bureaucrat stands between you and your doctor.

TAXES AND JOBS

We all know that keeping taxes low helps small businesses grow and create new jobs. Cutting the second-highest business tax rate in the world will help American companies compete and keep jobs from going overseas.

Doubling the child tax exemption from $3,500 to $7,000 will improve the lives of millions of American families.

Reducing government spending and getting rid of failed programs will let you keep more of your own money to save, spend and invest as you see fit.

Opening new markets and preparing workers to compete in the world economy is essential to our future prosperity.

I know some of you have been left behind in the changing economy, and it often seems that your government hasn't even noticed. Government assistance for the unemployed workers was designed for the economy of the 1950s. That's going to change on my watch.

Now, my opponent promises to bring back old jobs by wishing away the global economy. We're going to help workers who've lost a job that won't come back find a new one that won't go away. We will prepare them for the jobs of today. We will use our community colleges to help train people for new opportunities in their communities.

For workers in industries that have been hard-hit, we'll help make up part of the difference in wages between their old job and a temporary, lower-paid one, while they receive re-training that will help them find secure new employment at a decent wage.

EDUCATION

Education is the civil rights issue of this century. Equal access to public education has been gained, but what is the value of access to a failing school?

We need to shake up failed school bureaucracies with competition, empower parents with choice. Let's remove barriers to qualified instructors, attract and reward good teachers, and help bad teachers find another line of work.

When a public school fails to meet its obligations to students, parents deserve a choice in the education of their children. And I intend to give it to them.

Some may choose a better public school. Some may choose a private one. Many will choose a charter school. But they will have the choice, and their children will have that opportunity.

Sen. Obama wants our schools to answer to unions and entrenched bureaucrats. I want schools to answer to parents and students.

And when I'm president, they will.

ENERGY

My fellow Americans, when I'm president, we're going to embark on the most ambitious national project in decades. We're going to stop sending $700 billion a year to countries that don't like us very much, and some of that money . . . .

We'll attack the problem on every front. We'll produce more energy at home. We will drill new wells offshore, and we'll drill them now. We'll drill them now.

We'll, my friends, we'll build more nuclear power plants. We'll develop clean-coal technology. We'll increase the use of wind, tide, solar and natural gas. We'll encourage the development and use of flex-fuel, hybrid and electric automobiles.

Sen. Obama thinks we can achieve energy independence without more drilling and without more nuclear power. But Americans know better than that.

We must use all resources and develop all technologies necessary to rescue our economy from the damage caused by rising oil prices and restore the health of our planet.

My friends, it's an ambitious plan, but Americans are ambitious by nature, and we've faced greater challenges. It's time for us to show the world again how Americans lead.

This great national cause will create millions of new jobs, many in industries that will be the engine of our future prosperity, jobs that will be there when your children enter the workforce.

FOREIGN POLICY

Today, the prospect of a better world remains within our reach. But we must see the threats to peace and liberty in our time clearly and face them as Americans before us did: with confidence, wisdom and resolve. We have dealt a serious blow to al Qaeda in recent years, but they're not defeated, and they'll strike us again, if they can. Iran remains the chief state sponsor of terrorism and is on the path to acquiring nuclear weapons.

Russia's leaders, rich with oil wealth and corrupt with power, have rejected democratic ideals and the obligations of a responsible power. They invaded a small, democratic neighbor to gain more control over the world's oil supply, intimidate other neighbors and further their ambitions of re-assembling the Russian empire. And the brave people of Georgia need our solidarity and our prayers. As president, I'll work to establish good relations with Russia so that we need not fear a return to the Cold War.

But we can't turn a blind eye to aggression and international lawlessness that threatens the peace and stability of the world and the security of the American people. We face many dangerous threats in this dangerous world, but I'm not afraid of them. I'm prepared for them.

I know how the military works, what it can do, what it can do better and what it shouldn't do. I know how the world works. I know the good and the evil in it. I know how to work with leaders who share our dreams of a freer, safer and more prosperous world, and how to stand up to those who don't. I know how to secure the peace.

My friends, when I was 5 years old, a car pulled up in front of our house. A Navy officer rolled down the window and shouted at my father that the Japanese had bombed Pearl Harbor. I rarely saw my father again for four years.

My grandfather came home from that same war exhausted from the burdens he had borne and died the next day. In Vietnam, where I formed the closest friendships of my life, some of those friends never came home with me. I hate war. It's terrible beyond imagination.

I'm running for president to keep the country I love safe and prevent other families from risking their loved ones in war as my family has. I will draw on all my experience with the world and its leaders, and all the tools at our disposal—diplomatic, economic, military—and the power of our ideals to build the foundations for a stable and enduring peace.

POWER OF CHANGE

In America, we change things that need to be changed. Each generation makes its contribution to our greatness. The work that is ours to do is plainly before us; we don't need to search for it. We need to change the way government does almost everything—from the way we protect our security to the way we compete in the world economy, from the way we respond to disasters to the way we fuel our transportation network, from the way we train our workers to the way we educate our children.

All these functions of government were designed before the rise of the global economy, the information technology revolution and the end of the Cold War. We have to catch up to history, and we have to change the way we do business in Washington.

The constant partisan rancor that stops us from solving these problems isn't a cause. It's a symptom. It's what happens when people go to Washington to work for themselves and not for you.

Again and again—again and again, I've worked with members of both parties to fix problems that need to be fixed. That's how I will govern as president. I will reach out my hand to anyone to help me get this country moving again.

My friends, I have that record and the scars to prove it. Sen. Obama does not.

Instead of rejecting good ideas because we didn't think of them first, let's use the best ideas from both sides. Instead of fighting over who gets the credit, let's try sharing it.

This amazing country can do anything we put our minds to. I'll ask Democrats and independents to serve with me. And my administration will set a new standard for transparency and accountability.

We're going to finally start getting things done for the people who are counting on us, and I won't care who gets the credit.

My friends, I've been an imperfect servant of my country for many years. But I've been her servant first, last and always. And I've never lived a day, in good times or bad, that I didn't thank God for the privilege.

PRISONER OF WAR

Long ago, something unusual happened to me that taught me the most valuable lesson of my life. I was blessed by misfortune. I mean that sincerely. I was blessed because I served in the company of heroes, and I witnessed a thousand acts of courage and compassion and love.

On an October morning, in the Gulf of Tonkin, I prepared for my 23rd mission over North Vietnam. I hadn't any worry I wouldn't come back safe and sound. I thought I was tougher than anyone. I was pretty independent then, too.

I liked to bend a few rules and pick a few fights for the fun of it. But I did it for my own pleasure, my own pride. I didn't think there was a cause that was more important than me.

Then I found myself falling toward the middle of a small lake in the city of Hanoi, with two broken arms, a broken leg and an angry crowd waiting to greet me.

I was dumped in a dark cell and left to die. I didn't feel so tough anymore. When they discovered my father was an admiral, they took me to a hospital. They couldn't set my bones properly, so they just slapped a cast on me. And when I didn't get better and was down to about a hundred pounds, they put me in a cell with two other Americans.

I couldn't do anything. I couldn't even feed myself. They did it for me. I was beginning to learn the limits of my selfish independence. Those men saved my life.

I was in solitary confinement when my captors offered to release me. I knew why. If I went home, they would use it as propaganda to demoralize my fellow prisoners.

Our code said we could only go home in the order of our capture, and there were men who had been shot down long before me. I thought about it, though. I wasn't in great shape, and I missed everything about America, but I turned it down.

A lot of prisoners had it much worse. A lot of prisoners had it a lot worse than I did. I'd been mistreated before but not as badly as many others. I always liked to strut a little after I'd been roughed up to show the other guys I was tough enough to take it.

But after I turned down their offer, they worked me over harder than they ever had before—for a long time—and they broke me.

When they brought me back to my cell, I was hurt and ashamed, and I didn't know how I could face my fellow prisoners. The good man in the cell next door to me, my friend, Bob Craner, saved me.

Through taps on a wall, he told me I had fought as hard as I could. No man can always stand alone. And then he told me to get back up and fight again for my country and for the men I had the honor to serve with, because every day they fought for me.

I fell in love with my country when I was a prisoner in someone else's. I loved it not just for the many comforts of life here. I loved it for its decency, for its faith in the wisdom, justice and goodness of its people.

I loved it because it was not just a place but an idea, a cause worth fighting for. I was never the same again; I wasn't my own man anymore; I was my country's.

I'm not running for president because I think I'm blessed with such personal greatness that history has anointed me to save our country in its hour of need.

My country saved me. My country saved me, and I cannot forget it. And I will fight for her for as long as I draw breath, so help me God.

A GREATER CAUSE

My friends, if you find faults with our country, make it a better one. If you're disappointed with the mistakes of government, join its ranks and work to correct them. Enlist in our Armed Forces. Become a teacher. Enter the ministry. Run for public office. Feed a hungry child. Teach an illiterate adult to read. Comfort the afflicted. Defend the rights of the oppressed.

Our country will be the better, and you will be the happier, because nothing brings greater happiness in life than to serve a cause greater than yourself.

I'm going to fight for my cause every day as your president. I'm going to fight to make sure every American has every reason to thank God, as I thank him, that I'm an American, a proud citizen of the greatest country on Earth. And with hard work, strong faith and a little courage, great things are always within our reach.

Fight with me. Fight with me.

Fight for what's right for our country. Fight for the ideals and character of a free people. Fight for our children's future. Fight for justice and opportunity for all.

Stand up to defend our country from its enemies. Stand up for each other, for beautiful, blessed, bountiful America. Stand up, stand up, stand up and fight.

Nothing is inevitable here. We're Americans, and we never give up. We never quit. We never hide from history. We make history.

Thank you, and God bless you, and God bless America.

Obama Election Victory Speech

Following is a transcript of the speech given by Sen. Barack Obama at a rally Nov. 4, 2008, in Chicago's Grant Park after winning the presidential election.

Hello, Chicago. If there is anyone out there who still doubts that America is a place where all things are possible, who still wonders if the dream of our founders is alive in our time, who still questions the power of our democracy, tonight is your answer.

It's the answer told by lines that stretched around schools and churches in numbers this nation has never seen, by people who waited three hours and four hours, many for the first time in their lives, because they believed that this time must be different, that their voices could be that difference.

It's the answer spoken by young and old, rich and poor, Democrat and Republican, black, white, Hispanic, Asian, Native American, gay, straight, disabled and not disabled. Americans who sent a message to the world that we have never been just a collection of individuals or a collection of red states and blue states.

We are, and always will be, the United States of America.

It's the answer that led those who've been told for so long by so many to be cynical and fearful and doubtful about what we can achieve to put their hands on the arc of history and bend it once more toward the hope of a better day.

It's been a long time coming, but tonight, because of what we did on this date in this election at this defining moment, change has come to America.

A little bit earlier this evening, I received an extraordinarily gracious call from Sen. McCain.

Sen. McCain fought long and hard in this campaign. And he's fought even longer and harder for the country that he loves. He has endured sacrifices for America that most of us cannot begin to imagine. We are better off for the service rendered by this brave and selfless leader.

I congratulate him; I congratulate Gov. Palin for all that they've achieved. And I look forward to working with them to renew this nation's promise in the months ahead.

I want to thank my partner in this journey, a man who campaigned from his heart, and spoke for the men and women he grew up with on the streets of Scranton and rode with on the train home to Delaware, the vice president-elect of the United States, Joe Biden.

And I would not be standing here tonight without the unyielding support of my best friend for the last 16 years, the rock of our family, the love of my life, the nation's next first lady, Michelle Obama.

Sasha and Malia, I love you both more than you can imagine. And you have earned the new puppy that's coming with us to the White House.

And while she's no longer with us, I know my grandmother's watching, along with the family that made me who I am. I miss them tonight. I know that my debt to them is beyond measure.

To my sister Maya, my sister Alma, all my other brothers and sisters, thank you so much for all the support that you've given me. I am grateful to them.

And to my campaign manager, David Plouffe, the unsung hero of this campaign, who built the best—the best political campaign, I think, in the history of the United States of America.

To my chief strategist, David Axelrod, who's been a partner with me every step of the way.

To the best campaign team ever assembled in the history of politics, you made this happen, and I am forever grateful for what you've sacrificed to get it done.

But above all, I will never forget who this victory truly belongs to. It belongs to you. It belongs to you.

I was never the likeliest candidate for this office. We didn't start with much money or many endorsements. Our campaign was not hatched in the halls of Washington. It began in the back yards of Des Moines and the living rooms of Concord and the front porches of Charleston. It was built by working men and women who dug into what little savings they had to give $5 and $10 and $20 to the cause.

It grew strength from the young people who rejected the myth of their generation's apathy, who left their homes and their families for jobs that offered little pay and less sleep.

It drew strength from the not-so-young people who braved the bitter cold and scorching heat to knock on doors of perfect strangers, and from the millions of Americans who volunteered and organized and proved that more than two centuries later a government of the people, by the people and for the people has not perished from the Earth.

"THIS IS YOUR VICTORY"

And I know you didn't do this just to win an election. And I know you didn't do it for me.

You did it because you understand the enormity of the task that lies ahead. For even as we celebrate tonight, we know the challenges that tomorrow will bring are the greatest of our lifetime—two wars, a planet in peril, the worst financial crisis in a century.

Even as we stand here tonight, we know there are brave Americans waking up in the deserts of Iraq and the mountains of Afghanistan to risk their lives for us.

There are mothers and fathers who will lie awake after the children fall asleep and wonder how they'll make the mortgage or pay their doctors' bills or save enough for their child's college education.

There's new energy to harness, new jobs to be created, new schools to build, and threats to meet, alliances to repair.

The road ahead will be long. Our climb will be steep. We may not get there in one year or even in one term. But, America, I have never been more hopeful than I am tonight that we will get there. I promise you, we as a people will get there.

There will be setbacks and false starts. There are many who won't agree with every decision or policy I make as president. And we know the government can't solve every problem.

But I will always be honest with you about the challenges we face. I will listen to you, especially when we disagree. And, above all, I will ask you to join in the work of remaking this nation, the only way it's been done in America for 221 years—block by block, brick by brick, calloused hand by calloused hand.

What began 21 months ago in the depths of winter cannot end on this autumn night.

This victory alone is not the change we seek. It is only the chance for us to make that change. And that cannot happen if we go back to the way things were.

It can't happen without you, without a new spirit of service, a new spirit of sacrifice.

So let us summon a new spirit of patriotism, of responsibility, where each of us resolves to pitch in and work harder and look after not only ourselves but each other.

Let us remember that, if this financial crisis taught us anything, it's that we cannot have a thriving Wall Street while Main Street suffers.

In this country, we rise or fall as one nation, as one people. Let's resist the temptation to fall back on the same partisanship and pettiness and immaturity that has poisoned our politics for so long.

Let's remember that it was a man from this state who first carried the banner of the Republican Party to the White House, a party founded on the values of self-reliance and individual liberty and national unity.

Those are values that we all share. And while the Democratic Party has won a great victory tonight, we do so with a measure of humility and determination to heal the divides that have held back our progress.

As Lincoln said to a nation far more divided than ours, we are not enemies but friends. Though passion may have strained, it must not break our bonds of affection.

And to those Americans whose support I have yet to earn, I may not have won your vote tonight, but I hear your voices. I need your help. And I will be your president, too.

And to all those watching tonight from beyond our shores, from parliaments and palaces, to those who are huddled around radios in the forgotten corners of the world, our stories are singular, but our destiny is shared, and a new dawn of American leadership is at hand.

To those—to those who would tear the world down: We will defeat you. To those who seek peace and security: We support you. And to all those who have wondered if America's beacon still burns as bright: Tonight we proved once more that the true strength of our nation comes not from the might of our arms or the scale of our wealth, but from the enduring power of our ideals—democracy, liberty, opportunity and unyielding hope.

That's the true genius of America: that America can change. Our union can be perfected. What we've already achieved gives us hope for what we can and must achieve tomorrow.

"YES, WE CAN"

This election had many firsts and many stories that will be told for generations. But one that's on my mind tonight's about a woman who cast her ballot in Atlanta. She's a lot like the millions of others who stood in line to make their voice heard in this election except for one thing: Ann Nixon Cooper is 106 years old.

She was born just a generation past slavery, a time when there were no cars on the road or planes in the sky, when someone like her couldn't vote for two reasons: because she was a woman and because of the color of her skin.

And tonight, I think about all that she's seen throughout her century in America: the heartache and the hope; the struggle and the progress; the times we were told that we can't, and the people who pressed on with that American creed—yes, we can.

At a time when women's voices were silenced and their hopes dismissed, she lived to see them stand up and speak out and reach for the ballot. Yes, we can.

When there was despair in the Dust Bowl and depression across the land, she saw a nation conquer fear itself with a New Deal, new jobs, a new sense of common purpose. Yes, we can.

When the bombs fell on our harbor and tyranny threatened the world, she was there to witness a generation rise to greatness, and a democracy was saved. Yes, we can.

She was there for the buses in Montgomery, the hoses in Birmingham, a bridge in Selma, and a preacher from Atlanta who told a people that "we shall overcome." Yes, we can.

A man touched down on the moon, a wall came down in Berlin, a world was connected by our own science and imagination.

And this year, in this election, she touched her finger to a screen and cast her vote, because after 106 years in America, through the best of times and the darkest of hours, she knows how America can change.

Yes, we can.

America, we have come so far. We have seen so much. But there is so much more to do. So tonight, let us ask ourselves: If our children should live to see the next century, if my daughters should be so lucky to live as long as Ann Nixon Cooper, what change will they see? What progress will we have made?

This is our chance to answer that call. This is our moment.

This is our time, to put our people back to work and open doors of opportunity for our kids; to restore prosperity and promote the cause of peace; to reclaim the American dream and reaffirm that fundamental truth, that, out of many, we are one; that while we breathe, we hope. And where we are met with cynicism and doubts and those who tell us that we can't, we will respond with that timeless creed that sums up the spirit of a people: Yes, we can.

Thank you. God bless you. And may God bless the United States of America.

McCain Concedes Presidential Race

Following is the speech that Sen. John McCain gave to a crowd of supporters at Phoenix's Biltmore Hotel Nov. 4, 2008, in which he conceded his defeat in the presidential election.

Thank you. Thank you, my friends. Thank you for coming here on this beautiful Arizona evening.

My friends, we have—we have come to the end of a long journey. The American people have spoken, and they have spoken clearly. A little while ago, I had the honor of calling Sen. Barack Obama to congratulate him on being elected the next president of the country that we both love.

In a contest as long and difficult as this campaign has been, his success alone commands my respect for his ability and perseverance. But that he managed to do so by inspiring the hopes of so many millions of Americans who had once wrongly believed that they had little at stake or little influence in the election of an American president is something I deeply admire and commend him for achieving.

This is an historic election, and I recognize the special significance it has for African Americans and for the special pride that must be theirs tonight.

I've always believed that America offers opportunities to all who have the industry and will to seize it. Sen. Obama believes that, too. But we both recognize that though we have come a long way from the old injustices that once stained our nation's reputation and denied some Americans the full blessings of American citizenship, the memory of them still had the power to wound.

A century ago, President Theodore Roosevelt's invitation of Booker T. Washington to visit—to dine at the White House was taken as an outrage in many quarters. America today is a world away from the cruel and prideful bigotry of that time. There is no better evidence of this than the election of an African American to the presidency of the United States. Let there be no reason now for any American to fail to cherish their citizenship in this, the greatest nation on Earth.

Sen. Obama has achieved a great thing for himself and for his country. I applaud him for it, and offer him my sincere sympathy that his beloved grandmother did not live to see this day, though our faith assures us she is at rest in the presence of her creator and so very proud of the good man she helped raise.

Sen. Obama and I have had and argued our differences, and he has prevailed. No doubt many of those differences remain. These are difficult times for our country, and I pledge to him tonight to do all in my power to help him lead us through the many challenges we face.

I urge all Americans who supported me to join me in not just congratulating him, but offering our next president our good will and earnest effort to find ways to come together, to find the necessary compromises, to bridge our differences, and help restore our prosperity, defend our security in a dangerous world, and leave our children and grandchildren a stronger, better country than we inherited.

Whatever our differences, we are fellow Americans. And please believe me when I say no association has ever meant more to me than that.

"WE MUST MOVE BEYOND"

It is natural—it's natural tonight to feel some disappointment, but tomorrow we must move beyond it and work together to get our country moving again. We fought as hard as we could. And though we fell short, the failure is mine, not yours.

I am so deeply grateful to all of you for the great honor of your support and for all you have done for me. I wish the outcome had been different, my friends. The road was a difficult one from the outset. But your support and friendship never wavered. I cannot adequately express how deeply indebted I am to you.

I am especially grateful to my wife, Cindy, my children, my dear mother and all my family and to the many old and dear friends who have stood by my side through the many ups and downs of this long campaign. I have always been a fortunate man, and never more so for the love and encouragement you have given me.

You know, campaigns are often harder on a candidate's family than on the candidate, and that's been true in this campaign. All I can offer in compensation is my love and gratitude, and the promise of more peaceful years ahead.

I am also, of course, very thankful to Gov. Sarah Palin, one of the best campaigners I have ever seen. One of the best campaigners I have ever seen and an impressive new voice in our party for reform and the principles that have always been our greatest strength. Her husband, Todd, and their five beautiful children, with their tireless dedication to our cause, and the courage and grace they showed in the rough-and-tumble of a presidential campaign. We can all look forward with great interest to her future service to Alaska, the Republican Party and our country.

To all my campaign comrades, from Rick Davis and Steve Schmidt and Mark Salter, to every last volunteer who fought so hard and valiantly month after month in what at times seemed to be the most challenged campaign in modern times, thank you so much. A lost election will never mean more to me than the privilege of your faith and friendship.

I don't know what more we could have done to try to win this election. I'll leave that to others to determine. Every candidate makes mistakes, and I'm sure I made my share of them. But I won't spend a moment of the future regretting what might have been.

This campaign was and will remain the great honor of my life. And my heart is filled with nothing but gratitude for the experience and to the American people for giving me a fair hearing before deciding that Sen. Obama and my old friend Sen. Joe Biden should have the honor of leading us for the next four years.

I would not be an American worthy of the name should I regret a fate that has allowed me the extraordinary privilege of serving this country for a half a century. Today, I was a candidate for the highest office in the country I love so much. And tonight, I remain her servant. That is blessing enough for anyone, and I thank the people of Arizona for it.

Tonight—tonight, more than any night, I hold in my heart nothing but love for this country and for all its citizens, whether they supported me or Sen. Obama. I wish Godspeed to the man who was my former opponent and will be my president.

And I call on all Americans, as I have often in this campaign, to not despair of our present difficulties but to believe always in the promise and greatness of America, because nothing is inevitable here.

Americans never quit. We never surrender. We never hide from history; we make history.

Thank you, and God bless you, and God bless America. Thank you all very much.

Political Charts

Summary of Presidential Elections, 1789–2008

Year	No. of states	Candidates	Party	Electoral vote	Popular vote
1789[1]	10	**George Washington**	**Fed.**	**69**	—[2]
		John Adams	Fed.	34	
1792[1]	15	**George Washington**	**Fed.**	**132**	—[2]
		John Adams	Fed.	77	
1796[1]	16	**John Adams**	**Fed.**	**71**	—[2]
		Thomas Jefferson	Dem.-Rep.	68	
1800[1]	16	**Thomas Jefferson**	**Dem.-Rep.**	**73**	—[2]
		Aaron Burr	Dem.-Rep.	73	
		John Adams	Fed.	65	
		Charles Cotesworth Pinckney	Fed.	64	
1804	17	**Thomas Jefferson**	**Dem.-Rep.**	**162**	—[2]
		George Clinton			
		Charles Cotesworth Pinckney	Fed.	64	
		Rufus King			
1808	17	**James Madison**	**Dem.-Rep.**	**122**	—[2]
		George Clinton			
		Charles Cotesworth Pinckney	Fed.	64	
		Rufus King			
1812	18	**James Madison**	**Dem.-Rep.**	**128**	—[2]
		Elbridge Gerry			
		George Clinton	Fed.	89	
		Jared Ingersoll			
1816	19	**James Monroe**	**Dem.-Rep.**	**183**	—[2]
		Daniel D. Tompkins			
		Rufus King	Fed.	34	
		John Howard			
1820	24	**James Monroe**	**Dem.-Rep.**	**231**[3]	—[2]
		Daniel D. Tompkins			
1824[4]	24	**John Quincy Adams**	**Dem.-Rep.**	**99**	**113,122 (30.9%)**
		John C. Calhoun			
		Andrew Jackson	Dem.-Rep.	84	151,271 (41.3%)
		Nathan Sanford			
1828	24	**Andrew Jackson**	**Dem.-Rep.**	**178**	**642,553 (56.0%)**
		John C. Calhoun			
		John Quincy Adams	Nat.-Rep.	83	500,897 (43.6%)
		Richard Rush			
1832[5]	24	**Andrew Jackson**	**Dem.**	**219**	**701,780 (54.2%)**
		Martin Van Buren			
		Henry Clay	Nat.-Rep.	49	484,205 (37.4%)
		John Sergeant			
1836[6]	26	**Martin Van Buren**	**Dem.**	**170**	**764,176 (50.8%)**
		Richard M. Johnson			
		William Henry Harrison	Whig	73	550,816 (36.6%)
		Francis Granger			
1840	26	**William Henry Harrison**	**Whig**	**234**	**1,275,390 (52.9%)**
		John Tyler			
		Martin Van Buren	Dem.	60	1,128,854 (46.8%)
		Richard M. Johnson			
1844	26	**James K. Polk**	**Dem.**	**170**	**1,339,494 (49.5%)**
		George M. Dallas			
		Henry Clay	Whig	105	1,300,004 (48.1%)
		Theodore Frelinghuysen			
1848	30	**Zachary Taylor**	**Whig**	**163**	**1,361,393 (47.3%)**
		Millard Fillmore			
		Lewis Cass	Dem.	127	1,223,460 (42.5%)
		William O. Butler			
1852	31	**Franklin Pierce**	**Dem.**	**254**	**1,607,510 (50.8%)**
		William R. King			
		Winfield Scott	Whig	42	1,386,942 (43.9%)
		William A. Graham			
1856[7]	31	**James Buchanan**	**Dem.**	**174**	**1,836,072 (45.3%)**
		John C. Breckinridge			
		John C. Fremont	Rep.	114	1,342,345 (33.1%)
		William L. Dayton			
1860[8]	33	**Abraham Lincoln**	**Rep.**	**180**	**1,865,908 (39.8%)**
		Hannibal Hamlin			
		Stephen A. Douglas	Dem.	12	1,380,202 (29.5%)
		Herschel V. Johnson			
1864[9]	36	**Abraham Lincoln**	**Rep.**	**212**	**2,218,388 (55.0%)**
		Andrew Johnson			
		George B. McClellan	Dem.	21	1,812,807 (45.0%)
		George H. Pendleton			
1868[10]	37	**Ulysses S. Grant**	**Rep.**	**214**	**3,013,650 (52.7%)**
		Schuyler Colfax			
		Horatio Seymour	Dem.	80	2,708,744 (47.3%)
		Francis P. Blair Jr.			
1872	37	**Ulysses S. Grant**	**Rep.**	**286**	**3,598,235 (55.6%)**
		Henry Wilson			
		Horace Greeley	Dem.	—[11]	2,834,761 (43.8%)
		Benjamin Gratz Brown			
1876	38	**Rutherford B. Hayes**	**Rep.**	**185**	**4,034,311 (47.9%)**
		William A. Wheeler			
		Samuel J. Tilden	Dem.	184	4,288,546 (51.0%)
		Thomas A. Hendricks			

Year	No. of states	Candidates	Party	Electoral vote	Popular vote
1880	38	**James A. Garfield**	**Rep.**	**214**	**4,446,158 (48.3%)**
		Chester A. Arthur			
		Winfield S. Hancock	Dem.	155	4,444,260 (48.2%)
		William H. English			
1884	38	**Grover Cleveland**	**Dem.**	**219**	**4,874,621 (48.5%)**
		Thomas A. Hendricks			
		James G. Blaine	Rep.	182	4,848,936 (48.2%)
		John A. Logan			
1888	38	**Benjamin Harrison**	**Rep.**	**233**	**5,443,892 (47.8%)**
		Levi P. Morton			
		Grover Cleveland	Dem.	168	5,534,488 (48.6%)
		Allen G. Thurman			
1892[12]	44	**Grover Cleveland**	**Dem.**	**277**	**5,551,883 (46.1%)**
		Adlai E. Stevenson			
		Benjamin Harrison	Rep.	145	5,179,244 (43.0%)
		Whitelaw Reid			
1896	45	**William McKinley**	**Rep.**	**271**	**7,108,480 (51.0%)**
		Garret A. Hobart			
		William J. Bryan	Dem.	176	6,511,495 (46.7%)
		Arthur Sewall			
1900	45	**William McKinley**	**Rep.**	**292**	**7,218,039 (51.7%)**
		Theodore Roosevelt			
		William J. Bryan	Dem.	155	6,358,345 (45.5%)
		Adlai E. Stevenson			
1904	45	**Theodore Roosevelt**	**Rep.**	**336**	**7,626,593 (56.4%)**
		Charles W. Fairbanks			
		Alton B. Parker	Dem.	140	5,028,898 (37.6%)
		Henry G. Davis			
1908	46	**William Howard Taft**	**Rep.**	**321**	**7,676,258 (51.6%)**
		James S. Sherman			
		William J. Bryan	Dem.	162	6,406,801 (43.0%)
		John W. Kern			
1912[13]	48	**Woodrow Wilson**	**Dem.**	**435**	**6,293,152 (41.8%)**
		Thomas R. Marshall			
		William Howard Taft	Rep.	8	3,486,333 (23.2%)
		James S. Sherman			
1916	48	**Woodrow Wilson**	**Dem.**	**277**	**9,126,300 (49.2%)**
		Thomas R. Marshall			
		Charles E. Hughes	Rep.	254	8,546,789 (46.1%)
		Charles W. Fairbanks			
1920	48	**Warren G. Harding**	**Rep.**	**404**	**16,133,314 (60.3%)**
		Calvin Coolidge			
		James M. Cox	Dem.	127	9,140,884 (34.2%)
		Franklin D. Roosevelt			
1924[14]	48	**Calvin Coolidge**	**Rep.**	**382**	**15,717,553 (54.1%)**
		Charles G. Dawes			
		John W. Davis	Dem.	136	8,386,169 (28.8%)
		Charles W. Bryan			
1928	48	**Herbert C. Hoover**	**Rep.**	**444**	**21,411,991 (58.2%)**
		Charles Curtis			
		Alfred E. Smith	Dem.	87	15,000,185 (40.8%)
		Joseph T. Robinson			
1932	48	**Franklin D. Roosevelt**	**Dem.**	**472**	**22,825,016 (57.4%)**
		John N. Garner			
		Herbert C. Hoover	Rep.	59	15,758,397 (39.6%)
		Charles Curtis			
1936	48	**Franklin D. Roosevelt**	**Dem.**	**523**	**27,747,636 (60.8%)**
		John N. Garner			
		Alfred M. Landon	Rep.	8	16,679,543 (36.5%)
		Frank Knox			
1940	48	**Franklin D. Roosevelt**	**Dem.**	**449**	**27,263,448 (54.7%)**
		Henry A. Wallace			
		Wendell L. Willkie	Rep.	82	22,336,260 (44.8%)
		Charles L. McNary			
1944	48	**Franklin D. Roosevelt**	**Dem.**	**432**	**25,611,936 (53.4%)**
		Harry S. Truman			
		Thomas E. Dewey	Rep.	99	22,013,372 (45.9%)
		John W. Bricker			
1948[15]	48	**Harry S. Truman**	**Dem.**	**303**	**24,105,587 (49.5%)**
		Alben W. Barkley			
		Thomas E. Dewey	Rep.	198	21,970,017 (45.1%)
		Earl Warren			
1952	48	**Dwight D. Eisenhower**	**Rep.**	**442**	**33,936,137 (55.1%)**
		Richard M. Nixon			
		Adlai E. Stevenson II	Dem.	89	27,314,649 (44.4%)
		John J. Sparkman			
1956[16]	48	**Dwight D. Eisenhower**	**Rep.**	**457**	**35,585,245 (57.4%)**
		Richard M. Nixon			
		Adlai E. Stevenson II	Dem.	73	26,030,172 (42.0%)
		Estes Kefauver			
1960[17]	50	**John F. Kennedy**	**Dem.**	**303**	**34,221,344 (49.7%)**
		Lyndon B. Johnson			
		Richard Nixon	Rep.	219	34,106,671 (49.5%)
		Henry Cabot Lodge			
1964	50*	**Lyndon B. Johnson**	**Dem.**	**486**	**43,126,584 (61.1%)**
		Hubert H. Humphrey			
		Barry Goldwater	Rep.	52	27,177,838 (38.5%)
		William E. Miller			
1968[18]	50*	**Richard Nixon**	**Rep.**	**301**	**31,785,148 (43.4%)**
		Spiro T. Agnew			
		Hubert H. Humphrey	Dem.	191	31,274,503 (42.7%)
		Edmund S. Muskie			
1972[19]	50*	**Richard Nixon**	**Rep.**	**520**	**47,170,179 (60.7%)**
		Spiro T. Agnew			
		George McGovern	Dem.	17	29,171,791 (37.5%)
		Sargent Shriver			
1976[20]	50*	**Jimmy Carter**	**Dem.**	**297**	**40,830,763 (50.1%)**
		Walter F. Mondale			
		Gerald R. Ford	Rep.	240	39,147,793 (48.0%)
		Robert Dole			
1980	50*	**Ronald Reagan**	**Rep.**	**489**	**43,904,153 (50.7%)**
		George Bush			

Year	*No. of states*	*Candidates*	*Party*	*Electoral vote*	*Popular vote*
		Jimmy Carter	Dem.	49	35,483,883 (41.0%)
		Walter F. Mondale			
1984	50*	**Ronald Reagan**	**Rep.**	**525**	**54,455,074(58.8%)**
		George Bush			
		Walter F. Mondale	Dem.	13	37,577,137 (40.6%)
		Geraldine Ferraro			
1988[21]	50*	**George Bush**	**Rep.**	**426**	**48,881,278 (53.4%)**
		Dan Quayle			
		Michael S. Dukakis	Dem.	111	41,805,374 (45.6%)
		Lloyd Bentsen			
1992	50*	**Bill Clinton**	**Dem.**	**370**	**44,908,233 (43.0%)**
		Al Gore			
		George Bush	Rep.	168	39,102,282 (37.4%)
		Dan Quayle			
1996	50*	**Bill Clinton**	**Dem.**	**379**	**47,402,357 (49.2%)**
		Al Gore			
		Bob Dole	Rep.	159	39,198,755 (40.7%)
		Jack Kemp			
2000[22]	50*	**George W. Bush**	**Rep.**	**271**	**50,455,156 (47.9%)**
		Richard B. Cheney			
		Al Gore	Dem.	266	50,992,335 (48.4%)
		Joseph I. Lieberman			
2004[23]	50*	**George W. Bush**	**Rep.**	**286**	**62,040,610 (50.7%)**
		Richard B. Cheney			
		John Kerry	Dem.	251	59,028,439 (48.3%)
		John Edwards			
2008[24]	50*	**Barack Obama**	**Dem.**	**365**	**69,498,516 (52.9%)**
		Joseph R. Biden Jr.			
		John McCain	Rep.	173	59,948,323 (45.7%)
		Sarah Palin			

SOURCES: Harold W. Stanley and Richard G. Niemi, *Vital Statistics on American Politics,* 5th ed. (Washington, D.C.: CQ Press, 1995), table 3-13; Richard M. Scammon, Alice V. McGillivray, and Rhodes Cook, *America Votes 24* (Washington, D.C.: CQ Press, 2001), 9, 13.

NOTES: Bold indicates victors. In the elections of 1789, 1792, 1796, and 1800, each candidate ran for the office of president. The candidate with the second highest number of electoral votes became vice president. For elections after 1800, italic indicates vice-presidential candidates. Dem.-Rep.—Democratic-Republican; Fed.—Federalist; Nat.-Rep.—National-Republican; Dem.—Democratic; Rep.—Republican. 1. Elections of 1789–1800 were held under rules that did not allow separate voting for president and vice president. 2. Popular vote returns are not shown before 1824 because consistent, reliable data are not available. 3. Monroe ran unopposed. One electoral vote was cast for John Adams and Richard Stockton, who were not candidates. 4. 1824: All four candidates represented Democratic-Republican factions. William H. Crawford received 41 electoral votes, and Henry Clay received 37 votes. Since no candidate received a majority, the election was decided (in Adams's favor) by the House of Representatives. 5. 1832: Two electoral votes were not cast. 6. 1836: Other Whig candidates receiving electoral votes were Hugh L. White, who received 26 votes, and Daniel Webster, who received 14 votes. 7. 1856: Millard Fillmore, Whig-American, received 8 electoral votes. 8. 1860: John C. Breckinridge, Southern Democrat, received 72 electoral votes. John Bell, Constitutional Union, received 39 electoral votes. 9. 1864: Eighty-one electoral votes were not cast. 10. 1868: Twenty-three electoral votes were not cast. 11. 1872: Horace Greeley, Democrat, died after the election. In the electoral college, Democratic electoral votes went to Thomas Hendricks, 42 votes; Benjamin Gratz Brown, 18 votes; Charles J. Jenkins, 2 votes; and David Davis, 1 vote. Seventeen electoral votes were not cast. 12. 1892: James B. Weaver, People's Party, received 22 electoral votes. 13. 1912: Theodore Roosevelt, Progressive Party, received 86 electoral votes. 14. 1924: Robert M. La Follette, Progressive Party, received 13 electoral votes. 15. 1948: J. Strom Thurmond, States' Rights Party, received 39 electoral votes. 16. 1956: Walter B. Jones, Democrat, received 1 electoral vote. 17. 1960: Harry Flood Byrd, Democrat, received 15 electoral votes. 18. 1968: George C. Wallace, American Independent Party, received 46 electoral votes. 19. 1972: John Hospers, Libertarian Party, received 1 electoral vote. 20. 1976: Ronald Reagan, Republican, received 1 electoral vote. 21. 1988: Lloyd Bentsen, the Democratic vice-presidential nominee, received 1 electoral vote for president. 22. 2000: One District of Columbia elector did not vote. 23. 2004: A Democratic elector in Minnesota cast a vote for Edwards rather than Kerry. 24. 2008: Nebraska split its 5 electoral votes, with 4 going to John McCain and 1 to Barack Obama. Nebraska is one of two states, along with Maine, that splits electoral votes between congressional districts. Nebraska has three. The winner of each district receives that district's vote; the statewide winner receives the other two. The 2008 election was the first time that a split electoral vote occurred in either state. * Fifty states plus the District of Columbia.

Victorious Party in Presidential Races, 1860–2008

State	*1860*	*1864*	*1868*	*1872*	*1876*	*1880*	*1884*	*1888*	*1892*	*1896*	*1900*	*1904*	*1908*	*1912*	*1916*	*1920*	*1924*	*1928*	*1932*
Alabama	SD	[2]	R	R	D	D	D	D	D	D	D	D	D	D	D	D	D	D	D
Alaska																			
Arizona														D	D	R	R	R	D
Arkansas	SD	[2]	R	[4]	D	D	D	D	D	D	D	D	D	D	D	D	D	D	D
California	R	R	R	R	R	D[6]	R	R	D[7]	R[12]	R	R	R	PR	D	R	R	R	D
Colorado					R	R	R	R	PP	D	D	R	D	D	D	R	R	R	D
Connecticut	R	R	R	R	D	R	D	D	D	R	R	R	R	D	R	R	R	R	R
Delaware	SD	D	D	R	D	D	D	D	D	R	R	R	R	D	R	R	R	R	R
Dist. of Columbia																			
Florida	SD	[2]	R	R	R	D	D	D	D	D	D	D	D	D	D	D	D	R	D
Georgia	SD	[2]	D	D[5]	D	D	D	D	D	D	D	D	D	D	D	D	D	D	D
Hawaii																			
Idaho									PP	D	D	R	R	D	D	R	R	R	D
Illinois	R	R	R	R	R	R	R	R	D	R	R	R	R	D	R	R	R	R	D
Indiana	R	R	R	R	D	R	D	R	D	R	R	R	R	D	R	R	R	R	D
Iowa	R	R	R	R	R	R	R	R	R	R	R	R	R	D	R	R	R	R	D
Kansas		R	R	R	R	R	R	R	PP	D	R	R	R	D	D	R	R	R	R
Kentucky	CU	D	D	D	D	D	D	D	D	R[13]	D	D	D	D	D	D	R	R	D
Louisiana	SD	[2]	D	[4]	R	D	D	D	D	D	D	D	D	D	D	D	D	D	D
Maine	R	R	R	R	R	R	R	R	R	R	R	R	R	D	R	R	R	R	R
Maryland	SD	R	D	D	D	D	D	D	D	R	R	D[14]	D[15]	D	D	R	R	R	D
Massachusetts	R	R	R	R	R	R	R	R	R	R	R	R	R	D	R	R	R	D	D
Michigan	R	R	R	R	R	R	R	R	R[8]	R	R	R	R	PR	R	R	R	R	D
Minnesota	R	R	R	R	R	R	R	R	R	R	R	R	R	PR	R	R	R	R	D
Mississippi	SD	[2]	[3]	R	D	D	D	D	D	D	D	D	D	D	D	D	D	D	D
Missouri	D	R	R	D	D	D	D	D	D	D	D	R	R	D	D	R	R	R	D
Montana									R	D	D	R	R	D	D	R	R	R	D
Nebraska			R	R	R	R	R	R	R	D	R	R	D	D	D	R	R	R	D
Nevada		R	R	R	R	R	D	R	PP	D	D	R	D	D	D	R	R	R	D
New Hampshire	R	R	R	R	R	R	R	R	R	R	R	R	R	D	D	R	R	R	R
New Jersey	R[1]	D	D	R	D	D	D	D	D	R	R	R	R	D	R	R	R	R	D
New Mexico														D	D	R	R	R	D
New York	R	R	D	R	D	R	D	R	D	R	R	R	R	D	R	R	R	R	D
North Carolina	SD	[2]	R	R	D	D	D	D	D	D	D	D	D	D	D	D	D	R	D
North Dakota									[9]	R	R	R	R	D	D	R	R	R	D
Ohio	R	R	R	R	R	R	R	R	R[10]	R	R	R	R	D	D	R	R	R	D
Oklahoma													D	D	D	R	D	R	D
Oregon	R	R	D	R	R	R	R	R	R[11]	R	R	R	R	D	R	R	R	R	D
Pennsylvania	R	R	R	R	R	R	R	R	R	R	R	R	R	PR	R	R	R	R	R
Rhode Island	R	R	R	R	R	R	R	R	R	R	R	R	R	D	R	R	R	D	D
South Carolina	SD	[2]	R	R	D	D	D	D	D	D	D	D	D	D	D	D	D	D	D
South Dakota									R	D	R	R	R	PR	R	R	R	R	D
Tennessee	CU	[2]	R	D	D	D	D	D	D	D	D	D	D	D	D	R	D	R	D
Texas	SD	[2]	[3]	D	D	D	D	D	D	D	D	D					D	R	D
Utah											D	R	R	R	D	R	R	R	D
Vermont	R	R	R	R	R	R	R	R	R	R	R	R	R	R	R	R	R	R	R
Virginia	CU	[2]	[3]	R	D	D	D	D	D	D	D	D	D	D	D	D	D	R	D
Washington									R	D	R	R	R	PR	D	R	R	R	D
West Virginia		R	R	R	D	D	D	D	D	R	R	R	R	D	R[16]	R	R	R	D
Wisconsin	R	R	R	R	R	R	R	R	D	R	R	R	R	D	R	R	PR	R	D
Wyoming									R	D	R	R	R	D	D	R	R	R	D
Winning Party	R	R	R	R	R	R	D	R	D	R	R	R	R	D	D	R	R	R	D

NOTE: With the exception of the District of Columbia, blanks indicate states not yet admitted to the Union. The District of Columbia received the presidential vote in 1961.

KEY: AI-American Independent Party; CU-Constitutional Union Party; D-Democratic Party; PP-People's Party; PR-Progressive (Bull Moose) Party; R-Republican Party; SD-Southern Democratic Party; SR-States' Rights Democratic Party.

1. Four electors voted Republican; three, Democratic.
2. Confederate states did not vote in 1864.
3. Did not vote in 1868.
4. Votes were not counted.
5. Three votes for Greeley not counted.
6. Five electors voted Democratic; one, Republican.
7. Eight electors voted Democratic; one, Republican.
8. Nine electors voted Republican; five, Democratic.
9. One vote each for Democratic, Republican and People's parties.
10. Twenty-two electors voted Republican; one, Democratic.
11. Three electors voted Republican; one, People's Party.
12. Eight electors voted Republican; one, Democratic.

1936	*1940*	*1944*	*1948*	*1952*	*1956*	*1960*	*1964*	*1968*	*1972*	*1976*	*1980*	*1984*	*1988*	*1992*	*1996*	*2000*	*2004*	*2008*	*Dems*	*Reps*	*Other*
D	D	D	SR	D	D[18]	D[19]	R	AI	R	D	R	R	R	R	R	R	R	R	22	12	3
						R	D	R	R	R	R	R	R	R	R	R	R	R	1	12	0
D	D	D	D	R	R	R	R	R	R	R	R	R	R	R	D	R	R	R	8	17	0
D	D	D	D	D	D	D	D	AI	R	R	R	R	R	D	D	R	R	R	26	8	2
D	D	D	D	R	R	R	D	R	R	R	R	R	R	D	D	D	D	D	14	23	1
D	R	R	D	R	R	R	D	R	R	R	R	R	R	D	R	R	R	D	11	22	1
D	D	D	R	R	R	D	D	D	R	R	R	R	R	D	D	D	D	D	16	22	0
D	D	D	R	R	R	D	D	R	R	D	R	R	R	D	D	D	D	D	19	18	1
							D	D	D	D	D	D	D	D	D	D[26]	D	D	12	0	0
D	D	D	D	R	R	R	D	R	R	D	R	R	R	R	D	R	R	D	21	15	1
D	D	D	D	D	D	D	R	AI	R	D	D	R	R	D	R	R	R	R	27	8	2
						D	D	D	R	D	D	R	D	D	D	D	D	D	11	2	0
D	D	D	D	R	R	R	D	R	R	R	R	R	R	R	R	R	R	R	10	19	1
D	D	D	D	R	R	D	D	R	R	R	R	R	R	D	D	D	D	D	14	24	0
D	R	R	R	R	R	R	D	R	R	R	R	R	R	R	R	R	R	D	8	30	0
D	R	R	D	R	R	R	D	R	R	R	R	R	D	D	D	D	R	D	10	28	0
R	R	R	R	R	R	R	D	R	R	R	R	R	R	R	R	R	R	R	6	30	1
D	D	D	D	D	R	R	D	R	R	D	R	R	R	D	D	R	R	R	24	13	1
D	D	D	SR	D	R	D	R	AI	R	D	R	R	R	D	D	R	R	R	23	10	3
R	R	R	R	R	R	R	D	D	R	R	R	R	R	D	D	D	D	D	8	30	0
D	D	D	R	R	R	D	D	D	R	D	D	R	R	D	D	D	D	D	25	12	1
D	D	D	D	R	R	D	D	D	D	D	R	R	D	D	D	D	D	D	18	20	0
D	R	D	R	R	R	D	D	D	R	R	R	R	R	D	D	D	D	D	11	26	1
D	D	D	D	R	R	D	D	D	R	D	D	D	D	D	D	D	D[27]	D	17	20	1
D	D	D	SR	D	D	[20]	R	AI	R	D	R	R	R	R	R	R	R	R	21	11	4
D	D	D	D	R	D	D	D	R	R	D	R	R	R	D	D	R	R	R	22	16	0
D	D	D	D	R	R	R	D	R	R	R	R	R	R	D	R	R	R	R	11	19	0
D	R	R	R	R	R	D	R	R	R	R	R	R	R	R	R	R	R	R[28]	7	29	0
D	D	D	D	R	R	D	D	R	R	R	R	R	R	D	D	R	R	D	16	20	1
D	D	D	R	R	R	R	D	R	R	R	R	R	R	D	D	R	D	D	10	28	0
D	D	D	R	R	R	D	D	R	R	R	R	R	R	D	D	D	D	D	19	19	0
D	D	D	D	R	R	D	D	R	R	R	R	R	R	D	D	D	R	D	13	12	0
D	D	D	R	R	R	D	D	D	R	D	R	R	D	D	D	D	D	D	19	19	0
D	D	D	D	D	D	D	D	R[22]	R	D	R	R	R	R	R	R	R	D	24	12	1
D	R	R	R	R	R	R	D	R	R	R	R	R	R	R	R	R	R	R	5	24	1
D	D	R	D	R	R	R	D	R	R	D	R	R	R	D	D	R	R	D	11	27	0
D	D	D	D	R	R	R[21]	D	R	R	R	R	R	R	R	R	R	R	R	10	16	0
D	D	D	R	R	R	R	D	R	R	R	R	R	D	D	D	D	D	D	13	25	0
D	D	D	R	R	R	D	D	D	R	D	R	R	R	D	D	D	D	D	12	25	1
D	D	D	D	R	R	D	D	D	R	D	D	R	D	D	D	D	D	D	18	20	0
D	D	D	SR	D	D	D	R	R	R	D	R	R	R	R	R	R	R	R	21	14	2
D	R	R	R	R	R	R	D	R	R	R	R	R	R	R	R	R	R	R	4	25	1
D	D	D	D[17]	R	R	R	D	R	R	D	R	R	R	D	D	R	R	R	22	14	1
D	D	D	D	R	R	D	D	D	R	D	R	R	R	R	R	R	R	R	23	12	1
D	D	D	D	R	R	R	D	R	R	R	R	R	R	R	R	R	R	R	8	21	0
R	R	R	R	R	R	R	D	R	R	R	R	R	R	D	D	D	D	D	6	32	0
D	D	D	D	R	D	D	D	D	R[23]	R	R	R	R	R	R	R	R	D	20	15	1
D	D	D	D	R	R	R	D	D	R	R[24]	R	R	D	D	D	D	D	D	15	14	1
D	D	D	D	D	R	D	D	D	R	D	D	R	D[25]	D	D	R	R	R	20	17	0
D	D	R	D	R	R	R	D	R	R	D	R	R	D	D	D	D	D	D	14	23	1
D	D	R	D	R	R	R	D	R	R	R	R	R	R	R	R	R	R	R	8	22	0
D	D	D	D	R	R	D	D	R	R	D	R	R	R	D	D	R	R	D	15	23	0

13. Twelve electors voted Republican; one, Democratic.
14. Seven electors voted Democratic; one, Republican.
15. Six electors voted Democratic; two, Republican.
16. Seven electors voted Republican; one, Democratic.
17. Eleven electors voted Democratic; one, States' Rights.
18. One elector voted for Walter B. Jones.
19. Six of eleven electors voted for Harry F. Byrd.
20. Eight independent electors voted for Byrd.
21. One vote cast for Byrd.
22. Twelve electors voted Republican; one, American Independent.
23. One elector voted Libertarian.
24. One elector voted for Ronald Reagan.
25. One elector voted for Lloyd Bentsen.
26. One elector did not vote.
27. One elector voted for John Edwards.
28. Obama won the vote of one elector.

2004 Presidential Election

State	Total vote	George W. Bush (Republican)		John Kerry (Democrat)		Other		Plurality	
		Votes	%	Votes	%	Votes	%		
Alabama	1,883,449	1,176,394	62.5	693,933	36.8	13,122	0.7	482,461	R
Alaska	312,598	190,889	61.1	111,025	35.5	10,684	3.4	79,864	R
Arizona	2,012,585	1,104,294	54.9	893,524	44.4	14,767	0.7	210,770	R
Arkansas	1,054,945	572,898	54.3	469,953	44.5	12,094	1.2	102,945	R
California	12,421,852	5,509,826	44.4	6,745,485	54.3	166,541	1.3	1,235,659	D
Colorado	2,130,330	1,101,255	51.7	1,001,732	47.0	27,343	1.3	99,523	R
Connecticut	1,578,769	693,826	43.9	857,488	54.3	27,455	1.8	163,662	D
Delaware	375,190	171,660	45.8	200,152	53.3	3,378	0.9	28,492	D
Florida	7,609,810	3,964,522	52.1	3,583,544	47.1	61,744	0.8	380,978	R
Georgia	3,301,875	1,914,254	58.0	1,366,149	41.4	21,472	0.6	548,105	R
Hawaii	429,013	194,191	45.3	231,708	54.0	3,114	0.7	37,517	D
Idaho	598,447	409,235	68.4	181,098	30.3	8,114	1.3	228,137	R
Illinois	5,274,322	2,345,946	44.5	2,891,550	54.8	36,826	0.7	545,604	D
Indiana	2,468,002	1,479,438	59.9	969,011	39.3	19,553	0.8	510,427	R
Iowa	1,506,908	751,957	49.9	741,898	49.2	13,053	0.9	10,059	R
Kansas	1,187,756	736,456	62.0	434,993	36.6	16,307	1.4	301,463	R
Kentucky	1,795,860	1,069,439	59.6	712,733	39.7	13,688	0.7	356,706	R
Louisiana	1,943,106	1,102,169	56.7	820,299	42.2	20,638	1.1	281,870	R
Maine	740,752	330,201	44.6	396,842	53.6	13,709	1.8	66,641	D
Maryland	2,386,678	1,024,703	42.9	1,334,493	55.9	27,482	1.2	309,790	D
Massachusetts	2,912,388	1,071,109	36.8	1,803,800	61.9	37,479	1.3	732,691	D
Michigan	4,839,252	2,313,746	47.8	2,479,183	51.2	46,323	1.0	165,437	D
Minnesota	2,828,387	1,346,695	47.6	1,445,014	51.1	36,678	1.3	98,319	D
Mississippi	1,152,145	684,981	59.5	458,094	39.8	9,070	0.7	226,887	R
Missouri	2,731,364	1,455,713	53.3	1,259,171	46.1	16,480	0.6	196,542	R
Montana	450,445	266,063	59.1	173,710	38.6	10,672	2.3	92,353	R
Nebraska	778,186	512,814	65.9	254,328	32.7	11,044	1.4	258,486	R
Nevada	829,587	418,690	50.5	397,190	47.9	13,707	1.6	21,500	R
New Hampshire	677,738	331,237	48.9	340,511	50.2	5,990	0.9	9,274	D
New Jersey	3,611,691	1,670,003	46.2	1,911,430	52.9	30,258	0.9	241,427	D
New Mexico	756,304	376,930	49.8	370,942	49.0	8,432	1.2	5,988	R
New York	7,391,036	2,962,567	40.1	4,314,280	58.4	114,189	1.5	1,351,713	D
North Carolina	3,501,007	1,961,166	56.0	1,525,849	43.6	13,992	0.4	435,317	R
North Dakota	312,833	196,651	62.9	111,052	35.5	5,130	1.6	85,599	R
Ohio	5,627,903	2,859,764	50.8	2,741,165	48.7	26,974	0.5	118,599	R
Oklahoma	1,463,758	959,792	65.6	503,966	34.4		0.0	455,826	R
Oregon	1,836,782	866,831	47.2	943,163	51.3	26,788	1.5	76,332	D
Pennsylvania	5,769,590	2,793,847	48.4	2,938,095	50.9	37,648	0.7	144,248	D
Rhode Island	437,134	169,046	38.7	259,760	59.4	8,328	1.9	90,714	D
South Carolina	1,617,730	937,974	58.0	661,699	40.9	18,057	1.1	276,275	R
South Dakota	388,215	232,584	59.9	149,244	38.4	6,387	1.7	83,340	R
Tennessee	2,437,319	1,384,375	56.8	1,036,477	42.5	16,467	0.7	347,898	R
Texas	7,410,765	4,526,917	61.1	2,832,704	38.2	51,144	0.7	1,694,213	R
Utah	927,844	663,742	71.5	241,199	26.0	22,903	2.5	422,543	R
Vermont	312,309	121,180	38.8	184,067	58.9	7,062	2.3	62,887	D
Virginia	3,198,367	1,716,959	53.7	1,454,742	45.5	26,666	0.8	262,217	R
Washington	2,859,084	1,304,894	45.6	1,510,201	52.8	43,989	1.6	205,307	D
West Virginia	755,887	423,778	56.1	326,541	43.2	5,568	0.7	97,237	R
Wisconsin	2,997,007	1,478,120	49.3	1,489,504	49.7	29,383	1.0	11,384	D
Wyoming	243,428	167,629	68.9	70,776	29.1	5,023	2.0	96,853	R
District of Columbia	227,586	21,256	9.3	202,970	89.2	3,360	1.5	181,714	D
Totals	122,295,345	62,040,610	50.7	59,028,439	48.3	1,226,296	1.0	3,012,171	R

2004 Electoral Votes

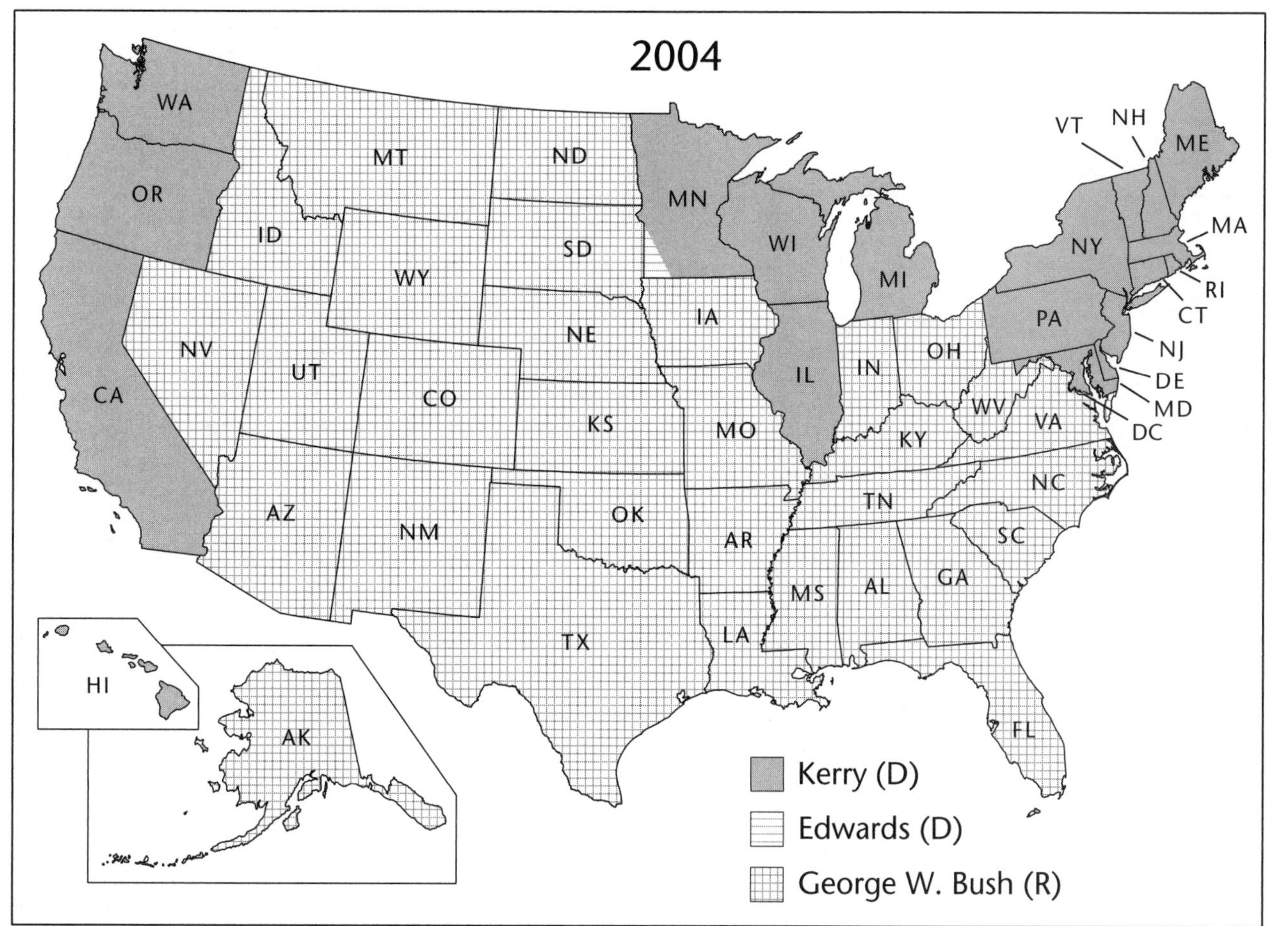

Key: D—Democrat; R—Republican

State	Electoral votes	Bush	Kerry	Edwards
Alabama	(9)	9	–	–
Alaska	(3)	3	–	–
Arizona	(10)	10	–	–
Arkansas	(6)	6	–	–
California	(55)	–	55	–
Colorado	(9)	9	–	–
Connecticut	(7)	–	7	–
Delaware	(3)	–	3	–
District of Columbia	(3)	–	3	–
Florida	(27)	27	–	–
Georgia	(15)	15	–	–
Hawaii	(4)	–	4	–
Idaho	(4)	4	–	–
Illinois	(21)	–	21	–
Indiana	(11)	11	–	–
Iowa	(7)	7	–	–
Kansas	(6)	6	–	–
Kentucky	(8)	8	–	–
Louisiana	(9)	9	–	–
Maine	(4)	–	4	–
Maryland	(10)	–	10	–
Massachusetts	(12)	–	12	–
Michigan	(17)	–	17	–
Minnesota[1]	(10)	–	9	1
Mississippi	(6)	6	–	–
Missouri	(11)	11	–	–
Montana	(3)	3	–	–
Nebraska	(5)	5	–	–
Nevada	(5)	5	–	–
New Hampshire	(4)	–	4	–
New Jersey	(15)	–	15	–
New Mexico	(5)	5	–	–
New York	(31)	–	31	–
North Carolina	(15)	15	–	–
North Dakota	(3)	3	–	–
Ohio	(20)	20	–	–
Oklahoma	(7)	7	–	–
Oregon	(7)	–	7	–
Pennsylvania	(21)	–	21	–
Rhode Island	(4)	–	4	–
South Carolina	(8)	8	–	–
South Dakota	(3)	3	–	–
Tennessee	(11)	11	–	–
Texas	(34)	34	–	–
Utah	(5)	5	–	–
Vermont	(3)	–	3	–
Virginia	(13)	13	–	–
Washington	(11)	–	11	–
West Virginia	(5)	5	–	–
Wisconsin	(10)	–	10	–
Wyoming	(3)	3	–	–
Totals	(538)	286	251	1

1. A Democratic elector cast a vote for John Edwards rather than John Kerry.

2008 Presidential Election

State	Total vote	Barack Obama (Democrat)		John McCain (Republican)		Other		Dem.-Rep.	
		Votes	%	Votes	%	Votes	%	Plurality	
Alabama	2,099,819	813,479	*38.7*	1,266,546	*60.3*	19,794	*0.9*	**453,067**	**R**
Alaska	326,197	123,594	*37.9*	193,841	*59.4*	8,762	*2.7*	**70,247**	**R**
Arizona	2,293,475	1,034,707	*45.1*	1,230,111	*53.6*	28,657	*1.2*	**195,404**	**R**
Arkansas	1,086,617	422,310	*38.9*	638,017	*58.7*	26,290	*2.4*	**215,707**	**R**
California	13,561,900	8,274,473	*61.0*	5,011,781	*37.0*	275,646	*2.0*	**3,262,692**	**D**
Colorado	2,401,462	1,288,633	*53.7*	1,073,629	*44.7*	39,200	*1.6*	**215,004**	**D**
Connecticut	1,646,797	977,772	*60.6*	629,428	*38.2*	19,597	*1.1*	**368,344**	**D**
Delaware	412,412	255,459	*61.9*	152,374	*36.9*	4,579	*1.1*	**103,085**	**D**
Florida	8,390,744	4,282,074	*51.0*	4,045,624	*48.2*	63,046	*0.8*	**236,450**	**D**
Georgia	3,924,486	1,844,123	*47.0*	2,048,759	*52.2*	31,604	*0.8*	**204,636**	**R**
Hawaii	453,568	325,871	*71.8*	120,566	*26.6*	7,131	*1.6*	**205,305**	**D**
Idaho	655,122	236,440	*36.1*	403,012	*61.5*	15,670	*2.4*	**166,572**	**R**
Illinois	5,522,371	3,419,348	*61.9*	2,031,179	*36.8*	71,844	*1.3*	**1,388,169**	**D**
Indiana	2,751,054	1,374,039	*49.9*	1,345,648	*48.9*	31,367	*1.1*	**28,391**	**D**
Iowa	1,537,123	828,940	*53.9*	682,379	*44.4*	25,804	*1.7*	**146,561**	**D**
Kansas	1,235,872	514,765	*41.7*	699,655	*56.6*	21,452	*1.7*	**184,890**	**R**
Kentucky	1,826,620	751,985	*41.2*	1,048,462	*57.4*	26,173	*1.4*	**296,477**	**R**
Louisiana	1,960,761	782,989	*39.9*	1,148,275	*58.6*	29,497	*1.5*	**365,286**	**R**
Maine	731,163	421,923	*57.7*	295,273	*40.4*	13,967	*1.9*	**126,650**	**D**
Maryland	2,631,596	1,629,467	*61.9*	959,862	*36.5*	42,267	*1.6*	**669,605**	**D**
Massachusetts	3,080,985	1,904,097	*61.8*	1,108,854	*36.0*	68,034	*2.2*	**795,243**	**D**
Michigan	5,001,766	2,872,579	*57.4*	2,048,639	*41.0*	80,548	*1.6*	**823,940**	**D**
Minnesota	2,910,369	1,573,354	*54.1*	1,275,409	*43.8*	61,606	*2.1*	**297,945**	**D**
Mississippi	1,289,865	554,662	*43.0*	724,597	*56.2*	10,606	*0.8*	**169,935**	**R**
Missouri	2,925,205	1,441,911	*49.3*	1,445,814	*49.4*	37,480	*1.3*	**3,903**	**R**
Montana	490,302	231,667	*47.3*	242,763	*49.5*	15,872	*3.2*	**11,096**	**R**
Nebraska	801,281	333,319	*41.6*	452,979	*56.5*	14,983	*1.9*	**119,660**	**R**
Nevada	967,848	533,736	*55.1*	412,827	*42.7*	21,285	*2.2*	**120,909**	**D**
New Hampshire	710,970	384,826	*54.1*	316,534	*44.5*	9,610	*1.4*	**68,292**	**D**
New Jersey	3,868,237	2,215,422	*57.3*	1,613,207	*41.7*	39,608	*1.0*	**602,215**	**D**
New Mexico	830,158	472,422	*56.9*	346,832	*41.8*	10,904	*1.3*	**125,590**	**D**
New York	7,640,931	4,804,945	*62.9*	2,752,771	*36.0*	83,215	*1.1*	**2,052,174**	**D**
North Carolina	4,310,789	2,142,651	*49.7*	2,128,474	*49.4*	39,664	*0.9*	**14,177**	**D**
North Dakota	316,621	141,278	*44.6*	168,601	*53.3*	6,742	*2.1*	**27,323**	**R**
Ohio	5,708,350	2,940,044	*51.5*	2,677,820	*46.9*	90,486	*1.6*	**262,224**	**D**
Oklahoma	1,462,661	502,496	*34.4*	960,165	*65.6*	0	—	**457,669**	**R**
Oregon	1,827,864	1,037,291	*56.7*	738,475	*40.4*	52,098	*2.9*	**298,816**	**D**
Pennsylvania	6,013,272	3,276,363	*54.5*	2,655,885	*44.2*	81,024	*1.0*	**620,478**	**D**
Rhode Island	471,766	296,571	*62.9*	165,391	*35.1*	9,804	*1.7*	**131,180**	**D**
South Carolina	1,920,969	862,449	*44.9*	1,034,896	*53.9*	23,624	*1.2*	**172,447**	**R**
South Dakota	381,975	170,924	*44.7*	203,054	*53.2*	7,997	*2.1*	**32,130**	**R**
Tennessee	2,599,749	1,087,437	*41.8*	1,479,178	*56.9*	33,134	*1.3*	**391,741**	**R**
Texas	8,077,795	3,528,633	*43.7*	4,479,328	*55.5*	69,834	*0.9*	**950,695**	**R**
Utah	952,370	327,670	*34.4*	596,030	*62.6*	28,670	*3.0*	**268,360**	**R**
Vermont	325,046	219,262	*67.5*	98,974	*30.4*	6,810	*2.1*	**120,288**	**D**
Virginia	3,723,260	1,959,532	*52.6*	1,725,005	*46.3*	38,723	*1.0*	**234,527**	**D**
Washington	3,036,878	1,750,848	*57.7*	1,229,216	*40.5*	56,814	*1.9*	**521,632**	**D**
West Virginia	713,451	303,857	*42.6*	397,466	*55.7*	12,128	*1.7*	**93,609**	**R**
Wisconsin	2,983,417	1,677,211	*56.2*	1,262,393	*42.3*	43,813	*1.5*	**414,818**	**D**
Wyoming	254,658	82,868	*32.5*	164,958	*64.8*	6,832	*2.7*	**82,090**	**R**
District of Columbia	265,853	245,800	*92.5*	17,367	*6.5*	2,686	*1.0*	**228,433**	**D**
Totals	**131,313,820**	**69,498,516**	***52.9***	**59,948,323**	***45.7***	**1,866,981**	***1.4***	**9,550,193**	**D**

2008 Electoral Votes

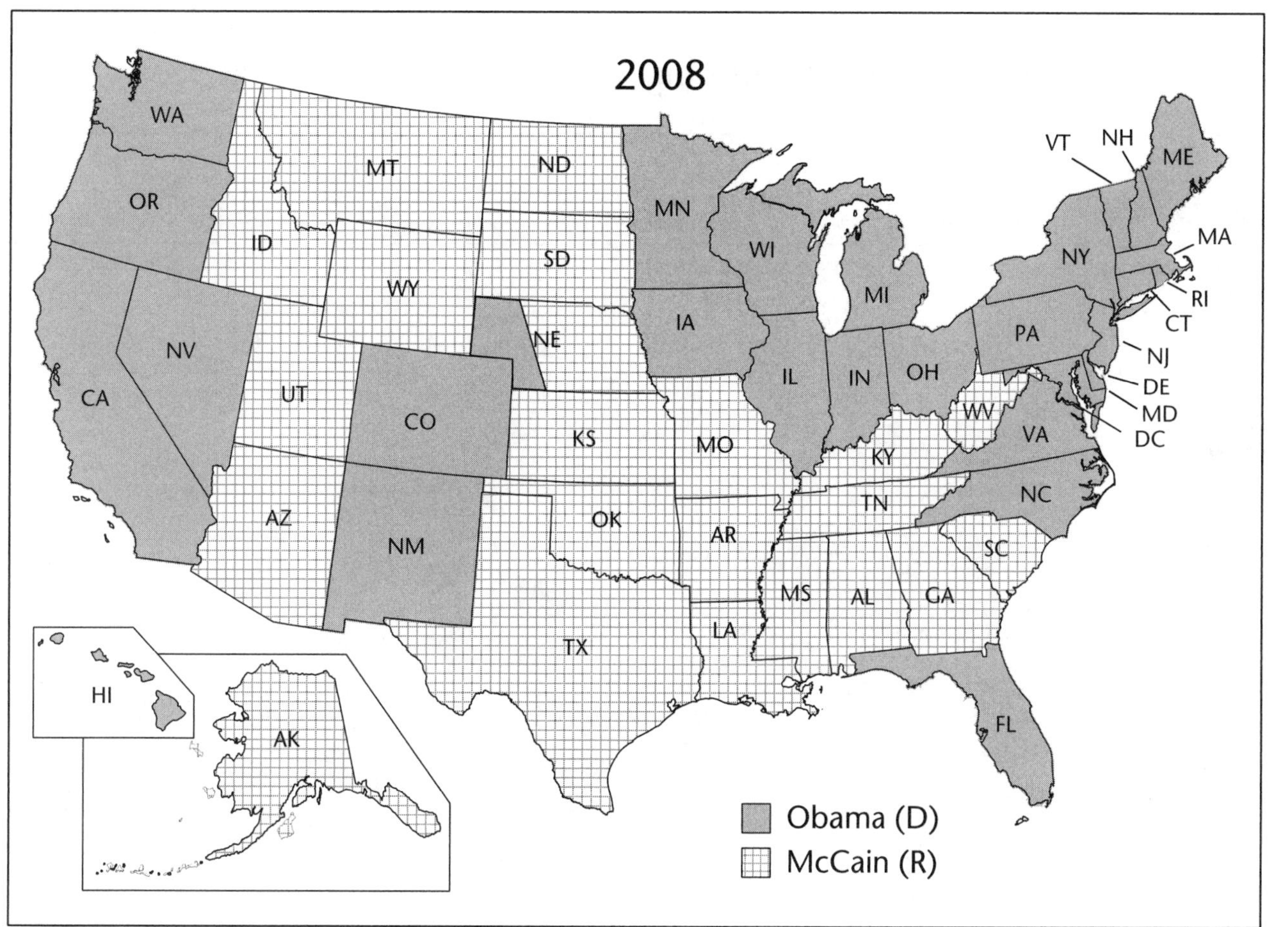

Key: D—Democrat; R—Republican

States	*Electoral votes*	*Obama*	*McCain*
Alabama	(9)	–	9
Alaska	(3)	–	3
Arizona	(10)	–	10
Arkansas	(6)	–	6
California	(55)	55	–
Colorado	(9)	9	–
Connecticut	(7)	7	–
Delaware	(3)	3	–
District of Columbia	(3)	3	–
Florida	(27)	27	–
Georgia	(15)	–	15
Hawaii	(4)	4	–
Idaho	(4)	–	4
Illinois	(21)	21	–
Indiana	(11)	11	–
Iowa	(7)	7	–
Kansas	(6)	–	6
Kentucky	(8)	–	8
Louisiana	(9)	–	9
Maine	(4)	4	–
Maryland	(10)	10	–
Massachusetts	(12)	12	–
Michigan	(17)	17	–
Minnesota	(10)	10	–
Mississippi	(6)	–	6
Missouri	(11)	–	11
Montana	(3)	–	3
Nebraska[1]	(5)	1	4
Nevada	(5)	5	–
New Hampshire	(4)	4	–
New Jersey	(15)	15	–
New Mexico	(5)	5	–
New York	(31)	31	–
North Carolina	(15)	15	–
North Dakota	(3)	–	3
Ohio	(20)	20	–
Oklahoma	(7)	–	7
Oregon	(7)	7	–
Pennsylvania	(21)	21	–
Rhode Island	(4)	4	–
South Carolina	(8)	–	8
South Dakota	(3)	–	3
Tennessee	(11)	–	11
Texas	(34)	–	34
Utah	(5)	–	5
Vermont	(3)	3	–
Virginia	(13)	13	–
Washington	(11)	11	–
West Virginia	(5)	–	5
Wisconsin	(10)	10	–
Wyoming	(3)	–	3
Totals	(538)	365	173

1. Barack Obama won one electoral vote. Nebraska divides three of its five votes by the winner in a congressional districts; the other two go to the statewide winner.

2008 Republican Convention Balloting

State	*Total votes*	*McCain*	*Paul*	*Romney*	*Not voting*
Alabama	48	48			
Alaska	29	24	5		
Arizona	53	53			
Arkansas	34	34			
California	173	173			
Colorado	46	46			
Connecticut	30	30			
Delaware	18	18			
Florida	57	57			
Georgia	72	72			
Hawaii	20	20			
Idaho	32	26			6
Illinois	70	70			
Indiana	57	57			
Iowa	40	40			
Kansas	39	39			
Kentucky	45	45			
Louisiana	47	47			
Maine	21	20			1
Maryland	37	37			
Massachusetts	43	43			
Michigan	30	30			
Minnesota	41	35			6
Mississippi	39	39			
Missouri	58	58			
Montana	25	25			
Nebraska	33	31			2
Nevada	34	34			
New Hampshire	12	12			
New Jersey	52	52			
New Mexico	32	32			
New York	101	101			
North Carolina	69	65			4
North Dakota	26	26			
Ohio	88	88			
Oklahoma	41	39	2		
Oregon	30	26	4		
Pennsylvania	74	73			1
Rhode Island	20	20			
South Carolina	24	24			
South Dakota	27	27			
Tennessee	55	55			
Texas	140	140			
Utah	36	34		2	
Vermont	17	17			
Virginia	63	63			
Washington	40	36	4		
West Virginia	30	28	2		
Wisconsin	40	40			
Wyoming	14	14			
District of Columbia	19	19			
Puerto Rico	23	23			
Virgin Islands	9	9			
American Samoa	9	9			
Guam	9	9			
Northern Marianas	9	9			
Totals	2,380	2,341	17	2	20

2008 Democratic Convention Balloting

State	*Total allocated votes*	*Obama*	*Clinton*	*Abstain/ not voting*
Alabama	60	48	5	7
Alaska	18	15	3	
American Samoa	9	9		
Arizona	67	40	27	
Arkansas	47	47		
California				
Colorado	70	55	15	
Connecticut	60	38	21	1
Delaware	23	23		
Democrats Abroad	11	8.5	2.5	
District of Columbia	40	33	7	
Florida	211	136	51	24
Georgia	102	82	18	2
Guam	9	4	3	2
Hawaii	29	26	1	2
Idaho	23	20	3	
Indiana	85	75	6	4
Iowa	57	48	9	
Illinois				
Kansas	41	34	6	1
Kentucky	60	36	24	
Louisiana	67	43	7	17
Maine	32	24	8	
Maryland	100	94	6	
Massachusetts	121	65	52	4
Michigan	157	125	27	5
Minnesota	88	78	8	2
Mississippi	41	33	8	
Missouri	88	82	6	
Montana	25	18	7	
Nebraska	31	28	3	
Nevada	34	25	8	1
New Hampshire	30	30		
New Jersey	127	127		
New Mexico				
New York				

SOURCE: Rhodes Cook Letter, August 2008.

NOTE: At the Democrat's 2008 convention Barack Obama of Illinois was nominated by acclamation Aug. 27, 2008. Before the acclamation vote occurred, however, some states cast ballots. The motion to suspend the roll call and nominate Obama by acclamation was made by his principal opponent, Hillary Rodham Clinton of New York. This came in a carefully orchestrated manner. California and Illinois passed; when the voting reached New Mexico it yielded to Illinois, which in turn yielded to New York, allowing Clinton to make her motion. The table shows the state-by-state vote count up to that point.

Distribution of House Seats and Electoral Votes

State	U.S. House seats									Electoral votes					
	1963–1973	1970 Census changes	1973–1983	1980 Census changes	1983–1993	1990 Census changes	1993–2003	2000 Census changes	2003–2013	1952, 1956, 1960	1964, 1968	1972, 1976, 1980	1984, 1988	1992, 1996, 2000	2004, 2008
Alabama	8	–1	7	—	7	—	7	—	7	11	10	9	9	9	9
Alaska	1	—	1	—	1	—	1	—	1	3	3	3	3	3	3
Arizona	3	+1	4	+1	5	+1	6	+2	8	4	5	6	7	8	10
Arkansas	4	—	4	—	4	—	4	—	4	8	6	6	6	6	6
California	38	+5	43	+2	45	+7	52	+1	53	32	40	45	47	54	55
Colorado	4	+1	5	+1	6	—	6	+1	7	6	6	7	8	8	9
Connecticut	6	—	6	—	6	—	6	–1	5	8	8	8	8	8	7
Delaware	1	—	1	—	1	—	1	—	1	3	3	3	3	3	3
Dist. of Col.	—	—	—	—	—	—	—	—	—	—	3	3	3	3	3
Florida	12	+3	15	+4	19	+4	23	+2	25	10	14	17	21	25	27
Georgia	10	—	10	—	10	+1	11	+2	13	12	12	12	12	13	15
Hawaii	2	—	2	—	2	—	2	—	2	3	4	4	4	4	4
Idaho	2	—	2	—	2	—	2	—	2	4	4	4	4	4	4
Illinois	24	—	24	–2	22	–2	20	–1	19	27	26	26	24	22	21
Indiana	11	—	11	–1	10	—	10	–1	9	13	13	13	12	12	11
Iowa	7	–1	6	—	6	–1	5	—	5	10	9	8	8	7	7
Kansas	5	—	5	—	5	–1	4	—	4	8	7	7	7	6	6
Kentucky	7	—	7	—	7	–1	6	—	6	10	9	9	9	8	8
Louisiana	8	—	8	—	8	–1	7	—	7	10	10	10	10	9	9
Maine	2	—	2	—	2	—	2	—	2	5	4	4	4	4	4
Maryland	8	—	8	—	8	—	8	—	8	9	10	10	10	10	10
Massachusetts	12	—	12	–1	11	–1	10	—	10	16	14	14	13	12	12
Michigan	19	—	19	–1	18	–2	16	–1	15	20	21	21	20	18	17
Minnesota	8	—	8	—	8	—	8	—	8	11	10	10	10	10	10
Mississippi	5	—	5	—	5	—	5	–1	4	8	7	7	7	7	6
Missouri	10	—	10	–1	9	—	9	—	9	13	12	12	11	11	11
Montana	2	—	2	—	2	–1	1	—	1	4	4	4	4	3	3
Nebraska	3	—	3	—	3	—	3	—	3	6	5	5	5	5	5
Nevada	1	—	1	+1	2	—	2	+1	3	3	3	3	4	4	5
New Hampshire	2	—	2	—	2	—	2	—	2	4	4	4	4	4	4
New Jersey	15	—	15	–1	14	–1	13	—	13	16	17	17	16	15	15
New Mexico	2	—	2	+1	3	—	3	—	3	4	4	4	5	5	5
New York	41	–2	39	–5	34	–3	31	–2	29	45	43	41	36	33	31
North Carolina	11	—	11	—	11	+1	12	+1	13	14	13	13	13	14	15
North Dakota	2	–1	1	—	1	—	1	—	1	4	4	3	3	3	3
Ohio	24	–1	23	–2	21	–2	19	–1	18	25	26	25	23	21	20
Oklahoma	6	—	6	—	6	—	6	–1	5	8	8	8	8	8	7
Oregon	4	—	4	+1	5	—	5	—	5	6	6	6	7	7	7
Pennsylvania	27	–2	25	–2	23	–2	21	–2	19	32	29	27	25	23	21
Rhode Island	2	—	2	—	2	—	2	—	2	4	4	4	4	4	4
South Carolina	6	—	6	—	6	—	6	—	6	8	8	8	8	8	8
South Dakota	2	—	2	–1	1	—	1	—	1	4	4	4	3	3	3
Tennessee	9	–1	8	+1	9	—	9	—	9	11	11	10	11	11	11
Texas	23	+1	24	+3	27	+3	30	+2	32	24	25	26	29	32	34
Utah	2	—	2	+1	3	—	3	—	3	4	4	4	5	5	5
Vermont	1	—	1	—	1	—	1	—	1	3	3	3	3	3	3
Virginia	10	—	10	—	10	+1	11	—	11	12	12	12	12	13	13
Washington	7	—	7	+1	8	+1	9	—	9	9	9	9	10	11	11
West Virginia	5	–1	4	—	4	–1	3	—	3	8	7	6	6	5	5
Wisconsin	10	–1	9	—	9	—	9	–1	8	12	12	11	11	11	10
Wyoming	1	—	1	—	1	—	1	—	1	3	3	3	3	3	3

NOTE: Table is based on the censuses of 1950, 1960, 1970, 1980, 1990, and 2000.

Party Affiliations in Congress and the Presidency, 1789–2011

Year	Congress	House: Majority party	House: Principal minority party	Senate: Majority party	Senate: Principal minority party	President
1789–1791	1st	AD-38	Op-26	AD-17	Op-9	F (Washington)
1791–1793	2nd	F-37	DR-33	F-16	DR-13	F (Washington)
1793–1795	3rd	DR-57	F-48	F-17	DR-13	F (Washington)
1795–1797	4th	F-54	DR-52	F-19	DR-13	F (Washington)
1797–1799	5th	F-58	DR-48	F-20	DR-12	F (J. Adams)
1799–1801	6th	F-64	DR-42	F-19	DR-13	F (J. Adams)
1801–1803	7th	DR-69	F-36	DR-18	F-13	DR (Jefferson)
1803–1805	8th	DR-102	F-39	DR-25	F-9	DR (Jefferson)
1805–1807	9th	DR-116	F-25	DR-27	F-7	DR (Jefferson)
1807–1809	10th	DR-118	F-24	DR-28	F-6	DR (Jefferson)
1809–1811	11th	DR-94	F-48	DR-28	F-6	DR (Madison)
1811–1813	12th	DR-108	F-36	DR-30	F-6	DR (Madison)
1813–1815	13th	DR-112	F-68	DR-27	F-9	DR (Madison)
1815–1817	14th	DR-117	F-65	DR-25	F-11	DR (Madison)
1817–1819	15th	DR-141	F-42	DR-34	F-10	DR (Monroe)
1819–1821	16th	DR-156	F-27	DR-35	F-7	DR (Monroe)
1821–1823	17th	DR-158	F-25	DR-44	F-4	DR (Monroe)
1823–1825	18th	DR-187	F-26	DR-44	F-4	DR (Monroe)
1825–1827	19th	AD-105	J-97	AD-26	J-20	DR (J.Q. Adams)
1827–1829	20th	J-119	AD-94	J-28	AD-20	DR (J.Q. Adams)
1829–1831	21st	D-139	NR-74	D-26	NR-22	DR (Jackson)
1831–1833	22nd	D-141	NR-58	D-25	NR-21	D (Jackson)
1833–1835	23rd	D-147	AM-53	D-20	NR-20	D (Jackson)
1835–1837	24th	D-145	W-98	D-27	W-25	D (Jackson)
1837–1839	25th	D-108	W-107	D-30	W-18	D (Van Buren)
1839–1841	26th	D-124	W-118	D-28	W-22	D (Van Buren)
1841–1843	27th	W-133	D-102	W-28	D-22	W (W. Harrison); W (Tyler)
1843–1845	28th	D-142	W-79	W-28	D-25	W (Tyler)
1845–1847	29th	D-143	W-77	D-31	W-25	D (Polk)
1847–1849	30th	W-115	D-108	D-36	W-21	D (Polk)
1849–1851	31st	D-112	W-109	D-35	W-25	W (Taylor); W (Fillmore)
1851–1853	32nd	D-140	W-88	D-35	W-24	W (Fillmore)
1853–1855	33rd	D-159	W-71	D-38	W-22	D (Pierce)
1855–1857	34th	R-108	D-83	D-40	R-15	D (Pierce)
1857–1859	35th	D-118	R-92	D-36	R-20	D (Buchanan)
1859–1861	36th	R-114	D-92	D-36	R-26	D (Buchanan)
1861–1863	37th	R-105	D-43	R-31	D-10	R (Lincoln)
1863–1865	38th	R-102	D-75	R-36	D-9	R (Lincoln)
1865–1867	39th	U-149	D-42	U-42	D-10	R (Lincoln); R (A. Johnson)
1867–1869	40th	R-143	D-49	R-42	D-11	R (A. Johnson)
1869–1871	41st	R-149	D-63	R-56	D-11	R (Grant)
1871–1873	42nd	R-134	D-104	R-52	D-17	R (Grant)
1873–1875	43rd	R-194	D-92	R-49	D-19	R (Grant)
1875–1877	44th	D-169	R-109	R-45	D-29	R (Grant)
1877–1879	45th	D-153	R-140	R-39	D-36	R (Hayes)
1879–1881	46th	D-149	R-130	D-42	R-33	R (Hayes)
1881–1883	47th	R-147	D-135	R-37	D-37	R (Garfield); R (Arthur)
1883–1885	48th	D-197	R-118	R-38	D-36	R (Arthur)
1885–1887	49th	D-183	R-140	R-43	D-34	D (Cleveland)
1887–1889	50th	D-169	R-152	R-39	D-37	D (Cleveland)
1889–1891	51st	R-166	D-159	R-39	D-37	R (B. Harrison)
1891–1893	52nd	D-235	R-88	R-47	D-39	R (B. Harrison)
1893–1895	53rd	D-218	R-127	D-44	R-38	D (Cleveland)
1895–1897	54th	R-244	D-105	R-43	D-39	D (Cleveland)
1897–1899	55th	R-204	D-113	R-47	D-34	R (McKinley)

(continued)

Year	Congress	House: Majority party	House: Principal minority party	Senate: Majority party	Senate: Principal minority party	President
1899–1901	56th	R-185	D-163	R-53	D-26	R (McKinley)
1901–1903	57th	R-197	D-151	R-55	D-31	R (McKinley); R (T. Roosevelt)
1903–1905	58th	R-208	D-178	R-57	D-33	R (T. Roosevelt)
1905–1907	59th	R-250	D-136	R-57	D-33	R (T. Roosevelt)
1907–1909	60th	R-222	D-164	R-61	D-31	R (T. Roosevelt)
1909–1911	61st	R-219	D-172	R-61	D-32	R (Taft)
1911–1913	62nd	D-228	R-161	R-51	D-41	R (Taft)
1913–1915	63rd	D-291	R-127	D-51	R-44	D (Wilson)
1915–1917	64th	D-230	R-196	D-56	R-40	D (Wilson)
1917–1919	65th	D-216	R-210	D-53	R-42	D (Wilson)
1919–1921	66th	R-240	D-190	R-49	D-47	D (Wilson)
1921–1923	67th	R-301	D-131	R-59	D-37	R (Harding)
1923–1925	68th	R-225	D-205	R-51	D-43	R (Coolidge)
1925–1927	69th	R-247	D-183	R-56	D-39	R (Coolidge)
1927–1929	70th	R-237	D-195	R-49	D-46	R (Coolidge)
1929–1931	71st	R-267	D-167	R-56	D-39	R (Hoover)
1931–1933	72nd	D-220	R-214	R-48	D-47	R (Hoover)
1933–1935	73rd	D-310	R-117	D-60	R-35	D (F. Roosevelt)
1935–1937	74th	D-319	R-103	D-69	R-25	D (F. Roosevelt)
1937–1939	75th	D-331	R-89	D-76	R-16	D (F. Roosevelt)
1939–1941	76th	D-261	R-164	D-69	R-23	D (F. Roosevelt)
1941–1943	77th	D-268	R-162	D-66	R-28	D (F. Roosevelt)
1943–1945	78th	D-218	R-208	D-58	R-37	D (F. Roosevelt)
1945–1947	79th	D-242	R-190	D-56	R-38	D (F. Roosevelt); D (Truman)
1947–1949	80th	R-245	D-188	R-51	D-45	D (Truman)
1949–1951	81st	D-263	R-171	D-54	R-42	D (Truman)
1951–1953	82nd	D-234	R-199	D-49	R-47	D (Truman)
1953–1955	83rd	R-221	D-211	R-48	D-47	R (Eisenhower)
1955–1957	84th	D-232	R-203	D-48	R-47	R (Eisenhower)
1957–1959	85th	D-233	R-200	D-49	R-47	R (Eisenhower)
1959–1961	86th	D-283	R-153	D-64	R-34	R (Eisenhower)
1961–1963	87th	D-263	R-174	D-65	R-35	D (Kennedy)
1963–1965	88th	D-258	R-177	D-67	R-33	D (Kennedy); D (L. Johnson)
1965–1967	89th	D-295	R-140	D-68	R-32	D (L. Johnson)
1967–1969	90th	D-247	R-187	D-64	R-36	D (L. Johnson)
1969–1971	91st	D-243	R-192	D-57	R-43	R (Nixon)
1971–1973	92nd	D-254	R-180	D-54	R-44	R (Nixon)
1973–1975	93rd	D-239	R-192	D-56	R-42	R (Nixon); R (Ford)
1975–1977	94th	D-291	R-144	D-60	R-37	R (Ford)
1977–1979	95th	D-292	R-143	D-61	R-38	D (Carter)
1979–1981	96th	D-276	R-157	D-58	R-41	D (Carter)
1981–1983	97th	D-243	R-192	R-53	D-46	R (Reagan)
1983–1985	98th	D-269	R-165	R-54	D-46	R (Reagan)
1985–1987	99th	D-252	R-182	R-53	D-47	R (Reagan)
1987–1989	100th	D-258	R-177	D-55	R-45	R (Reagan)
1989–1991	101st	D-259	R-174	D-55	R-45	R (G. Bush)
1991–1993	102nd	D-267	R-167	D-56	R-44	R (G. Bush)
1993–1995	103rd	D-258	R-176	D-57	R-43	D (Clinton)
1995–1997	104th	R-230	D-204	R-53	D-47	D (Clinton)
1997–1999	105th	R-227	D-207	R-55	D-45	D (Clinton)
1999–2001	106th	R-222	D-211	R-55	D-45	D (Clinton)
2001–2003	107th	R-221	D-212	R-50	D-50	R (G.W. Bush)
2003–2005	108th	R-229	D-205	R-51	D-48	R (G.W. Bush)
2005–2007	109th	R-232	D-202	R-55	D-44	R (G.W. Bush)
2007–2009	110th	D-233	R-202	D-49[1]	R-49	R (G.W. Bush
2009–2011	111th	D-236	R-199	D-57[2]	R-41	D (Obama)

SOURCES: U.S. Bureau of the Census, *Historical Statistics of the United States, Colonial Times to 1970* (Washington, D.C.: Government Printing Office, 1975); and U.S. Congress, Joint Committee on Printing, *Official Congressional Directory* (Washington, D.C.: Government Printing Office, 1967–); and *America Votes 26 and 27* (Washington, D.C,: CQ Press, 2007 and 2009.

NOTE: Figures are for the beginning of the first session of each Congress. Key to abbreviations: AD—Administration; AM—Anti-Masonic; D—Democratic; DR—Democratic-Republican; F—Federalist; J—Jacksonian; NR—National Republican; Op—Opposition; R—Republican; U—Unionist; W—Whig.

1. The 110th Congress had two independent senators who caucused with the Democrats, giving that party control of the chamber.

2. The 111th Congress had two independent senators who caucused with the Democrats.

109th Congress Special Elections, 2005 Gubernatorial Elections

Special House Elections, 109th Congress

	Vote total	*Percent*
California 5th CD–March 8, 2005		
Doris Matsui (D)	56,175	68.2
Julie Padilla (D)	7,158	8.7
John Thomas Flynn (no party)	6,559	8.0
California 48th CD–Dec. 6, 2005		
John Campbell (R)	46,148	44.4
Steve Young (D)	28,853	27.8
Jim Gilchrist (AMI)	26,507	25.5
California 50th CD–June 6, 2006		
Brian P. Bilbray (D)	78,341	49.6
Francine Busby (D)	71,146	45.0
New Jersey 13th CD–Nov. 7, 2006		
Albio Sires (D)	75,403	96.7
Ohio 2nd CD–Aug. 2, 2005		
Jean Schmidt (R)	59,671	51.6
Paul Hackett (D)	55,886	48.8
Texas 22nd CD–Nov. 7, 2006		
Shelly Sekula Gibbs (R)	76,924	62.1
M. Bob Smither (LIBERT)	23,425	18.9
Steve Stockman (R)	13,600	11.0
Don Richardson (R)	7,405	6.0

Special Senate Elections, 109th Congress

None

2005 Gubernatorial Elections

New Jersey		
Jon Corzine (D)	1,224,551	53.5
Doug Forrester (R)	985,271	43.0
Virginia		
Timothy M. Kaine (D)	1,025,942	51.7
Jerry W. Kilgore (R)	912,327	46.0

NOTE: Vote totals are included for all candidates listed on the ballot who received 5 percent or more of the total vote.

2006 Elections Returns for Governor, Senate, and House

Following are the official vote returns for the gubernatorial, Senate, and House races based on figures supplied by the fifty state election boards.

Vote totals are included for all candidates listed on the ballot who received 5 percent or more of the total vote. For candidates who received under 5 percent, consult *America Votes 26* (2005–2006), published by CQ Press. The percent column shows the percentage of the total vote cast.

An asterisk (*) indicates an incumbent.

An "X" denotes candidates without major part opposition; no votes were tallied.

An "AL" indicates an at-large member of Congress in a state with a single congressional district.

Alabama

		Vote total	*Percent*
Governor			
	Bob Riley (R)*	718,327	57.4
	Lucy Baxley (D)	519,827	41.6
House			
1	Jo Bonner (R)*	112,944	68.1
	Vivian Sheffield Beckerle (D)	52,770	31.8
2	Terry Everett (R)*	124,302	69.5
	Charles D. "Chuck" James (D)	54,450	30.4
3	Mike D. Rogers (R)*	98,257	59.4
	Greg A. Pierce (D)	63,559	38.4
4	Robert B. Aderholt (R)*	128,484	70.2
	Barbara Bobo (D)	54,382	29.7
5	Robert E. "Bud" Cramer (D)*	143,015	98.2
6	Spencer Bachus (R)*	163,514	98.3
7	Artur Davis (D)*	133,870	99.0

Alaska

		Vote total	*Percent*
Governor			
	Sarah Palin (R)	114,697	48.3
	Tony Knowles (D)	97,238	41.0
	Andrew Halcro (I)	22,443	9.5
House			
AL	Don Young (R)*	132,743	56.6
	Diane E. Benson (D)	93,879	40.0

Arizona

		Vote total	*Percent*
Governor			
	Janet Napolitano (D)*	959,830	62.6
	Len Munsil (R)	543,528	35.4
Senate			
	Jon Kyl (R)	814,398	53.3
	Jim Pederson (D)	664,141	43.5
House			
1	Rick Renzi (R)*	105,646	51.8
	Ellen Simon (D)	88,691	43.4
2	Trent Franks (R)*	135,150	58.6
	John Thrasher (D)	89,671	38.9
3	John Shadegg (R)*	112,519	59.3
	Herb Paine (D)	72,586	38.2
4	Ed Pastor (D)*	56,464	72.5
	Don Karg (R)	18,627	23.9
5	Harry E. Mitchell (D)	101,838	50.4
	J.D. Hayworth (R)*	93,815	46.4
6	Jeff Flake (R)*	152,201	74.8
	Jason M. Blair (LIBERT)	51,285	25.2
7	Raœl M. Grijalva (D)*	80,354	61.1
	Ron Drake (R)	46,498	35.4
8	Gabrielle Giffords (D)	137,655	54.3
	Randy Graf (R)	106,790	42.1

Arkansas

		Vote total	*Percent*
Governor			
	Mike Beebe (D)	430,765	55.6
	Asa Hutchinson (R)	315,040	40.7
House			
1	Marion Berry (D)*	127,577	69.3
	Mickey Stumbaugh (R)	56,611	30.7
2	Vic Snyder (D)*	124,871	60.5
	Andy Mayberry (R)	81,432	39.5
3	John Boozman (R)*	125,039	62.2
	Woodrow Anderson (D)	75,885	37.8
4	Mike Ross (D)*	128,236	74.7
	Joe Ross (R)	43,360	25.3

California

		Vote total	*Percent*
Governor			
	Arnold Schwarzenegger (R)*	4,850,157	55.9
	Phil Angelides (D)	3,376,732	38.9
Senate			
	Dianne Feinstein (D)*	5,076,289	59.4
	Richard "Dick" Mountjoy (R)	2,990,822	35.0
House			
1	Mike Thompson (D)*	144,409	66.2
	John W. Jones (R)	63,194	29.0
2	Wally Herger (R)*	134,911	64.2
	A.J. Sekhon (D)	68,234	32.5
3	Dan Lungren (R)*	135,709	59.5
	Bill Durston (D)	86,318	37.8
4	John T. Doolittle (R)*	135,818	49.0
	Charlie Brown (D)	126,999	45.9
	Dan Warren (LIBERT)	14,076	5.1
5	Doris Matsui (D)*	105,676	70.8
	Claire Yan (R)	35,106	23.5
6	Lynn Woolsey (D)*	173,190	70.2
	Todd Hooper (R)	64,405	26.1
7	George Miller (D)*	118,000	84.0
	Camden McConnell (LIBERT)	22,486	16.0
8	Nancy Pelosi (D)*	148,435	80.4
	Mike DeNunzio (R)	19,800	10.7
	Krissy Keefer (GREEN)	13,653	7.4
9	Barbara Lee (D)*	167,245	86.3
	John "J.D." denDulk (R)	20,786	10.7
10	Ellen O. Tauscher (D)*	130,859	66.4
	Darcy Linn (R)	66,069	33.5
11	Jerry McNerney (D)*	109,868	53.3
	Richard W. Pombo (R)	96,396	46.7
12	Tom Lantos (D)*	138,650	76.0
	Michael Moloney (R)	43,674	23.9
13	Pete Stark (D)*	110,756	74.9
	George I. Bruno (R)	37,141	25.1
14	Anna G. Eshoo (D)*	141,153	71.1
	Rob Smith (R)	48,097	24.2
15	Michael M. Honda (D)*	115,532	72.3
	Raymond L. Chukwu (R)	44,186	27.7
16	Zoe Lofgren (D)*	98,929	72.7
	Charel Winston (R)	37,130	27.3
17	Sam Farr (D)*	120,750	75.8
	Anthony R. De Maio (R)	35,932	22.6
18	Dennis Cardoza (D)*	71,182	65.5
	John A. Kanno (R)	37,531	34.5
19	George Radanovich (R)*	110,246	60.6
	TJ Cox (D)	71,748	39.4
20	Jim Costa (D)*	61,120	100.0

ABBREVIATIONS FOR PARTY DESIGNATIONS

C	Conservative	INDC	Independence
CFL:	Connecticut for Lieberman		
CNSTP	Constitution	L	Liberal
D	Democratic	LIBERT	Libertarian
GREEN	Green	R	Republican
I	Independent	REF	Reform

		Vote total	Percent
21	Devin Nunes (R)*	95,214	66.7
	Steven Haze (D)	42,718	29.9
22	Kevin McCarthy (R)	133,278	70.7
	Sharon M. Beery (D)	55,226	29.3
23	Lois Capps (D)*	114,661	65.2
	Victor D. Tognazzini (R)	61,272	34.8
24	Elton Gallegly (R)*	129,812	62.0
	Jill M. Martinez (D)	79,461	38.0
25	Howard P. "Buck" McKeon (R)*	93,987	60.0
	Robert Rodriguez (D)	55,913	35.7
26	David Dreier (R)*	102,028	57.0
	Cynthia Rodriguez Matthews (D)	67,878	37.9
27	Brad Sherman (D)*	92,650	68.8
	Peter Hankwitz (R)	42,074	31.2
28	Howard L. Berman (D)*	79,866	73.9
	Stanley Kimmel Kesselman (R)	20,629	19.1
29	Adam B. Schiff (D)*	91,014	63.5
	William J. Bodell (R)	39,321	27.4
	William M. Paparian (GREEN)	8,197	5.7
30	Henry A. Waxman (D)*	151,284	71.5
	David Nelson Jones (R)	55,904	26.4
31	Xavier Becerra (D)*	64,952	100.0
32	Hilda L. Solis (D)*	76,059	83.0
	Leland Faegre (LIBERT)	15,627	17.0
33	Diane Watson (D)*	113,715	100.0
34	Lucille Roybal-Allard (D)*	57,459	76.8
	Wayne Miller (R)	17,359	23.2
35	Maxine Waters (D)*	82,498	83.7
	Gordon Michael Mego (AMI)	8,343	8.5
	Paul T. Ireland (LIBERT)	7,665	7.8
36	Jane Harman (D)*	105,323	63.4
	Brian Gibson (R)	53,068	31.9
37	Juanita Millender-McDonald (D)*	80,716	82.4
	Herb Peters (LIBERT)	17,246	17.6
38	Grace F. Napolitano (D)*	75,181	75.3
	Sidney W. Street (R)	24,620	24.7
39	Linda T. Sánchez (D)*	72,149	65.9
	James L. Andion (R)	37,384	34.1
40	Ed Royce (R)*	100,995	66.8
	Florice Orea Hoffman (D)	46,418	30.7
41	Jerry Lewis (R)*	109,761	66.9
	Louie A. Contreras (D)	54,235	33.1
42	Gary G. Miller (R)*	129,720	100.0
43	Joe Baca (D)*	52,791	64.5
	Scott Folkens (R)	29,069	35.5
44	Ken Calvert (R)*	89,555	60.0
	Louis Vandenberg (D)	55,275	37.0
45	Mary Bono (R)*	99,638	60.7
	David Roth (D)	64,613	39.3
46	Dana Rohrabacher (R)*	116,176	59.6
	Jim Brandt (D)	71,573	36.7
47	Loretta Sanchez (D)*	47,134	62.3
	Tan Nguyen (R)	28,485	37.7
48	John Campbell (R)*	120,130	59.9
	Steve Young (D)	74,647	37.2
49	Darrell Issa (R)*	98,831	63.3
	Jeeni Criscenzo (D)	52,227	33.4
50	Brian P. Bilbray (R)*	118,018	53.1
	Francine Busby (D)	96,612	43.551
Bob Filner (D)*		78,114	67.4
	Blake L. Miles (R)	34,931	30.2
52	Duncan Hunter (R)*	123,696	64.6
	John Rinaldi (D)	61,208	32.0
53	Susan A. Davis (D)*	97,541	67.6
	John "Woody" Woodrum (R)	43,312	30.0

Colorado

		Vote total	Percent
Governor			
	Bill Ritter Jr. (D)	888,096	57.0
	Bob Beauprez (R)	625,886	40.2
House			
1	Diana DeGette (D)*	129,446	79.8
	Thomas D. Kelly (GREEN)	32,825	20.2
2	Mark Udall (D)*	157,850	68.2
	Rich Mancuso (R)	65,481	28.3
3	John Salazar (D)*	146,488	61.6
	Scott Tipton (R)	86,930	36.5
4	Marilyn Musgrave (R)*	109,732	45.6
	Angie Paccione (D)	103,748	43.1
	Eric Eidsness (REF)	27,133	11.3
5	Doug Lamborn (R)	123,264	59.6
	Jay Fawcett (D)	83,431	40.3
6	Tom Tancredo (R)*	158,806	58.6
	Bill Winter (D)	108,007	39.9
7	Ed Perlmutter (D)	103,918	54.9
	Rick O'Donnell (R)	79,571	42.1

Connecticut

		Vote total	Percent
Governor			
	M. Jodi Rell (R)*	710,048	63.2
	John DeStefano (D)	398,220	35.4
Senate			
	Joseph I. Lieberman (CFL)*	564,095	49.7
	Ned Lamont (D)	450,844	39.7
	Alan Schlesinger (R)	109,198	9.6
House			
1	John B. Larson (D)*	154,539	74.4
	Scott MacLean (R)	53,010	25.5
2	Joe Courtney (D)	121,248	50.0
	Rob Simmons (R)	121,165	50.0
3	Rosa DeLauro (D)*	150,436	76.0
	Joseph Vollano (R)	44,386	22.4
4	Christopher Shays (R)*	106,510	51.0
	Diane Farrell (D)	99,450	47.6
5	Christopher S. Murphy (D)	122,980	56.5
	Nancy L. Johnson (R)*	94,824	43.5

Delaware

		Vote total	Percent
Senate			
	Thomas R. Carper (D)*	170,567	67.1
	Jan Ting (R)	69,734	27.4
House			
AL	Michael N. Castle (R)*	143,897	57.2
	Denni Spivack (D)	97,565	38.8

Florida

		Vote total	Percent
Governor			
	Charlie Crist (R)*	2,519,845	52.2
	Jim Davis (D)	2,178,289	45.1
Senate			
	Bill Nelson (D)*	2,890,548	60.3
	Katherine Harris (R)	1,826,127	38.1
House			
1	Jeff Miller (R)*	135,786	68.5
	Jeff Roberts (D)	62,340	31.5
2	Allen Boyd (D)*	X	X
3	Corrine Brown (D)*	X	X
4	Ander Crenshaw (R)*	141,759	69.7
	Robert J. Harms (D)	61,704	30.3
5	Ginny Brown-Waite (R)*	162,421	59.9
	John Russell (D)	108,959	40.1
6	Cliff Stearns (R)*	136,601	59.9
	David E. Bruderly (D)	91,528	40.1
7	John L. Mica (R)*	149,656	63.1
	John F. Chagnon (D)	87,584	36.9
8	Ric Keller (R)*	95,258	52.8
	Charlie Stuart (D)	82,526	45.7
9	Gus Bilirakis (R)	123,016	55.9
	Phyllis Busansky (D)	96,978	44.1
10	C.W. Bill Young (R)*	131,488	65.9
	Samm Simpson (D)	67,950	34.1
11	Kathy Castor (D)	97,470	69.7
	Eddie Adams Jr. (R)	42,454	30.3
12	Adam H. Putnam (R)*	124,452	69.1
	Jo Viscusi (No party affiliation)	34,976	19.4
	Ed Bowlin (No party affiliation)	20,636	11.5
13	Vern Buchanan (R)	119,309	50.1
	Christine Jennings (D)	118,940	49.9
14	Connie Mack (R)*	151,615	64.4
	Robert M. Neeld (D)	83,920	35.6
15	Dave Weldon (R)*	125,965	56.3
	Bob Bowman (D)	97,834	43.7
16	Tim Mahoney (D)	115,832	49.5
	Joe Negron (R) (Mark Foley, R)[1]	111,415	47.7
17	Kendrick B. Meek (D)*	90,663	100.0
18	Ileana Ros-Lehtinen (R)*	79,631	62.1
	David "Big Dave" Patlak (D)	48,499	37.9
19	Robert Wexler (D)*		
20	Debbie Wasserman-Schultz (D)*		
21	Lincoln Diaz-Balart (R)*	66,784	59.5
	Frank J. Gonzalez (D)	45,522	40.5
22	Ron Klein (D)	108,688	50.9
	E. Clay Shaw Jr. (R)*	100,663	47.1
23	Alcee L. Hastings (D)*		
24	Tom Feeney (R)*	123,795	57.9
	Clint Curtis (D)	89,863	42.1
25	Mario Diaz-Balart (R)*	60,765	58.5
	Michael Calderin (D)	43,168	41.5

Georgia

		Vote total	Percent
Governor			
	Sonny Perdue (R)*	1,229,724	57.9
	Mark Taylor (D)	811,049	38.2

House

		Vote total	Percent
1	Jack Kingston (R)*	94,961	68.5
	Jim Nelson (D)	43,668	31.5
2	Sanford D. Bishop Jr. (D)*	88,662	67.9
	Bradley C. Hughes (R)	41,967	32.1
3	Lynn Westmoreland (R)*	130,428	67.6
	Mike McGraw (D)	62,371	32.4
4	Hank Johnson (D)	106,352	75.3
	Catherine Davis (R)	34,778	24.6
5	John Lewis (D)*	122,380	100.0
6	Tom Price (R)*	144,958	72.4
	Steve Sinton (D)	55,294	27.6
7	John Linder (R)*	130,561	70.9
	Allan Burns (D)	53,553	29.1
8	Jim Marshall (D)*	80,660	50.5
	Mac Collins (R)	78,908	49.5
9	Nathan Deal (R)*	128,685	76.6
	John D. Bradbury (D)	39,240	23.4
10	Charlie Norwood (R)*	117,721	67.4
	Terry Holley (D)	57,032	32.6
11	Phil Gingrey (R)*	118,524	71.1
	Patrick Samuel Pillion (D)	48,261	28.9
12	John Barrow (D)*	71,651	50.3
	Max Burns (R)	70,787	49.7
13	David Scott (D)*	103,019	69.2
	Deborah Travis Honeycutt (R)	45,770	30.8

Hawaii

		Vote total	Percent
Governor			
	Linda Lingle (R)*	215,313	62.5
	Randy Iwase (D)	121,717	35.4
Senate			
	Daniel K. Akaka (D)*	210,330	61.3
	Cynthia Thielen (R)	126,097	36.8
House			
1	Neil Abercrombie (D)*	112,904	69.4
	Richard "Noah" Hough (R)	49,890	30.6
2	Mazie K. Hirono (D)	106,906	61.0
	Bob Hogue (R)	68,244	39.0

Idaho

		Vote total	Percent
Governor			
	C. L. "Butch" Otter (R)	237,437	52.7
	Jerry M. Brady (D)	198,845	44.1
House			
1	Bill Sali (R)	115,843	49.9
	Larry E. Grant (D)	103,935	44.8
2	Mike Simpson (R)*	132,262	62.0
	Jim Hansen (D)	73,441	34.4

Illinois

		Vote total	Percent
Governor			
	Rod R. Blagojevich (D)*	1,736,731	49.8
	Judy Baar Topinka (R)	1,369,315	39.3
	Rich Whitney (GREEN)	361,336	10.4
House			
1	Bobby L. Rush (D)*	146,623	84.1
	Jason E. Tabor (R)	27,804	15.9
2	Jesse L. Jackson Jr. (D)*	146,347	84.8
	Robert Belin (R)	20,395	11.8
3	Daniel Lipinski (D)*	127,768	77.1
	Raymond G. Wardingley (R)	37,954	22.9
4	Luis V. Gutierrez (D)*	69,910	85.8
	Ann Melichar (R)	11,532	14.2
5	Rahm Emanuel (D)*	114,319	78.0
	Kevin Edward White (R)	32,250	22.0
6	Peter Roskam (R)	91,382	51.4
	Tammy Duckworth (D)	86,572	48.6
7	Danny K. Davis (D)*	143,071	86.7
	Charles Hutchinson (R)	21,939	13.3
8	Melissa Bean (D)*	93,355	50.9
	David McSweeney (R)	80,720	44.0
	William C. Scheurer	9,312	5.1
9	Jan Schakowsky (D)*	122,852	74.6
	Michael P. Shannon (R)	41,858	25.4
10	Mark Steven Kirk (R)*	107,929	53.4
	Daniel J. Seals (D)	94,278	46.6
11	Jerry Weller (R)*	109,009	55.1
	John Pavich (D)	88,846	44.9
12	Jerry F. Costello (D)*	157,802	100.0
13	Judy Biggert (R)*	119,720	58.3
	Joseph Shannon (D)	85,507	41.7
14	J. Dennis Hastert (R)*	117,870	59.8
	Jonathan "John" Laesch (D)	79,274	40.2
15	Timothy V. Johnson (R)*	116,810	57.6
	David Gill (D)	86,025	42.4
16	Donald Manzullo (R)*	125,951	63.6
	Richard D. Auman (D)	63,627	32.1
17	Phil Hare (D)	115,025	57.2
	Andrea Zinga (R)	86,161	42.8
18	Ray LaHood (R)*	150,194	67.3
	Steve Waterworth (D)	73,052	32.7
19	John Shimkus (R)*	143,491	60.7
	Danny L. Stover (D)	92,861	39.3

Indiana

		Vote total	Percent
Senate			
	Richard G. Lugar (R)*	1,171,553	87.4
	Steve Osborne (LIBERT)	168,820	12.6
House			
1	Peter J. Visclosky (D)*	104,195	69.7
	Mark J. Leyva (R)	40,146	26.8
2	Joe Donnelly (D)	103,561	54.0
	Chris Chocola (R)	88,300	46.0
3	Mark Souder (R)*	95,421	54.3
	Thomas Hayhurst (D)	80,357	45.7
4	Steve Buyer (R)*	111,057	62.4
	David Sanders (D)	66,986	37.6
5	Dan Burton (R)*	133,118	65.0
	Katherine Fox Carr (D)	64,362	31.4
6	Mike Pence (R)*	115,266	60.0
	Barry A. Welsh (D)	76,812	40.0
7	Julia Carson (D)*	74,750	53.8
	Eric Dickerson (R)	64,304	46.2
8	Brad Ellsworth (D)	131,019	61.0
	John Hostettler (R)*	83,704	39.0
9	Baron P. Hill (D)	110,454	50.0
	Mike Sodrel (R)*	100,469	45.5

Iowa

		Vote total	Percent
Governor			
	Chet Culver (D)	569,021	54.0
	Jim Nussle (R)	467,425	44.4
House			
1	Bruce Braley (D)	114,322	55.1
	Mike Whalen (R)	89,725	43.2
2	Dave Loebsack (D)	107,683	51.4
	Jim Leach (R)*	101,707	48.5
3	Leonard L. Boswell (D)*	115,769	51.8
	Jeff Lamberti (R)	103,722	46.5
4	Tom Latham (R)*	121,650	57.2
	Selden E. Spencer (D)	90,982	42.8
5	Steve King (R)*	105,580	58.5
	Joyce Schulte (D)	64,181	35.6

Kansas

		Vote total	Percent
Governor			
	Kathleen Sebelius (D)*	491,993	57.9
	Jim Barnett (R)	343,586	40.4
House			
1	Jerry Moran (R)*	156,728	78.6
	John Doll (D)	39,781	19.9
2	Nancy Boyda (D)	114,139	50.6
	Jim Ryun (R)*	106,329	47.1
3	Dennis Moore (D)*	153,105	64.6
	Chuck Ahner (R)	79,824	33.7
4	Todd Tiahrt (R)*	116,386	63.5
	Garth J. McGinn (D)	62,166	33.9

Kentucky

		Vote total	Percent
House			
1	Edward Whitfield (R)*	123,618	59.6
	Tom Barlow (D)	83,865	40.4
2	Ron Lewis (R)	118,548	55.4
	Mike Weaver (D)	95,415	44.6
3	John Yarmuth (D)	122,489	50.6
	Anne M. Northup (R)*	116,568	48.2
4	Geoff Davis (R)*	105,845	51.7
	Ken Lucas (D)	88,822	43.4
5	Harold Rogers (R)*	147,201	73.8
	Kenneth Stepp (D)	52,367	26.2
6	Ben Chandler (D)*	158,765	85.5
	Paul Ard (LIBERT)	27,015	14.5

Louisiana

		Vote total	Percent
House			
1	Bobby Jindal (R)*	130,508	88.1
	David Gereighty (D)	10,919	7.4
2	*Nov. 7 general*		
	William J. Jefferson (D)*	28,283	30.1
	Karen Carter (D)	20,364	21.7
	Derrick Shephard (D)	16,799	17.9
	Joseph "Joe" Lavigne (R)	12,511	13.3
	Troy C. Carter (D)	11,304	12.0
2	*Dec. 9 runoff*		
	William J. Jefferson (D)*	35,153	56.5
	Karen Carter (D)	27,011	43.5
3	Charlie Melancon (D)*	75,023	55.0
	Craig Romero (R)	54,950	40.3
4	Jim McCrery (R)*	77,078	57.4
	Artis R. Cash Sr. (D)	22,757	16.9

		Vote total	Percent
	Patti Cox (D)	17,788	13.2
	Chester T. Kelley (R)	16,649	12.4
5	Rodney Alexander (R)*	78,211	68.3
	Gloria Williams Hearn (D)	33,233	29.0
6	Richard H. Baker (R)*	94,658	82.8
	Richard M. Fontanesi (LIBERT)	19,648	17.2
7	Charles Boustany Jr. (R)*	113,720	70.7
	Mike Stagg (D)	47,133	29.3

Maine

		Vote total	Percent
Governor			
	John Baldacci (D)*	209,927	38.1
	Chandler E. Woodcock (R)	166,425	30.2
	Barbara Merrill (IMC)	118,715	21.6
	Patricia H. LaMarche (GREEN)	52,690	9.6
Senate			
	Olympia J. Snowe (R)*	402,598	74.0
	Jean M. Hay Bright (D)	111,984	20.6
	William H. Slavick (I)	29,220	5.4
House			
1	Tom Allen (D)*	170,949	60.8
	Darlene J. Curley (R)	88,009	31.3
	Dexter J. Kamilewicz (I)	22,029	7.8
2	Michael H. Michaud (D)*	179,732	70.5
	Laurence S. D'Amboise (R)	75,146	29.5

Maryland

		Vote total	Percent
Governor			
	Martin O'Malley (D)	942,279	52.7
	Robert L. Ehrlich Jr. (R)*	825,464	46.2
Senate			
	Benjamin L. Cardin (D)	965,477	54.2
	Michael S. Steele (R)	787,182	44.2
House			
1	Wayne T. Gilchrest (R)*	185,177	68.8
	Jim Corwin (D)	83,738	31.1
2	C.A. Dutch Ruppersberger (D)*	135,818	69.2
	Jimmy Mathis (R)	60,195	30.7
3	John Sarbanes (D)	150,142	64.0
	John White (R)	79,174	33.8
4	Albert R. Wynn (D)*	141,897	80.7
	Michael Moshe Starkman (R)	32,792	18.6
5	Steny H. Hoyer (D)*	168,114	82.7
	Steve Warner (GREEN)	33,464	16.5
6	Roscoe G. Bartlett (R)*	141,200	59.0
	Andrew Duck (D)	92,030	38.4
7	Elijah E. Cummings (D)*	158,830	98.1
8	Chris Van Hollen (D)*	168,872	76.5
	Jeffrey M. Stein (R)	48,324	21.9

Massachusetts

		Vote total	Percent
Governor			
	Deval L. Patrick (D)	1,234,984	55.6
	Kerry Healey (R)	784,342	35.3
	Christy Mihos (I)	154,628	7.0
Senate			
	Edward M. Kennedy (D)*	1,500,738	69.3
	Kenneth G. Chase (R)	661,532	30.5
House			
1	John W. Olver (D)*	158,057	76.4
	William H. Szych	48,574	23.5
2	Richard E. Neal (D)*	164,939	98.7
3	Jim McGovern (D)*	166,973	98.8
4	Barney Frank (D)*	176,513	98.5
5	Martin T. Meehan (D)*	159,120	98.7
6	John F. Tierney (D)*	168,056	69.5
	Richard W. Barton (R)	72,997	30.2
7	Edward J. Markey (D)*	171,902	98.3
8	Michael E. Capuano (D)*	125,515	90.7
	Laura Garza (SW)	12,449	9.0
9	Stephen F. Lynch (D)*	169,420	78.1
	Jack E. Robinson III (R)	47,114	21.7
10	Bill Delahunt (D)*	171,812	64.3
	Jeffrey K. Beatty (R)	78,439	29.4
	Peter A. White (I)	16,808	6.3

Michigan

		Vote total	Percent
Governor			
	Jennifer M. Granholm (D)*	2,142,513	56.4
	Dick DeVos (R)	1,608,086	42.3
Senate			
	Debbie Stabenow (D)*	2,151,278	57.0
	Mike Bouchard (R)	1,559,597	41.4
House			
1	Bart Stupak (D)*	180,448	69.4
	Don Hooper (R)	72,753	28.0
2	Peter Hoekstra (R)*	183,006	66.5
	Kimon Kotos (D)	86,950	31.6
3	Vernon J. Ehlers (R)*	171,212	63.1
	James Rinck (D)	93,846	34.6
4	Dave Camp (R)*	160,041	60.6
	Mike Huckleberry (D)	100,260	37.9
5	Dale E. Kildee (D)*	176,171	72.9
	Eric J. Klammer (R)	60,967	25.2
6	Fred Upton (R)*	142,125	60.6
	Kim Clark (D)	88,978	37.9
7	Tim Walberg (R)	122,348	49.9
	Sharon Marie Renier (D)	112,665	46.0
8	Mike Rogers (R)*	157,237	55.3
	Jim Marcinkowski (D)	122,107	42.9
9	Joe Knollenberg (R)*	142,390	51.6
	Nancy Skinner (D)	127,620	46.2
10	Candice S. Miller (R)*	179,072	66.2
	Robert Denison (D)	84,689	31.3
11	Thaddeus McCotter (R)*	143,658	54.1
	Tony Trupiano (D)	114,248	43.0
12	Sander M. Levin (D)*	168,494	70.2
	Randell J. Shafer (R)	62,689	26.1
13	Carolyn Cheeks Kilpatrick (D)*	126,308	100.0
14	John Conyers Jr. (D)*	158,755	85.3
	Chad Miles (R)	27,367	14.7
15	John D. Dingell (D)*	181,946	88.0

Minnesota

		Vote total	Percent
Governor			
	Tim Pawlenty (R)*	1,028,568	46.7
	Mike Hatch (D)	1,007,460	45.7
Senate			
	Amy Klobuchar (D)	1,278,849	58.1
	Mark Kennedy (R)	835,653	37.9
House			
1	Tim Walz (D)	141,556	52.7
	Gil Gutknecht (R)	126,486	47.1
2	John Kline (R)*	163,269	56.2
	Coleen Rowley (D)	116,343	40.0
3	Jim Ramstad (R)*	184,333	64.8
	Wendy Wilde (D)	99,588	35.0
4	Betty McCollum (D)*	172,096	69.5
	Obi Sium (R)	74,797	30.2
5	Keith Ellison (D)	136,060	55.6
	Alan Fine (R)	52,263	21.3
	Tammy Lee (INDC)	51,456	21.0
6	Michele Bachmann (R)	151,248	50.1
	Patty Wetterling (D)	127,144	42.1
	John Paul Binkowski (INDC)	23,557	7.8
7	Collin C. Peterson (D)*	179,164	69.7
	Michael J. Barrett (R)	74,557	29.0
8	James L. Oberstar (D)*	180,670	63.6
	Rod Grams (R)	97,683	34.4

Mississippi

		Vote total	Percent
Senate			
	Trent Lott (R)*	388,399	63.6
	Eric Fleming (D)	213,000	34.9
House			
1	Roger Wicker (R)*	95,098	65.9
	James K. "Ken" Hurt (D)	49,174	34.1
2	Bennie Thompson (D)*	100,160	64.3
	Yvonne E. Brown (R)	55,672	35.7
3	Charles W. "Chip" Pickering Jr. (R)*	125,421	77.7
	Jim Giles (I)	25,999	16.1
	Lamonica L. Magee (REF)	10,060	6.2
4	Gene Taylor (D)*	110,996	79.8
	Randy McDonnell (R)	28,117	20.2

Missouri

		Vote total	Percent
Senate			
	Claire McCaskill (D)	1,055,255	49.6
	Jim Talent (R)*	1,006,941	47.3
House			
1	William Lacy Clay (D)*	141,574	72.9
	Mark J. Byrne (R)	47,893	24.7
2	Todd Akin (R)*	176,452	61.3
	George D. "Boots" Weber (D)	105,242	36.6
3	Russ Carnahan (D)*	145,219	65.6
	David Bertelsen (R)	70,189	31.7
4	Ike Skelton (D)*	159,303	67.6
	James A. "Jim" Noland Jr. (R)	69,254	29.4
5	Emanuel Cleaver II (D)*	136,149	64.2
	Jacob Turk (R)	68,456	32.3
6	Sam Graves (R)*	150,882	61.6
	Mary Jo Shettles (D)	87,477	35.7

		Vote total	*Percent*
7	Roy Blunt (R)*	160,942	66.7
	Jack Truman (D)	72,592	30.1
8	Jo Ann Emerson (R)*	156,164	71.6
	Veronica J. Hambacker (D)	57,557	26.4
9	Kenny Hulshof (R)*	149,114	61.4
	Duane N. Burghard (D)	87,145	35.9

Montana

		Vote total	*Percent*
Senate			
	Jon Tester (D)	199,845	49.2
	Conrad Burns (R)*	196,283	48.3
House			
AL	Denny Rehberg (R)*	239,124	58.9
	Monica Lindeen (D)	158,916	39.1

Nebraska

		Vote total	*Percent*
Governor			
	Dave Heineman (R)*	435,507	73.4
	David Hahn (D)	145,115	24.5
Senate			
	Ben Nelson (D)*	378,388	63.9
	Pete Ricketts (R)	213,928	36.1
House			
1	Jeff Fortenberry (R)*	121,015	58.4
	Maxine Moul (D)	86,360	41.6
2	Lee Terry (R)*	99,475	54.7
	Jim Esch (D)	82,504	45.3
3	Adrian Smith (R)	113,687	55.0
	Scott Kleeb (D)	93,046	45.0

Nevada

		Vote total	*Percent*
Governor			
	Jim Gibbons (R)	279,003	47.9
	Dina Titus (D)	255,684	43.9
Senate			
	John Ensign (R)*	322,501	55.4
	Jack Carter (D)	238,796	41.0
House			
1	Shelley Berkley (D)*	85,025	64.8
	Kenneth Wegner (R)	40,917	31.2
2	Dean Heller (R)	117,168	50.3
	Jill Derby (D)	104,593	44.9
3	Jon Porter (R)*	102,232	48.5
	Tessa Hafen (D)	98,261	46.6

New Hampshire

		Vote total	*Percent*
Governor			
	John Lynch (D)*	298,760	74.0
	Jim Coburn (R)	104,288	25.8
House			
1	Carol Shea-Porter (D)	100,691	51.3
	Jeb Bradley (R)*	95,527	48.6
2	Paul W. Hodes (D)	108,743	52.7
	Charles Bass (R)*	94,088	45.6

New Jersey

		Vote total	*Percent*
Senate			
	Robert Menendez (D)*	1,200,843	53.4
	Thomas H. Kean Jr. (R)	997,775	44.3
House			
1	Robert E. Andrews (D)*	140,110	100.0
2	Frank A. LoBiondo (R)	111,245	61.6
	Viola Thomas-Hughes (D)*	64,279	35.6
3	H. James Saxton (R)*	122,559	58.4
	Rich Sexton (D)	86,113	41.0
4	Christopher H. Smith (R)*	124,482	65.7
	Carol E. Gay (D)	62,905	33.2
5	Scott Garrett (R)*	112,142	54.9
	Paul Aronsohn (D)	89,503	43.8
6	Frank Pallone Jr. (D)*	98,615	68.6
	Leigh-Ann Bellew (R)	43,539	30.3
7	Mike Ferguson (R)*	98,399	49.4
	Linda Stender (D)	95,454	48.0
8	Bill Pascrell Jr. (D)*	97,568	70.9
	Jose M. Sandoval (R)	39,053	28.4
9	Steven R. Rothman (D)*	105,853	71.5
	Vincent Micco (R)	40,879	27.6
10	Donald M. Payne (D)*	90,264	100.0
11	Rodney Frelinghuysen (R)*	126,085	71.6
	Tom Wyka (D)	47,414	26.9
12	Rush D. Holt (D)*	125,468	65.7
	Joseph S. Sinagra (R)	65,509	34.3
13	Albio Sires (D)	77,238	77.5

New Mexico

		Vote total	*Percent*
Governor			
	Bill Richardson (D)*	384,806	68.8
	John Dendahl (R)	174,364	31.2
Senate			
	Jeff Bingaman (D)*	394,365	70.6
	Allen W. McCulloch (R)	163,826	29.3
House			
1	Heather A. Wilson (R)*	105,986	50.2
	Patricia Madrid (D)	105,125	49.8
2	Steve Pearce (R)*	92,620	59.4
	Albert D. Kissling (D)	63,119	40.5
3	Tom Udall (D)	144,880	74.6
	Ronald L. Dolin (R)	49,219	25.4

New York

		Vote total	*Percent*
Governor			
	Eliot Spitzer (D)	3,086,709	69.6
	John J. Faso (R)	1,274,335	28.7
Senate			
	Hillary Rodham Clinton (D)*	3,008,428	67.0
	John Spencer (R)	1,392,189	31.0
House			
1	Timothy H. Bishop (D)*	104,360	62.2
	Italo A. Zanzi (R)	63,328	37.8
2	Steve Israel (D)*	105,276	70.4
	John W. Bugler (R)	44,212	29.6
3	Peter T. King (R)*	101,787	56.0
	David L. Mejias (D)	79,843	44.0
4	Carolyn McCarthy (D)*	101,861	64.9
	Martin W. Blessinger (R)	55,050	35.1
5	Gary L. Ackerman (D)*	77,190	100.0
6	Gregory W. Meeks (D)*	69,405	100.0
7	Joseph Crowley (D)*	63,997	84.0
	Kevin Brawley (R)	12,220	16.0
8	Jerrold Nadler (D)*	108,536	85.0
	Eleanor Friedman (R)	17,413	13.6
9	Anthony Weiner (D)*	71,762	100.0
10	Edolphus Towns (D)*	72,171	92.2
	Jonathan H. Anderson (R)	4,666	6.0
11	Yvette D. Clarke (D)	88,334	90.0
	Stephen Finger (R)	7,447	7.6
12	Nydia M. Velázquez (D)*	62,847	89.7
	Allan Romaguera (R)	7,182	10.3
13	Vito J. Fossella (R)*	59,334	56.8
	Stephen A. Harrison (D)	45,131	43.2
14	Carolyn B. Maloney (D)*	119,582	84.5
	Danniel Maio (R)	21,969	15.5
15	Charles B. Rangel (D)*	103,916	94.0
	Edward Daniels (R)	6,592	6.0
16	José E. Serrano (D)*	56,124	95.3
17	Eliot L. Engel (D)*	93,614	76.4
	Jim Faulkner (R)	28,842	23.6
18	Nita M. Lowey (D)*	124,256	70.7
	Richard A. Hoffman (R)	51,450	29.3
19	John Hall (D)	100,119	51.2
	Sue W. Kelly (R)*	95,359	48.8
20	Kirsten Gillibrand (D)	125,168	53.1
	John E. Sweeney (R)*	110,554	46.9
21	Michael R. McNulty (D)*	167,604	78.2
	Warren Redlich (R)	46,752	21.8
22	Maurice D. Hinchey (D)*	121,683	100.0
23	John M. McHugh (R)*	106,781	63.1
	Robert J. Johnson (D)	62,318	36.9
24	Michael Arcuri (D)	109,686	53.9
	Ray Meier (R)	91,504	45.0
25	James T. Walsh (R)*	110,525	50.8
	Dan Maffei (D)	107,108	49.2
26	Thomas M. Reynolds (R)*	109,257	52.0
	Jack Davis (D)	100,914	48.0
27	Brian Higgins (D)*	140,027	79.3
	Michael J. McHale (R)	36,614	20.7
28	Louise M. Slaughter (D)*	111,386	73.2
	John E. Donnelly (R)	40,844	26.8
29	John R. "Randy" Kuhl Jr. (R)*	106,077	51.4
	Eric Massa (D)	100,044	48.5

North Carolina

		Vote total	*Percent*
House			
1	G.K. Butterfield (D)*	82,510	100.0
2	Bob Etheridge (D)*	85,993	66.5
	Dan Mansell (R)	43,271	33.5
3	Walter B. Jones (R)*	99,519	68.6
	Craig Weber (D)	45,458	31.4
4	David E. Price (D)*	127,340	65.0
	Steve Acuff (R)	68,599	35.0
5	Virginia Foxx (R)*	96,138	57.2
	Roger Sharpe (D)	72,061	42.8
6	Howard Coble (R)*	108,433	70.8
	Rory Blake (D)	44,661	29.2
7	Mike McIntyre (D)*	101,787	72.8
	Shirley Davis (R)	38,033	27.2
8	Robin Hayes (R)*	60,926	50.1
	Larry Kissell (D)	60,597	49.9

		Vote total	*Percent*
9	Sue Myrick (R)*	106,206	66.5
	Bill Glass (D)	53,437	33.5
10	Patrick T. McHenry (R)*	94,179	61.8
	Richard Carsner (D)	58,214	38.2
11	Heath Shuler (D)	124,972	53.8
	Charles H. Taylor (R)*	107,342	46.2
12	Melvin Watt (D)*	71,345	67.0
	Ada M. Fisher (R)	35,127	33.0
13	Brad Miller (D)*	98,540	63.7
	Vernon L. Robinson (R)	56,120	36.3

North Dakota

		Vote total	*Percent*
Senate			
	Kent Conrad (D)*	150,146	68.8
	Dwight Grotberg (R)	64,417	29.5
House			
AL	Earl Pomeroy (D)*	142,934	65.7
	Matt Mechtel (R)	74,687	34.3

Ohio

		Vote total	*Percent*
Governor			
	Ted Strickland (D)	2,435,384	60.5
	J. Kenneth Blackwell (R)	1,474,285	36.6
Senate			
	Sherrod Brown (D)	2,257,369	56.2
	Mike DeWine (R)*	1,761,037	43.8
House			
1	Steve Chabot (R)*	105,680	52.2
	John Cranley (D)	96,584	47.8
2	Jean Schmidt (R)*	120,112	50.5
	Victoria Wulsin (D)	117,595	49.4
3	Michael R. Turner (R)*	127,978	58.5
	Richard Chema (D)	90,650	41.5
4	Jim Jordan (R)	129,958	60.0
	Richard E. Siferd (D)	86,678	40.0
5	Paul E. Gillmor (R)*	129,813	56.8
	Robin Weirauch (D)	98,544	43.1
6	Charlie Wilson (D)	135,628	62.1
	Chuck Blasdel (R)	82,848	37.9
7	David L. Hobson (R)*	137,899	60.6
	William R. Conner (D)	89,579	39.4
8	John A. Boehner (R)*	136,863	63.8
	Mort Meier (D)	77,640	36.2
9	Marcy Kaptur (D)*	153,880	73.6
	Bradley S. Leavitt (R)	55,119	26.4
10	Dennis J. Kucinich (D)*	138,393	66.4
	Michael D. Dovilla (R)	69,996	33.6
11	Stephanie Tubbs Jones (D)*	146,799	83.4
	Lindsey N. String (R)	29,125	16.6
12	Pat Tiberi (R)*	145,943	57.3
	Bob Shamansky (D)	108,746	42.7
13	Betty Sutton (D)	135,639	61.2
	Craig Foltin (R)	85,922	38.8
14	Steven C. La Tourette (R)*	144,069	57.6
	Lewis R. Katz (D)	97,753	39.1
15	Deborah Pryce (R)*	110,714	50.1
	Mary Jo Kilroy (D)	109,659	49.6
16	Ralph Regula (R)*	137,167	58.3
	Thomas Shaw (D)	97,955	41.7
17	Tim Ryan (D)*	170,369	80.3
	Don Manning II (R)	41,925	19.7
18	Zack Space (D)	129,646	62.1
	Joy Padgett (R)	79,259	37.9

Oklahoma

		Vote total	*Percent*
Governor			
	Brad Henry (D)*	616,135	66.5
	Ernest Istook (R)	310,327	33.5
House			
1	John Sullivan (R)*	116,920	63.6
	Alan Gentges (D)	56,724	30.9
	Bill Wortman (I)	10,085	5.5
2	Dan Boren (D)*	122,347	72.7
	Patrick K. Miller (R)	45,861	27.3
3	Frank D. Lucas (R)*	128,042	67.5
	Sue Barton (D)	61,749	32.5
4	Tom Cole (R)*	118,266	64.6
	Hal Spake (D)	64,775	35.4
5	Mary Fallin (R)	108,936	60.4
	David Hunter (D)	67,293	37.3

Oregon

		Vote total	*Percent*
Governor			
	Theodore R. Kulongoski (D)*	699,786	50.7
	Ron Saxton (R)	589,748	42.8
House			
1	David Wu (D)*	169,409	62.8
	Derrick Kitts (R)	90,904	33.7
2	Greg Walden (R)*	181,529	66.8
	Carol Voisin (D)	82,484	30.4
3	Earl Blumenauer (D)*	186,380	73.5
	Bruce Broussard (R)	59,529	23.5
4	Peter A. DeFazio (D)*	180,607	62.2
	Jim Feldkamp (R)	109,105	37.6
5	Darlene Hooley (D)*	146,973	54.0
	Mike Erickson (R)	116,424	42.8

Pennsylvania

		Vote total	*Percent*
Governor			
	Edward G. Rendell (D)*	2,470,517	60.4
	Lynn Swann (R)	1,622,135	39.6
Senate			
	Bob Casey (D)	2,392,984	58.7
	Rick Santorum (R)*	1,684,778	41.3
House			
1	Robert A. Brady (D)*	137,987	100.0
2	Chaka Fattah (D)*	165,867	88.6
	Michael Gessner (R)	17,291	9.2
3	Phil English (R)*	108,525	53.6
	Steven Porter (D)	85,110	42.1
4	Jason Altmire (D)	131,847	51.9
	Melissa A. Hart (R)	122,049	48.1
5	John E. Peterson (R)*	115,126	60.1
	Donald L. Hilliard (D)	76,456	39.9
6	Jim Gerlach (R)*	121,047	50.7
	Lois Murphy (D)	117,892	49.3
7	Joe Sestak (D)	147,898	56.4
	Curt Weldon (R)*	114,426	43.6
8	Patrick J. Murphy (D)	125,656	50.3
	Michael G. Fitzpatrick (R)*	124,138	49.7
9	Bill Shuster (R)*	121,069	60.3
	Tony Barr (D)	79,610	39.7
10	Christopher Carney (D)	110,115	52.9
	Don Sherwood (R)*	97,862	47.1
11	Paul E. Kanjorski (D)*	134,340	72.5
	Joseph F. Leonardi (R)	51,033	27.5
12	John P. Murtha (D)*	123,472	60.8
	Diana Irey (R)	79,612	39.2
13	Allyson Y. Schwartz (D)*	147,368	66.1
	Raj Peter Bhakta (R)	75,492	33.9
14	Mike Doyle (D)*	161,075	90.1
	Titus North (GREEN)	17,720	9.9
15	Charlie Dent (R)*	106,153	53.6
	Charles Dertinger (D)	86,186	43.5
16	Joe Pitts (R)*	115,741	56.6
	Lois K. Herr (D)	80,915	39.5
17	Tim Holden (D)*	137,253	64.5
	Matthew A. Wertz (R)	75,455	35.5
18	Tim Murphy (R)*	144,632	57.8
	Chad Kluko (D)	105,419	42.2
19	Todd R. Platts (R)*	142,512	64.0
	Philip J. Avillo Jr. (D)	74,625	33.5

Rhode Island

		Vote total	*Percent*
Governor			
	Donald L. Carcieri (R)*	197,366	51.0
	Charles J. Fogarty (D)	189,562	49.0
Senate			
	Sheldon White**House** (D)	206,110	53.5
	Lincoln Chafee (R)*	179,001	46.4
House			
1	Patrick J. Kennedy (D)*	124,676	69.2
	Jonathan P. Scott (R)	41,856	23.2
	Kenneth A. Capalbo (I)	13,638	7.6
2	Jim Langevin (D)*	140,352	72.6
	Rodney D. Driver (I)	52,743	27.3

South Carolina

		Vote total	*Percent*
Governor			
	Mark Sanford (R)*	601,868	55.1
	Tommy Moore (D)	489,076	44.8
House			
1	Henry E. Brown Jr. (R)*	115,766	59.7
	Randy Maatta (D)	73,218	37.7
2	Joe Wilson (R)*	127,811	62.6
	Michael Ray Ellisor (D)	76,090	37.3
3	J. Gresham Barrett (R)*	111,882	62.9
	Lee Ballenger (D)	66,039	37.1
4	Bob Inglis (R)*	115,553	64.2
	William Griff Griffith (D)	57,490	31.9
5	John M. Spratt Jr. (D)*	99,669	56.9
	Ralph Norman (R)	75,422	43.1
6	James E. Clyburn (D)*	100,213	64.4
	Gary McLeod (R)	53,181	34.1

South Dakota

		Vote total	*Percent*
Governor			
	Michael Rounds (R)*	206,990	61.7
	Jack Billion (D)	121,226	36.1

	Vote total	Percent
House		
AL Stephanie Herseth-Sandlin (D)*	230,468	69.1
Bruce W. Whalen (R)	97,864	29.3

Tennessee

	Vote total	Percent
Governor		
Phil Bredesen (D)	1,247,491	68.6
Jim Bryson (R)	540,853	29.7
Senate		
Bob Corker (R)	929,911	50.7
Harold E. Ford Jr. (D)	879,976	48.0
House		
1 David Davis (R)	108,336	61.1
Rick Trent (D)	65,538	37.0
2 John J. "Jimmy" Duncan Jr. (R)*	157,095	77.7
John Greene (D)	45,025	22.3
3 Zach Wamp (R)*	130,791	65.7
Brent Benedict (D)	68,324	34.3
4 Lincoln Davis (D)*	123,666	66.4
Kenneth Martin (R)	62,449	33.5
5 Jim Cooper (D)*	122,919	69.0
Thomas F. Kovach (R)	49,702	27.9
6 Bart Gordon (D)*	129,069	67.1
David R. Davis (R)	60,392	31.4
7 Marsha Blackburn (R)*	152,288	66.0
Bill Morrison (D)	73,369	31.8
8 John Tanner (D)*	129,610	73.2
John Farmer (R)	47,492	26.8
9 Steve Cohen (D)	103,341	59.9
Jake Ford (I)	38,243	22.2
Mark White (R)	31,002	18.0

Texas

	Vote total	Percent
Governor		
Rick Perry (R)*	1,716,792	39.0
Chris Bell (D)	1,310,337	29.8
Carole Keeton Strayhorn (I)	796,851	18.1
Richard S. "Kinky" Friedman (I)	547,674	12.4
Senate		
Kay Bailey Hutchison (R)*	2,661,789	61.7
Barbara Ann Radnofsky (D)	1,555,202	36.0
House		
1 Louie Gohmert (R)*	104,099	68.0
Roger L. Owen (D)	46,303	30.2
2 Ted Poe (R)*	90,490	65.6
Gary E. Binderim (D)	45,080	32.7
3 Sam Johnson (R)*	88,690	62.5
Dan Dodd (D)	49,529	34.9
4 Ralph M. Hall (R)*	106,495	64.4
Glenn Melancon (D)	55,278	33.4
5 Jeb Hensarling (R)*	88,478	61.8
Charlie Thompson (D)	50,983	35.6
6 Joe L. Barton (R)*	91,927	60.5
David T. Harris (D)	56,369	37.1
7 John Culberson (R)*	99,318	59.2
Jim Henley (D)	64,514	38.5
8 Kevin Brady (R)*	105,665	67.3
James "Jim" Wright (D)	51,393	32.7
9 Al Green (D)*	60,253	100.0
10 Michael McCaul (R)*	97,726	55.3
Ted Ankrum (D)	71,415	40.4
11 K. Michael Conaway (R)*	107,268	100.0
12 Kay Granger (R)*	98,371	66.9
John R. Morris (D)	45,676	31.1
13 William M. "Mac" Thornberry (R)*	108,107	74.4
Roger J. Waun (D)	33,460	23.0
14 Ron Paul (R)*	94,380	60.2
Shane Sklar (D)	62,429	39.8
15 Rubén Hinojosa (D)*	43,236	61.8
Paul B. Haring (R)	16,601	23.7
Eddie Zamora (R)	10,150	14.5
16 Silvestre Reyes (D)*	61,116	78.7
Gordon R. Strickland (LIBERT)	16,572	21.3
17 Chet Edwards (D)*	92,478	58.1
Van Taylor (R)	64,142	40.3
18 Sheila Jackson-Lee (D)*	65,936	76.6
Ahmad R. Hassan (R)	16,448	19.1
19 Randy Neugebauer (R)*	94,785	67.7
Robert Ricketts (D)	41,676	29.8
20 Charlie Gonzalez (D)*	68,348	87.4
Michael Idrogo (LIBERT)	9,897	12.6
21 Lamar Smith (R)*	122,486	60.1
John Courage (D)	49,957	24.5
Gene Kelly (D)	18,355	9.0
22 Nick Lampson (D)	76,775	51.8
Shelley Sekula-Gibbs (R)	61,938	41.8
M. Bob Smither (LIBERT)	9,009	6.1
23 *Nov. 7 general*		
Henry Bonilla (R)*	60,175	48.6
Ciro D. Rodriguez (D)	24,594	19.9
Albert Uresti (D)	14,552	11.8
Lukin Gilliland (D)	13,728	11.1
23 *Dec. 12 runoff*		
Ciro D. Rodriguez (D)	38,256	54.3
Henry Bonilla (R)*	32,217	45.7
24 Kenny Marchant (R)*	83,835	59.8
Gary R. Page (D)	52,075	37.2
25 Lloyd Doggett (D)*	109,911	67.3
Grant Rostig (R)	42,975	26.3
26 Michael C. Burgess (R)*	94,219	60.2
Tim Barnwell (D)	58,271	37.2
27 Solomon P. Ortiz (D)*	62,058	56.8
William "Willie" Vaden (R)	42,538	38.9
28 Henry Cuellar (D)*	52,574	67.6
Frank Enriquez (D)	15,798	20.3
Ron Avery (C)	9,383	12.1
29 Gene Green (D)*	37,174	73.5
Eric Story (R)	12,347	24.4
30 Eddie Bernice Johnson (D)*	81,348	80.2
Wilson Aurbach (R)	17,850	17.6
31 John Carter (R)*	90,869	58.5
Mary Beth Harrell (D)	60,293	38.8
32 Pete Sessions (R)*	71,461	56.4

Utah

	Vote total	Percent
Senate		
Orrin G. Hatch (R)*	356,238	62.4
Pete Ashdown (D)	177,459	31.1
Scott N. Bradley (CNSTP)	21,526	3.8
House		
1 Rob Bishop (R)*	112,546	63.1
Steven Olsen (D)	57,922	32.5
2 Jim Matheson (D)*	133,231	59.0
LaVar Christensen (R)	84,234	37.3
3 Chris Cannon (R)*	95,455	57.7
Christian Burridge (D)	53,330	32.2
Jim Noorlander (CNSTP)	14,533	8.8

Vermont

	Vote total	Percent
Governor		
Jim Douglas (R)*	148,014	56.4
Scudder Parker (D)	108,090	41.2
Senate		
Bernard Sanders (I)*	171,638	65.4
Rich Tarrant (R)	84,924	32.4
House		
AL Peter Welch (D)	139,815	53.2
Martha Rainville (R)	117,023	44.5

Virginia

	Vote total	Percent
Senate		
Jim Webb (D)	1,175,606	49.6
George Allen (R)*	1,166,277	49.2
House		
1 Jo Ann Davis (R)*	143,889	63.0
Shawn M. O'Donnell (D)	81,083	35.5
2 Thelma Drake (R)*	88,777	51.3
Phil Kellam (D)	83,901	48.5
3 Robert C. Scott (D)*	133,546	96.1
4 J. Randy Forbes (R)*	150,967	76.1
Albert P. Burckard Jr. (IGREEN)	46,487	23.4
5 Virgil H. Goode Jr. (R)*	125,370	59.1
Al Weed (D)	84,682	39.9
6 Robert W. Goodlatte (R)*	153,187	75.1
Barbara Jean Pryor (I)	25,129	12.3
Andre D. Peery (I)	24,731	12.1
7 Eric Cantor (R)*	163,706	63.9
James M. Nachman (D)	88,206	34.4
8 James P. Moran (D)*	144,700	66.4
Tom M. O'Donoghue (R)	66,639	30.6
9 Rick Boucher (D)*	129,705	67.8
C.W. "Bill" Carrico (R)	61,574	32.2
10 Frank R. Wolf (R)*	138,213	57.3
Judy M. Feder (D)	98,769	41.0
11 Thomas M. Davis III (R)*	130,468	55.5
Andrew L. Hurst (D)	102,511	43.6

Washington

	Vote total	Percent
Senate		
Maria Cantwell (D)*	1,184,659	56.9
Mike McGavick (R)	832,106	39.9
House		
1 Jay Inslee (D)*	163,832	67.7
Larry W. Ishmael (R)	78,105	32.3
2 Rick Larsen (D)*	157,064	64.2
Doug Roulstone (R)	87,730	35.8
3 Brian Baird (D)*	147,065	63.1
Michael Messmore (R)	85,915	36.9

	Vote total	Percent
4 Doc Hastings (R)*	115,246	59.9
Richard Wright (D)	77,054	40.1
5 Cathy McMorris Rodgers (R)*	134,967	56.4
Peter J. Goldmark (D)	104,357	43.6
6 Norm Dicks (D)*	158,202	70.6
Doug Cloud (R)	65,883	29.4
7 Jim McDermott (D)*	195,462	79.4
Steve Beren (R)	38,715	15.7
8 Dave Reichert (R)*	129,362	51.5
Darcy Burner (D)	122,021	48.5
9 Adam Smith (D)*	119,038	65.7
Steven C. Cofchin (R)	62,082	34.3

West Virginia

	Vote total	Percent
Senate		
Robert C. Byrd (D)*	296,276	64.4
John R. Raese (R)	155,043	33.7
House		
1 Alan B. Mollohan (D)*	100,939	64.3
Chris Wakim (R)	55,963	35.6
2 Shelley Moore Capito (R)*	94,110	57.2
Mike Callaghan (D)	70,470	42.8
3 Nick J. Rahall II (D)*	92,413	69.4
Kim Wolfe (R)	40,820	30.6

Wisconsin

	Vote total	Percent
Governor		
James E. Doyle (D)*	1,139,115	52.7
Mark Green (R)	979,427	45.3
Senate		
Herb Kohl (D)*	1,439,214	67.3
Robert Gerald Lorge (R)	630,299	29.5
House		
1 Paul D. Ryan (R)*	161,320	62.6
Jeffrey C. Thomas (D)	95,761	37.2
2 Tammy Baldwin (D)*	191,414	62.8
Dave Magnum (R)	113,015	37.1
3 Ron Kind (D)*	163,322	64.8
Paul R. Nelson (R)	88,523	35.1
4 Gwen Moore (D)*	136,735	71.3
Perfecto Rivera (R)	54,486	28.4
5 F. James Sensenbrenner Jr. (R)*	194,669	61.8
Bryan Kennedy (D)	112,451	35.7
6 Tom Petri (R)*	201,367	98.9
7 David R. Obey (D)*	161,903	62.2
Nick Reid (R)	91,069	35.0
8 Steve Kagen (D)	141,570	50.9
John Gard (R)	135,622	48.8

Wyoming

	Vote total	Percent
Governor		
Dave Freudenthal (D)*	135,516	70.0
Ray Hunkins (R)	58,100	30.0
Senate		
Craig Thomas (R)*	135,174	70.1
Dale Groutage (D)	57,671	29.9
House		
AL Barbara Cubin (R)*	93,336	48.3
Gary Trauner (D)	92,324	47.8

1. Mark Foley resigned from the House in late September 2006, too late to have his name removed from the ballot. Votes cast for Foley were credited to Joe Negron, the candidate selected by the Republican Party to replace Foley.

110th Congress Special Elections, 2007 Gubernatorial Elections

Special House Elections, 110th Congress

	Vote total	Percent
California 12th CD–April 8, 2008		
Jackie Speier (D)	66,279	77.7
Greg Conlon (R)	7,990	11.0
Mike Maloney (R)	4,517	6.4
Michelle T. McMurry (D)	4,546	5.9
California 37th CD–Aug. 21, 2007		
Laura Richardson (D)	15,559	67.0
John M. Kanaley (R)	5,837	25.1
Daniel Brezenoff (GREEN)	1,274	5.5
Georgia 10th CD–July 17, 2007		
Paul Broun (R)	23,529	50.4
Jim Whitehead (D)	23,135	49.6
Illinois 14th CD–March 8, 2008		
Bill Foster (D)	52,205	52.5
Jim Oberweis (R)	47,180	47.5
Indiana 7th CD–March 11, 2008		
Andre Carson (D)	45,668	54.0
Jon Elrod (R)	36,415	43.1
Louisiana 1st CD–May 3, 2008		
Steve Scalise (R)	33,867	75.1
Gilda Reed (D)	10,142	22.5

Louisiana 6th CD–May 3, 2008	Vote total	Percent
Don Cazayoux (D)	49,703	49.2
Louis "Woody" Jenkins (R)	46,746	46.3
Maryland 4th CD–June 17, 2008		
Donna Edwards (D)	16,481	80.5
Peter James (R)	3,638	17.8
Massachusetts 5th CD–Oct. 16, 2007		
Niki Tsongas (D)	54,359	51.3
Jim Ogonowski (R)	47,782	45.1
Mississippi 1st CD–May 13, 2008		
Travis W. Childers (D)	58,037	53.8
Greg Davis (R)	49,877	46.2
Ohio 5th CD–Dec. 11, 2007		
Robert Latta (R)	56,114	57.0
Robin Weirauch (D)	42,229	42.9
Ohio 11th CD–Nov. 18, 2008		
Marcia L. Fudge (D)	8,597	100.0
Virginia 1st CD–Dec. 11,2007		
Robert J. Wittman (R)	42,772	60.8
Philip R. Forgit (D)	26,282	37.3

Special Senate Elections, 110th Congress

None

2007 Gubernatorial Elections

	Vote total	Percent
Kentucky		
Steve Beshear (D)	619,552	58.7
Ernie Fletcher (R)	435,773	41.3
Louisiana[1]		
Bobby Jindal (R)	699,275	53.9
Democratic candidates	397,755	30.6
Mississippi		
Haley Barbour (R)	430,807	57.9
John A. Eaves (D)	313,232	45.8

NOTE: Vote totals are included for all candidates listed on the ballot who received 5 percent or more of the total vote.

1. In Louisiana for state offices such as governor, all candidates regardless of party ran together on the October 2007 ballot. Jindal, the only Republican on the ballot, won a majority of the vote and was elected. The other five candidates were all Democrats. Together they collected 397,755 votes.

2008 Elections Returns for Governor, Senate, and House

Following are the official vote returns for the gubernatorial, Senate, and House races based on figures supplied by the fifty state election boards.

Vote totals are included for all candidates listed on the ballot who received 5 percent or more of the total vote. For candidates who received under 5 percent, consult *America Votes 27* (2007–2008), published by CQ Press. The percent column shows the percentage of the total vote cast.

An asterisk (*) indicates an incumbent.

An "X" denotes candidates without major part opposition; no votes were tallied.

An "AL" indicates an at-large member of Congress in a state with a single congressional district.

		Vote total	*Percent*
Alabama			
Senate			
	Jeff Sessions (R)*	1,305,383	63.4
	Vivian Davis Figures (D)	752,391	36.5
House			
1	Jo Bonner (R)*	210,660	98.3
2	Bobby N. Bright (D)	144,368	50.2
	Jay Love (R)	142,578	49.6
3	Mike D. Rogers (R)*	142,708	54.0
	Joshua Segall (D)	121,080	45.8
4	Robert B. Aderholt (R)*	196,741	74.8
	Nicholas B. Sparks (D)	66,077	25.1
5	Parker Griffith (D)	158,324	51.5
	Wayne Parker (R)	147,314	47.9
6	Spencer Bachus (R)*	280,902	67.8
7	Artur Davis (D)*	228,518	98.6
Alaska			
Senate			
	Mark Begich (D)	151,767	47.8
	Ted Stevens (R)*	147,814	46.5
House			
AL	Don Young (R)*	158,939	50.1
	Ethan Berkowitz (D)	142,560	45.0
Arizona			
House			
1	Ann Kirkpatrick (D)	155,790	55.9
	Sydney Hay (R)	109,924	39.4
2	Trent Franks (R)*	200,918	59.4
	John Thrasher (D)	125,611	37.2
3	John Shadegg (R)*	148,800	54.1
	Bob Lord (D)	115,759	42.1
4	Ed Pastor (D)*	89,729	72.1
	Don Karg (R)	26,435	21.2
5	Harry E. Mitchell (D)*	149,033	53.2
	David Schweikert (R)	122,165	43.6
6	Jeff Flake (R)*	208,582	62.4
	Rebecca Schneider (D)	115,457	34.5
7	Raúl M. Grijalva (D)*	124,304	63.3
	Joseph Sweeney (R)	64,425	32.8
8	Gabrielle Giffords (D)*	179,629	54.7
	Timothy S. Bee (R)	140,533	42.8
Arkansas			
Senate			
	Mark Pryor (D)	804,678	79.5
	Rebekah Kennedy (GREEN)	207,076	20.5
House			
1	Marion Berry (D)*	X	X
2	Vic Snyder (D)*	212,303	76.5
	Deb McFarland (GREEN)	65,063	23.2
3	John Boozman (R)*	215,196	78.5
	Abel Noah Tomlinson (GREEN)	58,850	21.5
4	Mike Ross (D)*	203,178	86.2
	Joshua Drake (GREEN)	32,603	13.8
California			
House			
1	Mike Thompson (D)*	197,812	68.1
	Zane Starkewolf (R)	67,853	23.4
	Carol Wolman (GREEN)	24,793	8.5
2	Wally Herger (R)*	163,459	57.9
	Jeff Morris (D)	118,878	42.1
3	Dan Lungren (R)*	155,424	49.5
	Bill Durston (D)	137,971	43.9
4	Tom McClintock (R)	185,790	50.2
	Charlie Brown (D)	183,990	49.8
5	Doris Matsui (D)*	164,242	74.3
	Paul A. Smith (R)	46,002	20.8
6	Lynn Woolsey (D)*	229,672	71.7
	Mike Halliwell (R)	77,073	24.1
7	George Miller (D)*	170,692	72.8
	Roger Allen Petersen (R)	51,166	21.8
8	Nancy Pelosi (D)*	204,966	71.9
	Cindy Sheehan (I)	46,118	16.2
	Dana Walsh (R)	27,614	9.7
9	Barbara Lee (D)*	238,915	86.1
	Charles Hargrave (R)	26,917	9.7
10	Ellen O. Tauscher (D)*	192,226	65.1
	Nicholas Gerber (R)	91,877	31.1
11	Jerry McNerney (D)*	164,500	55.3
	Dean Andal (R)	133,104	44.7
12	Jackie Speier (D)*	200,442	75.1
	Greg Conlon (R)	49,258	18.5
13	Pete Stark (D)*	166,829	76.4
	Raymond Chui (R)	51,447	23.6
14	Anna G. Eshoo (D)*	60,610	69.8
	Ronny Santana (R)	21,855	22.2
15	Michael M. Honda (D)*	170,977	71.7
	Joyce Stoer Cordi (R)	55,489	23.3
	Peter Myers (GREEN)	12,123	5.1
16	Zoe Lofgren (D)*	146,481	71.3
	Charel Winston (R)	49,399	24.1
17	Sam Farr (D)*	168,907	73.9
	Jeff Taylor (R)	59,037	25.8
18	Dennis Cardoza (D)*	130,192	100.0
19	George Radanovich (R)*	179,245	98.4
20	Jim Costa (D)*	93,023	74.3
	Jim Lopez (R)	32,118	25.7
21	Devin Nunes (R)*	143,489	68.4
	Larry Johnson (D)	66,317	31.6
22	Kevin McCarthy (R)*	224,549	100.0
23	Lois Capps (D)*	171,403	68.1
	Matt T. Kokkonen (R)	80,385	31.9
24	Elton Gallegly (R)*	174,495	58.2
	Marta Ann Jorgensen (D)	125,560	41.8
25	Howard P. "Buck" McKeon (R)*	144,660	57.7
	Jackie Conaway (D)	105,929	42.3
26	David Dreier (R)*	140,615	52.6
	Russ Warner (D)	108,039	40.4
	Ted Brown (LIBERT)	18,476	6.9
27	Brad Sherman (D)*	145,812	68.5
	Navraj Singh (R)	52,852	24.8
	Tim Denton (LIBERT)	14,171	6.7
28	Howard L. Berman (D)*	137,471	99.9
29	Adam B. Schiff (D)*	146,198	68.9
	Charles Hahn (R)	56,727	26.7
30	Henry A. Waxman (D)*	242,792	100.0

ABBREVIATIONS FOR PARTY DESIGNATIONS

C	Conservative	INDC	Independence
CNSTP	Constitution	L	Liberal
D	Democratic	LIBERT	Libertarian
GREEN	Green	R	Republican
I	Independent		

		Vote total	Percent
31	Xavier Becerra (D)*	110,955	100.0
32	Hilda L. Solis (D)*	130,142	100.0
33	Diane Watson (D)*	186,924	87.6
	David C. Crowley II (R)	26,536	12.4
34	Lucille Roybal-Allard (D)*	98,503	77.1
	Christopher Balding (R)	29,266	22.9
35	Maxine Waters (D)*	150,778	82.6
	Ted Hayes (R)	24,169	13.2
36	Jane Harman (D)*	171,948	68.6
	Brian Gibson (R)	78,543	31.4
37	Laura Richardson (D)*	131,342	74.9
	Nicholas "Nick" Dibs (I)	42,774	24.4
38	Grace F. Napolitano (D)*	130,211	81.7
	Christopher M. Agrella (LIBERT)	29,113	18.3
39	Linda T. Sánchez (D)*	125,289	69.7
	Diane A. Lenning (R)	54,533	30.3
40	Ed Royce (R)*	144,923	62.5
	Christina Avalos (D)	86,772	37.5
41	Jerry Lewis (R)*	159,486	61.6
	Tim Prince (D)	99,214	38.4
42	Gary G. Miller (R)*	158,404	60.2
	Edwin "Ed" Chau (D)	104,909	39.8
43	Joe Baca (D)*	108,259	69.1
	John Roberts (R)	48,312	30.9
44	Ken Calvert (R)*	129,937	51.2
	Bill Hedrick (D)	123,890	48.8
45	Mary Bono Mack (R)*	155,166	58.3
	Julie Bornstein (D)	111,026	41.7
46	Dana Rohrabacher (R)*	149,818	52.5
	Debbie Cook (D)	122,891	43.1
47	Loretta Sanchez (D)*	85,878	69.5
	Rosemarie "Rosie" Avila (R)	31,432	25.4
	Robert Lauten (AMI)	6,274	5.1
48	John Campbell (R)*	171,658	55.6
	Steve Young (D)	125,537	40.7
49	Darrell Issa (R)*	140,300	58.3
	Robert Hamilton (D)	90,138	37.5
50	Brian P. Bilbray (R)*	157,502	50.2
	Nick Leibham (D)	141,635	45.2
51	Bob Filner (D)*	148,281	72.7
	David Lee Joy (R)	49,345	24.2
52	Duncan Hunter (R)	160,724	56.4
	Mike Lumpkin (D)	111,051	38.9
53	Susan A. Davis (D)*	161,315	68.5
	Michael Crimmins (R)	64,658	27.5

Colorado

Senate

		Vote total	Percent
	Mark Udall (D)	1,231,049	52.8
	Bob Schaffer (R)	990,784	42.5

House

		Vote total	Percent
1	Diana DeGette (D)*	203,755	71.9
	George C. Lilly (R)	67,345	23.8
2	Jared Polis (D)	215,571	62.6
	Scott Starin (R)	116,591	33.9
3	John Salazar (D)*	203,455	61.6
	Wayne Wolf (R)	126,762	38.4
4	Betsy Markey (D)	187,347	56.2
	Marilyn Musgrave (R)*	146,028	43.8
5	Doug Lamborn (R)*	183,178	60.0
	Hal Bidlack (D)	113,025	37.0
6	Mike Coffman (R)	250,877	60.7
	Hank Eng (D)	162,639	39.3
7	Ed Perlmutter (D)*	173,931	63.5
	John W. Lerew (R)	100,055	36.5

Connecticut

House

		Vote total	Percent
1	John B. Larson (D)*	211,493	71.6
	Joe Visconti (R)	76,860	26.0
2	Joe Courtney (D)*	212,148	65.7
	Sean Sullivan (R)	104,574	32.4
3	Rosa DeLauro (D)*	230,172	77.4
	Bo Itshaky (R)	58,583	19.7
4	Jim Himes (D)	158,475	51.3
	Christopher Shays (R)*	146,854	47.6
5	Christopher S. Murphy (D)*	179,327	59.3
	David J. Cappiello (R)	117,914	39.0

Delaware

Governor

		Vote total	Percent
	Jack Markell (D)	266,858	67.5
	William Swain Lee (R)*	126,660	32.0

Senate

		Vote total	Percent
	Joseph R. Biden Jr. (D)*	257,539	64.7
	Christine O'Donnell (R)	140,595	35.3

House

		Vote total	Percent
AL	Michael N. Castle (R)*	235,437	61.1
	Karen Hartley-Nagle (D)	146,434	38.0

Florida

		Vote total	Percent
1	Jeff Miller (R)*	232,559	70.2
	James "Jim" Bryan (D)	98,797	29.8
2	Allen Boyd (D)*	216,804	61.9
	Mark Mulligan (R)	133,404	38.1
3	Corrine Brown (D)*	X	X
4	Ander Crenshaw (R)*	224,112	65.3
	Jay McGovern (D)	119,330	34.7
5	Ginny Brown-Waite (R)*	265,186	61.2
	John Russell (D)	168,446	38.8
6	Cliff Stearns (R)*	228,302	60.9
	Tim Cunha (D)	146,655	39.1
7	John L. Mica (R)*	238,721	62.0
	Faye Armitage (D)	146,292	38.0
8	Alan Grayson (D)	172,854	52.0
	Ric Keller (R)*	159,490	48.0
9	Gus Bilirakis (R)*	216,591	62.2
	Bill Mitchell (D)	126,346	36.3
10	C.W. Bill Young (R)*	182,781	60.7
	Bob Hackworth (D)	118,430	39.3
11	Kathy Castor (D)*	184,106	71.7
	Eddie Adams Jr. (R)	72,825	28.3
12	Adam H. Putnam (R)*	185,698	57.5
	Doug Tudor (D)	137,465	42.5
13	Vern Buchanan (R)*	204,382	55.5
	Christine Jennings (D)	137,967	37.5
	Jan Schneider (No party affiliation)	20,289	7.0
14	Connie Mack (R)*	224,602	59.4
	Robert M. Neeld (D)	93,560	24.8
	Burt Saunders (No party affiliation)	54,750	15.8
15	Bill Posey (R)	192,151	53.1
	Stephen Blythe (D)	151,951	42.0
16	Tom Rooney (R)	209,874	60.1
	Tim Mahoney (D)*	139,373	39.9
17	Kendrick B. Meek (D)*		
18	Ileana Ros-Lehtinen (R)*	140,617	57.9
	Annette Taddeo (D)	102,372	42.1
19	Robert Wexler (D)*	202,465	66.2
	Edward J. Lynch (R)	83,357	27.2
	Ben Graber (No party affiliation)	20,214	6.6
20	Debbie Wasserman-Schultz (D)*	202,832	77.5
	Margaret Hostetter (No party affiliation)	58,958	22.5
21	Lincoln Diaz-Balart (R)*	137,226	57.9
	Raúl L. Martinez (D)	99,776	42.1
22	Ron Klein (D)*	169,041	54.7
	Allen West (R)	140,104	45.3
23	Alcee L. Hastings (D)*	172,835	82.2
	Marion D. Thorpe Jr. (R)	37,431	17.8
24	Suzanne Kosmas (D)	211,284	57.2
	Tom Feeney (R)*	151,863	41.1
25	Mario Diaz-Balart (R)*	130,891	53.1
	Joe Garcia (D)	115,820	46.9

Georgia

Senate

		Vote total	Percent
	Saxby Chambliss (R)	1,867,097	49.8
	Jim Martin (D)	1,757,393	46.8
Dec. 2 runoff[†]			
	Saxby Chambliss (R)	1,228,033	57.4
	Jim Martin (D)	909,923	42.6

House

		Vote total	Percent
1	Jack Kingston (R)*	165,890	66.5
	Bill Gillespie (D)	83,444	33.5
2	Sanford D. Bishop Jr. (D)*	158,435	68.9
	Lee Ferrell (R)	71,351	31.1
3	Lynn Westmoreland (R)*	225,055	65.7
	Stephen Camp (D)	117,522	34.3
4	Hank Johnson (D)*	224,494	99.9
5	John Lewis (D)*	231,368	100.0
6	Tom Price (R)*	231,520	68.5
	Bill Jones (D)	106,551	31.5
7	John Linder (R)*	209,354	62.0
	Doug Heckman (D)	128,159	38.0
8	Jim Marshall (D)*	157,241	57.2
	Rick Goddard (R)	117,446	42.8
9	Nathan Deal (R)*	217,493	75.5
	Jeff Scott (D)	70,537	24.5
10	Paul Broun (R)*	177,265	60.7
	Bobby Saxon (D)	114,638	39.3
11	Phil Gingrey (R)*	204,082	68.2
	Hugh "Bud" Gammon (D)	95,220	31.8
12	John Barrow (D)*	164,562	66.0
	John Stone (R)	84,773	34.0
13	David Scott (D)*	205,919	69.0
	Deborah Honeycutt (R)	92,320	31.0

Hawaii

House

		Vote total	Percent
1	Neil Abercrombie (D)*	154,208	77.1
	Steve Tataii (R)	38,115	19.1

	Vote total	Percent
2 Mazie K. Hirono (D)*	165,748	76.1
Roger B. Evans (R)	44,425	20.4

Idaho

	Vote total	Percent
Senate		
Jim Risch (R)	371,744	57.6
Larry LaRocco (D)	219,903	34.1
Rex Rammell (I)	34,510	5.4
House		
1 Walt Minnick (D)	175,898	50.6
Bill Sali (R)*	171,687	49.4
2 Mike Simpson (R)*	205,777	71.0
Deborah Holmes (D)	83,878	29.0

Illinois

	Vote total	Percent
Senate		
Richard J. Durbin (D)*	3,615844	67.8
Steve Sauerberg (R)	1,520,621	28.5
House		
1 Bobby L. Rush (D)*	233,036	85.9
Antoine Members (R)	38,361	14.1
2 Jesse L. Jackson Jr. (D)*	251,052	89.4
Anthony W. Williams (R)	29,721	10.6
3 Daniel Lipinski (D)*	172,581	73.3
Michael Hawkins (R)	50,336	21.4
Jerome Pohlen (GREEN)	12,607	5.4
4 Luis V. Gutierrez (D)*	112,529	80.6
Daniel Cunningham (R)	16,024	11.5
Omar López (GREEN)	9,283	7.9
5 Rahm Emanuel (D)*	170,728	73.9
Tom Hanson (R)	50,881	22.0
6 Peter Roskam (R)*	147,906	57.6
Jill Morgenthaler (D)	109,007	42.4
7 Danny K. Davis (D)*	235,343	85.0
Steve Miller (R)	41,474	15.0
8 Melissa Bean (D)*	179,444	60.7
Steve Greenberg (R)	116,081	39.3
9 Jan Schakowsky (D)*	181,948	74.7
Michael Benjamin Younan (R)	53,593	22.0
10 Mark Steven Kirk (R)*	153,082	52.6
Dan Seals (D)	138,176	47.4
11 Debbie Halvorson (D)	185,652	58.4
Marty Ozinga (R)	109,608	34.5
Jason M. Wallace (GREEN)	22,635	7.1
12 Jerry F. Costello (D)*	212,891	71.4
Timmy Jay Richardson Jr. (R)	74,382	24.9
13 Judy Biggert (R)*	180,888	53.6
Scott Harper (D)	147,430	43.6
14 Bill Foster (D)*	185,404	57.7
Jim Oberweis (R)	135,653	42.3
15 Timothy V. Johnson (R)*	187,121	64.2
Steve Cox (D)	104,393	35.8
16 Donald Manzullo (R)*	190,039	60.9
Robert G. Abboud (D)	112,648	36.1
17 Phil Hare (D)*	220,961	99.8
18 Aaron Schock (R)	182,589	58.9
Colleen Callahan (D)	117,642	37.9
19 John Shimkus (R)*	203,434	64.5
Daniel Davis (D)	105,338	37.9

Indiana

	Vote total	Percent
Governor		
Mitch Daniels (R)*	1,563,885	57.8
Jill Long Thompson (D)	1,082,463	40.0
House		
1 Peter J. Visclosky (D)*	199,954	70.9
Mark Leyva (R)	76,647	27.2
2 Joe Donnelly (D)*	187,416	67.1
Luke Puckett (R)	84,455	30.2
3 Mark Souder (R)*	155,693	55.0
Michael Montagano (D)	112,309	39.7
William Larsen (LIBERT)	14,877	5.3
4 Steve Buyer (R)*	192,526	59.9
Nels Ackerson (D)	129,038	40.1
5 Dan Burton (R)*	234,705	65.5
Mary Etta Ruley (D)	123,357	34.5
6 Mike Pence (R)*	180,608	64.0
Barry A. Welsh (D)	94,265	33.4
7 André Carson (D)*	172,650	65.1
Gabrielle Campo (R)	92,645	34.9
8 Brad Ellsworth (D)*	188,693	64.7
Greg Goode (R)	102,840	35.3
9 Baron P. Hill (D)*	181,281	64.7
Mike Sodrel (R)	120,517	38.4

Iowa

	Vote total	Percent
Senate		
Tom Harkin (D)*	941,665	62.7
Christopher Reed (R)	560,006	37.3
House		
1 Bruce Braley (D)*	186,991	64.6
David Hartsuch (R)	102,439	35.4
2 Dave Loebsack (D)*	176,904	57.2
Mariannette Miller-Meeks (R)	118,778	38.8
3 Leonard L. Boswell (D)*	176,904	56.3
Kim Schmett (R)	132,136	42.1
4 Tom Latham (R)*	185,458	60.5
Becky Greenwald (D)	120,746	39.4
5 Steve King (R)*	159,430	59.8
Rob Hubler (D)	99,601	37.4

Kansas

	Vote total	Percent
Senate		
Pat Roberts (R)*	727,121	60.1
Jim Slattery (D)	441,399	36.5
House		
1 Jerry Moran (R)*	214,549	81.9
James Bordonaro (D)	34,377	13.3
2 Lynn Jenkins (R)	155,532	50.6
Nancy Boyda (D)*	142,013	46.2
3 Dennis Moore (D)*	202,541	56.4
Nick Jordan (R)	142,307	39.7
4 Todd Tiahrt (R)*	177,617	63.4
Donald Betts Jr. (D)	90,706	39.7

Kentucky

	Vote total	Percent
Senate		
Mitch McConnell (R)*	953,816	53.0
Bruce Lunsford (D)	847,005	47.0
House		
1 Ed Whitfield (R)*	178,107	64.3
Heather A. Ryan (D)	98,674	35.7
2 Brett Guthrie (R)	158,936	52.6
David E. Boswell (D)	143,379	47.4
3 John Yarmuth (D)*	203,843	59.4
Anne M. Northup (R)	139,527	40.6
4 Geoff Davis (R)*	190,210	63.0
Michael Kelley (D)	111,549	37.0
5 Harold Rogers (R)*	177,024	84.1
Jim Holbert (I)	33,444	15.9
6 Ben Chandler (D)*	203,764	64.7
Jon Larson (R)	111,378	35.3

Louisiana

	Vote total	Percent
Senate		
Mary L. Landrieu (D)*	988,298	52.1
John Kennedy (R)	867,177	45.7
House		
1 Steve Scalise (R)*	189,168	65.7
Jim Harlan (D)	98,839	34.3
2 William J. Jefferson (D)*[2]	92,921	56.8
Helena Moreno (D)	70,705	43.2
Anh "Joseph" Cao (R)	X	X
Dec. 6 runoff		
Anh "Joseph" Cao (R)	33,132	49.5
William J. Jefferson (D)*	31,318	46.8
3 Charlie Melancon (D)*	X	X
4 Paul J. Carmouche (D)[3]	93,093	62.0
Willie Banks (D)	57,078	38.1
Dec. 6 runoff		
John Fleming (R)	44,501	48.1
Paul J. Carmouche (D)	44,151	47.7
5 Rodney Alexander (R)*	X	X
6 Bill Cassidy (R)	150,332	48.1
Don Cazayoux (D)*	125,866	40.3
Michael Jackson (I)	36,198	11.6
7 Charles Boustany Jr. (R)*	177,173	61.9
Donald "Don" Cravins Jr. (D)	98,280	34.3

Maine

	Vote total	Percent
Senate		
Susan Collins (R)*	444,300	61.3
Tom Allen (D)	279,510	38.6
House		
1 Chellie Pingree (D)	205,629	54.9
Charlie Summers (R)	168,930	45.1
2 Michael H. Michaud (D)*	226,274	67.4
John N. Frary (R)	109,268	32.6

Maryland

	Vote total	Percent
House		
1 Frank M. Kratovil Jr. (D)	177,065	49.1
Andy Harris (R)	174,213	48.3
2 C.A. Dutch Ruppersberger (D)*	198,578	71.9
Richard Pryce Matthews (R)	68,561	24.8
3 John Sarbanes (D)*	230,711	69.7
Thomas "Pinkston" Harris (R)	87,971	30.1
4 Donna Edwards (D)*	28,704	85.8
Peter James (R)	38,739	12.9
5 Steny H. Hoyer (D)*	253,854	73.6
Collins Bailey (R)	82,631	24.0

		Vote total	Percent
6	Roscoe G. Bartlett (R)*	190,926	57.8
	Jennifer P. Dougherty (D)	128,207	38.8
7	Elijah E. Cummings (D)*	227,379	79.5
	Michael T. Hargadon (R)	53,147	18.6
8	Chris Van Hollen (D)*	229,740	75.1
	Steve Hudson (R)	66,351	21.7

Massachusetts

Senate

		Vote total	Percent
	John Kerry (D)*	1,971,974	65.9
	Jeffrey K. Beatty (R)	926,044	30.9

House

		Vote total	Percent
1	John W. Olver (D)*	215,696	72.8
	Nathan A. Bech (R)	80,067	27.0
2	Richard E. Neal (D)*	234,369	98.5
3	Jim McGovern (D)*	227,619	98.5
4	Barney Frank (D)*	203,032	68.0
	Earl Henry Sholley (R)	75,571	25.3
	Susan Allen (I)	19,848	6.8
5	Niki Tsongas (D)*	225,947	98.7
6	John F. Tierney (D)*	226,216	70.4
	Richard A. Baker (R)	94,845	29.5
7	Edward J. Markey (D)*	212,304	75.6
	John Cunningham (R)	67,978	24.2
8	Michael E. Capuano (D)*	185,530	98.6
9	Stephen F. Lynch (D)*	242,166	98.7
10	Bill Delahunt (D)*	272,899	98.6

Michigan

Senate

		Vote total	Percent
	Carl Levin (D)	3,038,386	62.7
	Jack Hoogendyk Jr. (R)	1,641,070	33.8

House

		Vote total	Percent
1	Bart Stupak (D)*	213,216	65.0
	Tom Casperson (R)	107,340	32.7
2	Peter Hoekstra (R)*	214,100	62.4
	Fred Johnson (D)	119,506	34.8
3	Vernon J. Ehlers (R)*	203,799	61.1
	Henry Sanchez (D)	117,961	35.4
4	Dave Camp (R)*	204,259	61.9
	Andrew D. Concannon (D)	117,665	35.7
5	Dale E. Kildee (D)*	221,841	70.4
	Matt Sawicki (R)	85,017	27.0
6	Fred Upton (R)*	188,157	58.9
	Don Cooney (D)	123,257	38.6
7	Mark Schauer (D)	157,213	48.8
	Tim Walberg (R)*	149,781	46.5
8	Mike Rogers (R)*	204,408	56.6
	Robert D. Alexander (D)	145,491	40.2
9	Gary Peters (D)	183,311	52.1
	Joe Knollenberg (R)*	150,035	42.6
10	Candice S. Miller (R)*	230,471	66.3
	Robert Denison (D)	108,354	31.2
11	Thaddeus McCotter (R)*	177,461	51.4
	Joseph W. Larkin (D)	156,625	45.4
12	Sander M. Levin (D)*	225,094	72.1
	Bert Copple (R)	74,565	23.9
13	Carolyn Cheeks Kilpatrick (D)*	167,481	74.1
	Edward J. Gubics (R)	43,098	19.1
14	John Conyers Jr. (D)*	227,841	92.4
15	John D. Dingell (D)*	231,784	70.7
	John J. Lynch (R)	81,802	25.0

Minnesota

Senate

		Vote total	Percent
	Al Franken (D)	1,212,629	42.0
	Norm Coleman (R)	1,212,317	42.0
	Dean Barkley (INDC)	437,505	15.2

House

		Vote total	Percent
1	Tim Walz (D)*	207,753	62.5
	Brian J. Davis (R)	109,453	32.9
2	John Kline (R)*	220,924	57.3
	Steve Sarvi (D)	164,093	42.6
3	Erik Paulsen (R)	178,932	48.5
	Ashwin Madia (D)	150,787	40.9
	David Dillon (INDC)	38,970	10.7
4	Betty McCollum (D)*	216,267	68.4
	Ed Matthews (R)	98,939	31.3
5	Keith Ellison (D)*	228,766	70.9
	Barb Davis White (R)	71,020	22.0
	Bill McGaughey (INDC)	22,318	6.9
6	Michele Bachmann (R)*	187,817	46.4
	El Tinklenberg (D)	175,786	43.4
	Bob Anderson (INDC)	40,643	10.0
7	Collin C. Peterson (D)*	227,187	72.2
	Glen Menze (R)	87,062	27.7
8	James L. Oberstar (D)*	241,831	67.7
	Michael Cummins (R)	114,871	32.2

Mississippi

Senate

		Vote total	Percent
	Roger Wicker (R)	683,409	55.0
	Ronnie Musgrove (D)	560,064	45.0
	Thad Cochran (R)	766,111	61.4
	Erik Fleming (D)	480,915	38.6

House

		Vote total	Percent
1	Travis W. Childers (D)*	185,959	54.5
	Greg Davis (R)	149,818	49.3
2	Bennie Thompson (D)*	201,646	69.1
	Richard Cook (R)	90,364	30.9
3	Gregg Harper (R)	213,171	62.5
	Joel Gill (D)	127,698	37.5
4	Gene Taylor (D)*	216,542	74.5
	John McCay III (R)	73,977	25.5

Missouri

Governor

		Vote total	Percent
	Jay Nixon (D)	1,680,611	58.4
	Kenny Hulshof (R)	1,136,364	39.5

House

		Vote total	Percent
1	William Lacy Clay (D)*	242,570	86.9
	Robb E. Cunningham (LIBERT)	36,700	13.1
2	Todd Akin (R)*	232,276	62.3
	William C. "Bill" Haas (D)	132,068	35.4
3	Russ Carnahan (D)*	202,470	66.4
	Chris Sander (R)	92,759	30.4
4	Ike Skelton (D)*	200,009	65.9
	Jeff Parnell (R)	103,446	34.1
5	Emanuel Cleaver II (D)*	197,249	64.4
	Jacob Turk (R)	109,166	35.6
6	Sam Graves (R)*	196,526	59.4
	Kay Barnes (D)	121,894	36.9
7	Roy Blunt (R)*	219,016	67.8
	Richard Monroe (D)	91,010	28.2
8	Jo Ann Emerson (R)*	198,798	71.4
	Joe Allen (D)	72,790	26.2
9	Blaine Luetkemeyer (R)	161,031	50.0
	Judy Baker (D)	152,956	47.5

Montana

Governor

		Vote total	Percent
	Brian Schweitzer (D)	316,670	65.5
	Roy Brown (R)	158,268	32.5

Senate

		Vote total	Percent
	Max Baucus (D)*	348,289	72.9
	Bob Kelleher (R)	129,369	27.1

House

		Vote total	Percent
AL	Denny Rehberg (R)*	307,177	64.2
	John Driscoll (D)	154,710	32.4

Nebraska

Senate

		Vote total	Percent
	Mike Johanns (R)	455,854	57.5
	Scott Kleeb (D)	317,456	40.1

House

		Vote total	Percent
1	Jeff Fortenberry (R)*	184,923	70.4
	Max Yashirin (D)	77,897	29.6
2	Lee Terry (R)*	142,473	51.9
	Jim Esch (D)	131,901	48.1
3	Adrian Smith (R)*	183,117	76.9
	Jay C. Stoddard (D)	55,087	23.1

Nevada

House

		Vote total	Percent
1	Shelley Berkley (D)*	154,860	67.6
	Kenneth Wegner (R)	64,837	28.3
2	Dean Heller (R)*	170,771	51.8
	Jill Derby (D)	136,548	41.4
3	Dina Titus (D)	165,192	48.1
	Jon Porter (R)*	147,940	43.1

New Hampshire

Governor

		Vote total	Percent
	John Lynch (D)*	479,042	70.1
	Joe Kenney (R)	188,555	27.6

Senate

		Vote total	Percent
	Jeanne Shaheen (D)	358,438	51.6
	John E. Sununu (R)*	314,403	45.3

House

		Vote total	Percent
1	Carol Shea-Porter (D)*	176,435	51.8
	Jeb Bradley (R)	156,338	45.8
2	Paul W. Hodes (D)*	188,332	56.4
	Jennifer M. Horn (R)	138,222	41.4

New Jersey

Senate

		Vote total	Percent
	Frank R. Lautenberg (D)*	1,951,218	56.0
	Dick Zimmer (R)	1,461,025	42.0

House

		Vote total	Percent
1	Robert E. Andrews (D)*	206,453	72.4
	Dale M. Glading (R)	74,001	26.0
2	Frank A. LoBiondo (R)*	167,701	59.1
	David Kurkowski (D)	110,990	39.1
3	John Adler (D)	166,390	52.1
	Chris Myers (R)	153,122	47.9

		Vote total	*Percent*
4	Christopher H. Smith (R)*	202,972	66.2
	Joshua M. Zeitz (D)	100,036	32.6
5	Scott Garrett (R)*	172,653	55.9
	Dennis Shulman (D)	131,033	42.4
6	Frank Pallone Jr. (D)*	164,077	66.9
	Robert McLeod (R)	77,469	31.6
7	Leonard Lance (R)	148,461	50.2
	Linda Stender (D)	124,818	42.2
	Michael P. Hsing (I)	16,419	5.6
8	Bill Pascrell Jr. (D)*	159,279	71.1
	Roland Straten (R)	63,107	28.2
9	Steven R. Rothman (D)*	151,182	67.5
	Vincent Micco (R)	69,503	31.0
10	Donald M. Payne (D)*	169,945	98.9
11	Rodney Frelinghuysen (R)*	189,696	61.8
	Tom Wyka (D)	113,510	37.0
12	Rush D. Holt (D)*	193,732	63.1
	Alan R. Bateman (R)	108,400	35.3
13	Albio Sires (D)*	120,382	75.4
	Joseph Turula (R)	34,735	21.7

New Mexico

		Vote total	*Percent*
Senate			
	Tom Udall (D)	505,128	61.3
	Steve Pearce (R)	318,522	38.7
House			
1	Martin Heinrich (D)	166,271	55.7
	Darren White (R)	132,485	44.3
2	Harry Teague (D)	129,572	56.0
	Ed Tinsley (R)	101,980	44.0
3	Ben Ray Luján (D)	161,292	56.7
	Daniel K. East (R)	86,618	30.5
	Carol Miller (I)	36,348	12.8

New York

		Vote total	*Percent*
House			
1	Timothy H. Bishop (D)*	162,083	58.4
	Lee M. Zeldin (R)	115,545	41.6
2	Steve Israel (D)*	161,279	66.9
	Frank J. Staltzer (R)	79,641	33.1
3	Peter T. King (R)*	172,774	63.9
	Graham E. Long (D)	97,525	36.1
4	Carolyn McCarthy (D)*	164,028	64.0
	Jack M. Martins (R)	92,242	36.0
5	Gary L. Ackerman (D)*	112,724	71.0
	Elizabeth Berney (R)	43,039	27.1
6	Gregory W. Meeks (D)*	141,180	100.0
7	Joseph Crowley (D)*	118,459	84.6
	William E. Britt Jr. (R)	21,477	15.3
8	Jerrold Nadler (D)*	160,775	80.5
	Grace Lin (R)	39,062	19.5
9	Anthony Weiner (D)*	112,205	93.0
	Alfred F. Donohue (C)	8,384	7.0
10	Edolphus Towns (D)*	155,090	94.2
	Salvatore Grupico (R)	9,565	5.8
11	Yvette D. Clarke (D)*	168,562	92.8
	Hugh C. Carr (R)	11,644	6.4
12	Nydia M. Velázquez (D)*	123,053	89.9
	Allan Romaguera (R)	13,748	10.0
13	Michael E. McMahon (D)	114,219	60.9
	Robert A. Straniere (R)	62,441	33.3
14	Carolyn B. Maloney (D)*	183,239	79.9
	Robert G. Heim (R)	43,385	18.9
15	Charles B. Rangel (D)*	177,151	89.2
	Edward Daniels (R)	15,676	7.9
16	José E. Serrano (D)*	127,179	96.6
17	Eliot L. Engel (D)*	161,594	79.9
	Robert Goodman (R)	40,707	20.1
18	Nita M. Lowey (D)*	174,791	68.5
	Jim Russell (R)	80,498	31.5
19	John Hall (D)*	164,859	58.7
	Kieran Michael Lalor (R)	116,120	41.3
20	Kirsten Gillibrand (D)*	193,651	62.1
	Sandy Treadwell (R)	118,031	37.9
21	Paul Tonko (D)	171,286	62.1
	James Buhrmaster (R)	96,599	35.0
22	Maurice D. Hinchey (D)*	168,558	66.4
	George K. Phillips (R)	85,126	33.6
23	John M. McHugh (R)*	143,029	65.3
	Michael P. Oot (D)	75,871	34.7
24	Michael Arcuri (D)*	130,799	52.0
	Richard Hanna (R)	120,880	48.0
25	Dan Maffei (D)	157,375	54.8
	Dale A. Sweetland (R)	120,217	41.9
26	Christopher Lee (R)	148,607	54.8
	Alice Kryzan (D)	109,615	41.9
27	Brian Higgins (D)*	185,713	74.4
	Daniel J. Humiston (R)	56,354	22.6
28	Louise M. Slaughter (D)*	172,655	78.0
	David W. Crimmen (R)	48,690	22.0
29	Eric Massa (D)	140,529	51.0
	John "Randy" Kuhl Jr. (R)*	135,199	49.0

North Carolina

		Vote total	*Percent*
Governor			
	Beverly Perdue (D)	2,146,189	50.3
	Pat McCrory (R)	2,001,168	46.9
Senate			
	Kay Hagan (D)	2,249,311	52.7
	Elizabeth Dole (R)*	1,887,510	44.2
House			
1	G.K. Butterfield (D)*	192,765	70.3
	Dean Stephens (R)	81,506	29.7
2	Bob Etheridge (D)*	199,730	66.9
	Dan Mansell (R)	93,323	31.3
3	Walter B. Jones (R)*	201,686	65.9
	Craig Weber (D)	104,364	34.1
4	David E. Price (D)*	265,751	63.3
	William "B. J." Lawson (R)	153,947	36.7
5	Virginia Foxx (R)*	190,820	58.4
	Roy Carter (D)	136,103	41.6
6	Howard Coble (R)*	221,018	67.0
	Teresa Sue Bratton (D)	108,873	33.3
7	Mike McIntyre (D)*	215,383	68.8
	Will Breazeale (R)	97,472	31.2
8	Larry Kissell (D)	157,185	55.4
	Robin Hayes (R)*	126,634	44.6
9	Sue Myrick (R)*	241,053	62.4
	Harry Taylor (D)	138,719	35.9
10	Patrick T. McHenry (R)*	171,774	57.6
	Daniel Johnson (D)	126,699	42.4
11	Heath Shuler (D)*	122,087	62.0
	Carl Mumpower (R)	211,112	35.8
12	Melvin Watt (D)*	215,908	71.6
	Ty Cobb Jr. (R)	85,814	28.4
13	Brad Miller (D)*	221,379	65.9
	Hugh Webster (R)	114,373	34.1

North Dakota

		Vote total	*Percent*
Governor			
	John Hoeven (R)*	235,009	74.4
	Tim Mathern (D)	74,279	23.5
House			
AL	Earl Pomeroy (D)*	194,175	62.1
	Duane Sand (R)	118,519	37.9

Ohio

		Vote total	*Percent*
House			
1	Steve Driehaus (D)	155,455	52.5
	Steve Chabot (R)*	140,683	47.5
2	Jean Schmidt (R)*	148,671	44.8
	Victoria Wulsin (D)	124,213	37.5
	David H. Krikorian (I)	58,740	17.7
3	Michael R. Turner (R)*	200,204	63.3
	Jane Mitakides (D)	115,976	36.7
4	Jim Jordan (R)*	186,154	65.2
	Mike Carroll (D)	99,499	34.8
5	Robert E. Latta (R)*	188,905	64.1
	George F. Mays (D)	105,840	35.9
6	Charlie Wilson (D)*	176,330	62.3
	Richard D. Stobbs (R)	92,968	32.8
7	Steve Austria (R)	174,915	58.2
	Sharen Swartz Neuhardt (D)	125,547	41.8
8	John A. Boehner (R)*	202,063	67.9
	Nicholas A. Von Stein (D)	95,510	32.1
9	Marcy Kaptur (D)*	222,054	74.4
	Bradley S. Leavitt (R)	76,512	25.6
10	Dennis J. Kucinich (D)*	157,268	57.0
	Jim Trakas (R)	107,918	39.1
11	Marcia L. Fudge (D)	212,667	85.2
	Thomas Pekarek (R)	36,708	14.7
12	Pat Tiberi (R)*	197,447	54.8
	David Robinson (D)	152,234	42.2
13	Betty Sutton (D)*	192,593	64.7
	David Potter (R)	105,050	35.3
14	Steven C. LaTourette (R)*	188,488	58.3
	Bill O'Neill (D)	125,214	38.7
15	Mary Jo Kilroy (D)	139,584	45.9
	Steve Stivers (R)	137,272	45.2
16	John Boccieri (D)	169,044	55.4
	Kirk Schuring (R)	136,293	44.6
17	Tim Ryan (D)*	218,896	78.1
	Duane V. Grassell (R)	61,216	21.9
18	Zack Space (D)*	164,187	78.2
	Fred Dailey (R)	110,031	40.1

Oklahoma

		Vote total	*Percent*
Senate			
	James M. Inhofe (R)*	763,375	56.7
	Andrew Rice (D)	527,736	39.2
House			
1	John Sullivan (R)*	193,404	66.2
	Georgianna W. Oliver (D)	98,890	33.8
2	Dan Boren (D)*	173,757	70.5
	Raymond J. Wickson (R)	72,815	29.5
3	Frank D. Lucas (R)*	184,306	69.7
	Frankie Robbins (D)	62,297	23.6
	Forrest Michael (I)	17,756	6.7

	Vote total	Percent
4 Tom Cole (R)*	180,080	66.0
Blake Cummings (D)	79,674	29.2
5 Mary Fallin (R)*	171,925	65.9
Steven L. Perry (D)	88,966	34.1

Oregon

	Vote total	Percent
Senate		
Jeff Merkley (D)	864,392	48.9
Gordon H. Smith (R)*	805,159	45.6
David Brownlow (CNSTP)	92,565	5.2
House		
1 David Wu (D)*	237,567	71.5
Joel Haugen (R)	58,279	17.5
2 Greg Walden (R)*	236,560	69.5
Noah Lemas (D)	87,649	25.8
3 Earl Blumenauer (D)*	254,235	74.5
Delia Lopez (R)	71,063	20.8
4 Peter A. DeFazio (D)*	275,143	82.3
Jaynee Germond (CONST)	43,133	12.9
5 Kurt Schrader (D)	181,577	54.3
Mike Erickson (R)	128,297	38.3

Pennsylvania

	Vote total	Percent
House		
1 Robert A. Brady (D)*	242,799	90.8
Mike Muhammed (R)	24,714	9.2
2 Chaka Fattah (D)*	276,870	88.9
Adam A. Lang (R)	34,466	11.1
3 Kathy Dahlkemper (D)	146,846	51.2
Phil English (R)*	139,757	48.8
4 Jason Altmire (D)*	186,536	55.9
Melissa A. Hart (R)	147,411	44.1
5 Glenn Thompson (R)	155,513	56.7
Mark B. McCracken (D)	112,509	41.0
6 Jim Gerlach (R)*	179,423	52.1
Bob Roggio (D)	164,952	47.9
7 Joe Sestak (D)*	209,955	59.6
W. Craig Williams (R)	142,362	40.4
8 Patrick J. Murphy (D)*	197,869	56.8
Tom Manion (R)	145,103	41.6
9 Bill Shuster (R)*	174,951	63.9
Tony Barr (D)	98,735	36.1
10 Christopher Carney (D)*	160,837	56.3
Chris Hackett (R)	124,681	43.7
11 Paul E. Kanjorski (D)*	146,379	51.6
Lou Barletta (R)	137,151	48.4
12 John P. Murtha (D)*	155,268	57.9
William Russell (R)	113,120	42.1
13 Allyson Y. Schwartz (D)*	196,868	62.8
Marina Kats (R)	108,271	34.5
14 Mike Doyle (D)*	242,326	91.3
Titus North (GREEN)	23,214	8.7
15 Charlie Dent (R)*	181,433	58.6
Sam Bennett (D)	128,333	41.4
16 Joe Pitts (R)*	170,329	55.8
Bruce A. Slater (D)	120,193	39.4
17 Tim Holden (D)*	192,699	63.7
Toni Gilhooley (R)	109,909	36.3
18 Tim Murphy (R)*	213,349	64.1
Steve O'Donnell (D)	119,661	35.9
19 Todd R. Platts (R)*	218,862	66.6
Philip J. Avillo Jr. (D)	109,533	33.4

Rhode Island

	Vote total	Percent
Senate		
Jack Reed (D)*	320,644	73.1
Robert G. Tingle (R)	116,174	26.5
House		
1 Patrick J. Kennedy (D)*	145,254	68.5
Jonathan P. Scott (R)	51,340	24.2
Kenneth A. Capalbo (I)	15,108	7.2
2 Jim Langevin (D)*	158,416	70.1
Mark S. Zaccaria (R)	67,433	29.9

South Carolina

	Vote total	Percent
Senate		
Lindsey Graham (R)*	1,076,534	57.5
Bob Conley (D)	790,621	42.2
House		
1 Henry E. Brown Jr. (R)*	177,540	51.9
Linda Ketner (D)	163,724	47.9
2 Joe Wilson (R)*	184,583	53.7
Rob Miller (D)	158,627	46.2
3 J. Gresham Barrett (R)*	186,799	64.7
Jane Ballard Dyer (D)	101,724	35.2
4 Bob Inglis (R)*	184,440	60.1
Paul Corden (D)	113,291	36.9
5 John M. Spratt Jr. (D)*	188,785	61.6
Albert F. Spencer (R)	113,282	37.0
6 James E. Clyburn (D)*	193,378	67.5
Nancy Harrelson (R)	93,059	32.5

South Dakota

	Vote total	Percent
Senate		
Tim Johnson (D)*	237,889	62.5
Joel Dykstra (R)	142,784	37.5
House		
AL Stephanie Herseth* Sandlin (D)	256,041	67.6
Chris Lien (R)	122,966	32.4

Tennessee

	Vote total	Percent
Senate		
Lamar Alexander (R)*	1,579,477	65.1
Robert D. Tuke (D)	767,236	31.6
House		
1 Phil Roe (R)	168,343	71.8
Rob Russell (D)	57,525	24.5
2 John J. "Jimmy" Duncan Jr. (R)*	227,120	78.1
Bob Scott (D)	63,639	21.9
3 Zach Wamp (R)*	184,964	69.4
Doug Vandagriff (R)	73,059	27.4
4 Lincoln Davis (D)*	146,776	58.8
Monty J. Lankford (R)	94,447	37.8
5 Jim Cooper (D)*	181,467	65.8
Gerard Donovan (R)	85,471	31.0
6 Bart Gordon (D)*	194,264	74.4
Chris Baker (I)	66,764	25.6
7 Marsha Blackburn (R)*	217,332	68.6
Randy G. Morris (D)	99,549	31.4
8 John Tanner (D)*	180,465	100.0
9 Steve Cohen (D)*	198,798	87.9

Texas

	Vote total	Percent
Senate		
John Cornyn (R)*	4,337,469	54.8
Richard J. "Rick" Noriega (D)	3,389,365	42.9
House		
1 Louie Gohmert (R)*	189,012	87.6
Roger L. Owen (I)	26,814	12.4
2 Ted Poe (R)*	175,101	88.9
Craig Wolfe (LIBERT)	21,813	11.1
3 Sam Johnson (R)*	170,742	59.7
Tom Daley (D)	108,693	59.7
4 Ralph M. Hall (R)*	206,906	68.8
Glenn Melancon (D)	88,067	29.3
5 Jeb Hensarling (R)*	162,894	83.6
Ken Ashby (LIBERT)	31,967	16.4
6 Joe L. Barton (R)*	174,008	62.0
Ludwig Otto (D)	99,919	35.6
7 John Culberson (R)*	162,635	55.9
Michael Skelly (D)	123,242	42.4
8 Kevin Brady (R)*	207,128	72.6
Kent Hargett (D)	70,758	24.8
9 Al Green (D)*	143,868	93.6
Brad Walters (LIBERT)	9,760	6.4
10 Michael McCaul (R)*	179,493	53.9
Larry Joe Doherty (D)	143,719	43.1
11 K. Michael Conaway (R)*	189,625	88.3
James R. Strohm (LIBERT)	25,051	11.7
12 Kay Granger (R)*	181,662	67.6
Tracey Smith (D)	82,250	30.6
13 William M. "Mac" Thornberry (R)*	180,078	77.6
Roger James Waun (D)	51,841	22.4
14 Ron Paul (R)*	191,293	100.0
15 Rubén Hinojosa (D)*	107,578	65.7
Eddie Zamora (R)	52,303	31.9
16 Silvestre Reyes (D)*	130,375	82.1
Benjamin Eloy Mendoza (I)	16,384	10.3
Mette A. Baker (LIBERT)	12,000	7.6
17 Chet Edwards (D)*	134,592	53.0
Rob Curnock (R)	115,581	45.5
18 Sheila Jackson Lee (D)*	148,617	77.3
John Faulk (R)	39,095	20.3
19 Randy Neugebauer (R)*	168,501	72.4
Dwight Fullingim (D)	58,030	24.9
20 Charlie Gonzalez (D)*	127,298	71.9
Robert Litoff (R)	44,585	25.2
21 Lamar Smith (R)*	243,471	80.0
James Arthur Stohm (LIBERT)	60,879	20.0
22 Pete Olson (R)	161,996	52.4
Nick Lampson (D)*	140,160	45.4
23 Ciro D. Rodriguez (D)*	134,090	55.8
Lyle Larson (R)	100,799	41.9
24 Kenny Marchant (R)*	151,434	56.0
Tom Love (D)	111,089	41.1
25 Lloyd Doggett (D)*	191,755	65.8
George L. Morovich (R)	88,693	30.4
26 Michael C. Burgess (R)*	195,181	60.2
Ken Leach (D)	118,167	36.4
27 Solomon P. Ortiz (D)*	104,864	58.0
William "Willie" Vaden (R)	69,458	38.4
28 Henry Cuellar (D)*	123,494	68.7
Jim Fish (R)	52,524	29.2
29 Gene Green (D)*	79,718	74.6
Eric Story (R)	25,512	23.9

		Vote total	*Percent*
30	Eddie Bernice Johnson (D)*	168,249	82.5
	Fred Wood (R)	32,361	15.9
31	John Carter (R)*	175,563	60.3
	Brian P. Ruiz (D)	106,559	36.6
32	Pete Sessions (R)*	116,283	57.3
	Eric Roberson (D)	82,406	40.6

Utah

		Vote total	*Percent*
Governor			
	Jon Huntsman Jr. (R)*	682,409	77.7
	Bob Springmeyer (D)	172,646	19.7
House			
1	Rob Bishop (R)*	196,799	64.9
	Morgan Bowen (D)	92,469	30.5
2	Jim Matheson (D)*	220,666	63.4
	Bill Dew (R)	120,083	34.5
3	Jason Chaffetz (R)	187,038	65.6
	Bennion L. Spencer (D)	80,626	28.3
	Jim Noorlander (CNSTP)	17,408	6.1

Vermont

		Vote total	*Percent*
Governor			
	Jim Douglas (R)*	170,492	53.4
	Anthony Pollina (I)	69,791	21.9
	Gaye Symington (D)	69,534	21.1
House			
AL	Peter Welch (D)*	248,203	83.2

Virginia

		Vote total	*Percent*
Senate			
	Mark Warner (D)	2,369,327	65.0
	James S. Gilmore III (R)	1,228,830	34.7
House			
1	Rob Wittman (R)*	203,839	56.6
	Bill S. Day Jr. (D)	150,432	41.8
2	Glenn Nye (D)	141,857	52.4
	Thelma Drake (R)*	128,486	47.5
3	Robert C. Scott (D)*	239,911	97.0
4	J. Randy Forbes (R)*	199,075	59.5
	Andrea Miller (D)	135,041	40.4
5	Tom Perriello (D)	158,810	50.1
	Virgil H. Goode Jr. (R)*	158,083	49.9
6	Robert W. Goodlatte (R)*	192,350	61.6
	S. "Sam" Rasoul (D)	114,367	36.6
7	Eric Cantor (R)*	233,531	62.7
	Anita Hartke (D)	138,123	37.1
8	James P. Moran (D)*	222,986	67.9
	Mark W. Ellmore (R)	97,425	29.7
9	Rick Boucher (D)*	207,306	97.1
10	Frank R. Wolf (R)*	223,140	58.8
	Judy M. Feder (D)	147,357	38.8
11	Gerald E. Connolly (D)	196,598	54.7
	Keith Fimian (R)	154,758	43.0

Washington

		Vote total	*Percent*
Governor			
	Christine Gregoire (D)	1,598,738	53.2
	Dino Rossi (R)	1,404,124	46.8
House			
1	Jay Inslee (D)*	233,780	67.8
	Larry Ishmael (R)	111,240	32.2
2	Rick Larsen (D)*	217,416	62.4
	Rick Bart (R)	131,051	37.6
3	Brian Baird (D)*	216,701	64.0
	Michael Delavar (R)	121,828	36.0
4	Doc Hastings (R)*	169,940	63.1
	George Fearing (D)	99,430	36.9
5	Cathy McMorris Rodgers (R)*	211,305	65.3
	Mark Mays (D)	112,382	34.7
6	Norm Dicks (D)*	205,991	66.3
	Doug Cloud (R)	102,081	33.1
7	Jim McDermott (D)*	291,963	83.7
	Steve Beren (R)	57,054	16.3
8	Dave Reichert (R)*	191,568	52.8
	Darcy Burner (D)	171,358	47.2
9	Adam Smith (D)*	176,295	65.4
	James Postma (R)	93,080	34.6

West Virginia

		Vote total	*Percent*
Governor			
	Joe Manchin III (D)*	492,697	69.8
	Russ Weeks (R)	181,612	25.7
Senate			
	John D. Rockefeller IV (D)*	447,560	63.7
	Jay Wolfe (R)	254,629	36.3
House			
1	Alan B. Mollohan (D)*	187,734	99.9
2	Shelley Moore Capito (R)*	1147,334	57.1
	Anne Barth (D)	110,819	42.9
3	Nick J. Rahall II (D)*	133,522	66.9
	Marty Gearhart (R)	66,005	33.1

Wisconsin

		Vote total	*Percent*
House			
1	Paul D. Ryan (R)*	231,009	64.0
	Marge Krupp (D)	125,268	34.7
2	Tammy Baldwin (D)*	277,914	69.3
	Peter Theron (R)	122,513	30.6
3	Ron Kind (D)*	225,208	63.2
	Paul Stark (R)	122,760	34.4
4	Gwen Moore (D)*	222,728	87.6
	Michael D. LaForest (I)	29,282	11.5
5	F. James Sensenbrenner Jr. (R)*	275,271	63.7
	Robert R. Raymond (I)	69,715	20.2
6	Tom Petri (R)*	221,875	63.7
	Roger A. Kittelson (D)	126,090	36.2
7	David R. Obey (D)*	212,666	60.8
	Dan Mielke (R)	136,938	39.1
8	Steve Kagen (D)*	193,662	54.0
	John Gard (R)	164,621	45.9

Wyoming

		Vote total	*Percent*
Senate			
	John Barrasso (R)*	183,063	73.4
	Nick Carter (D)	66,202	26.5
	Michael B. Enzi (R)*	189,046	75.6
	Chris Rothfuss (D)	60,631	24.3
House			
AL	Cynthia M. Lummis (R)	131,244	52.6
	Gary Trauner (D)	106,758	42.8

NOTE: Vote totals are included for all candidates listed on the ballot who received 5 percent or more of the total vote.

1. In the general election neither candidate received a majority of the vote, requiring a runoff election on Dec. 2.

2. Incumbent Rep. William Jefferson (D) received 25 percent of the vote in a primary contest in October 2008, requiring that he face the next highest vote recipient, Helena Moreno, on Nov. 4. Jefferson won this contest with 56.8 percent of the vote, allowing him to proceed to the special runoff election on Dec. 6, 2008, against three other candidates: Green, Libertarian, and Republican. In the Dec. 6 contest the Green and Libertarian candidates received less than 5 percent of the vote and are not included in this volume.

3. Paul J. Carmouche (D) received 48 percent of the vote in a primary contest in October 2008, requiring him to face the next higher vote recipient, Willie Banks (D) on Nov. 4. Carmouche won this contest with 62 percent of the vote, allowing him to proceed to the special runoff election on Dec. 6, 2008.

Results of House Elections, 1928–2008

	1928	1930	1932	1934	1936	1938	1940	1942	1944	1946	1948	1950	1952	1954	1956	1958	1960	1962	1964	1966
Totals																				
Democrats	165	217	313	322	334	262	268	222	242	188	263	235	213	232	234	283	263	259	295	248
Republicans	269	217	117	103	88	169	162	209	191	246	171	199	221	203	201	153	174	176	140	187
Alabama																				
Democrats	10	10	9[1]	9	9	9	9	9	9	9	9	9	9	9	9	9	9	8[1]	3	
Republicans	0	0	0	0	0	0	0	0	0	0	0	0	0	0	0	0	0	0	5	
Alaska																				
Democrats	—	—	—	—	—	—	—	—	—	—	—	—	—	—	—	1	1	1	1	
Republicans	—	—	—	—	—	—	—	—	—	—	—	—	—	—	—	0	0	0	0	1
Arizona																				
Democrats	1	1	1	1	1	1	1	2[2]	2	2	2	2	1	1	1	1	1	2[2]	2	1
Republicans	0	0	0	0	0	0	0	0	0	0	0	0	1	1	1	1	1	1	1	2
Arkansas																				
Democrats	7	7	7	7	7	7	7	7	7	7	7	7	6[1]	6	6	6	6	4[1]	4	3
Republicans	0	0	0	0	0	0	0	0	0	0	0	0	0	0	0	0	0	0	0	1
California																				
Democrats	1	1	11[2]	13	15	12	11	12[2]	16	9	10	10	11[2]	11	13	16	16	25[2,3]	23	21
Republicans	10	10	9	7	4	8	9	11	7	14	13	13	19	19	17	14	14	13	15	17
Colorado																				
Democrats	1	1	4	4	4	4	2	1	0	1	3	2	2	2	2	3	2	2	4	3
Republicans	3	3	0	0	0	0	2	3	4	3	1	2	2	2	2	1	2	2	0	1
Connecticut																				
Democrats	0	2	2[2]	4	6	2	6	0	4	0	3	2	1	1	0	6	4	5	6	5
Republicans	5	3	4	2	0	4	0	6	2	6	3	4	5	5	6	0	2	1	0	1
Delaware																				
Democrats	0	0	1	0	1	0	1	0	1	0	0	0	0	1	0	1	1	1	1	0
Republicans	1	1	0	1	0	1	0	1	0	1	1	0	1	0	0	0	0	0	0	1
Florida																				
Democrats	4	4	5[2]	5	5	5	5	6[2]	6	6	6	6	8[2]	7	7	7	7	10[2]	10	9
Republicans	0	0	0	0	0	0	0	0	0	0	0	0	0	1	1	1	1	2	2	3
Georgia																				
Democrats	12	12	10[1]	10	10	10	10	10	10	10	10	10	10	10	10	10	10	10	9	8
Republicans	0	0	0	0	0	0	0	0	0	0	0	0	0	0	0	0	0	0	1	2
Hawaii																				
Democrats	—	—	—	—	—	—	—	—	—	—	—	—	—	—	—	—	1	2[2]	2	2
Republicans	—	—	—	—	—	—	—	—	—	—	—	—	—	—	—	—	0	0	0	0
Idaho																				
Democrats	0	0	2	2	2	1	1	1	1	0	1	0	1	1	1	1	2	2	1	0
Republicans	2	2	0	0	0	1	1	1	1	2	1	2	1	1	1	1	0	0	1	2
Illinois																				
Democrats	6	13[4]	19	21	21	17	11	7[1]	11	6	12	8	9[1]	12	11	14	14	12[1]	13	12
Republicans	21	14	8	6	6	10	16	19	15	20	14	18	16	13	14	11	11	12	11	12
Indiana																				
Democrats	3	9	12[1]	11	11	5	4	2[1]	2	2	7	2	1	2	2	8	4[4]	4	6	5
Republicans	10	4	0	1	1	7	8	9	9	9	4	9	10	9	9	3	7	7	5	6
Iowa																				
Democrats	0	1	6[1]	6	5	2	2	0[1]	0	0	0	0	0	0	1	4	2	1[1]	6	2
Republicans	11	10	3	3	4	7	7	8	8	8	8	8	8	8	7	4	6	6	1	5
Kansas																				
Democrats	1	1	3[1]	3	2	1	1	0[1]	0	0	0	0	1	0	1	3	1	0[1]	0	0
Republicans	7	7	4	4	5	6	6	6	6	6	6	6	5	6	5	3	5	5	5	5
Kentucky																				
Democrats	2	9	9[1]	8	8	8	8	8	8	6	7	7	6[1]	6	6	7	7	5[1]	6	4
Republicans	9	2	0	1	1	1	1	1	1	3	2	2	2	2	2	1	1	2	1	3
Louisiana																				
Democrats	8	8	8	8	8	8	8	8	8	8	8	8	8	8	8	8	8	8	8	8
Republicans	0	0	0	0	0	0	0	0	0	0	0	0	0	0	0	0	0	0	0	0
Maine																				
Democrats	0	0	2[1]	2	0	0	0	0	0	0	0	0	0	0	1	2	0	0[1]	1	2
Republicans	4	4	1	1	3	3	3	3	3	3	3	3	3	3	2	1	3	2	1	0

1. State lost seats due to reapportionment.

2. State gained seats due to reapportionment.

3. Alaska 1972, California 1962, and Louisiana 1972: national and state totals reflect the reelection of a Democrat who died before the election but whose name remained on the ballot.

4. Illinois 1930, Indiana 1960 and 1984, and New Hampshire 1936: national and state totals reflect the final outcome of a contested election in which a Republican was first certified the winner, but the House decided to seat the Democrat.

	1968	*1970*	*1972*	*1974*	*1976*	*1978*	*1980*	*1982*	*1984*	*1986*	*1988*	*1990*	*1992*	*1994*	*1996*	*1998*	*2000*	*2002*	*2004*	*2006*	*2008*
Totals																					
Democrats	243	255	243	291	292	277	243	269	253	258	260	267	258	204	207	211	212	205	202	233	255
Republicans	192	180	192	144	143	158	192	166	182	177	175	167	176	230	227	223	221	229	232	202	180
Alabama																					
Democrats	5	5	4[1]	4	4	4	4	5	5	5	5	5	4	4	2	2	2	2	2	2	3
Republicans	3	3	3	3	3	3	3	2	2	2	2	2	3	3	5	5	5	5	5	5	4
Alaska																					
Democrats	0	1	1[3]	0	0	0	0	0	0	0	0	0	0	0	0	0	0	0	0	0	0
Republicans	1	0	0	1	1	1	1	1	1	1	1	1	1	1	1	1	1	1	1	1	1
Arizona																					
Democrats	1	1	1[2]	1	2	2	2	2[2]	1	1	1	1	3[2]	1	1	1	1	2	2	4	3
Republicans	2	2	3	3	2	2	2	3	4	4	4	4	3	5	5	5	5	6	6	4	5
Arkansas																					
Democrats	3	3	3	3	3	2	2	2	3	3	3	3	2	2	2	2	3	3	3	3	3
Republicans	1	1	1	1	1	2	2	2	1	1	1	1	2	2	2	2	1	1	1	1	1
California																					
Democrats	21	20	23[2]	28	29	26	22	28[2]	27	27	27	26	30[2]	27	29	28	32	33	33	34	34
Republicans	17	18	20	15	14	17	21	17	18	18	18	19	22	25	23	24	20	20	20	19	19
Colorado																					
Democrats	3	2	2[2]	3	3	3	3	3[2]	2	3	3	3	2	2	2	2	2	2	3	4	5
Republicans	1	2	3	2	2	2	2	3	4	3	3	3	4	4	4	4	4	5	4	3	2
Connecticut																					
Democrats	4	3	3	4	4	5	4	4	3	3	3	3	3	3	4	4	3	2	2	4	5
Republicans	2	2	3	2	2	1	2	2	3	3	3	3	3	3	2	2	3	3	3	1	0
Delaware																					
Democrats	0	0	0	0	0	0	0	1	1	1	1	1	0	0	0	0	0	0	0	0	0
Republicans	1	1	1	1	1	1	1	0	0	0	0	0	1	1	1	1	1	1	1	1	1
Florida																					
Democrats	9	9	11[2]	10	10	12	11	13[2]	12	12	10	9	10[2]	8	8	8	8	7	7	9	10
Republicans	3	3	4	5	5	3	4	6	7	7	9	10	13	15	15	15	15	18	18	16	15
Georgia																					
Democrats	8	8	9	10	10	9	9	9	8	8	9	9	7[2]	4	3	3	3	5	6	7	6
Republicans	2	2	1	0	0	1	1	1	2	2	1	1	4	7	8	8	8	8	7	6	7
Hawaii																					
Democrats	2	2	2	2	2	2	2	2	2	1	1	2	2	2	2	2	2	2	2	2	2
Republicans	0	0	0	0	0	0	0	0	0	1	1	0	0	0	0	0	0	0	0	0	0
Idaho																					
Democrats	0	0	0	0	0	0	0	0	1	1	1	2	1	0	0	0	0	0	0	2	1
Republicans	2	2	2	2	2	2	2	2	1	1	1	0	1	2	2	2	2	2	2	0	1
Illinois																					
Democrats	12	12	10	13	12	11	10	12[1]	13	13	14	15	12[1]	10	10	10	10	9	10	10	12
Republicans	12	12	14	11	12	13	14	10	9	9	8	7	8	10	10	10	10	10	9	9	7
Indiana																					
Democrats	4	5	4	9	8	7	6	5[1]	5[4]	6	6	8	7	4	4	4	4	3	2	5	5
Republicans	7	6	7	2	3	4	5	5	5	4	4	2	3	6	6	6	6	6	7	4	4
Iowa																					
Democrats	2	2	3[1]	5	4	3	3	3	2	2	2	2	1[1]	0	1	1	1	1	1	3	3
Republicans	5	5	3	1	2	3	3	3	4	4	4	4	4	5	4	4	4	4	4	2	2
Kansas																					
Democrats	0	1	1	1	2	1	1	2	2	2	2	2	2[1]	0	0	1	1	1	1	2	1
Republicans	5	4	4	4	3	4	4	3	3	3	3	3	2	4	4	3	3	3	3	2	3
Kentucky																					
Democrats	4	5	5	5	5	4	4	4	4	4	4	4	4[1]	2	1	1	1	1	1	2	2
Republicans	3	2	2	2	2	3	3	3	3	3	3	3	2	4	5	5	5	5	5	4	4
Louisiana																					
Democrats	8	8	7[3]	6[5]	6	5	6	6	6	5	4	4	4[1]	4	2	2	2	3	2	2	1
Republicans	0	0	1	2	2	3	2	2	2	3	4	4	3	3	5	5	5	4	5	5	6
Maine																					
Democrats	2	2	1	0	0	0	0	0	0	1	1	1	1	1	2	2	2	2	2	2	2
Republicans	0	0	1	2	2	2	2	2	2	1	1	1	1	1	0	0	0	0	0	0	0

5. Louisiana 1974: national and state totals reflect the final outcome of a contested election in which no winner was declared, followed by a special election won by the Republican.

	1928	*1930*	*1932*	*1934*	*1936*	*1938*	*1940*	*1942*	*1944*	*1946*	*1948*	*1950*	*1952*	*1954*	*1956*	*1958*	*1960*	*1962*	*1964*	*1966*
Maryland																				
Democrats	4	6	6	6	6	6	6	4	5	4	4	3	3[2]	4	4	7	6	6[2]	6	5
Republicans	2	0	0	0	0	0	0	2	1	2	2	3	4	3	3	0	1	2	2	3
Massachusetts																				
Democrats	3	4	5[1]	7	5	5	6	4[1]	4	5	4	6	6	7	7	8	8	7[1]	7	7
Republicans	13	12	10	8	10	10	9	10	10	9	8	8	8	7	7	6	6	5	5	5
Michigan																				
Democrats	0	0	10[2]	6	8	5	6	5	6	3	5	5	5[2]	7	6	7	7	8[2]	12	7
Republicans	13	13	7	11	9	12	11	12	11	14	12	12	13	11	12	11	11	11	7	12
Minnesota																				
Democrats	0	0	1[1]	1	1	1	0	0	2	1	4	4	4	5	5	4	3	4[1]	4	3
Republicans	9	9	3	5	3	7	8	8	7	8	5	5	5	4	4	5	6	4	4	5
Mississippi																				
Democrats	8	8	7[1]	7	7	7	7	7	7	7	7	7	6[1]	6	6	6	6	5[1]	4	5
Republicans	0	0	0	0	0	0	0	0	0	0	0	0	0	0	0	0	0	0	1	0
Missouri																				
Democrats	6	12	13[15]	12	12	12	10	5	7	4	12	10	7	9	10	10	9	8[1]	8	8
Republicans	10	4	0	1	1	1	3	8	6	9	1	3	4	2	1	1	2	2	2	2
Montana																				
Democrats	1	1	2	2	2	1	1	2	1	1	1	1	1	1	2	2	1	1	1	1
Republicans	1	1	0	0	0	1	1	0	1	1	1	1	1	1	0	0	1	1	1	1
Nebraska																				
Democrats	2	4	5[1]	4	4	2	2	0[1]	0	0	1	0	0	0	0	2	0	0[1]	1	0
Republicans	4	2	0	1	1	3	3	4	4	4	3	4	4	4	4	2	4	3	2	3
Nevada																				
Democrats	0	0	1	1	1	1	1	1	1	0	1	1	0	0	1	1	1	1	1	1
Republicans	1	1	0	0	0	0	0	0	0	1	0	0	1	1	0	0	0	0	0	0
New Hampshire																				
Democrats	0	0	1	1	1[4]	0	0	0	0	0	0	0	0	0	0	0	0	0	1	0
Republicans	2	2	1	1	1	2	2	2	2	2	2	2	2	2	2	2	2	2	1	2
New Jersey																				
Democrats	2	3	4[2]	4	7	3	4	3	2	2	5	5	5	6	4	5	6	7[2]	11	9
Republicans	10	9	10	10	7	11	10	11	12	12	9	9	9	8	10	9	8	8	4	6
New Mexico																				
Democrats	0	1	1	1	1	1	1	2[2]	2	2	2	2	2	2	2	2	2	2	2	2
Republicans	1	0	0	0	0	0	0	0	0	0	0	0	0	0	0	0	0	0	0	0
New York																				
Democrats	23	23	29[2]	29	29	25	25	23	22	16	24	23	16[1]	17	17	19	22	20[1]	27	26
Republicans	20	20	16	16	16	19	19	21	22	28	20	22	27	26	26	24	21	21	14	15
North Carolina																				
Democrats	8	10	11[2]	11	11	11	11	12[2]	12	12	12	12	11	11	11	11	11	9[1]	9	8
Republicans	2	0	0	0	0	0	0	0	0	0	0	0	1	1	1	1	1	2	2	3
North Dakota																				
Democrats	0	0	0[1]	0	0	0	0	0	0	0	0	0	0	0	0	1	0	0	1	0
Republicans	3	3	2	2	2	2	2	2	2	2	2	2	2	2	2	1	2	2	1	2
Ohio																				
Democrats	3	9	18[2]	18	22	9	12	3[1]	6	4	12	7	6	6	6	9	7	6[2]	10	5
Republicans	19	13	6	6	2	15	12	20	17	19	11	15	16	17	17	14	16	18	14	19
Oklahoma																				
Democrats	5	7	9[2]	9	9	9	8	7[1]	6	6	8	6	5[1]	5	5	5	5	5	5	4
Republicans	3	1	0	0	0	0	1	1	2	2	0	2	1	1	1	1	1	1	1	2
Oregon																				
Democrats	0	1	2	1	2	1	1	0[2]	0	0	0	0	0	1	3	3	2	3	3	2
Republicans	3	2	1	2	1	2	2	4	4	4	4	4	4	3	1	1	2	1	1	2
Pennsylvania																				
Democrats	1	3	11[1]	23	27	15	19	14[1]	15	5	16	13	11[1]	14	13	16	14	13[1]	15	14
Republicans	35	33	23	11	7	9	15	19	18	28	19	20	19	16	17	14	16	14	12	13
Rhode Island																				
Democrats	1	1	2[1]	2	2	0	2	2	2	2	2	2	2	2	2	2	2	2	2	2
Republicans	2	2	0	0	0	2	0	0	0	0	0	0	0	0	0	0	0	0	0	0
South Carolina																				
Democrats	7	7	6[1]	6	6	6	6	6	6	6	6	6	6	6	6	6	6	6	6	5
Republicans	0	0	0	0	0	0	0	0	0	0	0	0	0	0	0	0	0	0	0	1
South Dakota																				
Democrats	0	0	2[1]	2	1	0	0	0	0	0	0	0	0	0	1	1	0	0	0	0
Republicans	3	3	0	0	1	2	2	2	2	2	2	2	2	2	1	1	2	2	2	2

	1968	*1970*	*1972*	*1974*	*1976*	*1978*	*1980*	*1982*	*1984*	*1986*	*1988*	*1990*	*1992*	*1994*	*1996*	*1998*	*2000*	*2002*	*2004*	*2006*	*2008*
Maryland																					
Democrats	4	5	4	5	5	6	7	7	6	6	6	5	4	4	4	4	4	6	6	6	7
Republicans	4	3	4	3	3	2	1	1	2	2	2	3	4	4	4	4	4	2	2	2	1
Massachusetts																					
Democrats	7	8	9[6]	10	10	10	10	10[1]	10	10	10	10	8[1]	8	10	10	10	10	10	10	10
Republicans	5	4	3	2	2	2	2	1	1	1	1	1	2	2	0	0	0	0	0	0	0
Michigan																					
Democrats	7	7	7	12	11	13	12	12[1]	11	11	11	11	10[1]	9	10	10	9	6	6	6	8
Republicans	12	12	12	7	8	6	7	6	7	7	7	7	6	7	6	6	7	9	9	9	7
Minnesota																					
Democrats	3	4	4	5	5	4	3	5	5	5	5	6	6	6	6	6	5	4	4	5	5
Republicans	5	4	4	3	3	4	5	3	3	3	3	2	2	2	2	2	3	4	4	3	3
Mississippi																					
Democrats	5	5	3	3	3	3	3	3	3	4	4	5	5	4	2	3	3	2	2	2	3
Republicans	0	0	2	2	2	2	2	2	2	1	1	0	0	1	3	2	2	2	2	2	1
Missouri																					
Democrats	9	9	9	9	8	8	6	6[1]	6	5	5	6	6	6	5	5	4	4	4	4	4
Republicans	1	1	1	1	2	2	4	3	3	4	4	3	3	3	4	4	5	5	5	5	5
Montana																					
Democrats	1	1	1	2	1	1	1	1	1	1	1	1	1[1]	1	1	0	0	0	0	0	0
Republicans	1	1	1	0	1	1	1	1	1	1	1	1	0	0	0	1	1	1	1	1	1
Nebraska																					
Democrats	0	0	0	0	1	1	0	0	0	0	1	1	1	0	0	0	0	0	0	0	0
Republicans	3	3	3	3	2	2	3	3	3	3	2	2	2	3	3	3	3	3	3	3	3
Nevada																					
Democrats	1	1	0	1	1	1	1	1[2]	1	1	1	1	1	0	0	1	1	1	1	1	2
Republicans	0	0	1	0	0	0	0	1	1	1	1	1	1	2	2	1	1	2	2	2	1
New Hampshire																					
Democrats	0	0	0	1	1	1	1	1	0	0	0	1	1	0	0	0	0	0	0	2	2
Republicans	2	2	2	1	1	1	1	1	2	2	2	1	1	2	2	2	2	2	2	0	0
New Jersey																					
Democrats	9	9	8	12	11	10	8	9[1]	8	8	8	8	7[1]	5	6	7	7	7	7	7	8
Republicans	6	6	7	3	4	5	7	5	6	6	6	6	6	8	7	6	6	6	6	6	5
New Mexico																					
Democrats	0	1	1	1	1	1	0	1[2]	1	1	1	1	1	1	1	1	1	1	1	1	3
Republicans	2	1	1	1	1	1	2	2	2	2	2	2	2	2	2	2	2	2	2	2	0
New York																					
Democrats	26	24	22[1]	27	28	26	22	20[1]	19	20	21	21	18[1]	17	18	18	19	19	20	23	26
Republicans	15	17	17	12	11	13	17	14	15	14	13	13	13	14	13	13	12	10	9	6	3
North Carolina																					
Democrats	7	7	7	9	9	9	7	9	6	8	8	7	8[2]	4	6	5	5	6	6	7	8
Republicans	4	4	4	2	2	2	4	2	5	3	3	4	4	8	6	7	7	7	7	6	5
North Dakota																					
Democrats	0	1	0[1]	0	0	0	1	1	1	1	1	1	1	1	1	1	1	1	1	1	1
Republicans	2	1	1	1	1	1	0	0	0	0	0	0	0	0	0	0	0	0	0	0	0
Ohio																					
Democrats	6	7	7[1]	8	10	10	11	10[1]	11	11	11	11	10[1]	6	8	8	8	6	6	7	10
Republicans	18	17	16	15	13	13	12	11	10	10	10	10	9	13	11	11	11	12	12	11	8
Oklahoma																					
Democrats	4	4	5	6	5	5	5	5	5	4	4	4	4	1	0	0	1	1	1	1	1
Republicans	2	2	1	0	1	1	1	1	1	2	2	2	2	5	6	6	5	4	4	4	4
Oregon																					
Democrats	2	2	2	4	4	4	3	3[2]	3	3	3	4	4	3	4	4	4	4	4	4	4
Republicans	2	2	2	0	0	0	1	2	2	2	2	1	1	2	1	1	1	1	1	1	1
Pennsylvania																					
Democrats	14	14	13[1]	14	17	15	13[6]	13[1]	13	12	12	11	11[1]	11	11	11	10	7	7	11	12
Republicans	13	13	12	11	8	10	12	10	10	11	11	12	10	10	10	10	11	12	12	8	7
Rhode Island																					
Democrats	2	2	2	2	2	2	1	1	1	1	0	1	1	2	2	2	2	2	2	2	2
Republicans	0	0	0	0	0	0	1	1	1	1	2	1	1	0	0	0	0	0	0	0	0
South Carolina																					
Democrats	5	5	4	5	5	4	2	3	3	4	4	4	3	2	2	2	2	2	2	2	2
Republicans	1	1	2	1	1	2	4	3	3	2	2	2	3	4	4	4	4	4	4	4	4
South Dakota																					
Democrats	0	2	1	0	0	1	1	1[1]	1	1	1	1	1	1	0	0	0	0	1	1	1
Republicans	2	0	1	2	2	1	1	0	0	0	0	0	0	0	1	1	1	1	0	0	0

6. Massachusetts 1972 and Pennsylvania 1980: national and state Democratic totals reflect the election of an Independent candidate who previously announced he would serve as a Democrat.

	1928	*1930*	*1932*	*1934*	*1936*	*1938*	*1940*	*1942*	*1944*	*1946*	*1948*	*1950*	*1952*	*1954*	*1956*	*1958*	*1960*	*1962*	*1964*	*1966*
Tennessee																				
Democrats	8	8	7[1]	7	7	7	7	8[2]	8	8	8	8	7[1]	7	7	7	7	6	6	5
Republicans	2	2	2	2	2	2	2	2	2	2	2	2	2	2	2	2	2	3	3	4
Texas																				
Democrats	17	17	21[2]	21	21	21	21	21	21	21	21	21	22[2]	21	21	21	21	21[2]	23	21
Republicans	1[7]	1	0	0	0	0	0	0	0	0	0	0	0	1	1	1	1	2	0	2
Utah																				
Democrats	0	0	2	2	2	2	2	2	2	1	2	2	0	0	0	1	2	0	1	0
Republicans	2	2	0	0	0	0	0	0	0	1	0	0	2	2	2	1	0	2	1	2
Vermont																				
Democrats	0	0	0[1]	0	0	0	0	0	0	0	0	0	0	0	0	1	0	0	0	0
Republicans	2	2	1	1	1	1	1	1	1	1	1	1	1	1	1	0	1	1	1	1
Virginia																				
Democrats	8	9	9[1]	9	9	9	9	9	9	9	9	9	7[2]	8	8	8	8	8	8	6
Republicans	2	1	0	0	0	0	0	0	0	0	0	0	3	2	2	2	2	2	2	4
Washington																				
Democrats	1	1	6[2]	6	6	6	6	3	4	1	2	2	1[2]	1	1	1	2	1	5	5
Republicans	4	4	0	0	0	0	0	3	2	5	4	4	6	6	6	6	5	6	2	2
West Virginia																				
Democrats	1	2	6	6	6	5	6	3	5	2	6	6	5	6	4	5	5	4[1]	4	4
Republicans	5	4	0	0	0	1	0	3	1	4	0	0	1	0	2	1	1	1	1	1
Wisconsin																				
Democrats	0	1	5[1]	3	3	0	1	3	2	0	2	1	1	3	3	5	4	4	5	3
Republicans	11	10	5	0	0	8	6	5	7	10	8	9	9	7	7	5	6	6	5	7
Wyoming																				
Democrats	0	0	0	1	1	0	1	0	0	0	0	0	0	0	0	0	0	1	0	0
Republicans	1	1	1	0	0	1	0	1	1	1	1	1	1	1	1	1	1	1	0	1

7. Texas 1928: national and state totals reflect the final outcome of a contested election in which a Democrats was at first certified the winner, but the House decided to seat the Republican.

	1968	*1970*	*1972*	*1974*	*1976*	*1978*	*1980*	*1982*	*1984*	*1986*	*1988*	*1990*	*1992*	*1994*	*1996*	*1998*	*2000*	*2002*	*2004*	*2006*	*2008*
Tennessee																					
Democrats	5	5	3[1]	5	5	5	5	6[2]	6	6	6	6	6	4	4	4	4	5	5	5	5
Republicans	4	4	5	3	3	3	3	3	3	3	3	3	3	5	5	5	5	4	4	4	4
Texas																					
Democrats	20	20	20[2]	21	22	20	19	22[2]	17	17	19	19	21[2]	19	17	17	17	17	11	13	12
Republicans	3	3	4	3	2	4	5	5	10	10	8	8	9	11	13	13	13	15	21	19	20
Utah																					
Democrats	0	1	2	2	1	1	0	0[2]	0	1	1	2	2	1	0	0	1	1	1	1	1
Republicans	2	1	0	0	1	1	2	3	3	2	2	1	1	2	3	3	2	2	2	2	2
Vermont																					
Democrats	0	0	0	0	0	0	0	0	0	0	0	0	0	0	0	0	0	0	0	1	1
Republicans	1	1	1	1	1	1	1	1	1	1	1	0	0	0	0	0	0	0	0	0	0
Virginia																					
Democrats	5	4	3	5	4	4	1	4	4	5	5	6	7[2]	6	6	6	4	3	3	3	6
Republicans	5	6	7	5	6	6	9	6	6	5	5	4	4	5	5	5	6	8	8	8	5
Washington																					
Democrats	5	6	6	6	6	6	5	5[2]	5	5	5	5	8[2]	2	3	5	6	6	6	6	6
Republicans	2	1	1	1	1	1	2	3	3	3	3	3	1	7	6	4	3	3	3	3	3
West Virginia																					
Democrats	5	5	4[1]	4	4	4	2	4	4	4	4	4	3[1]	3	3	3	2	2	2	2	2
Republicans	0	0	0	0	0	0	2	0	0	0	0	0	0	0	0	0	1	1	1	1	1
Wisconsin																					
Democrats	3	5	5[1]	7	7	6	5	5	5	5	5	4	4	3	5	4	5	4	4	5	5
Republicans	7	5	4	2	2	3	4	4	4	4	4	5	5	6	4	5	4	4	4	3	3
Wyoming																					
Democrats	1	1	1	1	0	0	0	0	0	0	0	0	0	0	0	0	0	0	0	0	0
Republicans	1	0	0	0	0	1	1	1	1	1	1	1	1	1	1	1	1	1	1	1	1

NOTES: State totals reflect the number of Democrats and Republicans in each House delegation at the start of each Congress. The above totals do not include "other" representatives elected as independent or third-party candidates. Those numbers are California: Progressive 1936 (1). (No formal party. The representative became a Democrat in 1938.) Minnesota: Farmer-Labor 1928–1930 (1), 1932 (5), 1934 (3), 1936 (5), 1938–1942 (1). (Merged with D in 1944.) New York: American Labor 1938–1948 (1). (Party disbanded after 1954.) Ohio: Independent 1950–1952 (1). (Defeated by Democrat in 1954.) Wisconsin: Progressive 1934 (7), 1936–1938 (2), 1940 (3), 1942 (2) and 1944 (1). (Disbanded after 1944. The last Progressive became a Republican in 1946.) Vermont: Independent 1990–2000 (1). Virginia: Independent 2000 (1). National totals: 1928–1930 (1), 1932 (5), 1934 (10), 1936 (13), 1938 (4), 1940 (5), 1942 (4), 1944 (2), 1946–1952 (1), 1990–1998 (1), and 2000 (2).

Governors, 2005–2009

Following is a list of governors who served during the period of President George W. Bush's second term, 2005–2009. All governors serve four-year terms except those representing New Hampshire and Vermont, where they serve two-year terms.

Party designations appear in parentheses following the governor's name. The following abbreviations were used: (D) Democrat; (I) Independent; (R) Republican. (Governors, 1981–1984, *Congress and the Nation Vol. VI*, p. 1122; 1985–1988, *Congress and the Nation Vol. VII*, p. 1143; 1989–1992, *Congress and the Nation Vol. VIII*, p. 1259; 1993–1996, *Congress and the Nation Vol. IX*, p. 1211; 1997–2001, *Congress and the Nation Vol. X*, p. 1094; 2001–2005, *Congress and the Nation Vol. XI*, p. 1026)

	Dates of Service
Alabama	
Bob Riley (R)	Jan. 21, 2003–
Alaska	
Frank H. Murkowski (R)	Dec. 2, 2002–Dec. 4, 2006
Sarah H. Palin (R)	Dec. 4, 2006–July 26, 2009
Arizona	
Janet Napolitano (D)	Jan. 6, 2003–Jan. 20, 2009
Arkansas	
Mike Huckabee (R)	July 15, 1996–Jan. 9, 2007
Mike Beebe (D)	July 9, 2007–
California	
Arnold Schwarzenegger (R)	Nov. 17, 2003–
Colorado	
Bill Owens (R)	Jan. 12, 1999–Jan. 9, 2007
Bill Ritter Jr. (D)	Jan. 9, 2007–
Connecticut	
M. Jodi Rell (R)	July 1, 2004–
Delaware	
Ruth Ann Miner (D)	Jan. 3, 2001–Jan. 20, 2009
Florida	
Jeb Bush (R)	Jan. 5, 1999–Jan. 2, 2007
Charlie Crist (R)	Jan. 2, 2007–
Georgia	
Sonny Perdue (R)	Jan. 13, 2003–
Hawaii	
Linda Lingle (R)	Dec. 2, 2002–
Idaho	
Dirk Kempthorne (R)	Jan. 8, 1999–Jan 1, 2007
C. L. "Butch" Otter (R)	Jan. 1, 2007–
Illinois	
Rod R. Blagojevich (D)	Jan. 13, 2003–Jan. 29, 2009

	Dates of Service
Indiana	
Mitchell E. Daniels Jr. (R)	Jan. 10, 2005–
Iowa	
Tom Vilsack (D)	Jan. 15, 1999–Jan. 12, 2007
Chet Culver (D)	Jan. 12, 2007–
Kansas	
Kathleen Sebelius (D)	Jan. 13, 2003–April 28, 2009
Kentucky	
Ernest L. Fletcher (R)	Dec. 9, 2003–Dec. 11, 2007
Steven L. Beshear (D)	Dec. 11, 2007–
Louisiana	
Kathleen B. Blanco (D)	Jan. 12, 2004–Jan. 15, 2008
Bobby Jindal (R)	Jan. 15, 2008–
Maine	
John E. Baldacci (D)	Jan. 8, 2003–
Maryland	
Robert L. Ehrlich Jr. (R)	Jan. 15, 2003–Jan. 17, 2007
Martin O'Malley (D)	Jan. 17, 2007–
Massachusetts	
Mitt Romney (R)	Jan. 2, 2003–Jan. 4, 2007
Deval Patrick (D)	Jan. 4, 2007–
Michigan	
Jennifer Granholm (D)	Jan. 1, 2003–
Minnesota	
Tim Pawlenty (R)	Jan. 6, 2003–
Mississippi	
Haley Barbour (D)	Jan. 13, 2004–
Missouri	
Matt Blunt (R)	Jan. 10, 2005–Jan. 12, 2009
Montana	
Brian Schweitzer (D)	Jan. 3, 2005–

	Dates of Service
Nebraska	
Dave Heineman (R)	Jan. 21, 2005–
Nevada	
Kenny Guinn (R)	Jan. 4, 1999–Jan. 2, 2007
Jim Gibbons (R)	Jan. 2, 2007–
New Hampshire	
John Lynch (D)	Jan. 6, 2005–
New Jersey	
Richard J. Codey (D)	Jan. 16, 2004–Jan. 17, 2006
Jon Corzine (D)	Nov. 17, 2006–
New Mexico	
William "Bill" Richardson (D)	Jan. 1, 2003–
New York	
George E. Pataki (R)	Jan. 1, 1995–Jan 1, 2007
Eliot Spitzer (D)	Jan. 1, 2007–March 17, 2008
David Patterson (D)	March 18, 2008–
North Carolina	
Michael Easley (D)	Jan. 6, 2001–Jan. 10, 2009
North Dakota	
John Hoeven (R)	Dec. 15, 2000–
Ohio	
Robert A. Taft II (R)	Jan. 11, 1999–Jan. 8, 2007
Ted Strickland (D)	Jan. 8, 2007–
Oklahoma	
Brad Henry (D)	Jan 13, 2003–
Oregon	
Ted Kulongoski (D)	Jan. 13, 2003–
Pennsylvania	
Edward G. Rendell (D)	Jan. 21, 2003–

	Dates of Service
Rhode Island	
Don Carcieri (R)	Jan. 7, 2003–
South Carolina	
Mark Sanford (R)	Jan. 15, 2003–
South Dakota	
M. Michael Rounds (R)	Jan. 7, 2003–
Tennessee	
Phil Bredesen (D)	Jan. 18, 2003–
Texas	
Rick Perry (R)	Dec. 21, 2000–
Utah	
Olene S. Walker (R)	Nov. 5, 2003–Jan. 3, 2005
Jon M. Huntsman Jr. (R)	Jan. 3, 2005–
Vermont	
James H. Douglas (R)	Jan. 9, 2003–
Virginia	
Mark R. Warner (D)	Jan. 12, 2002–Jan. 14, 2006
Timothy M. Kaine (D)	Jan. 14, 2006
Washington	
Christine Gregoire (D)	Jan. 12, 2005–
West Virginia	
Joe Manchin III (D)	Jan. 17, 2005–
Wisconsin	
James E. Doyle (D)	Jan. 6, 2003–
Wyoming	
David Freudenthal (D)	Jan. 6, 2003–

Public Laws 2005–2008

Public Laws 2005–2008

Following are the public laws passed by the 109th Congress and 110th Congress and signed by President George W. Bush from 2005 through 2008.

109th Congress—2005

PL 109-1 (HR 241) Accelerate the income tax benefits for charitable cash contributions for the relief of victims of the Dec. 26, 2004, tsunami in South Asia. Introduced by Thomas, R-Calif., on Jan. 6, 2005. House Ways and Means discharged. House passed Jan. 6. Senate passed Jan. 6. President signed Jan. 7, 2005.

PL 109-2 (S 5) Expand federal court jurisdiction over class action lawsuits, require courts to review noncash settlements and limit attorney fees in such cases. Introduced by Grassley, R-Iowa, on Jan. 25, 2005. Senate Judiciary reported Feb. 3 (S Rept 109-14). Senate passed Feb. 10. House passed Feb. 17. President signed Feb. 18, 2005.

PL 109-3 (S 686) Provide for the relief of the parents of Theresa Marie Schiavo. Introduced by Frist, R-Tenn., on March 20, 2005. Senate passed March 20. House passed, under suspension of the rules, March 21. President signed March 21, 2005.

PL 109-4 (HR 1160) Reauthorize the Temporary Assistance for Needy Families block grant program through June 30, 2005. Introduced by Herger, R-Calif., on March 8, 2005. House passed, under suspension of the rules, March 14. Senate passed March 15. President signed March 25, 2005.

PL 109-5 (S 384) Extend the existence of the Nazi War Crimes and Japanese Imperial Government Records Interagency Working Group for two years. Introduced by DeWine, R-Ohio, on Feb. 15, 2005. Senate passed Feb. 16. House Government Reform ordered reported March 10 (no written report). House passed, under suspension of the rules, March 14. President signed March 25, 2005.

PL 109-6 (HR 1270) Amend the Internal Revenue Code of 1986 to extend the Leaking Underground Storage Tank Trust Fund financing rate. Introduced by Thomas, R-Calif., on March 14, 2005. House passed, under suspension of the rules, March 16. Senate passed March 17. President signed March 31, 2005.

PL 109-7 (HR 1134) Amend the Internal Revenue Code of 1986 to provide for the proper tax treatment of certain disaster mitigation payments. Introduced by Foley, R-Fla., on March 7, 2005. House passed, under suspension of the rules, March 14. Senate Finance discharged. Senate passed, with amendment, April 13. House agreed to Senate amendment April 14. President signed April 15, 2005.

PL 109-8 (S 256) Amend Title 11 of the U.S. Code to make it more difficult for consumers to escape repaying debts through bankruptcy. Introduced by Grassley, R-Iowa, on Feb. 1, 2005. Senate Judiciary reported, amended, Feb. 17 (no written report). Senate passed, amended, March 10. House Judiciary reported April 8 (H Rept 109-31, Part 1). House Financial Services discharged. Passed House April 14. President signed April 20, 2005.

PL 109-9 (S 167) Provide intellectual property protection for movies, legalize movie-filtering technology, expand libraries' access to copyrighted works and reauthorize a Library of Congress film-preservation program. Introduced by Hatch, R-Utah, on Jan. 25, 2005. Senate Judiciary discharged. Senate passed, amended, Feb. 1. House Judiciary reported April 12 (H Rept 109-33, Part 1). House Administration discharged. House passed, under suspension of the rules, April 19. President signed April 27, 2005.

PL 109-10 (HR 787) Designate the U.S. courthouse located at 501 I St., Sacramento, Calif., as the "Robert T. Matsui United States Courthouse." Introduced by Thompson, D-Calif., on Feb. 10, 2005. House passed, under suspension of the rules, April 13. Senate passed April 14. President signed April 29, 2005.

PL 109-11 (H J Res 19) Appoint Shirley Ann Jackson as a citizen regent of the Board of Regents of the Smithsonian Institution. Introduced by Johnson, R-Texas, on Feb. 15, 2005. House passed, under suspension of the rules, April 19. Senate Rules and Administration discharged. Senate passed April 28. President signed May 5, 2005.

PL 109-12 (H J Res 20) Appoint Robert P. Kogod as a citizen regent of the Board of Regents of the Smithsonian Institution. Introduced by Johnson, R-Texas, on Feb. 15, 2005. House passed, under suspension of the rules, April 19. Senate Rules and Administration Committee discharged. Senate passed April 28. President signed May 5, 2005.

PL 109-13 (HR 1268) Make emergency supplemental appropriations for defense, the global war on terror and tsunami relief for the fiscal year ending Sept. 30, 2005. Introduced by Lewis, R-Calif., on March 11, 2005. House Appropriations reported March 11 (H Rept 109-16). House passed, amended, March 16. Senate Appropriations reported, amended, April 6 (S Rept 109-52). Senate passed, amended, April 21. Conference report filed in the House May 3 (H Rept 109-72). House agreed to the conference report May 5. Senate agreed to the conference report May 10. President signed May 11, 2005.

PL 109-14 (HR 2566). Extend highway, highway safety, motor safety, transit, and other programs funded out of the Highway Trust Fund through July 1, 2005. Introduced by Young, R-Alaska, on May 24, 2005. House passed, under suspension of the rules, May 25. Senate passed May 26. President signed May 31, 2005.

PL 109-15 (HR 1760) Designate the facility of the U.S. Postal Service located at 215 Martin Luther King, Jr. Blvd., Madison, Wis., as the "Robert M. La Follette, Sr. Post Office Building." Introduced by Baldwin, D-Wis., on April 21, 2005. House Government Reform ordered reported May 5 (no written report). House passed, under suspension of the rules, May 16. Senate Homeland Security and Government Affairs discharged. Senate passed May 26. President signed June 17, 2005.

PL 109-16 (HR 483) Designate a U.S. courthouse in Brownsville, Texas, as the "Reynaldo G. Garza and Filemon B. Vela United States Courthouse." Introduced by Ortiz, D-Texas, on Feb. 1, 2005. House passed, under suspension of the rules, April 13. Senate Environment and Public Works reported June 9 (no written report). Senate passed June 15. President signed June 29, 2005.

PL 109-17 (S 643) Amend the Agricultural Credit Act of 1987 to reauthorize state mediation programs through fiscal 2010. Introduced by Roberts, R-Kan., on March 16, 2005. Senate Agriculture, Nutrition and Forestry discharged. Senate passed April 21. House passed, under suspension of the rules, June 13. President signed June 29, 2005.

PL 109-18 (HR 1812) Amend the Public Health Service Act to authorize grants through fiscal 2010 to develop and operate pilot "patient navigator" programs to improve patient-health outcomes. Introduced by Menendez, D-N.J., on April 25, 2005. House Energy and Commerce reported June 7 (H Rept 109-104). House passed, amended, under suspension of the rules, June 13. Senate Health, Education, Labor and Pensions discharged. Senate passed June 22. President signed June 29, 2005.

PL 109-19 (HR 3021) Reauthorize the Temporary Assistance for Needy Families block grant program through Sept. 30, 2005. Introduced by Herger, R-Calif., on June 22, 2005. House passed, amended, under suspension of the rules, June 29. Senate passed June 30. President signed July 1, 2005.

PL 109-20 (HR 3104) Extend highway, highway safety, motor carrier safety, transit, and other programs funded out of the Highway Trust Fund through July 19, 2005. Introduced by Young, R-Alaska, on June 29, 2005. House committees on Transportation, Ways and Means, Science, and Resources discharged. House passed June 30. Senate passed June 30. President signed July 1, 2005.

PL 109-21 (S 714) Amend the Communications Act of 1934 to prohibit unsolicited advertisements by fax unless the sender has an "established business relationship" with the recipient, obtains the fax number either voluntarily through that relationship or from a publicly available source and provides an opt-out opportunity. Introduced by Smith, R-Ore., on April 6, 2005. Senate Commerce, Science and Transportation reported, amended, June 7 (S Rept 109-76). Senate passed, amended, June 24. House passed, under suspension of the rules, June 28. President signed July 9, 2005.

PL 109-22 (HR 120) Designate the facility of the U.S. Postal Service located at 30777 Rancho California Rd., Temecula, Calif., as the "Dalip Singh Saund Post Office Building." Introduced by Issa, R-Calif., on Jan. 4, 2005. House passed, under suspension of the rules, Feb. 1. Senate Homeland Security and Governmental Affairs ordered reported June 22 (no written report). Senate passed June 29. President signed July 12, 2005.

PL 109-23 (HR 289) Designate the facility of the U.S. Postal Service located at 8200 South Vermont Ave. in Los Angeles, Calif., as the "Sergeant First Class John Marshall Post Office Building." Introduced by Waters, D-Calif., on Jan. 6, 2005. House passed, amended, under suspension of the rules, Feb. 1. Senate Homeland Security and Governmental Affairs ordered reported June 22 (no written report). Senate passed June 29. President signed July 12, 2005.

PL 109-24 (HR 324) Designate the facility of the U.S. Postal Service located at 321 Montgomery Rd., Altamonte Springs, Fla., as the "Arthur Stacey Mastrapa Post Office Building." Introduced by Feeney, R-Fla., on Jan. 25, 2005. House passed, under suspension of the rules, Feb. 15. Senate Homeland Security and Governmental Affairs ordered reported June 22 (no written report). Senate passed June 29. President signed July 12, 2005.

PL 109-25 (HR 504) Designate the facility of the U.S. Postal Service located at 4960 West Washington Blvd., Los Angeles, Calif., as the "Ray Charles Post Office Building." Introduced by Watson, D-Calif., on Feb. 1, 2005. House Government Reform ordered reported April 13 (no written report). House passed, under suspension of the rules, April 20. Senate Homeland Security and Governmental Affairs ordered reported June 22 (no written report). Senate passed June 29. President signed July 12, 2005.

PL 109-26 (HR 627) Designate the facility of the U.S. Postal Service located at 40 Putnam Ave., Hamden, Conn., as the "Linda White-Epps Post Office." Introduced by DeLauro, D-Conn., on Feb. 8, 2005. House Government Reform ordered reported May 5 (no written report). House passed, under suspension of the rules, May 16. Senate Homeland Security and Governmental Affairs ordered reported June 22 (no written report). Senate passed June 29. President signed July 12, 2005.

PL 109-27 (HR 1072) Designate the facility of the U.S. Postal Service located at 151 West End St., Goliad, Texas, as the "Judge Emilio Vargas Post Office Building." Introduced by Hinojosa, D-Texas, on March 3, 2005. House Government Reform ordered reported April 13 (no written report). House passed, under suspension of the rules, April 20. Senate Homeland Security and Governmental Affairs ordered reported June 22 (no written report). Senate passed June 29. President signed July 12, 2005.

PL 109-28 (HR 1082) Designate the facility of the U.S. Postal Service located at 120 East Illinois Ave., Vinita, Okla., as the "Francis C. Goodpaster Post Office Building." Introduced by Boren, D-Okla., on March 3, 2005. House Government Reform ordered reported April 13 (no written report). House passed, under suspension of the rules, May 4. Senate Homeland Security and Governmental Affairs ordered reported June 22 (no written report). Senate passed June 29. President signed July 12, 2005.

PL 109-29 (HR 1236) Designate the facility of the U.S. Postal Service located at 750 4th St., Sparks, Nev., as the "Mayor Tony Armstrong Memorial Post Office." Introduced by Gibbons, R-Nev., on March 10, 2005. House Government Reform ordered reported April 13 (no written report). House passed, under suspension of the rules, April 26. Senate Homeland Security and Government Affairs ordered reported June 22 (no written report). Senate passed June 29. President signed July 12, 2005.

PL 109-30 (HR 1460) Designate the facility of the U.S. Postal Service located at 6200 Rolling Rd., Springfield, Va., as the "Captain Mark Stubenhofer Post Office Building." Introduced by J. Davis, R-Va., on April 5, 2005. House passed, under suspension of the rules, April 6. Senate Homeland Security and Governmental Affairs ordered reported June 22 (no written report). Senate passed June 29. President signed July 12, 2005.

PL 109-31 (HR 1524) Designate the facility of the U.S. Postal Service located at 12433 Antioch Rd., Overland Park, Kan., as the "Ed Eilert Post Office Building." Introduced by Moore, D-Kan., on April 6, 2005. House Government Reform ordered reported April 13 (no written report). House passed, under suspension of the rules, April 26. Senate Homeland Security and Governmental Affairs ordered reported June 22 (no written report). Senate passed June 29. President signed July 12, 2005.

PL 109-32 (HR 1542) Designate the facility of the U.S. Postal Service located at 695 Pleasant St., New Bedford, Mass., as the "Honorable Judge George N. Leighton Post Office Building." Introduced by Frank, D-Mass., on April 12, 2005. House Government Reform ordered reported April 13 (no written report). House passed, under suspension of the rules, May 4. Senate Homeland Security and Governmental Affairs ordered reported June 22 (no written report). Senate passed June 29. President signed July 12, 2005.

PL 109-33 (HR 2326) Designate the facility of the U.S. Postal Service located at 614 West Old County Rd., Belhaven, N.C., as the "Floyd Lupton Post Office." Introduced by Jones, R-N.C., on May 12, 2005. House Government Reform ordered reported May 26 (no written report). House passed, under suspension of the rules, June 13. Senate Homeland Security and Governmental Affairs ordered reported June 22 (no written report). Senate passed June 29. President signed July 12, 2005.

PL 109-34 (S 1282) Amend the Communications Satellite Act of 1962 to strike the privatization criteria for INTELSAT separated entities, remove certain restrictions on separated and successor entities to INTELSAT, and preserve the space segment of the Global Maritime Distress and Safety System. Introduced by Burns, R-Mont., on June 21, 2005. Senate passed June 21. House Energy and Commerce discharged. House passed June 29. President signed July 12, 2005.

PL 109-35 (HR 3332) Extend highway, highway safety, motor carrier safety, transit, and other programs funded out of the Highway Trust Fund through July 21, 2005. Introduced by Young, R-Alaska, on July 19, 2005. House committees on Transportation and Infrastructure, Ways and Means, Science, and Resources discharged. House passed July 19. Senate passed July 19. President signed July 20, 2005.

PL 109-36 (HR 1001) Designate the facility of the U.S. Postal Service located at 301 South Heatherwilde Blvd. in Pflugerville, Texas, as the "Sergeant Byron W. Norwood Post Office Building." Introduced by McCaul, R-Texas, on March 1, 2005. House Government Reform ordered reported April 13 (no written report). House passed, under suspension of the rules, April 20. Senate Homeland Security and Governmental Affairs ordered reported June 22 (no written report). Senate passed June 29. President signed July 21, 2005.

PL 109-37 (HR 3377) Extend highway, highway safety, motor carrier safety, transit, and other programs funded out of the Highway Trust Fund through July 27, 2005. Introduced by Young, R-Alaska, on July 21, 2005. House committees on Transportation and Infrastructure, Ways and Means, Science, and Resources discharged. House passed July 21. Senate passed July 21. President signed July 22, 2005.

PL 109-38 (HR 3071) Permit the individuals currently serving as executive director, deputy executive directors, and general counsel of Congress' Office of Compliance to serve one additional term. Introduced by Ney, R-Ohio, on June 27, 2005. House Administration discharged. House passed June 30. Senate passed July 13. President signed July 27, 2005.

PL 109-39 (H J Res 52) Approve the renewal of import restrictions contained in the Burmese Freedom and Democracy Act of 2003. Introduced by Lantos, D-Calif., on May 26, 2005. House passed, under suspension of the rules, June 21. Senate passed July 19. President signed July 27, 2005.

PL 109-40 (HR 3453) Extend highway, highway safety, motor carrier safety, transit, and other programs funded out of the Highway Trust Fund through July 30, 2005. Introduced by Young, R-Alaska, on July 27, 2005. House committees on Transportation and Infrastructure, Ways and Means, Science, and Resources discharged. House passed July 27. Senate passed July 27. President signed July 28, 2005.

PL 109-41 (S 544) Establish procedures for voluntary confidential reporting of medical errors to independent patient safety organizations, which then would submit the information to a national database for analysis and recommendations on improving patient safety and reducing errors. Introduced by Jeffords, I-Vt., on March 8, 2005. Senate Health, Education, Labor and Pensions ordered reported March 9 (no written report). Senate passed, amended, July 21. House passed, under suspension of the rules, July 27. President signed July 29, 2005.

PL 109-42 (HR 3512) Extend administrative expenses for highway, highway safety, motor carrier safety, transit, and other programs funded out of the Highway Trust Fund through Aug. 14, 2005. Introduced by Young, R-Alaska, on July 28, 2005. House committees on Transportation and Infrastructure, Ways and Means, Science, and Resources discharged. House passed July 29. Senate passed July 29. President signed July 30, 2005.

PL 109-43 (HR 3423) Amend the Medical Device User Fee and Modernization Act to preserve fees paid by medical device manufacturers to help fund Food and Drug Administration reviews and speed up the approval process. Introduced by Pitts, R-Pa., on July 25, 2005. House Energy and Commerce discharged. House passed July 26. Senate passed July 27. President signed Aug. 1, 2005.

PL 109-44 (HR 38) Designate a portion of the White Salmon River as a component of the National Wild and Scenic Rivers System. Introduced by Baird, D-Wash., on Jan. 4, 2005. House Resources reported June 14 (H Rept 109-125). House passed, amended, under suspension of the rules, June 27. Senate Energy and Natural Resources discharged. Senate passed July 26. President signed Aug. 2, 2005.

PL 109-45 (HR 481) Authorize the Cheyenne and Arapaho Tribes of Oklahoma to convey approximately 1,465 acres to the secretary of the interior to be held in trust for the tribes, and thus allow the National Park Service to formally establish the Sand Creek Massacre National Historic Site. Introduced by Musgrave,

R-Colo., on Feb. 1, 2005. House Resources reported, amended, June 8 (H Rept 109-107). House passed, amended, under suspension of the rules, June 27. Senate Energy and Natural Resources discharged. Senate passed July 26. President signed Aug. 2, 2005.

PL 109-46 (HR 541) Direct the secretary of agriculture to convey certain land to Lander County, Nev., and the secretary of the interior to convey certain land to Eureka County, Nev., for continued use as cemeteries. Introduced by Gibbons, R-Nev., on Feb. 2, 2005. House passed, under suspension of the rules, April 12. Senate Energy and Natural Resources discharged. Senate passed July 26. President signed Aug. 2, 2005.

PL 109-47 (HR 794) Correct the south boundary of the Colorado River Indian Reservation in Arizona. Introduced by Grijalva, D-Ariz., on Feb. 14, 2005. House passed, under suspension of the rules, April 12. Senate Indian Affairs discharged. Senate passed July 26. President signed Aug. 2, 2005.

PL 109-48 (HR 1046) Authorize the secretary of the interior to contract with the city of Cheyenne, Wyo., for the storage of the city's water in the Kendrick Project in Wyoming. Introduced by Cubin, R-Wyo., on March 2, 2005. House passed, under suspension of the rules, May 16. Senate passed July 26. President signed Aug. 2, 2005.

PL 109-49 (H J Res 59) Express the sense of Congress that women suffragists should be revered and celebrated for working to ensure the right of women to vote in the United States. Introduced by Berkley, D-Nev., on July 14, 2005. House passed, amended, under suspension of the rules, July 25. Senate passed July 28. President signed Aug. 2, 2005.

PL 109-50 (S 571) Designate the facility of the U.S. Postal Service located at 1915 Fulton St., Brooklyn, N.Y., as the "Congresswoman Shirley A. Chisholm Post Office Building." Introduced by Schumer, D-N.Y., on March 9, 2005. Senate Homeland Security and Governmental Affairs ordered reported June 22 (no written report). Senate passed June 29. House passed, under suspension of the rules, July 25. President signed Aug. 2, 2005.

PL 109-51 (S 775) Designate the facility of the U.S. Postal Service located at 123 W. 7th St., Holdenville, Okla., as the "Boone Pickens Post Office." Introduced by Inhofe, R-Okla., on April 13, 2005. Senate Homeland Security and Governmental Affairs ordered reported June 22 (no written report). Senate passed June 29. House passed, under suspension of the rules, July 25. President signed Aug. 2, 2005.

PL 109-52 (S 904) Designate the facility of the U.S. Postal Service located at 1560 Union Valley Rd., West Milford, N.J., as the "Brian P. Parrello Post Office Building." Introduced by Lautenberg, D-N.J., on April 26, 2005. Senate Homeland Security and Governmental Affairs ordered reported June 22 (no written report). Senate passed June 29. House passed, under suspension of the rules, July 26. President signed Aug. 2, 2005.

PL 109-53 (HR 3045) Approve and implement the Central American Free Trade Agreement between the United States, Costa Rica, the Dominican Republic, El Salvador, Guatemala, Honduras, and Nicaragua—also known as CAFTA. Introduced by DeLay, R-Texas, on June 23, 2005. House Ways and Means reported July 25 (H Rept 109-182). House passed July 28. Senate passed July 28. President signed Aug. 2, 2005.

PL 109- 54 (HR 2361) Make appropriations for the Interior Department, the EPA, and cultural programs and institutions for the fiscal year ending Sept. 30, 2006, and provide supplemental funding for veterans' health care. Introduced by Taylor, R-N.C., on May 13, 2005. House Appropriations reported May 13 (H Rept 109-80). House passed, amended, May 19. Senate Appropriations reported, amended, June 10 (S Rept 109-80). Senate passed, amended, June 29. Conference report filed in the House July 26 (H Rept 109-188). House agreed to the conference report July 28. Senate agreed to the conference report July 29. President signed Aug. 2, 2005.

PL 109-55 (HR 2985) Make appropriations for the legislative branch, including the House of Representatives, the Senate, and related agencies for the fiscal year ending Sept. 30, 2006. Introduced by Lewis, R-Calif., on June 20, 2005. House Appropriations reported June 20 (H Rept 109-139). House passed, amended, June 22. Senate Appropriations reported, amended, June 24 (S Rept 109-89). Senate passed, amended, June 30. Conference report filed in the House on July 26 (H Rept 109-189). House agreed to the conference report July 28. Senate agreed to the conference report July 29. President signed Aug. 2, 2005.

PL 109-56 (S 45) Amend the Controlled Substances Act to lift the patient limitation on prescribing drug addiction treatments by medical practitioners in group practices. Introduced by Levin, D-Mich., on Jan. 24, 2005. Senate committees on Health, Education, Labor and Pensions and the Judiciary discharged. Senate passed July 19. House passed, under suspension of the rules, July 27. President signed Aug. 2, 2005.

PL 109-57 (S 1395) Amend the Controlled Substances Import and Export Act to provide authority for the attorney general to authorize the export of controlled substances from the United States to another country for subsequent export from that country to a second country, if certain conditions and safeguards are satisfied. Introduced by Hatch, R-Utah, on July 13, 2005. Senate passed July 13. House passed, under suspension of the rules, July 27. President signed Aug. 2, 2005.

PL 109-58 (HR 6) Overhaul the nation's energy policies. Introduced by Barton, R-Texas, on April 18, 2005. House passed, amended, April 21. Senate passed, amended, June 28. Conference report filed in the House July 27 (H Rept 109-190). House agreed to the conference report July 28. Senate agreed to the conference report July 29. President signed Aug. 8, 2005.

PL 109-59 (HR 3) Authorize funds for federal highway, highway safety, and transit programs. Introduced by Young, R-Alaska, on Feb. 9, 2005. House Transportation and Infrastructure reported, amended, March 7 (H Rept 109-12, Part 1), and filed a supplemental report March 8 (H Rept 109-12, Part 2). House passed, amended, March 10. Senate passed, amended, May 17. Conference report filed in the House on July 28 (H Rept 109-203). House agreed to the conference report July 29. Senate agreed to the conference report July 29. President signed Aug. 10, 2005.

PL 109-60 (HR 1132) Provide for the establishment of a controlled substance monitoring program in each state. Introduced by Whitfield, R-Ky., on March 3, 2005. House Energy and Commerce reported, amended, July 27 (H Rept 109-191). House passed, amended, under suspension of the rules, July 27. Senate passed July 29. President signed Aug. 11, 2005.

PL 109-61 (HR 3645) Make emergency supplemental appropriations to meet immediate needs arising from the consequences of Hurricane Katrina, for the fiscal year ending Sept. 30, 2005. Introduced by Lewis, R-Calif., on Sept. 2, 2005. House passed Sept. 2. Senate passed Sept. 2. President signed Sept. 2, 2005.

PL 109-62 (HR 3673) Make further emergency supplemental appropriations to meet immediate needs arising from the consequences of Hurricane Katrina, for the fiscal year ending Sept. 30, 2005. Introduced by Lewis, R-Calif., Sept. 7, 2005. House passed, under suspension of the rules, Sept. 8. Senate passed Sept. 8. President signed Sept. 8, 2005.

PL 109-63 (HR 3650) Allow United States courts to conduct business during emergency conditions. Introduced by Sensenbrenner, R-Wis., on Sept. 6, 2005. House passed, under suspension of the rules, Sept. 7. Senate passed Sept. 8. President signed Sept. 9, 2005.

PL 109-64 (HR 804) Exclude from consideration as income certain payments under the national flood insurance program. Introduced by Baker, R-La., on Feb. 15, 2005. House Financial Services reported, April 14 (H Rept 109-44). House passed, amended, under suspension of the rules, July 12. Senate Banking, Housing, and Urban Affairs reported July 29 (no written report). Senate passed Sept. 8. President signed Sept. 20, 2005.

PL 109-65 (HR 3669) Temporarily increase the borrowing authority of the Federal Emergency Management Agency for carrying out the national flood insurance program. Introduced by Ney, R-Ohio, on Sept. 7, 2005. House passed, under suspension of the rules, Sept. 8. Senate passed Sept. 12. President signed Sept. 20, 2005.

PL 109-66 (HR 3169) Provide the secretary of education with waiver authority for students eligible for Pell grants who are adversely affected by a natural disaster. Introduced by Keller, R-Fla., on June 30, 2005. House passed, amended, under suspension of the rules, Sept. 7. Senate passed Sept. 15. President signed Sept. 21, 2005.

PL 109-67 (HR 3668) Provide the secretary of education with waiver authority for students eligible for federal higher education grants who are adversely affected by a natural disaster. Introduced by Jindal, R-La., on Sept. 7, 2005. House passed, amended, under suspension of the rules, Sept. 8. Senate passed Sept. 15. President signed Sept. 21, 2005.

PL 109-68 (HR 3672) Provide assistance to families affected by Hurricane Katrina through the Temporary Assistance for Needy Families. Introduced by McCrery, R-La., on Sept. 7, 2005. House passed, amended, under suspension of the rules, Sept. 8. Senate passed Sept. 15. President signed Sept. 21, 2005.

PL 109-69 (S 252) Direct the secretary of the interior to convey certain land in Washoe County, Nev., to the Board of Regents of the University and Community College System of Nevada. Introduced by Reid, D-Nev., on Feb. 1, 2005. Senate Energy and Natural Resources reported March 14 (S Rept 109-38). Senate passed July 26. House passed, under suspension of the rules, Sept. 13. President signed Sept. 21, 2005.

PL 109-70 (S 264) Amend the Reclamation Wastewater and Groundwater Study and Facilities Act to authorize certain projects in the state of Hawaii. Introduced by Akaka, D-Hawaii, on Feb. 2, 2005. Senate Energy and Natural Resources reported March 10 (S Rept 109-33). Senate passed, amended, July 26. House passed, under suspension of the rules, Sept. 13. President signed Sept. 21, 2005.

PL 109-71 (S 276) Revise the boundary of the Wind Cave National Park in South Dakota. Introduced by Johnson, D-S.D., on Feb. 3, 2005. Senate Energy and Natural Resources reported March 8 (S Rept 109-21). Senate passed July 26. House passed, under suspension of the rules, Sept. 13. President signed Sept. 21, 2005.

PL 109-72 (HR 3761) Provide special rules for disaster relief employment under the 1988 Workforce Investment Act for individuals displaced by Hurricane Katrina. Introduced by Boustany, R-La., on Sept. 14, 2005. House passed, amended, under suspension of the rules, Sept. 20. Senate passed Sept. 21. President signed Sept. 23, 2005.

PL 109-73 (HR 3768) Provide emergency tax relief for persons affected by Hurricane Katrina. Introduced by McCrery, R-La., on Sept. 14, 2005. House passed, amended, under suspension of the rules, Sept. 15. Senate passed, amended, Sept. 15. House agreed to Senate amendment with an amendment Sept. 21. Senate agreed to House amendment Sept. 21. President signed Sept. 23, 2005.

PL 109-74 (HR 3649) Ensure funding for sport fishing and boating safety programs funded out of the Highway Trust Fund through the end of fiscal 2005. Introduced by Young, R-Alaska, on Sept. 6, 2005. House passed, under suspension of the rules, Sept. 13. Senate passed, amended, Sept. 15. House agreed to Senate amendment, under suspension of the rules, Sept. 20. President signed Sept. 29, 2005.

PL 109-75 (S 1340) Amend the Pittman-Robertson Wildlife Restoration Act to extend the date after which surplus funds in the wildlife restoration fund become available for apportionment. Introduced by Inhofe, R-Okla., on June 30, 2005. Senate Environment and Public Works reported Aug. 31 (S Rept 109-125). Senate passed Sept. 9. House passed, under suspension of the rules, Sept. 20. President signed Sept. 29, 2005.

PL 109-76 (S 1368) Extend the existence of the Parole Commission. Introduced by Specter, R-Pa., on July 1, 2005. Senate passed July 1. House passed, under suspension of the rules, Sept. 21. President signed Sept. 29, 2005.

PL 109-77 (H J Res 68) Make continuing appropriations for fiscal 2006. Introduced by Lewis, R-Calif., on Sept. 27, 2005. House passed Sept. 29. Senate passed Sept. 30. President signed Sept. 30, 2005.

PL 109-78 (HR 2132) Extend the waiver authority of the secretary of education with respect to student financial assistance during a war or other military operation or national emergency. Introduced by Kline, R-Minn., on May 5, 2005. House passed, under suspension of the rules, Sept. 20. Senate Health, Education, Labor and Pensions Committee discharged. Senate passed Sept. 27. President signed Sept. 30, 2005.

PL 109-79 (HR 2385) Extend for ten years the statutory authority for the secretary of commerce, rather than the Federal Trade Commission, to produce the quarterly financial report. Introduced by Turner, R-Ohio, on May 17, 2005. House Government Reform Committee reported, amended, July 12 (H Rept 109-164). Senate Commerce, Science, and Transportation Committee discharged. Senate Homeland Security and Governmental Affairs Committee discharged. Senate passed Sept. 26. President signed Sept. 30, 2005.

PL 109-80 (HR 3200) Permanently increase, to $400,000, the maximum federally subsidized life insurance payment that families of military personnel may receive if a service member is killed in the line of duty. Introduced by Miller, R-Fla., on July 11, 2005. House Committee on Veterans' Affairs reported July 20 (H Rept 109-177). House passed, under suspension of the rules, Sept 26. Senate Veteran's Affairs Committee discharged. Senate passed Sept. 27. President signed Sept. 30, 2005.

PL 109-81 (HR 3784) Extend through Dec. 31, 2005, the authorization of appropriations for, and the duration of, each program authorized under the Higher Education Act of 1965. Introduced by Boehner, R-Ohio, on Sept. 15, 2005. House passed, amended, under suspension of the rules, Sept. 20. Senate Health, Education, Labor, and Pensions Committee discharged. Senate passed, amended, Sept. 26. House passed, under suspension of the rules, Sept. 28. President signed Sept. 30, 2005.

PL 109-82 (HR 3864) Provide vocational rehabilitation services to individuals with disabilities affected by Hurricane Katrina or Hurricane Rita. Introduced by Boustany, R-La., on Sept. 22, 2005. House passed, amended, under suspension of the rules, Sept. 28. Senate passed Sept. 28. President signed Sept. 30, 2005.

PL 109-83 (S 1754) Extend the U.S. Grain Standards Act of 1916 (PL 64-190), which sets marketing and inspection standards for grains and oilseeds. Introduced by Chambliss, R-Ga., on Sept. 22, 2005. Senate passed Sept. 22. House passed, under suspension of the rules, Sept. 28. President signed Sept. 30, 2005.

PL 109-84 (HR 3667) Designate the facility of the U.S. Postal Service located at 200 South Barrington St., Los Angeles, as the "Karl Malden Station." Introduced by Waxman, D-Calif., on Sept. 7, 2005. House passed, under suspension of the rules, Sept. 21. Senate Homeland Security and Government Affairs discharged. Senate passed Sept. 27. President signed Oct. 4, 2005.

PL 109-85 (HR 3767) Designate the facility of the U.S. Postal Service located at 2600 Oak St. in St. Charles, Ill., as the "Jacob L. Frazier Post Office Building." Introduced by Hastert, R-Ill., on Sept. 14, 2005. House passed, under suspension of the rules, Sept. 21. Senate passed Sept. 27. President signed Oct. 4, 2005.

PL 109-86 (HR 3863) Provide the secretary of education with waiver authority for the reallocation rules in the Campus-Based Aid programs and extend the deadline by which funds have to be reallocated to institutions of higher education due to a natural disaster. Introduced by Jindal, R-La., on Sept. 22, 2005. House passed, amended, under suspension of the rules, Sept. 27. Senate passed Sept. 30. President signed Oct. 7, 2005.

PL 109-87 (S 1786) Authorize the secretary of transportation to make emergency airport improvement project grants-in-aid under title 49, U.S. Code, for repairs and costs related to damage from hurricanes Katrina and Rita. Introduced by Lott, R-Miss., on Sept. 28, 2005. Senate passed Sept. 28. House passed, under suspension of the rules, Oct. 6. President signed Oct. 7, 2005.

PL 109-88 (S 1858) Permit use of $750 million for a program to lend money to local governments to maintain essential services in the aftermath of hurricanes Katrina and Rita. Introduced by Vitter, R-La., on Oct. 7, 2005. Senate passed Oct. 7. House passed Oct. 7. President signed Oct. 7, 2005.

PL 109-89 (S 1413) Redesignate the Crowne Plaza in Kingston, Jamaica, as the Colin L. Powell Residential Plaza. Introduced by Lugar, R-Ind., on July 15, 2005. Senate passed July 15. House passed, under suspension of the rules, Oct. 6. President signed Oct. 13, 2005.

PL 109-90 (HR 2360) Make appropriations for the Department of Homeland Security for fiscal 2006. Introduced by Rogers, R-Ky., on May 13, 2005. House Appropriations reported May 13 (H Rept 109-79). House passed, amended, May 17. Senate Appropriations reported, amended, June 16 (S Rept 109-83). Senate passed, amended, July 14. Conference report filed in the House Sept. 29 (H Rept 109-241). House agreed to the conference report Oct. 6. Senate agreed to the conference report Oct. 7. President signed Oct. 18, 2005.

PL 109-91 (HR 3971) Provide assistance to individuals and states affected by Hurricane Katrina. Introduced by Deal, R-Ga., on Oct. 6, 2005. House passed, under suspension of the rules, Oct. 6. Senate passed, amended, Oct. 7. House agreed to Senate amendment with amendments pursuant to H Res 501 on Oct. 19. Senate agreed to House amendments Oct. 19. President signed Oct. 20, 2005.

PL 109-92 (S 397) Prohibit civil liability actions from being brought or continued against manufacturers, distributors, dealers or importers of firearms or ammunition for damages, injunctive or other relief resulting from the misuse of their products by others. Introduced by Craig, R-Idaho, on Feb. 16, 2005. Senate passed, amended, July 29. House passed Oct. 20. President signed Oct. 26, 2005.

PL 109-93 (S 55) Adjust the boundary of Rocky Mountain National Park in Colorado to include 5.9 acres of nonfederal land received in exchange for 70 acres of federal land. Introduced by Allard, R-Colo., on Jan. 24, 2005. Senate Energy and Natural Resources reported March 8 (S Rept 109-19). Senate passed July 26. House passed, under suspension of the rules, Oct. 18. President signed Oct. 26, 2005.

PL 109-94 (S 156) Designate the 11,183 acres of the Ojito Wilderness Study Area in New Mexico as wilderness, take 11,514 acres of land into trust for the Pueblo of Zia. Introduced by Bingaman, D-N.M., on Jan. 25, 2005. Senate Energy and Natural Resources reported, amended, Feb. 28 (S Rept 109-13). Senate passed, amended, July 26. House passed, under suspension of the rules, Oct. 18. President signed Oct. 26, 2005.

PL 109-95 (HR 1409) Amend the Foreign Assistance Act of 1961 to provide assistance for orphans and other vulnerable children in developing countries. Introduced by Lee, D-Calif., on March 17, 2005. House passed, amended, under suspension of the rules, Oct. 18. Senate passed Oct. 24. President signed Nov. 8, 2005.

PL 109-96 (S 172) Amend the Federal Food, Drug and Cosmetic Act to provide for the regulation of all contact lenses as medical devices. Introduced by DeWine, R-Ohio, on Jan. 26, 2005. Senate Health, Education, Labor, and Pensions reported, amended, July 27 (S Rept 109-110). Senate passed, amended, July 29. House passed, under suspension of the rules, Oct. 26. President signed Nov. 9, 2005.

PL 109-97 (HR 2744) Make appropriations for Agriculture, Rural Development, Food and Drug Administration, and Related Agencies for fiscal 2006. Introduced by Bonilla, R-Texas, on June 3, 2005. House Appropriations reported June 2 (H Rept 109-102). House passed, amended, June 8. Senate Appropriations reported, amended, June 27 (S Rept 109-92). Senate passed, amended, Sept. 22. Conference report filed in the House Oct. 26 (H Rept 109-255). House agreed to the conference report Oct. 28. Senate agreed to the conference report Nov. 3. President signed Nov. 10, 2005.

PL 109-98 (HR 2967) Designate the federal building located at 333 Mt. Elliott St. in Detroit as the "Rosa Parks Federal Building." Introduced by Kilpatrick, D-Mich., on June 17, 2005. House passed, under suspension of the rules, Oct. 26. Senate passed Nov. 1. President signed Nov. 11, 2005.

PL 109-99 (HR 3765) Extend through March 31, 2006, the authority of the secretary of the army to accept and expend funds contributed by nonfederal public entities and to expedite the processing of permits. Introduced by Baird, D-Wash., on Sept. 14, 2005. House passed, under suspension of the rules, Sept. 20. Senate Environment and Public Works discharged. Senate passed, amended, Oct. 7. House agreed to Senate amendments, under suspension of the rules, Oct. 18. President signed Nov. 11, 2005.

PL 109-100 (S 37) Extend the special postage stamp for breast cancer research for two years. Introduced by Feinstein, D-Calif., on Jan. 24, 2005. Senate Homeland Security and Governmental Affairs reported Sept. 26 (S Rept 109-140). Senate passed Sept. 27. House Government Reform, Energy and Commerce, and Armed Services discharged Oct. 27. House passed Oct. 27. President signed Nov. 11, 2005.

PL 109-101 (S 1285) Designate the federal building located at 333 Mt. Elliott St. in Detroit as the "Rosa Parks Federal Building" and designate the annex located on the 200 block of 3rd St. NW in the District of Columbia as the "William B. Bryant Annex." Introduced by Stabenow, D-Mich., on June 22, 2005. Senate Environment and Public Works reported Oct. 26 (no written report). Senate passed, amended, Oct. 26. House passed, under suspension of the rules, Nov. 2. President signed Nov. 11, 2005.

PL 109-102 (HR 3057) Make appropriations for foreign operations, export financing, and related programs for fiscal 2006. Introduced by Kolbe, R-Ariz., on June 24, 2005. House Appropriations reported June 24 (H Rept 109-152). House passed, amended, June 28. Senate Appropriations reported, amended, June 30 (S Rept 109-96). Senate passed, amended, July 20. Conference report filed in the House Nov. 2 (H Rept 109-265). House agreed to the conference report Nov. 4. Senate agreed to the conference report Nov. 10. President signed Nov. 14, 2005.

PL 109-103 (HR 2419) Make appropriations for energy and water development for fiscal 2006. Introduced by Hobson, R-Ohio, on May 18, 2005. House Appropriations reported May 18 (H Rept 109-86). House passed, amended, May 24. Senate Appropriations reported, amended, June 16 (S Rept 109-84). Senate passed, amended, July 1. Conference report filed in the House Nov. 7 (H Rept 109-275). House agreed to the conference report Nov. 9. Senate agreed to the conference report Nov. 14. President signed Nov. 19, 2005.

PL 109-104 (HR 4326) Authorize the secretary of the navy to enter into a contract for the nuclear refueling and complex overhaul of the USS *Carl Vinson* (CVN-70). Introduced by J. Davis, R-Va., on Nov. 15, 2005. House passed, under suspension of the rules, Nov. 16. Senate passed Nov. 18. President signed Nov. 19, 2005.

PL 109-105 (H J Res 72) Make further continuing appropriations for fiscal 2006. Introduced by Lewis, R-Calif., on Nov. 16, 2005. House passed Nov. 17. Senate passed Nov. 18. President signed Nov. 19, 2005.

PL 109-106 (HR 4133) Temporarily increase the borrowing authority of the Federal Emergency Management Agency for carrying out the national flood insurance program. Introduced by Fitzpatrick, R-Pa., on Oct. 25, 2005. House Financial Services reported Nov. 7 (H Rept 109-274). House passed, under suspension of the rules, Nov. 16. Senate passed, amended, Nov. 18. House agreed to Senate amendment Nov. 18. President signed Nov. 21, 2005.

PL 109-107 (HR 2490) Designate the facility of the U.S. Postal Service located at 442 West Hamilton St., Allentown, Pa., as the "Mayor Joseph S. Daddona Memorial Post Office." Introduced by Dent, R-Pa., on May 19, 2005. House passed, under suspension of the rules, June 27. Senate Homeland Security and Governmental Affairs discharged. Senate passed Nov. 8. President signed Nov. 22, 2005.

PL 109-108 (HR 2862) Make appropriations for science, the departments of State, Justice, and Commerce, and related agencies for fiscal 2006. Introduced by Wolf, R-Va., on June 10, 2005. House Appropriations reported June 10 (H Rept 109-118). House passed, amended, June 16. Senate Appropriations reported, amended, June 23 (S Rept 109-88). Senate passed, amended, Sept. 15. Conference report filed in the House Nov. 7 (H Rept 109-272). House agreed to the conference report Nov. 9. Senate agreed to the conference report Nov. 16. President signed Nov. 22, 2005.

PL 109-109 (HR 3339) Designate the facility of the U.S. Postal Service located at 2061 South Park Ave, in Buffalo, N.Y., as the "James T. Molloy Post Office Building." Introduced by Higgins, D-NY., on July 19, 2005. House passed, under suspension of the rules, July 26. Senate Homeland Security and Governmental Affairs discharged. Senate passed Nov. 8. President signed Nov. 22, 2005.

PL 109-110 (S 161) Provide for a land exchange in the state of Arizona between the secretary of agriculture and the Yavapai

Ranch Limited Partnership. Introduced by McCain, R-Ariz., on Jan. 25, 2005. Senate Energy and Natural Resources reported March 16 (S Rept 109-40). Senate passed July 26. House passed, under suspension of the rules, Nov. 15. President signed Nov. 22, 2005.

PL 109-111 (S 1234) Increase, effective Dec. 1, 2005, the rates of compensation for veterans with service-connected disabilities and the rates of dependency and indemnity compensation for survivors of certain disabled veterans. Introduced by Craig, R-Idaho, on June 14, 2005. Senate Veterans' Affairs reported Sept. 21 (S Rept 109-138). Senate passed, amended, Nov. 16. House passed Nov. 16. President signed Nov. 22, 2005.

PL 109-112 (S 1713) Make amendments to the Iran Nonproliferation Act of 2000 related to International Space Station payments. Introduced by Lugar, R-Ind., on Sept. 15, 2005. Senate Foreign Relations discharged. Senate passed Sept. 21. House passed, amended, under suspension of the rules, Oct. 26. Senate agreed to House amendments Nov. 8. President signed Nov. 22, 2005.

PL 109-113 (S 1894) Amend part E of Title IV of the Social Security Act to allow foster care maintenance payments to private for-profit agencies. Introduced by Inhofe, R-Okla., on Oct. 19, 2005. Senate passed Oct. 19. House passed, under suspension of the rules, Nov. 8. President signed Nov. 22, 2005.

PL 109-114 (HR 2528) Make appropriations for military quality of life functions of the Department of Defense, military construction, the Department of Veterans Affairs and related agencies for fiscal 2006. Introduced by Walsh, R-N.Y., on May 23, 2005. House Appropriations reported May 23 (H Rept 109-95). House passed, amended, May 26. Senate Appropriations reported, amended, July 21 (S Rept 109-105). Senate passed, amended, Sept. 22. Conference report filed in the House Nov. 18 (H Rept 109-305). House agreed to the conference report Nov. 18. Senate agreed to the conference report Nov. 18. President signed Nov. 30, 2005.

PL 109-115 (HR 3058) Make appropriations for the departments of Transportation, Treasury, and Housing and Urban Development, the judiciary, District of Columbia, and independent agencies for fiscal 2006. Introduced by Knollenberg, R-Mich., on June 24, 2005. House Appropriations reported June 24 (H Rept 109-153). House passed, amended, June 30. Senate Appropriations reported, amended, July 26 (S Rept 109-109). Senate passed, amended, Oct. 20. Conference report filed in the House Nov. 18 (H Rept 109-307). House agreed to the conference report Nov. 18. Senate agreed to the conference report Nov. 21. President signed Nov. 30, 2005.

PL 109-116 (HR 4145) Direct the Joint Committee on the Library to obtain a statue of Rosa Parks and place the statue in the National Statuary Hall of the U.S. Capitol. Introduced by Jackson, D-Ill., on Oct. 26, 2005. House Administration discharged. House passed, amended, Nov. 18. Senate passed Nov. 18. President signed Dec. 1, 2005.

PL 109-117 (HR 126) Amend Public Law 89-366 to allow for an adjustment in the number of free-roaming horses permitted in Cape Lookout National Seashore. Introduced by Jones, R-N.C., on Jan. 4, 2005. House passed, under suspension of the rules, March 14. Senate Energy and Natural Resources reported Oct. 19 (S Rept 109-154). Senate passed Nov. 16. President signed Dec. 1, 2005.

PL 109-118 (HR 539) Designate certain National Forest System land in the Commonwealth of Puerto Rico as components of the National Wilderness Preservation System. Introduced by Fortu, R-P.R., on Feb. 2, 2005. House Resources reported, amended, June 14 (H Rept 109-126). House passed, amended, under suspension of the rules, Sept. 13. Senate Energy and Natural Resources reported Oct. 19 (S Rept 109-155). Senate passed Nov. 16. President signed Dec. 1, 2005.

PL 109-119 (HR 606) Authorize appropriations to the secretary of the interior for the restoration of the Angel Island Immigration Station in California. Introduced by Woolsey, D-Calif., on Feb. 2, 2005. House passed, under suspension of the rules, May 23. Senate Energy and Natural Resources reported Oct. 19 (S Rept. 109-157). Senate passed Nov. 16. President signed Dec. 1, 2005.

PL 109-120 (HR 1972) Direct the secretary of the interior to conduct a special resource study to determine the suitability and feasibility of including in the National Park System certain sites in Williamson County, Tenn., relating to the Battle of Franklin. Introduced by Blackburn, R-Tenn., on April 28, 2005. House Resources reported, amended, Nov. 10 (H Rept 109-289). House passed, amended, under suspension of the rules, Nov. 15. Senate passed Nov. 16. President signed Dec. 1, 2005.

PL 109-121 (HR 1973) Make access to safe water and sanitation for developing countries a specific policy objective of U.S. foreign assistance programs. Introduced by Blumenauer, D-Ore., on April 28, 2005. House International Relations reported, amended, Oct. 28 (H Rept 109-260). House passed, amended, under suspension of the rules, Nov. 7. Senate passed Nov. 16. President signed Dec. 1, 2005.

PL 109-122 (HR 2062) Designate the facility of the U.S. Postal Service located at 57 West St. in Newville, Pa., as the "Randall D. Shughart Post Office Building." Introduced by Shuster, R-Pa., on May 3, 2005. House passed, under suspension of the rules, Sept. 27. Senate Homeland Security and Governmental Affairs discharged. Senate passed Nov. 18. President signed Dec. 1, 2005.

PL 109-123 (HR 2183) Designate the facility of the U.S. Postal Service located at 567 Tompkins Ave. in Staten Island, N.Y., as the "Vincent Palladino Post Office." Introduced by Fossella, R-N.Y., on May 5, 2005. House passed, under suspension of the rules, July 13. Senate Homeland Security and Governmental Affairs discharged. Senate passed Nov. 18. President signed Dec. 1, 2005.

PL 109-124 (HR 3853) Designate the facility of the U.S. Postal Service located at 208 South Main St. in Parkdale, Ark., as the "Willie Vaughn Post Office." Introduced by Ross, D-Ark., on Sept. 21, 2005. House passed, under suspension of the rules, Oct. 18. Senate Homeland Security and Governmental Affairs discharged. Senate passed Nov. 18. President signed Dec. 1, 2005.

PL 109-125 (HR 584) Authorize the secretary of the interior to recruit volunteers to assist with or facilitate the activities of various agencies and offices of the Department of the Interior. Introduced by Pombo, R-Calif., on Feb. 2, 2005. House passed, under suspension of the rules, March 14. Senate Energy and Natural

Resources reported Oct. 19 (S Rept 109-156). Senate passed Nov. 16. President signed Dec. 7, 2005.

PL 109-126 (HR 680) Direct the secretary of the interior to convey certain land held in trust for the Paiute Indian Tribe of Utah to the City of Richfield, Utah. Introduced by Cannon, R-Utah, on Feb. 9, 2005. House passed, under suspension of the rules, March 14. Senate Indian Affairs reported Nov. 7 (S Rept 109-175). Senate passed Nov. 18, 2005. President signed Dec. 7, 2005.

PL 109-127 (HR 1101) Revoke a public land order with respect to approximately 140 acres of lands erroneously included in the Cibola National Wildlife Refuge, Calif. Introduced by Hunter, R-Calif., on March 3, 2005. House passed, under suspension of the rules, May 23. Senate Energy and Natural Resources reported Oct. 27 (S Rept 109-172). Senate passed Nov. 16. President signed Dec. 7, 2005.

PL 109-128 (H J Res 75) Make further continuing appropriations for fiscal year 2006. Introduced by Lewis, R-Calif., on Dec. 17, 2005. House passed, amended, under suspension of the rules, Dec. 17. Senate passed Dec. 17. President signed Dec. 18, 2005.

PL 109-129 (HR 2520) Provide for the collection and maintenance of human cord blood stem cells for the treatment of patients and research, and amend the Public Health Service Act to authorize the C.W. Bill Young Cell Transplantation Program. Introduced by Smith, R-N.J., on May 23, 2005. House passed, under suspension of the rules, May 24. Senate passed, amended, Dec. 16. House agreed to Senate amendment, under suspension of the rules, Dec. 17. President signed Dec. 20, 2005.

PL 109-130 (S 52) Direct the secretary of the interior to convey approximately 200 acres of real property to Beaver County, Utah. Introduced by Hatch, R-Utah, on Jan. 24, 2005. Senate Energy and Natural Resources reported March 30 (S Rept 109-43). Senate passed July 26. House passed, under suspension of the rules, Dec. 6. President signed Dec. 20, 2005.

PL 109-131 (S 136) Authorize the secretary of the interior to provide supplemental funding and other services that are necessary to assist certain local school districts in the state of California in providing education services for students attending schools located within Yosemite National Park. Also, authorize the secretary of the interior to adjust the boundaries of the Golden Gate National Recreation Area and Redwood National Park. Introduced by Feinstein, D-Calif., on Jan. 24, 2005. Senate Energy and Natural Resources reported, amended, April 28 (S Rept 109-63). Senate passed, amended, July 26. House passed, under suspension of the rules, Dec. 6. President signed Dec. 20, 2005.

PL 109-132 (S 212) Amend the Valles Caldera Preservation Act to improve the preservation of the Valles Caldera. Introduced by Domenici, R-N.M., on Jan. 31, 2005. Senate Energy and Natural Resources reported Feb. 23 (S Rept 109-10). Senate passed July 26. House passed, under suspension of the rules, Dec. 6. President signed Dec. 20, 2005.

PL 109-133 (S 279) Amend the Pueblo Land Act of 1924, to provide for the exercise of criminal jurisdiction. Introduced by Domenici, R-N.M., on Feb. 3, 2005. Senate Indian Affairs discharged. Senate passed, amended, July 26. House passed, under suspension of the rules, Dec. 6. President signed Dec. 20, 2005.

PL 109-134 (S 1886) Authorize the transfer of naval vessels to certain foreign recipients. Introduced by Lugar, R-Ind., on Oct. 18, 2005. Senate passed Oct. 18. House passed, under suspension of the rules, Dec. 6. President signed Dec. 20, 2005.

PL 109-135 (HR 4440) Amend the Internal Revenue Code of 1986 to provide tax benefits for the Gulf Opportunity Zone and certain areas affected by hurricanes Rita and Wilma. Introduced by McCrery, R-La., on Dec. 6, 2005. House passed, under suspension of the rules, Dec. 7. Senate passed, amended, Dec. 16. House agreed to Senate amendment Dec. 16. President signed Dec. 22, 2005.

PL 109-136 (HR 797) Amend the Native American Housing Assistance and Self-Determination Act of 1996 and other acts to improve housing programs for Indians. Introduced by Renzi, R-Ariz., on Feb. 14, 2005. House passed, under suspension of the rules, April 6. Senate Indian Affairs reported Oct. 27 (S Rept 109-160). Senate passed, amended, Nov. 8. House agreed to Senate amendments, under suspension of the rules, Dec. 18. President signed Dec. 22, 2005.

PL 109-137 (HR 3963) Amend the Federal Water Pollution Control Act to extend the authorization of appropriations for Long Island Sound. Introduced by Simmons, R-Conn., on Sept. 29, 2005. House Transportation and Infrastructure reported Nov. 14 (H Rept 109-293). House passed, under suspension of the rules, Dec. 7. Senate passed Dec. 16. President signed Dec. 22, 2005.

PL 109-138 (HR 4195) Authorize early repayment of obligations to the Bureau of Reclamation within Rogue River Valley Irrigation District or within Medford Irrigation District. Introduced by Walden, R-Ore., on Nov. 1, 2005. House Resources reported Dec. 6 (H Rept 109-323). House passed, under suspension of the rules, Dec. 6. Senate Energy and Natural Resources discharged. Senate passed Dec. 16. President signed Dec. 22, 2005.

PL 109-139 (HR 4324) Amend the Robert T. Stafford Disaster Relief and Emergency Assistance Act to reauthorize the predisaster mitigation program. Introduced by Shuster, R-Pa., on Nov. 15, 2005. House Transportation and Infrastructure discharged. House passed Nov. 18. Senate Homeland Security and Governmental Affairs discharged. Senate passed Dec. 15. President signed Dec. 22, 2005.

PL 109-140 (HR 4436) Provide certain specific authorities for the Department of State. Introduced by Smith, R-N.J., on Dec. 6, 2005. House passed, amended, under suspension of the rules, Dec. 14. Senate passed Dec. 15. President signed Dec. 22, 2005.

PL 109-141 (HR 4508) Commend the outstanding efforts in response to Hurricane Katrina by members and employees of the Coast Guard and provide temporary relief for personnel and vessels affected by the hurricane. Introduced by Young, R-Alaska, on Dec. 13, 2005. House passed, under suspension of the rules, Dec. 14. Senate passed Dec. 16. President signed Dec. 22, 2005.

PL 109-142 (H J Res 38) Recognize Commodore John Barry as the first flag officer of the United States Navy. Introduced by King, R-N.Y., on March 17, 2005. House passed, under suspension of the rules, Dec. 14. Senate passed Dec. 16. President signed Dec. 22, 2005.

PL 109-143 (S 335) Reauthorize the Congressional Award Act. Introduced by Lieberman, D-Conn., on Feb. 9, 2005. Senate Homeland Security and Governmental Affairs reported June 23 (S Rept 109-87). Senate passed July 14. House passed, under suspension of the rules, Dec. 14. President signed Dec. 22, 2005.

PL 109-144 (S 467) Extend the applicability of the Terrorism Risk Insurance Act of 2002. Introduced by Dodd, D-Conn., on Feb. 18, 2005. Senate Banking, Housing and Urban Affairs reported, amended. Nov. 16 (no written report). Senate passed, amended, Nov. 18. House passed, amended, under suspension of the rules, Dec. 7. Senate agreed with amendment to the House amendment Dec. 16. House agreed to Senate amendment to House amendment, under suspension of the rules, Dec. 17. President signed Dec. 22, 2005.

PL 109-145 (S 1047) Require the secretary of the Treasury to mint coins in commemoration of each of the past presidents and their spouses, respectively, improve circulation of the $1 coin and create a new bullion coin. Introduced by Sununu, R-N.H., on May 17, 2005. Senate Banking, Housing and Urban Affairs reported July 29 (no written report). Senate passed, amended, Nov. 18. House passed, under suspension of the rules, Dec. 13. President signed Dec. 22, 2005.

PL 109-146 (HR 358) Require the secretary of the Treasury to mint coins in commemoration of the 50th anniversary of the desegregation of the Little Rock Central High School in Little Rock, Ark. Introduced by Snyder, D-Ark., on Jan. 25, 2005. House Financial Services reported, amended, June 15 (H Rept 109-134, Part I). House Ways and Means discharged. House passed, amended, under suspension of the rules, June 27. Senate Banking, Housing and Urban Affairs discharged. Senate passed, amended, Nov. 18. House agreed to Senate amendment, under suspension of the rules, Dec. 18. President signed Dec. 22, 2005.

PL 109-147 (HR 327) Allow binding arbitration clauses to be included in all contracts affecting land within the Gila River Indian Community Reservation. Introduced by Grijalva, D-Ariz., on Jan. 25, 2005. House passed, under suspension of the rules, Dec. 7. Senate passed Dec. 14. President signed Dec. 22, 2005.

PL 109-148 (HR 2863) Make appropriations for the Department of Defense for fiscal 2006. Introduced by Young, R-Fla., on June 10, 2005. House Appropriations reported June 10 (H Rept 109-119). House passed, amended, June 20. Senate Appropriations reported, amended, Sept. 29 (S Rept 109-141). Senate passed, amended, Oct. 7. Conference report filed in the House Dec. 18 (H Rept 109-359). House agreed to the conference report Dec. 19. Senate agreed to the conference report Dec. 21. President signed Dec. 30, 2005.

PL 109-149 (HR 3010) Make appropriations for the departments of Labor, Health and Human Services, and Education, and related agencies for fiscal 2006. Introduced by Regula, R-Ohio, on June 21, 2005. House Appropriations reported June 21 (H Rept 109-143). House passed, amended, June 24. Senate Appropriations reported, amended, July 14 (S Rept 109-103). Senate passed, amended, Oct. 27. Conference report filed in the House Nov. 16 (H Rept 109-300). House rejected the conference report Nov. 17. New conference report filed in the House Dec. 13 (H Rept 109-337). House agreed to the conference report Dec. 14. Senate agreed to the conference report Dec. 21. President signed Dec. 30, 2005.

PL 109-150 (HR 4525) Temporarily extend programs under the Higher Education Act of 1965. Introduced by Boehner, R-Ohio, on Dec. 14, 2005. House passed, amended, under suspension of the rules, Dec. 17. Senate passed Dec. 22. President signed Dec. 30, 2005.

PL 109-151 (HR 4579) Amend Title I of the Employee Retirement Income Security Act of 1974, Title XXVII of the Public Health Service Act, and the Internal Revenue Code of 1986 to extend by one year provisions requiring parity in the application of certain limits to mental health benefits. Introduced by Boehner, R-Ohio, on Dec. 16, 2005. House passed, under suspension of the rules, Dec. 17. Senate passed Dec. 22. President signed Dec. 30, 2005.

PL 109-152 (S 205) Authorize the American Battle Monuments Commission to establish in the state of Louisiana a memorial to honor the Buffalo Soldiers. Introduced by Landrieu, D-La., on Jan. 31, 2005. Senate Energy and Natural Resources reported, amended, March 9 (S Rept 109-24). Senate passed, amended, July 26. House Resources discharged. House passed Dec. 19. President signed Dec. 30, 2005.

PL 109-153 (S 652) Provide financial assistance for the rehabilitation of the Benjamin Franklin National Memorial in Philadelphia, Pa., and the development of an exhibit to commemorate the 300th anniversary of the birth of Benjamin Franklin. Introduced by Specter, R-Pa., on March 17, 2005. Senate Energy and Natural Resources reported Oct. 19 (S Rept 109-147). Senate passed Nov. 16. House Resources discharged. House passed Dec. 19. President signed Dec. 30, 2005.

PL 109-154 (S 1238) Amend the Public Lands Corps Act of 1993 to provide for the conduct of projects that protect forests. Introduced by Feinstein, D-Calif., on June 14, 2005. Senate Energy and Natural Resources reported, amended, Oct. 19 (S Rept 109-152). Senate passed, amended, Nov. 16. House passed Dec. 19. President signed Dec. 30, 2005.

PL 109-155 (S 1281) Authorize appropriations for the National Aeronautics and Space Administration for science, aeronautics, exploration, exploration capabilities, and the inspector general, for fiscal years 2006, 2007, 2008, 2009, and 2010. Introduced by Hutchison, R-Texas, on June 21, 2005. Senate Commerce, Science and Transportation reported, amended, July 26 (S Rept 109-108). Senate passed, amended, Sept. 28. House passed, amended, Nov. 18. Conference report filed in the House Dec. 16 (H Rept 109-354). House agreed to the conference report, under suspension of the rules, Dec. 17. Senate agreed to the conference report Dec. 22. President signed Dec. 30, 2005.

PL 109-156 (S 1310) Authorize the secretary of the interior to allow the Columbia Gas Transmission Corp. to increase the diameter of a natural gas pipeline located in the Delaware Water Gap National Recreation Area. Introduced by Santorum, R-Pa., on June 24, 2005. Senate Energy and Natural Resources reported, amended, Dec. 8 (S. Rept. 109-194). Senate passed, amended, Dec. 16. House passed Dec. 19. President signed Dec. 30, 2005.

PL 109-157 (S 1481) Amend the Indian Land Consolidation Act to provide for probate reform. Introduced by McCain, R-Ariz., on July 26, 2005. Senate passed July 26. House Resources discharged. House passed Dec. 19. President signed Dec. 30, 2005.

PL 109-158 (S 1892) Amend Public Law 107-153 to modify a certain date. Introduced by McCain, R-Ariz., on Oct. 19, 2005. Senate Indian Affairs reported Dec. 8 (S Rept 109-201). Senate passed, amended, Dec. 16. House passed Dec. 19. President signed Dec. 30, 2005.

PL 109-159 (S 1988) Authorize the transfer of items in the War Reserves Stockpile to the Republic of Korea. Introduced by Lugar, R-Ind., on Nov. 9, 2005. Senate passed Nov. 9. House passed, under suspension of the rules, Dec. 18. President signed Dec. 30, 2005.

PL 109-160 (S 2167) Amend the USA PATRIOT Act to extend to Feb. 3, 2006, the sunset of certain provisions of that act and the "lone wolf" provision of the Intelligence Reform and Terrorism Prevention Act of 2004. Introduced by Sununu, R-N.H., on Dec. 21, 2005. Senate passed Dec. 21. House passed, amended, Dec. 22, 2005. Senate agreed to House amendment Dec. 22, 2005. President signed Dec. 30, 2005.

PL 109-161 (HR 4635) Reauthorize the Temporary Assistance for Needy Families block grant program through March 31, 2006. Introduced by Herger, R-Calif., on Dec. 18, 2005. House Ways and Means discharged. House passed Dec. 19. Senate passed Dec. 22. President signed Dec. 30, 2005.

109th Congress—2006

PL 109-162 (HR 3402) Authorize appropriations for the Department of Justice for fiscal years 2006 through 2009. Introduced by Sensenbrenner, R-Wis., on July 22, 2005. House Judiciary reported, amended, Sept. 22 (H Rept 109-233). House passed, amended, Sept. 28. Senate Judiciary discharged. Senate passed, amended, Dec. 16. House agreed to Senate amendment, under suspension of the rules, Dec. 17. President signed Jan. 5, 2006.

PL 109-163 (HR 1815) Authorize appropriations for fiscal 2006 for military activities of the Department of Defense and prescribe military personnel strengths for fiscal 2006. Introduced by Hunter, R-Calif., on April 26, 2005. House Armed Services reported, amended, May 20 (H Rept 109-89). House passed, amended, May 25. Senate Armed Services discharged. Senate passed, amended, Nov. 15. Conference report filed in the House Dec. 18 (H Rept 109-360). House agreed to conference report Dec. 19. Senate agreed to conference report Dec. 21. President signed Jan. 6, 2005.

PL 109-164 (HR 972) Authorize appropriations for fiscal years 2006 and 2007 for the Trafficking Victims Protection Act of 2000. Introduced by Smith, R-N.J., on Feb. 17, 2005. House International Relations reported, amended, Nov. 18 (H Rept 109-317, Part I). House Armed Services and House Energy and Commerce discharged. House Judiciary reported, amended, Dec. 8 (H Rept 109-317, Part II). House passed, amended, under suspension of the rules, Dec. 14. Senate passed Dec. 22. President signed Jan. 10, 2006.

PL 109-165 (HR 2017) Amend the Torture Victims Relief Act of 1998 to authorize appropriations to provide assistance for domestic and foreign programs and centers for the treatment of victims of torture. Introduced by Smith, R-N.J., on April 28, 2005. House passed, under suspension of the rules, Dec. 6. Senate passed Dec. 22. President signed Jan. 10, 2006.

PL 109-166 (HR 3179) Reauthorize and amend the Junior Duck Stamp Conservation and Design Program Act of 1994. Introduced by Ortiz, D-Texas, on June 30, 2005. House Resources discharged. House passed Dec. 19. Senate passed Dec. 22. President signed Jan. 10, 2006.

PL 109-167 (HR 4501) Amend the Passport Act of June 4, 1920, to authorize the secretary of state to establish and collect a surcharge to cover the costs of meeting the increased demand for passports as a result of actions taken to comply with section 7209(b) of the Intelligence Reform and Terrorism Prevention Act of 2004. Introduced by Hyde, R-Ill., on Dec. 13, 2005. House passed, amended, under suspension of the rules, Dec. 18. Senate passed Dec. 22. President signed Jan 10, 2006.

PL 109-168 (HR 4637) Make technical corrections in amendments made by the Energy Policy Act of 2005. Introduced by Gillmor, R-Ohio, on Dec. 18, 2005. House Energy and Commerce discharged. House passed Dec. 19. Senate passed Dec. 22. President signed Jan 10, 2006.

PL 109-169 (HR 4340) Implement the United States-Bahrain Free Trade Agreement. Introduced by Blunt, R-Mo., on Nov. 16, 2005. House Ways and Means reported Dec. 6 (H Rept 109-318). House passed Dec. 7. Senate passed Dec. 13. President signed Jan. 11, 2006.

PL 109-170 (HR 4659) Amend the USA PATRIOT Act to extend the sunset of certain provisions. Introduced by Sensenbrenner, R-Wis., on Jan. 31, 2006. House passed, under suspension of the rules, Feb. 1. Senate passed Feb. 2. President signed Feb. 3, 2006.

PL 109-171 (S 1932) Provide for reconciliation pursuant to Section 202(a)of the fiscal 2006 budget resolution (H Con Res 95). Introduced by Gregg, R-N.H., on Oct. 27, 2005. Senate Budget reported Oct. 27 (no written report). Senate passed, amended, Nov. 3. House passed, amended, Nov. 18. Conference report filed in the House Dec. 19 (H Rept 109-362). House agreed to the conference report Dec. 19. Conference report defeated in the Senate on Dec. 21, 2005. Senate agreed to House amendment with amendment Dec. 21. House agreed to Senate amendment to House amendment pursuant to H. Res. 653 on Feb. 1, 2006. President signed Feb. 8, 2006.

PL 109-172 (HR 4519) Amend the Public Health Service Act to extend funding for the operation of state high-risk health insurance pools. Introduced by Shadegg, R-Ariz., on Dec. 13, 2005. House passed, under suspension of the rules, Dec. 17. Senate Health, Education, Labor, and Pensions discharged. Senate passed Feb. 1, 2006. President signed Feb. 10, 2006.

PL 109-173 (HR 4636) Enact the technical and conforming amendments necessary to implement the Federal Deposit Insurance Reform Act of 2005. Introduced by Oxley, R-Ohio, on Dec. 18, 2005. House Financial Services discharged. House passed Dec. 19. Senate passed Dec. 22. President signed Feb. 15, 2006.

PL 109-174 (HR 4745) Make supplemental appropriations for fiscal 2006 for the Small Business Administration's disaster loans program. Introduced by Lewis, R-Calif., on Feb. 14, 2006. House passed, under suspension of the rules, Feb. 15. Senate passed Feb. 17. President signed Feb. 18, 2006.

PL 109-175 (S 1989) Designate the facility of the U.S. Postal Service located at 57 Rolfe Square in Cranston, R.I., as the "Holly A. Charette Post Office." Introduced by Reed, D-R.I., on Nov. 10, 2005. Senate Homeland Security and Governmental Affairs discharged. Senate passed Nov. 18. House passed, under suspension of the rules, Feb. 14, 2006. President signed Feb. 27, 2006.

PL 109-176 (S 1777) Provide relief for the victims of Hurricane Katrina. Introduced by Collins, R-Maine, on Sept. 27, 2005. Senate Homeland Security and Governmental Affairs reported Sept. 27 (no written report). Senate passed, amended, Feb. 15, 2006. House passed, amended, March 2. Senate agreed to House amendment March 3. President signed March 6, 2006.

PL 109-177 (HR 3199) Amend the USA PATRIOT Act to extend the sunset of certain provisions and make certain modifications. Introduced by Sensenbrenner, R-Wis., on July 11, 2005. House Judiciary reported, amended, July 18 (H Rept 109-174, Part 1). House Intelligence reported, amended, July 18 (H Rept 109-174 Part 2). House passed, amended, July 21. Senate passed, amended, July 29. Conference report filed in the House Dec. 8 (H Rept 109-333). House agreed to conference report Dec. 14. Senate agreed to conference report March 2, 2006. President signed March 9, 2006.

PL 109-178 (S 2271) Clarify that individuals who receive FISA orders can challenge nondisclosure requirements, that individuals who receive national security letters are not required to disclose the name of their attorney, that libraries are not wire or electronic communication service providers unless they provide specific services. Introduced by Sununu, R-N.H., on Feb. 10, 2006. Senate passed, amended, March 1. House passed, under suspension of the rules, March 7. President signed March 9, 2006.

PL 109-179 (S 449) Facilitate shareholder consideration of proposals to make Settlement Common Stock under the Alaska Native Claims Settlement Act available to missed enrollees, eligible elders, and eligible persons born after Dec. 18, 1971. Introduced by Murkowski, R-Alaska, on Feb. 17, 2005. Senate Indian Affairs reported July 28 (S Rept 109-112). Senate passed Dec. 14. House passed, under suspension of the rules, Feb. 28, 2006. President signed March 13, 2006.

PL 109-180 (HR 4515) Designate the facility of the U.S. Postal Service located at 4422 West Sciota St., Scio, N.Y., as the "Cpl. Jason L. Dunham Post Office." Introduced by Kuhl, R-N.Y., on Dec. 13, 2005. House Government Reform discharged. House passed Dec. 19. Senate passed March 3, 2006. President signed March 14, 2006.

PL 109-181 (HR 32) Amend Title XVIII, U.S. Code, to provide criminal penalties for trafficking in counterfeit marks. Introduced by Knollenberg, R-Mich., Jan. 4, 2005. House Judiciary reported, amended, May 3 (H Rept 109-68). House passed, amended, under suspension of the rules, May 23. Senate Judiciary discharged. Senate passed, with amendment, Feb. 15, 2006. House agreed to Senate amendment, under suspension of the rules, March 7. President signed March 16, 2006.

PL 109-182 (H J Res 47). Increase the statutory limit on the public debt. House passed pursuant to rule XXVII and H Con Res 95 on April 28, 2005. Senate Finance discharged. Senate passed March 16, 2006. President signed March 20, 2006.

PL 109-183 (S 1578) Reauthorize the Upper Colorado and San Juan River Basin Endangered Fish Recovery Programs. Introduced by Allard, R-Colo., July 29, 2005. Senate Energy and Natural Resources reported Dec. 8 (S Rept 109-196). Senate passed Dec. 16. House passed, under suspension of the rules, March 8, 2006. President signed March 20, 2006.

PL 109-184 (HR 1287) Designate the facility of the U.S. Postal Service located at 332 South Main St. in Flora, Ill., as the "Robert T. Ferguson Post Office Building." Introduced by Shimkus, R-Ill., on March 14, 2005. House Government Reform discharged. House passed, amended, Dec. 19. Senate passed March 3, 2006. President signed March 20, 2006.

PL 109-185 (HR 2113) Designate the facility of the U.S. Postal Service located at 2000 McDonough St. in Joliet, Ill., as the "John F. Whiteside Joliet Post Office Building." Introduced by Weller, R-Ill., on May 5, 2005. House passed, under suspension of the rules, July 13. Senate Homeland Security and Governmental Affairs reported Dec. 16 (no written report). Senate passed March 3, 2006. President signed March 20, 2006.

PL 109-186 (HR 2346) Designate the facility of the U.S. Postal Service located at 105 NW Railroad Ave. in Hammond, La., as the "John J. Hainkel Jr. Post Office Building." Introduced by Jindal, R-La., on May 12, 2005. House passed, amended, under suspension of the rules, June 27. Senate Homeland Security and Governmental Affairs reported Dec. 16 (no written report). Senate passed March 3, 2006. President signed March 20, 2006.

PL 109-187 (HR 2413) Designate the facility of the U.S. Postal Service located at 1202 1st St. in Humble, Texas, as the "Lillian McKay Post Office Building." Introduced by Poe, R-Texas, on May 17, 2005. House passed, under suspension of the rules, Nov. 1. Senate Homeland Security and Governmental Affairs reported Dec. 16 (no written report). Senate passed March 3, 2006. President signed March 20, 2006.

PL 109-188 (HR 2630) Redesignate the facility of the U.S. Postal Service located at 1927 Sangamon Ave. in Springfield, Ill., as the "J.M. Dietrich Northeast Annex." Introduced by LaHood, R-Ill., on May 25, 2005. House passed, under suspension of the rules, July 13. Senate Homeland Security and Governmental Affairs reported Dec. 16 (no written report). Senate passed, March 3, 2006. President signed March 20, 2006.

PL 109-189 (HR 2894) Designate the facility of the U.S. Postal Service located at 102 South Walters Ave. in Hodgenville, Ky., as the "Abraham Lincoln Birth Place Post Office Building." Introduced by Lewis, R-Ky., on June 14, 2005. House passed, under suspension of the rules, July 26. Senate Homeland Security and Governmental Affairs reported Dec. 16 (no written report). Senate passed March 3, 2006. President signed March 20, 2006.

PL 109-190 (HR 3256) Designate the facility of the U.S. Postal Service located at 3038 West Liberty Ave. in Pittsburgh, Pa., as the "Congressman James Grove Fulton Memorial Post Office Building." Introduced by Murphy, R-Pa., on July 12, 2005. House passed, under suspension of the rules, Oct. 25. Senate Homeland Security and Governmental Affairs reported Dec. 16 (no written report). Senate passed March 3, 2006. President signed March 20, 2006.

PL 109-191 (HR 3368) Designate the facility of the U.S. Postal Service located at 6483 Lincoln St. in Gagetown, Mich., as the "Gagetown Veterans Memorial Post Office." Introduced by Kildee, D-Mich., on July 20, 2005. House passed, under suspension of the rules, Oct. 25. Senate Homeland Security and Governmental Affairs reported Dec. 16 (no written report). Senate passed March 3, 2006. President signed March 20, 2006.

PL 109-192 (HR 3439) Designate the facility of the U.S. Postal Service located at 201 North 3rd St. in Smithfield, N.C., as the "Ava Gardner Post Office." Introduced by Etheridge, D-N.C., on July 26, 2005. House passed, under suspension of the rules, Oct. 6. Senate Homeland Security and Governmental Affairs reported Dec. 16 (no written report). Senate passed March 3, 2006. President signed March 20, 2006.

PL 109-193 (HR 3548) Designate the facility of the U.S. Postal Service located on Franklin Ave. in Pearl River, N.Y., as the "Heinz Ahlmeyer Jr. Post Office Building." Introduced by Engel, D-N.Y., on July 28, 2005. House passed, under suspension of the rules, Nov. 1. Senate Homeland Security and Governmental Affairs reported Dec. 16 (no written report). Senate passed March 3, 2006. President signed March 20, 2006.

PL 109-194 (HR 3703) Designate the facility of the U.S. Postal Service located at 8501 Philatelic Dr. in Spring Hill, Fla., as the "Staff Sgt. Michael Schafer Post Office Building." Introduced by Brown-Waite, R-Fla., on Sept. 8, 2005. House passed, under suspension of the rules, Sept. 27. Senate Homeland Security and Governmental Affairs reported Dec. 16 (no written report). Senate passed March 3, 2006. President signed March 20, 2006.

PL 109-195 (HR 3770) Designate the facility of the U.S. Postal Service located at 205 West Washington St. in Knox, Ind., as the "Grant W. Green Post Office Building." Introduced by Chocola, R-Ind., on Sept. 14, 2005. House passed, under suspension of the rules, Nov. 8. Senate Homeland Security and Governmental Affairs reported Dec. 16 (no written report). Senate passed March 3, 2006. President signed March 20, 2006.

PL 109-196 (HR 3825) Designate the facility of the U.S. Postal Service located at 770 Trumbull Dr. in Pittsburgh, Pa., as the "Clayton J. Smith Memorial Post Office Building." Introduced by Murphy, R-Pa., on Sept. 19, 2005. House passed, under suspension of the rules, Nov. 8. Senate Homeland Security and Governmental Affairs reported Dec. 16 (no written report). Senate passed March 3, 2006. President signed March 20, 2006.

PL 109-197 (HR 3830) Designate the facility of the U.S. Postal Service located at 130 East Marion Ave. in Punta Gorda, Fla., as the "U.S. Cleveland Post Office Building." Introduced by Foley, R-Fla., on Sept. 20, 2005. House passed, under suspension of the rules, Oct. 18. Senate Homeland Security and Governmental Affairs reported Dec. 16 (no written report). Senate passed March 3, 2006. President signed March 20, 2006.

PL 109-198 (HR 3989) Designate the facility of the U.S. Postal Service located at 37598 Goodhue Ave. in Dennison, Minn., as the "Albert H. Quie Post Office." Introduced by Kline, R-Minn., on Oct. 6, 2005. House passed, amended, under suspension of the rules, Nov. 1. Senate Homeland Security and Governmental Affairs reported Dec. 16 (no written report). Senate passed March 3, 2006. President signed March 20, 2006.

PL 109-199 (HR 4053) Designate the facility of the U.S. Postal Service located at 545 North Rimsdale Ave. in Covina, Calif., as the "Lillian Kinkella Keil Post Office." Introduced by Solis, D-Calif., on Oct. 7, 2005. House passed, under suspension of the rules, Nov. 8. Senate Homeland Security and Governmental Affairs reported Dec. 16 (no written report). Senate passed March 3, 2006. President signed March 20, 2006.

PL 109-200 (HR 4107) Designate the facility of the U.S. Postal Service located at 1826 Pennsylvania Ave. in Baltimore, Md., as the "Maryland State Delegate Lena K. Lee Post Office Building." Introduced by Cummings, D-Md., on Oct. 20, 2005. House passed, under suspension of the rules, Dec. 13. Senate Homeland Security and Governmental Affairs discharged. Senate passed March 3, 2006. President signed March 20, 2006.

PL 109-201 (HR 4152) Designate the facility of the U.S. Postal Service located at 320 High St. in Clinton, Mass., as the "Raymond J. Salmon Post Office." Introduced by McGovern, D-Mass., on Oct. 26, 2005. House passed, under suspension of the rules, Feb. 14, 2006. Senate passed March 3, 2006. President signed March 20, 2006.

PL 109-202 (HR 4295) Designate the facility of the U.S. Postal Service located at 12760 South Park Ave. in Riverton, Utah, as the "Mont and Mark Stephensen Veterans Memorial Post Office Building." Introduced by Cannon, R-Utah, on Nov. 10, 2005. House passed, under suspension of the rules, Dec. 13. Senate Homeland Security and Governmental Affairs discharged. Senate passed March 3, 2006. President signed March 20, 2006.

PL 109-203 (S 2089) Designate the facility of the U.S. Postal Service located at 1271 North King St. in Honolulu, Hawaii, as the "Hiram L. Fong Post Office Building." Introduced by Akaka, D-Hawaii, on Dec. 13, 2005. Senate Homeland Security and Governmental Affairs reported Dec. 16 (no written report). Senate passed March 3, 2006. House passed, under suspension of the rules, March 7, 2006. President signed March 20, 2006.

PL 109-204 (S 2320) Make available funds included in the Deficit Reduction Act of 2005 for the Low-Income Home Energy Assistance Program for fiscal year 2006. Introduced by Snowe, R-Maine, on Feb. 16, 2006. Senate passed, amended, March 7. House passed, under suspension of the rules, March 16, 2006. President signed March 20, 2006.

PL 109-205 (HR 1053) Authorize the extension of nondiscriminatory treatment (normal trade relations) to the products of Ukraine. Introduced by Gerlach, R-Pa., on March 2, 2005. House passed, amended, under suspension of the rules, March 8, 2006. Senate passed March 9. President signed March 23, 2006.

PL 109-206 (HR 1691) Designate the Department of Veterans Affairs outpatient clinic in Appleton, Wis., as the "John H. Bradley Department of Veterans Affairs Outpatient Clinic." Introduced by Green, R-Wis., on April 19, 2005. House passed, under suspension of the rules, Nov. 2. Senate Veterans' Affairs discharged. Senate passed March 13, 2006. President signed March 23, 2006.

PL 109-207 (S 2064) Designate the U.S. Postal Service facility located at 122 South Bill St. in Francesville, Ind., as the "Malcolm Melville 'Mac' Lawrence Post Office." Introduced by Lugar, R-Ind., on Nov. 18, 2005. Senate Homeland Security and Governmental

Affairs reported Dec. 16 (no written report). Senate passed March 3, 2006. House passed, under suspension of the rules, March 14. President signed March 23, 2006.

PL 109-208 (S 2275) Temporarily increase the borrowing authority of the Federal Emergency Management Agency for carrying out the national flood insurance program. Introduced by Shelby, R-Ala., on Feb. 10, 2006. Senate passed Feb. 10. House passed, amended, under suspension of the rules, Feb. 15. Senate agreed to House amendment March 16. President signed March 23, 2006.

PL 109-209 (HR 4826) Extend through Dec. 31, 2006, the authority of the secretary of the army to accept and expend funds contributed by nonfederal public entities to expedite the processing of permits. Introduced by Baird, D-Wash., on March 1, 2006. House passed, under suspension of the rules, March 14. Senate passed March 16. President signed March 24, 2006.

PL 109-210 (S 1184) Waive the passport fees for a relative of a deceased member of the armed forces proceeding abroad to visit the grave of the member or to attend a funeral or memorial service for the member. Introduced by Biden, D-Del., on June 7, 2005. Senate Foreign Relations reported Nov. 4, 2005 (no written report). Senate passed Dec. 22. House passed, under suspension of the rules, March 14, 2006. President signed March 24, 2006.

PL 109-211 (S 2363) Extend the educational flexibility program under Section 4 of the Education Flexibility Partnership Act of 1999. Introduced by Burr, R-N.C., on March 2, 2006. Senate passed March 2. House passed, under suspension of the rules, March 14. President signed March 24, 2006.

PL 109-212 (HR 4911) Temporarily extend the programs under the Higher Education Act of 1965. Introduced by McKeon, R-Calif., on March 9, 2006. House passed, under suspension of the rules, March 14. Senate passed March 28. President signed April 1, 2006.

PL 109-213 (HR 1259) Authorize the president to award a gold medal on behalf of the Congress, collectively, to the Tuskegee Airmen in recognition of their unique military record, which inspired reform in the armed forces. Introduced by Rangel, D-N.Y., on March 10, 2005. House passed, amended, under suspension of the rules, Feb. 28, 2006. Senate Banking, Housing, and Urban Affairs discharged. Senate passed March 27. President signed April 11, 2006.

PL 109-214 (S 2116) Transfer jurisdiction of certain real property (the small triangular piece of land between the Hart Senate Office Building and the Supreme Court) to the Supreme Court. Introduced by Lott, R-Miss., on Dec. 15, 2005. Senate passed Dec. 15. House passed, under suspension of the rules, March 28, 2006. President signed April 11, 2006.

PL 109-215 (S 2120) Ensure regulatory equity between and among all dairy farmers and handlers for sales of packaged fluid milk in federally regulated milk marketing areas and into certain nonfederally regulated milk marketing areas from federally regulated areas. Introduced by Kyl, R-Ariz., on Dec. 16, 2005. Senate passed Dec. 16. House passed, under suspension of the rules, March 28, 2006. President signed April 11, 2006.

PL 109-216 (H J Res 81) Provide for the appointment of Phillip Frost as a citizen regent of the Board of Regents of the Smithsonian Institution. Introduced by Regula, R-Ohio, on March 7, 2006. House passed, under suspension of the rules, April 4. Senate passed April 5. President signed April 13, 2006.

PL 109-217 (H J Res 82) Provide for the reappointment of Alan G. Spoon as a citizen regent of the Board of Regents of the Smithsonian Institution. Introduced by Regula, R-Ohio, on March 7, 2006. House passed, under suspension of the rules, April 4. Senate passed April 5. President signed April 13, 2006.

PL 109-218 (HR 4979) Amend the Robert T. Stafford Disaster Relief and Emergency Assistance Act to clarify the preference for local firms in the award of certain contracts for disaster relief activities. Introduced by Pickering, R-Miss., on March 16, 2006. House passed, amended, under suspension of the rules, March 28. Senate passed April 6. President signed April 20, 2006.

PL 109-219 (S 592) Extend the contract for the Glendo Unit of the Missouri River Basin Project in Wyoming. Introduced by Thomas, R-Wyo., on March 10, 2005. Senate Energy and Natural Resources reported, amended, Oct. 27 (S Rept 109-167). Senate passed, amended, Nov. 16. House passed, under suspension of the rules, April 25, 2006. President signed May 5, 2006.

PL 109-220 (S J Res 28) Approve the location of the commemorative work in the District of Columbia honoring former President Dwight D. Eisenhower. Introduced by Stevens, R-Alaska, on Feb. 7, 2006. Senate Energy and Natural Resources reported April 3 (S Rept 109-227). Senate passed April 4. House passed, under suspension of the rules, April 25. President signed May 5, 2006.

PL 109-221 (HR 3351) Make technical corrections to laws relating to Native Americans. Introduced by Pombo, R-Calif., on July 19, 2005. House Resources reported, amended, Nov. 16 (H Rept 109-298, Part 1). House Transportation and Infrastructure discharged. House passed, amended, under suspension of the rules, Nov. 16. Senate Indian Affairs discharged. Senate passed, amended, April 7, 2006. House agreed to Senate amendment, under suspension of the rules, May 2. President signed May 12, 2006.

PL 109-222 (HR 4297) Provide for reconciliation pursuant to Section 201(b) of the concurrent resolution on the budget for fiscal 2006. Introduced by Thomas, R-Calif., on Nov. 10, 2005. House Ways and Means reported, amended, Nov. 17 (H Rept 109-304). House passed, amended, Dec. 8. Senate passed, amended, Feb. 2, 2006. Conference report filed in the House May 9 (H Rept 109-455). House agreed to conference report May 10. Senate agreed to conference report May 11. President signed May 17, 2006.

PL 109-223 (H J Res. 83) Memorialize and honor the contribution of Chief Justice William H. Rehnquist. Introduced by Pombo, R-Calif., on April 4, 2006. House passed, under suspension of the rules, April 25. Senate passed May 4. President signed May 18, 2006.

PL 109-224 (S 1382) Require the secretary of the interior to accept the conveyance of certain land to be held in trust for the benefit of the Puyallup Indian tribe. Introduced by Cantwell, D-Wash., on July 12, 2005. Senate passed Oct. 24. House passed, under suspension of the rules, May 9, 2006. President signed May 18, 2006.

PL 109-225 (S 1165) Provide for the expansion of the James Campbell National Wildlife Refuge, Honolulu County, Hawaii. Introduced by Inouye, D-Hawaii, on June 6, 2005. Senate Environment and Public Works reported, amended, Dec. 8 (S Rept 109-191). Senate passed, amended, Dec. 16. House Resources reported April 25, 2006 (H Rept 109-429). House passed, under suspension of the rules, May 16. President signed May 25, 2006.

PL 109-226 (S 1869) Reauthorize the Coastal Barrier Resources Act. Introduced by Inhofe, R-Okla., on Oct. 17, 2005. Senate Environment and Public Works reported, amended, Nov. 15 (S Rept 109-179). Senate passed, amended, Dec. 16. House Resources reported April 25, 2006 (H Rept 109-428). House passed, under suspension of the rules, May 16. President signed May 25, 2006.

PL 109-227 (HR 1499) Amend the Internal Revenue Code of 1986 to allow members of the armed forces serving in a combat zone a deduction for contributions to their individual retirement plans even if the compensation on which the contribution is based is excluded from gross income. Introduced by Foxx, R-N.C., on April 6, 2005. House passed, amended, under suspension of the rules, May 23. Senate Finance discharged. Senate passed, amended, Nov. 15. House agreed to Senate amendment with amendment pursuant to H Res 803 on May 9, 2006. Senate agreed to House amendment to Senate amendment May 18. President signed May 29, 2006.

PL 109-228 (HR 5037) Amend Titles XXXVIII and XVIII, U.S. Code, to prohibit certain demonstrations at cemeteries under the control of the National Cemetery Administration and at Arlington National Cemetery. Introduced by Rogers, R-Mich., on March 29, 2006. House passed, under suspension of the rules, May 9. Senate passed, amended, May 24. House agreed to Senate amendment, under suspension of the rules, May 24. President signed May 29, 2006.

PL 109-229 (S 1736) Provide for the participation of judicial branch employees in the federal leave transfer program for disasters and emergencies. Introduced by Collins, R-Maine, on Sept. 20, 2005. Senate Homeland Security and Governmental Affairs reported Sept. 27 (S Rept 109-158). Senate passed Oct. 19. House Government Reform reported May 2, 2006 (H Rept 109-449). House passed, under suspension of the rules, May 22. President signed May 31, 2006.

PL 109-230 (HR 1953) Require the secretary of the Treasury to mint coins in commemoration of the Old Mint at San Francisco, otherwise known as the "Granite Lady." Introduced by Pelosi, D-Calif., on April 28, 2005. House passed, amended, under suspension of the rules, Nov. 10. Senate Banking, Housing and Urban Affairs discharged. Senate passed May 25, 2006. President signed June 15, 2006.

PL 109-231 (HR 3829) Designate the Department of Veterans Affairs medical center in Muskogee, Okla., as the "Jack C. Montgomery Department of Veterans Affairs Medical Center." Introduced by Boren, D-Okla., on Sept. 20, 2005. House passed, under suspension of the rules, May 9, 2006. Senate Veterans' Affairs discharged. Senate passed May 26. President signed June 15, 2006.

PL 109-232 (HR 5401) Amend section 308 of the Lewis and Clark Expedition Bicentennial Commemorative Coin Act to make clarifying and technical amendments. Introduced by Emerson, R-Mo., on May 17, 2006. House passed, under suspension of the rules, May 22. Senate passed May 25. President signed June 15, 2006.

PL 109-233 (S 1235) Amend Title XXXVIII, U.S. Code, to improve and extend housing, insurance, outreach, and benefits programs administered by the secretary of veterans affairs and to improve and extend employment programs for veterans administered by the secretary of labor. Introduced by Craig, R-Idaho, on June 14, 2005. Senate Veterans' Affairs reported, amended, Sept. 21 (S Rept 109-139). Senate passed, amended, Sept. 28. House passed, amended, under suspension of the rules, May 22, 2006. Senate agreed to House amendments May 25. President signed June 15, 2006.

PL 109-234 (HR 4939) Make emergency supplemental appropriations for the fiscal year ending Sept. 30, 2006. Introduced by Lewis, R-Calif., on March 13, 2006. House Appropriations reported March 13, 2006 (H Rept 109-388). House passed, amended, March 16. Senate Appropriations reported, amended, April 5 (S Rept 109-230). Senate passed with amendment May 4. Conference report filed in the House June 8 (H Rept 109-494). House agreed to conference report June 13. Senate agreed to conference report June 15. President signed June 15, 2006.

PL 109-235 (S 193) Increase the penalties for violations by television and radio broadcasters of the prohibitions against transmission of obscene, indecent, and profane language. Introduced by Brownback, R-Kan., on Jan. 26, 2005. Senate Commerce, Science and Transportation discharged. Senate passed May 18, 2006. House passed, under suspension of the rules, June 7. President signed June 15, 2006.

PL 109-236 (S 2803) Amend the Federal Mine Safety and Health Act of 1977 to improve the safety of mines and mining. Introduced by Enzi, R-Wyo., on May 16, 2006. Senate Health, Education, Labor and Pensions reported, amended, May 23 (no written report). Senate passed, amended, May 24. House passed, under suspension of the rules, June 7. President signed June 15, 2006.

PL 109-237 (S 1445) Designate the facility of the U.S. Postal Service located at 520 Colorado Ave., Arriba, Colo., as the "William H. Emery Post Office." Introduced by Salazar, D-Colo., on July 21, 2005. Senate Homeland Security and Governmental Affairs reported Dec. 16 (no written report). Senate passed March 3, 2006. House passed, under suspension of the rules, June 12. President signed June 23, 2006.

PL 109-238 (HR 5603) Temporarily extend the programs under the Higher Education Act of 1965. Introduced by Keller, R-Fla., on June 14, 2006. House passed, under suspension of the rules, June 21. Senate passed June 23. President signed June 30, 2006.

PL 109-239 (HR 5403) Improve protections for children and hold states accountable for the safe and timely interstate placement of children. Introduced by DeLay, R-Texas, on May 17, 2006. House passed, under suspension of the rules, May 24. Senate passed June 23. President signed July 3, 2006.

PL 109-240 (HR 4912) Amend Sect. 242 of the National Housing Act to extend the exemption for critical access hospitals under the FHA program for mortgage insurance for hospitals. Introduced by Ney, R-Ohio, on March 9, 2006. House Financial Services reported April 25 (H Rept 109-424). House passed, under suspension of the rules, May 9. Senate Banking, Housing and Urban Affairs discharged. Senate passed June 28. President signed July 10, 2006.

PL 109-241 (HR 889) Authorize appropriations for the Coast Guard for fiscal 2006. Introduced by Young, R-Alaska, on Feb. 17, 2005. House Transportation and Infrastructure reported, amended, July 28 (H Rept 109-204, Part 1). House Homeland Security discharged. House passed, amended, Sept. 15. Senate Commerce, Science and Transportation discharged. Senate passed, amended, Oct. 27. Conference report filed in the House on April 6, 2006 (H Rept 109-413). House agreed to the conference report, under suspension of the rules, June 27. Senate agreed to the conference report June 27. Senate vitiated action on the conference report June 27 and agreed to the conference report June 28. President signed July 12, 2006.

PL 109-242 (S 3504) Amend the Public Health Service Act to prohibit the solicitation or acceptance of tissue from fetuses gestated for research purposes. Introduced by Santorum, R-Pa., on June 13, 2006. Senate Health, Education, Labor and Pensions discharged July 17. Senate passed July 18. House passed, under suspension of the rules, July 18. President signed July 19, 2006.

PL 109-243 (HR 42) Ensure that the right of an individual to display the flag of the United States on residential property not be abridged. Introduced by Bartlett, R-Md., on Jan. 4, 2005. House passed, under suspension of the rules, June 27, 2006. Senate Banking, Housing and Urban Affairs discharged. Senate passed July 17. President signed July 24, 2006.

PL 109-244 (S J Res 40) Authorize the printing and binding of a supplement to, and revised edition of, Senate Procedure. Introduced by Frist, R-Tenn., on June 29, 2006. Senate passed June 29. House Administration discharged. House passed July 11. President signed July 25, 2006.

PL 109-245 (S 655) Amend the Public Health Service Act with respect to the National Foundation for the Centers for Disease Control and Prevention. Introduced by Isakson, R-Ga., on March 17, 2005. Senate Health, Education, Labor and Pensions reported, amended, June 27 (S Rept 109-91). Senate passed, amended, July 27. House Energy and Commerce reported, amended, June 20, 2006 (H Rept 109-510). House passed, amended, under suspension of the rules, July 11. Senate agreed to House amendment July 13. President signed July 26, 2006.

PL 109-246 (HR 9) Reauthorize and amend the Voting Rights Act of 1965. Introduced by Sensenbrenner, R-Wis., on May 2, 2006. House Judiciary reported, amended, May 22 (H Rept 109-478). House passed, amended, July 13. Senate passed July 20. President signed July 27, 2006.

PL 109-247 (HR 2872) Require the secretary of the Treasury to mint coins in commemoration of Louis Braille. Introduced by Ney, R-Ohio, on June 13, 2005. House passed, amended, under suspension of the rules, Feb. 28, 2006. Senate Banking, Housing and Urban Affairs discharged. Senate passed July 12. President signed July 27, 2006.

PL 109-248 (HR 4472) Protect children; secure the safety of judges, prosecutors, law enforcement officers, and their family members; and reduce and prevent gang violence. Introduced by Sensenbrenner, R-Wis., on Dec. 8, 2005. House passed, amended, under suspension of the rules, March 8, 2006. Senate passed, amended, July 20. House agreed to Senate amendments, under suspension of the rules, July 25. President signed on July 27, 2006.

PL 109-249 (HR 5117) Exempt persons with disabilities from the prohibition against providing Section 8 rental assistance to college students. Introduced by Pryce, R-Ohio, on April 6, 2006. House Financial Services reported June 13 (H Rept 109-500). House passed, amended, under suspension of the rules, June 13. Senate passed July 18. President signed July 27, 2006.

PL 109-250 (HR 5865) Amend Section 1113 of the Social Security Act to temporarily increase funding for the program of temporary assistance for U.S. citizens returned from foreign countries. Introduced by Thomas, R-Calif., on July 24, 2006. House passed, under suspension of the rules, July 25. Senate passed, amended, July 26. House agreed to Senate amendment July 26. President signed July 27, 2006.

PL 109-251 (H J Res 86) Approve the renewal of import restrictions contained in the Burmese Freedom and Democracy Act of 2003. Introduced by Lantos, D-Calif., on May 19, 2006. House passed, under suspension of the rules, July 11. Senate passed July 26. President signed Aug. 1, 2006.

PL 109-252 (HR 2977) Designate the facility of the U.S. Postal Service located at 306 2nd Ave., Brockway, Mont., as the "Paul Kasten Post Office Building." Introduced by Rehberg, R-Mont., on June 17, 2005. House passed, under suspension of the rules, July 26. Senate Homeland Security and Governmental Affairs reported June 22, 2006 (no written report). Senate passed July 20. President signed Aug. 1, 2006.

PL 109-253 (HR 3440) Designate the facility of the U.S. Postal Service located at 100 Avenida RL Rodriguez, Bayamon, P.R., as the "Dr. Jose Celso Barbosa Post Office Building." Introduced by Fortuño, R-P.R., on July 26, 2005. House passed, under suspension of the rules, March 28, 2006. Senate Homeland Security and Governmental Affairs reported June 22 (no written report). Senate passed July 20. President signed Aug. 1, 2006.

PL 109-254 (HR 3549) Designate the facility of the U.S. Postal Service located at 210 West 3rd Ave., Warren, Pa., as the "William F. Clinger Jr. Post Office Building." Introduced by English, R-Pa., on July 28, 2005. House passed, under suspension of the rules, Oct. 18. Senate Homeland Security and Governmental Affairs reported June 22, 2006 (no written report). Senate passed July 20. President signed Aug. 1, 2006.

PL 109-255 (HR 3934) Designate the facility of the U.S. Postal Service located at 80 Killian Rd., Massapequa, N.Y., as the "Gerard A. Fiorenza Post Office Building." Introduced by King, R-N.Y., on Sept. 28, 2005. House passed, under suspension of the rules, March 7, 2006. Senate Homeland Security and Governmental

Affairs reported June 22 (no written report). Senate passed July 20. President signed Aug. 1, 2006.

PL 109-256 (HR 4101) Designate the facility of the U.S. Postal Service located at 170 East Main St., Patchogue, N.Y., as the "Lieutenant Michael P. Murphy Post Office Building." Introduced by Bishop, D-N.Y., on Oct. 20, 2005. House passed, under suspension of the rules, May 2, 2006. Senate Homeland Security and Governmental Affairs discharged. Senate passed July 20. President signed Aug. 1, 2006.

PL 109-257 (HR 4108) Designate the facility of the U.S. Postal Service located at 3000 Homewood Ave., Baltimore, Md., as the "State Senator Verda Welcome and Dr. Henry Welcome Post Office Building." Introduced by Cummings, D-Md., on Oct. 20, 2005. House Government Reform discharged. House passed Dec. 19. Senate Homeland Security and Governmental Affairs reported June 22, 2006 (no written report). Senate passed July 20. President signed Aug. 1, 2006.

PL 109-258 (HR 4456) Designate the facility of the U.S. Postal Service located at 2404 Race St., Jonesboro, Ark., as the "Hattie Caraway Station." Introduced by Berry, D-Ark., on Dec. 7, 2005. House passed, amended, under suspension of the rules, Feb. 8, 2006. Senate Homeland Security and Governmental Affairs reported June 22 (no written report). Senate passed July 20. President signed Aug. 2, 2006.

PL 109-259 (HR 4561) Designate the facility of the U.S. Postal Service located at 8624 Ferguson Rd., Dallas, Texas, as the "Francisco 'Pancho' Medrano Post Office Building." Introduced by Johnson, D-Texas, on Dec. 15, 2005. House passed, under suspension of the rules, April 5, 2006. Senate Homeland Security and Governmental Affairs reported June 22 (no written report). Senate passed July 20. President signed Aug. 2, 2006.

PL 109-260 (HR 4688) Designate the facility of the U.S. Postal Service located at 1 Boyden St., Badin, N.C., as the "Mayor John Thompson 'Tom' Garrison Memorial Post Office." Introduced by Hayes, R-N.C., on Feb. 1, 2006. House passed, under suspension of the rules, April 5. Senate Homeland Security and Governmental Affairs reported June 22 (no written report). Senate passed July 20. President signed Aug. 2, 2006.

PL 109-261 (HR 4786) Designate the facility of the U.S. Postal Service located at 535 Wood St., Bethlehem, Pa., as the "H. Gordon Payrow Post Office Building." Introduced by Dent, R-Pa., on Feb. 16, 2006. House passed, under suspension of the rules, March 28. Senate Homeland Security and Governmental Affairs reported June 22 (no written report). Senate passed July 20. President signed Aug. 2, 2006.

PL 109-262 (HR 4995) Designate the facility of the U.S. Postal Service located at 7 Columbus Ave., Tuckahoe, N.Y., as the "Ronald Bucca Post Office." Introduced by Lowey, D-N.Y., on March 16, 2006. House passed, under suspension of the rules, May 2. Senate Homeland Security and Governmental Affairs reported June 22 (no written report). Senate passed July 20. President signed Aug. 2, 2006.

PL 109-263 (HR 5245) Designate the facility of the U.S. Postal Service located at 1 Marble St., Fair Haven, Vt., as the "Matthew Lyon Post Office Building." Introduced by Sanders, I-Vt., on April 27, 2006. House passed, under suspension of the rules, June 6. Senate Homeland Security and Governmental Affairs reported June 22 (no written report). Senate passed July 20. President signed Aug. 2, 2006.

PL 109-264 (HR 4019) Amend Title IV of the U.S. Code to clarify the treatment of self-employment for purposes of the limitation on state taxation of retirement income. Introduced by Cannon, R-Utah, on Oct. 7, 2005. House Judiciary reported, amended, June 29, 2006 (H Rept 109-542). House passed, amended, under suspension of the rules, July 17. Senate Finance discharged. Senate passed July 24. President signed Aug. 3, 2006.

PL 109-265 (S 310) Direct the secretary of the interior to convey the Newlands Project Headquarters and Maintenance Yard Facility to the Truckee-Carson Irrigation District in the state of Nevada. Introduced by Ensign, R-Nev., on Feb. 8, 2005. Senate Energy and Natural Resources reported Dec. 8 (S Rept 109-188). Senate passed Dec. 16. House passed, under suspension of the rules, July 24, 2006. President signed Aug. 3, 2006.

PL 109-266 (S 1496) Direct the secretary of the interior to conduct a pilot program under which up to 15 states may issue electronic federal migratory-bird hunting stamps. Introduced by Crapo, R-Idaho, on July 26, 2005. Senate Environment and Public Works reported, amended, Dec. 8 (S Rept 109-187). Senate passed, amended, Dec. 16. House Resources reported July 13, 2006 (H Rept 109-556). House passed, under suspension of the rules, July 24. President signed Aug. 3, 2006.

PL 109-267 (HR 5877) Amend the Iran and Libya Sanctions Act of 1996 and reauthorize it until Sept. 29, 2006. Introduced by Ros-Lehtinen, R-Fla., on July 25, 2006. House passed, under suspension of the rules, July 26. Senate passed July 31. President signed Aug. 4, 2006.

PL 109-268 (S 3741) Provide funding authority to facilitate the evacuation of persons from Lebanon. Introduced by Lugar, R-Ind., on July 26, 2006. Senate passed July 26. House passed, amended, July 28. Senate agreed to House amendment, July 31. President signed Aug. 4, 2006.

PL 109-269 (HR 3682) Redesignate the Mason Neck National Wildlife Refuge in Virginia as the Elizabeth Hartwell Mason Neck National Wildlife Refuge. Introduced by T. Davis, R-Va., on Sept. 7, 2005. House Resources reported April 25, 2006 (H Rept 109-433). House passed, under suspension of the rules, May 16. Senate Environment and Public Works discharged. Senate passed Aug. 1. President signed Aug. 12, 2006.

PL 109-270 (S 250) Reauthorize and amend the Carl D. Perkins Vocational and Technical Education Act of 1998. Introduced by Enzi, R-Wyo., on Feb. 1, 2005. Senate Health, Education, Labor and Pensions reported, amended, March 9 (S Rept 109-65). Senate passed, amended, March 10. House passed, amended, July 12, 2006. Conference report filed in the House July 25 (H Rept 109-597). Senate agreed to the conference report July 26. House agreed to the conference report July 29. President signed Aug. 12, 2006.

PL 109-271 (S 3693) Make technical corrections to the Violence Against Women and Department of Justice Reauthorization

Act of 2005. Introduced by Specter, R-Pa., on July 19, 2006. Senate passed July 19. House passed July 29. President signed Aug. 12, 2006.

PL 109-272 (HR 5683) Preserve the Mt. Soledad Veterans Memorial in San Diego, Calif., by providing for the immediate acquisition of the memorial by the United States. Introduced by Hunter, R-Calif., on June 26, 2006. House passed, amended, under suspension of the rules, July 19. Senate passed Aug. 1. President signed Aug. 14, 2006.

PL 109-273 (HR 4646) Designate the facility of the U.S. Postal Service located at 7320 Reseda Blvd., Reseda, Calif., as the "Coach John Wooden Post Office Building." Introduced by Sherman, D-Calif., on Dec. 18, 2005. House passed, under suspension of the rules, April 5, 2006. Senate Homeland Security and Governmental Affairs reported Aug. 1 (no written report). Senate passed Aug. 2. President signed Aug. 17, 2006.

PL 109-274 (HR 4811) Designate the facility of the U.S. Postal Service located at 215 West Industrial Park Rd., Harrison, Ark., as the "John Paul Hammerschmidt Post Office Building." Introduced by Boozman, R-Ark., on Feb. 28, 2006. House passed, under suspension of the rules, May 2. Senate Homeland Security and Governmental Affairs reported Aug. 1 (no written report). Senate passed Aug. 2. President signed Aug. 17, 2006.

PL 109-275 (HR 4962) Designate the facility of the U.S. Postal Service located at 100 Pitcher St., Utica, N.Y., as the "Captain George A. Wood Post Office Building." Introduced by Boehlert, R-N.Y., on March 15, 2006. House passed, under suspension of the rules, July 18. Senate Homeland Security and Governmental Affairs reported Aug. 1 (no written report). Senate passed Aug. 2. President signed Aug. 17, 2006.

PL 109-276 (HR 5104) Designate the facility of the U.S. Postal Service located at 1750 16th St. South, St. Petersburg, Fla., as the "Morris W. Milton Post Office." Introduced by Davis, D-Fla., on April 5, 2006. House passed, under suspension of the rules, June 19. Senate Homeland Security and Governmental Affairs reported Aug. 1 (no written report). Senate passed Aug. 2. President signed Aug. 17, 2006.

PL 109-277 (HR 5107) Designate the facility of the U.S. Postal Service located at 1400 West Jordan St., Pensacola, Fla., as the "Earl D. Hutto Post Office Building." Introduced by Miller, R-Fla., on April 5, 2006. House passed, under suspension of the rules, May 2. Senate Homeland Security and Governmental Affairs reported Aug. 1 (no written report). Senate passed Aug. 2. President signed Aug. 17, 2006.

PL 109-278 (HR 5169) Designate the facility of the U.S. Postal Service located at 1310 Highway 64 NW, Ramsey, Ind., as the "Wilfred Edward 'Cousin Willie' Sieg Sr. Post Office." Introduced by Sodrel, R-Ind., on April 25, 2006. House passed, under suspension of the rules, June 12. Senate Homeland Security and Governmental Affairs reported Aug. 1 (no written report). Senate passed Aug. 2. President signed Aug. 17, 2006.

PL 109-279 (HR 5540) Designate the facility of the U.S. Postal Service located at 217 Southeast 2nd St., Dimmitt, Texas, as the "Sergeant Jacob Dan Dones Post Office." Introduced by Neugebauer, R-Texas, on June 7, 2006. House passed, under suspension of the rules, June 19. Senate Homeland Security and Governmental Affairs reported Aug. 1 (no written report). Senate passed Aug. 2. President signed Aug. 17, 2006.

PL 109-280 (HR 4) Overhaul the pension system in the United States. Introduced by Boehner, R-Ohio, on July 28, 2006. House passed July 28. Senate passed Aug. 3. President signed Aug. 17, 2006.

PL 109-281 (S 3534) Amend the Workforce Investment Act of 1998 to provide for a YouthBuild program. Introduced by Enzi, R-Wyo., on June 16, 2006. Senate passed, amended, Aug. 3. House passed, under suspension of the rules, Sept. 6. President signed Sept. 22, 2006.

PL 109-282 (S 2590) Require full disclosure of all entities and organizations receiving federal funds. Introduced by Coburn, R-Okla., on April 6, 2006. Senate Homeland Security and Governmental Affairs reported, amended, Aug. 2 (S Rept 109-329). Senate passed, amended, Sept. 7. House passed, under suspension of the rules, Sept. 13. President signed Sept. 26, 2006.

PL 109-283 (HR 5684) Implement the United States-Oman Free Trade Agreement. Introduced by Boehner, R-Ohio, on June 26, 2006. House Ways and Means reported July 17 (H Rept 109-574). House passed July 20. Senate passed Sept. 19. President signed Sept. 26, 2006.

PL 109-284 (HR 866) Make technical corrections to the U.S. Code. Introduced by Sensenbrenner, R-Wis., on Feb. 16, 2005. House Judiciary reported April 19 (H Rept 109-48). House passed, under suspension of the rules, Nov. 16. Senate Judiciary reported Sept. 7, 2006 (no written report). Senate passed Sept. 12. President signed Sept. 27, 2006.

PL 109-285 (HR 2808) Require the secretary of the Treasury to mint coins in commemoration of the bicentennial of the birth of Abraham Lincoln. Introduced by LaHood, R-Ill., on June 8, 2005. House passed, amended, under suspension of the rules, Sept. 6, 2006. Senate passed Sept. 8. President signed Sept. 27, 2006.

PL 109-286 (S 1773) Resolve certain Native American claims in New Mexico. Introduced by Domenici, R-N.M., on Sept. 26, 2005. Senate Indian Affairs reported, amended, May 3, 2006 (S Rept 109-252). Senate passed, amended, May 24. House Resources reported Sept. 6 (H Rept 109-633). House passed, under suspension of the rules, Sept. 12. President signed Sept. 27, 2006.

PL 109-287 (S 2784) Award a Congressional Gold Medal to Tenzin Gyatso, the 14th Dalai Lama, in recognition of his many enduring and outstanding contributions to peace, nonviolence, human rights, and religious understanding. Introduced by Feinstein, D-Calif., on May 11, 2006. Senate Banking, Housing and Urban Affairs reported May 23 (no written report). Senate passed May 25. House passed, under suspension of the rules, Sept. 13. President signed Sept. 27, 2006.

PL 109-288 (S 3525) Amend Title IV-B, Subpart 2, of the Social Security Act to improve outcomes for children in families affected by methamphetamine abuse and addiction and reauthorize the Promoting Safe and Stable Families program. Introduced by Grassley, R-Iowa, on June 15, 2006. Senate Finance reported June 15 (S Rept 109-269). Senate passed, amended, July 13. House passed, amended, under suspension of the rules, July 25. Senate agreed to House amendments with amendments Sept. 20. House agreed to Senate amendments to House amendments, under suspension of the rules, Sept. 26. President signed Sept. 29, 2006.

PL 109-289 (HR 5631) Make appropriations for the Department of Defense for fiscal 2007. Introduced by Young, R-Fla., on June 16, 2006. House Appropriations reported June 16 (H Rept 109-504). House passed, amended, June 20. Senate Appropriations reported, amended, July 25 (S Rept 109-292). Senate passed, amended, Sept. 7. Conference report filed in the House Sept. 25 (H Rept 109-676). House agreed to the conference report Sept. 26. Senate agreed to the conference report Sept. 29. President signed Sept. 29, 2006.

PL 109-290 (S 418) Protect members of the armed forces from unscrupulous practices regarding sales of insurance, financial, and investment products. Introduced by Enzi, R-Wyo., on Feb. 17, 2005. Senate Banking, Housing and Urban Affairs reported, amended, July 13, 2006 (S Rept 109-282). Senate passed, amended, July 19. House passed, under suspension of the rules, Sept. 21. President signed Sept. 29, 2006.

PL 109-291 (S 3850) Foster accountability, transparency, and competition in the credit rating agency industry. Introduced by Shelby, R-Ala., on Sept. 6, 2006. Senate Banking, Housing and Urban Affairs reported Sept. 6 (S Rept 109-326). Senate passed, amended, Sept. 22. House passed, under suspension of the rules, Sept. 27. President signed Sept. 29, 2006.

PL 109-292 (HR 6138) Temporarily extend programs under the Higher Education Act of 1965. Introduced by Keller, R-Fla., on Sept. 21, 2006. House passed, amended, under suspension of the rules, Sept. 27. Senate passed Sept. 30. President signed Sept. 30, 2006.

PL 109-293 (HR 6198) Hold the current regime in Iran accountable for its threatening behavior and support a transition to democracy in Iran. Introduced by Ros-Lehtinen, R-Fla., on Sept. 27, 2006. House passed, amended, under suspension of the rules, Sept. 28. Senate passed Sept. 30. President signed Sept. 30, 2006

PL 109-294 (S 260) Authorize the secretary of the interior to provide technical and financial assistance to private landowners to restore, enhance, and manage private land to improve fish and wildlife habitats through the Partners for Fish and Wildlife program. Introduced by Inhofe, R-Okla., on Feb. 2, 2005. Senate Environment and Public Works reported, amended, June 22 (S Rept 109-86). Senate passed, amended, June 27. House Resources reported July 13, 2006 (H Rept 109-562). House passed, under suspension of the rules, Sept. 20. President signed Oct. 3, 2006.

PL 109-295 (HR 5441) Make appropriations for the Department of Homeland Security for fiscal 2007. Introduced by Rogers, R-Ky., on May 22, 2006. House Appropriations reported May 22 (H Rept 109-476). House passed, amended, June 6. Senate Appropriations reported, amended, June 29 (S Rept 109-273). Senate passed, amended, July 13. Conference report filed in the House on Sept. 28 (H Rept 109-699). House agreed to the conference report Sept. 29. Senate agreed to the conference report Sept. 29. President signed Oct. 4, 2006.

PL 109-296 (HR 3408) Reauthorize the Livestock Mandatory Reporting Act of 1999 and amend the swine reporting provisions. Introduced by Goodlatte, R-Va., on July 22, 2005. House passed, amended, under suspension of the rules, Sept. 14. Senate Agriculture, Nutrition and Forestry discharged. Senate passed Sept. 20, 2006. President signed Oct. 5, 2006.

PL 109-297 (S 176) Extend the deadline for commencement of construction of a hydroelectric project in the state of Alaska. Introduced by Murkowski, R-Alaska, on Jan 26, 2005. Senate Energy and Natural Resources reported March 10 (S Rept 109-29). Senate passed July 26. House Energy and Commerce reported Sept. 26, 2006 (H Rept 109-681). House passed, under suspension of the rules, Sept. 26. President signed Oct. 5, 2006.

PL 109-298 (S 244) Extend the deadline for commencement of construction of a hydroelectric project in the state of Wyoming. Introduced by Thomas, R-Wyo., on Feb. 1, 2005. Senate Energy and Natural Resources reported March 10 (S Rept 109-32). Senate passed July 26. House Energy and Commerce reported Sept. 26, 2006 (H Rept 109-682). House passed, under suspension of the rules, Sept. 26. President signed Oct. 5, 2006.

PL 109-299 (S 1025) Authorize the secretary of the interior to assist in the funding and implementation of the Equus Beds Aquifer Storage and Recharge Project as a division of the Wichita Federal Reclamation Project. Introduced by Roberts, R-Kan., on May 12, 2005. Senate Energy and Natural Resources reported, amended, Dec. 8 (S Rept 109-192). Senate passed, amended, Dec. 16. House passed, under suspension of the rules, Sept. 20, 2006. President signed Oct. 5, 2006.

PL 109-300 (S 1275) Designate the facility of the U.S. Postal Service located at 7172 North Tongass Highway, Ward Cove, Alaska, as the "Alice R. Brusich Post Office Building." Introduced by Stevens, R-Alaska, on June 21, 2005. Senate Homeland Security and Governmental Affairs discharged. Senate passed July 1. House passed, under suspension of the rules, Sept. 25, 2006. President signed Oct. 5, 2006.

PL 109-301 (S 1323) Designate the facility of the U.S. Postal Service located on Lindbald Ave., Girdwood, Alaska, as the "Dorothy and Connie Hibbs Post Office Building." Introduced by Stevens, R-Alaska, on June 28, 2005. Senate Banking, Housing and Urban Affairs discharged. Senate passed July 1. House passed, under suspension of the rules, Sept. 25, 2006. President signed Oct. 5, 2006.

PL 109-302 (S 2690) Designate the facility of the U.S. Postal Service located at 8801 Sudley Rd., Manassas, Va., as the "Harry J. Parrish Post Office." Introduced by Allen, R-Va., on May 2, 2006. Senate Homeland Security and Governmental Affairs reported June 22 (no written report). Senate passed July 20. House passed, under suspension of the rules, Sept. 25. President signed Oct. 5, 2006.

PL 109-303 (HR 1036) Amend Title XVII U.S. Code, to make technical corrections relating to copyright royalty judges. Introduced by Smith, R-Texas, on March 2, 2005. House Judiciary reported April 28 (H Rept 109-64). House passed, amended, under suspension of the rules, Nov. 16. Senate Judiciary reported, amended, July 13, 2006 (no written report). Senate passed, amended, July 19. House agreed to Senate amendment, under suspension of the rules, Sept. 25. President signed Oct. 6, 2006.

PL 109-304 (HR 1442) Complete the codification of Title XLVI, U.S. Code, "Shipping," as positive law. Introduced by Sensenbrenner, R-Wis., on March 17, 2005. House Judiciary reported, amended, July 14 (H Rept 109-170). House passed, amended, under suspension of the rules, Nov. 16, 2006. Senate Judiciary reported Sept. 7, 2006 (no written report). Senate passed Sept. 13. President signed Oct. 6, 2006.

PL 109-305 (HR 5074) Amend the Railroad Retirement Act of 1974 to provide for continued payment of railroad retirement annuities by the Department of the Treasury. Introduced by Young, R-Alaska, on April 4, 2006. House Transportation and Infrastructure reported July 17 (H Rept 109-569). House passed, under suspension of the rules, July 25. Senate Health, Education, Labor and Pensions reported Sept. 21 (no written report). Senate passed Sept. 25. President signed Oct. 6, 2006.

PL 109-306 (HR 5187) Amend the John F. Kennedy Center Act to authorize additional appropriations for the John F. Kennedy Center for the Performing Arts for fiscal year 2007. Introduced by Oberstar, D-Minn., on April 25, 2006. House Transportation and Infrastructure reported June 20 (H Rept 109-514). House passed, under suspension of the rules, July 25. Senate Environment and Public Works reported Sept. 21 (no written report). Senate passed Sept. 26. President signed Oct. 6, 2006.

PL 109-307 (HR 5574) Amend the Public Health Service Act to reauthorize support for graduate medical education programs in children's hospitals. Introduced by Deal, R-Ga., on June 9, 2006. House Energy and Commerce reported, amended, June 20 (H Rept 109-508). House passed, amended, under suspension of the rules, June 21, 2006. Senate Health, Education, Labor and Pensions discharged. Senate passed, amended, Sept. 26. House agreed to Senate amendment, under suspension of the rules, Sept. 28. President signed Oct. 6, 2006.

PL 109-308 (HR 3858) Amend the Robert T. Stafford Disaster Relief and Emergency Assistance Act to ensure that state and local emergency preparedness operational plans address the needs of individuals with household pets and service animals after a major disaster or emergency. Introduced by Lantos, D-Calif., on Sept. 22, 2005. House passed, under suspension of the rules, May 22, 2006. Senate Homeland Security and Governmental Affairs discharged. Senate passed, amended, Aug. 3. House agreed to Senate amendment, under suspension of the rules, Sept. 20. President signed Oct. 6, 2006.

PL 109-309 (HR 4841) Amend the Ojito Wilderness Act to make a technical correction. Introduced by Udall, D-N.M., on March 1, 2006. House passed, under suspension of the rules, March 14. Senate Energy and Natural Resources discharged. Senate passed Sept. 29. President signed Oct. 6, 2006.

PL 109-310 (S 3187) Designate the Post Office located at 5755 Post Rd., East Greenwich, R.I., as the "Richard L. Cevoli Post Office." Introduced by Reed, D-R.I., on May 25, 2006. Senate Homeland Security and Governmental Affairs reported June 22 (no written report). Senate passed July 20. House passed, under suspension of the rules, Sept. 28. President signed Oct. 6, 2006.

PL 109-311 (S 3613) Designate the facility of the U.S. Postal Service at 2951 New York Highway 43, Averill Park, N.Y., as the "Major George Quamo Post Office Building." Introduced by Clinton, D-N.Y., on June 29, 2006. Senate Homeland Security and Governmental Affairs reported Aug. 1 (no written report). Senate passed Aug. 2. House passed, under suspension of the rules, Sept. 28. President signed Oct. 6, 2006.

PL 109-312 (HR 683) Amend the Trademark Act of 1946 with respect to dilution by blurring or tarnishment. Introduced by Smith, R-Texas, on Feb. 9, 2005. House Judiciary reported, amended, March 17 (H Rept 109-23). House passed, amended, under suspension of the rules, April 19. Senate Judiciary reported, amended, Feb. 27, 2006 (no written report). Senate passed, amended, March 8. House agreed to Senate amendment, under suspension of the rules, Sept. 25. President signed Oct. 6, 2006.

PL 109-313 (HR 2066) Amend Title XL, U.S. Code, to establish a Federal Acquisition Service and replace the General Supply Fund and the Information Technology Fund with an Acquisition Services Fund. Introduced by T. Davis, R-Va., on May 4, 2005. House Government Reform reported, amended, May 23 (H Rept 109-91). House passed, amended, under suspension of the rules, May 23. Senate Homeland Security and Governmental Affairs reported, amended, May 25, 2006 (S Rept 109-257). Senate passed, amended, Sept. 6. House agreed to Senate amendments, under suspension of the rules, Sept. 25. President signed Oct. 6, 2006.

PL 109-314 (HR 2107) Modify authority for the use of the National Law Enforcement Officers Memorial Maintenance Fund. Introduced by Saxton, R-N.J., on May 4, 2005. House passed, under suspension of the rules, May 16. Senate Judiciary discharged. Senate Energy and Natural Resources reported April 20, 2006 (S Rept 109-247). Senate passed Sept. 29. President signed Oct. 6, 2006.

PL 109-315 (HR 5664) Designate the facility of the U.S. Postal Service at 110 Cooper St., Babylon, N.Y., as the "Jacob Samuel Fletcher Post Office Building." Introduced by King, R-N.Y., on June 21, 2006. House passed, amended, under suspension of the rules, Sept. 20. Senate Homeland Security and Governmental Affairs discharged. Senate passed Sept. 30. President signed Oct. 10, 2006.

PL 109-316 (HR 6159) Extend temporarily certain authorities of the Small Business Administration. Introduced by Manzullo, R-Ill., on Sept. 25, 2006. House passed, under suspension of the rules, Sept. 26. Senate passed Sept. 30. President signed Oct. 10, 2006.

PL 109-317 (HR 318) Authorize the secretary of the interior to study the suitability and feasibility of designating Castle Nugent Farms located on St. Croix, Virgin Islands, as a unit of the National Park System. Introduced by Christensen, D-Virgin Is., on Jan. 25, 2005. House passed, under suspension of the rules, Nov. 15. Senate Energy and Natural Resources reported April 20, 2006 (S Rept 109-241). Senate passed Sept. 29. President signed Oct. 11, 2006.

PL 109-318 (HR 326) Amend the Yuma Crossing National Heritage Area Act of 2000 to adjust the boundary of the heritage area and extend the authority of the secretary of the interior to provide assistance under the act. Introduced by Grijalva, D-Ariz., on Jan. 25, 2005. House Resources reported, amended, Nov. 15 (H Rept 109-294). House passed, amended, under suspension of the rules, Nov. 15. Senate Energy and Natural Resources reported April 20, 2006 (S Rept 109-242). Senate passed Sept. 29. President signed Oct. 11, 2006.

PL 109-319 (HR 1728) Authorize the secretary of the interior to study the suitability and feasibility of designating the French Colonial Heritage Area in Missouri as a unit of the National Park System. Introduced by Carnahan, D-Mo., on April 20, 2005. House Resources reported, amended, Dec. 13 (H Rept 109-338). House passed, amended, under suspension of the rules, Feb. 28, 2006. Senate Energy and Natural Resources reported April 20 (S Rept 109-246). Senate passed Sept. 29. President signed Oct. 11, 2006.

PL 109-320 (HR 2720) Direct the secretary of the interior, acting through the commissioner of reclamation, to carry out an assessment and demonstration program to control the spread of salt cedar and Russian olive trees in the West. Introduced by Pearce, R-N.M., on May 26, 2005. House Resources reported Dec. 13 (H Rept 109-341, Part 1). House Agriculture discharged. House passed, under suspension of the rules, May 2, 2006. Senate passed Sept. 29. President signed Oct. 11, 2006.

PL 109-321 (HR 3443) Direct the secretary of the interior to convey certain water distribution facilities to the Northern Colorado Water Conservancy District. Introduced by Musgrave, R-Colo., on July 26, 2005. House Resources reported Nov. 10 (H Rept 109-290). House passed, amended, under suspension of the rules, Dec. 13. Senate Energy and Natural Resources reported April 20, 2006 (S Rept 109-248). Senate passed Sept. 29. President signed Oct. 11, 2006.

PL 109-322 (HR 5539) Reauthorize the North American Wetlands Conservation Act. Introduced by Pombo, R-Calif., on June 7, 2006. House Resources reported, amended, Sept. 6 (H Rept 109-639). House passed, amended, under suspension of the rules, Sept. 12. Senate passed Sept. 30. President signed Oct. 11, 2006.

PL 109-323 (HR 6106) Extend the waiver authority for the secretary of education under Title IV, Section 105, of Public Law 109-148. Introduced by Jindal, R-La., on Sept. 19, 2006. House passed, under suspension of the rules, Sept. 27. Senate passed Sept. 30. President signed Oct. 11, 2006.

PL 109-324 (S 213) Direct the secretary of the interior to convey certain federal land to Rio Arriba County, N.M. Introduced by Bingaman, D-N.M., on Jan. 31, 2005. Senate Energy and Natural Resources reported, amended, Oct. 27 (S Rept 109-166). Senate passed, amended, Nov. 16. House passed, under suspension of the rules, Sept. 27, 2006. President signed Oct. 11, 2006.

PL 109-325 (S 2146) Extend relocation expenses test programs for federal employees. Introduced by Collins, R-Maine, on Dec. 20, 2005. Senate Homeland Security and Governmental Affairs reported July 21, 2006 (S Rept 109-289). Senate passed Aug. 1. House passed, under suspension of the rules, Sept. 28. President signed Oct. 11, 2006.

PL 109-326 (S 2430) Amend the Great Lakes Fish and Wildlife Restoration Act of 1990 to provide for implementation of recommendations of the U.S. Fish and Wildlife Service contained in the Great Lakes Fishery Resources Restoration Study. Introduced by DeWine, R-Ohio, on March 16, 2006. Senate Environment and Public Works reported, amended, June 27 (S Rept 109-270). Senate passed, amended, July 11. House passed, amended, under suspension of the rules, Sept. 27. Senate agreed to House amendment Sept. 30. President signed Oct. 11, 2006.

PL 109-327 (HR 4109) Designate the facility of the U.S. Postal Service at 6101 Liberty Rd., Baltimore, Md., as the "U.S. Rep. Parren J. Mitchell Post Office." Introduced by Cummings, D-Md., on Oct. 20, 2005. House Government Reform discharged. House passed Dec. 19. Senate Homeland Security and Governmental Affairs discharged. Senate passed Sept. 30, 2006. President signed Oct. 12, 2006.

PL 109-328 (HR 4674) Designate the facility of the U.S. Postal Service at 110 North Chestnut St., Olathe, Kan., as the "Gov. John Anderson Jr. Post Office Building." Introduced by Moore, D-Kan., on Jan. 31, 2006. House passed, under suspension of the rules, May 2. Senate Homeland Security and Governmental Affairs discharged. Senate passed Sept. 30. President signed Oct. 12, 2006.

PL 109-329 (HR 5224) Designate the facility of the U.S. Postal Service at 350 Uinta Dr., Green River, Wyo., as the "Curt Gowdy Post Office Building." Introduced by Cubin, R-Wyo., on April 27, 2006. House passed, under suspension of the rules, Sept. 25. Senate passed Sept. 30. President signed Oct. 12, 2006.

PL 109-330 (HR 5504) Designate the facility of the U.S. Postal Service at 6029 Broadmoor St., Mission, Kan., as the "Larry Winn Jr. Post Office Building." Introduced by Moore, D-Kan., on May 25, 2006. House passed, under suspension of the rules, June 19. Senate Homeland Security and Governmental Affairs discharged. Senate passed Sept. 30. President signed Oct. 12, 2006.

PL 109-331 (HR 5546) Designate the federal courthouse to be constructed in Greenville, S.C., as the "Carroll A. Campbell Jr. United States Courthouse." Introduced by Inglis, R-S.C., on June 7, 2006. House passed, amended, under suspension of the rules, Sept. 27. Senate passed Sept. 30. President signed Oct. 12, 2006.

PL 109-332 (HR 5606) Designate the federal building and U.S. courthouse at 221 and 211 W. Ferguson St., Tyler, Texas, as the "William M. Steger Federal Building and U.S. Courthouse." Introduced by Hall, R-Texas, on June 14, 2006. House passed, under suspension of the rules, Sept. 27. Senate passed Sept. 30. President signed Oct. 12, 2006.

PL 109-333 (HR 5929) Designate the facility of the U.S. Postal Service at 950 Missouri Ave., East St. Louis, Ill., as the "Katherine Dunham Post Office Building." Introduced by Costello, D-Ill., on July 27, 2006. House passed, under suspension of the rules, Sept. 28. Senate passed Sept. 30. President signed Oct. 12, 2006.

PL 109-334 (HR 6033) Designate the facility of the U.S. Postal Service at 39-25 61st St., Woodside, N.Y., as the "Thomas J. Manton Post Office Building." Introduced by Crowley, D-N.Y., on Sept 6, 2006. House passed, under suspension of the rules, Sept. 14. Senate Homeland Security and Governmental Affairs discharged. Senate passed Sept. 30. President signed Oct. 12, 2006.

PL 109-335 (HR 6051) Designate the federal building at 2 South Main St., Akron, Ohio, as the "John F. Seiberling Federal

Building and United States Courthouse." Introduced by Ryan, D-Ohio, on Sept. 8, 2006. House passed, amended, under suspension of the rules, Sept. 27. Senate passed Sept. 30. President signed Oct. 12, 2006.

PL 109-336 (HR 6075) Designate the facility of the U.S. Postal Service at 101 East Gay St., West Chester, Pa., as the "Robert J. Thompson Post Office Building." Introduced by Pitts, R-Pa., on Sept. 14, 2006. House passed, under suspension of the rules, Sept. 28. Senate passed Sept. 30. President signed Oct. 12, 2006.

PL 109-337 (S 56) Establish the Rio Grande Natural Area in Colorado. Introduced by Allard, R-Colo., on Jan. 24, 2005. Senate Energy and Natural Resources reported March 30 (S Rept 109-45). Senate passed July 26. House passed, under suspension of the rules, Sept. 27, 2006. President signed Oct. 12, 2006.

PL 109-338 (S 203) Temporarily reduce the royalty payment for sodium produced on federal lands. Introduced by Thomas, R-Wyo., on Jan. 31, 2005. Senate Energy and Natural Resources reported Feb. 16 (S Rept 109-4). Senate passed, amended, July 26. House passed, amended, under suspension of the rules, July 24, 2006. President signed Oct. 12, 2006.

PL 109-339 (HR 315) Designate the U.S. courthouse at 300 N. Hogan St., Jacksonville, Fla., as the "John Milton Bryan Simpson U.S. Courthouse." Introduced by Brown, D-Fla., on Jan. 25, 2005. House passed, under suspension of the rules Feb. 8. Senate Environment and Public Works discharged. Senate passed Sept. 30, 2006. President signed Oct. 13, 2006.

PL 109-340 (HR 562) Authorize the government of Ukraine to establish a memorial on federal land in the District of Columbia to honor the victims of the man-made famine that occurred in Ukraine in 1932-33. Introduced by Levin, D-Mich., on Feb. 2, 2005. House passed, amended, under suspension of the rules, Nov. 16. Senate Energy and Natural Resources reported April 20, 2006 (S Rept 109-244). Senate passed Sept. 29. President signed Oct. 13, 2006.

PL 109-341 (HR 1463) Designate a portion of the federal building at 2100 Jamieson Ave., Alexandria, Va., as the "Justin W. Williams United States Attorney's Building." Introduced by T. Davis, R-Va., on April 5, 2005. House passed, under suspension of the rules, April 13. Senate Environment and Public Works reported Sept. 28, 2006 (no written report). Senate passed Sept. 30. President signed Oct. 13, 2006.

PL 109-342 (HR 1556) Designate a parcel of land located on the site of the Thomas F. Eagleton United States Courthouse in St. Louis, Mo., as the "Clyde S. Cahill Memorial Park." Introduced by Clay, D-Mo., on April 12, 2005. House passed, under suspension of the rules, Sept. 27, 2006. Senate passed Sept 30. President signed Oct. 13, 2006.

PL 109-343 (HR 2322) Designate the federal building at 320 N. Main St., McAllen, Texas, as the "Kika de la Garza Federal Building." Introduced by Doggett, D-Texas, on May 12, 2005. House passed, under suspension of the rules, Sept. 27, 2006. Senate passed Sept. 30. President signed Oct. 13, 2006.

PL 109-344 (HR 3127) Impose sanctions against individuals responsible for genocide, war crimes, and crimes against humanity in the Darfur region of Sudan; support measures for the protection of civilians and humanitarian operations; and support peace efforts. Introduced by Hyde, R-Ill., on June 30, 2005. House International Relations reported, amended, March 14, 2006 (H Rept 109-392, Part 1). House Judiciary reported, amended, March 29 (H Rept 109-392, Part 2). House passed, amended, under suspension of the rules, April 5. Senate Foreign Relations discharged. Senate passed, amended, Sept. 21. House agreed to Senate amendment, under suspension of the rules, Sept. 25. President signed Oct. 13, 2006.

PL 109-345 (HR 4768) Designate the facility of the U.S. Postal Service at 777 Corporation St., Beaver, Pa., as the "Robert Linn Memorial Post Office Building." Introduced by Hart, R-Pa., on Feb. 16, 2006. House passed, under suspension of the rules, Sept. 20. Senate Homeland Security and Governmental Affairs discharged. Senate passed Sept. 30. President signed Oct. 13, 2006.

PL 109-346 (HR 4805) Designate the facility of the U.S. Postal Service at 105 N. Quincy St., Clinton, Ill., as the "Gene Vance Post Office Building." Introduced by Johnson, R-Ill., on Feb. 28, 2006. House passed, under suspension of the rules, March 28. Senate Homeland Security and Governmental Affairs discharged. Senate passed Sept. 30. President signed Oct. 13, 2006.

PL 109-347 (HR 4954) Improve maritime and cargo security through enhanced layered defenses. Introduced by Lungren, R-Calif., on March 14, 2006. House Homeland Security reported, amended, April 28 (H Rept 109-447, Part 1). House Transportation and Infrastructure discharged. House passed, amended, May 4. Senate passed, amended, Sept. 14. Conference report filed in the House Sept. 29 (H Rept 109-711). House agreed to the conference report Sept. 30. Senate agreed to the conference report Sept. 30. President signed Oct. 13, 2006.

PL 109-348 (HR 5026) Designate the Investigations Building of the Food and Drug Administration at 466 Fernandez Juncos Ave., San Juan, P.R., as the "Andres Toro Building." Introduced by Fortuño, R-P.R., on March 28, 2006. House passed, under suspension of the rules, Sept. 27. Senate passed Sept. 30. President signed Oct. 13, 2006.

PL 109-349 (HR 5428) Designate the facility of the U.S. Postal Service at 202 E. Washington St., Morris, Ill., as the "Joshua A. Terando Morris Post Office Building." Introduced by Weller, R-Ill., on May 19, 2006. House passed, amended, under suspension of the rules, Sept. 12. Senate Homeland Security and Governmental Affairs discharged. Senate passed Sept. 30. President signed Oct. 13, 2006.

PL 109-350 (HR 5434) Designate the facility of the U.S. Postal Service at 40 S. Walnut St., Chillicothe, Ohio, as the "Larry Cox Post Office." Introduced by Ney, R-Ohio, on May 19, 2006. House passed, under suspension of the rules, Sept. 12. Senate Homeland Security and Governmental Affairs discharged. Senate passed Sept. 30. President signed Oct. 13, 2006.

PL 109-351 (S 2856) Provide regulatory relief and improve productivity for insured depository institutions. Introduced by Crapo, R-Idaho, on May 18, 2006. House Banking, Housing and Urban Affairs reported May 18 (H Rept 109-256). Senate passed May 25. House passed, amended, under suspension of the rules, Sept. 27. President signed Oct. 13, 2006.

PL 109-352 (S 3661) Amend Section 29 of the International Air Transportation Competition Act of 1979 relating to air transportation to and from Love Field, Texas. Introduced by Hutchison, R-Texas, on July 13, 2006. Senate Commerce, Science and Transportation reported, amended, Aug. 1 (S Rept 109-317). Senate passed Sept. 29. House passed, under suspension of the rules, Sept. 29. President signed Oct. 13, 2006.

PL 109-353 (S 3728) Promote nuclear nonproliferation in North Korea. Introduced by Frist, R-Tenn., on July 25, 2006. Senate passed July 25. House passed Sept. 30. President signed Oct. 13, 2006.

PL 109-354 (HR 138) Revise the boundaries of John H. Chafee Coastal Barrier Resources System Jekyll Island Unit GA-06P. Introduced by Kingston, R-Ga., on Jan. 4, 2005. House Resources reported, amended, Sept. 6, 2006 (H Rept 109-618). House passed, amended, under suspension of the rules, Sept. 12. Senate passed Sept. 30. President signed Oct. 16, 2006.

PL 109-355 (HR 479) Replace a Coastal Barrier Resources System map relating to Coastal Barrier Resources System Grayton Beach Unit FL-95P in Walton County, Florida. Introduced by Miller, R-Fla., on Feb. 1, 2005. House Resources reported, amended, Sept. 6, 2006 (H Rept 109-620). House passed, amended, under suspension of the rules, Sept. 12. Senate passed Sept. 30. President signed Oct. 16, 2006.

PL 109-356 (HR 3508) Authorize improvements in the operation of the government of the District of Columbia. Introduced by T. Davis, R-Va., on July 28, 2005. House Government Reform reported, amended, Nov. 3 (H Rept 109-267). House passed, amended, under suspension of the rules, Dec. 14. Senate Homeland Security and Governmental Affairs reported, amended, July 25, 2006 (no written report). Senate passed, amended, Aug. 3. House agreed to Senate amendment, under suspension of the rules, Sept. 25. President signed Oct. 16, 2006.

PL 109-357 (HR 4902) Award a Congressional Gold Medal to Byron Nelson in recognition of his significant contributions to the game of golf as a player, a teacher, and a commentator. Introduced by Burgess, R-Texas, on March 8, 2006. House passed, under suspension of the rules, May 9. Senate Banking, Housing and Urban Affairs discharged. Senate passed Sept. 30. President signed Oct. 16, 2006.

PL 109-358 (HR 5094) Require the conveyance of Mattamuskeet Lodge and surrounding property, including the Mattamuskeet National Wildlife Refuge headquarters, to the state of North Carolina to permit the state to use the property as a public facility dedicated to the conservation of the natural and cultural resources of North Carolina. Introduced by Jones, R-N.C., on April 5, 2006. House Resources reported July 13 (H Rept 109-560). House passed, under suspension of the rules, Sept. 12. Senate passed Sept. 30. President signed Oct. 16, 2006.

PL 109-359 (HR 5160) Establish the Long Island Sound Stewardship Initiative. Introduced by Simmons, R-Conn., on April 6, 2006. House passed, amended, under suspension of the rules, Sept. 27. Senate passed Sept. 30. President signed Oct. 16, 2006.

PL 109-360 (HR 5381) Establish a volunteer program and promote community partnerships for the benefit of national fish hatcheries and fisheries program offices. Introduced by Saxton, R-N.J., on May 11, 2006. House Resources reported Sept. 6 (H Rept 109-638). House passed, amended, under suspension of the rules, Sept. 12. Senate passed Sept. 30. President signed Oct. 16, 2006.

PL 109-361 (S 2562) Increase, effective as of Dec. 1, 2006, the rates of compensation for veterans with service-connected disabilities and the rates of dependency and indemnity compensation for the survivors of certain disabled veterans. Introduced by Craig, R-Idaho, on April 6, 2006. Senate Veterans' Affairs reported July 27 (S Rept 109-296). Senate passed, amended, Sept. 21. House passed Sept. 30. President signed Oct. 16, 2006.

PL 109-362 (HR 233) Designate certain National Forest System lands in the Mendocino and Six Rivers National Forests and certain Bureau of Land Management lands in Humboldt, Lake, Mendocino and Napa counties in California as wilderness; designate the Elkhorn Ridge Potential Wilderness Area; and designate certain segments of the Black Butte River in Mendocino County, Calif., as a wild or scenic river. Introduced by Thompson, D-Calif., on Jan. 4, 2005. House passed, amended, under suspension of the rules, July 24, 2006. Senate passed Sept. 29. President signed Oct. 17, 2006.

PL 109-363 (HR 4957) Direct the Secretary of the interior to convey the Tylersville division of the Lamar National Fish Hatchery and Fish Technology Center to the state of Pennsylvania. Introduced by Peterson, R-Pa., on March 14, 2006. House Resources reported, amended, July 28 (H Rept 109-612). House passed, amended, under suspension of the rules, Sept. 20. Senate passed Sept. 30. President signed Oct. 17, 2006.

PL 109-364 (HR 5122) Authorize appropriations for fiscal year 2007 for military activities of the Department of Defense, to prescribe military personnel strengths for fiscal year 2007. Introduced by Hunter, R-Calif., on April 6, 2006. House Armed Services reported, amended, May 5 (H Rept 109-452). House passed, amended, May 11. Senate passed, amended, June 22. Conference report filed in the House Sept. 29 (H Rept 109-702). House agreed to conference report Sept. 29. Senate agreed to conference report Sept. 30. President signed Oct. 17, 2006.

PL 109-365 (HR 6197) Amend the Older Americans Act of 1965 to authorize appropriations for fiscal years 2007 through 2011. Introduced by Tiberi, R-Ohio, on Sept. 27, 2006. House passed, under suspension of the rules, Sept. 28. Senate passed Sept. 30. President signed Oct. 17, 2006.

PL 109-366 (S 3930) Authorize trial by military commission for violations of the law of war. Introduced by McConnell, R-Ky., on Sept. 22, 2006. Senate passed Sept. 28. House passed Sept. 29. President signed Oct. 17, 2006.

PL 109-367 (HR 6061) Establish operational control over the international land and maritime borders of the United States. Introduced by King, R-N.Y., on Sept. 13, 2006. House passed, amended, Sept. 14. Senate passed Sept. 29. President signed Oct. 26, 2006.

PL 109-368 (HR 6326) Clarify the provision of nutrition services to older Americans. Introduced by Tiberi, R-Ohio, on Nov. 15, 2006. House Education and the Workforce discharged. House passed Nov. 15. Senate passed Nov. 15. President signed Nov. 17, 2006.

PL 109-369 (H J Res 100) Make further continuing appropriations for fiscal 2007. Introduced by Lewis, R-Calif., on Nov. 14, 2006. House passed Nov. 15. Senate passed Nov. 15. President signed Nov. 17, 2006.

PL 109-370 (S 435) Amend the Wild and Scenic Rivers Act to designate a segment of the Farmington River and Salmon Brook in Connecticut for study for potential addition to the National Wild and Scenic Rivers System. Introduced by Dodd, D-Conn., on Feb. 17, 2005. Senate Energy and Natural Resources reported, amended, Dec. 8 (S Rept 109-189). House passed, under suspension of the rules, Nov. 13, 2006. Senate passed, amended, Dec. 16. President signed Nov. 27, 2006.

PL 109-371 (S 819) Authorize the secretary of the interior to reallocate costs of the Pactola Dam and Reservoir in South Dakota to reflect increased demand for municipal, industrial, and fish and wildlife purposes. Introduced by Johnson, D-S.D., on April 15, 2005. Senate Energy and Natural Resources reported Oct. 27 (S Rept 109-168). House passed, under suspension of the rules, Nov. 13, 2006. Senate passed Nov. 16. President signed Nov. 27, 2006.

PL 109-372 (S 1131) > Authorize the exchange of certain federal lands in Idaho. Introduced by Craig, R-Idaho, on May 26, 2005. Senate Energy and Natural Resources reported, amended, April 20, 2006 (S Rept 109-232). Senate passed, amended, Sept. 29. House passed, under suspension of the rules, Nov. 13. President signed Nov. 27, 2006.

PL 109-373 (S 2464) Revise a provision relating to a repayment obligation of the Fort McDowell Yavapai Nation under the Fort McDowell Indian Community Water Rights Settlement Act of 1990. Introduced by McCain, R-Ariz., on March 28, 2006. Senate Indian Affairs reported July 19 (S Rept 109-284). Senate passed, amended, Sept. 13. House passed, under suspension of the rules, Sept. 28. President signed Nov. 27, 2006.

PL 109-374 (S 3880) Give the Department of Justice the necessary authority to apprehend, prosecute, and convict individuals who commit animal-enterprise terror. Introduced by Inhofe, R-Okla., on Sept. 8, 2006. Senate Judiciary discharged. Senate passed, amended, Sept. 30. House passed, under suspension of the rules, Nov. 13. President signed Nov. 27, 2006.

PL 109-375 (HR 409) Provide for the exchange of land within the Sierra National Forest in California. Introduced by Radanovich, R-Calif., on Jan. 26, 2005. House passed, under suspension of the rules, Sept. 20. Senate Energy and Natural Resources reported, amended, April 20, 2006 (S Rept 109-243). Senate passed, amended, Sept. 29. House agreed to Senate amendment, under suspension of the rules, Nov. 13. President signed Dec. 1, 2006.

PL 109-376 (HR 860) Provide for the conveyance of the reversionary interest of the United States in certain lands to the Clint Independent School District, El Paso County, Texas. Introduced by Reyes, D-Texas, on Feb. 16, 2005. House passed, under suspension of the rules, July 18, 2006. Senate Foreign Relations discharged. Senate passed Nov. 13. President signed Dec. 1, 2006.

PL 109-377 (HR 1129) Authorize the exchange of certain lands in Colorado. Introduced by Udall, D-Colo., on March 3, 2005. House Resources reported, amended, Oct. 25 (H Rept 109-252). House passed, amended, under suspension of the rules, Dec. 6. Senate Energy and Natural Resources reported, amended, April 20, 2006 (S Rept 109-245). Senate passed, amended, Sept. 29. House agreed to Senate amendment, under suspension of the rules, Nov. 13. President signed Dec. 1, 2006.

PL 109-378 (HR 3085) Amend the National Trails System Act to update the feasibility and suitability study originally prepared for the Trail of Tears National Historic Trail and provide for the inclusion of new trail segments, land components, and campgrounds associated with the trail. Introduced by Wamp, R-Tenn., on June 28, 2005. House Resources reported, amended, July 10, 2006 (H Rept 109-549). House passed, amended, under suspension of the rules, July 17. Senate Energy and Natural Resources discharged. Senate passed, amended, Sept. 29. House agreed to Senate amendment, under suspension of the rules, Nov. 13. President signed Dec. 1, 2006.

PL 109-379 (HR 5842) Compromise and settle all claims in the case of Pueblo of Isleta v. United States, to restore, improve, and develop the valuable on-reservation land and natural resources of the Pueblo. Introduced by Pearce, R-N.M., on July 19, 2006. House passed, under suspension of the rules, Sept. 27. Senate passed Nov. 13. President signed Dec. 1, 2006.

PL 109-380 (S 101) Convey to the town of Frannie, Wyo., certain land withdrawn by the commissioner of reclamation. Introduced by Enzi, R-Wyo., on Jan. 24, 2005. Senate Energy and Natural Resources reported March 30 (S Rept 109-46). Senate passed July 26. House passed, under suspension of the rules, Nov. 15, 2006. President signed Dec. 1, 2006.

PL 109-381 (S 1140) Designate the State Route 1 Bridge in Delaware as the "Sen. William V. Roth, Jr. Bridge." Introduced by Carper, D-Del., on May 26, 2005. Senate Environment and Public Works reported June 9 (no written report). Senate passed June 15. House passed, under suspension of the rules, Nov. 13, 2006. President signed Dec. 1, 2006.

PL 109-382 (S 4001) Designate certain land in New England as wilderness for inclusion in the National Preservation System and designate certain land as a National Recreation Area. Introduced by Sununu, R-N.H., on Sept. 29, 2006. Senate passed Sept. 29. House passed, under suspension of the rules, Nov. 15. President signed Dec. 1, 2006.

PL 109-383 (H J Res 102) Make further continuing appropriations for fiscal 2007. Introduced by Lewis, R-Calif., on Dec. 7, 2006. House passed Dec. 8. Senate passed Dec. 9. President signed Dec. 9, 2006.

PL 109-384 (HR 2383) Redesignate the facility of the Bureau of Reclamation located at 19550 Kelso Rd. in Byron, Calif., as the "C. W. 'Bill' Jones Pumping Plant." Introduced by Nunes, R-Calif., on May 16, 2005. House Resources reported Oct. 17 (H Rept 109-247). House passed, under suspension of the rules, March 8, 2006. Senate Energy and Natural Resources discharged. Senate passed Nov. 16. President signed Dec. 12, 2006.

PL 109-385 (HR 3817) Withdraw the Valle Vidal Unit of the Carson National Forest in New Mexico from mineral exploration or development. Introduced by Udall, D-N.M., on Sept. 15, 2005. House Resources reported July 20, 2006 (H Rept 109-583). House passed, under suspension of the rules, July 24. Senate Energy and Natural Resources discharged. Senate passed Nov. 16, 2006. President signed Dec. 12, 2006.

PL 109-386 (HR 4000) Authorize the secretary of the interior to revise certain repayment contracts with the Bostwick Irrigation District in Nebraska, the Kansas Bostwick Irrigation District No. 2, the Frenchman-Cambridge Irrigation District, and the Webster Irrigation District No. 4, all part of the Pick-Sloan Missouri Basin Program. Introduced by Moran, R-Kan., on Oct. 6, 2005. House Resources discharged. House passed Dec. 19. Senate Energy and Natural Resources reported July 31, 2006 (S Rept 109-315). Senate passed Nov. 16. President signed Dec. 12, 2006.

PL 109-387 (HR 4559) Provide for the conveyance of certain National Forest System land to the towns of Laona and Wabeno, Wis. Introduced by Green, R-Wis., on Dec. 15, 2005. House passed, amended, under suspension of the rules, Sept. 26, 2006. Senate passed Nov. 16. President signed Dec. 12, 2006.

PL 109-388 (HR 5061) Direct the secretary of the interior to convey Paint Bank National Fish Hatchery and Wytheville National Fish Hatchery to the state of Virginia. Introduced by Boucher, D-Va., on March 30, 2006. House Resources reported June 28 (H Rept 109-533). House passed, under suspension of the rules, July 10. Senate Environment and Public Works reported Sept. 20 (S Rept 109-341). Senate passed Nov. 16. President signed Dec. 12, 2006.

PL 109-389 (HR 5103) Provide for the conveyance of the former Konnarock Lutheran Girls School in Smyth County, Va., federally owned and administered by the Forest Service, and facilitate the restoration and reuse of the property. Introduced by Boucher, D-Va., on April 5, 2006. House passed, amended, under suspension of the rules, Sept. 26. Senate passed Nov. 16. President signed Dec. 12, 2006.

PL 109-390 (HR 5585) Improve the netting process for financial contracts. Introduced by McHenry, R-N.C., on June 12, 2006. House Financial Services reported Sept. 12 (H Rept 109-648, Part 1). House Judiciary discharged. House passed, amended, under suspension of the rules, Sept. 27. Senate passed, amended, Sept. 30. House agreed to Senate amendments, under suspension of the rules, Nov. 15. President signed Dec. 12, 2006.

PL 109-391 (HR 5690) Adjust the boundaries of the Ouachita National Forest in Oklahoma and Arkansas. Introduced by Boren, D-Okla., on June 27, 2006. House passed, under suspension of the rules, Sept. 27. Senate passed Nov. 16. President signed Dec. 12, 2006.

PL 109-392 (HR 6121) Amend the Federal Water Pollution Control Act to reauthorize a program relating to the Lake Pontchartrain Basin. Introduced by Baker, R-La., on Sept. 20, 2006. House passed, under suspension of the rules, Nov. 13. Senate passed Nov. 16. President signed Dec. 12, 2006.

PL 109-393 (HR 4377) Extend the time required for construction of a hydroelectric project at the Arrowrock Dam on the Boise River in Idaho. Introduced by Otter, R-Idaho, on Nov. 17, 2005. House Energy and Commerce reported Sept. 26, 2006 (H Rept 109-684). House passed, under suspension of the rules, Sept. 26. Senate passed Nov. 16. President signed Dec. 13, 2006.

PL 109-394 (HR 4766) Amend the Native American Programs Act of 1974 to provide for the revitalization of Native American languages through immersion programs. Introduced by Wilson, R-N.M., on Feb. 15, 2006. House passed, amended, under suspension of the rules, Sept. 27. Senate Indian Affairs discharged. Senate passed Dec. 6. President signed Dec. 14, 2006.

PL 109-395 (S 2250) Award a congressional gold medal to Dr. Norman E. Borlaug, a Nobel laureate and father of the "Green Revolution." Introduced by Grassley, R-Iowa, on Feb. 7, 2006. Senate Banking, Housing, and Urban Affairs discharged. Senate passed Sept. 27. House passed, under suspension of the rules, Dec. 6. President signed Dec. 14, 2006.

PL 109-396 (HR 3699) Provide for the sale, acquisition, conveyance, and exchange of certain real property in the District of Columbia to facilitate the utilization, development, and redevelopment of the property. Introduced by T. Davis, R-Va., on Sept. 8, 2005. House Government Reform reported, amended, Nov. 18 (H Rept 109-316, Part 1). House Transportation and Infrastructure reported, amended, Dec. 16 (H Rept 109-316, Part 2). House Energy and Commerce reported, amended, Feb. 3, 2006 (H Rept 109-316, Part 3). House Resources discharged. House passed, amended, Sept. 30. Senate Homeland Security and Governmental Affairs discharged. Senate Energy and Natural Resources discharged. Senate passed Nov. 16. President signed Dec. 15, 2006.

PL 109-397 (HR 1472) Designate the facility of the U.S. Postal Service located at 167 East 124th St. in New York as the "Tito Puente Post Office Building." Introduced by Rangel, D-N.Y., on April 5, 2005. House passed, under suspension of the rules, Sept. 28, 2006. Senate Homeland Security and Governmental Affairs discharged. Senate passed Dec. 6. President signed Dec. 18, 2006.

PL 109-398 (HR 4246) Designate the facility of the U.S. Postal Service located at 8135 Forest Lane in Dallas as the "Dr. Robert E. Price Post Office Building." Introduced by Sessions, R-Texas, on Nov. 7, 2005. House Government Reform discharged. House passed Dec. 19. Senate Homeland Security and Governmental Affairs discharged. Senate passed Dec. 6, 2006. President signed Dec. 18, 2006.

PL 109-399 (HR 4720) Designate the facility of the U.S. Postal Service located at 200 Gateway Drive in Lincoln, Calif., as the "Beverly J. Wilson Post Office Building." Introduced by Doolittle, R-Calif., on Feb. 8, 2006. House passed, under suspension of the rules, Sept. 28. Senate Homeland Security and Governmental Affairs discharged. Senate passed Dec. 6. President signed Dec. 18, 2006.

PL 109-400 (HR 5108) Designate the facility of the U.S. Postal Service located at 1213 East Houston St. in Cleveland, Texas, as the "Lance Cpl. Robert A. Martinez Post Office Building." Introduced by Poe, R-Texas, on April 5, 2006. House passed, under suspension of the rules, Sept. 28. Senate Homeland Security and Governmental Affairs discharged. Senate passed Dec. 6. President signed Dec. 18, 2006.

PL 109-401 (HR 5682) Exempt from certain requirements of the Atomic Energy Act of 1954 a proposed agreement on nuclear cooperation with India. Introduced by Hyde, R-Ill., on June 26, 2006. House International Relations reported, amended, July 21 (H Rept 109-590, Part 1). House Rules discharged. House passed, amended, July 26. Senate passed, amended, Nov. 16. Conference report filed in the House Dec. 7 (H Rept 109-721). House agreed to the conference report Dec. 8. Senate agreed to the conference report Dec. 9. President signed Dec. 18, 2006.

PL 109-402 (HR 5736) Designate the facility of the U.S. Postal Service located at 101 Palafox Place in Pensacola, Fla., as the "Vincent J. Whibbs Sr. Post Office Building." Introduced by Miller, R-Fla., on June 29, 2006. House passed, under suspension of the rules, Sept. 28. Senate Homeland Security and Governmental Affairs discharged. Senate passed Dec. 6. President signed Dec. 18, 2006.

PL 109-403 (HR 5857) Designate the facility of the U.S. Postal Service located at 1501 South Cherrybell Ave. in Tucson, Ariz., as the "Morris K. 'Mo' Udall Post Office Building." Introduced by Grijalva, D-Ariz., on July 20, 2006. House passed, under suspension of the rules, Sept. 25. Senate Homeland Security and Governmental Affairs discharged. Senate passed Dec. 6. President signed Dec. 18, 2006.

PL 109-404 (HR 5923) Designate the facility of the U.S. Postal Service located at 29-50 Union St. in Flushing, N.Y., as the "Dr. Leonard Price Stavisky Post Office." Introduced by Ackerman, D-N.Y., on July 27, 2006. House passed, under suspension of the rules, Sept. 25. Senate Homeland Security and Governmental Affairs discharged. Senate passed Dec. 6. President signed Dec. 18, 2006.

PL 109-405 (HR 5989) Designate the facility of the U.S. Postal Service located at 10240 Roosevelt Road in Westchester, Ill., as the "John J. Sinde Post Office Building." Introduced by Davis, D-Ill., on July 28, 2006. House passed, under suspension of the rules, Sept. 28. Senate Homeland Security and Governmental Affairs discharged. Senate passed Dec. 6. President signed Dec. 18, 2006.

PL 109-406 (HR 5990) Designate the facility of the U.S. Postal Service located at 415 South 5th Ave. in Maywood, Ill., as the "Wallace W. Sykes Post Office Building." Introduced by Davis, D-Ill., on July 28, 2006. House passed, under suspension of the rules, Sept. 28. Senate Homeland Security and Governmental Affairs discharged. Senate passed Dec. 6. President signed Dec. 18, 2006.

PL 109-407 (HR 6078) Designate the facility of the U.S. Postal Service located at 307 West Wheat St. in Woodville, Texas, as the "Chuck Fortenberry Post Office Building." Introduced by Brady, R-Texas, on Sept. 14, 2006. House passed, under suspension of the rules, Sept. 28. Senate Homeland Security and Governmental Affairs discharged. Senate passed Dec. 6. President signed Dec. 18, 2006.

PL 109-408 (HR 6102) Designate the facility of the U.S. Postal Service located at 200 Lawyers Road NW in Vienna, Va., as the "Capt. Christopher P. Petty and Maj. William F. Hecker III Post Office Building." Introduced by T. Davis, R-Va., on Sept. 19, 2006. House passed, amended, under suspension of the rules, Sept. 25. Senate Homeland Security and Governmental Affairs discharged. Senate passed Dec. 6. President signed Dec. 18, 2006.

PL 109-409 (HR 6151) Designate the facility of the U.S. Postal Service located at 216 Oak St. in Farmington, Minn., as the "Hamilton H. Judson Post Office." Introduced by Kline, R-Minn., on Sept. 21, 2006. House passed, under suspension of the rules, Sept. 28. Senate Homeland Security and Governmental Affairs discharged. Senate passed Dec. 6. President signed Dec. 18, 2006.

PL 109-410 (S 1219) Authorize certain tribes in Montana to enter into a lease or other temporary conveyance of water rights to meet the water needs of the Dry Prairie Rural Water Association, Inc. Introduced by Burns, R-Mont., on June 9, 2005. Senate Indian Affairs reported Jan. 24, 2006 (S Rept 109-213). Senate passed Feb. 1. House passed, under suspension of the rules, Dec. 5. President signed Dec. 18, 2006.

PL 109-411 (S 1820) Designate the facility of the U.S. Postal Service located at 6110 East 51st Place in Tulsa, Okla., as the "Dewey F. Bartlett Post Office." Introduced by Inhofe, R-Okla., on Oct. 5, 2005. Senate Homeland Security and Governmental Affairs reported Dec. 16 (no written report). Senate passed March 3, 2006. House passed, under suspension of the rules, Dec. 6. President signed Dec. 18, 2006.

PL 109-412 (S 3759) Name the Armed Forces Readiness Center in Great Falls, Mont., in honor of Capt. William Wylie Galt, a recipient of the Medal of Honor. Introduced by Burns, R-Mont., on July 27, 2006. Senate Armed Services discharged. Senate passed Nov. 16. House passed, under suspension of the rules, Dec. 7. President signed Dec. 18, 2006.

PL 109-413 (S 4050) Designate the facility of the U.S. Postal Service located at 103 East Thompson St. in Thomaston, Ga., as the "Sgt. 1st Class Robert Lee 'Bobby' Hollar Jr. Post Office Building." Introduced by Isakson, R-Ga., on Nov. 14, 2006. Senate Homeland Security and Governmental Affairs discharged. Senate passed Dec. 6. House passed, under suspension of the rules, Dec. 8. President signed Dec. 18, 2006.

PL 109-414 (S 4073) Designate the outpatient clinic of the Department of Veterans Affairs located in Farmington, Mo., as the "Robert Silvey Department of Veterans Affairs Outpatient Clinic." Introduced by Talent, R-Mo., on Nov. 16, 2006. Senate passed Nov. 16. House passed, under suspension of the rules, Dec. 6. President signed Dec. 18, 2006.

PL 109-415 (HR 6143) Amend Title XXVI of the Public Health Service Act to revise and extend the program for providing life-saving care for those with HIV/AIDS. Introduced by Bono, R-Calif., on Sept. 21, 2006. House Energy and Commerce reported Sept. 28 (H Rept 109-695). House passed, amended, under suspension of the rules, Sept. 28. Senate Health, Education, Labor and Pensions discharged. Senate passed, amended, Dec. 6. House agreed to Senate amendment Dec. 9. President signed Dec. 19, 2006.

PL 109-416 (S 843) Amend the Public Health Service Act to combat autism through research, screening, intervention, and education. Introduced by Santorum, R-Pa., on April 19, 2005. Senate Health, Education, Labor and Pensions reported, amended,

Aug. 3, 2006 (S Rept 109-318). Senate passed, amended, Aug. 3. House passed, amended, under suspension of the rules, Dec. 6. Senate agreed to House amendment Dec. 7. President signed Dec. 19, 2006.

PL 109-417 (S 3678) Amend the Public Health Service Act with respect to public health security and all-hazards preparedness and response. Introduced by Burr, R-N.C., on July 18, 2006. Senate Health, Education, Labor and Pensions reported, amended, Aug. 3 (S Rept 109-319). Senate passed, amended, Dec. 5. House passed Dec. 9. President signed Dec. 19, 2006.

PL 109-418 (HR 5466) Amend the National Trails System Act to designate the Capt. John Smith Chesapeake National Historic Trail. Introduced by J. Davis, R-Va., on May 24, 2006. House passed, amended, under suspension of the rules, Dec. 5. Senate passed Dec. 7. President signed Dec. 19, 2006.

PL 109-419 (HR 394) Direct the secretary of the interior to conduct a boundary study to evaluate the significance of the Col. James Barrett Farm in Massachusetts, as well as the suitability and feasibility of its inclusion in the National Park System as part of the Minute Man National Historical Park. Introduced by Meehan, D-Mass., on Jan. 26, 2005. House Resources reported, amended, June 16 (H Rept 109-135). House passed, amended, under suspension of the rules, Sept. 20. Senate Energy and Natural Resources reported July 31, 2006 (S Rept 109-311). Senate passed Dec. 7. President signed Dec. 20, 2006.

PL 109-420 (HR 758) Establish an interagency aerospace revitalization task force to develop a national strategy for aerospace workforce recruitment, training, and cultivation. Introduced by Ehlers, R-Mich., on Feb. 10, 2005. House passed, under suspension of the rules, Oct. 25. Senate Commerce, Science and Transportation discharged. Senate passed Dec. 6, 2006. President signed Dec. 20, 2006.

PL 109-421 (HR 854) Provide for certain lands to be held in trust for the Utu Utu Gwaitu Paiute Tribe. Introduced by McKeon, R-Calif., on Feb. 16, 2005. House Resources reported, amended, July 13, 2006 (H Rept 109-557). House passed, amended, under suspension of the rules, July 24. Senate Indian Affairs reported Sept. 20 (S Rept 109-342). Senate passed Dec. 6. President signed Dec. 20, 2006.

PL 109-422 (HR 864) Provide for programs and activities aimed at preventing underage drinking. Introduced by Roybal-Allard, D-Calif., on Feb. 16, 2005. House passed, amended, under suspension of the rules, Nov. 14, 2006. Senate passed, amended, Dec. 6. House agreed to Senate amendment, under suspension of the rules, Dec. 7. President signed Dec. 20, 2006.

PL 109-423 (HR 1285) Provide a three-year extension of the changes in requirements for admission of nonimmigrant nurses in health professional shortage areas made by the Nursing Relief for Disadvantaged Areas Act of 1999. Introduced by Rush, D-Ill., on March 14, 2005. House passed, amended, under suspension of the rules, June 20, 2006. Senate Judiciary discharged. Senate passed Dec. 6. President signed Dec. 20, 2006.

PL 109-424 (HR 1674) Authorize and strengthen the tsunami detection, forecasting, warning, and mitigation program of the National Oceanic and Atmospheric Administration, to be carried out by the National Weather Service. Introduced by Boehlert, R-N.Y., on April 18, 2005. House Science reported, amended, Sept. 28, 2006 (H Rept 109-698). House passed, amended, under suspension of the rules, Dec. 6. Senate passed Dec. 8. President signed Dec. 20, 2006.

PL 109-425 (HR 4057) Provide that attorneys employed by the Department of Justice shall be eligible for compensatory time off for travel under Section 5550b of Title V, U.S. Code. Introduced by Porter, R-Nev., on Oct. 17, 2005. House Government Reform reported March 14, 2006 (H Rept 109-390). House passed, amended, under suspension of the rules, March 28. Senate Homeland Security and Governmental Affairs discharged. Senate passed Dec. 6. President signed Dec. 20, 2006.

PL 109-426 (HR 4416) Reauthorize the use of penalty and franked mail in efforts related to the location and recovery of missing children. Introduced by Millender-McDonald, D-Calif., on Nov. 18, 2005. House passed, under suspension of the rules, June 26, 2006. Senate Homeland Security and Governmental Affairs discharged. Senate passed Dec. 7. President signed Dec. 20, 2006.

PL 109-427 (HR 4510) Direct the Joint Committee on the Library to accept the donation of a bust depicting Sojourner Truth and to display it in a suitable location in the rotunda of the Capitol. Introduced by Jackson-Lee, D-Texas, on Dec. 13, 2005. House Administration discharged. House passed, amended, Dec. 19. Senate Rules and Administration discharged. Senate passed Dec. 6, 2006. President signed Dec. 20, 2006.

PL 109-428 (HR 4583) Amend the Wool Products Labeling Act of 1939 to revise the requirements for labeling of certain wool and cashmere products. Introduced by Blackburn, R-Tenn., on Dec. 16, 2005. House Energy and Commerce reported, amended, Sept. 8, 2006 (H Rept 109-644). House passed, amended, under suspension of the rules, Sept. 19. Senate Commerce, Science and Transportation discharged. Senate passed Dec. 6. President signed Dec. 20, 2006.

PL 109-429 (HR 5132) Direct the secretary of the interior to conduct a special resource study to determine the suitability and feasibility of including in the National Park System certain sites in Monroe County, Mich., relating to the Battles of the River Raisin during the War of 1812. Introduced by Dingell, D-Mich., on April 6, 2006. House Resources reported, amended, Sept. 6 (H Rept 109-637). House passed, amended, under suspension of the rules, Sept. 25. Senate passed Dec. 7. President signed Dec. 20, 2006.

PL 109-430 (HR 5136) Establish a National Integrated Drought Information System within the National Oceanic and Atmospheric Administration to improve drought monitoring and forecasting capabilities. Introduced by Hall, R-Texas, on April 6, 2006. House Science reported, amended, June 15 (H Rept 109-503). House passed, amended, under suspension of the rules, Sept. 26. Senate Commerce, Science and Transportation discharged. Senate passed Dec. 6. President signed Dec. 20, 2006.

PL 109-431 (HR 5646) Study and promote the use of energy-efficient computer servers in the United States. Introduced by Rogers, R-Mich., on June 20, 2006. House Energy and Commerce reported June 28 (H Rept 109-538). House passed, amended, under suspension of the rules, July 12. Senate Energy and Natural

Resources discharged. Senate passed Dec. 7. President signed Dec. 20, 2006.

PL 109-432 (HR 6111) Amend the Internal Revenue Code of 1986 to provide that the Tax Court may review claims for equitable innocent-spouse relief and to suspend the running on the period of limitations while such claims are pending. Introduced by Tauscher, D-Calif., on Sept. 19, 2006. House passed, amended, under suspension of the rules, Dec. 5. Senate passed, amended, Dec. 7. House agreed to Senate amendment with amendments Dec. 8. Senate agreed to House amendments to Senate amendment Dec. 9. President signed Dec. 20, 2006.

PL 109-433 (HR 6131) Permit certain expenditures from the Leaking Underground Storage Tank Trust Fund. Introduced by Chocola, R-Ind., on Sept. 21, 2006. House passed, under suspension of the rules, Sept. 26. Senate Finance discharged. Senate passed Dec. 8. President signed Dec. 20, 2006.

PL 109-434 (HR 6316) Extend through Dec. 31, 2008, the authority of the secretary of the army to accept and expend funds contributed by nonfederal public entities to expedite the processing of permits. Introduced by Baird, D-Wash., on Nov. 13, 2006. House passed, under suspension of the rules, Dec. 5. Senate passed Dec. 6. President signed Dec. 20, 2006.

PL 109-435 (HR 6407) Improve the operations and accountability of the U.S. Postal Service. Introduced by T. Davis, R-Va., on Dec. 7, 2006. House passed, amended, under suspension of the rules, Dec. 8. Senate passed Dec. 9. President signed Dec. 20, 2006.

PL 109-436 (S 1346) Direct the secretary of the interior to conduct a study of maritime sites in Michigan. Introduced by Stabenow, D-Mich., on June 30, 2005. Senate Energy and Natural Resources reported, amended, April 20, 2006 (S Rept 109-234). Senate passed, amended, Sept. 29. House passed, under suspension of the rules, Dec. 6. President signed Dec. 20, 2006.

PL 109-437 (S 1998) Amend Title XVIII, U.S. Code, to enhance protections relating to the reputation and meaning of the Medal of Honor and other military decorations and awards. Introduced by Conrad, D-N.D., on Nov. 10, 2005. Senate Judiciary discharged. Senate passed Sept. 7, 2006. House passed, under suspension of the rules, Dec. 6. President signed Dec. 20, 2006.

PL 109-438 (S 3938) Reauthorize the Export-Import Bank of the United States. Introduced by Crapo, R-Idaho, on Sept. 26, 2006. Senate Banking, Housing and Urban Affairs reported Sept. 26 (no written report). Senate passed, amended, Sept. 30. House passed, amended, under suspension of the rules, Dec. 6. Senate agreed to House amendment Dec. 6. President signed Dec. 20, 2006.

PL 109-439 (S 4044) Clarify the treatment of certain charitable contributions under Title XI, U.S. Code. Introduced by Hatch, R-Utah, on Sept. 29, 2006. Senate passed Sept. 30. House passed, under suspension of the rules, Dec. 6. President signed Dec. 20, 2006.

PL 109-440 (S 4046) Extend oversight and accountability related to U.S. reconstruction funds and efforts in Iraq by extending the termination date of the Office of the Special Inspector General for Iraq Reconstruction. Introduced by Collins, R-Maine, on Nov. 13, 2006. Senate Homeland Security and Governmental Affairs reported Nov. 16 (no written report). Senate passed Dec. 6. House passed, under suspension of the rules, Dec. 8. President signed Dec. 20, 2006.

PL 109-441 (HR 1492) Provide for the preservation of the historic confinement sites where Japanese Americans were detained during World War II. Introduced by Thomas, R-Calif., on April 6, 2005. House Resources reported, amended, June 21 (H Rept 109-142). House passed, amended, under suspension of the rules, Nov. 16. Senate Energy and Natural Resources reported, amended, July 31, 2006 (S Rept 109-314). Senate passed, amended, Nov. 16. House agreed to Senate amendments, under suspension of the rules, Dec. 5. President signed Dec. 21, 2006.

PL 109-442 (HR 3248) Amend the Public Health Service Act to establish a program to assist family caregivers in accessing affordable and high-quality respite care. Introduced by Ferguson, R-N.J., on July 12, 2005. House Energy and Commerce reported, amended, Dec. 5, 2006 (H Rept 109-716). House passed, amended, under suspension of the rules, Dec. 6. Senate passed Dec. 8. President signed Dec. 21, 2006.

PL 109-443 (HR 5076) Amend Title XLIX, U.S. Code, to authorize appropriations for the National Transportation Safety Board for fiscal 2007 and 2008. Introduced by Young, R-Alaska, on April 4, 2006. House Transportation and Infrastructure reported June 20 (H Rept 109-512). House passed, amended, under suspension of the rules, Dec. 6. Senate passed Dec. 7. President signed Dec. 21, 2006.

PL 109-444 (HR 6342) Amend Title XXXVIII, U.S. Code, to extend certain expiring provisions administered by the secretary of veterans affairs and to expand eligibility for the Survivors' and Dependents' Educational Assistance program. Introduced by Buyer, R-Ind., on Dec. 5, 2006. House passed, under suspension of the rules, Dec. 6. Senate passed Dec. 7. President signed Dec. 21, 2006.

PL 109-445 (HR 6429) Treat payments by charitable organizations with respect to certain firefighters as exempt payments. Introduced by Bono, R-Calif., on Dec. 8, 2006. House Ways and Means discharged. House passed Dec. 9. Senate passed Dec. 9. President signed Dec. 21, 2006.

PL 109-446 (S 2370) Promote the development of democratic institutions in areas under the administrative control of the Palestinian Authority. Introduced by McConnell, R-Ky., on March 6, 2006. Senate Foreign Relations discharged. Senate passed, amended, June 23. House passed, under suspension of the rules, Dec. 7. President signed Dec. 21, 2006.

PL 109-447 (H J Res 101) Appoint the day for the convening of the first session of the 110th Congress. Introduced by Boehner, R-Ohio, on Nov. 15, 2006. House passed Nov. 15. Senate passed Dec. 9. President signed Dec. 22, 2006.

PL 109-448 (S 214) Authorize the secretary of the interior to cooperate with the states on the border with Mexico and other appropriate entities in conducting a hydrogeologic characterization, mapping, and modeling program for priority transboundary aquifers. Introduced by Bingaman, D-N.M., on Jan. 31, 2005. Senate Energy and Natural Resources reported March 7 (S Rept

109-17). Senate passed, amended, July 26. House passed, amended, under suspension of the rules, Dec. 6, 2006. Senate agreed to House amendment Dec. 9. President signed Dec. 22, 2006.

PL 109-449 (S 362) Establish a program within the National Oceanic and Atmospheric Administration (NOAA) and the U.S. Coast Guard to help identify, determine sources of, assess, reduce, and prevent marine debris and its adverse impacts on the marine environment and navigation safety, in coordination with nonfederal entities. Introduced by Inouye, D-Hawaii, on Feb. 10, 2005. Senate Commerce, Science and Transportation reported, amended, April 13 (S Rept 109-56). Senate passed, amended, July 1. House Resources reported, amended, Dec. 8 (H Rept 109-332, Part 1). House Transportation and Infrastructure reported, amended, July 25, 2006 (H Rept 109-332, Part 2). House passed, amended, under suspension of the rules, Sept. 27. Senate agreed to House amendment Dec. 9. President signed Dec. 22, 2006.

PL 109-450 (S 707) Reduce preterm labor and delivery, the risk of pregnancy-related deaths and complications, and infant mortality caused by prematurity. Introduced by Alexander, R-Tenn., on April 5, 2005. Senate Health, Education, Labor and Pensions reported, amended, July 31, 2006 (S Rept 109-298). Senate passed, amended, Aug. 1. House Energy and Commerce discharged. House passed, amended, Dec. 9. Senate agreed to House amendment Dec. 9. President signed Dec. 22, 2006.

PL 109-451 (S 895) Direct the secretary of the interior to establish a rural water-supply program in certain "reclamation states" to provide a clean, safe, affordable, and reliable water supply to rural residents. Introduced by Domenici, R-N.M., on April 25, 2005. Senate Energy and Natural Resources reported, amended, Oct. 1 (S Rept 109-148). Senate passed, amended, Nov. 16. House passed, amended, under suspension of the rules, Dec. 6, 2006. Senate agreed to House amendments Dec. 9. President signed Dec. 22, 2006.

PL 109-452 (S 1096) Amend the Wild and Scenic Rivers Act to designate portions of the Musconetcong River in New Jersey as a component of the National Wild and Scenic Rivers System. Introduced by Corzine, D-N.J., on May 23, 2005. Senate Energy and Natural Resources reported Dec. 8 (S Rept 109-193). Senate passed, amended, Dec. 16. House Resources discharged. House passed Dec. 9, 2006. President signed Dec. 22, 2006.

PL 109-453 (S 1378) Amend the National Historic Preservation Act to provide appropriation authorization and improve the operations of the Advisory Council on Historic Preservation. Introduced by Talent, R-Mo., on July 11, 2005. Senate Energy and Natural Resources reported, amended, April 20, 2006 (S Rept 109-235). Senate passed, amended, Sept. 29. House passed Dec. 9. President signed Dec. 22, 2006.

PL 109-454 (S 1529) Provide for the conveyance of certain federal land in Yuma, Ariz. Introduced by Kyl, R-Ariz., on July 28, 2005. Senate Energy and Natural Resources reported, amended, July 31, 2006 (S Rept 109-300). Senate passed, amended, Dec. 7. House passed Dec. 9. President signed Dec. 22, 2006.

PL 109-455 (S 1608) Enhance Federal Trade Commission enforcement against illegal spam, "spyware," and cross-border fraud and deception. Introduced by Smith, R-Ore., on July 29, 2005. Senate Commerce, Science and Transportation reported March 14, 2006 (S Rept 109-219). Senate passed March 16. House Energy and Commerce discharged. House passed, amended, Dec. 9. Senate agreed to House amendment Dec. 9. President signed Dec. 22, 2006.

PL 109-456 (S 2125) Promote relief, security, and democracy in the Democratic Republic of the Congo. Introduced by Obama, D-Ill., on Dec. 16, 2005. Senate Foreign Relations reported May 23, 2006 (no written report). Senate passed, amended, June 29. House passed, amended, under suspension of the rules, Dec. 6. Senate agreed to House amendment Dec. 9. President signed Dec. 22, 2006.

PL 109-457 (S 2150) Direct the secretary of the interior to convey certain Bureau of Land Management Land to the City of Eugene, Ore. Introduced by Wyden, D-Ore., on Dec. 20, 2005. Senate Energy and Natural Resources reported, amended, July 31, 2006 (S Rept 109-306). Senate passed, amended, Dec. 7. House passed Dec. 9. President signed Dec. 22, 2006.

PL 109-458 (S 2205) Direct the secretary of the interior to convey certain parcels of land acquired for the Blunt Reservoir and Pierre Canal features of the initial stage of the Oahe Unit, James Division, S.D., to the South Dakota Commission of Schools and Public Lands and the Department of Game, Fish and Parks for the purpose of mitigating lost wildlife habitat, on certain conditions. Introduced by Thune, R-S.D., on Jan. 26, 2006. Senate Energy and Natural Resources discharged. Senate passed, amended, Dec. 7. House passed Dec. 9. President signed Dec. 22, 2006.

PL 109-459 (S 2653) Direct the Federal Communications Commission to make efforts to reduce telephone rates for armed forces personnel deployed overseas. Introduced by Stevens, R-Alaska, on April 26, 2006. Senate Commerce, Science and Transportation discharged. Senate passed, amended, Dec. 6. House passed Dec. 9. President signed Dec. 22, 2006.

PL 109-460 (S 2735) Reauthorize the National Dam Safety Program Act. Introduced by Bond, R-Mo., on May 4, 2006. Senate Environment and Public Works reported, amended, July 10 (S Rept 109-276). Senate passed, amended, Dec. 6. House passed, under suspension of the rules, Dec. 9. President signed Dec. 22, 2006.

PL 109-461 (S 3421) Authorize major medical facility projects and leases for the Department of Veterans Affairs for fiscal 2006 and 2007. Introduced by Craig, R-Idaho, on June 6, 2006. Senate Veterans' Affairs reported, amended, Sept. 6 (S Rept 109-328). Senate passed, amended, Sept. 26. House passed, amended, under suspension of the rules, Dec. 8. Senate agreed to House amendments Dec. 9. President signed Dec. 22, 2006.

PL 109-462 (S 3546) Amend the Federal Food, Drug and Cosmetic Act with respect to dietary supplements and nonprescription drugs. Introduced by Hatch, R-Utah, on June 21, 2006. Senate Health, Education, Labor and Pensions reported, amended, Sept. 5 (S Rept 109-324). Senate passed, amended, Dec. 6. House passed, under suspension of the rules, Dec. 9. President signed Dec. 22, 2006.

PL 109-463 (S 3821) Authorize certain athletes to be admitted temporarily into the United States to compete or perform in an athletic league, competition or performance. Introduced by

Collins, R-Maine, on August 3, 2006. Senate Judiciary discharged. Senate passed, amended, Dec. 6. House passed, under suspension of the rules, Dec. 9. President signed Dec. 22, 2006.

PL 109-464 (S 4042) Amend Title XVIII, U.S. Code, to prohibit disruptions of funerals of members or former members of the armed forces. Introduced by Durbin, D-Ill., on Sept. 29, 2006. Senate Judiciary discharged. Senate passed Dec. 7. House passed, under suspension of the rules, Dec. 9. President signed Dec. 22, 2006.

PL 109-465 (S 4091) Provide authority for restoration of the Social Security Trust Funds from the effects of a clerical error. Introduced by Grassley, R-Iowa, on Dec. 6, 2006. Senate Finance discharged. Senate passed Dec. 7. House passed Dec. 9. President signed Dec. 22, 2006.

PL 109-466 (S 4092) Clarify certain land use in Jefferson County, Colo. Introduced by Allard, R-Colo., on Dec. 6, 2006. Senate passed Dec. 6. House passed Dec. 9. President signed Dec. 22, 2006.

PL 109-467 (S 4093) Amend the Farm Security and Rural Investment Act of 2002 to extend a suspension of limitation on the period for which certain borrowers are eligible for guaranteed assistance. Introduced by Harkin, D-Iowa, on Dec. 6, 2006. Senate passed Dec. 6. House passed, under suspension of the rules, Dec. 8. President signed Dec. 22, 2006.

PL 109-468 (HR 5782) Amend Title XLIX, U.S. Code, to reauthorize federal pipeline safety programs. Introduced by Young, R-Alaska, on July 13, 2006. House Transportation reported, amended, Dec. 5 (H Rept 109-717, Part 1). House Energy and Commerce reported, amended, Dec. 5 (H Rept 109-717, Part 2). House passed, amended, under suspension of the rules, Dec. 6. Senate passed Dec. 7. President signed Dec. 29, 2006.

PL 109-469 (HR 6344) Reauthorize the Office of National Drug Control Policy Act. Introduced by Souder, R-Ind., on Dec. 5, 2006. House passed, amended, under suspension of the rules, Dec. 7. Senate passed Dec. 8. President signed Dec. 29, 2006.

PL 109-470 (HR 486) Provide for a land exchange involving private owners and the Bureau of Land Management to remove private land from the required safety zone surrounding munitions storage bunkers at Holloman Air Force Base, N.M. Introduced by Pearce, R-N.M., on Feb. 1, 2005. House passed, under suspension of the rules, March 14. Senate Energy and Natural Resources reported, amended, July 31, 2006 (S Rept 109-313). Senate passed, amended, Dec. 7. House agreed to Senate amendment, Dec. 9. President signed Jan. 11, 2007.

PL 109-471 (HR 4588) Reauthorize grants for and require applied water supply research regarding the water resources research and technology institutes established under the Water Resources Research Act of 1984. Introduced by Doolittle, R-Calif., on Dec. 16, 2005. House Resources reported, amended, Sept. 6, 2006 (H Rept 109-630). House passed, amended, under suspension of the rules, Sept. 25. Senate passed, amended, Dec. 6. House agreed to Senate amendment, Dec. 9. President signed Jan. 11, 2007.

PL 109-472 (HR 6060) Authorize certain activities by the Department of State and the Broadcasting Board of Governors, including strengthening visa fraud investigations and protective functions of security officials, and resolving certain pay discrepancies. Introduced by Smith, R-N.J., on Sept. 13, 2006. House International Relations reported, Sept. 29 (H Rept. 109-706). House passed, amended, under suspension of the rules, Dec. 8. Senate passed Dec. 9. President signed Jan. 11, 2007.

PL 109-473 (HR 6345) Make a conforming amendment to the Federal Deposit Insurance Act with respect to examinations of certain insured depository institutions. Introduced by Bachus, R-Ala., on Dec. 5, 2006. House passed, under suspension of the rules, Dec. 7. Senate passed Dec. 8. President signed Jan. 11, 2007.

PL 109-474 (HR 482) Provide for a land exchange involving federal lands in the Lincoln National Forest in New Mexico. Introduced by Neugebauer, R-Texas, on Feb. 1, 2005. House passed, under suspension of the rules, April 12. Senate Energy and Natural Resources reported, amended, July 31, 2006 (S Rept 109-312). Senate passed, amended, Dec. 7. House agreed to Senate amendment, Dec. 9. President signed Jan. 12, 2007.

PL 109-475 (HR 1245) Provide for programs to increase the awareness and knowledge of women and health care providers with respect to gynecologic cancers. Introduced by Issa, R-Calif., on March 10, 2005. House passed, amended, under suspension of the rules, Nov. 14, 2006. Senate passed, amended, Dec. 8. House agreed to Senate amendment, Dec. 9. President signed Jan. 12, 2007.

PL 109-476 (HR 4709) Amend Title XVIII, U.S. Code, to strengthen protections for law enforcement officers and the public by providing criminal penalties for the fraudulent acquisition or unauthorized disclosure of phone records. Introduced by Smith, R-Texas, on Feb. 8, 2006. Judiciary Committee reported March 16 (H Rept. 109-395). House passed, amended, under suspension of the rules, April 25. Senate Judiciary discharged. Senate passed Dec. 8. President signed Jan. 12, 2007.

PL 109-477 (HR 4997) Extend for two years the authority to grant waivers of the foreign country residence requirement to certain international medical graduates. Introduced by Moran, R-Kan., on March 16, 2006. House Judiciary reported, amended, Dec. 5 (H Rept 109-715). House passed, amended, under suspension of the rules, Dec. 6. Senate passed, Dec. 9. President signed Jan. 12, 2007.

PL 109-478 (HR 5483) Increase the disability earning limitation under the Railroad Retirement Act and index the amount of allowable earnings consistent with increases in the substantial gainful activity dollar amount under the Social Security Act. Introduced by Young, R-Alaska, on May 25, 2006. House Transportation reported, Sept. 19 (H Rept 109-669). House passed, under suspension of the rules, Sept. 27. Senate Health, Education, Labor, and Pensions discharged. Senate passed Dec. 9. President signed Jan. 12, 2007.

PL 109-479 (HR 5946) Reauthorize and amend the Magnuson-Stevens Fishery Conservation and Management Act. Introduced by Pombo, R-Calif., on July 27, 2006. House passed, amended, under suspension of the rules, Sept. 27. Senate passed, amended,

Dec. 7. House agreed to Senate amendment, under suspension of the rules, Dec. 9. President signed Jan. 12, 2007.

PL 109-480 (HR 5948) Reauthorize the Belarus Democracy Act of 2004. Introduced by Smith, R-N.J. on July 27, 2006. House passed, amended, under suspension of the rules, Dec. 8. Senate passed Dec. 9. President signed Jan. 12, 2007.

PL 109-481 (HR 6338) Amend Title XVIII, U.S. Code, to prevent and repress the misuse of the distinctive Red Crescent and Third Protocol (Red Crystal) emblems. Introduced by Flake, R-Ariz., on Dec. 5, 2006. House passed, under suspension of the rules, Dec. 5. Senate passed Dec. 8. President signed Jan. 12, 2007.

PL 109-482 (HR 6164) Amend Title IV of the Public Health Service Act to revise and extend the authorities of the National Institutes of Health. Introduced by Barton, R-Texas, on Sept. 25, 2006. House Energy and Commerce reported Sept. 26 (H Rept 109-687). House passed, under suspension of the rules, Sept. 26. Senate Health, Education, Labor, and Pensions discharged. Senate passed, amended, Dec. 8. House agreed to Senate amendment, under suspension of the rules, Dec. 9. President signed Jan. 15, 2007.

110th Congress—2007

PL 110-1 (S 159) Redesignate the White Rocks National Recreation Area in Vermont as the "Robert T. Stafford White Rocks National Recreation Area." Introduced by Leahy, D-Vt., on Jan. 4, 2007. Senate passed Jan. 4. House Natural Resources discharged. House passed Jan. 5. President signed Jan. 17, 2007.

PL 110-2 (HR 475) Revise the composition of the House of Representatives Page Board to equalize the number of members representing the majority and minority parties, and include a member representing the parents of pages and a member representing former pages. Introduced by Kildee, D-Mich., on Jan. 16, 2007. House passed Jan. 19. Senate passed Jan. 23. President signed Feb. 2, 2007.

PL 110-3 (HR 188) Provide a new effective date for the applicability of certain provisions of law to Public Law 105-331. Introduced by Pallone, D-N.J., on Jan. 4, 2007. House passed, under suspension of the rules, Jan. 16. Senate Banking, Housing and Urban Affairs discharged. Senate passed Jan. 25. President signed Feb. 8, 2007.

PL 110-4 (HR 434) Provide for an additional temporary extension of programs under the Small Business Act and the Small Business Investment Act of 1958, through July 31, 2007. Introduced by Chabot, R-Ohio, on Jan. 12, 2007. House passed, under suspension of the rules, Jan. 17. Senate Small Business and Entrepreneurship discharged. Senate passed, amended, Feb. 1. House agreed to Senate amendments, under suspension of the rules, Feb. 7. President signed Feb. 15, 2007.

PL 110-5 (H J Res 20) Make further continuing appropriations for fiscal 2007. Introduced by Obey, D-Wis., on Jan. 29, 2007. House passed Jan. 31. Senate passed Feb. 14. President signed Feb. 15, 2007.

PL 110-6 (HR 742) Amend the Antitrust Modernization Commission Act of 2002, to extend the term of the Antitrust Modernization Commission. Introduced by Conyers, D-Mich., on Jan. 31, 2007. House passed, under suspension of the rules, Feb. 7. Senate passed Feb. 12. President signed Feb. 26, 2007.

PL 110-7 (HR 49) Designate the facility of the U.S. Postal Service located at 1300 North Frontage Rd. West in Vail, Colo., as the "Gerald R. Ford Jr. Post Office Building." Introduced by Udall, D-Colo., on Jan. 4, 2007. House passed, under suspension of the rules, Jan. 29. Senate Homeland Security and Governmental Affairs discharged. Senate passed Feb. 17. President signed March 7, 2007.

PL 110-8 (HR 335) Designate the facility of the U.S. Postal Service located at 152 North 5th St. in Laramie, Wyo., as the "Gale W. McGee Post Office." Introduced by Cubin, R-Wyo., on Jan. 9, 2007. House passed, under suspension of the rules, Jan 29. Senate Homeland Security and Governmental Affairs discharged. Senate passed Feb. 17. President signed March 7, 2007.

PL 110-9 (HR 433) Designate the facility of the U.S. Postal Service located at 1700 Main St. in Little Rock, Ark., as the "Scipio A. Jones Post Office Building." Introduced by Snyder, D-Ark., on Jan. 12, 2007. House passed, under suspension of the rules, Feb. 5. Senate Homeland Security and Governmental Affairs discharged. Senate passed Feb. 17. President signed March 7, 2007.

PL 110-10 (HR 514) Designate the facility of the U.S. Postal Service located at 16150 Aviation Loop Drive in Brooksville, Fla., as the "Sgt. Lea Robert Mills Brooksville Aviation Branch Post Office." Introduced by Brown-Waite, R-Fla., on Jan. 17. House passed, under suspension of the rules, Feb. 5. Senate Homeland Security and Governmental Affairs discharged. Senate passed Feb. 17. President signed March 7, 2007.

PL 110-11 (HR 577) Designate the facility of the U.S. Postal Service located at 3903 South Congress Ave. in Austin, Texas, as the "Sgt. Henry Ybarra III Post Office Building." Introduced by Doggett, D-Texas, on Jan. 19, 2007. House passed, under suspension of the rules, Feb. 5. Senate Homeland Security and Governmental Affairs discharged. Senate passed Feb. 17. President signed March 7, 2007.

PL 110-12 (HR 521) Designate the facility of the U.S. Postal Service located at 2633 11th St. in Rock Island, Ill., as the "Lane Evans Post Office Building." Introduced by Hare, D-Ill., on Jan. 17, 2007. House passed, under suspension of the rules, Jan. 29. Senate Homeland Security and Governmental Affairs discharged. Senate passed Feb. 17. President signed March 15, 2007.

PL 110-13 (HR 342) Designate the U.S. courthouse located at 555 Independence St. in Cape Girardeau, Mo., as the "Rush Hudson Limbaugh Sr. U.S. Courthouse." Introduced by Emerson, R-Mo., on Jan. 9, 2007. House Transportation reported, amended, Feb. 12 (H Rept 110-10). House passed, under suspension of the rules, Feb. 12. Senate Environment and Public Works discharged. Senate passed March 9. President signed March 21, 2007.

PL 110-14 (HR 544) Designate the U.S. courthouse at South Federal Place in Santa Fe, N.M., as the "Santiago E. Campos U.S. Courthouse." Introduced by Udall, D-N.M., on Jan. 17, 2007. House Transportation reported Feb. 16 (H Rept 110-18). House passed, under suspension of the rules, March 6. Senate passed March 9. President signed March 21, 2007.

PL 110-15 (HR 584) Designate the federal building located at 400 Maryland Ave. SW in the District of Columbia as the "Lyndon Baines Johnson Department of Education Building." Introduced by G. Green, D-Texas, on Jan. 19, 2007. House Transportation and Infrastructure reported, amended, Feb. 16 (H Rept 110-17). House passed, amended, under suspension of the rules, March 6. Senate passed March 9. President signed March 23, 2007.

PL 110-16 (HR 1129) Provide for the construction, operation, and maintenance of an arterial road in St. Louis County, Mo. Introduced by Carnahan, D-Mo., on Feb. 16, 2007. House passed, under suspension of the rules, Feb. 27. Senate passed March 13. President signed March 28, 2007.

PL 110-17 (S 494) Endorse further enlargement of the North Atlantic Treaty Organization (NATO) and facilitate the timely admission of new members. Introduced by Lugar, R-Ind., on Feb. 6, 2007. Senate Foreign Relations reported March 9 (S Rept 110-34). Senate passed, amended, March 15. House passed March 26. President signed April 9, 2007.

PL 110-18 (HR 1132) Amend the Public Health Service Act to provide waivers related to grants for preventive health measures with respect to breast and cervical cancers. Introduced by Baldwin, D-Wis., on Feb. 16, 2007. House Energy and Commerce reported, amended, March 27 (H Rept 110-76). House passed, under suspension of the rules, March 27. Senate passed March 29. President signed April 20, 2007.

PL 110-19 (S 1002) Amend the Older Americans Act of 1965 to reinstate certain provisions relating to the nutrition services incentive program. Introduced by Kennedy, D-Mass., on March 27, 2007. Senate passed, March 27. House Education and Labor discharged. House passed March 28. President signed April 23, 2007.

PL 110-20 (HR 753) Redesignate the federal building located at 167 North Main St. in Memphis, Tenn., as the "Clifford Davis and Odell Horton Federal Building." Introduced by Cohen, D-Tenn., on Jan. 31, 2007. House Transportation and Infrastructure reported, amended, March 26 (H Rept 110-72). House passed, under suspension of the rules, March 26. Senate passed April 10. President signed May 2, 2007.

PL 110-21 (HR 1003) Amend the Foreign Affairs Reform and Restructuring Act of 1998 to reauthorize the United States Advisory Commission on Public Diplomacy. Introduced by Watson, D-Calif., on Feb. 12, 2007. House passed, under suspension of the rules, March 13. Senate Foreign Relations reported April 12 (S Rept 110-55). Senate passed April 18. President signed May 2, 2007.

PL 110-22 (HR 137) Amend Title 18, U.S. Code, to strengthen prohibitions against animal fighting. Introduced by Gallegly, R-Calif., on Jan. 4, 2007. House Judiciary reported, amended, March 1 (H Rept 110-27, Part 1). House Agriculture discharged. House passed, under suspension of the rules, March 26. Senate passed April 10. President signed May 3, 2007.

PL 110-23 (HR 727) Amend the Public Health Service Act to add requirements regarding trauma care. Introduced by G. Green, D-Texas, on Jan. 30, 2007. House Energy and Commerce reported, amended, March 27 (H Rept 110-77). House passed, under suspension of the rules, March 27. Senate passed March 29. President signed May 3, 2007.

PL 110-24 (HR 1130) Amend the Ethics in Government Act of 1978 to extend the authority to withhold from public availability a financial disclosure report filed by an individual who is a judicial officer or judicial employee, to the extent necessary to protect the safety of the individual or of a family member. Introduced by Conyers, D-Mich., on Feb. 16, 2007. House Judiciary reported March 20 (H Rept 110-59). House passed, under suspension of the rules, March 21. Senate Homeland Security and Governmental Affairs discharged. Senate passed April 19. President signed May 3, 2007.

PL 110-25 (S 521) Designate the federal building and U.S. courthouse and customhouse located at 515 West First St. in Duluth, Minn., as the "Gerald W. Heaney Federal Building and United States Courthouse and Customhouse." Introduced by Klobuchar, D-Minn., on Feb. 7, 2007. Senate Environment and Public Works reported March 29 (no written report). Senate passed April 10. House passed, under suspension of the rules, April 23. President signed May 8, 2007.

PL 110-26 (HR 1681) Amend the Congressional Charter of The American National Red Cross to modernize its governance structure and enhance the ability of the board of governors to support the critical mission of the American National Red Cross in the 21st century. Introduced by Lantos, D-Calif., on March 26, 2007. House Foreign Affairs reported, amended, April 16 (H Rept 110-87). House passed, under suspension of the rules, April 17. Senate passed April 23. President signed May 11, 2007.

PL 110-27 (HR 988) Designate the facility of the U.S. Postal Service located at 5757 Tilton Ave. in Riverside, Calif., as the "Lieutenant Todd Jason Bryant Post Office." Introduced by Calvert, R-Calif., on Feb. 12, 2007. House passed, under suspension of the rules, April 16. Senate Homeland Security and Governmental Affairs reported May 22 (no written report). Senate passed May 23. President signed May 25, 2007.

PL 110-28 (HR 2206) Make emergency supplemental appropriations and additional supplemental appropriations for agricultural and other emergency assistance for the fiscal year ending Sept. 30, 2007. Introduced by Obey, D-Wis., on May 8, 2007. House passed May 10. Senate passed, amended, May 17. House agreed to the Senate amendment, with amendments, May 24. Senate agreed to House amendments May 24. President signed May 25, 2007.

PL 110-29 (HR 414) Designate the facility of the U.S. Postal Service located at 60 Calle McKinley West in Mayaguez, Puerto Rico, as the "Miguel Angel Garcia Mendez Post Office Building." Introduced by Fortuño, R-P.R., on Jan. 11, 2007. House passed, under suspension of the rules, Feb. 12. Senate Homeland Security and Governmental Affairs reported May 22 (no written report). Senate passed May 23. President signed June 1, 2007.

PL 110-30 (HR 437) Designate the facility of the U.S. Postal Service located at 500 West Eisenhower St. in Rio Grande City, Texas, as the "Lino Perez Jr. Post Office." Introduced by Cuellar, D-Texas, on Jan. 12, 2007. House passed, under suspension of the rules, Feb. 13. Senate Homeland Security and Governmental Affairs reported May 22 (no written report). Senate passed May 23. President signed June 1, 2007.

PL 110-31 (HR 625) Designate the facility of the U.S. Postal Service located at 4230 Maine Ave. in Baldwin Park, Calif., as the "Atanacio Haro-Marin Post Office." Introduced by Solis, D-Calif., on Jan. 22, 2007. House passed, under suspension of the rules, April 23. Senate Homeland Security and Governmental Affairs reported May 22 (no written report). Senate passed May 23, 2007. President signed June 1, 2007.

PL 110-32 (HR 1402) Designate the facility of the U.S. Postal Service located at 320 South Lecanto Highway in Lecanto, Fla., as the "Sergeant Dennis J. Flanagan Lecanto Post Office Building." Introduced by Brown-Waite, R-Fla., on March 8, 2007. House passed, under suspension of the rules, April 23. Senate Homeland Security and Governmental Affairs reported May 22 (no written report). Senate passed May 23. President signed June 1, 2007.

PL 110-33 (HR 2080) Amend the District of Columbia Home Rule Act to conform the District charter to revisions made by the Council of the District of Columbia relating to public education. Introduced by Norton, D-D.C., on May 1, 2007. House passed, under suspension of the rules, May 8. Senate passed May 22. President signed June 1, 2007

PL 110-34 (S 214) Amend Chapter 35, Title 28, U.S. Code, to preserve the independence of U.S. attorneys. Introduced by Feinstein, D-Calif., on Jan. 9, 2007. Senate Judiciary reported, amended, Feb. 12 (no written report). Senate passed, amended, March 20. House passed, under suspension of the rules, May 22. President signed June 14, 2007.

PL 110-35 (HR 1675) Suspend the requirements of the Department of Housing and Urban Development regarding electronic filing of previous participation certificates and the filing of such certificates with respect to certain low-income housing investors. Introduced by Bean, D-Ill., on March 26, 2007. House Financial Services reported April 23 (H Rept 110-106). House passed, under suspension of the rules, April 24. Senate Banking, Housing, and Urban Affairs reported May 17 (no written report). Senate passed May 24. President signed June 15, 2007.

PL 110-36 (S 1104) Increase the number of Iraqi and Afghani translators and interpreters who may be admitted to the United States as special immigrants. Introduced by Lugar, R-Ind., on April 12, 2007. Senate passed April 12. House Judiciary reported, amended, May 21 (H Rept 110-158). House passed, amended, under suspension of the rules, May 22. Senate agreed to House amendment May 24. President signed June 15, 2007.

PL 110-37 (HR 1676) Reauthorize the Housing and Urban Development program of loan guarantees for Indian housing. Introduced by Boren, D-Okla., on March 26, 2007. House Financial Services reported April 20 (H Rept 110-102). House passed, under suspension of the rules, April 24. Senate Banking, Housing, and Urban Affairs reported May 17 (no written report). Senate passed May 24. President signed June 18, 2007.

PL 110-38 (S 676) Provide that the executive director or the alternate executive director of the Inter-American Development Bank may serve on the board of directors of the Inter-American Foundation. Introduced by Biden, D-Del., on Feb. 17, 2007. Senate Foreign Relations reported March 9 (S Rept 110-35). Senate passed March 15. House passed, under suspension of the rules, June 11. President signed June 21, 2007.

PL 110-39 (S 1537) Authorize the transfer of certain funds from the Senate Gift Shop Revolving Fund to the Senate Employee Child Care Center. Introduced by Landrieu, D-La., on May 25, 2007. Senate passed May 25. House passed June 6. President signed June 21, 2007.

PL 110-40 (HR 57) Repeal a 1936 federal statute that limited the authority of the Virgin Islands government to assess and collect real property taxes in the territory. Introduced by Christensen, D-Virgin Is., on Jan. 4, 2007. House passed, under suspension of the rules, Jan. 17. Senate Energy and Natural Resources reported Feb. 15 (S Rept 110-19). Senate passed June 12. President signed June 29, 2007.

PL 110-41 (HR 692) Amend Title 4, U.S. Code, to authorize the governor of a U.S. state, territory, or possession to order that the national flag be flown at half-staff in that jurisdiction in the event that a member of the armed forces from that jurisdiction dies while serving on active duty. Introduced by Stupak, D-Mich., on Jan. 24, 2007. House Judiciary reported, amended, May 9 (H Rept 110-139). House passed, amended, under suspension of the rules, May 15. Senate Judiciary reported June 7 (no written report). Senate passed June 14. President signed June 29, 2007.

PL 110-42 (HR 1830) Extend the authorities of the Andean Trade Preference Act until Feb. 29, 2008. Introduced by Rangel, D-N.Y., on March 29, 2007. House passed, amended, under suspension of the rules, June 27. Senate passed June 28. President signed June 30, 2007.

PL 110-43 (S 1352) Designate the facility of the U.S. Postal Service located at 127 East Locust St. in Fairbury, Ill., as the "Dr. Francis Townsend Post Office Building." Introduced by Durbin, D-Ill., on May 10, 2007. Senate Homeland Security and Governmental Affairs reported May 22 (no written report). Senate passed May 23. House passed, under suspension of the rules, June 19. President signed July 3, 2007.

PL 110-44 (S 1704) Temporarily extend the programs under the Higher Education Act of 1965. Introduced by Kennedy, D-Mass., on June 27, 2007. Senate passed June 27. House passed June 28. President signed July 3, 2007.

PL 110-45 (S 229) Redesignate a federal building in Albuquerque, N.M., as the "Raymond G. Murphy Department of Veterans Affairs Medical Center." Introduced by Domenici, R-N.M., on Jan. 9, 2007. Senate Veterans' Affairs discharged. Senate passed April 12. House passed, under suspension of the rules, June 25. President signed July 5, 2007.

PL 110-46 (S 801) Designate a U.S. courthouse located in Fresno, Calif., as the "Robert E. Coyle U.S. Courthouse." Introduced by Boxer, D-Calif., on March 7, 2007. Senate Environment and Public Works reported March 29 (no written report). Senate passed April 10. House passed, under suspension of the rules, June 25. President signed July 5, 2007.

PL 110-47 (S 277) Modify the boundaries of Grand Teton National Park to include certain land within the park subdivision. Introduced by Thomas, R-Wyo., on Jan 12, 2007. Senate Energy and Natural Resources reported Feb. 15 (S Rept 110-16). Senate passed, amended, June 19. House Natural Resources discharged. House passed June 27. President signed July 13, 2007.

PL 110-48 (S 1701) Provide for the extension of transitional medical assistance and the abstinence education program through the end of fiscal year 2007. Introduced by Baucus, D-Mont., on June 27, 2007. Senate passed June 27. House passed, under suspension of the rules, July 11. President signed July 18, 2007.

PL 110-49 (HR 556) Overhaul the process by which such foreign investments are examined for any effect they may have on national security, and to establish the Committee on Foreign Investment in the United States. Introduced by Maloney, D-N.Y., on Jan. 18, 2007. House Financial Services reported, amended, Feb. 23 (H Rept 110-24, Part 1). House Energy and Commerce and Foreign Affairs discharged. House passed, amended, Feb. 28. Senate Banking, Housing, and Urban Affairs discharged. Senate passed, amended, June 29. House agreed to Senate amendment, under suspension of the rules, July 11. President signed July 26, 2007.

PL 110-50 (S 966) Enable the Department of State to respond to a critical shortage of passport processing personnel. Introduced by Schumer, D-N.Y., on March 22, 2007. Senate Foreign Relations reported, amended, June 27 (S Rept 110-109). Senate passed, amended, June 29. House passed, amended, under suspension of the rules, July 16. Senate agreed to House amendment July 18. President signed July 30, 2007.

PL 110-51 (S 1868) Temporarily extend the programs under the Higher Education Act of 1965. Introduced by Kennedy, D-Mass., on July 24, 2007. Senate passed July 24. House passed, under suspension of the rules, July 25. President signed July 31, 2007.

PL 110-52 (H J Res 44) Approve the renewal of import restrictions contained in the Burmese Freedom and Democracy Act of 2003. Introduced by Lantos, D-Calif., on May 24, 2007. House passed, amended, under suspension of the rules, July 23. Senate passed July 24. President signed Aug. 1, 2007.

PL 110-53 (HR 1) Implement recommendations of the National Commission on Terrorist Attacks Upon the United States. Introduced by Thompson, D-Miss., on Jan. 5, 2007. House passed Jan. 9. Senate Homeland Security and Governmental Affairs discharged. Senate passed, amended, July 9. Conference report filed in the House July 25 (H Rept 110-259). Senate agreed to the conference report July 26. House agreed to the conference report July 27. President signed Aug. 3, 2007.

PL 110-54 (HR 2429) Amend Title XVIII of the Social Security Act to provide an exception to the 60-day limit on Medicare reciprocal billing arrangements between two physicians during the period in which one of the physicians is ordered to active duty as a member of a reserve component of the Armed Forces. Introduced by Thompson, D-Calif., on May 22, 2007. House passed, under suspension of the rules, May 23. Senate Finance discharged. Senate passed July 24. President signed Aug. 3, 2007.

PL 110-55 (S 1927) Amend the Foreign Intelligence Surveillance Act of 1978 to provide additional procedures for authorizing certain acquisitions of foreign intelligence information. Introduced by McConnell, R-Ky., on Aug. 1, 2007. Senate passed, amended, Aug. 3. House passed Aug. 4. President signed Aug. 5, 2007.

PL 110-56 (HR 3311) Authorize additional funds for emergency repairs and reconstruction of the Interstate I-35 bridge located in Minneapolis that collapsed Aug. 1, and waive the $100 million limitation on emergency relief funds for those emergency repairs and reconstruction. Introduced by Oberstar, D-Minn., on Aug. 2, 2007. House passed, amended, under suspension of the rules, Aug. 3. Senate passed, amended, Aug. 3. House agreed to Senate amendment Aug. 4. President signed Aug. 6, 2007.

PL 110-57 (HR 3206) Provide for an additional temporary extension of programs under the Small Business Act and the Small Business Investment Act of 1958 through Dec. 15, 2007. Introduced by Velázquez, D-N.Y., on July 27, 2007. House passed, under suspension of the rules, July 30. Senate passed July 31. President signed Aug. 8, 2007.

PL 110-58 (HR 1260) Designate the facility of the U.S. Postal Service located at 6301 Highway 58 in Harrison, Tenn., as the "Claude Ramsey Post Office." Introduced by Wamp, R-Tenn., on March 1, 2007. House passed, under suspension of the rules, May 14. Senate Homeland Security and Governmental Affairs reported Aug. 1 (no written report). Senate passed Aug. 3. President signed Aug. 9, 2007.

PL 110-59 (HR 1335) Designate the facility of the U.S. Postal Service located at 508 East Main St. in Seneca, S.C., as the "S/Sgt. Lewis G. Watkins Post Office Building." Introduced by Barrett, R-S.C., on March 6, 2007. House passed, under suspension of the rules, May 14. Senate Homeland Security and Governmental Affairs reported Aug. 1 (no written report). Senate passed Aug. 3. President signed Aug. 9, 2007.

PL 110-60 (HR 1384) Designate the facility of the U.S. Postal Service located at 118 Minner St. in Bakersfield, Calif., as the "Buck Owens Post Office." Introduced by McCarthy, R-Calif., on March 7, 2007. House Oversight and Government Reform discharged. House passed, amended, July 30. Senate passed Aug. 3. President signed Aug. 9, 2007.

PL 110-61 (HR 1425) Designate the facility of the U.S. Postal Service located at 4551 East 52nd St. in Odessa, Texas, as the "Staff Sergeant Marvin 'Rex' Young Post Office Building." Introduced by Conaway, R-Texas, on March 9, 2007. House passed, under suspension of the rules, May 21. Senate Homeland Security and Governmental Affairs reported Aug. 1 (no written report). Senate passed Aug. 3. President signed Aug. 9, 2007.

PL 110-62 (HR 1434) Designate the facility of the U.S. Postal Service located at 896 Pittsburgh St. in Springdale, Pa., as the "Rachel Carson Post Office Building." Introduced by Altmire, D-Pa., on March 9, 2007. House passed, under suspension of the rules, April 23. Senate Homeland Security and Governmental Affairs reported Aug. 1 (no written report). Senate passed Aug. 3. President signed Aug. 9, 2007.

PL 110-63 (HR 1617) Designate the facility of the U.S. Postal Service located at 561 Kingsland Ave. in University City, Mo., as the "Harriett F. Woods Post Office Building." Introduced by Carnahan, D-Mo., on March 21, 2007. House passed, under suspension of the rules, May 14. Senate Homeland Security and Governmental Affairs reported Aug. 1 (no written report). Senate passed Aug. 3. President signed Aug. 9, 2007.

PL 110-64 (HR 1722) Designate the facility of the U.S. Postal Service located at 601 Banyan Trail in Boca Raton, Fla., as the "Leonard W. Herman Post Office." Introduced by Wexler, D-Fla., on March 27, 2007. House passed, under suspension of the rules, May 22. Senate Homeland Security and Governmental Affairs reported Aug. 1 (no written report). Senate passed Aug. 3. President signed Aug. 9, 2007.

PL 110-65 (HR 2025) Designate the facility of the U.S. Postal Service located at 11033 South State St. in Chicago, Ill., as the "Willye B. White Post Office Building." Introduced by Jackson, D-Ill., on April 25, 2007. House passed, under suspension of the rules, May 14. Senate Homeland Security and Governmental Affairs reported Aug. 1 (no written report). Senate passed Aug. 3. President signed Aug. 9, 2007.

PL 110-66 (HR 2077) Designate the facility of the U.S. Postal Service located at 20805 State Route 125 in Blue Creek, Ohio, as the "George B. Lewis Post Office Building." Introduced by Schmidt, R-Ohio, on April 30, 2007. House passed, under suspension of the rules, May 21. Senate Homeland Security and Governmental Affairs reported Aug. 1 (no written report). Senate passed Aug. 3. President signed Aug. 9, 2007.

PL 110-67 (HR 2078) Designate the facility of the U.S. Postal Service located at 14536 State Route 136 in Cherry Fork, Ohio, as the "Staff Sergeant Omer T. 'O.T.' Hawkins Post Office." Introduced by Schmidt, R-Ohio, on April 30, 2007. House passed, under suspension of the rules, May 21. Senate Homeland Security and Governmental Affairs reported Aug. 1 (no written report). Senate passed Aug. 3. President signed Aug. 9, 2007.

PL 110-68 (HR 2127) Designate the facility of the U.S. Postal Service located at 408 West 6th St. in Chelsea, Okla., as the "Clem Rogers McSpadden Post Office Building." Introduced by Boren, D-Okla., on May 3, 2007. House passed, under suspension of the rules, June 18. Senate Homeland Security and Governmental Affairs reported Aug. 1 (no written report). Senate passed Aug. 3. President signed Aug. 9, 2007.

PL 110-69 (HR 2272) Invest in innovation through research and development, and improve the competitiveness of the United States. Introduced by Gordon, D-Tenn., on May 10, 2007. House passed, under suspension of the rules, May 21. Senate passed, amended, July 19. Conference report filed in the House Aug. 1 (H Rept 110-289). House agreed to the conference report Aug. 2. Senate agreed to the conference report Aug. 2. President signed Aug. 9, 2007.

PL 110-70 (HR 2309) Designate the facility of the U.S. Postal Service located at 3916 Milgen Rd. in Columbus, Ga., as the "Frank G. Lumpkin Jr. Post Office Building." Introduced by Westmoreland, R-Ga., on May 14, 2007. House Oversight and Government Reform discharged. House passed July 30. Senate passed Aug. 3. President signed Aug. 9, 2007.

PL 110-71 (HR 2563) Designate the facility of the U.S. Postal Service located at 309 East Linn St. in Marshalltown, Iowa, as the "Major Scott Nisely Post Office." Introduced by Latham, R-Iowa, on June 5, 2007. House passed, under suspension of the rules, June 18. Senate Homeland Security and Governmental Affairs reported Aug. 1 (no written report). Senate passed Aug. 3. President signed Aug. 9, 2007.

PL 110-72 (HR 2570) Designate the facility of the U.S. Postal Service located at 301 Boardwalk Dr. in Fort Collins, Colo., as the "Dr. Karl E. Carson Post Office Building." Introduced by Musgrave, R-Colo., on June 5, 2007. House passed, under suspension of the rules, July 16. Senate Homeland Security and Governmental Affairs reported Aug. 1 (no written report). Senate passed Aug. 3. President signed Aug. 9, 2007.

PL 110-73 (HR 2688) Designate the facility of the U.S. Postal Service located at 103 South Getty St. in Uvalde, Texas, as the "Dolph S. Briscoe Jr. Post Office Building." Introduced by Rodriguez, D-Texas, on June 12, 2007. House Oversight and Government Reform discharged. House passed, amended, July 30. Senate passed Aug. 3. President signed Aug. 9, 2007.

PL 110-74 (S 1099) Amend Chapter 89 of Title 5, U.S. Code, to make individuals employed by the Roosevelt Campobello International Park Commission eligible to obtain federal health insurance. Introduced by Collins, R-Maine, on April 12, 2007. Senate Homeland Security and Governmental Affairs reported June 19 (no written report). Senate passed June 22. House Oversight and Government Reform discharged. House passed July 30. President signed Aug. 9, 2007.

PL 110-75 (HR 2863) Authorize the Coquille Indian Tribe of the state of Oregon to convey land and interests in land owned by the tribe. Introduced by DeFazio, D-Ore., on June 26, 2007. House Natural Resources reported, amended, July 30 (H Rept 110-274). House passed, amended, July 30. Senate passed Aug. 2. President signed Aug. 13, 2007.

PL 110-76 (HR 2952) Authorize the Saginaw Chippewa Tribe of Indians of the state of Michigan to convey land and interests in land owned by the tribe. Introduced by Kildee, D-Mich., on July 10, 2007. House Natural Resources reported, amended, July 30 (H Rept 110-275). House passed, amended, July 30. Senate passed Aug. 2. President signed Aug. 13, 2007.

PL 110-77 (HR 3006) Improve the use of a grant of a parcel of land to the state of Idaho for use as an agricultural college. Introduced by Simpson, R-Idaho, on July 11, 2007. House passed, under suspension of the rules, July 30, 2007. Senate passed Aug. 3. President signed Aug. 13, 2007.

PL 110-78 (S 375) Waive application of the Indian Self-Determination and Education Assistance Act to a specific parcel of real property transferred by the United States to two Indian tribes in the state of Oregon. Introduced by Smith, R-Ore., on Jan. 24, 2007. Senate Indian Affairs reported April 10 (S Rept 110-44). Senate passed May 22. House Natural Resources reported July 30 (H Rept 110-276). House passed July 30. President signed Aug. 13, 2007.

PL 110-79 (S 975) Grant the consent and approval of Congress to an interstate forest fire protection compact. Introduced by Thune, R-S.D., on March 23, 2007. Senate Judiciary discharged. Senate passed July 13. House passed, under suspension of the rules, July 30. President signed Aug. 13, 2007.

PL 110-80 (S 1716) Amend the U.S. Troop Readiness, Veterans' Care, Katrina Recovery and Iraq Accountability Appropriations Act of 2007 to strike a requirement relating to forage producers. Introduced by Thune, R-S.D., on June 27, 2007. Senate Agriculture, Nutrition, and Forestry discharged. Senate passed July 25. House passed, under suspension of the rules, July 30. President signed Aug. 13, 2007.

PL 110-81 (S 1) Provide greater transparency in the legislative process and greater lobbying disclosure. Introduced by Reid, D-Nev., on Jan. 4, 2007. Senate passed, amended, Jan. 18. House passed, amended, under suspension of the rules, July 31. Senate agreed to House amendment Aug. 2. President signed Sept. 14, 2007.

PL 110-82 (HR 2358) Require the secretary of the Treasury to mint and issue coins in commemoration of Native Americans and the important contributions made by tribes and individual Native Americans to the history and development of the United States. Introduced by Kildee, D-Mich., on May 17, 2007. House passed, under suspension of the rules, June 12. Senate Banking, Housing and Urban Affairs discharged. Senate passed, amended, Aug. 3. House agreed to Senate amendment, under suspension of the rules, Sept. 4. President signed Sept. 20, 2007.

PL 110-83 (S 377) Establish a United States-Poland parliamentary youth exchange program. Introduced by Lugar, R-Ind., on Jan. 24, 2007. Senate Foreign Relations reported March 9 (S Rept 110-33). Senate passed March 15. House passed, under suspension of the rules, Sept. 5. President signed Sept. 20, 2007.

PL 110-84 (HR 2669) Reduce the cost and expand the availability of loans and other financial aid for postsecondary students, using the reconciliation process. Introduced by Miller, D-Calif., on June 12, 2007. House Education and Labor reported, amended, June 25 (H Rept 110-210). House passed, amended, July 11. Senate passed, amended, July 20. Conference report filed in the House on Sept. 6 (H Rept 110-317). Senate agreed to the conference report Sept. 7. House agreed to the conference report Sept. 7. President signed Sept. 27, 2007.

PL 110-85 (HR 3580) Amend the Federal Food, Drug and Cosmetic Act to revise and extend the user-fee programs for prescription drugs and medical devices and enhance the postmarket authorities of the Food and Drug Administration with respect to the safety of drugs. Introduced by Dingell, D-Mich., on Sept. 19, 2007. House passed, under suspension of the rules, Sept. 19. Senate passed Sept. 20. President signed Sept. 27, 2007.

PL 110-86 (HR 3528) Provide authority to the Peace Corps to give separation pay for host country resident personal services contractors. Introduced by Lantos, D-Calif., on Sept. 14, 2007. House passed, under suspension of the rules, Sept. 17. Senate passed Sept. 19. President signed Sept. 27, 2007.

PL 110-87 (HR 954) Designate the facility of the U.S. Postal Service located at 365 West 125th St. in New York, N.Y., as the "Percy Sutton Post Office Building." Introduced by Rangel, D-N.Y., on Feb. 8, 2007. House passed, under suspension of the rules, Sept. 5. Senate Homeland Security and Governmental Affairs discharged. Senate passed Sept. 11. President signed Sept. 28, 2007.

PL 110-88 (HR 3218) Designate a portion of Interstate 395 in Baltimore, Md., as "Cal Ripken Way." Introduced by Sarbanes, D-Md., on July 27, 2007. House passed, under suspension of the rules, Sept. 5. Senate passed Sept. 12. President signed Sept. 28, 2007.

PL 110-89 (HR 3375) Extend the trade adjustment assistance program under the Trade Act of 1974 for three months. Introduced by Herger, R-Calif., on Aug. 3, 2007. House Ways and Means reported, amended, Sept. 24 (H Rept 110-345). House passed, amended, under suspension of the rules, Sept. 25. Senate passed Sept. 25. President signed Sept. 28, 2007.

PL 110-90 (HR 3668) Provide for the extension of transitional medical assistance, the abstinence education program, and the qualifying individuals program. Introduced by Dingell, D-Mich., on Sept. 26, 2007. House passed, under suspension of the rules, Sept. 26. Senate passed Sept. 27. President signed Sept. 29, 2007.

PL 110-91 (H J Res 43) Increase the statutory limit on the public debt. Introduced on May 17, 2007. House passed May 17. Senate Finance reported Sept. 24 (S Rept 110-184). Senate passed Sept. 27. President signed Sept. 29, 2007.

PL 110-92 (H J Res 52) Make continuing appropriations for fiscal 2008. Introduced by Obey, D-Wis., on Sept. 25, 2007. House passed, amended, Sept. 26. Senate passed Sept. 27. President signed Sept. 29, 2007.

PL 110-93 (HR 3625) Make permanent the waiver authority of the secretary of education with respect to student financial assistance during a war or other military operation or national emergency. Introduced by Sestak, D-Pa., on Sept. 20, 2007. House passed, under suspension of the rules, Sept. 25. Senate passed Sept. 27. President signed Sept. 30, 2007.

PL 110-94 (S 1983) Amend the Federal Insecticide, Fungicide and Rodenticide Act to renew and amend the provisions for the enhanced review of covered pesticide products, authorize fees for certain pesticide products, and extend and improve the collection of maintenance fees. Introduced by Harkin, D-Iowa, on Aug. 2, 2007. Senate passed Aug. 2. House passed, under suspension of the rules, Sept. 24. President signed Oct. 9, 2007.

PL 110-95 (S 474) Award a congressional gold medal to Michael Ellis DeBakey, M.D. Introduced by Hutchison, R-Texas, on Feb. 1, 2007. Senate Banking, Housing, and Urban Affairs discharged. Senate passed March 27. House passed, under suspension of the rules, Oct. 2. President signed Oct. 16, 2007.

PL 110-96 (S 1612) Amend the penalty provisions in the International Emergency Economic Powers Act. Introduced by Dodd, D-Conn., on June 13, 2007. Senate Banking, Housing, and Urban Affairs reported June 13 (S Rept 110-82). Senate passed, amended, June 26. House Foreign Affairs discharged. House passed, under suspension of the rules, Oct. 2. President signed Oct. 16, 2007.

PL 110-97 (HR 1124) Extend the District of Columbia College Access Act of 1999. Introduced by T. Davis, R-Va., on Feb. 16, 2007. House Oversight and Government Reform reported April

30 (H Rept 110-112). House passed, under suspension of the rules, May 14. Senate passed, amended, Sept. 18. House agreed to Senate amendment, under suspension of the rules, Oct. 9. President signed Oct. 24, 2007.

PL 110-98 (HR 2467) Designate the facility of the U.S. Postal Service located at 69 Montgomery St. in Jersey City, N.J., as the "Frank J. Guarini Post Office Building." Introduced by Stres, D-N.J., on May 23, 2007. House passed, under suspension of the rules, Sept. 10. Senate Homeland Security and Governmental Affairs reported Sept. 26 (no written report). Senate passed Oct. 3. President signed Oct. 24, 2007.

PL 110-99 (HR 2587) Designate the facility of the U.S. Postal Service located at 555 South 3rd St. Lobby in Memphis, Tenn., as the "Kenneth T. Whalum, Sr. Post Office Building." Introduced by Cohen, D-Tenn., on June 6, 2007. House passed, amended, under suspension of the rules, Sept. 10. Senate Homeland Security and Governmental Affairs reported Sept. 26 (no written report). Senate passed Oct. 3. President signed Oct. 24, 2007.

PL 110-100 (HR 2654) Designate the facility of the U.S. Postal Service located at 202 South Dumont Ave. in Woonsocket, S.D., as the "Eleanor McGovern Post Office Building." Introduced by Herseth-Sandlin, D-S.D., on June 11, 2007. House passed, under suspension of the rules, Sept. 10. Senate Homeland Security and Governmental Affairs reported Sept. 26 (no written report). Senate passed Oct. 3. President signed Oct. 24, 2007.

PL 110-101 (HR 2765) Designate the facility of the U.S. Postal Service located at 44 North Main St. in Hughesville, Pa., as the "Master Sergeant Sean Michael Thomas Post Office." Introduced by Carney, D-Pa., on June 18, 2007. House Oversight and Government Reform discharged. House passed July 30. Senate Homeland Security and Governmental Affairs reported Sept. 26 (no written report). Senate passed Oct. 3. President signed Oct. 24, 2007.

PL 110-102 (HR 2778) Designate the facility of the U.S. Postal Service located at 3 Quaker Ridge Rd. in New Rochelle, N.Y., as the "Robert Merrill Postal Station." Introduced by Lowey, D-N.Y., on June 19, 2007. House passed, under suspension of the rules, Sept. 10. Senate Homeland Security and Governmental Affairs reported Sept. 26 (no written report). Senate passed Oct. 3. President signed Oct. 24, 2007.

PL 110-103 (HR 2825) Designate the facility of the U.S. Postal Service located at 326 South Main St. in Princeton, Ill., as the "Owen Lovejoy Princeton Post Office Building." Introduced by Weller, R-Ill., on June 21, 2007. House passed, under suspension of the rules, Sept. 10. Senate Homeland Security and Governmental Affairs reported Sept. 26 (no written report). Senate passed Oct. 3. President signed Oct. 24, 2007.

PL 110-104 (HR 3052) Designate the facility of the U.S. Postal Service located at 954 Wheeling Ave. in Cambridge, Ohio, as the "John Herschel Glenn Jr. Post Office Building." Introduced by Space, D-Ohio, on July 16, 2007. House passed, under suspension of the rules, Sept. 5. Senate Homeland Security and Governmental Affairs reported Sept. 26 (no written report). Senate passed Oct. 3. President signed Oct. 24, 2007.

PL 110-105 (HR 3106) Designate the facility of the U.S. Postal Service located at 805 Main St. in Ferdinand, Ind., as the "Staff Sgt. David L. Nord Post Office." Introduced by Hill, D-Ind., on July 19, 2007. House Oversight and Government Reform reported Aug. 2. House passed, under suspension of the rules, Sept. 5. Senate Homeland Security and Governmental Affairs reported Sept. 26 (no written report). Senate passed Oct. 3. President signed Oct. 24, 2007.

PL 110-106 (HR 995) Amend PL 106-348 to extend the authorization for establishing a memorial in the District of Columbia or its environs to honor veterans who became disabled while serving in the U.S. armed forces. Introduced by Hare, D-Ill., on Feb. 12, 2007. House passed, under suspension of the rules, March 5, 2007. Senate Energy and Natural Resources reported Sept. 17 (S Rept 110-165). Senate passed Oct. 24. President signed Oct. 25, 2007.

PL 110-107 (HR 3233) Designate the facility of the U.S. Postal Service located at Highway 49 South in Piney Woods, Miss., as the "Laurence C. and Grace M. Jones Post Office Building." Introduced by Pickering, R-Miss., on July 31, 2007. House passed, under suspension of the rules, Oct. 1. Senate Homeland Security and Governmental Affairs discharged. Senate passed Oct. 19. President signed Oct. 26, 2007.

PL 110-108 (HR 3678) Amend the Internet Tax Freedom Act to extend the moratorium on certain taxes relating to the Internet and to electronic commerce. Introduced by Conyers, D-Mich., on Sept. 27, 2007. House Judiciary reported, amended, Oct. 12 (H Rept 110-372). House passed, amended, under suspension of the rules, Oct. 16. Senate passed, amended, Oct. 25. House agreed to Senate amendment, under suspension of the rules, Oct. 30. President signed Oct. 31, 2007.

PL 110-109 (S 2258) Temporarily extend the programs under the Higher Education Act of 1965 and amend the definition of an eligible not-for-profit holder. Introduced by Kennedy, D-Mass., on Oct. 30, 2007. Senate passed Oct. 30. House passed, under suspension of the rules, Oct. 30. President signed Oct. 31, 2007.

PL 110-110 (HR 327) Direct the secretary of veterans affairs to develop and implement a comprehensive program to reduce the incidence of suicide among veterans. Introduced by Boswell, D-Iowa, on Jan. 9, 2007. House Veterans' Affairs reported, amended, March 20 (H Rept 110-55). House passed, amended, under suspension of the rules, March 21. Senate Veterans' Affairs Committee discharged. Senate passed, amended, Sept. 27. House concurred in Senate amendment, under suspension of the rules, Oct. 23. President signed Nov. 5, 2007.

PL 110-111 (HR 1284) Increase, as of Dec. 1, 2007, the rates of compensation for veterans with service-connected disabilities and the rates of dependency and indemnity compensation for the survivors of certain disabled veterans. Introduced by Hall, D-N.Y., on March 1, 2007. House Veterans' Affairs reported March 20 (H Rept 110-56). House passed, under suspension of the rules, March 21. Senate Veterans' Affairs discharged. Senate passed Oct. 18. President signed Nov. 5, 2007.

PL 110-112 (HR 1808) Designate the Department of Veterans Affairs medical center in Augusta, Ga., as the "Charlie Norwood Department of Veterans Affairs Medical Center." Introduced by Kingston, R-Ga., on March 29, 2007. House passed, under suspension of the rules, Oct. 23. Senate Veterans' Affairs discharged. Senate passed Oct. 31. President signed Nov. 8, 2007.

PL 110-113 (S 2106) Provide nationwide subpoena authority for actions brought under the September 11 Victim Compensation Fund of 2001. Introduced by Biden, D-Del., on Sept. 27, 2007. Senate Judiciary discharged. Senate passed Oct. 3. House passed, under suspension of the rules, Oct. 30. President signed Nov. 8, 2007.

PL 110-114 (HR 1495) Provide for the conservation and development of water and related resources and authorize the secretary of the army to construct various projects for improvements to rivers and harbors of the United States. Introduced by Oberstar, D-Minn., on March 13, 2007. House Transportation and Infrastructure reported, amended, March 29 (H Rept 110-80). House passed, amended, April 19. Senate passed, amended, May 16. Conference report filed in the House on July 31 (Rept 110-280). House agreed to the conference report Aug. 1 Senate agreed to the conference report Sept. 24. President vetoed Nov. 2. House passed over presidential veto Nov. 6. Senate passed over presidential veto Nov. 8. Became law Nov. 9, 2007.

PL 110-115 (HR 2779) Recognize the Navy UDT-SEAL Museum in Fort Pierce, Fla., as the official national museum of Navy SEALS and their predecessors. Introduced by Mahoney, D-Fla., on June 19, 2007. House passed, under suspension of the rules, Oct. 1. Senate Armed Services discharged. Senate passed Oct. 31. President signed Nov. 13, 2007.

PL 110-116 (HR 3222) Make appropriations for the Department of Defense for fiscal 2008. Introduced by Murtha, D-Pa., on July 30, 2007. Appropriations reported July 30, 2007 (H Rept 110-279). House passed, amended, Aug. 5. Senate Appropriations reported, amended, Sept. 14 (S Rept 110-155). Senate passed, amended, Oct. 3. Conference report filed in the House on Nov. 6 (H Rept 110-434). House agreed to conference report Nov. 8. Senate agreed to conference report Nov. 8. President signed Nov. 13, 2007.

PL 110-117 (HR 2546) Designate the Department of Veterans Affairs medical center in Asheville, N.C., as the "Charles George Department of Veterans Affairs Medical Center." Introduced by Shuler, D-N.C., on May 24, 2007. House passed, under suspension of the rules, June 25. Senate Veterans' Affairs discharged. Senate passed Nov. 1. President signed Nov. 15, 2007.

PL 110-118 (HR 2602) Designate the Department of Veterans Affairs medical facility in Iron Mountain, Mich., as the "Oscar G. Johnson Department of Veterans Affairs Medical Facility." Introduced by Stupak, D-Mich., on June 6, 2007. House passed, under suspension of the rules, June 25. Senate Veterans' Affairs discharged. Senate passed Nov. 7. President signed Nov. 16, 2007.

PL 110-119 (S J RES 7) Provide for the reappointment of Roger W. Sant as a citizen regent of the Board of Regents of the Smithsonian Institution. Introduced by Leahy, D-Vt., on March 8, 2007. Senate Committee on Rules and Administration discharged. Senate passed June 31. House passed, under suspension of the rules, Nov. 5. President signed Nov. 16, 2007.

PL 110-120 (S 2206) Provide technical corrections to extend the time period for the Joint Committee on the Library to enter into an agreement to obtain a statue of Rosa Parks. Introduced by Feinstein, D-Calif., on Oct. 18, 2007. Senate passed Oct. 18. House passed, under suspension of the rules, Nov. 5. President signed Nov. 19, 2007.

PL 110-121 (HR 2089) Designate the facility of the U.S. Postal Service located at 701 Loyola Ave. in New Orleans, La., as the "Louisiana Armed Services Veterans Post Office." Introduced by Jefferson, D-La., on May 1, 2007. House passed, under suspension of the rules, Oct. 15. Senate Homeland Security and Governmental Affairs reported Nov. 14 (no written report). Senate passed Nov. 16. President signed Nov. 30, 2007.

PL 110-122 (HR 2276) Designate the facility of the U.S. Postal Service located at 203 North Main St. in Vassar, Mich., as the "Cpl. Christopher E. Esckelson Post Office Building." Introduced by Kildee, D-Mich., on May 10, 2007. House passed, under suspension of the rules, Oct. 1. Senate Homeland Security and Governmental Affairs reported Nov. 14 (no written report). Senate passed Nov. 16. President signed Nov. 30, 2007.

PL 110-123 (HR 3297) Designate the facility of the U.S. Postal Service located at 950 West Trenton Ave. in Morrisville, Pa., as the "Nate DeTample Post Office Building." Introduced by Murphy, D-Pa., on Aug. 1, 2007. House passed, under suspension of the rules, Oct. 15. Senate Homeland Security and Governmental Affairs reported Nov. 14 (no written report). Senate passed Nov. 16. President signed Nov. 30, 2007.

PL 110-124 (HR 3307) Designate the facility of the U.S. Postal Service located at 570 Broadway in Bayonne, N.J., as the "Dennis P. Collins Post Office Building." Introduced by Sires, D-N.J., on Aug. 1, 2007. House passed, under suspension of the rules, Oct. 30. Senate Homeland Security and Governmental Affairs reported Nov. 14 (no written report). Senate passed Nov. 16. President signed Nov. 30, 2007.

PL 110-125 (HR 3308) Designate the facility of the U.S. Postal Service located at 216 East Main St. in Atwood, Ind., as the "Lance Cpl. David K. Fribley Post Office." Introduced by Souder, R-Ind., on Aug. 1, 2007. House passed, under suspension of the rules, Oct. 9. Senate Homeland Security and Governmental Affairs reported Nov. 14 (no written report). Senate passed Nov. 16. President signed Nov. 30, 2007.

PL 110-126 (HR 3325) Designate the facility of the U.S. Postal Service located at 235 Mountain Rd. in Suffield, Conn., as the "Cpl. Stephen R. Bixler Post Office." Introduced by Courtney, D-Conn., on Aug. 2, 2007. House passed, under suspension of the rules, Oct. 1. Senate Homeland Security and Governmental Affairs reported Nov. 14 (no written report). Senate passed Nov. 16. President signed Nov. 30, 2007.

PL 110-127 (HR 3382) Designate the facility of the U.S. Postal Service located at 200 North William St. in Goldsboro, N.C., as the "Philip A. Baddour Sr. Post Office." Introduced by Butterfield, D-N.C., on Aug. 3, 2007. House passed, under suspension of the rules, Oct. 1. Senate Homeland Security and Governmental Affairs reported Nov. 14 (no written report). Senate passed Nov. 16. President signed Nov. 30, 2007.

PL 110-128 (HR 3446) Designate the facility of the U.S. Postal Service located at 202 East Michigan Ave. in Marshall, Mich., as the "Michael W. Schragg Post Office Building." Introduced by

Walberg, R-Mich., on Aug. 3, 2007. House passed, under suspension of the rules, Oct. 30. Senate Homeland Security and Governmental Affairs reported Nov. 14 (no written report). Senate passed Nov. 16. President signed Nov. 30, 2007.

PL 110-129 (HR 3518) Designate the facility of the U.S. Postal Service located at 1430 South Highway 29 in Cantonment, Fla., as the "Charles H. Hendrix Post Office Building." Introduced by Miller, R-Fla., on Sept. 10, 2007. House passed, amended, under suspension of the rules, Oct. 9. Senate Homeland Security and Governmental Affairs reported Nov. 14 (no written report). Senate passed Nov. 16. President signed Nov. 30, 2007.

PL 110-130 (HR 3530) Designate the facility of the U.S. Postal Service located at 1400 Highway 41 North in Inverness, Fla., as the "Chief Warrant Officer Aaron Weaver Post Office Building." Introduced by Brown-Waite, R-Fla., on Sept. 14, 2007. House passed, under suspension of the rules, Oct. 9. Senate Homeland Security and Governmental Affairs reported Nov. 14 (no written report). Senate passed Nov. 16. President signed Nov. 30, 2007.

PL 110-131 (HR 3572) Designate the facility of the U.S. Postal Service located at 4320 Blue Parkway in Kansas City, Mo., as the "Wallace S. Hartsfield Post Office Building." Introduced by Cleaver, D-Mo., on Sept. 18, 2007. House passed, under suspension of the rules, Oct. 15. Senate Homeland Security and Governmental Affairs reported Nov. 14 (no written report). Senate passed Nov. 16. President signed Nov. 30, 2007.

PL 110-132 (HR 50) Reauthorize the African Elephant Conservation Act and the Rhinoceros and Tiger Conservation Act of 1994. Introduced by Young, R-Alaska, on Jan. 4, 2007. House Natural Resources reported, amended, July 23 (H Rept 110-244). House passed, amended, under suspension of the rules, July 23. Senate Environment and Public Works reported Oct. 29 (S Rept 110-211). Senate passed Nov. 16. President signed Dec. 6, 2007.

PL 110-133 (HR 465) Reauthorize the Asian Elephant Conservation Act of 1997. Introduced by Saxton, R-N.J., on Jan. 12, 2007. House Natural Resources reported, amended, July 23 (H Rept 110-245). House passed, amended, under suspension of the rules, July 23. Senate Environment and Public Works reported Aug. 2 (S Rept 110-212). Senate passed Nov. 16. President signed Dec. 6, 2007.

PL 110-134 (HR 1429) Reauthorize the Head Start Act, to improve program quality and expand access. Introduced by Kildee, D-Mich., on March 9, 2007. House Education and Labor reported, amended, March 23 (H Rept 110-67). House passed, amended, May 2. Senate passed, amended, June 19. Conference report filed in the House on Nov. 9 (H Rept 110-439). House agreed to the conference report Nov. 14. Senate agreed to the conference report Nov. 14. President signed Dec. 12, 2007.

PL 110-135 (HR 4343) Amend Title 49, U.S. Code, to modify age standards for pilots engaged in commercial aviation operations. Introduced by Oberstar, D-Minn., on Dec. 11, 2007. House passed, under suspension of the rules, Dec. 11. Senate passed Dec. 12. President signed Dec. 13, 2007.

PL 110-136 (HR 4252) Provide for an additional temporary extension, through May 23, 2008, of programs under the Small Business Act and the Small Business Investment Act of 1958. Introduced by Chabot, R-Ohio, on Dec. 4, 2007. House passed, under suspension of the rules, Dec. 5. Senate passed Dec. 7. President signed Dec. 14, 2007.

PL 110-137 (H J Res 69) Make further continuing appropriations for fiscal year 2008. Introduced by Obey, D-Wis., on Dec. 12, 2007. House passed Dec. 13. Senate passed Dec. 13. President signed Dec. 14, 2007.

PL 110-138 (HR 3688) Implement the U.S.-Peru Trade Promotion Agreement. Introduced by Hoyer, D-Md., on Sept. 27, 2007. House Ways and Means reported Nov. 5 (H Rept 110-421). House passed Nov. 8. Senate passed Dec. 4. President signed Dec. 14, 2007.

PL 110-139 (HR 3315) Provide that the great hall of the Capitol Visitor Center shall be known as Emancipation Hall. Introduced by Wamp, R-Tenn., on Aug. 2, 2007. House Transportation and Infrastructure reported Nov. 8 (H Rept 110-436). House passed, under suspension of the rules, Nov. 13. Senate passed Dec. 6. President signed Dec. 18, 2007.

PL 110-140 (HR 6) Move the United States toward greater energy independence and security; increase the production of clean renewable fuels; protect consumers; increase the efficiency of products, buildings, and vehicles; promote research on and deploy greenhouse gas capture and storage options; and improve the energy performance of the federal government. Introduced by Rahall, D-W. Va., on Jan. 12, 2007. House passed Jan. 18. Senate passed, amended, June 21. House agreed to Senate amendments with amendments Dec. 6. Senate agreed to House amendments to Senate amendments with amendment Dec. 13. House agreed to Senate amendment to House amendments to Senate amendments Dec. 18. President signed Dec. 19, 2007.

PL 110-141 (HR 4118) Exclude from gross income payments from the Hokie Spirit Memorial Fund to the victims of the tragic event at Virginia Polytechnic Institute & State University. Introduced by Boucher, D-Va., on Nov. 8, 2007. House passed, amended, under suspension of the rules Dec. 4. Senate passed Dec. 6. President signed Dec. 19, 2007.

PL 110-142 (HR 3648) Amend the Internal Revenue Code of 1986 to exclude discharges of indebtedness on principal residences from gross income. Introduced by Rangel, D-N.Y., on Sept. 25, 2007. House Ways and Means reported, amended, Oct. 1 (H Rept 110-356). House passed, amended, Oct. 4. Senate Finance discharged. Senate passed, amended, Dec. 14. House agreed to Senate amendment, under suspension of the rules, Dec. 18. President signed Dec. 20, 2007.

PL 110-143 (HR 365) Provide for a research program for cleanup and remediation of closed methamphetamine production laboratories. Introduced by Gordon, D-Tenn., on Jan. 10, 2007. House Science and Technology reported Feb. 7 (H Rept 110-8). House passed, under suspension of the rules, Feb. 7. Senate Environment and Public Works discharged. Senate passed Dec. 11. President signed Dec. 21, 2007.

PL 110-144 (HR 710) Amend the National Organ Transplant Act to provide that criminal penalties do not apply to human organ paired donation. Introduced by Norwood, R-Ga., on Jan. 29, 2007. House passed, amended, under suspension of the rules, March 7. Senate passed, amended, July 9. House agreed to Senate amendment with amendments Dec. 4. Senate agreed to House amendments to Senate amendment Dec. 6. President signed Dec. 21, 2007.

PL 110-145 (HR 2408) Designate the Department of Veterans Affairs outpatient clinic in Green Bay, Wis., as the "Milo C. Huempfner Department of Veterans Affairs Outpatient Clinic." Introduced by Kagen, D-Wis., on May 21, 2007. House passed, under suspension of the rules, Oct. 23. Senate Veterans' Affairs discharged. Senate passed Dec. 13. President signed Dec. 21, 2007.

PL 110-146 (HR 2671) Designate the U.S. courthouse located at 301 North Miami Ave. in Miami, Fla., as the "C. Clyde Atkins United States Courthouse." Introduced by Ros-Lehtinen, R-Fla., on June 12, 2007. House Transportation and Infrastructure reported Sept. 14 (H Rept 110-326). House passed, under suspension of the rules, Oct. 29. Senate Environment and Public Works discharged. Senate passed Dec. 13. President signed Dec. 21, 2007.

PL 110-147 (HR 3703) Amend section 5112(p)(1)(A) of Title 31, U.S. Code, to allow an exception from the $1 coin dispensing capability requirement for certain vending machines. Introduced by Scott, D-Ga., on Sept. 27, 2007. House passed, under suspension of the rules, Nov. 13. Senate passed Dec. 17, 2007. President signed Dec. 21, 2007.

PL 110-148 (HR 3739) Amend the Arizona Water Settlements Act to modify the requirements for the statement of findings. Introduced by Grijalva, D-Ariz., on Oct. 3, 2007. House Natural Resources reported Dec. 11 (H Rept 110-484). House passed, under suspension of the rules, Dec. 11. Senate Indian Affairs discharged. Senate passed Dec. 14. President signed Dec. 21, 2007.

PL 110-149 (H J Res 72) Make further continuing appropriations for fiscal year 2008. Introduced by Obey, D-Wis., on Dec. 18, 2007. House passed Dec. 19. Senate passed Dec. 19. President signed Dec. 21, 2007.

PL 110-150 (S 597) Amend Title 39, U.S. Code, to extend the authority of the U.S. Postal Service to issue a fundraising, or "semi-postal," stamp to raise funds for breast cancer research. Introduced by Feinstein, D-Calif., on Feb. 14, 2007. Senate Homeland Security and Governmental Affairs reported Nov. 7 (S Rept 110-222). Senate passed, amended, Nov. 14. House passed, amended, under suspension of the rules, Dec. 11. Senate agreed to House amendments Dec. 13. President signed Dec. 21, 2007.

PL 110-151 (S 888) Amend section 1091 of Title 18, U.S. Code, to allow the prosecution of genocide in appropriate circumstances. Introduced by Durbin, D-Ill., on March 15, 2007. Senate Judiciary reported March 26 (no written report). Senate passed March 29. House passed, under suspension of the rules, Dec. 5. President signed Dec. 21, 2007.

PL 110-152 (S 2174) Designate the facility of the U.S. Postal Service located at 175 South Monroe St. in Tiffin, Ohio, as the "Paul E. Gillmor Post Office Building." Introduced by Voinovich, R-Ohio, on Oct. 17, 2007. Senate Homeland Security and Governmental Affairs reported Nov. 14 (no written report). Senate passed Nov. 16. House passed, under suspension of the rules, Dec. 17. President signed Dec. 21, 2007.

PL 110-153 (S 2371) Amend the Higher Education Act of 1965 to make technical corrections. Introduced by Kennedy, D-Mass., on Nov. 15, 2007. Senate passed Nov. 15. House passed, amended, under suspension of the rules, Dec. 5. Senate agreed to House amendment Dec. 6. President signed Dec. 21, 2007.

PL 110-154 (S 2484) Rename the National Institute of Child Health and Human Development as the Eunice Kennedy Shriver National Institute of Child Health and Human Development. Introduced by Hatch, R-Utah, on Dec. 13, 2007. Senate passed Dec. 13. House passed, under suspension of the rules, Dec. 17. President signed Dec. 21, 2007.

PL 110-155 (S J Res 8) Provide for the reappointment of Patricia Q. Stonesifer as a citizen regent of the Board of Regents of the Smithsonian Institution. Introduced by Leahy, D-Vt., on March 8, 2007. Senate Rules and Administration discharged. Senate passed July 31. House passed, under suspension of the rules, Dec. 5. President signed Dec. 21, 2007.

PL 110-156 (HR 366) Designate the Department of Veterans Affairs outpatient clinic in Tulsa, Okla., as the "Ernest Childers Department of Veterans Affairs Outpatient Clinic." Introduced by Sullivan, R-Okla., on Jan. 10, 2007. House passed, under suspension of the rules, June 25. Senate Veterans' Affairs discharged. Senate passed Dec. 19. President signed Dec. 26, 2007.

PL 110-157 (HR 797) Amend Title 38, U.S. Code, to improve compensation benefits for veterans in certain cases of impairment of vision involving both eyes. Introduced by Baldwin, D-Wis., on Feb. 5, 2007. House Veterans' Affairs reported, amended, March 20 (H Rept 110-57). House passed, amended, under suspension of the rules, March 21. Senate Veterans' Affairs discharged. Senate passed, with amendment, Nov. 2. House agreed to Senate amendment, with amendments pursuant to H Res 855 on Dec. 11. Senate agreed to House amendments to Senate amendment Dec. 17. President signed Dec. 26, 2007.

PL 110-158 (HR 1045) Designate the federal building located at 210 Walnut St. in Des Moines, Iowa, as the "Neal Smith Federal Building." Introduced by Boswell, D-Iowa, on Feb. 14, 2007. House Transportation and Infrastructure reported March 12 (H Rept 110-46). House passed, under suspension of the rules, March 13. Senate Environment and Public Works discharged. Senate passed Dec. 19. President signed Dec. 26, 2007.

PL 110-159 (HR 2011) Designate the federal building and U.S. courthouse located at 100 East 8th Ave. in Pine Bluff, Ark., as the "George Howard Jr. Federal Building and United States Courthouse." Introduced by Ross, D-Ark., on April 24, 2007. House Transportation and Infrastructure reported June 25 (H Rept 110-209). House passed, under suspension of the rules, June 25. Senate Homeland Security and Governmental Affairs discharged July 30. Senate Environment and Public Works discharged. Senate passed Dec. 19. President signed Dec. 26, 2007.

PL 110-160 (HR 2761) Extend the Terrorism Insurance Program of the Department of the Treasury. Introduced by Capuano, D-Mass., on June 18, 2007. House Financial Services reported, amended, Sept. 6 (H Rept 110-318). House passed, amended, Sept. 19. Senate Banking, Housing, and Urban Affairs discharged. Senate passed, with amendment, Nov. 16. House agreed to Senate amendment, under suspension of the rules, Dec. 18. President signed Dec. 26, 2007.

PL 110-161 (HR 2764) Make appropriations for the Department of State, foreign operations, and related programs for fiscal year 2008. Introduced by Lowey, D-N.Y., on June 18, 2007. House Appropriations reported June 18 (H Rept 110-197). House passed, amended, June 22. Senate Appropriations reported, amended, July 10 (S Rept 110-128). Senate passed, with amendment, Sept. 6. House agreed to Senate amendment, with first House amendment, Dec. 17. House agreed to Senate amendment, with second House amendment, Dec. 17. Senate agreed to second House amendment to Senate amendment, with amendment, Dec. 18. Senate agreed to first House amendment to Senate amendment Dec. 18. House agreed to Senate amendment to second House amendment to Senate amendment Dec. 19. President signed Dec. 26, 2007.

PL 110-162 (HR 3470) Designate the facility of the U.S. Postal Service located at 744 West Oglethorpe Highway in Hinesville, Ga., as the "John Sidney 'Sid' Flowers Post Office Building." Introduced by Kingston, R-Ga., on Sept. 4, 2007. House passed, under suspension of the rules, Nov. 13. Senate Homeland Security and Governmental Affairs discharged. Senate passed Dec. 19. President signed Dec. 26, 2007.

PL 110-163 (HR 3569) Designate the facility of the U.S. Postal Service located at 16731 Santa Ana Ave. in Fontana, Calif., as the "Beatrice E. Watson Post Office Building." Introduced by Baca, D-Calif., on Sept. 18, 2007. House passed, under suspension of the rules, Nov. 13. Senate Homeland Security and Governmental Affairs discharged. Senate passed Dec. 19. President signed Dec. 26, 2007.

PL 110-164 (HR 3571) Amend the Congressional Accountability Act of 1995 to permit individuals who have served as employees of the Office of Compliance to serve as executive director, deputy executive director, or general counsel of the office, and permit individuals appointed to such positions to serve one additional term. Introduced by Brady, D-Pa., on Sept. 18, 2007. House passed, under suspension of the rules, Oct. 2. Senate Homeland Security and Governmental Affairs reported Dec. 18 (no written report). Senate passed Dec. 19. President signed Dec. 26, 2007.

PL 110-165 (HR 3974) Designate the facility of the U.S. Postal Service located at 797 Sam Bass Rd. in Round Rock, Texas, as the "Marine Corps Cpl. Steven P. Gill Post Office Building." Introduced by Carter, R-Texas, on Oct. 25, 2007. House passed, under suspension of the rules, Nov. 13. Senate Homeland Security and Governmental Affairs discharged. Senate passed Dec. 19. President signed Dec. 26, 2007.

PL 110-166 (HR 3996) Amend the Internal Revenue Code of 1986 to extend certain expiring provisions. Introduced by Rangel, D-N.Y., on Oct. 30, 2007. House Ways and Means reported, amended, Nov. 6 (H Rept 110-431). House passed, amended, Nov. 9. Senate passed, amended, Dec. 6. House agreed to Senate amendment, under suspension of the rules, Dec. 19. President signed Dec. 26, 2007.

PL 110-167 (HR 4009) Designate the facility of the U.S. Postal Service located at 567 West Nepessing St. in Lapeer, Mich., as the "Turrill Post Office Building." Introduced by Miller, R-Mich., on Oct. 30, 2007. House passed, under suspension of the rules, Dec. 11. Senate Homeland Security and Governmental Affairs discharged. Senate passed Dec. 19. President signed Dec. 26, 2007.

PL 110-168 (S 1396) Authorize a major medical facility project to modernize inpatient wards at the Department of Veterans Affairs medical center in Atlanta, Ga. Introduced by Isakson, R-Ga., on May 15, 2007. Senate Veterans' Affairs discharged. Senate passed Dec. 13. House passed, under suspension of the rules, Dec. 19. President signed Dec. 26, 2007.

PL 110-169 (S 1896) Designate the facility of the U.S. Postal Service located at 11 Central St. in Hillsborough, N.H., as the "Officer Jeremy Todd Charron Post Office." Introduced by Sununu, R-N.H., on July 30, 2007. Senate Homeland Security and Governmental Affairs reported Aug. 1 (no written report). Senate passed Aug. 3. House passed, under suspension of the rules, Dec. 19. President signed Dec. 26, 2007.

PL 110-170 (S 1916) Amend the Public Health Service Act to modify the program for the sanctuary system for surplus chimpanzees by terminating the authority for the removal of chimpanzees from the system for research purposes. Introduced by Burr, R-N.C., on Aug. 1, 2007. Senate Health, Education, Labor, and Pensions reported, amended, Dec. 12 (no written report). Senate passed, amended, Dec. 13. House Energy and Commerce discharged. House passed Dec. 19. President signed Dec. 26, 2007.

PL 110-171 (S J Res 13) Grant the consent of Congress to the International Emergency Management Assistance Memorandum of Understanding entered into by the states of Maine, New Hampshire, Vermont, Massachusetts, Rhode Island and Connecticut, as well as several Canadian provinces. Introduced by Leahy, D-Vt., on May 21, 2007. Senate Judiciary reported Sept. 27 (no written report). Senate passed Oct. 2. House passed, under suspension of the rules, Dec. 17. President signed Dec. 26, 2007.

PL 110-172 (HR 4839) Amend the Internal Revenue Code of 1986 to make technical corrections. Introduced by Rangel, D-N.Y., on Dec. 19, 2007. House Ways and Means discharged. House passed Dec. 19. Senate passed Dec. 19. President signed Dec. 29, 2007.

PL 110-173 (S 2499) Amend Titles XVIII, XIX and XXI of the Social Security Act to extend provisions under Medicare, Medicaid, and the State Children's Health Insurance Program. Introduced by Baucus, D-Mont., on Dec. 18, 2007. Senate passed Dec. 18. House passed, under suspension of the rules, Dec. 19. President signed Dec. 29, 2007.

PL 110-174 (S 2271) Authorize state and local governments to divest assets in companies that conduct business operations in Sudan and prohibit U.S. government contracts with such companies. Introduced by Dodd, D-Conn., on Oct. 31, 2007. Senate Banking, Housing, and Urban Affairs reported Oct. 31 (S Rept 110-213). Senate passed, amended, Dec. 12. House passed, under suspension of the rules, Dec. 18. President signed Dec. 31, 2007.

PL 110-175 (S 2488) Promote accessibility, accountability, and openness in government by strengthening Section 552 of Title 5, U.S. Code (commonly referred to as the Freedom of Information Act). Introduced by Leahy, D-Vt., on Dec. 14, 2007. Senate passed Dec. 14. House passed, under suspension of the rules, Dec. 18. President signed Dec. 31, 2007.

110th Congress—2008

PL 110-176 (S 2436) Amend the Internal Revenue Code of 1986 to clarify the term of the commissioner of internal revenue. Introduced by Baucus, D-Mont., on Dec. 10, 2007. Senate passed Dec. 19. House passed Dec. 19. President signed Jan. 4, 2008.

PL 110-177 (HR 660) Amend Title 18, U.S. Code, to protect judges, prosecutors, witnesses, victims, and their family members. Introduced by Conyers, D-Mich., on Jan. 24, 2007. House Judiciary reported, amended, July 10 (H Rept 110-218, Part 1). House passed, amended, under suspension of the rules, July 10. Senate Judiciary discharged. Senate passed, amended, Dec. 17. House agreed to Senate amendment, under suspension of the rules, Dec. 19. President signed Jan. 7, 2008.

PL 110-178 (HR 3690) Provide for the transfer of the Library of Congress police to the U.S. Capitol Police. Introduced by Brady, D-Pa., on Sept. 27, 2007. House Administration reported, amended, Dec. 4 (H Rept 110-470, Part 1). House passed, amended, under suspension of the rules, Dec. 5. Senate passed, amended, Dec. 17. House agreed to Senate amendment, under suspension of the rules, Dec. 18. President signed Jan. 7, 2008.

PL 110-179 (S 863) Amend Title 18, U.S. Code, with respect to fraud in connection with major disaster or emergency funds. Introduced by Sessions, R-Ala., on March 13, 2007. Senate Judiciary reported May 22 (S Rept 110-69). Senate passed Dec. 4. House passed, under suspension of the rules, Dec. 19. President signed Jan. 7, 2008.

PL 110-180 (HR 2640) Improve the National Instant Criminal Background Check System. Introduced by McCarthy, D-N.Y., on June 11, 2007. House passed, under suspension of the rules, June 13. Senate Judiciary discharged. Senate passed, amended, Dec. 19. House agreed to Senate amendment Dec. 19. President signed Jan. 8, 2008.

PL 110-181 (HR 4986) Provide for the enactment of the National Defense Authorization Act for fiscal 2008, as previously enrolled, with certain modifications to address the foreign sovereign immunities provisions of Title 28, U.S. Code, with respect to the attachment of property in certain judgments against Iraq, the lapse of statutory authorities for the payment of bonuses, and special pay and similar benefits for members of the uniformed services. Introduced by Skelton, D-Mo., on Jan. 16, 2008. House passed, under suspension of the rules, Jan. 16. Senate passed Jan. 22. President signed Jan. 28, 2008.

PL 110-182 (HR 5104) Extend the Protect America Act of 2007 for 15 days. Introduced by Conyers, D-Mich., on Jan. 23, 2008. House passed, amended, under suspension of the rules, Jan. 29. Senate passed Jan. 29. President signed Jan. 31, 2008.

PL 110-183 (HR 3432) Establish the Commission on the Abolition of the Transatlantic Slave Trade. Introduced by Payne, D-N.J. on Aug. 3, 2007. House passed, amended, under suspension of the rules, Oct. 2. Senate Judiciary discharged. Senate passed, amended, Dec. 19. House agreed to Senate amendment, under suspension of the rules, Jan. 22, 2008. President signed Feb. 5, 2008.

PL 110-184 (S 2110) Designate the facility of the U.S. Postal Service located at 427 North St. in Taft, Calif., as the "Larry S. Pierce Post Office." Introduced by Feinstein, D-Calif., on Sept. 27, 2007. Senate Homeland Security and Governmental Affairs reported Nov. 14 (no written report). Senate passed Nov. 16. House passed, under suspension of the rules, Jan. 28, 2008. President signed Feb. 6, 2008.

PL 110-185 (HR 5140) Provide economic stimulus through tax rebates to individuals, incentives for business investment, and an increase in conforming and Federal Housing Administration loan limits. Introduced by Pelosi, D-Calif., on Jan. 28, 2008. House passed, under suspension of the rules, Jan. 29. Senate passed, amended, Feb. 7. House agreed to Senate amendment Feb. 7. President signed Feb. 13, 2008.

PL 110-186 (HR 4253) Improve and expand small-business assistance programs for veterans of the armed forces and military reservists. Introduced by Altmire, D-Pa., on Dec. 4, 2007. House passed, under suspension of the rules, Dec. 6. Senate passed, amended, Dec. 19. House agreed to Senate amendment, with amendment, Jan. 16, 2008. Senate agreed to House amendment to Senate amendment Jan. 31. President signed Feb. 14, 2008.

PL 110-187 (HR 3541) Amend the Do-Not-Call Implementation Act to eliminate the automatic removal of telephone numbers registered on the federal Do Not Call Registry. Introduced by Doyle, D-Pa., on Sept. 17, 2007. House Energy and Commerce reported, amended, Dec. 11 (H Rept 110-486). House passed, amended, under suspension of the rules, Dec. 11. Senate Commerce, Science and Transportation discharged. Senate passed Feb. 6, 2008. President signed Feb. 15, 2008.

PL 110-188 (S 781) Extend the authority of the Federal Trade Commission to collect Do Not Call Registry fees beyond fiscal 2007. Introduced by Pryor, D-Ark., on March 6, 2007. Senate Commerce, Science and Transportation reported, amended, Dec. 12 (S Rept 110-244). Senate passed, amended, Dec. 17. House passed, under suspension of the rules, Feb. 6, 2008. President signed Feb. 15, 2008.

PL 110-189 (HR 1216) Direct the secretary of transportation to issue regulations to reduce the incidence of child injury and death inside or outside light motor vehicles. Introduced by Schakowsky, D-Ill., on Feb. 27, 2007. House passed, amended, under suspension of the rules, Dec. 19. Senate Commerce, Science and Transportation discharged. Senate passed Feb. 14, 2008. President signed Feb. 28, 2008.

PL 110-190 (HR 5270) Amend the Internal Revenue Code of 1986 to extend the funding and expenditure authority of the Airport and Airway Trust Fund. Introduced by Rangel, D-N.Y., on Feb. 7, 2008. House passed, under suspension of the rules, Feb. 12. Senate passed Feb. 13. President signed Feb. 28, 2008.

PL 110-191 (HR 5264) Extend the Andean Trade Preference Act. Introduced by Rangel, D-N.Y., on Feb. 7, 2008. House Ways and Means reported, amended, Feb. 25 (H Rept 110-529). House passed, amended, under suspension of the rules, Feb. 27. Senate passed Feb. 28. President signed Feb. 29, 2008.

PL 110-192 (HR 5478) Provide for the continued minting and issuance of certain $1 coins in 2008. Introduced by Gutierrez, D-Ill., on Feb. 25, 2008. House passed, under suspension of the rules, Feb. 25. Senate Banking, Housing and Urban Affairs discharged. Senate passed Feb. 28. President signed Feb. 29, 2008.

PL 110-193 (S 2571) Make technical corrections to the Federal Insecticide, Fungicide and Rodenticide Act. Introduced by Harkin, D-Iowa, on Jan. 29, 2008. Senate passed Jan. 29. House passed, under suspension of the rules, Feb. 14. President signed March 6, 2008.

PL 110-194 (S 2478) Designate the facility of the U.S. Postal Service located at 59 Colby Corner in E. Hampstead, N.H., the "Capt. Jonathan D. Grassbaugh Post Office." Introduced by Sununu, R-N.H., on Dec. 13, 2007. Senate Homeland Security and Governmental Affairs discharged. Senate passed Dec. 19. House passed, under suspension of the rules, Feb. 28, 2008. President signed March 11, 2008.

PL 110-195 (S 2272) Designate the facility of the U.S. Postal Service known as the Southpark Station in Alexandria, La., the "John 'Marty' Thiels Southpark Station," in honor and memory of Thiels, a Louisiana postal worker who was killed in the line of duty on Oct. 4, 2007. Introduced by Vitter, R-La., on Oct. 31, 2007. Senate Homeland Security and Governmental Affairs reported Nov. 15 (no written report). Senate passed Nov. 16. House passed, under suspension of the rules, Feb. 28, 2008. President signed March 12, 2008.

PL 110-196 (S 2745) Extend agricultural programs until April 18, 2008, and suspend permanent price support authorities until that date. Introduced by Harkin, D-Iowa, on March 12, 2008. Senate passed March 12. House passed, under suspension of the rules, March 12. President signed March 14, 2008.

PL 110-197 (S J Res 25) Provide for the appointment of John W. McCarter as a citizen regent of the Board of Regents of the Smithsonian Institution. Introduced by Leahy, D-Vt., on Nov. 16, 2007. Senate Rules and Administration discharged. Senate passed Feb. 4, 2008. House passed, under suspension of the rules, March 5. President signed March 14, 2008.

PL 110-198 (S 2733) Temporarily extend the programs under the Higher Education Act of 1965. Introduced by Kennedy, D-Mass., on March 7, 2008. Senate passed March 7. House passed, under suspension of the rules, March 12. President signed March 24, 2008.

PL 110-199 (HR 1593) Reauthorize the grant program for reentry of offenders into the community under the Omnibus Crime Control and Safe Streets Act of 1968 and improve reentry planning and implementation. Introduced by Davis, D-Ill., on March 20, 2007. House Judiciary reported May 9 (H Rept 110-140). House passed, amended, under suspension of the rules, Nov. 13. Senate Judiciary discharged. Senate passed March 11, 2008. President signed April 9, 2008.

PL 110-200 (HR 5813) Amend PL 110-196 to temporarily extend programs authorized by the Farm Security and Rural Investment Act of 2002 until April 25, 2008. Introduced by Peterson, D-Minn., on April 16, 2008. House passed, under suspension of the rules, April 16. Senate passed April 17. President signed April 18, 2008.

PL 110-201 (S 550) Preserve existing judgeships on the Superior Court of the District of Columbia. Introduced by Akaka, D-Hawaii, on Feb. 12, 2007. Senate Homeland Security and Governmental Affairs reported Jan. 8, 2008 (S Rept 110-256). Senate passed Feb. 4. House passed, under suspension of the rules, April 1. President signed April 18, 2008.

PL 110-202 (S 845) Direct the secretary of Health and Human Services to expand and intensify programs related to research and other activities related to falls by the elderly. Introduced by Enzi, R-Wyo., on March 12, 2007. Senate Health, Education, Labor and Pensions reported, amended, March 29 (S Rept 110-110). Senate passed, amended, Aug. 1. House passed, under suspension of the rules, April 8, 2008. President signed April 23, 2008.

PL 110-203 (H J Res 70) Congratulate the Army Reserve on its centennial, to be formally celebrated on April 23, 2008, and commemorate the historic contributions of its veterans and continuing contributions of its soldiers to the vital national security interests and homeland defense missions of the United States. Introduced by Bishop, D-Ga., on Dec. 13, 2007. House passed, amended, under suspension of the rules, April 8, 2008. Senate passed April 14. President signed April 23, 2008.

PL 110-204 (S 1858) Amend the Public Health Service Act to establish grant programs for education and outreach on newborn screening and coordinated follow-up care once newborn screening has been conducted, and reauthorize programs under Part A of Title XI of the Act. Introduced by Dodd, D-Conn., on July 23, 2007. Senate Health, Education, Labor and Pensions reported, amended, Dec. 5 (S Rept 110-280). Senate passed, amended, Dec. 13. House passed, under suspension of the rules, April 8, 2008. President signed April 24, 2008.

PL 110-205 (S 2903) Amend PL 110-196 to provide for a temporary extension of programs authorized by the Farm Security and Rural Investment Act of 2002 until May 2, 2008. Introduced by Harkin, D-Iowa, on April 24, 2008. Senate passed April 24. House passed April 24. President signed April 25, 2008.

PL 110-206 (S 793) Provide for the expansion and improvement of traumatic brain injury programs. Introduced by Hatch, R-Utah, on March 7, 2007. Senate Health, Education, Labor and Pensions reported, amended, Aug. 1 (S Rept 110-140). Senate passed, amended, Dec. 11. House passed, amended, under suspension of the rules, April 8, 2008. Senate agreed to House amendment April 10. President signed April 28, 2008.

PL 110-207 (HR 1119) Amend Title 36, U.S. Code, to revise the congressional charter of the Military Order of the Purple Heart of the United States of America Inc., to authorize associate membership in the corporation for the spouse and siblings of a recipient of the Purple Heart medal. Introduced by Davis, D-Calif., on Feb. 16, 2007. House Judiciary reported, amended, Nov. 6 (H Rept 110-428). House passed, amended, under suspension of the rules, Nov. 6. Senate passed April 14, 2008. President signed April 30, 2008.

PL 110-208 (S 2954) Amend PL 110-196 to provide for a temporary extension of programs authorized by the Farm Security and Rural Investment Act of 2002 until May 16, 2008. Introduced by Harkin, D-Iowa, on May 1, 2008. Senate passed May 1. House passed, under suspension of the rules, May 1. President signed May 2, 2008.

PL 110-209 (HR 4286) Award a congressional gold medal to Daw Aung San Suu Kyi in recognition of her courageous and unwavering commitment to peace, nonviolence, human rights, and democracy in Burma. Introduced by Crowley, D-N.Y., on Dec. 5, 2007. House passed, under suspension of the rules, Dec. 17. Senate Banking, Housing and Urban Affairs discharged. Senate passed April 24, 2008. President signed May 6, 2008.

PL 110-210 (HR 3196) Designate the facility of the U.S. Postal Service located at 20 Sussex St. in Port Jervis, N.Y., the "E. Arthur Gray Post Office Building." Introduced by Hall, D-N.Y., on July 26, 2007. House passed, under suspension of the rules, March 10, 2008. Senate Homeland Security and Governmental Affairs reported April 10 (no written report). Senate passed April 22. President signed May 7, 2008.

PL 110-211 (HR 3468) Designate the facility of the U.S. Postal Service located at 1704 Weeksville Road in Elizabeth City, N.C., the "Dr. Clifford Bell Jones Sr. Post Office." Introduced by Butterfield, D-N.C., on Aug. 4, 2007. House passed, under suspension of the rules, Feb. 12, 2008. Senate Homeland Security and Governmental Affairs reported April 10 (no written report). Senate passed April 22. President signed May 7, 2008.

PL 110-212 (HR 3532) Designate the facility of the U.S. Postal Service located at 5815 McLeod St. in Lula, Ga., the "Pvt. Johnathon Millican Lula Post Office." Introduced by Deal, R-Ga., on Sept. 14, 2007. House passed, under suspension of the rules, Feb. 12, 2008. Senate Homeland Security and Governmental Affairs reported April 10 (no written report). Senate passed April 22. President signed May 7, 2008.

PL 110-213 (HR 3720) Designate the facility of the U.S. Postal Service located at 424 Clay Ave. in Waco, Texas, the "Army Pfc. Juan Alonso Covarrubias Post Office Building." Introduced by Edwards, D-Texas, on Oct. 2, 2007. House passed, under suspension of the rules, Jan. 22, 2008. Senate Homeland Security and Governmental Affairs reported April 10 (no written report). Senate passed April 22. President signed May 7, 2008.

PL 110-214 (HR 3803) Designate the facility of the U.S. Postal Service located at 3100 Cashwell Drive in Goldsboro, N.C., the "John Henry Wooten Sr. Post Office Building." Introduced by Butterfield, D-N.C., on Oct. 10, 2007. House passed, under suspension of the rules, Feb. 28, 2008. Senate Homeland Security and Governmental Affairs reported April 10 (no written report). Senate passed April 22. President signed May 7, 2008.

PL 110-215 (HR 3936) Designate the facility of the U.S. Postal Service located at 116 Helen Highway in Cleveland, Ga., the "Sgt. Jason Harkins Post Office Building." Introduced by Deal, R-Ga., on Oct. 23, 2007. House passed, under suspension of the rules, Feb. 28, 2008. Senate Homeland Security and Governmental Affairs reported April 10 (no written report). Senate passed April 22. President signed May 7, 2008.

PL 110-216 (HR 3988) Designate the facility of the U.S. Postal Service located at 3701 Altamesa Blvd. in Fort Worth, Texas, the "Master Sgt. Kenneth N. Mack Post Office Building." Introduced by Granger, R-Texas, on Oct. 29, 2007. House passed, under suspension of the rules, Jan. 22, 2008. Senate Homeland Security and Governmental Affairs reported April 10 (no written report). Senate passed April 22. President signed May 7, 2008.

PL 110-217 (HR 4166) Designate the facility of the U.S. Postal Service located at 701 E. Copeland Drive in Lebanon, Mo., the "Steve W. Allee Carrier Annex." Introduced by Skelton, D-Mo., on Nov. 13, 2007. House passed, under suspension of the rules, March 10, 2008. Senate Homeland Security and Governmental Affairs reported April 10 (no written report). Senate passed April 22. President signed May 7, 2008.

PL 110-218 (HR 4203) Designate the facility of the U.S. Postal Service located at 3035 Stone Mountain St. in Lithonia, Ga., the "Spc. Jamaal RaShard Addison Post Office Building." Introduced by Johnson, D-Ga., on Nov. 15, 2007. House passed, under suspension of the rules, amended, Feb. 12, 2008. Senate Homeland Security and Governmental Affairs reported April 10 (no written report). Senate passed April 22. President signed May 7, 2008.

PL 110-219 (HR 4211) Designate the facility of the U.S. Postal Service located at 725 Roanoke Ave. in Roanoke Rapids, N.C., the "Judge Richard B. Allsbrook Post Office." Introduced by Butterfield, D-N.C., on Nov. 15, 2007. House passed, under suspension of the rules, Jan. 22, 2008. Senate Homeland Security and Governmental Affairs reported April 10 (no written report). Senate passed April 22. President signed May 7, 2008.

PL 110-220 (HR 4240) Designate the facility of the U.S. Postal Service located at 10799 W. Alameda Ave. in Lakewood, Colo., the "Felix Sparks Post Office Building." Introduced by Perlmutter, D-Colo., on Nov. 15, 2007. House passed, under suspension of the rules, Jan. 28, 2008. Senate Homeland Security and Governmental Affairs reported April 10 (no written report). Senate passed April 22. President signed May 7, 2008.

PL 110-221 (HR 4454) Designate the facility of the U.S. Postal Service located at 3050 Hunsinger Lane in Louisville, Ky., the "Iraq and Afghanistan Fallen Military Heroes of Louisville Memorial Post Office Building" in honor of the service members from Louisville who died in service during Operation Enduring Freedom and Operation Iraqi Freedom. Introduced by Yarmuth, D-Ky., on Dec. 11, 2007. House passed, under suspension of the rules, Feb. 28, 2008. Senate Homeland Security and Governmental Affairs reported April 10 (no written report). Senate passed April 22. President signed May 7, 2008.

PL 110-222 (HR 5135) Designate the facility of the U.S. Postal Service located at 201 W. Greenway St. in Derby, Kan., as the "Sgt. Jamie O. Maugans Post Office Building." Introduced by Tiahrt, R-Kan., on Jan. 23, 2008. House passed, under suspension of the rules, Feb. 12. Senate Homeland Security and Governmental Affairs reported April. 10 (no written report). Senate passed April 22. President signed May 7, 2008.

PL 110-223 (HR 5220) Designate the facility of the U.S. Postal Service located at 3800 SW 185th Ave. in Beaverton, Ore., the "Maj. Arthur Chin Post Office Building." Introduced by Wu, D-Ore., on

Jan. 29, 2008. House passed, under suspension of the rules, March 5. Senate Homeland Security and Governmental Affairs reported April 10 (no written report). Senate passed April 22. President signed May 7, 2008.

PL 110-224 (HR 5400) Designate the facility of the U.S. Postal Service located at 160 E. Washington St. in Chagrin Falls, Ohio, the "Sgt. Michael M. Kashkoush Post Office Building." Introduced by LaTourette, R-Ohio, on Feb. 12, 2008. House passed, under suspension of the rules, March 5. Senate Homeland Security and Governmental Affairs reported April 10 (no written report). Senate passed April 22. President signed May 7, 2008.

PL 110-225 (HR 5472) Designate the facility of the U.S. Postal Service located at 2650 Dr. Martin Luther King Jr. St., Indianapolis, Ind., the "Julia M. Carson Post Office Building." Introduced by Visclosky, D-Ind., on Feb. 14, 2008. House passed, under suspension of the rules, April 9. Senate passed April 22. President signed May 7, 2008.

PL 110-226 (HR 5489) Designate the facility of the U.S. Postal Service located at 6892 Main St. in Gloucester, Va., the "Congresswoman Jo Ann S. Davis Post Office." Introduced by Wittman, R-Va., on Feb. 26, 2008. House passed, under suspension of the rules, April 9. Senate passed April 22. President signed May 7, 2008.

PL 110-227 (HR 5715) Ensure continued availability of access to the federal student loan program for students and families. Introduced by Miller, D-Calif., on April 8, 2008. House Education and Labor reported April 14 (H Rept 110-583). House passed, amended, April 17. Senate passed, amended, April 30. House agreed to Senate amendments, under suspension of the rules, May 1. President signed May 7, 2008.

PL 110-228 (S 2457) Provide for extensions of leases of certain land by Mashantucket Pequot (Western) Tribe. Introduced by Lieberman, I-Conn., on Dec. 12, 2007. Senate Indian Affairs discharged. Senate passed, amended, Feb. 5, 2008. House Natural Resources reported April 29 (H Rept 110-611). House passed, under suspension of the rules, April 29. President signed May 8, 2008.

PL 110-229 (S 2739) Authorize certain programs and activities in the Department of the Interior, the Forest Service, and the Department of Energy; further implement the act approving the Covenant to Establish a Commonwealth of the Northern Mariana Islands in Political Union with the United States of America; and amend the Compact of Free Association Amendments Act of 2003. Introduced by Bingaman, D-N.M., on March 10, 2008. Senate passed April 10. House passed, under suspension of the rules, April 29. President signed May 8, 2008.

PL 110-230 (S 2929) Temporarily extend the programs under the Higher Education Act of 1965. Introduced by Kennedy, D-Mass., on April 29, 2008. Senate passed April 29. House passed, amended, under suspension of the rules, May 6. Senate agreed to House amendment May 7. President signed May 13, 2008.

PL 110-231 (HR 6051) Amend PL 110-196 to provide for a temporary extension of programs authorized by the Farm Security and Rural Investment Act of 2002 until May 23, 2008, or the date of the enactment of the Food, Conservation and Energy Act of 2008, whichever occurs first. Introduced by Peterson, D-Minn., on May 14, 2008. House passed May 14. Senate passed May 14. President signed May 18, 2008.

PL 110-232 (HR 6022) Suspend the acquisition of petroleum for the Strategic Petroleum Reserve. Introduced by Welch, D-Vt., on May 12, 2008. House passed, under suspension of the rules, May 13. Senate passed May 14. President signed May 19, 2008.

PL 110-233 (HR 493) Prohibit discrimination on the basis of genetic information with respect to health insurance and employment. Introduced by Slaughter, D-N.Y., on Jan. 16, 2007. House Education and Labor reported, amended, March 5 (H Rept 110-28, Part 1). House Ways and Means reported, amended, March 26 (H Rept 110-28, Part 2). House Energy and Commerce reported, amended, on March 29 (H Rept 110-28, Part 3). House Energy and Commerce filed a supplemental report April 19 (H Rept 110-28, Part 4). House passed, amended, under suspension of the rules, April 25. Senate passed, amended, April 24, 2008. House agreed to Senate amendment May 1. President signed May 21, 2008.

PL 110-234 (HR 2419) Provide for the continuation of agricultural programs through fiscal 2012. Introduced by Peterson, D-Minn., on May 22, 2007. House Agriculture reported, amended, July 23 (H Rept 110-256, Part 1). House Foreign Affairs discharged. House passed, amended, July 27. Senate passed, amended, Dec. 14. Conference report filed in the House on May 13, 2008 (H Rept 110-627). House agreed to conference report May 14. Senate agreed to conference report May 15. President vetoed May 21. House passed over president's veto, May 21. Senate passed over president's veto, May 22. Became law without president's signature May 22, 2008.

PL 110-235 (S 3029) Provide for an additional temporary extension of programs under the Small Business Act and the Small Business Investment Act of 1958. Introduced by Kerry, D-Mass., on May 15, 2008. Senate passed May 15. House passed, under suspension of the rules, May 20. President signed May 23, 2008.

PL 110-236 (HR 3522) Ratify a conveyance of a portion of the Jicarilla Apache Reservation to Rio Arriba County, N.M., pursuant to the settlement of litigation between the Jicarilla Apache Nation and Rio Arriba County, authorize issuance of a patent for said lands, and change the exterior boundary of the Jicarilla Apache Reservation accordingly. Introduced by Udall, D-N.M., on Sept. 10, 2007. House Natural Resources reported April 29, 2008 (H Rept 110-610). House passed, under suspension of the rules, April 29. Senate passed May 1. President signed May 27, 2008.

PL 110-237 (HR 5919) Make technical corrections regarding the Newborn Screening Saves Lives Act of 2007. Introduced by Roybal-Allard, D-Calif., on April 29, 2008. House passed, under suspension of the rules, April 30. Senate passed May 2. President signed May 27, 2008.

PL 110-238 (S 3035) Temporarily extend the programs under the Higher Education Act of 1965. Introduced by Kennedy, D-Mass., on May 20, 2008. Senate passed May 20. House passed, under suspension of the rules, May 20. President signed May 30, 2008.

PL 110-239 (HR 2356) Amend Title 4, U.S. Code, to encourage the display of the U.S. flag on Father's Day. Introduced by Scott, D-Ga., on May 17, 2007. House passed, under suspension of the rules, June 11. Senate Judiciary discharged. Senate passed May 15, 2008. President signed June 3, 2008.

PL 110-240 (HR 2517) Amend the Missing Children's Assistance Act to authorize appropriations. Introduced by Lampson, D-Texas, on May 24, 2007. House passed, amended, under suspension of the rules, Dec. 5. Senate Judiciary discharged. Senate passed May 20, 2008. President signed June 3, 2008.

PL 110-241 (HR 4008) Amend the Fair Credit Reporting Act to make technical corrections to the definition of willful noncompliance with violations involving the printing of an expiration date on certain credit and debit card receipts before the date of enactment of this act. Introduced by Mahoney, D-Fla., on Oct. 30, 2007. House passed, under suspension of the rules, May 13, 2008. Senate passed May 20. President signed June 3, 2008.

PL 110-242 (S 2829) Make technical corrections to Section 1244 of the fiscal 2008 National Defense Authorization Act, which provides special immigrant status for certain Iraqis. Introduced by Kennedy, D-Mass., on April 8, 2008. Senate Judiciary discharged. Senate passed April 28. House passed, under suspension of the rules, May 21. President signed June 3, 2008.

PL 110-243 (S J Res 17) Direct the United States to initiate international discussions and take necessary steps with other nations to negotiate an agreement for managing migratory and transboundary fish stocks in the Arctic Ocean. Introduced by Stevens, R-Alaska, on Aug. 3, 2007. Senate Foreign Relations discharged. Senate Commerce, Science and Transportation reported Oct. 4 (no written report). Senate passed Oct. 4. House passed, under suspension of the rules, May 21, 2008. President signed June 3, 2008.

PL 110-244 (HR 1195) Amend the Safe, Accountable, Flexible, Efficient Transportation Equity Act: A Legacy for Users to make technical corrections. Introduced by Oberstar, D-Minn., on Feb. 27, 2007. House Transportation and Infrastructure reported, amended, March 21 (H Rept 110-62). House passed, amended, under suspension of the rules, March 26. Senate Environment and Public Works reported, amended, March 7, 2008 (no written report). Senate passed, amended, April 17. House agreed to Senate amendment, under suspension of the rules, April 30. President signed June 6, 2008.

PL 110-245 (HR 6081) Amend the Internal Revenue Code of 1986 to provide benefits for military personnel. Introduced by Rangel, D-N.Y., on May 16, 2008. House passed, amended, under suspension of the rules, May 20. Senate passed May 22. President signed June 17, 2008.

PL 110-246 (HR 6124) Reauthorize agricultural, nutrition, conservation, and other programs through fiscal 2012. Introduced by Peterson, D-Minn., on May 22, 2008. House passed, under suspension of the rules, May 22. Senate passed June 5. President vetoed June 18. House passed over president's veto June 18. Senate passed over president's veto June 18. Became law without president's signature on June 18, 2008.

PL 110-247 (S 2420) Encourage executive contracts to provide for the donation of excess food to nonprofit organizations that provide assistance to needy people. Introduced by Schumer, D-N.Y., on Dec. 6, 2007. House Homeland Security and Governmental Affairs reported, amended, May 22, 2008 (S Rept 110-338). Senate passed, amended, May 22. House passed, under suspension of the rules, June 3. President signed June 20, 2008.

PL 110-248 (HR 3179) Amend Title 40, U.S. Code, to authorize the use of federal supply schedules for the acquisition of law enforcement, security, and certain other related items by state and local governments. Introduced by Towns, D-N.Y., on July 25, 2007. House Oversight and Government Reform reported Dec. 17 (H Rept 110-494). House passed, under suspension of the rules, Dec. 17. Senate Homeland Security and Governmental Affairs reported June 5, 2008 (S Rept 110-344). Senate passed June 10. President signed June 26, 2008.

PL 110-249 (HR 3913) Amend the International Center Act to authorize the lease or sublease of certain property to an entity other than a foreign government or international organization if certain conditions are met. Introduced by Ros-Lehtinen, R-Fla., on Oct. 22, 2007. House Transportation and Infrastructure reported Jan. 28, 2008 (H Rept 110-518). House passed, under suspension of the rules, Jan. 28. Senate Foreign Relations reported June 2 (S Rept 110-343). Senate passed June 5. President signed June 26, 2008.

PL 110-250 (S 1245) Reform mutual aid agreements for the National Capital Region. Introduced by Cardin, D-Md., on April 26, 2007. Senate Homeland Security and Governmental Affairs reported Dec. 6 (S Rept 110-237). Senate passed Dec. 12. House passed, under suspension of the rules, June 9, 2008. President signed June 26, 2008.

PL 110-251 (S 2516) Assist certain members of the armed forces in obtaining U.S. citizenship. Introduced by Mikulski, D-Md., on Dec. 18, 2007. Senate Judiciary discharged. Senate passed, amended, March 11, 2008. House passed, under suspension of the rules, June 9. President signed June 26, 2008.

PL 110-252 (HR 2642) Make emergency supplemental appropriations for U.S. operations in Iraq and Afghanistan and other purposes. Introduced by Edwards, D-Texas, on June 11, 2007. House Appropriations reported June 11 (H Rept 110-186). House passed, amended, June 15. Senate passed, amended, Sept. 6. House agreed to Senate amendment, with amendments, May 15, 2008. Senate agreed to House amendment No. 2 to Senate amendment, with amendment, May 22. Senate agreed to House amendment No. 1 to Senate amendment, with amendment, May 22. House agreed to Senate amendment to House amendment No. 1 on June 19. House agreed to Senate amendment to House amendment No. 2, with an amendment, June 19. Senate agreed to House amendment to Senate amendment to House amendment No. 2 on June 26. President signed June 30, 2008.

PL 110-253 (HR 6327) Amend the Internal Revenue Code of 1986 to extend the funding and expenditure authority of the Airport and Airway Trust Fund. Introduced by Rangel, D-N.Y., on June 20, 2008. House passed, amended, under suspension of the rules, June 24. Senate passed June 26. President signed June 30, 2008.

PL 110-254 (S 1692) Grant a federal charter to the Korean War Veterans Association Inc. Introduced by Cardin, D-Md., on June 25, 2007. Senate Judiciary reported Sept. 7 (no written report). Senate passed Sept. 12. House passed, under suspension of the rules, June 17, 2008. President signed June 30, 2008.

PL 110-255 (S 2146) Authorize the administrator of the Environmental Protection Agency to accept, as part of a settlement, diesel emission reduction supplemental environmental projects. Introduced by Carper, D-Del., on Oct. 4, 2007. Senate Environment and Public Works reported Feb. 28, 2008 (S Rept 110-266). Senate passed Feb. 29. House passed, amended, under suspension of the rules, June 12. Senate agreed to House amendment June 17. President signed June 30, 2008.

PL 110-256 (S 3180) Temporarily extend the programs under the Higher Education Act of 1965. Introduced by Kennedy, D-Mass., on June 23, 2008. Senate passed June 23. House passed, under suspension of the rules, June 25. President signed June 30, 2008.

PL 110-257 (HR 5690) Exempt the African National Congress from treatment as a terrorist organization for certain acts or events, and provide relief for certain members of the African National Congress to enter the country without regard to activities undertaken in opposition to apartheid rule in South Africa. Introduced by Berman, D-Calif., on April 3, 2008. House Judiciary reported, amended, May 5 (H Rept 110-620, Part 1). House Foreign Affairs discharged. House passed, amended, under suspension of the rules, May 8. Senate Judiciary reported, amended, June 26 (no written report). Senate passed, amended, June 26. House agreed to Senate amendment June 26. President signed July 1, 2008.

PL 110-258 (S 188) Revise the short title of the Fannie Lou Hamer, Rosa Parks, and Coretta Scott King Voting Rights Act Reauthorization and Amendments Act of 2006. Introduced by Salazar, D-Colo., on Jan. 4, 2007. Senate Judiciary reported, amended, Feb. 8 (no written report). Senate passed, amended, Feb. 15. House passed, under suspension of the rules, June 17, 2008. President signed July 1, 2008.

PL 110-259 (S 254) Award a congressional gold medal posthumously to Constantino Brumidi. Introduced by Enzi, R-Wyo., on Jan. 10, 2007. Senate Banking, Housing, and Urban Affairs reported, amended, May 17 (no written report). Senate passed, amended, May 21. House passed, under suspension of the rules, June 10, 2008. President signed July 1, 2008.

PL 110-260 (S 682) Award a congressional gold medal to Edward William Brooke III in recognition of his unprecedented and enduring service to the nation. Introduced by Kennedy, D-Mass., on Feb. 17, 2007. Senate Banking, Housing, and Urban Affairs discharged. Senate passed March 29. House passed, under suspension of the rules, June 10, 2008. President signed July 1, 2008.

PL 110-261 (HR 6304) Amend the Foreign Intelligence Surveillance Act of 1978 to establish a procedure for authorizing certain acquisitions of foreign intelligence. Introduced by Reyes, D-Texas, on June 19, 2008. House passed June 20. Senate passed July 9. President signed July 10, 2008.

PL 110-262 (HR 430) Designate the U.S. bankruptcy courthouse located at 271 Cadman Plaza E., Brooklyn, N.Y., as the "Conrad Duberstein United States Bankruptcy Courthouse." Introduced by Towns, D-N.Y., on Jan. 11, 2007. House Transportation and Infrastructure reported, amended, Feb. 16 (H Rept 110-21). House passed, amended, under suspension of the rules, March 13. Senate Environment and Public Works discharged. Senate passed June 24, 2008. President signed July 15, 2008.

PL 110-263 (HR 781) Redesignate Lock and Dam No. 5 of the McClellan-Kerr Arkansas River Navigation System near Redfield, Ark., authorized by the Rivers and Harbors Act of 1946, as the "Col. Charles D. Maynard Lock and Dam." Introduced by Ross, D-Ark., on Jan 31, 2007. House Transportation and Infrastructure reported July 11 (H Rept 110-229). House passed, under suspension of the rules, July 16. Senate Environment and Public Works reported June 4, 2008 (no written report). Senate passed June 24. President signed July 15, 2008.

PL 110-264 (HR 2728) Designate the station of the U.S. Border Patrol located at 25762 Madison Ave. in Murrieta, Calif., as the "Theodore L. Newton Jr. and George F. Azrak Border Patrol Station." Introduced by Issa, R-Calif., on June 14, 2007. House Transportation and Infrastructure reported Sept. 14 (H Rept 110-327). House passed, under suspension of the rules, Oct. 29. Senate Environment and Public Works discharged. Senate passed June 24, 2008. President signed July 15, 2008.

PL 110-265 (HR 3721) Designate the facility of the U.S. Postal Service located at 1190 Lorena Road in Lorena, Texas, as the "Marine Gunnery Sgt. John D. Fry Post Office Building." Introduced by Edwards, D-Texas, on Oct. 2, 2007. House passed, under suspension of the rules, April 23, 2008. Senate Homeland Security and Governmental Affairs reported June 25 (no written report). Senate passed June 27. President signed July 15, 2008.

PL 110-266 (HR 4140) Designate the Port Angeles Federal Building in Port Angeles, Wash., as the "Richard B. Anderson Federal Building." Introduced by Dicks, D-Wash., on Nov. 9, 2007. House Transportation and Infrastructure reported Jan. 28, 2008 (H Rept 110-515). House passed, under suspension of the rules, Jan. 28. Senate Environment and Public Works reported June 4 (no written report). Senate passed June 24. President signed July 15, 2008.

PL 110-267 (HR 4185) Designate the facility of the U.S. Postal Service located at 11151 Valley Blvd. in El Monte, Calif., as the "Marisol Heredia Post Office Building." Introduced by Solis, D-Calif., on Nov. 14, 2007. House passed, under suspension of the rules, April 23, 2008. Senate Homeland Security and Governmental Affairs reported June 25 (no written report). Senate passed June 27. President signed July 15, 2008.

PL 110-268 (HR 5168) Designate the facility of the U.S. Postal Service located at 19101 Cortez Blvd. in Brooksville, Fla., as the "Cody Grater Post Office Building." Introduced by Brown-Waite, R-Fla., on Jan 29, 2008. House passed, under suspension of the rules, April 1. Senate Homeland Security and Governmental Affairs reported June 25 (no written report). Senate passed June 27. President signed July 15, 2008.

PL 110-269 (HR 5395) Designate the facility of the U.S. Postal Service located at 11001 Dunklin Drive in St. Louis as the

"William 'Bill' Clay Post Office Building." Introduced by Carnahan, D-Mo., on Feb. 12, 2008. House passed, under suspension of the rules, April 9. Senate Homeland Security and Governmental Affairs reported June 25 (no written report). Senate passed June 27. President signed July 15, 2008.

PL 110-270 (HR 5479) Designate the facility of the U.S. Postal Service located at 117 N. Kidd St. in Ionia, Mich., as the "Alonzo Woodruff Post Office Building." Introduced by Ehlers, R-Mich., on Feb. 25, 2008. House passed, under suspension of the rules, April 23. Senate Homeland Security and Governmental Affairs reported June 25 (no written report). Senate passed June 27. President signed July 15, 2008.

PL 110-271 (HR 5517) Designate the facility of the U.S. Postal Service located at 7231 FM 1960 in Humble, Texas, as the "Texas Military Veterans Post Office." Introduced by Poe, R-Texas, on Feb. 28, 2008. House passed, under suspension of the rules, April 15. Senate Homeland Security and Governmental Affairs reported June 25 (no written report). Senate passed June 27. President signed July 15, 2008.

PL 110-272 (HR 5528) Designate the facility of the U.S. Postal Service located at 120 Commercial St. in Brockton, Mass., as the "Rocky Marciano Post Office Building." Introduced by Lynch, D-Mass., on March 4, 2008. House passed, under suspension of the rules, April 23. Senate Homeland Security and Governmental Affairs reported June 25 (no written report). Senate passed June 27. President signed July 15, 2008.

PL 110-273 (HR 5778) Preserve the independence of the District of Columbia Water and Sewer Authority. Introduced by Van Hollen, D-Md., on April 10, 2008. House passed, amended, under suspension of the rules, June 9. Senate passed June 16. President signed July 15, 2008.

PL 110-274 (HR 6040) Amend the Water Resources Development Act of 2007 to clarify the authority of the secretary of the army to provide reimbursement for travel expenses incurred by members of the Committee on Levee Safety. Introduced by Mica, R-Fla., on May 13, 2008. House passed, under suspension of the rules, June 23. Senate passed June 25. President signed July 15, 2008.

PL 110-275 (HR 6331) Amend Titles XVIII and XIX of the Social Security Act to extend expiring provisions under the Medicare Program, improve beneficiary access to preventive and mental health services, enhance low-income benefit programs, and maintain access to care in rural areas, including pharmacy access. Introduced by Rangel, D-N.Y., on June 20, 2008. House passed, amended, under suspension of the rules, June 24. Senate passed July 9. President vetoed July 15. House passed over president's veto July 15. Senate passed over president's veto July 15. Became law without president's signature July 15, 2008.

PL 110-276 (HR 1019) Designate the U.S. customhouse building located at 31 Gonzalez Clemente Ave. in Mayaguez, P.R., as the "Rafael Martinez Nadal United States Customhouse Building." Introduced by Fortuño, R-P.R., on Feb. 13, 2007. House Transportation and Infrastructure reported March 26 (H Rept 110-70). House passed, under suspension of the rules, March 26. Senate Environment and Public Works reported June 4, 2008 (no written report). Senate passed June 24. President signed July 15, 2008.

PL 110-277 (HR 634) Require the secretary of the Treasury to mint coins in commemoration of veterans who became disabled for life while serving in the U.S. armed forces. Introduced by Moore, D-Kan., on Jan 23, 2007. House passed, amended, under suspension of the rules, May 15, 2007. Senate Banking, Housing, and Urban Affairs reported, amended, June 2, 2008 (no written report). Senate passed, amended, June 10. House agreed to Senate amendment, under suspension of the rules, June 18. President signed July 17, 2008.

PL 110-278 (HR 814) Require the Consumer Product Safety Commission to issue regulations mandating child-resistant closures on all portable gasoline containers. Introduced by Moore, D-Kan., on Feb. 5, 2007. House Energy and Commerce reported, amended, Oct. 9 (H Rept 110-367). House passed, amended, under suspension of the rules Oct. 9. Senate Commerce, Science and Transportation discharged. Senate passed June 16, 2008. President signed July 17, 2008.

PL 110-279 (S 2967) Provide for the continuation of certain federal employee benefits for certain employees of the Senate restaurants after operations of the restaurants are contracted out to a private business concern. Introduced by Feinstein, D-Calif., on May 1, 2008. Senate Rules and Administration discharged. Senate passed June 3. House passed July 10. President signed July 17, 2008.

PL 110-280 (HR 802) Amend the Act to Prevent Pollution from Ships to require the U.S. Coast Guard and the Environmental Protection Agency to prescribe regulations to implement vessel air emission standards outlined under Annex VI to the MARPOL Convention. Introduced by Oberstar, D-Minn., on Feb. 5, 2007. House Transportation and Infrastructure reported, amended, March 20 (H Rept 110-54). House passed, amended, under suspension of the rules March 26. Senate Commerce, Science and Transportation reported, amended, June 23, 2008 (S Rept 110-394). Senate passed, amended, June 26. House agreed to Senate amendment, under suspension of the rules, July 8. President signed July 21, 2008.

PL 110-281 (HR 3891) Amend the National Fish and Wildlife Foundation Establishment Act to increase the number of directors on the foundation's board of directors. Introduced by Brown, R-S.C., on Oct. 18, 2007. House Natural Resources reported March 31, 2008 (H Rept 110-552). House passed, amended, under suspension of the rules, March 31. Senate Environment and Public Works reported June 27 (S Rept 110-405). Senate passed July 7. President signed July 21, 2008.

PL 110-282 (S 3145) Designate a portion of U.S. Route 20A, located in Orchard Park, N.Y., as the "Timothy J. Russert Highway." Introduced by Clinton, D-N.Y., on June 18, 2008. Senate Homeland Security and Governmental Affairs discharged. Senate Environment and Public Works discharged. Senate passed June 24. House passed, under suspension of the rules, July 15. President signed July 23, 2008.

PL 110-283 (HR 3403) Promote and enhance public safety by facilitating the rapid deployment of IP-enabled 911 and E-911 services, encouraging the nation's transition to a national IP-enabled emergency network and improving 911 and E-911 access to those with disabilities. Introduced by Gordon, D-Tenn., on Aug. 3, 2007. House Energy and Commerce reported, amended, Nov. 13 (H Rept 110-442). House passed, amended, under suspension of the rules, Nov. 13. Senate Commerce, Science and Transportation discharged. Senate passed, amended, June 16, 2008. House agreed to Senate amendment June 23. President signed July 23, 2008.

PL 110-284 (HR 3712) Designate the federal building and U.S. courthouse located at 1716 Spielbusch Ave. in Toledo, Ohio, as the "James M. & Thomas W.L. Ashley Customs Building and United States Courthouse." Introduced by Kaptur, D-Ohio, on Oct. 1, 2007. House Transportation and Infrastructure reported, amended, Nov. 15 (H Rept 110-455). House passed, amended, under suspension of the rules June 4, 2008. Senate Environment and Public Works discharged. Senate passed June 24. President signed July 23, 2008.

PL 110-285 (HR 1553) Amend the Public Health Service Act to advance medical research and treatments of pediatric cancers to ensure that patients and families have access to the current treatments and information regarding pediatric cancers, establish a population-based national childhood cancer database, and promote public awareness of pediatric cancers. Introduced by Pryce, R-Ohio, on March 15, 2007. House Energy and Commerce reported, amended, June 10, 2008 (H Rept 110-706). House passed, amended, under suspension of the rules June 12. Senate passed July 16. President signed July 29, 2008.

PL 110-286 (HR 3890) Amend the Burmese Freedom and Democracy Act of 2003 to waive the requirement for annual renewal resolutions on import sanctions, impose import sanctions on Burmese gemstones, expand the number of individuals against whom the visa ban is applicable, and expand the blocking of assets and other prohibited activities. Introduced by Lantos, D-Calif., on Oct. 18, 2007. House Foreign Affairs reported, amended, Oct. 31 (H Rept 110-418, Part 1). House Judiciary discharged. House passed, amended, under suspension of the rules, Dec. 11. Senate Foreign Relations discharged. Senate passed, amended, Dec. 19. House agreed to Senate amendments, with amendments pursuant to H Res 1341, on July 15, 2008. Senate agreed to House amendments to Senate amendments July 22. President signed July 29, 2008.

PL 110-287 (H J Res 93) Approve the renewal of import restrictions in the Burmese Freedom and Democracy Act of 2003. Introduced by Crowley, D-N.Y., on June 5, 2008. House passed, amended, under suspension of the rules, July 23. Senate passed July 24. President signed July 29, 2008.

PL 110-288 (S 2766) Amend the Federal Water Pollution Control Act to address certain discharges incidental to the normal operation of a recreational vessel. Introduced by Nelson, D-Fla., on March 13, 2008. Senate Environment and Public Works reported June 23 (S Rept 110-398). Senate passed July 22. House passed, under suspension of the rules, July 22. President signed July 29, 2008.

PL 110-289 (HR 3221) Move the United States toward greater energy independence and security, develop innovative technologies, reduce carbon emissions, create green jobs, protect consumers, increase clean renewable-energy production, and modernize the U.S. energy infrastructure. Introduced by Pelosi, D-Calif., on July 30, 2007. House passed, amended, Aug. 4. Senate passed, amended, April 10, 2008. House agreed to Senate amendments, with amendments, May 8. Senate agreed to House amendments to Senate amendments, with amendments, July 11. House agreed to Senate amendment to House amendments to Senate amendment, with amendments, July 23. Senate agreed to House amendment to Senate amendment to House amendments to Senate amendment July 26. President signed July 30, 2008.

PL 110-290 (HR 3564) Amend Title 5, U.S. Code, to authorize appropriations for the Administrative Conference of the United States through fiscal 2011. Introduced by Cannon, R-Utah, on Sept. 18, 2007. House Judiciary reported Oct. 18 (H Rept 110-390). House passed, under suspension of the rules, Oct. 22. Senate passed, amended, June 27, 2008. House agreed to Senate amendment, under suspension of the rules, July 14. President signed July 30, 2008.

PL 110-291 (HR 3985) Amend Title 49, U.S. Code, to direct the secretary of transportation to register a person providing transportation by an over-the-road bus as a motor carrier of passengers only if the person is willing and able to comply with certain accessibility requirements in addition to other existing requirements. Introduced by DeFazio, D-Ore., on Oct. 29, 2007. House Transportation and Infrastructure reported Nov. 15, 2007 (H Rept 110-456). House passed, under suspension of the rules, Dec. 12. Senate Commerce, Science and Transportation reported June 23, 2008 (S Rept 110-395). Senate passed July 14. President signed July 30, 2008.

PL 110-292 (HR 4289) Name the Department of Veterans Affairs outpatient clinic in Ponce, P.R., as the "Euripides Rubio Department of Veterans Affairs Outpatient Clinic." Introduced by Fortuño, R-P.R., on Oct. 29, 2007. House passed, under suspension of the rules, June 24, 2008. Senate Veterans' Affairs discharged. Senate passed July 11. President signed July 30, 2008.

PL 110-293 (HR 5501) Authorize appropriations for fiscal 2009 through 2013 to provide assistance to foreign countries to combat HIV/AIDS, tuberculosis, and malaria. Introduced by Berman, D-Calif., on Feb. 27, 2008. House Foreign Affairs reported March 10 (H Rept 110-546, Part 1). Financial Services discharged. Foreign Affairs filed supplemental report March 11 (H Rept 110-546, Part 2). House passed, amended, April 2. Senate Foreign Relations discharged. Senate passed, amended, July 16. House agreed to Senate amendment July 24. President signed July 30, 2008.

PL 110-294 (S 231) Authorize the Edward Byrne Memorial Justice Assistance Grant Program at fiscal year 2006 levels through fiscal 2012. Introduced by Feinstein, D-Calif., on Jan. 9, 2007. Senate Judiciary reported May 23 (no written report). Senate passed May 24. House passed, under suspension of the rules, July 14, 2008. President signed July 30, 2008.

PL 110-295 (S 2607) Make a technical correction to Section 3009 of the Deficit Reduction Act of 2005. Introduced by Snowe, R-Maine, on Feb. 7, 2008. Senate Commerce, Science and Transportation reported June 10 (S Rept 110-348). Senate passed, amended, June 19. House passed, under suspension of the rules, July 9. President signed July 30, 2008.

PL 110-296 (S 3218) Extend the pilot program for volunteer groups to obtain criminal history background checks. Introduced by Biden, D-Del., on June 26, 2008. Senate passed June 26. House passed, under suspension of the rules, July 14. President signed July 30, 2008.

PL 110-297 (HR 4841) Approve, ratify, and confirm the settlement agreement entered into to resolve claims by the Soboba Band of Luiseño Native Americans relating to alleged interferences with the water resources of the tribe, and authorize and direct the secretary of the interior to execute the settlement agreement and related waivers. Introduced by Bono Mack, R-Calif., on Dec. 19, 2007. House Natural Resources reported, amended, May 15, 2008 (H Rept 110-649). House passed, amended, under suspension of the rules, May 21. Senate passed July 23. President signed July 31, 2008.

PL 110-298 (S 2565) Establish an awards mechanism to honor exceptional acts of bravery in the line of duty by federal law enforcement officers. Introduced by Biden, D-Del., on Jan. 29, 2008. Judiciary reported, amended, June 24 (no written report). Senate passed, amended, June 26. House passed, under suspension of the rules, July 22. President signed July 31, 2008.

PL 110-299 (S 3298) Clarify the circumstances during which the administrator of the Environmental Protection Agency and applicable states may require permits for discharges from certain vessels, and require the administrator to conduct a study of discharges incidental to the normal operation of vessels. Introduced by Murkowski, R-Alaska, on July 22, 2008. Senate passed July 22. House passed, under suspension of the rules, July 22. President signed July 31, 2008.

PL 110-300 (S 3352) Temporarily extend the programs under the Higher Education Act of 1965. Introduced by Kennedy, D-Mass., on July 28, 2008. Senate passed July 28. House passed, under suspension of the rules, July 30. President signed July 31, 2008.

PL 110-301 (S 3370) Resolve pending claims against Libya by U.S. nationals. Introduced by Biden, D-Del., on July 31, 2008. Senate passed July 31. House passed July 31. President signed Aug. 4, 2008.

PL 110-302 (HR 2245) Designate the Department of Veterans Affairs outpatient clinic in Wenatchee, Wash., as the "Elwood 'Bud' Link Department of Veterans Affairs Outpatient Clinic." Introduced by Hastings, R-Wash., on May 9, 2007. House passed, under suspension of the rules, June 26, 2008. Senate Veterans' Affairs discharged. Senate passed Aug. 1. President signed Aug. 12, 2008.

PL 110-303 (HR 4210) Designate the facility of the U.S. Postal Service located at 401 Washington Ave. in Weldon, N.C., as the "Dock M. Brown Post Office Building." Introduced by Butterfield, D-N.C., on Nov. 15, 2007. House passed, under suspension of the rules, Dec. 17. Senate Homeland Security and Governmental Affairs reported July 30, 2008 (no written report). Senate passed Aug. 1. President signed Aug. 12, 2008.

PL 110-304 (HR 4918) Designate the Department of Veterans Affairs medical center in Miami as the "Bruce W. Carter Department of Veterans Affairs Medical Center." Introduced by Ros-Lehtinen, R-Fla., on Dec. 19, 2007. House passed, under suspension of the rules, June 26, 2008. Senate Veterans' Affairs discharged. Senate passed Aug. 1. President signed Aug. 12, 2008.

PL 110-305 (HR 5477) Designate the facility of the U.S. Postal Service located at 120 S. Del Mar Ave. in San Gabriel, Calif., as the "Chi Mui Post Office Building." Introduced by Schiff, D-Calif., on Feb. 21, 2008. House passed, under suspension of the rules, June 3. Senate Homeland Security and Governmental Affairs reported July 30 (no written report). Senate passed Aug. 1. President signed Aug. 12, 2008.

PL 110-306 (HR 5483) Designate the facility of the U.S. Postal Service located at 10449 White Granite Drive in Oakton, Va., as the "Pfc. David H. Sharrett II Post Office Building." Introduced by Davis, R-Va., on Feb. 25, 2008. House passed, under suspension of the rules, April 23. Senate Homeland Security and Governmental Affairs reported July 30 (no written report). Senate passed Aug. 1. President signed Aug. 12, 2008.

PL 110-307 (HR 5631) Designate the facility of the U.S. Postal Service located at 1155 Seminole Trail in Charlottesville, Va., as the "Cpl. Bradley T. Arms Post Office Building." Introduced by Goode, R-Va., on March 13, 2008. House passed, under suspension of the rules, April 29. Senate Homeland Security and Governmental Affairs reported July 30 (no written report). Senate passed Aug. 1. President signed Aug. 12, 2008.

PL 110-308 (HR 6061) Designate the facility of the U.S. Postal Service located at 219 E. Main St. in West Frankfort, Ill., as the "Kenneth James Gray Post Office Building." Introduced by Costello, D-Ill., on May 14, 2008. House passed, under suspension of the rules, July 9. Senate Homeland Security and Governmental Affairs reported July 30 (no written report). Senate passed Aug. 1. President signed Aug. 12, 2008.

PL 110-309 (HR 6085) Designate the facility of the U.S. Postal Service located at 42222 Rancho Las Palmas Drive in Rancho Mirage, Calif., as the "Gerald R. Ford Post Office Building." Introduced by Bono Mack, R-Calif., on May 20, 2008. House passed, under suspension of the rules, June 18. Senate Homeland Security and Governmental Affairs reported July 30 (no written report). Senate passed Aug. 1. President signed Aug. 12, 2008.

PL 110-310 (HR 6150) Designate the facility of the U.S. Postal Service located at 14500 Lorain Ave. in Cleveland as the "John P. Gallagher Post Office Building." Introduced by Kucinich, D-Ohio, on May 22, 2008. House passed, under suspension of the rules, June 18. Senate Homeland Security and Governmental Affairs reported July 30 (no written report). Senate passed Aug. 1. President signed Aug. 12, 2008.

PL 110-311 (HR 6340) Designate the federal building and U.S. courthouse located at 300 Quarropas St. in White Plains, N.Y., as the "Charles L. Brieant Jr. Federal Building and United States Courthouse." Introduced by Lowey, D-N.Y., on June 20, 2008. House passed, amended, under suspension of the rules, July 29. Senate passed Aug. 1. President signed Aug. 12, 2008.

PL 110-312 (S 3294) Provide for the continued performance of the functions of the U.S. Parole Commission. Introduced by Leahy, D-Vt., on July 21, 2008. Senate passed July 21. House passed, under suspension of the rules, July 31. President signed Aug. 12, 2008.

PL 110-313 (S 3295) Amend Title 35, U.S. Code, and the Trademark Act of 1946 to provide that the secretary of commerce, in consultation with the director of the U.S. Patent and Trademark Office, shall appoint administrative patent judges and administrative trademark judges. Introduced by Leahy, D-Vt., on July 21, 2008. Senate Judiciary discharged. Senate passed July 22. House passed, under suspension of the rules, July 31. President signed Aug. 12, 2008.

PL 110-314 (HR 4040) Establish consumer product safety standards and other safety requirements for children's products and reauthorize and modernize the Consumer Product Safety Commission. Introduced by Rush, D-Ill., on Nov. 1, 2007. House Energy and Commerce reported, amended, Dec. 19 (H Rept 110-501). House passed, amended, under suspension of the rules, Dec. 19. Senate passed, amended, March 6, 2008. Conference report filed in the House July 29 (H Rept 110-787). House agreed to the conference report, under suspension of the rules, July 30. Senate agreed to the conference report July 31. President signed Aug. 14, 2008.

PL 110-315 (HR 4137) Amend and extend the Higher Education Act of 1965. Introduced by Miller, D-Calif., on Nov. 9, 2007. House Education and Labor reported, amended, Dec. 19 (H Rept 110-500, Part 1). House Judiciary, Science and Technology, and Financial Services discharged. House passed Feb. 7, 2008. Senate Health, Education, Labor and Pensions discharged. Senate passed, amended, July 29. Conference report filed in the House July 30 (H Rept 110-803). House agreed to the conference report July 31. Senate agreed to the conference report July 31. President signed Aug. 14, 2008.

PL 110-316 (HR 6432) Amend the Federal Food, Drug, and Cosmetic Act to revise and extend the animal drug user fee program. Introduced by Pallone, D-N.J., on July 8, 2008. House Energy and Commerce reported, amended, July 30 (H Rept 110-804). House passed, under suspension of the rules, July 30. Senate passed Aug. 1. President signed Aug. 14, 2008.

PL 110-317 (HR 6580) Ensure the fair treatment, including continued payment of bonuses and similar benefits, for members of the armed forces who receive sole survivorship discharges. Introduced by Kind, D-Wis., on July 23, 2008. House passed, under suspension of the rules, July 29. Senate passed Aug. 1. President signed Aug. 29, 2008.

PL 110-318 (HR 6532) Amend the Internal Revenue Code of 1986 to restore the Highway Trust Fund balance. Introduced by Rangel, D-N.Y., on July 17, 2008. House passed, under suspension of the rules, July 23. Senate Finance discharged. Senate passed, amended, Sept. 10. House agreed to Senate amendment, under suspension of the rules, Sept. 11. President signed Sept. 15, 2008.

PL 110-319 (S 2837) Designate the U.S. courthouse located at 225 Cadman Plaza E., Brooklyn, N.Y., as the "Theodore Roosevelt United States Courthouse." Introduced by Schumer, D-N.Y., on April 9, 2008. Senate Environment and Public Works reported June 4 (no written report). Senate passed June 24. House Transportation and Infrastructure reported Sept. 8 (H Rept 110-823). House passed, under suspension of the rules, Sept. 8. President signed Sept. 17, 2008.

PL 110-320 (S 2403) Designate the new federal courthouse, located in the 700 block of East Broad Street, Richmond, Va., as the "Spottswood W. Robinson III and Robert R. Merhige Jr. Federal Courthouse." Introduced by Warner, R-Va., on Dec. 3, 2007. Senate Environment and Public Works reported June 4, 2008 (no written report). Senate passed June 24. House Transportation and Infrastructure reported, amended, Sept. 8 (H Rept 110- 824). House passed, amended, under suspension of the rules, Sept. 8. Senate agreed to House amendments Sept. 9. President signed Sept. 18, 2008.

PL 110-321 (HR 6456) Provide for extensions of certain authorities of the Department of State. Introduced by Berman, D-Calif., on July 10, 2008. House passed, amended, under suspension of the rules, July 30. Senate Foreign Relations discharged Sept. 8. Senate passed Sept. 8. President signed Sept. 19, 2008.

PL 110-322 (S 2450) Amend the federal rules of evidence to address the waiver of the attorney-client privilege and the work product doctrine. Introduced by Leahy, D-Vt., on Dec. 11, 2007. Senate Judiciary reported Feb. 25, 2008 (S Rept 110-264). Senate passed Feb. 27. House passed, under suspension of the rules, Sept. 8. President signed Sept. 19, 2008.

PL 110-323 (HR 5683) Make certain reforms with respect to the Government Accountability Office. Introduced by Davis, D-Ill., on April 2, 2008. House Oversight and Government Reform reported, amended, May 22 (H Rept 110-671). House passed, amended, under suspension of the rules, June 9. Senate Homeland Security and Governmental Affairs reported, amended, July 26 (no written report). Senate passed, amended, Aug. 1. House agreed to Senate amendment, under suspension of the rules, Sept. 9. President signed Sept. 22, 2008.

PL 110-324 (S 2617) Increase, effective Dec. 1, 2008, the rates of compensation for veterans with service-connected disabilities and the rates of dependency and indemnity compensation for the survivors of certain disabled veterans. Introduced by Akaka, D-Hawaii, on Feb. 8, 2008. Senate Veterans' Affairs reported, amended, July 24 (S Rept 110-430). Senate passed, amended, July 30. House passed, under suspension of the rules, Sept. 10. President signed Sept. 24, 2008.

PL 110-325 (S 3406) Reauthorize and revise the Americans with Disabilities Act of 1990. Introduced by Harkin, D-Iowa, on July 31, 2008. Senate passed Sept. 11. House passed, under suspension of the rules, Sept. 17. President signed Sept. 25, 2008.

PL 110-326 (HR 5938) Amend Title 18, U.S. Code, to provide Secret Service protection to former vice presidents. Introduced by Conyers, D-Mich., on May 1, 2008. House Judiciary reported June 5 (H Rept 110-696). House passed, under suspension of the rules, June 9, 2008. Senate Judiciary discharged. Senate passed, amended, July 30. House agreed to Senate amendments, under suspension of the rules, Sept. 15. President signed Sept. 26, 2008.

PL 110-327 (HR 1777) Amend the Improving America's Schools Act of 1994 to make permanent the favorable treatment of need-based educational aid under antitrust laws. Introduced by Delahunt, D-Mass., on March 29, 2007. House Judiciary reported April 10, 2008 (H Rept 110-577). House passed, amended, under suspension of the rules, April 30. Senate Judiciary discharged. Senate passed, amended, Sept. 25. House agreed to Senate amendment, under suspension of the rules, Sept. 27. President signed Sept. 30, 2008.

PL 110-328 (HR 2608) Amend Section 402 of the Personal Responsibility and Work Opportunity Reconciliation Act of 1996 to extend supplemental security income for refugees, asylees, and certain other humanitarian immigrants, and amend the Internal Revenue Code to collect unemployment compensation debts resulting from fraud. Introduced by McDermott, D-Wash., on June 7, 2007. House passed, under suspension of the rules, July 11. Senate Finance discharged. Senate passed, amended, Aug. 1, 2008. House agreed to Senate amendments, under suspension of the rules, Sept. 17. President signed Sept. 30, 2008.

PL 110-329 (HR 2638) Make appropriations for the departments of Homeland Security, Defense, and Veterans Affairs and for military construction in fiscal 2009. Provide continuing appropriations for all agencies and activities covered by the remaining nine unfinished fiscal 2009 appropriations bills until March 6, 2009. Introduced by Price, D-N.C., on June 8, 2007. House Appropriations reported June 8 (H Rept 110-181). House passed, amended, June 15. Senate passed, amended with the continuing appropriations bill, July 26. House agreed to Senate amendment, with an amendment, Sept. 24, 2008. Senate agreed to House amendment to Senate amendment Sept. 27. President signed Sept. 30, 2008.

PL 110-330 (HR 6984) Amend Title 49, U.S. Code, to extend authorizations for the airport improvement program, and amend the Internal Revenue Code of 1986 to extend the funding and expenditure authority of the Airport and Airway Trust Fund. Introduced by Oberstar, D-Minn., on Sept. 22, 2008. House passed, under suspension of the rules, Sept. 23. Senate passed Sept. 23. President signed Sept. 30, 2008.

PL 110-331 (S 171) Designate the facility of the U.S. Postal Service located at 301 Commerce St. in Commerce, Okla., as the "Mickey Mantle Post Office Building." Introduced by Inhofe, R-Okla., on Jan. 4, 2007. Senate Homeland Security and Governmental Affairs discharged. Senate passed Feb. 17. House passed, under suspension of the rules, Sept. 18, 2008. President signed Sept. 30, 2008.

PL 110-332 (S 2339) Designate the Department of Veterans Affairs clinic in Alpena, Mich., as the "Lt. Col. Clement C. Van Wagoner Department of Veterans Affairs Clinic." Introduced by Stabenow, D-Mich., on Nov. 13, 2007. Senate Veterans' Affairs discharged. Senate passed Dec. 13. House passed, under suspension of the rules, Sept. 17, 2008. President signed Sept. 30, 2008.

PL 110-333 (S 3241) Designate the facility of the U.S. Postal Service located at 1717 Orange Ave. in Fort Pierce, Fla., as the "CeeCee Ross Lyles Post Office Building." Introduced by Martinez, R-Fla., on July 10, 2008. Senate Homeland Security and Governmental Affairs reported July 30 (no written report). Senate passed Aug. 1. House Oversight and Government Reform discharged. House passed Sept. 24. President signed Sept. 30, 2008.

PL 110-334 (S 3009) Designate the FBI building under construction in Omaha, Neb., as the "J. James Exon Federal Bureau of Investigation Building." Introduced by Nelson, D-Neb., on May 12, 2008. Senate Environment and Public Works reported June 4 (no written report). Senate passed June 24. House Transportation reported Sept. 24 (H Rept 110-878). House passed, under suspension of the rules, Sept. 24. President signed Oct. 1, 2008.

PL 110-335 (HR 5551) Amend Title 11, District of Columbia Official Code, to implement the increase provided under the District of Columbia Appropriations Act of 2008, in the amount of funds made available for the compensation of attorneys representing indigent defendants in the District of Columbia courts. Introduced by Davis, D-Ill., on March 6, 2008. House Oversight and Government Reform reported March 31 (H Rept 110-560). House passed, under suspension of the rules, April 1. Senate Homeland Security and Governmental Affairs reported July 25 (S Rept 110-432). Senate passed Sept. 16. President signed Oct. 2, 2008.

PL 110-336 (HR 5893) Reauthorize the sound recording and film preservation programs of the Library of Congress. Introduced by Brady, D-Pa., on April 24, 2008. House Administration reported, amended, June 4 (H Rept 110-683, Part 1). House Judiciary discharged June 4. House passed, amended, under suspension of the rules, June 4. Senate Rules and Administration discharged. Senate passed Sept. 16. President signed Oct. 2, 2008.

PL 110-337 (S 996) Amend Title 49, U.S. Code, to expand passenger facility fee eligibility for certain noise compatibility projects. Introduced by Feinstein, D-Calif., on March 27, 2007. Senate Commerce, Science and Transportation discharged. Senate passed Feb. 28, 2008. House passed, under suspension of the rules, Sept. 17. President signed Oct. 2, 2008.

PL 110-338 (HR 3986) Amend the John F. Kennedy Center Act to authorize appropriations for the John F. Kennedy Center for the Performing Arts. Introduced by Oberstar, D-Minn., on Oct. 29, 2007. House Transportation and Infrastructure reported Dec. 10 (H Rept 110-480). House passed, amended, under suspension of the rules, Dec. 11. Senate Environment and Public Works reported, amended, June 4, 2008 (S Rept 110-406). Senate passed, amended, June 26. House agreed to Senate amendment, under suspension of the rules, Sept. 18, 2008. President signed Oct. 3, 2008.

PL 110-339 (S 1760) Amend the Public Health Service Act with respect to the Healthy Start Initiative. Introduced by Brown, D-Ohio, on July 10, 2007. Senate Health, Education, Labor and Pensions reported, amended, April 29, 2008 (no written report). Senate passed, amended, April 30. House passed, under suspension of the rules, Sept. 23. President signed Oct. 3, 2008.

PL 110-340 (S 2135) Prohibit the recruitment or use of child soldiers, designate persons who recruit or use child soldiers as inadmissible aliens, and allow the deportation of those who recruit or use child soldiers. Introduced by Durbin, D-Ill., on Oct. 3, 2007. Senate Judiciary reported, amended, Dec. 11 (no written report). Senate passed, amended, Dec. 19. House passed, under suspension of the rules, with amendment, Sept. 8, 2008. Senate agreed to House amendment Sept. 15. President signed Oct. 3, 2008.

PL 110-341 (S J Res 35) Amend Public Law 108-331 to provide for construction and related activities in support of the Very Energetic Radiation Imaging Telescope Array System (VERITAS) project in Arizona. Introduced by Leahy, D-Vt., on May 22, 2008. Senate Rules and Administration discharged. Senate passed July 17. House Transportation and Infrastructure reported Sept. 15 (H Rept 110-850). House passed, under suspension of the rules, Sept. 18. President signed Oct. 3, 2008.

PL 110-342 (S J Res 45) Express the consent and approval of Congress to an interstate compact regarding water resources in the Great Lakes-St. Lawrence River Basin. Introduced by Levin, D-Mich., on July 23, 2008. Senate Judiciary discharged. Senate passed, amended, Aug. 1. House passed, under suspension of the rules, Sept. 23. President signed Oct. 3, 2008.

PL 110-343 (HR 1424) Provide authority for the federal government to purchase and insure certain types of troubled assets for the purposes of providing stability to and preventing disruption in the economy and financial system and protecting taxpayers, to amend the Internal Revenue Code of 1986 to provide incentives for energy production and conservation, extend certain expiring provisions, and provide individual income tax relief. Introduced by Kennedy, D-R.I., on March 9, 2007. House Education and Labor reported, amended, Oct. 15 (H Rept 110-374, Part 1). House Ways and Means reported, amended, Oct. 15 (H Rept 110-374, Part 2). House Energy and Commerce reported, amended, March 4, 2008 (H Rept 110-374, Part 3). House passed, amended, March 5. Senate passed, amended, Oct. 1. House agreed to the Senate amendments Oct. 3. President signed Oct. 3, 2008.

PL 110-344 (HR 923) Designate a deputy chief in the Civil Rights Division of the Department of Justice responsible for unsolved criminal civil rights cases and a supervisory special agent in the Civil Rights Unit of the FBI. Introduced by Lewis, D-Ga., on Feb. 8, 2007. House Judiciary reported, amended, June 19 (H Rept 110-200). House passed, amended, under suspension of the rules, June 20. Senate passed Sept. 24, 2008. President signed Oct. 7, 2008.

PL 110-345 (HR 1199) Extend a grant program for drug-endangered children. Introduced by Cardoza, D-Calif., on Feb. 27, 2007. House Judiciary reported Sept. 24 (Rept 110-341, Part 1). House Energy and Commerce discharged. House passed, under suspension of the rules, Sept. 24. Senate Judiciary discharged. Senate passed Sept. 24, 2008. President signed Oct. 7, 2008.

PL 110-346 (HR 5834) Amend the North Korean Human Rights Act of 2004 to promote respect for the fundamental human rights of the people of North Korea. Introduced by Ros-Lehtinen, R-Fla., on April 17, 2008. House Foreign Affairs reported, amended, May 13 (H Rept 110-628). House passed, amended, under suspension of the rules, May 15. Senate Foreign Relations discharged. Senate passed, amended, Sept. 22. House agreed to Senate amendments, under suspension of the rules, Sept. 23. President signed Oct. 7, 2008.

PL 110-347 (HR 5975) Designate the facility of the U.S. Postal Service located at 101 W. Main St. in Waterville, N.Y., as the "Cpl. John P. Sigsbee Post Office." Introduced by Arcuri, D-N.Y., on May 6, 2008. House passed, under suspension of the rules, July 8. Senate Homeland Security and Governmental Affairs reported Sept. 24 (no written report). Senate passed Sept. 26. President signed Oct. 7, 2008.

PL 110-348 (HR 6092) Designate the facility of the U.S. Postal Service located at 101 Tallapoosa St. in Bremen, Ga., as the "Sgt. Paul Saylor Post Office Building." Introduced by Gingrey, R-Ga., on May 20, 2008. House passed, under suspension of the rules, July 8. Senate Homeland Security and Governmental Affairs reported Sept. 24 (no written report). Senate passed Sept. 26. President signed Oct. 7, 2008.

PL 110-349 (HR 6437) Designate the facility of the U.S. Postal Service located at 200 N. Texas Ave. in Odessa, Texas, as the "Cpl. Alfred Mac Wilson Post Office." Introduced by Conway, R-Texas, on July 8, 2008. House passed, under suspension of the rules, July 31. Senate Homeland Security and Governmental Affairs reported Sept. 24 (no written report). Senate passed Sept. 26. President signed Oct. 7, 2008.

PL 110-350 (HR 6889) Extend the authority of the secretary of education to purchase guaranteed student loans for an additional year. Introduced by Miller, D-Calif., on Sept. 15, 2008. House passed, under suspension of the rules, Sept. 15. Senate passed Sept. 17. President signed Oct. 7, 2008.

PL 110-351 (HR 6893) Amend Parts B and E of Title IV of the Social Security Act to connect and support relative caregivers, improve outcomes for children in foster care, provide for tribal foster care and adoption access, and improve incentives for adoption. Introduced by McDermott, D-Wash., on Sept. 15, 2008. House passed, under suspension of the rules, Sept. 17. Senate passed Sept. 22. President signed Oct. 7, 2008.

PL 110-352 (S 3015) Designate the facility of the U.S. Postal Service located at 18 S. G St., Lakeview, Ore., as the "Dr. Bernard Daly Post Office Building." Introduced by Smith, R-Ore., on May 14, 2008. Senate Homeland Security and Governmental Affairs reported June 25 (no written report). Senate passed June 27. House Oversight and Government Reform discharged. House passed Sept. 27. President signed Oct. 7, 2008.

PL 110-353 (S 3082) Designate the facility of the U.S. Postal Service located at 1700 Cleveland Ave. in Kansas City, Mo., as the "Rev. Earl Abel Post Office Building." Introduced by McCaskill, on D-Mo., June 4, 2008. Senate Homeland Security and Governmental Affairs reported June 25 (no written report). Senate passed June 27. House Oversight and Government Reform discharged. House passed Sept. 27. President signed Oct. 7, 2008.

PL 110-354 (HR 1157) Amend the Public Health Service Act to authorize the director of the National Institute of Environmental Health Sciences to make grants for the development and operation of research centers regarding environmental factors that may be related to the etiology of breast cancer. Introduced by Lowey, D-N.Y., on Feb. 16, 2007. House Energy and Commerce reported, amended, Sept. 25, 2008 (H Rept 110-889). House passed, amended, under suspension of the rules, Sept. 25. Senate passed Sept. 27. President signed Oct. 8, 2008.

PL 110-355 (HR 1343) Amend the Public Health Service Act to provide additional authorization of appropriations for the health centers program under Section 330 of the act. Introduced by G. Green, D-Texas, on March 6, 2007. House Energy and Commerce reported, amended, June 4, 2008 (H Rept 110-680). House passed, amended, under suspension of the rules, June 4. Senate Health, Education, Labor and Pensions discharged. Senate passed, amended, Sept. 24. House agreed to Senate amendment, under suspension of the rules, Sept. 25. President signed Oct. 8, 2008.

PL 110-356 (HR 3068) Prohibit awarding contracts to provide guard services under the contract security guard program of the Federal Protective Service to a business concern that is owned, controlled, or operated by an individual who has been convicted of a felony. Introduced by Norton, D-D.C., on July 17, 2007. House Transportation and Infrastructure reported, amended, Sept. 14 (H Rept 110-328). House passed, amended, under suspension of the rules, Oct. 2. Senate Homeland Security and Governmental Affairs reported, amended, Sept. 11, 2008 (S Rept 110-455). Senate passed, amended, Sept. 23. House agreed to Senate amendment, under suspension of the rules, Sept. 27. President signed Oct. 8, 2008.

PL 110-357 (HR 3229) Require the secretary of the Treasury to mint coins in commemoration of the legacy of the U.S. Army Infantry and the establishment of the National Infantry Museum and Soldier Center. Introduced by Westmoreland, R-Ga., on July 30, 2007. House passed, amended, under suspension of the rules, June 10, 2008. Senate Banking, Housing and Urban Affairs discharged. Senate passed Sept. 27. President signed Oct. 8, 2008.

PL 110-358 (HR 4120) Amend Title 18, U.S Code, to provide for more effective prosecution of cases involving child pornography. Introduced by Boyda, D-Kan., on Nov. 8, 2007. House passed, under suspension of the rules, Nov. 14. Senate Judiciary discharged. Senate passed, amended, Sept. 23, 2008. House agreed to Senate amendment, under suspension of the rules, Sept. 26. President signed Oct. 8, 2008.

PL 110-359 (HR 5001) Authorize the administrator of General Services to provide for the redevelopment of the Old Post Office Building located in the District of Columbia. Introduced by Norton, D-D.C., on Jan. 16, 2008. House Transportation and Infrastructure reported, amended, June 19 (H Rept 110-724). House passed, amended, under suspension of the rules, June 23. Senate Environment and Public Works reported Sept. 24 (S Rept 110-501). Senate passed Sept. 26. President signed Oct. 8, 2008.

PL 110-360 (HR 5057) Reauthorize the Debbie Smith DNA Backlog Grant Program. Introduced by Maloney, D-N.Y., on Jan. 17, 2008. House Judiciary reported, amended, July 14 (H Rept 110-757). House passed, amended, under suspension of the rules, July 14. Senate Health, Education, Labor and Pensions discharged. Senate Judiciary discharged. Senate passed, amended, Sept. 25. House agreed to Senate amendment, under suspension of the rules, Sept. 27. President signed Oct. 8, 2008.

PL 110-361 (HR 5265) Amend the Public Health Service Act to provide for research with respect to various forms of muscular dystrophy, including Becker, congenital, distal, Duchenne, Emery-Dreifuss facioscapulohumeral, limb-girdle, myotonic, and oculopharyngeal. Introduced by Engel, D-N.Y., on Feb. 7, 2008. House passed, amended, under suspension of the rules, Sept. 24. Senate passed, amended, Sept. 26. House agreed to Senate amendment Sept. 27. President signed Oct. 8, 2008.

PL 110-362 (HR 5571) Extend for five years the program allowing for a waiver of the foreign country residence requirement for international medical graduates. Introduced by Lofgren, D-Calif., on March 10, 2008. House Judiciary reported May 15 (H Rept 110-646). House passed, amended, under suspension of the rules, May 21. Senate Judiciary discharged. Senate passed, amended, Sept. 26. House agreed to Senate amendment, under suspension of the rules, Sept. 27. President signed Oct. 8, 2008.

PL 110-363 (HR 5872) Require the secretary of the Treasury to mint coins in commemoration of the centennial of the Boy Scouts of America. Introduced by Sessions, R-Texas, on April 22, 2008. House passed, amended, under suspension of the rules, May 15. Senate Banking, Housing and Urban Affairs discharged. Senate passed Sept. 27. President signed Oct. 8, 2008.

PL 110-364 (HR 6370) Transfer excess federal property administered by the Coast Guard to the Confederated Tribes of the Coos, Lower Umpqua, and Siuslaw Indians. Introduced by DeFazio, D-Ore., on June 25, 2008. House Transportation and Infrastructure reported Sept. 22 (H Rept 110-865). House passed, under suspension of the rules, Sept. 22. Senate passed Sept. 24. President signed Oct. 8, 2008.

PL 110-365 (HR 6460) Amend the Federal Water Pollution Control Act to provide for the remediation of sediment contamination in areas of concern. Introduced by Ehlers, R-Mich., on July 10, 2008. House Transportation and Infrastructure reported, amended, Sept. 15 (H Rept 110-849, Part 1). House Science and Technology discharged. House passed, amended, under suspension of the rules, Sept. 18. Senate passed, amended, Sept. 25. House agreed to Senate amendment, under suspension of the rules, Sept. 28. President signed Oct. 8, 2008.

PL 110-366 (HR 6890) Extend the waiver authority for the secretary of education under Section 105, Subtitle A of Title IV of Division B of PL 109-148, relating to hurricane relief for elementary and secondary schools. Introduced by Melancon, D-La., on Sept. 15, 2008. House passed, amended, under suspension of the rules, Sept. 22. Senate passed Sept. 25. President signed Oct. 8, 2008.

PL 110-367 (HR 6894) Extend and reauthorize the Defense Production Act of 1950. Introduced by Gutierrez, D-Ill., on Sept. 15, 2008. House passed, under suspension of the rules, Sept. 23. Senate passed Sept. 25. President signed Oct. 8, 2008.

PL 110-368 (HR 6946) Make a technical correction in the NET 911 Improvement Act of 2008. Introduced by Dingell, D-Mich., on Sept. 18, 2008. House Energy and Commerce discharged. House passed Sept. 25. Senate passed Sept. 27. President signed Oct. 8, 2008.

PL 110-369 (HR 7081) Approve the U.S.-India Agreement for Cooperation on Peaceful Uses of Nuclear Energy. Introduced by Berman, D-Calif., on Sept. 25, 2008. House passed, under suspension of the rules, Sept. 27. Senate passed Oct. 1. President signed Oct. 8, 2008.

PL 110-370 (H J Res 62) Honor the achievements and contributions to the United States by Native Americans. Introduced by Baca, D-Calif., on Nov. 13, 2007. House passed, under suspension of the rules, Nov. 13. Senate Indian Affairs reported, amended, July 31, 2008 (S Rept 110-435). Senate passed, amended, Sept. 22. House agreed to Senate amendment Sept. 26. President signed Oct. 8, 2008.

PL 110-371 (S 496) Reauthorize and improve the program authorized by the Appalachian Regional Development Act of 1965. Introduced by Voinovich, R-Ohio, on Feb. 6, 2007. Senate Environment and Public Works reported, amended, May 7 (S Rept 110-63). Senate passed, amended, Aug. 3. House passed, amended, under suspension of the rules, July 15, 2008. Senate agreed to House amendment Sept. 26. President signed Oct. 8, 2008.

PL 110-372 (S 1046) Modify pay provisions relating to certain senior-level positions in the federal government. Introduced by Voinovich, R-Ohio, on March 29, 2007. Senate Homeland Security and Governmental Affairs reported April 22, 2008 (S Rept 110-328). Senate passed, amended, July 11. House passed, under suspension of the rules, Sept. 26. President signed Oct. 8, 2008.

PL 110-373 (S 1382) Amend the Public Health Service Act to provide for the establishment of an Amyotrophic Lateral Sclerosis Registry. Introduced by Reid, D-Nev., on May 14, 2007. Senate Health, Education, Labor and Pensions reported, amended, Dec. 4 (no written report). Senate passed, amended, Sept. 23, 2008. House passed, under suspension of the rules, Sept. 26. President signed Oct. 8, 2008.

PL 110-374 (S 1810) Amend the Public Health Service Act to increase the provision of scientifically sound information and support services to patients receiving a positive test diagnosis for Down syndrome or other prenatally and postnatally diagnosed conditions. Introduced by Brownback, R-Kan., on July 18, 2007. Senate Health, Education, Labor and Pensions reported, amended, April 21, 2008 (no written report). Senate passed, amended, Sept. 23. House passed, under suspension of the rules, Sept. 25. President signed Oct. 8, 2008.

PL 110-375 (S 2482) Repeal the provision of Title 46, U.S. Code, requiring a license for employment in the business of salvaging on the coast of Florida. Introduced by Nelson, D-Fla., on Dec. 13, 2007. Senate Commerce, Science and Transportation reported May 22, 2008 (S Rept 110-340). Senate passed June 5. House passed, under suspension of the rules, Sept. 27. President signed Oct. 8, 2008.

PL 110-376 (S 2606) Reauthorize the U.S. Fire Administration. Introduced by Dodd, D-Conn., on Feb. 7, 2008. Senate Homeland Security and Governmental Affairs reported, amended, July 10 (S Rept 110-411). Senate passed, amended, Sept. 18. House passed, under suspension of the rules, Sept. 24. President signed Oct. 8, 2008.

PL 110-377 (S 2932) Amend the Public Health Service Act to reauthorize the national poison center toll-free number, national media campaign, and grant program to provide assistance for poison prevention, sustain the funding of poison centers, and enhance the public health of people of the United States. Introduced by Murray, D-Wash., on April 29, 2008. Senate Health, Education, Labor and Pensions discharged. Senate passed, amended, Sept. 23. House passed, under suspension of the rules, Sept. 26. President signed Oct. 8, 2008.

PL 110-378 (S 2982) Amend the Runaway and Homeless Youth Act to authorize appropriations. Introduced by Leahy, D-Vt., on May 6, 2008. Senate Judiciary reported, amended, May 22 (no written report). Senate passed, amended, Sept. 25. House passed Sept. 26. President signed Oct. 8, 2008.

PL 110-379 (S 3560) Amend Title XIX of the Social Security Act to provide additional funds for the qualifying individual program. Introduced by Baucus, D-Mont., on Sept. 24, 2008. Senate Finance discharged. Senate passed Sept. 25. House passed, under suspension of the rules, Sept. 27. President signed Oct. 8, 2008.

PL 110-380 (S 3597) Provide that funds allocated for community food projects for fiscal 2008 remain available until Sept. 30, 2009. Introduced by Harkin, D-Iowa, on Sept. 25, 2008. Senate passed Sept. 25. House passed, under suspension of the rules, Sept. 27. President signed Oct. 8, 2008.

PL 110-381 (HR 2851) Amend the Employee Retirement Income Security Act of 1974, the Public Health Service Act, and the Internal Revenue Code of 1986 to ensure that dependent students who take a medically necessary leave of absence do not lose health insurance coverage. Introduced by Hodes, D-N.H., on June 25, 2007. House Energy and Commerce reported, amended, July 30, 2008 (H Rept 110-806, Part 1). House Education and Labor and House Ways and Means discharged. House passed, amended, under suspension of the rules, July 30. Senate Health, Education, Labor and Pensions discharged. Senate passed Sept. 25. President signed Oct. 9, 2008.

PL 110-382 (S 2840) Establish a liaison with the FBI in U.S. Citizenship and Immigration Services to expedite naturalization applications filed by members of the armed forces and to establish a deadline for processing such applications. Introduced by Schumer, D-N.Y., on April 10, 2008. Senate Judiciary reported, amended, Aug. 1 (S Rept 110-440). Senate passed, amended, Sept. 24. House passed, under suspension of the rules, Sept. 28. President signed Oct. 9, 2008.

PL 110-383 (HR 2963) Transfer certain land in Riverside County, Calif., and San Diego County, Calif., from the Bureau of Land Management to the United States to be held in trust for the Pechanga Band of Luiseño Mission Indians. Introduced by Issa, R-Calif., on July 10, 2007. House Natural Resources discharged. House passed July 30. Senate Indian Affairs reported, amended, Sept. 25, 2008 (S Rept 110-503). Senate passed, amended, Sept. 26. House agreed to Senate amendments Sept. 29. President signed Oct. 10, 2008.

PL 110-384 (HR 3480) Direct the U.S. Sentencing Commission to ensure appropriate punishment enhancements for those involved in receiving stolen property consisting of veterans' grave markers. Introduced by Carney, D-Pa., on Sept. 6, 2007. House Judiciary reported, amended, May 15, 2008 (H Rept 110-647). House passed, amended, under suspension of the rules, May 21. Senate Judiciary reported June 12 (no written report). Senate passed Oct. 2. President signed Oct. 10, 2008.

PL 110-385 (S 1492) Improve the quality of federal and state data on the availability and quality of broadband services and promote the deployment of affordable broadband services to all parts of the nation. Introduced by Inouye, D-Hawaii, on May 24,

2007. Senate Commerce, Science and Transportation reported, amended, Oct. 24 (S Rept 110-204). Senate passed, amended, Sept. 26, 2008. House Energy and Commerce discharged. House passed, amended, Sept. 29. Senate agreed to House amendments Sept. 30. President signed Oct. 10, 2008.

PL 110-386 (S 1582) Reauthorize and amend the Hydrographic Services Improvement Act. Introduced by Inouye, D-Hawaii, on June 7, 2007. Senate Commerce, Science and Transportation reported, amended, Nov. 2 (S Rept 110-218). Senate passed, amended, Sept. 6, 2008. House passed Sept. 29. President signed Oct. 10, 2008.

PL 110-387 (S 2162) Improve the treatment and services provided by the Department of Veterans Affairs to veterans with post-traumatic stress disorder and substance use disorders. Introduced by Akaka, D-Hawaii, on Oct. 15, 2007. Senate Veterans' Affairs reported, amended, April 8, 2008 (S Rept 110-281). Senate passed, amended, June 3. House passed, amended, under suspension of the rules, Sept. 24. Senate agreed to House amendment Sept. 27. President signed Oct. 10, 2008.

PL 110-388 (S 2816) Provide for the secretary of homeland security to appoint a chief human capital officer for the department. Introduced by Voinovich, R-Ohio, on April 3, 2008. Senate Homeland Security and Governmental Affairs reported Sept. 16 (S Rept 110-466). Senate passed Sept. 23. House passed, under suspension of the rules, Sept. 27. President signed Oct. 10, 2008.

PL 110-389 (S 3023) Amend Title 38, U.S. Code, to improve and enhance compensation; pensions; and housing, labor, education, and insurance benefits for veterans. Introduced by Akaka, D-Hawaii, on May 15, 2008. Senate Veterans' Affairs reported, amended, Sept. 9 (S Rept 110-449). Senate passed, amended, Sept. 16. House passed, amended, under suspension of the rules, Sept. 24. Senate agreed to House amendment Sept. 27. President signed Oct. 10, 2008.

PL 110-390 (S 3128) Direct the secretary of the interior to provide a loan to the White Mountain Apache Tribe for use in planning, engineering, and designing a certain water system project. Introduced by Kyl, R-Ariz., on June 12, 2008. Senate Indian Affairs reported, amended, Sept. 24 (S Rept 110-502). Senate passed, amended, Sept. 25. House Natural Resources discharged. House passed Sept. 29. President signed Oct. 10, 2008.

PL 110-391 (S 3606) Extend the special immigrant nonminister religious worker program. Introduced by Hatch, R-Utah, on Sept. 26, 2008. Senate passed Sept. 26. House passed, under suspension of the rules, Sept. 27. President signed Oct. 10, 2008.

PL 110-392 (HR 1532) Amend the Public Health Service Act with respect to making progress toward eliminating tuberculosis. Introduced by G. Green, D-Texas, on March 15, 2007. House Energy and Commerce reported, amended, Sept. 23, 2008 (H Rept 110-873). House passed, amended, under suspension of the rules, Sept. 24. Senate passed Sept. 27. President signed Oct. 13, 2008.

PL 110-393 (HR 5350) Authorize the secretary of commerce to sell or exchange certain National Oceanic and Atmospheric Administration property located in Norfolk, Va. Introduced by Scott, D-Va., on Feb. 12, 2008. House Natural Resources reported, amended, Aug. 1 (H Rept 110-822, Part 1). House Oversight and Government Reform discharged. House passed, amended, under suspension of the rules, Sept. 17. Senate passed, amended, Sept. 26. House agreed to Senate amendment Sept. 29. President signed Oct. 13, 2008.

PL 110-394 (HR 5618) Reauthorize and amend the National Sea Grant College Program Act. Introduced by Bordallo, D-Guam, on March 13, 2008. House Natural Resources reported, amended, June 9 (H Rept 110-701, Part 1). House Science and Technology reported, amended, July 11 (H Rept 110-701, Part 2). House passed, amended, under suspension of the rules, July 14. Senate Commerce, Science and Transportation discharged. Senate passed, amended, Sept. 26. House agreed to Senate amendment Sept. 29. President signed Oct. 13, 2008.

PL 110-395 (HR 6199) Designate the facility of the U.S. Postal Service located at 245 N. Main St. in New City, N.Y., as the "Kenneth Peter Zebrowski Post Office Building." Introduced by Engel, D-N.Y., on June 5, 2008. House Oversight and Government Reform discharged. House passed Sept. 24. Senate passed Sept. 30. President signed Oct. 13, 2008.

PL 110-396 (HR 6229) Designate the facility of the U.S. Postal Service located at 2523 7th Ave. East in North St. Paul, Minn., as the "Mayor William 'Bill' Sandberg Post Office Building." Introduced by McCollum, D-Minn., on June 10, 2008. House passed, under suspension of the rules, Sept. 18. Senate passed Sept. 30. President signed Oct. 13, 2008.

PL 110-397 (HR 6338) Designate the facility of the U.S. Postal Service located at 4233 W. Hillsboro Blvd. in Coconut Creek, Fla., as the "Army Spc. Daniel Agami Post Office Building." Introduced by Klein, D-Fla., on June 20, 2008. House passed, under suspension of the rules, Sept. 18. Senate passed Sept. 30. President signed Oct. 13, 2008.

PL 110-398 (HR 6849) Amend the commodity provisions of the Food, Conservation and Energy Act of 2008 to permit producers to aggregate base acres and reconstitute farms to avoid the prohibition on receiving direct payments, countercyclical payments, or average crop revenue election payments when the sum of the base acres of a farm is 10 acres or less. Introduced by Etheridge, D-N.C., on Sept. 9, 2008. House Agriculture reported, amended, Sept. 24 (H Rept 110-881). House passed, amended, under suspension of the rules, Sept. 24. Senate passed, amended, Sept. 29. House agreed to Senate amendment Sept. 29. President signed Oct. 13, 2008.

PL 110-399 (HR 6874) Designate the facility of the U.S. Postal Service located at 156 Taunton Ave. in Seekonk, Mass., as the "Lance Cpl. Eric Paul Valdepenas Post Office Building." Introduced by McGovern, D-Mass., on Sept. 11, 2008. House Oversight and Government Reform discharged. House passed Sept. 24. Senate passed Sept. 30. President signed Oct. 13, 2008.

PL 110-400 (S 431) Require convicted sex offenders to register online identifiers. Introduced by Schumer, D-N.Y., on Jan. 30, 2007. Senate Judiciary reported, amended, April 22, 2008 (S Rept 110-332). Senate passed, amended, May 20. House passed, amended, Sept. 27. Senate agreed to House amendment Sept. 30. President signed Oct. 13, 2008.

PL 110-401 (S 1738) Establish a National Strategy for Child Exploitation Prevention and Interdiction within the Office of the Deputy Attorney General to improve the Internet Crimes Against Children Task Force, to increase resources for regional computer forensic labs, and to make other improvements to increase the ability of law enforcement agencies to investigate and prosecute predators. Introduced by Biden, D-Del., on June 28, 2007. Senate Judiciary reported, amended, July 7, 2008 (no written report). Senate passed, amended, Sept. 25. House passed, under suspension of the rules, Sept. 27. President signed Oct. 13, 2008.

PL 110-402 (S 3296) Extend the authority of the U.S. Supreme Court Police to protect court officials off the Supreme Court grounds and change the title of the administrative assistant to the chief justice to counselor to the chief justice. Introduced by Leahy, D-Vt., on July 21, 2008. Senate Judiciary reported Sept. 11 (no written report). Senate passed, amended, Sept. 25. House passed, under suspension of the rules, Sept. 29. President signed Oct. 13, 2008.

PL 110-403 (S 3325) Enhance remedies for violations of intellectual property laws. Introduced by Leahy, D-Vt., on July 24, 2008. Senate Judiciary reported, amended, Sept. 15 (no written report). Senate passed, amended, Sept. 28. House passed, under suspension of the rules, Sept. 28. President signed Oct. 13, 2008.

PL 110-404 (S 3477) Amend Title 44, U.S. Code, to authorize grants for Presidential Centers of Historical Excellence. Introduced by Warner, R-Va., on Sept. 11, 2008. Senate Homeland Security and Governmental Affairs reported, amended, Sept. 25 (no written report). Senate passed, amended, Sept. 26. House passed, under suspension of the rules, Sept. 27. President signed Oct. 13, 2008.

PL 110-405 (S 3536) Amend section 5402 of Title 39, U.S. Code, to modify the authority relating to U.S. Postal Service air transportation contracts. Introduced by Carper, D-Del., on Sept. 22, 2008. Senate Homeland Security and Governmental Affairs discharged. Senate passed Sept. 26. House passed, under suspension of the rules, Sept. 29. President signed Oct. 13, 2008.

PL 110-406 (S 3569) Make improvements in the operation and administration of the federal courts. Introduced by Schumer, D-N.Y., on Sept. 24, 2008. Senate Judiciary discharged. Senate passed Sept. 27. House passed, under suspension of the rules, Sept. 27. President signed Oct. 13, 2008.

PL 110-407 (S 3598) Amend titles 46 and 18, U.S. Code, with respect to the operation of submersible vessels and semi-submersible vessels without nationality. Introduced by Inouye, D-Hawaii, on Sept. 25, 2008. Senate passed Sept. 25. House passed, under suspension of the rules, Sept. 29. President signed Oct. 13, 2008.

PL 110-408 (S 3605) Extend the pilot program for volunteer groups to obtain criminal history background checks. Introduced by Biden, D-Del., on Sept. 26, 2008. Senate passed Sept. 26. House Judiciary discharged. House passed Sept. 27. President signed Oct. 13, 2008.

PL 110-409 (HR 928) Amend the Inspector General Act of 1978 to enhance the independence of inspectors general and to create a Council of the Inspectors General on Integrity and Efficiency. Introduced by Cooper, D-Tenn., on Feb. 8, 2007. House Oversight and Government Reform reported, amended, Sept. 27 (H Rept 110-354). House passed, amended, Oct. 3. Senate Homeland Security and Governmental Affairs discharged. Senate passed, amended, Sept. 24, 2008. House agreed to Senate amendment, under suspension of the rules, Sept. 27. President signed Oct. 14, 2008.

PL 110-410 (HR 1594) Designate the Department of Veterans Affairs outpatient clinic in Hermitage, Pa., as the "Michael A. Marzano Department of Veterans Affairs Outpatient Clinic." Introduced by English, R-Pa., on March 20, 2007. House passed, under suspension of the rules, Sept. 17, 2008. Senate passed Sept. 30. President signed Oct. 14, 2008.

PL 110-411 (HR 2786) Reauthorize programs for housing assistance for American Indians. Introduced by Kildee, D-Mich., on June 20, 2007. House Financial Services reported Aug. 3 (H Rept 110-295). House passed, amended, Sept. 6. Senate Indian Affairs discharged. Senate passed, amended, Sept. 25, 2008. House agreed to Senate amendment, under suspension of the rules, Sept. 27. President signed Oct. 14, 2008.

PL 110-412 (HR 6098) Amend the Homeland Security Act of 2002 to improve the financial assistance provided to state, local, and tribal governments for information-sharing activities. Introduced by Reichert, R-Wash., on May 20, 2008. House Homeland Security reported, amended, July 10 (H Rept 110-752). House passed, amended, under suspension of the rules, July 29. Senate Homeland Security and Governmental Affairs reported, amended, Sept. 24 (no written report). Senate passed, amended, Sept. 27. House agreed to Senate amendment Sept. 29. President signed Oct. 14, 2008.

PL 110-413 (HR 7198) Establish the Stephanie Tubbs Jones Gift of Life Medal for organ donors and the families of organ donors. Introduced by Stark, D-Calif., on Sept. 28, 2008. House Financial Services and House Energy and Commerce discharged. House passed Sept. 29. Senate passed Oct. 1. President signed Oct. 14, 2008.

PL 110-414 (S 906) Prohibit the sale, distribution, transfer, and export of elemental mercury. Introduced by Obama, D-Ill., on March 15, 2007. Senate Environment and Public Works reported, amended, Sept. 22, 2008 (S Rept 110-477). Senate passed, amended, Sept. 26. House passed, under suspension of the rules, Sept. 29. President signed Oct. 14, 2008.

PL 110-415 (S 1276) Establish a grant program to facilitate the creation of methamphetamine precursor electronic logbook systems. Introduced by Durbin, D-Ill., on May 3, 2007. Senate Judiciary reported, amended, Sept. 15, 2008 (no written report). Senate passed, amended, Sept. 25. House Energy and Commerce and House Judiciary discharged. House passed Sept. 29. President signed Oct. 14, 2008.

PL 110-416 (S 2304) Amend Title I of the Omnibus Crime Control and Safe Streets Act of 1968 to provide grants for the mental health treatment and services provided to offenders with mental illnesses. Introduced by Domenici, R-N.M., on Nov. 5, 2007. Senate Judiciary reported, amended, April 1, 2008 (no written report). Senate passed, amended, Sept. 26. House passed, under suspension of the rules, Sept. 29. President signed Oct. 14, 2008.

PL 110-417 (S 3001) Authorize appropriations for fiscal 2009 for military activities of the Department of Defense, military construction, and defense activities of the Department of Energy and to prescribe military personnel strengths for the fiscal year. Introduced by Levin, D-Mich., on May 12, 2008. Senate Armed Services reported May 12 (S Rept 110-335). Senate passed, amended, Sept. 17. House passed, amended, under suspension of the rules, Sept. 24. Senate agreed to House amendment Sept. 27. President signed Oct. 14, 2008.

PL 110-418 (S 3550) Designate a portion of the Rappahannock River in the Commonwealth of Virginia as the "John W. Warner Rapids." Introduced by Boxer, D-Calif., on Sept. 24, 2008. Senate Environment and Public Works reported Sept. 24 (no written report). Senate passed Sept. 24. House Natural Resources discharged. House passed Sept. 29. President signed Oct. 14, 2008.

PL 110-419 (HR 1714) Clarify the boundaries of Coastal Barrier Resources System Clam Pass Unit FL-64P. Introduced by Mack, R-Fla., on March 27, 2007. House passed, under suspension of the rules, July 14, 2008. Senate Environment and Public Works discharged. Senate passed Sept. 30. President signed Oct. 15, 2008.

PL 110-420 (HR 4544) Require the issuance of medals to recognize the dedication and valor of Native American code talkers. Introduced by Boren, D-Okla., on Dec. 13, 2007. House passed, amended, Sept. 25, 2008. Senate passed Sept. 30. President signed Oct. 15, 2008.

PL 110-421 (HR 6045) Amend Title I of the Omnibus Crime Control and Safe Streets Act of 1968 to extend the authorization of the Bulletproof Vest Partnership Grant Program through fiscal 2012. Introduced by Visclosky, D-Ind., on May 13, 2008. House passed, under suspension of the rules, Sept. 26. Senate passed Sept. 30. President signed Oct. 15, 2008.

PL 110-422 (HR 6063) Authorize the programs of the National Aeronautics and Space Administration. Introduced by Udall, D-Colo., on May 15, 2008. House Science and Technology reported, amended, June 9 (H Rept 110-702). House passed, amended, June 18. Senate Commerce, Science and Transportation discharged. Senate passed, amended, Sept. 25. House agreed to Senate amendment, under suspension of the rules, Sept. 27. President signed Oct. 15, 2008.

PL 110-423 (HR 6073) Provide that federal employees receiving their pay by electronic funds transfer shall be given the option of receiving their pay stubs electronically. Introduced by Foxx, R-N.C., on May 15, 2008. House Oversight and Government Reform reported July 28 (H Rept 110-780). House passed, under suspension of the rules, July 30. Senate Homeland Security and Governmental Affairs reported Sept. 24 (no written report). Senate passed Sept. 30. President signed Oct. 15, 2008.

PL 110-424 (HR 6083) Authorize funding to conduct a national training program for state and local prosecutors. Introduced by Spratt, D-S.C., on May 19, 2008. House Judiciary reported July 29 (H Rept 110-784). House passed, under suspension of the rules, July 31. Senate Judiciary discharged. Senate passed Sept. 30, 2008. President signed Oct. 15, 2008.

PL 110-425 (HR 6353) Amend the Controlled Substances Act to address online pharmacies. Introduced by Stupak, D-Mich., on June 24, 2008. House Energy and Commerce reported, amended, Sept. 23. (H Rept 110-869, Part 1). House Judiciary discharged. House passed, amended, under suspension of the rules Sept. 23. Senate passed Sept. 30. President signed Oct. 15, 2008.

PL 110-426 (HR 6469) Amend the Public Health Service Act to authorize increased federal funding for the Organ Procurement and Transplantation Network. Introduced by DeGette, D-Colo., on July 10, 2008. House passed, amended, under suspension of the rules Sept. 25. Senate passed, amended, Oct. 2. House agreed to Senate amendment Oct. 3. President signed Oct. 15, 2008.

PL 110-427 (HR 6524) Authorize the administrator of General Services to take certain actions with respect to parcels of real property located in Eastlake, Ohio, and Koochiching County, Minn. Introduced by LaTourette, R-Ohio, on July 16, 2008. House Transportation and Infrastructure reported Sept. 22 (H Rept 110-866, Part 1). House Armed Services discharged. House passed, under suspension of the rules, Sept. 22. Senate passed Sept. 30, 2008. President signed Oct. 15, 2008.

PL 110-428 (HR 7082) Amend the Internal Revenue Code of 1986 to permit the secretary of the Treasury to disclose certain prisoner-return information to the Federal Bureau of Prisons. Introduced by Ramstad, R-Minn., on Sept. 25, 2008. House passed, amended, under suspension of the rules, Sept. 27. Senate passed Oct. 2. President signed Oct. 15, 2008.

PL 110-429 (HR 7177) Authorize the transfer of naval vessels to certain foreign recipients. Introduced by Berman, D-Calif., on Sept. 27, 2008. House passed, under suspension of the rules, Sept. 27. Senate passed Oct. 1. President signed Oct. 15, 2008.

PL 110-430 (H J Res 100) Appointing the day for the convening of the first session of the 111th Congress and establishing the date for the counting of the electoral votes for president and vice president cast by the electors in December 2008. Introduced by Arcuri, D-N.Y., on Sept. 28, 2008. House passed Sept. 28. Senate passed Oct. 2. President signed Oct. 15, 2008.

PL 110-431 (S 3641) Authorize funding for the National Crime Victim Law Institute to provide support for victims of crime under Crime Victims Legal Assistance Programs as a part of the Victims of Crime Act of 1984. Introduced by Kyl, R-Ariz., on Sept. 27, 2008. Senate passed Sept. 27. House passed, under suspension of the rules, Oct. 2. President signed Oct. 15, 2008.

PL 110-432 (HR 2095) Amend Title 49, U.S. Code, to prevent railroad fatalities, injuries, and hazardous-materials releases and to authorize the Federal Railroad Safety Administration. Introduced by Oberstar, D-Minn., on May 1, 2007. House Transportation reported, amended, Sept. 19 (H Rept 110-336). House passed, amended, Oct. 17. Senate Commerce, Science and Transportation discharged. Senate passed, amended, Aug 1. House agreed to Senate amendment, with an amendment, Sept. 24. Senate agreed to House amendment to Senate amendment Oct. 1. President signed Oct. 16, 2008.

PL 110-433 (HR 6296) Extend through 2013 the authority of the Federal Election Commission to impose civil money penalties on the basis of a schedule of penalties established and published by the commission. Introduced by Brady, D-Pa., on June 18, 2008. House passed, under suspension of the rules, July 15. Senate Rules and Administration discharged. Senate passed Oct. 2. President signed Oct. 16, 2008.

PL 110-434 (HR 6531) Amend Chapter 13 of Title 17, U.S. Code to clarify the definitions of a vessel hull and a deck. Introduced by Berman, D-Calif., on July 17, 2008. House passed, under suspension of the rules, July 22. Senate passed Sept. 30. President signed Oct. 16, 2008.

PL 110-435 (HR 7084) Amend section 114 of Title 17, U.S. Code, to provide for agreements for the reproduction and performance of sound recordings by webcasters. Introduced by Inslee, D-Wash., on Sept. 25, 2008. House passed, under suspension of the rules, Sept. 27. Senate passed Sept 30. President signed Oct. 16, 2008.

PL 110-436 (HR 7222) Extend the Andean Trade Preference Act. Introduced by Rangel, D-N.Y., on Sept. 29, 2008. House Ways and Means discharged. House passed Sept. 29. Senate passed, amended, Oct. 2. House agreed to the Senate amendment Oct. 3. President signed Oct. 16, 2008.

PL 110-437 (HR 5159) Establish the Office of the Capitol Visitor Center within the Office of the Architect of the Capitol, headed by the chief executive officer for visitor services, to provide for the effective management and administration of the Capitol Visitor Center. Introduced by Brady, D-Pa., on Jan. 29, 2008. House Administration reported, amended, March 3 (H Rept 110-535). House passed, under suspension of the rules, March 5. Senate passed, amended, Sept. 27. House agreed to the Senate amendment Oct. 2. President signed Oct. 20, 2008.

PL 110-438 (S 3197) Amend Title 11, U.S. Code, to make it easier for members of the National Guard and reserve to file for bankruptcy by eliminating the means tests for those who serve for 90 days or more on active duty after Sept. 11, 2001. Introduced by Durbin, D-Ill., on June 25, 2008. Senate Judiciary reported, amended, Sept. 15 (no written report). Senate passed, amended, Sept. 30. House passed, under suspension of the rules, Oct. 3. President signed Oct. 20, 2008.

PL 110-439 (HR 3511) Designate the facility of the U.S. Postal Service located at 2150 East Hardtner Dr. in Urania, La., as the "Murphy A. Tannehill Post Office Building." Introduced by Alexander, R-La., on Sept. 10, 2007. House Oversight and Government Reform discharged. House passed Sept. 24, 2008. Senate passed Sept. 30. President signed Oct. 21, 2008.

PL 110-440 (HR 4010) Designate the facility of the U.S. Postal Service located at 100 West Percy St. in Indianola, Miss., as the "Minnie Cox Post Office Building." Introduced by Thompson, D-Miss., on Oct. 30, 2007. House passed, under suspension of the rules, July 14, 2008. Senate Homeland Security and Governmental Affairs discharged. Senate passed Oct. 2. President signed Oct. 21, 2008.

PL 110-441 (HR 4131) Designate a portion of California State Route 91 located in Los Angeles County, Calif., as the "Juanita Millender-McDonald Highway." Introduced by Richardson, D-Calif., on Nov. 9, 2007. House Transportation and Infrastructure reported Sept. 27, 2008 (H Rept 110-895). House passed, under suspension of the rules, Sept. 29. Senate passed Oct. 2. President signed Oct. 21, 2008.

PL 110-442 (HR 6558) Designate the facility of the U.S. Postal Service located at 1750 Lundy Ave. in San Jose, Calif., as the "Gordon N. Chan Post Office Building." Introduced by Honda, D-Calif., on July 21, 2008. House Oversight and Government Reform discharged. House passed Sept. 27. Senate passed Oct. 2. President signed Oct. 21, 2008.

PL 110-443 (HR 6681) Designate the facility of the U.S. Postal Service located at 300 Vine St. in New Lenox, Ill., as the "Jacob M. Lowell Post Office Building." Introduced by Weller, R-Ill., on July 30, 2008. House passed, under suspension of the rules, Sept. 18. Senate passed Sept. 30. President signed Oct. 21, 2008.

PL 110-444 (HR 6834) Designate the facility of the U.S. Postal Service located at 4 South Main St. in Wallingford, Conn., as the "Chief Warrant Officer Richard R. Lee Post Office Building." Introduced by DeLauro, D-Conn., on Sept. 8, 2008. House Oversight and Government Reform discharged. House passed Sept. 27. Senate passed Oct. 2. President signed Oct. 21, 2008.

PL 110-445 (HR 6847) Designate the facility of the U.S. Postal Service located at 801 Industrial Blvd. in Ellijay, Ga., as the "First Lieutenant Noah Harris Ellijay Post Office Building." Introduced by Deal, R-Ga., on Sept. 9, 2008. House passed, under suspension of the rules, Sept. 25. Senate passed Sept. 30. President signed Oct. 21, 2008.

PL 110-446 (HR 6902) Designate the facility of the U.S. Postal Service located at 513 6th Ave. in Dayton, Ky., as the "Staff Sergeant Nicholas Ray Carnes Post Office." Introduced by Davis, R-Ky., on Sept. 15, 2008. House Oversight and Government Reform discharged. House passed Sept. 27. Senate passed Oct. 2. President signed Oct. 21, 2008.

PL 110-447 (HR 6982) Designate the facility of the U.S. Postal Service located at 210 South Ellsworth Ave. in San Mateo, Calif., as the "Leo J. Ryan Post Office Building." Introduced by Speier, D-Calif., on Sept. 22, 2008. House Oversight and Government Reform discharged. House passed Sept. 27. Senate passed Oct. 2. President signed Oct. 21, 2008.

PL 110-448 (HR 6197) Designate the facility of the U.S. Postal Service located at 7095 Highway 57 in Counce, Tenn., as the "Pickwick Post Office Building." Introduced by Blackburn, R-Tenn., on June 5, 2008. House Oversight and Government Reform discharged. House passed Sept. 27. Senate passed Oct. 2. President signed on Oct. 22, 2008.

PL 110-449 (HR 6867) Provide for additional emergency unemployment compensation. Introduced by McDermott, D-Wash., Sept. 10, 2008. House passed, amended, under suspension of the rules, Oct. 3. Senate passed Nov. 20. President signed Nov. 21, 2008.

PL 110-450 (HR 5714) Require the secretary of the Treasury to mint coins in recognition and celebration of the establishment of the U.S. Army in 1775; to honor the American soldier of today and yesterday, in wartime and in peace; and to commemorate the traditions, history, and heritage of the U.S. Army and its role in American society. Introduced by Skelton, D-Mo., April 8, 2008. House Financial Services discharged. House passed, amended, Oct. 3. Senate passed Nov. 17. President signed Dec. 1, 2008.

PL 110-451 (HR 2040) Require the secretary of the Treasury to mint coins in commemoration of the semicentennial of the enactment of the Civil Rights Act of 1964. Introduced by Lewis, D-Ga., April 25, 2007. House passed, amended, under suspension of the rules, April 1, 2008. Senate Banking, Housing and Urban Affairs discharged. Senate passed Nov. 19. President signed Dec. 2, 2008.

PL 110-452 (S 602) Develop the next generation of parental-control technology. Introduced by Pryor, D-Ark., Feb. 15, 2007. Senate Commerce, Science and Transportation reported, amended, March 3, 2008 (S Rept 110-268). Senate passed, amended, Oct. 1. House Energy and Commerce discharged. House passed, amended, Oct. 3. Senate agreed to House amendment Nov. 17. President signed Dec. 2, 2008.

PL 110-453 (S 1193) Direct the secretary of the interior to take into trust two parcels of federal land for the benefit of certain Indian pueblos in the state of New Mexico. Introduced by Domenici, R-N.M., April 24, 2007. Senate Indian Affairs reported July 31, 2008 (S Rept 110-434). Senate passed Sept. 22. House Natural Resources discharged. House passed, amended, Sept. 29. Senate agreed to House amendments Nov. 19. President signed Dec. 2, 2008.

PL 110-454 (HR 6859) Designate the facility of the U.S. Postal Service located at 1501 S. Slappey Blvd. in Albany, Ga., as the "Dr. Walter Carl Gordon Jr. Post Office Building." Introduced by Bishop, D-Ga., Sept. 10, 2008. House Oversight and Government Reform discharged. House passed Sept. 27. Senate passed Nov. 20. President signed Dec. 19, 2008.

PL 110-455 (S J Res 46) Ensure that the compensation and other emoluments attached to the office of secretary of state are those that were in effect on Jan. 1, 2007. Introduced by Reid, D-Nev., Dec. 10, 2008. Senate passed Dec. 10. House passed Dec. 10. President signed Dec. 19, 2008.

PL 110-456 (HR 6184) Provide for a program circulating quarter-dollar coins that are emblematic of a national park or other national site in each state, the District of Columbia and each U.S. territory. Introduced by Castle, R-Del., June 4, 2008. House Financial Services reported July 8 (H Rept 110-748). House passed, under suspension of the rules, July 9. Senate Banking, Housing and Urban Affairs discharged. Senate passed Dec. 10. President signed Dec. 23, 2008.

PL 110-457 (HR 7311) Authorize appropriations for fiscal years 2008 through 2011 for the Trafficking Victims Protection Act of 2000 and enhance measures to combat trafficking in persons. Introduced by Berman, D-Calif., Dec. 9, 2008. House Foreign Affairs, Energy and Commerce, and Judiciary discharged. House passed Dec. 10. Senate passed Dec. 10. President signed Dec. 23, 2008.

PL 110-458 (HR 7327) Make technical corrections related to the Pension Protection Act of 2006. Introduced by Rangel, D-N.Y., Dec. 10, 2008. House Ways and Means and Education and Labor discharged. House passed Dec. 10. Senate passed Dec. 11. President signed Dec. 23, 2008.

PL 110-459 (S 3663) Require the Federal Communications Commission to provide for a short-term extension of the analog television broadcasting authority so that essential public safety announcements and digital television transition information may be provided for a short time during the transition to digital television broadcasting. Introduced by Rockefeller, D-W. Va., Oct. 1, 2008. Senate Commerce, Science and Transportation discharged. Senate passed, amended, Nov. 20. House Energy and Commerce discharged. House passed Dec. 10. President signed Dec. 23, 2008.

PL 110-460 (S 3712) Make a technical correction in the Paul Wellstone and Pete Domenici Mental Health Parity and Addiction Equity Act of 2008. Introduced by Kennedy, D-Mass., Nov. 20, 2008. Senate passed Nov. 20. House Energy and Commerce, Education and Labor, and Ways and Means discharged. House passed Dec. 10. President signed Dec. 23, 2008.

Index to Legislation by Name and by Public Law and Bill Number

The three indexes that follow are supplements to the primary index for this volume that begins on page 1205. These supplementary indexes are designed to give *Congress and the Nation* users a quick guide to articles on legislation, and related activity, considered during the 109th Congress and 110th Congress. The first index *(p. 1197)* is organized alphabetically by the name of the subject, in most cases the title used for the article on the subject. Most users may wish to consult the alphabetical index first. The second *(p. 1200)* is organized by the public law number for legislation enacted between 2005 and 2009 that is covered in the volume. The third index *(p. 1202)* is organized by bill number or Senate and House resolution numbers and includes legislation that did not become law. These two indexes will be useful to users who know a bill or public law number. They may be particularly helpful when researching legislation that Congress attached to an underlying but unrelated bill. The two congresses of this four year period, more so than in earlier years, enacted a variety of legislation by combining unrelated measures—such as tax cuts, minimum wage, unemployment compensation, and important economic measures—into a single bill. This use of omnibus legislation can be seen clearly in the second and third indexes organized by public law and bill number. Readers who need a more detailed guide to the volume's content will want to consult the full index.

Index to Legislation by Name

Index to Legislation by Congress and Public Law Number

Index to Legislation by Bill or Resolution Number

Legislation	Bill number	Public law Number	Page Number
FAA short-term authorization extensions (in fiscal 2008 omnibus appropriations)	HR 2764	PL 110-161	437, 439
Fiscal 2008 foreign aid appropriations (in fiscal 2008 omnibus appropriations)	HR 2764	PL 110-161	314
Fiscal 2008 Iraq/Afghanistan supplemental war appropriations (in fiscal 2008 omnibus appropriations)	HR 2764	PL 110-161	117, 386
Fiscal 2008 military construction appropriations (in fiscal 2008 omnibus appropriations)	HR 2764	PL 110-161	389
Fiscal 2008 omnibus appropriations (eleven unfinished bills and war supplemental)	HR 2764	PL 110-161	111, 112, 314
Passport requirements (in fiscal 2008 omnibus appropriations)	HR 2764	PL 110-161	255
Native American housing	HR 2786	PL 110-411	804
Brownfields (not cleared)	HR 280		629
Library, bookstore records (dropped from Commerce, Justice, State appropriations)	HR 2826	PL 109-108	236
Pension security: 2005 (not cleared)	HR 2830, S 1783, HR 4		654
Employment wage-gender discriminations (did not clear)	HR 2831, HR 1338		669, 670
Fiscal 2006 Commerce, Justice, Science, State appropriations	HR 2862	PL 109-108	76, 352
Detainee policies: Detainee Treatment Act (includes habeas corpus)	HR 2863	PL 109-148	364, 365, 399
Fiscal 2006 defense appropriations	HR 2863	PL 109-148	73, 344
Flu emergency (in fiscal 2006 defense appropriations)	HR 2863	PL 109-148	556
Habeas corpus petitions	HR 2863	PL 109-148	400
Katrina end of 2005 funding package (in fiscal 2006 defense appropriations bill)	HR 2863	PL 109-148	79, 344
Spyware controls (not cleared)	HR 29, HR 744		424
Capitol visitor center funding	HR 2985	PL 109-55	821
Congress Contingency Plans	HR 2985	PL 109-55	819
Fiscal 2006 legislative appropriations	HR 2985	PL 109-55	77
Surface transportation authorization	HR 3	PL 109-59	407
Fiscal 2006 Labor, HHS, Education, appropriations	HR 3010	PL 109-149	73
Environmental education (not cleared)	HR 3036		618
Fiscal 2006 foreign aid appropriations	HR 3057	PL 109-102	77, 282
Congressional pay (in fiscal 2006 Transportation, Treasury, HUD appropriations)	HR 3058	PL 109-115	849
D.C. gun law (in Transportation, Treasury, HUD appropriations)	HR 3058	PL 109-115	796
D.C. marriage promotion (in fiscal 2006 Transportation, Treasury, HUD appropriations	HR 3058	PL 109-115	795
Fiscal 2006 D.C. appropriations (in transportation, Treasury, HUD appropriations)	HR 3058	PL 109-115	76
Fiscal 2006 Transportation, Treasury, HUD appropriations	HR 3058	PL 109-115	78
Gun trace data (not cleared)	HR 3093		726
Military sales to China (bill rejected)	HR 3100		296
Sudan sanctions	HR 3127	PL 109-344	293
Drug imports (dropped from agriculture appropriations in omnibus bill)	HR 3161, HR 2764		578
Displaced student aid (Pell grants)	HR 3169	PL 109-66	608
Patriot Act	HR 3199	PL 109-177	222
Mortgage foreclosure relief, financial reform	HR 3221	PL 110-289	153
Mortgage relief	HR 3221	PL 110-289	630
Fiscal 2008 defense appropriations	HR 3222	PL 110-116	116, 380
Central American free trade accord	HR 3283	PL 109-53	202
National Indian Gaming Commission	HR 3351	PL 109-221	796
Small housing authorities (not cleared)	HR 3422, S 3620		629
Food and Drug Administration overhaul	HR 3580	PL 110-85	563
Mortgage relief: subprime (not cleared)	HR 3609		640
Katrina first supplemental appropriation	HR 3645	PL 109-61	79
Mortgage forgiveness	HR 3648	PL 110-142	639
Displaced student aid (campus-based aid)	HR 3668	PL 109-67	608

Legislation	Bill number	Public law Number	Page Number
Katrina second supplemental appropriations	HR 3673	PL 109-62	79
Internet taxation	HR 3678	PL 110-108	434
Employment sexual orientation discrimination (did not clear)	HR 3685		670
Peru free trade agreement	HR 3688	PL 110-138	209
Katrina tax relief bill for individuals, corporations	HR 3768	PL 109-73	80
Endangered species (not cleared)	HR 3824		481
Animal evacuation	HR 3858	PL 109-308	793
Campus-based aid program (Katrina related)	HR 3863	PL 109-86	607
Rural multifamily housing (not cleared)	HR 3873		647
Oil: refineries construction (not cleared)	HR 3893, S 1772		482
Rental assistance (not cleared)	HR 3895		629
Mortgage lender regulation (not cleared)	HR 3915		640
Restrictions on school districts (not cleared)	HR 3975		608
AMT: short-term extension	HR 3996	PL 110-166	91, 118
Pension Security: 2006	HR 4	PL 109-280	658
Consumer product, toy safety	HR 4040	PL 110-314	429
Eminent domain (not cleared)	HR 4128		705
Flood insurance funding	HR 4133	PL 109-106	792
Higher education overhaul	HR 4137	PL 110-315	611
Food uniformity (not cleared)	HR 4167		512
Fiscal 2006 tax reconciliation	HR 4297	PL 109-222	89
Bahrain trade pact	HR 4340	PL 109-169	205
Pilot Retirement Act	HR 4343	PL 110-135	439
Immigration (not cleared)	HR 4437, S 2611, S 1639		686, 711
Katrina second tax incentive bill (includes habeas corpus provisions)	HR 4440	PL 109-135	80
Commodity futures (not cleared)	HR 4473, S 1566		511
Property rights (not cleared)	HR 4772		707
Genetic discrimination	HR 493	PL 110-233	717
Fiscal 2006 Iraq/Afghanistan and disaster supplemental appropriations	HR 4939	PL 109-234	105, 350
Flu pandemic preparation: supplemental appropriations	HR 4939	PL 109-234	105
Hurricane recovery supplemental appropriations	HR 4939	PL 109-234	105
Internet Gambling	HR 4954	PL 109-347	422
U.S. ports security	HR 4954	PL 109-347	237
Fiscal 2008 defense authorization	HR 4986	PL 110-181	373
Wounded Warriors Act	HR 4986	PL 110-181	374, 593
Medical malpractice (not cleared)	HR 5		554
Student borrower interest rates (not cleared)	HR 5		617
Fiscal 2007 intelligence authorization (not cleared)	HR 5020, S 3237		292
Horse protection (not cleared)	HR 503, S 1915		513
College grant reauthorization (not cleared)	HR 509, HR 510		609
Section 8 voucher program (not cleared)	HR 5117, HR 1851, HR 3965		627, 644
FHA competitiveness (not cleared)	HR 5121		627
North Korea policy (in fiscal 2007 defense authorization)	HR 5122	PL 109-353	295
Fiscal 2007 defense authorization	HR 5122	PL 109-364	354
Campaign finance (not cleared)	HR 513		844
Economic stimulus package	HR 5140	PL 110-185	151
Telecommunications overhaul (not cleared)	HR 5252		426
Andean trade pact #1	HR 5264	PL 110-19	213
HOPE IV reauthorization (not cleared)	HR 5347, HR 3524		627, 644
Math, science competitiveness (not cleared 109th Congress)	HR 5356, HR 5358		609
D.C. representation (not cleared)	HR 5388, HR 1905, S 1257		820, 836
Coast Guard appropriations (in homeland security appropriations)	HR 5441	PL 109-295	229
FEMA overhaul (in fiscal 2007 homeland security appropriations)	HR 5441	PL 109-295	236
Fiscal 2007 homeland security appropriations	HR 5441	PL 109-295	102

Legislation	Bill number	Public law Number	Page Number
Prescription drug imports (in fiscal 2007 homeland security appropriations)	HR 5441	PL 109-295	556
NOAA reorganization (not cleared)	HR 5450		793
HIV/AIDS assistance	HR 5501	PL 110-293	312
Foreign investment review process	HR 556	PL 110-49	257
Fiscal 2007 defense appropriations	HR 5631	PL 109-289	102, 358
U.S.-India nuclear agreement	HR 5682	PL 109-401	277
Oman free trade agreement	HR 5684	PL 109-283	206
Student loan access	HR 5715	PL 110-227	615
Pipeline safety	HR 5782	PL 109-468	479
Starret City housing (not cleared)	HR 5937		648
Fisheries overhaul	HR 5946	PL 109-479	466
Fiscal 2009 intelligence authorization (not cleared)	HR 5959, S 2996		322
Energy overhaul	HR 6	PL 109-58	447
Energy policy	HR 6	PL 110-140	484
Border fence	HR 6061	PL 109-367	694
NASA reauthorization	HR 6063	PL 110-422	797
Health savings accounts (in tax breaks extension)	HR 6111	PL 109-432	554
Medicare physician payments (in tax breaks extension)	HR 6111	PL 109-432	553
Oil: Offshore drilling (in tax breaks extension)	HR 6111	PL 109-432	106, 471
Tax breaks extended	HR 6111	PL 109-432	105
Vietnam trade relations (in tax breaks extension)	HR 6111	PL 109-432	207
Alternative energy (in farm bill)	HR 6124	PL 110-246	493
Farm bill (vetoed twice; both overridden)	HR 6124	PL 110-246	514
National Institutes of Health reauthorization	HR 6141	PL 109-482	545
Ryan White AIDS reauthorization	HR 6143	PL 109-415	546
Older Americans Act	HR 6197	PL 109-365	582
Iran sanctions	HR 6198	PL 109-293	299
Public housing regulations (not cleared)	HR 6216		645
Disaster-damaged public housing (not cleared)	HR 6276		647
Electronic Surveillance: FISA reforms 2008	HR 6304	PL 110-261	251
Medicare physician payments	HR 6331	PL 110-275	571
Postal Service overhaul	HR 6407	PL 109-435	784
Highway trust fund financing	HR 6532	PL 110-318	439
Seller-financed down payments (not cleared)	HR 6649		647
Mortgage fraud coordinator (not cleared)	HR 6853		642
Unemployment benefits: Second extension	HR 6867	PL 110-449	668
U.S.-India nuclear agreement congressional approval	HR 7081	PL 110-369	311
Israel: aid for	HR 7177	PL 110-429	327
Middle East arms sales (Israel aid)	HR 7177	PL 110-429	327
Clean water (not cleared)	HR 720		504
Andean trade pact #2, Generalized System of Preferences extension	HR 7222	PL 110-436	213
Estate taxes (not cleared)	HR 8		96
Union check card (not cleared)	HR 800		668
Flood insurance grants	HR 804	PL 109-64	792
Stem cell research (vetoed)	HR 810, S 5, HR 3		542, 573
Hawaiian housing (not cleared)	HR 835		648
Homeless assistance (not cleared)	HR 840		648
Coast Guard authorization	HR 889	PL 109-241	228
Student loan subsidies (not cleared)	HR 890		618
Voting Rights Act	HR 9	PL 109-246	696
Inspectors General tenure	HR 928	PL 110-409	799
Human trafficking	HR 972	PL 109-164	710
SCHIP reauthorization (vetoed twice)	HR 976, HR 3963		558
Pell grant limit (not cleared; included in PL 109-171)	HR 990		618
Lobbying reform	S 1	PL 110-81	816, 830
Presidential dollar coin	S 1047	PL 109-145	795

Legislation	Bill number	Public law Number	Page Number
NASA reauthorization	S 1281	PL 109-155	786
Clean Air Act rewrite (not cleared)	S 131		480
Health information technology (not cleared)	S 1418, HR 4157		555
Broadband access	S 1492	PL 110-385	435
Iran sanctions	S 1612	PL 110-96	326
Space travel	S 1713	PL 109-112	787
Syria sanctions	S 1713	PL 109-112	301
Leave bank program/judiciary	S 1736	PL 109-229	793
Teachers and school supplies (not cleared)	S 1764		608
Guantanamo Bay detainees (habeas corpus rights; not cleared)	S 185		724
Electronic surveillance: FISA reforms 2007	S 1927	PL 110-55	249
Broadcasting indecency penalties	S 193	PL 109-235	421
Deposit insurance FDIC (in fiscal 2006 omnibus reconciliation bill)	S 1932	PL 109-171	148
Digital TV conversion (in fiscal 2006 omnibus reconciliation bill)	S 1932	PL 109-171	419
Fiscal 2006 omnibus reconciliation bill: mandatory entitlement cuts	S 1932	PL 109-171	81
Higher education reauthorization (in fiscal 2006 omnibus reconciliation bill)	S 1932	PL 109-171	602
Home energy aid: LIHEAP (in fiscal 2006 omnibus reconciliation bill)	S 1932	PL 109-171	628
Medicare, Medicaid, Children's Insurance (in fiscal 2006 omnibus reconciliation bill)	S 1932	PL 109-171	535
Pension plan premiums (in fiscal 2006 omnibus reconciliation bill)	S 1932	PL 109-171	81, 656
Welfare extension (in fiscal 2006 omnibus reconciliation bill)	S 1932	PL 109-171	579
Arctic National Wildlife Refuge ANWR (multiple bills, not cleared)	S 1932, HR 2863, S Con Res 83)		474
Fired U.S. attorneys	S 214	PL 110-34	721
Patriot Act short term extension	S 2167	PL 109-160	224
Sudan sanctions	S 2271	PL 110-174	323
Surplus food donations	S 2420	PL 110-247	799
Freedom of information	S 2488	PL 110-175	724
SCHIP extended to March 31, 2009	S 2499	PL 110-173	562
Vocational education reauthorization	S 250	PL 109-270	606
Bankruptcy reform	S 256	PL 109-8	142
Government online database	S 2590	PL 109-282	794
Mine safety	S 2803	PL 109-236	660
Financial services regulatory relief	S 2856	PL 109-351	150
Fiscal 2009 defense authorization	S 3001	PL 110-417	390
Americans with disabilities	S 3406	PL 110-325	716
Identity theft protections (veterans)	S 3421	PL 109-461	590
Flood insurance, national (not cleared)	S 3589, HR 311		791, 797
Dallas airport agreement	S 3661	PL 109-352	425
Bioterrorism	S 3678	PL 109-417	226
Credit rating agencies regulation	S 3850	PL 109-291	149
Guantanamo tribunals legislation	S 3930	PL 109-366	366
Military Commissions Act	S 3930	PL 109-366	364, 366
Gun liability	S 397	PL 109-92	699
Abortion: minors across state lens (not cleared)	S 403		549
Technology instruction at minority colleges (not cleared)	S 432, HR 921		608
Terrorism insurance	S 467	PL 109-144	240
Class action lawsuits	S 5	PL 109-2	695
Medical errors	S 544	PL 109-41	548
Army Corp of Engineers (not cleared)	S 728, HR 2864		469
Asbestos fund (not cleared)	S 852		703
Fiscal 2008 budget resolution	S Con Res 21		108
Fiscal 2009 budget resolution	S Con Res 70		121
Fiscal 2007 budget resolution (in fiscal 2006 war supplemental)	S Con Res 83 H Con Res 376	PL 109-234	97, 101

Index

Index

Alphabetization is letter-by-letter (e.g., "Aircraft carriers" precedes "Air Force").

C

G